Holidays and Anniversaries of the World

Holidays and Anniversaries of the World

A Comprehensive Catalog Containing Detailed Information on
Every Month and Day of the Year, with Coverage of more than 26,000
Holidays, Anniversaries, Fasts and Feasts, Holy Days of the Saints, the Blesseds,
and Other Days of Religious Significance, Birthdays of the Famous, Important
Dates in History, and Special Events and Their Sponsors

THIRD EDITION

Beth A. Baker, Editor

GALE

DETROIT • LONDON

HOLIDAYS AND ANNIVERSARIES OF THE WORLD, 3rd EDITION

Beth A. Baker, *Editor*

GALE RESEARCH STAFF:
Allison McNeill, *Project Manager*
Rita M. Runchock, *Managing Editor*

Tracey Rowens, *Art Director*
Cynthia Baldwin, *Product Design Manager*
Christine O'Bryan, *Desktop Publisher*
Barbara J. Yarrow, *Graphic Services Manager*

Deborah Milliken, *Production Assistant*
Evi Seoud, *Assistant Production Manager*
Mary Beth Trimper, *Production Director*

LIBRARY OF CONGRESS CATALOGING-IN-PUBLICATION DATA

Holidays and anniversaries of the world: a comprehensive catalogue
   containing detailed information on every month and day of the year
   . . . / Beth A. Baker, editor. — 3rd ed.
      p. cm.
      Includes index.
      ISBN 0-8103-5477-2 (hardcover)
      1. Calendar, Gregorian. 2. Holidays. 3. Chronology, Historical.
   I. Baker, Beth A., 1964-   .
   CE76.H65   1998   98-38866
   394.26—dc21   CIP

Printed in the United States of America

10 9 8 7 6 5 4 3 2 1

CONTENTS

Foreword . . . . *vii*

Introduction . . . . *ix*

Guide to Use . . . . *xi*

The Development of Our Modern Calendar . . . . *xiii*

Projection of Moveable Holidays, 1999-2004 . . . . *xviii*

Perpetual Calendar . . . . *xx*

Time Words . . . . *xxii*

Glossary of Time Words . . . . *xxiii*

   Date References . . . . *xxxi*

   Latin Terms of Time . . . . *xxxi*

   Clock Time . . . . *xxxii*

   Geologic Time . . . . *xxxii*

   Prescription Abbreviations Referring to Time . . . . *xxxiii*

   Time of Notes in Music . . . . *xxxiv*

   Anniversaries and Suggested Gifts . . . . *xxxiv*

HOLIDAYS AND ANNIVERSARIES

   JANUARY 1

   FEBRUARY 87

   MARCH 169

   APRIL 263

   MAY 347

   JUNE 429

   JULY 505

   AUGUST 583

   SEPTEMBER 665

   OCTOBER ͻ7

   NOVEMBER 909

   DECEMBER 983

Index . . . .

FOREWORD

For thousands of years, man has needed calendars; in the earliest times to enable him to predict the most propitious times for planting and harvesting, later on, to schedule religious observances that might not have coincided, as they had before, with agricultural needs. It is to the need for calendars that the development of astronomy can be traced, for men determined that the regularity of the positioning of the heavenly bodies would enable them to predict, with some accuracy, the seasons of the year. Early calculations were based on the moon, partly because it offered a readily observable, regular object on which to base observations. Most of the religions of the world developed calendars for holy days based on the moon's positions and the frequency of appearance of its several phases.

Despite the replacement of the lunar calendars in everyday life by more predictable solar, then astronomical, calendars, religions today still calculate many major holidays on the old "lunar month" —a term that is redundant, at least etymologically. Hence, it has become difficult for the layman to determine when Easter, Ramadan, or Yom Kippur falls without some help, as these moveable holidays, unlike Christmas, Bastille Day, and the Fourth of July, are not tied to a particular date in the modern calendar.

In more recent times, and especially since the beginning of the Christian Era, holy days have traditionally been linked with dates in the civil calendar, and most of the information in *Holidays and Anniversaries of the World* is organized in keeping with the January 1—December 31 year, which is recognized everywhere today and observed in most countries.

This book, though arranged in chronological sequence, is provided with a comprehensive index that enables the user to look up any particular event or name he or she may be seeking for reference to the date or dates of occurrence or significance. Saints' days, Blesseds' days, days of major events in world history, holidays and anniversaries of most nations are included, together with the birth dates of well-known people from every area of human endeavor. The user is thus enabled to look up a given day—say, his or her birthday—and learn the important events that took place on that day throughout history as well as the famous people born on that day.

For the practical, a given date can be checked to determine whether it is a bank holiday in Scotland, a national holiday in The Gambia, or a religious fast day in Saudi Arabia.

For businesses and institutions that attend to the many and various "Days," "Weeks," or "Months" such as have been established for promotional purposes, such Special Events are detailed in the pages at the beginning of a given month, along with the names of their sponsors. These, too, are included in the index. In addition, certain days, like Mother's Day and Election Day, are listed in the months when they occur, with information about how they are established—for example, "the first Sunday," "the first Tuesday after the first Monday," etc.

Historians, historical novelists, and science-fiction writers will find useful the Perpetual Calendar, which allows for the ready calculation of the day of every date (or the date of every day) for every year from 1753 through 2100. For those unable to recall it, the day of the week on which they were born can easily be determined.

Within the realm of practicality, every religious and civil observance in modern times has been documented, making *Holidays and Anniversaries of the World* an invaluable work of reference.

Laurence Urdang
Editor of First Edition

INTRODUCTION

to the
third
edition

Holidays and Anniversaries of the World is a book about time and the arbitrary standards that have been used to measure and mark it. Concentration is upon people and events of all periods, ancient and modern, with the arrangement of material based upon the Gregorian calendar system. Significant holidays, birthdates, historical events, beatification and saints' days are recorded for each date—January 1 through December 31. Whether for serious research or casual browsing, there is quick and convenient reference to pertinent information on every day of the year.

Included are regional, national, and international holidays: both civil and religious; birthdates of renowned individuals: political and religious leaders, artists, inventors, entrepreneurs, celebrities, and others who have influenced history or culture; and historical events of significance or interest. In addition, every month is treated individually, with a brief note on its history, name, and associations, as well as a list of special holidays, commemorations, and events celebrated, observed, or sponsored during that month in places around the world.

COVERAGE GREATLY EXPANDED

Since its initial publication in 1985, a great deal of additional material has been collected. The third edition contains approximately 26,000 entries, representing a 15 percent increase of new entries since the second edition. Additionally, extensive updating of existing material was undertaken for the third edition.

Thousands of birthdates have been added for prominent individuals throughout the world who have achieved recent success or notoriety. Examples include U.S. politician, Cynthia A. McKinney; Haitian president, René Préval; Croatian president, Franjo Tudjman; U.S. actor, Leonardo DiCaprio; U.S. actor, Cuba Gooding, Jr.; U.S. physician, Stanley B. Prusiner; U.S. basketball player, Shaquille O'Neal; and U.S. speed skater, Bonnie Blair.

Coverage of historical events has increased considerably, with emphasis upon the recent past. Among new entries collected since the last edition are the death of Diana, Princess of Wales; the bombing of the Alfred P. Murrah Building in Oklahoma City, Oklahoma; the unmanned spacecraft *Pathfinder* lands on Mars; the Berlin Wall is taken down; Nelson Mandela is sworn in as the first black president of South Africa; Terry Waite is released after four years of captivity by the Islamic Jihad in Lebanon; Bill Clinton becomes the first president in U.S. history to testify before a grand jury regarding his alleged misconduct.

Many new holidays have been added, some commemorating recent political developments. Examples include Day of Remembrance (Armenians remember those who perished in the earthquake catastrophe of 1988); Birthday of Japan's Emperor Akihito; Day of the Slav Apostles, St. Cyril and St. Methodius in Slovakia; Anniversary of the Battle of Vonnu (1919) in Estonia.

EXTENSIVE UPDATING REQUIRED

In addition to collecting thousands of previously unlisted items, hundreds of the previous editions' entries have been updated and enhanced by adding recent achievements, new responsibilities, and death dates for prominent individuals.

SPECIAL SECTIONS

To supplement the text and enhance overall usefulness of *Holidays and Anniversaries of the World*, several special sections have been included:

- An historical presentation on the development of our modern calendar. The Babylonian, Egyptian, Hebrew, Roman, Julian, and Gregorian systems are discussed.

- A projection of major movable holidays for the years 1999-2004.

- An easy-to-use perpetual calendar covering the years 1753 through 2100.

- A glossary of time words, including tables that present and explain common abbreviations and references to time.

ACKNOWLEDGMENTS

For suggestions, contributions of entries, permission to take material from personal or published sources, and for other courtesies extended during the preparation of the previous and present editions, the editors are indebted to the following individuals: The Reverend Harvey Blaise, Bethany Lutheran Church, West Hartford, CT; The Reverend Douglas T. Cooke, Archdiocese of Hartford, CT; Jean Dudley, Astronomer, U.S. Naval Observatory, Washington D.C.; Dr. Wadi Z. Haddad, Hartford Seminary Foundation, Hartford, CT; Peter Knapp, Head of Reference, Trinity College Library, Hartford, CT; Dr. David Menke, Director, Copernican Observatory, Central Connecticut State University, New Britain, CT; Dr. Abdel-Rahman Osman, Imam and Director, Islamic Cultural Center, New York, NY; Renae P. Reese, Yale-China Association, New Haven, CT; the reference staff, Royal Oak Public Library, Royal Oak, MI.

SUGGESTIONS ARE WELCOME

In spite of the considerable care that has been taken to keep errors and inconsistencies to a minimum, they have no doubt occurred. To assist in preparing revisions, it would be appreciated if users would send to the editor any information, suggestions, or corrections that might improve future editions.

GUIDE TO USE

Entries are arranged according to the Gregorian calendar, with each day subdivided into several sections. Holidays are listed alphabetically by country of origin, while birthdates and historical events are arranged chronologically. Users requiring information about a particular day should turn directly to the appropriate portion of the text. Questions such as "Which famous people share my birthday?" or "What holidays are celebrated on May 25?" can best be answered in this way.

For those who do not have a specific date in mind, a detailed index of personal names, terms, and events is provided. Users needing to know when Jane Austen was born, when the American Library Association was founded, or when Army Day is celebrated in Guatemala should begin by consulting the index.

SAMPLE ENTRIES

Typical entries may provide the following information:

HOLIDAYS

1   Country of origin

2   Name of holiday

3   Commemoration note

4   Other name for holiday

RELIGIOUS CALENDAR

5   Solemnities

6   The Saints

7   The Beatified

BIRTHDATES

8   Year of birth

9   Name of person

10 Brief identification (nationality, occupation, etc.)

11 Death date

HISTORICAL EVENTS

12 Year of event

13 Description of event

JANUARY 1

HOLIDAYS

[1] **Haiti**
[2] *Independence Day*
[3] Commemorates the declaration of independence of the island by Jean Jacques Dessalines, 1804. Also called
[4] *Heroes Day, Ancestors Day, or The Day of the Glorification of the Heroes of Independence.*

RELIGIOUS CALENDAR

[5] **Solemnities**
Octave of Christmas. Commemorates the Circumcision of Christ.

[6] **The Saints**
St. Concordius, martyr. Also called Concord. [d. c. 178]

[7] **The Beatified**
Blessed Zdislava, matron. Founded the Dominican priory of St. Laurence. [d. 1252]

BIRTHDATES

[8] [9] **1449** *Lorenzo de Medici,* Florentine
[10] statesman, merchant prince,
[11] patron of the arts. [d. April 8, 1492]

HISTORICAL EVENTS

[12] **1515** *Louis XII* of France dies and is
[13] succeeded by Francis I.

THE DEVELOPMENT

of our
modern
calendar

THE EGYPTIAN CALENDAR

The earliest calendar known, that of the Egyptians, was lunar-based, that is, dependent upon observation of one cycle of the moon's phases, say from one new moon to the next. One cycle is a lunar month, about 29.5 days in length (by solar reckoning). Although the observations required for lunar reckoning are fairly simple, reliance upon lunar months eventually leads to a problem: a lunar year, based upon 12 lunations (complete lunar cycles), is only 354 days, shorter than the solar year by more than 11 days. In any agricultural society (such as ancient Egypt), the solar-based seasons of the year are vitally important, as they are the most reliable guide for knowing when to plow, plant, harvest, store, etc. Hence the discrepancy between the lunar and solar year must somehow be addressed.

The Egyptian solution was to rely on a solar calendar to govern civil affairs and agriculture; this was put in place around the third millennium B.C. This calendar observed the same new year's day as the older lunar one, which for the Egyptians was the day, about July 3, of the heliacal rising (i.e., appearance on the horizon just before sunrise) of the star Sirius, the "Dog Star," called Sothis by the Egyptians. This event was significant for the Egyptians, for it was nearly coincidental with the annual flooding of the Nile, the key to their agricultural prosperity. The new Egyptian solar calendar also retained the division of days into months, although they were no longer based on lunar cycles. The Egyptian year in the reformed calendar contained 12 months of 30 days, with 5 intercalated days, bringing the total number of days to 365, only a fraction of a day different from the length of the solar year as determined by modern scientific means.

THE SUMERIAN CALENDAR

Like the early Egyptian calendar, the ancient Sumerian calendar, developed around the 27th century B.C., was lunar. To the Sumerians, however, the lunar cycles apparently had greater significance, for they retained lunar months and a 354-day year, making alignment with the seasons by means of intercalation, i.e., the addition of extra days outside the regular calendar, added as necessary to reconcile the lunar with the solar year. The calendar of the sacred city of Nippur, which became the Sumerian standard in the 18th century B.C., assigned names to the months, with the intercalary month designated by royal decree. (See also below.)

THE SEVEN-DAY WEEK

The ancient Babylonians, a Sumerian people, are thought to be the first people to observe a seven-day week. The concept apparently was based upon the periods between the distinct phases of the moon, which roughly correspond to seven days. They also regarded the number seven as sacred, probably because of the fact that the Babylonians, in their highly developed astronomy, knew of seven principal heavenly bodies. The Babylonians saw supernatural significance in the movements of the seven: Sun, Moon, Mars, Mercury, Jupiter, Venus, and Saturn. They referred to them as *bibbu,* "wild sheep," because of their irregular movements against a backdrop of fixed stars. The days of the week were named for these principal heavenly bodies, one assigned to each day according to which governed the first hour of that day. (See also below.)

In addition to their lunar calendar, the Babylonians also devised a solar calendar based upon the points at which the sun rises in relation to the constellations. This calendar is the basis for the zodiac system, the key to astrology.

From the Babylonians, the ancient Hebrews are believed to have adopted the practices of intercalation and observance of a seven-day week, probably during the time of Jewish captivity in Babylon beginning in 586 B.C. Babylonian influence may also have suggested or at least encouraged the practice of observing every seventh day as special—the Jewish concept of Sabbath. It should be mentioned, however, that evidence for an earlier Jewish calendar (from at least the 12th century B.C.) does exist, so the observance of a Sabbath may well antedate Babylonian influence. In any event, it is clear that the tradition of the seven-day week, as well as the retention of the concept of months, has much to do with the Western inheritance of Jewish calendar practices. (See also **The Hebrew Calendar,** below.)

The seven-day week as we know it today was carried into Christian use in the 1st century A.D. and was officially adopted by the Roman emperor Constantine in the 4th century. It is also worth noting that the English names for the days and their Romance equivalents still reflect, etymologically, their origin in the references to the seven principal heavenly bodies of the ancient Babylonian astronomy:

Sunday

Old English *Sunnan daeg,* a translation of Latin *dies solis* day of the sun.

Monday

Old English *Monan daeg,* a translation of Latin *lunae dies* day of the moon ; cf. French *lundi.*

Tuesday

Old English *Tiwes daeg* day of Tiw, an adaptation of Latin *dies Martis* day of Mars (the god Tiw being identified with the Roman Mars); cf. French *Mardi.*

Wednesday

Old English *Wodnes daeg* "Woden's Day," an adaptation of Latin *Mercurii dies* "day of Mercury" (the god Woden being identified with the Roman Mercury); cf. French *mercredi.*

Thursday

Old English *Thunres daeg* "Thunor's day" or "Thor's day," an adaptation of the Latin *dies Jovis* "day of Jove" (the god Thor being identified with the Roman Jove); cf. French *jeudi.*

Friday

Old English *Frize daeg* "Freya's Day," an adaptation of the Latin *dies Veneris* "day of Venus" (the goddess Freya being identified with the Roman Venus); cf. French *vendredi.*

Saturday

Old English *Saetern(es) daeg,* derived from the Latin *Saturni Dies* "day of Saturn."

THE HEBREW CALENDAR

Little is known of the Hebrew calendar prior to the Exodus from Egypt (c. 1250 B.C.) except that it appears to have contained four single and four double months called *yereah.* The early Hebrews apparently did not study the heavens and timekeeping as did their Sumerian and Egyptian neighbors. In fact, it was only after the period of Babylonian Exile (586-516 B.C.) that a more fully developed method of timekeeping was adopted to modify the ancient practices. After their return from captivity, the Hebrews employed a calendar very similar to that of the Babylonians, intercalating months in to the lunar calendar to keep it in correspondence with the solar year. However, despite the Babylonian practice of marking the beginning of the new year in the spring, the Hebrews retained the custom of recognizing the new year in the autumn, the time of their principal religious festivals of Rosh Hashanah (New Year), Yom Kippur, the Sukkoth, all falling in the month of Tishri (September/October). Still, similarities of the Jewish to the Babylonian calendar are clear from a comparison of the names used in each system for the months:

THE NAMES OF THE MONTHS IN THE BABYLONIAN AND JEWISH CALENDAR SYSTEMS:

BABYLONIAN	JEWISH	EQUIVALENT
Nisanu	Nisan	March/April
Aiaru	Iyar	April/May
Simanu	Sivan	May/June
Du uzu	Tammuz	June/July
Abu	Ab	July/Aug
Ululu	Elul	Aug/Sept
Tashritu	Tishri	Sept/Oct
Arahsamnu	Heshvan	Oct/Nov
Kislimu	Kislev	Nov/Dec
Tebetu	Tebet	Dec/Jan
Shabatu	Shebat	Jan/Feb
Adaru I	Adar	Feb/March
Adaru II	Veadar	(intercalary)

Thus, the year in the Jewish (and Babylonian) calendar consists of 12 lunar months, with the addition of the intercalary month, as necessary, to synchronize with the solar year.

The months contain alternately 29 or 30 days; the beginning of each is marked by the appearance of the new moon.

The Hebrew week ends with the observation of the Sabbath, lasting from sunset Friday to sunset Saturday, a day to rest and pay homage to God. The use of weeks and observation of a day of rest are primarily contributions from Jewish tradition to our present-day calendar. (See also **The Seven-day Week,** above.)

The Jewish Era, designated *A.M.* (for Latin *anno mundi,* year of the world), begins with the supposed date of Creation, which tradition sets at 3761 B.C.

After more than two thousand years, devout Jews still observe essentially the same calendar for religious purposes, although they follow other calendars for their business and social lives. With its Mosaic roots and later, though still ancient, modifications, the Hebrew calendar has remained a primary binding force of tradition and continuity throughout the long and varied history of the Jewish people.

THE EARLY ROMAN CALENDAR

Another source of significant influence in the development of our modern method of reckoning time was ancient Rome. The earliest known Roman calendar, created, according to legend, by the city's eponymous founder, Romulus, in the 8th century B.C., had 10 months totalling 304 days—6 months of 30 days and 4 months of 31 days. The new year began in March, the time when agricultural activities were revived and new military campaigns were initiated, and ended with December, which was followed by a winter gap that was used for intercalation. The Etruscan king Numa Pompilius (reigned 715-673 B.C.) reformed the primitive calendar of Romulus, instituting a lunar year of 12 months. The two new months following December were named *Januarius* and *Februarius,* and were respectively assigned 29 and 28 days.

While this reform was a clear improvement, it was set aside at Rome after the explusion of the kings in about 510 B.C. Still, its advantages were remembered, and in 153 B.C. the calendar of Numa Pompilius was once again adopted. At the same time the beginning of the Roman civil year was changed to January 1, which became the day that newly elected consuls assumed office.

DAYS OF THE ROMAN MONTH

The Romans had no serial method of numbering the days of their months.

They did, however, establish three fixed points from which other days could be reckoned. These three designations were: 1) *Kalends,* the first day of the month (ancestor of English *calendar*); 2) *Nones,* the ninth day (reckoned inclusively) before 3) *Ides,* originally the day of the full moon of the lunar month. In months of 31 days (March, May, July, October) the Nones were the seventh day and the Ides the fifteenth, while in the shorter months the Nones fell on the fifth and the Ides on the thirteenth day.

The Romans also recognized a market day, called *nundinae,* which occurred every eighth day. This established a cycle for agriculture in which the farmer worked for seven days in his field and brought his produce to the city on the eighth for sale.

THE JULIAN CALENDAR

It was not until the mid-first century B.C., by which time the reformed lunar calendar had shifted eight weeks out of phase with the seasons, that Julius Caesar took it upon himself to effect a truly long-term and scientific reform of the calendar. In order to accomplish this, he enlisted the aid of the Alexandrian astronomer Sosigenes

to devise a new calendar. The solar year was reckoned quite accurately at 365.25, and the calendar provided for years of 365 days with an additional day in February every fourth year. In 46 B.C. a total of 90 days were intercalated into the year, bringing the calendar back into phase with the seasons. As a result, what would have been March 1, 45 B.C. was, in the new system, referred to as January 1, 45 B.C. Thus 46 B.C. was a long year, containing 445 days, and was referred to by Romans as *ultimus annus confusionis,* the last year of the muddled reckoning.

In 10 B.C. it was found that the priests in charge of administering the new Roman calendar had wrongly intercalated the extra day every third year rather than every fourth. In order to rectify the situation, the emperor Augustus declared that no 366-day years should be observed for the next 12 years, and made certain that future intercalation would be properly conducted. With this minor adjustment, the Julian calendar was fully in place, so to remain for the next 1,626 years.

THE GREGORIAN CALENDAR

Since the Julian calendar year of 365.25 days (averaging in the leap-year day) was slightly longer than

the actual length of a solar year, 365.242199 days, over time even this system proved wanting, growing out of phase by about three or four days every four centuries. By the time of Pope Gregory XIII in the late 16th century, the difference between the calendar and the seasons had grown to 10 days; the vernal equinox of 1582 occurred on March 11. Left without change, the Julian calendar would have resulted in fixed holy days occurring in the wrong season, which bewildered church officials. Moreover, certain fixed holy days were also used to determine when to plant and harvest crops. Pope Gregory's reform, enunciated in the papal bull of February 24, 1582, consisted of deleting 10 days from the year (the day following October 5 was designated as October 15) and declaring that three out of every four century years (1700, 1800, etc.) would not be leap years; if a century year, such as 1600, were divisible by 400, it would be a leap year. These modifications established the form of our present calendar.

In spite of its superior accuracy, the Gregorian calendar met with resistance in various parts of the world, and was not utilized until the 18th century in Protestant Europe and the American colonies, and even later still in areas under strong Byzantine influence:

DATES OF ADOPTION OF THE GREGORIAN CALENDAR

COUNTRIES	DATE OF ADOPTION
Italy, France, Spain, Portugal, Luxembourg	1582
Germany (Protestant areas), Sweden, Norway	1700
Great Britain & colonies	1752
Japan	1873
Egypt	1876
Turkey	1908
China	1912
Bulgaria	1915
Russia, Finland	1918
Romania	1919
Greece	1923

Although the Gregorian calendar measures out a year that is slightly longer than the solar year (differing by about 25 seconds a year, or 3 days in every 10,000 years) its general workability and accuracy have led to its use worldwide for nearly all non-religious purposes.

PROJECTION

of movable
holidays
1999-2004

The holidays listed below are not fixed to particular dates on the Gregorian calendar, owing to their dependence upon a lunar-based calendar. Each is given with its date of incidence according to the Gregorian calendar for the years shown:

PRINCIPAL CHRISTIAN HOLIDAYS

Ash Wednesday
1999	February 17
2000	March 8
2001	February 28
2002	February 13
2003	March 5
2004	February 25

Easter Sunday
1999	April 4
2000	April 23
2001	April 15
2002	March 31
2003	April 20
2004	April 11

Ascension Thursday
1999	April 1
2000	April 20
2001	April 12
2002	March 28
2003	April 17
2004	April 8

Pentecost Sunday or Whitsunday
1999	May 23
2000	June 11
2001	June 3
2002	May 19
2003	June 8
2004	May 30

Trinity Sunday
1999	May 30
2000	June 18
2001	June 10
2002	May 26
2003	June 15
2004	June 6

Beginning of Advent
1999	November 28
2000	December 3
2001	December 2
2002	December 1
2003	November 30
2004	November 28

PRINCIPAL JEWISH HOLIDAYS

Purim
1999	March 2
2000	March 21
2001	March 9
2002	February 26
2003	March 18
2004	March 7

Passover
1999	April 1
2000	April 20
2001	April 8
2002	March 28
2003	April 17
2004	April 6

Shavuoth
1999	May 21
2000	June 9
2001	May 28
2002	May 17
2003	June 6
2004	May 26

Tish Ab B'ab
1999	July 22
2000	August 10
2001	July 29
2002	July 18
2003	August 7
2004	July 27

Rosh Hashanah
1999	September 11
2000	September 30
2001	September 18
2002	September 7
2003	September 27
2004	September 16

Yom Kippur
1999	September 20
2000	October 9
2001	September 27
2002	September 16
2003	October 6
2004	September 25

Sukkoth
1999	September 25
2000	October 14
2001	October 2
2002	September 21
2003	October 11
2004	September 30

Shemini Atzereth
1999	October 2
2000	October 21
2001	October 9

2002	*September 28*
2003	*October 18*
2004	*October 7*

Simhath Torah

1999	*October 3*
2000	*October 22*
2001	*October 10*
2002	*September 29*
2003	*October 19*
2004	*October 8*

Hanukkah

1999	*December 4*
2000	*December 22*
2001	*December 10*
2002	*November 30*
2003	*December 20*
2004	*December 9*

PRINCIPAL ISLAMIC HOLIDAYS

The dates shown are only approximations, since the months in the Islamic calendar do not begin until there has been a verified, visual sighting of the new moon.

I Ramadan

1999	*December 9*
2000	*November 28*
2001	*November 17*
2002	*November 6*
2003	*October 27*
2004	*October 15*

1 Shawwal

1999	*January 19*
2000	*January 8*
2000	*December 28*
2001	*December 17*
2002	*December 6*
2003	*November 26*
2004	*November 14*

1 Muharram

1999	*April 17*
2000	*April 6*
2001	*March 26*
2002	*March 15*
2003	*March 5*
2004	*February 22*

10 Muharram

1999	*April 26*
2000	*April 15*
2001	*April 4*
2002	*March 24*
2003	*March 14*
2004	*March 2*

12 Rabi'ul-Awwal

1999	*June 26*
2000	*June 15*
2001	*June 4*
2002	*May 24*
2003	*May 14*
2004	*May 2*

PERPETUAL CALENDAR 1753-2100

To find the calendar in use for any month or year from 1753 (the year in which Great Britain and its possessions adopted the Gregorian calendar) to 2100, simply select the desired year from the table at right, read the number next to it, and refer to the calendar so numbered.

For example, to find the day of the week on which *July 4, 1776*, occurred, look up *1776* in the table, take the number given there, *9*, refer to calendar number 9, and find that *July 4* was on a Thursday that year.

Calendar 1

January
S	M	T	W	T	F	S
1	2	3	4	5	6	7
8	9	10	11	12	13	14
15	16	17	18	19	20	21
22	23	24	25	26	27	28
29	30	31				

February
S	M	T	W	T	F	S
				1	2	3	4
5	6	7	8	9	10	11
12	13	14	15	16	17	18
19	20	21	22	23	24	25
26	27	28				

March
S	M	T	W	T	F	S
				1	2	3	4
5	6	7	8	9	10	11
12	13	14	15	16	17	18
19	20	21	22	23	24	25
26	27	28	29	30	31	

April
S	M	T	W	T	F	S
						1
2	3	4	5	6	7	8
9	10	11	12	13	14	15
16	17	18	19	20	21	22
23	24	25	26	27	28	29
30						

(Calendars 1–8 each display the twelve months January through December arranged in a standard seven-day grid; the numeral 1–8 labels each calendar block at the left and right margins.)

xx

Year	No.		Year	No.		Year	No.		Year	No.		Year	No.		Year	No.		Year	No.		Year	No.		Year	No.
1753	2		1792	8		1831	7		1870	7		1909	6		1948	12		1987	5		2026	5		2065	5
1754	3		1793	3		1832	8		1871	1		1910	7		1949	7		1988	13		2027	6		2066	6
1755	4		1794	4		1833	3		1872	9		1911	1		1950	1		1989	1		2028	14		2067	7
1756	12		1795	5		1834	4		1873	4		1912	9		1951	2		1990	2		2029	2		2068	8
1757	7		1796	13		1835	5		1874	5		1913	4		1952	10		1991	3		2030	3		2069	3
1758	1		1797	1		1836	13		1875	6		1914	5		1953	5		1992	11		2031	4		2070	4
1759	2		1798	2		1837	1		1876	14		1915	6		1954	6		1993	6		2032	12		2071	5
1760	10		1799	3		1838	2		1877	2		1916	14		1955	7		1994	7		2033	7		2072	13
1761	5		**1800**	4		1839	3		1878	3		1917	2		1956	8		1995	1		2034	1		2073	1
1762	6		1801	5		1840	11		1879	4		1918	3		1957	3		1996	9		2035	2		2074	2
1763	7		1802	6		1841	6		1880	12		1919	4		1958	4		1997	4		2036	10		2075	3
1764	8		1803	7		1842	7		1881	7		1920	12		1959	5		1998	5		2037	5		2076	11
1765	3		1804	8		1843	1		1882	1		1921	7		1960	13		1999	6		2038	6		2077	6
1766	4		1805	3		1844	9		1883	2		1922	1		1961	1		**2000**	14		2039	7		2078	7
1767	5		1806	4		1845	4		1884	10		1923	2		1962	2		2001	2		2040	8		2079	1
1768	13		1807	5		1846	5		1885	5		1924	10		1963	3		2002	3		2041	3		2080	9
1769	1		1808	13		1847	6		1886	6		1925	5		1964	11		2003	4		2042	4		2081	4
1770	2		1809	1		1848	14		1887	7		1926	6		1965	6		2004	12		2043	5		2082	5
1771	3		1810	2		1849	2		1888	8		1927	7		1966	7		2005	7		2044	13		2083	6
1772	11		1811	3		1850	3		1889	3		1928	8		1967	1		2006	1		2045	1		2084	14
1773	6		1812	11		1851	4		1890	4		1929	3		1968	9		2007	2		2046	2		2085	2
1774	7		1813	6		1852	12		1891	5		1930	4		1969	4		2008	10		2047	3		2086	3
1775	8		1814	7		1853	7		1892	13		1931	5		1970	5		2009	5		2048	11		2087	4
1776	9		1815	1		1854	1		1893	1		1932	13		1971	6		2010	6		2049	6		2088	12
1777	4		1816	9		1855	2		1894	2		1933	1		1972	14		2011	7		2050	7		2089	7
1778	5		1817	4		1856	10		1895	3		1934	2		1973	2		2012	8		2051	1		2090	1
1779	6		1818	5		1857	5		1896	11		1935	3		1974	3		2013	3		2052	9		2091	2
1780	14		1819	6		1858	6		1897	6		1936	11		1975	4		2014	4		2053	4		2092	10
1781	2		1820	14		1859	7		1898	7		1937	6		1976	12		2015	5		2054	5		2093	5
1782	3		1821	2		1860	8		1899	1		1938	7		1977	7		2016	13		2055	6		2094	6
1783	4		1822	3		1861	3		**1900**	2		1939	1		1978	1		2017	1		2056	14		2095	7
1784	12		1823	4		1862	4		1901	3		1940	9		1979	2		2018	2		2057	2		2096	8
1785	7		1824	12		1863	5		1902	4		1941	4		1980	10		2019	3		2058	3		2097	3
1786	1		1825	7		1864	13		1903	5		1942	5		1981	5		2020	11		2059	4		2098	4
1787	2		1826	1		1865	1		1904	13		1943	6		1982	6		2021	6		2060	12		2099	5
1788	10		1827	2		1866	2		1905	1		1944	14		1983	7		2022	7		2061	7		2100	13
1789	5		1828	10		1867	3		1906	2		1945	2		1984	8		2023	1		2062	1			
1790	6		1829	5		1868	11		1907	3		1946	3		1985	3		2024	9		2063	2			
1791	7		1830	6		1869	6		1908	11		1947	4		1986	4		2025	4		2064	10			

9
Perpetual calendar grid No. 9 — monthly calendars for January through December.

10
Perpetual calendar grid No. 10 — monthly calendars for January through December.

11
Perpetual calendar grid No. 11 — monthly calendars for January through December.

12
Perpetual calendar grid No. 12 — monthly calendars for January through December.

13
Perpetual calendar grid No. 13 — monthly calendars for January through December.

14
Perpetual calendar grid No. 14 — monthly calendars for January through December.

TIME WORDS

by Ethel Olicker

In this glossary are definitions of more than 200 time period terms, such as:

- *semiweekly* and *fortnightly,* terms that indicate recurrence

- *aeon* and *age,* terms that take the measure of a block of time

- A.H. and C.E., abbreviations that fix a year in a particular calendar

- *sesquicentennial* and *jubilee,* terms that mark particular anniversaries

- *ab initio, circa,* and *pro tempore,* Latin terms for relations of time

- terms that relate to specific fields, like *trecento* to art or *olympiad* to sports

Most of the terms have unambiguous definitions and are presented in this glossary for the convenience of the user. However, for many of the time period terms presented herein there is uncertainty regarding precise meaning. The meaning of *monthly* is fairly clear and consistently applied, but what about *bimonthly?* A word such as *annual* poses little difficulty, but *biannual* (or should it be *biennial?*) is used in two senses. Prior to and during the year 1976 in the United States, the popular use of the term *bicentennial* grew dramatically, and its meaning was quite clear, but other, similar terms are elusive. The word *triannual,* for example, does not appear in most dictionaries, yet it is used by publishers and others. Many of the time period terms that begin with *bi-* or *tri-* have two definitions, with the first having a meaning that is the inverse of the second. To compound the problem, dictionaries do not always agree as to which is the standard or which the second definition. Thus, to present a single definition as standard does not accurately describe the general use of many terms.

Books on usage discuss this matter and make recommendations; this glossary has attempted to address the problem by presenting, as the first meaning for certain ambiguous terms, the standard definition used by publishers in reference to periodicals and serials. The planning and revenues of the publishing industry are based upon the assumption of conventionally accepted meanings for frequency-of-issue terms. If an issue is promised every two months, all scheduling and costs are so predicated; the term *bimonthly,* for publishers, has a single meaning: once in (every) two months. Applying, then, the standards of publishing, this glossary defines ambiguous terms with the first meaning according to this convention and any other meanings following.

Most of the terms in the glossary are general, with application to the periodicity of events, publications, and divers temporal relations. A few items were drawn from specialized fields such as medicine, law, and art. In addition, various terms, abbreviations, and other temporal references that are the subject of frequent questions are conveniently presented in the tables that follow the glossary. Time-related subjects, such as relativity and clock time, which are (better) treated in special studies and encyclopedia articles, were mentioned as necessary, but without detailed coverage.

If other terms that may fit into the scope of this glossary are known or discovered by the reader, the editors would welcome being informed of them.

ab init., abbreviation for *ab initio* (Latin), 'from the beginning.'

absolute time, *n.* Newton's concept that time flows equally without relation to anything external, independent of all particular events and processes. This concept was shown to be inadequate and modified by Einstein's concepts of relativity of time and space-time in his Special and General Theories of Relativity.

A.D., abbreviation for *Anno Domini* (Latin), 'in the year of our Lord'; in reference to the count of years measured from the birth of Christ, arbitrarily fixed as A.D. 1. Properly, A.D. should precede references to a specific year, as A.D. 395, although it regularly follows words such as century, as in the fourth century A.D. When neither B.C. nor A.D. accompanies a date, it is usually understood that the year is part of our present calendar. Dating by A.D. was adopted in 525 by Christendom. See also **B.C.; C.E.; Table 1.**

ad inf., abbreviation for *ad infinitum* (Latin), 'to infinity, endlessly, without limit.'

ad init., abbreviation for *ad initium* (Latin), 'at the beginning.'

ad int., abbreviation for *ad interim* (Latin), 'in the meantime.'

aeon, *n.* Also **eon.** 1. an indefinitely long period of time. 2. *Geology.* the longest period of geologic time, comprising two or more eras. See also **Table 4.**
-aeonian, eonian, *adj.*

aet., aetat. See **anno aetatis suae.**

age, *n.* 1. the length of time during which a being or thing has existed. 2. a particular period of history as distinguished from others; a historical epoch. 3. a long, indeterminate span of time. 4. *Geology.* a period of time shorter than an epoch during which one particular stage of rock formation takes place.

A.H.1, abbreviation for *Anno Hejirae* (Latin), 'in the year of the Hegira,' i.e., A.D. 622, the year of the flight of Muhammad from Mecca, subsequently established as the first year of the Muslim era. See also **Table 1.**

A.H.2, abbreviation for *Anno Hebraico* (Latin), 'in the Hebrew year,' i.e., based upon the Hebrew reckoning of the year of creation as 3761 B.C. See also **Table 1.**

A.L., See **Anno Lucis.**

almanac, *n.* an annual publication that contains information on weather, tides, astronomy, events, and anniversaries for the coming year, and frequently gives useful information about the past year, as well as agricultural data, vital statistics, maps, prizes and awards in many fields, etc.

a.m., A.M. 1. abbreviation for *ante meridiem* (Latin) 'before noon.' 2. The period from 12 midnight to 12 noon, especially in reference to the daylight hours before noon.

A.M., See **Anno Mundi.**

anniversary, *n.* 1. the yearly recurrence of the date of a past event; the commemoration or celebration of an event on its recurring date. *-adj.* 2. pertaining to an anniversary, as *an anniversary dinner.*

anno aetatis suae, *Latin.* 'in the year of his (or her) life,' used in reference to an individual's age, as on gravestones. Abbreviated aet., aetat.

Anno Domini, See **A.D.**

Anno Lucis, *Latin.* 'in the year of light.' Abbreviated A.L. Used by Freemasons to indicate the number of years elapsed since 4000 B.C.; A.D. 1985 is A.L. 5984. See also **Table 1.**

Anno Mundi, *Latin.* 'in the year of the world,' used in reference to time since the date of creation in the chronology of Bishop Usher, i.e., 4004 B.C. Abbreviated A.M. See also **Table 1.**

Anno Regni, *Latin.* 'in the year of the reign,' used to designate the year in the reign of a king or queen, as A.R. Victoriae Reginae vicesimo secundo, 'in the 22nd year of the reign of Queen Victoria.' Abbreviated A.R. See also **Table 1.**

annual, *n.* 1. a publication issued once a year. 2. a plant that grows from seed to maturity in one growing season or year. *-adj.* 3. of, for, or pertaining to a year; occurring or returning once a year; happening during one year. -annually, *adv.*

ante meridiem, See **a.m., A.M.**

A.R., See **Anno Regni.**

atomic second, *n.* a standard for time measurement, defined in 1967 by the 13th General Conference on Weights and Measures, to replace reckoning based on astronomical measurements. The second is equal to 9,192,631,770 cycles or vibrations within a hyperfine electron level of the cesium atom. The accuracy of this cesium-based second is about one part in ten billion.

B.C., abbreviation for *before Christ.* Used in referring to dates before A.D. 1. B.C. follows the year, as in 1,000,000 B.C., as contrasted with A.D., which properly precedes. Use of B.C. was introduced in the 17th century. Dates followed by B.C. are reckoned from A.D. 1, the year set as that for the birth of Christ. The first century B.C. extends from 1 B.C. to 100 B.C.; the second century B.C. goes from 101 B.C. to 200 B.C., and so on. It is useful to note that, since there was no year 0, intervals that span from B.C. to A.D. are one year less than standard arithmetic would suggest: someone born in 4 B.C. would be seven years old on his birthday in A.D.4. See also **A.D.; B.C.E.; Table 1.**

B.C.E., abbreviation for *before the Common Era* or *before the Christian Era.* Used instead of B.C. as a secular date reference. See also **Table 1.**

bi-, prefix meaning 'twice' or 'once every two.' Usage: The confusion about the part played by the prefix bi- in words like *biweekly, bimonthly,* and *biyearly,* stems from the fact that its derivation can be tied to either of two related yet subtly different Latin words, the adjective *bini* 'two at a time, two together' and the adverb *bis* 'twice, two times.' Unfortunately, their similarity has led to confusion over the meaning of bi-, and the problem has affected English usage, where the question has not been consistently resolved. It has been the practice of some dictionaries to give both possible meanings, the first in a "standard definition," followed by a "loose" meaning which differs from the first. Another source of confusion is the fact that the established, "standard" sense of bi- in words such as biannual and biquarterly is 'twice per -,' and in other words like biennial and bimonthly it is 'once every two -.'

biannual, *adj.* occurring, appearing, being made, done, or acted upon twice a year, but not necessarily six months apart. Biannual exams, for instance, may be given in separate terms of a school year, but four or five months apart. - **biannually,** *adv.*

bicentenary, *n. Chiefly British.* bicentennial.

bicentennial, *n.* 1. a 200th anniversary or the celebration of such an anniversary. Also **bicentenary, bicentennium.** -*adj.* 2. pertaining to or acknowledging a 200th anniversary; consisting of or lasting 200 years; occurring every 200 years. -**bicentenially,** *adv.*

bicentennium, See **bicentennial.**

biennial, *n.* 1. an event, act, or publication with a frequency of once every two years. 2. a plant that takes two years to develop and mature; lasting or living for two years. -*adj.* 3. happening every two years.

Also **biyearly.** -**biennially,** *adv.*

biennium, *n.* (*pl.* -iums, -ia) a period of two years.

bihourly, *adj.* occurring every two hours, as *a bihourly medical bulletin.*

bimester, *n.* a two-month period. -**bimestrial,** *adj.*

bimillenary, *n.* 1. a 2000-year period. 2. an anniversary or celebration of an event that occurred 2000 years earlier. Also **bimillennial; bimillennium.**

bimillennial, *n.* 1. bimillenary. -*adj.* 2. of or relating to a 2000-year period or its celebration.

bimillennium, See **bimillenary.**

bimonthly, *n.* 1. an act, event, or publication with a frequency of once every two months; a period of two months. Cf. **semimonthly.** -*adj.* 2. of or pertaining to a two-month period. -*adv.* 3. every two months.

biquarterly, *adj.* occurring twice every three months.

biweekly, *n.* 1. a publication appearing once every two weeks; an event that takes place or lasts over a two week period. -*adj.* 2. occurring every two weeks. -*adv.* 3. every two weeks. Also **fortnightly.** Cf. **semiweekly.**

biyearly, *adj.* 1. of or pertaining to a two-year period. Also **biennial.** -*adv.* 2. every two years; biennially.

c, common abbreviation for circa. Also written **c., ca, ca., cir., circ.**

C.E., abbreviation for Common Era or Christian Era, a secular reference used in place of A.D. See also **Table 1.**

centenarian, *n.* 1. one who has lived to the age of 100 years. -*adj.* 2. pertaining to or having lived 100 years or longer.

centenary, *n.* 1. a period of 100 years. 2. esp. Brit. a commemoration 100 years after an event. Also **centennial, centennium, century.** -*adj.* 3. of or pertaining to a period of 100 years. Also **centennial.**

centennial, *n.* 1. a 100th anniversary or its celebration; centenary. Also **centennium.** -*adj.* 2. pertaining to a period of 100 years; lasting or aged l00 years. -**centennially,** *adv.*

centennium, See **centenary, centennial.**

centurial, ad;. relating to 100 years; marking or beginning a century ,as the centurial years of 1600 and 1700.

centuriate, *adj.* of or relating to, or divided in hundreds or centuries.

century, *n.* a period of 100 years. The first century included the years 1 to 100; 101 to 200 was the second century, etc. The twentieth century, which began in 1901, will technically end at the end of the year 2000.

Christian Era, See **C.E.**

cinquecento, *n.* the 16th century or 1500s, esp. with reference to art and literature in Italy [for Italian *mil cinque cento,* '1500']. -**cinquecentist,** *adj.*

circa, prep., adv. *Latin.* 'about, around' used especially in referring to approximate dates, as circa l850. Abbreviated **c, c., ca, ca., cir., circ.**

circadian, *adj.* 1. pertaining to a biological cycle that repeats itself at 24-hour intervals. -*n.* 2. a daily, 24-hour rhythm inherent in living organisms, with optimum times for waking, sleeping, and other activities.

Common Era, See **C.E.**

cycle of indiction, a recurring 15-year period in the Roman calendar, used as a basis for the revaluation of property.

daily, *n.* 1. an event or publication that occurs or appears everyday. -*adj.* 2. of, done, occur-

ring, or appearing each day, or on each weekday. Also diurnal. -*adv.* 3. on each day.

de die in diem, *Latin.* 'from day to day.'

decade, *n.* any period of ten years. Specific decades are usually thought to begin with the year ending in 0, as the Fifties ran from 1950-59. Also **decennary, decennial, decennium.**

decennary, *n.* 1. a period of ten years. Also **decade, decennial, decennium.** -*adj.* 2. pertaining to a ten-year span.

decennial, *n.* 1. a ten-year anniversary or its celebration. Also **decade, decennary, decennium.** -*adj.* 2. of or pertaining to ten years; occurring every ten years.

decennium, *n.* (*pl.* -iums; -ia) a period of ten years. Also **decade, decennary, decennial.**

demi-, prefix. 1. half. 2. shortened.

diurnal, *adj.* 1. of, belonging to, or occurring each day; daily. 2. of or occurring during the daytime; not nocturnal. 3. opening during the day, closing at night (of flowers and leaves of some plants). See **nocturnal.**

dominical letter, a letter from A-G assigned in church calendars to designate the Sundays of the liturgical year as an aid in determining the date for Easter Sunday.

duecento, the 13th century or 1200s, esp. with reference to art and literature in Italy [for Italian *mil due cento* '1200']. -**duecentist,** *adj.*

eon, See **aeon.**

epact, *n.* 1. the difference in days between a lunar and a solar year. 2. a period added to harmonize the lunar with the solar calendar. 3. the number of days since the new moon at the beginning of the calendar year.

epoch, *n.* 1. a characteristic,

remarkable, or memorable period of time. 2. the beginning of such a new period in time. 3. *Geology.* A unit of time shorter than a period, but longer than an age. See also **Table 4.** 4. a period of time during which a particular culture is dominant.

equinox, the time at which the sun crosses the plane of the earth's equator, so that day and night are of equal duration. The equinoxes occur approximately on March 21 (**vernal equinox**) and September 22 (**autumnal equinox**). -**equinoctial,** *adj.*

era, *n.* l. a period of time that utilizes a specific point in history as the basis of its chronology. 2. a period of time notable because of its memorable aspects, events, or personalities. 3. *Geology.* The longest period of named time. See also **Table 4.**

femtosecond, *n.* one quadrillionth of a second, used in measuring the briefest events known to physical science. Abbrev. **fsec.**

fin de siecle, French. 'end of the century,' esp. in reference to the end of the 19th century. Also **finde-siecle.**

fortnight, *n.* fourteen continuous days and nights; two weeks.

fortnightly, *n.* 1. a periodical or publication appearing once every two weeks or fourteen days. -*adj.* 2. occurring or appearing once every two weeks. -*adv.* 3. once in two weeks. Also **biweekly.**

generation, *n.* 1. the period between the birth of parents and that of their children, for humans, usually reckoned as 25 or 30 years. 2. a single step in natural descent.

Gregorian calendar, a calendar in use worldwide for civil, commercial, and political purposes, named for Pope Gregory XIII, who promulgated its use in

1582 to replace the Julian calendar. It differs from the Julian calendar in that no centennial year (e.g., 1800, 1900) is a leap year unless it is divisible by 400. See also **Julian calendar; leap year.**

hebdomad, *n.* 1. a group of seven. 2. a period of seven days; a week.

hebdomadal, *adj.* 1. taking place, coming together, or published once every seven days. Also **weekly.** 2. lasting seven days. -**hebdomadally,** *adv.*

hebdomadary, *adj.* occurring every seven days; weekly.

heliacal rising, the rising of a particular celestial object most nearly coincident with the rising of the sun.

hemi-, *prefix.* half.

horal, *adj.* relating to hours; hourly.

horary, *adj.* pertaining to, noting the hours; continuing or occurring hourly.

in pr., abbreviation for *in principio* (Latin), 'in the first place; in the beginning.'

instant, *n.* 1. an infinitesimal space of time; a moment. 2. the present or current month.

intercalate, to insert an extra period of time into a calendar.

isochronal, *adj.* of equal duration; occurring in, characterized by, or recurring in equal intervals of time; performed in equal intervals of time. -**isochronally,** *adv.*

jubilee, *n.* 1. the celebration of special anniversaries, such as the 25th (silver jubilee), 50th (golden jubilee), or 60th and 75th (diamond jubilee). See also **Table 7.** 2. any time of rejoicing and celebration. 3. Hebrew law. a year of celebration observed by Jews once every 50 years. 4. *Roman Catholic law.* a period of time proclaimed by the pope every 25

years as a time of rejoicing.

Julian calendar, a calendar in use in the Roman Empire and much of Europe from 45 B.C. until the 16th century or later, named after Julius Caesar, who established its use. Caesar consulted the Greek astronomer, Sosigenes, who drew up the calendar and based it on the Egyptian solar calendar with 365 days per year plus 1 extra day every fourth year. See also **Gregorian calendar.**

leap year, a year in which an extra day is inserted in order to precisely coordinate the calendar year with the solar-based seasons. In the Gregorian calendar, every fourth year is a leap year, with an extra day inserted at the end of February, except for centennial years (e.g., 1800, 1900) whose number is not divisible by 400.

lunar calendar, a system of reckoning the passing of the year based on the recurrence of the phases of the moon.

lunar year, *n.* a period of 12 complete lunations or revolutions of the moon around the earth; a period of roughly 354 days or 12 lunar months, each equaling 29.531 days.

lustrum, *n.* 1. *Roman history.* a ceremonial purification of the people, performed every five years, after the taking of the census. 2. any five-year period.

m., abbreviation for *meridies* (Latin), 'noon.'

Metonic Cycle, a cycle of 235 synodic months, very nearly 19 years, after which the new moon occurs on the same day as it had at the beginning of the cycle [After Meton, 5th-century B.C. Greek astronomer who discovered the cycle.]. See also *synodic month.*

microsecond, one millionth of a second.

millenarian, *adj.* 1. of or pertaining to a thousand years, especially to the thousand years of the prophesied Millennium. -*n.* 2. a believer in the millennium. See also **millenium,** def. 2.

millenary, *n.* 1. an aggregate of a thousand; millennium. 2. a 1000th anniversary or celebration. -*adj.* 3. consisting of or pertaining to a thousand, especially a thousand years.

millennium, *n.* (*pl.* -iums; -ia) 1. a period of a thousand years; an anniversary of an event that occurred a thousand years earlier. 2. *usu.* **The Millennium,** the predicted period of a thousand years during which Christ will reign on earth; a period of general righteousness and happiness. -**millennial,** *adj.*

millisecond, *n.* one thousandth of a second. Abbreviated msec.

monthly, *n.* 1. a periodical published once a month. 2. any event which occurs once a month. -*adj.* 3. done, happening, appearing once a month, or continuing or lasting a month. -*adv.* 4. by the month; once a month.

musical time, See **Table 6.**

myriad, *n.* 1. an immense number of persons or things. 2. ten thousand. *adj.* 3. of an indefinitely great number; countless.

nanosecond, *n.* one billionth of a second. Abbreviated nsec.

Nippur calendar, the standard calendar of the ancient Babylonians during the age of Hammurabi (late 18th century B.C.)

nocturnal, *n.* 1. of, belonging to, or occurring each night; nightly. 2. of or occurring during the night-time; not diurnal. 3. active at night, as a nocturnal predator. See **diurnal.**

nonage, *n.* 1. the period of legal minority. 2. the condition of not being of legal age to partake in certain activities. 3. any period of immaturity.

nonagenarian, *n.* 1. someone who has reached the age of 90 years, but is not yet 100. *-adj.* 2. between the ages of 90 and 100.

notes, musical. See **Table 6.**

novendial, *adj. Rare.* 1. lasting nine days. 2. on the ninth day after an event.

novena, *n. Roman Catholicism.* a prayer service lasting nine consecutive days.

novennial, *adj.* occurring every ninth year.

nychthemeron, *n.* 1. (*pl.* -ra) a full period of a night and a day; 24 hours. *-adj.* 2. pertaining to a 24-hour period. Also **nycthemeron.**

octennial, *adj.* 1. happening every eighth year. 2. lasting for an eight-year period.

octogenarian, *n.* 1. someone who has reached the age of 80 years, but is not yet 90. *-adj.* 2. between the ages of 80 and 90 years.

olympiad, *n.* 1. a period of four years reckoned from one celebration of the Olympic Games to the next, by which the ancient Greeks computed time from 776 B.C. 2. a quadrennial celebration of the modern Olympic Games, as in 1984, 1988, 1992, 1996, etc.

pentad, *n.* a period of five years. Also **quinquenniad, quinquennial, quinquennium.**

per annum, by the year; yearly [from Latin]. Often used in stating a yearly basis in accounting, as *$20,000 per annum.* Abbreviated **p.a., per an.**

per diem, 1. by the day; daily. 2. a daily allowance for living expenses. [from Latin]

perennial, *n.* 1. something that is continuing or recurrent for an indefinite number of years. 2. *Botany.* a plant that renews its

top growth every growing season and lives more than two years; trees, bushes, and plants such as chrysanthemums and strawberries are perennials. Cf. **annual; biennial.** *-adj.* 3. continuing or lasting for an indefinitely long time. 4. enduring, present all through the year; perpetual; recurrent. **-perennially,** *adv.*

period, *n.* 1. a division or unit of time marked by a beginning, a duration, and an end; a specified division or portion of time. 2. the duration of a cyclic occurrence. 3. an interval in time that can be characterized by certain conditions, events, technology, development, culture, or ideology. 4. Geology. The unit of time comprising several epochs and included with other periods in an era. See **Table 4.** -**periodic,** *adj.*

periodical, *n.* 1. a magazine or other publication whose issues appear at regular intervals, more often than once a year. 2. periodic.

photoperiodism, *n.* the biological responses of an organism such as a bird, flower, or animal to the period of daylight.

picosecond, *n.* one trillionth of a second. Abbreviated psec.

Platonic Year, the period of about 26,000 years that equals the time for one complete revolution of the equinoxes. See also *precession of the equinoxes.*

p.m., abbreviation for *post meridiem* (Latin), 'after noon,' in reference to the hours from 12 noon until midnight. Also written **P.M.**

precession of the equinoxes, the progressively earlier occurrence of the equinoxes each year caused by the gravitational force of the sun, moon, and planets on the earth's orbit. A cycle of gradually shifting

equinoxes (and seasons) takes approximately 26,000 years. See also **Platonic Year.**

pro tem, abbreviation for *pro tempore,* Latin 'for the time being,' i.e., temporary, or, *adverbially, temporarily.*

proximo, *adv.* in, of, or during the next or following month; occurring next month; e.g., in April, the 6th proximo is the 6th of May. See also *ultimo.*

quadragenarian, *n.* 1. someone who has reached the age of 40 years, but is not yet 50. *-adj.* 2. Also **quadragenarious.** between the ages of 40 and 50.

Quadragesima or Quadragesima Sunday, *n. Christian calendar.* the first Sunday in Lent, its name referring to the forty days (excepting Sundays) from Ash Wednesday to Easter.

Quadragesimal, *adj. Christian religion.* 1. of, pertaining to, or suitable for Lent; Lenten. 2. lasting 40 days, as the period of Lent.

quadrennial, *n.* 1. a fourth anniversary or its celebration. 2. an event occurring every four years. *-adj.* 3. occurring every four years, as a quadrennial election. *-adv.* **quadrennially.**

quadrennium, *n.* a period of four years.

Quadrennium Utile, n. *Scots Law.* a period of four years after reaching one's majority, during which a person is within his rights to avoid carrying out certain contracts and other obligations.

quadricentennial, *n.* 1. a 400th anniversary or its celebration. *-adj.* 2. of, pertaining to, or marking the completion of a 400-year period.

quartan, *n.* 1. a fever that recurs every fourth day. 2. something that is fourth after three others.

quattrocento, *n.* 1. the 15th century or 1400s, esp. with reference to art and literature in Italy [for Italian *mil quattro cento,* '1400']. **-quattrocentist,** *adj.*

quincentenary, *adj.* of or relating to a 500th anniversary. Also **quincentenary.**

quincentennial, *n.* 1. a 500th anniversary or its celebration. -*adj.* 2. of or relating to a 500th anniversary or to a 500-year period. Also **quincentenary.**

quindecennial, *n.* 1. a fifteenth anniversary. -*adj.* 2. of or pertaining to a period of 15 years or the 15th occurrence of a series, as an anniversary.

quinquagenarian, *n.* 1. someone who has reached the age of 50, but is not yet 60. -*adj.* 2. between the ages of 50 and 60 years.

quinquagenary, *n.* 1. a 50th anniversary or its celebration. -*adj.* 2. consisting of or containing 50 (years).

Quinquagesima or Quinquagesima Sunday, n. Christian calendar. the Sunday before Lent, approximately fifty days before Easter. Also called **Shrove Sunday.**

quinquagesimal, *adj.* occurring in a season of 50 days; consisting of 50 days.

quinquennial, *n.* 1. something that occurs every five years. 2. a five-year term of office. 3. a fifth anniversary. 4. Also **quinquennium, pentad, quinquenniad.** a period of five years. -*adj.* 6. of or for five years; lasting five years. 6. occurring every five years. -*adv.* **quinquennially.**

quinquenniad, See **quinquennial.**

quinquennium, See **quinquennial.**

quintan, *n.* 1. a fever that recurs every fifth day. 2. something that is the fifth after four others.

quotidian, *n.* 1. something occurring daily, like a report or fever. -*adj.* 2. daily. 3. everyday. 4. ordinary.

regnal year, a year calculated within the reign of a sovereign.

saros, the period of 223 synodic months, equalling about 18 years, after which eclipses repeat their cycle, but shifted 120 west.

score, *n.* a count, group, or set of 20, frequency referring to years, as in *four score and seven years ago.*

seicento, the 17th century or 1600s, esp. with reference to art and literature in Italy [for Italian *mil sei cento* '1600']. **-seicentist** *adj.*

semester, *n.* 1. a term comprising half of an academic year, lasting from 15 to 18 weeks. 2. *(in German universities)* an academic term lasting about six months including holidays.

semestral, *adj.* 1. of or perqaining to a semester. 2. of or pertaining to a six-month period. Also **semestrial.**

semi-, *prefix.* 1. half. 2. half of or occurring halfway through a time period.

semiannual, *n.* 1. a publication that is issued every six months or twice a year 2. *Botany.* a plant that lives for half a year. Also **semiyearly.** -*adj.* 3. occurring, done, or published every six months or twice a year; lasting for half a year. -**semiannually,** *adv.*

semicentenary, See **semicentennial.**

semicentennial, *n.* 1. a 50th anniversary or its celebration. Also, *Chiefly Brit.* **semicentenary.** -*adj.* 2. of or pertaining to the 50th year after an event.

semimonthly, *n.* 1. something that occurs twice a month. Cf. **bimonthly.** -*adj.* 2. made, done, occurring, or published twice a month. -*adv.* 3. twice a month.

semiweekly, *n.* 1. something which takes place twice a week, as a publication. -*adj.* 2. occurring, done, appearing, or being published twice a week. -*adv.* 3. twice a week.

semiyearly, *adj.* 1. occurring, done, or appealing every half year or twice a year. Also **semiannual.** *adv.* 2. twice a year. Also **semiannually.**

septenary, *n.* 1. a group or set of seven. 2. a period of seven years. Also **septennate; septennial; septennium.** -*adj.* 3. of or pertaining to the number seven or forming a group of seven. Also **septennial.**

septennate, *n.* a seven-years term of office; a period of seven years. Also **septenary; septennial; septennium.**

septennial, *n.* 1. something that occurs every seven years; a period of seven years. Also **septenary; septennate; septennium.** -*adj.* 2. Occurring every seven years: of or for seven years. Also **septenary.** -*adv.* **septennially.**

septennium, *n.* (*pl.* -ia) a period of seven years. Also **septenary; septennate; septennial.**

septicentennial, *n.* a 700th anniversary or its celebration.

septuagenarian, *n.* 1. someone who has reached the age of 70 years, but is not yet 80. -*adj.* 2. between the ages of 70 and 80 years. Also **septuagenary.**

Septuagesima or Septuagesima Sunday, *n. Christian calendar.* The third Sunday before Lent or the ninth Sunday before Easter, roughly seventy days before Easter.

sesquicentenary, See **sesquicentennial.**

sesquicentennial, *n.* 1. a 150th year anniversary or its celebration. -*adj.* 2. of or pertaining to or marking the completion of a period of 150 years. Also

sesquicentenary. -sesquicen-tennially, *adv.*

sesquimillennium, *n.* 1. a period of 1500 years or 15 centuries; the anniversary or celebration of such a span of time. -*adj.* 2. of or pertaining to a period of 1500 years.

sexagenarian, *n.* 1. someone who has reached the age of 60 years, but is not yet 70. -*adj.* 2. between the ages of 60 to 70 years. Also **sexagenary.**

Sexagesima or Sexagesima Sunday, *n. Christian calendar.* the second Sunday before Lent and the eighth before Easter, approximately sixty days before Easter.

sexcentenary, *n.* 1. a 600th anniversary or its celebration. -*adj.* 2. pertaining to the number 600 or a period of 600 years; marking the completion of 600 years.

sexennial, *adj.* 1. pertaining to six years or a period of six years; occurring every six years. 2. continuing or lasting for six years. -**sexennially,** *adv.*

ship's bells, *n.* a signal of the half-hour aboard a ship. There are six four-hour watches in one 24-hour day; at the end of the first half-hour of a watch, one bell is struck; at the end of the first hour, two bells, and so on to eight bells at the end of the watch. Watches begin at 8 p.m., midnight, 4 a.m., etc.

sidereal year, *n.* the time in which the earth completes one revolution in its orbit around the sun, measured with respect to the fixed stars: 365 days, 6 hours, 9 minutes, and 9.54 seconds of solar time.

sine die, *Latin.* 'without a day,' i.e., no time fixed for future action or meeting; indefinite. Abbreviated **s.d.** See **Table 2.**

solar calendar, a calendar based on the movement of the sun.

Measured from equinox to equinox or solstice to solstice.

solar cycle, n. a period of 28 years, at the end of which the days of the month return to the same days of the week.

solar day, the 24-hour interval from one midnight to the next.

solar year, *n.* a division of time equal to the interval between one vernal equinox and the next, equal to 365 days, 5 hours, 48 minutes, and 46 seconds. Also **astronomical year, equinoctial year, tropical year.**

solstice, the time at which the sun is at its greatest distance north (about June 21, the **summer solstice**) or south (about December 22, the **winter solstice**) of the plane of the earth's equator. -**solstitial,** *adj.*

sub anno, *Latin.* 'under a year,' i.e., within the span of a given year. Abbreviated **s.a.** See **Table 2.**

synodic month, period between two successive new moons, equal to 29.531 days. See also **Metonic cycle.**

tercentenary, *n.* a 300th anniversary or its celebration. -*adj.* 2. pertaining to a 300th anniversary or its celebration. Also **tercentennial, tricentenary, tricentennial.**

tercentennial, *adj.* or *n.* See **tercentenary.**

tertian, *n.* 1. a fever with paroxysms every other day. -*adj.* 2. recurring at approximately 48-hour intervals; recurring every third day.

trecento, *n.* 1. the 14th century or 1300s, esp. with reference to art and literature in Italy [for Italian *mil tre cento* '1300']. -**trecentist,** *adj.*

triannual, *adj.* an event or publication that occurs or appears three times a year. -**triannually,** *adj.*

tricenary, *adj.* of or pertaining to

thirty days or a month; containing or lasting thirty days.

tricennial, *n.* 1. a 30-year celebration. 2. a 30th anniversary or its celebration. -*adj.* 3. of or pertaining to thirty years; taking place every thirty years.

tricentenary, See **tercentenary.**

tricentennial, See **tercentenary.**

triennial, *n.* 1. a three-year period. 2. a third anniversary; something that occurs once in three years. Also **triennium.** -*adj.* 3. consisting of or lasting for three years. 4. being done or occurring once every three years. -**triennially,** *adv.*

triennium, *n.* (*pl.* -iums; -ia) a period of three years. Also **triennial.**

trimester, *n.* 1. a period of three months. 2. one of the three terms into which an academic year may be divided. -**trimestral, trimestrial,** *adj.*

trimonthly, *n.* 1. a publication or event appearing or occurring once every three months. -*adj.* 2. occurring, appearing, being made, done, or acted upon every three months.

triweekly, *n.* 1. a publication that is issued three times a week. 2. a publication that is issued every three weeks. -*adj.* 3. occurring or appearing three times a week. -*adv.* 4. three times a week.

tropical year, See **sidereal year.**

twenty-four-hour time, *n.* system of clock-time used by the military, airlines, and continental Europe. The first two digits stand for the hour, the next two for the minutes. The last minute of the day is 2359; 0000 is midnight; 0001 is the first minute of the new day.

ultimo, *adv.* in, of, or during the preceding month, e.g., in October, the 5th ultimo is the 5th of September. See also **proximo.**

vicennial, *adj.* 1. of or for twenty years. 2. occurring once every twenty years.

weekly, *n.* 1. a periodical or event appearing or occurring once a week. *-adj.* 2. being made, done, acted upon or appearing every week. Also **hebdomadal.** *-adv.* 3. once a week, by the week. Also **hebdomadally.**

yearly, *n.* 1. a publication appearing or an event occurring once a year; an annual. *-adj.* 2. reckoned by the year; occurring or recurring every year. Also **annual.** *-adv.* 3. from year to year; once a year; annually.

TABLES

TABLE 1
Date References

ABBREVIATION	FULL TERM	TRANSLATION
A.C.	*Anno Christi* (Latin)	in the year of Christ
A.D.	*Anno Domini* (Latin)	in the year of our Lord (Christ)
aet. or aetat.	*anno aetatis suae* (Latin)	in the year of his (or her) age
A.H.	*Anno Hebraico* (Latin)	in the Hebrew year (i.e., since 3761 B.C.)
A.H.	*Anno Hegirae* or Hejirae (Latin)	in the year of the Hegira (A.D. 622)
A.H.S.	*Anno Humanae Salutis* (Latin)	in the year of man's redemption (= A.D.)
A.L.	*Anno Lucis* (Latin)	in the year of light (i.e., since 4000 B.C.)
A.M.	*Anno Mundi* (Latin)	in the year of the world (i.e., since 4004 B.C.)
A.N.C.	*Ante Nativitatem Christi* (Latin)	before the birth of Christ (= B.C.)
A.P.C.N.	*Anno Post Christum Natum* (Latin)	in the year after the birth of Christ
A.P.R.C.	*Anno Post Roman Conditam* (Latin)	in the year after the founding of Rome (which took place 753 B.C.)
A.R.	*Anno Regni* (Latin)	in the year of the reign (of king, queen)
A.S.	*Anno Salutis* (Latin)	in the year of salvation (= A.D.)
A.U.C.	*Ab Urbe Condita* or *Anno Urbis Conditae* (Latin)	in the year of the founding of Rome (753 B.C.)
B.C.	Before Christ	
B.C.E.	Before the Common Era	
B.P.	Before the Present	
C.E.	Common Era	

TABLE 2
Latin Terms of Time

ABBREVIATION	LATIN	TRANSLATION
ab init. (continued)	*ab initio*	from the beginning

TABLE 2
Latin Terms of Time (continued)

ABBREVIATION	LATIN	TRANSLATION
ad an.	*ad annum*	up to the year
ad ex.	*ad extremum*	to the extreme, to the end
ad inf.	*ad infinitum*	to infinity, endlessly, no end
ad init.	*ad initium*	at the beginning
ad int.	*ad interim*	in the meantime
ca.	*circa*	about, approximately
in pr.	*in principio*	in the beginning
pro tem.	*pro tempore*	for the time being
prox.	*proximo*	of next month
s.a.	*sine anno*	without year or date
s.a.	*sub anno*	under the year
s.d.	*sine die*	without fixing a date for future action or future meeting
ult.	*ultimo*	of last month

TABLE 3
Clock Time

ABBREVIATION	LATIN	TRANSLATION
a.m./A.M.	*ante meridiem*	before noon
m./M.	*meridies*	noon, meridian
p.m./P.M.	*post meridiem*	after noon

TABLE 4
Geologic Time

The succession of eras, periods, and epochs as considered in historical geology pertaining to the physical history and age of the earth.
(B = billion years; M = million years)

YEARS AGO	ERA	PERIOD	EPOCH
5 B to 1-1/2 B	Precambrian-Archeozoic		
1-1/2 B to 600 M	Precambrian-Proterozoic		
600 M to 500 M		Cambrian	
500 M to 440 M		Ordovician	
440 M to 400 M		Silurian	
400 M to 350 M		Devonian	
350 M to 300 M	Paleozoic	Mississippian/ Carboniferous, Lower	

(continued)

TABLE 4
Geologic Time (continued)

YEARS AGO	ERA	PERIOD	EPOCH
300 M to 270 M		Pennsylvanian/ Carboniferous, Upper	
270 M to 220 M		Permian	
220 M to 180 M		Triassic	
180 M to 135 M	Mesozoic	Jurassic	
135 M to 70 M		Cretaceous	
70 M to 60 M		Tertiary/Paleogene	Paleocene
60 M to 40 M			Eocene
40 M to 25 M			Oligocene
25 M to 10 M	Cenozoic	Tertiary/Neogene	Miocene
10 M to 1 M			Pliocene
1 M to 10,000		Quaternary	Pleistocene
10,000 to present			Holocene

TABLE 5
Prescription Abbreviations Referring to Time

ABBREVIATION	EXPANDED FORM (LATIN)	MEANING
a.c.	*ante cibos*	before meals
ad lib.	*ad libitum*	at pleasure
alt. hor.	*alternis horis*	every other hour
b.	*bis*	twice
b.i.d.	*bis in die*	twice a day
C	*Centum*	a hundred
cito disp!	*cito dispensetur!*	let it be dispensed quickly!
d.	*dies*	day
dieb. alt.	*diebus alternis*	on alternate days
dieb. secund.	*diebus secundis*	every second day
h.s.	*hora somni*	at the hour of sleep, at bedtime
i.c.	*inter cibos*	between meals
m.	*mane*	in the morning
n. et m.	*nocte et mane*	night and morning
noct.	*nocte*	at night
non rep.	*non repetatur*	do not repeat
omn. hor.	*omni hora*	at every hour
omn. man.	*omni mane*	on every morning
p.c.	*post cibos*	after meals
p.r.n.	*pro re nata*	as occasion arises, as needed
pt.	*perstetur*	let it be continued
(continued)		

TABLE 5
Prescription Abbreviations Referring to Time (continued)

ABBREVIATION	EXPANDED FORM (LATIN)	MEANING
q., qq.	*quisque* (and related forms)	each, every
q.i.d.	*quater in die*	four times a day
qq. hor.	*quaque hora*	at every hour
quot. op. sit	*quoties opus sit*	as often as necessary
ren. sem.	*renovetur semel*	shall be renewed (only) once
rept.	*repetatur*	let it be repeated
sesquih.	*sesquihora*	an hour and a half
s.o.s.	*si opus sit*	if there is need
ss.	*semis*	one half
stat.	*statim*	immediately
t.i.d.	*ter in die*	three times a day
ult.	*ultime*	lastly
vesp.	*vespera*	in the evening

TABLE 6
Time of Notes in Music

WORD	DEFINITION
breve	twice as long as a whole note
whole note	the standard measure; also semibreve
half note	half the time of a whole note; also minim
quarter note	one-quarter the time of a whole note; also crotchet
eighth note	one-eighth the time of a whole note; also quaver
sixteenth note	one-sixteenth the time of a whole note; also semiquaver
thirty-second note	one thirty-second of a whole note; also demisemiquaver
sixty-fourth note	one sixty-fourth of a whole note; also hemidemisemiquaver

TABLE 7
Anniversaries and Suggested Gifts

YEAR	TRADITIONAL GIFT	MODERN GIFT
1st	Paper	Clock
2nd	Cotton	China
3rd	Leather	Crystal or Glass
4th	Fruit or Flowers	Appliances
5th	Wood	Silverware
(continued)		

TABLE 7

Anniversaries and Suggested Gifts (continued)

YEAR	TRADITIONAL GIFT	MODERN GIFT
6th	Candy or Ironware	Wood
7th	Copper or Wool	Pens, Pencils, Desk Sets
8th	Pottery or Bronze	Linens or Laces
9th	Pottery or Willow	Leather
10th	Aluminum or Tin	Diamond Jewelry
11th	Steel	Fashion Jewelry and Accessories
12th	Silk or Linen	Pearls or Colored Gems
13th	Lace	Textiles or Furs
14th	Ivory	Gold Jewelry
15th	Crystal	Watches
16th		Silver Hollow Ware
17th		Furniture
18th		Porcelain
19th		Bronze
20th	China	Platinum
25th (Jubilee)	Silver	Silver
30th	Pearl	Diamond
35th	Coral	Jade
40th	Ruby	Ruby
45th	Sapphire	Sapphire
50th (Jubilee)	Gold	Gold
55th	Emerald	Emerald
60th (Jubilee)	Diamond	Diamond
75th (Jubilee)	Diamond	Diamond

JANUARY

January is the first month of the Gregorian calendar and has 31 days. The early Roman calendar, discussed in the Introduction, was organized on the basis of ten months, with a winter gap occurring between December, the tenth month, and March, then the first month; January and February did not exist as months. During the reign of the Roman king Numa Pompilius (715–673 B.C.), the calendar was expanded from ten to twelve months, and *Januarius* and *Februarius* were the names given to the new months.

During the period of the Etruscan kings at Rome (616–510 B.C.), the beginning of the year was moved to January 1. With the expulsion of the kings in 510 B.C., the beginning of the year reverted to March 1, and so it remained through much of the Roman Republican period.

In 153 B.C., January 1 was officially set as the beginning of the new civil year at Rome, i.e., the day that newly elected consuls took office, and it has retained that position through both the Julian and Gregorian calendar reforms. However, popular usage long continued to regard March as the beginning of the year, primarily owing to the occurrence of the vernal equinox in that month, marking the beginning of a new agricultural season (see also at **March**).

January (Latin *Januarius*) is derived from the name of the ancient Roman deity, *Janus,* the god of gates and doors and, hence, all beginnings, whose image is of two faces, one looking forward and one back. Janus was also regarded as the protector of ships and trade, apparently as a sort of providential deity. January, the month which looked both to the past and the future, came to be important in Roman ritual and was consecrated by offerings of wine, salt, meal, and frankincense. On the first day of January, Romans exchanged gifts of small coins bearing the image of Janus on one side and a ship on the other.

In the astrological calendar, January spans the zodiacal signs of Capricorn, the Goat (December 22–January 19) and Aquarius, the Water Bearer (January 20–February 18).

The birthstone for January is the garnet, and the flower is the carnation or snowdrop.

STATE, NATIONAL, AND INTERNATIONAL HOLIDAYS

New Year's Day
January 1

George Washington Carver Day
(United States)
January 5

Three Kings' Day
(Puerto Rico)
January 6

Battle of New Orleans Day
(Louisiana)
January 8

DeHostos' Birthday
(Puerto Rico)
January 11

Feast of Christ of Esquipulas or the Black Christ Festival
(Guatemala)
January 15

Teacher's Day
(Venezuela)
January 15

Confederate Heroes' Day
(Texas)
January 19

Franklin D. Roosevelt's Birthday
(Kentucky)
January 30

Handsel Monday
(Scotland)
First Monday

Maitlisunntig
(Switzerland)
Second Sunday

Martin Luther King, Jr.'s Birthday
(United States)
Third Monday; an official national holiday beginning in 1986

Robert E. Lee's Birthday
(Alabama, Mississippi)
Third Monday
(Arkansas, Florida, Georgia, Kentucky, Louisiana, South Carolina)
January 19

Lee-Jackson Day
(Virginia)
Third Monday

SPECIAL EVENTS AND THEIR SPONSORS

Stamp Collector's Month
Franklin D. Roosevelt Philatelic Society

Weeks' Week
First Week
Richard R. Falk Associates

Man Watchers' Week
Second Week
Man Watchers, Inc.

International Printing Week
Third Week
International Association of Printing HouseCraftsmen

Printing Ink Day
Tuesday of International Printing Week, above
National Association of Printing Ink Manufacturers

National Jaycees Week
Third Week
United States Jaycees

World-wide Kiwanis Week
Third Week
Kiwanis International

Graphics Communication Week
Week of January 17
International Graphic Arts Education Association, Inc.

Junior Achievement Week
Final Week
Junior Achievement Inc.

Trivia Day
January 4
Puns Corp.

Benjamin Franklin's Birthday
January 17

Philately Day
January 20

Franklin D. Roosevelt's Birthday Anniversary
January 30
Franklin D. Roosevelt Philatelic Society

Handwriting Day
January 23
Writing Instrument Manufacturers Association

HOLIDAYS

New Year's Day
Observed in all countries of the world that follow the Gregorian calendar.

Albania
Anniversary Day

Cameroon
Independence Day

Cuba
Liberation Day or Anniversary of the Triumph of the Revolution
Commemorates the overthrow of the Batista government by Fidel Castro, 1959.

Haiti
Independence Day
Commemorates the declaration of independence of the island by Jean Jacques Dessalines, 1804. Also called *Heroes Day, Ancestors Day,* or *The Day of the Glorification of the Heroes of Independence.*

Palau
Independence Day

Somali Democratic Republic
Bank Holiday

Sudan
Independence Day
Celebrates Sudan's treaty of independence with Great Britain, 1956.

Taiwan
Founding of Republic of China
Celebrates the establishment of the Republic by Chiang Kaishek, 1949.

Western Samoa
Independence Day

RELIGIOUS CALENDAR

Solemnities
Octave of Christmas Commemorates the *Circumcision of Christ.*
Solemnity of Mary, Mother of God Sometimes called the *Birthday of Mary;* honors the divine motherhood of Mary. Celebrated on December 26 in the Byzantine and Syrian churches; on January 16 in the Coptic rite.

The Saints
St. Concordius, martyr. Also called *Concord.* [d. c. 178]
St. Almachius, martyr. Also called *Telemachus.* [d. c. 400]
St. Euphrosyne, virgin. Called *Our Mother* by the Greeks. [d. c. fifth century]
St. Eugendus, Abbot of the Monastery of Condat (Saint-Oyend). Also called *Oyend.* [d. c. 510]
St. Fulgentius, Bishop of Ruspe. [d. 533]
St. Felix of Bourges, bishop. [d. c. 580]
St. Clarus, Abbot of the Monastery of St. Marcellus at Vienne in Dauphine. First monk in the Abbey of St. Ferreol. [d. c. 660]
St. Peter of Atroa, abbot. [d. 837]
St. William of Saint Benignus, abbot; advocate of Cluniac reform. [d. 1031]

St. Odilo, abbot of the monastery at Cluny; instituted the annual commemoration of all the faithful departed on November 2, or All Souls' Day. Also called *Alou, Olon.* [d. 1049]
St. Zdislava, matron. Founded the Dominican priory of St. Laurence. [d. 1252]

The Beatified
Blessed Hugolino of Gualdo, abbot. [d. 1260]
Blessed Joseph Tommasi, Cardinal of the Holy Roman Church. Called the *Prince of Liturgists.* [d. 1713]

BIRTHDATES

1449 *Lorenzo de Medici,* Florentine statesman, merchant prince, patron of the arts. [d. April 8, 1492]

1484 *Huldrych (Ulrich) Zwingli,* Swiss Protestant reformer; leader of the Protestant Reformation. [d. October 11, 1531]

1618 *Bartolomé Esteban Murillo,* Spanish baroque religious painter. [d. April 13, 1682]

1697 *Joseph Dupleix,* Governor-General of French possessions in India, 1742–54. [d. November 10, 1763]

1735 *Paul Revere,* American patriot, silver-smith; his

famous ride (April 18, 1775) to warn the colonists of the arrival of the British made him a legend in American history. [d. May 10, 1818]

1745 *Anthony (Mad Anthony) Wayne,* American Revolutionary general; his capture of the fortress at *Stony Point, New York,* provided great inspiration for the colonial cause. [d. December 15, 1796]

1750 *Frederick Augustus Conrad Muhlenberg,* U.S. statesman, Lutheran clergyman; first president, *Muhlenberg College,* Pennsylvania, 1867–76. [d. June 4, 1801]

1752 *(Elizabeth) Betsy Ross,* American colonial patriot; reputed to have sewn the first American flag. [d. January 30, 1836]

1823 *Sandor Petofi (Petrovics),* Hungarian poet and revolutionary; among the first of Hungary's lyric poets; his lyrics for revolutionary patriotic songs won him recognition as the *national poet of Hungary.* [d. July 31, 1849]

1834 *Ludovic Halévy,* French dramatist, novelist, born in Turkey; known for his theory that the Sumerian people never existed and that their writings were merely secret codes of the Babylonian priesthood. [d. May 8, 1908]

1854 *Sir James George Frazer,* Scottish anthropologist, classicist; best known as the author of *The Golden Bough.* [d. May 7, 1941]

1859 *Michael J. Owens,* U.S. inventor of the automatic *bottle-making machine;* a

founder of the *Libbey-Owens Sheet Glass Co.,* 1916. [d. December 27, 1923]

1863 *Pierre Coubertin,* French sportsman; revived *Olympic Games* in 1894; President of the International Olympic Committee, 1894–1925. [d. September 1, 1937]

1864 *Alfred Stieglitz,* U.S. photographer; known as the *Father of Modern Photography.* [d. July 13, 1946]

1879 *E(dward) M(organ) Forster,* British novelist, critic. [d. June 7, 1970]

William Fox, U.S. film executive; founder of *Twentieth-Century Fox.* [d. 1952]

Ernest Jones, British psychoanalyst; popularizer, translator and biographer of Sigmund Freud. [d. February 11, 1958]

1883 *Roy Wilson Howard,* U.S. newspaperman; a founder of the *Scripps-Howard* newspaper chain. [d. November 20, 1964]

William Joseph (Wild Bill) Donovan, U.S. Army general, lawyer, public official; World War I hero; Congressional Medal of Honor; World War II Head of Office of Strategic Services, 1942–45. [d. February 8, 1959]

1887 *Wilhelm Franz Canaris,* German admiral; chief of military intelligence, anti-Hitler conspirator. [d. April 9, 1945]

1888 *John Cantius Garand,* U.S. rifle inventor, designer; designer of the *M-1 rifle,* the

basic weapon of U.S. infantry during World War II. [d. February 16, 1974]

1892 *Manuel Roxas y Acuna,* Philippine statesman, first president of the Philippines, 1946–48. [d. April 15, 1948]

Martin Niemöller, German priest; open opponent of Hitler in the 1930s; President of the World Council of Churches. [d. March 6, 1984]

1895 *J(ohn) Edgar Hoover,* U.S. government official, lawyer, criminologist; director of F.B.I., 1924–72. [d. May 1, 1972]

Red Allen, U.S. musician; Dixieland-jazz trumpet player. [d. April 17, 1967]

1900 *Xavier Cugat,* Spanish bandleader; popularized the rhumba, cha-cha, and mambo dances, 1940s–50s. [d. October 27, 1990]

1909 *Barry (Morris) Goldwater,* U.S. Senator, 1953–64, 1969–86; Republican Party nominee for President, 1964. [d. May 29, 1998]

1911 *Pierre Samuel DuPont, III,* U.S. business executive.

Hank Greenberg, U.S. baseball player; elected to Baseball Hall of Fame, 1956. [d. September 4, 1986]

1912 *Harold (Kim) Philby,* Soviet master-spy in British intelligence, 1933–63; defected and escaped to the Soviet Union. [d. May 11, 1988]

1913 *Eliot Janeway,* U.S. economist, author. [d. February 8, 1993]

1919 *J(erome) D(avid) Salinger,* U.S. novelist, short-story writer; author of *Catcher in the Rye, Franny and Zooey.*

1922 *Ernest Frederick (Fritz) Hollings,* U.S. politician; Senator, 1966– .

1923 *Milt(on) Jackson,* U.S. musician.

1930 *Goafar Mohammed Nimeiri,* Sudanese political leader; President, 1971–85; Prime Minister, 1977–85.

Frederick Wiseman, U.S. filmmaker.

1932 *Terry Moore (Helen Koford),* U.S. actress; wife of Howard Hughes.

1936 *Richard Vincent Allen,* U.S. government official; National Security Council advisor, 1981–82.

1940 *Frank Langella,* U.S. actor; Tony Award winner for *Seascape,* 1977.

1943 *Don Novello,* U.S. comedic actor; best known for his role as Father Guido Sarducci on television series, *Saturday Night Live.*

1953 *Afonso Dhlakama,* Mozambique politician.

1957 *Nancy Lopez,* U.S. golfer; named Rookie of the Year and Player of the year, 1978; set record (of $153,336) for rookie earnings.

HISTORICAL EVENTS

1515 *Louis XII* of France dies and is succeeded by *Francis I.*

1519 *Ulrich Zwingli,* Swiss religious reformer, is ordained at Zurich.

1531 *Rio de Janeiro (River of January),* in Brazil, is discovered by Portuguese navigators.

1547 *Michelangelo* is appointed chief architect of St. Peter's by *Pope Paul III.*

1596 The first Dutch colonists land on *Sumatra,* Indonesia, an ancient trade center.

1651 *King Charles II* is crowned King of Scotland, marking the last coronation at Scone.

1673 Dutch capture *St. Helena Island,* in the South Atlantic, from the British.

1776 First U.S. flag, *The Great Union,* is displayed by *George Washington;* it becomes the unofficial national flag, preceding the 13-star, 13-stripe version.

1801 Legislative Union of Great Britain with Ireland under the name of *United Kingdom* becomes effective.

1804 *Haiti* declares its independence from France.

1808 Importation of slaves into the U.S. is officially banned.

Sierra Leone becomes a crown colony of Great Britain.

1833 Great Britain gains sovereignty over the *Falkland Islands.*

1840 First recorded *ten-pin bowling match* is played at *Knickerbocker Alleys,* New York City.

1863 The *Emancipation Proclamation* becomes law, marking the end of legalized slavery in the U.S.

1871 *Church of Ireland* is established.

1873 Japan adopts the *Gregorian calendar.*

1876 Egypt adopts the *Gregorian calendar.*

1877 *Queen Victoria* is proclaimed Empress of Egypt and India.

1886 *Upper Burma* is annexed by the British.

1889 State of New York introduces use of the *electric chair* for capital punishment.

1890 Italian possessions on the Red Sea in *Eritrea* are united as a colony.

1892 The U.S. government opens an immigrant processing station at *Ellis Island, New York.*

1898 The five boroughs of New York are joined to form greater *New York.*

1900 *Upper Nigeria, Lower Nigeria,* and *Lagos* are proclaimed protectorates of Great Britain.

1901 The *Commonwealth of Australia* is proclaimed, consisting of New South Wales, Victoria, Queensland, South Australia, Western Australia, and Tasmania.

1902 First *Rose Bowl* football game is played at Pasadena, California.

1903 *King Edward VII* of Great Britain is proclaimed Emperor of India.

1908 *Gustav Mahler* makes his first American appearance, conducting the Metropolitan Opera in *Tristan und Isolde.*

1912 The *Chinese Republic* is declared; *Dr. Sun Yat-sen* is sworn in as provisional president.

1913 *U.S. Parcel Post* begins.

1914 The Colony and Protectorate of *Nigeria* is formed from ten old British protectorates of Southern and Northern Nigeria.

1915 The British battleship *Formidable* is sunk in the English Channel by a German submarine with the loss of 600 lives (*World War I*).

1917 *Rasputin's* body is taken from the Neva River in St. Petersburg, Russia, following his assassination by Russian noblemen.

1920 The *eight-hour workday* becomes law in Sweden.

1921 New *Elementary Education Act* goes into effect in the *Netherlands*.

Mauritania becomes a separate French colony.

1922 French and Flemish are declared official languages in *Belgium*.

1925 *Christiana*, the capital of Norway, resumes the name *Oslo*.

Damascus and *Aleppo* are united to form the state of *Syria* by decree of the French government.

1927 The *metric system* of weights and measures is adopted by the U.S.S.R.

1930 The *Indian National Congress* votes for complete independence.

1934 *Fiorello LaGuardia* is inaugurated as mayor of New York.

1937 The first *Cotton Bowl* football game is played in Dallas, Texas.

1942 *Atlantic Charter* officially proclaimed.

The Allied nations begin their *East Indies Campaign* (*World War II*).

1945 *British 14th Army* offensive in Burma begins (*World War II*).

1947 *Great Britain* nationalizes its coal mines and communications.

1948 *Great Britain* nationalizes its railways.

1950 The U.S. Navy commissions its first woman doctor, *Mary Sproul*.

1951 The *Saar* becomes independent from France but retains its economic union.

1956 *Sudan* gains independence from Great Britain and Egypt.

1957 The Saar region is officially transferred from French to West German control. *Saarland* becomes the 10th West German state.

1958 *European Economic Community*, referred to as the *Common Market*, is formed.

1960 *Cameroon* becomes independent of France.

1962 *Western Samoa* becomes independent.

1965 *Intermall*, an international steel trust made up of the U.S.S.R. and five Eastern European nations, begins operations from headquarters in Budapest, Hungary.

1966 *Col. Jean-Bedel Bokassa* assumes power in the Central African Republic after a coup d'état.

1968 *C(ecil) Day Lewis* is named Poet Laureate of Great Britain, succeeding John Masefield.

1969 New *Czechoslovak federal government* is inaugurated, marking the beginning of a massive Communist Party reorganization in that country.

1970 *Great Britain* lowers the age for voting, making contracts, and holding property to 18.

1972 *Kurt Waldheim* is inaugurated as secretary general of the United Nations.

1973 United Kingdom, Ireland, and Denmark become members of the *European Economic Community* or *Common Market*.

1975 *John Ehrlichman*, *H. R. Haldeman*, and *John Mitchell* are found guilty of obstructing justice in the *Watergate incident*.

1977 *Episcopal Church of U.S.* ordains its first woman priest.

1979 The *People's Republic of China* and the U.S. establish full diplomatic relations as the U.S. simultaneously severs diplomatic relations with Chinese Nationalists in Taiwan.

The Chinese government introduces *Pinyin*, a new transliteration system.

1981 *Premier Abdou Diouf* is named President of *Senegal*.

Greece officially becomes the tenth member of the *European Economic Community* (Common Market).

1984 *American Telephone & Telegraph Co.* officially divests itself of 22 Bell System subsidiaries.

Brunei becomes fully independent of Great Britain.

The last trade barriers for industrial goods between the member nations of the *European Community* and the *European Free Trade*

Association are officially removed. The elimination of quotas and tariffs on finished products creates a 17-country free trade area.

Major General *Mohammed Buhari* stages a bloodless coup in Nigeria.

France receives its first allotment of *natural gas* as part of a 25-year contract with the Soviet Union.

1986 *Aruba* becomes a self-governing island within the realm of the Kingdom of the Netherlands.

Spain and Portugal become official members of the *European Community*.

1987 Bolivia issues its new currency, the *boliviano,* which equals $1 million old pesos.

1990 *Poland* begins free-market rules, causing a glut of consumer goods on the market at high prices.

1992 *Boutros Boutros-Ghali* becomes secretary-general of the United Nations.

1993 The *European Community* permits free movement of goods across national borders.

The *Czech Republic* and *Slovakia* are formed after the division of Czechoslovakia.

1994 *Zapatista National Liberation Army* stages a rebellion in the Chiapas province of Mexico.

1995 The *World Trade Organization* comes into existence, succeeding the *General Agreement on Tariffs and Trade (GATT).*

1998 *Mongolia* begins a 40-hour, 5-day work week. Previous work weeks lasted 46 hours over 6 days.

Peter Treseder, Ian Brown, and *Keith Williams* become the first Australians to reach the South Pole.

january

JANUARY
2

HOLIDAYS

Botswana
Public holiday

Haiti
*Ancestry Day or Heroes of
Independence Day*

Japan
Bank Holiday

Mauritius
New Year's Day

New Zealand
New Year's Day

St. Lucia
Public holiday

Scotland
New Year's Day

Seychelles
Bank Holiday

Slovenia
New Year's Day

South Korea
New Year's Day

Switzerland
Berchtoldstag or Berchtold's Day.
Honors the 12th century *Duke
Berchtold V,* who founded the City
of *Berne.*

Taiwan
Founding of the Republic of China

RELIGIOUS CALENDAR

Solemnities
Feast of the Holy Name of Jesus
Celebrated January 2 when
there is no Sunday between
January 1 and January 6.
Otherwise, a moveable feast
falling on the Sunday between
January 1, the Circumcision,
and January 6, the Epiphany.
Suppressed 1970.

The Saints
St. Basil the Great, Archbishop of
Caesarea, Doctor of the
Church, and patriarch of
Eastern monks; founder of
the Order of Basilicans. Feast
formerly June 14. [d. 379]
Obligatory Memorial.
St. Gregory Nazianzen, Bishop of
Constantinople and Doctor of
the Church; one of the very
earliest of Christian poets.
Surnamed the *Theologian;*
also called *Nazianzus.* Feast
formerly May 9. [d. 390]
Obligatory Memorial.
St. Macarius of Alexandria, monk;
called the *Younger;* patron
saint of pastry cooks and
confectioners. [d. 394]
St. Munchin, bishop. Called the
Wise. Principal patron saint of
the Diocese of Limerick. Feast
celebrated throughout
Ireland. [d. 7th century]
St. Vincentian. [d. c. 672]
St. Adalhard, abbot; cousin to
Emperor *Charlemagne.*
Founder of Monastery of New
Corbie, or Corwey. Also called
Adalard, Adelard, Alard. [d.
827]
St. Caspar del Bufalo, priest;
founder of the Missioners of
the Precious Blood. [d. 1837]

The Beatified
Blessed Ayrald, Bishop of
Maurienne. [d. c. 1146]
Blessed Stephana Quinzani, virgin;
founder of the Convent at
Soncino. [d. 1530]

BIRTHDATES

1647 *Nathaniel Bacon,* American
colonial leader, pioneer;
leader of *Bacon's Rebellion*
against the Indians in Virginia,
1676. [d. October 1676]

1721 *John Manners,* Marquis of
Granby, British military
commander; commander in
chief of English forces during
the *Seven Years' War.* [d.
October 18, 1770]

1727 *James Wolfe,* British army
general; led the British
expedition against Quebec,
1759; completed British
conquest of North America.
[d. September 13, 1759]

1751 *Ferdinand IV,* King of Naples;
also, *Ferdinand III,* King of
Sicily; *Ferdinand I,* King of
the Two Sicilies, 1816–20. [d.
January 4, 1825]

1752 *Philip Morin Freneau,*
American poet, journalist;
known as the *Poet of the
American Revolution.* [d.
December 19, 1832]

1831 *Justin Winsor,* U.S. historian;
librarian of Boston Public

january

Library, 1866–77; and of Harvard College, 1877–97; a founder and first president of the *American Library Association*, 1876–88. [d. October 22, 1897]

1836 *Mendele Mokher Sforim*, writer, co-founder of modern Yiddish literature. [d. 1917]

1857 *Frederick Burr Opper*, U.S. cartoonist. [d. August 28, 1937]

Martha Carey Thomas, U.S. educator, suffragist; President of *Bryn Mawr College*, 1894–1922. [d. December 2, 1935]

1866 *(George) Gilbert Murray*, British classical scholar, translator; recognized as a guiding force in the creation of the *League of Nations*. [d. May 20, 1957]

1895 *Count Folke Bernadotte*, Swedish statesman, Red Cross official; UN mediator in Palestine during the partition of Palestine after British withdrawal. Assassinated by Israeli extremists. [d. September 17, 1948]

1904 *Sally Rand (Helen Beck)*, U.S. fan dancer. [d. August 31, 1979]

1920 *Isaac Asimov*, U.S. biochemist, author born in Russia; noted for his prolific work and clear style of writing on extremely complicated subjects. [d. April 16, 1992]

1922 *Renata Tebaldi*, Italian operatic lyric soprano.

1928 *Dan(iel David) Rostenkowski*, U.S. politician; Congressman, 1958–94.

1930 *Julius LaRosa*, U.S. singer.

1936 *Roger Dean Miller*, U.S. singer; 11 Grammy Awards. [d. October 25, 1992]

1938 *Lynn Conway*, U.S. electrical engineer; known for her simplification of the computer chip design.

1939 *James Orsen (Jim) Bakker*, U.S. clergyman, television personality; founded PTL Club Ministry; fired as president and defrocked after sex scandal and misuse of funds, 1987.

1968 *Cuba Gooding, Jr.*, U.S. actor; Academy Award winner (Best Supporting Actor) for his performance in *Jerry Maguire*, 1996.

HISTORICAL EVENTS

1492 Moors surrender *Granada* to Spain.

1788 *Georgia* ratifies *U.S. Constitution*.

1799 *Napoleon Bonaparte* advances into *Syria*.

1861 *Frederick William IV* of Prussia dies and is succeeded by *William I*.

1896 Men of the *Jameson Raid*, including *Starr Jameson*, are captured by the Boers at Doornkop, South African Republic *(Boer War)*.

1901 First municipal crematorium opens in England, at *Hull*.

1905 Russians are defeated at *Port Arthur* by the Japanese *(Russo-Japanese War)*.

1915 Turks are defeated by the Russians in the *Battle of Sarikamish* in the Caucasus *(World War I)*.

1922 *Ukraine* signs treaty with Turkey recognizing independence of the Ukraine.

1926 *Royal Academy of Italy* is created.

1942 Japanese invade and occupy *Manila* and the *Philippines* after successful attack on *Pearl Harbor*.

1945 *Japanese-American citizens* who were placed in internment camps during World War II are released.

1946 *King Zog* of Albania is deposed *in absentia*.

1955 *José Antonio Remón*, President of Panama 1951–1955, is assassinated.

1959 *Fidel Castro* and his followers capture *Santiago, Cuba*; *Fulgencio Batista* goes into exile.

Luna I, first Soviet moon probe, is launched.

1960 The U.S. Federal Trade Commission charges seven record companies and eight distribution firms with paying disc-jockeys to play certain songs *(Payola Incident)*.

1962 *King Hassan II of Morocco* signs decree creating a free zone in the port of *Tangier*.

1963 General *Lyman L. Lemnitzer* becomes the supreme commander of NATO.

1968 *Robert Clark* is seated as first black legislator in *Mississippi* in 74 years.

Philip Blaiberg becomes the third recipient of a transplanted heart.

1973 *Rafael Hernandez Colon* is inaugurated as fourth governor of Puerto Rico.

1975 *Elizabeth Domitien* is named the first woman premier in Africa by the President of the *Central African Republic,* Jean-Bedel Bokassa.

1988 President Ronald Reagan and Prime Minister Brian Mulroney sign the final version of the *U.S.-Canadian* *trade accord.* The pact provides for the elimination of tariffs on most goods within 10 years and creates a series of binational groups to regulate the agreement.

1989 *Ranasinghe Premadasa* is inaugurated as president of Sri Lanka.

U.S. President *Ronald Reagan* and Canadian Prime Minister *Brian Mulroney* sign trade agreement, ending tariffs and reducing other trade barriers.

1998 Premier *Josef Tosovsky* takes office in the Czech Republic.

HOLIDAYS

Burkina Faso
Revolution Day

Japan
Genshi-Sai or First Beginning
One of the four great holidays of the Emperor and his family; observed by the reading of the Imperial Proclamations.

Bank Holiday

U.S. (Alaska)
Admission Day
Celebrates Alaska's admission to the Union as the 49th state.

Upper Volta
Revolution Day

RELIGIOUS CALENDAR

The Saints
St. Antherus, Pope and martyr. Elected Bishop of Rome 235. Also called *Anterus.* [d. 236]
St. Peter Balsam, martyr. [d. 311]
St. Geneviève, virgin. Patroness of Paris, secretaries, actors, lawyers, and the Woman's Army Corps. Invoked against fever. Also called *Genovefa, Genoveffa.* [d. c. 500]
St. Bertilia of Mareuil, widow. [d. 8th century]

The Beatified
Blessed Alanus de Solminihac. [beatified 1981]

BIRTHDATES

106BC *Marcus Tullius Cicero,* Roman orator, statesman, philosopher. [d. 43 B.C.]

1698 *Pietro Antonio Domenico Buonaventura Metastasio,* Italian poet, dramatist; celebrated librettist. [d. April 12, 1782]

1793 *Lucretia (Coffin) Mott,* U.S. abolitionist, feminist, Quaker minister; with Elizabeth Cady Stanton (November 12) founded the women's rights movement in the U.S. [d. November 11, 1880]

1823 *Robert Whitehead,* British engineer; inventor of the *naval torpedo.* [d. November 14, 1905]

1835 *Larkin Goldsmith Mead,* U.S. sculptor; among his works are the statue of *Ethan Allen,* Montpelier, Vermont, and *Abraham Lincoln,* Springfield, Illinois. [d. October 15, 1910]

1840 *Joseph Damie de Veuster (Father Damien),* Belgian priest; known for his missionary work in the leper colony in Molokai, Hawaii. [d. April 15, 1889]

1876 *Wilhelm Pieck,* German Communist leader, President of German Democratic Republic (East Germany), 1949–60. [d. September 1960]

1879 *Grace Coolidge,* wife of U.S. President Calvin Coolidge. [d. July 8, 1957]

1883 *Clement (Richard) Attlee,* Viscount Prestwood, British politician; Prime Minister, 1945–52. [d. October 8, 1967]

1886 *Raymond Ames Spruance,* U.S. admiral; Ambassador to the Philippines, 1951–55. [d. December 13, 1969]

1892 *J(ohn) R(onald) R(euel) Tolkien,* British philologist, writer; known for his fantasy novels including *The Hobbit* and *The Lord of the Rings.* [d. September 2, 1973]

1897 *Marion Davies,* U.S. actress; mistress of William Randolph Hearst; affair depicted inn *Citizen Kane,* 1941. [d. September 22, 1961]

1898 *T(ubal) Claude Ryan,* U.S. aircraft manufacturer; established first year-round passenger air service in U.S.; responsible for design and construction of Charles A. Lindbergh's *Spirit of St. Louis.* [d. September 11, 1982]

1900 *Eliza Susan (Zasu) Pitts,* U.S. actress, comedienne. [d. June 7, 1963]

1901 *Ngo Dinh Diem,* Vietnamese leader; President of the Republic of Vietnam, 1954–63. [d. November 2, 1963]

1908 *Ray(mond Alton) Milland,* U.S. actor, director; Oscar Award for *The Lost Week-end,* 1945. [d. March 10, 1986]

1909 *Victor Borge,* Danish-American pianist, comedian.

1916 *Elizabeth Mary (Betty) Furness,* U.S. actress, public official; Chairman, Committee on Consumer Interests, 1967–69. [d. April 2, 1994]

1917 *Vernon Anthony Walters,* U.S. diplomat; Ambassador to the United Nations, 1985–89; Ambassador to Germany, 89–91.

1918 *Maxine Andrews,* U.S. singer; member of singing group, *The Andrews Sisters.* [d. October 21, 1995]

1926 *Joan Walsh Anglund,* U.S. author, illustrator; popular illustrator of children's books; wrote *A Friend is Someone Who Likes You,* 1958.

1932 *Dabney Coleman,* U.S. actor; known for his role as Bill Bittinger on television series, *Buffalo Bill,* 1983–84.

1933 *Richard W. Riley,* U.S. lawyer; U.S. Secretary of Education, 1993– .

1934 *Carla Anderson Hills,* U.S. government official; Secretary, Department of Housing and Urban Development, 1975–77.

1936 *Betty Rollin,* U.S. author, broadcast journalist; wrote *First, You Cry,* 1976.

Loret Miller Ruppe, U.S. government official; Director of Peace Corps, 1981–89; Ambassador to Norway, 89–93.

1939 *Robert Martin (Bobby) Hull,* Canadian hockey player, sportscaster; known for slap shot.

1944 *Robert Lacey,* British author; wrote *Ford: The Men and the Machine,* 1986.

Victoria Principal, U.S. actress; best known for her role as Pamela Ewing on television series, *Dallas,* 1978–87.

1945 *Stephen Stills,* U.S. musician, singer, songwriter; member of the rock group, *Crosby, Stills, Nash, and Young.*

1946 *John Paul Jones,* British musician; member of the rock group, *Led Zeppelin.*

1956 *Mel Gibson,* U.S. actor, director; known for roles in the *Lethal Weapon* movies. Academy Award for best picture, *Braveheart,* 1995.

HISTORICAL EVENTS

1322 *Philip V* of France dies and is succeeded by *Charles IV.*

1399 *Timur (Tamerlane)* and his Mongols, at the height of their power in Asia, defeat *Emperor Mahmud* of India and gain control of Delhi.

1521 *Martin Luther* is formally excommunicated from the Roman Catholic Church by *Pope Leo X.*

1661 In England, *female actresses* appear on stage for the first time.

1777 General *George Washington* defeats the British under *Lord Cornwallis* at the *Battle of Princeton.*

1847 *Yerba Buena,* a U.S. town of 200 people, is renamed *San Francisco.*

1857 *Archbishop Sebour* of Paris is assassinated by *Verger,* a priest.

1868 The *Emperor of Japan* assumes direct control of the government, precipitating civil war with forces of the shogunate.

1870 Construction begins on the *Brooklyn Bridge.*

1888 Waxed paper *drinking straws* are patented in the United States.

1895 *An Ideal Husband,* by *Oscar Wilde,* premieres at the Haymarket Theatre, London.

1903 *Shanghai* is evacuated by last detachment of German troops (*Boxer Rebellion*).

1921 First parliament in India meets.

1925 *Benito Mussolini* proclaims a Fascist dictatorship in Italy.

1928 *Leon Trotsky* and thirty other members of the opposition are banished to the provinces of the Soviet Union.

1938 *March of Dimes* anti-polio campaign is organized in the U. S.

1941 *Sergei Rachmaninoff's* suite, *Symphonic Dances,* premieres in Philadelphia; it is performed by the Philadelphia Orchestra, Eugene Ormandy conducting.

1946 *William Joyce,* nicknamed *Lord Haw-Haw,* British broadcaster of propaganda from Nazi Germany during World War II, is hanged in Great Britain for treason.

1951 U.S. President *Harry S. Truman* creates the *Defense Production Administration,* headed by William H. Harrison, to centralize various emergency production agencies.

1952 *Dragnet* makes it television debut.

1958 Members of the newly created *U.S. Civil Rights Commission* take office.

1959 *Alaska* is admitted to the Union as the 49th state.

1960 *Moscow State Symphony,* performs in New York City, becoming the first Russian orchestra to perform in the U.S.

1961 U.S. breaks diplomatic relations with *Cuba.*

1962 The Vatican excommunicates Cuban premier, *Fidel Castro,* from the Roman Catholic Church.

1967 *Jack Ruby,* who shot *Lee Harvey Oswald,* alleged assassin of U.S. President *John F. Kennedy,* dies in a Dallas hospital.

1970 *People's Republic of the Congo* is formed under a new constitution.

1972 *William Tolbert, Jr.,* is inaugurated as President of *Liberia.*

1974 Spain's new premier, *Carlos Arias Navarro,* forms a new cabinet, following the assassination of *Luis Carrero Blanco.*

The *Socialist Republic of the Union of Burma* is proclaimed.

1975 *Lopez Rega* becomes the most powerful man in Argentine government when President *Isabel Perón* gives him special powers.

1983 *Fernando Schwalb Lopez Aldana* is inaugurated as prime minister of Peru.

Times Beach, Missouri is declared a federal disaster area after fall floods spread dangerous amounts of the toxic chemical *dioxin.*

1985 *Leontyne Price* makes her farewell appearance at New York's Metropolitan Opera in the title role of Verdi's *Aida.*

1990 General *Manuel Noriega* is arrested by U.S. invasion forces in Panama (December 20, 1989).

1993 Presidents *George Bush* and *Boris Yeltsin* sign the Strategic Arms Reduction Treaty (START II) in Moscow.

january

JANUARY
4

HOLIDAYS

Burma
Independence Day
Commemorates achievement of
independence from Great Britain,
1948.

**Democratic Republic of the
Congo**
*Commemoration of the Martyrs of
Independence.*

U.S. (Utah)
Admission Day
Commemorates Utah's entry into
the Union, 1896.

RELIGIOUS CALENDAR

The Saints
St. Gregory, Bishop of Langes. [d.
539]
St. Pharaildis, virgin. Invoked by
mothers who are anxious
about their children's health.
Also called *Varelde, Veerle,
Verylde.* [d. c. 740]
St. Rigobert, Archbishop of Rheims.
Also called *Robert.* [d. c. 745]
St. Elizabeth Ann Seton, nun;
founder of the American
Sisters of Charity. First native-
born American citizen to be
canonized. [d. 1821]

The Beatified
Blessed Roger of Ellant, founder of
Monastery of Ellant in
Diocese of Rheims. [d. 1160]
Blessed Oringa, virgin. [d. 1310]

BIRTHDATES

1581 *James Ussher,* Irish scholar,
prelate of Ireland; Archbishop
of Armagh, 1625; known for
his scheme of Biblical
chronology which dated
creation at 4004 B.C. [d. March
21, 1656]

1643 *Sir Isaac Newton,* English
physicist, mathematician;
leader of 17th century
scientific revolution. [d.
March 20, 1727]

1710 *Giovanni Pergolesi,* Italian
composer; noted for his
influence in the development
of comic opera. [d. March 16,
1736]

1785 *Jacob Grimm,* German
philologist, folklorist, scholar,
fairy-tale collector; with his
brother Wilhelm (February
20) edited numerous
collections of folk and fairy
tales. [d. September 20, 1863]

1809 *Louis Braille,* French
musician, teacher; inventor of
Braille system used by the
blind. [d. January 6, 1852]

1813 *Sir Isaac Pitman,* British
printer, publisher; inventor of
shorthand. [d. January 12,
1897]

1831 *E(dward) P(ayson) Dutton,*
U.S. publisher; founded E.P.
Dutton Publishing House,
1858. [d. September 6, 1923]

1838 *General Tom Thumb,* U.S.
circus performer; 33 inch
midget; hired by P.T. Barnum,
1842. [d. July 15, 1883]

1858 *Carter Glass,* U.S. politician;
Secretary of the Treasury,
1918–20; U.S. Senator,
1920–46. [d. May 28, 1946]

1874 *Thornton W. Burgess,* U.S.
author of children's books;
noted for nature stories and
animal tales. [d. June 6, 1965]

1887 *Edwin Emil Witte,* U.S.
economist; author of *U.S.
Social Security Act of 1935.*
[d. May 20, 1960]

1895 *Leroy Randle Grumman,* U.S.
aircraft manufacturer. [d.
October 4, 1982]

1896 *Everett McKinley Dirksen,*
U.S. public official; U.S.
Senator, 1950–69. [d.
September 7, 1969]

1905 *Sterling Holloway,* U.S. actor;
known for his parts as the
voice of many *Walt Disney*
animated characters. [d.
November 22, 1992]

1914 *Jane Wyman (Sarah Jane
Fulks),* U.S. actress; Oscar
Award, 1948; first wife of
Ronald Reagan; lead role on
television series, *Falcon Crest,*
1981–90.

1920 *William Egan Colby,* U.S.
government official; Director
of Central Intelligence

Agency, 1973–76. [d. April 27, 1996]

1929 *Barbara Rush,* U.S. actress; known for roles on television series, *Peyton Place* and *Flamingo Road.*

1930 *Don Francis Shula,* U.S. football coach; co-owner and head coach, Miami Dolphins, 1970–95.

1935 *Floyd Patterson,* U.S. boxer; world heavyweight champion, 1956–59.

1937 *Grace Ann Jaeckel Bumbry,* U.S. opera singer.

1938 *Dyan Cannon (Samille Diane Friesen),* U.S. actress; former wife of Cary Grant.

1940 *Brian Davis Josephson,* British physicist; Nobel Prize in physics for research on the occurrence of *superconductivity* (with I. Esaki and I. Giaever), 1973. [d. March 13, 1978]

1941 *Maureen Reagan,* daughter of Ronald Reagan, 40th U.S. President, and Jane Wyman.

1957 *Patty Loveless,* U.S. singer.

HISTORICAL EVENTS

1717 *Triple alliance* is signed between England, France, and Holland.

1762 England declares war on Spain and Naples *(Seven Years' War).*

1805 Spain enters the *War of the Third Coalition* on the side of Napoleon and against the British and their allies.

1896 *Utah* is admitted to the Union as the 45th state.

1908 *Mulai Hafid* is proclaimed *Sultan of Morocco.*

1916 British make the first attempt to raise the Turkish siege of *Kut-el-Amara (World War I).*

1919 *Riga, Latvia,* is captured by the Bolsheviks *(Russian Revolution).*

1920 Polish troops capture *Dvinsk.*

1932 *Mahatma Gandhi* is arrested and begins a fast unto death to win suffrage for the untouchables.

1945 Allies bomb *Brenner Pass* in the Alps to prevent retreat of German troops *(World War II).*

1948 *Burma* becomes independent of Great Britain; Thakin Nu is appointed Prime Minister.

1951 *Seoul* is captured by Chinese Communists and North Koreans *(Korean War).*

1958 The first man-made satellite, *Sputnik I,* disintegrates on re-entry to the earth's atmosphere.

1960 Countries outside the Common Market form the *European Free Trade Association.*

1962 Council of *Organization of American States* lifts all diplomatic and economic sanctions against the *Dominican Republic.*

1965 President *Lyndon B. Johnson,* in his State of the Union message, outlines a sweeping program to move U.S. toward the *Great Society.*

1966 Reconstruction work begins on the ancient *Abu Simbel* temples in Egypt, salvaged during construction of *Aswan High Dam.*

Colonel *Sangoule Lamizana* assumes power in Upper Volta after a coup d'etat.

1967 *Swahili* is designated as the official language of *Tanzania.*

1974 *Burma* adopts a new constitution that establishes the country as a socialist republic.

1977 *Thomas (Tip) O'Neill* becomes Speaker of the U.S. House of Representatives.

1983 The *Orphan Drug Bill* is signed into law. It encourages pharmaceutical companies to produce drugs for unusual illnesses with limited markets.

The U.S. Department of Justice seeks a court order to force *Westinghouse Electric Corp.* to clean up two chemically contaminated Indiana sites in the first use of the "*superfund*" law.

1984 Doctors at the University of Miami and the Centers for Disease Control publish information on one of the first cases of heterosexual transmission of *AIDS* in the U.S.

1985 Secret Israeli airlifts of ten thousand Ethiopian Jews *(Falashas)* end after the operation is discovered by the Ethiopian government.

Shenuda III resumes duties as patriarch of Egypt's Coptic Church.

1987 The worst *Amtrak* accident in history occurs when a freight train collides with a passenger train.

1998 *Valdas Adamkus* is elected President of Lithuania.

january

JANUARY
5

HOLIDAYS

England

Twelfth Night
The last or 12th night of the
Christmas season according to the
Gregorian or New Style calendar; or
Wassail Eve, reflecting the tradition
celebrating the good health of
friends and neighbors by drinking a
spicy wine or ale from what is
commonly referred to as the *loving
cup;* or *Eve of Epiphany,* being the
evening before the *Epiphany* or
Manifestation of God or the *Feast of
the Three Kings.*

U.S.

George Washington Carver Day

RELIGIOUS CALENDAR

The Saints

St. Telesphorus, Pope and martyr.
Elected 7th bishop of Rome,
A.D. 125. [d. c. 136]

St. Apollinaris, virgin. [death date
unknown]

St. Syncletica, virgin. Also called
Syncletia. [d. c. 400]

St. Simon the Stylite, founder of an
order of solitary devotees
called *pillar-saints.* [d. 459]

St. Convoyon, founder and abbot of
the Monastery of Saint Savior
in Brittany. [d. 868]

St. Dorotheus the Younger, abbot.
Also called *Dorotheus of
Khiliokomos.* [d. 11th
century]

St. Gerlac, hermit. [d. c. 1170]

St. John Nepomucen Neumann,
Bishop of Philadelphia;

organized Catholic schools
into diocesan system. [d.
1860]

The Beatified

Blessed Maria Repetto. [beatified
1981]

BIRTHDATES

1592 *Shah Jahan (Prince
Khurram),* fifth Emperor of
Hindustan, 1628–58; ruler of
India during the golden age
of Mohammedan architecture;
builder of the *Taj Mahal.* [d.
January 22, 1666]

1744 *Gaspar Melchor de
Jovellanos,* Spanish statesman
and writer; Chief Justice of
the Spanish Court, 1778. [d.
July 29, 1811]

1745 *Benjamin Rush,* U.S.
physician, medical educator,
patriot, reformer; established
first free dispensary in
America, 1786; Treasurer of
the Mint of the U.S.,
1797–1813; author of the first
systematic treatment of the
subject of mental illness in
the U.S., 1812. [d. April 19,
1813]

1779 *Zebulon Montgomery Pike,*
U.S. army officer, explorer;
famous for his explorations of
the American southwest;
produced the first English
language account of the

region. *Pike's Peak* is named
for him; killed while leading
victorious attack on Toronto
(War of 1812). [d. April 27,
1813]

Stephen Decatur, U.S. naval
commodore; led one of the
greatest naval victories of the
War of 1812, capturing the
British frigate *Macedonian.*
Issued the famous quote,
"Our country! In her
intercourse with foreign
nations may she always be in
the right; but our country,
right or wrong." [d. March 22,
1820]

1789 *Thomas Pringle,* Scottish-
South African traveller, poet;
funder of parent publication
of *Blackwood's Magazine.* [d.
December 5, 1834]

1846 *Rudolph Christoph Eucken,*
German philosopher; Nobel
Prize in literature, 1908. [d.
September 14, 1926]

1855 *King C. Gillette,* U.S. inventor
of *safety razor;* founder and
head of Gillette Safety Razor
Company, 1901–32. [d. July 9,
1932]

1864 *George Washington Carver,*
U.S. botanist, chemist,
educator; discovered
industrial uses for peanut,
sweet potato, and soybean.
[d. January 5, 1943]

Byron Bancroft Johnson, U.S.
sportsman; organizer and first

president of *American Baseball League.* [d. October 4, 1902]

1874 *Joseph Erlanger,* U.S. physiologist; Nobel Prize in physiology or medicine for study of functions of nerve fibers (with H. S. Gasser), 1944. [d. December 5, 1965]

1876 *Konrad Adenauer,* German statesman; first chancellor of the *Federal Republic of Germany,* 1949–63. [d. April 19, 1967]

1882 *Herbert Bayard Swope,* U.S. journalist; Pulitzer Prize in reporting, 1917. [d. June 20, 1958]

1887 *Courtney Hicks Hodges,* U.S. army general; commander of Third and First Armies, World War II. [d. January 16, 1966]

1900 *Yves Tanguy,* U.S. artist; surrealist painter. [d. January 15, 1955]

1913 *Kemmons Wilson,* U.S. hotelier, founder of Holiday Inn chain.

Jean-Pierre Aumont (Jean-Pierre Salomons), French actor, in U.S. since 1941.

1918 *Jeane Pinckert Dixon,* U.S. psychic, author; began predicting the future at the age of eight. [d. January 25, 1997]

1921 *Friedrich Durrenmatt,* Swiss playwright, novelist. [d. December 4, 1990]

Grand Duke Jean, Head of State, Grand Duchy of Luxembourg, 1964– .

1923 *Sam Phillips,* U.S. record company executive; founded Sun Records, 1952; first to record Elvis Presley, Carl Perkins.

1926 *William Dewitt Snodgrass,* U.S. educator, poet; Pulitzer Prize in poetry, 1960.

1928 *Zulfikar Ali Bhutto,* Pakistani president, 1971–73; prime minister, 1973–77; deposed in a bloodless coup. [d. April 4, 1979]

Walter (Frederick) Mondale, U.S. politician, lawyer; U.S. Senator; Vice-President, 1977–81; Democratic Party nominee for President, 1984.

1931 *Alvin Ailey,* U.S. dancer and choreographer; founder of the Alvin Ailey American Dance Theater. [d. December 1, 1989]

Alfred Brendel, Austrian musician.

Robert Seldon Duvall, U.S. actor; best known for roles in *Lonesome Dove,* 1989, *Tender Mercies,* 1983, and *The Great Santini,* 1980.

1932 *Raisa Maximovna Gorbachev,* wife of Soviet General Secretary, Mikhail Gorbachev.

1938 *William McReynolds Agee,* U.S. business executive.

Juan Carlos I de Borbon y Borbon, King of Spain, 1975– .

1946 *Diane Keaton (Diane Hall),* U.S. actress; Oscar Award for *Annie Hall,* 1977.

1954 *Pamela Sue Martin,* U.S. actress; best known for her role as Fallon on the television series, *Dynasty,* 1981–84.

HISTORICAL EVENTS

1340 *Edward III* of England assumes title of King of

France. *(Hundred Years' War)*

1371 *Pierre Roger de Beaufort* is crowned *Pope Gregory XI.*

1537 *Alessandro de' Medici,* Duke of Florence and last male of elder branch of his family, is assassinated.

1762 *Elizabeth of Russia* dies and is succeeded by *Peter III.*

1887 First library school in the U.S. opens at *Columbia University.*

1905 *National Association of Audubon Societies* is incorporated.

1911 *Monaco* promulgates its constitution.

1919 *National Socialist (German Workers) Party* is founded.

Bolsheviks capture *Vilna (Russian Revolution).*

1925 *Nellie Taylor Ross* of Wyoming becomes first woman governor in American history.

1929 *King Alexander I* of Yugoslavia proclaims a dictatorship.

1940 Frequency modulation *(FM)* radio is successfully demonstrated by *Edwin H. Armstrong,* near Worcester, Massachusetts.

1960 *Francisco Sabater,* a guerrilla leader opposed to the Franco regime since 1939, is captured and killed by the Spanish Civil Guard.

1964 *Pope Paul VI* and *Athenagoras I,* ecumenical patriarch of Constantinople, meet in Jerusalem in the first meeting of leaders of the Roman Catholic and Orthodox churches since 1439.

january

1967 U.S. President *Lyndon B. Johnson* signs executive order cutting off virtually all trade between the U.S. and *Rhodesia*.

Harold Pinter's play, *The Homecoming*, opens in New York.

1968 *Alexander Dubček* succeeds *Antonin Novotny* as First Secretary of the Czechoslovak Communist Party.

1970 United Mine Workers official *Joseph A. Yablonski* and his wife and daughters are found slain in their Clarksville, Pennsylvania, home.

1971 *Chile* establishes diplomatic relations with *People's Republic of China*.

1972 U.S. President Nixon orders *National Aeronautics and Space Administration (NASA)* to begin work on a manned space shuttle.

1975 *The Wiz*, a play by Charlie Smalls and William Brown, premieres in New York.

1976 *Kumpuchea (Cambodia)* becomes a Communist people's republic.

1982 *Dr. Roberto Suazo Córdova* is inaugurated as President of Honduras.

1987 *President Ronald Reagan* submits the first $1 trillion budget to Congress.

1998 Tickets to visit the grave of *Diana, Princess of Wales*, go on sale (August 31, 1997). Diana's grave site is located on her family estate in Northampton, England.

Daniel T. arap Moi begins his fifth term as President of Kenya.

HOLIDAYS

Armenia
Christmas Day

Austria
Epiphany

Colombia
Epiphany

Cyprus
Epiphany Day

Ethiopia
Christmas
Marks the Nativity of Christ according to the Eastern Orthodox Church.

Germany
Epiphany

Greece
Epiphany

Iraq
Army Day

Italy
Epiphany

Laos
Pathet Lao Day

Mexico
Epiphany

Puerto Rico
Three Kings Day (Día de los Trés Magos)

Spain
Epiphany

Sweden
Epiphany

U.S. (New Mexico)
Admission Day
Commemorates New Mexico's admission as the 47th state, 1912.

Uruguay
Epiphany

Children's Day

Venezuela
Epiphany

RELIGIOUS CALENDAR

Solemnities

The Epiphany. Also called *The Adoration of the Magi* or *The Manifestation of God.* In the Christian Church in the East this day has long been recognized as the celebration of the Nativity of Our Lord. In the fourth century, December 25, the date of the Feast in the Western Christian Church, was adopted. It is believed that this early change in dates gave rise to the tradition of the *12 Days of Christmas.* In some records, Christmas and Epiphany were referred to as the first and second nativity; the second being Christ's manifestation to the world. Specifically, in present usage, the Epiphany celebrates four distinct events: 1) the nativity of Christ; 2) the manifestation of Christ to the Magi; 3) Christ's baptism by John the Baptist in the River Jordan; and 4) the miracle at Cana, in which Christ changed water into wine at the wedding feast.

The Saints

St. Wiltrudis, widow and abbess. [d. c. 986]

St. Erminold, Abbot of the Monastery of Prufening. [d. 1121]

St. Guarinus, Bishop of Sion. Also called *Guerin.* [d. 1150]

St. John De Ribera, Archbishop of Valencia. Founded and endowed the College of Corpus Christi. [d. 1611]

St. Carol Melchiori, priest. [d. 1670]

St. Raphaela Mary, virgin and founder of the Handmaids of the Sacred Heart, and *St. Corde Jesu,* virgin. [d. 1925]

The Beatified

Blessed Gertrude of Delft, virgin and mystic. Called *van Oosten.* [d. 1358]

Blessed Maria Angela Astorch. [beatified 1982]

Blessed Andrew Bessette. [beatified 1982]

BIRTHDATES

1367 *Richard II of Great Britain.* [d. February 1400]

1412 *Joan of Arc (Jeanne d'Arc),* French heroine; led troops to victory over English, 1429; captured by English and burned at stake for heresy. [d. May 30, 1431]

1799 *Jedediah Strong Smith,* U.S. explorer and fur trader; the first American explorer to enter *California* from the east, the first to explore the northern California-Oregon coast by land, the first to cross the Sierra Nevada from west to east. [d. May 27, 1831]

1811 *Charles Sumner,* U.S. politician, abolitionist; uncompromising in his opposition to slavery; U.S. Senator, 1851–74. [d. March 11, 1874]

1822 *Heinrich Schliemann,* German archaeologist; discovered the ruins of *Troy.* [d. December 26, 1890]

1842 *Clarence King,* U.S. geologist; founder of the *U.S. Geological Survey.* [d. December 24, 1901]

1878 *Carl Sandburg,* U.S. poet, historian, folklorist; Pulitzer Prize in poetry, 1918, 1951; Pulitzer Prize in biography, 1940. [d. July 22, 1967]

1880 *Tom Mix (Thomas Edwin Mix),* U.S. actor; leading box office attraction of the 1920s, starred in over 100 silent films. [d. October 12, 1940]

1882 *Sam Taliaferro Rayburn (Mr. Sam),* U.S. politician, lawyer; U.S. Congressman, 1912–61; Speaker of the House of Representatives, 1940–47; 1949–53; 1955–61. [d. November 16, 1961]

1883 *Khalil Gibran,* Syrian-American Symbolist poet. [d. April 10, 1931]

1903 *Zora Neale Hurston,* U.S. writer; wrote *Their Eyes Were Watching God.* [d. 1960]

1911 *Joey Adams (Joseph Abramowitz),* U.S. comedian.

1913 *Edward Gierek,* Polish communist leader; First Secretary of Central Committee, 1970–80.

Loretta Gretchen Young, U.S. actress.

1914 *Danny Thomas (Amos Jocobs),* U.S. actor, comedian, producer; known for his lead role in television series, *Make Room for Daddy,* 1953–64. [d. February 6, 1991]

1915 *Alan (Wilson) Watts,* British-American writer, lecturer, philosopher known for his study of Zen Buddhism. [d. November 16, 1973]

1920 *Sung Myung Moon (Yong Myung Moon),* Korean religious leader; founder of Unification Church with reported membership of three million, 1954.

1921 *Louis Harris,* U.S. pollster; founded marketing research firm, 1956.

1923 *Jacobo Timmerman,* Argentine author, journalist; imprisoned for political views, 1977–79; wrote *Prisoner Without a Name, Cell Without a Number,* 1981.

1924 *Kim Dae Jung,* Korean politician; opposition leader who has struggled to restore human rights to South Korea; President of the Peace and Democratic Party, 87–91.

Earl Scruggs, U.S. musician, songwriter; Grammy Award, 1969.

1925 *John Zachary DeLorean,* U.S. auto executive; founded DeLorean Motor Co, 1975; acquitted of drug trafficking charges, 1984.

1931 *E(dgar) L(aurence) Doctorow,* U.S. novelist, editor; author of *Ragtime.*

1944 *Bonnie Gail Franklin,* U.S. actress; known for her lead role on television series, *One Day at a Time.*

Rolf M. Zinkernagel, Swiss immunologist; Nobel Prize for Medicine (1996) along with Peter C. Doherty, Australian immunologist, for their study of virus-infected cells.

1950 *Louis J. Freeh,* U.S. lawyer; director of the Federal Bureau of Investigation (FBI), 1993– .

1957 *Nancy Lopez,* U.S. golfer; youngest woman inducted into the Ladies Professional Golf Association Hall of Fame, 1987.

1960 *Paul Azinger,* U.S. golfer.

1968 *John Singleton,* U.S. director.

HISTORICAL EVENTS

871 *Battle of Ashdown* is fought between Saxons and Danes.

1066 *Harold II* is crowned King of England.

1099 *Henry V* is elected King of Germany.

1169 Peace is established between *Henry II* of England and *Louis VII* of France.

1540 *Henry VIII* of England marries *Anne of Cleves.*

1622 *Sir Edward Coke* is sent to prison by *James I* of England for championing common law in face of royal prerogative.

1857 *Marthinius Pretorius* is inaugurated as first president of the *South African Republic (Transvaal).*

1797 *Albany* is designated the permanent capital of New York State.

1821 *Indianapolis* is designated as the capital of the State of Indiana.

1838 *S. F. B. Morse* demonstrates his completed *telegraph* at the Speedwell Iron Works.

1871 *Henry M. Stanley, New York Herald* journalist, arrives in Zanzibar to begin his search for *Dr. David Livingstone,* missing since 1867.

1883 *Pendleton Act* reforms *U.S. civil service,* initiating competitive examinations for placement.

1896 *Cecil Rhodes* resigns as Prime Minister of the *Cape Colony* following accusations of complicity in the *Jameson Raid* into Transvaal.

1912 *New Mexico* is admitted to the Union as the 47th state.

1916 British parliament passes its first compulsory *military service bill* despite much opposition *(World War I).*

1931 New *Sadler's Wells Theatre* opens in London.

1941 President *Franklin Roosevelt* delivers his "Four Freedoms" speech to the U.S. Congress, summarizing the goals Americans are ready to defend.

1942 First around-the-world commercial flight is completed by Pan American Airways.

1944 The U.S. army reveals the development of a propellerless plane powered by *jet propulsion.*

1946 *Poland* nationalizes basic industries.

1950 *Great Britain* gives official recognition to the *People's Republic of China.*

1959 Belgian paratroopers are sent to Leopoldville to subdue civil unrest in the *Belgian Congo* following the disruption of a banned nationalist group meeting.

1967 U.S. and South Vietnamese troops launch a major offensive against the *Viet Cong* stronghold in the *Mekong River delta,* the first direct commitment of U.S. troops to combat in that area *(Vietnam War).*

Angostura Bridge over the *Orinoco River,* the longest suspension bridge in Latin America, is opened by President *Raul Leoni* of Venezuela.

1971 *Human growth hormone* is synthesized by University of California Medical Center scientists.

1977 Czechoslovak intellectuals issue a manifesto demanding human rights as spelled out in the *Helsinki Agreement* of 1975.

1978 U.S. Secretary of State *Cyrus Vance* turns over the *Crown of St. Stephen* to Hungarian officials in Budapest.

1979 *Shahpur Bakhtiar* is inaugurated as premier of Iran, prompting antigovernment riots.

1983 *American Bell, Inc.,* one of the new companies created by the break up of American Telephone & Telegraph Co., introduces its first product line.

Argentina announces the issuance of a new peso note after years of triple-digit inflation had made the old currency virtually useless.

1984 First *quadruplets* to be conceived in a test tube are born to an Australian woman.

1985 Rock singer *Bob Geldof* arrives in Ethiopia to distribute famine relief funds raised by the proceeds from *Band Aid* record sales.

1994 President Bill Clinton's mother, *Virginia Clinton Kelley,* dies from breast cancer.

Figure skater *Nancy Kerrigan* is attacked after finishing a practice session (January 14, 1994). She eventually competes in the Winter Olympics in Lillehammer, Norway (February 12, 1994).

1996 President *Bill Clinton* signs a new budget that enables federal workers to return to their jobs after being away for 21 days, the longest government shutdown in U.S. history.

1998 *The World Food Program,* sponsored by the United Nations, appeals for monies from around the world to avert famine in North Korea.

NASA sends the unmanned *Lunar Prospector* into space for a geological survey of the moon.

january

JANUARY
7

HOLIDAYS

Russian Christmas
Celebrated by Eastern Orthodox
Churches that still use the Julian
calendar.

Kampuchea
Liberation Day
Commemorates the fall of Phnom-
Penh to the Vietnamese.

Liberia
Pioneers' Day
Commemorates the black pioneers,
mostly freed slaves from the U.S.
who settled there, the oldest of
Africa's independent republics, 1820.

RELIGIOUS CALENDAR

The Saints
St. Lucian of Antioch, priest and
  martyr. [d. 312]
St. Valentine, Bishop of Rhaetia. [d.
  c. 440]
St. Tillo, priest. Also called *Theau,
  Thillo* in France, *Tilloine* or
  Tilman in Flanders, *Hillonius*
  in Germany. [d. c. 702]
St. Kentigerna, matron and
  anchoress. Also called
  Caentigern, Quentigerna. [d.
  734]
St. Aldric, Bishop of Le Mans. [d.
  856]
St. Reinold, monk and martyr.
  Honored in some places as
  patron of stone masons. [d. c.
  960]
St. Canute Lavard, martyr. Also
  called *Knud Lavard, the Lord.*
  [d. 1131]

St. Raymond of Peñafort, Dominican
  friar. Also called *Raymund of
  Pennafort.* Feast formerly
  January 23. [d. 1275]

The Beatified
Blessed Edward Waterson, priest
  and martyr. [d. 1593]

BIRTHDATES

1502 *Pope Gregory XIII,* Pope,
  1572–85; issued the reformed
  (Gregorian) calendar. [d.
  1585]

1718 *Israel Putnam,* American
  Revolutionary general; known
  for his heroic and sometimes
  mythical exploits; a hero of
  the *Battle of Bunker Hill.* [d.
  May 29, 1790]

1745 *Jacques Etienne Montgolfier,*
  French inventor and
  balloonist; with his brother,
  Joseph Michel (August 26),
  developed the first practical
  hot air balloon, 1783. [d.
  August 2, 1799]

1768 *Joseph Bonaparte,* King of
  Naples, 1806–08, King of
  Spain, 1808–13; brother of
  Napoleon Bonaparte. [d. July
  28, 1844]

1794 *Eilhardt Mitscherlich,*
  German chemist; noted for
  experiments in chemical
  geology; produced artificial
  minerals. [d. August 28, 1863]

1800 *Millard Fillmore,* U.S. lawyer,
  politician, U.S. Vice-President,
  1849–50, U.S. President,
  1850–53. [d. March 8, 1874]

1830 *Albert Bierstadt,* German-U.S.
  landscape painter of the
  Hudson River School. [d.
  February 18, 1902]

1844 *Bernadette (Marie Bernarde
  Soubirous* or *Soubiroux),*
  French nun; her visions of
  the Virgin Mary resulted in
  Lourdes becoming a major
  Marian shrine; canonized,
  1933. [d. April 16, 1879]

1845 *King Louis III,* last King of
  Bavaria; reigned 1913–18;
  abdicated. [d. October 18,
  1921]

1863 *Konstantin Stanislavsky,*
  Russian actor, director; co-
  founder and director of
  Moscow Art Theater,
  1898–1938; developed a
  system of dramatic training
  now called "method acting."
  [d. August 7, 1938]

1873 *Charles Peguy,* French poet,
  philosopher, socialist; known
  for his studies of Joan of Arc,
  Victor Hugo, and Henri
  Bergson. Killed at the Battle
  of the Marne, World War I.
  [d. September 5, 1914]

  Adolph Zukor, U.S. film
  executive born in Hungary;
  founder of Famous Players
  Film Co., 1912; Chairman of
  the Board, Paramount
  Pictures, 1935–76. [d. June 10,
  1976]

1899 *Francis Poulenc,* French composer; member of *The Six,* ultramodern school of music in Paris. [d. January 30, 1963]

1903 *Zora Neale Hurston,* U.S. anthropologist, author. [d. January 28, 1960]

1910 *Orval Faubus,* U.S. politician, teacher, editor; as Governor of Arkansas (1955–67), led resistance to Supreme Court-mandated desegregation of educational institutions. [d. December 14, 1994]

Baron Alain de Rothschild, French banker; a leading member of the French banking family; president of the Representative Council of Jewish groups, 1957–82; member of the Legion of Honor. [d. October 20, 1982]

1911 *Thelma (Butterfly) McQueen,* U.S. actress; known for her role as Prissy in *Gone With the Wind,* 1939. [d. December 22, 1995]

1912 *Charles (Samuel) Addams,* U.S. cartoonist: noted for his cartoons in *New Yorker* magazine from 1935. [d. September 29, 1988]

1922 *Vincent Gardenia (Vincent Scognamiglio),* U.S. actor; Tony Award, 1971; Oscar Award, 1973. [d. December 9, 1992]

1922 *Jean-Pierre Louis Rampal,* French flautist.

1925 *Gerald Durrell,* Indian author, naturalist; noted for his contributions to magazines, lectures, and television series on wildlife; brother of Lawrence Durrell (February 27). [d. January 30, 1995]

1928 *William Peter Blatty,* U.S. author; wrote *The Exorcist,* 1971, which sold over 10 million copies and was on the best-seller list for 55 weeks.

1930 *Douglas Kiker,* U.S. broadcast journalist, author. [d. August 14, 1991]

1936 *Hunter Davies,* Scottish author, editor; wrote authorized biography for *The Beatles,* 1968.

1945 *Anthony Richard (Tony) Conigliaro,* U.S. baseball player; led the American League in home runs, 1965. [d. February 24, 1990]

1947 *Jann Wenner,* U.S. journalist, publisher.

1948 *Kenneth Clarke (Kenny) Loggins,* U.S. singer, musician, songwriter; Grammy Award for top male vocalist, 1980.

1957 *Katherine (Katie) Couric,* U.S. television broadcaster; co-host of the NBC show *Today,* 1991– .

1964 *Nicolas Cage (Nicholas Coppola),* U.S. actor; performed in *Moonstruck,* 1987 and *Con Air,* 1997.

HISTORICAL EVENTS

1450 *University of Glasgow* is founded.

1558 *Calais,* last English possession in France, is regained by the French.

1610 Major satellites of *Jupiter* are first seen by *Galileo.*

1714 First *typewriter* patent is issued in England.

1761 The *Mogul* rule in India ends.

1782 *Bank of North America,* first commercial bank in the U.S., opens in Philadelphia.

1785 *François Blanchard* and *John Jeffries* cross the English Channel from Dover to Calais by hot-air balloon; the first crossing of the Channel by air.

1789 First U.S. *presidential election* is held; *George Washington* is elected.

1807 British blockade the French coast *(Napoleonic Wars).*

1841 The British seize ten forts at Chuenpi, China, in the first of the *Opium Wars.*

1857 *London General Omnibus Company* begins operation.

1865 Indians attempt to ambush Cavalry of Iowa Volunteers at *Julesburg, Colorado.*

1888 *The Players,* a club for New York theatrical people, is founded.

1895 *Korea* declares its independence from China.

1902 The imperial Chinese court returns to Peking from its exile during the foreign occupation *(Boxer Rebellion).*

1920 The capital of the Don Cossacks, Novo 'Tcherksk, is taken by Soviet forces *(Russian Revolution).*

1927 *Transatlantic telephone service* begins between New York and London.

1933 Louis Gruenberg's opera *The Emperor Jones* is produced at the Metropolitan Opera House in New York.

1964 New constitution initiates self-government in the *Bahama Islands.*

1968 *Surveyor VII* lands on the moon, the last flight of the U.S. *Surveyor* series, and begins transmitting data and photographs.

1969 *France* bars the sale of military equipment to *Israel*.

1971 The U.S. Court of Appeals orders a ban on all usage of the pesticide *DDT,* until its effects on public health have been studied.

1972 *Lewis Powell* and *William Rehnquist* are confirmed as U.S. Supreme Court justices.

1977 A 347.5 per cent cost of living rise is reported during 1976 in *Argentina*.

1979 *Phnom Penh,* capital of Cambodia, falls to United Front insurgents.

1986 President Ronald Reagan bans trade and travel to *Libya* and calls for an international boycott because of its involvement in terrorist activities.

Soviet dissident *Anatoly Shcharansky* is sent to a labor camp for his participation in a hunger strike.

1989 Emperor *Hirohito* of Japan dies after the longest reign of any Japanese monarch (62 years), and is succeeded by his son, *Akihito*.

1997 *Newt Gingrich* is re-elected as Speaker of the House of Representatives.

1998 *Timothy McVeigh* escapes the death penalty when a jury fails to come to a unanimous decision. He receives life imprisonment for the Oklahoma City bombing (April 19, 1995).

HOLIDAYS

U.S. (Louisiana)

Battle of New Orleans Day
Commemorates U.S. troops, under General Andrew Jackson, and the defeat of the British at New Orleans, 1815.

RELIGIOUS CALENDAR

The Saints

St. Apollinaris, Bishop of Hieropolis. Called the *Apologist.* [d. c. 179]

St. Lucian of Beauvais, martyr. [d. c. 290]

St. Severinus of Noricum, missionary to Austria. [d. c. 480]

St. Severinus, Bishop of Septempeda; brother of *St. Victorinus.* [d. c. 550]

St. Erhard, Bishop of Ratisbon. [d. c. 686]

St. Gudula, virgin. Patron saint of Brussels. Also called *Ergoule, Gedula, Goelen, Goule.* [d. c. 712]

St. Pega, virgin, hermit; sister of *St. Guthlac.* [d. c. 719]

St. Wulsin, Bishop of Sherborne. Also called *Vulsin.* [d. 1005]

St. Thorfinn, Bishop of Hamar. [d. 1285]

BIRTHDATES

1081 *Henry V, Holy Roman Emperor* and King of Germany, 1106–25; last of the Franconian dynasty. [d. 1125]

1682 *Jonathan Belcher,* American merchant; colonial governor of Massachusetts, New Hampshire, and New Jersey. [d. August 31, 1757]

1735 *John Carroll,* U.S. clergyman; first Roman Catholic bishop in the U.S.; founded *Georgetown University.* [d. December 3, 1815]

1786 *Nicholas Biddle,* U.S. financier, lawyer, diplomat, publisher; director of the Bank of the United States, 1822–36. [d. February 27, 1844]

1791 *Jacob Collamer,* U.S. public official; U.S. Congressman, 1843–49; U.S. Senator, 1855–65; U.S. Postmaster General, 1849. [d. 1865]

1792 *Lowell Mason,* U.S. educator, hymn writer; known for his efforts to introduce musical education into U.S. public schools. [d. August 11, 1872]

1821 *James Longstreet,* Confederate general during U.S. Civil War; ill-reputed for his lack of aggressiveness during several major battles, resulting in Confederate defeats. [d. January 2, 1904]

1823 *Alfred Russel Wallace,* British naturalist, explorer; simultaneously theorized on *natural selection,* publishing his findings jointly with

Charles Darwin (February 12). [d. November 7, 1913]

1824 *(William) Wilkie Collins,* British novelist; collaborated with Charles Dickens (February 7). [d. September 23, 1889]

1825 *Henri Giffard,* French aeronaut, inventor; the first to build and fly a steerable airship. [d. April 15, 1882]

1862 *Frank Nelson Doubleday,* U.S. publisher and editor; founder of Doubleday & Co., 1897. [d. January 30, 1934)

1867 *Emily Green Balch,* U.S. economist, social scientist, pacifist; Nobel Peace Prize (with J. R. Mott), 1946. [d. January 9, 1961]

1871 *Viscount Craigavon (James Craig),* Irish statesman; first Prime Minister of Northern Ireland, 1921–40. [d. November 24, 1940]

1881 *William Thomas Piper,* U.S. aircraft manufacturer. [d. January 15, 1970]

1885 *John Curtin,* Australian editor, statesman; Prime Minister, 1941–45. [d. July 5, 1945]

1891 *William Kiplinger,* U.S. journalist; founder of *Kiplinger Washington Letters.* [d. August 6, 1967]

Walther Wilhelm Georg Franz Bothe, German

physicist; Nobel Prize in physics for development of coincidence method of time-telling (with Max Born), 1954. [d. February 8, 1957]

1899 *Sherman Llewellyn Adams,* U.S. politician; Governor of New Hampshire, 1949–53; White House Chief of Staff, 1953–58. [d. October 27, 1986]

1902 *Georgi Maximilianovich Malenkov,* Russian leader; Premier of the U.S.S.R., 1953–55; expelled from Communist Party, 1964. [January 14, 1988]

Carl Ransom Rogers, U.S. psychologist, author; wrote *On Becoming a Person,* 1961 and *A Way of Being,* 1980. [d. February 4, 1987]

1904 *Peter Arno (Curtis Arnoux Peters),* U.S. cartoonist, writer; known for his frequent cartoon contributions to *New Yorker* magazine. [d. February 22, 1968]

1910 *Galina Sergeyevna Ulanova,* Soviet prima ballerina. [d. March 21, 1998]

1912 *José Ferrer (José Vincente Ferrer y Centron),* Puerto Rican actor, director, producer. [d. January 26, 1992]

1914 *John Thomas Watson, Jr.,* U.S. business executive; Ambassador to U.S.S.R., 1979–81.

1928 *Sander Vanocur,* U.S. broadcast journalist; chief diplomatic correspondent, American Broadcasting Company, 1981– .

1930 *Soupy Sales (Milton Hines),* U.S. television personality;

best known for pie-throwing act on *Soupy Sales Show,* 1953–66.

1931 *Bill Graham (Wolfgang Grajonca),* U.S. producer; organized concert tours for rock performers. [d. October 25, 1991]

1933 *Charles Osgood (Charles Osgood Wood, III),* U.S. broadcast journalist, author; correspondent, Columbia Broadcasting System, 1971–; host of the TV show *Sunday Morning,* 1994– .

1935 *Elvis (Aron) Presley,* U.S. popular singer, actor; leader in the American and eventually the international *rock and roll* revolution. [d. August 16, 1977]

1939 *Shirley Bassey,* Welsh singer.

Caroline Herrera, Venezuelan fashion designer.

Yvette Carmen M. Mimieux, U.S. actress.

1941 *Graham Chapman,* British actor, writer; wrote and starred in Monty Python's satirical films. [d. October 4, 1989]

1942 *Stephen Hawking,* British scientist; called by many the greatest theoretical physicist since Albert Einstein.

1947 *David Bowie (David Robert Hayward-Jones),* British singer, songwriter, actor; starred in films, *The Man Who Fell to Earth,* 1976, and *Merry Christmas Mr. Lawrence,* 1983.

1948 *Kenneth A. Troutt,* U.S. businessman; founder of Excel Communications, 1988.

1949 *Wolfgang Puck,* Austrian-born chef; known for his celebrity-frequented restaurants.

1968 *R(obert) Kelly,* U.S. singer, producer.

HISTORICAL EVENTS

1107 *Alexander I of Scotland* accedes to the throne.

1790 First State of the Union message is delivered by *President George Washington.*

1798 The *11th Amendment* of the U.S. Constitution, modifying the power of the Supreme Court, is ratified.

1800 First *soup kitchens* are opened in London for the relief of the poor.

1806 British occupy the *Cape of Good Hope.*

1815 Andrew Jackson defeats the British at the *Battle of New Orleans (War of 1812).*

1870 *Joseph Lister* publishes the results of his study of antiseptic surgical methods. His use of carbolic acid to sterilize instruments and wounds trebles the survival rate of his patients.

1904 *Pope Pius X* sanctions the *cantus tradionalis* in preference to the reformed *Gregorian chant.*

1915 Turkish forces occupy *Tabriz,* northern Persia, after the Russians evacuate *(World War I).*

The *Battle of Soissons* breaks out along the Western Front *(World War I).*

1918 President *Woodrow Wilson* delivers his "Fourteen Points" speech, suggesting the creation of a *League of Nations.*

1926 *Ibn Saud* is proclaimed King of the *Hijaz* and sultan of *Nejd (Saudi Arabia).*

1952 *Jordan* promulgates a new constitution.

1961 *U.S. Civil War centennial* officially opens with ceremonies in New York City and in Lexington, Virginia.

1962 *El Salvador* promulgates a constitution.

1966 *Stephen Cardinal Wyszynski,* Roman Catholic primate of Poland, is barred by the Polish government from attending the Vatican celebration of the thousandth anniversary of Christianity in Poland.

1976 Countries of the *International Monetary Fund* agree to a monetary reform that would permit currencies to "float" in the world market.

E.L. Doctorow receives the first National Book Critics Circle Award for fiction for *Ragtime.*

1984 Foreign ministers of Costa Rica, Honduras, Nicaragua, Guatemala, and Venezuela agree in principle to the *Contadora Peace Proposal.*

South African troops begin withdrawal from *Angola* following a month-long offensive.

1985 General Motors announces plans for the *Saturn Corp.,* a subsidiary that will manufacture subcompact cars.

Lawrence Martin Jenco, head of the U.S. based Catholic Relief Services, is kidnapped in West Beirut by gunmen believed to represent the *Islamic Jihad Organization.*

1986 All Libyan government assets in the U.S. are frozen because of suspected involvement in terrorist activities.

1987 The *Dow Jones* industrial stock average passes the 2,000 mark.

1993 *Hakija Turajlic,* deputy Premier of Bosnia, is assassinated.

1998 *Ramzi Ahmed Yousef* receives a life sentence for his role in the World Trade Center bombing (February 26, 1993).

Scientists at the meeting of the *American Astronomical Society* announce that the universe is 15 billion years old.

january

JANUARY
9

HOLIDAYS

Panama
National-Mourning Day or Martyrs' Day

RELIGIOUS CALENDAR

The Saints

St. Marciana, virgin, martyr. [d. c. 303]

SS. Julian and *Basilissa,* companions, martyrs. Julian and Basilissa were man and wife; St. Julian is regarded as the patron of hospitality and hotelkeepers. [d. c. 304]

St. Peter, Bishop of Sebastea. Parents were *St. Basil the Elder* and *St. Emmelia.* Brother of *St. Basil, St. Gregory of Nyssa,* and *St. Macrina.* [d. 391]

St. Waningus. Assisted *St. Wandrille* in founding the *Abbey at Fontenelle.* Also called *Vaneng.* [d. c. 683]

St. Adrian, abbot of Canterbury. Abbot of the monastery of SS. Peter and Paul (afterwards called St. Augustine's), at Canterbury. [d. 710]

St. Berhtwald, Archbishop of Canterbury. Also called *Berctuald, Brithwald.* [d. 731]

The Beatified

Blessed Alix Le Clercq, virgin, cofounder of the *Augustinian Canonesses Regular of the Congregation of Our Lady.* [d. 1622]

BIRTHDATES

1554 *Pope Gregory XV,* pope, 1621–23. [d. July 8, 1623]

1735 *John Jervis,* Earl of St. Vincent, English admiral; First Lord of the Admiralty, 1801–4. [d. 1823]

1839 *John Knowles Paine,* U.S. composer; first professor of music in an American university, at Harvard, 1875–1906. [d. April 25, 1906]

1859 *Carrie Chapman Catt,* U.S. women's rights leader; founder of *National League of Women Voters,* 1919. [d. March 9, 1947]

1873 *Hayyim Nahman Bialik,* Hebrew writer, poet; strong supporter of Zionism; influenced revival of Hebrew. [d. July 4, 1934]

1878 *John Broadus Watson,* U.S. psychologist; founder of *behaviorist school* of psychology. [d. September 25, 1958]

Humbert I, King of Italy, 1844–1900. [assassinated July 29, 1900]

1898 *Gracie Fields (Gracie Stansfield),* British comedienne. [d. September 7, 1979]

1900 *Richard Halliburton,* U.S. traveler, author; traced routes of numerous great explorers, including Hannibal, Alexander the Great; lost at sea trying to sail a Chinese junk from Hong Kong to San Francisco. [d. March 23 or 24, 1939]

1902 *Sir Rudolph Bing,* Anglo-Austrian impresario; general manager, Metropolitan Opera, New York, 1950–72. [d. September 2, 1997]

1904 *George Balanchine* (Georgy Melitonovich Balanchivadze), Russian-American choreographer; director, New York City Ballet Co., 1948–1983. [d. April 30, 1983]

1908 *Simone de Beauvoir,* French novelist, essayist, existentialist; front runner in the movement toward equal rights for women. [d. April 14, 1986]

1913 *Richard Milhous Nixon,* U.S. lawyer, politician; U.S. Vice-President, 1953–61; 37th president of U.S.; first president to resign office. [d. April 22, 1994]

1914 *Gypsy Rose Lee (Rose Louise Hovick),* U.S. entertainer, author; burlesque dancer; perfected the art of the striptease. [d. April 26, 1970]

1922 *Har Gobind Khorana,* U.S. chemist; Nobel Prize in physiology or medicine for research on the role of enzymes in genetic development (with M. W. Nirenberg and R. W. Holley), 1968.

1925 *Fernando Lamas,* U.S. actor, director; famous for his roles as a 'Latin lover' in 1950's films. [d. October 8, 1982]

1928 *Judith Krantz (Judith Tarcher),* U.S. author; wrote *Scruples,* 1978 and *Princess Daisy,* 1980

1934 *Bryan B. (Bart) Starr,* U.S. football player, coach; quarterback, Green Bay Packers, 1956–71; elected to Hall of Fame, 1977.

1935 *Bob Denver,* U.S. actor; best known for his role as Gilligan on television series, *Gilligan's Island,* 1964–67.

1941 *Joan Baez,* U.S. singer, political activist.

Susannah York (Susannah Yolande Fletcher), British actress.

1944 *James Patrick (Jimmy) Page,* British musician; guitarist for the rock groups, *The Firm, Honey-drippers, Led Zeppelin,* and *Yardbirds.*

1950 *David Johansen,* U.S. rock singer; founding member of influential 1960s punk band *New York Dolls;* "re-made" himself in the 1980s as lounge singer *Buster Poindexter.*

1951 *Crystal Gayle,* U.S. singer; Grammy Award for *Don't It Make My Brown Eyes Blue,* 1978; sister of Loretta Lynn.

HISTORICAL EVENTS

1493 *Vladislav II* of Poland grants Polish noblemen *Habeas Corpus Constitution* of Cracow.

1570 *Ivan the Terrible* of Russia, suspecting a revolt in the city of Novgorod, captures city and executes many of its inhabitants.

1788 *Connecticut* becomes the fifth state to ratify the U.S. Constitution.

1792 *Peace of Jassy* between Russia and Turkey is signed; Russia obtains the coast of the Black Sea, including the Crimea.

1793 First successful U.S. balloon flight is completed in Philadelphia, Pennsylvania, by *François Blanchard.*

1809 U.S. issues *Non-Intercourse Act* against British commerce.

1861 *Mississippi* secedes from the Union (*U.S. Civil War*).

1867 *Emperor Mutsuhito (Meiji)* assumes throne as the Emperor of Japan, leading the nation into the modern period.

1875 *Alfonso XII* lands at Barcelona and is recognized as King of Spain.

1878 *Victor Emmanuel* of Italy dies and is succeeded by *Humbert I.*

1912 Russian troops begin to expel Chinese from Mongolia.

1917 The last Turkish troops are driven back across the Egyptian frontier (*World War I*).

1945 U.S. forces invade Luzon, Philippines (*World War II*).

1957 British Prime Minister *Anthony Eden* resigns from office.

1960 *Aswan High Dam* construction is initiated in ceremonies at Aswan, Egypt.

1962 U.S. and Japan conclude a formal agreement for the final settlement of U.S. post-war economic assistance to Japan.

1968 U.S. spacecraft *Surveyor VII* makes a successful landing on the moon.

1969 *Concorde,* a supersonic jetliner, is tested for the first time at Bristol, England.

1970 *Cuba* and *Soviet Union* sign technical assistance agreement for installation of a satellite communications station in Cuba.

1972 The *Queen Elizabeth,* luxury ocean liner, is gutted by fire in Hong Kong harbor.

1976 Twyla Tharp's ballet-jazz dance, *Push Comes to Shove,* premieres in New York.

1986 U.S. and Australian researchers report the discovery of *interferon alpha two,* a drug thought to be effective in preventing the common cold.

1987 Iran launches a major offensive against the southern Iraqi city of *Basra (Iran-Iraq War)*

1998 Scientists at the meeting of the *American Astronomical Society* announce the ability to calculate the amount of invisible light emitted from the universe.

JANUARY
10

RELIGIOUS CALENDAR

The Saints

St. Marcian. [d. 471]

St. Saethrith, abbess of Faremoutier-en-Brie. Also called *Saethryda.* [d. 7th century]

St. John the Good, Bishop of Milan. [d. 660]

St. Agatho, Pope. Elected Bishop of Rome 678. [d. 681]

St. Dermot Diarmaid, abbot; founder of the monastery on the island of Inchcleraun in Lough Ree. [d. 6th century]

St. Peter Orseolo, monk. Also called *Peter Urseolus.* [d. 987]

St. William, Archbishop of Bourges. [d. 1209]

The Beatified

Blessed Gregory X, pope. [d. 1276]

BIRTHDATES

1738 *Ethan Allen,* American patriot; best known for his leadership of the *Green Mountain Boys,* who fought for the independence and integrity of Vermont; performed heroically during American Revolution. [d. February 12, 1789]

1769 *Michel Ney,* Napoleonic military commander; commanded the Old Guard at the *Battle of Waterloo;* tried and condemned for treason, 1815. [d. December 7, 1815]

1834 *John Emerich Edward Dalberg-Acton, First Baron Acton,* British historian; planned *Cambridge Modern History.* [d. June 19, 1902]

1850 *John Wellborn Root,* U.S. architect; with his partner, Daniel H. Burnham (September 4), led the emergence of the *Chicago School* of American architecture, which was marked by design based on function. [d. January 15, 1892]

1880 *Grock (Adrien Wettach),* Swiss clown, entertainer. [d. July 14, 1959]

1882 *Aleksei Nikolaevich Tolstoi,* Russian novelist and short-story writer. [d. February 23, 1945]

1883 *Francis X(avier) Bushman,* U.S. silent-screen actor; considered the greatest leading man of the silent film era. [d. August 23, 1966]

1887 *(John) Robinson Jeffers,* U.S. poet; Pulitzer Prize for poetry, 1954. [d. January 20, 1962]

1892 *Dumas Malone,* U.S. author; Pulitzer Prize for *Jefferson and His Time,* 1975. [d. December 27, 1986]

1893 *Vicente Huidobro,* Chilean poet, novelist, literary theorist. [d. January 2, 1948]

1898 *Katharine Burr Blodgett,* U.S. physicist, chemist; first woman research scientist at General Electric Corp.; invented *non-reflecting (invisible) glass* used in optical equipment. [d. October 12, 1979]

1903 *Barbara Hepworth,* British sculptor. [d. 1975]

1904 *Ray Bolger,* U.S. actor, dancer; known for his role as the Scarecrow in *The Wizard of Oz,* 1939. [d. January 15, 1987]

1908 *Paul Henreid,* Italian actor, director; known for his role in *Casablanca,* 1943. [d. March 29, 1992]

1913 *Gustáv Husák,* Czechoslovak communist leader; First Secretary, Committee of Presidium, 1969–71; General Secretary, 1971–75; President, 1975–89. [d. November 18, 1991]

Mehmet Shehu, Albanian statesman; Premier of Albania, 1978–81; committed suicide. [d. December 17, 1981]

1915 *Dean Dixon,* U.S. musician; first black and youngest musician ever to conduct *New York Philharmonic Orchestra.* [d. November 4, 1976]

1916 *Sune K. Bergstrom,* Swedish biochemist; Nobel Prize in physiology or medicine (with John RiVane and Bengt I. Samuelsson), 1982.

1927 *Gisele MacKenzie (Marie Marguerite La Fleche),* Canadian singer, actress.

John Alvin (Johnnie) Ray, U.S. singer; known for his songs, *Cry* and *The Little Cloud that Cried.* [d. February 25, 1990]

Ron Galella, U.S. photographer; known for his attempts to photograph Jacqueline Onassis.

1931 *Marlene Sanders,* U.S. broadcasting journalist, educator.

1935 *Sherrill Eustace Milnes,* U.S. operatic baritone; most recorded American opera singer.

1936 *Robert Wilson,* U.S. physicist; Nobel Prize in physics for discovery of cosmic radiation that validates *Big Bang Theory.* (with A. A. Penzias and P. Kapitsa), 1978.

1938 *Francis William (Frank) Mahovlich,* Canadian hockey player; scored 533 goals in 18 National Hockey League seasons; elected to Hall of Fame, 1981.

1939 *David Joel Horowitz,* U.S. author; co-wrote *The Fords: An American Epic* with Peter Collier, 1986.

Sal Mineo, U.S. actor, singer; known for starring roles in *Rebel Without a Cause,* 1955 and *Exodus,* 1960. [d. February 12, 1976]

1941 *Philip Joseph Caputo,* U.S. author, journalist; Pulitzer Prize, 1972; wrote *Rumour of War,* an account of his experiences in Vietnam.

1943 *Jim Croce,* U.S. singer, songwriter; known for songs, *Operator,* 1972 and *Bad, Bad Leroy Brown,* 1973; died in airplane crash at the height of his career. [d. September 20, 1973]

1945 *Rod(erick David) Stewart,* Scottish singer; member of the rock groups, *Jeff Beck Group,* 1968–69 and *Faces,* 1969–75; known for raspy voice.

1949 *George Foreman,* U.S. boxer; world heavyweight champion, 1973–74.

1952 *Pat Benatar (Patricia Andrzejewski),* U.S. singer; known for songs, *Treat Me Right* and *Love is a Battlefield.*

1958 *Shawn Colvin,* U.S. pop singer; Grammy Award winner, 1998.

HISTORICAL EVENTS

1356 *Charles IV, Holy Roman Emperor,* issues *Golden Bull* at Nuremberg, settling procedure for election of German king and creating a constitution for the Empire.

1429 The *Order of the Golden Fleece,* famous chivalric order, is founded by Duke Philip the Good of Burgundy.

1757 Holy Roman Empire declares war on Prussia; Russia, Poland and Sweden also oppose Prussia *(Seven Years' War).*

1776 American *Thomas Paine* publishes his *Common Sense,* a pamphlet calling for independence from England.

1840 *Penny postage* begins in Great Britain.

1861 *Florida* secedes from the Union *(U.S. Civil War).*

1863 London's underground transportation system is inaugurated.

1870 *Standard Oil Company* is incorporated at Cleveland, Ohio.

1883 *Arabi Pasha* and other Egyptian rebels are exiled to Ceylon.

1900 Field-Marshal *Lord Roberts* and *Lord Kitchener* arrive at Cape Town to take command of British troops *(Boer War).*

1901 *Spindletop,* the first great Texas oil strike, is made.

1915 German airplanes bomb Dunkirk, France, and raid the east coast of England *(World War I).*

1918 Cossacks declare the independence of the *Republic of Don* with General Kaledin as president *(Russian Revolution).*

1919 Rumania annexes Transylvania.

1920 *League of Nations* is founded.

British mandate over German East Africa (Tanganyika) goes into effect.

1921 War trials begin in Leipzig, Germany, before the German Supreme Court.

1923 Burton Lane's musical *Finian's Rainbow* opens in New York.

Juan de la Cierva demonstrates the first *autogyro,* in Spain.

1946 *League of Nations* is dissolved.

First *United Nations General Assembly* meets in London.

World's first communication through space occurs as radar

pulses from Fort Monmouth, New Jersey, are echoed from the moon.

1949 *Columbia Inc.* and *Radio Corp. of America* introduce 33 1/3 r.p.m. and 45 r.p.m. vinyl records.

1956 Elvis Presley's first million-selling record, *Heartbreak Hotel,* is released.

1957 *Harold Macmillan* becomes Prime Minister of Great Britain after the resignation of *Anthony Eden.*

Tunisia and the *People's Republic of China* establish diplomatic relations.

1961 *Sinhalese* replaces English as the official language of Ceylon.

Two black students are admitted to the *University of Georgia,* marking the first step toward racial integration of the state's public school system.

1966 State Representative *Julian Bond* is denied a seat in the Georgia legislature because of his opposition to the Vietnam War.

1969 Sweden extends full diplomatic recognition to *North Vietnam.*

Saturday Evening Post announces suspension of publication effective in early fall of the year.

1983 *Jamaica* creates a two-tier currency system which

legitimizes black market rates for most transactions.

1984 *Benazir Bhutto,* opposition leader and daughter of former Pakistani prime minister, *Zulfikar Ali Bhutto,* is released after two years in detention.

U.S. and the *Vatican* reestablish full diplomatic relations after more than one hundred years.

1985 *Daniel Ortega* is inaugurated for a six-year term as president of Nicaragua.

1995 *Robert Rubin* is selected as the new Secretary of the Treasury.

HOLIDAYS

Albania
Proclamation of the Republic Day
Commemorates establishment of Albanian Republic, 1946.

Chad
Independence Day
Celebration of independence of Chad, August 11, 1960. Official observation is held in January to avoid the August rainy season.

Micronesia (Kosrae)
Constitution Day

Nepal
National Unity Day
Celebration dedicated to King Prithvinarayan, Shah 1773–75, who established this, the only Hindu kingdom in the world.

Puerto Rico
De Hostos' Birthday
Celebrates the birth of the philosopher and patriot, Eugenio Maria De Hostos, 1839.

RELIGIOUS CALENDAR

The Saints
St. Hyginus, Pope. Elected Bishop of Rome c. 138. [d. c. 142]
St. Theodosius the Cenobiarch. Appointed head of all Cenobites, or men living in community, throughout Palestine. [d. 529]
St. Salvius, Bishop of Amiens. Also called *Sauve*. [d. c. 625]

BIRTHDATES

1503 *Francesco Mazzola (Il Parmigiano)*, Italian Mannerist painter. [d. 1540]

1755 *Alexander Hamilton*, U.S. statesman, lawyer, author; first U.S. Secretary of the Treasury. [d. July 12, 1804]

1807 *Ezra Cornell*, U.S. capitalist and philanthropist; founder of *Cornell University*. [d. December 9, 1894]

1808 *Jean Gilbert Fialin Persigny*, French statesman; ardent Bonapartist; Minister of Interior, 1852–54; 1860–63; Ambassador to Great Britain, 1855–58; 1859–60. [d. January 11, 1872]

1815 *Sir John Macdonald*, Canadian statesman, first Prime Minister, 1867–73, 1878–91; regarded as the organizer of Canada as a Dominion. [d. June 6, 1891]

1839 *Eugenio Maria De Hostos*, Puerto Rican philosopher, educator, patriot. [d. August 11, 1903]

1842 *William James*, U.S. philosopher, teacher, psychologist; founder of *pragmatism*. [d. August 26, 1910]

1859 *George Nathaniel Curzon*, First Baron and First Marquis Curzon of Kedleston, British statesman; Viceroy of India, 1899–1905; Secretary of State for Foreign Affairs, 1919–24; leader of House of Lords, 1919–24. [d. March 20, 1925]

1864 *Harry Gordon Selfridge*, U.S.-British merchant; partner in Marshall Field & Co.; founded Selfridge & Co., Ltd., London, in 1909. [d. May 8, 1947]

1873 *Dwight Morrow Whitney*, U.S. diplomat; Ambassador to Mexico, 1927–30; Senator, 1930–31; father-in-law of Charles Lindbergh. [d. October 5, 1931]

1885 *Alice Paul*, U.S. feminist, lawyer, leader of the Equal Rights Amendment movement. [d. July 9, 1977]

1889 *Calvin Blackman Bridges*, U.S. geneticist. [d. December 17, 1938].

1897 *Bernard A. De Voto*, U.S. editor, critic, historian, novelist; editor, *Saturday Review of Literature*, 1936–38; Pulitzer Prize in history, 1947; one of the most widely read critics and historians of his time. [d. November 13, 1955]

1898 *George Francis Pierrot*, U.S. traveler, author, editor. [d. February 16, 1980]

1903 *Alan Stewart Paton*, South African novelist, political activist; author of *Cry, the*

Beloved Country. [d. April 12, 1988]

1905 *Manfred B. Lee,* U.S. mystery writer; with his cousin Frederic Dannay (October 20) wrote over 40 *Ellery Queen* novels, which became the most widely read mystery novels in the world, selling over 100 million copies by the 1950s. [d. September 3, 1982]

1907 *Pierre Mendes-France,* French political leader, economist; Premier, 1954–55. [d. October 18, 1982]

1911 *Zenko Suzuki,* Japanese statesman; Prime Minister, 1980–83.

1921 *Juanita Morris Kreps,* U.S. government official; Secretary of Commerce, 1977–79.

1924 *Roger Guillemin,* U.S. physiologist; Nobel Prize in physiology or medicine for research on the pituitary hormone (with A. Schally and R. S. Yalow), 1977.

1926 *Grant A. Tinker,* U.S. television executive, producer; President, MTM Enterprises, 1970–81.

1934 *Jean Chretien,* Canadian politician, prime minister of Canada, 1993– .

1946 *Naomi Judd,* U.S. country singer.

1952 *Ben Daniel Crenshaw,* U.S. golfer; Master's Tournament Champion, 1984, 1995.

HISTORICAL EVENTS

1360 *Treaty of Guillon* between *Edward III* of England and *Philip of Burgundy* of France is signed, in which the English renounce all claims to the French crown in exchange for Aquitaine *(Hundred Years' War).*

1851 The *Taiping Rebellion,* led by Hung Hsiu-Ch'uan, attempts to overthrow Manchu Dynasty.

1861 *Alabama* secedes from the Union *(U.S. Civil War).*

1864 *Charing Cross Railway Station* opens in London.

1904 The *Hereros* of South-West Africa begin a bloody and costly uprising against their German colonizers.

1916 The Russians begin a general offensive against the Turks in Armenia *(World War I).*

The French seize the Greek island of *Corfu* as a base for the Serbian army.

1925 *Symphony* by *Aaron Copland* is performed by the New York Symphony.

1940 *Sergei Prokofiev's* ballet *Romeo and Juliet* opens in Leningrad.

1944 Count *Galeazzo Ciano,* a member of the Fascist Supreme Council who helped force Mussolini's resignation, is executed for treason *(World War II).*

1954 Albert Camus' novel, *The Rebel,* is published in New York.

1960 *India* and *Pakistan* announce the designation of an exact border between the two countries to eliminate clashes.

1970 Owerri in *Biafra* is taken by federal Nigerian troops; the Biafran leader *General Ojukwu* leaves the country.

1975 President *Guillermo Rodriguez Lara* of Ecuador is overthrown in a military coup.

1984 The U.S. Centers for Disease Control publishes evidence that *AIDS* can be transmitted through blood transfusions.

1992 *Chadli Benjedid,* President of Algeria, announces his resignation.

1995 *Ryutaro Hashimoto* is elected as Premier by Japan's Diet.

HOLIDAYS

Tanzania
Zanzibar Revolution Day
Commemorates People's Revolution of 1964.

Turkmenistan
Commemoration Day

RELIGIOUS CALENDAR

The Saints
St. Arcadius, martyr. [d. c. 304]
SS. Tigrius, priest, and *Eutropius,* a reader, both martyrs. [d. 404]
St. Caesaria, virgin, abbess. Sister of *St. Caesarius.* [d. c. 529]
St. Victorian, abbot of Asan in Aragon. [d. 558]
St. Benedict, abbot of Wearmouth and Jarrow. Also called *Benet, Bennet, Biscop.* [d. 690]

The Beatified
Blessed Margaret Bourgeoys.
Blessed Anthony Pucci, priest. [d. 1892]

BIRTHDATES

1580 *Jan Baptist van Helmont,* Belgian chemist, physiologist, physician; the first to differentiate gas as a distinct form; conducted early research in digestive process of humans. [d. December 30, 1644]

1588 *John Winthrop,* British-born governor; Governor of Massachusetts Bay Colony, 1629–48. [d. March 26, 1649]

1628 *Charles Perrault,* French writer, especially known for his fairy tales. [d. May 16, 1703]

1729 *Edmund Burke,* British statesman, political writer, conservative political theorist; advocate of liberal treatment of American colonies. [d. July 9, 1797]

Lazzaro Spallanzani, Italian physiologist; noted for his experiments on human digestive process; disproved theory of spontaneous generation. [d. February 11, 1799]

1737 *John Hancock,* American Revolutionary leader; famed signer of the Declaration of Independence; first governor of state of Massachusetts. [d. October 8, 1793]

1746 *Johann H. Pestalozzi,* Swiss educator, reformer; his emphasis on the concrete approach to education strongly influenced elementary education throughout Europe and the U.S. [d. February 17, 1827]

1751 *Jakob Michael Reinhold Lenz,* German dramatist, poet, critic; a member of circle of writers who followed Johann Von Goethe (August 28). [d. May 24, 1792]

1810 *Ferdinand II,* King of the Two Sicilies, 1830–59. [d. May 22, 1859]

1850 *Charlotte Ray,* U.S. lawyer; first African American woman lawyer. [d. 1911]

1852 *Joseph Jacques Joffre,* Commander in Chief of French armies, World War I; a hero of the Battle of the Marne, 1914. [d. January 3, 1931]

1856 *John Singer Sargent,* U.S. artist; noted especially for his portraiture; also known for his decorative work, especially in the Boston Public Library and the Boston Museum of Fine Arts. [d. April 25, 1925]

1860 *Sir Charles Oman,* British military historian; noted for his exhaustive histories of military events in Europe from the fifth century through 1930. [d. 1946]

1873 *Frank Gerber,* U.S. manufacturer; founder of Gerber Products, 1917; his son, Daniel Gerber (May 6), introduced the strained baby food which ultimately made the company famous. [d. October 7, 1952]

1876 *Jack London,* U.S. novelist, short-story writer; well-known for his adventure stories which displayed a preoccupation with primitive strength, violence, and exciting action. [d. November 22, 1916]

1890 *Mordecai Johnson,* U.S. educator; president of Howard University. [d. 1976]

1893 *Hermann Wilhelm Göring,* prominent German Nazi leader; headed *Luftwaffe;* jailed for his activities after World War II; committed suicide. [d. October 15, 1946]

1894 *Georges Carpentier,* French boxer. [d. October 27, 1975]

1899 *Paul Müller,* Swiss chemist; Nobel Prize in physiology or medicine for research in DDT, 1948. [d. October 12, 1965]

Herbert Orin Crisler (Fritz), U.S. football coach; one of most innovative coaches in early football history; devised the platoon system. [d. August 19, 1982]

1902 *Joe E. Lewis,* U.S. comedian. [d. June 4, 1971]

1907 *Tex Ritter (Woodward Maurice Ritter),* U.S. cowboy songwriter, singer; starred in over 60 early American Western films; father of actor *John Ritter* (September 17). [d. January 2, 1974]

1908 *José Arcadio Limón,* Mexican-U.S. modern dancer, choreographer, teacher. [d. December 2, 1972]

1910 *Ernestine Potowski-Rose,* U.S. political activist for women's rights. [d. 1892]

1915 *Martin Zama Agronsky,* U.S. broadcast journalist; Emmy Award, 1969.

1916 *P(ieter) W(illem) Botha,* South African political leader;

Prime Minister, 1978–84; President, 84–89; staunch supporter of the apartheid political system.

1920 *James Leonard Farmer,* U.S. civil rights activist, union organizer, lecturer; a founder of the *Congress of Racial Equality (CORE),* 1942; recipient of the Medal of Freedom, 1998.

1930 *Miles Gilbert (Tim) Horton,* Canadian hockey player; 24 years in National Hockey League as defenseman; elected to Hall of Fame, 1977. [d. February 21, 1974]

Glenn Yarborough, U.S. singer.

1935 *Kreskin (George Joseph Kresge, Jr.),* U.S. psychic, entertainer, author; wrote *Use Your Head to Get Ahead,* 1977.

1942 *Bernadine Rae Dohrn,* U.S. radical activist; leader of *Weatherman* faction of *Students for a Democratic Society (SDS);* Director, Children and Family Justice Center at Northwestern University.

1949 *Wayne Wang,* Asian director.

1951 *William (Bill) Madlock, Jr.* U.S. baseball player; National League batting titles, 1975, 1976, 1981, 1983.

1952 *John Walker,* New Zealand runner; Olympic gold medalist in 1,500 meter race, 1976.

1954 *Howard Stern,* U.S. radio disc jockey; known for his outrageous "shock jock" style.

1955 *Kirstie Alley,* U.S. comedic actress; best known for her role as Rebecca Howe on TV's *Cheers.*

1960 *Dominique Wilkins,* U.S. basketball player.

HISTORICAL EVENTS

1701 The *Gregorian calendar* is adopted by Swiss Protestants.

1773 First museum in America is organized in *Charlestown, South Carolina.*

1777 *Mission Santa Clara de Asis* in California is established.

1816 Family of *Bonaparte* is excluded from France forever.

1848 Revolution against *Ferdinand II,* King of the Two Sicilies begins.

1866 *Aeronautical Society of Great Britain* is formed in London.

1875 *Kwang-su* becomes Emperor of China.

1879 *Zulu War* begins between the British of the Cape Colony and the natives of Zululand.

1907 *Histoires Naturelles* by *Maurice Ravel* premieres at a concert of Société Nationale de Musique in Paris.

1914 *Ford Motor Co.* becomes the first manufacturer to adopt profit-sharing and a forty-hour work week.

1918 *Latvia* declares its independence from Russia.

1949 *Arthur Godfrey and His Friends* makes its television debut.

1950 *Mustapha el Nahas Pasha* becomes premier of Egypt.

Restoration of the death penalty in the U.S.S.R. for treason, espionage, and sabotage is decreed by Presidium of the Supreme Council.

1954 Prince *Buu Loc* becomes premier of Vietnam.

Parliament in *New Zealand* is opened by *Queen Elizabeth II;* the first time the parliament is opened by a reigning monarch.

1962 U.S. State Department denies passports to *American Communist Party* members.

1964 African rebels overthrow the predominantly Arab government of *Zanzibar* and proclaim a republic.

1965 Prime ministers of 13 *Arab nations* announce agreement on a unified policy against foreign countries that have established relations with Israel.

1970 *Biafra* capitulates to the federal Nigerian government, ending the 31-month-old civil war.

Boeing 747 lands at Heathrow Airport in London after its first trans-atlantic proving flight from New York.

1971 *All in the Family* makes its television debut.

1972 *Mujibur Rahman* is inaugurated as prime minister of Bangladesh.

1985 China's *giant pandas* are added to the endangered species list.

january

JANUARY
13

HOLIDAYS

Ghana
Redemption Day
Commemorates military government takeover, 1972.

Lithuania
Defenders of Freedom Day

Norway
Tyvendedagen
The official end of Yuletide in Norway.

Sweden
Canutes (Knute's) Day
Swedish occasion for dismantling Christmas trees and celebrating the end of the Christmas season.

Togo
Liberation Day
Commemorates the overthrow of the *Grunitzky* government by *General Gnassingbé Eyadéma*, 1967.

U.S.
Stephen Foster Memorial Day
Commemorates the death of the composer of numerous popular romantic songs of the American South.

RELIGIOUS CALENDAR

The Saints
St. Agrecius, Bishop of Trier. Also called *Agritius*. [d. c. 329]
St. Berno, first Abbot of Cluny and founder of Abbey of Gigny. [d. 927]
St. Hilary, Bishop of Poitiers and Doctor of the Church. Feast formerly January 14. [d. c. 368]

The Beatified
Blessed Godfrey of Kappenberg, Count of Kappenberg. [d. 1127]
Blessed Jutta of Huy, widow and mystic. Also called *Juetta*. [d. 1228]
Blessed Veronica of Binasco, virgin. [d. 1497]

BIRTHDATES

1749 *Friedrich Müller* (called *Maler*), German poet, painter, and engraver. [d. April 23, 1825]

1808 *Salmon Portland Chase*, U.S. jurist, lawyer, teacher; U.S. Secretary of the Treasury, 1861–64; Chief Justice of U.S., 1864–73. [d. May 7, 1873]

1832 *Horatio Alger*, U.S. author, clergyman; wrote over one hundred rags-to-riches stories for boys. [d. July 18, 1899]

1867 *Francis Everett Townsend*, U.S. physician, social reformer; originator and head of Old-Age Revolving Pensions, Inc., the controversial forerunner to the Social Security Act of 1935. [d. September 1, 1960]

1870 *Ross Granville Harrison*, U.S. zoologist; discovered technique for culturing tissue cells outside of the body. [d. September 30, 1959]

1884 *Sophie Tucker (Sophia Abuza)*, U.S. singer, vaudeville star. [d. February 10, 1966]

1885 *Carl Alfred Fuller*, U.S. manufacturer; founder of Fuller Brush Co. [d. December 4, 1973]

1905 *Kay Francis (Katherine Gibbs)*, U.S. actress. [d. August 26, 1968]

1924 *Sir Brian Barratt Boyes*, New Zealand heart surgeon.

1919 *Robert Stack*, U.S. actor; known for his lead role on television series, *The Untouchables*, 1959–63.

1925 *Gwen Verdon (Gwyneth Evelyn Verdon)*, U.S. dancer, actress, musical performer; four-time Tony Award winner.

1927 *Brock(man) Adams*, U.S. lawyer, government official; Secretary of Transportation, 1977–79.

1931 *Charles Nelson Reilly*, U.S. comedic actor, director.

1949 *Brandon Tartikoff*, U.S. television executive; responsible for television series, *The Cosby Show* and *Cheers*. [d. August 27, 1997]

1964 *Penelope Ann Miller*, U.S. actress; known for her roles in *The Freshman*, 1990 and *Chaplin*, 1992.

HISTORICAL EVENTS

1842 A British force is massacred in the *Khyber Pass* by the Afghans.

1846 American troops are ordered into disputed territory between the Nueces and Rio Grande River, precipitating the *Mexican-American War*.

1864 The *Zemstous,* or provincial assemblies, are formed in Russia.

1874 Conscription is introduced in Russia.

1886 *Gold Coast of Africa* is divided into the two separate colonies of *Lagos* and the *Gold Coast* by British charter.

1893 *Independent Labour Party* is formed in Great Britain under the auspices of *Keir Hardie*.

1898 Emile Zola's *J'accuse,* about the *Dreyfus case,* first appears in a French newspaper.

1904 *Kossuth,* first truly symphonic work by *Béla Bartók,* is first performed in Budapest.

1916 Flooding of northern Holland occurs when the dikes of the *Zuider Zee* collapse.

Greek government refuses to permit Allied occupation of *Corfu (World War I)*.

1919 *Medina* is surrendered to *King Hussein* of the Hejaz.

1930 The *Mawson Antarctic Expedition* lands on

Proclamation Island, reaffirming British possession.

1959 *Inter-Governmental Maritime Commission* is established as an agency of the United Nations.

President *Sukarno* of Indonesia dissolves all opposition parties.

1961 *Brazil* and the U.S. sign their first extradition treaty.

1963 Military insurgents seize power in *Togo* after assassinating President *Sylvanus Olympio* and arresting most of his ministers; *Nikolas Grunitzky* is named president.

1964 U.S. and Canadian negotiators reach agreement on the *Columbia River* hydraulic and flood-control project.

1966 *Robert C. Weaver,* the first black ever nominated to the U.S. Cabinet, is named Secretary of the new *Department of Housing and Urban Development*.

1967 Army Chief of Staff Lt. Col. *Etienne Eyadéma* overthrows Grunitzky government of *Togo* and establishes the *Third Togalese Republic*.

1971 U.S. Department of the Interior approves construction of *Alaska pipeline*.

1976 *Sarah Caldwell* becomes the first woman to conduct at New York's Metropolitan Opera.

1977 The London Court of Appeals rules that mere possession of

cannabis leaves is not an offense under English law.

1982 Air Florida plane crashes into a Washington, D.C. bridge, killing 78 people.

1986 An attempted purge of political opponents by *Ali Nasser Muhammad* ignites civil unrest in the *People's Democratic Republic of Yemen*.

1987 Geneticists succeed in tracing the human lineage back to one common ancestor who lived approximately 200,000 years ago in Africa. Evidence is derived from a single gene that has evolved at a regular rate through time.

1988 *Lee Teng-hui* is inaugurated as president of Taiwan following the death of *Chiang Ching-Kuo*. Lee, the first native-born leader to assume the presidency, ends forty years of rule by the Chiang family.

The U.S. Supreme Court rules that public school officials can censor *student newspapers*.

1993 French, British, and U.S. air forces destroy Iraq air-defense missile stations that could threaten U.N. planes overseeing the "*no-fly zone*."

A treaty prohibiting the creation and use of *chemical weapons* is signed in Paris, France, by more than 100 countries.

1998 *Iraq* blocks United Nations inspectors from their mission to search for possible stockpiles of chemical and biological weapons.

january

JANUARY
14

HOLIDAYS

U.S.
Ratification Day
Celebrates the official ending of the
American Revolution.

RELIGIOUS CALENDAR

The Saints
St. Sava, Archbishop of the Serbs.
Patron saint of Serbia.
Orthodox Serbians consider
him the founder of their
national church. Also called
Savas. [d. 123]
St. Felix of Nola. Invoked against
perjury. [d. c. 260]
St. Macrina the Elder, widow. [d. c.
340]
St. Barbasymas, Bishop of Seleucia
and Ctesiphon, and his
companions, martyrs. Also
called *Barbasceminus,
Barbashemin, Barba'shmin.*
[d. 346]
The Martyrs of Mount Sinai. [d. 4th
century]
St. Datius, Bishop of Milan. [d. 552]
St. Kentigern, Bishop of Strathclyde.
Patron of Glasgow. Feast kept
throughout Scotland and also
in the dioceses of Liverpool,
Salford, Lancaster, and
Menevia. Also called *Mungo.*
[d. 603]
St. Anthony Pucci, priest. [d. 1892]

The Beatified
Blessed Odo of Novara, Carthusian
monk. [d. 1200]
Blessed Roger of Todi, monk. Also
called *Ruggiero.* [d. 1237]

Blessed Odoric of Pordenone,
monk. [d. 1331]
Blessed Giles of Lorenzana, lay-
brother. [d. 1518]
Blessed Maria Rivier.
Blessed Peter Donders.

BIRTHDATES

1131 *Waldemar I,* King of
Denmark (called *the Great*);
reigned 1157–82. [d. May 12,
1182]

1730 *William Whipple,* American
Revolutionary leader; member
of Continental Congress,
1776–77; a signer of the
Declaration of Independence.
[d. November 28, 1785]

1741 *Benedict Arnold,* American
Revolutionary War general
and traitor. [d. June 14, 1801]

1798 *Jan Rudolf de Thorbecke,*
Dutch statesman; Premier,
1849–53; 1862–66; 1871–72.
[d. June 4, 1872]

1806 *Matthew Fontaine Maury,*
U.S. oceanographer,
meteorologist; first to publish
a work defined as
contemporary *oceanography.*
[d. February 1, 1873]

1831 *William Drew Washburn,*
U.S. manufacturer;
government official; U.S.
Congressman 1879–85; U.S.
Senator, 1889–95. [d. July 29,
1912]

1841 *Berthe Morisot,* French
Impressionist painter; sister-
in-law of Edouard Manet
(January 23). [d. March 2,
1895]

1875 *Albert Schweitzer,* Alsatian
physician, missionary,
philosopher, musician; Nobel
Peace Prize, 1952. [d.
September 4, 1965]

1882 *Hendrik Van Loon,* Dutch-
American author, lecturer,
historian. [d. March 11, 1944]

1886 *Hugh Lofting,* British-
American writer of children's
stories; best known for the
Dr. Doolittle series. [d.
September 26, 1947]

1892 *Hal Roach,* U.S. film director
and producer. [d. November
2, 1992]

1896 *John (Roderigo) Dos Passos,*
U.S. novelist, journalist. [d.
September 18, 1970]

1898 *John Dos Passos,* U.S. writer;
wrote the trilogy, *U.S.A.* [d.
1976]

1904 *Cecil (Walter Hardy) Beaton,*
British photographer,
theatrical designer, writer. [d.
January 18, 1980]

1905 *Takeo Fukuda,* Japanese
politician; Prime Minister,
1976–78. [d. 1995]

1906 *William Bendix,* U.S. actor.
[d. December 14, 1964]

1919 *Giulio Andreotti,* Italian politician, journalist, editor; Prime Minister, 1972–73; 1976–78.

Andy Rooney, (Andrew Aitken), U.S. author, producer; feature commentator on television series, *60 Minutes,* 1978– .

1925 *Yukio Mishima (Kimitake Hiraoka),* Japanese novelist; noted for his novels relating the conflict between the older military traditions and the modern trends in Japan. [d. by seppuku (ritual suicide), November 25, 1970]

1926 *Thomas Tryon,* U.S. author and actor; known especially for his novels dealing with the supernatural. [d. September 4, 1991]

1935 *Loretta Lynn (Loretta Webb),* U.S. country-and-western singer.

1938 *Morihiro Hosokawa,* Japanese politician; Prime Minister of Japan, 1993–94.

Jack Jones, U.S. singer.

1940 *Julian Bond,* U.S. politician, poet, television commentator; gained national attention while challenging the Georgia delegation to the Democratic National Convention, 1968.

1941 *(Dorothy) Faye Dunaway,* U.S. actress; Oscar Award for *Network,* 1976.

1944 *Nina Totenberg,* U.S. journalist; legal affairs correspondent for National Public Radio, 1975– .

1945 *(Hugh) Marjoe (Ross) Gortner,* U.S. evangelist, actor; Oscar Award for autobiographical documentary, *Marjoe,* 1972.

1949 *Lawrence Edward Kasdan,* U.S. director, screenwriter; co-wrote the screenplays *Empire Strikes Back,* 1980 and *The Big Chill,* 1983.

Franklin Raines, U.S. politician; director of the U.S. Office of Management and Budget, 1996– .

HISTORICAL EVENTS

1604 The *Hampton Court Conference* begins in England to discuss Puritan requests for changes in the Church of England.

1639 *The Fundamental Orders of Connecticut* is ratified; considered the first constitution written in America.

1784 *Continental Congress* ratifies *Treaty of Paris* at the Maryland State House.

1797 *Napoleon Bonaparte* defeats Austrians at *Rivoli (Napoleonic Wars).*

1814 Norway is ceded to the King of Sweden by the King of Denmark (*Treaty of Kiel*).

1858 In France, Orsini's attempted assassination of *Napoleon III* fails.

1866 *Peru* declares war on *Spain.*

1868 *Boston Weekly Journal* is printed on paper derived from wood-pulp; first recorded instance of a U.S. newspaper's using the material.

1875 *Alfonso XII* is proclaimed king of Spain; reigned 1875–85.

1878 W. H. Preece first demonstrates A. G. Bell's *telephone* to Queen Victoria.

1897 *Mattias Zurbriggen* completes the first ascent of *Mount Aconcagua,* the highest peak of the Andes.

1900 *Tosca* by *Giacomo Puccini* has its world premiere at the Costanzi Theatre in Rome.

1902 Imperial Chinese edicts are issued protecting missionaries and native Christians.

1915 The *Battle of Soissons* is ended with the Germans gaining a bridgehead on the *Aisne (World War I).*

1922 The *Irish Free State* is established.

1929 *King Amanulla* of Afghanistan is forced to abdicate; his brother *Inayatullah* is named successor.

1943 *Casablanca Conference* begins; Allies agree on military strategy and demand for unconditional surrender of Axis nations.

1950 U.S. recalls all consular personnel from People's Republic of China.

1960 *John L. Lewis* resigns as president of the *United Mine Workers* after 40 years of service.

1961 U.S. President *Dwight D. Eisenhower* issues prohibition against holding of *gold* abroad by U.S. citizens and corporations.

1963 *George Wallace* is inaugurated as governor of Alabama and promises to fight for "segregation now, and ... forever."

1965 The Prime Ministers of *Northern Ireland* and the *Irish Republic* meet for the first time since the partition of Ireland in 1921.

1969 The *Enterprise,* a U.S. nuclear-powered aircraft carrier, suffers several explosions off the coast of Hawaii.

1972 Formation of a new government in the Yugoslav republic of *Croatia* is announced in a continuing purge of nationalism begun in 1971.

1985 A three-stage withdrawal plan from occupied *Lebanon* is decided upon by the Israeli cabinet.

Hun Sen is elected prime minister of Kampuchea.

1986 *Marco Vinicio Cerezo Arevalo* is inaugurated as president of Guatemala.

1987 *William Paley* and *Lawrence Tisch* are confirmed as chairman and president of *CBS.*

1994 *Jeff Gillooly,* ex-husband of figure skater Tonya Harding, is arrested for the attack on Nancy Kerrigan (January 6, 1994).

HOLIDAYS

Guatemala
Feast of Christ of Esquipulas or Black Christ Festival

Japan
Adults' Day
Day of tribute to young men and women who have reached adulthood.

Jordan
Arbor Day

Sri Lanka
Tamil Thai Pongal Day

Tibet
Lantern Festival

U.S. and Virgin Islands
Martin Luther King's Birthday
Commemorates the birth of the U.S. civil rights leader, assassinated in 1968.

Venezuela
Teacher's Day

RELIGIOUS CALENDAR

The Saints
St. Paul, first Christian hermit; patron saint of clothing industry workers, weavers. [d. 342]

St. Macarius the Elder, anchorite. One of the fathers of Egyptian monasticism. [d. 390]

St. Isidore of Alexandria, priest and hospitaler. [d. 404]

St. John Calybites. [d. c. 450]

St. Ita, abbess and virgin. Also called *Ida, Ide, Mida.* [d. c. 570]

St. Bonitus, Bishop of Clermont. Also called *Bonet, Bont.* [d. 706]

St. Ceolwulf, Northumbrian king and monk. [d. 1208]

The Beatified
Blessed Peter of Castelnau, martyr and monk. [d. 1208]

Blessed Francis de Capillas, priest and martyr. First beatified martyr in China. [d. 1648]

Blessed Arnold Janssen, priest. [d. 1909]

BIRTHDATES

1622 *Moliere (Jean Baptiste Pouquelin),* French dramatist, actor; wrote *The School for Wives,* 1662 and *The Imaginary Invalid,* 1673. [d. February 17, 1673]

1666 *Guru Gobind Singh,* Sikh's tenth master and teacher. Promoter of one community in India thereby abolishing the caste system. [d. 1708]

1716 *Philip Livingston,* American patriot, merchant, signer of Declaration of Independence. [d. June 12, 1778]

1785 *William Prout,* English chemist; discovered presence of *hydrochloric acid* in the stomach. [d. April 9, 1850]

1795 *Aleksandr Sergeievich Griboedov,* Russian poet; known for his satirical comedy discrediting the struggle between generations, *Woe from Wit.* [d. February 11, 1829]

1809 *Pierre Proudhon,* French socialist, anarchist, writer; called the *Father of Anarchism.* [d. January 19, 1865]

1812 *Peter Christen Asbjörnsen,* Norwegian folklorist. [d. January 1, 1885]

1842 *Josef Breuer,* Austrian physician, physiologist; known for his studies of the ear; with Sigmund Freud wrote work on hysteria. [d. June 20, 1925]

1844 *Thomas Coleman (Cole) Younger,* U.S. outlaw. [d. March 21, 1916]

1845 *Ella Flagg Young,* U.S. educator; associated with Jane Addams (September 6) in *settlement house movement.* [d. October 26, 1918]

1859 *Nathaniel Lord Britton,* U.S. botanist; long-time director of the New York Botanical Garden. [d. June 25, 1934]

1866 *Nathan Söderblom,* Swedish theologian; Nobel Peace Prize, 1930. [d. July 12, 1931] bank robbery, 1876; wrote *The Story of Cole Younger,* 1903. [d. March 21, 1916]

1870 *Pierre Samuel Du Pont,* U.S. industrialist; President and

Chairman of the Board, E. I. Du Pont de Nemours, 1915–40. [d. April 5, 1954]

1877 *Lewis Madison Terman,* U.S. psychologist; creator of the *I.Q. test,* 1916; advocate of superior educational opportunities for gifted children. [d. December 21, 1956]

1891 *Osip Emilyevich Mandelshtam,* Russian poet; known for impersonal, fatalistic poetry; died in a Russian labor camp. [d. December 28, 1938]

1895 *Artturi I. Virtanen,* Finnish biochemist; Nobel Prize in chemistry for research into plant synthesis of nitrogen compounds, conservation of fodder, 1945. [d. November 11, 1973]

1899 *Goodman Ace,* U.S. radio performer, humorist; co-starred with his wife Jane in 1930s radio comedy show, *Easy Aces.* [d. March 25, 1982]

1902 *Saud, King of Saudi Arabia,* 1953–64; deposed by Crown Prince Faisal in 1964. [d. February 23, 1969]

1908 *Edward Teller,* U.S. physicist, born in Hungary; known as the *Father of the Hydrogen Bomb.*

1909 *Gene Krupa,* U.S. drummer, bandleader. [d. October 16, 1973]

1912 *Leonid Kantorovich,* Russian mathematician; Nobel Prize in economics for development of theory of optimum allocation of resources, 1975. [d. April 7, 1986]

1913 *Lloyd Bridges (Lloyd Vernet II),* U.S. actor; known for his starring role on television series, *Sea Hunt.* [d. March 10, 1998]

1918 *Joao Baptista de Oliveira Figueiredo,* President of Brazil, 1979–85.

Gamal Abdel Nasser, President of Egypt, 1956–59; President of United Arab Republic 1958–70. [d. September 28, 1970]

1920 *Cardinal John Joseph O'Connor,* U.S. religious leader; Archbishop of New York, 1984– .

1926 *Chuck Berry (Charles Edward Anderson Berry),* U.S. singer, songwriter; one of earliest *rock and roll* stars.

Rod MacLeish, U.S. journalist.

1929 *Martin Luther King, Jr.,* U.S. civil rights leader; Nobel Peace Prize, 1964. [d. April 4, 1968]

1933 *Ernest J. Gaines,* U.S. author; Guggenheim Award, 1971; wrote *The Autobiography of Miss Jane Pittman* and *A Lesson Before Dying.*

1937 *Margaret O'Brien (Angela Maxine O'Brien),* U.S. actress.

1946 *Veronica Tennant,* Canadian dancer; joined the Canadian National Ballet Company as principal dancer in 1965.

1951 *Charo (Maria Rosario Pilar Martinez),* Spanish actress, dancer, singer.

1957 *Mario Van Peebles,* U.S. director and actor; directed *New Jack City,* 1991.

HISTORICAL EVENTS

1535 The *Act of Supremacy* is passed in England.

1549 *Uniformity Act* is issued in England, demanding consistency in order of divine worship.

1552 *Treaty of Chambord* is signed by *Henry II* of France and German Protestants, who cede Metz, Toul, and Verdun to France.

1559 Queen *Elizabeth I* of England is crowned.

1582 Peace of *Jam-Zapolski* between Russia and Poland is signed. Russia is cut off from Baltic Sea *(Livonian War).*

1701 *Prussia* is proclaimed a kingdom.

1759 *British Museum* opens in London.

1777 *Vermont* declares its independence as a republic called *New Connecticut.*

1844 *University of Notre Dame,* South Bend, Indiana, is founded.

1858 *Alexander II* of Russia begins emancipation of serfs.

1859 *National Portrait Gallery* opens in London.

1863 Confederate cruiser *Florida* leaves Mobile, Alabama, to begin its raids on Union shipping *(U.S. Civil War).*

1895 *Swan Lake,* Tchaikovsky's ballet, opens in St. Petersburg, Russia.

1910 The name of the *French Congo* is changed to *French Equatorial Africa.*

1925 *Leon Trotsky* is relieved of his duties as chairman of the Revolutionary War Council by the Central Executive Committee of the Russian Communist Party.

1936 *Ford Foundation* is incorporated to administer funds for scientific, educational, and charitable purposes.

1939 First *Pro Bowl* game in *National Football League* history is played at Los Angeles.

1943 *Pentagon Building* in Washington, D.C., is completed.

U.S. troops force the Japanese off *Guadalcanal (World War II).*

1950 Discovery of the 700-year old crown belonging to King *Alfonso X* of Spain is made public.

1951 U.S. Supreme Court rules invalid a New York City ordinance requiring police permits for preachers to hold religious services on city streets.

1952 *Jean Van Houtte* becomes premier of Belgium.

1963 *Kantanga* ends its two-and-a-half year secession from the Democratic Republic of the Congo.

1966 The *Mongolian Peoples' Republic* signs a 20-year friendship and mutual assistance pact with the USSR, aligning itself against China in the Sino-Soviet dispute.

1967 The Green Bay Packers defeat the Kansas City Chiefs in the first *Super Bowl* football game.

1969 Denmark, Finland, Norway, and Sweden propose a *Nordic Economic Union.*

General Gowan of Nigeria accepts unconditional surrender from Biafran commanders and officers.

1970 *Diana Ross* sings with the Supremes for the last time in Las Vegas.

Israeli archaeologists discover the first evidence of the demolition of *Jerusalem* by the Romans in 70 A.D.

The *Republic of Biafra* is formally disbanded as a independent state and reintegrated into *Nigeria.*

1971 *Aswan High Dam,* in Egypt, is formally dedicated.

1972 *Margrethe II* is proclaimed Queen of Denmark, following the death of her father, *King Frederick IX.*

1973 President *Richard Nixon* orders all offensive military operations against North Vietnam halted *(Vietnam War).*

Israeli Prime Minister *Golda Meir* and *Pope Paul VI* meet at the Vatican.

1974 *Happy Days* makes its television debut.

1981 *Hill Street Blues* makes it television debut.

1985 U.S. Supreme Court rules that public school officials can search students if there are reasonable grounds to suspect a violation of the law.

Tancredo de Almeida Neves is elected as the first civilian president of Brazil in 21 years.

1986 The National Institutes of Health declares the use of *snuff* and *chewing tobacco* to be a health risk.

1987 The U.S. Navy launches a *Trident II* intercontinental ballistic missile in its first land-based test.

1992 The *European Community* acknowledges Slovenia and Croatia.

1996 *Andreas Papandreou,* Prime Minister of Greece, announces his resignation. *Costas Simitis* is selected as the new Prime Minister.

1998 *Milo Djukanovic* takes office as the president of Montenegro.

january

JANUARY
16

HOLIDAYS

Benin
Martyrs' Day

RELIGIOUS CALENDAR

The Saints

St. Priscilla, matron. [d. c. 98 A.D.]

St. Marcellus I, Pope and martyr. Elected Bishop of Rome 309. [d. 309]

St. Honoratus, Archbishop of Arles. Founded Monastery of Lerins. Also called *Honaratus.* [d. 429]

St. Fursey, abbot. Also called *Fursa.* [d. c. 648]

St. Henry of Cocket, hermit. [d. 1127]

St. Berard and his companions, friars and martyrs. First martyrs of the Franciscan order. Berard also called *Berardus* or *Bernard.* Companions: *Adjutus; Odo* or *Otto; Peter.* [d. 1220]

The Beatified

Blessed Ferreolus, Bishop of Grenoble, martyr. [d. c. 670]

Blessed Gonsalo of Amarante, Dominican friar. Also called *Gundisalvus.* [d. c. 1259]

BIRTHDATES

1697 *Richard Savage,* English poet, satirist; friend and biographer of Samuel Johnson (September 18). [d. August 1, 1743]

1749 *Count Vittorio Alfieri,* Italian dramatic poet; his poetry is said to have inspired the revival of the Italian national spirit. [d. October 8, 1803]

1757 *Samuel McIntire,* U.S. architect and woodcarver; called the *architect of Salem;* best known for the exquisite detail of his carvings in the *Sheraton style.* [d. February 6, 1811]

1815 *Henry Wager Halleck,* U.S. military officer, Union Army; known for the brilliance of his administrative abilities during the U.S Civil War. [d. January 9, 1872]

1845 *Charles Dwight Sigsbee,* U.S. admiral during Spanish-American War; commander of U.S. battleship *Maine* when it was sunk in Havana, 1898. [d. July 19, 1923]

1853 *Andre Michelin,* French industrialist; developed the *pneumatic tire* for use on automobiles. [d. April 4, 1931]

1874 *Robert W. Service,* Canadian poet; best known for his poems about travels in the subarctic region. [d. September 11, 1958]

1878 *Henry Dewitt (Harry) Carey, II,* U.S. actor; known for his role as Cheyenne Harry in 26 of John Ford's western films. [d. September 21, 1947]

1901 *Fulgencio Batista y Zaldivar,* Cuban dictator, 1934–59; overthrown by *Fidel Castro.* [d. August 6, 1973]

1909 *Ethel Merman (Ethel Zimmerman),* U.S. singer, actress; regarded as the *First Lady of American Musical Comedy.* [d. February 15, 1984]

1911 *Eduard Frei,* Chilean politician; President of Chile, 1964–70. [d. Janury 22, 1982]

Dizzy Dean (Jerome Dean), U.S. baseball player, radio broadcaster. [d. July 17, 1974]

1934 *Marilyn Horne,* U.S. operatic mezzo-soprano; Director, Music Academy of the West, 1995– .

1928 *William Kennedy,* U. S. author; Pulitzer Prize for *Ironweed,* 1983.

1929 *Francesco Scavullo,* U. S. photographer; known for his cover photographs of models and celebrities.

1930 *Norman Podhoretz,* U.S. editor, critic.

1932 *Dian Fossey,* U.S. naturalist, author; became leading authority on gorillas, 1966–85; murdered in the Virunga Mountains, Rwanda, where she conducted her research. [d. December 27, 1985]

1935 *A(nthony) J(ames) Foyt,* U.S. auto racer.

1944 *Ronnie Milsap,* U.S. singer; Grammy Awards, 1974, 1976, 1981; known for songs, *Stand by My Woman Man* and *Lost in the Fifties Tonight.*

1948 *John Carpenter,* U.S. director; best known for his horror films which include, *Halloween,* 1978, and *Christine,* 1984.

1950 *Debbie Allen,* U.S. actress, dancer; known for starring role on television series, *Fame;* Emmy Awards for choreography, 1982, 1983.

1960 *Sade (Helen Folasade Adu),* Nigerian singer, model; her debut album, *Diamond Life,* which included the single *Smooth Operator,* sold over six million copies.

1974 *Kate Moss,* British model.

HISTORICAL EVENTS

1547 *Ivan IV* of Russia is crowned; first Russian leader to assume title of Tsar officially.

1556 *Charles V, Holy Roman Emperor,* resigns Spain to his son, *Philip II.*

1756 *Treaty of Westminster* between England and Prussia is signed, declaring England's neutrality (*Seven Years' War*).

1883 *Pendleton Act* is passed in the U.S., providing for competitive examinations for civil service.

1915 Germany refuses to give up *submarine warfare* against Allied merchant ships (*World War I*).

1920 *Prohibition* goes into effect in the U.S. one year after ratification of the *18th Amendment.*

1938 *Benny Goodman* and his band perform the first jazz concert at *Carnegie Hall.*

1940 *Frank Murphy* is confirmed as U.S. Supreme Court justice.

1944 General *Dwight D. Eisenhower* takes command of the Allied forces in London and prepares to invade Europe. (*World War II*).

1945 *Battle of the Bulge,* the final German offensive of *World War II* ends in allied victory.

1961 U.S. Department of State issues a ban on travel to *Cuba.*

1964 Jerry Herman's musical, *Hello Dolly,* opens in New York.

1967 *Lucius Amerson* of Tuskegee, Alabama, becomes the first black sheriff of a southern U.S. city in the twentieth century.

1967 All-black cabinet headed by Prime Minister *Lynden O. Pindling* takes office in the *Bahama Islands.*

1969 Two Soviet *Soyuz spacecrafts* dock in orbit, accomplishing the first transfer of men from one space vehicle to another.

Jan Palach, a Czech student, burns himself to death publicly in Prague to protest the Soviet occupation of *Czechoslovakia.*

Swiss Ambassador to Brazil, *Giovanni Enrico Bucher,* is released 40 days after being kidnapped by Brazilian terrorists.

1973 *Lunokhod 2,* unmanned Soviet lunar vehicle, lands on the moon.

1979 *Shah Mohammad Reza Pahlavi* leaves Iran, ending his 37-year reign.

1982 Great Britain establishes full diplomatic relations with the *Vatican.*

1987 A medical advisory panel to the Food and Drug Administration recommends the licensing of *azidothymidine (AZT)* for the treatment of *AIDS.*

San Francisco television station KRON becomes the first in U.S. to break the ban on *contraceptive advertising* due to the concern over *AIDS.*

Sir David Wilson is named British Governor of Hong Kong.

Zhao Ziyang replaces *Hu Yaobang* as general secretary of the Chinese Communist Party's Central Committee.

1991 *Operation Desert Storm* begins as allied and U.S. forces begin air attacks on Iraq in response to the invasion of Kuwait.

1992 *Mohammed Boudiaf* is sworn in as the new President of Algeria.

The government of *El Salvador* and rebel forces that have participated in the 12-year-old civil war sign a peace agreement.

1998 *NASA* announces that U.S. Senator *John Glenn* (D-OH) will return to space on the shuttle *Discovery* later in the the year. Glenn was the first American to orbit Earth (February 20, 1962).

Lithuania, Latvia, and *Estonia* sign a partnership treaty with the United States. The treaty will help their cause for membership in the *North Atlantic Treaty Organization (NATO).*

january

JANUARY
17

HOLIDAYS

U.S.
Benjamin Franklin's Birthday

RELIGIOUS CALENDAR

The Saints

SS. Speusippus, Eleusippus, and
   Meleusippus, martyrs. [d. c.
   155]
St. Genulf, bishop. Also called
   Genou, Gundulphus. [d. c.
   250]
St. Anthony the Abbot, hermit.
   Founder of monasticism.
   Patron saint of Italy, butchers,
   brushmakers, domestic
   animals, and cemetery
   workers. Invoked against the
   disease St. Antony's Fire. Also
   called *Antony, Antonius.* [d.
   356]. Feast celebrated by the
   Coptic, Syrian and Byzantine
   Rites. Obligatory Memorial.
St. Julian Sabas, hermit. [d. 377]
St. Sabinus, Bishop of Piacenza. [d.
   420]
St. Sulpicius II, Bishop of Bourges.
   Also called *Pius, Sulpice.* [d.
   647]
St Mildgyth, abbess of Eastry. [d. 7th
   century]
St. Richimir, abbot. Founder of the
   monastery at Saint-Rigomer-
   des-Bois. [d. c. 715]

The Beatified

Blessed Peter To Rot. [d. beatified
   1995]
Blessed Roseline, virgin and prioress.
   [d. 1329]

BIRTHDATES

1501 *Leonhard Fuchs,* German
   physician, botanist; the plant
   genus *fuchsia* is named for
   him. [d. May 10, 1566]

1504 *Pope St. Pius V,* ascetic and
   reformer; Pope, 1566–72;
   opponent of Queen Elizabeth
   I of England. [d. May 1, 1572]

1600 *Pedro Calderon de la Barca,*
   Spanish dramatist, priest;
   author of over 120 comedies.
   [d. May 25, 1681]

1612 *Thomas Fairfax, Third Baron
   Fairfax,* British nobleman and
   military leader; Commander
   in Chief of Parliamentary
   Army, 1645 (English Civil
   War). [d. November 12, 1671]

1706 *Benjamin Franklin* (b.
   January 6, Old Style),
   American statesman, inventor,
   diplomat, journalist;
   established first *subscription
   library* in America; founder of
   the *American Philosophical
   Society;* published *Poor
   Richard's Almanac,* the most
   popular publication in the
   colonies; invented the
   Franklin stove; proposed
   theories of *electricity;*
   organized the *U.S. Postal
   system;* invented *bifocals;*
   served as American delegate
   to France during American
   Revolution; described as "an
   harmonious human
   multitude" by his biographer,

Carl Van Doren. [d. April 17,
   1790]

1732 *Stanislas II* of Poland, last
   king of independent Poland,
   1764–95. [d. February 12,
   1798]

1761 *Sir James Hall,* Scottish
   scientist; founder of
   experimental geology. [d.
   June 23, 1832]

1820 *Anne Brontë,* English novelist,
   poet; author of *Agnes Grey;*
   sister of Emily Brontë (July
   30) and Charlotte Brontë
   (April 21). [d. May 28, 1849]

1834 *August Weismann,* German
   biologist; a pioneer in
   embryology; one of the
   founders of science of
   genetics. [d. November 5,
   1914]

1860 *Anton (Pavlovich) Chekhov,*
   Russian playwright; author of
   *The Sea Gull, The Cherry
   Orchard.* [d. July 2, 1904]

   Douglas Hyde, known as *An
   Craoibhin Aoibhinn* or *The
   Fair Branch,* Irish scholar,
   statesman; first president of
   Ireland, 1938–45. [d. July 12,
   1949]

1863 *David Lloyd George,* British
   statesman; Prime Minister,
   1916–22. [d. March 26, 1945]

1867 *Carl Laemmle,* German-
   American motion picture
   producer; founder of

Universal Picture Corporation; produced first full-length photoplay, 1912, first million dollar movie, 1922. [d. September 24, 1939]

1871 *David, Earl Beatty, First Earl of the Northsea and of Brooksby,* first Sea Lord of the Admiralty, 1919–27. [d. 1936]

1880 *Mack Sennett,* Canadian film comedian and producer; produced first American feature length comedy film; creator of *Keystone Kops;* prime promotor of such film greats as Charlie Chaplin, W. C. Fields, Buster Keaton. [d. November 5, 1960]

1884 *Noah Beery,* U.S. actor; best known for role in silent film, *Beau Geste,* 1926. [d. April 1, 1946]

1886 *Glenn Luther Martin,* U.S. aviation pioneer, manufacturer; beginning as a barn-storming pilot, became a pioneer in American aviation industry; early advocate of military use of aircraft; many of his planes played significant roles in World Wars I and II; designed *Martin flying boats,* the first transoceanic clippers. [d. December 4, 1955]

1891 *Pablo Manlapit,* Filipino activist; known for promoting laborer's rights in Hawaii. [d. 1969]

1892 *Harry Herbert Bennett,* U.S. auto executive; Henry Ford's henchman; fired by Henry Ford II, 1945. [d. January 4, 1979]

1896 *Loyal Davis,* U.S. surgeon; known for practicing and teaching brain surgery; stepfather of First Lady Nancy Reagan. [d. August 19, 1982]

1899 *Robert Maynard Hutchins,* U.S. lawyer, educator; was made president of University of Chicago at the age of 30, where he proceeded to make controversial changes in curriculum, 1929–51. [d. May 14, 1977]

Nevil Shute (Nevil Shute Norway), British novelist, aeronautical engineer; author of *On the Beach.* [d. January 12, 1960]

Alphonse (Scarface Al) Capone, U.S. gangster; one of the most notorious figures in America's gangland era. [d. January 25, 1947]

1911 *George J. Stigler,* U.S. economist; Nobel Prize in economics, 1982. [d. December 1, 1991]

1917 *Betty White,* U.S. actress; known for her roles as Sue Ann Nivens on television series, *The Mary Tyler Moore Show,* 1973–77 and Rose on *The Golden Girls,* 1985–92.

1922 *Luis Echeverria Alvarez,* Mexican leader; President, 1970–76. [d. September 1, 1988]

1926 *Moira Shearer,* Scottish ballerina.

1928 *Vidal Sassoon,* British hairstylist; wrote *A Year of Beauty and Health,* 1976.

1929 *Jacques Plante,* Canadian hockey player.

1931 *James Earl Jones,* U.S. actor.

L. Douglas Wilder, U.S. politician; first U.S. African American governor (Virginia), 1989–93.

1933 *Sheree North (Dawn Bethel),* U.S. actress; brought into the

limelight by Fox Studios with the hopes of having her replace Marilyn Monroe as lead sex symbol, but film career was limited.

1934 *Shari Lewis (Shari Hurwitz),* U.S. entertainer, ventriloquist, puppeteer.

1943 *René Préval,* Haitian politician; President of Haiti, 1996– .

1944 *Joe (Smokin' Joe) Frazier,* U.S. boxer; Olympic gold medalist, 1964; Professional Heavyweight champ, 1970–73.

1948 *Mick Taylor,* British musician; member of the rock group, *The Rolling Stones,* 1969–74.

1949 *Andy Kaufman,* U.S. actor, comedian; known for appearances on television series, *Saturday Night Live,* 1975–78 and for his role as Latka on *Taxi,* 1978–83. [d. May 16, 1984]

1952 *Darrell Ray Porter,* U.S. baseball player; Most Valuable Player, 1982 World Series.

1955 *Steve Earl,* U.S. country/pop singer.

1962 *Jim Carrey,* Canadian actor; best known for roles in *Ace Ventura: Pet Detective,* 1993; *The Mask,* 1994 and *Batman Forever,* 1995.

HISTORICAL EVENTS

1328 *Louis IV, the Bavarian,* is crowned Holy Roman Emperor at Rome.

1377 *Pope Gregory XI* returns to Rome, signalling the end of the *Avignonese papacy.*

1562 *Edict of St. Germain* formally recognizes French Protestantism.

1601 *Treaty of Lyons* between France and Savoy is signed; France gains Bresse, Bugey, Gex, and Valromey.

1781 *Daniel Morgan* and his sharpshooters are victorious over British at *Cowpens, South Carolina. (American Revolution).*

1837 The second party of Boers in the Great Trek from the British Cape Colony reaches the land of Zulu chief Mosilikatze and defeats him in battle.

1852 *Sand River Convention* is agreed upon, in which the British government recognizes the independence of the *Transvaal,* South Africa.

1912 *Robert Scott's* expedition reaches the *South Pole.*

1916 The *Professional Golfers Association of America* is formed.

1917 The *Original Dixieland Jazz Band,* first ensemble to call themselves a *jazz* band, opens at Reisenweber's Restaurant in New York City.

Virgin Islands are formally purchased from Denmark by United States.

1919 *Ignace Paderewski* becomes Premier of Poland, the first musician to become head of a modern state.

1929 *Bacha-i-Saquao* captures Kabul and proclaims himself king as *Amir Habibullah Ghazi* of Afghanistan.

1945 Soviet and Polish forces unite to capture *Warsaw* ending a five-year German occupation *(World War II).*

1950 The University of California reveals the development of *berkelium,* a new element with an atomic number of 97.

1961 President *Dwight D. Eisenhower* delivers his Farewell Address, warning against the growing power of the "military-industrial complex" in the U.S.

1966 Truman Capote's novel, *In Cold Blood,* is published.

1977 Capital punishment is reinstated in U.S. when *Gary Gilmore* is executed at Utah State Prison.

Catholic schools in South Africa defy racial segregation by admitting black and colored (mixed-race) students.

1983 Two million illegal immigrants are expelled from *Nigeria* to ease civil and economic difficulties.

1984 U.S. Commission on Civil Rights publicly renounces the use of *racial quotas* for the promotion of minorities.

1986 Massachusetts Institute of Technology scientists announce the first laboratory production of *artificial blood vessels* grown from cells.

1992 President *George Bush* officially declares January 20 as a national holiday honoring Martin Luther King, Jr.

1995 *Kobe, Japan* is hit by an *earthquake,* killing more than 5,000 people.

HOLIDAYS

Tunisia

National Revolution Day
Honors nationalist movements of the 1930s and 1940s; independence in 1956, and abolition of monarchy in 1957.

RELIGIOUS CALENDAR

Feasts

Confession of St. Peter the Apostle [major holy day, Episcopal Church; minor feast day, Lutheran Church]

The Saints

St. Volusian, Bishop of Tours. [d. 496]

St. Deicolus, abbot. Founder of Abbey of Lure. Also called *Deel, Desle.* [d. c. 625]

St. Bathan, bishop. Also called *Baithan, Bothanus.* [death date unknown]

St. Prisca, virgin and martyr. Also called *Priscian, Priscilla.* [death date unknown]

The Beatified

Blessed Beatrice D'Este of Ferrara, widow. [d. 1262]

Blessed Christina of Aquila, virgin. [d. 1543]

BIRTHDATES

1689 *Charles Louis de Secondat, Baron de La Brède et Montesquieu,* French lawyer, philosopher; author of *Lettres Persanes,* a criticism of French society of his day, and of *L'Esprit des Lois,* which greatly infuenced political thought on the Continent and in America. [d. February 10, 1755]

1779 *Peter Mark Roget,* English physician, author; creator of *Thesaurus of English Words and Phrases,* 1852. [d. September 12, 1869]

1782 *Daniel Webster,* U.S. statesman, lawyer, orator; a leader of the Whig Party, 1832–52; U.S. Secretary of State, 1841–43; 1850–52. [d. October 24, 1852]

1813 *Joseph Farwell Glidden,* U.S. farmer, inventor; inventor of *barbed wire. [d. October 9, 1906]*

1825 *Edward Frankland,* British chemist; discovered *helium* in the sun. [d. August 9, 1899]

1858 *Daniel Hale Williams,* U.S. surgeon; pioneer in *open heart surgery,* performing first successful repair of a wound of the heart. [d. August 4, 1931]

1867 *Rubén Dario (Félix Rubén García-Sarmiento),* Nicaraguan poet, government official; Nicaraguan Minister to Brazil, 1904; Minister to Madrid, 1908–11. [d. February 6, 1916]

1882 *A(lan) A(lexander) Milne,* British author, poet, playwright; best known as the creator of *Winnie the Pooh.* [d. January 31, 1956]

1888 Sir *Thomas Sopwith,* British aircraft designer; World War I aircraft, the *Sopwith Camel,* named for him. [d. January 27, 1989]

1892 *Oliver Hardy,* U.S. comedian; with his partner, Stan Laurel (June 16), comprised one of the great American comedy teams of all time; the team starred in over 200 films between 1926 and 1951. [d. August 7, 1957]

1904 *Cary Grant (Archibald Leach),* British-American actor. [d. November 29, 1986]

1910 *Kenneth Ewart Boulding,* U.S. economist, author, educator. [d. 1993]

1913 *Danny Kaye (David Daniel Kaminsky),* U.S. actor, comedian. [d. March 3, 1987]

1931 *Chun Doo Hwan,* Korean political leader; President of the Republic of Korea, 1980–88.

Fernando Henrique Cardoso, Brazilian educator, politician; president of Brazil, 1995– .

1933 *Ray Milton Dolby,* U.S. inventor; created Dolby

sound, a noise reduction system that revolutionized the recording industry, 1965; recipient of the National Medal of Technology.

1938 *Curt(is Charles) Flood,* U.S. baseball player; his 1970 lawsuit led to new rules on free agency. [d. January 20, 1997]

1942 *Muhammad Ali,* U.S. boxer; Olympic gold medalist, 1960; World Heavyweight Champion, 1964-67, 1974-78, and 1978-78.

1955 *Steve Earl,* U.S. country/pop singer.

1955 *Kevin Costner,* U.S. actor and director. Won an Academy Award for his film *Dances with Wolves,* 1990.

1961 *Mark Messier,* Canadian hockey player.

HISTORICAL EVENTS

1074 Imperial charter is issued for the *City of Worms.*

1401 *Poland* and *Lithuania* are formally united.

1562 *Gorboduc,* by *Thomas Norton* and *Thomas Sackville,* the first real English tragedy, is presented before Queen Elizabeth I.

1701 *Frederick of Brandenburg* is crowned King of Prussia, as *Frederick I.*

1871 *William I of Prussia* is proclaimed Emperor of Germany.

1919 The opening session of the Peace Conference ending *World War I* is held in Paris with *Georges Clemenceau* of France presiding.

1928 Norway annexes *Bounet Island.*

1962 *Rafael Bonnelly* succeeds *Joaquin Balaguer* as president of the Dominican Republic.

1963 British colony of *Aden* joins the Federation of *Saudi Arabia.*

Brazil and *International Telephone and Telegraph Corporation* sign an agreement whereby Brazil will compensate the company for property expropriated by Brazil in February 1962.

1967 *Albert DeSalvo,* the self-confessed *"Boston Strangler,"* is convicted for sex offenses.

1974 Disengagement agreement is reached on the *Suez Canal* between Egypt and Israel.

1977 Cause of *Legionnaires' Disease* is identified as a hitherto unknown bacterium.

Prime Minister *Indira Gandhi* calls for national elections in India, also freeing some of her imprisoned political opponents.

1982 Four members of the *U.S. Air Force Thunderbirds* flying team die while practicing aerial stunts over the Nevada desert.

1983 South Africa resumes direct control of *Namibia.*

The *International Monetary Fund* increases its General Arrangements to Borrow unit from $7.1 billion to $19 billion and opens the fund to Third World nations.

1989 *F. W. de Klerk* succeeds *Pieter W. Botha* as President of South Africa.

1991 *Iraqi forces* bomb Tel Aviv and Haifa.

1995 *Lamberto Dini* becomes the new Premier of Italy.

1998 *Milorad Dodik* is elected the new Premier of Bosnia-Herzegovina.

HOLIDAYS

Cyprus
Name Day of Archbishop Makarios

Ethiopia
Timket (Eastern Orthodox Epiphany)

Finland
Epiphany

Guyana
Youman Nabi

U.S. (Texas)
Confederate Heroes Day
Honors *Robert E. Lee*, Civil War leader; also honors *Jefferson Davis* and other Confederate heroes.

RELIGIOUS CALENDAR

The Saints
St. Germanicus, martyr. [d. c. 155]
SS. Marius, Martha, Audifax, and *Abachum*, martyrs. Marius also called *Maris*. [d. c. 260] Suppressed 1970.
St. Nathalan, bishop. [d. 678]
St. Albert of Cashel, bishop. [d. 7th century]
St. Fillan, abbot. Also called *Felan, Fillian, Foelan*. [d. 8th century]
St. Canute of Denmark. King and patron saint of Denmark. Also called *Cnut, Knut*. [d. 1086]
St. Wulfstan, Bishop of Worcester. Also called *Wulstan*. [d. 1095]
St. Henry, Bishop of Uppsala, martyr. Patron saint of Finland. [d. c. 1156]

St. Charles of Sezze, Franciscan Lay-Brother of the Observance. [d. 1670]

The Beatified
Blessed Andrew of Peschiera, missionary. [d. 1485]
Blessed Bernard of Corleone, Capuchin lay-brother. [d. 1667]
Blessed Margaret Bourgeoys, virgin, founder of the Congregation of Notre Dame of Montreal. First schoolmistress of Montreal. [d. 1700]
Blessed Mother Mary of the Cross MacKillop. [beatified 1995]
Blessed Thomas of Cori, Franciscan priest. [d. 1729]

BIRTHDATES

1544 *Francis II*, King of France. [d. December 5, 1560]

1736 *James Watt*, Scottish mechanical engineer, inventor; invented modern *condensing steam engine*; originated the word *horsepower*; the *watt* is named for him. [d. August 25, 1819]

1737 *Jacques Henri Bernardin de Saint-Pierre*, French novelist, naturalist; precursor of Romantic Movement in France. [d. January 21, 1814]

1747 *Johann Elert Bode*, German astronomer; catalogued over 12,000 stars; *Bode's Law* for expressing planets' relative distance from the sun is named for him. [d. November 23, 1826]

1798 *(Isidore) Auguste (Marie François) Comte*, French philosopher; founder of *positivism*. [d. September 5, 1857]

1807 *Robert E(dward) Lee*, Confederate Army general during U.S. Civil War; the outstanding military leader of the Confederacy. [d. October 12, 1870]

1809 *Edgar Allan Poe*, U.S. poet, short-story writer, critic; best known for his mystery stories and poems of a supernatural bent. [d. October 7, 1849]

1813 *Sir Henry Bessemer*, British engineer, inventor; developed industrial process for manufacturing steel from molten pig iron known as the Bessemer process. [d. March 15, 1898]

1837 *William Williams Keen*, U.S. surgeon; a pioneer in *neurosurgery*. [d. June 7, 1932]

1839 *Paul Cezanne*, French painter; a leader in the Post-Impressionistic era. [d. October 11, 1906]

1851 *David Starr Jordan*, U.S. biologist, educator,

philosopher; leading U.S. biologist; world renowned ichthyologist; first president of *Stanford University*. [d. September 19, 1931]

1887 *Alexander Woollcott*, U.S. journalist, critic, author; leading personality in literary circles; member of the literary *Round Table* at the New York Algonquin Hotel; exerted great influence on American culture. [d. January 23, 1943]

1905 *Ovetta Culp Hobby*, U.S. government official, newspaper publisher; Director, U.S. Women's (Auxiliary) Army Corps, 1942–45; former editor and chairperson, Houston Post Company. [d. August 16, 1995]

1918 *John Johnson*, U.S. publisher; founder and President, Johnson Publishing Co., Inc.; member of the board of a number of major U.S. corporations.

1920 *Javier Perez de Cuellar*, Peruvian statesman; Secretary-General of United Nations, 1982–92.

1923 *Jean Stapleton*, U.S. actress; known for her role as Edith on television series, *All in the Family*, 1971–79.

1926 *Fritz William Weaver*, U.S. actor; Tony Award for *Child's Play*, 1970.

1931 *Robert Breckenridge Ware MacNeil*, U.S. broadcast journalist; co-anchor of news show, *MacNeil/Lehrer NewsHour*, 1975–95; Emmy Award, 1974.

1932 *Richard Lester*, U.S. director; known for his direction of Beatles films *Help!*, 1965 and *A Hard Days Night*, 1964.

1935 *Natalie Kay (Tippi) Hedren*, U.S. actress; known for her starring role in Hitchcock's film, *The Birds*, 1963.

1939 *Phil Everly*, U.S. singer, musician; member of pop duo, *Everly Brothers*.

1942 *Michael Crawford (Patrick Dumble-Smith)*, British singer, actor; Tony Award winner for *Phantom of the Opera*, 1988.

1943 *Janis Joplin*, U.S. singer. [d. October 4, 1970]

1944 *Michelle Marie (Shelley) Fabares*, U.S. actress; known for her role on television series, *The Donna Reed Show*; also co-starred with Elvis Presley in *Girl Happy* and *Clambake*.

1946 *Dolly Parton*, U.S. country-and-western singer.

1947 *Ann Compton*, U.S. broadcast journalist, ABC

1949 *Robert Palmer*, British singer, musician; known for songs, *Some Like It Hot* and *Addicted to Love*.

1953 *Desi(derio Alberto) Arnaz, Jr.* U.S. actor; son of Desi Arnaz and Lucille Ball.

1954 *Cynthia Sherman*, U.S. photographer.

HISTORICAL EVENTS

1419 Rouen in France capitulates to *Henry V* of England *(Hundred Years' War)*.

1479 *Union of Aragon and Castile* is established under *Ferdinand the Catholic* and *Isabella*.

1493 *Peace of Barcelona* between France and Spain is signed, by which France cedes *Roussillon* and *Cerdagne*.

1874 *Morrison Remick Waite* is nominated as the Seventh Chief Justice of the U.S. Supreme Court.

1904 A serious anti-European uprising breaks out in the British protectorate of *Southern Nigeria*.

1915 The first major German air raid over England occurs with attacks on Yarmouth, Kings Lynn, and other Norfolk County towns *(World War I)*.

1921 *Pact of Union* is signed between *Costa Rica, Guatemala, Honduras,* and *Salvador* (dissolved in 1922).

1929 Communist leader *Leon Trotsky* is exiled from Russia.

1951 Viet-Minh Communist offensive in Indochina is defeated by French forces.

1961 U.S. Federal Communications Commission authorizes first space *satellite communications* link between U.S. and Europe on an experimental basis.

1962 Canadian Immigration Minister *Ellen Fairclough* announces new *immigration regulations* abolishing discrimination based on race, color, or religion.

Charles Van Doren and nine other television quiz show winners are given suspended sentences for perjury. The contestants falsely testified that they had not received answers prior to their television appearances.

Laotian premier, *Bon Oum*, neutralist *Souvanna Phouma*, and Prince *Souphanouvrong* of the Pathet Lao agree upon a coalition government for *Laos*.

1966 *Indira Gandhi,* daughter of *Jawaharlal Nehru,* is elected India's third prime minister.

1968 Great Britain and Russia sign agreement to cooperate in the fields of applied science and technology.

1970 U.S. Supreme Court rules that the *Selective Service System* lacks authority to accelerate the induction of persons violating *draft regulations.*

India's first (and Asia's largest) *nuclear power plant* at Tarapur is dedicated by Prime Minister *Indira Gandhi.*

1975 *Papua* New Guinea is declared a *Papua Republic* with an interim government by separatists who pledge to seize control of the island.

China publishes a new state constitution embodying the basic ideas of *Mao Tse-tung.*

1976 The U.S. Food and Drug Administration bans *Red Dye No. 2* in foods, drugs, and cosmetics, after it is linked to cancer in laboratory animals.

1977 President Gerald Ford pardons *Iva Toguri D'Aquino,* known as *Tokyo Rose* to U.S. servicemen during World War II.

Radio astronomers at the *Max Planck Institute* in West Germany report discovery of water molecules outside earth's galaxy.

Lake Erie freezes from bank to bank for the first time in modern history.

1989 *Ante Markovic* becomes premier of Yugoslavia.

1995 *Russian troops* take control of *Chechnya* after three years of rebel fighting.

1998 The *Food and Drug Administration (FDA)* announces it must approve any attempts to clone humans.

january

JANUARY
20

HOLIDAYS

Azerbaijan
Black January or Martyr's Day

Brazil (Rio de Janeiro)
St. Sebastian Day
Commemorates the founding of Rio de Janeiro.

Cape Verde Islands
National Heroes Day

Great Britain
St. Agnes Eve
Traditionally believed to be the night during which a maid dreams of her future spouse.

Guinea-Bissau
National Heroes Day

Laos
Day of the Army

Republic of Mali
Army Day

Award Day

U.S.
Inauguration Day
Twentieth Amendment to the U.S. Constitution declares that the term of newly elected President and Vice-President begin at noon on this day.

Philately Day

RELIGIOUS CALENDAR

The Saints

St. Fabian, Pope and martyr; elected Bishop of Rome, 236. [d. 250] Optional Memorial.

St. Sebastian, martyr; patron saint of Portugal, archers, soldiers, pinmakers, and athletes; invoked against plague. [d. c. 288] Optional Memorial.
St. Euthymius the Great, abbot. [d. 473]
St. Fechin, abbot. [d. 665]

The Beatified

Blessed Benedict of Coltiboni. [d. c. 1107]
Blessed Desiderius, Bishop of Thèrouanne. Also called *Didier.* [d. 1194]

BIRTHDATES

1716 *Charles III,* King of Spain, 1757–88. [d. December 14, 1788]

1724 *John Goddard,* U.S cabinetmaker; considered one of the finest furniture craftsmen that America has produced. [d. July 16, 1785]

1732 *Richard Henry Lee,* American Revolutionary patriot, lawyer, signer of the Declaration of Independence; first Senator from Virginia. [d. June 19, 1794]

1734 *Robert Morris,* American merchant, public official; signer of the Declaration of Independence; established the *Bank of North America.* [d. May 9, 1806]

1763 *Theobald Wolfe Tone,* Irish nationalist; persuaded French military to help overthrow English rule in Ireland. [d. November 19, 1798]

1812 *Sir William Fox,* New Zealand author, statesman; Prime Minister, 1856; 1861–62; 1869–72; 1873. [d. June 23, 1893]

1814 *Jean-François Millet,* French painter. [d. January 20, 1875]

1873 *Johannes Jensen,* Danish poet, novelist; Nobel Prize in literature, 1944. [d. November 25, 1950]

1879 *Ruth St. Denis,* U.S. dancer, choreographer; noted for her innovative dance concepts, based on cultures of the Far East; considered one of the great women of American dance. [d. July 21, 1968]

1889 *Huddie (Leadbelly) Ledbetter,* U.S. blues singer, guitarist; noted for his folk songs and stories, which he not only performed but also helped gather for the Library of Congress. [d. December 6, 1949]

1894 *Walter Piston,* U.S. composer, teacher; Pulitzer Prize in music, 1947, 1960. [d. November 12, 1976]

1896 *George Burns (Nathan Birnbaum),* U.S. comedian, actor; an institution in American comedy for decades. [d. March 9, 1996]

1904 *Alexandra Danilova,* Russian-born ballerina, choreographer. [d. July 13, 1997]

1906 *Aristotle Socrates Onassis,* Greek shipping magnate; married Jacqueline Kennedy, widow of U.S. President John F. Kennedy. [d. March 15, 1975]

1910 *Joy Adamson,* British author and naturalist; wrote *Born Free* and *Elsa.*

1912 *Walter Owen Briggs, Jr.,* U.S. baseball executive; former owner of Detroit Tigers; Tiger Stadium previously known as Briggs Stadium. [d. July 3, 1970]

1918 *Juan Esquivel,* Mexican musician.

1920 *Federico Fellini,* Italian screenwriter and film director; world renowned for such films as *La Dolce Vita* and *8 1/2.* [d. October 31, 1993]

Joy (Friederike Victoria) Adamson, Austrian wildlife conservationist; best known as author of *Born Free,* an account of her life in Kenya. [d. January 3, 1980]

1926 *Patricia Neal,* U.S. actress.

1930 *Edwin Eugene (Buzz) Aldrin, Jr.,* U.S. astronaut; crew member of *Apollo 11,* first manned spacecraft to land on the moon.

1931 *David M. Lee,* U.S. physicist; Nobel Prize for Physics in 1996. Lee shares the prize with Robert C. Richardson and Douglass D. Osheroff for their discovery of superfluidity in helium-3.

1945 *Susan Rothenbaerg,* U.S. artist; known for her work with rich colors on large-scale canvases.

1946 *David K. Lynch,* U.S. screenwriter, director; known for the films *The Elephant Man* and *Blue Velvet.*

1948 *Anatoly Borisovich Shcharansky,* Russian scientist; Jewish dissident who served nine years in Soviet prisons, 1977–86.

1949 *Paul Stanley (Paul Eisen),* U.S. singer, musician; member of the rock group, *Kiss.*

1956 *Bill Maher,* U.S. talk show host, comedian; host of *Politically Incorrect,* 1993– .

John Naber, U.S. swimmer; four-time Olympic gold medalist.

1958 *Lorenzo Lamas,* U.S. actor; known for his role as Lance Cumson on television series, *Falcon Crest;* son of Fernando Lamas and Arlene Dahl.

HISTORICAL EVENTS

1301 In England, *Parliament of Lincoln* rejects papal claims on Scotland.

1320 *Wladyslaw I,* known as the *Short,* is crowned King of Poland.

1327 *Edward II* of England resigns throne and is succeeded by *Edward III.*

1558 French, under the *Duke of Guise,* take *Calais,* the last English possession in France.

1612 *Rudolf II,* Holy Roman Emperor, dies, and is succeeded by *Matthias.*

1801 The *War of the Oranges* breaks out between Spain and Portugal.

1841 *Hong Kong* is ceded by China to the British.

1848 *Christian VIII* of Denmark dies and is succeeded by *Frederick VII.*

1874 *The Treaty of Pangkor* gives the British a protectorate over Perak in the Malay Peninsula.

1885 *Mersey Tunnel* between Birkenhead and Liverpool, England, opens.

1887 U.S. gains exclusive right to establish a fortified naval base at *Pearl Harbor* in Hawaii.

1892 First game of *basketball* is played at YMCA gym in Springfield, Massachusetts, with peach baskets nailed to balconies at each end of room.

1918 The *Breslau,* a German-Turkish cruiser, is sunk in the Dardanelles; the *Goeben* is beached in an action with British warships *(World War I).*

1920 The *American Civil Liberties Union (ACLU)* holds its first meeting in New York City.

1921 *Mustapha Kemal* issues the Fundamental Law providing for a parliament and responsible ministry, a president, and manhood suffrage for Turkey.

1924 The first *Kuo Min Tang National Congress* opens at Canton, China; *Sun Yatsen* is elected president.

1936 King *George V* of Great Britain dies and is succeeded by his son, *Edward VIII.*

1941 *Franklin D. Roosevelt* becomes the first U.S.

president to be inaugurated for a third term.

1942 Procedures for implementing the mass annihilation of Jews by the Nazi regime are formulated at the *Wannsee Conference.*

1949 *Margaret Chase Smith* is elected to the U.S. Senate, becoming the first woman to serve in both houses of Congress.

1949 *Harry S Truman* is inaugurated for his second term (first full term) as 33rd president of the U.S., *Alben W. Barkley* is sworn in as vice-president.

1950 A new constitution grants the Dutch colony of *Suriname* autonomy in its domestic affairs.

1953 *Dwight David Eisenhower* is inaugurated as 34th president of the U.S.; *Richard Nixon* is sworn in as vice-president.

1960 *William V. S. Tubman* is inaugurated for a fourth 4-year term as president of Liberia.

1961 *John Fitzgerald Kennedy* is inaugurated as 35th president of the U.S.; *Lyndon B. Johnson* takes the oath as vice-president.

1965 *Lyndon Baines Johnson* and *Hubert H. Humphrey* are inaugurated as president and vice-president of the U.S.

1966 Australian prime minister, *Rober Menzies,* resigns from office and is succeeded by *Harold Holt.*

1969 *Richard Milhous Nixon* is inaugurated as 37th president of the U.S.; *Spiro Agnew* is sworn in as vice-president.

1971 United Kingdom postal workers begin the first nationwide postal strike in the nation's history.

1977 *Jimmy Carter* is inaugurated as 39th president of the U.S.; *Walter Mondale* is sworn in as vice-president.

1981 The 52 *American hostages* in Iran are freed after 444 days in captivity and are flown to a U.S. Air Force base in Wiesbaden, West Germany.

Ronald Wilson Reagan is inaugurated as the 40th president of the U.S.; *George Bush* is sworn in as vice-president.

1985 *Ronald Wilson Reagan* is inaugurated for his second term as 40th president of the U.S.; at 73 years of age he is the oldest man ever elected to this office; *George Bush* is sworn in as vice-president.

1986 *Martin Luther King Day* is officially observed for the first time.

The government of Chief *Leabua Jonathan* of Lesotho

is overthrown in a military coup led by General *Justin Lekbonya.*

1987 Anglican Church envoy *Terry Waite* disappears in Lebanon during negotiations to free Western hostages.

1989 *George Bush* is inaugurated as the 41st president of the U.S.; *Dan Quayle* is sworn in as vice-president.

The *Soviet Union* begins the final withdrawal of its armed forces from *Afghanistan.*

1990 *Soviet troops,* in an attempt to quell a possible rebel uprising for independence, attack the city of Baku in *Azerbaijan,* killing hundreds of innocent people.

1993 *William Jefferson (Bill) Clinton* is sworn in as the forty-second president of the United States.

1996 *Yasir Arafat* is elected president of the Palestine Liberation Organization.

1997 President *Bill Clinton* takes the oath of office to begin his second term.

1998 *Vaclav Havel* is re-elected as President of the Czech Republic.

Scientists *James Robl* and *Steven Stice* announce the *cloning* of a calf.

january

HOLIDAYS

Bulgaria
Grandmother's Day

Barbados
Errol Barrow Day

Dominican Republic
Altagracia Day
Celebrated with processions to the shrine of St. Altagracia.

Lesotho
Army Day

RELIGIOUS CALENDAR

The Saints
St. Fructuosus, Bishop of Tarragona and martyr. [d. 259]
St. Patroclus, martyr. [d. c. 259]
St. Agnes, virgin and martyr. Patron of purity, virginity, young girls, girl scouts, and Cumana, Venezuela. [d. c. 304] Obligatory Memorial.
St. Epiphanius, Bishop of Pavia; called the *Peacemaker, the Glory of Italy, the Light of Bishops,* and also *Papa.* [d. 496]
St. Meinrad, hermit and martyr; patron of the Abbey of Einsiedeln in Switzerland; also called *Meginrat.* [d. 861]
St. Alban Roe, priest and martyr. [d. 1642]

The Beatified
Blessed Edward Stransham, priest and martyr. [d. 1586]
Blessed Joseph Vaz, priest. [d. 1711]

Blessed Thomas Reynolds, priest and martyr. [d. 1642]
Blessed Josepha of Beniganim, virgin and nun. [d. 1696]

BIRTHDATES

1337 *Charles V,* King of France (called the *Wise*); reigned, 1364–80. [d. September 16, 1380]

1721 *James Murray,* English soldier; Governor of Quebec, 1760; Governor of Canada, 1763–66. [d. June 18, 1794]

1743 *John Fitch,* U.S. inventor; an early pioneer in the development of steam-powered boats. [d. July 2, 1798]

1813 *John Charles Frémont,* U.S. explorer, public official, Union general, mapmaker; Republican presidential candidate; Territorial Governor of Arizona, 1878–81. [d. July 13, 1890]

1815 *Horace Wells,* U.S. dentist; one of the first to use *ether* and *nitrous oxide* as *anesthetic* in dental surgery. [d. January 24, 1848]

1821 *John Cabell Breckinridge,* U.S. politician, lawyer, railroad executive; U.S. Vice-President, 1857–61; Confederate Army general during U.S. Civil War, 1864–65. [d. May 17, 1875]

1823 *Imré Madách,* Hungarian poet, dramatist; author of *The Tragedy of Man,* a dramatic poem dealing with the fall of the human race. [d. October 5, 1864]

1824 *Thomas Jonathan (Stonewall) Jackson,* Confederate Army general during U.S. Civil War; known as a master of military tactics and a great military leader. [d. May 10, 1863]

1829 *Oscar II,* King of Sweden and Norway; reigned over both countries until Norway became independent in 1905. [d. December 8, 1907]

1884 *Roger Nash Baldwin,* U.S. social reformer; founder of *American Civil Liberties Union.* [d. August 26, 1981]

1887 *Wolfgang Köhler,* German-U.S. *Gestalt* psychologist; known especially for experiments in *animal psychology.* [d. June 11, 1967]

1895 *Cristobal Balenciaga,* Spanish fashion designer. [d. March 24, 1972]

1900 *J. Carroll Naish,* U.S. character actor. [d. January 24, 1973]

1905 *Christian Dior,* French fashion designer. [d. October 24, 1957]

1906 *Igor Alexandrovich Moiseyev,* Russian ballet dancer, choreographer, director; Ballet Master, Bolshoi Theater, 1924–39.

1912 *Konrad Emil Bloch,* U.S. biochemist; Nobel Prize in physiology or medicine for research on *cholesterol metabolism* (with F. Lynen), 1964.

1922 *Barney Clark,* U.S. dentist; the first human to receive a permanent *artificial heart.* [d. March 23, 1983]

1922 *Paul Scofield,* British stage and film actor.

1925 *Benjamin (Benny) Hill,* British comedian; known for his internationally sydicated television series, *The Benny Hill Show.* [d. April 20, 1992]

1927 *Telly Savalas (Aristotle Savalas),* U.S. actor. [d. February 22, 1994]

1928 *Reynaldo Benito Antonio Bignone,* Argentine statesman; President of Argentina, 1982–83.

1938 *Wolfman Jack (Robert Smith),* U.S. radio personality. [d. July 1, 1995]

1940 *Jack Nicklaus,* U.S. golfer; won more major tournaments than any golfer in history.

1941 *Plácido Domingo,* Spanish operatic tenor.

Richie Havens, U.S. singer; known for song, *Here Comes the Sun,* 1971.

1944 *(Rufus) Jack (Henry) Abbott,* U.S. author, convicted murderer; wrote *In the Belly of the Beast: Letters from Prison,* 1981.

1947 *Jill Eikenberry,* U.S. actress.

1950 *Billy Ocean,* Trinidad-born singer, songwriter; known for song, *Caribbean Queen,* 1984.

1957 *Geena Davis,* U.S. actress; won Best Supporting Actress Oscar for *The Accidental Tourist,* 1988.

HISTORICAL EVENTS

1528 England declares war on *Holy Roman Emperor Charles V.*

1645 In England, *Sir Thomas Fairfax* is appointed head of the Parliamentary army, opposing *Charles I (English Civil War).*

1793 *Louis XVI* of France is beheaded *(French Revolution).*

1896 *Dr. Starr Jameson* and those arrested with him for the raid into the Transvaal, leave Durban, South Africa, for trial in Britain.

1899 *Lord Kitchener* is appointed governor-general of the Sudan.

1908 New York City's *Sullivan Ordinance* makes it illegal for woman to smoke in public.

1911 *National Progressive Republican League,* led by *Robert La Follette,* is organized in U.S.

1915 *Kiwanis International* is founded in Detroit, Michigan.

1925 *Albania* is proclaimed a republic.

1929 *Leon Trotsky* is deported by *Josef Stalin* from the U.S.S.R. and goes to Istanbul, Turkey.

1930 *London Naval Conference* opens with Japan, the United States, Great Britain, France, and Italy attempting to reach agreement on naval limitations.

1949 Chinese president, *Chiang Kai-shek,* abandons the capital city of *Nanking* as Communist forces advance *(Chinese Civil War).*

1950 Treaty of friendship, commerce, and navigation between the U.S. and the *Republic of Ireland* is signed in Dublin.

Alger Hiss is found guilty of perjury by a U.S. federal jury in denying that he had passed confidential U.S. documents to *Whittaker Chambers.*

1954 *U.S.S. Nautilus,* world's first nuclear-powered submarine, is launched.

1965 *Indonesia* withdraws from the UN.

1970 North Vietnam refuses to publish the names of captured U.S. pilots, branding them criminals, not prisoners of war.

1977 *President Jimmy Carter* issues a pardon for U.S. draft evaders.

1979 *Pittsburgh Steelers* become the first football team to win three Super Bowls.

1993 President *Bill Clinton* reverses the previous restrictions set by Supreme Court on abortion (July 3, 1989).

1998 President *Bill Clinton* publicly denies allegations of an affair with former White House intern *Monica Lewinsky* (August 17, 1998).

Pope John Paul II visits Cuba.

HOLIDAYS

China
Sending Off the Kitchen God Day

New Zealand (Wellington)
Anniversary Day

St. Vincent
Discovery Day

Heros' Day

RELIGIOUS CALENDAR

The Saints
St. Vincent of Saragossa, martyr; patron of the wine industry. [d. 304] Optional Memorial.
St. Blesilla, widow. [d. 383]
St. Anastasius the Persian, martyr. [d. 628]
St. Dominic of Sora, abbot; invoked against thunderstorms. [d. 1031]
St. Berhtwald, Bishop of Ramsbury. [d. 1045]
St. Vincent Pallotti, founder of the Society of Catholic Apostolate, the Pallottine Fathers. [d. 1850]

The Beatified
Blessed William Patenson, priest and martyr. [d. 1592]
Blessed Joseph Freinademetz, priest. [d. 1908]

BIRTHDATES

1440 *Ivan III* (the *Great*), Grand Duke of Muskovy; ruler of Russia, 1462–1505; regarded as founder of the *Russian empire.* [d. October 27, 1505]

1561 *Sir Francis Bacon,* Baron Verulam, Viscount St. Albans, English philosopher, essayist, statesman; developed a new system of analysis of knowledge, designed to replace Aristotle's logic, published in Latin as *Novum Organum,* 1620. [d. April 9, 1626]

1592 *Pierre Gassendi,* French physicist, philosopher; opposed to Aristotelian philosophy; revived *Epicurean doctrine.* [d. October 24, 1655]

1729 *Gotthold Ephraim Lessing,* German critic, dramatist; author of the first German tragedy of middle-class life, *Miss Sara Sampson.* [d. February 15, 1781]

1775 *Andre Marie Ampere,* French scientist; made important discoveries in electricity and magnetism, now known as electro-dynamics. [d. June 10, 1836]

1783 *Henri Joseph Paixhans,* French artillery expert; inventor of one of the earliest shell-guns, the *Paixhans Gun,* 1837. [d. August 19, 1854]

1788 *George Gordon, Sixth Baron Byron (Lord Byron),* British Romantic poet, satirist; known for *Childe Harold's Pilgrimage, The Corsair,* and other romantic works; joined Greek struggle for independence; died of malaria. [d. April 19, 1824]

1802 *Richard Upjohn,* U.S. architect; known especially for his church designs; a founder and first president of *American Institute of Architects.* [d. August 17, 1878]

1849 *(Johan) August Strindberg,* Swedish playwright, novelist, short story writer; sometimes called the *Shakespeare of Sweden.* [d. May 14, 1912]

1850 *Robert Somers Brookings,* U.S. manufacturer, philanthropist; President of *Washington University,* 1897–1916; helped establish the *Brookings Institution,* famed research center named for him. [d. November 15, 1932]

1858 *Beatrice (Potter) Webb,* British socialist, economist; with her husband, Sidney Webb (July 13), founded the *London School of Economics.* [d. April 30, 1943]

1875 *D(avid) W(ark) Griffith,* U.S. film producer, director; renowned for his pioneering film epics *Birth of a Nation* and *Intolerance.* [d. July 23, 1948]

1877 *Hjalmar Schacht,* German financier; Minister of Economics under the Third Reich, 1934–37; acquitted of war crimes after participation in Reparations Commission deliberations. [d. June 4, 1970]

1882 *Louis Pergaud,* French novelist, short-story writer; best known for his animal stories. [d. April 8, 1915]

1890 *Frederick Moore Vinson,* U.S. politician, jurist; Director, Office of Stabilization, 1939–45; Chief Justice of U.S. Supreme Court, 1946–53. [d. September 8, 1953]

1897 *Rosa Melba Ponselle,* U.S. operatic soprano. [d. May 25, 1981]

1908 *Lev Davidovitch Landau,* Russian physicist; Nobel Prize in physics for studies on condensed gas, 1962. [d. April 1, 1968]

1909 *U Thant,* Burmese diplomat; Secretary-General of UN, 1962–72. [d. November 25, 1974]

1911 *Bruno Kreisky,* Austrian political leader; Federal Chancellor of Austria, 1970–83. [d. July 29, 1990]

1912 *Ann Sothern (Harriette Lake),* U.S. comedic actress.

1916 *Bill Durnan,* Canadian hockey player; elected to Hall of Fame, 1964.

1928 *Birch (Evans) Bayh,* U.S. politician, lawyer, farmer; U.S. Senator, 1963–80.

1932 *Piper Laurie (Rosetta Jacobs),* U.S. actress; best known for her role in *Carrie,* 1976.

1934 *Bill Bixby,* U.S. actor; known for his starring roles on television series, *My Favorite Martian, The Courtship of Eddie's Father,* and *The Incredible Hulk.* [d. November 21, 1993]

1935 *Sam Cooke,* U.S. singer, musician. [d. December 11, 1964]

Pierre Samuel (Pete) DuPont, IV, U.S. politician; Governor of Delaware, 1977–85.

1937 *Eden Pastora (Gomez),* Nicaraguan political leader; led 1979 revolt that toppled Anastasio Somoza.

Joseph Wambaugh, U.S. novelist; author of *The Onion Field, The Choir Boys.*

1940 *John Hurt,* British actor; known for his starring role in *The Elephant Man,* 1980.

1941 *Ed Bradley,* U.S. television journalist.

1945 *William Harris,* head of the *Symbionese Liberation Army,* responsible for the kidnapping of newspaper heiress Patricia Hearst.

Michael Christofer (Michael Anthony Procaccino), U.S. playwright, actor; Pulitzer Prize in drama, 1977.

1949 *Steve Perry,* U.S. singer; lead singer of the rock group, *Journey.*

1954 *Jim Jarmusch,* U.S. director; directed the popular *Stranger Than Paradise.*

1957 *Mike Bossy,* Canadian hockey player; elected to Hall of Fame, 1991.

1959 *Linda Denise Blair,* U.S. actress; known for her role as the demon-possessed girl in *The Exorcist,* 1973.

1965 *Diane Lane,* U.S. actress.

HISTORICAL EVENTS

1760 The French are defeated in the *Battle of Wandiwash,* India, by the British.

1771 Spain cedes the *Falkland Islands* to Great Britain.

1840 First British colonists in New Zealand land at *Port Nicholson.*

1901 *Queen Victoria* of Great Britain dies after the longest reign of any British monarch (63 years, 7 months), and is succeeded by her son, *Edward VII.*

1905 *Bloody Sunday* begins in St. Petersburg, Russia (*Revolution of 1905*).

1907 Richard Strauss' *Salome* has its American premiere in New York, outraging the moralistic American audience.

1917 U.S. President *Woodrow Wilson* makes his *peace without victory* address to the Senate, favoring establishment of a *League of Nations.*

1924 First Labour Cabinet gains power in Great Britain under *Ramsey MacDonald.*

1936 Paul Hindemith first performs his *Funeral Music* in memory of the death of King *George V* of Great Britain.

1944 The Allied forces begin *Operation Shingle,* a plan to capture Rome by landing troops in *Anzio* and *Neturno,* Italy (*World War II*).

1949 Communist forces capture *Peking,* the last stronghold of the Nationalist troops north of the Yangtze river (*Chinese Civil War*).

1953 Arthur Miller's play, *The Crucible*, premieres on Broadway.

1964 Canada and the U.S. sign agreements for the development of the *Columbia River* basin and for establishment of an international park at the former summer home of Franklin D. Roosevelt, Campobello Island.

Kenneth D. Kaunda is sworn in as first prime minister of Northern Rhodesia (Zambia).

1967 *Brazil* adopts a new constitution.

1968 *Rowan and Martin's Laugh-In* makes its television debut.

U.S. B-52 bomber carrying four unarmed hydrogen bombs crashes near *Thule, Greenland*.

1970 The first regularly scheduled commercial flight of the *Boeing 747* jumbo jet arrives in London.

1973 *George Foreman* knocks out *Joe Frazier* for world heavyweight boxing title.

Former U.S. President *Lyndon B. Johnson* dies of a heart attack.

U.S. Supreme Court rules that states may not prevent a woman from obtaining an *abortion* during the first six months of pregnancy.

1980 Soviet physicist and human rights advocate *Andrei Sakharov* is exiled to Siberia.

1998 *Theodore (Ted) J. Kaczynski* pleads guilty to bombing charges. Kaczynski, only known as the "unabomber" until his arrest, is charged with sixteen bombings over seventeen years.

Australia bans Japanese fishing boats from its waters due to a decline in the bluefin tuna population.

january

JANUARY
23

HOLIDAYS

Liechtenstein
National Holiday
Celebrates the formation of the principality, 1719.

U.S.
Handwriting Day
Sponsored by the Writing Instrument Manufacturers Association.

RELIGIOUS CALENDAR

The Saints
St. Asclas, martyr. [d. c. 3rd century]
St. Emerentiana, virgin and martyr. [d. c. 304]
SS. Clement and Agathangelus, martyrs. [d. c. 308]
St. John the Almsgiver, Patriarch of Alexandria; patron of the Order of St. John at Jerusalem, the Knights of Malta. [d. c. 619]
St. Ildephonsus, Archbishop of Toledo. Also called *Alfonso, Alphonsus, Alonzo, Hildephonsus, Ildefonsus.* [d. 667]
St. Bernard, Archbishop of Vienne. Also called *Barnard.* [d. 842]
St. Lufthildis, virgin. Also called *Leuchteldis, Liuthild, Lufthold.* [d. c. 850]
St. Maimbod, missionary and martyr. Also called *Mainboeuf.* [d. c. 880]

The Beatified
Blessed Margaret of Ravenna, virgin. [d. 1505]

BIRTHDATES

1688 *Ulrika Eleonora,* Queen of Sweden, reigned 1718–20; abdicated in favor of her husband who became *King Frederick I.* [d. November 24, 1741]

1730 *Joseph Hewes,* U.S. merchant; signer of Declaration of Independence. [d. November 10, 1779]

1783 *Stendahl (Marie Henri Beyle),* French novelist; author of biographies of Haydn, Rossini, and Napoleon; best known for his novels *Le Rouge et le Noir,* and *La Chartreuse de Parme.* [d. March 23, 1842]

1813 *Camilla Collett,* Norwegian novelist; a leader of the feminist movement in Norway. [d. March 6, 1895]

1832 *Edouard Manet,* French painter, print-maker; originator and leader of French Impressionism. [d. April 30, 1883]

1862 *David Hilbert,* German mathematician; known for his research on invariant theory. [d. February 14, 1943]

1876 *Otto Paul Hermann Diels,* German chemist; Nobel Prize in chemistry for studies in synthesizing of organic compound (with K. Adler), 1950. [d. March 7, 1954]

1898 *Sergei Mikhailovich Eisenstein,* Russian director; first film director to master the technique of montage; known for his direction of *Battleship Potemkin.* [d. February 10, 1948]

1899 *Thomas A. Dorsey,* U.S. gospel songwriter and singer; composed "Take My Hand, Precious Lord." [d. 1993]

1903 *Randolph Scott (Randolph Crance),* U.S. actor. [d. March 2, 1987]

1907 *Hideki Yukawa,* Japanese physicist; Nobel Prize in physics for theory of existence of *mesons,* 1949. [d. September 8, 1981]

1915 *Sir W. Arthur Lewis,* British agricultural economist; Nobel Prize in economics, 1979. [d. 1991]

Potter Stewart, U.S. jurist, lawyer; Associate Justice, U.S. Supreme Court, 1958–81. [d. December 7, 1985]

1918 *Gertrude Elion,* U.S. biochemist; Nobel Prize in physiology or medicine (with George Hitchings and Sir James Black), 1988.

1919 *Ernie Kovacs,* U.S. comedian. [d. January 13, 1962]

1921 *Sergio Leone,* Italian filmmaker. [d. April 30, 1989]

1928 *Jeanne Moreau,* French actress.

1929 *John Charles Polanyi,* Canadian chemist; Nobel Prize in chemistry for his research in reaction dynamics (with Dudley Robert Herschbach and Yuan T. Lee), 1986.

1930 *Derek Walcott,* West Indian poet; Nobel Prize for Literature in 1992.

1933 *Chita Rivera,* U.S. singer, dancer, comedienne; Tony Award for her role as Anna in *The Rink,* 1984.

1943 *Gil Gerard,* U.S. actor; known for his role as Buck on television series, *Buck Rogers in the 25th Century,* 1979–81.

1957 *Princess Caroline (Louise Marguerite Grimaldi),* Monacan princess; daughter of Princess Grace and Prince Rainier.

1963 *Akeem Abdul Ajibola Olajuwon,* Nigerian-born basketball player.

1974 *Tiffani-Amber Thiessen,* U.S. actress; known for her role on the TV drama *Beverly Hills 90210.*

HISTORICAL EVENTS

1516 *Ferdinand of Aragon* dies and is succeeded by *Charles V,* his grandson.

1668 *Alliance of the Hague,* a triple alliance of England, Holland, and Sweden against France, is signed.

1719 Principality of *Liechtenstein* is formed.

1793 Second partition of *Poland* by Russia and Prussia takes place.

1911 *International Oceanographic Institute* opens in Paris.

1913 A coup d'état of the *Young Turks* overthrows the Turkish Ministry of Kemal Pasha as a triumvirate of Enver, Talaat, and Jemal seizes power.

1916 Austrians seize *Scutaria, Albania,* and *Podgorica, Montenegro (World War I).*

1920 Holland refuses to bow to pressures to surrender the exiled *Kaiser Wilhelm* of Germany.

1924 Polish decree introduces a new national currency, the *zloty.*

1950 The Israeli parliament names *Jerusalem* as the nation's capital.

1958 *Jimmy Hoffa* assumes the presidency of the *Teamsters Union.*

1960 U.S. Navy bathyscape *Trieste* breaks all records by descending to a depth of 35,800 feet in the Pacific Ocean off Guam.

1961 *Venezuela* adopts a new constitution that provides for a strong central government.

1967 United Nation's *Outer Space Treaty* is signed.

1968 Israel and Egypt conclude their prisoner exchanges following the *Six-Day War.* 4,481 Egyptians are traded for 11 Israelis.

U.S.S. Pueblo, a U.S. Navy intelligence ship, is seized off the Korean coast by North Korean patrol boats.

1973 *Eldfell Volcano* in Iceland, dormant for thousands of years, erupts, forcing the evacuation of the town of *Vestmannaeyjax.*

1977 First episode of the television mini-series *Roots,* is aired.

1984 U.S. formally adds *Iran* to its list of nations exporting terrorism.

1985 Filipino armed forces chief *Fabian Ver* and 25 others are charged in the 1983 assassination of opposition leader *Benigno Aquino.*

1989 U.S. Supreme Court rules that most governmental set-aside programs for minority business-people are unconstitutional.

1991 *Peru* suffers an outbreak of *cholera,* resulting in the deaths of hundreds.

1997 *Madeleine Albright* becomes the first female U.S. Secretary of State.

january

JANUARY
24

HOLIDAYS

Romania
Union Day

Togo
Economic Liberation Day
Commemorates the failed attack at
Sarakawa.

RELIGIOUS CALENDAR

The Saints
St. Babylas, Bishop of Antioch and
martyr. First martyr of whom
a translation of relics is
recorded. [d. c. 250]
St. Felician, Bishop of Foligno and
martyr; patron of Foligno,
Italy. Original Apostle of
Umbria. [d. c. 254]
St. Macedonius, ascetic. [d. c. 430]
St. Francis de Sales, Bishop of
Geneva and Doctor of the
Church. Co-founder of the
Order of the Visitation. Feast
formerly January 29. [d. 1622]
Obligatory Memorial.
St. Timothy, pastor and confessor.
[minor Lutheran festival]

The Beatified
Blessed Marcolino of Forlì,
Dominican monk. [d. 1397]

BIRTHDATES

74   *Hadrian (Publius Aelius
Hadrianus),* Roman Emperor.
[d. 138 A.D.]

1670 *William Congreve,* English
dramatist; known for his wit

and refined dialogue; best
known for *The Way of the
World.* [d. January 19, 1729]

1712 *Frederick II (the Great),* King
of Prussia, 1740–86. [d.
August 17, 1786]

1732 *Pierre Augustin Caron de
Beaumarchais,* French
dramatist; author of *Le
Barbier de Sèville* and *Le
Mariage de Figaro,* later
inspiring operas by Rossini
and Mozart. [d. May 18, 1799]

1746 *Gustavus III,* King of Sweden;
his reign was known as the
Gustavian Enlightenment. [d.
March 29, 1792]

1749 *Charles James Fox,* English
statesman, orator; major
parliamentary opponent of
King George III. [d.
September 13, 1806]

1776 *Ernst Theodor Hoffmann,*
German writer, composer,
caricaturist; his novels are
among the finest produced
during the German Romantic
movement. [d. June 25, 1822]

1800 *Sir Edwin Chadwick,* British
social reformer; laid the
foundation for the
government inspection
system. [d. July 6, 1890]

1828 *Ferdinand Julius Cohn,*
Polish botanist; called the
Father of Bacteriology. [d.
June 25, 1898]

1836 *Nikolai Dobrolyubov,* Russian
radical, critic; looked upon as
a founder of the revolutionary
movement in Russia. [d.
November 17, 1861]

1855 *Charles Henry Niehaus,* U.S.
sculptor; responsible for
numerous sculptures in
rotunda of national capitol,
Washington, D.C., as well as
statues of many American
heroes in various state
capitols throughout the
country. [d. June 19, 1935]

1860 *Bernard Henry Kroger,* U.S.
grocer. [d. July 21, 1938]

1862 *Edith (Newbold) Wharton,*
U.S. novelist, short-story
writer; Pulitzer Prize in fiction,
1921. [d. August 11, 1937]

1874 *Arthur Alfonso Schomburg,*
Puerto Rican collecter;
collection of African American
culture was purchased by the
New York Library and named
the *Arthur A. Schomburg
Collection of Negro Literature
and Art.* [d. 1938]

1885 *Umberto Nobile,* Italian
aeronautical engineer;
pioneer in Arctic aviation;
flew with Amundsen and
Ellsworth across the North
Pole, 1926. [d. July 29, 1978]

1888 *Vicki Baum,* Austrian-
American novelist, dramatist;
author of *Grand Hotel.* [d.
August 29, 1960]

1915 *Mark Goodson,* U.S. producer; developed television game shows, *The Price is Right,* and *Family Feud* with Bill Todman. [d. December 18, 1992]

1917 *Ernest Borgnine (Ermes Borgnino),* U.S. actor.

1918 *(Granville) Oral Roberts,* U.S. evangelist.

1919 *Leon Kirchner,* U.S. composer, pianist; Pulitzer Prize in music, 1967.

1925 *Maria Tallchief,* U.S. ballerina; former wife of George Balanchine.

1927 *Paula Fickes Hawkins,* U.S. politician; Senator, 1980–86.

1934 *Leonard Goldberg,* U.S. producer; known for production of television series, *Charlie's Angels* and *Hart to Hart* with Aaron Spelling.

1936 *Doug(las James) Kershaw,* U.S. musician; cajun fiddler, known for classic, *Louisiana Man.*

1939 *Ray Stevens (Harold Ray Ragsdale),* U.S. musician, singer.

1941 *Giorgio Chinaglia,* Italian soccer player.

Neil Diamond, U.S. singer, songwriter.

Aaron Neville, U.S. country singer.

1947 *Warren Zebon,* U.S. singer, songwriter.

1949 *John Belushi,* U.S. actor, comedian. [d. March 5, 1982]

1960 *Nastassja Kinski (Nastassja Nakszynski),* German actress; known for her starring roles in *Tess,* 1978, and *Unfaithfully Yours,* 1984.

1968 *Mary Lou Retton,* U.S. gymnast; first American woman to win individual medal in gymnastics; Olympic gold medalist, 1984.

HISTORICAL EVENTS

661 *Caliph Ali of Arabia,* son-in-law of Muhammad, is murdered by anti-Shiite faction.

1076 *Synod of Worms* is held; German bishops challenge *Pope Gregory VII,* who dethrones and excommunicates *Henry IV* of Germany.

1446 *Pope Eugene IV* deposes archbishops of Cologne and Trier for their opposition to *Frederick III* of Germany.

1742 *Charles Albert,* Elector of Bavaria, is elected Holy Roman Emperor; he becomes *Charles VII.*

1848 Gold is discovered at *Sutter's Mill,* in the San Joaquin Valley of California, marking the beginning of the great *California Gold Rush.*

1857 *University of Calcutta* in India is established.

1867 *Schleswig* and *Holstein* are incorporated into *Prussia.*

1915 German cruiser *Blücher* is sunk by the British in the *Battle of Dogger Bank (World War I).*

1919 The *Catalonian Union* meets at Barcelona, Spain, drawing up a program for home rule.

1943 *Tripoli* falls to British Eighth Army *(World War II).*

1960 *General Maurice Challe,* Supreme French Commander in Algeria, declares a state of siege in *Algiers.*

1965 *Sir Winston Churchill,* British statesman and author, dies in London.

1966 *Indira Gandhi,* daughter of *Jawaharlal Nehru,* is sworn in as the third prime minister of India, following the January 11 death of Prime Minister *Lal Bahadun Shastri.*

1969 *Italy* recognizes the *People's Republic of China.*

1972 U.S.S.R. becomes the first major world power to recognize the newly formed nation of *Bangladesh.*

Japanese Army Sergeant *Shoichi Yokoi,* unaware that the war had ended in 1945, is found in the jungles of Guam where he has lived in hiding since U.S. troops seized the island in *World War II.*

1978 Fragments of Soviet reconnaissance satellite *Cosmos 954* land in a remote area of Canada's Northwest Territory.

1984 Apple Computer, Inc. introduces the *Macintosh personal computer.*

1985 The U.S. space shuttle *Discovery* begins its first military mission.

1986 The *Voyager-2* spacecraft transmits photographs from the planet *Uranus* and discovers new moons and rings.

1989 *Barbara Harris* is confirmed as the first female bishop in the history of the *Church of England.*

1989 Convicted serial killer *Ted Bundy* is executed in Florida.

1995 Touted as "the Trial of the Century," the trial of O. J.

january

Simpson for the murders of Nicole Brown Simpson and Ron Goldman begins.

1996 *Olestra* gains approval from the U.S. Food and Drug Administration as a new fat substitute. Some researchers object to Olestra's entry into the marketplace due to its ability to inhibit the absorption of nutrients.

HOLIDAYS

Brazil (Sao Paulo)
Founding of Sao Paulo Day

Scotland
Burns Night
Honors poet Robert Burns.

RELIGIOUS CALENDAR

Feasts
The Conversion of St. Paul, apostle
of the Gentiles. Baptism and
conversion took place in 34
A.D. [major holy day, Episcopal
Church; minor festival,
Lutheran Church]

The Saints
SS. *Juventinus* and *Maximinus,*
soldiers and martyrs. [d. 363]
St. *Publius,* abbot. [d. c. 380]
St. *Apollo,* abbot. [d. c. 395]
St. *Dwyn,* virgin and nun; Welsh
patron of lovers. Invoked to
cure sick animals. Also called
*Donwen, Donwenna,
Dunwen, Dwynwen.* [d.
5th–6th century]
St. *Praejectus,* Bishop of Clermont
and martyr. Also called *Prelis,
Prest, Priest, Prix.* [d. 676]
St. *Poppo,* abbot. [d. 1048]
St. *Artemas,* martyr. [death date
unknown]

BIRTHDATES

1627 *Robert Boyle,* Anglo-Irish
physicist, chemist; noted for
his early research in
chemistry and natural
philosophy; a founding
member of England's *Royal
Society.* [d. December 30,
1691]

1736 *Joseph Louis Lagrange,*
French mathematician,
astronomer; developer of the
calculus of variations. [d.
April 10, 1813]

1746 *Stéphanie Félicité du Crest de
Saint Aubin, Comtesse de
Genlis,* French novelist,
educator; governess of the
children of the *Duchesse de
Chartres.* [d. December 31,
1830]

1759 *Robert Burns,* Scottish poet;
the national poet of Scotland;
renowned throughout the
world for his ballads and
songs. [d. July 21, 1796]

1783 *William Colgate,* U.S.
manufacturer, philanthropist;
founder of the Colgate Soap
Company, 1804; founder of
Colgate University, which is
named for him. [d. March 25,
1857]

1813 *James Marion Sims,* U.S.
surgeon. [d. November 13,
1883]

1825 *George Edward Pickett,*
Confederate army general in
U.S. Civil War; led *Pickett's
Charge,* one of the most
celebrated military actions in
U.S. history. [d. July 30, 1875]

1851 *Arne Evenson Garborg,*
Norwegian novelist, poet,
playwright, essayist;
proponent of *Landsmaal,* a
Norwegian literary language
based on peasant dialect. [d.
January 14, 1924]

1860 *Charles Curtis,* U.S. politician,
lawyer; U.S. Vice President,
1929–33. [d. February 8,
1936]

1874 *W(illiam) Somerset
Maugham,* British novelist,
short-story writer, playwright;
known for the realism of his
novels, and his depiction of
the essential tragedies and
victories of human life. [d.
December 16, 1965]

1878 *Ernst Frederick Werner
Alexanderson,* U.S. electrical
engineer; with the General
Electric Company, received
over 300 patents for
developments in electrical
equipment; with Radio
Corporation of America, did
pioneer work in radio and
television. [d. May 14, 1975]

1882 *(Adeline) Virginia Woolf,*
British novelist, short-story
writer, playwright, screenwriter; master of the stream
of consciousness style of
writing. [d. March 18, 1941]

1891 *William Christian Bullitt,* U.S.
diplomat; first U.S.
Ambassador to the U.S.S.R.,
1933–36; U.S. Ambassador to

France, 1936–42. [d. February 15, 1967]

1899 *Paul Henri Spaak,* Belgian statesman; Premier, 1938–39, 1946; first President of UN General Assembly, 1946. [d. July 31, 1972]

1901 *Robert Ingersoll Wilder,* U.S. author, journalist; wrote *Flamingo Road,* 1942; *An Affair of Honor,* 1969. [d. August 22, 1974]

1917 *Ilya Prigogine,* Belgian chemist; Nobel Prize in chemistry for explanation of contradictory biological processes, 1977.

1918 *Ernie Harwell,* U.S. broadcaster, author; broadcaster for the Detroit Tigers; Baseball Hall of Fame, 1981.

1919 *Edwin (Harold) Newman,* U.S. news commentator, author.

1928 *Eduard Amvrosiyevich Shevardnadze,* Russian diplomat; Minister of Foreign Affairs, 1985–90; President, Republic of Georgia, 1992– .

1933 *Corazon Cojuangco (Cory) Aquino,* Philippine politician; widow of opposition leader Benigno Aquino; became president after Ferdinand Marcos fled the country, 1986–93.

1935 *Antonio dos Santos Ramalho Eanes,* Portuguese statesman; President, 1976–78.

1936 *Dean Jones,* U.S. actor; known for his starring roles in Disney films, *That Darn Cat,* 1965 and *The Love Bug,* 1968.

1938 *Etta James (Jamesetta Hawkins),* U.S. R & B singer.

HISTORICAL EVENTS

1327 *Edward III* of England seizes the throne of England.

1502 *Margaret,* daughter of *Henry VII* of England, marries *James IV* of Scotland.

1533 *Henry VIII* of England and *Anne Boleyn* are secretly married, he for the second time.

1909 *Elektra,* by Richard Strauss, premieres at the Dresden Royal Opera House.

1915 First *transcontinental telephone call* is made, between New York and San Francisco; Alexander Graham Bell and Dr. Thomas A. Watson exchange greetings.

1919 The Peace Conference of World War I adopts President Wilson's resolution for the creation of a *League of Nations* as part of the peace agreement.

1961 Presdent *John F. Kennedy* holds the first live televised news conference.

1966 *Constance Baker Motley* is named U.S. District Judge for southern New York, becoming the first black female federal judge.

1970 The Vatican refuses to accredit a West German diplomat. Mrs. *Elisabeth Mueller,* because she is a woman.

1971 General *Idi Amin Dada* creates the *Second Republic of Uganda* after a military coup.

1975 Prime Minister *Sheikh Mujiur Rahman* of *Bangladesh* is inaugurated as President.

1980 *Abolhassan Bani-Sadr* is elected President of the *Islamic Republic of Iran.*

1981 *Jiang Qing,* widow of chairman Mao Tse-tung, is sentenced to death for her role during the *Cultural Revolution* in China.

1983 The death sentence given to Chinese Communist leader, *Jiang Qing,* is commuted to life imprisonment.

The *Infrared Astronomical Satellite* is launched into orbit to gather information on distant stars and our solar system.

Nazi war criminal, *Klaus Barbie,* is arrested in Bolivia.

Pope *John Paul II* approves the first revision in Canon law since 1917.

1988 *Ramsewak Shankar* is inaugurated as the first civilian president of Suriname in eight years.

HOLIDAYS

Australia
Australia Day

Dominican Republic
Duarte's Birthday
Commemorates the birth of *Juan Pablo Duarte*, a founder of the Republic and leader in the fight for freedom from Haiti.

India
Basant Pancami or Independence Day
Celebrates the proclamation of the Republic, 1950.

Monaco
St. Dévote (patron saint of Monaco)

Uganda
Liberation Day

U.S. (Arkansas)
Douglas MacArthur Day

U.S. (Michigan)
Admission Day
Commemorates Michigan's admission to the Union, 1837.

RELIGIOUS CALENDAR

The Saints

St. Timothy, bishop and martyr. Disciple of the Apostle Paul. Patron of stomach patients. Feast formerly January 24. [d. c. 97] Obligatory Memorial.

St. Titus, Bishop in Crete. Feast formerly February 6. [d. 1st century] Obligatory Memorial. [minor Lutheran festival]

St. Paula, widow. [d. 404]

St. Conan, Bishop of Man. Also called *Conon.* [d. 7th century]

St. Alberic, Abbot of Citeaux; co-founder of the Cistercian Order. Also called *Aubrey.* [d. 1109]

St. Eystein, Archbishop of Nidaros. [d. 1188]

St. Margaret of Hungary, virgin and Dominican nun; daughter of Bela IV, King of Hungary. [d. 1270]

BIRTHDATES

1468 *Guillaume Budé* or *Budaeus,* French humanist; responsible for laying foundation of *Bibliothèque National.* [d. August 23, 1540]

1715 *Claude Adrien Helvetius,* French philosopher; exponent of *sensationalism* or *sensualism.* [d. December 26, 1771]

1763 *Charles XIV John (Jean Baptiste Jules Bernadotte),* French soldier and King of Sweden and Norway, 1818–44. [d. March 8, 1844]

1810 *Joseph Brown,* U.S. inventor; designed the first universal *milling machine,* a breakthrough in machinery, 1862; also devised precision *measuring instruments* (calipers, protractors). [d. July 23, 1876]

1826 *Julia Grant,* wife of U.S. President Ulysses S. Grant. [d. December 14, 1902]

1831 *Mary Elizabeth Dodge (Mary Elizabeth Mapes),* U.S. editor, author of children's books; author of *Hans Brinker or The Silver Skates;* pre-eminent figure in U.S. children's literature, 1864–84. [d. August 21, 1905]

1880 *Douglas MacArthur,* U.S. Army officer; one of the greatest but most controversial military leaders in U.S. history; U.S. Army Chief of Staff, 1930–35; Supreme Commander of Allied Forces in Southwest Pacific, 1942–45; 1950–51; relieved of duty after conflict with U.S. President Harry Truman. [d. April 5, 1964]

1904 *Sean MacBride,* Irish international civil servant; Nobel Peace Prize, 1974; Lenin Peace Prize, 1977. [d. January 15, 1988]

1905 *Maria Augusta von Trapp,* Austrian-American musician, member of the world famous *Trapp Family Singers;* the subject of *The Sound of Music.* [d. March 28, 1987]

1908 *Stephane Grappelli,* French musician. [d. December 1, 1997]

1911 *Polykarp Kusch,* U.S. physicist; Nobel Prize in

physics for measurement of electromagnetic properties of electrons, 1955. [d. March 20, 1993]

1913 *Jimmy Van Heusen (Edward Chester Babcock),* U.S. composer; known for his compositions, *Swinging on a Star, High Hopes,* and *The Second Time Around.* [d. February 7, 1990]

1918 *Nicolae Ceauşescu,* Rumanian political leader; first president of Socialist Republic of Rumania, 1974–89. [d. December 25, 1989]

Philip Jose Farmer, U.S. author; science-fiction writer known for novels, *To Your Scattered Bodies Go,* 1971; *Venus on the Half-Shell,* 1975.

1923 *Anne Jeffreys,* U.S. actress.

1925 *Paul Newman,* U.S. actor.

1928 *Eartha Kitt,* U.S. singer, actress.

Roger Vadim (Roger Vadim Plemmianikov), French film director; credited with discovery of *Brigitte Bardot* (September 28).

1929 *Jules Feiffer,* U.S. cartoonist, writer.

1930 *Thomas Gumbleton,* U.S. religious leader; archbishop of Detroit, 1968–; known for his visit to U.S. embassy hostages in Iran.

1935 *Robert George (Bob) Uecker,* U.S. baseball player, actor, broadcaster; famous for his mediocre baseball playing; known for his roles in beer commercials and on television series, *Mr. Belvedere,* 1984–89.

1936 *Samuel Chao Chung Ting,* U.S. physicist; Nobel Prize in

physics for discovery of subatomic particle known as *psi* or *J particle* (with B. Richter), 1976.

1942 *Scott Glenn,* U.S. actor; performed in *The Right Stuff,* 1983, *Backdraft,* 1991 and *Silence of the Lambs,* 1991.

1944 *Angela (Yvonne) Davis,* U.S. black militant; Communist activist.

1946 *Eugene Karl (Gene) Siskel,* U.S. movie critic; known for his film reviews on television with Roger Ebert.

1957 *Edward (Eddie) Van Halen,* U.S. musician, singer; member of the rock band, *Van Halen;* married to Valerie Bertinelli.

1961 *Wayne Gretzky,* Canadian-born hockey player; Edmonton Oilers, 1978–88; Los Angeles Kings, 1988–96; St. Louis Blues, 1996; and New York Rangers, 1996– ; all-time leader in goals, assists, and points.

HISTORICAL EVENTS

1699 The *Treaty of Karlowitz* is signed with the Turks giving up most of Hungary, Transylvania, Croatia, and Slavonia to Austria; Venice and Poland also receive territory.

1788 First settlers, including 717 convicts, arrive at *Sydney, Australia.*

1827 *Peru* secedes from Colombia.

1837 *Michigan* is admitted as the 26th state of the Union.

1885 *Khartoum,* the Sudan, falls to the Mahdi who massacre *General Gordon* and the Egyptian garrison.

1911 *Der Rosenkavalier* by Richard Strauss premieres at the Dresden Opera.

1915 Turkish forces led by Germans begin their advance across the Sinai towards the *Suez Canal (World War I).*

Russians open a counter-offensive against the Austrians in the *Battles of the Carpathian Passes (World War I).*

U.S. Congress establishes the *Rocky Mountain National Park* in Colorado.

1920 The U.S. recognizes the *Armenian Republic.*

1930 *Wireless telegraph service* is opened between Japan and London.

1931 The British release *Mahatma Gandhi* from prison after the second campaign of civil disobedience.

1936 *Barcelona* is captured by General Francisco Franco's troops *(Spanish Civil War).*

1942 First U.S. Expeditionary Force to Europe in *World War II* reaches Northern Ireland.

1950 *Jawaharlal Nehru* is inaugurated as the first prime minister of India.

1951 *Temple Beth Israel* of Meridian, Mississippi becomes the first Jewish congregation to allow women to perform the functions of a rabbi.

1960 *Cameroon* is admitted to the UN as the 83rd member.

1965 Military leaders of *South Vietnam* oust the civilian government of Premier *Tran Van Huong* and name Lieut. Gen. Hguyen Khanh to deal with the crisis caused by anti-government demonstrations.

Hindi is designated the official language of India, replacing English; the declaration results in riots in the southern part of the country; shortly afterwards, the Official Languages Act of 1963 is amended to confirm English as the "associate language."

1970 Poor Richard's Universal Life Church, a tax-exempt atheist church, is founded by *Madalyn Murray O'Hair.*

1971 *Charles Manson* and three of his followers are convicted on seven counts of murder, including the death of actress *Sharon Tate.*

1975 *Thailand* holds its first parliamentary elections since 1957.

1977 The Spanish government bans public demonstrations.

1978 Tunisian workers rise against President *Habib Bourguiba* in worst civil violence in decades.

1983 The *W particle,* a new subatomic particle, is discovered by Swiss physicists.

1988 Researchers release evidence that a single *aspirin* taken every other day can prevent heart attacks in healthy men.

1991 *Mohammed Siad Barre* is ousted as the President of Somalia by rebel forces of the *United Somali Congress.*

1992 The *Washington Redskins* win *Super Bowl XXVI,* defeating Buffalo Bills, 37-24.

1996 *Vaclav Havel* is elected President of the newly formed Czech Republic.

In an historic first, First Lady *Hillary Rodham-Clinton* testifies before a grand jury investigating the Whitewater affair.

january

JANUARY
27

HOLIDAYS

Monaco
St. Devote
Commemorates the patron saint of
Monte Carlo.

Vietnam
Vietnam Day
Celebrates peace agreement that
included the removal of U.S. forces.

RELIGIOUS CALENDAR

The Saints
St. Marius, abbot. Also called
Maurus, May. [d. c. 555]
St. Vitalian, Pope. Elected Bishop of
Rome, 657. [d. 672]
St. Angela Merici, [d. 1540] Optional
Memorial.
St. Julian, Bishop of Le Mans. [death
date unknown]

The Beatified
Blessed John of Warneton, Bishop of
Thérouanne. [d. 1130]
Blessed Henry de Osso y Cervello.
[beatified 1979]

BIRTHDATES

1756 *Wolfgang Amadeus
(Johannes Chrysostomus
Wolfgangus Theophilus)
Mozart*, Austrian composer;
one of the universal geniuses
of music; composed over 600
pieces, including *Idomeneo*,
said to have revolutionized
lyrical drama, and *Don
Giovanni* and *The Magic
Flute*, which were the
beginnings of romantic opera.
[d. December 5, 1791]

1775 *Friedrich Wilhelm Joseph von
Schelling*, German romantic
philosopher; espoused theory
recognizing *purpose* as the
guiding principle of the
universe. [d. August 20, 1854]

1814 *Giovanni Prati*, Italian poet,
patriot; ardent advocate of
Italian unity. [d. May 9, 1884]

1832 *Lewis Carroll (Charles
Lutwidge Dodgson)*, British
author of children's books,
mathematician; best known as
author of *Alice's Adventures
in Wonderland* and *Through
the Looking Glass.* [d. January
14, 1898]

1836 *Leopold von Sacher-Masoch*,
Austrian short-story writer,
novelist, dramatist; term
masochism was created to
describe the abnormal
behavior portrayed in his
novels. [d. March 9, 1895]

1850 *Samuel Gompers*, U.S. labor
union official; founder and
president of the American
Federation of Labor,
1886–1924. [d. December 13,
1924]

1859 *William II, (Kaiser Wilhelm)*,
Emperor of Germany and
King of Prussia, 1888–1918;
led Germany in World War I;
abdicated, 1918. [d. June 4,
1941]

1885 *Jerome (David) Kern*, U.S.
composer; widely acclaimed
for his show music;
composed 50 scores during
his career. [d. November 11,
1945]

1900 *Hyman George Rickover*,
Russian-born U.S. naval
officer; responsible for design
and development of the
Nautilus, the world's first
nuclear-powered submarine;
established nuclear power
educational facilities for the
U.S. Navy; known for his
outspokenness, especially his
criticism of American
education. [d. July 8, 1986]

1903 *Sir John Carew Eccles*,
Australian physiologist; Nobel
Prize in physiology or
medicine for research on
electrical charges and their
passage through nerve
membranes (with A. L.
Hodgkin and A. F. Huxley),
1963. [d. May 2, 1997]

1908 *William Randolph Hearst, Jr.*,
U.S. editor, publisher. [d. May
14, 1993]

1921 *Donna Reed (Donna
Mullenger)*, U.S. actress;
Academy Award for *From
Here to Eternity*, 1953. [d.
January 14, 1986]

1929 *Ingrid Thulin*, Swedish actress; appeared in *Wild Strawberries* and *Cries and Whispers*.

1934 *Edith Cresson*, French politician; Prime Minister of France, 1991–92.

1937 *Troy Donahue (Merle Johnson, Jr.)*, U.S. actor; teen idol of the 1960s; known for starring roles on television series, *Hawaiian Eye* and *Surfside 6*.

1944 *Mairead Corrigan*, Irish pacifist; co-founder of the *Community of the Peace People*; Nobel Peace Prize, 1976.

1956 *Mimi Rogers*, U.S. actress.

1964 *Bridget Fonda*, U.S. actress.

HISTORICAL DATES

1186 *Henry VI* of Germany marries Constance, heiress of Sicily, and assumes title of Caesar.

1822 *Greece* proclaims its independence from Turkey, setting off over a decade of conflict.

1943 First U.S. air attack on Germany is staged by the Eighth Air Force on the docks of Wilhemshaven *(World War II)*.

1945 German guards close the *Auschwitz-Birkenau* concentration camp as the Soviet army approaches, moving as many prisoners as possible to Western camps.

1950 *Somaliland* is declared a UN trust territory.

1952 *Aly Maher Pasha* replaces *Mustapha el Nahas Pasha* as premier of Egypt following anti-British riots and the imposition of martial law.

1961 *Georgia* legislature repeals the state's public school *segregation laws*.

1962 Soviet government confirms the removal of all place names in the U.S.S.R. designated *Molotov, Voroshilov, Kaganovich,* and *Malenkov*.

1964 France recognizes the *People's Republic of China*

and establishes diplomatic relations.

1967 Representatives of 60 nations including the U.S. and U.S.S.R. sign a UN treaty providing for the peaceful uses of outer space and banning weapons of mass destruction in space.

Three U.S. astronauts die in a flash fire at Cape Kennedy, Florida, while training for the first launch of the *Apollo* spacecraft.

1973 *Vietnam War Cease-Fire* is signed in Paris, ending U.S. combat role in *Vietnam*.

1983 *Babcock & Wilson Co.* agrees to rebate $37 million as a settlement for the nuclear reactor accident at *Three Mile Island*.

1986 *Jose Azcona* is inaugurated as president of Honduras.

1991 The *New York Giants* defeat the Buffalo Bills, 21-19, in *Super Bowl XXV*.

1998 *Carlos Flores Facusse* is sworn in as president of Honduras.

january

JANUARY
28

HOLIDAYS

Rwanda
Democracy Day

RELIGIOUS CALENDAR

The Saints

St. John Reomay, abbot. [d. c. 544]

St. Paulinus, Patriarch of Aquileia.
[d. 804]

St. John the Sage. [d. 11th century]

St. Amadeus, Bishop of Lausanne.
[d. 1159]

St. Peter Nolasco, founder of the
Order of Our Lady of Ransom
or Mercedarians; patron of
midwives. [d. 1258]

St. Thomas Aquinas, Doctor of the
Church; patron of Naples and
of all universities, colleges,
and schools. Invoked against
thunderstorms and sudden
death. Feast formerly March
7. [d. 1274] Obligatory
Memorial.

St. Peter Thomas, titular patriarch of
Constantinople, martyr. [d.
1366]

The Beatified

Blessed Charlemagne, first Holy
Roman Emperor. [d. 814]

Blessed James, the *Almsgiver.* [d.
1304]

Blessed Antony of Amandola,
Augustinian friar. [d. 1350]

Blessed Mary of Pisa, widow. [d.
1431]

Blessed Julian Maunoir, priest. [d.
1683]

BIRTHDATES

1457 *Henry VII,* King of England,
founder of the Tudor dynasty;
brought an end to the War of
the Roses; father of Henry
VIII. [d. April 21, 1509]

1600 *Pope Clement IX*; pope,
1667–69; credited with writing
first comic opera. [d.
December 9, 1669]

1608 *Giovanni Borelli,* Italian
physiologist, physicist,
mathematician, astronomer.
[d. December 31, 1679]

1768 *Frederick VI,* King of
Denmark, 1808–39, and of
Norway, 1808–14. [d.
December 3, 1839]

1822 *Alexander Mackenzie,*
Canadian statesman, first
Liberal premier of Canada,
1873–78. [d. April 17, 1892]

1833 *Charles George Gordon
(Chinese Gordon* or *Gordon
Pasha),* British officer sent to
rescue Egyptian garrison
before British abandoned the
region; trapped at *Khartoum*
by the Mahdi; defended the
position for ten months
before being killed when the
city fell. [d. January 26, 1885]

1841 *Henry Morton Stanley (John
Rowlands),* British-American
journalist; best known for his
expedition in search of
African explorer *David
Livingstone*; led several other
expeditions in which he
discovered *Lake Edward,*
circumnavigated *Lake
Victoria,* and surveyed *Lake
Tanganyika.* Published
several accounts of his travels
and explorations. [d. May 10,
1904]

1853 *José Marti,* Cuban poet,
patriot; leader in struggle for
Cuban independence. [d. May
19, 1895]

1855 *William Seward Burroughs,*
U.S. inventor; developed first
successful recording *adding
machine,* 1888. [d.
September 15, 1898]

1861 *Daniel Willard,* U.S. railroad
executive; President of
Baltimore and Ohio Railroad,
1910–42; Chairman of U.S.
War Industries Board,
1917–18. [d. July 6, 1942]

1864 *Charles William Nash,* U.S.
manufacturer, automobile
pioneer; developed the Nash
Motor Co., 1916; President of
the merged Nash-Kelvinator
Corporation, 1937–48. [d.
June 6, 1948]

1873 *Colette (Sidonie Gabrielle
Colette),* French novelist;
known for her fictional
romances built around an
autobiographical character,
Claudine. [d. August 3, 1954]

1884 *Auguste Piccard,* Swiss
physicist; made balloon

ascents into stratosphere in 1930s; made observations about *cosmic rays.* [d. March 24, 1962]

1887 *Arthur Rubinstein,* U.S. concert pianist, born in Poland; considered one of the towering musical figures of the 20th century. [d. December 20, 1982]

1912 *(Paul) Jackson Pollock,* U.S. painter; a founder of the *Abstract Expressionist* school. [d. August 11, 1956]

1922 *Robert William Holley,* U.S. chemist; Nobel Prize in physiology or medicine for studies in role of *enzymes* in genetic development (with H. G. Khorana and M. W. Nirenberg), 1968. [d. February 11, 1993]

1933 *Susan Sontag,* U.S. critic, essayist, novelist.

1936 *Alan Alda,* U.S. actor; best known for role as Hawkeye Pierce on TV's *M*A*S*H.*

1943 *Susan Howard (Jeri Lynn Mooney),* U.S. actress; known for her role as Donna Culver Krebs on television series, *Dallas.*

1948 *Mikhail Baryshnikov,* Soviet-American ballet dancer; former Artistic Director, American Ballet Theater.

1968 *Sarah McLachlan,* Canadian pop singer; driving force behind popular summer "Lilith Fair" concert tours.

1981 *Elijah Wood,* U.S. actor; featured in *Forever Young,* 1993, and *The War,* 1994.

HISTORICAL EVENTS

1077 *Henry IV,* King of Germany and Holy Roman Emperor, excommunicated by *Pope Gregory VII* over the issue of lay investiture, makes his pilgrimage to Canossa where he stands for three days, bareheaded and barefooted, awaiting an audience with the Pope.

1547 *Henry VIII* of England dies and is succeeded by *Edward VI.*

1871 Paris capitulates to Prussia (*Franco-Prussian War*).

1909 *Jose Miguel Gomez* is inaugurated as president of Cuba and the U. S. provisional government withdraws.

1915 The *William P. Frye,* a U.S. merchant ship, is sunk in the Atlantic by the German *Prince Eitel Friedrich.*

United States Coast Guard is established by Congress, combining the *Life Saving Service* and the *Revenue Cutter Service.*

1918 The *Ukraine* proclaims itself independent of Russia.

1932 Japanese troops seize *Shanghai* to force an end to intensive Chinese boycott of Japanese goods.

1941 Aaron Copland's instrumental suite, *Quiet City,* premieres in New York.

1944 *Leonard Bernstein* conducts the premiere of his first symphony *Jeremiah,* at Pittsburgh, Pennsylvania.

1950 *Alcide de Gasperi* becomes prime minister of Italy.

1951 *Shah Mohammad Riza Pahlavi* of Iran orders sale to peasants on favorable terms of all land he had inherited from his father.

1955 *Fulgencio Batista* ends military rule and becomes civilian president of Cuba.

1963 Black student *Harvey Gantt* enters Clemson College in South Carolina, thus breaking the barrier in the last state to hold out against *integration.*

1970 *Arthur Ashe,* U.S. black tennis star, is denied a visa to South Africa.

1982 U.S. army officer, *James Dozier,* is rescued from his *Red Brigade* captors in Padua, Italy.

1986 The space shuttle *Challenger* explodes shortly after take-off, killing all seven crew members. It represents the worst space disaster in U.S. history.

1988 The Canadian Supreme Court rules federal restrictions on abortions violate the constitution. The decision legalizes *abortion* on demand.

Public Service Co. of New Hampshire becomes the first public utility since the Depression to file for bankruptcy protection. The company had defaulted on millions of dollars in unsecured debt because it could not free the 70 percent of its assets invested in the *Seabrook nuclear power plant.*

JANUARY
29

HOLIDAYS

Nepal
Martyrs' Day

New Zealand (Auckland)
Anniversary Day

Singapore
Hari Raya Puasa

U.S. (Kansas)
Admission Day
Celebrates the admission of Kansas
to the Union, 1861.

RELIGIOUS CALENDAR

The Saints
St. Gildas the Wise, abbot. [d. c.
    570]
St. Sulpicius, Bishop of Bourges. Also
    called *Severus.* [d. 591]
St. Sabian, martyr.

The Beatified
Blessed Genoveva Torres Morales.
    [beatified 1995]
*Blessed Grimoaldo of the
    Purification.* [beatified 1995]
*Blessed Modestino of Jesus and
    Mary.* [beatified 1995]
Blessed Rafael Guizar Valencia.
    [beatified 1995]

BIRTHDATES

1688 *Emanuel Swedenborg,*
    Swedish scientist, mystic,
    philosopher, theologian;
    known for his voluminous

works of interpretations of
the Bible; his followers, who
founded the *New Jerusalem
Church,* are called
Swedenborgians. [d. March
29, 1772]

1737 *Thomas Paine,* American
    colonial political philosopher;
    patriot; pamphleteer; author
    of *Common Sense,* pamphlet
    calling for independence from
    England. [d. June 8, 1809]

1749 *Christian VII, King of
    Denmark and Norway,*
    1766–1808. [d. March 13,
    1808]

1759 *Henry (Light-Horse Harry)
    Lee,* American Revolutionary
    cavalry officer, public official;
    Governor of Virginia,
    1791–95. [d. March 25, 1818]

1761 *Albert Gallatin,* U.S.
    politician, banker, farmer;
    U.S. Secretary of the Treasury,
    1801–14, U.S. Minister to
    France, 1816–23, and Great
    Britain, 1826–27. [d. August
    12, 1849]

1773 *Friedrich Mohs,* German
    mineralogist; developed the
    scale of hardness still used in
    mineralogy. [d. September 29,
    1839]

1838 *Edward Williams Morley,*
    U.S. chemist, physicist;
    renowned for his experiment,
    (known as the *Michelson-
    Morley experiment*) with

Albert Michelson (December
19), on the behavior of light
waves, an experiment which
was used to test Einstein's
contention, in his *special
theory of relativity* that light
rays are bent by gravitational
force when passing near a
heavenly body. [d. February
24, 1923]

1843 *William McKinley,* U.S.
    lawyer, politician; 25th
    President of the United
    States, 1897–1901;
    assassinated. [d. September
    14, 1901]

1864 *Whitney Warren,* U.S.
    architect; known for his
    designs of *Grand Central
    Terminal,* New York City; the
    Ritz-Carlton Hotel, New York
    City; and the *Louvain
    Library,* Belgium. [d. January
    24, 1943]

1866 *Romain Rolland,* French
    novelist, dramatist,
    biographer, essayist; Nobel
    Prize in literature, 1914. [d.
    December 30, 1944]

1867 *Vincente Blasco Ibáñez,*
    Spanish novelist; best known
    internationally for his *Four
    Horsemen of the Apocalypse.*
    [d. January 28, 1928]

1874 *John Davison Rockefeller, Jr.,*
    U.S. industrialist,
    philanthropist. [d. May 11,
    1960]

1880 *W. C. Fields (William Claude Dukenfield),* U.S. comedian, film actor. [d. December 25, 1946]

1881 *Alice Evans,* U.S. bacteriologist; discovered connection between bacterium in cow milk can cause disease in humans, campaigned for pasteurization of milk. [d. September 5, 1975]

1892 *Reinhard Johannes Sorge,* German dramatist; a member of the ultramodern expressionist school. [d. July 20, 1916]

1895 *Adolf Augustus Berle,* U.S. lawyer, economist; an early expert in the study of the concentration of wealth in industry; a member of President Franklin D. Roosevelt's *Brain Trust;* Assistant Secretary of State, 1938–44; U.S. Ambassador to Brazil, 1945–46. [d. February 17, 1971]

1905 *Barnett Newman,* U.S. abstract expressionist painter. [d. July 3, 1970]

1912 *Martha Wright Griffiths,* U.S. politician, lawyer; Lieutenant-Governor of Michigan, 1982–90.

1916 *Victor Mature,* U.S. actor.

1918 *John Forsythe (John Lincoln Freund),* U.S. actor; known for his role as Blake Carrington on television series, *Dynasty,* 1981–89.

1923 *Paddy Chayefsky,* U.S. playwright; wrote screenplays for *Altered States* and *Network;* best-known television play, later a film, was *Marty.* [d. August 1, 1981]

1925 *Robert Crichton,* U.S. author; known for his novels, *The Great Imposter,* 1959 and *The Secret of Santa Vittoria,* 1966. [d. March 23, 1993]

1926 *Abdus Salam,* Pakistani scientist; Nobel Prize in physics for studies in electromagnetism as it relates to the weak force in subatomic particles, 1979. [d. November 21, 1996]

1939 *Germaine Greer,* Australian author, educator.

1942 *Claudine Georgette Longet,* French actress, singer; ex-wife of Andy Williams; accused of shooting Spider Sabich.

1943 *Katharine Ross,* U.S. actress.

1945 *Tom Selleck,* U.S. actor; known for his starring role on television series, *Magnum, P.I.;* also known for his role in the film *Three Men and a Baby,* 1987.

1948 *Cristina Saralegui,* Cuban-born talk show host.

1951 *Ann Jillian,* U.S. actress; known for starring roles in *Sugar Babies* and on television series, *It's a Living.*

1954 *Oprah Winfrey,* U.S. actress, talk show host.

1960 *Greg Louganis,* U.S. diver; Olympic gold medalist, 1984, 1988.

HISTORICAL EVENTS

1635 *Cardinal Richelieu* founds *Académie Française.*

1820 *George III* of Great Britain dies and is succeeded by *George IV.*

1850 *Slave trade* is abolished in the District of Columbia.

1857 Order of the *Victoria Cross* is instituted to reward persons of all ranks in the British army and navy.

1861 *Kansas* is admitted to the Union as the 34th state.

1896 U.S. physician *Emil H. Grube* becomes the first to use *X-ray treatment* for *breast cancer.*

1900 *American Baseball League* is formed in Chicago.

1914 *Academy of International Law* is founded at The Hague.

1932 George Gershwin's *Second Rhapsody,* for piano and orchestra, premieres at Boston.

1936 *Baseball Hall of Fame* is established at Cooperstown, New York, to honor distinguished players.

1941 *Alexander Korizis* is named premier of Greece following the death of *Ioannis Metaxas.*

1950 The Indochinese states of *Vietnam, Laos,* and *Cambodia* become independent states within the French union.

1953 *Jamil al-Madfai* becomes premier of Iraq.

1960 French President *Charles de Gaulle* calls on the French army to restore order in *Algeria,* marking the final struggle for Algerian independence, finally achieved in 1962.

1966 Cy Coleman and Dorothy Fields' musical, *Sweet Charity,* premieres in New York.

1967 *Pope Paul VI* and Soviet President *Podgorny* confer at the Vatican in the first meeting between the Roman Catholic pontiff and the head of a Communist state.

1968 *Nauru* adopts a constitution in preparation for its independence from Great Britain.

1986 *Yoweri Museveni* is inaugurated as president of Uganda after overthrowing the government of General *Tito Okello.*

1995 The *United Nations* sends troops to Haiti to ensure continued peace and help instruct the Haitian police force.

The *San Francisco 49ers* win *Super Bowl XXIX,* defeating the San Diego Chargers, 49-26.

1996 French President *Jacques Chirac* announces an end to France's nuclear testing in the South Pacific.

HOLIDAYS

Mauritius
Cavadee

U.S.
Franklin D. Roosevelt's Birthday
Sponsored by the Franklin D.
Roosevelt Philatelic Society.

RELIGIOUS CALENDAR

Feasts

Holy Day of the Three Hierarchs
Honors SS. Basil, Gregory,
and John Chrysostomos.
Celebrated in the Eastern
Orthodox Churches.

The Saints

St. Bersimaeus, Bishop of Edessa.
[d. c. 250]
St. Bathildis, widow, queen of
France. Also called
*Baldechilde, Baldhild,
Barthild, Barthildis,
Bathildas, Bathildes, Bauteur.*
[d. 680]
St. Aldegundis, virgin. Also called
Aldegondes. [d. 684]
St. Adelemus, abbot. Also called
Aleaume. [d. c. 1100]
St. Hyacintha Mariscotti, virgin and
nun. Also called *Giacinta.* [d.
1640]
St. Martina, virgin and martyr.
Patron of Rome.

The Beatified

Blessed Sebastian Valfré, priest. [d.
1710]

BIRTHDATES

1775 *Walter Savage Landor,* British
poet, writer; a quarrelsome
and temperamental artist who
lived in a storm of
controversy most of his life.
[d. September 17, 1864]

1816 *Nathaniel Prentiss Banks,*
Union Army general during
U.S. Civil War; U.S.
Congressman, 1852–88;
Governor of Massachusetts,
1858–61. [d. September 1,
1894]

1856 *Granville T. Woods,* U.S.
inventor of electrical
instruments.

1862 *Walter J(ohannes) Damrosch,*
U.S. conductor, composer,
born in Prussia; one of the
greatest American conductors;
Director of New York
Symphony Orchestra,
1885–1927; conducted the
first symphony to be
broadcast by radio, 1925;
introduced many new works
by old composers; son of
Leopold Damrosch (October
22). [d. December 22, 1950]

1882 *Franklin Delano Roosevelt,*
U.S. politician, statesman;
32nd President of the United
States, 1933–45; led the U.S.
out of the *Great Depression*
and through *World War II.*
[d. April 12, 1945]

1894 *Boris III, King of Bulgaria;*
reigned 1918–43; attempted
to steer a neutral course for
Bulgaria during World War II.
[d. August 28, 1943]

1899 *Max Theiler,* U.S.
microbiologist; Nobel Prize in
physiology or medicine for
discovery of a *yellow fever
vaccine,* 1951. [d. August 11,
1972]

1909 *Saul (David) Alinsky,* U.S.
social activist; renowned for
his adamant striving for
political and social equality;
established the *Industrial
Areas Foundation* to support
organizations in communities.
[d. June 12, 1972]

1912 *Barbara W(ertheim)
Tuchman,* U.S. historian;
Pulitzer Prize in general
nonfiction, 1963, 1972. [d.
February 6, 1989]

1914 *David Wayne (Wayne James
McMeekan),* U.S. actor;
known for his character
acting in *The Three Faces of
Eve* and *Front Page.* [d.
February 9, 1995]

1923 *Dick Martin,* U.S. comedian;
best known as co-host of
television series *Laugh-In,*
1967–73.

1925 *Dorothy Malone (Dorothy
Maloney),* U.S. actress; Oscar
Award for *Written on the
Wind,* 1956; starred on
television series, *Peyton
Place,* 1964–69.

1928 *Harold Smith Prince,* U.S. producer, director.

1931 *Gene Hackman,* U.S. actor.

1933 *Richard Brautigan,* U.S. author, poet; wrote *Trout Fishing in America,* 1967. [d. October 25, 1984]

Louis Richard Rukeyser, U.S. broadcast journalist, author; host of television series, *Wall Street Week,* 1970– ; wrote *How to Make Money in Wall Street.*

1937 *Vanessa Redgrave,* British actress, political activist; Oscar winner (Best Supporting Actress) for *Julia,* 1977.

Boris Spassky, Soviet chessmaster; world champion, 1969–72.

1939 *Eleanor Cutri Smeal,* U.S. feminist; President of National Organization of Women (NOW), 1977–83, 1985–87; co-founder of the Feminist Majority Foundation, 1987.

1943 *Marty Balin (Martyn Jerel Buchwald),* U.S. singer, songwriter; member of the rock group, *Jefferson Airplane/Starship,* 1965–70, 1975–85, 1994– .

David Allen (Dave) Johnson, U.S. baseball player, manager.

1951 *Phil Collins,* British singer, musician; Grammy Awards, 1984, 1985, 1990.

HISTORICAL EVENTS

1648 Peace is concluded between Spain and Netherlands, ending the *30 Years' War.*

1649 Charles I of Great Britain is beheaded; *Oliver Cromwell* takes control of the government.

1889 *Archduke Rudolph,* heir to the Austrian throne, commits suicide with his mistress, *Marie Vetsera,* at Mayerling.

1902 Great Britain and Japan sign treaty recognizing independence of *China* and *Korea.*

1915 The Russians take *Tabriz, Persia* (Iran) from the Turks (*World War I*).

1917 The *Original Dixieland Jazz Band* releases *Darktown Strutters' Ball,* the first commercial jazz recording.

1920 The White Russian government of General *Rozanov* at Vladivostok is overthrown by the Bolsheviks (*Russian Revolution*).

1933 *The Lone Ranger* makes its radio debut.

Adolf Hitler becomes Chancellor of Germany.

1948 *Mahatma Gandhi,* Indian spiritual leader, is assassinated by a young Hindu extremist, Nathuram Godse.

1962 U.S. President *John F. Kennedy* and *Aleksei I.*

Adzhubei, editor of *Izvestia,* principal Russian newspaper, hold conversations at the White House.

1965 Government of *Burundi* breaks diplomatic relations with the *People's Republic of China.*

1970 Prime Minister Chief *Leabua Jonathan* declares a state of emergency in *Lesotho* and orders the arrest of his political opponent, *Ntsu Mokhehle.*

1972 *Pakistan* becomes independent of Great Britain.

1979 U.S. citizens are evacuated from *Iran* following the departure of shah *Mohammad Reza Pahlavi* and increased anti-American demonstrations.

1984 Egypt rejoins the *Islamic Conference Organization* after a five-year suspension.

1985 *Jeane Kirkpatrick* resigns as United Nations ambassador due to foreign policy differences with the Reagan Administration.

1986 *Prince Felipe* of the House of Bourbon is appointed heir apparent to the Spanish throne.

1993 The first *subway* in *Los Angeles, California,* begins operation.

1994 The *Dallas Cowboys* win *Super Bowl XXVIII,* defeating the Buffalo Bills, 30-13.

HOLIDAYS

Nauru
Independence Day

RELIGIOUS CALENDAR

The Saints

SS. Cyrus and *John*, martyrs. [d. c. 303]

St. Marcella, widow. Organized a religious sisterhood, the beginnings of St. Jerome's famous following of cultivated ladies. [d. 410]

St. Aidan of Ferns, Bishop. Founded a monastery at Ferns in County Wexford and became the first bishop. Also called *Aidar, Aidus, Aiduus, Edan, Maedhog, Maedoc, Maidoc, Mogue, Maodhog.* [d. 626]

St. Adamnan of Coldingham, monk. Also called *Eunan.* [d. c. 680]

St. Ulphia, virgin and hermit. Also called *Olfe, Wulfe.* [d. c. 750]

St. Eusebius, martyr and hermit. [d. 884]

St. Nicetas, Bishop of Novgorod. Also called *Nikita.* [d. 1107]

St. Francis Xavier Bianchi, priest. [d. 1815]

St. John Bosco, founder of the Salesians of Don Bosco and the Daughters of Our Lady, Help of Christians. [d. 1888]

The Beatified

Blessed Paula Gambara-Costa, matron. [d. 1515]

BIRTHDATES

1734 *Robert Morris*, U.S. financier, Revolutionary patriot. [d. May 8, 1806]

1735 *Michael-Guillaume-Jean de Crèvecoeur* (Hector Saint-John de Crèvecoeur, J. Hector St. John, Agricola), French-American writer, naturalist. [d. November 12, 1813]

1752 *Gouverneur Morris*, American Revolutionary patriot, government official, delegate to Continental Congress, 1777–78, U.S. Minister of Finance, 1781–85, Senator, 1800–3. [d. November 6, 1816]

1785 *Charles Green*, British balloonist. [d. March 26, 1870]

1797 *Franz Peter Schubert*, Austrian composer. [d. November 19, 1828]

1798 *William Apess*, Native American; activist for equal rights among minorities. Wrote the first book ever published by a Native Amerian, *A Son of the Forest.* [d. c. 1840]

1812 *William Hepburn Russell*, U.S. businessman; founded *Pony Express* [d. September 10, 1872]

1830 *Victor-Henri Rochefort, Marquis de Rochefort-Luçay*, French polemical journalist, politician. [d. June 30, 1913]

James Gillespie Blaine, U.S. politician, newspaper editor. [d. January 27, 1893]

1831 *Rudolph Wurlitzer*, U.S. manufacturer. [d. January 14, 1914]

1848 *Nathan Straus*, U.S. merchant. [d. January 11, 1931]

1868 *Theodore William Richards*, U.S. chemist. Nobel Prize in chemistry, 1914. [d. April 2, 1928]

1872 *Zane Grey*, U.S. novelist. [d. October 23, 1939]

1881 *Irving Langmuir*, U.S. chemist; Nobel Prize in chemistry, 1932. [d. 1957]

1889 *Ella Cara Deloria*, Native American; researched the languages and cultures of Native Americans; author of *Waterlily.* [d. 1971]

1892 *Eddy Cantor (Edward Israel Iskowitz)*, U.S. comedian, song-and-dance man. [d. October 10, 1964]

1902 *Alva Reimer Myrdal*, Swedish diplomat; Nobel Peace Prize for her work toward disarmament (with Alfonso Garcia Robles), 1982. [d. February 1, 1986]

1903 *Tallulah (Brockman) Bankhead*, U.S. actress. [d. December 12, 1968]

1905 *John Henry O'Hara*, U.S. short-story writer, novelist. [d. April 11, 1970]

1913 *Don Hutson*, U.S. football player. [d. June 26, 1997]

1914 *Jersey Joe Walcott (Arnold Raymond Cream)*, U.S. boxer, world heavyweight champion, 1951–52. [d. February 25, 1994]

1915 *Bobby Hackett*, U.S. cornetist. [d. June 7, 1976]

Garry Moore (Thomas Garrison Morfit), U.S. television personality. [d. November 28, 1993]

1919 *Rudolf Ludwig Mössbauer*, German physicist; Nobel Prize in physics for discovery of the phenomenon known as the *Mössbauer effect* (with *R. Hofstadter*), 1961.

Jack(ie) Roosevelt Robinson, U.S. baseball player and civil-rights activist; first black to enter major leagues, with the Brooklyn Dodgers, 1947; Hall of Fame, 1962. [d. October 24, 1972]

1921 *Mario Lanza (Alfredo Arnold Cocozza)*, U.S. singer, actor. [d. October 7, 1959]

1923 *Carol Channing*, U.S. actress, singer.

Norman Mailer, U.S. novelist, journalist; Pulitzer Prize in general nonfiction, 1969.

1929 *Jean Simmons*, British actress.

1931 *Ernie Banks*, U.S. baseball player; Baseball Hall of Fame, 1977.

1934 *James Franciscus*, U.S. actor. [d. July 8, 1991]

1935 *Kenzaburo Oe*, Japanese novelist; Nobel Prize for Literature in 1994.

1937 *Philip Glass*, U.S. musician, composer; known for using electrically-amplified wind instruments.

Suzanne Pleshette, U.S. actress.

1944 *Jessica Walter*, U.S. actress; Emmy Award, 1975; known for her role in *Play Misty for Me*, 1971.

1947 *(Lynn) Nolan Ryan*, U.S. baseball player; all-time strikeout artist; pitched six no-hitters.

HISTORICAL EVENTS

1850 New Prussian constitution is promulgated.

1901 Anton Chekhov's play *Three Sisters* premieres at the Moscow Art Theatre.

1910 Slavery is abolished in China.

1915 A German air raid over England hits the industrial centers in the midland counties *(World War I)*.

1917 The German government informs U.S. that unrestricted submarine warfare will begin on February 1, 1917 *(World War I)*.

1918 The *Gregorian calendar* replaces the Julian in Russia.

1926 Italian law is enacted giving the prime minister the power to issue decrees with the force of law.

1946 *Eurico Gaspar Dutra* is inaugurated as president of Brazil.

Yugoslavia adopts its constitution and officially becomes a *people's republic*.

1950 President Truman directs *U.S. Atomic Energy Commission* to continue work on all forms of atomic weapons.

1951 *Getulio Vargas* is inaugurated as president of Brazil.

The U.S. releases 33 former Nazis incarcerated for war crimes, including *Alfred Krupp*. The death sentences of 21 others are commuted.

1958 *Explorer I*, first U.S. satellite, is launched.

1961 *Janio da Silva Quadros* is inaugurated as president of Brazil.

Ham, a male chimpanzee, is recovered alive in the Caribbean after being carried to a height of 155 miles in a U.S. space capsule launched from Cape Canaveral, Florida.

1962 Foreign ministers of the OAS, meeting at Punta del Este, vote to expel Cuba from participation in inter-American affairs.

1964 French President *Charles de Gaulle* in cooperation with the People's Republic of China, proposes the neutralization of Cambodia, Laos, and Vietnam.

1965 *Iraq* abolishes military tribunals and martial law and enacts a new public security regulation.

1967 *National Traffic Safety Agency* issues the first set of U.S. federal safety standards for vehicle safety.

1968 South Pacific island of *Nauru*, a former UN trust territory, becomes an independent republic.

West Germany and *Yugoslavia* resume diplomatic relations after a 10-year break.

North Vietnam launches the *Tet Offensive,* attacking South Vietnamese towns. The U.S. embassy in Saigon is held by a Viet Cong suicide squad for six hours *(Vietnam War).*

Kenya and *Somalia* resume diplomatic relations.

1971 Telephone service between *East and West Berlin* is re-established for the first time in 19 years.

Apollo 14 manned spacecraft is launched.

1972 King *Mahendra of Nepal* dies and is succeeded by his oldest son, Birendra.

1975 *Angola* adopts a transitional government.

1986 President *Jean-Claude Duvalier* declares a state of emergency in *Haiti* as protests against the

government grow increasingly violent.

1993 The *Dallas Cowboys* win *Super Bowl XXVII,* defeating the Buffalo Bills, 52-17.

1995 U.S. President *Bill Clinton* approves financial support (up to $20 billion) for *Mexico*'s failing economy.

january

FEBRUARY

February, the second month of the Gregorian calendar, has 28 days in the ordinary year of 365 days, and 29 days in every fourth year (leap year) of 366 days. Like January, February did not exist in the early Roman calendar, but was added as the twelfth month in approximately 700 B.C. under the calendar reform of the Etruscan King at Rome, Numa Pompilius. The Etruscan calendar reforms were abandoned at Rome for a time, but eventuallya 12-month year, including February, was permanently adopted. (See also at **January.**)

The Latin name *Februarius* is thought to be derived from the word *februa,* which means *rites of purification.* As the last month of the year in the early Roman calendar, it was dedicated to acts of purification in preparation for the coming of the new year in March. During the Feast of Lupercalia, February 15, women would be ritually struck with strips of skin from sacrificial goats, a ceremony honoring the god Faunus and thought to assure fertility and an easy delivery.

In the astrological calendar, February spans the zodiac sign of Aquarius, the Water Bearer (January 20–February 18), and Pisces, the Fishes (February 19–March 20).

The birthstone for February is the amethyst, and the flower is the violet or primrose.

STATE, NATIONAL, AND INTERNATIONAL HOLIDAYS

Lincoln's Birthday
(Delaware, Oregon)
First Monday

Lincoln Day
(Arizona)
Second Monday

Washington's Birthday
(United States)
Third Monday

Washington Day
(Arizona)
Third Monday

Presidents' Day
(Hawaii, Nebraska, Pennsylvania, South Dakota)
Third Monday

Washington-Lincoln Day
(Ohio, Wisconsin, Wyoming)
Third Monday

Pageant of Light
(Florida)
near Thomas Edison's Birthday
(February 11)

Race Relations Sunday
(United States)
Sunday nearest Lincoln's Birthday

Hamstrom
(Switzerland)
First Sunday

Bean-throwing Festival or Setsubun
(Japan)
February 3

SPECIAL EVENTS AND THEIR SPONSORS

American History Month
National Society Daughters of the American Revolution

National Afro-American (Black) History Month
Association for the Study of Afro-American Life and History, Inc.

World Understanding Month

World Understanding and Peace Day
February 23
Rotary International

Party Time is Pickle Time
Pickle Packers International, Inc.

International Friendship Month
Franklin D. Roosevelt Philatelic
Society

National Cherry Month
National Red Cherry Institute
Riverview Center

National Hobby Month
Hobby Industry of America

**National Children's Dental
Health Month**
American Dental Health Association

Potato Lover's Month
National Potato Promotion Board

National Crime Prevention Week
Week of Lincoln's Birthday
National Exchange Club

Engineer's Week
Week of Washington's Birthday
National Society of Professional
Engineers

**National Kraut & Frankfurter
Week**
Week containing February 14
National Kraut Packers Association

National Pay Your Bills Week
First Full Week
American Collectors Association

Brotherhood-Sisterhood Week
Week of Washington's Birthday
National Conference of Christians
and Jews

Scouting Anniversary
Week containing February 8
Boy Scouts of America

National FFA Week
*Week containing Washington's
Birthday*
Future Farmers of America

**FHA/HERO Week (Future
Homemakers of America/Home
Economics Related Occupations)**
Second Full Week
Future Homemakers of America

National Safety Sabbath
Second Weekend
National Safety Council

USO Anniversary
February 4
United Services Organization

february

HOLIDAYS

The Gambia, Senegal
Senegambia Confederation Day or Confederal Agreement Day
Commemorates merger of the Gambia and Senegal.

Malaysia
Federal Territory Day

Nicaragua
Air Force Day
Honors the achievements of the nation's airmen.

United States
National Freedom Day
Commemorates the ratification of the Thirteenth Amendment to the U.S. Constitution by President Abraham Lincoln, abolishing slavery.

RELIGIOUS CALENDAR

The Saints
St. Pionius, martyr. [d. c. 250]

St. Seiriol, abbot; founder of Penman church; patron of Anglesey. [d. 6th century]

St. Brigid, virgin, abbess of Kildare; patron of Ireland, Wales, Australia, and New Zealand, all Irish women, Irish nuns and dairy workers. Also called *Bride, the Mary of the Gael.* [d. c. 525]

St. Sigebert (King Sigebert III of Austrasia). [d. 656]

St. John of the Grating, Bishop of Saint-Malo. [d. c. 1170]

The Beatified
Blessed Antony the Pilgrim. [d. 1267]

BIRTHDATES

1552 *Sir Edward Coke,* English jurist, defender of the supremacy of the common law. [d. September 3, 1634]

1757 *John Philip Kemble,* English Shakespearean actor; director of *Drury Lane Theater,* 1783–1802. [d. February 26, 1823]

1797 *John Bell,* U.S. politician, lawyer; conservative Southern politician who supported the Union during the *U.S. Civil War.* [d. September 10, 1869]

1801 *Thomas Cole,* U.S. romantic landscape painter; a founder of the *Hudson River school* of painters. [d. February 8, 1848]

(Maximilien Paul) Emile Littré, French lexicographer and philosopher; successor to Auguste Comte as head of positivist school. [d. June 2, 1881]

1805 *Louis Auguste Blanqui,* French Revolutionary socialist; prominent activist in the revolutions of 1839, 1848, 1871. First advocate of a dictatorship of the proletariat. [d. January 1, 1881]

1828 *Meyer Guggenheim,* U.S. industrialist; known for his mining operations in Central and South America, from which he amassed a considerable fortune. [d. March 15, 1905]

1831 *Henry McNear Turner,* U.S. Methodist Episcopal bishop, government worker; advocate of return of blacks to Africa. [d. May 8, 1915]

1844 *Granville Stanley Hall,* U.S. psychologist; the first president of the *American Psychological Association.* [d. April 24, 1924]

1859 *Edward Aloysius Cudahy,* U.S. meat packer; partner, Armour & Co., 1875–87; founder of Cudahy Packing Co., 1890. [d. October 18, 1941]

Victor Herbert, U.S. virtuoso cellist, conductor, composer born in Ireland. [d. May 26, 1924]

1874 *Hugo von Hofmannsthal,* Austrian dramatist, poet. [d. July 15, 1919]

1878 *Hattie Wyatt Caraway,* U.S. politician, teacher; the first woman elected to the U.S. Senate. [d. December 21, 1950]

1882 *Louis Stephen St. Laurent,* Canadian lawyer and statesman; Prime Minister, 1948–57. [d. July 25, 1973]

1887 *Harry Scherman,* Canadian-American writer; originator of *Book-of-the-Month Club.* [d. November 12, 1969]

Charles Bernard Nordhoff, U.S. travel and adventure writer. [d. April 11, 1947]

1895 *John Ford (Sean O'Feeney),* U.S. film director. [d. August 31, 1973]

1896 *Nat Holman,* U.S. basketball player, coach. [d. February 12, 1995]

Anastasio Somoza Garcia, Nicaraguan leader; President, 1937–47, 1950–56. [d. September 29, 1956]

1901 *(William) Clark Gable,* U.S. actor. [d. November 16, 1960]

1902 *(James) Langston Hughes,* U.S. poet. [d. May 22, 1967]

1904 *S(idney) J(oseph) Perelman,* U.S. author, humorist. [d. October 17, 1979]

1905 *Emilio Segrè,* U.S. physicist born in Italy; Nobel Prize in physics for discovery of the *antiproton* (with O. Chamberlain), 1959. [d. April 22, 1989]

1906 *Hildegarde (Loretta Sell),* U.S. cabaret singer.

1918 *(Sarah) Muriel Spark,* Scottish novelist, critic, poet; author of *The Prime of Miss Jean Brodie,* 1961.

1923 *Stansfield Turner,* U.S. admiral; Commander in Chief of Allied Naval Forces in Southern Europe, 1975–77. Director of U.S. Central Intelligence Agency, 1977–80.

1928 *Stuart Whitman,* U.S. actor.

1931 *Boris Yeltsin,* Russian politician; president of Russian Federation, 1990– .

1937 *Don Everly,* U.S. singer, musician; member of pop duo, *Everly Brothers;* known for song, *Bye, Bye Love,* 1957.

1938 *Sherman Hemsley,* U.S. actor; known for his role as George Jefferson on television series, *The Jeffersons,* 1975–85.

1952 *Rick James (James Johnson),* U.S. singer; known for song, *Super Freak,* 1981.

1965 *Princess Stephanie (Marie Elisabeth Grimaldi),* Monacan princess; daughter of Princess Grace and Prince Rainier.

1965 *Sherilyn Fenn,* U.S. actress; played "Audrey Horne" on TV series, *Twin Peaks,* and performed in *Boxing Helena,* 1993.

1966 *Michelle Akers,* U.S. soccer player; winner of the Golden Boot Award and the Hermann Trophy, 1991.

1968 *Lisa Marie Presley,* U.S. celebrity relative; only child of Elvis and Priscilla Presley; married briefly to pop singer Michael Jackson.

1973 *Amy Van Dyken,* U.S. swimmer; four-time gold medalist at the 1996 summer Olympics.

HISTORICAL EVENTS

772 *Adrian I* is elected Pope; reigned 772–795.

1328 *Charles IV* of France, last of the Capets, dies and is succeeded by *Philip VI* of Valois.

1440 Frederick, Duke of Styria, is elected *Frederick III* of Germany.

1539 *Treaty of Toledo* between *Holy Roman Emperor* *Charles V* and *Francis I* of France is signed, temporarily halting the *Hapsburg-Valois Wars.*

1642 Holland signs the first treaties with chiefs of the *Gold Coast of Africa* for purchase of land.

1790 First meeting is held of the *U.S. Supreme Court,* Chief Justice *John Jay* presiding.

1793 *France* declares war on England, Holland, and Spain *(French Revolutionary period).*

1864 *Ferdinand de Lesseps* begins French effort to construct *Panama Canal.*

1884 First section of *Oxford English Dictionary* is published.

1896 *La Bohème,* by Giacomo Puccini, premieres in Turin, Italy.

1898 First *automobile insurance policy* is issued to Dr. Truman J. Martin of Buffalo, N.Y., protecting his automobile from damage caused by frightened horses.

1904 *Enrico Caruso* makes his first phonograph recording in America.

1908 *Carlos I* of Portugal and his eldest son are assassinated.

1914 The railroad from Dar-es-Salaam to Lake Tanganyika is completed.

1915 A German offensive renews the *Battle of Champagne* on the Western Front *(World War I).*

1917 Germany begins unrestricted *submarine warfare* on all neutral and belligerent shipping *(World War I).*

1924 Great Britain recognizes the *Bolshevik regime* in Russia.

1940 First official network *television broadcast* in the U.S. is aired.

1941 *British Air Training Corps* is founded.

1942 *Vidkun Quisling,* whose name became synonymous with traitor, is named Premier of Norway. His collaboration with the Germans during *World War II* led to his arrest and execution.

1946 The National Assembly declares *Hungary* a republic. *Zoltan Tildy* becomes president with *Ferenc Nagy* as premier.

1948 A group of British colonies on the Malay peninsula are joined to form the *Federation of Malaya.*

1949 Israel formally annexes *West Jerusalem.*

1950 Britain announces the formation of a provincial council and local government units in its trust territory of *Tanganyika.*

The Israeli government requires all men between the ages of 18 and 49 to register as military reservists. Women between the ages of 15 and 34 must also register.

1953 *General Electric Theater* makes its television debut.

1957 First *turbo-prop* airliner enters into scheduled service in Great Britain.

1958 Egypt and Syria unite to form the *United Arab Republic.*

1960 *William Lewis* is elected president of a racially integrated Teamsters Local, becoming the first black to hold such a position.

1960 *"Sit-Ins"* begin as African American students in Greensboro, North Carolina protest against the separation of blacks and white in public factilities.

1961 First U.S. *Intercontinental Ballistic Missile,* the *Minuteman,* is successfully fired from Cape Canaveral, Florida.

1963 *Hastings Banda* is sworn in as the first Prime Minister of *Nyasaland* (formerly *Malawi*).

1969 U.S.S.R. and Peru reestablish diplomatic relations following the overthrow of the *Fernando Belaúnde Terry* government.

1970 *Pope Paul VI* reiterates teaching of priestly celibacy as a fundamental principle of the Roman Catholic Church.

1976 First episode of the television mini-series, *Rich Man, Poor Man,* is aired.

1979 *Ayatollah Ruhollah Khomeini* returns to Iran after 15 years' exile in France to direct a revolution against the Iranian government and the overthrow of the Shah.

1982 The African nations of *Senegal* and *The Gambia* form a confederation, *Senegambia,* but they retain their sovereignties.

1985 *Greenland* withdraws from the *European Community.*

1987 Ethiopian voters approve a new constitution mandating a civilian Communist government in the first such referendum in the country's 2,500-year history.

1998 President *Bill Clinton* presents the first balanced budget in over 25 years to Congress.

Miguel Angel Rodriguez is elected as President of Costa Rica.

february

FEBRUARY
2

HOLIDAYS

Canada
Groundhog Day
Same as in the U.S. (see below); however, sometimes a bear is looked for instead of the groundhog.

Liechtenstein
Candlemas

Mexico
Dia de la Candelaria
Candlemas Day celebration in Mexico and other Latin American countries.

Scotland
Scottish Quarter Day
Fortieth day of Christmas.

U.S.
Groundhog Day
Traditionally, the day on which the groundhog appears from his hibernation. If he sees his shadow, it indicates another six weeks of winter are forthcoming. (Especially significant in Punxsutawney, Pa., where *the* groundhog is said to reside.)

RELIGIOUS CALENDAR

Feasts
Presentation of the Lord or
Candlemas or
Christ's Presentation or
Dia de la Candelaria or
Holiday of St. Simeon or
Purification of the Blessed Virgin Mary or

The Wives' Feast Celebration of the presentation of the Child Jesus to St. Simeon, and the Purification of Mary. Observed by Roman Catholics, Anglicans, and various Protestant churches.

The Saints
St. Adalbald of Ostrevant, martyr. [d. 652]
The Martyrs of Ebsdorf. [d. 880]
St. Joan de Lestonnac, widow and founder of the Religious of Notre Dame of Bordeaux. [d. 1640]

The Beatified
Blessed Maria Catherine Kasper. [beatified 1979]

BIRTHDATES

1208 *James I, the Conqueror,* King of Aragon. [d. 1276]

1649 *Pope Benedict XIII,* Pope 1724–30. [d. February 21, 1730]

1650 *Nell Gwyn (Eleanor Gwyn),* English actress; mistress of *Charles II.* [d. November 13, 1687]

1754 *Charles Maurice de Talleyrand-Périgord, Prince de Bénévet,* French statesman, diplomat, politician. [d. May 17, 1838]

1859 *(Henry) Havelock Ellis,* British scientist, man of letters; early advocate of sex education; pioneer in the study of the psychology of sex. [d. July 8, 1939]

1875 *Fritz Kreisler,* Austrian-American violin virtuoso. [d. January 29, 1962]

1882 *James Joyce,* Irish novelist, author of *Ulysses.* [d. January 13, 1941]

1886 *William Rose Benét,* U.S. poet, editor. [d. May 4, 1950]

1890 *Charles Correll,* U.S. comedic actor; best known as *Andy* in radio show *Amos 'n Andy.* [d. September 26, 1972]

1895 *George Halas,* U.S. football player, coach, executive; founder and coach of the *Chicago Bears* and one of founders of the *National Football League.* [d. October 31, 1983]

1901 *Jascha Heifetz,* Russian-American violin virtuoso. [d. December 10, 1987]

Louis Kahn I, U.S. architect. [d. March 17, 1974]

1905 *Ayn Rand,* U.S. novelist born in Russia; noted for her political and philosophical conservatism; originator of a doctrine called *Objectivism.* [d. March 6, 1982]

1906 *Gale Gordon (Charles Aldrich, Jr.),* U.S. actor;

known for his roles as Mr. Wilson on television series, *Dennis the Menace,* 1962–64, and Mr. Mooney on *The Lucy Show,* 1963–68, and Harrison Carter on *Here's Lucy,* 1968–74. [d. June 30, 1995]

1911 *Jussi Björling (Johan Jonaton Björling),* Swedish operatic tenor. [d. September 9, 1960]

1914 *Renato Dulbecco,* Italian-American molecular biologist; Nobel Prize in physiology or medicine for study of interaction between tumor viruses and genetic material (with D. Baltimore and H. Temin), 1975.

1915 *Abba Eban (Aubrey Solomon),* Israeli diplomat; Ambassador to the United Nations, 1949–59; to the U.S., 1950–59; wrote *Israel in the World,* 1966.

1919 *Anne Fogarty,* U.S. fashion designer; noted for her feminine designs during the early 1950s. [d. January 15, 1980]

Forrest Meredith Tucker, U.S. actor; known for his starring role on television series, *F-Troop,* 1965–67. [d. October 25, 1986]

1923 *James Dickey,* U.S. poet, critic; wrote *Deliverance,* 1970. [d. January 19, 1997]

Mary Elizabeth (Liz) Smith, U.S. journalist.

1926 *Valéry Giscard D'Estaing,* French political leader; President, 1974–81.

1927 *Stan Getz,* U.S. musician. [d. June 6, 1991]

1931 *Andreas van Agt,* Dutch politician; Prime Minister of the Netherlands, 1977–82.

Judith (Stahl) Viorst, U.S. author, poet; wrote *The Village Square,* 1965, and *People and Other Aggravations,* 1971.

1937 *Thomas Bolyn (Tommy) Smothers, III,* U.S. comedian, singer.

1942 *Bo Hopkins,* U.S. actor; known for tough guy roles in *The Wild Bunch,* 1969, and *American Graffiti,* 1973.

Graham Nash, British musician, singer; member of the rock group, *Crosby, Stills, Nash, and Young.*

1947 *Farrah Leni Fawcett,* U.S. actress, model; known for her role as Jill Monroe on television series, *Charlie's Angels,* which made her a superstar of the 1970s.

1948 *Jessica Beth Savitch,* U.S. broadcast journalist; National Broadcasting Company newscaster, 1977–83; wrote *Anchor Woman,* 1982. [d. October 23, 1983]

1953 *Christie Brinkley,* U.S. model, actress.

HISTORICAL EVENTS

962 *Otto I* is crowned *Holy Roman Emperor* at Rome.

1074 *Peace of Gerstungen* between *Henry IV* of Germany and the Saxons is promulgated.

1509 The Portuguese, under *Francisco de Almeida,* defeat Moslem fleet in the *Battle of Diu,* establishing Portuguese control of Indian waters.

1522 *Pope Leo X* bestows title *Defender of the Faith* on *Henry VIII* of England.

1775 British House of Commons declares *Massachusetts* to be in a state of rebellion.

1801 First parliament of the *United Kingdom of England and Ireland* meets.

1848 *Treaty of Guadalupe Hidalgo* ends the war with Mexico and provides for the cession of Texas, New Mexico, and California to the U.S. *(Mexican War).*

1872 The Netherlands cedes the *Gold Coast of Africa* to Great Britain.

1882 The *Knights of Columbus* are organized at New Haven, Connecticut.

1884 *Basutoland (Lesotho)* becomes a British Crown Colony.

1901 *Army Nurse Corps* is organized as a branch of the U.S. Army.

1913 *Grand Central Station,* one of the largest train terminals in the U.S., opens in New York City.

1914 Charlie Chaplin's first film *Making a Living* is released.

1916 British test armored motor cars, called *tanks,* for the first time *(World War I).*

1920 *Estonia* gains independence from Russia with the signing of the *Treaty of Dorpat.*

1922 *Ulysses* by *James Joyce* is published in Paris.

1932 *U.S. Reconstruction Finance Corporation* is established as a depression-relief measure.

1943 Last German troops surrender in Stalingrad pocket, completing Russian victory at *Stalingrad (World War II).*

february

1946 Norwegian diplomat *Trygve Lie* becomes the first Secretary-General of the United Nations.

1959 *Virginia schools* are desegregated, following Virginia State Supreme Court decision.

1960 Sit-in demonstrations begin in *Greensboro, N.C.,* to protest storekeepers' refusals to serve blacks.

1964 Soviet skater *Lidiya Skoblikova* wins her fourth gold medal in speed skating at the Innsbrook Winter Olympics. She is the first athlete to win four gold medals in any Olympic games competition.

U.S. lunar probe *Ranger 6* effects lunar landing and begins transmission of the first close-up photographs of the moon.

1967 *General Anastasio Somoza Debayle,* candidate of the ruling Nationalist Liberal Party, is elected president of *Nicaragua.*

American Basketball Association, the second major American league, is formed.

1971 Major-General *Idi Amin* declares himself absolute ruler in Uganda and maintains control until his government is overthrown in 1979.

1973 *Philippine President Ferdinand E. Marcos* offers amnesty to Communists and other "subversives" but not to their leaders.

Pope Paul VI nominates thirty new cardinals, bringing membership of the College of Cardinals to 145.

1974 A new *Cultural Revolution* begins in the *Peoples' Republic of China,* including an anti-Confucius campaign.

1979 *Chadli Benjedid* is elected president of Algeria.

1982 Photographs transmitted by U.S. space probe *Voyager 2* reveal four to six previously undiscovered moons orbiting *Saturn.*

1984 *Jaime Lusinchi* is inaugurated as president of Venezuela.

1988 *Carlos Andres Perez* is inaugurated as president of Venezuela.

1989 *Alfredo Stroessner,* Paraguay's dictator, is overthrown in a coup and General Andres Rodriguez declares himself president.

HOLIDAYS

Japan
Bean-throwing Festival or Setsbun

Mozambique
Heroes' Day
Commemorates the anniversary of President Mondlane's death.

Paraguay
St. Blas

Puerto Rico
Fiesta St. Blas
Feast of St. Blaise, patron of harvests.

São Tome and Principe
Day of Martyrs and Liberation

U.S.
Four Chaplains Memorial Day
Honors Chaplains *Alexander Goode* (Jewish), *John P. Washington* (Roman Catholic), *George L. Fox* and *Clark V. Poling* (Protestant) who gave their life jackets to others and perished when the *Dorchester,* U.S. troopship, was sunk off the coast of Greenland, 1943.

Vietnam
Founding Day
Commemorates the founding of the Communist Party of Vietnam.

RELIGIOUS CALENDAR

The Saints
St. Blaise, Bishop of Sebastea and martyr; patron of wool combers, wild animals, and all who suffer from afflictions of the throat. Also called *Blaize, Blase, Blasius.* [d. c. 316] (Optional Memorial)

St. Ia, virgin. [d. 6th century]

St. Laurence, Bishop of Spoleto. Also called The Enlightener. [d. 576]

St. Laurence, second Archbishop of Canterbury. [d. 619]

St. Werburga, virgin and abbess; patron of Chester. Daughter of King Wulfhere of Mercia. Also called *Werburgh, Wereburge, Wereburg.* [d. c. 700]

St. Anskar, Archbishop of Hamburg and Bremen. First missionary to northwestern Europe; patron of Norway, Sweden, and Denmark. Also called *Anscharius, Ansgar, Auscharius.* [d. 865] (Optional Memorial)

St. Margaret of England, virgin. [d. 1192]

The Beatified
Blessed Simon of Cascia, Augustinian friar. [d. 1348]

Blessed John Nelson, Jesuit priest and martyr. [d. 1578]

Blessed Stephen Bellesini, priest. [d. 1840]

Blessed Richard Pampuri. [beatified, 1981]

Blessed Maria Rivier. [beatified, 1982]

BIRTHDATES

590 *Pope St. Gregory I, the Great;* Pope, 590–604; responsible for sending St. Augustine to convert the Anglo-Saxons. [d. 604]

1735 *Count Ignacy Krasicki,* Polish poet and man of letters; a favorite of Frederick the Great. [d. March 14, 1801]

1793 *José Antonio de Sucre,* Venezuelan general and South American liberator; first President of Bolivia, 1826–28. [d. June 4, 1830]

1809 *Felix Mendelssohn (Jacob Ludwig Felix Mendelssohn-Bartholdy),* German composer, pianist; founder of the *Leipzig Conservatory of Music,* 1843. [d. November 4, 1847]

1811 *Horace Greeley,* U.S. journalist, editor, and politician; Congressman, 1848–52; nominated for president, 1872. [d. November 29, 1872]

1821 *Elizabeth Blackwell,* U.S. physician born in England; first woman in U.S. to gain an M.D. degree, 1849. [d. May 31, 1910]

1830 *Lord Robert Cecil, Third Marquess of Salisbury;* British Prime Minister, 1885–86, 1886–92, 1895–1902. [d. August 22, 1903]

1842 *Sidney Lanier,* U.S. poet, musician, and critic. [d. September 7, 1881]

1853 *Hudson Maxim,* U.S. inventor and explosives expert; developed and patented various powerful, increasingly stable explosive powders, which allowed for improvements in firearms and torpedoes. [d. May 6, 1927]

1873 *Hugh Montague Trenchard,* 1st Viscount Trenchard, British air marshal; principal organizer of the *Royal Air Force.* [d. February 10, 1956]

1874 *Gertrude Stein,* U.S. author, poet, novelist, critic; patron of the arts. [d. July 27, 1946]

1894 *Norman Rockwell,* U.S. illustrator, painter; known for his sentimental, realistic illustrations of American life. [d. November 8, 1978]

1895 *Carl Richard Soderbert,* Swedish-American engineer and educator; developer of the turbine engine. [d. October 17, 1979]

1897 *William White,* U.S. railroad executive. [d. April 6, 1967]

1898 *(Hugo) Alvar (Henrick) Aalto,* Finnish-American architect, city planner, furniture designer, and educator. [d. May 11, 1976]

1907 *James A(lbert) Michener,* U.S. novelist; Pulitzer Prize in fiction, 1947. [d. October 16, 1997]

1909 *Simone Weil,* French mystic, social philosopher; an activist in French resistance during World War II. [d. August 24, 1943]

1918 *Joey Bishop (Joseph Abraham Gottlieb),* U.S. comedian.

1926 *Sheldon Leonard (Shelley) Berman,* U.S. comedian, actor. [d. January 1, 1997]

1940 *Fran(cis Asbury) Tarkenton,* U.S. football player, television host; elected to Hall of Fame, 1986.

1943 *Blythe Katharine Danner,* U.S. actress; Tony Award for *Butterflies Are Free,* 1971.

1945 *Robert Allen (Bob) Griese,* U.S. football player; quarterback, Miami Dolphins, 1967–81.

1948 Bishop Carlos F. X. Belo; Nobel Prize for Peace in 1996, Belo shares the prize with Jos¤ Ramos-Horta, for their work toward peace in Timor.

1950 *Morgan Fairchild (Patsy Ann McClenny),* U.S. actress; known for starring role on television series, *Flamingo Road.*

1956 *Nathan Lane,* U.S. actor; Tony Award winner for *A Funny Thing Happened on the Way to the Forum,* 1996.

HISTORICAL EVENTS

1014 *Sweyn Forkbeard, King of the Danes,* dies and is succeeded by *Canute II (the Great),* his son.

1194 *Henry VI* of Germany releases King *Richard I* of England, captured while on the Third Crusade.

1388 *Merciless Parliament* in England meets in opposition to King *Richard II.*

1488 *Bartholomeu Dias,* Portuguese navigator, lands at *Mossal Bay, Cape of Good Hope.*

1518 *Pope Leo X* imposes silence on Augustinian monks.

1521 *Magellan* discovers *Shark Island* in the Pacific.

1766 *Benjamin Franklin* begins testifying to House of Commons in London on unenforceability of the *Stamp Act.*

1777 *Felipe de Neve,* Spanish governor, arrives at Monterey, designating it the capital of the *Californias.*

1831 *Louis Charles, Duc de Nemours,* third son of Louis-Philippe of France, is elected King of the Belgians.

U.S. copyright law is amended, making term of copyright twenty-eight years, with right of renewal for fourteen more. (This second term extension was increased to 47 years in 1976.)

1855 *Calcutta Railway* is opened.

1867 *Prince Mutsuhito* becomes Emperor of Japan at the age of 15 and reigns until 1912.

1915 Defeat of the last Boer rebels in South Africa brings an end to the *Boer War.*

1917 *S.S. Housatonic* is sunk by a German submarine, resulting in severing of diplomatic relations between Germany and the U.S. *(World War I).*

1925 The first *electric railway* in India opens in Bombay.

1954 *Battle of Dien Bien Phu* begins in French Indochina.

1958 *Benelux Economic Union* formally establishes the customs union of Belgium, Luxembourg, and the Netherlands, begun in 1948.

1960 British Prime Minister *Harold Macmillan* makes *Winds of*

Change speech in Cape Town, South Africa, condemning apartheid.

1962 U.S. President *John F. Kennedy* orders a ban on nearly all U.S. trade with *Cuba.*

1966 Soviet spacecraft *Luna 9* lands successfully on the moon and begins relaying signals.

1969 *Yasir Arafat* is elected chairman of the *Palestine Liberation Organization (PLO).*

1972 *XI Winter Olympics* open in *Sapporo,* Japan.

1977 Ethiopian chief of state Brigadier General *Teferi*

Bante is assassinated. Lieutenant Colonel *Mengistu Haile-Mariam* becomes the new government leader.

1978 China and the *European Economic Community* sign a five-year bilateral trade agreement.

1984 First baby is born to an infertile woman as the result of a *donated embryo.*

1985 *Desmond Tutu* becomes Johannesburg's first black Anglican bishop.

1989 General *Andres Rodriguez* is inaugurated as president of Paraguay after a military coup deposed *Alfredo Stroessner.*

1992 Haitian refugees temporarily housed at Guantanamo Bay,

Cuba, because of politicial unrest, return to *Haiti.*

1994 *William Perry* is selected as the new Defense Secretary.

U.S. President *Bill Clinton* ends the trade embargo with *Vietnam.*

The space shuttle *Discovery* launches into space with *Sergei Krikalev* aboard. Krikalev is the first Russian astronaut to fly on a U.S. spacecraft.

1997 *Nawaz Sharif* is elected President of Pakistan.

1998 *Karla Faye Tucker* becomes the first woman put to death in Texas since 1863.

Levon Ter-Petrossian resigns as President of Armenia.

february

FEBRUARY
4

HOLIDAYS

USO Anniversary
Sponsored by United Services Organization.

Angola

Commencement of the Armed Struggle
Celebrates the beginning of the struggle for freedom from Portugal, 1961.

Sri Lanka

Independence Commemoration Day or National Day
Celebrates independence from Great Britain, 1948.

United States

National Women in Sports Day

RELIGIOUS CALENDAR

The Saints

St. Phileas, Bishop of Thmuis and martyr. [d. 304]

St. Isidore of Pelusium, abbot. [d. c. 450]

St. Modan, abbot; titular saint of the High Church at Stirling, Scotland. [d. c. 550]

St. Aldate, bishop and martyr. [d. c. 577]

St. Nicholas Studites, abbot. [d. 863]

St. Rembert, Archbishop of Hamburg and Bremen. Also called *Rimbert*. [d. 888]

St. Andrew Corsini, Bishop of Fiesole. Invoked to settle quarrels and discords. [d. 1373]

St. Gilbert of Sempringham, founder of the Gilbertine's, only

medieval order of English origin. [d. 1189]

St. Joan of France, matron; founder of the Annonciades of Bourges. Daughter of Louis IX of France. Also called *Joan of Valois*. [d. 1505]

St. Joseph of Leonessa, Capuchin friar. [d. 1612]

St. John de Britto, Jesuit priest and martyr; missionary to India. [d. 1693]

St. Theophilus the Penitent. [death date unknown]

The Beatified

Blessed Rabanus Maurus, Bishop of Mainz. [d 856]

Blessed Thomas Plumtree, martyr. [d. 1570]

BIRTHDATES

1746 *Thaddeus Kosciusko (Tadeusz Andrzej Bonawentura Kościuszko)*, Polish general and national hero. [d. October 15, 1817]

1778 *Augustine Pyrame Candolle*, Swiss botanist, taxonomist; developed system of plant classification. [d. September 9, 1841]

1792 *James Gillespie Birney*, U.S. author, abolitionist; presidential candidate of the Liberty Party, 1840, 1844. [d. November 25, 1857]

1802 *Mark Hopkins*, U.S. educator, philosopher; chief proponent

of the *gospel of wealth*, which stressed individualism and pursuit of wealth. [d. June 17, 1887]

1848 *Francis Wayland Ayer*, U.S. advertising pioneer; standardized contract relations with clients; first to use *market research*; Ayer's *American Annual Newspaper Directory* is a product of his procedure. [d. March 5, 1923]

1871 *Friedrich Ebert*, first President of German Reich, 1919–25. [d. February 28, 1925]

1875 *Ludwig Prandtl*, German physicist; the *Father of Aerodynamics*. [d. August 15, 1953]

1881 *Kliment Efremovich Voroshilov*, Russian Army marshal and political leader; directed operations that broke German siege of Leningrad, 1943; President of U.S.S.R., 1953–60. [d. December 3, 1969]

Fernand Leger, French Cubist painter. [d. August 17, 1955]

1893 *Raymond Arthur Dart*, Australian anatomist, anthropologist; known for his research on early hominids; discovered the Taung child, 1924. [d. November 22, 1988]

1895 *Nigel Bruce*, British actor. [d. October 8, 1953]

1897 *Ludwig Erhard,* German statesman, economist; Chancellor of West Germany, 1963–66. [d. May 5, 1977]

1902 *Charles (Augustus) Lindbergh, (The Lone Eagle),* U.S. aviator; Pulitzer Prize for his autobiography, *The Spirit of St. Louis,* 1953. [d. August 26, 1974]

1904 *McKinlay Kantor,* U.S. novelist; Pulitzer Prize in fiction, 1955. [d. October 11, 1977]

1912 *Erich Leinsdorf,* U.S. conductor, born in Austria; conductor of the Metropolitan Opera Co., 1939–43; 1957–61; musical director of the Boston Symphony, 1962–68.

1913 *Rosa Lee Parks,* U.S. civil rights leader; initiated a bus boycott in Montgomery, Alabama, when she refused to give up her front seat in the bus to a white person, 1955.

1917 *Agha Muhammad Yahya Khan,* Pakistani statesman; President, 1969–71; responsible for first nation-wide elections based on universal suffrage, 1970. [d. August 8, 1980]

1918 *Ida Lupino,* British-born U.S. actress, director, producer. [d. August 3, 1995]

1921 *Betty Friedan (Naomi Goldstein),* U.S. feminist and writer; founder of the *National Organization of Women (NOW),* a civil rights group dedicated to equality of opportunity for women.

1923 *Conrad Stafford Bain,* Canadian actor; known for role on the television series, *Maude,* 1971–78; founded Actors Federal Credit Union, 1962.

1932 *Robert Coover,* U.S. author.

1938 *Donald Wayne Riegle, Jr.,* U.S. politician; Senator, 1976–94.

1940 *George Romero,* U.S. director. Directed *Silence of the Lambs,* 1991.

Allan Paul Bakke, U.S. student; famous for Supreme Court decision that upheld his charge of reverse discrimination against a medical school that denied him admission, 1978.

1945 *David Brenner,* U.S. comedian.

1947 *(James) Dan(forth) Quayle,* U.S. politician; Senator, 1981–; Vice-President, 1989–93.

1948 *Alice Cooper (Vincent Damon Furnier),* U.S. singer, songwriter; known for his ghoulish makeup and boa constrictors.

1962 *Clint Black,* U.S. country singer.

1973 *Oscar De La Hoya,* U.S. boxer; Olympic gold medalist, 1992.

HISTORICAL EVENTS

900 *Louis, the Child,* is crowned King of Germany.

1111 *Treaty of Sutri* is signed, in which Holy Roman Emperor *Henry V* renounces investiture of *Pope Paschal II.*

1629 Monopoly of trade in the *St. Lawrence River* and Gulf is granted to *Sir William Alexander* and his partners.

1787 *Daniel Shays'* forces, in rebellion against the government of Massachusetts, are routed in Petersham, Massachusetts (*Shays' Rebellion*).

1789 *George Washington* is elected the first President of the United States, with *John Adams* as Vice-President.

1830 Britain, France, and Russia formally recognize Greek independence under British protection (*Conference of London*).

1861 *Confederate States of America,* of Alabama, Georgia, Florida, Louisiana, Mississippi, and South Carolina, are organized.

1870 *Museum of Fine Arts* in Boston is incorporated.

1874 *Battle of Kumasi* ends the *Ashanti War* between Ghana and Britain.

1887 *Interstate Commerce Act* is passed by the U.S. Congress.

1899 The *Philippines* rebel against U.S. control.

1904 Japan lays siege to *Port Arthur* on the outbreak of the *Russo-Japanese War.*

1913 *National Institute of Arts & Letters* is incorporated to further the cause of literature and fine arts in the U.S.

1915 *Battle of Masuria* frees East Prussia from the Russians (*World War I*).

Germany announces that the waters around Great Britain are a war zone and that after February 18, 1915, enemy vessels will be destroyed without regard to safety of passengers or crew (*World War I*).

1919 The French government passes a law granting

citizenship to select Algerian natives.

Washington Conference delegates sign a treaty agreeing to respect China's sovereignty and maintain the *Open Door Policy.*

1924 British officials release *Mahatma Gandhi* from prison after two years.

1929 *Col. Charles A. Lindbergh* opens air mail service to Central America, carrying mail from Miami to Havana and to Belize, British Honduras.

1938 *Adolf Hitler* becomes German War Minister; von Ribbentrop appointed Foreign Minister.

1941 *United Service Organizations* is founded, to serve the social, educational, and religious needs of U.S. armed forces.

1945 *Yalta Conference* begins; President Franklin D. Roosevelt, Prime Minister Winston Churchill, and Premier Joseph Stalin meet to discuss post-war diplomacy.

1948 *Sri Lanka* (formerly Ceylon) becomes an independent member of the British Commonwealth of Nations.

1952 *United Nations Disarmament Commission* meets for the first time.

1962 *Francisco José Orlich Bolmarcich* is elected President of Costa Rica.

1964 *London Times* issues its first color Sunday supplement.

24th Amendment to U.S. Constitution is adopted, abolishing the poll tax.

1965 A federal judge bans the *literacy test* as a voting requirement in response to a month-long black voter registration drive led by *Martin Luther King, Jr.*

1971 *Rolls-Royce, Ltd.* of Great Britain declares bankruptcy.

1972 *Bangladesh* is officially recognized by Great Britain and seeks Commonwealth membership.

1974 *Symbionese Liberation Army* kidnaps *Patricia Hearst,* granddaughter of newspaper publisher William Randolph Hearst.

1976 A U.S. Senate subcommittee reveals that the *Lockheed Aircraft Corp.* paid $22 million in bribes to leaders in Japan, Turkey, Italy, and the Netherlands.

Earthquake in *Guatemala* kills 23,000.

XII Winter Olympic Games open in Innsbruck, Austria.

1978 *Sri Lanka* modifies its government to a presidential system. *Junius Richard Jay Awardene* is sworn in as the first president.

1981 *Gro Harlem Brundtland* becomes the first woman premier of Norway.

1987 *Carlos Enrique Lehder Rivas,* alleged leader of the world's largest drug ring, is arrested by Colombian police and extradited to the U.S.

Dennis Conner skippers the U.S. yacht, *Stars and Stripes,* to regain the *America's Cup.* The U.S. had lost the cup to Australia in 1983 after holding it for 132 years.

1988 The Soviet Supreme Court exonerates *Nikolai Bukharin,* a leading Communist theorist executed by Joseph Stalin.

1998 An *earthquake* in *Afghanistan* registering 6.1 on the Richter scale kills 4,500 people.

february

HOLIDAYS

Congo
President's Day

Finland
Runeberg's Day
Celebration of birthday of Johan Ludvig Runeberg, national poet of Finland.

Mauritius
Spring Festival

Mexico
Constitution Day
Celebrates anniversaries of Constitutions of 1857 and 1917.

San Marino
Anniversary of the Liberation of the Republic.

Tanzania
Chama Cha Mapenduzi (CCM Day)
Commemorates the foundation of the Chama Cha Mapenduzi Party, 1976.

U.S.
Roger Williams Day
Observed by American Baptists to celebrate the arrival of Roger Williams, their American founder, on the North American continent, 1631.

RELIGIOUS CALENDAR

The Saints
St. Avitus, Bishop of Vienne. [d. c. 525]

St. Bertulf. Also called *Bertoul.* [d. c. 705]

SS. Indractus and Dominica, martyrs. Dominica also called *Drusa.* [d. c. 710]

St. Vodalus. Also called *Voel.* [d. c. 720]

St. Adelaide of Bellich, virgin, abbess. Also called *Alice.* [d. 1015]

Martyrs of Japan 26 martyrs killed by Emperor Tagosama. [d. 1597]

St. Agatha, virgin, martyr; patron of Catania, Sicily, nurses, and bell-makers. Invoked against breast disease and any outbreak of fire. [death date unknown] Obligatory Memorial.

BIRTHDATES

1534 *Giovanni de' Bardi,* Italian scholar and music patron; creator of *Florentine camerata,* which eventually developed into *opera.* [d. 1612]

1723 *John Witherspoon,* Scottish-American Presbyterian clergyman; President of the College of New Jersey (later *Princeton University*), 1768–94; a signer of the Declaration of Independence. [d. November 15, 1794]

1725 *James Otis,* American Revolutionary leader; best known for his oratory skills and his pamphleteering. [d. May 23, 1783]

1744 *John Jeffries,* American physician, scientist; a pioneer in aerial scientific observations (balloons). [d. September 16, 1819]

1770 *Alexandre Brongniart,* French scientist; the first to arrange the geological formations of the Tertiary Period in chronological order. [d. October 7, 1847]

1788 *Sir Robert Peel,* British statesman; Prime Minister, 1834–35; founder of London *Metropolitan Police Force* (hence police referred to as *bobbies.*) [d. July 2, 1850]

1799 *Dr. John Lindley,* botanist; pioneer in the development of classification system for plants. [d. November 1, 1865]

1837 *Dwight Lyman Moody,* U.S. evangelist; built the first YMCA building in America, in Chicago. Founded *Chicago Bible Institute,* now known as the *Moody Bible Institute.* [d. December 22, 1899]

1840 *John Boyd Dunlop,* Scottish veterinary surgeon; developer of the *pneumatic rubber tire.* [d. 1921]

Sir Hiram Stevens Maxim, British inventor born in U.S.; known for the invention of the recoil-operated *machine gun.* [d. November 24, 1916]

1848 *Joris Karl Huysmans (Charles Marie George Huysmans),*

French novelist. [d. May 12, 1907]

Belle Starr (Myra Belle Shirley), U.S. outlaw. [d. February 3, 1889]

1888 *Cleveland Dodge,* U.S. businessman, philanthropist; Vice-President of Phelps Dodge Corporation, 1924–61. [d. November 24, 1982]

Bruce Austin Fraser, 1st Baron Fraser of North Cape, British naval officer; commander in chief of the Home Fleet, World War II; responsible for countering German U-boat attacks against Great Britain; First Sea Lord and Chief of Naval Staff, 1948–51 [d. February 12, 1981]

1898 *Ralph E. McGill,* U.S. journalist, spokesman for *Southern Progressive* position in politics; Pulitzer Prize in journalism, 1958. [d. February 3, 1969]

1900 *Adlai E(wing) Stevenson,* U.S. statesman and politician; Governor of Illinois, 1948–52; Democratic presidential candidate, 1952, 1956. [d. July 14, 1965]

1903 *Joan Whitney Payson,* U.S. philanthropist, sportswoman. [d. October 4, 1975]

1906 *John Richmond Carradine,* U.S. actor; starred in over 170 films. [d. November 27, 1988]

1914 *William (Seward) Burroughs,* U.S. author; noted for his picaresque, avante-garde, and sciene-fiction novels which were widely distributed in the U.S. literary underground long before they achieved popular recognition. [d. August 2, 1997]

Sir Alan Lloyd Hodgkin, British physiologist; Nobel Prize in physiology or medicine for research on nerve cells and the sodium-potassium exchange (with A. F. Huxley and J. C. Eccles), 1963.

1915 *Robert Hofstadter,* U.S. physicist; Nobel Prize in physics for research on subatomic particles (with R. L. Mossbauer), 1961. [d. November 17, 1990]

1919 *Red Buttons (Aaron Chwatt),* U.S. comedian, actor; Oscar Award for *Sayonara,* 1957.

Andreas George Papandreou, Greek politician; Prime Minister, 1981–89, 1993–96. [d. June 23, 1996]

1934 *Henry Louis (Hank) Aaron,* U.S. baseball player; broke Babe Ruth's home run record with 755 home runs; Hall of Fame, 1982.

1937 *Stuart Damon,* U.S. actor; known for his role as Dr. Alan Quartermaine on television soap opera, *General Hospital.*

1942 *Roger Thomas Staubach,* U.S. football player; Heisman Trophy, 1963; Dallas Cowboys' quarterback, 1969–79.

1943 *Stephen J. Cannell,* U.S. producer, writer; creator and producer of many television shows, including *Rockford Files* and *A-Team.*

1948 *Barbara Hershey (Barbara Herzstein),* U.S. actress.

David Wallechinsky, U.S. author.

1962 *Jennifer Jason Leigh,* U.S. actress; Golden Globe winner for *Short Cuts,* 1994.

1968 *Roberto Alomar,* Puerto Rican baseball player.

HISTORICAL EVENTS

1265 *Pope Clement IV* is elected.

1556 *Truce of Vaucelles* between *Henry II* of France and *Philip II* of Spain ends the *Hapsburg-Valois Wars.*

1725 *Bering Expedition* sets out from St. Petersburg, Russia.

1811 The insanity of *George III* of England leads to the *Regency Act* and the Prince of Wales (later George IV) becomes the Prince Regent.

1818 *Marshall Bernadotte* becomes King of Sweden as *Charles John XIV.*

1884 *Grolier Club* of New York book lovers is founded.

1885 Belgium settles the frontiers of the French and *Belgian Congo.*

1917 *Mexican Constitution* is adopted.

1918 Formal separation of church and state goes into effect in *Russia.*

1919 *League of Nations* meets for the first time in Paris, with U.S. President Woodrow Wilson as chairman.

1936 The *National Wildlife Federation* holds its first meeting.

1945 U.S. troops under the command of *General Douglas MacArthur* enter Manila *(World War II).*

1960 *Felipe Herrera* of Chile is elected first president of the Inter-American Development Bank.

1965 People's Republic of China forms a patriotic front to overthrow the *Thailand* government, forcing Thailand's withdrawal from SEATO.

1968 *Joe Kachingwe,* the first black diplomat assigned to South Africa, arrives in Cape Town.

1975 U.S. cuts off military aid to *Turkey* as a result of the Cyprus dispute.

1983 *Klaus Barbie* is extradited from Bolivia to France to be tried for crimes committed during World War II.

1988 Panamanian general *Manuel Noriega* is indicted by two U.S. grand juries on racketeering and drug trafficking charges.

1989 The *Soviet Union* completes the removal of its armed forces from *Afghanistan* after an occupying presence of nine years.

1993 The *Family and Medical Leave Act* is signed into law by President Bill Clinton. The act allows twelve unpaid weeks of leave due to a birth of a child or medical illness.

1994 *Byron De La Beckwith* is convicted of the 1963 murder of NAACP field secretary *Medgar Evers.*

1998 Animal and plant *fossils* are found in China dating back 580 million years.

february

FEBRUARY
6

HOLIDAYS

New Zealand
Waitangi Day or New Zealand Day
Commemorates the signing of the
Waitangi Treaty between the
European leaders and Maori
tribesmen, 1840.

U.S. (Arizona)
Arbor Day

RELIGIOUS CALENDAR

The Saints
St. Dorothy, virgin, martyr; patron of
gardeners and florists. Also
called *Dorothea*. [d. c. 303]
SS. Mel and *Melchu,* bishops. [d.
488]
St. Vedast, Bishop of Arras; patron of
children who are slow to
walk. Also called *Gaston,
Vaast*. [d. 539]
St. Aumand, missionary and bishop;
father of monasticism in
ancient Belgium; one of the
most imposing figures of the
Merovingian epoch. Also
called *Amand*. [d. c. 679]
St. Guarinus, Cardinal-Bishop of
Palestrina. [d. 1159]
St. Hildegund, widow and prioress.
[d. 1183]
St. Paul Miki and his companions,
first martyrs of the Far East.
Obligatory Memorial.

The Beatified
Blessed Raymund of Fitero, abbot.
Founded the military order of
the Knights of Calatrava. [d.
1163]

Blessed Angelo of Furcio. [d. 1327]

BIRTHDATES

1564 *Christopher Marlowe,* British
dramatist, poet; wrote *Dr.
Faustus*. [d. May 30, 1593]

1665 *Anne, Queen of England,*
1702–14. [d. August 1, 1714]

1756 *Aaron Burr,* U.S. politician;
U.S. Vice-President, 1801–5;
killed Alexander Hamilton in
duel; known for his
controversial attempts to
establish an independent
nation in the American West
as well as other schemes to
solicit foreign interest in the
western lands and Mexico. [d.
September 14, 1836]

1802 *Sir Charles Wheatstone,*
British physician; developer of
the *Wheatstone bridge,* a
device for precision
measurement of electrical
resistance. [d. October 19,
1875]

1820 *Thomas Clark Durant,* U.S.
railroad magnate; one of the
prime movers behind the
completion of the *Union
Pacific Railroad;* with Leland
Stanford (March 9), drove the
golden spike linking the
Union Pacific with the Central
Pacific at Promontory Point,
Utah. [d. October 5, 1885]

1833 *James (Jeb) Ewell Brown
Stuart,* Confederate cavalry

commander in U.S. Civil War.
[d. May 12, 1864]

1845 *Isidor Straus,* U.S. merchant
born in Germany; became
partner and eventually half-
owner of Macy's Department
Store in New York City. With
his wife, perished on the
Titanic. [d. April 15, 1912]

1878 *Walter Boughton Pitkin,* U.S.
psychologist, journalist,
editor; best known for his
book, *Life Begins at Forty*. [d.
January 25, 1953]

1887 *Ernest Gruening,* U.S.
politician, journalist, editor;
Governor of Alaska, 1939–53;
U.S. Senator, 1959–69. [d.
June 26, 1974]

1892 *William P. Murphy,* U.S.
physician; Nobel Prize in
physiology or medicine for
discovery of liver therapies
against *anemia* (with G. H.
Whipple and G. R. Minot),
1934.

1894 *Eric (Honeywood) Partridge,*
British lexicographer, author;
known for his *Dictionary of
Slang and Unconventional
Usage*. [d. June 1, 1979]

1895 *Robert Marion La Follette, Jr.,*
U.S. politician; Senator,
1925–47. [d. February 24,
1953]

George Herman (Babe) Ruth,
U.S. baseball player; elected
to Hall of Fame, 1936. [d.
August 16, 1948]

1902 *Louis Nizer,* U.S. lawyer, author, born in England; best known for his legal defense of American celebrities. [d. November 10, 1994]

1903 *Claudio Arrau,* Chilean-American concert pianist; a child prodigy. [d. June 9, 1991]

1905 *Wladyslaw Gomulka,* Polish political leader; First Secretary of Polish Communist Party, 1956. [d. September 1, 1982]

1911 *Ronald (Wilson) Reagan,* U.S. actor, politician; Governor of California, 1967–75; President of the United States, 1981–89.

1912 *Eva Braun,* mistress of Adolf Hitler. [d. April 30, 1945]

1913 *Mary Leakey,* British archaeologist; with her husband, Louis S(eymour) B(azett) Leakey (August 7), made significant discoveries in the Olduvai Gorge, Africa, of fossil evidence for early hominids. [d. December 9, 1996]

1919 *Zsa Zsa Gabor (Sari Gabor),* Hungarian-American actress. [d. July 4, 1994]

1922 *Patrick MacNee,* British actor; known for his role as John Steed on television series, *The Avengers,* 1966–69.

1926 *Barbara Stone Gelb,* U.S. author.

1931 *(Maria Estela) Isabel (Martinez) de Perón,* Argentine dancer, political leader; succeeded her husband, Juan Perón (October 8), as President of Argentina, 1974–76.

Elmore (Rip) Torn, Jr., U.S. actor; married to Geraldine Page.

1932 *Francois Truffaut,* French filmmaker, producer, director, writer, actor. [d. October 21, 1984]

1933 *Walter E. Fauntroy,* U.S. politician.

Mamie Van Doren (Joan Lucille Olander), U.S. actress; known for starring roles in *Untamed Youth* and *Ain't Misbehavin'.*

1939 *Mike Farrell,* U.S. actor; known for his role as B. J. Hunnicutt on television series, *M*A*S*H,* 1975–83.

1940 *Thomas John (Tom) Brokaw,* U.S. broadcast journalist; host, *The Today Show,* 1976–82; anchor, *NBC Nightly News,* 1982– .

1942 *Sarah Brady,* U.S. gun control activist; wife of James S. Brady.

1943 *Fabian (Fabian Forte),* U.S. singer, actor; teen-idol of the 1950–60's.

1945 *Bob Marley,* Jamaican musician known for reggae music. [d. May 11, 1981]

1949 *(Stephanie) Natalie Maria Cole,* U.S. singer; Grammy Award for debut album, *Inseparable,* 1976; daughter of Nat King Cole.

HISTORICAL EVENTS

46 B.C. *Gaius Julius Caesar* gains victory at Thapsus, in North Africa, over the adherents of Pompey under Cato, Metellus Scipio, and King Juba II.

337 *Julius I* is elected Pope.

1682 *Sieur de La Salle* sights the Mississippi River.

1685 *Charles II* of Great Britain dies and is succeeded by *James I.*

1778 *Britain* declares war on France.

France and the U.S. form an offensive and defensive alliance *(American Revolution).*

1788 *Massachusetts* ratifies the Constitution and joins the Union as the sixth state.

1838 Zulu warriors massacre Dutch settlers in *Natal, South Africa.*

1840 *Treaty of Waitangi* is signed, granting Queen Victoria sovereignty over New Zealand.

1862 *Battle of Fort Henry* (Kentucky) results in an early victory for Union troops under *General Ulysses S. Grant (U.S. Civil War).*

1865 *General Robert E. Lee* is appointed Commander in Chief of the Confederate armies *(U.S. Civil War).*

1899 U.S. Congress ratifies peace treaty ending the *Spanish-American War.*

1915 The British Cunard liner *Lusitania* flies the American flag as protection against German attack during its passage through the declared war zone of British waters *(World War I).*

1922 *Washington Conference,* with delegates from Japan, England, France, Italy, and U.S. ends after fixing the ratio of naval armaments and restricting *poison gas* and *submarine warfare.*

1933 *The 20th Amendment* to the U.S. Constitution is ratified, moving Inauguration Day from March 4 to January 20 and establishing rules of succession in the event of the death of the president.

1943 *General Dwight D. Eisenhower* is appointed Commander in Chief of all Allied forces in North Africa *(World War II).*

1950 President Harry S. Truman invokes national emergency provisions of the *Taft-Hartley Act* and appoints a fact-finding board to report to him in the soft-coal dispute.

85 persons are killed and about 500 injured when a railroad train plunges from a temporary wooden overpass in Woodbridge, New Jersey.

1952 *King George VI* of Great Britain dies and is succeeded by his daughter, *Elizabeth II.*

1956 First black student is enrolled in the *University of Alabama.*

Edwin O'Connor's political novel, *The Last Hurrah,* is published in Boston.

1961 Twenty-nine major U.S. manufacturing firms are fined $1.9 million for price-fixing.

1969 Peruvian President *Juan Velasco Alvarado* announces the seizure of all the assets of the *International Petroleum Co.*

1970 *European Economic Community* and *Yugoslavia* sign their first full-scale trade

pact, the first such agreement between the EEC and an Eastern European nation.

1973 *Dixy Lee Ray* becomes the first woman to head the Atomic Energy Commission.

1974 U.S. House of Representatives approves an *impeachment* inquiry against President *Richard M. Nixon* by the House Judiciary Committee.

Grenada proclaims its independence from Great Britain.

1977 *Queen Elizabeth II* observes the 25th anniversary of her accession to the throne of Great Britain.

HOLIDAYS

Grenada

Independence Day
Commemorates the achievement of independence from Great Britain, 1974.

RELIGIOUS CALENDAR

The Saints

St. Adaucus, martyr. Also called *Adauctus.* [d. 303]

St. Moses, bishop. Apostle of the Saracens, nomad tribes of the Syro-Arabian Desert. [d. c. 372]

St. Richard, King of the West Saxons. [d. 720]

St. Luke the Younger. Surnamed *Thaumaturgus* or the Wonderworker. [d. c. 946]

St. Ronan, Bishop of Kilmaronen. [death date unknown]

St. Theodore of Heraclea, martyr. Surnamed *Stratelates,* General of the Army. Also called *Theodorus.* [death date unknown]

The Beatified

Blessed Rizzerio, Franciscan friar. [d. 1236]

Blessed Antony of Stroncone, lay-brother. [d. 1461]

Blessed Thomas Sherwood, martyr. [d. 1578]

Blessed James Sales, Jesuit priest, and *Blessed William Saultemouche,* Jesuit lay-brother, martyrs. [d. 1593]

Blessed Giles Mary. Also called *Giles Mary-of-St.-Joseph.* [d. 1812]

Blessed Eugenia Smet, founder of the Helpers of the Holy Souls. Also called *Mother Mary of Providence.* [d. 1871]

BIRTHDATES

1478 *Sir Thomas More,* English statesman, humanist; well-known for his treatise *Utopia,* a description of a communal lifestyle that allowed equality for all members. Beheaded for treason, 1478, on order of King Henry VIII. Canonized, 1935. [d. July 6, 1535]

1693 *Anna, Empress of Russia,* 1730–40. [d. October 28, 1740]

1804 *John Deere,* U.S. manufacturer; introduced the *steel plow* in the U.S., 1837; founder of Deere & Co., 1868. [d. May 17, 1886]

1812 *Charles (John Huffon) (Boz) Dickens,* British novelist; noted for his graphic depiction of life of the poor in England; author of *Oliver Twist* and *David Copperfield,* among many others. [d. June 9, 1870]

1814 *George Palmer Putnam,* U.S. publisher. [d. December 20, 1872]

1824 *Sir William Huggins,* British astronomer; first to elucidate the similarity in structure between the sun and the stars. [d. May 12, 1910]

1834 *Dmitri Ivanovich Mendeleev,* Russian chemist; stimulated extensive use of the *periodic table of elements.* [d. February 2, 1907]

1837 *Sir James Augustus Murray,* Scottish lexicographer, philologist; chief work of his life was the *Oxford English Dictionary,* which he planned and edited, based on materials collected over many years. [d. July 26, 1915]

1867 *Laura Ingalls Wilder,* U.S. author of fiction for juveniles; best known for her stories of the pioneer life in the American West. [d. January 10, 1957]

1870 *Alfred Adler,* Austrian psychiatrist; advanced theories of *inferiority complex* as cause of psychopathic behavior. [d. May 28, 1937]

1883 *Eubie Blake,* U.S. pianist, singer, vaudeville performer; awarded Presidential Medal of Freedom, 1981. [d. February 12, 1983]

1885 *(Harry) Sinclair Lewis,* U.S. novelist; first American to win Nobel Prize in literature, 1930. [d. January 10, 1951]

1889 *H(aroldson) L(afayette) Hunt,* U.S. businessman; with

J. Paul Getty (December 15), considered one of the richest men in U.S. history. [d. February 17, 1974]

1899 *Arvid Y. Pelshe,* Russian military officer, statesman; last member of the Soviet leadership who took part in the Bolshevik Revolution of 1917. [d. June 1, 1983?]

1905 *Ulf Svante von Euler,* Swedish physiologist; Nobel Prize in physiology or medicine for investigations into substances found at the end of nerve fibers (with B. Katz and J. Axelrod), 1970. [d. March 10, 1983]

1909 *Buster Crabbe (Clarence Linden Crabbe),* U.S. athlete, actor; Olympic gold medalist, 1932; star of numerous movie series in the 1930s and 1940s including *Flash Gordon* and *Buck Rogers.* [d. April 23, 1983]

1920 *An Wang,* Chinese-born computer scientist; known for his research on magnetic core memories for computers; founder of the Wang Laboratories. [d. March 24, 1990]

1932 *Gay Talese,* U.S. author, journalist; wrote *Honour Thy Father,* 1971 and *Thy Neighbor's Wife,* 1980.

1937 *Peter Jay,* British diplomat, economist.

1953 *Dan(iel Raymond) Quisenberry,* U.S. baseball player; broke Major League record with forty-five saves as relief pitcher for the Kansas City Royals, 1983.

1960 *James Spader,* U.S. actor.

1962 *Garth Brooks,* U.S. country singer.

HISTORICAL EVENTS

1807 Napoleon engages Russians and Prussians at Battle of Eylau (*War of the Third Coalition.*)

1865 *Hampton Roads Conference* takes place aboard the *River Queen;* Lincoln meets with Confederate peace commissioners.

1868 *Shinto* is officially adopted as the state religion of Japan.

1883 First meeting of *Irish Nationalist League. John L. Sullivan* defeats *Paddy Ryan* in a bare knuckles contest to win the American heavyweight championship.

1904 Fire in *Baltimore* destroys 2600 buildings; it is the largest fire in the U.S. since the Chicago fire of 1871.

1924 The *Tangiers Convention* is signed by Britain, France, and Spain, providing for permanent neutralization of the *Tangier Zone* and government by international commission.

1925 Chinese delegates withdraw from the second *Opium Conference* at Geneva.

1940 Great Britain nationalizes its railroads.

1941 British capture *Benghazi* (*World War II*).

1945 *General Douglas MacArthur* enters *Manila* more than three years after he had been forced out by the Japanese (*World War II*).

1950 Great Britain and the U.S. recognize the governments of *Laos* and *Cambodia* and the Vietnam government headed by Bao Dai in *French Indochina.*

1953 *Claire Boothe Luce* is named U.S. ambassador to Italy. It is the first time a woman is appointed to a major diplomatic post.

1964 The *Beatles,* arrive in New York for their first tour of the U.S.

1968 All ten Canadian provincial premieres approve Prime Minister Lester Pearson's proposal to give the French language equal status with English throughout Canada.

Six Latin-American nations sign a convention at Bogotá, Colombia, establishing the *Andean Development Corporation.*

1969 *Diana Crump* becomes first woman jockey to race at a U.S. pari-mutuel track.

1970 Roman Catholic marchers in ten *Northern Ireland* cities defy the two-day-old *Public Order Act,* establishing conditions for demonstrations.

1971 Swiss voters approve a referendum giving women the right to vote in federal elections and to hold office.

1974 *Grenada* gains its independence within the British Commonwealth.

1981 Fire sweeps through 20 floors of the *Las Vegas Hilton* hotel, killing eight and injuring at least 200.

1982 *Luis Alberto Monage Alvarez* is elected President of Costa Rica.

1984 U.S. astronaut *Bruce McCandless* becomes the first human to fly in space with a jet backpack while untethered to a spacecraft.

1986 Philippine presidential elections are held, pitting *Ferdinand Marcos* against challenger *Corazon Aquino*.

President *Jean-Claude Duvalier* flees Haiti leaving a military-civilian council in control.

1988 *Leslie Manigat* is inaugurated as president of Haiti.

1996 *René Préval* is elected President of Haiti.

1998 The *XVIII Winter Olympics* begins in Nagano, Japan.

february

FEBRUARY
8

HOLIDAYS

Congo
Youth Day

Iraq
Eighth of February Revolution

Norway
Narvik Sun Pageant
Celebrates the return of the sun
after its winter absence.

Peru
Virgen de la Candelaria -Puno

Philippines
Constitution Day (1935)

Slovenia
Preseren Day
Honors poet Frances Preseren

Culture Day

U.S.
Boy Scout Day

RELIGIOUS CALENDAR

The Saints
St. Kew, virgin; patron of St. Kew,
Cornwall. Also called *Ciwa,
Kuet,* or *Kywere.* [d. c. 5th
cent.]
St. Nicetius, Bishop of Besancon.
Also called *Nizier.* [d. c. 611]
St. Elfleda, virgin and abbess of
Whitby; daughter of Oswy,
King of Northumbria. Also
called *Aelbfled, Aelfflaed.* [d.
714]
St. Cuthman. [d. c. 900]
St. Meingold, martyr; patron of
bakers and millers. [d. c. 892]

St. Stephen of Muret, abbot.
Sometimes called *Stephen of
Grandmont.* [d. 1124]
St. John of Matha, priest; co-founder
of the Order of the Most Holy
Trinity; also called the
Trinitarian Order for the
Redemption of Captives. [d.
1213]
St. Jerome Emiliani, founder of the
Somaschi; patron saint of
orphans and abandoned
children. Also called *Jerom
Miliani.* Feast formerly July
20. [d. 1537] Optional
Memorial.

The Beatified
Blessed Peter Igneus, Cardinal-
Bishop of Albano. [d. 1089]
Blessed Isaiah of Cracow,
Augustinian friar. [d. 1471]

BIRTHDATES

1577 *Robert Burton,* (Democritus
Junior), English clergyman
and author; noted for his
writings on melancholy, its
causes and cures. [d. January
25, 1640]

1819 *John Ruskin,* British writer,
art critic, reformer; noted for
his writings on art and
society. [d. January 20, 1900]

1820 *William Tecumseh Sherman,*
Union Army general in U.S.
Civil War. [d. February 14,
1891]

1825 *Henry Walter Bates,* British
naturalist, South American

traveler; known for his
expeditions and recovery of
unknown species in the
Amazon. [d. February 16,
1892]

1828 *Jules Verne,* French writer;
known especially for his
science fiction. Légion
d'Honneur, 1892. [d. March
24, 1905]

1834 *Dmitry Mendeleev,* Russian
chemist; developed the
periodic table of elements. [d.
February 2, 1907]

1851 *Kate O'Flaherty Chopin,* U.S.
novelist, short-story writer. [d.
August 22, 1904]

1878 *Martin Buber,* Austrian-Jewish
philosopher and theologian;
best known for his espousal
of *I-Thou* relationships. [d.
June 13, 1965]

1886 *Charles Ruggles,* U.S. comedic
character actor of the 1930s
and 1940s. [d. December 23,
1970]

1888 *Dame Edith Evans,* British
stage and film actress. [d.
October 14, 1976]

1894 *King Wallis Vidor,* U.S.
director; directed the first
Hollywood film with an all
black cast, *Hallelujah,* 1929.
[d. November 1, 1982]

1906 *Chester Carlson,* U.S.
physicist; inventor of
xerography, 1937. [d.
September 19, 1968]

1920 *Lana Turner,* U.S. actress. [d. June 29, 1995]

1924 *Khamtai Siphandon,* Laos politician; President of Laos, 1998– .

1925 *Jack Lemmon,* U.S. actor.

1930 *Alejandro Rey,* Argentine actor, director; known for his role as Carlos Ramirez on television series, *The Flying Nun,* 1967–70. [d. May 21, 1987]

1931 *James Dean (James Byron),* U.S. actor. [d. September 30, 1955]

1932 *John Williams,* U.S. conductor, composer; composer of numerous film scores, including that for *Star Wars;* conductor of Boston Pops Orchestra, 1980–93.

1937 *Harry Wu (Hongda),* Chinese-born human rights activist.

1942 *Robert Klein,* U.S. comedian, actor; Tony Award for *They're Playing Our Song,* 1979.

Nick Nolte, U.S. actor; known for his starring roles in *The Deep,* 1977, and *48 Hours,* 1983; Academy Award nominee for *Prince of Tides,* 1991.

1948 *Judith Light,* U.S. actress; two Emmy Awards for role as Karen Wolek on television soap opera, *One Life to Live;* known for her role as Angela on television series, *Who's the Boss?,* 1985–92.

1949 *Brooke Adams,* U.S. actress.

1953 *Mary Steenburgen,* U.S. actress; known for roles in *Melvin and Howard,* 1979 and *Parenthood,* 1989.

1968 *Gary Coleman,* U.S. actor; known for his role as Arnold on television series, *Different Strokes,* 1978–86.

1970 *Alonzo Mourning,* U.S. basketball player; member of the "Dream Team II" at the World Games, 1994.

HISTORICAL EVENTS

1587 *Mary, Queen of Scots,* is beheaded at Fotheringay Castle in England.

1690 French and Indians attack *Schenectady,* New York. *(French and Indian Wars)*

1693 *College of William and Mary,* the second oldest in the U.S., is chartered.

1725 *Peter the Great* of Russia dies and is succeeded by *Catherine I,* his Empress.

1849 *Roman National Assembly* divests the Pope of all governing power and proclaims a republic.

1861 *Jefferson Davis* is chosen president and *Alexander H. Stephens* vice-president of the *Confederate States of America.*

1862 Union forces take *Roanoke Island, N.C.,* from the Confederacy *(U.S. Civil War).*

1863 Prussia allies with Russia to suppress Polish insurrection *(Alvensleben Convention).*

1887 *Interstate Commerce Act* is passed in the U.S., chiefly to regulate railways.

1887 The U.S. passes the *Dawes General Allotment Act* stating that Native American tribes are no longer legal entities and corresponding lands are dispersed amount individuals owners.

1908 *Sergei Rachmaninoff* conducts premiere of his *Second Symphony in E Minor* with the orchestra of Moscow Philharmonic Society.

1910 *Boy Scouts of America* are incorporated.

1915 *Birth of a Nation,* one of the most celebrated films of its time, is first shown at Clune's Auditorium in Los Angeles.

1920 Odessa is taken by Bolshevik forces *(Russian Revolution).*

1936 *Jay Berwanger* of the University of Chicago becomes the first college football player to be drafted by the National Football League.

1937 *General Francisco Franco* captures *Malaga* with Italian support *(Spanish Civil War).*

1943 The U.S. Senate confirms the nomination of *Wiley Rutledge* as an associate justice of the Supreme Court.

1949 *Cardinal Mindszenty,* Primate of Hungary, is convicted of treason and espionage and sentenced to life imprisonment.

1950 The East German People's Chamber votes to establish the *State Security Ministry.* The new police will have unlimited powers to arrest citizens.

U.S. War Claims Commission rules that 120,000 former U.S. prisoners of war of Germany and Japan will receive $1 for each day of imprisonment because of substandard rations.

1962 *Argentina* breaks diplomatic relations with *Cuba.*

1965 South Vietnamese Air Force planes, accompanied by U.S.

february

jet fighters, bomb and strafe a military communications center in *North Vietnam*.

1966 *Declaration of Honolulu* is issued by U.S. President Lyndon Johnson and South Vietnamese Premier Ky outlining both nations' political and military policies in *South Vietnam*.

Vatican office charged with the censure of books is abolished.

1969 *The Saturday Evening Post* publishes its last issue, ending its 148-year history.

1973 *Sam Ervin* is appointed chairman of a Senate select committee to investigate the Watergate incident.

1974 *Skylab 4* crew returns to earth after a record 84 days, 1 hour, 16 minutes in space.

1977 *Larry C. Flynt,* publisher of *Hustler* magazine, is convicted in a test case of obscenity pandering.

1979 U.S. severs military ties with *Nicaragua*.

1984 Launch of three Soviet cosmonauts, along with the five-member U.S. *Challenger* crew, establishes record for the greatest number of people in space at one time.

1986 *Debi Thomas* becomes the first black skater to win the U.S. women's figure skating title in Uniondale, New York.

Haydar Abu Bakr al-Attas is confirmed as president of the People's Democratic Republic of Yemen.

A non-prescription *Tylenol capsule* is contaminated with potassium cyanide, causing the death of a random consumer who purchases the pain medication.

1996 President *Bill Clinton* signs the *Telecommunications bill* into law.

HOLIDAYS

Lebanon

St. Maron's Day or Feast of St. Maron
Commemorates massacres of Maronite Christians by Druze.

RELIGIOUS CALENDAR

The Saints

St. Apollonia, virgin and martyr; patron of dentists. Invoked against toothache and dental diseases. [d. 249]

St. Sabinus, Bishop of Canosa. [d. c. 566]

St. Ansbert, Bishop of Rouen. [d. c. 695]

St. Alto, abbot. [d. c. 760]

St. Teilo, bishop. [d. 6th cent.]

St. Nicephorus, martyr and layman. [death date unknown]

The Beatified

Blessed Marianus Scotus. [d. 1088]

BIRTHDATES

1773 *William Henry Harrison,* U.S. politician, statesman; President for only 32 days, March 4–April 4, 1841. First U.S. president to die in office. [d. April 4, 1841]

1814 *Samuel Jones Tilden,* U.S. politician, lawyer; best known for his participation in the overthrow of the Tweed Ring; U.S. presidential candidate, 1876 (lost the election by one electoral vote to Rutherford B. Hayes). [d. August 4, 1886]

1819 *Lydia Estes Pinkham,* U.S. patent-medicine manufacturer; creator of *Mrs. Lydia E. Pinkham's Vegetable Compound,* an advertising phenomenon of the time. [d. May 17, 1883]

1853 *Sir Leander Starr Jameson (Doctor Jameson),* Scottish physician, statesman in South Africa; leader of the Jameson Raid during the *Boer War* in South Africa; Prime Minister of Cape Colony, 1904–08. [d. November 26, 1917]

1865 *Mrs. Patrick Campbell (Beatrice Stella Tanner),* British stage actress, for whom George Bernard Shaw created the part of Eliza Doolittle in *Pygmalion.* [d. April 9, 1940]

1866 *George Ade,* U.S. humorist, playwright; noted for his short, humorous fables of the common man. [d. May 16, 1944]

1872 Paul Laurence Dunbar, U.S. author. [d. 1906]

1874 *Amy (Lawrence) Lowell,* U.S. poet, critic; Pulitzer Prize in poetry, 1925. [d. May 12, 1925]

1891 *Ronald Colman,* British actor. [d. May 19, 1958]

Pietro Nenni, Italian political leader; head of Italian Socialist Party, 1949–69. [d. January 1, 1980]

1907 *Victor (Dit) Clapper,* Canadian hockey player.

1909 *Carmen Miranda,* Brazilian singer, dancer, actress. [d. August 5, 1955]

Dean Rusk, U.S. government official; Secretary of State, 1961–69. [d. December 20, 1994]

1910 *Jacques Lucien Monod,* French biochemist; Nobel Prize in physiology or medicine for research in genetic control of enzymes, (with F. Jacob and A. M. Lwoff), 1965. [d. May 31, 1976]

1914 *Ernest (Ernie) Tubb,* U.S. singer, musician, songwriter; wrote over 150 country songs. [d. September 6, 1984]

1923 *Brendan (Francis) Behan,* Irish playwright. [d. March 20, 1964]

1928 *Frank Frazetta,* U.S. artist, cartoonist; drew Buck Rogers and Flash Gordon.

Roger Mudd, U.S. television newsman.

1932 *Gerhard Richter,* German artist.

1939 *Janet Suzman,* South African actress.

1941 *Carole King (Carole Klein),* U.S. singer, songwriter; four Grammy Awards for her album, *Tapestry,* 1972.

1943 *Joe Pesci,* U.S. actor; Academy Award nominee for *GoodFellas,* 1990.

1944 *Alice Walker,* U.S. author; Pulitzer Prize for *The Color Purple,* 1982.

1945 *Mia Villiers Farrow,* U.S. actress; known for her starring roles on television series, *Peyton Place,* 1964–67, and in the movie, *Hannah and Her Sisters,* 1985.

1946 *James H(enry) Webb,* U.S. author; known for his novels about the Vietnam War, including *Fields of Fire* and *A Sense of Honor;* Secretary of the Navy, 1987–88.

1961 *John Kruk,* former U.S. baseball player; National League All-Star 1991–93.

1963 *Travis Tritt,* U.S. country singer.

HISTORICAL EVENTS

1555 *Bishop John Hooper,* English prelate and martyr, is burned at the stake.

1674 *Treaty of Westminster* ends the war between Holland and Great Britain.

1798 France dissolves the *Swiss Confederation* and decrees the establishment of a *Helvetic Republic* in its place.

1801 *Peace of Lunéville* between France and Austria is signed, signalling the end of the *Holy Roman Empire.*

1849 Giuseppe Mazzini proclaims a Republic in *Rome.*

1861 Constitution of *Confederate States of America* is promulgated.

1870 *U.S. Weather Bureau* is established by Congress as part of *Signal Corps.*

1904 Russian cruisers *Variag* and *Korietz* are sunk off Korea by the Japanese *(Russo-Japanese War).*

1909 The Franco-German agreement over *Morocco* is signed, with Germany recognizing France's special position in Morocco in return for economic concessions.

1917 *Mata Hari* is arrested by the French and charged with passing Allied secrets to Germany *(World War I).*

1926 The Viceroy of India announces the creation of the *Royal Indian Navy* and reconstruction of the *Indian Mercantile Marine.*

1929 The *Litvinov Protocol,* an eastern pact for renunciation of war, is signed at Moscow by Russia, Poland, Romania, Estonia, and Latvia.

1934 *Balkan Pact* between Greece, Romania, Turkey, and Yugoslavia is signed.

1941 German troops cross to North Africa under command of *Marshal Erwin Rommel (World War II).*

1942 France's *Normandie* burns at the pier in New York City.

1943 The Japanese evacuate *Guadalcanal Island (World War II).*

1950 Senator *Joseph McCarthy* makes his first public accusations against alleged Communists in the U.S.

Department of State during a speech in Wheeling, West Virginia.

1964 *The Beatles,* British rock group, make their first appearance on the U.S. television program, *Ed Sullivan Show.*

1970 Forty-one persons are killed in an avalanche in *Val d'Isere,* France.

1971 Worst *earthquake* since 1933 strikes southern California, measuring 6.5 on the Richter scale; 60 lives are lost and several hundred people are injured.

1977 The dramatization of Alex Haley's *Roots* sets new television viewing records in the U.S.

1978 *Canada* expels 11 Soviet diplomats for operating a highly sophisticated spy ring.

1981 Polish Premier *Josef Pinkowski* is replaced by *Gen. Wojciech Jaruzelski* in the face of continuing labor unrest.

1984 Soviet leader *Yuri Andropov* dies after a long illness.

Sultan *Mahmood Iskander* becomes king of Malaysia.

1988 A panel of historians appointed by Austrian president *Kurt Waldheim* finds that he knew of World War II atrocities but did not personally commit any crimes.

1991 A *nuclear power plant* in *Japan* leaks radioactive water, but disaster is averted when an emergency system shuts down the plant, injecting water in the reactor core to prevent a meltdown.

1997 President *Abdal Bucaram* of Ecuador is removed from office due to unrest in the country. *Fabian Alarcon* is named interim president.

1998 *Eduard Shevardnadze,* President of the country of Georgia, survives an assassination attempt.

FEBRUARY
10

HOLIDAYS

Malta

St. Paul's Shipwreck
Commemorates wreck of the
Christian apostle St. Paul off the
coast of Malta in A.D. 60

RELIGIOUS CALENDAR

The Saints

St. Soteris, virgin and martyr. Also
    called *Coteris.* [d. 304]
St. Scholastica, virgin; sister of *St.
    Benedict,* and first
    Benedictine nun. Patron of
    Benedictine nuns and
    nunneries, and of children in
    convulsions. Invoked against
    storms. [d. 543] Obligatory
    Memorial.
St. Trumwin, Bishop of the Picts. [d.
    c. 690]
St. Austreberta, virgin. Also called
    Eustreberta. [d. 704]
St. Merewenna, Abbess of Romsey.
    [d. 10th cent.]
St. William of Maleval. [d. 1157]

The Beatified

Blessed Hugh of Fosses. [d. 1164]
Blessed Clare of Rimini, widow. [d.
    1346]

BIRTHDATES

1775 *Charles Lamb,* British essayist,
    critic; active in British literary
    circles during the late 18th
    century; close friend of S. T.
    Coleridge (October 21). [d.
    December 27, 1834]

1824 *Samuel Plimsall,* British
    social reformer leader of
    shipping reform; known as
    *The Sailors' Friend. Plimsall's
    mark,* the load line allowed
    by law on ships, is named for
    him. [d. 1898]

1846 *Ira Remsen,* U.S. chemist;
    discovered *saccharin.* [d.
    March 4, 1927]

1859 *Etienne Alexandre Mitterand,*
    French statesman; President
    of the French Republic,
    1920–24. [d. April 6, 1943]

1868 *William Allen White (the Sage
    of Emporia)* U.S. journalist,
    editor; Pulitzer Prize in
    editorial writing, 1923; in
    biography (posthumously),
    1947. [d. January 29, 1944]

1890 *Boris (Leonidovich)
    Pasternak,* Russian poet,
    novelist; Nobel Prize in
    literature, 1958 (refused). [d.
    May 30, 1960]

1892 *Ivo Andrié,* Yugoslav novelist,
    short story writer, poet;
    Nobel Prize in literature,
    1961. [d. March 13, 1975]

    *Alan Hale (Rufus Alan
    McKahan),* U.S. actor; known
    for his role as Errol Flynn's
    sidekick. [d. January 22, 1950]

1893 *Jimmy Durante,* U.S.
    comedian, vaudeville
    performer. [d. January 29,
    1980]

*William Tatem (Bill) Tilden,
    Jr.,* U.S. tennis player; first
    American to win a Wimbledon
    singles title. [d. June 5, 1953]

1894 *Harold Macmillan,* British
    statesman; Prime Minister,
    1957–63. [d. December 29,
    1986]

1897 *John Franklin Enders,* U.S.
    microbiologist; Nobel Prize in
    physiology or medicine for
    research on polio virus (with
    T.H. Weller and F.C.
    Robbins), 1954. [d.
    September 8, 1985]

1898 *Dame Judith Anderson,*
    Australian actress. [d. January
    3, 1992]

    Bertolt Brecht, German
    dramatist, poet. [d. August 11,
    1956]

1900 *Cevdet Sunay,* Turkish
    statesman, political leader;
    President of Turkish Republic,
    1960–66. [d. May 22, 1982]

1902 *Walter Houser Brattain,* U.S.
    physicist; Nobel Prize in
    physics for the development
    of the *electronic transistor*
    (with W. Shockley and J.
    Bardeen), 1956. [d. October
    13, 1987]

1905 *Lon Chaney, Jr. (Creighton
    Tull Chaney),* U.S. actor;
    known for his role as Lenny
    in *Of Mice and Men,* 1940.
    [d. July 12, 1973]

1913 *(Albert) Merriman Smith,* U.S. journalist; called the *Dean of the White Correspondents;* Pulitzer Prize in national reporting, 1964. [d. April 13, 1970]

1927 *Leontyne Price,* U.S. operatic soprano.

1930 *Robert John Wagner, Jr.,* U.S. actor; known for his starring roles on television series, *It Takes a Thief* and *Hart to Hart;* widower of Natalie Wood.

1940 *Roberta Flack,* U.S. singer; Grammy Awards for *The First Time Ever I Saw Your Face,* 1972 and *Killing Me Softly,* 1973.

1944 *Peter Woolnough Allen,* Australian songwriter, singer. [d. June 18, 1992]

1946 *Donovan (Donovan P. Leitch),* Scottish singer, songwriter.

1950 *Mark Spitz,* U.S. Olympic swimmer; first athlete to win seven gold medals in a single Olympic Games, 1972.

1955 *Greg Norman,* Australian golfer; first professional player to win one million dollars in one year, 1986.

1963 *Lenny Dykstra,* former U.S. baseball player.

1966 *Laura Dern,* U.S. actress; starred in *Jurassic Park,* 1993.

HISTORICAL EVENTS

1364 *Treaty of Brünn,* a family pact of succession between the *Luxemburgs* and the *Hapsburgs,* is signed.

1495 *Aberdeen University* in Scotland is founded.

1567 *Lord Darnley* dies in a gunpowder explosion; his wife, *Mary, Queen of Scots,* is suspected of murder.

1763 France cedes *Canada* to England at the *Treaty of Paris,* ending the *French and Indian War.*

The Seven Years' War between Great Britain and Spain ends with the signing of the *Treaty of Paris.*

1840 *Queen Victoria* of England marries *Prince Albert* of Saxe-Coburg-Gotha. *Upper and Lower Canada* are united.

1846 The *Mormon exodus* to the American West begins.

1899 The use of the *Revised Version of the Bible* in church services is authorized by the Church of England.

1916 German government informs the U.S. that after March 1, 1916, armed merchantmen will be treated as warships and attacked without warning (*World War I*).

1926 A treaty designed to control the smuggling of liquor is signed by the U.S. and Spain.

1944 *PAYE (pay-as-you-earn) system of income tax* is introduced in Britain.

1949 Arthur Miller's play *Death of a Salesman* premieres in New York.

1950 *Klaus E. J. Fuchs,* British atomic scientist, confesses to revealing atomic secrets to the Soviets.

1960 French President Charles de Gaulle dissolves the *Algerian Home Guard.*

1962 Soviets release U.S. U-2 pilot *Francis Gary Powers* in Berlin in exchange for convicted Soviet agent *Rudolf Abel.*

1963 *Third Afro-Asian People's Solidarity Conference,* at Moshi, Tanganyika, approves resolutions for the use of violence to end *apartheid* in South Africa and an economic boycott of Portugal.

1964 *Nationalist China* severs diplomatic relations with France.

1967 The *25th Amendment* to the U.S. Constitution is ratified, providing a contingency plan for *presidential succession.*

1970 *Arab terrorists* kill one Israeli and wound 11 persons in an attack at a *Munich,* West Germany, airport.

1974 British coal miners begin a strike which causes Prime Minister *Edward Heath* to dissolve Parliament and call for a general election.

1975 *The Eritrean Liberation Front* launches new offensives in northern Ethiopia.

National Awami (Opposition) *Party* is banned in Pakistan.

1977 Soviet dissident *Yuri Orlov* is arrested in the Soviet Union.

1978 *The National Organization of Cypriot Struggle* is dissolved.

1979 *Pakistan* adopts an Islamic legal system.

1983 American Telephone & Telegraph Co. inaugurates a *laser fiber-optics system* between New York City and Washington, D.C. It is the first of its kind linking two major cities.

february

1989 *Ronald Brown*, U.S. lawyer, becomes first African American chairman of the Democratic National Committee.

1990 *James "Buster" Douglas* defeats Mike Tyson to win the world heavyweight boxing title.

1998 *David Satcher* is selected as the new Surgeon General. His predessor, *Joycelyn Elders*, had resigned in 1994.

HOLIDAYS

Cameroon
Youth Day
Dedicated to children and young people of the nation.

Iran
National Day
Commemorates fall of Shah Mohammad Reza Pahlavi.

Japan
Empire Day or National Foundation Day
Commemorates founding of the nation in 660 B.C. by the first emperor, Jimmu Tenno.

Liberia
Armed Forces Day
Public holiday honoring professional army, navy, and militia.

Thailand
Makha Bucha Day

U.S.
National Inventors Day

U.S. (Michigan)
White Shirt Day
Observed as a day of recognition of the dignity of work and the anniversary of the 1937 sit-down strike in Flint, Michigan.

Vatican City State
Anniversary of Lateranensi
Commemorates the independence of the State of Vatican City and the recognition of the sovereignty of the Holy See, established by the Lateran Treaty, 1929.

RELIGIOUS CALENDAR

The Saints

St. Saturninus, priest, *St. Dativus,* senator, and other martyrs. [d. 304]

St. Lucius, Bishop of Adrianople and martyr. [d. 350]

St. Lazarus, Bishop of Milan. [d. c. 450]

St. Gobnet, virgin. [d. 5th cent.]

St. Severinus, abbot. [d. 507]

St. Caedmon, monk. *The Father of English Sacred Poetry.* [d. c. 680]

St. Benedict of Aniane, abbot. [d. 821]

St. Paschal I, Pope; elected Bishop of Rome 817. [d. 824]

Feast of the Appearing of Our Lady at Lourdes, celebrating the appearances of the Virgin to Bernadette Soubirous, her sister, and a friend at a grotto in Lourdes, France, 1858. Optional Memorial.

BIRTHDATES

1535 *Pope Gregory XIV,* pope 1590–91. [d. October 16, 1591]

1800 *William Talbot,* British physicist; first to produce *paper positives,* a landmark discovery in *photography,* 1841. [d. September 17, 1877]

1812 *Alexander Hamilton Stephens,* U.S. political leader, lawyer; Vice-President of the Confederacy during U.S. Civil War., 1861–65. [d. March 4, 1883]

1833 *Melville Weston Fuller,* U.S. lawyer; eighth Chief Justice of the U.S. Supreme Court. [d. July 4, 1910]

1839 *Josiah Willard Gibbs,* U.S. physicist; considered to be the greatest American theoretical scientist up to his time. [d. April 28, 1903]

1847 *Thomas Alva Edison* U.S. inventor; with over 1000 patents to his credit, including the electric light bulb, the phonograph, and an early version of the movie camera, he is the archetypical inventor. [d. October 18, 1931]

1863 *John Fitzgerald (Honey Fitz),* U.S. newspaper publisher, banker, insurance broker. [d. October 2, 1950]

1898 *Leo Szilard,* U.S. physicist; developed first method of separating isotopes of radioactive elements. [d. May 30, 1964]

1907 *William Jaird Levitt,* U.S. building executive; developer of Levittown, N.Y. [d. January 28, 1994]

1909 *Joseph Leo Mankiewicz,* U.S. writer, film director; director of *Cleopatra* and *Sleuth.* [d. February 5, 1993]

1912 *Rudolf Firkusny,* Czech-American pianist; a child prodigy, noted especially for his interpretation of Beethoven. [d. 1994]

1917 *Sidney Sheldon,* U.S. author; wrote *The Other Side of Midnight,* 1973 and *Rage of Angels,* 1980.

1920 *Faruk I (or Farouk),* King of Egypt, 1936–52; abdicated after a coup led by *Gamal Abdel Nasser.* [d. March 18, 1965]

1921 *Lloyd Millard Bentsen, Jr.,* U.S. politician, businessman; U.S. Senator, 1971–93; Vice Presidential candidate, 1988; U.S. Secretary of the Treasury, 1992–94.

    Eva Gabor, Hungarian actress; known for her starring role on television series, *Green Acres,* 1965–71. [d. July 4, 1995]

1925 *Virginia E. Johnson,* U.S. psychologist; wrote *Human Sexual Response,* with her husband, William Masters, 1966.

1926 *Paul Bocuse,* French chef; wrote *Paul Bocuse's French Cooking.*

    Leslie Nielsen, U.S. actor.

1936 *Burt Reynolds,* U.S. actor, director.

1937 *Tina Louise (Tina Blacker),* U.S. actress; known for her role as Ginger on television series, *Gilligan's Island,* 1964–67.

1941 *Sergio Mendes,* Brazilian musician.

1964 *Sheryl Crow,* U.S. singer.

1969 *Jennifer Aniston,* U.S. actress; known for her role on the TV sitcom *Friends.*

1979 *Brandy (Norwood),* U.S. singer, actress; stars in the TV sitcom, *Moesha.*

HISTORICAL EVENTS

1573 *Sir Francis Drake* of England first views the Pacific Ocean.

1730 *Peter II* of Russia dies and is succeeded by Anna, daughter of Ivan V.

1755 *Severndroog* and other strongholds on the coast of India are taken by British forces, providing for the establishment of the British Empire in *India.*

1768 *Massachusetts Circular Letter* is sent to assemblies of 12 other American colonies denouncing the *Townshend Acts* of Great Britain.

1809 *Robert Fulton* receives a patent for his *steamboat* invention.

1810 *Napoleon* marries *Maria-Luisa of Austria.*

1826 *London University* is chartered.

1836 *Mount Holyoke Seminary,* the first U.S. college for women, is founded in South Hadley, Massachusetts.

1873 *King Amadeo I* of Spain abdicates and Spain is declared a republic.

1875 *Boston University* in Massachusetts, *National University* in Greece, and *Royal University* in Italy reach an agreement to form the first joint American-European study program.

1922 *Honduras* is declared an independent republic.

1929 *Lateran Treaty* between Italy and the Holy See is made, establishing Vatican City as a separate, independent Papal state.

1945 *Yalta Conference* ends (see February 4).

1963 The first black-controlled television station begins broadcasting in Washington, D.C.

1965 People's Republic of China and Algeria sign an agreement providing for Chinese military aid to *Algeria.*

1970 *Japan* launches its first satellite into orbit from Uchinoura.

1971 Representatives from 63 countries sign a pact banning *nuclear weapons testing* on the ocean floor.

1975 *Margaret Thatcher* becomes head of Great Britain's Conservative Party, the first woman to ever head a political party in Britain.

    Col. *Richard Ratsimandrava,* President of the *Malagasy Republic,* is assassinated in the capital city of Tananarive.

1976 *Popular Movement for the Liberation of Angola* is recognized by the *Organization for African Unity.*

1979 *Ayatollah Ruhollah Khomeini* establishes an Islamic government in *Iran.*

1986 *Anatoly Shcharansky* and three other dissidents are allowed to leave the Soviet Union in exchange for five Eastern-bloc spies.

1988 Ethnic *Armenians,* advocating a reunification of the Nagorno-Karabakh Autonomous Region with the

Armenian Republic, demonstrate in the Soviet city of *Stepanakert*. The event touches off two weeks of violence between Soviet troops, Armenian protestors, and the area's Moslem majority.

1990 *Nelson R. Mandela,* South African human rights activist, is released from prison after serving twenty-seven years.

february

FEBRUARY 12

HOLIDAYS

Bangladesh
National Mourning Day

Burma
Union Day
Commemorates formation of Union of Burma, 1947.

Cameroon
Youth Day

U.S. (Georgia)
Georgia Day
Commemorates the anniversary of the founding of Georgia.

U.S.
Lincoln's Birthday
Commemorates the birth of U.S. President Abraham Lincoln. Observed as a legal holiday in some states. First celebrated in 1866 as a memorial service to the assassinated president. (See additional information in *Introduction to February*)

RELIGIOUS CALENDAR

The Saints
St. Meletius, Archbishop of Antioch. [d. 381]
St. Ethelwald, Bishop of Lindisfarne. [d. c. 740]
St. Anthony Kausleas, Patriarch of Constantinople. [d. 901]
St. Ludan. [d. c. 1202]
The Seven Founders of the Servite Order. Also called *Servants of Mary.* [d. 13th cent.]
St. Julian the Hospitaller; patron of innkeepers, travelers,

boatmen, violinists, jugglers, clowns, shepherds, pilgrims, and ferrymen. [death date unknown]
St. Marina, monk and virgin (her sex was not detected until her death). [death date unknown]

The Beatified
Blessed Thomas Hemerford and his companions, priests and martyrs. [d. 1584]

BIRTHDATES

1567 *Thomas Campion,* British poet, composer, and physician; noted for his musical lyrics; wrote *Cherry Ripe.* [d. March 1, 1620]

1663 *Cotton Mather,* American colonial clergyman; active in the promotion of the founding of Yale College; author of over 400 separate works on theology and science; some of his writings provoked the witchcraft trials at Salem, Massachusetts. [d. February 13, 1728]

1746 *Thaddeus Kosciuszko,* Polish soldier; fought for the American Revolution and used the money he received for his services to buy slaves and set them free. [d. November 15, 1817]

1768 *Francis II, Holy Roman Emperor,* 1792–1806; forced

to abdicate; his daughter, Maria Luisa, married Napoleon of France, 1810. [d. March 2, 1835]

1775 *Louisa Adams,* British-born wife of U.S. President John Quincy Adams. [d. May 14, 1852]

1785 *Pierre-Louis Dulong,* French chemist physicist; contributor to early *atomic theory.* [d. July 18, 1838]

1791 *Peter Cooper,* U.S. inventor, manufacturer, philanthropist; designed and constructed the first U.S. steam locomotive, the *Tom Thumb,* 1830. [d. April 4, 1883]

1809 *Abraham Lincoln,* U.S. lawyer, politician; 16th President of the U.S., 1860–65; led the Union through the Civil War; assassinated. [d. April 15, 1865]

Charles Robert Darwin, British naturalist; famed for his studies in *evolution* and *natural selection.* [d. April 19, 1882]

1828 *George Meredith,* British novelist, poet. [d. May 18, 1909]

1850 *William Morris Davis,* U.S. geographer, geologist; a principal founder of the science of *geomorphology.* [d. February 5, 1934]

1870 *Marie Lloyd (Matalida Alice Wood),* British musical entertainer; known for her impersonations of low-comedy characters. [d. October 7, 1922]

1880 *John L(lewellyn) Lewis,* U.S. labor leader; President of the *United Mine Workers,* 1920–60; first president of the *Congress of Industrial Organization,* 1935–41. [d. June 11, 1969]

1884 *Alice Lee Roosevelt Longworth,* U.S. socialite; daughter of U.S. President Theodore Roosevelt. [d. February 20, 1980]

1893 *Omar Nelson Bradley,* U.S. army general; Commander of 12th Army Group, the largest unit to serve under a single American field commander; first chairman of the Joint Chiefs of Staff, 1949–53. [d. April 18, 1981]

1898 *David K(ilpatrick) E(stes) Bruce,* U.S. diplomat; Ambassador to France, 1949–52; to West Germany, 1957–59; to Great Britain, 1961–69. [d. December 4, 1977]

1904 *Ted Mack (William E. Maguiness),* U.S. television host, musician; helped promote Frank Sinatra. [d. July 12, 1976]

1912 *Ronald Frederick Delderfield,* British author, dramatist. [d. June 24, 1972]

1915 *Lorne Greene,* U.S. actor; known for role as Ben Cartwright on television series, *Bonanza,* 1959–73. [d. September 11, 1987]

1918 *Julian Seymour Schwinger,* U.S. physicist; Nobel Prize in physics for research in *quantum electrodynamics* (with R. P. Feynman and S. I. Tomonaga), 1965. [d. July 16, 1994]

1923 *Franco Zeffirelli,* Italian stage, opera director and designer.

1926 *Joseph Henry (Joe) Garagiola,* U.S. baseball player, sportscaster.

1934 *William Felton (Bill) Russell,* U.S. basketball player, coach; five-time Most Valuable Player; first black coach in the National Basketball Association, 1966–69; elected to Hall of Fame, 1975.

1936 *Joe Don Baker,* U.S. actor; known for his role in *Walking Tall,* 1973.

1938 *Judy Blume,* U.S. author; wrote *Are You There God? It's Me Margaret,* 1970; *Wifey,* 1978.

1945 *Maud Adams (Maud Solveig Christina Wilkstrom),* Swedish actress, model; known for her roles in James Bond films, *Man with the Golden Gun,* 1974 and *Octopussy,* 1983.

1955 *Arsenio Hall,* U.S. talk show host, actor.

1980 *Christina Ricci,* U.S. actress; known for roles in *Mermaids,* 1990 and *Addams Family Values,* 1993.

HISTORICAL EVENTS

881 *Charles III* is crowned Holy Roman Emperor.

1111 *Henry V,* Holy Roman Emperor, imprisons *Pope Paschal II.*

1531 English clergy are ordered henceforth to regard the ruler of England as head of the Church.

1554 *Lady Jane Grey,* considered a rival for the English throne, is beheaded under orders of *Queen Mary I.*

1733 *James Oglethorpe* founds Savannah, Georgia.

1818 *Chile* declares independence from Spain after seven years of war.

1832 Ecuador annexes the *Galapagos Islands.*

1877 First public demonstration of Alexander Graham Bell's articulating *telephone* is made.

1895 Japanese destroy the Chinese army and navy and end the *Sino-Japanese War* in the *Battle of Weihaiwei.*

1909 *National Association for the Advancement of Colored People* is formed in the U.S.

1912 *Emperor Pu-Yi* of China abdicates, ending the rule of the *Manchu Dynasty; China* becomes a republic.

1915 Protocol of *Opium Convention of 1912* is signed at The Hague by China, the U.S., and the Netherlands.

1922 Indian Nationalist campaign of mass civil disobedience led by *Mahatma Gandhi* is suspended because of murders at *Chauri Chaura.*

1924 *Tutankhamen's sarcophagus* is opened, disclosing three sumptuously ornamented coffins. (See also February 16, 1923.)

George Gershwin is piano soloist in the premiere of his *Rhapsody in Blue* in New York.

1947 First launching of a *guided missile* from a submarine takes place off Ft. Mugo, California.

1961 Tribesmen kill *Patrice Lumumba,* Prime Minister of the *Republic of the Congo,* and two companions.

A space probe toward *Venus* is launched from a Soviet satellite. This is the first time that an orbiting satellite is used for such a mission.

1968 Eldridge Cleaver's book, *Soul On Ice,* is published.

1970 *Israel* bombs a *U.A.R.* steel plant, killing or wounding Egyptian civilian workers.

1973 First group of U.S. prisoners of war are freed by North Vietnam and flown from Hanoi to Clark Air Force Base in the Philippines *(Vietnam War).*

1978 The *Sandinista National Liberation Front,* a Nicaraguan guerilla organization, declares war on the *Somoza* government.

1994 The *XVII Olympic Winter games* begin in *Lillehammer, Norway.*

1998 The *Line Item Veto Act (1996)* is declared unconstitutional by a federal judge.

HOLIDAYS

Cyprus
Public Holiday
Commemorates founding of the Turkish Federated State of Cyprus (TFSC).

U.S. (Florida)
Fiesta de Menéndez
Observed to honor the birthday of the founder of St. Augustine, Pedro Menéndez de Avilés.

RELIGIOUS CALENDAR

The Saints
St. Polyeuctus, martyr. [d. 259]

St. Stephen of Rieti, abbot. [d. c. 560]

St. Modomnoc. Also called *Dominic, Dominick, Medomnoc, Modomnoe.* [d. 6th cent.]

St. Licinius, Bishop of Angers. Also called *Lésin.* [d. c. 616]

St. Huna, priest and monk. [d. 7th cent.]

St. Ermengild, Abbess of Ely and widow; daughter of King Ercombert of Kent. Also called *Ermenilda.* [d. 703]

St. Catherine dei Ricci, virgin, prioress, and mystic. Also called *Katherine dei Ricci.* [d. 1590]

St. Martinian the Hermit. Also called *Martinianus.* [death date unknown]

The Beatified
Blessed Beatrice of Ornacieu, virgin, Carthusian nun. [d. 309]

Blessed Christina of Spoleto. [d. 1458]

Blessed Eustochium of Padua, virgin and nun. [d. 1469]

Blessed Archangela Girlani, virgin and prioress. [d. 1494]

BIRTHDATES

1599 *Pope Alexander VII,* Pope, 1655–67. [d. May 22, 1667]

1728 *John Hunter,* British physician; incorporated the principles of science into surgery. [d. October 16, 1793]

1793 *Philipp Veit,* German painter; founder of the *Nazarenes.* [d. December 18, 1877]

1849 *Lord Randolph (Henry Spencer) Churchill,* British politician; developed a school of progressive conservatives called Tory Democrats; father of *Winston Churchill* (November 30). [d. January 24, 1895]

1873 *Fyodor Ivanovich Chaliapin,* Russian-French operatic bass; best known for popularization of *The Song of the Volga Boatmen.* [d. April 12, 1938]

1885 *Bess Truman,* U.S. First Lady; wife of President Harry S. Truman. [d. October 18, 1982]

1892 *Robert Houghwout Jackson,* U.S. jurist, lawyer; Associate Justice of the U.S. Supreme Court, 1941–45; 1946–54. [d. October 9, 1954]

Grant Wood, U.S. painter; best known for his painting *American Gothic.* [d. February 12, 1942]

1910 *William Bradford Shockley,* U.S. physicist; Nobel Prize in physics for development of the *transistor* (with J. Bardeen and W. H. Brattain), 1956. [d. August 11, 1989]

1919 *Tennessee Ernie Ford (Ernest Jennings Ford),* U.S. country singer. [d. October 17, 1991]

1920 *Eileen Farrell,* U.S. operatic soprano.

1923 *Charles Elwood (Chuck) Yeager,* U.S. pilot; first man to break the sound barrier.

1929 *Omar Torrijos-Herrera,* Panamanian leader, soldier; Chief of Government, 1972–78. [d. August 1, 1981]

1931 *Beate Klarsfeld,* German reformer; known for tracking down Nazi war criminals and bringing them to trial.

1934 *George Segal,* U.S. actor; known for his starring roles in *A Touch of Class* and *Fun with Dick and Jane.*

1938 *(Robert) Oliver Reed,* British actor.

1943 *Elaine Pagels,* U.S. educator, writer; author of the books

The Gnostic Gospels and *The Origin of Satan.*

1944 *Stockard Channing (Susan Stockard),* U.S. actress; known for her role in *Grease,* 1978, and *Six Degrees of Separation,* 1993.

Peter Tork, U.S. musician; member of the rock group, *The Monkees.*

1947 *Mike Krzyzewski,* U.S. collegiate basketball coach.

1948 *Teller,* U.S. magic performer; one half of the comedy duo Penn & Teller.

HISTORICAL EVENTS

1498 *Maximilian I,* Holy Roman Emperor, establishes the Imperial Council, Chancery, and Chamber.

1542 *Catherine Howard,* fifth wife of *Henry VIII* of England, is beheaded.

1566 *St. Augustine, Florida,* is founded.

1635 First *public school* in America, *Boston Latin School,* is opened.

1668 Spain recognizes the independence of *Portugal.*

1689 *William and Mary* are proclaimed joint rulers of Great Britain and reign together until December 27, 1694.

1692 *Glencoe Massacre* occurs in the Scottish Highlands; 38 members of Clan MacDonald are murdered by opposing clan leaders.

1706 *Charles XII* of Sweden defeats the Russians and Saxons at *Altranstädt.*

1779 *Captain James Cook,* English explorer, is murdered by

Hawaiian natives in a scuffle over a stolen boat.

1788 The trial of *Warren Hastings,* former governor of Bengal, for high crimes and misdemeanors, begins in England. His trial, in which Edmund Burke (January 12) and Richard Brinsley Sheridan (November 4) were among prosecuting counsel, achieved wide public attention and resulted in Hastings' acquittal, 1795.

1793 Coalition against France is formed by Prussia, Austria, Holland, Britain, Sardinia, and Spain *(French Revolutionary period).*

1795 *The University of North Carolina,* the first state university in the U.S., opens.

1858 *Sir Richard Burton* and *Captain John Speke,* British explorers, discover *Lake Tanganyika* in East Africa.

1886 Afghanistan gives *Penjdeh* up to Russia.

1895 *Louis Jean* and *Auguste Lumière* receive a French patent on their *motion-picture projector.*

1904 *Panama* adopts a constitution.

1906 *Lockhart Medical College* at Peking, China, opens.

1914 *The American Society of Composers, Authors, and Publishers (ASCAP)* is established.

1918 Cossack rebels marching on Moscow are defeated by the Bolshevik forces, and General Aleksei Kaledin, the Cossack leader, commits suicide *(Russian Revolution).*

1920 The *Declaration of London* of the Council of the League

of Nations recognizes the perpetual neutrality of *Switzerland.*

1945 Soviet troops conquer *Budapest* following a 50-day siege which inflicts enormous losses on the Allied forces *(World War II).*

1953 The Catholic Church in *Poland* is placed under state control.

1959 *Romulo Betancourt* is inaugurated as president of Venezuela.

1960 *Cuba* and the *U.S.S.R.* sign a $100 million trade agreement to take place over the next four years.

France explodes its first *atomic weapon* in the Sahara desert.

U.S. District Court in Tulsa, Oklahoma, acquits 29 large oil companies accused of conspiring to fix crude oil prices.

1967 *National Student Association* confirms that since 1952 it has received more than $3 million in secret funds from the U.S. *Central Intelligence Agency.*

1969 *U.S.S.R.* and *Japan* sign an agreement allowing commercial Japanese planes to fly across Siberia.

1970 World Jewish leaders and officials of the *World Council of Churches* announce the beginning of regular meetings.

Joseph L. Searles III becomes the first black member of the New York Stock Exchange.

1973 The *National Council of Catholic Bishops* announces that anyone undergoing or performing an *abortion* will be excommunicated from the Roman Catholic Church.

1974 *Alexander Solzhenitsyn,* Nobel Prize winning novelist, is expelled from Russia.

1975 *Turkish Cypriots* proclaim the northern 40 per cent of the island of *Cyprus* to be a separate state.

Anker Jorgensen is inaugurated as prime minister of Denmark.

1976 General *Murtala Mohammed,* Nigerian head of state, is assassinated in a failed coup attempt. Lieutenant-General *Olusegun Obasanjo* succeeds him.

1979 The *Guardian Angels* is founded in New York City by *Curtis Sliwa* to protect citizens against crime.

1984 The U.S. Federal Trade Commission gives preliminary approval to Texaco's acquisition of *Getty Oil Co.* in one of the largest business mergers in U.S. history.

Konstantin Chernenko replaces *Yuri Andropov* as general secretary of the Soviet Communist Party.

1989 *Michael Manley* is inaugurated as prime minister of Jamaica.

february

FEBRUARY 14

HOLIDAYS

St. Valentine's Day
Celebrates the two 3rd-century martyrs of this name. Also believed to be a continuation of the Roman festival of *Lupercalia*. Observed by the exchange of love messages and greetings.

Bulgaria
Viticulturists' Day or Trifon Zarenzan
Celebration of the viticulturists' art; based on ancient cult rituals honoring Dionysius.

Denmark
Fjartende Februar (Fourteenth of February)
Day for exchange of tokens and gifts among Danish school children.

Liberia
Literacy Day
Established to honor worldwide campaign to eliminate illiteracy and encourage adult education.

Mexico
Day of National Mourning
Commemorates the death of *Vincente Guerrero,* revolutionary war hero.

U.S. (Arizona)
Admission Day
Commemorates Arizona's admission to the Union, 1912.

U.S. (Oregon)
Admission Day
Commemorates the admission of Oregon, 1859.

RELIGIOUS CALENDAR

The Saints
St. Valentine, priest and martyr; patron of engaged couples. Invoked against plague, epilepsy, and fainting. [d. c. 269]
St. Abraham, Bishop of Carrhae. Also called *Abraames.* [d. c. 422]
St. Maro, abbot; patriarch of Maronites. [d. 433]
St. Auxentius, hermit. Also called *Augentius.* [d. 473]
St. Conran, bishop. [d. 6th cent.]
St. Antoninus of Sorrento, abbot; patron of Sorrento. [d. 830]
St. Cyril and *St. Methodius,* Archbishop of Sirmium, missionaries; apostles of the Slavs. St. Cyril developed an alphabet for the Slavs. Feast formerly July 7. [d. 869, 885] Obligatory Memorial.
St. Adolf, Bishop of Osnabrück. [d. 1224]

The Beatified
Blessed Conrad of Bavaria. [d. 1154]
Blessed Nicholas Paglia, prior. [d. 1255]
Blessed Angelo of Gualdo, solitary. [d. 1325]
Blessed John Baptist of Almodovar, founder. Founded the Barefooted, Reformed or Displaced Trinitarians. [d. 1613]

BIRTHDATES

1404 *Leon Battista Alberti,* Italian architect, scholar, art theorist, moral philosopher, mathematician. [d. April 25, 1472]

1760 *Richard Allen,* U.S. clergyman; founder and first bishop of *African Methodist Church.* [d. March 26, 1831]

1763 *Jean Victor Marie Moreau,* French Revolutionary general; bitter opponent of Napoleon. [d. September 2, 1813]

1766 *Thomas (Robert) Malthus,* British political economist; known for his theory of the ratio of population increase to the means of subsistence. [d. December 29, 1834]

1817 *Frederick Douglass (Frederick Augustus W. Bailey),* U.S. lecturer, author; after escaping the bonds of slavery, he became an antislavery activist, 1838. [d. February 20, 1895]

1819 *Christopher Latham Sholes,* U.S. inventor; patented first practical *typewriter.* [d. February 17, 1890]

1824 *Winfield Scott Hancock,* U.S. army general; with the Union Army during the U.S. Civil War. [d. February 9, 1886]

1847 *Anna Howard Shaw,* U.S. suffrage leader, physician, cleric; first woman ordained in the Methodist Church. [d. July 2, 1919]

1856 *Frank Harris (James Thomas Harris),* Irish-American editor, journalist, biographer; known for his frank biography of *Oscar Wilde.* [d. August 26, 1931]

1858 *Joseph Thomson,* Scottish geologist and naturalist; conducted explorations into Africa, which led to great discoveries of its natural life and geology. [d. August 2, 1895]

1869 *Charles T. R. Wilson,* British physicist; Nobel Prize in physics for experiments with *x rays* (with A. H. Compton), 1927. [d. November 15, 1959]

1882 *George Jean Nathan,* U.S. editor, critic; known as the most influential drama critic in America, 1906–58; with H. L. Mencken (September 12) founded *The American Mercury.* [d. April 8, 1958]

1894 *Jack Benny (Benjamin Kubelsky),* U.S. comedian. [d. December 26, 1974]

1896 *Andrei Alexandrovich Zhdanov,* Soviet government Communist Party official; a close associate of Joseph Stalin. [d. August 31, 1948]

1898 *Fritz Zwicky,* Swiss physicist in the U.S.; known for investigations of *cosmic rays.* [d. February 8, 1974]

1905 *Thelma Ritter,* U.S. character actress. [d. February 5, 1969]

1913 *Mel Allen (Melvin Allen Israel),* U.S. sportscaster; longtime host of *This Week in Baseball.* [d. June 16, 1996]

Wayne Woodrow (Woody) Hayes, U.S. football coach; head coach, Ohio State, 1951–79. [d. March 12, 1987]

James R(iddle) Hoffa, U.S. labor leader; President of the Teamsters Union, 1957–71 [disappeared July 30, 1975; presumed dead]

(James) Albert Pike, U.S. Episcopal priest, lawyer. [d. September 7, 1969]

1917 *Herbert A(aron) Hauptman,* U.S. physicist; Nobel Prize in chemistry for work done in determining crystal structures (with Jerome Karle), 1985.

1921 *Hugh Downs,* U.S. television personality; host of television news show, *20/20.*

1932 *Vic Morrow,* U.S. actor; known for his starring role on television series, *Combat,* 1962–67; died in a helicopter crash while making a movie. [d. July 23, 1982]

1932 *William Schroeder,* U.S. transplant patient; second person to receive an artificial heart, 1984. [d. August 6, 1986]

1934 *Florence Henderson,* U.S. actress, singer; known for her role as the mother on television series, *The Brady Bunch,* 1969–75.

1941 *Paul Efthemios Tsongas,* U.S. politician; Congressman, 1975–78; Senator, 1979–85. [d. January 18, 1997]

Donna Shalala, U.S. government official; Secretary of Health and Human Services, 1993– .

1944 *Carl Bernstein,* U.S. journalist, author; best known as a member of the *Washington Post's* reporting team during the *Watergate Incident.*

1946 *Gregory Oliver Hines,* U.S. dancer, actor; known for his starring roles in *Running Scared, White Nights,* and *The Cotton Club;* Tony Award winner for *Jelly's Last Jam,* 1992.

1956 *David Dravecky,* former U.S. baseball player; Willie McCovey Award winner, 1989.

1960 *Meg Tilly,* U.S. actress; Oscar nominee for *Agnes of God,* 1985.

Jim Kelly, U.S. football player.

1972 *Drew Bledsoe,* U.S. football player.

HISTORICAL EVENTS

1014 *Henry II, the Saint,* is crowned *Holy Roman Emperor.*

1130 *Innocent II* elected pope; reigns 1130–43.

1400 *Richard II* of England is murdered.

1674 *John III Sobieski* is crowned King of Poland.

1764 A patent on *spinning and carding machinery* is granted to *James Davenport.*

1859 *Oregon* is admitted to the Union as the 33rd state.

1903 *U.S. Department of Labor and Commerce* is established by Congress.

1912 *Arizona* is admitted to the Union as the 48th state.

1917 Sweden, Norway, and Denmark refuse to recognize the German submarine blockade *(World War I).*

1918 *Swanee,* by *George Gershwin,* premieres in New York.

february

1920 The *National League of Women Voters,* an organization for the promotion of political awareness, is founded in Chicago, Illinois.

1927 The *Strangest Love Story of All,* a film adaptation of Bram Stoker's *Dracula,* premieres.

1929 Seven die in a gangland massacre in *Chicago (St. Valentine's Day Massacre).*

Puerto Rico's legislature meets for the first time.

1939 German warship *Bismarck* is launched.

1944 *Teodoro Picado* is elected president of Costa Rica.

1949 *Chaim Weizmann* is elected first president of *Israel.*

1951 *Sugar Ray Robinson* defeats *Jake La Motta* to win the world middleweight boxing title.

1956 The *Twentieth Communist Party Congress* begins.

1958 The *Arab Federation of Iraq and Jordan* is proclaimed.

1962 Council of *Organization of American States* formally excludes Cuba from participation in any organizational activities.

1967 *Aretha Franklin* records the song *Respect.*

1969 Longest dock strike in *New York* history ends after 57 days.

1970 Indian Prime Minister *Indira Gandhi* renationalizes private banks.

President Richard Nixon orders a ban on the production and application of *chemical toxins* used in warfare.

Simon and Garfunkel's song, *Bridge Over Troubled Water*

hits number one on U.S. pop music charts.

1972 *Grease,* by Jim Jacobs and Warren Casey, premieres off-Broadway.

1979 U.S. Ambassador to Afghanistan, *Adolph Dubs,* is assassinated in Kabul by Muslim extremists.

1984 *Stormie Jones* becomes the first recipient of a *heart-liver transplant.*

1985 The U.S. *Rabbinical Assembly of Conservative Judaism* announces their decision to accept women as rabbis.

1989 Victims of the *Union Carbide* chemical plant leak that occurred in Bhopal, India (1984) were awarded $470 million.

february

HOLIDAYS

Canada
National Flag of Canada Day

China
Spring Festival

Iran
Revolution Day

South Korea
Folklore Day

U.S.
Susan B. Anthony Day
Celebrates the birthday of the pioneer crusader for women's rights, 1820.

U.S. (Maine and Massachusetts)
Maine Memorial Day
Commemorates sinking of U.S.S. *Maine* and beginning of the *Spanish-American War.*

RELIGIOUS CALENDAR

The Saints

St. Walfrid, abbot. Also called *Galfrido della Gherardesca.* [d. c. 765]

St. Tanco, Bishop of Verden and martyr. Also called *Tatta,* or *Tatto.* [d. 808]

St. Sigfrid, Bishop of Växjö; the Apostle of Sweden. Also called *Sigefride.* [d. c. 1045]

St. Agape, virgin and martyr; patron of Terni in Umbria. [death date unknown]

SS. Faustinus and Jovita, martyrs; patrons of Brescia. [death date unknown]

The Beatified

Blessed Jordan of Saxony, second master general of the Dominicans; the first university chaplain. [d. 1237]

Blessed Angelo of Borgo San Sepolcro, Augustinian hermit. [d. c. 1306]

Blessed Julia of Certaldo, virgin and anchoress. [d. 1367]

Blessed Claud la Colombière, Jesuit priest. [d. 1682]

BIRTHDATES

1368 *Sigismund, King of Hungary,* 1387–1437, Holy Roman Emperor, 1410. [d. December 9, 1437]

1497 *Philipp Melanchthon,* German theologian, Protestant reformer, educator; collaborator with Martin Luther in the Protestant Reformation. [d. April 19, 1560]

1519 *Pedro Menéndez de Avilés,* Spanish soldier, navigator; settled Florida as a Spanish colony. [d. September 17, 1574]

1564 *Galileo Galilei,* Italian physicist, astronomer; pioneered the use of the telescope for astronomical study; put forth the theory of *heliocentricity* of the universe; tried by the Inquisition for his teachings. [d. January 8, 1642]

1571 *Michael Praetorius (Schutheiss),* German composer, music historian [d. February 15, 1621]

1710 *Louis XV, King of France.* [d. May 10, 1774]

1748 *Jeremy Bentham,* English Utilitarian economist; proposed the theory that man makes ethical decisions on the basis of pleasure and pain. [d. June 6, 1831]

1782 *William Miller,* U.S. Protestant revivalist; founder of the *Millerites,* the forerunners of the Seventh-Day Adventist. [d. December 20, 1849]

1797 *Henry Engelhard Steinway,* German-U.S. piano manufacturer; founder of Steinway and Sons. [d. February 7, 1871]

1803 *John Augustus Sutter,* U.S. pioneer; his discovery of gold precipitated the California gold rush. [d. June 18, 1880]

1809 *Cyrus Hall McCormick,* U.S. inventor of farm machinery; founder of International Harvester Co. [d. May 13, 1884]

1812 *Charles Lewis Tiffany,* U.S. merchant; founder of Tiffany and Co., jewelers. [d. February 18, 1902]

1817 *Charles François Daubigny,* French landscape painter;

leader of the *Barbizon School.* [d. February 19, 1878]

1820 *Susan B(rownell) Anthony,* U.S. social reformer; a pioneer crusader for women's suffrage. [d. March 13, 1906]

1845 *Elihu Root,* U.S. Secretary of War, 1899–1904; U.S. Secretary of State, 1905–1909; awarded Nobel Peace Prize, 1912. [d. February 7, 1937]

1861 *Charles Edouard Guillaume,* Swiss-French physicist; Nobel Prize in physics for discovery of anomalies in nickel-steel alloys, 1920. [d. June 13, 1938]

Alfred North Whitehead, British mathematician, philosopher. [d. December 30, 1947]

1873 *Hans Karl August Simon Euler-Chelpin,* Swedish chemist born in Germany; Nobel Prize in chemistry for investigation into fermentation process (with A. Harden), 1929. [d. November 6, 1964]

1882 *John Barrymore,* U.S. actor; younger brother of Ethel and Lionel Barrymore; his portrayal of Hamlet is considered one of the best of all time. [d. May 29, 1942]

Felix Frankfurter, Jewish American lawyer and educator. Became a U.S. supreme court justice under Franklin Roosevelt.

1892 *James Vincent Forrestal,* U.S. government official; first U.S. Secretary of Defense. [d. May 22, 1949]

1907 *Cesar Romero,* U.S. actor; known for his role as the Joker on television series, *Batman.* [d. January 1, 1994]

1911 *Leonard (Freel) Woodcock,* U.S. government and labor union official; President of United Automobile Workers, 1970–77.

1914 *(Thomas) Hale Boggs,* U.S. politician; Congressman, 1941–43, 1947–72; lost in an Alaskan plane crash. [d. October, 1972]

1916 *Ian Keith Ballantine,* U.S. publishing executive. [d. March 9, 1995]

1929 *James Rodney Schlesinger,* U.S. government official and economist; U.S. Secretary of Defense, 1973–75.

1931 *Claire Bloom (Claire Blume),* British actress.

Maxine Singer, U.S. biochemist; known for her contributions to established guidelines in DNA research.

1935 *Roger Chaffee,* U.S. astronaut; one of astronauts killed aboard *Apollo 1.* [d. January 27, 1967]

Susan Brownmiller, U.S. author, feminist.

1942 *Kim Jong Il,* Russian-born politician; President of the Democratic People's Republic of Korea, 1994– .

1950 *Peter Gabriel,* British rock singer; founding member of the band *Genesis.*

1951 *Melissa Toni Manchester,* U.S. singer, songwriter; began career as back-up singer for Bette Midler; known for song *Don't Cry Out Loud.*

Jane Seymour (Joyce Penelope Frankenberg), British actress; known for her starring role in television movies, *East of Eden* and *The*

Scarlet Pimpernel; and for the TV series, *Dr. Quinn, Medicine Woman.*

1953 *Francisco Dallmeier,* U.S. wildlife biologist; known for his contribution to biodiversity.

1964 *Chris Farley,* U.S. comedian; known for his performances on *Saturday Night Live.* [d. December 18, 1997]

1972 *Jaromir Jagr,* Czechoslovakian-born hockey player; Art Ross Trophy winner, 1995.

HISTORICAL EVENTS

44BC *Julius Caesar* is offered the diadem of kingship by Antony and refuses it.

1637 *Ferdinand II, Holy Roman Emperor,* dies and is succeeded by *Ferdinand III.*

1763 *Treaty of Hubertusburg* between Prussia and Austria is signed. Prussia retains Silesia and emerges as a great military power.

1764 City of *St. Louis, Missouri* is founded by *Auguste Chouteau* under the direction of *Pierre Laclède.*

1876 U.S. patent is issued for the manufacture of *barbed wire.*

1898 *U.S.S. Maine* is mysteriously blown up in Havana harbor, leading U.S. to declare war on Spain *(Spanish-American War).*

1905 *Rimsky-Korsakov, Rachmaninoff, Taneyev, Gretchaninoff, Glière, Chaliapin, Siloti,* and 25 others sign a declaration protesting the political repression of the government of Czar Nicholas II.

1912 *Yüan Shih-kai* replaces *Sun Yat-sen* as provisional president of China.

1922 The *Permanent Court of International Justice* opens at The Hague.

1933 Assassin *Giuseppe Zangara* fires at President-elect Franklin Roosevelt's party in Miami, Florida, missing Roosevelt but fatally wounding Chicago Mayor *Anton Cermak.*

1938 Rebel forces under General Francisco Franco take *Teruel (Spanish Civil War).*

1942 *Singapore* is surrendered to the Japanese army *(World War II).*

1944 Allies bomb *Monte Cassino* monastery *(World War II).*

1948 *Romulo Gallego* is inaugurated as the first popularly elected president of Venezuela.

1950 The *Congress of Industrial Organizations (CIO)* expels three member unions for suspected Communist sympathies.

1965 *Canada* officially adopts a new flag; the Red Maple Leaf becomes the new symbol, replacing the Union Jack.

1971 *Britain* adopts the *decimal currency* system after 1200 years of a system based on 12-penny shillings.

1972 Brigadier General *Guillermo Rodriguez* assumes power in Ecuador after a bloodless coup d'etat.

1975 The government of *Ethiopia* declares a state of emergency in the northern province of *Eritrea* where fighting between the government and Eritrean secessionists has been going on for 13 years.

1989 A one million dollar contract is offered by the Khomeini leadership of Iran for the life of *Salman Rushdie. The Satanic Verses,* written by Rushdie, offended members of the Islam faith.

The last Soviet troops are withdrawn from *Afghanistan* after a nine-year military intervention.

1993 *Michal Kovac* is elected President of the newly formed Republic of Slovakia.

1998 *Glafcos Clerides* is elected for a second term as President of Cyprus.

february

FEBRUARY
16

HOLIDAYS

Canada (Alberta)
Family Day

Lithuania
Independence Day
Commemorates the adoption of the declaration of independence by the Council of Lithuania in 1918.

U.S. (Lithuanian Community)
Lithuanian Independence Day
Commemorates proclamation of independence, 1918.

RELIGIOUS CALENDAR

The Saints
St. Onesimus, martyr. [d. 1st cent.]
St. Juliana, virgin and martyr. [d. c. 305]
SS. Elias, Jeremy, Isaias, Samuel, and *Daniel,* martyrs. [d. 309]

The Beatified
Blessed Philippa Mareri, virgin and anchoress. [d. 1236]
Blessed Verdiana, virgin and recluse. Also called *Veridiana,* or *Viridiana.* [d. c. 1240]
Blessed Eustochium of Messina, virgin and abbess. [d. 1468]
Blessed Bernard Scammacca. [d. 1486]

BIRTHDATES

1740 *Giambattista Bodoni,* Italian printer and type designer. [d. November 29, 1813]

1812 *Henry Wilson,* U.S. politician, U.S. Vice-President, 1873–75; leader in the anti-slavery movement. [d. November 22, 1875]

1821 *Heinrich Barth,* German explorer and scholar; considered one of the greatest African explorers. [d. November 25, 1865]

1822 *Sir Francis Galton,* British anthropologist; founder of the science of *eugenics;* devised system for *fingerprint identification.* [d. January 17, 1911]

1831 *Nikolai Semyanovich Leskov,* Russian novelist. [d. March 5, 1895]

1834 *Ernst Heinrich Haeckel,* German biologist, philosopher; first German advocate of *organic evolution.* [d. August 9, 1919]

1838 *Henry Brooks Adams,* U.S. historian, novelist. [d. March 27, 1918]

1843 *Henry Martyn Leland,* U.S. manufacturer, auto-industry pioneer. [d. March 26, 1932]

1848 *Hugo Marie De Vries,* Dutch botanist; one of chief elucidators of Gregor Mendel's law of inheritance of characteristics. [d. May 21, 1935]

1886 *Van Wyck Brooks,* U.S. literary critic, cultural historian; Pulitzer Prize in history, 1937. [d. May 2, 1963]

1898 *Katharine Cornell,* U.S. stage actress. [d. June 8, 1974]

1903 *Edgar Bergen (John Edgar Bergren),* U.S. ventriloquist, actor; with his dummy, *Charlie McCarthy,* set a standard for American comedy during the 1930s and 1940s. Upon Bergen's death, McCarthy was placed in the Smithsonian Institution. [d. September 30, 1978]

1904 *George Frost Kennan,* U.S. diplomat, historian; Pulitzer Prize in history, 1957; Pulitzer Prize in biography, 1968.

1907 *Alec Wilder,* U.S. composer; composed hundreds of popular songs, as well as operas, operettas, and chamber music. [d. December 24, 1980]

1909 *Hugh Beaumont,* U.S. actor; known for his role as Ward Cleaver on television series, *Leave It to Beaver,* 1957–63. [d. May 14, 1982]

1920 *Patricia (Patti) Andrews,* U.S. singer; member of the singing group, *Andrews Sisters.*

1926 *Vera-Ellen (Rohe),* U.S. actress, dancer; one of the most renowned dancers of the 1940s. [d. August 30, 1981]

John Schlesinger, British director.

1940 *Salvatore Phillip (Sonny) Bono,* U.S. singer, actor, politician; co-hosted television series, *The Sonny and Cher Comedy Hour,* 1971–75; mayor of Palm Springs, California, 1988–94; U.S. representative, 1994–98. [d. January 5, 1998]

1955 *William Katt,* U.S. actor; known for his starring role on television series, *The Greatest American Hero,* 1981–83.

Sean McManus, U.S. broadcasting executive; Vice President, NBC Sports.

1956 *James Ingram,* U.S. singer, songwriter.

1957 *LeVar(dis Robert Martyn) Burton, Jr.,* U.S. actor; known for his role as Kunta Kinte on television mini-series, *Roots,* 1977.

1959 *John Patrick McEnroe, Jr.,* U.S. tennis player; famous for his tantrums on the court, giving him the nickname, *Superbrat.*

HISTORICAL EVENTS

1486 *Maximilian I* is elected King of Germany; ruled, 1486–1519.

1801 *William Pitt* resigns as Prime Minister of Great Britain.

1804 The U.S. frigate *Philadelphia,* captured by Tripolitans, is destroyed by an American party led by *Stephen Decatur.*

1808 France invades Spain *(Peninsular War).*

1862 Confederates surrender *Fort Donelson* in Tennessee to General *Ulysses S. Grant (U.S. Civil War).*

1868 *Benevolent and Protective Order of Elks* is founded in New York City.

1915 After small German gains, the French open a counter-offensive in the continuing *Battle of Champagne* on the Western Front *(World War I).*

1916 The Russian army, under Grand Duke Nicholas, seizes *Erzerum,* the strongest fortified city in Asiatic Turkey, from the Turks *(World War I).* The Allies (Great Britain, France, Russia, Serbia, and Italy) pledge to continue World War I until Belgium is restored to independence.

1923 *Bessie Smith* makes her first recording, *Downhearted Blues,* for Columbia Records.

British archaeologist *Howard Carter* opens *Tutankhamen's sepulchral chamber.* (See also February 12, 1924.)

1927 The first *railway* service between India and Nepal begins.

1944 Japanese naval base at *Truk* is raided by U.S. aircraft which destroy 201 enemy planes *(World War II).*

1945 *Corregidor* in Manila Day is bombarded by Allies *(World War II).*

1950 *What's My Line?* makes its television debut.

1959 *Fidel Castro* becomes Prime Minister of *Cuba.*

1965 Giant winged satellite called *Pegasus,* designed to measure the potential hazards of meteoroids to astronauts and spacecraft, is launched from Cape Kennedy, Florida.

1967 Legislation is enacted to give the British colonies of *Antigua, Dominica, Grenada, St. Kitts-Nevis* and *Anguilla,* and *St. Lucia* the status of states associated with the United Kingdom.

1970 *Joe Frazier* knocks out *Jimmy Ellis* in five rounds for world heavyweight boxing title.

1971 Highway between *West Pakistan* and *China* is formally opened.

1972 U.S. Census Bureau issues report showing steep decline in *U.S. birthrate.*

U.S. basketball player *Wilt Chamberlain* scores his 30,000th point in a game between the Los Angeles Lakers and Phoenix Suns. He is the first player in National Basketball Association history to amass 30,000 points.

1977 *American Buffalo,* a play by David Mamet, opens on Broadway.

1985 Israel begins the first stage of its withdrawal from Lebanon when three hundred troops leave the city of *Sidon.*

1992 *Yitzhak Rabin* becomes the new Prime Minister of Israel.

february

FEBRUARY
17

HOLIDAYS

U.S.
Frances E. Willard Memorial Day
In recognition of her work for the
Christian Temperance Union.

RELIGIOUS CALENDAR

Feasts
Seven Founders of the Servite
Order. Formerly February 12.
Optional Memorial.

The Saints
SS. Theodulus and *Julian,* martyrs.
[d. 309]
St. Loman, Bishop of Trim. Also
called *Luman.* [d. c. 450]
St. Fintan of Cloneenagh, abbot. [d.
603]
St. Finan, Bishop of Lindisfarne. [d.
661]
St. Silvin, bishop. [d. c. 720]
St. Evermod, Bishop of Ratzeburg;
Apostle of the Wends. [d.
1178]

The Beatified
Blessed Reginald of Orleans. [d.
1220]
Blessed Luke Belludi, Franciscan
friar. [d. c. 1285]
Blessed Andrew of Anagni, friar
minor. Also called *Andrea dei
Conti du Segni (Andrew of
the Counts of Segni), Andreas
de Comitibus.* [d. 1302]
Blessed Peter of Treia, Franciscan.
[d. 1304]
Blessed William Richardson, priest
and martyr; last martyr to

suffer death for his religion
during the reign of Queen
Elizabeth I. [d. 1603]
The Martyrs of China. [d. 19th
cent.]

BIRTHDATES

1653 *Arcangelo Corelli,* Italian
composer and violinist;
considered the creator of the
concerto grosso. [d. January
8, 1713]

1740 *Horace de Saussure,* Swiss
geologist; first scientific
explorer of the Alps. [d.
January 22, 1799]

1774 *Raphael Peale,* U.S. artist. [d.
March 4, 1825]

1781 *René Laënnec,* French
physician; inventor of the
stethoscope. [d. August 13,
1826]

1843 *Montgomery Ward,* founder
of Montgomery Ward & Co.,
first U.S. mail-order house. [d.
December 7, 1913]

1856 *Frederich Eugene Ives,* U.S.
inventor; perfected *half-tone
printing process.* [d. May 27,
1937]

1874 *Thomas John Watson,* U.S.
industrialist; introduced
*printing tabulator, electric
typewriter, electronic
calculator.* [d. June 19, 1956]

1877 *André Maginot,* French
statesman; responsible for

construction of *Maginot Line,*
a defensive barrier along the
eastern border of France
prior to World War II. [d.
January 7, 1932]

1879 *Dorothy Canfield Fisher,* U.S.
novelist; dealt especially with
stories of Vermont life. [d.
November 9, 1958]

1888 *Otto Stern,* U.S. physicist born
in Germany; Nobel Prize in
physics for studies in the
magnetic properties of atoms,
1943. [d. August 17, 1969]

1890 *Ronald A. Fisher,* British
biologist; the first to
demonstrate that Darwinian
evolution was compatible
with *genetics.* [d. July 29,
1962]

1902 *Marian Anderson,* U.S.
contralto, concert artist. [d.
April 8, 1993]

1907 *Marjorie Lawrence,*
Australian operatic soprano;
known especially for her
interpretation of Wagner. [d.
January 13, 1979]

1908 *Walter Lanier (Red) Barber,*
U.S. sportscaster. [October
22, 1992]

1924 *(Mary) Margaret Truman
Daniel,* daughter of Harry S.
Truman, 33rd U.S. president;
author of mysteries.

1925 *Harold Rowe (Hal)
Holbrook, Jr.,* U.S. actor;

Tony Award for *Mark Twain Tonight!*, 1966.

1929 *Chaim Potok*, U.S. novelist.

1934 *Alan Arthur Bates*, British actor; known for starring roles in *King of Hearts*, 1967, and *An Unmarried Woman*, 1978.

1936 *James Nathaniel (Jim) Brown*, U.S. actor, football player; running back, Cleveland Browns, 1957–65, social activist.

1947 *Tim Buckley*, U.S. singer, songwriter. [d. June 29, 1975]

1962 *Lou Diamond Phillips*, Philippine-born actor.

1963 *Michael Jordan*, U.S. basketball player.

1970 *Tommy Moe*, U.S. skier; Olympic medalist, 1994.

HISTORICAL EVENTS

1461 Queen Margaret of England defeats Warwick at *St. Albans* (War of the Roses).

1854 *Convention of Bloemfontein* constitutes the *Orange Free State* as the British government withdraws.

1864 First successful submarine attack takes place, in which Confederate ship *Hunley* sinks Union *Housatonic* with charge of gunpowder *(U.S. Civil War)*.

1865 *Columbia*, South Carolina, is burned by Union Army *(U.S. Civil War)*.

1880 An explosion rips through the dining room of the Winter Palace, St. Petersburg, Russia, during an attempt to assassinate *Czar Alexander II;* the Czar escapes injury because he and his family are late for dinner.

1897 *National Congress of Parents and Teachers* is founded in Washington, D.C.

1904 World premiere of *Madame Butterfly* by *Giacomo Puccini* takes place at the Teatro alla Scala in Milan.

1905 *Grand Duke Serge*, uncle of Czar Nicholas II, is killed when a bomb is thrown under his carriage in Moscow.

1913 Marcel Duchamp's controversial painting, *Nude Descending a Staircase*, scandalizes viewers at the 1913 Armory Show in New York City.

1915 German forces reoccupy Memel, pushing back the Russians in the *Battle of Masuria (World War I)*.

1916 The Allied forces occupy *Chios* in the Aegean Sea *(World War I)*.

1933 *Newsweek* magazine begins publication.

1934 *Albert I* of Belgium dies and is succeeded by *Leopold III*.

1936 Military revolt leads to overthrow of Paraguayan president *Eligio Ayala*.

1952 *Dorothy Maynor* becomes the first black to sing at Constitution Hall.

1960 *Mohammed Ayub Khan* is inaugurated as president of Pakistan.

1964 The U.S. Supreme Court rules that *congressional districts* should be made as equal as possible in population to ensure voter parity.

1965 *English language* is declared an associate official language in India after weeks of language riots in southern India.

1966 Pope Paul VI announces major liberalizing changes in the rules of *fasting and abstinence* for Roman Catholics.

1972 President *Richard M. Nixon* leaves Washington for his historic trip to China.

1976 President *Gerald Ford* announces a reorganization of U.S. intelligence agencies, the first since 1947.

1979 Chinese troops invade *Vietnam* as a punishment for Vietnam's intrusion into Cambodia and alleged violations of Chinese territory.

1998 The *U.S. women's hockey* team wins the gold medal at the Winter Olympics. This is the first time women's hockey is an Olympic event.

february

FEBRUARY
18

HOLIDAYS

Gambia
Republic Day
Commemorates day on which The
Gambia became self-governing
nation within British
Commonwealth, 1965.

Nepal
Democracy Day
Celebration of anniversary of 1952
Constitution.

RELIGIOUS CALENDAR

Feasts
Martin Luther, Doctor and
 Confessor. [Lutheran Minor
 Festival].

The Saints
St. Simeon, Bishop of Jerusalem and
 martyr; cousin of Jesus. Also
 called *Simon.* [d. c. 107]
St. Flavian, patriarch of
 Constantinople, martyr. [d.
 449]
St. Helladius, Archbishop of Toledo.
 [d. 633]
St. Colman, Bishop of Lindisfarne.
 [d. 676]
St. Angilbert, abbot. [d. 814]
St. Theotonius, Abbot of the
 Monastery of the Holy Cross.
 [d. 1166]
St. Leo and *St. Paregorius,* martyrs.
 [death date unknown]

The Beatified
Blessed William Harrington, priest,
 martyr. [d. 1594]
Blessed John Pibush, priest, martyr.
 [d. 1601]

BIRTHDATES

1516 *Mary I of England (Bloody
 Mary),* first English queen to
 rule in her own right;
 persecuted Protestants in an
 attempt to restore Roman
 Catholicism in England. [d.
 November 17, 1558]

1609 *Edward Hyde,* 1st Earl of
 Clarendon, British statesman,
 historian; brought Oliver
 Cromwell to power after
 English Civil War. [d.
 December 9, 1674]

1745 *Conte Alessandro Giuseppe
 Volta,* Italian physicist;
 invented the *electric battery.*
 [d. March 5, 1827]

1790 *Marshall Hall,* British
 physician, physiologist;
 discovered *reflex action.* [d.
 August 11, 1857]

1795 *George Peabody,* U.S.
 merchant, philanthropist;
 donated the *Peabody
 Museum* at Yale and at
 Harvard. Peabody,
 Massachusetts, is named for
 him. [d. November 4, 1869]

1836 *Ramakrishna,* Hindu teacher,
 writer, religious reformer;
 looked upon as a sainted wise
 man by the Hindus. [d.
 August 16, 1886]

1838 *Ernst Mach,* Austrian
 physicist, psychologist; noted
 for his research into the
 physiology and psychology of

the senses; developed
method of measuring
movement in terms of the
speed of sound (i.e. Mach
number). [d. February 19,
1916]

1848 *Louis Comfort Tiffany,* U.S.
 painter, craftsman, designer,
 glassmaker, and
 philanthropist; internationally
 known for his stained glass
 creations. [d. January 17,
 1933]

1853 *August Belmont,* U.S. banker;
 Belmont Stakes and *Belmont
 Racetrack* named in his
 family's honor. [d. December
 10, 1924]

1854 Solomon Rabinowitz, U.S.
 writer, psedonym Sholom
 Aleichem. Co-founder of
 modern Yiddish literature. [d.
 1916]

1859 *Sholem Aleichem (Solomon J.
 Rabinowitz),* Ukranian-
 Yiddish writer; known as the
 Yiddish Mark Twain. [d. May
 13, 1916]

1862 *Charles Michael Schwab,* U.S.
 manufacturer, considered the
 Boy Wonder of the American
 steel industry. [d. September
 18, 1939]

1890 *Adolphe Menjou,* U.S. actor.
 [d. October 29, 1963]

1892 *Wendell Lewis Willkie,* U.S.
 politician, business executive,
 lawyer; Republican

presidential candidate, 1940. [d. October 8, 1944]

1894 *Andres Segovia,* Spanish classical-guitar virtuoso. [d. June 2, 1987]

1896 *André Breton,* French poet, essayist, critic; one of the founders of the *Surrealist movement.* [d. September 28, 1966]

1898 *Luis Muñoz Marín,* Puerto Rican statesman; first governor of *Commonwealth of Puerto Rico.* [d. April 30, 1980]

1903 *Nikolai Viktorovich Podgorny,* Russian politician; President of U.S.S.R., 1965–1977. [d. January 11, 1983]

1909 *Wallace Earle Stegner,* U.S. author. [d. April 13, 1993]

1920 *Jack Palance (Walter Jack Palahnuik),* U.S. actor; hosted TV series, *Ripley's Believe It or Not,* Oscar winner (Best Supporting Actor) for the movie *City Slickers,* 1991

1922 *Helen Gurley Brown,* U.S. author, editor.

1925 *George Kennedy,* U.S. actor; Oscar Award for *Cool Hand Luke,* 1967; also known for his roles in the *Naked Gun* movies.

1927 *John William Warner,* U.S. politician; Senator, 1979–; husband of Elizabeth Taylor, 1976–82.

1929 *Leonard Cyril (Len) Deighton,* British cartoonist, author; wrote *The Ipcress File,* 1962.

1931 *Toni Morrison (Chloe Anthony Wofford),* U.S.

author; wrote *Song of Solomon,* 1977, and *Tar Baby,* 1981; Pulitzer Prize for *Beloved,* 1988; Nobel Prize for Literature, 1993.

1932 *Milos Forman,* Czechoslovak director; Oscar Awards for *One Flew Over the Cuckoo's Nest,* 1975, and *Amadeus,* 1984.

1933 *Kim (Marilyn) Novak,* U.S. actress; known for her starring role in *Vertigo,* 1959.

Yoko Ono, Japanese artist, musician; recorded album, *Double Fantasy,* with husband John Lennon, 1980.

1936 *Jean Marie Auel,* U.S. author; wrote *The Clan of the Cave Bear,* 1980, *The Valley of Horses,* 1982, and *The Mammouth Hunters,* 1986.

1945 *Michael Nader,* U.S. actor; known for his role as Dex on television series, *Dynasty,* 1983–89.

1950 *John Hughes,* U.S. director.

Cybill Shepherd, U.S. model, actress; known for her roles on the TV series, *Moonlighting* and *Cybill.*

1951 *Dick Stockton,* U.S. tennis player.

1952 *Juice Newton (Judy Cohen),* U.S. singer; known for songs, *Angel of the Morning* and *Queen of Hearts.*

1954 *John Travolta,* U.S. actor; known for his starring roles in *Saturday Night Fever, Grease, Pulp Fiction,* and *Michael.*

1964 *Matt Dillon,* U.S. actor.

1968 *Molly Ringwald,* U.S. actress; known for starring roles in *The Breakfast Club,* 1985, and *Pretty in Pink,* 1986.

HISTORICAL EVENTS

1248 Lombards defeat *Frederick II* of Germany, at Parma.

1405 *Timur Lenk (Tamerlane),* Mongul ruler, dies and is succeeded by *Shah Rokh.*

1678 *Pilgrim's Progress* by *John Bunyan* is published.

1804 *Ohio University,* the first federal land grant university, is founded in Athens, Ohio.

1861 The first *Italian parliament* meets.

1865 *Charleston,* South Carolina is taken by the Union fleet (*U.S. Civil War*).

1876 Direct *telegraphic line* between London and New Zealand is established.

1884 *Gen. Charles Gordon* arrives at *Khartoum* to suppress the rebellion led by the Mahdi in the Sudan against the Egyptian ruler.

1915 The Germans begin their *submarine blockade* of British waters (*World War I*).

1916 The Germans in *Cameroon* surrender to the Allies, ending that African campaign and German control of the Colony of Cameroon (*World War I*).

1918 Bolshevik forces capture *Kiev,* the capital of the newly-proclaimed *Republic of the Ukraine (Russian Revolution).*

1930 Planet *Pluto* is discovered by *Clyde Tombaugh* at Lowell Observatory in Flagstaff, Arizona.

1932 Japan establishes the independent nation of *Manchukuo* from seized Manchurian territory.

february

1943 *Carl Orff's Die Kluge* opens in Frankfurt, Germany.

1960 Foreign ministers of *Argentina, Brazil, Chile, Mexico, Paraguay, Peru,* and *Uruguay* sign a treaty providing for a free-trade zone linking the economies of their nations.

VIII Winter Olympic Games open at *Squaw Valley,* California.

1963 *U.S. Supreme Court* declares unconstitutional two acts of Congress depriving Americans of citizenship for leaving the country to avoid the draft.

1965 *The Gambia* becomes an independent state within the British Commonwealth.

1970 All defendants in the *Chicago Seven* trial are acquitted of charges of conspiring to incite a riot during the 1968 Democratic National Convention.

1984 Italy and the Vatican sign a new concordat removing Roman Catholicism as Italy's state religion.

1988 *Anthony Kennedy* is sworn in as an associate justice of the U.S. Supreme Court.

1995 *Myrlie Evers-Williams* is selected as the new chairwoman for the *National Association for the Advancement of Colored People (NAACP).*

HOLIDAYS

Cyprus
Green Monday

Nepal
National Democracy Day

Turkmenistan
Flag Day

U.S. (Kentucky)
Robert E. Lee Day

RELIGIOUS CALENDAR

The Saints

St. Mesrop, bishop. Principal colleague of St. Isaac the Great in developing the Armenian church. Also called *Mesrop the Teacher,* or *Mashtots.* [d. 441]

St. Barbatus, Bishop of Benevento; patron of Benevento. Also called *Barbas.* [d. 682]

St. Beatus of Liebana, priest. [d. c. 798]

St. Boniface, Bishop of Lausanne. [d. 1260]

St. Conrad of Piacenza, anchorite; invoked against ruptures. [d. 1351]

The Beatified

Blessed Alvarez of Cordova, Dominican friar. [d. c. 1430]

BIRTHDATES

1473 *Nicolaus Copernicus,* Polish astronomer; developed the mathematics and was first to propose the heliocentric solar system. [d. May 24, 1543]

1717 *David Garrick,* British actor, theatrical manager. [d. January 20, 1779]

1743 *Luigi Boccherini,* Italian composer, cellist; developed concept of string quartets and quintets. [d. May 28, 1805]

1792 *Roderick Impey Murchison,* Scottish geologist; developed *Silurian system of geology.* [d. October 27, 1871]

1817 *William III of the Netherlands,* ruled 1849–90. [d. November 23, 1890]

1833 *Elie Ducommun,* Swiss journalist, pacifist; led organization of *International League of Peace and Freedom.* Nobel Peace Prize (with C. A. Gobat), 1902. [d. December 7, 1906]

1859 *Svante August Arrhenius,* Swedish chemist; Nobel Prize in chemistry for development of the theory of *ionization,* 1903. [d. October 2, 1927]

1863 *Augusto Bernardino Leguía y Salcedo,* Peruvian politician; President 1908–13; dictator 1919–30. [d. February 6, 1932]

1865 *Sven Anders Hedin,* Swedish scientist and explorer of central and east Asia; explorations determined the source of the *Indus River.* [d. November 26, 1952]

1880 *Alvaro Obregón,* Mexican revolutionary and reformer; President of Mexico, 1920–24. [d. July 17, 1928]

1893 *Sir Cedric Hardwicke,* British actor. [d. August 6, 1964]

1911 *Merle Oberon,* British actress; especially noted for her leading roles in the 1930s and 1940s. [d. November 23, 1979]

1912 *Stan Kenton,* U.S. musician, arranger. [d. August 25, 1979]

Anton Buttigieg, President of Malta, 1976–82.

1916 *Eddie Arcaro,* U.S. jockey; winner of 4,779 races, including five Kentucky Derbies. [d. November 14, 1997]

1917 *Carson McCullers,* U.S. author and playwright; author of *The Heart Is a Lonely Hunter.* [d. September 29, 1967]

1924 *Lee Marvin,* U.S. actor. [d. August 29, 1987]

1930 *John Frankenheimer,* U.S. director; known for his film, *Birdman of Alcatraz.*

1940 *Jill Krementz,* U.S. photographer, author; wife of author Kurt Vonnegut.

William (Smokey) Robinson, Jr., U.S. singer, songwriter, producer; famous for songs, *Shop Around* and *Tracks of My Tears.*

1955 *Jeff Daniels,* U.S. actor.

1960 *Prince Andrew Albert Christian Edward,* second son of *Queen Elizabeth II* of England.

1963 *Hana Mandlikova,* Czechoslovak tennis player; defeated Chris Evert Lloyd and Martina Navratilova at the U.S. Open, 1985.

1966 *Justine Bateman,* U.S. actress; known for her role as Mallory Keaton on television series, *Family Ties,* 1982–89.

HISTORICAL EVENTS

1800 *Napoleon* centralizes French administration; establishes himself in the Tuileries as First Consul.

1864 *Knights of Pythias* are founded.

1878 Patent for first *gramophone* is awarded to *Thomas Alva Edison.*

1915 A combined British-French fleet begins the naval bombardment of the *Dardanelles (World War I).*

1918 Nationalization of all land, farm buildings, machinery, and livestock is announced in Russia.

1923 *Jean Sibelius* conducts the premiere of his *Sixth Symphony,* op. 104, in Helsinki.

1929 The entire artillery corps of the *Spanish army* is disbanded by royal decree following riots and mutiny of artillery garrisons.

1942 President Franklin D. Roosevelt authorizes the relocation of *Japanese-American citizens* to government-sponsored internment centers *(World War II).*

1945 U.S. Marines invade *Iwo Jima. (World War II)*

1962 *U.S. Senator Carl Hayden* completes fifty years of service in the U.S. Congress— the longest term in U.S. history.

Talks with France on ending the 7 1/2-year rebellion in *Algeria* conclude with full agreement on a cease-fire and accords on a provisional government.

1964 Detection of *omega-minus sub-atomic particle,* providing confirmation of a new theory of binding forces in the atomic nucleus, is announced.

1970 Detroit Tiger pitcher *Denny McLain* is suspended from baseball indefinitely for gambling.

1972 Five U.S. airmen, allegedly captured during intensive bombing raids of February 16–17, are publicly displayed in *Hanoi (Vietnam War).*

1976 *Iceland* severs diplomatic relations with Britain in dispute over fishing limits in Icelandic waters.

1977 *Lady Spencer-Churchill,* the 91-year-old widow of Britain's wartime leader Sir Winston Churchill, begins selling items of great sentimental value, citing serious financial difficulties.

1982 The *DeLorean Motor Co.* of Belfast, Northern Ireland, is put into receivership.

1997 *Deng Xiaoping,* Chinese communist leader, dies.

february

HOLIDAYS

Bangladesh
Shaheed Day or Martyrs' Day or National Mourning Day.

Canada (Yukon)
Heritage Day

RELIGIOUS CALENDAR

The Saints
SS. *Tyrannio,* Bishop of Tyre, *Zenobius,* priest and physician, and other martyrs. [d. 304 and 310]
St. *Sadoth,* Bishop of Seleucia-Ctesiphon, and martyr. Also called *Sadosh, Schiadurte, Shadost, Shahdost,* or *Shiadustes.* [d. c. 342]
St. *Eleutherius,* first Bishop of Tournai. [d. 532]
St. *Eucherius,* Bishop of Orleans. [d. 743]
St. *Wulfric,* anchoret. Also called *Ulric, Ulrich,* or *Ulrick.* [d. 1154]

The Beatified
Blessed Elizabeth of Mantua, virgin. [d. 1468]

BIRTHDATES

1726 *William Prescott,* American Revolutionary officer, hero of the *Battle of Bunker Hill,* 1775. [d. October 13, 1775]

1791 *Karl Czerny,* Austrian pianist, composer. [d. July 15, 1857]

1805 *Angelina Emily Grimké,* U.S. reformer, abolitionist; woman's rights advocate. [d. October 26, 1879]

1844 *Ludwig Boltzmann,* Austrian physicist; made great contributions to the development of *statistical mechanics.* [d. September 5, 1906]

Joshua Slocum, U.S. author, adventurer; sailed around the world alone, 1895–98. [d. 1910]

1887 *Vincent Massey,* Canadian statesman; first native-born Canadian to become governor-general of Canada, 1952–59. [d. December 30, 1967]

1898 *Enzo Ferrari,* Italian auto manufacturer. [d. 1988]

1901 *René Dubos,* U.S. microbiologist, environmentalist, educator, author; primarily concerned with environmental issues during his lengthy career. [d. February 20, 1982]

1902 *Ansel Adams,* U.S. landscape photographer; recognized as one of the foremost photographic artists in America. [d. April 24, 1984]

1904 *Alexei Nikolaevich Kosygin,* Russian communist leader; Russian premier, 1964–80. Led Soviet effort at economic modernization in 1960s. [d. December 18, 1980]

1912 *Pierre François Marie-Louis Boulle,* French novelist; best known for *Bridge over the River Kwai* and *Planet of the Apes.* [d. January 30, 1994]

1923 *Linden Forbes Burnham,* Guyana politician; President, 1964–85. [d. August 6, 1985]

1924 *Gloria Morgan Vanderbilt (Gloria Cooper),* U.S. artist, actress, designer.

1925 *Robert Altman,* U.S. film producer, director.

1927 *Roy Marcus Cohn,* U.S. lawyer; was chief counsellor to Senator Joseph McCarthy's Communist-hunting investigations subcommittee. [d. August 2, 1986]

Sidney Poitier, U.S. actor; Oscar winner for *Lillies of the Field,* 1963.

1931 *Amanda Blake (Beverly Louise Neill),* U.S. actress; known for her role as Miss Kitty on television series, *Gunsmoke,* 1955–75. [d. August 16, 1989]

1934 *Bobby Unser,* U.S. auto racer.

1937 Robert Huber, German biochemist; Nobel Prize for Chemistry (1988). Huber shares with fellow biochemists, Johann Deisenhofer and Hartmut Michel.

Nancy Wilson, U.S. singer.

1941 *Beverly (Buffy) Sainte-Marie,* Canadian singer, composer; Oscar Award for best song from *An Officer and a Gentleman,* 1982.

1942 *Phil(ip) Esposito,* Canadian hockey player; scored 717 career goals, fourth on the National Hockey League all-time list.

1945 *George F. Smoot,* U.S. astrophysicist; known for the discovery of ripples in cosmic radiation, 1992.

1946 *Sandy Duncan,* U.S. actress; known for her role as Peter Pan on Broadway.

1947 *Peter Strauss,* U.S. actor; Emmy Award for *The Jericho Mile,* 1979.

1949 *Jennifer O'Neill,* U.S. actress, model; known for her starring role in *The Summer of '42.*

Ivana Trump, Czechoslovakian-born businesswoman; former wife of Donald Trump.

1951 *Edward Albert,* U.S. actor, photographer; known for his starring role in *Butterflies Are Free,* 1972.

1954 *Patricia Campbell (Patty) Hearst,* U.S. kidnap victim, author; kidnapped by the Symbionese Liberation Army, February 5, 1974.

1961 *Steve Lundquist,* U.S. swimmer.

HISTORICAL EVENTS

1963 *Charles Barkley,* U.S. basketball player.

1437 *James I* of Scotland is murdered by *Sir Robert Graham* at Perth.

1471 *James III* of Scotland annexes *Orkney* and *Shetland Islands.*

1547 *Edward VI* of England ascends the throne.

1790 *Joseph II,* Holy Roman Emperor, dies and is succeeded by Leopold II.

1815 U.S. frigate *Constitution* captures the British *Cyane* and *Levant (War of 1812).*

1862 *William Wallace Lincoln,* the son of U.S. President Abraham Lincoln, dies in the White House.

1864 *Battle of Olustee* or *Ocean Pond,* Florida, results in a Confederate victory. *(U.S. Civil War).*

1915 *Liquid fire (flamethrower)* is first used as a weapon by the Germans in attacks against the French in the *Argonne (World War I).*

1916 *Battle of Verdun* begins *(World War I).*

1928 Treaty with Great Britain is signed providing for autonomous government in Trans-Jordan (now primarily *Jordan*).

1952 John Huston's film *The African Queen,* starring Katharine Hepburn and Humphrey Bogart, premieres in New York.

1960 Cuban cabinet approves a new law bringing all private enterprise in *Cuba* under control of a *Central Planning Board* headed by Premier *Fidel Castro.*

1962 U.S. astronaut *John Glenn* becomes first American to orbit the earth, in spaceship *Friendship VII.*

1965 U.S. spacecraft *Ranger 8* relays to earth 7,000 pictures of the moon before crashing into an area known as the *Sea of Tranquillity.*

1970 *Chile* agrees to sell $11 million worth of foodstuffs to *Cuba* despite the embargo imposed by members of the Organization of American States in 1964.

Construction begins on 5,118 foot *Bosporus Bridge,* linking Istanbul in Europe to Uskudar in Asia.

1994 U.S. citizens *Aldrich and Maria Hazen* are arrested on charges of spying for the Soviet government.

1996 *Kweisi Mfume* becomes the president of the *National Association for the Advancement of Colored People (NAACP).*

HOLIDAYS

Norway
Crown Prince Harald's Birthday

RELIGIOUS CALENDAR

The Saints
St. Severian, Bishop of Scythopolis and martyr. [d. 453]

St. Germanus of Granfel, abbot and martyr. Also called *German.* [d. c. 677]

St. George, Bishop of Amastris. [d. c. 825]

St. Peter Damian [d. 1072] Optional Memorial.

The Beatified
Blessed Pepin of Landen, mayor of the palace to Kings Clotaire II, Dagobert I, and Sigebert III of France. [d. 646]

Blessed Noel Pinot, priest and martyr. [d. 1794]

BIRTHDATES

1728 *Peter III, Emperor of Russia,* 1761–62; deposed in favor of his consort, *Catherine the Great.* [d. July 17, 1762]

1794 *Antonio Lopez de Santa Anna,* Mexican statesman and army officer; President of Mexico, 1833–36, 1846–47. [d. June 21, 1876]

1801 *St. John (Henry) Newman,* British Catholic cardinal, theologian, and writer. Canonized 1980. [d. August 11, 1890]

1821 *Charles Scribner,* U.S. publisher; publisher and founder *Scribner's Monthly;* also with Issac D. Baker founder of Baker & Scribner, publishers, 1846 (later Charles Scribner's Sons). [d. August 26, 1871]

1855 *Alice (Elvira) Freeman Palmer,* U.S. educator; president of Wellesley College, 1882–88; co-founder of the Association of Collegiate Alumnae (later the *American Association of University Women*); first dean of women at the *University of Chicago,* 1892–95. [d. December 6, 1902]

1863 *Rudolph Jay Schaefer,* U.S. brewery executive; introduced first *bottled beer* in U.S., 1891; founder of F. M. Schaefer Brewing Co., 1882. [d. November 9, 1923]

1866 *August von Wasserman,* German bacteriologist; developed the diagnostic test for *syphilis,* 1906. [d. March 15, 1925]

1867 *Otto Hermann Kahn,* U.S. banker, philanthropist; noted patron of the arts. [d. March 29, 1934]

1876 *Constantin Brancusi,* Rumanian-French sculptor; noted for his sculpture of abstract figures. [d. March 16, 1957]

1895 *Henrik C. P. Dam,* Danish biochemist; Nobel Prize in physiology or medicine for discovery of *Vitamin K,* 1943. [d. April 1976]

1903 *Anaïs Nin,* French-U.S. diarist, novelist, short-story writer; well-known for her diaries, especially those recounting bohemian life in war-torn Europe. [d. January 14, 1977]

1907 *W(ystan) H(ugh) Auden,* British-U.S. poet, dramatist, editor; Pulitzer Prize in poetry, 1947. [d. September 18, 1973]

1914 *Zachary Scott,* U.S. actor. [d. October 3, 1965]

1915 *Ann Sheridan (Clara Lou Sheridan),* U.S. actress. [d. January 21, 1967]

1921 *Jean-Bedel Bokassa,* African political leader; took control of Central African Republic, 1966; Life President, 1972–77; Emperor, 1977–79. [d. November 3, 1996]

1923 *William Forrest Winter,* U.S. politician; Governor of Mississippi, 1980–84.

1924 *Robert Mugabe,* Prime Minister of newly independent state of *Zimbabwe,* 1980–88; Executive President, 1988– .

1925 *(David) Sam(uel) Peckinpah,* U.S. film director; known for his artistic but violent films. [d. December 28, 1984]

1927 *Erma Bombeck,* U.S. newspaper columnist, author; known for her witty writings about the American domestic scene. [d. April 22, 1996]

Hubert de Givenchy, French fashion designer.

1936 *Barbara Jordan,* U.S. politician, orator; the first black woman to serve in the Texas legislature. [d. January 17, 1996]

1937 *Gary Lockwood (John Gary Yusolfsky),* U.S. actor; known for his role in *2001: A Space Odyssey,* 1968.

1943 *David Geffen,* U.S. producer; produced Tony Award-winning musical, *Cats.*

1944 *(Ellen) Tyne Daly,* U.S. actress; two Emmy Awards for role of Mary Beth Lacey on television series, *Cagney and Lacey.*

1945 *Kelsey Grammer,* U.S. actor; Emmy winner for his portrayal as Dr. Frasier Crane on the TV sitcoms *Cheers* and *Frasier.*

1958 *Alan Stuart Trammel,* U.S. baseball player; Most Valuable Player, 1984 World Series.

1961 *Christopher Atkins,* U.S. actor; known for his role in *The Blue Lagoon,* 1980.

HISTORICAL EVENTS

891 *Wido of Spoleto* is crowned Holy Roman Emperor and King of Italy.

1613 *Michael Romanov* is elected Tsar of Russia, marking the beginning of the reign of the Romanovs, which lasted until 1917.

1828 Publication of the *Cherokee Phoenix,* the first Native American newspaper published in a Native American language.

1849 British forces crush the Sikh army in the *Battle of Gujarat,* leading to annexation of the *Punjab (Second Sikh War).*

1885 *Washington Monument,* designed by *Robert Mills,* is dedicated in Washington, D.C.

1911 Treaty between U.S. and Japan is signed, affirming the Gentlemen's Agreement for Japanese restriction of labor emigration to the U.S.

1918 British troops capture *Jericho* as the Turks retreat beyond the Jordan *(World War I).*

1921 *Reza Khan,* an army officer, seizes Teheran, overthrowing the Persian government of the Kajars and marking the beginning of the *Pahlavi* dynasty.

1943 Allied Forces in North Africa are placed under the supreme command of *General Dwight D. Eisenhower (World War II).*

1950 U.S. Justice Department files a civil antitrust suit against *Lee and Jacob J. Shubert,* charging them with monopolizing the legitimate theater in the U.S.

1961 The constitution of *Gabon* is promulgated.

1964 The U.S. satellite, *Echo II,* relays a British broadcast to the Zimenki Observatory in the U.S.S.R. It is the first cooperative space effort between the U.S., U.S.S.R., and Great Britain.

1965 *Malcolm X (Malcolm Little),* U.S. black nationalist leader, is assassinated in New York City as he addresses the *Afro-American Unity Organization.*

1969 Philip Roth's novel, *Portnoy's Complaint,* is published.

1971 Brazilian diplomat *Aloysio Dias Gomide* is released by Uruguayan rebels almost seven months after his kidnapping.

1972 U.S. President *Richard M. Nixon* becomes the first U.S. President to visit the *People's Republic of China.*

1975 *John Ehrlichman, H. R. Haldeman,* and *John Mitchell* are sentenced for their participation in the *Watergate Incident.*

1976 Former president *Richard M. Nixon* begins an eight-day visit to the *People's Republic of China* at the invitation of the Chinese government.

1979 *St. Lucia,* a tiny island in the Caribbean, gains independence from Great Britain.

1988 *George Vassiliou* is elected president of Cyprus.

Television evangelist, *Jimmy Swaggert,* announces that he will leave his ministry for an unspecified length of time. Press reports of Swaggert's alleged sexual indiscretions prompted the decision.

1989 *Iran-Contra trial* begins in Washington, D.C.

HOLIDAYS

Bolivia (Oruro)
Public Holiday

Egypt
Unity Day
Celebrates the cooperation among Arab states.

India
Mothers' Day
Established as a memorial to *Mrs. Mahatma K. Gandhi,* wife of the Hindu religious leader, nationalist, and social reformer.

Mexico
Day of Mourning
Commemorates the death of *Francisco I. Madero,* leader of the campaign to overthrow the dictatorship of *Porfiro Díaz.*

Qatar
Public Holiday
Commemorates the Amir's accession.

St. Lucia
Independence Day
Commemorates independence from Great Britain in 1979.

Syria
Unity Day
Celebrates the cooperation among Arab states.

U.S.
George Washington's Birthday
Commemorates birthday of the commander-in-chief of the Continental Army and the first president of the U.S.

RELIGIOUS CALENDAR

Feasts
Chair of Peter Commemorates the founding of the See of Antioch by St. Peter. [1st century A.D.]

The Saints
St. Thalassius and *St. Limnaeus,* anchorets. [d. c. 450]
St. Baradates, anchoret. [d. c. 460]
St. Margaret of Cortona, penitent and founder of the Congregation of the Poverelle and the Confraternity of Our Lady of Mercy. [d. 1297]

BIRTHDATES

1403 *Charles VII* of France. [d. July 22, 1461]

1440 *Ladislas V,* King of Hungary, 1444–57 post-humous son of Albert II. [d. November 23, 1457]

1732 *George Washington,* first president of the United States, 1789–97; commander-in-chief of the Continental Army. [d. December 14, 1799]

1778 *Rembrandt Peale,* U.S. artist. [d. October 3, 1860]

1788 *Arthur Schopenhauer,* German philosopher. [d. September 21, 1860]

1796 *(Lambert) Adolphe Quetelet,* Belgian mathematician; a founder of the *London Statistical Society;* formulated the theory of the *average man.* [d. February 17, 1874]

1810 *Frédéric François Chopin,* Polish-French composer and pianist; noted for his lyric compositions; intimate of *George Sand* (July 1); (some sources give his birthdate as March 1). [d. October 17, 1849]

1819 *James Russell Lowell,* U.S. poet, critic, editor; co-founder of the *Atlantic Monthly;* a key figure in the New England literary renaissance; U.S. Minister to Great Britain, 1880–85. [d. August 12, 1891]

1857 *Robert (Stephenson Smyth) Baden-Powell,* First Baron Baden-Powell of Gilwell; British founder of the *Boy Scouts.* [d. January 8, 1941]

Heinrich Rudolf Hertz, German physicist; his theories of *electromagnetism* led to the discovery of *wireless telegraphy;* Hertzian waves are named for him. [d. January 1, 1894]

Frank Lebby Stanton, U.S. poet, journalist. [d. January 7, 1927]

1872 Santiago Iglesias, Puerto Rican politician/labor leader. President of the Federacion Libre de Trabajadores de

Puerto Rico for thirty-five years. Representative of Puerto Rico to U.S. Congress. [d. 1939]

1876 Zitkala-Sa (Gertrude Bonnin), Native American Sioux writer. Activist for Native American rights and preservation of their culture. [d. 1938]

1882 *(Arthur) Eric Gill,* British sculptor, type designer. [d. November 17, 1940.]

1886 *Hugo Ball,* German poet, theatrical producer, Catholic theologian; a founder of *Dadaism.* [d. September 14, 1927]

1892 *David Dubinsky,* U.S. labor leader, born in Poland; President of International Ladies Garment Worker's Union (ILGWU), 1932–66. [d. September 17, 1982]

Edna St. Vincent Millay, U.S. poet, dramatist; Pulitzer Prize in poetry, 1923. [d. October 19, 1950]

1900 *Luis Buñuel,* Spanish film director, working in France, 1920s–30s; in Mexico, 1945–60. [d. July 29, 1983]

Sean O'Faolain (Sean Whelan), Irish short-story writer, novelist, essayist, biographer. [d. April 21, 1991]

1907 *Sheldon Leonard (Sheldon Leonard Bershad),* U.S. actor, producer; produced television series, *The Dick Van Dyke Show* and *I Spy.* [d. January 10, 1997]

Robert Young, U.S. actor. [d. July 21, 1998]

1908 *Romulo Betancourt,* Venezuelan statesman; President, 1945–48, 1959–64. [d. September 28, 1981]

Eddie Albert (Edward Albert Heimberger), U.S. actor.

Sir John Mills, British actor.

1912 *Henry S. Reuss,* U.S. politician, lawyer; U.S. Congressman, 1954–82.

1917 *Sybil Leek (Sybil Falk),* British astrologer, author; known for her predictions of the Kennedy assassinations and election of Nixon to the presidency; wrote *Diary of a Witch,* 1968. [d. October 26, 1982]

1932 *Edward M(oore) Kennedy,* U.S. politician, U.S. Senator, 1963–; brother of President John F. Kennedy (May 29) and Robert F. Kennedy (November 20).

1918 *Sid Abel,* Canadian hockey player.

1934 *George Lee (Sparky) Anderson,* U.S. baseball manager; first manager to win World Series in both leagues; Cincinnati, 1975, 1976 and Detroit, 1984.

1936 J. Michael Bishop, U.S. virologist; Nobel Prize for Medicine in 1989, with fellow virologist, Harold E. Varmus.

1944 *Jonathan Demme,* U.S. film director, producer; Academy Award winner (Best Actor) for *Silence of the Lambs,* 1991.

1950 *Julius Winfield (Doctor J.) Erving,* U.S. basketball player; Most Valuable Player, 1974, 1976, and 1981.

1959 *Kyle MacLachlan,* U.S. actor; known for role on TV series *Twin Peaks.*

1972 *Michael Chang,* U.S. tennis player; winner of the 1989 French Open.

1975 Drew Barrymore, U.S. actress.

HISTORICAL EVENTS

1370 *Robert II* of Scotland accedes to the throne.

1418 *Pope Martin V* condemns the doctrines of *John Wycliffe* and *John Hus.*

1785 The merchant ship *Empress of China* leaves New York, inaugurating U.S. trade with the Orient.

1787 The first black settlers, freed slaves, sail from Portsmouth, England, to settle in *Sierra Leone,* Africa.

1819 Treaty between Spain and the U.S. is signed, in which Spain cedes *Florida* to the U.S.; the western boundaries of the *Louisiana Purchase* are fixed.

1847 *Battle of Buena Vista* begins in which Americans under *Zachary Taylor* defeat Mexicans led by *Santa Anna (Mexican War).*

1892 The *People's Party* (Populist Party) is organized at St. Louis, Missouri.

1912 *J. Vedrines,* a Frenchman, becomes the first man to fly over 100 m.p.h.

1913 Mexican President *Francisco I. Madero* is assassinated.

1966 *Prime Minister Milton Obote* of *Uganda* seizes all governmental power and arrests five cabinet members.

1967 A force of over 25,000 U.S. and South Vietnamese troops launch *Operation Junction City,* the largest offensive of the *Vietnam War.*

Donald B. Sangster is sworn in as Prime Minister of Jamaica.

1972 Sheik *Khalifa Bin Hamad Al Thani* assumes power in

Qatar after a bloodless coup d'etat.

Irish Republican Army kills seven people at *Aldershot*.

Jean-Bédel Bokassa is named President for Life of the *Central African Republic*.

1980 Martial law is declared in *Afghanistan* as Soviet army attempts to curb civilian unrest.

1983 U.S. government offers to buy all homes and businesses in *Times Beach, Mo.*, which was evacuated because of *dioxin* contamination.

1986 Iran receives the first secret shipment of U.S. arms *(Iran-contra affair)*.

1990 *Simplesse*, a fat substitute, is approved by the Food and Drug Administration (FDA).

1991 President *Ramiz Alia* of Albania appoints *Fatos Nano* as the new Premier in response to the public protest for government reform.

1993 The *U.N. Security Council* approves the creation of an international court to prosecute war crimes in Yugoslavia. This is the first international court since World War II.

february

FEBRUARY
23

HOLIDAYS

Brunei
National Day

Guyana
Republic Day
Commemorates Guyana's becoming a republic, 1970.

Republic of Georgia (Adjaria)
Men's Day

Tajikistan
Army Day

RELIGIOUS CALENDAR

The Saints

St. Polycarp, Bishop of Smyrna and martyr. Most famous of the Apostolic Fathers, the immediate disciples of the Apostles. Feast formerly January 26. [d. c. 155] Obligatory Memorial

St. Serenus the Gardener, ascetic and martyr. Also called *Cerneulf.* [d. 302]

St. Alexander Akimetes, monk. Instituted a form of choral service which was carried on night and day without interruption. [d. c. 430]

St. Dositheus, monk. [d. c. 530]

St. Milburga, abbess of Wenlock and virgin; founder of the nunnery of Wenlock in Shropshire. Invoked for the protection of crops against the ravages of birds. Also called *Milburge, Mildburga, Mildburb, Mildgytha,* or *Milgithe.*

St. Willigis, Archbishop of Mainz. [d. 1011]

St. Peter Damian, Cardinal-Bishop of Ostia and Doctor of the Church. One of the chief forerunners of the Hildebrandine reform in the Church. Patron of Faenza. [d. 1072]

BIRTHDATES

1400 *Johannes Gutenberg,* German inventor of printing from movable type; publisher of the first printed Bible, 1496. [d. February, 1468]

1417 *Pope Paul II,* Pope from 1464–71. [d. July 26, 1471]

1633 *Samuel Pepys,* English diarist, Secretary to the Admiralty, 1673; 1684–89; his diary offers a unique picture of life in England, 1660–69. [d. May 26, 1703]

1680 *Jean-Baptiste Le Moyne sieur de Bienville,* French-Canadian explorer and colonizer; founder of *New Orleans.* [d. March 7, 1767]

1685 *George Frederick Handel,* British composer born in Germany; noted for his oratorios, especially his *Messiah.* [d. April 14, 1759]

1743 *Meyer Rothschild,* German banker, financier; founder of the *House of Rothschild*

financial dynasty. [d. September 19, 1812]

1787 *Emma (Hart) Willard,* U.S. educator; established *Emma Willard School,* Troy, New York, 1821. [d. April 15, 1870]

1817 *George Frederic Watts,* British painter and sculptor; used grand allegorical themes in his work; noted for his fresco *George and the Dragon* in the British Parliament Hall of Poets; executed over 300 portraits of distinguished contemporaries. [d. July 1, 1904]

1832 *John Heyl Vincent,* U.S. Methodist bishop; noted for his development of the *Chatauqua* concept of training Methodist Sunday school teachers. [d. May 9, 1920]

1856 *George Cave,* British judge, political leader; Lord Chancellor, 1922–28. [d. March 29, 1928]

1868 *W(illiam) E(dward) B(urghardt) Dubois,* U.S. historian, reformer; a founder of the *Niagara Movement,* which eventually merged with the National Association for the Advancement of Colored People; editor of numerous books on the black experience; joined the Communist party, 1961; emigrated to Africa where he became a citizen of Ghana, 1962. [d. August 27, 1963]

1879 *Norman Lindsay,* Australian artist and novelist. [d. November 29, 1969]

1883 *Karl Theodor Jaspers,* German philosopher, existentialist. [d. February 26, 1969]

1884 Casimir Funk, U.S. scientist; best known for his work with vitamins. [d. 1967]

1904 *William (Lawrence) Shirer,* U.S. journalist; author of *Berlin Diary,* 1941, *The Rise and Fall of the Third Reich,* 1960. [d. December 28, 1994]

1907 *Constantine Karamanlis,* President of Greece, 1980–81. [d. April 23, 1998]

1911 *G(erhard) Mennen Williams,* U.S. politician; Governor of Michigan, 1949–60; Ambassador to Africa, 1961–66. [d. February 2, 1988]

1915 *Violet Weingarten,* U.S. journalist, author. [d. July 17, 1976]

1924 *Allan MacLeod Cormack,* U.S. physicist. Nobel Prize in physiology or medicine for development of *CAT (computerized axial tomography) scanning x-ray* technique (with G. N. Hounsfield), 1979. [d. May 7, 1998]

1938 *Sylvia Chase,* U.S. broadcast journalist; correspondent, American Broadcasting Companies News *20/20,* 1978–86; Emmy Awards, 1978, 1980.

1939 *Peter Fonda,* U.S. actor, director; wrote, co-produced, and starred in *Easy Rider,* 1969.

1944 *John Dawson (Johnny) Winter, III,* U.S. singer, musician.

1951 *Edward Lee (Too Tall) Jones,* U.S. football player, boxer.

1955 *Rodney E. Slater,* U.S. lawyer, politician; Secretary of Transportation, 1997– .

1963 *Bobby (Roberto) Bonilla,* U.S. baseball player.

HISTORICAL EVENTS

1660 *Charles X* of Sweden dies and is succeeded by *Charles XI.*

1820 *Cato Street Conspiracy* to murder members of the British Cabinet is uncovered in London.

1841 Hostilities between Britain and China resume in the *First Opium War.*

1854 Great Britain recognizes the independence of the *Orange Free State* in South Africa.

1863 Captains *John Speke* and *Richard Burton* publish the news of their discovery of the source of the *Nile River* in Lake Victoria.

1866 *King Alexander Cuza* of Rumania is dethroned and is succeeded by *Charles, Prince of Hohenzollern.*

1905 *Rotary Club International* is founded.

1915 The island of *Lemnos* in the Aegean Sea is seized by the British as a base in their attack on the *Dardanelles,* arousing the protests of the Greek government *(World War I).*

1921 Anti-Bolshevik mutiny by Russian sailors at *Kronstadt* naval base is crushed.

1927 The *Federal Radio Commission* is created as an independent U.S. regulatory agency to control stations' use of frequency and power.

1942 First enemy attack on the U.S. mainland in *World War II* occurs when a Japanese submarine shells an oil refinery near Santa Barbara, California.

1945 U.S. flag is raised on *Mt. Suribachi, Iwo Jima.*

1961 U.S. *National Council of Churches* approves the use of artificial methods for birth control in family planning.

1962 *Thalidomide,* a sedative introduced on the European market in 1957, is reported to have caused thousands of birth defects.

1964 *Libya* announces cessation of U.S. leases for military bases.

The revolutionary government of *Zanzibar* is officially recognized by the United Kingdom.

1966 Syrian premier Salah al-Bitar's moderate *Baath Party* government is overthrown by left-wing militants in a bloody coup.

1967 Council of the *Organization of American States* unanimously approves the admission of *Trinidad and Tobago.*

1970 *Guyana* formally ends over 150 years of British rule by declaring itself an independent republic.

The *Holy Eucharist* is distributed by women for the first time in a Roman Catholic service.

february

1971 *Rolls-Royce Ltd.* aircraft and marine divisions are nationalized.

1976 *Daniel Schorr*, U.S. television news correspondent, is suspended from his job at CBS News for disclosing a secret report of the House Select Committee on Intelligence.

1991 *Chatichai Choonhaven*, Prime Minister of Thailand, is overthrown by the military.

HOLIDAYS

Estonia
Independence Day

Lithuania
Estonia Independence Day

Mexico
Flag Day
Anniversary of proclamation of the *Plan of Iguala*, a proposal for independence from Spain.

RELIGIOUS CALENDAR

The Saints
SS. Montanus, Lucius, and their companions, martyrs. [d. 259]
St. Praetextatus, Bishop of Rouen and martyr. Also called *Pretextatus,* or *Prix.* [d. 586]
St. Matthias the Apostle. [Major Episcopal Holy Day; Minor Lutheran Feast Day]

BIRTHDATES

1440 *Matthias I,* of Hungary, 1458–90; brought the Renaissance to eastern Europe. [d. April 6, 1490]

1500 *Charles V,* Holy Roman Emperor, 1519–56, and (as Charles I), King of Spain, 1516–56. [d. September 21, 1558]

1536 *Pope Clement VIII,* pope 1592–1605. [d. March 5, 1605]

1619 *Charles Le Brun,* French painter; first to be appointed painter to the king. Responsible for decoration of *Palace of Versailles.* [d. February 12, 1690]

1709 *Jacques de Vaucanson,* French inventor; created early robot devices of significance for modern industry; noted for contributions to silk-weaving industry. [d. November 21, 1782]

1786 *Wilhelm Carl Grimm,* German philologist, folklorist, lexicographer; with his brother Jacob (January 4) authored the famous *Grimm's Fairy Tales.* [d. December 16, 1859]

1836 *Winslow Homer,* U.S. Romantic painter. [d. September 29, 1910]

1842 *Arrigo Boito,* Italian composer, librettist, poet; known chiefly for his opera *Mefistofele,* which marks a major transition in Italian opera. [d. June 10, 1918]

1852 *George Moore,* Irish novelist, dramatist, critic; with William Butler Yeats (June 13) created a revival in Irish literature. [d. January 21, 1933]

1885 *Chester William Nimitz,* U.S. admiral; commanded U.S. fleet in the Pacific during World War II, 1941–45. [d. February 20, 1966]

1921 *Abe Vigoda,* U.S. actor; known for his role as Detective Fish on television series, *Barney Miller.*

1928 *(Edward) Michael Harrington,* U.S. politician, author; wrote *The Other America,* 1962. [d. July 31, 1989]

1931 *James George Abourezk,* U.S. lawyer, politician; Senator, 1973–77.

1932 *Michel Jean Legrand,* French composer, conductor; five-time Grammy Award winner; three-time Academy Award winner; recipient of the Henry Mancini Lifetime Achievement Award, 1998.

1934 *Benedetto (Bettino) Craxi,* Italian politician; first socialist Prime Minister of Italy, 1983–86.

Renata Scotto, Italian opera singer.

1936 *Linda Cristal (Marta Victoria Moya Burges),* Argentine actress; known for her role on television series, *High Chaparral,* 1967–71.

1938 *James Farentino,* U.S. actor; known for his starring role on television series, *The Bold Ones,* 1970–72.

Phil(ip H.) Knight, U.S. business executive; co-founder, Nike, Inc., 1967.

1945 *Barry Bostwick,* U.S. actor; Tony Award for *The Robber Bridegroom,* 1977.

1947 *Rupert Holmes,* U.S. singer, songwriter.

Edward James Olmos, U.S. actor; Emmy winner for *Miami Vice* TV series and starred in *Stand and Deliver,* 1988.

1951 *Helen Shaver,* Canadian actress; known for roles in *The Amityville Horror* and *Supergirl.*

1955 *Steven Jobs,* U.S. electronics engineer; cofounder of Apple Computer, Inc.

Alain Marie Pascal Prost, French auto racer.

1956 *Eddie Clarence Murray,* U.S. baseball player; led American League in runs batted in and home runs, 1981.

Paula Zahn, U.S. television broadcaster.

1966 *Billy Zane,* U.S. actor.

HISTORICAL EVENTS

1389 Danes defeat *Albert* of Sweden at *Falköping,* paving way for union of Sweden, Denmark, and Norway.

1525 Germans and Spaniards defeat French and Swiss at Paris; *Francis I* of France is taken prisoner *(Hapsburg-Valois Wars).*

1582 *Pope Gregory XIII* issues a papal bull correcting the *Julian Calendar.* His new calendar, the *Gregarian Calendar* still in use today, became effective October 4, 1582.

1664 Confederation of Hamburg, Bremen, and Lübeck is formed as part of the *Hanseatic League.*

1777 *Joseph I* of Portugal dies and is succeeded by *Maria I.*

1785 *John Adams* is appointed the first U.S. Minister to Great Britain.

1803 U.S. Supreme Court delivers the *Marbury v. Madison* decision, establishing the concept of *judicial review.*

1848 Revolution in Paris succeeds; *Louis Philippe* abdicates, and the *Republic of France* is proclaimed.

1917 The Germans begin a strategic withdrawal along the Western Front to the fortified *Hindenburg Line (World War I).*

1956 Soviet leader, *Nikita Khruschshev,* delivers his seven-hour "Secret Speech," attacking Joseph Stalin's policies.

1960 The U.S. launches the *Titan,* an intercontinental ballistic missile.

1961 *Che Guevera* is appointed to head the newly established Cuban Ministry of Industry.

Major U.S. auto manufacturers announce the introduction of *seatbelts* as standard equipment for the 1962 model year.

1965 American pilots bomb Viet Cong sites in *South Vietnam* for the first time *(Vietnam War)*

1966 General *Joseph Ankrah* assumes power in Ghana after a coup d'etat.

1967 Malaysia, Indonesia, Thailand, Singapore, and the Philippines form the *Association of Southeast Asian Nations (ASEAN)* to promote economic progress and stability in Southeast Asia.

1970 Hawaii state legislature approves a bill legalizing *abortions* on demand.

1971 French oil companies and natural gas facilities are nationalized in *Algeria.*

1972 Rumania and Hungary sign a new 20-year friendship treaty proclaiming their independence and disregard of the *Brezhnev Doctrine.*

1974 Pakistan officially recognizes the nation of *Bangladesh* (formerly *East Pakistan*).

1975 *Birendra Bir Bikram Shah Dev* is crowned king of Nepal.

President *Mujibur Rahman* abolishes 13 political parties in Bangladesh, making his *Awami League* the only legal party.

The U.S. lifts a ten-year arms embargo on *Pakistan* and *India.*

1976 U.S. Secretary of State *Henry Kissinger* signs a foreign policy agreement with Brazil, the first such agreement with a Latin American country.

1981 *Jean Harris* is found guilty of murdering Dr. *Herman Tarnower,* developer of the popular Scarsdale Diet.

1991 The *U.S. military* begins a ground invasion of *Iraq,* known as *Operation Desert Storm,* in reponse to that country's invasion of Kuwait.

1993 *Brian Mulroney,* Prime Minister of Canada, announces his resignation.

1996 *Cuban air force* planes shoot down two U.S. civilian planes, which are part of the Brothers to the Rescue organization.

1998 *Khamtai Siphandon* becomes the President of Laos.

february

FEBRUARY
25

HOLIDAYS

Kuwait
National Day
Celebrates the accession of *Shaykh Sir 'Ab-dallah Al-Salim al-Sabah.*

Philippines
Freedom Day
Celebrates the peaceful overthrow of former president, Ferdinand Marcos, 1986.

Suriname
Day of Liberation and Renewal

RELIGIOUS CALENDAR

The Saints
SS. Victorinus and his companions, martyrs. [d. 284]
St. Caesarius of Nazianzus, physician. [d. 369]
St. Ethelbert, first Christian king of Kent. Also called *Albert.* [d. 616]
St. Walburga, virgin and abbess of Heidenheim. Also called *Falbourg, Gauburge, Vaubourg, Walburg, Waldburg, Walpurgis, Warpurg,* or *Wilburga.* [d. 779]
St. Gerland, Bishop of Girgenti. [d. 1100]
St. Tarasius, Patriarch of Constantinople. [d. 806]

The Beatified
Blessed Robert of Arbrissel, abbot of Fontevrault. [d. 1117]
Blessed Avertanus, Carmelite lay-brother, and *Romaeus.* [d. 1380]

Blessed Constantius of Fabriano. [d. 1481]
Blessed Sebastian Aparicio, friar. [d. 1600]

BIRTHDATES

1682 *Giovanni Battista Morgagni,* Italian anatomist; the *Father of Medical Pathology.* [d. December 6, 1771]

1707 *Carlo Goldoni,* Italian dramatist; the father of modern Italian comedy. [d. February 6, 1793]

1746 *Charles Cotesworth Pinckney,* U.S. statesman, diplomat; a prominent soldier in the American Revolution. [d. August 16, 1825]

1778 *José de San Martín,* South American statesman, soldier; with *Simon Bolivar* (July 24) was one of the leaders in the South American liberation movement. [d. August 17, 1850]

1823 *Li Hung-Chang,* leading 19th-century Chinese statesman; advocated modernization of China. [d. November 7, 1901]

1841 *Pierre Auguste Renoir,* French painter; one of the founders of *French Impressionism.* [d. December 3, 1919]

1848 *Edward Henry Harriman,* U.S. railroad magnate; one of the prime movers in the revitalization of the Union Pacific, the Southern Pacific, and the Central Pacific Railroads. [d. September 9, 1909]

1856 *Charles Lang Freer,* U.S. industrialist, philanthropist; made his fortune manufacturing railroad cars. [d. September 25, 1919]

1866 *Benedetto Croce,* Italian idealist philosopher, author, statesman, critic. [d. November 20, 1952]

1873 *Enrico Caruso,* Italian operatic lyric tenor; one of the all-time stars of the Metropolitan Opera, New York. [d. August 2, 1921]

1883 *Alice (Mary Victoria Augusta Pauline),* British princess; last surviving grandchild of Queen Victoria; wrote, *For My Grandchildren: Some Reminiscences.* [d. January 3, 1981]

1888 *John Foster Dulles,* U.S. government official, diplomat, lawyer; U.S. Secretary of State, 1953–59. [d. May 24, 1959]

1896 *John Little McClennan,* U.S. politician; Senator. [d. November 27, 1977]

Ida Tacke Noddack, German chemist; discovered element 75, rhenium, known for her contributions to nuclear fission. [d. 1979]

1901 *Herbert (Zeppo) Marx,* U.S. comedian; with his brothers Harpo (November 21), Groucho (October 2), Chico (March 26), and Gummo (date unknown), performed as an extremely popular vaudeville team. [d. November 30, 1979]

1903 *Frank (King) Clancy,* Canadian hockey player.

1904 *(Daisie) Adelle Davis,* U.S. nutritionist, author, natural-foods crusader. [d. May 31, 1974]

1908 *Frank G. Slaughter,* U.S. author, surgeon.

1910 *Millicent Hammond Fenwick,* U.S. politician; Congresswoman, 1975–82. [d. September 16, 1992]

1913 *James Gilmore (Jim) Backus,* U.S. actor; known as the voice of Mr. Magoo and for his role as the millionaire on television series, *Gilligan's Island,* 1964–67. [d. July 3, 1989]

1917 *Anthony Burgess,* British novelist, critic; known for his bizarre novels, usually with a linguistic twist; author of *Clockwork Orange.*

1918 *Robert Larimore (Bobby) Riggs,* U.S. tennis player, defeated by Billy Jean King in the Match of the Century, 1973. [d. October 25, 1995]

1920 *Philip Charles Habib,* U.S. diplomat; Ambassador to Korea, 1971–74; special Middle East envoy, 1981–83. [d. May 25, 1992]

1923 *Nathan Glazer,* U.S. author.

1928 *Larry Gelbart,* U.S. producer; comedy writer for Sid Caesar; creator of the television series, *M*A*S*H.*

1937 *Tom Courtenay,* British actor; known for his role in *The Dresser,* 1984.

1938 *Diane Baker,* U.S. actress; known for her roles in *Diary of Anne Frank,* 1959, and *Marnie,* 1969.

1943 *George Harrison,* British rock performer; member of the *Beatles,* 1963–70.

Sally Jessie Raphael, U.S. talk show host.

HISTORICAL EVENTS

1225 Third re-issue is made of the *Magna Carta,* this time in its final form.

1308 *Edward II* of England ascends the throne.

1455 The *Italian League* is formed under the protection of *Pope Nicholas V.*

1570 *Elizabeth I* of England is excommunicated by *Pope Pius V* for her severe persecution of Roman Catholics in England.

1803 *Diet of Ratisbon* reconstructs Germany, abolishing most ecclesiastical princedoms and imperial cities.

1863 *National Banking Act* is passed in the U.S., strengthening the national fiscal system.

1871 The Netherlands cedes all Dutch forts and towns on the *Gold Coast of Africa* to Great Britain in exchange for recognition of Dutch claims in the Far East.

1885 Germany annexes *Tanganyika* and *Zanzibar.*

1913 *Sixteenth Amendment* to U.S. Constitution is adopted, providing for an income tax.

1922 *Carnaval des Animaux* by *Camille Saint-Saëns* premieres in Paris.

1933 *U.S.S. Ranger,* the first true aircraft carrier, is commissioned.

1948 Communist cabinet members stage a coup in *Czechoslovakia,* forcing President Edvard Benes to remove all non-Communists from the government.

1951 *The 22nd Amendment* to the U.S. Constitution is ratified, providing for a maximum of two consecutive presidential terms.

1964 *Muhammed Ali* defeats *Sonny Liston* in seven rounds to win the world heavyweight boxing title.

1972 A one-party state is announced in *Zambia. Luna 20,* unmanned Soviet probe, returns to earth with samples from the moon's surface.

1973 Stephen Sondheim's *A Little Night Music* premieres in New York.

1986 *Corazon Aquino* is inaugurated as president of the Philippines. She replaces *Ferdinand Marcos,* who flees to the U.S.

1988 *Roh Tae Woo* is inaugurated as president of South Korea. It marks the country's first peaceful transition of power since independence.

1990 *Violetta Barrios de Chamorro* is elected president of Nicaragua.

1993 Federal trial begins for Los Angeles police officers in the beating case of *Rodney King.* The state trial ended in acquittal and sparked the

february

most severe rioting in U.S. history.

1994 Peace talks between *Israel* and *Palestine* break down after a Jewish extremist kills over thirty people in a mosque.

1998 *Kim Dae Jung* is sworn in as the President of South Korea.

HOLIDAYS

Kuwait

Liberation Day
Commemorates those killed or missing from Iraq's 1990 invasion.

RELIGIOUS CALENDAR

The Saints

St. Nestor, Bishop of Magydus, martyr. [d. 251]

St. Alexander, Bishop of Alexandria. [d. 328]

St. Porphyry, Bishop of Gaza. Also called *Porphyrius.* [d. 420]

St. Victor the Hermit, priest. Also called *Vittré.* [d. c. 610]

The Beatified

Blessed Leo of Saint-Bertin, abbot. [d. 1163]

Blessed Isabel of France, princess and virgin; daughter of Louis VIII. Founded the monastery of the Humility of the Blessed Virgin Mary. [d. 1270]

BIRTHDATES

1564 *Christopher Marlowe,* baptized on this date, English playwright; author of *Tamburlaine the Great* and *The Tragedy of Dr. Faustus.* [d. 1593]

1786 *François Arago,* French physicist; the first to work out the fundamental laws of *light waves.* [d. October 2, 1853]

1802 *Victor Hugo,* French poet, novelist, dramatist, politician; a leader in the Romantic movement in France. [d. May 22, 1885]

1808 *Honoré Daumier,* French caricaturist, painter, sculptor; known for his satirical cartoons. [d. February 11, 1879]

c1829 Levi Strauss, American businessman. Inventor of "Levi" jeans. [d. 1902]

1846 *William Frederick Cody (Buffalo Bill),* U.S. buffalo hunter, Army scout, Indian fighter, showman. [d. January 10, 1917]

1852 *John Harvey Kellogg,* U.S. physician; his experiments with health foods and dry breakfast cereals inspired brother *Will Kellogg* to found the Kellogg Cereal Co., 1906. [d. December 14, 1943]

1861 *Ferdinand I* of Bulgaria; first king of modern *Bulgaria.* [d. September 10, 1948]

1866 *Herbert Henry Dow,* U.S. chemist; founder of the Dow Chemical Co., 1897. [d. October 15, 1930]

1882 *Husband Edward Kimmel,* U.S. naval officer; commander of *Pearl Harbor* naval base at the time of the Japanese attack, 1941. [d. May 14, 1968]

1887 *Grover Cleveland Alexander,* U.S. baseball player; won 373 games as a pitcher, 1911–30; elected to Hall of Fame, 1938. [d. November 4, 1950]

Sir Bengal Narsing Rau, Indian jurist, diplomat; head of United Nations Security Council, 1950. [d. November 29, 1953]

1898 *Shields Warren,* U.S. pathologist; noted for his studies of the effects of radiation on humans. [d. July 1, 1980]

1903 *Giulio Natta,* Italian chemist; Nobel Prize in chemistry for the development of methods for converting simple hydrocarbons into complex polymeric structures (with K. Ziegler), 1963. [d. May 2, 1979]

Orde Charles Wingate, British Army general; led *Chindits,* or *Wingate's Raiders,* against Japanese Army in northern Burma during World War II. [d. March 24, 1944]

1906 *Umberto Romano,* U.S. artist born in Italy; noted for his portraits of such famous figures as Albert Einstein, Martin Luther King, Jr., and John F. Kennedy. [d. September 27, 1982]

1914 *Robert Alda (Alphonso Giovanni Giusseppi Roberto*

d'Abruzzo), U.S. actor; best known for his role as George Gershwin in *Rhapsody in Blue,* 1945; father of Alan Alda. [d. May 3, 1986]

1916 *Jackie Gleason,* U.S. comedian, actor. [d. February 26, 1987]

1917 *Robert Alphonso Taft, Jr.,* U.S. politician; Senator, 1971–76. [d. December 6, 1993]

1921 *Betty Hutton (Betty Thornberg),* U.S. actress; known for her lead role in *Annie Get Your Gun,* 1950.

1924 *Tony Randall,* U.S. actor; Emmy Award for his role as Felix Unger on television series, *The Odd Couple,* 1975.

1928 *Antoine (Fats) Domino,* U.S. singer; known for his song, *Blueberry Hill,* 1956.

1931 *Robert Novak,* U.S. journalist.

1932 *Johnny Cash,* U.S. country singer.

1933 *Godfrey Cambridge,* U.S. actor, comedian; known for his roles in *Purlie Victorious,* 1963, and *Cotton Comes to Harlem,* 1970. [d. November 29, 1976]

1943 *Brian Jones,* British singer, musician; member of the rock group, *The Rolling Stones.* [d. July 3, 1969]

1945 *Mitch Ryder (William S. Levise, Jr.),* U.S. singer; lead vocalist of the rock group, *Mitch Ryder and the Detroit Wheels.*

1953 *Michael Bolton (Bolotin),* U.S. songwriter, singer.

1956 *Adrian Delano Dantley,* U.S. basketball player; led the National Basketball Association in scoring, 1980–81.

HISTORICAL EVENTS

1443 *Alfonso V* of Aragon invades Naples.

1797 One-pound and two-pound bank notes are first used in England.

1876 *Korea* is opened to Japanese trade by the signing of a Korean-Japanese Treaty.

1913 *Deux Images* by *Béla Bartók* premieres in Budapest.

1919 *Grand Canyon National Park* in Arizona is established.

1926 *Tiger Flowers* defeats *Harry Greb* to win the world middleweight boxing title.

1929 *Grand Teton National Park* in Wyoming is established.

1935 *First Symphony* by *Georges Bizet* premieres in Basel, Switzerland.

1950 The Federal Trade Commission accuses the *American Dental Association,* six of its officers, and 143 dental supply companies of price fixing and orders them to move barriers to competition in the profession.

1961 *Crown Prince Mulay Hassan* is proclaimed King of Morocco.

1962 *Irish Republican Army* announces the end of its campaign of violence against the partition of Ireland with the laying down of its arms and disbanding of its volunteers.

1963 Data from Venus probe *Mariner II,* made public by NASA, indicates that the temperature of *Venus* is about 800 degrees Fahrenheit.

1965 *European Social Charter* comes into force, with Ireland, Norway, Sweden, the United Kingdom, and West Germany as initial parties.

1972 Agreement ending 26 years of civil war in *Sudan* is reached in Addis Ababa.

1980 *Egypt* and *Israel* exchange diplomatic ambassadors for the first time.

1984 President Ronald Reagan evacuates U.S. Marines from *Beirut* and places them on offshore ships in order to ensure their safety.

1986 *Robert Penn Warren* is named the first official U.S. poet laureate.

1987 The *Tower Commission* releases its report on the *Iran-contra affair* and faults the White House Staff for not monitoring policy decisions closely.

1988 Panama's National Assembly removes President *Eric Arturo Delvalle* after he attempts to fire General *Manuel Noriega. Manuel Solis Parma* is inaugurated as president.

1993 The *World Trade Center Building* in New York City is attacked by a bomb, killing six people and injuring more than one thousand.

HOLIDAYS

Bonaire
Carnival Rest Day

Dominican Republic
Independence Day
Commemorates 1844 revolt against Haiti, in which independence was regained and republic established under Pedro Santana.

St. Kitts-Nevis
Statehood Day
Celebrates joint independence of two countries, 1967.

RELIGIOUS CALENDAR

The Saints
SS. *Juliun, Cronion,* and *Besas,* martyrs. Cronion also called *Chronion.* [d. 250]
St. Thalelaeus the Hermit, surnamed *Epiklautos;* also called *Thaliloeus,* or *Thalelaeus the Cilician.* [d. c. 450]
St. Leander, Bishop of Seville. Honored in Spain as a Doctor of the Church. [d. 596]
St. Baldomerus, subdeacon; patron of locksmiths. Also called *Galmier.* [d. c. 660]
St. Alnoth, hermit. [d. c. 700]
St. John of Gorze, abbot. [d. 974]
St. Gabriel Possenti, priest. Also called *Gabriel-of-our-Lady-of-Sorrows.* [d. 1862]

The Beatified
Blessed Mark Barkworth, priest and martyr. Also called *Lambert.* [d. 1601]

BIRTHDATES

1807 *Henry Wadsworth Longfellow,* U.S. poet; the best-loved and best-known poet of his time; the first American to be honored with a memorial bust in Poets' Corner, Westminster Abbey. [d. March 24, 1882]

1848 Dame *Ellen Alice Terry,* British stage actress; famous for paper courtship with *George Bernard Shaw.* [d. July 21, 1928]

1850 *Henry Edwards Huntington,* U.S. capitalist; organized and financed the Los Angeles transit system and *Pacific Light & Power Co.* [d. May 23, 1927]

Laura Elizabeth Richards, U.S. novelist, short-story writer; Pulitzer Prize in biography, 1917. [d. January 14, 1943]

1861 *Rudolph Steiner,* Austrian educator, writer, social philosopher; founder of movement called *anthroposophy.* [d. March 30, 1925]

1863 *Joaquin Sorolla y Bastida,* Spanish painter; considered one of the foremost modern Impressionists. [d. August 11, 1923]

1881 *Sveinn Björnsson,* first President of Iceland upon its becoming a republic, in 1944. [d. January 25, 1952]

1882 *Burton K. Wheeler,* U.S. politician, lawyer; U.S. Senator, 1923–47; Progressive Party vice-presidential candidate, 1924. [d. January 7, 1975]

1886 *Hugo Lafayette Black,* U.S. jurist, lawyer; U.S. Senator, 1927–37. [d. September 24, 1971]

1891 *David Sarnoff,* U.S. communications executive; President of Radio Corporation of America, 1930–49; Chairman of the Board, 1947 70. [d. December 12, 1971]

1892 *William Demarest,* U.S. actor; known for his role on television series, *My Three Sons,* 1967–73. [d. December 27, 1983]

1896 *Arthur William Radford,* U.S. admiral; engaged in campaigns in Gilbert and Marshall Islands (World War II). [d. August 17, 1973]

1902 *John (Ernst) Steinbeck,* U.S. novelist; Novel Prize in literature, 1962. [d. December 20, 1968]

1904 *James Thomas Farrell,* U.S. novelist; author of *Studs Lonigan.* [d. August 22, 1979]

1910 *Joan Bennet,* U.S. actress; known for her role on

television soap opera, *Dark Shadows*. [d. December 78, 1990]

Peter DeVries, U.S. author; wrote *The Tunnel of Love*, 1954, and *Reuben, Reuben*, 1964. [d. September 28, 1993]

Eric Sloane (Everard Jean Hinrichs), U.S. artist. [d. March 6, 1985]

1912 *Lawrence (George) Durrell*, British novelist, poet, playwright, travel writer; author of *Alexandria Quartet*. [d. November 7, 1990]

1913 *Irwin Shaw*, U.S. novelist, short-story writer. [d. May 16, 1984]

1917 *John Bowden Connally*, U.S. politician, lawyer; Governor of Texas, 1963–69. [d. June 15, 1993]

1926 *David H. Hubel*, Canadian-born neurobiologist; Nobel Prize in physiology or medicine for his experimentation on the visual system of mammals (with Torsten N. Wiesel), 1981.

1930 *Joanne (Gignilliat) Woodward*, U.S. actress.

1932 *Elizabeth Taylor*, British-U.S. actress.

1934 *Ralph Nader*, U.S. lawyer, consumer advocate, author.

1936 *Sonia Johnson*, U.S. feminist; excommunicated from the Mormon Church because of her support for the Equal Rights Amendment, 1979; wrote *From Housewife to Heretic*, 1981.

1939 *Peter Jeffrey Revson*, U.S. auto racer; killed while practicing for auto race; nephew of the

cosmetic magnate, Charles Haskell Revson. [d. August 24, 1975]

1940 *Howard Hesseman*, U.S. actor; known for his role as Dr. Fever on television series, *WKRP in Cincinnati*, and his starring role on *Head of the Class*.

HISTORICAL EVENTS

380 *Emperor Theodosius* issues edict regarding the Catholic faith, suppressing *Arianism*, and promoting unity.

1386 Death of *Charles III* of Naples sets off war of succession between his son, *Ladislaus*, and *Louis II* of Anjou.

1844 *Dominican Republic* gains independence from Haiti.

1900 British forces under *Lord Horatio Herbert Kitchener* win the battle of Paardeberg, their first major victory. *(Boer War)*

1915 The *Battle of Przasnyz* in northern Poland ends in a Russian victory over the Germans *(World War I)*.

1933 The *Reichstag*, seat of the German parliament in Berlin, burns to the ground, allegedly the work of Nazi arsonists.

1939 France and Britain recognize the government of *General Francisco Franco* in Spain.

1942 Japan defeats the U.S. in the *Battle of the Java Sea*. *(World War II)*

1950 U.S. and Canada sign a 50-year treaty designed to increase the power output of the *Niagara River* and to protect the beauty of *Niagara Falls*.

1963 *Juan Bosch* takes office as the first constitutionally elected president of the *Dominican Republic* since 1924.

1967 *Antigua* in the Caribbean becomes an associated state within the United Kingdom.

1972 The *Shanghai Communique* outlines future plans to improve Sino-American relations. It is issued at the end of President Richard Nixon's historic trip to the *People's Republic of China*.

1973 *Wounded Knee*, on the *Oglala Sioux* reservation in South Dakota, is occupied by members of the *American Indian Movement*, who demand an investigation of federal treatment of Indians.

1974 A new constitution is promulgated in *Sweden*.

1976 *Polisario Republic (Saharan Arab Democratic Republic*, formerly the *Spanish Sahara)* is proclaimed.

1982 *Wayne B. Williams* is convicted of murdering two black youths in Atlanta, Georgia. He is suspected of more than 20 other murders over a two-year period.

1986 The U.S. Senate votes to allow television coverage on a trial basis.

1987 Former U.S. senator, *Howard Baker*, replaces *Donald Regan* as White House chief of staff. The Tower Commission had criticized Regan's management style.

The *Irish Sweepstakes* ends it 57-year operation, being unable to compete with state-run lotteries.

1991 U.S. tank forces defeat Iraqi tank forces and march into *Kuwait City, Kuwait.*

1998 The *United States* ends the 35-year moratorium on weapons sales to *South Africa.*

february

FEBRUARY
28

HOLIDAYS

Finland
Kalevala Day
National holiday dedicated to epic
poem *Kalevala*.

Spain
Day of Andalucia

RELIGIOUS CALENDAR

Feasts
*Feast of the Martyrs in the Plague of
    Alexandria.* [d. 261]

The Saints
St. Proterius, Patriarch of Alexandria
    and martyr. [d. 457]
St. Hilarus, pope. [d. 468]
SS. Romanus and *Lupicinus,*
    brothers and abbots; founders
    of the monasteries of Condat
    and Leuconne. Romanus is
    invoked for cure of insanity
    and protection from
    drowning. Lupicinus is
    commemorated separately on
    March 21. [d. c. 460 and 480]
St. Oswald of Worcester, Archbishop
    of York. [d. 992]

The Beatified
Blessed Angela of Foligno, widow
    and mystic. [d. 1309]
Blessed Villana of Florence, matron.
    [d. 1360]
Blessed Hedwig of Poland, matron.
    Also called *Jadwiga.* [d. 1399]
Blessed Antonia of Florence, widow
    and abbess. [d. 1472]
Blessed Louisa Albertoni, widow and
    nun. Also called *Lodovica.* [d.
    1533]

BIRTHDATES

1533 *Michel Eyquem de
    Montaigne,* French essayist;
    the founder of a new style in
    French literature. [d.
    September 13, 1592]

1683 *René A. F. de Réaumur,*
    French scientist,
    entomologist; devised the
    thermometric scale; wrote
    first technical treatise on iron.
    [d. October 17, 1757]

1712 *Louis Joseph Montcalm,*
    French army general;
    Commander in Chief of
    French forces in Canada,
    1756–59. [d. September 14,
    1759]

1797 *Mary Lyon,* U.S. educator;
    founder of *Mt. Holyoke
    College,* the first women's
    college in the U.S., 1837. [d.
    March 5, 1849]

1820 *Sir John Tenniel,* British
    cartoonist, artist; illustrated
    *Alice's Adventures in
    Wonderland;* cartoonist for
    Punch magazine. [d. February
    25, 1914]

1823 *(Joseph) Ernest Renan,*
    French theologian, religious
    writer; author of *Life of Jesus,*
    1863. [d. October 2, 1892]

1824 *Charles Blondin,* (Jean-
    François Gravelet), French
    tightrope walker; crossed
    above Niagara Falls many
    times. [d. February 19, 1897]

1833 *Alfred Graf von Schlieffen,*
    German army field marshal;
    Chief of General Staff,
    1891–1905. [d. January 4,
    1913]

1865 *Sir Wilfred Grenfell,* British
    medical missionary in
    Labrador; fitted out first
    hospital ship to serve
    fishermen in the North Sea;
    founder of *King George V
    Seamen's Institute.* [d.
    October 9, 1940]

1877 *Abbé Henri Edouard-Prosper
    Breuil,* French priest,
    archaeologist; authority on
    paleolithic art. [d. August 14,
    1961]

1894 *Ben Hecht,* U.S. journalist,
    playwright, novelist, short-
    story writer; author of *The
    Front Page, The Scoundrel.*
    [d. April 18, 1964]

1896 *Philip Showalter Hench,* U.S.
    physician; Nobel Prize in
    physiology or medicine for
    discovery of *cortisone* (with
    E.C. Kendall and T.
    Reichstein), 1950. [d. March
    31, 1965]

1901 *Linus Carl Pauling,* U.S.
    chemist; Nobel Prize in
    chemistry for studies of
    molecular bonding, 1954;
    Nobel Peace Prize, 1962. [d.
    August 19, 1994]

1906 *Benjamin (Bugsy) Siegel,* U.S.
    gangster; began syndicate-

controlled gambling in Las Vegas. [d. June 20, 1947]

1908 *Dee (Alexander) Brown,* U.S. author, historian; wrote *Bury My Heart at Wounded Knee,* 1971.

1909 *Stephen (Harold) Spender,* British poet, critic. [d. July 16, 1995]

1913 *Vincente Minnelli,* U.S. director; Oscar Award for *Gigi,* 1958; married to Judy Garland. [d. July 25, 1986]

1915 *Peter Brian Medawar,* British biologist; Nobel Prize in physiology or medicine for discovery of aquired immunity (with F.M. Burnet), 1960. [d. October 2, 1987]

Samuel Joel (Zero) Mostel, U.S. actor; known for his role as Tevye in *Fiddler on the Roof;* three Tony Awards. [d. September 8, 1977]

1919 *Sir Brian Urquhart,* British statesman; United Nations Under Secretary-General for Special Political Affairs, 1974–86; known as *Mr. Peacekeeper;* member of delegation accepting Nobel Peace Prize on behalf of peacekeeping forces, 1988.

1923 *Charles Durning,* U.S. actor; known for his co-starring role in *Tootsie,* 1982.

1924 *Christopher Columbus Kraft,* U.S. aeronautical engineer; flight director of U.S. manned space-flight program, 1959–70.

1930 *Leon N. Cooper,* U.S. physicist; Nobel Prize in physics for work in the field of superconductors (with J. Bardeen and J. R. Schrieffer), 1972.

Gavin MacLeod, U.S. actor; known for his roles on television series, *The Mary Tyler Moore Show,* 1970–77, and *The Love Boat,* 1977–86.

1939 *Thomas James (Tommy) Tune,* U.S. director, choreographer; Tony Awards for *A Day in Hollywood/A Night in the Ukraine,* 1980, and *Nine,* 1982.

1940 *Kenzo Takada,* Japanese fashion designer.

1945 *Charles Aaron (Bubba) Smith,* U.S. football player.

Mercedes Ruehl, U.S. actress; Oscar winner (Best Supporting Actress) for *The Fisher King,* 1991.

1947 *Stephanie Beacham,* British actress; known for her role as Sable Colby on television series, *The Colbys.*

1948 *Bernadette Peters (Bernadette Lazzara),* U.S. actress, singer; Tony Award for *Song and Dance,* 1986.

1953 *Cristina Raines,* U.S. actress; known for her role on television series, *Flamingo Road.*

1957 *John Turturro,* U.S. actor; known for roles in *Quiz Show,* 1994 and *Clockers,* 1995.

1960 *Dorothy Stratten (Dorothy Hoogstratten),* Canadian actress, model; Playboy centerfold shot to death by her estranged husband; was the subject of film, *Star '80.* [d. August 14, 1980]

1969 *Robert Sean Leonard,* U.S. actor; known for roles in *Dead Poet's Society,* 1989 and *The Age of Innocence,* 1994.

1973 *Eric Lindros,* Canadian hockey player.

HISTORICAL EVENTS

1474 *Peace of Utrecht* is signed between Hanseatic League and England.

1704 *Abenaki Indians* destroy *Deerfield, Massachusetts.*

1803 Swiss *Act of Mediation* is promulgated under Napoleon, establishing a centralized structure for the *Helvetic Republic* (Switzerland).

1825 Treaty between Britain and Russia is signed settling boundaries between Canada and Alaska.

1900 British forces under *Redvers Buller* raise the siege of *Ladysmith,* driving the Boers back *(Boer War).*

1921 Treaty of friendship between *Russia* and *Afghanistan* providing financial and political aid for the Afghans is signed.

1922 *Egypt* is declared independent, ending a seven-year British protectorate. *Fuad I* is recognized as ruler.

1952 *Vincent Massey* becomes the first Canadian-born Governor-General of Canada.

1971 Male voters in *Liechtenstein* defeat a referendum granting women voting rights.

1979 White minority rule in *Rhodesia* comes to an end with the adjournment of the country's parliament.

1986 Swedish prime minister, *Olof Palme,* is assassinated.

1993 *David Koresh,* leader of the *Branch Davidian* cult in Waco, Texas, clashes with agents from the Department of Alcohol, Tobacco, and

Firearms (ATF). Four ATF agents are killed and a fifty-one day stand-off begins.

1993 The United States begins aid relief air drops over war-torn *Bosnia*.

1996 *Prince Charles* and *Princess Diana* agree to divorce after fifteen years of marriage.

HOLIDAYS

Leap Year Day or Bachelor's Day
Day added to offset difference
between common year and
astronomical year. Occurs every
fourth year except centenary years
not divisible by 400.

BIRTHDATES

1468 *Pope Paul III,* Bishop of
Rome, 1534–40;
excommunicated Henry VIII
of England. [d. November 10,
1549]

1736 *Ann Lee,* English religious
leader; founder of American
sect of Shakers. [d.
September 8, 1784]

1792 *Karl Ernst von Baer,* Russian
naturalist, embryologist;
discovered the *human ovum.*
[d. November 28, 1876]

Gioacchino Antonio Rossini,
Italian opera composer; one
of the last masters of *opera
buffa.* [d. November 13,
1868]

1840 *John Philip Holland,* U.S.
inventor born in Ireland; a
pioneer in the development
of the modern submarine. [d.
August 12, 1914]

1904 *Jimmy Dorsey,* U.S. musician;
a key figure during the *Big
Band* era. [d. June 12, 1957]

1908 *Barthus (Comte Balthazar
Klossowski de Rola),* French
artist; self-taught painter.

1924 *David Stuart Beattie,* New
Zealand politician; Governor-
General, 1980–86.

1936 *Jack Lousma,* U.S. astronaut.

1948 *Willi Donnell Smith,* U.S.
fashion designer; Coty Award
for women's fashion, 1983.
[d. April 17, 1987]

HISTORICAL EVENTS

1720 *Ulrika Eleanora,* Queen of
Sweden, abdicates in favor of
her husband, *Frederick I.*

1868 British Prime Minister
Benjamin Disraeli begins his
first ministry.

1880 *Gotthard Railway Tunnel*
connecting Switzerland and
Italy is completed.

1956 *Islamic Republic* is
proclaimed in *Pakistan.*

1968 Discovery of the first *pulsar*
is announced at Cambridge,
England.

1984 Canadian prime minister,
Pierre Trudeau, announces
his resignation as head of the
government and the Liberal
Party.

1992 Voters in *Bosnia* and
Herzegovina cast their ballots
in favor of independence
from *Yugoslavia.*

february

MARCH

March, the third month in the Gregorian calendar, has 31 days. In the early Roman civil calendar March marked the beginning of the new year, since it corresponded with the revival of agriculture and of military campaigning. It was named *Martius* in honor of the Roman god of war, Mars.

In 153 B.C., January 1 was adopted as the day the Roman consuls assumed office and as the beginning of the new year, and March was then accepted as the third month for civil purposes. Nevertheless, popular sentiment still viewed March as the first month, so that even in medieval Europe the Christian feast of the Annunciation on March 25 was regarded as the beginning of the year. It was not until after 1582, with the Gregorian calendar reform, that January generally came to be accepted as the start of the year. It isalso the month of the vernal equinox (occuring about March 21), after which daylight is longer than darkness. This fact, too, may have contributed to the persistence of regarding March as the first month.

In the astrological calendar, March spans the zodiac signs of Pisces, the Fishes (February 19–March 20) and Aries, the Ram (March 21–April 19).

The birthstone for March is the bloodstone or aquamarine, and the flower is the jonquil or daffodil.

STATE, NATIONAL, AND INTERNATIONAL HOLIDAYS

St. Patrick's Day
(especially in Ireland)
March 17

Feast of St. Joseph
(Spain)
around March 19

Afghan New Year
(Afghanistan)
Day of vernal equinox

Vernal Equinox Day
(Japan)
usually March 21 or 22

Commonwealth Day
(Swaziland)
First Monday

Town Meeting Day
(Vermont)
First Tuesday

Youth Day
(Zambia)
Second Saturday

Tree Planting Day
(Lesotho)
during Third Week

Youth Day
(Taiwan)
Fourth Monday

Transfer Day
(Virgin Islands)
Final Monday

Seward's Day
(Alaska)
Final Monday

Decoration Day
(Liberia)
during Second Week

Youth Day
(Oklahoma)
First Day of Spring

Prince Johan Kuhio Kalanianaole Day
(Hawaii)
on or near March 26

SPECIAL EVENTS AND THEIR SPONSORS

National Nutrition Time
American Dietetic Association

Parents Without Partners Founder's Month
Parents Without Partners

National Peanut Month
National Peanut Council

Philatelic Literature Month
Franklin D. Roosevelt Philatelic
Society

National Youth Art Month
The Art and Craft Materials Institute,
Inc.

National Foreign Language Week
First Week
Alpha Mu Gamma

National Procrastination Week
First Week
Procrastinators' Club

National Save Your Vision Week
First Week
American Optometric Association

Volunteers of America Week
First Week
Volunteers of America

Camp Fire Birthday Week
Second Week
Camp Fire, Inc.

Girl Scout Week
Second Week
Girl Scouts of the U.S.A.

Music in our Schools Week
Second or Third Week
Music Education National
Conference

**National Poison Prevention
Week**
Third Week
Poison Prevention Week Council

National Wildlife Week
Third Week
National Wildlife Association

Art Week
Final Week
Richard R. Falk Associates

International Women's Day
March 8

World Maritime Day
March 17

World Meteorological Day
March 23
United Nations

Fireside Chat Anniversary Day
March 12
Franklin D. Roosevelt Philatelic
Society

Girl Scout Birthday
March 12
Girl Scouts of the U.S.A.

St. Urho's Day
March 16
Sauna Society of America

Camp Fire Founder's Day
March 17
Camp Fire, Inc.

Agriculture Day
March 21 or 22
Agriculture Council of America

Memory Day
March 21
Puns Corp.

Doctor's Day
March 30
McLaren Hospital

HOLIDAYS

Paraguay
Heroes' Day or National Defense Day

South Korea
Independence Movement Day
Anniversary of passive revolution against Japan, 1919.

Wales (United Kingdom)
St. David's Day

RELIGIOUS CALENDAR

The Saints
St. Felix II (III), pope. Elected 483. [d. 492]
St. Albinus, Bishop of Angers. Also called *Aubin*. [d. c. 550]
St. David, Bishop of Mynyw. Patron of Wales and of poets. Surnamed *The Waterman*. Also called *Dewi*. [d. c. 589]
St. Swithbert, bishop and missionary. Joint patron of St. Peter's Kaiserswerth. Also called *Suidbert, Swihert, Swidbert,* or *Swithbert the Elder*. [d. 713]
St. Rudesind, Bishop of Dumium and abbot. Founded monastery at Celanova. Also called *Rosendo*. [d. 977]

The Beatified
Blessed Roger Le Fort, Archbishop of Bourges. [d. 1367]
Blessed Bonavita, Franciscan tertiary. [d. 1375]
Blessed Christopher of Milan, Apostle of Liguria. [d. 1484]

Blessed Peter René Roque, priest and martyr. [d. 1796]

BIRTHDATES

1456 *Ladislas II, King of Bohemia*, 1490–1516; his rule was contested by the Hungarian king, *Matthias Corvinus*. [d. March 13, 1516]

1701 *Johann Jakob Breitinger*, Swiss critic, literary theorist; his anti-rationalism won him the recognition of Goethe and Schiller. [d. December 13, 1776]

1747 *Sir Samuel Romilly*, English lawyer, reformer; opposed harsh and irrational laws; agitated against slavery. [d. November 2, 1818]

1782 *Thomas Hart Benton*, U.S. politician, lawyer, teacher, editor, author; U.S. Senator, 1821–51. [d. April 10, 1858]

1810 *Frédéric François Chopin*, Polish-French composer, pianist; one of the foremost composers of all time; an intimate of George Sand (July 1); some sources give his birthdate as February 22. [d. October 17, 1849]

1812 *Augustus Welby Pugin*, British Victorian Gothic architect; made detail drawings for *Houses of Parliament*. [d. September 14, 1852]

1837 *William Dean Howells*, U.S. novelist, editor, critic; was commonly acknowledged as the *Dean of American Letters*. [d. May 11, 1928]

Georg Moritz Ebers, German Egyptologist, novelist; known for his acquisition of the 16th-century B.C. papyrus henceforth called the *Ebers papyrus*. [d. August 7, 1898]

1841 *Blanche Kelso Bruce*, first black to serve full term as U.S. Senator. [d. March 17, 1898]

1848 *Augustus Saint-Gaudens*, U.S. sculptor, born in Ireland; known for his sculptures of *Abraham Lincoln*, in Chicago, and *General Sherman*, New York City. [d. August 3, 1907]

1880 *(Giles) Lytton Strachey*, British biographer. [d. January 21, 1932]

1886 *Oskar Kokoschka*, Austrian expressionist artist; noted for his use of expressive distortion; condemned by the Nazis, 1937. [d. February 22, 1980]

1896 *Dimitri Mitropoulos*, U.S. symphony conductor; known for interpretations of twentieth-century music. [d. November 2, 1960]

1904 *Glenn Miller*, U.S. bandleader, trombonist. [d. December 16, 1944]

1906 *Joseph Edwin Curran,* U.S. labor leader. [d. August 14, 1981]

Pham van Dong, Vietnamese politician; Prime Minister of North Vietnam, 1955–76; Prime Minister of the Socialist Republic of Vietnam, 1976–87.

1910 *Archer John Porter Martin,* British biochemist; Nobel Prize in chemistry for *paper partition chromatography* (with Richard L. M. Synge), 1952.

David Niven, British actor; known for his roles as a sophisticated and debonair man-about-town. [d. July 29, 1983]

1914 *Ralph Waldo Ellison,* U.S. novelist; author of *The Invisible Man.* [d. April 16, 1994]

1917 *Robert Traill Spence Lowell,* U.S. poet; Pulitzer Prize in poetry, 1947. [d. September 12, 1977]

1920 *Howard Nemerov,* U.S. poet, critic, novelist, teacher; author of *The Salt Garden* and *Mirrors and Windows.* [d. July 5, 1991]

Dinah Shore, U.S. singer and actress. [d. February 24, 1994]

1921 *Dinah Shore (Frances Rose Shore),* U.S. singer, talkshow hostess. [d. February 24, 1993]

Richard Purdy Wilbur, U.S. poet; Pulitzer Prize in poetry, 1956.

1922 *Yitzhak Rabin,* Israeli politician; Ambassador to the U.S., 1968–73; Prime Minister, 1974–77; Nobel Peace Prize for his efforts to create peace in the Middle East, 1994. [d. November 4, 1995]

1926 *Alvin Ray (Pete) Rozelle,* U.S. football executive; brought about the merger of the National Football League and the American Football League, 1966. [d. December 6, 1996]

1927 *Harry Belafonte,* U.S. singer, actor.

Robert Heron Bork, U.S. lawyer, judge; known for carrying out the firing of Watergate prosecutor Archibald Cox, 1973; U.S. Appeals Court judge, 1981–88; his nomination to the Supreme Court was the subject of controversy until turned down by the Senate, 1987.

1929 *Sonny James (Jimmy Loden),* U.S. singer.

1930 *Edward Zigler,* U.S. psychologist; co-founder of the children's education organization Project Head Start, 1965.

1934 *Joan Hackett,* U.S. actress; known for her starring roles in *The Group,* 1966, and *Only When I Laugh,* 1982. [d. October 8, 1983]

1935 *Robert Conrad (Conrad Robert Falk),* U.S. actor; known for his starring roles on television series, *Hawaiian Eye,* 1959–63, and *The Wild, Wild West,* 1965–69.

Judith Rossner, U.S. author; wrote *Looking for Mr. Goodbar,* 1975.

1945 *Dirk Benedict (Dirt Niewoehner),* U.S. actor, singer; known for his role on television series, *The A-Team.*

Roger Daltrey, British singer; member of the rock group, *The Who.*

1954 *Catharine Bach (Catharine Bachman),* U.S. actress; known for her role as Daisy Duke on television series, *The Dukes of Hazzard,* 1979–85.

Ron Howard, U.S. actor, director; known for his roles as Opie on television series, *The Andy Griffith Show,* 1960–68, and Richie on television series, *Happy Days,* 1974–80; directed *Splash* and *Cocoon.*

1973 *Mayce Edward Christopher (Chris) Webber III,* U.S. basketball player.

HISTORICAL EVENTS

1498 *Vasco da Gama* arrives at *Mozambique,* Africa, on his voyage to India.

1562 Massacre of French Protestants at Vassy begins *Huguenot Wars.*

1692 *Salem Witch Trials* begin in Massachusetts with the conviction of West Indian slave, *Tituba,* for witchcraft.

1790 First *U.S. census* begins.

1792 Holy Roman Emperor *Leopold II* dies and is succeeded by his brother, *Francis II.*

1797 The *Jesuits* are expelled from Spain by *King Charles III.*

1803 *Ohio* is admitted to the Union as the 17th state.

1811 *Mohammed Ali,* Turkish governor of Egypt, massacres the *Mameluke* leaders, breaking their power and seizing supreme power for himself.

1815 *Georgetown College* is chartered, becoming the first Catholic college established in the U.S.

Napoleon returns to France from Elba.

1836 *Texas* declares its independence from Mexico.

1845 *Texas* is annexed to the U.S. by joint resolution of Congress.

1862 *Kingdom of Italy* is recognized by Prussia.

1865 Telegraph service between Europe and India begins.

1867 *Nebraska* is admitted to the Union as the 37th state.

1871 *Napoleon III* of France is deposed. The French people revolt against his dictatorial rule and unwise empire-building policies.

1872 *Yellowstone National Park,* first of the great U.S. national parks, is established.

1896 *Battle of Aduwa* is fought in which the Abyssinians under Menelik defeat Italians decisively, forcing Italy's withdrawal from the country.

1897 *Japan* adopts the gold standard.

1907 Debussy's *La Mer* premieres in Boston.

1915 The British naval blockade of German East Africa begins *(World War I).*

1917 *February Revolution* in Russia ends.

1919 A passive resistance movement against Japanese rule begins in *Korea.*

The new colony of *Upper Volta* (Burkina Faso) is formed by the French.

1921 The first imperial census of Japan is published.

1929 French Chamber of Deputies ratifies *Paris Peace Pact.*

1932 The 20-month old son of pilot *Charles A. Lindbergh* is kidnapped from his home in Hopewell, New Jersey.

1941 *Bulgaria* permits German troops to enter the country *(World War II).*

1947 *International Monetary Fund* begins operation.

1949 *Joe Louis,* undefeated heavyweight boxing champion, retires.

1950 Generalissimo *Chiang Kai-shek* resumes presidency of the Chinese Nationalist government.

1954 Several Puerto Rican nationalists open fire in the U.S. House of Representatives, injuring five Congressmen.

1961 President John F. Kennedy establishes the *Peace Corps,* composed of U.S. men and women volunteers for service in underdeveloped foreign countries.

1962 *Faustino Harrison* is inaugurated as president of Uruguay.

Benedicto Kiwanuka takes office as the first prime minister of Uganda, marking the beginning of self-government.

Pakistani President *Mohammed Ayub Khan* announces the adoption of a new constitution providing for a strong presidential form of government.

1965 Remains of *Sir Roger Casement,* Irish patriot hanged in England for treason in 1916, are reburied with state honors in Dublin.

1966 Russian spacecraft *Venus 3,* launched November 16, 1965,

crashes on Venus, the first man-made object to reach another planet.

Ghanaian National Liberation Council orders the expulsion of Soviet, East German, and Communist Chinese technicians and teachers from the country.

1967 *Oscar Diego Gestido* is inaugurated as President of Uruguay.

U.S. House of Representatives votes to exclude *Rep. Adam Clayton Powell, Jr.,* from the 90th Congress and declares his Harlem seat vacant.

Marshall McLuhan's study of mass communication, *The Medium is the Message,* is published.

1972 *Juan Maria Bordaberry* is inaugurated as president of Uruguay.

1974 Seven former White House and Nixon campaign officials are indicted by a grand jury investigating the *Watergate Incident.*

1975 A fact-finding delegation of the U.S. Congress visits *South Vietnam* and *Cambodia* at request of U.S. President *Gerald Ford* to determine whether Saigon and Phnom Penh require additional military aid.

1979 The Unión Centro Democrático, headed by *Premier Adolfo Suárez González,* is victorious in the first parliamentary elections held in Spain since the adoption of a new constitution in December 1978.

In a national referendum, Wales and Scotland reject

home rule. British *Prime Minister James Callaghan* suffers a political setback because of his strong support of the proposal.

U.S. spacecraft *Voyager 1* begins relaying information as it approaches *Jupiter*.

1985 *Julio Maria Sanguinetti* is inaugurated as president of Uruguay.

1991 Voters in the *Soviet Union* favor keeping the union intact.

1994 The governments of *Bosnia* and *Herzegovina* agree to form a federation.

1995 *Denver International Airport* opens.

HOLIDAYS

Burma
Peasants Day

Ethiopia
Victory of Aduwa Day
Celebrates Aduwa victory of 1896, which saved country from becoming possession of Italy.

Morocco
Independence Day

U.S. (Texas)
Independence Day
Commemorates the signing of a declaration of independence from Mexico, 1836.

RELIGIOUS CALENDAR

The Saints
St. Joavan, monk and bishop. [d. c. 562]
St. Chad, Bishop of Lichfield; patron saint of medicinal springs. Also called *Caedda, Ceada,* or *Ceadda.* [d. 672]
The Martyrs under the Lombards. [d. c. 579]

The Beatified
Blessed Charles the Good, Count of Flanders and Amiens, and martyr. Also called *the Dane.* [d. 1127]
Blessed Fulco of Neuilly, priest and missionary. [d. 1201]
Blessed Agnes of Bohemia, virgin and founder of first establishment of Poor Clares north of the Alps. Also called *Agnes of Prague.* [d. 1282]

Blessed Henry Suso, Dominican prior. [d. 1365]
Blessed Angela de la Cruz Guerrero Gonzalez. [beatified, 1982]

BIRTHDATES

1316 *Robert II, King of Scotland,* 1371–90, grandson of *Robert Bruce;* called *The Steward;* first of the so-called Stuart line. [d. April 19, 1390]

1459 *Pope Adrian VI,* the only Dutch Pope; reigned 1522–23. [d. September 14, 1523]

1705 *William Murray,* 1st Earl of Mansfield, English jurist; authority on *commercial law.* [d. March 20, 1793]

1769 *Dewitt Clinton,* U.S. political leader, lawyer, historian; Mayor of New York City, 1803–15; Governor of New York, 1817–21, 1825–28. [d. February 11, 1828]

1793 *Sam(uel) Houston,* U.S. politician, soldier, lawyer; U.S. Senator, 1846–59; chief military figure in Texas' fight for independence from Mexico; Governor of Texas, 1859–61. [d. July 26, 1863]

1810 *Pope Leo XIII;* reigned 1878–1903; known for willingness to compromise with civil governments; considered one of the most notable pontiffs in Church

history for his constant efforts to achieve world peace. [d. July 20, 1903]

1817 *János Arany,* Hungarian poet; known for his *Toldi* trilology and his epic poem, *King Buda's Death.* [d. October 22, 1882]

1820 *Eduard Douwes Dekker (Multatuli),* Dutch novelist, essayist, satirist; wrote works protesting Dutch colonial policies. [d. February 19, 1887]

1824 *Bedřich Smetana,* Czech composer; known as the *Father of Modern Czechoslovak Music.* [d. May 12, 1884]

1829 *Carl Schurz,* U.S. statesman, orator, writer, lawyer, reformer; U.S. Senator, 1869–75, U.S. Secretary of the Interior, 1877–81. [d. May 14, 1906]

1876 *Pius XII,* reigned 1939–58; proclaimed the dogma of the *Assumption of the Virgin Mary,* 1950. [d. October 9, 1958]

1880 *Ivar Kreuger,* Swedish financier, industrialist, swindler; known for his vast international match monopoly; after his empire collapsed, he committed suicide. [d. March 12, 1932]

1897 *William Miles (Webster) Thomas, Baron Thomas,*

British industrialist; President, International Air Transport Association, 1951–52; Chairman, Monsanto Chemicals, Ltd., 1956–63. [d. February 9, 1980]

1900 *Kurt Weill,* German composer; wrote *Threepenny Opera;* husband of Lotte Lenya (October 18). [d. April 3, 1950]

1902 *A(lmer) S(tilwell) Monroney,* U.S. journalist, politician; U.S. Congressman, 1939–50; U.S. Senator, 1951–68. [d. February 13, 1980]

1904 *Theodore Seuss Geisel (Dr. Seuss),* U.S. author and illustrator of children's books. [d. September 24, 1991]

1909 *Mel(vin Thomas) Ott,* U.S. baseball player; inducted into Baseball Hall of Fame, 1951. [d. November 21, 1958]

1917 *Desi Arnaz (Desiderio Alberto Arnaz de Acha, III),* U.S. bandleader, actor, singer; known for his role as Ricky Ricardo on television series, *I Love Lucy. [d. December 2, 1986]*

1919 *Jennifer Jones (Phyllis Isley),* U.S. actress; Academy Award for *The Song of Bernadette,* 1943.

1927 *John Brademas,* U.S. politician; Congressman, 1959–78; President, New York University, 1981–92; President emeritus, 1992– .

1931 *Mikhail S. Gorbachev,* Russian politician; General Secretary of Soviet Communist Party, 1985–91; President, 1990–91; Nobel Peace Prize winner, 1990.

Tom Wolfe (Thomas Kennerly Wolfe, Jr.), U.S. journalist;

leader in the *New Journalism* movement in the U.S.; author of *Kandy-Kolored Tangerine-Flake Streamline Baby, The Electric Kool-Aid Acid Test,* and *The Right Stuff.*

1942 *John Irving,* U.S. novelist; author of *The World According to Garp,* and *The Hotel New Hampshire.*

1944 *Lou Reed,* U.S. singer, songwriter; known for song, *Walk on the Wild Side,* 1973.

1949 *Rory Gallagher,* Irish musician; blues-rock guitarist.

1950 *Karen Ann Carpenter,* U.S. singer, musician; member of the rock duo, *The Carpenters;* sold over eighty million albums at time of death. [d. February 4, 1983]

HISTORICAL EVENTS

1476 The Swiss Confederacy defeats *Charles the Bold* of Burgandy at the *Battle of Granson.*

1765 *Stamp Act* is passed by the English Parliament, requiring American colonists to buy and affix British-issued stamps to most documents.

1801 Spain declares war on Portugal (*War of the Oranges*).

1835 *Francis I* of Austria dies and is succeeded by *Ferdinand I.*

1855 *Nicholas I* of Russia dies and is succeeded by *Alexander II.*

1865 First message by cable from Calcutta to London is sent.

1867 U.S. Congress passes *Reconstruction Act,* setting up conditions for reintegration of Southern states into the Union.

1877 *Rutherford B. Hayes* is declared U.S. President by a special Electoral Commission in the disputed election of 1876.

1887 *Hatch Act* providing for the promotion of U.S. agricultural science by creating *state agricultural experiment stations* becomes law.

1901 Congress adopts the *Platt Amendment,* establishing a U.S. protectorate over *Cuba.*

1917 *Puerto Rico* becomes U.S. territory and its inhabitants become U. S. citizens.

Hamadan is captured by the Russians in a new drive against the Turks in Persia (Iran) (*World War I*).

1939 *Pius XII* is elected pope.

1943 *Battle of Bismarck Sea* begins, resulting in major victory by U.S. over Japanese shipping and aircraft (*World War II*).

1949 U.S. Air Force Captain *James Gallagher* and 13 crew members complete the first round-the-world non-stop flight in a Boeing B-50 Superfortress, *Lucky Lady II.*

1956 *Morocco* gains independence from France.

1958 First crossing of *Antarctica* by land is made by *Sir Vivian Fuchs.*

1961 French troops complete the evacuation of all their military bases in Morocco.

1962 Coup d'état in *Burma* replaces the U Nu government with a military government.

1969 Soviet and Chinese border forces engage in heavy

fighting over *Damansky (Chanpao) Island,* a disputed territory in the Ussuri River.

1970 *Rhodesia* declares itself a republic, dissolving its last ties with Great Britain.

1972 *Pioneer 10,* unmanned U.S. interplanetary probe, is launched from Cape Kennedy, Florida.

Michael Manley is inaugurated as prime minister of Jamaica.

1973 Representatives of 80 countries agree to a treaty outlawing trade in 375 *endangered wildlife species.*

1974 Military rule ends in *Burma* with the adoption of a new constitution; U Ne Win is declared President.

1976 *Bubblin' Brown Sugar,* a musical featuring the songs of Eubie Blake, opens on Broadway.

1977 U.S. House of Representatives approves stringent *code of ethics* for itself.

1983 Iraqi air strikes damage a crippled Iranian oil installation, creating one of the largest oil spills in Middle East history *(Iran-Iraq War).*

1985 The first commercial blood test for *AIDS* is approved by the U.S. Department of Health and Human Services.

1986 Queen *Elizabeth II* of England signs a proclamation that frees *Australia* from remaining British Constitutional authority.

1989 The *European Community* agrees to a ban on the manufacturing of *chlorofluorocarbons (CFCs).*

1994 The Mexican government and the *Zapatista National Liberation Army* reach a peace accord stemming from the January 1994 rebellion in the Chiapas province of Mexico.

1996 U.S. President *Bill Clinton* signs a new law that intensifies the economic embargo currently used against Cuba.

march

MARCH
3

HOLIDAYS

Bulgaria
Liberation Day
Commemorates Bulgaria's release from Ottoman Rule, 1878.

Japan
Hina Matsuri or Dolls' Day or Peach Festival
A day on which ceremonial dolls are displayed throughout the country by young girls. The dolls are decorated with peach blossoms, the symbols of mildness and peacefulness, qualities the girls hope to achieve before marriage.

Malawi
Martyrs' Day
Honors the nation's heroes.

Morocco
Feast of the Throne or Morocco National Day or Fête du Trône
Marks accession to throne of *King Hassan II*, 1961.

Sudan
National Unity Day
Honors cooperation among Arab nations.

RELIGIOUS CALENDAR

The Saints
SS. *Marinus* and *Astyrius*, martyrs. Also called *Asterius* and *Marnan*. [d. c. 262]

SS. *Emeterius* and *Chelidonius*, soldiers and martyrs. Patrons of Santander, Spain. Emeterius also called *Madir*. [d. 304]

St. *Arthelais*, virgin. [d. c. 560]

St. *Non*. Also called *Nonnita*. [d. 6th century]

St. *Winwaloe*, abbot. Also called *Galnutius, Guénolé, Guignolé, Guingalois, Guinvaloeus, Wingalotus*, or *Winwalocus*. [d. 6th century]

St. *Anselm of Nonantola*, abbot. [d. 803]

St. *Cunegund*, Empress of Rome and widow. Also called *Cunegunda*, or *Cunegundes*. [d. 1033]

St. *Gervinus*, Abbot of Saint-Riquier. Also called the *Holy Abbot*. [d. 1075]

St. *Aelred*, Abbot of Rievaulx. Also called *Ailred*. [d. 1167]

The Beatified
Blessed *Serlo*, Abbot of Gloucester. [d. 1104]

Blessed *Jacopino of Canepaci*, Carmelite lay-brother. [d. 1508]

Blessed *Teresa Verzeri*, virgin and founder of the Daughters of the Sacred Heart. [d. 1852]

Blessed *Innocent of Berzo*, priest and Capuchin Friar Minor. [d. 1890]

BIRTHDATES

1606 *Edmund Waller*, English poet; political activist; popularized the *heroic couplet*. [d. October 21, 1687]

1748 *Kazimierz Pulaski*, activist against foreign domination in his homeland of Poland; fought in the American Civil War. [d. 1779]

1756 *William Godwin*, English philosopher; a noted proponent of English radicalism. [d. April 7, 1836]

1793 *Charles Sealsfield (Karl Anton Postl)*, Austrian novelist, short-story writer. [d. May 26, 1864]

William Charles Macready, English actor. theatrical manager; known for Shakespearean roles. [d. April 27, 1873]

1819 *Alexander Crummell*, U.S. religious leader; known for his writings regarding African American life. [d. 1898]

1826 *Joseph Wharton*, U.S. metals producer; developed process for making pure malleable nickel; a founder of *Swarthmore College*; *Wharton School of Business and Commerce* at University of Pennsylvania is named for him. [d. January 11, 1909]

1831 *George Mortimer Pullman*, U.S. manufacturer, inventor; developed first *Pullman railroad car*. [d. October 19, 1897]

1841 *John Murray*, Canadian scientist; one of the pioneers of *oceanography*. [d. March 16, 1914]

1845 *Georg Cantor,* German mathematician; founded *theory of sets* and *theory of irrational numbers.* [d. January 6, 1918]

1847 *Alexander Graham Bell,* U.S. inventor, born in Scotland; the first to patent and commercialize the *telephone.* [d. August 2, 1922]

1869 *Sir Henry Joseph Wood,* British conductor, composer; conductor of Queen's Hall Symphony (*London Symphony*), 1897–1944. [d. August 19, 1944]

1873 *William Green,* U.S. labor leader; President of American Federation of Labor, 1924–52. [d. November 21, 1952]

1877 *Garrett Morgon,* U.S. inventor; best known for his inventions of the gas mask and the traffic light. [d. 1963]

1883 *Clifford Milburn Holland,* U.S. civil engineer; *Holland Tunnel* in New York City is named for him. [d. October 27, 1924]

1895 *Ragnar Frisch,* Norwegian economist; Nobel Prize in economics for contributions to study of business cycles, 1969. [d. January 31, 1973]

Matthew Bunker Ridgway, U.S. Army general; Supreme Commander, Allied Forces in Europe, 1952–53; U.S. Army Chief of Staff, 1953–55. [d. July 26, 1993]

1899 *Alfred M. Gruenther,* U.S. Army general; gifted staff officer and administrator; remembered for his work with the North Atlantic Treaty Organization (NATO). [d. 1966]

1911 *Jean Harlow (Harlean Carpentier),* U.S. actress. [d. June 7, 1937]

1918 *Arthur Kornberg,* U.S. physician; Nobel Prize in physiology or medicine for discoveries concerning *DNA,* 1959.

1930 *Heiiti Aki,* U.S. scientist; discovered seismic moment to help measure earthquakes.

1933 *(Caroline) Lee Bouvier Radziwill Ross,* U.S. celebrity relative; wrote *One Special Summer* with sister, Jacqueline Onassis.

1940 *Perry Edwin Ellis,* U.S. fashion designer. [d. May 30, 1986]

1950 *Ed Marinaro,* U.S. actor, football player; known for his role as Joe Coffey on television series, *Hill Street Blues.*

1958 *Miranda Richardson,* British actress; known for roles in *Damage,* 1993 and *Tom & Viv,* 1994.

1962 *Jackie Joyner-Kersee,* U.S. athlete; Olympic gold medalist, 1988, 1992, 1996.

Herschel Walker, U.S. football player; Heisman Trophy, 1982.

HISTORICAL EVENTS

1812 First *U.S. foreign aid bill* authorizes $50,000 for relief of victims of an earthquake in Venezuela.

1815 U.S. declares war on *Algiers.*

1819 U.S. Congress authorizes war on pirates in Gulf of Mexico.

1820 *Missouri Compromise* is passed by U.S. Congress, admitting *Maine* as a free state and *Missouri* as a slave state.

1845 *Florida* is admitted to the Union as 27th state.

1861 Serfs are emancipated in Russia.

1863 Congress establishes the *National Academy of Science* to advise the government on scientific and technical issues.

1871 *Indian Appropriations Act* passes.

1875 *Carmen,* by *Georges Bizet,* premieres in Paris.

1878 Russia signs treaty of peace with the Turks at *San Stefano,* ending the *Russo-Turkish War; Serbia* gains its independence.

1879 *Belva Anna Bennett Lockwood* becomes first woman to try a case before the *U.S. Supreme Court.*

1886 Peace is established between Bulgaria and Serbia with the signing of *Treaty of Bucharest.*

1901 The *U.S. Steel Corp.* is formed.

1918 *Treaty of Brest-Litovsk* is signed by Russia and the Central Powers, ending World War I.

1921 *Crown Prince Hirohito* begins the first world tour by any member of the Japanese imperial family.

1924 *Turkish Caliphate* is abolished.

1931 *The Star-Spangled Banner* is officially designated *U.S. national anthem.*

1933 *Franklin Delano Roosevelt* is inaugurated as the 32nd president of the U.S. He tells Americans, "the only thing we have to fear is fear itself," referring to the Great Depression. *John Nance Garner* becomes vice-president.

1951 *Tran Van Huu* becomes premier of Vietnam.

1952 *Puerto Rico* becomes a U.S. commonwealth with autonomy in internal affairs.

1953 The first fatal *jetliner accident* occurs when a Canadian plane crashes in Karachi, Pakistan.

1960 *Pope John XXIII* names seven new cardinals of the Roman Catholic Church; among them the first Japanese, Filipino, and black cardinals.

1962 *George Borg Olivier* is sworn in as *Malta's* first prime minister under a constitution extending self-rule to the British colony.

1963 *Senegal* adopts a new constitution.

1964 *George C. Price* is sworn in as the first prime minister of *British Honduras* under a constitution providing internal self-government.

1967 Caribbean island of *Grenada* is granted internal self-government.

1969 *Apollo 9* spacecraft is launched from Cape Kennedy.

1980 *Pierre Trudeau* replaces *Joe Clark* as prime minister of Canada.

That's Incredible! makes its television debut.

1987 Premier *Bettino Craxi* resigns after three years and seven months, the longest term of service of any post-war Italian leader.

1988 The U.S. *Stars and Stripes* defeats New Zealand in the America's Cup yacht race.

1991 *Rodney King* is severly beaten by Los Angeles policemen. The beating is was caught on videotape and becomes an international symbol of police brutality.

1995 The *United Nations* removes its peacekeeping forces from *Somalia*.

1997 *Harold Nicholson* enters a plea of guilty to charges of spying for Russia. Nicholson was a former employee of the *Central Intelligence Agency (CIA)*.

HOLIDAYS

U.S.
Constitution Day
Celebration of the day when the U.S. Constitution came into effect, March 4, 1789.

U.S.(Vermont)
Admission Day
Celebrates Vermont's admission to the Union, 1791.

RELIGIOUS CALENDAR

The Saints
St. Lucius, pope; reigned 253–254; elected Bishop of Rome 253. Patron of Copenhagen. [d. 254]

St. Adrian, missionary bishop, and his companions, martyrs. [d. c. 875]

St. Peter of Cava, first bishop of Policastro. [d. 1123]

St. Casimir of Poland, prince. Patron of Poland. Son of Casimir IV, King of Poland. Also called the *Peacemaker.* [d. 1484] Optional Memorial.

The Beatified
Blessed Humbert III of Savoy, count. [d. 1188]

Blessed Christopher Bales, priest and martyr. Also called *Bayles.* [d. 1590]

Blessed Placida Viel, virgin and second superior general of the Sisters of the Christian Schools. [d. 1877]

BIRTHDATES

1394 *Prince Henry the Navigator,* Portuguese prince; sponsored voyages of discovery leading to foundation of the Portuguese Empire. [d. November 13, 1460]

1678 *Antonio Vivaldi,* Italian composer, violin virtuoso. [d. July 28, 1741]

1747 *Count Casimir Pulaski,* Polish cavalry general in the American Revolution. [d. October 11, 1779]

1754 *Benjamin Waterhouse,* U.S. physician; promoted scientific approach to *vaccination* in U.S. [d. October 2, 1846]

1782 *Johann Rudolf Wyss,* Swiss folklorist; edited his father's story, *Swiss Family Robinson.* [d. March 21, 1830]

1798 *Sigurdur Eirikson Breidfjord,* Icelandic poet. [d. July 21, 1846]

1826 *John Buford,* Union Army general during U.S Civil War, known for his brilliant command of Union infantry. [d. December 16, 1863]

1888 *Knute (Kenneth) Rockne,* U.S. football coach; famous for leadership in sport; best known for development of *Fighting Irish* of Notre Dame. [d. March 31, 1931]

1901 *Charles Henry Goren,* U.S. bridge expert, lawyer. [d. April 3, 1991]

1904 *George Gamow,* U.S.-Russian physicist; known for research in *stellar evolution.* [d. August 19, 1968]

1913 *John Garfield (Julius Garfinkle),* U.S. actor. [d. May 21, 1952]

1928 *Alan Sillitoe,* British novelist.

1931 *Alice Mitchell Rivlin,* U.S. government official; director, Congressional Budget Office, 1975–83; director, Office of Management and Budget, 1994– .

1932 *Miriam Makeba,* South African singer.

1937 *Barbara McNair,* U.S. singer.

1939 *Paula Prentiss (Paula Ragusa),* U.S. actress; known for her starring role on television series, *He and She,* 1967–68.

1941 *Adrian Lyne,* British director; directed the movies *Fatal Attraction,* 1987, and *Indecent Proposal,* 1993.

1953 *Kay Lenz,* U.S. actress; Emmy Award for *Heart in Hiding.*

1954 *Catherine O'Hara,* Canadian actress; known for roles in the *Home Alone* movies.

1959 *Kelly Lynch,* U.S. actress.

HISTORICAL EVENTS

1152 *Frederick I Barbarossa* is elected King of Germany.

1193 *Saladin of Damascus,* sultan and Muslim hero, one of the chief opponents of the Crusades, dies.

1461 *Henry VI* of England is deposed; succeeded by *Edward IV.*

1493 *Christopher Columbus* lands at Lisbon after completing his first voyage to the New World.

1510 *Afonso de Albuquerque,* Portuguese navigator, annexes *Goa,* on Indian subcontinent, for Portugal.

1681 *William Penn* is given a charter for lands in the New World by *King Charles II.*

1789 First meeting of *U.S. Congress* under the Constitution takes place.

1791 *Vermont* is admitted to the Union as the 14th state.

1793 *George Washington* is inaugurated for a second term as President of the United States, in Philadelphia; *John Adams* is Vice-President.

1794 *Eli Whitney* is granted a patent for his *cotton gin.*

1797 *John Adams* is inaugurated as the second President of the United States; *Thomas Jefferson* becomes Vice-President.

1801 *Thomas Jefferson* becomes the first president to be inaugurated in the new U.S. capital of *Washington, D.C.;* *Aaron Burr* becomes Vice-President.

1809 *James Madison* is inaugurated as fourth President of the United States; *Elbridge Gerry* is Vice-President.

1817 *James Monroe* is inaugurated as fifth President of the United States; *Daniel D. Tompkins* is Vice-President.

1825 *John Quincy Adams* is inaugurated as sixth President of the United States; *John C. Calhoun* is Vice-President.

1828 The *Baltimore & Ohio Railroad* is begun; it is the first public railroad in the U.S.

1829 *Andrew Jackson* is inaugurated as the seventh President of the United States; *John C. Calhoun* is Vice-President.

1837 *Martin Van Buren* is inaugurated as eighth President of the United States; *Richard M. Johnson* is Vice-President.

1841 *William H. Harrison* is inaugurated as ninth President of the United States; on his death a month later, the Vice-President, *John Tyler,* becomes the tenth President.

1845 *James Polk* is inaugurated as the 11th President of the United States; *George M. Dallas* is Vice-President.

1849 *Zachary Taylor* is inaugurated as the 12th President of the United States; *Millard Fillmore,* the Vice-President, becomes the 13th President following Taylor's death in 1850.

1853 *Franklin Pierce* is inaugurated as the 14th President of the United States; *William R. King* is Vice-President.

1857 *James Buchanan* is inaugurated as the 15th President of the U.S.; *John C. Breckinridge* is Vice-President.

1861 *Abraham Lincoln* is inaugurated as 16th President of the United States; *Hannibal Hamlin* is Vice-President.

U.S. Government Printing Office is established.

1865 *Abraham Lincoln* is inaugurated for a second term; his Vice-President, *Andrew Johnson,* becomes 17th President following Lincoln's assassination.

1869 *Ulysses S. Grant* is inaugurated as 18th President of the United States; *Henry Wilson* is Vice-President.

1871 *U.S. Civil Service Commission* is established by U.S. President *Ulysses S. Grant.*

1876 *Don Carlos,* pretender to the Spanish throne and leader of the *Carlist* forces, arrives in England, having given up his fight in Spain.

1877 *Rutherford B. Hayes* is inaugurated as 19th President of the United States; *William A. Wheeler* is Vice-President.

1878 *Pope Leo XIII* revives Roman Catholic hierarchy in Scotland.

1881 *James Garfield* is inaugurated as 20th President of the United States; *Chester A. Arthur,* Vice-President, becomes 21st President following Garfield's assassination.

1885 *Grover Cleveland* is inaugurated as 22nd President of the United States; *Thomas A. Hendricks* is Vice-President.

1889 *Benjamin Harrison* is inaugurated as 23rd President of the United States; *Levi P. Morton* is Vice-President.

1893 *Grover Cleveland* is inaugurated for a second term as 24th President of the United States; *Adlai E. Stevenson* is Vice-President.

1897 *William McKinley* is inaugurated as the 25th President of the United States; *Garret A. Hobart* is Vice-President.

1901 *William McKinley* is inaugurated for a second term as President of the United States; *Theodore Roosevelt,* his Vice-President, becomes 26th President following McKinley's assassination.

1905 *Theodore Roosevelt* is inaugurated after being elected President; *Charles Warren Fairbanks* is Vice-President.

1909 *William Howard Taft* is inaugurated as the 27th President of the United States; *James S. Sherman* is Vice-President.

1913 *(Thomas) Woodrow Wilson* is inaugurated as the 28th President of the United States; *Thomas R. Marshall* is Vice-President.

1915 Railroad passenger service across the Lower Ganges opens in India.

1917 *Joannette Rankin* becomes the first female member of the U.S. Congress.

(Thomas) Woodrow Wilson is inaugurated for a second term as President of the United States; *Thomas R. Marshall* remains his Vice-President.

1921 *Warren G. Harding* is inaugurated as 29th President of the United States; *Calvin Coolidge* is Vice-President.

1925 *Calvin Coolidge* is inaugurated as the 30th President of the United States; *Charles G. Dawes* is Vice-President.

1927 The rush for the *Grosfontein diamond field* in South Africa opens with about 25,000 runners participating.

1929 *Herbert C. Hoover* is inaugurated as the 31st President of the United States; *Charles Curtis* is Vice-President.

1931 Indian leader *Mahatma Gandhi* ends second *civil disobedience* campaign as British release nonviolent political prisoners.

1933 *Franklin Delano Roosevelt* is inaugurated as the 32nd President of the United States; *John Nance Garner* is Vice-President.

1942 U.S. Air Force strikes *Marcus Island,* 1200 miles southeast of Tokyo *(World War II).*

1958 The *Nautilus,* U.S. atomic submarine, passes under the polar ice cap.

1962 U.S. Atomic Energy Commission announces that the first *atomic power plant* in Antarctica is in operation at McMurdo Sound.

1964 The United Nations unanimously votes to send a peacekeeping force to *Cyprus* to end fighting between Greek and Turkish sectors.

Kentucky Fried Chicken Corp. is incorporated in Kentucky.

James R. Hoffa, President of the International Brotherhood of Teamsters, is found guilty in Chattanooga, Tennessee, of tampering with a federal jury in 1962.

1975 The government of Rhodesia arrests Methodist clergyman *Ndabaningi Sithole,* President of the militant *Zimbabwe African National Union,* on charges of plotting to murder black rivals.

1977 Earthquake destroys parts of *Bucharest, Rumania,* and nearby area, leaving 1,500 dead.

1980 *Robert Mugabe* is elected to head the newly-formed government of Zimbabwe.

1986 Austrian presidential candidate, *Kurt Waldheim,* is linked to German army units that committed atrocities in Greece and Yugoslavia during World War II.

1987 *Jonathan Pollard* is sentenced to life imprisonment for passing U.S. military secrets to Israel.

Great Britain becomes the first nation to grant permission for the commercial use of *azidothymidine (AZT),* a drug employed to treat *AIDS.*

1989 *Time Inc.* and *Warner Communications Inc.* announce that they will merge to form the world's largest media company.

1993 Scientists announce the discovery of the gene that causes *amyotrophic lateral sclerosis (Lou Gehrig's Disease).*

1997 *Koh Hun* is elected as the new Premier of South Korea.

march

1998 Federal lawyers bring a
lawsuit against six companies
for illegal gambling on the
Internet.

HOLIDAYS

French Polynesia
Missionary Day

RELIGIOUS CALENDAR

The Saints

SS. Adrian and *Eubulus,* martyrs. [d. 309]

St. Eusebius of Cremona. [d. c. 423]

St. Gerasimus, hermit and abbot. [d. 475]

St. Kieran of Saighir, first bishop of Ossory. The first native-born Irish saint. Also called *Ciaran, Kenerin,* or *Kiaran.* [d. c. 530]

St. Piran, abbot. [d. c. 6th century]

St. Virgil, Archbishop of Arles. [d. c. 610]

St. John Joseph of the Cross, Franciscan priest. [d. 1734]

St. Phocas of Antioch, martyr. [death date unknown]

BIRTHDATES

1133 *Henry II,* British ruler; first Plantagenet King of England, 1154–89. [d. 1189]

1326 *Louis I, King of Hungary,* reigned 1342–82. Joint ruler of Poland with *Casimir III.* [d. September 10, 1382]

1512 *Gerardus Mercator* (Gerhard Kremer), Flemish geographer; Mercator projection, used in cartography, is named for him. [d. December 5, 1594]

1658 *Antoine de la Mothe Cadillac,* French fur trader, explorer; founded the city of *Detroit, Michigan,* 1701. [d. October 15, 1730]

1696 *Giambattista (Giovanni Battista) Tiepolo,* Italian artist. [d. March 27, 1770]

1824 *James Merritt Ives,* U.S. painter, lithographer; with his partner, Nathaniel Currier (March 27), founded the firm *Currier & Ives,* which produced art prints extremely popular in the U.S. and in Europe, 1857–95. [d. January 3, 1895]

Elisha Harris, U.S. physician; pioneer in *public health* field in U.S. [d. January 31, 1884]

1830 *Charles Wyville Thomson,* British naturalist; led early oceanographic voyage, which circumnavigated the globe; described his findings in *The Voyage of the Challenge.* [d. March 10, 1882]

1836 *William Steinway,* U.S. piano manufacturer. [d. November 30, 1896]

1852 *Lady Isabella Gregory,* Irish writer, playwright; contributed greatly to the renaissance of *Irish literature* in the late 19th century. [d. May 22, 1932]

1853 *Howard Pyle,* U.S. illustrator, painter, author; noted for his highly popular children's books, usually dealing with medieval themes; also recognized for his renderings of American historical scenes; among his students were *Maxfield Parrish* (July 25) and *N. C. Wyeth* (October 22). [d. November 9, 1911]

1870 *(Benjamin) Franklin Norris,* U.S. novelist. [d. October 25, 1902]

1879 *William Henry Beveridge,* British economist; wrote *Beveridge Report* on social services in post-war Great Britain. [d. March 16, 1963]

1887 *Hector Villa-Lobos,* Brazilian composer, music educator; composed 12 symphonies; known for his espousal of nationalistic themes in his music. [d. November 17, 1959]

1908 *Rex Harrison,* British actor; Oscar winner for role in *My Fair Lady,* 1964. [d. June 2, 1990]

1918 *Mit Schmidt,* Canadian hockey player.

James Tobin, U.S. economist; Nobel Prize in economics, 1981.

1927 *Jack Cassidy,* U.S. actor, singer, dancer; Tony Award for *She Loves Me,* 1964. [d. December 12, 1976]

1936 *Cannan Banana,* Zimbabwean statesman, educator; President, 1980–87; professor, University of Zimbabwe, 1989– .

1940 *Samantha Eggar,* British actress; Cannes Film Festival Award for *The Collector,* 1965.

1941 *Paul Sand,* U.S. actor.

1942 *Felipe Gonzalez Marquez,* Spanish politician; former prime minister.

1946 *Robert Patrick (Rocky) Bleier,* U.S. football player; lost part of his right foot in Vietnam, 1969; running back for Pittsburgh Steelers, 1968, 1971–80.

1950 *Eugene Nicholas Fodor,* U.S. musician; first Westerner to win Moscow's Tchaikovsky Prize, 1974.

1955 *Penn Jillette,* U.S. magic performer; one half of the comedy duo Penn & Teller.

1958 *Andy Gibb,* British singer, songwriter, musician; known for song, *How Deep Is Your Love.* [d. March 10, 1988]

1966 *Michael Irvin,* U.S. football player.

HISTORICAL EVENTS

493 *Odoacer,* leader of German tribe, is defeated at *Ravenna* by *Theodoric* and his Ostrogoths.

1460 *Christian I* of Denmark becomes Duke of *Schleswig and Holstein,* which are declared forever indivisible.

1496 *Henry VII* of England gives his patronage to *John Cabot* for his voyages of exploration and discovery to *North America.*

1770 *Boston Massacre* occurs as a result of the American colonists' resentment of having British troops quartered in the city; several are killed as British troops fire into a mob.

1904 *String Quartet in F* by *Maurice Ravel* premieres in Paris.

1907 First *radio broadcast* of a musical composition takes place when *Lee De Forest* transmits a performance of Rossini's *William Tell Overture* from Telharmonic Hall in New York to the Brooklyn Navy Yard.

1916 *General Jan Smuts* of the *Union of South Africa* begins an advance on *Kilimanjaro,* German East Africa *(World War I).*

1920 *Norway* joins *League of Nations.*

1923 *Montana* and *Nevada* enact the first old-age pensions in the U.S.

The first *Workmen's Compensation Act* is passed in India.

1924 *Sweden* officially recognizes the government of *Soviet Russia.*

1928 A passive resistance strike begins in India against the *East Indian Railway.*

1931 The *Delhi Pact* between *Mahatma Gandhi* and *Edward Wood, Viceroy Irwin,* brings a halt to the *civil disobedience* campaign with Gandhi accepting the federal constitution plan adopted by the conference in return for British efforts to lessen repression.

1946 In a speech at Missouri's Westminster College, *Winston Churchill* introduces the phrase "*iron curtain*" to describe the repression of Soviet-dominated Europe.

1952 *Ghana* inaugurates its first cabinet with *Kwame Nkrumah* as prime minister.

1960 Indonesian President *Sukarno* suspends the Indonesian parliament.

Guinea becomes the first nation outside the Communist bloc to recognize *East Germany.*

1967 Colonel *Fidel Sanchez Hernandez* is elected president of El Salvador.

UN Secretary General *U Thant,* returning to New York from Burma, declares that "Peace is not yet in sight" in Vietnam, and predicts a "prolonged and bloody" conflict unless the U.S. halts bombing raids on *North Vietnam.*

1976 *Spain* moves towards democracy by allowing free political parties, except terrorists, anarchists, separatists, or Communists.

1977 In an unprecedented two-hour radio broadcast, U.S. President *Jimmy Carter* speaks over the telephone with 42 callers from 26 states.

1979 *Voyager 1* relays data from *Jupiter,* including photographs of its four largest moons.

China begins withdrawal of its troops from *Vietnam.*

1983 *Robert Hawke* is elected prime minister of Australia as his Labor Party wins an absolute majority in the House of Representatives.

The *United States Football League* begins its first season.

1984 *Standard Oil Company* of California and *Gulf Corp.* agree to merge in a $13.3 billion transaction.

1989 Buddhist monks lead an independence demonstration of over two thousand people in *Tibet*.

1994 *Byron de la Beckwith* receives life imprisonment for the 1963 murder of civil rights activist *Medgar Evers* (June 12, 1963).

1997 The Swiss government establishes a *Holocaust Victims Fund*.

march

MARCH
6

HOLIDAYS

Ethiopia
Victory Day

Ghana
Independence Day
Honors establishment of sovereignty of Ghana, 1957.

Guam
Discovery Day or Magellan Day
Commemorates discovery of island by Magellan on this date, 1521.

RELIGIOUS CALENDAR

The Saints
St. Chrodegang, Bishop of Metz. [d. 766]
St. Fridolin, abbot. Also called the *Traveller, Viator.* [d. c. 6th century]
SS. Cyneburga, abbess, *Cyneswide,* abbess, and *Tibba,* hermitess. Cyneburga founded the Convent of Cyneburgecester, or Castor. [d. 7th century]
St. Cadroe, abbot. Also called *Cadroc,* or *Cadroel.* [d. 976]
SS. Balred and *Bilfrid,* hermits. Balred also called *Baldrede,* or *Balther.* [d. 8th century]
St. Ollegarius, Archbishop of Tarragona. Also called *Olaguer,* or *Oldegar.* [d. 1137]
St. Cyril, Patriarch of Constantinople and prior-general of the Carmelites. Also called *Cyrillus.* [d. c. 1235]

St. Colette, virgin and superior of all convents of Minoresses. [d. 1447]

The Beatified
Blessed Jordan of Pisa, Dominican priest. [d. 1311]

BIRTHDATES

1475 *Michelangelo (surnamed Buonarroti),* Italian painter, sculptor, architect, poet; the consummate creative genius; known throughout the world for his mastery of several different art forms. [d. February 18, 1564]

1483 *Francesco Guicciardini,* Italian historian and statesman; prominent in the affairs of Florence. [d. May 22, 1540]

1492 Juan Luis Vives, Spanish humanist, philosopher; known especially as a proponent of induction as a philosophical method; *De Anima et Vita,* his chief work, is the first work dealing with psychology. [d. May 6, 1540]

1619 *(Savinien de) Cyrano de Bergerac,* French novelist, playwright; noted duelist. [d. July 28, 1655]

1787 *Joseph von Fraunhofer,* German astronomer; the first to chart lines of *solar spectrum,* naming the

principal ones. [d. June 7, 1826]

1806 *Elizabeth Barrett Browning,* English poet; best known for her *Sonnets from the Portuguese;* wife of Robert Browning (May 7). [d. June 29, 1861]

1812 *Aaron Lufkin Dennison,* U.S. watch manufacturer; dubbed *Father of the Watch Industry* in the U.S. [d. January 9, 1895]

1831 *Philip Henry Sheridan,* Union Army general during U.S. Civil War; known more for his aggressiveness and ability to inspire confidence in his troops than for his skill in military strategy; Commander-in-Chief of U.S. Army, 1883–88. [d. August 5, 1888]

1844 *Nicolai Rimski-Korsakov,* Russian composer, teacher; composed numerous operas; among his most popular symphonic poems is *Scheherazade.* [d. June 21, 1908]

1885 *Ring(old) Lardner,* U.S. humorist, short-story writer. [d. September 25, 1933]

1897 *John Donald MacArthur,* U.S. insurance executive. [d. January 6, 1978]

1906 *Lou Costello (Louis Cristillo),* U.S. comedian; partner of Bud Abbott (October 2);

made numerous comedy films in 1940s and 1950s. [d. March 3, 1959]

Lawrence (Lovell) Schoonover, U.S. author; wrote dozens of historical novels based on carefully researched fact; author of *The Burnished Blade.* [d. January 8, 1980]

1909 *Obafemi Awolowo,* Nigerian politician, writer; Chancellor of *University of Ife,* 1967; leader of *Unity Party of Nigeria,* 1979–1987. [d. May 9, 1987]

1923 *Ed(ward Lee) McMahon,* U.S. entertainer; known as the announcer on television series, *The Tonight Show,* 1962–92.

1924 *Sarah Caldwell,* U.S. conductor, director; founded Opera Company of Boston, 1957.

William Hedgcock Webster, U.S. government official; Director, Federal Bureau of Investigation, 1978–87; Director, Central Intelligence Agency, 1987–91.

1926 *Alan Greenspan,* U.S. economist, government official; Chairman, Council of Economic Advisers, 1974–77; Chairman, Federal Reserve Board, 1987– .

1927 *Leroy Gordon Cooper,* U.S. astronaut; commander pilot of *Gemini 5* spacecraft, 1965.

1928 *Gabriel Garcia Marquez,* Colombian author; wrote *One Hundred Years of Solitude,* 1970; Nobel Prize in literature, 1982.

1929 *Thomas S. Foley,* U.S. politician; Speaker of the House of Representatives, 1989–95.

1930 *Lorin Maazel,* French-born conductor, violinist.

1936 *Marion Barry,* U.S. politician; Mayor of Washington, D.C., 1979–91, 95– .

1937 *Valentina Vladimirovna Tereshkova,* Russian cosmonaut; the first woman to travel into space, 1963.

1941 *Willie Stargell,* U.S. baseball player.

1942 *Ben(jamin Edward) Murphy,* U.S. actor.

Flora Purim, Brazilian singer.

1947 *Kiki Dee (Pauline Matthews),* British singer; known for her duet, *Don't Go Breaking My Heart,* with Elton John.

Dick Fosbury, U.S. high jumper; originator of the *Fosbury Flop;* won Olympic gold medal, 1968.

David Gilmour, British singer, musician; member of the rock group, *Pink Floyd.*

Rob(ert) Reiner, U.S. actor, director; two Emmy Awards for his role as Michael Stivic on television series, *All in the Family,* 1971–78.

Dame Kiri Te Kanawa, New Zealand opera singer; known for performing at wedding of Prince Charles, 1981.

1959 *Tom Arnold,* U.S. comedian, actor.

1972 *Shaquille O'Neal,* U.S. basketball player.

HISTORICAL EVENTS

1480 *Treaty of Toledo* is signed, in which Spain recognizes conquest of *Morocco* by Portugal and Portugal cedes claims to *Canary Islands.*

1629 *Edict of Restitution* orders all church property secularized in Germany since 1552 to be restored to the Roman Church.

1714 *Peace of Rastatt* between France and Holy Roman Emperor, *Charles VI,* is signed; France recognizes Italian possessions of the Hapsburgs; Electors of Bavaria and Cologne are restored; Spain relinquishes possessions in Flanders, Luxembourg, and Italy.

1819 U.S. Supreme Court hands down landmark *M'Culloch v. Maryland* decision; Justice Marshall states doctrine of loose construction of U.S. Constitution.

1834 The city of *Toronto, Canada* is incorporated; William Lyon Mackenzie is its first mayor.

1836 Mexican troops under *Santa Anna* capture the *Alamo* and massacre the American garrison defending it, including *Davy Crockett* and *James Bowie.*

1882 *Milan IV* is proclaimed king of an independent *Serbia* by the Serbian assembly.

1889 *Milan, King of Serbia,* abdicates in favor of his young son *Alexander;* a liberal regency is established.

1898 *Sino-German Convention* is signed, giving Germany a 99-year lease on *Kiaochow Bay* and railway and mining privileges in *Shantung.*

1902 A permanent U.S. *Bureau of the Census* is established.

1912 The first use of *dirigibles* in warfare takes place in an Italian action against the Turks in *Tripoli (First Balkan War).*

march

1916 The *Battle of Verdun* is renewed with German attacks on both sides of the Meuse River *(World War I)*.

1933 A four-day *national bank holiday* begins in the U.S., marking the start of the administration of U.S. President *Franklin D. Roosevelt*.

1943 U.S. cruisers and destroyers bombard *Vila* and *Munda* in the *Solomon Islands (World War II)*.

1944 In an Allied air offensive, 600 U.S. planes bomb *Berlin (World War II)*.

1945 Allied troops capture *Cologne (World War II)*.

1947 U.S. Supreme Court upholds a fine against *John L. Lewis,* President of *United Mine Workers,* for a strike called in November 1946 in defiance of an injunction.

1962 U.S. pledges itself to defend *Thailand* without waiting for prior agreement on action by the Southeast Asia Treaty Organization.

1964 Crown Prince *Constantine* is proclaimed King of Greece following the death of his father, *Paul I.*

1967 *Svetlana Alliluyeva,* daughter of the late Soviet dictator *Joseph Stalin,* seeks asylum at the U.S. Embassy in New Delhi, India.

1986 Soviet spacecraft *Vega I* enters the atmosphere of *Halley's comet* and sends back pictures of the comet's icy nucleus.

1990 Soviet citizens are now allowed to own the means of production as the *Soviet Parliament* passes a new property law.

RELIGIOUS CALENDAR

The Saints

SS. Perpetua, Felicity, Revocatus, Saturninus, Saturus, and *Secundulus,* martyrs. Felicity patron of young children. [d. 203] Feast formerly March 6. Obligatory Memorial.

St. Paul the Simple, hermit. [d. c. 339]

St. Drausius, Bishop of Soissons. Also called *Drausin.* [d. c. 674]

St. Esterwine, Abbot of Wearmouth. Also called *Eosterwine.* [d. 686]

St. Ardo, priest. [d. 843]

St. Theophylact, Bishop of Nicomedia. [d. 845]

BIRTHDATES

1693 *Pope Clement XIII,* reigned 1758–69. [d. February 2, 1769]

1707 *Stephen Hopkins,* American patriot, farmer, merchant, signer of the Declaration of Independence; Governor of Rhode Island. [d. July 13, 1785]

1765 *Joseph Nicéphore Niepce,* French physicist, inventor; pioneer in development of *photography.* [d. July 5, 1833]

1785 *Alessandro (Francesco Tommaso Antonio de) Manzoni,* Italian novelist, poet; best known for his novel *I Promessi Sposi (The Betrothed),* a model of modern Italian prose. [d. April 28, 1873]

1792 *Sir John Frederick Herschel,* English astronomer; son of *Sir William Herschel* (November 15); continued his father's experiments and studies; discovered solvent powers of sodium hyposulfite, later used in *photography;* first to use terms *positive* and *negative* in photographic experiments. [d. May 11, 1871]

1814 *Kamehameha III (Kauikeaouli),* Hawaiian King, responsible for giving Hawaii a constitution, 1840; revised, 1852. [d. December 15, 1854]

1837 *Henry Draper,* U.S. astronomer, physician; noted for his pioneering experiments in *celestial photography* and *spectroscopy.* [d. November 20, 1882]

1844 *Anthony Comstock,* U.S. reformer, author; known for his anti-pornography crusades resulting in the Comstock Act of 1873. [d. September 21, 1915]

1849 *Luther Burbank,* U.S. botanist, horiculturist; known for his numerous experiments in hybridizing new species of hundreds of different vegetables and flowers. [d. April 11, 1926]

1850 *Champ Clark (James Beauchamp Clark),* U.S. politician; U.S. Congressman, 1892–1920; Speaker of the House of Representatives, 1911–19. [d. March 3, 1921]

Thomáš Garrigue Masaryk, Czech statesman, philosopher; member of Austrian Parliament, 1891–93, 1907–14; first President of the Czechoslovak Republic, 1918–35. [d. September 14, 1937]

1857 *Julius Wagner Von Jauregg,* Austrian scientist; Nobel Prize in physiology or medicine for treatment of paralysis by *malarial therapy,* 1927. [d. September 17, 1940]

1872 *Pieter Cornelis Mondrian (Mondriaan),* Dutch artist; representative of *ultramodern school.* [d. February 1, 1944]

1875 *Maurice Joseph Ravel,* French impressionist composer, best known for his *Boléro.* [d. December 28, 1937]

1904 *Reinhard Heydrich,* German Nazi official; deputy chief of Gestapo and administrator of Nazi *concentration camps.* [d. June 4, 1942]

1908 *Anna Magnani,* Italian actress. [d. September 26, 1973]

1930 *Antony Charles Robert Armstrong-Jones, Earl of Snowden,* British photographer; ex-husband of Princess Margaret; known for celebrity portraits.

1938 *David Baltimore,* U.S. microbiologist; Nobel Prize in physiology or medicine for research on *tumor viruses* (with R. Dulbecco and H. Temin), 1975.

Janet Guthrie, U.S. auto racer; the first woman to qualify for and race in the *Indianapolis 500.*

1940 *Daniel J(ohn) Travanti,* U.S. actor; two Emmys for his role as Frank Furillo on television series, *Hill Street Blues,* 1980–87.

1941 *Piers Paul Read,* British author.

1946 *John Heard,* U.S. actor; known role in the *Home Alone* movies.

Peter Wolf, U.S. singer; member of the rock group, *J. Geils Band.*

1950 *Franco Harris,* U.S. football player; Rookie of the Year, 1972.

1960 *Joe Carter,* U.S. baseball player.

Ivan Lendl, Czech tennis player.

1967 *Julio Bocca,* Argentine ballet dancer.

HISTORICAL EVENTS

1080 *Pope Gregory VII* excommunicates *Henry IV* of Germany for the second time over the issue of *lay investiture.*

1138 *Conrad III* is elected King of Germany.

1645 Swedes defeat army of Holy Roman Empire at *Jankau (Thirty Years' War).*

1792 French National Assembly adopts the *guillotine* as method of execution throughout France (*French Revolution*).

1793 France declares war on Spain (*French Revolution*).

1857 U.S. Supreme Court issues the *Dred Scott decision,* declaring that the *Missouri Compromise* is unconstitutional.

1876 *Alexander Graham Bell* is awarded patent for the *telephone.*

1917 World's first *jazz recording* is issued by the Victor Company, including *Livery Stable Blues* and *Dixieland Jazz Band One Step.*

1918 President Woodrow Wilson authorizes the *Distinguished Service Medal* to be given for outstanding service in the U.S. military.

1936 Germany denounces the *Locarno Pacts* of 1925 and reoccupies the Rhineland.

1945 U.S. troops capture *Bonn* (*World War II*).

U.S. troops capture the key *Remagen Bridge* across the *Rhine* (*World War II*).

1951 Premier *Ali Razmara* of Iran is assassinated by a religious fanatic in a mosque in Teheran.

U.S. *House Un-American Activities Committee* releases a list of subversive organizations and publications.

1954 *Al Amir Mohammed Farid Didi* becomes sultan of the Maldive Islands.

1965 *Pope Paul VI* celebrates mass in a parish church in Rome mainly in Italian instead of Latin, and facing the congregation, thus implementing the decisions of the *Ecumenical Council.*

1970 *Malaysia* and *Thailand* sign an agreement permitting their troops to combat Communist guerrillas in each other's territory.

1985 Major U.S. recording artists combine their talents and release *We Are the World.* Proceeds from record sales will be donated to *African famine relief.*

HOLIDAYS

Afghanistan
Women's Day

Azerbaijan
Women's Day

Belarus
Women's Day

British Virgin Islands
Commonwealth Day

Cape Verde Islands
Women's Day

China
Women's Day

Guinea-Bissau
Women's Day

Kyrgyzstan
Women's Holiday

Liberia
Decoration Day

Libya
National Day

Mauretania
Women's Day

Nepal
Women's Day

Russia
Women's Day

Swaziland
Commonwealth Day

Syria
Revolution Day
Commemorates the coming to power of the National Council of Revolution, 1963.

Zambia
Youth Day

UN Member Countries
International Women's Day
This day is recognized in many socialist countries as the counterpart to *Mother's Day*. Official greetings are conveyed by way of red and white banners hung from buildings and press, radio, and television messages.

RELIGIOUS CALENDAR

The Saints
St. Dontius. [d. 260]
SS. Philemon and *Apollonius,* martyrs. [d. c. 305]
St. Senan of Scattery Island, bishop. [d. 560]
St. Felix of Dunwich, Bishop and Apostle of the East Angles. [d. 648]
St. Julian, Archbishop of Toledo. [d. 690]
St. Humphrey, Bishop of Thérouanne. Also called *Hunfrid.* [d. 871]
St. Duthac, Bishop of Ross. Also called *Duthak.* [d. c. 1065]
St. Veremund, Abbot of Hyrache. [d. 1092]
St. Stephen of Obazine, abbot. [d. 1154]
St. John of God, founder of the Brothers Hospitallers; patron of all hospitals, sick people, nurses, and book and print sellers. [d. 1550] Optional Memorial.

The Beatified
Blessed Vincent, Bishop of Cracow. First Polish chronicler. [d. 1223]

BIRTHDATES

1714 *Karl Philipp Emanuel Bach,* German composer; the most gifted of *Johann Sebastian Bach's* 11 sons. [d. December 14, 1788]

1726 *Richard Howe, Earl Howe,* British admiral, commander of British forces in North America, 1776–78. [d. August 5, 1799]

1783 *Hannah Van Buren,* wife of U.S. President Martin Van Buren. [d. February 5, 1819]

1830 *João de Deus Ramos,* Portuguese lyric poet; the foremost poet of his time in Portugal. [d. January 11, 1896]

1841 *Oliver Wendell Holmes, Jr.* U.S. jurist; son of Oliver Wendell Holmes (August 29), U.S. poet; known as the *Great Dissenter.* [d. March 6, 1935]

1859 *Kenneth Grahame,* British author of children's books; known especially for *Wind in the Willows.* [d. July 6, 1932]

1865 *Frederic William Goudy,* U.S. type designer, printer; known as the designer of a number of new type faces, several of which bear his name, *Goudy, Goudy Old Style.* [d. May 11, 1947]

1879 *Otto Hahn,* German chemist; Nobel Prize in chemistry for discovery of *fission of heavy atomic nuclei,* 1944. [d. July 28, 1968]

1886 *Edward Calvin Kendall,* U.S. biochemist; Nobel Prize in physiology or medicine for discovery of *cortisone* (with P. Hench and T. Reichstein), 1950. [d. May 4, 1972]

1890 *George Magoffin Humphrey,* U.S. manufacturer, government official; Secretary of the Treasury, 1953–57. [d. January 20, 1970]

1900 *Howard Hathaway Aiken,* U.S. mathematician, inventor; developed first large-scale *computer, Mark I.* [d. March 14, 1973]

1902 *Jennings Randolph,* U.S. politician; Senator, 1958–85. [d. May 8, 1998]

1909 *Claire Trevor (Claire Wemlinger),* U.S. actress.

1917 *Leslie Fiedler,* U.S. literary critic, professor of English; known for his application of theories of Freud and Jung to contemporary literature.

1918 *Alan Hale, Jr.,* U.S. actor; known for his role as captain on television series, *Gilligan's Island,* 1964–67. [d. January 2, 1990]

1923 *Cyd Charisse,* U.S. dancer.

1927 *Stanislaw Kania,* Polish politician; head of Polish Communist Party, 1980–81.

1937 *Juvenal Habyarimana,* Rwandan statesman; President, Republic of Rwanda, 1973– [d. April 6, 1994]

1939 *James Alan (Jim) Bouton,* U.S. baseball player, author; wrote *Ball Four,* 1970.

1943 *Lynn Redgrave,* British actress; known for her starring role on television series, *House Calls.*

1945 *Mickey Dolenz,* U.S. singer; member of the rock group, *The Monkees.*

Anselm Kiefer, German artist.

1946 *Randy Meisner,* U.S. singer, musician; member of the rock group, *The Eagles,* 1971–77.

1947 *Carole Bayer Sager,* U.S. singer, songwriter.

1959 *Aidan Quinn,* U.S. actor.

1967 *John Harkes,* U.S. soccer player.

HISTORICAL EVENTS

1198 *Philip, Duke of Swabia,* and brother of *Emperor Henry VI,* is elected King of Germany.

1702 *William III* of Great Britain dies and is succeeded by *Queen Anne.*

1844 *Charles XIV John, King of Sweden and Norway,* dies and is succeeded by his son, *Oscar I.*

1862 Confederate ironclad frigate *Merrimac* sinks the Union *Cumberland* at *Hampton Roads,* Virginia *(U.S. Civil War).*

1916 The S.S. Kresge Co. (later *K Mart Corp.*) is incorporated in Michigan.

1917 Food riots break out in Petrograd (formerly St. Petersburg), Russia *(Russian Revolution).*

1920 *Switzerland* and *Denmark* join the *League of Nations.*

1921 Spanish Prime Minister *Eduardo Dato* is assassinated.

1922 *Wireless telephone service* is inaugurated between Peking and Tientsin.

1924 *Greece* officially recognizes the Soviet government of Russia.

1948 U.S. Supreme Court rules in *McCollum v. Board of Education* that religious instruction in public schools is unconstitutional.

1950 British government withholds recognition of *Seretse Khama* as tribal chief in *Bechuanaland* because of his marriage to a white woman.

1963 Pro-Nasser military elements seize control of the Syrian government in that country's third revolution in 18 months.

1967 Bernard Malamud's novel, *The Fixer,* wins the Pulitzer Prize.

1971 U.S. army Captain *Ernest L. Medina* is ordered court-martialed on murder charges in connection with the *My-Lai incident* of March 1968 *(Vietnam War).*

Muhammad Ali (Cassius Clay) is defeated by *Joe Frazier* in what is dubbed *The Fight of the Century* at Madison Square Garden. Frazier becomes undisputed world heavyweight boxing champion.

1973 *Northern Ireland* referendum favors maintenance of ties with the *United Kingdom.*

1976 *Meteorites* fall in northeastern China, with the largest fragment weighing about 3,900 pounds, perhaps largest in recorded history.

1996 *Dr. Jack Kevorkian* is found not guilty in the 1993 assisted suicides of his patients. This is the third time Kevorkian is acquitted of charges.

march

MARCH
9

HOLIDAYS

Belize

Baron Bliss Day
Commemorates the birth of Baron
Bliss, who left his fortune to Belize.

Gibraltar

Commonwealth Day

RELIGIOUS CALENDAR

The Saints

St. Pacian, Bishop of Barcelona. [d.
c. 390]

St. Gregory, Bishop of Nyssa. Also
called *Father of the Fathers.*
[d. c. 395]

St. Bosa, Bishop of York. [d. 705]

St. Frances of Rome, widow and
founder of the Oblates of Tor
de' Specchi. Also called
Francesca Romana or
Frances the Roman. [d. 1440]
Optional Memorial.

St. Catherine of Bologna, virgin and
Abbess of Corpo di Cristo.
Patron of artists. Also called
Katherine of Bologna. [d.
1463]

St. Dominic Savio. [d. 1857]

BIRTHDATES

1451 *Amerigo Vespucci (Americus
Vespucius),* Italian navigator;
early explorer of the New
World; the Americas named
for him. [d. February 22,
1512]

1749 *Gabriel Honoré Rigueti
Mirabeau,* French orator,
statesman; considered one of
most significant figures in
early French Revolutionary
period; President of French
National Assembly, 1791. [d.
April 2, 1791]

1753 *Jean Baptiste Kleber,* French
revolutionary. [d. June 14,
1800]

1773 *Isaac Hull,* U.S. naval
commodore; commander of
U.S.S. Constitution during War
of 1812; under his command,
the ship earned its nickname,
Old Ironsides. [d. February
13, 1843]

1791 *George Hayward,* U.S.
surgeon; credited with being
first surgeon to perform
major surgery using *ether* as
an *anesthetic.* [d. 1863]

1806 *Edwin Forrest,* U.S. actor;
famous for his Shakespearean
roles. [d. December 12, 1872]

1814 *Taras Grigorievich
Shevchenko,* Russian poet,
artist; considered the *Father
of Ukrainian National
Literature.* [d. March 10,
1861]

1824 *A(masa) Leland Stanford,*
U.S. financier, philanthropist,
major California pioneer;
Governor of California,
1861–63; U.S. Senator,
1885–93. *Stanford University*

was founded in memory of
his son, Leland Stanford, Jr.,
who died in 1884 at the age
of 15. [d. June 21, 1893]

1856 *Eddie Foy (Edward
Fitzgerald),* U.S. vaudeville
entertainer; known for his
vaudeville act with his
children, billed as *The Seven
Litle Foys,* 1913–20. [d.
February 16, 1928]

1881 *Ernest Bevin,* British
statesman, labor leader;
Minister of Labour, 1940–45;
Foreign Minister, 1945–51. [d.
April 14, 1951]

1890 *Vyacheslav Mikhailovich
Molotov (V.M. Skryabin),*
Soviet communist leader;
Chairman, Council of People's
Commissars, 1930–41;
Minister for Foreign Affairs,
1949–56; the *Molotov
cocktail* named for him. [d.
November 8, 1986]

1892 *Victoria Mary Sackville-West,*
British novelist, poet, critic.
[d. June 2, 1962]

1902 *Will Geer,* U.S. character
actor. [d. April 22, 1978]

Edward Durell Stone, U.S.
architect; known for his use
of traditional elements in
contemporary designs; early
works are classified as prime
examples of the *International
Style.* [d. August 6, 1978]

1910 *Samuel Barber,* U.S.
composer; Pulitzer Prize in

music, 1958, 1963. [d. January 23, 1981]

1918 *George Lincoln Rockwell,* U.S. political activist; organized American Nazi Party, 1958; advocated violence towards minorities; assassinated. [d. August 25, 1967]

Mickey Spillane (Frank Morrison Spillane), U.S. author; known for his detective novels.

1922 *Floyd (Bixler) McKissick,* U.S. civil rights activist, lawyer; National Director of *Congress of Racial Equality,* 1966–68; developer of *Soul City, North Carolina.* [d. April 28, 1991]

1923 *James Lane Buckley,* U.S. politician, author; Senator, 1971–77; wrote *If Men Were Angels,* 1975.

1925 *G(eorge) William Miller,* U.S. government official, lawyer, business executive; Chairman of Federal Reserve Board, 1978–79; U.S. Secretary of the Treasury, 1979–81.

1930 *Thomas Schippers,* U.S. conductor; conductor of Metropolitan Opera, 1955–77. [d. December 16, 1977]

1934 *Yuri Alekseyevich Gagarin,* Soviet cosmonaut; first man to travel into space, April 12, 1961. [d. March 27, 1968]

1936 *Mickey Leroy Gilley,* U.S. musician; his club, Gilley's, was the setting for the movie, *Urban Cowboy.*

1940 *Raul Julia (Raul Rafael Carlos Julia y Arcelay),* Puerto Rican-born actor. [d. October 24, 1994]

1943 *Robert James (Bobby) Fischer,* U.S. chess player; first American to hold world chess title.

1945 *Robin Trower,* British musician.

Trish Van Devere (Patricia Dressel), U.S. actress; known for starring roles in *Where's Poppa?* and *Day of the Dolphin.*

1947 *David Hume Kennerly,* U.S. photographer; Pulitzer Prize for feature photography of Vietnam War, 1972.

1971 *Emmanuel Lewis,* U.S. actor; known for his role as Webster on television series, *Webster.*

HISTORICAL EVENTS

1074 All *married priests* are excommunicated from Roman Catholic Church.

1551 Hapsburg family declares *Philip II* of Spain the sole heir of *Charles V,* Holy Roman Emperor.

1796 *Napoleon Bonaparte* marries *Josephine de Beauharnais.*

1846 *Kashmir* is ceded to the *British East India Company* by the *Treaty of Lahore,* ending the *First Sikh War.*

1858 The rule of the Mogul emperors ends in India with the banishment of *Bahadur Shah II* by the British for his part in the *Sepoy Mutiny.*

1864 *Ulysses S. Grant* is appointed commander-in-chief of the U.S. Union armies (*U.S. Civil War*).

1869 Great Britain buys the territories of the *Hudson Bay Company.*

1888 *Emperor William I* of Germany dies and is succeeded by *Frederick III.*

1916 Germany declares war on Portugal as a result of

Portugal's seizing German and Austrian shipping in Portuguese harbors (*World War I*).

1917 Capital of Russia is moved from *Leningrad (St. Petersburg, Petrograd)* to *Moscow.*

1920 *Sweden* and the *Netherlands* join the *League of Nations.*

1933 *Emergency Banking Relief Act* is passed by U.S. Congress, giving the President broad discretionary fiscal powers.

The *Hundred Days* begin. President Franklin Roosevelt pushes sweeping social and economic reforms of the *New Deal* through Congress within the next one hundred days.

1942 Great Britain surrenders *Burma* to Japanese troops (*World War II*).

Japanese complete conquest of *Java (World War II).*

1946 *Juho Paasikivi* is elected president of Finland.

1954 Journalist *Edward R. Murrow* accuses Senator *Joseph McCarthy* of misleading the U.S. public and persecuting Congressional witnesses.

1955 *East of Eden,* the film version of John Steinbeck's novel, premieres in New York.

1956 Archbishop *Makarios,* head of the Cypriot Orthodox Church and pro-Greek movement, is deported from Cyprus by British authorities.

Graham Greene's novel, *The Quiet American,* is published in New York.

1961 Radio Moscow announces that U.S.S.R. has orbited and

march

recovered a spaceship carrying a dog and other live biological specimens.

1962 U.S. Department of State confirms that U.S. pilots are flying combat training missions with South Vietnamese airmen over guerrilla-held areas.

1975 Work begins on the 789-mile *Alaskan oil pipeline,* the largest private construction project in U.S. history.

1978 Korean businessman *Park Tong Sun* testifies before the House Ethics Committee pertaining to allegations of South Korean influence-buying on Capitol Hill.

1983 *Anne M. Burford* is forced to resign her post as head of the U.S. *Environmental Protection Agency (EPA)* following a dispute with Congress over the agency's enforcement of toxic waste regulations.

1986 *Mario Soares* is inaugurated as Portugal's first civilian president in 60 years.

1987 *Chrysler Corp.* announces its decision to buy the 46 percent of *American Motors Corp.* owned by the French national auto company, Regie Nationale des Usines Renault. Chrysler also offers to purchase the remainder of the company by swapping its stock for that of AMC.

HOLIDAYS

Korea
Labor Day

RELIGIOUS CALENDAR

The Saints

St. Codratus and his companions, martyrs. [d. c. 258]
The Forty Martyrs of Sebastea, Roman soldiers of The Thundering Legion. [d. 320]
St. Macarius, Bishop of Jerusalem. [d. c. 335]
St. Simplicius, pope. Elected 468. [d. 483]
St. Droctoveus, abbot. Also called *Drotté.* [d. c. 580]
St. Kessog, bishop and martyr; patron of Lennox, Scotland. Also called *Mackessog,* or *Mackessoge.* [d. 6th century]
St. Attalas, abbot. [d. 627]
St. Himelin, priest [d. c. 750]
St. John Ogilvie, Jesuit priest and martyr. [d. 1615]
St. Anastasia Patricia, virgin and hermit. Also called *Anastasius the Eunuch.* [death date unknown]

The Beatified

Blessed Andrew of Strumi, Abbot of San Fedele. [d. 1097]
Blessed John of Vallombrosa, monk and hermit. Also called the *Hermit of the Cells.* [d. c. 1380]
Blessed Peter Geremia, Dominican priest. [d. 1452]

BIRTHDATES

1452 *Ferdinand V* of Castile (Ferdinand II of Aragon). King of Aragon who unified Spain by his marriage to *Isabella I,* Queen of Castile. [d. January 25, 1516]

1503 *Ferdinand I, King of Bohemia* 1526 and Hungary 1527; Holy Roman Emperor, 1558–64. [d. July 25, 1564]

1628 *Marcello Malpighi,* Italian physiologist; called *Founder of Microscopic Anatomy.* [d. November 30, 1694]

1748 *John Playfair,* Scottish geologist, mathematician; promoted and popularized theory of *uniformitarianism.* [d. July 20, 1819]

1749 *Lorenzo da Ponte,* Italian American opera singer, educator; aided the establishment of the Italian Opera House. [d. 1838]

1772 *Friedrich von Schlegel,* German critic, orientalist, poet. [d. January 12, 1829]

1787 *Francisco Martinez de la Rosa,* Spanish writer, statesman; Premier of Spain, 1820–23; 1834; Spanish Ambassador to France, 1847–51. [d. February 7, 1862]

1788 *Joseph Karl Eichendorff,* German poet; member of the Romantic religious group of poets including Friederich von Schlegel (above, 1772). [d. November 26, 1857]

1791 *Angel Saavedra (Ramírez de Baquedano),* Spanish poet, dramatist; the outstanding figure of *Spanish romanticism.* [d. June 22, 1865]

1810 *John McCloskey,* U.S. Roman Catholic clergyman; first president of *St. John's College (Fordham University),* 1841; first U.S. Roman Catholic cardinal, 1875. [d. October 10, 1885]

1833 *Pedro Antonio de Alarcón,* Spanish novelist, journalist; known especially for his short stories, sketches of rustic Spanish life. [d. July 20, 1891]

1845 *Alexander III, Emperor of Russia,* 1881–94; supporter of Russian nationalism; interfered in politics of Balkan States; formed close alliance with France. [d. November 1, 1894]

1867 *Lillian D. Wald,* U.S. social worker, public health nurse; responsible for establishment of first municipally sponsored *public school nursing program* in the world. [d. September 1, 1940]

1886 *Frederic Waller,* U.S. manufacturer, inventor;

developed the *Cinerama* process, 1938. [d. May 18, 1954]

1888 *Barry Fitzgerald (William Joseph Shields),* Irish character actor. [d. January 4, 1961]

Oscar Gottfried Mayer, U.S. meat packer; President, Oscar Mayer Co., 1928–55; Chairman, 1955–65. [d. March 5, 1965]

1891 *Shih-Chieh Wang,* Chinese government official, diplomat, educator; Minister of Foreign Affairs, 1945–48; one of Chiang Kai-shek's most valued and trusted advisers. [d. April, 1981]

1892 *Arthur Oscar Honegger,* French composer; identified as leader of *The Six,* an ultra-modern school of music. [d. November 27, 1955]

1903 *Leon Bismarck (Bix) Beiderbecke,* U.S. jazz cornetist, composer; one of leaders in world of jazz; strongly influenced style of later musicians. [d. August 7, 1931]

1918 *Heywood Hale Broun,* U.S. author, actor, broadcast journalist.

1923 *Val Fitch,* U.S. physicist; Nobel Prize in physics (with James Cronin), 1980.

1928 *James Earl Ray,* U.S. assassin; killed Martin Luther King, Jr., 1968; sentenced to 99 years in prison. [d. April 23, 1998]

1940 *David William Rabe,* U.S. dramatist.

1947 *Robert Bernard (Bob) Greene, Jr.,* U.S. journalist; wrote *Billion Dollar Baby,* 1974.

1958 *Sharon Stone,* U.S. actress.

1964 *Edward Antony Richard Louis,* British prince; third son of Queen Elizabeth II.

1965 *Rod Woodson,* U.S. football player.

1966 *Edie Brickell,* U.S. pop singer; formerly with Edie Brickell & the New Bohemians; wife of U.S. pop singer Paul Simon (October 13, 1941).

1977 *Shannon Miller,* U.S. gymnast; winner of five Olympic medals, 1992, 1996.

HISTORICAL EVENTS

1528 *Hubmaier,* leader of Austrian Anabaptists, is burned at the stake in Vienna.

1624 England declares war on France (*Thirty Years' War*).

1839 Imperial Commissioner *Lin Tse-hsu* arrives in Canton and is forced to surrender and burn opium shipments (*First Opium War*).

1862 Great Britain and France recognize the independence of *Zanzibar.*

1863 The Prince of Wales (later *Edward VII* of England) is married to Princess Alexandra of Denmark.

1876 *Alexander Graham Bell* transmits first complete intelligible sentence by *telephone.*

1880 George Scott Raiton presides over the first U.S. open air meeting of the *Salvation Army* in Battery Park, New York.

1893 The name of the *Rivières du Sud* colony is changed to *French Guinea.*

The *Ivory Coast* is constituted as a French colony.

1900 A definitive treaty is signed between *Uganda* and *Great Britain* regulating the form of government in Uganda.

1911 France adopts *Greenwich time* as legal standard.

1912 *Yüan Shih-K'ai* is installed as first President of the *Republic of China,* ending two millenia of monarchy and empire.

1914 Militant suffragists mutilate Velásquez's *Venus with the Mirror* in National Gallery, London.

1915 The British launch a vigorous attack on the Germans in the start of the *Battle of Neuve Chapelle (World War I).*

1917 The *Second Battle of Monastir* opens in Serbian Macedonia with an Allied offensive (*World War I*).

A general mutiny of Russian troops occurs in the capital of St. Petersburg (*Russian Revolution*).

1922 *Mahatma Gandhi* is arrested by the British government of India for sedition.

1944 General *Edelmiro Farrell* becomes the president of Argentina following the resignation of *Pedro Ramirez.*

1952 *Fulgencio Batista* executes a coup d'état in *Cuba,* preventing popular elections and assuming military control of the country.

1959 Tennessee Williams's play, *Sweet Bird of Youth,* opens on Broadway.

1966 Violent clashes among Hindus, Punjabi-speaking Sikhs, and police, break out following a decision by India's ruling Congress Party to create a Punjabi-speaking state within the existing state of Punjab.

1969 *James Earl Ray* pleads guilty to the assassination of the Rev. Martin Luther King, Jr., and is sentenced to 99 years in prison.

1971 *William McMahon* is inaugurated as prime minister of Australia.

1972 Morocco promulgates its Constitution.

1976 Critics of the South Korean government of President *Park Chung Hee* are arrested.

Former U.S. President *Richard M. Nixon* testifies that he ordered wiretapping in 1969 and that *Henry Kissinger* selected those to be tapped.

1987 Ireland's parliament elects *Charles Haughey* as prime minister.

The Vatican declares its opposition to *test-tube fertilization, embryo transfer,* and most other forms of scientific interference in procreation.

1998 President *Ahmad Tejan Kabbah* returns to power in Sierra Leone after ten months in exile.

march

MARCH
11

HOLIDAYS

Lithuania

Day of Independence Restored
Marks the date in 1990 when the Republic of Lithuania was reestablished breaking all ties with the former Soviet Union.

RELIGIOUS CALENDAR

The Saints

St. Constantine, King of Cornwall, Abbot of Govan, and first martyr of Scotland. [d. 6th century]

St. Sophronius, Patriarch of Jerusalem. Surnamed the *Sophist.* [d. c. 638]

St. Vindician, Bishop of Cambrai. [d. 712]

St. Benedict, Archbishop of Milan. [d. 725]

St. Oengus, abbot and bishop. Also called *Aengus, Culdee* or *Kele-De* [d. c. 824]

St. Eulogius of Córdova, priest and martyr; patron of carpenters. Wrote *The Memorial of the Saints,* a 7-year chronicle of the suffering of other martyrs. [d. 859]

St. Aurea, virgin and nun. [d. c. 1100]

St. Teresa Margaret Redi, virgin and Carmelite nun. Also called *Teresa-Margaret-of-the-Sacred-Heart.* [d. 1770]

The Beatified

Blessed John Larke, Jermyn Gardiner and *John Ireland,*
martyrs. Jermyn also called *German Gardiner.* [d. 1544]

Blessed Christopher Macassoli, Franciscan priest. [d. 1485]

Blessed John Baptist of Fabriano, priest. [d. 1539]

BIRTHDATES

1544 *Torquato Tasso,* Italian poet; best known for his heroic epic poem, *Jerusalem Delivered.* [d. April 25, 1595]

1731 *Robert Treat Paine,* American public official, judge; signer of the Declaration of Independence. [d. May 11, 1814]

1811 *Urbain Le Verrier,* French astronomer; one of the first to predict existence of planet *Neptune.* [d. September 23, 1877]

1822 *Marius Petipa,* French dancer, choreographer. [d. June 2, 1910]

1885 *Sir Malcolm Campbell,* British businessman, race-car driver; established numerous early speed records. [d. December 31, 1948]

1890 *Vannevar Bush,* U.S. electrical engineer; headed U.S. scientific war effort and early research on the *atomic bomb.* [d. June 28, 1974]

1892 *Thomas T(roy) Handy,* U.S. Army general; after World War
II, was commander of all American forces in Europe. [d. April 14, 1982]

Raoul Walsh, U.S. film director. [d. December 31, 1980]

1897 *Henry Dixon Cowell,* U.S. composer; a pioneer in *experimental music;* developed the *rhythmica,* an early electronic musical instrument. [d. December 10, 1965]

1898 *Dorothy Gish (Dorothy de Guiche),* U.S. silent-screen actress. [d. June 4, 1968]

1899 *Frederick IX, King of Denmark,* 1947–72; encouraged Danish resistance to the Nazi occupation during World War II. [d. January 14, 1972]

1903 *Lawrence Welk,* U.S. bandleader, television host. [d. May 17, 1992]

1916 *Sir (James) Harold Wilson,* British statesman, economist; Prime Minister, 1964–70, 1974–76. [d. May 24, 1995]

1919 *Mercer Ellington,* U.S. musician, band leader; son of Duke Ellington. [d. February 8, 1996]

1920 *Nicolaas Bloembergen,* Dutch physicist; Nobel Prize in physics for his work in spectroscopy (with Arthur L. Schawlow), 1981.

1921 *Charlotte Friend,* U.S. microbiologist; known for her research on cancer-causing viruses.

1926 *Ralph Abernathy,* U.S. civil rights leader, clergyman; President of *Southern Christian Leadership Conference.* [d. April 17, 1990]

1931 *(Keith) Rupert Murdoch,* Australian publisher.

1934 *Sam(uel Andrew) Donaldson,* U.S. broadcast journalist.

1936 *Antonin Scalia,* U.S. judge; Supreme Court Justice, 1986– .

1950 *Jerry Zucker,* U.S. director.

Bobby McFerrin, U.S. singer, musician.

1952 *Douglas Noel Adams,* British author; wrote *The Hitchhiker's Guide to the Galaxy,* 1979.

HISTORICAL EVENTS

1824 The *Bureau of Indian Affairs* is created in the U.S. War Department.

1898 The British reopen the *Khyber Pass* after quelling the *Afridi uprising.*

1915 The Germans begin a new offensive against the Russians near Przasnyz, Poland *(World War I).*

1917 *Baghdad* is captured by British forces *(World War I).*

1918 *Universal suffrage* is decreed in Portugal.

1920 *Faisal I* is proclaimed *King of Syria* by the Syrian National Congress.

1925 *No No Nanette* by Vincent Youmans opens in London.

1935 The *Bank of Canada* opens as a privately-owned and government-controlled corporation.

1936 Rafael Franco proclaims a totalitarian state in *Paraguay.*

1941 U.S. Congress maintains neutrality but passes *Lend-Lease Act* enabling England to borrow aircraft, weapons, and merchant ships.

1959 Lorraine Hansberry's play, *A Raisin in the Sun,* opens in New York. It is the first play by a black woman to appear on Broadway.

1960 *Pioneer V,* U.S. planetoid, is launched from Cape Canaveral, Florida, into orbit around the sun.

1964 *Raul Leoni* is inaugurated as president of Venezuela, succeeding *Romulo Betancourt.* It marks the first transition of power between popularly-elected presidents in Venezuelan history.

South Africa withdraws from the International Labour Organization.

1968 Major riots occur in *Poland* as tens of thousands of Poles protest government inference in cultural affairs.

1969 *Rafael Caldera Rodriguez* is inaugurated as president of Venezuela.

1970 *Iraq* recognizes the autonomy of the *Kurdish people,* ending over eight years of warfare.

Brazilian revolutionaries kidnap *Nobuo Okuchi,* Japanese consul general in São Paulo.

1973 Peronista presidential candidate *Héctor J. Cámpora* is the victor in the first Argentine election since 1965.

1976 The *Dow Jones* industrial stock average passes the 1,000 mark.

1981 *General Augusto Pinochet* declares himself President of Chile for an 8-year term.

1982 U.S. Senator *Harrison Williams* resigns his Senate seat as a result of being charged with misconduct; he is the first Senator to do so in over 60 years.

1985 *Bernard St. John* is inaugurated as prime minister of *Barbados.*

Mikhail Gorbachev is chosen to succeed *Konstantin Chernenko* as general secretary of the Soviet Communist Party.

1988 Former National Security Advisor, *Robert McFarlane,* pleads guilty to withholding information from Congress during the *Iran-contra affair.*

U.S. attorney general, Edward Meese, officially orders the closure of the *Palestine Liberation Organization* observer mission to the United Nations.

1990 The Parliament of *Lithuania* votes to secede from the Soviet Union. *Mikhail Gorbachev* stops oil shipments to Lithuania in an attempt to stop the country's independence movement.

1994 *Eduardo Frei* is sworn in as the president of Chile.

1996 The *Whitewater trial* begins in Little Rock, Arkansas. Governor Jim Guy Tucker and James and Susan McDougal are accused of obtaining money under false pretenses. U.S. President *Bill Clinton*

march

and his wife *Hillary Rodham Clinton* were partners with the defendants in the Whitewater Development Corporation.

1998 *President Suharto* is re-elected in Indonesia.

HOLIDAYS

Gabon Republic
Anniversary of Renewal or Renovation Day

Lesotho
Moshoeshoe's Day
Honors the tribal leader who consolidated the *Bosotho* nation, now Lesotho, in the 19th century.

Mauritius
Independence Day or National Day
Commemorates the attainment of independence from Great Britain, 1968.

Taiwan
Arbor Day
The death of Dr. Sun Yat-Sen on this day in 1925 is commemorated by the planting of trees.

RELIGIOUS CALENDAR

The Saints
St. Maximilian, martyr. [d. 295]
SS. Peter, Gorgonius, and *Dorotheus,* martyrs. [d. 303]
St. Paul Aurelian, Bishop of Léon. Also called *Paulinus,* or *Pol de Léon.* [d. c. 573]
St. Mura, abbot; founder of the monastery of Fahan. Also called *Muranus* or *Muru.* [d. 7th century]
St. Theophanes the Chronicler, Abbot of Mount Sigriana. [d. 817]
St. Alphege, Bishop of Winchester. Also called the *Bald Elder.* [d. 951]

St. Bernard of Capua, Bishop of Caleno. [d. 1109]
St. Fina, virgin. Also called *Seraphina.* [d. 1253]

The Beatified
Blessed Justina of Arezzo, virgin and anchoress. [d. 1319]
Blessed Aloisius Orione. [beatified, 1980]

BIRTHDATES

1613 *André LeNôtre,* French landscape gardener; called *Gardener of Kings and King of Gardeners.* [d. September 15, 1700]

1626 *John Aubrey,* English antiquary and author; known for his biographical sketches of Milton, Raleigh, and Hobbes, among others. [d. June 1697]

1685 *George Berkeley,* Irish philosopher, Anglican bishop; known for development of philosophy of *subjective idealism.* [d. January 14, 1753]

1710 *Thomas Augustine Arne,* English composer; composed *Rule Britannia.* [d. March 5, 1778]

1795 *William Lyon Mackenzie,* Canadian statesman. [d. August 28, 1861]

1806 *Jane Pierce,* wife of U.S. President Franklin Pierce. [d. December 2, 1863]

1831 *Clement Studebaker,* U.S. wagon, carriage, and auto manufacturer; founder of Studebaker Corporation, 1902. [d. November 27, 1901]

1832 *Charles Cunningham Boycott,* British land-estate manager; became subject of economic and social isolation practices of *Irish Land League* agitators. The term *boycott* comes from his name. [d. June 19, 1897]

1835 *Simon Newcomb,* U.S. astronomer, mathematician. Revised motion theories and position tables for all the major celestial reference objects; responsible for adoption of universal system of *astronomical constants;* a founder and first president of the *American Astronomical Society.* [d. July 11, 1909]

1838 *Sir William Henry Perkin,* British chemist; discovered and produced *mauve,* the first of the synthetic aniline dyes. [d. July 14, 1907]

1858 *Adolph Simon Ochs,* Publisher of the *New York Times,* 1896–1935; responsible for funding publication of the *Dictionary of American Biography.* [d. April 8, 1935]

1862 *Jane Delano,* U.S. nurse; organized *Red Cross Nursing Service,* 1911. [d. 1919]

1863 *Gabriele d'Annunzio,* Italian author, political leader, soldier; a popular hero of World War I; known for his voluminous output of poetry, short stories, and novels. [d. March 1, 1938]

1864 *William Halse Rivers,* British physiologist, anthropologist; founder of *Cambridge School of Experimental Psychology.* [d. June 4, 1922]

1866 *Sun Yat-sen,* founder of the Republic of China. [d. 1925]

1880 *Kemal Atatürk,* Turkish military leader; first President of the Turkish Republic, 1923–38. [d. November 10, 1938]

1890 *Vaslav Nijinsky,* Russian ballet dancer; member of Diaghilev's *Ballet Russe;* became insane during later life and was committed to an asylum. [d. April 8, 1950]

1910 *Masayoshi Ohira,* Japanese politician; Prime Minister, 1978–80. [d. June 12, 1980]

1912 *Les(ter Raymond) Brown,* U.S. band leader; known for accompanying Bob Hope; wrote *Sentimental Journey.*

1921 *Gordon MacRae,* U.S. actor, singer; known for his starring roles in *Oklahoma,* 1955, and *Carousel,* 1956. [d. January 24, 1986]

1922 *Jack Kerouac,* U.S. author; associated with the beat generation. [d. October 21, 1969]

(Joseph) Lane Kirkland, U.S. labor leader; President of AFL-CIO, 1979–95.

1923 *Walter Marty Schirra, Jr.,* U.S. astronaut; participated in Mercury *Sigma 7* space flight,

1962; commanded *Gemini 6,* 1965, and *Apollo 7,* 1968, space flights.

1925 *Leo Esaki,* Japanese physicist; Nobel Prize in physics for research on *superconductors* (with I. Giaever and B. D. Josephson), 1973; President, University of Tsukuba, Japan, 1992– .

1928 *Edward Franklin Albee,* U.S. dramatist; Pulitzer Prize in drama, 1967, 1975.

1932 *Andrew Young,* U.S. politician, clergyman; the first black to win a Democratic nomination for Congress from the South in over 100 years; Mayor of Atlanta, Georgia, 1982–89.

1940 *Al Jarreau,* U.S. singer; two Grammy Awards for best jazz vocalist, 1978, 1979.

1941 *Barbara Feldon,* U.S. actress; known for her role as Agent 99 on television series, *Get Smart,* 1965–70.

1942 *Paul Kantner,* U.S. singer, musician; member of the rock group, *Jefferson Airplane/Starship.*

1946 *Liza Minnelli,* U.S. singer, actress.

1948 *Mark DeWayne Mosely,* U.S. football player.

James Taylor, U.S. folk-rock singer, guitarist, composer.

1957 *Marlon David Jackson,* U.S. singer; member of the rock group, *The Jacksons.*

1962 *Darryl Eugene Strawberry,* U.S. baseball player; National League Rookie of the Year, 1983.

HISTORICAL EVENTS

1799 Austria declares war on France (*War of the Second Coalition*).

1814 *Duke of Wellington* takes Bordeaux (*Peninsular War*).

1849 *Sikhs* surrender to the British at Rawalpindi.

1854 Great Britain, France, and Turkey form an alliance against Russia (*Crimean War*).

1868 *Basutoland* is annexed by British Cape Colony.

1888 *The Great Blizzard of '88* hits the north-eastern United States, paralyzing all major cities and causing the deaths of more than 400 people.

1912 First patrol of *Girl Guides,* forerunner of *Girl Scouts,* is formed by *Juliet Low.*

1917 The *Petrograd Soviet of Workers and Soldiers Deputies* is organized as part of the continuing revolutionary unrest in Russia.

1922 Armenia, Azerbaijan, and Georgia establish the *Trans-Caucasian Soviet Socialist Republic.*

First transatlantic radio broadcast is made.

1930 Indian leader *Mahatma Gandhi* begins his second *civil disobedience* campaign to protest the British government's salt tax.

1933 U.S. President *Franklin D. Roosevelt* delivers his first *fireside chat,* a nationwide radio address.

1934 *Konstantin Paets,* aided by the military, sets up a virtual dictatorship in *Estonia.*

1938 Germany invades and annexes *Austria (World War II)*.

1940 *Russo-Finnish War* ends with significant territorial gains by the U.S.S.R.

1962 British ministries of Health and Education start a drive to inform the British public of the dangers of *cigarette smoking*.

1965 U.S. Marines in South Vietnam engage in their first skirmish with Viet Cong forces (*Vietnam War*).

1966 President *Ahmed Sukarno* transfers executive powers to General *Suharto* in the aftermath of an abortive coup staged by the Indonesian Communist Party.

1968 *Mauritius* achieves independence from Great Britain.

1970 U.S. lowers voting age to 18 years.

1971 Syrian Premier *Hafez al-Assad* is elected President of Syria in a national referendum.

1973 Syrian electorate approves a new permanent constitution.

1974 *Carlos Andres Perez* is inaugurated as president of Venezuela.

1979 *Luis Herrera Campins* is inaugurated as President of Venezuela.

1986 *Ingvar Carlsson* is inaugurated as prime minister of Sweden.

1993 *Janet Reno* is sworn in as the first female attorney general of the United States.

North Korea announces that it is withdrawing from the *Nuclear Nonproliferation Treaty*.

1994 The *Church of England* ordains the first women priests.

march

MARCH
13

HOLIDAYS

Grenada
National Day
Commemorates Grenada Revolution, 1979.

RELIGIOUS CALENDAR

The Saints
St. Euphrasia, virgin and nun. Also called *Eupraxia.* [d. c. 420]
St. Mochoemoc, abbot. [d. 7th century]
St. Gerald of Mayo, abbot. [d. 732]
St. Nicephorus, Patriarch of Constantinople. [d. 828]
St. Ansovinus, Bishop of Camerino; patron saint and protector of crops. [d. 840]
St. Heldrad, abbot. [d. c. 842]
SS. Roderic and *Solomon,* martyrs. [d. 857]

The Beatified
Blessed Agnello of Pisa, founder of the English Franciscan province. [d. 1236]

BIRTHDATES

1615 *Pope Innocent XII,* reigned 1691–1700. [d. September 17, 1700]

1720 *Charles Bonnet,* Swiss naturalist, philosopher; discovered *parthenogenesis.* [d. May 20, 1793]

1733 *Joseph Priestley,* English chemist, clergyman, political radical; research resulted in discovery of *oxygen, ammonia, sulfur dioxide, hydrogen chloride.* [d. February 6, 1804]

1741 *Josef II, King of Germany* and Holy Roman Emperor, 1765–90, one of the *enlightened despots* of 18th-century Europe. [d. February 20, 1790]

1764 *Charles Grey,* Second Earl Grey, English statesman; Foreign Secretary, 1806–07, Prime Minister, 1830–34. [d. July 17, 1845]

1798 *Abigail Fillmore,* first wife of U.S. President Millard Fillmore. [d. March 30, 1853]

1813 *Lorenzo Delmonico,* U.S. restaurateur, born in Switzerland; dubbed *Father of American Restaurants;* owner and operator of the first and largest restaurant in America, 1832–81. [d. September 13, 1881]

1855 *Percival Lowell,* U.S. astronomer; known for research on planet *Mars;* postulated the existence of a planet beyond *Neptune* which ultimately led to the discovery of *Pluto;* brother of the poet Amy Lowell. [d. November 12, 1916]

1857 *Herbert Charles Onslow Plumer,* 1st Viscount Plumer, British army field marshal; Governor of Malta, 1919–25. [d. July 16, 1932]

1860 *Hugo Wolf,* Austrian composer; a disciple of Wagner. [d. February 22, 1903]

1869 *Ramón Menéndez Pidal,* Spanish literary historian, linguist. [d. November 14, 1968]

1872 *Oswald Garrison Villard,* U.S. editor, journalist; founder of *The Nation,* a journal of social protest. [d. October 1, 1949]

1884 *Hugh Walpole,* British novelist. [d. 1941]

1887 *Alexander Archer Vandegrift,* U.S. Marine Corps general; in charge of troop landing at *Guadalcanal,* 1942. [d. May 8, 1973]

1892 *Janet Flanner,* U.S. journalist, correspondent for *The New Yorker* for nearly 50 years. [d. November 7, 1978]

1899 *John Hasbrouck Van Vleck,* U.S. physicist; Nobel Prize in physics for contributions to development of *solid state circuitry* (with N.F. Mott and P.W. Anderson), 1977. [d. November 28, 1980]

1900 *Giorgos Seferis (Giorgos Sefiriades),* Greek poet; Nobel Prize in literature, 1963. [d. September 20, 1971]

1908 *Walter Hubert Annenberg,* U.S. publisher, diplomat; Ambassador to Great Britain, 1969–75.

1911 *L(afayette) Ron(ald) Hubbard,* U.S. science fiction writer, religious leader; founder of *Scientology.* [d. January 24, 1986]

1913 *William Joseph Casey,* U.S. lawyer, author; Ronald Reagan's campaign manager, 1980; Director, Central Intelligence Agency, 1981–87. [d. May 6, 1987]

Sammy Kaye, U.S. bandleader. [d. June 2, 1987]

1914 *Edward Henry O'Hare,* U.S. Navy officer, aviator. Chicago's *O'Hare Airport* is named for him. [d. November 27, 1943]

1916 *Corinne C. (Lindy) Boggs,* U.S. politician; Congresswoman, 1973–91.

1939 *Neil Sedaka,* U.S. singer, songwriter.

1947 *Lyn St. James,* U.S. race car driver; named first woman rookie of the year, Indianapolis 500, 1992.

1953 *Deborah Raffin,* U.S. actress, model; known for her starring roles in *The Dove* and *Once Is Not Enough.*

1956 *Dana Delaney,* U.S. actress.

HISTORICAL EVENTS

1470 Yorkists defeat Lancastrians at *Battle of Stamford.*

1781 *Sir William Herschel,* English astronomer, discovers planet *Georgium Sidres,* later named *Uranus.*

1806 *Gustavus IV* of Sweden is deposed, and the crown is assumed by his uncle, who becomes *Charles XIII.*

1813 Sweden joins the *Grand Alliance* against Napoleon's France and its allies.

1848 *Prince Clemens Metternich* of Austria resigns under pressure of a mob in Vienna; the ruler of Austria since 1809, he maintained unprecedented stability there by repressing liberal ideas.

1861 Richard Wagner's opera, *Tannhäuser,* premieres in Paris.

1865 Confederate Congress agrees to the recruitment of *slaves* into the army *(U.S. Civil War).*

1881 *Czar Alexander II* of Russia dies in the explosion of a bomb thrown at him as he rides through the streets of St. Petersburg.

1884 *Somali Coast, Nigeria,* and *New Guinea* become British protectorates.

1900 *Bloemfontein,* the Orange Free State, surrenders to Lord Frederick Roberts in the *Boer War* and the government of the Free State retires to Kroonstad.

1904 *Christ of the Andes,* a bronze statue of Christ on the Argentine-Chile border, is dedicated.

1907 *New York stock market* drop sets off *Panic of 1907.*

1915 The *Battle of Neuve Chapelle* ends as a limited British victory. *(World War I).*

The Swedish vessel *Hana* becomes the first neutral ship to be sunk by a German submarine in World War I.

1917 Russian revolutionaries seize the *Winter Palace* in Petrograd (St. Petersburg).

1938 Hitler takes formal possession of Vienna *(World War II).*

Léon Blum forms the *Popular Front* Ministry in France.

1947 Frederick Loewe's musical fantasy *Brigadoon* premieres in New York.

1954 The *Viet-Minh* begin a successful siege of the French-held *Dien Bien Phu* in Vietnam.

1961 *Floyd Patterson* defeats *Ingemar Johansson* in professional heavyweight championship bout.

1963 Soviets establish *Supreme Council of National Economy* to coordinate national economic planning.

1968 Oil is discovered at *Prudhoe Bay* in Alaska.

1969 U.S. *Apollo 9* spacecraft splashes down in the Atlantic Ocean after a ten-day flight testing the *lunar module.*

1972 United Kingdom and People's Republic of China establish diplomatic relations at the ambassadorial level.

Clifford Irving and his wife, Edith, plead guilty to conspiring to defraud *McGraw-Hill* by selling it a fake autobiography of *Howard Hughes.*

1979 The *Common Market* officially inaugurates the new *European Monetary System* (EMS).

Sir Eric Gairy is ousted as Prime Minister of *Grenada. Maurice Bishop,* leader of the *New Jewel Movement,* takes power.

march

1988 *Irving Jordan, Jr.,* becomes the first deaf president of *Gallaudet University.* The appointment follows a week of student protests over a board of trustees decision to appoint *Elizabeth Zinser,* who is not hearing impaired and had no experience with deaf students.

1989 The space shuttle *Discovery* is launched to record global damage of Earth.

1996 In *Dunblane, Scotland,* sixteen children and a teacher are killed when *Thomas Hamilton* opens fire with handguns. Hamilton then kills himself.

RELIGIOUS CALENDAR

The Saints

St. Leobinus, Bishop of Chartres. Also called *Lubin.* [d. c. 558]

St. Eutychius, martyr. Also called *Eustathius.* [d. 741]

St. Matilda, Queen of Germany and widow. Also called *Mathilda, Mathildis,* or *Maud.* [d. 968]

The Beatified

Blessed James, Archbishop of Naples. [d. 1308]

BIRTHDATES

1681 *Georg Philipp Telemann,* German baroque composer; composed over 600 overtures and 40 operas. [d. June 25, 1767]

1750 *Caroline Lucretia Herschel,* English astronomer; discovered seven comets; sister of Sir William Herschel. [d. January 9, 1848]

1782 *Thomas Hart Benton,* U.S. politician; U.S. Senator, 1820–50; U.S. Representative, 1852–54; strongly opposed to the abolition of slavery. [d. April 10, 1858]

1800 *James Bogardus,* U.S. inventor; designed the world's first *cast-iron construction,* in New York City. [d. April 13, 1874]

1804 *Johann Strauss, the Elder,* Austrian composer, conductor; composed over 150 waltzes, 19 marches. [d. September 24, 1849]

1816 *William Marsh Rice,* U.S. merchant, philanthropist; bequeathed his fortune for founding of *Rice Institute,* Houston, Texas. [d. September 23, 1900]

1820 *Victor Emmanuel II,* first king of modern, united *Italy,* 1871–78. [d. January 9, 1878]

1835 *Giovanni Virginio Schiaparelli,* Italian astronomer, the discoverer of the canals on Mars. [d. July 4, 1910]

1837 *Charles Ammi Cutter,* U.S. librarian; devised *Cutter system* of book labeling by alphanumeric code. [d. September 6, 1903]

1844 *Sir Thomas Lauder Brunton,* Scottish pharmacologist, physician; best known for his research on *circulation.* [d. September 16, 1916]

1854 *Paul Ehrlich,* German bacteriologist; Nobel Prize in physiology or medicine for work in *immunology* (with E. Metchnikoff), 1908. [d. August 20, 1915]

Thomas Riley Marshall, U.S. politician; Governor of Indiana, 1909–13; U.S. Vice-President, 1913–21. [d. June 1, 1925]

1862 *Vilhelm F. K. Bjerknes,* Norwegian physicist; proposed theory of *electric resonance,* which aided development of *wireless telegraphy.* [d. April 9, 1951]

1864 *John Luther (Casey) Jones,* U.S. railroad engineer memorialized in *Ballad of Casey Jones.* [d. April 30, 1900]

1875 *Isadore Gilbert Mudge,* U.S. librarian, author, bibliographer; an award for distinguished service in bibliography is given in her name annually by the American Library Association. [d. May 17, 1957]

1879 *Albert Einstein,* German-American physicist; one of the foremost scientists of all time, responsible for the *theory of relativity;* Nobel Prize in physics for his explanation of the photoelectric effect, which verified the quantum theory proposed by Max Planck, 1921. [d. April 18, 1955]

1923 *Diane Arbus,* U.S. photographer. [Suicide July 26, 1971]

1925 *William Clay Ford,* U.S. auto executive; brother of Henry Ford, II; owner, Detroit Lions, 1964– .

1928 *Frank Borman,* U.S. astronaut, piloted first

manned flight around the moon, 1968; currently Chairman of the Board of Eastern Airlines.

Michael Caine (Maurice Micklewhite), British actor.

1933 *Quincy Delight Jones*, U.S. composer; known for writing scores for over 50 films including *The Wiz*, 1978.

1942 *Rita Tushingham*, British actress; known for her roles in *A Taste of Honey*, 1961, and *Dr. Zhivago*, 1965.

1947 *William (Billy) Crystal*, U.S. actor, comedian; known for his starring role in television series, *Soap*, 1977–81; also known for his performances in the movies *When Harry Met Sally*, 1989 and *City Slickers*, 1991.

1954 *Adrian Zmed*, U.S. actor; known for his starring roles in *Grease II* and on television series *T.J. Hooker*.

1958 *Albert (Alexandre Louis Pierre Grimaldi)*, Monacan prince; son of Prince Rainier and Princess Grace; heir to the Monacan throne.

1961 *Kirby Puckett*, U.S. baseball player; six-time Gold Glove winner.

1969 *Larry Johnson*, U.S. basketball player.

HISTORICAL EVENTS

1369 *Peter of Castile* is defeated at *Monteil (Hundred Years' War)*.

1489 *Catherine Cornaro, Queen of Cyprus*, cedes her kingdom to Venice.

1558 *Ferdinand I* assumes title of *Holy Roman Emperor*, the

first to do so without being crowned by the Pope.

1590 *Henry IV, King of Navarre (Henry III* of France), defeats the Catholic League at Ivry (Ypres).

1647 Treaty of neutrality between Bavaria, France, and Sweden, is signed at *Ulm (Thirty Years' War)*.

Frederick Henry, Dutch stadholder, dies and is succeeded by *William II* as Dutch ruler.

1794 *Eli Whitney* patents the *cotton gin*.

1849 The Sikhs surrender unconditionally to the British in India *(Second Sikh War)*.

1864 *Sir Samuel White Baker* discovers *Lake Albert Nyanza* in East Africa.

1872 *Sir Henry Morton Stanley* leaves *David Livingstone* at *Unyamwize* in Central Africa, bringing away his diary and other documents.

1885 *The Mikado*, a comic opera by *Gilbert and Sullivan*, premieres in London.

1888 *Sino-American treaty* is signed, allowing Chinese immigration to the U.S. for twenty years.

1891 The first submarine telephone line is put into place across the English channel.

1900 U.S. Congress adopts *gold standard*.

1904 The anti-European rebellion led by the native society, the *Silent Ones*, in Southern Nigeria is suppressed by the British.

1915 German cruiser *Dresden* is sunk *(World War I)*.

1917 Germany begins retreat to *Hindenburg Line (World War I)*.

The czar's train is stopped at Pskov, Russia, by revolutionaries, and *Czar Nicholas II* is placed under arrest.

1945 The U.S. Air Force begins bombing *Osaka, Japan (World War II)*.

1951 *Seoul*, capital of South Korea, is recaptured without opposition by UN forces *(Korean War)*.

1955 King *Tribhubana* of Nepal dies and is succeeded by his son, Crown Prince *Mahendra*.

1962 India annexes the former Portuguese enclaves of *Goa, Diu*, and *Damao*.

1964 *Jack Ruby* is found guilty in Dallas of the murder of *Lee Harvey Oswald*, accused assassin of U.S. President *John F. Kennedy*, and is sentenced to death.

1968 U.S. command in Saigon reports that the number of U.S. casualties in *Vietnam* has exceeded those in the *Korean War*.

1970 *Japanese World Exposition, Expo 70*, opens in Osaka.

1974 *Kurdish rebels* seize a large area on the Iraqi border with Turkey.

1978 By a unanimous vote, the UN Security Council rejects as illegal and unacceptable Rhodesia's plan for *black majority rule*. Great Britain, U.S., Canada, France, and West Germany abstain from voting.

1983 The *Organization of Petroleum Exporting*

Countries (OPEC) agrees to lower the benchmark price for crude oil by 15%. It marks the first price cut since the group's formation in 1960.

1988 The U.S. Senate unanimously ratifies an international treaty to limit the use of *chloroflurocarbons (CFCs),* which damage the earth's protective *ozone layer.*

MARCH
15

HOLIDAYS

Ides of March
Day on which Julius Caesar was
assassinated, 44 B.C.

Belarus
Constitution Day
(1994)

Hungary
Hungarian Revolution Anniversary
(1848–49)

Liberia
J. J. Roberts' Birthday
Honors Liberia's first president, born
on this day, 1809.

U.S. (Maine)
Admission Day
Commemorates Maine's admission
to the Union, 1820.

RELIGIOUS CALENDAR

The Saints
St. Longinus, martyr. [d. 1st century]
St. Zachary, pope. Elected 741. [d.
    752]
St. Leocritia, virgin and martyr. Also
    called *Lucretia.* [d. 859]
St. Louisa de Marillac, widow and
    cofounder of the Vincentian
    Sisters of Charity. Also called
    Louise de Marillac. [d. 1660]
St. Clement Hofbauer, priest;
    founder of the Redemptorists.
    [d. 1820]
St. Matrona, virgin and martyr.
    [death date unknown]

The Beatified
Blessed William Hart, martyr. [d.
    1583]

Blessed Placid Riccardi, Benedictine
    monk. [d. 1915]

BIRTHDATES

1767 *Andrew Jackson,* U.S. soldier,
    lawyer, military hero of the
    War of 1812; seventh
    President of the United
    States. [d. June 8, 1845]

1779 *William Lamb,* 2nd Viscount
    Melbourne, British statesman;
    Prime Minister, 1835–41;
    political advisor to Queen
    Victoria. [d. November 24,
    1848]

1794 *Friedrich Christian Diez,*
    German linguist; called
    *Founder of Romance
    linguistics.* [d. May 29, 1876]

1830 *Paul Johann Ludwig von
    Heyse,* German short-story
    writer, novelist, poet; Nobel
    Prize in literature, 1910. [d.
    April 2, 1914]

1838 *Alice Cunningham Fletcher,*
    U.S. ethnologist, author;
    pioneer in the study of
    American Indian music. [d.
    May 22, 1932]

1842 *Robert C. Delarge,* U.S.
    Congressman, 1871–73. [d.
    1874]

1854 *Emil von Behring,* German
    physician, immunologist;
    discoverer of *diphtheria
    antitoxin* and *bovovaccine;*

Nobel Prize in physiology or
    medicine for research in
    serum therapy, 1901. [d.
    March 31, 1917]

1858 *Liberty Hyde Bailey,* U.S.
    botanist, horticulturist;
    organized first college
    department of horticulture in
    U.S., 1884. [d. December 25,
    1954]

1874 *Harold LeClair Ickes,* U.S.
    public official. [d. February 3,
    1952]

1887 *Marjorie Merriweather Post,*
    U.S. business executive; Post
    Cereal heiress; wife of E.F.
    Hutton; mother of Dina
    Merrill. [d. September 12,
    1973]

1900 *Luigi Longo,* Italian political
    leader; Secretary General of
    Italian Communist Party,
    1964–72; a founder of the
    party, 1921; recognized as a
    major anti-Mussolini force in
    World War II. [d. October 16,
    1980]

1907 *Jimmy McPartland (James
    Dulgald McPartland),* U.S.
    jazz cornetist. [d. March 13,
    1991]

1912 *Sam (Lightnin') Hopkins,* U.S.
    songwriter, blues singer. [d.
    January 30, 1982]

1914 *(Edward) MacDonald Carey,*
    known for his role as Tom
    Horton on television soap
    opera, *Days of Our Lives.* [d.
    March 21, 1994]

1915 *David Franz Schoenbrun,* U.S. journalist. [d. May 23, 1988]

1916 *Harry James,* U.S. trumpeter, bandleader. [d. July 5, 1983]

1920 *Thomas E. Donnall,* U.S. physician; 1990 Nobel Prize for Medicine. Donnall shares the prize with Joseph E. Murray for their work on transplant techniques.

1926 *Norm Van Brocklin,* U.S. football player, coach. [d. May 2, 1983]

1932 *Alan L. Bean,* U.S. astronaut; with *Apollo 12,* landed in *Sea of Storms* on moon's surface in Lunar Module (with C. Conrad, Jr.). Flew *Skylab 3* mission, July 28, 1973.

1933 *Philippe Claude Alex de Broca,* French film director, producer.

Ruth Bader Ginsburg, U.S. lawyer, Supreme Court justice, 1993– .

1935 *Judd Hirsch,* U.S. actor; known for his role as Alex on television series, *Taxi,* 1978–85; Tony Award for *I'm Not Rappaport,* 1986.

1941 *Mike Love,* U.S. singer, musician; member of the rock group, *The Beach Boys,* 1961– .

1944 *Sly Stone (Sylvester Stewart),* U.S. singer, musician; member of the rock group, *Sly and the Family Stone.*

1947 *Ry(land Peter) Cooder,* U.S. musician.

1955 *(Daniel) Dee Snider,* U.S. singer, composer; member of the rock group, *Twisted Sister,* 1976–87.

1962 *Terence Trent D'Arby,* U.S. R & B singer.

HISTORICAL EVENTS

44BC *Ides of March; Julius Caesar* is assassinated by Brutus, Cassius, and others.

1077 Diet of *Forchheim* deposes *Henry IV, King of Germany and Holy Roman Emperor; Rudolf, Duke of Swabia,* is elected Emperor.

1341 Alliance is signed between Holy Roman Emperor *Louis IV* and *Philip VI* of France (*Hundred Years' War*).

1744 France declares war on England (*War of the Austrian Succession*).

1781 British army, under Lord Cornwallis, wins *Battle at Guilford Courthouse,* North Carolina (*American Revolution*).

1808 *U.S. Embargo Act* is repealed under pressure by New England states.

1815 *Joachim, King of Naples,* declares war on Austria.

1820 *Maine* is admitted to the Union as the 23rd state.

1915 A British order prohibits all traffic to and from Germany (*World War I*).

The German offensive in Poland is checked by a Russian victory at the *Battle of Augustovo Forest* near Przasnysz (*World War I*).

1916 Austria-Hungary declares war on Portugal (*World War I*).

U.S. troops enter Mexico in futile search for revolutionary bandit *Pancho Villa.*

1917 *Czar Nicholas II* of Russia abdicates for himself and his son in favor of his brother, *Grand Duke Michael.*

1919 The *American Legion* is founded by war veterans in Paris.

1922 The *Sultan of Egypt* is proclaimed king of the newly sovereign state of *Egypt* as *Fuad I.*

1924 The first parliament of an independent *Egypt* is opened by *King Fuad.*

1927 The British formally hand over their concessions at *Hankow* and *Kiukiang* to the Nationalist Chinese.

1939 Germany occupies *Bohemia* and *Moravia;* Slovakia remains nominally independent; Czech state becomes extinct (*World War II*).

Hungary occupies and annexes the *Carpatho-Ukraine* region (*World War II*).

1951 U.S. warships bombard *Wonsan,* killing 8,000 enemy troops (*Korean War*).

Iranian national assembly votes to nationalize the oil industry.

1955 Lerner and Loewe's *My Fair Lady* premieres in New York.

1960 *Syngman Rhee* is elected to a fourth consecutive four-year term as President of South Korea.

National Observatory at *Kitt Peak,* Arizona, site of the world's largest *solar telescope,* is dedicated.

Police in Orangeburg, South Carolina, arrest more than 350 blacks as *sit-in demonstrations* and sporadic racial violence spread throughout the South.

1961 Cuban government orders its citizens to surrender all foreign currency and securities and exchange them for Cuban pesos.

1964 *Elizabeth Taylor* marries her fifth husband, *Richard Burton.*

1967 *Artur da Costa e Silva* is inaugurated as president of Brazil.

1971 U.S. government lifts restrictions on travel to *China* by U.S. citizens.

1972 *The Godfather,* a film starring Marlon Brando and Al Pacino, premieres in New York.

1974 *Ernesto Geisel* is inaugurated as president of Brazil.

1975 The *High Council of the Revolution* in Portugal nationalizes the country's banks and insurance companies.

Brazil grants asylum to ex-President *António de Spinola* of Portugal.

1977 *Three's Company* makes its television debut.

1979 *Gen. João Baptista da Figueiredo* assumes the office of President of Brazil.

An agreement in Kano, Nigeria, ends civil war in *Chad;* France withdraws its troops.

1985 *Jose Sarnay* is inaugurated as president of Brazil.

march

HOLIDAYS

U.S.
St. Urho's Day
Sponsored by the Sauna Society of America, Washington, D.C.

RELIGIOUS CALENDAR

The Saints
St. Finnian Lobhar, abbot. Also called the *Leper.* [d. c. 560]
St. Abraham Kidunaia, hermit. [d. 6th century]
St. Eusebia, abbess. [d. c. 680]
St. Gregory Makar, Bishop of Nicopolis and recluse. [d. c. 1010]
St. Heribert, Archbishop of Cologne. Invoked for rain. Also called *Herbert.* [d. 1021]
St. Julian of Antioch, martyr. [death date unknown]

The Beatified
Blessed John, Bishop of Vicenza and martyr. [d. 1183]
Blessed Torello, hermit. [d. 1282]
Blessed John Amias and *Robert Dalby,* priests and martyrs. [d. 1589]

BIRTHDATES

1581 *Pieter (Corneliszoon) Hooft,* Dutch poet, humanist; leader of the Dutch Renaissance. [d. May 21, 1647]

1739 *George Clymer,* American merchant; signer of the Declaration of Independence and of the U.S. Constitution. [d. January 24, 1813]

1751 *James Madison,* U.S. lawyer; fourth President of the U.S.; known as the *Father of the U.S. Constitution.* [d. June 28, 1836]

1774 *Jethrow Wood,* U.S. inventor; developer of *cast-iron plow,* 1819. [d. September 18, 1834]

1787 *George Simon Ohm,* German physicist, pioneer in electricity; developed the unit for measurement of *electrical resistance,* the *ohm,* which is named for him. [d. July 7, 1854]

1803 *Nikolay Yazykov,* Russian poet. [d. January 7, 1846]

1822 *Rosa Bonheur,* French artist and painter of animals. [d. May 25, 1899]

John Pope, U.S. Union Army general during Civil War. [d. September 23, 1892]

1825 *Camillo Castello Branco,* Portuguese novelist. [d. June 1, 1890]

1839 *Sully Prudhomme (René François Armand Prudhomme),* French poet; Nobel Prize in literature, 1901. [d. September 7, 1907]

1868 *Maksim Gorki (Aleksei Maksimovich Peshkov),* Russian writer. [d. June 14, 1936]

1878 *Emile Cammaerts,* Belgian poet, writer, patriot. [d. November 2, 1953]

1897 *Conrad Nagel,* U.S. character actor. [d. February 24, 1974]

1903 *Michael Joseph (Mike) Mansfield,* U.S. politician, diplomat, engineer; Senate Majority Leader, 1961–76; U.S. Ambassador to Japan, 1977–88.

1908 *Robert Rossen,* U.S. screen writer, producer, director. [d. February 18, 1966]

1911 *Josef Mengele,* German Nazi leader; known for his medical experimentation at Auchwitz concentration camp. [d. February 7, 1979]

1912 *Thelma (Pat) Ryan Nixon,* wife of U.S. President Richard Nixon. [d. June 22, 1993]

1926 *Jerry Lewis (Joseph Levitch),* U.S. comedian, actor.

1918 *Frederick Reines,* U.S. physicist; one-half of the 1995 Nobel Prize for Physics for the discovery of the subatomic particle, neutrino. Martin L. Perl, U.S. physicist; other half of the 1995 Nobel Prize for Physics for the discovery of the subatomic particle tau.

1919 *Eugene M. Lang,* U.S businessman, philanthropist; founder of the minority student education program "I Have a Dream."

1921 *Anne Truitt,* U.S. artist.

1927 *Daniel Patrick Moynihan,* U.S. politician, professor; U.S. Ambassador to India, 1973–74, U.S. Senator, 1977– .

1928 *Christa Ludwig,* Austrian operatic mezzo-soprano.

1940 *Bernardo Bertolucci,* Italian film director; directed *Last Tango in Paris,* 1972.

1949 *Erik (Henry Enrique) Estrada,* U.S. actor; known for his role as Ponch on television series, *Chips,* 1977–83.

1951 *Kate (Patricia Colleen) Nelligan,* Canadian actress.

1955 *Isabelle Huppert,* French actress; Cannes Film Festival Award for *Violette Noziere,* 1978.

1957 *Joan Benoit,* U.S. runner; set women's record for the Boston Marathon with time, 2:22.24, 1983; winner of the first women's Olympic marathon, 1984.

HISTORICAL EVENTS

1322 *Edward II* of England defeats rebellious *Thomas of Lancaster* at *Boroughbridge.*

1517 The *Fifth Lateran Council* of the Roman Catholic Church ends after forbidding the printing of books without ecclesiastical authority.

1792 Count Ankerström assassinates *Gustavus III* of Sweden.

1802 U.S. Military Academy is founded at *West Point,* New York.

1827 *Freedom Journal,* the first black newspaper in the U.S., is printed in New York City.

1843 *Molly Maguire,* a secret society, is formed in Ireland.

1851 A concordat is signed between the papacy and Spain recognizing the *Roman Catholic* faith as the only authorized religion of *Spain* and giving the Church total control of education and censorship.

1881 The *Barnum and Bailey Circus* makes its debut in New York City.

1910 Foundation stone of *Hong Kong University* is laid.

1916 *Admiral Alfred von Tirpitz,* conductor of Germany's submarine campaign, resigns in disagreement over German policy *(World War I).*

1918 The Soviet Congress ratifies the *Treaty of Brest-Litovsk.*

1926 U.S. scientist *Robert Goddard* launches the first successful *liquid-fuel rocket,* at Worcester, Massachusetts.

1935 *Germany* abrogates the *Treaty of Versailles* by ordering universal military service. *Adolf Hitler* announces he will raise an army of 500,000 men.

1968 *My-Lai* and *My-Khe* villagers are killed by American troops in Vietnam *(Vietnam War).*

1977 Druze leader, *Kamal Jumblatt,* is assassinated near Baaklin, Lebanon.

1978 Former Italian premier *Aldo Moro* is kidnapped in Rome

by the *Red Brigade;* his five bodyguards are killed.

Two Russian cosmonauts return to earth in their *Soyuz 27* capsule after setting a new endurance record in space of 96 days.

1979 *Ayatollah Khomeini* orders a halt to the secret trials and summary executions by the *Revolutionary Council of Iran.*

1984 *William Buckley,* first secretary of the U.S. embassy's political section, is kidnapped in Beirut. U.S. government officials later admit that Buckley was also the Beirut station chief for the Central Intelligence Agency.

1988 Lieutenant Colonel *Oliver North,* Rear Admiral *John Poindexter, Richard Secord,* and *Albert Hakim* are indicted by a federal grand jury on charges of conspiring to defraud the U.S. government by funneling aid to the Nicaraguan contras *(Iran-contra affair).*

President Ronald Reagan dispatches 3,200 troops to *Honduras* after Sandinista forces had reportedly crossed the Nicaraguan border to attack a contra base camp.

1995 Mississippi's House of Representatives adopts *Thirteenth Amendment* to the state constitution.

HOLIDAYS

Ireland and many other countries in the West
St. Patrick's Day
Honors the patron saint of Ireland.

U.S.
Camp Fire Founders Day
Sponsored by Camp Fire, Inc.
Kansas City, Missouri

U.N. Member Countries
World Maritime Day

RELIGIOUS CALENDAR

Popularly regarded in the Middle Ages as the day *Noah* entered the Ark.

The Saints
St. Joseph of Arimathea, disciple who obtained the body of Jesus and buried it in his own tomb. [d. 1st century]
The Martyrs of the Serapeum. [d. 390]
St. Patrick, Archbishop of Armagh and Apostle of Ireland. Patron of Ireland. Also called *Patricius*. [d. 461] Optional Memorial.
St. Agricola, Bishop of Chalon-sur-Saône. Also called *Arègle*. [d. 580]
St. Gertrude of Nivelles, virgin and abbess. Patron of travelers and of souls on their journey from this world to the next. Invoked against mice and rats, for good quarters on a journey, and for gardens. [d. 659]

St. Paul of Cyprus, martyr. [d. c. 760]

The Beatified
Blessed John Sarkander, priest and martyr. [d. 1620]
Blessed Daniel Comboni, missionary. [d. 1881]
Blessed Guido Maria Conforti. [beatified 1996]

BIRTHDATES

1473 *James IV, King of Scotland*, 1489–1513; his marriage to the daughter of *Henry VII* of England led ultimately to the union of Scotland and England. [d. September 9, 1513]

1628 *François Girardon*, French baroque sculptor; under Charles Le Brun, decorated Palace at Versailles; executed the tomb of *Cardinal Richelieu* at the Sorbonne. [d. September 1, 1715]

1764 *William Pinkney*, U.S. diplomat. [d. December 25, 1822]

1777 *Roger Brooke Taney*, U.S. jurist, lawyer; Chief Justice of U.S. Supreme Court, 1836–64. [d. October 12, 1864]

1780 *Thomas Chalmers*, Scottish Presbyterian clergyman; a leader of the *Free Church of Scotland.* [d. May 31, 1837]

1787 *Edmund Kean*, English actor; the leading tragic actor of his day; best known for his portrayal of *Shylock* in Shakespeare's *Merchant of Venice.* [d. May 15, 1833]

1804 *James Bridger*, U.S. fur trapper, scout; the first white man to view the Great Salt Lake in Utah. [d. July 17, 1881]

1817 *Pasquale Stanislao Mancini*, Italian statesman, jurist; Minister of Justice, 1876–78; Minister of Foreign Affairs, 1881–85; responsible for Italian occupation of *Eritrea*. [d. December 26, 1888]

1834 *Gottlieb Wilhelm Daimler*, German inventor; developed high speed, gasoline burning *internal combustion engine.* [d. March 6, 1900]

1846 *(Catherine) Kate Greenaway*, British painter, illustrator; noted for her illustrations of children's books. [d. November 6, 1901]

1849 *Charles Francis Brush*, U.S. scientist, inventor; made numerous contributions to modern electrical engineering, including the *electric arc light* and a *storage battery.* [d. June 15, 1928]

1866 *Pierce Butler*, U.S. jurist; Associate Justice, U.S. Supreme Court, 1923–39. [d. November 16, 1939]

1873 *Margaret Grace Bondfield,* British labor leader; first woman minister in the British cabinet. [d. June 16, 1953]

1874 *Stephen Samuel Wise,* U.S. reform rabbi, Jewish leader; founder of *Zionist Organization of America,* 1906; a major anti-Hitler spokesman in the 1930s. [d. April 19, 1949]

1881 *Walter Hess,* Swiss physiologist; Nobel Prize in physiology or medicine for studies of the brain (with E. Moniz), 1949. [d. 1973]

1884 *Frank (Howard) Buck,* U.S. jungle explorer, adventurer, animal collector; author of *Bring 'em Back Alive;* idol of American men and boys during 1930s. [d. March 25, 1950]

1898 *Ella Winter,* U.S. journalist, social activist born in Australia; known for her writings on the post-revolutionary Russia; intimate of Donald Ogden Stewart, the black-listed Hollywood writer. [d. August 5, 1980]

1903 *Marquis William Childs,* U.S. journalist; Pulitzer Prize in commentary, 1969. [d. June 30, 1990]

1910 *Bayard Rustin,* U.S. civil rights activist; organized March on Washington, 1963. [d. August 24, 1987]

1912 Bayard Rustin, U.S. civil rights activist, known for his non-violent approach to solving social injustices. [d. 1987]

1918 *Mercedes McCambridge,* U.S. actress; Oscar Award for *All the King's Men,* 1949.

1919 *Nat (King) Cole (Nathaniel Adams Coles),* U.S. singer,

pianist. [d. February 15, 1965).

1933 *Myrlie Evers-Williams,* U.S. civil rights activist; widow of slain civil rights leader *Medgar Evers* (June 12, 1963).

1938 *Rudolf (Hametovich) Nureyev,* Russian-born ballet dancer; defected from U.S.S.R., 1961. [d. January 6, 1993]

1940 *Mark Wells White, Jr.,* U.S. politician; Governor of Texas, 1983–87.

1944 *John Sebastian,* U.S. singer; member of the rock group, *Lovin' Spoonful.*

1948 *William Gibson,* U.S. writer; author of *Neuromancer* and *Virtual Light.*

1949 *Patrick Duffy,* U.S. actor; known for his role as Bobby Ewing on television series, *Dallas,* 1978–85, 1986–91.

1951 *Kurt (Von Vogel) Russell,* U.S. actor; known for his starring roles in *Escape From New York* and *Silkwood.*

1954 *Lesley-Anne Down,* British actress; known for her starring role in Public Broadcasting System series, *Upstairs, Downstairs.*

1955 *Cynthia A. McKinney,* U.S. politician; U.S. representative for Georgia, 1992– .

1964 *Rob(ert Hepler) Lowe,* U.S. actor; known for his starring roles in *Hotel New Hampshire, St. Elmo's Fire,* and *Wayne's World.*

HISTORICAL EVENTS

45BC *Caesar* defeats Pompey's supporters at *Munda.*

1776 British, threatened by American artillery in *Dorchester Heights,* evacuate Boston *(American Revolution).*

1860 *Maori War* begins in New Zealand.

1861 *Kingdom of Italy* is proclaimed by the first Italian parliament, with *Victor Emmanuel* as first king.

1910 *Camp Fire Girls* are established in the United States.

1915 The first *Battle of Champagne* on the Western Front ends, with small gains by the French *(World War I).*

1917 *Nicholas II* of Russia abdicates; Russia becomes a republic *(Russian Revolution).*

1918 *Oliver Plunkett,* Archbishop of Armagh, Ireland, is beatified.

1921 *Lenin* inaugurates the New Economic Policy in Russia.

1929 The *University of Madrid* is closed by royal decree because of rioting by students and opposition to the government by intellectuals.

1941 *National Gallery of Art* opens in Washington, D.C.

1942 General *Douglas MacArthur* arrives in Australia to assume supreme command of the Allied forces *(World War II).*

1945 Battle of *Iwo Jima* ends with U.S. victory *(World War II).*

1948 *Brussels Pact,* a 50-year military alliance, is signed between Great Britain, France, Belgium, the Netherlands, and Luxembourg.

1950 The University of California announces the development of *californium,* a new element with the atomic number 98.

1951 The Iranian Senate votes to nationalize the country's oil industry.

Vatican excommunicates all persons connected with the persecution of the Roman Catholic Church in *Czechoslovakia.*

1958 *Vanguard I* spacecraft is launched by U.S. at Cape Canaveral.

1960 U.N. conference on the *Law of the Sea* opens at Geneva, Switzerland.

1963 *Mother Elizabeth Ann Bayley Seton,* U.S. founder of the *Sisters of Charity of St. Joseph,* is beatified by Pope John XXIII in Rome.

1968 Violent anti-Vietnam demonstrations outside U.S. embassy in London result in over 300 arrests.

1969 *Golda Meir* is sworn in as Israel's fourth Prime Minister.

1970 *Arthur Chung* is elected as the first president of Guyana.

1978 One of worst *oil spills* in history occurs when supertanker *Amoco Cadiz* breaks in two off the Brittany Coast in France, dumping more than 1.3 million barrels of crude oil into the sea.

Bolivian government severs diplomatic relations with Chile because of a dispute over giving *Bolivia* an outlet to the Pacific Ocean.

1998 *Zhu Rongji* is elected Premier of China.

march

MARCH 18

HOLIDAYS

Aruba
National Anthem & Flay Day

Congo
Day of Supreme Sacrifice
Commemorates President Ngouabi's
assassination.

RELIGIOUS CALENDAR

The Saints
St. Alexander, Bishop of Jerusalem
and martyr. [d. 251]
St. Cyril, Archbishop of Jerusalem
and Doctor of the Church. [d.
386] Optional Memorial.
St. Frigidian, Bishop of Lucca.
Patron of Lucca, Italy. Also
called *Erigdian, Frediano,
Fridian, Frigdian.* [d. c. 588]
St. Edward the Martyr, King of
England. [d. 979]
St. Anselm, Bishop of Lucca. Patron
of Mantua. [d. 1086]
St. Salvator of Horta, Franciscan
friar. [d. 1567]
St. Finan of Aberdeen. [death date
unknown]

The Beatified
Blessed Christian, Abbot of
Mellifont, the first Cistercian
monastery in Ireland. Also
called *Christian O'Conarchy,
Giolla Criost Ua Condoirche.*
[d. 1186]

BIRTHDATES

1578 *Adam Elsheimer,* German
painter. [d. December 1610]

1609 *Frederick III, King of
Denmark and Norway,*
1648–70; established the
absolute monarchy
maintained in Denmark until
1848. [d. February 9, 1670]

1733 *Christoph Friedrich Nicolai,*
German critic, novelist,
publisher; champion of the
Enlightenment in Germany.
[d. January 1, 1811]

1782 *John (Caldwell) Calhoun,*
U.S. statesman, proponent of
slavery; U.S. Secretary of War,
1817–24; U.S. Vice-President,
1825–32; U.S. Secretary of
State, 1844–45. [d. March 31,
1850]

1813 *Joshua Ballinger Lippincott,*
U.S. publisher; founded J.B.
Lippincott & Co., 1836. [d.
January 5, 1886]

1827 *Pierre Eugene Marcelin
Berthelot,* French chemist;
noted for his research in
thermochemistry; Foreign
Minister, 1895–96; Secretary
of French Academy, 1886–87.
[d. March 18, 1902]

1830 *Numa Denis Fustel de
Coulanges,* French historian;
known for his studies of
ancient and medieval history.
[d. September 12, 1889]

1837 *(Stephen) Grover Cleveland,*
U.S. attorney, politician; 22nd
and 24th President of the
U.S., 1885–89, 1893–97. [d.
June 24, 1908]

1838 *Sir William Randal Cremer,*
British jurist; Nobel Peace
Prize for advocating
international arbitration, 1903.
[d. July 22, 1908]

1842 *Stéphane Mallarmé,* French
poet, essayist, translator;
member of *Symbolist School*
of poets. [d. September 9,
1898]

1858 *Rudolf Diesel,* German
mechanical engineer; inventor
of the *diesel engine* (1897).
[d. September 30, 1913]

1869 *Neville Chamberlain,* British
statesman; Prime Minister,
1937–40. [d. November 9,
1940]

1875 *Lee Shubert,* U. S. theatrical
producer; with his brother
Jacob (August 15) controlled
the most powerful monopoly
of theaters in the U.S. [d.
December 25, 1953]

1877 *Edgar Cayce,* U.S. psychic;
diagnosed ailments and
prescribed remedies for
thousands of sick people;
founded Association for
Research and Enlightenment
to keep track of his cases,
1931. [d. January 3, 1945]

1892 *(Robert Peter) Tristram
Coffin,* U.S. writer; Pulitzer

Prize in poetry, 1935. [d. January 20, 1955]

1893 *Wilfred Owen,* British poet; wrote most of his poetry during World War I. [d. November 4, 1918]

1897 *Ray H(oward) Jenkins,* U.S. lawyer; acted as special counsel during U.S. Senate hearings of Senator Joseph McCarthy's accusations against the U.S. Army. [d. December 26, 1980]

1899 *Lavrenti Pavlovich Beriya,* Russian secret-police chief under Stalin. [d. December 23, 1953]

1905 *Robert Donat,* British actor. [d. June 9, 1958]

1910 *Chiang Ching-Kuo,* Chinese statesman; Head of State, Republic of China (Taiwan), 1978–88. [d. January 13, 1988]

Herman Tarnower, U.S. physician, author; wrote *The Complete Scarsdale Medical Diet,* 1979; murdered by his former lover, Jean Harris. [d. March 10, 1980]

1915 *Hamilton Shirley Amerasinghe,* Sri Lankan diplomat, statesman; chief delegate to UN General Assembly, 1967–80; President of General Assembly, 1967. [d. December 4, 1980]

Richard Condon, U.S. novelist; author of *Prizzi's Honor.* [d. April 9, 1996]

1926 *Peter Graves (Peter Aurness),* U.S. actor; known for his role as Jim Phelps on television series, *Mission Impossible,* 1967–73.

1927 *George Plimpton,* U.S. author; wrote *Out of My League,* 1961, and *Paper Lion,* 1966.

1930 *Adam J. Maida,* U.S. Roman Catholic Cardinal; head of the Archdiocese of Detroit, Michigan.

1932 *John (Hoyer) Updike,* U.S. novelist, shortstory writer, poet.

1936 *F. W. de Klerk,* South African president (1989–94); recipient of the Nobel Peace Prize in 1993 with Nelson Mandela.

1938 *Charley Pride,* U.S. singer; first black star of country music.

1941 *Wilson Pickett,* U.S. singer, songwriter.

1944 *Kevin Dobson,* U.S. actor; known for his role as Mac Mackenzie on television series, *Knot's Landing.*

1956 *Ingemar Stenmark,* Swedish skier; winner of several World Cup championships and Olympic events.

1959 *Irene Cara,* U.S. actress, singer; known for her starring role in *Fame,* 1980.

1962 *James McMurtry,* U.S. singer, songwriter.

1963 *Vanessa Williams,* U.S. actress, singer, beauty contest winner; first black Miss America, 1983; during her reign, photographs she had earlier posed for surfaced and caused her to give up her title.

1964 *Bonnie Blair,* U.S. speed skater; winner of five Olympic gold medals during her career.

HISTORICAL EVENTS

979 *King Edward the Martyr* of England is murdered by his stepmother; *Ethelred II,* the Unready, succeeds to throne.

1123 The First *Lateran Council* of the Roman Catholic Church begins.

1229 *Frederick II, Holy Roman Emperor,* crowns himself *King of Jerusalem* during the *Sixth Crusade.*

1438 *Albert of Austria* is elected King of Germany.

1766 British Parliament repeals the *Stamp Act* because of widespread opposition to it in America.

1848 Revolution breaks out in *Milan.*

1861 Widespread revolts and continued attacks from Haiti lead President *Pedro Santana* of *Santo Domingo* to place his country under Spanish rule.

1871 Commune uprising in *Paris* starts the brief rule of the socialist government.

1890 *Prince Bismarck* of Germany resigns offices of premier and foreign minister after frequent clashes with the new emperor, *William II.*

1891 Telephone communication between London and Paris is established.

1897 *Crete* proclaims union with *Greece.*

1913 *King George I* of Greece is assassinated at Solonika and is succeeded by his son, *Constantine I.*

1915 The *Russians* retake Memel, East Prussia, in their continuing counter-offensive against Germany on the Eastern Front *(World War I).*

1916 Dutch ship *Palembang* is sunk by a German torpedo *(World War I).*

march

The *Battle of Narock* marks the beginning of a Russian offensive against the Germans on the Eastern Front *(World War I)*.

1919 British Parliament passes *Rowlatt Acts,* drastically curbing civil liberties in India.

1921 *Treaty of Riga* concludes Russian-Polish war and defines frontiers.

1922 *Mahatma Gandhi* is sentenced to six years in jail after his first *civil disobedience* campaign against British rule in India.

1938 Mexican government expropriates properties of British and U.S. oil companies valued at $450 million.

1945 U.S. naval task force conducts carrier strike against military targets on *Kyushu, Japan (World War II)*.

1957 *Tales of Wells Fargo* makes its television debut.

1963 The U.S. Supreme Court rules that states must supply free *legal aid* to indigent clients charged with serious criminal offenses.

1965 Russian cosmonaut *Aleksei A. Leonov* becomes the first man to float freely in space, on a lifeline attached to Soviet spacecraft *Voskhod 2.*

1966 Fourteen *NATO* members (all except France) express their support for the North Atlantic Treaty and the principle of military integration.

1967 The tanker *Torrey Canyon* is wrecked near Cornwall, England, and discharges more than 30,000 tons of crude oil.

1969 *Apollo 10* spacecraft is launched from Cape Kennedy.

1970 Lieutenant General *Lon Nol* assumes power in Cambodia after a bloodless coup d'etat.

1974 Arab oil companies, except Libya and Syria, end oil embargo against U.S.

1975 The National Assembly of Tunisia appoints *Habib Bourguiba* as president-for-life.

1977 *Maj. Marien Ngouabi,* President of the *Congo,* is shot and killed in Brazzaville.

1978 Former Pakistani Prime Minister *Zulfikar Ali Bhutto,* removed from power by a military coup in July 1977, is convicted and sentenced to death; he is hanged April 4.

1985 *Capital Cities Communications, Inc.* announces the purchase of *American Broadcasting Companies* for $3.5 billion.

1986 Buckingham Palace announces the engagement of Prince *Andrew* to *Sarah Ferguson.*

1987 *Fleet Financial Corp.* and *Norstar Bancorp* swap stock in a $1.3 billion merger.

1994 *Michael Jordan* announces that he will return to the National Basketball Association as a member of the Chicago Bulls. Previously, on October 6, 1993, Jordan announced his retirement from basketball.

HOLIDAYS

Andorra, Colombia, Costa Rica, Lichtenstein, San Marino, Spain, Vatican City, Venezuela
St. Joseph's Day

U.S. (California)
Swallow Day
The day on which the swallows traditionally return to the Mission of San Juan Capistrano.

RELIGIOUS CALENDAR

Solemnities
St. Joseph, husband of the Virgin Mary; step-father of Christ; Patron of the Universal Church, also of carpenters, wheelwrights, and combatants against Communism. [d. 1st century]

The Saints
St. John of Panaca, abbot. [d. 6th century]
St. Landoald, [d. c. 668]
St. Alcmund, martyr. [d. c. 800]

The Beatified
Blessed Andrew of Siena, founder of the Society of Mercy. [d. 1251]

BIRTHDATES

1519 *Henry II, King of France;* husband of *Catherine de' Médicis.* [d. July 10, 1559]

1589 *William Bradford,* American colonial leader; Governor of *Plymouth Colony* for thirty years; author of *History of Plymouth Plantation.* [d. May 9, 1657]

1601 *Alonso Cano (El Granadino),* Spanish painter, sculptor, architect; chief architect of *Granada Cathedral.* [d. October 5, 1667]

1721 *Tobias George Smollett,* Scottish novelist; author of several picaresque novels; edited a *Universal History;* translated Voltaire's works. [d. September 17, 1771]

1725 *Richard Howe,* British admiral. [d. August 5, 1799]

1727 *Ferdinand Berthoud,* Swiss-French watchmaker, marine clockmaker, writer on horological subjects. [d. June 20, 1807]

1813 *David Livingstone,* British missionary, physician, explorer. [d. May 1, 1873]

1821 *Sir Richard Francis Burton,* British scholar, explorer; explored Somaliland, Lake Tanganyika region, and Gold Coast; published translations of *Arabian Nights.* [d. October 20, 1890]

1847 *Albert Pinkham Ryder,* U.S. painter; known for landscapes, marines; his *Toilers of the Sea* hangs in the Metropolitan Museum of Art, New York City. [d. March 28, 1917]

1848 *Wyatt Earp,* U.S. law officer, gunfighter; most famous for his participation at the gunfight at O.K. Corral. [d. January 13, 1929]

1849 *Alfred von Tirpitz,* German admiral; Secretary of the Navy, 1897–1916. [d. March 6, 1930]

1858 *K'ang Yu-wei,* Chinese scholar, reformer; known as the *Rousseau of China.* [d. March 31, 1927]

1860 *William Jennings Bryan,* U.S. politician, orator, lawyer, editor; Democratic presidential nominee, 1896, 1900, 1908; U.S. Secretary of State, 1912–13. [d. July 26, 1925]

1872 *Sergei Pavlovich Diaghilev,* Russian ballet master, theatrical impresario; revitalized ballet by integrating ideals of other art forms. [d. August 19, 1929]

1876 *Sir John Hubert Marshall,* British archaeologist; discoverer of the *Indus Valley civilization.* [d. August 17, 1958]

1883 *Sir Walter N. Haworth,* British chemist; Nobel Prize in chemistry for determining chemical structures of carbohydrates (with P. Karrer), 1937. [d. March 19, 1950]

Joseph Warren Stilwell (Vinegar Joe), U.S. Army general; commanded U.S. forces in the China-Burma-India theater during *World War II.* [d. October 12, 1946]

1891 *Earl Warren,* U.S. lawyer, jurist; Governor of California, 1943–53; 14th Chief Justice of U.S. Supreme Court, 1953–69. [d. July 9, 1974]

1894 *Jackie (Moms) Mabley (Loretta Mary Aiken),* U.S. singer, comedienne. [d. May 23, 1975]

1900 *Jean Frédéric Joliot-Curie* (originally Joliot), French nuclear physicist; Nobel Prize in chemistry for synthesis of new *radioactive elements* (with wife Irène, the daughter of Marie and Pierre Curie), 1935. [d. August 14, 1958]

1901 *Jo Mielziner,* U.S. stage designer. [d. March 15, 1976]

1904 *John J(oseph) Sirica,* Chief Judge of U.S. District Court, District of Columbia, 1971–74; presided over the Watergate trials, 1972–74. [d. August 14, 1997]

1905 *Albert Speer,* German architect; confidante of Hitler; sentenced at Nuremburg trials and imprisoned 1945–1966. [d. September 1, 1981]

1906 *(Karl) Adolf Eichmann,* German Nazi official held responsible for the execution of millions of Jews during World War II. [executed May 31, 1962]

1916 *Irving Wallace,* U.S. novelist. [d. June 20, 1990]

1928 *Hans Küng,* Swiss-German liberal Roman Catholic theologian, author; censured by Catholic Church in 1979.

Patrick McGoohan, U.S. actor; known for his roles in Disney films.

1930 *Ornette Coleman,* U.S. jazz saxophonist.

1933 *Philip Roth,* U.S. writer; author of *Goodbye Columbus* and *Portnoy's Complaint.*

1935 *Phyllis Newman,* U.S. actress, singer; Tony Award for *Subways are for Sleeping,* 1962.

1936 *Ursula Andress,* Swiss actress.

1943 *Mario Molina,* U.S. chemist; the Nobel Prize for Chemistry in 1995. Molina shares the award with fellow chemists, F. Sherwood Rowland and Paul Crutzen. The three chemists researched atmospheric chemistry.

1944 *Sirhan Bishara Sirhan,* Jordanian assassin; shot Robert Kennedy, 1968.

1955 *Bruce Willis (Walter Bruce),* U.S. actor; known for his role as David Addison on television series, *Moonlighting,* 1985–89; and for the *Die Hard* movies.

1967 *Vladimir Konstantinov,* Russian-born hockey player.

HISTORICAL EVENTS

72 The first *lunar eclipse* recorded in history is observed by the Babylonians (according to Ptolemy).

1284 The *Statute of Wales* is enacted making that land part of the Kingdom of England.

1286 *Margaret, Maid of Norway,* becomes Queen of Scotland under six guardians upon the death of her grandfather, *Alexander III* of Scotland.

1452 *Frederick III* is crowned Holy Roman Emperor.

1563 *Edict of Amboise* grants French Huguenots some freedom, ending first *Huguenot War.*

1782 English Prime Minister, *Lord North,* resigns and is replaced as by *Charles Watson-Wentworth, Marquis of Rockingham.*

1799 *Napoleon* lays siege to *Acre.*

1808 *Charles IV* of Spain abdicates in favor of his son, *Ferdinand.*

1853 The *Taiping rebels* seize *Nanking* and make it their capital (*Taiping Rebellion*).

1861 The *Maori insurrection* ends in New Zealand with surrender of the Maori.

1896 *Horatio Kitchener* begins an advance up the Nile with British troops to check the activity of the dervishes and to relieve *Kasala* in the Sudan.

1920 The U.S. Senate rejects the *Versailles Treaty.*

1921 *Georgia* proclaimed a Soviet Republic.

1942 *Netherlands East Indies* formally surrenders to Japan (*World War II*).

1950 *Indonesia* devalues its currency by 50 percent. The government also appropriates half of all circulating currency and bank accounts as a loan.

1951 France, West Germany, the Netherlands, Belgium, Italy, and Luxembourg establish the *European Coal and Steel Community.*

1957 Senate confirms the nominations of *William*

Brennan and *Charles Whittaker* to the U.S. Supreme Court.

1963 *Mohammed Yousef* is inaugurated as premier of Afghanistan.

1964 *Great St. Bernard Tunnel,* 3.4 miles long, between Italy and Switzerland in the Alps, is officially opened to automobile traffic.

1965 *Nicolae Ceausescu* becomes head of the Romanian Communist Party and government.

1968 President Johnson signs into law a bill eliminating the requirement that 25 per cent of U.S. currency be backed by *gold.*

1970 East German Premier Stoph and West German Chancellor Brandt confer in Erfurt, East Germany, at the first meeting of the heads of the *postwar German states.*

1972 *India* and *Bangladesh* sign a 25-year treaty of friendship and mutual defense in Dacca.

1987 Reverend *Jim Bakker* resigns as head of his television ministry, the *PTL Club,* after admitting to an affair with a church secretary.

1989 *Alfredo Christiani* is elected President of El Salvador.

1993 *Byron White,* associate justice on the Supreme Court, announces his retirement after serving thirty years.

1996 In the former Yugoslavia, *Sarejevo* is reunified when Grbavica, the last Sarejevo suburb, is now governed by a Moslem-Croat federation.

1998 *Atal Bihari Vajpayee* is sworn in as the new Prime Minister of India.

march

MARCH
20

HOLIDAYS

Japan
Vernal Equinox
Celebrates the beginning of spring.

Iran
Oil Nationalization Day

Tunisia
Independence Day
Commemorates the signing by the French of the March 20, 1956, treaty recognizing Tunisian autonomy.

RELIGIOUS CALENDAR

The Saints
St. Martin, Archbishop of Braga. [d. 579]

St. Cuthbert, Bishop of Lindisfarne. [d. 687]

St. Herbert, anchoret and priest. [d. 687]

St. Wulfram, Archbishop of Sens. [d. c. 703]

The Martyrs of Mar Saba, monks. [d. 796]

St. Photina and her companions, martyrs. [death date unknown]

The Beatified
Blessed Evangelist and *Peregrine,* hermits. [d. c. 1250]

Blessed Ambrose of Siena, Dominican friar. [d. 1286]

Blessed John of Parma, seventh minister general of the Franciscans. [d. 1289]

Blessed John Duns Scotus, priest. [d. 1308]

Blessed Maurice of Hungary, friar. [d. 1336]

Blessed Mark of Montegallo, Franciscan friar. [d. 1497]

Blessed Baptist of Mantua, prior general of the Carmelite Order. Surnamed *Spagnuolo,* the *Spaniard.* [d. 1516]

Blessed Hippolytus Galantini, founder of the Institute of Christian Doctrine or the Vanchetoni. [d. 1619]

Blessed Dina Belanger. [beatified 1993]

BIRTHDATES

43BC *Publius Ovidius Naso,* Latin poet, known as *Ovid.* [d. c. A.D. 17]

1741 *Jean Antoine Houdon,* French neoclassical sculptor; known for his sculptures of such renowned figures as *Voltaire, George Washington,* and *Thomas Jefferson.* [d. July 15, 1828]

1770 *Johann Friedrich Hölderlin,* German poet. [d. June 7, 1843]

1796 *Edward Gibbon Wakefield,* British colonizer of *South Australia* and *New Zealand.* [d. May 16, 1862]

1811 *George Caleb Bingham,* U.S. painter; best known for his works portraying river scenes, frontier life, and historical events in the Missouri River Valley. [d. July 7, 1879]

1823 *Ned Buntline (Edward Zane Carroll Judson),* U.S. novelist, adventurer; organized the *Know-Nothing Party,* 1850s. [d. July 16, 1886]

1828 *Henrik Ibsen,* Norwegian poet and playwright: author of *Hedda Gabler, A Doll's House,* and *The Wild Duck.* [d. May 23, 1906]

Prince Frederick Charles, the *Red Prince* of Prussia. [d. January 15, 1885]

1834 *Charles William Eliot,* U.S. educator; President, Harvard University, 1869–1909; a founder of *Radcliffe College.* [d. August 22, 1926]

1856 *Frederick Winslow Taylor,* U.S. engineer; particularly known for his *time and motion studies* which revolutionized production techniques and industrial management in the U.S. [d. March 21, 1915]

1890 *Beniamino Gigli,* Italian opera tenor. [d. November 30, 1957]

Lauritz (Lebrecht Hommel) Melchior, U.S. operatic tenor, born in Denmark; known for his Wagnerian roles. [d. March 18, 1973]

1892 *Max Brand (Frederick Faust),* U.S. novelist, screenwriter; under various pseudonyms, created such classic stories as *Destry Rides Again* and the *Dr. Kildare* series of the 1930s. Known as the *King of the Pulp Writers,* it is estimated that he produced more than 500 full-length novels before his death at the Battle of Santa Maria Infante in Italy during World War II. [d. May 16, 1944]

1897 *Frank (Joseph) Sheed,* U.S. publisher, lecturer, lay theologian; founder of Sheed and Ward publishing house. 1926; author of *Theology and Sanity,* 1953. [d. November 20, 1981]

1904 *B(urrhus) F(rederic) Skinner,* U.S. behavioral psychologist; known as the *Father of Programmed Instruction;* espoused principles of *behavioral engineering.* [d. August 18, 1990]

1908 Sir *Michael Redgrave,* British actor; father of Vanessa and Lynn Redgrave. [d. March 21, 1985]

Frank (Nicholas) Stanton, U.S. communications executive; Director, CBS Inc., 1945–78.

1906 *Oswald George (Ozzie) Nelson,* U.S. actor, band leader; known for his starring role on television series, *The Adventures of Ozzie and Harriet,* 1952–65. [d. June 3, 1975]

1909 *Kathryn Forbes (Kathryn Anderson McLean),* U.S. short-story writer; well known for her collection of stories which were dramatized as *I Remember Mama.* [d. May 15, 1966]

1911 *Alfonso Garcia Robles,* Mexican diplomat; Nobel

Peace Prize for his work toward disarmament (with Alva Myrdal), 1982.

1915 *Rudolf Kirchschlaeger,* Austrian statesman; President, 1974–86.

1920 *Pamela Harriman,* British-born diplomat; U.S. ambassador to France, 1993–96.

Marian Margaret McPartland, U.S. jazz pianist and composer, born in England.

1922 *Ray (Walter) Goulding,* U.S. comedian; with partner Bob Elliott formed the popular radio comedy team of *Bob and Ray.* [d. March 24, 1990]

Carl Reiner, U.S. actor, author; director, *The Dick Van Dyke Show,* 1961–66.

1925 *John D(aniel) Ehrlichman,* U.S. government official, lawyer; played a major role in the *Watergate Incident.* Convicted, 1975; released, 1978.

1928 *Fred McFeely Rogers,* U.S. educator, television personality; host of television show, *Mister Rogers Neighborhood,* 1965–75.

1931 *Hal Linden (Harold Lipschitz),* U.S. actor; known for his starring role on television series, *Barney Miller,* 1975–82; Tony Award for *The Rothchilds.*

1934 *Willie Brown, Jr.,* U.S. lawyer, politician; mayor of San Fransico, California, 1996– .

1937 *Jerry Reed (Jerry Hubbard),* U.S. actor, singer, songwriter.

1939 *(Martin) Brian Mulroney,* Canadian politician; Prime Minister, 1984–93.

1944 *Erwin Neher,* German physicist; Nobel Prize for Medicine in 1991. Neher shares the prize with Bert Sakmann for their research of cell functions.

1945 *Pat(rick) James Riley,* U.S. basketball coach; head coach of the Los Angeles Lakers, 1981–90; head coach of the New York Knicks, 1991– .

1948 *Robert Gordon (Bobby) Orr,* Canadian hockey player; Hall of Fame, 1979.

1950 *William Hurt,* U.S. actor; Academy Award for *Kiss of the Spider Woman,* 1985.

1951 *Carl Palmer,* British musician; member of the rock group, *Emerson, Lake, and Palmer,* 1970–79.

1956 *Spike Lee,* U.S. filmmaker and actor; directed *Malcolm X,* 1992.

1958 *Holly Hunter,* U.S. actress; Academy Award (Best Actress) for *The Piano,* 1993.

HISTORICAL EVENTS

1239 *Pope Gregory IX* excommunicates *Holy Roman Emperor Frederick II.*

1602 *Dutch East India Company* is established.

1604 *Charles IX* assumes title of King of Sweden.

1751 *Frederick, Prince of Wales,* son of *George II* of Great Britain, dies, leaving a son who becomes *George III.*

1806 The foundation stone of *Dartmoor Prison* in England is laid.

1815 The independence and perpetual neutrality of

Switzerland is secured by acts of the *Congress of Vienna*.

Napoleon arrives at Fontainebleau, the beginning of *The Hundred Days* in France.

1819 The *Burlington Arcade* is opened in London.

1848 *Ludwig I, King of Bavaria,* resigns.

1890 *General Federation of Women's Clubs* is founded in U.S.

1915 *Great Britain, France,* and *Russia* sign a secret agreement granting Constantinople (Istanbul) and the Dardanelles to Russia, and Persia (Iran) to Great Britain *(World War I)*.

General Botha defeats German forces at Pforteberg, South Africa *(World War I)*.

1919 *Wireless telephone service* is established between Ireland and Canada.

1920 The first successful flight across Africa, from Cairo to Cape Town, is completed by Col. H. A. van Rejneveld and Maj. C. J. Brand of the South African Air Force.

1922 First *U.S. aircraft carrier, U.S.S. Langley,* is commissioned.

1945 British troops capture Japanese-held *Mandalay (World War II)*.

1952 The peace treaty restoring Japanese sovereignty is

ratified, ending American occupation of Japan.

1956 *Tunisia* gains full independence from France.

1986 *Jacques Chirac* accepts the position of premier of France, replacing *Laurent Fabius.*

1987 The *Food and Drug Administration (FDA)* approves the drug AZT in the treatment of AIDS.

1995 Twelve passengers are killed and hundreds are injured after a nerve gas attack in *Tokyo, Japan,* subway.

1996 *Erik and Lyle Menendez* are found guilty for the murder of their parents in 1989.

1997 The tobacco company *Liggett Group, Inc.* publicly admits that smoking is addictive.

HOLIDAYS

Afghanistan
Now Rooz
Ancient Persian New Year
celebration marks the beginning of
spring.

Iran
Nawruz

Iraq
Spring Day or Nairuz

Mexico
Juárez Birthday
Honors the national hero and
former president Benito Juárez

Tajikistan
Navruz (New Day)

Turkmenistan
Novruz Bairam
Celebrates the first day of spring.

U.S.
Memory Day
Sponsored by Puns Corporation
Falls Church, Virginia.

Fragrance Day
Sponsored by Richard R. Falk
Associates

UN Member Countries
*International Day for the
Elimination of Racial
Discrimination*
in memory of victims of racial
discrimination at Sharpeville, South
Africa, and in other parts of the
world.

RELIGIOUS CALENDAR

The Saints
St. Serapion, Bishop of Thmuis.
Surnamed the *Scholastic* or
Sindonite. Also called
Sarapion. [d. c. 370]
St. Enda, abbot, and *St. Fanchea*,
virgin. Enda also called *Enna*,
or *Endeus*. Fanchea also
called *Faenche*, or *Faine*. [d.
c. 530]

The Beatified
Blessed Santuccia, matron. [d. 1305]

BIRTHDATES

1685 *Johann Sebastian Bach*,
German composer; founder
of a musical dynasty;
internationally renowned as a
master of *keyboard
compositions*. [d. July 28,
1750]

1713 *Francis Lewis*, American
merchant; signer of
Declaration of Independence.
[d. December 31, 1802]

1763 *Jean Paul Friedrich Richter
(Jean Paul)*, German novelist.
[d. November 14, 1825]

1768 *Joseph Jean Baptiste Fourier*,
French mathematician; first
conceived mathematic theory
of *heat conduction*. [d. May
16, 1830]

1806 *Benito Juárez*, Mexican
leader, revolutionary hero;
President, 1858–59, 1861–63,
1867–72. [d. July 18, 1872]

1831 *Dorothea Beale*, British
educator; a founder of *St.
Hilda's Hall* at Oxford. [d.
November 9, 1906]

1839 *Modest Petrovich Mussorgsky*,
Russian composer; composed
Boris Godunov. [d. March 28,
1881]

1869 *Albert Kahn*, U.S. architect;
noted for his design of office
and factory buildings. [d.
December 8, 1942]

Florenz Ziegfeld, U.S.
producer, particularly known
for extravagant stage shows,
Ziegfeld Follies. [d. July 22,
1932]

1882 *Gilbert (Bronco Billy)
Anderson (Max Aronson)*,
U.S. producer; star of silent
western movies. [d. January
20, 1971]

1884 *George David Birkoff*, U.S.
mathematician; renowned for
his research in theoretical
mathematics; developed the
ergodic theorem of the
kinetic theory of gases,
expanded on Einstein's theory
of relativity; Dean of Harvard
Faculty of Arts and Sciences,
1935–39. [d. November 12,
1944]

1889 *Frederick (Henry) Osborn*,
U.S. demographer, author;
known for his efforts on
behalf of atomic energy
control; Chairman of

Population Council, 1930–68.
[d. January 5, 1981]

1900 *Eugenie Leontovich,* Russian-U.S. actress, dramatic coach; founder of *Actors's Workshop,* 1953.

1905 *Phyllis McGinley,* U.S. poet; Pulitzer Prize in poetry, 1960. [d. February 22, 1978]

1906 *Helen Deutsch,* U.S. screenwriter, lyricist.

1920 *Eric Rohmer (Jean-Marie Maurice Schere),* French director; directed *Claire's Knee, Chloe in the Afternoon.*

1921 *Terence James Cooke,* U.S. Roman Catholic cardinal; Archbishop of New York, 1969–1983. [d. October 6, 1983].

1925 *Peter Brook,* British director; co-director of the Royal Shakespeare Theatre; N.Y. Drama Critics Award for the Best Director 1965–6; founded the Centre International de Créations Théâtrales, Paris, 1971.

1927 *Claurène duGran,* British author.

Hans-Dietrich Genscher, German diplomat.

1929 *James Coco,* U.S. actor. [d. February 25, 1987]

1930 *John Malcolm Fraser,* Australian politician, Prime Minister, 1975–83.

1932 *Walter Gilbert,* U.S. biologist; Nobel Prize in chemistry for his work with nucleic acids, 1980.

1944 *Timothy Dalton,* British actor.

1958 *Gary Oldman,* British actor.

1962 *Matthew Broderick,* U.S. actor.

Rosie O'Donnell, U.S. actress, talk show host.

HISTORICAL EVENTS

1098 Monastery at *Cîteaux* is founded.

1413 *Henry IV* of England dies and is succeeded by *Henry V* who ruled through August 31, 1422.

1556 *Thomas Cranmer,* Archbishop of Canterbury and supporter of Henry VIII, is burned at the stake under orders of Mary Tudor.

1791 *Bangalore,* India, is seized by the British under Lord Cornwallis in the *Third Mysore War.*

1847 *Union of Central American Republics* is formed.

1859 The *Scottish National Gallery* opens.

1871 The first *Reichstag* officially opens.

Sir Henry Morton Stanley embarks on African expedition to find *Dr. David Livingstone.*

1917 The provisional Russian government restores the Finnish Constitution and declares *Finland* a free and independent state in the Russian federation.

Czar Nicholas II and his wife, Alexandra, are ordered imprisoned at their residence by the provisional Russian government.

1918 The great *Somme offensive* begins as the Germans pierce British lines *(World War I).*

1919 The *Rowlatt Acts* is passed in India giving the government

far-reaching and arbitrary anti-sedition powers.

1927 *Shanghai* is taken by the Nationalist Chinese forces of Chiang Kai-shek.

1935 Persia is renamed *Iran.*

1944 Lieutenant General *George S(mith) Patton* is replaced as commander of the U.S. Seventh Army by Major General *Alexander Patch,* in part because of his inappropriate behavior towards several soldiers suffering from battle anxiety *(World War II).*

1946 U.S. Air Force establishes the *Strategic Air Command* and the *Tactical Air Command.*

1950 The *Academy of Radio and Television Arts and Sciences* presents its first annual awards.

1960 *Sharpeville Massacre* takes place in South Africa when blacks besiege Johannesburg police station protesting law requiring all blacks to carry papers *(Pass Law).*

1963 The federal prison on *Alcatraz Island,* California, is closed after 50 years of operation.

1965 *Martin Luther King, Jr.* and *Ralph Bunche* lead 300 civil rights activists on a 54-mile march from *Selma, Alabama* to the state capitol at Montgomery.

1968 Israelis capture *Karameh* in major assault on Jordan.

1983 *Barney Clark,* first human to receive a permanent artificial heart, dies 112 days after the operation from circulatroy collapse and multiorgan failure.

1986 U.S. figure skater, *Debi Thomas,* becomes the first black woman to win the world championship in Geneva, Switzerland.

National Aeronautics and Space Administration (NASA) officials announce that faulty rocket joint seals caused the space shuttle *Challenger* disaster.

1990 *Namibia* becomes an independent nation with *Sam Nujoma* as its president.

1998 *Julian Bond* is elected chairman of the NAACP, succeeding *Myrlie Evers-Williams.*

march

HOLIDAYS

Arab League Countries
Arab League Day
A holiday for all signatories in the March 22, 1945, formation of the Arab League.

Azerbaijan
Novruz Bayrom
Celebrates the beginning of spring.

Lesotho
National Tree Planting Day

Puerto Rico
Emancipation Day or Abolition Day
Commemorates the abolition of slavery on the island on March 22, 1873.

RELIGIOUS CALENDAR

The Saints
St. Paul of Narbonne, missionary. [d. c. 290]
St. Basil of Ancyra, priest and martyr. [d. 362]
St. Deogratias, Bishop of Carthage. [d. 457]
St. Benvenuto, Bishop of Osimo. [d. 1282]
St. Nicholas von Flüe, layman and hermit. Also called *Brother Klaus,* or *Bruder Klaus.* [d. 1487]

The Beatified
Blessed Isnardo of Chiampo, Dominican priest. [d. 1244]
Blessed Hugolino of Cortona, Augustinian hermit. [d. c. 1470]

BIRTHDATES

1459 *Maximilian I, Holy Roman Emperor,* 1493–1519. [d. January 12, 1519]

1599 *Sir Anthony Van Dyke,* Flemish artist; court painter under *Charles I* of England; his style influenced English art for more than 100 years. [d. December 9, 1641]

1785 *Adam Sedgwick,* English geologist; introduced term *Devonian.* [d. January 27, 1873]

1797 *Emperor William I* of Prussia (Kaiser Wilhelm I), 1871. [d. March 9, 1888]

1817 *Braxton Bragg,* Confederate Army general during the U.S. Civil War; responsible for Confederate victory at *Shiloh.* [d. September 27, 1876]

1839 *Robert Smalls,* U.S. politician. Served in the navy during the American Civil War. Member of the U.S. Congress. [d. 1915]

1846 *Randolph Caldecott,* British artist; illustrator; annual U.S. award for outstanding illustration in juvenile literature is presented in his honor (*Caldecott Award*). [d. February 12, 1886]

1857 *Paul Doumer,* French statesman; 13th President of the Third Republic, 1931–32; assassinated by *Paul Gorgouluv.* [d. May 7, 1932]

1868 *Robert Andrews Millikan,* U.S. physicist; Nobel Prize in physics for research on *photoelectricity,* 1923. [d. December 19, 1953]

1884 *Arthur Hendrick Vandenberg,* U.S. politician, editor, U.S. senator; played significant role in formation of *United Nations, NATO,* and the *Marshall Plan.* [d. April 18, 1951]

1907 *James Maurice Gavin,* U.S. army general, diplomat; Ambassador to France, 1960–62. [d. February 23, 1990]

1908 *Maurice Hubert Stans,* U.S. government official; Secretary of Commerce, 1969–72; a leading figure in *Watergate Incident.* [d. April 14, 1998]

1913 *Karl Malden (Maiden Sekulovich),* U.S. actor.

1920 *Werner Klemperer,* German actor; known for his role as Colonel Klink on television series, *Hogan's Heroes,* 1965–71.

1923 *Marcel Marceau,* French mime.

1930 *Derek Curtis Bok,* U.S. educator; President, Harvard University, 1971–91.

Stephen (Joshua) Sondheim, U.S. composer, lyricist.

1931 *Burton Richter,* U.S. physicist; Nobel Prize in physics for discovery of *subatomic particle J,* with S. C. C. Ting, 1976.

William Shatner, U.S. actor; known for his role as Captain Kirk on television series, *Star Trek,* 1966–69.

1933 *Abolhassan Bani-Sadr,* Iranian political leader; first President of the Islamic Republic of Iran, 1980–81.

1934 *Orrin Grant Hatch,* U.S. politician; Senator, 1977– .

J(oseph) P(riestly) McCarthy, U.S. radio personality. [d. 1995]

1935 *M. Emmet Walsh,* U.S. actor.

1943 *George Benson,* U.S. singer, musician; three Grammy Awards.

1948 *Andrew Lloyd Webber,* U.S. composer; known for musicals, *Jesus Christ Superstar,* 1970; *Evita,* 1976; *Cats,* 1981; and *Phantom of the Opera,* 1988.

1957 *Stephanie Mills,* U.S. singer, actress; known for her Broadway role as Dorothy in *The Wiz.*

HISTORICAL EVENTS

1312 *Pope Clement V* abolishes *Order of Templars.*

1621 Governor *John Carver* signs a friendship treaty with *Chief Massasoit* of the Wampanoag Indian Tribe. It is the first such agreement between American colonists and Indians.

1673 In England, the *Test Act* excludes Roman Catholics and dissenters from holding office.

1830 Richard and John Lander, British explorers, begin exploration of the *Niger River* establishing that its outlet is at the Bight of Benim.

1847 The first meeting of *Young Men's Hebrew Association* is held in New York.

1848 *Venetian Republic* proclaims its independence.

1915 Russians capture Austrians' fortress camp of *Przemyşl, Galicia,* taking 119,000 prisoners, the greatest number ever to surrender in war time *(World War I).*

1917 The U.S., Great Britain, France, Italy, Rumania, and Switzerland recognize the provisional government of *Russia.*

1919 A Bolshevik coup headed by *Béla Kun* overthrows the republican government of *Hungary.*

1929 *King Alexander of Yugoslavia* orders the replacement of the Cyrillic alphabet with the Latin alphabet in Yugoslavia.

1944 German troops occupy Hungary and set up a pro-German régime *(World War II).*

1946 First U.S. *rocket* to leave the earth's atmosphere, launched from White Sands, New Mexico, attains a height of 50 miles.

Great Britain announces the independence of *Transjordan.*

1960 *Arthur L. Schawlow* and *Charles Hard Towens* are granted the first patent for a LASER (light amplification by stimulated emission of radiation).

1962 *Louis B. Leakey* announces his discovery of a 14 million-year-old hominid in Kenya.

1966 Congolese President *Joseph D. Mobutu* abolishes Parliament's functions and assumes all national legislative powers.

1971 Argentine President *Roberto Marcelo Levingston* is deposed in a bloodless coup.

1972 U.S. Senate passes *Equal Rights Amendment* subject to ratification by the fifty states.

1978 *Karl Wallenda,* leader of the famous high-wire acrobatic troupe, dies of injuries sustained during a performance in San Juan, Puerto Rico.

1979 British ambassador to the Netherlands, *Sir Richard Sykes,* is assassinated at The Hague.

1982 U.S. space shuttle *Columbia* lifts off for its third voyage into outer space.

1988 U.S. Congress votes to override President Ronald Reagan's veto and reinstate the *Civil Rights Restoration Act.* The law, which was designed to replace protections voided by a 1984 U.S. Supreme Court decision, prohibits discrimination by any part of an institution receiving federal funds.

1990 Captain *Joseph Hazelwood* is found guilty of negligence in the *Exxon Valdez* oil spill in Alaska (March 24, 1989).

MARCH
23

HOLIDAYS

Japan
Spring Imperial Festival or Shunki-Koreisan
A day on which the Emperor pays special respect to his ancestors.

Pakistan
Pakistan Republic Day
Commemorates the establishment of Pakistan Republic on March 23, 1956.

UN Member Countries
World Meteorological Day

RELIGIOUS CALENDAR

The Saints
St. Victorian and his companions, martyrs. [d. 484]
St. Benedict the Hermit. [d. c. 550]
St. Ethelwald the Hermit. Also called *Edelwald, Ethelwold, Oidilwald.* [d. 699]
St. Turibius of Mongrovejo. [d. 1606] Optional Memorial.
St. Joseph Oriol, priest. [d. 1702]
St. Gwinear, missionary; patron of Gwinear, Cornwall. Also called *Fingar, Guigner.* [death date unknown]

The Beatified
Blessed Peter of Gubbio, Augustinian hermit. [d. c. 1250]
Blessed Sibyllina of Pavia, virgin and recluse. [d. 1367]

BIRTHDATES

1430 *Margaret of Anjou, Queen of England;* wife of Henry VI. [d. August 25, 1482]

1699 *John Bartram,* American botanist; called the *Greatest Contemporary Botanist* by Carolus Linnaeus; later recognized as the *Father of Botany in U.S.* [d. September 22, 1777]

1749 *Pierre Simon, Marquis de Laplace,* French astronomer, mathematician; noted for discovery of *invariability of planetary mean motions,* 1773. [d. March 5, 1827]

1760 *William Smith,* English geologist; founder of *stratigraphical geology.* [d. August 28, 1839]

1780 *Count Karl Robert Nesselrode,* Russian statesman; Chancellor of Russia, 1845–56. [d. 1862]

1823 *Schuyler Colfax,* U.S. politician, newspaper editor; U.S. Congressman,1854–69; U.S. Vice-President, 1869–73. [d. January 13, 1885]

1855 *Franklin Henry Giddings,* U.S. sociologist; author of *The Principles of Sociology.* [d. June 11, 1931]

1857 *Fannie (Merritt) Farmer,* U.S. cookery expert; noted for her standardization of measurements in recipes and the publication of her *Boston Cooking School Cookbook,* still a classic in its revised form as *Fannie Farmer Cookbook.* [d. January 15, 1915]

1858 *Ludwig Quidde,* German peace activist; Nobel Peace Prize (with F. E. Buisson), 1927. [d. March 5, 1941]

1872 *Michael Joseph Savage,* first Labour Prime Minister of New Zealand, 1935–40. [d. March 27, 1940]

1873 *Barron Gift Collier,* U.S. business executive, financier. [d. March 13, 1939]

1881 *Hermann Staudinger,* German chemist; Nobel Prize in chemistry for work on *giant molecules* and contributions to the development of *plastics,* 1953. [d. September 8, 1965]

Roger Martin du Gard, French novelist, dramatist; Nobel Prize in literature, 1937. [d. August 22, 1958]

1884 *Florence Ellinwood Allen,* U.S. jurist; first woman to be named to U.S. Circuit Court of Appeals, 1934. [d. September 12, 1966]

1887 *Juan Gris,* Spanish cubist painter. [d. 1927]

Sidney Hillman, U.S. labor leader, born in Lithuania; a

founder and president of *Amalgamated Clothing Workers of America*, 1915–46. [d. July 10, 1946]

1899 *Louis Adamic*, U.S. author, born in Yugoslavia; known for his expression of immigrants' ideals. [d. September 4, 1951]

1900 *Erich Fromm*, U.S. psychoanalyst, born in Germany; author of *The Art of Loving*. [d. March 18, 1980]

1907 *Daniel Bovet*, Swiss-Italian pharmacologist; Nobel Prize in physiology or medicine for development of *muscle-relaxing drugs*, 1957. [d. 1992]

1908 *Joan Crawford (Lucille Le Sueur)*, U.S. actress. [d. February 14, 1977]

1910 *Akira Kurosawa*, Japanese movie director. [d. September 6, 1998]

1912 *Werner (Magnus Maximilian) von Braun*, German-U.S. engineer; pioneer of rocketry; responsible for German development of *V-2 rockets*; the *Father of U.S. Space Exploration*. [d. June 16, 1977]

1929 *Roger Bannister*, British athlete, physician; first to run a mile in under four minutes, May 6, 1954.

1934 *Mark Rydell*, U.S. director; directed *On Golden Pond*, 1981 and *Havana*, 1990.

1937 *Robert Gallo*, U.S. physician; co-discoverer of AIDS.

1938 *Maynard Jackson*, U.S. politician, lawyer.

1951 *Ron(ald Vincent) Jaworski*, U.S. football player.

1952 *Teofilo Stevenson*, Cuban boxer; Olympic gold medalist, 1972, 1976.

1953 *Chaka Khan (Yvette Marie Stevens)*, U.S. singer, songwriter; member of the rock group, *Rufus*, 1972–78.

1955 *Moses Eugene Malone*, U.S. basketball player; three Most Valuable Player titles.

1957 *Amanda Plummer*, U.S. actress; Tony Award for *Agnes of God*, 1982.

HISTORICAL EVENTS

1324 *Pope John XXII* excommunicates *Louis IV* of Germany.

1509 *League of Cambrai* is formed, allying the Papacy, Holy Roman Empire, France, and Aragon against Venice.

1752 The first known example of printing in Canada, the *Halifax Gazette*, is produced by *John Bushell* in Nova Scotia.

1765 British Parliament passes the *Stamp Act*, imposing duties on the 13 American colonies.

1775 To encourage the arming of Virginia militia, *Patrick Henry* delivers *Give me liberty or give me death* speech to the second Virginia convention.

1801 *Paul I, Czar of Russia* is assassinated in the course of a palace revolution and succeeded by *Alexander I*.

1848 First officially organized settlers of New Zealand land at Dunedin.

1849 *Charles Albert, King of Sardinia*, abdicates in favor of his son, *Victor Emmanuel*.

1861 First tram cars in London begin operation at Bayside.

1877 *Mormon Bishop John D. Lee* is executed by a firing squad in Utah for his part in the September, 1857, *Mountain Meadow Massacre* of 120 emigrants bound for California.

1889 Lord Rosebery opens the *free steam ferry* at Woolwich in London.

1901 *Emilie Aguinaldo*, leader of a Philippine rebellion, is captured by U.S. forces.

1903 *Irish Bank Holiday* bill is passed, establishing *St. Patrick's Day* as bank holiday.

1918 The *German bombardment of Paris* by long-range guns begins from a distance of 75 miles *(World War I)*.

1919 *Benito Mussolini* founds the Fascist movement, *Fasci del Combattimento*, in Milan.

1933 *Adolf Hitler*, as Reich Chancellor and leader of the Nazi party, is formally given dictatorial powers by German Reichstag.

1935 The U.S.S.R. sells its share of the *Chinese Eastern Railway* to Manchuria, then ruled by Japan.

1942 First group of *Japanese-American citizens* are evacuated from the West Coast because of suspected disloyalty *(World War II)*.

1950 *Sophocles Venizelos* is inaugurated as premier of Greece.

World Meteorological Organization is established by United Nations to facilitate

march

an international system of coordinating weather data and observation.

1962 The world's first nuclear-powered merchant vessel, the *Savannah,* is launched at Camden, New Jersey.

1965 Maj. *Virgil I. Grissom* and Lieut. Comdr. *John Young* of the U.S. orbit the earth three times in a *Gemini* spacecraft and then land in the Atlantic off Grand Turk Island.

1966 *Arthur Michael Ramsey, Archbishop of Canterbury,* exchanges public greetings with *Pope Paul VI* in the first official visit to a Roman Catholic pontiff by a head of the Anglican Church in 400 years.

1982 General *Efrain Rios Montt* is named to head the government of Guatemala.

1985 *Muhammad Khan Junejo* is inaugurated as prime minister of Pakistan.

1994 Mexican presidential candidate *Luis Murrieta* is assassinated, causing unrest.

HOLIDAYS

Zambia
Africa Day

RELIGIOUS CALENDAR

The Saints

St. Irenaeus, Bishop of Sirmium and martyr. [d. 304]

St. Dunchad, Abbot of Iona; patron of sailors in Ireland. [d. 716]

St. Aldemar, abbot. Surnamed the *Wise.* [d. c. 1080]

St. Catherine of Vadstena, virgin and abbess. Invoked against miscarriages. Also called *Catherine of Sweden, Karin, Katherine.* [d. 1381]

SS. Simon of Trent, infant, and *William of Norwich,* martyrs. Simon also called *Simeon.* [d. 1475, 1144]

St. Gabriel the Archangel, the angel of the annunciation to Mary. Patron of postal, telegraph, and telephone workers.

The Beatified

Blessed Didacus of Cadiz, Franciscan priest; called the *Apostle of the Holy Trinity.* Also called *Diego.* [d. 1801]

BIRTHDATES

1494 *Georgius Agricola (Georg Bauer),* German mineralogist, physician; called the *Father of Mineralogy.* [d. November 21, 1555]

1607 *Michiel Adriaanszoon de Ruyter,* Dutch naval commander, hero in Dutch-English Wars. [d. 1676]

1754 *Joel Barlow,* U.S. poet, statesman; one of the *Hartford Wits.* [d. December 24, 1812]

1755 *Rufus King,* U.S. politician, diplomat, lawyer. U.S. senator, 1789–96 and 1813–25. [d. April 27, 1827]

1809 *Mariano José de Larra y Sanchez de Castro,* Spanish writer; considered one of the greatest Spanish satirists of the 19th century. [d. February 13, 1837]

1822 *Henry Murger,* French journalist, poet; known for his sketches of Bohemian life in Paris. [d. January 28, 1861]

1828 *Horace Gray,* U.S. judge; Supreme Court Justice, 1881–1902. [d. September 15, 1902]

1834 *William Morris,* British poet, artist; his work exerted great influence on decorating taste of Victorian England; considered a leader of the modern romantic school of English art. [d. October 1, 1896]

John Wesley Powell, U.S. geologist, ethnologist; explored *Grand Canyon;* an early director of the U.S. Geological Survey, 1881–94. [d. September 23, 1902]

1855 *Andrew William Mellon,* U.S. financier, government official, philanthropist; U.S. Secretary of the Treasury, 1921–32. [d. August 26, 1937]

1862 *Frank Weston Benson,* U.S. artist; known for his bird prints. [d. November 14, 1951]

1874 *Harry Houdini (Ehrich Weiss),* U.S. magician, escape artist, born in Hungary; renowned for his spectacular magic and escape tricks. [d. October 31, 1926]

1884 *Peter J. W. Debye,* Dutch chemist; Nobel Prize in chemistry for his investigations of dipole moments, 1936. [d. November 2, 1966]

1886 *Edward Weston,* U.S. photographer; known for his exceptional artistry as a nature photographer. [d. January 1, 1958]

1887 *Fatty Arbuckle (Roscoe Conkling Arbuckle),* U.S. film comedian. [d. June 29, 1953]

1893 *George Sisler,* U.S. baseball player. Baseball Hall of Fame, 1939. [d. March 26, 1973]

1897 *Wilhelm Reich,* Austrian-born psychoanalyst. [d. November 3, 1957]

1902 *Thomas E(dmund) Dewey,* U.S. politician, lawyer; Governor of New York, 1943–55; Republican candidate for President, 1944 and 1948. [d. March 16, 1971]

1903 *Adolf Friedrich Johann Butenandt,* German chemist; Nobel Prize in chemistry for studies of *sex hormones* (with L. Ruzicka), 1939.

1906 *Dwight MacDonald,* U.S. writer, critic; known for his sardonic wit and relentless standards in discussions of social issues; staff writer for *New Yorker,* and *Esquire.* [d. December 19, 1982]

1907 *Lauris Norstad,* U.S. Air Force general; Commander-in-Chief of U.S. Air Forces in Europe, 1951–56; Supreme Allied Commander in Europe, 1956–62. [d. September 12, 1988]

1909 *Clyde Barrow,* U.S. outlaw, robber, murderer; companion of Bonnie Parker (October 1). [d. May 23, 1934]

1917 *John C. Kendrew,* British scientist; Nobel Prize in chemistry for determining the structure of the muscle protein *myoglobin* (with M. F. Perutz), 1962. [d. August 23, 1997]

1919 *Lawrence (Monsanto) Ferlinghetti,* U.S. poet, publisher.

Robert Louis Heilbroner, U.S. economist.

1925 *Norman Fell,* U.S. actor; known for his role as Mr. Roper on television series, *Three's Company,* 1977–79.

1926 *Dario Fo,* Italian actor, playwright; Nobel Prize winner for literature, 1997.

1930 *Steve McQueen,* U.S. actor. [d. November 7, 1980]

1940 *Robert Gordon (Bob) Mackie,* U.S. fashion designer; Emmy Awards, 1969, 1976.

1941 *Joseph H. Taylor,* Jr., U.S. physicist; Nobel Prize for Physics with Russell A. Hulse for their discovery of binary pulsars, 1993.

1954 *Robert Reed Carradine,* U.S. actor; known for his starring role in *The Big Red One,* 1979.

Donna Pescow, U.S. actress; known for her starring role on television series, *Angie.*

1959 *Renaldo Nehemiah,* U.S. football player, track athlete.

1967 *Kathy Rinaldi,* U.S. tennis player.

1970 *Lara Flynn Boyle,* U.S. actress; got her start as Donna Hayward on the TV series *Twin Peaks.*

HISTORICAL EVENTS

1267 *Saint Louis of France* calls his knights to Paris to prepare for his *Second Crusade.*

1401 *Timur Lenk (Tamerlane),* Mongol ruler, conquers *Damascus.*

1449 English break truce, capturing *Fougères,* France, in *Hundred Years' War.*

1603 *Elizabeth I* of England dies and is succeeded by *James VI* of Scotland who is proclaimed *James I, King of England, Ireland, Scotland, and France.*

1644 A charter is granted to *Roger Williams* for the colony of *Rhode Island.*

1927 *Nationalist Chinese* troops seize Nanking.

1934 The U.S. adopts the *Tydings-McDuffie Act* providing for eventual independence for the *Philippines.*

1941 German General *Erwin Rommel* begins North African offensive *(World War II).*

Yugoslavia capitulates and signs pact with Germany *(World War II).*

1944 U.S. President *Franklin D. Roosevelt* issues statement appealing to Hungarians to help the Jews escape from Nazis *(World War II).*

1955 Tennessee Williams's play, *Cat on a Hot Tin Roof,* premieres on Broadway.

1958 Rock star, *Elvis Presley,* is inducted into the U.S. army.

1965 U.S. spacecraft *Ranger 9* crash-lands precisely on target in the Alphonsus crater of the moon after transmitting to earth 5,814 photographs of the crater region.

1976 The government of *Argentine President Isabel Perón* is overthrown by armed forces lead by Lt. General *Jorge Rafaél Videla.*

1977 *Morarji R. Desai* is sworn in as India's fourth prime minister, replacing *Indira Gandhi.*

1980 Salvadoran human rights activist, Archbishop *Oscar Romero,* is assassinated in San Salvador.

1982 Military coup in *Bangladesh* results in suspension of the constitution and imposition of martial law.

1986 Libyan and U.S. forces exchange gunfire after U.S.

naval planes enter a restricted area across the *Gulf of Sidra*.

1987 French premier, Jacques Chirac, signs a contract to build the first *Disneyland* amusement park in Europe on the outskirts of Paris.

1988 In an election that ends forty years of one-party rule, *Joe*

Bossano is elected chief minister of Gibraltar.

Mordechai Vanunu, a nuclear technician who leaked details of Israel's atomic weapons program to the British press, is convicted of espionage in Jerusalem.

1989 The oil tanker, *Exxon Valdez*, hits a reef off the coast of southern Alaska, causing the largest oil spill in U.S. history.

1998 The first legal *physician-assisted suicide* takes place in Oregon.

march

MARCH
25

HOLIDAYS

Cyprus
Greek Independence Day

Great Britain
Lady Day or Quarter Day
A day marking the end of the first quarter of the year (calculated from Christmas); also commemorates the appearance of the Angel Gabriel to the Virgin Mary announcing that she would be the mother of Christ.

Greece
Independence Day
Commemorates the day when the Greek flag was first raised in revolt against Ottoman domination, 1821.

San Marino
Universal Vote Day or Anniversary of the Arengo

Uganda
Public Holiday
Commemorates the formation of the Ugandan National Liberation Front (UNLF).

U.S. (Maryland)
Maryland Day
Commemorates the landing of Lord Baltimore and the first colonists on St. Clement's Island, 1634.

RELIGIOUS CALENDAR

Solemnities
The Annunciation of Our Lord to the Blessed Virgin Mary. [Also major Episcopal Holy Day; minor Lutheran festival.]

The Saints
The Good Thief, the thief who was crucified with Christ; patron of thieves. Also called *Dismas, Gestas,* or *Titus.* [d. 29 A.D.]

St. Barontius, monk and hermit. [d. c. 695]

St. Hermenland, abbot. [d. c. 720]

St. Alfwold, Bishop of Sherborne. [d. c. 1058]

St. Lucy Filippini, virgin. [d. 1732]

St. Ermelandus, abbot. [death date unknown]

The Beatified
Blessed Thomasius, hermit. Also called *Thomas.* [d. 1337]

Blessed James Bird, layman and martyr. [d. 1593]

BIRTHDATES

1252 *Conradin* (also called *Conrad V*), Holy Roman Emperor; King of Jerusalem and Sicily, 1266–68; last of the German Hohenstaufen dynasty; executed. [d. October 29, 1268]

1767 *Joachim Murat,* French cavalry leader; marshal with *Napoleon;* King of Naples, 1808–15; known as the *Dandy King.* [d. October 13, 1815]

1797 *John Winebrenner,* U.S. clergyman; founder of the *Church of God* denomination. [d. September 12, 1860]

1839 *William Bell Wait,* U.S. educator; devised an embossing machine for printing books for the blind. [d. October 25, 1916]

1862 *William Eugene Johnson (Pussyfoot Johnson),* U.S. reformer; militant Prohibitionist. [d. February 2, 1945]

1863 *Simon Flexner,* U.S. pathologist, bacteriologist; discoverer of the serum to treat *meningitis.* [d. May 2, 1946]

1867 *Arturo Toscanini,* U.S. conductor, born in Italy; one of the best known modern conductors. [d. January 16, 1957]

1871 *Gutzon Borglum (John Gutson de la Mothe Borglum),* U.S. sculptor; famed for his presidential sculptures on *Mt. Rushmore,* South Dakota. [d. March 6, 1941]

1881 *Béla Bartók,* Hungarian composer, pianist; recognized as the father of contemporary Hungarian music. [d. September 26, 1945]

1887 *Raymond Gram Swing,* U.S. radio commentator. [d. December 22, 1968]

1891 *Byron Price,* U.S. journalist, public official; U.S. Director of Censorship, 1941–45; Assistant Secretary General of UN, 1947–54. [d. August 6, 1981]

1901 *Ed(ward James) Begley,* U.S. actor; Academy Award for *The Unsinkable Molly Brown,* 1964. [d. April 28, 1970]

John Earl Fetzer, U.S. baseball executive, businessman; started Fetzer Broadcasting, 1930; owner, Detroit Tigers, 1956–83.

1908 *David Lean,* British director; two Oscar Awards for *Bridge on the River Kwai* and *Lawrence of Arabia.* [d. April 16, 1991]

1909 *Emil John (Dutch) Leonard,* U.S. baseball player; won 191 Major League games in twenty years of pitching.

1914 *Norman E. Borlaug,* U.S. agronomist; Nobel Peace Prize for his work in developing new varieties of *high-yield cereals,* 1970; U.S. Medal of Freedom, 1970.

1920 *Howard Cosell (Howard William Cohen),* U.S. sportscaster. [d. April 23, 1995]

Paul Mark Scott, British author; wrote *The Raj Quartet,* 1976. [d. March 1, 1978]

1921 *Simone Signoret (Simone-Henriette-Charlotte Kaminker),* French actress. [d. September 30, 1985]

1922 *Eileen Ford,* U.S. business executive.

1925 *(Mary) Flannery O'Connor,* U.S. short-story writer, novelist. [d. August 3, 1964]

1928 *James Arthur Lovell Jr.,* U.S. astronaut; aboard *Gemini 12* space mission.

1934 *Gloria Steinem,* U.S. feminist, writer, lecturer; founder and editor of *Ms.* magazine.

1937 *Tom Monaghan,* U.S. businessman; owner, Detroit Tigers, 1983–92, and Domino's Pizza.

1938 *Hoyt Wayne Axton,* U.S. singer, songwriter, actor; sold over twenty-five million records in twenty years.

1940 *Anita Bryant,* U.S. singer.

1942 *Paul Michael Glaser,* U.S. actor; known for his role as Starsky on television series, *Starsky and Hutch,* 1975–79.

1947 *Elton John (Reginald Kenneth Dwight),* British singer, songwriter; known for his outrageous stage costumes.

1948 *Bonnie Bedelia (Bonnie Culkin),* U.S. actress, singer, dancer; known for her starring role in *They Shoot Horses, Don't They?,* 1969.

1949 *Nick Lowe,* British singer, musician; known for song, *Cruel to Be Kind.*

1965 *Sarah Jessica Parker,* U.S. actress.

1971 *Sheryl Swoopes,* U.S. basketball player; Olympic gold medalist, 1994.

HISTORICAL EVENTS

1306 *Robert Bruce* is crowned *Robert I, King of Scotland.*

1634 Lord Baltimore's settlers arrive in *Maryland,* establishing the foundation of the new colony.

1799 Austrians defeat French at *Stokach* in *War of the Second Coalition.*

1821 Uprising occurs in the *Greek Peloponnesus,* initiating a decade of revolution against the Turks and civil war in Greece.

1900 Warfare breaks out anew between the *Ashantis* of West Africa and the British when the British seize the *Golden Stool,* a symbol of Ashanti royalty.

1904 *Armida,* the last opera of *Antonin Dvořák,* premieres in Prague.

1911 Fire in the Triangle Shirtwaist Co., near Washington Square, New York City, kills more than 150 persons, mostly young seamstresses who are unable to escape; the tragedy awakens New Yorkers to the misery and dangers of the *sweatshop* system.

1919 The Peace Conference of World War I is reduced to a *Council of Four* for decision making: Clemenceau of France, Lloyd George of Britain, President Wilson of the U.S., and Orlando of Italy.

1935 *Paul Van Zeeland* becomes premier of Belgium and is given decree powers for one year to cope with the nation's desperate financial situation.

1957 The *Treaty of Rome* is signed, establishing the *European Economic Community (Common Market).* Members are Belgium, France, West Germany, Italy, Luxembourg, and the Netherlands.

1965 About 25,000 *civil rights demonstrators* end a five-day march from Selma, to Montgomery, Alabama, with a rally demanding equal rights for blacks.

1966 U.S. Supreme Court declares the *poll tax* to be unconstitutional for all elections.

1972 Agreement to coordinate efforts to control the trade in

march

narcotic drugs is signed by 36 countries in Geneva.

1975 *King Faisal* of Saudi Arabia is assassinated in Riyadh by his nephew, Prince Faisal ibn Musad, who is subsequently beheaded publicly. *Crown Prince Khalid,* brother of the king, succeeds to the throne.

1983 Prince *Bhekimpi Dlamini* replaces Prince *Mabandla Dlamini* as prime minister of Swaziland.

1984 The first round of national elections is held in El Salvador. The centrist Christian Democratic Party candidate, *Jose Napoleon Duarte,* wins an absolute majority.

1985 *Vernon Walters* replaces *Jeane Kirkpatrick* as U.S. ambassador to the United Nations.

1986 Canadian officials announce the introduction of a one dollar coin planned to replace the Canadian paper dollar by 1989.

1987 The U.S. Supreme Court rules that an employer may voluntarily act to redress imbalances in the workforce through *affirmative action programs for women.* It is the first time that the court specifically addresses such programs for women.

1988 Representatives from the Sandinista government and contra forces sign a ceasefire accord in *Sapoa, Nicaragua.* The pact provides for a 60-day truce, a general amnesty, and continuing negotiations.

HOLIDAYS

Bangladesh
Independence Day
Commemorates the proclamation establishing Bangladesh, 1971.

Spain
Fiesta del Arbol or Arbor Day
Celebrated since 1895 when *King Alfonso XIII* planted a pine sapling at a ceremony near Madrid.

U.S. (Hawaii)
Prince Jonah Kuhio Kalanianaole Day or Regatta Day.
Commemorates the birth of the Prince.

RELIGIOUS CALENDAR

The Saints
St. Castulus, martyr. Also called *Castalus.* [d. 286]
St. Felix, Bishop of Trier. [d. c. 400]
St. Macartan, bishop. [d. c. 505]
St. Govan, hermit. Also called *Gowan.* [d. 6th century]
St. Braulio, Bishop of Saragossa; patron of Aragon; one of the most famous of the Spanish saints. [d. 651]
St. Ludger, Bishop of Münster; founder of the Monastery of Werden. Also called *Liudger.* [d. 809]
St. Basil the Younger, hermit. [d. 952]

BIRTHDATES

1516 *Konrad von Gesner,* Swiss naturalist; his *Historiae Animalium* is considered the basis of modern zoology. [d. December 13, 1565]

1749 *William Blount,* U.S. politician; one of first two senators of Tennessee; expelled from the Senate for attempting a conspiracy to increase illegally the value of western land. [d. March 21, 1800]

1753 *Sir Benjamin Thompson, Count Rumford,* American-English physicist; responsible for bringing Watt's steam engine into general use. [d. August 21, 1814]

1773 *Nathaniel Bowditch,* U.S. mathematician, navigator, astronomer. [d. March 16, 1838]

1819 *Louise Otto,* German writer; founder of the feminist movement in Germany. [d. March 13, 1895]

1840 *George Smith,* British Assyriologist; deciphered many cuneiform scripts. [d. August 19, 1876]

1850 *Edward Bellamy,* U.S. author; wrote *Looking Backward,* a utopian novel which gave rise to *Nationalist Clubs* throughout the U.S. devoted to achieving the ideals expressed in the novel. [d. May 22, 1899]

1859 *A(lfred) E(dward) Housman,* British poet, classical scholar. [d. April 30, 1936]

1868 *Ahmed Fuad Pasha, Fuad I, King of Egypt,* 1922–1936. [d. June 1936]

1873 *Sir Gerald du Maurier,* British theatrical manager and actor; father of novelist Daphne du Maurier. [d. April 11, 1934]

1874 *Robert Frost,* U.S. poet; Pulitzer Prize in poetry, 1921, 1924, 1937, 1943. [d. January 29, 1963]

Condé Nast, U.S. magazine publisher. [d. September 19, 1942]

1879 *Othmar H. Ammann,* U.S. engineer, bridge builder; designed the *George Washington, Golden Gate,* and *Mackinac* Bridges. [d. September 22, 1965]

1880 *Duncan Hines,* U.S. gourmet. [d. March 15, 1959]

1884 *Wilhelm Backhaus,* Swiss pianist; exponent of classical German music; professor of piano at Manchester Royal College. [d. July 5, 1969]

1891 *Leonard (Chico), Marx* U.S. comedian, member of the *Marx Brothers.* [d. October 11, 1961]

1892 *Paul Howard Douglas,* U.S. politician, educator; U.S. Senator, 1948–66. [d. September 24, 1976]

1893 *James Bryant Conant,* U.S. educator, diplomat; President of Harvard University, 1933–53; U.S. Ambassador to West Germany, 1955–57. [d. February 11, 1978]

Palmiro Togliatti, Italian political leader; Vice-Premier of Italy, 1945. [d. April 21, 1964]

1909 *Héctor José Cámpora,* Argentinian government official; President of Chamber of Deputies, 1946–55; ardent supporter of Juan D. Perón; President of Argentina for seven weeks (May–July, 1973) as stand-in for Perón who was in exile. [d. December 19, 1980]

1911 *Sir Bernard Katz,* British physiologist; Nobel Prize in physiology or medicine for discoveries of nature of substances found at the end of *nerve fibers* (with J. Axelrod and U. S. Von Euler), 1970.

Tennessee Williams (Thomas Lanier Williams), U.S. dramatist; Pulitzer Prize in drama, 1947, 1955. [d. February 25, 1983]

1914 *William Childs Westmoreland,* U.S. army general; commanded U.S. forces in Vietnam, 1964–68.

1916 *Christian Boehmer Anfinsen,* U.S. biochemist; Nobel Prize in chemistry (with S. Moore and W. H. Stein) for research on structure of *ribonuclease,* 1972.

Sterling Hayden (John Hamilton), U.S. actor, author; known for his roles in films, *The Asphalt Jungle,* 1950, and *Dr. Strangelove,* 1964. [d. May 23, 1986]

1919 *Strother Martin,* U.S. actor; known for his character acting in *Harper,* 1966; *Cool Hand Luke,* 1967; and *True Grit,* 1969.

1922 *William G(rawn) Milliken,* U.S. politician; Governor of Michigan, 1969–82.

1923 *Bob Elliot,* U.S. comedian.

1925 *Pierre Boulez,* French conductor, composer of abstract constructivist music.

1930 *Sandra Day O'Connor,* U.S. jurist; first woman U.S. Supreme Court justice, 1981; recipient of the ABA Medal, 1997.

1931 *Leonard Nimoy,* U.S. actor, director; known for his role as Mr. Spock on television series, *Star Trek,* 1966–69.

1934 *Alan Wolf Arkin (Roger Short),* U.S. actor, director; Tony Award for *Enter Laughing,* 1963.

1939 *James Caan,* U.S. actor; known for his roles in the movies, *Brian's Song,* 1971, *The Godfather,* 1972, and *Misery,* 1990.

1942 *Erica (Mann) Jong,* U.S. novelist, poet.

1943 *Robert (Upshur) Woodward,* U.S. journalist; with colleague Carl Bernstein (February 14) reported on the *Watergate Incident.*

1944 *Diana Ross,* U.S. actress, singer; member of the rock group, *The Supremes;* Tony Award, 1977.

1949 *Vicki Lawrence,* known for her roles on television series, *The Carol Burnett Show* and *Mama's Family.*

1950 *Theodore D. (Teddy) Pendergrass,* U.S. singer.

Martin Short, Canadian actor, comedian; cast member of television series, *Saturday Night Live,* 1984–85.

1954 *Curtis Sliwa,* U.S. social reformer; founder and president of a civil patrol group, the Guardian Angels, 1979.

1960 *Jennifer Grey,* U.S. actress; known for her performance in *Dirty Dancing,* 1987.

1962 *John Stockton,* U.S. basketball player.

HISTORICAL EVENTS

1027 *Conrad II* is crowned Holy Roman Emperor.

1780 The first British Sunday newspaper, *The British Gazette and Sunday Monitor,* is published.

1793 The Holy Roman Empire formally declares war on France.

1825 The *Republic of Mexico* is proclaimed at Monterey, California.

1871 The *Paris Commune,* the socialistic government of Paris which ruled until May 27, is formally established.

1913 Bulgarians take Adrianople in Turkey (*Balkan War*).

1917 The first *Battle of Gaza* begins (*World War I*).

1919 The *American Council on Education* is formally organized.

1934 The *British Road Traffic Act* requires *driving tests* for car owners.

1943 *Battle of Komandorskie Islands* is fought in Bering Sea *(World War II)*.

1946 The *United Nations Security Council* meets for the first time in New York.

1960 *Malagasy Republic (Madagascar)* becomes independent of France.

1964 The seven men accused in the *Great Train Robbery* are convicted in London.

1969 Sir *Learie Nicholas Constantine* becomes the first black member of the British House of Lords.

1971 Shaikh Mujibur Rahman declares East Pakistan independent as *Bangladesh*.

1975 North Vietnamese take *Hué (Vietnam War)*.

1979 President *Anwar el-Sadat* of Egypt and Prime Minister *Menachem Begin* of Israel sign a peace treaty ending more than 30 years of hostility between their nations.

1981 The *Social Democratic Party* gains official recognition in Great Britain.

1982 Groundbreaking takes place in Washington, D.C., for a memorial to honor American soldiers killed in *Vietnam*.

1987 The U.S. government sells its 85 percent ownership of *Conrail*, one of the nation's largest rail systems and earns $1.65 billion in one of the largest stock offerings in history.

1989 The first multicandidate election since 1917 is held in the Soviet Union.

1993 Scientists announce the discovery of the gene that causes *Huntington's Disease*.

march

MARCH
27

HOLIDAYS

Angola
Victory Day

Burma
Resistance Day or Armed Forces Day
Honors the movement of guerrilla forces to oppose invaders during World War II.

RELIGIOUS CALENDAR

The Saints
St. John of Egypt, desert hermit. [d. 394]

The Beatified
Blessed William Tempier, Bishop of Poitiers. [d. 1197]

BIRTHDATES

1676 *Ferenc Rákóczy II* Hungarian patriot; led insurrection in Hungary, 1703; defeated by Austrians, 1708. [d. April 8, 1735]

1753 *Andrew Bell,* Scottish educator, clergyman; introduced *Bell* or *monitorial system* of education. [d. January 27, 1832]

1785 *Louis XVII,* (Louis Charles) titular King of France, 1793–95. [d. June 8, 1795]

1797 *Alfred Victor, Comte de Vigny (Alfred de Vigny),* French poet, playwright, novelist; author of *Cinq-Mars,* 1826; elected to the French Academy, 1845. [d. September 17, 1863]

1809 *Georges Eugène Haussmann,* French architect; responsible for the replanning of *Paris.* [d. January 11, 1891]

1813 *Nathaniel Currier,* U.S. lithographer; partner with James Merritt Ives (March 5) in *Currier and Ives.* [d. November 20, 1888]

1844 *Adolphus Washington Greely,* U.S. Arctic explorer, soldier; supervised one of first successful meteorological expeditions to the Arctic; chief of U.S. Signal Service, responsible for laying thousands of miles of telephone and telegraph cables, 1886–1906; [d. October 20, 1935]

1845 *Wilhelm Konrad Röntgen,* German scientist; Nobel Prize in physics for discovery of *x rays,* 1901. [d. February 10, 1923]

1847 *Otto Wallach,* German organic chemist; Nobel Prize in chemistry for discovery of *alicyclic compounds,* 1910. [d. February 26, 1931]

1851 *Vincent d'Indy,* French composer; founder of *Schola Cantorum;* a leader in the radical modern school of French music. [d. December 1, 1931]

1857 *Karl Pearson,* British mathematician; developed *standard deviation theory,* 1893. [d. April 27, 1936]

1863 *Sir Frederick Henry Royce,* British automaker; with his partner C. S. Rolls founded Rolls Royce Ltd., 1904. [d. April 22, 1933]

1879 *Miller Huggins,* U.S. baseball manager; Baseball Hall of Fame, 1964. [d. December 25, 1929]

Edward Steichen, U.S. photographer; created such classics as *The Family of Man.* [d. March 25, 1973]

1880 *James Wares Bryce,* U.S. inventor; responsible for early developments in electronics and business machines; leader in development of visual display monitors for computers. [d. March 27, 1949]

1886 *(Ludwig) Mies van der Rohe,* prominent modern architect; Director of the Bauhaus 1930–1937. [d. August 17, 1969]

1892 *Ferde Grofé (Ferdinand Rudolph von Grofé),* U.S. composer and arranger; best known for *Grand Canyon Suite* and his arrangement of

Gershwin's *Rhapsody in Blue.*
[d. April 3, 1972]

1893 *Draža Mihajlovič (or Mikhailovitch),* Serbian soldier; organizer of guerrilla warfare against German and Italian armies *(World War II).* [d. July 17, 1946]

1899 *Gloria (May Josephine) Swanson,* U.S. actress. [d. April 4, 1983]

1901 *Eisako Sato,* Japanese statesman; Prime Minister, 1964–72; Nobel Peace Prize (with Sean MacBride), 1974. [d. June 3, 1975]

1906 *Pee Wee Russell (Charles Ellsworth Russell),* U.S. jazz clarinetist. [d. February 15, 1969]

1907 *Lucia Chase,* U.S. ballerina; principal dancer, American Ballet Theatre, 1940–60; co-director, 1945–80. [d. January 9, 1986]

1912 *(Leonard) James Callaghan,* British politician; Prime Minister, 1976–79.

1914 *Budd Schulberg,* U.S. writer, scriptwriter; author of *What Makes Sammy Run?*

1917 *Cyrus (Robert) Vance,* U.S. government official; U.S. Secretary of State, 1977–80.

1923 *Louis Simpson,* U.S. poet, teacher; Pulitzer Prize in poetry, 1963.

1924 *Sarah (Lou) Vaughan,* U.S. jazz vocalist. [d. April 3, 1990]

1927 *Anthony Lewis,* U.S. journalist; Pulitzer Prize in national reporting, 1955.

Mstislav Rostropovich, Russian-U.S. cello virtuoso, conductor; Music Director,

National Symphony Orchestra, Washington, D.C., 1977–94.

1930 *David Janssen (David Meyer),* U.S. actor. [d. February 13, 1980]

1934 *Arthur Mitchell,* U.S. dancer, choreography; founder of the Dance Theatre of Harlem, 1969.

1942 *Michael York (Michael York-Johnson),* British actor.

1953 *Annemarie Proell,* Austrian skier; World Cup champion, 1971–75, 1979.

1955 *Chris McCarron,* U.S. jockey; inducted into Racing Hall of Fame, 1989.

1958 *Susan Molinari,* U.S. politician; representative for New York, 1990–97.

1963 *Randall Cunningham,* U.S. football player.

Quentin Tarantino, U.S. director.

1970 *Mariah Carey,* U.S. pop singer.

HISTORICAL EVENTS

1625 *James I* of Great Britain dies and is succeeded by *Charles I.*

1794 U.S. President George Washington signs act officially establishing the *United States Navy.*

1802 England and France sign *Peace of Amiens* by which England receives *Trinidad* and *Ceylon.*

1854 France declares war on Russia *(Crimean War).*

1884 The first inter-city telephone link in the U.S. is put into

service between New York City and Boston.

1890 Spain adopts *universal suffrage.*

1899 First signals of *wireless telegraph* are sent across English Channel.

1917 The Russian grand dukes and royal princes renounce their hereditary rights and privileges *(Russian Revolution).*

1927 80,000 young Italian men are inducted into *Fascist party* and declared members of Fascist militia in Italy.

1943 The U.S. Army announces development of the *bazooka,* a portable antitank weapon.

1945 U.S. troops land on *Caballo Island* in the Philippines *(World War II).*

1951 *Khaled el Azam* becomes premier of Syria.

1961 *Gaston Eyskens* resigns as premier of Belgium after his Christian Social Party loses support in parliamentary elections.

1962 Archbishop Joseph Francis Rummel orders all Roman Catholic schools in the New Orleans diocese to end *segregation.*

1964 Alaska suffers the worst *earthquake* ever to hit North America. The city of Anchorage is destroyed.

1977 Two jumbo jets collide in *Tenerife,* Canary Islands, in the worst air disaster in history, killing 582 persons.

1980 *Mount St. Helens,* a volcano in Washington, dormant for 123 years, begins to erupt.

1987 Marine guards, Sergeant *Clayton Lonetree* and

march

Corporal *Arnold Bracy,* are accused of allowing Soviet agents access to top-security areas of the U.S. embassy in Moscow.

Wayne State University physicists reveal a ceramic compound which superconducts at -27 degrees Fahrenheit, the warmest temperature yet known.

1993 *Jiang Zemin* is elected president of China.

1996 *Yigal Amir* is sentenced to life imprisonment for the assassination of *Yitzhak Rabin* (November 4, 1991).

1998 *Sergie Kiriyenko* is selected as Russia's new prime minister.

HOLIDAYS

Libya

Evacuation Day
Commemorates the withdrawal of British troops and the end of Allied occupation after World War II, 1951.

RELIGIOUS CALENDAR

The Saints

St. Guntramnus, King of Burgundy. Also called *Gontran.* [d. 592]

St. Tutilo, Benedictine monk. [d. c. 915]

BIRTHDATES

1475 *Fra Bartolommeo (Baccio della Porta; Bartolommeo di Pagolo del Fattorino),* Italian painter; associated with Raphael, Bellini, and Giorgione; known for his *Apparition of the Virgin to St. Bernard.* [d. October 31, 1517]

1483 *Raphael (Raffaello Sanzio or Santi),* Italian painter; chief architect of St. Peter's in Rome; one of the great painters of the Italian Renaissance. [d. April 6, 1520]

1515 *Teresa of Avila (Teresa de Cepeda y Ahumda),* Spanish reformer, author; Carmelite nun famous for her mystical visions. [d. October 4, 1582]

1592 *Jan Amos Komenský (Johannes Amos Comenius),* Czech philosopher, educator; known for his innovations in education; devised the first textbook adapted for teaching children. [d. November 4, 1670]

1652 *Samuel Sewall,* American colonial jurist; presided over the *Salem witchcraft trials,* 1692. [d. January 1, 1730]

1660 *George I, King of Great Britain and Ireland,* 1714–27. [d. June 11, 1727]

1702 *Ignacio de Luzán,* Spanish critic, poet; known for his strict adherence to classical rules in composition. [d. May 19, 1754]

1750 *Francisco Antonio Gabriel Miranda,* Venezuelan revolutionary; led patriot army in Venezuela; dictator of Venezuela when it gained independence, 1811; forced to sign a treaty with Royalists, 1812. [d. July 14, 1816]

1793 *Henry Rowe Schoolcraft,* U.S. explorer, naturalist; wrote *The Myth of Hiawatha,* 1856. [d. December 10, 1864]

1811 *St. John Nepomucene Neumann,* U.S. Roman Catholic bishop; first male Roman Catholic saint from the U.S.; canonized, 1977. [d. January 5, 1860]

1817 *Francesco De Sanctis,* Italian critic; dubbed the *Father of Modern Literary Criticism in Italy.* [d. December 19, 1883]

1818 *Wade Hampton,* Confederate cavalry general during U.S. Civil War; Governor of South Carolina, 1876–79; U.S. Senator, 1879–91. [d. April 11, 1902]

1819 *Sir Joseph William Bazalgette,* British civil engineer; responsible for construction of London's main drainage system. [d. March 15, 1891]

1862 *Aristide Briand,* French statesman; prime minister seven times, 1909–32; Nobel Peace Prize (with G. Stresemann), 1926. [d. March 7, 1932]

1869 *William Allen Neilson,* U.S. educator, editor, author; President of *Smith College,* 1917–39. [d. February 13, 1946]

1871 *Willem Mengelberg,* Dutch orchestra conductor, pianist, composer; upon his suggestion the National Symphony Orchestra of New York merged with the New York Philharmonic Society to form the *New York Philharmonic-Symphony Orchestra.* [d. March 21, 1951]

1891 *Paul (Samuel) Whiteman,* U.S. musician, bandleader. [d. December 29, 1967]

march

1892 *Corneille J. F. Heymans,* Belgian physiologist; Nobel Prize in physiology or medicine for work on *respiration of sensory organs,* 1938. [d. July 18, 1968]

1895 *Christian Archibald Herter,* U.S. diplomat, journalist, politician; U.S. Secretary of State, 1959–61. [d. December 30, 1966]

Spencer Woolley Kimball, U.S. religious leader; President, Mormon Church, 1973–85. [d. November 5, 1985]

1902 *(Richard) Marlin Perkins,* U.S. television personality, adventurer; known for filming wild animals in their habitats on his television series, *Wild Kingdom,* 1963–85. [d. June 14, 1986]

1903 *Rudolf Serkin,* Austrian-U.S. pianist. [d. May 8, 1991]

1907 *Irving Paul (Swifty) Lazar,* U.S. businessman, literary agent. [d. December 30, 1993]

1909 *Nelson Algren,* U.S. novelist; author of *The Man with the Golden Arm* and *A Walk on the Wild Side.* [d. May 9, 1981]

1914 *Edmund (Sixtus) Muskie,* U.S. politician, lawyer; Democratic vice-presidential candidate, 1968; U.S. Secretary of State, 1980–81. [d. March 26, 1996]

1921 *Dirk Bogarde (Derek van den Bogaerd),* British actor, author.

1924 *Frederick Llewellyn (Freddie) Bartholomew,* U.S. actor; known for his starring role in *David Copperfield,* 1935. [d. January 23, 1992]

1928 *Zbigniew Brzezinski,* U.S. government official, political scientist, born in Poland; assistant to the President Jimmy Carter for national security affairs 1977–1981.

1930 *Jerome I. Friedman,* U.S. physicist; Nobel Prize for Physics with Richard Taylor and Henry Kendall, for their study of quarks, 1990.

1936 *(Jorge) Mario (Pedro) Vargas Llosa,* Peruvian author, politician; wrote *The Green House,* 1968.

1942 *Neil Gordon Kinnock,* Welsh politician; leader of Britain's Labor Party, 1983–92.

1944 *Ken(neth Joseph) Howard, Jr.,* U.S. actor, singer; known for his starring role on television series, *White Shadow,* 1978–81.

1948 *Dianne Wiest,* U.S. actress; Oscar winner (Best Supporting Actress) for *Hannah and Her Sisters,* 1986 and *Bullets Over Broadway,* 1994.

1954 *Reba McEntire,* U.S. country singer, actress.

1958 *Lucy Lawless,* New Zealand actress; known for her role as Xena on the TV series *Xena: Warrior Princess.*

HISTORICAL EVENTS

1774 British pass *Coercive Acts* against Massachusetts, one of the immediate causes of the *American Revolution.*

1849 *Frederick William IV* of Prussia is elected *Emperor of the Germans* by the German National Assembly.

1854 Great Britain declares war on Russia and France (*Crimean War.*)

1891 First world *weight-lifting* championship match is held in London.

1930 *Constantinople* is officially renamed *Istanbul, Angora* is renamed *Ankara,* and other Greek names are changed to Turkish ones by the government of Turkey.

1939 *Spanish Civil War* ends with the surrender of Madrid and Valencia to rebel forces under General *Francisco Franco.*

1941 King *Peter II* of Yugoslavia assumes the full powers of his office after the regency government of Prince *Paul* is deposed.

1942 British commandos raid *St. Nazaire* on the French coast (*World War II*).

1951 U.S. and United Nations officials sign agreement permitting the United Nations to issue its own postage stamps.

1960 *Pope John XXIII* creates ten new cardinals in a secret consistory, increasing the number of cardinals to a record 88.

1967 Pope *Paul VI* advocates land redistribution in his fifth encyclical letter.

1969 Czechoslovak victory over a Russian team in the world championship hockey tournament in Stockholm touches off anti-Soviet demonstrations in Czechoslovak cities.

Earthquake in Kutahya, Turkey, kills over 1000 and causes devastating damage.

1972 *Sir Dawda Jawara* is elected to a five-year term as president in The Gambia's first parliamentary elections.

1973 Egyptian President *Anwar el-Sadat* proclaims himself military governor-general of Egypt and assumes the duties of prime minister.

1974 Rumanian Communist Party leader *Nicolae Ceauşescu* is elected to the newly created post of President of Rumania.

1977 Sylvester Stallone's film, *Rocky,* wins an Academy Award for Best Picture.

1979 *Three Mile Island* nuclear power plant in southeastern Pennsylvania seriously malfunctions, raising fears of a meltdown of the reactor's core, causing the evacuation of thousands, and creating widespread concern about the safety of such facilities.

British Labour government falls when, for the first time in 55 years, the British House of Commons votes "no confidence" in Her Majesty's government.

1996 The British government orders a ban on the sale of cattle for meat products over the age of 30 months due to an outbreak of *mad cow disease*.

march

MARCH
29

HOLIDAYS

Central African Republic
Boganda Day
Anniversary of the death of *Barthelemy Boganda,* the nation's first president, 1959.

Malagasy Republic
Memorial Day
Commemorates the martyrs of the Malagasy Revolution of 1947.

Nationalist China (Taiwan)
Youth and Martyrs' Day

U.S.
Vietnam Veterans' Day
Commemorates the withdrawal of U.S. troops from Vietnam, 1973.

U.S. (Delaware)
Swedish Colonial Day
Celebrates the establishment of the first Swedish settlement in Delaware, 1638.

RELIGIOUS CALENDAR

The Saints
SS. Jonas and *Barachisius,* monks and martyrs. [d. 327]
SS. Mark, Bishop of Arethusa, and *Cyril,* deacon and martyr. [d. c. 365]
SS. Armogastes, Archinimus, and *Saturus,* martyrs. [d. c. 455]
SS. Gundleus, chieftain, and *Gwladys,* his wife. Gundleus also called *Gwynllyw,* or *Woolo.* [d. 6th century]
St. Rupert, Bishop of Salzburg; evangelized the Germans. [d. c. 710]

St. Berthold, priest, hermit; first superior of the Carmelite order. [d. c. 1195]
St. Ludolf, Bishop of Ratzeburg and martyr. [d. 1250]

The Beatified
Blessed Diemoda, virgin, nun, and recluse. Also called *Diemux.* [d. c. 1130]

BIRTHDATES

1769 *Nicolas Jean de Dieu Soult,* Duke of Dalmatia; Marshal of France under Napoleon. [d. November 26, 1851]

1790 *John Tyler,* U.S. lawyer, politician; tenth President of the U. S.; first vice-president to succeed to the presidency in U.S. history, upon the death of William Henry Harrison, 1841. [d. January 18, 1862]

1815 *Sir Henry Bartle Frere,* British statesman; colonial administrator; responsible for precipitating the *Zulu War.* [d. May 29, 1884]

1819 *Edwin Laurentine Drake,* U.S. oil-industry pioneer; drilled the first oil well in the world at Titusville, Pennsylvania. [d. November 8, 1880]

Isaac Mayer Wise, German-U.S. rabbi; the *Father of Reformed Judaism* in America. [d. March 26, 1900]

1853 *Elihu Thomson,* U.S. inventor; discovered alternating current (AC) repulsion phenomenon. [d. March 13, 1937]

1859 *Oscar Ferdinand Mayer,* U.S. businessman; founder of Oscar Mayer Co., meatpackers, 1888. [d. March 11, 1955]

1867 *Cy Young (Denton True Young),* U.S. baseball pitcher; Baseball Hall of Fame, 1937; annual award to outstanding pitcher in each major league named for him. [d. November 4, 1955]

1869 *Sir Edwin Landseer Lutyens,* British architect, artist; President of Royal Academy of Great Britain, 1938–44. [d. January 1, 1944]

Aleš Hrdlihčka, Bohemian-U.S. anthropologist, author; curator of physical anthropology department of the U.S. National Museum, Washington, D.C., 1910–43. [d. September 5, 1943]

1875 *Lou Hoover,* wife of U.S. President Herbert Hoover. [d. January 7, 1944]

1889 *Howard Lindsay,* U.S. playwright; Pulitzer Prize in drama, 1946. [d. February 11, 1968]

1892 *Joseph (Jozsef Pehm) Mindszenty,* Hungarian Roman Catholic cardinal;

known throughout the world for his adamant anti-Communist stand; imprisoned by Polish Communists, 1949–56. [d. May 6, 1975]

1902 *Sir William Walton,* British composer; first important work was *Façade* written to accompany poems by his patron, *Edith Sitwell.* [d. May 8, 1983]

1906 *E(dward George) Power Biggs,* British. U.S. organist; authority on J. S. Bach; popularized baroque organ music. [d. March 10, 1977]

1916 *Eugene McCarthy,* U.S. politician, Senator; contender for Democratic presidential nomination, 1968.

1918 *Pearl (Mae) Bailey,* U.S. singer. [d. August 17, 1990]

Sam Moore Walton, U.S. businessman; Chairman, Wal-Mart; one of the richest men in U.S. [d. April 5, 1992]

1927 *John R(obert) Vane,* British pharmacologist; Nobel Prize in physiology or medicine (with Sune K. Bergstrom and Bengt I. Samuelsson), 1982.

1936 *Judith Guest,* U.S. author; wrote *Ordinary People,* 1976.

1937 *Billy Carter,* brother of Jimmy Carter, 39th U.S. President. [d. September 25, 1988]

1942 *Larry Pressler,* U.S. politician; Senator, 1979– .

1943 *Eric Idle,* British actor, author; Cannes Film Festival Award for *Monty Python's Meaning of Life,* 1983.

Vangelis (Evangelos Papathanassiou), Greek composer; Academy Award for score of *Chariots of Fire,* 1982.

John Major, British politician; former Prime Minister of England, 1990–94.

1944 *Dennis Dale (Denny) McLain,* U.S. baseball player; two Cy Young Awards, 1968, 1969.

1945 *Walt Frazier,* U.S. basketball player.

1954 *Karen Ann Quinlan,* U.S. coma victim since 1975; her parents won a landmark court decision to remove life-support systems. [d. June 11, 1985]

1956 *Kurt Thomas,* U.S. gymnast; first U.S. male to win gold medal in world competition for gymnastics.

1957 *Christopher Lambert,* French actor.

1964 *Elle Macpherson,* Australian supermodel.

1976 *Jennifer Capriati,* U.S. tennis player.

HISTORICAL EVENTS

1461 *Edward IV* of York defeats former *King Henry VI* of Lancaster at Towton *(War of the Roses).*

1632 *Treaty of St. Germain-en-Laye;* England restores North American possessions of *Acadia* and the *St. Lawrence* to France *(Thirty Years' War).*

1638 The first Swedish colonists in America establish a Lutheran settlement at *Fort Christiana, Delaware.*

1792 *Gustavus III* of Sweden dies of gunshot wounds suffered 13 days earlier and is succeeded by *Gustavus IV.*

1804 Thousands of whites are massacred in *Haiti* as a result

of a proclamation by *Jean Jacques Dessalines.*

1809 *Gustavus IV* of Sweden is forced to abdicate and is succeeded by *Charles XIII.*

1847 *Vera Cruz* is besieged by U.S. troops and surrenders *(Mexican War).*

1849 The *British* formally annex the *Punjab* after the defeat of the Sikhs in India.

1871 Queen Victoria opens the *Royal Albert Hall* in London.

1882 *The Knights of Columbus* fraternal benefit society of Catholic men is chartered.

1923 A customs union is concluded between *Switzerland* and *Liechtenstein* under which Switzerland will operate postal and telegraph services and protect the foreign interests of Liechtenstein.

1925 *Japan* passes a universal *male suffrage* law.

1936 *Nazi* candidates win elections in Germany with *Adolf Hitler* receiving 99 per cent of the vote.

1938 *Eastern Air Lines* is incorporated in Delaware.

1959 *Some Like It Hot,* a film comedy starring Marilyn Monroe, Jack Lemmon, and Tony Curtis, premieres in New York.

Barthelemy Boganda, first President of the *Central African Republic,* is killed in a plane crash.

1961 The *23rd Amendment* to the U.S. Constitution, giving District of Columbia residents the right to vote in presidential elections, is ratified.

1963 United Kingdom grants *Northern Rhodesia* the right to secede from the *Federation of Rhodesia and Nyasaland.*

1965 The U.S. Supreme Court rules that a business may close in order to prevent a union from forming.

1967 *Le Redoutable,* France's first nuclear-powered submarine, is launched.

1971 U.S. army court-martial finds 1st Lieut. *William L. Calley,* *Jr.,* guilty of the premeditated murder of at least 22 South Vietnamese civilians at *My-Lai* in March 1968.

Ford Motor Co. recalls 220,000 *Pintos* to repair a defect responsible for fires in the engine compartment.

1973 Last U.S. prisoners of war held by Communist forces in *Vietnam* are released and the last U.S. troops withdrawn from *South Vietnam.*

1976 The film, *One Flew Over the Cuckoo's Nest,* wins four Academy Awards.

Argentinian Lt. General *Jorge Rafaél Videla* takes oath of office as president of Argentina five days after overthrow of the government of *Isabel Perón.*

1982 *El Chínchon* volcano in *Mexico* begins series of eruptions, killing and injuring hundreds.

HOLIDAYS

U.S. (Georgia)
Doctor's Day
Sponsored by McLaren General Hospital, Barrow County, Georgia

RELIGIOUS CALENDAR

The Saints
St. Regulus, first bishop of Senlis, France. Patron of the City and Diocese of Senlis. Also called *Rieul.* [d. c. 250]

St. John Climacus, hermit and Abbot of Mt. Sinai. Wrote the *Ladder to Perfection.* Also called *John the Scholastic.* [d. c. 649]

St. Zosimus, Bishop of Syracuse. Also called *Zozimus.* [d. c. 660]

St. Osburga, virgin and first abbess of Coventry. [d. c. 1016]

The Beatified
Blessed Dodo, solitary. [d. 1231]
Blessed Amadeus IX of Savoy, duke. [d. 1472]

BIRTHDATES

1135 *Moses Maimonides,* Spanish rabbi, physician, Arabic scholar, and Jewish philosopher; attempted to reconcile Judaism with Aristotelian philosophy. [d. December 13, 1204]

1746 *Goya, (Francisco José de Goya y Lucientas),* Spanish painter, etcher; known as the master of 18th-century Spanish school of art. [d. April 16, 1828]

1820 *Anna Sewell,* British author; wrote *Black Beauty,* 1877. [d. April 25, 1878]

1840 *Charles Booth,* British shipowner, sociologist, statistician, and reformer; known for efforts to obtain passage of *Old Age Pension Act.* [d. November 23, 1916]

1844 *Paul Verlaine,* French symbolist poet; recognized as the leader of the *Symbolist School* of French poetry. [d. January 8, 1896]

1853 *Vincent van Gogh,* Dutch painter; associated with *Post-Impressionist School.* [d. July 29, 1890]

1876 *Clifford Whittingham Beers,* U.S. mental hygienist; dubbed *Father of the Mental Hygiene Movement* in the U.S. [d. July 9, 1943]

1880 *Sean O'Casey (John O'Casey),* Irish dramatist. [d. September 18, 1964]

1883 *Jo Davidson,* U.S. sculptor; known for his portraits and sculptures of many of the leading figures of his time. [d. January 2, 1952]

1913 *Richard McGarrah Helms,* U.S. government official; Director, Central Intelligence Agency, 1966–73.

Frankie Laine (Frank Paul LoVecchio), U.S. singer.

1918 *Robert L. (Bob) Evans,* U.S. restaurateur; President, Bob Evans Farms, Inc.

1919 *McGeorge Bundy,* U.S. educator, government official; Dean, Faculty of Arts and Sciences, Harvard University, 1953–61; Special Assistant for National Security Affairs, 1961–66; President, Ford Foundation, 1966–79.

1930 *John Allen Astin,* U.S. actor, director; known for his role as Gomez Addams on television series, *The Addams Family,* 1964–66.

Peter Marshall (Pierre LaCock), U.S. actor, television host; known for hosting over five thousand shows of *The Hollywood Squares.*

1937 *Warren Beatty,* U.S. actor, director, screenwriter.

1945 *Eric Clapton,* British musician; member of the rock groups, *Cream, Yardbirds, Derrick and the Dominos,* and *Blind Faith.*

1957 *Paul Reiser,* U.S. comedian, actor; best known for his role as Paul Buchman on the TV sitcom *Mad About You.*

1968 *Celine Dion,* Canadian pop singer.

HISTORICAL EVENTS

1406 *James I* of Scotland is captured near *Flamborough Head* by the English and is imprisoned by *Henry IV* of England.

1492 The Jews are expelled from Spain by Inquisitor-General Tomás de Torquemada (*Spanish Inquisition*).

1806 *Joseph Bonaparte* is declared *King of Naples*.

1856 The *Crimean War* ends with the signing of the *Treaty of Paris*.

1863 *William, Prince of Denmark,* assumes the throne as king of *Greece*.

1867 U.S. purchases *Alaska* from Russia for $7,200,000. The purchase is referred to as *Seward's Folly*.

1869 *The 15th Amendment* to the U.S. Constitution is ratified, forbidding voting discrimination based on race, color, or previous condition of servitude.

1909 The *Queensboro Bridge* opens, linking the New York City boroughs of Queens and Manhattan.

1917 The independence of *Poland* is proclaimed by the Russian provisional government.

All imperial lands and lands belonging to monasteries are confiscated by the Russian provisional government.

1919 *Mahatma Gandhi* begins organized defiance of British government after passage of the *Rowlatt Acts* with a general strike and a campaign of peaceful *civil disobedience*.

1941 U.S. takes possession of all German, Italian, and Danish ships in the U.S. *(World War II)*.

1945 Soviet forces invade *Austria* from the east *(World War II)*.

1951 Rodgers and Hammerstein's *The King and I* premieres in New York.

1953 *Denmark* abolishes the Upper House of Parliament, lowers the voting age to 23, and promulgates a new constitution.

1962 *Jose Maria Guido* assumes power in Argentina after a bloodless coup d'etat.

1963 Colonel *Enrique Peralta Azurdia* assumes power in Guatemala after a bloodless coup d'etat.

1972 *Great Britain* imposes direct rule on *Northern Ireland*.

1975 North Vietnamese capture *Da Nang,* South Vietnam.

1981 U.S. president *Ronald Reagan* is wounded in an assassination attempt by *John W. Hinckley, Jr.*

1985 *Christos Sartzetakis* is inaugurated as president of Greece.

1994 After tribal warfare begins in *Rwanda,* refugees flee the violence and head for Tanzania. A few weeks later, two thousand of the refugees are massacred by Rwandan troops.

1998 *Robert Kocharyan* is elected president of Armenia.

Victor Ciorbea resigns as premier of Romania.

HOLIDAYS

Malta
National Day or Freedom Day
Commemorates Maltese achievement of independence from Great Britain, 1964.

U.S. (Virgin Islands)
Virgin Islands Transfer Day
Celebrates date the Virgin Islands were transferred from Danish to U.S. control.

RELIGIOUS CALENDAR

The Saints
St. Acacius, bishop. Also called *Achates,* or *Achatius.* [d. 3rd century]
St. Benjamin, deacon and martyr. [d. c. 421]
St. Guy of Pomposa, abbot. Also called *Guido, Guion, Wido, Wit,* or *Witen.* [d. 1046]
St. Balbina, virgin. [death date unknown]

The Beatified
Blessed Joan of Toulouse, virgin; founder of the Carmelite Tertiary Order [d. 14th century]
Blessed Bonaventure of Forli, Vicar General of the Order of Servites. [d. 1491]

BIRTHDATES

1499 *Pope Pius IV,* pope 1560–65. [d. December 9, 1565]

1596 *René Descartes,* French philosopher, mathematician, scientist; founder of *Rationalism;* his philosophy, *Cartesianism,* espoused the possibility of mathematical certitude in metaphysical issues. [d. February 1, 1650]

1675 *Pope Benedict XIV,* pope 1740–58. [d. May 3, 1758]

1723 *Frederick V, King of Denmark and Norway,* 1746–66. [d. January 14, 1766]

1732 *(Franz) Joseph Haydn,* Austrian composer. [d. May 31, 1809]

1809 *Edward Fitzgerald,* British poet, translator; especially noted for his translation of works of *Omar Khayyám.* [d. June 14, 1883]

Nikolai Vasilyevich Gogol, Russian short-story writer, novelist, dramatist. [d. February 21, 1852]

1811 *Robert Wilhelm Bunsen,* German chemist, inventor. [d. August 16, 1899]

1835 *John La Farge,* U.S. landscape and figure painter. [d. November 14, 1910]

1837 *Robert Ross McBurney,* U.S. YMCA leader; responsible for centralized system of leadership in *YMCA.* [d. December 27, 1898]

1838 *Léon Dierx,* French poet. [d. June 11, 1912]

1844 *Andrew Lang,* Scottish author, translator. [d. July 20, 1912]

1857 *Edouard Rod,* Swiss novelist, critic. [d. January 29, 1910]

1878 *Jack Johnson,* U.S. boxer; first black to hold world heavyweight title, 1908–15. [d. June 10, 1946]

1887 *St. John Perse (Marie René Auguste Alexis Léger),* French poet, diplomat; Nobel Prize in literature, 1960. [d. September 20, 1975]

1890 *Sir William Lawrence Bragg,* Australian-British physicist; Nobel Prize in physics (with W. H. Bragg), 1915; the youngest man ever to win a Nobel Prize. [d. July 1, 1971]

1906 *Sin-Itiro Tomonaga,* Japanese physicist; Nobel Prize in physics (with J. S. Schwinger and R. P. Feynman), 1965.

1908 *Red Norvo,* U.S. musician.

1912 *William (Julius) Lederer,* U.S. novelist, non-fiction writer.

1914 *Octavio Paz,* Mexican poet, critic, social philosopher. [d. April 19, 1998]

1925 *Felice Leonardo (Leo) Buscaglia,* U.S. educator, author; lecturer on interpersonal relationships; wrote *Living, Loving, Learning,* 1982.

1926 *John Fowles,* British novelist.

1927 *Cesar Estrada Chavez,* U.S. labor union organizer. [d. April 23, 1993]

William Daniels, U.S. actor; Emmy Award for his role as Dr. Mark Craig on television series, *St. Elsewhere,* 1984.

1928 *Gordon (Gordie) Howe,* Canadian-born hockey player.

1929 *Elisabeth (Liz) Claiborne,* U.S. fashion designer.

1932 *John Jakes,* U.S. author;wrote *The Bastard,* 1974, and *The Rebels,* 1975.

1934 *Shirley Jones,* U.S. actress, singer; Academy Award for *Elmer Gantry,* 1960; known for her starring role on television series, *The Partridge Family,* 1970–74.

Carlo Rubbia, Italian physicist; Nobel Prize in physics for demonstrating the existence of subatomic particles called intermediate vector bosons (with Simon van der Meere), 1984.

1935 *Herb Alpert,* U.S. musician, band leader; co-founder, A & M Records, 1962.

1940 *Patrick Joseph Leahy,* U.S. politician; Senator, 1974– .

1943 *Christopher Walken,* U.S. actor; Academy Award for *The Deer Hunter,* 1978.

1945 *Gabriel (Gabe) Kaplan,* U.S. actor, comedian; known for his starring role on television series, *Welcome Back, Kotter,* 1975–79.

1946 *Rhea Perlman,* U.S. actress; Emmy Award for her role as Carla on television series, *Cheers,* 1984.

HISTORICAL EVENTS

1084 *Clement III* (antipope) crowns *Henry IV* Holy Roman Emperor.

1146 *St. Bernard of Clairvaux* preaches the *Second Crusade* at Vezelay.

1282 A bloody uprising of the Sicilians against the French (Angevin) rule takes place; called the *Sicilian Vespers* because it breaks out at the hour of vespers.

1495 *Holy League,* consisting of Holy Roman Emperor Maximilian I, Pope Alexander VI, Spain, Venice, and Milan, is formed against *Charles VIII* of France who is forced to leave Italy.

1547 *Francis I* of France dies and is succeeded by *Henry II.*

1621 *Philip III* of Spain dies and is succeeded by *Philip IV.*

1657 *Humble Petition and Advice* offers title of King of England to *Oliver Cromwell.*

1814 *Paris* surrenders to Alliance of Austria, Russia, and Prussia *(Napoleonic Wars).*

1854 U.S. Commodore *Matthew Perry* signs *Treaty of Kanagawa,* the first treaty between Japan and the U.S., opening two Japanese ports and permitting regulated trade.

1861 Great Britain recognizes Italy as a kingdom under *Victor Emmanuel II.*

1901 A British proclamation outlaws *slave trade* in the Nigerian protectorates.

1917 *Danish West Indies* (Virgin Islands, St. Thomas, St. Croix, and St. John) purchased from Denmark by U.S. for $25 million.

1918 *Daylight Saving Time* first goes into effect in the U.S.

1933 *Civilian Conservation Corps* is established under the *Unemployment Relief Act* in U.S. to provide work for more than 3 million unemployed American men.

1943 Rodgers and Hammerstein's *Oklahoma!* premieres in New York.

1944 The *Soldier Vote bill* becomes law, enabling members of the U.S. armed forces stationed abroad to vote on absentee ballots *(World War II).*

1945 Tennessee Williams's play, *The Glass Menagerie,* premieres in New York.

1947 *Dodecanese Islands,* held by Italy from 1912 to 1943, are transferred to Greece.

1949 *Newfoundland* joins Canadian Federation as the tenth province.

1959 The *Dalai Lama,* fleeing Chinese occupation of Tibet, is given political asylum by India.

1967 *NATO Supreme Military Headquarters* formally opens in Casteau, Belgium.

1968 U.S. President *Lyndon B. Johnson* announces that he will neither seek nor accept another term as president.

1969 Kurt Vonnegut's novel, *Slaughterhouse Five,* is published.

1970 The first U.S. satellite, *Explorer I,* returns to the earth's atmosphere more than 12 years after its launch.

1970 *Lesotho* Prime Minister *Leabua Jonathan* orders *King Moshoeshoe II* into exile.

1971 U.S. army jury sentences Lt. *William Calley* to life imprisonment for murder of South Vietnamese civilians at *My Lai* in 1968.

1976 The New Jersey Supreme Court rules that a mechanical life sustaining system may be removed from *Karen Ann Quinlan.*

1977 Michael Christofer's play, *The Shadow Box,* opens on Broadway.

1983 Team owners and the *National Basketball Players Association* agree on a four-year labor contract which introduces *revenue sharing* for players for the first time in professional sports.

1987 New Jersey judge, Harvey R. Sorkow, awards custody of "*Baby M*" to William and Elizabeth Stern and rules that *surrogate parenting*

contracts are constitutionally protected.

1995 Mexican pop singer *Selena (Quintanliaa Perez),* known for her Tejano music, is killed by Yolanda Saldivar.

1996 Russian President *Boris Yeltsin* announces a peace plan for the Russian republic of Chechnya.

1998 The *United Nations* imposes a ban on the sale of weapons to *Yugoslavia* to ethnic unrest.

march

April is the fourth month in the Gregorian calendar and has 30 days. Prior to the reform of the calendar in 153 B.C., April was the second month of the Roman civil calendar. The Roman name for the month, *Aprilis,* is thought to be derived from the Latin verb aperire 'to open (as buds do)'; the precise etymology, however, is very uncertain.

The Roman emperor Nero (ruled 54–68) attempted unsuccessfully to have the name *Neronius* adopted for this month. In the time of Charlemagne April was referred to as the "Grass Month," one indication of its strong associations with the beginning of Spring and blossoming. The principal Christian and Jewish feasts, Easter and Passover, respectively, usually fall in April, and this parallels the celebration at this time of Spring festivals in many religions throughout history.

April spans the zodiac signs of Aries, the Ram (March 21–April 20) and Taurus, the Bull (April 20–May 20).

The birthstone for April is the diamond, and the flower is the sweet pea or daisy.

STATE, NATIONAL, AND INTERNATIONAL HOLIDAYS

Fast and Prayer Day
(Lesotho)
Second Friday

Fast and Prayer Day
(Liberia)
Second Friday

Patriot's Day
(Maine, Massachusetts)
Third Monday

Oklahoma Day
(Oklahoma)
April 22

Arbor Day
(Nebraska, Delaware)
April 22
(Wyoming)
Final Monday
(Utah)
Final Friday

Bird Day
(United States)
Last Friday

Confederate Memorial Day
(Alabama, Mississippi)
Final Monday
(Florida, Georgia)
April 26

SPECIAL EVENTS AND THEIR SPONSORS

Boost Your Home Town Month
Fraternal Order of Eagles

Correct Posture Month
American Chiropractic Association

Freedom Shrine Month
National Exchange Club

Glaucoma Alert Month
Society to Prevent Blindness

Philatelic Societies' Month
Franklin D. Roosevelt Philatelic Society

Red Cross Month
American Red Cross

National Drafting Week
First Week
American Institute for Design and Drafting

Publicity Stunt Week
First Week
Richard R. Falk Associates

Week of the Young Child
First Week
National Association for the Education of Young Children

National Bike Safety Week
Third Week
National Safety Council

Keep America Beautiful Week
Third Week
Keep America Beautiful, Inc.

National Library Week
Third Week
American Library Association

National Victims' Rights Week
Third Week
National Organization for Victim
Assistance

**General Federation of Womens'
Clubs Week**
Week containing April 24
General Federation of Womens'
Clubs

Canada-U.S. Goodwill Week
Final Week
Kiwanis International

Jewish Heritage Week
Final Week
Jewish Community Relations Council
of New York

National YWCA Week
Final Week
National Board of the YWCA of the
U.S.A.

Professional Secretaries' Week
Final Full Week
Professional Secretaries International

Grange Week
Final Full Week
The National Grange

Lion's Journey for Sight
Second Weekend
Lion's Club

**Death Anniversary of Franklin D.
Roosevelt**
April 12
Franklin D. Roosevelt Philatelic
Society

Arbor Day
April 22
National Arbor Day Foundation

Earth Day
April 22
Environmental Action, Inc.

**General Federation of Womens'
Clubs Day**
April 24
General Federation of Womens'
Clubs

World YWCA Day
Final Wednesday
National Board of the YWCA of the
U.S.A.

**World Day of Prayer for
Vocations**
*Final Sunday (or First Sunday in
May)*
National Catholic Vocation Council

HOLIDAYS

April Fools' Day or All Fools' Day
A day of practical jokes, intended to make fools of unsuspecting people.

Anguilla
Constitution Day

Popular Republic of Benin
Youth Day and Abdoulaye Issa Day

Cyprus
Cyprus National Day

Iran
Islamic Republic Day

San Marino
National Day or Captain Regents Day
The traditional date for the installation of *Capitani Regginti* or government officials.

RELIGIOUS CALENDAR

The Saints
St. Melito, Bishop of Sardis. [d. c. 180]
St. Walaricus, Abbot of Leuconaus and missionary. Also called *Valéry.* [d. c. 620]
St. Agilbert, Bishop of Paris. Also Bishop of Dorchester-on-Thames. [d. c. 690]
St. Tewdric, Prince and hermit. Also called *Theodoric.* [d. 5th–6th centuries]
St. Macarius the Wonder-worker, Abbot of Constantinople. [d. c. 830]
St. Hugh, Bishop of Grenoble. [d. 1132]

St. Gilbert of Caithness, bishop. [d. 1245]
St. Catherine of Palma, virgin. [d. 1574]

The Beatified
Blessed Ludovic Pavoni, founder of the Sons of Mary Immaculate of Brescia. [d. 1849]

BIRTHDATES

1578 *William Harvey,* English physician; *Father of Modern Physiology;* discovered that blood circulates. [d. June 3, 1657]

1616 *Charles de Marguetel de Saint-Denis, Sieur de Saint-Evremond,* French courtier, writer; exiled to England; an intimate of Hortense Mancini, Duchess of Mazarin. [d. September 20, 1703]

1697 *Antoine François Prévost (Abbé Prévost or Prévost d'Exiles),* French novelist, journalist; spent his life in travel and adventure. [d. December 23, 1763]

1730 *Salomon Gessner,* Swiss writer, painter, and etcher; wrote *Der Tod Abels,* which was translated into most European languages. [d. March 2, 1788]

1753 *Joseph Marie de Maistre,* French statesman, writer, and philosopher; opponent of the French Revolution. [d. February 26, 1821]

1755 *Anthelme Brillat-Savarin,* French politician, writer; best known for his *Physiologie du Goût,* a literary work on gastronomy. [d. 1825]

1815 *Otto von Bismarck (The Iron Chancellor),* German statesman; founder and first chancellor of the German Empire. Unified the German states into one empire under Prussian leadership. [d. July 20, 1898]

1823 *Simon Bolivar Buckner,* Confederate Army general during U.S. Civil War; Governor of Kentucky, 1887–91. [d. January 8, 1914]

1834 *James (Jim) Fisk,* U.S. financier. [d. January 7, 1872]

1852 *Edwin Austin Abbey,* U.S. artist, illustrator. [d. 1911]

1865 *Richard Adolf Zsigmondy,* German chemist; Nobel Prize in chemistry for research on *colloid solutions,* 1925. [d. September 23, 1929]

1866 *Sophonisba Breckinridge,* U.S. social reformer, social worker, educator; prominent activist for woman suffrage, child welfare, prison reform, labor legislation, and international peace. [d. July 30, 1948]

april

Ferruccio Benvenuto Busoni, Italian composer, transcriber, pianist, conductor. [d. July 27, 1924]

1868 *Edmond Rostand,* French dramatist; best known for his play, *Cyrano de Bergerac.* [d. December 2, 1918]

1873 *Sergei (Wassilievitch) Rachmaninoff,* U.S. piano virtuoso, composer, born in Russia. [d. March 28, 1943]

1883 *Lon Chaney,* U.S. silent-screen actor; known as the *Man of a Thousand Faces.* [d. August 26, 1930]

1885 *Eli Lilly,* U.S. drug manufacturer, philanthropist; President and Chairman of the Board, Eli Lilly & Co. [d. January 24, 1977]

1886 *Wallace Beery,* U.S. character actor. [d. April 15, 1949]

1887 *Leonard Bloomfield,* U.S. linguistic scholar, educator. [d. April 18, 1949]

1901 *(Jay David) Whittaker Chambers,* U.S. journalist; His testimony accusing *Alger Hiss* of espionage led to the latter's conviction for perjury in a *cause célèbre* of 1949–1950. [d. July 9, 1961]

1909 *Eddy Duchin (Edwin Frank Duchin),* U.S. pianist. [d. February 9, 1951]

1919 *Joseph E. Murray,* U.S. surgeon; Nobel Prize for Medicine. Murray shares the prize with Thomas E. Donnall for their work on transplant techniques, 1990.

1920 *Toshiro Mifune,* Japanese actor, director. [d. December 24, 1977]

1922 *William Manchester,* U.S. novelist, biographer; author of *The Death of a President,* 1967.

1929 *Milan Kundera,* Czechoslovak author; wrote *The Book of Laughter and Forgetting,* 1980, and *The Unbearable Lightness of Being,* 1984.

Jane Powell (Suzanne Burce), U.S. actress, singer; a leading lady in 1940s–1950s films.

Glenn Edward (Bo) Schembechler, former U.S. football coach, athletic administrator; head coach, University of Michigan, 1969–89.

1932 *Debbie (Marie Frances) Reynolds,* U.S. actress, singer; known for her starring roles in *The Unsinkable Molly Brown,* 1964, and *Singing in the Rain,* 1952.

1938 *Ali MacGraw,* U.S. model, actress; known for her starring role in *Love Story,* 1971.

1939 *Phil(ip Henry) Niekro,* U.S. baseball player.

1947 *David Eisenhower,* U.S. author, lawyer; grandson of Dwight David Eisenhower, thirty-fourth U.S. President.

1948 *Jimmy Cliff,* Jamaican singer.

HISTORICAL EVENTS

1406 *Robert III, of Scotland,* dies and is succeeded by his younger brother, *Robert Stewart,* Duke of Albany.

1810 *Napoleon* marries Archduchess *Marie Louise,* daughter of Francis I of Austria.

1865 The *Battle of Five Forks* proves to be the final and decisive battle of the *U.S. Civil War* as General Robert E. Lee's forces are defeated by the Union Army.

1906 Parliamentary elections for the first *Duma* (official assembly) are held in St. Petersburg, Russia, and result in a sweeping victory for the constitutional democrats.

1912 *Metric system* of weights and measures is adopted in *Denmark.*

Royal Flying Corps (later called the *Royal Air Force*) is established in Great Britain.

1924 The *Bank of Poland* is established.

1925 *Lord Balfour* dedicates *Hebrew University* at Jerusalem.

1929 The *Iraqi Army* is established.

1930 The *Child Marriage Act* prohibiting marriages of boys under 18 and girls under 14 comes into effect in India.

1933 An official *Anti-Semitic Day* is held in Germany as systematic persecution of German Jews begins.

1939 The United States recognizes Spanish rebel government of *Francisco Franco (Spanish Civil War).*

1942 Winthrop Chemical Co. reports the development of *Demerol,* a synthetic drug which can be used as a substitute for morphine.

1943 The U.S. air force bombs *Cagliari Harbor* and several Sardinian airfields in a major campaign against German troops in North Africa *(World War II).*

1945 U.S. invasion of *Okinawa* begins *(World War II).*

1947 *Paul I* is crowned King of Greece following the death of *George II.*

1950 *Indian government* centralizes control of post office, telegraph, customs, excise and income taxes, and armed forces.

1954 The *U.S. Air Force Academy* is established.

1960 *Tiros I,* first U.S. satellite designed to provide detailed photos of the earth's weather, is launched into orbit.

1961 *Emile Griffith* defeats *Benny Paret* to win the world welterweight boxing title.

1970 President Richard Nixon signs a bill banning television and radio *cigarette advertising.*

1977 The Spanish government disbands Francisco Franco's *National Movement* political organization.

1979 The last British sailors leave *Malta,* ending 179 years of a British military presence.

1998 The *Food and Drug Administration (FDA)* approves the artificial sweetener *sucralose.*

Radu Vasile is selected as the new premier of Romania after Victor Ciorbea resigns (March 30, 1998).

The *Paula Jones* sexual harassment lawsuit against U.S. President *Bill Clinton* is dismissed.

april

APRIL
2

HOLIDAYS

Iran
Revolution Day

U.S. (Florida)
Pascua Florida Day

RELIGIOUS CALENDAR

The Saints

SS. *Apphian of Palestine,* and
Theodosia, martyrs. Apphian
also called *Apian.* [d. 306]

St. *Mary of Egypt,* penitent; patron
of penitent women who
formerly lived in sin. Also
called *Mary Egyptica.* [d. c.
5th century]

St. *Nicetius,* Bishop of Lyons. Also
called *Nizier.* [d. 573]

St. *Francis of Paola.* Founded the
Minim Friars; patron saint of
sailors. [d. 1507] Optional
Memorial.

St. *Leopold of Gaiche,* priest. [d.
1815]

The Beatified

Blessed *Francis Coll.* [beatified,
1979]

BIRTHDATES

742 *Charlemagne (Charles the
Great, Charles I),* French
ruler; King of the Franks,
768–814; conquered and
united almost all of the
Christian lands of western
Europe and ruled as emperor
800–814. [d. 814]

1725 *Giovanni Casanova de
Seingalt (Casanova),* Italian
writer; adventurer whose
name has become
synonymous with roguery and
romantic exploits. [d. June 4,
1798]

1798 *August Heinrich Hoffmann
von Fallersleben,* German
poet, scholar; author of
*Deutschland, Deutschland
über Alles,* adopted as
national hymn, 1922. [d.
January 19, 1874]

1805 *Hans Christian Andersen,*
Danish fairy-tale writer, poet,
novelist. [d. August 4, 1875]

1814 *Erastus Brigham Bigelow,*
U.S. textile manufacturer;
inventor of several types of
looms for specialty work
(particularly carpets).
Founded Bigelow Carpet
Mills, 1850. A founder of
*Massachusetts Institute of
Technology.* [d. December 6,
1879]

1827 *(William) Holman Hunt,*
British painter; one of the
founders of *Pre-Raphaelite
Brotherhood,* 1848. [d.
September 7, 1910]

1834 *Frédéric-Auguste Bartholdi,*
French-Italian sculptor;
designer of *Statue of Liberty.*
[d. October 4, 1904]

1838 *Léon Gambetta,* French
political leader; one of the

chief founders of the Third
Republic. [d. December 31,
1882]

1840 *Émile Zola,* French novelist,
critic; considered one of the
great leaders of the
naturalistic movement in
French literature. [d.
September 1902]

1862 *Nicholas Murray Butler,* U.S.
educator; president of
Columbia University; Nobel
Peace Prize, 1931. [d.
December 7, 1947]

1875 *Walter Percy Chrysler,* U.S.
industrialist; developer of the
six-cylinder auto engine;
founder of Chrysler
Corporation; responsible for
construction of *Chrysler
Building* in New York City.
[d. August 18, 1940]

1891 *Max Ernst,* German
expressionist-surrealist
painter, sculptor; chief
exponent of *Dadaism* in
Germany. [d. April 1, 1976]

1893 *Harold Lloyd,* U.S. comedian,
actor; highest paid film star of
the 1920s. [d. March 8, 1971]

1903 *Orville Liscum Hubbard,* U.S.
politician; Mayor of Dearborn,
Michigan, 1941–77. [d.
December 16, 1982]

1908 *Buddy Ebsen (Christian
Ebson, Jr.),* U.S. actor, dancer;
known for his starring roles in
television series, *The Beverly*

Hillbillies, 1962–71, and *Barnaby Jones*, 1973–79.

1914 *Sir Alec Guinness*, British actor; received Tony award for Best Actor, 1964, and Academy Award for Best Actor, 1957.

1920 *Jack Webb*, U.S. actor, producer; prominent in *Dragnet* television series. [d. December 23, 1982]

1926 *Sir John Arthur Brabham*, Australian auto racer, auto builder; Grand Prix champion, 1959–60, 1960–61, 1966.

1927 *Kenneth (Peacock) Tynan*, British drama critic; noted for his provocative criticism; leader in the acceptance of *new realism* in the British theater. [d. July 26, 1980]

1939 *Marvin (Pentz) Gaye*, U.S. singer; two Grammy Awards; known for song, *I Heard it through the Grapevine*. [d. April 1, 1984]

1941 *Leon Russell*, U.S. singer, musician.

1945 *Don(ald Howard) Sutton*, U.S. baseball player.

1945 *Linda Hunt*, U.S. actress; Oscar winner (Best Supporting Actress) for *The Year of Living Dangerously*, 1983.

1947 *Camille Paglia*, U.S. educator, writer; author of *Sexual Personae*.

1948 *Emmylou Harris*, U.S. singer, songwriter; two Grammy Awards, 1976, 1977.

1949 *Pamela Reed*, U.S. actress; known for role in *Kindergarten Cop*, 1990.

1955 *Dana Carvey*, U.S. actor; best known for his performances on the TV show *Saturday Night Live* and the movie, *Wayne's World*, 1992.

HISTORICAL EVENTS

1513 *Juan Ponce de León* discovers *Florida* and claims it for the King of Spain.

1792 *U.S. Mint* is established.

1801 *Lord Nelson* of England destroys the Danish fleet off Copenhagen.

1832 *Dom Pedro* proclaims himself regent of *Portugal*.

1849 Great Britain annexes the *Punjab* in India.

1860 First *Italian Parliament* meets at Turin.

1895 *The East India Railway* is opened by the lieutenant governor of Bengal.

1917 The Russian provisional government repeals all laws abridging religious freedom.

President *Woodrow Wilson* requests a declaration of war on Germany from the U.S. Congress, insisting that "the world must be made safe for democracy" *(World War I)*.

1921 *Armenian Soviet Socialist Republic* is proclaimed.

1942 *Juan Antonio Rios* is inaugurated as president of Chile.

1945 U.S. troops land on *Sanga Sanga* and *Bangao Islands*, Philippines (World War II).

1951 *United Nations Food and Agriculture Organization* opens its new headquarters in Rome.

1956 *Khim Tit* is appointed premier of Cambodia.

1960 *France* and *U.S.S.R.* sign agreements on trade, scientific and cultural exchanges, and peaceful uses of atomic energy.

1970 U.S. grand jury in Chicago indicts 12 members of the *Weatherman* faction of the *Students for a Democratic Society* on charges of conspiring to incite riot in October 1969.

Massachusetts Governor *Francis W. Sargent* signs a bill providing that servicemen from that state do not have to fight in an undeclared war.

1978 *Dallas* makes its television debut.

1982 Argentina seizes the *Falkland Islands*, held by Great Britain since 1833.

1985 *A.H. Robins Co.* announces the creation of a $615 million fund to settle suits of women injured by the *Dalkon Shield* contraceptive device.

1992 *Edith Cresson*, first female prime minister of France, resigns after only eleven months in office. *Pierre Beregovoy* is selected to replace her.

april

APRIL
3

HOLIDAYS

Guinea
Celebration of the Second Republic
Commemorates the 1984 coup.

RELIGIOUS CALENDAR

The Saints
St. Pancras, first bishop of Taormina and martyr. Also called *Pancratius.* [d. c. 90 A.D.]

St. Sixtus I, pope and martyr. Elected pope c. 119. Also called *Xistus,* or *Xystus.* [d. c. 127]

SS. Agape, Chionia, and *Irene,* virgins and martyrs. [d. 304]

St. Burgondofara, virgin and abbess; founder of Benedictine Abbey of Faremoutiers. Also called *Fare.* [d. 657]

St. Nicetas, abbot and martyr. [d. 824]

St. Richard of Wyche, Bishop of Chichester, ascetic. Also called *Richard of Burford.* [d. 1253]

The Beatified
Blessed Gandulf of Binasco, Franciscan friar. [d. 1260]

Blessed John of Penna, Franciscan friar. [d. 1271]

BIRTHDATES

1245 *Philip III,* also called *Philip the Bold,* King of France, 1270–85. [d. October 5, 1285]

1367 *Henry IV,* King of England, (surnamed *Bolingbroke*)

1399–1413. [d. March 21, 1413]

1593 *George Herbert,* English clergyman, poet; best known for his poem *The Temple.* [d. March 1, 1633]

1715 *John Hanson,* U.S. farmer, politician; first president under the Articles of Confederation, 1781–82. Considered by some as the first president of the U.S. [d. November 15, 1783]

1737 *Arthur St. Clair,* American Revolutionary general, public official; president of Continental Congress, 1787. [d. August 31, 1818]

1783 *Washington Irving,* U.S. essayist, historian, and "spinner of tales," his most notable works are *Legend of Sleepy Hollow* and *Rip Van Winkle.* [d. November 28, 1859]

1798 *Charles Wilkes,* U.S. naval officer, explorer; led round-the-world expedition that explored Antarctic area now known as *Wilkes Land,* 1838–42. [d. February 8, 1877]

1822 *Edward Everett Hale,* U.S. clergyman; author of *The Man Without a Country.* [d. June 10, 1909]

1823 *William Marcy (Boss) Tweed,* U.S. politician; Democratic

political boss. [d. April 12, 1878]

1837 *John Burroughs,* U.S. essayist, naturalist. [d. March 29, 1921]

1866 *James Barry Munnik Hertzog,* Afrikaans nationalist; Prime Minister of South Africa, 1924–39. [d. 1942]

1881 *Alcide de Gasperi,* Italian politician; as Prime Minister, 1945–53, led the reconstruction of Italy after World War II. [d. August 19, 1954]

1893 *Leslie Howard (Leslie Stainer),* British actor. [d. June 1, 1943]

1898 *George Jessel,* U.S. vaudevillian entertainer. [d. May 24, 1981]

Henry Robinson Luce, U.S. editor and publisher; founded *Time, Fortune,* and *Life* magazines. [d. February 28, 1967]

1923 *Jan Sterling (Jane Sterling Adriance),* U.S. actress.

1924 *Marlon Brando,* U.S. actor; known for his *method acting* in dramatic roles; Academy Award (Best Actor) for *The Godfather,* 1972 (refused).

Doris Day (Doris von Kappelhoff), U.S. singer, dancer, actress.

1925 *Tony Benn,* British political leader, cabinet minister; head of Labour Party, 1971–72.

1926 *Virgil Ivan (Gus) Grissom,* U.S. astronaut, killed in *Apollo I* when fire broke out during a simulation exercise. [d. January 27, 1967]

1930 *Lawton Mainor Chiles, Jr.* U.S. politician; Senator, 1971–89.

1934 *Jane Goodall (Baroness Jane Van Lawick-Goodall),* British ethologist; noted for studies on chimpanzees.

1942 *Marsha Mason,* U.S. actress.

Wayne Newton, U.S. singer; popular for his nightclub performances in Las Vegas.

1944 *Tony Orlando (Michael Anthony Orlando Cassavitis),* U.S. singer; known for song *Tie a Yellow Ribbon Round the Old Oak Tree,* 1973.

1948 *Carlos Salinas de Gortari,* Mexican politician; President of Mexico, 1988–95.

1959 *David Hyde Pierce,* U.S. actor; known for his role as Dr. Niles Crane on the TV sitcom *Frasier.*

1958 *Alec Baldwin,* U.S. actor.

1961 *Eddie Murphy,* U.S. comedian; known for his starring roles in *Trading Places* and the *Beverly Hills Cop* movies.

HISTORICAL EVENTS

1189 *Peace of Strasbourg* is signed, effecting a reconciliation between *Emperor Frederick Barbarossa* of Germany and *Pope Clement III.*

1559 The *Treaty of Cateau-Cambrésis* ends *Hapsburg-Valois Wars* between France and Spain; reaffirms Spanish possession of its Italian states and the *Franche-Conté* and France's ownership of *Saluzzo.*

1696 *Sir John Friend* and *Sir William Parkyns* are executed for attempted assassination of *William III* of England.

1860 The first *Pony Express* leaves St. Joseph, Missouri, bound for Sacramento, California, with the U.S. mail.

1861 *Czar Alexander II* of Russia issues the *Emancipation Edict,* liberating the Russian serfs.

1865 *Richmond, Virginia,* the capital of the U.S. Southern Confederacy, is surrendered to the Army of the Potomac under General Ulysses S. Grant (*U.S. Civil War*).

1903 U.S. President *Theodore Roosevelt* inaugurates East Room musicals in the *White House* with a special concert given by *Ignace Paderewski.*

1930 *Ras Tafari* is proclaimed Emperor of Ethiopia under the throne-name *Haile Selassie I.*

1941 German forces under General Wavell capture *Benghazi, Libya (World War II).*

1944 The U.S. Supreme Court rules that political parties cannot exclude voters in primary elections on the basis of race.

1948 U.S. Congress passes *Marshall Plan,* authorizing spending over $17 billion in economic aid to 16 European countries.

1949 *Israel* and *Transjordan* sign armistice; Transjordan gains control of West Bank and part of Jerusalem.

1962 U.S. Department of Defense orders full and effective *racial integration* in military reserve units exclusive of National Guard.

1964 *U.S.* and *Panama* sign a joint declaration providing for immediate resumption of diplomatic relations.

1966 Soviet spacecraft *Luna 10* becomes the first man-made object to achieve a lunar orbit.

1968 Stanley Kubrick's film, *2001: A Space Odyssey,* is released.

1970 U.S. President Richard Nixon signs the *Water Quality Improvement Act of 1970.*

1974 Some 350 persons are killed as *tornadoes* sweep from Georgia in the U.S. to Ontario Province in Canada; nearly 1,200 are injured and property damage is set at $1 billion.

1977 Colonel *Joachim Yombi-Opango* is appointed president of the Congo.

1978 *Park Tong Sun* reveals to a Congressional committee that he gave $850,000 to U.S. politicians (*Koreagate scandal*).

Woody Allen's film, *Annie Hall,* wins three Academy Awards.

1979 *Wilfried Martens,* Chairman of the Social Christian Party, becomes Prime Minister of Belgium following six months of political crisis.

1984 Guinea's military seizes power in a bloodless coup and disbands the ruling *Guinean Democratic Party.*

april

1988 *Ethiopia* and *Somalia* sign a peace agreement officially ending their war over the Ethiopian border region of *Ogaden*.

1996 U.S. Commerce Secretary *Ron Brown* dies in plane crash while touring Croatia and Bosnia-Herzegovina.

HOLIDAYS

Hungary
Liberation Day
Commemorates the day when the last German soldier was driven from Hungarian soil, 1945.

Senegal
National Day
Commemorates completion of agreements with France giving sovereignty to Senegal, 1960.

RELIGIOUS CALENDAR

The Saints
SS. *Agathopus* and *Theodulus,* martyrs. [d. 303]
St. *Tigernach,* bishop. Also called *Tierney.* [d. 549]
St. *Isidore,* Bishop of Seville and Doctor of the Church. [d. 636] Optional Memorial.
St. *Plato,* abbot. [d. 814]
St. *Benedict the Black,* Franciscan lay brother; patron saint of North American blacks and the town of Palermo. [d. 1589]

The Beatified
Blessed Peter, Bishop of Poitiers. [d. 1115]

BIRTHDATES

1648 *Grinling Gibbons,* English woodcarver, sculptor; under *Sir Christopher Wren,* carved stalls in *St. Paul's Cathedral,* London. [d. 1720]

1752 *Nicola Antonio Zingarelli,* Italian composer; *maestro di cappella,* St. Peter's, Rome, 1804–11. [d. 1837]

1780 *Edward Hicks,* U.S. folk painter; painted *Peaceable Kingdom.* [d. August 23, 1849]

1792 *Thaddeus Stevens,* U.S. statesman; a radical anti-slavery spokesman in Congress, 1849–53, 1859–68. [d. August 11, 1868]

1793 *Jean François Casimir Delavigne,* French poet and dramatist. [d. December 11, 1843]

1802 *Dorothea (Lynde) Dix,* U.S. social reformer; pioneer in the movement for specialized treatment of the insane. [d. July 17, 1887]

1809 *Benjamin Peirce,* U.S. mathematician, astronomer; active in U.S. Coast Survey; a founding member of *Smithsonian Institution.* [d. October 6, 1880]

1819 *Maria II (da Gloria),* Queen of Portugal, 1834–53. [d. November 15, 1853]

1823 *Sir William Siemens (Wilhelm Siemens),* British inventor, industrialist; a steel-making process is named after him. [d. November 18, 1883]

1826 *Zénobe Théophile Gramme,* Belgian engineer; developer of the first practical dynamo. [d. January 20, 1901]

1843 *Hans Richter,* Hungarian conductor. [d. November 21, 1916]

1846 *Le Comte de Lautréamont (Isidore Lucien Ducasse),* French prose-poet, born in Uruguay; recognized as precursor of surrealism. [d. November 24, 1870]

1863 *Samuel Shannon Childs,* U.S. restaurateur; founder of Childs Restaurant chain in U.S. [d. March 17, 1925]

1866 *George Pierce Baker,* U.S. teacher of playwrighting; founded *47 Workshop* at Harvard, 1905; students included Eugene O'Neill, Philip Barry, Thomas Wolfe, and John Dos Passos. Founded *Yale Drama School.* [d. January 6, 1935]

1875 *Pierre Monteux,* U.S. orchestra conductor born in France; conductor of Metropolitan Opera, 1917–19; Boston Symphony Orchestra, 1919–24; Paris Symphony Orchestra, 1930–38; San Francisco Symphony Orchestra, 1935–64. [d. July 1, 1964]

1877 *Georg Kolbe,* German sculptor. [d. November 21, 1947]

1884 *Isoroku Yamamoto,* Japanese admiral; planned and led attack on *Pearl Harbor,* 1941. [d. April 18, 1943]

1888 *Tris(tram) Speaker,* U.S. baseball player. [d. December 8, 1958]

1895 *Arthur Murray,* U.S. dancing teacher; founded the *Arthur Murray School of Dancing.* [d. March 3, 1991]

1896 *Robert Sherwood,* U.S. dramatist; winner of four Pulitzer Prizes, 1936, 1939, 1941, 1949. [d. November 14, 1955]

1906 *John Cameron Swayze, Sr.,* U.S. news correspondent. [d. August 15, 1995]

1908 *Antony Tudor,* British choreographer. [d. April 19, 1987]

1913 *Jules Léger,* Canadian statesman; Governor-General of Canada, 1974–79. [d. November 22, 1980]

1914 *Marguerite (Donnadieu) Duras,* French novelist, playwright, screenwriter. [d. March 3, 1996]

1915 *Muddy Waters (McKinley Morganfield),* U.S. singer, musician; five Grammy Awards. [d. April 30, 1983]

1922 *Elmer Bernstein,* U.S. composer.

1924 *Gil(bert Raymond) Hodges,* U.S. baseball player, manager. [d. April 2, 1972]

1928 *Maya Marguerita Angelou,* U.S. actress, author, journalist; wrote *I Know Why the Caged Bird Sings,* 1970, and *All God's Children Need Traveling Shoes,* 1986.

1931 *Bobby Ray Inman,* U.S. government official,

businessman; Deputy Director, Central Intelligence Agency, 1981–82; Chairman, Westmark Systems Inc., 1986–89.

1932 *Richard Green Lugar,* U.S. politician; Senator, 1977– .

Anthony Perkins, U.S. actor. [d. September 12, 1992]

1938 *A(ngelo) Bartlett Giamatti,* U.S. educator, baseball executive; President of Yale University, 1978–86; Commissioner of Baseball, 1989. [d. September 1, 1989]

1942 *Kitty Kelley,* U.S. tell-all biographer.

1946 *Craig T. Nelson,* U.S. actor; played Hayden Fox on *Coach* TV series.

1950 *Christine Lahti,* U.S. actress; known for roles in *Swing Shift,* 1984, and *Just Between Friends,* 1986; plays Dr. Kathryn Austin on the TV drama *Chicago Hope.*

1965 *Robert Downey, Jr.,* U.S. actor; starred in *Chaplin,* 1992.

1966 *Nancy McKeon,* U.S. actress; known for her role as Jo on television series, *Facts of Life.*

HISTORICAL EVENTS

1406 *James I of Scotland* officially accedes to the throne although not crowned until May 21, 1424.

1541 *Ignatius Loyola* is elected first General of *Jesuit Order.*

1581 *Elizabeth I* of England confers knighthood on *Francis Drake,* first Englishman to circumnavigate the globe.

1611 *Denmark* declares war on *Sweden.*

1841 *William Henry Harrison,* U.S. President, dies after only one month in office; he is succeeded by his Vice-President, *John Tyler.*

1884 *Bolivia* cedes her coast to *Chile.*

1892 Anarchist plot to blow up the royal palace and the Chamber of Deputies is discovered in *Spain.*

1905 A severe *earthquake* hits northern *India;* 20,000 people are believed killed.

1911 The *Masai* sign a treaty with Great Britain, giving up their lands in *Laikipia,* East Africa, to European colonization.

1917 *Union of Polish Falcons Societies* votes to form *Army of Kosciuszko* to fight with U.S. for liberty and independence of Poland.

1928 *Mussolini's* ten commandments are promulgated to govern activities of *Fascists* abroad.

1939 *Faisal II* becomes child-king of Iraq on the death of his father, *King Ghazi I.*

1942 Japanese naval task force enters Bay of Bengal and strikes *Ceylon (World War II).*

1949 *North Atlantic Treaty* is signed; U.S., Canada, and Western European powers agree on common defense.

1953 The first *Phi Beta Kappa* chapter at a black college is organized at *Fisk University.*

1960 *Ben Hur* wins a record 11 Academy Awards, including best picture and best actor.

France and *Mali Federation* sign accords granting

independence to the Federation's two constituent republics, *Senegal* and *Sudan*.

1968 U.S. civil rights leader Rev. *Martin Luther King, Jr.* is shot and killed by a sniper in Memphis, Tennessee.

1969 The world's first totally artificial heart is implanted in a human by U.S. surgeon Dr. *Denton A. Cooley.* The patient, *Haskell Karp,* lives only 38 hours, dying of pneumonia and kidney failure.

1975 Prime Minister *Ian Smith* of Rhodesia releases the Rev. *Ndabaningi Sithole,* Zimbabwe African National Union leader accused of plotting the murder of black leaders in Rhodesia.

1978 Cuban troops lead Angolan attack on pro-western *National Union for the Total Independence of Angola.*

1979 Former Pakistani Prime Minister *Zulfikar Ali Bhutto* is hanged on charges of conspiring to murder a political opponent.

1983 *U.S. Space Shuttle Challenger* is launched into orbit for a five-day mission which includes the deploying of a tracking and data relay satellite, the world's largest communications satellite, and a *space walk* by two of the four astronauts aboard.

1988 Governor Evan Mecham is impeached by the Arizona Senate on charges of official misconduct and is formally removed from office.

1992 Mafia boss *John Gotti* is found guilty of murder and sentenced to life imprisonment.

april

APRIL
5

HOLIDAYS

China
Respect for Ancestors Day

Hong Kong, Taiwan
Ching Ming

South Korea
Arbor Day

Taiwan
Tomb Sweeping Day

Anniversary of the Death of Chiang Kai-shek

RELIGIOUS CALENDAR

The Saints
St. Derfel Gadarn, monk and warrior. [d. 6th century]

St. Ethelburga, Abbess of Lyminge and matron. Daughter of King Ethelbert of Kent, who did much to convert her husband, King Edwin, and his realm, Northumbria, to Christianity. Also called *Tata.* [d. c. 647]

St. Gerald of Sauve-Majeure, abbot. [d. 1095]

St. Albert, Bishop of Montecorvino in Apulia. [d. 1127]

St. Vincent Ferrer, Dominican preacher, missionary; patron of brick and tile manufacturers, plumbers, and pavement workers. [d. 1419] Optional Memorial.

The Beatified
Blessed Juliana of Mount Cornillon, virgin. Responsible for introducing the Feast of Corpus Christi. [d. 1258]

Blessed Crescentia of Kaufbeuren, virgin. [d. 1744]

BIRTHDATES

1588 *Thomas Hobbes,* English philosopher; exiled to France for his political convictions; known for his theory of *social contracts.* [d. December 4, 1679]

1649 *Elihu Yale,* British businessman, philanthropist; endowed Yale University. [d. July 8, 1721]

1684 *Catherine I,* Empress of Russia, 1725–27; widow of Peter the Great; she ruled in her own right for two years. [d. 1727]

1732 *Jean-Honoré Fragonard,* French painter, engraver. [d. August 22, 1806]

1784 *Louis Spohr,* German violin virtuoso, composer. [d. 1859]

1795 *Sir Henry Havelock,* British colonial officer in India; distinguished himself during *Sepoy Mutiny.* [d. 1857]

1801 *Vincenzo Gioberti,* Italian patriot, author, philosopher; Premier of Sardinia, 1848–49; Ambassador at Paris, 1849–51. [d. October 26, 1852]

1804 *Matthias Schleiden,* German biologist, botanist; evolved an important theory concerning *origin of plant cells.* [d. June 23, 1881]

1811 *Jules Dupré,* French landscape painter; regarded as one of the founders of modern French school of landscape painting. [d. October 6, 1889]

1821 *Linus Yale,* U.S. inventor and lock manufacturer. [d. December 25, 1868]

1827 *Joseph Lister, Baron Lister of Lyme Regis,* British surgeon; responsible for practice of *antiseptic medicine.* [d. February 10, 1912]

1832 *Jules François Camille Ferry,* French statesman; Premier, 1880–81, 1883–85. [d. March 16, 1893]

1835 *Vítezslav Hálek,* Czech poet, novelist, dramatist; considered the *Father of Modern Czech Poetry.* [d. October 8, 1874]

1837 *Algernon Charles Swinburne,* British poet and critic; a leader in lyric poetry. [d. April 10, 1909]

1839 *Robert Smalls,* U.S. Congressman, 1875–79, 1881–87; only black naval captain during U.S. Civil War. [d. 1916]

1856 *Booker (Taliaferro) Washington,* U.S. educator,

social reformer; founder of *Tuskegee Institute*, 1881. [d. November 14, 1915]

1858 *W(ashington) Atlee Burpee,* U.S. seed-products executive, born in Canada; founded first successful mail-order seed business. [d. November 26, 1915]

1893 *David Burpee,* U.S. horticulturist; president of world's largest mail order seed company; son of W. Atlee Burpee (see above). [d. June 24, 1980]

1900 *Spencer Tracy,* U.S. actor. [d. June 10, 1967]

1901 *Chester Bowles,* U.S. diplomat, advertising executive; Governor of Connecticut, 1949–51. [d. May 26, 1986]

Melvyn Douglas (Melvyn, Hesselberg), U.S. actor. [d. August 4, 1981]

1904 *Richard Ghormley Eberhart,* U.S. poet; Pulitzer Prize in poetry, 1966.

1908 *Bette (Ruth Elizabeth) Davis,* U.S. actress; one of the foremost dramatic actresses in film history. [d. October 6, 1989]

Hebert von Karajan, Austrian orchestral and operatic conductor. [d. July 16, 1989]

1916 *Gregory Peck,* U.S. actor; Hollywood leading man for more than 30 years.

1920 *Arthur Hailey,* Canadian author; wrote *Hotel*, 1965, *Airport*, 1968, and *Wheels*, 1971.

1923 *Nguyen Van Thieu,* Vietnamese politician; President, Republic of Vietnam, 1967–75.

1929 *Ivar Giaevar,* U.S. physicist born in Norway; Nobel Prize in physics for research in *semi-conductor and superconductor electronics* (with L. Esaki and B. D. Josephson), 1973.

1930 *Maxine Cheshire,* U.S. journalist; reporter, *Washington Post;* columnist, *Los Angeles Times.*

1937 *Joseph S. Lelyveld,* U.S. newspaper editor; Pulitzer Prize winner, 1986.

Colin Powell, U.S. military leader; Chairman of the Joint Chiefs of Staff, 1989–93.

1941 *Eric Burdon,* British singer; member of the rock group, *The Animals.*

1942 *Michael Moriarty,* U.S. actor; Emmy Award for *Holocaust*, 1978; featured on the TV drama *Law & Order.*

1943 *Max(well Towbridge) Gail, Jr.,* U.S. actor; known for his role as Sergeant Wojciehowicz on television series, *Barney Miller*, 1975–81.

1949 *Judith (Judy) Resnik,* U.S. astronaut; second American woman in space; died in the space shuttle *Challenger* explosion. [d. January 28, 1986]

1957 *Vince Gill,* U.S. country singer.

HISTORICAL EVENTS

1355 *Charles IV* is crowned Holy Roman Emperor at Rome.

1513 *Treaty of Mechlin* between *Maximilian I,* Holy Roman Emperor, *Henry VIII* of England, *Ferdinand* of Aragon, and *Pope Leo X* is signed.

1614 *Pocahontas,* daughter of Indian chief *Powhatan,* marries *John Rolfe,* English colonist at Virginia.

1873 The *Ashanti War* breaks out between African natives and the British along the *Gold Coast.*

1879 *Chile* declares war on *Bolivia* and *Peru,* beginning what is called the *Saltpetre War* in which Chile hopes to acquire the saltpeter mines in Bolivia and Peru.

1881 The *Treaty of Pretoria* ends the rebellion of the Transvaal Boers; the South African Republic attains independence under British suzerainty (*Boer War*).

1897 The *Czech language* is granted equal status with the German language in *Bohemia.*

1915 *Jess Willard* knocks out *Jack Johnson* to win world heavyweight boxing title.

1917 The German strategic retreat along the Western Front to the *Hindenburg Line* is completed (*World War I*).

1919 *Eamon de Valera* is named President of Ireland's *Sinn Fein.*

1949 *Fireside Theatre* makes its television debut.

1951 *Julius and Ethel Rosenberg* are sentenced to death by U.S. federal court after being found guilty of treason in passing *atomic bomb* secrets to Soviet agents.

1955 *Herbert von Karajan* is appointed conductor of the Berlin Philharmonic Orchestra.

april

Richard J. Daley is elected to his first term as mayor of Chicago.

1960 The South African government outlaws non-white political organizations, including the *African National Congress (ANC)* and the *Pan Africanist Congress (PAC)*.

1960 *U Nu* succeeds Gen. Ne Win as Premier of *Burma*. [d. February 14, 1995]

1963 *J. Robert Oppenheimer*, U.S. physicist, declared a security risk in 1954, is named winner of the Atomic Energy Commission's Fermi award.

1964 *Jigme Dorji*, Prime Minister of *Bhutan*, is assassinated.

1967 *Great Britain* launches its first satellite from Vandenberg Air Force Base.

1968 Czechoslovakia's Communist Party Secretary *Alexander Dubček* issues liberal reform program.

The assassination of *Martin Luther King, Jr.* provokes riots in Baltimore, Pittsburgh, Chicago, and Washington, D.C. U.S. troops are called in to protect government offices in the District of Columbia.

1970 Count *Karl von Spreti*, West German Ambassador to Guatemala, is found slain after the Guatemalan government refuses to grant demands of his kidnappers.

1973 *American Indian Movement* leaders and representatives of the U.S. government agree to a cease-fire in the 37-day siege of *Wounded Knee*, South Dakota.

A new system is adopted for numbering football jerseys by player positions.

1974 A coalition government is formed in *Laos;* Prince Souvana Phouma continues as premier.

1976 Riots break out in *Beijing* directed against the radical wing of the Chinese Communist Party leadership and in support of *Deng Xiaoping.*

Foreign Secretary *James Callaghan* becomes the new Prime Minister of Great Britain, succeeding Harold Wilson.

1985 The U.S. Geological Survey issues its first official earthquake forecast,

predicting a strike in California's *Cholame Valley* by 1993.

1986 Two people are killed in the bombing of a West German discotheque filled with U.S. servicemen. Officials suspect Libyan involvement.

1988 Reputed drug trafficker, *Juan Ramon Matta*, is seized by military personnel in Honduras and flown to the U.S. Matta's arrest provokes rioting in Tegucigalpa.

1989 Polish opposition leaders and the Communist Party reach an agreement to legalize the trade union, *Solidarity*, and hold free elections for a new Senate.

1989 The *Vietnamese* government begins the withdrawal of its armed forces from Cambodia. The military presence was begun over ten years earlier in an attempt to end the brutal rule of the *Khmer Rouge* and *Pol Pot.*

1992 Peru President *Alberto Fujimori* suspends the constitution as he struggles with the Maoist Sendera Luminosa guerrillas and government corruption.

HOLIDAYS

Ethiopia
Patriots' Victory Day

Republic of South Africa
Van Riebeeck Day or Founders Day
Honors Dutch explorer Jan van
Riebeeck, who founded Cape Town,
South Africa, 1652.

Thailand
Chakri Memorial Day
Commemorates the founding of the
ruling dynasty by King Rama I, 1782.

RELIGIOUS CALENDAR

The Saints
120 Persian martyrs put to death for
    refusing to worship the sun.
    [d. 345]
St. Marcellinus, martyr. [d. 413]
St. Celestine I, pope. Elected 422. [d.
    432]
St. Eutychius, Patriarch of
    Constantinople. [d. 582]
St. Prudentius, Bishop of Troyes. [d.
    861]
St. Elstan, Bishop of Ramsbury. Also
    called *Elfstan.* [d. 981]
St. William of Eskill, abbot. [d.
    1203]
St. Brychan, Welsh king. [death date
    unknown]

The Beatified
Blessed Notker Balbulus, monk,
    poet, and musician. [d. 912]
Blessed Catherine of Pallanza,
    virgin. [d. 1478]

BIRTHDATES

1671 *Jean-Baptiste Rousseau,*
French poet, dramatist; exiled
because of satires aimed at
prominent political and
literary figures. [d. March 17,
1741]

1773 *James Mill,* Scottish
economist, historian,
philosopher in England;
father of *John Stuart Mill.* [d.
June 23, 1836]

1818 *Aasmund Olavssen Vinje,*
Norwegian poet, essayist,
journalist; active in
Landsmaal movement. [d.
July 30, 1870]

1826 *Gustave Moreau,* French
painter; donated his home to
the city of Paris (Musée
Gustave Moreau). [d. 1898]

1852 *Timothy Cole,* U.S. wood
engraver, born in England;
known for his engravings of
the old masters. [d. May 17,
1931]

1866 *(Joseph) Lincoln Steffens,* U.S.
journalist; one of the
foremost *muckraking*
journalists of the early 20th
century. [d. August 9, 1936]

1867 *Butch Cassidy (George Leroy
Parker),* U.S. outlaw; subject
of the film, *Butch Cassidy
and the Sundance Kid,* 1969.
[d. 1912]

1869 *Louis Raemaekers,* Dutch
political cartoonist, artist;

known for his anti-German
cartoons during World War I.
[d. 1956]

1870 *Oscar Straus,* Austrian
composer; widely known for
his comic operas and
operettas; wrote *Der Tapfere
Soldat.* [d. 1954]

1884 *Walter Huston (Walter
Houghston),* Canadian
character actor. [d. April 7,
1950]

1890 *Anthony Herman Gerard
Fokker,* Dutch airplane
designer, builder;
manufacturer of German
pursuit planes during World
War I. [d. December 23,
1939]

1892 *Donald Willis Douglas,* U.S.
aircraft manufacturer;
founded Douglas Aircraft,
1920. [d. February 1, 1981]

Lowell (Jackson) Thomas,
U.S. traveler, author, radio
news commentator. [d.
August 29, 1981]

1906 *Sir John Betjeman,* British
poet; named Poet Laureate of
England, 1972. [d. 1984]

1910 *Olin E(arl) Teague,* U.S.
politician; Congressman,
1946–77; frequently identified
with issues related to
American veterans. [d.
January 23, 1981]

1911 *Feodor Lynen,* German
biochemist; Nobel Price in

physiology or medicine for work on the metabolism of *cholesterol and fatty acids* (with K. E. Bloch), 1964. [d. 1979]

1918 *Alfredo Ovanda Candia,* Bolivian statesman; President of Bolivia, 1966; 1969–70; Led military campaign against Cuban-backed guerrillas in which *Che Guevara* was killed; his government overthrown, 1970. [d. January 24, 1982]

1920 Edmond H. Fischer, U.S. biochemist; Nobel Prize for Medicine along with Edwin G. Krebs. They discover the reversible protein phosphorylation process, 1992.

1926 *Alexander Porter Butterfield,* U.S. government official; assistant to Richard Nixon, 1969–73; administrator, Federal Aviation Administration, 1973–75.

Ian Richard Kyle Paisley, Irish clergyman, political leader; hard-line Protestant minister.

1927 *Gerry Mulligan,* U.S. jazz musician. [d. January 20, 1996]

1928 *James Dewey Watson,* U.S. biochemist; Nobel Prize in physiology or medicine for discovery of molecular structure of *DNA* (with F. H. C. Crick and M. H. F. Wilkins), 1962.

1929 *André Previn,* U.S. composer, conductor.

1930 *Lonnie Bristow,* U.S. physician; first African American to head the American Medical Association.

1937 *Merle Ronald Haggard,* U.S. singer.

Billy Dee Williams, U.S. actor; known for his roles in *Lady Sings the Blues,* 1972, and *The Empire Strikes Back,* 1980.

1944 *Michelle Gillam Phillips,* U.S. actress, singer; member of the rock group, *The Mamas and the Papas.*

1948 *Mary Fisher,* U.S. AIDS activist; founder of the Family AIDS Network, Inc.

1951 *Bert (Rikalbert) Blyleven,* Netherlands-born baseball player.

1953 *Marilu Henner,* U.S. actress; known for her role as Elaine on television series, *Taxi.*

1965 *Sterling Sharpe,* former U.S. football player; National Football League reception record holder, 1993.

HISTORICAL EVENTS

6 B.C. Day believed by some scientists to be the real date of the Nativity of Jesus Christ.

1199 *Richard I of England* dies in battle; succeeded by his brother, *John Lackland.*

1490 *Matthias Corvinus, King* of Hungary, dies; succeeded by *Ladislas II* of Bohemia, the son of *Casimir IV* of Poland.

1652 A Dutch East India Company expedition, led by *Jan van Riebeeck,* reaches Table Bay and establishes the *Cape Colony,* first permanent European settlement in South Africa.

1793 *Committee of Public Safety* assumes dictatorial powers in France (*French Revolution*).

1830 The *Mormon Church* is organized by *Joseph C. Smith* and *Oliver Crowdy* at Fayette, New York.

1862 The *Battle of Shiloh* begins at Pittsburg Landing, Tennessee, with the Union Army under General U. S. Grant and the Confederate forces under Generals Albert Johnston and Pierre Beauregard (*U.S. Civil War*).

1868 *Brigham Young, Mormon Church* leader, marries his 27th and last wife.

Emperor Meiji proclaims the *Charter Oath,* promising *Japan* a deliberative assembly and an open attitude to the West.

1896 *James Connolly* becomes the first U.S. Olympic gold medal winner.

The first modern *Olympic Games* begin at *Athens, Greece.*

1909 Expedition of *Admiral Robert Peary* reaches the *North Pole.*

1917 The U.S. declares war on Germany (*World War I*).

George M. Cohan composes *Over There* as U.S. declares war on Germany; the song is copyrighted on June 1, 1917.

1918 The *First Battle of the Somme* ends with the German offensive stopped after driving 40 miles into the British lines (*World War I*).

1929 The *City of Glasgow* arrives in Karachi, opening weekly air mail service between Great Britain and India.

1930 *Mahatma Gandhi* and his followers begin taking salt from the sea in defiance of the British monopoly on salt production.

1941 British and South African troops capture the Ethiopian capital of *Addis Ababa,* from Italy. (*World War II*)

Germany invades Greece and Yugoslavia (*World War II*).

1945 The Japanese begin *Operation Ten-Go,* a massive Kamikaze attack on the U.S. naval fleet near Okinawa, causing severe damage. *(World War II)*

1948 Finland and the Soviet Union sign a *Mutual Security and Friendship Pact,* agreeing to defend each other in the event of an attack.

1951 *Oscar Collazo,* Puerto Rican nationalist, is sentenced to death after being found guilty of murdering a White House guard in an attempt to assassinate President *Harry S. Truman* on November 1, 1950.

1955 *Sir Anthony Eden* becomes Prime Minister of Great Britain.

1964 The U.S. Supreme Court applies the *Sherman Anti-Trust Law* to banks for the first time when it declares a planned merger between the First National Bank and the Security Trust Co. in violation of the act.

1965 *Early Bird,* the world's first commercial *communications satellite,* is launched from Cape Kennedy, Florida.

1968 Canadian Justice Minister *Pierre Elliott Trudeau* is elected to succeed Prime Minister Pearson as leader of the Liberal Party.

1972 *Egypt* severs diplomatic relations with *Jordan.*

1973 *Sweden* becomes the first Western nation to recognize *North Korea.*

1975 *Yen Chia-kan* is inaugurated as president of Taiwan.

1977 U.S. President *Jimmy Carter* signs legislation that restores to the White House authority for government reorganization.

1978 U.S. President *Jimmy Carter* signs into law legislation raising *mandatory retirement age* from 65 to 70 for private industry and eliminating it for most federal workers.

1984 Voters in the *Cocos Islands* choose to become fully integrated with Australia, rejecting the independence option in a referendum.

1985 General *Abdel Rahman Siwar el-Dahab* overthrows Sudanese president, *Gaafar Nimeiri,* in a military coup.

1994 Presidents *Juvenal Habyarimana* of Rwanda and *Cyprien Ntaryamira* of Burundi are killed in a plane crash.

april

APRIL
7

HOLIDAYS

World Health Day
Marks the anniversary of the
establishment of the World Health
Organization, 1948. Sponsored by
the United Nations.

People's Republic of Mozambique
Women's Day

U.S. (New York)
Verrazano Day
Celebrates the discovery of New
York Harbor by Giovanni da
Verrazano, 1524.

Yugoslavia
Yugoslav Republic Day
Anniversary of formation of Socialist
Federal Republic of Yugoslavia, 1963.

RELIGIOUS CALENDAR

The Saints
St. Hegesippus, church historian. [d.
   c. 180]
St. Aphraates. [d. c. 345]
St. George the Younger, Bishop of
   Mitylene, Greece. [d. c. 816]
St. Celsus, Archbishop of Armagh.
   Also called *Ceallach.* [d.
   1129]
St. Aybert. Also called *Aibert, Albert.*
   [d. 1140]
St. John Baptist de La Salle, founder
   of the Brothers of the
   Christian Schools for the
   training of teachers. [d. 1719].
   Feast formerly May 15.
   Obligatory Memorial.
St. Goran, hermit; patron of Gorran,
   Cornwall. Also called *Goron,*

or *Gorran.* [death date
   unknown]

The Beatified
Blessed Herman Joseph, mystic. [d.
   1241]
Blessed Ursulina, virgin. [d. 1410]
Blessed William of Scicli, Franciscan
   tertiary. [d. 1411]
Blessed Alexander Rawlins and
   Henry Walpole, martyrs. [d.
   1595]
Blessed Edward Oldcorne and *Ralph
   Ashley,* martyrs. [d. 1606]
Blessed Mary Assunta Pallotta,
   religious of the Franciscan
   Missionaries of Mary. [d.
   1905]

BIRTHDATES

1506 *Saint Francis Xavier
   (Francisco Javier),* Spanish
   Jesuit missionary to the
   Orient. [d. 1552]

1640 *Louis Hennepin,* French
   explorer; explored the Great
   Lakes with LaSalle, 1678–79;
   wrote *Description de la
   Louisiane,* 1682. [d. 1701]

1652 *Clement XII,* pope 1730–40.
   [d. February 6, 1740]

1770 *William Wordsworth,* English
   poet; leader of the English
   Romantic movement. [d. April
   23, 1850]

1772 *François Marie Fourier,*
   French philosopher, social
   reformer; developed

cooperative society concept
called *Fourierism,* of which
Brook Farm in the U.S. is an
example. [d. October 10,
1837]

1780 *William Ellery Channing,*
   U.S. religious leader; founder
   of American Unitarianism. [d.
   October 2, 1842]

1786 *William Rufus de Vane King,*
   U.S. politician; Vice-President,
   1853. [d. April 18, 1853]

1859 *Jacques Loeb,* U.S.
   physiologist and experimental
   biologist, born in Germany;
   known for his rigorously
   scientific studies of
   reproduction and
   regeneration. [d. February 11,
   1924]

1860 *Will Keith Kellogg,* U.S. food-
   products manufacturer;
   founded W. K. Kellogg Co. [d.
   October 6, 1951]

1873 *John Joseph McGraw (Little
   Napoleon),* U.S. baseball
   player, manager; coach of the
   New York Giants, 1902–32.
   [d. February 25, 1934]

1884 *Bronislaw Kasper
   Malinowski,* Polish social
   anthropologist; known for his
   studies of the societies of the
   western Pacific islands. [d.
   May 16, 1942]

1889 *Gabriela Mistral (Lucila
   Godoy Alcayaga),* Chilean
   poet; first Latin-American

woman to win Nobel Prize in literature, 1945. [d. January 10, 1957]

1891 *Sir David Alexander Cecil Low,* British political cartoonist, caricaturist; created character *Colonel Blimp.* [d. September 19, 1963]

1893 *Irene Castle,* U.S. dancer; formed popular dance team with her husband, Vernon. Created *Turkey Trot* and *Castle Walk.* [d. January 25, 1969]

Allen Dulles, U.S. government official, diplomat, lawyer; brother of *John Foster Dulles* (February 25). [d. January 29, 1959]

1897 *Walter Winchell,* U.S. journalist, syndicated columnist. [d. February 20, 1972]

1899 *Robert Casadesus,* French concert pianist, composer. [d. September 19, 1972]

1908 *Frank Fitzsimmons,* U.S. labor leader; President of Teamsters Union in U.S., 1971–81. [d. May 6, 1981]

1915 *Billie Holiday (Lady Day),* U.S. jazz singer. [d. July 17, 1959]

1920 *Ravi Shankar,* Indian musician, sitar player.

1928 *James Garner (James Baumgardner),* U.S. actor.

Alan Jay Pakula, U.S. director; known for direction of *Klute, All the President's Men,* and *Sophie's Choice.*

1931 *Donald Barthelme,* U.S. novelist, short-story writer. [d. July 23, 1989]

1931 *Daniel Ellsberg,* U.S. author, economist; provided the

"Pentagon Papers" to the *New York Times;* wrote *Papers on the War,* 1972.

1933 *Wayne Rogers,* U.S. actor, businessman; known for his role as Trapper John on television series, *M*A*S*H* and for his starring role on television series, *House Calls.*

1935 *(William) Hodding Carter, III,* U.S. government official, journalist; spokesman, State Department, 1977–80; anchorman, *Inside Story,* 1981–84.

1938 *Edmund Gerald (Jerry) Brown, Jr.,* U.S. politician; Governor of California, 1975–82; Mayor of Oakland, California, 1988– .

1939 *Francis Ford Coppola,* U.S. film director, producer, writer; Academy Award (Director) for *The Godfather, Part II* 1974.

David (Parradine) Frost, British television personality.

1944 *Julia Phillips,* U.S. writer, producer; Academy Award for *The Sting,* 1974.

1949 *John Oates,* U.S. singer, one half of *Hall & Oates.*

1954 *Jackie Chan,* Chinese actor; known for his action movies.

Anthony Drew (Tony) Dorsett, U.S. football player; Heisman Trophy, 1976.

HISTORICAL EVENTS

1118 *Pope Gelasius II* excommunicates *Henry V,* Holy Roman Emperor.

1348 *Prague University* (Czechoslovakia) is founded by Holy Roman Emperor *Charles IV.*

1763 *George, Lord Grenville,* succeeds John Stuart, Earl of Bute, as British prime minister.

1782 George Washington establishes the *Badge of Military Merit* for U.S. soldiers injured in action. It later became known as the *Purple Heart.*

1823 War between France and Spain begins as 100,000 *Sons of St. Louis* invade Spain.

1831 *Pedro I* of Brazil abdicates in favor of his son, *Pedro II.*

1862 Union forces under General *Ulysses S. Grant* win *Battle of Shiloh* in *U.S. Civil War* (see April 6).

1907 Provincial government is instituted in *Manchuria* by China.

1921 *Sun Yat-sen* is elected president of China by the rebel parliament at Canton.

1934 *Mahatma Gandhi* of India suspends his civil disobedience campaign.

1936 *President Niceto Alcalá Zamora y Torres* of Spain is deposed (*Spanish Civil War*).

1939 Italians bombard *Albania* and overrun the country (*World War II*).

1945 In South China Sea, U.S. carrier-based planes sink the Japanese battleship *Yamato,* one of the largest enemy ships sunk during World War II.

1948 The *World Health Organization* is established by the United Nations.

1949 *Rodgers and Hammerstein's* musical, *South Pacific,* premieres in New York City.

april

1951 Vietnamese Communist leader *Ho Chi Minh* orders his forces to revert to guerrilla warfare (*French-Indo-Chinese War*).

1953 Swedish diplomat and author, *Dag Hammarskjold,* is elected Secretary General of the United Nations.

1962 A Cuban military court sentences 1,179 persons involved in the *Bay of Pigs invasion* to 30 years in prison for treason.

1963 *Jack Nicklaus* wins the Masters Golf Tournament, becoming the youngest player ever to win.

By proclamation the Socialist Federal Republic of *Yugoslavia* is established, and *Marshal Tito* becomes president for life.

1978 Philippine President *Ferdinand E. Marcos* permits the first national elections since his imposition of martial law on September 23, 1972.

1980 U.S. breaks diplomatic ties with *Iran* over the seizure of Americans as hostages at the U.S. embassy in Tehran.

1983 Scientists at the *Smithsonian Institution* detail the discovery, in 1982, in Egypt, of a human skeleton 60–80,000 years old, a significant link in the study of human evolution.

1985 Soviet leader, *Mikhail Gorbachev,* announces a unilateral moratorium on the deployment of *intermediate range nuclear missiles* and encourages the U.S. to do the same.

1990 *John Poindexter* is found guilty for his involvement in the *Iran-Contra affair.* Poindexter was the national security advisor under President Ronald Reagan.

The *Scandinavian Star* ferry catches fire, killing over 175 people.

1992 The United States and the Europe Community recognize *Bosnia-Herzegovina* as an independent republic.

1998 *Mary Bono* is elected to the U.S. House of Representatives, replacing her husband, Sonny Bono, who died earlier in the year (February 16, 1940).

HOLIDAYS

Japan
Hana Matsuri or Flower Festival,
Buddha's Birthday
Commemorates the birth of the
founder of Buddhism, Gautama
Buddha.

Korea
Buddha's Birthday

RELIGIOUS CALENDAR

The Saints
St. Dionysius, Bishop of Corinth. [d.
   c. 180]
St. Perpetuus, Bishop of Tours. [d. c.
   494]
St. Walter of Pontoise, abbot. [d.
   1095]

The Beatified
Blessed Clement of Osimo,
   Augustinian prior. [d. 1291]
Blessed Julian of St. Augustine,
   Franciscan monk. [d. 1606]
Blessed Julia Billiart, virgin and
   cofounder of the Institute of
   Notre Dame of Namur. [d.
   1816]

BIRTHDATES

c563BC *Gautamu Buddha,* Indian
   religious leader, philosopher;
   founder of Buddhism. [d. c.
   483 B.C.]

1460 *Juan Ponce de Leon,* Spanish
   explorer; famous for his
   search for the legendary
   fountain of youth; discovered
   Florida, 1513. [d. 1521]

1605 *Philip IV,* King of Spain,
   1621–65, during its decline as
   a great world power. [d.
   September 17, 1665]

1726 *Lewis Morris,* American
   colonist; member of
   Continental Congress; signer
   of the Declaration of
   Independence. [d. January 22,
   1798]

1783 *John Claudius Loudon,*
   Scottish horticulturist, writer.
   [d. 1843]

1798 *Dionysius Solomos,* Greek
   poet; author of *Hymn to*
   Liberty, from which come
   words to Greek National
   Anthem. [d. February 21,
   1857]

1817 *Charles Edouard Brown-*
   Séquard, French physiologist,
   physician; known for
   experiments in life-prolonging
   injections of serum extracted
   from sheep. [d. April 2, 1894]

1818 *Christian IX* of Denmark. [d.
   January 29, 1906]

   August Wilhelm von
   Hofmann, German organic
   chemist; noted for work on
   coaltar products. [d. 1892]

1827 *Ram n Betances,* Puerto Rican
   writer and social activist;
   promoter of independence
   for Puerto Rico, wrote *Ten*
   Commandments of Free Men.
   [d. 1898]

1850 *William Henry Welch,* U.S.
   physician, bacteriologist,
   teacher; developed first
   pathology laboratory in U.S.,
   1879; influential in founding
   of *Johns Hopkins University.*
   [d. April 30, 1934]

1859 *Edmund Husserl,* German
   philosopher; founder of
   phenomenology. [d. April 26,
   1938]

1869 *Harvey Williams Cushing,*
   U.S. neuro-surgeon, a
   specialist on the pituitary
   gland; introduced *blood*
   pressure determination in
   U.S. [d. October 7, 1939]

1875 *Albert I,* of Belgium, acceded
   to throne 1909; led the
   Belgian Army during World
   War I and guided his
   country's economic recovery
   afterwards. [d. February 17,
   1934]

1888 *Dennis Chávez,* U.S. politician
   serving in both the House of
   Representatives and the
   Senate. Founder of the Fair
   Employment Practices
   Commission. [d. 1962]

1889 *Sir Adrian Cedric Boult,*
   British conductor; knighted,
   1937; known for his
   persistence in broadcasting
   BBC Symphonies throughout

World War II, in spite of air raids and other disruptions. [d. February 23, 1983]

1893 *Mary Pickford (Gladys Marie Smith),* U.S. actress; leading lady of the silent screen, then talkies. Helped establish United Artists Co. with her husband, Douglas Fairbanks, and Charlie Chaplin and D. W. Griffith. [d. May 29, 1979]

1896 *E(dgar) Y. (Yip) Harburg,* U.S. lyricist, librettist; wrote lyrics for Broadway musicals and films. [d. March 5, 1981]

Lansing Peter Shield, U.S. business executive; President of Grand Union, 1947–60. [d. January 6, 1960]

1897 *Louis Skidmore,* U.S. architect; partner in Skidmore, Owings, and Merrill, an architectural firm that pioneered in commercial and institutional design and structure. [d. September 27, 1962]

1904 *Sir John R. Hicks,* British economist; Nobel Prize in economics for contributions to general equilibrium (with K. J. Arrow), 1972.

1908 *Donald Ford Whitehead,* U.S. journalist; known for coverage of the major battles of World War II in Europe and North Africa; Pulitzer Prize in international reporting, 1951. [d. January 12, 1981]

1912 *Sonja Henie,* U.S. figure skater, born in Norway; Olympic gold medalist, 1928, 1932, and 1936. [d. October 12, 1969]

1914 *Robert Giroux,* U.S. publisher; partner, Farrar, Straus, and Giroux, Inc., 1955– .

1918 *Elizabeth (Betty) Ford,* wife of U.S. President Gerald Ford.

1919 *Ian (Douglas) Smith,* Rhodesian political leader; led Rhodesian move to independence from Great Britain; opponent of black equality in *Rhodesia* (Zimbabwe).

1921 *Franco Corelli,* Italian operatic tenor.

1929 *Jacques Brel,* Belgian composer, singer. [d. Oct. 9, 1978]

1932 *John Gavin (Jack Golenor),* U.S. actor, diplomat; Ambassador to Mexico, 1981–86.

1934 *Vartan Gregorian,* Iranian-born educator; President of the New York Public Library, 1981–89; President of Brown University, 1989– .

1937 *Seymour Hersh,* U.S. journalist; Pulitzer Prize for international reporting on the My Lai massacre, 1970.

1940 *John Havlicek,* U.S. basketball player; elected to Hall of Fame, 1983.

Peggy Lennon, U.S. singer; member of the singing group, *Lennon Sisters.*

1943 *Michael Bennett (Michael Bennett DiFiglia),* U.S. choreographer; two Tony Awards for creating, directing, and choreographing *A Chorus Line,* 1975. [d. July 2, 1987]

1954 *John Schneider,* U.S. actor, singer; known for his role as Bo on television series, *The Dukes of Hazzard.*

1955 *Ricky Lynn Bell,* U.S. football player. [d. November 28, 1984]

1963 *(John Charles) Julian Lennon,* British singer, musician; son of John Lennon (December 8, 1980).

1966 *Robin Wright,* U.S. actress; featured in the film *Forrest Gump,* 1994.

HISTORICAL EVENTS

1341 *Francesco Petrarch,* Italian lawyer and diplomat, is crowned poet laureate in Rome.

1364 *John II* of France dies in England and is succeeded by *Charles V.*

1838 The *Great Western,* British passenger steamer, leaves Bristol, England, on its maiden trans-Atlantic voyage to New York.

1904 *Entente Cordiale* between Great Britain and France settles colonial disputes over Egypt and Moroccan interests.

1913 Convocation of the first elected parliament of the *Chinese Republic* is held at Peking.

1915 Turkish government begins the deportation and massacre of *Armenians* accused of aiding the Russians in the Caucasus (*World War I*).

1917 *Austria-Hungary* severs diplomatic relations with the U.S. (*World War I*).

1926 *Benito Mussolini* embarks on visit to *Tripoli;* first visit of Italian premier to African colonies.

1934 U.S. Congress enacts the *Emergency Relief Appropriation Act,* which leads to the *Works Progress Administration.*

1939 *King Zog of Albania* abdicates the day after Mussolini's forces seize Albania (*World War II*).

1940 The *bald eagle* is placed under federal protection as an endangered species in the U.S.

1943 President Franklin D. Roosevelt orders a nationwide *wage freeze* in an effort to curb inflation.

1974 Baseball's *Hank Aaron* surpasses Babe Ruth's career home run record of 714.

1977 Israeli Prime Minister *Yitzhak Rabin* plunges the country into political turmoil when he admits violating Israeli currency laws; Defense Minister *Shimon Peres* takes over the government.

1984 U.S. presidential candidate, *Jesse Jackson,* refuses to repudiate the support of controversial Black Muslim leader, *Louis Farrakhan.*

1985 The Indian government files suit against *Union Carbide Corp.* for a gas leak in *Bhopal* that killed 1,700 people.

1987 Paraguayan president, Alfredo Stroessner, lifts a state of emergency that had been in effect since 1954.

1988 President Ronald Reagan invokes the *Emergency Economic Powers Act* to prohibit U.S. citizens and companies from making payments to the Panamanian government. Income taxes, import duties, and other fees are to be placed in an escrow account in an attempt to weaken the government of General *Manuel Noriega.*

1993 *Macedonia* becomes a member of the United Nations.

1994 Japanese Prime Minister *Morihiro Hosokawa* announces his resignation after revelation of financial improprieties.

april

APRIL
9

HOLIDAYS

Bolivia
National Day
Commemorates popular uprising and reestablishment of National Revolutionary Movement, 1952.

Tunisia
Martyrs' Day

RELIGIOUS CALENDAR

The Saints
St. Mary of Cleophas, matron. [d. 1st century]

St. Waldetrudis, widow; patron of Mons, Belgium. Also called *Vaudru, Vautrude, Waltrude,* or *Waudru.* [d. c. 688]

St. Hugh, Bishop of Rouen. [d. 730]

St. Gaucherius, abbot. Also called *Gaucher, Gautier.* [d. 1140]

The Beatified
Blessed Ubald of Florence. [d. 1315]

Blessed Thomas of Tolentino, martyr and missionary. [d. 1321]

Blessed Anthony Pavoni, martyr. [d. 1374]

Blessed Juan Diego. [beatified 1990]

BIRTHDATES

1798 *Giuditta Pasta,* Italian operatic soprano. [d. April 1, 1865]

1802 *Elias Lönnrot,* Finnish folklorist, philologist, and physician. [d. March 19, 1884]

1806 *Isambard Kingdom Brunel,* British engineer; designer and builder of bridges, railroads, and steamships. [d. 1859]

1815 *Alphonse Beau de Rochas,* French engineer; developed early *internal combustion engine.* [d. March 27, 1893]

1821 *Charles Baudelaire,* French poet, critic, translator; much of his work was banned during his lifetime; known for his decadent, bohemian lifestyle. [d. August 31, 1867]

1830 *Eadweard (Edward) Muybridge,* U.S. motion picture pioneer born in England; known for developments in *rapid sequence photography.* [d. May 8, 1904]

1835 *Leopold II, of Belgium,* 1865–1909; leader of first European efforts to develop Africa's Congo Basin, which was annexed in 1908 as the *Belgian Congo.* [d. December 17, 1909]

1848 *Helene Lange,* German feminist educator, author, and editor. [d. May 13, 1930]

1864 *William George Stuber,* U.S. business executive; succeeded George Eastman as president of Eastman Kodak Co., 1925–34. [d. June 17, 1959]

1865 *Erich Friedrich Wilhelm Ludendorff,* German Army general; launched unlimited *submarine warfare* that drew U.S. into World War I. [d. December 20, 1937]

Charles Proteus Steinmetz (Karl August Rudolf Steinmetz), U.S. electrical engineer born in Germany; established the mathematical methods of *electrical engineering.* [d. October 26, 1923]

1870 *Nikolai Lenin (Vladimir Ilich Ulyanov),* Russian Communist leader; Premier of Russia, 1918–24. [d. January 21, 1924]

1872 *Léon Blum,* French socialist statesman; Premier, 1936–37; provisional President, 1946. [d. 1950]

1887 *Frank (Earl) Adair,* U.S. surgeon; a leader in research in cancer of the breast; led in the development of the clinical section of Sloan-Kettering Institute for Cancer Research. [d. December 31, 1981]

1888 *Sol(omon) Hurok,* U.S. impresario born in Russia; considered one of most influential figures in development of knowledge and appreciation of music and dance in the U.S. [d. March 5, 1974]

1889 *Efrem Zimbalist,* Russian violinist, composer. [d. February 22, 1985]

1898 *Curly Lambeau (Earl Louis Lambeau),* U.S. football coach; founder of *Green Bay Packers.* [d. June 1, 1965]

Paul Leroy Robeson, U.S. singer, actor, political activist; known for the song *Ol' Man River* in *Show Boat,* 1936. [d. January 23, 1976]

1903 *Ward Bond,* U.S. character actor; appeared in many Westerns in movies and on TV. [d. November 5, 1960]

Gregory Pincus, U.S. biologist; responsible for development of the *birth control pill.* [d. August 22, 1967]

1905 *J. William Fulbright,* U.S. politician, lawyer, teacher; U.S. Senator, 1942–74; founded the *Fulbright Scholarship Program.* [d. February 9, 1995]

1906 *Antal Dorati,* Hungarian-born composer, conductor; Music Director, Washington National Symphony Orchestra, 1970–77; Principal Conductor, Royal Philharmonic Orchestra, 1975–78. [d. November 13, 1988]

1910 *Abraham A. Ribicoff,* U.S. lawyer, politician; Congressman, 1948–52; Governor of Connecticut, 1954–61; Secretary of U.S. Dept. of Health, Education and Welfare, 1961–62, U.S. Senator, 1962–80. [d. February 22, 1998]

1925 *Frank Joseph Shakespeare, Jr.,* U.S. government official; broadcast executive; President, CBS Television Service Division, 1967–69; Head, U.S. Information Agency, 1969–73; President, RKO General, 1975–85.

1926 *Hugh Hefner,* U.S. editor; publisher of *Playboy.*

1929 *Michael Learned,* U.S. actress; known for her role as Olivia on television series, *The Waltons,* 1972–79; three Emmy Awards.

1932 *Carl Perkins,* U.S. songwriter; author of the song "Blue Suede Shoes." [d. January 9, 1998]

1933 *Jean-Paul Belmondo,* French actor.

1935 *Avery Schreiber,* U.S. actor, comedian.

1954 *Dennis Quaid,* U.S. actor; known for his starring role in *The Right Stuff,* 1983.

1957 *Severiano Ballesteros,* Spanish golfer.

1971 *Jacques Villeneuve,* Canadian race car driver; winner of the Indianapolis 500, 1995.

HISTORICAL EVENTS

1241 Mongols defeat Polish princes under *Batu* at *Liegnitz,* Silesia; *Henryk II, Duke of Silesia,* is killed.

1454 *Peace of Lodi* is signed between Venice and Milan; Venice secures Brescia, Bergamo, Crema, and Treviglio.

1483 *Edward V* of England accedes to throne on death of Edward IV.

1609 *Truce of Antwerp* grants independence of the United Provinces (*Netherlands*).

1682 *Sieur de La Salle,* French explorer, claims vast interior of North America for France, naming it *Louisiana.*

1705 The *Haymarket Theater* is established in London.

1865 Confederate general *Robert E. Lee* surrenders to Union general *Ulysses S. Grant* at *Appomattox Court House,* ending *U.S. Civil War.*

1891 *Pan-German League* is formed.

1909 *Lee De Forest* engineers first wireless transmission of the human voice singing, of *Enrico Caruso* in the Metropolitan Opera House in New York.

1917 Canadians storm *Vimy Ridge* in northern France (*World War I*).

1918 Germans break through Allied lines in *Flanders* but are halted by British and French reenforcements (*World War I*).

The *Moldavian Republic (Bessarabia)* proclaims its union with *Rumania.*

1928 *Turkey* ends legal status of *Islam* as the state religion.

1938 Civil disobedience campaign begins in *Tunisia,* organized by *Habib Bourguiba.*

1939 *Marian Anderson* performs on the steps of the Lincoln Memorial in Washington, D.C. First lady Eleanor Roosevelt arranges the concert after the *Daughters of the American Revolution* deny Anderson the use of Constitution Hall, because she is black.

1940 The first public demonstration of *stereophonic sound* is performed at Carnegie Hall in New York.

German troops invade Denmark and Norway by sea and air (*World War II*).

april

1941 The Professional Golfers Association establishes the *Golf Hall of Fame* in U.S.

1942 *Bataan* in the Philippines falls to the Japanese after more than three months of siege (*World War II*).

1952 *Victor Paz Estenssoro* seizes power in Bolivian revolution, reestablishing the *National Revolutionary Movement.*

1963 *Sir Winston Churchill* is proclaimed an honorary U.S. citizen in ceremony televised internationally from the White House.

1974 *India, Pakistan,* and *Bangladesh* sign Indian subcontinent accord in New Delhi.

1977 Communist Party is legalized in *Spain* after a 38-year ban.

1992 Deposed Panamanian leader *Manuel Noriega* is found guilty by a Florida court of drug trafficking.

1993 U.S. planes patrolling the "*no-fly zone*" in Iraq are fired upon by Iraqi forces. The United States responds by destroying the Iraqi anti-aircraft gun positions.

1996 *President Bill Clinton* signs the *Line-Item Veto Act* in law. It is later declared unconstitutional.

RELIGIOUS CALENDAR

The Saints

St. Bademus, abbot. [d. 376]

The Martyrs under the Danes, Anglo-Saxon monks. [d. c. 870]

St. Macarius of Ghent. Invoked against epidemic diseases. Also called *Macaire.* [d. 1012]

St. Fulbert, Bishop of Chartres. [d. 1029]

St. Paternus of Abdinghof. [d. 1058]

St. Michael de Sanctis, priest and convent superior. [d. 1625]

The Beatified

Blessed Antony Neyrot, martyr. [d. 1460]

Blessed Mark Fantucci, Franciscan monk and missionary. [d. 1479]

BIRTHDATES

1512 *James V* of Scotland, 1513–42; upheld Roman Catholicism and allied his country with France against England. [d. December 24, 1542]

1583 *Hugo Grotius,* Dutch theologian, jurist; called the *Father of Modern International Law.* [d. August 28, 1645]

1755 *Samuel Christian Friedrich Hahnemann,* German physician; the founder of *homeopathy.* [d. July 2, 1843]

1778 *William Hazlitt,* English critic, essayist. [d. September 18, 1830]

1794 *Matthew Calbraith Perry,* U.S. Navy commodore; negotiated *Treaty of Kanagawa,* which opened U.S. trade with Japan. [d. March 4, 1858]

1827 *Lew(is) Wallace,* U.S. soldier, lawyer, diplomat, novelist; *Ben Hur.* [d. February 15, 1905]

1829 *William Booth,* British social reformer; founder of the *Salvation Army.* [d. August 20, 1912]

1835 *Henry Villard (Ferdinand Heinrich Gustav Hilgard),* U.S. journalist, railroad magnate, born in Germany; President of Northern Pacific Railroad, 1881–84. [d. November 12, 1900]

1847 *Joseph Pulitzer,* U.S. newspaper publisher; called the *Father of Modern American Journalism.* Established and endowed the School of Journalism at Columbia University and the *Pulitzer Prize,* which is awarded for excellence in journalism, letters, and music. [d. October 29, 1911]

1857 *Lucien Lévy-Bruhl,* French philosopher, sociologist, anthropologist. [d. March 13, 1939]

1862 *Wilbur Lucius Cross,* U.S. educator, politician; Governor of Connecticut, 1931–39. [d. October 5, 1948]

1864 *Eugen Francis Charles d'Albert,* German-French pianist, composer, born in Scotland; best known for his operas. [d. March 3, 1932]

1867 *George William Russell (AE),* Irish author. [d. 1935]

1868 *George Arliss (Augustus George Andrews),* British actor. [d. February 5, 1946]

1882 *Frances Perkins,* U.S. Secretary of Labor, 1933–45; first woman to serve in a presidential cabinet. [d. May 14, 1965]

1885 *Bernard Feustman Gimbel,* U.S. retailer; president of Gimbel Brothers, 1927–53. [d. September 29, 1966]

1887 *Bernardo Alberto Houssay,* Argentine physiologist; Nobel Prize in physiology or medicine for research on *pituitary hormone* (with C. F. and G. T. Cori), 1947. [d. September 21, 1971]

1894 *Ben Nicholson,* British artist; known especially for his all-white reliefs of *absolute form* executed in the 1930's. [d. February 6, 1982]

1897 *Eric Mowbray Knight,* British-U.S. writer; best known for his children's classic, *Lassie Come Home.* [d. January 21, 1943]

1903 *Claire Booth Luce,* U.S. author, journalist, politician, diplomat; Congresswoman, 1943–47; U.S. Ambassador to Italy, 1953–56. [d. October 9, 1987]

1906 *Thomas S(overeign) Gates, Jr.,* U.S. businessman, politician; U. S. Secretary of the Navy, 1957–59; U.S. Secretary of Defense, 1959–60. [d. March 25, 1983]

1915 *Harry Morgan (Harry Bratsburg),* U.S. actor; known for his starring roles on television series, *Dragnet,* 1967–70, and *M*A*S*H,* 1975–83.

1917 *Robert Burns Woodward,* U.S. chemist; Nobel Prize in chemistry for work in chemical synthesis, particularly of *chlorophyll,* 1965. [d. July 8, 1979]

1921 *Kevin Joseph (Chuck) Connors,* U.S. actor; known for his starring role on television series, *The Rifleman,* 1957–62.

1923 *Marshall Warren Nirenberg,* U.S. biochemist; Nobel Prize in physiology or medicine for research in *genetic development* (with H. G. Khorana and R. W. Holley), 1968.

1929 *Max (Carl Adolf) von Sydow,* Swedish actor.

1930 *Dolores Huerta,* U.S. labor activist; co-founder of the United Farm Workers.

1931 *James Lee Dozier,* U.S. military leader; five-star general who was kidnapped by the Red Brigade terrorists and rescued 42 days later by the Italian police, 1981.

1932 *Omar Sharif (Michel Shalhouz),* Egyptian actor.

1934 *David Halberstam,* U.S. author, journalist; Pulitzer Prize, 1964; wrote *The Best and the Brightest,* 1972.

1936 *John Madden,* U.S. sportscaster; two Emmys for his analyses of National Football League games during telecasts, 1982, 1983.

1938 *(Joseph) Don(ald) Meredith,* U.S. football player, sportscaster; quarterback, Dallas Cowboys, 1960–69; co-host, *Monday Night Football,* 1970–73, 1977–86.

1941 *Paul Theroux,* U.S. novelist.

1951 *Steven Seagal,* U.S. actor.

HISTORICAL EVENTS

1302 First meeting of the *French States-General.*

1606 First *Charter of Virginia* is issued to London and Plymouth Companies by *James I* of England.

1741 *Frederick II* of Prussia defeats Austrians at *Mollwitz* and conquers *Silesia.*

1854 The constitution of the *Orange Free State* is adopted.

1861 Confederates demand evacuation of *Fort Sumter* in Charleston, S. C., leading to outbreak of the *U.S. Civil War.*

1864 Archduke *Maximilian of Austria,* supported by the French army, accepts the Mexican crown.

1866 *American Society for the Prevention of Cruelty to Animals* is founded.

1906 O. Henry's short story *The Gift of the Magi* is published.

1916 The first *Professional Golfers Association* tournament begins at Siwanoy course in Bronxville, New York.

1922 The *Genoa Conference* opens to discuss reconstruction of Europe following World War I; it marks the first international involvement with Communist Russia since the war.

1930 *London Naval Conference Treaty* is signed between Great Britain, U.S., France, Italy, and Japan, regulating submarine warfare and tonnage on all classes of ships.

1932 *Paul von Hindenburg* defeats *Adolf Hitler* in German presidential election.

1963 *U.S.S. Thresher,* nuclear-powered submarine, is lost in the Atlantic with 129 men on board.

Papal encyclical *Pacem in Terris,* devoted to world peace and addressed to all men of good will, is issued by *Pope John XXIII.*

1968 *Algeria, Mali, Mauritania,* and the *Congo* resume diplomatic ties with *Great Britain,* broken during the dispute over *Rhodesia* in December 1965.

1970 *Paul McCartney* announces that he is leaving *The Beatles* for personal reasons.

1972 A treaty prohibiting the stockpiling of *biological weapons* is signed by more than 70 nations in ceremonies in Washington, London, and Moscow.

1974 *Golda Meir* resigns as Israeli prime minister.

1977 *Zaire,* under invasion from neighboring Angola, receives military aid from Morocco, France, and the U.S.

1978 The United Nation's highest-ranking Russian official,

Arkady N. Shevchenko, renounces his Russian citizenship and applies for political asylum in the U.S.

1984 *Shearson/American Express Inc.* announces plan to purchase *Lehman Brothers,* an investment banking firm.

1993 *Chris Hani,* a leader in the African National Congress, is assassinated.

1995 The first *subway* in Shanghai opens.

1998 *Northern Ireland* and *Britain* come to terms over a peace settlement that would transfer legislative powers back to Northern Ireland and the creation of a North-South Ministerial Council.

april

APRIL
11

HOLIDAYS

Costa Rica
National Heroes Day
Commemorates Costa Rican triumph over invaders from Nicaragua, 1856. Also called *Battle of Rivas Day, Juan Santamaria Day.*

Liberia
Fast and Prayer Day

RELIGIOUS CALENDAR

The Saints
St. Barsanuphius [d. c. 550]
St. Isaac of Spoleto, monk. [d. c. 550]
St. Godeberta, virgin. Invoked against all kinds of calamities, especially drought and epidemics. [d. c. 700]
St. Guthlac, hermit. Also called *Guthlake.* [d. 714]
St. Stanislaus, Bishop of Cracow and martyr; patron of Poland. [d. 1079] Feast formerly May 7. Optional Memorial.
St. Gemma Galgani, virgin and laywoman. [d. 1903]

The Beatified
Blessed Waltman, abbot. [d. 1138]
Blessed Rainerius Inclusus of Osnabruck, recluse. Also called *Rayner.* [d. 1237]
Blessed George Gervase, priest and martyr. Also called *Jervis.* [d. 1608]
Blessed Helen Guerra, founder of the Congregation of St. Rita, later called the Oblates of the Holy Spirit. [d. 1914]

BIRTHDATES

1492 *Margaret of Navarre (Margaret of Angoulême),* outstanding figure of French Renaissance; active in politics, supporter of Protestantism. [d. December 21, 1549]

1770 *George Canning,* English statesman; Foreign Secretary; Prime Minister, 1822–27. [d. August 8, 1827]

1794 *Edward Everett,* U.S. statesman, orator; President of Harvard College, 1846–49; the speaker who immediately preceded Abraham Lincoln at the dedication of the National Cemetery at *Gettysburg.* [d. January 15, 1865]

1825 *Ferdinand Lassalle,* German socialist leader; founder of *German Social Democratic Party.* [d. August 31, 1864]

1862 *William Wallace Campbell,* U.S. astronomer; President, University of California, 1923–30; President, National Academy of Sciences, 1931–35. [d. June 14, 1938]

Charles Evans Hughes, U.S. jurist, lawyer; Governor of New York, 1907–10; Republican presidential nominee, 1916; U.S. Secretary of State, 1921–25; Chief Justice, U.S. Supreme Court, 1930–41. [d. August 27, 1948]

1879 *Clarence Cannon,* U.S. politician, lawyer, history

professor; a noted parliamentarian. [d. May 12, 1964]

1893 *Dean G. Acheson,* U.S. lawyer, statesman; Secretary of State, 1949–53; the principal creator of the U.S. foreign policy aimed at containment of Communist expansion after World War II. [d. October 12, 1971]

1899 *Percy Lavon Julian,* U.S. chemist and steroid researcher; most noted for development of *steroids* used in treatment of *arthritis.* [d. April 19, 1975]

1907 *Paul Douglas,* U.S. actor. [d. September 11, 1959]

1910 *António de Spinola,* Portuguese leader, army officer; provisional President of Portugal, May–September, 1974.

1911 *Stella Walsh (Stanislawa Walasiewicz),* Polish-born athlete; won over forty U.S. track-and-field titles and set many world records. [d. December 4, 1980]

1913 *Oleg Lolewski Cassini,* French fashion designer; official White House designer for Jacqueline Kennedy, 1961–63.

1917 *Morton Sobell,* U.S. spy; co-defendant with *Julius* and *Ethel Rosenberg* in U.S. atomic secrets spy trial, 1951.

Found guilty and sentenced to thirty years in prison; released, 1969.

1919 *Hugh (Leo) Carey,* U.S. politician, lawyer; U.S. Congressman, 1960–75; Governor of New York, 1975–82.

1932 *Joel Grey (Joe Katz),* U.S. actor; Academy Award (Best Supporting Actor) for *Cabaret,* 1972.

1941 *Ellen Holtz Goodman,* U.S. journalist; Pulitzer Prize for commentary, 1980.

HISTORICAL EVENTS

1512 The French are defeated in the *Battle of Ravenna* and are expelled from Italy.

1677 In Dutch war with France, *William of Orange* is defeated at *Cassel.*

1713 *Peace of Utrecht* between France and Prussia ends *War of the Spanish Succession.*

1764 Treaty is signed between *Russia* and *Prussia* to control *Poland.*

1805 Russia joins Great Britain, Austria, and Sweden in the *Third Coalition* against France and its leader, *Napoleon.*

1814 Defeated by the English, *Napoleon* abdicates and is banished to *Elba.*

1894 *Uganda* is declared a British protectorate.

1900 The U.S. Navy buys its first submarine, the *U.S.S. Holland.*

1905 The *Victoria Falls Bridge* over the Zambezi River, 2,875 feet above sea level, is completed, providing a link in the Cape to Cairo Railway.

1919 *Geneva,* Switzerland, is chosen as the headquarters of the *League of Nations.*

1939 Under German pressure, *Hungary* withdraws from the *League of Nations.*

1944 *John Milius,* U.S. director; directed *Red Dawn,* 1984 and *Clear and Present Danger,* 1994.

1947 *Peter Riegart,* U.S. actor; known for roles in *Animal House,* 1978 and *Crossing Delancey,* 1989.

Jackie Robinson signs a contract with the Brooklyn Dodgers, becoming the first black major league baseball player in U.S. history.

1951 U.S. General *Douglas MacArthur* is relieved of command in the Korean conflict by President *Harry Truman* after a dispute over the former's exercise of authority.

1958 U.S. pianist *Van Cliburn* wins the Tchaikovsky International Piano and Violin Competition held in Moscow.

1961 Trial of *Adolf Eichmann* begins in an Israeli court in Jerusalem.

1963 British government rejects the request of the all-white government of *Southern Rhodesia's* for early independence.

1967 Tom Stoppard's tragicomedy, *Rosencrantz and Guildenstern Are Dead,* premieres in London.

1968 U.S. President Lyndon B. Johnson signs a *civil rights bill* prohibiting racial discrimination in the sale or rental of U.S. housing.

1970 *Apollo 13* is launched, manned by astronauts James A. Lovell, Jr., John L. Swipert, and Fred W. Haise, Jr.

1979 *Kampala,* the capital of Uganda, is captured by Tanzanians and rebellious Ugandans.

1982 British explorers *Charles Burton* and *Sir Ranulph Fiennes* become the first to cross both poles in a single journey around the earth.

1984 The U.S. Federal Trade Commission gives final approval to *General Motors Corp.* and *Toyota Motors Corp.* to jointly produce a small car at a California plant.

1985 First secretary of the Albanian Communist Party, *Enver Hoxha,* dies and is replaced by *Ramiz Alia.*

1996 Forty-three African countries sign the *African Nuclear Weapons Free Zone Treaty.*

april

APRIL
12

HOLIDAYS

Liberia
National Redemption Day
Commemorates the coup by the People's Redemption Council, 1980.

U.S. (North Carolina)
Anniversary of the Signing of the Halifax Resolves

U.S.
Franklin Delano Roosevelt
Death Anniversary Sponsored by Franklin D. Roosevelt Philatelic Society, St. Augustine Shores, Florida

RELIGIOUS CALENDAR

The Saints
St. Julius I, pope. Elected 337. Fixed December 25 as the date of the birth of Jesus Christ. [d. 352]

St. Zeno, Bishop of Verona. [d. 371]

St. Sabas the Goth, martyr. [d. 372]

St. Alferius, Abbot of La Cava; founder of the Abbey of La Cava. [d. 13th century]

The Beatified
Blessed Andrew of Montereale. [d. 1480]

Blessed Angelo of Chivasso, priest and evangelical. [d. 1495]

BIRTHDATES

1539 *Garcilaso de la Vega, El Inca,* Peruvian historian. [d. 1616]

1577 *Christian IV* of Denmark and Norway; led his country into the *Thirty Years' War.* [d. February 28, 1648]

1777 *Henry Clay,* U.S. statesman; known as *The Great Compromiser.* [d. June 29, 1852]

1791 *Francis Preston Blair,* U.S. journalist, politician. [d. October 18, 1876]

1823 *Alexander Nikolaevich Ostrovsky,* [O.S., March 31] Russian playwright; considered the greatest representative of Russian realism. [d. June 14 [O.S., June 2], 1886]

1825 *Richard Harvey Cain,* U.S. Congressman, 1873–75, 1877–79. [d. 1887]

1831 *Constantin Emile Meunier,* Belgian painter, sculptor; known for his paintings of mines and factories. [d. April 4, 1905]

1838 *John Shaw Billings,* U.S. Army surgeon, librarian; responsible for organization of *New York Public Library* system. [d. March 11, 1913]

1857 *John Thomas Underwood,* U.S. manufacturer. [d. July 2, 1937]

1871 *Johannes Metaxas,* Greek statesman, general; dictator of Greece, 1936–41. [d. January 29, 1941]

1879 *Frederick G. Melcher,* U.S. book publisher, editor; founder of *Children's Book Week,* 1919. [d. March 9, 1963]

1883 *Imogen Cunningham,* U.S. photographer. [d. June 24, 1976]

1884 *Otto F. Meyerhof,* German biochemist; Nobel Prize in physiology or medicine for research on the chemical reactions of metabolism in the muscle (with A. V. Hill), 1922. [d. October 6, 1951]

1903 *Jan Tinbergen,* Dutch economist; Nobel Prize in economics for developing mathematical models to measure economic change (with R. Frisch), 1969. [d. June 4, 1994]

1905 *Warren G. Magnuson,* U.S. politician, lawyer; U.S. Senator, 1944–81. [d. May 20, 1989]

1913 *Lionel Hampton,* U.S. jazz musician, bandleader.

1922 *Tiny Tim (Herbert Buckingham Khaury),* U.S. singer; known for his song, *Tiptoe Through the Tulips.* [d. November 30, 1996]

1923 *Ann Miller (Lucille Ann Collier),* U.S. dancer.

1924 *Raymond Barre,* French politician; Vice-President of

Commission of European Communities, 1967–72; Prime Minister, 1976–81.

1932 *Moishe Rosen,* U.S. religious leader; founded Jews for Jesus.

1933 *Montserrat Caballe,* Spanish operatic soprano.

1939 *Alan Ayckbourn,* British dramatist.

1940 *Herbert Jeffrey (Herbie) Hancock,* U.S. jazz musician; Grammy Award for *Rockit,* 1984.

1947 *David Letterman,* U.S. television host; known for television series, *Late Night with David Letterman,* 1982–93; Late Show with David Letterman, 1993– .

1950 *David Bruce Cassidy,* U.S. singer, actor; known for television series, *The Partridge Family,* 1970–74.

1956 *Andy Garcia,* U.S. actor; born in Cuba, Garcia is known for his roles in *The Godfather Part III,* 1990 and *When a Man Loves a Woman,* 1994.

1963 *Garry Kasparov,* Azerbaijan chess player; youngest world chess champion, 1985 (see November 9, 1985), first ranked player defeated by a computer, Deep Blue, in 1997.

1971 *Shannen Doherty,* U.S. actress; starred for four years on the TV series *Beverly Hills, 90210.*

HISTORICAL EVENTS

1204 Crusaders capture *Constantinople* and establish the Latin Empire (*Fourth Crusade*).

1500 *Peace of Basel* establishes Swiss independence from Holy Roman Empire.

1533 *Thomas Cromwell* is appointed Privy Councillor and Secretary of State of England.

1654 Scotland and Ireland are united with *England* by the *Ordinance of Union.*

1859 First U.S. *billiards* championships match is played in Detroit, Michigan, between *Michael Phelan* and *John Seereiter;* Phelan is the winner.

1861 The *U.S. Civil War* begins with an attack on *Fort Sumter* by South Carolina forces (see also April 10).

1877 Great Britain annexes the Boer South African Republic as the *Transvaal.*

1907 A new *Swiss Army* bill passes, reorganizing military forces and designating the army as a standing militia with required training biennially.

1915 The *Battle of Shaiba* begins with a Turkish attack on British positions in Mesopotamia (*World War I*).

1929 The *Trades Disputes Act* and the *Public Safety Act* are enacted in India.

1945 U.S. President *Franklin D. Roosevelt* dies and is succeeded by his vice-president, *Harry S. Truman.*

1955 The polio vaccine developed by Dr. *Jonas Salk* found to be successful after subjection to a year of clinical trials.

1956 *Solomon Bandaranaike* is inaugurated as prime minister of Ceylon.

1959 Archibald MacLeish's *J.B.* wins the Tony Award for best Broadway play of the season.

1961 The U.S. Atomic Energy Commission (AEC) announces the development of *Lawrencium,* a new element with the atomic number of 103.

Yuri Gagarin, Russian astronaut, is first man in space, orbiting the earth in *Vostok I.*

1965 The *Houston Astrodome* hosts the first major league baseball game ever played in an indoor stadium.

1971 *East Pakistan* declares its independence as *Bangladesh.*

1978 Transitional government of *Rhodesia* replaces its cabinet with an 18-member Council of Ministers; Prime Minister Ian D. Smith is the only white on the four-man Executive Council.

1980 *Samuel K. Doe* and the *People's Redemption Party* oust Liberian president *William Tolbert.*

1981 *Columbia,* U.S. *space shuttle,* is first launched from Kennedy Space Center in Florida.

1983 *Harold Washington* is elected mayor of Chicago, the first black to win that office.

U.S. embassy in *Beirut, Lebanon* is destroyed by a car bomb. 17 Americans are among the 63 people killed by the blast, for which a pro-Iranian terrorist group, the *Islamic Jihad Organization,* claims responsibility.

An Egyptian administrative court upholds a presidential

april

decree removing Pope *Shenouda III* as spiritual leader of the nation's *Coptic Orthodox Church*.

1984 The U.S. House of Representatives votes to condemn the mining of *Nicaragua*'s harbors. A similar resolution was passed by the Senate two days earlier.

1987 *Texaco Inc.* becomes the largest U.S. company in history to file for bankruptcy after it is ordered to pay *Pennzoil* $8.53 billion in damages for unfair business practices.

1988 The first U.S. law mandating *universal health insurance* is signed in Massachusetts.

1990 *Lothar de Maizière* is selected Premier of East Germany.

The *H. J. Heinz, Van Camp Seafood,* and *Bumble Bee Seafoods companies* agree to ban the purchase of tuna that have been caught with nets. Protests from environmentalists had pushed the agreement through after they proved that a serious decline in the dolphin population resulted from the use of net fishing.

HOLIDAYS

U.S. (Alabama, Oklahoma, Virginia)
Thomas Jefferson's Birthday

RELIGIOUS CALENDAR

The Saints

SS. Carpus, Papylus, and *Agathonice,* martyrs. Carpus, bishop from Lydia; Papylus, deacon from Thyateria; and Agathonice, matron. [d. c. 170]

St. Martius, Abbot of Clermont. Also called *Mars.* [d. c. 530]

St. Hermenegild, martyr. [d. 585]

St. Martin I, pope and martyr. Elected 649. [d. 655] Feast formerly November 12. Optional Memorial.

St. Guinoch, counsellor of King Kenneth. Also called *Guinochus.* [d. 838]

The Beatified

Blessed Ida of Boulogne, widow; founded the Monastery of Saint-Wulmer at Boulogne and Vasconvilliers. [d. 1113]

Blessed James of Certaldo, abbot. [d. 1292]

Blessed Ida of Louvain, virgin. [d. c. 1300]

Blessed Margaret of Cittœa-di-Castello, virgin. [d. 1320]

Blessed John Lockwood and *Blessed Edmund Catherick,* priests and martyrs. [d. 1642]

BIRTHDATES

1519 *Catherine de Medici,* queen consort of Henry II of France; regent of France, 1560–63. [d. January 5, 1589]

1593 *Sir Thomas Wentworth, 1st Earl of Strafford,* English statesman; supporter of *Charles I;* Lord Deputy of Ireland, 1632–38. [d. May 11, 1641]

1732 *Frederick North, 2nd Earl of Guilford,* English statesman; Prime Minister, 1770–82; his policies led to the *American Revolution* and British loss of the American colonies. [d. August 5, 1792]

1739 *Christian Friedrich Daniel Schubart,* German poet; under patronage of *Frederick the Great.* [d. October 10, 1791]

1743 *Thomas Jefferson,* U.S. politician, educator, architect; U.S. Vice-President, 1797–1801; third President of the U.S.; a principal intellectual force behind the founding of the American republic. [d. July 4, 1826]

1748 *Joseph Bramah,* English machinist; inventor of the modern *toilet.* [d. December 9, 1814]

1769 *Sir Thomas Lawrence,* English portrait painter; principal painter to the King of England after Sir Joshua Reynolds (July 16). [d. January 7, 1830]

1771 *Richard Trevithick,* English engineer; built first *steam locomotive* to be tried on a railway, 1804. [d. April 22, 1833]

1795 *James Harper,* U.S. publisher; with his brother John (January 22), founded *Harper's Monthly, Harper's Weekly,* and *Harper's Bazaar.* Founded J.J. Harper Co. publishers (later Harper & Row). [d. March 27, 1869]

1852 *Frank Winfield Woolworth,* U.S. merchant; founder of F. W. Woolworth Co., 1879. [d. August 8, 1919]

1869 *Tully Marshall (William Phillips),* U.S. silent film actor. [d. 1943]

1892 *Sir Robert Alexander Watson-Watt,* Scottish physicist; responsible for development of U.S. and British *radar systems.* [d. December 5, 1973]

1901 *Robert Lee Dennison,* U.S. naval officer; naval aide to U.S. President Harry S. Truman, 1948–53; Commander-in-Chief, U.S. Atlantic Fleet and Supreme Allied Commander of the Atlantic forces for NATO, 1960–63. [d. March 14, 1980]

april

1906 *Samuel Beckett,* British-French Irish playwright, novelist; Nobel Prize in literature, 1969. [d. December 22, 1989]

1907 *Harold Edward Stassen,* U.S. lawyer, politician; Governor of Minnesota, 1938–45.

1909 *Eudora Welty,* U.S. short-story writer, novelist; Pulitzer Prize winner for *The Optimist's Daughter,* 1973.

1917 *Robert Orville Anderson,* U.S. oil industry executive; chief financial officer of the Board of Atlantic Richfield Co., 1965– .

1919 *Madalyn (Mays) O'Hair,* U.S. lawyer; well-known for atheist beliefs. As Madalyn Murray, filed suit that resulted in Supreme Court ruling (1963) for the removal of Bible reading and prayer recitation in public schools.

1932 *Orlando Letelier,* Chilean diplomat; assassinated while in exile in the U.S. [d. September 21, 1976]

1933 *Ben Nighthorse Campbell,* U.S. politician; U.S. senator, 1993– .

1935 *Lyle Waggoner,* U.S. actor; known for his roles on television series, *The Carol Burnett Show,* 1967–74, and *Wonder Woman,* 1977–79.

1937 *Edward Fox,* British actor; known for his roles in *The Day of the Jackal,* 1973, and *Gandhi,* 1984.

1939 *Seamus Heaney,* Irish poet; Nobel Prize for Literature, 1995.

1941 *Michael Stuart Brown,* U.S. physician; Nobel Prize in physiology or medicine for research in cholesterol metabolism (with Joseph L. Goldstein), 1985.

1942 *Bill Conti,* U.S. composer; Academy Award for the score of *The Right Stuff,* 1983.

1945 *Tony Dow,* U.S. actor; known for his role as Wally Cleaver on television series, *Leave It to Beaver,* 1957–63.

1946 *Al Green,* U.S. R & B singer.

1951 *(Robert) Peabo Bryson,* U.S. singer.

1964 *Bret William Saberhagen,* U.S. baseball player; Cy Young Award, 1985.

1970 *Ricky Schroder,* U.S. actor; known for his role on television series, *Silver Spoons.*

HISTORICAL EVENTS

1059 *Pope Nicholas II* decrees that future popes will be elected by cardinals only.

1111 *Henry V* is crowned Holy Roman Emperor at Rome.

1346 *Pope Clement VI* excommunicates and dethrones *Holy Roman Emperor Louis IV.*

1598 *Henry IV* of France promulgates the *Edict of Nantes,* granting toleration to *Huguenots.*

1640 *Short Parliament* is convened by *Charles I* of England.

1742 Handel's *Messiah* premieres in Dublin, Ireland.

1749 *Radcliffe Library, Oxford University,* is opened.

1752 *Philadelphia Contributionship,* the first *fire insurance company* in colonial America, is established.

1848 *Sicily* declares itself independent of Naples.

1862 *Treaty of Saigon* between France and Annam is signed; France annexes *Cochin-China.*

1870 The *Metropolitan Museum of Art* is incorporated in New York City.

1913 An attempt on the life of *King Alfonso XIII* of Spain by the Catalonian anarchist, S. Alegre, fails.

1919 The *Amritsar Massacre* occurs in India, as a British commander orders his troops to fire on an unarmed assembly, killing 379 and wounding 1200.

1932 German government under Chancellor *Heinrich Brüning* imposes ban on Nazi storm troops.

1941 The *U.S.S.R.* and *Japan* sign a five-year neutrality pact which enables both nations to fight one-front wars until 1945 *(World War II).*

1943 The *Jefferson Memorial* in Washington, D.C., is dedicated by President Franklin D. Roosevelt on the two hundredth anniversary of Thomas Jefferson's birth.

1945 Nearly five square miles of *Tokyo* are destroyed in attacks by Allied bombers *(World War II).*

Soviet forces enter *Vienna,* ending Austria's seven-year union with Germany. *Karl Renner* is appointed to head a coalition interim government *(World War II).*

1960 *Transit I-B,* 265-pound U.S. experimental *space lighthouse,* designed as an aid to navigation, is placed in orbit from Cape Canaveral, Florida.

1961 The United Nations votes to condemn South Africa's *apartheid* policies.

1962 *Ahti Karjalainen* becomes Finland's youngest prime minister at the age of 39.

1964 *Ian D. Smith* is named Prime Minister of Southern Rhodesia, succeeding Winston J. Field.

1967 *Rosemary's Baby,* Ira Levin's novel of the supernatural, is published.

1968 Tanzania becomes the first country to grant recognition to the Nigerian secessionist state of *Biafra.*

1972 First players' strike in the history of *baseball* ends in its thirteenth day, forcing delay of the opening of the season until April 15.

1975 *President François Tombalbaye* of *Chad* is assassinated and his regime is overthrown by the army.

1988 *Ciriaco De Mita* is inaugurated as premier of Italy.

1997 *Tiger Woods,* age 21, becomes the youngest golfer to win the Masters Tournament.

april

APRIL
14

HOLIDAYS

Pan American Day
Commemorates the first
International Conference of
American States, 1890.

Angola
Youth Day

Chad
Independence Day
Commemorates the promulgation of
the nation's constitution, 1962.

Honduras
Day of the Americas

Peru (Lima)
National Contest of Paso Horses

RELIGIOUS CALENDAR

The Saints
St. Ardalion, martyr. [d. c. 300]
St. Lambert, Archbishop of Lyons.
  [d. 688]
St. Bernard of Tiron, abbot. Also
  called *Bernard of Abbeville.*
  [d. 1117]
St. Caradoc, hermit. [d. 1124]
St. Bénezet; one of the patrons of
  Avignon. Also called *Benedict,
  Little Benedict the Bridge
  Builder.* [d. 1184] SS. *John,
  Antony,* and *Eustace,* martyrs.
  [d. 1342] SS. *Tiburtius,
  Valerius,* and *Maximus,*
  martyrs. [death date
  unknown]

The Beatified
Blessed Lanvinus, Carthusian monk.
  [d. 1120]

Blessed Peter Gonzalez; patron of
  mariners. Also called *St. Elm,
  Elmo, Telm, Telmo.* [d. 1246]
Blessed Lydwina of Schiedam,
  virgin; patron of those who
  lead lives of intense suffering
  to expiate others' sins. Also
  called *Lidwina, Lydwid.* [d.
  1433]

BIRTHDATES

1527 *Ortelius (Abraham Oertel),*
  Flemish geographer,
  cartographer, and engraver.
  [d. 1598]

1578 *Philip III* of Spain, 1598–21;
  his reign was characterized by
  a peaceful foreign policy in
  western Europe. [d. March
  31, 1621]

1629 *Christian Huygens,* Dutch
  physicist, mathematician,
  astronomer; developed many
  improvements in production
  of telescopes, including a new
  method of grinding lenses,
  negative eyepieces; also
  discovered a satellite and a
  ring of *Saturn;* with his
  brother was first to use
  pendulum to regulate clock
  movements. [d. June 8, 1695]

1812 *Sir George Grey,* British
  Colonial Governor of New
  Zealand, 1845–54, 1861–67.
  [d. September 20, 1898]

1813 *Junius Spencer Morgan,* U.S.
  merchant, philanthropist. [d.
  April 8, 1890]

1842 *Adna Chaffee,* U.S. Army
  Chief of Staff, 1904–06. [d.
  November 1, 1914]

1866 *Anne Sullivan (Macy),* U.S.
  teacher; best known for her
  work with *Helen Keller.* [d.
  October 20, 1936]

1868 *Peter Behrens,* German
  architect, artist; an early
  proponent of the use of steel
  and glass; developed modern
  industrial architectural style.
  [d. March 2, 1940]

1878 *George Malvin Holley,* U.S.
  industrialist; manufacturer of
  first practical *motorcycle,*
  1899. [d. June 26, 1963]

1879 *James Branch Cabell,* U.S.
  novelist; wrote about first
  families of Virginia. [d. May 5,
  1958]

1886 *Edward Chace Tolman,* U.S.
  psychologist; a leader in the
  behaviorist movement. [d.
  November 19, 1959]

1889 *Arnold Toynbee,* British
  historian; analyzed cyclical
  development and decline of
  civilizations. [d. October 22,
  1975]

1892 *Vere Gordon Childe,*
  Australian archaeologist. [d.
  1957]

1896 *Arthur Bartlett Homer,* U.S.
  industrialist, Bethlehem Steel
  Corporation's president and
  chief executive officer. [d.
  June 18, 1972]

1904 *Sir John Gielgud,* British actor, director; particularly distinguished as a Shakespearean actor.

1906 *Hastings Kamuzu Banda,* Malawian statesman; President, Republic of Malawi, 1966–94.[d. November 25, 1997]

1907 *François Duvalier (Papa Doc),* Haitian leader; President, 1957–71. [d. April 21, 1971]

1914 *Richard Salant,* U.S. communications executive. [d. February 16, 1993]

1917 *Norman Luboff,* U.S. composer; conductor, Norman Luboff Choir.

1925 *Rod Steiger,* U.S. actor; Academy Award (Best Actor) for *In the Heat of the Night,* 1967.

Abel Mozorewa, Zimbabwean statesman; Prime Minister of Zimbabwe, 1979–80; the first black to occupy the position.

1929 *Chadli Bendjedid,* Algerian leader; President, 1979–91.

1932 *William Richards Bennett,* Canadian politician, businessman; Premier of British Columbia, 1975–86.

Anthony Perkins, U.S. actor; known for his role as Norman Bates in *Psycho.* [d. September 12, 1992]

1935 *Erich von Däniken,* Swiss author.

1936 *Francisco Vincent (Frank) Serpico,* U.S. police officer; exposed police corruption in New York City; subject of the book and film, *Serpico.*

1940 *Julie Christie,* British actress; Academy Award for *Darling,* 1965.

1941 *Pete(r Edward) Rose,* U.S. baseball player, manager; Ball Player of the Decade, 1979; banned from baseball for gambling, 1989.

1954 *Bruce Sterling,* U.S. writer; author of *The Hacker Crackdown: Law and Disorder on the Electronic Frontier,* 1992.

1966 *Greg Maddux,* U.S. baseball player; winner of the Cy Young Award, 1992, 1993, and 1994.

1968 *Anthony Michael Hall,* U.S. actor; known for roles in *Sixteen Candles,* 1984 and *The Breakfast Club,* 1985

HISTORICAL EVENTS

979 *Ethelred II* is crowned King of England.

1028 *Henry III* is elected King of Germany.

1191 *Henry VI* is crowned Holy Roman Emperor.

1471 In England the rebellious *Warwick* is defeated and killed by *Edward IV* at Barnet (*War of the Roses*).

1528 *Pánfilo de Narváez,* Spanish soldier, lands near *Tampa, Florida,* with group of 400 colonists.

1800 *Banque de France* is founded.

1828 *Noah Webster* obtains copyright for the first edition of his *American Dictionary of the English Language.*

1849 *Hungary* declares itself independent of *Austria.*

1865 U.S. President *Abraham Lincoln* is assassinated at Ford's Theater in Washington by *John Wilkes Booth.*

1879 An attempt to assassinate Russian *Czar Alexander II* is made by *Alexander Solovieff.*

1915 The *Battle of Shaiba* in Mesopotamia ends when British forces repel and rout a Turkish attack (*World War I*).

1918 Lieutenant *Douglas Campbell* becomes the first U.S. ace pilot after gunning down his fifth German aircraft (*World War I*).

1929 Nationalist Chinese take control of *Manchuria.*

1930 *Jawarhalal Nehru* is arrested by the British government of India for abetting the manufacture of contraband salt.

1931 The *Republic of Spain* is established.

1937 *Richard Rodgers'* Musical comedy, *Babes in Arms,* with lyrics by *Lorenz Hart,* premieres in New York.

1947 *Small Fry Club,* the first television program designed specifically for children, begins broadcasting.

1955 *Hungarian premier Imre Nagy* is stripped of his government and Communist party positions after attempting to introduce reforms.

1956 Ampex Corp. demonstrates the first commercially practical magnetic *videotape recording machine.*

1959 *Taft Memorial Bell Tower* is dedicated in Washington, D.C., in memory of Robert Alphonso Taft, son of President *William Howard Taft.*

1960 Charles Strouse and Lee Adams' musical, *Bye, Bye*

april

Birdie, premieres in New York.

1962 *Georges Pompidou* is named Premier of France by President *Charles de Gaulle.*

Chad promulgates its constitution.

1976 Morocco and Mauritania agree to divide the territory of the *Spanish Sahara.*

1979 Liberian demonstration over food prices ends in rioting and granting of emergency powers to President *William R. Tolbert* for one year.

1981 U.S. *space shuttle Columbia* lands safely after a 36-orbit mission, its first.

1984 Anti-Sandinista rebels led by *Eden Pastora* seize the southern Nicaraguan town of *San Juan del Norte.* Although they are forced to withdraw after three days, the action is the first confirmed capture of a Nicaraguan town by the contras.

1986 Russian-born pianist, *Vladimir Horowitz,* returns to his native country for two performances after a 61-year absence.

U.S. aircraft attack Libyan targets in retaliation for Libya's suspected bombing of a West German discotheque that killed two and injured fifty U.S. servicemen.

1988 The *U.S.S.R.* agrees to withdraw its troops from Afghanistan and restore an Afghan state.

HOLIDAYS

Bangladesh
Bengali New Year

Bolivia (Tarija)
Public Holiday

Niger
Assumption of Power by the Supreme Military Council, 1974.

North Korea
Kim Il-Sung's Birthday

Tibet
Anniversary of the Enlightenment of Sakyamuni, founder of Buddhism.

RELIGIOUS CALENDAR

The Saints
SS. *Basilissa* and *Anastasia,* martyrs. [d. c. 65 A.D.]
St. *Padarn,* Bishop in Ceredigion; missionary and monastery founder. Also called *Patern.* [d. c. 5th–6th centuries]
St. *Ruadan of Lothra,* abbot, monastery founder; one of the Apostles of Ireland. Also called *Ruadhan.* [d. c. 584]
St. *Hunna,* matron. Also called the *Holy Washerwoman, Huva.* [d. c. 679]

BIRTHDATES

1452 *Leonardo da Vinci,* Italian artist, architect, musician, scientist; considered one of the most versatile talents of all time, the ultimate Renaissance man. [d. May 2, 1519]

1469 *Nanak,* founder of *Sikhism,* an Indian religious sect. [d. 1538]

1646 *Christian V* of Denmark and Norway. [d. August 25, 1699]

1672 *Etienne (Geoffroy) Saint-Hilaire,* French naturalist; published first table of chemical affinities, 1718. [d. June 19, 1744]

1707 *Leonhard Euler,* Swiss mathematician; established many of the mathematical notations used today. [d. September 18, 1783]

1741 *Charles Wilson Peale,* U.S. painter; best known for portraits of American Revolutionary figures. [d. February 22, 1827]

1793 *Friedrich Georg Wilson von Struve,* German-Russian astronomer; pioneer in the study of *binary stars.* [d. November 23, 1864]

1797 *Louis Adolphe Thiers,* French statesman, historian; a founder and the first president of the Third Republic, 1871–73. [d. September 3, 1877]

1800 *Sir James Clark Ross,* British polar explorer; the first to explore *Antarctica,* 1839. [d. April 3, 1862]

1801 *Edouard Armand Isidore Hippolyte Lartet,* French paleontologist; regarded as one of the founders of *paleontology.* [d. January 28, 1871]

1809 *Hermann Günther Grassmann,* German mathematician, Sanskritist; laid foundation of modern *vector analysis.* [d. September 26, 1877]

1817 *Benjamin Jowett,* British theologian, classical scholar, and educational reformer; renowned for his translations of Plato and Aristotle. [d. October 1, 1893]

1820 *Mariano Melgarejo,* Bolivian ruler; President of Bolivia, 1864–71. [d. November 23, 1872]

1832 *Wilhelm Busch,* German poet, painter; originator of the *comic strip.* [d. January 9, 1908]

1843 *Henry James,* U.S.-British novelist, renowned for his prose style; became naturalized British citizen, 1915. [d. February 28, 1916]

1856 *Jean Moréas (Ioannes Papadiamantopoulos),* French symbolist poet, born in Greece; organized *École Romane.* [d. March 30, 1910]

1858 *Émile Durkheim,* French sociologist; one of founders of modern sociology. [d. November 15, 1917]

1874 *Johannes Stark,* German physicist; Nobel Prize in physics for discoveries concerning electricity and light, 1919. [d. June 21, 1957]

1880 *Max Wertheimer,* U.S. psychologist; co-founder, Gestalt movement, 1912. [d. October 12, 1943]

1887 *(Helen) Violet Bonham Carter,* British public official; wrote *Winston Churchill as I Knew Him,* 1965. [d. February 19, 1969]

1889 *Thomas Hart Benton,* U.S. painter, muralist; created an American artistic style called *Regionalism.* [d. January 19, 1975]

Asa Philip Randolph, U.S. labor leader; a pioneer in the unionization of blacks in America. [d. May 16, 1979]

1890 *Wallace Reid,* U.S. actor; leading man in silent films. [d. January 18, 1923]

1892 *Corrie Ten Boom,* Dutch author, lecturer; sentenced to a concentration camp for hiding Jews during World War II; wrote *The Hiding Place,* 1971. [d. April 15, 1983]

1894 *Bessie Smith (The Empress of the Blues),* U.S. singer; legendary blues singer of 1920s–1930s. [d. September 26, 1937]

1896 *Nikolay Nikolaevich Semenov,* Russian physical chemist; Nobel Prize in chemistry for study of kinetics of chemical reactions (with C. N. Hinshelwood), 1956. [d. 1986]

1903 *Waverley L(ewis) Root,* U.S. writer, journalist; best known as author of *The Foods of France,* 1958, and *Contemporary French Cooking,* 1962. [d. October 31, 1982]

1907 *Nikolaas Tinbergen,* British ethologist; Nobel Prize in physiology or medicine for research in ethology (with K. Z. Lorenz and K. von Frisch), 1973. [d. December 21, 1988]

1912 *Kim Il-Sung,* Korean political leader; organized Korean People's Revolutionary Army in Korean struggle against Japan; President of North Korea, 1972–94. [d. July 8, 1994]

1916 *Alfred S. Bloomingdale,* U.S. business executive; founded Diner's Club Credit Card Co., 1950. [d. August 20, 1982]

1922 *Harold Washington,* U.S. politician; Mayor of Chicago, 1983–87. [d. November 27, 1987]

1924 *Neville Marriner,* British conductor, musician.

1930 *Vigdís Finnbogadóttir,* Icelandic politician; President of Iceland, 1980–96; first woman to hold that position.

1933 *Roy Linwood Clark,* U.S. singer, songwriter, musician.

Elizabeth Montgomery, U.S. actress; known for her role as Samantha on television series, *Bewitched,* 1964–72. [d. May 18, 1995]

1938 *Claudia Cardinale,* Italian actress.

1940 *Jeffrey Howard Archer,* British author, politician; Member of Parliament, 1969–74; wrote *Kane and*

Abel, 1979, and *First Among Equals,* 1984.

1944 *Dave Edmunds,* Welsh musician, producer; member of the rock group, *Rockpile.*

1947 *Linda Bloodworth-Thomason,* U.S. writer, director; creator of the TV shows *Designing Women* and *Evening Shade.*

1957 *Evelyn Ashford,* U.S. track athlete; Olympic gold medalist, 1984, 1988.

1959 *Emma Thompson,* British actress; Academy Award (Best Actress) for *Howard's End,* 1992

HISTORICAL EVENTS

1450 French defeat English at *Formigny (Hundred Years' War).*

1861 U.S. President *Abraham Lincoln* calls for 75,000 volunteers to serve for three months in the Union Army *(U.S. Civil War).*

1891 *Katanga Company* is formed in Brussels to develop and settle the Katanga area in Central Africa.

1892 *General Electric Co.* is incorporated in New York.

1904 The *National Child Labor Committee (NCLC)* is organized to reform U.S. child labor laws.

1912 *Titanic,* largest passenger liner afloat, supposedly unsinkable, strikes an iceberg and sinks on its maiden voyage; over 1500 drown.

Albert Einstein, during a lecture at Columbia University on his theory of relativity, speaks of *time* as the Fourth Dimension.

1927 *Chiang Kai-Shek* and conservative members of the Kuomintang split with the Communists at Hankow.

1938 Gen. Francisco Franco's forces capture *Vinaroz (Spanish Civil War).*

1942 The entire population of *Malta* is awarded the George Cross of Great Britain for gallantry under heavy fire (*World War II*).

1945 Prisoners of war in *Belsen,* a German concentration camp, are liberated by the British Second Army.

1947 *Rudolf Hoess* is executed at Auschwitz, the concentration camp which he had directed during World War II.

1952 *Salah Eddine Baccouche* becomes premier of Tunisia after French authorities depose *Mohammed Chenik.*

1953 Nikos Kazantakis's novel, *Zorba the Greek,* is published in New York.

1963 About 70,000 persons participate in a *Ban the Bomb* rally in London, during which the British government's secret emergency plan is circulated.

1965 *West Germany* finishes paying reparations to *Israel* for crimes committed against Jews during the Nazi era.

1967 Peace demonstrators numbering over 100,000 march through the streets of New York City and assemble before the United Nations in protest against the *Vietnam War.*

1968 Two unmanned Russian satellites in earth orbit find each other by radar, maneuver together, and dock automatically.

1971 Yugoslav Ambassador to Sweden *Vladimir Lolovic* dies of gunshot wounds received a week earlier in an attack by Croatian separatists.

1974 *Hamani Diori,* President of Niger, is deposed.

1985 A U.S. grand jury indicts 23 members of the neo-Nazi group, *The Order,* on crimes ranging from racketeering to involvement in the murder of radio personality, *Alan Berg.*

The South African government announces that it will legalize *interracial marriage.*

1987 The *Stanford Linear Collider,* a device that splits atoms, is unveiled by scientists at Stanford University.

1986 U.S. forces bomb Libyan leader *Muammar Qaddafi's* headquarters. The bombing is in retaliation for the German bombing of a dance club.

1989 Former Politburo member *Hu Yaobang* dies. Students gather in Tiananmen Square to mourn his death, which eventually turns into a democracy movement demonstration. The demonstration ends in violence as hundreds are killed in the *Tiananmen Square massacre* (June 4, 1989).

Ninety-five soccer fans are killed in *Sheffield, England,* when fans begin pushing to enter the stadium, crushing those ahead.

april

APRIL
16

HOLIDAYS

Denmark
Queen Margrethe's Birthday
Celebrates the queen's birth, 1940.

Puerto Rico
de Diego's Birthday
Commemorates the birthday of José de Diego, poet and statesman, 1867.

RELIGIOUS CALENDAR

The Saints
SS. Optatus and his companions, and *St. Encratis,* virgin, martyrs. St. Encratis also called *Engratia.* [d. 304]

St. Turibius, Bishop of Astorga. [d. c. 450]

St. Paternus, Bishop of Avranches. Also called *Pair.* [d. 564]

St. Fructuosus, Archbishop of Braga. [d. 665]

St. Magnus of Orkney, martyr. Son of king of Orkneys. Patron saint of fishmongers. Also called *Mans.* [d. 1116]

St. Drogo. Patron of shepherds. Invoked against ruptures, hernias, and unpleasant births. Also called *Drugo, Druon.* [d. 1189]

St. Contardo, the pilgrim. [d. 1249]

St. Benedict Joseph Labre, mendicant. Patron of displaced persons. Also called the *Beggar of Rome.* [d. 1783]

St. Bernadette, virgin and visionary. [d. 1879]

The Beatified
Blessed Joachim of Siena. [d. 1305]
Blessed William of Polizzi, mendicant religious; patron of Castelbuono. [d. c. 1317]
Blessed Archangelo of Bologna. [d. 1513]

BIRTHDATES

1319 *John II (the Good)* of France, acceded to the throne 1350. [d. April 8, 1364]

1646 *Jules Hardouin-Mansart,* French architect; designed the *Galerie de Glaces* at *Versailles.* Building superintendent and architect of Louis XIV. [d. May 11, 1708]

1660 *Sir Hans Sloane,* English physician, naturalist; his museum and library formed the nucleus of the *British Museum.* [d. 1753]

1661 *Charles Montagu, 1st Earl of Halifax,* English politician and poet; first Lord of Treasury and Prime Minister. [d. 1715]

1728 *Joseph Black,* Scottish chemist; evolved theory of *latent heat.* [d. December 6, 1799]

1786 *Sir John Franklin,* English naval officer, explorer; lost in the Arctic while searching for the *Northwest Passage.* [d. June 11, 1847]

1821 *Ford Madox Brown,* British romantic painter; teacher of *Dante Gabriel Rossetti.* [d. October 11, 1893]

1838 *Ernest Solvay,* Belgian industrial chemist; patented the *Solvay ammonia process* for the manufacture of sodium carbonate, 1861. [d. May 26, 1922]

1844 *Anatole France (Jacques Anatole Thibault),* French novelist, poet, critic; Nobel Prize in literature, 1921. [d. October 13, 1924]

1850 *Herbert Baxter Adams,* U.S. historian; a founder and first secretary of *American Historical Association.* [d. July 30, 1901]

1854 *Jacob Sechler Coxey,* U.S. reformer; leader of the 1894 march of the unemployed on Washington, D.C. called *Coxey's Army.* [d. May 18, 1951]

1856 *Albert Blake Dick,* U.S. inventor of *mimeograph process* and machines; founder of A. B. Dick Co. [d. August 15, 1934]

1865 *Grace Livingstone Hill,* U.S. author; wrote *April Gold,* 1936. [d. February 23, 1947]

José de Diego, Puerto Rican poet, supportor of independence for his homeland. [d. 1918]

1867 *Wilbur Wright,* U.S. aviation pioneer; with his brother Orville (August 19) made first powered, controlled, sustained airplane flight on December 17, 1903, at *Kitty Hawk, North Carolina.* [d. May 30, 1912]

1871 *John Millington Synge,* Irish dramatist, poet; noted for his portrayal of primitive life. [d. March 24, 1909]

1881 *Edward Wood, Earl of Halifax,* British statesman, diplomat; Viceroy of India, 1925–31; British Foreign Secretary, 1938–40. [d. December 23, 1959]

1889 *Charlie (Sir Charles Spencer) Chaplin,* English comedian, producer, director; the beloved *Little Tramp* of the silent-film era. [d. December 25, 1977]

1904 *Lily Pons (Alice Josephine Pons),* U.S. operatic soprano. [d. February 13, 1976]

1915 *Walter Washington,* U.S. politician, lawyer; Mayor of Washington, D.C., 1975–79.

1918 *Terence Alan (Spike) Milligan,* British director, author.

1919 *Merce Cunningham,* U.S. dancer, choreographer.

1921 *Peter (Alexander) Ustinov,* British actor, producer, writer.

1922 *Kingsley Amis,* British author. [d. October 22, 1995]

1923 *Arch Alfred Moore, Jr.,* U.S. politician; Governor of West Virginia, 1969–77, 1985–89.

1924 *Henry Mancini,* U.S. composer. [d. June 14, 1994]

1929 *Edie Adams (Elizabeth Edith Enke),* U.S. singer, actress; known for her role in *It's a Mad, Mad, Mad, Mad World,* 1963.

1930 *Herbie Mann (Herbert Jay Solomon),* U.S. jazz musician.

1933 *Ike Pappas,* U.S. broadcast journalist.

1934 *Robert C. Stigwood,* Australian producer; Tony Award for *Evita,* 1980.

1935 *Stanley Robert (Bobby) Vinton,* U.S. singer; known for his song, *Blue Velvet.*

1939 *Dusty Springfield (Mary Isobel Catherine O'Brien),* British singer.

1940 *Margrethe II* of Denmark; acceded to throne January 14, 1972; first woman to rule Denmark.

1947 *Kareem Abdul-Jabbar (Ferdinand Lewis Alcindor, Jr.),* U.S. basketball player; six Most Valuable Player titles.

HISTORICAL EVENTS

1175 *Treaty of Montebello* is signed between *Frederick I, Holy Roman Emperor,* and the Lombard League.

1712 The *Peace of Constantinople* ends war between Russia and the Ottoman Empire.

1746 *Battle of Culloden,* in Scotland, results in final defeat of Jacobites by the English.

1853 The first *Indian railway,* from Bombay to Tannah, is opened.

1883 *Paul Kruger,* Boer leader, is elected President of the *South African Republic.*

1912 *Harriet Quimby* becomes first woman to fly across the English Channel.

1917 The *Second Battle of the Aisne* opens between Soissons and Reims (*World War I*).

1922 The *Treaty of Rapallo* is signed by Germany and the Soviet Union resulting in resumption of diplomatic relations and renunciation of reparations for World War I.

1941 German raider *Atlantis* attacks and sinks an Egyptian passenger liner with 138 Americans aboard, arousing great anti-German sentiment in the U.S. (*World War II*).

1945 U.S. troops land on Ie Shima in Ryuku Islands (*World War II*).

1952 *Victor Paz Estenssoro* becomes president of Bolivia after his followers overthrow the country's military junta.

1972 Two giant pandas, given to the U.S. by China in return for a pair of musk oxen, arrive at the National Zoo in Washington, D.C.

1986 The Philippine government charges former president, *Ferdinand Marcos,* with embezzlement and misappropriation of funds.

1987 The U.S. Department of Commerce permits the patenting of new forms of animal life developed through *gene splicing* and *genetic engineering.* Such patents are not extended to human applications.

1988 *Khalil Walid,* military head of the *Palestine Liberation Organization,* is assassinated in Tunisia, by alleged Israeli commandos.

april

APRIL
17

HOLIDAYS

American Samoa
Flag Day
Commemorates signing of Instrument of Cession, 1900, and establishment of Samoan constitutional government, 1960.

Burma
New Year's Day

Cambodia
Victory over American Imperialism Day

Japan
Children's Protection Day
Commemorates passage of laws protecting juveniles.

Syria
Evacuation Day or Independence Day
Commemorates withdrawal of French troops, 1946.

RELIGIOUS CALENDAR

The Saints
St. Anicetus, pope and martyr. Elected 155. [d. c. 165]
SS. Mappalicus and his companions, martyrs. [d. c. 250]
St. Innocent, Bishop of Tortona. [d. c. 350]
SS. Donnan and his companions, monks and martyrs. [d. 618]
SS. Robert of Chaise-Dieu, abbot; founder of Benedictine abbey in Auvergne. Also called *Robert de Turlande.* [d. 1067]

St. Stephen Harding, Abbot of Cîteaux; co-founder of Cistercian Order. [d. 1134]

The Beatified
Blessed Eberhard of Marchthal, abbot. [d. 1178]
Blessed James of Cerqueto, Augustinian monk. [d. 1367]
Blessed Clare of Pisa, widow and prioress. [d. 1419]
Blessed Kateri Tekakwitha. [d. 1680]

BIRTHDATES

1586 *John Ford,* English playwright. [death date unknown]

1622 *Henry Vaughan,* Welsh mystic poet, translator. [d. 1695]

1676 *Frederick I* of Sweden, 1720–51; his rule superseded by a powerful parliament. [d. March 25, 1751]

1741 *Samuel Chase,* U.S. jurist, lawyer; signer of the Declaration of Independence; U.S. Supreme Court Justice, 1796–1811. [d. June 19, 1811]

1806 *William Gilmore Simms,* U.S. poet; wrote numerous histories of the American South. [d. June 11, 1870]

1837 *John Pierpont Morgan,* U.S. financier, philanthropist; controlled one of the most prosperous and powerful financial empires in the world. [d. March 31, 1913]

1842 *Charles Henry Parkhurst,* U.S. clergyman; remembered for denunciation of crime in New York City government. President of *Society for the Prevention of Crime.* [d. September 8, 1933]

1845 *Isabel Barrows,* U.S. editor; early penologist. [d. October 25, 1913]

1849 *William Rufus Day,* U.S. judge; Supreme Court Justice, 1903–22. [d. July 9, 1923]

1851 *(Adrian) Cap Anson,* pioneer U.S. baseball player. [d. April 14, 1922]

1859 *Walter (Chauncey) Camp,* U.S. football player, coach, athletic director; called the Father of American Football. [d. March 14, 1925]

1866 *Ernest Henry Starling,* British physiologist; with W. M. Bayliss, discovered hormone *secretin,* 1902. [d. May 2, 1927]

1874 *Charles Hungerford Mackay,* U.S. financier, art patron. [d. November 12, 1938]

1880 *Sir Charles Leonard Woolley,* British archaeologist; excavated *Ur of the Chaldees.* [d. 1960]

1885 *Isak Dinesen (Baroness Karen Christentze Blixen),* Danish author; known for her memoirs of life in Kenya, *Out* *of Africa,* 1937. [d. September 7, 1962]

1886 *Alfonso XIII,* King of Spain. [d. February 28, 1941]

1894 *Nikita Khrushchev,* Russian Communist leader; Premier of the Soviet Union, 1958–64. [d. September 11, 1971]

1897 *Thornton (Niven) Wilder,* U.S. playwright, and novelist. [d. December 7, 1975]

1915 *Rebekah (West) Harkness,* U.S. philanthropist, patron of dance; President and Director of William Hale Harkness Foundation; supported Robert Joffrey Ballet and Jerome Robbins Ballet; President and Artistic Director, Harkness Ballet, 1970–75. [d. June 17, 1982]

1916 *Sirimavo Bandaranaike,* Sri Lankan stateswoman; first woman to hold position of Prime Minister, 1960–65, 1970–77, 1994– .

1918 *William Holden (William Beedle),* U.S. actor. [d. November 16, 1981]

1923 *Harry Reasoner,* U.S. television news correspondent. [d. August 6, 1991]

1934 *Don Kirshner,* U.S. publisher.

1946 *Georges J. F. Kohler,* German immunologist; Nobel Prize in physiology or medicine for development of the production of antibodies (with Cesar Milstein), 1984.

1951 *Olivia Hussey,* British actress; known for her role as Juliet in *Romeo and Juliet,* 1969.

1961 *Norman (Boomer) Esiason,* former U.S. football player; broadcaster on *Monday Night Football.*

1967 *Elizabeth (Liz) Phair,* U.S. singer, songwriter.

HISTORICAL EVENTS

1194 Second coronation of *Richard I* of England takes place upon his return from the *Third Crusade.*

1492 *Christopher Columbus* receives his commission from the Spanish monarchy to explore the western ocean.

1521 *Martin Luther* is excommunicated by *Diet of Worms.*

1555 Spaniards capture *Siena* and sell it to *Cosimo de Medici.*

1711 *Josef I, Holy Roman Emperor,* dies and is succeeded by *Charles VI.*

1895 The Sino-Japanese *Treaty of Shimonoseki* is signed, ending warfare and recognizing the independence of *Korea.*

1916 The *American Academy of Arts and Letters* is chartered by an act of Congress.

1922 *Dom Miguel of Portugal* renounces succession in favor of *Dom Duarte Nuna.*

1923 The Chicago Motor Coach Co. (later *The Hertz Corp.*) is incorporated.

1941 *Yugoslavia* surrenders unconditionally to *Germany (World War II).*

Yugoslavian army surrenders to invading Germans (*World War II*).

1942 The first issue of the U.S. army newspaper, *Stars and Stripes,* is published.

1946 *Syria* gains independence.

1961 *Bay of Pigs,* attempted invasion of *Cuba* by American-backed troops, begins.

The U.S. Supreme Court rules that restaurants conducting business on publicly-owned property cannot refuse service to blacks.

1965 Demonstrators from throughout the U.S. march on Washington in protest against the *Vietnam War.*

1969 *Alexander Dubcek* is replaced as First Secretary of the Czechoslovakian Communist Party by *Gustav Huzak.*

Sirhan Bishara Sirhan is convicted by a Los Angeles jury of first-degree murder for the slaying of Senator *Robert F. Kennedy.*

1972 *Nina Kuscsik* outruns women contestants in the first Boston Marathon open to women runners.

1974 Nigerois army, under Chief of Staff Lieutenant Colonel *Seyni Kountche,* takes power in Niger.

1975 War in *Cambodia* ends with the takeover of *Phnom Penh* by *Khmer Rouge* troops.

1977 Women vote in *Liechtenstein* for the first time.

1980 *Zimbabwe,* formerly *Rhodesia,* gains its independence.

1982 Queen Elizabeth II proclaims *Constitution Act,* supplanting British North America Act of 1867 and bringing *Canada* solely under its own jurisdiction.

april

1985 The last South African combat troops withdraw from southern *Angola*, ending 10 years of military intervention in that region.

1992 *Serbia* and *Montenegro* form a new *Yugoslavia*.

HOLIDAYS

Zimbabwe

Independence Day
Commemorates end of white minority rule, 1980.

RELIGIOUS CALENDAR

The Saints

St. Apollonius, the Apologist, martyr. [d. c. 185]

St. Laserian, Bishop of Leighlin. Also called *Laisren, Molaisre,* or *Molaisse.* [d. 639]

St. Deicola, Abbot of Bosham. Also called *Dicuill, Dicul.* [d. 7th century]

St. Idesbald, Abbot of Our Lady of the Dunes Abbey, in France. [d. 1167]

St. Galdinus, Archbishop of Milan and Cardinal; patron of *Milan.* [d. 1176]

SS. Eleutherius and his companions, martyrs. [death date unknown]

The Beatified

Blessed James of Lodi, Franciscan priest. [d. 1404]

Blessed Andrew Hibernon, layman. [d. 1602]

Blessed Mary of the Incarnation, widow. Helped establish the Ursuline and Oratorian orders in Paris and introduced the Teresian Carmelites to France. [d. 1618]

Blessed Ludovico of Casoria. [beatified 1993]

Blessed Paula Montal Fornés. [beatified 1993]

Blessed Faustina Kowalska. [beatified 1993]

Blessed Mary Angela Truszkowska. [beatified 1993]

BIRTHDATES

1480 *Lucrezia Borgia,* Duchess of Ferrara, Italian noblewoman; her name, long associated with vice and crime, has recently been vindicated. [d. June 24, 1519]

1740 *Sir Francis Baring,* English banker, merchant; director of *East India Company.* [d. 1810]

1759 *Thomas Thorild,* Swedish poet, critic, and philosopher; sympathizer with revolutionary leaders in France. [d. October 1, 1808]

1789 *John Young Mason,* U.S. politician, jurist, diplomat; U.S. Congressman, 1831–37; U.S. Secretary of the Navy, 1844–45; 1846–49; U.S. Attorney General, 1845–46. [d. October 3, 1859]

1817 *George Henry Lewes,* British critic, philosopher; associated with *Marian Evans (George Eliot).* [d. November 28, 1878]

1842 *Antero de Quental,* Portuguese poet, philosopher; known for his extremely pessimistic works. [d. September 11, 1891]

1857 *Clarence (Seward) Darrow,* U.S. labor and criminal lawyer; served as defense counsel in many notable trials. [d. March 13, 1938]

1864 *Richard Harding Davis,* U.S. author, journalist; best-known and most influential U.S. reporter of his era. [d. April 11, 1916]

1882 *Leopold Stokowski,* British-U.S. conductor. [d. September 13, 1977]

1902 *Giuseppe Pella,* Italian economist, legislator; Prime Minister of Italy, 1953–54 (for five months); his administration marked by crisis with Yugoslavia over Trieste. [d. May 31, 1981]

1905 *George Hitchings,* U.S. biochemist; Nobel Prize in physiology or medicine (with Gertrude Elion and Sir James Black), 1988.

1907 *Rául Roa y García,* Cuban government official, lawyer; responsible for strengthening Cuban ties with the Soviet Union. [d. July 6, 1982]

1911 *Maurice Goldhaber,* Austrian-U.S. physicist; responsible for breakthroughs in study of *neutron physics* and nuclear reactor technology.

1918 *Frederika (Louise),* consort of *Paul I,* King of the Hellenes, mother of former King

Constantine of Greece and Queen Sofia of Spain. [d. February 6, 1981]

1934 *George Shirley,* U.S. operatic tenor.

1937 *Robert Hooks,* U.S. actor; founder, Negro Ensemble Co.

1940 *Joseph L(eonard) Goldstein,* U.S. physician; Nobel Prize in physiology or medicine for research in cholesterol metabolism (with Michael S. Brown), 1985.

1946 *James Augustus (Catfish) Hunter,* U.S. baseball player.

Hayley (Catherine Rose Vivian) Mills, British actress; Oscar Award for *Pollyanna,* 1960.

1947 *James Woods,* U.S. actor; known for his roles in *Onion Field,* 1979, *Salvador,* 1986, and *The Ghosts of Mississippi,* 1996.

1954 *Rick Moranis,* U.S. actor; known for *Honey, I Shrunk the Kids,* 1989 and *The Flintstones,* 1994.

HISTORICAL EVENTS

1328 *Holy Roman Emperor Louis IV* of Bavaria deposes *Pope John XXII* for heresy and lese majesty.

1775 *Paul Revere,* American patriot, makes his famous midnight ride to warn colonists of advance of British troops.

1847 U.S. General *Winfield Scott* wins *Battle of Cerro Gordo (Mexican War).*

1897 *Greece* declares war on *Turkey.*

1906 *San Francisco* is destroyed by the most devastating *earthquake* in U.S. history.

1909 *Joan of Arc* is beatified in ceremony held at St. Peter's in Rome.

1916 Russians capture port of *Trebizond* on the Black Sea from the Turks (*World War I*).

1922 *Vilna* is incorporated into Poland.

1923 *Yankee Stadium* opens in New York City.

1927 *Chiang Kai-shek* inaugurates moderate Nationalist government of China at Nanking.

1942 Sixteen American bombers under the command of *Col. James Doolittle* successfully attack *Tokyo, Yokohama,* and *Nagoya (World War II).*

Pierre Laval takes the title premier of France and forms a new cabinet in which he is recognized as leader of the Vichy government.

1945 *League of Nations* votes to dissolve, transferring its material property to the *United Nations.*

1949 Eire breaks its allegiance to the British crown and its association with the Commonwealth of Nations, becoming the *Republic of Ireland.*

1951 France, West Germany, Italy, Belgium, the Netherlands, and Luxembourg sign a treaty establishing a single market for coal and steel; this constitutes an important first step in the direction of *European economic union.*

1953 *Mohammed Ali* takes office as prime minister of Pakistan

after food shortages and religious conflict force the resignation of *Khwaja Nazimuddin.*

1954 Colonel *Gamal Abdel Nasser* succeeds General *Mohammed Naguib* as premier of Egypt.

1955 The *Bandung Conference* of Asian and African states begins in Indonesia. During the week-long meeting, delegates condemn colonialism and lay the groundwork for the nonaligned nations movement.

1960 *Tangier* is reintegrated financially and economically with *Morocco.*

1963 Successful *transplants of human nerves* are reported by *James B. Campbell* of the New York University Medical Center.

1975 U.S. President Gerald Ford initiates the *American Revolution Bicentennial,* a nationwide celebration, on the 200th anniversary of Paul Revere's famous ride.

1978 U.S. Senate ratifies second *Panama Canal Treaty* providing for operation and defense of the canal until 1999.

1986 The South African government rescinds its *Pass Law,* that required blacks to carry identification and obtain authorization to enter white-designated areas.

1987 *Amintore Fanfani* is inaugurated as premier of Italy.

1998 The second *Summit of the Americas* takes place in Santiago, Chile. Leaders at the summit begin work on a *Free Trade Area of the Americas (FTAA)* agreement.

april

APRIL
19

HOLIDAYS

Sierra Leone
Republic Anniversary Day
Commemorates the founding of the
Republic, 1971.

Swaziland
King's Birthday

Uruguay
*Landing of the 33 Orientales, or 33
Immortals*
Commemorates landing of 33
patriotic exiles in 1825, an event that
ultimately resulted in independence
of Uruguay from Brazil.

Venezuela
Independence Day
Commemorates the birth of the
Republic, 1830.

RELIGIOUS CALENDAR

The Saints
St. Ursmar, abbot and bishop. [d.
713]
St. Geroldus, recluse. [d. 978]
St. Alphege, Archbishop of
Canterbury and martyr. Also
called *Aelfheah,* or *Elphege.*
[d. 1012]
St. Leo IX, pope. Elected 1049.
Originator of the Crusades.
[d. 1054]

The Beatified
Blessed Bernard the Penitent. [d.
1181]
Blessed Conrad of Ascoli, Franciscan
and papal legate. [d. 1289]

Blessed James Duckett, martyr.
Patron of booksellers and
publishers. [d. 1602]

BIRTHDATES

1721 *Roger Sherman,* U.S.
statesman, lawyer, surveyor;
signer of the Declaration of
Independence, the Articles of
Association, the Articles of
Confederation, and the
Constitution; the only person
who signed all four
documents. [d. July 23, 1793]

1772 *David Ricardo,* English
political economist; founder
of the classical school of
economics. [d. September 11,
1823]

1793 *Ferdinand I,* Emperor of
Austria. [d. June 29, 1875]

1795 *Christian Ehrenberg,* German
naturalist; founder of
protozoology. [d. 1876]

1832 *José Echegaray y Eizaguirre,*
Spanish dramatist,
mathematician; Nobel Prize in
literature, 1904. [d.
September 14, 1916]

Lucretia Garfield, wife of U.S.
President James Garfield. [d.
March 13, 1918]

1836 *Augustus D. Juilliard,* U.S.
merchant, philanthropist;
founded Juilliard School of
Music. [d. April 25, 1919]

1865 *May Robson (Mary Robison),*
U.S. character actress. [d.
October 20, 1942]

1877 *Gertrude Vanderbilt Whitney,*
U.S. sculptor; conceived and
financed *Whitney Museum of
American Art,* 1931. [d. April
18, 1942]

1883 *Getulio Dorneles Vargas,*
Brazilian leader; President,
1930–45, 1951–54. [d. August
24, 1954]

1900 *Richard Hughes,* British
novelist. [d. April 28, 1976]

1901 *Edith (Clara) Summerskill,
Baroness Summerskill,* British
politician, physician; a
founder of the *Socialist
Medical Association,* which
led to the establishment of
the National Health Service,
1948. [d. February 4, 1980]

1903 *Eliot Ness,* U.S. government
agent; headed investigation of
Al Capone, notorious Chicago
gangster, 1929–32. [d. May 7,
1957]

1912 *Glenn T. Seaborg,* U.S.
nuclear chemist, physicist;
Nobel Prize in chemistry for
isolating and identifying
elements heavier than
uranium (with E. M.
McMillan), 1951; element 106
(Seaborgium) named for him,
1994.

1921 *Yitzhak Navon,* Israeli
statesman; President,
1978–83.

1927 *Don Adams (Donald James Yarmy),* U.S. actor, comedian; known for his role as Maxwell Smart on television series, *Get Smart,* 1965–70.

1932 *Fernando Botero (Angulo),* Colombian artist; known for his sensual paintings and sculptures.

Jayne Mansfield (Vera Jayne Palmer), U.S. actress; sex symbol of the 1950's. [d. June 29, 1967]

1933 *Dick Sargent,* U.S. actor; known for his role as Darrin on television series, *Bewitched,* 1969–72.[d. July 8, 1994]

1935 *Dudley Stuart John Moore,* U.S. actor, musician; known for his starring roles in *10* and *Arthur.*

1937 *Elinor Donahue,* U.S. actress; known for her role as Betty Anderson on television series, *Father Knows Best,* 1954–62.

1946 *Tim Curry,* British actor.

1949 *Paloma Picasso,* French designer; designs jewelry for Tiffany and Co.; daughter of Pablo Picasso.

1962 *Al Unser, Jr.,* U.S. auto racer.

1967 *Dar Williams,* U.S. folk singer.

1968 *Ashley Judd,* U.S. actress; sister of country singer Wynonna Judd.

HISTORICAL EVENTS

1012 In England, Danes murder *Archbishop Elfheah* and are bought off by *King Ethelred.*

1428 *Peace of Ferrara* is signed, in which Milan cedes *Brescia* and *Bergamo* to Venice.

1539 *Truce of Frankfort* between *Holy Roman Emperor Charles V* and his rebellious Protestant subjects is signed.

1587 *Sir Francis Drake* of England attacks *Cadiz,* destroying 33 Spanish vessels and escaping unscathed.

1713 *Charles VI, Holy Roman Emperor,* issues *Pragmatic Sanction,* giving females the right of succession in Hapsburg possessions.

1770 *Captain James Cook* sights the eastern coast of *Australia.*

1775 The *American Revolution* begins with the battles of *Lexington* and *Concord.*

1839 *Treaty of London* is signed, establishing recognition of *Kingdom of Belgium* by all the states of Europe.

1850 *Clayton-Bulwer Treaty* between U.S. and Great Britain is signed, providing that neither country may obtain exclusive control over proposed interoceanic canal in Central America.

1853 Russia claims protectorate over Turkey in a prelude to the *Crimean War.*

1861 Blockade of Confederate ports is proclaimed by Union forces (*U.S. Civil War*).

1901 The Philippine rebellion against U.S. forces is ended by proclamation.

1917 The *Second Battle of Gaza* ends in British failure to dislodge the Turks (*World War I*).

The first American shot of *World War I* is fired from the steamer *Mongolia* in repulsing a German submarine attack.

1919 *Jozef Pilsudski* and Polish army drive Bolsheviks out of *Vilna.*

1928 *Oxford English Dictionary* is completed.

1932 The U.S. officially abandons the *gold standard.*

1945 U.S. troops liberate *Buchenwald,* a Nazi concentration camp near Weimar, Germany.

Rodgers' and Hammerstein's Carousel premieres in New York.

1950 The first successful use of *cardiac massage* to treat heart attack victims is demonstrated at St. John's Episcopal Hospital in Brooklyn, New York.

1951 General *Douglas MacArthur* delivers his "old soldiers never die" speech to the U.S. Congress after being relieved of duty by President Harry Truman.

1956 Samuel Beckett's play, *Waiting for Godot,* opens on Broadway.

1960 *Pho Preung* is chosen to succeed Prince Norodom Sihanouk as premier of Cambodia.

1961 U.S. soldiers officially assume positions as advisors to *Laotian army.*

1970 *Gustavo Rojas Pinilla* is defeated in Colombian presidential election.

1971 *Sierra Leone* declares itself a republic within the British Commonwealth.

1984 A U.S. court rules that *Standard Oil Company* and its subsidiaries are

april

responsible for damages incurred when the supertanker, *Amoco Cadiz,* broke apart off of the French coast in 1978.

1985 The *People's Republic of China* announces plans to reduce their armed forces by one million troops.

1987 Biologists capture the last wild *condor* in California. The bird is on the endangered species list and will join other captured condors in a breeding program.

1989 An explosion aboard the *USS Iowa* kills forty-seven sailors.

1993 The fifty-one day stand-off in *Waco, Texas,* between *David Koresh,* leader of the Branch Davidian cult, and the *U.S. Department of Alcohol,* *Tobacco, and Firearms (ATF)* ends when ATF agents storm the compound. More than eighty members of the cult are killed, including Koresh.

1995 The *Alfred P. Murrah federal building* in Oklahoma City, Oklahoma, is bombed. Over one hundred sixty are killed.

1998 *Thomas Klestil* is reelected president of Austria.

RELIGIOUS CALENDAR

The Saints

St. Marcellinus, first bishop of Embrun. [d. c. 374]

St. Marcian, monk. Also called *Marian.* [d. c. 488]

St. Caedwalla, King of the West Saxons. [d. 689]

St. Hildegund, virgin. [d. 1188]

St. Agnes of Montepulciano, virgin and founder of Dominican nunnery at Montepulciano. [d. 1317]

The Beatified

Blessed Hugh of Anzy, prior. [d. c. 930]

Blessed Simon of Todi, Augustinian prior. [d. 1322]

Blessed James Bell and *Blessed John Finch,* martyrs. [d. 1584]

Blessed Robert Watkinson and *Blessed Francis Page,* priests and martyrs. [d. 1602]

BIRTHDATES

121 *Marcus Aurelius,* Roman Emperor. [d. A.D. 180]

1492 *Pietro Aretino,* Italian man of letters, notorious libertine. [d. October 21, 1556]

1745 *Philippe Pinel,* French physician; primary founder of *psychiatry;* first to call insanity a disease rather than result of possession by demons. [d. October 26, 1826]

1786 *Marc Séguin,* French engineer; inventor of the wire-cable *suspension bridge* and the tubular steam-engine boiler. [d. February 24, 1875]

1807 *Louis Jacques Napoleon Bertrand (Aloysius),* French writer of prose poems. [d. April 29, 1841]

1808 *Napoleon III (Louis Napoleon),* Emperor of France, 1852–70. [d. January 9, 1873]

1839 *Carol I,* first king of Romania; ruled 1866–1914. [d. October 10, 1914]

1850 *Daniel Chester French,* U.S. sculptor; created statue of Lincoln in the *Lincoln Memorial.* [d. October 7, 1931]

1868 *Charles Maurras,* French writer, philosopher; founder of *Action Française.* [d. 1952]

1880 *Sol Harry Goldberg,* U.S. manufacturer. [d. June 4, 1940]

1882 *Holland McTyeire (Howlin' Mad) Smith,* U.S. Marine Corps general during World War II. [d. January 12, 1967]

1889 *Adolf Hitler,* German politician; leader of the National Socialist Workers' (Nazi) Party, 1921–45; dictator of Germany, 1933–45. [d. April 30, 1945]

1893 *Harold Lloyd,* U.S. comedian, actor. [d. March 8, 1971]

Joan Miró, Spanish Surrealist painter. [d. December 25, 1983]

1900 *Norman Norell,* U.S. clothing designer. [d. October 25, 1972]

1903 *Gregor Piatigorsky,* U.S. cello virtuoso born in Russia. [d. August 6, 1976]

1904 *Edward Louis Bartlett,* U.S. politician, gold miner, newspaperman. [d. December 11, 1968]

1905 *Harold Stanley Marcus,* U.S. retailer; President of Nieman-Marcus Co., 1950–72.

1910 *Robert (Ferdinand) Wagner, Jr.,* U.S. politician, diplomat; Mayor of New York City, 1954–65. [d. February 12, 1991]

1918 *Kai M. Siegbahn,* Swedish physicist; Nobel Prize in physics for his work in spectroscopy, 1981.

1920 *John Paul Stevens,* U.S. jurist; Associate Justice of Supreme Court, 1975– .

1924 *Nina Foch,* Dutch actress.

1941 *Ryan O'Neal,* U.S. actor; known for his starring role on television series, *Peyton Place,* and in the movie, *Love Story,* 1970.

1947 *Andrew Tobias,* U.S. financial author, business executive; wrote *The Funny Money Game,* 1971, and *My Vast Fortune,* 1997.

1949 *Jessica Lange,* U.S. actress; Academy Award (Best Supporting Actress) for *Tootsie,* 1982; Academy Award (Best Actress) for *Blue Sky,* 1994.

Timothy E. Quill, U.S. physician; doctor-assisted suicide advocate.

1951 *Luther Vandross,* U.S. singer, musician.

1961 *Don(ald Arthur) Mattingly,* U.S. baseball player; American League Most Valuable Player, 1985.

HISTORICAL EVENTS

1534 *Jacques Cartier,* French explorer, reaches *Labrador.*

1653 In England, *Oliver Cromwell* expels *Long Parliament* for attempting to pass *Perpetuation Bill* which would have kept parliament in the hands of only a few members.

1657 Spanish West Indian fleet is destroyed by the English under Admiral *Robert Blake* in the harbor of *Santa Cruz de Tenerife.*

1792 *France* declares war on Austria, Prussia, and Sardinia.

1890 The *Haka Road* connecting Burma and India is completed.

1902 French scientists *Pierre* and *Marie Curie* succeed in isolating pure radium.

1911 Decree for separation of church and state in *Portugal* is issued.

1915 The *Armenians* revolt against Turkish atrocities and seize the fortress at *Van* in the Caucasus *(World War I).*

1916 The French counter-attack German positions on the east bank of the Meuse at the *Battle of Verdun (World War I).*

Sir Roger Casement lands in Ireland to incite rebellion against British involvement in *World War I;* subsequently, he is hanged as a traitor.

1920 *Montenegro* becomes part of *Yugoslavia.*

1935 The weekly radio program, *Your Hit Parade,* begins regular broadcasts. It ranks the most popular songs, based upon sheet music sales and radio air play.

1939 *Radio Corp. of America* offically reveals the modern system of television broadcasting at the New York World's Fair.

1941 German troops occupy *Belgrade,* Yugoslavia *(World War II).*

1941 King *George II* of Greece becomes premier following the suicide of *Alexander Korizis.*

1943 Germans massacre Jews in *Warsaw ghetto.*

1944 W. Somerset Maugham's novel, *The Razor's Edge,* is published.

1947 *King Christian X* of Denmark dies and is succeeded by his son, *Frederick IX.*

1951 Australia completes its trials of Japanese citizens charged with war crimes *(World War II).*

1961 *Fidel Castro* proclaims a victory after last of the Cuban rebel invaders are captured at *Playa Giron* near the original landing point of the *Bay of Pigs* invasion.

1969 Terrorists attack nine post offices and a bus station in a weekend of violence among Roman Catholics, Protestants, and police in *Northern Ireland.*

1978 A South Korean Boeing 707 is shot down, killing two persons and injuring 13, when the plane strays into Russian territory.

1979 *Palace of the Senators* on Capitoline Hill in Rome is bombed by a neo-Fascist organization and a previously unknown group, the *Italian Popular Movement.*

1982 Spain reopens its border with British-owned *Gibraltar* after a lapse of 12 years.

1984 Foreign Secretary Sir *Geoffrey Howe* announces that Great Britain will withdraw from *Hong Kong* when its 99-year lease expires in 1997.

1987 *Karl Linnas,* accused of heading an Estonian concentration camp during World War II, is deported from the U.S. to stand trial for war crimes in the Soviet Union.

1989 Dissident physicist *Andrei Sakharov* is elected to the Soviet Congress of People's Deputies.

HOLIDAYS

Brazil
Independence Hero Tiradentes (Tiradentes Day)
Commemorates the execution of Joaquim José de Silva Xavier, conspirator in revolt against Portugal, 1789.

Indonesia
Kartini Day
A day of tribute to Baden Adjeng Kartini, leader in the emancipation of Indonesian women.

U.S. (Texas)
San Jacinto Day
Commemorates the Battle of San Jacinto, 1836.

RELIGIOUS CALENDAR

The Saints
SS. Simeon Barsabae, Bishop of Seleucia-Ctesiphon, and his companions, martyrs. [d. 341]
St. Anastasius I, Patriarch of Antioch. [d. 599]
St. Beuno, Abbot of Clynnog. Also called *Beunor.* [d. c. 640]
St. Malrubius, abbot. Also called *Maelrubha.* [d. 722]
St. Anselm, Archbishop of Canterbury and Doctor of the Church. Also called *Anselem, Father of Scholasticism.* [d. 1109] Optional Memorial.
St. Conrad of Parzham, Capuchin lay-brother. [d. 1894]

The Beatified
Blessed Clara Bosatta. [beatified 1991]
Blessed Annunciata Cocchetti. [beatified 1991]
Blessed Marie Therese Haze. [beatified 1991]

BIRTHDATES

1488 *Ulrich von Hutten,* German author, humanist, and soldier. [d. September 1523]

1555 *Ludovico Carracci,* Italian painter; a pioneer of Italian baroque painting. [d. November 13, 1619]

1634 *Jan van Riebeeck,* Dutch surgeon; founder of *Cape Town, South Africa.*

1729 *Catherine the Great (Catherine II),* Empress of Russia. [d. November 6, 1796]

1816 *Charlotte (Currer Bell) Brontë (Mrs. A. B. Nicholls),* British novelist, poet; best known as the author of *Jane Eyre;* sister of Ann (January 17) and Emily Brontë (July 30). [d. March 31, 1855]

1828 *Hippolyte Adolphe Taine,* French literary critic, historian, positivist philosopher. [d. March 5, 1893]

1837 *Fredrik Bajer,* Danish statesman, writer; Nobel Peace Prize for his work in helping found the International Peace Bureau, 1908. [d. January 22, 1922]

1838 *John Muir,* U.S. naturalist; primary force behind U.S. *land conservation* movement. [d. December 24, 1914]

1843 *Walther Flemming,* German anatomist; discovered *chromosomes* and process of *mitosis.* [d. August 5, 1905]

1864 *Max Weber,* German sociologist; founder of modern *sociology.* [d. June 14, 1920]

1865 *Frederick Albert Cook,* U.S. physician, Arctic explorer; claimed to have been the first person to reach the *North Pole.* [d. August 5, 1940]

1872 *Friedrich Wilhelm Froebel,* German educator; founder of the *kindergarten system.* [d. June 21, 1952]

1882 *Percy Williams Bridgman,* U.S. physicist; philosopher of science; Nobel Prize in physics for development of high pressure chambers for study of matter at extreme pressure, 1946. [d. August 20, 1961]

1889 *Paul Karrer,* Swiss chemist; Nobel Prize in chemistry for investigations into chemistry of *carotenoids, flavins,* and *Vitamins A and B2,* 1937. [d. June 18, 1971]

1905 *(Edmund Gerald) Pat Brown,* U.S. politician, lawyer;

Governor of California, 1958–66. Father of Edmund G. (Gerry) Brown, Jr. (July 7).

1911 *Leonard Warren (Leonard Vaarenov),* U.S. operatic baritone. [d. March 4, 1960]

1915 *Anthony (Rudolph) Quinn,* U.S. actor; a specialist in ethnic roles.

1926 *Elizabeth II,* Queen of Great Britain and Northern Ireland, 1952– .

1932 *Elaine May (Elaine Berlin),* U.S. actress, director.

1935 *Charles Grodin,* U.S. actor, director, writer; known for his roles in *The Heartbreak Kid,* 1972, *The Woman in Red,* 1984, and *Beethoven,* 1992.

1941 *David Lyle Boren,* U.S. politician; Governor of Oklahoma, 1975–79; Senator, 1979–94; President, University of Oklahoma, 1994– .

1942 *Anne McGill Gorsuch Burford,* U.S. lawyer, government official; administrator, Environmental Protection Agency, 1981–83.

1947 *Iggy Pop (James Osterberg),* U.S. punk icon of the 1960s; founding member of *The Stooges.*

1949 *Patti LuPone,* U.S. actress; Tony Award for *Evita,* 1980.

1951 *Tony Danza,* U.S. actor, boxer; known for his starring roles on television series, *Taxi,* 1982–85 and *Who's the Boss?,* 1984–92.

1958 *Andie MacDowell,* U.S. actress; known for roles in *sex, lies and videotape* and *Four Weddings and a Funeral.*

HISTORICAL EVENTS

1408 *Ladislaus, King of Naples,* seizes Rome for the first time in attempt to conquer Italy.

1509 *Henry VII* of England dies and is succeeded by *Henry VIII.*

1538 *John Calvin,* Protestant religious reformer, is banished from Geneva, Switzerland.

1836 Texans under General *Sam Houston* defeat the Mexican forces of *Santa Anna* at *San Jacinto.*

1912 *Tibet* becomes a province of China.

1914 U.S. Marines occupy port of *Veracruz, Mexico* in effort to prevent German ship from unloading munitions there. The incident nearly causes war between Mexico and the U.S.

1918 *Manfred von Richthofen, the Red Baron* German air ace, dies in battle over France (*World War I*).

1922 Civil war begins in *China* between the War Lord of Manchuria and the War Lord of the Yangtze.

1927 *Fascist Charter of Labor* is promulgated by *Benito Mussolini* of Italy.

1945 U.S. forces capture *Nuremberg, Germany (World War II).*

1960 *Brasilia,* the new city in Brazil's interior, is proclaimed the national capital.

1963 *Bruno M. Pontecorvo,* atomic scientist who defected from Britain to the U.S.S.R. in 1950, is named a winner of the Lenin Prize in science.

1966 Opening of the *British Parliament* is telecast for the first time.

1967 *George Papadopoulos* stages a coup d'état, gaining control of the government of Greece.

1969 The U.S. Supreme Court rules that residency requirements for welfare recipients are unconstitutional.

1970 *Bruno Kreisky* is sworn in as Chancellor of Austria.

1972 U.S. *Apollo 16* astronauts *Charles M. Duke, Jr.* and *John W. Young* walk on surface of moon and collect 214 pounds of lunar rocks and soil.

1975 South Vietnamese president *Nguyen Van Thieu* resigns after ten years in office.

1977 *Annie,* by Martin Charnin and Charles Strouse, premieres in New York.

General *Ziaur Rahman* is inaugurated as president of Bangladesh.

1979 *United African National Council* wins Rhodesia's first universal suffrage elections; *Bishop Abel Muzorewa* is elected prime minister.

1983 Members of the *Ku Klux Klan* and *American Nazi Party* are indicted on charges of conspiring to disrupt a 1979 demonstration in North Carolina. Five people had been killed in the confrontation.

1984 The U.S. Centers for Disease Control announce that French researchers at the Pasteur Institute have identified the *AIDS* virus.

1996 The *Olive Tree coalition* wins the general elections in Italy.

HOLIDAYS

Spain

Queen Isabella Day
Honors the birth of the Spanish queen who sponsored Christopher Columbus's voyage to the New World.

U.S. (Delaware, Nebraska)

Arbor Day
Commemorates birthday of J. Sterling Morton, Nebraska politician and agriculturist.

U.S. (Oklahoma)

Oklahoma Day
Commemorates the opening of the Oklahoma Territory for settlement, 1889.

U.S.

Earth Day
Sponsored by Environmental Action, Inc., Washington, D.C.

RELIGIOUS CALENDAR

The Saints

SS. Soter and *Caius,* popes and martyrs. Elected, respectively, c. 173 and 283. *Caius* also called *Gaius.* [d. 174 and 296]

SS. Epipodius and *Alexander,* martyrs. [d. 178]

St. Leonides, martyr. [d. 202]

St. Agapitus I, pope. Elected 535. Also called *Agapetus.* [d. 536]

St. Theodore of Sykeon, Bishop of Anastasiopolis. [d. 613]

St. Opportuna, virgin and abbess. [d. c. 770]

The Beatified

Blessed Wolfhelm, abbot. [d. 1091]

Blessed Francis of Fabriano, Franciscan friar. First Franciscan to form a library. [d. c. 1322]

Blessed Bartholomew of Cervere, martyr. [d. 1466]

BIRTHDATES

1451 *Isabella I,* Queen of Castile, 1474–1504; patron of *Christopher Columbus.* [d. November 26, 1504]

1707 *Henry Fielding,* English novelist, playwright; among his best known works are *Tom Jones* and *Joseph Andrews.* [d. October 8, 1754]

1711 *Eleazar Wheelock,* U.S. educator; founder of *Hanover, New Hampshire,* and of *Dartmouth College;* first president of Dartmouth, 1770–79. [d. April 24, 1779]

1724 *Immanuel Kant,* German philosopher; one of foremost thinkers of the Enlightenment. [d. February 12, 1804]

1766 *Anne Louise Germaine,* Baroness of Staël-Holstein *(Madame de Staël),* French novelist, critic; an enemy of Napoleon; exiled during French Revolution. [d. July 14, 1817]

1832 *Julius Sterling Morton,* U.S. politician, agriculturist; responsible for establishment of *Arbor Day* in several U.S. states.

1854 *Henri La Fontaine,* Belgian lawyer, politician; Nobel Peace Prize for establishing *Permanent Court of International Justice,* 1913. [d. May 14, 1943]

1861 *Count Nobuaki Makino,* Japanese statesman; Japanese representative at Paris Peace Conference, 1919. [d. January 25, 1949]

1874 *Ellen Glasgow,* U.S. novelist. [d. November 21, 1945]

1876 *Robert Bárány,* Austrian otologist; Nobel Prize in physiology or medicine for his work on the physiology and pathology of the inner ear, 1914. [d. April 8, 1936]

O(le) E(dvart) Rolvaag, U.S. novelist, educator, born in Norway; author of *Giants in the Earth.* [d. November 5, 1931]

1881 *Aleksandr Feodorovich Kerenski,* Russian revolutionary leader; prime minister of post-revolutionary Russia; overthrown by Bolsheviks. [d. June 11, 1970]

1887 *James Hall,* U.S. novelist, short-story writer; collaborator with C. B.

Nordhoff (February 1) on *Mutiny on the Bounty* and *Pitcairn's Island*. [d. July 5, 1951]

1891 *Nicola Sacco,* U.S. radical, factory worker; with Bartolomeo Vanzetti (July 11), was tried, convicted, and executed for a 1920 robbery and shooting; became martyrs representing an aggrieved Italian-American community. They were pardoned in 1977 by proclamation of the Governor of Massachusetts. [d. by electrocution August 23, 1927]

1899 *Vladimir Nabokov,* U.S. novelist, short-story writer, born in Russia; gained international attention with his 1950s novel *Lolita*. [d. July 2, 1977]

1904 *J. Robert Oppenheimer,* U.S. physicist; headed Los Alamos, New Mexico laboratories during development of first *atomic bombs*. [d. February 18, 1967]

1914 *Jan Deltartog,* Dutch author; Tony Award for *The Fourposter,* 1952.

1916 *Yehudi Menuhin,* U.S. violin virtuoso.

1919 *Donald J. Cram,* U.S. chemist; Nobel Prize in chemistry (with C.J. Pedersen and J.M. Lehn), 1987.

1922 *Charles Mingus,* U.S. jazz musician; a major figure in jazz of the 1950s and 1960s. [d. January 12, 1979]

1925 *Aaron Spelling,* U.S. producer; known for his production of television series, *Charlie's Angels, Dynasty,* and *Hotel*.

1926 *Charlotte Rae (Charlotte Rae Lubotsky),* U.S. actress;

known for her starring roles on television series, *Diff'rent Strokes* and *Facts of Life*.

1938 *Glen Campbell,* U.S. country-rock singer.

1939 *Jason Miller,* U.S. playwright, actor.

1946 *John Waters,* U.S. filmmaker.

1950 *Peter Frampton,* British born singer, songwriter; his album, *Frampton Comes Alive!* sold over twelve million copies, 1976.

1954 *Joseph Bottoms,* U.S. actor.

HISTORICAL EVENTS

1124 *Alexander I* of Scotland dies and is succeeded by *David I*.

1500 *Pedro Alvarez Cabral* reaches the coast of *Brazil* and claims the territory for Portugal.

1529 *Treaty of Saragossa* defines Spanish-Portuguese frontier in Pacific; Spain gives up *Molucca Islands*.

1793 *George Washington,* U.S. president, issues proclamation of neutrality in effort to keep the U.S. from becoming embroiled in war between Britain and France.

1834 The *Quadruple Alliance* is formed between Great Britain, France, Portugal, and Spain, supporting *Isabella II* of Spain against the pretender, Don Carlos.

The island of *Saint Helena* is placed under the direct administration of the British government.

1884 The U.S. becomes the first nation to recognize the *International Association of the Congo* as a federal state.

1889 Unoccupied land in *Oklahoma,* formerly in Indian hands, is opened to white settlers.

1900 French are victorious over the Muslims in the battle for control of *Chad*.

1915 The first use of *poison gas* (chlorine) as a battle weapon is instituted by the Germans against French colonial troops in the *Second Battle of Ypres (World War I)*.

1918 Women in *Denmark* vote for the first time.

1920 *Leningrad* becomes the new name of *Petrograd* (formerly *St. Petersburg*).

1953 *J.O. Bowers* becomes the first black Roman Catholic bishop in the U.S.

1960 *American Lutheran Church* is formed in Minneapolis by the merger of three major Lutheran denominations-Evangelical Lutheran, American Lutheran, and United Evangelical Lutheran churches.

1963 *Lester Pearson* is inaugurated as prime minister of Canada.

1969 Doctors in Houston, Texas perform the first total human *eye transplant*.

1970 *Earth Day* observances focus attention on environmental problems in communities throughout the U.S.

1971 Death of Haitian President *François Duvalier* is announced; his son Jean-Claude is sworn in as President for Life.

1975 A bloodless military coup d'état ousts Honduran chief of state General *Oswaldo López Arellano*.

1990 *Robert Polhill* is freed from his kidnappers in Lebanon after three years of captivity.

1993 *Jim Folsom, Jr.,* becomes the governor of Alabama after his predecessor, *Guy Hunt,* is found guilty of misuse of funds.

1995 Over 2,000 Hutu civilians housed in refugee camps are killed by Rwandan government forces attempting to force them out.

april

APRIL
23

HOLIDAYS

Bermuda
Peppercorn Day
Commemorates payment of one peppercorn to Bermuda governor for use of Old State House by Masonic Lodge, 1816.

Cyprus, Turkey
National Sovereignty Day
Commemorates inauguration of Grand National Assembly, 1923.

England
St. George's Day
Celebrates St. George, patron saint of England.

Spain
Feast of St. George

Turkey
Children's Day

RELIGIOUS CALENDAR

The Saints
SS. Felix, Fortunatus, and *Achilleus,* martyrs. [d. 212]
St. George, martyr. Protector of the Kingdom of England; patron of Portugal, soldiers, and Boy Scouts. Invoked against skin diseases. [d. c. 303] Optional Memorial.
St. Ibar, Bishop of Beggery. Also called *Ivor.* [d. 5th century]
St. Gerard, Bishop of Toul. [d. 994]
St. Adalbert, Bishop of Prague, martyr and founder of the Abbey of Brevnov in Prague. [d. c. 997]

The Beatified
Blessed Giles of Assisi, Franciscan and companion to St. Francis of Assisi. [d. 1262]
Blessed Helen of Udine, widow. [d. 1458]

BIRTHDATES

1484 *Julius Caesar Scaliger,* Italian-French literary critic. [d. October 21, 1558]

1564 *William Shakespeare,* England's most renowned playwright. [d. April 23, 1616]

1697 *George Anson,* English admiral; effected reforms in naval administration, raising navy to high efficiency. [d. June 6, 1762]

1720 *Elijah Ben Solomon,* Hebrew religious writer born in Lithuania. [d. October 17, 1797]

1775 *J(oseph) M(allard) W(illiam) Turner,* English romantic painter; best known for impressionistic landscapes and seascapes. [d. December 19, 1851]

1791 *James Buchanan,* U.S. lawyer; 15th President of the United States, 1857–61; the only bachelor president. [d. June 1, 1868]

1804 *Maria Taglioni,* Italian ballet dancer born in Sweden; popularized dancing *sur les pointes.* [d. April 24, 1884]

1813 *Stephen (Arnold) Douglas,* U.S. politician, lawyer; a distinguished orator noted for his debates with Abraham Lincoln during the 1858 Senate campaign. [d. June 3, 1861]

1839 *James Bartlett Hammond,* U.S. inventor; developed the modern *typewriter keyboard,* patented 1880. [d. January 27, 1913]

1844 *Sanford Ballard Dole,* U.S. lawyer, political leader; President, Republic of Hawaii, 1894–1900; Governor, Territory of Hawaii, 1900–03. [d. June 9, 1926]

1852 *Edwin Charles Markham,* U.S. poet, lecturer; known for his poem *Man with the Hoe,* which became a standard statement of exploitation of the working classes. [d. March 7, 1940]

1853 *Alphonse Bertillon,* French criminologist; founded a system for identifying people through bodily measurements (*anthropometry*). [d. February 13, 1914]

1856 *Arthur Twining Hadley,* U.S. economist, educator; President of Yale University, 1899–1921. [d. March 6, 1930]

1858 *Max (Karl Ernst Ludwig) Planck,* German physicist; Nobel Prize in physics for development of *quantum theory*, 1918. [d. October 3, 1947]

1861 *Edmund Henry Hynman Allenby, 1st Viscount Allenby of Megiddo,* British field marshal; led Egyptian Expeditionary Force in World War I. [d. May 14, 1936]

1867 *Johannes A. G. Fibiger,* Danish pathologist; Nobel Prize in physiology or medicine for his work in cancer research, 1926. [d. January 20, 1928]

1891 *Serge Prokofiev,* Russian composer; known especially for *Peter and the Wolf.* [d. March 5, 1953]

1897 *Lucius Clay,* U.S. army general; Commander in Chief of U.S. Forces in Germany, 1945–49; administered Berlin airlift, 1948–49. [d. April 16, 1978]

Lester (Bowles) Pearson, Canadian statesman, diplomat; president of U.N. General Assembly; Nobel Peace Prize for his role in settlement of the *Suez Crisis,* 1957. [d. December 27, 1972]

1899 *Dame Ngaio Marsh,* New Zealand novelist; known especially for mysteries featuring *Inspector Roderick Alleyn of Scotland Yard.* [d. February 18, 1982]

1909 *Rita Levi-Montalcini,* Italian embryologist; Nobel Prize in chemistry for her discovery of a natural substance that promotes the growth of nerve cells (with Stanley Cohen), 1986.

1921 *Warren Spahn,* U.S. baseball player.

1926 *J(ames) P(atrick) Donleavy,* U.S.-Irish novelist.

1928 *Shirley Temple Black,* U.S. actress, diplomat; child film star; Academy Award for outstanding contribution, 1934; U.S. representative to the United Nations, 1969–70; Ambassador to Ghana, 1974–76; Ambassador to Czechoslovakia, 1989– .

1932 *James Fuller Fixx,* U.S. author, runner; wrote best-selling book, *Complete Book of Running;* collapsed and died while jogging. [d. July 20, 1984]

1932 *(Roy) Halston (Frowick),* U.S. fashion designer. [d. March 26, 1990]

1936 *Roy Orbison,* U.S. country-rock musician, singer. [d. December 6, 1988]

1938 *Steven Douglas Symms,* U.S. politician; Senator, 1981–91.

1940 *David Edwin Birney,* U.S. actor; known for his starring role on television series, *Bridget Loves Bernie,* 1972.

Lee Majors (Harvey Lee Yeary), U.S. actor, producer; known for his starring roles on television series, *The Big Valley, The Six Million Dollar Man,* and *The Fall Guy.*

1942 *Sandra Dee (Alexandra Zuck),* U.S. actress, singer; known for her starring roles in *Gidget,* 1959, and *Tammy Tell Me True,* 1961.

1943 *Herve Jean Pierre Villechaize,* French actor; known for his role as Tattoo on television series, *Fantasy Island,* 1978–83. [d. September 4, 1993]

1944 *Anthony James (Tony) Esposito,* Canadian hockey player; set National Hockey League record for number of shutouts in a season with 15, 1969–70; elected to Hall of Fame, 1988.

1947 *Bernadette (Josephine) Devlin (McAliskey),* Irish civil rights leader; youngest woman ever elected to *British Parliament.*

1960 *Valerie Bertinelli,* U.S. actress, producer; known for her role as Barbara on television series, *One Day at a Time,* 1975–84.

HISTORICAL EVENTS

1014 *Brian Borormke,* King of Ireland, defeats Danes at *Clantarf* but is himself slain.

1348 *Order of the Garter,* oldest and most famous order of British knighthood, is established by *Edward III.*

1616 *William Shakespeare* dies.

1625 *Maurice of Nassau* dies and is succeeded by *Frederick Henry* as *stadholder* (ruler of the Netherlands).

1633 *League of Heilbronn* is established, creating a union of South German Protestants with Sweden and France.

1661 *Charles II* of England, (the *Merry Monarch*), is crowned.

1795 *Warren Hastings* is acquitted of charges of high crimes and misdemeanors during his term as governor of Bengal.

1850 *Alfred Lord Tennyson* becomes British poet laureate.

1860 *Savoy* is annexed to France by its own vote.

1895 *Tongoland* is annexed by Great Britain.

april

1896 The first *motion picture* to be commercially exhibited is shown in New York City.

1904 *American Academy of Arts and Letters* is founded by *National Institute of Arts and Letters,* with membership limited to 50 chosen from among members of the Institute.

1909 Villages of *Benevente* and *Samora* in Portugal are destroyed by an *earthquake*.

Theodore Roosevelt sails for Africa on a scientific expedition under the auspices of the Smithsonian Institution.

1910 *Mount Etna,* on the island of Sicily, erupts.

1923 The *Second Lausanne Conference* opens between the Allied Powers and Turkey to settle disputes in the Mid-East and Turkey.

1941 Greek army surrenders to Germany (*World War II.*)

1944 *George Papandreou* is named premier of Greece following the resignation of *Sophocles Venizelos.*

1945 U.S. uses *guided missiles* for only time in *World War II* as two BAT missiles are released at Balikiapen, Borneo.

1950 *Hainan Island* is abandoned to Chinese Communist troops by Nationalist forces.

1952 The *High Court of Parliament* is created by the government of South Africa. The new court can overrule decisions made by the Supreme Court which had recently found an apartheid law unconstitutional.

1964 Official celebration of the four hundredth anniversary of *William Shakespeare's birth* begins at Stratford-on-Avon, England, his birthplace.

1969 *Sirhan Beshara Sirhan* is sentenced to death in the gas chamber for the murder of *Robert F. Kennedy.*

1970 *The Gambia* is proclaimed a republic within the British Commonwealth.

James Dickey's novel, *Deliverance,* is published.

1984 U.S. researchers at the National Cancer Institute identify the *AIDS* virus, and reveal a test to detect the virus in blood. French scientists had announced a similar discovery two days earlier.

1988 *Kanellos Kanellopoulos* sets two flight records when he pedals the *Daedalus 88,* a human-powered aircraft, from Crete to Santorini.

1992 The discovery of clusters of galaxies by astrophysicist *George Smoot* promotes the *Big Bang theory*.

The United Nations accepts *Slovenia* as a member country.

1993 The *U.S. Defense Department* releases the report of misconduct during the *TailHook Association convention* in 1991.

Ranasinghe Premadasa, President of Sri Lanka, is assassinated. Then-Prime Minister *Dingiri Banda Wijetunge* is sworn in as the new president.

1998 *Tsakhiagiin Elbegdorj* is elected premier of Mongolia.

HOLIDAYS

Armenia
Genocide Memorial Day
Commemorates the Armenian genocide of 1915.

Sweden
Vega Day
Commemorates first successful navigation of Northeast Passage by Nils Adolf Nordenskjöld on ship *Vega*, 1880.

Togo
Victory Day

U.S.A.
General Federation of Women's Clubs Day
Sponsored by General Federation of Women's Clubs, Washington, D.C.

RELIGIOUS CALENDAR

The Saints
St. Mellitus, Archbishop of Canterbury. Built St. Mary's Church at Canterbury. [d. 624]

St. Egbert, bishop. [d. 729]

St. William Firmatus of Tours, hermit. [d. c. 1090]

St. Fidelis of Sigmaringen, martyr. [d. 1622] Optional Memorial.

St. Mary Euphrasia Pelletier, virgin and founder of the Institute of Our Lady of Charity of the Good Shepherd. [d. 1868]

St. Ivo, bishop; patron of lawyers, civilians, and of St. Ive, England. Also called *Ive, Ivia,* or *Yves.* [death date unknown]

The Beatified
Blessed Isidore Bakanja. [beatified 1994]

Blessed Gianna Beretta Molla. [beatified 1994]

Blessed Elizabeth Canori Mora. [beatified 1994]

BIRTHDATES

216 *Manes (Mani, Manichaeus),* Persian religious leader; founder of Manichaean sect. [d. c. 274]

1533 *William I, the Silent,* Prince of Orange and Count of Nassau; founder of the Dutch Republic which proclaimed its independence in 1581. [d. July 1584]

1703 *José Francisco Isla,* Spanish novelist, satirist; known for his scathing satires on pulpit oratory; his works were banned by the Inquisition. [d. November 2, 1781]

1719 *Giuseppe Marc'antonio Baretti,* Italian writer, critic, lexicographer; intimate of Dr. Johnson, Burke, and Garrick in England. [d. May 5, 1789]

1743 *Edmund Cartwright,* English clergyman; invented the *power loom,* 1785. [d. October 30, 1823]

1815 *Anthony Trollope,* British novelist; known for his novels of Victorian life. [d. December 6, 1882]

1845 *Carl Friedrich George Spitteler (Felix Tandem),* Swiss poet, novelist; Nobel Prize in literature, 1919. [d. December 29, 1924]

1856 *Henri (Philippe Omer) Pétain,* French army marshal, chief of state; his defense of Verdun in 1916 made him a national hero; Premier of unoccupied France, 1940–44; later convicted of conspiring with the enemy; sentence commuted from death to life imprisonment. [d. July 23, 1951]

1876 *Erich Raeder,* German admiral; Naval Commander-in-Chief, 1928–43. [d. November 6, 1960]

1882 *Hugh Caswall Tremenheere Dowding, 1st Baron Dowding,* British general; head of Royal Air Force fighter command, 1936–40. [d. February 13, 1970]

1902 *Halldor Kiljan Laxness,* Icelandic novelist, poet, playwright; Nobel Prize for Literature, 1955. [d. February 8, 1998]

1904 *Willem DeKooning,* Netherlands-born artist; known for his distorted portraits of women. [d. March 19, 1997]

1905 *Robert Penn Warren,* U.S. novelist, poet, critic,

educator; Pulitzer Prize in fiction, 1947; Pulitzer Prize in poetry, 1958, 1979. [d. September 15, 1989]

1923 *Albert King,* U.S. blues musician. [d. December 21, 1992]

1934 *Shirley Maclaine (Shirley Beaty),* U.S. dancer, actress, author.

1935 *Louis Keith,* U.S. physician; founded the Center for the Study of Multiple Births in 1977, along with his brother, Donald.

1936 *Jill Ireland,* British-born actress; leading lady of the 1950s; wife of Charles Bronson. [d. May 18, 1990]

1942 *Richard M. Daley,* U.S. lawyer, politician; Mayor of Chicago, 1989–; son of Mayor Richard J. Daley.

Barbra (Joan) Streisand, U.S. actress, singer, director.

1952 *Jean-Paul Gaultier,* French fashion designer.

1953 *Eric Bogosian,* U.S. playwright, actor; Obie Award winner for *Drinking in America,* 1986.

1954 *Vince Ferragamo,* U.S. football player.

HISTORICAL EVENTS

1558 *Mary, Queen of Scots* marries Dauphin Francis of France.

1704 The *Boston News-Letter* begins publication, the first successful newspaper in the American colonies.

1800 U.S. *Library of Congress* is established.

1898 Spain declares war on U.S. (*Spanish-American War*).

1916 *Sinn Fein* rebellion (*Great Easter Rebellion*) begins in *Ireland,* with rebels declaring the establishment of a republic.

1921 The *Tyrol* region votes for union with Germany.

1945 *Dachau,* German concentration camp, is liberated by Allies (*World War II*).

Russian troops enter *Berlin* (*World War II*).

1950 The state of *Jordan* is formed by union of Jordanian-occupied Palestine and the Kingdom of Transjordan.

1954 The stage revival of Sir J. M. Barrie's *Peter Pan* premieres.

1960 Riots break out in *Biloxi, Mississippi* after blacks attempt to swim at city's beaches.

1962 The first television pictures ever to be transmitted by a satellite are relayed by *Echo I* from California to Massachusetts.

1965 All foreign-owned enterprises in *Indonesia* are seized by the Sukarno government.

1968 *Mauritius* is admitted to the United Nations.

1970 *The Gambia* Constitution is promulgated.

China launches its first earth satellite.

1971 *Soyuz 10,* Soviet spacecraft carrying three cosmonauts, docks in space with *Salyut,* a previously launched space station.

1975 Terrorists attack the West German embassy in Stockholm, killing the military attaché and demanding the release of 26 anarchists in West Germany.

1979 *Manhattan,* a film starring Woody Allen and Diane Keaton, premieres in New York.

1980 U.S. attempt to rescue its hostages in *Iran* is aborted because of malfunctioning helicopters.

1989 *Richard M. Daley,* son of former Mayor Richard J. Daley, is inaugurated as mayor of Chicago.

1990 The space shuttle *Discovery* is launched into space with the *Hubble Space Telescope* among its payload.

Michael Milken, also known as the "Junk Bond King," pleads guilty to securities fraud. Milken was employed by the securities firm Drexel Burnham Lambert, Inc.

1996 The *Palestine National Council* shows its commitment to the Israeli-PLO peace process by rescinding its charter causes which called for the destruction of Israel.

HOLIDAYS

Australia, New Zealand, Samoa, Tonga
ANZAC Day
(Australia, New Zealand Army Corps)
Marks the day on which the combined Army Corps landed at Gallipoli during World War I, 1915.

Denmark
All Prayer's Day

Italy
Liberation Day
Celebrates the Allied Victory of World War II, 1945.

Papua New Guinea
Remembrance Day

Portugal
Portugal Day or Liberty Day
Commemorates seizing of power by Portuguese Armed Forces and establishment of provisional military government, 1974.

Swaziland
National Flag Day

RELIGIOUS CALENDAR

Feasts
St. Mark, evangelist and martyr; patron of Venice, lawyers, and glaziers. Invoked against sudden and unexpected death. [d. c. 74] [minor festival, Lutheran church; major holy day, Episcopal Church]

The Saints
St. Anianus, Bishop of Alexandria. [d. 1st century]
St. Heribald, Bishop of Auxerre. [d. c. 857]

The Beatified
Blessed Robert Anderton and *Blessed William Marsden,* priests and martyrs. [d. 1586]
Blessed Peter de Betancur. [beatified 1980]

BIRTHDATES

1214 *Louis IX (Saint Louis)* of France. [d. August 25, 1270]

1228 *Conrad IV, Holy Roman Emperor,* 1250–54; lost lower Italy to *Charles of Anjou.* [d. May 21, 1254]

1284 *Edward II* of England, 1307–27; lost power to baronial committee; overthrown and imprisoned by *Roger de Mortimer,* protégé of *Queen Isabella;* forced to resign throne, 1327; murdered. [d. September 1327]

1599 *Oliver Cromwell,* English statesman, soldier; led the parliamentary forces in the English Civil War; installed as Lord Protector of England, Scotland, and Ireland, 1653–58. [d. September 3, 1658]

1769 *Sir Marc Isambard Brunel,* U.S. engineer, inventor born in France; solved the problem of *underwater tunnelling* with his invention of the cast iron tunnel shield, 1818. [d. December 12, 1849]

1825 *Sebastián Lerdo de Tejada,* Mexican lawyer, statesman; President of Mexico, 1872–76. [d. April 21, 1889]

1873 *Walter de la Mare,* British poet. [d. June 23, 1956]

1874 *Guglielmo Marconi,* Italian physicist; inventor of the *radio.* [d. July 20, 1937]

1891 *Sid Richardson,* U.S. oil executive. [d. September 29, 1959]

1900 *Wolfgang Pauli,* U.S. physicist born in Austria; Nobel Prize in physics for explaining the behavior of a class of atomic particles, 1945. [d. December 15, 1958]

1906 *William Joseph Brennan, Jr.,* U.S. jurist, lawyer; Associate Justice of U.S. Supreme Court, 1956–90. [d. July 24, 1997]

1908 *Edward R(oscoe) Murrow,* U.S. broadcast journalist; Director, U.S. Information Agency, 1961–64. [d. April 27, 1965]

1914 *Marcos Perez Jiminez,* Venezuelan politician; president of Venezuela, 1953–58.

1918 *Ella Fitzgerald,* U.S. jazz singer. [d. June 15, 1996]

1923 *Melissa Hayden (Mildred Herman),* Canadian ballerina.

Arnold Ray Miller, U.S. labor leader. [d. July 12, 1985]

1925 *Alhaji Shehu Shagari,* Nigerian statesman; President of Nigeria, 1979–83.

1928 *Cy (Edward Parker) Twombly,* U.S. artist; inducted in the American Academy and Institute of Arts and Letters, 1987.

1930 *Paul Mazursky,* U.S. director, writer.

1932 *Meadow George (Meadowlark) Lemon, III,* U.S. basketball player; center, Harlem Globetrotters, 1954–78.

1939 *Patrick Lichfield (Earl Thomas Patrick John Anson),* British photographer; cousin of Queen Elizabeth II.

1940 *Al Pacino,* U.S. actor; Academy Award (Best Actor) for *Scent of a Woman,* 1992.

1946 *Talia Shire,* U.S. actress.

HISTORICAL EVENTS

1284 *Edward Plantagenet* (later *King Edward II*), son of *Edward I* of England, is born at Caernarvon Castle, Wales and is proclaimed the first *Prince of Wales.*

1792 *Guillotine* is first used in France (*French Revolution*).

1859 Work is started on the *Suez Canal.*

1867 Edo (*Tokyo*) is opened to foreign trade by *Japan.*

1903 First stone of new *Campanile* at Venice is laid.

1905 *Jean Sibelius* conducts the premiere performance of chamber-orchestra version of *Valse Triste.*

1910 *Charles Evans Hughes* is appointed associate justice of the U.S. Supreme Court.

1915 *Australian-New Zealand* troops make first invasion of Turkey, beginning *Gallipoli Campaign (World War I).*

1920 The Supreme Council of the Paris Peace Conference mandates *Syria* to France and *Iraq* and *Palestine* to Great Britain.

1926 *Reza Shah Pahlavi* is crowned Shah of Persia at Teheran.

1944 The *United Negro College Fund* is founded in New York.

1945 U.S. and Soviet troops, advancing from opposite directions, meet at *Torgau* on the banks of the Elbe River, cutting Germany in half (*World War II*).

1950 U.S. government orders *Rumania* to close its commercial attaché office in New York City.

1953 *DNA* (deoxyribose nucleic acid) structure is first presented in the British publication *Nature* in an article by U.S. scientist *James Dewey Watson* and British geneticist *Francis H. C. Crick.*

1961 U.S. and West Germany exchange notes effecting a $587 million partial settlement of Germany's post-World War II debt to the U.S.

1964 General *Paul Harkins* is replaced by Lieutenant General *William*

Westmoreland as leader of the U.S. Military Assistance Command in South Vietnam.

1965 Civilian government in the *Dominican Republic* collapses, leaving army factions struggling for control.

1974 In military coup in Portugal, Dr. *Marcelo Caetano* is overthrown and *General Antonio de Spinola* becomes president.

1975 *Prince Norodom Sihanouk,* head of a government-in-exile since 1970, is named chief of state for life by the Khmer Rouge's Royal Government of National Union of *Cambodia.*

1976 New constitution of *Portugal* goes into effect.

Vietnamese elect joint National Assembly to seal the reunification of the two *Vietnams* into one country.

1980 *Liberia* is taken over by a 17-member *People's Redemptive Council,* and the constitution is suspended.

1982 Israel returns the *Sinai,* captured in 1967, to Egypt as part of the 1979 *Camp David agreement.*

British troops retake *South Georgia Island* from Argentina in first military action in battle over *Falkland Islands.*

1983 Portugal's Social Democrat Party, led by former Prime Minister *Mario Soares,* wins national elections.

Pioneer 10, U.S. space probe launched on March 2, 1972, hurtles past the orbit of the planet *Pluto,* becoming the first man-made object to reach such a distance from the earth.

1986 Prince Makhosetive Dlamini, 18, is made King *Mswati III* of Swaziland after four years of preparation for his accession following his father's death.

1989 More than a quarter of the Soviet Communist Party Central Committee, including former President *Andrei Gromyko,* resign their posts under pressure from reformers.

Japanese prime minister *Noboru Takeshita* announces that he will resign after he is implicated in a government bribery scandal.

1990 The *Hubble Space Telescope* is sent into orbit by the space shuttle *Discovery.*

1991 The U.S. launches the *Hubble Space Telescope.*

APRIL
26

HOLIDAYS

Egypt
Sinai Liberation Day

Tanzania
Union Day
Commemorates the unification of *Zanzibar* and *Tanganyika*, 1964.

U.S. (Florida, Georgia)
Confederate Memorial Day

RELIGOUS CALENDAR

The Saints
SS. Cletus and *Marcellinus,* popes and martyrs. Cletus, elected 76. Marcellinus elected 296. Cletus also called *Anacletus,* or *Anencletus.* [d. c. 91 and 304]
St. Peter, Bishop of Braga; patron of Braga, Portugal. [d. c. 350]
St. Richarius, abbot. Also called *Riquier.* [d. c. 645]
St. Paschasius Radbertus, Abbot of Corbie. [d. c. 860]
St. Franca of Piacenza, virgin and abbess. [d. 1218]
St. Stephen, Bishop of Perm; linguist; translated the liturgy and scriptures into Russian. [d. 1396]

The Beatified
Blessed John I, Bishop of Valenca. [d. 1146]
Blessed Dominic and *Blessed Gregory,* Dominican missionaries. [d. 1300]
Blessed Alda, widow and visionary. Also called *Aldobrandesca.* [d. 1309]

BIRTHDATES

121AD *Marcus Aurelius,* Roman emperor; author of *Meditations.* [d. 180 A.D.]

1564 Christening date of *William Shakespeare,* England's most renowned playwright. [d. April 23, 1616]

1661 *Daniel Defoe,* British author; wrote *Robinson Crusoe,* 1719. [d. April 26, 1731]

1711 *David Hume,* Scottish philosopher; developed philosophy of *skepticism.* [d. August 25, 1776]

1718 *Esek Hopkins,* American Revolutionary naval commander; first Commander-in-Chief of *American Navy.* [d. February 26, 1802]

1774 *Leopold von Buch,* German geologist, geographer; noted for early research on *volcanic processes.* [d. March 4, 1853]

1785 *John James Audubon (Jean Rabine),* U.S. naturalist, painter, born in Santo Domingo; renowned for his ornithological illustrations. [d. January 27, 1851]

1798 *Eugene Delacroix,* French Romantic painter; recognized as a leader in the development of Romanticism in France. [d. August 13, 1863]

1812 *Alfred Krupp,* German armaments manufacturer; considered the *Father of Modern Armaments.* [d. July 14, 1887]

1822 *Frederick Law Olmsted* (or Olmstead), U.S. landscape architect; designer of New York's *Central Park.* [d. August 28, 1903]

1828 *Martha Finley,* U.S. novelist; wrote novels for young girls, including the *Elsie Dinsmore* stories. [d. January 30, 1909]

1834 *Charles Farrar Browne (Artemus Ward),* U.S. humorist, lecturer. [d. March 6, 1867]

1868 *Harold Sidney Harmsworth, Viscount Rothmere,* Irish newspaper publisher; founded British newspaper empire. [d. November 26, 1940]

1875 *Syngman Rhee,* Korean statesman; President of Korean provisional government in exile, 1919–39; first president of the *Republic of Korea* (South Korea). [d. July 19, 1965]

1879 *Sir Owen Willans Richardson,* British physicist; Nobel Prize in physics for study of electron emissions from heated bodies, 1928. [d. February 15, 1959]

1880 *Michel Fokine,* U.S. dancer, choreographer, born in

Russia; called the *Father of Modern Ballet*. [d. August 22, 1942]

1886 *William L. Dawson,* U.S. Congressman, 1943–70. [d. November 9, 1970]

Ma Rainey (Gertrude Melissa Nix Pridgett), U.S. musician, jazz singer. [d. December 22, 1939]

1889 *Ludwig Josef Johann Wittgenstein,* British philosopher, born in Austria; early student of logical positivism; known for studies of philosophical significance of ordinary language. [d. April 19, 1951]

1893 *Anita Loos,* U.S. screenwriter, novelist; author of *Gentlemen Prefer Blondes.* [d. August 18, 1981]

1894 *(Walther Richard) Rudolf Hess,* German Nazi official; Hitler's deputy and second in line of succession to Hitler, until his defection in 1941; imprisoned for life after World War II. [d. August 17, 1987]

1896 *Jules (Caesar) Stein,* U.S. businessman; founder and president of Music Corporation of America, 1924–46; fought for creation of *National Eye Institute.* [d. April 29, 1981]

1897 *Cass Canfield,* U.S. publishing executive; Senior Editor, Harper & Row. [d. March 27, 1986]

1898 *Vicente Aleixandre,* Spanish poet; Nobel Prize in literature, 1977. [d. December 14, 1984]

1900 *Charles Francis Richter,* U.S. seismologist; developed method of measuring earthquake intensity; the *Richter scale* is named for him. [d. September 30, 1985]

1902 *Jonathan (Worth) Daniels,* U.S. journalist, author, government official; member of U.S. President Franklin D. Roosevelt's administration; later wrote biographies of Roosevelt, disclosing his love affair with *Lucy Page Mercer.* [d. November 6, 1981]

1914 *Bernard Malamud,* U.S. novelist, short-story writer; Pulitzer Prize in fiction, 1966. [d. March 18, 1986]

1916 *Morris (Langlo) West,* Australian novelist; author of *The Naked Country* and *The Shoes of the Fisherman.*

1917 *I(eoh) M(ing) Pei,* U.S. architect, born in China; known for innovative modernist structures.

1930 *Bruce Friedman,* U.S. novelist, short-story writer, playwright; author of *Steambath.*

1932 *Michael Smith,* British biochemist; one-half of the Nobel Prize for Chemistry in 1993. Smith did research on oligonucleotide-based site-directed mutagenesis. *Kary B. Mullis,* U.S. biochemist; other half of the prize for inventing the polymerase chain reaction.

1933 *Arno Allan Penzias,* U.S. physicist; Nobel Prize in physics for discovery of *cosmic microwave background radiation,* lending support to Big Bang theory (with R. W. Wilson), 1978.

1936 *Carol Burnett,* U.S. comedienne.

1942 *Bobby Rydell (Robert Ridarelli),* U.S. singer.

1943 *Gary Wright,* U.S. musician; member of the rock band, *Spooky Tooth.*

1946 *Vladimir Zhirinovsky,* Russian politician; founder of the Liberal Democratic Party of Russia, 1990.

1955 *Michael Warren (Mike) Scott,* U.S. baseball player.

1961 *Joan Chen,* Chinese-born actress; known for her performance on the TV drama *Twin Peaks* and the film *The Last Emperor.*

HISTORICAL EVENTS

1798 *Geneva, Switzerland* is annexed by France.

1819 The first U.S. *Independent Order of Odd Fellows* lodge is established at Baltimore, Maryland.

1849 *Civita Vecchia* is occupied by French forces.

1865 *John Wilkes Booth,* assassin of Abraham Lincoln, is shot by federal troops at a farm-house near Washington, D.C.

1915 *Italy* signs a secret treaty with the Allies in London, gaining territorial concessions at the expense of Austria-Hungary and Turkey and joining the Allies (*World War I*).

1922 The U.S. recognizes the newly independent state of *Egypt.*

1937 German planes begin bombing *Guernica, Spain.* Immortalized in a painting by Pablo Picasso, the event becomes a symbol of the Republican cause (*Spanish Civil War*).

1943 U.S. task force bombards Japanese installations at *Attu* in the Aleutians (*World War II*).

1962 First *international satellite*, carrying British experiments and propelled aloft by a U.S. rocket, is launched from Cape Canaveral.

1964 Tanganyika and Zanzibar unite to form the *United Republic of Tanganyika and Zanzibar;* it is renamed *Tanzania* on October 29, 1964.

1966 *Aleksandr Pushkin,* the first Soviet transatlantic liner, arrives in Quebec on her maiden voyage.

1977 *Tanzanian Constitution* is promulgated.

1986 The *Chernobyl* nuclear power reactor in the Soviet Union experiences a hydrogen explosion and core meltdown. Dangerous amounts of radiation are released into the atmosphere causing 23 deaths and requiring the evacuation of 100,000 local residents.

1994 South African blacks vote for the first time in the history of the *Republic of South Africa.*

HOLIDAYS

Afghanistan
Saur Revolution Day
Commemorates the creation of the People's Republic upon the upset of the government by Marxist rebels, 1978.

Sierra Leone
Independence Day
Commemorates achievement of independence from Great Britain, 1961.

Slovenia
National Resistance Day

Sudan
Sham el Nassim

Togo
Independence Day
Commemorates establishment of Togo as a sovereign nation, 1960.

Yugoslavia
Slovenian Liberation Front Day

RELIGIOUS CALENDAR

The Saints
St. Anthimus, Bishop of Nicomedia. [d. 303]

St. Asicus, Bishop of Elphin; patron of *Elphin* in County Roscommon, Ireland. Also called *Tassach*. [d. c. 470]

St. Maughold, Bishop of Man. Also called *Macallius, Maccul*, or *Macul*. [d. c. 498]

St. Floribert, Bishop of Liège. [d. 746]

St. Stephen Pechersky, Bishop of Vladimir. [d. 1094]

St. Zita, virgin; patron of domestic workers. [d. 1278]

St. Turibius, Archbishop of Lima and missionary. First saint of the New World; founded college at Lima, first seminary for training clergy in the Americas. [d. 1606]

The Beatified
Blessed Peter Armengol. [d. 1304]

Blessed Antony of Siena, hermit. [d. 1311]

Blessed James of Bitetto, lay-brother of Observant Franciscan Friars. [d. c. 1485]

Blessed Osanna of Cattaro, virgin and anchoress. [d. 1565]

BIRTHDATES

1733 *Josef Gottlieb Kölreuter*, German botanist; a pioneer in field of *hybridization*. [d. November 12, 1806]

1737 *Edward Gibbon*, British historian; best known for his classic *The History of the Decline and Fall of the Roman Empire*. [d. January 16, 1794]

1744 *Nikolay Ivanovich Novikov*, Russian writer, publisher; attempted to popularize good literature by publishing inexpensive volumes of classics. [d. July 31, 1818]

1748 *Adamantios Koraës*, Greek physician, philologist, patriot, educator; contributed to purification of Greek language in contemporary literature. [d. April 6, 1833]

1759 *Mary (Wollstonecraft) Godwin*, English writer, feminist; an early advocate of women's rights; mother of Mary Shelley (August 30). [d. September 10, 1797]

1791 *Samuel F(inley) B(reese) Morse*, U.S. inventor; invented first practical *telegraph*. Devised *Morse Code* for use in telegraph communications. [d. April 2, 1872]

1818 *Amasa Stone*, U.S. philanthropist, railroad tycoon; built Cleveland, Columbus, and Cincinnati Railroad, 1846; Chicago and Milwaukee Railroad, 1858. [d. May 11, 1883]

1820 *Herbert Spencer*, British naturalist philosopher; a primary formulator of *Social Darwinism*. Popularized idea of *survival of the fittest*. [d. December 8, 1903]

1822 *Ulysses S(impson) Grant*, U.S. army general for the Union, 18th President of United States; his presidential administration was characterized by corruption and bitter partisan politics. [d. July 23, 1885]

1855 *Benjamin Newton Duke*, U.S. tobacco-products

april

manufacturer, philanthropist; with his brother, James Buchanan (December 23), founded American Tobacco Company and Imperial Tobacco Company. *Duke University* is named for the two brothers. [d. January 8, 1929]

1893 *Norman Bel Geddes,* U.S. theatrical and industrial designer; noted for stage designs and airplane, train, and automobile interiors. [d. May 8, 1958]

1896 *Wallace Hume Carothers,* U.S. chemist; invented first form of *nylon* and *neoprene* (synthetic rubber), 1931. [d. April 29, 1937]

Rogers Hornsby (The Rajah), U.S. baseball player; elected to Baseball Hall of Fame, 1942. [d. January 5, 1963]

1898 *Ludwig Bemelmans,* U.S. writer, illustrator, born in Austria. [d. October 1, 1962]

1904 *Arthur Burns,* U.S. government official, economist; Chairman, Federal Reserve Board, 1950–78. [d. June 26, 1987]

C(ecil) Day Lewis (Nicholas Blake), British poet; Poet Laureate of England, 1967–72. [d. May 22, 1972]

1922 *Jack Klugman,* U.S. actor; two Emmy Awards; known for his role as Oscar Madison on television series, *The Odd Couple,* 1970–75.

1927 *Coretta (Scott) King,* U.S. civil rights leader, lecturer, writer, concert singer; widow of *Martin Luther King, Jr.*

1932 *Anouk Aimee (Françoise Sorya),* French actress; leading lady in 1960s films.

1932 *Roelof Pik Botha,* South African politician.

1937 *Sandy Dennis,* U.S. actress; Oscar Award for *Who's Afraid of Virginia Woolf?,* 1966. [d. March 2, 1992]

1939 *Judy Carne (Joyce A. Botterill),* British actress, comedienne; known for her appearances on television series, *Laugh In,* 1968–70.

1959 *Sheena Easton (Sheena Shirley Orr),* Scottish singer.

1967 *Prince Willem-Alexander Claus* of the Netherlands, oldest son of Queen Beatrix.

HISTORICAL EVENTS

1124 *David I (the Saint)* of Scotland accedes to the throne.

1296 *Edward II* of England defeats the Scots at the *Battle of Dunbar.*

1521 *Ferdinand Magellan* is killed by natives of the Philippine Islands during his circumnavigation of the globe.

1773 *Tea Act* is passed by British Parliament, setting stage for conflict with Americans over the tea tax; leads to *Boston Tea Party* of December 16.

1784 *Le Mariage de Figaro* by Beaumarchais premieres in Paris.

1805 U.S. naval forces capture *Derne, Tripoli,* in a combined land-sea assault, and raise U.S. flag over foreign soil for the first time.

1914 Sino-Tibetan convention is signed recognizing independence of *Tibet* under Chinese suzerainty.

1916 The *University of Capetown, Stellenbosch University,* and the *University of South Africa* are established by the Union of South Africa.

1919 *Korean nationalists* declare a republic and begin rebellion against Japan.

1935 *U.S. Soil Conservation Service* is established by Congress.

1939 British government begins *conscription (World War II).*

1941 German troops enter *Athens* and raise the Swastika over the Acropolis (*World War II*).

1950 The state of *Israel* is recognized by the British government.

1960 United Nations trust territory of *Togoland* becomes the independent *Republic of Togo.*

1961 *Sierra Leone* gains independence from Great Britain.

1965 Soviet communications satellite *Molniya 1* is first used for a scheduled telecast.

1969 Bolivian President *René Barrientos* is killed in a helicopter crash; Vice-President *Luis Adolfo Siles Salinas* succeeds him.

1970 Scientists at the University of California - Berkeley synthesize a new element, *unnilpentium,* with an atomic number of 105.

1972 *Apollo 16* spacecraft comes down in the Pacific after a successful mission during which U.S. astronauts *John Young* and *Charles Duke* spend a record 71 hours and 2 minutes on the moon.

1973 *L. Patrick Gray* resigns as acting director of the *F.B.I.* *(Watergate Incident)*.

1978 President *Sardar Mohammad Daud Khan* of Afghanistan is killed in a military coup.

1983 President Ronald Reagan addresses a joint session of Congress to appeal for military and economic aid to *Central America*. U.S. presidents traditionally call joint sessions only in cases of national emergency or to deliver the annual State of the Union address.

1987 The Department of Justice prohibits Austrian president, *Kurt Waldheim*, from entering the U.S. after a year-long investigation links him to Nazi war crimes.

april

APRIL
28

HOLIDAYS

Libya
Evacuation Day (British)

RELIGIOUS CALENDAR

The Saints

SS. Vitalis and *Valeria*, martyrs. [d. c. second century]

St. Pollio, martyr. [d. 304]

SS. Theodora and *Didymus*, martyrs. [d. c. 304]

St. Cronan of Roscrea, abbot. [d. c. 626]

St. Pamphilus, Bishop of Sumona. [d. c. 700]

St. Cyril, Bishop of Turov, Biblical scholar. Considered one of outstanding figures in early Russian Christian culture. [d. 1182]

St. Louis Mary of Montfort, founder of the Company of Mary and of the Daughters of Wisdom. [d. 1716]

St. Peter Mary Chanel, missionary and martyr. First martyr in the South Seas. [d. 1841] Optional Memorial.

The Beatified

Blessed Luchesio, the first Franciscan tertiary of Italy. [d. 1260]

BIRTHDATES

1442 *Edward IV* of England, a major participant in the *War of the Roses*. [d. April 9, 1483]

1630 *Charles Cotton*, English poet, burlesque writer; completed a second part to Walton's *Compleat Angler*, 1676; produced standard translation of Montaigne's *Essays*. [d. February 16, 1687]

1665 *Pier Iacopo Martello* (Martelli), Italian poet, man of letters; attempted to create classical Italian tragedy. [d. May 10, 1727]

1758 *James Monroe*, U.S. politician, diplomat; fifth President of the United States; established the *Monroe Doctrine*. [d. July 4, 1831]

1795 *Charles Stuart*, English explorer in Australia; responsible for much early knowledge of the interior of the continent. [d. June 16, 1869]

1838 *Tobias M. C. Asser*, Dutch jurist; Nobel Peace Prize for helping form the *Permanent Court of Arbitration* at the first Hague peace conference, 1911. [d. July 29, 1913]

1869 *Bertram Grosvenor Goodhue*, U.S. architect; best known for his Gothic revival designs. [d. April 23, 1924]

1874 *Sidney Toler*, U.S. character actor. [d. February 12, 1947]

1878 *Lionel Barrymore*, U.S. actor; leading character actor, often in sentimental roles. [d. November 15, 1954]

1889 *António de Oliveira Salazar*, Portuguese dictatorial leader, 1932–68. [d. July 27, 1970]

1892 *Walter Nathan Rothschild*, U.S. merchant; President of Abraham & Straus department store, 1937–55. [d. October 8, 1960]

John Jacob Niles, U.S. folk singer, folklorist; collected American folk songs, ballads; composed musical accompaniment to the poems of Trappist monk Thomas Merton. [d. May 1, 1980]

1900 *Jan Hendrik Oort*, Dutch astronomer; President, International Astronomical Union, 1959–61. [d. November 5, 1992]

1924 *Kenneth David Kaunda*, Zambian leader; President of Zambia, 1964–91.

1926 *(Nelle) Harper Lee*, U.S. novelist; author of *To Kill a Mockingbird*.

1930 *James Addison Baker, III*, U.S. government official; White House Chief of Staff, 1981–85, 1992–93; Secretary of Treasury, 1985–88; Secretary of State, 1989–92; Special envoy to Western Sahara, 1997– .

1933 *Carolyn Jones*, U.S. actress; known for her role as Morticia on television series, *The Addams Family*, 1964–66. [d. August 3, 1983]

1937 *Saddam Hussein,* Iraqi statesman; President, 1979– .

Jack Nicholson, U.S. actor; Oscar winner (Best Actor) for *One Flew Over the Cuckoo's Nest* and *As Good As It Gets,* also Oscar winner (Best Supporting Actor) for *Terms of Endearment.*

1941 *Ann-Margret (Ann Margret Olsson),* U.S. dancer, singer, actress.

1950 *Jay Leno,* U.S. comedian; host of the *Tonight Show,* 1992– .

HISTORICAL EVENTS

1521 *Ferdinand,* brother of *Holy Roman Emperor Charles V,* obtains Austrian dominions of the Hapsburgs.

1770 *Captain James Cook* lands at Cape Everard, Botany Bay, *Australia,* and claims possession for Great Britain.

1788 *Maryland* becomes seventh state to ratify U.S. Constitution.

1789 Crew members of the English ship *H.M.S. Bounty* stage a mutiny against *Captain William Bligh.*

1864 *Ionian Islands* are turned over to Greece by England.

1915 The great Austro-German offensive begins under the command of *Gen. von Machensen* against the Russian army in *Galicia (World War I).*

The *U.S.S. Cushing* is bombed by German planes in the North Sea *(World War I).*

1919 The Covenant of the *League of Nations* is adopted by the Peace Conference at Paris *(World War I).*

1936 *King Fuad I of Egypt* dies and is succeeded by *Farouk I.*

1941 The U.S. Supreme Court rules that withholding services and accommodations from blacks on passenger trains is unlawful discrimination.

1945 *Benito Mussolini,* Italian dictator, is captured and killed by Italian partisans *(World War II).*

1950 *Frédéric Joliot-Curie,* Nobel Prize winner and well-known French Communist, is dismissed as High Commissioner for Atomic Energy by French cabinet.

1952 General *Matthew Ridgway* succeeds *Dwight D. Eisenhower* as supreme commander of Allied forces in Europe. General *Mark Clark* is named commander of U.S. troops in the Far East.

1964 Japan becomes the 21st full member of the *Organization for Economic Cooperation and Development.*

Yemeni government promulgates a new constitution declaring *Yemen* to be an Islamic Arab state.

1969 French President *Charles de Gaulle* resigns; Senate president *Alain Poher* becomes interim president.

1970 French doctors announce the implantation of the first nuclear-powered *pacemaker.*

1976 *The Bell of Amherst,* a one-character play about Emily Dickinson, opens in New York.

1977 U.S. Secretary of Health, Education, and Welfare, *Joseph A. Califano,* signs regulations prohibiting discrimination against the *handicapped* in institutions receiving federal support.

1993 *Les Aspin,* U.S. Defense Secretary, approves women for service in aerial combat.

april

APRIL
29

HOLIDAYS

Japan
Greenery Day

RELIGIOUS CALENDAR

The Saints

St. Endellion, virgin. Also called
  Endelient. [d. c. 6th century]
St. Wilfrid the Younger, Bishop of
  York. [d. c. 744]
St. Hugh the Great, Abbot of Cluny;
  advisor to nine popes.
  Invoked against fevers. [d.
  1109]
St. Robert of Molesmes, abbot; a
  founder of the Cistercian
  Order. [d. 1110]
St. Peter of Verona, martyr. [d.
  1252]
St. Catherine of Siena, virgin, papal
  advisor, and Doctor of the
  Church. Patron of Italian
  nurses. [d. 1380] Feast
  formerly April 30. Obligatory
  Memorial.
St. Joseph Cottolengo, founder of the
  Societies of the Little House
  of Divine Providence. [d.
  1842]

The Beatified

Blessed Manuel Barbal Cosan.
  [beatified 1990]
Blessed Mercedes Prat. [beatified
  1990]
Blessed Philip Rinaldi. [beatified
  1990]

BIRTHDATES

1745 *Oliver Ellsworth,* U.S. jurist;
  third Chief Justice of the U.S.
  Supreme Court. [d.
  November 26, 1807]

1818 *Alexander II,* Emperor of
  Russia, 1855–81. [d. March 13,
  1881]

1854 *Jules Henri Poincaré,* French
  mathematician; made
  significant contributions in
  areas of probability, calculus,
  and analytics. [d. July 17,
  1912]

1860 *Lorado Taft,* U.S. sculptor;
  known for his monumentalal
  sculptures, including
  Fountain of Time in Chicago.
  [d. October 30, 1936]

1863 *William Randolph Hearst,*
  U.S. editor, publisher; creator
  of *Hearst Newspapers,* one of
  largest newspaper chains in
  U.S. [d. August 14, 1951]

1875 *Rafael Sabatini,* Italian
  author, dramatist; wrote
  Scaramouche, 1921, and
  Captain Blood, 1922. [d.
  February 13, 1950]

1879 *Sir Thomas Beecham,* British
  conductor; founder of the
  *London Philharmonic
  Orchestra,* 1932. [d. March 8,
  1961]

1885 *Frank Jack Fletcher,* U.S.
  admiral; led U.S. naval forces
  in Pacific in World War II. [d.
  April 25, 1973]

1893 *Harold Clayton Urey,* U.S.
  chemist; Nobel Prize in
  chemistry for discovery of
  heavy hydrogen (deuterium),
  1934. [d. January 5, 1981]

1899 *Duke Ellington (Edward
  Kennedy Ellington),* U.S.
  musician, bandleader. [d. May
  24, 1974]

1901 *Hirohito,* Emperor of Japan,
  1926–89. [d. January 7, 1989]

1907 *Fred Zinnemann,* U.S. film
  director; established Neo-
  Realist movement in U.S.
  cinema. [d. March 14, 1997]

1919 *Celeste Holm,* U.S. actress.

1929 *Maurice Strong,* Canadian
  environmentalist.

  (John) Jeremy Thorpe, British
  politician; member of
  Parliament, 1959–79.

1936 *Zubin Mehta,* Indian-born
  conductor; Music Director,
  New York Philharmonic.

1938 *Rod McKuen,* U.S. poet.

1957 *Daniel Day-Lewis,* British
  actor; Academy Award (Best
  Actor) for *My Left Foot,* 1989.

1959 *Michelle Pfeiffer,* U.S. actress.

1970 *Uma Thurman,* U.S. actress.

  Andre Agassi, U.S. tennis
  player; Wimbledon
  Champion, 1992.

HISTORICAL EVENTS

1091 *Alexius I Comnenus,* Byzantine Emperor, defeats the invading Patzinaks and Kumans by the River Leburnium.

1854 *Lincoln University,* the first black college in the U.S., is founded.

1870 The Atlantic Refining Co. (later *Atlantic Richfield Co.*) is incorporated in Pennsylvania.

1916 The British garrison of 10,000 at *Kut-el-Amara* surrenders to the Turks after repeated failures to lift the siege (*World War I*).

1930 The world's largest lock, at the point where North Sea channel cuts across North Holland, is opened.

1942 Japanese forces capture *Lashio* and cut the *Burma Road,* the only viable route between India and China (*World War II*).

1944 Aircraft from 12 U.S. carriers bomb *Truk* in the Caroline Islands (*World War II*).

1951 *Mohammed Mossadegh* becomes premier of Iran after a cabinet crisis precipitated by nationalization of the oil industry.

1952 President *Harry Truman's* attempt to nationalize the steel industry is declared to be illegal by a U.S. court.

1962 *Milton Obote* is inaugurated as prime minister of Uganda.

1965 *Malta* becomes the 18th member of the *Council of Europe.*

1975 U.S. presence in *Vietnam* comes to an end; thousands of Vietnamese and Americans are evacuated.

1979 *Jaime Roldós Aquilera,* of the Concentración de Fuerzas Populares party, is elected President of *Ecuador;* he rules until his death in a plane crash, May 24, 1981.

1988 The first *condor* to be conceived in captivity is hatched at the San Diego Wild Animal Park.

1992 Los Angeles police officers are acquitted in the *Rodney King* beating. The acquittal of the officers starts the most severe riot in U.S. history.

april

APRIL
30

HOLIDAYS

Finland
May Day Eve

Germany and Scandinavian Countries
Walpurgis Night
Ancient rituals for warding off witches and evil spirits are traditionally performed on this night, particularly in the Harz Mountains of Germany.

Netherlands and Netherlands Antilles
Queen's Birthday
Commemorates the birthday of Queen Juliana, 1909.

Vietnam
Liberation of Saigon

RELIGIOUS CALENDAR

The Saints
St. Maximus, martyr. [d. 250]
SS. Marian and James, martyrs. [d. 259]
St. Eutropius, Bishop of Saintes and martyr. [d. 3rd century]
St. Forannan, Abbot of Waulsort in France. [d. 982]
St. Gualfardus, hermit-monk. Also called *Wolfhard.* [d. 1127]
St. Pius V, pope. Elected 1565. [d. 1572] Feast formerly May 5. Optional Memorial.

The Beatified
Blessed Hildegard, matron and wife of Charlemagne. [d. 783]

Blessed Francis Dickenson and *Blessed Miles Gerard,* priests and martyrs. [d. 1590]
Blessed Benedict of Urbino, friar. [d. 1625]
Blessed Johann Nepomuk von Tschiderer. [beatified 1995]

BIRTHDATES

1309 *Casimir III (the Great),* King of Poland, 1333–70. [d. November 5, 1370]

1651 *Jean Baptiste de La Salle,* French educator, Roman Catholic saint; feast day celebrated April 7. [d. April 7, 1719]

1770 *David Thompson,* Canadian explorer, geographer, born in England; the first European to explore the Columbia River; head of British Commission for demarcating borders between Canada and U.S., 1816–26. [d. February 10, 1857]

1771 *Hosea Ballou,* U.S. preacher, an early leader of the Universalists. [d. June 7, 1852]

1777 *Karl Friedrich Gauss (Johann Friedrich Karl Gauss),* German mathematician; developed concept of complex numbers and proved the fundamental algebraic theorems; considered one of the greatest mathematicians of all time. [d. February 23, 1855]

1858 *Mary (Mamie) Harrison,* wife of U.S. President Benjamin Harrison. [d. January 5, 1948]

1870 *Franz Lehár,* Hungarian composer; best known for his operetta, *The Merry Widow.* [d. October 24, 1948]

1877 *Alice B(abette) Toklas,* U.S. secretary; secretary and lover of novelist Gertrude Stein. [d. March 7, 1967]

1883 *Jaroslav Hašek,* Czech novelist, short-story writer; known for his satire *The Good Soldier Schweik.* [d. January 3, 1923]

1888 *John Crowe Ransom,* U.S. poet, critic; founder of *Kenyon Review* and proponent of *New Criticism,* which focused on close textual reading of poetry. [d. July 3, 1974]

1893 *Joachim von Ribbentrop,* German diplomat; Ambassador to Great Britain, 1936–38; played key role in German attack on Poland which started *World War II.* [d. October 16, 1946]

1901 *Simon Kuznets,* U.S. economist; Nobel Prize in economics for extensive research on the economic growth of nations, 1971. [d. July 8, 1985]

1902 *Theodore W. Schultz,* U.S. economist; Nobel Prize in economics for his work in agricultural economics, 1979.[d. February 26, 1998]

1909 *Juliana,* Queen of the Netherlands, 1948–80; abdicated in favor of her daughter, Beatrix.

1912 *Eve Arden (Eunice Quedens),* U.S. actress; known for her starring role on radio and television series, *Our Miss Brooks,* 1948–56. [d. November 12, 1990]

1916 *Claude Elwood Shannon,* U.S. mathematician.

1925 *Cloris Leachman,* U.S. actress; Oscar Award for *The Last Picture Show,* 1971.

1933 *Willie Nelson,* U.S. musician, singer; two Grammy Awards for *Blue Eyes Crying in the Rain,* 1975, and *Georgia on My Mind,* 1978.

1939 *Ellen Zwilich,* U.S. violinist, composer.

1943 *Frederick Chiluba,* Zambian politician; President of the Republic of Zambia, 1991– .

1944 *Jill Clayburgh,* U.S. actress; Cannes Film Festival Award for *An Unmarried Woman,* 1978.

1945 *Annie Doak Dillard,* U.S. author; Pulitzer Prize for *Pilgrim at Tinker Creek,* 1975.

1946 *Carl XVI Gustaf,* King of Sweden, 1973– .

1948 *Perry King,* U.S. actor; known for his starring role on television series, *Riptide.*

1961 *Isiah Thomas,* U.S. basketball player, general manager, sports analyst.

HISTORICAL EVENTS

1789 *George Washington* is inaugurated at New York City as the first U.S. president under the Constitution.

1803 U.S. purchases *Louisiana Territory* from France, more than doubling the size of the country.

1812 *Louisiana* is admitted to the Union as the 18th state.

1815 Central provinces are designated *Kingdom of Poland* under Alexander of Russia.

1900 U.S. railroad engineer *Casey Jones* dies at the throttle, slowing down his crashing *Cannonball* to save his passengers' lives.

1902 Debussy's opera *Pelléas et Mélisande* premieres at the Opéra-Comique in Paris.

1934 New constitution in Austria sets up a dictatorship under *Engelbert Dollfuss.*

1937 The *Wilderness Society* is founded in Washington, D.C. for the preservation of wilderness areas.

1945 *Adolf Hitler* commits suicide in Berlin as Russian troops capture the city.

Women are given the right to vote in *France.*

Arthur Godfrey Time, one of the most popular radio programs of the fifties, begins broadcasting.

1961 Cuban Prime Minister *Fidel Castro* is awarded the 1960 *Lenin Peace Prize.*

1963 New Hampshire legalizes the first state-sponsored *lottery* since 1894.

1965 *Basutoland (Lesotho)* attains internal self-government.

1973 U.S. Attorney General *Kleindienst* and presidential advisors *H. R. Haldeman* and *John Ehrlichman* resign; *John Dean,* presidential counsel, is dismissed (*Watergate Incident*).

1975 *Saigon,* Vietnam, is renamed *Ho Chi Minh City.*

1979 The cargo ship *Ashdod* passes through the *Suez Canal,* becoming the first Israeli ship to sail there since 1948.

1980 Iranian embassy in London is seized by five armed *Iranian dissidents.*

Juliana, Queen of the Netherlands, abdicates in favor of her daughter, *Beatrix.*

1990 *Frank Reed* is freed from his kidnappers in Lebanon after four years of captivity.

1991 *Bangladesh* suffers tragic losses as a cyclone claims over 138,000 lives and much of the country's livestock.

april

May is the fifth month of the Gregorian calendar and has 31 days. In the early Roman calendar, May was the third month of the year.

The name has two possible origins: from the Greek goddess Maia, the mother of Hermes, or from the Italian goddess of spring, Maia Maiesta, to whom sacrifices were made to insure the growth of crops.

The "merry month of May" has traditionally been associated with dancing, singing, love, and general rejoicing over the return of spring. During early Roman times, the month was regarded as being under the protection of the god Apollo, and Romans celebrated by gathering boughs and blossoms to adorn temples, statues, or sweethearts' homes, continuing the spirit of the Floralia, honoring Flora, goddess of flowers, whose festival commenced at theend of April. The Druids instituted sacrificial May bonfires to assure successful planting and rich harvests. In medieval England, May poles and May queens reflected a spirit similar to that of the Romans' Floralia.

In the astrological calendar, May spans the signs of Taurus, the Bull (April 20–May 20) and Gemini, the Twins (May 21–June 21).

The birthstone for May is the emerald, and the flower is the lily of the valley or hawthorn.

STATE, NATIONAL, AND INTERNATIONAL HOLIDAYS

May Day
May 1

Loyalty Day
(United States)
May 1

Independence Day
(Rhode Island)
May 4

Bird Day
(Oklahoma)
May 1

Truman Day
(Missouri)
May 8

Minnesota Day
(Minnesota)
May 11

Mecklenburg Independence Day
(North Carolina)
May 20

National Maritime Day
(United States)
May 22

Constitution Day
(Japan)
First Monday

King's Birthday
(Lesotho)
First Monday

Prayer Day
(Denmark)
First or Second Saturday

Simbra Oilor at Oas
(Romania)
First Sunday

Mother's Day
(United States)
Second Sunday
(Central African Republic)
Final Saturday

Discovery Day
(Cayman Islands)
Third Monday

Battle of Las Piedras
(Uruguay)
Third Monday

Primary Election Day
(Pennsylvania)
Third Tuesday
(Indiana)
First Tuesday after First Monday

Armed Forces Day
(United States)
Third Saturday

Confederate Memorial Day
(North Carolina, South Carolina)
May 10
(Virginia)
May 30

Commonwealth Day
(Belize)
Fourth Monday

Victoria Day
(Scotland)
Fourth Monday
(Canada)
Monday before May 25

Memorial Day
(most of the United States)
Final Monday
except:
(New Mexico)
May 25
(Puerto Rico)
May 28
(Delaware, Illinois, Maryland, New
Hampshire South Dakota,Vermont)
May 30

Africa Freedom Day
(Zambia)
Last Tuesday

Carnival in Valletta
(Malta)
Second Weekend

Windmill Day
(The Netherlands)
Second Saturday

**Gabrovo's Biannual Comedic
Extravaganza**
(Bulgaria)
mid-May (odd years)

SPECIAL EVENTS AND THEIR SPONSORS

Arthritis Month
Arthritis Foundation

**Better Hearing and Speech
Month**
Council for Better Hearing and
Speech

National Barbecue Month
Barbecue Industry Association

Bike Safety Month
National Safety Council

**National Home Decorating
Month**
National Decorating Products
Association

National Hope Chest Month
National Multiple Sclerosis Society

Older Americans Month
National Safety Council

National Mental Health Month
National Mental Health Association

Philatelic Exhibitions Month
The Philatelic Journalist

Touring Theater Month
Richard R. Falk Associates

Be Kind to Animals Week
First Week
American Humane Society

**International Classified
Advertising Week**
First Week
Association of Newspaper Classified
Advertising Managers,Inc.

**National Extension Homemaker
Council Week**
First Week
National Extension Homemakers
Council

National Pet Week
First Week
Auxiliary to the American Veterinary
MedicalAssociation

National Girls Club Week
Second Week
Girls Clubs of America

**National Historic Preservation
Week**
Second Week
National Trust for Historic
Preservation

National Nursing Home Week
Second Week
American Health Care Association

National Salvation Army Week
Second Week
The Salvation Army

National White Cane Week
Third Week
National Federation of the Blind

Pickle Weeks
Final Two Weeks
Pickle Packers International, Inc.

Public Relations Week
Final Full Week
Richard R. Falk Associates

Law Day
May 1
American Bar Association

**Anniversary of the First Postage
Stamp**
May 6
The Philatelic Journalist

**Birthday Anniversary of Jean
Henri Dunant**
May 8
Franklin D. Roosevelt Philatelic
Society

**World Day of Prayer for
Vocations**
*First Sunday (or last Sunday in
April)*
National Catholic Vocation Council

HOLIDAYS

Labor Day or Worker's Day
(except U.S. and Canada)
Recognizes the alliance of working
people in most nations of the world.
Recognized as a workers' holiday in
most socialist countries.

May Day
Traditionally a day of flower festivals;
celebrated with hanging of May
Baskets and dancing around May
Poles in England and some sections
of U.S.

Bulgaria
Labor Day

Chechnia
Day of International Socialism

Cyprus
Makarios Memorial Day

Mongolia
International Solidarity Day

Singapore
Vesak Day

Slovenia
Labor Day

Spain, Vatican City
St. Joseph the Worker Day

Turkey
Spring Day

Russia
Spring Day

U.S.
Law Day
Established to enhance citizen
awareness of the benefits of law and
order.

Loyalty Day

U.S. (Oklahoma)
Bird Day

RELIGIOUS CALENDAR

Feasts
SS. Philip and *James,* apostles. Philip
is considered the first of
Christ's disciples. James is
also called *Minor,* or *The Less,*
[d. 1st century] [Major holy
day, Episcopal Church; minor
festival, Lutheran Church.]
(Transferred to May 11.)

The Saints
St. Amator, Bishop of Auxerre. Also
called *Amatre.* [d. 418]
St. Sigismund of Burgundy, King of
Burgundy. [d. 524]
St. Marculf. Invoked to cure skin
diseases. Also called *Marcon,
Marcoul, Marculfus.* [d. c.
558]
St. Brieuc, abbot of monastery in
Brittany. Also called *Briocus.*
[d. 6th century]
St. Corentin, first bishop of
Cornouaille. Also called *Cury.*
[d. 6th century]
St. Theodard, Archbishop of
Narbonne. Also called
Audard. [d. 893]
St. Peregrine Laziosi, Servite friar.
[d. 1345]

BIRTHDATES

1218 *Rudolf I,* founder of the
Hapsburg Dynasty; became
King of Germany, 1273. [d.
July 1291]

1672 *Joseph Addison,* English poet,
essayist, critic, playwright. [d.
June 17, 1719]

1764 *Benjamin Henry Latrobe,*
U.S. architect. [d. September
3, 1820]

1769 *Arthur Wellesley, 1st Duke of
Wellington,* British Army field
marshal, public official;
defeated Napoleon at
Waterloo. British Prime
Minister, 1829–30. [d.
September 14, 1852]

1824 *Alexander William
Williamson,* British chemist;
first to describe principle of
dynamic equilibrium and
function of catalyst in
chemical reaction. [d. May 6,
1904]

1825 *George Inness,* U.S. painter;
landscapist of the *Hudson
River School.* [d. August 3,
1894]

1827 *Jules Adolphe Breton,* French
painter. [d. July 4, 1906]

1828 *Adelardo López de Ayala y
Herrera,* Spanish dramatist,
politician; President, Chamber
of Deputies, 1878. [d.
December 30, 1879]

1830 *Mary Jones (Mother Jones),*
U.S. labor leader; famous as

an agitator in behalf of Appalachian coal miners. [d. November 30, 1930]

1839 *Louis Marie Chardonnet,* French chemist; invented *rayon,* the first common artificial fiber. [d. March 12, 1924]

1852 *Santiago Ramón y Cajal,* Spanish histologist; Nobel Prize in physiology or medicine for work establishing the neuron as the basic unit of the nervous system (with C. Golgi), 1906. [d. October 17, 1934]

Martha Jane Burke (Calamity Jane), U.S. frontier adventuress, legendary dance-hall girl and Indian fighter. [d. August 1, 1903]

1880 *Albert Davis Lasker,* U.S. advertising executive; created ads telling consumers why to buy products. [d. May 30, 1952]

1881 *Pierre Teilhard de Chardin,* French Roman Catholic priest, paleontologist, philosopher; synthesized theories of Christianity and evolution. [d. April 10, 1955]

1896 *Mark Wayne Clark,* U.S. army general; commanded United Nations forces in Korea, 1952–53. [d. April 17, 1984]

1909 *Kate Smith,* U.S. singer. [d. June 17, 1986]

1912 *Winthrop Rockefeller,* U.S. politician; Governor of Arizona, 1967–71. [d. February 22, 1973]

1916 *Glenn Ford (Gwyllyn Ford),* U.S. actor, born in Canada.

1918 *Jack Paar,* U.S. entertainer; pioneer talk show host; host of *The Tonight Show,* 1957–62.

1923 *Joseph Heller,* U.S. novelist; author of *Catch 22.*

1925 *(Malcolm) Scott Carpenter,* U.S. astronaut, oceanographer.

1939 *Judith (Judy) Collins,* U.S. singer.

1940 *Elsa Peretti,* U.S. model, designer.

1945 *Rita Coolidge,* U.S. singer.

1954 *Ray Parker, Jr.,* U.S. singer, musician, songwriter.

1960 *Steve Cauthen,* U.S. jockey; first jockey to win U.S. Triple Crown, 1978, and British Epsom Derby, 1985.

1967 *Tim McGraw,* U.S. country singer.

HISTORICAL EVENTS

1429 *Joan of Arc,* inspiring loyal French troops, raises siege of Orlèans, driving back the English and Burgundian attackers.

1703 *Charles XII of Sweden* defeats *Peter the Great of Russia* at Pultusk.

1707 Union of *England* and *Scotland* under the name of *Great Britain* becomes effective.

1808 *Napoleon* forces both *Charles IV of Spain* and his son *Ferdinand* to relinquish the Spanish crown in his favor.

1809 *Napoleon* annexes *Papal States;* Pope *Pius VII* is held prisoner at Savona.

1847 The *Smithsonian Institution* in Washington, D.C., is formally dedicated.

1851 First *Great Exhibition* of industries of all nations opens in Hyde Park, London.

1862 *New Orleans* falls to Union troops after naval bombardment by *Admiral Farragut (U.S. Civil War).*

1876 *Queen Victoria* of Great Britain is proclaimed Empress of India.

1893 *Columbian Exhibition* opens in Chicago.

1898 *Battle of Manila Bay* ends with destruction of Spanish fleet by U.S. Navy commanded by Admiral *George Dewey (Spanish-American War).*

1907 *Metered taxi cabs* make their first appearance in New York City.

1911 U.S. Supreme Court, acting under the *Sherman Anti-Trust Act,* orders dissolution of *Standard Oil Co.* and *American Tobacco Co.*

1915 The American merchant ship, the tanker *Gulflight,* is first to be torpedoed and sunk by a German submarine (*World War I*).

1920 Longest major league baseball game, 26 innings, ends in a tie, called because of darkness (Brooklyn 1, Boston 1).

1922 The first *National Labor Congress of China* opens in Canton.

1924 *Greece* is proclaimed a republic after overthrow of *King George II.*

1931 The *Empire State Building,* then the world's tallest building, is dedicated in New York.

1943 The *Netherlands* is placed under martial law by Nazi officials.

1947 The *Smithsonian Institution* in Washington, D.C. celebrates the one hundredth anniversary of its dedication.

1948 The prime minister of Nepal, General *Padma Rana,* resigns and is replaced by his son Maharaja *Chandra Rana.*

1957 *Luis Somoza* is inaugurated as president of Nicaragua.

1960 U.S. *U-2 reconnaissance plane* is shot down near Sverdlovsk, central U.S.S.R., and pilot *Francis Gary Powers* is captured.

1961 Cuban Prime Minister *Fidel Castro* declares *Cuba* to be a socialist nation.

Tanganyika, British protectorate, achieves full internal self-government; *Julius Nyerere* becomes first prime minister.

Harper Lee wins the Pulitzer Prize for her novel, *To Kill a Mockingbird.*

1971 *Amtrak* (National Railroad Passenger Corporation) takes over operation of most U.S. passenger trains.

1975 U.S. baseball player, *Hank Aaron,* surpasses Babe Ruth's career record of 2,209 runs batted in.

Communist victory in *South Vietnam* is completed.

1981 Japan voluntarily limits its automobile exports to the U.S. for two years.

New Jersey Senator *Harrison Williams* is convicted of criminal charges related to the *Abscam investigation.*

1986 American *Ann Bancroft* becomes the first woman to reach the North Pole. She achieves this feat by dogsled.

1993 Sri Lanka President *Ranasinghe Premadas* is assassinated.

1997 *Tony Blair* is elected prime minister of Britain.

may

MAY
2

HOLIDAYS

Belize
Labor Day

Israel
Martyrs and Heroes Remembrance Day
Commemorates the six million Jews who died during the Holocaust.

Slovenia
Labor Day

RELIGIOUS CALENDAR

The Saints
SS. *Exsuperius* and *Zoë*, husband and wife, martyrs. [d. c. 135]
St. *Athanasius, Archbishop of Alexandria* and Doctor of the Church. [d. 373] Obligatory Memorial.
St. *Waldebert*, Abbot of Luxeuil. Also called *Gaubert, Walbert*. [d. c. 665]
St. *Ultan*, Abbot of Fosses. Also called *Ultain*. [d. 686]
St. *Wiborada*, virgin, recluse, and martyr. Also called *Guiborat, Weibrath*. [d. 926]
St. *Mafalda*, princess and nun. Also called *Matilda*. [d. 1252]

The Beatified
Blessed Conrad of Seldenbüren, founder of Benedictine Abbey of Engelberg. [d. 1126]

BIRTHDATES

1551 *William Camden,* English antiquary, historian. [d. November 9, 1623]

1660 *Alessandro Scarlatti,* Italian composer; considered the *Father of Modern Opera.* [d. October 24, 1725]

1729 *Catherine II, the Great,* (Sophia Augusta Frederika), Empress of Russia, 1762–96. [d. November 17, 1796]

1750 *John André,* British army officer; conspired with Benedict Arnold for surrender of West Point during American Revolution. [d. October 2, 1780]

1837 *Henry Martyn Robert,* U.S. military engineer, parliamentarian; author of *Robert's Rules of Order,* the standard work on parliamentary procedure. [d. May 11, 1923]

1851 *Graham Taylor,* U.S. clergyman, sociologist; founder of forerunner of *University of Chicago School of Social Work.* [d. September 26, 1938]

1860 *Theodor Herzl,* Austrian Jewish writer born in Hungary; founder of modern *Zionism.* [d. July 3, 1904]

Sir William Maddock Bayliss, British physiologist; discovered (with E. H. Starling) hormone *secretin* manufactured by glands on wall of small intestine. [d. August 27, 1924]

1866 *Jesse William Lazear,* U.S. bacteriologist, army surgeon; served with Walter Reed on Yellow Fever Commission, 1900. [d. September 25, 1900]

1879 *James Francis Byrnes,* U.S. politician, lawyer, editor; U.S. Senator, 1931–41; Associate Justice of U.S. Supreme Court, 1941–42; Director, Office of Economic Stability, 1941–42; Director, Office of War Mobilization 1943–45; U.S. Secretary of State, 1945–47; Governor of South Carolina, 1951–55. [d. April 9, 1972]

1887 *Vernon Castle (Vernon Castle Blythe),* U.S. dancer; with wife *Irene Castle* formed famous dancing team in period before World War I. [d. February 15, 1918]

1892 *Manfred (Freiherr) von Richthofen (The Red Baron),* German aviator, World War I fighter ace. [d. April 21, 1918]

1895 *Lorenz (Milton) Hart,* U.S. lyricist; collaborator with Richard Rodgers (June 28) on musical scores for numerous plays. [d. November 22, 1943]

1902 *Brian (Delacy) Aherne,* U.S. actor. [d. February 10, 1986]

1903 *Benjamin (McLane) Spock,* U.S. pediatrician; major influence on modern U.S. child-rearing practices and health care. [d. March 15, 1998]

1904 *Bing Crosby (Harry Lillis Crosby),* U.S. singer, actor; leading crooner of the 1930s and 1940s. [d. October 14, 1977]

1921 *Satyajit Ray,* Indian director. [d. April 23, 1992]

1923 *Patrick J. Hillery,* Irish statesman; President, Irish Republic, 1976–90.

1938 *Moshoeshoe II, King of Lesotho,* 1960–70, 1970–89, 1995–96.[d. January 17, 1996]

1946 *Lesley Gore,* U.S. singer.

1949 *Larry Wayne Gatlin,* U.S. singer, songwriter; member of country group, *Gatlin Brothers.*

HISTORICAL EVENTS

1316 *Edward Bruce,* brother of the Scottish king, is crowned King of Ireland.

1322 *Parliament of York* declares that all legislation must be approved by both the king and parliament.

1670 *Hudson Bay Company* receives a charter from English crown and is given a monopoly of the trade in Hudson Bay region.

1912 *B.F. Goodrich Co.* is incorporated in New York.

1913 *Republic of China* is recognized by the United States and Mexico.

1915 The *Battle of Gorlice-Tarnow* begins (*World War I*).

1936 *Prokofiev's Peter and the Wolf* premieres at a children's concert in Moscow.

1945 *Berlin* falls to the Allied armies (*World War II*).

German forces in Italy surrender to the Allies (*World War II*).

1951 *German Federal Republic* becomes a full member of the *Council of Europe.*

Iran nationalizes its oil industry.

1957 Teamsters Union president, *Dave Beck,* is indicted by a U.S. grand jury on charges of income tax evasion.

Eugene O'Neill's last play, *A Moon for the Misbegotten,* opens on Broadway.

1953 King *Faisal II* of Iraq officially ascends to the throne upon his 18th birthday.

1953 King *Hussein I* of Jordan formally assumes the throne.

1961 Argentina, Brazil, Chile, Mexico, Peru, and Uruguay ratify the *Treaty of Montevideo,* which creates the *Latin American Free Trade Association.*

1965 Fourteen thousand U.S. troops arrive in the *Dominican Republic* to prevent Communists from seizing control of the unstable government.

Early Bird, the world's first commercial satellite, begins transmission.

1966 Arthur Schlesinger's account of the Kennedy administration, *A Thousand Days,* wins a Pulitzer Prize.

1974 Former U.S. Vice-President *Spiro Agnew* is barred from practicing law in Maryland, the only state where he was licensed.

1983 Australian doctors announce the world's first human pregnancy using a fertilized egg which had been frozen before implantation.

1985 One of the largest U.S. brokerage companies, *E.F. Hutton,* pleads guilty to charges of bank fraud.

1989 *Yasser Arafat* declares the 1964 charter of the *Palestinian Liberation Organization* "null and void" on French television.

1989 *Hungary* opens a border with Austria when it tears down a fence that had been erected in 1969.

1992 Federal troops are sent into Los Angeles, California, to help restore order after a day of rioting caused by the acquittal of police officers in the *Rodney King* beating case.

may

MAY
3

HOLIDAYS

Japan
Constitution Memorial Day

Poland
Constitution Day
Commemorates the adoption of Poland's first constitution, ratified on this day in 1794.

RELIGIOUS CALENDAR

The Saints
SS. Alexander, Eventius, and *Theodolus,* martyrs. [d. c. 113]

SS. Timothy and *Maura,* martyrs. [d. c. 286]

St. Juvenal, Bishop of Narni. [d. c. 376]

St. Philip of Zell, priest and recluse. [d. 8th century]

St. Glywys, monk; patron of St. Gluvias, Cornwall. Also called *Gluvias.* [death date unknown]

BIRTHDATES

1469 *Niccolò di Machiavelli,* Italian statesman, author; one of the outstanding figures of the Renaissance; best known for *The Prince,* a pragmatic guide to the use and furtherance of political power. [d. June 21, 1527]

1748 *Emmanuel Joseph Sieyès (Abbé Sieyès),* French Revolutionary leader; one of chief figures in Napoleon's rise to power. [d. June 20, 1836]

1791 *Count Henryk Rzewuski (J. Bejla),* Polish novelist. [d. February 28, 1866]

1826 *Charles XV, King of Sweden and Norway,* 1859–72. [d. September 18, 1872]

1827 *John Hanning Speke,* British African explorer; confirmed theory that Lake Victoria is one source of the Nile. [d. September 15, 1864]

1844 *(Richard) D'Oyly Carte,* British operatic impresario; founded the Savoy Theatre, home of *Gilbert and Sullivan* productions. [d. April 3, 1901]

1848 *Francisco Teixeira de Queiroz,* Portuguese short-story writer, novelist. [d. 1919]

1849 *Jacob August Riis,* U.S. journalist, reformer, author; a crusader for urban reforms. [d. May 26, 1914]

Prince Bernhard von Bulow, German statesman; Chancellor of Germany, 1900–09. [d. October 28, 1929]

1874 *François Coty,* French industrialist, newspaper owner, parfumier. [d. 1934]

1892 *Sir George Paget Thomson,* British physicist; Nobel Prize in physics for discovery of diffraction of electrons by crystals (with C. J. Davisson), 1937. [d. September 10, 1975]

1898 *Septima Clark,* U.S. civil rights activist. [d. 1987]

Golda Meir, Israeli stateswoman; first woman premier of Israel, 1969–74. [d. December 8, 1978]

1902 *Alfred Kastler,* French physicist; Nobel Prize in physics for research in atomic structure, 1966. [d. January 9, 1984]

Walter Slezak, U.S. actor. [d. April 22, 1983]

1906 *Roberto Rossellini,* Italian film director. [d. June 3, 1977]

1907 *Earl Wilson,* U.S. syndicated columnist.

1912 *Virgil (Keel) Fox,* U.S. organist; known for his flamboyant, popular presentation style. [d. October 25, 1980]

May Sarton, U.S. author, poet. [d. July 16, 1995]

1913 *(Samuel) Earl Blackwell, Jr.,* U.S. author, publisher; organizer, Theater Hall of Fame, 1972.

William Motter Inge, U.S. playwright. [d. June 10, 1973]

1919 *Pete Seeger,* U.S. folksinger, composer.

1920 *(Sugar) Ray Robinson (Walker Smith, Jr.),* U.S. boxer; five-time middleweight champion, 1951–60. [d. April 12, 1989]

1933 *Steven Weinberg,* U.S. physicist; Nobel Prize in physics for formulating theory concerning interaction of elementary particles (with S. L. Glashow), 1979.

1934 *James Brown,* U.S. singer; Grammy Award, 1965; has thirty-eight gold records in twenty years.

1936 *Engelbert Humperdinck (Arnold Gerry Dorsey),* British singer.

1937 *Frankie Valli (Francis Castelluccio),* U.S. singer; member of the rock group, *The Four Seasons.*

1947 *Doug(las James) Henning,* Canadian magician.

HISTORICAL EVENTS

1616 *Treaty of Loudun* ends second civil war in France and rebellion of Henry, Prince de Condé.

1660 *John II Casimir of Poland* signs the *Treaty of Oliva,* abandoning his claim to the throne of Sweden and ending the *Northern War.*

1765 Dr. *John Morgan* is granted permission to begin the first medical school in the U.S. at the College of Philadelphia.

1841 *New Zealand* becomes a British colony.

1859 France, under *Napoleon III,* declares war on Austria.

1895 The name of *Rhodesia* is given to the territories of the British South Africa Company.

1915 The Austrian army under Archduke Josef Ferdinand takes *Tarnow* as the Russians fall back from the Austro-German offensive in Galicia (*World War I*).

1939 Drastic anti-Jewish laws are introduced in *Hungary.*

1945 British troops capture *Rangoon,* insuring the Allied conquest of Burma (*World War II*).

U.S. troops land at *Santa Cruz, Philippines.* (*World War II*)

1947 *Japan* promulgates its constitution.

1950 The Chinese Communist government bans *polygamy* and the sale of women.

The first round of prisoner exchanges between Communist and United Nations forces in Korea ends (*Korean War*).

1954 *Bruce Catton* receives a Pulitzer Prize for the final volume of his Civil War trilogy, *Stillness at Appomattox.*

1960 *Cyrus Eaton,* U.S. industrialist, is awarded the Lenin Peace Prize.

Harvey Schmidt and Tom Jones' musical, *The Fantasticks,* premieres in New York.

1965 *Cambodia* severs diplomatic relations with U.S.

1968 South African House of Assembly votes to abolish parliamentary representation for the country's blacks.

1971 *Erich Honecker* becomes First Secretary of the East German Communist Party.

1972 U.S. Assistant Attorney General, *L. Patrick Gray III,* is named acting director of the FBI, succeeding J. Edgar Hoover, who died May 2.

1979 *Margaret Thatcher,* the 53-year old head of the Conservative Party, becomes the first woman Prime Minister of Great Britain.

Headquarters of the ruling Christian Democrats in Rome are bombed by the terrorist *Red Brigade.*

1990 The *Food and Drug Administration* approves the AIDS drug *AZT* for use in children

may

MAY
4

HOLIDAYS

Tonga
Birthday of Crown Prince Tupouto'a

U.S. (Rhode Island)
Independence Day
Commemorates day on which Rhode Island proclaimed its independence from Great Britain, 1776.

RELIGIOUS CALENDAR

The Saints
St. Cyriacus, bishop; principal patron of Ancona. Also called *Judas Quiriacus.* Believed to have aided St. Helena in the recovery of the cross of Christ. [d. c. 133]
St. Florian, Roman army officer and martyr; patron of Poland, Linz, and Upper Austria. Invoked in danger from fire or water. [d. 304]
St. Pelagia of Tarsus, virgin and martyr. [d. c. 304]
St. Venerius, Bishop of Milan. [d. 409]
St. Godehard, Bishop of Hildesheim. Also called *Godard, Gothard.* [d. 1038]
The Martyrs of England and Wales. [d. 1535–1681]

The Beatified
Blessed Catherine of Parc-aux-Dames, virgin and visionary. [d. early 13th century]

Blessed Gregory of Verucchio. Invoked when rain is needed. [d. 1343]
Blessed Michael Giedroyé, Augustinian monk. [d. 1485]
Blessed John Martin Moye, missionary priest and founder of the Sisters of Divine Providence. [d. 1793]
Blessed Florentino Asensio Barroso, bishop. [beatified 1997]
Blessed Gaetano Catanoso. [beatified 1997]
Blessed Ceferino Gimenez Malla. [beatified 1997]
Blessed Enrico Rebuschini. [beatified 1997]
Blessed Sr. Maria Enarnacion Rosal of the Sacred Heart. [beatified 1997]

BIRTHDATES

1654 *K'ang-hsi,* second emperor of the *Manchu Dynasty.* [d. December 20, 1722]

1655 *Bartolommeo Cristofori,* Italian maker of harpsichords; credited with development of hammer action later used in modern pianos. [d. 1731]

1796 *Horace Mann,* U.S. educator, public official; established model for U.S. public education system. [d. August 2, 1859]

1806 *William F. Cooke,* British technician; with Charles Wheatstone, patented a *telegraph,* 1837.

1820 *Julia Tyler,* second wife of U.S. President John Tyler. [d. July 10, 1889]

1825 *Thomas Henry Huxley,* British philosopher, biologist. [d. June 29, 1895]

Henry Browne Blackwell, U.S. social reformer. [d. September 7, 1909]

1826 *Frederick Edwin Church,* U.S. painter. [d. April 7, 1900]

1846 *Henryk Sienkiewicz,* polish writer; Nobel Prize for literature in 1905. [d. 1916]

1866 *William Ellis Corey,* U.S. industrialist; second president of U.S. Steel Corp. [d. May 11, 1934]

1889 *Francis Joseph Spellman,* U.S. Roman Catholic Cardinal; Archbishop of New York, 1939–67. [d. December 2, 1967]

1896 *(Edward William) Alton Ochsner,* U.S. physician; one of first to present evidence that cigarette smoking is a major cause of lung cancer; founder of the *Alton Ochsner Clinic* at Tulane University. [d. September 24, 1981]

Mary Ellis (Opdycke) Peltz, U.S. journalist, author, editor; first editor of *Opera News,* 1936–57; author of several books on the history of opera in America. [d. October 24, 1981]

1909 *Howard DaSilva (Harold Silverblatt),* U.S. actor, director, producer; known for his role as Benjamin Franklin in the Broadway musical, *1776,* 1969. [d. February 16, 1986]

1918 *Kakuei Tanaka,* Japanese statesman; Prime Minister, 1972–74. [d. December 16, 1993]

1919 *Heloise (Heloise Bowles Reese),* U.S. journalist, author; wrote syndicated column, *Hints from Heloise,* 1961–77. [d. December 28, 1977]

1925 *Luis Herrera Campins,* Venezuelan statesman; President, 1979–84.

1928 *Maynard Ferguson,* Canadian musician.

Hosni Mubarak, Egyptian leader; President, 1981– .

1929 *Audrey Hepburn (Audrey Hepburn-Ruston),* Belgian-born U.S. actress. [d. January 20, 1993]

1930 *Roberta Peters,* U.S. operatic soprano.

1940 *Robin Cook,* U.S. physician, writer; author of *Coma* and *Terminal.*

1941 *George F. Will,* U.S. journalist; Pulitzer Prize, 1977; commentator, American Broadcasting Companies News.

1942 *Tammy Wynette (Wynette Pugh),* U.S. singer. [d. April 6, 1998]

1957 *Richard Max (Rick) Leach,* U.S. baseball player.

1959 *Randy Travis,* U.S. country singer.

HISTORICAL EVENTS

1041 The Lombards and Normans defeat the Greeks at *Montemaggiore.*

1256 *Pope Alexander IV* founds *Order of Augustine Hermits.*

1328 *Treaty of Northampton* is signed between England and Scotland; *Robert Bruce* is recognized as King of Scotland.

1471 *Edward, Prince of Wales,* son of *Henry VI of England,* is slain at the *Battle of Tewksbury (War of the Roses).*

1493 *Pope Alexander VI* divides the New World between Spain and Portugal.

1702 England, Holland, and the Holy Roman Empire declare war on France.

1776 *Rhode Island* is first American colony to renounce allegiance to *King George III.*

1780 *American Academy of Arts and Sciences* is chartered at Boston.

1824 The *First Burma War* breaks out; the British take Rangoon.

1863 *Battle of Chancellorsville* ends with Union forces defeated by Confederates (*U.S. Civil War*).

1886 *Haymarket Riot* occurs in Chicago when an anarchist's bomb kills several policemen and injures many other policemen and civilians.

1919 Students in Peking protest the Versailles Peace Conference decision that Japan (rather than China) should retain Germany's possessions in Shantung Province. The *May Fourth Movement* marks the beginning of the *Chinese Communist Party.*

1938 *Douglas Hyde* is elected first president of Ireland under the new constitution.

1942 *Battle of the Coral Sea,* first carrier-vs.-carrier sea battle, begins (*World War II*).

The British Royal Air Force begins the first in a series of air raids on *Hamburg (World War II).*

1943 *William Tubman* is elected president of Liberia.

1950 A 100-day strike of United Automobile Workers against the *Chrysler Corporation* ends.

1953 William Inge's drama, *Picnic,* wins a Pulitzer Prize.

1961 *Freedom Rides* depart from Washington, D.C., to test bus desegregation throughout the South.

1970 National Guardsmen fire on antiwar demonstrators at *Kent State University.* Four people are killed and at least nine are wounded.

1982 Argentina's computer-guided missile destroys British destroyer *Sheffield* in battle over *Falkland Islands.*

1986 *Babrak Karmal* resigns as general secretary of the Afghan Communist Party and is replaced by *Najibullah,* former head of the secret police.

1987 *Rashid Karami* resigns as premier of Lebanon.

1989 *Lt. Col. Oliver North* is found guilty of obstruction of justice for his part in the Iran-Contra affair.

may

1996 *Jose Maria Aznar* is selected as the new premier of Spain.

1998 *Theodore (Ted) Kaczynski* is sentenced to four life prison terms for the *unabomber bombings.*

HOLIDAYS

Iran
Jerusalem Day
A day set aside for protesting the annexation of Jerusalem by Israel.

Japan
Children's Day or Kodomo-No-Hi
A day set aside to honor all children of the country and to wish them happiness.

Kyrgyzstan
Constitution Day

Mexico
Puebla Battle Day or Cinco de Mayo
Commemorates defeat of Napoleon III's forces, 1867.

The Netherlands
Liberation Day
Commemorates the liberation from German occupation, 1945.

South Korea
Children's Day

Thailand
Coronation Day
Celebrates the coronation of *King Bhumibol Adulyades,* the titular head of state, 1946.

RELIGIOUS CALENDAR

The Saints
St. Hilary, Bishop of Arles. [d. 449]
St. Mauruntius, abbot. Also called *Mauront.* [d. 701]
St. Avertinus. Invoked against dizziness and headache. Also called *Avertin.* [d. c. 1180]
St. Angelo, martyr and Carmelite. Also called *Angelus.* [d. 1220]
St. Jutta, widow and recluse; patroness of Prussia. Also called *Judith.* [d. 1260]
St. Hydroc, hermit. Also called *Hydoc.* [death date unknown]

BIRTHDATES

1282 *Juan Manuel,* Infante de Castile, Spanish soldier, statesman, writer; his writings provided models for the works of Chaucer, Boccaccio, and Lope de Vega. [d. c. 1349]

1809 *Frederick Augustus Porter Barnard,* U.S. educator; established *Barnard College for Women,* thus extending Columbia University's educational opportunities to women. [d. April 27, 1889]

1813 *Sören Kierkegaard,* Danish philosopher, theologian; called the *Father of Existentialism.* [d. November 11, 1855]

1818 *Karl Marx,* German social philosopher; chief theorist of modern *socialism* and *communism.* [d. March 14, 1883]

1832 *Hubert Howe Bancroft,* U.S. historian; directed the creation of *Western American Historical Series,* a 39-volume history of the American West. [d. March 2, 1918]

1846 *Henryk Sienkiewicz,* Polish novelist, short-story writer; Nobel Prize in literature, 1905. [d. November 15, 1916]

1852 *Pietro Gasparri,* Italian cardinal; Papal Secretary of State, 1914–34. [d. November 18, 1934]

1867 *Nellie Bly (Elizabeth Cochrane Seaman),* U.S. journalist; well known for her unorthodox and aggressive journalistic procedures. [d. January 27, 1922]

1882 *Sir Douglas Mawson,* Australian explorer of Antarctica; made some of most important discoveries regarding that region in the early twentieth century. [d. October 14, 1958]

1883 *Archibald Percival Wavell, 1st Earl Wavell,* British Army field marshal during World War II. [d. May 24, 1950]

1897 *Jacob Shapiro (Jake Gurrah),* U.S. mobster. [d. June 9, 1947]

1899 *Freeman Gosden,* U.S. radio comedian; played Amos in *Amos n' Andy* radio show. [d. December 10, 1982]

1903 *James Beard,* U.S. cooking authority, cook-book author. [d. January 23, 1985]

Sally Stanford (Marcia Busby), U.S. politician; ran

San Francisco brothel; Mayor of Sausalito, California, 1976–78. [d. February 2, 1982]

1906 *Mary Astor (Lucille Langebanke),* U.S. actress. [d. September 25, 1987]

1908 *Rex Harrison (Reginald Carey),* British stage and film actor. [d. June 1, 1990]

1913 *Tyrone (Edmund) Power,* U.S. actor. [d. November 15, 1958]

1915 *Alice Faye (Ann Leppert),* U.S. actress, singer.[d. May 9, 1998]

Richard H(alworth) Rovere, U.S. journalist, author; best known for the commentaries he contributed to the *New Yorker* called "Letter from Washington," 1948–79. [d. November 23, 1979]

1916 *Giani Zail Singh,* Indian statesman; President, 1982–87.[d. December 25, 1994]

1921 *Arthur L. Schawlow,* U.S. physicist; Nobel Prize in physics for his work in spectroscopy (with Nicolaas Bloembergen), 1981.

1925 *Leo Joseph Ryan,* U.S. politician; Congressman, 1973–78; murdered by a member of Jim Jones' Peoples Temple. [d. November 19, 1978]

1927 *Pat(ricia Ann Angela Bridgit) Carroll,* U.S. actress, comedian; Tony Award for *Catch a Star,* 1955; Emmy Award for *Caesar's Hour,* 1956–57.

1941 *Jane Ellen Brody,* U.S. author, journalist; wrote *Jane Brody's Nutrition Book,* 1981.

1943 *Michael Palin,* British actor, author; member of *Monty Python's Flying Circus* comedy group.

1958 *Annette Bening,* U.S. actress; won Academy Award for her performance in *The Grifters,* 1990.

1961 *George Clooney,* U.S. actor.

1962 *Patrick Aloysius Ewing,* U.S. basketball player.

1973 *Tina Yothers,* U.S. actress; known for her role as Jennifer Keaton on television series, *Family Ties,* 1982–89.

HISTORICAL EVENTS

1292 *Adolf, Count of Nassau,* is elected King of Germany.

1645 *Charles I* surrenders to Scottish army at Newark (*English Civil War*).

1705 Holy Roman Emperor *Leopold I* dies and is succeeded by *Josef I.*

1811 British defeat French at *Fuentes d'Oñoro,* Portugal (*Napoleonic Wars*).

1821 *Napoleon I of France* dies at St. Helena, where he has been in exile since 1815.

1860 *Giuseppe Garibaldi* and his thousand Redshirts sail from Genoa to Sicily (*Italian Revolution*).

1867 Mexican army, led by Gen. *Ignacio Zaragoza,* defeats a large French force near *Puebla,* Mexico.

1893 Stocks on *New York Stock Exchange* drop sharply, setting off *Panic of 1893.*

1904 *Cy Young* of Boston Americans Baseball Team becomes first major league pitcher to pitch a perfect game.

1930 *Mahatma Gandhi* is arrested by the British for violating India's salt-tax law in his *civil disobedience* campaign.

1936 Italy captures *Addis Ababa,* ending Ethiopian resistance.

1941 *Isaias Medina Angarita* is inaugurated as president of Venezuela.

1945 Nazi occupation of *Denmark* ends *(World War II).*

A Japanese balloon bomb lands in *Lake-view, Oregon,* killing six people. They represent the first recorded casualties resulting from an enemy attack on the U.S. mainland. *(World War II)*

Poet *Ezra Pound* is charged with treason for making broadcasts on behalf of the Italian Facist regime (*World War II*).

1950 *Gwendolyn Brooks* becomes the first black American to win the Pulitzer Prize for poetry.

The *National Science Foundation* is created as an independent government agency to grant research funds and promote science.

Phumiphon Adundet is crowned King of Thailand as *Rama IX* in ceremonies at Bangkok.

1954 Paraguayan president, *Federico Chaves,* is overthrown in a coup led by army officers including General *Alfredo Stroessner.*

1955 Adler and Ross's *Damn Yankees* premieres in New York.

1957 *Adolf Schaerf* is elected president of Austria.

1958 James Agee is awarded a Pulitzer Prize posthumously for his only novel, *A Death in the Family*.

1959 Senate confirms the nomination of *Potter Stewart* to the U.S. Supreme Court.

1961 *Alan B. Shepard* makes 15-minute flight in *Freedom 7* from Cape Canaveral, reaching altitude of 116 miles and becoming first American in space.

1964 Israel's pipeline from the Sea of Galilee to the southern Negev Desert begins operation.

1973 The University of Miami awards the first female athletic scholarship in the U.S. to *Terry Williams*.

1981 Irish Republican Army hunger striker, *Bobby Sands*, dies in Maze Prison, Belfast.

1987 The U.S. Immigration and Naturalization Service begins accepting applications for work authorization from aliens previously classified as illegal. Under the terms of the amnesty program those who entered the U.S. illegally prior to 1982 will be given legal status.

U.S. Senate and House committees investigating the *Iran-contra affair* begin joint public hearings.

1989 The space shuttle *Atlantis* is launched. Its mission is to send off the *Magellan* spacecraft that will explore Venus.

Manuel Noriega loses the presidential elections in Panama but refuses to acknowledge the loss.

1994 *Yasser Arafat* and Israeli Prime Minister *Yitzhak Rabin* sign an accord that ends Israel's occupation of the Gaza Strip and Jericho.

1996 The *U.S.-Mexico Binational Commission* meets and agrees to eleven pacts between the two countries, most significantly the *Migrants' Rights pact*.

may

MAY
6

HOLIDAYS

Lebanon
Martyrs' Day

Phillipines
Kagitingan Day

Syria
Martyrs' Day

U.S.
Anniversary of the First Postage Stamp
Sponsored by The Philatelic Journalist.

RELIGIOUS CALENDAR

The Saints
St. Evodius, Bishop of Antioch; first to use the word *Christian.* [d. c. 64]
St. John before the Latin Gate, patron of booksellers. [d. c. 94]
St. Edbert, Bishop of Lindisfarne. Also called *Eadbert.* [d. 698]
St. Petronax, Abbot of Monte Cassino. [d. c. 747]

The Beatified
Blessed Prudence, virgin and nun. [d. 1492]
Blessed Edward Jones and *Blessed Anthony Middleton,* martyrs. [d. 1590]
Blessed Francis de Montmorency-Laval. [beatified 1980]
Blessed Jose Maria de Yermo y Porres. [beatified 1990]

BIRTHDATES

1501 *Pope Marcellus II,* pope 1555. [d. May 1, 1555]

1758 *Maximilien François Marie Isidore de Robespierre,* French revolutionary leader; a major figure in the Reign of Terror of the French Revolution. [d. July 28, 1794]

Due André Massena, Prince d'Essling, French Army marshal during French Revolutionary and Napoleonic Wars. [d. April 4, 1817]

1806 *Chapin Aaron Harris,* U.S. dentist; leader in founding *American Journal of Dental Science* and *American Society of Dental Surgeons.*

1812 *Martin Delany,* African American physician and scientist. [d. 1885]

1837 *John Mahlon Marlin,* U.S. firearms inventor, manufacturer. [d. July 1, 1901]

1843 *Grove Karl Gilbert,* U.S. geologist. [d. May 1, 1918]

1853 *Philander Chase Knox,* U.S. politician, lawyer; U.S. Secretary of State, 1909–13. [d. October 12, 1921]

1856 *Sigmund Freud,* Austrian neurologist; the founder of *psychoanalysis.* [d. September 23, 1939]

Robert Edwin Peary, U.S. Arctic explorer; leader of the first expedition to reach the *North Pole,* 1909. [d. February 20, 1920]

1859 *Luis María Drago,* Argentine statesman; famous mainly for his support of the principle of international law known as the *Drago Doctrine,* providing that a nation may not use armed force to collect debts from another nation. [d. 1921]

1867 *Wladislaw Stanislaw Reymont,* Polish novelist; Nobel Prize in literature, 1924. [d. December 5, 1924]

1868 *Nicholas II (Nikolai Aleksandrovich), Czar of Russia,* 1894–1917; his efforts led to *International Peace Conference* at the Hague, 1899; the founding of the *Hague Tribunal;* his rule was terminated by *Russian Revolution* of 1917, Abdicated March 15, 1917. [Executed July 16/17, 1918]

1870 *Amadeo Peter Giannini,* U.S. banker; organized California's Bank of America. [d. June 3, 1949]

John McCutcheon, U.S. cartoonist; Pulitzer Prize in editorial cartooning, 1932. [d. June 10, 1949]

1871 *Victor Grignard,* French chemist; Nobel Prize in

chemistry for developing the *Grignard reaction* (with P. Sabatier), 1912. [d. December 13, 1935]

1875 *William Daniel Leahy,* U.S. admiral during World War II; Chief of Staff to Presidents Franklin Roosevelt and Harry Truman, 1942–49. [d. July 20, 1959]

1888 *Emmanuel Celler,* U.S. politician, lawyer; U.S. Congressman, 1923–72; wrote and guided passage of *U.S. Civil Rights Act.* [d. January 15, 1981]

1895 *Rudolph Valentino (Rodolpho d'Antonguolla),* U.S. actor born in Italy; one of the film idols of the 1920s. [d. August 23, 1926]

1898 *Daniel Gerber,* U.S. baby food manufacturer; President and Chairman of the Board of Gerber Products; responsible for introducing strained baby food into U.S. [d. March 16, 1974]

1902 *Harry (Lewis) Golden,* U.S. author; known for his humorous as well as historical studies of Jews in America. [d. October 2, 1981]

1904 *Harry Edmund Martinson,* Swedish novelist, poet; Nobel Prize in literature, 1974. [d. February 11, 1978]

1909 *Edwin H. Land,* U.S. businessman and inventor, founder of the Polaroid Company. [d. 1991]

1913 *Stewart Granger (James Stewart),* British actor. [d. August 16, 1993]

1914 *Randall Jarrell,* U.S. poet, critic, novelist; recipient of two National Book Awards. [d. October 14, 1965]

1915 *Orson Welles,* U.S. actor, director, producer. [d. October 10, 1985]

Theodore (Harold) White, U.S. journalist, author, chronicler of U.S. presidential campaigns; Pulitzer Prize in nonfiction, 1962. [d. May 15, 1986]

1917 *John (Black Jack) Stewart,* Canadian hockey player; elected to Hall of Fame, 1964.

1926 *Ross Hunter (Martin Fuss),* U.S. film producer. [d. March 10, 1996]

1931 *Willie (Howard) Mays,* U.S. baseball player. Inducted into Baseball Hall of Fame, 1979.

1945 *Bob Seger,* U.S. singer, musician; known for songs, *Night Moves* and *Main Street.*

1950 *Joel Hyatt (Joel Zylberberg),* U.S. lawyer; co-founder, Hyatt Legal Services, 1977.

1952 *Samuel K. Doe,* Liberian statesman; President,

1953 *Tony Blair,* British politician; Prime Minister of England, 1994– .

1959 *Mare Winningham,* U.S. actress.

HISTORICAL EVENTS

1432 *Jan van Eyck* finishes altarpiece for St. John's in Ghent, Belgium.

1527 Spanish and German mercenaries under *Charles V, Holy Roman Emperor,* sack Rome, bringing an end to the *Roman Renaissance.*

1757 *Frederick II of Prussia* captures Prague (*Seven Years' War*).

1840 First adhesive postage stamps, *Penny Blacks,* go on sale in England.

1861 *Arkansas* becomes the ninth state to secede from the Union (*U.S. Civil War*).

1877 *Crazy Horse* and one thousand of his Sioux followers surrender to U.S. troops near Camp Robinson, Nebraska.

1882 The *Chinese Exclusion Act* bars Chinese laborers from entering the U.S.

Fenians murder Chief Secretary of Ireland, *Lord Frederick Cavendish,* and his under-secretary, *Thomas Burke,* in Dublin's Phoenix Park.

1889 *Eiffel Tower* in Paris is completed for the opening of the Universal Exhibition.

1910 *King Edward VII of Great Britain* dies and is succeeded by *George V.*

1919 *Togoland* in West Africa becomes a mandate of France and Great Britain.

1930 Riots and uprisings against British rule break out all over *India* following the arrest of *Mahatma Gandhi.*

1937 The dirigible *Hindenburg* bursts into flames while landing at Lakehurst, N.J., killing 36 persons.

1941 Soviet general secretary *Joseph Stalin* increases his political power by assuming the additional title and responsibilities of premier.

1942 U.S. General *Jonathan Wainwright* surrenders *Corregidor* in the Philippines to the Japanese (*World War II*).

may

Bataan in the Philippines falls to Japan (*World War II*).

1954 *Dr. Roger Bannister* of Great Britain becomes the first person to run the mile in less than four minutes.

1960 U.S. President Dwight D. Eisenhower signs the *Civil Rights Act* of 1960.

Princess Margaret Rose, sister of Queen Elizabeth II of England, is married in Westminster Abbey to *Antony Armstrong-Jones.*

1962 U.S. *Polaris* missile, armed with a nuclear warhead, is launched from the nuclear submarine *Ethan Allen* and successfully explodes near Christmas Island. It is the first test of a nuclear warhead carried by a long-range missile and the first launched from a submarine.

1968 Norman Mailer's book, *The Armies of the Night,* is published.

1974 West German Chancellor *Willy Brandt* resigns in connection with an East German spy affair.

1976 An earthquake measuring 6.5 on the Richter scale kills an estimated 1,000 people in northeastern Italy.

1979 Austrian Chancellor *Bruno Kreisky* wins an unprecedented fourth term of office.

1984 Christian Democratic Party candidate, *Jose Napoleon Duarte,* wins El Salvador's first presidential election in 50 years with no military interference.

Leon Febres Cordero Rivadeneira is elected president of Ecuador.

1994 The *Eurotunnel,* an underground tunnel linking France and England, opens.

RELIGIOUS CALENDAR

Feasts
C. F. W. Walter, Doctor. Minor Lutheran festival.

The Saints
St. Domitian, Bishop of Maestricht. Patron of Huy on the Meuse River, Belgium. [d. c. 560]
St. Liudhard, bishop. [d. c. 602]
SS. Serenicus and *Serenus,* brothers, recluses. Serenicus also called *Cerenicus* and *Seneridus.* [d. c. 669 and 680]
St. John of Beverly, Bishop of York. [d. 721]

The Beatified
Blessed Rose Venerini, virgin. Founder of many schools. [d. 1728]
Blessed Maria Domenica Brun Barbantini. [beatified 1995]
Blessed Guiseppina Bonino. [beatified 1995]
Blessed Maria Alvarado Cardoza. [beatified 1995]
Blessed Angostino Roscelli. [beatified 1995]
Blessed Maria Helena Stollenwerk. [beatified 1995]

BIRTHDATES

1426 *Giovanni Gioviano Pontano,* Italian poet, humanist; State Secretary to Ferdinand I of Naples, 1486–94. [d. September 1503]

1574 *Pope Innocent X,* pope, 1644–55. [d. January 7, 1655]

1812 *Robert Browning,* British poet; husband of Elizabeth Barrett; buried in Westminster Abbey. [d. December 12, 1889]

1833 *Johannes Brahms,* German composer; called one of the great musicians of all times. [d. April 3, 1897]

1836 *Joseph Gurney Cannon (Uncle Joe),* U.S. politician, lawyer; U.S. Congressman for 50 years, from 1873, except for 1891–93 and 1913–15. [d. November 12, 1926]

1840 *Peter Ilyich Tchaikovsky,* Russian composer; renowned for his symphonic works and ballet music. [d. November 6, 1893]

1851 *Adolf von Harnack,* German Protestant theologian; noted for his work on Martin Luther, *Luthers Theologie.* [d. June 10, 1930]

1861 *Rabindranath Tagore,* Bengali poet, playwright, essayist, novelist; Nobel Prize in literature, 1913; knighted, 1915. [d. August 7, 1941]

1870 *Harry Vardon,* British golfer; considered one of the greatest golfers who ever lived; won six British Opens. [d. March 21, 1937]

1885 *Gabby Hayes (George Hayes),* U.S. character actor. [d. February 9, 1969]

1892 *Archibald MacLeish,* U.S. poet, playwright; Pulitzer Prize, 1932, 1953, 1959; Librarian of Congress, 1939–44. [d. April 20, 1982]

Marshall (Josip Broz) Tito, Yugoslav communist leader; created the modern state of *Yugoslavia.* [d. May 4, 1980]

1901 *Gary Cooper (Frank James Cooper),* U.S. actor. [d. May 13, 1961]

1909 *Edwin Herbert Land,* U.S. inventor; invented the Polaroid lens, 1932 and the *Polaroid Land* instant camera, 1947. [d. March 1, 1991]

1919 *Eva Duarte de Perón,* Argentine political leader; as wife of Argentine dictator *Juan Perón,* brought about numerous social reforms. [d. July 26, 1952]

1920 *Elizabeth Lindley Post,* U.S. author; updates and edits the etiquette guides of her husband's grandmother, Emily Post.

1922 *Darren McGavin,* U.S. actor; known for his starring role on television series, *The Night Stalker,* 1974–75.

1923 *Anne Baxter,* U.S. actress; known for her roles in *The Razor's Edge,* 1946, and *All About Eve,* 1950. [d. December 12, 1985]

1927 *Ruth Prawer Jhabvala,* British author.

1928 *Marvin M(orris) Mitchelson,* U.S. lawyer; known for the palimony trial involving Lee Marvin and Michelle Triola Marvin.

1930 *Totie Fields (Sophie Feldman),* U.S. comedienne. [d. August 2, 1978]

1931 *Theresa Brewer,* U.S. singer, actress.

1932 *Pete V(ichi) Domenici,* U.S. politician; Senator, 1972– .

Johnny Unitas (John Constantine), U.S. football player; named greatest quarterback of all time at the fiftieth anniversary of the National Football League.

1934 *Willard Herman Scott, Jr.,* Weatherman for the *Today Show,* 1980– .

1938 *Lester Carl Thurow,* U.S. economist.

1939 *Sidney Altman,* U.S. molecular biologist; Nobel Prize for Chemistry with Thomas R. Cech, 1989.

1950 *Janis Ian (Janis Fink),* U.S. singer, songwriter; Grammy Award for *At Seventeen,* 1975.

HISTORICAL EVENTS

1847 *American Medical Association* is founded in Philadelphia.

1902 *Mt. Soufrière volcano* in Guadeloupe erupts, killing two thousand people.

1915 The *Lusitania* is torpedoed by a German submarine off the coast of Ireland and sinks with a loss of 1198 lives, including 139 Americans, bringing the U.S. and Germany to the brink of war (*World War I*).

1918 *Treaty of Bucharest* is signed between Rumania, Germany, and Austro-Hungary with Rumanian indemnities and cession of territory (*World War I*).

1919 The Supreme Council of the Allies of World War I assigns *German East Africa (Tanganyika)* to the mandate of Great Britain.

1925 *Leon Trotsky* returns from exile in the Caucasus.

1936 First airborne piano recital is given aboard the dirigible *Hindenburg* by *Franz Wagner* on an aluminum grand piano.

1942 The Japanese army forces eleven thousand U.S. and Philippine soldiers and civilians to walk through *Bataan.* Called the "*Death March,*" the journey kills between seven and ten thousand people. (*World War II*)

1953 Cole Porter's musical comedy *Can Can* premieres in New York.

1954 *Dien Bien Phu* is captured from the French by Communist Vietnamese.

Construction begins on the *Mackinac Bridge,* connecting Michigan's upper and lower peninsulas.

1956 *Richard Hofstadter* wins the Pulitzer Prize for his history of U.S. political thought, *The Age of Reform; MacKinlay Kantor* receives the fiction award for *Andersonville.*

1960 U.S. government concedes that U.S. plane shot down by U.S.S.R. was equipped for intelligence purposes; Soviet Premier Khrushchev reports the captured pilot, *Francis Gary Powers,* has confessed to being on a photo-reconnaissance mission.

Leonid I. Brezhnev is chosen by the Soviet Supreme Council as president of the U.S.S.R.

1975 Rally in Saigon celebrates emergence of new military authorities one week after the city's surrender, and marks the 21st anniversary of the communist victory over the French at *Dien Bien Phu.*

1989 Panamanian voters elect *Guillermo Endara* as their new president, but General *Manuel Noriega,* leader of the military regime then ruling the country, nullifies the election.

1993 The *Polish government* approves the *privatization* of over 500 state-owned businesses.

1995 *Jacques Chirac* is elected president of France, ending fourteen years of socialist rule.

1996 The *International Criminal Tribunal* begins the Bosnia-Herzegovina war crimes trial.

1998 *Daimler-Benz,* the German company that produces the Mercedes Benz automobile, announces a merger with the *Chrysler Corporation.* The resulting company name is *Daimler-Chrysler.*

HOLIDAYS

Red Cross Day
Celebrates the birth of Henri Dunant, founder of the International Red Cross, 1828.

V-E Day
Commemorates the end of World War II in Europe and the surrender of the Germans.

France, French Polynesia
Liberation Day

Slovakia
Liberation Day

U.S.
Jean Henri Dunant's Birthday
Sponsored by the Franklin D. Roosevelt Philatelic Society.

U.S. (Missouri)
Harry S. Truman's Birthday

RELIGIOUS CALENDAR

Feasts
The Appearing of St. Michael the Archangel.

The Saints
St. Victor Maurus, martyr Patron of Milan, Italy. [d. c. 303]
St. Acacius, soldier and martyr. One of only two genuine ancient martyrs of Byzantium. Also called *Agathus.* [d. c. 303]
St. Gibrian, priest and hermit. Also called *Gobrian, Gybrian.* [d. c. 515]
St. Desideratus, Bishop of Bourges. Also called Désiré. [d. c. 550]

St. Boniface IV, pope. Elected 608. Converted the Pantheon in Rome into a Christian church. [d. 615]
St. Benedict II, pope. Elected 684. Streamlined the procedure of papal elections. [d. 685]
SS. Wiro and *Plechelm,* bishops, and *St. Otger,* missionary. [d. 8th century]
St. Peter, Archbishop of Tarentaise. [d. 1175]

BIRTHDATES

1668 *Alain René Lesage,* French novelist, dramatist; author of *L'Historie de Gil Blas de Santellane.* [d. November 17, 1747]

1753 *Miguel Hidalgo y Costilla,* Mexican priest, revolutionary leader; known as the *Father of Mexican Independence.* [d. August 1, 1811]

1821 *William Henry Vanderbilt,* U.S. financier; son of Cornelius Vanderbilt (May 27), and successor to his empire. [d. December 8, 1885]

1828 *Jean Henri Dunant,* Swiss philanthropist; founded *International Red Cross.* Recipient of the first Nobel Peace Prize (with F. Passy), 1901. [d. October 30, 1910]

1829 *Louis Moreau Gottschalk,* U.S. pianist, composer; renowned in international music circles of the period for both his classical style and his own compositions. [d. December 18, 1869]

1847 *Oscar Hammerstein,* U.S. producer; pioneer opera impresario; grandfather of composer Oscar Hammerstein II (July 12). [d. August 1, 1919]

1861 *Rabindranath Tagore;* Nobel Prize for literature in 1913. [d. 1941]

1864 *John Galen Howard,* U.S. architect. [d. July 18, 1931]

1877 *Oscar Bloch,* French linguist. [d. April 15, 1937]

1884 *Harry S Truman,* U.S. politician, U.S. Vice-President, 1945; U.S. President, 1945–1953, succeeding to presidency upon the death of Franklin D. Roosevelt; served as president during end of World War II; responsible for the decision to drop atomic bombs on Hiroshima and Nagasaki. His term also encompassed the Korean War and the era of McCarthyism. [d. December 26, 1972]

1885 *Thomas B(ertram) Costain,* U.S. historical novelist; author of *The Silver Chalice.* [d. October 8, 1965]

1895 *Fulton J(ohn) Sheen,* U.S. Roman Catholic bishop; well known for radio and television broadcasts during 1950s. [d. December 9, 1979]

Edmund Wilson, U.S. literary and social critic; noted for his criticisms of Ernest Hemingway's works. [d. June 12, 1972]

1897 *Philip F. La Follette,* U.S. politician, lawyer; Governor of Wisconsin, 1931–33; 1935–39. [d. August 18, 1965]

Roscoe H(enry) Hillenkoetter, U.S. naval officer, government official; first director of Central Intelligence Agency, 1947–50; helped establish CIA as vanguard anti-Communist espionage organization. [d. June 18, 1982]

1899 *Friedrich August von Hayek,* British economist born in Austria; Nobel Prize in economics (with G. Myrdal), 1974. [d. March 23, 1992]

1902 *André Michael Lwoff,* French microbiologist; Nobel Prize in physiology or medicine for research in genetics and enzymes and virus synthesis (with J. Monod and F. Jacob), 1965.[d. September 30, 1994]

1905 *Red Nichols (Ernest Loring Nichols),* U.S. musician, cornetist and bandleader; formed a group, *The Five Pennies,* very popular during 1930s and 1940s. [d. June 28, 1965]

1910 *Mary Lou Williams,* U.S. pianist, composer, arranger; known as the *Queen of Jazz;* composed "What's Your Story, Morning Glory?" [d. May 28, 1981]

1920 *Sloan Wilson,* U.S. novelist; author of *The Man in the Gray Flannel Suit.*

1926 *David Frederick Attenborough,* British author, naturalist; travel writer, broadcaster for Public Broadcasting System; wrote television series, *Zoo Quest,* 1956–82.

Don Rickles, U.S. comedian; known for his comedy style based on insults.

1928 *Theodore Chaikin (Ted) Sorensen,* U.S. lawyer, government official; special counsel to the president, 1961–64.

1932 *Charles (Sonny) Liston,* U.S. boxer, actor; Heavyweight champ who lost his title to Muhammed Ali, 1962–64. [d. January 5, 1971]

1936 *James Robert Thompson,* U.S. politician; Governor of Illinois, 1977–79, 1983–87.

1937 *Dennis Webster DeConcini,* U.S. politician; Senator, 1976–94.

Thomas Pynchon, U.S. novelist; author of *Gravity's Rainbow.*

1940 *Peter (Bradford) Benchley,* U.S. novelist; author of *Jaws.*

Rick (Eric Hilliard) Nelson, U.S. singer, actor; known for his role on television series, *The Adventures of Ozzie and Harriet;* sold thirty-five million records before the age of twenty-one. [d. December 31, 1985]

1942 *Angel Thomas Cordero,* Puerto Rican jockey; first jockey to win over ten million dollars in one year.

1943 *Toni Tennille,* U.S. singer; member of the singing duo, *Captain and Tennille.*

1945 *Keith Jarrett,* U.S. composer, musician.

1948 *Marc Bolan (Mark Field),* British musician; member of the rock group, *T. Rex.* [d. September 16, 1977]

1952 *Beth Henley,* U.S. dramatist; Pulitzer Prize for *Crimes of the Heart,* 1981.

1955 *Alex Van Halen,* U.S. musician; member of the rock group, *Van Halen.*

1964 *Melissa Gilbert,* U.S. actress; known for her role as Laura Ingalls Wilder on television series, *Little House on the Prarie,* 1974–82.

HISTORICAL EVENTS

1559 Elizabeth of England assents to new *Act of Supremacy* defining crown's authority in the church and establishing use of *Book of Common Prayer.*

1794 *U.S. Post Office* is established.

1846 *Zachary Taylor* and his American troops defeat Mexicans at the *Battle of Palo Alto (Mexican War).*

1852 *Treaty of London* is signed by Great Britain, France, Russia, Austria, Sweden, and Prussia, guaranteeing the integrity of *Denmark.*

1918 *Ferdinand Foch* of France is appointed Allied Commander-in-Chief at the *Conference of Doullens (World War I).*

1929 Norway annexes *Jan Mayen Island.*

1940 *Rafael Angel Caldron Guardia* is inaugurated as president of Costa Rica.

1942 U.S. carrier-based planes inflict heavy damage on Japanese fleet in the *Coral Sea (World War II).*

1945 The German High Command surrenders unconditionally to the Allies (*World War II*).

1952 U.S. planes bomb *Suan, Korea* (*Korean War*).

1962 Stephen Sondheim's musical, *A Funny Thing Happened on the Way to the Forum,* premieres in New York.

1964 Former U.S. President *Harry S Truman,* on his 80th birthday, becomes the first former president to address a regular session of the Senate.

1967 Heavyweight boxing champion *Muhammad Ali (Cassius Clay)* is indicted by a federal grand jury in Houston, Texas, after refusing induction into the U.S. armed forces.

1968 *Catfish Hunter* of the Kansas City A's pitches a perfect game against the Minnesota Twins.

1970 Construction workers disrupt student *antiwar demonstrations* in New York City's Wall Street.

The Beatles release *Let It Be,* their final album recorded as a group.

Jose Figueres Ferrer is inaugurated as president of Costa Rica.

1972 President Richard Nixon orders the mining of North Vietnamese ports and a naval blockade of the country (*Vietnam War*).

1973 Siege of *Wounded Knee* ends after 70 days as occupying Indians surrender under terms of a new cease-fire.

1974 *Daniel Oduber Quiros* is inaugurated as president of Costa Rica.

1976 *Clarence M. Kelly,* Director of the *FBI,* apologizes to the public for some of the FBI's activities during J. Edgar Hoover's 48-year term as director.

1986 *Oscar Arias* is inaugurated as president of Costa Rica.

1987 U.S. politician, *Gary Hart,* withdraws from the presidential race amidst allegations of marital infidelity.

1988 *Rodrigo Borja Cevallos* is elected president of Ecuador.

1996 *South Africa* adopts a new constitution.

may

MAY
9

HOLIDAYS

Armenia
Peace Day

Belarus
Victory Day

Czech Republic
Anniversary of Liberation

Poland
Victoria Day
Celebrates the end of World War II
in Europe.

Romania
Independence Day

Russia (Bashkir)
Victory Day

Thailand
Ploughing Ceremony

United Kingdom (Channel Islands)
Liberation Day

RELIGIOUS CALENDAR

The Saints
St. Beatus, priest and hermit. [d. c. 112]
St. Pachomius, abbot. Founder of Christian monasticism. Also called *the Elder.* [d. 348]
St. Gerontius, Bishop of Cervia. [d. 501]

The Beatified
Blessed Nicholas Albergati, Bishop of Bologna and Cardinal. [d. 1443]

BIRTHDATES

1775 *Jacob Jennings Brown,* U.S. general; prominent in War of 1812. [d. February 24, 1828]

1785 *James Pollard Espy,* U.S. meteorologist; a pioneer in the scientific methods of predicting weather. [d. January 24, 1860]

1800 *John Brown,* U.S. abolitionist; legendary antislavery figure. [d. December 2, 1859]

1845 *Gustav de Laval,* Swedish scientist; developed first successful *steam turbines* for small engines. [d. February 2, 1913]

1860 *Sir J(ames) M(atthew) Barrie,* Scottish dramatist, novelist; author of *Peter Pan.* [d. June 19, 1937]

1873 *Howard Carter,* British Egyptologist; discovered tomb of *Tutankhamen,* 1922. [d. 1939]

1874 *Dame Lilian Baylis,* British theatrical manager; associated with *Old Vic Theatre* and *Sadler's Wells Theatre.* [d. 1937]

1882 *Henry John Kaiser,* U.S. industrialist; built *San Francisco Bay Bridge,* 1933; *Bonneville Dam,* 1934; *Grand Coulee Dam,* 1939. Built "Liberty Ships" in World War II: laying of keel to

launching was only 30 days. [d. August 24, 1967]

1883 *José Ortega y Gasset,* Spanish philosopher; one of foremost Spanish thinkers of the 20th century. [d. October 18, 1955]

1886 *Francis Beverly Biddle,* U.S. lawyer, government official; first chairperson, National Labor Relations Board; was the judge at Nuremberg trials. [d. October 4, 1968]

1904 *Gregory Bateson,* U.S. author, anthropologist; married to Margaret Mead. [d. July 4, 1980]

1910 *Barbara Blackburn Woodhouse,* U.S. author, television personality; wrote *Dog Training My Way,* 1981. [d. July 9, 1988]

1914 *Hank Snow,* U.S. singer.

1918 *Mike Wallace,* U.S. television interviewer, commentator; correspondent for the TV news show *60 Minutes,* 1968– .

1921 *Daniel J. Berrigan,* U.S. poet, priest; convicted of destroying draft records with his brother Philip, 1968.

Mona Van Duyn, U.S. poet; first woman named as U.S. poet laureate, 1992.

1927 *Manfred Eigen,* German physicist; Nobel Prize in

chemistry for research on high-speed chemical reactions (with R. G. Norrish and G. Porter), 1967.

1928 *Richard Alonzo (Pancho) Gonzalez,* U.S. tennis player, coach; world professional tennis champion eight times. [d. July 3, 1995]

1936 *Albert Finney,* British actor.

1937 *Glenda Jackson,* British actress; two Oscar Awards for *Women in Love,* 1970, and *A Touch of Class,* 1973.

Jose Rafael Moneo, Spanish architect, Pritzker Architecture Prize winner, 1996.

1940 *James L. Brooks,* U.S. producer, director, actor; co-created television series, *The Mary Tyler Moore Show.*

1946 *Candice Bergen,* U.S. actress, photojournalist.

1947 *Josie Natori,* Philippine-born fashion designer.

1949 *Billy Joel,* U.S. singer, songwriter, musician.

1960 *Tony Gwynn,* U.S. baseball player; Gold Glove Award winner 1986–87, 1989–91.

1965 *Stevie Yzerman,* Canadian hockey player.

HISTORICAL EVENTS

1846 Americans under Zachary Taylor defeat Mexicans in the *Battle of Resaca de la Palma (Mexican War).*

1901 *Australia* opens its first parliament at Melbourne.

1911 All Chinese railroads are nationalized.

1915 Portugal declares war on Germany (*World War I*).

The *Second Battle of Artois* starts on the Western Front with simultaneous French and British attacks on German positions (*World War I*).

1916 The *American Federation of Teachers* is founded.

1926 Rear Admiral *Richard Byrd* of the U.S. Navy and Floyd Bennett complete the first flight over the *North Pole.*

1936 *Ethiopia* is formally annexed to Italy (*World War II*).

1937 The coronation march by *William Walton, Crown Imperial,* is first performed by the BBC in London in anticipation of the coronation of *George VI.*

1940 British troops occupy *Iceland* (*World War II*).

1942 U.S. carrier *Wasp* launches British aircraft to reinforce troops in *Malta (World War II).*

1944 Soviet troops regain the Black Sea port of *Sevastopol* which had been occupied by Germany for two years (*World War II*).

1951 *Matthew Ridgway* is named Far Eastern commander and head of United Nations forces in Korea (*Korean War*).

Panama's Congress names *Alcibiades Arosemena* to replace President *Arnulfo Arias,* who had attempted to void the constitution and set up a dictatorship.

1960 U.S. Food and Drug Administration approves the sale of *birth control pills.*

Federation of Nigeria is admitted to the British Commonwealth.

1961 Shah *Mohammad Pahlavi* dissolves the Iranian Parliament and renders power to the newly appointed premier, *Ali Amini.*

1965 U.S.S.R. launches an instrumented space station, *Lunik 5,* from a rocket previously placed in orbit around the Earth.

1969 Roman Catholic Church issues a revised calendar which eliminates more than 200 saints.

1974 U.S. House of Representatives begins committee hearings on possibility of impeachment of *Richard M. Nixon.*

1978 The body of former Italian prime minister *Aldo Moro,* kidnapped by *Red Brigade* terrorists, is found in Rome.

1979 U.S. and U.S.S.R. complete *SALT II* agreement to limit strategic arms.

1983 *Pope John Paul II* announces the reversal of the Catholic Church's condemnation of *Galileo Galilei,* the 17th-century scientist who espoused the heliocentric nature of the solar system.

1986 Norwegian prime minister, *Gro Harlem Bruntland,* announces her cabinet appointments. Eight women are selected, representing a world record for female cabinet representation.

MAY
10

HOLIDAYS

Guatemala
Mother's Day

Romania
Independence Day

U.S. (North Carolina, South Carolina)
Confederate Memorial Day

RELIGIOUS CALENDAR

The Saints

St. Calepodius, martyr. Also called *Galepodius.* [d. 222]

SS. Alphius and his companions, martyrs; principal patrons of Vaste in the diocese of Otranto and of Lentini, in Sicily. [d. 251]

SS. Gordian and *Epimachus,* martyrs. [d. c. 362 and 250]

St. Catald, Bishop of Taranto, and *St. Conleth,* Bishop of Kildare. Also called *Cataldus* and *Conlaed.* [d. c. 685 and c. 520]

St. Solangia, virgin and martyr; patron of Berry Province, France. Also called *Genevieve of Berry, Solange.* [d. 880]

St. Antoninus, Archbishop of Florence. Also called *Antonino, Little Antony.* [d. 1459]

The Beatified

Blessed Beatrice of Este, virgin and nun. [d. 1226]

Blessed John of Avila, priest; one of the most influential and eloquent religious leaders of sixteenth-century Spain. [d. 1569]

BIRTHDATES

1755 *Robert Gray,* U.S. sailor, explorer; captained the first U.S. ship to circumnavigate the world, 1787–90; discovered the *Columbia River* in the American northwest. [d. 1806]

1770 *Louis Nicolas Davout,* Marshal of France during Napoleonic period, 1804; Minister of War during Hundred Days. [d. June 1, 1823]

1788 *Augustin Fresnel,* French physicist; established the transverse wave theory of light; designed *Fresnel lens.* [d. July 14, 1827]

1808 *Elisha Root,* U.S. mechanic, inventor; one of first to use principle of interchangeable parts in production. [d. August 31, 1865]

1813 *Montgomery Blair,* U.S. politician; Postmaster General, 1861–64. [d. July 27, 1883]

1823 *John Sherman,* U.S politician, government official; leading financial expert. [d. October 22, 1900]

1826 *Henry Clifton Sorby,* British geologist; discovered the microstructure of steel, marking the beginning of modern metallurgical science. [d. March 9, 1908]

1838 *John Wilkes Booth,* U.S. actor; assassin of President Abraham Lincoln. [d. April 26, 1865]

1841 *James Gordon Bennett,* U.S. publisher; founder of Paris edition of the New York *Herald.* [d. May 14, 1918]

1843 *Kaufmann Kohler,* U.S. rabbi; leader of Reformed Judaism. [d. January 28, 1926]

1850 *Sir Thomas Johnstone Lipton,* British merchant; founder of a financial empire based on tea, coffee, and cocoa. [d. October 2, 1931]

1878 *Gustav Stresemann,* German statesman; Nobel Peace Prize (with A. Briand), 1926. [d. October 3, 1929]

1886 *Karl Barth,* Swiss theologian. [d. December 9, 1968]

1888 *Max Steiner,* U.S. composer, born in Austria. [d. December 28, 1971]

1890 *Alfred Jodl,* German army general; helped plan most of Germany's World War II military campaigns. [d. October 16, 1946]

1898 *Ariel Durant (Ada Kaufman Durant),* U.S. historian, writer; co-author with husband Will Durant of numerous works which provided detailed, comprehensive history of civilization in a popularized format. [d. October 25, 1981]

1899 *Fred Astaire (Frederick Austerlitz),* U.S. dancer and actor. [d. June 22, 1987]

1902 *David O. Selznick,* U.S. film producer. [d. June 22, 1965]

1908 *Carl Albert,* U.S. lawyer, politician; Congressman, 1947–82; Speaker of the House, 1971–76.

1909 *Maybell (Mother) Carter,* U.S. singer, songwriter; member of the country singing group, *The Carter Family.* [d. October 23, 1978]

1918 *T(homas) Berry Brazelton,* U.S. physician, author; wrote *On Becoming a Family.*

1919 *Ella Tambussi Grasso,* U.S. politician; Governor of Connecticut, 1975–81. [d. February 5, 1981]

1921 *Nancy Walker (Anne Myrtle Swoyer),* U.S. actress, singer; known for her supporting roles on television series, *McMillan and Wife,* 1971–76, and *Rhoda,* 1974–76. [d. March 25, 1992]

1934 *Judith Jamison,* U.S. dancer.

1940 *Wayne Dyer,* U.S. author; wrote *Your Erroneous Zones,* 1976, and *The Sky's the Limit,* 1980.

1946 *Donovan (Leitch),* Scottish folk-rock singer.

Dave Mason, British musician; member of the rock group, *Traffic.*

1955 *Mark David Chapman,* U.S. murderer; shot and killed

John Lennon, December 8, 1980.

1958 *Ellen Ochoa,* U.S. astronaut; flew aboard the space shuttle *Discovery,* 1993, becoming the first female Hispanic astronaut.

HISTORICAL EVENTS

1307 *Robert Bruce,* Scottish king, defeats English at *Ayrshire.*

1774 *Louis XV of France* dies and is succeeded by his grandson, *Louis XVI.*

1775 *Second Continental Congress* convenes in Philadelphia.

Ethan Allen and his *Green Mountain Boys* capture *Fort Ticonderoga* from the British *(American Revolution).*

1796 Bonaparte of France defeats Austrians at *Lodi (Napoleonic Wars).*

1849 *Astor Place Riot* takes place in New York City, following a controversial performance of *Macbeth;* 22 people are killed and 36 hurt.

1869 *Golden Spike* is driven at Promontory, Utah, to complete the first transcontinental railroad in the U.S.

1871 Franco-German peace treaty is signed at Frankfurt; France cedes Alsace and Lorraine *(Franco-German War).*

1876 *U.S. Centennial Exposition* opens in Philadelphia.

1908 The first *Mothers' Day* is observed in Philadelphia, based on the suggestions of *Julia Ward Howe* and *Anne Jarvis.*

1917 Major General *John J. Pershing* is named to

command the U.S. forces in France *(World War I).*

1921 *Greenland* is officially declared a Danish possession.

1940 Germany invades *Luxembourg, Netherlands,* and *Belgium* by land and air *(World War II).*

Winston Churchill becomes Prime Minister of Great Britain.

1941 Nazi party leader, *Rudolf Hess,* parachutes into Glasgow in an unauthorized attempt to negotiate peace between Great Britain and Germany *(World War II).*

1943 German troops in *Tunisia* surrender unconditionally to the Allied Forces *(World War II).*

1950 Haitian president *Dumarasais Estime* is forced to resign in favor of a military junta led by General *Paul Magloire.*

1951 Veterans of *Korean War* are officially acknowledged by U.S. Congress, thus entitling them to veteran's benefits.

1957 *Gabriel Paris* stages a military coup against President *Gustavo Rojas Pinilla* in Colombia. The new junta repeals censorship laws and frees political prisoners.

1960 U.S. atomic submarine *Triton* completes an 84-day submerged voyage around the world.

Lunch counters at four national and two local stores in Nashville, Tennessee, are desegregated without incident after a month of negotiations.

1962 Engineers at the Massachusetts Institute of

Technology bounce a *laser beam* off the moon's surface, producing the first artificial light to appear on another celestial body.

1972 Irish voters overwhelmingly approve entry into the *European Economic Community* in a national referendum.

1981 *François Mitterand,* a Socialist, defeats incumbent

Val éry Giscard in French presidential election.

1984 A district court rules that the U.S. government was negligent in conducting above-ground *nuclear tests* in Nevada from 1951 to 1962. The government is held liable for cancer among residents exposed to the radioactive fallout from these tests.

1988 *Michel Rocard* is appointed premier of France.

1994 *Nelson Mandela* is sworn in as the first black president of South Africa after the first free elections in the country's history.

1998 *Raul Cubas Grav* is elected president of Paraguay.

HOLIDAYS

U.S. (Minnesota)
Minnesota Day
Commemorating the state's admission into the Union in 1858.

RELIGIOUS CALENDAR

Feasts
SS. Philip and *James,* (Formerly May 1, which see.)

The Saints
St. Mamertus, Bishop of Vienne. Author of the Rogation processions. Also called *Mammertus.* [d. c. 475]

St. Tudy, monk and abbot. Also called *Tudec.* [d. 6th century]

St. Comgall, Abbot of Bangor. One of the founders of Irish monasticism. [d. 603]

St. Asaph, bishop. Founded the church of Llanasa in Flintshire and at Llanelwy. [d. 7th century]

St. Gengulf, a Burgundian knight. Also called *Gengoul.* [d. 760]

St. Fremund, hermit and martyr. [d. 866]

St. Majolus, Abbot of Cluny. Also called *Maieul, Maiolus, Mayeul.* [d. 994]

St. Ansfrid, Bishop of Utrecht. [d. 1010]

St. Walter of L'Esterp, abbot. [d. 1070]

The English Carthusian Martyrs, with Blessed John Haile, monk. London community of monks martyred under the Tudor persecution. General feast kept in Archdiocese of Westminster and by the Carthusians. [d. 1540]

St. Francis di Girolamo, Jesuit priest. [d. 1716]

St. Ignatius of Laconi, Franciscan monk. [d. 1781]

The Beatified
Blessed Albert of Bergamo, Dominican tertiary. [d. 1279]

Blessed Vivaldo, a solitary. Also called *Ubaldo.* [d. 1300]

Blessed Benincasa, hermit. [d. 1426]

Blessed Aloysius Rabata, Carmelite prior. [d. 1490]

Blessed Ladislaus of Gielniow, Franciscan missioner; one of the principal patrons of Poland. [d. 1505]

BIRTHDATES

1720 *Karl Friedrich Hieronymous, Baron von Munchhausen,* German soldier, huntsman; reputedly a great storyteller whose name is now commonly associated with absurdly exaggerated stories. [d. February 22, 1797]

1722 *Pieter Camper,* Dutch naturalist, anthropologist; known for early experiments in *comparative anatomy;* discovered the comparatively large air content of bird bones. [d. April 7, 1789]

1752 *Johann Friedrich Blumenbach,* German naturalist, anthropologist; recognized as the *Father of Modern Anthropology.* [d. January 22, 1840]

1811 *George Whitfield Scranton,* U.S. manufacturer; developed process for smelting iron ore with anthracite coal; *Scranton, Pennsylvania* is named for him. [d. March 24, 1861]

1852 *Charles W. Fairbanks,* U.S. Vice-President, 1905–9. [d. June 4, 1918]

1854 *Ottmur Mergenthaler,* U.S. inventor of *Linotype machine.* [d. October 28, 1899]

1880 *George Edmund Haynes,* U.S. sociologist, civil rights leader; one of founders of the *National Urban League,* 1910. [d. January 8, 1960]

1888 *Irving Berlin (Israel Baline),* U.S. composer, songwriter; writer of over 800 popular songs as well as dozens of Broadway musical scores. [d. September 22, 1989]

1891 *Henry Morgenthau, Jr.,* U.S. government official, conservationist; as Secretary of the Treasury under Franklin D. Roosevelt, was responsible for engineering support and financing of the

New Deal programs, as well as the unparalleled expansion of the U.S. budget during World War II. [d. February 6, 1967]

1892 *Dame Margaret Rutherford,* British character actress. [d. May 22, 1972]

1893 *Martha Graham,* U.S. dancer, teacher, and choreographer of modern dance. [d. April 1, 1991]

1894 *Ellsworth Bunker,* U.S. diplomat; U.S. Ambassador-at-Large, 1966–67; 1973–78; Ambassador to Vietnam, 1967–73. [d. September 28, 1984]

1895 *William Grant Still,* U.S. musician, conductor, and composer. First African American to conduct a symphony orchestra. [d. 1978]

1897 *Robert Ellsworth Gross,* U.S. industrialist. [d. September 3, 1961]

1904 *Salvador Dali,* Spanish surrealist painter. [d. January 23, 1989]

1906 *Jay C. Higginbotham,* U.S. jazz trombonist, singer. [d. May 26, 1973]

1911 *Phil Silvers (Philip Silversmith),* U.S. comedian. [d. November 1, 1985]

1912 *Foster Murrell Brooks,* U.S. comedian, actor.

1916 *Camilo Jose Cela,* Spanish writer; Nobel Prize for Literature (1989). Author of La Familia de Pascual Duarte.

1918 *Richard Philips Feynman,* U.S. physicist; Nobel Prize for research in quantum electrodynamics (with J.S. Schwinger and S. I. Tomonaga), 1965. [d. February 15, 1988]

1924 *Antony Hewish,* British radio astronomer; Nobel Prize in physics for developing revolutionary *radio telescope systems* (with Sir M. Ryle), 1974.

1927 *Mort (Lyon) Sahl,* U.S. comedian.

1932 *Valentino (Valentino Garavani),* Italian fashion designer.

1933 *Louis Farrakhan,* U.S. religious leader.

1938 *Doug McClure,* U.S. actor; known for his role as Trampas on television series, *The Virginian,* 1962–71. [d. February 5, 1995]

1946 *Robert Koffler Jarvik,* U.S. physician; designed the Jarvik-7, an artificial heart first used in Barney Clark, 1982.

1950 *Randy Quaid,* U.S. actor.

1963 *Natasha Richardson,* British actress.

HISTORICAL EVENTS

330 *Constantinople* becomes new capital of the Roman Empire.

973 English *King Edgar* is crowned at Bath.

1258 *Treaty of Corbeil* between *Louis IX of France* and *James of Aragon* regulates the Pyrenees frontier.

1812 British Prime Minister *Spencer Percival* is assassinated in the lobby of the House of Commons by a bankrupt broker, *John Bellingham.*

1858 *Minnesota* enters the Union as the 32nd state.

1867 Grand Duchy of *Luxembourg* is declared independent by the Treaty of London.

1894 *Pullman strike* in U.S. ends in defeat for organized labor.

1910 *Glacier National Park* in Montana is established.

1931 The failure of the Austrian *Credit-Anstalt* (Austria's largest bank) marks the beginning of the financial collapse of central Europe.

1935 U.S. President Franklin D. Roosevelt creates the *Rural Electrification Administration* to extend electricity into rural areas of the U.S.

1938 Richard Rodgers' and Lorenz Hart's *I Married an Angel* premieres in New York.

1943 U.S. amphibious force lands on *Attu* in the Aleutians and annihilates 2,350 Japanese defenders (*World War II*).

1949 *Israel* is admitted to the United Nations.

Siam is officially renamed *Thailand.*

1950 *Grand Coulee Dam* in the State of Washington is dedicated by U.S. President Harry S. Truman.

1960 The *S.S. France,* the world's longest passenger ship, is launched at St. Nazaire, France.

1972 The *F.B.I.* announces that women will be recruited for special agent positions for the first time.

1973 Formal relations between *East* and *West Germany* are established by a treaty ratified by the West German Bundestag.

1976 President Gerald Ford signs the *Federal Election*

Campaign Act into law. It limits individual contributions and the amount that candidates can spend on primaries.

1978 Anti-government rioting spreads to Iranian capital where religious Muslim demonstrators demand the removal of *Shah Mohammad Reza Pahlavi.*

Secessionist guerrillas of the *Congo National Liberation Front* invade Zaire's Shaba province with the active support of Angolan and Cuban forces.

1983 A recently discovered comet, *IRAS-Araki-Alcock,* passes 2.9 million miles from Earth, the closest of any comet in two hundred years.

1987 The trial of former Nazi chief, *Klaus Barbie,* begins in Lyons, France. He is charged with crimes committed during World War II as leader of the German Gestapo in Lyons.

1989 *Kenya* appeals for a ban on ivory as the existence of the African elephant is threatened.

1998 *India* conducts underground *nuclear testing* in the state of Rajasthan.

Joseph Estrada is elected president of the Philippines.

may

HOLIDAYS

Italy
Festival of the Tricolor

RELIGIOUS CALENDAR

The Saints

SS. Nereus, Achilleus and *Domitilla,* martyrs. [d. c. 1st century] Optional Memorial.

St. Pancras, martyr; in Middle Ages regarded as protector against false oaths and as the avenger of perjury. [d. c. 304] Optional Memorial.

St. Epiphanius, Bishop of Salamis. [d. 403]

St. Modoaldus, Bishop of Trier and advisor to King Dagobert. Also called *Modowaldus.* [d. c. 640]

St. Rictrudis, widow and abbess. Founded the double Monastery at Marchiennes. Also called *Rictrudes.* [d. 688]

St. Germanus, Patriarch of Constantinople. [d. 732]

St. Dominic of the Causeway, hermit and hospice-builder. [d. c. 1109]

The Beatified

Blessed Francis Patrizzi, member of Servite Order. [d. 1328]

Blessed Gemma of Solmona, virgin and recluse. [d. 1429]

Blessed Jane of Portugal, virgin and Dominican lay-sister. Daughter of King Alphonso V of Portugal. [d. 1490]

Blessed Maria Antonia Bandres. [beatified 1996]

Blessed Maria Raffaella Cimatti. [beatified 1996]

Blessed Candida Maria de Jesus Cipitria y Barriola. [beatified 1996]

Blessed Gennaro Sarnelli, priest. [beatified 1996]

Blessed Alfredo Ildefonso Schuster. [beatified 1996]

Blessed Filippo Smaldone, priest. [beatified 1996]

BIRTHDATES

1803 *Baron Justus von Liebig,* German organic chemist; established first practical teaching laboratory for study of chemistry. Discovered chloroform, aldehyde; considered the founder of agricultural chemistry. [d. April 10, 1873]

1804 *Robert Baldwin,* Canadian statesman; formed first Canadian administration after Act of Union. [d. December 9, 1858]

1812 *Edward Lear,* British author, artist; best known for limericks and nonsense verse. [d. January 29, 1888]

1816 *Sir Edmund Beckett, 1st Baron Grimthorpe,* British lawyer, author, inventor, architect; superintended construction of *Big Ben.* [d. April 29, 1905]

1820 *Florence Nightingale,* British nurse, hospital reformer, philanthropist. First woman to receive British Order of Merit. [d. August 13, 1910]

1828 *Dante Gabriel Rossetti (Gabriel Charles Dante),* British poet, painter; founder of *Pre-Raphaelite Brotherhood.* [d. April 9, 1882]

1842 *Jules Emile Frédéric Massenet,* French composer; winner of *Prix de Rome,* 1863. [d. August 13, 1912]

1850 *Henry Cabot Lodge,* U.S. politician, historian; grandfather of Henry Cabot Lodge, Jr. (July 5). [d. November 9, 1924]

1857 *William Archibald Dunning,* U.S. historian, educator; instructor in history, Columbia University, 1886–1922. [d. August 25, 1922]

1859 *Lillian Nordica,* U.S. operatic soprano, best known for Wagnerian roles. [d. May 10, 1914]

1871 *Oscar de Priest,* U.S. politician, served in the House of Representatives. [d. 1951]

1880 *Lincoln Ellsworth,* U.S. polar explorer, scientist; first man to accomplish air crossings of both the Arctic, 1926, and Antarctic, 1933. [d. May 26, 1951]

1895 *William Francis Giauque,* U.S. chemist; Nobel Prize in chemistry for studies of properties of substances at extremely low temperatures, 1949. [d. March 29, 1982]

1901 Sir *Christopher Hinton, Lord Hinton of Bankshire, Baron of Dulwich,* British nuclear engineer; built first large scale nuclear power plant in England, 1956. [d. June 22, 1983]

1902 *Philip Wylie,* U.S. novelist, critic; best known for *Generation of Vipers,* an attack on traditional American institutions. [d. October 25, 1971]

1903 *Wilfred Hyde-White,* British character actor. [d. May 6, 1991]

1906 *William Maurice Ewing,* U.S. geologist, oceanographer; best known for studies of ocean floor and underwater exploration with seismic waves.[d. May 7, 1974]

1910 *Dorothy C. Hodgkin,* British chemist; Nobel Prize in chemistry for work determining structure of *Vitamin B-12,* 1964. [d. July 29, 1994]

1914 *Howard K. Smith,* U.S. news commentator.

c1915 *Mary Kay Ash,* U.S. businesswoman; founder of Mary Kay Cosmetics.

1918 *Julius Rosenberg;* he and his wife, Ethel, were first U.S. civilians to be executed for espionage. [d. June 19, 1953]

1921 *Farley McGill Mowat,* Canadian author; known for his books about Northern Canadian Eskimos which have sold seven million copies.

1925 *(Lawrence Peter) Yogi Berra,* U.S. baseball player, manager, coach. Elected to Baseball Hall of Fame, 1972.

1929 *Burt Bacharach,* U.S. composer, pianist.

Samuel D. Nujoma, Namibian politician; President of Namibia, 1990– .

1936 *Tom Snyder,* U.S. broadcast journalist; known as host of television news show, *Tomorrow,* 1973–81.

Frank Stella, U.S. artist; known for his abstract and three-dimensional art.

1937 *George Carlin,* U.S. comedian, actor.

1938 *Andrei (Alekseyevich) Amalrik,* Soviet author, dissident, historian; outspoken in his criticism both of Russian and western policies. Died in an automobile accident. [d. November 11, 1980]

1942 *Susan Hampshire,* British actress; three Emmy Awards, 1970, 1971, and 1973.

1944 *Christopher Patten,* British politician; governor of Hong Kong, 1992–97.

1948 *Lindsay Ann Crouse,* U.S. actress.

Steve (Stevie) Winwood, British musician, singer; member of the rock groups, *Traffic, Spencer Davis Group,* and *Blind Faith.*

1950 *Billy Squier,* U.S. singer, musician.

1951 *Bruce Boxleitner,* U.S. actor; known for his starring role on television series, *Scarecrow and Mrs. King.*

1957 *Lou(is Rodman) Whitaker,* U.S. baseball player.

1962 *Emilio Estevez (Emilio Sheen),* U.S. actor; known for starring roles in *The Breakfast Club,* 1985, *St. Elmo's Fire,* 1985, and *The Mighty Ducks,* 1992; son of Martin Sheen.

1973 *Mackenzie Alexander Astin,* U.S. actor; known for his role as Andy on television series, *Facts of Life.*

HISTORICAL EVENTS

1843 *Natal* in South Africa is proclaimed a British colony.

1846 U.S. declares war on Mexico (*Mexican War*).

1873 *King Oscar II* and his wife *Sophia* are crowned as rulers of *Sweden.*

1888 British establish protectorates over *North Borneo, Brunei,* and *Sarawak.*

1898 Louisiana adopts constitution disenfranchising blacks under property and literacy tests and the *grandfather clause.*

1902 *Joe Gans* defeats *Frank Erne* in one round to win the world lightweight boxing title.

1917 *Thoroughbred Omar Khayyam* becomes first horse not born in America to win the *Kentucky Derby.*

1922 A twenty-ton *meteor* falls near Blackstone, Virginia, causing a 500-square-foot breach in the earth.

1926 *Joseph Pilsudski* leads successful military revolt against the Polish government.

Roald Amundsen, Umberto Nobile, and *Lincoln Ellsworth* fly over the *North Pole* in a 71-hour flight in the dirigible *Norge.*

may

1933 U.S. President Franklin D. Roosevelt signs the *Agricultural Adjustment Act* providing subsidies for farmers and establishing parity prices.

1936 Broadcast of the coronation of *George VI of England* is the first worldwide radio broadcast heard in the U.S. George VI succeeds his brother, *Edward VIII*, who has abdicated in order to marry U.S. divorcèe *Wallis Warfield Simpson*.

1943 German and Italian troops numbering 252,000 surrender to the Allies in *North Africa* (*World War II*).

Trident Conference in Washington, D.C., opens as *Franklin D. Roosevelt* and *Winston Churchill* plan global strategy and prepare for a second front in Europe (*World War II*).

1962 U.S. President *John F. Kennedy* orders troops into *Thailand* to defend the country against insurgents from Laos.

1963 *Betty Miller* becomes the first female pilot to complete a solo flight across the Pacific Ocean.

1967 *H. Rap Brown* succeeds *Stokely Carmichael* as head of the *Student Nonviolent Coordinating Committee* (*SNCC*).

1975 Cambodia seizes U.S. merchant ship *Mayaguez*.

1987 *Eddie French Adami* is inaugurated as premier of Malta.

HOLIDAYS

Liberia
National Rally Day

Portugal
Lady of Fatima Day

RELIGIOUS CALENDAR

The Saints

St. Glyceria, virgin and martyr. [d. c. 177]

St. Mucius, martyr. Also called *Mocius*. [d. 304]

St. Servatius, Bishop of Tongres. Invoked against rodents and leg diseases, and for the success of enterprises. Also called *Servais, Servatus*. [d. 384]

St. John the Silent, hermit. Also called *the Sabaïte*. [d. 558]

St. Erconwald, Bishop of London and monastery founder. Also called *Earconwald, Erkenwald, Erkonwald*. [d. c. 693]

St. Euthymius the Enlightener, abbot. [d. 1028]

St. Peter Regalatus, Franciscan monk. Also called *Peter Regalati*. [d. 1456]

St. Andrew Hubert Fournet, co-founder of the Daughters of the Cross, also called the Sisters of St. Andrew. [d. 1834]

The Beatified

Blessed Imelda, virgin. [d. 1333]
Blessed Julian of Norwich, virgin and mystic. [d. c. 1423]

BIRTHDATES

1655 *Pope Innocent XIII*, pope 1721–24. [d. March 7, 1724]

1713 *Alexis Clairaut*, French mathematician; conducted mathematical investigations regarding the shape of the earth. [d. May 17, 1765]

1717 *Maria Theresa, Empress of Austria*, 1740–80; Archduchess of Austria, Queen of Hungary and Bohemia. [d. November 29, 1780]

1753 *Lazare Nicolas Carnot*, French general, statesman, author; military genius of the French revolutionary wars; known as *le grand Carnot*. [d. 1823]

1767 *John VI, King of Portugal* 1816–26. [March 10, 1826]

1792 *Pope Pius IX*, pope 1846–78; during his term the dogma of *infallibility* was promulgated. [d. February 7, 1878]

1842 *Sir Arthur S(eymour) Sullivan*, British composer, conductor; best known as collaborator with W. S. Gilbert (November 18) in popular satiric operettas. [d. November 22, 1900]

1845 *Gabriel Urbain Fauré*, French composer; credited with moving away from German influence in modern French music. [d. November 4, 1924]

1850 *Oliver Heaviside*, British physicist; *Heaviside layer* in the ionosphere (now called *E-layer*) was named after him. [d. February 3, 1925]

1857 *Sir Ronald Ross*, British bacteriologist; Nobel Prize in physiology or medicine for discovery of life cycle of *malaria* parasite, 1902. [d. September 16, 1932]

1882 *Georges Braque*, French painter, sculptor, stage designer; a principal figure in modern art. [d. August 31, 1963]

1883 *George Nicholas Papanicolaou*, U.S. physiologist; developer of *Pap smear* test for detection of cervical cancer. [d. February 19, 1962]

1907 *Daphne Du Maurier*, British novelist; author of *Rebecca*. [d. April 19, 1989]

1913 *William R(ichard) Tolbert, Jr.*, Liberian statesman; President of Liberia, 1972–80; President of Baptist World Alliance, 1965–70. Killed in a coup. [d. April 12, 1980]

1914 *Joe Louis (Joseph Louis Barrow)*, U.S. boxer; World Heavyweight Champion, 1937–49, longest reign in history; known as the *Brown Bomber*. [d. April 12, 1981]

may

1926 *Bea(trice) Arthur (Bernice Frankel)*, U.S. actress; known for her starring roles on television series, *Maude*, 1972–78, and *The Golden Girls*, 1985–92.

1927 *Clive Alexander Barnes*, British journalist; dance and drama critic, *New York Post*.

Herbert David Ross, U.S. director; known for *The Turning Point*, 1977, and *Footloose*, 1984.

1929 *John R. Galvin*, U.S. military leader; NATO Supreme Allied Commander, 1987–92.

1939 *Harvey Keitel*, U.S. actor; known for his performances in *Reservoir Dogs*, 1992, and *The Piano*, 1993.

1941 *Richie Valens (Richard Vanlenzuela)*, U.S. singer; known for his song, *La Bamba;* died in a plane crash with Buddy Holly and The Big Bopper. [d. February 3, 1959]

1943 *Mary Wells*, U.S. singer; known for song, *My Guy*. [d. July 26, 1992]

1950 *Peter Gabriel*, British singer, songwriter; member of the rock group, *Genesis*, 1968–75.

Stevie Wonder (Steveland Morris), U.S. singer, composer.

1961 *Dennis Rodman*, U.S. basketball player.

HISTORICAL EVENTS

1532 *Scottish College of Justice* is established.

1568 *Mary, Queen of Scots*, is defeated by English at Langside.

1783 *Society of the Cincinnati* is founded at Newburgh, New York, by a group of Continental Army officers.

1888 *Serfdom* is abolished in Brazil.

1907 Legislation establishing *universal suffrage* is passed in Sweden.

1927 *Black Friday* signals the collapse of the German economic structure.

1954 Jerry Ross and Richard Adler's musical, *The Pajama Game*, premieres in New York.

1965 The *Rolling Stones*, British rock group, finish recording the song, *(I Can't Get No) Satisfaction*.

West Germany and *Israel* open full diplomatic relations; Algeria, Iraq, Jordan, Saudi Arabia, Syria, the United Arab Republic, and Yemen sever relations with West Germany.

1967 About 70,000 persons march down Fifth Avenue in New York City in support of the U.S. soldiers fighting in Vietnam (*Vietnam War*).

1968 U.S. and North Vietnamese negotiators open talks aimed at ending *Vietnam War*.

1981 *Pope John Paul II* is shot and wounded in an assassination attempt in Rome; a Turkish terrorist is arrested.

1983 *Braniff International Corp.* files for reorganization under chapter 11 of the Federal Bankruptcy Act.

HOLIDAYS

Guinea
Anniversary of the Guinean Democratic Party

Israel
Independence Day
Commemorates end of British rule and establishment of the State of Israel.

Liberia
National Unification Day
A day set aside to recognize the National Unification Party, which is dedicated to a unified Liberia.

Malawi (Nyasaland)
Kamuzu Day
Commemorates the birthday of Dr. Kamuzu Banda, first president of the republic, 1906.

Paraguay
National Flag Day
Beginning of a two-day celebration marking the achievement of independence from Spain, 1811.

RELIGIOUS CALENDAR

Feasts

St. Matthias, apostle and martyr. Took the place among the twelve apostles left vacant by Judas Iscariot. Patron of carpenters, tailors, and reformed drunks. Invoked against smallpox. Feast formerly February 24. [d. 1st century]

St. Pontius, martyr. [d. c. 3rd century]

St. Boniface of Tarsus, martyr. [d. c. 306]

St. Carthage, bishop. Founded one of most famous of all Irish monastic schools, that of Lismore. Also called *Carthach, Carthagh, Mochuda, Mochudu.* [d. 637]

St. Erembert, Bishop of Toulouse. [d. c. 672]

St. Michael Garicoïts, founder of the Priests of the Sacred Heart of Bétharram. [d. 1863]

St. Mary Mazzarello, virgin and co-founder of the Daughters of Our Lady Help of Christians, founded for educating children. [d. 1881]

The Beatified

Blessed Giles of Portugal, Dominican friar. [d. 1265]

Blessed Petronilla of Moncel, virgin and abbess. [d. 1355]

Blessed Magdalen di Canossa, virgin and founder of the Canossian Daughters of Charity. [d. 1835]

BIRTHDATES

1316 *Charles IV of Luxemburg,* Holy Roman Emperor 1355–78; known as a patron of the arts and sciences. [d. November 29, 1378]

1686 *Gabriel Daniel Fahrenheit,* German physicist; devised *Fahrenheit scale* which bears his name. [d. September 16, 1736]

1710 *Adolf Frederick, King of Sweden,* 1751–71. [d. February 12, 1771]

1727 *Thomas Gainsborough,* baptized on this day; English painter of landscapes and idyllic scenes. [d. August 2, 1788]

1752 *Timothy Dwight,* U.S. educator, theologian; one of *Hartford Wits;* President, Yale University, 1795–1817; grandson of Jonathan Edwards. [d. January 11, 1817]

1771 *Robert Owen,* Welsh sociologist; pioneer of cooperation in industry; founder of socialism in Great Britain; founder of *New Harmony, Indiana,* a utopian community. [d. November 17, 1858]

1827 *Jean Baptiste Carpeaux,* French sculptor; sculpted *The Dance,* now in the Louvre, Paris. [d. October 11, 1875]

1853 *Sir Thomas Henry Hall Caine,* British novelist, playwright. [d. August 31, 1931]

1872 *Mikhail Semenovich Tsvett,* Russian botanist; inventor of *chromatography,* 1906. [d. May 1920]

1885 *Otto Klemperer,* German conductor; known especially for interpretations of German

Romantic works. [d. July 3, 1973]

1894 *Frank (Francis Marion) Folsom,* U.S. electronics executive; President of Radio Corp. of America, 1949–57. [d. January 22, 1970]

1922 *Franjo Tudjman,* Croatian politician; President of Croatia, 1990– .

1925 *Patrice Munsel,* U.S. soprano; the youngest singer ever to become a member of the Metropolitan Opera Company (at age 18).

1929 *Lorne (Gump) Worsley,* Canadian hockey player; elected to Hall of Fame, 1980.

1936 *Bobby Darin (Walden Robert Cassotto),* U.S. singer. [d. Dec. 20, 1973]

1937 *Richard Dalton (Dick) Howser,* U.S. baseball player, baseball manager. [d. June 17, 1987]

1944 *George Lucas,* U.S. director; directed *American Graffiti* and the *Star Wars* movies.

1951 *Robert Zemeckis,* U.S. director; directed *Forrest Gump,* 1994.

Season Hubley, U.S. actress; known for her role as Priscilla Presley in the television movie, *Elvis.*

1952 *David Byrne,* Scottish musician; member of the rock group, *Talking Heads.*

1961 *Tim Roth,* British actor; known for roles in *Reservoir Dogs,* 1992 and *Pulp Fiction,* 1994.

HISTORICAL EVENTS

1509 *Venetians* are defeated at Agnadello by the *League of*

Cambrai, consisting of Holy Roman Empire, France, Aragon, and the Papacy.

1607 *Jamestown, Virginia,* the first permanent English settlement in America, is founded.

1619 *Jan van Barneveldt,* Dutch statesman and champion of Dutch independence, is executed for treason.

1643 *Louis XIV of France* accedes to the throne (with *Anne of Austria* as Regent).

1796 *Dr. Edward Jenner* begins experiments which ultimately result in development of *vaccination.*

1801 *Yusef, Pasha of Tripoli,* declares war on the U.S. *(Tripolitan War).*

1804 *Meriwether Lewis* and *William Clark* leave St. Louis to explore the Louisiana Territory and establish a land route to the Pacific Ocean *(Lewis and Clark Expedition).*

1852 *Antioch College* is chartered as the first coeducational and nonsectarian institution in the U.S.

1900 *Sanford Ballard Dole* is appointed as the first governor of *Hawaii.*

1913 The *Rockefeller Foundation* is established as a charitable organization by John D(avison) Rockefeller.

1930 *Carlsbad Caverns* in New Mexico becomes a national park.

1938 League of Nations recognizes unconditional neutrality of *Switzerland.*

1950 *Celal Bayar* becomes president of Turkey when his

Democratic Party wins a landslide victory in the nation's first free elections. *Adnan Menderes* becomes prime minister.

1955 Eight Eastern European countries sign the *Warsaw Pact,* a mutual defense treaty.

1958 U.S. and Great Britain dispatch troops and arms to *Lebanon* following violence between Moslem and Christian factions.

1963 *Kuwait* becomes the 111th member of the United Nations.

1965 *Queen Elizabeth II* donates three acres of land at Runnymede to the U.S. for a memorial to assassinated U.S. President *John F. Kennedy.*

1973 The *National Right to Life Committee,* an organization opposed to abortion and euthanasia, is founded in Washington, D.C.

Skylab, first orbiting U.S. space laboratory, is launched.

1974 *Archbishop Donald Coggan* is named 101st Archbishop of Canterbury by Queen Elizabeth II, succeeding Archbishop *Michael Ramsey.*

1978 *Franz Oppurg,* an Austrian climber, makes first successful solo ascent of *Mount Everest.*

1979 The U.S. establishes formal trade relations with the *People's Republic of China.*

1987 Lieutenant Colonel *Sitiveni Rabuka* assumes power in Fiji after a coup d'etat.

1989 *Carlos Menem* is elected president of Argentina.

HOLIDAYS

Paraguay
Independence Day
Celebrates the achievement of independence from Spain, 1811. The second day of a two-day celebration. (See Flag Day, May 14.)

U.S.
Peace Officers Memorial Day
Commemorates all those law enforcement persons who have lost their lives in the line of duty.

RELIGIOUS CALENDAR

The Saints
SS. Torquatus and his companions, martyrs. First Christian missionaries in Spain. [d. c. 1st century]

St. Isidore of Chios, martyr. [d. c. 251]

SS. Peter of Lampsacus and his companions, martyrs. [d. 251]

St. Hilary of Galeata, abbot and founder of the Monastery at Galeata. [d. 558]

SS. Dympna and *Gerebernus,* martyrs. Dympna is now regarded as patron saint of the insane. [d. c. 650]

St. Bertinus, abbot. Also called *Bercthun, Bertin, Brithun.* [d. c. 709]

SS. Bertha and *Rupert,* mother and son who established several hospices for the poor. [d. c. 840]

St. Hallvard, martyr; patron of Oslo, Norway. Invoked in defense of an innocent person. [d. 1043]

St. Isaias, Bishop of Rostov. [d. 1090]

St. Isidore the Husbandman, layman; patron of Madrid, Spain. [d. 1130]

The Beatified
Blessed Magdalen Albrizzi, virgin and superior of Convent at Brunate. [d. 1465]

BIRTHDATES

1567 *Claudio Giovanni Antonio Monteverdi,* baptized on this day; Italian composer, music reformer; responsible for many innovations in musical compositions, including the elaboration on recitative forms; composed many madrigals. [d. November 29, 1643]

1633 *Sebastien le Prestre de Vauban,* French military engineer; Marshal of France, 1703. [d. March 30, 1707]

1773 *Klemens Wenzel Nepomuk Lothar von Metternich,* Austrian diplomat and statesman; played key role in making Austria a leading power of the 19th century. [d. June 11, 1859]

1788 *James Gadsden,* U.S. statesman; responsible for the *Gadsden Purchase* from Mexico by which the U.S. acquired southern *Arizona* and *New Mexico.* [d. December 25, 1858]

1803 *Edward George Earl Lytton Bulwer-Lytton, First Baron Lytton,* British author, poet; wrote *The Last Days of Pompeii,* 1834. [d. January 18, 1873]

1808 *Michael William Balfe,* Irish operatic composer; composed *The Bohemian Girl,* which contains *I Dreamed I Dwelt in Marble Halls.* [d. October 20, 1870]

1814 *Stephen Heller,* Hungarian composer, pianist; intimate of Chopin, Liszt, and Berlioz. [d. January 14, 1888]

1845 *Elie Metchnikoff (Ilya Ilich Mechnikov),* French bacteriologist born in Russia; discovered *white corpuscles* in living cells; Nobel Prize in physiology or medicine for work on immunology (with P. Ehrlich), 1908. [d. July 15, 1916]

1855 *Louis Bamberger,* U.S. merchant. [d. March 11, 1944]

1856 *L(yman) Frank Baum,* U.S. writer of children's stories; known chiefly for the *Oz* books. [d. May 6, 1919]

1859 *Pierre Curie,* French chemist; Nobel Prize in physics for work on spontaneous radioactivity (with his wife Marie Curie and A. H. Becquerel), 1903. [d. April 19, 1906]

1860 *Ellen Louise Wilson,* first wife of President Woodrow Wilson. [d. August 6, 1914]

1862 *Arthur Schnitzler,* Austrian playwright, novelist. [d. October 21, 1931]

1870 *Henry Latham Doherty,* U.S. industrialist; founder of Cities Service Corporation, 1910. [d. December 26, 1939]

1889 *Bessie Hillman,* U.S. labor leader; founder of the *Amalgamated Clothing Workers of America.* [d. December 23, 1970]

1890 *Katherine Anne Porter,* U.S. short-story writer, novelist. [d. September 18, 1980]

1902 *Richard J. Daley,* U.S. political leader; Mayor of Chicago, 1955–76; called the last of the big-city bosses. [d. December 20, 1976]

1904 *Clifton Fadiman,* U.S. literary critic, author.

1905 *Joseph Cotten,* U.S. actor. [d. February 16, 1992]

1909 *James Mason,* British actor. [d. July 27, 1984]

1910 *Constance Cummings (Constance Halverstadt),* U.S. stage and film actress.

1914 *Walter (Turk) Broda,* Canadian hockey player; elected to Hall of Fame, 1967.

1915 *Paul Anthony Samuelson,* U.S. economist; Nobel Prize in economics, 1970.

1918 *Eddy Arnold,* U.S. singer.

1921 *Erroll Garner,* U.S. jazz pianist, composer. [d. January 2, 1977]

1923 *Richard Avedon,* U.S. photographer.

1926 *(Levin) Peter Shaffer,* British playwright.

1930 *Jasper Johns,* U.S. artist.

1936 *Anna Maria Alberghetti,* U.S. operatic soprano born in Italy.

Paul Zindel, U.S. author, dramatist; Pulitzer Prize for drama, 1971.

1937 *Madeleine Albright,* Czechoslovakian-born government official; U.S. ambassador to the United Nations, 1993– .

Trini(dad) Lopez, III, U.S. singer; known for song, *If I Had a Hammer,* 1963.

1943 *Jack Bruce,* Scottish musician; member of the rock group, *Cream.*

David Cronenberg, Canadian filmmaker; known for the movies *The Fly,* 1985, and *Dead Ringers,* 1988.

1944 *George Lucas,* U.S. director; known for his direction of *American Graffiti, Star Wars,* and *The Empire Strikes Back.*

1948 *Brian Eno,* British musician, producer; member of the rock group, *Roxy Music.*

1951 *Chazz Palminteri,* U.S. actor; Oscar nominee for *Bullets Over Broadway.*

1953 *George Howard Brett,* U.S. baseball player.

1954 *James Belushi,* U.S. actor.

1955 *Lee Horsley,* U.S. actor; known for his starring role on television series, *Matt Houston,* 1982–84.

1969 *Emmitt Smith,* U.S. football player.

1970 *Desmond Howard,* U.S. football player; 1991 Heisman Trophy winner.

HISTORICAL EVENTS

1004 *Henry II of Germany* is crowned King of Lombardy.

1213 *King John of England* submits to *Pope Innocent III,* and England and Ireland become papal fiefs.

1455 Crusade against the Turks and for the capture of *Constantinople* is proclaimed by *Pope Calixtus III.*

1567 *Mary, Queen of Scots* marries *James Hepburn, Earl of Bothwell.*

1860 *Giuseppe Garibaldi* defeats Neapolitan army at Calatafimi (*War of Italian Unification*).

1867 Russia ratifies the treaty selling *Alaska* to the U.S. for $7 million.

1900 *Paderewski Fund* is established by Ignace Paderewski to award American orchestral composers.

1916 Austro-Hungarians successfuly launch offensive at Trentino, Italy (*World War I*).

1920 English army of occupation, known as the *Black and Tans,* arrives in Ireland.

1924 The *Emergency Quota Act* is passed, excluding Oriental immigrants from the U.S.

1934 Coup d'état in *Latvia* is led by *Karlis Ulmanis,* the Prime Minister.

1940 Dutch army capitulates to Germany (*World War II*).

1941 *Elie Lescot* is inaugurated as president of Haiti.

1947 The first *Arab-Israeli War* begins. Egypt, Syria, Lebanon, and Iraq join forces to attack Israel.

1951 *American Telephone & Telegraph Co.* becomes the world's first corporation to have one million stockholders.

1955 *Austria* and *Russia* conclude a state treaty restoring Austrian independence and ending Russian occupation.

1958 Vincente Minnelli's film musical, *Gigi,* opens in New York.

1967 U.S. Supreme Court rules that children are entitled to the same constitutional protections extended to adults.

1969 Students and others occupying *People's Park* on the campus of the University of California at Berkeley are attacked by police and national guardsmen during *Vietnam War protest.*

Justice Abe Fortas resigns from the U.S. Supreme Court because of criticism of his financial dealings.

1970 At *Jackson State College,* Mississippi, two students are killed when city and state police open fire on demonstrators.

1972 Alabama governor *George Wallace* is seriously wounded in an assassination attempt while campaigning in the Maryland Democratic presidential primary.

1980 *Max Anderson* completes first nonstop flight across the U.S. in a hot-air balloon.

1985 *Radovan Vlajkovic* is inaugurated as president of Yugoslavia.

1988 The U.S.S.R. begins withdrawing its troops from *Afghanistan.*

1991 *Edith Cresson* is appointed the first female premier of France by President François Mitterrand.

may

MAY
16

RELIGIOUS CALENDAR

The Saints

St. Peregrine, Bishop of Auxerre, martyr. Evangelized much of his part of France. [d. c. 261]

St. Possidius, Bishop of Calama; a pupil and close associate of St. Augustine. [d. c. 440]

St. Germerius, Bishop of Toulouse. Also called *Germier.* [d. c. 560]

St. Brendan, Abbot of Clonfert. [d. 577 or 583]

St. Domnolus, Bishop of Le Mans. Builder of several churches and a hospice. [d. 581]

St. Carantoc, abbot. Also called *Carannog.* [d. 6th century]

St. Honoratus, Bishop of Amiens. In France regarded as patron of bakers and all trades that deal with flour. Also called *Honorius.* [d. c. 600]

St. Ubald, Bishop of Gubbio. Also called *Ubaldo, Ubaldus.* [d. 1160]

St. Simon Stock, Carmelite friar; responsible for the tradition of wearing the scapular. [d. 1265]

St. John Nepomucen, martyr; principal patron of Bohemia and patron of bridges. His name is invoked against floods and slander, as well as for help in making a good confession. Also called *Nepomuc, Nepomucene, Nepomuk.* [d. 1393]

The Beatified

Blessed Florida Cevoli. [beatified 1993]

Blessed Columba Gabriel. [beatified 1993]

Blessed Maurice Tornay. [beatified 1993]

Blessed Marie-Louise Trichet. [beatified 1993]

BIRTHDATES

1782 *John Sell Cotman,* English painter; among his most famous pieces are *Silver Birches* and *Waterfall.* [d. July 24, 1842]

1801 *William Henry Seward,* U.S. politician, statesman; responsible for U.S. acquisition of *Alaska,* then known as *Seward's Folly.* [d. October 10, 1872]

1804 *Elizabeth Palmer Peabody,* U.S. educator; founded first *kindergarten* in U.S., 1860. [d. January 3, 1894]

1824 *Edmund Kirby-Smith,* Confederate Army officer during U.S. Civil War; the last Confederate commander to surrender. [d. March 28, 1893]

Levi P. Morton, U.S. Vice-President, 1889-93. [d. May 16, 1920]1831

David Edward Hughes, U.S. inventor of type-printing telegraph and *microphone.* [d. January 22, 1900]

1832 *Philip Danforth Armour,* U.S. meat-packing executive; President of Armour & Co., 1875–1901. [d. January 6, 1901]

1892 *Richard Tauber,* Austrian-born opera singer. [d. January 8, 1948]

1905 *Henry Fonda,* U.S. actor. [d. August 12, 1982]

1909 *Deighton Ward,* Governor-General of Barbados, 1976–84. [d. January 9, 1984]

1911 *Margaret (Brooke) Sullavan,* U.S. actress. [d. January 1, 1960]

1912 *Studs (Louis) Terkel,* U.S. writer; noted for books based on extensive personal interviews with average people.

1913 *Woody Herman (Woodrow Charles),* U.S. musician, orchestra leader. [d. October 29, 1987]

1919 *Liberace (Wladziu Valentino),* U.S. entertainer. [d. February 4, 1987]

1923 *Merton H. Miller,* U.S. economist; Nobel Prize for Economics. Miller shares the award with William F. Sharpe and Harry M. Markowitz, for their work on the theory of financial economics, 1990

1924 *Dawda Kairaba Jawara,* Gambian statesman; President, 1965–94.

Frank Fabian Mankiewicz, U.S. lawyer, journalist.

1928 *Alfred Manuel (Billy) Martin,* U.S. baseball player, baseball manager. [d. December 25, 1989]

1929 *Adrienne Rich,* U.S. poet.

1931 *Lowell Palmer Weicker, Jr.,* U.S. politician; Governor of Connecticut, 1990–94; Senator, 1971–89; member, Senate Watergate Committee, 1973–74.

1940 *Lainie Kazan (Lanie Levine),* U.S. singer.

1947 *Bob Edwards,* U.S. radio personality; host of National Public Radio's *Morning Edition.*

1953 *Pierce Brosnan,* Irish actor; known for his starring role on television series, *Remington Steele,* 1982–86 and for his performances in the James Bond movies.

1955 *Olga Korbut,* Russian gymnast; Olympic gold medalist, 1972.

1956 *Jack (John Scott) Morris,* U.S. baseball player.

1960 *Yannick Noah,* French tennis player.

1966 *Janet Jackson,* U.S. singer, actress.

Thurman Thomas, U.S. football player.

1970 *Gabriela Sabatini,* Argentine tennis player.

HISTORICAL EVENTS

1568 *Mary, Queen of Scots,* flees to England for sanctuary after her defeat at *Langsides* (now Glasgow).

1763 *Samuel Johnson,* the great British lexicographer, meets his future biographer, *James Boswell,* for the first time.

1770 The French Dauphin, 15, (the future *Louis XVI*) marries *Marie Antoinette,* 14, at Versailles.

1866 U.S. Congress authorizes the issuance of the *nickel.*

1868 U.S. Senate in impeachment trial of President *Andrew Johnson* votes for acquittal.

1915 The *Battle of the San* begins as Russians attempt to halt the advancing Austro-German army in Galicia (*World War I*).

1918 The *Sedition Act* goes into effect in the U.S., providing stiff penalties for hindering the war effort (*World War I*).

1920 *Joan of Arc* is canonized.

1939 *Food stamps* are first introduced in the U.S.

1942 *Rafael Leonidas Trujillo Molina* is elected president of the Dominican Republic.

1946 Irving Berlin's musical comedy, *Annie Get Your Gun,* premieres in New York.

1950 *Vladimir Houdek,* Czechoslovak delegate to the United Nations, resigns and seeks asylum in the U.S.

1951 Bolivian president, *Mamerto Urriolagoiti,* resigns in favor of a military junta in order to prevent President-elect *Victor Paz Estenssoro* from assuming power.

1956 Alfred Hitchcock's film, *The Man Who Knew Too Much,* premieres in New York.

1960 Alain Resnais' film, *Hiroshima Mon Amour,* premieres in New York.

1963 U.S. astronaut *Gordon Cooper* in *Faith 7* capsule is recovered near Midway after orbiting the earth 22 times.

1966 *Stokely Carmichael* is named head of the *Student Nonviolent Coordinating Committee (SNCC).*

1974 *Helmut Schmidt* is sworn in as West German Chancellor.

1979 The problem of *boat people* and other peoples displaced by conflict in Southeast Asia is first addressed by the Association of Southeast Asian Nations.

1989 *China* and the *U.S.S.R.* normalize relations after a 30-year lapse.

1997 *Laurent Kabila* leads a rebellion and overthrows Mobutu Sese Seko, president of Zaire.

may

MAY
17

HOLIDAYS

World Telecommunications Day
Sponsored by United Nations.

Nauru
Constitution Day
Commemorates the adoption of the country's constitution and achievement of independence from Australia, 1968.

Norway
Constitution Day or Independence Day
Commemorates the adoption of Norway's constitution, 1814.

RELIGIOUS CALENDAR

The Saints
St. Madron. Springs in the ruins of St. Madron's Church in Cornwall are noted for their curing powers, supposedly effective in helping skin diseases. Also called *Maden, Madern.* [d. c. 6th century]
St. Bruno, Bishop of Würzburg. Built cathedral of St. Kilian. [d. 1045]
St. Paschal Baylon, Friar Minor; patron of eucharistic congresses and organizations. Also called *Paschal Babylon.* [d. 1592]

The Beatified
Blessed Ratho of Andechs; a Bavarian monastery-builder, his name is invoked by invalids, especially those suffering from hernia and stone. [d. 953]

Blessed Andrew Abellon, Dominican prior. [d. 1450]
Blessed Josephine Bakhita. [beatified 1992]
Blessed Josemarie Escriva de Balaguer. [beatified 1992]

BIRTHDATES

1749 *Edward Jenner,* English physician; developed vaccination for *smallpox.* [d. January 24, 1823]

1836 *Sir Joseph Norman Lockyer,* British astronomer; pioneered *solar spectroscopy.* [d. August 16, 1920]

1845 *Jacinto Verdaguer,* Catalan poet. [d. June 10, 1902]

1855 *Timothy Michael Healy,* Irish political leader; first Governor-General of the *Irish Free State.* [d. March 26, 1931]

1864 *Harry Chandler,* U.S. newspaper publisher. [d. September 23, 1944]

1866 *Erik Alfred-Leslie Satie,* French composer. [d. July 1, 1925]

1868 *Horace Elgin Dodge,* U.S. manufacturer; responsible for the initial success of the Dodge Company, automobile manufacturer. [d. December 10, 1920]

1875 *Joel Elias Springarn,* U.S. educator, literary critic, civil rights leader; co-founder of *National Association for the Advancement of Colored People;* President, 1930–39; *Spingarn Medal,* established and endowed by Springarn, is awarded annually to a black in recognition of service to his race. [d. July 26, 1939]

1886 *Alphonso XIII, King of Spain;* ruled during Spanish-American War when Spain lost Cuba, Puerto Rico, and the Philippines. Spanish Revolution forced his resignation, 1931. [d. February 28, 1941]

1897 *Odd Hassel,* Norwegian chemist; Nobel Prize in chemistry for helping establish conformational analysis (with D. Barton), 1969.[d. May 11, 1981]

1900 *Ruholla Khomeini (Ruhollah Hendi),* Iranian ayatollah, Moslem religious and revolutionary leader; the chief political figure in Iran since 1979. [d. June 4, 1989]

1904 *Jean Gabin (Alexis Moncourge),* French actor. [d. November 15, 1976]

1905 *John Patrick (Goggan),* U.S. playwright. [d. November 7, 1995]

1911 *Maureen O'Sullivan,* U.S. actress.[d. June 23, 1998]

1912 *Archibald Cox,* U.S. lawyer, professor; special prosecutor in *Watergate* investigation 1973.

1914 *Stewart Johonnot Oliver Alsop,* U.S. journalist, editor. [d. May 26, 1974]

1917 *John (Papa) Creach,* U.S. musician. [d. February 22, 1994]

1918 *Birgit Nilsson,* Swedish operatic soprano.

1936 *Dennis Hopper,* U.S. actor, director; known for his starring role in *Easy Rider,* 1969.

1937 *Hazel O'Leary,* U.S. politician; Secretary of Energy, 1993– .

1944 *Jesse (James Ridout) Winchester,* U.S. singer, songwriter.

1955 *Debra Winger,* U.S. actress; known for her starring roles in *An Officer and a Gentleman,* 1982, *Terms of Endearment,* 1983, and *Shadowlands,* 1993.

1956 *(Sugar) Ray Leonard,* U.S. boxer.

1961 *Enya (Eithne Ni Bhraonain),* Irish new age singer.

HISTORICAL EVENTS

1198 *Frederick II, Holy Roman Emperor,* is crowned King of Sicily.

1540 *Humayun,* Sultan of Delhi, is defeated at Kanauj and is driven out of India by Sher Shah.

1579 Southern Netherlands recognizes *Philip II of Spain* in the *Peace of Arras (Dutch War of Liberation).*

1792 The *New York Stock Exchange (NYSE)* is established at Merchants Coffee House, New York City.

1814 *Norway* declares independence from Sweden.

1875 First *Kentucky Derby* is held at Churchill Downs, Kentucky. *Aristides* is the winner of the $2850 purse.

1885 Apaches under *Geronimo* rise in revolt in Arizona and New Mexico.

1902 *Alfonso XIII* reaches his majority and is recognized as constitutional monarch in Spain, ending the long regency of his mother.

1904 *Shéhérazade* by Maurice Ravel premieres in Paris.

1925 *St. Thérèse of Lisieux* is canonized.

1930 The British administration restricts Jewish immigration to *Palestine.*

1944 British forces take *Cassino, Italy* from the Germans *(World War II).*

1954 U.S. Supreme Court issues *Brown v. Board of Education* decision, ruling that segregated schools are unconstitutional.

1962 *Hong Kong* begins construction of a barbed-wire wall across its border with the *People's Republic of China* to curb the flow of illegal Chinese immigrants.

1966 The first *heart bypass pump,* created by Dr. *Michael DeBakey,* is implanted in Houston, Texas.

1971 West German president, *Gustav Heinemann,* visits Romania. He is the first West German official to visit an Eastern European Communist nation.

1973 The U.S. Senate Select Committee on Presidential Campaign Activities begins hearings *(Watergate Incident).*

1983 *Israel* and *Lebanon* sign an agreement providing for the withdrawal of Israeli troops and a normalization of relations. The Israelis are permitted to retain a security zone in southern Lebanon.

1984 The U.S. Federal Deposit Insurance Corp. and the Federal Reserve Board agree to a financial rescue package for *Continental Illinois Corp.,* the nation's ninth largest bank holding company. A week-long run on the bank, triggered by depositor uneasiness over questionable loans, had forced Continental to take heavy losses.

1987 An Iraqi warplane bombs the missile frigate, *U.S.S. Stark,* killing 37 U.S. sailors in the *Persian Gulf.*

1989 The Polish government legalizes the *Roman Catholic Church* and restores its property confiscated after World War II.

1997 *Laurent Kabila* announces himself as the new ruler of Zaire and renames the country *The Democratic Republic of the Congo* (May 16, 1997).

may

MAY
18

HOLIDAYS

Haiti
Flag Day

Uruguay
La Piedras Battle Day
Commemorates the end of conflict between Uruguay and Brazil and the achievement of Uruguayan Independence; 1828.

RELIGIOUS CALENDAR

The Saints
St. Venantius, martyr. Also called *Verantius.* [d. c. 257]

SS. Theodotus, Thecusa, and their companions, martyrs. [d. c. 304]

St. Potamon, Bishop of Heraclea, martyr. Also called *Potamion.* [d. c. 340]

St. John I, pope and martyr. [d. 526] Feast formerly May 27. Optional Memorial.

St. Elgiva, founder of the Shaftesbury nunnery. Also called *Ælgifu, Ælgytha, Algyva.* [d. 944]

St. Eric of Sweden, King of Sweden and martyr. Did much to establish Christianity in Upper Sweden. Until Reformation was considered patron of Sweden. His banner is regarded as a portent of victory. [d. 1161]

St. Felix of Cantalice, Capuchin lay-brother and visionary. [d. 1587]

The Beatified
Blessed William of Toulouse, hermit and preacher. [d. 1369]

BIRTHDATES

1692 *Joseph Butler,* English clergyman, moralist, writer; Dean of St. Paul's, 1740; Bishop of Durham, 1750. [d. June 16, 1752]

1788 *Hugh Clapperton,* one of first European explorers of *Nigeria.* [d. April 13, 1827]

1814 *Mikhail Aleksandrovitch Bakunin,* Russian anarchist; leading revolutionary figure in Europe, 1861–76; his philosophy, *Bakuninism,* is based on atheism, destruction of the state, and extremes of individual rights. [d. July 13, 1876]

1830 *Karl Goldmark,* Hungarian composer. [d. January 2, 1915]

1852 *I. L. Peretz,* polish writer, co-founder of modern Yiddish literature. [d. 1915]

1872 *Bertrand (Arthur William) Russell, 3rd Earl Russell,* British philosopher, mathematician, writer. [d. February 2, 1970]

1883 *Walter (Adolph) Gropius,* German architect; founder of *Bauhaus* school of architecture. [d. July 5, 1969]

1889 *Thomas Midgley,* U.S. engineer, chemist; developer of *tetraethyl lead,* anti-knock additive for gasoline. [d. November 2, 1944]

1892 *Ezio Pinza,* Italian operatic bass. [d. May 9, 1957]

1897 *Frank Capra,* U.S. film director; a leading film director of 1930s and 1940s. [d. September 3, 1991]

1901 *Vincent Du Vigneaud,* U.S. chemist; Nobel Prize in chemistry for work on *pituitary hormones* and first synthesis of *polypeptide hormone,* 1955. [d. December 11, 1978]

1902 *Meredith Willson,* U.S. composer; composed *The Music Man.* [d. June 15, 1984]

1904 *Jacob (Koppel) Javits,* U.S. politician, lawyer; Congressman, 1946–54; Senator, 1956–80. [d. March 7, 1986]

1907 *Clifford Curzon,* British pianist; knighted, 1977. [d. September 1, 1982]

1912 *Perry Como (Pierino Como),* U.S. singer.

Richard Brooks, U.S. film director; wrote and directed screenplays for *Cat on a Hot Tin Roof, Elmer Gantry, Sweet Bird of Youth,* and *In*

Cold Blood. [d. March 11, 1992]

1914 *Pierre Aléxandre Balmain,* French fashion designer. [d. June 29, 1982]

1919 *Margot Fonteyn (Margaret Hookham),* British prima ballerina. [d. February 21, 1991]

1920 *Pope John Paul II (Karol Wojtyla),* pope, elected 1978; the first non-Italian pope in 455 years.

1922 *Bill Macy,* U.S. actor; known for his starring role on television series, *Maude.*

1930 *Pernell Roberts,* U.S. actor; known for his roles on television series, *Bonanza,* 1959–65, and *Trapper John, M.D.,* 1979–86.

1937 *Brooks Calbert Robinson, Jr.,* U.S. baseball player, sportscaster; elected to Hall of Fame, 1983.

1946 *Reggie (Reginald) Jackson,* U.S. baseball player.

1949 *Rick Wakeman,* British musician; member of the rock group, *Yes.*

1951 *James Howard (Jim) Sundberg,* U.S. baseball player.

1952 *George Strait,* U.S. country singer.

HISTORICAL EVENTS

1291 *Mamelukes* conquer *Acre,* bringing end to Christian rule in the East.

1412 *Henry IV of England* abandons Duke of Burgundy and forms alliance with Duke of Orléans (*Hundred Years' War*).

1652 *Rhode Island* becomes the first U.S. colony to pass a law limiting slavery by prohibiting perpetual servitude.

1803 Great Britain declares war on France (*Napoleonic Wars*).

1804 *France* becomes an empire with *Napoleon Bonaparte* as Emperor.

1900 The *Tonga Islands* become a British protectorate.

1917 *U.S. Selective Service Act* is passed, providing for registration of men between ages of 21 and 31.

1918 The first British retaliatory air raid on German towns is carried out against *Cologne* (*World War I*).

1920 *Iceland* adopts universal suffrage.

1933 *Tennessee Valley Authority* is created in U.S. to improve agriculture in that region.

1951 UN General Assembly, by unanimous vote, requests all nations to impose arms embargo against Communist China and North Korea.

1953 *Jacqueline Cochran* becomes the first woman to fly faster than the speed of sound.

James Baldwin's first novel, *Go Tell It on the Mountain,* is published.

1973 Harvard Law School professor, *Archibald Cox,* is appointed as special prosecutor (*Watergate Incident*).

1974 *India* explodes its first nuclear device, marking its entry into the nuclear age as the sixth nuclear power.

1978 Despite strong opposition from the Vatican, the Italian senate votes in favor of legalized *abortion.*

1980 *Mount St. Helens,* in Washington state, erupts, devastating a 122-square mile area, killing at least 60 people.

1983 *Owen Bieber* is elected president of the *United Automobile Workers* union.

1989 One million students and workers flood *Tiananmen Square* in Beijing during the fifth day of a pro-democracy rally. It is the largest popular protest against the government since 1949.

1990 *East Germany* and *West Germany* approve a shared monetary economy.

1996 *Romano Prodi* becomes Italy's new prime minister.

may

MAY
19

HOLIDAYS

Cyprus, Turkey
Youth and Sports Day

Turkey
Birthday of Atatürk
Commemorates the birthday of Atatürk, Turkish nationalist leader

RELIGIOUS CALENDAR

The Saints

SS. Pudentiana and *Pudens,* martyrs. Pudentiana also called *Pudenziana.* Pudentiana's feast suppressed 1969. [d. c. 1st century]

SS. Calocerus and *Parthenius,* martyrs. Brothers and eunuchs in the household of Emperor Decius' wife. [d. 304]

St. Dunstan, Archbishop of Canterbury; most famous of Anglo-Saxon saints. Regarded as father of English Benedictines. Patron of goldsmiths, jewelers, and locksmiths. [d. 988]

St. Celestine V, pope. Elected 1294; abdicated after five months; kept prisoner by the next pope, Boniface VIII. Also called *St. Peter Celestine.* Regarded as patron of book industry workers. [d. 1296]

St. Ivo of Kermartin, priest and lawyer; patron of lawyers, jurists, notaries, bailiffs, and orphans. Also called *Ives, Yves.* [d. 1303]

The Beatified

Blessed Alcuin, abbot. [d. 804]
Blessed Augustine Novello, Augustinian lay-brother; papal legate. [d. 1309]
Blessed Peter Wright, Jesuit priest and martyr. [d. 1651]

BIRTHDATES

1593 *Jacob Jordaens,* Flemish painter; a follower of Rubens. [d. October 18, 1678]

1611 *Pope Innocent XI,* pope 1676–89. [d. August 12, 1689]

1762 *Johann Fichte,* German philosopher; developer of *ethical idealism.* [d. January 29, 1814]

1795 *Johns Hopkins,* U.S. merchant, philanthropist; left his fortune to found *Johns Hopkins University* and *Johns Hopkins Medical Hospital.* [d. December 24, 1873]

1861 *Nellie Melba (Helen Porter Mitchell),* Australian operatic soprano. [d. February 23, 1931]

1864 *Carl Akeley,* U.S. animal sculptor, naturalist; renowned for his African life exhibitions at Chicago's Field Museum and at New York City's American Museum of Natural History. [d. November 17, 1926]

1879 *Viscountess Nancy Witcher Langhorne Astor,* British politician; first woman member of the British House of Commons. [d. May 2, 1964]

1890 *Ho Chi Minh (Nguyen That Thanh),* Vietnamese leader; President of Democratic Republic of Vietnam (North Vietnam), 1954–69. [d. September 3, 1969]

1898 *Alan Frank Guttmacher,* U.S. physician, birth control advocate. [d. March 18, 1974]

1901 *Dorothy Buffum Chandler,* U.S. journalist. [d. July 6, 1997]

1914 *Max Perutz,* British biochemist; Nobel Prize in chemistry for determination of the structure of *hemoproteins* (with J. C. Kendrew), 1962; recipient of the Lewis Thomas Prize, 1997

1925 *Malcolm X (Malcolm Little),* U.S. militant black leader. [assassinated February 21, 1965]

1928 *Pol Pot (Saloth Sar),* Cambodian politician; Prime Minister, 1975–79; associated with the atrocities of the Khmer Rouge. [d. April 15, 1998]

1930 *Lorraine Hansberry,* U.S. playwright. [d. January 12, 1965]

1932 *Paul E. Erdman,* Canadian economist, author.

1935 *David (Downs) Hartman,* U.S. actor, talk show host.

1936 *John Wilson Jenrette, Jr.,* U.S. politician; Congressman; convicted in ABSCAM scandal and served two years in prison, 1984–86.

1939 *James Fox* (William Fox), British actor; performed in *Those Magnificent Men in Their Flying Machines,* 1965, *Remains of the Day,* 1993, and *Patriot Games,* 1992.

Nancy Kashen Kwan, Chinese actress; known for her starring roles in *The World of Suzie Wong,* 1960, and *Flower Drum Song,* 1961.

Francis Richard (Dick) Scobee, U.S. astronaut; spacecraft commander who died in the explosion of the *Challenger* space shuttle. [d. January 28, 1986]

1941 *Nora Ephron,* U.S. author; wrote *Heartburn.*

1945 *Peter Dennis Blanford (Pete) Townshend,* British musician; member of the rock group, *The Who.*

1947 *Glenn Close,* U.S. actress; performed in the movies *The World According to Garp,* 1982, *The Big Chill,* 1983, and *Fatal Attraction,* 1987.

1950 *Pat(rick Hayward) Caddell,* U.S. pollster; President, Cambridge Survey Research.

1952 *Grace Jones,* Jamaican singer, actress, model; known for avante-garde appearance and music.

HISTORICAL EVENTS

1536 *Anne Boleyn,* second wife of *Henry VIII* of England, is beheaded.

1588 The *Spanish Armada* sets sail from Lisbon, bound for England.

1635 France declares war on Spain (*Thirty Years' War*).

1643 French defeat Spaniards at *Rocroi (Thirty Years' War);* considered end of supremacy of the Spanish forces.

New England Confederation is formed of representatives from Massachusetts, Plymouth, Connecticut, and New Haven colonies.

1802 *French Legion of Honor* is instituted.

1828 U.S. Congress passes *tariff of abominations,* raising duties on imports.

1849 Residents of *Colony of Cape of Good Hope,* Africa, successfully resist British attempt to make the Cape a penal colony.

1861 Spain annexes *Santo Domingo.*

1906 *Simplon Tunnel* through the Alps is opened in ceremonies by the King of Italy and the President of the Swiss Republic.

Federated Boys' Clubs of America is founded.

1918 *Codex Juris Canonici,* official collection of general Roman Catholic Church law, becomes effective.

1923 Cardinal *Robert Bellarmine* is beatified.

1934 Coup d'état of army officers under Gen. *Kimon Guerorguiev* takes place in Bulgaria.

1949 Martial law is imposed in *Taiwan.*

1956 *Abdullah Issa* becomes the first premier of Somalia.

1977 *Kenya* issues ban on big-game hunting.

1994 *Jacqueline Kennedy Onassis,* wife of U.S. President John F. Kennedy, dies in New York City from Hodgkin's disease.

1998 *Momir Bulatovic* is selected as the new premier of Yugoslavia.

France approves a 35-hour work week, replacing the current 39-hour work week.

may

HOLIDAYS

Cameroon
National Day
Commemorates achievement of
independence of the country, 1972.

Democratic Republic of the Congo
*Anniversary of the Popular
Movement of the Revolution*

U.S. (North Carolina)
*Anniversary of Mecklenburg
Declaration of Independence, 1775.*
The Declaration contained five
resolutions of independence from
England.

RELIGIOUS CALENDAR

The Saints
St. Thalelaceus, martyr. Called *the
Merciful* by the Greeks. [d. c.
284]
St. Basilla, virgin and martyr. Also
called *Basilissa.* [d. 304]
St. Baudelius, martyr; principal
patron of Nîmes, France. Also
called *Baudille.* [d. c. 380]
St. Austregisilus, Bishop of Bourges.
Also called *Outril.* [d. 624]
St. Ethelbert, King of the East Angles,
martyr. Invoked against
thieves. Also called *Aethelbert.*
[d. 794]
St. Bernardino of Siena, Franciscan
friar, apostle, reformer, and
missionary throughout Italy.
Called *the People's Preacher.*
Also called *Bernardin of
Siena, Bernardine.* [d. 1444]

The Beatified
Blessed Columba of Rieta, virgin;
patron of Perugia, Italy. [d.
1501]
Blessed Pierre Giorgio Frassati.
[beatified 1990]

BIRTHDATES

1470 *Pietro Bembo,* Italian
humanist, man of letters,
papal secretary. [d. January
18, 1547]

1537 *Hieronymous Fabricius,*
Italian humanist, surgeon;
known especially for work in
comparative anatomy and
embryology. [d. 1619]

1759 *William Thornton,* U.S.
architect born in West Indies.
Designed the *Capitol
Building,* Washington, D.C.
[d. March 28, 1828]

1768 *Dolley Madison,* U.S. First
Lady; wife of President James
Madison. [d. July 12, 1849]

1780 *Bernardino Rivadavia,* first
President of the Argentine
Republic, 1826–27. [d.
September 2, 1845]

1799 *Honoré de Balzac,* French
novelist; founder of school of
realism in French literature;
considered the greatest
novelist in French literature;
authored a comprehensive
picture of French society, *La
Comèdie Humaine.* [d.
August 18, 1850]

1806 *John Stuart Mill,* British
utilitarian economist,
philosopher; first a champion
of *utilitarianism;* later
espoused more radical social
philosophies. [d. May 8, 1873]

1818 *William George Fargo,* U.S.
transportation executive;
founder of American Express
Co. and Wells Fargo & Co. [d.
August 3, 1881]

1822 *Frederic Passy,* French
economist; awarded first
Nobel Peace Prize (with J.
Dunant), 1901. [d. June 12,
1912]

1825 *Antoinette Louisa Blackwell,*
U.S. clergywoman; first
ordained woman minister in
U.S. (Congregational), 1853.
[d. November 5, 1921]

1826 *Potter Palmer,* U.S. merchant;
a founder of Marshall Field &
Co. [d. May 4, 1902]

1846 *Alexander von Kluck,*
German Army general;
headed First German Army in
siege of Paris, 1914 (*World
War I*). [d. October 19, 1934]

*Sir George Dashwood
Taubman Goldie,* British
administrator; founder of
Nigeria. [d. August 22, 1928]

1851 *Emile Berliner,* U.S. inventor
of the flat (disk) *phonograph
record.* [d. August 3, 1929]

1860 *Eduard Buchner,* German
chemist; Nobel Prize in

chemistry for discovery of *cell-free fermentation*, 1907. [d. August 24, 1917]

1882 *Sigrid Undset,* Norwegian novelist; Nobel Prize in literature, 1928. [d. June 10, 1949]

1890 *Allan Nevins,* U.S. historian; a prolific writer noted for his masterful political biographies; Pulitzer Prize in biography, 1933, 1937. [d. March 3, 1971]

1891 *Earl Russell Browder,* U.S. political leader; head of *U.S. Communist party.* [d. June 27, 1973]

1894 *Adela Rogers St. Johns,* U.S. journalist; noted for coverage of Lindbergh baby kidnapping and Bruno Hauptmann trial. [d. August 10, 1988]

1899 *John Marshall Harlan,* U.S. judge; Supreme Court Justice, 1955–71. [d. December 29, 1971]

1908 *James (Maitland) Stewart,* U.S. actor. [d. July 2, 1997]

1913 *William Hewlett,* U.S. businessman, engineer; founded Hewlett-Packard, 1939.

1915 *Moshe Dayan,* Israeli public official and general; led invasion of Sinai Peninsula, 1956; Israeli Foreign Minister, 1977–79. [d. October 16, 1981]

1918 *Edward B. Lewis,* U.S. geneticist; Nobel Prize for Medicine. Lewis shares with award with Christiane N¤sslein-Volhard and Eric F. Wieschaus. They discovered the influence of genetics in embryonic development, 1995.

1919 *George Leslie Gobel,* U.S. comedian. [d. February 24, 1991]

1920 *Peggy Lee (Norma Delores Egstrom),* U.S. singer, actress.

1935 *Ted Bessell,* U.S. actor; known for his role as Donald Hollinger on television series, *That Girl,* 1966–71. [d. 1997]

1944 *Joe (Robert John) Cocker,* British musician, singer.

1946 *Cher (Cherilyn Sarkisian),* U.S. singer, actress; Academy Award for *Moonstruck,* 1988.

1950 *Wei Jingsheng,* Chinese human rights activist, educator.

HISTORICAL EVENTS

1303 *Treaty of Paris* restores Gascony to England (*Hundred Years' War*).

1498 *Vasco da Gama* arrives at *Calicut,* completing his voyage around Africa to India.

1571 A great armada of the *Holy League* begins assembling at Messina under *Don John of Austria* to break Turkish sea power in the Mediterranean.

1774 English parliament passes *Quebec Act,* providing permanent and highly centralized civil government for Canada.

1862 U.S. President Abraham Lincoln signs into law the *Homestead Act,* which entitles every U.S. citizen who is over 21 and the head of a family to acquire 160 acres of land in the public domain by residing on it for five years and paying a nominal price per acre.

1882 *St. Gotthard Tunnel,* first great railroad tunnel through the Alps, opens, providing a link between Lucerne, Switzerland and Milan, Italy.

1902 U.S. troops withdraw from *Cuba,* ending three-year military occupation.

1927 Treaty between Great Britain and *King Ibn Saud* recognizes the complete independence of the *Nejd-Hejaz (Saudi-Arabia).*

1929 Japanese evacuation of *Shantung Province* in China is completed.

1939 Italian and German forces are withdrawn from Spain (*Spanish Civil War*).

1941 German troops invade *Crete* (*World War II*).

1943 The British Royal Air Force begins the first in a series of air raids on *Berlin* (*World War II*).

1955 The Argentine Senate votes to abolish Roman Catholicism as the state religion at the behest of President *Juan Peron.*

1958 *Japanese-American citizens* who renounced U.S. citizenship during World War II regain full citizenship.

1961 U.S. marshals are sent to *Alabama* to help settle racial unrest.

1966 U.S. makes its first sale of tactical military aircraft to *Israel.*

1969 U.S. and South Vietnamese troops capture *Hamburger Hill* after 10 days of bloody fighting (*Vietnam War*).

1970 *Wilfred Jenkins* is elected president of the *International Labor Organization.*

may

1972 *Cameroon* promulgates its constitution.

1973 Swiss voters, in a national referendum, repeal two anti-Catholic articles that had been in the constitution since 1874.

1978 *Chiang Ching-Kuo,* the 68-year old son of the late Chiang Kai-shek and Premier since June 1972, becomes President of the Nationalist Chinese government in Taiwan.

1985 *Israel* releases 1,150 Arab prisoners in exchange for three Israelis held by a Palestinian guerrilla group.

Retired U.S. Navy chief warrant officer, *John Walker,* is charged with spying for the Soviet Union. Other members of his family are later arrested on similar charges.

HOLIDAYS

Chile

Battle of Iquique
Commemorates the naval battle at Iquique, 1879.

Navy Day

RELIGIOUS CALENDAR

The Saints

St. Godric, hermit. Earliest known lyrical poet in English; author of earliest known musical settings of English words. Also called *Godrick.* [d. 1170]

St. Andrew Bobola, Jesuit priest, missionary, and martyr. [d. 1657]

St. Theophilus of Corte, Franciscan priest noted for his oratory. [d. 1740]

St. Crispin of Viterbo, Capuchin brother. His life symbolized values of goodness. [d. 1750] Canonized May 21, 1982 by Pope John Paul II.

St. Collen, patron and founder of the Llangollen Church. Also called *Colan.* [death date unknown]

The Beatified

Blessed Benvenuto of Recanati, Franciscan lay-brother. [d. 1289]

BIRTHDATES

1471 *Albrecht Dürer,* German painter, graphic artist; one of the geniuses of the Renaissance in Germany. [d. April 6, 1528]

1527 *Philip II, King of Spain.* [d. September 13, 1598]

1688 *Alexander Pope,* English poet of the Augustan period; powerful figure in English literature. [d. May 30, 1744]

1759 *Joseph Fouché, Duke of Otranto,* French statesman, public official; known for his elaborate system of spies throughout the government; led provisional government after Napoleon's abdication. [d. December 25, 1820]

1796 *Reverdy Johnson,* U.S. public official; U.S. Senator, 1845–49; 1863–68; Attorney General, 1849–50; U.S. Minister to Great Britain, 1868–69. [d. February 10, 1876]

1817 *Rudolf Hermann Lotze,* German philosopher; influential in founding of science of *physiological psychology.* [d. July 1, 1881]

1843 *Charles A. Gobat,* Swiss lawyer, statesman; Nobel Peace Prize for work with *Bureau International Permanent de la Paix* (with E. Ducommun), 1902. [d. March 16, 1914]

1844 *Henri Rousseau,* French painter of the primitivist school of post-impressionism; known as *Le Douanier.* [d. September 2, 1910]

1851 *Léon V. A. Bourgeois,* French statesman; Nobel Peace Prize for promotion of the *League of Nations,* 1920. [d. September 29, 1925]

1856 *José Batlle Ordóñez,* Uruguayan statesman; President of Uruguay, 1902–1907. [d. October 20, 1929]

1860 *Willem Einthoven,* Dutch physiologist; Nobel Prize in physiology or medicine for development of the *electrocardiograph,* 1924. [d. September 29, 1927]

1878 *Glenn (Hammon) Curtiss,* U.S. inventor, aviator; made first public airplane flight in U.S., 1908; invented the *hydroplane.* [d. July 23, 1930]

1895 Lázaro Cárdenas, president of Mexico, 1934-40. [d. 1970]

1898 *Armand Hammer,* U.S. oil executive, art patron; Chairman, Occidental Petroleum Corp. [d. December 10, 1990]

1902 *Marcel Lajos Breuer,* U.S. architect born in Hungary; recognized for his streamlined design and international style in architecture and the invention of the tubular metal chair that bears his name. [d. July 1, 1981]

1904 *Fats (Thomas) Waller,* U.S. musician; jazz pianist. [d. December 15, 1943]

Robert Montgomery, U.S. actor, producer. [d. September 27, 1981]

1909 *Baron Guy Edouard Alphonse Paul de Rothschild,* French banker.

1916 *Harold Robbins,* U.S. novelist. [d. October 14, 1997]

1917 *Raymond Burr,* Canadian actor. [d. September 12, 1993]

1921 *Andrei Sakharov,* Russian physicist; one of the leaders of the dissident movement in the U.S.S.R.; Nobel Peace Prize, 1975. [d. December 14, 1989]

1923 *Ara (Raoul) Parseghian,* U.S. football coach; head coach, University of Notre Dame, 1964–75.

1925 *Peggy Cass (Mary Margaret Cass),* U.S. actress; Tony Award for *Auntie Mame,* 1956.

1934 *Bengt I. Samuelsson,* Swedish biochemist; Nobel Prize in physiology or medicine (with John R. Vane and Sune K. Bergstrom), 1982.

1935 *Gerald Anthony (Gerry) Faust, Jr.,* U.S. football coach.

1939 *David Lawrence Groh,* U.S. actor; known for his role as Joe Girard on television series, *Rhoda.*

1944 *Mary Robinson,* Irish politician; president of Ireland, *1990– .*

1948 *Leo (Gerald) Sayer,* British singer.

1952 *Mr. T (Lawrence Tero),* U.S. actor; former celebrity bodyguard; known for his starring role on television series, *The A-Team.*

1956 *Judge Reinhold,* U.S. actor; known for role in *Beverly Hills Cop* movies.

HISTORICAL EVENTS

996 *Otto III* is crowned Holy Roman Emperor at Rome.

1369 *Charles V of France* declares war on England (*Hundred Years' War*).

1424 *James I* is crowned King of Scotland at Scone.

1471 *Henry VI, King of England,* dies in the Tower of London, supposedly murdered by order of his rival, *Edward IV.*

1502 The island of *Saint Helena* is discovered by *Juan de Nova Castella,* on a return voyage from India.

1856 Proslavery border ruffians from Missouri ravage the free-soil town of *Lawrence, Kansas.*

1881 The *American Red Cross Society* is organized with *Clara Barton* as president.

1900 The British annex the *Orange Free State* to the British Empire as the *Orange River Colony (Boer War).*

1927 *Charles Lindbergh,* U.S. aviator, completes the first non-stop solo flight across the Atlantic (New York to Paris) in 33 hours, 29 minutes.

1932 *Amelia Earhart* completes first solo flight by a woman across the Atlantic.

U.S. Socialist Party convention nominates *Norman Thomas* for president.

1941 U.S. freighter *Robin Moor* is sunk by German submarine (*World War II*).

1950 General *Anastasio Somoza Garcia* resumes the Presidency of Nicaragua following the death of his uncle.

1955 South Vietnamese National Revolutionary Committee removes *Bao Dai* as chief of state.

1959 Jule Styne and Stephen Sondheim's musical, *Gypsy,* premieres in New York. It is based on the life of Gypsy Rose Lee.

1961 Military rule is introduced in *South Korea* as 14-man military cabinet is sworn in.

1964 World's first *nuclear-powered lighthouse* goes into operation in Chesapeake Bay.

1968 Attempt by exiles to invade *Haiti* and overthrow the government of *President François Duvalier* is crushed by the Haitian government.

1971 *Barbara McClintock* receives the U.S. Medal of Science for her work in the field of genetics. She is the first woman awarded the nation's highest honor for scientific achievement.

1978 Tokyo's new international airport at *Narita* is opened.

1980 President Jimmy Carter orders the evacuation of residents from the *Love Canal* area of New York after it is found that residents suffered chromosomal damage from leaking toxic chemical waste.

1985 Patti Frustaci gives birth to *septuplets* - the largest multiple birth in U.S. history.

1986 The Teamsters Union reelects *Jackie Presser* as president for a five-year term despite his indictment on racketeering charges.

The U.S. Justice Dept. allows *General Electric Co.* to buy *RCA Corp.* for $6.28 billion.

1991 *Mengistu Haile Mariam,* dictator of Ethiopia, resigns and goes into exile.

Rajiv Gandhi, former prime minister of India, is assassinated while campaigning for his reelection.

1994 *Bakili Muluzi* is elected president of Malawi.

1998 *President Suharto* of Indonesia resigns after serving 32 years in office. Vice-President *Bacharuddin Jusuf Habibe* is sworn in as the new president.

may

MAY
22

HOLIDAYS

Haiti

National Sovereignty and Thanksgiving Day

Day set aside to honor customs and rulers of Haiti.

Sri Lanka

National Heroes Day (formerly Republic Day)

Commemorates ratification of Sri Lanka's constitution, 1972.

U.S.

National Maritime Day

Commemorates the first transatlantic voyage by a steam-driven vessel, the *S.S. Savannah,* 1819.

Yemen

National Unity Day

RELIGIOUS CALENDAR

The Saints

SS. Castus and *Æmilius,* martyrs. [d. 250]

St. Quiteria, virgin and martyr. Invoked against the bites of mad dogs. [d. c. 5th century]

St. Romanus, monk. Befriended St. Benedict; founded Monastery at Fontrouge, France. [d. c. 550]

St. Julia, martyr. [d. c. 6th century]

St. Aigulf, Bishop of Bourges. Also called *Ayoul.* [d. 836]

St. Margaret of Hulme, martyr. [d. 1170]

St. Humility, widow. Founder of Vallombrosan nuns. [d. 1310]

St. Rita of Cascia, widow and nun; patron of the impossible and

advocate of desperate cases. [d. 1457]

St. Joachima des Mas y de Vedruna, widow and founder of the Carmelites of Charity. [d. 1854]

The Beatified

Blessed John Forest, martyr, priest, and confessor of Catherine of Aragon, first wife of Henry VIII. [d. 1538]

BIRTHDATES

1783 *William Sturgeon,* British investor, electrician; developed first *electromagnet.* [d. 1850]

1813 *Richard Wagner,* German opera composer; best known for *Tannhäuser, Lohengrin,* and *The Ring of the Nibelung.* [d. February 13, 1883]

1844 *Mary Cassatt,* U.S. impressionist painter and printmaker in France; noted for her paintings of mothers and children. [d. June 14, 1926]

1851 *Emil Gustav Hirsch,* U.S. rabbi; a representative of the extreme wing of Reform Judaism. [d. January 7, 1923]

1859 *Sir Arthur Conan Doyle,* British novelist; creator of the fictional detective *Sherlock Holmes.* [d. July 7, 1930]

1871 *William McDougall,* U.S. psychologist born in England. [d. November 28, 1938]

1902 *Al Simmons (Aloys Szymanski),* U.S. baseball player; elected to Baseball Hall of Fame, 1953. [d. May 26, 1956]

1907 *Laurence (Kerr) Olivier,* British stage and film actor, especially well known for Shakespearean roles; knighted in 1947; in 1970 became the first actor in English history to be named a baron. [d. July 11, 1989]

1912 *Herbert Brown,* U.S. physicist; Nobel Prize in chemistry for development of substances that facilitate very difficult chemical reactions (with G. Wittig), 1979.

Janos Kadar, Hungarian Communist leader; Premier, 1956–58, 1961–65; General Secretary of the Politburo, 1956–88. [d. July 6, 1989]

1914 *Vance (Oakley) Packard,* U.S. author. [d. December 12, 1996]

1927 *Michael Constantine (Constantine Joanides),* U.S. actor; Emmy Award for his role as Seymour Kaufman on television series, *Room 222,* 1970.

Quinn Martin, U.S. producer; known for the production of

television series, *The Untouchables* and *The Fugitive.* [d. September 5, 1987]

George A. Olah, U.S. chemist; Nobel Prize for Chemistry in 1994 for his work with carbocations.

1928 *T(homas) Boone Pickens, Jr.,* U.S. corporate executive; founded Mesa Petroleum Co., 1964.

1934 *Peter Nero,* U.S. pianist.

Garry Wills, U.S. author.

1938 *Susan Strasberg,* U.S. actress.

1940 *Michael Sarrazin (Jacques Michel Andre Sarrazin),* Canadian actor.

1941 *Paul Edward Winfield,* U.S. actor.

1943 *Thomas Edward (Tommy) John, Jr.,* U.S. baseball player; pitcher who had his left elbow surgically reconstructed in 1974 and went on to win twenty games in 1977.

Betty Williams, Irish peace activist; Nobel Peace Prize for helping start *Northern Ireland Peace Movement* (with M. Corrigan), 1976.

1948 *Benjamin Chavis,* U.S. social activist.

1950 *Bernie Taupin,* British lyricist; known for his songs written for Elton John.

1970 *Naomi Campbell,* British model, actress.

HISTORICAL EVENTS

1200 *Peace of Le Goulet* between *King John of England* and *Philip II of France* is signed.

1455 *War of the Roses* begins in England as Richard, Duke of York, defeats royal forces at *St. Albans.*

1526 *League of Cognac* between the pope, France, Venice, Florence, and Milan is established against *Charles V of Germany.*

1629 Peace of Lübeck between *Ferdinand II, Holy Roman Emperor,* and *Christian IV of Denmark* ends hostilities between the Empire and Denmark.

1900 *Associated Press* is founded in the U.S.

1911 The *gold escudo* becomes the official currency in Portugal.

1913 The *American Cancer Society* is founded in New York City.

1969 Canadian government decides to admit U.S. military deserters on the same basis as other immigrants.

Apollo 10 astronauts bring their lunar module, *Snoopy,* to within 9.4 miles of the moon and return it to the command ship, *Charlie Brown.*

1970 *Leonard Woodcock* is chosen to succeed Walter Reuther as president of the *United Automobile Workers.*

1972 *Ceylon* officially becomes *Sri Lanka,* an independent republic.

U.S. President *Richard Nixon* arrives in Moscow to begin the first official visit of a U.S. president to the U.S.S.R.

1977 After 94 years of service, the famed *Orient Express* makes its last regularly scheduled run across Europe.

1979 *Joe Clark,* the Progressive Conservative leader, replaces *Pierre Trudeau* as prime minister of Canada, thereby ending the 11-year rule of the Liberals.

1988 Premier *Karoly Grosz* replaces *Janos Kadar* as general secretary of Hungary's Communist Party.

1989 The first approved transfer of a gene to a melanoma patient for *gene therapy* takes place.

1992 *Herzegovina, Bosnia, Croatia,* and *Slovenia* become members of the United Nations.

Johnny Carson hosts his last *Tonight Show* after twenty-nine years.

1998 *Irish voters* approve the peace plan referendum (April 10, 1998).

may

MAY
23

HOLIDAYS

Jamaica
Labour Day

RELIGIOUS CALENDAR

The Saints

St. Desiderius, Bishop of Vienne and martyr. Also called *Didier.* [d. 607]

St. Guibert, monk and missionary. Founded celebrated Benedictine Monastery at Gembloux. Also called *Guilbert, Wibert.* [d. 962]

St. Leontius, Bishop of Rostov, martyr. [d. 1077]

St. Ivo, Bishop of Chartres. Also called *Yvo.* [d. 1116]

St. Euphrosyne of Polotsk, virgin and recluse. [d. 1173]

St. William of Rochester, martyr. [d. 1201]

St. John Baptist Rossi, priest. [d. 1764]

The Beatified

Blessed Gerard of Villamagna, hermit who joined the Third Crusade to the Holy Land. [d. 1245]

Blessed Bartholomew of Montepulciano, Franciscan monk. [d. 1330]

BIRTHDATES

1707 *Carolus Linnaeus,* (Carl von Linné) Swedish botanist; founder of modern *taxonomy.* [d. January 10, 1778]

1729 *Giuseppe Parini,* Italian didactic poet; best known for his epic satire *Il Giorno.* [d. August 15, 1799]

1734 *Franz Anton Mesmer,* Austrian physician; his discovery of cures by suggestion led to discovery of *hypnotism* and *mesmerism.* [d. March 5, 1815]

1795 *Sir Charles Barry,* English architect; designed the *Houses of Parliament* in London. [d. May 12, 1860]

1810 *Sarah Margaret Fuller, Marchioness Ossoli,* U.S. journalist, writer, foreign correspondent, critic; associated with Ralph Waldo Emerson and the Brook Farm experimental community. [d. July 19, 1850]

1824 *Ambrose Everett Burnside,* U.S. Civil War army general, political leader; was assigned to head Army of the Potomac during Civil War; Governor of Rhode Island, 1866–69; U.S. Senator, 1874–81. His style of facial whiskers led to the term *burnsides,* or *sideburns.* [d. September 13, 1881]

1848 *Otto Lilienthal,* German inventor, aeronautical engineer; contributed to improvement of wing designs of early planes. [d. August 9, 1896]

1873 *Leo Baeck,* German rabbi, leader of World Union of Progressive Judaism. [d. 1956]

1883 *Douglas Fairbanks (Douglas Ullman),* U.S. actor, silent-screen star. [d. December 12, 1939]

1886 *James Gleason,* U.S. character actor, writer, director. [d. April 12, 1959]

1891 *Pär Fabian Lagerkvist,* Swedish novelist, poet, dramatist; Nobel Prize in literature, 1951. [d. July 11, 1974]

1908 *John Bardeen,* U.S. physicist; Nobel Prize in physics for development of *electronic transistors* (with W. B. Shockley and W. H. Brattain), 1956; Nobel Prize in physics for development of *theory of superconductivity* (with L. N. Cooper and J. R. Schrieffer), 1972. [d. January 30, 1991]

1910 *Benjamin Sherman (Scatman) Crothers,* U.S. actor, musician, singer. [d. November 22, 1986]

Artie Shaw (Arthur Arshawsky), U.S. bandleader, clarinetist.

1914 *Barbara Mary Ward, Baroness Jackson of*

Lodsworth, British economist; author of *Spaceship Earth*. [d. May 31, 1981]

1920 *Helen O'Connell*, U.S. singer. [d. September 9, 1993]

1923 *Alicia De Larrocha*, Spanish concert pianist; child prodigy who debuted at the age of four. Known for interpretations of Chopin.

1925 *Joshua Lederberg*, U.S. geneticist; Nobel Prize in physiology or medicine for studies on genetic function in *hereditary characteristic transfers* (with E. L. Tatum and G. W. Beadle), 1958.

1928 *Rosemary Clooney*, U.S. actress, singer; known for song, *Come on-a My House*, 1951.

1933 *Joan Collins*, British actress; known for her role as Alexis Carrington Colby on television series, *Dynasty*.

1934 *Robert Moog*, U.S. inventor; established R. A. Moog Co., 1954.

1944 *John Newcombe*, Australian tennis player.

1951 *Anatoly Yevgenyevich Karpov*, Russian chess player; International Grandmaster, 1970.

1952 *(Marvelous) Marvin Nathaniel Hagler*, U.S. boxer; middleweight champion, 1980–87.

1962 *Karen Duffy*, U.S. model, actress; best known for her work on MTV, 1991–94.

1974 *Jewel (Jewel Kilcher)*, U.S. rock singer.

HISTORICAL EVENTS

1430 *Joan of Arc* is captured by Burgundians at Compiègne.

1474 *Pope Sixtus IV* confirms Order of the Hermits of St. Francis of Assisi, founded by *Francis of Padua*.

1493 *Treaty of Senlis* is signed between France and Hòly Roman Empire; France renounces Netherlands and Burgundy.

1498 *Girolamo Savonarola*, Italian reformer and preacher of penitence, is burned to death at Florence.

1533 *Henry VIII* is divorced from *Catherine of Aragon*.

1611 *Matthias*, brother of Holy Roman Emperor *Rudolf II*, becomes King of Bohemia.

1618 *Defenestration of Prague* takes place as Protestants begin Bohemian revolt against Hapsburg *Emperor Ferdinand II*, starting the *Thirty Years' War*.

1701 Captain *William Kidd* is hanged for murder and piracy in London.

1706 Marlborough of England defeats French at *Ramillies* and conquers Spanish Netherlands (*War of the Spanish Succession*).

1788 *South Carolina* is admitted to the Union as the 8th state.

1890 The *Colonial Dames of America* is organized in New York.

1895 *New York Public Library* is incorporated.

1903 *Wisconsin* becomes the first state in the U.S. to adopt the *direct primary system*.

1915 Italy, previously neutral, declares war on Austria-Hungary (*World War I*).

1945 The Allies officially disband the Nazi government still headquartered in the northern German town of *Flensburg*. Admiral *Karl Doenitz*, head of state since Hitler's death, is arrested.

1950 *Harry Gold*, confederate of *Klaus Fuchs*, is arrested on espionage charges in U.S. for his dealings with Fuchs and passing of atomic secrets to the Russians.

1960 Israeli Prime Minister *David Ben-Gurion* reports the capture by Israeli agents of *Adolf Eichmann*, alleged leader in carrying out the Nazi program for extermination of the Jews.

1969 *Z*, a film directed by Henri Costa-Gavras, wins the Golden Palm at the Cannes Film Festival.

1971 Body of *Ephraim Elrom*, Israeli Consul General in Istanbul, is found six days after being kidnapped by Turkish leftists who were demanding the release of political prisoners.

1973 U.S. agrees to grant commonwealth status to the *Mariana Islands*.

1977 South Moluccan extremists seize 100 children as hostages in the Netherlands.

University of California researchers announce the successful use of the recombinant DNA technique to produce the *insulin gene* in large quantities.

1983 Seven Afghan guerrilla organizations merge to form a unified front, the *Islamic Alliance of Afghan Mujahedeen,* to better combat Soviet activities in Afghanistan.

1984 U.S. surgeon general, C. Everett Koop, releases a report linking *passive*

smoking to lung disease. Nonsmokers who are regularly exposed to cigarette smoke are found to be at greater risk of developing lung disease.

1990 The unification of the People's Democratic Republic

of Yemen with the Yemen Arab Republic resulting in the newly created *Republic of Yemen.*

1997 *Mohammed Khatami* is elected president of Iran.

1998 *Daniel Ortega* is reelected president of Nicaragua.

HOLIDAYS

Belize
Commonwealth Day (Emancipation Day)

Bulgaria
Day of Slav Letters or Education Day
A day of tribute to the nation's literature and culture.

SS. Cyril & Methodius Day

Ecuador
Battle of Pichincha Day
Commemorates the battle during the war for independence from Spain, 1822.

Korea
Buddha's Birthday

RELIGIOUS CALENDAR

The Saints
SS. Donatian and *Rogatian*, martyrs. Greatly venerated at Nantes and known there as *Les Enfants Nantais*. [d. 289 or 304]
St. Vincent of Lérins, hermit. [d. c. 445]
St. David I of Scotland, King of Scotland 1124–53. [d. 1153]
St. Nicetas of Pereaslau, martyr. Also called *the Wonder-Worker* for his miracles of healing. [d. 1186]

The Beatified
Blessed Lanfranc, Archbishop of Canterbury. [d. 1089]

Blessed John of Prado, Franciscan missionary and martyr. [d. 1613]

BIRTHDATES

1494 *Jacopo da Pontormo (Jacopo Carrucci)*, Italian painter of Florentine school; pupil of Leonardo da Vinci and Andrea del Sarto. [d. January 2, 1557]

1544 *William Gilbert*, English physician, physicist; known as *Father of Electricity*. First to use terms *electric force, magnetic pole*. [d. December 10, 1603]

1743 *Jean Paul Marat*, French Revolutionary politician born in Switzerland; advocate of extreme violence. [d. at the hand of *Charlotte Corday*, July 13, 1793]

1810 *Abraham Geiger*, German rabbi, scholar, author; leader of the second generation of Reform Judaism in Germany. [d. October 23, 1874]

1819 *(Alexandrina) Victoria, Queen of Great Britain and Ireland*, 1837–1901; Empress of India, 1876–1901. Ruled in dignified manner which created new concept of monarchy in the Empire. [d. January 22, 1901]

1854 *Richard Mansfield*, U.S. actor; known for his portrayal of the

lead role in *Cyrano de Bergerac*. [d. August 30, 1907]

1855 *Alfred Cort Haddon*, British ethnologist, anthropologist; one of founders of modern *anthropology*. [d. April 20, 1940]

Arthur Wing Pinero, British playwright; his works marked the beginning of a new era in British drama, characterized by *problem plays*. [d. November 23, 1934]

1863 *George Grey Barnard*, U.S. sculptor; sculpted more than 30 pieces for state capitol at Harrisburg, Pennsylvania. [d. April 24, 1938]

1870 *Benjamin Nathan Cardozo*, U.S. jurist, lawyer; Justice of U.S. Supreme Court, 1932–38. Profound legal philosopher. [d. July 9, 1938]

Jan Christiaan Smuts, South African statesman, soldier; played a significant role in the creation of *Union of South Africa*. [d. September 11, 1950]

1878 *Harry Emerson Fosdick*, U.S. Protestant minister; stimulated healed controversy between liberals and fundamentalists. [d. October 5, 1969]

1879 *Ines Mexia*, U.S. botanical scientist. [d. 1938]

1883 *Elsa Maxwell,* U.S. journalist, socialite; known for organizing parties for socially prominent people. [d. November 1, 1963]

1888 *Jim (James Francis) Thorpe,* U.S. Olympic athlete. [d. 1953]

1891 *William F. Albright,* U.S. orientalist, archaeologist; authority on Dead Sea Scrolls. [d. September 19, 1971]

1898 *Helen Brooke Taussig,* U.S. physician; developed surgical procedure for treating "blue babies"; led fight against Thalidomide in U.S. [d. May 20, 1986]

1899 *Suzanne Lenglen,* French tennis player; called the *Pavlova of Tennis.* [d. July 4, 1938]

1905 *Mikhail Aleksandrovich Sholokhov,* Russian novelist; Nobel Prize in literature, 1965. [d. February 21, 1984]

1907 *Douglas Leigh,* U.S. advertising executive; best known for *Coca-Cola* and *Camel Cigarette* signs in Times Square, New York City.

1909 *Wilbur Daigh Mills,* U.S. politician; Congressman, 1939–77. [d. May 2, 1992]

1914 *Lilli Palmer,* German-born actress, author. [d. January 27, 1986]

1918 *Coleman A(lexander) Young,* U.S. politician; Mayor of Detroit, 1974–93. [d. November 29, 1997]

1922 *Siobhan McKenna,* Irish actress.

1934 *Jane Byrne,* U.S. politician; Mayor of Chicago, 1979–82.

1940 *Joseph Alexandrovich Brodsky,* Russian-born author,

poet; Nobel Prize in literature, 1987. [d. January 28, 1996]

1941 *Bob Dylan (Robert Zimmerman),* U.S. singer, songwriter.

1943 *Gary Burghoff,* U.S. actor; known for his role as Radar on television series, *M*A*S*H.*

1944 *Patti LaBelle (Patricia Holt),* U.S. singer; known for songs, *New Attitude,* 1985, and *On My Own,* 1986.

1946 *Priscilla Ann Beaulieu Presley,* U.S. actress; married to Elvis Presley, 1967–73; known for her role as Jena on television series, *Dallas.*

1955 *Roseanne Cash,* U.S. singer; daughter of Johnny Cash.

HISTORICAL EVENTS

1153 *King David I of Scotland* dies and is succeeded by his grandson, *Malcolm IV.*

1370 *Peace of Stralsund* between Denmark-Norway and Hansa secures Hanseatic predominance in Northern Europe.

1822 *Ecuador* achieves independence.

1844 *Samuel F. B. Morse* transmits the first telegraphic message from the U.S. Supreme Court room in the Capitol, Washington, D.C., to Baltimore. The message: *What hath God wrought.*

1846 U.S. General *Zachary Taylor* captures *Monterey (Mexican War).*

1856 *John Brown,* U.S. abolitionist, leads retaliatory massacre at *Pottawatomie Creek, Kansas,* in revenge for Quantril's raid on *Lawrence, Kansas* (see May 21).

1883 The *Brooklyn Bridge* opens, linking Manhattan to Brooklyn, New York.

1915 The U.S. proclaims its neutrality in the war between Italy and Austria-Hungary (*World War I*).

1917 Russians peasants rise against large land owners and Germans living in Russia (*Russian Revolution*).

1928 *Umberto Nobile,* in his last exploratory flight in the dirigible *Italia,* crashes on a return flight from the North Pole.

1930 *Amy Johnson* arrives in Australia, becoming first woman to complete solo flight from England to Australia.

1935 First major league *baseball night game* is played at Crosley Field, Cincinnati, Ohio, between Cincinnati Reds and the Philadelphia Phillies.

1941 German battleship *Bismarck* sinks the British battle cruiser *Hood.* British air and naval forces subsequently sink the *Bismarck* (*World War II*).

1960 U.S. Air Force launches *Midas II,* a 5,000 pound experimental satellite designed to give early warning of surprise missile attacks.

1962 *M(alcolm) Scott Carpenter* successfully completes second U.S. manned orbital space flight with three trips around the earth.

1966 Jerry Herman's musical, *Mame,* premieres in New York.

1968 *Bob Foster* defeats *Dick Tiger* in four rounds to win the world light heavyweight boxing title.

1976 Supersonic *Concorde* jets begin regular flights, less than four hours in duration, from London and Paris to Dulles International Airport near Washington, D.C., on a 16-month trial basis.

1978 *Princess Margaret of Great Britain* and her husband, the Earl of Snowden, are granted a divorce after 18 years of marriage.

1983 Dr. *Fred Sinowatz* is inaugurated as chancellor of Austria.

The U.S. Supreme Court rules that the *Internal Revenue Service* can deny tax exemptions to *private schools* that discriminate against minorities in admissions and other policies.

1984 Five former Salvadoran National Guardsmen are found guilty of aggravated homicide and robbery in the 1980 murders of three U.S. nuns and one lay person.

1992 The U.S. Coast Guard begins returning *Haitian refugees* from Guantanamo, Cuba, due to overcrowding.

1993 *Eritrea* becomes an independent nation.

may

MAY
25

HOLIDAYS

Argentina
National Holiday (Revolución de Mayo)
Commemorates the revolution of 1810.

Bermuda
Bermuda Day

Bolivia (Sucre)
Public Holiday

Chad, Gabon, Liberia, Mali, Mauretania, Zambia, Zimbabwe
Liberation of Africa Day
Commemorates the formation of the *Organization of African Unity,* 1963, and celebrates freedom and productivity.

Eritrea
Independence Day

Equatorial Guinea
OAU Day
Commemorates the founding of the Organization for African Unity.

Jordan
Independence Day
Celebrates the coming to full independence of Jordan, 1949.

Libya
National Day of Sudan or Revolution Day in the Sudan
Commemorates the overthrow of the government of King Idris I, 1969 (see below).

Sudan
Revolution Day
Commemorates the military coup and takeover by Col. Jaafar al-Nimeiry, 1969.

U.S. (New Mexico)
Memorial Day

RELIGIOUS CALENDAR

The Saints
St. Urban I, pope and martyr. Elected 222 or 223. [d. c. 230]
St. Dionysius, Bishop of Milan. [d. c. 360]
St. Zenobius, Bishop of Florence; principal patron of the city of Florence, Italy. [d. c. 390]
St. Leo, Abbot of Monastery at Mantenay. Also called *Lyé.* [d. c. 550]
St. Aldhelm, first Bishop of Sherborne. Called the first English scholar of distinction. Also called *Adhelm.* [d. 709]
St. Bede the Venerable, Doctor of the Church. Known for his *Ecclesiastical History of the English People,* and for the first martyrology with historical notes. Also called *Beda.* [d. 735] Feast formerly May 27. Optional Memorial.
St. Gennadius, Bishop of Astorga; invoked by the Spaniards against fever. [d. 936]
St. Gregory VII, pope. Elected 1073. [d. 1085]
St. Mary Magdalen dei Pazzi, virgin, Carmelite nun, and mystic. [d.

1607] Feast formerly May 29. Optional Memorial.
St. Madeleine Sophie Barat, virgin, founder of the Society of the Sacred Heart, which provided for girls' education. [d. 1865]

The Beatified
Blessed Claritus, founder of convent of Augustinian nuns in Florence. Also called *Chiarito.* [d. 1348]

BIRTHDATES

1803 *Ralph Waldo Emerson,* U.S. philosopher, poet, essayist; leader of the *transcendental movement* in the U.S. [d. April 27, 1882]

1847 *John Alexander Dowie,* Scottish religious leader; established *Zion City* in Illinois; eventually deposed by his followers. [d. March 9, 1907]

1848 *Helmuth Johannes Ludwig, Graf von Moltke (Moltke the Younger),* German Army general; Chief of General Staff, 1906–16. [d. June 18, 1916]

1865 *Pieter Zeeman,* Dutch physicist; Nobel Prize in physics for research on influence of magnetism on radiation (with H. A. Lorentz), 1902. [d. October 9, 1943]

John Raleigh Mott, U.S. evangelist, Methodist layman;

Nobel Peace Prize for his work in international church and missionary movements (with E. G. Balch), 1946. [d. January 31, 1955]

1878 *Bill (Bojangles) Robinson,* U.S. dancer. [d. November 25, 1949]

1879 *Lord Beaverbrook (William Maxwell Aitken),* British publisher, statesman; accumulated his fortune by investments in cement manufacturing plants. [d. June 9, 1964]

1886 *Philip Murray,* U.S. labor leader; President of CIO, 1940–52. [d. November 9, 1952]

1889 *Igor Ivanovich Sikorsky,* U.S. aviation engineer born in Russia; developed first successful *helicopter,* 1939. [d. October 26, 1972]

1898 *Gene Tunney,* U.S. boxer; World Heavyweight Champion, 1926–28. [d. November 7, 1978]

Bennett (Alfred) Cerf, U.S. publisher, editor, columnist; publisher of Modern Library; founder of Random House. [d. August 27, 1971]

James Joseph (Gene) Tunney, U.S. boxer, businessman; beat Jack Dempsey to become the heavyweight champ, 1922. [d. November 7, 1978]

1908 *Theodore Roethke,* U.S. poet; Pulitzer Prize in poetry, 1954. [d. August 1, 1963]

1910 *James N. Demaret,* U.S. golfer; first to win three Masters titles (1940, 1947, 1950). [d. December 28, 1983]

1913 *Joseph Peter Grace,* U.S. business executive; President of W. R. Grace & Co., major manufacturer of chemicals, and owner of Grace Line, major shipping company. [d. April 19, 1995]

1917 *Theodore Martin Hesburgh,* U.S. author, educator; President, Notre Dame, 1952–86.

1921 *Hal David,* U.S. lyricist; Oscar Award for *Raindrops Keep Fallin' on My Head,* 1969; President, American Society of Composers, Authors, and Publishers, 1980–86.

Jack Steinberger, U.S. physicist; Nobel Prize for Physics (1988), with Leon M. Lederman and Melvin Schwartz. The three physicists researched neutrinos.

1922 *Enrico Berlinguer,* Italian politician; General Secretary of the Italian Communist Party, 1972–84. [d. June 11, 1984]

1926 *Miles (Dewey) Davis, Jr.,* U.S. jazz musician, trumpeter. [d. September 28, 1991]

1927 *Robert Ludlum,* U.S. author; wrote *The Osterman Weekend,* 1972.

1929 *Beverly Sills (Belle Silverman),* U.S. coloratura soprano.

1932 *John Gregory Dunne,* U.S. author; wrote *True Confessions,* 1977.

1934 *Ron(ald Harold) Nessen,* U.S. journalist; Press Secretary, 1974–76.

1936 *Tom T. Hall,* U.S. singer, storyteller; known for his song, *Harper Valley PTA.*

1939 *Ian Murray McKellen,* British actor, director; Tony Award for his role as Salieri in *Amadeus,* 1981.

1943 *Leslie Uggams,* U.S. singer, actress.

1947 *Jessie Colter (Miriam Johnson),* U.S. singer.

Karen Valentine, U.S. actress; known for her starring role on television series, *Room 222,* 1969–74.

1955 *Connie Sellecca,* U.S. actress; known for her role as Christine Francis on television series, *Hotel.*

1963 *Mike Myers,* Canadian comedian and actor; starred in *Wayne's World* movies and *Austin Powers.*

HISTORICAL EVENTS

1085 *Alfonso VI of Castile* captures *Toledo,* thus bringing the Moorish center of science into Christian hands.

1659 *Richard Cromwell,* Lord Protector of England and son of *Oliver Cromwell,* resigns under pressure from Parliament.

1780 Mutiny by two Connecticut regiments at Washington's winter quarters, Morristown, N.J., is suppressed (*American Revolution*).

1787 The American *Constitutional Convention* meets in first session in Philadelphia to draw up a constitution for the new nation.

1810 Revolution occurs in *Argentina,* initiating the move toward independence, finally achieved July 9, 1816.

1909 The *India Councils Act* is enacted, providing some reform concerning powers of legislative councils in India.

1911 Mexican President *Porfirio Diaz* resigns after

may

revolutionist *Francisco Madero's* forces defeat government troops (*Mexican Civil War*).

1915 *The Second Battle of Ypres,* begun April 22, ends with total casualties to all sides of about 105,000 (*World War I*).

German airplane raid on *Kent* and *Folkestone,* England, produces 290 casualties (*World War I*).

1921 The *League of Nations* assigns the *Aaland Islands* to Finland.

1933 Walt Disney's film, *Three Little Pigs,* with popular song *Who's Afraid of the Big Bad Wolf?* premieres in New York.

1944 *Marshal Tito* escapes unharmed from his headquarters near Drvar, Bosnia, when it is captured by

German troops *(World War II).*

1946 *Abdullah ibn Hussein* is crowned king of Transjordan.

1950 *Brooklyn-Battery Tunnel,* the longest roadway tunnel in the U.S., is formally opened to traffic.

1960 A team from the People's Republic of China completes the first ascent of *Mt. Everest* from the northern side.

1965 *Cassius Clay (Muhammad Ali)* knocks out *Sonny Liston* in the first round of a bout at Lewiston, Maine, to retain the world heavyweight boxing title.

1969 John Schlesinger's film, *Midnight Cowboy,* is released.

1969 Sudanese coalition government led by Prime

Minister *Muhammad Ahmed Mahgoub* is overthrown by leftist military coup; *Abubakr Awadallah* is named prime minister and foreign minister.

1971 Soviet supersonic jetliner, the *Tu-144,* makes its western debut, arriving in Paris for an air show.

1979 A *DC-10* jetliner crashes at Chicago's O'Hare International Airport, killing 274 persons.

1986 Nearly five and a half million people join hands to form a human chain across the U.S. The event, *Hands Across America,* is designed to raise funds for the poor and homeless.

1997 *Ahmed Tejan Kabbah,* president of Sierra Leone, is removed from power by a military coup.

HOLIDAYS

Republic of Georgia
Independence Day

RELIGIOUS CALENDAR

The Saints

St. Quadratus, Bishop of Athens;
first of great line of Christian
apologists. Also called
Codratus. [d. c. 129]
SS. Priscus and his companions,
martyrs. Also called *Prix.* [d.
c. 272]
St. Augustine, Archbishop of
Canterbury; Apostle of the
English. Also called *Austin.* [d.
c. 605] Feast formerly May 28.
St. Lambert, Bishop of Vence,
France. [d. 1154]
St. Philip Neri, priest; founder of the
Congregation of the Oratory
and of Trinity Hospital in
Rome. Also called the *Apostle
of the city of Rome.* [d. 1595]
Obligatory Memorial.
St. Mariana of Quito, virgin. Also
called the *Lily of Quito.* [d.
1645]

The Beatified

Blessed Eva of Liège, virgin and
prioress of Mount Cornillon.
[d. c. 1265]
Blessed Peter Sanz, bishop, and his
companions, martyrs;
missionaries in China. [d.
1747 and 1748]

BIRTHDATES

1478 *Pope Clement VII,* Pope
1523–34. [d. September 25,
1534]

1602 *Philippe de Champagne,*
Belgian painter of the Flemish
school. [d. August 12, 1674]

1650 *John Churchill, 1st Duke of
Marlborough,* British general,
politician; English leader
during the *War of the
Spanish Succession.* [d. June
16, 1722]

1689 *Lady Mary Wortley Montagu,*
British author; known for her
letters of Middle Eastern life
published posthumously,
1763. [d. August 21, 1762]

1784 *Joseph Stevens Buckminster,*
U.S. clergyman; founder of
the *Boston Atheneum.* [d.
June 9, 1812]

1814 *Heinrich Geissler,* German
glassblower, inventor;
produced first *Geissler tubes*
(most effective vacuum tubes
created to that time), and the
Geissler pump. [d. January 24,
1879]

1822 *Edmond Louis Antoine Huot
de Goncourt,* French novelist,
historian, art critic; brother of
Jules Alfred Huot de
Goncourt (December 17).
Popularized naturalistic style
of novel writing. By his will,
established the *Académie des
Goncourt,* which makes an

annual award for imaginative
fiction. [d. July 16, 1896]

1837 *Washington Augustus
Roebling,* U.S. engineer and
bridge builder born in
Germany; with brother John,
designed and constructed the
Brooklyn Bridge. [d. July 21,
1926]

1854 *Susette LaFlesche Tibbles,*
Native American activist. [d.
1903]

1859 *A(lfred) E(dward) Housman,*
British classical scholar and
poet. [d. April 30, 1936]

1863 *Shailer Mathews,* U.S.
theologian, educator, writer;
dean of Divinity School of
University of Chicago. [d.
October 23, 1941]

1876 *Robert Merans Yerkes,* U.S.
psychologist; pioneer and
leading authority on the great
apes, particularly the
chimpanzee. [d. February 3,
1956]

1884 *Charles Winninger,* U.S.
character actor. [d. January
1969]

1886 *Al Jolson (Asa Yoelson),* U.S.
singer, actor born in Russia;
sang in blackface (his
trademark), in vaudeville and
minstrel companies,
1899–1926. Starred in first
feature-length talking motion
picture, *The Jazz Singer,*
1927. [d. October 23, 1950]

1891 *Paul Lukas,* U.S. actor born in Hungary. [d. August 15, 1971]

1897 *Norma Talmadge,* U.S. actress; silent-film star. [d. December 24, 1957]

1907 *John Wayne (Marion Michael Morrison),* known as *the Duke,* U.S. actor. [d. June 11, 1979]

1908 *Robert Morley,* British actor, dramatist; known for his starring role in *Pygmalion,* 1937; spokesman for British Airways. [d. June 5, 1992]

1910 *Laurance Spelman Rockefeller,* U.S. executive; known for his numerous donations of land to U.S. government for parks, in particular the *Grand Teton Park,* Colorado. Chairman of Rockefeller Center, Inc., 1953–56, 1958–66.

1913 *Peter Cushing,* British actor; known for his roles in horror films.

1920 *Peggy Lee (Norma Egstrom),* U.S. singer.

1923 *James Arness (James Aurness),* U.S. actor; played Marshall Dillon on the TV show *Gunsmoke.*

1926 *Miles Davis,* U.S. jazz trumpeter. [d. September 28, 1991]

1939 *Brent Woody Musburger,* U.S. sportscaster, CBS Sports, 1974–90; ABC Sports, 1990– .

1943 *Levon Helm,* U.S. musician, singer, actor; known for his role as Loretta Lynn's father in *Coal Miner's Daughter,* 1980; member of the rock group, *The Band.*

1948 *Stephanie (Stevie) Nicks,* U.S. singer, songwriter; member of the rock group, *Fleetwood Mac.*

1949 *Pamela Suzette Grier,* U.S. actress; known for her roles in *Something Wicked This Way Comes,* 1983, and *Jackie Brown,* 1997.

Philip Michael Thomas, U.S. actor; known for his role as Ricardo Tubbs on television series, *Miami Vice,* 1984–89.

Hank Williams, Jr., U.S. singer.

1951 *Sally Ride,* astronaut, first U.S. woman in space.

1962 *Genie Francis,* U.S. actress; known for her role as Laura on television soap opera, *General Hospital.*

1964 *Lenny Kravitz,* U.S. pop singer.

1966 *Helena Bonham-Carter,* British actress; best known for *A Room with a View,* 1985, and *Howard's End,* 1992.

HISTORICAL EVENTS

1521 *Edict of Worms* outlaws *Martin Luther* and his followers.

1659 *Aurangzeb* formally ascends throne of Mogul dynasty, succeeding his deposed father, *Shah Jahan;* assumes title *Alamcir, conqueror of the world.*

1805 *Napoleon* crowns himself King of Italy in the Cathedral of Milan.

1834 *Dom Miguel of Portugal* capitulates to troops of *Dom Pedro,* ending the six-year *Portuguese Civil War.*

1879 The *Treaty of Gandamak* is signed by the British and Afghans giving the British occupation of the *Khyber Pass.*

1896 *Nicholas II,* destined to be the last Russian czar, is crowned in the Cathedral of the Assumption in Moscow.

1913 The *Actors' Equity Union* is founded in New York City.

1919 Women achieve full suffrage in *Sweden.*

1924 *Johnson-Reed Immigration Bill* is signed by U.S. President Calvin Coolidge, limiting number of immigrants from any one country to 2 percent of 1890 population of that nationality; Japanese are excluded entirely.

1932 Drainage of the *Zuider Zee* in the Netherlands is completed.

1947 Nicaraguan National Guard ousts President *Leonardo Arguello. Anastasio Somoza Garcia* regains the presidency.

1950 The *Journal of the American Medical Association* publishes research findings which show heavy smokers have much higher rates of *lung cancer* than do light smokers and nonsmokers.

1961 U.S. *B-58* jet bomber flies from New York to Paris in record time of 3 hours 19 minutes 41 seconds.

1963 *Organization of African Unity* charter is adopted by heads of all 50 independent African states except those dominated by whites in the south.

1966 *Guyana* adopts a constitution and gains independence within the British

Commonwealth. Constitution remains in effect until 1980, when the black majority *People's National Congress* takes power.

1967 The Vatican announces that Protestants and members of the Eastern Orthodox Church may partake of the sacraments in the Roman Catholic faith under special circumstances.

1968 *Sir Henry Tucker* of the United Bermuda Party is named Bermuda's first prime minister.

1978 Legalized *casino gambling* begins in *Atlantic City,* New Jersey, the first legal casino in the U.S. outside of Nevada.

Dominican Republic President *Joaquin Balaguer* is unseated by Dominican Revolutionary Party candidate *Antonio Guzmán Fernandez.*

1979 Finnish president *Urho K. Kekkonen* names Social Democrat *Mauno Koivisto* prime minister of a new four-party coalition government; Koivisto assumes the presidency, 1982.

1987 Scientists successfully transplant a human gene into a monkey's bone marrow cells.

may

MAY
27

RELIGIOUS CALENDAR

Feasts

Feast of the Immaculate Heart of Mary. Formerly celebrated August 22. Optional Memorial.

The Saints

St. Restituta of Sora, virgin and martyr; principal patron of the Italian town of Sora. [d. c. 271]

SS. Julius and his companions, soldiers and martyrs. [d. c. 302]

St. Eutropius, Bishop of Orange. [d. c. 476]

St. John I, pope and martyr. Elected pope 523. [d. 526]

St. Melangell, virgin. Also called *Monacella.* [date unknown]

BIRTHDATES

1265 *Dante Alighieri,* Italian poet; wrote *The Divine Comedy.* [d. September 14, 1321]

1794 *Cornelius Vanderbilt,* U.S. financier, railroad builder; founder of the Vanderbilt empire. [d. January 4, 1877]

1799 *Jacques François Fromental Elie Levy (Halévy),* French opera composer; teacher of Gounod and Bizet. [d. March 17, 1862]

1818 *Amelia Bloomer,* U.S. social reformer, women's rights advocate; published the *Lily,* the first U.S. newspaper to be edited entirely by a woman, providing a forum for women's rights advocates as well as temperance reformers. Became involved in dress reform movement, and, by wearing trousers under a short skirt, gave rise to the term, and the fashion, called *bloomers.* [d. December 30, 1894]

1819 *Julia Ward Howe,* U.S. poet, writer, social reformer; author of the words for *The Battle Hymn of the Republic.* [d. October 17, 1910]

1835 *Charles Francis Adams, Jr.,* U.S. historian, lawyer. [d. March 20, 1915]

1836 *Jay Gould (Jason Gould),* U.S. financier, railroad executive; his gold speculations caused the *Black Friday* panic of 1869. [d. December 2, 1892]

1837 *James Butler (Wild Bill) Hickok,* U.S. frontier scout, marshal 1855–71; member of Buffalo Bill Cody's Wild West Show, 1872–73. [d. August 2, 1876]

1849 *Adolph Lewisohn,* U.S. financier, philanthropist; dedicated to reform of child labor laws and prisons. [d. August 17, 1938]

1867 *(Enoch) Arnold Bennett,* British novelist, dramatist; noted as a master of fiction; treated sordid aspects of English industrial life with infinite detail. [d. March 27, 1931]

1878 *Isadora Duncan,* U.S. dancer; her innovations in dance freed ballet from its previous restrictions and set the stage for the development of modern dance. [d. September 14, 1927]

1879 *Lucile Watson,* U.S. character actress. [d. June 24, 1962]

1894 *Louis-Ferdinand Celine (Louis-Ferdinand Destouches),* French author; wrote *Journey to the End of Night,* 1932, and *Death on the Installment Plan,* 1936. [d. July 4, 1961]

(Samuel) Dashiell Hammett, U.S. writer of "tough-guy" detective stories; author of *The Maltese Falcon.* [d. January 10, 1961]

1897 *Sir John Douglas Cockcroft,* British physicist; first to cause *nuclear reaction* with artificially accelerated atomic particles. Knighted, 1948; Nobel Prize in physics (with E. T. S. Walton), 1951. [d. September 18, 1967]

1902 *Peter Marshall,* U.S. Presbyterian clergyman;

Chaplain to the U. S. Senate, 1947–48; subject of the book and film, *A Man Called Peter*. [d. January 25, 1949]

1903 *John Barth*, U.S. novelist; author of *The Sot-Weed Factor*.

1907 *Rachel Carson*, U.S. biologist, author. Her final book, *Silent Spring*, stimulated widespread national controversy about the use of chemical herbicides and pesticides and their potential danger to world ecological balance. [d. April 14, 1964]

1908 *Harold (Jacob) Rome*, U.S. composer of musicals; composed scores for *Pins and Needles, I Can Get It for You Wholesale.*

1911 *Hubert (Horatio) Humphrey*, U.S. politician; U.S. Senator; Vice-President, 1965–69; Democratic presidential candidate, 1968. [d. January 13, 1978]

Vincent Price, U.S. stage and screen actor. [d. October 25, 1993]

1912 *(Slammin') Sam Snead*, U.S. golfer.

John Cheever, U.S. writer; Pulitzer Prize in fiction, 1979. [d. June 18, 1982]

1915 *Herman Wouk*, U.S. novelist; author of *The Caine Mutiny, Marjorie Morningstar, The Winds of War* trilogy.

1918 *Yasuhiro Nakasone*, Japanese politician; Premier, 1982–87.

1921 *Caryl (Whittier) Chessman*, U.S. criminal, author. Wrote four books which won him support by such figures as Albert Schweitzer, Aldous Huxley. [d. by electrocution,

after eight stays of execution, May 2, 1960]

1922 *Christopher (Frank Carandini) Lee*, British actor; known for his roles in horror films. [d. March 31, 1993]

1923 *Henry Kissinger*, U.S. government official, diplomat, scholar, born in Germany; U.S. Secretary of State, 1973–77; Nobel Peace Prize, 1973.

1930 *John Simmons Barth*, U.S. author; wrote *The Open Decision*, 1970.

1934 *Harlan Jay Ellison*, U.S. writer, known for his fantasy and speculative fiction; wrote numerous stories for *Star Trek* television series.

1935 *Ramsey Lewis*, U.S. musician, pianist, song-writer.

Lee Meriwether, U.S. actress; Miss America, 1955; known for her role on television series, *Barnaby Jones*, 1973–80.

1936 *Lou(is) Gossett, Jr.*, U.S. actor; Oscar Award for *An Officer and a Gentleman*, 1983.

1943 *Bruce Peter Weitz*, U.S. actor; Emmy Award for his role as Mick Belker on television series, *Hill Street Blues*, 1984.

1944 *Christopher John Dodd*, U.S. politician; Senator, 1980– .

1945 *Bruce Cockburn*, Canadian folk/rock singer.

1968 *Frank Thomas*, U.S. baseball player; American League MVP, 1993.

HISTORICAL EVENTS

1471 *Ladislas*, son of *Casimir IV* of Poland, becomes King of Bohemia and Hungary.

1536 First *Helvetian Confession* is issued by Swiss Protestants.

1679 *Habeas Corpus Act* for protection against false arrest and imprisonment is passed in England.

1703 *St. Petersburg* (later *Leningrad*) is founded at the mouth of the Neva River by *Peter the Great*.

1860 *Giuseppe Garibaldi* takes Palermo and sets up a provisional government (*Unification of Italy*).

1883 *Czar Alexander III* and his consort, Marie, are crowned with great ceremony at Moscow.

1885 A new ship canal from St. Petersburg to Kronstadt in Russia is opened.

1905 Russian fleet is annihilated in the *Battle of Tsushima Strait* (*Russo-Japanese War*).

1918 *Third Battle of the Aisne* begins as Germans drive to Marne River, 13 miles from Paris (*World War I*).

1919 First west to east airplane crossing of the Atlantic is completed by *A. C. Read* and his U.S. Navy crew.

1933 U.S. Congress passes *Federal Securities Act* compelling full disclosure to investors.

1935 In *Schechter Poultry Corp. v. United States,* the U.S. Supreme Court unanimously rules that the *National Industrial Recovery Act* is unconstitutional.

1937 San Francisco's *Golden Gate Bridge* is opened.

1941 A state of *unlimited national emergency* is declared by U.S.

may

President Franklin Roosevelt in response to sweeping German victories in Europe (*World War II*).

1944 U.S. troops land on *Biak,* off New Guinea (*World War II*).

1951 *Tibet* is incorporated into China by forced agreement of Dalai Lama, Panchen Lama, and the people's government.

1958 John Kenneth Galbraith's *The Affluent Society,* is published in New York.

1960 Lieutenant General *Cemal Gursel* assumes power in

Turkey after a bloodless coup d'etat.

U.S. ends economic aid to *Cuba.*

1966 First French cabinet since 1948 to include Communists is sworn in.

1986 *George S. K. Wong* of the National Research Council of Canada discovers that the accepted *speed of sound* used for the past 40 years is incorrect due to a 1942 miscalculation.

1988 *Mohammed Hassan Sharq* replaces *Soltan Ali*

Keshtmand as premier of Afghanistan.

1990 *César Gaviria Trujillo* is elected President of Colombia.

1996 Russian Premier *Viktor Chernomyrdin* and Chechen leader *Zelimkhan Yandarbiyev* sign a cease-fire agreement.

1998 The *Democratic Republic of the Congo* announces plans to create a legislative body whose job would be to form a constitution for the new democratic political system.

HOLIDAYS

Azerbaijan
Day of the Republic

Armenia
Independence Day
Anniversary of the declaration of the first Armenian Republic in 1918.

Puerto Rico
Memorial Day

RELIGIOUS CALENDAR

St. Senator, Bishop of Milan. Served as papal legate. [d. 475]

St. Justus, Bishop of Urgel. [d. c. 550]

St. Germanus, Bishop of Paris. Founded famous church of Saint-Germain-des-Prés, royal burial place for several generations. Also called *Germain.* [d. 576]

St. William of Gellone, founder of the Monastery at Gellone. [d. 812]

St. Bernard of Montjoux. Founded the two celebrated Alpine hospices of Great and Little Bernard which have saved the lives of many mountaineers. Known as patron of Alpinists and other mountaineers. [d. c. 1081]

St. Ignatius, Bishop of Rostov. [d. 1288]

The London martyrs of 1582, three priests, hanged, drawn, and quartered for denying that Elizabeth I was head of the Church. [d. 1582]

The Beatified
Blessed Margaret Pole, widow and cousin of *Henry VIII,* martyr; beheaded for denying Henry's supremacy over the Church in England. [d. 1541] *Blessed Mary Bartholomea of Florence,* virgin. [d. 1577]

BIRTHDATES

1660 *George I,* King of Great Britain; his reign saw the emergence of the prime minister as a powerful figure. [d. June 11, 1727]

1738 *Joseph Ignace Guillotin,* French politician, physician; defender of *capital punishment* as means of preventing crime. Proposed use of beheading machines (i.e., the *guillotine*) as most humane form of capital punishment [d. March 26, 1814]

1759 *William Pitt,* English statesman; Prime Minister of England, 1783–1801. [d. January 23, 1806]

1764 *Edward Livingston,* U.S. statesman, law reformer; U.S. Congressman, 1794–1801; 1823–29; Mayor of New York City, 1801–03; U. S. Senator, 1829–31; known throughout the world for his *System of Penal Law for the United States of America.* [d. May 23, 1836]

1779 *Thomas Moore,* Irish poet, patriot; known for his lyrical, patriotic songs. [d. February 25, 1852]

1789 *Bernhard Severin Ingemann,* Danish poet, playwright, novelist. [d. February 24, 1862]

1807 *Jean Louis Rodolphe Agassiz,* U.S. naturalist, educator, zoologist, geologist, born in Switzerland; founder of *Harvard's Museum of Comparative Zoology.* Innovator in teaching techniques for natural history. [d. December 14, 1873]

1818 *P(ierre) G(ustave) T(outant) Beauregard,* Confederate Army general during U.S. Civil War; ordered bombardment of *Fort Sumter,* which opened the war. [d. February 20, 1893]

1853 *Carl (Olof) Larsson,* Swedish artist, author; wrote and illustrated *A Farm.* [d. January 22, 1919]

1884 *Edvard Beneš,* Czechoslovak statesman; founder of modern Czechoslovakia. [d. September 3, 1948]

1888 *Jim (James Francis) Thorpe,* U.S. athlete; winner of pentathlon and decathlon at 1912 Olympics, he was later stripped of medals when he was declared a professional;

the decision was reversed on January 18, 1983, when the medals Thorpe won were returned to his children. [d. March 28, 1953]

1908 *Ian (Lancaster) Fleming,* British writer of adventure novels; created *Secret Agent 007, James Bond.* [d. August 12, 1964]

1912 *Patrick White,* Australian novelist; Nobel Prize in literature, 1973. [d. September 30, 1990]

1916 *Walker Percy,* U.S. essayist, novelist. [d. May 10, 1990]

1917 *Barry Commoner,* U.S. biologist, environmentalist.

Gerald C. Cash, Bahamian statesman; Governor General, 1979–88.

1919 *May Swenson,* U.S. poet.

1925 *Dietrich Fischer-Dieskau,* German operatic baritone.

1930 *Edward Phillip George Seaga,* Jamaican politician; Prime Minister, 1980–89.

1931 *Stephen Birmingham,* U.S. author; known for his nonfiction books about the wealthy.

1934 *Dionne Quintuplets* (Marie, Emilie, Yvonne, Annette, and Cecile), world's first recorded surviving quintuplets. The quintuplets were delivered of *Oliva Dionne,* already the mother of six. [Marie d. February 27, 1970; Emilie d. August 5, 1954]

1935 *Carroll Baker,* U.S. actress.

Darryl D. Rogers, U.S. football coach.

1941 *Beth Howland,* U.S. actress; known for her role as Vera on television series, *Alice.*

1942 *Stanley B. Prusiner,* U.S. physician, Nobel Prize for Medicine in 1997 for his discovery of prions, a disease causing agent.

1944 *Rudolph Giuliani,* U.S. politician; Mayor of New York City, 1994– .

Gladys Maria Knight, U.S. singer; two Grammy Awards for *Midnight Train to Georgia,* 1973.

1945 *John Fogerty,* U.S. rock singer; was founding member of *Creedence Clearwater Revival.*

1947 *Sondra Locke,* U.S. actress; known for her co-starring roles with Clint Eastwood in films such as *Any Which Way You Can,* 1980.

1957 *Kirk Gibson,* U.S. baseball player.

HISTORICAL EVENTS

1037 Holy Roman Emperor *Conrad II* issues *Constitutis de Feudis,* which makes fiefs of small Italian land holders hereditary.

1156 *William of Sicily* destroys Byzantine fleet at *Brindisi.*

1167 *Frederick I (Frederick Barbarossa)* of Germany defeats Romans at Tusculum; enters Rome and enthrones the antipope, *Paschal III.*

1892 The *Sierra Club,* dedicated to the conservation of natural resources, is founded.

1916 *Sir Julian Byng* becomes commander of the Canadian Corps (*World War I*).

1918 *Armenia* and *Azerbaijan* are declared republics independent of Russia.

U.S. forces in France score their first military success by the capture of *Cantigny* and hold it during three counterattacks (*World War I*).

1919 *R.H. Macy & Co.* is incorporated in New York.

1929 *On With the Show,* the first all-color talking picture, premieres in New York.

1940 *Belgium* capitulates to Germany (*World War II*).

1954 President Dwight Eisenhower signs a bill which adds the words "under God" to the *Pledge of Allegiance.*

Alfred Hitchcock's film, *Dial M for Murder,* premieres in New York.

1957 The *National Academy of Recording Arts and Sciences,* known for its presentation of the Grammy Awards, is founded in Hollywood, California.

1958 United Presbyterian Church of North America and Presbyterian Church of the U.S.A. merge to form the *United Presbyterian Church in the U.S. A.*

1959 *Able* and *Baker,* a pair of squirrel monkeys, become the first U.S. animals in space when they are launched on a *Jupiter* rocket.

1963 *Jomo Kenyatta* is named first prime minister of *Kenya.*

1972 U.S. President *Richard Nixon* expresses his desire for peace in an unprecedented televised address to the Russian people during his visit in Moscow.

1976 Martin Scorsese's film, *Taxi Driver,* wins a Golden Palm, the top award at the Cannes Film Festival.

1979 *Greece* is formally admitted to membership in the European Economic Community (Common Market).

1984 The only unidentified U.S. soldier killed during the *Vietnam War* is buried with military honors in the *Tomb of the Unknown Soldier* in Arlington, Virginia.

1998 *Pakistan* conducts five underground nuclear tests following reports that India was developing nuclear weapons (May 11, 1998).

may

MAY
29

HOLIDAYS

U.S. (Rhode Island)
Admission Day
Celebrates Rhodes Island's
ratification of the Constitution, 1790.

RELIGIOUS CALENDAR

The Saints
St. Cyril of Caesarea, martyr. [d. c.
251]
St. Maximinus, Bishop of Trier. [d.c.
347]
SS. Sisinnius, Martyrius, and
Alexander, missionaries and
martyrs. [d. 397]
St. Theodosia, virgin, nun, and
martyr. [d. 745]
*SS. William, Stephen, Raymund, and
their companions,* martyrs.
[d. 1242]

The Beatified
Blessed Peter Petroni of Siena; held
in great veneration by the
Carthusian order. [d. 1361]
Blessed Richard Thirkeld, priest and
martyr. [d. 1583]

BIRTHDATES

1630 *Charles II,* King of Great
Britain. [d. February 6, 1685]

1736 *Patrick Henry,* American
patriot, lawyer, merchant;
Governor of Virginia,
1776–79; 1784–86. Great
orator of the American
Revolution. [d. June 6, 1799]

1826 *Ebenezer Butterick,* U.S.
inventor; invented
standardized paper patterns
for clothes. [d. March 31,
1903]

1830 *Clémence Louise Michel,*
French revolutionary,
anarchist, agitator; took part
in the *Paris Commune,* 1871;
exiled; returned to France
and continued to pursue
anarchist activities. [d. January
10, 1905]

1859 *James Henry Rand,* U.S.
business-equipment
manufacturer; founder of
Remington Rand, Inc., 1890.
[d. September 15, 1944]

1874 *G(ilbert) K(eith) Chesterton,*
British essayist, novelist,
journalist, poet; created the
priest-sleuth, *Father Brown.*
[d. June 14, 1936]

1878 *Winford Lee Lewis,* U.S.
chemist; discoverer of
Lewisite, a poison gas. [d.
January 1, 1943]

1880 *Oswald Spengler,* German
writer on philosophy of
history; proposed a theory
that Western culture, like all
other great cultures, follows a
definite cycle, destined
ultimately to decline. [d. May
8, 1936]

1898 *Beatrice Lillie (Constance
Sylvia Munston),* English-
Canadian comedienne,
actress. [d. January 20, 1989]

1903 *Bob (Leslie Townes) Hope,*
U.S. comedian, actor; four
Oscar Awards.

1906 *T(erence) H(anbury) White,*
Irish author; wrote *The Once
and Future King,* 1958. [d.
January 18, 1964]

1912 *Pamela Hansford Johnson,*
British author; noted for her
witty, often satirical fiction;
wife of C.P. Snow (October
15). [d. June 18, 1981]

1917 *John Fitzgerald Kennedy,* U.S.
politician, World War II naval
hero, 35th President of the
U.S. [assassinated November
22, 1963]

1918 *Herb Shriner,* U.S. television
personality. [d. April 23, 1970]

1920 *John C. Harsanyi,* U.S.
economist; Nobel Prize for
Economics with John F. Nash
and Reinhard Selten, 1994.

1932 *Paul Ralph Ehrlich,* U.S.
biologist.

1938 *Francis (Fran) T. Vincent, Jr.,*
U.S. lawyer; commissioner of
Major League Baseball,
1989–91.

1939 *Al Unser,* U.S. auto racer.

1944 *Maurice Bishop,* Grenadian
political leader; Prime
Minister, 1979–83. [d.
October 19, 1983]

1948 *Anthony Geary,* U.S. actor;
known for his role as Luke

Spencer on television soap opera, *General Hospital.*

1955 *John Warnock Hinckley, Jr.,* U.S. would-be assassin; shot President Ronald Reagan, March 30, 1981.

1961 *Melissa Etheridge,* U.S. rock singer.

1963 *Lisa Whelchel,* U.S. actress; known for her role as Blair on television series, *Facts of Life.*

HISTORICAL EVENTS

1453 Siege and fall of Constantinople takes place as *Mohammed II* and his Turkish forces capture the city and kill *Byzantine Emperor Constantine.*

1660 *Charles II* of England, an exile in France during the Cromwellian period, returns to England.

1765 *Patrick Henry* introduces resolutions in the Virginia House of Burgesses, challenging the British government.

1790 *Rhode Island* ratifies the U.S. Constitution, becoming the last of the 13 original states in the federal union.

1848 *Wisconsin* is admitted to the Union as the 30th state.

1889 Trial by jury is first introduced in Spain.

1913 Igor Stravinsky's *Rite of Spring* is first performed by the Diaghileff Ballet Russe in Paris.

1921 *Edith Wharton* receives a Pulitzer Prize for her novel, *The Age of Innocence.* She is the first woman to win this award.

Salzburg region votes for union with Germany.

1944 *U.S.S. Block Island,* torpedoed by a German submarine, becomes the only U.S. carrier lost in the Atlantic during *World War II.*

1953 *Sir Edmund Hillary* of New Zealand and Nepalese Sherpa tribesman *Tenzing Norgay* are the first men to reach the summit of *Mt. Everest.*

1961 U.S. Supreme Court upholds the constitutionality of state *blue laws* prohibiting commercial activity on Sunday.

1962 *John O'Neil* joins the Chicago Cubs, becoming the first black to coach a Major League baseball team.

1964 The *Palestine Liberation Organization,* a group aimed at recovering the Palestinian homeland from Israel, is formed in Jerusalem.

1986 *Errol Barrow* is elected prime minister of Barbados.

1990 *Boris Yeltsin* is elected president of Russia.

1996 *Benjamin Netanyahu* becomes Israel's new prime minister.

may

MAY
30

HOLIDAYS

Anguilla
Anguilla Day

Croatia
Republic Day

U.S.
Memorial Day
Established as legal holiday to commemorate the U.S. war dead, 1868.

U.S. (Virginia)
Confederate Memorial Day

RELIGIOUS CALENDAR

The Saints
St. Eleutherius, pope. Elected c. 174. [d. c. 189]
St. Felix I, pope. Elected 269. [d. 274]
St. Isaac of Constantinople, hermit and abbot. Founded Dalmatian Monastery, the oldest in Constantinople. [d. c. 410]
St. Exuperantius, Bishop of Ravenna. Built the town of Argenta, so called because it paid a tribute in silver to the church of Ravenna. Also called *Superantius.* [d. 418]
St. Madelgisilus, recluse. Also called *Madelgisilus, Maguil, Maguille, Mauguille.* [d. c. 655]
St. Walstan, confessor. Invoked to cure fevers, palsies, lameness, and blindness. [d. 1016]
St. Ferdinand III of Castile, king. Reign of most importance in Spanish history because of great territorial gains. Founded the University of Salamanca. [d. 1252]
St. Joan of Arc, virgin, martyr, and patron of France. Also called *Jeanne la Pucelle, Joan the Maid,* and the *Maid of Orléans.* [d. 1431]

The Beatified
Blessed Andrew, Bishop of Pistola. [d. 1401]
Blessed James Bertoni, a Servite. [d. 1483]
Blessed William Scott and *Blessed Richard Newport,* priests and martyrs. [d. 1612]

BIRTHDATES

1845 *Amadeus I,* King of Spain, 1870–73; forced to abdicate. [d. January 18, 1890]

1846 *Peter Carl Fabergé (Karl Gustavovich Faberge),* Russian goldsmith, jeweler. [d. September 24, 1920]

1859 *Pierre Marie Félix Janet,* French psychopathologist, neurologist; known for research on hysteria. [d. February 24, 1947]

1879 *Vanessa Bell,* British artist; sister of Virginia Woolf. [d. April 7, 1961]

1887 *Alexander Archipenko,* U.S. sculptor born in Russia; one of first Cubists. [d. February 25, 1964]

1888 *James A(loysius) Farley,* U.S. politician; head of Democratic National Committee, 1932–40; U.S. Postmaster General, 1933–40. [d. June 9, 1976]

1896 *Howard Hawks,* U.S. film director; gained reputation for excellence in both comedy and drama in films during 1930s and 1940s. [d. December 26, 1977]

1899 *Irving Grant Thalberg,* U.S. producer; head of MGM production, 1923–36. [d. September 14, 1936]

1901 *Cornelia Otis Skinner,* U.S. actress, author; known for her play, *The Pleasure of His Company* and her book *Our Hearts Were Young and Gay;* daughter of stage actor *Otis Skinner* (June 28). [d. July 9, 1979]

1904 *Billy Baldwin,* U.S. fashion designer. [d. November 25, 1983]

1908 *Hannes Alfvén,* Swedish physicist; Nobel Prize in physics for contributions in the study of plasmas, 1970. [d. April 2, 1995]

Mel(vin Jerome) Blanc, U.S. actor, musician; voice of cartoon characters, Bugs Bunny, Porky Pig, and Daffy Duck. [d. July 10, 1989]

1909 *Benny Goodman (Benjamin David Goodman),* U.S.

orchestra leader, clarinetist. [d. June 13, 1986]

1912 *Julian Gustave Symons,* British novelist, poet, biographer, critic; especially known for his crime novels.

Julius Axelrod, U.S. biochemist; Nobel Prize in physiology or medicine for research on composition of nerve fibers (with B. Katz and U.S. Von Euler), 1970.

1915 *Frank Blair,* U.S. broadcast journalist; newscaster on television news show, *Today Show,* 1952–75. [d. March 14, 1995]

1920 *Godfrey Binaisa,* President of Uganda, 1979; successor to Idi Amin; ousted by a six-man military commission.

1934 *Aleksei Arkhipovich Leonov,* Russian cosmonaut; the first man to accomplish a *space walk,* 1965.

1944 *Meredith MacRae,* U.S. actress; known for her starring role on television series, *Petticoat Junction,* 1966–70.

1946 *Candy Lightner,* U.S. reformer; founded Mothers Against Drunk Driving, 1980.

1964 *Wynonna Judd,* U.S. country singer.

HISTORICAL EVENTS

1431 *Joan of Arc* is burned at the stake at Rouen, France, by the English.

1536 *Henry VIII* of England marries *Jane Seymour,* his third wife.

1574 *Charles IX* of France dies and is succeeded by *Henry III.*

1814 *Malta* is annexed by Great Britain.

1848 U.S. acquires *New Mexico, Texas, California, Nevada, Utah, Arizona,* and parts of *Colorado* and *Wyoming* from Mexico; this constitutes more than 30 per cent of Mexico's territory.

1854 *Kansas-Nebraska Act* is passed in U.S., opening Nebraska territory to settlement with popular sovereignty on issue of slavery.

1868 *Memorial Day* is first celebrated in U.S.

1901 *Hall of Fame for Great Americans,* founded in 1900, is dedicated at New York University.

1911 First 500-mile automobile race at *Indianapolis Speedway* is held.

1913 *First Balkan War* between Bulgaria, Greece, Serbia, and Montenegro and the Turks, ends with signing of *Treaty of London.*

1915 Italian forces capture *Cortina* in the Venetian Alps (*World War I*).

1918 The first American troops arrive in *Italy* (*World War I*).

1922 *Lincoln Memorial* in Washington is dedicated.

1942 British send 1,000 bombers in raid on Cologne, Germany (*World War II*).

1961 Dominican strongman *Rafael Leonidas Trujillo Molina,* dictator of the Republic since 1930, is assassinated.

1967 *Biafra* secedes from Nigeria.

Jordan and *Egypt* sign a joint defense pact and the Jordanian Army is placed under Egyptian control. (*Six-Day War*)

1975 Ten European nations establish the *European Space Agency.*

1981 President *Ziaur Rahman* of Bangladesh is killed in an unsuccessful coup attempt by a group of military leaders.

1982 *Spain* becomes a member of NATO.

may

MAY
31

HOLIDAYS

Brunei
Public Holiday
Commemorates the revelation of the Koran.

Anniversary of the Royal Brunei Regiment

Madagascar
Memorial Day

Republic of South Africa, Namibia
Republic Day
Commemorates the formation of the South African Republic, 1961.

RELIGIOUS CALENDAR

Feasts
Visitation of the Virgin Mary to her cousin Elizabeth. [Major holy day, Episcopal Church]

The Saints
St. Petronilla, virgin and martyr. [d. c. 251]
SS. Cantius, Cantianus, and *Cantianella,* martyrs. [d. c. 304]
St. Mechtildis of Edelstetten, virgin and abbess. [d. 1160]

The Beatified
Blessed James the Venetian, friar and mystic. [d. 1314]

BIRTHDATES

1557 *Fyodor I, Emperor of Russia,* 1584–98; his brother-in-law, *Boris Godunov,* held real power. [d. January 7, 1598]

1750 *Prince Karl August von Hardenberg,* Prussian statesman; active in Prussian War against France, 1792–95; made a prince in recognition of service during War of Liberation, 1813–14. [d. November 26, 1822]

1819 *William Worrall Mayo,* U.S. physician, surgeon; father of William James and Charles Horace Mayo, who founded the *Mayo Clinic,* Rochester, Minnesota. [d. March 6, 1911]

Walt(er) Whitman, U.S. poet; renowned for his free-form use of words, which gave rise to a new generation of poetry, and for his celebration of the individual and of democracy. [d. March 26, 1892]

1857 *Pope Pius XI,* a tireless worker for world peace. [d. February 10, 1939]

1861 *Emily Perkins Bissell,* U.S. welfare worker; responsible for concept and use of *Christmas seals* to aid tubercular children. [d. March 8, 1948]

1887 *Alexis Saint-Leger Leger (Marie-Rene Alexis St. Leger),* French poet, diplomat; Nobel Prize, 1960. [d. September 20, 1975]

Saint-John Perse, French poet, diplomat; Nobel Prize in literature, 1960. [d. September 20, 1975]

1894 *Fred Allen (John Florence Sullivan),* U.S. comedian, radio personality of the 1930s and 1940s; introduced Jack Benny (February 14) to American radio audiences. [d. March 17, 1956]

1898 *Norman Vincent Peale,* U.S. clergyman, author; well known for his national radio program, *The Art of Living.* [d. December 24, 1993]

1908 *Don Ameche (Dominic Felix Amici),* U.S. actor. [d. December 6, 1993]

1911 *Maurice Allais,* French economist; author of *In Search of an Economic Discipline;* Nobel Prize in Economics, 1988.

1912 *Henry (Martin) "Scoop" Jackson,* U.S. politician, lawyer; U.S. Congressman, 1941–52; U.S. Senator, 1953–1983. [d. September 1, 1983]

c1912 *Chien-Shiung Wu,* Chinese-born nuclear physicist; known for her research on beta decay and nuclear fission.

1919 *(Rupert) Vance Hartke,* U.S. politician; U.S. Senator, 1959–77.

1920 *Edward Bennett Williams,* U.S. criminal lawyer, sports franchise owner.

1923 *Ellsworth Kelly,* U.S. artist.

Rainier III, Prince of Monaco.

1924 *Patricia Roberts Harris,* U.S. government official, lawyer; Secretary of Housing and Urban Development, 1977–79; Secretary of Health, Education, and Welfare; first black woman to reach both ambassadorial and cabinet rank. [d. March 23, 1985]

1930 *Clint Eastwood,* U.S. actor, director; Academy Award (Director, Best Picture) for *Unforgiven,* 1992.

1931 *John Robert Schrieffer,* U.S. physicist; Nobel Prize in physics for experiments in superconductivity (with J. Bardeen and L. Cooper), 1972.

1938 *Jim Hutton,* U.S. actor; known for his starring roles in *Where the Boys Are,* 1960, and *The Trouble with Angels,* 1966. [d. June 2, 1979]

Peter Yarrow, U.S. singer, member of folk-singing group, *Peter, Paul, and Mary.*

1939 *Terence Hardy (Terry) Waite,* British clergyman; known for his negotiations with terrorists for hostages; disappeared in Beirut while negotiating with terrorists, January 20, 1987; released by the Islamic Jihad in Lebanon after four years in captivity (November 18, 1991).

1941 *Johnny Paycheck (Don Lytle),* U.S. singer; known for song, *Take This Job and Shove It.*

1943 *Sharon Gless,* U.S. actress; known for her role as Chris

Cagney on television series, *Cagney and Lacey.*

Joe Namath, U.S. football player, actor.

1946 *Rainer Werner Fassbinder,* German actor, author, director; known for films *The Marriage of Maria Braun,* 1978, *Lili Marleen,* 1980, and *Lola,* 1981. [d. June 10, 1982]

1949 *John Henry Bonham,* British musician; member of the rock group, *Led Zeppelin.* [d. September 25, 1980]

1950 *Thomas (Tom) Berenger,* U.S. actor; known for his roles in *The Big Chill* and *Platoon.*

Gregory Harrison, U.S. actor; known for his role as Gonzo Gates on television series, *Trapper John, MD,* 1979–86.

1951 *David Kessler,* U.S. physician; commissioner of the Food and Drug Administration, 1990– .

1957 *Jim Craig,* U.S. hockey player; goalie for 1980 U.S. hockey team which defeated the Soviets and won gold medal in Olympic competition.

1961 *Lea Thompson,* U.S. actress; known for roles in *All the Right Moves,* 1983 and the *Back to the Future* films.

1965 *(Christa) Brooke (Camille) Shields,* U.S. model, actress; known for her starring roles in *The Blue Lagoon* and *Endless Love;* stars in the TV sitcom *Suddenly Susan.*

1967 *Kenny Lofton,* U.S. baseball player; American League Gold Glove winner, 1993–96.

HISTORICAL EVENTS

1433 *Sigmund of Germany* is crowned Holy Roman Emperor by *Pope Eugene IV.*

1639 *Rev. Thomas Hooker* and his fellow settlers reach *Hartford, Connecticut.*

1653 *Pope Innocent X* declares propositions of *Cornelis Jansen* to be heretical; Jansen teaches that Augustinian interpretation of grace, free will, and predestination is against the teaching of Jesuit schools.

1740 *Frederick William I* of Prussia dies and is succeeded by *Frederick II.*

1775 *American Continental Army* is formed from the colonial troops assembled against the British at Boston.

1793 *Reign of Terror* begins in France.

1821 First Catholic cathedral in U.S., *Cathedral of the Assumption of the Blessed Virgin Mary,* is dedicated in Baltimore.

1868 First official *bicycle race* is held at *Parc de St. Cloud,* outside of Paris. It is won by *James Moore,* an Englishman.

1891 Construction of the *Trans-Siberian Railway,* linking Moscow with the Pacific Coast of Russia, begins.

1900 The British seize *Johannesburg (Boer War).*

1902 *Boer War* ends with the signing of the *Treaty of Vereeniging* in Pretoria, South Africa.

1910 *Union of South Africa* is inaugurated, uniting the *Cape*

may

of *Good Hope, Natal,* the *Transvaal,* and the *Orange Free State.*

1913 *The 17th Amendment* to U.S. Constitution, providing for direct popular election of U.S. senators, goes into effect.

1915 German *Zeppelins* drop nearly a hundred incendiary bombs on London (*World War I*).

1916 *Battle of Jutland,* a naval battle between Germany and Britain, is fought, with both sides claiming victory. Britain retains command of the seas, but the German fleet escapes (*World War I*).

1918 The German advance in the *Third Battle of the Aisne* reaches the Marne, only 37 miles from Paris (*World War I*).

1935 An estimated 50,000 die in an *earthquake* in *Quetta, India.*

1938 *Henry Armstrong* defeats *Barney Ross* to win the world welterweight boxing title.

1942 Germany bombs *Canterbury, England,* causing severe damage to the cathedral, in retaliation for Britain's assault on Cologne *(World War II).*

1945 *T.V. Soong* becomes premier of China following the resignation of Chiang Kai-shek.

1947 *Lajos Dinnyes* becomes premier of Hungary.

1961 *Union of South Africa* secedes from the British Commonwealth and becomes an independent republic.

1966 The Kuwaiti National Assembly confirms Prime Minister *Jaber al-Ahmed al-Sabah* as crown prince.

1970 A devastating *earthquake* in the Andes destroys entire cities in Peru; death toll is estimated to exceed 50,000.

1975 *Darryl Dawkins* joins the Philadelphia 76ers, becoming the first U.S. high school player to sign a professional basketball team contract.

1979 *Bishop Abel Muzorewa* becomes Prime Minister of the new black-dominated government in *Rhodesia,* which later changed its name to *Zimbabwe.*

1982 *Belisario Betancur* is elected president of Colombia.

1989 Speaker of the House *Jim Wright* announces his resignation over ethics charges of financial wrongdoings.

JUNE

June is the sixth month of the Gregorian calendar and has 30 days. It was the fourth month of the early Roman 10-month calendar.

The Roman name for the month, *Junius,* probably derives from Juno, one of the most important goddesses in the Roman pantheon, consort of Jupiter and the patroness of women, invoked for propitious marriage and childbirth.

In the northern hemisphere the summer solstice, the day of the year with the longest daylight, occurs on June 21 or 22; this fact led to the celebration of Midsummer's Day, June 24, one of the quarter days in Great Britain. June is also a popular month for marriages, and marks the end of the school year in many countries and the beginning of the vacation season.

In the astrological calendar, June spans the zodiac signs of Gemini, the Twins (May 21–June 21) and Cancer, the Crab (June 22–July 22).

The birthstone for June is the pearl, moonstone, or alexandrite, and the flower is the rose or the honeysuckle.

STATE, NATIONAL, AND INTERNATIONAL HOLIDAYS

Rose Harvest Festival
(Bulgaria)
First Sunday

Bank Holiday
(Ireland)
First Monday

Jefferson Davis's Birthday
(Alabama, Mississippi)
First Monday
(Florida, Georgia, South Carolina)
June 3

Labor Day
(Bahamas)
First Friday

Jack Jouett Day
(Virginia)
First Saturday

Queen's Official Birthday
(Great Britain, St. Lucia)
Third Saturday
(Australia, Belize, Bermuda, Cayman Islands, Fiji, and Papua New Guinea)
Second Monday
(New Zealand)
First Saturday
(Tuvalu)
First Monday

Flag Day
(United States)
June 14

Labor Day
(Trinidad and Tobago)
Third Saturday

Holland Festival
(The Netherlands)
First Three Weeks

Midsummer's Day
(Great Britain)
June 24

Midsummer Celebrations
(Finland, Sweden)
Weekend closest to summer solstice

Father's Day
(United States)
Third Sunday

SPECIAL EVENTS AND THEIR SPONSORS

National Dairy Month
American Dairy Association

National Pest Control Month
National Pest Control Association

Philatelic Writers' Month
Franklin D. Roosevelt Philatelic Society

National Ragweed Month
Air Pollution Control League of Cincinnati

National Safe Boating Week
Second Week
National Safety Council

Fan Fair Celebration
Second Full Week
International Fan Club Organization,
Tri-Son, Inc.

National Little League Week
Second Week
Little League Baseball, Inc.

Great Hudson River Revival
Third Weekend
Hudson River Sloop Clearwater, Inc.

Philatelic Journalists Day
June 6
Franklin D. Roosevelt Philatelic
Society

Portuguese Day-Dia de Camões
Sunday nearest June 10
Luso-American Education
Foundation

HOLIDAYS

Cape Verde Islands
Children's Day

Kenya
Madaraka Day
A freedom celebration.

Western Samoa
Independence Holiday
Celebrates the coming to independence, 1962. First day of a three-day celebration.

Tunisia
Constitution Day or Victory Day
Commemorates promulgation of Tunisia's constitution, 1959. First day of a two-day celebration.

RELIGIOUS CALENDAR

The Saints

St. Justin, philosopher and martyr. First great Christian apologist. Feast formerly April 14. [d. 165] Obligatory Memorial.

St. Proculus, The Soldier, and St. Proculus, Bishop of Bologna, martyrs. [d. c. 304 and 542]

St. Pamphilus and his companions, martyrs. St. Pamphilus, a priest, was the greatest Biblical scholar of his day. [d. 309]

St. Caprasius, Abbot of Lérins in France. Also called *Caprais.* [d. 430]

St. Wistan, prince and martyr. [d. 849]

St. Simeon of Syracuse, monk. [d. 1035]

St. Eneco, Abbot of Oña, in Castile. Also called *Iñigo.* [d. 1057]

St. Theobald of Alba, patron of cobblers and porters. [d. 1150]

St. Angela Merici, virgin; founder of the Company of St. Ursula, the first teaching order of women. [d. 1540]

The Martyrs of Japan. Numbering about 205, included many Dominican and Jesuit missionaries and many Japanese Christians, put to death in an effort to root out Christianity in Japan. [d. 1617–32]

St. Gwen Teirbron of Brittany. [death date unknown]

St. Ronan, bishop. [death date unknown]

St. Wite. One of two English saints to remain in their shrines undisturbed by the Protestant Reformation. Also called *Candida.* [death date unknown]

The Beatified

Blessed John Pelingotto, Franciscan monk. [d. 1304]

Blessed Herculanus of Piegaro, Franciscan preacher. [d. 1451]

Blessed John Storey, martyr. [d. 1571]

Blessed Felix of Nicosia, Capuchin monk. [d. 1787]

BIRTHDATES

1637 *(Père) Jacques Marquette,* French Jesuit missionary explorer in North America. [d. May 18, 1675]

1780 *Karl Maria von Clausewitz,* Prussian Army general, military strategist. [d. November 16, 1831]

1796 *Nicolas Leonard Sadi Carnot,* French physicist; his work formed foundation for study of thermodynamics. [d. August 24, 1832]

1801 *Brigham Young,* U.S. religious leader; one of the fathers of the *Mormon Church* in the U.S. Led migration to Utah and oversaw founding of *Salt Lake City.* [d. August 29, 1877]

1804 *Mikhail Ivanovich Glinka,* Russian composer; wrote first Russian national opera, *A Life for the Czar.* [d. February 15, 1857]

1813 *Evariste Régis Huc,* French Vincentian missionary to China, Mongolia, and Tibet. [d. April 26, 1860]

1814 *Philip Kearny,* U.S. soldier, cavalry expert; served as brigadier general of New Jersey militia during U.S. Civil War. [d. September 1, 1862]

1831 *John Bell Hood,* Confederate general in U.S. Civil War. [d. August 30, 1879]

1833 *John Marshall Harlan,* U.S. jurist, lawyer; Associate Justice

june

of U.S. Supreme Court, 1877–1911. [d. October 14, 1911]

1849 *Francis Edgar Stanley,* U.S. inventor; with his twin brother, Freelan, developed first successful steam-powered automobile, the *Stanley Steamer.* [d. July 31, 1918]

1855 *Edward Hartley Angle,* U.S. orthodontist; founder of modern *orthodontics.* [d. August 11, 1930]

1862 *Simon Iturri Patino,* Bolivian mining executive; developer of world's richest tin reserves. [d. April 20, 1947]

1878 *John Masefield,* British poet; Poet Laureate, 1930–67. [d. May 12, 1967]

1882 *John Drinkwater,* British dramatist. [d. March 25, 1937]

1909 *James Henry Rowe, Jr.,* U.S. government official; assistant to Franklin Delano Roosevelt. [d. June 17, 1984]

1921 *Nelson Riddle,* U.S. musician, composer; Oscar Award for the score of *The Great Gatsby,* 1974. [d. October 6, 1985]

1924 *William Sloane Coffin,* U.S. liberal clergyman; active in Vietnam War peace movement.

1926 *Andrew (Andy) Griffith,* U.S. actor; known for his starring role on television series, *The Andy Griffith Show* and *Matlock.*

Marilyn Monroe (Norma Jean Baker), U.S. actress, sex symbol of the 1950s. [d. August 5, 1962]

1930 *Frank Whittle,* British inventor; first developed *gas*

turbine unit for jet propulsion in aircraft. [d. August 8, 1996]

1934 *Pat Boone (Charles Eugene Boone),* U.S. pop singer.

1937 *Morgan Freeman,* U.S. actor; known for roles in *Driving Miss Daisy,* 1989 and *The Shawshank Redemption,* 1994.

Colleen McCullough, Australian author; wrote *The Thorn Birds,* 1977.

1939 *Cleavon Jake Little,* U.S. actor; Tony Award for musical, *Purlie,* 1970. [d. October 22, 1992]

1940 *Rene Murat Auberjonois,* U.S. actor; Tony Award for *Coco,* 1969; known for his role as Clayton Endicott on television series, *Benson.*

1945 *Frederica von Stade,* U.S. operatic mezzosoprano.

1947 *Ron(ald) Wood,* British musician; member of the rock group, *The Rolling Stones.*

1948 *Thomas Edsol (Tom) Sneva,* U.S. auto racer.; Indianapolis 500 winner, 1983.

1949 *Powers Boothe,* U.S. actor; Emmy Award for his starring role on television movie, *Guyana Tragedy: The Story of Jim Jones,* 1980.

1953 *David Berkowitz,* U.S. murderer; committed "Son of Sam" murders in New York City, 1976–77.

1961 *Paul Coffey,* Canadian hockey player.

1970 *Alexi Lalas,* U.S. soccer player; member of the U.S. Olympic Team, 1992.

1974 *Alanis Morissette,* Canadian rock singer; released

Grammay Award-winning *Jagged Little Pill* album in 1995.

HISTORICAL EVENTS

1783 *Bank of Ireland* is established.

1792 *Kentucky* is admitted to the Union as the 15th state.

1796 *Tennessee* is admitted to the Union as the 16th state.

1882 First scheduled train of *Gotthard Railway* makes trip from Lucerne, Switzerland, to Milan, Italy.

1896 *Macmillan Inc.* is incorporated in New York.

1918 American forces are rushed into battle at *Château-Thierry* to stem German advance on Paris in the *Third Battle of the Aisne (World War I).*

1932 *Franz von Papen* becomes German chancellor.

1936 *Victor Emmanuel III* is made emperor of Ethiopia.

1946 Former premier *Ion Antonescu* is executed on treason charges for leading Romania into the Axis alliance during World War II.

1958 *Charles de Gaulle* becomes premier of France with almost unlimited authority, following a military revolt in Algeria and the collapse of the *Fourth Republic.*

1959 Tunisian Constitution goes into effect, establishing Tunisia's independence from France.

1961 *Northern Cameroon,* a former British UN trust territory, merges with *Nigeria.*

1966 *Joaquín Balaguer* is elected President of the Dominican Republic and remains in power until 1978.

1967 *The Beatles* release their *Sgt. Pepper's Lonely Hearts Club Band* album.

1973 Greek cabinet abolishes Greek monarchy, naming *George Papadopoulos* as Premier.

British Honduras officially changes its name to *Belize*.

1983 Swiss scientists announce confirmation of the existence of the *Z-zero* sub-nuclear particle. The announcement follows the January, 1983 announcement of the discovery of the sub-atomic *W particles*.

1993 President *Jorge Serrano Elías* is ejected president of

Guatemala by armed forces after public outcry over corruption.

1996 *Ukraine* transfers the last of its nuclear warheads to Russia in agreement with the 1994 nuclear disarmament pact with Russia.

1997 *Necmettin Erbakan,* premier of Turkey, resigns.

june

JUNE
2

HOLIDAYS

Italy
Proclamation of the Republic
Commemorates the abolition of
monarchy in 1946.

Western Samoa
Independence Holiday
Second day of a three-day
celebration.

Tunisia
Victory Day or Youth Day
Second day of a two-day celebration.

RELIGIOUS CALENDAR

The Saints
St. Pothinus, Bishop of Lyons and
his companions, the *Martyrs
of Lyons and Vienne.* [d. 177]
St. Erasmus, bishop and martyr;
patron of sailors who regard
the corona discharge (St.
Elmo's fire) seen before and
after storms as manifestations
of his protection. Invoked
against cramp or colic,
especially in children. Also
called *Elmo, Ermo.* [d. c. 303]
SS. Marcellinus and *Peter,* martyrs.
[d. 304] Optional Memorial.
St. Eugenius I, pope. Elected 654.
[d. 657]
St. Stephen, Bishop in Sweden and
martyr. Called *Apostle of the
Helsings.* [d. c. 1075]
St. Nicholas the Pilgrim. Also called
Peregrinus. [d. 1094]

The Beatified
Blessed Sadoc and his companions,
martyrs. [d. 1260]

Blessed Jozef Sebastian Pelczar.
[beatified 1991]

BIRTHDATES

1535 *Pope Leo XI,* pope, 1605. [d.
April 27, 1605]

1624 *John III Sobieski,* King of
Poland, 1674–96. [d. June 17,
1696]

1740 *Donatien Alphonse François
de Sade, Marquis de Sade,*
French man of letters; noted
for his scandalous sex life,
which inspired the term
sadism. [d. December 2,
1814]

1743 *Count Alessandro Cagliostro,*
Italian charlatan; with his
wife, traveled widely through
Europe posing as physician,
alchemist, necromancer, and
freemason. [d. August 26,
1795]

1773 *John Randolph,* U.S.
politician, advocate of states'
rights. [d. May 24, 1833]

1811 *Henry James,* U.S. theologian;
father of William James
(January 11), and Henry
James (April 15). [d.
December 18, 1882]

1835 *St. Pius X,* pope 1903–14;
maintained a deep interest in
social questions and in
bettering the life of the poor.
Beatified in 1951; canonized
1954. [d. August 20, 1914]

1840 *Thomas Hardy,* British
novelist, poet; his works were
major influence in poetry and
novel writing of the late 19th
and early 20th centuries. [d.
January 11, 1928]

1845 *Arthur MacArthur,* U.S. Army
officer; Congressional Medal
of Honor for heroism at
Battle of Missionary Ridge
(Spanish-American War);
father of Douglas MacArthur
(January 26). [d. September 5,
1912]

1849 *Paul Albert Besnard,* French
painter, etcher. [d. December
4, 1934]

1857 *Sir Edward William Elgar,*
British composer; best known
for his composition, *Pomp
and Circumstance,* 1902. [d.
February 23, 1934]

Karl Adolf Gjellerup, Danish
poet, novelist; Nobel Prize in
literature (with H.
Pontoppidan, 1917). [d.
October 11, 1919]

1861 *Helen Taft,* wife of U.S.
President William Howard
Taft. [d. May 22, 1943]

1875 *Charles Stewart Mott,* U.S.
industrialist; founded Mott
Foundation, 1926. [d.
February 18, 1973]

1890 *Hedda Hopper,* U.S. actress,
journalist, best known for her
syndicated column about
Hollywood, begun in 1938.
[d. February 1, 1966]

1897 *R(euben) H(erbert) Mueller,* U.S. clergyman; leader in interfaith movement in the U.S.; President, National Council of Churches of Christ, 1963–66. [d. July 6, 1982]

1899 *Edwin Way Teale,* U.S. naturalist, writer, photographer; Pulitzer Prize for work entitled *Wandering Through Winter,* 1966. [d. June 2, 1899]

1904 *Johnny Weissmuller,* U.S. swimmer, actor; won 52 national championships, 3 Olympic gold medals (1924 and 1928 Olympic Games), and set 67 world records during 1920's. Played role of *Tarzan* in 19 films between 1930 and 1947. [d. January 22, 1984]

1907 *Michael Todd (Avron Hirsch Golbogen),* U.S. producer; husband of Elizabeth Taylor. [d. March 22, 1958]

1915 *Lester Del Rey (Ramon Alvarez del Rey),* U.S. science-fiction writer. [d. May 19, 1993]

1929 *Chuck Barris,* U.S. television host, producer; known for his production of television game shows, *The Dating Game, The Newlywed Game,* and *The Gong Show.*

1930 *Charles (Pete) Conrad, Jr.,* U.S. astronaut on flight of *Gemini 5,* August 23, 1965; *Gemini 11,* September 12, 1966; and *Apollo 12,* November 14, 1969. Conrad, aboard Lunar Module, landed in Sea of Storms (with A. Bean). Also aboard first manned flight to *Skylab* space station, May 25, 1973.

1932 *Barry Levinson,* U.S. director, producer; Academy Award

(Director) for *Rain Man,* 1988.

1937 *Sally Kellerman,* U.S. actress.

1939 *Peter Collier,* U.S. author; co-wrote *The Fords: An American Epic,* 1986.

1941 *Stacy Keach,* U.S. actor.

Charles Robert (Charlie) Watts, British singer, musician; member of the rock group, *The Rolling Stones.*

1944 *Marvin Hamlisch,* U.S. composer, musician; wrote scores for *The Way We Were, The Sting,* and *A Chorus Line.*

1948 *Jerry Mathers,* U.S. actor, businessman; known for his role as Beaver on television series, *Leave It to Beaver,* 1957–63.

1951 *Larry Robinson,* Canadian hockey player; elected to Hall of Fame, 1995.

1953 *Diana Canova (Diana Canova Rivero),* U.S. actress; known for her role on television series, *Soap.*

Cornel West, U.S. educator, writer; author of *Race Matters,* 1993.

HISTORICAL EVENTS

1420 *Henry V* of England marries *Catherine* of France.

1734 Russians take *Danzig* and expel *Stanislus Leszczinski* from Poland (*War of the Polish Succession*).

1774 *Quartering Act,* passed by British Parliament, legalizes quartering of troops in occupied dwellings; one of events precipitating *American Revolution.*

1793 The arrest of 31 Girondist deputies to national assembly

leads to *Reign of Terror* during the French Revolution (see June 4).

1899 Spain cedes the *Carolinas, Pelews, Ladrones,* and *Mariannas Islands* to Germany.

1902 *Oregon* is first state to adopt *initiative* and *referendum* procedures on a general scale.

1916 Russians break through Austrian lines on eastern front and capture fortresses of *Lutzk* and *Dubno (World War I).*

1941 *Charles Evans Hughes,* Chief Justice of the U.S. Supreme Court, resigns.

1946 Italian voters abolish the monarchy in favor of a republican government through a nationwide referendum. *Alcide de Gasperi* becomes head of state.

1951 U.S. government prohibits all travel by U.S. citizens in *Czechoslovakia.*

1952 Communist Party leader, *Gheorge Gheorghiu-Dej,* assumes power in Romania.

1953 *Elizabeth II* of Great Britain is crowned by the Archbishop of Canterbury in Westminster Abbey, London.

1964 *Lal Bahadun Shastri* is elected prime minister of India, succeeding the late *Jawaharlal Nehru.*

1966 U.S. spacecraft *Surveyor I* makes successful soft landing on the moon and begins to relay first closeup pictures of the moon.

1967 U.S. Federal Communications Commission rules that radio

june

and television stations must provide time for programming presenting the possible dangers of smoking as a balance to cigarette advertising.

Benno Ohnesorg, a West German student, is killed by police during a protest demonstration against a visit by the Shah of Iran in West Berlin.

1989 *Sousuke Uno* is elected Prime Minister of Japan.

HOLIDAYS

Western Samoa
Independence Day
Third day of a three-day celebration.

U.S. (Florida, Georgia, South Carolina)
Jefferson Davis's Birthday

U.S. (Kentucky, Louisiana)
Confederate Memorial Day

RELIGIOUS CALENDAR

The Saints
St. Cecilius, priest. [d. c. 248]
SS. Pergentinus and *Laurentius,* martyrs. Patrons of Arezzo. [d. 251]
SS. Lucillian and his companions, martyrs. [d. 273]
St. Clotilda, Queen of France and widow. Converted her husband, Clovis, King of the Franks, to Christianity. Also called *Clotildis.* [d. 545]
SS. Liphardus and *Urbicius,* abbots and monks. Liphardus also called *Liéfard, Liphardus.* [d. 6th century]
St. Kevin, Abbot of Glendalough. Founder of Monastery at Glendalough, one of four principal pilgrimage-places of Ireland. One of the principal patrons of Ireland. Also called *Coemgen.* [d. c. 618]
St. Genesius, Bishop of Clermont. Also called *Genesis, Genêt.* [d. c. 660]
St. Isaac of Cordova, martyr. [d. 852]

St. Morand, missionary priest in Alsace. Patron of wine growers. [d. c. 1115]
SS. Charles Lwanga, Joseph Mkasa, and their companions, the Martyrs of Uganda, the first martyrs of Black Africa. [d. 1886] Optional Memorial.

The Beatified
Blessed Andrew of Spello, a disciple of St. Francis of Assisi. Called *Andrew of the Waters* because a providential rain resulted from a petition to him. [d. 1254]
Blessed John the Sinner, hospitaler. [d. 1600]

BIRTHDATES

1726 *James Hutton,* Scottish geologist; one of founders of modern geology; proposed principle of *uniformitarianism* which suggested that forces changing earth's crust are uniform and constant in nature, 1785. [d. March 26, 1797]

1793 *Antoni Malczewski,* Polish poet; intimate of Lord Byron; chief work was *Marja.* [d. May 2, 1826]

1804 *Richard Cobden,* British statesman, economist; known as the *Apostle of Free Trade.* [d. April 2, 1865]

1808 *Jefferson Davis,* U.S. political leader; President of the *Confederate States of America,* 1861–65 (U.S. Civil War). [d. December 6, 1889]

1819 *Thomas Ball,* U.S. sculptor; sculpted equestrian statue of George Washington now in Public Garden, Boston, Daniel Webster, now in Central Park, New York, plus numerous others. [d. December 11, 1911]

Johan Barthold Jongkind, Dutch luminist painter and etcher of Fontainebleau school. [d. February 9, 1891]

1843 *Frederick VIII,* King of Denmark, 1906–12. [d. May 14, 1912]

1844 *Garret Augustus Hobart,* U.S. lawyer, legislator; Vice-President of U.S., 1897–99. [d. November 21, 1899]

1864 *Ransom Eli Olds,* U.S. inventor, auto manufacturer; manufactured first Oldsmobile, 1895. Developed principles and methods for *assembly line* method of manufacturing. [d. August 26, 1950]

1865 *George V,* King of Great Britain. [d. January 20, 1936]

1873 *Otto Loewi,* U.S. physiologist born in Germany; Nobel Prize in physiology or medicine for discovery of chemical transmission of nerve impulses (with H. H. Dale), 1936. [d. December 25, 1961]

1877 *Raoul Dufy,* French painter, designer, associated with Fauvists. [d. March 23, 1953]

1887 *Roland Hayes,* U.S. tenor; one of first black American concert artists to achieve international fame. [d. December 31, 1976]

1899 *Georg von Békésy,* U.S. physiologist; Nobel Prize in physiology or medicine for findings concerning the cochlea of the ear, 1961. [d. June 13, 1972]

1901 *Maurice Evans,* British actor. [d. March 12, 1989]

1904 *Jan Peerce,* U.S. operatic tenor; first American singer to appear at the Bolshoi Opera in Russia. [d. December 15, 1984]

Charles Drew, U.S. physician, researcher in area of blood plasma; developed efficient way to store blood plasma in blood banks. [d. April 1, 1950]

1906 *Josephine Baker,* U.S.-French dancer; star of the Folies-Bergère; owned her own club in Paris; traveled widely; well-known throughout Europe for her eccentric style, both on and off stage. [d. April 12, 1975 during 50th anniversary of her Paris debut]

1911 *Paulette Goddard (Marian Levee),* U.S. actress; known for her role in *Modern Times;* married to Charlie Chaplin, 1936–42. [d. April 23, 1990]

1913 *Ellen Corby (Ellen Hansen),* U.S. actress; known for her role as Grandma on television series, *The Waltons.*

1922 *Alain Resnais,* French film director.

1924 *Torsten N. Wiesel,* Swedish neurobiologist; Nobel Prize in physiology or medicine for his experimentation on the visual system of mammals (with David H. Hubel), 1981.

1925 *Tony Curtis (Bernard Schwartz),* U.S. actor.

1926 *Allen Ginsburg,* U.S. poet of the beat generation. [d. April 5, 1997]

1931 *Raul Castro,* Cuban politician; Vice Premier of Cuba; brother of Fidel Castro.

1933 *Celso Torrelio Villa,* Bolivian statesman; President, 1981–82.

1936 *Larry Jeff McMurtry,* U.S. author; Pulitzer Prize for *Lonesome Dove,* 1986.

1939 *Kathleen E. Woodiwiss,* U.S. author; wrote *Shanna,* 1977, and *Ashes in the Wind,* 1979.

1945 *Hale Irwin,* U.S. golfer.

1950 *Suzi Quatro,* U.S. singer.

1951 *Deniece Williams,* U.S. singer; known for song, *Let's Hear It for the Boy,* 1984.

HISTORICAL EVENTS

1083 *Henry IV* of Germany storms Rome, making *Pope Gregory VII* a virtual prisoner.

1098 Crusaders take Antioch (*First Crusade*).

1539 *Fernando de Soto* claims *Florida* for Spain.

1621 *Dutch West Indies Company* is chartered.

1818 In India, the last *Marantha War* ends with British defeat of the resisting Maranthas.

1916 The Allies assume the administration of *Salonika,* *Greece* and proclaim martial law (*World War I*.)

1918 *Ernest Pool* becomes the first novelist to win a Pulitzer Prize.

1942 Japanese launch carrier-borne air attack on U.S. Naval base in the *Aleutians (World War II).*

1952 *Nguyen Van Tam* replaces *Tran Van Huu* as premier of Vietnam.

1963 *Pope John XXIII* dies at age 81; he is later succeeded by Cardinal Giovanni Battista Montini, *Pope Paul VI.*

1965 *Major Edward H. White II* spends 20 minutes outside the *Gemini 4* spacecraft launched earlier in the day from Cape Kennedy, Florida, completing the first American *space walk.*

Silver is eliminated from coining of U.S. dimes and quarters, and percentage is reduced in half-dollars, in first major change in *U.S. coinage* since 1792.

1969 U.S. destroyer *Frank E. Evans* collides with Australian aircraft carrier *Melbourne* in the South China Sea; 73 U.S. seamen are killed.

1970 Scientists at the University of Wisconsin announce the first complete synthesis of a *gene.*

1971 U.S. novelist, *Julien Green,* is elected to the French Academy. He is the first American elected to the prestigious institution.

1972 *Sally Jane Preisand* becomes the first female to be ordained as a rabbi.

1989 *Ayatollah Ruhollah Khomeini* of Iran dies.

1992 The *Earth Summit* opens in Rio de Janeiro, Brazil, with global warming as a main issue.

june

JUNE
4

HOLIDAYS

Finland

Flag Day
Finnish armed forces commemorate birthday of Carl Gustaf Mannerheim, Finnish military leader in fight for independence from Russia, 1867.

Tonga

Emancipation Day or Independence Day
Commemorates Tonga's achievement of independence, 1970.

RELIGIOUS CALENDAR

The Saints

St. Quirinus, Bishop of Siscia, martyr. [d. 308]

St. Metrophanes, Bishop of Byzantium. [d. c. 325]

St. Optatus, Bishop of Milevis or Milevum. One of most illustrious champions of the Church during the 4th century. [d. c. 387]

St. Petroc, abbot. Also called *Pedrog, Perreuse.* [d. 6th century]

St. Edfrith, Bishop of Lindisfarne. Wrote the Lindisfarne Gospels. Also called *Eadfrith.* [d. 721]

St. Francis Caracciolo, founder of the Minor Clerks Regular. [d. 1608]

St. Vincentia Gerosa, virgin; co-founder of the Sisters of Charity of Lovere. [d. 1847]

St. Ninnoc, nun. Also called *Ninnocha, Gwengusetle.* [death date unknown]

The Beatified

Blessed Damien de Veuster.
[beatified 1995]

BIRTHDATES

1694 *François Quesnay,* French economist, physician; his theories formed the basis of the physiocratic approach to economics. [d. December 16, 1774]

1718 *Aleksandr Petrovich Sumarokov,* Russian playwright, poet; director of first permanent theater in St. Petersburg. [d. September 1, 1777]

1738 *George III,* King of Great Britain (1760–1820); ruled during the revolt of the American colonies. [d. January 29, 1820]

1744 *Jeremy Belknap,* U.S. clergyman, historian; founder of the *Massachusetts Historical Society.* [d. June 20, 1798]

1867 *Carl Gustav Emil, Baron von Mannerheim,* Finnish Field Marshal, public official; President of Finland, 1944–46. [d. January 27, 1951]

1877 *Heinrich Otto Wieland,* German chemist; Nobel Prize in chemistry for studies of bile acids, 1927. [d. 1957]

1879 *Alla Nazimova,* Russian actress; best known for interpretation of Ibsen roles. [d. July 13, 1945]

1911 *Rosalind Russell,* U.S. actress. [d. November 28, 1976]

1917 *Charles Cummings Collingwood,* U.S. broadcast journalist; first U.S. network journalist to be admitted to North Vietnam, 1968. [d. October 3, 1985]

Howard M(orton) Metzenbaum, U.S. politician; Senator, 1974, 1977–95.

1919 *Robert Merrill,* U.S. operatic baritone.

1922 *Gene Barry (Eugene Klass),* U.S. actor; known for his starring roles on television series, *Bat Masterson, Burke's Law,* and *Name of the Game.*

1925 *Dennis Weaver,* U.S. actor; known for his starring roles on television series, *Gunsmoke,* 1955–64, and *McCloud,* 1970–77.

1936 *Bruce MacLeish Dern,* U.S. actor; known for his starring role in *Coming Home,* 1978.

1937 *Robert Fulghum,* U.S. writer; author of *All I Really Need to Know I Learned in Kindergarten.*

1946 *Bettina Louise Gregory,* U.S. journalist.

1951 *Parker Stevenson,* U.S. actor; known for his starring role on television series, *Hardy Boys Mysteries*, 1978–79.

1965 *Andrea Jaegar,* U.S. tennis player.

1966 *Cecilia Bartoli,* Italian opera singer.

1971 *Noah Wyle,* U.S. actor; known for his role as Dr. John Carter on the TV drama *ER.*

HISTORICAL EVENTS

1133 *Lothair of Saxony* is crowned Holy Roman Emperor and is invested with Tuscany by *Pope Innocent II.*

1249 *Louis IX* of France, leader of the *Sixth Crusade,* lands in Egypt.

1316 *Louis X* of France dies and is succeeded by *Philip V.*

1793 *Robespierre* is declared President of France, marking the beginning of the *Reign of Terror* (see June 2).

1832 *Reform Act* passes Britain's House of Lords, redistributing parlimentary seats to favor growing industrial areas and, by lowering property qualifications, admitting the industrial middle class to the electorate.

1892 The *Sierra Club* is organized in San Francisco, California.

1942 *Battle of Midway* begins, leading to a great American naval victory over Japan (*World War II*). German Nazi leader *Reinhard Heydrich* dies in Prague after being shot by Czech patriots *(World War II).*

1943 Argentine army troops overthrow President *Ramon Castillo* in a coup staged by General *Arturo Rawson* and War Minister *Pedro Ramirez,* who becomes president three days later.

1944 U.S. troops liberate *Rome (World War II).*

1946 *Juan Peron* is inaugurated as president of Argentina.

1950 *Nazem el-Kodsi* is appointed premier of Syria.

1954 Vietnamese premier *Buu Loc* and French premier *Joseph Laniel* sign agreements granting *Vietnam* complete independence within the French Union.

1970 *Tonga* becomes an independent kingdom and member of the British Commonwealth.

1977 The *Soviet Union* releases for publication the draft of its most recent constitution, the fourth since the Russian

Revolution of 1917, which states for the first time the dominant role of the Communist Party in ruling the U.S.S.R.

1986 Former U.S. Navy intelligence analyst, *Jonathan Pollard,* pleads guilty to participating in an espionage conspiracy on behalf of Israel.

1989 A Democracy Movement demonstration held in *Tiananmen Square* in China ends in disaster as the People's Liberation Army (PLA) guns down hundreds of unarmed student protestors.

Polish voters participate in *free elections* for the first time in over forty years.

The fifth *International Conference on Acquired Immune Deficiency Syndrome (AIDS)* is held in Montreal, Quebec, Canada.

The United States launches the largest *unmanned rocket,* a Titan 4, into space.

1998 *Terry Nichols* is sentenced to life imprisonment for the Oklahoma City bombing (April 19, 1995).

june

JUNE 5

HOLIDAYS

World Environment Day
Commemorates anniversary of
opening day of United Nations
Conference on Human Environment,
1972.

Denmark
Constitution Day
Designated as day to remember
signing of constitutions of 1849,
1953.

Seychelles
Liberation Day
Commemorates the 1977 coup.

RELIGIOUS CALENDAR

The Saints
St. Dorotheus of Tyre, priest and
    martyr. [d. c. 362]
St. Boniface, martyr and Archbishop
    of Mainz; patron of England
    and Apostle of Germany.
    Compiled first Latin grammar
    written in England. Also called
    Winfrid. [d. 754] Obligatory
    Memorial.
St. Eoban, bishop and martyr. [d.
    754]
St. Sanctius. Aso called *Sancho.* [d.
    851]

The Beatified
Blessed Meinwerk, Bishop of
    Paderborn. Made cathedral
    school of Paderborn famous
    throughout Germany. [d.
    1036]
Blessed Ferdinand of Portugal,
    prince. Called the *Constant.*
    [d. 1443]

Blessed Boleslava Lament. [beatified
    1991]

BIRTHDATES

1718 *Thomas Chippendale,* English
    cabinet-maker, furniture
    designer, baptized on this
    day. [d. November, 1779]

1723 *Adam Smith,* Scottish
    economist, philosopher;
    author of *The Wealth of
    Nations.* [d. July 17, 1790]

1819 *John Couch Adams,* British
    astronomer, most noted for
    his discovery of *Neptune.* [d.
    January 21, 1892]

1826 *Ivar Christian Hallström,*
    Swedish composer of operas,
    ballets, and folk songs;
    composed *The Mountain
    King.* [d. April 11, 1901]

1854 *James Carroll,* U.S.
    bacteriologist, Army surgeon;
    noted for his work on *yellow
    fever.* [d. September 16,
    1907]

1862 *Allvar Gullstrand,* Swedish
    ophthamologist, physicist;
    Nobel Prize for physiology or
    medicine for work on the
    dioptrics of the eye, 1911. [d.
    July 28, 1930]

1867 *Paul Jean Toulet,* French
    poet, novelist; his
    Contrerimes exerted
    significant influence on
    French poetry. [d. September
    6, 1920]

1877 *John Henry Breck,* U.S.
    cosmetics manufacturer; best
    known for hair-care products.
    [d. February 16, 1965]

1878 *Francisco (Pancho) Villa*
    Mexican guerrilla leader and
    revolutionary. [d. June 20,
    1923]

1883 *John Maynard Keynes,* British
    economist; proposed theory
    of economics whereby
    economic depression could
    be avoided by increased
    governmental investment in
    public works, encouragement
    of capital goods production,
    and stimulation of
    consumption. [d. April 21,
    1946]

1887 *Ruth (Fulton) Benedict,* U.S.
    anthropologist; best known
    for her study of the
    influences of culture on
    personality development
    published as *Patterns of
    Culture.* Her study was
    translated into 14 languages
    and served to popularize
    anthropology. [d. September
    17, 1948]

1892 *Dame Ivy Compton-Burnett,*
    British author; wrote *Mother
    and Son,* 1955. [d. August 27,
    1969]

1895 *William Boyd,* U.S. actor; best
    known for his role as
    Hopalong Cassidy. [d.
    September 12, 1972]

1896 *Allyn Cox*, U.S. mural painter; known for the completion of the 300-foot mural depicting American historical scenes on great rotunda of U.S. capitol building. [d. September 26, 1982]

1899 *Federico García Lorca*, Spanish poet, playwright; known for the violence and passion of his works. Killed during Spanish Civil War. [d. August 1936]

1900 *Dennis Gabor*, British physicist born in Hungary; Nobel Prize in physics for invention of holography, 1971. [d. February 8, 1979]

1920 *Cornelius John Ryan*, U.S. novelist, journalist born in Ireland; author of *The Longest Day, A Bridge Too Far*. [d. November 23, 1974]

1929 *Tony Richardson*, British producer, director; known for *Taste of Honey* and *Tom Jones*. [d. November 14, 1991]

1933 *Katherine Helmond*, U.S. actress; known for her roles on television series, *Soap* and *Who's the Boss?*

1934 *Bill Moyers*, U.S. journalist, editor, television news correspondent.

1936 *Bruce Dern*, U.S. actor.

1939 *Charles Joseph (Joe) Clark*, Canadian politician; Prime Minister, 1979–80.

Margaret Drabble, British author; wrote *A Summer Bird-Cage*, 1964, and *The Needle's Eye*, 1972.

1941 *Harry Nilsson (Harry Edward Nelson III)*, U.S. singer, songwriter. [d. January 15, 1994]

1942 *Teodoro Obiang Nguema Mbasogo*, Guinean statesman; President, Supreme Military Council, Republic of Equatorial Guinea, 1979– .

1949 *Ken(neth Martin) Follett*, Welsh author; wrote *Eye of the Needle*, 1978.

1971 *Mark Wahlberg*, U.S. singer, actor.

HISTORICAL EVENTS

1806 *The Netherlands* is declared a kingdom; *Louis Bonaparte*, brother of Napoleon Bonaparte, is made king.

1864 *Greece* regains sovereignty over *Ionian Islands* after fifty years under British protection.

1873 *Sultan Barghash* of Zanzibar, under British pressure, signs treaty abolishing *slave trade*.

1900 The British under *Redvers Buller* capture *Pretoria*, Transvaal *(Boer War)*.

1916 Field Marshal *Lord Kitchener*, on secret mission to Russia, is drowned when his ship is torpedoed off the Orkney Islands *(World War I)*.

1918 The *New York Times* is awarded a Pulitzer Prize, becoming the first newspaper to receive this honor.

1944 King *Victor Emmanuel III* of Italy relinquishes all power to his son, *Umberto II*.

1945 Allied Control Council partitions *Berlin* into four sections to be administered by Great Britain, France, the U.S., and U.S.S.R. *(World War II)*.

Germany is placed under an Allied Control Council and divided into four occupation zones *(World War II)*.

Marshall Plan is announced by U.S. Secretary of State *George C. Marshall* in address at Harvard University.

1950 U.S. Supreme Court rules that *segregation* of blacks in railroad dining cars violates the *Interstate Commerce Act*.

1953 *Danish Constitution* is adopted, making *Greenland* an integral part of Denmark.

1961 U.S. Supreme Court sustains constitutionality of 1950 *Internal Security Act* requiring registration of Communist organizations.

1963 British War Minister *John Dennis Profumo* resigns after admitting association with call girl *Christine Keeler,* who has also been involved with a known Soviet spy.

1965 U.S. State Department acknowledges combat activity in *South Vietnam* for the first time.

1967 Fighting breaks out between Israel and Egypt, Syria and Jordan *(Six-Day War)*.

1968 *Robert F. Kennedy,* while campaigning for the presidential nomination, is shot by *Sirhan Bishara Sirhan,* a Jordanian-American, and dies the following day.

1975 *Suez Canal* reopens to shipping after eight years. The Canal has been closed since the *Arab-Israeli War of 1967*.

First national referendum in Great Britain is held; citizens vote to remain in *Common Market*.

1976 *Teton Dam* in Idaho collapses, resulting in a flood

june

that kills 11 persons and leaves 30,000 homeless. The flood causes an estimated $1 billion damage and nearly wipes out the Idaho cattle industry.

1977 *Park Tong Sun* is identified as the agent who illegally spent millions of dollars to influence American policy toward *South Korea*.

1978 China releases 110,000 persons arrested during the 1957 antirightist campaign and the *Cultural Revolution* of the late 1960s.

1984 U.S. Supreme Court rules that aliens must show a clear probability of persecution in their homelands, rather than simply a fear, to avoid deportation.

1993 The Guatemalan congress elects *Ramiro de Leon Carpio* as the country's new president. Former president *Jorge Serrano Elías* was forcibly removed from power (June 1, 1993).

HOLIDAYS

South Korea
Memorial Day
Day set aside in commemorate
Korean war dead.

Sweden
Flag Day
Commemorates ascension of
Gustavus Eriksson Vasa to throne of
Sweden as Gustavus I, 1523; marks
signing of Swedish constitution,
1809.

U.S.
Philatelic Journalists Day
Sponsored by Franklin Delano
Roosevelt Philatelic Society, St.
Augustine Shores, Florida.

RELIGIOUS CALENDAR

The Saints
St. Philip the Deacon. Surnamed *the
Evangelist* because of his
great zeal in spreading the
faith, especially in Samaria. [d.
1st century]
St. Ceratius, Bishop of Grenoble.
Also called Cérase [d. c. 455]
St. Eustorgius II, Bishop of Milan. [d.
518]
St. Jarlath, Bishop of Tuam, in
Galway; opened a famous
school in connection with the
monastery. Principal patron of
Tuam. Feast is kept
throughout Ireland. [d. c.
550]
St. Gudwal. One of earliest
missionaries to Brittany. Also
called *Gudwall, Gurval.* [d. c.
6th century]
St. Claud, Bishop of Besançon. Also
called *Claude.* [d. c. 699]
St. Norbert, Archbishop of
Magdeburg, founder of the
Canons Regular of Prémontré.
[d. 1134] Optional Memorial.

The Beatified
Blessed Gerard of Monza. Principal
patron of Monza, the ancient
capital of Lombardy. [d. 1207]
Blessed Laurence of Villamagna,
one of the greatest preachers
of his age. [d. 1535]
Blessed Marcellinus Champagnat,
founder of the teaching
congregation of Little
Brothers of Mary, or Marist
Brothers. [d. 1840]
*Blessed Bernardina Maria
Jablonski.* [beatified 1997]
Blessed Maria Karlowska. [beatified
1997]

BIRTHDATES

1436 *Regiomontanus (Johann
Müller),* German astronomer,
mathematician; recognized for
his careful study of planetary
motion. First to observe
Halley's Comet; advanced
study of algebra, trigonometry
in Germany. [d. July 6, 1476]

1502 *John III* of Portugal (*the
Pious*), instituted the
Inquisition, 1531. [d. June 6,
1557]

1599 *(Diego Rodriguez de Silva y)
Velázquez,* Spanish baroque
painter; known for his
portraits of Spanish
noblemen, as well as dwarfs
and jesters. [d. August 6,
1660]

1606 *Pierre Corneille,* French
dramatist; called *Father of
French Tragedy.* [d.
September 30, 1684]

1755 *Nathan Hale,* American
Revolutionary hero; hanged
by British as a spy. Famous
for his dying words: "I only
regret that I have but one life
to lose for my country." [d.
September 22, 1776]

1756 *John Trumbull,* U.S. painter;
best known for his scenes of
the American Revolution. His
most famous work, *The
Declaration of
Independence,* included more
than 48 portraits, mostly
painted from life. [d.
November 10, 1843]

1799 *Alexander Sergeyevich
Pushkin,* Russian poet,
novelist, dramatist, short-story
writer; the *Father of Modern
Russian Literature.* [d.
February 10, 1837]

1804 *Louis Antoine Godey,* U.S.
publisher; best known as
publisher of *Godey's Lady's
Book,* most popular American
periodical of mid-19th
century. [d. November 29,
1878]

june

1850 *Karl F. Braun,* German physicist; Nobel Prize in physics for development of the wireless telegraph (with G. Marconi), 1909. [d. April 20, 1918]

1860 *William Ralph Inge,* British theologian; referred to as the *Gloomy Dean* because of his pessimism. [d. February 26, 1954]

1868 *Robert Falcon Scott,* British Antarctic explorer; reached South Pole January 18, 1912, shortly after Amundsen expedition; perished on return trip because of bad weather and lack of food. [d. c. March 19, 1912]

1875 *Thomas Mann,* German writer, exiled, 1933; became U.S. citizen in 1944; best-known novel: *The Magic Mountain;* Nobel Prize in literature, 1929. [d. August 12, 1955]

1886 *Paul Dudley White,* U.S. physician; leading heart specialist. [d. October 31, 1973]

1892 *Ted Lewis (Theodore Leopold Friedman),* U.S. bandleader, clarinetist. [d. August 25, 1971]

1896 *Italo Balbo,* Italian aviator, statesman; developer of Italy's Air Force under Benito Mussolini. [d. June 28, 1940]

1898 *Ninette de Valois (Edris Stannus),* British dancer, choreographer, ballet director.

1901 *Ahmed Sukarno,* Indonesian statesman; leader of the Indonesian independence movement and the nation's first president, 1949–66. [d. June 21, 1970]

1902 *Jimmie Lunceford,* U.S. bandleader, saxophonist. [d. July 13, 1947]

1903 *Aram Ilich Khachaturian,* Russian composer; *Saber Dance* is among his best-known works. [d. May 1, 1978]

1904 *Peter Lorre,* Hungarian actor; known for his roles in the *Mr. Moto* series.

1918 *Edwin G. Krebs,* U.S. biochemist; Nobel Prize for Medicine along with Edmond H. Fischer. They discover the reversible protein phosphorylation process, 1992.

1925 *Maxine Winokur Kumin,* U.S. poet, novelist, children's book writer; Pulitzer Prize in poetry, 1972.

1926 *Colleen Dewhurst,* Canadian actress. [d. August 22, 1996]

1928 *George Deukmejian, Jr.,* U.S. lawyer, politician; Governor of California, 1983–91.

1933 *Heinrich Rohrer,* Swiss physicist; Nobel Prize in physics for his development of the scanning tunneling microscope (with Gerd Binnig), 1986.

1934 *Roy Innis,* U.S. civil rights leader, editor; National Director, Congress of Racial Equality.

1939 *Gary U.S. Bonds (Gary Anderson),* U.S. singer, songwriter.

Marian Wright Edelman, U.S. lawyer; president and founder of the Children's Defense Fund, 1973– .

1949 *Robert Englund,* U.S. actor; known for his portrayal of

Freddy Krueger in the *Nightmare on Elmstreet* movies.

1954 *Harvey Forbes Fierstein,* U.S. dramatist, actor; Tony Award for *Torch Song Trilogy,* 1983.

1955 *Sandra Bernhard,* U.S. comedian and actress.

1956 *Bjorn Borg,* Swedish tennis player; Wimbledon Champion, 1976–80.

Chris Isaak, U.S. singer.

HISTORICAL EVENTS

1513 Swiss papal forces defeat the French at *Novara (War of the Holy League).*

1654 *Christina of Sweden,* a convert to Catholicism, abdicates the Swedish throne to devote the remainder of her life to religion and art.

1660 *Treaty of Copenhagen* is signed, whereby Denmark surrenders southern half of Scandinavian peninsula to Sweden.

1801 War between Spain and Portugal ends with signing of *Treaty of Badajoz;* Portugal cedes part of *Guiana* to Spain.

1806 *Sweden* adopts a representative constitution.

1844 *YMCA* is organized in London by George Williams to combat unhealthy conditions arising from the Industrial Revolution.

1884 The *Treaty of Hué* establishes French control over *Annum* and places *Tonkin* under a French protectorate.

1904 The *American Lung Association* holds its first

meeting in Atlantic City, New Jersey.

1913 First ascent of *Mount McKinley* in Alaska is made by *Hudson Stuck.*

1917 The first annual *Pulitzer Prizes* are awarded.

1918 *Battle of Belleau Wood,* first sizable U.S. action of World War I, begins; battle results in American recapture of *Vaux, Bouresches,* and *Belleau Wood.*

1919 *Finland* declares war on Russia.

1934 *Securities & Exchange Commission* is created in U.S. to limit bank credit for speculators and to regulate the securities industry.

1939 The first *Little League Baseball* game is played in Williamsport, Pennsylvania.

1942 *Battle of Midway* ends with first major defeat of Japanese naval forces *(World War II).*

The *Congress of Racial Equality (CORE)* is organized in Nyack, New York.

1944 Allied forces invade *Normandy* on *D-Day,* the largest amphibious invasion in history. *(World War II).*

1952 King Talal agrees to the appointment of a regency council to rule Jordan after his alleged mental illness worsens.

1961 *Sony Corp.* begins selling $3.5 million worth of shares on the U.S. market, the first sale of a Japanese company's common stock in the U.S.

1966 *Gemini 9* splashes down after three-day, 44-orbit trip and a record space walk of 2 hours 9 minutes by *Eugene A. Cernan, Gemini* co-pilot.

1967 Egypt closes the *Suez Canal* to all shipping and breaks diplomatic relations with the U.S. and Great Britain after an Israeli attack demolishs the Egyptian Air Force *(Six-Day War).*

1971 *Ramon Ernesto Cruz* is inaugurated as the first freely-elected president of Honduras in 22 years.

1977 U.S. Supreme Court rules that *capital punishment* for rape is unconstitutional.

1978 California voters overwhelmingly endorse *Proposition 13,* a state constitutional amendment to reduce property taxes by 57 percent.

1982 *Israel* invades *Lebanon* to destroy Palestine Liberation Organization strongholds.

1984 Indian troops confront Sikh extremists entrenched in the *Golden Temple of Amritsar,* Sikhism's holiest site. Sikh leader, *Jarnail Singh,* and several hundred of his followers are killed in the battle.

1988 Protesting the repression of *antiapartheid groups,* South African blacks go on strike.

june

JUNE
7

HOLIDAYS

Chad
National Liberation Day
Commemorates independence from
Libya.

RELIGIOUS CALENDAR

The Saints
St. Paul I, Bishop of Constantinople.
[d. c. 350]
St. Colman, first Bishop of Dromore
in County Down, Ireland. [d.
6th century]
St. Meriadoc, bishop. Subject of only
complete miracle play written
in English based on a saint.
Also called *Meriadec,
Meriasek.* [d. c. 6th century]
St. Vulflagius, hermit priest. Also
called *Wulphy.* [d. c. 643]
St. Willibald, first Bishop of
Eichstätt. First known English
pilgrim to the Holy Land. [d.
786]
St. Gottschalk, Prince of the Western
Vandals. Also called
Godeschalc. [d. 1066]
St. Robert, Abbot of Newminster. [d.
1159]
St. Antony Gianelli, Bishop of
Bobbio; founder of the
Missioners of St. Alphonsus
and the Sisters of St. Mary
dell'Orto. [d. 1846]

The Beatified
Blessed Baptista Varani, virgin and
mystic. [d. 1527]
Blessed Anne of St. Bartholomew,
virgin. [d. 1626]

BIRTHDATES

1502 *Gregory XIII (Ugo
Buoncompagni),* pope,
1572–85. Responsible for
reformation of Julian
calendar, promulgation of
Gregorian calendar. [d. April
10, 1585]

1761 *John Rennie,* English
engineer; builder of three
bridges over the Thames in
London. [d. October 4, 1821]

1778 *George Bryan (Beau)
Brummell,* English dandy and
wit; friend of Prince of Wales,
later George IV of England.
[d. March 30, 1840]

1811 *Sir James Young Simpson,*
Scottish obstetrician; founder
of modern *gynecology.*
Discovered anesthetic
properties of *chloroform;* first
to use anesthesia (ether) in
obstetric practice. [d. May 6,
1870]

1840 *Carlota (Marie-Charlotte
Amélie Augustine Victoire
Clémentine Léopoldine),*
Empress of Mexico, 1864–67.
Wife of Emperor Maximilian,
Archduke of Austria, later
imperial ruler of Mexico. [d.
January 19, 1927]

1848 *(Eugène-Henri) Paul
Gauguin,* French painter; one
of the founders of the
Symbolist school. From his
studio in Tahiti, he sent many

brilliant, primitive paintings to
Paris. [d. May 8, 1903]

1862 *Philipp E. A. von Lenard,*
German physicist; Nobel Prize
in physics for research on
cathode rays, 1905. [d. May
20, 1947]

1877 *Charles G. Barkla,* British
physicist; Nobel Prize in
physics for his work on x ray
scattering, 1917. [d. October
23, 1944]

1879 *Knud Johan Victor
Rasmussen,* Danish explorer;
first to cross the Northwest
Passage by dog sled. [d.
December 21, 1933]

1896 *Robert S. Mulliken,* U.S.
chemist; Nobel Prize in
chemistry for fundamental
investigations regarding
molecules, 1966. [d. October
31, 1986]

Imre Nagy, Hungarian
communist leader; Premier,
1953–55; executed for anti-
Soviet activities during
Hungarian revolution, 1956.
[d. June 16, 1958]

1899 *Elizabeth Bowen (Dorothea
Cole),* British novelist, short-
story writer. [d. February 22,
1973]

1909 *Peter Wallace Rodino, Jr.,*
U.S. politician; Congressman,
1948–89.

Jessica Tandy, British actress;
Academy Award (Best Actress)

for *Driving Miss Daisy*, 1989.
[d. September 11, 1994]

1917 *Gwendolyn (Elizabeth)
Brooks*, U.S. poet; the first
black woman to win a Pulitzer
Prize, 1950.

1922 *Rocky Graziano*, U.S. boxer,
television personality; World
Middleweight Boxing
Champion, 1947–48. [d. May
22, 1990]

1928 *Charles Strouse*, U.S.
composer; best known for
scores of *Bye Bye Birdie*,
Applause, and *Annie*.

1940 *Tom Jones (Thomas Jones
Woodward)*, Welsh musician,
singer; known for songs, *It's
Not Unusual*, 1964, and
What's New Pussycat, 1965.

1943 *Nikki Giovanni (Yolande
Cornelia, Jr.)*, U.S. author,
poet; wrote *My House*, 1972,
and *The Women and the
Men*, 1975.

1946 *Jenny Jones (Janina
Stronski)*, U.S. talk show host.

1947 *Thurman Lee Munson*, U.S.
baseball player; Most Valuable
Player, 1976. [d. August 2,
1979]

1952 *Liam Neeson*, Irish actor;
starred in *Schindler's List* and
Rob Roy.

1958 *Prince (Prince Roger Nelson)*,
U.S. musician, singer,
songwriter; Oscar Award for
score of *Purple Rain*, 1985.

HISTORICAL EVENTS

1329 *Robert Bruce*, King of
Scotland, dies and is
succeeded by *David II*.

1492 *Casimir IV* of Poland dies and
is succeeded in Poland by
John Albert; in Lithuania by
Alexander.

1494 Spain and Portugal divide
New World between
themselves in the *Treaty of
Tordesillas*.

1523 A victorious *Gustavus Vasa* is
proclaimed *King Gustavus I*
by the Swedish Riksrand after
he frees the country of the
Danes.

1840 *Frederick William III* of
Prussia dies and is succeeded
by *Frederick William IV*.

1905 *Union of Norway and
Sweden* is dissolved.

1917 The *Battle of Messines*, a
British offensive, opens in
Flanders with the British
capturing Messines Ridge, a
German position overlooking
British lines *(World War I)*.

1955 *The $64,000 Question* makes
its television debut.

1965 U.S. Supreme Court strikes
down 1879 Connecticut law
prohibiting sale of birth-
control devices, establishing
new constitutional precedent
for *right to privacy*.

1971 *Soyuz II*, Soviet spacecraft,
docks in earth orbit with the
Salyut space station; its three
cosmonauts begin laboratory
experiments.

1979 The first direct elections for
the *European Parliamentary
Assembly* are held with an
increase in seats from 198 to
410.

1981 Israeli fighter planes attack
and destroy the *Osirak
nuclear reactor* near
Baghdad, Iraq.

june

JUNE
8

RELIGIOUS CALENDAR

The Saints

St. Maximinus of Aix. Legend calls him one of Christ's 72 disciples who accompanied the Three Marys to evangelize Provence. Principal patron of Aix, France. Also called *Maximus.* [d. c. 5th century]

St. Medard, Bishop of Vermandois; weather on his day is used to forecast weather for next 40 days. Invoked to cure toothache. [d. c. 560]

St. Clodulf, Bishop of Metz. Also called *Clodulphus, Clou, Cloud.* [d. c. 692]

St. William, Archbishop of York. Also called *William Fitzherbert* or *William of Thwayt.* [d. 1154]

The Beatified

Blessed John Rainuzzi. Also called *John Raynutius* or *John of Todi.* [d. c. 1330]

Blessed Pacifico of Cerano, Franciscan friar. [d. 1482]

BIRTHDATES

1625 *Jean Dominique Cassini,* French astronomer; first director of Paris Observatory. Discovered four of Saturn's satellites, eccentricity of earth's orbit. [d. September 11, 1712]

1724 *John Smeaton,* English engineer, innovator in lighthouse building, canal construction, and pumping engines; noted for rediscovering *hydraulic cement,* unknown since Roman times. [d. October 28, 1792]

1772 *Robert Stevenson,* Scottish engineer; designed and built numerous *lighthouses;* invented the system of intermittent or flashing lights used in lighthouses. [d. 1850]

1810 *Robert Schumann,* German composer; regarded as one of greatest followers of Franz Schubert. [d. July 29, 1856]

1813 *David Dixon Porter,* Union admiral during U.S. Civil War. [d. February 13, 1891]

1814 *Charles Reade,* British novelist; known for his novels exposing social abuses. Best known for *The Cloister and the Hearth,* a novel about the father of Erasmus. [d. April 11, 1884]

1821 *Sir Samuel White Baker,* British traveler, explorer; discovered *Lake Albert;* explored tributaries of the *Nile.* [d. December 30, 1893]

1829 *Sir John Everett Millais,* British painter; originator, with Holman Hunt and D. G. Rossetti, of the *Pre-Raphaelite Movement.* [d. August 23, 1896]

1847 *Ida McKinley,* wife of U.S. President William McKinley. [d. May 26, 1907]

1867 *Frank Lloyd Wright,* U.S. architect, writer; recognized for his highly unorthodox approach to building design, an approach which integrated color, form, and texture. [d. April 9, 1959]

1877 *Robert Ferdinand Wagner,* U.S. politician, public official born in Germany. Drafted numerous *New Deal* measures, including the *National Labor Relations Act,* which gave rise to the *National Labor Relations Board,* 1935. [d. May 4, 1953]

1916 *Francis Harry Compton Crick,* British biologist, biochemist, physicist; Nobel Prize in physiology or medicine for determining molecular structure of *DNA* (with J. D. Watson and M. H. F. Wilkins), 1962.

1917 *Byron Raymond White,* U.S. athlete, jurist; All-American and later professional football player (University of Colorado, Pittsburgh Pirates, Detroit Lions); Associate Justice of U.S. Supreme Court, 1962–93.

1918 *Robert Preston (Robert Preston Meservey),* U.S. actor; known for his starring role in *The Music Man* on Broadway;

Victor/Victoria, 1982. [d. March 21, 1987]

1921 *Alexis Smith,* U.S. actress.

Raden Suharto, Indonesian military officer, politician. Responsible for overthrow of President *Ahmed Sukarno.* President of Indonesia, 1968–98.

1923 *Malcolm Boyd,* U.S. Episcopal priest, author.

1924 *Lyn (Franklin Curran) Nofziger,* U.S. government official; assistant to President Reagan for political affairs.

1925 *Barbara Bush,* wife of U.S. President George Bush.

1926 *LeRoy Neiman,* U.S. artist; known for paintings of athletes.

Jerry Stiller, U.S. comedian, actor; member of comedy team Stiller and Meara with his wife, Anne Meara.

1936 *James Darren,* U.S. actor, singer; known for his starring role on television series, *The Time Tunnel,* 1966–67.

Kenneth G. Wilson, U.S. physicist; Nobel Prize in physics for theories about changes in matter, 1982.

1937 *Bruce McCandless, II,* U.S. astronaut; made the first untethered spacewalk on the tenth shuttle flight, 1984.

1938 *Martin Lee (Chu-Ming Lee),* Hong Kong politician.

1939 *William Simon Rukeyser,* U.S. editor; managing editor, *Money* magazine.

1942 *Andrew Weil,* U.S. physician, author; known for his books on alternative medicine.

1944 *William Royce (Boz) Scaggs,* U.S. musician, singer;

Grammy Award for *Lowdown,* 1976.

1947 *Eric F. Wieschaus,* U.S. biologist; Nobel Prize for Medicine. Wieschaus shares with award with Edward B. Lewis and Christiane Nüsslein-Volhard. They discover the influence of genetics in embryonic development, 1995.

1953 *Bonnie Tyler (Gaynor Hopkins),* Welsh singer; known for her song, *Total Eclipse of the Heart,* 1983.

1958 *Keenen Ivory Wayans,* U.S. comedian, actor.

HISTORICAL EVENTS

632 *Muhammad* whose teachings converted all of Arabia to Islamic faith, dies. [born c. 570]

1042 *Hardecanute,* King of England, dies and is succeeded by *Edward the Confessor.*

1536 *Articles of Religion* are published by English clergy in support of Henry VIII's declarations.

1912 *Daphnis et Chloë,* a ballet by Maurice Joseph Ravel, premieres in Paris.

1915 *William Jennings Bryan,* U.S. Secretary of State and a pacifist, resigns in disagreement with President Wilson over U.S. policy on handling the *Lusitania* crisis *(World War I).*

1928 *Peking* is captured by Nationalist Chinese troops.

1937 *Carmina Burana* by *Carl Orff* premieres in Frankfurt.

1948 *Texaco Star Theater* makes its television debut.

1953 Benjamin Britten's opera, *Gloriana,* premieres in London.

1963 *American Heart Association* becomes the first U.S. voluntary public agency to open a drive against *cigarette smoking.*

1966 Plans to merge the *National Football League (NFL)* and *American Football League (AFL)* are announced. Provisions include a common player draft, one commissioner, and a league divided into two conferences.

1968 *James Earl Ray,* alleged assassin of the *Rev. Martin Luther King, Jr.,* is arrested by Scotland Yard detectives at Heathrow Airport in London.

Bermuda promulgates a new constitution placing most of the island's executive powers in the hands of the premier, while the British-appointed governor retains control over external affairs.

1969 President Richard Nixon announces the withdrawal of 25,000 U.S. troops from South Vietnam *(Vietnam War).*

1973 Generalissimo *Francisco Franco (Bahamonde)* resigns as Premier of Spain, appointing Admiral *Luis Carrero Blanco* to succeed him, but retaining the title of Chief of State.

1981 Striking coal miners of the *United Mine Workers* end a 72-day strike, the second longest in the industry's history.

1987 A federal panel recommends the complete overhaul of a new U.S. chancery building in Moscow, after Soviet listening

june

devices are discovered in the concrete pillars and beams.

President *Raul Alfonsin* signs a bill legalizing *divorce* in Argentina.

1990 The first free elections in over forty years are held in *Czechoslovakia,* with the Civic Forum party proving victorious.

1995 Air Force pilot *Scott O'Grady* is rescued by U.S. forces after being shot down by Serbian missiles over Bosnia-Herzegovina. O'Grady spent six days in hiding behind Serbian lines.

1998 *Gen. Sani Abacha,* military ruler of Nigeria, dies.

HOLIDAYS

Iran
Twelfth Imam's Birthday

U.S. (Oklahoma)
Senior Citizens Day

RELIGIOUS CALENDAR

The Saints

SS. Primus and *Felician*, martyrs. Felician also called *Felicianus.* [d. c. 297]

St. Vincent of Agen, martyr. [d. c. 300]

St. Pelagia of Antioch, virgin and martyr. [d. c. 311]

St. Ephraem, Doctor of the Church. Writer and theologian. Also called *Ephrem.* [d. c. 373] Feast formerly June 18. Optional Memorial.

St. Columba, Abbot of Iona. The most famous of Scottish saints; actually an Irish missionary on Isle of Iona. Patron of Scotland. Also called *Colmcille, Columkille, Colum Cille.* [d. 597]

St. Richard, first Bishop of Andria in Apulia. [d. c. 12th cent.]

The Beatified

Blessed Diana, Cecilia, and *Amata,* virgins and Dominican nuns. [d. 1236 and 1290]

Blessed Silvester of Valdiseve, lay-brother. [d. 1348]

Blessed Henry the Shoemaker, founder of the Frères Cordonniers, a religious society for shoemakers. [d. 1666]

Blessed Anne Mary Taigi, matron. [d. 1837]

Blessed Rafael Chylinski. [beatified 1991]

BIRTHDATES

1672 *Peter I,* Emperor of Russia, 1682–1725, known as *Peter the Great.* Introduced Western European civilization into Russia; founded *St. Petersburg* (now *Leningrad*). [d. February 8, 1725]

1768 *Samuel Slater,* U.S. textile manufacturer; one of the founders of the U.S. textile industry. [d. April 21, 1835]

1776 *Count Amedeo Avogadro,* Italian chemist; proposed theory (*Avogadro's Law*) which states that all gases at same pressure and temperature contain equal number of molecules. [d. July 9, 1856]

1781 *George Stephenson,* British inventor, credited with developing first successful *steam locomotive.* [d. August 12, 1848]

1785 *Sylvanus Thayer,* U.S. Army engineer, general, and educator. Controversial superintendent of U.S. military academy at West Point, 1817–33. Known as the *Father of the Military Academy.* [d. September 7, 1872]

1791 *John Howard Payne,* U.S. dramatist; composer of song *Home, Sweet Home;* known for the play *Clari: or, The Maid of Milan.* [d. April 9, 1852]

1812 *Johann Galle,* German astronomer; first to sight planet *Neptune,* 1846. [d. July 10, 1910]

1843 *Baroness Bertha von Suttner,* Austrian humanitarian; Nobel Peace Price, 1905; probably responsible for influencing Alfred Nobel to establish the Nobel Prize for Peace. [d. June 21, 1914]

1850 *Wilhelm Roux,* German zoologist, anatomist; founder of modern experimental embryology. [d. September 15, 1924]

1865 *Carl August Nielsen,* Danish composer; composed opera, *Saul and David.* [d. 1931]

1875 *Sir Henry H. Dale,* British physiologist; Nobel Prize in physiology or medicine for discoveries in the chemical transmission of nerve impulses (with O. Loewi), 1936. [d. July 23, 1968]

1892 *Cole Porter,* U.S. composer, lyricist; wrote some of the most popular, enduring music and lyrics of his time, including many musicals. [d. October 25, 1964]

1900 *Fred M. Waring,* U.S. orchestra conductor. [d. July 29, 1984]

1901 *Nelson Eddy,* U.S. singer, actor; mostly known for duet roles in operetta films with Jeanette MacDonald (June 18). [d. March 6, 1967]

1913 *Patrick Christopher Steptoe,* British physician; developer of in vitro fertilization with Robert Edwards. [d. March 21, 1988]

1916 *Robert (Strange) McNamara,* U.S. banker, businessman, government official; U.S. Secretary of Defense, 1961–68; President of World Bank, 1968–81.

1930 *Marvin Leonard Kalb,* U.S. broadcast journalist, professor.

1932 *Jackie Wilson,* U.S. singer. [d. January 21, 1984]

1939 *Dick Vitale,* U.S. sports commentator.

1946 *Kenneth Lee Adelman,* U.S. government official; Director, Arms Control and Disarmament Agency, 1983–87.

1961 *Michael J. Fox,* Canadian actor; starred in television series' *Family Ties* and *Spin City.* Known for film roles in the *Back to the Future* movies.

1963 *Johnny Depp,* U.S. actor; starred in *Edward Scissorhands,* 1990, and *Ed Wood,* 1994.

HISTORICAL EVENTS

1549 English Parliament establishes uniformity of religious services and the first *prayer book.*

1732 Royal charter is granted to *James Oglethorpe* for formation of colony of *Georgia,* the last of the 13 original colonies to be settled.

1902 *Gustav Mahler* conducts the first complete performance of his *Third Symphony.*

1904 The *London Symphony Orchestra* presents its inaugural concert, *Hans Richter* conducting.

1918 The *Battle of the Metz* begins in German attempt to link the Soissons and Noyen salients, taken in the last two offensives *(World War I).*

1930 *King Carol II* assumes throne of Rumania.

1940 The Cuban Constituent Assembly drafts a new constitution providing for a Parliamentary system with a premier appointed by the president.

1951 Joseph Haydn's opera, *Orfeo et Euridice,* premieres in Florence, Italy, 160 years after it was written.

1970 *Harry Blackmun* is sworn in as associate justice of the U.S. Supreme Court.

1973 *Secretariat* wins the Belmont Stakes, becoming the first horse since 1948 to win thoroughbred racing's *Triple Crown.*

1976 Spanish parliament passes legislation allowing for the establishment of independent political parties. It is the first time since 1939 that groups opposed to the right-wing *National Movement* are allowed to organize.

1978 *Mormon Church* (The Church of Jesus Christ of the Latter-Day Saints) votes to allow blacks to become priests, thus ending a 148-year-old exclusionary policy.

1981 *Mardiros Jamkodjian,* an Armenian dissident, is arrested in Switzerland for the murder of a Turkish consular employee.

1983 *Mario Soares* is inaugurated as premier of Portugal.

1986 A U.S. presidential panel commissioned to investigate the space shuttle *Challenger* accident, issues a report blaming the *National Aeronautics and Space Administration (NASA)* for not detecting the gas leak from a faulty seal that caused the explosion.

1993 *Masako Owada* marries *Prince Naruhito* of Japan.

HOLIDAYS

Argentina
Sovereignty Day

Macao
*Camoëns and Portuguese
Communities Day*
Commemorates death of Luiz Vaz de
Camoëns, Portugal's national poet,
1580.

Portugal
Portugal Day

RELIGIOUS CALENDAR

The Saints
SS. Getulius and his companions,
martyrs. [d. c. 120]
St. Ithamar, Bishop of Rochester, the
first Englishman to become a
Bishop. [d. c. 656]
St. Landericus, Bishop of Paris.
Founded the first real
hospital in Paris. Also called
Landry. [d. c. 660]
St. Bogumilus, Archbishop of
Gniezno, Poland. Founder of
the Cistercian Monastery of
Coronowa. [d. 1182]

The Beatified
Blessed Olive of Palermo, virgin and
martyr. Feast observed in
dioceses of Carthage and
Palermo. [d. 9th century]
Blessed Henry of Treviso. Also called
Henry of San Rigo. [d. 1315]
Blessed Bonaventure of Peraga. The
first Augustinian hermit to
become a cardinal of the
Roman Church. [d. 1386]

Blessed John Dominici, Archbishop
of Ragusa and cardinal. [d.
1419]

BIRTHDATES

1735 *John Morgan,* American
physician; responsible for
establishment of first medical
school in the American
colonies (College of
Philadelphia, later *University
of Pennsylvania*), 1765.
Appointed Director-General
of Hospitals and Physician-in-
Chief to the American Army
by the Continental Congress,
1775–77. [d. October 15,
1789]

1741 *Joseph Warren,* American
Revolutionary general,
physician. Active in American
revolutionary politics;
member of three provisional
congresses held in
Massachusetts. Dispatched
Paul Revere and *William
Dawes* to Lexington to warn
of British approach. Killed at
Battle of Bunker Hill, [d
June 17, 1775]

1819 *Gustave Courbet,* French
realist painter, revolutionary;
associated with the
Commune, revolutionary
regime in Paris, 1871. [d.
December 31, 1877]

1832 *Nikolaus August Otto,*
German inventor; responsible

for early form of *internal
combustion engine* and first
four-cycle gasoline engine.
[d. January 26, 1891]

1841 *George Wallace Melville,* U.S.
naval engineer, Arctic
explorer. [d. March 17, 1912]

1850 *David Jayne Hill,* U.S.
diplomat, author, historian,
and educator. [d. March 2,
1932]

1854 *George Earle Buckle,* British
editor of *The Times* of
London, 1884–1912. [d.
March 3, 1935]

1887 *Harry Flood Byrd, Jr.,* U.S.
politician; Governor of
Virginia, 1926–30; Senator,
1933–65. [d. October 20,
1966]

1895 *Hattie MacDonald,* U.S.
actress; Oscar Award for *Gone
with the Wind,* 1939. [d.
October 26, 1952]

Immanuel Velikovsky, U.S.
writer born in Russia;
proposed controversial theory
that Earth has been visited
numerous times by beings
from outer space. [d.
November 17, 1979]

1904 *Frederick Loewe,* U.S.
composer; most noted for
works created in collaboration
with A. J. Lerner (August 31);
composed music for
*Brigadoon, Paint Your
Wagon,* and *My Fair Lady.* [d.
February 14, 1988]

june

1910 *Howlin' Wolf (Chester Burnett),* U.S. singer; known for songs, *The Little Red Rooster* and *Back Door Man.* [d. January 10, 1976]

1911 *Sir Terence (Mervyn) Rattigan,* British playwright; knighted 1971. [d. November 30, 1977]

1915 *Saul Bellow,* U.S. novelist; Nobel Prize in literature, 1976.

1921 *Prince Philip, Duke of Edinburgh,* husband and consort of *Queen Elizabeth II* of England.

1922 *Judy Garland (Frances Gumm),* U.S. singer, actress. [d. June 22, 1969]

1928 *Maurice (Bernard) Sendak,* U.S. author, illustrator of children's books.

1929 *James Alton McDivitt,* U.S. astronaut. Commanded *Gemini 4* space flight, 1965, and participated in *Apollo 9* flight, 1969.

Edward O. Wilson, U.S. environmentalist, biologist, entomologist; known for his contributions to sociobiology.

1933 *F(rancis) Lee Bailey,* U.S. criminal lawyer; member of defense team in the O. J. Simpson trial (January 24, 1995).

Samuel K. Skinner, U.S. lawyer; Secretary of Transportation, 1989–91; White House Chief of Staff, 1991–93.

1955 *Andrew Stevens,* U.S. actor.

1966 *Doug McKeon,* U.S. actor; known for his role as Jane Fonda's son in *On Golden Pond.*

HISTORICAL EVENTS

1190 *Frederick I,* Holy Roman Emperor, drowns in the river Saleph in Cilicia.

1376 *Wenceslas,* son of *Charles IV,* Holy Roman Emperor, is elected King of the Romans.

1791 *Canada Constitution Act* is passed by British Parliament; Canada is divided into *Upper Canada* and *Lower Canada.*

1868 *Prince Michael III Obrenović* of Serbia is assassinated in Belgrade, after freeing Serbia from Ottoman rule.

1903 *King Alexander* and *Queen Draga* of Serbia are massacred along with aides and members of the palace guard in their palace at Belgrade in a radical coup d'état and revolution led by the military.

1906 The first *Church of Christ, Scientist* is dedicated in Boston.

1921 The *General Accounting Office (GAO)* is established as an independent U.S. government agency.

1924 *Giacomo Matteotti,* Italian Socialist Deputy, is kidnapped and murdered by Fascists.

1935 *Alcoholics Anonymous* is established in New York by ex-alcoholic *Bill Wilson* and *Dr. Robert H. Smith.*

1940 *Italy* declares war on France and Great Britain *(World War II).*

1942 *Lidice, Czechoslovakia* is destroyed and all the residents murdered or tortured by Nazis in reprisal for assassination of *Reinhard Heydrich.*

1948 U.S. Air Force Captain *Charles Yeager,* flying a rocket-powered jet, becomes the first person to break the *sound barrier.*

1962 Archdiocese of *Atlanta, Georgia,* announces nonracial admission policy for coming school year.

1963 U.S. President *John F. Kennedy* signs into law a bill guaranteeing equal pay for equal work, regardless of sex.

1966 Ugandan president, *Milton Obote,* dissolves the *Kingdom of Buganda* and brings it under the authority of the central Ugandan government.

1967 Soviet Union breaks diplomatic relations with *Israel.*

1969 Pope Paul VI arrives in *Geneva.* He is the first pope to visit the city since the Protestant Reformation.

1970 U.S. military attaché in Amman, Major *Robert Perry,* is shot to death by commandos.

1971 U.S. President *Richard Nixon* removes the 21-year old embargo on trade with *China.*

1977 *Rules of War Conference,* held to update 1949 Geneva conventions, approves a provision by which guerrillas have the same rights as soldiers engaged in international wars.

1983 The United Presbyterian Church in the U.S.A. and the Presbyterian Church in the United States reunite to form the *Presbyterian Church (U.S.A.).* The church had divided in 1861 over the issues of slavery and states' rights.

1985 *Israel* completes its three-stage withdrawal of troops from *Lebanon,* leaving advisers within the security zone.

1996 The *Chechen pullout accord* is signed, which calls for the removal of Russian troops and the disarmament of rebel forces.

Peace talks between *Northern Ireland* and Britain begin.

june

JUNE
11

HOLIDAYS

Libya
Evacuation Day
Commemorates the closing of U.S.
Air Force bases and the evacuation
of U.S. military personnel, 1967.

U.S. (Hawaii)
Kamehameha Day
Celebrates King Kamehameha's
unification of the Hawaiian Islands.

RELIGIOUS CALENDAR

The Saints
St. Barnabas, Apostle. Not one of
Christ's first 12 disciples but
closely associated with St.
Paul. Regarded as apostle
because of his great
dedication to apostolic works.
[d. 1st century] Obligatory
Memorial. [major holy day,
Episcopal Church; minor
festival, Lutheran Church.]
SS. Felix and *Fortunatus,* martyrs.
[d. c. 296]
St. Parisio, priest, prophet, and
miracle-worker. [d. 1267]

The Beatified
Blessed Paula Frassinetti, virgin,
founder of the Sisters of St.
Dorothy. [d. 1882]

BIRTHDATES

1572? *Ben(jamin) Jonson,* English
playwright, poet; best known
for his satires, comedies, and
poetry. [d. August 6, 1637]

1776 *John Constable,* English
landscape painter; known for
his realistic landscapes and
studies of rustic life. [d.
March 31, 1837]

1815 *Otto von Böhtlingk,* German
Sanskrit scholar; associated
with Rudolf von Roth in effort
to introduce Vedic studies
into Germany. [d. April 1,
1904]

1842 *Carl von Linde,* German
chemist, engineer; credited
with developing first
successful compression
system using liquid ammonia
as a refrigerant, 1873. [d.
November 16, 1934]

1864 *Richard Strauss,* German
composer, conductor; best
known for his operas.
Regarded as leader of the
New Romantic School. [d.
September 8, 1949]

1880 *Jeanette Rankin,* U.S.
politician, social worker; first
woman member of U.S.
Congress, 1916–18; 1940–42.
Maintained active role in
social reform and women's
liberation movements until
her death at age 92. [d. May
18, 1973]

1895 *Nikolai Aleksandrovich
Bulganin,* Russian political
leader; Minister of Defense,
1947–49, 1953–55; Premier of
Soviet Union, 1955–58. [d.
February 24, 1975]

1899 *Kawabata Yasunari,*
Japanese novelist; Nobel Prize
in literature, 1968. [d. April
16, 1972]

1903 *Ernie Nevers,* U.S. football
and baseball player. [d. May 3,
1976]

1904 *Clarence (Pinetop) Smith,*
U.S. musician; originator of
boogie-woogie, a musical form
based on blues piano playing.
[d. March 14, 1929]

1910 *Jacques-Yves Cousteau,*
French marine explorer,
writer, film producer; partly
responsible for invention of
aqualung, 1943. Creator of
numerous award-winning
documentary films. [d. June
25, 1997]

1913 *Vince Lombardi,* U.S. football
coach; elected to Pro Football
Hall of Fame, 1971. [d.
September 3, 1970]

Risé Stevens (Risé Steenberg),
U.S. operatic mezzo-soprano.

1919 *Richard Todd,* British actor,
producer.

1920 *Irving Howe,* U.S. literary and
social critic. [d. May 5, 1993]

Hazel (Dorothy) Scott, U.S.
jazz pianist, singer; known for
her numerous benefit
performances on behalf of
civil rights; wife of U.S.
Congressman Adam Clayton
Powell, Jr. (November 29). [d.
October 2, 1981]

1925 *William Clark Styron, Jr.,* U.S. author; Pulitzer Prize for *The Confessions of Nat Turner,* 1968.

1932 *Athol Fugard,* South African playwright; author of the plays *The Blood Knot* and *Master Harold.*

1935 *Gene Wilder (Jerry Silberman),* U.S. comedic actor, writer, and director.

1937 Chad Everett (Raymon Lee Cramton), U.S. actor; known for his role as Joe Gannon on television series, *Medical Center,* 1969–76.

1939 *Jackie Stewart,* Scottish auto racer, sportscaster.

1945 *Adrienne Barbeau,* U.S. actress; known for her role on television series, *Maude,* 1972–78.

1947 *Henry G. Cisneros,* U.S. politician.

1956 *Joseph C. (Joe) Montana,* U.S. football player; Most Valuable Player, 1982.

HISTORICAL EVENTS

1258 English barons, headed by *Simon de Montfort,* force *Henry III* to issue *Provisions of Oxford,* guaranteeing three Parliaments annually (*Mad Parliament*).

1488 *James III* of Scotland is murdered after *Battle of Bannockburn.* He is succeeded by *James IV.*

1917 *Constantine,* King of Greece, abdicates and is succeeded by his son, *Alexander.*

1926 General *Chiang Kai-shek* becomes Commander in Chief of the Nationalist Chinese army.

1927 U.S. pilot, *Charles A. Lindbergh* receives the first *Distinguished Flying Cross,* a medal for heroism.

1962 *Students for a Democratic Society,* a national student organization concerned with social issues, is formally established.

1963 Governor *George Wallace* blocks a University of Alabama doorway, barring two black students from registering for classes.

Quang Duc, Buddhist monk, commits suicide by burning himself to death as protest against government of *South Vietnam.*

1967 The *Six-Day War* ends with the Israeli capture of the Sinai Peninsula, Gaza Strip, Golan Heights, West Bank, and East Jerusalem.

1970 U.S. Army Colonels, *Anna Mae Hays* and *Elizabeth Hoisington,* are promoted to brigadier generals. They are the first women promoted to the rank of general officer.

1975 The first oil flows from Britain's *North Sea oil fields.*

1988 *Daimler-Benz* becomes the last German firm to pay reparations to Jews used as forced laborers during World War II.

june

JUNE
12

HOLIDAYS

Paraguay
Peace with Bolivia Day or Peace of Chaco Day
Commemorates end of Chaco War between Paraguay and Bolivia, 1935

Philippines
Independence Day
Commemorates Philippine declaration of independence from Spain, 1898.

Russia
State Sovereignty Day

RELIGIOUS CALENDAR

The Saints
SS. Basilides and his companions, martyrs. [d. 3rd century] Feast suppressed in 1969.
St. Antonina, martyr. [d. c. 304]
St. Onuphrius, hermit. [d. c. 400]
St. Ternan, Bishop of the Picts. [d. 5th or 6th century]
St. Peter of Mount Athos, hermit. [d. c. 8th century]
St. Leo III, pope. Elected 795. Famous for crowning Charlemagne Holy Roman Emperor at St. Peter's in 800. [d. 816]
St. Odulf, evangelizer of Friesland. [d. c 855]
St. Eskil, bishop and martyr. Honored as one of the most illustrious martyrs of Scandinavia. [d. c. 1080]
St. John of Sahagun, priest and Augustinian hermit. [d. 1479]

The Beatified
Blessed Stephen Bandelli, Dominican preacher. [d. 1450]

BIRTHDATES

1519 *Cosimo I de Medici (the Great),* Florentine statesman; Duke of Florence, 1537–74. [d. April 21, 1574]

1802 *Harriet Martineau,* British novelist, economist. [d. June 27, 1876]

1806 *John Augustus Roebling,* U.S. civil engineer, industrialist born in Germany; established first factory to manufacture *wire rope* in America. Pioneered design of *suspension bridges,* including one over Niagara Falls. Conceived preliminary plans for *Brooklyn Bridge,* built after his death. [d. July 22, 1869]

1819 *Charles Kingsley,* British clergyman, novelist, chaplain to Queen Victoria; professor of modern history, Cambridge, 1860–69; author of *Westward Ho!* and *The Water Babies.* [d. January 23, 1875]

1827 *Johanna Heuser Spyri,* Swiss author; wrote *Heidi,* 1880. [d. July 7, 1901]

1851 *Sir Oliver Joseph Lodge,* British physicist, author. Conducted considerable investigation in field of electromagnetics, wireless telegraphy. [d. August 22, 1940]

1864 *Frank Michler Chapman,* U.S. ornithologist, editor; Curator of Ornithology at American Museum of Natural History, New York, 1908–42. Founded magazine *Bird Lore* which later became *Audubon Magazine.* [d. November 15, 1945]

1897 *Sir Anthony Eden, First Earl of Avon,* British statesman; Foreign Secretary, 1935–38, 1940–45, 1951–55; Prime Minister, 1955–57. [d. January 14, 1977]

1899 *Fritz Albert Lipmann,* U.S. biochemist born in Russia; Nobel Prize in physiology or medicine for studies on biochemical activity in cell metabolism, including discovery of *coenzyme A* (with H.A. Krebs), 1953. [d. July 24, 1986]

1915 *David Rockefeller,* U.S. banker, philanthropist; chairman, Chase Manhattan Bank, 1969–81; one of most powerful financiers in the world.

1916 *Irwin Allen,* U.S. director, producer, writer; Oscar Award for *The Sea Around Us,* 1952. [d. November 2, 1991]

1919 *Uta Hagen,* German actress, teacher.

1924 *George Bush,* U.S. politician; Vice-President, 1981–89; President, 1989–93.

1928 *Vic Damone (Vito Farinola),* U.S. singer, actor; known for his starring role in *From Here to Eternity,* 1960.

1929 *Anne Frank,* Dutch writer; her diary, written during two years of hiding with her Jewish family from Nazis during World War II, won acclaim after her death. [d. c. March 1945]

1932 *Rona Jaffe,* U.S. author; wrote *The Last Chance* and *Class Reunion.*

Jim Nabors (James Thurston), U.S. singer, actor; known for his role as Gomer Pyle on television series, *The Andy Griffith Show* and *Gomer Pyle, USMC.*

1941 *Armando (Chick) Corea,* U.S. jazz musician; four Grammy Awards.

1942 *Bert Sakmann,* German physicist; Nobel Prize for Medicine in 1991. Sakmann shares the prize with Erwin Neher for their research of cell functions.

HISTORICAL EVENTS

1727 *George I* of England dies and is succeeded by *George II.*

1898 *Philippines* declares independence from Spain.

1900 *Second German Naval Law* initiates program to double the number of German battleships, thus challenging England's supremacy at sea.

1901 *Cuba* becomes an unofficial protectorate of the U.S.

U.S. military rule of the *Philippines* ends, and a civil government is established.

1917 Allied troops seize *Corinth* and *Larissa, Greece (World War I).*

1930 *Max Schmeling* defeats *Jack Sharkey* for world heavyweight boxing title.

1935 Armistice between *Bolivia* and *Paraguay* ends *Chaco War.*

1937 *Marshal Michael Tukhachevski* and seven other high-ranking generals are executed after a secret court martial in Russia.

1939 *Baseball Hall of Fame,* Cooperstown, New York, is dedicated.

1941 *James Francis Byrnes* is nominated to the U.S. Supreme Court.

U.S. Naval Reserves are called to active duty *(World War II).*

1944 Aircraft from 15 U.S. carriers begin bombing the *Mariana Islands (World War II).*

V-1 rocket is first used by Germans but is shot down by Allied gunners *(World War II).*

1948 U.S. Congress makes *Women's Army Corps* a permanent part of the army and creates the *Women's Air Force.*

1950 The first *nuclear engineering* college course in the U.S. is offered at the University of North Carolina at Raleigh.

1952 *Anne Frank: The Diary of a Young Girl* is published.

1962 *Dawda K. Jawara* is inaugurated as the first premier of the Gambia.

1963 U.S. civil rights activist *Medgar Evers* is murdered. *Byron De La Beckwith* will not be convicted of the crime until 1994.

1971 *Tricia Nixon,* elder daughter of U.S. President Nixon, is married to Edward Finch Cox in the White House rose garden.

1973 Metal industry workers in *Natal, South Africa* establish the country's first black trade union.

1974 *Little League Baseball, Inc.* announces that girls will be allowed to play on its teams.

1975 Indian Prime Minister *Indira Gandhi* is convicted of election violations in 1971 but refuses to resign.

1979 First man-powered flight across the English Channel is made by Bryan Allen in the *Gossamer Albatross.*

1988 The *Russian Orthodox Church* celebrates its one thousandth anniversary at a special mass in Moscow.

1989 *Raúl Alfonsín* announces his resignation as President of Argentina, as the country's economy spirals downward

1991 *Boris Yeltsin* is elected president of the Russian Republic.

1993 Canada elects its first female prime minister, *Kim Campbell.*

june

JUNE
13

HOLIDAYS

Portugal (Lisbon)
St. Anthony's Day
Commemorates feast of St. Anthony of Padua, born in Lisbon, 1195.

Yemen Arab Republic
Reform Movement's Anniversary or Corrective Movement Anniversary

RELIGIOUS CALENDAR

The Saints
St. Felicula, martyr. [d. c. 90]
St. Aquilina, martyr. [d. c. end of 3rd century]
St. Triphyllius, Bishop of Nicosia. [d. c. 370]
St. Anthony of Padua, Doctor of the Church. A great preacher and biblical scholar; patron of Padua, Italy, of the poor and the illiterate; alms given to obtain his intercession are known as *St. Anthony's bread.* Also invoked for help in finding lost articles. Also called *Antonio, Antony.* [d. 1231] Obligatory Memorial.

The Beatified
Blessed Gerard of Clairvaux, brother and assistant of St. Bernard. [d. 1138]

BIRTHDATES

823 *Charles II (the Bald),* King of France, 843–877. [d. October 6, 877]

1752 *Frances (Fanny) Burney,* English novelist, also known as *Madame d'Arblay;* author of *Evelina, Camilla,* and *The Wanderer.* [d. January 6, 1840]

1773 *Thomas Young,* English physicist, physician, Egyptologist; first to describe and measure *astigmatism,* explain nature of color sensation in the human eye. Involved in translation of Egyptian hieroglyphics, especially the *Rosetta stone.* [d. May 10, 1829]

1786 *Winfield Scott (Old Fuss and Feathers),* U.S. army general, 1807–61; foremost military figure of the period. Saw action in War of 1812, Mexican War, pre-Civil War period. [d. May 29, 1866]

1795 *Thomas Arnold,* English educator; greatly influenced development of modern public school system in England, 1828–42. As headmaster of *Rugby,* introduced mathematics, modern history, and foreign languages into school's curriculum. [d. June 12, 1842]

1854 *Sir Charles Algernon Parsons,* British inventor, engineer; developed *compound steam turbine* used in ships, 1897. [d. February 11, 1931]

1865 *William Butler Yeats,* Irish poet, playwright, politician; considered leader of Irish literary revival; one of first senators of Irish Free State, 1922–28; Nobel Prize in literature, 1923. [d. January 28, 1939]

1870 *Jules Jean Baptiste Vincent Bordet,* Belgian bacteriologist, noted for his work in immunology, serology. Developed theories that laid basis for *Wasserman test* for syphilis; Nobel Prize in physiology or medicine, 1919. [d. April 6, 1961]

1879 *Robert Elkington Wood,* U.S. army officer, World War I; President, Sears, Roebuck and Company, 1928–54. Responsible for developing Sears from mail order house to largest merchandising company in the world. [d. November 6, 1969]

1881 *Mary Antin,* U.S. writer, best known work, The Promised Land. [d. 1949]

1884 *John McCormack,* U.S. operatic tenor. [d. September 16, 1945]

1892 *(Philip St. John) Basil Rathbone,* British actor. [d. July 21, 1967]

1893 *Dorothy L(eigh) Sayers,* British novelist; best known for sophisticated mystery stories. [d. December 17, 1957]

1894 *Mark Van Doren,* U.S. critic, poet, educator; film critic of *The Nation,* 1935–38; Pulitzer Prize in poetry, 1940. [d. December 10, 1972]

1897 *Paavo Nurmi,* Finnish long-distance runner; Olympic gold medalist, 1920 (10,000 meter run); 1924 (5,000 meter run); 1928 (10,000 meter run). [d. October 2, 1973]

1899 *Carlos Chávez,* Mexican composer, conductor; organized Mexican Symphony Orchestra, 1928. [d. August 2, 1978]

1903 *Harold Edward (Red) Grange,* U.S. football player, known as *The Galloping Ghost.* [d. January 28, 1991]

1911 *Luis Walter Alvarez,* U.S. physicist; developed ground-controlled approach system for aircraft (with Lawrence Johnston), 1940–43. Renowned for his investigations into physics of subatomic particles. Albert Einstein Award, 1961; Nobel Prize in physics, 1968. [d. September 1, 1988]

1915 *Don Budge,* U.S. tennis player. Elected to Tennis Hall of Fame, 1964.

1926 *Paul (Edward) Lynde,* U.S. comedian, actor; well-known for his quirky, sneering characterizations. [d. January 9, 1982]

1935 *Christo (Christo Javacheff),* Bulgarian artist.

1937 *Eleanor Holmes Norton,* U.S. government official, lawyer; Chairman, Equal Employment Opportunities Commission, 1977–81.

1945 *Levi Watkins Jr.,* U.S. physician; first surgeon to implant the Automatic Implantable Defibrilator device. Also known for his research on congestive heart failure and heart disease.

1948 *Joe Roth,* U.S. director.

1951 *Richard Earl Thomas,* U.S. actor; known for his role as John Boy on television series, *The Waltons.*

1953 *Tim Allen,* U.S. comedian, actor. Known for his role on the hit TV sitcom *Home Improvement.*

HISTORICAL EVENTS

1515 *Martin Luther* marries *Catherine von Bora.*

1541 *John Calvin,* French religious reformer, begins organization of *Geneva* as theocratic state. Geneva becomes focal point for defense of Protestantism throughout Europe.

1898 *Yukon Territory* is formed from the *Northwest Territory* in Canada.

1911 Igor Stravinsky's ballet *Petrouchka* premieres in Paris.

1917 General *John J. Pershing,* leader of the American Expeditionary Force, arrives in France *(World War I).*

1935 *James J. Braddock* defeats *Max Baer* for world heavyweight boxing title.

1951 *Eamon De Valera* becomes prime minister of Ireland.

1953 The military seizes power in Colombia, replacing President *Laureano Gomez* with General *Gustavo Rojos Pinilla.*

1959 *Robert Schwartz* and *William Damashek* report the discovery of a drug that suppresses the immune system in animals. It is the first such agent to be of use in *organ transplants.*

1965 Military triumvirate led by Major General *Nguyen Van Thieu* takes control of the South Vietnam government.

1967 Attorney General *Thurgood Marshall* is appointed to *U.S. Supreme Court,* becoming the first black to be seated on the Supreme Court bench.

1971 *The New York Times* begins publishing the *Pentagon papers,* ending Daniel Ellsberg's long attempt to get those documents made public.

1974 Colonel *Ibrahim al-Hamdi* assumes power in the Yemen Arab Republic after a coup d'etat.

1979 The U.S. Court of Claims awards the *Sioux Nation* $17.5 million for land in the Black Hills of South Dakota that was taken from them in 1877.

1983 *Pioneer 10,* an unmanned U.S. space probe, crosses the orbit of Neptune and becomes the first man-made object to leave the solar system.

1988 A New Jersey jury holds *Liggett Group Inc.* partially responsible for the cancer death of *Rose Cipollone.* It is the first time a cigarette manufacturer is held liable for a smoking-related illness.

june

JUNE 14

HOLIDAYS

U.S.

Flag Day
Commemorates Continental
Congress's adoption of flag for the
13 United States, consisting of 13
stripes, 7 red and 6 white, and 13
white stars arranged in a circle on a
field of blue, 1777.

RELIGIOUS CALENDAR

The Saints

SS. Valerius and *Rufinus,* martyrs.
[d. c. 287]

St. Dogmael. In Britanny, mothers
often invoke him to help
their small children walk. Also
called *Docmael, Dogfael,
Dogwell;* and in Britanny,
Dogméel and *Toël.* [d. c. 6th
century]

St. Methodius I, Patriarch of
Constantinople; greatly
venerated in the East for his
important role in the final
overthrow of Iconoclasm. Also
called *the Confessor* and *the
Great.* [d. 847]

The Beatified

Blessed Castora Gabrielli, widow
and Franciscan tertiary. [d.
1391]

BIRTHDATES

1736 *Charles Augustin de
Coulomb,* French physicist;

known for work on friction,
electricity, and magnetism.
The electrical unit, the
coulomb, is named for him.
[d. August 23, 1806]

1798 *Frantisek Palacký,* Czech
historian, political leader;
worked for creation of
autonomous Czech nation. [d.
April 26, 1876]

1811 *Harriet (Elizabeth) Beecher
Stowe,* U.S. writer; best
known for her novel, *Uncle
Tom's Cabin,* 1852, which
stimulated anti-slavery
sentiment prior to U.S. Civil
War. [d. July 1, 1896]

1820 *John Bartlett,* U.S. editor,
bookseller; compiler of
Familiar Quotations, a classic
reference work. [d. December
3, 1905]

1838 *Yamagata Aritomo,* Japanese
prince, army general; Premier
of Japan, 1889–91, 1898–1900.
[d. February 1, 1922]

1855 *Robert Marion La Follette,
Sr.,* U.S. public official,
political leader; U.S. Senator,
1907–25. Introduced
resolution calling for
investigation of *Teapot Dome
Scandal.* [d. June 18, 1925]

1862 *John Joseph Glennon,* U.S.
Roman Catholic cardinal. [d.
March 9, 1946]

1868 *Karl Landsteiner,* U.S.
physician born in Austria;

Nobel Prize in physiology or
medicine for discovery of
human blood groups, 1930.
[d. June 26, 1943]

1895 *José Carlos Mariátegui,*
Peruvian writer, reformer. [d.
April 16, 1930]

1906 *Margaret Bourke-White,* U.S.
photographer; noted for her
photographs of numerous
world events, including U.S.
campaigns into North Africa,
Italy, and Germany during
World War II, and photo-
essays on Russia, India, the
American South. A founding
editor of *Life* magazine. [d.
August 27, 1971]

1909 *Burl Ives (Burl Icle Ivanhoe),*
U.S. folk singer, character
actor. [d. April 14, 1995]

1918 *Dorothy McGuire,* U.S.
actress; known for her
starring role in *Claudia,* 1941.

1924 *Sir James W. Black,* British
pharmacologist; Nobel Prize
in Medicine. Black shares this
award with fellow
pharmacologists, Gertrude
Elion and George H.
Hitchings, for their study of
drugs in the treatment of
diseases, 1988.

1925 *Pierre Salinger,* U.S.
politician, journalist; Press
Secretary to President John F.
Kennedy, 1961–63.

1928 *Che Guevera (Ernesto
Guevera de la Serna),* Latin

American guerrilla, revolutionary theoretician and tactician; served as aide to Fidel Castro (August 13) during Cuban Revolution, 1959. [d. October 9, 1967]

1954 *Will Patton,* U.S. actor; *Desperately Seeking Susan,* 1985 and *The Client,* 1994.

1958 *Eric Heiden,* U.S. speed skater; winner of five gold medals in 1980 Winter Olympics.

1961 *Boy George (George O'Dowd),* British singer; member of the rock group, *Culture Club;* known for his avante-garde appearance.

1969 *Steffi Graf,* German tennis player.

HISTORICAL EVENTS

1800 *Napoleon* defeats Austrians at *Marengo.*

1846 *Bear Flag Revolt* begins with proclamation of *Republic of California* by a group of settlers. California is annexed to U.S. on August 17, 1846.

1900 The *Hawaiian Islands* become the Territory of Hawaii, part of the United States.

1918 The *Battle of the Metz* ends in the failure of the German offensive *(World War I).*

1934 *Max Baer* knocks out *Primo Carnera* for world heavyweight boxing title.

The U.S. Congress creates the *Federal Communications Commission.*

1940 *Auschwitz,* the largest of the Nazi concentration camps, opens near Krakow, Poland.

1940 German troops enter *Paris (World War II).*

1942 Japanese garrisons arrive by sea and seize the Aleutian islands of *Kiska, Attu,* and *Agattu (World War II).*

1956 Great Britain officially ends its 74-year occupation of the *Suez Canal* Zone.

1962 The *European Research Organization* is established to develop a joint satellite system for Western European nations.

1978 *Sierra Leone* ratifies a new constitution, making the All People's Congress the only recognized political party.

1982 Argentine troops surrender to British, ending fighting over *Falkland Islands.*

1985 Argentine officials announce the introduction of a new currency called the *austral,* which is one thousand times greater than the peso it replaced.

june

JUNE
15

HOLIDAYS

U.S. (Delaware)
Separation Day

U.S. (Idaho)
Pioneer Day
Commemorates first white
settlement at Franklin, 1860.

RELIGIOUS CALENDAR

The Saints

SS. Vitus, Modestus, and *Crescentia,*
martyrs. Vitus is patron of
Germany, Saxony, Bohemia,
and Sicily. St. Vitus is
especially venerated in
Germany as the special
protector of epileptics;
regarded as patron of dancers
and actors; invoked against *St.
Vitus's dance* or chorea,
storms, over-sleeping, the
bites of mad dogs and
serpents, and other injuries of
animals against man. Vitus
also called *Guy.* [d. c. 300]

St. Hesychius, martyr. [d. 302]

St. Tatian Dulas, martyr. [d. c. 310]

St. Orsiesius, Abbot of Tabennisi in
the Egyptian desert. [d. c.
380]

St. Landelinus, abbot. Founder of
the great abbeys of Lobbes
and Crespin. Also called
Landelin. [d. c. 686]

St. Edburga of Winchester, virgin
and abbess. Granddaughter of
the Anglo-Saxon King Alfred.
[d. 960]

St. Bordo, Archbishop of Mainz. [d.
1053]

St. Aleydis, virgin, Cistercian nun,
and mystic. Also called
Aleydia or *Alice.* [d. 1250]

St. Germaine of Pibrac, virgin. [d.
1601]

The Beatified

Blessed Jolenta of Hungary, widow.
Founder of convent at
Gnesen. Also called *Helena.*
[d. 1299]

Blessed Aloysius Palazzolo, priest
and founder of the Brothers
of the Holy Family and the
Sisters of the Poor. [d. 1886]

BIRTHDATES

1330 *Edward the Black Prince,*
son of *King Edward III* of
England. One of the
outstanding commanders
during the *Hundred Years'
War;* accompanied Edward III
on two successive campaigns
to recover throne of France.
Father of *King Richard II* of
England. [d. June 8, 1376]

1767 *Rachel Jackson,* wife of U.S.
President Andrew Jackson. [d.
December 22, 1828]

1843 *Edvard (Hagerup) Grieg,*
Norwegian composer; based
many of his compositions on
Norwegian folk songs. [d.
September 4, 1907]

1856 *Edward Channing,* U.S.
historian, educator; began the
History of the United States, a

monumental single-handed
work detailing the
development of the U.S.
beginning in A.D. 1000. Seven
volumes were completed
upon his death. Volume 6
awarded the Pulitzer Prize in
history, 1926. [d. January 7,
1931]

1882 *Marshall Ion Antonescu,*
Rumanian statesman, soldier;
dictator of German-controlled
government of Rumania,
1940–44; removed from
office, 1944; executed as war
criminal. [d. June 1, 1946]

1894 *Robert Russell Bennett,* U.S.
composer, arranger,
conductor; a leading
orchestrator of Broadway
musicals; scored more than
300 shows, including *Show
Boat, Porgy and Bess, Annie
Get Your Gun,* and *My Fair
Lady.* [d. August 18, 1981]

1914 *Yuri Vladimirovich
Andropov,* Russian political
leader; General Secretary,
Communist Party, 1982–84.
[d. February 9, 1984]

Saul Steinberg, U.S. artist,
architect, cartoonist.

1915 *Thomas Huckle Weller,* U.S.
microbiologist; Nobel Prize in
physiology or medicine for
successful growth of *polio
virus* in laboratory cultures
and discovery of more
effective methods of polio

detection (with J. F. Enders and F. C. Robbins), 1954.

1916 *Herbert A. Simon,* U.S. economist; Nobel Prize in economics for research in the decision-making process within economic organizations, 1978.

1920 *Carol Fox,* U.S. opera producer; a founder of the Lyric Theatre of Chicago (frequently called *La Scala West*); introduced such famous European opera stars as Tito Gobbi and Maria Callas to American audiences. [d. July 21, 1981]

1922 *Morris (King) Udall,* U.S. lawyer; U.S. Congressman, 1961–91

1932 *Mario Matthew Cuomo,* U.S. politician; Governor of New York, 1983–94.

1937 *Waylon Jennings,* U.S. singer.

1941 *Harry Nilsson,* U.S. songwriter, singer. [d. January 15, 1994]

1943 *Malcolm McDowell,* British actor.

1956 *Lance Michael Parrish,* U.S. baseball player; set American League record for home runs by a catcher with thirty-two, 1982.

1958 *Wade Anthony Boggs,* U.S. baseball player; two American League batting titles, 1983, 1985.

1963 *Helen Hunt,* U.S. actress; known for role in TV series *Mad About You*; Academy Award (Best Actress) for *As Good as it Gets*, 1997.

1964 *Courteney Cox,* U.S. actress; known for role on the TV series, *Friends.*

1969 *Ice Cube (Oshea Jackson),* U.S. rap singer, actor.

HISTORICAL EVENTS

1215 *Magna Carta* is signed at Runnymede as *King John* comes to terms with the English barons, laying foundation for English political and personal liberties.

1498 *Niccolò Machiavelli* is appointed Florentine secretary to the *Deici di Libertá e Pace.*

1520 *Pope Leo X* issues papal bull condemning *Martin Luther's* teaching on 41 counts.

1567 *Mary, Queen of Scots,* is imprisoned by her nobles and forced to abdicate in favor of her 13-month old son who is proclaimed *James VI* of Scotland.

1775 *George Washington* is appointed commander-in-chief of the *Continental Army* by the *Continental Congress.*

1836 *Arkansas* is admitted to the Union as the 25th state.

1844 *Charles Goodyear* is granted a patent for *rubber vulcanization.*

1846 *Oregon Treaty* with Great Britain is signed by U.S., setting boundaries between U.S. and British Northwest Territory at 49th parallel.

1866 *Prussia* declares war against Hanover and Saxony (*European War*).

1888 Emperor *Frederick III* of Germany dies and is succeeded by *William II.*

1895 The territory of *Kenya* is made a British protectorate, the British government taking over for the British East Africa Company.

1898 U.S. ships destroy the fort and take possession of the outer bay at *Guantanamo, Cuba (Spanish-American War).*

1919 First nonstop aircraft crossing of the Atlantic is completed by Englishmen *J. W. Alcock* and *A. Whitten-Brown.*

1944 U.S. Marines land on *Saipan,* Mariana Islands *(World War II).*

1964 The last remaining French troops leave *Algeria,* two years after the country gained its independence.

1969 *Georges Pompidou* is elected president of France.

1977 The first free parliamentary elections in *Spain* since 1936 result in a victory for the *Union of the Democratic Center.*

Spain holds first free elections in 41 years, with distinct turn toward democracy despite its status as a monarchy.

1978 U.S. Supreme Court rules that the *snail darter* is protected by the *Endangered Species Act* of 1973; as a consequence, the $100 million *Tellico Dam,* already 80 percent complete, cannot be finished.

1997 *Franjo Tudjman* is elected for a third term as president of Croatia.

JUNE
16

HOLIDAYS

International Day of Solidarity with the Struggling People of South Africa or Soweto Day
Commemorates the start of uprising in Soweto and other areas, 1976, and expresses outrage at apartheid policies and other racist policies in South Africa. Sponsored by the United Nations.

RELIGIOUS CALENDAR

The Saints

SS. Ferreolus and *Ferrutio,* missionaries and martyrs. Probably missionaries in area of Besançon, France. Also called *Fargeau* and *Ferrutius.* [d. c. 212]

SS. Cyricus and *Julitta,* martyrs. Cyricus also called *Circicus, Ciriacus, Cirycus, Quiricus,* and, in France, *Cirgues* or *Cyr.* [d. c. 304]

St. Aurelian, Bishop of Arles. Founded monastery and convent at Arles. [d. 551]

St. Ismael, bishop. Also called *Osmail, Ysfael.* [d. 6th cent.]

St. Tychon, very early Bishop of Amarthus on Cyprus; patron of vine growers. Also called *Tikhon.* [d. c. 5th century]

St. Benno, Bishop of Meissen. [d. 1106]

St. Lutgardis, virgin, Cistercian nun, and mystic. Also called *Lutgard.* [d. 1246]

St. John Francis Regis, Jesuit missionary. [d. 1640]

The Beatified

Blessed Guy of Cortona; an early disciple of St. Francis of Assisi. [d. c. 1245]

BIRTHDATES

1514 *Sir John Cheke,* English classical scholar, embroiled in political unrest; imprisoned by *Queen Mary* for serving as secretary of state to *Lady Jane Grey.* [d. September 13, 1557]

1858 *Gustavus V,* King of Sweden, 1907–50; responsible for maintaining Swedish neutrality during World War I. [d. October 29, 1950]

1874 *Arthur Meighen,* Canadian lawyer, statesman; Prime Minister, 1920–21; 1926. [d. August 5, 1960]

1889 *Nelson Doubleday,* U.S. publisher. [d. January 11, 1949]

1890 *Stan Laurel (Arthur Stanley Jefferson),* British comedian, best known for his film comedies with Oliver Hardy (January 18). Together they pioneered era of film comedy. [d. February 23, 1965]

1892 *Jennie Grossinger,* U.S. hotelier born in Austria [d. November 20, 1972]

1897 *Georg Wittig,* German chemist; Nobel Prize in chemistry for his work with phosphorus compounds, 1979. [d. August 26, 1987]

1899 *John L(awrence) Sullivan,* U.S. government official; U.S. Secretary of the Navy, 1947–59; resigned in protest over funding policies of the Truman administration. [d. August 8, 1982]

1902 *Barbara McClintock,* U.S. geneticist; Nobel Prize for physiology or medicine, 1983. [d. September 2, 1991]

1910? *Jack Albertson,* U.S. actor. [d. November 25, 1982]

1917 *Katharine (Meyer) Graham,* U.S. publisher of the *Washington Post,* 1968–78; Chairman and Chief Executive Officer of Washington Post Co., 1973–.

1920 *José Lopez Portillo,* Mexican lawyer, statesman; President of Mexico, 1976–82.

John Howard Griffin, U.S. writer, musicologist; best known as author of *Black Like Me,* an account of discrimination in America written while traveling through the South disguised as a black man. [d. September 9, 1980]

1923 *Joseph Anthony Colombo,* U.S. gangster. [d. May 23, 1978]

1934 *William F. Sharpe,* U.S. economist; Nobel Prize for Economics. Sharpe shares the award with Merton H. Miller and Harry M. Markowitz, for their work on the theory of financial economics, 1990.

1937 *Erich Segal,* U.S. novelist, classical scholar.

1938 *Joyce Carol Oates,* U.S. novelist, short-story writer, poet, critic, teacher.

1940 *Billy (Crash) Craddock,* U.S. singer.

1946 *Derek Michael Sanderson,* Canadian hockey player.

Joan Van Ark, U.S. actress; known for her role as Val Ewing on television series, *Knot's Landing.*

1948 *Ron(ald) LeFlore,* U.S. baseball player.

1951 *Roberto Duran,* Panamanian boxer; world lightweight champion, 1972–79.

1952 *Gino Vannelli,* Canadian singer; known for songs, *Wheels of Life* and *Living Inside Myself.*

1955 *Laurie Metcalf,* U.S. actress; portrayed Jackie Harris on the TV series *Roseanne.*

1962 *Wallace Keith (Wally) Joyner,* U.S. baseball player.

HISTORICAL EVENTS

1654 *Queen Christina,* a convert to Catholicism, abdicates the Swedish throne to devote the remainder of her life to religion and art.

1919 Irving Berlin's *A Pretty Girl Is Like a Melody* premieres in New York at Ziegfeld Follies.

1920 *International Telephone and Telegraph Corporation* is incorporated in Maryland.

1922 *Henry Berliner* completes first successful helicopter flight.

1933 U.S. Congress passes *Farm Credit Act,* an antidepression measure.

1941 U.S. State Department closes all German consulates in U.S. *(World War II).*

1949 *Jake LaMotta* defeats *Marcel Cerdan* to win the world middleweight boxing title.

1951 The U.S. Public Health Service reports that *fluoride* added to public water supplies decreases the occurence of tooth decay by two-thirds.

1960 Alfred Hitchcock's film, *Psycho,* is released in New York.

1961 Soviet dancer, *Rudolph Nureyev,* leaves the touring Kirov Opera ballet group and asks for political asylum in France.

1963 First female in space, *Valentina V. Tereshkova,* is launched into orbit in Soviet *Vostok VI.*

1969 U.S. Supreme Court rules that *Adam Clayton Powell's* rights were violated when he was prohibited from taking his seat in Congress due to alleged misuse of public funds.

1970 Chicago Bears football player, *Brian Piccolo,* dies of cancer.

1976 Violence erupts in the black South African township of *Soweto* after the government announces the mandatory use of Afrikaans in schools.

1977 Russian Communist Party general secretary, *Leonid I. Brezhnev,* is elected chief of state, becoming the first leader in the U.S.S.R. to occupy both posts concurrently.

1979 Executions of former leaders in *Ghana* begin in an anticorruption campaign by Flight Lieut. *Jerry Rawlings,* in control of the government since June 4.

1987 *Bernhard Goetz,* charged with the attempted murder of four black youths on a subway train in New York City, is acquitted by a New York State Supreme Court jury on grounds of self-defense.

1992 U.S. President *George Bush* and Soviet President *Boris Yeltsin* agree to reduce their countries' nuclear arsenals.

Fidel Ramos is elected president of the Philippines.

june

JUNE
17

HOLIDAYS

Federal Republic of Germany
National Day or Day of German Unity

Iceland
Independence Day
Commemorates Iceland's separation from Denmark and independent status, 1944.

U.S. (Boston, Massachusetts)
Bunker Hill Day

RELIGIOUS CALENDAR

The Saints

SS. *Nicander* and *Marcian*, martyrs. Nicander also called *Nicandeo, Nicanor.* [d. c. 303]

St. *Bessarion,* hermit. [d. 4th century]

St. *Hypatius,* abbot. Invoked as a protector against harmful beasts. [d. c. 446]

St. *Avitus,* abbot. Also called *Avy.* [d. c. 530]

St. *Hervé,* blind abbot. One of the most popular saints of Brittany. Invoked for eye troubles of all sorts. Also called *Harvey.* [d. 6th century]

St. *Nectan,* hermit. Also called the *Headless Saint, Nighton.* [d. c. 6th century]

St. *Botulf,* abbot, and St. *Adulf.* Botulf also called *Botolph* [d. c. 680]

St. *Moling,* Bishop of Leinster. One of the four prophets of Ireland. Also called *Daircheall, Dairchilla, Molingus, Mulling.* [d. 697]

St. *Rainerius,* patron saint of Pisa. Also called *Raniero* and nicknamed *de Aqua.* [d. 1160]

SS. *Teresa* and *Sanchia* of Portugal. [d. 1250 and 1229]

St. *Gregory Barbarigo,* Bishop of Padua and cardinal. [d. 1697]

St. *Emily de Vialar,* virgin; founder of the Sisters of Saint Joseph of the Apparition. [d. 1856]

St. *Briavel,* hermit; patron of St. Briavels. [death date unknown.]

The Beatified

Blessed Peter of Pisa, founder of the Poor Brothers of St. Jerome. [d. 1435]

BIRTHDATES

1239 *Edward I,* King of England; noted for strengthening the crown against the feudal nobility. [d. July 7, 1307]

1682 *Charles XII,* King of Sweden. Invaded Russia and Poland; was finally defeated at Poltava in 1709. [d. November 30, 1718]

1703 *John Wesley,* English evangelist, theologian; founder of the *Methodist movement.* [d. March 2, 1791]

1714 *César Cassini de Thury,* French surveyor; directed the first national geographical survey. [d. September 4, 1784]

1808 *Everhardus Johannes Potgieter,* Dutch poet, essayist, critic; founder and editor of *De Gids (The Guide),* leading literary monthly of the Netherlands. [d. February 3, 1875]

Henrik Arnold Wergeland, Norwegian poet, playwright, and prose writer. [d. July 12, 1845]

1818 *Charles François Gounod,* French composer; especially well known for opera *Faust.* [d. October 18, 1893]

1832 *Sir William Crookes,* British physicist, chemist; discovered thallium, 1861; invented *Crookes' tube,* a high-exhaustion vacuum tube. [d. April 4, 1919]

1860 *Charles Frohman,* U.S. theatrical manager; developed Empire Theatre Stock Company, 1891, where such actors as Maude Adams, Ethel Barrymore, and William Gillette gained prominence. [d. May 7, 1915]

1865 *Susan LaFlesche Picotte,* Native American doctor. [d. 1915]

1871 *James Weldon Johnson,* poet, teacher, critic, civil rights leader; first black to serve as executive secretary of NAACP. [d. June 26, 1933]

1882 *Igor Fyodorovich Stravinsky,* U.S. composer born in Russia; controversial, avantgarde composer of symphonies, ballets, concertos; recognized as one of most influential composers of 20th century. [d. April 6, 1971]

1888 *Heinz Wilhelm Guderian,* German general; commander in chief of armored units, 1939–41. [d. May 15, 1954]

1904 *Ralph Bellamy,* U.S. actor; Tony Award for *Sunrise at Campobello,* 1958. [d. November 29, 1991]

1907 *Charles Eames,* U.S. designer; best known for chair design developed with Eero Saarinen (August 20), which opened way for new approach to production of furniture and the coming of age of *industrial design.* [d. August 21, 1978]

1914 *John (Richard) Hersey,* U.S. educator, novelist, journalist; *A Bell for Adano* won Pulitzer Prize for fiction, 1945; also wrote *The Wall* and *Hiroshima,* an account based on survivors' documentation of atomic bombing of that city. [d. May 24, 1993]

1917 *Dean Martin (Dino Crocetti),* U.S. singer, actor; known for his comedy films with Jerry Lewis, 1948–57. [d. December 25, 1995]

1919 *Kingman Brewster,* U.S. educator, diplomat; President of Yale University, 1963–77; U.S. Ambassador to Great Britain, 1977–80. [d. November 8, 1988]

1920 *François Jacob,* French biologist; Nobel Prize in

physiology or medicine for discovery of body processes which contribute to genetic control of enzymes and virus synthesis (with J. L. Monod and A. M. Lwoff), 1965.

1928 *James Brown,* U.S. singer.

1943 *Newt Gingrich,* U.S. politician; Speaker of the House of Representatives, 1994– .

1946 *Barry Manilow,* U.S. singer, songwriter; Grammy Award for *The Copacabana,* 1978, two Emmy Awards, and Tony Award.

1951 *Joseph Charles (Joe) Piscopo,* U.S. actor, comedian; known for his roles on television series, *Saturday Night Live.*

1965 *Dan Jansen,* U.S. speed skater; Olympic gold medalist, 1994.

1980 *Venus Williams,* U.S. tennis player.

HISTORICAL EVENTS

656 *Caliph Othman* of Arabia is murdered by Mohammed, son of *Abu-Bakr.*

1040 *Hardecanute (Harthacnut),* King of Denmark, becomes King of England, 1040–42.

1775 American forces meet British at *Breed's Hill* near Boston. The battle, known as the *Battle of Bunker Hill,* ends in an American defeat but only after heavy British losses.

1789 The French Third Estate declares itself the National Assembly and vows *Tennis Court Oath* not to disband until it has created a constitution for France *(French Revolution).*

1903 *Babes in Toyland* by Victor Herbert premieres in Chicago.

1925 The *Geneva Protocol* prohibiting use of poison gases in warfare is signed.

1944 Allied task force lands French troops on *Elba, Italy (World War II).*

Iceland becomes a republic independent of Denmark.

Iceland severs its ties with Denmark and becomes a republic. *Sveinn Bjornsson* is named the country's first president.

1950 Dr. *Richard Lawler* performs the first human *kidney transplant.*

1957 *John Diefenbaker* succeeds *Louis St. Laurent* as prime minister of Canada, ending 22 years of Liberal Party rule.

1967 The *People's Republic of China* announces its first successful hydrogen bomb test.

1968 U.S. Supreme Court upholds 1866 law prohibiting racial discrimination in sales and rental of property.

1970 *Oh, Calcutta!,* created by Kenneth Tynan, Samuel Beckett, Jules Feiffer and John Lennon, premieres off-Broadway.

1971 *Dominic Mintoff* is inaugurated as prime minister of Malta.

1972 Five men are seized while apparently trying to install eavesdropping equipment in the Democratic National Committee headquarters at the Watergate building in Washington, D.C. (*Watergate Incident*).

1976 Eighteen teams from the *National Basketball*

june

Association merge with four of the remaining six teams of the defunct *American Basketball Association.*

1981 The U.S. Navy's first Trident submarine, *U.S.S. Ohio,* is launched at Groton, Connecticut.

1991 South Africa repeals the discriminatory *Population Registration Act.*

1994 *Orenthal James "O.J." Simpson* leads police on a car chase before surrendering to police for the murders of his ex-wife Nicole Brown and her friend, Ron Goldman. Simpson was later acquitted of murder charges.

1996 The United States and China sign an *antipiracy agreement,* thereby avoiding a trade war.

HOLIDAYS

Egypt

Evacuation Day

Celebrates evacuation of French, British, and Israeli troops, who invaded after nationalization of Suez Canal in 1956.

RELIGIOUS CALENDAR

The Saints

SS. Mark and *Marcellian,* martyred brothers. Also called *Marcus* and *Marcellianus.* [d. c. 287]

St. Amandus, Bishop of Bordeaux. Also called *Amand.* [d. c. 431]

St. Elizabeth of Schönau, virgin, visionary, and abbess. Also called *Elizabeth of Sconage.* [d. 1164]

BIRTHDATES

1754 *Anna Maria Lenngren,* Swedish satirical poet. [d. March 8, 1817]

1769 *Robert Stewart, Viscount Castlereagh,* British statesman; Chief Secretary for Ireland, 1799–1801; British Foreign Secretary and leader of House of Commons, 1812–22. [d. August 12, 1822]

1845 *Sir Sidney Colvin,* British art critic, biographer; intimate friend of Robert Louis Stevenson, and editor of Stevenson's works. [d. May 11, 1927]

Charles Louis Alphonse Laveran, French army surgeon; Nobel Prize in physiology or medicine for studies of protozoa-caused diseases, 1907. [d. May 18, 1922]

1850 *Cyrus Hermann Kotzschmar Curtis,* U.S. publisher, philanthropist; founder of Curtis Publishing Co., publishers of *Ladies Home Journal, Saturday Evening Post,* and the *Philadelphia Inquirer.* [d. June 7, 1933]

1854 *E(dward) W(yllis) Scripps,* U.S. newspaper publisher; with his brother, James Edmund Scripps, formed the Scripps-McRae League of Newspapers, which evolved into Scripps-Howard Newspapers. Also developed company to disseminate news by telegraph to subscriber newspapers, United Press International (UPI). [d. March 12, 1926]

1857 *Henry Clay Folger,* U.S. industrialist, philanthropist; Chairman, Standard Oil Co. of New York; avid collector of Shakespeare's works; built and endowed *Folger Shakespeare Library,* Washington, D.C. [d. June 11, 1930]

1869 *Miklos von Nagybanya Horthy,* Hungarian military officer; Commander in Chief of Austro-Hungarian fleet during World War I; commander in chief of national army in Hungary, 1919. Regent of Hungary, 1920–44. [d. February 9, 1957]

1883 *Baltasar Brum,* Uruguayan statesman, journalist, jurist; President of Uruguay, 1919–23. [d. March 31, 1933]

1884 *Edouard Daladier,* French politician; Premier of France 1933, 1934, 1938–40. [d. October 10, 1970]

1907 *Jeanette MacDonald,* U.S. singer, actress; best known for series of film operettas with Nelson Eddy (June 9). [d. January 14, 1965]

1913 *Sammy Cahn,* U.S. songwriter; two Oscar Awards for *The Three Coins in a Fountain* and *All the Way.* [d. January 15, 1993]

Sylvia (Field) Porter, U.S. journalist, financial adviser; author of *The Money Book.* [d. June 5, 1991]

1917 *Richard Boone,* U.S. actor; known for his starring role in television series, *Medic,* 1954–56 and *Have Gun Will Travel,* 1957–63. [d. 1981]

1918 *Jerome Karle,* U.S. physicist; Nobel Prize in chemistry for

june

work done in determining crystal structures (with Herbert A. Hauptman), 1985.

Franco Modigliani, U.S. economist; Nobel Prize for theories of savings and corporate finance, 1985.

1926 *Thomas Grey (Tom) Wicker (Paul Connelly),* U.S. journalist, author; wrote *Kennedy Without Tears: The Man Behind the Myth,* 1964.

1932 *Dudley Robert Herschbach,* U.S. chemist; Nobel Prize in chemistry for his research in reaction dynamics (with Yuan T. Lee and John C. Polanyi), 1986.

1937 *John D(avison) Rockefeller IV,* U.S. politician; Secretary of State for West Virginia, 1969–72; President of West Virginia Wesleyan College, 1973–75; Governor of West Virginia, 1977–85.

1942 *Paul McCartney,* British musician; bass guitarist, vocalist and songwriter with John Lennon (October 9) for *The Beatles,* 1962–70.

1952 *Carol Kane,* U.S. actress; Emmy Award for her role as Simka on television series, *Taxi,* 1982.

Isabella Rossellini, Italian actress, model; known for her starring role in *White Nights;* daughter of Ingrid Bergman and Roberto Rossellini.

HISTORICAL EVENTS

1155 *Frederick I (Barbarossa)* is crowned Holy Roman Emperor, beginning a period of great advancements in intellectual areas and exploration.

1812 The U.S. declares war on Great Britain (*War of 1812*).

1815 Napoleon's troops are defeated at the *Battle of Waterloo* by the combined forces of the Duke of Wellington and General von Blücher.

1872 Suffragist *Susan B. Anthony* is arrested for voting in a Rochester, New York, local election.

1910 Congress passes the *Mann-Elkins Act,* placing all U.S. telegraph, telephone, and cable companies under *Interstate Commerce Commission* jurisdiction.

1915 *Second Battle of Artois* ends with enormous numbers of British and French casualties (*World War I*).

1933 The *Nazi party* is dissolved in Austria.

1934 The *Indian Reorganization Act (Wheeler-Howard Act)* is passed by the U.S. Congress, allowing Indians to return to their reservations and providing some local self-government.

1941 *Joe Louis* defeats *Billy Conn* to retain the world heavyweight boxing title.

1944 *Battle of the Philippine Sea* begins; Japan's defeat in this battle marks end of effective Japanese carrier power in the Pacific (*World War II*).

1948 First public demonstration of the 12-inch vinyl *long-playing phonograph record* is made in New York by CBS engineer Peter Goldmark.

1953 *Egypt* is declared a republic with *General Mohammed Naguib* as President.

1965 Air Vice-Marshal *Nguyen Cao Ky* is named Premier of South Vietnam under the new military regime of General *Nguyen Van Thieu.*

1966 Premier *Chou En-lai* announces that a cultural revolution directed against anti-socialist elements is taking place in the *People's Republic of China.*

1975 *Prince Faisal ibn Musad* is beheaded in Riyadh, Saudi Arabia, for the assassination of his uncle *King Faisal.*

1979 U.S. President Jimmy Carter and Russian President Leonid Brezhnev sign the *Strategic Arms Limitation Treaty (SALT) II* in Vienna.

1983 *Li Xiamian* is named first president of the People's Republic of China since 1960.

1987 Vietnam's premier, *Phram Van Dong,* and president, *Truong Chinh,* are ousted from office and replaced by *Phram Hung* and *Vo Chi Cong.*

HOLIDAYS

Algeria
Righting Day or Revolutionary Recovery Day
Commemorates overthrow of government of President Ahmed Ben Bella, 1965.

Trinidad and Tobago
Labour Day

Uruguay
Artigas Day
Commemorates the birthday of General José Gervasio Artigas, 1764.

U.S. (Texas)
Emancipation Day

RELIGIOUS CALENDAR

The Saints
St. Deodatus, Bishop of Nevers. Also called *Dié* or *Didier.* [d. c. 679]

St. Bruno of Querfurt, bishop, missionary, and martyr; Apostle of Russia. Also called *Boniface.* [d. 1009]

St. Romualdo, abbot. Founder of the Camaldolese Benedictines. Also called *Romuald.* [d. 1027] Feast formerly February 7. Optional Memorial.

St. Juliana Falconieri, virgin, founder of the Servite order. [d. 1341]

St. Gervase and *St. Protase,* martyrs. Venerated as the first martyrs of Milan. Also called *Gervasius* and *Protasius.* [death date unknown]

The Beatified
Blessed Odo, Bishop of Cambrai. [d. 1113]
Blessed Thomas Woodhouse, martyr. [d. 1573]

BIRTHDATES

1566 *James I,* King of Great Britain, 1603–25 (King James VI of Scotland, 1567–1625); first king to rule both England and Scotland. [d. March 27, 1625]

1623 *Blaise Pascal,* French scientist, philosopher; contributed significantly to development of mathematical theories including *differential calculus.* Pascal's literary works, especially *Provinciales* and *Pensées,* are recognized as masterpieces of ironical style. [d. August 19, 1662]

1754 *Jean Baptiste Marie Meusnier,* French general, aeronautical theorist; his studies contributed to knowledge of aeronautical principles of balloons. [d June 13, 1793]

1764 *Sir John Barrow,* English geographer; Secretary of the Admiralty, 1804–06; 1807–45. Founder of *Royal Geographical Society,* 1830. [d. November 23, 1848]

1783? *Thomas Sully,* U.S. painter born in England; among his best-known works are portraits of the Marquis de Lafayette, Thomas Jefferson, James Madison, and Andrew Jackson. [d. November 5, 1872]

1861 *Douglas Haig, 1st Earl Haig,* British army officer; Commander in Chief of expeditionary forces in France, 1915–19 (World War I). [d. January 29, 1928]

José Mercado Rizal, Philippine patriot, author; leader of a nationalist movement. [d. December 30, 1896]

1877 *Charles Coburn,* U.S. actor. [d. August 30, 1961]

1880 *Jóhann Sigurjónsson,* Icelandic dramatist, poet. [d. August 31, 1919]

1881 *James (John) Walker,* U.S. politician, lawyer; Mayor of New York City, 1925–32. [d. November 18, 1946]

1896 *(Bessie) Wallis Warfield, Duchess of Windsor,* U.S. socialite divorcee for whom King *Edward VIII* of England renounced his throne.[d. 1986]

1897 *Sir Cyril Norman Hinshelwood,* British physical chemist; Nobel Prize in chemistry for research into the kinetics of chemical reactions (with N. N.

june

Semenov), 1956. [d. October 9, 1967]

Moe Howard, U.S. comedian; member of the comedy group, *The Three Stooges.* [d. May 24, 1975]

1900 *Laura Z(ametkin) Hobson,* U.S. author; wrote *Gentlemen's Agreement,* about anti-Semitism in U.S., 1947. [d. February 28, 1986]

1902 *Guy Lombardo,* U.S. bandleader born in Canada; leader of *Royal Canadians* band whose New Year's Eve musical countdown became a U.S. radio and television tradition. [d. November 5, 1977]

1903 *(Henry) Lou(is) Gehrig,* U.S. baseball player; inducted into Baseball Hall of Fame, 1939. [d. June 2, 1941]

1906 *Ernst Boris Chain,* British biochemist born in Germany; Nobel Prize in physiology or medicine for discovery of *penicillin* (with A. Fleming and H.W. Florey), 1945. [d. September 14, 1979]

1908 *Mildred Natwick,* U.S. character actress. [d. October 25, 1994]

1910 *Abe Fortas,* U.S. jurist, lawyer; Associate Justice of U.S. Supreme Court, 1965–69. [d. April 5, 1982]

Paul J. Flory, U.S. chemist; Nobel Prize in chemistry for his investigations of synthetic and natural macromolecules, 1974. [d. September 9, 1985]

1914 *Alan MacGregor Cranston,* U.S. politician; Senator, 1969–91.

1918 *Morris Berthold Abram,* U.S. lawyer; first head of Peace Corps legal department, 1961.

1919 *Pauline Kael,* U.S. author, movie critic; wrote *When the Lights Go Down,* 1980.

1921 *Louis Jourdan (Louis Gendre),* French actor.

1922 *(Aage) Niels Bohr,* Danish physicist; Nobel Prize in physics for discovery of connection between collective motion and particle motion in atomic nucleus (with J. Rainwater and B. Mottelson), 1975.

1928 *Nancy Marchand,* U.S. actress; known for her role as Mrs. Pynchon on television series, *Lou Grant,* 1977–81; two Emmy Awards.

1936 *Gena Rowlands,* U.S. actress; known for her role in *Gloria,* 1980.

1945 *Aung San Suu Kyi,* Myanmar human rights activist; Nobel Prize for Peace in 1991.

1954 *Kathleen Turner,* U.S. actress; known for her starring roles in *Romancing the Stone,* 1984, *Jewel of the Nile,* 1985, and *Peggy Sue Got Married,* 1986.

1963 *Paula Abdul,* U.S. singer, choreographer.

HISTORICAL EVENTS

1464 *Louis XI,* King of France, establishes *Poste Royale,* pioneering concept of national *postal service.*

1669 *Michael Wisniowiecki* is elected King of Poland following abdication of *John Casimir.*

1842 The British seize *Shanghai* in the *First Opium War* with China.

1846 First real *baseball game* with set rules is played at the Elysian Fields in Hoboken, New Jersey, between the *Knickerbocker Baseball Club* and the *New York Nine.* Knickerbocker Club is defeated by a score of 23-1.

1867 Mexico's *Emperor Maximilian* is executed by a firing squad, thus ending France's hopes for establishing an empire in Central America.

1910 *Father's Day* is observed for the first time under the sponsorship of the Spokane, Washington, Ministerial Association and YMCA.

1934 *U.S. Federal Communications Commission* is created to regulate interstate and foreign communications by telegraph, radio, and cable.

1961 U.S. Supreme Court rules that evidence produced from an illegal search or seizure is inadmissible in a state court.

Kuwait gains independence from Great Britain.

1963 *Levi Eshkol* replaces *David Ben-Gurion* as prime minister of Israel.

1965 Algerian President *Ahmed ben Bella* is ousted from office in a coup d'état headed by Defense Minister *Houari Boumedienne.*

1967 *Gamal Abdel Nasser* names himself Prime Minister of the *United Arab Republic.*

1968 *Poor People's Campaign* comes to an end in Washington, D.C., as more than 50,000 persons take part in a *Solidarity Day* march on the capital.

1970 Russian spacecraft *Soyuz 9* returns to earth concluding a record-breaking 17-day flight.

1977 *John Nepomucene Neumann* becomes the first U.S. prelate to be canonized.

1987 The U.S. Supreme Court strikes down a Louisiana law which requires public schools to teach *creationism* if they teach *evolutionism*, stating it violates the First Amendment.

june

JUNE
20

HOLIDAYS

Argentina
Flag Day

Eritrea
Martyr's Day

U.S. (West Virginia)
West Virginia Day
Commemorates admission of West
Virginia to the Union, 1863.

RELIGIOUS CALENDAR

The Saints
St. Silverius, pope and martyr.
    Elected 536. [d. c. 537]
St. Goban, priest and martyr. Also
    called *Gobain, Gobian*. [d. c.
    670]
St. Bagnus, Bishop of Thérouanne;
    principal patron of Calais.
    Also called *Bain*. [d. c. 710]
*Translation of St. Edward the
    Martyr*, King of England, from
    Wareham to Shaftsbury, 980.
St. Adalbert, Archbishop of
    Magdeburg. [d. 981]
St. John of Matera, Abbot of
    Pulsano. [d. 1139]
*The English Martyrs of the Oates
    Plot* [1678–1680],

The Beatified
Blessed Michelina of Pesaro, widow.
    [d. 1356]
Blessed Osanna of Mantua, virgin.
    [d. 1505]

BIRTHDATES

1389 *John of Lancaster, Duke of
    Bedford*, third son of *Henry
    IV* of England; English military
    leader. [d. September 14,
    1435]

1700 *Peter Faneuil*, American
    merchant; donated *Faneuil
    Hall* in Boston to the city. [d.
    March 3, 1743]

1793 *Count Alexander Fredro*,
    Polish playwright, poet; called
    the *Polish Molière*. [d. July
    15, 1876]

1819 *Jacques Offenbach (Jakob
    Eberst)*, French composer
    born in Germany; best known
    for operettas and *opéra
    bouffe* written for his own
    theater in Paris as well as
    others; wrote *Gaiété
    Parisienne*, which contains
    traditional music for the can-
    can. [d. October 5, 1880]

1832 *Benjamin Helm Bristow*, U.S.
    lawyer, public official; highly
    effective in his opposition to
    the Ku Klux Klan and as
    protector of blacks' rights.
    Served as second president of
    American Bar Association. [d.
    June 22, 1896]

1833 *Léon Joseph Florentin
    Bonnat*, French painter, art
    collector; noted for his
    religious paintings. [d.
    September 8, 1922]

1858 *Charles Waddell Chestnutt*,
    U.S. lawyer, novelist; first

black to have work published
in *Atlantic Monthly*. Noted
for his various fictional works
on the lives and attitudes of
blacks in America, as well as
his successes as a lawyer. [d.
November 15, 1932]

1863 *John Miller Turpin Finhey*,
    U.S. surgeon, author,
    educator. [d. May 30, 1942]

1873 *Alberto Santos-Dumont*,
    Brazilian aeronaut; known for
    his experiments with balloons
    and early airships; built first
    airship station in France,
    1903. [d. July 25, 1932]

1883 *Royal Eason Ingersoll*, U.S.
    naval officer; commanded
    U.S. Atlantic fleet, 1942–44
    (World War II). [d. May 20,
    1976]

1894 *Lloyd A. Hall*, U.S. chemist;
    discover method for the
    preservation and sterilization
    of food. [d. January 2, 1971]

1899 *Helen Traubel*, U.S. operatic
    soprano; member of
    Metropolitan Opera
    Company, 1940–53. [d. July
    28, 1972]

1900 *Julian (Edwin) Levi*, U.S.
    artist, educator; known for his
    seascapes; member of the
    faculty of the New School for
    Social Research, 1945–66. [d.
    February 28, 1982]

1905 *Lillian Hellman*, U.S.
    playwright; plays include

Children's Hour, The Little Foxes, Watch on the Rhine, as well as other dramas and plays written for or adapted for the screen. [d. June 30, 1984]

1909 Errol Flynn, U.S. actor. [d. October 14, 1959]

1924 Chet Atkins (Chester B. Atkins), U.S. country-and-western guitarist.

Audie Murphy, U.S. soldier, actor; most highly decorated U.S. soldier of World War II. [d. May 28, 1971]

1929 Edgar Miles Bronfman, Canadian distiller; Chairman and Chief Executive Officer, Seagrams Co., Ltd.

1931 Olympia Dukakis, U.S. actress; Oscar winner for Moonstruck, 1987.

1934 Martin Landau, U.S. actor; played Rollin Hand on TV series Mission Impossible; Oscar winner for Ed Wood, 1994.

1942 Brian Douglas Wilson, U.S. singer, songwriter, member of the rock group, The Beach Boys.

1945 (Morna) Anne Murray, Canadian singer; known for her song, Snowbird, 1970.

1946 Andre Watts, German-born musician.

1952 John Goodman, U.S. actor.

1953 Cynthia (Cyndi) Lauper, U.S. singer; Grammy Award, 1984; she broke the record for most top ten singles from a debut album with She's So Unusual, 1984.

1967 Nicole Kidman, Australian actress.

HISTORICAL EVENTS

1624 Treaty of Compiègne is signed between France and the Netherlands (Thirty Years' War).

1756 The Nawab of Bengal, Surāj-ud-Dawlah, captures Calcutta and imprisons 146 English residents in what is later called The Black Hole of Calcutta. Allegedly, only 23 prisoners survive the overnight imprisonment.

1782 U.S. Congress adopts the Great Seal of the United States.

1792 French mob marches on the Tuileries (French Revolution).

1837 William IV of England dies and is succeeded by Queen Victoria.

Hanover is separated from England upon the accession of Queen Victoria because Hanoverian law forbids the succession of a woman to the throne (Salic Law).

1840 A patent for the telegraph is granted to Samuel F. B. Morse.

1863 West Virginia is admitted to the Union as the 35th state.

1900 Boxer Rebellion begins in China as one Chinese faction attempts to rid the nation of foreign control and interference.

1941 The British Royal Air Force bombs Damascus. (World War II)

Archaeologists open the tomb of Mongol ruler Timur (Tamerlane), who died in 1405 at Samarkand.

1944 Battle of the Philippine Sea ends with heavy losses inflicted by U.S. planes on the Japanese fleet (World War II).

1946 Frederick Vinson becomes Chief Justice of the U.S. Supreme Court.

1948 The Ed Sullivan Show makes its television debut.

1960 Floyd Patterson knocks out Ingemar Johansson in the 5th round to become the first man to regain the world heavyweight boxing championship.

Senegal and Sudanese Republic, former French territories in Africa, obtain independence as Federation of Mali.

1963 France announces the withdrawal of its naval units from NATO.

1977 The first oil from Alaska's frozen north slope begins flowing into the trans-Alaska pipeline.

1979 Ugandan president Jusufu Lule is forced from office and Godfrey Binasia is appointed in his place.

1988 Lieutenant General Henri Namphy declares himself president of Haiti and dissolves the legislature after overthrowing President Leslie Manigat in a military coup.

The U.S. Supreme Court unanimously upholds a New York law requiring most private men's clubs to begin admitting women.

1990 Former South African political prisoner Nelson Mandela arrives in New York City and is given a ticker-tape parade.

june

JUNE 21

HOLIDAYS

Togo
Pya Martyrs Day

RELIGIOUS CALENDAR

The Saints

St. Eusebius, Bishop of Samosata. [d. c. 379]

St. Alban of Mainz, martyr. Also called *Albinus.* [d. 5th century]

St. Méen, abbot. Famous as a healer of skin diseases. Also called *Main, Melanus, Mevennus, Mewan.* [d. c. 6th century]

St. Engelmund, abbot and missionary. [d. c. 720]

St. Leutfridus, abbot. Also called *Leufredus, Leufroi, Leufroy.* [d. 738]

St. Ralph, Archbishop of Bourges. Also called *Radolphus, Radulf, Raoul.* [d. 866]

St. Aloysius, patron of Catholic youth. Also called *Luigi Gonzaga.* [d. 1591] Obligatory Memorial.

The Beatified

Blessed Francesco Spinelli. [beatified 1992]

BIRTHDATES

1639 *Increase Mather,* American colonial religious leader; father of *Cotton Mather.* Pastor of Boston's Second Church, 1664–1723; President of Harvard College, 1685–1701. [d. August 23, 1723]

1676 *Anthòny Collins,* English deist, theological controversialist; intimate of John Locke. [d. December 13, 1729]

1731 *Martha Washington,* U.S first lady; wife of President George Washington. [d. May 22, 1802]

1757 *Alexander James Dalls,* U.S. lawyer, public official; U.S. Secretary of the Treasury, 1814–16. [d. January 16, 1817]

1774 *Daniel Thompkins,* U.S. Vice-President, 1817–25. [d. June 11, 1825]

1781 *Siméon-Denis Poisson,* French mathematician; known for innovative applications of mathematical laws to physics. [d. April 25, 1840]

1792 *Ferdinand Christian Baur,* German theologian; founder of Tübingen School of Theology. [d. December 2, 1860]

1805 *Charles Thomas Jackson,* U.S. chemist, geologist; first state geologist of Maine, Rhode Island, and New Hampshire. Controversial for his claims of precedence of discovery of *electric telegraph* over Samuel F. B. Morse, and *ether* as an anesthetic over William T. G. Morton. [d. August 28, 1880]

1832 *Joseph Hayne Rainey,* U.S. banker, politician; first black to serve in U.S. House of Representatives. [d. August 2, 1887]

1850 *Daniel Carter Beard,* U.S. artist, naturalist; inaugurated first class in animal drawing at Woman's School of Applied Design, New York. Founder of *Sons of Daniel Boone,* 1905, which later merged with *Boy Scouts of America.* [d. June 11, 1941]

1880 *Arnold Lucius Gesell,* U.S. psychologist; developed standards for child development which outlined progressive stages of child development from infancy through adolescence (*Gesell Development Schedules*). Founded Yale Psycho-Clinic (Yale Clinic of Child Development), 1908. [d. May 29, 1961]

1882 *Rockwell Kent,* U.S. painter, illustrator; one of most successful American artists of his period, with works in permanent collections of many museums, both in U.S. and Europe. [d. March 13, 1971]

1884 *Sir Claude (John Eyre) Auchinleck,* British field

marshal; commander of British forces in Egypt and Mesopotamia, World War I; commander of British forces in the Middle East, World War II; dismissed by Winston Churchill for refusal to pursue Erwin Rommel after British recapture of Tobruk. [d. March 23, 1981]

1891 *Pier (Luigi) Nervi,* Italian architect, engineer; a pioneer in the use of *reinforced concrete.* [d. January 9, 1979]

1892 *Reinhold Niebuhr,* U.S. theologian. His teachings and writings marked the beginning of the *neo-orthodox movement* in U.S. [d. June 1, 1971]

1902 *Howie Morenz,* Canadian hockey player; elected to Hall of Fame, 1945.

1903 *Albert Hirschfeld,* U.S. caricaturist, author; inducted into the Illustrators Club Hall of Fame, 1986.

1905 *Jean-Paul Sartre,* French existentialist philosopher, novelist, playwright. [d. April 15, 1980]

1912 *Mary (Therese) McCarthy,* U.S. novelist, critic.

1914 *William Vickrey,* U.S. economist; Nobel Prize for Economics, 1996. Vickrey shares with award with fellow economist, James A. Mirrlees. [d. 1996]

1921 *Jane Russell,* U.S. actress.

Judy Holliday (Judith Tuvim), U.S. actress. [d. June 7, 1965]

1925 *Maureen Stapleton,* U.S. character actress.

1927 *Carl Burton Stokes,* U.S. politician; Mayor of Cleveland, 1960s. [d. April 3, 1996]

1931 *Margaret Mary Heckler,* U.S. government official; Secretary of Health and Human Services, 1983–85; Ambassador to Ireland, 1985–89.

1933 *Bernard Morton (Bernie) Kopell,* U.S. actor; known for his role as Dr. Adam Bricker on television series, *The Love Boat,* 1976–86.

1935 *Monte Markham,* U.S. actor; known for his roles on television series, *Second Hundred Years* and *Mr. Deeds Goes to Town.*

Françoise Sagan (Françoise Quoirez), French novelist.

1940 *Mariette Hartley,* U.S. actress.

1941 *Ginny Foat (Virginia Galluzzo),* U.S. feminist; President, California National Organization for Women; arrested on an eighteen-year-old murder charge in 1983 and later acquitted.

1944 *Ray(mond Douglas) Davies,* British singer, musician; member of the rock group, *The Kinks.*

1947 *Meredith Baxter,* U.S. actress; known for her starring roles on television series, *Family,* 1976–80, and *Family Ties,* 1982–89.

Michael Gross, U.S. actor; known for his role as Steven Keaton on television series, *Family Ties,* 1982–89.

1951 *Nils Lofgren,* U.S. musician, singer; member of the rock group, *E Street Band.*

1953 *Benazir Bhutto,* Pakistani politician; daughter of Zulfikar Ali Bhutto; first female Prime Minister 1988–90, 1993–96.

1956 *Richard Lee (Rick) Sutcliffe,* U.S. baseball player; National

League Cy Young Award, 1984.

1982 *Prince William* of Great Britain, first child of Prince Charles and Princess Diana, and second generation heir to British throne, is born.

HISTORICAL EVENTS

1377 *Edward III* of England dies and is succeeded by his grandson, *Richard II.*

1684 *Massachusetts Bay Colony* charter is annulled by British Court of Chancery.

1788 *New Hampshire* ratifies the U.S. Constitution.

1791 *Louis XVI* and the royal family are arrested at Varennes and brought back to Paris after attempting to escape (*French Revolution*).

1813 Duke of Wellington defeats French at *Vitoria,* ending France's presence in Spain (*Napoleonic Wars*).

1834 *Cyrus H. McCormick* is awarded a U.S. patent for his *reaper.*

1868 Richard Wagner's comic opera, *Die Meistersinger,* premieres at Munich.

1887 *Queen Victoria* celebrates her golden jubilee.

Zululand is annexed to the British Empire.

1919 The German High Seas Fleet is scuttled by ships' crews at *Scapa Flow* after surrendering to the British (*World War I*).

1932 *Jack Sharkey* defeats *Max Schmeling* to gain world heavyweight championship.

1940 *France* surrenders to Germany. (*World War II*)

june

1942 *Tobruk* in Libya is taken by German Field Marshal *Erwin Rommel (World War II)*.

1943 Gestapo chief *Heinrich Himmler* orders the liquidation of Jewish ghettos in German-occupied areas of the U.S.S.R. *(World War II)*

1951 *Theodor Koerner* is inaugurated as president of Austria.

1956 U.S. Atomic Energy Commission announces the discovery of the *neutrino,* an atomic particle with no electric charge.

1960 *Patrice Lumumba* is named to form the first government of the *Belgian Congo*.

1963 *Giovanni Battista Cardinal Montini* is elected as 262nd pope of the Roman Catholic Church, taking the name *Paul VI.*

1964 *Jim Bunning* of the Philadelphia Phillies pitches the first perfect baseball game in the National League's history.

Haitian National Assembly affirms presidency of *François (Papa Doc) Duvalier* and proclaims a new constitution. Duvalier governs Haiti until his death in 1971.

1977 *Menachem Begin* becomes Prime Minister of Israel; resigns September 15, 1983.

1978 *Evita,* a musical by Tim Rice and Andrew Lloyd Webber, opens in London.

1982 *John Hinckley* is found not guilty by reason of insanity in the attempted assassination of President *Ronald Reagan*.

Charles, Prince of Wales and his wife Diana, announce the birth of their first child, *Prince William*. The infant will be second in line to the British throne.

1984 The first amendment to the Canadian constitutuion guarantees the properties and constitutional rights of *Indians* and the *Inuit.*

1985 The skeletal remains of Nazi war criminal, Dr. *Josef Mengele,* are identified. Mengele reportedly escaped to South America after World War II and drowned in Brazil in 1979.

1990 An *earthquake* registering 7.7 on the Richter scale hits *Iran,* killing 40,000 people.

P. V. Narasimha Rao is named the new prime minister of India.

1997 The *Women's National Basketball Association (WNBA)* begins its first season.

1998 *Andres Pastrana Arango* is elected president of Colombia.

HOLIDAYS

Croatia
National Day

People's Democratic Republic of Yemen
Corrective Move Day

RELIGIOUS CALENDAR

The Saints

St. Nicetas, Bishop of Remesiana, missionary and writer. [d. c. 414]

St. Paulinus of Nola, bishop and poet. [d. 431] Optional Memorial.

St. Ebbe the Younger, martyr. [d. 870]

St. Eberhard, Archbishop of Salzburg. [d. 1164]

St. John Fisher, Bishop of Rochester and cardinal, martyr. [d. 1535] Feast formerly July 9. Optional Memorial.

St. Thomas More, martyr. [d. 1535] Feast formerly July 9. Optional Memorial.

St. Acacius, martyr. [death date unknown]

St. Alban, martyr. Protomartyr of Britain. [death date unknown]

The Beatified

Blessed Innocent V, pope. Elected 1276. Commonly known as *Peter of Tarentaise.* [d. 1277]

BIRTHDATES

1748 *Thomas Day,* English reformer, author; attempted to reconcile Rousseau's doctrines with conventional morality. [d. September 28, 1789]

1757 *George Vancouver,* British navigator; explored coasts of Australia, New Zealand, Hawaiian Islands, 1791–92; led expedition along Pacific Coast of North America, 1792–94. *Vancouver Island* and city of *Vancouver, British Columbia,* are named for him. [d. May 10, 1798]

1767 *Wilhelm von Humboldt,* German scholar, statesman, philologist; influential in developing science of comparative philology. [d. April 8, 1835]

1805 *Giuseppe Mazzini,* Italian patriot, political theorist, and critic; devoted most of his life to unification of Italy. Helped organize Garibaldi's expeditions. [d. March 10, 1872]

1837 *Paul Morphy,* U.S. chessmaster; defeated world's best players of his era, gaining unofficial world chess championship, 1857. [d. July 10, 1884]

1844 *Harriet Mulford Lothrop (Margaret Sidney),* U.S. children's book writer. [d. August 2, 1924]

1856 *Sir Henry Rider Haggard,* British novelist; author of *She, King Solomon's Mines, Alan Quatermain.* [d. May 14, 1925]

1861 *Count Maximilian von Spee,* German admiral; defeated British squadron at Coronel, off Chilean coast, 1914. Went down with his ship when German fleet was destroyed near Falkland Islands, 1914 (World War I). [d. December 8, 1914]

1869 *Hendrik Colijn,* Dutch anti-Fascist leader, statesman; Minister of War, 1911–13; Premier, 1925–26; 1933–39. [d. September 15, 1944]

1887 *Julian Huxley,* British biologist, author; first director of UNESCO, 1946–48; proponent of evolutionary humanism; knighted, 1958; brother of Aldous Huxley (July 26). [d. February 14, 1975]

1888 *Harold Hitz Burton,* U.S. lawyer, jurist; Associate Justice, U.S. Supreme Court, 1945–58. [d. October 28, 1964]

Alan Seeger, U.S. poet; author of *I Have a Rendezvous with Death* and *Ode in Memory of the American Volunteers*

Fallen in France. Killed in World War I. [d. July 4, 1916]

1898 *Erich Maria Remarque (Erich Paul Remark),* German-U.S. anti-militaristic novelist; author of *All Quiet on the Western Front.* [d. September 25, 1970]

1903 *John Dillinger,* U.S. outlaw; designated as public enemy number one in the early 1930s; betrayed by mysterious "woman in red," shot to death by FBI agents. [d. July 22, 1934]

Carl Hubbell, U.S. baseball player; Baseball Hall of Fame, 1947. [d. November 21, 1988]

1906 *Ann Morrow Lindbergh,* U.S. writer, poet; wife of Charles A. Lindbergh (February 4).

Billy Wilder, U.S. film writer, producer, director born in Austria.

1910 *Katherine Dunham,* U.S. dancer, choreographer, anthropologist; leading dancer and dance authority deriving much of her inspiration from primitive rituals of the Caribbean. Founded *Katherine Dunham Dance Company,* 1945 (later the *Katherine Dunham School of Cultural Arts*).

1921 *Gower Champion,* U.S. dancer, choreographer, director. [d. August 25, 1980]

Joseph Papp (Papirofsky), U.S. theatrical producer; founder, head of New York Shakespeare Festival. [d. October 31, 1991]

1922 *Bill Blass,* U.S. fashion designer.

1928 *Ralph Waite,* U.S. actor; known for his role as John

Walton on television series, *The Waltons.*

1933 *Dianne Feinstein,* U.S. politician; Mayor of San Francisco, 1978–87; selected as mayor after the murder of George Moscone; Senator, 1992– .

1936 *Kris Kristofferson,* U.S. actor, singer, songwriter.

1941 *Ed Bradley,* U.S. broadcast journalist; co-anchor on television news show, *60 Minutes,* 1981–.

1944 *Peter Asher,* British singer, producer; member of the singing duo, *Peter and Gordon.*

1947 *Jerry Rawlings,* Ghanaian statesman; President, Republic of Ghana, 1981–.

1948 *Pete Maravich,* U.S. basketball player. [d. January 5, 1988]

1949 *Meryl Streep,* U.S. actress; Academy Award (Best Supporting Actress) for *Kramer vs. Kramer* and (Best Actress) for *Sophie's Choice,* 1982.

Lindsay Wagner, U.S. actress; known for her starring role on television series, *Bionic Woman,* 1976–78.

1954 *Freddie Prinze,* U.S. comedian. [d. January 29, 1977]

1962 *Clyde Drexler,* U.S. basketball player.

HISTORICAL EVENTS

1377 *Richard II,* King of England, is crowned after the death of his grandfather, *Edward III.*

1812 French troops of the *Grande Armée* begin invasion of

Russia under leadership of *Napoleon.*

1815 *Napoleon Bonaparte* abdicates for the second time.

1870 *U.S. Department of Justice* is established by Congress.

1894 *Dahomey* becomes a French colony.

1910 *Count Zeppelin* inaugurates first airship passenger service, with the *Deutschland.*

1912 President Theodore Roosevelt forms the *Progressive* or *Bull Moose Party* whose platform calls for broad social reform.

1921 First session of *Northern Ireland* Parliament is opened by *King George V.*

1922 *Sir Henry Wilson,* opponent of the *Sinn Fein* (Irish separatist radical group) is murdered by members of that group.

1938 *Joe Louis* knocks out *Jim Braddock,* becoming the world heavyweight boxing champion.

1940 France signs armistice with Germany at Compiègne *(World War II).*

1941 Finnish troops, under the leadership of Marshal *Carl Gustav Mannerheim,* attack the Soviet Union *(World War II).*

German armies invade *Russia* on a 2000-mile front *(World War II).*

1944 President Franklin D. Roosevelt signs the *GI Bill of Rights,* providing education, disability pay, government loans, and job training to World War II veterans.

1949 *Ezzard Charles* defeats *Jersey Joe Walcott* to win the world heavyweight boxing title.

1962 The American Medical Association announces the successful testing of a chemical *pacemaker* in a dog's heart.

1965 *Japan* and *Korea* sign treaty and normalize relations after a lapse of 55 years.

1973 Three *Skylab 2* astronauts, Charles Conrad, Jr., Joseph P. Kerwin and Paul J. Weitz return safely to earth after spending a record 28 days in space during which they make two major repairs to the orbiting *Skylab*.

1981 *Abolhassan Bani-Sadr* is dismissed as President of Iran by *Ayatollah Ruhollah Khomeini*.

1983 Former Israeli defense minister, *Ariel Sharon*, files a $50 million libel suit in New York City against *Time Magazine*. An article appearing in the publication charged that Sharon had encouraged Lebanese Phalangists to attack two Beirut refugee camps.

The U.S. Federal Reserve Board approves the merger of two West Coast bank holding companies, *BankAmerica Corp.* and *Seafirst Corp.*

1984 Former Argentine president, *Roberto Viola*, is arrested on charges related to his part in the "dirty war" of the 1970's. The action is one of several measures undertaken by President *Raul Alfonsin* to assert civilian control over the military.

1989 The warring factions in Angola, led by President *José Eduardo dos Santos* and the leader of the rebel opposition, *Jonas Savimbi*, agree to a peace accord after fourteen years of fighting.

june

JUNE
23

HOLIDAYS

Estonia
Anniversary of the Battle of Vonnu (1919)

Luxembourg
National Holiday
Celebration of the Grand Duke's birthday.

RELIGIOUS CALENDAR

The Saints
St. Agrippina, virgin and martyr. Invoked against evil spirits, thunderstorms, and leprosy. [d. c. 262]

St. Etheldreda, Abbess of Ely and widow. Founded double monastery for monks and nuns at the *Isle of Ely.* Also called *Aethelthryth, Audrey, Audry.* [d. 679]

St. Lietbertus, Bishop of Cambrai. Also called *Libert, Liébert.* [d. 1076]

St. Joseph Cafasso, priest of Turin; patron saint of prisons. [d. 1860]

The Beatified
Blessed Peter of Jully. [d. 1136]
Blessed Lanfranc, Bishop of Pavia. [d. 1194]
Blessed Mary of Oignies, virgin. [d. 1213]
Blessed Thomas Corsini, monk. [d. 1345]
Blessed Bernhard Lichtenberg. [beatified 1996]
Blessed Karl Leisner. [beatified 1996]

BIRTHDATES

1668 *Giovanni Battista Vico,* Italian philosopher, historian, critic, poet; pioneer in the study of esthetics. [d. January 23, 1744]

1763 *Josephine (Beauharnais),* Empress of France, wife of Napoleon Bonaparte; divorced by him because she did not provide him with an heir. [d. May 29, 1814]

1775 *Etienne Louis Malus,* French engineer, physicist; pioneer in field of *optics.* First to describe polarization of light by reflection. [d. February 23, 1812]

1876 *Irvin S(hrewsbury) Cobb,* U.S. journalist, humorist, short-story writer, playwright. [d. March 10, 1944]

1894 *Edward VIII,* King of England; the only British king to abdicate voluntarily (reigned January 20 to December 11, 1936), to marry American divorcee Wallace Warfield (Simpson); became Duke of Windsor. [d. May 27, 1972]

Alfred Charles Kinsey, U.S. zoologist and student of human sexual behavior. Most famous for his *Sexual Behavior in the Human Male,* 1948, a study based on interviews with 18,000 people; the study stirred up national controversy and brought great attention to the subject of human sexual activity, an area previously considered taboo. [d. August 25, 1956]

1904 *Carleton S(tevens) Coon,* U.S. anthropologist, archaeologist, educator; author of *The Story of Man,* in which he put forward a theory that the apes are descended from a species of "ground-living" mammals that almost became man. [d. June 3, 1981]

1907 *James E. Meade,* British economist; Nobel Prize in economics for contributions to theory of international trade (with B. Ohlin), 1977. [d. December 22, 1995]

1910 *Jean Anouilh,* French playwright; plays include *Antigone, La Valse des Toreadors,* (translated into English as *The Waltz of the Toreadors).* [d. October 3, 1987]

1911 *David Mackenzie Ogilvy,* British advertising executive; wrote *Confessions of an Advertising Man,* 1964.

1912 *Alan Turing,* British mathematician; known for his contributions toward the development of working computers. [d. June 7, 1954]

1927 *Bob Fosse,* U.S. director, choreographer. [d. September 23, 1987]

1936 *Richard (Davis) Bach,* U.S. author, aviator.

1940 *Wilma Rudolph,* U.S. sprinter; winner of three gold medals in 1960 Olympics. [d. November 12, 1994]

1943 *Donald Johanson,* U.S. anthropologist; discovered "Lucy," human-like skeleton over three million years old in Ethiopia.

James Levine, U.S. conductor, pianist; Music Director of the Metropolitan Opera, New York.

1946 *Ted Shackelford,* U.S. actor; known for his role as Gary Ewing on television series, *Knot's Landing.*

1947 *Bryan Brown,* Australian actor; played Luke O'Neill in *The Thorn Birds* TV miniseries.

1948 *Clarence Thomas,* U.S. lawyer; Supreme Court justice, 1991– .

1957 *Frances McDormand,* U.S. actress; Academy Award (Best Actress) for *Fargo,* 1996.

HISTORICAL EVENTS

1372 French and Castilians defeat English off *La Rochelle, France (Hundred Years' War).*

1501 *Pedro Cabral* completes voyage establishing Portuguese trade with East Indies; he accomplishes this by traveling west, reaching *Brazil,* which he claims for Portugal, 1500.

1919 The Estonian national army wins battle of Vonnu in the *War of Independence.*

1925 The *Lenin Peace Prize* is established in Moscow.

1930 *Iceland* celebrates the 1,000th anniversary of the *Alting,* the oldest parliament in the world.

1947 U.S. Congress adopts the *Taft-Hartley Law* over President Truman's veto, prohibiting closed shops and restricting union activity.

1950 East Germany abandons claims to the *Sudetenland* and accepts the expulsion of two million ethnic Germans from Czechoslovakia.

1955 Walt Disney's animated film, *Lady and the Tramp,* premieres in New York.

1966 *Secular Affairs Institute,* Buddhist antigovernment stronghold, is seized by South Vietnamese troops (*Vietnam War*).

1967 *Pope Paul VI* issues encyclical *Sacerdotalis Caelibatus,* reaffirming church ruling on priestly *celibacy.*

1969 *Warren Earl Burger* is sworn in as Chief Justice of the U.S. Supreme Court.

1970 Prince *Charles* receives a bachelor's degree from Cambridge University. He is the first British heir to the throne to earn a university degree.

1983 The U.S. Supreme Court rules unconstitutional the *legislative veto* used by Congress to override decisions made by the President and federal agencies. Incorporated into as many as 200 laws, the legislative veto had given Congress a greater influence over foreign and regulatory policies.

june

JUNE
24

HOLIDAYS

Andorra
Feast of St. John

Canada (Quebec)
St. Jean Day

Democratic Republic of the Congo
Constitution Day

Great Britain
Midsummer's Day

Ireland
St. John's Day

Latvia
St. John's Day

Peru
Countryman's Day

Puerto Rico
San Juan Day

Spain
King Juan Carlos' Saint's Day

Venezuela
Battle of Carabobo
Commemorates Bolivar's victory at Carabobo, the final battle in war for independence against Spain, 1821.

RELIGIOUS CALENDAR

Solemnities

The Nativity of St. John the Baptist, forerunner and herald of Jesus Christ; sanctified in his mother's womb; invoked against hail, epilepsy, convulsions, and spasms, and for the protection of lambs. [d. c. 30] [major holy day, Episcopal Church; minor festival, Lutheran Church]

The Saints

The Martyrs under Nero. [d. 64 A.D.]
St. Simplicius, Bishop of Autun. [d. 4th or 5th century]
St. Bartholomew of Farne, hermit. [d. 1193]

BIRTHDATES

1450 *John Cabot (Giovanni Caboto),* Italian navigator, explorer; credited with discovery of the North American continent after setting out on a westward voyage to the Orient. [d. 1498]

1485 *Johann Bugenhagen,* German Protestant reformer; assisted Martin Luther (November 10) in translating the Bible. [d. April 20, 1558]

1542 *Saint John of the Cross* (in Spain, *Juan de la Cruz*), Spanish monk, lyric poet, mystic; one of greatest mystical poets; wrote *The Dark Night of the Soul.* [d. December 24, 1591]

1616 *Ferdinand Bol,* Dutch painter; a student of Rembrandt. [d. July 24, 1680]

1753 *William Hull,* U.S. army general, lawyer; court-martialed for uncontested surrender of *Detroit* to British, 1812. Death sentence stayed by President James Madison. [d. November 29, 1825]

1771 *Eleuthère Irénée Du Pont de Nemours,* U.S. industrialist born in France; established gunpowder manufacturing plant near Wilmington, Delaware, that his descendants developed into E. I. Du Pont de Nemours and Co., one of the world's largest chemical and industrial firms. [d. October 31, 1834]

1795 *Ernst Heinrich Weber,* German physiologist, anatomist; known for his research on the human senses. Developed theory that least noticeable increase of a stimulus is a constant directly proportionate to original stimulus (*Weber's Law*). [d. January 26, 1878]

1813 *Henry Ward Beecher,* U.S. religious leader, social reformer; famous for his oratorical style. [d. March 8, 1887]

1839 *Gustavus Franklin Swift,* U.S. meat packer, founder of Swift & Co., 1885. [d. March 29, 1903]

1848 *Brooks Adams,* U.S. historian; wrote *Emancipation of Massachusetts,* 1887; *Theory* *of Social Revolution,* 1913. [d. February 13, 1927]

1850 *Horatio Herbert Kitchener, 1st Earl Kitchener of Khartoum,* British soldier; Governor-General of Sudan, 1886, 1898; Commander in Chief of British forces in India, 1902–09; Secretary of War, 1914. Organized British forces for World War I, 1914–16. [d. June 5, 1916]

1864 *Walther Hermann Nernst,* German physicist, chemist; researcher in areas of thermodynamics, theories of ions, chemical equilibrium and solutions; Nobel Prize in chemistry for application of thermodynamics to chemistry, 1920. [d. November 18, 1941]

1883 *Victor F. Hess,* U.S. physicist born in Austria; Nobel Prize in physics for discovery of *cosmic rays* (with C. D. Anderson), 1936. [d. December 17, 1964]

1895 *Jack Dempsey (William Harrison Dempsey),* U.S. boxer; world heavyweight champion, 1919–26. [d. May 31, 1983]

1915 *Norman Cousins,* U.S. editor, author; editor of *Saturday Review,* 1940–77. [d. November 30, 1990]

1916 *John Anthony Ciardi,* U.S. poet, author; known for his English translation of Dante's *Inferno,* 1954. [d. April 1, 1986]

1923 *Jack Carter (Jack Chakrin),* U.S. comedian.

1927 *Martin L. Perl,* U.S. physicist; one-half of the 1995 Nobel Prize for Physics. Perl discovered a subatomic particle, tau. Frederick Reines;

other half for discovering the subatomic particle the neutrino.

1935 *William (Pete) Hamill,* U.S. journalist; wrote *The Gift,* 1973, and *Flesh and Blood,* 1977.

1936 *Antoine Predock,* U.S. architect; known for his buildings that reflect an awareness for the environment.

1942 *Mick Fleetwood,* British singer, musician; member of the rock group, *Fleetwood Mac.*

Michele Lee (Michele Lee Dusiak), U.S. actress, dancer; known for her role as Karen Fairgate MacKenzie on television series, *Knot's Landing.*

1944 *Jeff Beck,* British musician; member of the rock groups, *Yardbirds* and *Honeydrippers.*

1945 *George Pataki,* U.S. lawyer, politician; governor of New York, 1995– .

1946 *Ellison Onizuka,* U.S. astronaut; crew member who died in space shuttle *Challenger* explosion. [d. January 28, 1986]

Robert Reich, U.S. lawyer; U.S. secretary of labor, 1993–97.

1947 *Peter Weller,* U.S. actor; known for roles in *Robocop* films.

1949 *Nancy Allen,* U.S. actress; known for her starring roles in *Dressed to Kill,* 1980, and *Blowout,* 1981.

HISTORICAL EVENTS

1314 The *Battle of Bannockburn* is won by the Scottish forces

under *Robert Bruce,* completely defeating the English under *Edward II,* and establishing Bruce on the throne of Scotland.

1340 English defeat French off *Sluys,* giving England control of the English Channel until 1372 (*Hundred Years' War*).

1497 *John Cabot,* Italian-born explorer sailing from England, lands on North American soil (exact location is subject of debate, but it was probably Newfoundland, Labrador, or Cape Breton Island).

1916 *Battle of the Somme* begins in France as British artillery bombards German lines (*World War I*).

1922 American Professional Football Association becomes *National Football League.*

1947 First sightings of *unidentified flying objects* are publicized.

1948 Soviet Union imposes total blockade on all land traffic between *Berlin* and West Germany.

U.S. President Harry Truman signs the *Selective Service Act,* requiring men between 18 and 25 to register for military service.

1963 Internal self-government is informally introduced in *Zanzibar,* with Sheikh Mohammed Shamte Hamadi as Prime Minister.

1967 *Zaire* ratifies a new constitution, providing for a federal system of government with a strong president and unicameral legislature.

1976 *Manila* formally replaces Quezon City as capital of the Philippines.

june

1978 President *Ahmed Hussein al Gashmi* of North Yemen is assassinated by a South Yemeni envoy.

1983 Yasir Arafat closes the offices of the *Palestine Liberation Organization* and *AlFatah* in Damascus, Syria, shortly before he is expelled from Syria in a policy dispute.

U.S. space shuttle *Challenger* lands at Edwards Air Force Base, completing its second flight. Crew member *Sally K. Ride* is the first U.S. woman astronaut to go into space.

1985 *Francesco Cossiga* is elected president of Italy.

1987 *James V. Moore,* a prison inmate and *AIDS* carrier, is found guilty of assault with a deadly weapon by a federal jury after biting two prison guards in an attempt to infect them with the virus.

HOLIDAYS

Mozambique
Independence Day
Commemorates Mozambique's achievement of independence from Portugal, 1975.

Slovenia
National Statehood Day

RELIGIOUS CALENDAR

Feasts
Presentation of the Augsburg Confession. [minor festival, Lutheran Church]

The Saints
St. Febronia, virgin and martyr. [d. c. 304]
St. Gallicanus. [d. c. 352]
St. Prosper of Aquitaine, layman, poet, and author. Secretary to Pope St. Leo the Great. [d. c. 465]
St. Prosper, Bishop of Reggio; principal patron of Reggio. [d. c. 466]
St. Maximus, Bishop of Turin. [d. c. 467]
St. Molaug, abbot. Founded Scottish Monastery of Lismore. Invoked for cures from madness. Also called *Lugaid, Molloch.* [d. 592]
St. Adalbert of Egmond, missionary. Also called *Adelbert.* [d. 8th century]
St. Eurosia, virgin and martyr. Honored as protector of the fruits of the field and invoked against bad weather. Also called *Eurosis.* [d. 8th century]
St. Gohard, Bishop of Nantes, and his companions, martyrs. [d. 843]
St. William of Vercelli, Abbot of Monte Vergine. [d. 1142]
St. Cyneburga of Gloucester, princess. [death date unknown]

The Beatified
Blessed Henry Zdik, Bishop of Olomuc. [d. c. 1150]
Blessed John the Spaniard, prior. [d. 1160]
Blessed Guy Maramaldi, theologian and preacher. [d. 1391]

BIRTHDATES

1768 *Lazare Hoche,* French Revolutionary general. [d. September 19, 1797]

1860 *Gustave Charpentier,* French composer. [d. February 18, 1956]

1865 *Robert Henri,* U.S. painter, art teacher; influential artist of the period who, with Maurice Prendergast (October 10) and others, attempted to convey *new realism;* group became known as the *Ashcan School.* [d. July 12, 1929]

1886 *Henry Harley (Hap) Arnold,* U.S. Air Force five-star general; as commander of U.S. forces, 1941–46, was responsible for building the world's largest air force. Planned massive air strikes against Germany in World War II. [d. January 15, 1950]

1887 *George Abbot,* U.S. producer, director, and playwright. [d. January 31, 1995]

1900 *Louis Mountbatten, First Earl Mountbatten of Burma,* British naval officer, government official; great-grandson of Queen Victoria; last viceroy of India; killed in an Irish Republican Army bomb explosion. [d. August 27, 1979]

1903 *George Orwell (Eric Arthur Blair),* British author, critic; wrote *Animal Farm,* 1946, and *1984,* 1949. [d. January 21, 1950]

1907 *J. Hans Daniels Jensen,* German physicist; Nobel Prize in physics for discoveries of atomic nucleus shell structure (with M. Goeppert-Mayer and E. P. Wigner), 1963. [d. February 11, 1973]

1911 *William Howard Stein,* U.S. biochemist; Nobel Prize in chemistry for research related to chemical structure of ribonuclease (with C.B. Anfisen and S. Moore), 1972. [d. February 2, 1980]

1916 *William Bart Saxbe,* U.S. politician; Senator, 1969–74;

june

Ambassador to India, 1975–77.

1921 *Celia Franca,* British ballet dancer, director, choreographer; founder of *National Ballet of Canada.*

1924 *Sidney Lumet,* U.S. director; known for the direction of *Twelve Angry Men, Dog Day Afternoon, Network, Serpico,* and *Prince of the City.*

1925 *June Lockhart,* U.S. actress; known for her starring roles on television series, *Lassie,* 1958–64, and *Lost in Space,* 1965–68.

1933 *James Howard Meredith,* U.S. political activist; first black student, University of Mississippi, 1962; wrote *Three Years in Mississippi,* 1966.

1935 *Larry Kramer,* U.S. author, AIDS activist; founded AIDS Coalition to Unleash Power (ACT-UP), 1987.

1936 *Bacharuddin Jusuf Habibe,* Indonesian politician; President, 1998– .

1937 *Marabel Morgan,* U.S. author; wrote *The Total Woman.*

1945 *Carly Simon,* U.S. singer, songwriter.

1948 *James Carter (Jimmie) Walker,* U.S. actor, comedian; known for his role as J.J. on television series, *Good Times,* 1974–78.

1949 *Phyllis George,* U.S. broadcaster; Miss America, 1971.

1963 *Doug Gilmour,* Canadian hockey player; Frank J. Selke Trophy winner, 1993.

George Michael, British singer; member of the rock group, *Wham!,* 1982–86; solo performer, 1984– .

HISTORICAL EVENTS

1080 *Synod of Brixen* elects imperial anti-pope *Clement III* after *Pope Gregory VII* is deposed.

1115 *Abbey of Clairvaux* is founded with St. Bernard as its first abbot.

1580 *Book of Concord,* official collection of Lutheran confessional treatises, is published.

1788 *Virginia* ratifies the U.S. constitution.

1857 *Prince Albert,* husband of *Queen Victoria* of England, is named Prince Consort.

1861 The *Order of the Star of India* is instituted by the British.

1870 *Queen Isabella II* of Spain abdicates in favor of her son, *Alfonso XII.*

1876 Gen. *George Custer* and his men are massacred by *Sitting Bull* and his Sioux at *Little Big Horn,* South Dakota.

1910 *Igor Stravinsky's* first ballet, *The Firebird,* premieres in Paris, performed by Ballet Russe.

U.S. Congress passes *Mann Act (White Slave Traffic Act),* prohibiting interstate transportation of women for immoral purposes.

1918 U.S. Marine brigade captures *Belleau Wood* after weeks of fighting *(World War I).*

1938 U.S. Congress passes the *Fair Labor Standards Act,* providing for a 40-hour work week.

1944 U.S. troops capture *Cherbourg, France,* from the Germans *(World War II).*

1950 People's Army of North Korea drives across the 38th parallel in invasion of *South Korea (Korean War).*

1957 Congregational Christian, Evangelical, and Reformed denominations merge to form the *United Church of Christ.*

1962 U.S. Supreme Court rules that *prayer in public schools* is unconstitutional.

1975 After 470 years of colonial rule, *Portuguese East Africa* becomes the independent *People's Republic of Mozambique.*

1983 The U.S. grants $183.7 million in damages to the *Marshall Islands* for problems caused by nuclear weapons testing in the 1940s and 1950s.

1991 *Croatia* and *Slovenia* announce their independence from Yugoslavia.

1997 The Russian space station *Mir* collides with an unmanned cargo ship causing significant damage (September 25, 1997).

1998 The U.S. Supreme Court rules that the *Line Item Veto Act (1996)* is unconstitutional.

HOLIDAYS

United Nations
Charter Day
Commemorates the signing of the Charter, 1945.

Guyana
Caribbean Day

Madagascar
Independence Day

Somalia (Northern Region)
Independence Day

RELIGIOUS CALENDAR

The Saints
St. John and *St. Paul,* martyrs. [d. c. 362] Feast suppressed in 1969.

St. Vigilius, Bishop of Trent, martyr. First martyr to be canonized by the Holy See. Principal patron of Trentino and the Italian Tirol. [d. 405]

St. Maxentius, abbot. [d. c. 515]

St. Salvius, bishop, and *St. Superius,* martyrs. Salvius also called *Sauve.* [d. c. 768]

St. John, Bishop of the Goths. [d. c. 800]

St. Pelagius, boy martyr. Also called *Pelayo.* [d. 925]

St. Anthelm, Bishop of Belley. First minister general of the Carthusian monks. [d. 1178]

BIRTHDATES

1730 *Charles Messier,* French astronomer; credited with discovery of numerous comets. His catalog of nebulae gave rise to system of identification called *Messier numbers.* [d. April 11, 1817]

1742 *Arthur Middleton,* U.S. politician; signed the Declaration of Independence, 1776. [d. January 1, 1787]

1819 *Abner Doubleday,* U.S. sportsman, soldier; legendary originator of game of *baseball* (a story now debunked). Manned the guns at Fort Sumter when first shots of Civil War were fired. [d. January 26, 1893]

1824 *William Thomson, 1st Baron Kelvin,* British engineer, mathematician, physicist; established the *absolute (Kelvin) scale* of temperature, 1848. [d. December 17, 1907]

1854 *Robert Laird Borden,* Canadian statesman; Prime Minister, 1917–20. [d. June 10, 1937]

1865 *Bernard Berenson,* U.S. art critic, author; wrote *Drawings of the Florentine Painters,* 1903. [d. October 6, 1959]

1891 *Sidney (Coe) Howard,* U.S. playwright; best known for screenplay version of *Gone With the Wind.* [d. August 23, 1939]

1892 *Pearl (Sydenstricker) Buck,* U.S. author; educator; well-known expert on life in China, the basis for most of her writing; wrote *The Good Earth,* later a film; Nobel Prize in literature, 1938. [d. March 6, 1973]

1894 *Pyotr Kapitsa,* Russian scientist; Nobel Prize in physics for his work in low-temperature physics, 1978. [d. April 8, 1984]

1898 *Willy (Wilhelm) Messerschmitt,* German aviation engineer. [d. September 15, 1978]

Lewis Burwell Puller, U.S. Marine Corps general, World War II. [d. October 11, 1971]

1901 *Stuart Symington,* U.S. politician, businessman; President of Emerson Manufacturing Co., 1938–45; U.S. Secretary of the Air Force, 1947–50; U.S. Senator, 1952–77. [d. December 14, 1988]

1902 *Antonia Brico,* U.S. conductor, teacher; first woman to conduct Berlin Philharmonic, 1935; founder of *Brico Symphony,* 1935. [d. 1989]

1904 *Peter Lorre (Laszlo Loewenstein),* Hungarian-born actor; known for his roles in *The Maltese Falcon* and *Casablanca.* [d. March 24, 1964]

june

1914 *(Mildred Ella) Babe Didrikson Zaharias,* U.S. athlete; winner of two gold medals, 1932 Olympics. Leading woman golfer, 1932–55. Recognized as one of greatest woman athletes of all time. [d. September 27, 1956]

1922 *Eleanor Parker,* U.S. actress; known for her roles in *Caged, Detective Story,* and *Interrupted Melody.*

1934 *John Varick Tunney,* U.S. politician; Senator, 1971–77.

1937 *Robert C. Richardson,* U.S. physicist; Nobel Prize for Physics in 1996. Richardson shares the prize with David Lee and Douglass D. Osheroff for their discovery of superfluidity in helium-3.

1939 *Charles Spittal Robb,* U.S. politician; Governor of Virginia, 1981–86; Senator, 1989–; husband of Lynda Bird Johnson.

1940 *Billy Davis, Jr.,* U.S. singer; member of the rock group, *Fifth Dimension.*

1946 *Pamela Bellwood,* U.S. actress; known for her role as Claudia Carrington on television series, *Dynasty.*

1966 *John Cusack,* U.S. actor.

1970 *Chris O'Donnell,* U.S. actor.

HISTORICAL EVENTS

1306 The English are victorious over Robert Bruce, Scottish king, at *Methuen.*

1483 *Richard of Gloucester* assumes the English throne, succeeding *Edward V,* who was murdered in the Tower of London on June 23. Richard reigns as *Richard III.*

1794 Austrians are defeated by French at *Fleurus* and lose Belgium (*French Revolutionary period*).

1830 *George IV* of England dies and is succeeded by *William IV.*

1858 The *Treaty of Tientsin* is signed, ending hostilities between China and Great Britain and giving diplomatic and trade rights to Britain.

1900 Imperial edict declares war on all foreigners and orders their expulsion from China (*Boxer Rebellion*).

1917 First U.S. troops arrive in France (*World War I*).

1935 U.S. President Franklin D. Roosevelt establishes *National Youth Administration* to provide jobs for those aged 16–25.

1945 *United Nations* charter is signed in San Francisco, to become effective October 24, 1945.

1959 *St. Lawrence Seaway,* connecting the Great Lakes with the Atlantic, officially opens.

Ingemar Johansson defeats *Floyd Patterson* for world heavyweight boxing title.

1960 *Malagasy Republic* (formerly *Madagascar,* a French possession) and *Somaliland* (formerly British protectorate) become independent.

1963 President *John F. Kennedy,* visiting *West Berlin* to demonstrate U.S. support for the city, declares, "Ich bin ein Berliner (I am a Berliner)."

1966 Drs. *Maurice Hilleman* and *Eugene Buynak* announce the development of a live-virus *mumps vaccine.*

1967 John Kenneth Galbraith's book, *The New Industrial State,* is published.

1968 The *Bonin Islands,* including *Iwo Jima,* are returned to Japan by the U.S.

1971 The U.S. Supreme Court overturns the draft evasion conviction and prison sentence of boxer *Muhammad Ali.*

1972 *Roberto Duran* defeats *Ken Buchanan* to win the world lightweight boxing title.

1975 State of emergency is declared in *India* in an attempt to control critics of Prime Minister *Indira Gandhi.*

1986 *U.S. Congress* approves monies to support the military overthrow of the Sandinista regime in Nicaragua.

1993 The *U.S. Navy* launches tomahawk missiles at Iraqi intelligence headquarters after learning of a plot to assassinate *George Bush.*

1997 *Bertie Ahern* is selected as the new prime minister of Ireland.

HOLIDAYS

Djibouti

Independence Feast Day
Commemorates achievement of independence from France, 1977.

RELIGIOUS CALENDAR

The Saints

St. Zoilus and his companions, martyrs. [d. c. 304]

St. Cyril, Archbishop of Alexandria and Doctor of the Church; called *Doctor of the Incarnation.* [d. 444] Feast formerly February 9.

St. Samson of Constantinople, physician and priest. [d. 5th century]

St. John of Chinon, hermit. Also known in France as *Jean de Tours,* or *St. Jean du Moustier.* [d. 6th century]

St. George Mtasmindeli, Abbot of Iviron. [d. 1066]

St. Ladislaus of Hungary, King of Hungary. Helped organize First Crusade. [d. 1095]

The Beatified

Blessed Benvenuto of Gubbio, monk. [d. 1232]

Blessed Madeleine Fontaine and her companions, virgins and martyrs. [d. 1794]

BIRTHDATES

1462 *Louis XII,* King of France, 1498–1515; called the *Father of his People.* [d. January 1, 1515]

1550 *Charles IX,* King of France; remembered for ordering the massacre of Protestants on *St. Bartholomew's Day,* August 24, 1572. [d. May 30, 1574]

1838 *Bankim Chandra Chatterjee,* Indian novelist; creator of an Indian school of fiction based on European model. [d. April 8, 1894]

Peter Paul Mauser, German arms inventor and manufacturer; invented the Mauser magazine rifle. [d. May 29, 1914]

1846 *Charles Stewart Parnell,* Irish nationalist leader; advocate of Irish Home Rule. [d. October 6, 1891]

1849 *Harriet Hubbard Ayer,* U.S. manufacturer of cosmetics; author. [d. November 23, 1903]

1850 *Lafcadio Hearn,* U.S. journalist born in Greece of British parents, wrote extensively on Japan in attempt to interpret Japan to English-speaking people. Became a Japanese citizen, writing under name of *Yakumo Koizumi.* [d. September 26, 1904]

1869 *Hans Spemann,* German zoologist; Nobel Prize in physiology or medicine for discovery of organizing effect in embryonic development, 1935. [d. September 12, 1941]

Emma Goldman, U.S. anarchist born in Lithuania; active in organizing laborers in New York, working against U.S. involvement in World War I and military conscription of U.S. citizens. Founded and edited *Mother Earth,* an anarchist journal suppressed in 1917. Died while working on behalf of antifascist cause in Spanish Civil War. [d. May 14, 1940]

1872 *Paul Lawrence Dunbar,* U.S. poet, shortstory writer, novelist. The son of former slaves, he wrote of the lives of blacks in America. [d. February 9, 1906]

1876 *Percy Selden Straus,* U.S. merchant; co-owner of *Macy's* Department Store, New York, with his brother, Jesse Isidor Straus. [d. April 6, 1944]

1880 *Helen Adams Keller,* U.S. author, lecturer; overcame her blindness and deafness by learning to speak and write with the help of Anne Sullivan; her story was told in *The Miracle Worker,* 1962. [d. June 1, 1968]

1888 *Antoinette Perry,* U.S. actress, director; the Tony Award is named for her. [d. June 28, 1946]

1899 *Juan (Terry) Trippe,* U.S. commercial airline pioneer; founder of Pan American Airways. [d. April 3, 1981]

1913 *Philip Guston,* U.S. artist; leading representative of abstract expressionist school; best known for his depiction of the plight of blacks in America. [d. June 7, 1980]

1927 *Bob Keeshan (Captain Kangaroo),* U.S. television personality; known for his starring role on *Captain Kangaroo,* 1955–81, the longest-running children's program in network history.

1929 *Peter Maas,* U.S. author; wrote *The Valachi Papers, Serpico,* and *King of the Gypsies.*

1930 *(Henry) Ross Perot,* U.S. businessman, philanthropist; founder, owner, Electronic Data Systems, 1962–86; U.S. independent presidential candidate, 1992.

1934 *Anna Moffo,* U.S. operatic soprano.

1936 *John Shalikashvili,* Polish-born military leader; chairman of the U.S. Joint Chiefs of Staff, 1993– .

1938 *Bruce Edward Babbitt,* U.S. politician, author; Governor of Arizona, 1977–87; U.S. Secretary of the Interior, 1993– .

1945 *Norma Kamali,* U.S. fashion designer.

1955 *Isabelle Adjani,* French actress; known for her role in *The Story of Adele H.,* 1975.

1966 *Jason Patric* (Jason Patric Miller), U.S. actor.

HISTORICAL EVENTS

1375 Anglo-French *Truce of Bruges* confines English to Bordeaux, Bayonne, and Calais (*Hundred Years' War*).

1450 *Cade's Insurrection* begins when *Jack Cade* and 20,000 Kentsmen defeat and slay *Sir Humphry Stafford* at Sevenoaks, enter London and behead the Lord Treasurer, Lord Saye, in an attempt to stop oppressive taxation and corruption at the court of *Henry VI.*

1743 *George II* of England and his allies defeat French at *Dettingen (First Silesian War).*

1844 *Joseph Smith,* leader of the *Mormons,* is murdered by a mob in Carthage, Illinois.

1864 *Battle of Kennesaw Mountain,* Georgia, results in Confederate victory, temporarily checking Sherman's march to Atlanta (*U.S. Civil War*).

1905 The *Industrial Workers of the World* holds its founding convention.

1941 *Harlan Fiske Stone* is confirmed as Chief Justice of the U.S. Supreme Court.

Hungary declares war against the *U.S.S.R. (World War II).*

1950 U.S. President *Harry S. Truman* orders U.S. forces into battle in aid of South Korea (*Korean War*).

1955 First state law requiring that automobiles be equipped with *seat belts* is passed in Illinois.

1961 *Arthur Michael Ramsey* is enthroned as the 100th Archbishop of Canterbury.

1971 The U.S.S.R. announces the opening of a *trans-Siberian oil pipeline,* ranging from Irkutsk to the Pacific port of Nakhodka.

1977 *Republic of Djibouti* is proclaimed.

1983 U.S. balloonists, *Maxie Anderson* and *Don Ida,* are killed in West Germany while competing in the Gordon Bennett International Balloon Race.

1986 The *International Court of Justice* finds the U.S. guilty of violating international law and Nicaraguan sovereignty by supplying aid to the contras.

1988 Michigan becomes the first U.S. state to ban *surrogate parenting* for a fee.

1991 *Thurgood Marshall,* the first African American to serve on the U.S. Supreme Court, retires after serving twenty-four years.

JUNE
28

RELIGIOUS CALENDAR

The Saints

St. Irenaeus, bishop and martyr. [d. c. 202] Obligatory Memorial.

SS. Plutarch, Potamiaena and their companions, martyrs. [d. c. 202]

St. Austell, monk. [d. 6th century]

Pope St. Paul I. Elected pope 757. [d. 767]

St. Heimrad. [d. 1019]

St. Sergius and *St. Germanus* of Valaam, abbots. Germanus also called *Herman.* [death date unknown]

BIRTHDATES

1476 *Pope Paul IV,* pope 1555–59. [d. August 18, 1559]

1491 *Henry VIII,* King of England, 1509–47. Notorious for his conflicts with Roman Catholic Church over issue of divorce. Married six times in an attempt to father a male heir to the throne. Separated Anglican Church from Roman Catholic Church. [d. January 28, 1547]

1577 *Peter Paul Rubens,* Flemish painter; renowned for excellence of his coloring and for painting plump female nudes as well as historical and sacred subjects. [d. May 30, 1640]

1712 *Jean-Jacques Rousseau,* French philosopher, educator, author whose theories greatly influenced the development of the French Revolution and Romanticism. [d. July 2, 1778]

1819 *Carlotta Gris,* Italian ballerina; cousin of *Girdetta* and *Guilio Grisi,* famous Italian operatic singers. [d. May 20, 1899]

1824 *Pierre Paul Broca,* 19th-century French anthropologist, surgeon; *convolution of Broca* (area of the brain) named for him. [d. July 9, 1880]

1831 *Joseph Joachim,* Hungarian violinist, composer; Director of musical *Hochschule* at Berlin, 1868–1907. [d. August 15, 1907]

1858 *Otis Skinner,* U.S. stage actor. [d. January 4, 1942]

1865 *Sir David Young Cameron,* British painter and etcher. [d. September 16, 1945]

1867 *Luigi Pirandello,* Italian playwright, novelist, short-story writer; Nobel Prize in literature, 1934. [d. December 10, 1936]

1873 *Alexis Carrel,* U.S. surgeon, born in France; Nobel Prize in physiology or medicine for development of vascular suture and surgical transplantation of blood vessels and organs. [d. November 5, 1944]

1875 *Henri Lebesque,* French mathematician; revolutionized integral calculus. [d. July 26, 1941]

1883 *Pierre Laval,* French lawyer, politician; Premier of France, 1931–32; 1935–36; 1942–45; executed for treason for collaborationist policy toward Germans. [d. October 15, 1945]

1889 *Harold W(illis) Dodds,* U.S. educator; president, Princeton University, 1933–57. [d. October 25, 1980]

1891 *Carl Spaatz,* U.S. air force general; led U.S. troops in World Wars I and II both in European and Pacific theaters. Orchestrated strategic bombings of Japan which ended with dropping of atomic bombs on Hiroshima and Nagasaki. [d. July 14, 1974]

1902 *Richard Rodgers,* U.S. composer; famous for his music for the theater, written in collaboration with Lorenz Hart (May 2), and Oscar Hammerstein II (July 12). [d. December 30, 1979]

1905 *Ashley Montagu (Montague Francis),* British-U.S. anthropologist, writer.

1906 *Marie Goeppert-Mayer,* German-U.S. physicist; Nobel Prize in physics for

june

HOLIDAYS AND ANNIVERSARIES OF THE WORLD, 3RD EDITION   497

discoveries regarding atomic nucleus shell structure (with J. Hans D. Jensen), 1963. [d. February 20, 1972]

1909 *Eric Ambler,* British novelist; a specialist in novels of international intrigue.

1914 *Lester Raymond Flatt,* U.S. musician, singer. [d. May 11, 1979]

1921 *P. V. Narasimba Rao,* Indian politician; Prime Minister of India, 1991– .

1926 *Mel Brooks (Melvin Kaminsky),* U.S. filmmaker, comedian.

1927 *F. Sherwood Rowland,* U.S. chemist; Nobel Prize for Chemistry in 1995. Rowland shares the award with fellow chemists, Mario Molina and Paul Crutzen. The three chemists researched atmospheric chemistry.

1934 *Carl Milton Levin,* U.S. politician; Senator, 1979–.

1936 *Pat Morita,* U.S. actor; played Arnold on TV series *Happy Days* and starred in the *Karate Kid* movies.

1937 *Ron(ald Michael) Luciano,* U.S. baseball umpire; wrote *The Umpire Strikes Back,* 1982. [d. January 18, 1995]

1938 *Leon Panetta,* U.S. lawyer; White House Chief of Staff for the Clinton administration, 1994–96.

1943 *Klaus von Klitzing,* German physicist; Nobel Prize in physics for the discovery of the quantized Hall effect, 1985.

1946 *Gilda Radner,* U.S. actress, comedienne; known for her roles on television series, *Saturday Night Live.* [d. May 20, 1989]

1947 *Laura D'Andrea Tyson,* U.S. educator; chief economic adviser for President Clinton, 1993– .

1948 *Kathy Bates (Kathleen Doyle Bates),* U.S. actress; Academy Award (Best Actress) for *Misery,* 1990.

1960 *John Albert Elway,* U.S. football player.

1966 *Mary Stuart Masterson,* U.S. actress; known for roles in *Fried Green Tomatoes* and *Benny & Joon.*

1969 *Danielle Brisebois,* U.S. actress; known for her roles on television series, *Archie Bunker's Place* and *Knot's Landing.*

HISTORICAL EVENTS

1098 Crusaders defeat Turks at *Antioch (First Crusade).*

1519 *Charles I* of Spain is elected Holy Roman Emperor assuming the name *Charles V.*

1629 *Peace of Alais* ends *Huguenot Wars.* Huguenots obtain religious freedom and dissolve their political organization.

1840 British fleet blockades *Canton (First Opium War).*

1841 Jean Coralli's ballet, *Giselle,* premieres in Paris at the Théâtre de l'Académie Royale de Musique. It is destined to become one of the classic tragedies of ballet.

1894 U.S. Congress establishes the first Monday in September as *Labor Day.*

1914 *Archduke Francis Ferdinand,* heir to the Austrian throne,

and his wife are murdered at *Sarajevo, Bosnia* by a student, *Gavrilo Princip,* acting as an agent of the Serbian terrorist group *The Black Hand.* The incident touches off *World War I.*

1919 The *Treaty of Versailles,* ending World War I, is signed in the Hall of Mirrors at Versailles.

China refuses to sign the *Treaty of Versailles* because of a stipulation awarding Shantung Concessions to Japan.

1934 *Federal Housing Administration* is created to insure loans for new construction in an effort to stimulate activity in the U.S. housing industry.

1939 First commercial *trans-Atlantic passenger air service* begins with Pan American Airways *Yankee Clipper* flight from Port Washington, New York, to Marseilles, France.

1948 The *Cominform* (Communist Information Bureau) expels *Yugoslavia* from membership for doctrinal errors and hostility to the Soviet Union.

Independence National Historical Park in Philadelphia, Pennsylvania becomes part of the U.S. National Park System. The Park includes the *Liberty Bell Pavilion* and *Independence Hall.*

1950 *Seoul, South Korea* is captured by invading North Korean Communist troops. President *Syngman Rhee* escapes to Taejon (*Korean War*).

1951 *Amos n' Andy* makes its television debut.

First commercial *color television* broadcast is aired in New York City by Columbia Broadcasting System.

1967 Israel annexes Jerusalem's "Old City," captured from Jordan during the Six-Day War.

All tariffs on industrial goods moving within the *European Economic Community* member countries are abolished.

1978 The U.S. Supreme Court rules that *Alan Bakke* is a victim of reverse discrimination and orders his admission to the University of California Medical School.

june

JUNE
29

HOLIDAYS

Chile, Colombia, Costa Rica, Italy, Malta, Peru, San Marino, Spain, Vatican City, Venezuela
Feast of SS. Peter and Paul

Seychelles
Independence Day
Commemorates Seychelles' proclamation of independence from Great Britain, 1976.

RELIGIOUS CALENDAR

The Saints
St. Peter, Apostle and martyr. One of the 12 original disciples of Jesus Christ, first Bishop of Rome, leader of Christian community after Christ's death. Patron of fishermen, locksmiths, cobblers. [d. c. 64] [major holy day, Episcopal Church; minor festival, Lutheran Church]

St. Paul, Apostle of the Gentiles. Through his letters he has had a profound and lasting influence on the development of Christianity. Patron of Rome and of ropemakers. Invoked against hail and snakebite. [d. c. 67] [major holy day, Episcopal Church; minor festival, Lutheran Church]

St. Cassius, Bishop of Narni. [d. 538]

St. Salome and *St. Judith.* [d. 9th century]

St. Emma, widow. Also called *Hemma.* [d. c. 1045]

St. Elwin, Bishop of Lindsey. Also called *Æthelwine.* [death date unknown]

BIRTHDATES

1721 *Johann, Baron de Kalb,* French army officer born in Germany; accompanied Lafayette to America; he died in Battle of Camden (American Revolution). [d. August 16, 1780]

1798 *Count Giacomo Leopardi,* Italian poet, scholar; leading Italian poet of *pessimism.* [d. June 14, 1837]

1849 *Count Sergei Yulievich Witte,* Russian statesman; first constitutional Russian premier, 1905–06. [d. March 13, 1915]

1852 *John Bach McMaster,* U.S. historian, educator; noted for his eight-volume *Volumes of the History of the People of the United States from the Revolution to the Civil War,* as well as numerous historical textbooks which focus on social and economic forces influencing history. [d. May 24, 1932]

1858 *George Washington Goethals,* U.S. army officer; engineer in charge of construction of *Panama Canal,* 1907–14. Appointed first Governor of Canal Zone, 1914. [d. January 21, 1928]

Julia Clifford Lathrop, U.S. social worker; chief of U.S. Dept. of Labor, Children's Bureau, 1912–25. Member of Advisory Committee on Child Welfare for League of Nations, 1925–32. Friend and co-worker of Jane Addams (September 6). [d. April 15, 1932]

1861 *William James Mayo,* U.S. surgeon; with his brother, Charles Horace Mayo (July l9), founded the Mayo Foundation for Medical Education and Research (*Mayo Clinic*), 1915. [d. July 28, 1939]

1863 *James Harvey Robinson,* U.S. historian, educator; co-founder of the *New School for Social Research.* Author of *The Mind in the Making,* a study of the intellectual history of mankind. [d. February 16, 1936]

1865 *William Edgar Borah,* U.S. lawyer, politician; U.S. Senator, 1907–40; maintained an isolationist policy toward all proposed American involvement in foreign relations during his political career; strongly opposed U.S. joining League of Nations. [d. January 19, 1940]

1868 *George Ellery Hale,* U.S. astronomer; influential in establishment of *Yerkes Observatory,* Wisconsin;

director of *Mt. Wilson Observatory*, California, where he pioneered solar research; responsible for securing funding for construction of *Mt. Palomar Observatory*, California. Invented *spectroheliograph* for photographing surface of the sun. [d. February 21, 1938]

1871 *Luisa Tetrazzini*, Italian operatic coloratura soprano. [d. April 28, 1940]

1875 *Edwin Walter Kemmerer*, U.S. economist; financial adviser to numerous foreign governments. [d. December 16, 1945]

1910 Frank Loesser, U.S. composer, lyricist; noted for his musical film and stage scores, including *Guys and Dolls, Most Happy Fella.* Also achieved fame for war songs, including *Praise the Lord and Pass the Ammunition,* 1942. [d. July 28, 1969]

1911 *Prince Bernhard (Bernhard Leopold Friedrich Eberhard Julius Kurt Karl Gottfried Peter),* husband and consort of Queen Juliana of the Netherlands.

1912 *John Willard Toland,* U.S. journalist, author, historian; Pulitzer Prize for *The Rising Sun, 1970.*

1919 *Slim Pickens (Louis Bert Lindley),* U.S. character actor, principally in 1940s westerns. [d. December 8, 1983]

1930 *Robert (Bob) Evans,* U.S. actor, producer; known for the production of *Love Story,* 1970, and *The Godfather,* 1972.

Oriana Fallaci, Italian journalist, writer; frequent contributor to *New York Times Magazine, Life, Look;* well-known for her in-depth interviews of world famous persons.

1936 *Harmon (Clayton) Killebrew,* U.S. baseball player; elected to Baseball Hall of Fame, 1984.

1941 *Stokely Carmichael,* U.S. black militant leader; Chairman of *Student Nonviolent Coordinating Committee,* 1966; Prime Minister of *Black Panther Party,* 1967–69. Proponent of Black Power and militant tactics to achieve racial equality in U.S.

1944 *Gary Busey,* U.S. actor; Oscar nominee for his performance in *The Buddy Holly Story,* 1978.

1957 *Leslie Browne,* U.S. ballerina, actress; soloist, American Ballet Theater, 1976–; known for her starring role in *The Turning Point,* 1977.

1963 *Anne-Sophie Mutter,* German violinist.

1972 *Samantha Smith,* U.S. student, actress; visited the U.S.S.R. as a guest of Yuri Andropov after writing the Soviet leader a letter, 1982; died in a plane crash. [d. August 25, 1985]

HISTORICAL EVENTS

1236 *Ferdinand III* of Castile recaptures *Cordoba* from the Moors after 400 years of Moorish possession.

1312 *Henry VII* is crowned Holy Roman Emperor at Rome.

1408 *Council of Pisa* is called to end schism in Catholic Church, hearing charges against *Gregory XII* at Rome and *Benedict XII* at Avignon. Both are deposed and *Peter Philarges* is elected *Pope Alexander V.*

1767 *Townshend Revenue Acts* are passed by British parliament, establishing duties on tea, glass, paint, oil, lead, and paper imported into American colonies.

1880 France annexes *Tahiti* in South Pacific.

1906 *Mesa Verde National Park* in Colorado is established by an act of Congress. The park contains prehistoric cliff dwellings.

1916 *Sir Roger Casement,* the Irish leader, is convicted of high treason by a British court and sentenced to death for conspiracy with Germany *(World War I).*

1933 *Primo Carnera* knocks out *Jack Sharkey* at Madison Square Garden and becomes world heavyweight boxing champion.

1949 The *South African Nationalist Party* bans interracial marriages between blacks and whites.

1966 Lieutenant General *Juan Carlos Ongania* assumes power in Argentina after a coup d'etat.

U.S. aircraft bombs oil installations near *Hanoi* and *Haiphong* for the first time *(Vietnam War).*

1976 *Seychelles* gain independence.

1981 *Hu Yaobang* succeeds *Hua Guofeng* as Chinese Communist Party Chairman.

1988 U.S. Supreme Court upholds the *special prosecutor law*

june

allowing the appointment of independent counsels to prosecute high-ranking federal officials accused of wrong-doing.

1992 Algerian president *Mohammed Boudiaf* is assassinated.

1995 The U.S. space shuttle *Atlantis* successfully docks

with the Russian space station *Mir*.

1996 A department store in *Seoul, Korea,* collapses, killing hundreds.

HOLIDAYS

Democratic Republic of the Congo
Independence Day

Guatemala
Army Day
Commemorates revolution for agrarian reform, 1871.

RELIGIOUS CALENDAR

The Saints
Martyrs of Rome. Feast of the protomartyrs of Roman Church who died in the persecution of Nero in the late 1st century. Optional Memorial.
St. Martial, Bishop of Limoges and missionary. [d. c. 250]
St. Bertrand, Bishop of Le Mans. Also called *Bertichramnus.* [d. 623]
St. Erentrude, virgin and abbess. [d. c. 718]
St. Theobald of Provins, hermit. Also called *Thibaud.* [d. 1066]

The Beatified
Blessed Arnulf of Villers, lay-brother, Also called *Arnoul Cornebout.* [d. 1228]
Blessed Philip Powell, martyr. [d. 1646]

BIRTHDATES

1470 *Charles VIII,* King of France. [d. April 7, 1498]

1755 *Count Paul François Jean Nicolas Barras,* French revolutionary. [d. January 29, 1829]

1768 *Elizabeth Monroe,* wife of U.S. President James Monroe. [d. September 23, 1830]

1819 *William A. Wheeler,* U.S. Vice-President, 1877–81. [d. June 4, 1887]

1861 *Sir Frederick Gowland Hopkins,* British biochemist; Nobel Prize in physiology or medicine for discovery of *vitamins A and B* (with C. Eijkman), 1929. [d. May 16, 1947]

1893 *Harold Joseph Laski,* British political scientist, educator; Professor at London School of Economics, 1926–50. [d. March 24, 1950]

1896 *Wilfrid Pelletier,* Canadian conductor, pianist; founder of *Société des Concerts Symphoniques de Montréal,* 1935. [d. April 9, 1982]

1909 *Juan Bosch,* Dominican political leader; elected President of Dominican Republic, 1962.

1911 *Czeslaw Milosz,* U.S. writer born in Poland; Nobel Prize for literature, 1980.

1917 *Lena Horne,* U.S. singer.

Buddy Rich (Bernard Rich), U.S. jazz drummer. [d. April 2, 1987]

1919 *Susan Hayward (Edythe Marrener),* U.S. actress. [d. March 14, 1975]

1925 *Dorothy Malone,* U.S. actress.

1926 *Paul Berg,* U.S. biochemist; Nobel Prize in chemistry for his work with nucleic acids, 1980.

1936 *Nancy Dussault,* U.S. actress, singer; known for her role as Muriel Rush on television series, *Too Close for Comfort.*

1942 *Robert D. Ballard,* U.S. geologist; developed the Argo-Jason system used in deep sea exploration.

1943 *Florence Ballard,* U.S. singer; member of the rock group, *The Supremes. [d. February 22, 1976]*

HISTORICAL EVENTS

1815 U.S. Captain *Stephen Decatur* concludes treaty for U.S. with Dey of Algiers, ending war declared on March 3, 1815. War was the result of Dey's harrassing U.S. ships and insisting upon tribute payments.

1854 Treaty is signed between Mexico and U.S. providing for the purchase of territory now comprising *Arizona* and *New Mexico* by the U.S. (*Gadsden Purchase*).

june

1892 *Homestead (Steel) Plant* strike in U.S. ends in violence and use of state troops to protect Carnegie property; the state troops remain in Homestead for 95 days protecting the plant.

1903 *Harry Lawrence Freeman,* U.S. black composer, conducts the premiere of his opera, *African Kraal,* with an all-black cast.

1906 *U.S. Pure Food and Drug Act* is passed, prohibiting the misbranding and adulteration of foods.

1908 *Meteorites* fall along the *Stony Tunguska River* in northern Siberia, creating the only meteorite craters known to have been formed in historic times.

1913 *Second Balkan War* begins as Bulgaria attacks Greece and Serbia.

1921 President *William Howard Taft* is confirmed as Chief Justice of the U.S. Supreme Court, becoming the only American to have served in the highest executive and judicial offices.

1934 *Great Blood Purge* takes place in Germany as 77 Reichstag leaders are executed because of an alleged plot against Hitler.

1936 Ethiopian Emperor *Haile Selassie* addresses League of Nations, denouncing Mussolini's bombing of Ethiopia. He utters the often repeated threat "*God and history will remember your judgment.*"

1943 U.S. Marines and Army land in New Georgia area, *Solomon Islands (World War II).*

1949 *Alexander Diomedes* becomes premier of Greece following the death of *Themistocles Sophoulis.*

1951 The peso becomes the only monetary unit in *Cuba* after the government withdraws the U.S. dollar as legal tender.

1953 General Motors unveils its *Corvette,* the first sports car with a fiberglass body.

1960 Independence of the *Democratic Republic of the Congo,* formerly *Zaire,* is proclaimed in Léopoldville by King Baudouin of Belgium.

1964 United Nations forces depart from the *Democratic Republic of the Congo* after four years of military operation.

1969 Spain returns southern Atlantic region of *Ifni* to Morocco after 35 years of occupation.

1971 In pursuit of a nonalignment policy, Malta cancels its *Mutual Defense and Assistance Agreement* with Great Britain.

Russian *Soyuz 11* cosmonauts Georgi T. Dobrovolsky, Victor I. Volkov, and Vladislav N. Patsayev complete a flight setting a new space endurance record of 570 hours, 22 minutes (although all 3 cosmonauts died 30 minutes before landing due to a sudden drop in air pressure when the ship's seals failed.)

The *26th Amendment* to the U.S. Constitution, extending full voting rights to 18-year-olds, receives necessary ratification when Ohio legislature approves it.

1977 *The Southeast Asia Treaty Organization,* a regional defense league founded in 1954, is dissolved after 23 years.

1984 *John Turner* is inaugurated as prime minister of Canada.

1988 Ultraconservative Archbishop *Marcel Lefebvre* is excommunicated when he ordains four bishops in defiance of the Pope. The act results in the Roman Catholic Church's first schism in over a century.

1992 General *Fidel V. Ramos* is elected as the new president of the Philippines.

July is the seventh month of the Gregorian Calendar and has 31 days. In the early Roman 10-month calendar it was named *Quintilis* 'fifth,' designating the position it occupied in that calendar. The name of the month was changed to *Julius* (hence our *July*) in honor of Julius Caesar; ironically, the adoption of the change took effect in 44 B.C., the year of Caesar's assassination.

The "dog days" of summer, the hottest part of the year in the northern hemishpere, were recognized by the Romans as corresponding to the heliacal rising of the star they called *Canicula*, 'Little Dog,' which is now known as Sirius. This star, in the constellation Canis Major, rises above the horizon before sunrise during the period of July 3 to August 11. Its brightness apparently suggested that it added to the heat from the sun, hence, the "dog days," with allusion to the Roman name for Sirius.

In the astrological calendar, July spans the zodiac signs of Cancer, the Crab (June 22–July 22) and Leo, the Lion (July 23–August 22).

The birthstone for July is the ruby, and the flower is the larkspur or water lily.

STATE, NATIONAL, AND INTERNATIONAL HOLIDAYS

Independence or Decoration Day
(United States)
July 4

Kadooment Day
(Barbados)
First Monday

Constitution Day
(Cayman Islands)
First Monday

Caribbean Day
(Barbados, Guyana)
First Monday

Family Day
(Lesotho)
First Monday

Heroes Day
(Zambia)
First Monday

Feria de San Fermin
(Spain)
Second Week

Unity Day
(Zambia)
Second Tuesday

Girls' Fair
(Romania)
Third Sunday

Il Redentore
(Venice; gondola race and procession)
Third Sunday

President's Day
(Botswana)
Second or Third Monday

SPECIAL EVENTS AND THEIR SPONSORS

July Belongs to Blueberries
North American Blueberry Council

Eye Safety Month
American Society for the Prevention of Blindness

Hitch Hiking Month
Richard R. Falk Associates

National Hot Dog Month
National Hot Dog and Sausage Council

Man Watchers' Compliment Week
First Week
Man Watchers, Inc.

National Ice Cream Week
Week containing July 15
Dairymen, Inc.

Carnation Day
July 4
Puns Corp. c/o Robert L. Birch

HOLIDAYS

Bangladesh
Bank Holiday

British Virgin Islands
Territory Day

Burundi and Rwanda
Independence Day
Commemorates their independence
from Belgian trust territory of
Rwanda-Urundi, 1962.

Canada (except Newfoundland)
Dominion Day or Canada Day
Celebrates the establishment of
Dominion of Canada by the British
North American Act, 1867.

Ghana
First Republic Day
Commemorates Ghana's gaining
republic status within British
Commonwealth, 1960.

Guatemala
Bank Employees Day

Hong Kong
Half-year Holiday

Somalia
Foundation of the Republic Day

Sudan
Decentralization Day

Surinam
*Day of Freedom or National Union
Day*

Taiwan
Bank Holiday

RELIGIOUS CALENDAR

The Saints

St. Shenute, abbot. Also called
Shenoudi. [d. c. 466]

St. Theodoric, abbot. Also called
Thieri, Thierry. [d. 533]

St. Carilefus, abbot. Also called
Calais, Carilephus. [d. c. 540]

St. Gall, Bishop of Clermont. [d.
551]

St. Eparchius. Also called *Cybar,
Cybard, Separcus.* [d. 581]

St. Simeon Salus, monk and hermit.
[d. c. 590]

St. Serf, bishop; patron of the
Orkney Islands off the coast
of Scotland. Also called
Servanus, Suranus. [d. 6th
century]

The Beatified

Blessed Thomas Maxfield, priest and
martyr. Also called
Macclesfield. [d. 1616]

Blessed Oliver Plunket, Archbishop
of Armagh and martyr. [d.
1681] Feast Formerly July 11.

BIRTHDATES

1481 *Christian II,* King of Denmark
and Norway, 1513–23, and of
Sweden, 1520–22. [d. January
25, 1559]

1506 *Louis II* of Hungary, 1516–26.
[d. August 29, 1526]

1534 *Frederick II* of Denmark and
Norway. [d. April 4, 1588]

1646 *Gottfried Wilhelm von
Leibniz,* German philosopher,
mathematician, diplomat. [d.
November 14, 1716]

1725 *Jean Baptiste Donatien de
Vimeur, Comte de
Rochambeau,* French Army
marshal; commanded French
forces in America during the
American Revolution. [d. May
10, 1807]

1804 *George Sand (Amandine
Aurore Lucie Dupin),* French
writer; known for her
controversial writings and
lifestyle. Liaisons, both
romantic and artistic, were
formed with Jules Sandeau,
Alfred de Musset, and
Frédéric Chopin. [d. June 8,
1876]

1846 *William Howard Brett,* U.S.
librarian; responsible for
many innovations in library
science. [d. August 24, 1918]

1854 *Albert Bushnell Hart,* U.S.
historian, professor, and
editor; leading contributor to
field of American history;
Professor of History, Harvard
College, 1883–1926. [d. June
16, 1943]

1872 *Louis Blériot,* French aviator;
first to cross the *English
Channel* in a heavier-than-air
machine. [d. August 2, 1936]

1877 *Benjamin Oliver Davis,* U.S.
army general; first black
general in U.S. Army. [d.
November 26, 1970]

july

1879 *Léon Jouhaux,* French labor leader, politician; Secretary-General of Confèdèration Gènèrale du Travail, 1909–40, 1945–47; Nobel Peace Prize, 1951. [d. April 28, 1954]

1892 *Jean Marie Hurcat,* French artist. [d. January 6, 1966]

1893 *Walter Francis White,* U.S. author, civil rights leader; Secretary of NAACP, 1930–35. [d. March 21, 1955]

1899 *Charles Laughton,* British actor. [d. December 15, 1962]

1902 *William Wyler,* U.S. film director, producer. [d. July 27, 1981]

José Luis Sert, U.S. architect born in Spain; Dean, Harvard University Graduate School of Design, 1953–69. [d. March 15, 1983]

1908 *Estee Lauder,* U.S. cosmetics executive; Chairman, Estee Lauder Inc.

1912 *David Brower,* U.S. conservationist; founder of Friends of the Earth, 1969.

1916 *Olivia de Havilland,* British actress, born in Toykyo, Japan.

1921 *Sir Seretse M. Khama,* Botswanean statesman; Prime Minister of Bechuanaland, 1965–66; President of Botswana, 1966–80. [d. July 13, 1980]

1925 *Farley Granger,* U.S. actor.

1926 *Robert W. Fogel,* U.S. economist; Nobel Prize for Economics with Douglass C. North, for their work on cliometrics, 1993

1929 *Gerald Maurice Edelman,* U.S. biochemist; Nobel Prize

in physiology or medicine for research into chemical structure of *antibodies,* 1972.

1931 *Leslie Clare Margaret Caron,* French actress, dancer; starred in *An American in Paris,* 1951, and *Gigi,* 1958.

1934 *Jamie Farr,* U.S. actor; known for his role as Corporal Klinger on television series, *M*A*S*H,* 1972–83.

Jean Lyndsey Torren Marsh, British actress; known for her role as Rose in the television series, *Upstairs, Downstairs;* Emmy Award, 1975.

Sydney Pollack, U.S. film director.

1936 *Wally Amos,* U.S. business executive; known for Famous Amos chocolate chip cookie shops.

1941 *Alfred G. Gilman,* U.S. pharmacologist; Nobel Prize for Medicine, 1994. Gilman and Martin Rodbell (who shares the prize with Gilman) discovered G proteins.

Sally Quinn, U.S. journalist; wrote best-selling novel, *Regrets Only;* wife of Ben Bradlee.

Twyla Tharp, U.S. choreographer, dancer; organized modern dance troupe, 1965–; created the dance, *Push Comes to Shove.*

1942 *Genevieve Bujold,* French-Canadian actress.

Karen Black (Karen Ziegler), U.S. actress.

1945 *Debbie Harry,* U.S. singer; lead vocalist of rock group, *Blondie.*

1952 *Dan Aykroyd,* Canadian actor, comedian.

1954 *Lee Edward (Chip) Hanauer,* U.S. hydroplane racer; American Powerboat Association Gold Cup, 1982–85.

1958 *Nancy Lieberman-Cline,* U.S. basketball player; first woman to be given a try-out with a National Basketball Association team; Women's National Basketball Association (WNBA), head coach and general manager of the Detroit Shock, 1997– .

1960 *Evelyn (Champagne) King,* U.S. singer.

1961 *Diana, Princess of Wales,* wife of Prince Charles, heir apparent to British throne. [d. August 31, 1997]

Carl Lewis, U.S. athlete.

1978 *Liv Tyler (Rundgren),* U.S. actress.

HISTORICAL EVENTS

1097 Crusaders defeat Turks at *Dorylaeum (First Crusade).*

1190 *Richard I* of England and *Philip II* of France start on the *Third Crusade.*

1543 *Peace of Greenwich* between England and Scotland provides that *Prince Edward* will marry *Mary, Queen of Scotland.*

1569 *Union of Lublin* merges *Poland* and *Lithuania.*

1810 *Louis Bonaparte,* King of Holland, abdicates.

1863 *Battle of Gettysburg,* one of the decisive battles of the *U.S. Civil War,* begins.

1867 *Dominion of Canada* is created by the *British North*

America Act; the Dominion consists of Nova Scotia, New Brunswick, Lower and Upper Canada.

1873 *Prince Edward Island* becomes a province of Canada.

1885 *King Leopold* of Belgium is proclaimed sovereign of the state of the *Congo.*

1898 The *Battle of San Juan Hill,* Cuba, is fought between the Americans and Spanish forces, with Col. *Theodore Roosevelt* commanding the *Rough Riders. (Spanish-American War).*

1899 *International Gideons,* an organization that places Bibles in hotels, hospitals, etc., is founded in Boscobel, Wisconsin.

1916 *Battle of the Somme,* Allied offensive on the Western front, opens with bombardment of German positions *(World War I).*

1927 *First Piano Concerto* by *Béla Bartók* premieres in Frankfurt.

1931 First trip around the world by airplane is completed by *Wiley Post,* pilot, and *Harold Gatty,* navigator (New York to New York in 8 days, 15 hours).

Benguela-Katanga railway, the first trans-Africa line, is completed.

1942 *Sevastopol* falls to Germans after an 8-month siege *(World War II).*

1944 *Bretton Woods Conference,* a UN conference making financial plans for the post-war world, begins.

1950 U.S. senator, *Margaret Chase Smith,* condemns *McCarthyism* in her "Declaration of Conscience" speech.

1951 Great Britain promulgates a new constitution for *Nigeria,* including provisions for home rule.

1960 *Ghana* becomes an independent republic within the British Commonwealth. *Kwame Nkrumah* is inaugurated as the country's first president.

Italian Somaliland and *British Somaliland* are united to form the independent *Somali Democratic Republic.*

1962 Lieutenant Colonel *Julio Adalberto Rivera* is inaugurated as president of El Salvador.

Kingdom of Burundi, Republic of Rwanda become independent.

1968 Sixty-two nations sign the *Nuclear Non-Proliferation Treaty* aimed at limiting the spread of nuclear weapons.

1969 *Queen Elizabeth II* invests her son, Prince Charles, as *Prince of Wales* in ceremonies at Caernarvon Castle, Wales.

U.S. Truth-in-Lending Law goes into effect.

1970 Colonel *Carlos Arana Osorio* is inaugurated as president of Guatemala.

1974 *Isabel Perón* becomes the first woman chief of state in the Americas when she assumes presidency of Argentina upon the death of her husband, *Juan Perón.*

Kjell Laugerud Garcia is inaugurated as president of Guatemala.

1980 *Ó Canada* is officially proclaimed Canada's national anthem.

1988 *Wyoming* raises its legal drinking age to 21. It is the last U.S. state to comply with federal laws.

1990 The shared monetary economy between *East Germany* and *West Germany* begins (May 18, 1990).

1997 China regains control of *Hong Kong* after 99 years under British rule.

july

JULY
2

HOLIDAYS

Dominica
Caricom Day

Italy (Siena)
Il Palio
A day of medieval sport, featuring horse racing and flag throwing in medieval garb.

RELIGIOUS CALENDAR

The Saints
St. Monegundis, widow. Also called *Monegoude.* [d. 570]
St. Otto, Bishop of Bamberg. Also called *Otho.* [d. 1139]
St. Processus and Martinian, martyrs. [death date unknown]

The Beatified
Blessed Peter of Luxemburg, Bishop of Metz and Cardinal; patron of *Avignon.* [d. 1387]

BIRTHDATES

1489 *Thomas Cranmer,* English churchman, reformer; Archbishop of Canterbury, 1533–55. Adviser to Henry VIII, especially in Henry's divorces and declaration of supremacy over the Church of England. One of the principal authors of *Book of Common Prayer.* Convicted of heresy during reign of Queen Mary I; burned at the stake. [d. March 21, 1556]

1714 *Christoph Willibald (Ritters von) Gluck,* German composer; innovator in operatic composition, his masterpieces such as *Orfeo ed Eurydice* (Italian libretto) revolutionized opera. [d. November 15, 1787]

1724 *Friedrich Gottlieb Klopstock,* German poet; first to use free verse in German; reformer of German literature. [d. March 14, 1803]

1821 *Sir Charles Topper,* Canadian statesman; Prime Minister, 1896; responsible for Nova Scotia's becoming a province of Canada. [d. October 30, 1915]

1861 *John Sanburn Phillips,* U.S. editor, publisher. [d. February 28, 1949]

1862 *Sir William Henry Bragg,* British physicist; with his son, W. L. Bragg, pioneered study of *molecular structures of crystals;* Nobel Prize in physics (with W. L. Bragg), 1915.

1877 *Hermann Hesse,* German author living in Switzerland, whose works include *Siddhartha,* and *Steppenwolf;* Nobel Prize in literature, 1946. [d. August 9, 1962]

1893 *Emanuel Neumann,* U.S. Zionist leader, lawyer, business executive; key figure in establishment of *Israel;* founder of *Tarbuth Foundation for the Advancement of Hebrew Culture.* [d. October 26, 1980]

1898 *Anthony Clement McAuliffe,* U.S. army general; distinguished himself during World War II, particularly during *Battle of the Bulge.* [d. August 11, 1975]

1903 *Alexander Frederick Douglas-Home,* British politician; Prime Minister, 1963–64. [d. October 9, 1995]

Olaf V, King of Norway, 1957–91.[d. January 17, 1991]

1905 *(Jean-) Rene Lacoste,* French tennis player; called *the Crocodile.* [d. October 14, 1996]

1906 *Hans Albrecht Bethe,* U.S. physicist born in Germany; Nobel Prize in physics for contributions to theory of *nuclear reaction,* 1967; professor, Cornell University, 1935– .

1908 *Thurgood Marshall,* U.S. jurist, lawyer; Associate Justice, U.S. Supreme Court, 1967–91. First black to serve on Supreme Court. [d. January 24, 1993]

1911 *Dorothy Horstmann,* U.S. virologist; known for her contributions toward the polio vaccine.

1918 *Robert William Sarnoff,* U.S. electronics and communications executive; President, RCA Corp., 1966–71; Chairman, RCA Corp., 1970–75; Director, RCA Global Communications. [d. February 22, 1997]

1922 *Dan Rowan,* U.S. comedian; co-star of television series, *Laugh-In.* [d. September 22, 1987]

1923 *Wislawa Szymborsha,* Polish poet; Nobel Prize for Literature in 1996.

1924 *Laurence Swinburne,* U.S. author; writes children's books and educational materials; Notable Book Award for Children's Book, American Library Association, 1977.

1925 *Medgar Evers,* U.S. civil rights leader; field secretary, NAACP, 1954–63. Assassinated. [d. June 12, 1963]

Patrice Lumumba, African nationalist; leader and first premier of *Republic of the Congo,* 1960. [d. February 12, 1961]

1931 *Imelda Marcos,* Philippine political leader; wife of Phillipine president Ferdinand Marcos; became known for her extravagance after her departure from the Philippines.

1932 *Fred Begay,* U.S. nuclear physicist.

Dave Thomas, U.S. businessman; founder of Wendy's International, Inc.

1937 *Polly Dean Holliday,* U.S. actress; known for her role as Flo on television series, *Alice,* 1976–80.

Richard Petty, U.S. auto racer.

1952 *Cheryl Ladd,* U.S. actress; known for her role as Kris on television series, *Charlie's Angels,* 1977–81.

1961 *Jimmy McNichol,* U.S. actor.

1964 *Jose Canseco,* Cuban-born baseball player.

HISTORICAL EVENTS

1819 *Factory Act* is passed in Great Britain, prohibiting employment of children under 9 years of age in cotton mills.

1853 Russian army crosses Pruth River, invading Turkey and beginning *Crimean War.*

1862 *Morrill Act* is passed by U.S. Congress, providing for endowment of at least one agricultural (land-grant) college in each state.

1865 General *William Booth* presides over the first meeting of the *Salvation Army* in London.

1871 The government of newly unified *Italy* establishes its seat at Rome.

1881 *James A. Garfield,* U.S. president, is shot by *Charles J. Guiteau;* Garfield dies on September 19.

1890 *Sherman Anti-Trust Law* is enacted in U.S., curtailing the powers of U.S. business monopolies.

1900 *Finlandia* by *Jean Sibelius* premieres.

1917 The pro-Allied Greek government under King *Alexander* declares war on Germany and Austria-Hungary, Bulgaria, and Turkey *(World War I).*

1932 *Franklin Delano Roosevelt,* accepting Democratic presidential nomination, pledges a *New Deal* for the American people.

1937 U.S. aviator *Amelia Earhart* disappears over the Pacific during an attempt to circumnavigate the globe.

1940 *Lake Washington* floating bridge in Seattle, the greatest floating structure ever built, opens to traffic.

1947 The U.S.S.R. rejects U.S. *Marshall Plan* for European recovery.

1955 *The Lawrence Welk Show* makes its television debut.

1963 *Seyyid Iamshid bin Abdullah* succeeds his father as sultan of Zanzibar.

1964 U.S. President *Lyndon B. Johnson* signs the *Civil Rights Act* of 1964, prohibiting discrimination on the basis of race, sex, or national origin in public accommodations and federally assisted programs.

1976 U.S. Supreme Court finds that the *death penalty* does not violate the Constitution's prohibition of "cruel and unusual" punishment.

North and South Vietnam are reunited, with *Hanoi* as the capital. The country had been divided since the 1954 Geneva Agreement following the French defeat at Dien Bien Phu.

1992 *Ali Kafi* is named president of Algeria following the assassination of President *Mohammed Boudiaf* (June 29, 1992).

july

1994 The *Citadel*, an historically male military educational institution, is ordered to admit women.

HOLIDAYS

Antigua and Barbuda
CARICOM Day

Virgin Islands
Danish West Indies Emancipation Day

RELIGIOUS CALENDAR

Feasts
St. Thomas, Apostle of the Indies and martyr; patron of architects, builders, and divines; surnamed *Didymus* or *the Twin.* [d. 1st century] Feast formerly December 21.

The Saints
St. Anatolius, Bishop of Laodicea. [d. c. 283]
St. Julius and *St. Aaron,* martyrs. [d. 304]
St. Heliodorus, Bishop of Altino. [d. c. 400]
St. Anatolius, Bishop and Patriarch of Constantinople. [d. 458]
St. Germanus of Man, bishop. Also called *Garmon, German.* [d. c. 475]
St. Leo II, pope; elected 682. [d. 683]
St. Rumold, martyr and bishop. Also called *Rombaut.* [d. c. 775]
St. Bernardino Realino, Jesuit. [d. 1616]

BIRTHDATES

1728 *Robert Adam,* English architect, furniture designer, decorator. [d. March 3, 1792]

1738 *John Singleton Copley,* American painter; known for his direct, realistic portraits of New Englanders, biblical scenes, and historical events; one of first great American painters. [d. September 9, 1815]

1746 *Henry Grattan,* Irish statesman; worked for Irish independence and Catholic emancipation. [d. June 6, 1820]

1854 *Leoš Janáček,* Czech composer; most of his works are based upon Czech folk music. [d. August 12, 1928]

1878 *George M(ichael) Cohan,* U.S. composer, playwright, actor, producer; known as much for his exuberant stage presence as for his talents; received Congressional Medal of Honor for spirited efforts in elevating morale in World War I, especially for song, *Over There!.* [d. November 5, 1942]

1883 *Franz Kafka,* Austrian novelist; his psychological and philosophical works display a desperation in man's awareness of his plight in modern society. Most of his works were published posthumously. [d. June 3, 1924]

1909 *Stavros Spyros Niarchos,* Greek shipping executive; pioneer of *supertanker shipping.* [d. April 15, 1996]

1927 *Ken Russell,* British film director; achieved worldwide acclaim for his BBC film documentaries of famous people including Henri Rousseau, Isadora Duncan, Richard Strauss.

1930 *Peter Dewey (Pete) Fountain, Jr.,* U.S. jazz musician; clarinetist; member of the Lawrence Welk Orchestra, 1957–60.

1935 *Harrison (Jack) Schmitt,* U.S. politician, geologist, astronaut; U.S. Senator, 1977–83.

1937 *Tom Stoppard (Thomas Straussler),* British writer born in Czechoslovakia; noted for such award winning plays as *Rosencrantz and Guildenstern Are Dead.*

1940 *Lamar Alexander,* U.S. lawyer, politician; Governor of Tennessee, 1979–87; U.S. Secretary of Education, 1990–93.

John Patrick Sears, U.S. lawyer; campaign manager, Reagan for President, 1975–76, 1979–80.

1947 *Betty Buckley,* U.S. actress; known for her role on television series, *Eight is Enough, 1977–81;* Tony Award for *Cats,* 1982.

Michael Burton, U.S. swimmer. Olympic gold medalist, 1968 and 1972.

1949 *Jan Smithers,* U.S. actress; known for her role as Bailey on the television series, *WKRP in Cincinnati, 1978–82.*

1951 *Jean-Claude (Baby Doc) Duvalier,* Haitian leader; President, 1971–86.

1953 *Frank Daryl Tanana,* U.S. baseball player.

1957 *Laura Branigan,* U.S. singer.

1958 *Aaron Tippin,* U.S. country singer.

1962 *Tom Cruise,* U.S. actor.

HISTORICAL EVENTS

1608 *Samuel de Champlain* establishes European settlement on site of city of *Quebec.*

1775 *George Washington* takes command of *Continental Army* at Cambridge, Massachusetts (*American Revolution*).

1866 *Venetia* is ceded to Italy, marking a major step in the unification of *Italy.*

Battle of Königgrätz or *Sadowa,* decisive battle of the *Seven Weeks' War* between the Prussians and Austrians, ends in a tactical victory for the Prussians.

1880 *Madrid Convention* is signed by leading European powers and the U.S., recognizing independence and integrity of Morocco.

1890 *Idaho* joins the Union as the 43rd state.

1930 *U.S. Veterans Administration* is created by *Veterans Administration Act.*

1946 *Klement Gottwald* is named premier of Czechoslovakia.

1962 France formally proclaims the independence of *Algeria.*

1970 *Portugal* recalls its ambassador to the Vatican and delivers a formal protest over the meeting of *Pope Paul VI* with leaders of independence movements in Portugal's African territories.

1976 Israeli commandos storm *Entebbe Airport* in Uganda, rescuing 103 passengers aboard an Air France plane held by Arab hijackers.

King Juan Carlos of Spain replaces Premier *Carlos Arias Navarro* with *Adolfo Suarez Gonzales.*

1979 West German government votes to continue prosecution of *Nazi war criminals* by removing the statute of limitations on murder.

1984 European researchers announce the discovery of the *top quark,* one of the basic building blocks of larger subatomic particles. The finding further supports the *unified field theory* of nature.

1986 The U.S. begins its celebration of the 100th anniversary of the *Statue of Liberty.* The extravaganza includes fireworks, boat parades, and naturalization ceremonies for 38,000 new citizens.

1987 *Richard Branson* and *Per Lindstrand* cross the Atlantic and establish a world record for the longest distance travelled in a *hot air balloon.*

1988 The *U.S.S. Vincennes* shoots down an Iranian passenger plane over the Persian Gulf, believing it to be a hostile fighter. All 290 civilians aboard the airbus are killed.

1989 The Supreme Court rules in favor of restrictions on *abortion* and sends the authority to set limitations to the state level.

1996 *Boris Yeltsin* is reelected president of Russia.

HOLIDAYS

Denmark
Rebildfest
Largest celebration of America's independence held outside U.S.

Philippines
Philippine-American Friendship Day

Tonga
Birthday of His Majesty, King Taufa'ahau Tupou IV

U.S. (including Guam, Puerto Rico, Virgin Islands)
Independence Day
Celebrates the signing of the Declaration of Independence, 1776.

U.S.
Carnation Day
Sponsored by Puns Corp.

U.S. (Wisconsin)
Indian Rights Day

RELIGIOUS CALENDER

The Saints
St. Bertha, widow and abbess. [d. c. 725]
St. Andrew of Crete, Archbishop of Gortyn; preacher, and poet. Also called *St. Andrew of Jerusalem.* [d. c. 740]
St. Oda, Archbishop of Canterbury. Also called *Oda* or *Odo the Good.* [d. 959]
St. Ulric, Bishop of Augsburg. Also called *Udalric.* [d. 973]
St. Elizabeth, widow and queen of Portugal. Also called *Isabel,*

Isabella. [d. 1336] Feast formerly July 8. Optional Memorial.

The Beatified
Blessed William of Hirschau, abbot. [d. 1091]
Blessed John Cornelius and his companions, the Dorchester martyrs. [d. 1594]
Blessed William Andleby and his companions, martyrs. William Andleby also called *Anlaby.* [d. 1597]

BIRTHDATES

1610 *Paul Scarron,* French comic poet, novelist, and dramatist. [d. October 6, 1660]

1736 *Robert Raikes,* British publisher, philanthropist; developer of concept of *Sunday School.* [d. April 5, 1811]

1793 *Friedrich Bleek,* German theologian, Bible scholar. [d. February 27, 1859]

1799 *Oscar I, King of Sweden,* 1844–59. [d. July 8, 1859]

1804 *Nathaniel Hawthorne,* U.S. author of *The Scarlet Letter;* member of the *Concord Circle* of great American writers. His work is marked by a preoccupation with evil and the dark side of man's nature. [d. May 19, 1864]

1807 *Giuseppe Garibaldi,* Italian military leader; key figure in the movement of *Italian unification;* with his Redshirts, defeated the Kingdom of the Two Sicilies, 1860, by expelling Francis II from Naples. Marched against Rome twice, 1862, 1867, but was defeated both times. [d. June 2, 1882]

1816 *Hiram Walker,* U.S. distiller; opened Hiram Walker and Sons, Canada; town of Walkerville, Ontario, named for him. [d. January 12, 1899]

1819 *Edward Robinson Squibb,* U.S. manufacturer; founded E.R. Squibb, 1858. [d. October 25, 1900]

1826 *Stephen (Collins) Foster,* U.S. composer; most famous for his ballads and minstrel songs inspired by a romantic view of life in the *Old South.* Some of his best known works are: *Oh, Susannah, My Old Kentucky Home,* and *Beautiful Dreamer.* [d. January 13, 1864]

1845 *Jan Hendrik Hofmeyr,* South African politician, editor; member of Cape Parliament, 1879–95; firm supporter of federation in South Africa. [d. October 16, 1909]

1858 *Emmeline Pankhurst,* British suffragist, barrister, radical; known for her unorthodox, often extreme methods of achieving attention for her cause, including arson, bombing, and hunger strikes. [d. June 14, 1928]

1862 *Gustav Klimt,* Austrian artist; recognized as the foremost Viennese painter of art nouveau; paintings include *The Kiss.* [d. February 6, 1918]

1872 *(John) Calvin Coolidge, (Silent Cal)* U.S. lawyer; Vice-President, 1921–23; President, 1923–29; administration was marked by conservative economic policies and nonaggressive foreign policies. [d. January 5,1933]

1883 *Reuben Lucius (Rube) Goldberg,* U.S. cartoonist; created the comic strips, *Mike & Ike* and *Lucifer Butts;* known for his drawings of absurb mechanical contraptions. [d. December 7, 1970]

1885 *Louis B(urt) Mayer,* U.S. film producer born in Russia; his fortune was based on the establishment of the *motion picture* as the foundation of American entertainment; founded Louis B. Mayer Picture Corporation, which eventually evolved into Metro-Goldwyn-Mayer Studio. [d. October 29, 1957]

1898 *Gertrude Lawrence,* British actress. [d. September 6, 1952]

1900 *(Daniel) Louis (Satchmo) Armstrong,* U.S. jazz musician. [d. July 6, 1971]

1902 *Meyer Lansky (Maier Suchowljansky),* U.S. crime figure; called the *Financial Genius of the Underworld* and *Meyer the Bug.* [d. January 15, 1983]

1905 *Lionel Trilling,* U.S. critic, author. [d. November 5, 1975]

1916 *Tokyo Rose (Iva Toguri D'Aquino),* U.S. propagandist during World War II.

1918 *Ann Landers (Esther Pauline Friedman),* U.S. journalist; syndicated columnist of extremely popular advice-to-the-love-lorn column. Twin sister of Abigail Van Buren.

Abigail Van Buren (Pauline Esther Friedman), U.S. journalist; syndicated advice columnist, creator of *Dear Abby.* Twin sister of Ann Landers.

King Taufa'ahau Tupou IV, King of Tonga, 1965– .

1921 *Adam Smith,* French-born economist; Nobel Prize for economics, 1983.

1924 *Eva Marie Saint,* U.S. actress.

1927 *Neil Simon,* U.S. playwright; author of highly successful comedies for stage and screen.

1928 *Gina Lollobrigida,* Italian actress.

1930 *George Michael Steinbrenner, III,* U.S. baseball executive; principal owner of New York Yankees, 1973– .

1935 *Paul Scoon,* Governor-General, State of Grenada, 1978–92.

1938 *Bill Withers,* U.S. singer, songwriter.

1943 *Geraldo Rivera,* U.S. journalist; known for his investigative reporting; host of the *Geraldo Rivera Show.*

1955 *John Waite,* British singer, songwriter.

1958 *Cristina Garcia,* Cuban-born writer; author of *Dreaming in Cuban* and *The Aguero Sisters.*

1962 *Pamela (Pam) Shriver,* U.S. tennis player; doubles partner of Martina Navratilova.

HISTORICAL EVENTS

1776 In Philadelphia, American *Declaration of Independence* is adopted by delegates to the Continental Congress.

1804 *U.S. Military Academy* at *West Point* formally opens.

1817 Construction of *Erie Canal* begins; the canal officially opens on October 26, 1825.

1828 *Baltimore and Ohio Railroad,* the first public railroad in the U.S., is begun.

1863 *Vicksburg* surrenders to Union forces, giving Union control of the Mississippi River *(U.S. Civil War).*

1881 The *Tuskeegee Institute,* one of the first black educational institutions, is founded by *Booker T. Washington.*

1884 The *Statue of Liberty* is formally presented to the U.S. by France.

1903 First Pacific *telegraph cable,* between San Francisco and Manila, is put into operation.

1910 *Jack Johnson* defeats *Jim Jeffries* to retain the world heavyweight boxing title.

1919 *Jack Dempsey* knocks out *Jess Willard* to win the heavyweight boxing championship.

1946 *Republic of the Philippines* is proclaimed with *Manuel A. Roxas* as first president.

1953 *Imre Nagy* becomes premier of Hungary.

1960 New 50-star *U.S. flag* is officially flown for the first time.

1966 *Queen Elizabeth II* and *Prince Philip* of Great Britain escape injury in Belfast, Northern Ireland, when a 30-pound concrete block drops on the car in which they are riding.

1976 The U.S. celebrates its *Bicentennial* with pageantry, prayer, games, parades, picnics, and fireworks. In New York City millions watch an armada of tall-masted sailing ships from 31 countries pass in review on the Hudson River.

Jose Lopez Portillo is elected president of Mexico.

1979 Former Algerian President, *Ahmed Ben Bela,* is released after 14 years of house arrest; he is considered by many a national hero for his role in Algeria's struggle for independence.

1982 *Miguel de la Madrid* is elected president of Mexico.

1987 Former Nazi Gestapo chief, *Klaus Barbie,* is convicted of crimes committed during World War II and sentenced to life imprisonment.

1994 *Tutsi rebel forces* declare victory in the bloody Rwandan civil war that claims more than 500,000 victims.

1997 The U.S. unmanned spacecraft *Pathfinder* lands on Mars for exploration purposes.

july

HOLIDAYS

Algeria
Independence Day
Celebrates Algeria's achievement of independence from France, 1962.

Cape Verde Islands
Independence Day
Commemorates Cape Verde's coming to independence from Portugal, 1975.

Rwanda
Peace Day or National Peace Unity Day
Commemorates the 1973 coup.

Slovakia
Day of the Slav Apostles, St. Cyril and St. Methodius

United Kingdom (Isle of Man)
Tynwald Day

Venezuela
Independence Anniversary
Celebrates Venezuelan declaration of independence from Spain, 1811.

Zambia
Heroes Day

RELIGIOUS CALENDAR

The Saints
St. Athanasius the Athonite, abbot. Built first monastery at Mount Athos. [d. c. 1000]

St. Antony Zaccaria, founder of Clerks Regular of St. Paul; founded the Congregation of St. Paul (*Barnabites*). [d. 1539]

BIRTHDATES

1731 *Samuel Huntington,* American jurist; signer of the Declaration of Independence. [d. January 5, 1796]

1755 *Sarah Siddons (Sarah Kemble),* Welsh actress; renowned for her portrayal of various Shakespearean roles, especially Lady Macbeth. [d. June 8, 1831]

1801 *David Glasgow Farragut,* U.S. naval officer; Union admiral during U.S. Civil War; first person to hold rank of admiral in U.S. history. Renowned for his aggressive naval tactics. [d. August 14, 1870]

1803 *George Henry Borrow,* British linguist, writer, traveler; especially known for his Romany lexicon. [d. July 26, 1881]

1810 *P(hineas) T(aylor) Barnum,* U.S. showman. Formed *Barnum and Bailey Circus, the Greatest Show on Earth,* basing his success on the gullibility of audiences. Specialized in human and animal curiosities and extravagant exaggerations. [d. April 7, 1871]

1820 *William John McQuorn Rankine,* Scottish civil engineer, physicist; best known for research in

molecular physics. [d. December 24, 1872]

1841 *William Collins Whitney,* U.S. businessman, government official; influential in breaking up the Tweed Ring; U.S. Secretary of the Navy, 1885–89. [d. February 2, 1904]

1853 *Cecil John Rhodes,* British administrator, financier; acquired fortune in Kimberley diamond fields; formed De Beers Consolidated Mines, 1888; Prime Minister of Cape Colony, 1890–96; endowed 70 scholarships for education at Oxford University (*Rhodes Scholarships*). [d. March 26, 1902]

1870 *Richard Bedford Bennett,* Canadian statesman; Prime Minister, 1930–35. [d. June 26, 1947]

1872 *Edouard Herriot,* French statesman; Prime Minister, 1924–25, 1932; served in nine different cabinets. [d. March 26, 1957]

1877 *Wanda Landowska,* Polish harpsichordist, musicologist, in France. [d. August 16, 1959]

1879 *Dwight Filley Davis,* U.S. sportsman; donor of the *Davis Cup,* trophy awarded to the winner of an international tennis tournament. [d. November 28, 1945]

1888 *Herbert Spencer Gasser,* U.S. physiologist; Nobel Prize in physiology or medicine for discovery of highly differentiated functions of nerve fibers (with E. J. Erlanger), 1944. [d. May 11, 1963]

1889 *Jean Cocteau,* French poet, novelist (*Les Enfants Terribles*), playwright, essayist, filmmaker (*Orpheus*), craftsman, artist. [d. October 11, 1963]

1891 *John Howard Northrop,* U.S. biochemist; Nobel Prize in chemistry for preparation of enzymes and virus proteins in pure form (with W.M. Stanley), 1946. [d. May 27, 1987]

1902 *Henry Cabot Lodge, Jr.,* U.S. politician, diplomat; Senator, 1936–44, 1946–52; Chief, U.S. Mission to the United Nations, 1953–60; Ambassador to South Vietnam, 1963–64, 1965–67; Ambassador to Federal Republic of Germany, 1968–69; chief U.S. negotiator at Paris peace talks on Vietnam. [d. February 27, 1985]

1911 *Georges Pompidou,* French statesman; Premier of France, 1962–68; President of Fifth Republic, 1969–74. [d. April 2, 1974]

1915 *Barbara Cushing (Babe) Paley,* U.S. socialite; known as one of the world's great beauties; married to William S. Paley. [d. July 6, 1978]

1926 *Salvador Jorge Blanco,* Dominican statesman; President, Dominican Republic, 1982–86.

1928 *Warren Oates,* U.S. actor.

1936 *James A. Mirrlees,* Scottish economist; Nobel Prize for Economics, 1996. Mirrlees shares with award with fellow economist, William Vickrey.

1937 *Brooke Hayward,* U.S. actress, author; wrote *Haywire;* daughter of Leland Hayward and Margaret Sullavan.

Shirley Knight, U.S. actress; Academy Award nominee for *The Dark at the Top of the Stairs,* 1959; Tony Award for *Kennedy's Children,* 1975.

1942 *Eliot Feld,* U.S. choreographer, dancer.

1944 *Jaime (Robbie) Robertson,* Canadian musician, actor; former member of the rock group, *The Band.*

1948 *Julie Nixon Eisenhower,* daughter of Richard Milhous Nixon, 37th U.S. President.

1951 *Huey Lewis,* U.S. singer; leads the rock group, *Huey Lewis and the News;* Platinum Album Award for *Sports,* 1984.

Richard Michael (Goose) Gossage, U.S. baseball player; known for his highly successful relief pitching.

HISTORICAL EVENTS

1809 Napoleon defeats Austrians at *Wagram.*

1821 *Venezuela* gains independence under *Simón Bolívar.*

1830 A French expeditionary force captures *Algiers* and deposes the ruler.

1884 A treaty with the king of *Togo* puts that African area under German sovereignty.

1932 *António de Oliveira Salazar* becomes Premier of Portugal.

1935 The U.S. *Wagner-Connery Act* establishes a new *National Labor Relations Board,* protecting employees' right to collective bargaining.

1943 U.S. warships bombard *Vila, Kolombangara,* and *Bairoko Harbor, New Georgia, Solomon Islands (World War II).*

1954 *Elvis Presley* is given his first recording session in Memphis, Tennessee.

1962 *Algeria* gains its independence from France.

1972 *Kakuei Tanaka* is elected premier of Japan.

1975 *Arthur Ashe* defeats Jimmy Connors at Wimbledon, becoming the first black male to win the British tennis title.

Cape Verde Islands achieve independence from Portugal.

1977 General *Mohammad Zia ul-Haq* replaces *Zulfikar Ali Bhutto* as prime minister of Pakistan.

Leaders of 48 nations, all members of the *Organization of African Unity,* conclude a four-day meeting in Gabon endorsing the efforts for black rule in *Rhodesia.*

1984 The U.S. Supreme Court finds that evidence gathered in good faith by police may be used in trials, even if their search warrant was legally flawed. The ruling limits the application of the *exclusionary rule* which prohibits the use of evidence obtained in violation of suspects' constitutional rights.

july

1996 British scientist *Ian Wilmut* clones a sheep called *"Dolly."*

1998 *Pete Sampras* wins his fifth Wimbledon title.

HOLIDAYS

Comoros
Independence Day

Czech Republic
Day of the Apostles, St. Cyril and St. Methodius Day

Lithuania
Anniversary of the Coronation of Grand Duke Mindaugas

Malawi
Republic Day
Commemorates Malawi's (Nyasaland) declaration of independence from Great Britain, 1967.

RELIGIOUS CALENDAR

The Saints
St. Romulus, Bishop of Fiesole, martyr. [d. c. 90]
St. Dominica, virgin and martyr. [d. c. 303]
St. Sisoes, hermit. Also called *Sisoy.* [d. c. 429]
St. Monenna, abbess and founder of nunnery at Killeevy. Also called *Bline, Darerca.* [d. c. 518]
St. Gour, solitary. [d. c. 575]
St. Sexburga, Abbess of Ely, widow. Also called *Sexburgh.* [d. 699]
St. Modwenna, virgin. Also called *Modwena, Modwina,* or *Monenna.* [d. 7th century]
St. Godeleva, laywoman and martyr. Locally invoked against sore throats. Also called *Godeleine, Godelive.* [d. 1070]
St. Mary Goretti, virgin and martyr. Also called *Maria.* [d. c. 1902] Optional Memorial.

The Beatified
Blessed Thomas Alfield, martyr. [d. 1585]

BIRTHDATES

1747 *John Paul Jones,* American naval officer, born in Scotland; known for his highly successful campaign against the British; honored with the only gold medal awarded by Congress to a naval officer in the Revolution, 1787. [d. July 18, 1792]

1755 *John Flaxman,* English sculptor; as designer with Josiah Wedgewood's pottery company, was responsible for the cameo-like decorations which became the *Wedgewood* trademark. [d. December 7, 1826]

1759 *Joshua Barney,* U.S. naval officer, prominent in American Revolution and War of 1812. [d. December 1, 1818]

1766 *Alexander Wilson,* U.S. ornithologist born in Scotland; pioneered science of *ornithology* in America, collecting and recording specimens for entire East Coast; published multi-volume work considered a pioneering effort in the field. [d. August 23, 1813]

1796 *Nicholas I,* Emperor of Russia, 1825–55, a reactionary ruler whose reign was marked by militarism and bureaucracy. [d. March 2, 1855]

1831 *Daniel Coit Gilman,* U.S. educator; first president of *Johns Hopkins University;* first president of *Carnegie Institution,* Washington, D.C. [d. October 13, 1908]

1832 *Maximilian (Ferdinand Maximilian Joseph),* Archduke of Austria, 1864–67; Emperor of Mexico, 1864–67 under auspices of French Emperor Napoleon III. Condemned by court martial and shot to death. [d. June 19, 1867]

1858 *José Miguel Gómez,* Cuban soldier, patriot; president, 1909–13. [d. June 13, 1921]

1859 *Verner von Heidenstam,* Swedish author, poet; Nobel Prize in literature, 1916. [d. May 20, 1940]

1863 *Ronald McKenna,* British politician; first Lord of Admiralty, 1908–11; Chairman of Midland Bank, Ltd., 1919–43. [d. September 6, 1943]

1875 *Roger Ward Babson,* U.S. statistician, economist; pioneered in developing charts to forecast business trends (*Babson charts*); presidential candidate, 1940. Founded *Babson Institute,* 1919; *Webber College,* 1927; *Utopia College,* 1946. [d. March 5, 1967]

1877 *Robert Morris Ogden,* U.S. psychologist, educator. [d. March 2, 1959]

1896 *James Spencer Love,* U.S. textile manufacturer; founder of Burlington Industries, 1923. [d. January 20, 1962]

1903 *(Alex) Hugo (Teodor) Theorell,* Swedish biochemist; Nobel Prize in physiology or medicine for his work on enzymes, 1955. [d. August 15, 1982]

1907 *Frida Kahlo,* Mexican artist; known for her self-portraits. [d. July 13, 1954]

1909 *Andrei Gromyko,* Russian diplomat; long-time Minister of Foreign Affairs; President of the U.S.S.R., 1985–88. [d. July 2, 1989]

1915 *LaVerne Andrews,* U.S. singer; member of the musical group, *Andrews Sisters.* [d. May 8, 1967]

1918 *Sebastian Cabot,* British actor; known for his role as Mr. French on television series, *Family Affair,* 1966–71. [d. August 23, 1977]

1921 *Nancy Davis Reagan,* U.S. First Lady; wife of Ronald Wilson Reagan, 40th U.S. President.

1923 *Wojciech Witbold Jaruzelski,* Polish political leader, soldier; Chairman, Council of Ministers, 1981–85; President, Council of State, 1985–90.

1925 *Merv Griffin,* U.S. entertainer, talk-show host, businessman.

Bill Haley (William John Clifford, Jr.), U.S. singer, musician; known for his song *Rock Around the Clock.* [d. February 9, 1981]

1927 *Janet Leigh (Jeanette Morrison),* U.S. actress.

Pat Paulsen, U.S. comedian. [d. April 25, 1997]

1932 *Della Reese (Delloreese Patricia Early),* U.S. entertainer; plays Tess on the TV drama *Touched by an Angel,* 1994– .

1937 *Vladimir Ashkenazy,* Russian pianist; international concert star.

Ned Beatty, U.S. actor.

1946 *George Walker Bush,* U.S. politician; governor of Texas, 1994– .

Sylvester Stallone, U.S. film actor, writer, director.

1948 *Brad Park,* Canadian hockey player; elected to Hall of Fame, 1988.

1952 *Shelley Hack,* U.S. model, actress.

1957 *Ronald (Ron) Duguay,* Canadian hockey player.

Susan Elizabeth Ford, daughter of Gerald Rudolph Ford, 38th U.S. president.

HISTORICAL EVENTS

1189 *Henry II* of England, dies and is succeeded by *Richard I.*

1415 *Jan Hus,* Bohemian religious reformer and nationalist, is burned at the stake for heresy.

1535 *Sir Thomas More* is beheaded for refusal to recognize *Henry VIII* of England as the supreme head of the church.

1540 The marriage of *Henry VIII* of England and *Anne of Cleves* is declared invalid.

1553 *Edward VI* of England dies and is succeeded by *Queen Mary I.*

1777 British troops capture *Fort Ticonderoga (American Revolution).*

1854 First state convention of the *Republican Party* is held in Jackson, Michigan.

1898 By a joint resolution of Congress, *Hawaii* is declared a U.S. territory.

1917 Col. *T. E. Lawrence (Lawrence of Arabia)* leads a force of Arabs in capturing *Aqaba* from the Turks (*World War I*).

1919 First Atlantic crossing by *dirigible* is completed by Major *G. H. Scott* in British dirigible *R-34.*

1933 First major league all-star *baseball game* is played at Chicago's Comiskey Park.

1936 The *United Steelworkers of America* is formed.

1943 U.S. naval forces are victorious over Japanese in *Battle of Kula Gulf* in the *Solomon Islands (World War II).*

1955 *Marcelo Caetano* is appointed president of Portugal.

1957 *Althea Gibson* becomes the first black woman to win the All-England Championship in singles tennis at Wimbledon.

1958 *Adolfo Lopez Mateos* is elected president of Mexico.

1962 The first *hydrogen bomb* to be tested in the continental U.S. is detonated at an underground test site in Nevada.

1964 *Nyasaland* gains independence from Great Britain as the African state of *Malawai. H. Kamazu Banda* is named prime minister.

1966 *H. Kamazu Banda* is inaugurated as the first president of Malawi.

1967 Civil war breaks out in *Nigeria* after the eastern region declares its independence as the *Republic of Biafra.*

1975 *The Comoros Islands* in the Indian Ocean declare their independence from France.

1978 A Roman Catholic mass is held in the House of Commons Chapel in *Westminster Palace* for the first time since the Reformation.

1983 The U.S. Supreme Court rules that *retirement plans* must pay the same monthly pension benefits to both men and women.

1990 *President Petar Mladenov* of Bulgaria resigns.

july

JULY
7

HOLIDAYS

Belgium
Ommegang Pageant
Medieval pageant presented in the Grand Place in Brussels recreating an entertainment given in honor of *Charles V* and his court.

Solomon Islands
Independence Day
Commemorates the gaining of independence from British rule, 1978.

Tanzania
Saba Saba Peasants Day

Yugoslavia
Serbian Uprising Day

RELIGIOUS CALENDAR

The Saints
St. Pantaenus, one of the Fathers of the Church. Nicknamed the *Sicilian Bee.* [d. c. 200]
St. Palladius, bishop and missionary. Apostle of the Scots. [d. 432]
St. Felix, Bishop of Nantes. [d. 582]
St. Ethelburga, St. Ercongota, and *St. Sethrida,* virgins. Ethelburga is also called *Aubierge* or *Edelburge* by the French. [d. c. 664 and 660]
St. Hedda, Bishop of Winchester. [d. 705]
St. Maelruain, abbot and founder of the *Monastery of Tallaght.* Most influential figure in the reform movement of the Culdees, a monastic community in Ireland between 8th and 10th century. [d. 792]
St. Boisil, Abbot of Melrose. Also called *Boswell.* [d. 664] Feast formerly February 23.

The Beatified
Blessed Benedict XI, pope. Elected 1303. [d. 1304]
Blessed Roger Dickenson and his companions, martyrs. [d. 1591]

BIRTHDATES

1586 *Thomas Hooker,* American clergyman, colonist; founded *Hartford, Connecticut;* called the *Father of Connecticut.* [d. July 19, 1647]

1673 *George Graham,* English watchmaker; developed many specialized astronomical instruments for Edmund Halley, James Bradley, and the French Academy. [d. November 16, 1751]

1752 *Joseph Marie Jacquard,* French inventor of first *machine loom* to weave intricate patterns; the machine was controlled by cards containing patterned perforations, very much like the Hollerith cards later developed for computers. [d. August 7, 1834]

1843 *Camillo Golgi,* Italian physician; known for study of nervous system; Nobel Prize in physiology or medicine for study of *nervous system* and cell distribution (with R. C. Santiago), 1906. [d. January 21, 1926]

1860 *Gustav Mahler,* Bohemian composer, conductor. [d. May 18, 1911]

1887 *Marc Chagall,* Russian-born artist; works include paintings and engravings, murals, costumes, ceramics, stained-glass windows; avante-garde style influenced by Fauvism and Cubism. [d. March 28, 1985]

1895 *Julius Jennings Hoffman,* U.S. judge; presided over the controversial *Chicago Seven* trial, 1969–70. [d. July 1, 1983]

1899 *George Cukor,* U.S. film director; director for Metro Goldwyn Mayer, 1933–82. [d. January 24, 1983]

1901 *Vittorio De Sica,* Italian film director. [d. November 13, 1974]

1906 *(Leroy Robert) Satchel Paige,* U.S. baseball player; generally regarded as one of professional baseball's greatest pitchers; elected to Baseball Hall of Fame, 1971. [d. June 8, 1982]

1907 *Robert A(nson) Heinlein,* U.S. science fiction writer. [d. May 8, 1988]

1908 *Harriette Louisa Simpson Arnow,* U.S. author; wrote novels about Appalachian life; author of *The Dollmaker.* [d. March 22, 1986]

1911 *Gian Carlo Menotti,* Italian composer, librettist, producer; Pulitzer Prize in music, 1950 and 1954. Composer of *The Medium, The Telephone,* and *Amahl and the Night Visitors,* the first opera written for television, 1951; recipient of the Lifetime Achievement Award (Kennedy Center), 1984.

1917 *Lawrence O'Brien,* U.S. government official, politician; active in presidential campaigns of John F. Kennedy and George McGovern; U.S. Postmaster General, 1965–68. [d. September 28, 1990]

1919 *William Kunstler,* U.S. lawyer, noted for his flamboyant style and defense of U.S. political activists. [d. September 4, 1995]

1922 *Pierre Cardin,* French fashion designer.

1927 *Carl H. (Doc) Severinsen,* U.S. musician, bandleader; known for his musical direction on the *Tonight Show, 1967–92.*

1928 *Vince Edwards (Vincent Edward Zoino),* U.S. actor; starred in the television series, *Ben Casey, 1961–66.* [d. March 11, 1996]

1938 *Edmund G. Brown, Jr.,* U.S. politician, lawyer; Governor of California, 1959–82. [d. February 16, 1996]

1940 *Ringo Starr (Richard Starkey),* British musician; drummer for The Beatles.

1946 *Joe Spano,* U.S. actor; known for his role as Henry Goldblum on television series, *Hill Street Blues.*

1949 *Shelley Duvall,* U.S. actress.

1954 *Andre Nolan Dawson,* U.S. baseball player; outfielder, Montreal Expos and Chicago Cubs; National League Most Valuable Player, 1987.

1955 *Leonard Harold (Len) Barker, II,* U.S. baseball player; pitched perfect game, 1981.

1960 *Ralph Sampson,* U.S. basketball player; forward, Houston Rockets; National Basketball Association Rookie of the Year, 1984.

Lisa Leslie, U.S. basketball player; Olympic gold medalist for basketball, 1996.

HISTORICAL EVENTS

1307 *Edward I* of England dies and is succeded by *Edward II.*

1572 *Sigismund II* of Poland dies, ending the *Jagellon Dynasty;* Poland becomes an elective kingdom.

1807 *Treaty of Tilsit* is signed by Russia, Prussia, and France, ending the fighting among them and bringing Russia into secret alliance with Napoleon.

1839 The murder of Chinese villagers by drunken British seamen precipitates the *First Opium War.*

1875 The E. Anheuser Brewing Association (later *Anheuser-Busch Companies*) is incorporated in Missouri.

1912 *Jim Thorpe* wins his first Olympic gold medal in the pentathlon event.

1919 The German government ratifies the *Versailles Treaty* ending *World War I.*

1946 *Mother Frances Xavier Cabrini* is canonized in ceremonies conducted by Pope Pius XII; she is the first American to be canonized.

1948 First *WAVE* enlisted women (Women Appointed for Voluntary Emergency) are sworn into Regular *U.S. Navy.*

1968 President Lyndon Johnson signs a bill making it a federal crime to desecrate a *U.S. flag.*

1969 French and English are designated as official languages of *Canada.*

1978 *Joseph Conombo* is elected premier of Upper Volta.

Solomon Islands gain independence from Great Britain.

1979 First civilian elections since 1966 take place in *Nigeria.*

1981 U.S. President Ronald Reagan nominates *Sandra Day O'Connor* to become a Supreme Court justice; she becomes the first woman member of the *U.S. Supreme Court.*

Solar Challenger, the first solar-powered airplane without storage batteries, flies across the English Channel.

1985 West German tennis player, *Boris Becker,* becomes the youngest male ever to win the Wimbledon singles title.

1987 Lieutenant Colonel *Oliver North* begins testimony at Congressional hearings concerning his involvement in the diversion of funds generated from Iranian arms sales to Nicaraguan contra rebels. *(Iran-contra affair)*

july

JULY
8

RELIGIOUS CALENDAR

The Saints

St. Aquila and *St. Prisca.* Prisca also called *Priscilla.* [d. first century]

St. Procopius, martyr. [d. 303]

St. Kilian, bishop, *and his companions,* martyrs. [d. c. 689]

St. Withburga, virgin. Also called *Withburge.* [d. c. 743]

St. Adrian III, pope. Elected 884. [d. 885]

St. Grimbald, monk. Also called *Grimald.* [d. 903]

St. Sunniva and her companions. [d. c. 10th century]

St. Raymund of Toulouse, Canon Regular. [d. 1118]

St. Urith of Chittlehampton, virgin and founder of Church of Chittlehampton. Also called *Erth,* or *Hieritha.* [death date unknown]

The Beatified

Blessed Eugenius III, pope. Elected 1145. [d. 1153]

BIRTHDATES

1478 *Giangiorgio Trissino,* Italian writer, scholar; protègè of Popes Leo X, Clement VII, and Paul III; urged the standardization of Italian language, made up of parts from various Italian dialects. [d. December 8, 1550]

1621 *Jean de La Fontaine,* French poet, fabulist; created 12 volumes of fables, 1668–94. [d. March 13, 1695]

1838 *Count Ferdinand von Zeppelin,* German soldier, aeronautical engineer; responsible for construction of first rigid-bodied airship, 1900. [d. March 8, 1917]

1857 *Alfred Binet,* French psychologist; with Thèodore Simon, developed standard for measuring degrees of intelligence (*Binet* or *Binet-Simon* test). [d. October 18, 1911]

1867 *Käthe Kollwitz,* German printmaker, sculptor, etcher, and painter. [d. April 22, 1945]

1887 *Hermann Rauschning,* German statesman; noted for his strong anti-Nazi stance during World War II; immigrated to the U.S., 1942; author of *The Revolution of Nihilism* and other anti-Nazi works. [d. 1982]

1892 *Richard Aldington,* British novelist, poet. [d. July 27, 1962]

1895 *Igor Yevgenyevich Tamm,* Russian physicist; Nobel Prize in physics for discovery of *Cherenkov effect* in which radiated electrons accelerate in water to speeds greater than that of light in the same medium (with P. A. Cherenkov and I. M. Frank), 1958. [d. April 12, 1971]

1898 *Alec (Alexander Raban) Waugh,* British novelist; brother of Evelyn Waugh. [d. September 3, 1981]

1899 *David E(li) Lilienthal,* U.S. government official, lawyer; director of the Tennessee Valley Authority, 1933–45, seeing it become the largest producer of electricity in America; Chairman, Atomic Energy Commission, 1947–50. [d. January 15, 1981]

1906 *Philip (Cortelyou) Johnson,* U.S. architect, theorist; developer and proponent of *International Style* of architecture.

1907 *George Wilcken Romney,* U.S. businessman, politician; Governor of Michigan, 1962–69. [d. July 26, 1995]

1908 *Louis Jordan,* U.S. musician. [d. February 4, 1975]

Nelson Aldrich Rockefeller, U.S. politician; Governor of New York, 1959–73; U.S. Vice-President, 1974–77. [d. January 26, 1979]

1913 *Walter Francis Kerr,* U.S. journalist, playwright; drama critic for *New York Herald Tribune,* 1951–56, and *New York Times.* [d. October 9, 1996]

1917 *Faye Emerson*, U.S. actress; noted for her starring film roles during the 1940s; one of the pioneers of early television; hosted a late-night interview show which set precedent for later shows of the same type. [d. March 9, 1983]

1926 *John David Dingell, Jr.,* U.S. politician; Congressman, 1956–; Chairman, Energy and Commerce Commission.

Elisabeth Kubler-Ross, U.S. psychiatrist, author; known for books and research on death and dying.

1929 *Shirley Ann Grau,* U.S. author; Pulitzer Prize for *The Keeper of the House,* 1965.

1931 *Roone Pinckney Arledge,* U.S. television executive; President, American Broadcasting Company News and Sports; inducted into the Academy of Television, Arts, and Science Hall of Fame, 1990.

1932 *Jerry Vale (Gerano Louis Vitaliamo),* U.S. singer; known for his renditions of *Innamorata,* 1956, and *Dommage, Dommage,* 1966.

1933 *Marty Feldman,* British comic actor. [d. December 2, 1982]

1935 *Steve Lawrence,* U.S. singer, actor.

1942 *William Philip (Phil) Gramm,* U.S. economist, politician; Senator, 1984–; co-author of Gramm-Rudman law for balancing the federal budget, 1985.

1946 *Cynthia Kathleen Gregory,* U.S. ballerina; principal dancer, American Ballet Theatre.

1948 *Kim Darby,* U.S. actress.

1952 *John Harold (Jack) Lambert,* U.S. football player.

Anna Quindlen, U.S. journalist; Pulitzer Prize winner for commentary in 1992.

1958 *Kevin Bacon,* U.S. actor; known for his performances in *The River Wild,* 1994 and *Apollo 13,* 1995.

1962 *Joan Osborne,* U.S. pop singer.

HISTORICAL EVENTS

1497 *Vasco da Gama* leaves Lisbon on his voyage to India during which he discovers the *Cape of Good Hope.*

1709 *Battle of Poltava* is a resounding victory for *Peter the Great* over *Charles XII* of Sweden and marks Russia's emergence as the dominant power in northern Europe *(Great Northern War).*

1853 U.S. Commodore *Matthew Perry* and his fleet arrive at *Edo Bay* with first formal bid for trade and diplomatic relations with *Japan.*

1859 *Oscar I* of Sweden dies and is succeeded by *Charles XV.*

1889 Last bare-knuckles championship *boxing* match is staged between *John L. Sullivan* and *Jake Kilrain.* Kilrain is defeated after 75 rounds.

1895 The *Delagoa Bay Railway* is opened from Johannesburg and Pretoria to the sea, giving the Boers in the Transvaal an economic outlet free of British influence.

1896 *William Jennings Bryan* delivers his "Cross of Gold"

speech to the Democratic National Convention.

1907 *Follies of 1907,* the first edition of what later became known as the *Ziegfeld Follies,* premieres in New York.

1937 *Peel Report* of Great Britain recommends dividing *Palestine* into Arab and Jewish states.

1944 U.S. naval bombardment of Japanese-held *Guam* begins *(World War II).*

U.S. troops capture *Saipan Island* from the Japanese in one of the bloodiest battles of the Pacific war zone *(World War II).*

1950 U.S. President *Harry S. Truman* appoints General *Douglas MacArthur* commander-in-chief of all U.N. forces in Korea.

1951 Celebrations marking the city's 2,000th birthday are held in *Paris.*

1954 Colonel *Carlos Castillo Armas* becomes president of Guatemala.

1963 U.S. government bans all financial transactions with *Cuba.*

1966 King *Mwambutsa* is deposed by his son, Prince *Charles Ndinzeye,* after a fifty-year reign in Burundi.

1971 *Frank Fitzsimmons* is elected president of the *International Brotherhood of Teamsters.*

1975 Argentine cabinet of President *Isabel Perón* resigns.

1976 Former U.S. President *Richard M. Nixon* is ordered disbarred by a New York

july

court for obstructing the due administration of justice during his presidency.

Indonesia launches a communications satellite from Cape Canaveral in the U.S.; the spacecraft links 40 Indonesian cities with telephone and television signals. (The only other countries with domestic satellite systems are the U.S., Canada, and the Soviet Union.)

1978 *Alessandro Pertini* is elected the first Socialist president of Italy. He succeeds *Giovanni Leone* who resigns amidst charges of corruption.

1979 New constitution is approved in the *Congo*.

1986 *Kurt Waldheim* is inaugurated as president of Austria amidst allegations of his involvement in Nazi war crimes.

1988 *President François Mitterand* of France is reelected.

HOLIDAYS

Argentina
Independence Day
Commemorates Argentina's declaration of independence from Spain, 1816.

RELIGIOUS CALENDAR

The Saints
St. Everild, virgin. Also called *Everildis.* [d. c. 700]
St. Nicholas Pieck and his companions, the martyrs of Gorkum. [d. 1572]
St. Veronica Giuliani, virgin, abbess, and mystic. [d. 1727]
The Martyrs of Orange. [d. 1794]
The Martyrs of China, under the Boxers. [d. 1900]

The Beatified
Blessed Jane of Reggio, virgin. [d. 1491]

BIRTHDATES

1578 *Ferdinand II, Holy Roman Emperor,* 1619; deposed by Bohemian Protestants, beginning *Thirty Years' War.* [d. February 15, 1637]

1764 *Ann Radcliffe,* English gothic novelist. [d. February 7, 1823]

1775 *Matthew Gregory (Monk) Lewis,* English gothic novelist, playwright, poet; inspired by Ann Radcliffe (see above). [d. May 14, 1818]

1777 *Henry Hallam,* English historian; his son Arthur is subject of Alfred Lord Tennyson's *In Memoriam.* [d. January 21, 1859]

1819 *Elias Howe,* U.S. inventor; developed the *sewing machine,* for which he was awarded patent rights after lengthy conflict with *Isaac M. Singer,* 1854. [d. October 3, 1867]

1835 *Tomàs Estrada Palma,* first president of Cuba, 1902–1906. [d. November 4, 1908]

1839 *John D(avison) Rockefeller,* U.S. industrialist, philanthropist; founder of Standard Oil Co., 1870; built a financial empire; devoted more than $500 million to philanthropic causes. [d. May 23, 1937]

1845 *Sir George Howard Darwin,* British astronomer, mathematician; authority on tidal friction as cause of decrease in earth's rotation and angular momentum; son of *Charles Darwin.* [d. December 7, 1912]

1856 *Nikola Tesla,* U.S. electrical engineer, inventor born in Yugoslavia; developed induction, synchronous, and split-phase motors; conceived and built new types of generators and transformers which constituted basis of *alternating-current* electric power system. [d. January 7, 1943]

Daniel Guggenheim, U.S. industrialist; son of *Meyer Guggenheim;* responsible for development and management of American Smelting and Refining Company, which became the largest and most modern mining enterprise in the world, 1905–19. Established *Daniel and Florence Guggenheim Foundation* and *Daniel Guggenheim Fund for the Promotion of Aeronautics.* [d. September 28, 1930]

1858 *Franz Boas,* U.S. anthropologist born in Germany; Columbia University's first professor of anthropology; greatly influenced many subsequently great anthropologists such as Margaret Mead and Ruth Benedict. His careful study and documentation destroyed the theory of innate racial differences. [d. December 22, 1942]

Richard Achilles Ballinger, U.S. lawyer, administrator; Secretary of the Interior, 1909–11. [d. June 6, 1922]

1878 *H.V. (Hans von) Kaltenborn,* U.S. journalist, radio commentator, news analyst; chief news commentator for

july

Columbia Broadcasting System, 1929–40; chief commentator for National Broadcasting Company, 1940–55; noted for his coverage of world news events. [d. June 14, 1965]

1887 *Samuel Eliot Morison*, U.S. historian; Professor of History, Harvard University, 1925–55; historian of naval operations in World War II, 1942–45; prolific writer whose 25 works in various aspects of American history won him wide acclaim; Pulitzer Prizes in biography, 1941, 1959. [d. May 15, 1976]

1894 *Dorothy Thompson*, U.S. journalist; syndicated columnist with *New York Herald Tribune*, 1936–42; one of the most widely-read columnists of the 1930s and 1940s. [d. January 31, 1961]

1901 *Barbara Hamilton Cartland*, British author, dramatist; considered to be the best-selling novelist in the world; has written over 350 books; called the *Queen of Romance*.

1908 *Paul Brown*, U.S. football coach, executive; elected to Pro Football Hall of Fame, 1967. [d. August 5, 1991]

1916 *Edward (Richard George) Heath*, British statesman; Prime Minister, 1970–74.

1919 *Helen Lenore Vogt Van Slyke*, U.S. author; wrote the best-sellers, *A Necessary Woman*, 1979, and *No Love Lost*, 1979. [d. July 3, 1979]

1926 *Ben Ray Mottelson*, Danish physicist; Nobel Prize in physics for discovery of connection between collective and particle motion in *atomic*

nucleus (with J. Rainwater and A. N. Bohr), 1975.

1927 *Ed Ames (Edmund Dantes Urick)*, U.S. singer, actor, producer; member of the vocal group, the *Ames Brothers*.

Leonard Patrick (Red) Kelly, Canadian hockey player.

1929 *Hassan II*, King of Morocco, 1961– .

1932 *Donald Rumsfeld*, U.S. government official, business executive; Secretary of Defense, 1975–77.

1933 *Oliver Wolf Sacks*, British writer, neurologist; known for his book, *Awakenings*, which was later made into a film starring Robin Williams.

1937 *David Hockney*, British artist; best known for his double portraits and California-inspired paintings of water and swimming pools.

1939 *Brian Dennehy*, U.S. actor.

1945 *Dean Koontz*, U.S. writer; author of *Watchers*.

1947 *O(renthal) J(ames) Simpson*, U.S. football player, actor.

1951 *Angelica Huston*, U.S. actress; Oscar winner for *Prizzi's Honor*, 1985.

1952 *John Tesh*, U.S. TV broadcaster, musician.

1954 *Debbie Sledge*, U.S. singer; member of the rock group, *Sister Sledge*.

Jimmy Smits, U.S. actor; known for roles on TV dramas *LA Law* and *NYPD Blue*.

1956 *Tom Hanks*, U.S. actor; Academy Award (Best Actor) for both *Philadelphia*, 1994, and *Forrest Gump*, 1995.

HISTORICAL EVENTS

1386 *Leopold III* of Austria is defeated and killed by the Swiss at *Sempach* during Swiss struggle for independence.

1686 *League of Augsburg* is created, setting the Holy Roman Empire, Spain, Sweden, Saxony, and Palatinate against *Louis XIV* of France.

1755 English General *Edward Braddock* is defeated near *Ft. Duquesne* by French and Indians at *Battle of the Wilderness (French and Indian War)*.

1810 *Holland* is annexed to France after the abdication of Holland's King *Louis Bonaparte*, brother of France's Napoleon Bonaparte.

1816 *Argentina* gains independence from Spain.

1850 U.S. President *Zachary Taylor* dies in office and is succeeded by *Millard Fillmore*.

1944 British and Canadian forces unite to capture *Caen, France*, forcing back the German defense line *(World War II)*.

1962 *Trans-Tasman submarine telephone cable* linking Sydney, Australia, and Auckland, New Zealand, is formally opened.

1963 An agreement creating the *Federation of Malaysia* is signed by Malaya, Sarawak, Sabah, and Singapore.

1973 *Clarence M. Kelley*, former Kansas City, Missouri, police chief, is sworn in as Director of the *FBI*.

HOLIDAYS

Bahamas

Independence Day
Commemorates Bahamas' achievement of independence from Great Britain, 1973.

Japan

Bon or O-Bon or Feast of Fortune

Mauritania

Armed Forces Day

RELIGIOUS CALENDAR

The Saints

The Seven Brothers and *St. Felicity,* their mother, martyrs. Invoked for the birth of male children. Felicity also called *Felicitas.* [d. 2nd century]

St. Rufina and *St. Secunda,* virgins and martyrs. [d. c. 257]

St. Amalburga of Sustern, widow. Also called *Amelberga, Amelia.* [d. c. 690]

St. Anthony and *St. Theodosius Pechersky,* abbots of the caves of Kiev; founders of the first Russian monastery. [d. 1073, 1074]

The Beatified

Blessed Emmanuel Ruiz, Francis Masabki, and their companions, the *Martyrs of Damascus.* [d. 1860]

BIRTHDATES

1509 *John Calvin (Jean Chauvin),* French theologian,
ecclesiastical reformer; brought into focus the scattered reform theologies of Europe. Founder of *Calvinism.* [d. May 27, 1564]

1723 *Sir William Blackstone,* English jurist; author of *Commentaries on the Law of England,* a history of the fundamental doctrines of law, 1765–69. [d. February 14, 1780]

1752 *David Humphreys,* American Revolutionary war officer, diplomat, poet. [d. February 21, 1818]

1792 *George Mifflin Dallas,* U.S. Vice-President, 1845–49. [d. December 31, 1864]

1825 *Richard King,* U.S. rancher, steamboatman; developed and controlled the *King Ranch,* the largest cattle ranch in the U.S. [d. April 14, 1885]

1830 *Camille Pissarro,* French Impressionist painter. [d. November 13, 1903]

1834 *Jan Neruda,* Czech poet, story writer, journalist, and critic. [d. August 22, 1891]

James (Abott) McNeill Whistler, U.S. painter, etcher; his *Arrangement in Gray and Black, No. 1: The Artist's Mother* (later known as *Whistler's Mother*) is among his most famous works. [d. July 17, 1903]

1839 *Adolphus Busch,* U.S. brewery executive; founded Anheuser-Busch Brewery in St. Louis. [d. October 10, 1913]

1867 *Finley Peter Dunne,* U.S. humorist, creator of *Mr. Dooley,* a nationally syndicated column whose main character issued pithy, humorous observations on the people and events of his time. [d. April 24, 1936]

1871 *Marcel Proust,* French novelist, known for his autobiographical *Remembrance of Things Past.* [d. November 18, 1922]

1875 *Mary McLeod Bethune,* U.S. educator, government administrator; first black woman to hold administrative position in U.S. federal government (Office of Minority Affairs). [d. May 18, 1955]

1885 *Mary O'Hara,* U.S. novelist; most famous for her novel *My Friend Flicka,* (1941) which was later adapted for the screen. [d. October 15, 1980]

1891 *Edith H. Quimby,* U.S. biophysicist; known for her contributions to the field of radiology. [d. October 11, 1982]

1895 *Carl Orff,* German composer; known for his neo-medieval style in such compositions as

july

Carmina Burana. [d. March 29, 1982]

Nahum Goldmann, German Zionist leader born in Lithuania; noted for his efforts at establishing the state of Israel; President of World Jewish Congress, 1951–78; President of World Zionist Organization, 1956–68. [d. August 29, 1982]

1897 *John Gilbert (John Pringle),* U.S. silent-screen actor. [d. January 9, 1936]

Manlio (Giovanni) Brosio, Italian statesman; leader of the Liberal party; Ambassador to Soviet Union, 1947–52; to Great Britain, 1952–54; to U.S. 1955–60; and to France, 1961–64; Secretary General of NATO, 1964–71. [d. March 14, 1980.]

1902 *Kurt Adler,* German organic chemist; Nobel Prize in chemistry for developing method for synthesizing organic compounds of the *diene group* (with O. P. H. Diels), 1950. [d. June 20, 1958]

Nicolás Guillén, Cuban poet. [d. 1989]

1917 *Magda Gabor,* Hungarian-born actress. [d. June 6, 1997]

1920 *David (McClure) Brinkley,* U.S. television news correspondent and commentator.

Owen Chamberlain, U.S. physicist; Nobel Prize in physics for discovery of *antiproton* (with E. G. Segræe), 1959.

1921 *Jacob (Jake) LaMotta,* U.S. boxer; portrayed by Robert DeNiro in 1981 film, *Raging Bull.*

1923 *Earl Henry Hamner, Jr.,* U.S. author; created the television series, *The Waltons* and *Falcon Crest.*

1926 *Hugo Banzer-Suarez,* Bolivian political leader; President of Bolivia, 1971–78.

Fred Gwynne, U.S. actor, author; known for his role as Herman Munster on the television show, *The Munsters,* 1964–68; Obie Award for *Grand Magic,* 1979. [d. July 2, 1993]

1927 *David N. Dinkins,* U.S. politician; Mayor of New York City, 1990–93.

1931 *Alice Munro,* Canadian writer; author of *Dance of the Happy Shades.*

1943 *Arthur Ashe,* U.S. professional tennis player. [d. February 6, 1993]

1945 *Ron Glass,* U.S. actor; known for his role as Ron Harris on television series, *Barney Miller,* 1975–82.

Virginia Wade, British tennis player; Wimbledon Women's Singles champion, 1977.

1947 *Arlo Guthrie,* U.S. folk-rock singer, son of Woody Guthrie (July 14); best known for his epic narrative *Alice's Restaurant.*

1960 *Roger Timothy Craig,* U.S. football player; fullback who became the first National Football League player to run, catch passes for 1,000 yards, 1985.

HISTORICAL EVENTS

1460 *Richard of York* defeats *Henry VI* of England at Northampton and takes him prisoner (*War of the Roses*).

1584 *William of Orange,* stadtholder of Holland and Zealand, is assassinated; he is succeeded by his son *Maurice of Nassau.*

1898 U.S. troops begin bombardment of *Santiago Harbor,* Cuba (*Spanish-American War*).

1913 Rumania declares war on Bulgaria (*Second Balkan War*).

1925 The trial of educator *John Scopes* begins in Tennessee. *Clarence Darrow* defends Scopes from charges of unlawfully teaching evolution in his classroom.

1934 *Franklin D. Roosevelt* becomes first U.S. president to visit South America.

1944 First jet combat plane begins operational service (*World War II*).

1945 Aircraft from 14 U.S. carriers begin striking mainland Japan (*World War II*).

1949 Soviet scientists detonate their first experimental *nuclear warhead* in the Ust-Urt desert.

1953 Soviet officials reveal that the head of internal security forces, *Lavrenti Beriya,* has been removed from office.

1962 *Kim Hyun Chul* is appointed premier of South Korea.

Telstar I, experimental communications satellite developed by American Telephone and Telegraph Co., is launched from Cape Canaveral and later relays live television pictures from Andover, Maine, to France and Great Britain.

1973 *Bahamas* become
  independent of Great Britain.

1994 *Leonid Kuchma* is elected
  president of Ukraine.

july

JULY
11

Mongolia
National Day

RELIGIOUS CALENDAR

The Saints

St. Pius I, pope and martyr. Elected 142. [d. c. 155]

St. Benedict, abbot; patriarch of Western monks. Founded the Benedictine order. Invoked against the devil, fever, and inflammatory and kidney diseases. Also called *Bennett.* [d. c. 547] Feast formerly March 21. Obligatory Memorial.

St. Drostan, Abbot of Deer. [d. c. 610]

St. John, Bishop of Bergamo. [d. c. 690]

St. Hildulf, bishop. Also called *Hidulphus.* [d. c. 707]

St. Olga, widow. [d. 969]

The Martyrs of Indo-China, I. [d. 1745–1840]

The Beatified

Blessed Adrian Fortescue, martyr. [d. 1539]

BIRTHDATES

1274 *Robert I (the Bruce),* King and liberator of Scotland; defeated the forces of *Edward III* of England numerous times, finally forcing Edward to recognize Scotland's independence, 1328. Died of leprosy. [d. June 7, 1329]

1657 *Frederick I,* first King of Prussia, 1701–13. [d. February 25, 1713]

1767 *John Quincy Adams,* U.S. politician, diplomat, political writer; sixth President of U.S., 1825–29. [d. February 23, 1848]

1838 *John Wanamaker,* U.S. merchant, government official; founded one of first major department stores in U.S.; Postmaster General, 1889–93. [d. December 12, 1922]

1861 *George William Norris,* U.S. politician, lawyer; drafted the *20th Amendment* to U.S. Constitution, specifying the terms of the president and the Congress, as well as determining succession to presidency in case of death of the president. [d. August 29, 1944]

1888 *Bartolomeo Vanzetti,* Italian fish merchant, political radical; accused with *Nicola Sacco* (April 22) of murder of factory workers in South Braintree, Massachusetts, during a robbery attempt. Their cause won world-wide sympathy and roused protests against the system of justice that had condemned them. [executed August 23, 1927]

1890 *Arthur William Tedder, 1st Baron Tedder,* British air chief marshal; active in World War I in France and Egypt; instrumental in development of Royal Air Force training and development; Chief of Air Staff, 1946–50. [d. June 3, 1967]

1893 *Thomas B(ayard) McCabe,* U.S. business executive; president, Scott Paper Company, 1927–67; Chairman, Federal Reserve Board, 1948–51. [d. May 27, 1982]

1897 *Theophilus Eugene (Bull) Connor,* U.S. police officer; Commissioner of Public Safety during the Alabama Freedom Ride and civil rights demonstrations. [d. March 8, 1973]

1899 *E(lwyn) B(rooks) White,* U.S. author, editor; frequent contributor to *New Yorker* magazine, 1938–43; famous children's books include *Stuart Little* and *Charlotte's Web.* [d. October 1, 1985]

1906 *Harry Von Zell,* U.S. entertainer; known for his mellow voice; provided support for such early entertainers as George Burns, Jack Benny, Fred Allen, and Eddie Cantor. [d. November 21, 1981]

1916 *Aleksander Prokhorov,* Russian scientist; Nobel Prize in physics for research in *quantum electronics,* leading to development of *maser principle* (with C. H. Towne and N. G. Basov), 1964.

1920 *Yul Brynner,* U.S. actor. [d. October 10, 1985]

1925 *Nikolai Gedda (Nikolai Ustinov),* Swedish operatic tenor.

1927 *Theodore Maiman,* U.S. physicist; developed the first working model of the laser in the United States.

1931 *Tab Hunter,* U.S. actor; teen idol of the 1950's.

1951 *Bonnie Pointer,* U.S. singer; former member of the rock group, *Pointer Sisters.*

1953 *Leon Spinks,* U.S. boxer; Olympic gold medalist, 1976; defeated Muhammed Ali in a heavyweight title bout, 1977.

1958 *Mark Lester,* British actor; starred in the film, *Oliver,* 1968.

HISTORICAL EVENTS

1302 *Philip IV* of France is defeated by the Flemish at *Courtrai.*

1533 *Pope Clement VII* excommunicates *Henry VIII* of England.

1804 *Alexander Hamilton* is fatally wounded in pistol duel with *Aaron Burr,* former U.S. Vice-President.

1890 *Wyoming* is admitted to Union as the 44th state.

1921 *Mongolian People's Republic* is established.

1934 *Franklin D. Roosevelt* becomes the first U.S. President to sail through the *Panama Canal.*

1946 King *George VI* becomes the first British monarch since Charles II to visit *Canterbury Cathedral.* He attends a thanksgiving service for the building's preservation.

1955 *U.S. Air Force Academy* is dedicated at its temporary location at Lowry Air Force Base, Colorado.

1960 Czechoslovakian constitution is adopted, signifying a liberalizing of Czechoslovakian society and government.

Katangan provincial premier, *Moise Tshombe,* proclaims his state's secession from the *Republic of the Congo.*

1962 The first underwater crossing of the *English Channel* is completed by U.S. scuba diver, *Fred Baldasare.*

1963 Ecuadoran president, *Carlos Arosemena Monroy,* is overthrown in a coup d'etat.

1966 Canada and the U.S.S.R. sign agreement providing for first direct air service between Soviet Union and North America.

1967 The Vatican reports that *Albania* has closed its last Roman Catholic church.

1974 *Burundi* adopts its constitution, amid hostilities between Tutsis and Hutus.

1979 U.S. space station *Skylab,* in orbit since 1973, returns to earth and disintegrates over Indian Ocean.

1985 *Nolan Ryan,* of the Houston Astros baseball team, becomes the first major league pitcher to strike out 4,000 batters.

1995 U.S. President *Bill Clinton* offers full diplomatic recognition to *Vietnam* after twenty-two years.

july

JULY
12

HOLIDAYS

Kiribati
Independence Day

São Tome and Principe
Anniversary of National Independence
Commemorates the coming of independence after 500 years of Portuguese rule, 1975.

Northern Ireland
Orangeman's Day
Commemorates the Battle of the Boyne, 1690.

RELIGIOUS CALENDAR

The Saints
St. Hermagoras and *St. Fortunatus,* martyrs. [d. 1st century]

St. Jason. [d. 1st century]

St. Veronica, said to have wiped the brow of Jesus on his way to Calvary. [d. 1st century]

SS. Nabor and Felix, martyrs. [d. c. 303]

St. John the Iberian, abbot. [d. c. 1002]

St. John Gualbert, abbot. Founder of the Vallombrosan Benedictines; patron of foresters. [d. 1073]

The Beatified
Blessed Andrew of Rinn, [d. 1462]

BIRTHDATES

100BC *Gaius Julius Caesar,* Roman general, statesman, writer, soldier. [Assassinated March 15, 44 B.C.]

1590 *Pope Clement X,* pope 1670–76. [d. July 22, 1676]

1730 *Josiah Wedgwood,* English potter, inventor; baptized on this day; his pottery techniques gained him renown; developed *queen's ware,* a cream colored domestic earthenware, and *jasperware.* Maternal grandfather of Charles Darwin (February 12). [d. January 3, 1795]

1805 *Constantine Brumidi,* U.S. painter; best known work "The Apotheosis of Washington." [d. 1880]

1811 *Vissarion Grigorievich Belinski,* Russian critic; first widely publicized literary critic; his works are the foundation of Russian literary criticism. (Born June 30, Old Style calandar.) [d. June 7, 1848 (May 26, Old Style calandar)]

1813 *Claude Bernard,* French physiologist; noted for discoveries related to the liver and pancreas. [d. February 10, 1878]

1817 *Henry David Thoreau,* U.S. essayist, poet, naturalist; associated with *transcendentalist school* of 19th-century American literature. [d. May 6, 1862]

1828 *Nikolay Gavrilovich Chernyshevsky,* Russian revolutionary, philsopher, economist, novelist, critic; spent 24 years in exile in Siberia. [d. October 17, 1889]

1852 *Hipòlito Irigoyen,* Argentine President, 1916–22, 1928–30. [d. July 3, 1933]

1854 *George Eastman,* U.S. inventor, industrialist, philanthropist; founder of Eastman Kodak Company, which for many years held a virtual monopoly in the film and camera industry. Contributed more than $75 million to various institutions, including Massachusetts Institute of Technology and Tuskegee Institute. [d. March 14, 1932]

1884 *Amedeo Modigliani,* Italian modernist painter, sculptor. [d. January 24, 1920]

1895 *R(ichard) Buckminster Fuller,* U.S. engineer, architect, author; developer of *geodesic dome.* [d. July 1, 1983]

Kirsten Flagstad, Norwegian operatic soprano; renowned for Wagnerian interpretations. [d. December 7, 1962]

Oscar Hammerstein II, U.S. lyricist; collaborator with Richard Rodgers in numerous Broadway musicals. [d. August 23, 1960]

1904 *Pablo Neruda,* Chilean poet; Nobel Prize in literature, 1971. [d. September 23, 1973]

1908 *Milton Berle (Milton Berlinger),* U.S. television comedian; became known as *Mr. Television.*

1913 *Willis E. Lamb,* U.S. physicist; Nobel Prize in physics for experimental work in *electromagnetic phenomena,* 1955.

1917 *Andrew Wyeth,* U.S. painter; renowned for his disciplined and symbolic style and depth of feeling.

1922 *Mark Hatfield,* U.S. politician, political scientist; Governor of Oregon, 1959–67; U.S. Senator, 1967– .

1925 *Roger Bonham Smith,* U.S. auto executive.

1928 *Elias James Corey,* U.S. chemist; Nobel Prize for Chemistry, 1990.

1934 *Van Cliburn (Harvey Levan, Jr.),* U.S. concert pianist; won first prize at International Tchaikovsky Piano Competition, Moscow, 1958.

1937 *Bill Cosby,* U.S. comedian, actor.

Robert Carl (Bud) McFarlane, U.S. government official; National Security advisor to Ronald Reagan, 1983–85.

1943 *Christine Perfect McVie,* British singer, songwriter; member of the rock group, *Fleetwood Mac.*

1948 *Richard Simmons,* U.S. television personality, author; known for his health and fitness expertise.

1971 *Kristi Yamaguchi,* U.S. figure skater; Olympic gold medalist, 1992.

HISTORICAL EVENTS

1174 *Henry II* of England, does penance at Canterbury for the murder of *Thomas à Becket.*

1191 *Richard I, the Lion-Hearted* and his Crusaders capture *Acre (Third Crusade).*

1542 *Henry VIII* of England marries *Catherine Parr,* his sixth wife.

1690 *Battle of the Boyne* in Ireland is fought with *William III* of Orange victorious over *James II,* whom he had just driven from the throne of England.

1862 U.S. Congress authorizes *Congressional Medal of Honor* for gallantry in action by noncommissioned officers.

1906 In France, controversial *Dreyfus affair* (in which *Alfred Dreyfus,* a French Army officer, had been convicted of treason), ends with Dreyfus' conviction being overthrown after it is proven that he has been condemned on the basis of forged documents.

Émile Zola is primarily responsible for Dreyfus' retrial and release, especially through his *J'accuse.*

1941 British forces occupy *Syria (World War II).*

1948 The Democratic Party convenes in Philadelphia and nominates *Harry S. Truman* and *Alben W. Barkley* for president and vice president.

1953 United Nations fleet launches heavy air and sea attack on *Wonsan (Korean War).*

1975 *São Tomè* and *Principe,* tiny islands off the west coast of Africa, are the fourth independent country to emerge from the decolonization of Portugal's African territories.

1984 U.S. presidential candidate, Walter Mondale, selects *Geraldine Ferraro* as his running mate on the Democratic ticket. She is the first female vice-presidential candidate for a major party in U.S. history.

1998 *Jamal Mahuad Witt* is elected president of Ecuador.

july

JULY
13

HOLIDAYS

Tahiti
National Day Eve

Yugoslavia (Montenegro)
Public Holiday

RELIGIOUS CALENDAR

The Saints

St. Silas, companion and fellow worker of St. Paul. Also called *Silvanus.* [d. 1st century]

St. Maura and *St. Brigid.* Brigid also called *Britta.* [d. c. 5th century]

St. Eugenius, Bishop of Carthage. [d. 505]

St. Mildred, Abbess of Minister-in-Thanet and virgin. Also called *Mildthryth.* [d. c. 700]

St. Henry the Emperor, Holy Roman Emperor, 1014–1024; patron of Benedictine oblates. [d. 1024] Feast formerly July 15.

St. Francis Solano, Franciscan friar and missionary to Peru. [d. 1610]

The Beatified

Blessed James of Voragine, Archbishop of Genoa. [d. 1298]

Blessed Thomas Tunstal, martyr. [d. 1616]

BIRTHDATES

1608 *Ferdinand III* of Hungary, 1625–57; Holy Roman Emperor, 1637–57; signed Peace of Westphalia, 1648, ending *Thirty Years' War.* [d. April 2, 1657]

1793 *John Clare,* English poet; known as *Northamptonshire peasant poet.* [d. May 20, 1864]

1808 *Marie-Edmé-Patrice-Maurice MacMahon,* Comte de Mac-Mahon, duc de Magenta French politician, soldier; second president of Third Republic, 1873–79. [d. October 17, 1893]

1816 *Gustav Freytag,* German novelist, playwright; champion of German liberalism and the middle class. [d. April 30, 1895]

1821 *Nathan Bedford Forrest,* Confederate general in U.S. Civil War; First Grand Wizard of original *Ku Klux Klan.* [d. October 29, 1877]

1826 *Stanislao Cannizzaro,* Italian chemist; first to clearly define distinction between atomic and molecular weights. [d. May 10, 1910]

1859 *Sidney James Webb,* British socialist, economist; cofounder of the *London School of Economics* with wife, Beatrice, 1895. [d. October 13, 1947]

1886 *Edward Joseph Flanagan,* U.S. Roman Catholic priest; founder of *Boys Town,* Nebraska, a school and hostel for rehabilitating delinquent boys. [d. May 15, 1948]

1898 *Sidney Blackmer,* U.S. actor. [d. October 5, 1973]

1905 *F. Bosley Crowther,* U.S. film critic; film critic for the *New York Times,* 1940–67; an influential authority on motion-picture art. [d. March 7, 1981]

1913 *Dave Garroway,* U.S. television personality. [d. July 21, 1982]

1922 *Anker Joergensen,* Danish statesman; Prime Minister of Denmark, 1975–82.

1927 *Simone Veil,* French lawyer, politician; President of the Parliament of the European Community.

1928 *Bob Crane,* U.S. actor; known for his role as Robert Hogan on television series, *Hogan's Heroes,* 1965–71. [d. June 29, 1978]

1934 *Wole Soyinka,* Nigerian poet, dramatist; Nobel Prize in literature, 1986.

1935 *Jack French Kemp,* U.S. politician, football player; Congressman, 1970–88; Secretary of Housing and Urban Development, 1989–93; board member of Empower America, 1993– .

1940 *Patrick Stewart,* British actor.

1942 *Harrison Ford,* U.S. actor; known for leading roles in *Star Wars* and *Raiders of the Lost Ark.*

Roger McGuinn, U.S. musician; member of the rock group, *The Byrds.*

1946 *Richard (Cheech) Marin,* U.S. actor; starred in the *Cheech and Chong* movies and currently stars in the TV series *Nash Bridges.*

1963 *Bobby Carpenter,* U.S. hockey player; first American-born player to score over 50 goals in season, 1984–85.

HISTORICAL EVENTS

1787 The American Continental Congress passes the *Northwest Ordinance,* establishing the procedure for the creation of new states.

1793 *Jean Paul Marat,* French revolutionary leader, is assassinated by *Charlotte Corday.*

1841 *Straits Convention* is signed by major European powers, guaranteeing independence of *Turkey.*

1878 *Berlin Congress* provides for the dissolution of the *Ottoman Empire* after almost 600 years. *Montenegro, Romania,* and *Serbia* become independent.

1931 All banks in Germany close following failure of Germany's *Danatbank.*

1960 Massachusetts Senator *John F. Kennedy* is named the Democratic party's presidential candidate.

1962 *Eugene McNeely,* President of American Telephone and Telegraph Co., and *Jacques Marette,* French Minister of Communications, hold the first official trans-Atlantic telephone conversation via *Telstar.*

1965 The British House of Commons votes to eliminate *hanging* as a method of execution.

1970 The *Black Academy of Arts and Letters* establishes a black Hall of Fame. Historian *W.E.B. Dubois,* educator *Carter Woodson,* and artist *Henry Tanner* are the first inductees.

1977 *Blackout* strikes *New York City* at 9:34 p.m. and lasts until the next day. The sweltering evening turns into a night of near-total chaos. Police arrest some 3,200 looters.

1985 *Live Aid,* a benefit rock concert to raise money for *African famine relief,* is staged simultaneously in London and Philadelphia, with worldwide broadcast via satellite.

1992 *Global Forum of Women* holds four-day meeting in Ireland.

1998 Premier *Ryutaro Itashimoto* of Japan announces his resignation.

july

JULY
14

HOLIDAYS

France, French Guiana, French Polynesia, New Caledonia, St. Pierre, Miquelon, Wallis and Futuna Islands
Bastille Day
Commemorates the fall of the Bastille and overthrow of the regime of King Louis XVI, 1789.

French West Indies, Monaco, Tahiti
National Holiday

Iran
Martyrdom of Imam Ali

Iraq
14th of July Revolution
Commemorates overthrow of King Faisal and proclamation of the republic, 1958.

Senegal
Day of Association

RELIGIOUS CALENDAR

The Saints
St. Deusdedit, Archbishop of Canterbury. [d. 664]
St. Marchelm, missionary. Also called *Marceaumes, Marcellinus, Marculf.* [d. c. 762]
St. Ulric of Zell, abbot. [d. 1093]
St Camillus de Lellis, priest and founder of the Ministers of the Sick; patron of nurses and the sick. [d. 1614] Optional Memorial.

The Beatified
Blessed Hroznata, martyr. [d. 1217]

Blessed Humbert of Romans, cardinal. [d. 1277]
Blessed Boniface of Savoy, Archbishop of Canterbury. [d. 1270]
Blessed Caspar de Bono, friar. [d. 1604]
Blessed Edoardo Giuseppe Rosaz. [beatified 1991]

BIRTHDATES

1602 *Jules Mazarin (Giulio Mazarini),* French cardinal, statesman born in Italy; succeeded *Richelieu* (September 9) as prime minister of France; greatly increased France's position as a European power. [d. March 9, 1661]

1743 *Gavrila Derzhavin,* Russian poet; considered one of the most influential and significant poets before Aleksander Pushkin. [d. July 21, 1816]

1794 *John Gibson Lockhart,* Scottish critic, editor, novelist, and biographer of Sir Walter Scott (August 15) and Robert Burns (January 25). Married to Scott's oldest daughter, Charlotte Sophia. [d. November 25, 1854]

1816 *Joseph Arthur Gobineau,* French writer, diplomat; first to propose the theory of *Aryan supremacy*

(Gobinism). [d. October 13, 1882]

1829 *Edward White Benson,* British theologian; Archbishop of Canterbury, 1882–96. [d. October 11, 1896]

1857 *Frederick Louis Maytag,* U.S. manufacturer; founder of Maytag Co., manufacturers of washing machines, 1907. [d. March 26, 1937]

1868 *Gertrude Bell,* British traveler, archaeologist, government official; an authority on Arabian culture; influential in molding administration of post-World War I *Mesopotamia.* [d. July 11/12, 1926]

1869 *Owen Wister,* U.S. novelist; his writings on life in Wyoming did much to create the popular romantic image of the American cowboy. [d. July 21, 1938]

1898 *Alexander Brook,* U.S. artist; known for his portraits of famous people of his period; called the *Unstruggling Artist.* [d. February 26, 1980]

1903 *Irving Stone,* U.S. author. [d. August 26, 1989]

1904 *Isaac Bashevis Singer,* U.S. author, born in Poland; novels are based on his life in the Jewish ghettos of eastern Europe; Nobel Prize in literature, 1978. [d. July 25, 1991]

1910 *William Denby Hanna*, U.S. cartoonist; created *Yogi Bear* and *The Flintstones* with Joseph Barbera.

1912 *Woody Guthrie (Woodrow Wilson Guthrie)*, U.S. folksinger, composer; father of Arlo Guthrie (July 10). [d. October 3, 1967]

1913 *Gerald (Rudolph J.) Ford*, U.S. lawyer, politician; Vice-President, 1973–74; 38th President of U.S., 1974–77. Succeeded to the presidency upon resignation of Richard M. Nixon; defeated in his bid for presidency, 1976.

1917 *Douglas Edwards*, U.S. radio performer, television personality. [d. October 13, 1990]

1918 *(Ernst) Ingmar Bergman*, Swedish film director, screenwriter.

1920 *Bella Abzug*, U.S. lawyer, politician; spokeswoman for peace, full employment, women's rights, environmental programs. [d. March 31, 1998]

1921 *Sir Geoffrey Wilkinson*, British chemist; Nobel Prize in chemistry for research in merger of organic and metallic atoms (with E. O. Fischer), 1973. [d. September 26, 1996]

1927 *John (William) Chancellor*, U.S. journalist, television newscaster; anchored the *Nightly News* for NBC, 1970–1982. [d. July 12, 1996]

1930 *Polly Bergen (Nellie Bergen)*, U.S. actress, executive of beauty products company.

1932 *Roosevelt (Rosey) Grier*, U.S. football player, actor.

1933 *Robert Bourassa*, Canadian politician; Premier of Quebec, 1970–76, 1985–93. [d. October 2, 1996]

1938 *Jerry Rubin*, U.S. political activist, author. [d. November 28, 1994]

HISTORICAL EVENTS

1223 *King Philip II Augustus* of France dies and is succeeded by *Louis VIII*.

1789 After two days of fighting in Paris, the *Bastille*, symbol of the power of *Louis XVI*, falls to revolutionaries, marking the end of the monarchy and the feudal system in France (*French Revolution*).

1865 First ascent of the *Matterhorn* is completed by Englishman *Edward Whymper*.

1890 *Sherman Act* is passed by Congress, regulating silver coinage in U.S.

1921 *Nicola Sacco* and *Bartolomeo Vanzetti* are convicted of robbery and murder. The controversial trial, in which both defendants plead innocent, incites worldwide protests against the U.S. justice system.

1933 In Germany the *National Socialist German Workers (Nazi) Party* is declared the only political party.

1940 General *Fulgencio Batista* becomes President of Cuba.

1958 *Iraq* overthrows its monarchy and becomes a revolutionary republic.

1960 The United Nations Security Council authorizes deployment of troops to *Katanga*, a province in the *Republic of the Congo*, to end fighting between Congolese rebels and Belgian forces.

1961 *Pope John XXIII* issues papal encyclical *Mater et Magistra* calling for aid to under-developed nations.

1964 *Iraq* nationalizes all private and foreign banks and insurance companies and 30 industrial and commercial concerns; foreign oil companies are not affected.

1972 *Jean Westwood* is appointed national chairperson of the Democratic National Committee. She is the first woman to head a major U.S. political party.

1978 Russian dissident *Anatoly B. Shcharansky* is convicted of treason, espionage, and anti-Soviet agitation and sentenced to three years in prison, to be followed by ten years in a labor camp.

1984 *David Lange* replaces *Robert Muldoon* as prime minister of New Zealand when the Labour Party wins a clear majority in parliamentary elections.

1986 *Truong Chinh* is elected secretary general of Vietnam's Communist Party.

1987 President *Chiang Ching-Kuo* ends 38 years of martial law in Taiwan.

july

JULY
15

HOLIDAYS

Botswana
President's Day

Brunei
Sultan's Birthday

RELIGIOUS CALENDAR

The Saints

St. James, first Bishop of Nisibis. One of the principal Doctors of the Armenian National Church. [d. 338]

St. Barhadbesaba, martyr. [d. 355]

St. Donald. [d. 8th century]

St. Swithin, Bishop of Winchester; patron of *Winchester.* Superstition says that if it rains on his feast day it will rain for 39 more. Also called *Swithun.* [d. 862]

St. Athanasius, Bishop of Naples. [d. 872]

St. Edith of Polesworth. [d. c. 10th century]

St. Vladimir of Kiev, Russian prince. He and his grandmother, St. Olga, are regarded as the first Russian-born Christians. [d. 1015]

St. David of Munktorp, bishop. [d. c. 1080]

St. Bonaventure, Cardinal-Bishop of Albano, Doctor of the Church, and head of the Franciscans. Also called *Bonaventura.* [d. 1274] Feast formerly July 14. Optional Memorial.

St. Pompilio Pirrotti, priest and teacher. [d. 1756]

The Beatified

Blessed Bernard of Baden. [d. 1458]

Blessed Ignatius Azevedo and his companions, martyrs. [d. 1570]

Blessed Anne Mary Javouhey, virgin. Founder of the Congregation of St. Joseph of Cluny. [d. 1851]

BIRTHDATES

1606 *Rembrandt (Rembrandt Harmenszoon van Rijn or Ryn),* Dutch artist; one of the leaders of the Dutch school and regarded as one of the greatest artists of all time. [d. October 4, 1669]

1779 *Clement (Clarke) Moore,* U.S. writer, poet, lexicographer; most widely recognized work is *A Visit from St. Nicholas;* devoted his life to teaching Greek and Oriental literature. [d. July 10, 1863]

1796 *Thomas Bulfinch,* U.S. author; published *The Age of Fable,* also called *Bulfinch's Mythology,* 1855. [d. May 27, 1867]

1808 *Henry Edward Manning,* British archdeacon in Church of England; converted to Catholicism, becoming supervisor of Oblates of St. Charles, 1857. Eventually became Roman Catholic cardinal, 1875. [d. January 14, 1892]

1809 *Pierre Joseph Proudhoun,* French journalist, politician, and social theorist; sometimes called the *Father of Anarchism.* [d. January 16, 1865]

1813 *George Peter Alexander Healy,* U.S. portrait painter; responsible for series of the presidents of the U.S. in Corcoran Art Gallery, Washington, D.C., as well as portraits of Daniel Webster and Henry Wadsworth Longfellow. [d. July 24, 1894]

1817 *Sir John Fowler,* British civil engineer; pioneer in underground railway construction. [d. November 20, 1898]

1848 *Vilfredo Pareto,* Italian economist, sociologist; developed methods of applying mathematics to economic and social phenomena; his theories formed the basis of *Italian fascism.* [d. August 20, 1923]

1850 *Saint Frances Cabrini (Mother Cabrini),* Italian missionary; became naturalized U.S. citizen, 1909. Her work with the poor Italians in America and her campaign to establish convents, schools, orphanages, and hospitals throughout the Americas led to her canonization in 1946; first U.S. citizen to be canonized. [d. December 22, 1917]

1865 *Alfred Charles William Harmsworth, Viscount Northcliffe,* British publisher, politician; established publishing empire that included *Answers,* 1888, *Evening News,* 1894, *Daily Mail,* 1896, *Daily Mirror,* 1903, and the *Times,* 1908. Outspoken enemy of Germany; led many special missions during and after World War I. [d. August 14, 1922]

1918 *Bertram N. Brockhouse,* Canadian physicist; one-half of the Nobel Prize in Physics for his contributions to the development of the neutron spectroscopy, 1994. Clifford G. Shull, U.S. physicist; other half of the prize.

1919 *(Jean) Iris Murdoch,* British novelist, university lecturer.

1921 *R(obert) Bruce Merrifield,* U.S. biochemist; Nobel Prize in chemistry for his synthesis of proteins, 1984.

1922 *Leon Lederman,* U.S. physicist; director of the Fermi National Accelerator Laboratory; Nobel Prize in physics for research into particle physics (with Melvin Schwartz and Jack Steinberger), 1988.

1933 *Julian Bream,* British guitarist, lutist; his research into Elizabethan lute music led to revival of interest in that instrument.

1935 *Alex(ander G.) Karras,* U.S. football player, actor.

Ken Kercheval, U.S. actor; known for his role as Cliff Barnes on television series, *Dallas.*

1939 *Patrick Wayne,* U.S. actor; son of John Wayne; appeared in *McClintock,* 1963, and *The Green Berets,* 1968.

1943 *Jocelyn Bell Burnell,* Irish astronomer; discovered pulsars.

1944 *Jan-Michael Vincent,* U.S. actor.

1946 *Linda Ronstadt,* U.S. singer.

1953 *Jean-Bertrand Aristide,* Haitian priest, politician; President of Haiti, 1991–96.

1960 *Willie Aames,* U.S. actor; known for his role as Tommy Bradford on television series, *Eight is Enough,* 1977–84.

1961 *Forest Whitaker,* U.S. actor, director; known for his performances in *The Crying Game,* 1992; directed *Waiting to Exhale,* 1995.

HISTORICAL EVENTS

455 *Rome* is pillaged by *Genseric the Vandal.*

1099 Crusaders take *Jerusalem (First Crusade).*

1662 *Royal Society for the Improvement of Science* (later the *Royal Society of London*)is chartered at London and becomes center of English scientific activity in the 17th and 18th centuries.

1815 *Napoleon* surrenders to British Captain *Frederick Lewis Maitland* of the *Bellerophon* at Rochefort; he is sent to St. Helena, where he lives out his life in exile.

1918 The *Second Battle of the Marne* begins with a German offensive from both sides of

Reims which meets strong resistance from French and American forces (*World War I*).

1945 U.S. warships bombard steel and iron works at *Muroran, Japan (World War II).*

1953 *Gentlemen Prefer Blondes,* a Howard Hawks film starring Marilyn Monroe, premieres.

1955 Sixteen Nobel laureates sign a resolution that condemns the development of *nuclear weapons.*

1960 *Gabon Republic* is granted full independence from France.

1968 First direct air service between U.S.S.R. and U.S. is opened by Aeroflot and Pan American World Airways.

Jean-Jacques Servan Schreiber's book, *The American Challenge,* is published.

1974 President *Makarios* of Cyprus is overthrown, marking the beginning of long-term fighting between Greek and Turkish sectors.

1977 U.S. President *Jimmy Carter* approves admittance of Indochinese *boat people* into U.S.

1981 U.S. Food and Drug Administration approves the artificial sweetener, *aspartame,* for use in food under the trade name, "Nutrasweet."

july

1987 Former U.S. presidential advisor, Admiral *John Poindexter,* testifies at Congressional hearings that he authorized funds generated from Iranian arms sales to be diverted to contra rebels in Nicaragua, without informing President Ronald Reagan. *(Iran-contra affair)*

HOLIDAYS

Bolivia (La Paz)
Public Holiday

Dominican Republic
Public Holiday
Commemorates the founding of
Sociedad la Trinitaria.

RELIGIOUS CALENDAR

The Saints

Feast of Our Lady of Mount Carmel,
commemorates day on which
Our Lady appeared to St.
Simon Stock and gave him
the scapular. Optional
Memorial.

St. Athenogenes, bishop and martyr.
[d. c. 305]

St. Eustathius, Bishop of Antioch. [d.
c. 340]

St. Helier, martyr. Also called *Elier.*
[d. 6th century]

St. Reineldis, virgin and martyr. Also
called *Raineld.* [d. c. 680]

St. Tenenan, Bishop of Lèon. Also
called *Tinibor.* [d. 7th
century]

St. Fulrad, Abbot of Saint Denis
monastery. [d. 784]

St. Mary Magdalen Postel, virgin.
Founder of the Sisters of the
Christian Schools of Mercy.
[d. 1846]

The Beatified

Blessed Ermengard, virgin. [d. 866]
Blessed Milo of Sèlincourt, Bishop of
Thèrouanne. [d. 1158]

BIRTHDATES

1486 *Andrea del Sarto (Andrea
Domenico d'Agnolo di
Francesco Vannucci),*
Florentine painter; best
known for his frescoes; called
the *Faultless Painter.* [d.
September 29, 1530]

1661 *Pierre Le Moyne, Sieur
d'Iberville,* French-Canadian
explorer, commander;
founder of French colony in
Louisiana. [d. July 9, 1706]

1723 *Sir Joshua Reynolds,* English
painter; foremost portrait
painter in England, 1752–90.
Responsible for establishment
of the *Literary Club,* of which
Dr. Samuel Johnson, David
Garrick, and others were
members. [d. February 23,
1792]

1746 *Giuseppe Piazzi,* Italian
astronomer; discovered and
named the first asteroid,
Ceres, 1801. [d. July 22, 1826]

1773 *Josef Jungmann,* Czech
philologist, critic, poet;
produced 5-volume Czech-
German dictionary which
formed foundation for
modern Czech lexicography;
considered by some the
*Father of Modern Czech
Literature.* [d. November 14,
1847]

1796 *Jean Baptiste Camille Corot,*
French landscape painter. [d.
February 22, 1875]

1821 *Mary (Morse) Baker Eddy,*
U.S. religious leader; founder
of *Christian Science*
movement, 1866. [d.
December 3, 1910]

1845 *Theodore Newton Vail,* U.S.
communications executive;
first president of American
Telephone and Telegraph
Co., 1885–87, 1907–19;
responsible for instituting first
employees' pension plan in
U.S., 1912. [d. April 16, 1920]

1860 *(Jens) Otto (Harry) Jespersen,*
Danish linguist; authority on
English grammar; proposed
an international language,
Nonial. [d. April 30, 1943]

1862 *Ida B. Wells-Barnet,* U.S.
journalist and civil rights
activist. [d. 1931]

1872 *Roald Amundsen,* Norwegian
polar explorer; navigated
Northwest Passage and
discovered *South Pole,* 1911;
disappeared during flight to
rescue Umberto Nobile on his
return from North Pole. [d.
June 1928]

1882 *Millicent Wilson Hearst,* U.S.
philanthropist; wife of William
Randolph Hearst, Sr. [d.
December 6, 1974]

1888 *Frits Zernike,* Dutch physicist;
Nobel Prize in physics for his
invention of *phase contrast
microscope,* 1953. [d. March
10, 1966]

july

1896 *Trygve Lie,* Norwegian government official; first Secretary-General of the United Nations, 1946–53. [d. December 30, 1968]

1907 *Barbara Stanwyck (Ruby Stevens),* U.S. actress. [d. January 20, 1990]

1911 *Ginger Rogers (Virginia Katherine McMath),* U.S. actress; associated with Fred Astaire (May 10) as his frequent dance partner in several films. [d. April 25, 1995]

1924 *Bess Myerson,* U.S. government official, author; Miss America, 1945.

1926 *Sergie Kiriyenko,* Russian politician; Prime Minister, 1998– .

1942 *Margaret Court,* Australian tennis player; Wimbledon champion, 1963, 1965, 1970.

1943 *Jimmy Johnson,* U.S. football coach.

1948 *Ruben Blades,* Panamanian-born actor, singer.

1952 *Stewart Copeland,* Egypt-born drummer; best known for work the band *Police.*

1953 *Mickey Rourke,* U.S. actor.

1954 *Nanci Griffith,* U.S. folk singer.

1959 *Stanley Shapiro,* U.S. writer, producer.

1964 *Miguel Induráin,* Spanish bicycle racer; Tour de France winner, 1991–92.

1965 *Claude Lemieux,* Canadian hockey player; Conn Smythe Trophy winner, 1995.

1968 *Barry Sanders,* U.S. football player.

1971 *Corey Feldman,* U.S. actor.

HISTORICAL EVENTS

1048 *Benedict IX (Boy Pope)* resigns from papacy; had been elected by simony; considered anti-pope to Clement II.

1917 The *Bolsheviks* attempt to seize power from the Russian provisional government but are defeated. *Trotsky* is arrested and *Lenin* goes into hiding in Finland.

1918 Russian *Czar Nicholas II* and his family are executed by order of Bolsheviks.

1937 The Nazi concentration camp at *Buchenwald* opens.

1945 First *atomic bomb* is exploded in a test at Alamogordo, New Mexico.

1947 U.S. President *Harry Truman* signs the *National Security Act,* creating a national military establishment and uniting the Army, Navy, and Air Force.

1948 *Key Largo,* a film starring Humphrey Bogart and Lauren Bacall, premieres in New York.

1951 J.D. Salinger's novel, *The Catcher in the Rye,* is published.

1965 *Mont Blanc Tunnel,* a seven-mile vehicular tunnel through the heart of Mont Blanc and connecting France and Italy, is opened.

1969 *Apollo 11,* U.S. manned spacecraft, is launched, carrying astronauts Armstrong, Aldrin, and Collins into moon orbit, from which Armstrong and Aldrin will launch *lunar module* for 21-hour *moon landing* (see July 20).

The *South African Students' Organization* is formed by black university students.

1979 *Ahmed Hassan al-Bakr* resigns as president of Iraq and is replaced by *Saddam Hussein.*

1982 *George Schultz* becomes U.S. Secretary of State.

Reverend *Sun Myung Moon,* founder of the *Unification Church,* is sentenced to 18 months in prison for tax fraud and conspiracy to obstruct justice.

HOLIDAYS

Iraq

17th of July Revolution or Baath Revolution Day
Commemorates the overthrow of the government by Revolutionary Command Council under General Ahmed Hassan al-Bakr, 1968.

Puerto Rico

Muñoz Rivera's Birthday
Commemorates the birthday of Luis Muñoz Rivera, Puerto Rican patriot and leader in gaining Puerto Rico's independence from Spain.

South Korea

Constitution Day
Commemorates the adoption of the constitution, 1963.

Venice

Feast of the Redeemer
Procession of gondolas and other craft commemorating the end of the epidemic of 1575.

RELIGIOUS CALENDAR

The Saints

St. Speratus and his companions, the Scillitan martyrs. [d. 180]
St. Marcellina, virgin. [d. c. 398]
St. Alexis, called the *Man of God;* patron saint of the Alexian Brothers. Also called *Alexius.* [d. 5th century]
St. Ennodius, Bishop of Pavia. [d. 521]
St. Kenelm, martyr. Also called *Cynehelm* or *Kenelm.* [d. c. 812]

St. Leo IV, pope. Elected 847. [d. 855]
St. Clement of Okhrida and his companions, the *Seven Apostles of Bulgaria.* [d. 9th–10th century]
St. Nerses Lampronatsi, Archbishop of Tarsus. Also called *Narsus of Lampron.* [d. 1198]
The Carmelite Martyrs of Compiegne, sixteen victims of the French Revolution. [d. 1794]

The Beatified

Blessed Ceslaus. [d. 1242]

BIRTHDATES

1698 *Pierre Louis Moreau Maupertius,* French mathematician, astronomer; led expedition sent by *Louis XV* to Lapland to make accurate measurements of longitude. [d. July 27, 1759]

1744 *Elbridge Gerry,* U.S. statesman; signer of Declaration of Independence; Vice-President of U.S., 1812–14. [d. November 23, 1814]

1763 *John Jacob Astor,* U.S. businessman, born in Germany; the founder and promoter of one of the greatest financial dynasties in the U.S. [d. March 29, 1848]

1797 *Hippolyte Paul Delaroche,* French historical and portrait painter. [d. November 4, 1856]

1827 *Sir Frederick Augustus Abel,* British chemist; developed *cordite* with James Dewar (September 20), the first *smokeless gun powder;* chemist to British War Department, 1854–88. [d. September 6, 1902]

1859 *Luis Muñoz Rivera,* Puerto Rican poet, politician, and journalist. [d. 1916]

1862 *Oscar Ivan Levertin,* Swedish poet, novelist, man of letters. [d. September 22, 1906]

1871 *Maxim Litvinov,* Russian revolutionary, statesman. [d. December 31, 1951]

1888 *Shmuel Yosef Halevi Agnon,* Israeli novelist, short-story writer. [d. February 17, 1970]

1889 *Erle Stanley Gardner,* U.S. lawyer, author of detective stories; developed the character *Perry Mason,* the hero of over 100 books and stories and a television series. [d. May 11, 1970]

1894 *Georges Lemaître,* Belgian astrophysicist, mathematician; first to introduce the concept of the *expanding universe,* 1927. [d. June 20, 1966]

1899 *James Cagney,* U.S. actor, dancer, active in American theater and films for over fifty years. [d. March 30, 1986]

july

1902 *Christina Ellen Stead,* British novelist. [d. March 31, 1983]

1905 *William Gargan,* U.S. actor; leading man in 1930s and 1940s films. [d. February 16, 1979]

1912 *Art Linkletter,* U.S. radio and television personality, born in Canada.

1917 *Phyllis Diller,* U.S. actress, comedienne; famous for her outrageous costumes.

1920 *William Blanc (Bill) Monroe, Jr.,* U.S. broadcast journalist; moderator and executive producer of the television series, *Meet the Press.*

1934 *Donald Sutherland,* Canadian actor.

1935 *Diahann Carroll (Carol Diahann Johnson),* U.S. singer, actress.

 Benjamin R. Civiletti, U.S. government official; Attorney General, 1979–81.

1951 *Lucie Desiree Arnaz,* U.S. actress, singer.

1952 *Phoebe Lamb Snow,* U.S. singer; Gold Album Award for *Phoebe Snow,* 1975.

 David Hasselhof, U.S. actor; known for his leading roles on television series, *Knight Rider* and *Baywatch.*

1956 *Bryan Trottier,* Canadian hockey player.

1965 *Alex Winter,* British actor; featured in *Bill and Ted's Excellent Adventure,* 1989.

HISTORICAL EVENTS

1245 *Pope Innocent IV* declares German *King Frederick II* deposed and orders Germans to elect a new king; war breaks out throughout the German territories.

1453 French defeat English under *John Talbot,* Earl of Shrewsbury, at *Castillon (Hundred Years' War).*

1841 *Punch,* the British humor magazine, begins publication.

1868 *Edo,* renamed *Tokyo,* becomes the capital of *Japan.*

1890 *Cecil Rhodes* becomes Prime Minister of the Cape Colony of South Africa.

1898 The Spanish formally surrender *Santiago, Cuba,* to American forces (*Spanish-American War*).

1945 Churchill, Stalin, and Truman arrange the terms of Germany's occupation and demand an unconditional surrender from Japan at the *Potsdam Conference. (World War II)*

1948 *Dixiecrats* opposed to U.S. President Harry Truman's strong civil rights stand, form the *States Rights Party* and nominate *J. Strom Thurmond* for president.

1951 *Leopold III* of Belgium abdicates and is succeeded by his son, *Baudouin I.*

1955 The *Disneyland* amusement park opens in Anaheim, California.

1969 *Luna 15,* Soviet unmanned space craft, is launched into orbit.

1973 *Afghanistan* monarchy is abolished when Lieut. Gen. *Mohammad Daud Khan* deposes his brother-in-law, *King Mohammad Zahir Shah* and proclaims himself president.

1975 U.S. *Apollo 18* and U.S.S.R. *Soyuz 19* linkup in space takes place as a dramatic goodwill gesture between Russia and the United States.

1979 *Anastasio Somoza* resigns and leaves *Nicaragua* as Sandinistas take control of Managua, ending civil war.

1981 *Wayne B. Williams* is indicted on charges of murdering two black youths in Atlanta, Georgia. He is suspected of murdering more than 20 other black youths over a two-year period.

1984 *Laurent Fabius* is named prime minister of France.

1992 *Vaclav Havel,* president of Czechoslovkia, resigns after voters decide to create two independent republics.

1996 *TWA flight 800,* bound for Paris, France, plunges into the Atlantic Ocean after only thirty minutes into the flight, killing all 230 persons.

HOLIDAYS

Mexico
Benito Juárez Memorial Day
Commemorates the death of Mexican statesman who led the revolt against Maximilian and the French, 1872.

Uruguay
Constitution Day

RELIGIOUS CALENDAR

The Saints
St. Pambo, monk. [d. c. 390]
St. Philastrius, Bishop of Brescia. [d. c. 397]
St. Arnulf, Bishop of Metz. Also called *Arnoul.* [d. c. 643]
St. Edburga of Bicester, nun. Also called *Eadburh of Aylesbury.* [d. c. 650]
St. Frederick, Bishop of Utrecht, martyr. Also called *Frederic.* [d. 838]
St. Bruno, Bishop of Segni. [d. 1123]
St. Symphorosa and her seven sons, martyrs. [death date unknown]

BIRTHDATES

1504 *Heinrich Bullinger,* Swiss religious reformer; head of Reformation in German Switzerland after the death of Zwingli. [d. September 17, 1575]

1635 *Robert Hooke,* English experimental scientist; proposed numerous theories of physics which were later substantiated by more sophisticated scientific techniques: theories of combustion, center of gravity of earth and moon, elasticity. [d. March 3, 1703]

1757 *Royall Tyler,* U.S. playwright; wrote the first commercially successful American play, *The Contrast.* [d. August 26, 1826]

1811 *William Makepeace Thackeray,* British novelist; known for his pointed satires on upper class society of London, including *Vanity Fair;* contributed regularly to *Punch,* 1842–54. [d. December 24, 1863]

1853 *Hendrik A. Lorentz,* Dutch physicist; Nobel Prize in physics for his theory of electromagnetic radiation (with P. Zeeman), 1902. [d. February 4, 1928]

1864 *Philip Snowden, 1st Viscount Snowden of Ickornshaw,* British politician, socialist; Chairman of Independent Labor Party, 1903–06, 1917–20. [d. May 15, 1937]

1883 *Lev Borisovich Kamenev,* Russian revolutionary, politician; Vice-President of U.S.S.R., 1923. After Lenin's death became member of ruling triumvirate with Stalin (December 21) and Zinoviev (September 11). [d. August 25, 1936]

1887 *Vidkun Quisling,* Norwegian politician, public official; founded National Union Party in Norway; collaborated with Germany in conquest of Norway; executed as a traitor. [d. October 24, 1945]

1890 *Charles Erwin Wilson,* U.S. industrialist, public official; President of General Motors Corporation, 1941–46; U.S. Secretary of Defense, 1952–57. [d. September 26, 1961]

1902 *Jessamyn West,* U.S. author; many of her works were based on the lives of her Quaker ancestors; wrote *The Friendly Persuasion* and *Except for Me and Thee.* [d. February 23, 1984]

Chill Wills, U.S. character actor. [d. December 15, 1978]

1903 *Victor (David) Gruen,* U.S. architect, urban planner, born in Austria; known for his large-scale planned commercial projects (mainly shopping centers) which integrated architecture, art, and landscape design. [d. February 14, 1980]

1906 *Clifford Odets,* U.S. playwright; a leading writer of the Depression era; helped found the Group Theatre in

New York with Lee Strasberg. [d. August 14, 1963]

S(amuel) I(chiye) Hayakawa, U.S. educator, semanticist, politician, born in Canada; President of San Francisco State College, 1968–73; U.S. Senator, 1976–82. [d. February 27, 1992]

1911 *Hume Cronyn (Hume Blake),* Canadian actor.

1912 *Harriet Nelson,* U.S. actress, singer; began career as a vocalist in husband Ozzie Nelson's Orchestra; starred in the television series, *The Adventures of Ozzie and Harriet,* 1952–65. [d. October 2, 1994]

1913 *(Richard) Red Skelton,* U.S. comedian, actor. [d. September 17, 1997]

1915 *Philip Leslie Graham,* U.S. newspaper executive; publisher of *Washington Post,* 1946–63. [d. August 3, 1963]

1918 *Nelson Rolihlahla Mandela,* South African political activist; imprisoned for conspiracy to overthrow the government, 1964; symbol of international opposition to apartheid; release from prison in 1990; Nobel Prize for Peace in 1993, along with F. W. de Klerk, former South African president (1989-94); President of South Africa, 1994– .

1921 *John (Herschel) Glenn, Jr.,* U.S. astronaut, politician; first American to complete earth orbit, February 22, 1962; U.S. Senator, 1975– .

1929 *Dick Button,* U.S. figure skater, broadcaster; Olympic gold medalist in figure skating, 1948, 1952; world titlist, 1948–52.

1933 *Yevgeny Aleksandrovich Yevtushenko,* Russian poet.

1937 *Roald Hoffmann,* Polish-born chemist; Nobel Prize in chemistry, 1981.

1938 *Paul Verhoeven,* Dutch director; directed *Basic Instinct,* 1992 and *Showgirls,* 1995.

1939 *Dion (DiMucci),* U.S. singer.

Hunter S(tockton) Thompson, U.S. author, journalist; wrote *Hell's Angels: A Strange and Terrible Saga,* 1966, and *Fear and Loathing in Las Vegas,* 1972.

1940 *Joe Torre,* U.S. baseball manager; managed the 1996 New York Yankees' World Championship team.

1941 *James Brolin,* U.S. actor; Emmy Award for *Marcus Welby, MD;* known for leading role on television series, *Hotel.*

Martha Reeves, U.S. singer; lead vocalist of *Martha and the Vandellas,* 1962–72.

1947 *(Malcolm) Steve(nson) Forbes, Jr.,* U.S. businessman; Republican presidential candidate, 1996.

1948 *Hartmut Michel,* German biochemist; Nobel Prize for Chemistry along with fellow biochemists, Johann Deisenhofer and Robert Huber, 1988.

1952 *Nicolette Larson,* U.S. singer.

1954 *Ricky Skaggs,* U.S. singer.

1957 *Nick Faldo,* British golfer.

1961 *Elizabeth McGovern,* U.S. actress; Oscar nomiee for *Ragtime.*

1971 *Anfernee (Penny) Hardaway,* U.S. basketball player.

HISTORICAL EVENTS

1536 Authority of *Bishop of Rome* (the Pope) is declared void in England.

1870 Dogma of *papal infallibility* is declared by Vatican Council.

1915 The *Second Battle of Isonzo* begins with the Italians again attacking Austrian bridgeheads (*World War I*).

1918 *Second Battle of the Marne:* a turning point of *World War I* as French and Allies halt German offensive.

1928 The *Somport Tunnel,* connecting Spain and France through the Pyrenees, opens.

1936 *Spanish Civil War* begins with a revolt of the army chiefs, led by *General Francisco Franco,* at Melilla in Spanish Morocco.

1942 First jet combat plane is tested. *(World War II)*

1947 President Harry S. Truman signs the *Presidential Succession Act,* designating the Speaker of the House of Representatives and the President Pro Tempore of the Senate as next in line of succession after the Vice-President.

1951 Hundreds of manuscripts by William Butler Yeats, Sean O'Casey, and other prominent Irish writers are destroyed in a fire in Dublin's *Abbey Theater.*

Jersey Joe Walcott defeats *Ezzard Charles* in seven rounds for the world heavyweight boxing championship.

1955 Sloan Wilson's novel, *The Man in the Gray Flannel Suit,* is published.

1960 *Hayoto Ikeda* is inaugurated as premier of Japan.

1968 *U.S. B-52 bombers* are first used during air raids of missile sites in North Vietnam (*Vietnam War*).

1971 *Pele (Edson Arantes do Nascimento)* ends his career with the Brazilian national soccer team. He led his country to three World Cup victories in his 13 years of play.

1974 U.S. baseball player, *Bob Gibson,* strikes out his three thousandth batter, becoming the first National League pitcher to amass that many strikeouts.

1976 A new virus, spread by ticks and frequently causing arthritic symptoms in its victims, is found in Connecticut. It is called *Lyme Disease* after the town in which the first cases were discovered.

july

JULY
19

HOLIDAYS

Burma
Martyrs' Day

Nicaragua
Anniversary of the Sandinista Revolution or Liberation Day
Commemorates the coming to power of the Sandinist National Liberation Front over the the forces of President Somoza, 1979.

RELIGIOUS CALENDAR

The Saints
St. Justa and St. Rufina, virgins and martyrs. [d. c. 287]
St. Macrina the Younger, virgin. [d. 379]
St. Arsenius the Great, scholar and monk. [d. c. 450]
St. Symmachus, pope. Elected 498. [d. 514]
St. Ambrose Autpert, abbot. [d. c. 778]

The Beatified
Blessed Stilla, virgin. [d. c. 1140]

BIRTHDATES

1573 *Inigo Jones,* baptized on this day; influential early English designer; responsible for design of the restoration of St. Paul's Cathedral in London (1634–1642). [d. June 21, 1652]

1698 *Johann Jakob Bodmer,* Swiss scholar, critic, poet; contributed to the development of an original German literature in Switzerland. [d. January 2, 1783]

1800 *Juan José Flores,* Ecuadorian general; first president, 1830–35. [d. October 1, 1864]

1814 *Samuel Colt,* U.S. inventor, businessman; developed the repeating firearm (*six-shooter*), which he put into production in the U.S. in a sophisticated production line technique; his invention is said to be one of the most influential of the 19th century. [d. January 10, 1862]

1819 *Gottfried Keller,* Swiss novelist, short-story writer, poet. [d. July 15, 1890]

1834 *(Hilaire Germaine) Edgar Degas,* French Impressionist painter; known for his depiction of theater life, especially of ballet dancers. [d. September 27, 1917]

1840 *José Manuel Balmaceda,* Chilean statesman; president, 1851–61. [d. September 18, 1891]

1860 *Lizzie (Andrew) Borden,* U.S. accused murderer; alleged to have murdered her father and step-mother in a brutal ax-slaying. [d. June 1, 1927]

1865 *Charles Horace Mayo,* U.S. surgeon; co-founder of the Mayo Foundation for Medical Education and Research (Mayo Clinic). Brother of William James Mayo (June 29). [d. May 26, 1939]

1875 *Alice Dunbar-Nelson,* U.S. author and educator. [d. 1935]

1878 *Don(ald Robert Perry) Marquis,* U.S. author, journalist; leading humorist of his period; known for his characters *Archy* and *Mehitabel.* [d. December 29, 1937]

1885 *Malcolm King,* U.S. publisher; President of McGraw-Hill, Inc., 1928–37; President of Newsweek, Inc., 1937–61. [d. January 30, 1979]

1893 *Vladimir Vladimirovich Mayakovsky,* Russian poet; leading futurist writer of Russian Revolutionary period. [d. April 14, 1930]

1896 *A(rchibald) J(oseph) Cronin,* U.S. writer; formerly a physician in Scotland; turned to writing and gained enormous success with *The Keys of the Kingdom, The Citadel.* [d. January 6, 1981]

1898 *Herbert Marcuse,* U.S. philosopher, born in Germany; considered the prophet of the *New Left,* his writings became the foundation for political thought of radical students during the 1960s; lectured at Columbia University, 1940; Brandeis University, 1954–65. [d. July 29, 1979]

1917 *William Warren Scranton,* U.S. lawyer, politician, diplomat; U.S. Congressman, 1961–63; Governor of Pennsylvania, 1963–67; Special Envoy to Middle East, 1968.

1921 *Rosalyn Yalow,* U.S. medical physicist; Nobel Prize in physiology or medicine for development of method for using isotopes for diagnostic purposes, 1977.

1922 *George (Stanley) McGovern,* U.S. politician; U.S. Senator, 1963–81; Democratic presidential candidate, 1972.

1924 *Martin Patterson (Pat) Hingle,* U.S. actor; featured in the movies, *Splendor in the Grass,* 1961, and *Norma Rae,* 1979.

1938 *Richard Jordan,* U.S. actor. [d. August 30, 1993]

1941 *Vikki Carr (Florencia Bisenta de Casillas),* U.S. singer.

1945 *George Dzundza,* German actor.

Nancy S. Wexler, U.S. psychologist; known for her research on hereditary diseases.

1946 *Ilie Nastase,* Romanian-born tennis player.

1947 *Brian May,* British singer, musician; member of the rock group, *Queen.*

1962 *Anthony Edwards,* U.S. actor; known for TV series *ER.*

HISTORICAL EVENTS

1101 *Robert of Normandy* invades England in attempt to take English throne from his younger brother, *Henry I;* forestalled by *Treaty of Alton.*

1333 *Edward III* of England defeats Scots army at *Halidon Hill* in struggle to place *Edward Balliol* on the throne of Scotland.

1821 *George IV* of England is crowned king; refuses to allow his estranged queen, Caroline, to attend coronation.

1848 First *women's rights convention* is held at *Seneca Falls, New York,* under the leadership of *Elizabeth Cady Stanton* and *Lucretia Coffin Mott.*

1862 *Garibaldi* calls for volunteers with watchword "Rome or death!" in his first attempt to capture the city.

1870 France declares war on Prussia (*Franco-Prussian War*).

1919 *Ford Motor Co.* is reincorporated in Delaware, with the sale of major stockholder *James Couzens's* interest in the 16-year-old firm to *Henry Ford.*

1934 The Boeing Airplane Co. (later the *Boeing Co.*) is incorporated in Delaware.

1940 *Tony Zale* defeats *Al Hostak* to win the world middleweight boxing title.

1943 Allied forces attack *Rome* for the first time, bombing major railroad yards and airports (*World War II*).

1949 *Laos* becomes independent sovereign state within the French Union.

1968 The first international *Special Olympics* begins in Chicago with over one thousand mentally retarded competitors.

1969 U.S. Senator *Edward Kennedy* reports to police that his car has plunged off *Chappaquiddick Island* bridge in Edgartown, Massachusetts, drowning a woman passenger, *Mary Jo Kopechne.*

1985 A New Hampshire high school teacher, *Sharon Christa McAuliffe,* is selected to be the first private citizen in space flight.

1989 *Wojciech Jaruzelski* is elected president of Poland.

1996 Opening ceremonies for the summer *Olympics* begin in Atlanta, Georgia.

1997 *Charles Taylor* is elected president of Liberia.

july

JULY
20

HOLIDAYS

Colombia
Independence Day

RELIGIOUS CALENDAR

The Saints

St. Joseph Barsabas, one of the disciples of Christ. [d. 1st century]

St. Aurelius, Bishop of Carthage. [d. 429]

St. Flavian, Patriarch of Antioch, and *St. Elias,* Patriarch of Jerusalem. [d. 518]

St. Vulmar, abbot and hermit. Also called *Ulmar, Wulmar.* [d. c. 700]

St. Ansegisus, abbot and advisor to Charlemagne. [d. 833]

St. Arild, virgin. Also called *Alkelda.* [death date unknown]

St. Margaret, virgin and martyr; patron of women. Invoked in childbirth and for the cure of kidney diseases. Also called *Marina.* Feast suppressed in 1969. [death date unknown]

St. Wilgefortis, princess. Invoked against troublesome husbands. Also called *Kümmernis, Liberta, Livrade, Ontkommer, Regentledis,* or *Uncumber.* [death date unknown]

The Beatified

Blessed Gregory Lopez, hermit. [d. 1596]

Blessed Leo Ignatius Mangin, Ann Wang, and their

companions, martyrs. Four French Jesuits and 52 Chinese lay people martyred by the Boxers in 1900. [d. 1900]

BIRTHDATES

1304 *Petrarch (Francesco Petrarca),* Italian poet, humanist; known for his collection of sonnets and odes written to Laura, his beloved. [d. July 18, 1374]

1519 *Pope Innocent IX,* pope in 1591 for two months. [d. December 30, 1591]

1591 *Anne Hutchinson,* American colonial religious leader, baptized on this day. Proposed a theology based on a covenant of grace; excommunicated from Puritan community and banished from Massachusetts. [d. August, 1643]

1656 *Johann Bernard Fischer von Erlach,* Austrian architect; responsible for original plans for *Schönbrunn Castle,* 1695, and *Royal Library in Vienna,* 1722. [d. April 5, 1723]

1785 *Mahmud II,* Sultan of Turkey. [d. July 1, 1839]

1830 *Sir Clements Robert Markham,* British geographer, historical writer. [d. January 30, 1916]

1847 *Max Liebermann,* German Postimpressionist painter. [d. February 8, 1935]

1850 *John Graves Shedd,* U.S. merchant; partner with Marshall Field (September 3) in development of Marshall Field & Co. President of Marshall Field & Co., 1906–22; donated *Shedd Aquarium* in Chicago. [d. October 22, 1926]

1864 *Erik Axel Karlfeldt,* Swedish poet; Nobel Prize in literature (posthumously), 1931. [d. April 8, 1931]

1890 *George II,* King of Greece. [d. April 1, 1947] *Theda Bara (Theodosia Goodman),* U.S. silent screen star; created the role of the vamp. [d. April 7, 1955]

1893 *Alexander,* King of Greece, 1917–20; became king when his father was forced to abdicate; died of blood poisoning after being bitten by a pet monkey. [d. October 25, 1920]

1894 *Edmond H(arrison) Leavey,* U.S. army officer, businessman; Assistant Chief of Staff, Supreme Headquarters, Allied Powers in Europe, 1952–56; President, ITT, 1956–59. [d. February 11, 1980]

1897 *Tadeusz Reichstein,* Swiss chemist; Nobel Prize in physiology or medicine for research in hormones and discovery of *cortisone* (with P. S. Hench and E. C. Kendall), 1950.

1919 *Benson Ford,* U.S. auto executive. [d. July 27, 1978]

Sir *Edmund (Percival) Hillary,* New Zealand mountain climber, Arctic explorer, author; with *Tenzing Norkay* was first to reach summit of *Mt. Everest,* 1953; reached South Pole, January 4, 1958.

1920 *Juan Antonio Samaranch,* Spanish diplomat; president of International Olympic Committee, 1980– .

Elliot (Lee) Richardson, U.S. lawyer, government official, diplomat; U.S. Secretary of Health, Education and Welfare, 1970–72; Attorney General of U.S., 1973; Ambassador to United Kingdom, 1975–76; U.S. Secretary of Commerce, 1976–77.

1924 *Elias Sarkis,* Lebanese statesman; President, 1976–82. [d. July 27, 1985]

1925 *Jacques Delors,* French businessman; president of the European Economic Community, 1985–94.

1929 *Mike Ilitch,* U.S. businessman, hockey executive; owner, Detroit Red Wings hockey team; established Little Caesar's pizza franchises.

1933 *John (Champlin) Gardner,* U.S. author, educator; noted for his experimental style of novel writing; author of *Grendel,* and *October Light.* [d. September 14, 1982]

1934 *Sally Ann Howes,* British actress, singer; child star of films in the 1940's; appeared in *Chitty, Chitty, Bang, Bang,* 1968.

1936 *Elizabeth (Liddy) Hanford Dole,* U.S. government official; first female Secretary of Transportation, 1983–87; Secretary of Labor, 1989–90.

1938 *Barbara Ann Mikulski,* U.S. politician; Congresswoman, 1976–87; Senator from Maryland, 1987– .

Diana Rigg, British actress; known for her role as Emma Peel on television series, *The Avengers,* 1965–68.

Natalie Wood (Natasha Gurdin), U.S. actress. [d. November 29, 1981]

1939 *Judy Chicago (Judy Cohen),* U.S. artist, feminist; works include *The Dinner Party.*

1946 *Kim Carnes,* U.S. singer, songwriter; Grammy Award, 1981.

1947 *Gerd Binnig,* German-born physicist; Nobel Prize in physics for the development of the scanning tunneling microscope (with Heinrich Rohrer), 1986.

Carlos Santana, Mexican rock musician.

HISTORICAL EVENTS

1402 The *Battle of Angora* (Ankara) is won by *Timur (Tamerlane)* who defeats and captures *Bazazid I,* Sultan of Turkey.

1810 *Colombia* defies Spanish authority and declares its independence.

1866 Austria and France destroy Italian fleet off *Lissa,* setting back Italy's unification efforts.

1917 The *Pact of Corfu* declares that Serbs, Croats, and Slovenes will form a single nation to be called *Yugoslavia.*

1927 *Ferdinand I* of Rumania dies and is succeeded by Michael.

1942 U.S. Congress authorizes *Legion of Merit* medal to recognize meritorious efforts by armed forces members.

1944 Lieutenant Colonel *Klaus von Stauffenberg* and other high-ranking German officials attempt to assassinate *Adolf Hitler* by bombing his East Prussian headquarters. Hitler escapes with minor injuries.

1951 *King Abdullah ibn Hussein* of Jordan is assassinated; he is succeeded by his son Talal.

1953 The *United Nations International Children's Emergency Fund (UNICEF)* is granted permanent status as a UN agency. It was originally designated as an emergency measure to aid Chinese and European children after World War II.

1960 *Polaris missile* is launched for the first time from a submerged submarine near Cape Canaveral, Florida.

1965 President Lyndon Johnson appoints *Arthur Goldberg* as U.S. Ambassador to the United Nations, replacing the late *Adlai Stevenson.*

1969 U.S. astronauts *Neil A. Armstrong* and *Edwin E. Aldrin,* during the mission of *Apollo 11,* land their lunar excursion module *Eagle* on the moon. Armstrong becomes the first man to set foot on the moon.

july

1976 *Viking 1,* U.S. robot spacecraft, lands on *Mars* in the *Plain of Chryse.*

The last U.S. military personnel are withdrawn from *Vietnam,* marking an end to American military involvement begun in 1965.

1977 *CIA* experiments in behavior control from 1949 through the mid-1960s are revealed; experiments were conducted through the use of chemical, biological, and radiological agents on human subjects, including prisoners and mental patients.

1990 *William Brennan,* Supreme Court justice, announces his retirement after serving thirty-four years.

JULY
21

HOLIDAYS

Belgium
National Day or Independence Day
Commemorates accession of first king of independent Belgium, Leopold I, 1831.

French West Indies
Schoelcher Day
Commemorates the birthday of Victor Schoelcher, French politician devoted to elimination of slavery in French possessions.

Guam
Liberation Day
Commemorates liberation of the island by U.S. forces, 1944.

RELIGIOUS CALENDAR

The Saints
St. Praxedes, virgin. Also called *Praxedis.* [d. 1st–2nd century] Feast suppressed 1969.
St. Victor of Marseilles, martyr; patron of cabinet-makers. Invoked against lightning. [d. c. 290]
St. Arbogast, Bishop of Strasburg. Also called *Arbogastus.* [d. 6th century]
St. Lawrence of Brindisi, theologian, missionary, and doctor of the church. [d. 1619]

The Beatified
Blessed Oddino of Fossano, parish priest. [d. 1400]
Blessed Angelina of Marsciano, widow and abbess. [d. 1435]

BIRTHDATES

810 *Mohammed Ibn Ismail Al-Bukhari,* Arabic scholar, author of one of the sacred books of Islam, the *Sahih,* which ranks next to the *Koran* in importance for Sunni Muslims. [d. August 31, 870]

1414 *Pope Sixtus IV,* pope 1471–84. [d. August 12, 1484]

1816 *Baron Paul Julius von Reuter,* German pioneer in gathering and disseminating news. His carrier pigeon and telegraph outpost in France, 1849, became the foundation of *Reuter's News Service.* [d. February 25, 1899]

1821 *Vasile Alexandri,* Rumanian poet, playwright, politician; Minister of Foreign Affairs for Rumania, 1859–85; Ambassador to France, 1885–90. [d. 1890]

1851 *Sam Bass,* U.S. outlaw; had a short but spectacular career as a train robber and cattle thief; killed in a gunfight with Texas Rangers. [d. July 21, 1878]

1863 *Sir C(harles) Aubrey Smith,* British character actor. [d. December 20, 1948]

1864 *Frances Cleveland,* wife of U.S. President Grover Cleveland. [d. October 29, 1947]

1885 *Frances Parkinson Keyes,* U.S. novelist. [d. July 3, 1970]

1899 *Ernest (Miller) Hemingway,* U.S. novelist, short-story writer; Nobel Prize in literature, 1954. [d. July 2, 1961]

(Harold) Hart Crane, U.S. poet. [d. April 27, 1932]

1905 *Diana Rubin Trilling,* U.S. author, literary critic. [d. October 23, 1996]

1911 *(Herbert) Marshall McLuhan,* Canadian author, educator; contemporary expert on theories of *mass communication.* [d. December 31, 1980]

Ralph Lane Polk, U.S. publisher; President of R.L. Polk, 1949–63; Chairman, 1963–83. [d. February 9, 1984]

1920 *Isaac Stern,* U.S. violinist, born in Russia.

1923 *Rudolph A. Marcus,* U.S. chemist; Nobel Prize for Chemistry for his development of the electron-transfer reactions theory, 1992.

1924 *Don Knotts,* U.S. comedian, actor; five Emmy Awards for his role as Barney Fife on television series, *The Andy Griffith Show,* 1960–68.

Kay Starr (Kathryn Stark), U.S. singer.

july

1926 *Norman Jewison,* U.S. director; directed *Fiddler on the Roof,* 1971, and *Moonstruck,* 1988.

1934 *Jonathan Wolfe Miller,* British physician, stage and film director; co-author of and actor in *Beyond the Fringe,* 1961; directed numerous plays for National Theatre of London, 1970–78.

1938 *Leslie (Les) Aspin, Jr.,* U.S. politician; Congressman; Chairman, House Armed Services Committee. [d. May 21, 1995]

Janet Reno, U.S. lawyer; Attorney General, 1993– .

1943 *Edward Herrmann,* U.S. actor; Tony Award for *Mrs. Warren's Profession,* 1976; played President Franklin Roosevelt in the television special, *Eleanor and Franklin.*

1947 *Cat Stevens (Steven Georgiou, now known as Yusef Islam),* British singer, songwriter.

1952 *Robin Williams,* U.S. comedian, actor; starred in the television series, *Mork and Mindy,* 1979–81; featured in the movies, *The World According to Garp, Good Morning, Vietnam,* and *Mrs. Doubtfire*; Academy Award (Best Supporting Actor) for *Good Will Hunting,* 1997.

1957 *Jon Lovitz,* U.S. comic actor.

1962 *Rob Morrow,* U.S. actor; known for role as Dr. Joel Fleischman on *Northern Exposure* series.

HISTORICAL EVENTS

1773 *Pope Clement XIV* suppresses *Jesuit Order.*

1796 *Mungo Park,* British explorer, reaches the *Niger River,* in Africa, and starts his trip downstream to trace the course of the river.

1798 French defeat the Mamluk cavalry and take *Cairo* during the *Battle of the Pyramids* in Bonaparte's Egyptian expedition.

1861 Union General Irvin McDowell is defeated at *First Battle of Bull Run.*

1941 German troops invade *Moscow (World War II).*

1944 U.S. Marines and Army troops land on *Guam (World War II).*

1954 French and Viet Minh representatives agree to partition *Vietnam* along the 17th parallel. The northern part will be controlled by the Communists, while the southern region is to be governed by the pro-French Bao Dai regime.

1960 Ceylon's first woman prime minister, Mme. *Sirimavo Bandaranaike,* is sworn in at ceremonies in Colombo.

1966 *Gemini 10,* U.S. spacecraft carrying astronauts *John Young* and *Michael Collins,* achieves rendezvous with two space targets, and Collins accomplishes two walks in space.

1970 The National Better Business Bureau and the Association of Better Business Bureaus merge to form the *Council of Better Business Bureaus.*

1976 Christopher T.E. Ewart-Briggs, British ambassador to *Ireland,* and others are killed by a land mine set off under their car.

An American Legion convention begins in Philadelphia. Twenty-three participants eventually die from *Legionnaire's Disease,* a previously unknown malady later traced to bacteria in the hotel cooling system.

1978 *Juan Pereda Asbún* declares himself President of Bolivia after deposing President *Hugo Banzer Suárez* in a military coup.

HOLIDAYS

Poland
National Liberation Day

Swaziland
Birthday of King Sobhuza II

RELIGIOUS CALENDAR

The Saints
St. Mary Magdalen, a follower of Christ and the first to see the Risen Christ; patron of perfumers, glove-makers, tanners, and repentant women. Also called *Mawdleyn.* [d. 1st century] Obligatory Memorial [major holy day, Episcopal Church; minor festival, Lutheran Church].

St. Joseph of Palestine, scholar. Also called *Count Joseph.* [d. c. 356]

St. Wandregisilus, abbot. Also called *Vandrille, Wandrille.* [d. 668]

The Beatified
Blessed Benno, Bishop of Osnabrück. [d. 1088]

BIRTHDATES

1621 *Anthony Ashley Cooper Shaftesbury, First Earl of Shaftesbury, 1st Baron Ashley,* English statesman; a leading politician under Oliver Cromwell (April 25). [d. January 21, 1683]

1784 *Friedrich Wilhelm Bessel,* Prussian astronomer; calculated path of Halley's Comet; invented mathematical functions (*Bessel functions*) used in mathematical physics. [d. March 17, 1846]

1803 *Eugene Louis Gabriel Isabey,* French painter; known for his marine paintings. [d. April 25, 1886]

1822 *Gregor Johann Mendel,* Austrian botanist, Augustinian monk; described laws of biological inheritance (*Mendel's laws*). [d. January 6, 1884]

1849 *Emma Lazarus,* U.S. poet, essayist; her sonnet, *The New Colossus,* is inscribed on the base of the *Statue of Liberty.* [d. November 19, 1887]

1878 *Ernest Ball,* U.S. vaudeville actor, composer of such early 20th-century songs as *Mother Machree.* [d. May 3, 1927]

1882 *Edward Hopper,* U.S. painter; known as *Painter of Loneliness* because of his portrayal of stark, realistic scenes of contemporary life. [d. May 15, 1967]

1887 *Gustav Ludwig Hertz,* German physicist; Nobel Prize in physics for discovery of laws governing the collision of electron with an atom (with J. Franck), 1925. [d. October 30, 1975]

1888 *Selman Abraham Waksman,* U.S. microbiologist, born in Russia; Nobel Prize in physiology or medicine for discovery of uses for *streptomycin* in treating tuberculosis, 1952. [d. August 16, 1973]

1890 *Rose Kennedy,* mother of U.S. President John F. Kennedy (May 29), Senators Robert F. (November 20) and Edward M. (February 22) Kennedy. [d. January 22, 1995]

1891 *Ely Culbertson,* U.S. bridge expert born in Rumania; world champion *contract bridge* player; responsible for popularity of the game, especially during 1930s and 1940s. Became deeply involved in world peace activities during his later years, 1949–55. [d. December 17, 1955]

1892 *Arthur Seyss-Inquart,* German politician, Nazi leader; Chancellor of Austria, 1938–39; German High Commissioner of the Netherlands, 1940–45. Hanged for war crimes. [d. October 16, 1946]

1893 *Karl Augustus Menninger,* U.S. psychiatrist; with his father, Charles Frederich Menninger and his brother,

july

William Claire, created the *Menninger Foundation*, 1941, a national center for training of psychiatrists and treatment and research in mental health. [d. July 18, 1990]

1898 *Stephen Vincent Benét*, U.S. poet, short-story writer, novelist; Pulitzer Prize in poetry, 1928, 1943. [d. March 13, 1943]

Alexander Calder, U.S. sculptor; best known for his mobiles and stabiles. Also recognized for his watercolors, jewelry, tapestries, and carving. [d. November 11, 1976]

1899 *King Sobhuz II*, King of Swaziland, 1921–82. [d. August 21, 1982]

1908 *Amy Vanderbilt*, U.S. journalist, etiquette expert, author. [d. December 27, 1974]

1913 *Charles B(ates) Thornton*, U.S. industrialist; head of Ford Motor Company's "Whiz Kids," who set up modern management systems at the company, 1948–53; a founder of Litton Industries; Chairman and Chief Executive Officer of Litton, 1953–81. [d. November 24, 1981]

1922 *Jason (Nelson) Robards, Jr.*, U.S. actor.

1923 *Robert J. Dole*, U.S. politician, lawyer; Senator, 1969–91; presidential candidate, 1996.

1924 *Margaret Whiting (Madcap Maggie)*, U.S. singer, big band era star.

1928 *Orson Bean (Dallas Frederick Burrows)*, U.S. actor, comedian.

1932 *Oscar de la Renta*, U.S. fashion designer.

1940 *George Clinton*, U.S. R & B singer; best known for years with *Parliament* and *Funkadelic*

Terence Stamp, British actor.

Alex Trebek, Canadian-born television performer; known for hosting television game show, *Jeopardy!*, 1984– .

1945 *Bobby Sherman*, U.S. singer, actor.

1947 *Danny Glover*, U.S. actor; known for role in the *Lethal Weapon* movies with Mel Gibson.

Don Henley, U.S. singer, musician; member of the rock group, *The Eagles*.

1955 *Willem Dafoe*, U.S. actor.

1965 *John Leguizamo*, Colombian comedian and actor.

HISTORICAL EVENTS

1194 *Richard I* of England defeats *Philip Augustus* of France at Frèteval.

1298 *Edward I* of England defeats Scottish leader *William Wallace* at Falkirk.

1812 The *Battle of Salamanca* ends in the defeat of the French by the British under *Wellesley* during British drive into Spain.

1847 First large *Mormon* company enters Salt Lake Valley.

1876 *Maria Spelterina* walks across *Niagara Falls* on a tightrope.

1913 Turkey recaptures Adrianople and forces Bulgaria to capitulate (*Second Balkan War*).

1917 The reorganized Rumanian army joins with the Russians

in launching an attack on the Germans in the *Battle of Marasesti (World War I)*.

Siam declares war on Germany and Austria-Hungary (*World War I*).

1932 U.S. Congress adopts the *Federal Home Loan Bank Act* to help financial institutions lend money to homeowners.

1943 U.S. forces liberate *Palermo, Sicily (World War II)*.

1944 The *Ziegfeld Follies* closes after 553 performances on Broadway.

1946 Bolivian students and laborers overthrow the government, killing President *Gualberto Villarroel*. *Tomas Monje Gutierrez* becomes provisional president.

Zionists bomb the British military headquarters at the *King David Hotel* in Jerusalem.

1963 *Sonny Liston* defeats *Floyd Patterson* in the first round to retain the world heavyweight championship.

1969 Prince *Juan Carlos (Alfonso Victor María de Borbón y) Borbón* is named legal successor and heir to the Spanish throne by General *Francisco Franco*. Juan Carlos assumes the throne upon the death of Franco, November 20, 1975.

1976 The International Amateur Athletic Federation bans *South Africa* from participation in track and field events because of its apartheid policies.

Romanian gymnast, *Nadia Comaneci*, becomes the first Olympic athlete to score a perfect ten.

1977 Officials reveal that *Deng Xiaoping* has been restored to power in the Chinese Communist Party.

1981 *Mehmet Ali Agca* is sentenced to life imprisonment for the attempted assassination of Pope John Paul II.

1983 The Polish government officially lifts *martial law* after 19 months, but new restrictions further restrict the press and demonstrations.

1987 The U.S. Navy begins escorting reflagged Kuwaiti oil tankers through the *Strait of Hormuz* and across the *Persian Gulf* as a protective measure against Iranian attacks.

1995 U.S. astronomers *Alan Hale* and *Thomas Bopp,* working separately, discover the Hale-Bopp Comet.

july

JULY
23

HOLIDAYS

Egypt
Revolution Anniversary
Commemorates the overthrow of
the monarchy, 1952.

Libya
A.R.E. National Day
Commemorates the overthrow of
the monarchy in Egypt, 1952.

Oman
Accession of the Sultan

Papua New Guinea
Remembrance Day

Syria
Egyptian Revolution Day

RELIGIOUS CALENDAR

The Saints
The Three Wise Men, patrons of
Cologne and of travellers. [d.
1st century]
St. Liborius, Bishop of Le Mans.
Invoked against gravel and
the stone and allied
complaints. [d. 4th century]
St. John Cassian, abbot. Founded
two monasteries at Marseilles.
Commonly known as *Cassian.*
[d. c. 433]
St. Romula and her companions,
virgins. [d. 6th century]
St. Anne, virgin. Also called
Susanna. [d. c. 918]
St. Bridget of Sweden, widow and
founder of the Order of the
Most Holy Savior, or the
Bridgettines. Patron of
Sweden. [d. 1373]

St. Apollinaris, Bishop of Ravenna
and martyr. [death date
unknown]

The Beatified
Blessed Joan of Orvieto, virgin. [d.
1306]

BIRTHDATES

1649 *Pope Clement XI,* pope
1700–21. [d. March 19, 1721]

1816 *Charlotte Saunders
Cushman,* U.S. actress; best
known for her portrayals of
Lady Macbeth. [d. February
12, 1876]

1823 *Coventry Kersey Dighton
Patmore,* British poet,
political reactionary; assistant
librarian of British Museum,
1846–65. [d. November 26,
1896]

1834 *James Gibbons,* U.S. Roman
Catholic cardinal; founder of
*Catholic University of
America.* [d. March 24, 1921]

1863 *Samuel Henry Kress,* U.S.
merchant, philanthropist;
founder of S. H. Kress & Co.,
5, 10, and 25 cent store.
Established the *Samuel H.
Kress Foundation* to
distribute his significant art
collection to selected
museums throughout the U.S.
[d. September 22, 1955]

Kelly Miller, U.S. black
academician, editor; dean of

Howard University School of
Arts & Letters. [d. December
29, 1939]

1883 *Sir Alan Francis Brooke, 1st
Viscount Alanbrooke,* British
soldier; Commander in Chief
of British home forces,
1940–41; Chief of Imperial
General Staff, 1941; Field
Marshal, 1944. [d. June 17,
1963]

1884 *Albert Warner,* U.S. film
executive born in Poland;
brother of Harry (December
12) and Jack (August 2); with
his brothers, founded Warner
Brothers Studios. [d.
November 26, 1967]

1885 *Vincent Sardi, Sr.,* U.S.
restaurateur; opened Sardi's
restaurant in Manhattan's
theater district, 1921. [d.
November 19, 1969]

1886 *Arthur W. Brown,* British
aviator; with *John Alcock*
made the first flight across
the Atlantic, 1919. [d. October
4, 1948]

1888 *Raymond (Thornton)
Chandler,* U.S. short-story
writer, novelist; author of
numerous detective stories
revolving around the
escapades of detective *Philip
Marlowe.* [d. March 26, 1959]

1892 *Haile Selassie (Tafari
Makonnen),* called the *Lion
of Judah,* Emperor of

Ethiopia, 1930–74. [d. August 27, 1975]

1894 *Arthur Treacher,* British actor; famous for his roles as a haughty butler. [d. December 14, 1975]

1906 *Vladimir Prelog,* Yugoslav-Swiss chemist; Nobel Prize in chemistry for his work in *stereochemistry* (with J. W. Cornforth), 1975. [d. January 7, 1998]

1911 *Penitala Fiatau Teo,* Tuvaluan statesman; Governor-General, 1978–86.

1912 *Michael Wilding,* British actor. [d. July 8, 1979]

1913 *Michael Foot,* British political leader; head of the Labour Party, 1980–83.

1919 *Harold Henry (Pee Wee) Reese,* U.S. baseball player; shortstop, 1940–58; collected 2,170 hits in career; elected to Hall of Fame, 1984.

1925 *Gloria DeHaven,* U.S. actress.

Dr. Quett Ketumile Joni Masire, Botswanan statesman; President, 1980– .

1930 *Moon Landrieu,* U.S. politician; Mayor of New Orleans, 1970–78, Secretary of Housing and Urban Development, 1979–81.

1931 *Arata Isozaki,* Japanese architect.

1934 *Bert Convy,* actor; host of television game shows. [d. July 15, 1991]

1936 *Donald Scott (Don) Drysdale,* U.S. baseball player, sportscaster; holder of Major League pitching record for most consecutive scoreless innings. [d. July 3, 1993]

Anthony Kennedy, U.S. jurist; associate justice of the Supreme Court, 1988– .

1940 *Don Imus,* radio talk show host.

1947 *David Essex (David Cook),* British rock singer, actor.

1961 *Woody Harrelson,* U.S. actor; portrayed Woody Boyd on TV series *Cheers.*

1962 *Eriq La Salle,* U.S. actor; known for his role as Dr. Peter Benton on the TV drama *ER.*

HISTORICAL EVENTS

1840 *Union Act* is passed by British Parliament, uniting *Upper* and *Lower Canada* into one government with one governor, one council, and one popularly elected assembly.

1920 *British East Africa* becomes crown colony of *Kenya.*

1950 *King Leopold III* of Belgium returns after six years in exile and is met by Socialist demonstrations which force his abdication on July 17, 1951.

1952 Egypt's Lt. Col. *Gamal Abdel Nasser* and a group of military officers stage a coup d'état and exile *King Farouk.*

1956 The U.S. Public Health Service releases results of a 10-year survey showing that *fluoridation of drinking water* dramatically decreases tooth decay.

1960 *Cuba* signs a major trade agreement involving the sale of sugar to the *People's Republic of China.*

1967 U.S. National Guard troops are called into *Detroit* to quell racial violence.

1970 *Sultan Sa'īd ibn Taimur* of Oman is deposed by his son, *Qabus ibn Sa'īd,* in a palace coup.

1971 *William R. Tolbert, Jr.,* is sworn in as President of *Liberia* upon the death of William Tubman.

1976 *Mario Soares* is inaugurated as premier of Portugal.

1977 Muslim leader *Hamaas Abdul Khaalis* and two followers are found guilty of kidnapping, conspiracy, and second-degree murder during their seizure in March of three buildings in Washington, D.C.

Junius Jayewardene is inaugurated as prime minister of Sri Lanka.

1979 *Ayatollah Khomeini,* Islamic religious leader of Iran, issues a ban on music and reaffirms bans on most Western movies, alcoholic drink, singing by women, and swimming of men and women in the same pool or at the same beaches.

1986 *Andrew, Duke of York,* and *Sarah Ferguson* are married at Westminster Abbey in London.

1988 General *Ne Win* resigns as chairman of the Burma Socialist Program Party, following several months of student disturbances.

1997 *Sali Berisha* resigns as president of Albania over financial scandals.

july

1997 *Slobodan Milosevic* takes office as the new president of Yugoslavia. Milosevic is the former president of Serbia (December 20, 1992).

HOLIDAYS

Ecuador, Venezuela
Bolívar's Birthday
Commemorates birth of Simón Bolívar, the *George Washington of South America,* 1783.

Fiji
Constitution Day

U.S. (Utah)
Pioneer Day

RELIGIOUS CALENDAR

The Saints
St. Declan, first Bishop of Ardmore. [d. 6th century]
St. Boris and *St. Gleb,* martyrs; patrons of Muscovy. Sometimes referred to by their christening names, *Romanus and David.* Gleb is also called *Cliba, Hliba.* [d. 1015]
St. Christina the Astonishing, virgin. [d. 1224]
St. Cunegund, virgin. Also called *Cunegundes* or *Kinga.* [d. 1292]
St. Christina, virgin and martyr. Also called *Christine.* [death date unknown]
St. Lewina, virgin and martyr. Also called *Lewine.* [death date unknown]
St. Wulfhad and *St. Ruffin,* brothers, princes, and martyrs. [death date unknown]

The Beatified
Blessed Nicholas, Bishop of Linköping. [d. 1391]
Blessed Felicia of Milan, virgin and abbess. [d. 1444]
Blessed John of Tossignano, Bishop of Ferrara. [d. 1446]
Blessed Augustine of Biella. [d. 1493]
The Durham Martyrs of 1594: Blessed John Speed (or *Spence*); *Blessed John Boste,* priest; *Blessed George Swallowell; Blessed John Ingram,* priest.

BIRTHDATES

1738 *Elisabeth Wolff-Bekker, (Silviana),* Dutch novelist, essayist, poet, translator. [d. November 5, 1804]

1783 *Simón Bolívar,* South American soldier, statesman, revolutionary leader; leader of struggle for independence from Spain in Venezuela, Peru, and Colombia. [d. December 17, 1830]

1798 *John Adams Dix,* U.S. politician, soldier; U.S. Secretary of the Treasury, 1861; Governor of New York, 1872–74. [d. April 21, 1879]

1802 *Aléxandre Dumas (Dumas père),* French novelist, playwright; author of: *Les Trois Mousquetaires, Le Comte de Monte Cristo,* as well as numerous other novels and plays. [d. December 5, 1870]

1817 *Adolphus William,* Grand Duke of Luxembourg; the first ruler of the autonomous duchy. [d. November 17, 1905]

1827 *Francisco Solano López,* president of Paraguay, 1862–70. [d. March 1, 1870]

1842 *Ambrose (Gwinett) Bierce,* U.S. journalist, short-story writer; known for his scathing wit and preoccupation with the supernatural. His tales of the Civil War and *Devil's Dictionary* gained him wide recognition, especially by American writers like O. Henry and Stephen Crane. [d. 1914?]

1855 *William (Hooker) Gillette,* U.S. dramatist, actor; best known for his stage portrayals of legendary detective *Sherlock Holmes.* [d. April 29, 1937]

1857 *Juan Vincente Gómez,* Venezuelan soldier, political leader; dictator of Venezuela and commander-in-chief of its army, 1908–35. [d. December 17, 1935]

Henrik Pontoppidan, Danish novelist, short-story writer; Nobel Prize in literature (with K. Gjellerup), 1917. [d. August 21, 1943]

1898 *Amelia Earhart,* U.S. aviator; pioneer in development of

july

U.S. aviation industry; first woman to cross the Atlantic by plane; disappeared over the Pacific during a flight from New Guinea to Howland Island. [d. July 2, 1937?]

1900 *Zelda Fitzgerald,* U.S. author; wife of F. Scott Fitzgerald. [d. March 10, 1948]

1914 *Kenneth Bancroft Clark,* U.S. educator, psychologist; developed methods of evaluating anti-poverty programs; author of *Dark Ghetto.*

1916 *John D. MacDonald,* U.S. mystery novelist, short story writer. [d. December 28, 1986]

1920 *Alexander H. Cohen,* U.S. theater and television producer.

1921 *Billy Taylor (William Edward Taylor),* U.S. musician, jazz pianist.

1922 *Charles McCurdy Mathias, Jr.,* U.S. politician, Senator, 1969–87.

1927 *Alex Katz,* U.S. artist; known for his portrait paintings.

1929 *Peter Yates,* British film director; known for his 1979 film, *Breaking Away.*

1934 *William Doyle Ruckleshaus,* U.S. government official; Administrator, Environmental Protection Agency.

1935 *Patrick Bruce Oliphant,* U.S. cartoonist; Pulitzer Prize for editorial cartooning, 1967.

1936 *Ruth Ann Buzzi,* U.S. actress, comedienne; known for her appearances on television series, *Laugh-In,* 1968–73.

1940 *Dan Hedaya,* U.S. actor; played Nick Tortelli on TV series *Cheers.*

1942 *Chris Sarandon,* U.S. actor; starred in the movie, *Dog Day Afternoon,* 1975.

1951 *Lynda Carter,* U.S. actress.

1963 *Julie Krone,* U.S. jockey; first woman to win horse racing's Triple Crown.

Karl Malone, U.S. basketball player.

1964 *Barry Bonds,* U.S. baseball player.

HISTORICAL EVENTS

1758 British take *Louisburg* in Canada from the French (*French and Indian War*).

1918 Cornerstone of the *Hebrew University* in Jerusalem is laid by *Dr. Chaim Weizmann.*

1923 *Treaty of Lausanne* is concluded, by which *Turkey* gives up all claims to non-Turkish territories lost in

World War I, but retains control over areas still regarded as modern Turkey.

1943 British and U.S. air forces begin concentrated bombing of *Hamburg,* Germany (*World War II*).

1963 Cuban government expropriates the U.S. embassy building and grounds in *Havana.*

Victor Marijnen is inaugurated as prime minister of the Netherlands.

1972 *Jigme Singye Wangchuk* is crowned king of Bhutan.

1974 U.S. Supreme Court orders President *Richard Nixon* to surrender 64 tapes to Washington district court (*Watergate Incident*).

1975 The three *Apollo 18* astronauts return to earth, ending an age of U.S. space exploration that began in 1961. The next U.S. venture into space does not occur until the launch of U.S. space shuttle *Columbia,* April 12, 1981.

1989 *Prime Minister Sousuke Uno* of Japan announces his resignation after only seven weeks in office.

1997 *Rexhep Mejdani* is elected president of Albania.

HOLIDAYS

Costa Rica
Annexation of Guanacaste

Cuba
National Revolutionary Festival
The first day of a three-day
celebration.

Ecuador (Guayaquil)
Public Holiday
Commemorates the founding of
Guayaquil).

Puerto Rico
Constitution Day

Spain
St. James Day

Tunisia
Republic Day
Commemorates the proclamation of
the Republic, 1957.

RELIGIOUS CALENDAR

Feasts
St. James the Greater, Apostle. First
apostle to be martyred.
Patron saint of Spain and
Chile. Also called *James
Major, Santiago.* [d. 44]
[Major holy day, Episcopal
Church; minor festival,
Lutheran Church.]

The Saints
St. Thea, St. Valentina and *St. Paul,*
martyrs. [d. 308]
St. Magnericus, Bishop of Trier. [d.
596]
St. Christopher, martyr; patron of
archers, fruit dealers,

travelers, mariners, and
motorists. Invoked against
water, tempest, plagues and
sudden death. Also called
Christoper, or *Christophorus.*
[death date unknown]

BIRTHDATES

1750 *Henry Knox,* American
Revolutionary general;
considered an artillery genius.
[d. October 25, 1806]

1775 *Anna Harrison,* wife of U.S.
President William Henry
Harrison. [d. February 25,
1864]

1839 *Francis Garnier,* French
explorer of mainland China.
[d. December 21, 1873]

1844 *Thomas (Cowperthwait)
Eakins,* U.S. artist; recognized
posthumously as one of the
greatest American artists;
noted for his realism and use
of geometrical perspective.
[d. June 25, 1916]

1848 *Arthur James Balfour, 1st
Earl of Balfour,* British
statesman; Prime Minister,
1902–05. [d. March 19, 1930]

1849 *Richard Lydekker,* British
naturalist, geologist, author.
[d. April 16, 1915]

1853 *David Belasco,* U.S. producer,
playwright; known for his
innovations in staging

techniques and technical
precision. Author of *Madame
Butterfly,* later made into an
opera by Giacomo Puccini. [d.
May 14, 1931]

1870 *Maxfield (Frederick) Parrish,*
U.S. painter, illustrator;
known for his use of
sentimental, romantic, and
dreamlike qualities in
paintings. [d. March 30, 1966]

1880 *Morris Raphael Cohen,* U.S.
philosopher, author; known
for his independent thought
that drew upon pragmatism,
logical positivism, and
linguistic analysis; recognized
for his work in the area of
legal philosophy. [d. January
28, 1947]

1884 *Davidson Black,* Canadian
anatomist; discoverer of
Peking Man, whose fossils
date back to between 300,000
and 400,000 B.C. [d. 1934]

1894 *Walter Brennan,* U.S.
character actor. [d.
September 21, 1974]

1895 *Gavrilo Princip,* Serbian
assassin of Archduke *Francis
Ferdinand* (December 18)
and his wife Sophie, 1914.
This assassination triggered
World War I. [d. April 28,
1918]

1902 *Eric Hoffer,* U.S. philosopher,
author; representative of the
working class in the area of

july

social and political thought. [d. May 21, 1983]

1905 *Elias Canetti,* Bulgarian author; works include *Auto-da-Fe,* 1935, and *Crowds and Power,* 1960; Nobel Prize, 1981. [d. August 13, 1994]

1906 *Johnny Hodges (John Cornelius Hodges),* U.S. jazz alto saxophonist of the 1930s and 1940s. [d. May 11, 1970]

1915 *Mario Del Monaco,* Italian opera singer; appeared with the Metropolitan Opera more than 100 times between 1951 and 1959. [d. October 16, 1982]

1920 *Rosalind Franklin,* British geneticist; known for her contributions toward the discovery of the molecular structure of DNA. [d. April 16, 1958]

1924 *Frank Church,* U.S. politician and lawyer; U.S. Senator, 1957–1981. [d. April 7, 1984]

1925 *Jerry Paris,* U.S. actor, director; known for his role as the neighbor on television series, *The Dick Van Dyke Show,* 1961–66. [d. April 2, 1986]

1935 *Adnan Khashoggi,* Saudi businessman; once considered to be the richest man in the world.

1954 *Walter Payton,* U.S. football player; running back, Chicago Bears, 1975–88; set National Football League career record in rushing, 1984.

HISTORICAL EVENTS

1139 *Alfonso Henriques* defeats the Moors in the *Battle of Ourique* and becomes King of Portugal.

1261 *Michael VIII Palaeologus,* Byzantine emperor, recovers Constantinople and overthrows *Latin Empire,* which had been established by the successful Crusaders in 1204.

1415 *Prince Henry* of Portugal sails for Morocco, the first of a series of voyages of exploration and conquest in Africa by Europeans.

1564 *Ferdinand I, Holy Roman Emperor,* dies and is succeeded by *Maximilian II.*

1712 The Protestant cantons led by the city of Bern win a decisive victory over the Catholic cantons at the *Battle of Villmergen,* ending the religious wars in *Switzerland.*

1848 In *Battle of Custozza,* Austrians defeat forces of *Charles Albert,* King of Sardinia, suppressing first efforts toward Italian independence.

1914 Austria and Serbia mobilize against one another in the wake of the assassination at Sarajevo of the Austrian heir, Archduke *Francis Ferdinand.*

1929 *Pope Pius XI* makes an appearance outside the Vatican; this is the first public appearance of a pope since the fall of the Papal States, 1870.

1934 *Franklin D. Roosevelt* reaches Hilo, Hawaii, on board *U.S.S.*

Houston, becoming the first U.S. president to visit Hawaii.

Austrian Chancellor *Engelbert Dollfuss* is assassinated by Nazi adherents.

1941 Radio Corp. of America announces the development of a high voltage *electron microscope* with the ability to magnify objects 100,000 times.

1943 Premier *Benito Mussolini* of Italy and his cabinet resign.

1956 Italian ocean liner *Andrea Doria* sinks after collision with the Swedish ship *Stockholm* off Cape Cod, killing approximately 50 people.

1957 The Tunisian monarchy is abolished and *Habib Bourguiba* assumes leadership of a new republic.

1967 Pope *Paul VI,* visiting Turkey, becomes the first pontiff to worship in an Eastern Orthodox Church.

1975 *A Chorus Line,* by Marvin Hamlisch and Edward Kleban, premieres on Broadway.

1978 The first documented *test-tube baby* is born in Lancashire, England. The five pound, 12-ounce girl, *Louise Joy Brown,* is delivered by Caesarean section.

1984 Soviet cosmonaut, *Svetlana Savitskaya,* becomes the first woman to walk in space.

1988 The first peace talks of the 10-year-old Cambodian conflict begin in *Bogor, Indonesia.*

HOLIDAYS

Cuba
National Revolutionary Festival
The second day of a three-day celebration.

Liberia
Independence Day
Commemorates ratification of Liberian constitution, 1847.

Maldives
Independence Day
Commemorates achievement of independence from Great Britain, 1965.

RELIGIOUS CALENDAR

The Saints
St. Joachim, father of the Virgin Mary, and *St. Anne,* matron, mother of the Virgin Mary. Anne is patron of women in labor, miners, dealers in used clothing, seamstresses, carpenters, stablemen, and broommakers. Invoked against poverty and to find lost objects. [d. 1st century B.C.]
St. Simeon the Armenian, pilgrim. [d. 1016]
St. Bartholomea Capitanio, virgin and co-founder of the Sisters of Charity of Lovene. [d. 1833]

The Beatified
Blessed William Ward, martyr. [d. 1641]

BIRTHDATES

1739 *George Clinton,* U.S. Revolutionary soldier, public official; Governor of New York, 1777–95, 1800–04; U.S. Vice-President, 1805–12. [d. April 20, 1812]

1779 *Thomas Birch,* U.S. artist; noted for his marine paintings. [d. January 13, 1851]

1796 *George Catlin,* U.S. painter, author; created a knowledgeable, first-hand account, in words and pictures, of the life and details of the American Indian. He produced numerous illustrated texts, the greatest of which is *Letters and Notes on the Manners, Customs, and Conditions of the North American Indians,* 1841. [d. December 23, 1872]

1799 *Isaac Babbitt,* U.S. inventor, metallurgist; founded the company which was to become Reed & Barton silversmiths; developed a new alloy ("Babbitt metal") for use in bearings. [d. May 26, 1862]

1805 *Constantino Brumidi,* U.S. painter born in Italy; artist of the frescoes in the Capitol, Washington, D.C. [d. 1880]

1829 *Auguste Marie François Beernaert,* Belgian diplomat; Nobel Peace Prize for his work as member of international peace conferences of 1899 and 1907 (with P. H. B. Estournelles de Constant), 1909. [d. October 6, 1912]

1856 *William Rainey Harper,* U.S. educator, scholar; first President of *University of Chicago,* 1891–1906. [d. January 10, 1906]

George Bernard Shaw, British playwright, critic; Nobel Prize in literature, 1925. [d. November 1, 1950]

1858 *Edward Mandell House,* U.S. statesman; most trusted adviser of President *Woodrow Wilson.* [d. March 28, 1938]

1860 *Philippe Jean Bunau-Varilla,* French engineer, diplomat; involved in early French efforts to construct *Panama Canal,* 1884–89, 1894. Negotiated *Hay-Bunau-Varilla Treaty* by which U.S. gained control of Canal Zone, 1903. [d. May 18, 1940]

1870 *Ignacio Zuloaga y Zabaleta,* Spanish painter; noted for his use of Spanish folklore themes. [d. October 31, 1945]

1874 *Serge Alexandrovitch Koussevitzky,* U.S. conductor, born in Russia; Director, Russian State Symphony Orchestra, 1918–20;

july

Conductor, Boston Symphony Orchestra, 1924–49. Established *Berkshire Symphonic Festival,* 1934. [d. June 4, 1951]

1875 *Carl Gustav Jung,* Swiss psychologist, psychiatrist; founded analytical psychology. [d. June 6, 1961]

1885 *André Maurois (Émile Salomon Wilhelm Herzog),* French writer; known for his biographies of Balzac, Disraeli, Byron, and others. [d. October 9, 1967]

1886 *Emil Jannings (Theodor Friedrich Emil Janenz),* U.S. actor; Academy Award for *The Last Command.* [d. January 3, 1950]

1894 *Aldous (Leonard) Huxley,* British novelist, essayist; best known for his works *Brave New World, Point Counter Point,* and *Eyeless in Gaza.* [d. November 22, 1963]

1895 *Robert Ranke Graves,* British poet, author; wrote over 135 books, known for his novel of ancient Rome, *I, Claudius,* 1934. [d. December 7, 1985]

1897 *Paul William Gallico,* U.S. novelist, journalist. [d. July 15, 1976]

1903 *(Carey) Estes Kefauver,* U.S. politician, lawyer; Congressman, 1939–63. [d. August 10, 1963]

1906 *Gracie Allen (Grace Ethel Cecile Rosalie Allen),* U.S. comedienne; always performed with husband, *George Burns* (January 20). [d. August 27, 1964]

1908 *Salvador Allende Gossens,* Chilean politician, physician; first Marxist to be elected president of Chile, 1970–73. [d. September 11, 1973]

1912 *Vivian Vance,* U.S. actress; known for her role as Ethel Mertz in the television series, *I Love Lucy,* 1951–59; featured in the television series, *The Lucy Show,* 1962–65. [d. August 17, 1979]

1919 *James E. Lovelock,* British climatologist; known for his Gaia hypothesis.

1922 *Blake Edwards (William Blake McEdwards),* U.S. film director; noted for the *Pink Panther* film series.

1928 *Stanley Kubrick,* U.S.-born filmmaker, writer, producer, director.

1940 *Mary Jo Kopechne,* U.S. secretary; drowned in a car accident off Chappaquiddik Island bridge involving Senator Edward Kennedy. [d. July 19, 1969]

1943 *Mick Jagger (Michael Philip Jagger),* British rock singer; lead singer of *The Rolling Stones* since 1962.

1954 *Vitas Gerulaitis,* U.S. tennis player. [d. September 18, 1994]

1959 *Kevin Spacey,* U.S. actor; Academy Award (Best Supporting Actor) for *The Usual Suspects,* 1996.

HISTORICAL EVENTS

1648 Swedes and French, allied against the Holy Roman Emperor, capture *Prague (Thirty Years' War).*

1757 French defeat English at *Hastenbeck (Seven Years' War).*

British generals Amherst and Wolfe capture Louisburg,

taking more than 6,000 French prisoners (*French and Indian War*).

1788 *New York State* ratifies the new Constitution and becomes the 11th of the 13 original American states.

1803 In England the *Surrey Iron Railway,* first public freight-carrying railroad, opens from Wandsworth to Croydon with horses supplying motive power.

1847 *Liberia* is established as the first free and independent republic in Africa.

1858 *Sir Nathan Meyer, 1st Baron Rothschild,* becomes the first Jew admitted to the House of Lords.

1941 U.S. President *Franklin D. Roosevelt* names *Gen. Douglas MacArthur* Commander in Chief of U.S. forces in the Far East.

President Roosevelt freezes all Japanese credit in the U.S., virtually stopping Japanese-American trade.

1945 *Clement Attlee* becomes prime minister of Great Britain.

1951 U.S. Army disbands its oldest and last remaining all-black unit, the *24th Infantry Regiment.*

1952 *Eva Peron,* wife of Argentine president Juan Peron, dies in Buenos Aires.

1953 *Fidel Castro* leads an armed opposition in an unsuccessful attack on the Moncado army barracks.

1956 Egypt nationalizes the *Suez Canal.*

1957 President *Carlos Castillo Armas* of Guatemala is

assassinated by a palace guard.

1964 The *Organization of American States* votes to impose economic sanctions and end diplomatic relations with *Cuba*.

1965 *Maldives* becomes independent of Great Britain.

1971 *Apollo 15,* U.S. manned lunar spacecraft, is launched, carrying astronauts *Scott, Worden,* and *Irwin* to the moon's surface, where they will perform experiments and explore in the lunar rover.

1973 U.S. President *Richard Nixon* refuses to comply with subpoenas ordering him to release the Watergate tapes (*Watergate Incident*).

1976 Nitrogen is found in Martian atmosphere by *Viking 1,* unmanned explorer, but there are no signs of life present.

1990 U.S. President *George Bush* signs the *Americans with Disabilities Act* into law.

1993 *Disaster areas* are declared in ten midwestern states due to what is later called "The Great Flood of 1993."

july

JULY
27

HOLIDAYS

Belarus
Independence Day

Bosnia and Herzegovina
Labor Day

Cuba
National Revolutionary Festival
The third day of a three-day celebration.

Maldives
Independence Day
The second day of the two-day national celebration.

Puerto Rico
Barbosa's Birthday
Commemorates the birth of José Barbosa, political leader, 1857.

Yugoslavia
Croatian and Bosnian Uprising Day

RELIGIOUS CALENDAR

The Saints

St. Pantaleon, martyr; patron of doctors and midwives. Invoked against tuberculosis. Also called *Panteleimon.* [d. c. 305]

St. Aurelius, St. Natalia, and their companions, martyrs. [d. c. 852]

St. Theobald of Marly, abbot. [d. 1247]

The Seven Sisters of Ephesus. Legend says they were sealed into a cave while still alive. Invoked against sleeplessness. [death date unknown]

The Beatified

Blessed Berthold of Garsten, abbot. [d. 1142]
Blessed Lucy of Amelia, virgin and prioress. [d. 1350]
Blessed Rudolf Aquaviva and his companions, martyrs. [d. 1583]
Blessed Mary Magdalen Martinengo, virgin and abbess. [d. 1737]

BIRTHDATES

1768 *Charlotte Corday (Marie Anne Charlotte Corday d'Armont),* French patriot; assassin of French revolutionary leader Jean Paul Marat (May 24). [d. July 17, 1793]

1777 *Thomas Campbell,* Scottish poet, biographer; his biography of S. T. Coleridge (October 21) is considered the standard. [d. June 25, 1844]

1801 *Sir George Biddell Airy,* British mathematician, astronomer, physicist; discoverer of basis for study of astigmatism. [d. January 2, 1892]

1824 *Aléxandre Dumas (Dumas fils),* French dramatist, novelist; son of Aléxandre Dumas (père) (July 24). Author of *La Dame aux Camèlias,* 1848. [d. November 27, 1895]

1835 *Giosuè Carducci,* Italian poet, critic; Nobel Prize in literature, 1906. [d. February 16, 1907]

1852 *George Foster Peabody,* U.S. merchant, banker, philanthropist; amassed fortune in international commercial trade; established and endowed many institutions and funds. Founded Peabody Museum of natural history and science at Yale University. [d. March 4, 1938]

1857 *Jose Celso Barbosa,* Puerto Rican journalist, politician, [d. September 21, 1921]

Sir Ernest Alfred Wallis Budge, British orientologist, archaeologist; keeper of Egyptian and Assyrian antiquities at British Museum, 1893–1924. [d. November 23, 1934]

1870 *(Joseph-Pierre) Hilaire Belloc,* British writer, born in France; journalist, member of Parliament, 1906–10. [d. July 16, 1953]

1881 *Hays Fischer,* German chemist; Nobel Prize in chemistry for research into constitution of *hemin* and *chlorophyll,* 1930. [d. March 31, 1945]

1901 *George D(avid) Woods,* U.S. banker; President and Chief

Executive Officer, World Bank, 1963–68; Chairman of J. Kaiser Foundation, 1968–82. [d. August 20, 1982]

1906 *Leo Ernest Durocher,* U.S. baseball player, manager; known both for his outstanding performances with the St. Louis Cardinals and Brooklyn Dodgers and for his flamboyant management style. [d. October 7, 1991]

1912 *Igor Markevitch,* Russian-born conductor; began as a composing prodigy; later known as a master of conducting precision. [d. March 7, 1983]

1916 *Elizabeth Hardwick,* U.S. author; first female recipient of the Nathan Drama Criticism Award, 1967; author of *Sleepless Nights.*

Keenan Wynn, U.S. actor. [d. October 14, 1986]

1922 *Norman Lear,* U.S. television producer, director.

1924 *Vincent Canby,* U.S. journalist, critic; *New York Times* film critic.

1931 *Jerry Van Dyke,* U.S. actor; brother of Dick Van Dyke; known for his role as Luther Van Dam on the TV sitcom *Coach.*

1937 *Don Galloway,* U.S. actor; known for his role as Sergeant Ed Brown on the television series, *Ironside,* 1967–75.

1938 *John Deutch,* Belgium-born educator; director for the Central Intelligence Agency, 1995– .

1942 *Bobbie Gentry (Roberta Streeter),* U.S. singer, songwriter.

1948 *Peggy Fleming,* U.S. figure skater; Olympic gold medalist, 1968; world champion, 1966–68.

Betty Thomas (Betty Thomas Nienhauser), U.S. actress; known for her role as Lucy Bates on the television series, *Hill Street Blues,* 1981–87.

1949 *Maureen Therese McGovern,* U.S. singer.

1953 *Rick Inatome,* U.S. business executive; founder, Computer Mart, 1976; President and Chief Executive Officer of Inacomp Computer Centers, 1982– .

HISTORICAL EVENTS

1054 *Siward of Northumbria* and *Malcolm* defeat *Macbeth* at *Dunsinane* in Scotland.

1214 *Battle of Bouvines* establishes France as a major European power, as Philip II of France, allied with Frederick II of Germany, defeats anti-Capetian coalition of England, Flanders, Belgium, Lorraine, and Holy Roman Emperor.

1689 Scottish Jacobites are defeated at *Killiecrankie.*

1694 *Bank of England* is incorporated.

1789 Congress establishes the U.S. *Department of State.*

1866 *Atlantic cable* is completed, establishing communication by telegraph between England and U.S.

1900 *H. J. Heinz Co.* is incorporated in Pennsylvania.

1941 Senate confirms the nomination of *Robert Jackson* to the U.S. Supreme Court.

1944 U.S. regains control of *Guam* after bitter fighting (*World War II*).

1953 Armistice is signed by United Nations and Communist delegates, ending *Korean War.*

1965 Belgium's longest governmental crisis since World War II is ended by the formation of a coalition cabinet by *Pierre Harmel* of the Social Christian Party.

1967 President Lyndon Johnson creates the *National Advisory Commission on Civil Disorders* to investigate the cause and recommend prevention of riots.

1979 The family of political activist *Steven Biko* is awarded $76,000 in an out-of-court settlement. They accused the government of negligence in the death of Biko.

1980 *Mohammed Reza Pahlavi,* the deposed Shah of Iran, dies in Cairo.

1985 Ugandan president, *Milton Obote,* is overthrown in a military coup by Brigadier *Basilio Olara Okello.*

1996 A bomb explodes in *Centennial Olympic Park* in Atlanta, Georgia, during the summer Olympics, killing one person.

july

JULY
28

HOLIDAYS

Peru
Independence Day
Commemorates Peru's declaration of independence from Spain, 1821. The first day of a two-day celebration.

San Marino
Public Holiday
Commemorates the fall of Fascism.

RELIGIOUS CALENDAR

The Saints
St. Victor I, pope and martyr; elected 189. [d. c. 199] Rome 189.

St. Innocent I, pope; elected 402. [d. 417]

St. Samson, Bishop of Dol. Important figure in the evangelization of Cornwall and the Channel Islands. Also called *Sampson.* [d. c. 565]

St. Botvid, martyr; venerated as one of the apostles of Sweden.

St. Nazarius and *St. Celsus,* martyrs. [death date unknown]

The Beatified
Blessed Antony Della Chiesa, friar and prior. [d. 1459]

BIRTHDATES

1804 *Ludwig Andreas Feuerbach,* German philosopher; after abandoning Hegelian idealism, adopted a philosophy of *naturalistic materialism* which culminated in the teaching that God is merely the outward projection of man's own nature. [d. September 13, 1872]

1812 *Józef Ignacy Kraszewski,* Polish writer of novels, plays, verse, criticism, and history; one of the most influential and prolific Polish authors of the 19th century. [d. March 19, 1887]

1830 *Charles Franklin Dunbar,* U.S. editor, economist; first professor of political economy at Harvard, 1870–1900. [d. January 29, 1900]

1844 *Gerard Manley Hopkins,* British Jesuit priest, poet; developed poetic techniques of *sprung rhythm, counterpoint,* and *inscape.* [d. June 8, 1889]

1859 *Ballington Booth,* U.S. reformer, born in England; son of William Booth (April 10), founder of the Salvation Army. Ballington headed the *Salvation Army* in Australia, 1885–87 and in U.S., 1887–96. After disagreement with his father, left organization and founded *Volunteers of America.* [d. October 5, 1940]

1866 *Beatrix Potter,* British author of children's books, illustrator; the creator of *Peter Rabbit.* [d. December 22, 1943]

1887 *Marcel Duchamp,* U.S. painter born in France; a founder of *Dadaism.* [d. October 2, 1968]

1892 *Joe E. Brown,* U.S. comedian. [d. July 6, 1973]

1901 *Rudy Vallee (Hubert Prior Vallee),* U.S. entertainer; first to popularize the singing style known as *crooning;* introduced Edgar Bergen (February 16) and Charlie McCarthy, George Burns (January 20), and Grace Allen (July 16). [d. July 3, 1986]

1902 *Kenneth Flexner Fearing,* U.S. novelist, poet; noted for his radical style in poetry, marked by unconventional structure and use of vernacular phrases. [d. June 26, 1961]

1906 *Maria Goeppert-Mayer,* U.S. physicist; Nobel Prize for Physics (1963) for her theory of nuclear shells.

1909 *(Clarence) Malcolm Lowry,* British author, poet; wrote autobiographical novel, *Under the Volcano,* 1947. [d. June, 1957]

1915 *Charles Hard Townes,* U.S. physicist; Nobel Prize in physics for development of *maser-laser principle* (with N. G. Basov and Aleksander M. Prokhorov), 1964.

1916 *David Brown,* U.S. producer, writer, journalist; produced the films, *The Sting, Jaws,* and *Cocoon.*

1925 *Baruch S. Blumberg,* U.S. physician; Nobel Prize in physiology or medicine for discoveries relating to origin and spread of infectious diseases (with D. C. Gajdusek), 1976.

1929 *Jacqueline Bouvier Kennedy Onassis,* former U.S. First Lady; widow of U.S. President John F. Kennedy (May 29); widow of Greek shipping magnate Aristotle Onassis. [d. May 19, 1994]

1937 *Peter (Oelrichs) Duchin,* U.S. musician; pianist and orchestra leader; son of Eddy Duchin (April 1).

1938 *Alberto Fujimori,* Peruvian educator, politician; President of Peru, 1990– .

1943 *(William Warren) Bill Bradley,* U.S. politician, basketball player for New York Knickerbockers, 1967–77; U.S. Senator, 1979–96.

1945 *James Robert (Jim) Davis,* U.S. cartoonist; created comic strip character, Garfield.

1948 *Georgia Bright Engel,* U.S. actress; known for her role as Georgette on the television series, *The Mary Tyler Moore Show,* 1972–77.

Sally Ann Struthers, U.S. actress; known for her role as Gloria on the television series, *All in the Family,* 1971–78; two Emmy Awards.

1949 *Vida Rochelle Blue,* U.S. baseball player; Cy Young and Most Valuable Player Awards, 1971

1958 *Terrance Stanley (Terry) Fox,* Canadian runner; after losing his leg to cancer, began a marathon run across Canada to raise money for research; died before completing run. [d. June 28, 1981]

HISTORICAL EVENTS

1402 *Timur Link (Tamerlane)* and his Mongols defeat and capture Ottoman ruler *Bajazet I* at the *Battle of Angora* (Ankara).

1461 *Charles VII* of France dies and is succeeded by *Louis XI.*

1540 *Thomas Cromwell, Earl of Essex,* is beheaded for heresy in the Tower of London after alienating *Henry VIII;* he had arranged Henry's brief and unsuccessful marriage to *Anne of Cleves.*

Henry VIII of England marries *Catherine Howard,* his fifth wife.

1588 *Spanish Armada,* anchored in Calais, is dispersed by English ships.

1637 A combined force from Plymouth, Massachusetts and Connecticut destroys remnants of *Pequot Indians* near New Haven (*Pequot War*).

1794 *Robespierre* and 71 others are guillotined, ending the *Reign of Terror (French Revolution).*

1821 *Peru,* under the leadership of *José de San Martín* declares itself independent of Spain.

1868 The *14th Amendment to U.S. Constitution* is ratified, granting citizenship to U.S. blacks.

1904 *Vyacheslav Plehwe,* Russian Minister of the Interior, is assassinated.

1914 *Austria-Hungary* declares war on *Serbia (World War I).*

1916 *Battle of Kovel* renews the successful Russian offensive against Austria in southern Galicia (*World War I*).

1926 Panama-U.S. Treaty is signed, protecting *Panama Canal* in time of war.

1932 *Bonus March* on Washington, D.C. is disbanded by federal troops; the march resulted from dissatisfaction on the part of soldiers over U.S. government's honoring of soldiers' bonus certificates.

1945 *Jose Luis Bustamante Rivero* becomes president of Peru.

1954 Elia Kazan's film, *On the Waterfront,* premieres in New York.

France begins evacuating its citizens and Vietnamese supporters from *Hanoi* after the mandated ceasefire takes effect. Under the terms of the partition treaty, the city belongs to the Viet Minh.

1956 *Manuel Prado Ugarteche* is inaugurated as president of Peru after the nation's first free election in 11 years.

1963 *Fernando Belaúnde Terry* is inaugurated as president of Peru.

1965 President Lyndon Johnson requests that fifty thousand additional soldiers be sent to Vietnam and doubles the draft (*Vietnam War*).

1972 Mexican President *Luis Echeverría* decrees the expropriation of some

july

500,000 acres of private estates and distribution of the land to peasants.

1973 U.S. astronauts *Alan L. Bean, Owen K. Garriott,* and *Jack R. Lousma* are launched into space for a 59-day mission in *Skylab,* demonstrating man's ability to withstand long periods in space.

1976 Two major *earthquakes,* occurring 16 hours apart and measuring 8.2 and 7.9 on the Richter scale, strike northeast *China,* resulting in nearly 750,000 deaths.

1977 First oil through the *Alaskan Pipeline* reaches Valdez, Alaska.

1979 The leader of a breakaway faction of the *Janata Party,* 77-year old *Charan Sinph,* is sworn in as Prime Minister of India but resigns within one month as Gandhi government regains power.

1985 *Alain Garcia Perez* is inaugurated as president of Peru.

1989 *Ali Akbar Rafsanjani* is elected president of Iran.

HOLIDAYS

Peru
Independence Day
The second day of a two-day celebration.

RELIGIOUS CALENDAR

The Saints

St. Martha, virgin; sister of Mary and Lazarus; ministered to Jesus. Patron of hotelkeepers, laundresses, housewives, cooks, and those of service to the needy. [d. 1st century]

St. Simplicius, St. Faustinus and *St. Beatrice,* martyrs. Beatrice is also called *Viatrix.* [d. c. 304]

St. Felix II, antipope. [d. 365]

St. Lupus, Bishop of Troyes. Also called *Loup.* [d. 478]

St. Sulian, founder of Luxulyan Monastery. Also called *Silin.* [d. 6th century]

St. Olaf of Norway, King of Norway and martyr; patron and national hero of Norway. Also called *Olaus,* or *Olave.* [d. 1030]

St. William Pinchon, Bishop of Saint-Brieuc. [d. 1234]

The Beatified

Blessed Urban II, pope. Elected 1088. [d. 1099]

BIRTHDATES

1793 *Jan Kollár,* Slovak poet, philologist born in Hungary. [d. January 4, 1852]

1794 *Thomas Corwin,* U.S. lawyer, legislator; U.S. Secretary of the Treasury, 1850–53. [d. December 18, 1865]

1796 *Christian Winther,* Danish romantic poet; author of epic poem *Hjortens Flugt.* [d. December 30, 1876]

1805 *Alexis de Tocqueville,* French writer; noted for his writings on American democracy; author of *La Dèmocratie en Amérique.* [d. April 26, 1859]

1820 *Clement Laird Vallandigham,* U.S. public official, lawyer; leader of the *Peace Democrats* or *Copperheads* during the U.S. Civil War; vehemently opposed President Abraham Lincoln's policies during the Civil War; opposition resulted in his banishment to the Confederacy. [d. June 17, 1871]

1828 *John Sargent Pillsbury,* U.S. manufacturer, politician; co-owner of C.A. Pillsbury Co.; Governor of Minnesota, 1876–82. [d. October 18, 1901]

1861 *Alice Roosevelt,* first wife of U.S. President Theodore Roosevelt. [d. February 14, 1884]

1869 *(Newton) Booth Tarkington,* U.S. author; popular for his novels portraying boyhood

and life in the American Midwest; author of *Penrod* and *Seventeen.* [d. May 19, 1946]

1877 *(Charles) William Beebe,* U.S. naturalist, author; Director of Tropical Research, New York Zoological Society; with Otis Barton developed the *bathysphere,* which was capable of record depth exploration of the ocean. [d. June 4, 1962]

1883 *Benito Mussolini,* Italian dictator; founder of Fascism with the creation of *Fascio di Combattimento,* 1919; dictator of Italy, 1922–43. [d. April 28, 1945]

1887 *Sigmund Romberg,* U.S. composer; composed nearly 80 scores for stage plays and more than 2,000 songs; considered one of the most popular U.S. composers; wrote *The Student Prince.* [d. November 9, 1951]

1892 *William Powell,* U.S. actor. [d. March 5, 1984]

1896 *Clark M(ell) Eichelberger,* U.S. international relations specialist; director of *League of Nations Association* (later *American Association for the United Nations),* 1934–64. [d. January 26, 1980]

1898 *I(sidor) I(saac) Rabi,* Polish-born physicist; Nobel Prize in

july

physics for discoveries in *spectroscopy,* 1944. [d. Janaury 11, 1988]

1900 *Eyvind Johnson,* Swedish novelist, short-story writer; Nobel Prize in literature, 1974. [d. 1976]

1905 *Dag Hammarskjöld,* Swedish political economist; Secretary-General of United Nations, 1953–61; Nobel Peace Prize, 1961. [d. September 18, 1961]

1907 *Melvin (Mouron) Belli,* U.S. lawyer; known for his dramatic style and controversial status of his clients. [d. July 9, 1996]

1908 *Edgar F(osburgh) Kaiser,* U.S. industrialist; head of Kaiser Industries Corporation; son of Henry J. Kaiser (May 9). [d. December 11, 1981]

1914 *Marcel Bich,* U.S.-French manufacturer, born in Italy; founder of Bic Pen Corporation, 1950. [d. May 30, 1994]

1918 *Edwin (Greene) O'Connor,* U.S. novelist. [d. March 23, 1968]

1925 *Ted Lindsey,* Canadian hockey player; elected to Hall of Fame, 1966.

1930 *Paul (Belville) Taylor,* U.S. modern dancer, choreographer; director of the Paul Taylor Dance Co., 1950– .

1932 *Nancy Landon Kassebaum,* U.S. politician; Senator, 1979–96; daughter of Alf Landon.

1938 *Peter Charles Jennings,* Canadian-born journalist; Anchorman, *ABC World News Tonight,* 1983– .

1953 *Kenneth L. Burns,* U.S. historian, filmmaker; creator of the PBS series *The Civil War.*

1956 *Michael Spinks,* U.S. boxer; Olympic gold medalist, 1976; World Heavyweight Champion, 1985.

HISTORICAL EVENTS

1030 *Olaf Haraldson,* Norwegian pretender, is defeated at the *Battle of Stiklestad* by *King Canute II.*

1565 *Mary, Queen of Scots* is married to her cousin, *Henry Stuart, Lord Darnley.*

1830 *Charles X* abdicates during the *Revolution of 1830* in France. He is replaced by the Bourbon Duc d'Orléans who will reign as *Louis-Philippe.*

1844 The *New York Yacht Club* is founded.

1848 *O'Brien's Rebellion,* the result of severe food shortages, is suppressed in Ireland, and rebellion leader *Smith O'Brien* is jailed.

1900 *Humbert I* of Italy is assassinated by anarchist *Gaetano Bresci.*

1946 Delegates from the Allied nations meet at the *Paris Peace Conference* to draft peace terms and establish boundaries for Axis powers and the countries which they occupied during World War II.

1953 Robert Heilbroner's classic survey of economic thought, *The Worldly Philosophers,* is published.

1958 President Dwight D. Eisenhower establishes the

National Aeronautics and Space Administration (NASA) to conduct space exploration research.

1967 The aircraft carrier *U.S.S. Forrestal* is severely damaged off Vietnam by a fire; 134 lives are lost and 60 planes and helicopters destroyed or damaged (*Vietnam War*).

1968 *Pope Paul VI,* in an encyclical, *Humanae Vitae,* upholds the Roman Catholic Church's prohibition against all artificial means of contraception.

Virtually all the governing bodies of the Soviet and Czechoslovak Communist parties meet in *Cierna,* Czechoslovakia, to try to bridge the divisions between them.

1970 Alvin Toffler's book, *Future Shock,* is published.

1975 Nigerian president, *Yakubu Gowan,* is overthrown in a bloodless coup.

The *Organization of American States* lifts economic and diplomatic sanctions imposed on *Cuba* in 1964.

1981 *Charles, Prince of Wales,* and *Lady Diana Spencer* are married in St. Paul's Cathedral, in London.

1987 Six former officials at the *Chernobyl* nuclear power reactor are convicted of gross safety violations that led to the April 26th accident in the Soviet Ukraine.

Giovanni Goria is inaugurated as premier of Italy, replacing *Bettino Craxi.*

HOLIDAYS

U.S. (Louisiana)
Huey P. Long Day

Vanuatu
Independence Day
Commemorates the achievement of independence from Great Britain and France, 1980.

RELIGIOUS CALENDAR

The Saints
St. Julitta, widow and martyr. [d. c. 303]

St. Abdon and *St. Sennen,* martyrs. Abdon also called *Abden.* [d. c. 303]

St. Peter Chrysologus, Archbishop of Ravenna and Doctor of the Church. [d. c. 450] Feast formerly December 4. Optional Memorial.

The Beatified
Blessed Mannes, Augustinian monk. [d. c. 1230]

Blessed Archangelo of Calatafimi, hermit. [d. 1460]

Blessed John Soreth, Carmelite prior and reformer. [d. 1471]

Blessed Simon of Lipnicza, Franciscan Friar Minor. [d. 1482]

Blessed Peter of Mogliano, Observant Franciscan Friar. [d. 1490]

Blessed Edward Powell and *Richard Fetherston,* martyrs. [d. 1540]

Blessed Thomas Abel, priest and martyr. [d. 1540]

Blessed Everard Hanse, priest and martyr. [d. 1581]

BIRTHDATES

1511 *Giorgio Vasari,* Italian painter, architect, art historian; author of *Lives of the Painters,* 1551, which provides a detailed account of the lives of the great Italian masters; referred to in several of Robert Browning's poems on Renaissance artists. [d. June 27, 1574]

1818 *Emily Jane (Ellis Bell) Brontë,* British novelist, poet; author of *Wuthering Heights.* Sister of Anne (January 17) and Charlotte Brontë (April 21). [d. December 19, 1848]

1856 *Richard Burdon Haldane, Viscount Haldane of Cloan,* British statesman, author; member of Parliament, 1885–1911; Lord Chancellor, 1912–15, 1924. [d. August 19, 1928]

1857 *Thorstein (Bunde) Veblen,* U.S. social scientist, economist; author of *Theory of the Leisure Class,* 1899. [d. August 3, 1919]

1863 *Henry Ford,* U.S. industrialist; founder and President of the Ford Motor Co.; introduced standardization and mass-production techniques in the automobile industry; established the *Ford Foundation,* 1936. [d. April 7, 1947]

1870 *Lavrenti Georgievich Kornilov,* Russian general; commander of Russian Army after Revolution of 1917. [d. April 13, 1918]

1880 *Robert Rutherford (Colonel) McCormick,* U.S. editor; publisher of *Chicago Tribune,* 1910–55; President of Tribune Co., 1911–55; founder, with his cousin Robert W. Patterson, of the *New York Daily News,* 1919. [d. April 1, 1955]

1881 *Smedley Darlington Butler,* U.S. Marine commander, prominent in World War I. [d. June 21, 1940]

1889 *Vladimir Kosma Zworykin,* U.S. engineer, inventor, born in Russia; developed the *iconoscope,* which made possible the development of *television.* Called the *Father of Television.* [d. July 29, 1982]

1891 *Casey (Charles Dillon) Stengel,* U.S. baseball player and manager; as manager of New York Yankees, 1949–60, led his team to 10 American League pennants and 7 World Series championships; elected to Baseball Hall of Fame, 1966. [d. September 30, 1975]

july

1898 *Henry Moore,* British sculptor. [d. August 31, 1986]

1934 *Bud (Allan H.) Selig,* U.S. businessman; interim, then permanent, commissioner of Major League Baseball, 1991– .

1939 *Peter Bogdanovich,* U.S. film director, producer, writer.

1940 *Patricia Scott (Pat) Schroeder,* U.S. politician; Congresswoman, 1973–96.

1941 *Paul Anka,* Canadian singer composer.

1947 *Arnold Schwarzenegger,* Austrian-born body-builder, actor, author; Mr. Universe title, five times; Mr. Olympia title, six times; starred in *Conan the Barbarian, Twins,* and the *Terminator* movies.

1956 *Anita Hill,* U.S. lawyer, educator; known for her testimony during the Supreme Court nominee Clarence Thomas hearings.

1958 *Kate Bush,* British singer, songwriter.

Daley Thompson, British athlete; winner of 1980 and 1984 Olympic decathlon events.

1961 *Laurence Fishburne,* U.S. actor; known for roles in *Boyz N the Hood,* 1991;

Searching for Bobby Fischer, 1993; and *What's Love Got to Do with It?,* 1993.

1963 *Lisa Kudrow,* U.S. actress; known for her role as Phoebe on the TV show *Friends.*

HISTORICAL EVENTS

1178 *Frederick I, Holy Roman Emperor,* is crowned King of Burgundy.

1619 First legislative assembly in America, the *House of Burgesses,* is convened at *Jamestown, Virginia.*

1866 Armistice between Austria and Prussia ends the *Seven Weeks' War.*

1907 Foundation stone of Carnegie *Palace of Peace* at The Hague is laid.

1945 U.S. cruiser *Indianapolis* is sunk by Japanese submarine in the Philippine Sea with a loss of 880 lives (*World War II*).

1952 Peerage titles of pasha and bey are abolished in *Egypt.* Prisoners jailed for showing disrespect towards the nobility are freed.

Chesapeake Bay Bridge is dedicated in Washington, D.C.

1965 President Lyndon Johnson signs legislation establishing

the *Medicare* and *Medicaid* health insurance programs.

1974 The U.S. House Judiciary Committee votes three articles of *impeachment* against President *Richard Nixon (Watergate Incident).*

The Quebec National Assembly passes the *Official Language Act,* making French the official language of the province.

1975 Leaders of 35 nations sign the *Helsinki accords,* agreeing on security, economic, and human rights issues.

1980 The *Republic of Vanuatu* (formerly *New Hebrides* attains independence from Great Britain and France.

1981 Researchers report in the *New England Journal of Medicine* that the drug, *cyclosporin,* reduces the mortality rate in organ transplant patients by selectively depressing the immune system.

1989 The *Organization of the Oppressed of the World* announces the killing of Lieutenant Colonel *William Higgins.* Higgins had been a member of the U.N. Truce Supervision Organization stationed in Lebanon when he was kidnapped in 1988.

HOLIDAYS

Congo
Revolution Day

RELIGIOUS CALENDAR

The Saints

St. Germanus, Bishop of Auxerre. Also called *Germain.* [d. 448] Feast formerly August 3.

St. Helen of Skövde, widow and martyr. [d. c. 1160]

St. Ignatius of Loyola, founder of the Society of Jesus; patron of spiritual exercises and retreats. [d. 1556] Obligatory Memorial.

St. Neot, monk. Also called *Niet.* [death date unknown]

St. Sidwell, virgin. Also called *Sativola.* [death date unknown]

The Beatified

Blessed John Colombini, founder of the Apostolic Clerics of St. Jerome. [d. 1367]

Blessed Justin de Jacobis, titular Bishop of Nilopolis and missionary. [d. 1860]

BIRTHDATES

1763 *James Kent,* U.S. jurist, legal writer; first professor of law at Columbia College 1793; produced first systematic work on Anglo-American law, 1830. [d. December 12, 1847]

1803 *John Ericsson,* U.S. engineer, inventor, born in Sweden; invented *screw propeller;* developed first propeller-driven commercial ship; designed U.S. Union warship *Monitor,* which defeated the *Merrimack* in the *Battle of Hampton Roads;* responsible for revolutionizing naval warfare. [d. March 8, 1889]

1814 *Amos Adams Lawrence,* U.S. merchant, philanthropist; partner in firm of Mason and Lawrence, leading Boston textile merchants; benefactor of *Lawrence University,* Appleton, Wisconsin, and a college at Lawrence, Kansas, that later became the *University of Kansas;* adamant anti-slavery figure. [d. August 22, 1886]

1816 *George Henry Thomas,* Union Army general during U.S. Civil War; known as the *Rock of Chickamauga* after his success at the *Battle of Chickamauga* during the Chattanooga Campaign. Inflicted heaviest losses of entire war on Confederates at *Battle of Nashville,* 1864. [d. March 28, 1870]

1822 *Abram Stevens Hewitt,* U.S. businessman, political figure, philanthropist; built first open hearth smelting furnace; U.S. Congressman, 1874–79, 1881–87; Mayor of New York City, 1886–88. [d. January 18, 1903]

1839 *William Clarke Quantrill,* U.S. guerrilla leader, outlaw; loosely attached to Confederate Army, he and his band of guerrillas carried out many bloody attacks on towns and organizations sympathetic to the Union; most notoriety gained from his raid on *Lawrence, Kansas,* during which he killed more than 180 citizens and burned the town. [d. June 6, 1865]

1859 *Theobald Smith,* U.S. pathologist; first to demonstrate that parasites could act as vectors of disease; pioneer in field of immunology; established distinction between bacillus of human tuberculosis and that of bovine strain. [d. December 10, 1934]

1867 *Sebastian Spering Kresge,* U.S. merchant; founded the S.S. Kresge Co. which became K-Mart. [d. October 18, 1966]

1899 *Robert T(en Broeck) Stevens,* U.S. government official, industrialist; U.S. Secretary of the Army, 1953–55; President and Chairman of the Board, J.P. Stevens Company, 1929–74. [d. January 30, 1983]

1900 *Antoine (Marie-Roger) de Saint-Exupéry,* French aviator, author; noted for his fable

The Little Prince and for his novels, *Wind, Sand, and Stars* and *Night Flight* ("Vol de Nuit"). [disappeared, presumed deceased July 31, 1944]

1912 *Milton Friedman,* U.S. economist, author; leading conservative economist; anti-Keynesian and advocate of *laissez-faire* economics; Nobel Prize in economics, 1976.

1919 *Curt Gowdy,* U.S. sportscaster.

1921 *Whitney Moore Young, Jr.,* U.S. civil-rights leader; advocate of a total spectrum black coalition. [d. March 11, 1971]

1943 *William John Bennett,* U.S. government official; Chairman, National Endowment for the Humanities, 1981–85; Secretary of Education, 1985–88; administrator of federal anti-drug policies, 1989–93.

Susan Flannery, U.S. actress; Emmy Award for her role on the soap opera, *Days of Our Lives,* 1975.

1944 *Geraldine Chaplin,* U.S. actress; daughter of Charlie Chaplin (April 16); granddaughter of Eugene O'Neill (October 16).

Sherry Lee Lansing, U.S. film executive; first woman in charge of production at a major studio, 20th Century Fox, 1980–82; co-producer of *Fatal Attraction,* 1987.

1946 *Bob Welch,* U.S. musician; member of the rock group, *Fleetwood Mac.*

1951 *Evonne Goolagong,* Australian tennis player.

1962 *Wesley Snipes,* U.S. actor.

HISTORICAL EVENTS

1559 *University of Lille* in France is authorized by a papal bull.

1790 *U.S. Patent Office* opens and issues its first patent to *Samuel Hopkins* of Vermont for new method of making potash and pearlash.

1877 *Thomas A. Edison* receives a U.S. patent on his *phonograph.*

1897 *Guglielmo Marconi* is awarded patent for his *wireless telegraph.*

1914 Germany declares war on Russia (*World War I*).

France mobilizes its army and navy (*World War I*).

General mobilization is ordered for the *Austro-Hungarian Empire* (*World War I*).

1917 The *Third Battle of Ypres* opens in Flanders as a British offensive (*World War I*).

1919 The *Weimar Constitution* is adopted in Germany, establishing a new republic.

1942 U.S. President Franklin Roosevelt creates the *U.S. Army Transportation Corps* (*World War II*).

1960 War betweeen the Malaysian government and Communist insurgents officially ends.

1964 U.S. lunar probe *Ranger 7* crashes on moon's surface after transmitting some 4,000 photographs back to earth.

1971 *Apollo 15* astronauts make the first of three planned excursions on the moon in their lunar rover.

1975 Former Teamsters Union President *James R. Hoffa* is reported missing; Hoffa is declared legally dead December 8, 1982.

1978 Argentine president, *Jorge Rafael Videla,* retires from the military junta, effectively turning over rule to General *Roberto Viola.*

1988 Jordan severs legal and administrative ties to the Israeli-occupied *West Bank,* granting responsibility for the territory to the *Palestine Liberation Organization.*

1991 The U.S. Senate approves of *women pilots* serving in combat missions.

August is the eighth month of the Gregorian calendar and has 31 days. In the early Roman 10-month calendar, it was called *Sextilis,* a reference to its position as the sixth month in that calendar. In 8 B.C., Augustus Caesar, the adopted son and heir to Julius Caesar, consented to have a month named in his honor. Rather than the month of his birth, September, he chose Sextilis, acknowledging the many events favorable to his political-career that occurred during that month, e.g., his first election to the consulship in 43 B.C. and the conquest of Egypt in 31 B.C., the latter marking the end of protracted civil war. Also at this time, in a move designed in part to make his month equal in length to Julius Casear's month of July, Augustus instituted changes in the number of days in certain months: the new *Augustus* was increased to 31 days (equaling July) from its traditional 30, while February was reduced to 28 days (except in leap years). The length of the months following August were also set, with an alternationof 30-day and 31-day months through December. Hence, the months of the year were assigned the number of days that they still retain today.

In the astrological calendar, August spans the zodiac signs of Leo, the Lion (July 23–August 22) and Virgo, the Virgin (August 23–September 22).

The birthstone for August is the carnelian, sardonyx, or peridot, and the flower is the poppy or gladiolus.

STATE, NATIONAL, AND INTERNATIONAL HOLIDAYS

American Family Day
(Arizona, Minnesota)
First Sunday

Fiesta de Andorra la Vieja
(Andorra)
First Saturday, Sunday, and Monday

Colorado Day
(Colorado)
First Monday

Discovery Day
(Trinidad and Tobago)
First Monday

August Monday
(Dominica)
First Monday

Bank Holiday
(St. Lucia)
First Monday

Bank Holiday
(Botswana, Canada, Fiji, Grenada, Guyana, Hong Kong, Ireland,Malawi)
First Monday

Emancipation Day
(Bahamas)
First Monday

Freedom Day
(Guyana)
First Monday

Independence Day
(Jamaica)
First Monday

Hora de la Prisiop
(Romania)
Second Sunday

Victory Day
(Rhode Island)
Second Monday

Admission Day
(Hawaii)
Third Friday

Liberation Day
(Hong Kong)
Final Monday

SPECIAL EVENTS AND THEIR SPONSORS

Florida Appreciation Month
California Depopulation Commission

National Clown Week
First Week
Clowns of America, Inc.

Beauty Queen Week
First Week
Richard R. Falk Associates

All American Soap Box Derby
Second Week
International Soap Box Derby, Inc.

National Hosiery Week
Week containing August 15
National Association of Hosiery
Manufacturers

Bald Eagle Days
Third Week
Eagle Valley Environmentalists, Inc.

Family Day
August 7
Kiwanis International

HOLIDAYS

Angola
Armed Forces Day

Benin
Independence Day

People's Republic of China
Army Day

Democratic Republic of the Congo
Parents' Day

England
Lammas Day
From Middle English *Lammasse* or *loaf mass,* celebrating occasion of blessing of first bread made from new wheat or corn; associated with celebration of deliverance of St.Peter from imprisonment. See Religious Calendar below.

Iceland
Bank Holiday

People's Republic of China
Army Day

Rwanda
Public Holiday

Switzerland
National Day or Confederation Day
Commemorates the formation of the Swiss confederation, 1291.

RELIGIOUS CALENDAR

The Saints

St. Peter ad Vincula; commemorates chains binding Peter when he was imprisoned in Rome. Also called *St. Peter's Chains.* Feast day now in recession.

The Holy Machabees, martyrs. Also called *Maccabees.* [d. 168 B.C.] Feast suppressed 1969.

St. Aled, virgin and martyr. Also called *Almedha,* or *Eiluned.* [d. 6th century]

St. Kyned, monk and hermit. Also called *Cenydd, Kened,* or *Keneth.* [d. c. 6th century]

St. Ethelwold, Bishop of Winchester. Also called *Etholwold.* [d. 984]

St. Alphonsus de' Liguori, Bishop of Sant' Agata Dei Goti, Doctor of the Church and founder of the Congregation of the Most Holy Redeemer. [d. 1787] Feast formerly August 2.

SS. Faith, Hope, and Charity and their mother, St. Wisdom, martyrs. [death date unknown]

The Beatified

Blessed Thomas Welbourn and Blessed William Brown, martyrs. [d. 1605]

BIRTHDATES

10 B.C. *Claudius (Tiberius Claudius Drusus Nero Germanicus),* Roman emperor. [d. October 13, A.D. 54]

1749 *Jean Baptiste Pierre Antoine de Monet, chevalier de Lamarck,* French naturalist; forerunner of Darwin; first to categorize animals into *vertebrates* and *invertebrates.* [d. December 18, 1829]

1770 *William Clark,* U.S. soldier, explorer; shared command with Meriwether Lewis (August 18) of the expedition to *Northwest Territory;* upon return, gathered all records from exploration, providing documentation for the journals published in 1814. [d. September 1, 1838]

1779 *Francis Scott Key,* U.S. poet, lawyer; author of the poem which eventually became the verse for the *Star-Spangled Banner,* the *U.S. national anthem.* [d. January 11, 1843]

1815 *Richard Henry Dana, Jr.,* U.S. lawyer, author; his novel, *Two Years before the Mast,* recounts his life as a crew member aboard the ship *Pilgrim.* As a lawyer, specialized in maritime law and published *The Seaman's Friend,* a guide to the law for common seamen. [d. January 6, 1882]

1818 *Maria Mitchell,* U.S. astronomer; was recognized in scientific circles for her discovery of a comet; became first woman member of the American Academy of Arts and Sciences; Professor of Astronomy, Vassar College, 1865–69. [d. June 28, 1889]

august

1819 *Herman Melville,* U.S. novelist; author of *Moby Dick.* [d. September 28, 1891]

1843 *Robert Todd Lincoln,* U.S. lawyer, cabinet officer, diplomat; the oldest son of President Abraham Lincoln. [d. July 25, 1926]

1863 *Gaston Doumergue,* French statesman; 12th president of French Republic, 1924–31. [d. June 18, 1937]

1881 *Rose Macaulay,* British novelist. [d. 1958]

1885 *Georg Hevesy,* Hungarian chemist; Nobel Prize in chemistry for discovery of use of isotopes as *tracer elements,* 1943. [d. July 5, 1966]

1892 *Hugh Macdiarmid (Christopher Murray Grieve),* Scottish poet, critic. [d. August 11, 1892]

1899 *William F(riske) Dean,* U.S. Army major general; highest ranking U.S. military person to be taken prisoner during *Korean War.* [d. August 25, 1981]

Joseph (Herman) Hirshhorn, U.S. financier, art patron; amassed multi-million dollar fortune through speculation in mining and stock market; owner of one of largest private art collections in the world, later donated, with a museum to house it, to U.S., 1966. [d. August 31, 1981]

1924 *Georges Charpak,* French physicist; Nobel Prize for Physics, 1992. Invented subatomic particle detectors.

1931 *Harold Connolly,* U.S. athlete; Olympic Gold Medal for hammer throw, 1956.

1933 *Dom DeLuise,* U.S. comedian, actor.

1936 *Yves (Mathieu) St. Laurent,* French fashion designer.

1937 *Alfonse Marcello D'Amato,* U.S. politician; Senator, 1980– .

1941 *Ronald Harmon Brown,* U.S. lawyer, government official; Secretary of Commerce, 1993–96. [d. April 3, 1996]

1942 *Jerome John (Jerry) Garcia,* U.S. musician, singer; member of the rock group, *The Grateful Dead.* [d. August 9, 1995]

Giancarlo Giannini, Italian actor, known for his role in *Love and Anarchy.*

1945 *Douglass D. Osheroff,* U.S. physicist; Nobel Prize for Physics in 1996. Osheroff shares the prize with David Lee and Robert Richardson for their discovery of superfluidity in helium-3.

1953 *Robert Cray,* U.S. blues musician.

1958 *Ernest Maurice (Kiki) Vandeweghe,* U.S. basketball player; forward, Denver and Portland; two-time All Star.

1963 *Coolio (Artis Ivey, Jr.),* U.S. rapper.

HISTORICAL EVENTS

1137 *Louis VI* of France dies and is succeeded by *Louis VII.*

1291 *Swiss Confederation* is formed by the Forest Cantons of Uri, Unterwalden, and Schwyz for defense against the Austrians.

1658 *Leopold I* is elected Holy Roman Emperor.

1714 *Queen Anne* of England dies and is succeeded by George Lewis, Elector of Hanover, who becomes *George I.*

1798 British Admiral *Horatio Nelson* destroys Napoleon's French fleet in harbor at Abukir, Egypt (*Battle of the Nile*).

1808 English expedition lands in Portugal to oppose French (*Napoleonic Wars*).

1834 *Slavery* is abolished throughout the British Empire.

1849 *Dr. David Livingstone,* British explorer and missionary, becomes the first European to reach *Lake Ngami* in Africa.

1876 *Colorado* is admitted to the Union as the 38th state.

1894 China and Japan declare war on each other (*Sino-Japanese War*).

1935 The *Federal Music Project* is organized in Washington to provide work for unemployed American musicians.

1943 U.S. aircraft based at Libya stage successful low-level attack on Romanian oil refineries at *Ploesti (World War II).*

1944 *Sergio Osmena* becomes president of the Philippines following the death of *Manuel Quezon y Molina.*

1946 U.S. President Harry S. Truman signs the *McMahon Act* creating the U.S. *Atomic Energy Commission.*

President Truman signs the *Fulbright Act,* funding an international educational exchange in the form of *Fulbright Scholarships.*

1950 President Harry Truman signs legislation giving U.S. citizenship and limited self-government to the inhabitants of *Guam*.

1952 U.S. troops capture *Old Baldy,* a hill near Chorwon, Korea, after two weeks of fighting *(Korean War)*.

1960 *Benin* (formerly *Dahomey*) proclaims its independence as a republic within the French Community.

1966 Lieut. Col. *Yakubu Gowon,* Nigerian Army Chief of Staff, assumes power following the overthrow of the government in a bloody coup d'état that sees thousands of Ibo tribesmen massacred and more than a million driven from homes in the northern sector of the country.

1976 Nearly one million Roman Catholics participate in the *41st International Eucharistic Congress.* The first such congress was held in Lille, France, in 1881.

1979 *Maria de Lurdes Pintas-Silgo* is inaugurated as premier of Portugal, becoming the country's first woman head of state.

1990 *Zhelyu Zhelov* is selected as the new president of Bulgaria after *Petar Mladenov* resigns (July 6, 1990).

august

AUGUST
2

HOLIDAYS

Costa Rica
Our Lady of the Angels

Macedonia
National Holiday

St. Lucia, St. Vincent, Turks and Caicos Islands
Emancipation Day or Freedom Day
Joint celebration of emancipation from Great Britain.

Yugoslavia
Macedonian Uprising Day

RELIGIOUS CALENDAR

The Saints
St. Stephen I, pope. Elected 254. Patron of Vienna. [d. 257]
St. Theodata, martyr. [d. c. 304]
St. Etheldritha, recluse. Also called *Ælfryth* or *Alfreda.* [d. c. 835]
St. Plegmund, Archbishop of Canterbury. [d. 914]
St. Thomas of Dover, monk. [d. 1295]

BIRTHDATES

1754 *Pierre Charles L'Enfant,* French engineer, architect, urban designer; responsible for the design and layout of *Washington, D.C.* [d. June 14, 1825]

1820 *John Tyndall,* British physicist; responsible for discoveries in transmission and absorption of heat; discovered that the sky appeared blue owing in part to dust particles in the atmosphere. [d. December 4, 1893]

1823 *Edward Augustus Freeman,* British historian; Professor of Modern History at Oxford, 1884–92. [d. March 16, 1892]

1835 *Elisha Gray,* U.S. inventor; founder of Gray & Barton Co., the basis of Western Electric Company, 1872. Filed for patent on a telephone device only hours after Alexander Graham Bell filed for his patent; was granted 70 patents during his lifetime. [d. January 21, 1901]

1854 *Francis Marion Crawford,* U.S. author born in Italy; son of expatriate sculptor Thomas Crawford; advocate of romanticism in fiction. [d. April 9, 1909]

1865 *Irving Babbitt,* U.S. author, educator; with Paul Elmer More (December 12) founded the *neo-humanist* movement in the U.S. [d. July 15, 1933]

1868 *Constantine I, King of Greece;* deposed in 1917 as a result of his neutral stance on World War I; recalled 1920, but once again forced to abdicate, 1922, after a disastrous campaign against Turkey. [d. January 11, 1923]

1871 *John French Sloan,* U.S. artist; one of the founders of the *Ashcan School* of art. [d. September 7, 1951]

1884 *Romulo Gallegos,* Venezuelan politician, author, educator; President of Venezuela, 1948–52. [d. April 4, 1969]

1892 *John Kieran,* U.S. writer, analyst; first by-lined columnist of the *New York Times;* wrote *Sports of the Times* column, 1927–43; member of the radio quiz panel of *Information Please;* editor of *Information Please Almanac,* 1947–80. [d. December 10, 1981]

Jack Warner, U.S. motion picture executive; with his brothers, Harry (December 12) and Albert (July 23), founded Warner Brothers Pictures, Inc. [d. September 9, 1978]

1900 *Helen Morgan,* U.S. singer, actress. [d. October 8, 1941]

1905 *Myrna Loy (Myrna Williams),* U.S. actress. [d. December 14, 1993]

1915 *Gary Franklin Merrill,* U.S. actor; starred in the movie, *All About Eve,* 1950; former husband of Bette Davis. [d. March 5, 1990]

1920 *Lonnie (William) Coleman,* U.S. author; wrote novel *Beulah Land,* 1963. [d. August 13, 1982]

1922 *Paul Laxalt,* U.S. politician, lawyer; Governor of Nevada, 1967–71; Senator, 1974–87.

1924 *James Baldwin,* U.S. novelist, essayist; leading spokesman for the black community in the U.S. as well as an outstanding figure in contemporary American literature. [d. November 30, 1987]

Carroll O'Connor, U.S. actor; best known for his role as Archie Bunker on television series, *All in the Family* and played Bill Gillespie in the series *In the Heat of the Night,* 1988–94

1925 *Jorge Rafael Videla,* Argentine government official, general; President, 1976–81.

1932 *Peter (Seamus) O'Toole,* Irish actor; known for his roles in *Lawrence of Arabia* and *The Lion in Winter.*

1939 *Wes Craven,* U.S. director; known for the films *Nightmare on Elm Street,* 1984, and *Scream,* 1997.

1951 *Andrew Gold,* U.S. singer.

1960 *Linda Fratianne,* U.S. figure skater; Olympic silver medalist, 1980.

1964 *Mary-Louise Parker,* U.S. actress; known for role in *Fried Green Tomatoes.*

1967 *Aaron Krickstein,* U.S. tennis player; youngest player to advance in the United States Open competition, 1983.

HISTORICAL EVENTS

1100 *William II,* King of England, is killed in New Forest in a hunting accident and is succeeded by *Henry I.*

1589 *Henry III* of France is murdered; the House of Valois becomes extinct and *Henry of Navarre* claims throne.

1858 *India Bill* is passed, ending the rule of the *British East India Company.*

1909 First *Lincoln penny* is issued in U.S.

1914 *Germany* begins its invasion of France near Sirez-sur-Vezouze and other frontier posts (*World War I*).

1923 *Warren G. Harding* dies; Vice-President Calvin Coolidge is sworn in as President of U.S. the following morning at 2:30 a.m.

1935 The *Government of India Act* is passed by British parliament, separating *Burma* and *Aden* from India.

1967 Norman Jewison's film, *In the Heat of the Night,* is released.

1990 *Kuwait* is invaded by Iraqi military.

august

AUGUST
3

HOLIDAYS

El Salvador
Employee's Day

Equatorial Guinea
Armed Forces Day

Grenada
Emancipation Day

Guinea-Bissau
Martyrs of Colonialism Day

Niger
Independence Day
Celebrates the achievement of independence from France, 1960.

Tunisia
President Bourguiba's Birthday
Celebrates the birth of Habib Bourguiba, 1903.

RELIGIOUS CALENDAR

Feasts
The Finding of St. Stephen. Also called *The Invention of St. Stephen.* Relics discovered 415. This feast day is now in recession.

The Saints
St. Waltheof, Abbot of Melrose. Also called *Walthen,* or *Walthenus.* [d. c. 1160]
St. Peter Julian Eymard, founder of the Priests of the Blessed Sacrament. [d. 1868]
St. Manaccus, bishop. Also called *Mancus.* [death date unknown]

The Beatified
Blessed Augustine, Bishop of Lucera. [d. 1323]

BIRTHDATES

1746 *James Wyatt,* English romantic architect; responsible for revival of *Gothic architecture* in England. [d. September 4, 1813]

1770 *Frederick William III,* King of Prussia, 1797–1846. [d. June 7, 1840]

1801 *Sir Joseph Paxton,* British architect, horticulturist; designed *Crystal Palace,* site of London exhibition, 1851. [d. June 8, 1865]

1808 *Hamilton Fish,* U.S. politician, lawyer; U.S. Secretary of State, 1869–77. [d. September 6, 1893]

1811 *Elisha Graves Otis,* U.S. inventor; developed the first safe passenger *elevator.* [d. April 8, 1861]

1867 *Stanley Baldwin, 1st Earl Baldwin,* British statesman; Prime Minister, 1923–29, 1935–37. [d. December 14, 1947]

1872 *Haakon VII,* King of Norway, 1905–57; first king of Norway after the restoration of its independence from Denmark. [d. September 21, 1957]

1887 *Rupert Brooke,* British poet; died of blood poisoning at beginning of World War I. [d. April 23, 1915]

1900 *Ernest (Ernie) Pyle,* U.S. journalist; managing editor of *Washington Daily News,* 1932–35; noted for his reporting of events in World War II, which eventually won him the Pulitzer Prize, 1944. Killed by enemy machine gun fire on Ie Shima, in the Pacific. [d. April 18, 1945]

John Thomas Scopes, U.S. teacher; tried for teaching evolution in a Tennessee public school; defended by Clarence Darrow in the famous "monkey trial" of 1925. [d. October 21, 1970]

1901 *Stefan Cardinal Wyszynski,* Roman Catholic cardinal; Primate of Poland; renowned for his staunch anti-Communist position. [d. May 28, 1981]

John Cornelius Stennis, U.S. politician, lawyer; Senator, 1947–89. [d. April 23, 1995]

1903 *Habib Bourguiba,* first president of Tunisia, 1957–87.

1905 *Dolores Del Rio,* U.S. actress, born in Mexico. [d. April 11, 1983]

1906 *George Sanders,* U.S. actor, born in Russia. Committed suicide. [d. April 25, 1972]

1909 *Walter van Tilburg Clark,* U.S. author; wrote *The Ox-Bow Incident,* 1940, and *The Watchful Gods, and Other Stories,* 1950; O. Henry Memorial Award, 1945. [d. November 10, 1971]

1920 *P(hyllis)D(orothy) James,* British author; known for her mystery novels including *Innocent Blood* and *The Skull Beneath the Skin;* Crime Writers Association Prize, 1967.

1922 *John Sheldon Doud Eisenhower,* U.S. author, diplomat.

1923 *Anne Klein,* U.S. fashion designer; known for her sophisticated sportswear. [d. March 19, 1974]

1926 *Tony Bennett (Anthony Benedetto),* U.S. singer.

1934 *Jonas Malheiro Savimbi,* Angolan political leader; led UNITA forces in Angolan civil war.

1935 *Richard D. Lamm,* U.S. politician; Governor of Colorado, 1974–87; wrote *The Immigration Time Bomb,* 1985.

1940 *Martin Sheen (Ramon Estevez),* U.S. actor, social activist.

1950 *John David Landis,* U.S. director.

1952 *Jay North,* U.S. actor; known for his role as Dennis the Menace in the television series of the same name, 1959–63.

HISTORICAL EVENTS

1347 *Calais* in France surrenders to *Edward III* of England (*Hundred Years' War*).

1460 *James II* of Scotland is killed at Roxburgh; he is succeeded by *James III.*

1492 *Christopher Columbus* embarks from Palos, Spain, on his first voyage of exploration aboard the *Santa Maria.*

1858 Captain *John Speke* discovers *Lake Victoria,* which he recognizes as the source of the *White Nile.*

1880 *American Canoe Association* is organized at Lake George, New York.

1914 *Germany* and *France* declare war on each other (*World War I*).

1916 Sir Roger Casement, Irish nationalist leader in the *Easter Rebellion,* is hanged in London for treason.

1917 Mutiny breaks out in the German fleet at *Wilhemshaven* (*World War I*).

1923 *Calvin Coolidge* is inaugurated as U.S. president following the death of *Warren G. Harding.*

1942 First U.S. woman naval officer, *Mildred McAfee,* is commissioned.

1945 All Germans and Hungarians in *Czechoslovakia* are deprived of their citizenship and subsequently expelled.

1958 U.S. atomic submarine *Nautilus* reaches the *North Pole.*

1960 *Niger* gains its independence from France.

1967 *West Germany* and *Czechoslovakia* resume diplomatic relations, which have been severed since World War II.

1976 Former Philippine legislator, *Benigno Aquino,* is arraigned before a military court on subversion charges.

1979 President *Masie Nguema Biyogo* of Equatorial Guinea is overthrown in a coup led by his nephew, *Teodoro Obiang Nguema Mbasogo.*

1983 *Upper Volta* is renamed *Burkina Faso* by the nation's military government.

1993 *Ruth Bader Ginsburg* is appointed to the U.S. Supreme Court, becoming the second female jurist.

august

AUGUST
4

HOLIDAYS

Barbados
Caricom Day

Burkina Faso
National Day

Cook Island (New Zealand Dependency)
Constitution Day
Commemorates the attainment of internal self-government, 1965.

El Salvador
San Salvador's Feast (1st day)

Kiribati
Youth Day

Tuvalu
National Children's Day

RELIGIOUS CALENDAR

The Saints
St. Ia and her companions, martyr. Ia also called *Is.* [d. c. 360]
St. John Vianney; principal patron saint of parish clergy throughout the world. Also known as the *Holy Curé of Ars* and *John-Baptist Vianney.* [d. 1859]Formerly celebrated August 8. Obligatory Memorial.
St. Sithney; patron of Sithney and mad dogs. Also called *Sezni.* [death date unknown]

BIRTHDATES

1521 *Urban VII,* pope in 1590 (one month). [d. September 27, 1590]

1792 *Percy Bysshe Shelley,* English Romantic poet; the most aberrant of the English Romantics, both in his social and philosophical activities and opinions. Died at the age of 29, at the height of his career, in a boating accident. [d. July 8, 1822]

1805 *Sir William Rowan Hamilton,* Irish mathematician; pioneer in the science of *quantum mechanics;* discovered the phenomenon of *conical refraction.* [d. September 2, 1865]

1816 *Russell Sage,* U.S. financier, public official; U.S. Congressman, 1850–57. Built his fortune through investments in the stockmarket and railroading; his fortune used by his widow, Margaret Slocum Sage, to endow many philanthropic institutions including *Russell Sage Foundation* for study of social conditions. [d. July 22, 1906]

1839 *Walter (Horatio) Pater,* British essayist; associated with pre-Raphaelite school; devoted his life to interpretation of the humanism of the Renaissance. [d. July 30, 1894]

1841 *William Henry Hudson,* British naturalist, writer; author of *The Purple Land* and *Green Mansions.* [d. August 18, 1922]

1859 *Knut Hamsun (Knut Pedersen),* Norwegian novelist; wrote *Hunger* and *Growth of the Soil;* Nobel Prize in literature, 1920. [d. February 19, 1952]

1870 *Sir Harry Lauder,* Scottish entertainer; popular balladeer of British music halls and U.S. vaudeville theaters. [d. February 26, 1950]

1899 *Ezra Taft Benson,* U.S. agriculturist, religious leader; Secretary of Agriculture, 1953–61; President, Church of Jesus Christ of Latter-day Saints, 1985–94. [d. May 30, 1994]

1900 *Elizabeth, the Queen Mother,* British consort; wife of King George VI; mother of Queen Elizabeth II and Princess Margaret.

Arturo (Umberto) Illia, Argentinian physician, statesman; President of Argentina, 1963–66. [d. January 18, 1983]

1901 *Louis Armstrong,* U.S. musician, singer, trumpeter. [d. July 6, 1971]

1912 *Rauol Gustav Wallenberg,* Swedish diplomat; saved over 100,000 Budapest Jews during World War II. [d. July 17, 1947]

1913 *Jerome Weidman,* U.S. novelist, short-story writer; author of *I Can Get It for You Wholesale.*

1920 *Helen A. Thomas,* U.S. journalist.

1921 *Joseph Henri Maurice (Rocket Richard),* Canadian hockey player; elected to Hall of Fame, 1961.

1943 *Tina Cole,* U.S. actress, vocalist; member of the singing group, *The King Family.*

1949 *John Riggins,* U.S. football player; running back, 1971–85; Most Valuable Player, 1983 Super Bowl.

1958 *Mary Decker Slaney,* U.S. track athlete.

1962 *(William) Roger Clemens,* U.S. baseball player; broke Major League record with 20 strikeouts in one game, 1986.

1971 *Jeff Gordon,* U.S. stock car racer.

HISTORICAL EVENTS

1060 *Henry I,* King of France, dies and is succeeded by *Philip I.*

1213 The *Council of St. Albans,* a precursor of the British parliament, is convened.

1265 *Prince Edward* of England represses barons' rebellion by defeating and killing *Simon de Montfort* at Evesham. Simon is henceforth revered as a martyr and called *Simon the Righteous.*

1704 English capture *Gibraltar* from Spain (*War of the Spanish Succession*).

1789 The *Declaration of the Rights of Man* is adopted in France.

1846 *Santa Barbara, California,* is taken by U.S. Marines and sailors (*Mexican War*).

1914 *Great Britain* declares war on *Germany (World War I).*

Germany declares war on *Belgium* as Belgian forces resist German advancement through Belgium (*World War I*).

U.S. President *Woodrow Wilson* declares neutrality in the European war (*World War I*).

1916 Denmark cedes *Danish West Indies,* including the *Virgin Islands,* to U.S. for $25 million.

1936 *Ioannis Metaxas* seizes power in Greece; his dictatorship will last into World War II and invasion by Italy, until his death. [d. January 29, 1941]

1954 Alfred Hitchcock's film, *Rear Window,* premieres in New York.

1955 Alfred Hitchcock's film, *To Catch a Thief,* premieres in New York.

1972 *Arthur Bremer* is found guilty of having shot Governor *George Wallace* of Alabama and three other persons on May 15; he is sentenced to 63 years in prison.

1977 *U.S. Department of Energy* is created by presidential proclamation.

1983 *Bettino Craxi* is inaugurated as the first Socialist premier of Italy.

1987 The Federal Communications Commission rescinds the *Fairness Doctrine* on the grounds that it restricts free speech. In effect since 1949, it required U.S. broadcasters to present both sides of controversial issues.

august

AUGUST
5

HOLIDAYS

Burkina Faso
Independence Day

El Salvador
San Salvador's Feast (2nd day)

Zambia
Farmer's Day

RELIGIOUS CALENDAR

The Saints
St. Addai and *St. Mari,* bishops. Addai also called *Thaddeus.* [d. c. 180]
St. Afra, martyr. Venerated in Germany. [d. 304]
St. Nonna, matron. [d. 374]
St. Cassyon, bishop. Also called *Cassian.* [d. 4th century]
The Dedication of the Basilica of St. Mary Major. Also called *St. Mary ad Nives* or *of the Snow,* and *St. Mary ad Praesepe.* [dedicated 5th century] Optional Memorial.

BIRTHDATES

1540 *Joseph Justus Scaliger,* French scholar; laid the basis for modern *textual criticism.* [d. January 21, 1609]

1802 *Niels Henrik Abel,* Norwegian mathematician; known for his research in the theory of *elliptic functions.* [d. April 6, 1829]

1829 *Manuel Deodoro da Fonseca,* first president of the Republic of Brazil, 1889–91. [d. August 23, 1892]

1850 *Guy de Maupassant,* French short-story writer, novelist; considered a master of the short story. [d. July 6, 1893]

1856 *Asher Ginzberg (Ahab Ha'am),* Russian essayist, editor; expounded *cultural Zionism.* [d. January 2, 1927]

1889 *Conrad (Potter) Aiken,* U.S. poet; Pulitzer Prize in poetry, 1930. [d. August 17, 1973]

1906 *John Huston,* U.S. film director, actor; known for his direction of many action-adventure films. [d. August 28, 1987]

Wassily Leontief, U.S. economist, born in Russia; Nobel Prize in economics for development of *input-output system of economic planning,* 1973.

1911 *Robert Taylor (Spangler Arlington Brugh),* U.S. actor. [d. June 8, 1969]

1923 *Richard Gordon Kleindienst,* U.S. government official; Attorney General, 1972–73.

Chengara Veetil Devan Nair, President, Republic of Singapore, 1981–85.

1924 *Ahmadou Ahidjo,* President, United Republic of Cameroon, 1960–82. [d. 1989]

1928 *Bogdan C. Maglich,* Yugoslavian-born physicist; known for his research on migma fusion reactors.

1930 *Neil Alden Armstrong,* U.S. astronaut; first man to set foot on the moon, July 20, 1969; Professor of Engineering, University of Cincinnati, 1971–79.

1935 *John Saxon (Carmen Orrico),* U.S. actor.

1937 *Manuel Pinto da Costa,* President, Democratic Republic of São Tomé and Principe, 1975–91.

1946 *Loni Anderson,* U.S. actress; known for her role as Jennifer on television series, *WKRP in Cincinnati,* 1978–80.

Shirley Ann Jackson, U.S. physicist; known for her contributions to the study of subatomic particles.

Erika Slezak, U.S. actress; two Emmy Awards for her role as Victoria Lord Buchanan in the soap opera, *One Life to Live.*

1953 *Samantha Sang,* Australian singer.

1956 *David Scott (Dave) Rozema,* U.S. baseball player.

1962 *Patrick Ewing,* U.S. basketball player.

1966 *Jonathan Silverman,* U.S. actor.

HISTORICAL EVENTS

1529 *Peace of Cambrai* is signed between *Charles V,* Holy Roman Emperor, and *Francis I* of France; Francis renounces claims in Italy; Charles renounces claims in Burgundy.

1850 *Australian Constitution Act* is passed, providing for redistricting of country and representative government for South Australia and Tasmania.

1857 *Atlantic cable* is completed, establishing means of telegraphic communication between U.S. and Great Britain.

1864 Union forces under Admiral *David Farragut* defeat the Confederate troops at *Battle of Mobile Bay (U.S. Civil War);* Farragut's battle cry, "Damn the torpedoes!" has become famous.

1884 Cornerstone of the *Statue of Liberty* is laid on Bedloe's (now Liberty) Island in New York Harbor.

1914 Cuba, Uruguay, Mexico, and Argentina all proclaim their separate neutralities in the start of *World War I; Montenegro* declares war on Austria-Hungary.

1915 *Warsaw,* evacuated by the Russians, is occupied by the Germans (*World War I*).

1933 *National Labor Board* is established by U.S. President Franklin D. Roosevelt to enforce the right to collective bargaining.

1949 Severe earthquake in *Ecuador* razes 50 towns and kills about 6,000.

Upper Volta (Burkina Faso) gains independence from France; Maurice Yameozo is named president.

1953 *From Here to Eternity,* a film starring Burt Lancaster and Deborah Kerr, premieres.

1961 *Bolivia* adopts a new constitution that separates church and state and increases presidential power.

1962 *Marilyn Monroe* is found dead of an apparent overdose of sleeping pills in her Los Angeles home.

1963 The U.S., U.S.S.R., and Great Britain sign a *limited test ban treaty,* which bans nuclear testing in all environments except underground.

1964 Leftist rebels in the *Democratic Republic of the Congo* gain control of *Stanleyville,* the nation's third largest city.

U.S. navy bombs *North Vietnam* for the first time in retaliation for the bombing of U.S. destroyers in the *Gulf of Tonkin. (Vietnam War)*

1983 Captain *Thomas Sankara* overthrows the regime of Major *Jean-Baptiste Ouedraogo* in Upper Volta (Burkina Faso).

august

AUGUST
6

HOLIDAYS

Bolivia
Independence Day
Commemorates Bolivia's achievement of independence from Spain, 1825.

El Salvador
San Salvador's Feast (3rd day)

Abu Dhabi, United Arab Emirates
Anniversary of the Accession of Sheik Zaid Bin Sultan Al-Nahayan
Commemorates the accession of the sheik, 1971.

RELIGIOUS CALENDAR

Feasts
The Transfiguration of Our Lord Jesus Christ. Celebrates Christ's revelation of his holiness to Saints Peter, James, and John on Mount Tabor. [Major holy day, Episcopal Church]

The Saints
St. Justus and St. Pastor, martyrs. [d. 304]

St. Hormisdas, pope. Elected 514. [d. 523]

BIRTHDATES

1638 *Nicolas de Malebranche,* French philosopher, metaphysicist; espoused the belief that man cannot know anything external to himself except through his relation to God. [d. October 13, 1715]

1651 *François de Salignac de la Mothe Fénelon,* French religious writer; tutor to the grandson of Louis XIV of France. His writings were condemned, in part, by the papacy. [d. January 7, 1715]

1697 *Charles VII,* Holy Roman Emperor. [d. January 20, 1745]

1766 *William Hyde Wollaston,* British chemist; first observed dark lines in solar spectrum; the *Wollaston Medal,* awarded for mineralogical research, is given in his honor. [d. December 22, 1828]

1775 *Daniel O'Connell,* Irish leader; originated *Catholic Association,* 1823. [d. May 15, 1847]

1809 *Alfred, 1st Baron Tennyson (Alfred, Lord Tennyson),* British poet; Poet Laureate of England, 1850–92; recognized as the greatest English poet of the Victorian age. [d. October 6, 1892]

1811 *Judah Philip Benjamin,* U.S. lawyer, politician, statesman; outstanding secessionist leader during American Civil War; Attorney General and Secretary of State of the Confederacy; escaped to England after the war, where he achieved great success as an appeals lawyer. [d. May 6, 1884]

1861 *Edith Roosevelt,* second wife of U.S. President Theodore Roosevelt. [d. September 30, 1948]

1868 *Paul (Louis-Marie) Claudel,* French diplomat, dramatist, poet; member of French diplomatic corps, 1892–55; associated with Symbolist school of poetry. [d. February 23, 1955]

1881 *Sir Alexander Fleming,* British bacteriologist; discoverer of penicillin, 1928; Nobel Prize in physiology or medicine for discovery of penicillin (with H. W. Florey and E. B. Chain), 1945. [d. March 11, 1955]

Louella O. Parsons, U.S. journalist; known for her flamboyant Hollywood gossip column, which was syndicated and appeared regularly in more than 400 Hearst newspapers, 1934–65. [d. December 9, 1972]

1889 *George Churchill Kenney,* U.S. military officer; Army Air Force general; commander of Allied air forces in the southwest Pacific during World War II. [d. August 9, 1977]

1892 *(Edward) Hoot Gibson,* U.S. silent-film actor. [d. August 23, 1962]

1893 *Wright Patman,* U.S. politician, lawyer; U.S.

Congressman, 1928–76. [d. March 7, 1976]

1895 *F(rancis) W(ilton) Reichelderfer,* U.S. meteorologist; Chief, U.S. Weather Bureau, 1938–63; implemented air-mass theory in forecasting services; first president, *World Meteorological Organization.* [d. January 25, 1983]

1902 *Dutch Schultz (Arthur Flegenheimer),* U.S. gangster; ran bootlegging syndicate during prohibition era in U.S. [d. October 24, 1934]

1905 *Clara Bow,* U.S. actress; star of jazz age silent films; acquired the name the *It Girl* after her starring role in the Elinor Glyn movie *It.* [d. September 26, 1965]

1909 *Karl Ulrich Schnabel,* U.S. concert pianist, born in Germany.

1911 *Lucille Ball,* U.S. actress; renowned comedienne; President, Desilu Productions, 1962–67; President of Lucille Ball Productions. [d. April 26, 1989]

1916 *Richard Hofstadter,* U.S. historian; Pulitzer Prize for *The Age of Reform,* 1955. [d. October 24, 1970]

1917 *Robert Mitchum,* U.S. actor. [d. July 1, 1997]

1922 *Frederick Alfred (Freddie) Laker,* British airline executive; founded Laker Airways, 1976; created the inexpensive, no-reservation Skytrain between London and New York.

1926 *Frank Finlay,* British actor; featured in *The Three Musketeers,* 1973.

Jackie Presser, U.S. labor union official; President, Teamsters Union, 1983–88. [d. July 9, 1988]

1927 *Andy Warhol,* U.S. artist; famous for *pop art;* produced numerous commercial silk screens on canvas, including pictures of Campbell's tomato soup cans and portaits of Marilyn Monroe and Elvis Presley; experimented in film medium and rock music. [d. February 22, 1987]

1957 *James Robert (Bob) Horner,* U.S. baseball player; 11th Major League player to hit four home runs in one game, 1986.

1958 *Randy DeBarge,* U.S. singer, musician.

1965 *David Robinson,* U.S. basketball player.

HISTORICAL EVENTS

1825 *Bolivia* declares its independence from Spain.

1890 The first U.S. execution by electrocution takes place at *Auburn Prison,* New York.

1896 *Madagascar* is proclaimed a French colony.

1914 *Austria* declares war on Russia (*World War I*).

Serbia declares war on Germany (*World War I*).

1918 General *Ferdinand Foch* is appointed Marshal of France (*World War I*).

1923 Direct railroad connection between the east and west coasts of New Zealand is established with the opening of the *Otira Tunnel.*

1926 *Gertrude Ederle,* U.S. swimmer, becomes first

woman to swim the *English Channel* (14 hours, 34 minutes).

Harry Houdini performs his most famous magic act, remaining under water, in a sealed tank, for 91 minutes.

1927 *Metropolitan University* is created at Peking, China, by union of nine government universities.

1930 The body of Swedish balloonist and explorer *S. A. Andrée,* who died in an 1897 attempt to cross the North Pole by balloon, is found on White Island in the Barents Sea by a Norwegian scientific expedition.

1944 Harvard University announces that an automatic *calculator* capable of solving any mathematical problem has been developed by *Howard Aikin* in collaboration with IBM.

1945 U.S. drops first-ever atomic bomb on *Hiroshima, Japan* (*World War II*).

1950 *Laureano Gomez Castro* is inaugurated as president of Colombia.

1956 *Hernan Siles Zuazo* assumes the presidency of Bolivia.

1959 Alfred Hitchcock's film, *North by Northwest,* premieres in New York.

1962 *Jamaica* becomes an independent member of the British Commonwealth.

1965 President Lyndon Johnson signs the *Voting Rights Act,* allowing black voters to register with federal examiners if they are turned down by state officials.

1966 Lieutenant General *Rene Barrientos* is inaugurated as president of Bolivia.

1978 *Pope Paul VI* dies of a heart attack at age 80.

1985 *Victor Paz Estenssoro* is inaugurated as president of Bolivia.

Desmond Hoyte is inaugurated as president of Guyana.

1990 *Ghulam Ishaq Khan,* President of Pakistan, removes Prime Minister *Benazir Bhutto* from her position. President Khan cites corruption as the reason.

HOLIDAYS

Colombia
Battle of Boyacá

Guyana
Freedom Dayá

U.S.
Family Day
Sponsored by Kiwanis International, Indianapolis, Indiana.

RELIGIOUS CALENDAR

The Saints
St. Claudia, matron. [d. 1st century]

St. Sixtus II, pope, *St. Felicissimus*, and *St. Agapitus*, with their companions, martyrs. Sixtus elected pope in 257. Sixtus also called *Xystus*. [d. 258] Optional Memorial.

St. Dometius the Persian, martyr. [d. c. 362]

St. Victricius, Bishop of Rouen. [d. c. 407]

St. Albert of Trapani. Also called *St. Albert of Sicily*. [d. c. 1307]

St. Cajetan, co-founder of the Theatine Clerks Regular. Also called *Gaetano*. [d. 1547]

The Beatified
Blessed Agathangelo and Cassian, martyrs. [d. 1638]

BIRTHDATES

1533 *Alonso de Ercilla y Zúñiga*, Spanish soldier; author of *La Araucana*, an epic poem immortalizing the Araucanian heroes of the resistance to Spanish supremacy. This work is considered by some as one of first significant literary works in the Americas. [d. November 29, 1594]

1578 *Georg Stiernhielm (Georgius Olai)*, Swedish poet, scholar; known as the *Father of Swedish Poetry*. [d. April 22, 1672]

1742 *Nathanael Greene*, American Revolutionary general; second in command of American army under General George Washington; largely responsible for the triumph of the American campaigns in the South. [d. June 19, 1786]

1805 *Ira Aldridge*, U.S. actor. [d. 1867]

1876 *Mata Hari (Margartha Geertruida Macleod)*, Dutch dancer; convicted and executed as a spy during World War I for passing Allied secrets to Germany. [d. October 15, 1917]

1886 *Billie Burke (Mary William Ethelberg Appleton)*, U.S. actress; known for her role as Glinda, the Good Witch, in *The Wizard of Oz*, 1939. [d. May 14, 1970]

1887 *Carl Eric Wickman*, U.S. transportation executive; founder of Greyhound Bus Corporation; President of Greyhound, 1930–46. [d. February 5, 1954]

1890 *Elizabeth Gurley Flynn*, U.S. labor leader; first chairperson of *U.S. Communist Party National Committee*, 1961. [d. September 5, 1964]

1896 *John J(oseph) Bergen*, U.S. financier; responsible for relocation of New York's *Madison Square Garden*, 1968, from 50th Street and Eighth Avenue to the lower stories of a building over Pennsylvania Station. [d. December 11, 1980]

1903 *L(ouis) S(eymour) B(azett) Leakey*, British archaeologist, anthropologist; discovered evidence of early humanoid existence in Africa, weakening theory that earliest man came from Asia. [d. October 1, 1972]

1904 *Ralph Bunche*, U.S. diplomat, educator; Nobel Peace Prize for negotiating peace between Arabs and Israel, 1950. [d. December 9, 1971]

1927 *Edwin Washington Edwards*, U.S. politician; Governor of Louisiana, 1972–80, 1984–88; acquitted of fraud charges, 1986.

1928 *James Randi (The Amazing Randi)*, Canadian magician, author; known for discrediting parapsychologists and faith healers; wrote *The Magic of Uri Geller,* 1975.

1938 *Helen Caldicott,* Australian physician and antinuclear activist.

1942 *B(illy) J(oe) Thomas,* U.S. singer.

Garrison Keillor (Gary Edward Keillor), U.S. radio performer, author, producer; known for his radio program, *A Prarie Home Companion;* wrote *Lake Wobegon Days,* 1985.

1950 *Alan L. Keyes,* U.S. politician, radio personality; candidate for 1996 Republican nomination for presidency.

1954 *Steve(n F.) Kemp,* U.S. baseball player.

1960 *David Duchovny,* U.S. actor; known for his role on the TV series *The X Files.*

HISTORICAL EVENTS

1803 *Second Maratha War* begins as British under Sir Arthur Wellesley attack Ahmadnagar, India.

1830 *Louis-Philippe* is elected king of France; known as the *Citizen King* during his six-year reign.

1914 City of *Liège, Belgium,* falls to invading Germans (*World War I*).

First troops of the *British Expeditionary Force* arrive in France (*World War I*).

1918 The *Second Battle of the Marne* ends with the Allies forcing a German retreat over the Marne (*World War I*).

1942 *Alfonso Lopez* is inaugurated president of Colombia.

First U.S. land offensive in Pacific Theater of World War II begins in *Solomon Islands* as Marines land on Japanese-held *Guadalcanal.*

1946 *Mariano Ospina Perez* is inaugurated president of Colombia.

1948 *Alice Coachman* becomes the first black woman to win an Olympic gold medal for her performance in the high jump.

1950 *David Hurrah* and *James Maxwell* become the first climbers to reach the summit of Peru's *Mount Yerupaja.*

1958 *Alberto Lleras Camargo* is inaugurated as president of Colombia.

Nuclear-powered U.S. submarine *Nautilus* completes history-making cruise under the Arctic ice pack and across the North Pole, traveling 1,830 miles in 4 days under the polar ice.

1960 *Ivory Coast* achieves full independence from France.

1964 U.S. Congress passes a joint resolution approving U.S. action in Southeast Asia (*Tonkin Gulf Resolution*).

1966 Dr. *Carlos Lleras Restrepo* is inaugurated as president of Colombia.

1970 *Misael Pastrana Borrero* is inaugurated as president of Colombia.

1972 A Protestant militiaman becomes the 500th victim in three years of sectarian violence in North Ireland when he is shot down outside his home in Armagh.

1974 *Alfonso Lopez Michelsen* is inaugurated as president of Colombia.

1978 Honduran president *Juan Alberto Melgar Castro* is overthrown in a military coup.

Julio Cesar Turbay Ayala is inaugurated as president of Colombia.

The *Love Canal* region of Niagara Falls, New York, is declared to be a disaster area due to chemical contamination.

1986 *Virgilio Barco Vargas* is inaugurated as president of Colombia.

1987 A Central American peace plan proposed by Costa Rican president, *Oscar Arias,* is signed by five nations in the region. It calls for an end to hostilities and democratic reforms.

1998 *U.S. embassies* in Kenya and Tanzania are hit by terrorist bombs, killing over 300 people (August 20, 1998).

HOLIDAYS

Iceland
Bank Holiday

RELIGIOUS CALENDAR

The Saints

The Fourteen Holy Helpers, a group of 14 German saints with special intercessory powers.

St. Hormisdas, martyr. Also called *Hormidz,* or *Hormizd.* [d. c. 420]

St. Altman, Bishop of Passau. [d. 1091]

St. Dominic, founder of the Order of Preachers. This order also called Blackfriars, or Dominicans. [d. 1221] Feast formerly August 4. Obligatory Memorial.

St. Lide, Celtic hermit. Also called *Elid,* or *Elidius.* [death date unknown]

The Beatified

Blessed Joan of Aza, matron. Mother of *St. Dominic.* [d. c. 1190]

Blessed John Felton, martyr. [d. 1570]

BIRTHDATES

1646 *Sir Godfrey Kneller (Gottfried Kniller),* English portrait painter; court painter to *William III, Anne,* and *George I.* [d. October 8, 1723]

1694 *Francis Hutcheson,* Irish teacher, philosopher. [d. 1746]

1763 *Charles Bulfinch,* U.S. architect; designed the *Beacon Hill Monument, Connecticut State House;* served as architect of the Capitol, 1817–30. [d. April 4, 1844]

1799 *Nathaniel Brown Palmer,* U.S. explorer; discovered *Antarctica,* 1820. [d. June 21, 1877]

1807 *Emilie Flygare-Carlèn,* Swedish novelist, feminist. [d. February 5, 1892]

1839 *Nelson Appleton Miles,* U.S. army officer; fought in the Civil War, the Indian wars, and the Spanish-American War. [d. May 15, 1925]

1846 *Samuel Milton (Golden Rule) Jones,* U.S. inventor, businessman, philanthropist, reform politician. [d. July 12, 1904]

1876 *Patrick A. McCarran,* U.S. politician, lawyer; U.S. Senator, 1932–54. [d. September 28, 1954]

1879 *Robert Holbrook Smith,* U.S. reformer; founder of *Alcoholics Anonymous,* 1935. [d. November 6, 1950]

1882 *Edward John Noble,* U.S. business executive; one of

founders of American Broadcasting Company. [d. December 28, 1958]

1883 *Emiliano Zapata,* Mexican revolutionary leader; championed agrarian movements, 1911–16. [d. April 10, 1919]

1884 *Sara Teasdale,* U.S. poet; Pulitzer Prize in poetry, 1918. [d. January 29, 1933]

1896 *Marjorie Kinnan Rawlings,* U.S. novelist; best known for her novel, *The Yearling,* 1939. [d. December 14, 1953]

1901 *Ernest Orlando Lawrence,* U.S. physicist; Nobel Prize in physics for development of *cyclotron,* 1939. [d. August 27, 1958]

1902 *Paul Adrien Maurice Dirac,* British physicist, mathematician; Nobel Prize in physics for development of new atomic theories (with E. Schrödinger), 1933.

1907 *Benny Carter (Bennett Lester Carter),* U.S. jazz musician, composer; composed music for *Stormy Weather* and *Guns of Navarone.*

Jesse Stuart, U.S. writer, educator; author of works dealing with mountain regions of Kentucky. [d. February 17, 1984]

1908 *Arthur Joseph Goldberg,* U.S. lawyer, government official, diplomat; U.S. Secretary of Labor, 1961–62; Associate Justice, U.S. Supreme Court, 1962–65; U.S. Representative to United Nations, 1965–68. [d. January 19, 1990]

1910 *Sylvia Sidney (Sophia Koskow),* U.S. actress, author.

1919 *Dino De Laurentiis,* Italian film producer.

1922 *Rudi Gernreich,* U.S. fashion designer. [d. April 21, 1985]

1923 *Rory Calhoun (Francis Timothy Durgin),* U.S. actor; appeared in Western films including *Ticket to Tomahawk* and *Treasure of Pancho Villa.*

Esther Williams, U.S. swimmer/actress; starred in many movies with an aquatic theme; widow of Fernando Lamas.

1925 *Alija Izetbegovic,* Bosnian politician; president of Bosnia and Herzegovina, 1990–96, member of the three-member presidency of Bosnia and Herzegovina, 1996– .

1930 *Jerry Tarkanian,* U.S. basketball coach.

1932 *Mel(vin) Tillis,* U.S. singer, songwriter.

1937 *Dustin Hoffman,* U.S. actor; Academy Award (Best Actor) for both *Kramer vs. Kramer,* 1979 and *Rain Man,* 1988.

1938 *Connie Stevens,* U.S. actress, singer.

1942 *James J. Blanchard,* U.S. politician; Governor of Michigan, 1982–90.

Roberta Cooper Ramo, U.S. lawyer; first woman president of the American Bar Association, 1995– .

1944 *Peter Weir,* Australian director; films include *The Year of Living Dangerously* and *Witness.*

1947 *Ken Dryden,* Canadian hockey player.

Larry Dee Wilcox, U.S. actor; known for his starring role on television series *CHIPs,* 1977–83.

1950 *Keith Ian Carradine,* U.S. actor, singer.

1953 *Donny Most,* U.S. actor; known for his role as Ralph Malph on television series *Happy Days,* 1974–80.

HISTORICAL EVENTS

1502 *James IV* of Scotland marries *Margaret Tudor,* daughter of *Henry VII* of England.

1570 *Peace of St. Germain* grants *Huguenots* in France general amnesty.

1588 *Spanish Armada* is defeated by England; decline of Spanish power follows.

1786 First ascent of *Mont Blanc* is accomplished by *Dr. Michel Paccard* and *Jacques Balmat.*

1815 *Napoleon* is banished to *St. Helena* after his final defeat.

1881 *Pretoria Convention* restores South African Republic to British suzerainty.

1890 National Society of the *Daughters of the American Revolution* is organized in Washington, D.C.

1919 Great Britain signs the *Treaty of Rawalpindi* which recognizes the independence of *Afghanistan.*

1940 German bombers begin major offensive designed to destroy British air power (*World War II*).

1942 U.S. captures the Japanese Air Force base at *Guadalcanal,* renaming it *Henderson Field* (*World War II*).

U.S. Marines win control of *Tulagi, Gavutu,* and *Tanambogo* in the Solomon Islands (*World War II*).

1945 The U.S.S.R. declares war against *Japan* in an attempt to hasten an unconditional surrender to the Allied forces (*World War II*).

1963 Bandits rob the Glasgow-London mail train and escape with approximately $7 million in banknotes.

1967 *Association of Southeast Asian Nations* is established by Thailand, Indonesia, Singapore, the Philippines, and Malaysia, to promote regional growth, social progress, and cultural development.

1969 U.S. actress, *Sharon Tate,* is brutally murdered by followers of *Charles Manson.*

1974 President *Richard Nixon* announces his resignation, marking the culmination of events known as the *Watergate Incident.* The resignation occurs six years to the day after he was nominated by the Republican party as its presidential candidate.

1983 Brigadier General *Oscar Humberto Mejia Victores* overthrows the government of General *Efrain Rios Montt* in Guatemala.

1988 The Chicago Cubs play their first night game at *Wrigley*

Field, the last major league baseball stadium to install lights.

1994 *Cesar Chavez* is presented with the Medal of Freedom by President Bill Clinton.

august

AUGUST
9

HOLIDAYS

Singapore
National Day
Celebrates Singapore's achievement of independence from Malaysia, 1965.

RELIGIOUS CALENDAR

Feasts
Feast of St. Matthias Celebrated by Eastern Orthodox Churches.

The Saints
St. Romanus, martyr. [d. 258]
St. Nathy and *St. Felim,* bishops. Felim also called *Fedhlimidh, Fedlemid,* or *Felimy.* [d. c. 6th century]
St. Oswald, King of Northumbria, martyr. Patron of Zug, Switzerland. [d. 642]

The Beatified
Blessed John of Salerno, Dominican monk. [d. 1242]
Blessed John of Rieti. [d. c. 1350]

BIRTHDATES

1593 *Izaak Walton,* English biographer, author; author of *The Compleat Angler or the Contemplative Man's Recreation* and of biographies of John Donne and George Herbert. [d. December 15, 1683]

1613 *John Dryden,* English poet, dramatist, critic; Poet Laureate of England, 1670–1700. [d. May 1, 1700]

1757 *Thomas Telford,* Scottish civil engineer; designer of the *Menai suspension bridge,* and of numerous canals and bridges in northern Scotland. [d. September 2, 1834]

1809 *William Barret Travis,* Texas lawyer, soldier; leader in the revolt against Mexico. Commander of Texan forces at the *Battle of the Alamo,* 1836. [d. March 6, 1836]

1819 *William Thomas Green Morton,* U.S. dentist; pioneered in use of *anesthetics (ether)* for surgery. [d. July 15, 1868]

1830 *Franz Josef,* Austro-Hungarian emperor. [d. November 21, 1916]

1896 *Jean Piaget,* Swiss psychologist; famous for his theories of child's cognitive development; Professor of Psychology, University of Lausanne, 1937–54; Director of International Bureau of Education, 1929–67. [d. September 17, 1980]

A(loysius) M(ichael) Sullivan, U.S. poet, businessman, editor; Editor, *Dun's Review,* 1954–61; moderator, *New Party Program,* 1932–40, a broadcast of readings by prominent poets of the period. [d. June 10, 1980]

1898 *(Lawrence) Brooks Hays,* U.S. politician; U.S. Congressman, 1943–59; noted for his efforts at compromise in civil rights issues. [d. October 11, 1981]

1905 *Robert C. Nix,* U.S. politician, judge; Congressman, 1958–72. [d. June 22, 1987]

1911 *William A. Fowler,* U.S. physicist; Nobel Prize in physics for his research of nuclear reactions in the formation of stars, 1983.

1913 *Herman Eugene Talmadge,* U.S. lawyer, politician; Governor of Georgia, 1948–55; U.S. Senator, 1957–80.

1922 *Philip (Arthur) Larkin,* British poet, novelist, editor, librarian. [d. December 2, 1985]

1927 *Marvin Minsky,* U.S. scientist; known for his research in artificial intelligence.

Robert Shaw, British actor; known for his starring role in 1975 film, *Jaws.* [d. August 28, 1978]

1928 *Bob Cousy (Robert Joseph Cousy),* U.S. basketball player, coach, sportscaster; inducted into Basketball Hall of Fame, 1970.

1930 *Jacques Parizeau,* Canadian politician; Premier of Quebec, 1994– .

1938 *Rod(ney George) Laver,* Australian tennis player; 1962 and 1969 winner of tennis Grand Slam: U.S., Australian, French, and British championships.

1940 *Jill Saint John,* U.S. actress.

1942 *David Steinberg,* Canadian comedian.

1944 *Sam Elliott,* U.S. actor.

1945 *Ken Norton,* U.S. boxer, world heavyweight champion, 1978.

1957 *Melanie Griffith,* U.S. actress.

1963 *Whitney Houston,* U.S. singer, actress; Grammy Award for top female vocalist, 1986; known for her performances in *The Bodyguard,* 1992 and *Waiting to Exhale,* 1995.

1964 *Brett Hull,* Canadian hockey player.

1967 *Deion Sanders,* U.S. football, baseball player.

1968 *Gillian Anderson,* U.S. actress; known for her role as Agent Dana Scully on the TV show *The X Files.*

HISTORICAL EVENTS

378 *Roman Emperor Valens* is killed at *Adrianople* as the mounted Visigoths easily defeat Roman footsoldiers.

870 *Treaty of Mersen* divides Lorraine between Germany and France.

1757 French army under *Montcalm* captures *Fort William Henry* from British; on August 10 many British are killed by Indians allied with the French (*French and Indian War*).

1807 Robert Fulton's steam boat, *Clermont,* begins regular service on Hudson River from New York to Albany.

1842 The *Webster-Ashburton Treaty* settles the boundary between the U.S. and British Canada from Maine to beyond the Great Lakes.

1851 The *Australian Gold Rush* is triggered by the discovery of large nuggets of gold at Bathhurst, New South Wales.

1903 *Pope Pius X* is anointed Bishop of Rome and Pope of the Roman Catholic Church.

1905 *Portsmouth Peace Conference* brings an end to the *Russo-Japanese War;* Japan secures recognition of its rights in *Korea* and consolidates its position in *Manchuria.*

1935 The *U.S. Motor Carrier Act* is adopted, giving the *Interstate Commerce Commission* regulatory power over trucks and buses.

1936 *Jessie Owens* becomes the first Olympic athlete to win four gold medals.

1942 *Mahatma Gandhi* is arrested for the fourth and final time for protesting against British rule in India.

1945 The U.S. drops an atomic bomb on *Nagasaki, Japan,* causing over 40,000 deaths (*World War II*)

1965 *Singapore* withdraws from the Federation of Malaysia.

1974 *Gerald Ford* is inaugurated as 38th U.S. president following the resignation of Richard Nixon.

august

AUGUST
10

HOLIDAYS

Ecuador
Independence Day
Celebrates Ecuador's achievement of independence, 1822.

Nicaragua (Managua)
Public Holiday

RELIGIOUS CALENDAR

The Saints
St. Laurence, martyr. Patron of cooks, vintners, and restaurateurs; invoked against lumbago and fire. Also called *Lawrence*. [d. 258] [Minor festival, Lutheran Church]

St. Bettelin, patron of Stafford. [death date unknown]

St. Philomena. Also called *Philumena*. [death date unknown] Feast suppressed, 1961.

BIRTHDATES

1729 *William Howe, 5th Viscount Howe*, British Army general; Commander in Chief of British army in North America, 1776–78. [d. July 12, 1814]

1753 *Edmund Jennings Randolph*, U.S. lawyer, politician; Attorney General, 1789–94; Secretary of State, 1794–95. [d. September 12, 1813]

1790 *George McDuffie*, U.S. politician; Congressman, 1821–34; Governor of South Carolina, 1834–36; greatly influenced John C. Calhoun on issue of nullification. [d. March 11, 1851]

1810 *Camillo Benso, Comte de Cavour*, Italian statesman; Premier of Sardinia, 1852–59, 1860–61; one of main figures in the campaign for Italian unity. [d. June 6, 1861]

1821 *Jay Cooke*, U.S. financier; founder of Jay Cooke & Co., a banking house; responsible for U.S. bond selling during Civil War; speculator in railroad construction. [d. February 18, 1905]

1848 *William Michael Harnett*, U.S. still-life painter; executed painfully detailed, realistic paintings of common objects. [d. October 29, 1892]

1856 *Edward Lawrence Doheny*, U.S. oilman; major figure in the *Teapot Dome Scandal* of 1921. [d. September 8, 1935]

1861 *Sir Almroth E. Wright*, British physician; introduced immunization against *typhoid fever* by means of inoculation. [d. April 30, 1947]

1865 *Aleksandr Konstantinovich Glazunov*, Russian composer. [d. March 21, 1936]

1869 *Laurence Binyon*, British poet, art critic; supervisor of Oriental prints and drawings at British Museum, 1913–32. [d. March 10, 1943]

1873 *William E. Hocking*, U.S. Idealist philosopher; Professor of Philosophy, Harvard University, 1914–43. [d. June 12, 1966]

1874 *Herbert (Clark) Hoover*, 31st President of the U.S., 1929–33. [d. October 20, 1964]

1887 *Sam(uel Louis) Warner*, U.S. film executive; co-founded Warner Brothers, 1923. [d. October 5, 1927]

1894 *V(arahagiri) V(enkata) Giri*, Indian statesman; President of India, 1969–74; key figure in organization of India's government after independence from Great Britain. [d. June 25, 1980]

1895 *Harry Richman*, U.S. singer, vaudeville sensation. [d. November 3, 1972]

1900 *Jack Haley*, U.S. actor; known for his role as the Tin Man in the film, *The Wizard of Oz*, 1939. [d. June 6, 1979]

1902 *Arne W. K. Tiselius*, Swedish biochemist; Nobel Prize in chemistry for discoveries in biochemistry and the invention of important laboratory apparatus for separating and detecting *colloids* and *serum proteins*, 1948. [d. October 29, 1971]

1904 *Norma Shearer,* U.S. actress. [d. June 12, 1983]

Pavel Alekseyevich Cherenkov, Soviet physicist; Nobel Prize in physics for discovery of *Cherenkov effect* (radiated electrons accelerate in water to speeds greater than speed of light in that medium) (with I. M. Frank and I. Y. Tamm), 1958. [d. 1990]

1910 *Mohammed V (Sidi Mohammed Ben Moulay Youssef),* Moroccan king. [d. February 26, 1961]

1913 *Noah Beery, Jr.,* U.S. actor.

Wolfgang Paul, German physicist; Nobel Prize for Physics, 1989. Paul shares one-half of the prize with U.S. physicist, Hans Georg Dehmelt, for their study of ions. Norman F. Ramsey; other half of the prize for his work on shifting the energy levels of atoms. [d. 1993]

1922 *Rhonda Fleming (Marilyn Louis),* U.S. actress.

1928 *Eddie Fisher (Edwin Jack Fisher),* U.S. singer.

1938 *Diana Charlton Muldaur,* U.S. actress.

1942 *Betsey Johnson,* U.S. fashion designer.

1947 *Ian Anderson,* British musician, singer; lead vocalist of the rock group, *Jethro Tull.*

1948 *Patti Austin,* U.S. singer.

1959 *Rosanna Arquette,* U.S. actress.

1960 *Antonio Banderas,* Spanish actor.

HISTORICAL EVENTS

955 *Otto I* of Germany defeats the Magyars at *Battle of Lechfeld,* ending the threat of Magyar invasion of the West.

1557 England and Spain defeat France at *Battle of St. Quentin,* thereby driving France from Italy.

1759 *Ferdinand V* of Spain dies and is succeeded by *Charles III.*

1792 A Parisian mob storms the *Tuileries* and massacres 5,000 Swiss Guards; the legislative assembly suspends the monarchy (*French Revolution*).

1821 *Missouri* is admitted to the Union as the 24th state.

1913 *Treaty of Bucharest* is signed between Bulgaria and the Balkan allies, Greece, Serbia, Montenegro, and Rumania, ending the *Second Balkan War.*

1920 *Crazy Blues,* the first authentic blues recording, is released.

Treaty of Sevres, stripping Turkey of a major portion of her possessions, is signed by Allied and Associated Powers.

1941 *Dean Dixon,* first black to lead a major U.S. orchestra, conducts a concert by the *New York Philharmonic Orchestra.*

1944 U.S. troops recapture *Guam* (*World War II*).

1948 *Candid Camera* makes its television debut.

1949 U.S. President Harry S. Truman signs the *National Security Act,* which creates the *Department of Defense.*

1950 The first shipment of U.S. arms for *South Vietnam* arrives in Saigon.

1954 The union of the *Netherlands* and *Indonesia* is dissolved.

1964 *Pope Paul VI* issues the encyclical *Ecclesiam Suam,* which states his readiness to mediate in international disputes.

1966 U.S. air base at *Sattahid, Thailand* is dedicated, officially acknowledging cooperation between Thailand and the U.S. in the *Vietnam War.*

1970 Colonel *Harland Sanders,* founder of *Kentucky Fried Chicken Corp.,* resigns from the board of directors.

Sultan *Qabus ibn Said* of Muscat and Oman changes the name of his country to *Sultanate of Oman.*

1977 *David Berkowitz* is identified as "*Son of Sam*", responsible for a year-long series of murders in the New York City area.

1979 *Jaime Roldos Aguilera* is inaugurated as president of Ecuador.

1981 U.S. announces its decision to produce *neutron weapons.*

1988 *Lauro Cavazos* is nominated as U.S. Secretary of Education. He is the first Hispanic to be nominated for a cabinet position.

President Ronald Reagan signs legislation offering $20,000 in reparations to *Japanese American citizens* who were incarcerated during World War II.

President *George Bush* nominates General *Colin*

Powell as the new chairman of the Joint Chiefs of Staff.

1993 President *Bill Clinton* signs the *Revenue Reconciliation Act* into law.

1995 *Timothy McVeigh* and *Terry Nichols* are indicted for the bombing of the Alfred P. Murrah federal building in Oklahoma City, Oklahoma.

HOLIDAYS

Chad
Independence Day

Jordan
Accession of H. M. King Hussein
Celebrates the accession to the throne of Hussein, 1952.

Zimbabwe
Heroes' Day
Honors those who died in the struggle against white minority rule.

RELIGIOUS CALENDAR

The Saints
St. Alexander the Charcoal-Burner, bishop of Comana, martyr; patron of charcoal burners. [d. c. 275]
SS. Tiburtius and Susanna, martyrs. Susanna also called *Susan.* [d. c. 3rd cent.]
St. Equitius, abbot. [d. c. 560]
St. Blaan, bishop. Aso called *Blane,* or *Blaun.* [d. c. 590]
St. Attracta, virgin; patron of diocese of Achonry, Ireland. Also called *Araght,* or *Tarahata.* [d. c. 6th cent.]
St. Lelia, virgin. [d. c. 6th cent.]
St. Clare, virgin and foundress of the Poor Clares or Minoresses. Patron of embroidery workers, guilders, washerwomen. Invoked against eye diseases. Feast formerly August 12. [d. 1253] Obligatory Memorial.

The Beatified
Blessed Peter Favre. Also called *Peter Faber.* [d. 1546]
Blessed Innocent XI, pope. Elected 1676. [d. 1689]

BIRTHDATES

1778 *Friedrich Ludwig Jahn,* German educator; opened the first gymnasium in Berlin, 1811; called the *Father of Gymnastics.* [d. October 15, 1852]

1821 *Octave Feuillet,* French novelist, dramatist. [d. December 29, 1890]

1833 *Robert Green Ingersoll,* U.S. lawyer, orator, and lecturer; Attorney General of Illinois, 1867–69; major advocate of scientific and humanistic rationalism in the debates over Darwin's theory of evolution. Lectured widely, presenting a clear and logical summary of agnosticism. [d. July 21, 1899]

1837 *Marie François Sadi Carnot,* French statesman; fourth president of the French Republic, 1887–94; assassinated by Italian anarchist. [d. June 25, 1894]

1858 *Christiaan Eijkman,* Dutch physician; Nobel Prize in physiology or medicine for discovery of *Vitamin B,* 1929. [d. November 5, 1930]

1903 *Joseph Edward Frowde Seagram,* Canadian distiller. [d. November 28, 1979]

1921 *Alex (Palmer) Haley,* U.S. author; Pulitzer Prize, 1977 (special citation for his fictional biography, *Roots*). [d. February 10, 1992]

1925 *Mike Douglas (Michael Delaney Dowd, Jr.),* U.S. television performer, singer; Hosted *The Mike Douglas Show,* 1960s–70s; four Emmy Awards.

Carl T. Rowan, U.S. journalist, columnist.

1926 *Aaron Klug,* South African biologist; Nobel Prize in chemistry for his research in molecular biology, 1982.

Claus Von Bulow, Danish-born businessman; acquitted of injecting his wife with insulin, resulting in an irreversible coma, 1985.

1928 *Arlene Dahl,* U.S. actress, beauty columnist, model.

1932 *Peter Eisenman,* U.S. educator, architect; designed the Wexner Center for the Visual Arts (Ohio State University), 1989.

1933 *Jerry Falwell,* U.S. clergyman; founded Moral Majority, Inc.

1941 *Elizabeth Holtzman,* U.S. politician; Congresswoman, 1974–80.

august

1955 *Joe Jackson,* British singer; known for hit single, *Steppin' Out,* 1982.

HISTORICAL EVENTS

1332 *Edward Balliol* deposes *King David II* and assumes the throne of Scotland by his victory at *Dupplin.*

1863 *Cambodia* becomes French protectorate.

1914 The invasion of *Serbia* by Austria-Hungary begins (*World War I*).

1949 U.S. General *Omar Bradley* is appointed the first chairman of the *Joint Chiefs of Staff.*

1965 Rioting by blacks begins in the *Watts* section of Los Angeles. The 6 days of looting and burning result in 34 deaths and more than $40 million worth of property damage.

1966 The three-year undeclared war between *Indonesia* and *Malaysia* ends with the signing of a peace treaty at Jakarta.

1979 *Morocco* formally annexes *Tiris el-Gharbia,* an area of the Western Sahara, formerly part of Spain.

1983 Several Milwaukee youths are charged with gaining illegal access to sophisticated computer systems, including those at the *Sloan Kettering Cancer Center* and a government nuclear research facility. The incident renews concern about *computer security.*

1984 *Desmond Hoyte* replaces *Ptolemy Reid* as prime minister of Guyana.

HOLIDAYS

Thailand
Queen's Birthday

U.S. (Massachusetts)
Indian Day

Zimbabwe
Heroes' Day
Honors those who died in the struggle against white minority rule.

RELIGIOUS CALENDAR

The Saints

St. Euplus, martyr. Also called *Euplius.* [d. 304]

St. Murtagh, bishop. Also called *Muredach.* [d. c. sixth century]

SS. Porcarius and his Companions, martyrs. [d. c. 732]

St. Jambert, Archbishop of Canterbury. Also called *Jaenbeorht.* [d. 792]

BIRTHDATES

1503 *Christian III,* King of Denmark and Norway; called the *Father of the People;* introduced the Reformation to Denmark. [d. January 1, 1559]

1753 *Thomas Bewick,* English engineer, book illustrator; stimulated a rebirth of interest in wood engraving as an art form.

1762 *George IV,* King of Great Britain and Ireland, 1820–30. [d. June 26, 1830]

1781 *Robert Mills,* U.S. architect; Architect of Public Buildings 1830–51; designed the Washington Monument, although it was not built until 30 years after his death. [d. March 3, 1855]

1815 *Benjamin Pierce Cheney,* U.S. business executive; founder of New England stage-coach business that evolved into American Express Co., 1879. [d. July 23, 1895]

1856 *James Buchanan (Diamond Jim) Brady,* U.S. salesman of railroad carriages; bon vivant, flamboyant U.S. businessman known widely for his phenomenal selling ability, extravagant habits, and philanthropic leanings. Donated funds to *Johns Hopkins University* for establishment of its Urological Institute. [d. April 13, 1917]

1859 *Katherine Lee Bates,* U.S. author, educator; wrote the poem *America the Beautiful,* on which the song is based. [d. March 28, 1929]

1866 *Jacinto Benavante y Martínez,* Spanish dramatist; noted for his realistic and satirical plays of Spanish life; Nobel Prize in literature, 1922. [d. July 14, 1954]

1867 *Edith Hamilton,* U.S. author, mythology expert; author of *The Greek Way* and *The Roman Way.* [d. May 31, 1963]

1872 *Louis Loucheur,* French industrialist, statesman; French Minister of Labor, 1928–30; Minister of Commerce, 1930–31. [d. November 22, 1931]

1876 *Mary Roberts Rinehart,* U.S. novelist; noted for her popular mystery novels which appeared between 1908–53 and sold more than 10 million copies by the time of her death; a founder of Farrar & Rinehart, publishers. [d. September 22, 1958]

1880 *Christy Mathewson,* U.S. baseball player; inducted into Baseball Hall of Fame, 1936. [d. October 7, 1925]

1881 *Cecil B(lount) De Mille,* U.S. director, producer, Hollywood pioneer in production of films; first to establish the medium as a serious dramatic form. Noted for his extravagant large-scale productions on universally appealing themes such as Bible stories and American growth and expansion. [d. January 21, 1959]

1882 *George Wesley Bellows,* U.S. painter; exponent of realism; he brought modern art to

America with his efforts at organizing the *Armory Show of 1913*. Renowned for his bold and vigorous paintings of city life, boxing events, and World War II. Among his most famous works are *Stag at Sharkey's* and *Forty-two Kids*. [d. January 8, 1925]

Vincent Bendix, U.S. inventor, industrialist; founder of Bendix Company, a pioneer in car manufacturing. Established Bendix Brake Company, the first mass producer of four-wheel brakes, and Bendix Aviation Corporation. [d. March 27, 1945]

1887 *Erwin Schrödinger*, Austrian physicist; Nobel Prize in physics for development of new forms of atomic theory (with P. Dirac), 1933. [d. January 4, 1961]

1904 *Alexis, Czarevitch of Russia*, son of Nicholas II and Alexandra. Executed with his parents and sisters by Bolsheviks. [d. July 16, 1918]

1919 *E. Margaret Burbidge*, U.S. astrophysicist; known for her research on quasars with her husband, Geoffrey Burbidge.

1924 *Mohammad Zia ul-Haq*, Pakistani statesman; President, Islamic Republic of Pakistan, 1977–88; died in a suspicious plane crash. [d. August 17, 1988]

1925 *Dale Bumpers*, U.S. politician, lawyer; Governor of Arkansas, 1971–75; U.S. Senator, 1975– .

Norris Dewar McWhirter and *(Alan) Ross McWhirter*, British editors and authors; twin brothers; creators and editors of *Guinness Book of World Records*, 1955–75.

McWhirter was killed in an Irish Republican Army terrorist attack on November 27, 1975.

1926 *John Derek*, U.S. actor; starred in *The Ten Commandments*, 1956; former husband of Linda Evans, Ursula Andress; present husband of Bo Derek. [d. May 22, 1998]

1927 *Porter Wagoner*, U.S. singer; three Country Music Awards (with Dolly Parton).

1929 *Alvis E. (Buck) Owens*, U.S. singer, musician; starred in the television series *Hee Haw*, 1969–86.

1931 *William Goldman*, U.S. author, screenwriter; wrote the film scripts for *Marathon Man* and *Butch Cassidy and the Sundance Kid*.

1932 *John Richard Lane*, U.S. artist, author; Creative Director (1969–75), editorial cartoonist (1975–78), Art Director (1978–) for Newspaper Enterprise Association (now NEA-United Features Syndicate); illustrated such books as *Rockin' Steady* (1974) and *Secret Hidy Holes* (1979).

1936 *Andre Kolingba*, Head of State, Central African Republic, 1981–93.

1939 *George Hamilton*, U.S. actor; starred in and produced *Love at First Bite* and *Zorro, the Gay Blade*.

1949 *Mark Knopfler*, Scottish musician, composer; member of the rock group, *Dire Straits*; Grammy Award for *Money for Nothing*, 1986.

Fernando Collor de Mello, Brazilian politician; President of Brazil, 1990– .

1971 *Pete Sampras*, U.S. tennis player; youngest player to win the U.S. Open, 1990; won fifth Wimbledon title in 1998.

HISTORICAL EVENTS

1099 Crusaders defeat Egyptians at *Ascalon (First Crusade)*.

1450 French recover *Cherbourg* from English (*Hundred Years' War*).

1876 *Benjamin Disraeli* is created Earl of Beaconsfield by Queen Victoria.

1877 *Henry M. Stanley*, journalist, explorer, reaches the mouth of the Congo River in his search for explorer David Livingstone.

1898 The *Hawaiian Islands* are formally annexed by the United States.

Spanish-American War ends with the signing of a protocol by Spain and the United States. Spain relinquishes *Cuba* and cedes *Puerto Rico* to the U.S.

1914 Great Britain declares war on Austria-Hungary (*World War I*).

1922 German stock market collapses, with the *Deutschmark* declining in value from 162:1 U.S. dollar to 7,000:1 U.S. dollar.

1954 The first issue of *Sports Illustrated* is published.

1960 *Echo I*, U.S. balloon communications satellite (100 feet in diameter) is placed in orbit from Cape Canaveral.

1967 *Pope Paul VI* announces changes in the structure of the Roman Catholic Church's central administrative organ, the Curia, including the appointment of non-Italian bishops from all parts of the world to Curia posts.

1970 President Richard Nixon signs the *Postal Reorganization bill* replacing the Department of the Post Office with a government-owned postal service under executive authority.

1972 The last U.S. combat troops depart from South Vietnam. *(Vietnam War)*.

1978 The first papal funeral ever held outdoors is conducted for *Pope Paul VI* in St. Peter's Square, Rome.

China and Japan sign an historic treaty of peace and friendship in Peking.

1985 A *Japan Air Lines* jet slams into a mountain, killing 520 passengers in history's worst single-plane accident.

august

AUGUST
13

HOLIDAYS

Central African Republic
Proclamation of Independence
Commemorates the adoption of a parliamentary form of government, 1960.

Congo
Three Glorious Days
First day of a three-day celebration.

Tunisia
Women's Day

RELIGIOUS CALENDAR

The Saints
St. Hippolytus, martyr; patron of horses and their riders. Also called *Hippolytas.* [d. c. 235] Optional Memorial.

St. Pontian, pope and martyr. Elected to papacy 230. [d. c. 236] Optional Memorial. Feast formerly November 19.

St. Radegund, Queen of the Franks, matron. Founder of the nunnery at Poitiers. Also called *Radegundes.* [d. 587]

St. Maximus the Confessor, abbot. [d. 662]

St. Wigbert, abbot. [d. c. 738]

St. Nerses Klaiëtsi, Primate of the Armenians; foremost writer and poet of his time. Also called *Narses,* or *Narses III.* Also known as *Shnorhali,* or *the Gracious.* [d. 1173]

St. Benildus, teaching brother. [d. 1862]

St. Cassian of Imola, martyr. [death date unknown]

The Beatified
Blessed Novellone. [d. 1280]
Blessed Gertrude of Altenberg, virgin. [d. 1297]
Blessed John of Alvernia. Also called *John of Fermo.* [d. 1322]
Blessed William Freeman, martyr. Also called *William Mason.* [d. 1595]
Blessed Angela Salawa. [beatified 1991]

BIRTHDATES

1422 *William Caxton,* British author, printer; first to print books translated into English. [d. 1491]

1740 *Ivan VI,* Emperor of Russia, 1740–41; forced to abdicate; kept in prison after abdication; murdered, 1764. [d. July 15, 1764]

1814 *Anders Jonas Ångström,* Swedish physicist, astronomer; *Ångstrom unit,* used in measuring length of *light waves,* is named for him. [d. June 21, 1874]

1818 *Lucy Stone,* U.S. social reformer; leader in women's rights movement; founded American Woman Suffrage Association, 1869; founded *Woman's Journal,* a leading publication promoting woman's suffrage, 1870–1917. [d. October 18, 1893]

1820 *Sir George Grove,* British musicologist; editor of *Dictionary of Music and Musicians,* a standard work which bears his name even after numerous revisions by other editors. [d. May 28, 1900]

1860 *Annie Oakley (Phoebe Anne Oakley Mozee),* U.S. markswoman, entertainer; member of *Buffalo Bill Cody's Wild West Show* which toured America for over 17 years. [d. November 3, 1926]

1871 *Karl Liebknecht,* German Communist leader, lawyer; led opposition to Germany's involvement in World War I; murdered with Rosa Luxemburg (December 25) after *Spartacist Rebellion,* 1919. [d. January 15, 1919]

1872 *Richard M. Willstätter,* German chemist; Nobel Prize in chemistry for study of *chlorophyll* and other plant pigments, 1915. [d. August 3, 1942]

1888 *John Logie Baird,* Scottish engineer, an early contributor to science of visual transmission; developed first apparatus for transmitting visual record of moving objects, a forerunner of *television,* 1924. [d. June 14, 1946]

1895 *Bert Lahr (Irving Lahrheim),* U.S. comedian. [d. December 4, 1967]

1897 *Detlev Wulf Bronk,* U.S. biophysicist, educator; President of Johns Hopkins University, 1949–53; President of National Academy of Sciences, 1950–62; President of Rockefeller Institute for Medical Research, 1953–68. Received Presidential Medal of Freedom, 1964. [d. November 17, 1975]

1899 *Alfred (Joseph) Hitchcock,* British film director; master of the suspense film. [d. April 29, 1980]

1912 *(William) Ben(jamin) Hogan,* U.S. golfer; inducted into PGA Hall of Fame, 1953. [d. July 25, 1998]

Salvador Edward Luria, U.S. biologist, educator, university professor, born in Italy; Nobel Prize in physiology or medicine for discoveries in genetic structure of viruses (with M. Delbrück and A. D. Hershey), 1969. [d. February 6, 1991]

Jane Wyatt, U.S. actress; appeared in the television series, *Father Knows Best,* 1954–62.

1913 *Makarios III (Mikhail Khristodolou Mouskos),* Cypriot leader; first president of Cyprus, 1960–74; Archbishop of the Orthodox Church of Cyprus, 1950–77. [d. August 2, 1977]

(John) Richard (Nicholas) Stone, British economist; Nobel Prize in economics for his development of an accounting system that measures national incomes. [d. December 6, 1991]

1916 *Daniel (Louis) Schorr,* U.S. news correspondent; commentator for CBS TV

news, 1966–76; aroused national controversy by passing secret congressional report on the CIA to the *Village Voice.*

1917 *Philip Handler,* U.S. biochemist, educator; head of Department of Biochemistry, Duke University, 1950–69; Chairman, National Science Board, 1966–69. [d. December 29, 1981]

1918 *Frederick Sanger,* British biochemist; Nobel Prize in chemistry for determination of the structure of the *insulin* molecule, 1958.

1919 *Rex Humbard,* U.S. evangelist.

George Shearing, British musician; blind since birth; his jazz quintet has maintained great popularity for nearly 40 years.

1924 *Leon (Marcus) Uris,* U.S. novelist; best known for his novels *Exodus* and *Trinity.*

1926 *Fidel Castro,* Cuban political leader; Premier of Cuba, 1959– . Leader in establishing Cuba as the first Communist nation in the Western Hemisphere.

1929 *(Daniel) Pat(rick) Harrington,* U.S. actor; known for his role as Schneider on the television series, *One Day at a Time.*

1930 *Don Ho,* U.S. singer.

Robert Culp, U.S. actor; starred in the television series, *I Spy* and *The Greatest American Hero.*

1948 *Kathleen Battle,* U.S. opera singer; Grammy winner, 1987, 1988.

1951 *Dan(iel Grayling) Fogelberg,* U.S. composer, singer; hit

songs include *Part of the Plan* and *Leader of the Band.*

1967 *Quinn Cunningham,* U.S. actress; Academy Award nominee for *The Goodbye Girl,* 1977.

HISTORICAL EVENTS

1624 *Cardinal Richelieu* becomes first Chief Minister of France.

1704 *Battle of Blenheim* is fought, in which French troops are routed by a combined English and Austrian force (*War of the Spanish Succession*).

1814 *The Colony of the Cape of Good Hope* in South Africa is formally ceded to the British by the Dutch.

1831 *Nat Turner* slave insurrection begins in Southampton County, Virginia. During the uprising 55 whites and about 100 blacks are killed.

1889 *London Dock Strike,* which lasts for more than one month, begins the spread of trade unionism in Great Britain.

1898 U.S. forces capture *Manila* (*Spanish-American War*).

1914 *France* declares war on Austria-Hungary (*World War I*).

1918 *Czechoslovakia* declares war on Germany (*World War I*).

1943 In the heaviest attacks on Italy, U.S. and British planes bomb *Rome, Turin,* and *Milan* (*World War II*).

1960 *Chad,* the *Congo,* and the *Central African Republic* gain independence from France.

august

1961 Construction by the Soviets of
the *Berlin Wall*, which blocks
passage between East and
West Berlin, is begun.

HOLIDAYS

Congo
Three Glorious Days
Second day of a three-day celebration.

Morocco
Oued Eddahab Day
Commemorates the 1979 annexation of Western Sahara (Oued Eddahab).

Pakistan
Independence Day

San Marino
Summer Holiday or Bank Holiday
First day of a three-day celebration.

Vatican City
Mid-August Holiday

RELIGIOUS CALENDAR

The Saints
St. Marcellus, Bishop of Apamaea, martyr. [d. c. 389]
St. Eusebius (Vercelli) of Rome, priest. [d. 371]
St. Fachanan, Bishop; patron of diocese of Ross, Ireland. Also called *Eachanan,* or *Fachtna.* [d. 6th cent.]
St. Athanasia, matron. [d. c. 860]
St. Maximilian Kolbe. [canonized 1982]

The Beatified
Blessed Anthony Primaldi and his Companions, martyrs. [d. 1480]

BIRTHDATES

1742 *Pius VII,* pope, 1800–23; imprisoned by Napoleon, 1809–14; restored Jesuit order. [d. August 20, 1823]

1840 Baron *Richard Krafft-Ebbing,* German neurologist; noted for studies of *forensic psychiatry* and *aberrant sexual practices.* [d. December 22, 1902]

1860 *Ernest Thompson Seton,* Canadian artist, author, lecturer; one of originators of *American Boy Scout* movement; Chief Scout of Boy Scouts of America, 1910–15. [d. October 23, 1946]

1867 *John Galsworthy (John Sinjohn),* British novelist, dramatist; Nobel Prize in literature, 1932. [d. January 31, 1933]

1883 *Ernest Everett Just,* U.S. biologist, educator; recipient of the first Spingarn Medal awarded by the National Association for the Advancement of Colored People for his dedication to improvement of medical education for black students, 1914. [d. October 27, 1941]

1920 *Nehemiah Persoff,* U.S. character actor, born in Israel.

1925 *Russell (Wayne) Baker,* U.S. journalist; Pulitzer Prize in commentary, 1979.

1928 *Lina von Eigg Wertmuller (Arcangela Felice Assunta Wertmuller von Eigg),* Italian director; films include *Seven Beauties, Swept Away* and *Seduction of Mimi.*

1930 *Earl Weaver,* U.S. baseball player, manager; managed the Baltimore Orioles, 1968–82, 1985–86; won four pennants and a World Series.

1933 *Richard R. Ernst,* Swiss educator; Nobel Prize for Chemistry for his research on nuclear magnetic resonance spectroscopy, 1991.

1940 *Arthur Betz Laffer,* U.S. economist; supply-side theorist who promoted Reaganomics; devised Laffer Curve; called the *Guru of Tax Revolt.*

1941 *David Crosby,* U.S. singer, songwriter; member of the rock groups, *The Byrds* and *Crosby, Stills, Nash and Young.*

1944 *Robyn Carolina Smith,* U.S. jockey; first woman jockey to win major race; widow of Fred Astaire.

1945 *Steve Martin,* U.S. comedian, actor.

1946 *Susan Saint James,* U.S. actress; appeared in the television series, *The Name of the Game, McMillan and Wife* and *Kate and Allie.*

august

1952 *Debbie Meyer,* U.S. swimmer; Olympic gold medalist, 1968.

1954 *Mark (The Bird) Fidrych,* U.S. baseball player; pitcher for the Detroit Tigers, 1976–80; famous for talking to baseball; Rookie of the Year, 1976.

1959 *Earvin (Magic) Johnson,* U.S. basketball player.

1968 *Halle Berry,* U.S. actress.

HISTORICAL EVENTS

1040 *Duncan* is slain by *Macbeth,* who becomes king of Scots, reigning for 17 years.

1385 *John I* of Portugal defeats *John I* of Castile and secures independence of his country.

1765 American colonists challenge British governor in Boston by hanging effigies on what is later called the *Liberty Tree.*

1900 The *Imperial Court* flees Peking as international forces march on the city (*Boxer Rebellion*).

As consequence of *Boxer Rebellion,* Russian forces seize both banks of the Amur River and drive thousands of Chinese civilians to their death.

1912 U.S. Marines begin 21-year military presence in *Nicaragua* to protect American interests there.

1935 U.S. President *Franklin D. Roosevelt* signs *Social Security Act,* establishing Social Security Board to supervise payments of old-age benefits.

1941 The *Atlantic Charter* is signed by U.S. President *Franklin D. Roosevelt* and British Prime Minister *Winston Churchill;* the Charter forms the basis for the *United Nations Declaration.*

1945 Japanese acceptance of terms of surrender is announced to the American citizenry by President *Harry Truman,* touching off celebration known as *V-J Day.*

1947 *Indian Independence Act* is enacted by British parliament, dividing Indian subcontinent into *Pakistan* and *India.*

Manuel Roman y Reyes is elected president of Nicaragua.

1960 First broadcast via satellite is made from Bell Laboratories in New Jersey to the Jet Propulsion Laboratory in California.

1962 A gang of thieves holds up a U.S. mail truck in Plymouth, Massachusetts, and escapes with more than $1.5 million.

1970 The Food and Drug Administration issues a ban on all *cyclamates,* an artificially prepared salt used as a sweetener.

After nearly 18 years of separation, *Yugoslavia* and the *Vatican* resume full diplomatic relations.

1984 Governor *Mario Cuomo* of New York signs legislation mandating the reduction of chemical emissions from power plants which have been linked to *acid rain.* It is the first law in the U.S. to limit acid-rain pollution.

1989 *Pieter Botha* resigns as president of South Africa.

1995 *Shannon Faulkner* becomes the first woman admitted to the Citadel, historically an all-male military educational institution. Four days later Faulkner resigns from the cadet corps.

HOLIDAYS

Congo
Three Glorious Days
Third day of a three-day celebration.

India
Independence Day
Commemorates the independence of India from Great Britain, 1947.

Lebanon
Assumption Day

Malta
Assumption Day

Panama (Panama City)
Founding of Panama City

Republic of Korea
Liberation Day
Celebrates Korea's liberation from Japan, 1945, and the establishment of the Republic, 1948.

San Marino
Summer Holiday or Bank Holiday
Second day of a three-day celebration.

Senegal
Assumption Day

Vatican City
Mid-August Holiday

Roman Catholic Countries
Assumption Day
Celebrates the taking of the Blessed Virgin Mary, body and soul, into heaven, A.D. 40.

RELIGIOUS CALENDAR

Feasts
Feast of the Assumption of the Blessed Virgin Mary. [major holy day, Episcopal Church; minor festival, Lutheran Church]

The Saints
St. Tarsicius, martyr. [d. 3rd cent.]
St. Arnulf, Bishop of Soissons. Also called *Arnoul,* or *Arnulphus.* [d. 1087]

BIRTHDATES

1688 *Frederick William,* King of Prussia, 1713–40; helped transform Prussia into a prosperous modern state; was himself illiterate and hostile to cultural development. [d. May 31, 1740]

1740 *Matthias Claudius,* German poet; known for his lyric poems. [d. January 21, 1815]

1769 *Napoleon I (Bonaparte),* called *le Petit Corporal* or *the Little Corporal* as well as *the Corsican;* French military and political leader; one of the foremost historical figures of Europe; established the basis of the current French legal system; controlled much of central Europe during his reign. Defeated by alliance of European powers; exiled to Elba, where he plotted his return to power (*Hundred Days*); utterly defeated at Waterloo and exiled to St. Helena, where he died. [d. May 5, 1821]

1771 *Sir Walter Scott,* Scottish novelist, historian; wrote many historical romances, including *Ivanhoe.* [d. September 21, 1832]

1785 *Thomas DeQuincy,* English essayist, critic; noted for his genius in exposition, particularly in his personal account, *Confessions of an English Opium Eater.* [d. December 8, 1859]

1807 *François Paul Jules Grévy,* French politician; President of the Third Republic, 1879–87. [d. September 9, 1891]

1824 *John Simpson Chisum,* U.S. rancher; largest cattle owner in the U.S.; instrumental in the death of Billy the Kid. [d. December 23, 1884]

1858 *Emma Calvé (Emma de Roquer),* French operatic soprano. [d. January 6, 1942]

1860 *Florence Harding,* wife of U.S. President Warren G. Harding. [d. November 21, 1924]

1875 *Robert Abram (Captain Bob) Bartlett,* Canadian Arctic explorer; commander of the *Roosevelt* on Robert Peary's expedition, 1905–09. Led

august

numerous other expeditions to Greenland, Siberia, Labrador, and the Arctic. [d. April 28, 1946]

1879 *Ethel Barrymore,* U.S. actress; sister of Lionel and John Barrymore. [d. June 18, 1959]

1885 *Edna Ferber,* U.S. novelist, short-story writer, playwright; Pulitzer Prize in fiction, 1925. [d. April 16, 1968]

1888 *T(homas) E(dward) Lawrence (Lawrence of Arabia),* British archaeologist, soldier, author; led Arab revolt against Turks, 1917–18; noted for his controversial military strategies. Killed in a motorcycle accident. [d. May 19, 1935]

1889 *Leo T. Crowley,* U.S. businessman, public official. [d. April 15, 1972]

1892 Prince *Louis-Victor (Pierre-Raymond) de Broglie,* French physicist; Nobel Prize in physics for his revolutionary theory of the wave nature of electrons, 1929. [d. 1970]

1896 *Gerty T. Cori,* Czechoslovakian physician; known for her research in sugar metabolism with her husband, Carl Cori, (December 5, 1896).

(Sol) Sheldon Glueck, U.S. criminologist; noted for his research into prevention of *juvenile delinquency;* author of *The Problem of Delinquency,* 1958. [d. March 10, 1980]

1898 *Lillian Carter (Miss Lillian),* mother of Jimmy Carter, 39th U.S. President; served as a Peace Corps volunteer in India at the age of 68. [d. October 30, 1983]

1912 *Julia Child,* U.S. cooking expert, author, TV personality; known for her knowledge of and ability to teach the art of French cooking.

1917 *Oscar Arnulfo Romero y Galdamez,* Salvadoran religious leader; Archbishop of San Salvador; advocate of human rights. [assassinated March 24, 1980]

1919 *Robert Francis Goheen,* U.S. educator, diplomat; Ambassador to India, 1977–81.

1924 *Robert (Oxton) Bolt,* British playwright; noted for his stage play *A Man for All Seasons,* later adapted for film, and filmscript for *Lawrence of Arabia* and *Dr. Zhivago.* [d. February 20, 1995]

Phyllis Schlafly, U.S. political activist, author; led opposition to Equal Rights Amendment.

1925 *Mike Connors (Krekor Ohanian),* U.S. actor; known for his role on the television series, *Mannix,* 1967–74.

Oscar (Emanuel) Peterson, Canadian jazz pianist.

1930 *Tom Mboya,* Kenyan political leader; active in Kenyan struggle for independence. Assassinated by member of opposition political party (Kikuyu) while serving as Economics Minister. [d. July 5, 1969]

1935 *Abby Dalton,* U.S. actress, singer; known for role as Julia Cumson on the television series, *Falcon Crest.*

Vernon E. Jordan, Jr., U.S. civil rights spokesman, lawyer;

president of National Urban League, 1972–81.

1938 *Stephen G. Breyer,* U.S. lawyer; Supreme Court justice, 1994– .

1944 *Linda Ellerbee,* U.S. broadcast journalist, author.

1945 *(Eu)gene Upshaw,* U.S. football player; executive director of the National Football League Players Association, 1983.

1950 *Princess Anne* of Great Britain.

HISTORICAL EVENTS

1057 *Malcolm* kills *Macbeth of Scotland;* Macbeth's stepson *Lulach* succeeds him as king of Scotland.

1169 *Henry VI* is elected Holy Roman Emperor.

1307 *Henry of Carinthia* is elected king of Bohemia.

1534 *Jesuit Order* is founded at Paris as *Ignatius Loyola* and six companions take their vows.

1684 *Truce of Ratisbon* is signed between Holy Roman Empire and France, guaranteeing peace for 20 years.

1812 Indians massacre settlers and soldiers at *Fort Dearborn* (now *Chicago*).

1824 The colony on the West African coast for freed U.S. slaves is named *Liberia.*

1850 *Queen's University* in Ireland is established.

1867 *Second Reform Act* in Great Britain extends suffrage to householders and landowners, nearly doubling the electorate.

1914 The French repulse the Germans at the *Battle of Dinant (World War I).*

Panama Canal is opened to international commercial vessels.

1917 *Czar Nicholas II* and his family are moved from their residence at Tsarskoe Selo to further imprisonment in Tobolsk, Siberia (*Russian Revolution*).

1943 U.S. and Canadian troops reoccupy *Kiska* in the Aleutian Islands after Japanese withdrawal (*World War II*).

1945 Marshal *Henri Petain,* former premier of France's Vichy government, is sentenced to death for collaborating with Germany during World War II. His sentence is later commuted to life imprisonment.

1947 *India* becomes independent, self-governing dominion within the Commonwealth of Nations.

1948 *Syngman Rhee* becomes first President of the new *Republic of Korea.*

1950 Severe earthquake affects 30,000 square miles in *Assam, India,* killing 20,000 to 30,000 persons.

Joseph Pholien becomes premier of Belgium.

Federico Chaves is inaugurated as president of Paraguay.

1953 The religious powers of Sultan *Mohammed Ben Youssef* of Morocco are revoked.

1960 *Republic of the Congo* is proclaimed an independent nation within the French community in ceremonies at Brazzaville.

1966 *Gunther Schuller* is named president of the New England Conservatory of Music.

1967 *Rev. Martin Luther King, Jr.,* issues his call for massive campaigns of *civil disobedience.*

1969 *Woodstock Music and Art Fair,* held in Bethel, New York, begins.

1970 *Pat Palinkas* plays in an Atlantic Coast League game for the Orlando Panthers. She is the first woman to play in a professional football game.

1971 *Bahrain* gains independence from Great Britain.

1975 Bangladesh president, *Sheikh Mujibur Rahman,* is assassinated in an army coup. *Khandakar Mustaque Ahmed* is sworn in as president of the civilian regime.

Joanne Little, a black 21-year-old, is acquitted in Raleigh, N.C., of second degree murder in the death of her jailer, a white man, contending she defended herself against rape.

1979 *Andrew Young* resigns as U.S. Ambassador to the U.N. as a result of disagreement with the U.S. policy in the Middle East.

1984 Universal direct suffrage is introduced in *Macao* when the Chinese majority is allowed to vote, irrespective of residency length, for the first time.

august

AUGUST
16

HOLIDAYS

Dominican Republic
Restoration of the Republic
Celebrates the 1963 restoration to independence and first free elections since 1924.

Gabon Republic
Independence Anniversary
Celebrates Gabon's achievement of independence from France, 1960. A three-day holiday.

Liechtenstein
Birthday of Prince Franz Josef II

San Marino
Summer Holiday or Bank Holiday
Third day of a three-day celebration.

U.S. (Vermont)
Bennington Battle Day
Commemorates the defeat of the British at Bennington, 1777.

Vatican City
Mid-August Holiday

RELIGIOUS CALENDAR

The Saints
St. Arsacius. Also called *Ursacius.* [d. 358]
St. Armel, abbot. Also called *Arkel, Arthmael, Arzel, Erme, Ermel,* or *Ermyn.* [d. c. 570]
St. Stephen of Hungary, first Christian king of Hungary. Also called *Stephens.* Feast formerly September 2. [d. 1038] Optional Memorial.
St. Rock, patron of surgeons and tile makers. Invoked against plague, knee afflictions, and cattle diseases. Also called *Roch,* or *Roche.* [d. c. 1378]

The Beatified
Blessed Laurence Loricatus. [d. 1243]

BIRTHDATES

1397 *Albert II,* King of Germany, 1438–39; also king of Hungary and Bohemia. [d. October 27, 1439]

1557 *Agostino Carracci,* Italian painter; one of the pioneers of the *Italian baroque.* [d. February 23, 1602]

1645 *Jean de La Bruyère,* French moral satirist. [d. May 11, 1696]

1794 *Jean Henri Merle d'Aubigné,* Swiss theological historian. [d. October 21, 1872]

1798 *Mirabeau Buonaparte Lamar,* U.S. soldier; second president of the Republic of Texas; founded the capital at *Austin,* 1840. [d. December 19, 1859]

1813 *Sarah Porter,* U.S. educator; founder of *Miss Porter's School for Girls* in Connecticut; sister of *Noah Porter,* editor of first two editions of Noah Webster's unabridged dictionary. [d. February 17, 1900]

1821 *Arthur Cayley,* British mathematician; Professor of Pure Mathematics, Cambridge University, 1863–95; contributed significantly to development of mathematical theory; published more than 900 papers during his career. [d. January 26, 1895]

1830 *Diego Barros Arana,* Chilean historian, educator; renowned expert on Chilean history; wrote *Historia General de Chile,* 16 volumes, 1884–1902. [d. November 4, 1907]

1832 *Wilhelm Wundt,* German physiologist; founder of first laboratory of *experimental psychology,* 1879. [d. August 31, 1920]

1845 *Gabriel Lippmann,* French physicist; Nobel Prize in physics for producing the first *color photographic plate,* 1908. [d. July 13, 1921]

1861 *Edith Kermit Carow Roosevelt,* second wife of U.S. President Theodore Roosevelt. [d. September 30, 1948]

1862 *(Amos) Alonzo Stagg,* U.S. football coach; member of first all-American football team; coach of University of Chicago, 1892–1933; first college coach to achieve full faculty status; known as the *Grand Old Man of Football.* [d. March 17, 1965]

1892 *Otto Messmer,* U.S. film animator; created Felix the Cat character. [d. October 28, 1983]

1894 *George Meany,* U.S. labor union leader; President of AFL-CIO, 1955–79; awarded Presidential Medal of Freedom, 1964. [d. January 10, 1980]

1904 *Wendell Meredith Stanley,* U.S. biochemist; Nobel Prize in chemistry for preparation of pure forms of *enzymes* and *virus proteins* (with J. H. Northrop), 1946. [d. June 15, 1971]

1906 *Franz Josef II,* Crown Prince of Liechtenstein, 1938–89. [d. 1989]

1912 *H(enry) Ryan Price,* British hores trainer; four Schweppes Gold Trophies. [d. August 16, 1986]

1913 *Menachem Begin,* Israeli political leader; Prime Minister of Israel, 1977–83. [d. March 9, 1992]

1919 *Merce Cunningham,* U.S. dancer, choreographer; member of Martha Graham Dance Co., 1939–45; founder of *Merce Cunningham School of Dance,* 1959.

1923 *Shimon Peres,* Israeli statesman, politician; Prime Minister, 1984–86, 1995–96.

Lee Kuan Yew, Prime Minister, Republic of Singapore, 1959–90.

1925 *Fess Parker,* U.S. actor.

1928 *Ann Blyth,* U.S. actress.

1930 *Frank Gifford,* U.S. football player, broadcaster; elected to Football Hall of Fame, 1975.

1932 *Eydie Gorme,* U.S. singer; seven Emmy and two Grammy Awards; wife and singing partner of Steve Lawrence.

1938 *Bill (Bat) Masterton,* Canadian hockey player; first player in the National Hockey League to die from injuries suffered in game; trophy for sportsmanship, hard work named for him. [d. January 15, 1968]

1945 *Suzanne Farrell,* U.S. ballerina.

1946 *Lesley Ann Warren,* U.S. singer, dancer.

1947 *Carol Moseley Braun,* U.S. politician.

1953 *Kathie Lee Gifford,* U.S. talk show host; wife of sportscaster Frank Gifford.

1954 *James Cameron,* Canadian director; Academy Award (Director, Best Picture) for *Titanic,* 1997.

1955 *Helene D. Gayle,* U.S. epidemiologist; known for her AIDS research in children and teenagers.

1959 *Madonna (Louise Ciccone),* U.S. singer, actress; songs include *Like a Virgin* and *Material Girl;* starred in *Evita.*

1960 *Timothy James Hutton,* U.S. actor; Academy Award for *Ordinary People,* 1980.

1968 *L. L. Cool J (James Todd Smith),* U.S. rap singer.

HISTORICAL EVENTS

1513 *Battle of Spurs* is fought, in which Holy Roman Emperor *Maximilian I* and *Henry VIII* of England defeat French at *Guinegate.*

1773 *Jesuits* are expelled from Rome by *Pope Clement XIV.*

1777 American patriots defeat the British at the *Battle of Bennington (American Revolution).*

1780 Americans are defeated by British at Camden, New Jersey *(American Revolution).*

1807 *Gas street-lights* are first introduced in London at Golden Lane.

1812 U.S. forces at Detroit surrender to British *(War of 1812).*

1819 *Peterloo Massacre* in Manchester, England, results in several deaths and hundreds of injuries as British soldiers attempt to break up gathering listening to speakers on parliamentary reform and repeal of Corn Laws.

1896 *Klondike gold rush* is set off as gold is discovered on *Bonanza Creek,* near Dawson, Canada, 50 miles east of Alaska border.

1914 *Fort Flemalle,* the last of the fortresses at Liège, falls to the Germans; the Belgian government and royal family leave Brussels for Antwerp *(World War I).*

1921 *King Peter* of Yugoslavia dies and is succeeded by his son, *Alexander I*

1925 Charlie Chaplin's most celebrated film, *The Gold Rush,* premieres.

1943 *Messina, Sicily* is taken by U.S. Seventh Army *(World War II).*

1960 *Cyprus* proclaims its independence from Great Britain, which has held the island since 1878.

august

1966 *Declaration of Bogatá* is issued by presidents of Colombia, Chile, and Venezuela, calling for economic integration of Latin America.

1977 *Elvis Presley* dies of a heart attack in Memphis, Tennessee.

Soviet ship *Arktika* becomes the first surface craft in history to reach the *North Pole*.

1984 Former auto executive, *John De Lorean,* is acquitted of drug distribution charges by a Los Angeles jury.

HOLIDAYS

Argentina
Anniversary of the Death of General San Martin
Commemorates the event which occurred in 1850.

Gabon Republic
Independence Anniversary
Second day of a three-day celebration.

Indonesia
Independence Day
Commemorates establishment of the republic, 1945.

RELIGIOUS CALENDAR

The Saints
St. Mamas, martyr. Also called *Manus.* [d. c. 275]
St. Eusebius, pope. Elected 310. [d. 310]
SS. Liberatus and his Companions, martyrs. Also called *Libertas.* [d. 484]
St. Hyacinth, Dominican missionary and apostle of Poland. Also called *Jacek.* [d. 1257]
St. Clare of Montefalco, virgin. Also called *Chiara,* or *Claire.* [d. 1308]
St. Joan Delanoue, virgin and founder of the Sisters of St. Anne of The Providence of Saumur. [d. 1736] [canonized 1982]

BIRTHDATES

1601 *Pierre de Fermat,* French mathematician, referred to as the *Founder of Modern Number Theory;* developer of differential calculus and probability theory.

1603 *Lennart Torstenson, Count of Ortala,* Swedish soldier; Commander in Chief of Swedish Army, 1641. [d. April 7, 1651]

1629 *John III Sobieski,* King of Poland, 1674–96; responsible for saving his country from Turks; Polish hero and patron of arts and sciences. [d. June 17, 1696]

1786 *Davy Crockett,* U.S. frontiersman, politician; U.S. Congressman, 1827–31, 1833–35; hero of Texas war for independence from Mexico; killed at *Battle of the Alamo.* [d. March 6, 1836]

1801 *Fredrika Bremer,* Swedish novelist, women's rights advocate. [d. December 31, 1865]

1819 *Jón Árnason,* Icelandic folklorist; author of *Popular Legends of Iceland,* 1862. [d. September 4, 1888]

1837 *Charlotte Forten Grimké,* U.S. educator and author. [d. 1914]

1840 *Wilfrid Scawen Blunt,* British poet; severe critic of *white supremacy* policies and British exploitation of native races. Supported nationalist movements in Egypt, Ireland, and India. [d. September 11, 1922]

1847 *Alice Meynell,* British poet, essayist; wife of *Wilfred Meynell,* British journalist, biographer. [d. November 27, 1922]

1868 *Gene(ra) Grace Stratton Porter,* U.S. novelist; author of numerous books for children, nature books; at the time of her death, more than 10 million of her books had been sold. [d. December 6, 1924]

1887 *Charles I,* last Emperor of Austria and King of Hungary, abdicated November 11, 1918. [d. April 1, 1922]

Marcus (Moziah) Garvey, U.S. social reformer, black nationalist leader; advocate of black pride and *back to Africa* movement. [d. June 10, 1940]

1888 *Monty Woolley (Edgar Montillion Woolley),* U.S. actor, director. [d. May 6, 1963]

1890 *Harry (Lloyd) Hopkins,* U.S. public official; head of U.S. Emergency Relief Administration, 1933–38. Served as U.S. Secretary of

august

Commerce, 1938–40; member of Roosevelt's *Little War Cabinet*. [d. January 29, 1946]

1892 *Mae West*, U.S. actress, burlesque queen; stage career extended from 1897–1969; considered the embodiment of the Gay Nineties femme fatale. [d. November 22, 1980]

1904 *John Hay Whitney*, U.S. financier, diplomat, publisher; chairman, Selznick-International Pictures, producers of *Gone with the Wind*, 1936–40; U.S. Ambassador to Great Britain, 1956–61; publisher, *New York Herald Tribune*, 1957–66. [d. February 8, 1982]

1906 *Marcello (Jose) Gaetano*, Portuguese statesman; Prime Minister, 1968–74; protégé of Dictator Antonio Salazar; ousted by revolution of the Army; exiled to Brazil. [d. October 26, 1980]

Hazel (Gladys) Bishop, U.S. chemist, cosmetics manufacturer; founder of Hazel Bishop, Inc.; Director of Marketing, Fashion Institute of Technology.

1914 *Franklin Delano Roosevelt, Jr.*, U.S. politician; Congressman, 1949–53. [d. 1988]

1918 *George Scratchley Brown*, U.S. Air Force general; member of Chiefs of Staff, 1973–74; Chairman of Joint Chiefs of Staff, 1974–78. [d. December 5, 1978]

1921 *Maureen O'Hara (Maureen Fitzsimmons)*, U.S. actress, born in Ireland.

1923 *Larry Rivers (Yitzroch Loiza Grossberg)*, U.S. artist.

1926 *Jiang Zemin*, Chinese politician; president of the

People's Republic of China, 1993– .

1927 *Bernard Cornfeld*, U.S. financier; Chairman, Investors Overseas Services, 1958–71.

1929 *Francis Gary Powers*, U.S. pilot; shot down over Soviet territory in his U-2 reconnaissance plane, setting off an international diplomatic crisis, 1960; imprisoned by Russians; exchanged for Soviet agent, Rudolf Abel, 1962. [d. August 1, 1977]

1932 *V(idiadhar) S(urajpresad) Naipaul*, West Indian writer; BBC broadcaster; recorded cultural portraits of the Carribbean area.

1943 *Robert De Niro*, U.S. actor.

1952 *Guillermo Vilas*, Argentine tennis player.

1954 *Andres Pastrana Arango*, Colombian politician; president of Colombia, 1998– .

1958 *Belinda Carlisle*, U.S. singer; former lead vocalist of the rock group, *The Go-Go's*.

1960 *Sean Penn*, U.S. actor; appeared in *Fast Times at Ridgemont High* and *Dead Man Walking*.

1969 *Christian Laettner*, U.S. basketball player.

1970 *Jim Courier*, U.S. tennis player.

HISTORICAL EVENTS

1585 *Duke of Parma* takes Antwerp and regains Flanders and Brabant (*Dutch War of Liberation*).

1648 *Oliver Cromwell* defeats the Scots at the *Battle of Preston*.

1786 *Frederick the Great* of Prussia dies and is succeeded by *Frederick William II*.

1850 Denmark cedes all forts and property rights on the *Gold Coast of Africa* to Great Britain.

1900 International force of 19,000 British, French, Russian, American, German, and Japanese troops lift the seige of the imperial compound in Peking (*Boxer Rebellion*).

1938 *Henry Armstrong* defeats *Lou Ambers* to win the world lightweight boxing title.

1942 First U.S. strategic bombing in Europe takes place as American B-17s attack German-controlled *Rouen, France* (World War II).

1945 *Indonesia* proclaims itself an independent republic.

1961 U.S. and all Latin American nations except Cuba formally proclaim *Alliance for Progress*.

1962 German citizen *Peter Fechter* is killed at the Berlin Wall, stimulating anti-East German demonstrations.

1967 *Stokely Carmichael*, militant U.S. black leader, calls for U.S. blacks to arm for *total revolution*.

1969 *Hurricane Camille*, the most violent storm to strike the U.S. since 1935, devastates the Gulf Coast of Mississippi, killing more than 300.

1975 Heir to the *Seagram* dynasty is released by kidnappers after payment of $2.3 million ransom.

1976 A severe *earthquake* shakes the island of *Mindanao* in the Philippines, producing tidal waves that kill more than 8,000 persons and leave 175,000 homeless.

1978 Three American balloonists cross the Atlantic in their helium-filled *Double Eagle II,* establishing an endurance record of 137 hours, 3 minutes and a distance record of 5,023 km (3,120 miles).

Max Anderson, Ben Abruzzo, and *Larry Newman* complete the first successful transatlantic crossing in a *hot-air balloon.*

1995 *Maeve Leakey* discovers human-like fossils estimated to be over four million years old in Kenya.

The first summit meeting of the *Association of Caribbean States* takes place.

1998 *Bill Clinton* becomes the first president in U.S. history to testify before a grand jury, during the *Monica Lewinsky* investigation. President Clinton addresses the nation later that evening and admits to having a relationship with the former White House intern (January 21, 1998).

august

AUGUST
18

HOLIDAYS

Afghanistan
Independence Day

Gabon Republic
Independence Anniversary
Third day of the celebration.

RELIGIOUS CALENDAR

The Saints

St. Helen, widow and empress.
Mother of Constantine the
Great. Also called *Helena.* [d.
c. 330]

St. Alipius, Bishop of Tagaste,
companion of St. Augustine.
[d. c. 430]

St. Agapitus, martyr. Also called
Agapitue, or *Agapetus.* [death
date unknown]

SS. Florus and Laurus, martyrs.
[death dates unknown]

The Beatified

*Blessed Angelo Augustine of
Florence.* [d. 1438]

Blessed Beatrice da Silva, virgin and
foundress of the
Conceptionist Nuns. Also
called *Brites.* [d. 1490]

Blessed Haymo of Savigliano. [d.
1495]

BIRTHDATES

1564 *Federigo Borromeo,* Italian
cardinal, archbishop; founder
of the *Ambrosian Library* at
Milan, 1609. [d. September
22, 1631]

1587 *Virginia Dare,* first English
child to be born in colonial
America. She and all other
members of the *Roanoke
settlement,* in Virginia,
disappeared, the group being
later referred to as the *lost
colony of Roanoke.* [d. c.
1587]

1685 *Brook Taylor,* British
mathematician; published the
first treatise on *finite
differences in calculus,* 1715.
[d. December 29, 1731]

1774 *Meriwether Lewis,* U.S.
explorer, soldier, public
official; private secretary to
President Thomas Jefferson,
1801–03; head of the great
Lewis and Clark Expedition
into the Northwest Territory
of the U.S., 1803–06;
Governor of Louisiana
Territory, 1807–09. [d.
October 11, 1809]

1807 *Charles Francis Adams,* U.S.
statesman, economist; son of
U.S. President John Quincy
Adams; candidate for vice-
presidency, 1848; U.S.
Congressman, 1858–61; U.S.
Ambassador to Great Britain,
1861–68. [d. November 21,
1886]

1830 *Francis Joseph I,* Emperor of
Austria-Hungary; father of
Archduke Francis Ferdinand,
whose assassination in 1914
precipitated World War I. [d.
November 21, 1916]

1834 *Marshall Field,* U.S.
businessman, philanthropist;
founder of Marshall Field &
Co., 1881; donated large sums
of money to the University of
Chicago; established the *Field
Museum of Natural History.*
[d. January 16, 1906]

1854 *James Hervey Hyslop,* U.S.
psychologist, philosopher,
and educator; founder of
*American Society of Psychical
Research.* [d. June 17, 1920]

1900 *Vijaya Lakshmi Pandit,*
Indian politician, diplomat;
first woman Minister of Uttar
Pradesh government,
1937–39; 1946–47; head of
Indian delegation to UN,
1946–51, 1963; President of
UN General Assembly,
1953–54. [d. December 1,
1990]

1917 *Casper Willard (Cap)
Weinberger,* U.S. government
official; Secretary of Health,
Education and Welfare,
1973–75; Secretary of
Defense, 1981–87; called *Cap
the Knife.*

1922 *Alain Robbe-Grillet,* French
author, filmmaker,
agronomist; Chargé de
Mission, Institute Nationale de
la Statistique, 1945–48; author
of numerous *nouveau roman*
works.

Shelley Winters, U.S. actress.

1925 *Brian (Wilson) Aldiss,* award-winning British science fiction writer; literary editor of *Oxford Mail,* 1957–69.

1927 *Rosalynn Carter,* wife of former U.S. President Jimmy Carter (October 1).

1931 *Irene Chamie Kassorla,* U.S. psychologist, author; famous for treating Hollywood stars; wrote best-selling sex manual, *Nice Girls Do.*

1933 *Roman Polanski,* film director; known for *Repulsion, Rosemary's Baby,* and *Tess.*

1934 *Vincent T. Bugliosi,* U.S. lawyer, author; prosecutor in Manson family murder trials, wrote *Helter Skelter.*

Roberto Clemente, U.S. baseball player; inducted into Baseball Hall of Fame, 1973. Killed in plane crash. [d. December 31, 1972]

1935 *Gail Fisher,* U.S. actress; known for role as Peggy Fair in the television series, *Mannix,* 1968–74.

Rafer Johnson, U.S. athlete; Olympic decathlon champion, 1960.

1937 *Robert Redford,* U.S. actor, director; Academy Awards (Best Picture, Director) for *Ordinary People,* 1980.

1943 *Martin Mull,* U.S. actor, comedian; appeared in *Mr. Mom;* starred in the television series, *Mary Hartman, Mary Hartman* and *Fernwood 2-Night.*

1955 *Patrick Swayze,* U.S. actor, dancer; appeared as Orry Main in television mini-series, *North and South;* starred in the movies, *Dirty Dancing* and *Ghost.*

1958 *Madeleine Stowe,* U.S. actress.

1969 *Christian Slater,* U.S. actor.

1970 *Malcolm-Jamal Warner,* U.S. actor; known for his role as Theo Huxtable on *The Cosby Show,* 1984–92.

HISTORICAL EVENTS

1765 Holy Roman Emperor *Francis I* dies and is succeeded by *Josef II.*

1821 The first issue of the *Saturday Evening Post* is published.

1825 *Alexander Gordon Laing* becomes the first European to reach *Timbuktu* in Africa.

1846 U.S. troops occupy *Santa Fé (Mexican War).*

1873 A U.S. expedition climbs *Mount Whitney,* the highest mountain in the continental U.S. outside of Alaska.

1896 France annexes *Madagascar.*

1903 First U.S. transcontinental automobile trip is completed in 61 days, from San Francisco to New York, by *Tom Fitch* and *Marcus Kraarup.*

1917 First two-way *radiotelephone communication* between a plane and the ground is established.

1938 Benjamin Britten's *First Piano Concerto* premieres in London.

1947 *Hewlett-Packard Co.* is incorporated in California.

1955 *Shukri al-Kuwaitly* becomes president of Syria.

1987 *Charles Glass,* an American journalist kidnapped in Beirut, escapes from his Shiite Moslem captors.

august

AUGUST
19

HOLIDAYS

U.S.

National Aviation Day
Celebrates the progress made in manned flight.

RELIGIOUS CALENDAR

The Saints

St. Andrew the Tribune, martyr. [d. c. 300]

SS. Timothy, Agapius, and Thecla, martyrs. [d. 304]

St. Sixtus III, pope. Elected 432. [d. 440]

St. Mochta, abbot; last of St. Patrick's personal disciples. Also called *Mochteus.* [d. c. 535]

St. Bertulf, abbot. [d. 640]

St. Credan, Abbot of Evesham. [d. 8th cent.]

St. Sebald, patron of Nuremberg, Bavaria. [d. 8th cent.]

St. John Eudes, founder of the Congregations of Jesus and Mary and of Our Lady of Charity of the Refuge. Also called *John of Eudes.* [d. 1680]

St. Louis of Anjou, Bishop of Toulouse. Also called *Lewis.* [d. 1297]

The Beatified

Blessed Emily of Vercelli, virgin. [d. 1314]

BIRTHDATES

1398 *Iñigo López de Mendoza,* Marquis of Santillana, Spanish poet, humanist; noted for his contributions to Spanish poetry; composed sonnets imitating *Petrarch.* [d. March 25, 1458]

1560 *James Crichton,* Scottish prodigy; known as the *Admirable Crichton;* disputed scientific and philosophical questions in major centers of learning in France and Italy. [d. July 3, 1582]

1646 *John Flamsteed,* English astronomer; contributed to the discoveries of Sir Isaac Newton; established observatory at Greenwich, marking *prime meridian.* [d. December 31, 1719]

1689 *Samuel Richardson,* English novelist, baptized on this day; noted for his contributions to development of modern English novel; wrote *Pamela: or, Virtue Rewarded.* [d. July 4, 1761]

1743 *Comtesse Du Barry (Marie Jeanne Bécu),* French adventuress and mistress of *King Louis XV,* 1768–74; arrested by Robespierre, 1793, and executed. [d. December 7, 1793]

1793 *Samuel Griswold Goodrich (Peter Parley),* U.S. author, educator; famous for his series of *Peter Parley* books, of which over 7 million copies were sold between 1827–56. [d. May 9, 1860]

1808 *James Nasmyth,* British engineer; invented the *steam hammer,* 1839. [d. May 7, 1890]

1830 *Julius Lothar Meyer,* German chemist; known for his independent studies related to *periodic law.* [d. April 11, 1895]

1843 *Charles Montagu Doughty,* British poet, traveler; author of *Travels in Arabia Deserta,* 1888, a graphic narration describing his travels through Saudi Arabia disguised as an Arab. [d. January 20, 1926]

1853 *Aleksei Alekseevich Brusilov,* Russian general; highly successful military leader in World War I; appointed to Russian Supreme Command, 1917. [d. March 17, 1926]

1859 *Henry Ives Cobb,* U.S. architect; noted for his expertise in steel construction. [d. March 27, 1931]

1870 *Bernard M(annes) Baruch,* U.S. financier, public official; adviser to and confidant of every U.S. president from Woodrow Wilson to John F. Kennedy. [d. June 20, 1965]

1871 *Orville Wright,* U.S. inventor, aviator; with his brother Wilbur (April 16), succeeded in developing first machine capable of powered flight,

December 17, 1903. [d. January 30, 1948]

1876 *Manuel Quezon,* Filipino politician. [d. 1944]

1877 *Thomas Terry (Tom) Connally,* U.S. politician; Senator, 1929–53; intermittent chairman of the Senate Foreign Relations Committee. [d. October 28, 1963]

1878 *Manuel Luis Quezon y Molina,* first president, Commonwealth of Philippines, 1935–44; head of Philippine government in exile after Japanese conquest, 1942–44. [d. August 1, 1944]

1882 *Gabrielle (Coco) Chanel,* French fashion designer; famous for the simplicity and elegance of her designs, especially suits; created Chanel No. 5 perfume, 1924; subject of Broadway musical, *Coco.* [d. January 10, 1971]

1892 *Alfred Lunt,* U.S. actor; co-starred with wife Lynn Fontaine in over 24 plays including *The Visit.* [d. August 2, 1977]

1902 *(Frederic) Ogden Nash,* U.S. poet; member, editorial staff of *New Yorker* magazine; noted for his humorous, often satirical verse and witty observations on light subjects. [d. May 19, 1971]

1903 *James Gould Cozzens,* U.S. novelist; most popular novel was *By Love Possessed.* [d. August 9, 1978]

Claude Le Grand Maria Eugene Dauphin, French actor; known for his role in *April in Paris,* 1952. [d. November 17, 1978]

1907 *Thurston Ballard Morton,* U.S. politician; Congressman,

1946–52; Senator, 1957–69. [d. August 14, 1982]

1915 *Ring Wilmer Lardner, Jr.,* U.S. screenwriter; Academy Awards for *Woman of the Year,* 1942, and *M*A*S*H,* 1970; one of *The Hollywood Ten,* a group of writers and actors who refused to cooperate with the House Un-American Activities Committee.

1919 *Malcolm Stevenson Forbes,* U.S. publisher, editor; publisher of *Forbes* magazine; wrote *The Sayings of Chairman Malcolm,* 1978. [d. February 24, 1990]

1921 *Eugene Wesley (Gene) Roddenberry,* U.S. producer; creator of the television series, *Star Trek.* [d. October 24, 1991]

1930 *Frank McCourt,* U.S. author; Pulitzer Prize winner for *Angela's Ashes,* 1997.

1931 *Willie Shoemaker,* U.S. jockey; rode Kentucky Derby winners, 1955, 1959, 1965.

1934 *David Ferdinand Durenberger,* U.S. politician; Senator, 1978–94.

Renee Richards (Richard Raskin), U.S. tennis player, physician; known for playing on women's tennis circuit as a transsexual.

1938 *Wilson Goode,* U.S. politician; first black mayor of Philadelphia, 1984–92; deputy assistant secretary, Office of Intergovernmental and Interagency Affairs, 1997– .

Robert Graham, U.S. sculptor.

1940 *Peter (Ginger) Baker,* British musician, singer; former

percussionist for the rock group, *Blind Faith;* formed the rock group, *Cream,* with Eric Clapton, 1967–69.

Johnny Nash, U.S. singer; brought reggae music to attention of American public; had number one record, *I Can See Clearly Now,* 1972.

Jill St. John, U.S. actress.

1942 *Fred Thompson,* former U.S. actor; politician; U.S. senator, 1994– .

1946 *William Jefferson (Bill) Clinton,* U.S. politician; Governor of Arkansas, 1979–81, 1983–92; President of the United States, 1993– .

1948 *Gerald McRaney,* U.S. actor; known for role as Rick Simon on the television series *Simon and Simon,* 1981–88.

1955 *Peter Gallagher,* U.S. actor; known for roles in *sex, lies and videotape,* 1989 and *The Player,* 1992.

1960 *Ron(ald Maurice) Darling, Jr.,* U.S. baseball player; pitcher; member of the National League All-Star team, 1985.

1969 *Matthew Perry,* U.S. actor; featured on the TV sitcom *Friends.*

HISTORICAL EVENTS

1388 *Scots,* under the Earl of Douglas, defeat the English forces under Hotspur, Lord Percy, at the *Battle of Chevy Chase* at Otterburn.

1477 *Maximilian,* son of Holy Roman Emperor Frederick III, marries Mary of Burgundy.

1493 Holy Roman Emperor *Frederick III* dies and is succeeded by *Maximilian I.*

august

1561 *Mary Queen of Scots* arrives in Scotland to assume the throne.

1587 *Sigismund III,* son of John of Sweden, is elected king of Poland.

1772 Revolution in Sweden, backed by France, re-establishes *Gustavus III* as monarch. He abolishes torture, improves code of laws, and establishes religious tolerance.

1812 The *U.S.S. Constitution,* captained by *Isaac Hull,* defeats *H.M.S. Guerrière* (*War of 1812*).

1839 Academy of Sciences in Paris makes public the details of Louis Daguerre's first practical *photographic process.*

1914 The Germans occupy *Louvain* after a battle with the Belgian army (*World War I*).

1918 *Yip, Yip, Yaphank,* revue with book, music, and lyrics by Irving Berlin, is first performed at Camp Upton, New York; contains songs *Oh, How I Hate to Get Up in the Morning* and *God Bless America.*

1919 *Korea* becomes a Japanese province under a new plan of civil government.

1934 German plebiscite approves Hitler's assumption of the presidency in addition to being chancellor.

1936 In an attempt to consolidate his power, *Joseph Stalin* begins the first in a series of Soviet purge trials.

1942 British and Canadian troops launch suicidal attack on *Dieppe* (*World War II*).

1953 Israel's parliament confers citizenship posthumously on all Jews killed by the Nazis during the *Holocaust.*

1958 Studebaker-Packard announces that it will drop its luxury line of *Packard* automobiles.

1960 Two puppies become the first animals to survive launch, orbit, and landing aboard a spacecraft.

1968 Tom Wolfe's book, *The Electric Kool-Aid Acid Test,* is published.

1969 British army assumes full responsibility for security in *Northern Ireland.*

1972 King *Hassan II* of Morocco takes command of the armed forces, abolishing the posts of defense minister and army chief of staff.

1973 *Georgios Papadopoulos* is sworn in as the first president of Greece; vestiges of martial law in effect since 1967 are lifted and amnesty is granted to some political prisoners. He is unseated by military junta in Nov., 1973.

1976 U.S. President *Gerald Ford* is nominated as the Republican Party's presidential candidate.

1978 Theater fire set by Muslim extremists in *Abadan, Iran,* kills 430 people. The arrested suspects espouse belief that movie theaters are incompatible with Islamic teachings.

1991 The government of Soviet president *Mikhail Gorbachev* survives a military coup attempt; *Boris Yeltsin* leads resistance against the coup.

HOLIDAYS

Hungary

Constitution Day
Commemorates the establishment of the People's Republic, 1949.

RELIGIOUS CALENDAR

The Saints

St. Oswin, king of Deria in Britain, and martyr. [d. 651]

St. Philibert, abbot. The filbert (fruit or nut of the cultivated hazel) derived its name from being ripe near St. Philibert's day. [d. c. 685]

St. Bernard, abbot of Clairvaux, Doctor of the Church, founder of the Cistercian Order. Called *Doctor mellifluus,* the *Honey-sweet Doctor.* [d. 1153]

St. Amadour, hermit. [death date unknown]

The Beatified

Blessed Mary de Mattias, virgin and founder of the Sisters Adorers of the Precious Blood. [d. 1866]

Blessed Teresa Jornet Ihars, founder of the Little Sisters of the Aged Poor. [d. 1897]

BIRTHDATES

1632 *Louis Bourdaloue,* French Jesuit theologian; known for his saintly character. [d. May 13, 1704]

1745 *Francis Asbury,* U.S. religious leader; only English missionary in U.S. at outbreak of Revolutionary War; first bishop of *Methodist Episcopal Church* ordained in America, 1784; established Methodism as one of principal U.S. denominations. [d. March 31, 1816]

1749 *Aleksandr Nikolayevich Radishchev,* Russian poet, reformer; noted for his *Voyage from Petersburg to Moscow,* 1790, in which he criticized serfdom, government absolutism and religion; exiled to Siberia as a result of his criticism. [d. September 12, 1802]

1779 *Baron Jons Jakob Berzelius,* Swedish chemist; determined molecular weights of many substances; introduced system of *chemical symbols* in use today; advocated using chemical composition as method of classifying minerals. [d. August 7, 1848]

1808 *Narcisse Virgile Diaz de la Peña,* French landscape painter; member of Barbizon school; noted for his nymphs, Venuses, and cupids. [d. November 18, 1876]

1832 *Thaddeus S. C. Lowe,* U.S. inventor; developed the *compression ice machine,* leading to the mechanical refrigerator, 1865. [d. January 16, 1913]

1833 *Benjamin Harrison,* 23rd president of the U.S., 1889–93; noted for his achievements in foreign affairs. [d. March 13, 1901]

1847 *Boleslaw Prus (Alexander Glowacki),* Polish novelist and short-story writer. [d. May 19, 1912]

1860 *Raymond Poincaré,* French statesman, writer; 9th president of French Republic, 1913–20; member of French cabinet, 1893–1903; Prime Minister, 1912–13; 1922–24. [d. October 15, 1934]

1864 *Ion Bratianu,* Romanian statesman; Prime Minister, several terms, 1909–27. [d. November 24, 1927]

1873 *Eliel Saarinen,* Finnish architect; achieved his greatest recognition with his son Eero (below) for designs executed in the U.S.; exerted enormous influence on American architecture, particularly in the development of the *skyscraper.* [d. July 1, 1950]

1881 *Edgar A(lbert) Guest,* U.S. poet, journalist born in England; noted for his *Breakfast Table Chat,* daily verse column which was syndicated in more than 300

august

newspapers at its peak. Published numerous collections of folksy verse. [d. August 5, 1959]

1886 *Paul Tillich*, U.S. philosopher, theologian, born in Germany; outspoken critic of the Nazis; spokesman for Religious Socialism in the 1920s; developed a systematic theology that included psychology, philosophy, and art. [d. October 22, 1965]

1890 *H(oward) P(hillips) Lovecraft*, U.S. author; best known for horror and science fiction stories. [d. March 15, 1937]

1901 *Salvatore Quasimodo*, Italian poet, writer; Nobel Prize in literature for his lyrical poetry, 1959. [d. June 14, 1968]

1904 *Rose Hum Lee*, U.S. educator and author. [d. 1964]

1905 *Jack Weldon Lee Teagarden*, U.S. trombonist, orchestra leader. [d. January 15, 1964]

1910 *Eero Saarinen*, U.S. architect born in Finland; with his father Eliel (above), achieved wide recognition for his flamboyant steel and glass structures. [d. September 1, 1961]

1913 *Roger W. Sperry*, U.S. zoologist; Nobel Prize in physiology or medicine for his work that led to a greater understanding of how the brain works, 1981. [d. April 17, 1994]

1916 *Van Johnson*, U.S. actor.

1917 *Terry Sanford*, U.S. educator, politician; Governor of North Carolina, 1961–65; Senator, 1986–92. [d. April 18, 1998]

1921 *Jacqueline Susann*, U.S. novelist; author of *The Valley of the Dolls*. [d. September 21, 1974]

1933 *George John Mitchell*, U.S. politician; Senator, 1980–94.

1936 *Wilt(on Norman) Chamberlain*, U.S. basketball player.

Carla Fracci, Italian prima ballerina.

1941 *Slobodan Milosevic*, Serbian politician; president of Serbia 1990– .

1942 *Isaac Hayes*, U.S. singer, composer, actor.

1944 *Rajiv Ratna Gandhi*, Indian political leader; India's sixth and youngest prime minister, 1984–89; son of former prime minister, Indira Gandhi. [d. May 21, 1991 (assassinated)]

Graig Nettles, U.S. baseball player.

1946 *Connie Chung (Constance Yu-Hwa)*, U.S. broadcast journalist.

1947 *James Pankow*, U.S. musician; trombonist with the rock group, *Chicago*.

1948 *Robert Anthony Plant*, U.S. singer; member of the rock groups, *Led Zeppelin* and *Honeydrippers*.

1956 *Joan Allen*, U.S. actress; known for her performances in *Nixon* and *The Crucible*.

HISTORICAL EVENTS

636 *Syria* is lost to the Arabs at the *Battle of Yarmuk*.

1846 U.S. General Winfield Scott defeats the Mexicans at the *Battle of Churubusco (Mexican War)*.

1914 400,000 German soldiers under General Von Kluck enter Brussels, and the Belgian Army retreats to Antwerp (*World War I*).

1917 The French under General Pètain launch an offensive at *Verdun (World War I)*.

1920 First *commercial radio broadcast* featuring musical numbers is made by WWJ in Detroit; this claim is disputed by some, who say that KDKA, Pittsburgh, on November 2, was the first to broadcast commercially.

1942 German army crosses *Don River* in Russia (*World War II*).

1944 U.S. and British forces destroy the German Seventh Army at *Falaise-Argentan Gap*, west of Paris, capturing some 50,000 Germans (*World War II*).

1960 *Mali Federation* of Senegal and Sudan is split by a Senegalese declaration of secession, resulting from irreconcilable political differences.

1968 Warsaw Pact troops invade and occupy *Czechoslovakia*.

1971 Chiefs of state of Egypt, Syria, and Libya sign a constitution forming the *Confederation of Arab Republics*.

Malawian president, *Hastings Kamazu Banda*, completes an official visit to South Africa. He is the first black head of state to visit the racially segregated country.

1974 Former New York governor *Nelson Rockefeller* is nominated as Vice-President by President *Gerald Ford*, who has assumed the presidency of the U.S. upon the resignation of *Richard M. Nixon*.

1979 *Diana Nyad* becomes the first person to swim the 89 miles between the Bahamas and the U.S.

1980 First successful ascent of *Mt. Everest* by a solo climber is completed by *Reinhold Messner* of Italy.

1988 A United Nations-sponsored ceasefire between Iran and Iraq takes effect *(Iran-Iraq War)*.

1991 The Supreme Council of the *Republic of Estonia* issues its decision for the reestablishment of its independence from the Soviet Union.

1998 U.S. forces bomb targeted terrorist sites in Sudan and Afghanistan in retaliation for the embassy bombings in Kenya and Tanzania earlier in the month (August 7, 1998).

august

AUGUST
21

RELIGIOUS CALENDAR

The Saints

SS. Luxorius, Cisellus and Camerinus, martyrs. [d. c. 303]

SS. Bonosus and Maximian, martyrs. Maximian also called *Maxmilian.* [d. 363]

St. Sidonius Apollinaris, Bishop of Clermont. [d. 479]

St. Abraham of Smolensk, abbot. [d. 1221]

St. Pius X, pope. Elected 1903. Feast formerly September 3. [d. 1914]

The Beatified

Blessed Humbeline, matron. Sister of St. Bernard, whose feast is celebrated on August 20. [d. 1135]

Blessed Bernard Tolomei, abbot and founder of the Benedictines of Monte Oliveto. Also called *Bernard Ptolemy.* [d. 1348]

BIRTHDATES

1165 *Philip II,* King of France; one of the chief consolidators of the French monarchy. [d. July 14, 1223]

1609 *Jean de Rotron,* French dramatist; one of Cardinal Richelieu's *Fine Poets.* [d. June 27, 1650]

1789 *Augustin-Louis Cauchy,* French mathematician; developed *calculus of residues;* conducted research in applied and pure mathematics. [d. May 23, 1857]

1796 *Asher Brown Durand,* U.S. painter, illustrator, engraver; one of founders of National Academy of Design, 1826; credited with being one of the founders of the *Hudson River School* of landscape painting. [d. September 17, 1886]

1798 *Jules Michelet,* French historian, essayist; head of Historical Division, National Archives of France, 1831; noted for his extensive treatment of French history, 1838–72. [d. February 10, 1874]

1823 *John Fritz,* U.S. metallurgist, industrialist; one of first to introduce *Bessemer process* of steel-making in U.S. [d. February 13, 1913]

1826 *Karl Gegenbauer,* German comparative anatomist; pioneer in using evolutionary approach to *anatomical development.* [d. June 14, 1903]

1872 *Aubrey (Vincent) Beardsley,* British illustrator, noted for his black-and-white drawings; illustrated Malory's *Morte d'Arthur,* Oscar Wilde's *Salome,* Pope's *Rape of the Lock,* and Jonson's *Volpone.* [d. March 16, 1898]

1896 *Roark Bradford,* U.S. writer, humorist; author of *Ol' Man Adam an' His Chillun.* [d. November 13, 1948]

1904 *(William) Count Basie,* U.S. jazz and blues musician, pianist, composer. [d. April 26, 1984]

1912 *Robert John Donovan,* U.S. journalist.

1914 *Paul Hall,* U.S. labor union official; a founding member of *Seafarers' International Union,* 1938; renowned for his efforts to improve working conditions of merchant seamen. [d. June 22, 1980]

1920 *Christopher Robin Milne,* British author; known for his autobiographies; son of British author, A. A. Milne; made famous as the character Christopher Robin in the *Winnie-the-Pooh* stories. [d. April 20, 1996]

1924 *Chris(topher Eugene) Schenkel,* U.S. sportscaster.

1930 *Princess Margaret Rose* of Great Britain, sister of Queen Elizabeth II.

1938 *Kenny Rogers,* U.S. country-rock singer and actor.

1944 *Jackie DeShannon,* U.S. singer, songwriter.

1950 *Arthur Herman Bremer,* U.S. attempted assassin; wounded presidential candidate, George Wallace, during the 1972 campaign.

1954 *Archie (Mason) Griffin,* U.S. football player; only player to win Heisman Trophy twice: 1974, 1975.

1957 *Kim Sledge,* U.S. singer; member of the rock group, *Sister Sledge.*

1958 *Steve Case,* U.S. businessman; chief executive officer and chairman for America Online, Inc.

1959 *James Robert (Jim) McMahon,* U.S. football player.

1962 *Matthew Broderick,* U.S. actor; Tony Award for *Brighton Beach Memoirs,* 1983; starred in the films, *Ferris Bueller's Day Off* and *War Games.*

HISTORICAL EVENTS

1808 Arthur Wellesley and his British troops defeat the French at *Battle of Vimiera (Peninsular War).*

1810 Marshall *Bernadotte,* one of Napoleon's generals, is elected Crown Prince of Sweden under the name of *Charles John.*

1878 *American Bar Association* is created by a meeting of lawyers at Saratoga, New York.

1914 *Battle of Charleroi* opens with the Germans attacking the French and forcing their way over the Sambre River (*World War I*).

1915 *Gallipoli Campaign* ends in defeat for the British at the Battle of Scimitar Hill (*World War I*).

1918 The *Second Battles of the Somme* and of *Arras* open, extending the Allied offensive from Soissons to Arras (*World War I*).

1940 *Leon Trotsky,* a former leader of the Soviet Communist Party, is murdered in Mexico, reportedly by an agent of *Joseph Stalin.*

1944 *Dumbarton Oaks Conference,* in Washington, D.C., begins outlining plans for the *United Nations.*

1953 Sidi *Moulay Mohammed Ben Arafa* becomes sultan of Morocco after Berber tribesmen depose Sidi *Mohammed Ben Youssef.*

1956 Joshua Logan's film, *Bus Stop,* premieres in New York.

1959 *Hawaii* is admitted to the Union as the 50th state.

1961 *Jomo Kenyatta,* African nationalist leader imprisoned in Kenya since 1952, is released.

U.S. and El Salvador sign the first *Food for Peace* agreement.

1963 Martial law is declared in South Vietnam following raids on Buddhist pagodas and arrests of 100 Buddhist monks (*Vietnam War*).

1965 U.S. spacecraft *Gemini 5* is launched from Cape Kennedy, Florida, for a projected eight-day flight.

1971 *NATO* officials announce that their Mediterranean headquarters will be moved to *Naples.*

1982 The *Palestine Liberation Organization* begins its evacuation from West Beirut.

1983 Philippine opposition leader *Benigno S. Aquino Jr.* is assassinated in Manila moments after stepping off the plane that returned him to the island after a three-year exile in the U.S.

1986 Poisonous gas erupts from *Lake Nios* in *Cameroon,* killing more than 1700 people. Scientists believe that a landslide or earth tremor caused fumes trapped in layers of sediment below the lake to rise to the surface.

1987 Sergeant *Clayton Lonetree* becomes the first U.S. marine to be convicted of spying for the Soviet Union.

1991 *Latvia* adopts a new constitutional law stating its independence from the Soviet Union.

1994 *Ernesto Zedillo* is elected president of Mexico.

august

AUGUST
22

RELIGIOUS CALENDAR

Feasts

Queenship of Mary. Formerly celebrated May 31. Obligatory Memorial.

The Saints

SS. Timothy, Hippolytus, and Symphorian, martyrs. Feast suppressed in 1969. [d. 2nd to 4th cent.]

St. Sigfrid, Abbot of Wearmouth. [d. 690]

St. Andrew of Fiesole, deacon. [d. c. 9th cent.]

St. Arnulf, hermit. [death date unknown]

The Beatified

Blessed William Lacey and *Blessed Richard Kirkman,* martyrs. [d. 1582]

Blessed Frederic Ozanam, one of the founders of the Vincent de Paul Society. [d. 1853]

BIRTHDATES

1647 *Denis Papin,* French physicist; invented the *pressure cooker* with safety valve; suggested the first cylinder and piston steam engine. [d. c. 1712]

1741 *Jean François de Galaup,* Comte de La Pérouse, French naval officer; led exploration of Asiatic waters; lost with his entire expedition by shipwreck. [d. 1788]

1760 *Leo XII,* pope 1823–29. [d. February 10, 1829]

1771 *Henry Maudslay,* British engineer; invented the *metal-cutting lathe;* considered *Father of the Machine-tool Industry.* [d. February 14, 1831]

1811 *William Kelly,* U.S. inventor; developed, simultaneously with Sir Henry Bessemer, what became known as the *Bessemer process* for steel-making. [d. February 11, 1888]

1834 *Samuel Pierpont Langley,* U.S. astronomer, aviation pioneer; pioneer in *solar research* and of flight of heavier-than-air craft. [d. February 27, 1906]

1847 *Sir John Forrest,* Australian explorer; first premier of Western Australia, 1890–1901; first Australian to be honored by a peerage. [d. September 3, 1918]

Sir Alexander Campbell Mackenzie, Scottish composer, conductor, teacher; conductor of London Philharmonic Society, 1892–99; knighted, 1895. [d. April 28, 1935]

1852 *Alfredo Oriani,* Italian writer; forerunner of Fascist theorists in Italy. [d. October 18, 1909]

1862 *Claude (Achille) Debussy,* French Romantic composer; leader of French *ultramodernist school of music.* [d. March 25, 1918]

1887 *Walter McLennan Citrine,* First Baron Citrine of Wembly, British labor union leader; General Secretary, British Trade Union Congress, 1925–46; knighted, 1935; raised to peerage, 1946. [d. January 22, 1983]

1893 *Dorothy (Rothschild) Parker,* U.S. author; associated with *The New Yorker,* 1927–33; member of the Algonquin Round Table, a group of renowned American wits who gathered at New York's Algonquin Hotel to lunch and discuss literary goings-on. [d. June 7, 1967]

1894 *Cecil Kellaway,* British character actor. [d. February 28, 1973]

1900 *Charles A. Halleck,* U.S. politician; Congressman, 1935–68; Conservative leader during 1950s and 1960s. [d. March 3, 1986]

1908 *Henri Cartier-Bresson,* French photographer noted for his documentary photographs.

1917 *John Lee Hooker,* U.S. singer; sold one million copies of the rhythm and blues record, *Boogie Chillin';* recipient of the Lifetime Achievement

Award (Blues Foundation), 1996.

1920 *Ray (Douglas) Bradbury,* U.S. author, known for his science-fiction stories.

1928 *F. Ray Marshall,* U.S. government official and economist; Secretary of Labor, 1977–81.

1934 *H. Norman Schwarzkopf,* U.S. military leader; commander-in-chief of Operation Desert Storm, 1990.

1935 *E. Annie Proulx,* U.S. writer; Pulitzer Prize for *The Shipping News,* 1994.

1939 *Carl (Yaz) Yastrzemski,* U.S. baseball player.

1941 *Valerie Harper,* U.S. actress; four Emmy Awards for the role of Rhoda on the television series, *The Mary Tyler Moore Show* and *Rhoda.*

1942 *Kathy Lennon,* U.S. singer; member of the group, the *Lennon Sisters.*

1948 *Cindy Williams,* U.S. actress; starred in the television series, *Laverne and Shirley,* 1976–82.

1949 *Diana Nyad,* U.S. long-distance swimmer; the first person to swim the 89 miles between the Bahamas and the U.S.

1963 *James DeBarge,* U.S. singer, musician; member of the rock group, *DeBarge.*

Tori Amos (Mira Ellen Amos), U.S. singer.

1964 *Mats Willander,* Swedish tennis player; won 1982 French Open.

HISTORICAL EVENTS

1138 *Stephen,* King of England, defeats *David I* of Scotland near Northallerton at the *Battle of the Standard.*

1244 Egyptians and Khwarezmians capture *Jerusalem,* which never again falls in any subsequent Crusades.

1350 *Philip VI* of France dies and is succeeded by *John II.*

1485 *Richard III* of England is defeated and killed at *Bosworth.*

1642 *English Civil War* begins as Charles I sends Cavaliers against the Puritan parliament at York.

1787 Inventor *John Fitch* demonstrates the first *steamboat* to Constitutional Convention delegates in Philadelphia.

1791 Blacks in *San Domingo* revolt in effort to secure rights recently granted them by the French National Assembly.

1818 The *Savannah,* the first steamship to cross the Atlantic, is launched.

1851 The U.S. schooner, *America,* triumphs at the Royal Yacht Squadron in England, causing the international race to be renamed the *America's Cup.*

1864 Geneva Convention for Protection of the Wounded (*International Red Cross*) is founded.

1910 *Korea* is annexed by Japan after five years as a protectorate.

1914 *Austria-Hungary* declares war on Belgium (*World War I*).

The first air battle of the war occurs over Maubeuge, France, between British and German airplanes (*World War I*).

General *Paul von Hindenburg* is appointed commander of the German Eighth Army with *Erich von Ludendorff* as his chief of staff (*World War I*).

1922 *Michael Collins,* head of the Irish Free State Provisional Government, is killed by Republicans.

1945 U.S. destroyer escort *Levy* accepts surrender of first Japanese garrison to capitulate in World War II.

1948 The first assembly of the *World Council of Churches* is held in Amsterdam.

1953 Shah *Mohammed Reza Pahlevi* returns to Iran from a brief exile following the Royalist overthrow of Premier *Mohammed Mossadegh.*

1956 Bell Telephone Laboratories reports its development of a phone that transmits pictures as well as voices.

1962 U.S. nuclear ship *Savannah,* the world's first nuclear-powered cargo ship, completes her maiden voyage from Yorktown, Virginia, to Savannah, Georgia.

1968 Pope *Paul VI* arrives in Colombia, beginning the first papal visit to South America.

1971 *Hugo Banzer Suarez* assumes power in Bolivia after a coup d'etat.

1972 *International Olympic Committee,* in a move to head off a boycott by African and other black athletes, bars Rhodesia from participating in the forthcoming games.

august

1973 *Henry Kissinger* is named U.S. Secretary of State, replacing William Rogers, who has resigned.

1978 Twenty-five *Sandinista National Liberation Front* members take control of the national palace in Managua,

Nicaragua, killing six guards and holding 1,000 persons captive

1986 *Kerr-McGee Corp.* agrees to pay $1.38 million to the estate of former employee, *Karen Silkwood.* Foul play was suspected in the death of

Silkwood, who had raised public concern over contamination hazards in the nuclear power plant.

1992 *Hurricane Andrew* strikes the Bahamas, killing four people.

HOLIDAYS

Romania
Liberation Day

RELIGIOUS CALENDAR

The Saints

SS. Claudius, Asterius, Neon, Domnina, and Theonilla, martyrs. [d. c. 303]

St. Eugene, bishop. Also called *Eoghan, Eugenius,* or *Owen.* [d. 6th cent.]

St. Philip Benizi, Servite friar. Also called *Beniti,* or *Benize.* [d. 1285]

St. Rose of Lima, virgin; first South American saint, patron of Lima, Peru. Feast formerly August 30. [d. 1617]

The Beatified

Blessed James of Bevagna, Dominican friar. [d. 1301]

BIRTHDATES

1754 *Louis XVI,* King of France, 1774–93, during the French Revolution; with his wife, *Marie Antoinette,* was imprisoned and later executed. [d. January 21, 1793]

1761 *Jedediah Morse,* American religious leader, geographer; author of the first American geography textbooks. [d. June 9, 1826]

1769 *Baron Georges Jean-Léopold-Nicolas-Frédéric Cuvier,* French anatomist; *Father of Comparative Anatomy;* considered by some as founder of modern *paleontology;* developed natural system of animal classification. [d. May 13, 1832]

1785 *Oliver Hazard Perry,* U.S. naval officer; responsible for securing Great Lakes region for U.S. during the War of 1812; issued the famous message, "We have met the enemy and they are ours." Recognized as American naval hero. [d. August 23, 1819]

1849 *William Ernest Henley,* British poet; collaborated with Robert Louis Stevenson on four plays; author of numerous volumes of verse. [d. June 11, 1903]

1864 *Eleutherios Venizelos,* Greek statesman, diplomat; Prime Minister of Greece, 1910–15, 1917–20, 1924, 1928–32, 1933; led Greece during World War I. [d. March 18, 1936]

1869 *Edgar Lee Masters,* U.S. poet, biographer; best known for his poetic monologues of persons speaking from the graveyard of Spoon River, Illinois, a fictitious town. The volume, *Spoon River Anthology,* was widely acclaimed and went through 70 editions between 1915 and 1940. [d. March 5, 1950]

1883 *Jonathan (Mayhew) Wainwright,* U.S. Army general; defender of Corregidor and Bataan; succeeded Douglas MacArthur as commander-in-chief of U.S. forces. [d. September 2, 1953]

1884 *Will(iam Jacob) Cuppy,* U.S. humorist; famous for satirical works, including *How to Become Extinct.* [d. September 19, 1949]

1901 *John Sherman Cooper,* U.S. politician, lawyer; U.S. Senator, 1946–48, 1952–54, 1956–73; U.S. Ambassador to India and Nepal, 1955–56; U.S. Ambassador to East Germany, 1974–76. [d. February 21, 1991]

1904 *William Primrose,* U.S. violist; considered one of the greatest violists of his time. [d. May 1, 1982]

1912 *Gene (Curran) Kelly,* U.S. dancer, movie star, choreographer. [d. February 2, 1996]

1917 *Tex Williams,* U.S. singer, songwriter, band leader; popular country-western singer, 1930s–40s. [d. October 11, 1985]

1921 *Kenneth J. Arrow,* U.S. economist; Nobel Prize in economics for his contributions to the general equilibrium theory (with J. R. Hicks), 1972.

1922 *George Clyde Kell,* U.S. baseball player, sportscaster; third baseman, 1943–57; American League batting title, 1949; elected to Hall of Fame, 1983.

1924 *Robert M. Solow,* U.S. economist; Nobel Prize in economics for his contributions to the theory of economic growth, 1987.

1930 *Vera Miles (Vera Helena Hruba Ralston),* U.S. actress.

1931 *Hamilton O. Smith,* U.S. biochemist; Nobel Prize in physiology or medicine for discoveries in restriction enzymes control of genes on chromosomes (with D. Nathans and W. Arber), 1978.

1932 *Houari Boumedienne,* Algerian president. [d. December 27, 1978]

Mark Russell (Mark Ruslander), U.S. comedian; famous for political satires set to music.

1933 *Robert F. Curl, Jr.,* U.S. chemist; co-winner of the Nobel Prize for Chemistry, 1996, for the discovery of fullerenes. Curl shared the award with Sir Harold W. Kroto and Richard E. Smalley.

Peter B. Wilson, U.S. politician; Senator, 1983–91; Governor of California, 1991– .

1934 *Barbara Eden (Barbara Huffman),* U.S. actress.

Sonny Jurgenson (Christian Adolf Jurgenson III), U.S. football player.

1944 *Antonia Novello,* U.S. physician; first female surgeon general in the United States.

1946 *Keith Moon,* British musician; drummer for the rock group, *The Who.* [d. September 7, 1978]

1949 *Rick Springfield,* Australian actor, musician, singer; former star of the soap opera, *General Hospital;* Grammy Award for the song, *Jessie's Girl,* 1981.

Shelley Long, U.S. actress; Emmy Award for *Cheers,* 1983.

1951 *Mark Jeffrey Anthony Hudson,* U.S. singer, musician; member of the rock group, *Hudson Brothers.*

Queen Noor (Lisa Najeeb Halaby), U.S.-born wife of Jordan's King Hussein; plays major role in education, social welfare, and arts in Jordan.

1971 *River Phoenix,* U.S. actor. [d. October 31, 1993]

HISTORICAL EVENTS

1305 *William Wallace,* Scottish rival of *Edward I* of England, is executed at Smithfield after being convicted of treason by an English court.

1628 *Duke of Buckingham, George Villiers,* is assassinated as he prepares to lead a relief expedition to save *La Rochelle,* seat of power of the Huguenots.

1645 Denmark loses her possessions in Sweden with the signing of the *Peace of Brömsebro.*

1833 Act for abolition of *slavery* throughout the British colonies is passed by Parliament.

1866 *Treaty of Prague* brings an end to *Germanic Confederation of 1815.*

1914 German troops execute 664 Belgian civilians at *Dinant,* then sack and burn the town *(World War I).*

Japan declares war on Germany *(World War I).*

1940 Germany conducts its first night air raid on *London (World War II).*

1942 *Battle of the Eastern Solomons* begins a three-day naval engagement against the Japanese, which is finally won by the Americans *(World War II).*

1944 Coup in Romania overthrows pro-Axis government of *Ion Antonescu.*

Soviet armies invade *Romania* forcing Germans to begin their withdrawal *(World War II).*

1961 *Ranger I,* first in a series of successful lunar probes is launched from Cape Canaveral, Florida.

1979 *Aleksandr Godunov,* a principal dancer with the Bolshoi Ballet, defects to the U.S.

1984 *Yumjbagiyen Tsedenbal* resigns as chairman of the Presidium and secretary general of the Mongolian People's Revolutionary Party after 32 years in power.

1989 On the fiftieth anniversary of the *1939 Hitler-Stalin pact* that brought Lithuania, Lativia, and Estonia under Soviet rule, over one million people form a human chain to protest the pact.

1990 *Armenia* votes in favor of
   independence from the Soviet
   Union.

AUGUST
24

HOLIDAYS

Liberia
National Flag Day

Romania
National Holiday

Swaziland
Umhlanga or Reed Dance Day

Ukraine
Independence Day

RELIGIOUS CALENDAR

The Saints

St. Bartholomew, apostle; patron of
butchers, tanners, and
bookbinders. [d. 1st cent.]
The Martyrs of Utica. [d. c. 258]
St. Audoenus, Bishop of Rouen. Also
called *Audoen, Dado,* or
Ouen. [d. 684]
St. Bregwine, Archbishop of
Canterbury. [d. 764]

BIRTHDATES

1113 *Geoffrey, Count of Anjou,*
called *Geoffrey Plantagenet.*
[d. September 7, 1151]

1198 *Alexander II, King of
Scotland,* 1214–49;
maintained peace with
England and strengthened
Scottish monarchy. [d. July 8,
1249]

1724 *George Stubbs,* English animal
painter; known especially for
his accurate drawings of
horses. [d. July 10, 1806]

1759 *William Wilberforce,* English
statesman and reformer;
instrumental in abolition of
slavery in Great Britain, 1833.
[d. July 29, 1833]

1772 *William I (William the
Silent), King of Holland,*
1815–40. [d. December 12,
1843]

1787 *James Weddell,* British
Antarctic explorer; discovered
Weddell Sea, which was
named for him. [d.
September 9, 1834]

1817 *Count Alexey Tolstoy,* Russian
poet, dramatist, and satirist.
[d. September 28, 1875]

1846 *Henry Gannett,* U.S.
geographer; called the *Father
of American Mapmaking.* [d.
November 5, 1914]

1847 *Charles Follen McKim,* U.S.
architect; founder of McKim,
Mead and White, one of
foremost architectural firms in
U.S.; designed *Boston Public
Library;* leading exponent of
Neo-classical style in U.S. [d.
September 14, 1909]

1865 *Ferdinand I, King of
Romania,* 1914–27. [d. July
20, 1927]

1872 *Sir Max Beerbohm,* British
essayist, caricaturist, critic;
noted for his satirical stories
and parodies. [d. May 20,
1956]

1894 *Jean Rhys,* British author;
wrote *After Leaving Mr.
MacKenzie* and *Good
Morning, Midnight.* [d. May
14, 1979]

1895 *Richard James Cushing,* U.S.
Roman Catholic cardinal;
archbishop of Boston,
1944–70. [d. November 2,
1970]

1898 *Malcolm Cowley,* U.S. writer,
critic, and editor; literary
editor of *The New Republic,*
1929–40; literary advisor to
Viking Press, 1948–85. [d.
March 27, 1989]

1899 *Jorge Luis Borges,* Argentine
author, educator; Director,
National Library of Buenos
Aires, 1955–73; winner of
numerous prizes for his
original fictional narratives.
[d. June 14, 1986]

Albert Claude, Belgian-born
microbiologist; Nobel Prize in
physiology or medicine for
research in cell biology (with
C.R. de Duve and G. E.
Palade), 1974. [d. May 20,
1983]

1901 *Preston Foster,* U.S. actor. [d.
July 14, 1970]

1902 *Fernand Paul Braudel,*
French historian; influential
member of the Annales
school of historiography;
wrote *The Mediterranean
and the Mediterranean*

World in Age of Philip II and *Civilization and Capitalism, 15th–18th Centuries.* [d. November 28, 1985]

1903 *Graham (Vivian) Sutherland,* British artist; best known for his controversial portrait of Winston Churchill, which was eventually destroyed by Lady Spencer Churchill. [d. February 17, 1980]

1905 *Siaka P. Stevens,* President, Republic of Sierra Leone, 1971–85. [May 29, 1988]

1922 *Rene Levesque,* Canadian government official; Parti Quebecois premier of Quebec, 1976–85; famous for leading separtist movement; call *Rene the Red.* [d. November 1, 1987]

1924 *Louis Teicher,* U.S. pianist, composer; part of the Ferrante and Teicher piano team.

1925 *Shirley Hufstedler,* U.S. jurist; first U.S. Secretary of Education, 1979–81.

1927 *Harry M. Markowitz,* U.S. educator, co-winner of the Nobel Prize for Economics. Markowitz shares the award with Merton H. Miller and William F. Sharpe, for their work on the theory of financial economics, 1990.

1929 *Yasir Arafat,* Palestinian leader.

1956 *Gerald Arthur (Gerry) Cooney,* U.S. boxer; heavyweight contender defeated by Larry Holmes, 1982; known as the *Great White Hope;* lost to Michael Spinks, 1987.

1958 *Steve Guttenberg,* U.S. actor; known for his roles in

Cocoon, 1985 and *Three Men and a Baby,* 1987.

1960 *Cal(vin Edwin) Ripkin, Jr.,* U.S. baseball player; infielder for the Baltimore Orioles, 1982–; American League Rookie of the Year, 1982; Most Valuable Player, 1983; broke the record for most consecutive games played in 1995 (September 6, 1995).

1965 *Marlee Matlin,* U.S. actress; Oscar winner for *Children of a Lesser God.*

Reggie Miller, U.S. basketball player; member of the "Dream Team II" at the World Games, 1994.

HISTORICAL EVENTS

79 *Mount Vesuvius* on the Bay of Naples erupts, burying the cities of *Herculaneum* and *Pompeii* and killing 200,000 citizens.

410 *Rome* is sacked by *Alaric.*

1572 *St. Bartholemew's Day Massacre* of the Huguenots begins in Paris; up to 70,000 were eventually put to death throughout France.

1814 *Washington, D.C.* is captured and burned by the British (*War of 1812*).

1918 Bolshevik forces are defeated by the Allies at the *Battle of Dukhouskaya.*

1944 Romanian government surrenders as Soviet troops capture *Jassy* and *Kishinev* (*World War II*).

1949 *Thomas Campbell Clark* is sworn in as U.S. Supreme Court justice.

1950 *Edith Sampson* becomes the first black named to the U.S. delegation to the United Nations.

1954 Brazilian president *Getulio Vargas* commits suicide after being forced by the military to resign in favor of *Joao Cafe Filho.*

1958 Submarine *U.S.S. Nautilus* completes record setting six and one-half day underwater trans-Atlantic crossing.

1960 U.S. Surgeon General approves the live-virus oral *polio vaccine* developed by Dr. *Albert Sabin.*

1964 The Reverend Frederick McManus of Catholic University celebrates the first full *Roman Catholic Mass* in English at St. Louis, Missouri.

1968 France explodes its first *hydrogen bomb* in the South Pacific, becoming the world's fifth nuclear power.

1970 Massachusetts governor, Francis Sargent, signs the first U.S. *no-fault automobile insurance* plan into law.

1989 Baseball great *Pete Rose* is banned from the game by commissioner A. Bartlett Giamatti. Giamatti cites Rose's gambling on games he played or managed in as the reason for the ban.

1991 *Mikhail Gorbachev* resigns as the general secretary of the Communist party.

1992 *Hurricane Andrew* hits Miami, Florida, causing over $20 billion in damages and killing fifteen people.

august

AUGUST
25

HOLIDAYS

Paraguay
Constitution Day
Commemorates the adoption of the constitution of 1967.

Uruguay
Independence Day
Commemorates Uruguay's achievement of independence from Brazil, 1825.

RELIGIOUS CALENDAR

The Saints
St. Genesius of Arles, martyr. Also called *Genes.* [d. c. 303]

St. Mennas, Patriarch of Constantinople. [d. 552]

St. Ebba, Abbess of Coldingham and virgin. Also called *Aebba, Ebba the Elder,* or *Tabbs.* [d. 683]

St. Gregory of Utrecht, abbot. [d. c. 775]

St. Louis of France, (King Louis IX); patron of builders, haberdashers, distillers, embroidery workers, hairdressers, and barbers. [d. 1270]

St. Joseph Calasanctius, founder of the Clerks Regular of the Religious Schools, commonly called Piarists or Scolopi. Also called *Joseph Calasanz.* Feast formerly August 27. [d. 1648]

St. Joan Antide-Thouret, virgin; founder of the Sisters of Charity under St. Vincent's Protection. [d. 1826]

St. Mary Michaela Desmaisières, virgin and founder of the Handmaids of the Blessed Sacrament. [d. 1865]

St. Genesius the Comedian, martyr. Also called *Gelasinus,* or *Genesius the Actor.* [death date unknown]

St. Patricia, virgin. [death date unknown]

BIRTHDATES

1530 *Ivan IV,* Emperor of Russia, 1547–84; known as *Ivan the Terrible,* he became czar at the age of 3. [d. March 18, 1584]

1744 *Johann Gottfried von Herder,* German critic, philosopher, author; influenced Goethe and development of German Romanticism. [d. December 18, 1803]

1745 *Henry Mackenzie,* Scottish novelist and essayist; known as the *Man of Feelings* and the *Addison of the North.* [d. January 14, 1831]

1819 *Allan Pinkerton,* U.S. detective, born in Scotland; founder of *Pinkerton National Detective Agency,* 1850; established first counterespionage unit in U.S. government, 1861. [d. July 1, 1884]

1836 *(Francis) Bret(t) Harte,* U.S. author; noted for his use of Western local color subjects, such as scenes from the exotic California gold-mining era, descriptions of pioneer characters, etc. His works include *The Luck of Roaring Camp* and *The Outcasts of Poker Flat.* [d. May 5, 1902]

1841 *Emil Theodar Kocher,* Swiss surgeon; Nobel Prize in physiology or medicine for his research on the *thyroid gland,* 1909. [d. July 27, 1917]

1850 *Charles R. Richet,* French physiologist; Nobel Prize in physiology or medicine for his work on *anaphylaxis,* 1913. [d. December 4, 1935]

1862 *William Cooper Procter,* U.S. manufacturer; founder and president of Procter & Gamble Co., 1907–34. [d. May 2, 1934]

1873 *John North Willys,* U.S. manufacturer, diplomat; founder of Willys-Overland Auto Co., 1907, developers of the "Jeep"; U.S. Ambassador to Poland, 1930–32. [d. August 26, 1935]

1880 *Joshua Lionel Cowen,* U.S. businessman; founder of Lionel Corporation, manufacturers of toy electric trains, 1945; invented the *flashlight* and the *dry cell battery.* [d. September 8, 1965]

1889 *Waldo Frank,* U.S. author. [d. 1967]

1900 Sir *Hans Adolf Krebs,* British biochemist; Nobel Prize in physiology or medicine for biochemical studies of cell metabolism (with F.A. Lipmann), 1953. [d. November 22, 1981]

1909 *Ruby Keeler (Ethel Keeler),* U.S. dancer, actress. [d. February 28, 1993]

1912 *Erich Honecker,* Chairman, East German Democratic Republic, 1976–94. [d. May 29, 1994]

1913 *Eugene Victor Rostow,* U.S lawyer, economist; headed Arms Control Disarmament Agency; ousted by Ronald Reagan over a policy dispute, 1983.

1916 *Frederick Chapman Robbins,* U.S. microbiologist; Nobel Prize in physiology or medicine for successful growth of polio virus in tissue cultures and discoveries in polio detection (with J. F. Enders and T. Weller), 1954.

1917 *Mel Ferrer,* U.S. actor.

1918 *Leonard Bernstein,* U.S. composer, conductor; wrote music for *West Side Story;* Conductor of New York Philharmonic orchestra, 1957–58; Musical Director, 1958–69; Laureate Conductor for Life, 1969–; highly diversified in his approach to bringing music to the masses. [d. October 14, 1990]

1919 *George (Corley) Wallace,* U.S. politician, lawyer; U.S. presidential candidate, American Independent Party, 1968; victim of assassination attempt which left him partially paralyzed, 1972. [d. September 13, 1998]

1924 *Monty Hall,* Canadian-born television performer; hosted *Let's Make a Deal* and *Beat the Clock.*

1927 *Althea Gibson,* U.S. tennis player; first black player to win a major U.S. tennis championship.

1930 *Sean Connery (Thomas Connery),* Scottish actor; portrayed Ian Fleming's James Bond, Agent 007; Academy Award for *The Untouchables,* 1988.

1931 *Cecil D. Andrus,* U.S. politician; Governor of Idaho, 1971–77; U.S. Secretary of the Interior, 1977–81.

1933 *Thomas Roy (Tom) Skerritt,* U.S. actor.

1938 *Frederick Forsyth,* British author; known for best-selling thrillers; author of *Day of the Jackal* and *The Odessa File.*

1944 *Jacques Demers,* Canadian hockey coach; coached National Hockey League teams in Quebec, St. Louis, and Detroit.

1947 *Anne Archer,* U.S. actress; starred in the film, *Fatal Attraction.*

1949 *Gene Simmons (Gene Klein),* U.S. singer, musician; co-founded the rock group, *Kiss;* famous for dressing as fire-breathing, blood-spewing ghoul in public appearances.

1955 *Elvis Costello (Declan Patrick McManus),* British singer, songwriter; albums include *Armed Forces* and *Spike.*

1962 *Taslima Nasrin,* Bengali physician, author, feminist activist.

1964 *Joanne Whalley,* British actress.

1966 *Albert Belle,* U.S. baseball player; Player of the Year, 1995.

HISTORICAL EVENTS

325 *Council of Nicaea* ends after establishing the method of calculating the day on which *Easter* would be celebrated (the first Sunday after the first full moon after the spring equinox), and making decrees regarding several other theologically significant issues.

1270 *Louis IX* of France dies and is succeeded by *Philip III.*

1786 *Punctation of Ems,* a congress of German bishops, meets with the aim of creating a National Catholic Church.

1825 *Uruguay* establishes its independence from Brazil.

1830 Revolt of French-speaking provinces of the Netherlands (now *Belgium*) begins.

1875 *Captain Matthew Webb* becomes the first person to swim across the *English Channel* (21 hours, 45 minutes).

1883 France assumes protectorate over *Annam* and *Tonkin* with the signing of the *Treaty of Huè.*

1914 Japan declares state of war with Austria-Hungary (*World War I*).

British first employ the *aircraft patrol* in their retreat from Mons (*World War I*).

1916 *U.S. National Park Service* is established as part of the Department of Interior.

august

1921 The U.S. and Germany sign a peace treaty ending the state of war between them (*World War I*).

1940 *Lithuania, Latvia,* and *Estonia* are incorporated into the U.S.S.R.

1943 *Lord Louis Mountbatten* is appointed Supreme Allied Commander in Southeast Asia (*World War II*).

1944 U.S. and French troops liberate *Paris.* German forces surrender unconditionally (*World War II*).

1958 T.H. White's novel, *The Once and Future King,* is published in New York.

1960 *XVII Summer Olympics* open in Rome.

1963 More than 100 countries sign a *limited test ban treaty,* which bans nuclear testing in all environments except underground.

1967 *American Nazi Party* leader, *George Lincoln Rockwell,* is shot to death in Arlington, Virginia.

Paraguay promulgates a new constitution.

1976 French premier *Jacques Chirac* resigns. *Raymond Barre* is appointed to succeed him.

1981 U.S. *Voyager 2* spacecraft speeds past Saturn, transmitting photos of the planet's rings and moons.

1996 *Tiger Woods* wins U.S. Amateur Golf Tournament for the third consecutive year.

HOLIDAYS

U.N. Member Nations
Namibia Day

U.S.
Women's Equality Day
Commemorates the date women were given the right to vote.

RELIGIOUS CALENDAR

The Saints
St. Zephyrinus, pope and martyr. Elected bishop of Rome 198. Feast suppressed 1969. [d. c. 217]
St. Pandonia, virgin. Also called *Pandwyna.* [d. c. 904]
St. Elizabeth Bichier des Ages, virgin and cofounder of the Daughters of the Cross or Sisters of St. Andrew. [d. 1838]

The Beatified
Blessed Herluin, abbot. [d. 1078]
Blessed Timothy of Montecchio. [d. 1504]
Blessed Thomas Percy, martyr. [d. 1572]
Blessed Bernard of Offida. [d. 1694]

BIRTHDATES

1676 *Robert Walpole,* English statesman; Prime Minister, 1721–42; first to unify cabinet under leadership of a prime minister; established basis for Britain's colonial policy. [d. March 18, 1745]

1728 *Johann Heinrich Lambert,* German mathematician, physicist; devised methods of measuring light intensity and absorption; demonstrated *irrationality of pi.* [d. September 25, 1777]

1740 *Joseph Michel Montgolfier,* French inventor; with his brother, Jacques Etienne Montgolifer (January 7), invented the *hot air balloon,* 1783. [d. June 26, 1810]

1743 *Antoine Laurent Lavoisier,* French chemist, known as the *Founder of Modern Chemistry;* explained phenomenon of combustion; theorized on compounding of chemicals; executed by the Convention during the French Revolution. [d. May 8, 1794]

1819 *Prince Albert of Saxe-Coburg-Gotha,* Prince Consort of England, husband of Queen Victoria. [d. December 14, 1861]

1827 *Annie Turner Wittenmyer,* U.S. social reformer; first president of the National Woman's Christian Temperance Union, 1874–79. [d. February 2, 1906]

1873 *Lee De Forest,* U.S. inventor; developed the triode amplifier tube, thereby ushering in the electronics age; known as the *Father of Radio.* [d. June 30, 1961]

1875 *Sir John Buchan,* Scottish writer known for his adventure stories such as *The 39 Steps* and *Prester John.* [d. 1940]

1876 *James Joseph Couzens, Jr.,* U.S. businessman, politician; Ford Motor Co. executive, 1903–15; Mayor of Detroit, 1919–22. [d. October 22, 1936]

1882 *James Franck,* U.S. physicist born in Germany; Nobel Prize in physics for discovery of laws related to impact of electrons in an atom (with G. Hertz), 1925. [d. May 21, 1964]

1884 *Earl Derr Biggers,* U.S. mystery-story writer and novelist; noted for his *Charlie Chan* stories. [d. April 5, 1933]

1895 *Earl Kemp Long,* U.S. politician; Lieutenant Governor of Louisiana, 1936–38; Governor of Louisiana, 1939–40. [d. September 5, 1960]

1898 *Peggy Guggenheim,* U.S. art patron and collector. [d. December 23, 1979]

1901 *Maxwell (Davenport) Taylor,* U.S. general, diplomat; Chairman, Joint Chiefs of Staff, 1962–64; Ambassador to South Vietnam, 1964–65. [d. April 19, 1987]

august

1903 *Jimmy Rushing,* U.S. jazz-blues singer, member of Count Basie's orchestra, 1935–50. [d. June 8, 1982]

1904 *Christopher Isherwood,* British novelist; noted for his novel, *Goodbye to Berlin,* 1935, which was adapted to the stage as *I am a Camera,* 1951, and as a musical, *Cabaret,* 1966; frequently collaborated with *W.H. Auden.* [d. January 4, 1986]

1906 *Albert Bruce Sabin,* U.S. immunologist, born in Poland; developed the *Sabin vaccine* for polio, which resulted in significant reduction of the disease on an international scale. [d. March 3, 1993]

1916 *Jim Davis,* U.S. actor; known for his role as Jock Ewing on the television series, *Dallas,* 1978–81. [d. April 26, 1981]

1921 *David Begelman,* U.S. film executive; involved in money scandal which resulted in the book, *Indecent Exposure.*

Benjamin Crowninshield (Ben) Bradlee, U.S. journalist, editor; vice-president, executive editor of the *Washington Post,* 1968– .

1922 *Irving R. Levine,* U.S. broadcast journalist.

1933 *Ben J. Wattenberg,* U.S. demographer, author; wrote *The Good News is the Bad News is Wrong,* 1984, and *The Birth Dearth,* 1987.

1935 *Geraldine Anne Ferraro,* U.S. politician; first woman vice-presidential candidate; ran on Democratic ticket with Walter Mondale, 1984.

1960 *Branford Marsalis,* U.S. musician.

1980 *Macaulay Caulkin,* U.S. actor. Starred in *Home Alone* movies.

HISTORICAL EVENTS

1346 English longbowmen under *Edward III* rout the French crossbowmen at the *Battle of Crécy.* England is established as a dominant military power (*Hundred Years' War*).

1541 Conquest of *Hungary* by the Turks is completed.

1791 *John Fitch* is granted a U.S. patent for his invention of the *steamboat.*

1857 The *National Education Association (NEA)* is organized in Philadelphia, Pennsylvania.

1858 *Treaty of Edo* opens Japan to British trade.

1883 *Krakatoa volcano* in the South Pacific explodes, destroying its island, causing catastrophic tidal waves, killing more than 30,000 people, and destroying hundreds of villages.

1896 Attack on the Ottoman Bank at *Constantinople* by Armenian revolutionaries results in a massacre of Armenians: 6,000 killed.

1914 *First Battle of Lemberg* between Russia and Austria opens in the Austrian province of *Galicia (World War I).*

World's largest power dam to date, *Keokuk Dam,* is opened, across Mississippi River from Keokuk, Iowa.

Germans crush the Russian army at the *Battle of Tannenberg (World War I).*

1920 *19th Amendment* to the U.S. Constitution is ratified, giving women the right to vote.

1924 The Kuomintang, Chinese national congress, creates a *Labor Corps* in Canton which becomes the *Red Army.*

1935 The *United Automobile Workers (UAW)* labor union is founded.

1946 George Orwell's novel, *Animal Farm,* is published in New York.

1957 The Soviet Union announces its first successful test of an *intercontinental ballistic missile.*

1961 *Buddhism* becomes the official religion of *Burma.*

1964 President *Lyndon B. Johnson* and Senator *Hubert H. Humphrey* are selected as the Democratic candidates for president and vice-president.

1972 *XX Summer Olympics* open at Munich, Germany.

1976 *Prince Bernhard* of the Netherlands, husband of Queen Juliana, resigns most of his military and business posts because of his disgrace in a scandal involving bribes by Lockheed Aircraft Company.

1977 *Quebec* assembly passes bill intended to extend and encourage the use of French in the province.

1978 Albino Cardinal Luciani, patriarch of Venice, is elected pope of the Roman Catholic Church and chooses the name *John Paul I.* He served in the position for only 34 days [d. Sept. 29, 1978]

1981 *Queen Juliana* of the Netherlands becomes the first ruling sovereign of the House of Orange to visit *Indonesia*.

1984 Grand Duke *Franz Josef II* of Liechtenstein transfers executive authority to his son, Crown Prince *Hans Adam*.

august

AUGUST
27

HOLIDAYS

Guinea
Anniversary of Women's Revolt

Moldova
Independence Day

U.S. (Texas)
Lyndon B. Johnson's Birthday
Commemorates the birth of the 36th President of the U.S., 1908.

RELIGIOUS CALENDAR

The Saints
St. Marcellus and his Companions, martyrs. Marcellus also called *Marcellinus.* [d. 287]
St. Monica, widow. Mother of St. Augustine; patroness of the Augustinian nuns. Feast formerly May 4. [d. 387] Obligatory Memorial.
St. Poemen, abbot. Also called *Pastor.* [d. 5th cent.]
St. Caesarius, Bishop of Arles. Founded first women's convent in Gaul. [d. 543]
St. Decuman, monk and hermit; patron of Watchet and St. Decumans. [d. 6th cent.]
St. Syagrius, Bishop of Autun. [d. 600]
Little St. Hugh of Lincoln. His martyrdom is subject of Chaucer's *Prioress's Tale.* [d. 1255]
St. Rufus of Capua, martyr. Also called *Rufinus.* [death date unknown]

The Beatified
Blessed Angelo of Foligno, Augustinian friar. [d. 1312]
Blessed Gabriel Mary, Franciscan friar. [d. 1532]
Blessed Dominic Barberi, priest. [d. 1849]

BIRTHDATES

551BC *Confucius (Kung Fu-Tzu),* Chinese philosopher; developed religious system for management of society; emphasized good family relationships for social stability. [d. 479 B.C.]

1545 *Alessandro Farnese, Duke of Parma,* Spanish soldier; greatest military expert of his time; recovered provinces of the Netherlands for his uncle, Philip II of Spain. [d. December 3, 1592]

1730 *Johann Georg Hamann,* German philosophical writer; known as the *Magus of the North.* [d. June 21, 1788]

1770 *Georg Wilhelm Friedrich Hegel,* German Idealist philosopher; established a system of metaphysics based on the concept of the *Absolute;* profoundly influenced the development of philosophy during the middle of the 19th century. [d. November 14, 1831]

1797 *Ramón Castilla,* Peruvian soldier, President of Peru, 1845–51. [d. August 29, 1867]

1809 *Hannibal Hamlin,* U.S. politician, lawyer, farmer; U.S. Congressman, 1842–47; U.S. Senator, 1848–57; U.S. Vice-President, 1861–65. [d. July 4, 1891]

1865 *Charles Gates Dawes,* U.S. politician, diplomat, financier; Nobel Peace Prize (with Sir Austen Chamberlain), 1925; U.S. Vice-President under Calvin Coolidge; 1925–29; U.S. Ambassador to Great Britain 1929–32. [d. April 23, 1951]

James Henry Breasted, U.S. Egyptologist, archaeologist, and historian; professor of Egyptology and Oriental History, University of Chicago, 1905–19; head of University's archaeological expedition to Egypt, 1905–07; published many volumes of history of Egypt and dictionaries of ancient languages. First archaeologist elected to National Academy of Sciences, 1920. [d. December 2, 1935]

1871 *Theodore (Herman Albert) Dreiser,* U.S. novelist; controversial proponent of naturalism in novel writing; his first work, *Sister Carrie,* aroused widespread controversy and was suppressed by its publisher;

achieved recognition finally with *An American Tragedy.* [d. December 28, 1945]

1874 *Carl Bosch,* German industrial chemist; Nobel Prize for chemistry for development of chemical high-pressure methods (with F. Bergius), 1931. [d. April 26, 1940]

1877 *Lloyd C(assel) Douglas,* U.S. novelist, teacher of religion; known for his popular, religiously oriented novels, including *Magnificent Obsession, The Robe,* and *A Time to Remember.* [d. February 13, 1951]

Charles Stewart Rolls, British auto manufacturer; formed Rolls-Royce Ltd. (with F. Royce), 1906. [d. July 12, 1910]

1878 *Baron Petr Nikolayevich Wrangel,* Russian general; leader of counter-revolutionary forces in Russia, 1917–20. [d. April 25, 1928]

1884 *Samuel Goldwyn (Samuel Goldfish),* U.S. motion-picture industry pioneer, born in Poland; founded Goldwyn Pictures, 1917, which became Metro-Goldwyn-Mayer Studios, 1924. [d. January 31, 1974]

1890 *Man Ray (Emmanuel Radinski),* U.S. painter, photographer; with Marcel Duchamp founded Dadaism; one of first members of Surrealist movement; noted for his innovative, unpredictable style. [d. November 18, 1976]

1899 *C(ecil) S(cott) Forester,* British novelist; noted for *Horatio Hornblower* novels. [d. April 2, 1966]

1904 *Norah Robinson Lofts,* British author; wrote over fifty historical romances and biographies; author of *I Met a Gypsy* and *Day of the Butterfly.* [d. September 10, 1983]

1908 *Lyndon Baines Johnson,* U.S. teacher, politician; Vice-President, 1961–63; 36th President of U.S., 1963–69; became president upon assassination of John F. Kennedy; served during period of civil strife, racial unrest, and Vietnam War. [d. January 22, 1973]

1909 *Lester Young,* U.S. jazz musician. [d. March 15, 1959]

1910 *Mother Teresa* of Calcutta, the *Saint of the Gutters,* Italian-born humanitarian; Nobel Peace Prize for her work with the poor of India, 1979. [d. September 5, 1997]

1913 *Martin David Kamen,* U.S. biochemist, born in Canada; discovered carbon-14 isotope, used in archaeological research; recipient of the Enrico Fermi Award, 1995. Also known as the world's foremost amateur viola player.

1915 *Walter Wolfgang Heller,* U.S. economist, government official; Chairman, Council of Economic Advisors, 1961–64; architect of 1964 tax cut. [d. June 15, 1987]

Norman F. Ramsey, U.S. physicist; one-half of the Nobel Prize for Physics for his work on shifting the energy levels of atoms. Hans Georg Dehmelt, U.S. physicist, and Wolfgang Paul, German physicist share the other half of the prize for their study of ions, 1989.

1916 *Martha Raye (Maggie Yvonne O'Reed),* U.S. actress. [d. October 19, 1994]

1929 *Ira Levin,* U.S. novelist, playwright; author of *No Time for Sergeants, The Boys from Brazil,* and *Deathtrap.*

1932 *Lady Antonia Fraser,* British author; best known for her biographies of British royalty and statesmen.

1935 *Frank Yablans,* U.S. producer; films include *The Other Side of Midnight* and *Mommie Dearest.*

1939 *William Least Heat Moon (William Lewis Trogdon),* U.S. author; wrote critically acclaimed travel memoir, *Blue Highways,* 1983.

1943 *J. Robert Kerrey,* U.S. politician; Governor of Nebraska, 1983–87; U.S. senator, 1988– .

Tuesday Weld (Susan Ker Weld), U.S. actress.

1947 *Barbara Bach (Barbara Goldbach),* U.S. actress; starred in the movie, *Caveman;* wife of Ringo Starr.

1952 *Pee-Wee Herman,* U.S. comedian and actor.

1954 *John Lloyd,* British tennis player; Wimbledon Mixed-Doubles Champion, 1983.

1985 *Alexandra Nechita,* Romanian-born artist; child prodigy known for her Cubist style.

HISTORICAL EVENTS

1664 *New Amsterdam* surrenders to the English under Col. Richard Nicolls.

1828 *Uruguay* becomes a sovereign nation under the

Treaty of Rio de Janeiro, which ends war between Brazil and Argentina.

1859 U.S. prospector *Edwin Drake* drills first successful oil well in U.S. at Titusville, Pennsylvania, striking oil at 69 feet.

1916 *Romania* declares war on Austria-Hungary (*World War I*).

Italy declares war on Germany (*World War I*).

1928 *Kellogg-Briand Pact* is signed by 62 nations at Paris, outlawing war as an instrument of national policy.

1936 *Egypt* and *Great Britain* sign a treaty providing for withdrawal of British forces except in Suez Canal area.

1942 Oxford University announces the discovery of *penicillin* by British scientist, Sir *Alexander Fleming.*

1946 France concludes agreement with *Laos,* establishing a kingdom under French domination.

1952 High Court of Parliament removes non-whites from electoral rolls in *South Africa.*

1962 Spacecraft *Mariner II* is launched from Cape Canaveral on a projected 15-week trajectory toward the planet *Venus.*

1964 Walt Disney's film, *Mary Poppins,* premieres at Grauman's Chinese Theatre in Hollywood.

1976 Scientists at the *Massachusetts Institute of Technology* synthesize a gene and implant it in a living bacterial cell.

1977 Philippine military authorities release 500 prisoners imprisoned since the imposition of martial law on September 23, 1972.

1979 *Louis Mountbatten, 1st Earl Mountbatten of Burma,* is killed when a bomb planted by I.R.A. destroys his boat off the Irish coast.

1983 An estimated 250,000 people gather in Washington D.C. to commemorate the 20th anniversary of the march on Washington and Rev. Martin Luther King's "I have a dream" speech.

1985 Major General *Ibrahim Babangida* assumes power in Nigeria after a bloodless coup d'etat.

RELIGIOUS CALENDAR

The Saints

St. Hermes, martyr. [d. c. 2nd cent.]

St. Julian of Brioude, martyr. Also called *Julian of Auvergne.* [d. 3rd cent.]

SS. Alexander, John III, and Paul IV, Patriarchs of Constantinople. [d. 340, 577, 784]

St. Moses the Black, one of the Fathers of the Desert. [d. c. 405]

St. Augustine, Bishop of Hippo, and Doctor of the Church; patron of theologians and scholars. Also called *Austin* and the *Greatest of the Fathers.* [d. 430]

The London Martyrs of 1588. Fifteen or sixteen victims of anti-Catholic repression in England. [d. 1588]

BIRTHDATES

1481 *Francisco de Sá de Miranda,* Portuguese poet, playwright; author of first Portuguese prose comedy; first classical tragedy. [d. 1558]

1592 *George Villiers, 1st Duke of Buckingham,* English courtier, royal favorite; led British to relieve Rochelle. Assassinated. [August 23, 1628]

1728 *John Stark,* American Revolutionary War general; hero of the *Battle of Bennington,* 1777. [d. May 8, 1822]

1735 *Count Andreas Peter von Bernstorff,* Danish statesman, diplomat; leader in Danish reform movement, liberation of Danish peasants. [d. June 21, 1797]

1749 *Johann Wolfgang von Goethe,* German poet, dramatist, novelist; inaugurated German *Sturm and Drang* literary movement introduced Romanticism and Modernism in literary development of Germany. Author of *Faust.* [d. March 22, 1832]

1774 *Elizabeth Ann Seton,* U.S. educator, religious leader; founder of Sisters of St. Joseph; canonized, 1975; first U.S.-born saint. [d. January 4, 1821]

1814 *Joseph Sheridan Le Fanu,* Irish novelist; editor of *Dublin Evening Mail,* 1838–58; noted for his stories of the supernatural. [d. February 7, 1873]

1823 *James Oliver,* U.S. inventor, born in Scotland; invented the *chilled plow,* which used *annealed steel* for hardness, 1868. [d. March 2, 1908]

1831 *Lucy Webb Hayes,* wife of Rutherford B. Hayes, 19th U.S. President; first president's wife to graduate from college; refused to serve alcohol at the White House; known as *Lemonade Lucy.* [d. June 25, 1889]

1833 *Sir Edward Coley Burne-Jones,* British painter; student of Rossetti; noted for his large oil paintings, frequently done in series: *The Golden Stairs,* 1880. [d. June 17, 1898]

1878 *George H. Whipple,* U.S. physiologist; Nobel Prize in physiology or medicine for discoveries concerning treatment of *pernicious anemia,* then a fatal disease (with G. R. Minot and W. P. Murphy), 1934. [d. February 1, 1976]

1894 *Karl Böhn,* Austrian musician, conductor; Director, Dresden State Opera, 1934–42; Director, Vienna State Opera, 1943–45; 1954–56; Conductor of Vienna Philharmonic Orchestra, 1933–81. [d. August 14, 1981]

1898 *James Wong Howe,* U.S. cinematographer. [d. 1976]

1899 *Charles Boyer,* French actor. [d. August 26, 1978]

1903 *Bruno Bettelheim,* Austrian-born psychologist, author; Director, Sonia Shankman Orthogenic School at the University of Chicago, 1944–73; expert on emotionally disturbed children. [d. March 13, 1990]

august

1905 *Sam Levene,* U.S. comic character actor; [d. December 29, 1980]

1910 *Tjalling Koopmans,* U.S. economist, born in the Netherlands; Nobel Prize in economics for contributions to the theory of optimum allocation of resources (with F. A. von Hayek), 1975. [d. 1985]

1914 *Richard Tucker (Reuben Ticker),* U.S. operatic tenor; sang with Metropolitan Opera, 1945–75. [d. January 8, 1975]

1919 *Godfrey Newbold Hounsfield,* British scientist; Nobel Prize in physiology or medicine for development of computer-assisted tomography, *CAT scan* (with A.M. Cormack), 1979. [d. February 26, 1985]

1921 *Nancy Kulp,* U.S. actress; known for her role as Jane Hathaway on the television series, *The Beverly Hillbillies,* 1962–71. [d. February 3, 1991]

1925 *Donald O'Connor,* U.S. actor, singer, dancer.

1929 *Roxie Roker,* U.S. actress; known for her role as Helen Willis on the television series, *The Jeffersons,* 1975–84. [d. December 2, 1995]

1930 *Ben Gazzara,* U.S. actor.

1939 *Catherine Patricia (Cassie) Mackin,* U.S. broadcast journalist; first woman to anchor nighttime network newscast. [d. November 20, 1982]

1940 *William Cohen,* U.S. politician, lawyer; U.S. Congressman, 1973–77; U.S. Senator, 1979–97; U.S. Secretary of Defense, 1997– .

1943 *Louis Victor (Lou) Piniella,* U.S. baseball player, baseball manager; outfielder, 1964–68; managed the New York Yankees.

1946 *David Soul,* U.S. actor, singer; starred in the television series, *Here Come the Brides* and *Starsky and Hutch.*

1950 *Ron(ald Ames) Guidry,* U.S. baseball player.

1952 *Rita Dove,* U.S. educator, poet; Pulitzer Prize winner for poetry, 1987.

1958 *Scott Hamilton,* U.S. figure skater; Olympic gold medalist, 1984; known for virtuoso stunts and triple jumps.

1960 *Leroy Chiano,* U.S. astronaut; flew aboard the space shuttle *Columbia.*

1965 *Shania Twain,* Canadian country singer; Grammy winner for the album *The Woman in Me,* 1996.

1967 *Jason Priestly,* Canadian actor; featured on TV drama *Beverly Hills 90210.*

1982 *LeAnn Rimes,* U.S. country singer.

HISTORICAL EVENTS

1619 *Ferdinand II* is elected Holy Roman Emperor.

1850 Richard Wagner's *Lohengrin* premieres under the direction of *Franz Liszt* at Weimar, Germany.

1913 *Palace of Peace* at the Hague is dedicated.

1914 First major encounter between British and German naval forces occurs off *Heligoland (World War I).*

1916 Germany declares war on Rumania *(World War I).*

The Romanians begin an invasion of *Transylvania.*

1943 King *Boris III* of Bulgaria dies and is succeeded by King *Simeon II.*

1944 U.S. Third Army reaches *Marne River* in France *(World War II).*

1950 U.S. Senate ratifies the Charter of the *Organization of American States.*

1955 The *sudden death overtime* rule is invoked in a game between Los Angeles and New York. It is the first time the rule is used in professional football.

1957 Prince *Abdul Rahman* becomes prime minister of Malaya.

1963 Approximately 200,000 demonstrators, supporting the demands for *civil rights* for U.S. blacks, march on Washington; Dr. *Martin Luther King, Jr.* delivers his "I have a dream" speech.

1968 U.S. Vice-president *Hubert H. Humphrey* is nominated as Democratic candidate for U.S. president.

Violence erupts between Chicago police and demonstrators at the headquarters for the Democratic National Convention.

John Gordon Mein, U.S. Ambassador to Guatemala, is assassinated by terrorists.

1992 *Shin Kanemaru,* Vice-President of the Liberal Democratic Party in Japan, resigns after admission of financial wrongdoings.

1994 *Tiger Woods,* age eighteen, becomes the youngest person

to win the U.S. Amateur Golf
Championship.

1995 *Chase Manhattan Corp.* and
Chemical Banking Corp.
announce a merger, resulting
in the largest U.S. bank.

august

AUGUST
29

HOLIDAYS

Slovakia
Anniversay of the Slovak National Uprising Day

RELIGIOUS CALENDAR

Feasts
The Beheading of St. John the Baptist. [d. c. 30] Obligatory Memorial.

The Saints
St. Medericus, abbot. Also called *Merri,* or *Merry.* [d. c. 700]
St. Edwold of Cerne, hermit. Also called *Eadwold.* [d. 9th cent.]
St. Sabina, martyr. [death date unknown]

The Beatified
Blessed Richard Herst, martyr. [d. 1628]
Blessed Joanna Jugan. [beatified 1982]

BIRTHDATES

1619 *Jean Baptiste Colbert,* French government official, businessman; minister to Louis XIV; a financial reformer and organizer; responsible for creation of French Navy. [d. September 6, 1683]

1632 *John Locke,* English philosopher; known as the *Father of English Empiricism.* [d. October 28, 1704]

1780 *Jean-Auguste-Dominique Ingres,* French painter; recognized as a leader among French classicists; best known as a historical painter. [d. January 14, 1867]

Jean Laffite, French pirate; known as the *Pirate of the Gulf;* after British requested his aid, revealed the plans for attack on New Orleans to Americans, assuring U.S. victory in the Battle of New Orleans, 1814. [d. 1825]

1805 *John Frederick Denison Maurice,* British writer and clergyman; founder of *Christian Socialism.* [d. April 1, 1872]

1809 *Oliver Wendell Holmes,* U.S. physician, educator, author; key figure in U.S. literary development; author of *Breakfast Table* series of essays. [d. October 7, 1894]

1826 *George Frisbie Hoar,* U.S. lawyer, public official; U.S. Congressman, 1877–1904; frequent crusader for civil service reform and honesty in government. [d. September 30, 1904]

1862 *Andrew Fisher,* Australian statesman, political leader; Prime Minister, 1908–09; 1910–13; 1913–15. [d. October 22, 1928]

Maurice (Polydore Marie Bernard) Maeterlinck,

Belgian poet, dramatist, and essayist. [d. May 6, 1949]

1871 *Albert Lebrun,* 14th president of France, 1932–40; author of scientific works. [d. March 6, 1950]

1876 *Charles Franklin Kettering,* U.S. engineer, inventor; perfected the *electric self-starter* for automobiles. [d. November 25, 1958]

1899 *Lyman L. Lemnitzer,* U.S. Army general; U.S. Chief of Staff, 1959–60; Chairman, Joint Chiefs of Staff, 1960–62; Supreme Allied Commander, 1963. [d. November 12, 1989]

1904 *Werner Forssmann,* German surgeon; Nobel Prize for physiology or medicine for research into *heart disease* (with D. W. Richards and A. F. Cournand), 1956. [d. June 1, 1979]

1915 *Ingrid Bergman,* Swedish actress; international star of stage and screen. [d. August 29, 1982]

Nathan Pritikin, U.S. nutritionist; Director, Longevity Research Institute, 1976–85; author of diet, exercise, cookbooks. [d. February 21, 1985]

1916 *George Montgomery (George Montgomery Letz),* U.S. actor; known for portraying Western heroes; films include *Riders* *of the Purple Sage* and *Texas Rangers;* starred in the television show, *Cimarron City,* 1958–60.

1920 *Charlie (Bird) Parker,* U.S. jazz musician, composer; helped develop musical form called *bebop.* [d. March 12, 1955]

1923 *Sir Richard (Samuel) Attenborough,* British actor, producer, and film director.

1924 *Dinah Washington,* U.S. jazz singer. [d. December 14, 1963]

1933 *Isabel Gwendolyn Sanford,* U.S. actress; known for her role as Louise Jefferson on the television series, *The Jeffersons,* 1974–85.

1937 *James J. Florio,* U.S. politician; governor of New Jersey, 1990–94.

1938 *Elliott Gould (Elliot Goldstein)* U.S. actor.

1939 *Sir Julius Chan,* Papua-New Guinea statesman; Prime Minister 1980–82.

William Friedkin, U.S. director; Academy Award for *The French Connection,* 1971; directed *The Exorcist* and *To Live and Die in L.A.*

1940 *James S. Brady,* former U.S. press secretary wounded during assassination attempt of President Ronald Reagan in 1981; gun control activist; known for his contributions toward the passage of the Brady Bill.

1945 *Wyomia Tyus,* U.S. sprinter; gold medalist in 1964 and 1968 Olympics.

1946 *Jean Baptiste Bagaza,* President, Republic of Burundi, 1976–87.

1949 *Richard Gere,* U.S. actor; appeared in *An Officer and a Gentleman, American Gigolo,* and *Looking for Mr. Goodbar.*

1958 *Michael Jackson,* U.S. entertainer.

1961 *Rebecca de Mornay,* U.S. actress.

HISTORICAL EVENTS

1268 *Conradin,* the 16-year-old ruler of Germany, is defeated by Charles of Anjou at Tagliacozzo. Conradin is beheaded, setting off waves of disapproval throughout Europe and creating long-lasting alienation between Germany and the Roman Church whose leader, *Pope Clement IV,* approved of the execution.

1475 *Peace of Picquigny* between *Edward IV* of England and *Louis XI* of France is signed, guaranteeing Edward an annual subsidy and stipulating the marriage of his daughter to the French dauphin.

1521 *Sultan Suleiman I,* the Magnificent, of Turkey conquers Belgrade as the Ottomans move across Hungary.

1664 English annex *New Netherlands,* which becomes *New York.*

1708 A party of French and Indians kill 16 inhabitants of *Haverhill, Massachusetts,* and capture 35 more (*Haverhill Massacre*).

1756 *Seven Years' War* breaks out as *Frederick II* of Prussia invades Saxony.

1820 Portuguese rebel against the regency and adopt a

democratic constitution under King *John VI.*

1825 Portugal recognizes the independence of *Brazil.*

1833 *Shaftesbury Factory Act* is passed in Great Britain, authorizing factory inspection and forbidding employment of children under age 9.

1842 *Treaty of Nanking* ends the First Opium War; *Hong Kong* is ceded to Great Britain.

1871 Emperor *Meiji* orders the abolition of feudalism in *Japan.*

1898 *Goodyear Tire & Rubber Co.* is incorporated in Ohio.

1916 *General von Hindenburg* becomes German Chief of the General Staff, with Gen. Ludendorff as first quartermaster general.

1939 German forces invade the Free City of *Danzig* (now Gdansk, Poland) *(World War II).*

1940 *Ramon Castillo* assumes the duties of president of Argentina following the resignation of *Roberto Ortiz.*

1950 *Althea Gibson* becomes the first black woman to compete in a national tennis tournament.

1960 *Hazza El-Majali,* Premier of Jordan, is assassinated.

1961 Aerial reconnaissance photos reveal the presence of Soviet missiles in *Cuba.*

1975 *General Juan Velasco Alvarado,* President of the leftist military government in Peru, is overthrown in a bloodless coup.

august

AUGUST
30

HOLIDAYS

Cyprus, Turkey
Victory Day
Commemorates Turkish victory at
Battle of Dumlupinar, 1922.

Peru
St. Rose of Lima
Commemorates feast of St. Rose, a
native of Peru and the first South
American to be canonized.

U.S. (Louisiana)
Huey P. Long Day.

RELIGIOUS CALENDAR

The Saints
SS. Felix and Adauctus, martyrs. [d.
c. 304]
St. Pammachius, layman. [d. 410]
St. Rumon. Also called *Ruan.* [d. c.
6th century]
St. Fantinus, abbot. [d. 10th
century]

The Beatified
Blessed Bronislava, virgin. [d. 1259]

BIRTHDATES

1494 *Antonio Allegri da Correggio,*
Italian artist; famous works
include *The Assumption of
the Virgin* in the dome of
Parma's cathedral.

1705 *David Hartley,* English
philosopher, physician. [d.
August 28, 1757]

1748 *Jacques-Louis David,* French
artist; founder of French

Classical school of painting;
painter to Napoleon. [d.
December 29, 1825]

1794 *Stephen Watts Kearny,* U.S.
Army general; commanded
American Army of the West
during Mexican War. [d.
October 31, 1948]

1797 *Mary Wollstonecraft Shelley,*
English novelist; author of
Frankenstein, 1818; wife of
Percy Bysshe Shelley. [d.
February 1, 1851]

1811 *Theophile Gautier,* French
poet and novelist. [d. October
23, 1872]

1837 *Ellen Arthur,* wife of U.S.
President Chester A. Arthur.
[d. January 12, 1880]

1852 *Jacobus H. Van't Hoff,* Dutch
physical chemist; Nobel Prize
in chemistry for work on
rates of reaction, chemical
equilibrium, and osmotic
pressure, 1901. [d. March 1,
1911]

1871 *Ernest Rutherford,* 1st Baron
Rutherford of Nelson, British
physicist; Nobel Prize in
chemistry for discoveries in
chemistry of *radioactive
elements,* 1908. [d. October
19, 1937]

1879 *Yoshihito (Taisho),* Japanese
emperor, 1912–26, father of
Hirohito. [d. December 25,
1926]

1884 *Theodor H. E. Svedberg,*
Swedish chemist; Nobel Prize
in chemistry for work on
colloids, 1926. [d. February
26, 1971]

1893 *Huey P(ierce) Long (The
Kingfish),* U.S. politician,
lawyer; Governor of
Louisiana, 1928–32; U.S.
Senator, 1932–35.
Assassinated [d. September
10, 1935]

1896 *Raymond Massey,* U.S. actor,
born in Canada. [d. July 29,
1983]

1901 *John Gunther,* U.S. journalist,
author, radio and television
commentator; noted for his
series of books providing
analyses of various countries
and regions: *Inside Europe,*
1936, *Inside Russia Today,*
1958, etc. [d. May 29, 1970]

Roy Wilkins, U.S. civil rights
leader; Executive Director,
NAACP, 1964–77. [d.
September 8, 1981]

1904 *Charles E. (Chip) Bohlen,* U.S.
diplomat; Soviet affairs
specialist; U.S. Ambassador to
U.S.S.R., 1953–57; U.S.
Ambassador to the
Philippines, 1957–59; U.S.
Ambassador to France,
1962–68. [d. January 2, 1974]

1907 *Shirley Booth (Thelma Booth
Ford),* U.S. actress. [d.
October 16, 1992]

1908 *Fred(erick Martin) Macmurray,* U.S. actor. [d. November 5, 1991]

1909 *Joan Blondell,* U.S. comedic actress. [d. December 25, 1979]

1912 *Edward Mills Purcell,* U.S. physicist; Nobel Prize in physics for development of methods for precise measurement of atomic nucleic magnetic fields (with F. Bloch), 1952. [d. March 7, 1997]

1927 *Geoffrey Beene,* U.S. fashion designer; President and designer, Geoffrey Beene Incorporated, 1962– .

1930 *Warren Buffet,* U.S. businessman; known for his investment abilities.

1934 *Gary Collins,* U.S. actor.

1935 *Sylvia A. Earle,* U.S. oceanographer; known for her development of self-contained underwater breathing apparatus along with her husband Graham Hawkes.

John Phillips, U.S. singer; former member of the rock group, *The Mamas and the Papas.*

1939 *Elizabeth Ashley (Elizabeth Ann Cole),* U.S. actress; Tony Award, 1962; films include *The Carpet Baggers,* 1963.

1943 *Jean-Claude Killy,* French skier. Olympic gold medalist, 1968; World Cup championship, 1967, 1968.

1944 *Frank Edwin (Tug) McGraw,* U.S. baseball player.

1947 *Peggy Lipton,* U.S. actress; starred in the television series, *The Mod Squad,* 1968–73.

1951 *Timothy Bottoms,* U.S. actor; starred in the film, *The Last Picture Show;* brother of Joseph and Sam Bottoms.

HISTORICAL EVENTS

1125 *Lothair of Saxony* is elected king of Germany.

1483 *Louis XI* of France dies and is succeeded by Charles VIII.

1757 Russians win at Gross Jägersdorf and occupy East Prussia (*Seven Years' War*).

1914 The German 8th Army under Von Hindenburg envelops and practically annihilates a Russian army in the *Battle of Tannenberg.* General Samsonov, the Russian commander, commits suicide (*World War I*).

Germans make first air raid on Paris (*World War I*).

1916 Turkey joins her allies, Germany and Austria, and declares war against Romania (*World War I*).

1918 Lenin survives an assassination attempt by social revolutionary *Dora Kaplan.*

1928 *Jawaharlal Nehru* founds *Independence of India League* to work toward freedom from British rule.

1942 U.S. Naval and Army forces occupy *Adak* in the Aleutian Islands.

1944 Soviet troops capture the oil refineries at *Ploesti, Romania,* cutting off Germany's only remaining oil supply (*World War II*).

1945 U.S. occupation forces land at Tokyo Bay and begin U.S. occupation of Japan (*World War II*).

1957 U.S. Senator *Strom Thurmond* of South Carolina sets a new filibuster record in the U.S. Congress when he speaks for 24 hours, 27 minutes against a civil rights bill.

1963 A "*hot-line*" is established between leaders of the U.S. and U.S.S.R. to facilitate emergency communication.

1966 *The Beatles* perform their last concert as a group.

1983 A crew member on the space shuttle, *Challenger,* Lieutenant Colonel *Guion Bluford,* becomes the first black astronaut in space.

1988 *Vicki Keith* becomes the first person to swim all five of the Great Lakes when she sets a distance record across Lake Ontario.

1989 *Leona Helmsley,* U.S. hotel business owner, is convicted of tax evasion and tax fraud.

1992 *Marie Jepsen* becomes the first female Lutheran bishop.

1995 *United Nations forces* attack Bosnian Serb targets in retaliation for the bombing of Sarejevo.

august

AUGUST
31

HOLIDAYS

Afghanistan
Pushtoonistan Day

Kyrgyzstan
Independence Day

Malaysia
National Day
Celebrates Malaysia's achievement of independent status in British Commonwealth, 1957.

Trinidad and Tobago
Independence Day
Celebrates the achievement of independence and membership in the Commonwealth of Nations, 1962, and the promulgation of a new constitution, 1976.

RELIGIOUS CALENDAR

The Saints
St. Paulinus, Bishop of Trier. [d. 358]
St. Aidan, Bishop of Lindisfarne. Also called *Ædan.* [d. 651]
St. Cuthburga, Abbess of Wimborne, and widow. Feast formerly September 3. [d. c. 725]
St. Quenburga, nun. Also called *Coenburga.* [d. c. 735]
St. Raymund Nonnatus, cardinal; patron saint of midwives, women in labor, and little children. [d. 1240]

The Beatified
Blessed Laurence Nerucci and his companions, martyrs. [d. 1420]

Blessed Juvenal Ancina, Bishop of Saluzzo. [d. 1604]

BIRTHDATES

12 *Caligula (Gaius Caesar Augustus Germanicus),* Roman emperor, 37–41; great-grandson of Augustus Caesar. [d. January 24, 41]

1821 *Hermann Ludwig Ferdinand von Helmholtz,* German physiologist, physicist; known for numerous contributions to science; one of the formulators of the principle of the *conservation of energy.* [d. September 8, 1894]

1822 *Fitz-John Porter,* Union Army general during U.S. Civil War. [d. May 21, 1901]

1838 *Abel Bergaigne,* French linguist, philologist, and Sanskrit scholar. [d. August 6, 1888]

1870 *Maria Montessori,* Italian physician, educator; first woman in Italy to receive medical degree (1894); developed *Montessori method* of child education. [d. May 6, 1952]

1880 *Wilhelmina,* Queen of the Netherlands, 1890–1948; abdicated in favor of her daughter, Beatrix. [d. November 28, 1962]

1885 *Du Bose Heyward,* U.S. poet, novelist, and playwright;

author of novel *Porgy* from which opera *Porgy and Bess* was developed. [d. June 16, 1940]

1897 *Fredric March (Frederic McIntyre Bickel),* U.S. actor; popular leading dramatic actor during 1930s and 1940s. [d. April 14, 1975]

1903 *William Saroyan,* U.S. short-story writer, playwright, known for his light-hearted, poignant stories; declined the 1940 Pulitzer Prize for *The Time of Your Life.* [d. May 18, 1981]

Arthur Godfrey, U.S. broadcaster and entertainer; his audience reached over 82 million in the 1950s. [d. March 16, 1983]

1907 *Ramón Magsaysay,* President of the Philippine Republic, 1953–57. [d. March 17, 1957]

1913 *Sir Alfred Charles Bernard Lovell,* British astronomer; front-runner in development of radio telescopic devices; responsible for development of the first major *radio telescope,* for Nuffield Radio Astronomy Labs, 1957.

1914 *Richard Basehart,* U.S. actor. [d. September 18, 1984]

1918 *Alan Jay Lerner,* U.S. playwright, lyricist; frequent collaborator with Frederick Loewe (June 10) for

Broadway musical scores. [d. June 14, 1986]

(Theodore Samuel) Ted Williams, U.S. baseball player; last major leaguer to hit over .400 (.406 in 1941); inducted into Baseball Hall of Fame, 1966.

1924 *Buddy Hackett (Leonard Hucker),* U.S. comedian.

1928 *James Coburn,* U.S. actor.

1930 *Raymond James Donovan,* U.S. government official, U.S. Secretary of Labor, 1981–85.

1931 *Jean Beliveau,* Canadian hockey player.

1935 *Frank Robinson,* U.S. baseball player, manager; first black to manage a major league team (Cleveland Indians, 1974); elected to Baseball Hall of Fame, 1982.

1936 *Marva Deloise Nettles Collins,* U.S. teacher, reformer; started Chicago school, Westside Preparatory, 1975.

1939 *Paul Winter,* U.S. musician, composer.

1945 *Itzhak Perlman,* Israeli violinist.

Van Morrison, Irish-born singer, songwriter.

1955 *Edwin Moses,* U.S. hurdler; Olympic gold medalist, 1976, 1984.

1968 *Hideo Nomo,* Japanese-born baseball player; rookie of the year (National League), 1995.

HISTORICAL EVENTS

1422 *Henry V* of England dies and is succeeded by *Henry VI,* 9 months old.

1823 *Battle of Trocadero* is lost by Spanish revolutionaries, bringing the revolution to an end and restoring the repressive *Ferdinand VII* to the throne.

1895 First U.S. *professional football game* is played at *Latrobe, Pennsylvania,* between the Latrobe team of profit-sharing players and the *Jeannette, Pennsylvania* team. In hiring a substitute quarterback for $10 in expenses, Latrobe employed the first professional player, *John Brallier.*

1907 Anglo-Russian agreement is signed aligning Russia, Britain, and France against the *Triple Alliance* of Germany, Austria-Hungary, and Italy.

1914 *Greece* declares her neutrality in *World War I.*

1919 *Communist Labor Party of America* is founded at Chicago, Illinois.

1928 *Die Dreigroschenoper (The Threepenny Opera)* premieres in Berlin, starring Lotte Lenya, with music by Kurt Weill, and lyrics by Bertolt Brecht.

1935 U.S. President Franklin D. Roosevelt signs the *Neutrality Act* of 1935.

1942 *Battle of Alam El Halfa* in Egypt begins, with Rommel's German forces attacking the superior British (*World War II*).

1944 U.S. naval ships and aircraft attack *Iwo Jima* and the Bonin Islands (*World War II*).

1952 *Jose Maria Velasco Ibarra* is inaugurated as president of Ecuador.

1957 *Malaya* becomes an independent member of the British Commonwealth.

1962 Colony of *Trinidad and Tobago* becomes an independent member of the Commonwealth of Nations.

1964 U.S. President Lyndon B. Johnson signs the *Food Stamp Act,* designed to aid needy families by establishing a cooperative federal-state food assistance program.

1970 *Edward Akufo-Addo* is inaugurated as president of Ghana.

1976 *Trinidad and Tobago* adopts a new constitution under which it becomes a republic.

1994 The *Irish Republican Army (IRA)* enters into peace talks with England.

1997 *Diana, Princess of Wales,* is killed in an automobile accident in Paris, France.

august

September is the ninth month of the Gregorian calendar and has 30 days. The name is derived from the Latin *septem,* 'seven,' designating its position as the seventh month in the early Roman calendar. As with the other numerically named months, October, November and December, September has retained this anachronistic designation; attempts by the Roman Senate to change the name after *Januarius* was adopted as the first month of the 12-month calendar met with failure, and the misleading etymology remains today.

In the northern hemisphere, September is the month of the autumnal equinox, occurring about September 22, after which nighttime is longer than daylight. September is also associated with harvest festivals, cider-making, the southerly migration of birds, the beginning of the school year, and the end of the summer vacation period.

In the astrological calendar, September spans the zodiac signs of Virgo, the Virgin (August 23–September 22) and Libra, the Balance (September 23–October 22).

The birthstone for September is the sapphire, and the flower is the aster or the morning glory.

STATE, NATIONAL, AND INTERNATIONAL HOLIDAYS

Labor Day
(Canada, South Africa, United States)
First Monday

Primary Election Day
(Wisconsin)
First Tuesday
(Wyoming)
Second Tuesday

Rose of Tralee Festival
(Ireland)
Early in the Month

Sherry Wine Harvest
(Jerez de la Frontera, Spain)
Mid-Month
Third Sunday

SPECIAL EVENTS AND THEIR SPONSORS

Cable TV Month
Richard R. Falk Associates

Philatelic Publications Month
Franklin D. Roosevelt Philatelic Society

Sight Saving Month
American Society to Prevent Blindness

Youth Activities Month
Rotary International

National Rub a Bald Head Week
Second Week
Bald Headed Men of America, Inc.

Constitution Week
Third Week
National Society of the Daughters of the AmericanRevolution

National Farm Safety Week
Third Week
National Safety Council

National Rehabilitation Week
Third Week
Allied Services for the Handicapped, Inc.

Tolkien Week
Week containing September 22
American Tolkien Society

Snack a Pickle Time
Final Two Weeks
Pickle Packers International, Ltd.

Be Late for Something Day
September 5
Procrastinators' Club of America

Swap Ideas Day
September 10
Puns Corp.

National Play-Doh Day
September 16
Kenner Products

Constitution Day
September 17
Federal Union, Inc.

Hobbit Day
September 22
American Tolkien Society

Kids' Day
September 24
Kiwanis International

National Grandparents' Day
First Sunday after Labor Day
Marion McQuade Founder National
Grandparents Day

Defenders' Day
Sunday nearest Sunday 13–14
Star-Spangled Banner Flag House
and 1812 Museum

National Hunting and Fishing Day
Fourth Saturday
National Shooting Sports Foundation

National Good Neighbor Day
Fourth Sunday
Good Neighbor Day Foundation

SEPTEMBER
1

HOLIDAYS

Cameroon
Union Nationale Camerounaise Day

Libya
National Day or Revolution Day

Mexico
Public Holiday
President presents his annual messages.

Syria
Public Holiday
Commemorates the union of Syria, Egypt, and Libya.

Tanzania
Heroes' Day

Uzbekistan
Independence Day

RELIGIOUS CALENDAR

The Saints

St. Lupus, Bishop of Sens. Also called *Leu.* [d. 623]

St. Fiacre, hermit; invoked against all kinds of physical ills, including hemorrhoids and venereal disease; patron saint of gardeners and of cab drivers in Paris. Also called *Fefre, Fiachra,* or *Fiaker.* [d. c.670]

St. Sebbe, co-ruler of the East Saxons. Also called *Sebba, Sebbi.* [d. c. 694]

St. Drithelm, layman and visionary. [d. c. 700]

St. Giles, abbot; patron of Edinburgh, the indigent and crippled, and of spurmakers. Invoked against cancer, sterility in women, insanity, and night dangers. Also called *Aegidius.* [death date unknown]

St. Priscus of Capua, martyr. [death date unknown]

The Twelve Brothers, martyrs. [death date unknown]

St. Verena, virgin. [death date unknown]

The Beatified

Blessed John of Perugia and Blessed Peter of Sassoferrato, martyrs. [d. 1231]

Blessed Joan Soderini, virgin. [d. 1367]

Blessed Hugh More, martyr. [d. 1588]

Blessed Gabra Michael, martyr. Also called *Gabra Mika'el, Gilmichael, Michel Ghæebræe.* [d. 1855]

BIRTHDATES

1653 *Johann Pachelbel,* German composer, organist; composed *Hexachordum Apollinis,* 1699. [d. March 3, 1706]

1792 *Chester Harding,* U.S. portrait painter; noted for portraits of such famous Americans as Daniel Boone, Daniel Webster, and John C. Calhoun. [d. April 1, 1866]

1795 *James Gordon Bennett,* U.S. journalist, publisher, born in Scotland; founder of the *New York Herald,* 1834. [d. June 1, 1872]

1813 *Mark Hopkins,* U.S. railroad organizer, executive. [d. March 29, 1878]

1822 *Hiram Rhodes Revels,* U.S. clergyman, educator, politician; first black member of U.S. Congress, 1870–71. [d. January 16, 1901]

1854 *Engelbert Humperdinck,* German composer, best known for his fairy-tale operas, *Hansel und Gretel* and *Die Königskinder.* [d. September 27, 1921]

1864 *Sir Roger David Casement,* British civil servant, Irish rebel; knighted, 1910; later sought German assistance for Irish nationalist cause; hanged as a traitor by the British. [d. August 3, 1916]

1866 *James J. (Gentleman Jim) Corbett,* U.S. boxer; commonly regarded as the first scientific boxer, a reputation he earned by the techniques he developed to compensate for his small hands. [d. February 18, 1933]

1875 *Edgar Rice Burroughs,* U.S. novelist, known especially for his *Tarzan* novels, 1914–49, which had sold more than 35 million copies by the time of his death. [d. March 19, 1950]

1877 *Francis William Aston,* British chemist; Nobel Prize in chemistry for discovery of *isotopes* using the mass spectrograph, 1922. [d. November 20, 1945]

1878 *John Frederick Charles Fuller,* British military officer, theorist; wrote numerous books dealing with concept of mechanized warfare; greatly influenced military theories of post-World War I Europe. [d. February 10, 1966]

1892 *Leverett Saltonstall,* U.S. politician; Governor of Massachusetts, 1939–44; Senator, 1944–67. [d. June 17, 1979]

1900 *Don Wilson,* U.S. entertainer, radio and television announcer, producer; known for his role as Jack Benny's straight man. [d. April 25, 1982]

1907 *Joaquin Balaguer,* Dominican political leader; President of the Dominican Republic, 1960, 1966–78, 1986–

Walter (Philip) Reuther, U.S. labor leader; President, United Auto Workers, 1946–70; President, Congress of Industrial Organization, 1952–70; played significant role in formation of AFL-CIO, 1955. [d. May 10, 1970]

1920 *Elizabeth Sutherland (Liz) Carpenter,* U.S. journalist; Press Secretary, Staff Director for Lady Bird Johnson, 1963–69.

1922 *Vittorio Gassman,* Italian actor.

Melvin (Robert) Laird, U.S. politician, government official; Congressman, 1953–69; Secretary of Defense,

1967–73; espoused reduction of size of U.S. armed forces; Counsellor for National and International Affairs, Reader's Digest Association.

1923 *Rocky Marciano (Rocco Marchegiano),* U.S. boxer; undefeated world heavyweight champion, 1952–56. [d. August 31, 1969]

1924 *Yvonne De Carlo (Peggy Middleton),* Canadian actress.

1930 *Geoffrey Holder,* Trinidadian-born actor, director; Tony Awards as director and costume designer for the Broadway play, *The Wiz.*

1933 *George Maharis,* U.S. actor; appeared in the television series, *Route 66* and *Most Deadly Game.*

Conway Twitty, U.S. country-and-western singer. [d. June 5, 1993]

1935 *Seiji Ozawa,* Japanese orchestra conductor; Musical Director, Boston Symphony Orchestra.

1936 *Lily Tomlin,* U.S. actress, comedienne.

1944 *Leonard Slatkin,* U. S. conductor; Music Director, St. Louis Symphony Orchestra; Grammy Award, 1985.

1946 *Douglas (Barry) Gibb,* British singer, songwriter, guitarist; member of the rock group, *The Bee Gees;* featured on *Saturday Night Fever* soundtrack which sold 50 million copies, 1976–79.

1951 *Mary Elizabeth Cunningham,* U.S. business executive; President, Semper Corporation; wrote autobiography, *Powerplay,* 1984.

1957 *Gloria Estefan,* Cuban-born pop singer.

HISTORICAL EVENTS

891 *Arnulf,* Holy Roman Emperor, defeats the Normans at *Louvain.*

1192 *Richard I* of England *(the Lion-Hearted)* and *Saladin* of Damascus sign a truce, allowing the Crusaders free access to the Holy Sepulchre *(Third Crusade).*

1494 *Charles VIII* of France invades Italy in support of *Lodovico the Moor.*

1715 *Louis XIV of France* dies and is succeeded by his great-grandson, *Louis XV.*

1836 The party of *Marcus Whitman* reaches *Fort Walla Walla* on the Columbia River, establishing the first U.S. settlement in (what was then) Territory of Northern Oregon.

1858 *East India Company's* government of India ends with the British Crown taking over its territories and duties.

1864 *Charlottetown Conference* is convened on Prince Edward Island, representing the beginning of steps toward Canadian confederation.

1888 *Pontifical College Josephinum,* the first papal seminary in the U.S., is founded in Worthington, Ohio.

1900 *South African Republic* is annexed by Great Britain.

1905 Canadian Provinces of *Alberta* and *Saskatchewan* are established.

1916 U.S. Federal *Child Labor Act (Keating-Owen Act)* bars the products of *child labor* from interstate commerce.

Bulgaria declares war against Romania (*World War I*).

1923 Great *earthquake* in Japan completely destroys *Yokohama* and nearly destroys *Tokyo;* more than 100,000 lives are lost.

The *Royal Australian Air Force* is established.

1929 *Graf Zeppelin* completes first aerial circumnavigation of globe by a *dirigible.*

1937 *National Housing Act (Wagner-Steagall Act)* establishes *U.S. Housing Authority.*

1939 *George C. Marshall* is appointed U.S. Army chief of staff.

Germany, invades Poland without warning, precipitating *World War II.*

1951 The U.S., Australia, and New Zealand sign the *ANZUS Treaty,* providing for their mutual defense.

1966 California grape pickers elect *Cesar Chavez,* leader of the *Farm Workers Union,* to represent them as chief bargaining agent.

1969 Military officers overthrow government of *Libya;* Libyan Arab Republic is proclaimed under Colonel *Mu'ammar al-Qadhafi.*

1971 *Qatar* gains its independence from Great Britain.

1972 *Bobby Fischer* becomes the first American to hold the world chess title by defeating Soviet player, *Boris Spassky.*

1977 *Cuba* and the U.S. exchange low-level missions, a step toward restoration of full diplomatic relations.

1979 The U.S. unmanned spacecraft *Pioneer 11,* launched in 1973, transmits data to earth after coming within 20,200 km (12,560 miles) of Saturn's clouds; it surveyed Jupiter in 1974.

1980 *Sandy Hawley,* U.S. jockey, wins his 4,000th race, the 11th jockey in thoroughbred racing history to do so.

1981 A bloodless coup ousts President *David Dacko* of Central African Republic; General *Andrè Kolingba* is new government head.

1983 Korean Air Line *Flight 007,* an unarmed commercial airliner, crosses into Soviet airspace and is shot down over the Sea of Japan by a Soviet fighter; all 269 aboard perish.

1985 U.S. and French explorers discover the sunken remains of the *Titanic* luxury liner 500 miles off the coast of Newfoundland.

1987 *Lovastatin,* a highly effective drug for reducing cholesterol in the bloodstream, is approved for marketing by the U.S. Food and Drug Administration.

1985 The remains of the ocean luxury liner *Titanic* are discovered in the North Atlantic.

1995 The *Rock and Roll Hall of Fame and Museum* opens in Cleveland, Ohio.

september

SEPTEMBER
2

HOLIDAYS

Vietnam
National Day
First day of a two-day celebration.

RELIGIOUS CALENDAR

The Saints
St. Antoninus, martyr. [d. 4th cent.]
St. Castor, Bishop of Apt. [d. c. 425]
St. Agricolus, Bishop of Avignon; invoked to bring both rain and fair weather. [d. 7th cent.]
St. William, Bishop of Roskilde. Also called Bishop of Roschild. [d. c. 1070]
St. Brocard, cofounder of the Order of Carmelite Friars. Also called *Burchard.* [d. c. 1231]

The Beatified
Blessed Margaret of Louvain, virgin and martyr. [d. c. 1225]
Blessed John du Lau, Archbishop of Arles, and his Companions, the martyrs of September. Victims of the French Revolution. [d. 1792]

BIRTHDATES

1778 *Louis Bonaparte,* brother of Napoleon I and King of the Netherlands, 1806–10. [d. July 25, 1846]

1837 *James Harrison Wilson,* Union Army general during U.S. Civil War. [d. February 23, 1925]

1838 *Lydia Kamekeha Liluokalani,* Queen of Hawaiian Islands; last sovereign to rule Hawaii before annexation by U.S.; deposed, 1893. [d. November 11, 1917]

1839 *Henry George,* U.S. economist, social reformer, journalist; noted for his theories of economics based on land ownership. [d. October 29, 1897]

1840 *Giovanni Verga,* Italian novelist; leader of Sicilian realist school. [d. January 27, 1922]

1841 *Prince Hirobumi Ito,* Japanese statesman; Prime Minister, 1886–1901; assassinated by a Korean radical. [d. October 26, 1909]

1850 *Eugene Field,* U.S. poet, journalist; pioneer of personal feature column. [d. November 4, 1895]

Albert Goodwill Spalding, U.S. baseball player, businessman; Hall of Fame pitcher; first in major league baseball to win 200 games; founded sporting goods firm, 1876. [d. September 9, 1915]

1853 *Friedrich Wilhelm Ostwald,* German chemist; Nobel Prize in chemistry for work on *rates of chemical reaction,* 1909. [d. April 4, 1932]

1864 *Miguel de Unamuno y Jugo,* Spanish philosopher, writer, educator; subject of controversy because of his pro-republican leanings. [d. December 31, 1936]

1866 *Hiram Warren Johnson,* U.S. lawyer, politician; governor of California, 1911–17; U.S. Senator, 1917–45; favored U.S. neutrality in World War I. [d. August 6, 1945]

1877 *Frederick Soddy,* British chemist; Nobel Prize in chemistry for his work with *radioactive substances,* 1921. [d. Sept. 22, 1956]

1917 *Cleveland Amory,* U.S. journalist, author.

1918 *Allen Smart Drury,* U.S. novelist, journalist; known for his penetrating novels about U.S. politics; Pulitzer Prize in fiction, 1960, for *Advise and Consent.* [d. September 2, 1998]

Fania Fenelon (Fanny Goldstein), French author, musician, singer; autobiography, *Playing for Time,* tells of horrors as inmate of Nazi concentration camps. [d. December 20, 1983]

Martha Elizabeth Beall Mitchell, wife of John Mitchell, U.S. Attorney General, 1969–72; known for calling reporters in the middle of the night with

Washington gossip. [d. May 31, 1976]

1923 *Marge Champion (Marjorie Celeste Belcher)*, U.S. dancer, actress; with her husband, Gower (June 22), appeared in numerous musical films during 1930s and 1940s.

1924 *Daniel arap Moi*, Kenyan politician; president of Kenya, 1978– .

1928 *Horace Ward Martin Tavares Silver*, U.S. jazz musician, pianist, composer (*Senor Blues, Sister Sadie*); leader of *Horace Silver Quintet*.

1933 *Mathieu Kerekou*, President, People's Republic of Benin, 1972–91, 1996– .

1937 *Peter Victor Ueberroth*, U.S. businessman, baseball executive; President, Los Angeles Olympic Organizing Committee, 1979–84; Baseball Commissioner, 1984–89.

1948 *Terry Paxton Bradshaw*, U.S. football player, sports anchor; quarterback, Pittsburgh Steelers, 1970–83; led Steelers to four Super Bowl victories.

(Sharon) Christa Corrigan McAuliffe, U.S. teacher; first teacher in space; died in the explosion of the space shuttle, *Challenger*. [d. January 28, 1986]

1951 *Mark Harmon*, U.S. actor; starred in the television series, *St. Elsewhere*, 1984–86 and *Chicago Hope*, 1996–; son of Tom Harmon; husband of Pam Dawber.

1952 *Jimmy Connors*, U.S. tennis player.

1955 *Linda Purl*, U.S. actress; featured in the films, *W.C. Fields and Me* and *The High Country*; appeared in the television series, *Matlock*, 1986.

1960 *Eric Demetric Dickerson*, U.S. football player; National Football League records for the most yards rushing by a rookie and most yards rushing in season.

1964 *Keanu Reeves*, U.S. actor.

1972 *Dineh Mohajer*, U.S. businesswoman; founder of Hard Candy (nail polish company).

HISTORICAL EVENTS

31BC *Mark Antony* is defeated at *Actium* by Roman legions under Octavian (Augustus Caesar).

1644 In England, the army of the 3rd earl of Essex surrenders to *Charles I* at *Lostwithiel (English Civil War)*.

1666 *Great Fire of London* begins, lasting four days and destroying almost all of the City of London.

1789 *U.S. Department of the Treasury* is established.

1864 Union forces under *General Sherman* occupy Atlanta, Georgia (*U.S. Civil War*).

1870 *Napoleon III* capitulates to Prussians at *Sedan (Franco-Prussian War)*.

1898 *Lord Kitchener* decisively defeats the Dervishes at the *Battle of Omdurman* in the Sudan.

1914 The French government moves to *Bordeaux* as German troops move toward Paris (*World War I*).

1918 U.S. recognizes *Czechoslovakia* as a nation.

1930 Captain *Dieudonne Coste* and *Maurice Ballante* complete first nonstop flight from Paris to New York.

1945 Japanese premier and military leaders sign formal surrender on board the *U.S.S. Missouri* in Tokyo Bay, ending *World War II*. The Viet-Minh coalition proclaims the *Democratic Republic of Vietnam*, with *Ho Chi Minh* as president.

1957 *Abubakar Tafawa Balewa* becomes the first prime minister of the Nigerian Federation.

1969 Rock music festival on the *Isle of Wight* attracts more than 250,000 spectators.

1985 *Son Sen* is chosen to replace former Kampuchean prime minister, *Pol Pot*, as commander-in-chief of the guerrilla group, *Khmer Rouge*.

september

SEPTEMBER
3

HOLIDAYS

France, Monaco
Liberation of Monaco

Qatar
Independence Day
Commemorates Qatar's achievement of independence from Great Britain, 1971.

San Marino
St. Marinus Day or Republic Day
Official Foundation Day. A celebration of the patron saint of the country.

Tunisia
Commemoration of September 3, 1934
Commemorates the beginning of the Tunisian independence movement, 1934.

Vietnam
National Day
Second day of a two-day celebration.

RELIGIOUS CALENDAR

The Saints
St. Phoebe. [d. 1st cent.]
St. Macanisius, bishop. Also called *Aengus Mac Nisse, Macrisius.* [d. 514]
St. Simeon Stylites the Younger, [d. 592]
St. Aigulf, martyr. [d. c. 676]
St. Hildelitha, Abbess of Barking and virgin. Also called *Hildilid.* [d. c. 717]

The Beatified
Blessed Guala, Bishop of Brescia. [d. 1244]

Blessed Andrew of Borgo San Sepolcro, Servite friar. [d. 1315]

BIRTHDATES

1803 *Prudence Crandall,* U.S. educator; arrested after she admitted black girls to her Connecticut school in 1833. [d. January 28, 1890]

1827 *Gísli Brynjúlfsson,* Icelandic poet; spread the influences of European romanticism in Icelandic literature. [d. May 29, 1888]

1849 *Sarah Orne Jewett,* U.S. novelist, shortstory writer. [d. June 24, 1909]

1856 *Louis H. Sullivan,* U.S. architect; considered the *Father of Modern American Architecture,* especially noted for early *skyscraper* design. [d. April 14, 1924]

1859 *Jean Léon Jaures,* French Socialist leader; founder and editor of *L'Humanité,* 1904–14. [d. July 31, 1914]

1860 *Edward Albert Filene,* U.S. merchant, philanthropist; founder of Filene's, one of Boston's leading department stores; promoter of credit union movement in U.S. [d. September 26, 1937]

1869 *Fritz Pregl,* Austrian chemist; Nobel Prize in chemistry for

development of methods of *microanalysis of organic substances,* 1923. [d. December 13, 1930]

1875 *Ferdinand Porsche,* Austrian auto manufacturer, inventor; invented the German Volkswagon. [d. January 30, 1951]

1899 Sir *Frank Macfarlane Burnet,* Australian physician; Nobel Prize in physiology or medicine for discovery of *acquired immunity* (with P.B. Medawar), 1960. (d. August 31, 1985]

1900 *Sally Benson,* U.S. novelist, short-story writer; author of *Meet Me in St. Louis,* an autobiographical novel that was made into a highly successful film, 1944. [d. July 19, 1972]

1905 *Carl David Anderson,* U.S. physicist; Nobel Prize in physics for discovery of the *positron,* 1936.

1907 *Loren C(orey) Eiseley,* U.S. anthropologist, naturalist; noted for his writings on early human habitations of North America and interpretations of Darwin's influence on scientific development in the 20th century. [d. July 9, 1977]

1913 *Alan Ladd,* U.S. actor. [d. January 29, 1964]

1914 *Dixy Lee Ray,* U.S. politician, marine biologist; chairperson of Atomic Energy Commission, 1973–75; U.S. Assistant Secretary of State, 1975–77; Governor of Washington, 1977–80. [d. January 2, 1994]

1915 *Kitty Carlisle (Katherine Conn),* U.S. actress, singer; appeared in the film, *A Night at the Opera;* known as a panelist on the television series, *To Tell the Truth,* 1956–67; wife of Moss Hart.

1920 *Marguerite Higgins,* U.S. journalist; Pulitzer Prize for her coverage of front-line action during Korean War, 1951; reported on Vietnam War, 1960s. [d. January 3, 1966]

1926 *Alison Lurie,* U.S. author; Pulitzer Prize for *Foreign Affairs,* 1984.

Irene Papas, Greek actress.

1927 *Hugh Swanson Sidey,* U.S. author; columnist for *Time* magazine.

1936 *Anne Jackson,* U.S. actress.

1937 *Eileen Regina Brennan,* U.S. actress; starred in the television series and movie version of *Private Benjamin.*

1943 *Valerie Perrine,* U.S. actress; appeared in the films, *Lenny* and *Superman II.*

1947 *Marilyn McCoo,* U.S. singer, actress; member of the musical group, *The Fifth Dimension,* 1966–73; co-host of the television series, *Solid Gold.*

1965 *Charlie Sheen (Carlos Irwin Estavez),* U.S. actor; appeared in the films *Wall Street* and *Platoon;* son of Martin Sheen; brother of Emilio Estevez.

HISTORICAL EVENTS

1650 *Oliver Cromwell* of England defeats Scots at *Dunbar.*

1651 *Oliver Cromwell* defeats royal army of *Charles I* at *Worcester.*

1654 *First Protectorate* Parliament under *Oliver Cromwell* meets in England.

1658 *Oliver Cromwell,* Protector of England, dies and is succeeded by his son, Richard.

1783 *Treaty of Paris,* signed between the U.S. and Great Britain, recognizes the independence of the *United States.*

1826 *Nicholas I* is crowned czar of all the Russias at Moscow.

1879 British residents of *Kabul* are massacred by native Afghans.

1903 The *Humane Society* holds its first meeting in Newark, New Jersey.

1914 *Pope Benedict XV* is elected.

1918 *Second Battles of the Somme and of Arras* end with the Germans being pushed back behind the Hindenburg Line from which they had first advanced in March (*World War I*).

1919 *John J. Pershing* is named U.S. General of the Armies.

1939 Great Britain and France declare war against Germany following Germany's invasion of Poland (*World War II*).

1943 British 8th Army invades Italy from Sicily (*World War II*).

1944 U.S. naval task group attacks *Wake Island (World War II).*

1962 *Jens Otto Krag* is named prime minister of Denmark.

1967 Military ticket of *Nguyen Van Thieu* and *Nguyen Cao Ky* wins by an overwhelming majority in South Vietnamese presidential and vice-presidential elections.

1976 U.S. satellite, *Viking 2,* lands on *Mars* and begins sending back photographs of the Martian landscape.

1984 The Vatican issues its first report on *liberation theology.* The document reasserts the Catholic Church's commitment to the poor but condemns the political radicalization of some of its clergy in the Third World.

september

SEPTEMBER
4

HOLIDAYS

Venezuela
Civil Servants' Day

RELIGIOUS CALENDAR

The Saints

SS. Marcellus and Valerian, martyrs. [d. c. 178]

St. Marinus, deacon. [d. c. 4th cent.]

St. Boniface I, pope. Elected 418; patron of *Germany.* [d. 422]

St. Ultan, bishop. [d. 657]

St. Ida of Herzfeld, widow. [d. 825]

St. Rosalia, virgin; principal patron of *Palermo.* [d. c. 1160]

St. Rose of Viterbo, virgin. Also called *Rosa.* [d. c.1252]

The Beatified

Blessed Catherine of Racconigi, virgin. [d. 1547]

BIRTHDATES

1241 *Alexander III,* King of Scotland, 1249–86; responsible for consolidating royal power in Scotland. [d. March 18 or 19, 1286]

1768 *François-René Vicomte de Châteaubriand,* French writer, statesman; author of *René,* a seminal work in the French Romantic movement. [d. July 4, 1848]

1793 *Edward Bates,* U.S. politician; the first U.S. cabinet member (Attorney General, 1861–1864 from west of the Mississippi. [d. March 25, 1869]

1802 *Marcus Whitman,* U.S. Congregational missionary, pioneer, physician; responsible for the settlement of a large part of the *Northwest Territory;* massacred by Cayuse Indians. [d. November 29, 1847]

1803 *Sarah Childress Polk,* wife of James Polk, 11th U.S. President; served as her husband's official secretary; banned dancing and liquor from the White House. [d. August 14, 1891]

1824 *Anton Bruckner,* Austrian composer, organist; composed nine symphonies and three grand masses in the Romantic tradition. [d. October 11, 1896]

1846 *Daniel Hudson Burnham,* U.S. architect, city planner; member of the architectural firm, Burnham and Root, which designed the first building to be called a *skyscraper;* designed the site of the World's Columbian Exposition in Chicago, 1893; his *Report on Washington, D.C.,* which outlined a long-range plan of development for the city, marked the beginning of *city planning* in the U.S. [d. June 1, 1912]

1848 *Lewis Howard Latimer,* U.S. inventor, draftsman, engineer; associate of Alexander Graham Bell (March 3). [d. 1928]

1851 *John Dillon,* Irish nationalist politician; member of the British Parliament, 1880–83, 1885–1918. [d. August 4, 1927]

1899 *Ida Kaminska,* Polish actress, producer, director; head of government sponsored Jewish State Theatre of Poland, 1946–68; emigrated to U.S., 1968. [d. May 21, 1980]

1905 *Mary Renault (Mary Challens),* British novelist; noted for her historical novels of ancient Greece; author of *The King Must Die, The Nature of Alexander.* [d. December 13, 1983]

1906 *Max Delbrück,* U.S. biologist, physicist, born in Germany; Nobel Prize in physiology or medicine for discoveries in *genetic structure of viruses* (with A. D. Hershey and S. E. Luria), 1969. [d. March 9, 1981]

1908 *Richard Wright,* U.S. novelist, short-story writer; author of *Native Son,* 1940. [d. November 28, 1960]

1909 *Johannes Willebrands,* Dutch ecclesiastic; created cardinal, 1969; appointed Archbishop of Utrecht, 1975–83.

1913 *Stanford Moore,* U.S. biochemist; Nobel Prize in chemistry for research in life proceses at the molecular level and the biological activity of enzyme ribonuclease (with C.B. Anfinsen and W.H. Stein), 1972. [d. August 23, 1982]

1917 *Henry Ford II,* U.S. auto executive; Chairman, Ford Motor Co., 1960–80; Chief Executive Officer, 1960–79. [d. September 29, 1987]

1918 *Paul Harvey (Paul Harvey Aurandt),* U.S. broadcast journalist.

1920 *Craig Claiborne,* U.S. cookery expert and author.

1924 *Joan Delano Aiken,* British author; writes popular juvenile and adult mysteries; author of *Night Fall,* 1969.

Joseph Kraft, U.S. journalist, author; internationally syndicated political columnist known for non-ideological approach to world affairs. [d. January 10, 1986]

1926 *Donald Eugene Petersen,* U.S. auto executive; President, Ford Motor Company.

1928 *Richard Allen (Dick) York,* U.S. actor; starred as Darren in the television series, *Bewitched,* 1964–69. [d. February 20, 1992]

1931 *Mitzi Gaynor (Francesca Mitzi von Gerber),* U.S. dancer, actress.

1937 *Dawn Fraser,* Australian swimmer; Olympic gold medal winner, 1956, 1960, 1964.

1949 *Tom Watson,* U.S. professional golfer.

HISTORICAL EVENTS

1439 *Pope Eugene IV* condemns reform decrees of *Basel Council* and excommunicates the members of the Council.

1882 *Thomas Edison* opens his first commercial electric station in New York City, thus beginning the *electric lighting industry* in the U.S.

1918 The would-be assassin of Lenin, *Dora Kaplan,* is executed at Moscow.

1939 *Argentina* proclaims her neutrality in *World War II.*

1944 *Brussels* and *Antwerp* in Belgium are liberated by British and Canadian troops (*World War II*).

1948 *Wilhelmina,* Queen of the Netherlands, abdicates in favor of her daughter, *Juliana.*

1951 The one millionth U.S. soldier to die in action since the Battle of Lexington in 1775 is killed in Korea.

1954 First transit of *McClure Strait (Northwest Passage)* is made by the U.S. Navy icebreaker, *Burton Island,* and U. S. Coast Guard icebreaker, *Northwind.*

1957 Governor *Orval E. Faubus* orders the Arkansas National Guard to prohibit nine black students from entering Central High School in *Little Rock.*

Ford Motor Co. introduces a new automobile model, the *Edsel.*

1961 The *Agency for International Development* is established by the U.S. to consolidate foreign economic aid programs.

1969 U.S. Food and Drug Administration issues final approval of *oral contraceptives.*

1972 *Mark Spitz,* U.S. swimmer becomes the first person to win seven gold medals in a single Olympics.

1974 Diplomatic ties are established between the U.S. and *East Germany.*

1984 *Brian Mulroney* is inaugurated as prime minister of Canada.

1995 The United Nation's fourth *World Conference on Women* takes place in China.

september

SEPTEMBER
5

HOLIDAYS

U.S.
Be Late for Something Day
Sponsored by the Procrastinators'
Club of America, Philadelphia,
Pennsylvania.

Macao
Republic Day

Namibia, South Africa
Settlers' Day

RELIGIOUS CALENDAR

The Saints
St. Laurence Giustiniani, patriarch
of Venice. Also called
Laurence Justinian. [d. 1455]

The Beatified
Blessed Gentilis, martyr. [d. 1340]
Blessed Raymund Lull, martyr. [d.
1316]

BIRTHDATES

1568 *Tommaso Campanella,*
Italian philosopher, poet;
intimate of *Louis XIII* of
France and *Cardinal
Richelieu;* author of *Civitas
Solis,* a utopian work similar
to Plato's *Republic.* [d. May
21, 1639]

1638 *Louis XIV,* of France (*the Sun
King,*) called *the Great;*
reigned from 1643 to 1715,
longest reign in European

history; created an absolute
monarchy in France; built the
Palace at Versailles; in later
years, as a result of great
extravagances, brought France
to financial ruin. [d.
September 1, 1715]

1704 *Maurice Quentin de La Tour,*
French painter; best known
for pastel portraits. [d.
February 17, 1788]

1733 *Christoph Martin Wieland,*
German poet, novelist; called
the *German Voltaire.* [d.
January 20, 1813]

1735 *Johann Christian Bach,*
German composer, organist,
affiliated with the English
royal family, 1759–82; called
the *Milan* or *London Bach.*
Composed many operas,
sonatas, symphonies. Son of
Johann Sebastian Bach
(March 21). [d. January 1,
1782]

1847 *Jesse (Woodson) James,* U.S.
outlaw; executed many daring
robberies, 1866–82; murdered
by a member of his own
gang. [d. April 3, 1882]

1875 *Napoleon Lajoie,* U.S.
baseball player; inducted into
Baseball Hall of Fame, 1937.
[d. February 7, 1959]

1897 *A(rthur) C(harles) Nielsen,*
U.S. market researcher;
initiated ratings for television
programs, 1950. [d. June 1,
1980]

1901 *Florence Eldridge,* U.S.
actress; wife of Fredric March
(August 31).

1902 *Darryl F(rancis) Zanuck,*
U.S. film producer; President
and Chief Executive Officer of
20th-Century Fox Corp.,
1962–79. [d. December 22,
1979]

1905 *Arthur Koestler,* British
author, born in Hungary;
noted for his anti-Communist
writings and scientific and
fictional novels. Author of
*Darkness at Noon, The Art of
Creation, Life After Death.* [d.
March 3, 1983]

1912 *John Milton Cage, Jr.,* U.S.
composer; subject of
controversy because of his
use of novel instruments and
chance sounds in a style
known as *aleatory music.* [d.
August 12, 1993]

1916 *Frank (Garvin) Yerby,* U.S.
novelist. [d. November 29,
1992]

1921 *Jack Joseph Valenti,* U.S. film
executive, government
official; assistant to President
Lyndon Johnson, 1963–66;
President, Motion Picture
Association, 1966–.

1927 *Paul A. Volcker,* U.S. banker;
Chairman, Federal Reserve
Board, 1979–87.

1929 *Thomas Francis Eagleton,*
U.S. lawyer, politician;

Senator, 1969–87; withdrew as Democratic vice-presidential candidate after past bouts of nervous exhaustion became a campaign issue, 1972.

George Robert (Bob) Newhart, U.S. comedian; actor; known for low-key style; starred in the television series, *The Bob Newhart Show* and *Newhart.*

1934 *Ricardo de la Espriella,* President, Republic of Panama, 1982–84.

1935 *Werner Erhard (John Paul Rosenberg),* U.S. educator; developed Erhard Seminars Training, an individual, social transformation technique.

Carol Lawrence (Carol Maria Laraia), U.S. singer, dancer; played the role of Maria in the Broadway version of *West Side Story,* 1957–60.

1936 *John Claggett Danforth,* U.S. politician; Senator, 1976–94; heir to Ralston Purina fortune.

Joan Bennett Kennedy, former wife of Senator Edward M. Kennedy; active in the Joseph Kennedy Jr. Foundation for Mental Retardation.

Jonathan Kozol, U.S. author, educator; wrote *Illiterate America* and *Rachel and her Children.*

1937 *William Devane,* U.S. actor; stars in the television series, *Knots Landing,* 1983–93

1939 *Susumu Tonegawa,* Japanese molecular biologist; Nobel Prize in physiology or medicine for his research on the immune system, 1987.

1940 *Raquel Welch,* U.S. actress.

1950 *Cathy Lee Guisewaite,* U.S. cartoonist; created syndicated comic strip, *Cathy.*

1951 *Michael Keaton,* U.S. actor; known for roles in *Mr. Mom,* 1983; *Batman,* 1989; and *Batman Returns,* 1992.

HISTORICAL EVENTS

1338 *Louis IV,* Holy Roman Emperor, and *Edward III* of England conclude *Alliance of Coblenz,* which recognizes Edward's title to French throne.

Diet at Frankfurt declares that the Holy Roman Empire is divorced from the papacy.

1698 *English East India Company* (The General Society) is chartered.

1774 *First Continental Congress* opens at Philadelphia with all colonies except Georgia represented.

1905 A treaty of peace is signed at Portsmouth, New Hampshire, by Witte for the Russians and Baron Komura, the Japanese agent, ending the *Russo-Japanese War.*

1942 U.S.S.R. begins the first in a series of air raids on *Budapest (World War II).*

1950 The Syrian government approves a new constitution. *Hashem al-Atassi* becomes president.

1957 Jack Kerouac's novel *On the Road,* is published.

1958 Boris Pasternak's novel, *Dr. Zhivago,* is published in New York after being banned in the U.S.S.R.

1961 *Cheddi Jagan* is inaugurated as premier of British Guiana.

1972 *Black September* Palestinian terrorists attack an Israeli dormitory in the Olympic Village in *Munich,* shooting two members of the Israeli team. Nine other Israelis, five terrorists, and a West German policeman die at a shoot-out at the Munich airport as the Palestinians attempt to escape.

1975 *Lynette (Squeaky) Fromme,* 26, attempts to assassinate U.S. President *Gerald Ford* at Sacramento, California.

1984 Researchers announce conclusive evidence that *drug-resistant bacteria* promoted by antibiotics in livestock feed can cause serious illness in humans.

1991 The *Commonwealth of Independent States* is formed from the former U.S.S.R.

1995 *France* begins nuclear testing in French Polynesia, which violates a 1992 test moratorium.

september

SEPTEMBER
6

HOLIDAYS

Pakistan
Defense of Pakistan Day

São Tomé and Principe
National Heroes Day

Swaziland
Somblolo Day or Independence Day

RELIGIOUS CALENDAR

The Saints
SS. Donatian, Laetus and Others, bishops and martyrs. Donatian also called *Donation.* [d. c. 484]
St. Eleutherius, abbot. [d. 6th cent.]
St. Chainoaldus, Bishop of Laon. Also called *Cagnoald, Cagnou.* [d. c. 633]
St. Bega, virgin and nun. Also called *Bee, Bees,* or *Begh.* [d. 7th cent.]

The Beatified
Blessed Bertrand of Garrigues, Dominican prior. [d. c. 1230]
Blessed Peregrine of Falerone, layman. [d. 1240]
Blessed Liberatus of Loro, hermit. [d. c. 1258]

BIRTHDATES

1711 *Heinrich Melchior Muhlenberg,* U.S. Lutheran clergyman, born in Germany; known as the founder of Lutheranism in America. [d. October 7, 1787]

1729 *Moses Mendelssohn,* German philosopher, Biblical scholar, translator, and critic; called the *German Socrates.* [d. January 4, 1786]

1757 *Marie Joseph Paul, Marquis de Lafayette,* French soldier, statesman; entered American Army during Revolutionary War, 1777; responsible for securing French aid to American cause. After his return to France, 1789, remained active in politics; served in Chamber of Deputies, 1815, 1818–24; leader of opposition, 1825–30. [d. May 20, 1834]

1766 *John Dalton,* English scientist; established the *quantitative atomic theory* in chemistry, 1808. [d. July 27, 1844]

1795 *Frances (Fanny) Wright,* U.S. social reformer, born in Scotland; author of *Views of Society and Manners in America,* 1821; established *Nashoba Community* in Indiana; espoused radical views on religion, politics, education, women's rights, and marriage. [d. December 13, 1852]

1800 *Catharine Esther Beecher,* U.S. educator; established the *Hartford Female Seminary;* devoted her life to attainment of equal education for women, although she

opposed women's suffrage. [d. May 12, 1878]

1805 *Horatio Greenough,* U.S. sculptor, author; noted for his large-scale sculptures of famous Americans, especially the statue of George Washington at the Smithsonian Institution. [d. December 18, 1852]

1814 *Sir George Etienne Cartier,* Canadian statesman; Prime Minister of Canada, 1858–62. [d. May 20, 1873]

1817 *Alexander Tilloch Galt,* Canadian businessman and politician; first Minister of Finance, 1867–72; High Commissioner in England, 1880–83. [d. September 19, 1893]

1819 *William Starke Rosecrans,* Union Army general during U.S. Civil War; responsible for one of most disastrous Union defeats of the war, at *Chickamauga;* U.S. Minister to Mexico, 1868–69; U.S. Congressman, 1881–85. [d. March 11, 1898]

1820 *Marie E. Zakrzewska,* U.S. physician; "Mother of the Playground Movement," founder of first american school for nurses. [d. 1902]

1828 *Aleksandr Mikhailovich Butlerov,* Russian chemist; one of chief developers of theory of structure of organic compounds; recognized as discoverer of *tertiary alcohols*. [d. August 17, 1886]

1869 *Jane Addams,* U.S. social reformer, social worker; founder of *Hull House,* one of first settlement houses in U.S.; Nobel Peace Prize (with N. M. Butler), 1931. [d. May 21, 1935]

1876 *John James Rickard Macleod,* Scottish physiologist; Nobel Prize in physiology or medicine for production of *insulin* and discovery of its effectiveness in combating diabetes (with F. G. Banting), 1923. [d. March 16, 1935]

1878 *Henry Seidel Canby,* U.S. editor, critic; a founder of *Saturday Review of Literature.* [d. April 5, 1961]

1885 *Otto Kruger,* U.S. actor. [d. September 6, 1974]

1888 *Joseph Patrick Kennedy,* U.S. financier, diplomat; patriarch of Kennedy political dynasty; first chairman of *Securities and Exchange Commission;* U.S. Ambassador to Great Britain, 1937–40; father of John F. Kennedy, Robert Kennedy, and Edward M. Kennedy. [d. November 18, 1969]

1890 *Claire Lee Chennault,* U.S. Army Air Force general, creator of the *Flying Tigers,* a World War II combat unit in Southeast Asia. [d. July 27, 1958]

1892 *Sir Edward Victor Appleton,* British physicist; knighted, 1941; Nobel Prize in physics for investigations of physics of upper atmosphere, 1947. [d. April 21, 1965]

1895 *Walter R(obert) Dornberger,* German missile expert; led Nazi guided missile program during World War II; later became adviser to U.S. Air Force; Vice-President, Bell Aerosystems, 1960–65. [d. June 1980]

1899 *Billy Rose (William Samuel Rosenberg),* U.S. entrepreneur, songwriter; produced numerous variety shows, 1931–44, and Aquacade at New York World's Fair, 1939. [d. February 10, 1966]

1906 *Luis F. Leloir,* Argentinian chemist, born in France; Nobel Prize in chemistry for investigations into the breakdown of complex sugars, 1970. [d. December 2, 1987]

1915 *Franz Josef Strauss,* German politician. [d. October 3, 1988]

1937 *Jo Anne Worley,* U.S. comedienne; starred in the television series, *Laugh-In,* 1968–73.

1943 *Richard J. Roberts,* British molecular biologist; Nobel Prize for Medicine in 1993 with Phillip A. Sharp for their discovery of split genes.

1944 *Swoosie Kurtz,* U.S. actress; Tony Award for the play, *Fifth of July,* 1980; starred in the TV drama *Sisters.*

1947 *Jane Therese Curtin,* U.S. actress, comedienne; starred in the television series, *Saturday Night Live* and *Kate and Allie;* Emmy Awards, 1984, 1985.

1958 *Jeff Foxworthy,* U.S. comedian, actor; star of *The Jeff Foxworthy Show,* 1996.

1964 *Rosie Perez,* U.S. actress.

HISTORICAL EVENTS

1512 The constitution of *Florence* is altered, restoring the Medici family to power.

1898 *Queen Wilhelmina* of the Netherlands is crowned.

1901 U.S. President *William McKinley* is shot by *Leon Czolgosz,* an anarchist; dies September 14.

1914 *First Battle of the Marne (World War I)* opens with a general offensive by French and British forces against the German advance.

1940 U.S. transfers the first destroyers to Great Britain under the destroyers-for-bases agreement (*Lend-Lease Act*).

1941 A decree is issued in *Germany* requiring all Jews over the age of six to wear the Star of David with the inscription "Jew" over their left breast.

1947 U.S. successfully fires first *V-2 rocket* launched from a ship.

1950 *Yongchong, Korea,* is recaptured by UN forces (*Korean War*).

U.S.S.R. vetoes a Security Council resolution condemning North Korea for continued defiance of the UN and asking all nations to withhold aid to North Korea.

1951 *Prince Talal,* elder son of King Abdullah, takes oath as King of Jordan.

An agreement is signed in Lisbon giving U.S. additional rights in the Azores and including the islands in the defense framework of *NATO*.

1961 *Afghanistan* breaks off diplomatic relations with

september

Pakistan, closing its embassy, consulates, and trade agencies there.

1966 South African prime minister, *Hendrik Verwoerd,* is assassinated during a session of Parliament.

1968 *Swaziland* becomes independent, ending Britain's colonial links with Africa.

1970 *Philibert Tsiranana* is elected President of the *Malagasy Republic.*

Arab commandos hijack three jetliners that eventually land in the Jordanian desert, where the planes are blown up.

1975 Violent earthquake in eastern *Turkey* kills more than 2,000 people.

1976 A *Soviet MiG-25 jet,* believed to be the Soviet Union's most advanced fighter, is flown to Japan by a pilot seeking U.S. asylum; President Ford grants him asylum; after a long delay, the plane is shipped back to the U.S.S.R.

1977 Korean businessman *Park Tong Sun,* in the U.S., is indicted on 36 felony charges and is also accused of making illegal campaign contributions and failing to register as a foreign agent.

1982 The Communist Party of *China* adopts a new party constitution which abolishes the post of Chairman and creates a new central Advisory Committee.

All private Mexican banks are nationalized and placed under the control of the *Bank of Mexico.*

Labor Day centennial is celebrated in the U.S.

1995 *Cal Ripkin, Jr.,* sets a new baseball record when he plays in his 2,131st consecutive game. Lou Gehrig had held the record since 1939.

1997 The funeral of *Diana, Princess of Wales,* is broadcast worldwide.

Two new moons are discovered around *Uranus* by scientists at the Mount Palomar Observatory in California.

HOLIDAYS

Brazil
Independence Day

Mozambique
Victory Day
Commemorates the end of armed struggle against the Portuguese.

RELIGIOUS CALENDAR

The Saints
St. John of Nicomedia, martyr. Also called *Euetios, Euhtis.* [d. 303]

St. Clodoald, Frankish prince. Venerated in France as patron of nail makers. Also called *Cloud.* [d. c. 560]

St. Evurtius, Bishop of Orlèans. Also called *Enurchus, Evortius.* [d. 4th cent.]

SS. Alcmund and Tilbert, bishops of Hexham. Alcmund also called *Alchmund;* Tilbert also called *Tilberht.* [d. 781 and 789]

St. Grimonia, virgin and martyr. Also called *Germana.* [death date unknown]

St. Regina, virgin and martyr. Also called *Reine.* [death date unknown]

St. Sozon, martyr. [death date unknown]

The Beatified
Blessed Mark, Stephen, and Melchior, martyrs. [d. 1619]

Blessed John Duckett and Ralph Corby, martyrs. [d. 1644]

BIRTHDATES

1533 *Elizabeth I* of England, 1558–1603, ruled England during the literary Renaissance later identified as the *Elizabethan period;* as regent, defeated Mary, Queen of Scots; oppressed the Roman Catholics of England; defeated Philip of Spain and the Spanish Armada. [d. March 23, 1603]

1677 *Stephen Hales,* English scientist; conducted early studies on physiological phenomena; known as the *Founder of Science of Physiology.* [d. January 4, 1761]

1707 *Georges Louis Leclerc du Buffon,* French naturalist; Director of Jardin du Roi and Royal Museum, 1739; member, French Academy, 1753–88; published *Histoire Naturelle,* a 44-volume catalog of nature, 1749–1804 (portions published posthumously). [d. April 16, 1788]

1819 *Thomas Hendricks,* U.S. Vice-President, 1885. [d. November 25, 1885]

1829 *Friedrich August Kekule von Stradonitz,* German organic chemist; known for his work on the constitution of organic compounds; first to propose theory of leaking carbon atoms; first to theorize on the ring formation of the benzene molecule. [d. July 13, 1896]

1860 *Anna Mary Robertson (Grandma) Moses,* U.S. painter; renowned as one of America's finest primitive painters; began painting in her seventies; produced over 2000 paintings by the time of her death. [d. December 13, 1961]

1867 *J. P. Morgan Jr.,* U.S. financier; son of John Pierpont Morgan (April 17); prime successor to the financial empire left by his father. [d. March 13, 1943]

1873 *Carl Lotus Becker,* U.S. historian, educator; noted for his popular analyses of American institutions and events; author of *The Declaration of Independence;* President, American Historical Society, 1931–41. [d. April 10, 1945]

1884 *Charles Tomlinson Griffes,* U.S. composer; impressionistic in his style and exotic in his themes; directly influenced by Debussy and Ravel. [d. April 8, 1920]

1887 *Dame Edith Sitwell,* British poet, author; known for her wit and eccentricity. [d. December 9, 1964]

september

1900 *(Janet Miriam) Taylor Caldwell,* U.S. novelist. [d. August 30, 1985]

1908 *Michael Ellis Debakey,* U.S. heart surgeon; noted for his advanced techniques in heart surgery and heart transplants; recipient of the Ellis Island Medal of Honor, 1993.

1909 *Elia Kazan,* U.S. director, producer, author, born in Turkey. [d. 1990]

1911 *Todor Zhivkov,* President, People's Republic of Bulgaria, 1971–89. [d. August 5, 1998]

1912 *David Packard,* U.S. business executive; founded Hewlett-Packard with William Hewlett (May 20). [d. March 26, 1996]

1913 *Sir (John) Anthony Quayle,* British actor, director, known for his Shakespearean roles. [d. October 20, 1989]

1914 *James Alfred Van Allen,* U.S. physicist; discovered the *Van Allen belt* of radiation around the earth; pioneer in high-altitude rocket research.

1917 *John Cornforth,* Australian-British chemist; Nobel Prize in chemistry for contributions to *stereochemistry* (with V. Prelog), 1975.

1921 *Arthur Ferrante,* U.S. pianist, composer; part of the Ferrante and Teicher piano team.

1923 *Peter Lawford,* British actor. [d. December 24, 1984]

Louise Suggs, U.S. golfer; winner of 50 tournaments on the Ladies' PGA Tour, two-time winner of U.S. Open.

1924 *Daniel Ken Inouye,* U.S. politician, lawyer; U.S. Congressman, 1959–62; U.S. Senator, 1963–.

1925 *Laura Mountney Ashley,* Welsh designer, business executive; known for romantic textile and clothing designs inspired by English country gardens. [d. September 17, 1985]

Robert Jastrow, U.S. author, astronomer.

1928 *Al McGuire,* U.S. basketball coach, sportscaster; National Collegiate Athletic Association Championship for Marquette University, 1977.

1930 *Baudouin I* of Belgium; acceded to throne in 1951 on his father's abdication; helped restore confidence in the Belgian monarchy. [d. July 31, 1993]

Theodore Walter (Sonny) Rollins, U.S. musician, composer; tenor saxophone player; his album, *The Bridge,* is considered a jazz classic.

1935 *Abdou Diouf,* President, Republic of Senegal, 1981–.

1936 *(Charles Harden) Buddy Holly,* U.S. singer, guitarist; had significant influence on rock n' roll music worldwide. [d. February 3, 1959]

1942 *Richard Roundtree,* U.S. actor; starred in the movie, *Shaft,* 1971.

1948 *Susan Blakely,* U.S. actress; appeared in the movies, *The Way We Were* and *Towering Inferno.*

1949 *Gloria Gaynor,* U.S. singer; hit records include *Never Can Say Goodbye,* 1974, and *I Will Survive,* 1979; known as the *Queen of Disco.*

1950 *Peggy Noonan,* U.S. author; former White House speechwriter; wrote *What I Saw at the Revolution: A Political Life in the Reagan Era.*

1951 *Christine Elaine (Chrissie) Hynde,* U.S. singer, songwriter; founded the rock group, *The Pretenders,* 1978.

Julie Deborah Kavner, U.S. actress; played Brenda Morgenstern on the television series, *Rhoda,* 1974–78; Emmy Award, 1978; featured on the television series, *The Tracey Ullman Show,* 1987–90; voice of Marge Simpson on the TV show *The Simpsons.*

1954 *Corbin Bernsen,* U.S. actor; played Arnie Becker on TV series *LA Law.*

HISTORICAL EVENTS

1714 *Peace of Baden* between France and Holy Roman Empire is achieved; France keeps Alsace.

1812 *Battle of Borodino,* fought 70 miles west of Moscow, is a costly victory over the Russians for Napoleon's Grand Army.

1822 *Brazil* declares its independence from *Portugal.*

1848 *Serfdom* in *Austria* is abolished.

1856 *Alexander II* is crowned Czar of Russia in Moscow.

1860 *Garibaldi* and his troops take *Naples;* the unification of Italy ensues.

1892 *John L. Sullivan* defeats *James J. Corbett* in the first modern *boxing* match to be held using *Marquis of Queensbury rules.*

1901 *Boxer Rebellion,* led by anti-foreign element in China, ends as 12 nations sign *Boxer Protocol.*

1941 U.S. merchant ship, the *Steel Seafarer,* is the first to be lost to air attack (*World War II*).

1944 Germans fire first *V-2 rocket* on London (*World War II*).

1945 *General Douglas MacArthur* enters Tokyo as Supreme Commander for the Allied Powers in Japan.

1961 *Joao Goulart* replaces *Janio da Silva Quadros* as president of Bolivia.

1978 *Sri Lanka* adopts a new constitution, establishing a strong presidency, and abandoning the former name of the country, *Ceylon* to *Sri Lanka.*

1979 *Robert Runcie,* Bishop of St. Albans, is named 102nd *Archbishop of Canterbury.*

1987 Chairman *Erich Honecker* is the first East German leader to visit West Germany. The visit is intended to improve relations between the two countries.

1993 *Joycelyn Elders* becomes the first African American surgeon general.

1997 *Mobutu Sese Seko,* ousted president of Zaire, dies in exile (May 16, 1997).

september

SEPTEMBER
8

HOLIDAYS

International Literacy Day
Sponsored by the United Nations,
New York, New York.

Andorra
Our Lady of Meritxell
Celebrates the finding of a
madonnalike figure under an
almond tree which was in bloom
out of season.

Macedonia
Day of Referendum

RELIGIOUS CALENDAR

Feasts
*The Birthday of the Blessed Virgin
Mary.* Feast observed in the
West since about A.D. 600.

The Saints
SS. Adrian and Natalia, martyrs.
Adrian is patron of soldiers
and butchers, invoked against
plagues. [d. c. 304]
*SS. Eusebius, Nestabus, Zeno, and
Nestor,* martyrs. [d. c. 362]
St. Kinemark. Also called *Cynfarch
Oer.* [d. 5th cent.]
St. Ethelburga, princess of Kent and
Abbess of Lyming. Also called
Aedilburh, Tata. [d. 647]
St. Disibod, Irish monastery-founder.
Also called *Disen, Disibode.*
[d. c. 674]
St. Sergius I, pope. Elected 687. [d.
701]
St. Corbinian, bishop. [d. 725]

BIRTHDATES

1157 *Richard I (the Lion-Hearted),*
King of England, 1189–99; led
the *Third Crusade,* 1189–92;
kidnapped by Austrians, 1191;
ransomed and returned to
England, 1194; the subject of
numerous legends. [d. April
6, 1199]

1474 *Ludovico Ariosto,* Italian poet,
famous for his *Orlando
Furioso.* [d. July 6, 1533]

1767 *August Wilhelm Schlegel,*
German translator, critic,
orientalist, and poet; founder
of literary journal *Athenaeum,*
the primary organ of the
German Romantic school;
best known for his poetical
translation, with Ludwig
Tieck, of Shakespeare. [d.
May 12, 1845]

1778 *Clemens Maria Brentano,*
German poet, novelist;
described the visions of
German nun and visionary
Anna Katharina Emmerick.
[d. July 28, 1842]

1828 *Margaret Olivia Sage,* U.S.
philanthropist; wife of Russell
Sage (August 4); established
the *Russell Sage Foundation*
for the improvement of social
conditions, 1907. [d.
November 4, 1918]

1830 *Frédéric Mistral,* Provençal
poet and writer; Nobel Prize
in literature, 1904. [d. March
25, 1914]

1837 *Joaquin Miller (Cincinnatus
Hiner Miller),* U.S. poet,
journalist; best known in
Europe for his flamboyant
and romantic poems of the
Old West; his poetry was
regarded as overly
sentimental by American
critics. [d. February 17, 1913]

1841 *Antonín Dvořák,* Czech
composer; Director, National
Conservatory of Music, New
York, 1892–95; composed
numerous symphonies,
including *New World
Symphony.* [d. May 1, 1904]

1848 *Viktor Meyer,* German
chemist; noted for his
research in organic
compounds and physical
chemistry. [d. August 8, 1897]

1863 *W(illiam) W(ymark) Jacobs,*
British short-story writer;
known for his sea stories. [d.
September 1, 1943]

1886 *Siegfried (Lorraine) Sassoon,*
British poet; known for his
anti-war poetry and semi-
autobiographical fiction,
especially *Memoirs of a Fox-
Hunting Man.* [d. September
1, 1967]

1889 *Robert A(lphonso) Taft,* U.S.
politician; Senator, 1939–53;
drafted the *Taft-Hartley Act,*
aimed at preventing labor
strikes that could endanger
the public good; son of
William Howard Taft

(September 15). [d. July 31, 1953]

1892 *Theodore V. Houser,* U.S. business executive; Chairman of the Board of Sears, Roebuck & Co. [d. December 17, 1963]

1900 *Claude Denson Pepper,* U.S. politician; Senator, 1936–51; Congressman, 1963–89. [d. May 30, 1989]

1911 *Euell Gibbons,* U.S. author, naturalist; known for books on wild foods, including *Stalking the Good Life.* [d. December 29, 1975]

1922 *Sid Caesar,* U.S. actor, comedian.

Lyndon H. LaRouche, Jr., U.S. politician; controversial right-wing activist; convicted of mail fraud, 1988.

1924 *Grace Metalious,* U.S. novelist; wrote *Peyton Place.* [d. February 25, 1964]

1925 *Peter Sellers,* British comedian, actor; best known for his portrayal of *Inspector Clouseau* in the *Pink Panther* film series. [d. July 24, 1980]

1932 *Patsy Cline (Virginia Patterson Hensley),* U.S. singer. [d. March 5, 1963]

1938 *Samuel Augustus (Sam) Nunn, Jr.,* U.S. politician; Senator, 1973–96.

1946 *Kenneth Roth (Ken) Forsch,* U.S. baseball player

Freddie Mercury (Frederick Bulsara), British singer, musician; member of the rock group, *Queen.* [d. November 24, 1991]

1947 *Rita Marie Lavelle,* U.S. government official; former

head of the Environmental Protection Agency toxic waste clean-up program; indicted for conflict of interest and mismanagement.

HISTORICAL EVENTS

1565 The first permanent settlement in what is now the U.S., *St. Augustine, Florida,* is established by Don Pedro Menéndez.

1755 William Johnson achieves British victory at *Battle of Lake George (French and Indian War).*

1760 English capture Montreal from French *(French and Indian War).*

1847 *Battle of Molino del Rey* results in U.S. victory *(Mexican War).*

1883 *Northern Pacific Railroad* across the U.S. is completed as the final spike is driven in at Gold Creek, Montana, after 13 years of construction.

1892 The *Pledge of Allegiance* first appears in the magazine, *Youth's Companion.* It is later adopted as a national symbol.

1919 An agreement between the British and French recognizes the French right to all territory west of the Nile basin, including most of the *Sahara.*

1935 *Huey P. Long,* Louisiana Senator, is fatally wounded by an assassin in Baton Rouge, Louisiana; he dies two days later.

1943 *Italy* accepts Allied terms of unconditional surrender *(World War II).*

1944 *Bulgaria* surrenders to the Allies *(World War II).*

1950 U.S. Secretary of State, *Dean Acheson,* is appointed to head the *Point Four program* for helping underdeveloped countries.

1951 *San Francisco Treaty of Peace* with Japan is signed, establishing mutual assistance between the U.S. and Japan.

1952 Ernest Hemingway's novel, *The Old Man and the Sea,* is published.

1954 The *Southeast Asia Treaty Organization* is created to defend Asian states from Communist aggression.

1964 Public schools in *Prince Edward County, Virginia,* reopen for the first time since 1959 with seven whites and 1,400 blacks attending classes. The county kept its schools closed for five years to avoid *desegregation.*

1966 *Star Trek* makes its television debut.

1971 The *John F. Kennedy Center for the Performing Arts* opens in Washington, D.C.

1974 U.S. President *Gerald Ford* grants former President *Richard M. Nixon* an unconditional pardon for all federal crimes committed while in office.

1994 A *USAir* jet crashes near Pittsburgh, Pennsylvania, killing all 132 people aboard.

1998 *Mark McGwire* sets a new baseball record when he hits his 62nd homerun in a single season. Roger Maris had held the record of 61 since 1961.

september

SEPTEMBER
9

HOLIDAYS

Bulgaria
Liberation Day

China
Teachers' Day

Japan
Choxo-no-Sekku or Chrysanthemum Day

Korea
National Foundation Day

Tajikistan
Independence Day

U.S. (California)
Admission Day

RELIGIOUS CALENDAR

The Saints

St. Isaac, Primate of the Armenian Church. Also called *Isaac the Great, Sahak I.* [d. 439]

St. Kieran, Abbot of Clonmacnois. Also called *Ciaran, Kiaran,* or *Kieran the Younger.* [d. c. 556]

St. Audomarus, Bishop of Thèrouanne. Also called *Omer.* [d. c. 670]

St. Bettelin, hermit; patron of Stafford. Also called *Beccelin* or *Berthelm.* [d. 8th cent.]

St. Wulfhilda, Abbess of Barking. Also called *Wulfhildis.* [d. c. 1000]

St. Peter Claver, Jesuit priest. Missionary to Negro slaves in South America. [d. 1654]

St. Gorgonius, martyr. [death date unknown]

The Beatified
Blessed Seraphina Sforza, widow. [d. c. 1478]
Blessed Louisa of Savoy, widow. [d. 1503]
Blessed James D. Laval. [beatified 1979]

BIRTHDATES

1585 *Richelieu,* Armand Jean de Plessis, Duc de *Eminence Rouge,* French statesman, cardinal; chief minister of Louis XIII; directed domestic and foreign policies of France, 1624–42. [d. December 4, 1642]

1711 *Thomas Hutchinson,* American colonial official; Governor of Massachusetts Bay Colony, 1771–74; opposed revolutionary elements in America and returned to England as adviser to George III. [d. June 3, 1780]

1737 *Luigi Galvani,* Italian physician, physicist; known for his research into function of electrical current on muscle movements. [d. December 4, 1798]

1754 *William Bligh,* English naval officer; master of *H.M.S. Bounty;* cast adrift by mutinous sailors, sailed 4000 miles to East Indies with a crew of 18 men; Governor of New South Wales, 1805–08. [d. December 7, 1817]

1778 *Fabian Gottlieb von Bellingshausen,* Russian naval officer and Antarctic explorer; commanded *Antarctic expedition* which discovered Peter I Island and Alexander I Island. [d. January 13, 1852]

1789 *William Cranch Bond,* U.S. astronomer; the first director of the Harvard College Observatory; took the first photograph of a star, 1850. [d. January 29, 1859]

1828 *Leo Nikolayevich Tolstoi,* Russian novelist, philosopher, religious mystic; regarded as one of the great authors of all time; known not only for such works as *War and Peace,* but also for his system of *Christian anarchism;* founded sect of Tolstoyists who believed in nonresistance to evil. [d. November 20, 1910]

1887 *Alfred Mossman (Alf) Landon,* U.S. businessman, politician; presidential candidate who lost overwhelmingly to Franklin Roosevelt, 1936. [d. October 12, 1987]

1890 *Harland Sanders,* U.S. businessman; founder of Kentucky Fried Chicken Corporation, 1956. [d. December 16, 1980]

1900 *James Hilton*, British novelist; author of *Lost Horizon, Goobye, Mr. Chips,* and *Random Harvest.* [d. December 20, 1954]

1901 *Granville Hicks*, U.S. writer, literary critic; known for his Marxist writings; author of *The Great Tradition.* [d. June 18, 1982]

1919 *Jimmy the Greek (Demetrius George Synodinos),* U.S. journalist, sportscaster; former professional gambler; handicapper and analyst for television sports shows. [d. April 21, 1996]

1922 *Hans Georg Dehmelt,* U.S. physicist; Nobel Prize for Physics, 1989. Dehmelt shares one-half of Prize with Wolfgang Paul, German physicist, for their study of ions. Norman F. Ramsey received the other half of the prize for his work on shifting the energy levels of atoms.

1923 *Daniel C. Gajdusek,* U.S. physician; Nobel prize in physiology or medicine for discoveries concerning mechanisms involved in the origin and spread of *infectious diseases* (with B. S. Blumberg), 1976.

Cliff Robertson, U.S. actor, director.

1928 *Julian Edwin (Cannonball) Adderley,* U.S. musician; alto-saxophonist who played with Miles Davis; hit songs included *Mercy, Mercy, Mercy.* [d. August 8, 1975]

1932 *Sylvia Miles,* U.S. actress, comedienne; appeared in the movies, *Midnight Cowboy* and *Farewell My Lovely.*

1941 *Otis Redding,* U.S. singer, songwriter; hits include *Dock of the Bay* and *Respect.* [d. December 10, 1967]

1946 *William Everett (Billy) Preston,* U.S. singer, musician, songwriter; hits include *You are So Beautiful,* 1975, and *With You I'm Born Again,* 1979.

1949 *Joseph Robert (Joe) Theismann,* U.S. football player; former quarterback, Washington Redskins; led the National Football Conference in passing, 1982.

1951 *Tom Wopat,* U.S. actor; co-star of the television series, *The Dukes of Hazzard,* 1979–85.

1952 *Angela Cartwright,* U.S. actress; appeared in the television series, *Danny Thomas Show* and *Lost in Space.*

1960 *Hugh Grant,* British actor; known for roles in *Four Weddings and a Funeral,* 1994 and *Sense and Sensibility,* 1995.

1962 *Kristy McNichol,* U.S. actress; Emmy Award for her role as Buddy in the series, *Family,* 1977.

1966 *Adam Sandler,* U.S. comedian and actor.

1971 *Henry Thomas,* U.S. actor; known for role as Elliot in the movie *ET,* 1982.

HISTORICAL EVENTS

1513 *James IV* of Scotland is defeated by the English and killed at the *Battle of Flodden Field;* he is succeeded by *James V.*

1850 *California* is admitted to the Union as the 31st state.

1884 *American Historical Association* is founded at Saratoga, New York.

1895 *American Bowling Congress* is organized at New York.

1914 *First Battle of the Marne* ends with the Germans beginning a retreat to the *Aisne River (World War I).*

1942 The only aerial bombing of the continental U.S. during *World War II* takes place from plane launched by Japanese submarine off the Oregon coast. Only damage is a small forest fire.

1943 U.S. Fifth Army under General Mark Clark makes amphibious landings at *Salerno, Italy (World War II).*

1948 *Democratic People's Republic of Korea (North Korea)* is established.

1954 Canadian swimmer, *Marilyn Bell,* becomes the first to cross *Lake Ontario.*

1957 The first modern civil rights legislation in U.S. history is signed into law. The *Civil Rights Act of 1957* establishes a Civil Rights Commission and a Civil Rights Division at the Department of Justice.

1961 *Long Beach,* the U.S. Navy's first nuclear surface vessel, is commissioned.

1967 William Styron's novel of a slave rebellion, *The Confessions of Nat Turner,* is published.

1968 *Arthur Ashe* wins the U.S. Open tennis title at Forest Hills, New York, in the first tournament open to both professionals and amateurs.

1979 University of North Carolina graduate, *Karen Stevenson,*

september

wins a Rhodes Scholarship, becoming the first black American woman to receive the grant.

1985 The U.S. imposes trade sanctions against *South Africa* in reaction to that country's apartheid policy.

1990 President *Samuel K. Doe* of *Liberia* is shot by rebel assassins and the country is in turmoil as rival forces fight for control. Doe dies the next day.

HOLIDAYS

Belize
National Day or St. George's Cay Day

Bulgaria
Liberation Day

RELIGIOUS CALENDAR

The Saints

SS. Nemesian and companions, martyrs. [d. 257]

St. Pulcheria, virgin and Empress of Byzantium. [d. 453]

St. Finnian of Moville, bishop. Also called *Finian.* [d. c. 579]

St. Theodard, Bishop of Tongres-Maastricht [d. c. 670]

St. Aubert, Bishop of Avranches; founder of Church of Mont-Saint-Michel. [d. c. 725]

St. Frithestan, Bishop of Winchester. [d. c. 932]

St. Nicholas of Tolentino, Augustinian friar; patron of souls in purgatory. [d. 1305]

St. Barloc, hermit. [death date unknown]

The Beatified

Blessed Apollinaris Franco, Charles Spinola, and their companions, martyrs in the great martyrdom in Japan. [d. 1622]

BIRTHDATES

1487 *Julius III,* Pope 1550–55; resumed session of *Council of Trent,* 1551. [d. March 23, 1555]

1753 *Sir John Soane,* English architect; redesigned *Bank of England* in Roman Corinthian style; donated his antiquarian paintings, sculptures, drawings to the English nation as the basis of the *Soane Museum in London.* [d. January 20, 1837]

1771 *Mungo Park,* Scottish-born African explorer, surgeon; discovered the source and course of the *Nile River,* 1796. [d. 1806]

1787 *John Jordan Crittenden,* U.S. politician, lawyer; U.S. Senator, 1817–19; 1835–41; 1842–48; 1855–61. U.S. Attorney General, 1841; 1850–53. Governor of Kentucky, 1848–50. [d. July 26, 1863]

1835 *William Torrey Harris,* U.S. Hegelian philosopher, educator; U.S. Commissioner of Education, 1889–1906; Editor-in-Chief of the first edition of *Webster's New International Dictionary,* 1909. [d. November 5, 1909]

1836 *Joseph (Fighting Joe) Wheeler,* U.S. Union and Confederate Army general (served in Union Army for two years, then resigned his commission to fight for the Confederacy); saw continuous action during the entire Civil War; U.S. Congressman, 1881–1900; returned to the army during the Spanish-American War. [d. January 25, 1906]

1839 *Isaac (Kauffman) Funk,* U.S. editor, publisher, lexicographer; founder, with Adam Willis Wagnalls, of the *Standard Series* publications, and editors and producers of the *Standard Dictionary of the English Language.* [d. April 4, 1912]

Charles Santiago Sanders Peirce, U.S. mathematician, logician, philosopher; *Father of Pragmatism;* from 1867 to 1914 was probably the world's leading logician. [d. April 19, 1914]

1847 *John R. Lynch,* U.S. Congressman, 1873–77; 1881–83; first black to preside over a national convention of the Republican Party, 1884. [d. November 2, 1939]

1852 *Alice Brown Davis,* Native American civil rights activist for the Seminoles. [d. 1935]

1856 *Elbridge Amos Stuart,* U.S. manufacturer; founder of Carnation Co.; President, 1899–1932; Chairman of the Board, 1932–44. [d. January 14, 1944]

1885 *Carl Van Doren,* U.S. author, editor; while at Columbia

University, 1911–30, greatly influenced the revival of interest in American literature; author of Pulitzer Prize winning biography of Benjamin Franklin, 1939. [d. July 18, 1950]

1886 *Hilda Doolittle,* U.S. poet; major voice in the Imagist movement. [d. September 27, 1961]

1890 *Elsa Schiaparelli,* Italian fashion designer; known for using novel textures, colors, and accessories; introduced shocking pink for women's attire. [d. November 14, 1973]

Franz Werfel, Austrian poet, playwright, and novelist; member of Expressionist movement. [d. August 26, 1945]

1892 *Arthur Holly Compton,* U.S. physicist; Nobel Prize in physics for discovery of *Compton effect,* the change in wave length of x rays colliding with electrons, 1927. [d. March 25, 1962]

1898 *Adele Astaire (Adele Austerlitz),* U.S. dancer; with her brother, Fred Astaire (May 10), formed a famous dance team of the 1920s. [d. January 25, 1981]

1907 *Fay Wray,* Canadian actress; starred in *King Kong,* 1933.

1914 *Robert (Earl) Wise,* U.S. film director, producer; noted for his films, *Run Silent, Run Deep, West Side Story, The Sound of Music.*

1915 *Edmond O'Brien,* U.S. actress. [d. May 8, 1985]

1929 *Arnold Palmer,* U.S. golfer; winner of 79 professional titles; first $1 million winner in golf.

1934 *Charles Bishop Kuralt,* U.S. broadcast journalist; known for *On the Road* book, radio segments, and television specials. [d. July 4, 1997]

Roger Maris, U.S. baseball player; hit record 61 home runs in 1961. [d. December 14, 1985]

1938 *Karl Lagerfeld,* German fashion designer; associated with the House of Chloe.

1939 *Greg Mullavey,* U.S. actor; starred in the television series, *Mary Hartman, Mary Hartman.*

1941 *Stephen Jay Gould,* U.S. paleontologist, author; wrote *The Panda's Thumb, The Mismeasure of Man,* and *Hen's Teeth and Horse's Toes.*

Christopher Hogwood, British conductor, musician; founded Academy of Ancient Music, 1974.

1944 *John Entwistle,* British musician, singer; bassist for the rock group, *The Who.*

1945 *José Feliciano,* U.S. composer, guitarist.

1948 *Robert Jerry (Bob) Lanier, Jr.,* U.S. basketball player; scored average of 20 points per game; called *Bob-A-Dob.*

Margaret Joan Sinclair Trudeau, Canadian author, socialite; wrote *Beyond Reason,* 1979; former wife of Pierre Trudeau (October 18).

1951 *Gary Danielson,* U.S. football player.

William Charles (Bill) Rogers, U.S. golfer; 1981 British Open Champion.

1953 *Amy Irving,* U.S. actress.

1963 *Randall (Randy) David Johnson,* U.S. baseball player;

Cy Young Award winner, 1995.

HISTORICAL EVENTS

1721 *Treaty of Nystad* is signed, in which Russia obtains territories from Sweden: Livonia, Estonia, Ingria, and Eastern Karelia. (Old Style: August 30).

1794 *Blount College,* the first U.S. nondenominational college, is founded in Knoxville, Tennessee. It later became the University of Tennessee.

1813 *Battle of Lake Erie* results in important American victory as *Oliver Perry* defeats the British (*War of 1812*).

1846 *Elias Howe* patents his first *sewing machine.*

1893 Women are granted the right to vote in *New Zealand.*

1919 Austria signs the *Treaty of St. Germain,* ending *World War I* with the Allies and recognizing the independence of Czechoslovakia, Yugoslavia, Poland, and Hungary.

1921 The first *Miss America Pageant* is held in Atlantic City, New Jersey.

1942 Great Britain attacks *Madagascar,* launching an all out confrontation aimed at three west coast ports (*World War II*).

1943 German troops seize *Rome* (*World War II*).

1955 *Gunsmoke* makes its television debut.

1967 *Gibraltar* votes to remain under British sovereignty rather than return to Spanish rule.

1980 Coup d'état led by *General Kenan Evren* in Turkey gives power to the military.

1984 Ethiopia establishes the *Workers' Party of Ethiopia* as the only legal political party and officially declares itself a Communist nation.

1990 The fighting parties in *Cambodia*'s civil war agree to sign a United Nations proposal for peace.

september

SEPTEMBER
11

HOLIDAYS

Chile
National Liberation Day

Ethiopia
Ethiopian New Year and Reunion of Eritrea with Ethiopia
Commemorates the New Year of the Coptic Calendar, and the reunification of Eritrea, former Italian colony, with Ethiopia by U.N. mandate, 1952.

Pakistan
Anniversary of the Death of Quaid-e-Azam
Commemorates the death of *Mohammed Ali Jinnah,* founder and first leader of Pakistan, 1948.

Philippines
Barangay Day

RELIGIOUS CALENDAR

The Saints
St. Paphnutius, bishop. [d. c. 350]
St. Patiens, Bishop of Lyons. [d. c. 480]
St. Deiniol, bishop. Also called *Daniel of the Bangors, Deinoil.* [d. c. 584]
St. Peter of Chavanon, priest and monastery founder. [d. 1080]
SS. Protus and Hyacinth, martyrs. Hyacinth also called *Hyacinthus.* [death date unknown]
St. Theodora of Alexandria. [death date unknown]

The Beatified
Blessed Louis of Thuringia, king. Also called *Ludwig.* [d. 1227]
Blessed Bonaventure of Barcelona, Franciscan lay brother and hermitage-founder. [d. 1684]
Blessed John Gabriel Perboyre, martyr. [d. 1840]

BIRTHDATES

1524 *Pierre de Ronsard,* French poet; head of group of poets known as *Pléiade,* who were devoted to revitalizing the use of French language in great literature; called the *Father of Lyric Poetry in France.* [d. December 27, 1585]

1611 *Henri de La Tour d'Auvergne, Vicomte de Turenne,* French Army marshal; active during the Thirty Years' War, 1618–48; sided with the Fronde in rebellion against the French monarchy, 1648–53; led French troops in war in Holland, the Palatinate, and Alsace, 1672–75. Considered by Napoleon to be one of history's greatest military leaders. [d. July 27, 1675]

1723 *Johann Bernhard Basedow (Bernhard Nordalbingen),* German educator, educational reformer; established the *Philanthropinum,* a model school for children, 1774. [d. July 25, 1790]

1821 *Erastus Flavel Beadle,* U.S. publisher; his experiments in publication of *cheap* books led to the first *dime novel,* which was based on thrills, violence, suspense, and improbable narrative; this literary form became the most popular in 19th-century America. [d. December 21, 1894]

1862 *O. Henry (William Sidney Porter),* U.S. short-story writer; prolific master of the tightly plotted, superbly executed short story with a surprise ending. [d. June 5, 1910]

1877 *Sir James Hopwood Jeans,* British physicist, astronomer, author; noted for his work on *kinetic theory of gases and radiations;* knighted, 1928. [d. September 17, 1946]

1883 *D(avid) H(erbert) Lawrence,* British novelist, short-story writer, poet; noted for his passionate, primitive handling of controversial subjects. [d. March 2, 1930]

Grigori Evsevich Zinoviev, Russian political leader and associate of Lenin in forming Bolshevik party; member of ruling triumvirate with Kamenev and Stalin after Lenin's death; accused of plotting against Stalin; expelled from office; accused of complicity in the murder of Sergei Kirov. [executed August 25, 1936]

1895 *Vinoba Bhave,* Indian mystic, social reformer; heir to the spiritual empire of Mahatma Gandhi; after assassination of Gandhi, assumed leadership in movement for social reform and economic revolution begun by Gandhi. [d. November 15, 1982]

1896 *Robert Samuel Kerr,* U.S. politician, oilman; Governor of Oklahoma, 1943–47; U.S. Senator, 1949–63. [d. January 1, 1963]

1898 *Sir Gerald (Walter Robert) Templer,* British army officer; Chief of Imperial General Staff, 1935–54; knighted, 1949. [d. October 25, 1979]

1909 *Anne Eckert Seymour,* U.S. actress; starred in the radio serial, *Story of Mary Marlin,* 1934–44. [d. December 8, 1988]

1913 *Paul (Bear) Bryant,* U.S. football coach; coach for University of Alabama, 1958–82. [d. January 26, 1983]

Hedy Lamarr (Hedwig Eva Marie Kiesler), U.S. actress; gained notoriety for her ten-minute nude sequence in the film *Ecstasy,* 1933; billed as the world's most beautiful woman.

1917 *Ferdinand Edralin Marcos,* Philippine leader; President of Philippines, 1965–73; Prime Minister, 1973–86. [d. September 28, 1989]

Jessica Mitford, British-born journalist, author; wrote *The American Way of Death,* 1963; called *Queen of the Muckrakers.* [d. July 23, 1996]

1922 *James Charles Evers,* U.S. political, civil rights leader; Mayor of Fayette, Mississippi.

1923 *Betsy Drake,* U.S. actress; appeared in *Room for One More,* 1952.

1924 *Tom Landry,* U.S. football coach; head coach of Dallas Cowboys, 1960–89.

1928 *Reubin O'Donovan Askew,* U.S. government official, politician; Governor of Florida, 1971–79; sought Democratic presidential nomination, 1984.

William Xavier Kienzle, U.S. author; known for mysteries frequently set in the Catholic parishes of Detroit; wrote *The Rosary Murders* and *Death Wears a Red Hat.*

1932 *Robert William (Bob) Packwood,* U.S. politician; Senator, 1969–95.

1939 *Earl Holliman (Anthony Numkena),* U.S. actor; starred in the television series, *Police Woman,* 1974–78.

1940 *Brian Russell DePalma,* U.S. director; known for his horror films, including *Carrie* and *The Fury.*

Zandra Rhodes, British designer; unusual fashions of silk, chiffon, and jersey revolutionized dress design.

1943 *Lola Falana,* U.S. actress, singer, dancer; Theatre World Award, 1975; Tony Award nomination for *Doctor Jazz.*

1951 *Amy Madigan,* U.S. actress; Academy Award nominee for *Twice in a Lifetime.*

1963 *Virginia Madsen,* U.S. actress.

HISTORICAL EVENTS

1297 Scots under *William Wallace* defeat an English army of more than 50,000 at *Sterling Bridge.*

1649 *Oliver Cromwell* of England sacks *Drogheda* in Ireland, suppressing an Irish uprising led by the Marquis of Ormonde, James Butler.

1700 *Battle of Malplaquet* is fought as British, Dutch, and Austrian forces defeat the French in the last great battle of the *War of the Spanish Succession.*

1814 *Battle of Lake Champlain* (sometimes called *Battle of Plattsburg Bay*) results in American naval victory over the British (*War of 1812*).

1855 *Sebastopol* capitulates to England, France, and Turkey (*Crimean War*).

1941 U.S. President *Franklin D. Roosevelt* issues shoot-on-sight order to warships in U.S. defensive waters (*World War II*).

1943 Italian fleet surrenders to Allies (*World War II*).

1952 Dr. *Charles Hufnagel* performs the first artificial *aortic valve implant.*

1962 *The Beatles,* British rock group, make their first recordings, *Love Me, Do,* and *P.S., I Love You.*

1972 *Bay Area Rapid Transit,* first new *mass transit system* in the U.S. since 1907, begins limited service in the San Francisco Bay area.

1973 Leftist government of Chilean President *Salvador Allende* is overthrown by a military coup; Allende is reported to have committed suicide.

september

1975 Former United Mine Workers' president, *Tony Boyle,* is sentenced to three consecutive life prison terms for the murder of union rival, *Joseph Yablonski* and his family.

1985 The U.S. spacecraft, *International Cometary Explorer,* passes through a comet's tail and transmits first pictures of its nucleus.

1992 *Hurricane Iniki* hits the island of Kauai, Hawaii, killing two people.

1996 The United Nations approves the *Nuclear Test-Ban Treaty.*

HOLIDAYS

Cape Verde Islands
Nationality Day

Ethiopia
Popular Revolution Commemoration Day
Commemorates the coup which removed Emperor Haile Selassie from power, 1974.

Guinea-Bissau
National Day

U.S. (Maryland)
Defenders' Day

RELIGIOUS CALENDAR

Feasts
The Holy Name of Mary. Feast originated in 14th century. Suppressed 1969.

The Saints
St. Ailbhe, bishop. Also called *Ailbe, Albeus.* [d. c. 526]
St. Eanswida, virgin. Also called *Eanswide, Eanswitho.* [d. c. 640]
St. Guy of Anderlecht. Also called *Guidon, Guy of Anderlent,* or *Wye.* [d. c. 1012]

The Beatified
Blessed Victoria Fornari-Strata, widow and foundress of the Blue Nuns of Genoa. [d. 1617]

BIRTHDATES

1494 *Francis I* of France, 1515–47. [d. March 31, 1547]

1575 *Henry Hudson,* British navigator; made several attempts to find the Northwest Passage; first white man to go up the Hudson River, which was named for him. [d. June 23, 1611]

1788 *Alexander Campbell,* U.S. editor, clergyman born in Ireland. Founder of Bethany College; son of Thomas Campbell, with whom he founded the *Churches of Christ* in the U.S. [d. March 4, 1866]

1806 *Andrew Hull Foote,* U.S. naval officer; prominent in the U.S. Civil War, distinguishing himself at the battles of Fort Henry and Fort Donelson. [d. June 26, 1863]

1812 *Richard March Hoe,* U.S. inventor; perfected a *rotary printing press,* which revolutionized the newspaper publishing business in the U.S. [d. June 7, 1886]

1818 *Richard Jordan Gatling,* U.S. inventor; developed the *Gatling gun,* the first *machine gun,* for use during the U.S. Civil War. [d. February 26, 1903]

1852 *Herbert Henry Asquith, 1st Earl of Oxford and Asquith,* British statesman; Prime Minister, 1908–16; achieved passage of Parliament Act, Home Rule Bill for Ireland, and Welsh Disestablishment Act. [d. February 15, 1928]

1855 *William Sharp,* Scottish poet; promoter of Celtic literary revival; wrote under the pseudonym *Fiona Macleod.* [d. December 14, 1905]

1880 *H(enry) L(ouis) Mencken,* U.S. journalist, critic, editor; noted social observer and expert on the American language. [d. January 29, 1956]

1888 *Maurice Chevalier,* French singer, actor. [d. January 1, 1972]

1891 *Arthur Hays Sulzberger,* U.S. newspaper publisher; publisher of *New York Times,* 1935–68; a director of Associated Press, 1943–52. [d. December 11, 1968]

1892 *Alfred A. Knopf,* U.S. publisher; founder of Alfred A. Knopf, Inc., 1915; recognized as one of the foremost publishers of all time. [d. August 11, 1984]

1893 *Lewis Blaine Hershey,* U.S. army general; Director, U.S. Selective Service System, 1941–70. [d. May 20, 1977]

1897 *Irène Joliot-Curie,* French physicist; Nobel Prize in chemistry for synthesizing new radioactive elements, including radioactive nitrogen and phosphorus (with F. Joliot-Curie), 1935. [d. March 17, 1956]

1898 *Ben(jamin) Shahn,* U.S. painter, graphic artist, born in Russia; devoted his art to social and political causes; responsible for murals at Rockefeller Center, New York (with Diego Rivera), Bronx Central Annex Post Office, and the Social Security Building, Washington, D.C., as well as numerous posters, oils, gouaches, and book illustrations. [d. March 14, 1969]

1901 *Ben Blue,* U.S. comedian. [d. March 7, 1975]

1902 *Margaret Hamilton,* U.S. actress; known for her role as the Wicked Witch of the West in *The Wizard of Oz,* 1939. [d. May 16, 1985]

1904 *George K(ung) C(hao) Yeh,* Chinese National statesman, educator; Foreign Minister, 1949–58; Ambassador to U.S., 1958–62. [d. November 20, 1981]

1909 *Robert E(dmonds) Kintner,* U.S. broadcasting company executive; President, American Broadcasting Co., 1950–56; President, National Broadcasting Co., 1958–65. [d. December 20, 1980]

1913 *Jessie Owens,* U.S. athlete; winner of four gold medals at the 1936 Olympics in Berlin. [d. March 31, 1980]

1917 *Han Suyin,* Chinese-born author; wrote *A Many-Splendoured Thing,* 1952.

1920 *Irene Dailey,* U.S. actress; Emmy Award for soap opera *Another World,* 1979.

1931 *Ian Holm (Ian Holm Cuthbert),* British actor; Academy Award nomination for *Chariots of Fire,* 1981.

George Jones, U.S. singer; Country Music Association Best Male Vocalist, 1980; married to Tammy Wynette, 1968–75; called *The Crown Prince of Country Music.*

1940 *Michael Stephen (Mickey) Lolich,* U.S. baseball player.

1941 *Linda Gray,* U.S. actress; known for her role as Sue Ellen Ewing on the television series, *Dallas.*

1943 *Maria Muldaur,* U.S. singer.

1944 *Leonard Peltier,* U.S. Native American activist.

HISTORICAL EVENTS

490 B.C. Athenian force defeats the Persian army at the *Battle of Marathon.*

1683 The Turkish siege of *Vienna* is raised by a German-Polish army under the command of *John III Sobieski* of Poland.

1848 A new federal constitution, closely modeled on that of the United States, is adopted in *Switzerland.*

1908 *Lusitania,* world's largest steamship, arrives in New York on her maiden voyage.

1919 Gabriele d'Annunzio, with volunteer troops, seizes *Fiume,* under dispute between Yugoslavia and Italy, for Italy.

1934 Lithuania, Latvia, and Estonia sign the *Baltic Pact* to defend their independence.

1954 *Lassie* makes its television debut.

1959 *Bonanza* makes its television debut.

1966 U.S. spacecraft *Gemini 11* is launched from Cape Kennedy, Florida.

1973 Eleven black miners are killed by South African police at the Western Deep Levels gold mine in *Carletonville* during a riot over wages.

1974 *Haile Selassie,* Emperor of Ethiopia since 1930, is deposed in an army coup.

1977 South African political activist, *Steven Biko,* dies of unexplained head injuries while in police custody.

1987 Mexican neurosurgeon, *Ignacio Navarro Madrazo,* transplants brain tissue from an aborted fetus to treat *Parkinson's disease* patients. It represents the first human brain tissue transplant.

1990 Allied powers from World War II (Great Britain, United States, Soviet Union, France, West Germany, and East Germany) sign the *Treaty on the Final Settlement with Respect to Germany,* giving a reunited Germany complete control over its own domestic and international activities (October 3, 1990).

1992 Astronauts *Jan Davis* and *Mark Lee* begin a mission aboard the space shuttle *Endeavor,* as the first married couple in space.

Dr. Mae C. Jemison becomes the first African American woman in space aboard the space shuttle *Endeavour* (mission Spacelab-J).

RELIGIOUS CALENDAR

The Saints

St. John Chrysostom, archbishop of Constantinople and Doctor of the Church. Patron of preachers. Invoked against epilepsy. Surnamed Chrysostomus, 'golden-mouthed,' because of his eloquence. [d. 407] Obligatory Memorial.

St. Maurilius, Bishop of Angers. [d. 453]

St. Eulogius, Patriarch of Alexandria. [d. c. 607]

St. Amatus, abbot. Also called *Ameè*. [d. c. 630]

BIRTHDATES

1520 *William Cecil, Baron Burghley,* English statesman under Queen Elizabeth I; carried out execution of *Mary, Queen of Scots.* [d. August 4, 1598]

1722 *François Joseph Paul de Grasse, Marquis de Grasse-Tilly,* French admiral; aided America in its war for independence; supported General Washington at Yorktown, leading to the defeat of Cornwallis. [d. January 11, 1788]

1755 *Oliver Evans,* U.S. inventor; patented *high-pressure steam engine,* 1797; his work anticipated both the *steamboat* and the *automobile.* [d. April 15, 1819]

1851 *Walter Reed,* U.S. physician, bacteriologist; responsible for discovery of method to prevent *yellow fever.* [d. November 23, 1902]

1857 *Milton Snavely Hershey,* U.S. manufacturer; founded Hershey Chocolate Corp., the largest U.S. producer of chocolate products. [d. October 13, 1945]

1860 *John Joseph (Black Jack) Pershing,* U.S. Army general; led an unsuccessful pursuit of Mexican revolutionary Pancho Villa, 1915–17; headed American Expeditionary Force during World War I. Awarded the Pulitzer Prize for his memoirs, *My Experiences in the World War,* 1931. [d. July 15, 1948]

1863 *Baron Franz von Hipper,* German admiral prominent in World War I; Commander-in-Chief of German High Seas Fleet, 1918. [d. May 25, 1932]

Cyrus Adler, U.S. religious leader, educator; President, Dropsie College for Hebrew and Cognate Learning, 1908–40; President Jewish Theological Seminary, 1924–40; recognized as a major force in conservative Judaism in the U.S. [d. April 7, 1940]

Arthur Henderson, British diplomat; Nobel Peace Prize for work as head of World Disarmament Conference, 1934. [d. October 20, 1935]

1866 *Adolf Meyer,* U.S. psychiatrist, neurologist, born in Switzerland; *Father of the Mental Hygiene Movement* in the U.S.; developed the theory of objective psychobiology. [d. March 17, 1950]

1874 *Arnold Schönberg,* Austrian composer; revolutionized modern music through use of a 12-tone system. [d. July 13, 1951]

1876 *Sherwood Anderson,* U.S. author; known for his book, *Winesburg, Ohio,* 1919, [d. March 8, 1941]

1883 *Lewis Edward Lawes,* U.S. penologist; warden of Sing Sing Prison, 1919–40; firm advocate of reform rather than punishment of prison inmates; opposed capital punishment. [d. April 23, 1947]

1886 *Sir Robert Robinson,* British chemist; Nobel Prize in chemistry for his work with *alkaloids* and other plant products, 1947. [d. February 8, 1975]

1887 *Leopold Ruzicka,* Swiss chemist; Nobel Prize in

september

chemistry for work on *ringed molecules* and *terpenes, 1939.* [d. September 1976]

1894 *J(ohn) B(oynton) Priestley,* British novelist, dramatist, essayist; noted for his evocation of *déjàvu* in his writings. [d. August 14, 1984]

1902 *Leland Hayward,* U.S. producer; films include *Mister Roberts,* 1955, and *The Old Man and the Sea,* 1958. [d. March 18, 1971]

1916 *Roald Dahl,* British short-story and children's book writer; best known for his *Charlie and the Chocolate Factory.* [d. November 23, 1990]

1917 *Richard (Dick) Haymes,* U.S. singer; noted for his mellow voice; popular vocalist of the early 1940's. [d. March 28, 1980]

1924 *Maurice Jarre,* French composer; Academy Awards for movie scores to *Lawrence of Arabia,* 1962, and *Doctor Zhivago,* 1966.

1925 *Mel Torme,* U.S. singer.

1928 *Robert Indiana (Robert Clarke),* U.S. artist; creates art of words; his arrangement of red letters LOVE on a blue and green background was one of the most widely reproduced images of the 1960's.

1932 *Barbara Bain,* U.S. actress; known for her role as Cinnamon Carter on the television series, *Mission Impossible,* 1966–69.

1937 *Fred Silverman,* U.S. television executive; only man to run all three major television networks' entertainment divisions.

1938 *Judith Martin,* U.S. author, journalist; writes syndicated newspaper column, *Miss Manners,* 1978–; author of *Miss Manners Guide to Excruciatingly Correct Behavior,* 1982.

1939 *Larry Melvin Speakes,* U.S. government official; Deputy Press Secretary, 1981–87.

Joel-Peter Witkin, U.S. photographer.

1941 *Oscar Arias Sanchez,* Costa Rican politician; President of Costa Rica, 1986–; Nobel Peace Prize for his efforts to restore peace in Nicaragua between the Contra rebels and the government, 1987.

1944 *Jacqueline Fraser Bisset,* British actress; starred in the movies, *The Deep* and *Rich and Famous.*

Peter Cetera, U.S. singer, musician; lead vocalist for the rock group, *Chicago;* solo hit, *Glory of Love,* 1986.

1948 *Nell Carter,* U.S. actress, singer; known for her role on the television series, *Gimme a Break;* starred on stage in *Ain't Misbehavin'.*

1949 *John Rikard (Rick) Dempsey,* U.S. baseball player; catcher, Baltimore Orioles; Most Valuable Player of the World Series, 1983.

1956 *Joni Sledge,* U.S. singer; member of the rock group, *Sister Sledge.*

HISTORICAL EVENTS

1515 *Battle of Marignano* results in a French victory over the Swiss in the *War of the Holy League.*

1598 *Philip II* of Spain dies and is succeeded by *Philip III.*

1609 *Henry Hudson,* sailing for the Netherlands, enters harbor at New York and sails up Hudson River as far as Albany, thus establishing Dutch claims to this region.

1635 General Court of Massachusetts Bay Colony banishes *Roger Williams,* who leaves to establish the colony of *Rhode Island.*

1788 *New York* is declared the first federal capital and seat of U.S. Congress.

1816 *René Laennec,* using a rolled-up sheet of paper to better hear a patient's heart, invents the *stethoscope.*

1846 U.S. General *Winfield Scott* defeats Mexicans at the *Battle of Chapultepec (Mexican War).*

1899 First successful climb of *Mt. Kenya,* over 17,058 feet, is accomplished by *H. J. Mackinder.*

1942 German army enters *Stalingrad,* Russia (*World War II*).

1953 *Nikita Khruschshev* becomes First Secretary of the Soviet Communist Party's Central Committee.

1966 *Balthazar Vorster* is elected prime minister of South Africa by the ruling National Party.

1968 *Albania* withdraws from the *Warsaw Pact.*

1971 Prisoners riot at the state prison in *Attica, New York;* 28 prisoners are killed.

1973 General *Augusto Pinochet Ugarte* becomes President of Chile.

1974 *Chico and the Man* makes its television debut.

1978 *Ford Motor Co.* is indicted in the death of three accident victims whose *Pinto* fuel tank exploded upon impact.

1979 The Black enclave of *Venda* gains its independence from South Africa.

1987 An unmarked canister of radioactive cesium chloride found in an abandoned laboratory in *Goiania, Brazil,* is accidentally opened. Hundreds of people are contaminated and many are expected to develop cancer.

september

SEPTEMBER 14

HOLIDAYS

Bolivia (Cocha-bamba)
Public Holiday

Nicaragua
Battle of San Jacinto

RELIGIOUS CALENDAR

Feasts
The Exaltation of the Holy Cross,
commonly called *Holy Cross
Day.* Also known as *Holyrood
Day.* [major holy day,
Episcopal Church; minor
festival, Lutheran Church]

The Saints
St. Maternus, Bishop of Cologne. [d.
4th century]
St. Notburga, virgin; patroness of
poor peasants and hired
servants. [d. c. 1313]

BIRTHDATES

1547 *Jan van Olden Barnveldt,*
Dutch statesman; a champion
of Dutch independence. [d.
May 13, 1619]

1742 *James Wilson,* U.S. Supreme
Court justice. [d. August 21,
1798]

1769 *Alexander von Humboldt,*
German scientist and
explorer; conducted
numerous experiments
dealing with the earth's

magnetic field, climatic
conditions, rock formations
and volcanic activity; noted
for his *Kosmos,* a description
of the physical universe,
1845–62. [d. May 6, 1859]

1791 *Franz Bopp,* German
philologist; founder of the
science of *comparative
philology.* [d. October 23,
1867]

1843 *Lola Rodr guez de Tio,*
Puerto Rican poet and
supporter of independence
movement. [d. 1924]

1849 *Ivan Petrovich Pavlov,*
Russian physiologist; best
known for his studies of
conditioned reflexes in dogs;
Nobel Prize in physiology or
medicine, 1904. [d. February
27, 1936]

1860 *(Hannibal) Hamlin Garland,*
U.S. short-story writer,
novelist, essayist; Pulitzer
Prize in autobiography for *A
Daughter of the Middle
Border,* 1922. [d. March 4,
1940]

1864 *Edgar Algernon Robert, 1st
Viscount Cecil of Chelwood,*
British statesman; Nobel
Peace Prize, 1919, for his
work in drafting the 1919
League of Nations pact. [d.
November 24, 1958]

1867 *Charles Dana Gibson,* U.S.
artist, illustrator; best known

for his creation of the *Gibson
girl,* a model for women's
fashion and hair style from
1890–1914. [d. December 23,
1944]

1883 *Margaret Higgins Sanger,*
U.S. nurse, social reformer;
founder of birth control
movement in U.S.;
responsible for establishment
of the first birth control clinic
in the U.S.; first president of
*International Planned
Parenthood Federation,*
1953–66; worked in India and
Japan, as well as the U.S., to
further the cause of
intelligent contraceptive
practices. [d. September 6,
1966]

1886 *Jan (Garrigue) Masaryk,*
Czechoslovakian statesman;
Minister to Great Britain,
1925–38; Foreign Minister,
1940–48; Vice-Premier of
Czechoslovak provisional
government in London,
1941–45. [d. March 10, 1948]

1887 *Karl Taylor Compton,* U.S.
educator, physicist; President,
M.I.T., 1930–46. [d. June 22,
1954]

1895 *Robert Abercrombie Lovett,*
U.S. government official;
Secretary of Defense,
1951–53; Presidential Medal
of Freedom, 1963. [d. May 7,
1986]

1896 *John Robert Powers,* U.S.
model agency pioneer;

founder of *John Robert Powers Agency,* 1921. [d. July 19, 1977]

1898 *Hal (Brent) Wallis,* U.S. motion picture producer; in charge of production for Warner Brothers Studios, 1930–44; founded Hal Wallis Productions, 1944. [d. October 5, 1986]

1914 *Clayton Moore,* U.S. actor; starred in the television series, *The Lone Ranger,* 1949–56.

1917 *Sydney Justin Harris,* U.S. journalist; writes syndicated column, *Strictly Personal.* [d. 1986]

1920 *Lawrence R. Klein,* U.S. economist; Nobel Prize for economics for developing *forecasting models,* 1980.

1927 *Edmund Casimir Szoka,* U.S. religious leader; Archbishop of Detroit, 1981–88; Cardinal, 1988–.

1928 *Albert Shanker,* U.S. teacher, labor union official; President, American Federation of Teachers. [d. February 22, 1997]

1929 *John Lawrence (Larry) Collins,* U.S. author, journalist; co-wrote *Is Paris Burning?,* 1965, and *Freedom at Midnight,* 1975.

1934 *Katherine Murray (Kate) Millett,* U.S. feminist, author, artist; wrote *Sexual Politics,* 1970.

1938 *Nicol Williamson,* Scottish actor, known for his Shakespearean roles.

1942 *John Francis Lehman, Jr.,* U.S. government official; Secretary of the Navy, 1981–87.

1944 *Joey Heatherton,* U.S. actress, singer, dancer.

1959 *Mary Frances Crosby,* U.S. actress; known for her role as Kristen Shepard, who shot J.R. Ewing, in the television series, *Dallas,* 1980; daughter of Bing Crosby.

HISTORICAL EVENTS

1262 *Alfonso X* of Castile captures *Cadiz* from the Moors, thus ending a 500-year Moorish occupation of the city.

1752 England adopts the *Gregorian calendar;* September 14 of this year was preceded by September 3, thus effectively causing the loss of 11 days in the English calendar and sparking much unrest.

1770 *Censorship* is abolished in Denmark.

1814 *Francis Scott Key,* Maryland lawyer, is inspired to write the words to the song that is to become the American national anthem, *The Star-Spangled Banner,* as he witnesses the bombardment of *Fort McHenry (War of 1812).*

1829 *Peace of Adrianople* is signed between Russia and the Turks with Russia securing the mouth of the Danube and the eastern coast of the Black Sea (*Russo-Turkish War*).

1846 U.S. General *Winfield Scott* captures *Mexico City,* effectively ending the *Mexican War.*

1854 Allied armies (Britain, France, Turkey) land in the Crimea to oppose Russia (*Crimean War*).

1886 The *American Philatelic Society* holds its first meeting in Chicago, Illinois.

1901 U.S. President *William McKinley* dies from an assassin's bullet (see September 6); Vice-President *Theodore Roosevelt,* 42, becomes the youngest president ever to occupy the office.

1911 Russian premier *Peter Stolypin* is fatally wounded at a theater in Kiev by a reputed agent of the secret police.

1914 *General von Moltke* is succeeded as German Chief of Staff by *General von Falkenhayn (World War I).*

1926 The *National Broadcasting Co.* airs its first radio broadcast.

1930 General election in Germany gives *National Socialist Party (Nazis)* a majority in the Reichstag.

1939 First successful *helicopter* is flown by designer *Igor Sikorsky,* an American inventor born in Russia.

1950 Colonel *Oscar Osorio* is inaugurated as president of El Salvador.

1953 The *New York Yankees* capture the American League pennant, becoming the first major league baseball team to win five consecutive championships.

1957 *Have Gun Will Travel* makes its television debut.

1961 The Cuban government issues a ban on emigration.

1964 *New York City* begins busing students in an effort to desegregate its public

september

schools. Approximately 170,000 white students boycott classes for the first two days.

1969 The *U.S.S. Manhattan* becomes the first commercial vessel to sail through the *Northwest Passage*.

1972 *The Waltons* makes its television debut.

1975 *Mother Elizabeth Ann Bayley Seton*, first U.S.-born saint, is

canonized in Rome by Pope Paul VI.

1978 *Mork and Mindy* makes its television debut.

1984 *Shimon Peres* is inaugurated as prime minister after Israel's parliament votes to allow the Labor Party and Likud block of political organizations to rotate cabinet positions over a four-year period. No group had won enough votes in a

July election to form a government.

1994 Interim baseball commissioner *Bud Selig* announces the cancellation of the *World Series* due to the ongoing players strike. It is the first time in over ninety years that a World Series is not played.

HOLIDAYS

Costa Rica, El Salvador, Guatemala, Honduras, Nicaragua
Independence Day
Commemorates the achievement of independence from Spain, 1821.

Japan
Respect for the Aged Day

RELIGIOUS CALENDAR

Feasts
The Seven Sorrows of the Blessed Virgin Mary. Also called the *Compassion of Our Lady,* or *Our Lady of Sorrows.* Obligatory Memorial.

The Saints
St. Nicetas the Goth, martyr. [d. 375]
St. Aichardus, abbot. Also called *Achard, Achart, Aicard.* [d. c. 687]
St. Mirin. Irish missionary to Scotland. Also called *Meadhran.* [d. c. 7th century]
St. Adam, Bishop of Caithness and martyr. [d. 1222]
St. Catherine of Genoa, widow and mystic. [d. 1510]
St. Nicomedes, monk, religious writer, and martyr. [death date unknown]

BIRTHDATES

1584 *Georg Rodolf Weckherin,* German poet, translator, and parliamentary secretary to two English kings; responsible for introduction of Renaissance verse forms into German literature. [d. February 13, 1653]

1613 *François, duc de La Rochefoucauld,* French moralist and maxim writer; involved in plot against Richelieu; joined the Fronde; noted for his *Réflexions ou Sentences et Maximes Morales,* 1665. [d. March 16, 1680]

1765 *Manuel Maria Barbosa du Bocage,* Portuguese poet; leader of *Nova Arcádia group of poets.* [d. December 21, 1805]

1789 *James Fenimore Cooper,* U.S. author; the first truly American novelist; the Cooper hero, a woodsman characterized by an almost poetic solitude, courage, and stalwartness, can be seen in the characters of *Natty Bumppo, Leather-Stocking, Path-finder,* and *Hawkeye.* [d. September 14, 1851]

1830 *Porfirio Diaz,* Mexican statesman; President of Mexico, 1877–80; 1884–1911; ruled as a dictator, advancing the material status of the country but not improving the lot of the masses; exiled, 1911. [d. July 2, 1915]

1834 *Heinrich Gotthard von Treitschke,* German historian and patriot; contributed to rise of anti-British sentiment in Germany. [d. April 28, 1896]

1852 *Jan Ernst Matzeliger,* U.S. inventor; developed the *shoe-lasting machine,* which totally revolutionized the shoe manufacturing industry. [d. August 24, 1889]

1857 *William Howard Taft,* U.S. jurist; 17th President of the U.S., 1909–13; represented the conservative wing of a divided Republican party; actively supported anti-trust legislation; Chief Justice of U.S. Supreme Court, 1921–30. [d. March 8, 1930]

1876 *Frank Ernest Gannett,* U.S. newspaper publisher. [d. September 3, 1957]

Bruno Walter (Schlesinger), German conductor; conductor of Vienna Imperial Opera, 1901–12; Vienna State Opera, 1935–38; guest conductor in New York, 1922–26, 1932–35, and London, 1924–32. [d. February 17, 1962]

1879 *Sir Joseph Aloysius Lyons,* Australian statesman; Premier of Tasmania, 1923–28; Prime Minister of Australia, 1932–39. [d. April 7, 1939]

september

1889 *Robert Charles Benchley,* U.S. humorist, critic; on the staff of *Life* magazine, 1920–30; drama critic, *New Yorker,* 1930–40; noted for his depiction of the struggles of an ordinary man; author of *My Ten Years in a Quandary.* [d. November 21, 1945]

1890 *Dame Agatha (Mary Clarissa) Christie,* British novelist, playwright; known for her popular mystery novels; created crime-solving characters of Belgian detective *Hercule Poirot* and eccentric spinster *Miss Jane Marple.* [d. January 12, 1976]

1894 *Jean Renoir,* French film director; son of Pierre Auguste Renoir (February 25). [d. February 12, 1979]

1903 *Roy Acuff,* U.S.singer; sold over 30 million records including *Wabash Cannonball;* called *The King of Country Music.* [d. November 23, 1992]

1904 *Umberto II* of Italy, assumed throne upon the abdication of his father, *Victor Emmanuel III,* 1946; third king of united Italy; exiled 1946 when Italy became a republic. [d. March 18, 1983]

1914 *Creighton Williams Abrams,* U.S. Army general; active in Vietnam War, 1968–72; U.S. Army Chief of Staff, 1972–74. [d. September 4, 1974]

1915 *Fawn McKay Brodie,* U.S. author; wrote biographies of Sir Richard Burton, Joseph Smith, and Thomas Jefferson; Knopf Biography Award, 1943. [d. January 10, 1981]

1916 *Margaret Lockwood,* British actress.

1922 *Jackie Cooper,* U.S. actor, television director, producer.

1923 *Hank Williams,* U.S. country-music singer, songwriter. [d. January 1, 1953]

1926 *Robert Waltrip (Bobby) Short,* U.S. musician; pianist known for supper-club singing; specializes in songs of the 1920s–30s; wrote his autobiography, *Black and White Baby,* 1971.

1927 *Norman Lawrence (Norm) Crosby,* U.S. comedian; known for his routines which feature malapropisms.

1929 *Murray Gell-Mann,* U.S. physicist; Nobel Prize in physics for development of *Eight-fold Way,* a system of grouping nuclear particles, 1969; proposed the existence of the quark.

1937 *Robert E. Lucas, Jr.,* Nobel Prize for Economics, 1995.

1938 *Gaylord Jackson Perry,* U.S. baseball player; pitcher, 1962–83; 3,000 strikeouts; won the Cy Young Award in both the American and National Leagues.

1940 *Merlin Olsen,* U.S. football player, sports-caster, actor; Hall of Fame defensive lineman; featured on the TV series *Little House on the Praire* and *Father Murphy.*

1946 *Tommy Lee Jones,* U.S. actor; Academy Award (Best Supporting Actor) for *The Fugitive,* 1993.

Oliver Stone, U.S. filmmaker; Academy Award (Director) for both *Platoon,* 1986, and *Born on the Fourth of July,* 1989.

1961 *Daniel Constantine (Dan) Marino, Jr.,* U.S. football player; quarterback, Miami Dolphins; led the Natonal Football League in passing, 1983, 1984.

1984 *Henry (Harry) of Wales,* British prince; second son of Charles, Prince of Wales; third in line to the British throne behind his father and brother, William of Wales.

HISTORICAL EVENTS

1776 British troops, under General Howe, seize *New York City,* which had been recently evacuated by Washington's troops (*American Revolution*).

1812 *Moscow* is burned by the Russians in an attempt to make the city untenable for Napoleon and the French army.

1821 *Costa Rica, El Salvador, Guatemala, Honduras, and Nicaragua* achieve independence from Spain.

1830 *Liverpool and Manchester Railway* in England opens, launching the railroad era.

The first *National Convention of African Americans* is held.

1884 The anesthetic qualities of *cocaine* in eye and oral surgery are revealed in a paper presented to the German Ophthalmological Society in Heidelberg.

1914 *Battle of the Aisne* marks the end of the Allied advance and the beginning of trench warfare in World War I.

1916 The first use of *tanks* in battle, by the British in an Allied attack at *Flers-Courcelette* during the *Battle of the Somme* (*World War I*).

1935 *Nürnberg Laws* deprive Jews of citizenship in Germany.

1944 Allied forces begin *Rhineland Campaign* in Germany (*World War II*).

1949 *The Lone Ranger* makes its television debut.

1950 Amphibious UN landing at *Inchon* proves decisive in defeat of North Korean troops (*Korean War*).

1963 *Ahmed Ben Bella* is elected as the first constitutional president of Algeria.

1964 *Hungary* and the *Vatican* sign an agreement that restores the church's right to establish a Roman Catholic hierarchy in Hungary.

1972 U.S.S.R. and Spain sign a trade agreement, the first between the two countries since the 1936–39 Spanish Civil War.

1973 *King Gustaf VI Adolf* of Sweden dies at the age of 90 and is succeeded by his grandson, *Carl XVI Gustaf*.

East and West Germany and the *Bahamas* are accepted as members of the UN at the opening session of the 28th General Assembly.

1977 1,200 South African students, who have gathered to commemorate the death of *Steven Biko*, the country's best known young black leader, are arrested for violating the *Riotous Assemblies Act*.

1978 *Muhammad Ali* defeats *Leon Spinks* in 15 rounds in New Orleans to win an unprecedented fourth world heavyweight boxing title.

1983 Israeli prime minister, *Menachem Begin*, resigns his government and Herut Party posts.

september

SEPTEMBER 16

HOLIDAYS

Mexico, Papua New Guinea
Independence Day

U.S. (Oklahoma)
Cherokee Strip Day
Commemorates the opening of the
Cherokee Strip, 1893.

RELIGIOUS CALENDAR

The Saints

St. Cornelius, pope and martyr.
    Elected 251. [d. 253]
    Obligatory Memorial.
St. Cyprian, bishop of Carthage,
    martyr. Primate of the African
    church. Also known as
    Caecilius Cyprianus, or
    Thascius. [d. 258] Obligatory
    Memorial.
St. Euphemia, virgin and martyr. [d.
    c. 303]
*SS. Abundius, Abundantius, and
    their Companions,* martyrs.
    [d. c. 304]
St. Ninian, bishop. Missionary in
    Scotland. Also called *Ninias,
    Ninnidh, Ninyas, Nynia,* or
    Ringan. [d. c. 432]
St. Ludmila, martyr. [d. 921]
St. Edith of Wilton, virgin and nun.
    Also called *Eadgyth, Editha.*
    [d. 984]

The Beatified

Blessed Victor III, pope. Elected
    1086. [d. 1087]
Blessed Vitalis of Savigny, abbot. [d.
    1122]
Blessed Louis Allemand, Archbishop
    of Arles and cardinal. Also
called *Louis Aleman.* [d.
1450]

BIRTHDATES

1387 *Henry V* of England; began
    the *Hundred Years' War*
    against France. [d. August 31,
    1422]

1678 *Henry St. John, 1st Viscount
    Bolingbroke,* English
    politician, historian,
    philosopher; supporter of
    James Stuart, the *Old
    Pretender;* associated with
    Pope and Swift, he
    contributed the philosophical
    basis for the former's *Essay
    on Man,* 1730. [d. December
    12, 1751]

1685 *John Gay,* English playwright,
    poet; author of *The Beggar's
    Opera,* later adapted by
    Bertold Brecht and Kurt Weill
    for *The Threepenny Opera.*
    [d. December 4, 1732]

1745 *Prince Mikhail Illarionovich
    Golenishchev Kutuzov,*
    Russian Army field marshal;
    commander of army in
    Russian war against Poland,
    1805–12; defeated at
    Austerlitz; military governor of
    Kiev, 1805–12; his defeat at
    Battle of Borodino allowed
    Napoleon to enter Moscow.
    [d. April 28, 1813]

1777 *Nathan Mayer, 1st Baron
    Rothschild,* British financier,
born in Germany; son of
Meyer Amschel Rothschild;
head of financial institution's
branch at London; made
loans to European countries
fighting Napoleon. [d. July 28,
1836]

1785 *Thomas Barnes,* Editor of *The
    (London) Times* 1817–41. [d.
    May 7, 1841]

1822 *Charles Crocker,* U.S. railroad
    executive; founder of the
    Central Pacific Railroad Co.,
    1861, and of Southern Pacific
    Railroad, 1871. [d. August 14,
    1888]

1823 *Francis Parkman,* U.S.
    historian, author; compiled
    the massive *France and
    England in North America.*
    [d. November 8, 1893]

1837 *Pedro V,* King of Portugal,
    1853–61. [d. November 11,
    1861]

1838 *James Jerome Hill,* U.S.
    railroad magnate, financier;
    organized the Great Northern
    Railway; developed the
    Mesabi Range iron ore mines
    in Minnesota, 1904–16. [d.
    May 29, 1916]

1853 *Albrecht Kossel,* German
    biochemist; Nobel Prize in
    physiology or medicine for
    contributions to the
    knowledge of *cellular
    chemistry,* 1910. [d. July 5,
    1927]

1858 *Andrew Bonar Law,* British politician; Prime Minister of Great Britain, 1922–23. [d. October 30, 1923]

1875 *James Cash Penney,* U.S. merchant; founded the J.C. Penney Co., retail store; Chairman of the Board, 1917–58. [d. February 12, 1971]

1877 *Jacob Schick,* U.S. manufacturer; developed the *Schick razor.* [d. July 3, 1937]

1880 *Alfred Noyes,* British poet, author. [d. June 28, 1958]

1881 *Clive Bell,* British art critic; wrote *Art,* 1914, and *Since Cezanne,* 1922. [d. September 18, 1964]

1883 *T(homas) E(rnest) Hulme,* British critic, philosopher, poet; developed *Imagist theory* later popularized by T. S. Eliot and Ezra Pound. [d. September 28, 1917]

1885 *Karen Horney,* Norwegian-Dutch psychoanalyst, writer, teacher. [d. December 4, 1952]

1887 *Hans (or Jean) Arp,* French painter, sculptor, poet; founder of *Dadaism,* 1916; became member of Surrealist group, 1925. [d. June 7, 1966]

Nadia Juliette Boulanger, French music teacher, conductor; first woman conductor of Boston Symphony and New York Philharmonic. [d. October 22, 1979]

1888 *Frans Eemil Sillanpää,* Finnish novelist, short-story writer; Nobel Prize in literature, 1939. [d. June 3, 1964]

1891 *Karl Doenitz,* German admiral; commander-in-chief of German navy, 1943–45; Chancellor of Germany after Hitler's death, 1945; unconditionally surrendered to Allies. [d. December 24, 1980]

1893 *Sir Alexander Korda (Sandor Kellner),* Hungarian-born producer, director; developed British film industry with the creation of London Films Company; made 112 films including *The Thief of Baghdad* and *The Third Man.* [d. January 23, 1956]

Albert Szent-Györgyi, U.S. biochemist, born in Hungary; Nobel Prize in physiology or medicine for studies of effects of *Vitamins A and C,* 1937. [d. October 22, 1986]

1896 *Lester B. Granger,* U.S. social worker; Director, National Urban League, 1941–61. [d. January 9, 1976]

1914 *Allen Funt,* U.S. producer; creator and host of the television series, *Candid Camera.*

1919 *Lawrence (Johnston) Peter,* U.S. educator, author, born in Canada; developed the *Peter Principle* of competence in organizations. [d. January 12, 1990]

1923 *Lee Kuan Yew,* Singaporean politician, lawyer; Prime Minister, 1959–90.

Janis Paige (Donna Mae Jaden), U.S. singer, actress.

1924 *Lauren Bacall (Betty Joan Perske),* U.S. actress.

1925 *B. B. King (Riley B. King),* U.S. blues musician and guitarist.

1926 *John Knowles,* U.S. novelist; author of *A Separate Peace.*

Robert Harold Schuller, U.S. evangelist, author.

1927 *Peter Falk,* U.S. actor.

1930 *Anne Francis,* U.S. actress; played child roles on radio; starred in the television series, *Honey West,* 1965–66; called *The Little Queen of Soap Opera.*

1948 *Kenny Jones,* British musician; joined the rock group, *The Who,* as its drummer, 1979.

1949 *Ed Begley, Jr.,* U.S. actor; known for his role as Dr. Victor Ehrlich on the television series, *St. Elsewhere.*

1957 *Eric Ellsworth Hipple,* U.S. football player.

1958 *Maura O'Connell,* Irish singer.

1959 *Tim(othy) Raines,* U.S. baseball player.

1962 *Jennifer Tilly,* Canadian actress; Oscar nominee for *Bullets Over Broadway,* 1994.

HISTORICAL EVENTS

1380 *Charles V* of France dies and is succeeded by *Charles VI.*

1620 *Mayflower* sails from Plymouth, England.

1810 *Mexico* claims independence from Spain.(The republic is established December 6, 1822.)

1824 *Louis XVIII* of France dies and is succeeded by *Charles X.*

1859 *David Livingstone,* British explorer, discovers *Lake Nyasa* in Africa.

1893 *Cherokee Strip,* land between Kansas and Oklahoma, is opened for *land rush* settlement.

september

1908 *General Motors Corp.* is incorporated in New Jersey.

1915 *Haiti* becomes a U.S. protectorate as Marines occupy the island to quell civil disorder.

1941 Iranian leader, *Reza Shah Pahlavi,* abdicates in favor of his son, *Mohammad Reza Pahlavi.*

1944 U.S. forces land on Anguar, beginning their attack on the *Palau Islands (World War II).*

1963 Malaya, Sarawak, Sabah, and Singapore officially form the *Federation of Malaysia. Abdul Rahman* is inaugurated as premier.

1966 New *Metropolitan Opera House* in New York City's Lincoln Center opens with the world premiere of Samuel Barber's *Antony and Cleopatra.*

1974 Under a proclamation signed by U.S. President Gerald Ford, thousands of *Vietnam War deserters* and draft evaders become eligible for clemency if they swear allegiance to the U.S. and submit to alternate public service.

Mary Louise Smith of Iowa becomes the first woman to head the U.S. Republican National Committee.

1975 *Papua New Guinea* gains full independence from Australia.

1976 The *Episcopal Church* approves the ordination of woman priests and bishops.

1979 *Hafizullah Amin* is inaugurated as president of Afghanistan.

1982 Lebanese Christian militiamen massacre civilians in the *Sabra and Shatila refugee camps* in Israeli-controlled West Beirut.

1987 Twenty-four countries sign an international *ozone treaty* to protect the atmosphere by reducing global air pollution caused by *chlorofluorocarbons.*

HOLIDAYS

Angola
Day of the National Hero

U.S.
Citizenship Day

Constitution Day
Sponsored by Federal Union, Inc.,
Washington, D.C.

RELIGIOUS CALENDAR

Feasts
*The Impression of the Stigmata
    upon St. Francis* (1224).
    Celebrates stigmata that
    appeared on hands and feet
    of *St. Francis of Assisi* at La
    Verna.

The Saints
St. Satyrus, brother of St. Ambrose.
    [d. c. 379]
St. Lambert, Bishop of Maestricht,
    martyr. Also called *Landebert.*
    [d. c. 705]
St. Columba, virgin and martyr. [d.
    853]
St. Hildegard, virgin. First of the
    great German mystics. Also
    called *Hildegardis.* [d. 1179]
St. Peter Arbues, martyr. [d. 1485]
St. Robert Ballarmine, Archbishop
    of Capua, cardinal, and
    Doctor of the Church. Feast
    formerly May 13. [d. 1621]
    Optional Memorial.
SS. Socrates and Stephen, martyrs.
    [death date unknown]

BIRTHDATES

879 *Charles III* of France; called
    Charles the Simple. [d.
    October 7, 929]

1552 *Paul V,* pope 1605–21. [d.
    January 28, 1621]

1580 *Franscisco Gómez de
    Quevedo y Villegas,* Spanish
    satirist, novelist; renowned
    author of Spain's Golden Age
    of Literature. [d. September 8,
    1645]

1730 *Baron Friedrich Wilhelm
    Augustus von Steuben,*
    American Revolutionary
    general, born in Prussia;
    responsible for training
    Continental Army during
    American Revolution. [d.
    November 28, 1794]

1740 *John Cartwright,* English
    parliamentary reformer; called
    the *Father of Reform.* [d.
    September 23, 1824]

1743 *Marie-Jean-Antoine-Nicolas
    Caritat, Marquis de
    Condorcet,* French
    philosopher, educational
    theorist, mathematician,
    political economist; leading
    thinker of the Enlightenment.
    [d. March 25 or 29, 1794]

1800 *Franklin Buchanan,* U.S.
    naval officer; fought with the
    Confederate Navy; officer in
    charge of the *Merrimac* but
    not active in its historic battle
    with the *Monitor* because of a

battle wound; captured at the
    Battle of Mobile Bay, 1864;
    released, 1865. [d. May 11,
    1874]

1826 *Georg Friedrich Bernhard
    Riemann,* German
    mathematician; developed
    new, non-Euclidean geometry;
    conceptualized the Riemann's
    surface. [d. July 20, 1866]

1854 *David Dunbar Buick,* U.S.
    pioneer automobile builder;
    developed the Buick
    automobile; lost control of his
    company and died in
    obscurity as a clerk in a trade
    school. [d. March 5, 1929]

1857 *Konstantin Eduardovich
    Tsiolkovsky,* Soviet physicist;
    pioneer in development of
    Soviet rockets and space
    science. [d. September 19,
    1935]

1869 *Christian Louis Lange,*
    Norwegian pacifist and
    historian; Nobel Peace Prize
    for his guidance of the Inter-
    Parliamentary Union, 1921. [d.
    December 11, 1938]

1883 *William Carlos Williams,* U.S.
    poet, physician; noted for his
    objective poetic form,
    utilizing idiomatic speech and
    informal structure; he viewed
    his style as an extension of
    the Imagism of Ezra Pound.
    [d. March 4, 1963]

1896 *Samuel James (Sam) Ervin,
    Jr.,* U.S. politician, lawyer;

Senator, 1954–75; major opponent of Richard Nixon's claim of *executive privilege* during the *Senate Watergate Hearings.* [d. April 23, 1985]

1900 *John Willard Marriott,* U.S. hotel and restaurant executive; founder of the Marriott Hotel chain. [d. August 13, 1985]

1901 *Sir Francis Charles Chichester,* British adventurer, sportsman; made solo trip around the world in his yacht, *Gipsy Moth,* 1966–67. [d. August 26, 1972]

1904 *Sir Frederick Ashton,* British choreographer, dancer; principal choreographer, Royal Ballet, 1935–70; [d. August 18, 1988]

1906 *Junius Richard Jayewardene,* President, Democratic Socialist Republic of Sri Lanka, 1978–. [d. November 1, 1997]

1907 *Warren Earl Burger,* U.S. jurist, lawyer; Justice of U.S. Court of Appeals for the District of Columbia, 1955–69; Chief Justice of U.S. Supreme Court, 1969–87. [d. June 25, 1995]

1916 *Mary Stewart,* British novelist; author of romantic suspense novels.

Yumzhagiyen Tsedenbal, Chairman, Mongolian People's Republic, 1974–84.

1918 *Chaim Herzog,* Israeli statesman; Ambassador to UN, 1975–78; President, 1983–93. [d. April 17, 1997]

1927 *Ted Weiss,* U.S. politician; Congressman, 1977–92. [d. September 14, 1992]

1928 *Roderick Andrew (Roddy) McDowall,* British actor;

starred in *My Friend Flicka* and *Planet of the Apes.*

1929 *Pat Crowley,* U.S. actress; starred in the television series, *Please Don't Eat the Daisies,* 1965–67.

1930 *Edgar D. Mitchell,* U.S. astronaut; participant in *Apollo 14* moon landing.

Thomas Patten Stafford, U.S. astronaut; participated in the following flights: *Gemini 6,* 1965; *Gemini 9,* 1966; *Apollo 10,* 1969.

1931 *Anne Bancroft (Anna Maria Italiano),* U.S. actress; noted for her dramatic roles on stage and in films; married to Mel Brooks (June 28).

1934 *Maureen Connolly,* U.S. tennis player; U.S. singles champion, 1951–53; Wimbledon champion, 1952–54; Associated Press Woman Athlete of the Year, 1952–54. [d. June 21, 1969]

1935 *Ken Kesey,* U.S. novelist, editor; author of *One Flew Over the Cuckoo's Nest.*

1945 *Phil(ip) Jackson,* U.S. basketball coach; coach of the Chicago Bulls, 1989–98.

1948 *Jonathan Southworth (John) Ritter,* U.S. actor; starred as Jack Tripper in the television series, *Three's Company,* 1977–83; son of Tex Ritter.

1960 *Anthony Carter,* U.S. football player.

1962 *Donald Lavert (Don) Rogers,* U.S. football player; safety who was the first round draft pick of the Cleveland Browns, 1984; died of a cocaine overdose. [d. June 27, 1986]

HISTORICAL EVENTS

1631 *Battle of Breitenfeld,* fought near Leipzig, Germany, results in victory for Swedish and Protestant German forces under *Gustavus Adolphus* over Catholic troops led by the *Count of Tilly (Thirty Years' War).*

1665 *Philip IV* of Spain dies and is succeeded by *Charles II.*

1787 *U.S. Constitution* is signed by the delegates to the Constitutional Convention.

1796 U.S. President *George Washington* delivers his Farewell Address to the American people.

1806 Sweden cedes *Finland* to Russia by the *Peace of Frederikshamm.*

1838 *Great Western Railroad* from Liverpool to London is opened.

1862 *Battle of Antietam* halts Confederate advance into the North; known as the bloodiest battle of the Civil War (*U.S. Civil War*).

1908 *Thomas Selfridge* becomes the first airplane passenger to be killed in a crash.

1920 *American Professional Football Association,* forerunner of *NFL,* is formed at Canton, Ohio.

1930 Construction of *Boulder Dam* (now *Hoover Dam*) begins near Las Vegas, Nevada. The dam is completed in 1936.

1935 *Manuel Quezon y Molina* is elected first president of the Philippines.

1939 *U.S.S.R.* invades *Poland.*

1944 *Operation Market-Garden,* an Allied push to enter Germany and quickly end the war, begins with one of the largest airborne invasions in history.

1947 *James V. Forrestal* is sworn in as first U.S. Secretary of Defense.

1948 UN mediator Count *Folke Bernadotte* is assassinated in Jerusalem.

1964 *Bewitched* makes its television debut.

1970 *The Flip Wilson Show* makes its television debut.

1972 *M*A*S*H* makes its television debut.

1978 Egyptian President *Anwar al Sadat* and Israeli Prime Minister *Menachem Begin* sign documents providing machinery for peaceful relations, thus fulfilling purpose of Middle East summit at Camp David supported by U.S. President *Jimmy Carter*.

1980 *General Anastasio Somoza Debayle*, former president of Nicaragua, is assassinated in Paraguay.

Iraq abrogates the *Algiers Treaty,* igniting conflict with Iran. *(Iran-Iraq War)*

1986 *William Rehnquist* is confirmed as chief justice of the U.S. Supreme Court.

1988 Haitian president *Henri Namphy* is overthrown in a military coup. Lieutenant General *Prosper Avril* is named as his successor.

1991 The *Republic of Estonia* is accepted as a full member of the United Nations.

september

SEPTEMBER
18

HOLIDAYS

Burundi

Victory of UPRONA
Commemorates creation of the UPRONA (Unity and National Progress) Party, 1958.

Chile

Independence Day
Commemorates the end of Chile's allegiance to Spain, 1810, and independence, 1818.

RELIGIOUS CALENDAR

The Saints

St. Ferreolus, martyr. Also called *Ferreol.* [d. c. 3rd cent.]

St. Methodius of Olympus, bishop and martyr. [d. c. 311]

St. Richardis, widow. [d. c. 895]

St. Joseph of Cupertino, Franciscan friar and ecstatic. [d. 1663]

The Beatified

Blessed John Massias, Dominican brother of Lima, Peru. Also called *Masias.* [d. 1645]

BIRTHDATES

1709 *Samuel Johnson,* English author, critic, essayist, lexicographer; one of the great figures of English literature; renowned for his learned works, among which were the *Dictionary of the English Language,* 1755, and the *Lives of the Poets,* 1779–81. [d. December 13, 1784]

1765 *Gregory XVI,* pope 1831–46. [d. June 1, 1846]

1779 *Joseph Story,* U.S. jurist, legal writer; Associate Justice, U.S. Supreme Court, 1811–45; noted for his opinions on *patent law.* [d. September 10, 1845]

1786 *Christian VIII,* King of Denmark, 1839–48. [d. January 20, 1848]

1819 *Jean Bernard Léon Foucault,* French physicist; developed the *Foucault pendulum,* which visually demonstrated the rotation of the earth; invented the *gyroscope.* [d. February 11, 1868]

1857 *John Hessin Clarke,* U.S. jurist; associate justice of U.S. Supreme Court, 1916–22; noted for his liberal interpretations of the Constitution. [d. March 22, 1945]

1883 *Elmer Henry Maytag,* U.S. manufacturer; developer of the modern *washing machine;* founder, president, and chairman of the board of the Maytag Co., 1926–40. [d. July 20, 1940]

1886 *Powel Crosley, Jr.,* U.S. industrialist; developed radio *vacuum tube socket;* established Crosley Corporation, 1921. [d. March 28, 1961]

1895 *John George Diefenbaker,* Canadian lawyer, political leader; Prime Minister of Canada, 1957–63. [d. August 16, 1979]

1901 *Harold Clurman,* U.S. director, critic; founded *Group Theater,* which introduced the *Stanislavsky Method* of acting; discovered Lee Strasberg, Elia Kazan, John Garfield, Lee J. Cobb; first to produce plays by Clifford Odets, William Saroyan, and Irwin Shaw. [d. September 9, 1980]

1905 *Eddie (Rochester) Anderson,* U.S. character actor, best known for his role as Jack Benny's butler on radio and television, 1953–65. [d. February 28, 1977]

Claudette Colbert (Lily Claudette Chauchoin), U.S. actress, born in France; Oscar winner for *It Happened One Night,* 1934. [d. July 30, 1996]

Agnes George DeMille, U.S. dancer, author; choreographed the musicals, *Oklahoma, Carousel,* and *Brigadoon* during the 1940's.

Greta Garbo (Greta Lovisa Gustafsson), born in Sweden, one of the most glamorous and popular stars in motion-picture history; has lived in seclusion since 1941. [d. April 15, 1990]

1907 *Edwin Mattison McMillan,* U.S. physicist; Nobel Prize in chemistry for work in *synthetic transuranic elements* (with Glenn T. Seaborg), 1951. [d. September 7, 1991]

1916 *John J. Rhodes,* U.S. politician, lawyer; U.S. Congressman, 1952–81.

1918 *Derek Harold Richard Barton,* British organic chemist; Nobel Prize in chemistry for studies on *conformation analysis* (with O. Hassel), 1969. [d. March 16, 1998]

1919 *Pal Losonczi,* President, Hungarian People's Republic, 1967–87.

1920 *Jack Warden,* U.S. actor; Academy Award nominee for *Shampoo* and *Heaven Can Wait.*

1938 *Robert Blake (Michael Gubitosi),* U.S. actor; starred as a child in the series of short films, *Our Gang;* Emmy Award for *Baretta,* 1975.

1940 *Frankie Avalon (Francis Thomas Avalone),* U.S. actor, singer, entertainer; teen idol of the 1960's; starred with Annette Funicello in the series of *Beach* movies.

1950 *Darryl Glen Sittler,* Canadian hockey player.

1951 *Benjamin S. Carson,* U.S. neurosurgeon; known for his pediatric surgery techniques.

1955 *Billy Ray Sims,* U.S. football player; Heisman Trophy, 1978; selected as first pick in the National Football League draft by Detroit, 1980; running back, 1980–84.

1968 *Toni Kukoc,* Croatian-born basketball player.

HISTORICAL EVENTS

1180 *Louis VII* of France, dies and is succeeded by his son *Philip II.*

1502 *Christopher Columbus* lands at *Costa Rica* on his fourth and last voyage to the New World.

1544 *Treaty of Crespy* between *Charles V* of Germany and *Francis I* of France is signed; France abandons claims to Naples.

1679 *New Hampshire* province is separated from Massachusetts.

1810 *Chile* gains independence from Spain.

1873 *Panic of 1873,* financial depression caused partly by unbridled railroad speculation, causes widespread depression in U.S.

1900 Minneapolis holds first direct *primary election* in U.S.

1914 The Germans begin bombarding *Rheims,* France (*World War I*).

General *von Hindenburg* is named Commander in Chief of the German armies on the Eastern Front (*World War I*).

1917 *Ukulele* is patented by the Honolulu Ad Club.

1922 Hungary is admitted to the League of Nations.

1927 The *United Independent Broadcasters* (later CBS) airs its first radio broadcast.

1931 *Mukden Incident,* a bomb explosion damaging part of the South Manchurian railroad, provides a pretext for military action by the Japanese in *Manchuria.*

1934 The *U.S.S.R.* joins the League of Nations.

1950 General *Omar N. Bradley,* Chairman of the U.S. Joint Chiefs of Staff, is promoted to the rank of 5-Star General of the Army.

1953 Saul Bellow's novel, *The Adventures of Augie March,* is published.

1957 *Wagon Train* makes its television debut.

1961 U.N. Secretary-General *Dag Hammarskjöld* and 12 others are killed when their plane crashes in Northern Rhodesia.

1975 Fugitive *Patricia Hearst* is arrested in San Francisco after spending more than six months with the *Symbionese Liberation Army.*

1988 General *Saw Maung* stages a military coup in Burma, becoming the nation's fourth ruler in two months.

1996 U.S. President *Bill Clinton* signs the order creating the *Grand Staircase-Escalante National Monument* in Utah. The new national park encompasses over a million and a half acres.

september

SEPTEMBER
19

HOLIDAYS

Chile
Armed Forces Day

St. Christopher and Nevis
Independence Day
Commemorates independence from Great Britain.

RELIGIOUS CALENDAR

The Saints
St. Januarius, Bishop of Benevento, and his Companions, martyrs. Januarius is patron of Naples. Januarius also called *Gennaro.* [d. c. 305] Optional Memorial.

St. Peleus and his Companions, martyrs. [d. 310]

St. Sequanus, abbot. Also called *Seine.* [d. c. 580]

St. Goericus, Bishop of Metz. Also called *Abbo.* [d. 647]

St. Theodore, Archbishop of Canterbury. First bishop of all England. [d. 690]

St. Mary of Cerevellon, virgin. [d. 1290]

SS. Theodore, David, and Constantine. Theodore also called *the Black.* [d. 1299, 1321]

St. Emily de Rodat, virgin and foundress of the Congregation of the Holy Family of Villefranche. Also called *Emilie.* [d. 1852]

The Beatified
Blessed Alphonsus de Orozco, Augustinian friar. Also called *Alonso.* [d. 1591]

BIRTHDATES

1551 *Henry III,* King of France, 1574–89; last king of the *House of Valois.* [d. August 2, 1589]

1802 *Lajos Kossuth,* Hungarian statesman, patriot; President of Hungary, 1848–49; imprisoned in Turkey, 1849–51; lived in exile in U.S. and England, 1851–94. [d. March 20, 1894]

1851 *William Hesketh Lever, 1st Viscount Leverhulme,* British manufacturer; founded Lever Brothers, Inc., a soap manufacturer; established Port Sunlight, a model community for Lever Brothers employees. [d. May 7, 1925]

1867 *Arthur Rackham,* British artist; renowned for his book illustrations, especially for Grimm's *Fairy Tales.* [d. September 6, 1939]

1879 *Irvin Ferdinand Westheimer,* U.S. businessman; credited with the idea for Big Brothers, 1903; started Big Brothers organization, Cincinnati, 1912. [d. December 29, 1980]

1894 *Rachel (Lyman) Field,* U.S. author of New England novels and children's books: *Hitty, Her First Hundred Years, Time Out of Mind, All This and Heaven Too, And Now Tomorrow.* [d. March 15, 1942]

1895 *J(oseph) B(anks) Rhine,* U.S. psychologist; pioneer in research on *extrasensory perception* and *psychic phenomena;* author of *New Frontiers of the Mind,* 1937. [d. February 20, 1980]

1904 *Bergen Evans,* U.S. grammarian, educator, critic; author, with his sister, Cornelia, of *Dictionary of Contemporary American Usage,* 1957. [d. February 4, 1978]

1905 *Leon Jaworski,* U.S. lawyer; Watergate Special Prosecutor, 1973–74. [d. December 9, 1982]

1907 *Lewis F. Powell, Jr.,* U.S. jurist, lawyer; Associate Justice, U. S. Supreme Court, 1972–90. [d. August 25, 1998]

1909 *Ferdinand Porsche,* Austrian auto manufacturer, author; President, F. Porsche KG, Stuttgart; wrote *We at Porsche,* 1976. [d. March 27, 1998]

1911 *William (Gerald) Golding,* British novelist; author of

Lord of the Flies, 1954; Nobel Prize in Literature, 1984. [d. June 19, 1993]

1912 *(Elbert) Clifton Daniel, Jr.,* U.S. journalist, foreign correspondent; editor, *The New York Times;* married to Margaret Truman, daughter of former U.S. president Harry S. Truman.

1914 *Frances Farmer,* U.S. actress; stage and film star who spent most of the 1940's in mental institutions; her life was portrayed by Jessica Lange in *Frances,* 1983. [d. August 1, 1970]

Rogers C. B. Morton, U.S. politician; U.S. Congressman, 1962–71; U.S. Secretary of the Interior, 1971–75; U.S. Secretary of Commerce, 1975–76. [d. April 19, 1979]

1915 *Oscar Handlin,* U.S. historian; Pulitzer Prize in history, 1952.

1926 *Lurleen Burns Wallace,* U.S. governor; succeeded husband George Wallace to become first woman governor of Alabama, 1967. [d. May 7, 1968]

1927 *Harold Brown,* U.S. government official; President, California Institute of Technology, 1969–77; U.S. Secretary of Defense, 1977–81.

1930 *Rosemary Harris,* British actress; Tony Award for *Lion in Winter,* 1966.

1932 *Mike Royko,* U.S. journalist; Pulitzer Prize in commentary, 1972. [d. April 29, 1997]

1933 *David McCallum,* Scottish actor; known for his role as Illya Kuryakin on the television series, *The Man from U.N.C.L.E.,* 1964–67.

1934 *Brian Epstein,* British manager; handled the rock group, *The Beatles,* 1961–67. [d. August 27, 1967]

1936 *Al Oerter,* U.S. discus thrower; gold medalist, four consecutive Olympics, 1956–68.

1940 *Paul Williams,* U.S. singer, composer.

1941 *Cass Elliott,* U.S. singer; member of *The Mamas and the Papas.* [d. July 29, 1974]

1943 *Joseph Leonard (Joe) Morgan,* U.S. baseball player; second baseman; considered the National League's most complete player during his peak in the 1970's.

1945 *Jane Blalock,* U.S. professional golfer.

Freda Payne, U.S. singer; hit record, *Band of Gold,* 1970.

1948 *Jeremy Irons,* British actor; appeared in the television series, *Brideshead Revisited;* starred in the film, *The French Lieutenant's Woman,* 1981; Tony Award for *The Real Thing;* Academy Award (Best Actor) for *Reversal of Fortune,* 1990.

1964 *Trisha Yearwood,* U.S. country singer.

HISTORICAL EVENTS

1370 *Black Prince of England sacks Limoges,* France *(Hundred Years' War).*

1783 First balloon to carry a cargo (a sheep, a duck, and a rooster) makes its ascent in France.

1881 U.S. President *James Garfield* dies two months after being shot; Vice-President *Chester A. Arthur* becomes president.

1914 *Reims Cathedral* is badly damaged by German bombardment (*World War I*).

1928 The cartoon character later to be known as *Mickey Mouse* is introduced in a *Walt Disney* animated feature called *Steamboat Willie.*

1941 German troops conquer *Kiev,* capital of the Ukranian S.S.R. (*World War II*).

1955 Argentine President *Juan Perón* resigns and goes into exile after his government is overthrown.

1957 First underground *atomic explosion* is set off near Las Vegas, Nevada.

U.S. *bathyscaphe Trieste* reaches record depth of 3,200 meters in Mediterranean.

1961 *Jamaica* votes to secede from the West Indies Federation.

1966 *Guyana* is admitted to the United Nations.

1970 *The Mary Tyler Moore Show* makes its television debut.

1973 *India* and *Pakistan* begin an exchange of the more than 250,000 persons isolated by the 1971 war.

1983 *St. Kitts-Nevis,* Great Britain's oldest Caribbean colony, becomes independent.

1986 U.S. health officials announce the successful test results of *azidothymide (AZT),* a drug that adds months to the lives of some *AIDS* patients.

1994 *U.S. forces* occupy Haiti after unrest breaks out when elected *President Jean-Bertrand Aristide* is ousted by General *Raoul Cédras.*

september

SEPTEMBER 20

HOLIDAYS

U.S.
International Day of Peace
Sponsored by Franklin Delano
Roosevelt Philatelic Society.

RELIGIOUS CALENDAR

The Saints
St. Vincent Madelgarius, abbot. Also
called *Vincent Madelgaire* or
Mauger, and *Vincent of
Soignies.* [d. c. 687]
SS. Eustace and his companions,
martyrs. St. Eustace patron of
hunters. Invoked against fires
and for protection from hell.
St. Eustace also called
*Eustachius, Eustasius,
Eustathius,* or *Eustochius.*
[death date unknown]

The Beatified
Blessed Francis de Posadas,
Dominican priest. [d. 1713]

BIRTHDATES

356BC *Alexander the Great,*
Macedonian ruler; king who
forged the largest western
empire of the ancient world;
called *The Conqueror of the
World.* [d. June 13, 323 B.C.]

1737 *Charles Carroll,* American
Revolutionary leader; member
of Continental Congress,
1776–78; signer of Declaration
of Independence; U.S.
Senator, 1789–92. [d.
November 14, 1832]

1833 *David Ross Locke (Petroleum
V. Nasby),* U.S. political
satirist, journalist; creator of
the *Nasby letters* which
maintained a running attack
on slavery, the Democratic
Party, etc.; his work was
favored by President Abraham
Lincoln. [d. February 15,
1888]

Ernesto T. Moneta, Italian
journalist; Nobel Peace Prize
for his activities fostering
disarmament and
international arbitration, 1907.
[d. February 10, 1918]

1842 *Sir James Dewar,* Scottish
physicist, chemist; first to
produce liquid hydrogen,
1898; invented the *Dewar
vessel,* a forerunner of the
vacuum bottle; with
Frederick A. Abel invented
the explosive, *cordite.* [d.
March 27, 1923]

1849 *George Bird Grinnel,* U.S.
naturalist, author; editor of
Forest and Stream, a leading
journal of natural history and
conservation, 1880–1911; a
founder of the *Audubon
Society;* responsible, in large
part, for the establishment of
Glacier National Park, 1910.
[d. April 11 1938]

1878 *Upton (Beall) Sinclair,* U.S.
novelist, politician; author of
The Jungle and other novels
aimed at social reform;
instrumental in establishment
of *American Civil Liberties
Union* in California. [d.
November 25, 1968]

1884 *Maxwell (Evarts) Perkins,*
U.S. editor; as editor for
Charles Scribner's Sons
(1910–47), edited and
promoted the work of F.
Scott Fitzgerald, Ernest
Hemingway, and Thomas
Wolfe. [d. June 17, 1947]

1885 *Jellyroll Morton (Ferdinand
Morton),* U.S. jazz musician,
composer; noted as a pioneer
in *ragtime music* and one of
the great innovators in *jazz* in
the U.S. [d. July 10, 1941]

1886 Sister *Elizabeth Kenny,*
Australian nurse; developed
method of treating *infantile
paralysis.* [d. November 30,
1952]

1899 *Dilip Sindh Saund,* U.S.
politician; founding member
of the Indian Association of
America. [d. 1973]

1917 *Arnold Jacob (Red)
Auerbach,* U.S. basketball
coach; Coach of the Year,
1965; career record of
1,037–548; elected to the Hall
of Fame, 1968.

1924 *James Galanos,* U.S. fashion
designer; known for expense
and workmanship of his

fashions; elected to the Hall of Fame, 1959.

Anne Meara, U.S. actress, comedienne; played Veronica Rooney on the television series, *Archie Bunker's Place*, 1979–82.

1927 *John Philip William Dankworth*, British composer, conductor.

1934 *Sophia Loren (Sophia Scicoloni)*, Italian actress.

1936 *Sam Church, Jr.*, U.S. labor leader; head of United Mine Workers, 1979–82.

1938 *Pia Lindstrom*, U.S. journalist; daughter of Ingrid Bergman.

1941 *Dale P. Chihuly*, U.S. sculptor; known for his glass sculptures.

1951 *Guy Damien Lafleur*, Canadian hockey player; scored 50 or more goals in six consecutive seasons, 1974–80.

HISTORICAL EVENTS

622 *Muhammad* arrives at *Yathrib (Medina)* after completing his flight ("hegira") from Mecca. This year marks the beginning of the Muhammadan era.

1066 *Harald Haardraade, King of Norway* and *Tostig, Earl of Northumbria,* defeat troops loyal to *Harold II* of Engand at *Fulford.*

1697 *Treaty of Ryswyck* between France, Holland, England, and Spain is signed; Spain cedes some of West Indies possessions to France; this constitutes end of 11-year *War of the League of Augsburg.*

1819 *Carlsbad Decrees* to check revolutionary and liberal movements in Germany are enacted in reaction to the murder of *August von Kotzebue,* reactionary journalist, by university student *Karl Ludwig Sand.*

1850 *Compromise of 1850* becomes law as U.S. Congress passes resolution abolishing the *slave trade* in Washington, D.C.

1862 The Russian monarchy celebrates the 1,000th anniversary of its founding at *Novgorod.*

1927 Rightist *National Revolutionary Government* is formed by *Chiang Kai-shek* at Nanking, marking the end of the warlord era of Chinese history.

1949 Government of the *Federal Republic of Germany* is established.

1952 *The Jackie Gleason Show* makes its television debut.

1955 U.S.S.R. abolishes the office of High Commissioner for *East Germany* and grants the country full sovereignty.

1973 *Billie Jean King* defeats *Bobby Riggs,* 6-4, 6-3, 6-3, in a $100,000 tennis match in Houston, Texas, billed as the *Battle of the Sexes.*

1974 *Hurricane Fifi* strikes *Honduras,* killing thousands and leaving millions of dollars worth of devastation in its wake.

1976 Social Democratic Party of *Sweden* is narrowly defeated in parliamentary elections after more than 40 years in power.

1977 *Vietnam* and *Djibouti* are admitted to the UN.

1979 Central African *Emperor Bokassa I* is deposed by former president *David Dacko,* who returns the country to the status of a republic.

september

SEPTEMBER
21

HOLIDAYS

Armenia
Public Holiday

Belize
Independence Day
Commemorates the achievement of independence from England, 1981.

Philippines
National Thanksgiving Day

RELIGIOUS CALENDAR

Feasts
St. Matthew, apostle and evangelist. Patron of bankers, tax collectors, and customs officers. Probably originally called *Levi.* [d. 1st cent.] [major holy day, Episcopal Church; minor festival, Lutheran Church]

The Saints
St. Maura of Troyes, virgin. [d. c. 850]
St. Michael of Chernigov and *St. Theodore,* martyrs. [d. 1246]

The Beatified
Blessed Laurence Imbert and his companions, the *Martyrs of Korea.* [d. 1839]

BIRTHDATES

1415 *Frederick III,* Holy Roman Emperor, 1452–93; laid the foundations for the greatness of the Habsburgs. [d. August 19, 1493]

1452 *Girolamo Savonarola,* Italian reformer, member of Dominican order; drove Pietro de' Medici from power; dictatorial leader of Florence, 1494–97; excommunicated, tried for sedition and heresy; tortured and burned. [d. May 23, 1498]

1645 *Louis Joliet,* French-Canadian explorer; with Father Jacques Marquette, explored the northern portions of the Mississippi River between the Fox River confluence and the Arkansas River, 1673; explored Hudson Bay and Labrador coast; appointed Royal Hydrographer of New France, 1697. [d. May 1700]

1708 *Prince Dimitrie Cantemir,* Russian author, diplomat; Prince of Moldavia, 1710–11; joined with Peter the Great in war against Turks. [d. April 11, 1744]

1722 *John Home,* Scottish dramatist, clergyman; Minister at Athelstaneford, 1747–57; secretary to Prime Minister John Stuart, 3rd Earl of Bute, 1762; tutor to the Prince of Wales. [d. September 5, 1808]

1737 *Francis Hopkinson,* U.S. public official, judge, author; member of the Continental Congress; signer of the Declaration of Independence; known for his political satire;

one of the designers of first U.S. flag. [d. May 9, 1791]

1756 *John Loudon McAdam,* Scottish engineer; developed process for building roads of crushed stone, called *macadamized roads.* [d. November 26, 1836]

1788 *Margaret Taylor,* wife of U.S. President Zachary Taylor. [d. August 14, 1852]

1792 *Johann Peter Eckermann,* German writer; friend and literary assistant to *Goethe;* helped him prepare final editions of his work. [d. December 3, 1854]

1832 *Louis Paul Cailletet,* French physicist; credited with discovery of process for liquefying oxygen, nitrogen, etc., 1877–78. [d. January 5, 1913]

1849 *Sir Edmund William Gosse,* British poet, critic, and biographer; noted for his literary criticism and introduction of Scandinavian literature to the English reading public; on staff of British Museum, 1865–75; librarian to House of Lords, 1904–14. [d. May 16, 1928]

1853 *Heike Kamerlingh-Onnes,* Dutch physicist; Nobel Prize in physics for experiments in properties of matter at low temperatures, 1913. [d. February 21, 1926]

1866 *H(erbert) G(eorge) Wells,* British writer; renowned for his science fiction writings, which combined scientific kowledge, bold imagination, and high adventure. Among his works are *The Time Machine, The War of the Worlds,* and *Outline of History.* [d. August 13, 1946]

Charles J. H. Nicolle, French bacteriologist; Nobel Prize in physiology or medicine for discovery that typhus is transmitted by the body louse, 1928. [d. February 28, 1936]

1867 *Henry Lewis Stimson,* U.S. government official; U.S. Secretary of War, 1911–13, 1940–45; made final recommendation to President Harry Truman to drop the *atomic bomb* on Japan. [d. October 20, 1950]

1874 *Gustav Theodore Holst,* British composer, teacher; best known for his orchestral suite, *The Planets.* [d. May 25, 1934]

1895 *Juan de la Cierva,* Spanish aeronautical engineer; inventor of the *autogiro* aircraft; killed in an airplane accident. [d. December 9, 1936]

1902 *Sir Allen Lane (Williams),* British publisher; founder of Penguin Books, Ltd., the first paperback book publisher in England. [d. July 7, 1970]

1909 *Kwame Nkrumah,* Ghanaian politician, President; the first man to lead an African nation to independence from colonial rule. [d. April 27, 1972]

1921 *Robert David Muldoon,* Prime Minister of New Zealand, 1975–84. [d. August 5, 1992]

1926 *Donald Arthur Glaser,* U.S. physicist; Nobel Prize in physics for invention of *bubble chamber* for studying subatomic particles, 1960.

1930 *Tore Lokoloko,* Governor-General, Papua New Guinea, 1977–83.

1931 *Larry Hagman,* U.S. actor; starred in the television series, *I Dream of Jeannie,* 1965–68, and *Dallas,* 1978–91; son of Mary Martin.

1934 *Leonard Cohen,* Canadian author, songwriter, singer; songs include *Suzanne* and *Hey, That's No Way to Say Goodbye.*

1940 *William Horton (Bill) Kurtis,* U.S. broadcast journalist; co-anchor and correspondent of the *CBS Morning News,* 1982–86.

1944 *Frances Carlton (Fannie) Flagg,* U.S. comedienne, actress.

1947 *Donald William (Don) Felder,* U.S. musician, singer, songwriter; lead guitarist for the rock group, *The Eagles.*

Stephen King, U.S. novelist; author of *Carrie, The Shining,* and other horror stories, many of which have become films achieving considerable box-office success.

1950 *Bill Murray,* U.S. actor, comedian, writer; starred in the television series, *Saturday Night Live;* appeared in the movies, *Meatballs, Caddyshack,* and *Ghostbusters.*

1951 *Joan Lunden,* U.S. broadcast journalist; reporter and interviewer, *Good Morning, America,* 1980–97.

1952 *David Stewart,* British musician; member of the rock group, *The Eurythmics.*

1963 *Cecil Fielder,* U.S. baseball player.

1967 *Faith Hill,* U.S. country singer.

1971 *David,* U.S. patient; born without any immunity to disease; spent all but the last fifteen days of his life in a sterile, plastic bubble. [d. February 22, 1984]

HISTORICAL EVENTS

1435 *Peace of Arras* is formalized between *Charles VII* of France and *Philip* of Burgundy who obtains Macon, Auxerre, and part of Picardy.

1870 Italian army invades Rome following withdrawal of French troops; the *unification of the Kingdom of Italy* under Victor Emmanuel II is completed.

1914 German troops in New Guinea surrender to the Australians (*World War I*).

1915 *Stonehenge,* prehistoric British landmark, is sold by auction to C. H. E. Chubb of Salisbury, England, for the equivalent of $6,600.

1930 Great Britain abandons the *gold standard.*

1938 Devastating hurricane hits *New England,* causing widespread destruction and loss of nearly 500 lives.

1944 Aircraft from 12 U.S. carriers attack Japanese shipping and airfield on *Luzon, Philippines* (*World War II*).

september

1948 *Marcel Cerdan* defeats *Tony Zale* to win the world middleweight boxing title.

1956 Nicaraguan president, *Anastasio Somoza,* is shot by Rigoberto Lopez Perez. He dies of his wounds eight days later in Panama.

1957 *Haakon VII* of Norway dies and is succeeded by *Olaf V.*

Perry Mason makes its television debut.

1963 Indonesian president, *Ahmed Sukarno,* places an embargo on all trade with the newly formed *Federation of Malaysia.*

1964 *Malta* becomes an independent nation within the British Commonwealth.

1965 *The Gambia,* the *Maldive Islands,* and *Singapore* are admitted to the UN.

Great Britain discovers gas in the *North Sea.*

1970 The New York Jets compete against the Cleveland Browns in the first televised *NFL Monday Night Football* game.

1972 *Philippines* are placed under martial law by President Ferdinand Marcos.

1973 *Henry Kissinger* becomes U.S. secretary of state.

1976 Former Chilean cabinet minister, *Orlando Letelier,* is killed in Washington, D.C., by a bomb placed in his car.

1978 *Nigeria* lifts a ban on political parties which had been in effect since 1966.

1981 *Belize* (formerly *British Honduras*) becomes fully independent from Great Britain.

1982 *Amin Gemayel* is elected president of Lebanon.

National Football League players begin a strike after failing to agree on a new contract. This represents the first in-season strike in NFL history.

1989 *Hurricane Hugo* hits Charleston, South Carolina, causing massive destruction. Fifty-one people perish.

HOLIDAYS

Republic of Mali
National Holiday
Celebrates Mali's independence from France, 1960.

U.S.
Hobbit Day
Sponsored by American Tolkien Society, Union Lake, Michigan.

RELIGIOUS CALENDAR

The Saints
SS. Maurice and his companions, martyrs of the Theban Legion. Maurice is patron of infantrymen, weavers, and sword-makers. Invoked against gout. [d. c. 287]

St. Felix III (IV), pope. Elected 526. [d. 530]

St. Laudus, Bishop of Coutances. Also called *Lo.* [d. 6th century]

St. Salaberga, matron, and *St. Bodo,* bishop. [d. c. 665 and c. 670]

St. Emmeramus, bishop. Also called *Emmeram, Emmeran,* or *Haimhrammus.* [d. 7th cent.]

St. Thomas of Villanova, Archbishop of Valencia. Also called *Thomas of Villanueva.* [d. 1555]

St. Phocas, martyr; patron of sailors. [death date unknown]

BIRTHDATES

1606 *Richard Busby,* English scholar, grammarian; headmaster of Westminster School, 1638–95, numbering Dryden, South, Locke, and others among his students. [d. April 6, 1695]

1694 *Philip Dormer Stanhope, 4th Earl of Chesterfield (Lord Chesterfield),* English author; famous for his advice to his natural son, Philip, regarding the manners and standards of a man of the world. [d. March 24, 1773]

1791 *Michael Faraday,* English physicist, chemist; noted for his discovery of *benzene* and *carbon chloride;* did extensive research in field of *electricity* and *electromagnetism;* published numerous pioneering papers which led to the practical use of electricity. [d. August 25, 1867]

1882 *Wilhelm Keitel,* German Army Field Marshal; commanded German troops at Russian front during World War II; tried and executed as a war criminal, 1946. [d. October 16, 1946]

1885 *Erich von Stroheim,* U.S. film director, born in Austria. [d. May 2, 1957]

1895 *Paul Muni,* U.S. actor, born in Austria. [d. August 25, 1967]

1901 *Charles Brenton Huggins,* U.S. surgeon, born in Canada; Nobel Prize in physiology or medicine for discovering hormonal treatment of prostate cancer, 1966. [d. January 12, 1997]

1902 *John Houseman (Jacques Haussman),* U.S. actor, producer, director. [d. October 30, 1988]

Howard Arnold Jarvis, U.S. political activist; force behind California's Proposition 13, which reduced property taxes by 57%, 1978. [d. August 11, 1986]

1904 *Joseph M. (Joe) Valachi,* U.S. criminal; hit man turned informer for the Department of Justice, 1963. [d. April 3, 1971]

1922 *Chen Ning Yang,* U.S. physicist, born in China; Nobel Prize in physics for discovery of *parity conservation* law in physics (with T. D. Lee), 1957.

1927 *Thomas Charles (Tom) Lasorda,* U.S. baseball player, manager; managed the Los Angeles Dodgers, 1977–96; National League Manager of the Year, 1983.

1948 *Mark Anthony Peter Phillips,* husband of Anne, Princess Royal; aide-de-camp to Queen Elizabeth II, 1974– .

1954 *Shari Belafonte-Harper,* U.S. actress; known for her role as

september

Julie on the television series, *Hotel;* daughter of Harry Belafonte.

1956 *Deborah Ann (Debby) Boone,* U.S. singer; Platinum Record Award for *You Light Up My Life,* 1977; daughter of Pat Boone (June 1).

1960 *Tai Reina Babilonia,* U.S. figure skater.

Joan Jett (Joan Larkin), U.S. singer, musician, actress; member of the rock group, *Joan Jett and the Blackhearts;* Gold Record Award for *I Love Rock 'n Roll,* 1982.

1961 *Scott Vincent Baio,* U.S. actor; played Chachi on the television series, *Happy Days,* 1977–82; featured in the TV sitcom *Charles in Charge,* 1984–85.

HISTORICAL EVENTS

1499 Swiss independence is acknowledged in fact by Holy Roman Emperor Maximilian I with the signing of the *Treaty of Basel.*

1586 *Sir Philip Sidney* is mortally wounded at the *Battle of Zutphen.*

1776 American patriot and spy *Nathan Hale* is executed by the British. Before he is hanged he issues his famous statement, "I only regret that I have but one life to lose for my country," (*American Revolution*)

1792 *French Republic* is proclaimed (*French Revolution*).

1862 U.S. President *Abraham Lincoln* declares all slaves in rebellious states to be free as of January 1, 1863.

1914 A German U-boat sinks the English cruisers *Hogue, Cressy,* and *Aboukir* in the North Sea (*World War I*).

First Battle of Picardy opens in another Allied attempt to dislodge the Germans along the Western Front (*World War I*).

1915 *Second Battle of Champagne* opens with one of the heaviest artillery bombardments of World War I preceding the French attack.

1927 *Gene Tunney* defeats *Jack Dempsey* to retain the world heavyweight boxing title.

1940 Japanese attack French forces in Vietnam and bomb *Haiphong (World War II).*

1960 *Sudanese Republic* renames itself the *Republic of Mali* as it gains independence from France.

1961 *Peace Corps* becomes permanent agency of U.S. government.

Antonio Abertondo, of Argentina, makes first two-way, nonstop swim of the *English Channel* (43 hours, 5 minutes).

1964 Jerry Bock, Sheldon Harnick, and Joseph Stein's musical, *Fiddler on the Roof,* premieres in New York.

1969 San Francisco Giant outfielder *Willie Mays* becomes the second player (the other, *Babe Ruth*) to hit 600 career home runs.

1975 U.S. President *Gerald Ford* is the target of an attempt assassination by *Sara Jane Moore,* California radical. He is not hurt.

1980 War breaks out between *Iran* and *Iraq.*

1992 *Yugoslavia* is voted out of the *United Nations* for its involvement in the ongoing civil strife in Bosnia-Herzegovina. It is the first time in the history of the United Nations that a country has been removed.

1993 An *Amtrak passenger train* derails near Mobile, Alabama, killing forty-seven.

HOLIDAYS

Japan
Autumnal Equinox

Puerto Rico
Grito de Lares

Saudi Arabia
National Day
Commemorates unification of the kingdom in 1932.

RELIGIOUS CALENDAR

The Saints
St. Thecla of Iconium, virgin and martyr. [d. 1st century]
St. Linus, pope and martyr. First successor of St. Peter. Feast suppressed in 1969. [d. c. 79]
St. Adamnan, Abbot of Iona. Also called *Adomnan, Eunan.* [d. 704]

The Beatified
Blessed Mark of Modena, Franciscan prior. [d. 1498]
Blessed Helen of Bologna, widow. [d. 1520]

BIRTHDATES

480 BC *Euripides,* Greek dramatist; wrote about ninety tragedies; author of *Medea* and *Electra.* [d. c. 406 B.C.]

63 BC *Julius Caesar Octavianus Augustus (Octavian),* first Roman Emperor, 27 B.C.–A.D. 14; adopted son and heir to Julius Caesar; his reign was known as the *Augustan Age* and was marked by the flowering of Roman literature, art, and imperial administration. [d. August 19, A.D. 14]

1713 *Ferdinand VI,* King of Spain, 1746–59; supported economic and military reforms. [d. August 10, 1759]

1728 *Mercy Otis Warren,* U.S. playwright, historian; noted for her chronicles of the American Revolution; wrote a three-volume history of the Revolution, *A History of the Rise, Progress, and Fermentation of the American Revolution.* [d. October 19, 1814]

1738 *Moses Brown,* U.S. manufacturer; perfected the first *water mill* in America. [d. September 7, 1836]

1745 *John Sevier,* U.S. frontiersman, soldier, public official, member of North Carolina legislature, 1789–90; first governor of Tennessee, serving from 1796–1801; U.S. Congressman, 1811–15. [d. September 24, 1815]

1800 *William Holmes McGuffey,* U.S. educator, author; noted for his development of the *Eclectic Reader* which was destined to become one of the most influential early textbooks in America. [d. May 4, 1873]

1819 *Armand Fizeau,* French physicist; first to successfully measure speed of light without using astronomical calculations. [d. September 18, 1896]

1829 *George Crook,* U.S. soldier, Indian fighter; fought in U.S. Civil War, distinguishing himself at *Battle of Chickamauga;* led American troops in conflicts with Indians in Idaho and Arizona; responsible for capturing *Geronimo* and placing him and his tribe on their Arizona reservation. [d. March 21, 1890]

1838 *Victoria Woodhull,* U.S. social reformer, radical; with the support of *Cornelius Vanderbilt,* established herself in the forefront of the women's liberation movement in the U.S.; responsible for the libelous accusations against *Henry Ward Beecher* which brought him to trial on charges of adultery; was first female candidate for U.S. presidency, running on Equal Rights Party ticket, 1872. [d. June 10, 1927]

1852 *William Stewart Halsted,* U.S. surgeon; discovered anesthetic properties of *cocaine;* performed the first

september

blood transfusion in the U.S.; established the first school of surgery in the U.S. at *Johns Hopkins University*, 1890; contributed extensively to development of surgical procedures. [d. September 7, 1922]

1863 *Mary Church Terrell*, U.S. civil rights activist. [d. 1954]

1867 *John Avery Lomax*, U.S. folklorist; made significant contributions to the study of *folk music;* first curator of Archives of American Folk Song in Library of Congress. [d. January 26, 1948]

1880 *Lord John Boyd-Orr of Brechin Mearns*, British nutritionist; Nobel Peace Prize for his work on diet, nutrition, and world food supply, 1949. [d. June 25, 1971]

1884 *Adna Romanza Chaffee, Jr.,* U.S. army general; developed strategies for the use of tanks in warfare; called *Father of the Armored Force.* [d. August 22, 1941]

Eugene Talmadge, U.S. politician; Governor of Georgia, 1933–37, 1940–43. [d. December 21, 1946]

1889 *Walter Lippmann,* U.S. journalist, editor; noted for his penetrating political criticism; through his syndicated news column, became a prime source of political and social analysis between 1931 and 1962, being syndicated in more than 200 newspapers worldwide. [d. December 24, 1974]

1898 *Walter Pidgeon,* Canadian actor. [d. September 25, 1984]

1899 *Thomas Campbell Clark,* U.S. jurist; Associate Justice, U.S. Supreme Court, 1949–67; U.S. Attorney General, 1945–49; father of Ramsey Clark. [d. June 13, 1977]

1901 *Jaroslav Seifert,* Czechoslovak poet; Nobel Prize for literature, 1984. [d. January 10, 1984]

1910 *Elliot Roosevelt,* U.S. politician; Mayor of Miami Beach, 1965–69; Brigadier General, Army Air Corps, 1940–46; son of Franklin Delano Roosevelt. [d. October 27, 1990]

1915 *Clifford G. Shull,* U.S. physicist; one-half of the Nobel Prize for Physics in 1994 for significant contributions to the neutron spectroscopy. Bertram N. Brockhouse, Canadian physicist; other half of the Nobel Prize, 1994.

1916 *Aldo Moro,* Italian statesman; Prime Minister of Italy, 1963–68, 1974–76; kidnapped and killed by Red Brigade leftist terrorists. [d. May 9, 1978]

1920 *Mickey Rooney (Joe Yule, Jr.),* U.S. actor.

1930 *Ray Charles (Ray Charles Robinson),* U.S. singer, composer; widely regarded for his jazz, pop, and country music.

1938 *Romy Schneider,* Austrian actress. [d. May 29, 1982]

1943 *Julio Iglesias (Julio Iglesias de la Cueva),* Spanish singer, songwriter; known for his love songs; sold more than 100 million albums.

1947 *Mary Kay Place,* U.S. actress, singer, writer; starred in *The*

Big Chill, 1983; Emmy Award for *Mary Hartman, Mary Hartman,* 1977.

1949 *Bruce Springsteen,* U.S. rock singer, songwriter, musician; called *The Boss.*

HISTORICAL EVENTS

1122 Holy Roman Emperor *Henry V* renounces right of investiture in the *Concordat of Worms.*

1719 *Liechtenstein* becomes independent principality within the Holy Roman Empire.

1780 British agent *Major John André* is captured bearing incriminating papers near Tarrytown, N.Y. (*American Revolution*).

1806 *Meriwether Lewis* and *William Clark* return from their two-year exploration of the Louisiana Territory, having completed the first overland crossing of the continent (*Lewis and Clark Expedition*).

1862 *Otto von Bismarck* becomes Premier of Prussia.

1926 *Gene Tunney* wins world heavyweight boxing title from *Jack Dempsey.*

1932 The Kingdom of Hijaz and Nejd is renamed *Saudi Arabia.*

1947 Women are granted the right to vote in *Argentina.*

1952 *Camille Chamoun* becomes president of Lebanon.

Rocky Marciano gains world heavyweight boxing title by knocking out *Jersey Joe Walcott.*

1964 *Charles Helou* is inaugurated as president of Lebanon.

1969 *Marcus Welby, M.D.* makes its television debut.

1973 *Juan Perón* and his wife Isabel are elected President and Vice-President of Argentina.

1976 *Elias Sarkis* is inaugurated as president of Lebanon.

1979 American baseball player, *Lou Brock*, steals his 935th base, setting a new record.

1988 Outgoing Lebanese president *Amin Gemayel* appoints a Christian government in *East Beirut*, while Moslem members of Gemayel's cabinet form a rival regime in *West Beirut*.

september

SEPTEMBER
24

HOLIDAYS

Bolivia (Santa Cruz and Cobija)
Public Holiday

Dominican Republic and Peru
Feast of Our Lady Mary

Ghana
Third Republic Day
Recognizes the coming to power of Flight Lieutenant Jerry Rawlings, 1981.

Guinea-Bissau
Establishment of the Republic
Commemorates independence from Portugal and creation of the Republic, 1974.

New Caledonia
Territorial Day

Trinidad and Tobago
Republic Day

U.S.
Kids' Day
Sponsored by Kiwanis International.

Venezuela
Day of the Public Functionary

RELIGIOUS CALENDAR

Feasts
Our Lady of Ransom. Celebrates founding of Order for the Redemption of Captives in Spain in 13th century.

The Saints
St. Geremarus, abbot. Also called *Geremar, Germer.* [d. c. 658]
St. Gerard, Bishop of Csanad, martyr. Protomartyr of Venice.

Also called *Gerard Sagredo.* [d. 1046]
St. Pacifico of San Severino, Friar Minor. [d. 1721]

The Beatified
Blessed Robert of Knaresborough, hermit. [d. c. 1218]
Blessed Antonius Gonzdez, one of the Martyrs of Nagasaki. [beatified 1981]

BIRTHDATES

1501 *Girolamo Cardano,* Italian mathematician, physician; noted for his development of *algebraic solutions.* [d. 1576]

1583 *Albrecht Eusebius Wenzel von Wollenstein,* Duke of Friedland and Mecklenburg, Prince of Sagan, Austrian general; led Austrian forces during Thirty Years' War 1625–30, 1632–34; subject of jealousy of the princes of the empire; assassinated. [d. February 25, 1634]

1625 *Jan De Witt,* Dutch statesman; led Dutch in war against England, 1665–67; concluded Triple Alliance with Sweden and England against France, 1668. Upon invasion of the United Provinces by France, was forced to resign position as Grand Pensionary; killed by a rioting mob. [d. August 20, 1672]

1717 *Horace Walpole, 4th Earl of Orford,* English novelist,

letter-writer; wrote thousands of letters describing Georgian England, 1732–97; his fictional works were forerunners of the *supernatural romance.* [d. March 2, 1797]

1755 *John Marshall,* U.S. jurist; U.S. Secretary of State, 1800–01; Chief Justice, U.S. Supreme Court, 1801–35; established the Supreme Court's precedent for *judicial review* of statutes not in conformity with the Constitution; established practice of allowing only one opinion to be presented by the court, thus keeping dissension from the public view; primarily responsible for establishing unity of the federal court system in the U.S. [d. July 6, 1835]

1825 *Frances Ellen Watkins Harper,* U.S. author and civil rights activist. [d. 1911]

1834 *Marcus Alonzo Hanna,* U.S. merchant, politician; backed William McKinley's successful bid for U.S. presidency; U.S. Senator, 1897–1904. [d. February 15, 1904]

1884 *Ismet Inönü,* Turkish general, statesman; President 1938–1950. [d. December 25, 1973]

1895 *André F. Cournand,* U.S. physician; Nobel Prize in physiology or medicine for development of catheter that can be inserted into heart to diagnose circulatory problems (with D. W. Richards and W. Forssmann), 1956. [d. February 19, 1988]

1896 *F(rancis) Scott Fitzgerald,* U.S. novelist, short-story writer. [d. December 21, 1940]

1898 *Howard Walter Florey, Baron Florey of Adelaide,* British pathologist, born in Australia; Nobel Prize in physiology or medicine for discovery of *penicillin* (with A. Fleming and E. B. Chain), 1945. [d. February 22, 1968]

1899 *Georges Frederic Doriot,* U.S. educator, businessman; professor of Industrial Management, Harvard Business School; Chairman, American Research & Development Corp. [d. June 2, 1987]

1905 *Severo Ochoa,* U.S. biochemist, born in Spain; Nobel Prize in physiology or medicine for synthesis of *RNA* and *DNA* (with A. Kornberg), 1959. [d. November 1, 1993]

1911 *Konstantin Chernenko,* Russian politician; Soviet premier, 1984–85. [d. March 10, 1985]

1915 *Joseph Manuel Montoya,* U.S. politician; Senator. [d. June 5, 1978]

1918 *Audra Lindley,* U.S. actress; known for her role as Mrs. Roper in the television series *Three's Company,* 1977–79, and *The Ropers,* 1979–80. [d. October 16, 1997]

1921 *Jim McKay (James Kenneth McManus),* U.S. sportscaster; longtime host of the television series, *Wide World of Sports;* eight Emmy Awards.

1923 *Sheila MacRae,* U.S. actress, singer; starred in the television series, *Jackie Gleason Show,* 1966–70; first husband was Gordon MacRae.

1925 *Geoffrey Burbidge,* British astrophysicist; known for research on quasars with his wife, E. Margaret Burbidge.

1930 *John (Watts) Young,* U.S. astronaut; on *Gemini 3, Gemini 10,* and *Apollo 10* flights.

1931 *Anthony Newley,* British actor, singer.

John M.G. (Tom) Adams, Prime Minister, Barbados, 1976–85. [d. March 11, 1985]

1932 *Svetlana Beriosova,* British ballerina; performed with Metropolitan Ballet, Sadler's Wells Theatre Ballet, and Sadler's Wells Ballet (Royal Ballet).

1936 *James (Maury) Henson,* U.S. puppeteer, television producer; creator of the *Muppets.* [d. May 16, 1990]

1942 *Linda McCartney,* U.S. musician, photographer; member of the rock group, *Wings;* wife of Paul McCartney (June 18). [d. April 17, 1998]

1946 *Joseph (Joe) Greene,* U.S. football player; tackle, Pittsburgh Steelers, 1969–81; starred in award-winning Coca-Cola commercial; called *Mean Joe Greene.*

1948 *Phil Hartman,* Canadian-born comedian, actor. [d. May 28, 1998]

1952 *Joseph Patrick Kennedy, III,* U.S. politician; Congressman,

1987–98; holds the former seat of his uncle, John F. Kennedy; son of Robert Kennedy.

HISTORICAL EVENTS

787 *Second Council of Nicaea* convenes to limit the veneration of icons.

1326 *Queen Isabella* of England and *Roger Mortimer* rebel against *King Edward II.*

1834 *Dom Pedro* of Portugal dies and is succeeded by *Queen Maria da Gloria.*

1869 *Jay Gould* and *James Fisk* create a financial panic in the U.S. (by attempting unsuccessfully to corner the gold market) in what is subsequently referred to as *Black Friday.*

1916 The French conduct an air raid on the *Krupp Works* at Essen, Germany (*World War I*).

1922 *Battling Siki* defeats *Georges Carpentier* to win the world light heavyweight boxing title.

1950 The first Latin American stock exchange opens in *San Jose, Costa Rica.*

1953 Discovery of the antibiotic, *tetracycline,* is reported by the American Chemical Society.

1956 Grace Metalious's novel, *Peyton Place,* is published in New York.

1957 President *Dwight D. Eisenhower* federalizes the Arkansas National Guard and sends 1,000 paratroopers to *Little Rock* to enforce court-ordered *racial integration* of schools.

september

1960 *U.S.S. Enterprise,* first U.S. atomic-powered aircraft carrier, is launched at Newport News, Virginia.

1968 *60 Minutes* makes its television debut.

Swaziland is admitted to the United Nations.

1969 The trial of the *Chicago Seven,* radical leaders accused of inciting riots during the 1968 Democratic National Convention, begins.

1973 At the first *United Farm Workers'* convention, a constitution is adopted, and *Cesar Chavez* is elected president.

1979 *Hilla Limann* is inaugurated as president of Ghana.

1983 *Continental Airlines* files for bankruptcy.

1993 *Prince Norodom Sihanoik* of Cambodia is restored to power after being removed by a military coup in 1970.

HOLIDAYS

Mozambique

Day of the Armed Forces
Commemorates the launching of
armed struggle against the
Portuguese.

Rwanda

Kamarampaka Day
Commemorates the 1961
referendum.

RELIGIOUS CALENDAR

The Saints

St. Ferminus, bishop and martyr.
   Also called *Firmin.* [d. c. 4th
   cent.]
St. Cadoc, abbot. Also called *Cadog,*
   Catwg. [d. c. 575]
St. Aunacharius, Bishop of Auxerre.
   Also called *Aunaire.* [d. 605]
St. Finbar, first bishop of Cork. Also
   called *Bairre, Barr, Barrocus,*
   Barrus. [d. c. 633]
St. Ceolfrid, Abbot of Wearmouth.
   Also called *Ceufroy.* [d. 716]
St. Albert, Patriarch of Jerusalem. [d.
   1214]
St. Sergius of Radonezh, most
   beloved of all Russian saints.
   [d. 1292]
St. Vincent Strambi, Bishop of
   Macerata and Tolentino. [d.
   1824]

The Beatified

Blessed Herman the Cripple. [d.
   1054]

BIRTHDATES

1599 *Francesco Borromini,* Italian
architect, sculptor; master of
the baroque style. [d. August
3, 1667]

1711 *Ch'ien Lung,* 4th Manchu
emperor. [d. February 7,
1799]

1725 *Nicholas Cugnot,* French
engineer; designed and built
the world's first *automobile,*
a steam-driven vehicle, 1769.
[d. October 2, 1804]

1744 *Frederick William II* of
Prussia; responsible for
significant territorial
expansion of Prussia. [d.
November 16, 1797]

1832 *William Le Baron Jenney,*
U.S. civil engineer, architect;
pioneer in steel skeletal
construction with curtain-wall
exteriors, which made
possible the *skyscraper* form
of architecture. [d. June 15,
1907]

1866 *Thomas Hunt Morgan,* U.S.
geneticist; Nobel Prize in
physiology or medicine for
discoveries related to bone-
marrow's production of red
blood cells, 1933. [d.
December 4, 1945]

1877 *Plutarco Elias Calles,*
Mexican statesman; President
of Mexico, 1924–28. [d.
October 19, 1945]

1896 *Alessandro Pertini,* Italian
statesman; President of Italy,
1978–.

1897 *William (Harrison)*
Faulkner, U.S. author; noted
for his novels about the
American South; Nobel Prize
in literature, 1949. [d. July 6,
1962]

1898 *Robert Brackman,* U.S. artist;
widely recognized for his
portraits of the rich and
famous, such as the
Rockefellers and Lindberghs.
[d. July 16, 1980]

1902 *Elliott V(allance) Bell,* U.S.
publisher, editor; editor and
publisher, *Business Week,*
1950–67. [d. January 11, 1983]

1903 *Mark Rothko,* U.S. painter,
born in Russia; a leader in
school of Abstract
Expressionism; committed
suicide. [d. February 25,
1970]

1905 *Walter Wellesley (Red) Smith,*
U.S. journalist; sports
columns appeared in over 500
newspapers; Pulitzer Prize,
1976. [d. January 15, 1982]

1906 *Dimitri Shostakovich,* Russian
composer; his style and pro-
Soviet political leanings made
him a source of controversy.
[d. August 9, 1975]

1909 *Florizel A. Glasspole,*
Jamaican statesman;
Governor-General of Jamaica,
1973–91.

september

1911 *Eric (Eustace) Williams,* Prime Minister, Trinidad and Tobago, 1962–80. [d. March 29, 1981]

1922 *Hammer DeRoburt,* President, Republic of Nauru, 1978–92. [d. July 15, 1992]

1929 *Kevin Hagan White,* U.S. politician, lawyer; Mayor of Boston, 1967–84.

1931 *Barbara Walters,* U.S. newscaster, interviewer.

1932 *Adolfo Suarez Gonzalez,* Spanish lawyer, political leader; Prime Minister and President of Council of Ministers, 1976–1982.

Glenn Gould, Canadian composer, musician; first North American musician invited to play in the Soviet Union; retired from highly successful concert career to concentrate on recording, which he considered to be a distinct and even superior art form. [d. October 4, 1982]

1936 *Juliet Prowse,* U.S. dancer, actress; debuted in the film, *Can-Can,* 1960; appeared the television series, *Mona McClusky,* 1966. [d. September 14, 1996]

Moussa Traore, President, Republic of Mali, 1968–91.

1943 *Robert M. Gates,* U.S. government official; Director of the Central Intelligence Agency, 1991–93.

Robert Walden, U.S. actor; known for his role as Joe Rossi on the television series, *Lou Grant.*

1944 *Michael Douglas,* U.S. actor, producer; Academy Award for *Wall Street;* son of Kirk Douglas.

1947 *Cheryl Tiegs,* U.S. actress, model; highest paid model of 1970's.

1952 *Mark Hamill,* U.S. actor; known for his role as Luke Skywalker in *Star Wars,* 1977, and *The Empire Strikes Back,* 1980.

Christopher Reeve, known for his role in the *Superman* film series; spokesperson for spinal cord injuries.

1961 *Heather Locklear,* U.S. actress; known for her roles in the TV series, *Dynasty, T.J. Hooker,* and *Melrose Place.*

1965 *Scottie Pippen,* U.S. basketball player.

1968 *Will(ard) Smith Jr.,* U.S. singer, actor; known for his performances in the movies *Independence Day,* 1996, and *Men in Black,* 1997.

HISTORICAL EVENTS

1066 *Harold II* of England, defeats invading forces of Harald Haardraade of Norway and Tostig, Earl of Northumbria at *Stamford Bridge.*

1493 *Christopher Columbus* embarks on his second voyage of discovery to the New World.

1513 *Vasco Núñez de Balboa* crosses Isthmus of Panama and sights the *Pacific Ocean.*

1555 *Religious Peace of Augsburg* is signed, resolving bitter disputes between Protestants and Catholics in the German states.

1629 *Truce of Altmark* is signed by Sweden and Poland; Sweden obtains Livonia and parts of Prussia.

1780 Treason of *Benedict Arnold* is exposed; Arnold flees New York in British warship (*American Revolution*).

1804 The *12th Amendment* to the U.S. Constitution is adopted, requiring separate ballots for presidential and vice-presidential candidates in the electoral college.

1846 Zachary Taylor's troops defeat the Mexicans at the *Battle of Monterey (Mexican War).*

1915 *Third Battle of Artois* begins as a British diversion to the *Battle of Champagne (World War I).*

1932 *Catalonia,* in Spain, is granted autonomy.

1943 Russians liberate *Smolensk (World War II).*

1944 *Harvard University*'s medical school admits women for the first time.

1956 First *transatlantic telephone cable* is put into service.

1959 Ceylonese prime minister, *Solomon Bandaranaike,* is assassinated by a Buddhist monk in Colombo.

1962 *Sonny Liston* knocks out *Floyd Patterson* in first round of world heavyweight championship fight in Chicago.

1964 *Gomer Pyle, U.S.M.C.* makes its television debut.

1973 *Skylab 2* astronauts return to earth after 59 1/2 days in orbit.

1977 The funeral of *Steven Biko,* a 30-year-old black leader who died in police custody on September 12, attracts unprecedented support for South African blacks.

1997 The space shuttle *Atlantis* is launched into space carrying supplies to repair the Russian space station *Mir* (June 25, 1997).

SEPTEMBER
26

HOLIDAYS

Yemen Arab Republic
Revolution Day
Commemorates the 1962 revolution.

RELIGIOUS CALENDAR

The Saints
St. Colman of Lann Elo, abbot. Also called *Coarb of MacNisse, Colman Elo.* [d. 611]

St. Nilus of Rossano, abbot. Also called *Nil* or *Nilus the Younger.* [d. 1004]

St. John of Meda, layman. [d. c. 1159]

The Martyrs of North America. Commemorates 8 French Jesuit missionaries slain by Indians in North America. [d. 1642–49]

St. Francis of Camporosso, Capuchin laybrother. Feast formerly September 17. [d. 1866]

SS. Cosmas and Damian, martyrs; patrons of physicians, druggists, and midwives. Invoked for good health. Feast formerly September 27. [death dates unknown]

SS. Cyprian and Justina, martyrs. Cyprian also called *Cyprian the Magician* and *Cyprian of Antioch.* [death dates unknown]

The Beatified
Blessed Lucy of Caltagirone, virgin. [d. 13th century]

Blessed Dalmatius Moner, Friar, preacher. [d. 1341]

Blessed Teresa Couderc, virgin and co-foundress of the Congregation of Our Lady of the Retreat in the Cenacle. [d. 1885]

Blessed Giuseppe Marello. [beatified 1993]

BIRTHDATES

1774 *John Chapman (Johnny Appleseed),* U.S. farmer; reputed planter of apple orchards from the Allegheny Mountains of Pennsylvania to Indiana; stories of him usually have a legendary quality and tell of his numerous brave and generous acts. [d. March 1845]

1791 *(Jean Louis André) Theodore Gèricault,* French Romantic painter. [d. January 26, 1824]

1842 *George Frederick Baer,* U.S. lawyer, businessman; President, Philadelphia and Reading Railway Co. and Central Railroad Company; represented business interests in the U.S. which were shaken by the upstart labor movement. [d. April 26, 1914]

1862 *Arthur B(owen) Davies,* U.S. painter, printmaker, tapestry designer; member of the *Ashcan School;* led young American artists in a revolt against the conservatism and traditionalism of the National Academy. [d. October 24, 1928]

1870 *Christian X* of Denmark, acceded to throne 1912; symbolized nation's resistance to German occupation during World War II. [d. April 20, 1947]

1886 *Archibald Vivian Hill,* British physiologist; Nobel Prize in physiology or medicine for discoveries concerning the production of heat in muscles, 1922. [d. June 3, 1977]

1888 *T(homas) S(tearns) Eliot,* U.S.-born poet; noted for his original use of metrics and diction; responsible for a revolution in poetry; Nobel Prize in literature, 1948. [d. January 4, 1965]

James Frank Dobie, U.S. folklorist, educator; known for his expertise in and writing about the folklore of the Southwest; editor of publications of the Texas Folklore Society, 1922–42. [d. September 18, 1964]

1889 *Martin Heidegger,* German philosopher; chief existential philosopher of the 1920s and 1930s. [d. May 26, 1976]

1891 *Charles Munch,* French conductor; cofounder and conductor, Paris Philharmonic Orchestra, 1935–38;

conductor, Boston Symphony Orchestra, 1949–62; conductor, Tanglewood Berkshire Music Center, 1951–62. [d. November 6, 1968]

1894 *Bessie Smith,* U.S. blues singer, known as the "Empress of the Blues." [d. 1937]

1895 *George Raft (George Ranft),* U.S. actor; best known for gangster roles. [d. November 24, 1980]

1897 *Pope Paul VI* (born Giovanni Battista Montini), pope 1963–78; noted for his efforts toward social justice and church reunion. [d. August 6, 1978]

1898 *Richard Lockridge,* U.S. novelist, short-story writer; creator of the husband and wife detective team, *The Norths.* [d. June 19, 1982]

George Gershwin, U.S. composer; Pulitzer Prize, 1931, for *Of Thee I Sing,* the first musical to win the Pulitzer; wrote numerous scores for motion pictures. [d. July 11, 1937]

1902 *Albert Anastasia,* U.S. organized crime figure, murderer; joined Louis Buchalter and Murder, Inc., the mob's enforcement arm, 1931; extorted sweetheart contracts from unions. [d. October 29, 1957]

1914 *Jack LaLanne,* U.S. physical fitness expert, bodybuilder.

1915 *Frankie (Mr. Zero) Brimsek,* U.S. hockey player; elected to Hall of Fame, 1966.

1925 *Marty Robbins (Martin David Robinson),* U.S. singer;

Grammy Award for country-western hit, *El Paso,* 1959. [d. December 8, 1982]

1926 *John William (Trane) Coltrane,* U.S. jazz musician; Jazzman of the Year, 1965; played tenor saxophone with Dizzy Gillespie and Miles Davis. [d. July 17, 1967]

1927 *Patrick O'Neal,* U.S. actor; appeared in the television series, *Kaz,* 1978, and *Emerald Point,* 1983.

1929 *Meredith Gourdine,* U.S. inventor; known for his inventions based on electrogasdynamic technology.

1934 *Greg Morris,* U.S actor; starred in the television series, *Mission Impossible,* 1966–73. [d. August 27, 1996]

1942 *Kent McCord,* U.S. actor; starred in the television series, *Adam-12,* 1968–75

1945 *Bryan Ferry,* British singer, songwriter; lead vocalist for the rock group, *Roxy Music.*

1947 *Lynn Anderson,* U.S. singer; Grammy Award for *Rose Garden,* 1970.

1948 *Olivia Newton-John,* British-born singer, actress; starred in the film musicals, *Grease* and *Xanadu;* Grammy Award for *Let Me Be There,* 1973.

1949 *Jane Smiley,* U.S. educator, writer; Pulitzer Prize winner for *A Thousand Acres,* 1992.

1957 *Linda Hamilton,* U.S. actress; known for roles in the *Terminator* movies.

1962 *Melissa Sue Anderson,* U.S. actress; known for her role as Mary Ingalls on the television series, *Little House on the Prairie,* 1973–81.

HISTORICAL EVENTS

1687 The Venetian army bombards *Athens* and destroys the Parthenon and Propylaea.

1872 The *Shriners,* a fraternal and charitable organization, opens its first temple.

1901 *Ashanti* is formally annexed by Great Britain and placed under the administration of the *Gold Coast Colony.*

1907 *New Zealand* becomes a dominion rather than a colony of Great Britain.

1914 The *U.S. Federal Trade Commission* is established to encourage competition and prevent the growth of monopolies in commerce.

1918 *Battle of the Argonne,* the final Allied offensive of *World War I,* begins.

1919 U.S. President *Woodrow Wilson* is paralyzed by a stroke.

1950 *Seoul, Korea* falls to U.S. troops (*Korean War*).

1957 *West Side Story* by Leonard Bernstein premieres in New York.

1960 U.S. presidential candidates, *Richard Nixon* and *John Kennedy* confront each other in the first televised presidential debate.

1962 Algerian national assembly designates *Ahmed Ben Bella* to form the first regular government of *Algeria.*

The Beverly Hillbillies makes its television debut.

Imam *Saif-al-Islam Mohammed Bin Ahmed al-Badr* of Yemen is overthrown in a military coup d'etat.

september

1963 *Emilio da Los Santos* assumes power in the Dominican Republic after a bloodless coup d'etat.

1968 *Hawaii Five-O* makes its television debut.

1973 The *Rehabilitation Act* is passed by the U.S. Congress. It prohibits discrimination against those who are disabled.

1977 *Laker Airways* begins cheap trans-Atantic flights with its 345-seat DC-10 *Skytrain*.

1983 *Australia II* defeats the U.S. yacht, *Liberty,* to win the *America's Cup*. It is the first time that a country other than the U.S. has won in 132 years.

1986 *William Rehnquist* is sworn in as chief justice and *Antonin Scalia* as associate justice of the U.S. Supreme Court.

1989 The *Vietnamese army* exits from Cambodia and the country erupts into violence as the *Khmer Rouge* fight for power.

1990 The *Supreme Soviet* ends religious repression by allowing citizens to study religion without government interference.

1991 Six people begin a two-year, self-imposed existence in *Biosphere 2,* a man-made environment.

1993 Occupants of *Biosphere 2* emerge after a successful two-year existence inside the man-made environment.

HOLIDAYS

Ethiopia
Feast of the Finding of the True Cross

RELIGIOUS CALENDAR

The Saints
St. Barry, hermit. Also called *Barnic,* or *Barruc.* [d. 6th century]
St. Elzear and *Blessed Delphina,* his wife. Elzear also called *Eleazar.* [d. 1323 and 1360]
St. Vincent de Paul, founder of the Congregation of the Mission (Vincentians, or Lazarists) and the Sisters of Charity. Patron of all charitable societies. Feast formerly July 19. [d. 1660] Obligatory Memorial.

The Beatified
Blessed Rafael Arnáiz Baron. [beatified 1992]
Blessed Nazaria Ignacia March Mesa. [beatified 1992]
Blessed Léonie Françoise de Sales Aviat. [beatified 1992]
Blessed Maria Josefa Sancho de Guerra. [beatified 1992]

BIRTHDATES

1389 *Cosimo de Medici,* Italian ruler; first of the Medici family to rule Florence, 1433; known for his patronage of scholars and artists; called *Cosimo the Elder.* [d. August 1, 1464]

1601 *Louis XIII* of France, *the Just;* reigned during the *Thirty Years' War.* [d. May 14, 1643]

1627 *Jacques Bénigne Bossuet,* French bishop, historian, and orator; tutor to the Dauphin; renowned for his oratorical skills. [d. April 12, 1704]

1722 *Samuel Adams,* American Revolutionary patriot, statesman; helped instigate Stamp Act riots; leader of the Boston Tea Party; signer of the Declaration of Independence; member of Congress, 1776–81; Governor of Massachusetts, 1794–97. [d. October 2, 1803]

1772 *Martha Jefferson,* daughter of Thomas Jefferson, third U.S. President; served as her father's White House hostess. [d. October 10, 1836]

Sándor Kisfaludy, Hungarian poet, the *Father of Lyric Poetry in Hungary.* [d. October 28, 1844]

1783 *Peter Joseph von Cornelius,* German painter; known as the *Founder of the German School of Painting.* [d. March 6, 1867]

Agustin de Iturbide, Mexican soldier; Emperor of Mexico, 1822–23. [d. July 19, 1824]

1791 *Michael Faraday,* British scientist; discovered electromagnetism. [d. Aug. 27, 1867]

1792 *George Cruikshank,* British artist, illustrator; known for his satirical sketches in *Oliver Twist* and Grimm's *Popular Stories.* [d. February 1, 1878]

1809 *Raphael Semmes,* Confederate naval commander; responsible for the destruction or capture of 64 Union ships; after the Civil War, he lectured and wrote several books based on his war experiences. [d. August 30, 1877]

1818 *Adolph Wilhelm Hermann Kolbe,* German organic chemist; responsible for development of methods of synthesizing organic compounds, especially *acetylsalicylic acid (aspirin),* 1859. [d. November 25, 1884]

1839 *Henry Phipps,* U.S. manufacturer, philanthropist; Director, U.S. Steel Corporation, 1901–30. [d. September 22, 1930]

1840 *Alfred Thayer Mahan,* U.S. admiral, naval historian, and theorist; author of numerous classic studies of naval history and strategy; his works influenced the direction of naval development in most major countries of the world prior to World War II. [d. December 1, 1914]

Thomas Nast, U.S. cartoonist, illustrator, born in Germany;

september

his pointed political cartoons led to the fall of the *Tweed Ring* in New York City's *Tammany Hall*, 1869–72; conceived the Democratic Party's donkey symbol and the Republicans' elephant. [d. December 7, 1902]

1855 *Joy Morton,* U.S. manufacturer; founder and president of the Morton Salt Company. [d. May 9, 1934]

1862 *Louis Botha,* South African statesman, soldier; Premier of Transvaal, 1907–10; first Prime Minister of Union of South Africa, 1910–19. [d. August 27, 1919]

1875 *Grazia Deledda,* Italian novelist; Nobel Prize in literature for sympathetic portrayal of Sardinian life, 1926. [d. August 16, 1936]

1898 *Vincent (Millie) Youmans,* U.S. composer; wrote *Tea for Two, Great Day.* [d. April 5, 1946]

1914 *(Sarah) Catherine Marshall,* U.S. nonfiction writer, editor; known for her biography of her husband, Peter Marshall, entitled *A Man Called Peter.* [d. March 18, 1983]

1917 *Louis Stanton Auchincloss,* U.S. novelist, short-story writer.

1918 Sir *Martin Ryle,* British radio astronomer; Nobel Prize in physics for developing revolutionary *radio telescope systems* (with Anthony Hewish), 1974. [d. October 14, 1984]

1919 *Charles Harting Percy,* U.S. politician, business executive; President, Bell & Howell Co., 1949–61; U.S. Senator, 1967–84.

1920 *William Conrad,* U.S. actor, director, producer; starred in the television series, *Cannon,* 1971–76, and *Jake and the Fatman,* 1987–92. [d. February 11, 1994]

1922 *Arthur Penn,* U.S. director of plays and films such as *The Miracle Worker, Two for the Seesaw, Alice's Restaurant,* and *Bonnie and Clyde.*

1924 *Bud Powell,* U.S. pianist, composer, and modern jazz pioneer. [d. August 1, 1966]

1926 *Jayne Cotter Meadows,* U.S. actress; appeared in the television series, *I've Got a Secret,* 1952–58, and *Medical Center,* 1969–72; married to Steve Allen.

1929 *Sada Carolyn Thompson,* U.S. actress; known for her role as Kate Lawrence in the television series, *Family,* 1976–79.

1943 *Randy Bachman,* Canadian singer, musician; guitarist with the rock groups, *Guess Who* and *Bachman-Turner Overdrive.*

1947 *Meat Loaf (Marvin Lee Anday),* U.S. musician, actor; former member of the rock group, *Amboy Dukes;* appeared in the cult film, *Rocky Horror Picture Show;* Platinum Record Award for solo album, *Bat Out of Hell,* 1978.

1958 *Shaun Paul Cassidy,* U.S. singer, actor; starred in the television series, *Hardy Boy Mysteries* and *General Hospital.*

HISTORICAL EVENTS

1825 The world's first public *railroad* to use locomotive

traction opens in England between Stockton and Darlington.

1831 *British Association for the Advancement of Science* is formed.

1914 *First Battle of Artois* opens another Allied attempt to dislodge the Germans along the Western Front (*World War I*).

1939 *Warsaw* falls to invading Germans (*World War II*).

1940 German-Italian-Japanese pact is concluded at Berlin, providing for 10-year military and economic alliance (*World War II*).

1946 Emperor *Hirohito* visits General Douglas MacArthur at the U.S. embassy in Tokyo, becoming the first Japanese monarch in history to appear publicly.

1947 Colombia cedes the *San Miguel Triangle* to Ecuador, ending a 25-year land dispute.

1950 *Ezzard Charles* defeats *Joe Louis* to regain the world heavyweight boxing title.

1954 *The Tonight Show* makes its television debut.

1961 Former U.S. Vice-President *Richard Nixon* announces his candidacy for governorship of California.

Sierra Leone is admitted to the United Nations.

1964 *Warren Report* on the assassination of U.S. President *John F. Kennedy* is issued.

1969 South Vietnamese President Thieu states that the withdrawal of U.S. troops would take "years and years" because his country had "no ambition" to take over the fighting (*Vietnam War*).

1988 *Greg Louganis* becomes the first diver in Olympic history to win gold medals in consecutive Olympics.

Poland's parliament confirms *Mieczyslaw Rakowski* as premier.

1991 *Prime Minister Petre Roman* of Romania announces his resignation after public unrest over the country's weak economy.

1997 *Thailand*'s government approves a new constitution.

september

SEPTEMBER
28

HOLIDAYS

Guinea
Referendum Day

Taiwan
Birthday of Confucius or Teachers Day

U.S. (Minnesota)
Frances Willard Day

RELIGIOUS CALENDAR

The Saints
St. Exsuperius, Bishop of Toulouse. Also called *Exuperius.* [d. c. 412]
St. Eustochium, virgin. [d. c. 419]
St. Faustus, Bishop of Riez. [d. c. 493]
St. Machan, bishop. Also called *Manchan.* [d. 6th century]
St. Annemund, Bishop of Lyons. Also called *Dalfinus.* [d. 658]
St. Lioba, virgin. Also called *Leoba, Liobgetha.* [d. 780]
St. Wenceslaus of Bohemia, martyr; patron of *Czechoslovakia.* Also called *Vaclav, Wenceslas,* or *Wenzel.* [d. 929] Optional Memorial.

The Beatified
Blessed Laurence of Ripafratta, Dominican friar. [d. 1457]
Blessed John of Dukla, Franciscan friar. [d. 1484]
Blessed Bernardino of Feltre, Franciscan friar. Also called *Bernardino Tomitani.* [d. 1494]
Blessed Francis of Calderola, Friar Minor. [d. 1507]

Blessed Simon de Rojas. [d. 1624]

BIRTHDATES

1573 *Caravaggio,* Italian painter; founder of naturalistic school of Italian painting. [d. July 18, 1610]

1803 *Prosper Mérimée,* French man of letters; Senator, 1853–70; noted for his translations of Russian classics, which brought literature of Russia to the French; author of *Carmen.* [d. September 23, 1870]

1839 *Frances Willard,* U.S. reformer; organizer and first president of *World Woman's Christian Temperance Union,* 1883–98. [d. February 18, 1898]

1841 *Georges Clemenceau,* known as the *Tiger,* French statesman; member of Chamber of Deputies, 1876–93; Senator, 1902–06; Premier of France, 1906–09, 1917. [d. November 24, 1929]

1852 *Henri Moissan,* French chemist; Nobel Prize in chemistry for isolation of the element *fluorine* and the development of the *Moissan furnace,* 1906. [d. February 20, 1907]

1856 *Kate (Douglas) Wiggin,* U.S. educator, author; organized

first free *kindergarten* in the Far West, 1898; author of *Rebecca of Sunnybrook Farm,* one of the best-selling books of the 20th century. [d. August 24, 1923]

1887 *Avery Brundage,* U.S. sports figure; President, U.S. Olympic Association, 1929–53; President, International Olympic Committee, 1952–72. [d. May 8, 1975]

1888 *Herman Cyril McNeile (Sapper),* British novelist; author of a series of crime and adventure novels featuring *Bulldog Drummond.* [d. August 14, 1937]

1892 *Elmer (Leopold) Rice,* U.S. playwright; author of *The Adding Machine, Street Scene,* for which he won the 1929 Pulitzer Prize in drama. [d. May 8, 1967]

1893 *Marshall Field III,* U.S. publisher, philanthropist; established the Chicago *Sun* (later the *Sun-Times*). [d. November 8, 1956]

1895 *Wallace Kirkman Harrison,* U.S. architect; partner in architecture firm Harrison and Abramovitz, 1941–78; designer of Rockefeller Center, 1930, United Nations Headquarters, 1947, and Metropolitan Opera House, Lincoln Center, New York,

1955, New York State Capitol, South Mall, Albany, New York. [d. December 2, 1981]

1901 *William S. Paley,* U.S. communications executive; founder of CBS Inc.; President, 1928–46; Chairman, Museum of Modern Art. [d. October 26, 1990]

1902 *Ed(ward Vincent) Sullivan,* U.S. journalist, TV host; Broadway gossip columnist, 1929–39; radio columnist, 1929–48; television emcee of CBS's *Toast of the Town* (later known as the *Ed Sullivan Show*); on his television show, introduced nearly every major show-business personality of the period. His program was on CBS for 23 years. [d. October 13, 1974]

1905 *L(ucius) Mendel Rivers,* U.S. Congressman, 1941–70. [d. December 28, 1970]

Max Schmeling, German boxer; World Heavyweight Champion, 1930–32.

1909 *Al Capp,* U.S. cartoonist; creator of *Li'l' Abner,* satirical comic strip set in Dogpatch, U.S.A., and featuring various hillbilly citizens whose lives were occasionally interjected with visits from famous political figures of the day. [d. November 5, 1979]

1911 *Sydney Harris (Syd) Howe,* Canadian hockey player; center, 1929–46; three Stanley Cups with Detroit; Hall of Fame, 1965.

1913 *Alice Marble,* U.S. tennis player; U.S. singles champion, 1936, 1938–40; Wimbledon singles champion, 1939. [d. December 13, 1990]

1915 *Ethel Rosenberg,* U.S. traitor; arrested and convicted with her husband, Julius (May 12) of passing secrets to the Russians; executed for espionage. [d. June 19, 1953]

1916 *Peter Finch (William Mitchell),* British actor; posthumous Academy Award for *Network,* 1978. [d. January 14, 1977]

1917 *Michael Somes,* British ballet dancer; principal of Sadler's Wells Ballet Co., 1938–63; director of Royal Ballet Co., 1963–70.

1919 *Thomas D. (Tom) Harmon,* U.S. football player, sportscaster; Heisman Trophy, 1940; father of Mark Harmon (September 2). [d. March 15, 1990]

1924 *Marcello Mastroianni,* Italian actor; starred in *La Dolce Vita; Yesterday, Today, and Tomorrow.* [d. December 19, 1996]

1925 *Seymour Cray,* U.S. electronics engineer; known for his contributions to computer design and the supercomputer industry. [d. October 5, 1995]

1934 *Brigitte Bardot,* French actress; sex symbol.

1939 *Kurt Mamre Luedtke,* U.S. journalist, screenwriter; Academy Award for *Out of Africa,* 1985.

1947 *Jeffrey Jones,* U.S. actor; known for roles in *Amadeus,* 1984 and *Beetlejuice,* 1989.

1952 *Sylvia Kristel,* Dutch actress; starred in the erotic French film, *Emmanuelle,* 1974.

1962 *Grant Fuhr,* U.S. hockey player.

1964 *Janeane Garofalo,* U.S. comedian, actress.

1972 *Gwyneth Paltrow,* U.S. actress; known for her performances in *Flesh and Bone,* 1993, and *Emma,* 1996.

HISTORICAL EVENTS

1066 *Norman Conquest* of England begins when *William of Normandy* lands at Pevensey.

1914 Germans lay siege to *Antwerp (World War I).*

1916 The British take the fortress of *Kut-el-Amara* from the Turks (*World War I*).

1918 *Battle of Ypres* begins (*World War I*).

1928 *William S. Paley* purchases a controlling interest in *Columbia Broadcasting System* for $300,000.

1935 *Protestant Church* in Germany is placed under state control.

1941 *Ted Williams* of the Boston Red Sox finishes baseball season with .406 batting average.

1950 *Indonesia* is admitted to the United Nations.

1953 The Polish government suspends *Stephen (Cardinal) Wyszynski* as Roman Catholic primate, claiming that he abused his authority.

1958 *Fifth Republic* is established in *France.*

1960 *Mali and Senegal* are admitted to the United Nations.

1971 *Joszef Cardinal Mindszenty* arrives at the Vatican after spending 15 years as a virtual prisoner of the state in the U.S. Embassy in Hungary.

september

1976 U.S. Congress passes the *Toxic Substances Control Act,* requiring testing of new chemicals for health and environmental dangers before they are marketed.

1977 Cambodian leader *Pol Pot* is received in Peking by top Chinese leaders as the secretary of the Central Committee of the *Cambodian Communist Party,* whose existence had never been acknowledged before. The 17th anniversary of its founding was announced simultaneously by a Phnom Penh radio station.

1978 *Pieter Willem Botha* is elected prime minister of South Africa.

1994 Over nine hundred people are killed when an *Estonian ferry* capsizes in the Baltic Sea.

HOLIDAYS

Brunei
Constitution Day
Commemorates the promulgation of the constitution, 1959.

Paraguay
Battle of Boqueron Day

RELIGIOUS CALENDAR

Feasts
St. Michael and All the Angels.
Commonly called *Michaelmas Day.* Feast originated in the sixth century. [major holy day, Episcopal Church; minor festival, Lutheran Church]

The Saints
SS. Rhipsime, Gaiana, and their Companions, virgins and martyrs. Protomartyrs of the Armenian Church. Rhipsime also called *Arepsima,* [d. c. 312]
St. Theodata, martyr. [d. c. 318]

The Beatified
Blessed Richard of Hampole, hermit. Also called *Richard Rolle.* [d. 1349]
Blessed Charles of Blois. [d. 1364]
Blessed Guillelmus Courtet, Michael de Aozaraza, Vincentius Schiwozuka, Laurentius Ruiz and Lazarus de Kyoto, the Martyrs of Nagasaki. [beatified 1981]

BIRTHDATES

1547 *Miguel de Cervantes (Saavedra),* Spanish novelist, dramatist, poet; nicknamed *The Handless One* because of injury to his left hand. Author of *Don Quixote,* the burlesque novel of a country lord and his squire and their chivalric misadventures. [d. April 23, 1616]

1640 *Antoine Coysevox,* French sculptor; noted for his sculptural decorations at Versailles and his busts of such prominent figures as King Louis XIV, Richelieu, Mazarin, and Condé. [d. October 10, 1720]

1703 *François Boucher,* French painter, tapes-try and porcelain designer and engraver; a favorite of Madame Pompadour; known for his historical and pastoral painting. [d. May 30, 1770]

1725 *Robert Clive, Baron Clive of Plassey,* English administrator, soldier; obtained sovereignty over Bengal for East India Company; his governorship of India, 1758–59, was marked by corruption. Committed suicide after dishonorable return to Engand. [d. November 22, 1774]

1758 *Viscount Horatio Nelson,* British naval hero; won great victories in wars with Revolutionary and Napoleonic France; recognized for conspicuous bravery at *Battle of Cape St. Vincent,* 1797; defeated Danish fleet at Copenhagen; most famous for defeat of French fleet at *Trafalgar,* 1805. [d. October 21, 1805]

1838 *Henry Hobson Richardson,* U.S. architect, noted for his neo-Romanesque style; examples of his work are Trinity Church, Boston, and Harvard University Law School. [d. April 27, 1886]

1865 *Elizabeth Cleghorn Gaskell,* British novelist; wrote about life in the manufacturing cities of the English Midlands; biographer of Charlotte Brontë. [d. November 12, 1865]

1871 *Gerardo Machado y Morales,* Cuban patriot, president 1924–33. [d. March 29, 1939]

Emma Wold, U.S. lawyer, reformer; women's rights activist. [d. July 21, 1950]

1896 *Jolie Gabor (Jancsi Tilleman),* Hungarian-born mother of Eva, Magda, and Zsa Zsa Gabor. [d. April 1, 1997]

1897 *Herbert (Sebastian) Agar,* U.S. journalist, author; Pulitzer Prize in history, 1933; after World War II, lived in

september

London. [d. November 24, 1980]

1901 *Enrico Fermi,* U.S. physicist born in Italy; pioneer in research on *man-made nuclear chain reaction;* Nobel Prize in physics for work on *radioactive elements,* including artificial ones produced by neutron bombardment, 1938. [d. November 28, 1954]

1907 *(Orvon) Gene Autry,* U.S. actor, business executive; known as *The Singing Cowboy,* starred in over 80 Westerns, 1934–54.

1908 *Greer Garson,* U.S. actress; Academy Award for *Mrs. Miniver,* 1942. [d. April 6, 1996]

1910 *Virginia Bruce,* U.S. actress of the 1930s. [d. February 24, 1982]

1912 *Michelangelo Antonioni,* Italian film director, scriptwriter, noted for his surrealistic films such as *The Red Desert, Zambriskie Point, Blow Up.*

1913 *Stanley Kramer,* U.S. producer, director; noted for his production of such classics as *Death of a Salesman, High Noon,* and *The Caine Mutiny.*

1916 *Trevor (Wallace) Howard,* British actor. [d. January 7, 1988]

1920 *Peter Mitchell,* British chemist; Nobel Prize in chemistry for study of energy reception of human cells, 1978.

1922 *Lizabeth Scott (Emma Matzo),* U.S. actress; appeared in the film, *You Came Along,* 1945.

1925 *John Goodwin Tower,* U.S. politician, political scientist; Senator, 1961–85. [d. April 5, 1991]

1927 *Paul N. McCloskey, Jr.,* U.S. politician, lawyer; Congressman, 1967–83.

1931 *James Cronin,* U.S. physicist; Nobel Prize in physics (with Val Fitch), 1980.

Anita Ekberg, Swedish actress; films include *La Dolce Vita* and *Boccaccio '70;* called the *Ice Maiden.*

1933 *Samora Machel,* President, People's Republic of Mozambique, 1975–.

1935 *Jerry Lee Lewis,* U.S. musician; one of the early rock stars.

1939 *Larry Lavon Linville,* U.S. actor; known for his role as Frank Burns on the television series, *M*A*S*H,* 1972–77.

1942 *Madeline Gail Kahn,* U.S. actress; Academy Award nominee for *Paper Moon;* often associated with Mel Brooks' films including *Young Frankenstein* and *Blazing Saddles.*

Jean-Luc Ponty, French composer, violinist; jazz, rock, and fusion musician who popularized the use of violin in jazz.

1943 *Lech Walesa,* Polish labor leader, political figure; founder of *Solidarity* union; leader of the political opposition to the Communist Party; Nobel Peace Prize, 1983.

1948 *Bryant Charles Gumbel,* U.S. broadcast journalist; hosted *NBC Sports,* 1975–82; Emmy Awards, 1976, 1977; host of the television series, *Today Show,* 1982–96.

1956 *Sebastian Coe,* British distance runner.

HISTORICAL EVENTS

1829 *Robert Peel* remodels London police, henceforth known as *bobbies.*

1833 *King Ferdinand VII* of Spain dies and his wife becomes regent for their infant daughter, *Isabella II.*

1868 *Queen Isabella II* of Spain flees to France in the wake of a revolution and is declared deposed.

1879 A proclamation of the British government declares the *Transvaal* in South Africa a British Territory.

1911 *Italy* declares war on Turkey over Tripoli and Cyrenaica.

1913 *Fuller Brush Co.* is incorporated in Connecticut.

1918 The British pierce the *Hindenburg Line* of German defense between Cambrai and St. Quentin in the final offensive of *World War I.*

1938 European leaders sign the *Munich Pact,* allowing Germany to occupy Sudetenland in exchange for peace in Europe.

1948 Lawrence Olivier's film version of Shakespeare's *Hamlet* premieres in New York.

1950 General Douglas MacArthur, on behalf of the UN command, hands over the city of *Seoul* to President Syngman Rhee of the Republic of *Korea.*

1953 *The Danny Thomas Show* makes its television debut.

1964 Roman Catholic Church's Ecumenical Council approves admission of married men to the deaconate.

1970 The *New American Bible* is published by St. Anthony Guild Press. It represents the first English translation of a Roman Catholic bible.

1972 *China* and *Japan* agree to end the legal state of war existing between them since 1937 and to establish diplomatic relations.

1978 *Pope John Paul I* dies after a reign of only 34 days.

1979 China condemns the *Cultural Revolution of 1966–69.*

Equatorial Guinea executes deposed President *Macias Nquema* after a trial attended by international observers.

1981 The U.S. *federal debt ceiling* is raised to $1 trillion.

1983 Lady *Mary Donaldson* is elected as the first woman Lord Mayor of London in the 800-year history of the position.

1986 The Soviet Union releases U.S. reporter, *Nicholas*

Daniloff, who had been arrested one month earlier on charges of espionage.

1991 *President-elect Jean-Bertrand Aristide* is overthrown in a military coup.

1992 *Fernando Collor de Mello,* president of Brazil, is impeached for financial wrongdoings. *Itamar Augusto Cautiero Franco* becomes the new president.

1993 An earthquake devastates central *India,* killing an estimated 20,000 people.

september

SEPTEMBER
30

HOLIDAYS

Botswana
Botswana Day
Commemorates Botswana's coming to independence, 1966.

São Tomé and Principe
Nationalization Day

RELIGIOUS CALENDAR

The Saints
St. Gregory the Enlightener, bishop of Ashtishat. Also surnamed the *Apostle of Armenia* and the *Illuminator.* [d. c. 330]
St. Jerome, Doctor of the Church. One of greatest Biblical scholars; patron of students. [d. 420]
St. Honorius, Archbishop of Canterbury. [d. 653]
SS. Tancred, Torthred, and Tova, hermits and martyrs; venerated at Thorney. [d. 870]
St. Simon of Creèpy, royal monk. [d. 1082]

BIRTHDATES

1207 *Jalal ad-Din ar-Rumi (Mawlana),* Persian poet. [d. 1273]

1714 *Etienne Bonnot de Condillac,* French philosopher; exponent of doctrine of *sensationalism.* [d. April 2, 1780]

1732 *Jacques Necker,* French financier, statesman, born in Switzerland; appointed Director of Finances, 1776; dismissed, 1781; supervised establishment of the States-General, 1788; exiled, 1790; father of Madame de Stäel (April 22) [d. April 9, 1804].

1765 *Jose Morelos,* Mexican politician and military leader. [d. 1815]

1788 *Fitzroy James Henry Somerset Raglan, 1st Baron Raglan,* British Army field marshal; commander of British troops during Crimean War, 1853–55; responsible for loss of the *Light Brigade* at *Battle of Balaklava,* 1854. His name survives in the *raglan* sleeve, styled after the slit potato sacks his men were forced to wear. [d. June 28, 1855]

1861 *William Wrigley, Jr.,* U.S. manufacturer; founder of the Wrigley Chewing Gum Company, 1891. [d. January 26, 1932]

1870 *Jean Baptiste Perrin,* French physicist; Nobel Prize in physics for confirming the *atomic nature of matter* through studies of *Brownian movement,* 1926. [d. April 17, 1942]

1882 *(Johannes) Hans Wilhelm Geiger,* German physicist; invented the *Geiger counter,* the first device to successfully detect *radioactivity.* [d. September 24, 1945]

1905 *Sir Nevill Francis Mott,* British physicist; Nobel Prize in physics for advancement of *solid state circuitry* and basic theories of magnetism and conduction (with P. W. Anderson and J. H. Van Vleck), 1977.

1915 *Lester Maddox,* U.S. politician; Governor of Georgia, 1967–71; American Independent Party candidate, 1976 presidential election; avowed segregationist.

1917 *Park Chung Hee,* South Korean leader, military officer; President of South Korea, 1963–79; assassinated. [d. October 26, 1979]

1921 *Deborah Jane Kerr,* U.S. actress; starred in *From Here to Eternity,* 1953, and *Tea and Sympathy,* 1956.

1924 *Truman Capote,* U.S. novelist, short-story writer; author of *In Cold Blood.* [d. August 24, 1984]

1928 *Elie(zer) Wiesel,* U.S. journalist, author; Holocaust survivor whose work frequently involves Jewish themes; wrote *The Town beyond the Wall* and *Souls on Fire;* Nobel Peace Prize, 1986.

1929 *Robert Duvall,* U.S. actor; Academy Award (Best Actor) for *Tender Mercies,* 1983.

1931 *Angie Dickinson (Angeline Brown),* U.S. actress; starred in the television series, *Police Woman*, 1974–78.

1935 *Johnny Mathis*, U.S. singer.

1936 *James Ralph (Jim) Sasser*, U.S. politician, lawyer; Senator, 1977–94; Ambassador to China, 1996– .

1939 *Leonard (Len) Cariou*, Canadian-born actor, singer, director; Tony Award for *Sweeney Todd*, 1979.

Jean-Marie Lehn, French scientist; Nobel Prize in chemistry (with Charles J. Pedersen and Donald J. Cram), 1987.

1943 *Johann Deisenhofer*, German biochemist; Nobel Prize for Chemistry, 1988. Deisenhofer shares with prize with fellow biochemists, Hartmut Michel and Robert Huber.

1946 *Ibrahim Moussa*, Egyptian producer, talent agent; husband of Nastassja Kinski (January 24).

1953 *Deborah Allen*, U.S. singer, songwriter; known for her hit country-western record, *Baby I Lied*, 1983.

HISTORICAL EVENTS

1174 *Treaty of Montlouis* between *Henry II* of England and *Louis VII* of France ends family conspiracy against Henry.

1399 *Henry IV* of England, son of *John of Gaunt*, succeeds to English throne after *Richard II* is deposed.

1877 First *U.S. swimming championship* is held on Harlem River, New York.

1918 *Bulgaria* signs armistice with Allies (*World War I*).

1927 *Leon Trotsky* is expelled from the executive body of the Communist International.

1935 *Porgy and Bess*, George Gershwin's folk opera, premieres in Boston.

1949 *Berlin air lift* ends its successful operation after 277,264 flights.

1951 *The Red Skelton Show* makes its television debut.

1953 Baseball team owners approve the transfer of the *St. Louis Browns* to Baltimore, where the team is renamed the "Orioles."

1954 First atomic powered submarine, *U.S.S. Nautilus*, is commissioned at Groton, Connecticut.

1955 Actor *James Dean* is killed in a California auto accident.

1958 Governor *Orval E. Faubus* of Arkansas defies Supreme Court ruling against *segregation* by closing four high schools in Little Rock.

1962 Black student *James H. Meredith* is escorted onto the formerly white-only campus of the University of Mississippi by deputy U.S. marshals.

1962 *National Farm Workers Association* is founded.

1966 *Bechuanaland* gains its independence from Great Britain as the nation of *Botswana*.

1974 Establishment of year-round *Daylight Saving Time* is rescinded; it was instituted on January 1 as an energy-saving measure.

General *Francisco da Costa Gomes* replaces *Antonio de Spinola* as president of Portugal's ruling military junta.

1976 *California* becomes the first U.S. state to recognize the *right to die*.

1986 Accused Soviet spy, *Gennadi Zakharov*, is freed by the U.S. just one day after the Soviet Union releases U.S. reporter *Nicholas Daniloff*.

1990 World leaders meet in New York City for the *World Summit for Children*.

september

OCTOBER

October is the tenth month of the Gregorian calendar and has 31 days. The name is derived from the Latin *octo,* 'eight,' designating the position October held in the early Roman 10-month calendar. Following the adoption of January as the first month in the 12-month calendar (see also **September**), various attempts to rename the month in honor ofcelebrated Romans all met with failure.

October was a month of notable Roman festivals honoring Mars, the god of war. On the Ides of October, October 15, one ritual involved the *Equus October* 'October Horse,' consisting of a horse race after which one horse was sacrificed to Mars. On October 19 the *Armilustrium* involved a ritual purification of arms prior to their being put away for the winter; winter campaigning was virtually unknown in the ancient world.

In the New England region, the frost and snow flurries of the beginning of October came to be called "Squaw Winter," and the warm days that generally followed were known as "Indian Summer," expressions which remain in use in colder climes throughout the United States.

In the astrological calendar, October spans the zodiac signs of Libra, the Balance (September 23-October 22) and Scorpio, the Scorpion (October 23-November 21).

The birthstone for October is the opal or tourmaline, and the flower is the calendula or cosmos.

STATE, NATIONAL, AND INTERNATIONAL HOLIDAYS

Child Health Day
(United States)
First Monday

Thanksgiving Day
(St. Lucia)
First Monday

United Nations' Day
(Barbados)
First Monday

National Sports' Day
(Lesotho)
during First Week

Foundation of Workers' Party
(North Korea)
during First Week

Columbus Day
(most of the United States)
Second Monday

except:
(Maryland, Puerto Rico)
October 12

Fraternal Day
(Alabama)
Second Monday

Discoverers' Day
(Hawaii)
Second Monday

Farmers' Day
(Florida)
Second Monday

Fiji Day
(Fiji)
Second Monday

Pioneer's Day
(South Dakota)
Second Monday

Thanksgiving Day
(Canada)
Second Monday

Heroes' Day
(Jamaica)
Third Monday

Chulalongkorn's Day
(Thailand)
Fourth Monday

Independence Day
(Zambia)
Fourth Monday

Angam Day
(Nauru)
Fourth Wednesday

Bank Holiday
(Ireland)
Last Monday

Labor Day
(New Zealand)
Last Monday

SPECIAL EVENTS AND THEIR SPONSORS

National Apple Month
National Apple Month

National B'nai B'rith Month
B'nai B'rith International

Country Music Month
Country Music Association

Episcopal School Month
National Association of Episcopal Schools

Lazy Eye Alert Month
American Society to Prevent Blindness

Pizza Festival Time
Richard R. Falk Associates

National Popcorn Month
The Popcorn Institute

National Pretzel Month
National Pretzel Bakers Institute

National Spinal Health Month
American Chiropractic Association

Vocational Service Month
Rotary International

National Spinning and Weaving Week
First week
The Weaving and Spinning Council

National 4-H Week
Week of the First Sunday
Extension Service

National Fire Prevention Week
Second Week
National Fire Protection Association
The National Exchange Club
National Safety Council

International Letter Writing Week
Second Week
Franklin D. Roosevelt Philatelic Society

National Newspaper Week
Second Week
Newspaper Association Managers

National YWCA Teen Week
Second Week
National Board of the YWCA of the United States

National Vocation Awareness Week
Mid-Month
National Catholic Vocation Council

National Sunshine Week
Week of the Third Sunday
National Society for Shut-ins

National Handicapped Awareness Week
Third Week
National Easter Seal Society

National Lupus Week
Third Week
American Lupus Society

National Safety on the Streets Week
Fourth Week
National Safety Council

National Cleaner Air Week
Final Full Week
Air Pollution Control League of Greater Cincinnati

National Storytelling Festival
First Full Weekend
National Association for the Preservation and Perpetuation of Storytelling

Eleanor Roosevelt Birthday Anniversary
October 11
Franklin D. Roosevelt Philatelic Society

National Poetry Day
October 15
National Poetry Day Committee, Inc., and World Poetry Day Committee, Inc.

Good Bears of the World Day
October 27
Good Bears of the World

Sweetest Day
Third Saturday

Boss's Day
Third Sunday

National Shut-in Day
Third Sunday
National Society for Shut-ins

Mother-in-Law's Day
Fourth Sunday

HOLIDAYS

Botswana
Botswana Day
Continuation of the celebration of Botswana Day, September 30.

Cyprus
Independence Day

People's Republic of China
National Day

Lesotho
Independence Day

Nigeria
National Holiday
Celebrates Nigeria's achievement of independent status within the British Commonwealth, 1960, and establishment of the Republic, 1963.

San Marino
Captain Regents' Day

South Korea
Armed Forces Day

Tuvalu
Tuvalu Day
Commemorates the separation from the Gilbert Islands, 1975. First day of a two-day celebration.

U.S.
Agricultural Fair Day
The basis for this celebration is in the first agricultural fair in the U.S., at Pittsfield, Massachusetts, and the formation of the first permanent agricultural association, 1810.

RELIGIOUS CALENDAR

The Saints
St. Remigius, Bishop of Rheims. Apostle of France. Also called *Remi, Remigus.* [d. c. 530]

St. Romanus the Melodist, Byzantine hymn-writer. [d. 6th century]

St. Bavo, hermit and penitent; patron of Ghent and Haarlem. Also called *Allowin.* [d. c. 655]

St. Francis of Pesaro, hermit. Also called *Cecco.* [d. c. 1350]

The Canterbury Martyrs of 1588 and others.

St. Melorus, martyr. Also called *Melar, Mylor.* [death date unknown]

Theresa of the Child Jesus (St. Teresa of Lisieux), virgin; patron of all foreign missions. [d. 1897] Feast formerly October 3. Obligatory Memorial.

The Beatified
Blessed Nicholas of Forca Palena, hermit. [d. 1449]

Blessed Pietro Casini. [beatified 1995]

BIRTHDATES

1207 *Henry III* of England, 1216–72. [d. November 16, 1272]

1685 *Charles VI,* Holy Roman Emperor. [d. October 20, 1740]

1746 *John Peter Gabriel Muhlenberg,* American Revolutionary clergyman, general, congressman; commanded first American light infantry brigade, 1777; member of first U.S. Congress, 1788–1801. [d. October 1, 1807]

1754 *Paul I,* Emperor of Russia, 1796–1801; successor to Catherine the Great; assassinated. [d. March 23, 1801]

1781 *James Lawrence,* U.S. naval captain; commander of the *Hornet,* which defeated the British *Peacock* in the War of 1812, and of the *Chesapeake,* which was defeated by the British outside of Boston Harbor, 1813; issued the rallying cry, "Don't give up the ship." [d. June 1, 1813]

1799 *Rufus Choate,* U.S. lawyer, statesman; leading trial lawyer of his time; Massachusetts state attorney general, 1853–54. [d. July 13, 1859]

1832 *Caroline Harrison,* wife of U.S. President Benjamin Harrison. [d. October 25, 1892]

1847 *Annie Besant,* British theosophist, reformer, Indian political leader; President, *Theosophical Society,* 1907–33; organized Indian Home Rule League; President, Indian National Congress, 1917. [d. September 20, 1933]

october

1881 *William Edward Boeing,* U.S. airplane manufacturer; founded Boeing Aircraft, 1916, and United Aircraft and Transport, 1928. [d. September 28, 1956]

1885 *Louis Untermeyer,* U.S. poet, editor; compiled popular poetry anthologies. [d. December 18, 1977]

1893 *Faith (Cuthrell) Baldwin,* U.S. author; known for popular romantic novels. [d. March 19, 1978]

1904 *Vladimir Horowitz,* U.S. pianist, born in Russia; internationally recognized for his virtuosity. [d. November 5, 1990]

Otto Robert Frisch, British physicist; responsible for significant work on uranium atom, which led to the development of the *atomic bomb.* [d. September 22, 1979]

1910 *Bonnie Parker,* U.S. outlaw; with Clyde Barrow (March 24) carried out a two-year crime spree in the U.S. Southwest that resulted in 12 murders and numerous robberies; died in an ambush by Texas Rangers. [d. May 23, 1934]

1911 *Fletcher Knebel,* U.S. author, journalist; wrote *Night of Camp David,* 1965, and *Dark Horse,* 1972. [d. February 26, 1993]

1914 *Daniel J. Boorstin,* U.S. historian, author, librarian; Director of National Museum of History and Technology, 1969–73; Pulitzer Prize for history, 1974; Librarian of Congress, 1975–87.

1920 *Walter Matthau,* U.S. actor; starred in *The Odd Couple,*

The Sunshine Boys, and *Grumpy Old Men.*

1921 *James (Allen) Whitmore,* U.S. actor; noted for his impersonations of such famous figures as Will Rogers, Harry Truman.

1924 *Jimmy (James Earl) Carter,* 39th president of U.S.; first president from the deep South since the Civil War.

William Rehnquist, U.S. jurist, lawyer; Associate Justice, U.S. Supreme Court, 1972–87; Chief Justice, 1987–.

1927 *Tom Bosley,* U.S. actor; Tony Award for the title role in *Fiorello,* 1959; starred in the television series, *Happy Days,* 1974–84

1928 *Laurence Harvey, (Larushka Mischa Skikne)* British actor, born in Lithuania. [d. November 25, 1973]

George Peppard, U.S. actor, writer; starred in the television series, *Banacek* and *The A-Team;* films include *Breakfast at Tiffany's,* 1961. [d. May 8, 1994]

Zhu Rongji, Chinese politician; Premier of China, 1998– .

1930 *Richard (St. John) Harris,* British actor.

1935 *Julie Andrews (Julia Elizabeth Wells),* British singer and actress; Academy Award winner for *Mary Poppins,* 1964.

1936 *Edward Villella,* U.S. ballet dancer; principal dancer with New York City Ballet and other major dance companies, from 1957.

1938 *Mary Josephine McFadden,* U.S. fashion designer; known

for using bright colors and fine pleating in her clothing to create a distinctive, dramatic look.

Stella Stevens (Estelle Egglestone), U.S. actress.

1945 *Rod(ney Cline) Carew,* U.S. baseball player; infielder, 1967–86; seven batting titles; .328 career batting average; over 3,000 hits.

1950 *Randy Quaid,* U.S. actor.

1953 *Grete Waitz,* Norwegian runner; seven-time New York City Marathon winner.

HISTORICAL EVENTS

1810 First *agricultural fair* in the U.S. is held at Pittsfield, Massachusetts.

1869 First *postcards* are introduced in Austria by the government.

1890 *McKinley Tariff Act* is passed by Congress, significantly raising import tariffs.

1896 First *Rural Free Delivery* of U.S. mail begins.

1908 Henry Ford's *Model T* automobile is introduced at a price of $850.

1912 Edgar Rice Burroughs' first *Tarzan* story is published in *All Story* magazine.

1914 Turkey closes the *Dardanelles* to the Allies (*World War I*).

1918 *Damascus* is seized by the British and Arabs (*World War I*).

1923 *Southern Rhodesia* becomes a self-governing colony within the British Commonwealth.

1928 U.S.S.R. inaugurates its first *Five-Year Plan.*

1936 General *Francisco Franco Bahamonde* is appointed Chief of the Spanish State by the insurgents (*Spanish Civil War*).

1942 The first U.S. turbojet aircraft makes its initial flight at *Muroc Dry Lake, California.*

1943 U.S. troops enter *Naples,* burned by the departing Germans (*World War II*).

1946 International Military Tribunal in *Nuremberg* sentences 12 Nazi leaders to death.

1949 The *People's Republic of China* is proclaimed as the Communist Party takes control of the government. *Mao Tse-tung* becomes head of state and *Chou En-lai* is named premier.

1955 *The Honeymooners* makes its television debut.

1956 *Ernesto de la Guardia* is inaugurated as president of Panama.

1957 First meeting of the *International Atomic Energy Agency* in Vienna, Austria.

1958 *The Ugly American,* by William Lederer and Eugene Burdick, is published in New York.

1960 *Roberto Chiari* is inaugurated as president of Panama.

Nigeria becomes an independent member of the British Commonwealth.

1961 *Roger Maris* of New York Yankees breaks *Babe Ruth's* record by hitting 61st home run in one season.

1962 *The Lucy Show* makes its television debut.

1963 *Nnamdi Azikiwe* is inaugurated as president of Nigeria.

1966 *Albert Speer,* minister for armaments and war production in Nazi German

government, and *Baldur von Schirach,* leader of Hitler Youth, are released from Spandau War Crimes Prison in Berlin after 20 years' imprisonment.

1974 *Watergate* coverup trial opens in Washington, D.C.

1979 *Pope John Paul II* arrives in U.S. on visit.

The U.S. relinquishes control of the *Panama Canal* in adherence to treaty provisions.

Alhaji Shehu Shagari is inaugurated as president of Nigeria.

1988 *Mikhail Gorbachev* becomes president of the U.S.S.R. in a major reorganization of the Soviet government.

1995 *Britain* adopts the *metric system.*

october

OCTOBER
2

HOLIDAYS

People's Republic of China
National Day

Guinea
Anniversary of Guinean Independence
Celebrates Guinea's achievement of independence from France, 1958.

India
Mahatma Gandhi's Birthday

Tuvalu
Tuvalu Day
Commemorates the separation from the Gilbert Islands, 1975. Second day of a two-day celebration.

RELIGIOUS CALENDAR

Feasts
Feast of the Guardian Angels
   Obligatory Memorial.

The Saints
St. Leodegarius, Bishop of Autun and martyr. Also called *Leger, Leodegar.* [d. 679]
St. Eleutherius, martyr. [death date unknown]

BIRTHDATES

1452 *Richard III* of England, 1483–85; upon death of his predecessor, *Edward IV,* assumed power as protector of the young *Edward V;* allegedly had Edward V slain, claiming the crown for himself; suppressed rebellion by Duke of Buckingham but was killed by Earl of Richmond who became *Henry VII,* first in the Tudor line. [d. August 22, 1485]

1791 *Alexis Petit,* French physicist; developed methods for determining *atomic weights;* studied phenomenon of *thermal expansion* and *specific heat.* [d. June 21, 1820]

1800 *Nat Turner,* U.S. slave; led insurrection at Southampton, Va. which resulted in murder of more than 50 whites; the rebellion failed. Turner, his followers, and many innocent blacks were killed in retaliation, and most Southern states passed even harsher slave laws. [d. November 11, 1831]

1830 *Charles Pratt,* U.S. oil magnate; founder of one of first oil operations in Pennsylvania; bought out by John D. Rockefeller; executive with Standard Oil Co.; founded *Pratt Institute,* New York City; established Pratt Institute Free Library, the first free public library in New York City. [d. May 4, 1891]

1847 *Paul von Hindenburg,* German statesman, soldier; during World War I, led Germans in East Prussian campaign; commanded successful campaign against Russians in Poland, 1915; Chief of Staff for German army, 1917–18; second president of Germany, 1925–32; re-elected, 1932–34; forced to appoint Adolf Hitler as chancellor. [d. August 2, 1934]

1851 *Ferdinand Foch,* French Army marshal; Supreme Commander of Allied Armies, 1918. [d. March 20, 1929]

1852 *Sir William Ramsay,* Scottish chemist; Nobel Prize in chemistry for discovery of *helium, xenon,* and *krypton,* 1904. [d. July 23, 1916]

1865 *Dan(iel Maurice) Casey,* U.S. baseball player; pitcher, 1884–90; probable inspiration for Ernest Thayer's poem, *Casey at the Bat.* [d. February 8, 1943]

1869 *Mahatma Gandhi (Mohandas Karamchand Gandhi),* leader of the Indian nationalist movement against British rule; known for advocacy of nonviolent civil disobedience to achieve political and social progress. Assassinated by a Hindu fanatic. [d. January 30, 1948]

1871 *Cordell Hull,* U.S. statesman, diplomat, lawyer; U.S. Secretary of State, 1933–44; developed *Good Neighbor*

Policy between U.S. and Latin America; Nobel Peace Prize, 1945. [d. July 23, 1955]

1877 *Carl Trumbull Hayden,* U.S. politician; U.S. Congressman, 1912–69, the longest term in the nation's history. [d. January 25, 1972]

1879 *Wallace Stevens,* U.S. poet, businessman; Vice-President of Hartford Accident and Indemnity Co.; Pulitzer Prize in poetry, 1954. [d. August 2, 1955]

1885 *Ruth Bryan Rohde,* U.S. politician, diplomat; U.S. Congresswoman, 1929–33; U.S. Minister to Denmark, 1933–36; first woman diplomat appointed by U.S. government. [d. July 26, 1954]

1890 *Julius (Groucho) Marx,* U.S. comedian. With his brothers Chico (March 26), Harpo (November 21), Zeppo (February 25), formed one of the most outrageously funny comedy teams of the 1930s and 1940s. [d. August 20, 1977]

1895 *Bud Abbot (William Abbott),* U.S. comedian; with his partner, Lou Costello (March 6), formed popular comedy team of the 1940s and 1950s. [d. April 24, 1974]

1901 *(Ignatius) Roy (Dunnachie) Campbell,* South African poet. [d. April 22, 1957]

1904 *Graham Greene,* British novelist, short story writer, playwright; noted for his works set in exotic locations and dealing with major moral questions. [d. April 3, 1991]

1906 *Willy Ley,* German-U.S. scientist, engineer;

responsible for research leading to development of German *V-2 rocket* during World War II; defected to U.S., 1935; contributed significantly to U.S. entry into space age. [d. June 24, 1969]

1907 *Alexander Robertus Todd, Baron Todd of Trumpington,* Scottish biochemist; Nobel Prize in chemistry for studies of the compounds comprising *nucleic acid,* 1957. [d. January 10, 1997]

1917 *Christian Renè de Duve,* Belgian physiologist; Nobel Prize in physiology or medicine for research in cell biology (with A. Claude and G. E. Palade), 1974.

1919 *James M. Buchanan,* U.S. economist, author, educator; Nobel Prize in economics for his *public choice theory,* the application of economic principles to the study of political decision-making, 1986.

1921 *Robert Runcie,* British clergyman; Archbishop of Canterbury, 1980–91.

1937 *Johnnie L. Cochran,* U.S. lawyer; member of the defense team for the O. J. Simpson trial, 1995.

1939 *Rex Reed,* U.S. movie critic, journalist.

1945 *Don McLean,* US. singer, songwriter; Best Selling Single of the Year for *American Pie,* 1972.

1946 *Edward Finch Cox,* U.S. lawyer, son-in-law of Richard Nixon, 37th U.S. President.

1948 *Donna Faske Karan,* U.S. fashion designer; co-designer for Anne Klein and Company; Coty American Fashion Critics Winnie Award, 1977.

1949 *Annie Leibovitz,* U.S. photographer.

1950 *Persis Khambatta,* Indian-born actress; starred in *Star Trek: The Movie,* 1979.

1951 *Sting (Gordon Matthew Sumner),* British singer, musician, actor; former member of the rock group, *The Police;* appeared in the films *Dune* and *Plenty;* Platinum Record Award for *Dream of the Blue Turtles,* 1985.

1962 *Mark Rypkin,* U.S. football player; Most Valuable Player in Super Bowl XXVI, 1992.

HISTORICAL EVENTS

1187 *Saladin* of Damascus takes *Jerusalem.*

1889 First *Pan-American Conference* takes place in Washington, D. C.

1940 *S.S. Empress of Britain,* carrying children being evacuated from England to Canada, is sunk (*World War II*).

1944 U.S. First Army begins operations against the West Wall near *Aachen, Germany* (World War II).

1955 *Alfred Hitchcock Presents* makes its television debut.

1958 *Guinea* achieves its independence from France. *Sekou Toure* is appointed premier.

1959 *The Twilight Zone* makes its television debut.

1968 President Lyndon Johnson signs a bill establishing the *Redwood National Park* in California.

october

1970 The *Environmental Protection Agency (EPA)* is established as an independent U.S. government agency.

1984 *Elizabeth Kopp* becomes the first woman elected to the Swiss Federal Council, the executive branch of the government.

Richard Miller becomes the first FBI agent in U.S. history to be arrested and charged with spying.

1994 *Fernando Cardoso* is elected president of Brazil.

1995 *France* proceeds with its second nuclear test in French Polynesia.

HOLIDAYS

Germany
German Unity Day

Honduras
Francisco Morazán's Birthday
Commemorates the birth of the Honduran responsible for the establishment of government after Honduras gained independence from Spain and who sought a unified Central America.

South Korea
National Foundation Day
Celebrates the foundation of Korea in 2333 B.C.

RELIGIOUS CALENDAR

The Saints
St. Hesychius, monk. [d. 4th cent.]
The Two Ewalds, missionaries and martyrs. Patrons of Westphalia. Also called *Hewald.* [d. c. 695]
St. Gerard of Brogne, abbot. [d. 959]
St. Froilan, Bishop of Leon, and *St. Attilanus,* bishop of Zamora. Froilan also called *Foilan, Froylan.* [d. 10th cent.]
St. Thomas Cantelupe, Bishop of Hereford. [d. 1282]

The Beatified
Blessed Dominic Spadafora, priest and missionary. [d. 1521]

BIRTHDATES

1554 *Sir Fulke Greville, 1st Baron Brooke,* English statesman and poet in Queen Elizabeth I's court; Secretary of principality of Wales, 1583–1628; member of Parliament, 1592–1620; Chancellor of the Exchequer, 1614–21. [d. September 30, 1628]

1784 *Ithiel Town,* U.S. architect, engineer; known for his designs of custom house, Wall Street, New York; capitol buildings for states of Indiana and North Carolina; his collection of books on art and architecture was the best in the country. [d. June 13, 1844]

1800 *George Bancroft,* U.S. diplomat, historian; author of the *History of the United States,* 10 volumes, 1834–74; U.S. Secretary of the Navy, 1845–46; U.S. Minister to England, 1846–49. [d. January 17, 1891]

1802 *George Ripley,* U.S. journalist, social reformer; founder and editor of *The Dial,* the organ of the New England transcendentalists, 1840–44; instrumental in organizing *Brook Farm,* a utopian community which attempted to bring into effect the social ideals of transcendentalism; a founder of *Harper's New Monthly Magazine,* 1850. [d. July 4, 1880]

1804 *Townsend Harris,* U.S. merchant, diplomat; first U.S. consul general to Japan, 1855–60; responsible for securing first commercial trade agreement with Japan; achieved nearly legendary importance in Japan after his return to U.S. [d. February 25, 1878]

1809 *Alexey Vasilyevich Koltsov,* Russian poet. [d. October 19, 1842]

1844 *Sir Patrick Manson,* British physician, parasitologist; first to hypothesize on the mosquito's role in spread of malaria; called the *Father of Tropical Medicine.* [d. April 9, 1922]

1854 *William Crawford Gorgas,* U.S. army officer, physician; Surgeon General of U.S. Army, 1914–18; responsible for major break-throughs in prevention of *yellow fever.* [d. July 3, 1920]

1858 *Percy Faraday Frankland,* British chemist; known for his work on fermentation and stereochemistry, purification of water, and bacterial treatment of sewage. [d. October 28, 1946]

1859 *Eleanora Duse,* Italian actress; international star, best

october

known for playing Marguerite Gautier in *La Dame Aux Camélias*. [d. April 21, 1924]

1886 *Alain-Fournier (Henri Alban Fournier),* French author; completed only one novel, *Le Grand Meaulnes,* 1913; called one of the most outstanding books of the twentieth century. [d. September 22, 1914]

1888 *Carl von Ossietzky,* German journalist; Nobel Peace Prize for his exposure of Nazi secret rearmament before World War II, 1935; incarcerated in a concentration camp, where he died. [d. May 4, 1938]

1889 *Gertrude Berg (Gertrude Edelstein),* U.S. comedic actress and writer; noted for her portrayal of Molly Goldberg of *The Goldbergs,* radio and television series. [d. September 14, 1966]

1895 *Sergei Aleksandrovich Esenin,* Soviet poet; founder of Imagist school of Russian poetry; poet laureate of Russian Revolution; married to Isadora Duncan (May 27). [committed suicide December 27, 1925]

1897 *Louis Aragon,* French poet, novelist, critic; member of the Dadaist and Surrealist schools. [d. December 22, 1982]

1898 *Leo McCarey,* U.S. producer, director; known for films *Duck Soup* and *Going My Way.* [d. July 5, 1969]

1900 *Thomas (Clayton) Wolfe,* U.S. novelist; known for his novels *Look Homeward, Angel, Of Time and the River,* and *You Can't Go Home Again.* [d. September 15, 1938]

1902 *Arthur da Costa e Silva,* Brazilian army officer, politician; led the 1964 revolution; President, 1967–69. [d. December 17, 1969]

1904 *Charles J. Pedersen,* U.S. chemist; Nobel Prize in chemistry (with D.J. Cram and J.M. Lehn), 1987. [d. October 26, 1989]

1908 *Johnny Burke,* U.S. songwriter; known for *Pennies from Heaven* and *Moonlight Becomes You,* among others. [d. February 25, 1964]

1916 *Angeles Alvarino,* Spanish biologist; known for her numerous discoveries of ocean species.

James Herriot (James Wight), Scottish veterinarian, author; wrote *All Creatures Great and Small,* 1972, and *All Things Bright and Beautiful,* 1974. [d. February 23, 1995]

1925 *Gore Vidal,* U.S. novelist, playwright, critic.

1928 *Erik Bruhn (Belton Evers),* Danish ballet dancer; artistic director of National Ballet of Canada. [d. April 1, 1986]

Kaare Isaachsen Willoch, Norwegian statesman; Prime Minister, 1981–86.

1931 *Glenn (Mr. Goalie) Hall,* Canadian hockey player; elected to Hall of Fame, 1975.

1938 *Eddie Cochran,* U.S. singer, songwriter; hits included *Summertime Blues* and *C'Mon Everybody.* [d. April 17, 1960]

1941 *Chubby Checker (Ernest Evans)* U.S. rock-'n'-roll singer; popularized the *Twist.*

1947 *Lindsey Buckingham,* U.S. musician; member of the rock group, *Fleetwood Mac.*

1951 *David Mark (Dave) Winfield,* U.S. baseball player; joined the New York Yankees in 1981 with a $20 million, 10-year contract.

1954 *Stevie Ray Vaughan,* U.S. blues/rock guitarist, singer. [d. August 26, 1990]

1959 *Fred Couples,* U.S. golfer.

Jack Peter Wagner, U.S. actor, singer; known for his roles on *General Hospital* and *Melrose Place;* hit record, *All I Need,* 1984.

1969 *Gwen Stefani,* U.S. singer; member of band No Doubt.

1973 *Neve Campbell,* U.S. actress; featured in the TV drama *Party of Five* and starred in the movie *Scream.*

HISTORICAL EVENTS

1691 *Treaty of Limerick* is signed, ending the *Irish Rebellion.*

1777 Washington is defeated by English troops at *Germantown (American Revolution).*

1866 Treaty of peace between Italy and Austria is signed, ending the *Seven Weeks' War.*

1884 The *Palace at Christiansborg,* Denmark, the Danish National Gallery, Parliament, and royal reception rooms, are destroyed by fire.

1895 *Bechuanaland* is annexed to the British Cape Colony in South Africa.

1910 First *National Assembly* meets in Peking, China.

1929 *Yugoslavia* becomes the official name of the Kingdom of the Serbs, Croats and Slovenes.

1932 *Iraq* becomes one of the first Arab countries to free itself from Western Europe.

1935 Italian fascist forces begin invasion of *Ethiopia,* forcing exile of *Haile Selassie.*

1948 *Philco TV Playhouse* makes its television debut.

1952 Great Britain explodes its first *atomic weapon* on Monte Bello Island, near Australia.

The first *magnetic videotape recording* is produced by Bing Crosby Enterprises.

1953 *Peter Medawar* publishes the results of experiments which show that immunologic tolerance can be acquired in utero. It is the first evidence that rejection of *organ transplants* can be overcome.

1957 *Willy Brandt* is elected mayor of West Berlin.

1960 *The Andy Griffith Show* makes its television debut.

1961 *The Dick Van Dyke Show* makes its television debut.

1962 U.S. astronaut *Walter M. Schirra, Jr.,* makes third U.S. orbital flight, circling the earth six times in 10 hours, 46 minutes.

1963 *Oswaldo Lopez Arellano* assumes power in Honduras after a coup d'etat.

1965 *Harold Perry* is appointed bishop by Pope Paul VI. He is the first black American to become a bishop.

U.S. *immigration quota system* is abolished.

1968 General *Juan Velasco Alvarado* assumes power in Peru after a coup d'etat.

1974 *Frank Robinson* is appointed manager of the Cleveland Indians, becoming the first black manager in U.S. major league history.

1980 Two Armenian dissidents are injured at a Swiss hotel while preparing a bomb.

1989 Panama's General *Manuel Noriega* and his military regime survive an attempted coup.

1990 *East Germany* and *West Germany* are reunited as *Germany* after 43 years of separation.

1995 *O. J. Simpson* is acquitted in the murder of his ex-wife, Nicole Simpson and her friend, Ron Goldman, in the "trial of century."

october

OCTOBER
4

HOLIDAYS

Greece (Xanthi)
Liberation of Xanthi

Lesotho (Basutoland)
Independence Day
Celebrates attainment of independence from Great Britain, 1966.

RELIGIOUS CALENDAR

The Saints

St. Ammon, hermit. [d. c. 350]

St. Petronius, Bishop of Bologna. [d. c. 445]

St. Francis of Assisi, founder of the Friars Minor, or Franciscans, or Lesser Brothers. Also called *St. Francis of Assisium* and the *Seraphic.* [d. 1226] Obligatory Memorial.

BIRTHDATES

1289 *Louis X,* King of France; (the *Headstrong*), 1314–16. [d. June 5, 1316]

1472 *Lucas Cranach,* German artist, designer; court painter to Elector Frederick the Wise of Saxony; known for his altarpieces, woodcuts, and many portraits of Protestant leaders. [d. October 16, 1553]

1550 *Charles IX,* King of Sweden, 1604–11. [d. October 30, 1611]

1626 *Richard Cromwell,* British statesman; Lord Protector of England, 1658–59; son of Oliver Cromwell; retired to France as *John Clark.* [d. July 13, 1712]

1787 *François Pierre Guillaume Guizot,* French historian, statesman; Premier of France, 1840–48. [d. September 13, 1874]

1797 *Albrecht Bitzius (Jeremias Gotthelf),* Swiss novelist, short-story writer; known for his novels depicting Swiss village life. [d. October 22, 1854]

1810 *Eliza Johnson,* wife of U.S. President Andrew Johnson. [d. January 15, 1876]

1814 *Jean Francois Millet,* member of the Barbizon school; known for his landscapes and genre paintings of rural life; works include *The Water Carriers* and *The Gleaners.* [d. January 20, 1875]

1819 *Francesco Crispi,* Sicilian revolutionist; first representative of Palermo to Italian parliament; leader of radical leftists; Premier, 1887–91, 1893–96. [d. August 11, 1901]

1822 *Rutherford B(irchard) Hayes,* 19th President of U.S.; his presidency marked the end of Reconstruction in the South;

fought to achieve reforms in government which lost him much support; became increasingly disillusioned with concentration of wealth and power in certain segments of the population. [d. January 17, 1893]

1861 *Frederic Remington,* U.S. painter, sculptor, illustrator; known for his depiction of life in the American West; prolific in his output, completed thousands of drawings. [d. December 26, 1909]

1862 *Edward L. Stratemeyer,* U.S. children's author; his syndicate produced *The Rover Boys, Hardy Boys, Bobbsey Twins,* and *Nancy Drew* series of books. [d. May 10, 1930]

1881 *Heinrich Alfred Walther Brauchitsch,* German field marshal; Commander in Chief of German Army, 1938–41; planned and carried out occupation of Austria, Czechoslovakia, and Poland. [d. October 18, 1948]

1884 *(Alfred) Damon Runyon,* U.S. short-story writer, journalist; known for his colorful, humorous, sentimental portrayals of the low life of New York City, capturing the character and language of those who frequented Broadway: horseplayers, gamblers, grifters. [d. December 10, 1946]

1891 *Henri Gaudier-Brzeska,* French sculptor; associated with Ultramodernists. [d. June 5, 1915]

1892 *Engelbert Dollfuss,* Austrian statesman; Dictator of Austria, 1932–34; came into conflict with Nazi regime when he attempted to maintain Austria's independence; assassinated by Austrian Nazi rebels. [d. July 25, 1934]

1895 *Buster Keaton (Joseph Francis Keaton),* U.S. comedian, actor; one of the great clowns of the silent movie era; his career declined with advent of talkies but experienced a revival in the 1950s. [d. February 1, 1966]

1906 *George I. Sánchez,* Mexican educator and author. [d. 1972]

1914 *Brendan Gill,* U.S. author, drama and film critic; reviewer, *New Yorker* magazine, 1936–97; National Book Award for *The Trouble of One House,* 1951. [d. 1997]

1917 *Jan Murray (Murray Janofsky),* U.S. comedian.

1918 *Kenichi Fukui,* Japanese chemist; Nobel Prize in chemistry, 1981. [d. January 9, 1998]

1921 *Francisco Morales Bermudez,* Peruvian government official, general; Prime Minister, 1975; President, 1975–80.

1922 *(Howard) Malcolm Baldrige, Jr.,* U.S. government official; Secretary of Commerce, 1981–87. [d. July 25, 1987]

1924 *Charlton Heston,* U.S. actor.

1928 *Alvin Toffler,* U.S. author; wrote *Future Shock,* 1970, and *The Third Wave,* 1980.

1941 *Anne Rice,* U.S. writer; known for her *Vampire Chronicles.*

1943 *H(ubert) Rap Brown (Jamiel Abdul Al-Amin),* U.S. civil rights activist; Chairman, Student National Coordinating Committee, 1967, 1969.

1945 *Clifton Davis,* U.S. actor, singer, composer; wrote the song, *Never Can Say Goodbye.*

1946 *Susan Abigail Sarandon (Susan Tomaling),* U.S. actress; starred in the films, *Rocky Horror Picture Show, Pretty Baby,* and *Bull Durham;* Academy Award (Best Actress) for *Dead Man Walking,* 1995

1949 *Armand Assante,* U.S. actor; starred in the television mini-series, *Rage of Angels,* 1983, and *Napoleon and Josephine,* 1987.

1962 *Bradley D. Wong,* U.S. actor, Asian American activist.

1976 *Alicia Silverstone,* U.S. actress.

HISTORICAL EVENTS

1190 *Richard I* of England *(the Lion-Hearted)* storms Messina *(Third Crusade).*

1209 *Otto IV* is crowned Holy Roman Emperor at Rome.

1511 *Holy League* is formed between Pope Julius II, Ferdinand of Aragon, Henry VIII of England, and Venice, against France.

1582 *Gregorian Calendar* is first introduced in Roman Catholic

countries by Pope Gregory XIII, who abolishes the Julian Calendar and restores the vernal equinox to March 21.

1777 *Battle of Germantown* results in a British victory over Washington's disorganized troops *(American Revolution).*

1830 *Belgium* declares its independence from the Netherlands.

1877 *Chief Joseph* surrenders, ending U.S. warfare with the *Nez Percé Indians.*

1895 First *U.S. Golfers Association Open* is held at 9-hole course, Newport, Rhode Island.

1914 Hindenburg's army begins its advance on *Warsaw (World War I).*

1922 The *University of the Witwatersrand* is established in the Union of South Africa.

1931 *Dick Tracy,* Chester Gould's popular detective comic strip, makes its debut in U.S. newspapers.

1951 Vincente Minnelli's film version of *An American in Paris* premieres in New York.

1957 *Leave It to Beaver* makes its television debut.

Sputnik I, the first artificial satellite, is launched from the Soviet Union.

1965 *Abe Fortas* is confirmed as an associate justice of the U.S. Supreme Court.

1966 *Lesotho,* formerly the British colony of *Basutoland,* becomes an independent nation.

1970 U.S. Commission on Campus Unrest issues its report describing the *Kent State* shooting as unwarranted.

october

1971 Egyptian president, *Anwar Sadat,* is elected president of the newly formed *Confederation of Arab Republics.*

1976 U.S. Secretary of Agriculture *Earl Butz* is forced to resign after a furor over a "gross indiscretion" in remarks made about blacks.

1982 *Helmut Kohl* is inaugurated as chancellor of West Germany.

OCTOBER
5

HOLIDAYS

Macao, Portugal
Republic Day
Commemorates the founding of the Republic in Portugal, 1910.

Vanuatu
Constitution Day
Commemorates the framing of a constitution for the former French possession, 1979.

RELIGIOUS CALENDAR

The Saints
St. Apollinaris, Bishop of Valence; patron of Valence. Also called *Aplonay.* [d. c. 520]
St. Maurus, Abbot of Glanfeuil, afterwards called *Saint-Mausur-Loire.* [d. 584]
St. Placid, monk and martyr. Also called *Placidus.* [d. 6th cent.]
St. Magenulf. Also called *St. Méen, Meinulf.* [d. c. 857]
St. Flora of Beaulieu, virgin. [d. 1347]

The Beatified
Blessed Raymund of Capua, spiritual guide and biographer of St. Catherine of Siena. [d. 1399]
Blessed Aloisius Scrosoppi. [beatified 1981]
Blessed Joseph de Anchieta. [beatified 1981]

BIRTHDATES

1703 *Jonathan Edwards,* American colonial theologian, philosopher. [d. March 22, 1758]

1713 *Denis Diderot (Pantophile),* French philosopher and writer. Created the *Encyclopédie,* a 20-year, 28-volume attempt to incorporate all human knowledge into one organized whole; his work stimulated much thinking during the age of the Enlightenment. [d. July 30, 1784]

1813 *Antonio García Gutiérrez,* Spanish dramatist; noted as the foremost dramatist of the romantic era of Spanish literature. [d. August 26, 1884]

1819 *Jon Thoroddsen,* pioneer Icelandic novelist and poet; produced the first Icelandic novel, 1850; regarded as a master of Icelandic prose. [d. March 8, 1868]

1829 *Chester A(lan) Arthur,* U.S. lawyer; Vice President, 1881; 21st president of the U.S. (assumed presidency upon the assassination of Garfield, 1881). [d. November 18, 1886]

1864 *Louis Lumière,* French inventor; with his brother, Auguste, invented a process for *color photography* and an early *motion-picture camera.* [d. June 6, 1948]

1879 *Francis Peyton Rous,* U.S. physician; Nobel Prize in physiology or medicine for discovery of a *cancer virus* (with C. B. Huggins), 1966. [d. February 16, 1970]

1882 *Robert Hutchings Goddard,* U.S. physicist; developed and built the first *liquid fuel rocket,* 1926; developed and patented more than 200 inventions in the field of *rocketry.* [d. August 10, 1945]

1887 *René Cassin,* French jurist; President, UN Human Rights Commission, 1946–68; Nobel Peace Prize, 1968. [d. February 20, 1976]

1902 *Ray A. Kroc,* U.S. businessman; founder of *McDonald's Corporation,* one of the first fast food chains in the U.S. [d. January 14, 1984]

1905 *Eugene Fodor,* U.S. editor, publisher; began issuing *Fodor's Travel Guides,* 1949. [d. February 18, 1991]

1908 *Joshua Logan,* U. S. producer, director, author; producer of *Mr. Roberts, South Pacific,* and *Bus Stop;* Pulitzer Prize for *South Pacific,* 1950. [d. July 12, 1988]

october

1911 *Brian O'Nolan (Flann O'Brien),* Irish author. [d. 1966]

1918 *Allen Ellsworth Ludden,* U.S. producer, performer; hosted the television game show, *Password,* 1961–80; married to Betty White. [d. June 9, 1981]

1919 *Donald Pleasence,* British actor, producer; known for his roles as villians; appeared in *Oh God* and *Halloween.* [d. February 2, 1995]

1923 *Philip Francis Berrigan,* U.S. author, political activist; first Catholic priest imprisoned for peace agitation in the United States, 1968.

Glynis Johns, British actress; known for her role as Mrs. Banks in *Mary Poppins,* 1964.

1929 *Richard F. Gordon,* U.S. astronaut; pilot of *Gemini II* mission, 1966.

1930 *Reinhard Selten,* German mathematician; Nobel Prize for Economics in 1994 with John C. Harsanyi and John F. Nash.

1936 *Vaclav Havel,* Czechoslovakian playwright, politician; President of Czechoslovakia, 1989–92; President of Czech Republic, 1996– .

1943 *Steve Miller,* U.S. musician, singer; founder of the *Steve Miller Band;* Platinum Album Award for *Fly Like an Eagle,* 1976.

1950 *Jeff Conaway,* U.S. actor; starred on Broadway in *Grease;* known for his role as Bobby on the television series *Taxi,* 1978–81.

1951 *Karen Allen,* U.S. actress; appeared in the film, *Animal House,* 1978, and *Raiders of the Lost Ark,* 1981.

1954 *Bob Geldorf,* Irish actor, musician, singer; member of the rock group, *Boomtown Rats;* organizer of Live-Aid; raised $84 million for African famine relief, 1985.

1965 *Mario Lemieux,* Canadian hockey player.

Patrick Roy, Canadian hockey player.

1971 *Grant Hill,* U.S. basketball player.

HISTORICAL EVENTS

1285 *Philip III* of France dies of the plague and is succeeded by *Philip IV (the Fair).*

1735 *Treaty of Vienna* ends *War of the Polish Succession* and assures Russian-Austrian dominance in Poland.

1813 *Tecumseh,* chief of the Shawnee and leader of the movement to establish an Indian confederation, is killed commanding British troops at the *Battle of the Thames (War of 1812).*

1853 Turks declare war on Russia, beginning the *Crimean War.*

Rebecca Mann Pennell, the first female college professor, begins teaching at Antioch College, Ohio.

1877 *Chief Joseph* of the Nez Percé tribe surrenders to the U.S. government. Delivers "I will fight no more forever" speech.

1908 *Bulgaria* proclaims its independence from the Ottoman Empire.

1910 *Portugal* is declared a republic after successful revolt against *King Manuel II,* who flees to England.

1918 The French seize *Beirut (World War I).*

1941 Women are allowed to vote in *Panama* for the first time in accordance with a new constitution.

1947 U.S. President Harry S. Truman delivers the first televised address from the White House.

1950 *You Bet Your Life* makes its television debut.

1953 *Earl Warren* is sworn in as Chief Justice of the U.S. Supreme Court.

1965 *Pope Paul VI* makes unprecedented 14-hour visit to New York to plead for world peace before the UN.

1970 French-Canadian separatists kidnap British diplomat *James R. Cross* in Montreal; he is freed December 3, unharmed, after his kidnappers fly to Cuba.

1978 *Norway* announces a strict austerity program to combat a large foreign debt and to improve the nation's economy.

Isaac Bashevis Singer wins the Nobel Prize for Literature.

1983 *Richard Noble* sets a world land speed record at 633.6 miles per hour in a jet-powered car.

Lech Walesa, founder of Solidarity, the federation of Polish Trade Unions, is awarded the Nobel Peace Prize.

1986 Nicaragua shoots down a U.S. plane carrying military supplies intended for the contras. A captured pilot, *Eugene Hosenfus,* admits that the operation was supervised by the CIA.

1988 Chileans reject another term for President *Augusto Pinochet* in a plebiscite.

1989 U.S. televangelist *Jim Bakker* is convicted of fraud and conspiracy.

october

OCTOBER
6

HOLIDAYS

Universal Children's Day
Sponsored by United Nations, New
York, New York 10017

Egypt
Armed Forces Day

Lesotho
National Sports Day

Syria
Public Holiday
Commemorates the beginning of the
1973 war With Israel.

RELIGIOUS CALENDAR

The Saints
St. Faith, virgin and martyr. Also
    called *Fides, Foi,* or *Foy.* [d.
    c. 3rd cent.]
St. Nicetas of Constantinople, monk.
    [d. c. 838]
St. Bruno, founder of the
    Carthusian Order. [d. 1101]
    Optional Memorial
St. Mary Frances of Naples, virgin.
    [d. 1791]

The Beatified
Blessed Maria Rosa Durocher.
    [beatified 1982]
Blessed Wincenty Lewoniuk.
    [beatified 1996]
Blessed Edmund Rice. [beatified
    1996]
*Blessed Maria Ana Mogas
    Fontcuberta.* [beatified 1996]
Blessed Marcelina Darowski.
    [beatified 1996]

BIRTHDATES

1744 *James McGill,* Canadian
    businessman, philanthropist,
    born in Scotland; his estate
    was left to found *McGill
    University.* [d. December 19,
    1813]

1767 *Henri Christophe,* Haitian
    statesman; first president of
    the Republic of Haiti. [d.
    October 8, 1820]

1769 *Sir Isaac Brock,* British
    general; forced surrender of
    Hall's forces at Detroit, War
    of 1812; known as *Hero of
    Upper Canada.* [d. October
    13, 1812]

1773 *Louis-Philippe,* King of
    France, 1830–48; known as
    the *Citizen King.* [d. August
    26, 1850]

1795 *Joshua Reed Giddings,* U.S.
    public official; Congressman,
    1838–59; outspoken
    abolitionist; Consul General
    to Canada, 1861–64. [d. May
    27, 1864]

1808 *Frederick VII,* King of
    Denmark, 1848–63; adopted a
    representative government,
    thus forfeiting absolute
    power; last of the *Oldenburg*
    line. [d. November 15, 1863]

1820 *Jenny Lind (Johanna Maria
    Lind),* Swedish soprano;
    known as the *Swedish
    Nightingale* because of her
    exquisite voice. [d. November
    2, 1887]

1824 *Henry Chadwick,* U.S.
    journalist; one of earliest
    sports writers in U.S.;
    member of first baseball rules
    committee; responsible for
    developing baseball's scoring
    system. [d. April 20, 1908]

1831 *Richard Dedekind,* German
    mathematician; produced first
    rigorous theory of irrationals.
    [d. February 12, 1916]

1836 *Heinrich Wilhelm Gottfried
    von Waldeyer,* German
    anatomist; noted for his
    theories of the composition
    of the nervous system. [d.
    January 23, 1921]

1846 *George Westinghouse,* U.S.
    engineer; inventor of the *air
    brake;* founder of
    Westinghouse Electric
    Corporation, 1886;
    responsible for
    standardization of electrical
    transmission in U.S. to
    alternating current. [d. March
    12, 1914]

1862 *Albert Jeremiah Beveridge,*
    U.S. politician, historian; U.S.
    Senator, 1899–1911. [d. April
    27, 1927]

1867 *George Horace Lorimer,* U.S.
    editor, writer; editor of the
    Saturday Evening Post,
    1899–1936. [d. October 22,
    1937]

1887 *Le Corbusier (Charles-
    Edouard Jeanneret Gris),*

French architect, designer, painter, and city planner born in Switzerland; the father of modern functional architecture. [d. August 27, 1965]

1897 *Florence Seibert,* U.S. biochemist; developed the protein PPD-S used to detect tuberculosis. [d. August 23, 1991]

1903 *Ernest Thomas Sinton Walton,* Irish physicist; Nobel Prize in physics for transmutation of atomic nuclei with artificially accelerated atomic particles (with J. D. Cockroft), 1951. [d. June 25, 1995]

Brien McMahon, U.S. politician, lawyer; U.S. Senator, 1944–52; sponsored the legislation that resulted in the establishment of the *Atomic Energy Commission.* [d. July 28, 1952]

1905 *Helen Wills,* U.S. tennis player; U.S. champion, 1923–25, 1927–29, 1931; Wimbledon champion, 1927–30, 1932–33, 1935, 1938. [d. January 1, 1998]

1906 *Janet Gaynor (Laura Gainer),* U.S. actress. [d. September 14, 1984]

1908 *Carole Lombard (Jane Peters),* U.S. actress; wife of Clark Gable (February 1). [d. January 16, 1942]

1914 *Thor Heyerdahl,* Norwegian anthropologist, explorer; led *Kon Tiki* expedition from Peru to Polynesia, to prove that Peruvian Indians could have settled Polynesia, 1947; led *Ra* expedition from Morocco to Barbados, to prove that Mediterranean civilization could have

reached the Americas, 1970; author of numerous books on early civilizations.

1917 *Fannie Lou Hamer,* U.S. civil rights leader. [d. 1977]

1925 *Shana Alexander,* U.S. author, lecturer.

1930 *Hafez al Assad,* Syrian political leader; Minister of Defense, 1966–70; President, 1971–.

1941 *Mark Stephen Fowler,* U.S. government official; Chairman, Federal Communications Commission.

1942 *Britt Ekland,* Swedish actress.

1963 *Elisabeth Shue,* U.S. actress; known for roles in *Cocktail,* 1988 and *Leaving Las Vegas,* 1995.

HISTORICAL EVENTS

1404 In England, the *Unlearned Parliament* of Canterbury demands appropriation of all Church property.

1876 *American Library Association* is founded in Philadelphia by Melvil Dewey, F. W. Poole, and Charles Cutter.

1884 *U.S. Naval War College* is established at Newport, Rhode Island.

1892 *Alfred Austin* is named poet laureate of England upon the death of *Alfred, Lord Tennyson.*

1913 Japan and Russia recognize the *Republic of China.*

1915 The great Austro-German offensive and invasion of *Serbia* begins under the direction of General von Mackensen (*World War I*).

1927 *The Jazz Singer,* starring Al Jolson, opens in New York City. It is the first commercially successful motion picture with pre-recorded sound.

1940 Premier *Ion Antonescu* assumes the dictatorship of the Iron Guard, making him the political leader of Romania.

1973 Egyptian and Syrian forces attack Israeli-held territory on the east bank of the Suez Canal and in the Golan Heights.

1976 The government of *Thailand* falls to a military coup after three years of democratic regimes.

1977 The play, *The Gin Game,* opens on Broadway.

1978 The U.S. Senate votes to extend, to June 30, 1982, the deadline for individual states to ratify the proposed *Equal Rights Amendment.* Despite the extension, the Amendment does not receive the necessary support and is not adopted.

1979 Pope *John Paul II* meets with President Jimmy Carter in Washington, becoming the first pope to visit the White House.

1981 Egyptian president, *Anwar Sadat,* is assassinated by Muslim fundamentalists in Cairo.

1989 The Nobel Peace Prize committee announces the selection of the *Dalai Lama* as its recipient, citing his efforts to gain freedom for Tibetans who have been ruled by the Chinese for over forty years.

october

1993 *Michael Jordan*, U.S. basketball player, announces retirement from the National Basketball Association.

HOLIDAYS

**German Democratic Republic
(East Germany)**
*Day of Foundation of the German
Democratic Republic*

Libya
Evacuation Day

Nambia
Day of Goodwill

RELIGIOUS CALENDAR

Feasts
Feast of Our Lady of the Rosary.
Previously celebrated on the
first Sunday of October.
Obligatory Memorial.

The Saints
St. Mark, pope. Elected 336. [d. 336]
St. Osyth, virgin, queen of the East
Saxons, and martyr. Also
called *Osith, Sythe.* [d. c. 675]
St. Artaldus, Bishop of Belley. Also
called *Arthaud.* [d. 1206]
St. Justina, virgin and martyr.
Patroness of Padua and
Venice. [death date
unknown]

The Beatified
Blessed Matthew of Mantua. [d.
1470]
Blessed Hanibal Maria De Francia.
[beatified 1990]
Blessed Joseph Allamano. [beatified
1990]

BIRTHDATES

1471 *Frederick I,* King of Denmark;
encouraged spread of
Lutheranism in Denmark. [d.
April 10, 1533]

1573 *William Laud,* Archbishop of
Canterbury; condemned and
beheaded for high treason.
[d. January 10, 1645]

1728 *Caesar Rodney,* American
Revolutionary statesman;
member of Continental
Congress, 1774–76, 1777,
1778; signer of Declaration of
Independence; President of
Delaware, 1778–82. [d. June
26, 1784]

1734 *Sir Ralph Abercromby,* British
Army general; led British
forces that conquered
Trinidad; defeated French at
Alexandria, 1801; contributed
to establishment of strict
discipline among British
troops. [d. March 28, 1801]

1745 *Henry Rutgers,* U.S. soldier,
philanthropist; Queen's
College changed its name to
Rutgers University in his
honor. [d. February 17, 1830]

1746 *William Billings,* U.S.
composer, hymn-writer;
composed religious and
patriotic songs during his
lifetime; a founder of the
Stoughton Musical Society,
the oldest extant society of its
type in the U.S. [d.
September 29, 1800]

1748 *Charles XIII,* King of Sweden
and Norway, 1809–18; first
King of the Union of Sweden
and Norway. [d. February 5,
1818]

1849 *James Whitcomb Riley (The
Hoosier Poet),* U.S. poet,
wrote poems representing
rustic life in middle America.
[d. July 22, 1916]

1854 *Christiaan Rudolph De Wet,*
Boer general, politician; one
of the Boer leaders in the war
against the British. [d.
February 3, 1922]

1885 *Niels Henrik David Bohr,*
Danish physicist; Nobel Prize
in physics for studies of
atomic structure, 1922. [d.
November 18, 1962]

1888 *Henry Agard Wallace,* U.S.
politician, editor, agricultural
expert; U.S. Secretary of
Agriculture, 1935–40; U.S.
Vice-President, 1941–45; U.S.
Secretary of Commerce,
1945–46. [d. November 18,
1965]

1898 *Alfred Wallenstein,* U.S.
conductor, cellist. [d.
February 8, 1983]

1900 *Heinrich Himmler,* German
Nazi official; Chief of Gestapo,
1936–45; captured by the
British; committed suicide. [d.
May 23, 1945]

1905 *Andy Devine,* U.S. character
actor; known for his unusual

october

voice; appeared in hundreds of movies between 1930 and 1975. [d. February 18, 1977]

1907 *Helen Clark MacInnes,* Scottish-born novelist; author of numerous suspense and espionage novels. [d. September 30, 1985]

1911 *Vaughn Monroe,* U.S. bandleader, popular singer of the 1940s. [d. May 21, 1973]

1912 *Fernando Belaunde Terry,* Peruvian political leader; President, 1963–68; 1980–85.

1914 *Alfred Drake (Alfred Capurro),* U.S. singer, actor; musical comedy star of the 1940s and 1950s. [d. July 25, 1992]

1916 *Walt Whitman Rostow,* U.S. government official, educator; Chairman, Department of State Policy Planning Council, 1961–66; Special Assistant to the President, 1966–69; Presidential Medal of Freedom with Distinction, 1969.

1923 *June Allyson (Ella Geisman),* U.S. actress.

1931 *Desmond Mpilo Tutu,* South African religious leader; first black Anglican Bishop of Johannesburg; Nobel Peace Prize, 1984.

1934 *Leroi Jones (Imamu Amiri Baraka),* U.S. poet, dramatist; wrote *Black Magic,* 1969, and *It's Nation Time,* 1971.

1939 *Sir Harold W. Kroto,* British chemist, co-winner of the Nobel Prize in Chemistry,

1996 for the discovery of fullerenes (form of carbon compounds). He shared the awarded with Robert F. Curl, Jr., and Richard E. Smalley.

1951 *John Cougar Mellencamp,* U.S. singer, songwriter; Platinum Album Award for *Uh-Huh,* 1983.

1955 *Yo-Yo Ma,* U.S. musician; cellist known for his superiority of technique, tone, and interpretive abilities; Avery Fisher Prize, 1978.

HISTORICAL EVENTS

1290 *Margaret,* the Maid of Norway, and heiress to the Scottish throne, dies en route to England to marry *Prince Edward,* son of *Edward I* of England.

1571 *Don John* of Austria and his Christian forces overwhelmingly defeat the Turkish Navy at the *Battle of Lepanto.*

1763 *George III* of Great Britain issues the *Proclamation of 1763,* closing lands in North America north and west of the Alleghenies to white settlement.

1765 *Stamp Act Congress* meets in New York to protest British Stamp Act, which requires purchase of revenue stamps for certain export items.

1780 The British are defeated at the *Battle of King's Mountain* in North Carolina (*American Revolution*).

1883 *Pope Leo XIII* recognizes *Italian unity.*

1915 *Cape Cod Canal* in Massachusetts is opened for navigation.

1916 *Georgia Tech* defeats Cumberland University in football, 222-0, the biggest margin of victory on record.

1949 A constitution for the *German Democratic Republic (East Germany)* is proclaimed.

1954 *Marian Anderson* becomes the first black singer to sign a contract with the *Metropolitan Opera Co.* in New York.

1958 President *Iskander Mirza* declares martial law in Pakistan. The constitution is abrogated and political parties dissolved.

1960 *Nigeria* is admitted to the United Nations.

1977 *Soviet Union* adopts a new constitution, replacing the one adopted in 1936.

1985 Four Palestinian terrorists seize the Italian cruise ship *Achille Lauro,* with four hundred people aboard. One passenger, *Leon Klinghoffer,* is killed during the two-day ordeal.

1986 The *rose* is chosen to be national floral emblem of the U.S.

1993 U.S. author *Toni Morrison* wins the Nobel Prize in Literature.

HOLIDAYS

Peru
Combat of Angamos

RELIGIOUS CALENDAR

The Saints

St. Holy Simeon. [d. 1st century]

SS. Sergius and Bacchus, martyrs; patrons of desert wanderers. [d. c. 303] Feast suppressed in 1969.

St. Keyne, virgin. Also called *Cain, Keyna.* [d. c. 6th century]

St. Iwi, monk, deacon, and hermit. Also called *Ywi.* [d. 7th cent.]

St. Demetrius, martyr; local patron of Salonika. Also patron of soldiers and chivalry. [death date unknown]

SS. Marcellus and Apuleius, martyrs. [death date unknown] Feast suppressed 1969.

St. Pelagia the Penitent. Also called *Margaret, Pelagius.* [death date unknown]

St. Reparata, virgin and martyr. [death date unknown]

St. Thais, penitent. [death date unknown]

St. Triduana, virgin and abbess. Patron of Kintradwell, Caithness. Invoked for curing diseases of the eyes. Also called called *Tradwell, Trollbaena.* [death date, unknown]

BIRTHDATES

1619 *Philipp von Zesen,* German novelist, lyric poet; founded a literary society to purify the language of barbarisms. [d. November 13, 1689]

1708 *Albrecht von Haller,* Swiss scientist, physician, and poet; known for enunciation of doctrine of irritability of living tissue. [d. December 12, 1777]

1810 *James Wilson Marshall,* U.S. pioneer; discoverer of gold on *Sutter's Creek* in California that started the Gold Rush, 1849. [d. August 10, 1885]

1838 *John Hay,* U.S. statesman, diplomat, author; close associate and private secretary to U.S. President Abraham Lincoln, 1861–65; U.S. Secretary of State, 1898–1905; promoted U.S. Open Door Policy with China. [d. July 1, 1905]

1846 *Elbert Henry Gary,* U.S. lawyer, businessman; led in organization of U.S. Steel Corporation, 1901; Chairman of Board of Directors U.S. Steel Corporation, 1901–27; *Gary, Indiana,* is named for him. [d. August 15, 1927]

1850 *Henri Louis Le Châtelier,* French physical chemist; known for his research on chemical equilibrium. [d. September 17, 1936]

1873 *Ejnar Hertzsprung,* Danish astronomer. [d. October 21, 1967]

1883 *Otto Heinrich Warburg,* German biochemist; Nobel Prize in physiology or medicine for discovery of character of respiratory enzyme, 1931. [d. August 1, 1970]

1890 *Edward (Vernon) Rickenbacker,* U.S. aviator, airline executive; noted for his aerial heroics during World War I; head of Eastern Airlines, 1938–63; special representative of War Department to South Pacific air bases, 1942. [d. July 23, 1973]

1895 *Juan (Domingo) Perón,* Argentine political leader; President, 1946–55; 1973–74. [d. July 1, 1974]

1899 *Bruce Catton,* U.S. historian, editor, journalist; Pulitzer Prize in history, 1954. [d. August 28, 1978]

1905 *Meyer Levin,* U.S. Zionist leader, novelist, scriptwriter; author of *Compulsion,* a novel of the Leopold and Loeb murder case. [d. July 9, 1981]

1912 *John William Gardner,* U.S. psychologist, educator, public official; President, Carnegie Corporation of New York,

october

1955–65; U.S. Secretary of Health, Education and Welfare, 1965–68; Chairman of *Common Cause*, 1970–77.

1917 *Billy Conn*, U.S. boxer; light-heavyweight champion, 1939–41; defeated by Joe Louis in heavyweight title bout, 1941. [d. May 29, 1993]

Walter Lord, U.S. author, historian; known for his works on the Titantic sinking; author of *A Night to Remember*, 1955, and *The Night Lives On*, 1986.

Rodney Robert Porter, British biochemist; Nobel Prize in physiology or medicine for research into chemical structure of antibodies, 1972. [d. September 7, 1985]

1920 *Frank Patrick Herbert*, U.S. author; wrote the *Dune* series of science fiction books; Nebula Award, 1965; Hugo Award, 1966. [d. February 11, 1986]

1925 *Alvaro Alfredo Magana*, President, Republic of El Salvador, 1982–84.

1927 *Cesar Milstein*, Argentine-born immunologist; Nobel Prize in physiology or medicine for development of the production of antibodies (with Georges J.F. Kohler), 1984.

1933 *Michael Vincent Korda*, U.S. editor, author; Editor-in-Chief, Simon and Schuster; wrote *Worldly Goods*, 1982.

1936 *Rona Barrett (Rona Burstein)*, U.S. journalist; fan magazines, *Rona Barrett's Hollywood* and *Rona Barrett's Gossip*, sold over one million copies, 1974.

1939 *Paul Hogan*, Australian actor; known for role in *Crocodile Dundee*, 1986.

1940 *David Carradine*, U.S. actor; starred in *Shane*, 1966, and *Kung Fu*, 1972; son of John Carradine.

1941 *Jesse Jackson*, U.S. politician, civil rights leader.

1943 *Chevy Chase (Cornelius Crane Chase)*, U.S. comedian.

1948 *Sarah Purcell (Sarah Pentecost)*, U.S. television personality; co-host of the TV series *Real People*, 1979–84.

1949 *Sigourney Weaver*, U.S. actress.

1956 *Stephanie Zimbalist*, U.S. actress; starred in the television series, *Remington Steele*, 1982–86; daughter of Efrem Zimbalist, Jr.

HISTORICAL EVENTS

1755 *Acadians*, refusing to swear loyalty to British crown, are expelled from *Nova Scotia*.

1856 *Arrow War* of Britain and France against China is instigated when Chinese police board the British vessel *Arrow*, arrest 12 Chinese crewmen, and lower the British flag.

1871 *Great Chicago Fire*, which kills 250, leaves nearly 100,000 homeless, and destroys $200 million worth of property, begins in a stable on the west side of the Chicago River, when, according to legend, Mrs. O'Leary's cow kicks over an oil lamp.

Entire community of *Peshtigo, Wisconsin* is destroyed by fire, killing more than 600 people.

1912 *Montenegro* declares war on Turkey and hostilities begin (*First Balkan War*).

1956 *Don Larsen* pitches the first perfect baseball game in World Series history.

1957 Stockholders of the *Brooklyn Dodgers* baseball team vote to move the franchise to Los Angeles, California.

1962 *Algeria* becomes a member of the United Nations.

1982 The Polish Parliament legalizes a ban on the trade union, *Solidarity*.

1990 *David Souter* is sworn in as the new justice of the Supreme Court.

HOLIDAYS

Universal Postal Union Day
Sponsored by United Nations.

Azerbaijan
Army Day

Ecuador
Independence of Guayaquil
Celebrates the declaration of
Guayaquil's independence from
Spain, 1820.

South Korea
*Korean Alphabet Day or Han'gu
Day*
Celebrates the promulgation of
Hangul alphabet, 1443.

Uganda
Independence Day
Commemorates attainment of
independence from Great Britain,
1962.

**U.S. (especially Wisconsin and
Minnesota)**
Leif Ericsson Day
Celebrates the landing of Erikson in
America, ca. 1000.

RELIGIOUS CALENDAR

The Saints
St. Dionysius the Areopagite. [d. 1st
century]
St. Demetrius, bishop of Alexandria.
[d. 231]
SS. Denys, Bishop of Paris, *Rusticus,*
and *Eleutherius,* martyrs.
Denys patron saint of France.
Also called *Dionysius, Denis.*
[d. c. 258] Optional Memorial.

St. Publia, widow. [d. c. 370]
SS. Andronicus and Athanasia. [d.
5th century]
St. Savin, Apostle of Lavedan. [d. c.
5th century]
St. Gislenus, abbot. Also called
Ghislain, Guislain. [d. c. 680]
St. Louis Bertrand, Dominican friar,
missionary. Principal patron
of Colombia. Also called *Lewis
Bertrand, Luis Bertran.* [d.
1581]
St. John Leonardi, founder of the
Clerks Regular of the Mother
of God. [d. 1609] Optional
Memorial.

The Beatified
Blessed Gunther, hermit. [d. 1045]

BIRTHDATES

1751 *Pierre Louis Lacretelle,*
French lawyer, journalist;
active in French Revolution;
member of Commune of
Paris, States General, and
Legislative Assembly; noted
for his treatises on France of
the Revolutionary period. [d.
1824]

1757 *Charles X,* King of France;
deposed by the July
Revolution of 1830 after
attempting to restore absolute
monarchy. [d. November 6,
1836]

1782 *Lewis Cass,* U.S. general,
government official; senator,
1845–57; U.S. Secretary of

State, 1857–60. [d. June 17,
1866]

1835 *(Charles) Camille Saint-
Saëns,* French composer,
pianist. [d. December 16,
1921]

1852 *Emil Hermann Fischer,*
German chemist; Nobel Prize
in chemistry for synthesizing
sugars and purines, 1902. [d.
July 15,1919]

1854 *Myron Timothy Herrick,* U.S.
banker, diplomat, and lawyer;
Governor of Ohio, 1903–04;
Ambassador to France,
1912–14; 1921–29; organized
ambulance corps in France
(World War I); active in U.S.
post-war relief efforts. [d.
March 31, 1929]

1860 *Leonard Wood,* U.S. soldier,
physician; with Theodore
Roosevelt, organized the
Rough Riders; Military
Governor of Cuba,
1899–1903; Chief of Staff of
U.S. forces, 1910–14. [d.
August 7, 1927]

1863 *Gamaliel Bradford,* U.S.
biographer, historian; author
of *Lee, the American.* [d.
April 11, 1932]

Edward William Bok, U.S.
editor, author, born in The
Netherlands; editor of *Ladies
Home Journal,* 1889–1919;
Pulitzer Prize in biography for
The Americanization of

Edward Bok. [d. January 9, 1930]

1873 *Charles Rudolph Walgreen,* U.S. merchant; founded the Walgreen drugstore chain, 1916. [d. December 11, 1939]

1879 *Max von Laue,* German physicist; Nobel Prize for his discovery of x-ray diffraction, 1914. [d. April 24, 1960]

1884 *Helene Deutsch,* U.S. psychoanalyst. [d. March 29, 1982]

1888 *Nikolai Ivanovich Bukharin,* Russian Communist leader; member of Politburo, 1918–29; head of Third International, 1926–29; expelled from Communist Party, 1937; executed with other Bolshevik leaders, 1938. [d. March 13, 1938]

1890 *Aimee Semple McPherson (A. Elizabeth Kennedy),* U.S. religious leader; founder of the *International Church of the Four-Square Gospel;* known for her extravagant, dramatic style of fundamentalist preaching. [d. September 27, 1944]

1906 *Leopold Sedar Senghor,* Senegalese poet, statesman; President of Senegalese Republic, 1960–80.

1908 *Jacques Tati,* French film director, writer, producer, actor; known for his characterization of *Monsieur Hulot,* a bumbling Frenchman, befuddled by modern life. [d. November 4, 1982]

1918 *E(verette) Howard Hunt,* U.S. presidential advisor, author; Consultant to President Nixon, 1971–72; jailed for his involvement in Watergate, 1973–74, 1975–77.

Robert Schwarz Strauss, U.S. government official, politician; special U.S. Envoy to the Middle East, 1979; chairman of President Carter's Campaign Committee, 1979.

1940 *John Lennon,* British singer, composer; member of *The Beatles.* [d. December 8, 1980]

1941 *Trent Lott,* U.S. politician; member of the U.S. Senate, 1989– ; Senate Majority Leader, 1996– .

1944 *John Entwistle,* British bassist for the rock group *The Who.*

Peter Tosh (Winston Hubert MacIntosh), Jamaican singer; original member of the reggae group, *Bob Marley and the Wailers.* [d. September 11, 1987]

1948 *Jeffrey Osbourne,* U.S. singer; songs include *On the Wings of Love,* 1982.

1950 *Jackson Browne,* U.S. singer, songwriter; wrote the songs, *Doctor My Eyes* and *Take It Easy;* Platinum Album Award for *Running on Empty,* 1978.

1955 *Steve Ovett,* British middle-distance runner; Great Britain's outstanding athlete of 1980.

HISTORICAL EVENTS

1651 *First Navigation Act* establishes English monopoly on shipping in foreign trade.

1701 *Yale University* is founded in New Haven, Connecticut.

1831 *Ioannes Capodistrias,* President of Greece, is assassinated.

1870 *Rome* is incorporated with Italy by royal decree.

1899 The *Kruger Telegram,* considered the immediate cause of the *Boer War,* is sent to the British government, demanding immediate withdrawal of British troops from South Africa.

1914 *Antwerp* falls to the Germans (*World War I*).

Battle of Warsaw, first German offensive against that city, opens (*World War I*).

1915 *Belgrade,* capital of Serbia, falls to the Germans and Austrians (*World War I*).

1918 Canadian troops take *Cambrai* (*WorldWar I*).

1921 *Taras Bulba* by Leoš Janáček premieres in Brno, Yugoslavia.

1941 *Ricardo Adolfo de la Guardia* is elected president of Panama.

1943 Yugoslav partisans under Marshal Tito begin assault against Axis forces near Trieste (*World War II*).

1946 Eugene O'Neill's play, *The Iceman Cometh,* premieres in New York.

1951 Researchers at the University of Illinois and the Hines Veterans Hospital announce the replacement of arteries in the legs affected by *arteriosclerosis* by normal blood vessels from other areas of the body.

1953 *Florence Chadwick* swims the Dardanelles in both directions, achieving her goal of swimming Europe's four major channels both ways.

1962 *Uganda* gains its independence from Great Britain.

1967 In Bolivia, *Che Guevara* is killed while leading a Cuban-sponsored guerrilla force.

1970 Cambodian leadership abolishes the monarchy.

1975 *Andrei Sakharov,* father of the Soviet hydrogen bomb, becomes the first Soviet citizen to win the Nobel Peace Prize.

1997 *Dean Smith* retires as head basketball coach at the University of North Carolina after 36 years.

october

OCTOBER
10

HOLIDAYS

Cuba
Beginning of Independence Wars

Fiji
Independence Day
Commemorates independence from Great Britain.

Japan
Physical Education Day or Sports Day

Namibia, South Africa
Kruger Day
Celebrates the birthday of *Paulus Kruger (Oom Paul)*, South African statesman, President of the Transvaal, 1825.

North Korea
Public Holiday
Commemorates the founding of the Korean Workers' Party.

Oklahoma
Oklahoma Historical Day
Commemorates first settlement of whites in Oklahoma Territory, 1802.

Taiwan
National Day or Double Tenth Day
Commemorates the proclamation of the Republic, 1912.

RELIGIOUS CALENDAR

The Saints
SS. Eulampius and Eulampia, martyrs. [d. c. 310]
St. Maharsapor, martyr. [d. 421]
St. Cerbonius, Bishop of Populonia; patron of the Diocese of Massa Marittima. [d. c. 575]

St. Paulinus, Bishop of York, and missionary. [d. 644]
SS. Daniel and his companions, martyrs. Second martyrs of the Franciscan Order. [d. 1227]
St. Francis Borgia, third Father General of the Jesuits, and 4th Duke of Gandia. [d. 1572]
St. Gereon and his companions, martyrs. [death date unknown]

The Beatified
Blessed Maria Francesca Rubatto. [beatified 1993]
Blessed Maria Satellico. [beatified 1993]

BIRTHDATES

1560 *Jacob Arminius,* Dutch theologian; originator of doctrine known as *Arminianism.* [d. October 19, 1609]

1684 *(Jean) Antoine Watteau,* French rococo painter. [d. July 18, 1721]

1731 *Henry Cavendish,* English chemist; determined specific gravity of hydrogen and carbon dioxide; first to isolate hydrogen as an element of water; first to isolate argon; his work led to later experiments on electricity by Faraday. [d. February 24, 1810]

1738 *Benjamin West,* U.S. painter; first American to study art in Italy; appointed charter member of Royal Academy in London; painter to King George III, 1771–92; although he never returned to U.S., he remained faithful to his Quaker religion and American heritage. [d. March 11, 1820]

1813 *Giuseppe Verdi,* Italian opera composer. [d. January 17, 1901]

1825 *Stephanus Johannes Paulus Kruger,* South African statesman; founder and President of *Transvaal,* 1883–1900. [d. July 14, 1904]

1830 *Isabella II,* Queen of Spain; came to throne at age 3 and ruled until deposed by Revolution of 1868. [d. April 9, 1904]

1833 *John Mohler Studebaker,* U.S. auto manufacturer. [d. March 16, 1917]

1861 *Fridtjof Nansen,* Norwegian Arctic explorer; Nobel Peace Prize for work in repatriating war prisoners, 1922. [d. May 13, 1930]

1870 *Ivan Alekseyevich Bunin,* Russian short-story writer, novelist, poet; Nobel Prize in literature, 1933. [d. November 8, 1953]

1892 *Ivo Andrić,* Yugoslavian novelist; Nobel Prize in literature, 1961. [d. March 13, 1975]

1895 *Lin Yutang,* Chinese educator and author. [d. 1976]

1897 *Elijah Muhammad,* U.S. religious leader; head of the Black Muslims. [d. February 25, 1975]

1900 *Helen Hayes (Helen Brown),* U.S. actress; known as the *First Lady of the American Stage.* [d. March 17, 1993]

1901 *Alberto Giacometti,* Swiss sculptor. [d. January 11, 1966]

1913 *Claude Simon,* French novelist; Nobel Prize in literature, 1985.

1914 *Dorothy Lamour (Dorothy Kaumeyer),* U.S. actress; leading lady of 1930–40's films. [d. September 22, 1996]

1918 *Yigal Allan,* Israeli statesman; a leader in the fight for Israeli independence, 1948. [d. February 29, 1980]

Theolonius (Sphere) Monk, U.S. musician; pianist, composer; noted for his jazz compositions and interpretations. [d. February 17, 1982]

1924 *James Dumaresq Clavell,* U.S. novelist, screenwriter, director, born in England; especially known for his novels of Japan. [d. September 6, 1994]

1930 *Adlai E(wing) Stevenson III,* U.S. politician, lawyer; U.S. Senator, 1970–81.

1946 *Ben Vereen,* U.S. actor, singer, dancer; Tony Award for *Pippin,* 1972; starred in the television mini-series, *Roots,* 1977.

1952 *Thor Robert (Bob) Nystrom,* Swedish-born hockey player; right wing, New York Islanders, 1972–86; four Stanley Cups.

1955 *David Lee Roth,* U.S. singer, musician; lead vocalist for *Van Halen,* 1974–76.

1956 *Martina Navratilova,* U.S. tennis player; Wimbleton Champion, 1978, 1979, 1982–87.

1958 *Tanya Tucker,* U.S. singer; had first country-western hit at age 14.

HISTORICAL EVENTS

1845 *U.S. Naval School* (later *U.S. Naval Academy*) opens at *Annapolis,* Maryland.

1874 *Fiji* is ceded to Great Britain.

1911 *Chinese Revolution* begins with revolt of military officers in Hankow.

1918 The Irish mail boat *Leinster* is sunk by a German submarine with the loss of 480 lives (*World War I*).

Battle of Argonne Forest ends with very costly American and French victory (*World War I*).

1928 General *Chiang Kai-shek* is inaugurated in Nanking as President of China.

1944 U.S. aircraft bomb *Okinawa* and other islands in the Ryukyus (*World War II*).

Ramon Grau San Martin is inaugurated as president of Cuba.

1948 *Carlos Prio Socarras* is inaugurated as president of Cuba.

1964 *XVIII Summer Olympic Games* open in Tokyo.

1965 Yale University discloses the existence of the *Vinland Map,* dating from about 1440, which contains indisputable cartographic representation of the Americas, including Greenland.

1970 *Fiji* gains independence from Great Britain.

Pierre Laporte, Quebec Labour Minister, is kidnapped from his Montreal home by French-Canadian separatists. Three suspects in his kidnap and murder are arrested on December 12.

1972 *Sir John Betjeman* is named Britain's Poet Laureate.

1973 U.S. Vice-President *Spiro Agnew* resigns, on the same day pleading *nolo contendere* to income-tax evasion; he is fined $10,000 and placed on probation for three years.

1977 Soviet cosmonauts abort space mission of their *Soyuz 25* spacecraft; no official explanation is given.

1991 The *Food and Drug Administration (FDA)* approves the drug DDI for treatment in the fight against AIDS.

1997 After a 6-year court battle the *tobacco industry* settles with flight attendants for $349 million for exposure to second hand smoke.

The United Nations begins the *International Campaign to Ban Landmines.*

october

OCTOBER
11

HOLIDAYS

Day of Solidarity with South African Political Prisoners.
Sponsored by the United Nations.

Panama
Revolution Anniversary
Commemorates the overthrow of the 11-day-old Arias government by the National Guard, 1968.

U.S. (Indiana)
General Pulaski Memorial Day
Commemorates death of Polish General *Casimir Pulaski,* American Revolutionary War hero, 1779.

U.S.
Eleanor Roosevelt's Birthday
Sponsored by the Franklin D. Roosevelt Philatelic Society.

Yugoslavia (Macedonia)
Public Holiday

RELIGIOUS CALENDAR

Feasts
Feast of the Motherhood of Our Lady, promoted by Pope Pius XI in 1931.

The Saints
SS. Tarachus, Probus, and Andronicus, martyrs. [d. 304]
St. Nectarius, Archbishop of Constantinople. [d. 397]
St. Canice, abbot. Also called *Cainnech, Canicus, Kenneth, Kenny.* [d. 599]
St. Agilbert, Bishop of Paris. [d. c. 685]

St. Gummarus. Also called *Gomar, Gommaire, Gummar.* [d. c. 774]
St. Bruno the Great, Archbishop of Cologne. [d. 965]
St. Alexander Sauli, Bishop of Pavia and Barnabite Clerk Regular. [d. 1592]

The Beatified
Blessed James of Ulm, laybrother. [d. 1491]
Blessed Mary Soledad, virgin and foundress of the Handmaids of Mary Serving the Sick. [d. 1887]

BIRTHDATES

1671 *Frederick IV,* King of Denmark and Norway, 1699–1730. [d. October 12, 1730]

1675 *Samuel Clarke,* English theologian, metaphysician; disciple of Isaac Newton; noted for his demonstration of the existence of God. [d. May 17, 1729]

1814 *John Baptist Lamy,* U.S. Roman Catholic priest born in France; established Catholic missions and schools in New Mexico, Arizona, and parts of Colorado, Utah, and Nevada. Was the model for the main character in Willa Cather's *Death Comes for the Archbishop.* [d. February 13, 1888]

1821 *Sir George Williams,* British philanthropist; founder of the Young Men's Christian Association, 1844. [d. 1905]

1844 *Henry John Heinz,* U.S. food-products manufacturer; founder of H. J. Heinz Co. [d. May 14, 1919]

1872 *Harlan Fiske Stone,* U.S. jurist; Associate Justice, U.S. Supreme Court, 1925–41; Chief Justice, U.S. Supreme Court, 1941–46. [d. April 22, 1946]

1882 *Robert Nathaniel Dett,* U.S. composer and educator. [d. 1943]

1884 *Friedrich Karl Rudolf Bergius,* German chemist; Nobel Prize in chemistry for development of chemical high pressure methods (with C. Bosch), 1931. [d. March 30, 1949]

(Anna) Eleanor Roosevelt, U.S. First Lady, syndicated columnist, diplomat; wife of U.S. President Franklin D. Roosevelt. [d. November 7, 1962]

1885 *François Mauriac,* French novelist, essayist, dramatist; Nobel Prize in literature, 1952. [d. September 1, 1970]

1887 *Willie Hoppe,* U.S. billiards player; winner of more than 50 world billiards titles. [d. February 1, 1959]

1897 *Nathan Farragut Twining,* U.S. Air Force general; Chairman, Joint Chiefs of Staff, 1957–60. [d. March 29, 1982]

1902 *Frances Lillian Ilg,* U.S. pediatrician, educator; cofounder and director, Gesell Institute for Human Development, 1950–70. [d. July 26, 1981]

1906 *Charles (Haskell) Revson,* U.S. cosmetics manufacturer; founder of Revlon, Inc., world's largest cosmetics manufacturer. [d. August 24, 1975]

1910 *Joseph Wright Alsop, Jr.,* U.S. journalist, author; with his brother, Stewart (May 17), wrote *Matter of Fact,* a syndicated column for the New York *Herald Tribune,* 1946–58; sole author of the same for Los Angeles *Times* Syndicate, 1958–74. [d. August 28, 1989]

1918 *Jerome Robbins,* U.S. ballet dancer, choreographer; associate artistic director, New York City Ballet, 1949–1959; ballet master, New York City Ballet. [d. July 29, 1998]

1925 *Elmore John (Dutch) Leonard, Jr.,* U.S. author, screenwriter; known for his crime fiction; works include *City Primeval,* 1980, and *Glitz,* 1985.

1927 *William Perry,* U.S. educator; U.S. Secretary of Defense, 1994– .

1928 *Ennio Morricone,* Italian composer.

1930 *Arkady Nikolayevich Shevchenko,* Russian diplomat; former United Nations official; defected to the United States, 1978; wrote *Breaking with Moscow,* 1985. [d. February 28, 1998]

1932 *Dottie West (Dorothy Marie Marsh),* U.S. singer; Grammy Award for Best Female Country Vocal Performance, 1964; Country Music Association Awards, 1978, 1979. [d. September 4, 1991].

1938 *Ron Leibman,* U.S. actor; starred in the movie, *Norma Rae,* 1979; Emmy Award for *Kaz,* 1979.

1939 *Maria Bueno,* Brazilian tennis player; Wimbledon Singles Champion, 1959, 1960, 1964.

1946 *Peter Martins,* Danish-born dancer, choreographer.

1948 *Daryl Hall,* U.S. singer, musician; member of the rock group, *Hall and Oates;* Platinum Album Award for *Bigger Than Both of Us,* 1976.

1961 *Steve Young,* U.S. football player.

1962 *Joan Cusack,* U.S. actress.

1965 *Luke Perry,* U.S. actor; known for role as Dillon McKay on TV drama *Beverly Hills 90210.*

HISTORICAL EVENTS

1531 The Catholic cantons of Switzerland win the *Battle of Kappel* against the city of Zurich and her Protestant allies, and *Ulrich Zwingli,* the Protestant reformer, is killed.

1614 *New Netherlands Company* is chartered.

1698 *First Partition Treaty* divides Spanish possessions between Bavaria and other German states.

1865 *Governor Edward John Eyre* is recalled to Great Britain after exercising unnecessary harshness in quelling an insurrection of Jamaican natives. Eyre had ordered the execution of 450 natives and more than 1,000 native homes burned.

1899 *Boers* of the Transvaal and Orange Free State, hoping to destroy British supremacy in South Africa, declare war (*Boer War*).

1906 *San Francisco* school board orders *segregation* of all Japanese, Chinese, and Korean children into a separate Oriental school.

1912 *Leopold Stokowski* makes his first appearance as Director of the Philadelphia Orchestra.

1914 Cathedral of *Notre Dame* suffers some damage in a German air raid on Paris (*World War I*).

1939 *Albert Einstein* and other American scientists inform U.S. President Franklin Roosevelt of the possibilities of developing an *atomic bomb.*

1942 The U.S. and Japan begin the *Battle of Cape Esperance* off the coast of Guadalcanal (*World War II*).

1950 *Columbia Broadcasting System* receives authorization from the Federal Communications Commission to begin transmission of *color television* broadcasts.

1961 U.S. Air Force Major Robert M. White flies an *X-15 rocket plane* to a height of 217,000 feet, a record for winged, man-controlled aircraft.

1962 *Pope John XXIII* opens the *Second Vatican Council* in Rome.

october

1972 *Panama* promulgates a new constitution.

1973 The U.S. Food and Drug Administration orders *cosmetics manufacturers* to list ingredients on labels on all products.

1977 *Col. Ibrahim al-Hamdi,* President of the Yemen Arab Republic, is killed by unidentified assassins.

1980 Two Soviet cosmonauts conclude longest *space*

mission up to that time, 185 days.

1987 *National Coming Out March* on Washington is held.

1992 American *April Larson* becomes the first female Lutheran bishop.

HOLIDAYS

Bahamas, Honduras
Discovery Day
Celebrates Columbus' discovery of
the New World.

Belize
Pan American Day

Brazil
Our Lady Aparecida
Commemorates the patroness of
Brazil

**Central America, South America,
Spain, United States (some
states)**
*Columbus Day or Day of the
Hispanidad*
Commemorates Columbus' first
landfall in the New World, 1492.

**Chile, Colombia, Costa Rica,
Paraguay, Spain, Uruguay**
Day of the Race
Celebrates Spanish influences and
contributions to the New World.

Equatorial Guinea
National Day
Celebrates end of Equatorial
Guinea's status as a Spanish colony,
1968.

Spain
National Day

RELIGIOUS CALENDAR

The Saints

St. Maximilian, Bishop of Lorch and
martyr. [d. c. 284]
*St. Felix and Cyprian and many
other martyrs.* [d. c. 484]

St. Edwin, first Christian king of
Northumbria, martyr. [d. 633]
St. Ethelburga, Abbess of Barking,
virgin. Also called *Ædilburh,
Æthelburh.* [d. c. 678]

BIRTHDATES

1710 *Jonathan Trumbull,* American
colonial leader; Governor of
Connecticut, 1769–84. [d.
August 17, 1785]

1775 *Lyman Beecher,* U.S. religious
leader, social reformer;
vigorous critic of Roman
Catholicism; adamant
abolitionist; father of Harriet
Beecher Stowe (June 14) and
Henry Ward Beecher (June
24). [d. January 10, 1863]

1798 *Pedro IV,* King of Portugal,
1826; abdicated in favor of his
daughter, Donna Maria da
Gloria. [d. September 24,
1834]

1844 *George Washington Cable,*
U.S. author, reformer; literary
voice of old New Orleans; a
leading figure in *Western
local color movement* in
American fiction. [d. January
31, 1925]

1860 *Elmer A(mbrose) Sperry,* U.S.
inventor; developed the
gyrocompass, gyroscopic
stabilizer, and nearly 400
other inventions to which he
held patents; a founder of the

American Institute of
Electrical Engineers and the
American Electro-Chemical
Society. [d. June 16, 1930]

1865 *Sir Arthur Harden,* English
biochemist; Nobel Prize in
chemistry for investigations
into fermentation and
fermentative enzymes (with
Hans von Euler-Chelpin),
1929. [d. June 17, 1940]

1866 *James Ramsay MacDonald,*
British statesman; Secretary of
Labor Party, 1900–12;
Treasurer of the Party,
1912–24; leader of Labor
Party, 1911–14; Prime Minister
of Great Britain, 1924,
1929–31; organized first Labor
ministry in British history. [d.
November 9, 1937]

1872 *Ralph Vaughan Williams,*
British composer; wrote
choral works, songs, and
symphonies; composed
London, 1914, and *Pastoral,*
1922. [d. August 26, 1958]

1874 *Abraham Arden Brill,* U.S.
psychiatrist; popularizer of
Sigmund Freud. [d. March 2,
1948]

1884 *Sir Godfrey Tearle,* British
actor. [d. June 9, 1953]

1891 *Pearl Mesta,* U.S. diplomat,
hostess; the unofficial hostess
of Washington, D.C., during
the 1940s; U.S. Envoy to
Luxembourg, 1949–53. [d.
January 11, 1975]

october

1896 *Eugenio Montale,* Italian poet; Nobel Prize in literature, 1975. [d. September 28, 1981]

1901 *F(elix) Edward Hebert,* U.S. politician; Congressman, 1947–76; wrote award winning exposé of Huey Long's political career in Louisiana. [d. December 29, 1979]

1927 *Charles Gordone,* U.S. playwright; Pulitzer Prize in drama, 1970. [d. November 17, 1995]

1932 *Edwin Jacob (Jake) Garn,* U.S. politician; Senator, 1974–; voyage on the space shuttle, *Discovery,* made him the first legislator in space, 1985.

Dick Gregory, U.S. comedian, political activist.

1935 *Luciano Pavarotti,* Italian opera singer.

William Raspberry, U.S. journalist.

Joan Rivers, U.S. comedian, TV host.

1947 *Chris Wallace,* U.S. broadcast journalist; son of Mike Wallace.

1948 *John Engler,* U.S. lawyer, politician; governor of Michigan, 1991– .

1950 *Susan Anton,* U.S. actress, singer; known for her nightclub performances; starred in the movie, *Golden Girl,* 1979.

Ronald McNair, U.S. astronaut; died in the explosion of the space shuttle, *Challenger.* [d. January 28, 1986]

1968 *Adam Rich,* U.S. actor; known for his role as Nicholas

Bradford on the television series, *Eight Is Enough,* 1977–81.

1970 *Kirk Cameron,* U.S. actor; known for his role as Mike Seaver on the television show, *Growing Pains;* starred in the film, *Werewolf Too.*

HISTORICAL EVENTS

1297 *Edward I* of England solemnly confirms *Magna Carta,* restricting sovereign's right to raise taxes.

1492 *Christopher Columbus* makes first landfall in the New World in what is today San Salvador.

1518 *Martin Luther* is interrogated at Augsburg and refuses to recant.

1576 Holy Roman Emperor *Maximilian II* dies and is succeeded by his brother, *Rudolf II.*

1811 *Paraguay* declares its independence from Spain and Argentina.

1822 *Brazil* declares its independence from Portugal.

1864 *Salmon Chase* becomes Chief Justice of the U.S. Supreme Court.

1908 The *Convention of the South African Union* opens at Durban, Natal, to prepare the way for the union of the Cape Colony, Natal, the Transvaal, and the Orange River Colony.

1914 The Germans enter *Lille, France* and begin an occupation that lasts until 1918 (*World War I*).

1915 *Edith Cavell,* a British nurse in Brussels, is shot by the Germans for aiding Allied soldiers (*World War I*).

1944 U.S. carrier-based planes bomb Formosa and northern Luzon in the Philippines (*World War II*).

1950 *The George Burns and Gracie Allen Show* makes its television debut.

1965 U.S. Navy formally concludes *Sealab II* program in which teams of aquanauts lived and worked in an underwater capsule submerged off the California coast.

1968 *Equatorial Guinea* achieves its independence from Spain.

1971 *Jesus Christ Superstar,* by Andrew Lloyd Webber and Tim Rice, premieres in New York.

Major General *Goafar Mohammed Nimeiri* is inaugurated as the first president of Sudan.

Celebration of the 2,500th anniversary of the *Persian Empire* begins in Persepolis, Iran.

1973 Judge John Sirica orders President Richard Nixon to release personal tapes of Oval Office conversations to a U.S. District Court (*Watergate Incident*).

1976 Mao Tse-tung's widow, *Chiang Ch'ing,* and three other radical leaders (the *Gang of Four*) are arrested for plotting a military takeover.

Hua Guofeng is chosen to succeed *Mao Tse-tung* as chairman of the Chinese Communist Party.

1983 Former Japanese prime minister, *Kakuei Tanaka,* is convicted of bribery for arranging the purchase of Lockheed aircraft by All Nippon Airways.

october

OCTOBER
13

RELIGIOUS CALENDAR

The Saints

SS. Faustus, Januarius, and Martial, martyrs. Martial also called *Martialis.* [d. c. 304]

St. Comgan, abbot. [d. 8th century]

St. Gerald of Aurillac. Also called *Gerard.* [d. 909]

St. Coloman, martyr. Also called *Colman.* [d. 1012]

St. Edward the Confessor, King of England. Patron of England, especially of Westminster. [d. 1066]

St. Maurice of Carnoët, abbot. [d. 1191]

The Beatified

Blessed Magdalen Panattieri, virgin. [d. 1503]

BIRTHDATES

1754 *Mary McCauley (Molly Pitcher),* American heroine; earned her nickname when she carried water to the soldiers at the *Battle of Monmouth* during the American Revolution. [d. January 22, 1832]

1807 *Hans Conon von der Gabelentz,* German historian and linguist; known for his studies of languages of remote areas of Africa, Asia, and Pacific Islands. [d. September 3, 1874]

1821 *Rudolph Virchow,* German pathologist; father of cellular pathology; a leader of the German Liberal Party; member of the Reichstag, 1880–93. [d. September 5, 1902]

1850 *Pellegrino Matteucci,* Italian explorer; the first European to traverse the whole of Africa north of the Equator from Egypt to the Gulf of Guinea, 1880–81. [d. August 8, 1881]

1853 *Lillie Langtry (Emilie Charlotte Le Breton),* British actress; toured the world as *the Jersey Lily.* [d. February 12, 1929]

1862 *John Rogers Commons,* U.S. labor economist; author of numerous multi-volume studies of American industrial society; professor of economics, University of Wisconsin, 1904–13; director of American Economic Association, 1920–28. [d. May 11, 1944]

1872 *Ralph Vaughan Williams,* British composer. [d. August 26, 1958]

1877 *Theodore Gilmore Bilbo,* U.S. politician; U.S. Senator, 1935–46; known for his bigotry and his filibustering, especially on Southern populist issues. [d. August 21, 1947]

1902 *Luther H(arris) Evans,* U.S. educator, librarian; Librarian of Congress, 1945–53; Director General, UNESCO, 1953–58. [d. December 23, 1981]

1909 *Herbert Lawrence Block (Herblock),* U.S. cartoonist; Pulitzer Prize for cartoons, 1942, 1954, 1979.

1910 *Ernest K(ellogg) Gann,* U.S. novelist; author of *The High and the Mighty, Fate Is the Hunter.* [d. December 19, 1991]

1918 *Cornel(ius Louis) Wilde,* U.S. actor. [d. October 16, 1989]

1924 *Nipsey Russell,* U.S. comedian, actor; co-hosted the television series, *The Les Crane Show.*

1925 *Margaret (Hilda) Thatcher,* British barrister, politician; first woman Prime Minister of Great Britain, 1979–90.

Lenny Bruce (Leonard Alfred Schneider), U.S. comedian, satirist. [d. August 3, 1966]

1936 *Donald F. McHenry,* U.S. diplomat; U.S. Ambassador to the United Nations, 1979–81.

1941 *Art(hur) Garfunkel,* U.S. singer, songwriter; known for his singing and songwriting efforts with partner Paul Simon (November 5).

1942 *Jerry (Jerral) Jones,* U.S. businessman; owner of the Dallas Cowboys.

1944 *Robert Lamm,* U.S. singer, musician; keyboardist for the rock group, *Chicago.*

1946 *Lacy J. Dalton,* U.S. singer; country-western albums include *Hard Times,* 1980, and *Lacy J. Dalton,* 1980.

1949 *Sammy Hagar,* U.S. singer, musician; released ten albums in a nine year solo career; famous for his concert acts; member of the rock group, *Van Halen,* 1984–96.

1951 *Beverly Johnson,* U.S. model; first black woman on the cover of *Vogue* magazine, 1975; Outstanding U.S. Model Award, 1975.

1953 *Pat Day,* U.S. jockey; inducted into Racing Hall of Fame, 1991.

1959 *Marie Osmond,* U.S. singer.

1962 *Kelly Preston,* U.S. actress.

Jerry Rice, U.S. football player.

1969 *Nancy Kerrigan,* U.S. figure skater.

HISTORICAL EVENTS

1501 *Peace of Trento* is signed between France and Holy Roman Emperor, Maximilian I, who recognizes French conquests in Upper Italy.

1792 The cornerstone of the *White House* is laid.

1843 *B'nai B'rith International* is organized in New York.

1851 Permanent telegraphic communications are first established between France and England.

1877 *Satsuma Rebellion* is crushed by a modern army of Japanese commoners, ending the power of the warrior class as a separate group.

1913 The *Anti-Defamation League* of B'nai B'rith is organized in Chicago, Illinois.

1914 Continuing German advance in Flanders forces Belgian government to move to *Havre, France* from Ostend (*World War I*).

1919 France ratifies the *Treaty of Versailles,* ending *World War I.*

1922 The Colony of the *Niger* is formed by the French government.

1953 *John Kotalawala* becomes prime minister of Ceylon.

1955 William Golding's novel, *Lord of the Flies,* is published in New York.

1964 Three Soviet cosmonauts manning the world's first multi-seat spacescraft, *Voskhod,* land safely after orbiting the earth 16 times.

1970 *Fiji* becomes the 127th member of the UN.

1976 Scientists at the University of Michigan announce the identification of the mummy of King Tutankhamun's grandmother, who lived from 1397 to 1360 B.C.

1978 *Ola Ullsten* becomes premier of Sweden.

1981 *Hosni Mubarak* is confirmed as president of Egypt in a national referendum, following the assassination of Anwar Sadat.

1983 The U.S. Department of Transportation orders automakers to mount a third brake light on the back of cars starting in 1985.

1997 *Thrust* becomes the first land vehicle to break the *sound barrier,* in the Black Rock Desert in Nevada.

october

OCTOBER
14

HOLIDAYS

Democratic Republic of the Congo
Birthday of President Mobutu

Youth Day

Yemen People's Democratic Republic
National Day
Celebrates the proclamation of the Republic, 1962.

RELIGIOUS CALENDAR

The Saints

St. Callistus I, pope and martyr. Elected c. 217. Also called *Calixtus, Callixtus I.* [d. c. 222] Optional Memorial.

St. Justus, Bishop of Lyons. [d. c. 390]

St. Manacca, abbess. [d. c. 5th–6th cent.]

St. Manechildis, virgin. Also called Ménéhould. [d. c. 6th century]

St. Angadrisma, virgin. Also called *Angadrê me.* [d. c. 695]

St. Burchard, Bishop of Würzburg. Also called *Burckard, Burkardi.* [d. 754]

St. Dominic Loricatus. [d. 1060]

BIRTHDATES

1633 *James II,* King of England (James VII of Scotland). His abdication in 1688 established Parliament's strength in England. [d. September 16, 1701]

1644 *William Penn,* English Quaker leader in America; founder of *Pennsylvania.* [d. July 30, 1718]

1696 *Samuel Johnson,* American clergyman; first president of King's College (now *Columbia University*). [d. June 6, 1772]

1712 *George Grenville,* English politician; first Lord of the Admiralty, 1762–63; first Lord of the Treasury, Chancellor of the Exchequer, and Prime Minister, 1763–65; best known for enactment of the Stamp Act; nicknamed the *Gentle Shepherd.* [d. November 13, 1770]

1734 *Francis Lightfoot Lee,* American Revolutionary leader; member of Virginia House of Burgesses, 1758–68; 1769–76; delegate to Continental Congress; signer of Declaration of Independence. [d. January 11, 1797]

1784 *Ferdinand VII,* King of Spain, 1808, 1814–33; repressive reign was marked by periodic rebellion and reaction; Spain lost all her possessions in North and South America during his reign. [d. September 29, 1833]

1857 *Elwood Haynes,* U.S. inventor; creator of an early practical automobile, 1894. Patented *Stellite,* a cobalt alloy. [d. April 13, 1925]

1873 *Ray Ewry,* U.S. track and field star; winner of eight Olympic gold medals, 1900, 1904, 1908. [d. September 29, 1937]

1882 *Eamon De Valera,* Irish statesman; led the Easter Rising of 1916; President of Sinn Fein, 1917–26; Prime Minister, 1937–48; 1951–54; 1957–59. [d. August 29, 1975]

1888 *Katherine Mansfield (Kathleen Murry),* British writer; masterful short-story writer; most of her works were published after her death. [d. January 9, 1923]

1890 *Dwight David Eisenhower,* U.S. Army general, statesman, university president; 34th President of the U.S., 1953–61; Supreme Commander of Allied Expeditionary Force in Europe during World War II. [d. March 28, 1969]

1892 *(Benjamin) Sumner Welles,* U.S. diplomat; laid foundation of U.S. Good Neighbor Policy with Latin America; U.S. Under-Secretary of State, 1933–43. [d. September 24, 1961]

1893 *Lois Lenski,* U.S. author, illustrator; John Newberry

Medal for Most Distinguished Contribution to Literature for American Children for *Strawberry Girl*, 1946. [d. September 11, 1974]

1894 *e(dward) e(stlin) cummings,* U.S. poet; noted for his unorthodox typography and experimental approach to style and diction. [d. September 3, 1962]

1896 *Lillian Gish,* U.S. silent-screen actress. [d. February 27, 1993]

1906 *Hannah Arendt,* U.S. political scientist born in Germany; known for her studies of totalitarianism; first woman to hold full professorship at Princeton; author of *Origins of Totalitarianism*, 1951; *The Human Condition*, 1958. [d. December 4, 1975]

1911 *Le Duc Tho (Phan Dinh Khai),* Vietnamese government official; founding member of the Communist Party of Indochina, 1930; Special Adviser to the North Vietnamese Delegate at the Paris Peace Talks, 1968–72; declined the Nobel Peace Prize, 1973. [d. October 13, 1990]

1916 *Charles Everett Koop,* U.S. government official; Surgeon-General of the United States, 1982–89.

1928 *Roger George Moore,* British actor; starred in the television series, *The Saint*, 1967–69; known for his movie role as James Bond, Agent 007.

1930 *Joseph Mobutu (Mobotu Sese Seko),* Congolese general; President of the Congo, now Zaire, 1965–97. [d. September 7, 1997]

1938 *Farah Diba Pahlevi,* Iranian Empress; descendent of

Mohammed; widow of former Shah Mohammed Pahlevi.

1939 *Ralph Lauren (Ralph Lifshitz),* U.S. fashion designer; known for his popular ready-to-wear interpretations of classic clothing; head of Polo Fashions Incorporated, 1969–.

1940 *Cliff Richard (Harry Roger Webb),* British singer, actor; popular rock star of the early 1960's; comeback hit single, *Devil Woman*, 1976.

1950 *Sheila Young,* U.S. speed skater; winner of three medals in 1976 Winter Olympics.

1952 *Harry Anderson,* U.S. actor, magician; known for his role as Judge Harry Stone on the television series, *Night Court.*

1958 *Thomas Dolby (Thomas Morgan Dolby Robertson),* British singer, musician; hit single, *She Blinded Me With Science*, 1983.

HISTORICAL EVENTS

1066 *King Harold* of England is defeated and killed by the Normans at the *Battle of Hastings.*

1322 *Robert Bruce,* King of Scotland, defeats *Edward II* of England at *Byland.*

1656 Massachusetts General Court passes the first punitive legislation against *Quakers* in the colony, imposing a 40 shilling fine on anyone harboring a Quaker.

1705 English navy captures *Barcelona (War of the Spanish Succession).*

1806 Napoleon defeats Prussians and Saxons at Jena and Auerstä dt.

1809 *Peace of Vienna* is signed; Austria cedes Trieste and Illyria to France; Galicia to Poland and Russia; Salzburg and Inn District to Bavaria.

1915 Bulgaria declares war on Serbia (*World War I*).

1920 *Treaty of Dorpat* is signed by Finland and Russia, ending war between the two and defining boundaries.

1923 First mechanical *telephone switchboard* is installed in New York City.

1926 A.A. Milne's classic *Winnie-the-Pooh* is published.

1930 *Girl Crazy* by George Gershwin opens in New York.

1933 Germany withdraws from the Disarmament Conference and from the League of Nations.

1937 Socialist party is banned in Germany.

1944 General *Erwin Rommel* is forced to commit suicide by German authorities for allegedly conspiring against *Adolf Hitler.*

1947 American rocket-propelled *Bell X-1* becomes the first aircraft to exceed the speed of sound in level flight.

1961 Frank Loesser's musical, *How to Succeed in Business Without Really Trying,* premieres in New York.

1966 U.S. extends its exclusive *coastal fishing zone* to 12 miles.

1974 *Palestine Liberation Organization* is recognized by the UN.

october

1983 The National Council of
Churches issues *The Inclusive
Language Lectionary,* the first
volume of a new, three-
volume Bible translation
designed to eliminate sexist
references.

HOLIDAYS

El Salvador
Revolution Day

Tunisia
Evacuation Day

U.S.
White Cane Safety Day
Day dedicated to the visually
handicapped citizens of the U.S.
Sponsored by National Federation of
the Blind.

World Poetry Day
Sponsored by National Poetry Day
Committee, Inc., and World Poetry
Day Committee.

RELIGIOUS CALENDAR

The Saints
St. Leonard of Vandoeuvre, abbot.
[d. c. 570]
St. Thecla, Abbess of Kitzingen, and
virgin. Also called *Heilga,
Tecla.* [d. c. 790]
St. Euthymius the Younger, abbot.
[d. 898]
St. Teresa of Avila, virgin. Founder
of the Discalced Carmelites,
and Doctor of the Church. [d.
1582] Obligatory Memorial.

The Beatified
Blessed Magdalena de Nagasaki
[one of the Martyrs of
Nagasaki] [beatified 1981]

BIRTHDATES

70BC *Vergil* or *(Virgil) (Publius
Vergilius Maro),* Roman poet;
the chief poet of the Golden
Age of Rome; wrote *The
Aeneid,* the epic poem
relating the story of Aeneas
and the founding of Rome.
[d. September 21, 19 B.C.]

1542 *Akbar (Jala ud-Din
Mohammad),* Emperor of
Hindustan, 1556–1605;
considered one of the
greatest Indian emperors. [d.
1605]

1608 *Evangelista Torricelli,* Italian
physicist, mathematician;
developed early barometer;
made improvements in
telescope; constructed simple
microscope. [d. October 25,
1647]

1758 *Johann Heinrich von
Dannecker,* German sculptor;
associate of Schiller, Goethe,
Herder, Canova; best known
for busts of Schiller, Gluck.
[d. December 8, 1841]

1767 *Gabriel Richard,* French-born
priest, educator, printer;
started first newspaper in
Michigan, 1809; founded the
University of Michigan, 1817.
[d. September 13, 1832]

1783 *François Magendie,* French
physiologist; pioneered in
research on functions of
spinal nerves, blood flow;

introduced morphine,
codeine and bromide
compounds into medical
practice. [d. October 7, 1855]

1795 *Frederick William IV,* King of
Prussia, 1840–61; forced to
promulgate a new
constitution by the Revolution
of 1848; suffered from
insanity; his reign carried out
by his brother William
(William I) as regent,
1858–61. [d. January 2, 1861]

1805 *Wilhelm von Kaulbach,*
German painter; noted for his
ceilings and wall murals,
including the grand staircase
of the Neves Museum in
Berlin. [d. April 7, 1874]

1814 *Mikhail Yurievich Lermontov,*
Russian poet, novelist; early
Romantic poet; exiled to
Caucasus, where he died. [d.
July 27, 1841]

1829 *Asaph Hall,* U.S. mathematical
astronomer; noted especially
for his discovery of the
moons of Mars, 1877. [d.
December 7, 1914]

1830 *Helen Hunt Jackson,* U.S.
novelist, poet, essayist; known
for her sympathetic portrayal
of the American Indian;
appointed by U.S.
government to investigate
condition of Mission Indians
of California; author of
Ramona. [d. August 12, 1885]

october

1844 *Friedrich Nietzsche,* German philosopher; noted for his philosophy of the perfectability of man, which has been said to have influenced the development of the Nazi movement of the 1930s; proposed theory of the superman (*Übermensch*); suffered mental breakdown, 1889, which affected him for remainder of his life. [d. August 25, 1900]

1847 *Ralph Albert Blakelock,* U.S. romantic painter; unnoticed during his lifetime, many of his works are now in the collections of leading U.S. galleries. [d. August 9, 1919]

1858 *John L. Sullivan,* U.S. boxer; last bareknuckle heavyweight champion, 1882–92. [d. February 2, 1918]

William Sowden Sims, U.S. admiral; developed new theories of naval warfare that contributed to Allied victories in World War I; Pulitzer Prize in history, 1920. [d. September 28, 1936]

1872 *Edith Wilson,* second wife of U.S. President Woodrow Wilson. [d. December 28, 1961]

1878 *Paul Reynaud,* French statesman; Minister of Finance, 1930, 1938–40; Premier of France at time of defeat by Germans; imprisoned by Germans, 1943–45. [d. September 21, 1966]

1881 *Sir P(elham) G(renville) Wodehouse,* British author; noted for his humorous stories of the life of English gentry; developed characters of *Jeeves, Bertie Wooster;* interned in Germany during World War II; became U.S. citizen, 1955. [d. February 14, 1975]

1905 *C(harles) P(ercy) Snow,* British novelist, scientist, government official; British Civil Service Commissioner, 1945–60; author of *Strangers and Brothers,* an 11-volume novel sequence, 1935–70. [d. July 1, 1980]

1908 *John Kenneth Galbraith,* U.S. economist, author, diplomat, born in Canada; noted for his work on the American economy, especially *The Affluent Society;* U.S. Ambassador to India, 1961–63; Chairman of Americans for Democratic Action, 1967–68.

1917 *Arthur M(eier) Schlesinger, Jr.,* U.S. historian, public official; author of Pulitzer Prize-winning *The Age of Jackson,* 1945; *A Thousand Days,* 1965; professor of history, Harvard University, 1946–61; a founder of Americans for Democratic Action; speech-writer for Adlai E. Stevenson and John F. Kennedy during their presidential campaigns.

1920 *Lee Iacocca,* U.S. businessman, auto manufacturing executive; President, Ford Motor Co., 1970–78; Chief Executive, Chrysler Corporation, 1979–92.

Mario Puzo, U.S. author; best known for his novel *The Godfather.*

1923 *Italo Calvino,* Italian author; wrote *The Non-Existent Knight and the Cloven Viscount* and *Invisible Cities;* honorary member of the American Academy and Institute of Arts and Letters, 1975. [d. September 19, 1985]

1924 *Jose Quintero,* Panamanian director; Tony Award for *A Moon for the Misbegotten,* 1973.

1926 *Evan Hunter,* U.S. novelist; author of *The Blackboard Jungle,* 1954.

Jean Peters, U.S. actress.

1938 *John Wesley Dean, III,* U.S. lawyer; counsel to President Richard Nixon; achieved notoriety as chief prosecution witness during Watergate hearings.

1939 *Linda Lavin,* U.S. singer, actress; starred in the television series, *Alice,* 1976–85; Tony Award for *Broadway Bound,* 1987.

1940 *Peter C. Doherty,* Australian immunologist; Nobel Prize for Medicine along with Rolf M. Zinkernagel, Swiss immunologist, for their study of virus-infected cells, 1996.

1945 *Penny Marshall,* U.S. actress, director; known for her role as Laverne on the television series, *Laverne and Shirley;* directed *Big,* 1988.

James Alvin (Jim) Palmer, U.S. baseball player; pitcher, Baltimore Orioles, 1965–84; led the American League in most games won, 1975–77.

1946 *Richard Lynn Carpenter,* U.S. singer, musician, songwriter; member of the pop music group, *The Carpenters.*

1951 *(Leonard) Roscoe Tanner III,* U.S. tennis player; serve timed at 155 miles per hour; lost to Bjorn Borg in a five set Wimbledon final, 1979; called the *Cannonball Kid.*

1953 *Toriano Adaryll (Tito) Jackson,* U.S. singer, musician; member of the rock group, *The Jacksons.*

1959 *Sarah Ferguson,* Duchess of York; former wife of Prince Andrew of England.

HISTORICAL EVENTS

1080 *Henry IV* of Germany is defeated and *Rudolf,* Duke of Swabia is killed at *Pegau.*

1581 *Ballet Comique de la Reine,* regarded as the first ballet, is performed in Paris.

1788 *Jean François Pilatre de Rozier,* French aeronautical designer, becomes the first human to ascend into the air by balloon; duration: 5 minutes; height: 60 feet.

1815 *Napoleon* arrives at *St. Helena,* where he remains for the rest of his life.

1900 Symphony Hall in Boston is inaugurated as the home of the *Boston Symphony Orchestra.*

1915 *Third Battle of Artois* ends with the British failing to reach the main objective of Lens and suffering some 60,000 casualties (*World War I*).

Great Britain declares war on *Bulgaria (World War I).*

1918 *Poland* declares itself free and independent with *Josef Pi lsudski* as Chief of State.

1919 The British and Italian governments ratify the *Treaty of Versailles.*

1943 U.S. establishes Naval Supply Depot at *Guantanamo Bay,* Cuba.

1945 *Pierre Laval,* former premier of the French Vichy government, is executed in Paris after being convicted of collaborating with the Germans during World War II.

1946 Dr. *Glenn Seaborg* announces his discovery of a new chemical element called neptunium.

1949 *Laslo Rajk,* leader of Hungary's Communists, is executed after a show trial arranged by the pro-Soviet group within his own party.

1951 *I Love Lucy* makes its television debut.

1953 *Winston Churchill* wins the Nobel Prize in literature for his multi-volume memoir, *The Second World War.*

1964 *Nikita S. Khrushchev* is removed from all government and Communist Party posts; *Aleksei N. Kosygin* is named Premier, and *Leonid I. Brezhnev* becomes First Party Secretary.

1965 *Mikhail Sholokhov* wins the Nobel Prize in literature.

1966 President Lyndon Johnson signs a bill creating the *Department of Transportation.*

1968 Alexander Solzhenitsyn's novel, *The Cancer Ward,* is published in the U.S.

1970 U.A.R. Acting President *Anwar al-Sadat* is elected president in a national plebiscite.

1978 General *João Baptista da Figueiredo* is elected president of Brazil.

1979 General *Carlos Humberto Romero* is overthrown as president of El Salvador in a coup d'etat

1997 NASA sends *Cassini,* an unmanned spacecraft, to explore the planet Saturn.

october

OCTOBER
16

HOLIDAYS

World Food Day
Sponsored by United Nations.

RELIGIOUS CALENDAR

The Saints

SS. Martinian and other martyrs,
and *Maxima.* [d. 458]
St. Gall, monk and missionary;
patron of Switzerland. [d. c.
635]
St. Mommolinus, Bishop of Noyon.
Also called *Mommolin,*
Mummolin. [d. c. 686]
St. Bercharius, abbot. [d. c. 696]
St. Lull, Bishop of Mainz. Also called
Lullon, Lullus. [d. 786]
St. Anastasius of Cluny. [d. c. 1085]
St. Bertrand, Bishop of Comminges.
[d. 1123]
St. Hedwig, widow and laywoman.
Also called *Jadwiga.* [d. 1243]
Optional Memorial
St. Margaret Mary Alacoque, virgin
and visionary. [d. 1690]
Optional Memorial.
St. Gerard Majella, Redemptorist lay
brother. [d. 1755]

The Beatified

Blessed Nicolas Roland. [beatified
1994]
Blessed Alberto Hurtado Cruchaga.
[beatified 1994]
Blessed Maria Rafols. [beatified
1994]
Blessed Petra of St. Joseph Perez
Florido. [beatified 1994]
Blessed Josephine Vannini.
[beatified 1994]

BIRTHDATES

1430 *James II,* King of Scotland,
1437–60. [d. August 3, 1460]

1708 *Albrecht von Haller,* Swiss
physiologist, anatomist,
botanist, poet; founder of
experimental physiology and
neurology. [d. December 12,
1777]

1758 *Noah Webster,* U.S.
lexicographer, writer; creator
of the first dictionary of
American English, *An*
American Dictionary of the
English Language, 1828. [d.
May 28, 1843]

1760 *Jonathan Dayton,* U.S.
politician, lawyer, American
Revolutionary soldier; U.S.
Congressman, 1791–99; U.S.
Senator, 1799–1805; city of
Dayton, Ohio, is named for
him. [d. October 9, 1824]

1806 *William Pitt Fessenden,* U.S.
politician, lawyer; played
major role in founding of
Republican Party, 1856; U.S.
Secretary of the Treasury,
1864–65; Chairman of Joint
Congressional Committee on
Reconstruction, 1866. [d.
September 9, 1869]

1826 *Giovanni Battista Donati,*
Italian astronomer; discovered
six comets, one of which is
named for him. [d.
September 20, 1873]

1851 *Frederick Huntington Gillett,*
U.S. Congressman,
1892–1925; responsible for
legislation which established
General Accounting Office of
U.S.; U.S. Senator, 1924–30.
[d. July 31, 1935]

1854 *Oscar (Fingall O'Flahertie*
Wills) Wilde, Irish poet,
dramatist; known for his light-
hearted, sparkling comedies
including *The Importance of*
Being Earnest; produced
French drama *Salome;*
convicted of sodomy and
jailed; while in jail wrote *De*
Profundis. [d. November 30,
1900]

1863 *Sir Joseph Austen*
Chamberlain, British
statesman; Nobel Peace Prize,
1925. [d. March 16, 1937]

1886 *David Ben-Gurion,* Israeli
statesman, born in Poland;
first Prime Minister of Israel,
1949–53; 1957–63. [d.
December 1, 1973]

1888 *Eugene (Gladstone) O'Neill,*
U.S. playwright; first American
to win Nobel Prize in
literature, 1936; awarded
Pulitzer Prize in drama, 1920,
1922, 1928, 1957. [d.
November 27, 1953]

1890 *Michael Collins,* Irish
revolutionary leader; Minister
of Finance of Sinn Fein
ministry, 1919–22;
Commander in Chief of
Military Forces. Killed in
revolutionary action, 1922. [d.
August 22, 1922]

1893 *Carl Carmer,* U.S. writer, folklorist. [d. September 11, 1976]

1898 *William O(rville) Douglas,* U.S. jurist; Associate Justice, U.S. Supreme Court, 1939–75. [d. January 19, 1980]

1900 *Leon Allen (Goose) Goslin,* U.S. baseball player; outfielder, 1921–38; elected to the Hall of Fame, 1968. [d. May 15, 1971]

1906 *Edward (Jeffrey Irving) Ardizzone,* British artist; known for his illustrations of more than 200 books, including works by Thackeray, Trollope, Cervantes, and Mark Twain. [d. November 8, 1979]

1908 *Robert Ardrey,* U.S. author; known for his controversial anthropological books including *African Genesis,* and *The Territorial Imperative.* [d. January 14, 1980]

1911 *Mahalia Jackson,* U.S. gospel singer. [d. 1972]

1915 *Judd Clifton Holdren,* U.S. actor; starred in the 1950's film series, *Captain Video, Last Planet,* and *Zombies of the Stratosphere.* [d. March 11, 1974]

1921 *Linda Darnell (Manetta Eloisa Darnell),* U.S. actress. [d. April 10, 1965]

1925 *Angela Lansbury,* U.S. actress, born in England.

1927 *Günter Grass,* German novelist; spokesman for post-Nazi German literary movement.

1929 *Nicholas VonHoffman,* U.S. journalist.

1931 *Charles W. Colson,* U.S. government official; gained notoriety during Watergate scandal, 1973–74; started prison ministry program.

1932 *Henry Lewis,* U.S. conductor. [d. 1996]

1941 *Baddeley Devesi,* Governor-General, Solomon Islands, 1978–88.

1946 *Suzanne Somers (Suzanne Mahoney),* U.S. actress; starred in the television series, *Three's Company,* 1977–81.

1954 *Lorenzo Carcaterra,* U.S. writer; author of *Sleepers.*

1958 *Tim Robbins,* U.S. actor; known for roles in *The Sure Thing,* 1985, *Top Gun,* 1986, and *Bull Durham,* 1988.

HISTORICAL EVENTS

1076 Princes opposed to *Henry IV* of Germany meet at *Trebur.*

1171 *Henry II* of England invades Ireland at the request of deposed King Dermot Macmurrough.

1793 *Marie Antoinette* is beheaded.

1813 Allies defeat Napoleon at the *Battle of Leipzig,* causing French retreat from Germany.

1846 *William Morton* demonstrates the effectiveness of *ether* as a surgical anesthetic at Massachusetts General Hospital.

1859 *John Brown,* U.S. abolitionist, leads unsuccessful raid on government arsenal at *Harper's Ferry.*

1904 French federal government is established in *Senegal.*

1915 France and Serbia declare war on *Bulgaria (World War I).*

1917 *Margaret Sanger* and others open the first *birth control clinic,* in Brooklyn, New York.

1938 Aaron Copland's ballet *Billy the Kid* opens in Chicago.

1941 German troops conquer *Odessa. (World War II)*

1942 Aaron Copeland's ballet, *Rodeo,* premieres in New York.

1946 *Joachim von Ribbentrop,* Nazi leader, convicted of war crimes by *Nuremberg Tribunal,* hanged; *Hermann Goering,* sentenced to hang with von Ribbentrop, commits suicide just prior to the scheduled execution.

1951 Pakistani prime minister, *Liaqual Ali Khan,* is assassinated by an Afghan extremist in Rawalpindi.

1963 *Ludwig Erhard* is elected chancellor of West Germany.

1964 *Harold Wilson* is inaugurated as prime minister of Great Britain.

The *People's Republic of China* detonates its first nuclear weapon in the *Taklamakan Desert.*

1965 *Singapore* formally becomes a member of the Commonwealth of Nations.

1967 Tom Stoppard's play, *Rosencrantz and Guildenstern Are Dead,* opens in New York.

1968 Two American black athletes at Olympic Games, *Tommie Smith* and *John Carlos,* demonstrate for *black power* during their victory celebration. The Olympic Committee suspends them two days later.

october

1970 Canadian prime minister Pierre Trudeau invokes the *Emergency War Measures Act* to deal with recent kidnappings of British and Canadian officials. It is the first time such measures have been taken during peacetime in Canada.

1975 Argentine President *Isabel Perón* returns to office in response to the nation's political and economic troubles.

1978 The Roman Catholic College of Cardinals elects fist non-Italian pope in 456 years, Cardinal *Karol Wojtyla* of Poland, who takes the name *John Paul II*.

1995 The *Million Man March* takes place in Washington, D.C.

HOLIDAYS

Haiti

Dessalines Memorial Day
Commemorates the assassination of *Jean Jacques Dessalines,* early black leader of the country, 1806.

Malawi

Mothers Day
A day of tribute to the mothers of the country.

RELIGIOUS CALENDAR

The Saints

St. Ignatius, Bishop of Antioch and martyr. Also called *Theophorous,* or *God Bearer.* [d. c. 107]. Feast formerly February 1. Obligatory Memorial.

St. John the Dwarf, hermit. [d. 5th century]

St. Anstrudis, virgin. Also called *Anstru, Austrude.* [d. c. 700]

St. Nothelm, Archbishop of Canterbury. [d. c. 740]

St. Seraphino, Capuchin laybrother. [d. 1604]

St. Margaret Mary, virgin and visionary. [d. 1690]

The Ursuline Martyrs of Valenciennes. [d. 1794]

The Beatified

Blessed John Baptist Turpin du Cormier, Blessed Mary L'Huilier, and their companions, martyrs. [d. 1794]

BIRTHDATES

1780 *Richard Mentor Johnson,* U.S. Vice-President, 1837–41. [d. November 19, 1850]

1803 *Ferencz Deák,* Hungarian statesman; generally acknowledged ruler of Hungary, 1861–67; effected restoration of Hungarian Constitution, 1867; responsible for establishment of dual monarchy of *Austria-Hungary.* [d. January 29, 1876]

1851 *Thomas Fortune Ryan,* U.S. financier; established first holding company in U.S. in order to gain control of New York City street railways; notorious for his shady financial operations and exploitation of U.S. companies and the Belgian Congo. [d. November 23, 1928]

1859 *Childe Hassam,* U.S. painter, printmaker; one of leading exponents of Impressionism; allowed substantial bequest to the American Academy of Arts and Letters, which provided its support for many years; known as the leader of the *Ten American Painters.* [d. August 27, 1935]

1864 *Robert Lansing,* U.S. lawyer, diplomat; leading American expert on international law; U.S. Secretary of State, 1915–20; responsible for U.S. purchase of *Virgin Islands.* [d. October 30, 1928]

1880 *Charles Herbert Kraft,* U.S. food-products manufacturer; founder of the J. L. Kraft Co., 1909, and Kraft Foods, Inc., 1945. [d. March 25, 1952]

1895 *Doris Humphrey,* U.S. dancer, choreographer, teacher; major influence in U.S. modern dance movement. [d. December 29, 1958]

1903 *Irene Noblette Ryan,* U.S. actress; known for her role as Granny Clampett on the television series, *Beverly Hillbillies,* 1962–71. [d. April 26, 1973]

Nathanael West (Nathan Wallenstein Weinstein), U.S. author; wrote *Miss Lonely-hearts,* 1933, and *The Day of the Locust,* 1939.

1909 *William Randolph (Cozy) Cole,* U.S. jazz drummer. [d. January 29, 1981]

1912 *Pope John Paul I (Albino Luciani),* pope for 34 days, 1978. [d. September 29, 1978]

1914 *Sarah Churchill,* British actress; daughter of Sir Winston Churchill (November 30). [d. September 24, 1982]

1915 *Arthur Miller,* U.S. dramatist; author of *Death of a Salesman, The Crucible, A*

View from The Bridge. Awarded Pulitzer Prize in drama, 1949.

1918 *Rita Hayworth (Margarita Carmen Cansino),* U.S. actress. [d. May 14, 1987]

1920 *Montgomery Clift,* U.S. actor. [d. July 23, 1966]

1926 *Beverly Garland (Beverly Lucy Fessenden),* U.S. actress; appeared in the television series, *My Three Sons* and *Scarecrow and Mrs. King.*

1930 *Jimmy Breslin,* U.S. journalist, novelist; noted for his Runyonesque syndicated column and novels. Wrote *The Gang that Couldn't Shoot Straight.*

1938 *(Robert Craig) Evel Knievel,* U.S. stunt motorcyclist.

1947 *Michael McKean,* U.S. actor; played Lenny Koznowski on TV series *Laverne and Shirley.*

1948 *Margot Kidder,* U.S. actress; known for her role as Lois Lane in the *Superman* film series.

George Wendt, U.S. actor; known for his role as Norm Peterson on the television series, *Cheers,* 1982–93.

1949 *William Louis (Bill) Hudson II,* U.S. singer, musician; member of the rock group, *Hudson Brothers.*

1950 *Howard Ellsworth Rollins, Jr.,* U.S. actor; starred in the films, *Ragtime,* 1981, and *A Soldier's Story,* 1984; played Virgil Tibbs on the TV drama *In the Heat of the Night.* [d. December 8, 1996]

1955 *Sam Bottoms,* U.S. actor; appeared in *Apocalypse Now,*

1979; starred in the television movie, *East of Eden,* 1981; brother of Joseph and Timothy Bottoms.

1956 *Mae C. Jemison,* U.S. physician, astronaut; first African American woman in space; flew aboard the space shuttle *Endeavour,* (September 12, 1992).

1957 *Vince(nt) Van Patten,* U.S. actor, tennis player; son of Dick Van Patten.

1958 *Alan Jackson,* U.S. country singer.

HISTORICAL EVENTS

1346 *Queen Philippa* of England, wife of *Edward III,* defeats and captures *David II* of Scotland at *Neville's Cross.*

1483 *Spanish Inquisition* is placed under joint direction of state and church.

1777 English *General John Burgoyne* capitulates to American troops at *Saratoga (American Revolution).*

1797 *Peace of Campo Formio* between France and Austria is signed; Austria cedes Belgium and Lombardy and obtains Istria, Dalmatia, and Venice.

1854 *Siege of Sebastopol* begins, pitting Allies (Turkey, Britain, France, Austria) against Russia (*Crimean War*).

1907 Wireless telegraph newspaper service between England and U.S. begins.

1918 *Hungary* declares independence from Austria.

1941 Prior to U.S. entry into World War II, U.S. destroyer *Kearny,*

escorting British ships, is torpedoed off Iceland; 11 men are lost.

All U.S. merchant ships in Asiatic waters are ordered into friendly ports.

1944 Chicago's first *subway* formally opens.

1945 Mass mobilization in *Argentina* begins the Peronist movement.

1960 U.S. variety store chains, Woolworth's, W. T. Grant's, and McCrory-McLellan, begin racial *integration* of their lunch counters in more than 100 southern cities.

1966 *Botswana* and *Lesotho* are admitted to the UN.

1973 Organization of Arab Petroleum Exporting Countries imposes a cut in the flow of oil to force the U.S. to change its Middle East policy, marking the beginning of the *Arab oil embargo.*

1977 U.S. Supreme Court permits the supersonic *Concorde* to begin test flights to New York's Kennedy International Airport.

1978 Egyptian president *Anwar Sadat* and Israeli prime minister *Menachem Begin* win the Nobel Peace Prize.

Full U.S. citizenship is restored posthumously to Confederate president Jefferson Davis.

1989 An *earthquake* measuring 7.1 on the Richter scale hits San Francisco, California, killing at least 90 people and causing $6 billion in damages.

HOLIDAYS

Azerbaijan
Day of State Sovereignty

U.S. (Alaska)
Alaska Day
Commemorates the transfer of
Alaska from Russia to the U.S., 1867.

RELIGIOUS CALENDAR

Feasts
St. Luke, evangelist. Patron of
doctors, painters,
glassmakers, lacemakers, and
artists. [d. 1st century] [major
holy day, Episcopal Church;
minor festival, Lutheran
Church.]

The Saints
St. Gwen of Cornwall. Also called
Wenn. [death date unknown]
St. Justus of Beauvais, martyr. Also
called *Justin.* [death date
unknown]

The Beatified
*Blessed Pauline of the Heart of Jesus
in Agony Visintainer.*
[beatified 1991]

BIRTHDATES

1405 *Pius II,* pope 1458–64. [d.
August 14 or 15, 1464]

1595 *Edward Winslow,* British-born
colonial leader; Mayflower
passenger; Governor,
Plymouth Colony, 1633, 1636,
1644. [d. May 8, 1655]

1631 *Michael Wigglesworth,*
American colonial poet,
clergyman; best known for his
224-stanza poem *The Day of
Doom: Or a Poetical
Description of the Great and
Last Judgment,* 1662, a
dramatic exposition of
Calvinist theology. [d. June
10, 1705]

1697 *Canaletto (Giovanni Antonio
Canal),* Italian painter,
etcher, known for his urban
scenes, especially of Venice.
[d. April 19, 1768]

1824 *Juan Valera y Alcalá
Galiano,* Spanish novelist,
man of letters; Minister of
Public Instruction, 1871–1905;
Ambassador to Washington,
1883–86; Minister to Lisbon,
1886–88; Ambassador to
Vienna, 1893–95. [d. April 18,
1905]

1831 *Thomas Hunter,* U.S.
educator; founder of Normal
College of City of New York
(later *Hunter College*). [d.
October 14, 1915]

Frederick III, King of Prussia,
1888; ruled for only 88 days.
[d. June 15, 1888]

1836 *Ellen Browning Scripps,* U.S.
newspaper publisher,
philanthropist; with her
brother E. W. Scripps (March
19) was active in family-
owned newspaper chain;
founder of *Scripps College for
Women* (later part of the
Claremont Colleges,
Claremont, California). [d.
August 3, 1932]

1844 *Harvey W. Wiley,* U.S.
chemist; responsible for
enactment of U.S. *Pure Food
& Drug Act of 1906.* [d. June
30, 1930]

1854 *(Salomon) August Andrée,*
Swedish balloonist; lost
during 1897 attempt to cross
the North Pole in a balloon.
[d. 1897]

1859 *Henri Bergson,* French
philosopher, founder of
Bergsonism, a philosophy
based on concept of time as
duration; Nobel Prize in
literature, 1927. [d. January 4,
1941]

1878 *James Truslow Adams,* U.S.
historian; Pulitzer Prize in
history, 1922; noted for his
popular books on American
history, including the six-
volume *Dictionary of
American History.* [d. 1849]

1889 *Fannie Hurst,* U.S. novelist,
short-story writer. [d.
February 23, 1968]

1900 *Lotte Lenya (Karoline
Blamauer),* Austrian actress,
singer; known for her
interpretation of first husband
Kurt Weill's songs and
characters, especially as Jenny
in *The Threepenny Opera.* [d.
November 27, 1981]

october

1903 *Evelyn (Arthur St. John) Waugh,* British novelist; noted for sophisticated, satirical portrayals of 20th-century society. [d. April 10, 1966]

1905 *Felix Houphouet-Boigny,* President, Republic of Ivory Coast, 1960–93. [d. December 7, 1993]

1918 *Robert William (Bobby) Troup,* U.S. actor, songwriter, musician, singer; wrote the hit song, *Route 66;* known for his role as Dr. Joe Early on the television series, *Emergency,* 1972–77.

1919 *Pierre Elliott Trudeau,* Canadian political leader; Prime Minister of Canada, 1968–79; 1980–84; leader of federal Liberal Party, 1968–84.

1921 *Jesse A. Helms,* U.S. politician, newspaper editor; Senator, 1973– .

1922 *Richard (Peter) Stankiewicz,* U.S. sculptor; a pioneer in *junk art;* his works are on display in most major American museums of art. [d. March 27, 1983]

1925 *Melina (Amalia) Mercouri,* Greek actress, political activist; Minister of Culture of Greece. [d. March 6, 1994]

1927 *George C(ampbell) Scott,* U.S. actor, director.

1930 *Frank Charles Carlucci III,* U.S. government official, diplomat; Deputy Director, Central Intelligence Agency, 1978–81; National Security Advisor, 1986–87; Secretary of Defense, 1987–88.

1932 *Vytautas Landsbergis,* Lithuanian educator, politician; President of Lithuania, 1990– .

1935 *Peter Boyle,* U.S. actor; appeared in *Joe,* 1970, *Young Frankenstein,* 1974, *Taxi Driver,* 1976, and *Malcolm X,* 1992.

1939 *Mike Ditka,* U.S. football player, football coach.

Lee Harvey Oswald, alleged assassin of U.S. President John F. Kennedy; was in turn killed by Jack Ruby two days after Kennedy's assassination. [d. November 24, 1963]

1942 *William Wattison (Willie) Horton,* U.S. baseball player; outfielder, Detroit Tigers, 1963–77; 325 career home runs.

1947 *Laura Nyro,* U.S. singer, songwriter. [d. April 7, 1997]

1948 *Joe Morton,* U.S. actor; known for role in *Terminator 2: Judgement Day,* 1991.

Ntozake Shange (Paulette L. Williams), U.S. dramatist, poet; wrote the choreopoem, *For Colored Girls Who Have Considered Suicide/When the Rainbow is Enuf,* 1975.

1951 *Pam Dawber,* U.S. actress; starred in the television series, *Mork and Mindy* and *My Sister Sam.*

1958 *Thomas (Tommy) Hearns,* U.S. boxer; only fighter to win four different boxing titles in his career; called the *Detroit Hit Man.*

1961 *Wynton Marsalis,* U.S. musician; classical and jazz trumpeter; first artist to win Grammy Awards in both categories, 1984.

Erin Moran, U.S. actress; known for her role as Joanie on the television series, *Happy Days,* 1974–83.

Jean-Claude Van Damme, Belgian actor.

HISTORICAL EVENTS

1469 *Isabella of Castile* marries *Ferdinand II of Aragon,* thus uniting nearly all of the Christian areas of Spain in one monarchy.

1685 *Louis XIV* of France revokes *Edict of Nantes,* which had given religious freedom to French Huguenots.

1748 *Peace of Aix-la-Chapelle* ends the *War of the Austrian Succession.*

1854 *Ostend Manifesto* of the U.S. declares that if Spain refuses to sell Cuba to the U.S., the U.S. can take it by force.

1904 *Gustav Mahler* conducts the premiere performance of his Fifth Symphony.

1912 *First Balkan War* escalates as Bulgaria, Serbia, and Greece Montenegro join against Turkey.

Italian-Turkey *Treaty of Lausanne* gives Italy control of Tripoli and Cyrenaica; Turkey gets Dodecanese.

1922 *British Broadcasting Co., Ltd.,* is established as a private corporation.

1933 *Commodity Credit Corporation* is established in U.S., primarily to extend loans to farmers.

1950 *Connie Mack* retires after 50 years as manager of the Philadelphia Athletics baseball team.

1989 The space shuttle *Atlantis* is sent into space to deploy the spacecraft *Galileo* that will explore the planet Jupiter.

1991 The *Republic of Azerbaijian* declares its independence from the Soviet Union.

OCTOBER
19

The Saints

SS. Ptolemaeus, Lucius, and Another, martyrs. Ptolemaeus also called *Ptolemy.* [d. c. 161]

St. Varus, martyr, and *St. Cleopatra,* widow. [d. c. 4th century]

St. Ethbin, abbot. Also called *Egbin.* [d. 6th century]

St. Aquilinus, Bishop of Eureux. [d. c. 695]

St. Frideswide, virgin and abbess. Also called *Frévisse.* Patron of Oxford, England and the University of Oxford. [d. c. 735]

St. Peter of Alcántara, hermit and mystic. Patron of night watchmen. [d. 1562]

St. Isaac Jogues and his Companions. [d. 1647] Optional Memorial.

St. Jean de Brébeuf, Jesuit priest and martyr. Protomartyr of North America. [d. 1649]

St. Paul of the Cross, founder of the Barefooted Clerks of the Holy Cross and Passion, also called the Passionist Congregation. Feast formerly April 28. [d. 1775] Optional Memorial.

The Beatified

Blessed Thomas of Bioille, deacon. [d. 1257]

BIRTHDATES

1433 *Marsilio Ficino,* Italian philosopher, scholar; known as translator of Plato into Latin. [d. October 1, 1499]

1605 *Sir Thomas Browne,* English physician; best known for book of reflections, *Religio Medici.* [d. October 19, 1682]

1748 *Martha Jefferson,* wife of U.S. President Thomas Jefferson. [d. September 16, 1782]

1784 *(James Henry) Leigh Hunt,* English critic, essayist, poet, and playwright; associate of the major British Romantic poets, Keats, Shelley, and Byron; best known for his essays and *Autobiography,* 1850. [d. August 28, 1859]

James McLaughlin, Canadian fur trader; known as the father of Oregon because of the assistance he gave American settlers in that region. [d. September 13, 1857]

1859 *Alfred Dreyfus,* Jewish French Army officer; victim of anti-Semitism, convicted of treason on false evidence and sent to Devil's Island; was championed by Emile Zola, who wrote *J'accuse* in his defense; it eventually won him his pardon. [d. July 11, 1935]

1862 *Auguste Lumière,* French inventor, with his brother Louis, of the *motion picture.* [d. April 10, 1954]

1895 *Lewis Mumford,* U.S. social critic, author; noted for his writing and teaching, particularly in the areas of art, architecture, urban planning, and conservation. [d. January 26, 1990]

1899 *Miguel Angel Asturias,* Guatemalan novelist, short-story writer; Nobel Prize in literature, 1967. [d. June 9, 1974]

Eddie Bauer, U.S. merchant; pioneered the quilted, goose-down insulated jacket; founded the mail order sporting goods company which bears his name. [d. April 18, 1986]

1901 *Arleigh Burke,* U.S. naval commander; Chief of U.S. Naval Operations, 1955–61. [d. January 1, 1996]

1910 *Subrahmanyan Chandrasekhar,* Indian-born physicist; Nobel Prize in physics for his research on the evolution of stars, 1983. [d. August 21, 1995]

1916 *Jean Dausset,* French physician; Nobel Prize in physiology or medicine for his work dealing with the relationship between heredity and blood transfusions, 1980.

1921 *Herbert Warren Kalmbach,* U.S. lawyer, Watergate participant.

1922 *Jack Anderson,* U.S. journalist; successor to Drew Pearson (December 13).

1931 *John Le Carré (David John Moore Cornwell),* British novelist; author of *The Spy Who Came in from the Cold, The Little Drummer Girl,* and other spy novels.

1932 *Robert Reed (John Robert Rietz),* U.S. actor; known for his role as Mike Brady on the television series, *The Brady Bunch,* 1969–74. [d. May 12, 1992]

1936 *Johnetta B. Cole,* U.S. anthropologist, educator; first female president of Spelman College, 1987– .

1937 *Peter Max,* U.S. artist, designer; best known for his colorful, psychedelic posters and murals in the 1960's.

1941 *Simon Ward,* British actor; appeared in the films, *Young Winston* and *The Three Musketeers.*

1945 *John Arthur Lithgow,* U.S. actor; appeared in *The World According to Garp* and *Terms of Endearment.*

Jeannie C. Riley (Jeannie C. Stephenson), U.S. singer; best known for her hit song, *Harper Valley PTA;* Grammy Award, 1968.

1960 *Jennifer Yvette Holliday,* U.S. singer, actress; Tony Award for *Dreamgirls,* 1982.

1967 *Amy Carter,* daughter of Jimmy Carter, 39th U.S. President.

HISTORICAL EVENTS

1216 *King John* of England dies and is succeeded by *Henry III.*

1453 Bordeaux surrenders to the French; English retain only Calais and the Channel Islands (*Hundred Years' War*).

1781 British General Lord Cornwallis surrenders to Americans at *Yorktown (American Revolution).*

1914 The Germans open the *First Battle of Ypres (World War I).*

1915 Russia and Italy declare war on Bulgaria (*World War I*).

Venustiano Carranza becomes provisional president of Mexico, and the U.S. recognizes his government.

1941 German submarine sinks U.S. merchant ship *Lehigh (World War II).*

1943 *Moscow Conference of Foreign Ministers* opens; it is the first Allied meeting of World War II.

1944 John Van Druten's play, *I Remember Mama,* premieres in New York.

1959 *The Miracle Worker,* a dramatization of Helen Keller's early life, opens on Broadway.

1963 British rock group, *The Beatles,* record *I Want to Hold Your Hand,* at EMI Studios in London.

1982 U.S. auto executive, *John DeLorean,* is charged with possession of cocaine.

1983 U.S. Senate passes a bill making *Martin Luther King Jr.'s* birthday an annual federal holiday, beginning in 1986.

Grenadan prime minister, *Maurice Bishop,* is killed in a coup led by extremist members of his New Jewel Movement.

1987 The Dow Jones average plummets 508 points, causing the worst day in Wall Street history. The federal budget deficit, rising interest rates, and the falling dollar are cited as causes of the 22.6 percent decline on what has become known as "*Black Monday.*"

1960 The U.S. imposes an embargo on all exports to *Cuba* in retaliation for Cuba receiving arms shipments from the Soviet Union.

1993 *Benazir Bhutto,* former prime minister of Pakistan, is re-elected.

The *United Nations* imposes an embargo against *Haiti* in retaliation for General *Raoul Cédras's* refusal to relinquish leadership to elected president *Jean-Bertrand Aristide.*

october

OCTOBER
20

HOLIDAYS

Guatemala
1944 Revolution Day
Commemorates the overthrow of military strongman, *General Federico Ponce,* 1944.

Kenya
Kenyatta Day
Commemorates *Jomo Kenyatta,* the nation's first president.

RELIGIOUS CALENDAR

The Saints
St. Caprasius, martyr. [d. 3rd century]
St. Artemius, martyr. [d. 363]
St. Acca, Bishop of Hexham. [d. 740]
St. Andrew of Crete, martyr. Also called the *Calybite* [d. 766]
St. Bertilla Boscardin, virgin and nursing sister. [d. 1922]

The Beatified
Blessed Mary Teresa de Soubiran, virgin and founder of the Society of Mary Auxiliatrix. [d. 1889]

BIRTHDATES

1616 *Thomas Bartholin,* Danish physician; noted for discovery of *lymphatic vessels.* [d. December 4, 1680]

1632 *Sir Christopher Wren,* English architect, astronomer; proposed plan for rebuilding London after Great Fire, 1666; designed more than 50 churches in London, especially *St. Paul's Cathedral,* London. [d. February 25, 1723]

1741 *Angelica Kauffman,* Swiss-Italian painter and engraver. [d. November 5, 1807]

1762 *André-Marie Chénier,* French poet; one of greatest French classical poets after Racine; guillotined during Reign of Terror, 1794. [d. July 25, 1794]

1784 *(Henry John Temple), Viscount Palmerston,* English statesman; known as *Pam;* Home Secretary, 1853–55; Prime Minister, 1855–65; effected independence of Belgium, 1830; annexed Hong Kong, 1840–41. [d. October 18, 1865]

1822 *Thomas Hughes,* English reformer, author, jurist; founder of *Working Men's College* and its principal, 1872–83; established a model community in America which failed, 1879; best known as author of *Tom Brown's School Days* and *Tom Brown at Oxford.* [d. March 22, 1896]

1854 *Patrick Geddes,* British biologist, sociologist, educator, and city planner; noted for his avante-garde theories of the interrelationships between biology and sociology. [d. April 17, 1932]

(Jean Nicolas) Arthur Rimbaud, French poet; known for his highly imaginative verse forms; associated with Symbolist School; wrote most of his poetry before the age of 20. [d. November 10, 1891]

1859 *John Dewey,* U.S. philosopher, educator, psychologist; head of Department of Philosophy, Psychology, and Pedagogy at the University of Chicago, 1894–1904; established Laboratory School to test his educational theories; a founder of the American Association of University Professors. [d. June 1, 1952]

1874 *Charles Edward Ives,* U.S. composer; Pulitzer Prize in music, 1947. [d. May 19, 1954]

1891 *Sir James Chadwick,* British physicist; Nobel Prize in physics for discovery of the *neutron,* 1935. [d. July 24, 1974]

Johnstone (Jomo) Kenyatta (Johstone Kamau), Kenyan government official; led the fight against Great Britain for independence; President, 1964–78. [d. August 22, 1978]

1900 *Wayne Morse,* U.S. politician, lawyer; U.S. Senator, 1944–69. [d. July 22, 1974]

1904 *George Woodcock,* British labor leader, union official; General Secretary, Trades Union Congress, 1960–69. [d. October 30, 1979]

1905 *Frederic Dannay,* U.S. mystery writer; with his partner, Manfred B. Lee (January 11), created the *Ellery Queen* series. [d. September 3, 1982]

1925 *Art Buchwald,* U.S. journalist; his syndicated columns describe current controversies in a humorous tone.

1928 *Joyce Diane Bauer Brothers,* U.S. psychologist, author; only woman to win $64,000 on *The $64,000 Question,* 1955–56; wrote *What Every Woman Should Know about Men,* 1982; syndicated magazine columnist for *Good Housekeeping.*

1931 *Mickey Mantle,* U.S. baseball player; by the time of his retirement, 1969, he had 536 home runs and more than 1700 strikeouts. Elected to Baseball Hall of Fame, 1974. [d. August 13, 1995]

1932 *Michael McClure,* U.S. poet, dramatist.

1942 *Christiane Nüsslein-Volhard,* German geneticist; Nobel Prize for Medicine. Nüsslein-Volhard shares with award with Edward B. Lewis, and Eric F. Wieschaus. They discover the influence of genetics in embryonic development, 1995.

1944 *William Albright,* U.S. composer; noted chiefly for experimental techniques.

1952 *Melanie Mayron,* U.S. actress; Emmy winner for her work as Melissa Steadman on the TV series *thirtysomething.*

Tom Petty, U.S. rock singer; leader of Tom Petty and the Heartbreakers.

1953 *Keith Hernandez,* US. baseball player.

HISTORICAL EVENTS

1740 *Charles VI,* last male heir to *Hapsburg empire,* dies; he is succeeded by his daughter *Maria Theresa,* Queen of Bohemia and Hungary.

1818 Boundary between Canada and U.S. from Lake of the Woods to crest of Rocky Mountains is set at *49th parallel.*

1827 *Battle of Navarino* results in the destruction of the Egyptian-Turkish fleet by British, French, and Russian squadrons.

1883 *Peace of Ancón* ends *Saltpeter War* between Peru and Chile.

1899 Boers launch attack on British garrison at *Ladysmith, Natal (Boer War).*

1928 *French Academy* rules that *celibacy* is no longer a *conditio sine qua non* for applicants for the *Prix de Rome.*

1944 Russian and Yugoslav forces capture *Belgrade (World War II).*

U.S. forces, under the leadership of General *Douglas MacArthur,* begin their invasion of the *Philippines (World War II).*

1950 *Pyongyang,* capital of North Korea, is captured by UN forces *(Korean War).*

1958 Field Marshall *Sarit Thanarat* regains control of the government of Thailand in a bloodless coup.

1968 *Jacqueline Kennedy* marries Greek shipping magnate, *Aristotle Onassis.*

1972 *John Bardeen* becomes the first person to win two Nobel Prizes in the same field. He received the awards for his theory of *superconductivity* (1972) and development of electronic *transistors* (1956).

1973 *Sydney (Australia) Opera House* is officially opened by *Queen Elizabeth II.*

U.S. Attorney General *Elliott Richardson* resigns in dispute with U.S. President Richard Nixon over Watergate special prosecutor *Archibald Cox.*

1978 *Leo Tindemans* is inaugurated as premier of Belgium.

U.S. Congress disbands the *Women's Army Corps* as a special branch of the armed forces.

1986 *Yitzhak Shamir* is inaugurated as prime minister of Israel.

1987 The *Tokyo and London stock exchanges* plunge to record lows, reflecting the effects of the U.S. stock market collapse of the previous day. In Tokyo the Nikkei average drops 14 percent and in London the 100 share index plummets more than 12 percent.

1996 *Arnoldo Aleman* is elected president of Nicaragua.

october

OCTOBER
21

HOLIDAYS

British Virgin Islands
St. Ursula's Day

Honduras
Armed Forces Day

Somali Democratic Republic
Revolution Anniversary
Commemorates the rise to power of *Major General Mohammed Siad Barre* and establishment of a Supreme Revolutionary Council, 1969.

RELIGIOUS CALENDAR

The Saints

St. Hilarion, abbot and hermit. [d. c. 371]

St. Malchus. Also called *Malek.* [d. 4th cent.]

St. Fintan of Taghmon, abbot. Also called *Munnu.* [d. c. 635]

St. Tuda, Bishop of Northumbria. [d. 664]

St. Condedus, hermit. Also called *Condé, Condède.* [d. c. 685]

St. John of Bridlington, Canon Regular. [d. 1379]

St. Ursula and her Maidens, martyrs; patron of educators of young girls. Invoked for a good death. Ursuline Order named in her honor. [death date unknown]

The Beatified

Blessed James Strepar, Archbishop of Galich. [d. c. 1409]

Blessed Peter of Tiferno, confessor. [d. 1445]

Blessed Matthew, Bishop of Girgenti. [d. 1450]

BIRTHDATES

1660 *Georg Ernst Stahl,* German physician, chemist; proposed theory of phlogiston to explain combustion; enunciated a doctrine of animism, wherein the soul is the vital principle in organic development. [d. May 14, 1734]

1760 *Katsushika Hokusai,* Japanese painter, printmaker; noted for his technical excellence; his work has had great influence on artists of other countries; among his works are *Hundred Views of Mount Fuji,* 1835, and the 15-volume *Ten Thousand Sketches,* through 1836. [d. May 10, 1849]

1772 *Samuel Taylor Coleridge,* English poet, critic, essayist; one of spokesmen of the Romantic movement in English literature. [d. July 25, 1834]

1785 *Henry Miller Shreve,* U.S. riverboat captain; initiated commercial transportation on America's rivers; developed the snagboat, which was used to clear rivers of debris and make them navigable; superintendent of river improvements in the West, 1827–42; *Shreveport, Louisiana* is named for him. [d. March 6, 1851]

1790 *Alphonse Marie Louis Prat de Lamartine,* French man of letters; his *Méditations Poétiques* greatly influenced the Romantic movement in French literature. [d. February 28, 1869]

1813 *Caroline Fillmore,* second wife of U.S. President Millard Fillmore. [d. August 11, 1881]

1833 *Alfred Bernhard Nobel,* Swedish industrialist, inventor, philanthropist; inventor of *dynamite;* his fortune was left to support the *Nobel Prizes* in peace, medicine, chemistry, physics, and literature, awarded annually since 1901. [d. December 10, 1896]

1861 *Prince Georgy Yevgenyevich Lvov,* first president of the Russian Provisional Government after Russian Revolution, 1917. [d. March 6, 1925]

1869 *William Edward Dodd,* U.S. educator, historian, and diplomat; U. S. Ambassador to Germany, 1933–37. [d. February 9, 1940]

1877 *Ostwald T. Avery,* Canadian bacteriologist; conducted early studies of DNA molecules. [d. February 20, 1955]

1911 *Peter Graves*, British actor; known for his leading roles in musical comedy films of the 1940s. [d. June 6, 1994]

1912 *Sir Georg Solti*, British conductor, born in Hungary; Music Director, Royal Opera House, Covent Garden, 1961–71; Principal Conductor, London Philharmonic Orchestra and the Chicago Symphony Orchestra. [d. September 5, 1997]

1917 *John Birks (Dizzy) Gillespie*, U.S. jazz musician. [d. January 6, 1993]

1921 *Ursula Kroeber Le Guin*, U.S. author; known for her works of science fiction and fantasy; wrote *Left Hand of Darkness*, 1969, and *Malafrena*, 1979.

1928 *Edward Charles (Whitey) Ford*, U.S. baseball player; pitcher, New York Yankees, 1950–67; ten game World Series winner; elected to the Hall of Fame, 1974.

1943 *Brian Piccolo*, U.S. football player; running back, Chicago Bears, 1965–69; 1973 movie, *Brian's Song* is based on his life. [d. June 16, 1970]

1949 *Benjamin Netanyahu*, Israeli politician; Prime Minister of Israel, 1996– .

1952 *Patti Davis (Patricia Reagan)*, U.S. actress; daughter of Ronald Reagan, 40th U.S. President; wrote *Home Front*, 1986.

1956 *Carrie Frances Fisher*, U.S. actress, author; starred in *Star Wars*, 1977, and *The Empire Strikes Back*, 1980; daughter of Debbie Reynolds and Eddie Fisher.

1971 *Jade Jagger*, daughter of Mick and Bianca Jagger.

HISTORICAL EVENTS

1345 English, under *Earl of Derby*, defeat French at *Auberoche* (Hundred Years' War).

1422 *Charles VI* of France dies and is succeeded by *Charles VII*.

1805 *Lord Horatio Nelson* of Great Britain destroys Franco-Spanish fleet in the *Battle of Trafalgar (Napoleonic Wars)*.

1879 *Thomas Edison* successfully demonstrates for the first time a carbon-filament *incandescent lamp*.

1914 British and Japanese forces take the German *Mariana and Marshall Islands* in the Pacific (*World War I*).

1915 First *transatlantic radio-telephone transmission* is made, from Arlington, Virginia, to Paris.

1918 *Czechoslovakia* declares its independence from Austria-Hungary.

1937 Franco's troops capture *Gijon*, completing the conquest of northwest Spain (*Spanish Civil War*).

1938 Japanese troops take Chinese city of *Canton*, which had been mercilessly bombed for months (*World War II*).

1944 U.S. First Army takes *Aachen*, after eight days of fierce fighting; it is the first large German city to fall to the Allies (*World War II*).

1959 The *Guggenheim Museum of Art*, designed by Frank Lloyd Wright, opens in New York.

1960 Queen Elizabeth II launches Britain's first nuclear submarine, the *Dreadnought*.

1966 A colliery slag heap slips and crushes more than 140 persons and buries a school and several other buildings in *Aberfan, Wales*.

1973 Kuwait, Bahrain, Qatar, and Dubai announce a boycott of oil shipments to the U.S., completing the *Arab oil embargo* begun on October 17.

1976 Americans win all five Nobel prizes for 1976.

Saul Bellow becomes the first American in 24 years to win the Nobel Prize in Literature.

Cincinnati Reds win the World Series against the New York Yankees, becoming the first National League baseball team in 54 years to win two consecutive series.

1979 Israeli Foreign Minister *Moshe Dayan* resigns cabinet post in controversy over Palestinian autonomy.

1981 *Andreas Papandreou* becomes prime minister of Greece.

1993 *Melchior Ndadaye*, president of Burundi, is assassinated.

october

OCTOBER
22

HOLIDAYS

Somali Democratic Republic
Revolution Anniversary
Second day of the celebration.

Vatican City
Anniversary of the Installation of Pope John Paul II.

RELIGIOUS CALENDAR

The Saints
St. Abercius, Bishop of Hieropolis. [d. c. 200]
SS. Philip, Bishop of Heraclea, and his companions, martyrs. [d. 304]
St. Mallonus, Bishop of Rouen. Also called *Melanius, Mello, Mellon.* [d. c. 4th cent.]
SS. Nunilo and Alodia, virgins and martyrs. Nunilo also called *Nunelo.* [d. 851]
St. Donatus, Bishop of Fiesole. [d. c. 876]

BIRTHDATES

1740 *Sir Philip Francis,* British politician; reputed author of *Letters of Junius,* 69 letters attacking prominent British figures of the day. [d. December 23, 1818]

1811 *Franz Liszt,* Hungarian piano virtuoso, composer; known for his advanced musical techniques and methods of composition; in later years, became member of Franciscan order; known as *Abbé Liszt.* [d. July 31, 1886]

1818 *Charles Marie René Leconte de Lisle,* French poet; identified with Parnassian school; wrote poetry of disillusionment and skepticism inspired by the works of the ancients. [d. July 17, 1894]

1844 *Sarah Bernhardt (Henriette Rosine Bernard),* French actress; known as *The Divine Sarah;* renowned for her dramatic portrayals of tragic heroines as well as for her flamboyant lifestyle; continued her stage career in spite of an amputated leg, 1914; named to Legion of Honor, 1914. [d. March 23, 1923]

1881 *Clinton Joseph Davisson,* U.S. physicist; Nobel Prize in physics for discovery of diffraction of electrons by crystals (with G. P. Thomson), 1937. [d. February 1, 1958]

1882 *N(ewell) C(onvers) Wyeth,* U.S. illustrator, artist; known for his popular illustrations of Robert Louis Stevenson's novels and *Robin Hood;* his murals appear in the Missouri State Capitol and the Federal Reserve Bank of Boston. [d. October 19, 1945]

1887 *John Reed,* U.S. poet, radical journalist; as a reporter for *Metropolitan* magazine, was sent to cover several world-famous events, including Pancho Villa's revolutionary activities in Mexico, World War I action on the Eastern Front, and the October Revolution in Russia, 1917, about which he wrote *Ten Days That Shook the World.* Became a close friend of V. I. Lenin. Was named as seditious radical in U.S. and was arrested numerous times; escaped to Finland; died in Russia at age of 33; buried in Kremlin. [d. October 19, 1920]

1900 *Edward Reilly Stettinius, Jr.,* U.S. statesman, industrialist; executive, U.S. Steel Corp., 1935–39; Chairman, War Resources Board, 1939–40; administrator of Lend-Lease, 1941–43; U.S. Secretary of State, 1944–45; Chairman of U.S. delegation to UN, 1945–46. [d. October 31, 1949]

1903 *George Wells Beadle,* U.S. geneticist; Nobel Prize in physiology or medicine for discovery that genes transmit hereditary traits (with E. L. Tatum), 1958. [d. June 8, 1989]

1904 *Constance Bennett,* U.S. actress; a leading lady of 1930s films. [d. July 4, 1965]

1905 *Karl Guthe Janksy,* U.S. radio engineer; his experiments in determining sources of radio waves led to the development of radio astronomy. [d. February 14, 1950]

1917 *Joan Fontaine,* U.S. actress, born in Japan of British parents; sister of Olivia de Haviland (July 1).

1919 *Doris Lessing,* British novelist, short-story writer.

1920 *Timothy Francis Leary,* U.S. psychologist, educator; at the forefront of the drug controversy of the 1960s in the U.S. [d. May 31, 1996]

1925 *Robert Rauschenberg,* U.S. artist; creates collages called combines; works include *Gloria,* 1956, and *Summer Rental,* 1960.

1938 *Derek Jacobi,* British actor; known for his role in the television series, *I, Claudius.*

Christopher Lloyd, U.S. actor; known for *Back to the Future* movies and as Reverend Jim on TV series *Taxi.*

1939 *David Anthony (Tony) Roberts,* U.S. actor; frequently featured in Woody Allen's films; appeared in *Serpico* and *Annie Hall;* Tony Award nominations for *How Now, Dow Jones* and *Play It Again, Sam.*

1942 *Annette Funicello,* U.S. actress, an original Disney Mousketeer in 1950s.

1943 *Catherine Deneuve,* French actress.

1952 *Jeff Goldblum,* U.S. actor; starred in the films, *The Big Chill,* 1983, *The Fly,* 1986, and *Jurassic Park,* 1993.

1955 *Bonnie Marie Anderson,* U.S. broadcast journalist.

1963 *Brian Boitano,* U.S. figure skater.

1966 *Valeria Golino,* Italian actress.

HISTORICAL EVENTS

1721 *Peter I* is proclaimed Emperor of All the Russias.

1797 *André Jacques Garnerin,* French aeronaut and inventor of the *parachute,* makes first parachute jump from a balloon, at height of 2000 feet.

1836 *Sam Houston* takes the oath of office as President of the *Texas Republic.*

1873 New York's *Metropolitan Opera House* opens with a performance of Gounod's *Faust.*

1881 *Boston Symphony Orchestra* is founded with Georg Henschel as its first conductor.

1911 Italy uses *aerial reconnaissance* during its dispute with Turkey in North Africa. This marks the first reported use of an airplane for a reconnaissance mission.

1916 *Constanza,* a Romanian port on the Black Sea, is captured by a German-Bulgarian force under von Mackensen (*World War I*).

1935 Mikhail Sholokhov's opera, *Quiet Flows the Don,* opens in Leningrad.

1938 First true *xerographic* image is produced by New York Law School student *Chester Carlson.*

1952 The complete *Torah* is published in English for the first time.

Great Britain grants a new constitution to the *Sudan,* permitting self-government in internal affairs.

1957 *Francois Duvalier* is inaugurated as president of Haiti.

1962 U.S. establishes naval blockade of *Cuba* to prevent introduction of Soviet nuclear weapons there.

1964 *Jean-Paul Sartre,* French writer and philosopher, rejects the Nobel Prize for literature. [d. April 15, 1980]

1968 *Apollo 7* manned space flight comes to a successful conclusion as astronauts Schirra, Eisele, and Cunningham splash down in the Atlantic.

1979 Iran's deposed Shah, *Reza Pahlavi,* arrives secretly in U.S. for medical treatment.

1986 President Ronald Reagan signs a new tax code into law that radically alters U.S. tax brackets, deductions, and corporate tax shelters.

1995 The *United Nations* celebrates its fiftieth anniversary in New York City.

october

OCTOBER
23

HOLIDAYS

Hungary
Proclamation of the Republic Day
Celebrates the revolt against the communist regime in 1956.

Thailand
Chulalongkorn Day

RELIGIOUS CALENDAR

Feasts
St. James of Jerusalem, Brother of Our Lord Jesus Christ, and martyr. [major holy day, Episcopal Church]

The Saints
St. Theodoret, martyr. [d. 362]

St. Severinus, Bishop of Bordeaux; patron of Bordeaux. Also called *Seurin, Surin.* [d. 420]

St. Severinus Boethius, martyr and philosopher. Also called *Severin.* [d. 524]

St. Romanus, Bishop of Rouen. [d. c. 640]

St. Ignatius, Patriarch of Constantinople. [d. 877]

St. Ethelfleda, Abbess of Romsey. Also called *Elfleda.* [d. c. 960]

St. Allucio, shepherd; patron of Pescia in Tuscany. [d. 1134]

St. John of Capistrano, Franciscan missionary priest. Feast formerly March 28. [d. 1456] Optional Memorial.

St. Antony Claret, Archbishop of Santiago de Cuba. Founder of the Missionary Sons of the Immaculate Heart of Mary,

and confessor to Queen Isabella II. [d. 1870]

The Beatified
Blessed John Buoni, penitent. [d. 1249]

Blessed Bartholomew, Bishop of Vicenza. [d. 1271]

BIRTHDATES

1715 *Peter II,* Emperor of Russia, 1727–30; died at age 14 of smallpox. [d. January 29, 1730]

1734 *Nicolas-Edme Restiff (de la Bretonne),* French novelist; known as the *Rousseau of the Gutter* and the *Voltaire of Chambermaids.* [d. February 3, 1806]

1773 *Francis Jeffrey,* Scottish critic and longtime editor of the *Edinburgh Review.* [d. January 26, 1850]

1817 *Pierre Athanase Larousse,* French lexicographer, encyclopedist; among his most notable accomplishments was the *Grand Dictionnaire Universal du XIX Siècle,* the great dictionary of France. [d. January 3, 1875]

1831 *Basil Lanneau Gildersleeve,* U.S. educator, philologist; recognized as one of the foremost classical scholars of the U.S. in the 19th century. [d. January 9, 1924]

1835 *Adlai E(wing) Stevenson,* U.S. Congressman, 1875–77; 1879–81; Vice-President of U.S., 1893–97; grandfather of Adlai E. Stevenson (February 5). [d. June 14, 1914]

1838 *Francis Hopkinson Smith,* U.S. author; wrote chiefly novels about the American South. [d. April 7, 1915]

1844 *Robert Seymour Bridges,* British poet; known for innovations in English verse, giving more freedom to accentuation and flexibility to rhythm; Poet Laureate, 1913–30. [d. April 21, 1930]

1861 *Marquis M. Converse,* U.S. manufacturer; began making basketball sneakers at the Converse Rubber Shoe Company, 1908. [d. February 9, 1931]

1869 *John William Heisman,* U.S. football player, coach; the Heisman Trophy, college football's award for the best player, is named for him. [d. October 3, 1936]

1873 *William David Coolidge,* U.S. physicist; invented ductile tungsten; developed *Coolidge tube* for production of x rays, 1913. [d. February 3, 1975]

1890 *Robert McGowan,* U.S. Army general, government official; Chief Quartermaster, U.S. forces, 1942–46; as such, was responsible for supplying food, clothing, and fuel for the two million U.S. combat troops during World War II. [d. May 6, 1982]

1899 *Bernt Balchen,* U.S. aviator, born in Norway; pilot of Richard Byrd's flight over the South Pole, November 28, 1929. [d. October 17, 1973]

1905 *Felix Bloch,* U.S. physicist; Nobel Prize in physics for development of nuclear precision measurements of magnetic fields of atomic nuclei (with E.M. Purcell), 1952. [d. September 10, 1983]

1906 *Gertrude Ederle,* U.S. swimmer; first woman to swim the English Channel, 1926.

1908 *Ilya Mikhaylovich Frank,* Russian physicist; Nobel Prize in physics for discovery of Cherenkov effect (with I. Y. Tamm and P. A. Cherenkov), 1958. [d. June 22, 1990]

1920 *Tetsuya Theodore Fujita,* U.S. meteorologist; developed the F Scale used to measure the intensity of tornadoes.

1923 *Ned Rorem,* U.S. composer; Pulitzer Prize in music, 1977.

1925 *Johnny Carson,* U.S. comedian; longtime host of TV's *Tonight Show,* 1962–92.

1931 *Diana Dors (Diana Fluck),* British actress. [d. May 4, 1984]

1932 *Paul Lionel Zimmerman,* U.S. rugby and football player, journalist, author; senior writer, *Sports Illustrated* magazine, 1979–83; author of *A Thinking Man's Guide to Pro Football.*

1934 *Juan (Chi-Chi) Rodriguez,* Puerto Rican golfer.

1938 *(Henry) John Heinz III,* U.S. politician; Senator, 1976–91. [d. April 4, 1991]

1940 *Pelé (Edson Arantes Do Nascimento),* Brazilian soccer player; led Brazilian national team to three World Cup championships, 1958, 1962, 1970.

1942 *(John) Michael Crichton,* U.S. novelist, filmmaker; well-known for his mystery stories, especially related to science and medicine; wrote *Andromeda Strain, Coma, Terminal Man,* and *Jurassic Park.*

1956 *Dwight Yoakam,* U.S. country singer.

1959 *Alfred Matthew (Weird Al) Yankovic,* U.S. singer, comedian; known for his satirical versions of rock hits.

1962 *Doug(las Richard) Flutie,* U.S. football player; Heisman Trophy, 1984.

1966 *Alex Zanardi,* Italian race car driver; *Automobile* magazine's Man of the Year, 1998.

HISTORICAL EVENTS

1385 *University of Heidelberg* is founded by *Pope Urban VI.*

1452 English recapture *Bordeaux* from France (*Hundred Years' War*).

1885 *Bryn Mawr College,* the first U.S. graduate school for women, is opened in Pennsylvania.

1915 First national championship of *horseshoe pitching* is held at Kellerton, Kansas.

1917 In Russia, a Red Guard unit takes control of *Fortress of*

Peter and Paul in Petrograd, beginning the Bolsheviks' *October Revolution.*

The *Battle of Malmaison,* a French offensive on the Western Front, opens against the Germans (*World War I*).

1927 *Trotsky* and *Linoviev* are expelled from the Central Committee of the Russian Communist Party for their opposition to Stalin's policies.

1942 British and German forces clash in North Africa as the *Battle of El Alamein* begins. (*World War II*)

1950 Researchers at the University of Toronto announce the development of an electronic *cardiac pacemaker.*

1952 *Jomo Kenyatta* and suspected Mau Mau terrorists are arrested as British troops crush a nationalist uprising in *Kenya.*

1955 Premier *Ngo Dinh Diem* wins national referendum establishing him as Chief of State of *South Vietnam.*

1956 *Imre Nagy* is reappointed premier of Hungary following several days of anti-Soviet demonstrations.

1962 *Dick Tiger* defeats *Gene Fullmer* to win the world middleweight boxing title.

1972 *Pippin,* by Stephen Schwartz, premieres in New York.

1973 North Vietnamese negotiator Le Duc Tho refuses to accept the Nobel Peace Prize because "peace has not yet really been established in South Vietnam."

1980 *Alexei Kosygin* resigns as Chairman of the U.S.S.R.

october

Council of Ministers and as a member of the Politburo for reasons of health.

1983 A terrorist driving a truck filled with explosives makes a suicide attack on *U.S. Marine Corps* headquarters in Beirut, Lebanon. The resulting explosion kills 239 Marines and destroys the building. A similar attack two miles away destroys a French barracks, killing 58.

1984 A panel convened by Philippine president Ferdinand Marcos, to investigate the murder of opposition leader *Benigno Aquino,* concludes that high-ranking members of the military were involved.

1987 U.S. Senate rejects the Supreme Court nomination of *Robert Bork.*

1989 *Hungary* is declared a free republic by *President Matyas Szuros.*

1992 U.S. President *George Bush* signs the *Cuban Democracy Act* into law, tightening the embargo against Cuba.

1995 *Yolanda Salidivar* is found guilty for the murder of Mexican pop singer Selena (March 31, 1995).

1997 *Paul Biya* is re-elected President of Cameroon.

HOLIDAYS

United Nations Day
Commemorates the effective date of
the UN Charter, 1945.

*World Development Information
Day*
Sponsored by United Nations.

Egypt
*Suez National Day or Popular
Resistance Day*

Venezuela (Maracaibo)
Public Holiday

Zambia
Independence Day
Commemorates gaining of
independence of *Northern Rhodesia*
as Zambia, 1964.

RELIGIOUS CALENDAR

The Saints
St. Martin, hermit. Also called *Mark.*
[d. c. 58]
St. Felix, Bishop of Thibiuca, martyr.
[d. 303]
St. Proclus, Archbishop of
Constantinople. [d. 446]
*St. Aretas and the Martyrs of
Najran,* and *St. Elesbaan.* [d.
523]
St. Senoch, abbot. Also called *Senou.*
[d. 576]
St. Maglorius, Bishop of Dol. Also
called *Maelor, Magloire.* [d.
6th century]
St. Martin of Vertou, abbot. [d. 6th
century]

St. Evergislus, Bishop of Cologne.
Also called *Ebregiselus.* [d. c.
600]

The Beatified
Blessed John Angelo Porro. Patron
of novice masters. [d. 1506]

BIRTHDATES

1618 *Aurangzeb (Aurungzeb,
Aurungzebe),* 6th emperor of
Hindustan; overthrew his
father, 1658; last of the great
Mughal emperors; conquered
Muhammadan kingdoms;
alienated both Muhammadans
and Hindus with his bigotry.
[d. March 3, 1707]

1632 *Anton van Leeuwenhoek,*
Dutch biologist; pioneer in
development of the
microscope, with which he
made discoveries about the
blood, muscle fibers, lens of
the human eye, and
numerous characteristics of
plants. [d. August 26, 1723]

1710 *Alban Butler,* English
hagiographer, professor;
compiler of *Lives of the
Principal Saints,* which
remains a classic source
today. [d. May 15, 1773]

1788 *Sarah Josepha Buell Hale,*
U.S. editor, writer, and
feminist; editor of *Godey's
Lady's Book,* most influential
women's magazine in America

of that time; advocate of
women's education. [d. April
30, 1879]

1830 *Belva Anna Bennett
Lockwood,* U.S. lawyer,
suffragist, and reformer; the
first woman to argue before
the U.S. Supreme Court. [d.
May 19, 1917]

1855 *James Schoolcraft Sherman,*
U.S. Vice-President, 1909-12.
[d. October 30, 1912]

1882 *Dame Sybil Thorndike,*
English actress; manager of
numerous London theaters;
created a Dame of the British
Empire, 1931. [d. June 9,
1976]

1889 *Arde Bulova,* U.S.
manufacturer; founder of
Bulova Watch Company. [d.
March 19, 1958]

1891 *Rafael Leonidas Trujillo
(Molina),* Dominican
politician; President, 1930–38,
1942–52; dominated national
politics until his assassination.
[d. May 30, 1961]

1904 *Moss Hart,* U.S. playwright;
collaborated with George S.
Kaufman (November 16), Ira
Gershwin (September 26),
and Kurt Weill (March 2);
Awarded the Pulitzer Prize in
drama, 1937. [d. December
20, 1961]

1911 *Clarence M. Kelley,* U.S.
government official; FBI

Director, 1973–78. [d. August 5, 1997]

1923 *Denise Levertov,* U.S. poet; Bess Hokins Prize, 1959; Morton Dauwen Zabel Memorial Prize, 1965. [d. December 20, 1997]

1930 *The Big Bopper (J.P. Richardson),* U.S. radio performer, singer; known for his song, *Chantilly Lace,* 1958; killed with Buddy Holly and Ritchie Valens in a plane crash. [d. February 3, 1959]

1932 *Pierre-Gilles de Gennes,* French physicist; Nobel Prize for Physics, 1991.

1940 *F. Murray Abraham,* U.S. actor; Academy Award for *Amadeus,* 1983.

1941 *William George (Bill) Wyman,* British musician; bass guitarist for the rock group, *The Rolling Stones.*

1942 *Michael Crichton,* U.S. writer and producer.

1947 *Kevin Kline,* US. actor; Tony Awards for *On the Twentieth Century,* 1978, *The Pirates of Penzance,* 1981; Academy Award for *A Fish Called Wanda,* 1989.

1948 *Kweisi Mfume,* U.S. politician; president, National Association for the Advancement of Colored People (NAACP), 1996– .

HISTORICAL EVENTS

1260 *Chartres Cathedral* in France is consecrated.

1360 Final *Peace of Calais* is signed, allowing *Edward III* of England to keep Calais, Angoulême, Channel Islands, and other formerly-French territories *(Hundred Years' War).*

1604 *James I* is declared King of Great Britain, France, and Ireland.

1648 *Peace of Westphalia* is signed, ending *Thirty Years' War* and guaranteeing independence of Switzerland, Netherlands, and all German states.

1795 *Poland* ceases to exist as an independent state when Russia, Prussia, and Austria divide remaining Polish territory in the *Third Partition of Poland.*

1820 *Spain* cedes *Florida* to U.S.

1901 *Eastman Kodak Co.* is incorporated in New Jersey.

1910 *Naughty Marietta,* a light opera by Victor Herbert, premieres in Syracuse, New York.

1911 *Winston Churchill* is appointed First Lord of Admiralty.

1917 *Battle of Caporetto* in Italy ends in defeat of the Italians by the Austrian and German armies *(World War I).*

1922 *Irish Free State* constitution is adopted; the Irish Free State is officially proclaimed on December 6, 1922.

1929 *Black Thursday* at the New York Stock Exchange, so named because of panic selling that resulted from downward trend in the market during previous several weeks, marks the beginning of the collapse of the stock market on October 29.

1933 Work begins on the *Ft. Peck Dam* on the Missouri River in Montana, the biggest earth-filled hydroelectric dam in the world at that time.

1944 During *Battle of Leyte Gulf,* U.S. planes sink Japanese battleship *Musashi,* one of the largest ships sunk during *World War II.*

1964 *Republic of Zambia* gains independence from Great Britain.

1976 A Justice Department investigation of South Korean bribes to U.S. legislators is made public *(Koreagate Scandal).*

1989 Television evangelist *Jim Bakker* is sentenced to 45 years in prison for his fraud conviction (October 5, 1989).

1990 Secretary of Labor *Elizabeth Dole* resigns.

HOLIDAYS

Kazakstan
Independence Day

Taiwan
Taiwan Restoration Day or Retrocession Day
Commemorates the return of Taiwan to the possession of China after 50 years of occupation by the Japanese, 1945.

RELIGIOUS CALENDAR

The Saints
St. Gaudentius, Bishop of Brescia. [d. c. 410]

SS. Chrysanthus and Daria, martyrs. [death date unknown]

SS. Crispin and Crispinian, martyrs; patron saints of shoemakers, cobblers, and other workers in leather. [death date unknown]

SS. Fronto and George, bishops. [death date unknown]

The Beatified
Blessed Christopher of Romagnola, Friar Minor. [d. 1272]

Blessed Thomas of Florence, lay brother. [d. 1447]

Blessed Balthasar of Chiavari, Friar Minor. Patron of playing card makers. Invoked against epilepsy. [d. 1492]

Blessed Thaddeus, Bishop of Cork and Cloyne. [d. 1497]

The Martyrs of England and Wales, a festival of all 200 beatified English and Welsh martyrs, 1535–1681; includes *London Martyrs of 1588.*

Blessed Narcisa Martillo Moran. [beatified 1992]

BIRTHDATES

1759 *William Wyndham Grenville, Baron Grenville,* English politician; Foreign Secretary, 1791–1801; frequently associated with coalition government called the *All-the-Talents Administration,* 1806–07, which abolished the *English slave trade.* [d. January 12, 1834]

1767 *Henri Benjamin Constant de Rebecque,* French novelist, statesman; protégé of Madame de Staël; member of French Chamber of Deputies, 1819–30. [d. December 8, 1830]

1789 *Heinrich Samuel Schwabe,* German astronomer; discovered 11-year cycle of *sunspots,* 1843. [d. April 11, 1875]

1800 *Thomas Babington Macaulay,* British historian, statesman; member of Parliament, 1830–34; 1839–47; 1852–56; author of *History of England,* five volumes covering period 1848–61; noted for his numerous essays on Milton and others, as well as biographical sketches, speeches, etc. [d. December 28, 1859]

1811 *Evariste Galois,* French mathematician; a founder of *theory of groups* and modern *theory of functions.* [d. May 31, 1832]

1825 *Johann Strauss, (the Younger),* Austrian composer, known as the *Waltz King;* succeeded his father, Johann Strauss, as leader of orchestra of Vienna; toured widely before 1863; thereafter, devoted himself to composition; wrote *Die Fledermaus, The Blue Danube.* [d. June 3, 1899]

1838 *Georges (Aléxandre César Léopold) Bizet,* French composer; composed *Carmen, Jeux d'enfants.* [d. June 3, 1875]

1848 *William Henry Moore,* U.S. financier; founder of National Biscuit Co., 1898; American Can Co., 1901; and Rock Island Railroad Co., 1901. [d. January 11, 1923]

1864 *John Francis Dodge,* U.S. manufacturer; with his brother, Horace (May 17), founded the Dodge Automobile Co., 1901. [d. January 14, 1920]

1877 *Henry Norris Russell,* U.S. astronomer; developer of the method of determining stellar

october

types; with Ejnar Hertzsprung, after 1910, developed the *Hertzsprung-Russell Diagram* for illustrating relationship of spectral class and absolute magnitude of stars. [d. February 18, 1957]

1881 *Pablo Picasso,* Spanish painter, sculptor; one of foremost figures in modern art. [d. April 8, 1973]

1888 *Richard Evelyn Byrd,* U.S. admiral, aviator, explorer, author; made first flight over North Pole, 1926, and over South Pole, 1929; later conducted scientific expeditions to the South Pole. [d. March 11, 1957]

1890 *Floyd Bennett,* U.S. aviator; with Admiral Richard Byrd was the first to fly over the North Pole, 1926. [d. April 25, 1928]

1891 *Charles Edward Coughlin,* U.S. Roman Catholic priest, political activist; known for his opposition to the policies of the Roosevelt administration, expressing his reactionary and anti-Semitic views in the magazine *Social Justice* and on radio. [d. October 27, 1979]

1892 *Leo G. Carroll,* British character actor. [d. October 16, 1972]

Dolly Sisters (Rosie and Jenny), twins; a popular vaudeville dance act. [Rosie d. February 1, 1970; Jenny committed suicide June 1, 1941]

1902 *Henry Steele Commager,* U.S. historian; major interpreter of American history and development; author of *The American Mind, Documents of American History.* [d. March 2, 1998]

1912 *Minnie Pearl (Sarah Ophelia Colley Cannon),* U.S. country singer, comedienne. [d. March 5, 1996]

1914 *John Berryman,* U.S. poet; Pulitzer Prize in poetry, 1965, for *Dream Songs.* [committed suicide January 7, 1972]

1917 *Leland Stanford (Lee) MacPhail, Jr.,* U.S. baseball executive; President, American League.

1926 *Galina (Pavlovna) Vishnevskaya,* Russian-born opera singer; first Russian diva to sing with the Metropolitan Opera, 1961 U.S. tour; defected to the U.S., 1974; wrote best-selling memoirs, *Galina,* 1984; married to Mstislav Rostropovich (August 12).

1928 *Anthony Franciosa (Anthony Papaleo),* U.S. actor; starred in the television series, *Name of the Game* and *Matt Helm.*

1930 *Hanna Holborn Gray,* U.S. educator, born in Germany; acting president, Yale University, 1977–78; President, University of Chicago, 1978–93.

1940 *Robert Montgomery (Bobby) Knight,* U.S. basketball coach; head coach, Indiana University, 1971–; known for his tempermental outbursts.

1941 *Helen Reddy,* Australian singer.

Anne Tyler, U.S. author; Pulitzer Prize for *Breathing Lessons,* 1989.

1944 *James Carville,* U.S. political strategist; served as Bill Clinton's political strategist during his 1991 presidential campaign.

1950 *John Matuszak,* U.S. football player, actor. [d. June 17, 1989]

1966 *Wendel Clark,* Canadian hockey player; defenseman, Toronto Maple Leafs; first overall pick in the 1985 draft.

HISTORICAL EVENTS

732 *Charles Martel* defeats the Arabs at Poitiers, marking the total overthrow of Muslims in France.

1154 *King Stephen* of England dies and is succeeded by *Henry II,* establishing the house of *Plantagenet,* who rule England until 1399.

1415 *Henry V* of England defeats French at *Agincourt (Hundred Years' War).*

1555 *Charles V,* Holy Roman Emperor, resigns Italy and the Netherlands to his son, *Philip II* of Spain, in ceremonies at the Hall of the Golden Fleece in the Netherlands.

1760 *George II* of Great Britain dies and is succeeded by *George III,* his grandson.

1812 *Stephen Decatur,* in the *U.S.S. United States,* captures the *H.M.S. Macedonian (War of 1812).*

1854 *Battle of Balaclava* (in which the *Charge of the Light Brigade* occurs) between the Russians and Great Britain and her Turkish allies, begins (*Crimean War.*).

1874 Great Britain annexes *Fiji Islands.*

1900 The British formally annex the *South African Boer Republic* during the course of the Boer War and rename it *Transvaal Colony.*

1918 *Battle of Vittorio Veneto,* the final Italian offensive against the Austrians, opens between the Brenta and Piave Rivers (*World War I*).

1920 *Terence MacSweney,* Lord Mayor of Cork, dies on 74th day of hunger strike in Brixton jail, Cork.

1938 *Mussolini* declares *Libya* a part of Italy. Chinese city of *Hankow* falls to Japanese.

1944 *Battle of Leyte Gulf* (last and greatest naval engagement of World War II) ends in decisive defeat for Japanese.

1950 Chinese Communist forces invade *Tibet.*

1955 *Austria* becomes free and independent for the first time since 1938 as the *Austrian State Treaty* ends the Soviet-administered four power (Potsdam) occupation.

1961 *Outer Mongolia* and *Mauritania* are admitted to *United Nations.*

1962 *Uganda* becomes a member of the *United Nations.*

1971 UN General Assembly approves admission of *People's Republic of China* to the UN and expels *Nationalist China (Taiwan).*

1976 The *National Theatre* complex in London officially opens.

1983 An assault force led by U.S. Marines and Army Rangers invades the Caribbean island of *Grenada.*

1985 *Lazarus Salii* is inaugurated as president of the Pacific island republic of Palau.

1990 *Evander Holyfield* defeats James "Buster" Douglas to win the world heavyweight boxing title.

1995 *John J. Sweeney* is elected new president of the national labor federation AFL-CIO.

1997 The *Million Woman March* takes place in Philadelphia, Pennsylvania.

Denis Sassou-Nguesso becomes the President of the Congo Republic.

october

OCTOBER
26

HOLIDAYS

Austria
National Holiday

Benin, Rwanda
Armed Forces Day

Greece (Thessaloniki)
St. Dimitrios Day

RELIGIOUS CALENDAR

The Saints
St. Evaristus, pope and martyr. Elected 97 or 99. [d. c. 107]

SS. Lucian and Marcian, martyrs. [d. c. 250]

St. Rusticus, Bishop of Narbonne. Also called *Rotiri.* [d. c. 461]

St. Cedd, Bishop of the East Saxons. [d. 664]

St. Eata, Bishop of Hexham. [d. 686]

St. Bean, Bishop of Mortlach. [d. 11th century]

The Beatified
Blessed Damian of Finario, Dominican priest. [d. 1484]

Blessed Bonaventure of Potenza, Conventual Friar Minor. [d. 1711]

BIRTHDATES

1466 *Desiderius Erasmus,* Dutch scholar; regarded as the leader of the Renaissance in northern Europe. [d. July 12, 1536]

1673 *Dimitrie Kantemir (Cantemir),* Hospodar of Moldavia, historian and writer; author of *History of the Growth and Decay of the Ottoman Empire.* [d. August 21, 1723]

1685 *(Giuseppe) Domenico Scarlatti,* Italian composer; especially noted for harpsichord music. [d. July 23, 1757]

1757 *Charles Pinckney,* U.S. politician, diplomat; one of most important contributors to U.S. constitution; creator of the *Pinckney Draught;* Governor of South Carolina, 1790–96; U.S. Senator, 1798–1801; U.S. Minister to Spain, 1801–04. [d. October 29, 1824]

1759 *Georges Jacques Danton,* French revolutionary leader; a founder of the *Cordelier;* overthrown by *Robespierre* and leaders of the *Reign of Terror;* condemned and guillotined. [d. April 5, 1794]

1786 *Henry Deringer,* U.S. firearms inventor, manufacturer; invented the short-barreled pocket pistol called the *derringer.* [d. 1868]

1787 *Vuk Stefanović Karadžić,* Serbian lexicographer, folklorist; credited with simplifying Cyrillic alphabet used in Serbia; expert on Serbian grammar; published anthology of Serbian folk songs. [d. January 26, 1864]

1800 *Count Helmuth von Moltke,* Prussian soldier, field marshal; Chief of Staff of Prussian Army, 1858–88. [d. April 24, 1891]

1802 *Dom Miguel,* King of Portugal, 1828–33. [d. November 14, 1866]

1854 *Charles William Post,* U.S. breakfast food manufacturer; founder of C. W. Post Co., 1894. [d. May 9, 1914]

1858 *Take Ionescu,* Romanian politician, writer, and orator; Prime Minister of Romania, 1921–22. [d. June 21, 1922]

1876 *H(erbert) B(ryan) Warner,* British actor. [d. December 24, 1958]

1879 *Leon Trotsky,* Russian Communist leader; People's Commissar for Foreign Affairs, 1917; Commissar of War, 1918; close associate of Lenin; exiled after defeat by Stalin in conflict for control of Party, 1929; murdered in Mexico. [d. August 21, 1940]

1889 *Millar Burrows,* U.S. clergyman; authority on Dead Sea Scrolls. [d. April 29, 1980]

1894 *John S(hively) Knight,* U.S. newspaper publisher; founder of Knight-Ridder Newspapers, Inc.; Pulitzer Prize in editorial writing, 1968. [d. June 16, 1981]

1902 *Beryl Markham,* British-born aviatrix; first woman to fly solo across the Atlantic from east to west; wrote autobiography, *West With the Night,* 1942. [d. August 3, 1986]

1909 *Igor Gorin,* U.S. operatic baritone, composer, born in Russia; well known for his showmanship as well as his musicianship. [d. March 24, 1982]

1912 *Don Siegel,* U.S. director; known for Invasion of the *Body Snatchers,* 1955 and *Dirty Harry,* 1971.

1914 *Jackie Coogan (John Leslie),* U.S. actor. [d. March 1, 1984]

1916 *François Mitterand,* French statesman; President, 1981–95. [d. January 9, 1996]

1917 *Mario Biaggi,* U.S. politician; Congressman, 1969–89; secured major federal loans to restore New York City to fiscal health, 1978; convicted of crimes in the Wedtech scandal, 1988.

1919 *Shah Mohammed Reza Pahlavi,* Shah of Iran, 1941–79; forced into exile by fundamentalist Shi'ite Moslems led by Ayatollah Khomeini, 1979. [d. July 27, 1980]

Edward W. Brooke, U.S. Senator, 1966–80; first black senator to be elected since 1876.

1938 *Ralph Bakshi,* U.S. cartoonist; produced and directed animated version of J.R.R. Tolkien's *Lord of the Rings,* 1978.

1942 *Bob Hoskins,* British actor; Cannes Film Festival Best Actor Award for *Mona Lisa,* 1986.

1947 *Hillary Rodham Clinton,* U.S. lawyer; wife of President Bill Clinton.

1948 *Jaclyn Smith,* U.S. actress; starred in the television series, *Charlie's Angels,* 1976–80.

1951 *Julian Schnabel,* U.S. painter, director.

1962 *Cary Elwes,* British actor.

Dylan McDermott, U.S. actor; known for roles in *Steel Magnolias, In the line of Fire,* and *Miracle on 34th Street.*

1963 *Natalie Merchant,* U.S. singer; member of the group 10,000 Maniacs, 1981–93.

HISTORICAL EVENTS

1825 *Erie Canal* is opened in New York State.

1856 First Portuguese railway is opened.

1863 *International Committee of the Red Cross* is established at a meeting of nations in Geneva, Switzerland.

1881 U.S. law officer, *Wyatt Earp,* and his brothers, kill the *Clanton Gang* and *McLowery Brothers* at *O.K. Corral* in Tombstone, Arizona.

1896 *Treaty of Addis Ababa* is signed, establishing peace between Italy and Abyssinia (Ethiopia), and recognizing the independence of *Abyssinia.*

1905 Russian workers in St. Petersburg establish first *soviet* (assembly).

A treaty of separation, nullifying the 91-year-old *Union of Sweden and Norway,* is signed.

1951 *Winston Churchill* is appointed Prime Minister of Great Britain, for the second time, by King George VI.

1954 The city of *Trieste* is placed under Italian control following Marshal Tito's renunciation of a Yugoslav claim to the area.

1955 The film, *Rebel Without a Cause,* premieres in New York.

Republic of South Vietnam is established. *Ngo Dinh Diem* proclaims himself President under a provisional constitutional act.

1967 First unmanned docking in space is accomplished between two Russian *Cosmos* satellites.

1973 Widespread violence in *Northern Ireland* includes at least 17 bomb explosions and more than 50 bomb scares.

1976 The first of South Africa's black homelands, the *Republic of Transkei,* is given its independence.

1979 South Korean President *Park Chung Hee* is assassinated by *Kim Jae Kyu,* head of Korean Central Intelligence.

1983 The U.S. Senate rejects an appropriations amendment for the *Clinch River Breeder Reactor* in Tennessee. The measure ends construction of the nuclear power plant, which critics had contended was environmentally unsafe, poorly managed, and a probable target for terrorists seeking the plutonium to be produced there.

1984 Doctors at Loma Linda University Hospital transplant

october

a *baboon heart* into a 12-day-old baby girl. "Baby Fae" dies 15 days later.

1990 *African American Marketing & Media Association* is founded.

1994 *Israel* and *Jordan* agree to a peace treaty in the area between Eilat and Aqaba.

HOLIDAYS

Democratic Republic of the Congo
Anniversary of Zaire

St. Vincent
Thanksgiving and Independence Day
Commemorates achievement of independence from Great Britain, 1979.

Turkmenistan
Independence Day

U.S.
Good Bears of the World Day

RELIGIOUS CALENDAR

The Saints
St. Frumentius, Bishop of Aksum. Apostle of Ethiopia. [d. c. 380]
St. Otteran, abbot. Also called *Odhran, Odhuran.* [d. 563]

The Beatified
Blessed Contardo Ferrini, scholar. [d. 1902]
Blessed Adolph Kolping. [beatified 1991]

BIRTHDATES

1728 *James Cook,* British navigator; known for his exploration of the South Pacific, especially *Australia, New Zealand,* and the *Hawaiian Islands.* [d. February 14, 1779]

1736 *James Macpherson,* Scottish poet, historian; claimed to have discovered Gaelic epic *Fingal,* which he translated and published; his discovery was disputed by Dr. Johnson and never rebutted by Macpherson; member of Parliament, 1780–96. [d. February 17, 1796]

1760 *August Wilhelm, Count Neithardt von Gneisenau,* Prussian field marshal; noted for his participation in campaigns against Napoleon. [d. August 24, 1831]

1782 *Niccolo Paganini,* Italian composer, violin virtuoso. [d. May 27, 1840]

1811 *Isaac M. Singer,* U.S. inventor; invented the first practical domestic *sewing machine,* 1851. [d. July 23, 1875]

1827 *Marcelin Berthelot,* French chemist; noted for contributions to the field of thermochemistry and his investigations into explosives, dyestuffs, and synthesis of organic compounds. [d. March 18, 1907]

1838 *John Davis Long,* U.S. lawyer, statesman, and author; Governor of Massachusetts, 1880–82; Congressman, 1883–89; U.S. Secretary of the Navy, 1897–1902. [d. August 28, 1915]

1842 *Giovanni Giolitti,* Italian politician; Prime Minister of Italy 1892–93; 1903–05; 1906–09; 1911–14; 1920–21. [d. July 17, 1928]

1844 *Klas P. Arnoldson,* Swedish writer, politician; Nobel Peace Prize for his work in solving problems of the Norwegian-Swedish Union, 1908. [d. February 20, 1916]

1856 *Kenyon Cox,* U.S. mural and figure painter, conservative art critic. [d. March 17, 1919]

1858 *Theodore Roosevelt,* U.S. politician, Vice-President, 1901; 26th President of the U.S., 1901–09; as commander of the First U.S. Volunteers Cavalry (the *Rough Riders*) in Cuba, became national hero; as President, pursued antitrust legislation; awarded Nobel Peace Prize for negotiating end of Russo-Japanese War, 1905. [d. January 6, 1919]

1870 *Roscoe Pound,* U.S. educator; Dean, Harvard Law School, 1916–37; wrote on legal philosophy and practice. [d. July 1, 1964]

1872 *Emily Post,* U.S. journalist; wrote a definitive book of *etiquette* and a syndicated column on that subject. [d. September 25, 1960]

1889 *Enid Bagnold (Lady Roderick Jones),* British novelist,

october

playwright; best known for her novel *National Velvet.* [d. March 31, 1981]

1910 *Jack Carson,* U.S. actor; teamed with Dennis Morgan in a series of 1940's musicals. [d. January 2, 1963]

1911 *Leif Erickson,* U.S. singer, actor; known for his role as Big Jon Cannon on the television series, *The High Chaparral.* [d. January 30, 1986]

1914 *Dylan (Marlais) Thomas,* Welsh poet, author; known for his innovative poetic style based on rhythm and sound; author of *A Child's Christmas in Wales* and *Under Milk Wood.* [d. November 9, 1953]

1918 *Teresa Wright,* U.S. actress; Academy Award for *Mrs. Miniver,* 1941; nominated in the same year for *Pride of the Yankees.*

1920 *Nanette Fabray (Ruby Nanette Fabares),* U.S. actress; Tony Award for *Love Life,* 1949; appeared in the television series, *One Day at a Time.*

1922 *Carlos Andres Perez,* Venezuelan politician; President of Venezuela, 1974–79, 1989–93.

1923 *Roy Lichtenstein,* U.S. painter, a leader in the *pop art* movement. [d. September 29, 1997]

1924 *Ruby Dee (Ruby Ann Wallace),* U.S. actress; starred in the stage and screen productions of *Raisin in the Sun;* married to Ozzie Davis.

1925 *Warren Christopher,* U.S. lawyer, politician; U.S. Secretary of State, 1993– .

1926 *H(arry) R. Haldeman,* U.S. government official, advertising executive; Chief of Staff of U.S. President Nixon's presidential campaign; convicted of wrongdoing in *Watergate incident.* [d. November 12, 1993]

1927 *Lee Grant,* U.S. actress.

1932 *Sylvia Plath,* U.S. poet; became famous posthumously for her volume of poetry, *Ariel,* which was written shortly before her suicide but not published until 1968; author of *The Bell Jar.* [d. February 11, 1963]

1939 *Russell Chatham,* U.S. artist; known for his western landscape paintings.

John Cleese, British actor, writer, director; created the comedy team, *Monty Python's Flying Circus,* 1969; directed and starred in *A Fish Called Wanda.*

1940 *Maxine Hong Kingston,* U.S. author; National Book Critics Circle General Nonfiction Award for *The Woman Warrior,* 1976; American Book Award for *China Men,* 1981.

1942 *Lee Greenwood,* U.S. singer, songwriter; sang the country-western single, *IOU,* 1983.

1946 *Ivan Reitman,* Czechoslovakian director.

Carrie Snodgress, U.S. actress; Academy Award nominee for *Diary of a Mad Housewife,* 1970.

1950 *Fran(ces Ann) Lebowitz,* U.S. author, columnist; noted for satirical essays on urban life; wrote *Social Studies,* 1981.

1958 *Simon Le Bon,* British singer; lead vocalist with the rock

group, *Duran Duran;* considered a teen idol.

HISTORICAL EVENTS

1553 *Michael Servetus,* Spanish physician, theologian, and anti-Trinitarian, is convicted of heresy and blasphemy and burned at the stake at Geneva.

1659 Massachusetts, having outlawed *Quakers,* hangs two who defiantly return to the colony.

1662 *Charles II* of England sells *Dunkirk* to France.

1795 *Treaty of San Lorenzo,* or *Pinckney's Treaty,* is signed between the U.S. and Spain, establishing southern boundary of U.S. at 31st parallel and giving Americans right to navigate the Mississippi.

1807 *Treaty of Fontainebleau,* whereby Napoleon would help Spain conquer Portugal, is signed between Spain and France.

1871 Great Britain annexes diamond fields of *Kimberley* in South Africa.

1904 New York City opens the first section of a *subway system.*

1905 *King Oscar II* of Sweden announces his renunciation of the Norwegian throne and his recognition of *Norway* as an independent and separate nation.

1914 The Belgians open the flood gates at *Nieuport,* allowing sea water to flood their front, thereby halting the German advance (*World War I*).

British superdreadnought *Audacious* is sunk by a

German mine off the north coast of Ireland (*World War I*).

1916 Earliest mention of jazz bands in print occurs in *Variety* (spelled *jass*).

1918 *General Ludendorff,* mastermind of the German offensives on the Western Front during 1918, resigns his command.

1936 *Adolf Hitler* and *Benito Mussolini* form an alliance known as the *Rome-Berlin Axis.*

1952 *Jigme Dorji Wangchuk* becomes king of Bhutan.

1954 *Disneyland* makes its television debut.

1956 *Suleiman Nabulski* becomes premier of Jordan.

1958 Pakistani president *Iskander Mirza* resigns in favor of *Mohammed Ayub Khan.*

1961 U.S. and Soviet tanks confront each other at the crossing point between East and West Berlin as U.S. insists on free entry to *East Berlin* by U.S. citizens.

The *Mongolian People's Republic* is admitted to the United Nations.

1963 Dr. *Michael DeBakey* of Baylor University Medical School announces the first successful use of an implanted *heart-pumping device.* His patient was kept alive for four days.

1971 *Congo* government announces change of the name of the country to *Republic of Zaire.*

1972 Major *Mathieu Kerekou* assumes power in Dahomey after a bloodless coup d'etat.

1979 *St. Vincent and the Grenadines* gain independence from Great Britain.

1987 South Korean voters ratify a new constitution that provides for presidential elections and specifies that the military remain politically neutral.

october

OCTOBER
28

HOLIDAYS

Cyprus, Greece
Greek National Day or Ochi Day
Commemorates Greek defiance of
Italy's 1940 ultimatum.

RELIGIOUS CALENDAR

Feasts
SS. Simon and Jude, apostles.
Simon, patron of curriers;
Jude, patron of the
impossible. Jude also called
*Judas, Lebbaeus, Lebbeaus,
Libbius, Thaddeus.* Simon
also called the *Cananaean,*
the *Zealot.* [d. 1st century]
[major holy day, Episcopal
Church; minor festival,
Lutheran Church]

The Saints
St. Fidelis of Como, martyr. [d. c.
303]
St. Salvius, hermit. Also called *Saire.*
[d. c. 6th cent.]
St. Faro, Bishop of Meaux. [d. c.
672]
SS. Anastasia and Cyril, martyrs.
[death date unknown]

BIRTHDATES

1017 *Henry III (the Black),* Holy
Roman Emperor 1039–56;
deposed three rival popes,
appointing *Clement II;* a
patron of learning. [d.
October 5, 1056]

1585 *Cornelis Jansen,* Dutch
theologian; Bishop of Ypres
and founder of the
theological system called
Jansenism. [d. May 6, 1638]

1846 *Georges Auguste Escoffier,*
French chef. [d. February 12,
1935]

1847 *J(ames) Walter Thompson,*
U.S. advertising executive;
responsible for raising the
level of respectability of
advertising in the eyes of the
public. [d. October 16, 1928]

1866 *Philip Jaisohn (So Jae-P'il),*
U.S. physician; active in the
Korean independence
movement. [d. 1951]

1885 *Per Albin Hansson,* Swedish
statesman; Premier, 1932–46.
[d. October 5, 1946]

1891 *Hans Driesch,* German
embryologist; conducted early
investigations of development
of cells. [d. April 16, 1941]

1896 *Howard Harold Hanson,* U.S.
composer, conductor; Pulitzer
Prize in music, 1944. [d.
February 26, 1981]

1902 *Elsa Lanchester (Elizabeth
Sullivan),* British character
actress. [d. December 26,
1986]

1907 *Edith Head,* U.S. fashion
designer; noted in the film
industry since the 1930s. [d.
October 24, 1981]

1909 *Francis Bacon,* British
painter; noted for
expressionistic style,
especially in portraits marked
by terror.

1914 *Jonas Edward Salk,* U.S.
microbiologist; developed the
first *polio vaccine,* 1953. [d.
June 23, 1995]

*Richard Laurence Millington
Synge,* British biochemist;
Nobel Prize in chemistry for
development of method for
separating and identifying
chemical substances (with A.
J. P. Martin), 1952. [d. August
18, 1994]

1915 *Jack Soo (Goro Suzuki),* U.S.
actor; known for his role as
Yemana on the television
series, *Barney Miller,*
1975–79. [d. January 11, 1979]

1926 *Bowie Kuhn,* U.S. sports
executive; U.S. Commissioner
of Baseball, 1969–1984.

1927 *Cleo Laine (Clementina
Dinah Campbell),* British
singer, actress; only artist to
be nominated in the Female
Popular, Jazz, and Classical
categories for Grammy
Awards; appeared in the
Broadway musical, *The
Mystery of Edwin Drood,*
1985.

1929 *Dody Goodman,* U.S. actress,
dancer; appeared in the
television series, *Mary
Hartman, Mary Hartman.*

Joan (Anne) Plowright, British actress; wife of Sir Laurence Olivier (May 22).

1932 Spyros Kyprianou, President, Republic of Cyprus, 1977–88.

1933 Suzy Parker (Cecilia Parker), U.S. model; defined the look of the 1950s.

1936 Charlie Daniels, U.S. musician, songwriter; founded The Charlie Daniels Band, 1973; Grammy Award, Devil Went Down to Georgia, 1979; frequently uses a country fiddle in his music.

1937 Lenny (Leonard Randolph) Wilkens, U.S. basketball coach; head coach of the Atlanta Hawks, 1993– .

1939 Jane Alexander (Jane Quigley), U.S. actress; Tony Award for Great White Hope, 1969; appeared in the films, Kramer vs. Kramer and Testament.

1944 Dennis Franz, U.S. actor; known for his role as Andy Sipowicz on the TV drama NYPD Blue.

1948 Telma Louise Hopkins, U.S. singer, actress; member of the former pop group, Tony Orlando and Dawn; appeared in the television series, Gimme a Break.

1949 Bruce Jenner, U.S. athlete, sportscaster; Olympic decathlon winner, 1976.

1952 Annie Potts, U.S. actress; played Mary Jo Shively on the TV sitcom Designing Women, 1986–93.

Marianna Alexsavena Tcherkassky, U.S. ballerina; principal dancer, American Ballet Theatre, 1976–; known for her purity of style.

1955 William (Bill) Henry Gates III, U.S. businessman; cofounder of Microsoft Corporation.

1963 Daphne Zuniga, U.S. actress; featured on the TV drama Melrose Place.

1966 Lauren Holly, U.S. actress; played Maxine Stewart on TV series Picket Fences.

1967 Julia Roberts, U.S. actress.

1972 Terrell Davis, U.S. football player; MVP of Super Bowl XXXII, 1998.

HISTORICAL EVENTS

1492 Christopher Columbus discovers Cuba and claims it for Spain.

1497 John II of Denmark defeats Swedes at Brunkeberg and revives Scandinavian Union.

1628 Siege of La Rochelle ends with Huguenot capitulation after 14 months' resistance.

1636 Harvard College is founded with the Rev. Henry Dunster as its first president; the College receives its official name on March 13, 1639.

1871 Meeting of David Livingstone and H. M. Stanley, British explorers, takes place in Ujiji, Africa.

1886 Statue of Liberty is dedicated by U.S. President Grover Cleveland.

1891 An earthquake in Japan kills 10,000 and leaves 300,000 homeless.

1918 Czechoslovakia proclaims itself a republic; Thomas G. Masaryk is elected first president.

The Italian offensive at Vittorio Veneto drives Austrians back (World War I).

1922 Benito Mussolini and his Fascist followers make their march on Rome, taking control of Italy.

1924 France officially recognizes the government of the U.S.S.R.

1950 Erik Eriksen becomes prime minister of Denmark.

The Jack Benny Show makes its television debut.

1954 Ernest Hemingway receives the Nobel Prize for literature.

1958 Angelo Giuseppe Cardinal Roncalli is elected pope of the Roman Catholic Church and takes the name John XXIII.

Truman Capote's novel, Breakfast at Tiffany's, is published.

1962 Soviet premier, Nikita Khruschshev, orders the removal of Soviet missiles from Cuba, one week after the U.S. imposed a naval blockade of the island.

1973 UN issues a report stating that a drought in Ethiopia has killed nearly 100,000 people.

1975 Violence in Beirut, Lebanon, intensifies, leaving the city in shambles; large foreign corporations relocate.

1981 West Germany and East Germany complete exchanges of convicted spies.

1997 The National Basketball Association (NBA) allows women to referee games when Dee Kantner and Violet Palmer are hired.

october

OCTOBER
29

HOLIDAYS

Cyprus, Turkey
Turkish National Day or Republic Day
Commemorates proclamation of Turkish Republic, 1923.

Liberia
National Youth Day

U.S.S.R
Komsomal Foundation Day,
marks foundation of Russian Communist Youth Organization

RELIGIOUS CALENDAR

The Saints
St. Narcissus, Bishop of Jerusalem. [d. c. 215]
St. Theuderius, abbot. Also called *Chef.* [d. c. 575]
St. Colman of Kilmacduagh, Bishop and solitary. [d. c. 632]
St. Abraham of Rostov, abbot. [d. 12th century]
The Martyrs of Douax, English missionary priests. [d. 16th and 17th century]

The Beatified
Blessed Mary Theresa Scherer. [beatified 1995]
Blessed Maria Bernarda Butler. [beatified 1995]
Blessed Marguerite Bays. [beatified 1995]

BIRTHDATES

1507 *Fernando Alvarez de Toledo, Duke of Alba;* Spanish soldier and statesman, remembered for his conquest of Portugal and tyranny while governor general of the Netherlands. [d. December 11, 1582]

1740 *James Boswell,* Scottish biographer; best known for *The Life of Samuel Johnson,* 1791. [d. May 19, 1795]

1811 *(Jean Joseph Charles) Louis Blanc,* French utopian socialist; considered to be the father of state socialism. [d. December 6, 1882]

1815 *Daniel Decatur Emmett,* U.S. minstrel, songwriter; organized one of first blackface minstrel shows in U.S., known as *Virginia Minstrels,* 1843; composed *Dixie,* 1859. [d. June 28, 1904]

1831 *Othniel Charles Marsh,* U.S. paleontologist; first professor of vertebrate paleontology in U.S., Yale University, 1866; established the *Peabody Museum of Natural History* with funds contributed by his uncle, George Peabody, 1868. [d. March 18, 1899]

1837 *Abraham Kuyper,* Dutch theologian; formed alliance between Calvinist and Catholic clerics; formed Christian Conservative ministry, 1901; Minister of Interior, 1901–05; Minister of State, 1907. [d. November 8, 1920]

1865 *Charles Henry Ingersoll,* U.S. manufacturer; with his brother Robert Hawley Ingersoll (December 26) founded firm of Robert H. Ingersoll and Brother, which created and distributed the *one dollar watch,* frequently referred to as *the watch that made the dollar famous.* [d. September 21, 1948]

1882 *(Hippolyte) Jean Giraudoux,* French dramatist, diplomat; Chief of Propaganda, 1939–40; author of *Siegfried,* 1882. [d. January 31, 1944]

1884 *Bela Lugosi,* U.S. actor, born in Hungary; best known for parts in horror films. [d. August 16, 1956]

1891 *Fanny Brice (Fannie Borach),* U.S. entertainer; known primarily as a star of the Ziegfeld Follies, 1910–36; featured as *Baby Snooks* on radio, 1936–51. [d. May 29, 1951]

1897 *Joseph (Paul) Goebbels,* German Nazi official; Minister of Propaganda, 1929–45; member of Adolf Hitler's cabinet, 1938–45; committed suicide at the end of World War II. [d. May 1, 1945]

1911 *Mahalia Jackson,* U.S. gospel singer. [d. January 27, 1972]

1920 *Baruj Benacerraf,* Venezuelan-born physician;

Nobel Prize in physiology or medicine for his work dealing with the relationship between heredity and disease, 1980.

1925 *Dominick Dunne,* U.S. journalist, writer.

1926 *Jon Vickers,* Canadian opera singer.

1945 *Melba Moore,* U.S. singer, actress; appeared in the Broadway musicals, *Hair* and *Purlie.*

1947 *Richard (Stephen) Dreyfuss,* U.S. actor; Academy Award winner for *The Goodbye Girl,* 1978.

1948 *Kate Jackson,* U.S. actress; starred in the television series, *Charlie's Angels,* and *Scarecrow and Mrs. King.*

1951 *Jesse Lee Barfield,* U.S. baseball player; outfielder, Toronto Blue Jays.

1953 *Denis Potvin,* Canadian hockey player; elected to Hall of Fame, 1991.

1959 *David Parsons,* U.S. dancer, choreographer.

1961 *Steven Randall (Randy) Jackson,* U.S. singer; member of the rock group, *The Jacksons.*

1971 *Winona Ryder,* U.S. actress.

HISTORICAL EVENTS

1814 U.S. launches its first steam warship, *U.S.S. Fulton.*

1888 *Suez Canal Convention,* signed at Constantinople, internationalizes and neutralizes the *Suez Canal.*

1889 *British South Africa Company,* headed by *Cecil Rhodes,* is granted a charter by the British government giving it almost unlimited powers and rights in the area that becomes Rhodesia.

1914 *Prince Louis of Battenberg (Mountbatten)* is replaced as First Lord of the British admiralty by Lord Fisher, primarily due to his German heritage (*World War I*).

1923 *Turkish Republic* is formally proclaimed, with *Mustapha Kemal* as president.

1929 *Black Tuesday* at the New York Stock Exchange marks the final collapse of the stock market.

1937 *Henry Armstrong* defeats *Petey Sarron* in six rounds to win the world featherweight boxing title.

1940 First peacetime *draft* in U.S. history goes into effect.

1950 *Gustavus V* of Sweden dies and is succeeded by his son, *Gustavus VI Adolf.*

1958 General *Ne Win* is inaugurated as premier of Burma.

Boris Pasternak refuses the Nobel Prize for literature under pressure from Soviet authorities.

1966 *National Organization of Women (NOW)* is founded in U.S.

1967 Galt MacDermott, Gerome Ragni, and James Rado's musical, *Hair,* opens in New York.

october

OCTOBER
30

RELIGIOUS CALENDAR

The Saints

St. Serapion, Bishop of Antioch. [d. c. 212]

St. Marcellus the Centurion, martyr. [d. 298]

St. Asterius, Bishop of Amasea. [d. c. 410]

St. Germanus, Bishop of Capua. [d. c. 540]

St. Ethelnoth, Archbishop of Canterbury. Also called *Ednoth, Eadnodus, Adelnodus.* [d. 1038]

St. Alphonsus Rodriguez, Jesuit lay brother. [d. 1617]

The Beatified

Blessed Benvenuta of Cividale, virgin. [d. 1292]

Blessed Dorothy of Montau, widow. Popularly regarded as the patroness of Prussia. [d. 1394]

Blessed John Slade, martyr. [d. 1583]

Blessed Angelo of Acri, Franciscan priest. [d. 1739]

BIRTHDATES

1632 *Jan Vermeer,* Dutch painter of landscapes and portraits; noted especially for composition. [d. December 15, 1675]

1735 *John Adams,* U.S. politician, diplomat, U.S. Vice-President, 1789–97, U.S. President, 1797–1801; father of John Quincy Adams (July 11). [d. July 4, 1826]

1815 *Elizabeth L. Comstock,* British religious leader, abolitionist; Quaker minister; operated stations for underground railroads. [d. August 3, 1891]

1839 *Alfred Sisley,* French impressionist painter. [d. January 29, 1899]

1840 *William Graham Sumner,* U.S. educator, sociologist, economist; professor of political and social science, Yale University, 1872–1910; champion of *laissez-faire* economics and government; author of *Folkways,* an in-depth study of customs and mores. [d. April 12, 1910]

1857 *Gertrude Franklin Atherton,* U.S. novelist; author of *The Californians.* [d. June 14, 1948]

1861 *Emile Antoine Bourdelle,* French sculptor, painter; collaborator with Auguste Rodin (November 12). [d. October 1, 1929]

1871 *Paul Ambroise Toussaint Jules Valery,* French man of letters; associated with symbolist school. [d. July 20, 1945]

1873 *Francisco Indalécio Madero,* Mexican patriot; president, 1911–13. [d. February 22, 1913]

1882 *William Frederick (Bull) Halsey, Jr.,* U.S. naval officer; commander of U.S. South Pacific fleet and South Pacific area, 1942–45; victor at *Battle of Leyte Gulf,* most overwhelming naval victory in history. [d. August 16, 1959]

1885 *Ezra (Loomis) Pound,* U.S. poet, critic; noted for his singularly profound influence on the development of modern poetry; responsible for recognition of Robert Frost, T. S. Eliot; diagnosed as mentally ill and committed to an institution, 1946–58; died an exile in Venice. [d. November 1, 1972]

1886 *Zoe Akins,* U.S. dramatist, screenwriter; Pulitzer Prize in drama, 1935. [d. October 29, 1958]

1895 *Gerhard Domagk,* German bacteriologist, pathologist; Nobel Prize in physiology or medicine for discoveries leading to introduction and use of first of *sulfa drugs,* 1939. [d. April 24, 1964]

Dickinson W. Richards, Jr., U.S. physiologist; Nobel Prize in physiology or medicine for research in heart disease and techniques for diagnosing circulatory ailments (with A. F. Cournand and W. Forssmann), 1956. [d. February 23, 1973]

1896 *Ruth Gordon,* U.S. stage and film actress, screenwriter. [d. August 28, 1985]

1900 *Ragnar Granit,* Swedish neurophysiologist; Nobel Prize in physiology or medicine for work on the physiology of vision (with H. K. Hartline and G. Wald), 1967.

1912 *Clement Furman Haynsworth, Jr.,* U.S. judge. [d. November 22, 1989]

1915 *Fred W. Friendly,* U.S. communications executive, educator; collaborator with Edward R. Murrow in radio and television series, *See It Now,* 1951–59; President of CBS News, 1964–66. [d. March 3, 1998]

1917 *Ruth Hussey (Ruth Carol O'Rourke),* U.S. actress.

1922 *Nicanor Costa Mendez,* Argentine government official; Foreign Minister who led Argentine attack on Falkland Islands, 1982.

1923 *Hershel Bernardi,* U.S. actor, singer; starred in the Broadway version of *Fiddler on the Roof;* appeared in the television series, *Peter Gunn,* 1958–60, and *Arnie,* 1970–71. [d. May 10, 1986]

1928 *Daniel Nathans,* U.S. biologist; Nobel Prize in physiology or medicine for research on restriction enzymes (with W. Arber and H. Smith), 1978.

1930 *Harold Pinter,* British playwright, actor; author of *The Birthday Party, The Homecoming.*

1932 *Louis Malle,* French film director. [d. November 23, 1995]

1936 *Richard Albert (Dick) Vermeil,* U.S. sportscaster; coach, Philadelphia Eagles, 1976–82; analyst for television sports shows, 1983–.

1937 *Rudolfo Anaya,* U.S. author; known for his contributions to Chicano literature.

Dick Gautier, U.S. actor; appeared in the television series, *Get Smart,* 1966–69, and *When Things Were Rotten,* 1975.

Claude Lelouch, French film director.

1943 *Grace Wing Slick (Grace Barnett Wing),* U.S. singer; lead vocalist for the rock group, *Starship* (formerly called *Jefferson Airplane*), 1965–72.

1945 *Henry Winkler,* U.S. actor.

1951 *Harry Hamlin,* U.S. actor; played Michael Kuzak on TV series *L.A. Law.*

HISTORICAL EVENTS

1340 *Alfonso XI* of Castile defeats Moors at *River Salado.*

1611 *Charles IX* of Sweden dies and is succeeded by *Gustavus II Adolphus.*

1769 *Captain Cook* makes landfall in *New Zealand* and claims it for Great Britain.

1864 *Peace of Vienna* is signed; Denmark cedes Schleswig, Holstein, and Lauenburg to Prussia.

1905 *October Manifesto* is issued at St. Petersburg by *Nicholas II* giving Russia a constitution, a legislative duma, civil liberties, and a prime minister.

1918 Turkey signs *Armistice of Mudros* with Allies, ending its participation in *World War I.*

1930 *Treaty of Ankara* between Turkey and Greece resolves property claims and agrees on naval equality.

1939 The broadcast in the U.S. of Orson Welles' radio drama, *War of the Worlds,* causes a national panic.

1944 British and U.S. troops complete the liberation of *Greece (World War II).*

1948 Communist forces capture the city of *Mukden,* driving the Nationalists out of *Manchuria (Chinese Civil War).*

1951 Fifteen thousand British troops arrive in the Middle East to protect the *Suez Canal* after Egypt abrogates a 1936 Anglo-Egyptian treaty.

1953 *George C. Marshall,* former U.S. Secretary of State and formulator of the Marshall Plan, wins the Nobel Peace Prize. Withheld for a year, the 1952 prize is awarded to *Albert Schweitzer.*

1956 *Ebbets Field,* home of the Brooklyn Dodgers baseball team, is sold as the site of a housing development.

1967 *Shah Mohammad Reza Pahlavi* of Iran formally crowns himself and his wife, Empress Farah, at a lavish ceremony in Teheran.

1974 *Mohammad Ali* knocks out *George Foreman* in 8 rounds for world heavyweight boxing title.

1975 *Prince Juan Carlos* assumes the powers of Spain's chief of state, marking the end of the 36-year-old Franco regime.

1981 British Parliament enacts *British Nationality Bill,*

october

creating three separate categories of citizenship.

1995 *Quebec* votes to remain part of Canada by a narrow margin.

1997 *Mary McAleese* is elected President of Ireland.

HOLIDAYS

National UNICEF Day
Sponsored by United Nations.

Slovenia
Reformation Day

Taiwan
Birthday of President Chiang Kai-shek
Celebrates the event which occurred 1887.

U.S. (Nevada)
Nevada Day
Commemorates Nevada's admission to the Union, 1864.

U.S.
National Magic Day
A day for meetings of magicians occasioned by the death of *Harry Houdini*, 1926.

Protestant Reformation Day
Commemorates the date Martin Luther posted his 95 theses.

RELIGIOUS CALENDAR

Feasts
All Hallow Even, Vigil of All Saints, All Hallow's Eve, or *Hallowe'en;* corresponds with the eve of *All Saints' Day,* November 1; based on ancient pagan festival of autumn and Roman festival of Pomona, goddess of gardens. *Halloween* is celebrated as a night of pranks and ghost stories.
Reformation Day Celebrated by many Protestant denominations as the day on which Martin Luther affixed his *95 Theses* to the church door at Wittenberg, 1517. [minor festival, Lutheran Church]

The Saints
St. Foillan, abbot. [d. c. 655]
St. Wolfgang, Bishop of Regensburg (Ratisbon). Invoked to heal the good and to keep sheep and oxen fat. [d. 994]
St. Bega, nun. Also called *Begu.* [death date unknown]
St. Quintinus, martyr. Invoked against coughs. Also called *Quentin, Quintin, Quintus.* [death date unknown]

BIRTHDATES

1705 *Clement XIV,* Pope 1769–74. [d. September 22, 1774]

1795 *John Keats,* British lyric poet. [d. February 23, 1821]

1802 *Benoit Fourneyron,* French inventor; developed the *water-turbine.* [d. July 31, 1867]

1815 *Karl Weierstrass,* German mathematician; developed many calculus innovations; founded theory of functions of a complex variable. [d. February 19, 1897]

1817 *Heinrich Graetz,* Jewish historian; author of *Geschichte der Juden von den Altesten Zeiten.* [d. September 7, 1891]

1821 *Karl Havlíček (Havel Borouský),* Czech critic, journalist, poet; imprisoned for his liberal opinions. [d. July 29, 1856]

1827 *Richard Morris Hunt,* U.S. architect; noted most for his advocacy of the Beaux-Arts design of the *Metropolitan Museum of Art,* New York, 1900; designed residences for Vanderbilts, Astors, Belmonts, and other wealthy Americans; designed The Breakers and Marble House, Newport, R.I., and the Biltmore estate, Asheville, N.C. [d. July 31, 1895]

1828 *Sir Joseph Wilson Swan,* British chemist; a pioneer in photographic chemistry; invented *dry plate photography,* 1871. [d. May 27, 1914]

1835 *Adolph von Baeyer,* German chemist; Nobel Prize in chemistry for his work with dye and uric acid derivatives, 1905. [d. August 20, 1917]

1838 *Luis I,* King of Portugal, ruled 1861–89; freed slaves in Portuguese colonies. [d. October 19, 1889]

1852 *Mary Eleanor Wilkins Freeman,* U.S. novelist and short-story writer; member of local color school. [d. March 13, 1930]

1860 *Juliette Gordon Low,* U.S. youth leader; established first American troop of *Girl Guides* (which later became the *Girl Scouts*). [d. January 17, 1927]

Andrew Joseph Volstead, U.S. politician; author of *Volstead Act,* enforcing *prohibition* in U.S. [d. January 20, 1947]

1863 *William Gibbs McAdoo,* U.S. government official, lawyer; U.S. Secretary of the Treasury, 1912–18; first chairman, Federal Reserve Board; U.S. Senator, 1932–38; son-in-law of U.S. President Woodrow Wilson (December 28). [d. February 1, 1941]

1887 *Chiang Kai-shek,* Chinese government leader; President, Republic of China, 1928–49; assumed presidency in exile in Taiwan, 1949–75. [d. April 5, 1975]

1888 *Sir George Hubert Wilkins,* Australian polar explorer; leader of a number of Arctic and Antarctic expeditions, 1913–39. Advanced use of airplane and submarine in polar research and exploration. [d. December 1, 1958]

1895 *B(asil) H(enry) Liddell Hart,* British military scientist; military editor of *Encyclopaedia Britannica;* wrote numerous books on defense that influenced British military strategy. [d. January 29, 1970]

1899 *Nadezhda Yakovlevna Mandelstam,* Russian author, scholar; wife of Osip Mandelstam; spent most of her life trying to preserve her

husband's work; wrote memoirs, *Hope Against Hope* and *Hope Abandoned.* [d. December 29, 1980]

1900 *Ethel Waters,* U.S. actress, singer. [d. September 1, 1977]

1912 *Oscar Dystel,* U.S. publisher; President and Chairman of the Board, Bantam Books, 1954–80.

Dale Evans (Frances Smith), U.S. actress, singer; with husband, Roy Rogers (November 5), starred in numerous 1940s Western films and on television's *The Roy Rogers Show,* 1951–57.

1918 *Griffin Boyette Bell,* U.S. lawyer; Attorney General, 1977–79.

1921 *Yves Montand (Ivo Levi),* French actor, born in Italy. [d. November 9, 1991]

1922 *Barbara Bel Geddes,* U.S. actress.

Prince Norodom Sihanouk, King of Cambodia, 1941–55; established government in exile; established Royal Government of National Union of Cambodia, 1970; restored as Head of State when CRUNC forces overthrew Khmer Republic, 1975; abdicated, 1976; special envoy of Khmer Rouge to UN, 1979; reinstated (second time) as King, 1993.

1925 *Robin Moore (Robert Lowell Moore, Jr.),* U.S. novelist; author of *The French Connection.*

1930 *Michael Collins,* U.S. astronaut; co-pilot of U.S. *Gemini 10* space flight; pilot of command module, *Apollo 11,* lunar exploration flight.

1931 *Lee Grant (Lyova Haskell Rosenthal),* U.S. actress, director; Emmy Award for *Peyton Place,* 1965; Academy Award for *Shampoo,* 1975.

Dan(iel) Rather, U.S. television broadcast journalist.

1937 *Michael Landon (Eugene Michael Orowitz),* U.S. actor, director, writer; starred in and produced the television series, *Little House on the Prairie* and *Highway to Heaven.* [d. July 1, 1991]

Thomas R. (Tom) Paxton, U.S. singer, musician, songwriter.

1939 *Melinda Dillon,* U.S. actress; appeared in the film, *Absence of Malice,* 1981.

1942 *David Ogden Stiers,* U.S. actor; known for his role as Major Winchester on the television series, *M*A*S*H.*

1947 *Frank Shorter,* U.S. distance runner; winner of Olympic marathon gold medal, 1972.

1950 *John Candy,* Canadian actor, comedian; appeared in the films, *Splash,* 1984, and *Trains, Planes, and Automobiles,* 1987. [d. March 4, 1994]

(Margaret) Jane Pauley, U.S. broadcast journalist; co-host of the daily television program, *The Today Show,* 1976–89; *Dateline,* 1992– ; wife of cartoonist Garry Trudeau.

1965 *Annabella (Annabella Lwin),* Burmese singer; lead vocalist for the rock group, *Bow Wow Wow,* 1980–83.

Rob Schneider, U.S. comedian, actor; known for his performances on

Saturday Night Live,
1990–1994.

HISTORICAL EVENTS

1517 *Martin Luther* affixes *95 Theses* to door of Wittenberg Palace Church.

1754 *King's College* (now *Columbia University*) in New York City is granted a charter by *King George II.*

1864 *Nevada* is admitted to Union as the 36th state.

1879 *Irish National Land League* is founded, with *Charles Parnell* as president, for the purpose of destroying English landlordism in Ireland and establishing *home rule.*

1922 *Benito Mussolini* becomes Prime Minister of Italy.

1928 *Graf Zeppelin* completes first round-trip crossing of the Atlantic.

1941 U.S. destroyer *Reuben James* is torpedoed and sunk in the North Atlantic, becoming the first U.S. Navy warship to be sunk in the Atlantic during *World War II.*

1956 British and French troops attack Egyptian installations along the *Suez Canal.* Israeli forces capture the Sinai Peninsula and reach the banks of the Canal *(Suez Crisis).*

Auntie Mame opens on Broadway.

1971 Eleven women are elected to the Swiss parliament in the first election in which women are allowed to vote and hold office.

1981 Caribbean islands of *Antigua* and *Barbuda* become a single independent nation, ending three centuries of British rule.

1984 Indian prime minister, *Indira Gandhi,* is assassinated by two of her Sikh bodyguards in New Delhi. *Rajiv Gandhi* is inaugurated as his mother's successor.

1991 *Frederick Chiluba* is elected president of Zambia.

october

NOVEMBER

November is the eleventh month of the Gregorian calendar and has 30 days. The name is derived from the Latin *novem*, 'nine,' designating the position November held in the early Roman ten-month calendar (see also at **September**).

November generally marks, in the temperate zones of the northern-hemisphere, the time when work on the land ceases and, in the United States, is the month for general elections, the Thanksgiving holiday, and preparation for December holidays, with the pre-Christmas shopping season beginning late in the month.

In the astrological calendar, November spans the zodiac signs of Scorpio, the Scorpion (October 23–November 21) and Sagittarius, the Archer (November 22–December 21).

The birthstone for November is the topaz, and the flower is the chrysanthemum.

STATE, NATIONAL, AND INTERNATIONAL HOLIDAYS

General Election Day
(United States)
First Tuesday after First Monday

Thanksgiving Day
(Liberia)
First Thursday

Sadie Hawkins Day
(United States)
First Saturday after November 11

Remembrance Day
(Cayman Islands)
Second Monday

Oklahoma Heritage Week
(Oklahoma)
Week containing November 16

Geography Awareness Week
(United States)
Third Week

Prince Charles' Birthday
(Fiji)
Third Monday

Thanksgiving Day
(United States)
Fourth Thursday

Nellie Taylor Ross's Birthday
(Wyoming)
November 29
(Nebraska, Illinois, New Hampshire)
Day after Thanksgiving

SPECIAL EVENTS AND THEIR SPONSORS

Alcohol Education Month
Parents Without Partners

National Epilepsy Month
Epilepsy Foundation of America

National Ice Skating Month
Ice Skating Institute of America

National Jewish Book Month
JWB Jewish Book Council

One Nation Under God Month
The National Exchange Club

Home and Family Month
from Thanksgiving to Christmas
Fraternal Order of Eagles

National Stamp Collecting Month
Franklin D. Roosevelt Philatelic Society

Rotary Foundation Month
Rotary International

National Notary Public Week
Week containing November 7
American Society of Notaries

World Mutual Service Week
Second Full Week
National Board of the YWCA of the U.S.A.

Holidays are Pickle Days
Final Two Weeks and Month of December
Pickle Packers International, Inc.

Christmas Seal Campaign
November 15–December 31
American Lung Association

National Children's Book Week
Third Week
Children's Book Council

National Farm City Week
Third Week
Kiwanis International

National Adoption Week
Week of Thanksgiving
North American Council on
Adoptable Children

National Bible Week
Week of Thanksgiving
Laymen's National Bible Committee,
Inc.

Latin American Week
Last Full Week
Richard R. Falk Associates

Death Anniversary of Eleanor Roosevelt
November 7
Franklin D. Roosevelt Philatelic
Society

National Notary Public Day
November 7
American Society of Notaries

National Thanksgiving Salute to Older Americans
Thanksgiving Day
No Greater Love

HOLIDAYS

Antigua and Barbuda
Independence Day or National Day
Commemorates independence from Great Britain.

Algeria
Anniversary of the Revolution
Commemorates the beginning of the struggle for independence from France by the National Liberation Front, 1954.

Christian Communities Worldwide
Day of the Dead or All Saints' Day

Lithuania
National Day of Hope and Mourning

Panama
National Anthem Day

Slovakia
Reconciliation Day

U.S. Virgin Islands
Liberty Day

Yugoslavia (Slovenia)
Public Holiday

RELIGIOUS CALENDAR

Solemnities
All Saints' Day, a feast in Roman Catholic countries, and a holy day of obligation in the Roman Catholic Church. Celebrates all the saints of the church. Also known as *All Hallows Day.* [major holy day, Episcopal Church; minor festival, Lutheran Church]

The Saints
St. Benignus of Dijon, martyr, apostle of Burgundy. [d. c. 3rd century]
St. Austremonius, first bishop of Clermont. Apostle of Auvergne. [d. c. 4th century]
St. Mary, virgin and martyr. [d. c. 4th century]
St. Maturinus, priest; patron of fools. Also called *Mathurin.* [d. 4th century]
St. Marcellus, Bishop of Paris. [d. c. 410]
St. Vigor, Bishop of Bayeux. [d. c. 537]
St. Cadfan, abbot; patron of warriors. [d. c. 6th century]
SS. Caesarius and Julian, martyrs. [death date unknown]
St. Dingad, Welsh church founder of the tribe of Brychan; patron of Llandingat, Wales. Also called *Digat.* [death date unknown]
St. Gwythian, patron of the parish of this name in North Cornwall. Also called *Gwithian,* or *Gothian.* [death date unknown]

BIRTHDATES

1530 *Étienne de La Boétie,* French poet, translator; intimate of Michel de Montaigne (February 28). [d. August 18, 1563]

1596 *Pietro Berretini da Cortona,* Italian painter, architect; noted for his individualistic style in architecture; designed numerous churches in Rome and Florence. [d. May 16, 1669]

1609 *Sir Matthew Hale,* English judge; active in bringing about the Restoration. [d. December 25, 1676]

1636 *Nicolas Boileau-Despréaux,* French poet, critic; regarded as the founder of principles upon which French classical literature is based. [d. March 11, 1711?]

1757 *Antonio Canova,* Italian sculptor; founder of modern classic school of sculpture. [d. October 13, 1822]

George Rapp, U.S. religious leader born in Germany; founded *Harmony, Pennsylvania, Harmony, Indiana,* and *Economy, Pennsylvania,* all communities founded on religious, communistic principles. [d. August 7, 1847]

1764 *Stephen Van Rensselaer,* U.S. army officer, politician; commander, New York Militia; attacked Queenstown, Canada, 1812; early supporter of Erie Canal construction; Congressman, 1822–29; founded Rensselaer Polytechnic Institute, 1826. [d. January 26, 1839]

november

1778 *Gustavus IV Adolphus,* King of Sweden, 1792–1809; exiled, 1809; died in poverty. [d. February 7, 1837]

1815 *Crawford Williamson Long,* U.S. surgeon; despite his failure to publish his results, he is generally recognized as first to use *ether* as an anesthetic in surgery, 1842. [d. June 16, 1878]

1818 *James Renwick,* U.S. architect; noted for Gothic Revival architecture; designed *St. Patrick's Cathedral,* New York City; *Smithsonian Institution* building, Washington, D.C.; facade of the New York Stock Exchange Building. [d. June 23, 1895]

1871 *Stephen (Townley) Crane,* U.S. novelist, short-story writer; best known for his novel, *The Red Badge of Courage.* [d. June 5, 1900]

1878 *Carlos de Saavedra Lamas,* Argentine statesman; Foreign Minister, 1932–38; Nobel Peace Prize, 1936. [d. May 5, 1959]

1880 *(Henry) Grantland Rice,* U.S. sportswriter; Chairman of Selection Committee for All-American Football Team, 1925–54; author of numerous books of verse; syndicated columnist, 1930–47. [d. July 13, 1954]

Sholem Asch, U.S. novelist, born in Poland; known for his novels with Biblical themes written in both English and Yiddish. [d. July 10, 1957]

Alfred Wegener, German geophysicist; one of first to clearly state the *continental drift theory,* 1915. [d. November 1930]

1889 *Philip J. Noel-Baker,* British politician; Nobel Peace Prize for his work in the League of Nations and disarmament conferences, 1959. [d. October 9, 1982]

1895 *George Joseph Hecht,* U.S. publisher; founder of *Parents' Magazine,* 1926–78. [d. April 23, 1980]

1912 *Leo Kerz,* U.S. theatrical designer, director, born in Germany.

1920 *James Jackson Kilpatrick,* U.S. journalist; nationally syndicated columnist.

1927 *Marcel Ophuls,* German-born director; known for his controversial documentary about France under Nazi occupation, *The Sorrow and the Pity,* 1971; son of Max Ophuls.

1935 *Gary Player,* South African golfer; first foreign player to win U.S. Open Championship, 1965.

1941 *Robert Foxworth,* U.S. actor; known for his role as Chase Gioberti on the television series, *Falcon Crest,* 1982–87

1942 *Larry Claxton Flynt,* U.S. magazine executive; publisher, *Hustler* magazine; paralyzed in an assassination attempt.

1944 *Keith Emerson,* British musician; keyboardist with the rock group, *Emerson, Lake, and Palmer;* known for his flamboyant performances.

1957 *Lyle Lovett,* U.S. singer, actor.

1960 *Fernando Valenzuela (Fernando Anguamea),* Mexican-born baseball player; called *El Toro.*

1972 *Jenny McCarthy,* U.S. actress.

HISTORICAL EVENTS

1700 *Philip of Anjou,* grandson of Louis XIV of France, is proclaimed King *Philip V* on the death of *Charles II* of Spain; marks the beginning of *War of Spanish Succession.*

1755 Great earthquake at *Lisbon,* Portugal, accompanied by fire and flood, kills tens of thousands and destroys city.

1762 French troops capitulate at *Cassel* and evacuate right bank of the Rhine (*Seven Years' War*).

1894 *Alexander III* of Russia dies and is succeeded by *Nicholas II.*

1914 *Persia* declares neutrality in *World War I.*

1917 *Battle of Malmaison* ends in victory for France (*World War I*).

British troops capture *Beersheba* in Palestine and begin to break the Turkish line in the *Third Battle of Gaza (World War I).*

Jesse Lynch Williams becomes the first playwright to receive the Pulitzer Prize for his comedy, *Why Marry?*

1918 The Serbs reclaim their capital of *Belgrade* while German-Austrian troops under von Mackensen begin a rapid retreat through Transylvania (*World War I*).

An independent Hungarian government is established under *Count Michael Karolyi* as *Austria-Hungary* breaks apart.

1922 *Mustapha Kemal (Ataturk)* of Turkey proclaims the abolition of the sultanate.

1925 First train passes through the *Khyber Pass.*

1941 *Rainbow Bridge,* an international bridge at Niagara Falls, opens to the public.

U.S. President *Franklin Roosevelt* places *United States Coast Guard* under Navy control.

1947 UN approves trusteeship arrangement for *Nauru,* to be administered jointly by Australia, New Zealand, and Great Britain.

1950 *Pope Pius XII,* in a papal bull, proclaims the *assumption of the Virgin Mary* as a dogma of the Roman Catholic Church.

Two Puerto Rican nationalists attempt to assassinate President *Harry Truman* following a week of political unrest on the island.

1951 Five thousand U.S. troops witness *Exercise Desert Rock,* the first atomic bomb maneuvers.

1952 First U.S. hydrogen bomb test is conducted on *Eniwetok Atoll.*

1954 Algerian nationalists begin a war for independence from France.

1956 *John Bardeen, Walter Brattain,* and *William Shockley* are awarded the Nobel Prize in physics for their invention of the *transistor.*

Hungary proclaims neutrality and withdraws from the Warsaw Pact during political uprisings within the Pact countries.

1957 The *Mackinac Bridge,* connecting Michigan's upper and lower peninsulas, is opened to traffic. It has the world's longest total suspension span.

1960 Economic union between Belgium, Luxembourg, and the Netherlands comes into effect.

1964 *Antigua, Barbados, Dominica, Montserrat, St.* *Kitts, St. Lucia,* and *St. Vincent* reach agreement on forming a new independent *West Indies Federation.*

1972 The Standard Oil Co. of New Jersey changes its name to Exxon Corp.

1976 Military coup overthrows the government of *Burundi;* Lt. Col. *Bagaza* gains control.

1981 *Antigua* and *Barbuda* gain independence from Great Britain. *Vere Bird* is named the first Prime Minister.

1989 *East Germany* opens its border with Czechoslovakia. Many East Germans immigrate to West Germany through Czechoslovakia (November 9, 1989).

1991 *Clarence Thomas* is sworn in as a U.S. Supreme Court justice.

1995 South Africans vote in their country's first democratic elections; the *African National Congress* is victorious.

november

NOVEMBER
2

HOLIDAYS

Belarus
Day of Commemoration

Brazil, Ecuador, El Salvador, Luxembourg, Macao, Mexico, San Marino, Sweden, Uruguay, Vatican City
All Souls' Day or Memorial Day

Dominica
Independence Day
Celebrates Dominica's achievement of independence from Great Britain, 1978. First day of a two-day celebration.

Mexico
Dia de Muertos or Day of the Dead

RELIGIOUS CALENDAR

Solemnities
The Commemoration of All the Faithful Departed, commonly called *All Souls' Day.* Optional Memorial. [minor festival, Lutheran Church]

The Saints
St. Victorinus, Bishop of Pettau and martyr. [d. c. 303]
St. Marcian, hermit. [d. c. 387]
St. Ernin, hermit. Invoked to cure headaches. [d. 6th century]
St. Erc, patron of St. Erth, Cornwall. Also called *Ercius, Ercus,* or *Erth.* [death date unknown]

The Beatified
Blessed Thomas of Walden. Confessor to King Henry V. [d. 1430]

Blessed John Bodey, martyr. [d. 1583]

BIRTHDATES

1699 *Jean Baptiste Simeon Chardin,* French artist; known for his mastery of color and composition; painted the middle-class and still-lifes; works include *The Buffet* and *The Young Violinist.* [d. December 6, 1779]

1734 *Daniel Boone,* American frontiersman, explorer; primarily responsible for expansion and development of lands west of the Alleghenies. [d. September 26, 1820]

1755 *Marie Antoinette,* Queen of France; wife of *King Louis XVI;* extremely unpopular with the French people because of insensitivity to miseries of the poor; imprisoned with the king and her children, 1792. Convicted of treason and beheaded. [d. October 16, 1793]

1766 *Joseph Wenzel Radetzky, Count Radetzky von Radetz,* Austrian field marshal, national hero; victorious over Sardinians at Custoza and Novara; responsible for Austria's capture of Venice. [d. January 5, 1858]

1795 *James Knox Polk,* U.S. lawyer, politician; 11th President of the U.S., 1845–49; the youngest man at that time ever to be elected to the presidency; led U.S. during Mexican War, 1846–48. [d. June 15, 1849]

1815 *George Boole,* British mathematician; helped establish modern symbolic logic; his algebra of logic, *Boolean algebra,* is basic to the design of digital computers. [d. December 8, 1864]

1849 *Friedrich von Bernhardi,* German soldier, military historian; gave distinguished service in Franco-Prussian War and World War I. [d. July 10, 1930]

1865 *Warren Gamaliel Harding,* U.S. teacher, journalist, politician; 29th President of the U.S., 1921–23. Died in office. [d. August 2, 1923]

1877 *Aga Khan III (Aga Sultan Sir Mahomed Shah),* Indian religious leader, statesman; descendant of Mohammed; spiritual leader of 80 million Ismaili Moslems, 1885–1957; President, League of Nations, 1937. [d. July 11, 1957]

1879 *Jacob Aall Bonnevie Bjerknes,* U.S. meteorologist, born in Norway. [d. July 7, 1975]

1885 *Harlow Shapley,* U.S. astronomer; known for his research into sizes of galaxies and composition of Milky Way. [d. October 20, 1972]

1897 *Richard B. Russell,* U.S. politician, lawyer; U.S. Senator, 1933–71; President *pro tempore* of Senate, 1969–71. [d. January 21, 1971]

1903 *Emile Zola Berman,* U.S. lawyer; noted for his defense of Sirhan Sirhan, assassin of Robert F. Kennedy. [d. July 3, 1981]

1905 *James Dunn,* U.S. actor. [d. September 3, 1967]

1906 *Luchino Visconti,* Italian film director. [d. March 17, 1976]

1911 *Odysseus Elytis,* Greek poet; Nobel Prize in literature, 1979. [d. March 18, 1996]

1913 *Burt Lancaster,* U.S. actor. [d. October 20, 1994]

1917 *Ann Rutherford,* U.S. actress, born in Canada.

Andrew Fielding Huxley, British physiologist; Nobel Prize in physiology or medicine for research on nerve cells (with A. L. Hodgkin and J. C. Eccles), 1963.

1929 *Richard E. Taylor,* U.S. physicist; Nobel Prize for Physics with Jerome Freidman and Henry Kendall, for their study of quarks, 1990.

1932 *Melvin Schwartz,* U.S. physicist; Nobel Prize in physics for particle physics research (with Leon Lederman and Jack Steinberger), 1988.

1934 *Ken Rosewall,* Australian tennis player.

1938 *Patrick Joseph Buchanan,* U.S. journalist; assistant to President Nixon, 1966–73; Director of Communications for President Reagan, 1985–87.

1939 *Richard Anthony Serra,* U.S. artist; most innovative of minimalist sculptors.

1941 *David Hemmings,* British actor.

David (Dave) Stockton, U.S. golfer.

1942 *Shere D. Hite,* U.S. author: *The Hite Report: A Nationwide Study of Female Sexuality,* 1976.

1958 *Willie Dean McGee,* U.S. baseball player; outfielder, St. Louis Cardinals; National League batting title and National League Most Valuable Player, 1985.

1961 *k. d. lang (Kathryn Dawn Lang),* Canadian singer.

HISTORICAL EVENTS

1164 *Thomas Becket,* Archbishop of Canterbury, opponent of *King Henry II* of England, flees to France.

1439 *Charles VII* of France establishes the *taille,* a permanent tax.

1642 Swedes defeat army of Holy Roman Empire at *Breitenfeld (Thirty Years' War).*

1687 *Mohammed IV* of Turkey is deposed; he is succeeded by *Suleiman III.*

1795 *French Directory,* a moderate government, is installed.

1841 British envoys are murdered during Afghan uprisings in Kabul, during the *First Afghan War.*

1852 *Second Empire* is established in France under *Emperor Napoleon III.*

1889 *North Dakota* and *South Dakota* are admitted to Union as 39th and 40th states.

1899 Boer forces begin the siege of *Ladysmith,* held by the British (*Boer War*).

1914 *Russia* declares war on *Turkey (World War I).*

1917 *Balfour Declaration* states the British objective of establishing a Jewish state in Palestine.

Lansing-Ishi Agreement between the U.S. and Japan recognizes Japanese interests in China but maintains China's sovereignty; the *Open Door Policy* is supported; and Japan joins the Allies in the war against Germany (*World War I*).

1920 Radio station *KDKA, Pittsburgh,* broadcasts the first commercial news, the returns of the Harding-Cox presidential election.

1923 *Union of Soviet Socialist Republics* is officially adopted as the name of the newly federated Russian republic.

1930 *Haile I Selassie* is crowned Emperor of Abyssinia (*Ethiopia*).

1938 Hungary acquires southern *Slovakia* following the dismemberment of *Czechoslovakia* after German invasion.

1942 British decisively defeat Rommel's German troops at *Tel-el Aqqaqir (World War II).*

1947 Howard Hughes's mammoth wooden flying boat, *The*

november

Spruce Goose, makes its first and only flight.

1964 *King Saud* of Saudi Arabia is dethroned and replaced by his younger half-brother, *Prince Faisal.*

1965 *John V. Lindsay* becomes the first Republican mayor of New York City since Fiorello H. LaGuardia (1933).

Norman R. Morrison, a Quaker, burns himself to death in front of the Pentagon as a protest against U.S. policy in *Vietnam.*

1978 *Dominica* gains full independence from Great Britain.

Lee Iacocca is appointed president and chief operating officer of Chrysler Corp.

Two Soviet cosmonauts descend to earth in the *Soyuz 31* spacecraft after setting a new endurance record of 139 days and 14 hours aboard the orbiting *Salyut 6* space station.

1983 South Africa's white voters approve a new constitution which permits Asians and people of mixed race to vote for representatives in a *tricameral parliament.* Blacks remain excluded from the electoral process.

1984 Joseph Stalin's daughter, *Svetlana Alliluyeva,* returns to the U. S.S.R. and denounces life in the West. She redefects 14 months later.

1988 *Ngiratkel Etpison* is elected president of Palau.

1992 *Earvin "Magic" Johnson* retires from the NBA for the second time. In 1991 he had announced his retirement but had staged a comeback after he revealed he had the HIV virus.

HOLIDAYS

Dominica

Independence Day
Celebrates Dominica's achievement of independence from Great Britain, 1978. Second day of a two-day celebration.

Ecuador

Independence of Cuenca
Commemorates declaration of the city, 1820.

Japan

Culture Day
A day for the people of Japan to reflect on liberty and peace and to emphasize the importance of promoting culture.

Panama

Independence from Colombia
Commemorates the event, 1903.

RELIGIOUS CALENDAR

The Saints

St. Clydog, king and martyr. Also called *Clitaucus,* or *Clodock.* [d. 6th cent.]

St. Winifred, virgin and martyr; patron of virgins. Also called *Gwenfrewi, Wenefride,* or *Winefride.* [d. c. 650]

St. Rumwald, patron of Brackley. Also called *Rumald.* [d. c. 7th century]

St. Hubert, Bishop of Liège; patron of Liège, and of hunters, foresters, furriers, smelters, and makers of precision instruments. He is invoked against rabies and for the protection of dogs. [d. 727]

St. Pirminus, bishop. [d. 753]

St. Amicus, solitary. [d. c. 1045]

St. Malachy, Archbishop of Armagh. Also called *Malachi.* [d. 1148]

St. Martin de Porres, Dominican lay brother; patron of workers for social justice. In U.S., patron of work for interracial justice and harmony. Feast formerly November 5. [d. 1639] Optional Memorial.

St. Wulganus, confessor; patron of Lens. Also called *Wulgan.* [death date unknown]

The Beatified

Blessed Alpais, virgin. [d. 1211]

Blessed Ida of Toggenburg, matron. [d. 1226]

Blessed Simon of Rimini, lay brother. [d. 1319]

BIRTHDATES

1500 *Benvenuto Cellini,* Italian goldsmith, sculptor, writer; student of Michelangelo; protégé of Cosimo de' Medici; his *Autobiography* is a record of Renaissance life in Italy. [d. February 13, 1571]

1560 *Annibale Carracci,* Italian artist; with brother and cousin, painted the frescoes in the Farnese Palace, 1597–1604; co-founder of the Eclectic School. [d. July 15, 1609]

1611 *Henry Ireton,* English general; a close ally of Oliver Cromwell. [d. November 26, 1651]

1793 *Stephen Fuller Austin,* U.S. colonizer, public official; leader in settlement of Texas by Americans. Austin, Texas is named for him. [d. December 27, 1836]

1794 *William Cullen Bryant,* U.S. poet, critic, editor, and part owner of the New York *Evening Post;* author of *Thanatopsis,* 1817. [d. June 12, 1878]

1801 *Karl Baedeker,* German publisher; wrote travel books which did away with formal tour guides. [d. October 4, 1859]

Vincenzo Bellini, Italian composer; composed operas *La Sonnambula* and *Il Pirata.* [d. September 23, 1835]

1816 *Jubal Anderson Early,* U.S. Confederate Army general during U.S. Civil War; led a raid on Washington, D.C., during war but was turned back by General U.S. Grant. [d. March 2, 1894]

1834 *Charles Louis Fleischmann,* U.S. manufacturer; sold first compressed, non-liquid yeast in the U.S., 1868; also produced vinegar and

november

margarine. [d. December 10, 1897]

Paul Arrell Brown Widener, U.S. financier, philanthropist; supported development of transit systems in New York, Philadelphia, and Chicago; noted for his art collection, which was bequeathed to city of Philadelphia. [d. November 6, 1915]

1845 *Edward Douglass White,* U.S. jurist; Associate Justice, U.S. Supreme Court, 1894–1910; Chief Justice, U.S. Supreme Court, 1910–21; responsible for *White Doctrine* of incorporated and unincorporated territories; issued the *rule of reason* in interpretation of antitrust laws. [d. May 19, 1921]

1852 *Mutsuhito,* Emperor of Japan, 1867–1912. [d. July 30, 1912]

1879 *Vilhjalmur Stefansson,* U.S. explorer, ethnologist, born in Canada; noted for his extensive Arctic expeditions and adaptation to Eskimo life; spent five years living north of the Arctic Circle. [d. August 26, 1962]

1901 *Leopold III,* King of Belgium, 1934–51; abdicated in favor of son Baudouin in 1951. [d. September 25, 1983]

André Malraux, French novelist, art historian, public official; leader of French resistance during World War II; Minister of Cultural Affairs, 1959–69. [d. November 23, 1977]

1903 *Julian (Parks) Boyd,* U.S. editor, historian; edited 19 volumes of the 60 volumes of Thomas Jefferson's works, one of the most ambitious projects in the history of U.S. publishing. [d. May 21, 1980]

1908 *Giovanni Leone,* Italian politician, professor; President of Chamber of Deputies, 1948–49; President, 1955–63; President of Italian Republic, 1971–78.

1909 *James Barrett (Scotty) Reston,* U.S. journalist, born in Scotland; *New York Times* columnist, 1953–64; editor, 1964–69; Pulitzer Prize in national correspondence, 1944, 1957.[d. December 6, 1995]

1912 *Alfredo Stroessner,* President, Republic of Paraguay, 1954–89.

1914 *Yitzhak Shamir (Yitzak Yezernitsky),* Israeli government official; Deputy Prime Minister and Minister of Foreign Affairs, 1980–83, 1984–86; Prime Minister, 1983–84, 1986–92.

1918 *Russell (Billiu) Long,* U.S. politician, lawyer; Senator, 1948–86; son of Huey P. Long (August 30).

1930 *Philip Miller Crane,* U.S. politician, dentist; Congressman, 1969–.

1931 *Andrew Lindsay (Drew) Lewis, Jr.,* U.S. government official; Secretary of Transportation, 1981–83.

1933 *Ken Berry,* U.S. actor, singer, dancer; starred in the television series, *F-Troop,* 1965–67, and *Mayberry RFD,* 1968–71.

Michael Stanley Dukakis, U.S. politician; Governor of Massachusetts, 1975–79, 1983–91; Democratic nominee for president, 1988.

Louis Sullivan, U.S. physician; first African American physician to head the U.S. Department of Health and Human Services, 1989–93.

1936 *Roy Emerson,* Australian tennis player.

1938 *Bette Bao Lord,* Chinese-born author, pro-democracy activist; chairwoman of the human rights organization Freedom House, 1993– .

1942 *Martin Cruz Smith,* U.S. author; wrote *Gorky Park,* 1981.

1948 *Lulu (Marie McDonald McLaughlin Lawrie),* Scottish singer, actress; known for her hit single, *To Sir With Love,* 1967.

Thomas William (Tom) Shales, U.S. journalist; television editor, *Washington Post,* 1977–; film critic, National Public Radio's *Morning Edition.*

1949 *Larry Holmes,* U.S. boxer; World Boxing Council heavyweight champion, 1978–84.

1952 *David Ho,* Taiwan-born molecular biologist; known for his research on AIDS.

1953 *Jeffrey Banks,* U.S. fashion designer.

Dennis Miller, U.S. comedian, actor; known for his performances on TV's *Saturday Night Live.*

Roseanne (Roseanne Barr, Roseanne Arnold), U.S. comedian and actress.

1954 *Adam Ant (Stewart Goddard),* British singer, musician; former member of the rock group, *Adam and the Ants;* hit solo single, *Goody Two Shoes,* 1982.

1956 *Robert Lynn (Bob) Welch,* U.S. baseball player.

1959 *Dolph Lundgren,* Swedish actor.

HISTORICAL EVENTS

1492 *Peace of Etaples* is signed between England and France.

1760 *Frederick the Great* of Prussia scores brilliant victory over a superior Austrian force at *Torgau (Seven Years' War).*

1839 *First Opium War* between China and Great Britain begins; *Hong Kong* is taken by British.

1903 Under U.S. instigation and backing, *Panama* revolts and declares itself independent of Colombia.

1917 American forces are involved in trench fighting in *World War I* for the first time.

1918 Mutiny breaks out in the German fleet at *Kiel* and rapidly spreads through northwestern Germany (*World War I*).

Polish Republic is declared at Warsaw.

An *armistice* is signed at Belgrade between the Allies and Austria-Hungary (*World War I*).

The Italian army seizes *Trieste* and *Trent* at the end of the successful offensive of *Vittorio Veneto* against the Austrians (*World War I*).

1928 Roman alphabet is adopted by *Turkey.*

1948 *Irvin Mollison* is sworn in as U.S. Customs Court judge, becoming the first black to serve on a federal bench.

The *Chicago Tribune* prints its famous headline declaring *Thomas Dewey* to be the winner in the previous day's presidential election. *Harry Truman* actually wins, scoring one of the greatest upsets in U.S. political history.

1952 General *Carlos Ibanez del Campo* becomes president of Chile.

1954 German physicists, *Max Born* and *Walther Bothe,* receive the Nobel prize for their contributions to the theory of *quantum mechanics.*

1956 Soviet forces invade *Hungary* and crush a national uprising against the Communist coalition government; nearly 200,000 Hungarians flee the country.

1957 *Laika,* a small dog, becomes the first animal sent into space aboard the Soviet *Sputnik 2.*

1958 *Jorge Alessandri Rodriguez* is inaugurated as president of Chile.

1960 *Ivory Coast* adopts its constitution.

1962 *Barbara Salt* is appointed ambassador to Israel, becoming the first British woman to be given a top diplomatic post.

1964 *Eduardo Frei* is inaugurated as president of Chile.

1986 A Beirut magazine reports that the U.S. has been secretly supplying Iran with arms. (*Iran-contra affair*).

Joaquim Alberto Chissano is elected president of Mozambique.

1992 *William J. (Bill) Clinton* is elected as the forty-second president of the United States, defeating incumbent George Bush.

1996 *Petar Stoyanov* is elected president of Bulgaria.

november

NOVEMBER
4

HOLIDAYS

Andorra
Feast of St. Charles Borromeo

Iran
Death to America Day
Commemorates the seizure of the
U.S. Embassy in Teheran, 1979.

Italy
National Unity Day

Panama
Flag Day

Tonga
Constitution Day
Commemorates the granting of the
constitution by George I, 1875.

U.S. (Oklahoma)
Will Rogers Day
Commemorates the birth of the
world-famous actor and humorist,
1879.

RELIGIOUS CALENDAR

The Saints
St. Pierius, priest. [d. c. 310]
*St. John Zedazneli and his
    Companions,* Fathers of the
    Iberian church. [d. c. 580]
St. Clether, hermit. Also called
    Clanis, or *Cleer.* [d. c. 6th
    century]
St. Clarus, martyr. [d. c. 8th century]
St. Joannicius, monk and hermit. [d.
    846]
St. Charles Borromeo, archbishop of
    Milan and cardinal; patron of
    libraries, religious education.
    [d. 1584] Obligatory
    Memorial.

SS. Vitalis and Agricola, martyrs.
    [death date unkown]
    [Celebrated in particular
    calendars.]

The Beatified
Blessed Emeric, Hungarian prince.
    Also called *Imre;* generally
    referred to as *St. Emeric.* [d.
    1031]
Blessed Frances D'Ambrose, widow.
    Established first Carmelite
    convent in France. [d. 1485]
Blessed Marthe Aimee LeBouteiller.
    [beatified 1990]
*Blessed Louise Therese de
    Montaignac de Chauvance.*
    [beatified 1990]
Blessed Maria Schinina. [beatified
    1990]
Blessed Elisabeth Vendramini.
    [beatified 1990]

BIRTHDATES

1569 *Guillén de Castro y Bellvís,*
    Spanish dramatist; author of
    Las Mocedades del Cid, the
    basis for Pierre Corneille's *Le
    Cid.* [d. July 28, 1631]

1575 *Guido Reni,* Italian artist;
    known for his dramatic
    images with metallic
    tonalities; works include the
    Vatican's *Crucifixion of St.
    Peter;* rival of Caravaggio. [d.
    August 18, 1642]

1751 *Richard Brinsley (Butler)
    Sheridan,* Irish playwright,
    politician, baptized on this

day; noted for his comedies
of manners, *The Rivals, The
School for Scandal,* and *The
Critic.* [d. July 7, 1816]

1790 *Carlos Antonio López,*
    President and Dictator of
    Paraguay, 1844–62. [d.
    September 10, 1862]

1809 *Benjamin Robbins Curtis,*
    U.S. jurist, lawyer; Associate
    Justice, U.S. Supreme Court,
    1851–57; issued dissenting
    opinion in the *Dred Scott
    Case,* 1857. [d. September 15,
    1874]

1812 *Aleardo Aleardi,* Italian poet,
    patriot; participated in
    insurrection against Austrian
    control in Lombardy, 1848.
    [d. July 17, 1878]

1837 *James Douglas,* U.S.
    metallurgist, mine executive,
    and philanthropist; achieved
    reforms in U.S. mining
    industry; town of *Douglas,
    Arizona* is named for him. [d.
    June 25, 1918]

1841 *B(enjamin) F(ranklin)
    Goodrich,* U.S. manufacturer;
    founder of B. F. Goodrich
    Rubber Co. [d. August 3,
    1888]

1876 *James (Earle) Fraser,* U.S.
    sculptor; known for his
    monumental sculptures of
    historical figures, as well as
    allegorical figures such as *Law
    and Justice* at U.S. Supreme

Court Building; designed the buffalo nickel. [d. October 11, 1953]

1879 *Will(iam Penn Adair) Rogers,* U.S. humorist, actor; known throughout the world for his wry wit and satirical observations; killed in plane crash in Alaska with Wiley Post (November 22) at height of his career. [d. August 15, 1935]

1906 *Robert Bernard Considine,* U.S. journalist. [d. September 25, 1975]

1911 *Dixie Lee (Wilma Winifred Wyatt),* U.S. actress; known for ingenue roles in early talking films; married Bing Crosby, 1930. [d. November 1, 1952]

1916 *Walter (Leland) Cronkite, Jr.,* U.S. broadcast journalist; anchored the popular *CBS Evening News,* telecast 1962–81.

1917 *Gig Young (Byron Barr),* U.S. actor. [d. October 19, 1978]

1918 *Cameron Mitchell (Cameron Mizell),* U.S. actor; appeared on stage and in the film, *Death of a Salesman;* starred in the television series, *High Chaparral.* [d. July 6, 1994]

Art(hur) Carney, U.S. actor.

1919 *Martin Henry Balsam,* U.S. actor; Academy Award for *A Thousand Clowns,* 1964. [d. February 3, 1996]

1920 *Douglass C. North,* U.S. economist; Nobel Prize for Economics with Robert W. Fogel, for their work on cliometrics, 1993.

1936 *Didier Ratsiraka,* President, Democratic Republic of Madagascar, 1975–.

1937 *Loretta Swit,* U.S. actress; known for her role as Margaret Houlihan in the television series, *M*A*S*H,* 1972–83.

1962 *Ralph George Macchio, Jr.,* U.S. actor; starred in the films, *The Karate Kid,* 1984, and *The Karate Kid II,* 1986.

1963 *Andrea McArdle,* U.S. singer, actress; known for performance in the title role in the original Broadway production of *Annie.*

1969 *Matthew McConaughey,* U.S. actor; known for his performance in the movie *A Time to Kill,* 1996.

HISTORICAL EVENTS

1307 *Swiss Confederation* declares its independence of Austria.

1520 *Christian II* of Denmark is crowned king of Sweden after defeating the Swedes in battle.

1854 *Florence Nightingale,* with a staff of 38 nurses, arrives at Scutari (*Crimean War*).

1890 The British protectorate over *Zanzibar* is formally announced.

1908 Belgium assumes sovereignty over the *Congo State* of Africa.

1909 *Sergei Rachmaninoff,* Russian pianist and composer, makes his American debut in a recital at Smith College, Northampton, Massachusetts.

1918 Italy and Austria-Hungary sign armistice, ending conflict between the two countries (*World War I*).

The Allies formally agree to the U.S. demand for peace

based on President Wilson's *Fourteen Points* (World War I).

1921 *Takashi Hara,* Premier of Japan, is assassinated.

1939 *U.S. Neutrality Act of 1939* repeals an arms embargo and authorizes *cash and carry* exports of arms and munitions.

1942 British defeat Germans at *El Alamein* in North Africa, forcing Rommel's troops to retreat (*World War II*).

1943 *Eighth Symphony* of *Dimitri Shostakovich* premieres at the Moscow Conservatory.

1946 *John F. Kennedy* wins his first election to the U.S. Congress.

United Nations Educational, Scientific, and Cultural Organization (*UNESCO*) is established.

1956 *Janos Kadar* becomes premier of Hungary and head of a pro-Soviet government following the collapse of the anti-Communist rebellion.

1964 General *Rene Barrientos* assumes power in Bolivia after a coup d'etat.

1966 Soviet-U.S. agreement for direct air service between New York City and Moscow is signed in Washington, D.C.

1970 *Salvador Allende* is inaugurated as president of Chile. He is the first Marxist head of state to be elected in the Western Hemisphere.

1977 The United Nations Security Council approves a ban on military aid to *South Africa.*

1979 *Iranian militants* seize U.S. Embassy in Teheran and take

november

90 hostages, who are not released until January 20, 1981.

1984 *Daniel Ortega* is elected president of Nicaragua in the first national election since the 1979 overthrow of Anastasio Somoza.

1991 *Imelda Marcos,* wife of former President Ferdinand Marcos, returns to the Philippines after five years in exile.

1993 *Jean Chrétien* takes office as prime minister of Canada.

1995 A joint *Israeli-Albanian concert* is held in Albania to commemorate the Albanians' protection of Jews from Nazi occupiers during the *Holocaust* (World War II).

1995 Israeli prime minister *Yitzhak Rabin* is assassinated.

HOLIDAYS

El Salvador
Anniversary of First Cry of Independence
Commemorates first battle for independence from Spain, 1811.

Great Britain
Guy Fawkes Day
Commemorates the thwarting of the attempt to blow up Parliament by Guy Fawkes and his fellow Roman Catholic conspirators, 1605.

Panama (Colon)
Independence Day

Sweden
All Saints' Day

RELIGIOUS CALENDAR

The Saints
SS. Zachary and Elizabeth, parents of St. John the Baptist. [d. 1st century]
St. Bertilla, virgin and Abbess of Chelles. Also called *Bertila,* or *Bertille.* [d. 705]
SS. Galation and Episteme, martyrs. [death date unknown]
St. Kea, monk and bishop; invoked for the cure of toothache. Also called *Ke,* or *Quay.* [death date unknown]

The Beatified
Blessed Gomidas Keumurgian, martyr. [d. 1707]
Blessed Maddalena Caterina Morano. [beatified 1994]

BIRTHDATES

1494 *Hans Sachs,* German poet, dramatist, meistersinger; composed more than 6000 musical works. [d. January 19, 1576]

1558 *Thomas Kyd,* English dramatist; author of *The Spanish Tragedy,* an early masterpiece of English drama. [d. December 1594]

1779 *Washington Allston,* U.S. painter, author; a leading U.S. Romantic painter, noted for his use of color; close friend of Samuel Taylor Coleridge (October 21) and teacher of Samuel F. B. Morse (April 27). [d. July 9, 1843]

1787 *Franz Xavier Gruber,* Austrian musician, composer of *Silent Night,* 1818. [d. June 7, 1863]

1818 *Benjamin Franklin Butler,* Union Army general during U.S. Civil War; Military Governor of New Orleans during Civil War; U.S. Congressman, 1867–75; 1877–79; Governor of Massachusetts, 1882–84. [d. January 11, 1893]

1854 *Paul Sabatier,* French chemist; Nobel Prize in chemistry for developing process for hydrogenating organic compounds, 1912. [d. August 14, 1941]

1855 *Eugene V(ictor) Debs,* U.S. socialist leader, labor organizer; Socialist party presidential candidate four times, 1900–1912; presidential candidate while in prison for sedition, 1920; released by presidential order, 1921. [d. October 20, 1926]

1857 *Ida Minerva Tarbell,* U.S. journalist; best known as a muckraker of the early 20th century; noted for her *History of the Standard Oil Company,* 1904. [d. January 6, 1944]

1863 *James Ward Packard,* U.S. manufacturer; creator of the Packard automobile, 1899; founder of Packard Motor Car Co. [d. March 20, 1928]

1869 *Nicholas Longworth,* U.S. lawyer, politician; husband of Alice Lee Roosevelt (February 12), daughter of U.S. President Theodore Roosevelt (October 27); prominent member of the Republican Party. [d. April 9, 1931]

1877 *George Houk Mead,* U.S. business executive; organized Mead Corporation, 1905. [d. January 1, 1963]

1885 *Will(iam James) Durant,* U.S. historian, philosopher, author; Pulitzer Prize in general nonfiction, 1968. [d. November 7, 1981]

november

1892 *J(ohn) B(urdon) S(anderson) Haldane,* British geneticist; performed early studies on sex linkage in chromosomes. [d. December 1, 1964]

1895 *Charles G(ordon) MacArthur,* U.S. journalist, playwright; married to actress Helen Hayes. [d. April 21, 1956]

1901 *Martin Dies,* U.S. politician; U.S. Congressman, 1931–45; 1953–59; first chairman of *Dies Committee,* pinpointing infiltration of Communism into U.S. organizations; the committee later became the *Committee on Un-American Activities.* [d. November 14, 1972]

1905 *Annunzio Mantovani,* Italian conductor. [d. March 30, 1980]

Joel McCrea, U.S. actor. [d. October 20, 1990]

1912 *Roy Rogers (Leonard Slye),* U.S. actor, singer; most famous for his role as cowboy hero in films from 1935–55; owner of Roy Rogers fast food restaurants. Husband of Dale Evans (October 31). [d. July 6, 1998]

1913 *John McGiver,* U.S. actor. [d. September 9, 1975]

Vivien Leigh (Vivien Hartley), British actress; best known for her portrayal of Scarlett O'Hara in *Gone with the Wind.* [d. July 8, 1967]

1930 *Moorehead Cowell Kennedy, Jr.,* U.S. diplomat; economic counselor at the U.S. embassy in Iran; held hostage for 444 days, 1979–81.

1931 *Ike Turner,* U.S. singer, songwriter; hit songs include *A Fool in Love,* 1960, and

Goodbye, So Long, 1971; former husband and musical partner of Tina Turner (November 26).

1934 *Jeb Stuart Magruder,* U.S. government official; gained notoriety during *Watergate Incident.*

1941 *Elke Sommer,* U.S. actress, born in Germany.

1942 *Paul Simon,* U.S. songwriter, singer, actor; two Grammy Awards, with Art Garfunkel (October 13), for *Bridge Over Troubled Waters,* 1970; Grammy Award for the album, *Graceland,* 1986; inducted into the Rock and Roll Hall of Fame, 1990.

1943 *Sam Shepard (Samuel Shepard Rogers),* U.S. author, playwright, actor; Pulitzer Prize for Drama for *Buried Child,* 1978; starred in the movies, *Frances, The Right Stuff,* and *Baby Boom.*

1946 *Gram Parsons (Cecil Connor),* U.S. singer, songwriter; member of the rock groups, *The Byrds* and *The Flying Burrito Brothers.* [d. September 19, 1973]

1947 *Peter Noone,* British singer, musician; known as Herman of the rock group, *Herman's Hermits,* 1963–71.

1952 *Bill Walton,* U.S. basketball player; National Basketball Association Most Valuable Player, 1978.

1958 *Jon-Erik Hexum,* U.S. actor; starred in the television series, *Cover-Up,* 1984. [d. October 18, 1984]

1959 *Bryan Adams,* Canadian singer, musician; Platinum Album Award for *Reckless,* 1985.

1963 *Tatum O'Neal,* U.S. actress; Oscar winner for *Paper Moon,* 1973.

HISTORICAL EVENTS

1414 Roman Catholic *Council of Constance* convenes in order to condemn heresy of *John Wyclif* and *John Hus.*

1556 *Akbar the Great,* Mogul leader, defeats Hindus at *Panipat.*

1605 *Gunpowder Plot* in England is discovered, a conspiracy of prominent Roman Catholics attempting to destroy the English government by blowing up Parliament; the affair ends with the arrest of conspirator *Guy Fawkes.*

1630 *Treaty of Madrid* ends war between England and Spain *(Thirty Years' War).*

1767 *John Dickinson* writes the first of his *Letters from a Farmer in Pennsylvania,* a popular series of pamphlets on colonial opposition to the Townshend Acts.

1903 *Minneapolis Symphony Orchestra* makes its first appearance as a permanent organization under the direction of *Emil Oberhoffer.*

1911 *Tripoli* is annexed by Italy.

1912 First U.S. *cross-country flight* by Calbraith P. Rogers is successfully completed, taking 82 hours, 4 minutes.

1914 Great Britain and France declare war on Turkey *(World War I).*

1921 *Mongolia* declares its independence from China.

1967 Yemen Arab Republic president, *Abdullah al-Salal,* is overthrown by the Republican Council.

1974 *District of Columbia* residents vote for the first time for a mayor and 14-member city council; previously the posts were filled by presidential appointments.

The U.S.S.R. announces the completion of an *oil pipeline* from the Volga-Ural industrial region to the Black Sea port of Novorossisk, providing easy access to import markets.

1975 *São Tomé and Príncipe* promulgate a constitution.

1985 *Ali Hassan Mwinyi* is inaugurated as president of Tanzania.

1991 *Kiichi Miyazawa* is elected premier of Japan.

1992 *Bobby Fischer* defeats Boris Spassky in a chess competition. It is the first time in over twenty years that Fischer played publicly.

1994 *George Foreman* wins world heavyweight boxing title by defeating *Michael Moore.* Foreman is the oldest boxer to win a title in any class.

1995 *Eduard Shevardnadze* is elected president of Georgia, the former Soviet republic.

1996 *Benazir Bhutto,* prime minister of Pakistan, is removed from power for the second time after rumors of corruption.

november

NOVEMBER
6

HOLIDAYS

Dominican Republic
Constitution Day

Morocco
Al-Missira Celebration Day or Anniversary of the Green March

Sweden
Gustavus Adolphus Day
Commemorates the death of the famous military leader, 1632.

RELIGIOUS CALENDAR

Feasts
Feast of All Saints of Ireland.
    [observed only in Ireland.]

The Saints
St. Melaine, Bishop of Rennes. Also
    called *Malanius.* [d. c. 530]
St. Illtud, abbot. Also called *Eltut,*
    Hildutus, Iltet, Iltut, Illtutus,
    or *Illtyd.* [d. 6th century]
St. Leonard of Noblac; patron of
    prisoners, coppersmiths,
    blacksmiths, locksmiths,
    porters, coalminers,
    greengrocers, barrelmakers,
    and women in labor. [d. 6th
    century]
St. Winnoc, abbot. Also called
    Winoc. [d. c. 717]
St. Demetrian, Bishop of Khytri. [d.
    c. 912]
St. Barlaam of Khutyn, abbot. Also
    called *Varlaam.* [d. 1193]
The Martyrs of Indo-China. [d.
    1862]

The Beatified
Blessed Christina of Stommeln,
    virgin. [d. 1312]
Blessed Joan Mary de Maillé,
    widow. [d. 1414]
Blessed Nonius, lay brother and a
    national hero of Portugal.
    Also called *Nuñes.* [d. 1431]
Blessed Margaret of Lorraine,
    widow. [d. 1521]

BIRTHDATES

1661 *Charles II,* King of Spain,
    1665–1700; his death
    signalled beginning of *War of
    Spanish Succession.* [d.
    November 1, 1700]

1671 *Colley Cibber,* English actor,
    playwright; known for
    eccentric parts he portrayed
    in early English theater;
    named Poet Laureate, 1730;
    source of much debate,
    especially in his interpretation
    of Shakespeare. [d. December
    11, 1757]

1771 *Aloys Senefelder,* Hungarian
    inventor; invented
    lithography, 1796; invented
    process of lithographing in
    color. [d. February 26, 1834]

1825 *Jean Louis Charles Garnier,*
    French architect; designed
    the Paris Opéra, the Nice
    Conservatory, Monte Carlo
    Casino, and tombs of Bizet
    and Offenbach. [d. August 3,
    1898]

1833 *Jonas Lauritz Idemil Lie,*
    Norwegian novelist,
    playwright, and poet. [d. July
    5, 1908]

1851 *Charles Henry Dow,* U.S.
    financier, publisher; co-
    founder of the *Wall Street
    Journal,* 1889; formulated the
    theory behind the Dow-Jones
    average. [d. December 4,
    1902]

1854 *John Philip Sousa,* U.S.
    conductor, composer;
    conductor of U.S. Marine
    Band, 1880–92; formed own
    band and became renowned
    for his marches; during World
    War I, directed all U.S. Navy
    bands; composed more than
    100 marches. [d. March 6,
    1932]

1861 *James Naismith,* Canadian
    educator, credited with
    inventing *basketball,* 1891. [d.
    November 28, 1939]

1890 *Henry Knox Sherrill,* U.S.
    clergyman; considered to be
    one of the most influential
    post-war church leaders in
    the U.S.; President, World
    Council of Churches,
    1954–61. [d. May 11, 1980]

1892 *John W. Alcock,* British
    aviator; with Arthur Brown,
    made pioneer flight across
    the Atlantic, 1919 [d.
    December 18, 1919]

1893 *Edsel Bryant Ford,* U.S. auto
    executive; only son of Henry

Ford (July 30); President of
Ford Motor Co., 1919–43. [d.
May 26, 1943]

1907 *Charles W(oodruff) Yost,* U.S.
diplomat; played significant
role in founding the *United
Nations;* chief UN delegate,
1969–71. [d. May 21, 1981]

1912 *George Cakobau,* Governor-
General, Dominion of Fiji,
1973–83. [d. 1989]

1916 *Ray Conniff,* U.S. band
leader; albums include
S'Wonderful, 1956.

1921 *James Jones,* U.S. novelist. [d.
May 9, 1977]

1923 *Robert P. Griffin,* U.S.
politician, lawyer; U.S.
Congressman, 1957–66; U.S.
Senator, 1966–78.

1931 *Mike Nichols (Michael Igor
Peschowsky),* U.S. stage and
film director, producer, born
in Germany; Academy Award
(Director) for *The Graduate,*
1967.

1942 *Jean Rosemary Shrimpton,*
British model.

1946 *Sally Margaret Field,* U.S.
actress; Academy Awards for
Norma Rae, 1979, and *Places
in the Heart,* 1985.

1948 *Glenn Frey,* U.S. musician,
songwriter, singer; member of
the former rock group, *The
Eagles;* solo album, *No Fun
Aloud,* 1982.

1955 *Maria Owings Shriver,* U.S.
broadcast journalist; co-
anchor of the *CBS Morning
News,* 1985–86; daughter of
Sargent and Eunice Kennedy
Shriver; wife of Arnold
Schwarzenegger.

1962 *Lori Singer,* U.S. actress;
known for roles in *Footloose,*
1984 and *Warlock,* 1991.

1970 *Ethan Hawke,* U.S. actor.

HISTORICAL EVENTS

1789 *John Carroll* is appointed the
first Roman Catholic bishop
in the U.S.

1860 *Abraham Lincoln* is elected
President of the U.S.

1869 First modern American
football game is played
between Rutgers and
Princeton; the teams field 25
players on each side; Rutgers
defeats Princeton, 6–4.

1911 *Francisco Madero,* having led
successful revolution in
Mexico, becomes president,
an office he occupies for only
two years.

1914 The U.S. declares its
neutrality in hostilities
between Great Britain and
Turkey (*World War I*).

Egypt declares war on Turkey
(*World War I*).

1915 *Second Battle of Champagne*
ends with appalling casualties
to the Allies and Germany
and almost no gain for the
French and British (*World
War I*).

1917 Bolsheviks in Petrograd,
Russia, take over telephone
exchanges, railway stations,
and electric power plants
(*Revolution of 1917*).

1918 *Sedan,* in northeast France, is
taken by French and
American forces (*Word War
I*).

1923 First *electric shaver* patent is
awarded to *Col. Jacob Schick.*

1935 *Edwin Armstrong* first
demonstrates *FM radio
transmission,* a method
which he developed in 1933
but which did not come into
popular use until 1940.

1943 Carl Orff's *Catulli Carmina* is
first performed in Leipzig.

The Soviet army retakes *Kiev,*
ending a two-year German
occupation of the Ukranian
capital *(World War II).*

1947 *Meet the Press* makes its
television debut.

1974 *Janet Gray Hayes* is elected
mayor of San Jose, California.
She is the first woman to
become mayor of a major
U.S. city.

1978 An 88-day strike against the
New York Times and the
Daily News ends.

1984 President *Ronald Reagan* is
reelected by 525 electoral
votes, the largest margin in
the history of the U.S.
electoral college.

1985 *Anibal Cavaco Silva* is
inaugurated as prime minister
of Portugal.

1987 *Noboru Takeshita* is elected
to succeed *Yasuhiro
Nakasone* as premier of
Japan.

The United Nations allows
public access to secret files of
World War II war criminals.

november

NOVEMBER
7

HOLIDAYS

Albania, Bulgaria, Hungary, Mongolia, Russia
October Revolution Day
Commemorates the socialist revolution of 1917.

Bangladesh
National Revolution Day
Commemorates the overthrow of the government of *Abdus Sattar*, 1982.

Nepal
Queen Aishworya's Birthday

U.S.
Death Anniversary of Eleanor Roosevelt
Sponsored by the Franklin D. Roosevelt Philatelic Society.

U.S.
National Notary Public Day
Sponsored by American Society of Notaries.

RELIGIOUS CALENDAR

The Saints
St. Herculanus, Bishop of Perugia, martyr. [d. c. 547]
St. Florentius, Bishop of Strasburg. [d. 7th century]
St. Willibrord, Bishop of Utrecht and missionary. Surnamed *Clement.* [d. 739]
St. Engelbert, Archbishop of Cologne, and martyr. [d. 1225]
St. Congar, patron of Hope, Wales. [death date unknown]

The Beatified
Blessed Helen of Arcella, virgin. [d. 1242]
Blessed Margaret Colonna, virgin. [d. 1280]
Blessed Matthia of Matelica, virgin and abbess. [d. 1300]
Blessed Peter of Ruffia, martyr. [d. 1365]
Blessed Antony Baldinucci, Jesuit priest. [d. 1717]

BIRTHDATES

1598 *Francisco de Zurbaran,* Spanish baroque painter, baptized on this day; noted for his religious paintings and monastic portraiture. [d. August 27, 1664]

1811 *Karel Jaromir Erben,* Czech poet and scholar; several composers have drawn inspiration from his ballads. [d. November 21, 1870]

1832 *Andrew Dickson White,* U.S. educator, diplomat; cofounder, with Era Cornell (January 11), of Cornell University, 1865; served as President of Cornell, 1868–85; U.S. Minister to Germany, 1879–81; Minister to Russia, 1892–94; U.S. Ambassador to Germany, 1897–1902; U.S. delegate to Hague Conference. [d. November 4, 1918]

1838 *Jean Marie Mathias Philippe Auguste, Comte de Villiers de l'Isle-Adam (Comte de l'Isle),* French short-story writer, dramatist; founder of the *Symbolist School* in French literature. [d. August 19, 1889]

1867 *Marie Curie,* French physical chemist, born in Poland; with her husband, Pierre Curie (May 15), pioneered in investigation of radioactivity; Nobel Prize in physics for study of radiation phenomenon (with P. Curie and A. H. Becquerel), 1903; Nobel Prize in chemistry for discovery of radium and polonium, 1911. [d. July 4, 1934]

1878 *Lise Meitner,* Swedish physicist, born in Austria; noted for work on disintegration products of radium, thorium, and protoactinium; with Otto Hahn and Fritz Strassman, accomplished fission of uranium, 1938. [d. October 17, 1968]

1888 *Sir Chandrasekhara Venkata Raman,* Indian physicist; Nobel Prize in physics for discoveries in light diffusion, called Raman effect, 1930. [d. November 21, 1970]

1895 *Clement D(ixon) Johnston,* U.S. business executive; President, U. S. Chamber of Commerce, 1954–55. [d. October 16, 1979]

1903 *Konrad Zacharias Lorenz,* Austrian ethologist; Nobel Prize in physiology or medicine (with K. von Frisch and N. Tinbergen), 1973. [d. February 27, 1989]

1904 *Isamu Noguchi,* U.S. sculptor. [d. 1988]

1905 *Dean Jagger (Dean Jeffries),* U.S. character actor.[d. February, 1991]

1913 *Albert Camus,* French philosopher, novelist, dramatist, journalist. [d. January 4, 1960]

1920 *Max M. Kampelman,* U.S. lawyer, diplomat; led U.S. negotiating team at arms reduction talks, 1985–88; chairman, Institute for the Study of Diplomacy, 1994– .

1922 *Al Hirt,* U.S. jazz musician.

1926 *Dame Joan Sutherland,* Australian coloratura soprano.

1927 *Al Martino (Alfred Cini),* U.S. singer, actor; sang the theme song for and starred in the movie, *The Godfather,* 1972.

1937 *Mary Travers,* U.S. author, composer, singer; member of the folk group, *Peter, Paul, and Mary.*

1938 *Barry Foster Newman,* U.S. actor; starred in the television series, *Petrocelli,* 1974–76.

1942 *Thomas J. Peters,* U.S. motivational speaker, writer; author of *In Search of Excellence: Lessons from America's Best-Run Companies.*

Johnny Rivers (John Ramistella), U.S. singer; hit singles include *Midnight Special,* 1965; developed the careers of *The Fifth Dimension* and Laura Nyro.

1943 *Joni Mitchell (Roberta Joan Anderson),* Canadian singer, songwriter; wrote over 100 songs; hits include *Both Sides Now* and *Woodstock.*

HISTORICAL EVENTS

680 *Sixth Council of Constantinople* is convened; it condemns *Monophysitism* and *Monotheletism.*

1153 *Treaty of Wallingford* is signed *Stephen,* King of England, recognizes *Henry II* as his successor.

1811 *General William Henry Harrison* defeats Indians at the *Battle of Tippecanoe.*

1837 A pro-slavery mob in Alton, Illinois, destroys printing press and kills abolitionist printer *Elijah Lovejoy.*

1860 *Victor Emmanuel* enters Naples as King.

1900 Spain cedes the *Cagayan and Sibutu Islands* in the *Philippines* to the U.S. for $100,000.

1914 *Tsingtao,* German leasehold in China, surrenders to Japanese and British forces (*World War I*).

1917 *Bolshevik* minority, led by *Lenin,* rises in revolution, capturing most of the government offices in Petrograd, seizing the Winter Palace, and arresting members of the provisional government except Premier Kerensky, who manages to escape (*Russian Revolution*).

The British capture Gaza from the Turks, ending the *Third Battle of Gaza (World War I).*

1934 Rachmaninoff's *Rhapsody on a Theme by Paganini*

premieres in Baltimore with Leopold Stokowski conducting the Philadelphia Orchestra and the composer as soloist.

1941 *Bette Davis* becomes the first woman elected president of the *Academy of Motion Picture Arts and Sciences* in Hollywood.

1944 U.S. President *Franklin D. Roosevelt* is reelected for a historic fourth term.

1956 Eugene O'Neill's play, *Long Day's Journey into Night,* opens on Broadway, three years after the author's death and 15 years after it was written.

1963 New York Yankees catcher, *Elston Howard,* becomes the first black to win the American League's Most Valuable Player Award.

1967 *Carl Stokes* is elected mayor of *Cleveland, Ohio.* He is the first black mayor of a major U.S. city.

1970 *Carlos Monzon* defeats *Nino Benvenuti* to win the world middleweight boxing title.

1975 General *Ziaur Rahman* assumes power in Bangladesh after a coup d'etat.

1987 Tunisian president, *Habib Bourguiba,* is overthrown in a coup staged by Premier *Zine el-Abidine Ben Ali.*

1990 *Mary Robinson* is elected as the first female president of Ireland.

Prime Minister *Vishwanath Pratap Singh* of India resigns.

1991 *Earvin "Magic" Johnson* announces his retirement from basketball after revealing that he has tested postive for HIV.

november

NOVEMBER
8

RELIGIOUS CALENDAR

The Saints

The Four Crowned Ones, martyrs. A feast in commemoration of four masons martyred when they refused to sculpt a pagan god for the Emperor Diocletian. [d. c. 306]

St. Cybi, abbot. Also called *Cuby,* or *Kebie.* [d. 6th cent.]

St. Deusdedit, pope. Elected in 615 under the name *Adeodatus I.* [d. 618]

St. Tysilio, abbot. Also called *Suliau.* [d. c. 7th century]

St. Willehad, Bishop of Bremen and missionary. [d. 789]

St. Gerardin, monk and hermit. Also called *Garnard, Garnat, Gernardius,* or *Gervardius.* [d. c. 934]

St. Godfrey, Bishop of Amiens. Also called *Geoffrey.* [d. 1115]

BIRTHDATES

1086 *Henry V,* Holy Roman Emperor, reigned 1106–1125. [d. May 23, 1125]

1622 *Charles X Gustav,* King of Sweden. [d. February 13, 1660]

1656 *Edmund Halley,* English astronomer; best known for his study of comets; *Halley's comet* is named for him. [d. January 14, 1742]

1711 *Mikhail Vasilievich Lomonosov,* Russian scientist, poet, scholar; considered the founder of modern literary Russian, and the *Father of Modern Russian Poetry.* [d. April 4, 1765]

1732 *John Dickinson,* American patriot, lawyer; called the *Penman of the Revolution.* [d. February 14, 1808]

1818 *Marca Minghetti,* Italian premier, 1863–64; 1873–76. [d. December 10, 1886]

1821 *George Henry Bissell,* U.S. oil executive; responsible for establishing the Pennsylvania Oil Co., the first oil company in the U.S. [d. November 19, 1884]

1830 *Oliver Otis Howard,* U.S. Army general, educator; founder of *Howard University,* 1867. [d. October 26, 1909]

1836 *Milton Bradley,* U.S. manufacturer, publisher; founded the Milton Bradley Co.; developed its first game, *The Checkered Game of Life.* [d. May 30, 1911]

1847 *Bram Stoker,* Irish author; wrote *Dracula.* [d. April 20, 1912]

1848 *Gottlob Frege,* German mathematician, philosopher; founder of modern mathematical logic. [d. July 26, 1925]

1869 *Joseph Franklin Rutherford,* U.S. religious leader, author; a leader of the Russellites (Jehovah's Witnesses) in the U.S., 1916–42; outspoken proponent of conscientious objection. [d. January 8, 1942]

1884 *Hermann Rorschach,* Swiss psychiatrist; developed the ink blot test for psychiatric analysis (*Rorschach Test*), 1921. [d. April 2, 1922]

1885 *Tomoyuki Yamashita,* Japanese Army general; commander of Japanese forces in Malayan Campaign during World War II; executed as war criminal. [d. February 23, 1946]

1897 *Dorothy Day,* U.S. reformer; a founder of the *Catholic Worker Movement* in the U.S. [d. November 29, 1980]

1900 *Margaret Mitchell,* U.S. novelist; wrote *Gone with the Wind;* Pulitzer Prize, 1937. [d. August 16, 1949]

1909 *Katharine Hepburn,* U.S. actress; star in films and on stage; winner of four Academy Awards as Best Actress.

1916 *Peter Weiss,* Swedish writer, born in Germany; an important post-war European experimental playwright; author of *The Persecution and Assassination of Jean*

Paul Marat, 1964. [d. May 10, 1982]

June Havoc (June Hovick), Canadian actress; sister of Gypsy Rose Lee (January 9).

1918 *Florence Chadwick,* U.S. professional distance swimmer; the first woman to swim the English Channel both ways.

1921 *Jerome Hines (Jerome Heinz),* U.S. operatic bass.

Gene Michael Saks, U.S. director; directed *Mame, The Odd Couple.*

1922 *Christiaan (Neethling) Barnard,* South African surgeon; performed first successful *heart transplant,* 1967.

1927 *Patti Page (Clara Anne Fowler),* U.S. singer.

1931 *Morley Safer,* U.S. broadcast journalist, born in Canada; featured on the news show *60 Minutes,* 1970– .

1933 *Esther Rolle,* U.S. actress; known for her role as Florida Evans in the television series, *Maude,* 1972–74, and *Good Times,* 1974–78.

1935 *Alain Delon,* French actor.

1948 *Minnie Riperton,* U.S. singer; Gold Record Award for *Lovin' You,* 1974; known for her five-octave voice range. [d. July 12, 1979]

1949 *Bonnie Raitt,* U.S. singer, songwriter; known for her blues-rock style; featured on the soundtrack to the film, *Urban Cowboy,* 1980; board

member, Musicians United for Safe Energy; daughter of John Raitt.

1952 *Christine Ann (Christie) Hefner,* U.S. business executive; President, Playboy Enterprises, 1982–; daughter of Hugh Hefner.

1953 *Alfre Woodard,* U.S. actress; known for roles in TV dramas *Hill Street Blues, L.A. Law* and *St. Elsewhere.*

1961 *Leif Garrett,* U.S. actor, singer; hit single with a remake of *Surfin' USA;* known as a teen idol.

HISTORICAL EVENTS

1519 *Montezuma* receives *Hernando Cortés* in Aztec capital.

1520 Invasion of Sweden by *Christian II* of Denmark results in *Blood Bath of Stockholm,* in which nobility of Stockholm are massacred.

1576 *Pacification of Ghent* unites all Dutch provinces against Spain (*Dutch War of Liberation*).

1830 *Ferdinand II* accedes to the throne of Naples.

1889 *Montana* is admitted to the Union as the 41st state.

1910 *Victor Berger* is elected to the U.S. House of Representatives, the first Socialist to serve in Congress.

1917 *Second Congress of Soviets* convenes in Petrograd, Russia,

and names Council of People's Commissars for the governing of the country with Lenin as chairman, Trotsky foreign commissar, and Stalin as commissar of nationalities.

Lenin issues a decree of nationalization, abolishing private ownership of land in Russia.

1933 *Nadir Shah,* ruler of Afghanistan, is assassinated and succeeded by his son, *Mohammed Zahir Shah.*

1942 Allied forces begin landings in North Africa, beginning *Algeria-Morocco Campaign (World War II).*

1953 *Jose Figueres* is inaugurated as president of Costa Rica.

1956 Cecil B. DeMille's film, *The Ten Commandments,* premieres in New York.

1958 Jeweler Harry Winston donates the *Hope Diamond* to the Smithsonian Institution.

1974 The eight National Guardsmen charged in the deaths of four people during an anti-war demonstration at *Kent State University* in 1970 are acquitted.

1983 *Wilson Goode* is elected the first black mayor of Philadelphia.

1988 Former Vice-President *George Bush* is elected as the forty-first president of the United States, defeating Democratic nominee *Michael Dukakis.*

The U.S. Senate approves an increase in the *minimum wage* to $4.25 per hour.

NOVEMBER
9

HOLIDAYS

Nepal
Constitution Day

Pakistan
Allama Iqbal Day

Turks and Caicos Islands
Remembrance Day
Day set aside to commemorate all
the Bahamian war dead.

RELIGIOUS CALENDAR

Feasts
*The Dedication of the Archbasilica
   of the Most Holy Savior,*
   commonly called *St. John
   Lateran,* the acknowledged
   mother of churches and
   cathedral of the popes.

The Saints
St. Theodore Tiro, martyr. One of
   the patrons of warriors. Also
   called *Theodore Tyro,
   Theodore the Recruit,* or
   Theodorus. [d. c. 306]
St. Benignus, bishop. Also called
   Benen, or *Binen.* [d. 467]
St. Vitonus, Bishop of Verdun. Also
   called *Vanne.* [d. c. 525]

The Beatified
Blessed George Napper, martyr. Also
   called *Napier.* [d. 1610]

BIRTHDATES

1731 *Benjamin Banneker,* U.S.
   inventor, mathematician,
   almanac maker. [d. 1806]

1801 *Robert Dale Owen,* U.S. social
   reformer, born in Scotland;
   U.S. Congressman, 1843–47; a
   founder of the *Smithsonian
   Institution,* 1845. [d. June 24,
   1877]

   Gail Borden, U.S. inventor,
   manufacturer; opened the
   first factory for the
   production of *evaporated
   milk,* 1860. [d. January 11,
   1874]

1802 *Elijah Parish Lovejoy,* U.S.
   abolitionist, newspaperman;
   killed during riot over slavery
   issue; known as the *martyr
   abolitionist.* [d. November 7,
   1837]

1818 *Ivan Sergeyevich Turgenev,*
   Russian novelist, short-story
   writer; author of *Fathers and
   Sons.* [d. September 3, 1883]

1825 *Ambrose Powell Hill,*
   Confederate general during
   U.S. Civil War; commanded
   the best division of troops in
   Confederacy. [d. April 2,
   1865]

1841 *King Edward VII* of Great
   Britain, ruled 1901–10. [d.
   May 6, 1910]

1853 *Stanford White,* U.S. architect;
   designed original *Madison
   Square Garden,* New York,
   1889. [d. June 25, 1906]

1865 *Frederick Funston,* U.S.
   soldier, army general;
   primarily known for his

guerrilla activities during
   Spanish American War. [d.
   February 19, 1917]

1869 *Marie Dressler (Leila von
   Koeber),* Canadian actress. [d.
   July 28, 1934]

1871 *Florence R. Sabin,* U.S.
   anatomist; known for her
   research on the lymphatic
   immune systems. [d. October
   3, 1953]

1873 *Fritz Thyssen,* German
   industrialist; controller of
   Vereingte Stahlwerke; early
   supporter of Hitler; later lost
   all his property after a falling
   out with Hitler over policies
   in Germany. [d. February 8,
   1951]

1886 *Ed Wynn (Isaiah Edwin
   Leopold),* U.S. comedic actor;
   father of Keenan Wynn. [d.
   June 19, 1966]

1888 *Jean Omer Marie Gabriel
   Monnet,* French economist,
   government official; founder
   of the *European Coal and
   Steel Community;* helped to
   rebuild European economy
   after World War II. [d. March
   16, 1979]

1897 *Ronald George Wreyford,*
   British chemist; Nobel Prize
   in chemistry for studies of
   chemical reactions affected by
   short energy pulsations (with
   M. Eigen and G. Porter) 1967.
   [d. June 7, 1978]

1915 *R. Sargent Shriver, Jr.,* U.S. government official, diplomat; Director of Peace Corps, 1961–66; U.S. Ambassador to France, 1968–70.

1918 *Spiro Agnew,* U.S. politician, lawyer; Governor of Maryland, 1967–68; U.S. Vice-President, 1969–73. Resigned as Vice-President when faced with charge of federal income tax evasion, 1973. [d. September 17, 1996]

1922 *Dorothy Dandridge,* U.S. actress. [d. September 8, 1965]

1928 *Anne Sexton,* U.S. poet; Pulitzer Prize in poetry, 1966. [d. October 4, 1974]

1931 *Eugene Lipscomb,* U.S. football player; defensive tackle, Baltimore Colts, 1956–60; called *Big Daddy.* [d. May 10, 1963]

1934 *Carl Sagan,* U.S. astronomer; popularized studies of astronomy through television series, *Cosmos.* Pulitzer Prize, 1978, for *The Dragons of Eden.* [d. December 20, 1996]

1936 *Daniel Robert (Bob) Graham,* U.S. politician; Governor of Florida, 1979–86; Senator, 1987–.

1952 *Lou Ferrigno,* U.S. actor; known for his role as the Hulk on the television series, *The Incredible Hulk,* 1977–81.

HISTORICAL EVENTS

1906 *Theodore Roosevelt* visits the Isthmus of Panama, becoming the first U.S. president to leave the country while in office.

1918 The German delegates are received by General Foch in the Compiègne Forest and given the Allies' armistice terms.

German *Kaiser Wilhelm II* is forced to abdicate (*World War I*).

Poland proclaims its independence as a free and reconstituted state with Marshal Jòzef Piłsudski as chief of state.

1924 *Robert Frank,* Swiss-born photographer.

1935 *John L. Lewis* creates the *Congress of Industrial Organizations* within the *American Federation of Labor.*

1938 The German National Socialists organize a night of vandalism called *Crystal Night (Kristalnacht),* in which Jews are attacked and their property destroyed.

1943 *United Nations Relief and Rehabilitation Administration* is established.

1944 U.S. General *George Patton* launches an all-out drive to capture *Metz, France (World War II).*

1949 *Costa Rica* promulgates its constitution.

1950 Twelve Soviet-made MIG-15s attack four U.S. aircraft over North Korea in the first dogfight involving *jet fighter planes* in history. (*Korean War*)

1953 King *Ibn Saud* of Saudi Arabia dies and is succeeded by Crown Prince *Saud.*

1960 *Robert McNamara* succeeds *Henry Ford II* as president of Ford Motor Co.

1961 *Julio Arosemena Monroy* is inaugurated as president of Ecuador.

1964 The Japanese Diet elects *Eisako Sato* as prime minister.

1965 Largest *power failure* in history blacks out New York City, parts of eight northeastern states, and parts of Ontario and Quebec for several hours.

1967 First *Saturn V* rocket carrying the unmanned *Apollo 4* spacecraft is launched from Cape Kennedy.

1984 The Statue, *Three Servicemen,* is unveiled as the final part of the *Vietnam Veterans Memorial* in Washington, D.C.

1985 Russian chess master, *Gary Kasparov,* becomes the youngest world champion by defeating *Anatoly Karpov* in a 24-game match in Moscow.

1989 The *Berlin Wall,* separating East and West Germany since 1961, is taken down.

november

NOVEMBER
10

HOLIDAYS

Bolivia (Potosi)
Public Holiday

Panama
Uprising of Los Santos or First Call of Independence

RELIGIOUS CALENDAR

The Saints

St. *Leo the Great,* pope (elected 440) and Doctor of the Church. Feast formerly April 11. [d. 461]Obligatory Memorial.

St. *Aedh Mac Bricc,* bishop. Popularly invoked to cure headaches. Also called *Aed, Aid,* or *MacBrice.* [d. 589]

St. *Justice,* Archbishop of Canterbury, missionary, and the first bishop of Rochester. [d. c. 627]

St. *Andrew Avellino,* priest. [d. 1608]

St. *Theoctista,* virgin. [death date unknown]

SS. *Trypho, Respicius, and Nympha,* martyrs. [death dates unknown] Feast suppressed 1969.

BIRTHDATES

1433 *Charles, Duke of Burgundy,* known as *Charles the Bold;* the last Duke of Burgundy. [d. January 5, 1477]

1483 *Martin Luther,* German religious reformer; father of the Protestant Reformation in Germany; founder of the Lutheran church. [d. February 18, 1546]

1493 *Paracelsus (Philippus Aureolus Theophrastus Bombastus von Hohenheim),* Swiss alchemist, physician; noted for his early theories of disease and medicine. [d. September 24, 1541]

1577 *Jacob Cats,* Dutch poet, statesman; known as Holland's *Household Poet.* [d. September 12, 1660]

1668 *François Couperin,* French composer, harpsichordist; first great composer of harpsichord music. [d. September 12, 1773]

1683 *George II,* King of Great Britain, 1727–60. [d. October 25, 1760]

1697 *William Hogarth,* English painter, engraver; noted for his pictorial satire; responsible for legislation (*Hogarth's Act,* 1735) protecting artists from piracy. [d. October 26, 1764]

1728 *Oliver Goldsmith,* English poet, playwright, novelist; author of *The Vicar of Wakefield* and *She Stoops to Conquer.* [d. April 4, 1774]

1759 *Johann Christoph Friedrich Schiller,* German dramatist, poet, historian, and philosopher. [d. May 9, 1805]

1801 *Samuel Gridley Howe,* U.S. humanitarian, physician, educator; Director, Perkins School for the Blind, 1831–65; a pioneer in education of the blind in the U.S.; husband of Julia Ward Howe (May 27), composer of *The Battle Hymn of the Republic.* [d. January 9, 1876]

1843 *Miguel Antonio Caro,* Colombian statesman; President, 1894–98. [d. August 5, 1909]

1874 *Donald Baxter Macmillan,* U.S. Arctic explorer; assisted Robert Peary during polar expedition, 1908–09; spent the rest of his life exploring Arctic region; author of *Four Years in the White North* and *How Peary Reached the Pole.* [d. September 7, 1970]

1879 *(Nicholas) Vachel Lindsay,* U.S. poet, noted for the rhythm and phonetics of his poetry. [d. December 5, 1931]

1887 *Arnold Zweig,* German novelist. [d. November 26, 1968]

1889 *Claude Rains,* U.S. actor, born in England [d. May 30, 1967]

1892 *John Merrill Olin,* U.S. manufacturer; head of Olin-Matheson Chemical Corporation, 1944–57.

1893 *J(ohn) P(hillips) Marquand,* U.S. novelist; Pulitzer Prize in fiction, 1938. [d. July 16, 1960]

1895 *John Knudsen Northrup,* U.S. aircraft manufacturer; a founder of Lockheed Aircraft Corp., 1927. [d. February 18, 1985]

1912 *Bernard Haring,* German theologian; active in reforms brought about by Vatican Council II.

1913 *Karl Jay Shapiro,* U.S. poet, critic; Pulitzer Prize in poetry, 1945.

1918 *Ernst Otto Fischer,* German chemist; Nobel Prize in chemistry for study of methods of merging organic and metallic atoms (with G. Wilkinson), 1973.

1919 *Moise (Kapenda) Tshombe,* Congolese political leader; President of Katanga State, 1960–63; exiled, 1965. [d. June 29, 1969]

1925 *Richard Burton (Richard Jenkins),* Welsh stage and screen actor. [d. Aug. 5, 1984]

1934 *Norm(an Dalton) Cash,* U.S. baseball player; first baseman, Detroit Tigers, 1960–74; batting title, 1961.

1935 *Roy (Richard) Scheider,* U.S. actor.

1946 *David Allen Stockman,* U.S. government official; Director, Office of Management and Budget, 1981–85; wrote memoirs, *Triumph of Politics,* 1986.

1947 *Bashir Gemayel,* Lebanese political leader; President-elect, 1982; killed in a bomb attack before taking office; brother of Amin Gemayel. [d. September 14, 1982]

1949 *Donna Fargo (Yvonne Vaughan),* U.S. singer, songwriter; known for her country-western hits, *Happiest Girl in the USA* and *Funny Face.*

Ann Reinking, U.S. dancer, actress; starred in the film, *Micki and Maude.*

1957 *Sinbad,* U.S. comedian, actor.

1959 *(Laura) MacKenzie Phillips,* U.S. actress; starred in the television series, *One Day at a Time.*

HISTORICAL EVENTS

1444 The Turks win a decisive victory at *Varna* over Christian crusaders led by *Ladislas of Hungary.*

1775 The American Continental Congress establishes a full-time, national *Marine Corps.*

1917 *Third Battle of Ypres* ends near Passchedaile with massive British losses (*World War I*).

1918 Professor *T. G. Masaryk,* President of National Council, is elected President of the *Republic of Czechoslovakia.*

1919 First *air mail service* is established between Paris and London.

1938 *Kemal Atatürk,* President of Turkey, dies and is succeeded by *Ismet Inönü.*

1941 First U.S.-escorted troop convoy of *World War II* sails from Halifax, Nova Scotia.

1942 U.S. warships and carrier aircraft engage French naval forces at *Casablanca, Morocco (World War II).*

1953 *How to Marry a Millionaire,* a film starring Marilyn Monroe, premieres.

1954 *Marine Memorial,* based on a photograph of troops raising the U.S. flag on Iwo Jima during World War II, is dedicated in Arlington, Virginia.

1965 *Ferdinand Marcos* is elected president of the Philippines.

1969 *Sesame Street* makes its television debut.

1971 U.S. ratifies the treaty returning *Okinawa* and the southern Ryukyus to Japan.

1975 The *Edmund Fitzgerald,* an ore boat with 29 crewmen aboard, sinks during a storm on Lake Superior.

The United Nations General Assembly adopts a resolution that defines *Zionism* as a form of racism.

1976 *Emperor Hirohito* celebrates the fiftieth anniversary of his ascension to the Japanese throne.

1980 Polish Supreme Court rules that independent trade unions such as *Solidarity* are legal.

1987 Colonel *Ali Seybou* becomes the acting president of Niger following the death of *Seyni Kountche.*

1989 *Todor Zhivkov* resigns as president of Bulgaria (1971-89).

november

NOVEMBER
11

HOLIDAYS

Angola
Independence Day
Commemorates the achievement of independence from Portugal, 1975.

Belgium, French Guiana, French Polynesia, Martinique, Tahiti, Wallis and Futuna Islands
Armistice Day
Commemorates the signing of the Armistice ending World War I, 1918.

Colombia
Independence of Cartagena

Bhutan
Birthday of His Majesty the King
Celebrates the birthday of King *Jigme Singye Wangchuk,* 1955.

Canada, Bermuda
Remembrance Day
Commemorates all who participated in the two world wars.

France, Guam, Puerto Rico, U.S., Virgin Islands
Veterans Day
Commemorates the signing of the Armistice ending World War I, 1918, and pays tribute to all members of the armed forces.

French West Indies, Monaco, New Caledonia
Victory Day

Maldives
Republic Day
Celebrates the establishment of the Republic, 1953.

U.S. (Washington)
Washington Admission Day
Commemorates the date Washington was admitted as a state.

RELIGIOUS CALENDAR

The Saints
St. Martin, Bishop of Tours; apostle of the Gauls, and patron of reformed drunkards. This day also called *Martinmas Day;* a Quarter Day in Scotland. [d. 397] Obligatory Memorial.
St. Theodore the Studite, abbot. [d. 826]
St. Bartholomew of Grottaferrata, abbot. [d. c. 1050]
St. Mennas, martyr. Also called *Menas.* [death date unknown]

BIRTHDATES

1050 *Henry IV,* Holy Roman Emperor, 1056–1106. [d. August 7, 1106]

1491 *Martin Bucer* (or *Butzer,*) German Protestant clergyman; a leader of the Reformation in Germany. [d. February 28, 1551]

1729 *Louis Antoine de Bougainville,* French navigator; commanded first French expedition around the world; an island and two straits in the South Pacific are named for him; the flowering vine *bougainvillaea* is also named for him. [d. April 31, 1811]

1744 *Abigail Adams,* U.S. First Lady; wife of President John Adams, mother of President John Quincy Adams. [d. October 28, 1818]

1748 *Charles IV,* King of Spain, 1788–1808; abdicated, 1808. [d. January 20, 1819]

1771 *Marie François Xavier Bichat,* French physician, founder of the science of *histology.* [d. July 22, 1802]

Ephraim McDowell, U.S. surgeon; performed first successful removal of an ovarian tumor, previously considered impossible, 1809. [d. June 25, 1830]

1821 *Fyodor Mikhailovich Dostoyevsky,* Russian novelist; his best-known works are *Crime and Punishment* and *The Brothers Karamazov.* [d. February 9, 1881]

1836 *Thomas Bailey Aldrich,* U.S. poet, editor; editor of *Atlantic Monthly,* 1881–90. [d. March 19, 1907]

1852 *Franz Conrad von Hötzendorf,* Austrian general during World War I; Chief of Staff of Austro-Hungarian army, 1914–17. [d. August 26, 1925]

1868 *(Jean) Edouard Vuillard,* French painter, graphic artist; developer of *intimist style;* known for his interiors, still lifes, and flowers. [d. June 21, 1940]

1869 *Victor Emmanuel III,* last king of Italy; reigned 1900–46; forced into exile, 1946. [d. December 28, 1947]

1872 *Maude Adams (Maude Kiskadden),* U.S. actress. [d. July 17, 1953]

1882 *Gustav VI Adolf,* King of Sweden, 1950–73; the last Swedish king to have any real political power. [d. September 15, 1973]

1883 *Ernest Alexandre Ansermet,* Swiss conductor, composer. [d. February 20, 1969]

1885 *George S(mith) Patton, Jr.,* U.S. army officer, armored-warfare tactician; prominent commander in World War II. [d. December 21, 1945]

1889 *Sir Alexander Fleck,* Scottish industrialist; helped develop polyethylene and Dacron. [d. August 6, 1968]

1891 *René Clair,* French filmmaker; first member of the French Academy elected solely for his contributions to the art of filmmaking. [d. March 15, 1981]

1896 *Charles (Lucky) Luciano (Salvatore Lucania),* U.S. gangster, born in Italy; an infamous figure of 1930s in U.S.; deported to Italy in 1946. [d. January 26, 1962]

1899 *Pat O'Brien,* U.S. actor. [d. October 15, 1983]

1904 *Alger Hiss,* U.S. public official; central figure in widely publicized spy case in U.S. in early 1950s; U.S. State Department official, 1936–46. [d. November 15, 1997]

1913 *Sun Yun-suan,* Chinese leader; Premier, Republic of China (Taiwan), 1978–84.

1914 *Howard Fast,* U.S. author; wrote *Spartacus,* 1952, and *The Immigrants,* 1977; American Library Association Notable Book Award for *The Hessian,* 1972.

1915 *Willaim Proxmire,* U.S. politician; Senator, 1957–89; gained national attention with his *Golden Fleece Awards* to government-sponsored groups or persons whose subsidization he deemed unwarranted.

1922 *Kurt Vonnegut, Jr.,* U.S. novelist.

1925 *Jonathan Winters,* U.S. comedian.

1928 *Carlos Fuentes,* Mexican author, critic; head of Mexico's Department of Culture, 1956–59; Ambassador to France, 1975.

Edward Zorinsky, U.S. politician; Senator, 1977–87. [d. March 6, 1987]

1935 *Bibi Andersson,* Swedish actress.

1937 *Richard F. Celeste,* U.S. politician; Governor of Ohio, 1983–91; Ambassador to India, 1997– .

1945 *Daniel Ortega (Saavedra),* Nicaraguan political leader; President, 1979–90.

1950 *Otis Armstrong,* U.S. football player.

1951 *Frank Urban (Fuzzy) Zoeller,* U.S. golfer.

1953 *Marshall Crenshaw,* U.S. pop singer.

1962 *Demi Moore,* U.S. actress.

1964 *Philip McKeon,* U.S. actor; known for his role as Tommy in the television series *Alice,* 1976–85.

1974 *Leonardo DiCaprio,* U.S. actor; known for his performances in *Romeo and Juliet,* 1996, and *Titanic,* 1997.

HISTORICAL EVENTS

1500 *Treaty of Granada* is signed by France and Spain, determining partition of Italy.

1630 *Cardinal Richelieu* overthrows conspiracy of *Maria de' Medici,* the Queen Mother; referred to as the *Day of Dupes.*

1861 *Peter V* of Portugal dies and is succeeded by *Louis I.*

1885 The founding grant of *Stanford University* is signed in Palo Alto, California.

1889 *Washington* is admitted to the Union as the 42nd state.

1918 *Armistice* ending *World War I* goes into effect.

1921 *Tomb of the Unknown Soldier* is dedicated at *Arlington, Virginia.*

1922 *British Broadcasting Company* begins wireless transmissions of musical programs.

1939 *Kate Smith* sings Irving Berlin's patriotic composition, *God Bless America,* for the first time.

1941 British navy attacks and badly damages Italian fleet in *Malta* (*World War II*).

1944 Naval assault on *Iwo Jima* begins (*World War II*).

november

1945 *Marshal Tito's* Communist-dominated National Front wins elections in *Yugoslavia*.

1961 *Stalingrad,* Soviet city on the Volga River, is renamed *Volgograd*.

1965 *Rhodesia* makes a unilateral declaration of independence from Great Britain.

1966 U.S. spacecraft *Gemini 12* with James A. Lovell, Jr., and Edwin E. Aldrin, Jr., aboard, is launched from Cape Kennedy and later makes a successful rendezvous and linkup with an Agena target vehicle.

Methodist and *Evangelical United Brethren* churches of the U.S. vote to merge into the *United Methodist Church*.

1975 *Angola* gains independence from Portugal.

John Malcolm Fraser is inaugurated as prime minister of Australia.

1987 Senior Soviet party official, *Boris Yeltsin,* is dismissed as head of the Moscow organization. Yeltsin had criticized the leadership for delaying reforms.

1992 Women priests are approved by the *Church of England*.

1993 *Evander Holyfield* wins the world heavyweight boxing title by defeating *Riddick Bowe*.

HOLIDAYS

Liberia
*Anniversary of the 1985 Coup
Attempt*

Maldives
Republic Day
Second day of the celebration.

Republic of China (Taiwan)
Birthday of Dr. Sun Yat-sen
Celebrates the birth of the famous
Chinese statesman and revolutionary
leader, 1866; he is called the *Father
of the Revolution.*

U.S.
Elizabeth Cady Stanton Day

RELIGIOUS CALENDAR

The Saints
St. Nilus the Elder, solitary. [d. c.
430]
St. Emilian Cucullatus, abbot. A
patron of Spain. [d. 574]
St. Machar, bishop. Also called
Mochumma. [d. 6th cent.]
St. Cunibert, Bishop of Cologne. [d.
c. 663]
St. Cadwaladr, Welsh king. Also
called *battle-shunner.* [d. 664]
St. Cumian, abbot. Also called
Cuimine Fota. [d. c. 665]
St. Lebuin, monk and missionary.
Also called *Lebwin,* or
Liafwine. Patron of Daventer
(Daventry), England [d. c.
773]
St. Benedict and his Companions,
martyrs. Venerated in Poland
as the *Five Polish Brothers.*
[d. 1003]

St. Astrik, Archbishop of the
Hungarians. Also called
Anastasius, Radla. [d. 1040]
St. Josaphat, Archbishop of Polotsk
and martyr. Feast formerly
November 14. [d. 1623]
Obligatory Memorial.
St. Livinus, bishop and martyr. Also
called *Livin.* [death date
unknown]

The Beatified
Blessed Rainerius of Arezzo,
Franciscan Friar Minor. [d.
1304]
Blessed John Della Pace, hermit. [d.
c. 1332]
Blessed Gabriel of Ancona,
Franciscan friar and
missionary. [d. 1456]

BIRTHDATES

1493 *Baccio Bandinelli,* Italian
Renaissance sculptor;
sculpture of *Adam and Eve*
and bas-relief in choir of the
Florence cathedral. [d.
February 7, 1560]

1651 *Sor Juana Inés de la Cruz,*
Mexican poet, nun; one of
the great women of Mexican
history. [d. 1695]

1746 *Jacques Alexandre César
Charles,* French physicist,
chemist, inventor; first to use
hydrogen for balloon
inflation; anticipated Gay-
Lussac's (December 6)
discovery of law governing

expansion of gases. [d. April
7, 1823]

1790 *Letitia Tyler,* first wife of U.S.
President John Tyler. [d.
September 10, 1842]

1815 *Elizabeth Cady Stanton,* U.S.
reformer; a leader in the
movement for women's
suffrage; with Lucretia Mott
(January 3) organized the
Seneca Falls Convention on
Women's Rights, 1848. [d.
October 26, 1902]

1817 *Baha'u'llah (Mirza Husayn-
Ali),* Iranian religious leader;
founded the Baha'i World
Faith. [d. May 29, 1892]

1833 *Aleksandr Profiryevich
Borodin,* Russian composer;
one of the *Mighty Five* figures
in Russian nationalist school.
[d. February 27, 1887]

1840 *Auguste Rodin,* French
sculptor; creator of *The
Burghers of Calais, The Kiss,*
and *The Thinker.* [d.
November 17, 1917]

1842 *John William Strutt, 3rd
Baron Rayleigh,* English
physicist; Nobel Prize in
physics for discovery of
argon, 1904. [d. June 30,
1919]

1866 *Sun Yat-sen,* Chinese
revolutionary leader and
national hero; led fight to
overthrow Manchu dynasty;
head of South Chinese

november

Republic, 1921. [d. March 12, 1925]

1889 *Dewitt Wallace,* U.S. publisher; with his wife, Lila Bell Acheson, founded and edited *Reader's Digest,* 1921–65. [d. March Acheson, 30, 1981]

1908 *Harry Andrew Blackmun,* U.S. jurist, lawyer; Associate Justice, U.S. Supreme Court, 1970–94.

1915 *Roland Barthes,* French critic, writer; noted especially for his theories of *semiology,* or the study of signs and symbols. [d. March 25, 1980]

1917 *Joseph Coors,* U.S. brewer; Chief Executive Officer, Adolph Coors Co., 1982–.

1922 *Kim Hunter (Janet Cole),* U.S. actress; Academy Award for *Streetcar Named Desire,* 1951.

1929 *Princess Grace* of Monaco *(Grace Kelly),* U.S. film star prior to her marriage to Prince Rainier III of Monaco, 1956. [d. September 14, 1982]

1934 *Charles (Milles) Manson,* U.S. criminal; convicted murderer of actress Sharon Tate and six others; leader of a radical cult of drifters.

1942 *Stefanie Powers (Stefania Zofia Ferderkievicz),* U.S. actress; starred in the

television series, *The Girl from U.N.C.L.E.* and *Hart to Hart,* 1979–84.

1945 *Neil Young,* Canadian-born rock musician.

1949 *André Laplante,* Canadian pianist; first Canadian to win a medal in the International Tchaikovsky Competition in Moscow, 1978.

1961 *Nadia Comaneci,* Romanian gymnast; winner of three Olympic gold medals, 1976.

HISTORICAL EVENTS

1893 *Durand Agreement* is signed between Great Britain and Afghanistan fixing the frontier with India from Chitral to Baluchistan.

1912 Spain's Liberal Prime Minister *JosèCanalejas* is assassinated by anarchist *Pardinas.*

1918 *Charles I* of Austria, last Hapsburg emperor of *Austria-Hungary,* abdicates; *Austria* and *Hungary* are proclaimed republics.

1921 *Washington Armament Conference,* set to discuss reduction of naval armaments after World War I, begins in Washington, D.C.

1942 Naval battle of *Guadalcanal* begins (*World War II*).

1951 Alan Jay Lerner and Frederick Loewe's musical, *Paint Your*

Wagon, premieres in New York.

1954 *Ellis Island* closes after 62 years as the processing site for immigrants to the U.S.

1958 *Guinea* promulgates its constitution.

1968 *Equatorial Guinea* becomes a member of the United Nations.

1969 U.S. Army Lieutenant *William L. Calley, Jr.,* is charged with the murder of an undetermined number of Vietnamese civilians in the village of *My Lai.*

1975 Ailing U.S. Supreme Court Justice *William O. Douglas* resigns from the court after 36 years of service.

1981 Second launching of U.S. space shuttle *Columbia* marks the first reuse of a space vehicle.

1982 *Yury Andropov* is chosen to succeed *Leonid Brezhnev* as general secretary of the Soviet Communist Party.

1987 American Medical Association guidelines state that doctors have an ethical obligation to treat *AIDS* patients.

1997 *Ramzi Ahmed Yousef* is found guilty for the World Trade Center bombing (February 26, 1993).

RELIGIOUS CALENDAR

The Saints

St. Arcadius and his Companions, martyrs. [d. 437]

St. Brice, Bishop of Tours; invoked against stomach diseases. Also called *Brictio,* or *Britius.* [d. 444]

St. Eugenius, Archbishop of Toledo. [d. 657]

St. Maxellendis, virgin and martyr. [d. c. 670]

St. Kilian, preacher. Also called *Chilianus, Chillen, Kilien,* or *Killian.* [d. 7th century]

St. Nicholas I, pope. Elected 858; patron of Russia, Aberdeen, mariners, thieves, and parish clerks. Called *the Great.* [d. 867]

St. Abbo of Fleury, abbot and martyr. [d. 1004]

St. Homobonus, merchant; patron of tailors, clothmakers, and Cremona, Italy. Also called *Gutman.* [d. 1197]

St. Didacus, Franciscan lay brother. Also called *Diego.* [d. 1463]

St. Stanislaus Kostka, Jesuit. A lesser patron of Poland. Also called *Stanislas.* [d. 1568]

The Beatified

St. Frances Xavier Cabrini, missionary. Feast formerly celebrated December 22, moved to this date. [d. 1917]

BIRTHDATES

354 *Saint Augustine,* early Christian philosopher, theologian, and Father of the Church. Feast day is August 28. [d. August 28, 430]

1312 *Edward III,* King of England; 1327–77; a brilliant military leader who commanded the finest army in medieval Europe. [d. June 21, 1377]

1567 *Maurice of Nassau,* stadtholder of Dutch Republic; the Dutch Republic's greatest military leader of 16th and 17th centuries. [d. April 23, 1625]

1729 *Aleksandr Vasilievich Suvorov,* Count Suvorov Rimniksy, Prince Itolsky, Russian field marshal and tactician. [d. May 6, 1800]

1782 *Esaias Tegner,* Swedish poet, scholar, bishop, and orator; representative of Gothic school of literature; one of great poets of Sweden. [d. November 2, 1846]

1785 *Lady Caroline Ponsonby Lamb,* British author; wrote *Glenarron, Graham Hamilton,* and *Ada Reis;* gained notoriety because of her affair with Lord Byron. [d. January 24, 1828]

1814 *Joseph Hooker,* Union Army general during U.S. Civil War; Commander of Army of the Potomac, 1863. [d. October 31, 1879]

1831 *James Clerk Maxwell,* Scottish mathematician, physicist; proposed electromagnetic nature of light, 1873; experimented in color perception, color blindness, and kinetic theory of gases. [d. November 5, 1879]

1833 *Edwin Booth,* U.S. actor; outstanding U.S. stage actor of 19th century; noted for his portrayal of Shakespeare's *Hamlet.* Brother of John Wilkes Booth (May 10). [d. June 7 1893]

1854 *George Whitefield Chadwick,* U.S. composer; Director, New England Conservatory of Music, 1897–1931. [d. April 4, 1931]

1856 *Louis (Dembitz) Brandeis,* U.S. jurist, lawyer; Associate Justice, U.S. Supreme Court, 1916–39; Brandeis University is named for him. [d. October 5, 1941]

1859 *Robert Louis (Balfour) Stevenson,* Scottish novelist, essayist, critic, poet; author of *Treasure Island* and *A Child's Garden of Verses.* [d. December 3, 1894]

1893 *Edward A. Doisy,* U.S. biochemist; Nobel Prize in physiology or medicine for research into antihemorrhagic substances and the discovery of *vitamin K* (with C.P.H. Dam), 1943. [d. October 24, 1986]

november

1913 *Alexander Scourby,* U.S. actor; appeared in *Giant,* 1956; known for his resonant bass voice; narrated the documentary *Victory at Sea* and several *National Geographic* television specials. [d. February 22, 1985]

1915 *Nathaniel (Goddard) Benchley,* U.S. novelist, editor, journalist; son of Robert Benchley (September 15); father of Peter Benchley (May 8). [d. December 14, 1981]

1917 *Robert Sterling (William Sterling Hart),* U.S. actor; leading man of the 1940's; appeared in the television series, *Topper,* 1953–55.

1922 *Oskar Werner,* Austrian-born actor. [d. October 23, 1984]

1930 *Fred Roy Harris,* U.S. politician, author; Senator, 1964–73.

1932 *Richard Mulligan,* U.S. actor; Emmy Award for his role as Burt Campbell on the television series, *Soap,* 1977–80 and featured on the sitcom *Empty Nest,* 1988–95.

1934 *Garry Kent Marshall,* U.S. producer; created the television series, *Happy Days, Laverne and Shirley,* and *Mork and Mindy.*

1935 *George Carey,* British priest; named the Archbishop of Canterbury, 1991– .

1938 *Jean Seberg,* U.S. actress; starred in *Paint Your Wagon,* 1969. [d. August 31, 1979]

1941 *Dack Rambo,* U.S. actor; known for his role as Jack Ewing on the television series *Dallas,* 1985–87.

1947 *Joe Mantegna,* U.S. actor; won Tony award for *Glengarry Glen Ross.*

1949 *Whoopi Goldberg,* U.S. actress; Academy Award (Best Supporting Actress) for *Ghost,* 1990.

HISTORICAL EVENTS

1002 Danish settlers in England are massacred at *St. Brice* on order of *Ethelred II.*

1092 *Malcolm III* of Scotland is defeated and killed near Alnwick.

1851 First submarine telegraph cable is completed from Dover to Calais.

1940 Walt Disney's *Fantasia* premieres at the Broadway Theater in New York; first film to attempt to use stereophonic sound.

1950 Colonel *Carlos Delgado Chalbaud,* head of Venezuela's military junta, is assassinated in Caracas.

1955 General *Pedro Eugenio Aramburu* stages a coup and assumes the presidency of Argentina.

1956 The U.S. Supreme Court upholds a lower court decision that *racial segregation* on buses violates the 15th Amendment.

1962 The name of *St. Joseph* is added to the canon of the Roman Catholic mass. This is the first alteration of that canon since the seventh century.

1966 U.S. astronaut *Edwin E. Aldrin, Jr.* completes *space walk* during *Gemini 12* mission.

1971 *Mariner 9,* unmanned U.S. spacecraft, goes into orbit around Mars, the first man-made object to orbit another planet.

1974 Kerr-McGee Corp. employee and work safety activist, *Karen Silkwood,* dies in an automobile crash on her way to a meeting with a *New York Times'* reporter and union official.

1985 Volcano *Nevado del Ruiz* erupts in Colombia, killing almost twenty-three thousand people.

1986 President *Ronald Reagan* admits selling arms to Iran, but denies that the sale was an attempt to exchange arms for hostages *(Iran-contra affair).*

1987 The U.S. Food and Drug Administration approves the marketing of *tissue plasminogen activator,* a blood clot dissolver designed to aid heart attack victims.

NOVEMBER
14

HOLIDAYS

British Virgin Islands, St. Kitts, Tuvalu
Prince of Wales' Birthday
Celebrates the occasion of the prince's birth, 1948.

Jordan
H. M. King Hussein's Birthday
Commemorates the event, 1935.

RELIGIOUS CALENDAR

The Saints
St. Dubricius, bishop. Also called *Dyfrig.* [d. 6th century]
St. Laurence O'Toole, Archbishop of Dublin. Also called *Lawrence,* or (in Gaelic) *Lorcan Ua Tuathail.* [d. 1180]

The Beatified
Blessed Serapion, martyr. [d. 1240]
Blessed John Liccio, Dominican preacher, prior. [d. 1511]

BIRTHDATES

1650 *William III,* Stadholder of Holland, 1672–1702; King of Great Britain, 1689–1702. [d. March 19, 1702]

1668 *Johnann Lucus von Hildebrandt,* Austrian baroque architect, military engineer. [d. November 16, 1745]

1765 *Robert Fulton,* U.S. inventor; developed first practical

steamship, 1807. [d. February 24, 1815]

1779 *Adam Gottlob Oehlenschläger,* Danish poet, dramatist; named Danish national poet, 1849; leader of Romantic movement in Danish poetry. [d. January 20, 1850]

1797 *Sir Charles Lyell,* Scottish geologist; the father of modern geology. [d. February 22, 1875]

1820 *Anson Burlingame,* U.S. legislator, diplomat; noted for his great achievements as U.S. Minister to China, 1860–67; appointed by Chinese government to head a three-man mission to U.S. and Europe in 1868, charged with establishing diplomatic relations with the U.S., Great Britain, and Russia; (resulted in the *Burlingame Treaty,* July 28, 1868.) [d. February 23, 1870]

1828 *Charles Louis de Saulces de Freycinet,* French statesman, Premier of France, 1879–80; 1882; 1886; 1890–92. [d. May 14, 1923]

1840 *Claude Monet,* French artist; Impressionist painter. [d. December 5, 1926]

1861 *Frederick Jackson Turner,* U.S. historian; noted for his revolutionary interpretation of

American history; author of *The Significance of Sections in American History,* for which he received the Pulitzer Prize, 1933. [d. March 14, 1932]

1862 *Count Johann-Heinrich von Bernstorff,* German diplomat; German Ambassador to U.S., 1908–17; Chairman, German League of Nations Union; Vice-Chairman, League of Nations. [d. October 6, 1939]

1863 *Leo Hendrik Baekeland,* U.S. chemist, born in Belgium; developed *bakelite,* one of first widely used *plastics.* [d. February 23, 1944]

1885 *Sonia Delaunay,* French-Russian artist; influenced creative and applied arts, 1920–70; experimented with *infinite rhythm* in her paintings. [d. December 5, 1979]

1889 *Jawaharlah Nehru,* Indian statesman; first Prime Minister of India, 1947–64; became known throughout the world for his exercise of civil disobedience while striving for independence of India. [d. May 27, 1964]

1891 *Sir Frederick Grant Banting,* Canadian physiologist; Nobel Prize in physiology or medicine for production of *insulin* (with J. J. R. Macleod), 1923. [d. February 21, 1941]

1895 *Frank J. Lausche,* U.S. statesman; U.S. Senator, 1956–68. [d. April 21, 1990]

Wilmarth Sheldon Lewis, U.S. author, editor; his extensive works related to Horace Walpole; senior editor of projected 50-volume edition of Walpole's correspondence. [d. October 7, 1979]

1896 *Mamie Doud Eisenhower,* U.S. First Lady; wife of Dwight David Eisenhower, 34th U.S. President. [d. November 1, 1979]

1900 *Aaron Copland,* U.S. composer; Pulitzer Prize in music, 1945. [d. December 2, 1990]

1904 *Dick Powell,* U.S. actor, producer, director. [d. January 3, 1963]

1906 *Louise Brooks,* U.S. actress; appeared in the films *Pandora's Box* and *Diary of a Lost Child.* [d. August 8, 1985]

1907 *Astrid Lindgren,* Swedish author; wrote the *Pippi Longstocking* stories for children.

1908 *Joseph (Raymond) McCarthy,* U.S. politician, lawyer, farmer; U.S. Senator, 1947–57; responsible for controversial hearings into Communism in U.S., which became known as a witch-hunt because of the terrorizing tactics of him and his staff; slandered many people using unsubstantiated evidence. [d. May 2, 1957]

Harrison (Evans) Salisbury, U.S. journalist; editor and writer for *The New York Times,* 1949–73; Pulitzer Prize in international correspondence, 1955. [d. July 5, 1993]

1912 *Barbara Hutton,* U.S. heiress. [d. May 11, 1979]

1913 *George Armistead Smathers,* U.S. government official; Congressman, 1947–50; Senator, 1951–58.

1919 *Veronica Lake (Constance Ockleman),* U.S. actress. [d. July 7, 1973]

1921 *Brian Keith (Robert Keith, Jr.),* U.S. actor; known for his roles in Disney films and several television series. [d. June 24, 1997]

1922 *Boutros Boutros-Ghali,* Egyptian political leader; secretary general of the United Nations, 1992– .

1929 *McLean Stevenson,* U.S. actor; known for his role on the television series, *M*A*S*H,* 1972–75. [d. February 15, 1996]

1930 *Edward White,* U.S. astronaut; first man to walk in space (during *Gemini 4* mission, 1965). Killed in fire aboard *Apollo I.* [d. January 27, 1967]

1935 *Hussein ibn Talal,* King of Jordan, 1953– .

1948 *Charles, Prince of Wales,* oldest son of Queen Elizabeth II and Prince Philip; heir apparent to British throne.

1955 *Guillermo Villanueva (Willie) Hernandez,* Puerto Rican-born baseball player; relief pitcher, Detroit Tigers; Cy Young Award and American League Most Valuable Player Award, 1984.

HISTORICAL EVENTS

1784 *Samuel Seabury* is consecrated in Scotland as Bishop of Connecticut and Rhode Island, becoming the first Anglican bishop in America.

1847 *Chloroform* is first used as an anesthetic by Scottish physician *James Y. Simpson.*

Civil war breaks out in *Switzerland* between the federal government and the Sonderbund of the seven Catholic cantons.

1863 Great Britain cedes *Ionian Islands* to Greece.

1888 *St. Andrew's Golf Club,* Yonkers, New York, is organized, the first American golf club.

1914 First issue of *Popolo d'Italia,* edited by *Benito Mussolini,* is published.

1962 The former Italian colony of *Eritrea* is annexed to Ethiopia as a province.

1968 *Yale University* announces that it will begin admitting women as undergraduate students in 1969.

1969 *Apollo 12* spacecraft is successfully launched from Cape Kennedy, Florida.

1973 *Princess Anne* of Britain and Captain Mark Phillips are married in Westminster Abbey.

1979 President Jimmy Carter freezes Iranian assets in response to the seizure of U.S. hostages in *Iran.*

1986 U.S. securities speculator, *Ivan Boesky,* pleads guilty to criminal charges for engaging in *insider trading* and will pay a record $100 million in fines.

1988 *Spain* and *Portugal* formally
join the Western European
Union.

NOVEMBER
15

HOLIDAYS

Belgium
Dynasty Day

Brazil
Proclamation of the Republic
Commemorates the event, 1889.

Cyprus
TRNC Day
Commemorates the independence of the Turkish Republic of Northern Cyprus (TRNC).

RELIGIOUS CALENDAR

The Saints

SS. Gurius, Samonas, and Abibus, martyrs. Venerated as avengers of unfulfilled contracts. [d. 4th century]

St. Disiderius, Bishop of Cahors. Also called *Didier,* or *Géry.* [d. 655]

St. Malo, Bishop of Aleth. Also called *Machutus, Maclou, Maclovius,* or *Mallou.* [d. 7th century]

St. Fintan of Rheinau, solitary. Also called *Findan* [d. 879]

St. Leopold of Austria, prince; patron of Austria. Also called *the Good.* [d. 1136]

St. Albert the Great, Bishop of Regensburg and Doctor of the Church. Patron of Prussia and of students of the natural sciences. Called *the Universal Teacher.* [d. 1280] Optional Memorial.

BIRTHDATES

1397 *Nicholas V,* pope from 1447–55. [d. 1455]

1708 *William Pitt, the Elder,* English statesman; Secretary of State, 1756–61; 1766–68; led England during the Seven Years' War, 1756–63; responsible for England's rise to power and acquisition of Canada and other territories. Called *The Great Commoner.* [d. May 11, 1778]

1738 *Sir William Herschel (Friedrich Wilhelm Herschel),* English astronomer, born in Germany; refined telescope quality; discovered *Uranus.* [d. August 25, 1822]

1741 *Johann Kaspar Lavater,* Swiss philosopher, mystic, writer; founder of science of *physiognomy.* [d. January 2, 1801]

1816 *Isidore Kalish,* U.S. rabbi, author, leader; pioneer of Reform Judaism in the U.S. [d. May 11, 1886]

1849 *James O'Neill,* U.S. actor, born in Ireland; father of Eugene O'Neill (October 16). [d. August 10, 1920]

1862 *Gerhart Hauptmann,* German dramatic poet; one of most noted German writers of the early twentieth century; Nobel Prize in literature, 1912. [d. June 8, 1946]

1874 *Schack August Steenberg Krogh,* Danish physiologist; Nobel Prize in physiology or medicine for discovery of regulating mechanism in blood capillary action. [d. September 13, 1949]

1882 *Felix Frankfurter,* U.S. jurist; Associate Justice, U.S. Supreme Court, 1939–62. [d. February 22, 1965]

1887 *Marianne (Craig) Moore,* U.S. poet; noted for her highly personal subject matter, strict adherence to set metrical form, wit, and concern for abiding moral issues. Pulitzer Prize in poetry, 1952. [d. February 5, 1972]

Georgia O'Keeffe, U.S. painter; known for her abstract style and intensity of her images and colors. Married to Alfred Stieglitz (January 1). [d. March 6, 1986]

1891 *Erwin (Johannes Eugin) Rommel,* German field marshall; head of Nazi forces in Africa, 1941–43. [d. October 14, 1944]

W(illiam) Averell Harriman, U.S. statesman, diplomat, banker; special representative of the U.S. government to Great Britain and the U.S.S.R., 1941–43; Ambassador to the U.S.S.R., 1943–46; Ambassador to Great Britain, 1946; Secretary of Commerce, 1946–48; Chief Representative of the U.S. to the Paris Peace Talks (Vietnam War), 1968–69. [d. July 26, 1986]

1897 *Aneurin Bevan,* British political leader, Labour Party leader; Minister of Health, 1945–51; responsible for establishment of National Health Service in Great Britain. [d. July 6, 1960]

1906 *Curtis (Emerson) Lemay,* U.S. Air Force general; U.S. Commander of Strategic Air Command (SAC), 1957–61; U.S. Air Force Chief of Staff, 1961–65; ran for Vice President on Wallace ticket, 1968. [d. October 1, 1990]

1912 *Albert Baez,* U.S. physicist; built the first x-ray microscope.

1925 *Howard Henry Baker, Jr.,* U.S. politician, lawyer; Senator, 1967–85; President Ronald Reagan's Chief of Staff, 1987–89.

1929 *Edward Asner,* U.S. actor.

1931 *John Kerr,* U.S. actor, lawyer.

1932 *Petula Clark,* British singer, actress; Grammy Awards for *Downtown* and *I Know a Place.*

1940 *Sam(uel Atkinson) Waterston,* U.S. actor; Drama Desk Award for *Much Ado About Nothing,* 1972–73; Academy Award nominee for *The Killing Fields,* 1984.

1946 *Janet Lennon,* U.S. singer; member of the vocal group, *The Lennon Sisters.*

HISTORICAL EVENTS

1315 *Battle of Morgarten* is won by the Swiss, throroughly defeating *Leopold of Austria* and beginning the brilliant career of the *Swiss infantry.*

1635 *University of Budapest* opens.

1715 Austria obtains *Spanish Netherlands* in the *Barrier Treaty* with Holland.

1777 *Continental Congress* adopts the *Articles of Confederation* for the American colonies.

1806 *Pike's Peak* is first sighted by Zebulon M. Pike.

1853 *Maria II* of Portugal dies and is succeeded by *Pedro V.*

1863 *Frederick VII* of Denmark dies and is succeeded by *Christian IX.*

1864 *General William Sherman* and 60,000 Union troops leave Atlanta, beginning their famous *March to the Sea* (*U.S. Civil War*).

1889 *Pedro II* of Brazil abdicates and a republic is proclaimed.

1908 *Congo Free State* becomes the *Belgian Congo.*

1914 *Battle of Cracow* begins in the second Russian offensive in Galicia (*World War I*).

1920 First meeting of the Assembly of the *League of Nations,* with 42 member nations, takes place in London.

1921 *Russian State Bank* opens in Moscow and is granted a monopoly on purchase and sale of foreign currency and precious metals.

1942 *Battle of Guadalcanal* ends with decisive U.S. victory over the Japanese (*World War II*).

1948 *Louis St. Laurent* becomes prime minister of Canada

following the resignation of *William Lyon Mackenzie King.*

1950 *Arthur Dorrington* signs with the Atlantic City Seagulls, becoming the first black to play organized hockey.

U.S. Marines occupy *Hagaru, Korea (Korean War).*

1956 Gene de Paul and Johnny Mercer's musical, *Li'l Abner,* premieres in New York.

1960 *U.S.S. George Washington,* the first U.S. submarine armed with *thermonuclear missiles,* sails from Charleston, S.C., on its first patrol.

1971 *People's Republic of China* delegation, headed by Deputy Foreign Minister Chiao Kuan-hua, assumes its seats in the UN General Assembly.

1976 U.S. Supreme Court upholds *Allan Bakke's* claim of reverse discrimination in the admissions policy of the University of California Medical School.

1979 *Sir Anthony Blunt,* knight of the British Empire, advisor on art to Queen Elizabeth II, is discovered to be a spy for the Soviet Union and is stripped of his knighthood.

1985 Great Britain and the Republic of Ireland sign an agreement which gives Ireland a consultative role in the governing of *Northern Ireland.*

1988 The legislative arm of the *Palestinian Liberation Organization* votes to proclaim a Palestinian state and accept United Nations Resolution 242.

1990 U.S. President *George Bush* signs the *Clean Air Act* into law.

1993 The *World Health Organization* announces a tuberculosis global emergency as new drug-resistant strains increase.

1994 *Helmut Kohl* is reelected as chancellor of Germany.

HOLIDAYS

Syria
National Day

RELIGIOUS CALENDAR

The Saints

St. Eucherius, Bishop of Lyons. [d. c. 449]

St. Afan, bishop. Also called *Avan, Avanus,* or *Llanafan.* [d. c. 6th century]

St. Margaret of Scotland, queen and matron. Wife of Malcolm of Scotland. Patroness of Scotland. [d. 1093] Optional Memorial.

SS. Gertrude the Great and Mechtildis, virgins and mystics. [d. 1302 and 1298] Optional Memorial.

St. Edmund of Abingdon, Archbishop of Canterbury. Also called *St. Edme.* [d. 1240]

St. Agnes of Assisi, virgin and abbess. [d. 1253]

The Beatified

Blessed Louis Morbioli, Carmelite tertiary. [d. 1485]

Blessed Gratia of Cattaro, Augustinian lay brother. [d. 1508]

Blessed Lucy of Narni, virgin and mystic. [d. 1544]

BIRTHDATES

42BC *Tiberius (Tiberius Claudius Nero Caesar),* second Emperor of Rome, A.D. 14–37. [d. March 16, A.D. 37]

1758 *Peter Andreas Heiberg,* Danish poet, playwright; author of many satirical pieces aimed at Danish government; exiled, 1799; accompanied Talleyrand (February 2) on numerous diplomatic missions. [d. April 30, 1841]

1807 *Jónas Hallgrímsson,* Icelandic poet, patriot, scientist; exerted great influence in purifying the Icelandic language. [d. May 26, 1845]

1810 *Karel Hynek Mácha,* Czech poet, novelist; a leader in the Czech romantic movement. [d. November 6, 1836]

1811 *John Bright,* British politician, orator; leading proponent of Irish independence. [d. March 27, 1889]

1836 *David Kalakaua,* 7th King of the Hawaiians, 1874–91, elected by the Hawaiian assembly. [d. January 30, 1891]

1839 *Louis-Honoré Fréchette,* Canadian poet, journalist; preeminent French-Canadian poet of 19th century. [d. May 31, 1908]

1873 *W(illiam) C(hristopher) Handy,* U.S. composer; regarded by many as the father of the blues; wrote *Memphis Blues, St. Louis Woman.* [d. March 28, 1958]

1881 *Joel Hildebrand,* U.S. chemist, educator; member of the faculty, University of California at Berkeley for nearly 70 years. It is estimated that he taught over 40,000 students during his career. [d. May 2, 1983]

1889 *George S(imon) Kaufman,* U.S. dramatist, drama critic, director; Pulitzer Prize in drama, 1932, 1937. [d. June 2, 1961]

1890 *George (Henry) Seldes,* U.S. journalist; correspondent, *Chicago Tribune* and *New York Post;* editor of the books, *The Great Quotations* and *The Great Thoughts.* [d. July 2, 1995]

1895 *Paul Hindemith,* U.S. composer born in Germany; noted for his ultramodern style of composition. [d. December 23, 1963]

1896 *Sir Oswald Ernald Mosely,* British politician; founder of British Union of Fascists; member of House of Commons, 1918–31. [d. December, 2 1980]

1898 *Ben Pearson,* U.S. archery promoter. [d. March 2, 1971]

1899 *Mary Margaret McBride,* U.S. radio commentator. [d. April 7, 1976]

1909 *Burgess Meredith,* U.S. actor. [d. September 9, 1997]

1919 *Anatoliy F. Dobrynin,* Russian diplomat; Ambassador to the U. S., 1962–86.

1935 *France-Albert Rene,* President, Republic of Seychelles, 1977–.

1942 *Donna Ruth McKechnie,* U.S. dancer; Tony award, 1975, for role of Cassie in *A Chorus Line.*

1943 *Donald David DeFreeze,* U.S. revolutionary; leader of the Symbionese Liberation Army; kidnapped Patricia Hearst, 1974; killed in confrontation with police. [d. May 24, 1974]

1944 *Joanna Pettet,* U.S. actress; films include *The Group* and *Casino Royale.*

1956 *Bo Derek (Mary Cathleen Collins),* U.S. actress; starred in the movie, *10,* 1979; widow of John Derek.

1958 *Attalah Shabazz,* U.S. social activist; daughter of Malcolm X (May 19).

1959 *Corey Pavin,* U.S. golfer; PGA America Player of the year, 1991, U.S. Open winner, 1995.

1964 *Dwight Eugene Gooden,* U.S. baseball player; pitcher, New York Mets; won 24 games, 1985; Cy Young Award, 1985.

1977 *Oksana Baiul,* Ukrainian figure skater; Olympic gold medalist, 1994.

HISTORICAL EVENTS

1272 *Henry III* of England dies and is succeeded by *Edward I.*

1621 *Papal Chancery* first adopts *January 1* as beginning of the year.

1632 *Battle of Lützen* is fought, in which Protestant forces under Swedish *King Gustavus Adolphus* are victorious over Imperialist Catholic troops; Gustavus Adolphus is killed (*Thirty Years' War*).

1797 *Frederick William II* of Prussia dies and is succeeded by *Frederick William III.*

1900 *Philadelphia Orchestra* presents its inaugural concert.

1907 *Oklahoma* is admitted to Union as the 46th state.

1908 Italian-born conductor, *Arturo Toscanini,* gives his first performance at the Metropolitan Opera House in New York.

1914 *Battle of Lódź* begins in the second German offensive against the Russians at *Warsaw (World War I).*

1918 *Hungarian Republic* is proclaimed in the break-up of the Austro-Hungarian Empire (*World War I*). (See November 13)

The Allied armies begin their march into Germany (*World War I*).

1944 The U.S. First and Ninth Armies begin coordinated drive to the *Roer River* in western Germany (*World War II*).

1959 Rodgers & Hammerstein's musical comedy, *The Sound of Music,* premieres in New York.

1972 Pepsico Inc. announces that it will begin manufacturing and marketing the *Pepsi Cola* soft drink in the U.S.S.R.

1973 U.S. President Richard Nixon signs a bill authorizing construction of a *trans-Alaska oil pipeline.*

Skylab 3, with a crew of 3, is launched from Kennedy Space Center for a 60-day mission.

1992 The *United Nations* votes in favor of a naval blockade against Yugoslavia in response to the ethnic fighting in Bosnia and Herzegovina.

The *Roman Catholic Church* announces a new catechism after taking six years to revise the 400-year-old text.

1995 The *Yugoslav War Crimes Tribunal* indicts *Kadovan Daradzic* and *Ratko Mladic,* leaders of the Bosnian Serbs.

Liamine Zeroul is reelected to a five-year term as president of Algeria.

Roh Tae Woo, former president of South Korea (1988–93), is arrested for bribery.

HOLIDAYS

Azerbaijan
Day of National Revival

Democratic Republic of the Congo
Army Day

Germany
Day of Penance

RELIGIOUS CALENDAR

The Saints

St. Dionysius, Bishop of Alexandria. Also called *the Great.* [d. 265]

St. Gregory the Wonderworker, Bishop of Neocaesarea. Invoked in time of earthquake and flood. Also called *Thaumaturgus.* [d. 268]

SS. Alphaeus and Zachaeus, martyrs. Also called *Alphoeus* and *Zachoeus.* [d. 303]

SS. Acisclus and Victoria, martyrs. [d. c. 4th century]

St. Anianus, Bishop of Orleans. Also called *Agnan, Aignan,* or *Anian.* [d. c. 453]

St. Gregory, Bishop of Tours and historian. [d. 594]

St. Hilda, Abbess of Whitby and virgin. Also called *Hild;* patron saint of business and professional women. [d. 680]

St. Hugh, Bishop of Lincoln. [d. 1200]

St. Elizabeth of Hungary, widow and Landgravine (countess) of Thuringia. Feast formerly November 19. [d. 1231] Obligatory Memorial.

The Beatified

Blessed Salome, widow. [d. 1268]

Blessed Joan of Signa, virgin. [d. 1307]

Blessed Elizabeth the Good, virgin and mystic. [d. 1420]

Blessed Roque Gonzalez and His Companions, the martyrs of Paraguay. [d. 1628]

Blessed Philippine Duchesne, virgin. [d. 1852]

Blessed Hyacinthus Ansalone, one of the Martyrs of Nagasaki. [beatified 1981]

Blessed Thomas Hioji Rokuzayemon Nishi, one of the Martyrs of Nagasaki. [beatified 1981]

BIRTHDATES

1612 *Pierre Mignard,* French painter; preeminent court portrait painter of the mid-seventeenth century. [d. May 30, 1695]

1685 *Pierre Gaultier de Varennes, Sieur de La Verendrye,* French Canadian fur trader, explorer; discoverer of *Manitoba,* the *Dakotas,* and *western Minnesota.* [d. December 5, 1749]

1717 *Jean Le Rond d'Alembert,* French mathematician and scientist; one of the leading figures of the French Enlightenment. [d. October 29, 1783]

1755 *Louis XVIII,* King of France; first king to rule France after the restoration of the monarchy, 1814. [d. September 16, 1824]

1790 *August Ferdinand Möbius,* German mathematician, astronomer; *Möbius strip,* a three-dimensional, one-sided band with a continuous surface, is named for him. [d. September 26, 1868]

João Carlos Saldanha, Portuguese general and statesman; Premier, 1846–49; 1851–56; 1870. [d. November 21, 1876]

1794 *George Grote,* English historian of Greece; primarily known for his 8-volume *History of Greece.* [d. June 18, 1871]

1799 *Titian Ramsay Peale,* U.S. artist; member of the first party to climb Pike's Peak; known for his paintings of animals seen on the expedition; contributor to Charles Bonaparte's *American Ornithology.* [d. March 13, 1885]

1867 *Henri Joseph Eugène Gourand,* French soldier. [d. September 14, 1946]

1878 *Grace Abbott,* U.S. social worker, public administrator; chief of U.S. Children's Bureau, 1921–34; leader in

november

movement to legislate child labor and immigrant exploitation; author of *The Child and the State,* 1938. [d. June 19, 1939]

1887 *Bernard Law Montgomery, 1st Viscount of Alamein,* British Army field marshal; responsible for defeat of *Erwin Rommel* (November 15) at *El Alamein* in World War II. [d. March 24, 1976]

1901 *Lee Strasberg,* U.S. theatrical director, prominent acting teacher, born in Austria; cofounder of the Group Theatre. [d. February 17, 1982]

Walter Hallstein, German diplomat, lawyer; Secretary of Foreign Affairs, West Germany, 1951–58; a founder and first president of the *European Economic Community,* 1958–67. [d. March 29, 1982]

1902 *Eugene Paul Wigner,* U.S. physicist, born in Hungary; Nobel Prize in physics for research on structure of atom and its nucleus (with M. G. Mayer and J. H. D. Jensen), 1963. [d. January 1, 1995]

1904 *Isamu Noguchi,* U.S. sculptor, designer. [d. December 30, 1988]

1912 *Charles Gregory (Bebe) Rebozo,* U.S. real estate executive, banker; close friend of Richard Nixon. [d. May 8, 1998]

1918 *(William Franklin) Billy Graham,* U.S. Baptist clergyman, evangelist.

1919 *Hershy Kay,* U.S. composer, arranger; arranged scores for *Candide, Once Upon a Mattress, A Chorus Line,* and *Evita.* [d. December 2, 1981]

1922 *Stanley Cohen,* U.S. biochemist; Nobel Prize in physiology or medicine for his work with nerve and epidermal growth factors (with Rita Levi-Montalcini), 1986. [d. April 28, 1995]

1923 *Aristide Pereira,* President, Republic of Cape Verde, 1975–91.

1925 *Rock Hudson (Roy Fitzgerald),* U.S. actor [d. October 2, 1985]

1930 *Bob Mathias,* U.S. athlete; U.S. Olympic decathlon winner, 1948, 1952; U.S. Congressman, 1967–73.

1938 *Gordon Lightfoot,* Canadian singer.

1942 *Martin Scorsese,* U.S. director, writer; films include *Woodstock, Taxi Driver, Raging Bull,* and *The Last Temptation of Christ.*

1943 *Lauren Hutton,* U.S. model, actress.

1944 *George Thomas (Tom) Seaver,* U.S. baseball player; pitcher; won 300 games, 1985.

1953 *Dean Paul (Dino, Jr.) Martin,* U.S. actor; member of the pop group, *Dino, Desi, and Billy;* starred in the film, *Players,* 1979; killed while flying for the U.S. Air National Guard. [d. March 21, 1987]

HISTORICAL EVENTS

1292 *Edward I* of England awards vacant Scottish throne to *John Baliol.*

1558 *Queen Mary I* of England dies and is succeeded by *Elizabeth I.*

1637 *Anne Hutchinson,* American religious leader, is banished from Massachusetts by the General Court.

1796 *Catherine the Great,* Empress of Russia, dies and is succeeded by her son, *Paul.*

1800 The *U.S. Congress* meets for the first time in Washington, D.C.

1855 *Dr. David Livingstone* discovers *Victoria Falls* in Africa and names it for the British Queen.

1869 *Suez Canal* opens for navigation.

1870 *Amadeus,* Duke of Aosta, is proclaimed king of Spain as *Amadeo I* upon election by the Cortes.

1933 U.S. recognizes *Soviet government* in Russia.

1941 U.S. Congress amends the *Neutrality Act* to allow arming of U.S. merchant ships.

1958 Civilian government of *Sudan* is overthrown in a military coup.

1968 Unmanned Soviet spacecraft *Zond 6* completes its circumlunar flight.

1970 *Luna 17,* Soviet unmanned spacecraft, lands a *lunokhod,* a self-propelled, 8-wheel vehicle, on the moon.

1972 *Juan Perón* arrives in Buenos Aires from Rome, ending 17 years of exile.

1996 *Emil Constantinescu* is elected president of Romania.

HOLIDAYS

Bolivia (Beni)
Public Holiday

Haiti
Vertieres Day or Army Day
Commemorates the *Battle of Vertieres,* 1803.

Latvia
National Day

Proclamation of the Republic

Morocco
Independence Celebration Day
Celebrates achievement of independence from France, 1956.

Oman
National Day

U.S. (Latvian Community)
National Day or Independence Day
Commemorates 1918 proclamation of independence from Germany and Russia.

RELIGIOUS CALENDAR

Feasts
The Dedication of the Basilicas of St. Peter and of St. Paul, 1626 and 1854.

The Saints
St. Romanus of Antioch, martyr. [d. 304]
St. Mabyn, nun. [d. c. 6th century]
St. Mawes, abbot. Also called *Maudez.* [d. c. 6th century]
St. Odo of Cluny, abbot. Invoked for rain. Also called *Odo of Cluni.* [d. 942]

BIRTHDATES

1647 *Pierre Bayle,* French philosopher, critic; founder of 18th-century rationalism. [d. December 28, 1706]

1743 *Johannes Ewald,* Danish poet, playwright; author of the first original Danish tragedy, *Rolf Krage,* 1770. [d. March 17, 1781]

1768 *Zacharias Werner,* German dramatist, preacher; author of one of the first *fate tragedies,* 1810. [d. January 17, 1823]

Carl Maria von Weber, German composer; the founder of German Romantic opera. [d. June 5, 1826]

1786 *Sir Henry Rowley Bishop,* English conductor and composer of operas; composed music incidental to Shakespearean plays; known especially for refrain of *Home Sweet Home.* [d. April 30, 1855]

1789 *Louis Jacques Mandé Daguerre,* French artist, inventor; invented the *daguerreo-type process,* an early photographic technique. [d. July 10, 1851]

1810 *Asa Gray,* U.S. botanist; author of *Manual of the Botany of the Northern United States,* the fundamental resource in the area; chief advocate of Darwin's theory of evolution in the U.S. [d. January 30, 1888]

1832 *(Nils) Adolf Nordenskiöld,* Swedish Arctic explorer, scientist; first to successfully navigate the *Northeast Passage,* 1878–80. [d. August 12, 1901]

1836 *Sir William Schwenck Gilbert,* British poet and librettist; with his partner, Sir Arthur Sullivan (May 13), composed numerous comic operas. [d. May 29, 1911]

1860 *Ignace Jan Paderewski,* Polish statesman, pianist, composer; leader in Polish cause during World War I; Prime Minister of Polish coalition government, January–November, 1919; preeminent pianist, known for his interpretations of Schumann, Chopin, Liszt, and Rubinstein. [d. June 29, 1941]

1862 *William Ashley (Billy) Sunday,* U.S. evangelist, baseball player; conducted over 300 revivals with an audience of 100 million. [d. November 6, 1935]

1870 *Elizabeth Meriwhether Gilmer,* U.S. journalist; known for her syndicated advice to the lovelorn column written under byline *Dorothy Dix.* [d. December 16, 1951]

1871 *Jessie Bonstelle,* U.S. director, actress; tutored Broadway stars; founded civic theatre in Detroit, 1925. [d. October 14, 1932]

1874 *Clarence (Shepard) Day, Jr.,* U.S. essayist; author of series of essays upon which stage play *Life with Father* was based. [d. December 28, 1935]

1875 *Walter Seymour Allward,* Canadian sculptor; creator of massive Canadian war memorial on Vimy Ridge in France. [d. April 24, 1955]

1882 *Jacques Maritain,* French philosopher; representative of liberal apologist school of Catholic thought; author of numerous influential works, including *Art and Scholasticism* and *True Humanism.* [d. April 28, 1973]

1883 *Carl Vinson,* U.S. politician; U.S. Congressman, 1914–64, and Chairman House Armed Services Committee. [d. June 1, 1981]

1884 *(Percy) Wyndham Lewis,* British novelist, artist; representative of Post-Impressionist Vorticist school; author of *The Art of Being Ruled, Time and Western Man,* and *The Apes of God.* [d. March 7, 1957]

1886 *James S(cott) Kemper,* U.S. insurance executive; Chairman and Chief Executive Officer, Kemper Group, one of the world's largest underwriting organizations, 1945–66; U.S. Ambassador to Brazil, 1953–54. [d. September 17, 1981]

1894 *(Justin) Brooks Atkinson,* U.S. drama critic; preeminent U.S.

critic, 1920–40; Pulitzer Prize in correspondence, 1947. [d. January 13, 1984]

1897 *Lord Patrick Maynard Stuart Blackett,* British physicist; Nobel Prize in physics for discoveries in *cosmic radiation,* 1948. [d. July 13, 1974]

1899 *Euguene Ormandy,* Hungarian-born conductor; toured Europe as child prodigy violinist; conductor of Minneapolis Symphony, 1931–36; conductor of Philadelphia Symphony Orchestra, 1936–80; exercised great influence on development of U.S. symphony orchestras during 1930s and 1940s. [d. March 12, 1985]

1901 *George Horace Gallup,* U.S. public-opinion statistician; creator of the *Gallup Poll;* innovator in area of scientific analysis of public opinion. [d. July 27, 1984]

1906 *George Wald,* U.S. chemist; Nobel Prize in physiology or medicine for experimentation and discovery of processes in human eye, including color reception process (with H. K. Hartline and R. A. Granit), 1967. [d. April 12, 1997]

1909 *Johnny Mercer,* U.S. lyricist; composer of numerous popular songs, 1940s–1960s. [d. June 25, 1976]

1912 *Clement John Zablocki,* U.S. politician; Congressman, 1949–83; Chairman, House Foreign Affairs Committee, 1977–83. [d. December 3, 1983]

1923 *Alan (Bartlett) Shepard, Jr.,* U.S. astronaut; first American in space, May 1961; Chief,

Astronaut Office, 1965–74; commander *Apollo XIV* mission, 1971. [d. July 21, 1998]

Theodore Fulton (Ted) Stevens, U.S. politician, lawyer; Senator, 1968– .

1939 *Margaret Eleanor Atwood,* Canadian author, poet; wrote *The Handmaid's Tale,* 1986; Governor General's Award for *The Circle Game,* 1966.

Brenda Vaccaro, U.S. actress.

1942 *Linda Evans (Linda Evenstad),* U.S. actress; appeared in the television series, *Big Valley* and *Dynasty;* former wife of John Derek.

Qabus ibn Said, Sultan, Sultanate of Oman, 1970– .

1943 *Keith Richards,* British rock guitarist; member of *The Rolling Stones.*

1944 *Susan Sullivan,* U.S. actress; known for her role as Maggie Gioberti on the television series, *Falcon Crest.*

1950 *Jameson Parker,* U.S. actor; known for his role as A. J. Simon on the television series, *Simon & Simon,* 1981–88.

1954 *Rickie Lee Jones,* U.S. pop singer; best known for hit *Chuck E's In Love.*

1956 *Warren Moon,* U.S. football player.

1960 *Elizabeth Perkins,* U.S. actress; known for roles in *Big,* 1988 and *The Flintstones,* 1994.

1963 *Len Bias,* U.S. basketball player; number one draft choice of Boston Celtics; died of cocaine overdose. [d. June 19, 1986]

1968 *Gary Sheffield,* U.S. baseball player.

HISTORICAL EVENTS

1188 Richard (later *Richard I* of England), the rebellious son of *King Henry II* of England, allies with *Philip II* of France against his father.

1189 *William II* of Sicily dies and is succeeded by *Tancred the Bastard.*

1210 *Pope Innocent III* excommunicates Holy Roman Emperor *Otto IV.*

1901 *Hay-Pauncefote Treaty* is signed, giving the U.S. control of the *Isthmian Canal.*

1905 *Prince Charles* of Denmark is elected King of Norway; assumes the title *King Haakon VII.*

1914 The Russians are defeated at *Soldau,* East Prussia, in their second invasion of that German province (*World War I*).

1918 Belgian army reoccupies *Brussels* for the first time in more than four years (*World War I*).

Sovereign free state of *Latvia* is proclaimed.

1928 The first animated talking cartoon movie, *Steamboat Willie,* is shown in New York featuring the character of *Mickey Mouse,* the creation of *Walt Disney.*

1936 Germany and Italy recognize the government of Gen. Francisco Franco (*Spanish Civil War*).

1943 Planes from 11 U.S. carriers attack *Gilbert Islands* in the Pacific (*World War II*).

1959 *Ben Hur,* the film epic starring Charlton Heston, premieres in New York.

Rick Besoyan's musical, *Little Mary Sunshine,* premieres in New York.

1960 The Chrysler Corp. announces the discontinuation of its *DeSoto* line of cars, in production since 1928.

The International Court of Justice in The Hague awards three hundred square miles of disputed Nicaraguan-Honduran border territory to *Honduras.*

1966 U.S. spacecraft *Lunar Orbiter 2* begins transmission of photographs of moon's surface, allowing analysis of possible landing sites for future lunar craft.

1978 Murder of U.S. congressman Leo J. Ryan and four other Americans in *Jamestown, Guyana* triggers mass suicides and murders of more than 900 members of the *People's Temple* and their leader, *Jim Jones.*

1987 *CBS* agrees to sell its record division to *Sony Corp.* of Japan.

Final report of the congressional committees investigating the *Iran-contra affair* is released. President *Ronald Reagan* is held responsible for policies within his administration that reflected disregard for the law.

1989 Pennsylvania approves a bill severely restricting *abortions,* becoming the first state to do so following the Supreme Court ruling (July 3, 1989).

1991 *Terry Waite* is released after four years of captivity by the Islamic Jihad in Lebanon.

1993 Representatives from various political parties in *South Africa* approve a new constitution.

november

NOVEMBER
19

HOLIDAYS

Belize
Garifuna Settlement Day

France, Monaco
Prince of Monaco Holiday
Celebrates the official birthday of
Prince Rainier III.

Mali
Liberation Day

Oman
Sultan's Birthday

Puerto Rico
Discovery of Puerto Rico
Commemorates discovery of the
island by Christopher Columbus on
his second voyage of discovery,
1493.

RELIGIOUS CALENDAR

The Saints
St. Nerses I, Primate of the
Armenians and martyr. Also
called *Narses I* and *the Great.*
[d. c. 373]
St. Barlaam, martyr of Antioch. [d.
c. 4th century]
St. Ermenburga, abbess. Also called
Domneva, or *Eormenburh.*
[d. c. 700]

BIRTHDATES

1600 *Charles I,* King of England,
1625–49; his authoritarian
rule provoked a civil war that
led to his execution. [d.
January 30, 1649]

1752 *George Rogers Clark,* U.S.
frontiersman, army general;
known for his capture of
Vincennes during American
Revolution. [d. February 13,
1818]

1805 *Ferdinand De Lesseps,* French
diplomat, engineer; the
builder of the *Suez Canal.* [d.
December 7, 1894]

1812 *Franz Felix Adalbert Kuhn,*
German linguist, mythologist;
a pioneer of *comparative
mythology.* [d. May 5, 1881]

1831 *James Abram Garfield,*
college president, lay
preacher; U.S. Congressman,
1863–80; 20th President of
U.S.; shot July 2, 1881, after
six months in office. [d.
September 9, 1887]

1839 *Emil von Skoda,* Czech
industrialist; founder of *Skoda
Works,* famous for its
manufacture of munitions,
especially heavy artillery and
cannons. [d. August 8, 1900]

1853 *Albert Auguste Gabriel
Hanotaux,* French historian
and statesman; Minister of
Foreign Affairs, 1894–95;
1896–98; author of several
excellent histories of France.
[d. April 11, 1944]

1859 *Mihail Mihailovich Ippolitov-
Ivanov,* Russian composer;
noted especially for his
Sketches from the Caucasus.
[d. January 28, 1935]

1862 *(William Ashley) Billy
Sunday,* U.S. revivalist,
professional baseball player.
[d. November 6, 1935]

1875 *Mikhail Ivanovich Kalinin,*
Russian revolutionary and
Soviet official; President,
U.S.S.R., 1923–46. [d. June 3,
1946]

1887 *James Batcheller Sumner,*
U.S. biochemist; Nobel Prize
in chemistry for crystallizing
enzymes (with J. H. Northrop
and W. M. Stanley), 1946. [d.
August 12, 1955]

1896 *Clifton Webb,* U.S. character
actor. [d. October 13, 1966]

1899 *(John Orley) Allen Tate,* U.S.
critic, poet, novelist; a major
figure in New Criticism. [d.
February 9, 1979]

1905 *Tommy Dorsey,* U.S.
musician; major figure in U.S.
Big Band era; performed with
brother Jimmy (February 29)
and in own band. [d.
November 26, 1956]

1912 *George Emil Palade,* U.S.
physiologist born in Rumania;
Nobel Prize in physiology or
medicine for research in
science of *cell biology* (with
A. Claude and C. R. de Duve),
1974.

1915 *Earl Wilbur Sutherland,* U.S.
biochemist; Nobel Prize in
physiology or medicine for
discoveries in *chromosome*

research, 1971. [d. March 9, 1974]

1917 *Indira Gandhi,* Indian stateswoman; Prime Minister of India, 1966–77; 1980–84; assassinated. [d. October 31, 1984]

1918 *Hendrik van de Hulst,* Dutch astronomer; his discoveries contributed to mapping structure of *Milky Way.*

1921 *Roy Campanella,* U.S. baseball player; catcher, Brooklyn Dodgers, 1948–57; paralyzed in an automobile accident, 1958; elected to the Hall of Fame, 1969. [d. June 26, 1993]

1922 *Emil Zatopek,* Czech distance runner; winner of 3 Olympic gold medals, 1952.

1926 *Jeane Duane Jordan Kirkpatrick,* U.S. diplomat, educator; U.S. permanent representative to the United Nations, 1981–85.

1933 *Larry King (Larry Zeiger),* U.S. radio performer, television personality; hosts *Larry King Live,* 1985– .

1936 *Dick Cavett,* U.S. entertainer, talk-show host.

1937 *Penelope Leach,* British child-care expert, author; host of the TV show *Your Baby and Child.*

1938 *Robert Edward (Ted) Turner III,* U.S. sportsman, businessman; developed the first all-news cable network; owns the sports teams, the Atlanta Braves and the Atlanta Hawks; won America's Cup as captain of the *Courageous,* 1977.

1941 *Dan Haggerty,* U.S. actor; starred in the television series, *Life and Times of Grizzly Adams,* 1977–78.

1942 *Calvin Klein,* U.S. fashion designer.

1954 *Kathleen Quinlan,* U.S. actress; appeared in the movie, *I Never Promised You a Rose Garden* and *The Promise.*

1961 *Meg Ryan,* U.S. actress.

1962 *Alicia Christian (Jodie) Foster,* U.S. actress; starred in the movies, *Taxi Driver,* 1976, and *Foxes,* 1980; Academy Award (Best Actress) for both *The Accused,* 1988, and *Silence of the Lambs,* 1991.

1966 *(Yoland) Gail Devers,* U.S. track athlete: Olympic gold medalist, 1992.

1973 *Savion Glover,* U.S. choreographer, actor; Tony Award winner in choreography for *Bring in 'Da Noise, Bring in 'Da Funk,* 1996.

1977 *Kerri Strug,* U.S. gymnast; Olympic gold medalist, 1996.

HISTORICAL EVENTS

1794 *Jay's Treaty* between the U.S. and Great Britain is concluded, settling remaining disputes between the two countries.

1863 Abraham Lincoln delivers the *Gettysburg Address.*

1873 *William Marcy Tweed* is found guilty of defrauding New York City of millions of dollars.

1918 *Metz, Alsace* is occupied by the French (*World War I*).

Antwerp, Belgium is reoccupied by Belgian troops (*World War I*).

1942 Russian counteroffensive against Germans begins on the *Stalingrad front* (*World War II*).

1949 *Rainier III* is crowned Prince of Monaco.

1951 *Oscar Torp* is inaugurated as premier of Norway.

1952 *Alexander Papagos* is inaugurated as premier of Greece.

1957 *Leonard Bernstein* is appointed musical director of the New York Philharmonic Orchestra.

1959 Ford Motor Co. suspends production of its *Edsel* model. The car was never accepted by the general public, and its name became synonymous with failure.

1962 The Bulgarian National Assembly appoints *Todor Zhivkov* to replace *Anton Yugov* as premier of Bulgaria.

1965 *Ecumenical Council* of Roman Catholic Church declares *freedom of conscience* is official Church doctrine.

1968 Mali's first president, *Mobido Keita,* is overthrown in a military coup d'etat.

1969 U.S. astronauts *Charles Conrad, Jr.,* and *Alan L. Bean* land on the moon in the *Apollo 12* lunar module and begin the first of two scheduled moon walks.

Pelé (Edson Arantes do Nascimento), Brazilian soccer star, scores his 1000th goal, at the Maracaña Stadium, Rio de Janeiro.

november

1976 *Algeria* promulgates a new constitution.

1977 Egyptian president, *Anwar Sadat,* visits Israel's capital city and addresses its parliament, in an attempt to end 30 years of hostility between the two nations.

1979 *Lane Kirkland* is elected president of the American Federation of Labor-Congress of Industrial Organization (AFL-CIO).

1990 The *Conventional Forces in Europe treaty* is signed; participating countries agree to downsize their weapon stockpiles.

1991 The city of Vukovar, Croatia, falls to *Serbian forces.*

1995 *Aleksandr Kwasniewski* wins the presidential elections in Poland, defeating *Lech Walesa.*

The *Asia-Pacific Economic Cooperation (APEC)* agrees to the creation of a free trade policy.

HOLIDAYS

Mexico
Mexican Revolution Anniversary
Anniversary of the overthrow of the dictatorship of Porfirio Diaz, 1910.

RELIGIOUS CALENDAR

The Saints
St. Dasius, martyr. [d. c. 303]
SS. Nerses, Bishop of Sahgerd, and other martyrs. [d. 343]
St. Edmund the Martyr, King of the East Angles. [d. 870]
St. Bernward, bishop of Hildesheim. [d. 1022]
St. Felix of Valois, co-founder of the Order of the Most Holy Trinity. [d. 1212]
St. Maxentia, virgin and martyr. Also called *Masentia.* [death date unknown]

The Beatified
Blessed Ambrose of Camaldoli, abbot. [d. 1439]
Blessed Hyacinthe Marie Cormier. [beatified 1994]
Blessed Claudio Granzotto. [beatified 1994]
Blessed Agnes de Jesus Galand. [beatified 1994]
Blessed Eugenia Joubert. [beatified 1994]
Blessed Marie Poussepin. [beatified 1994]

BIRTHDATES

1602 *Otto von Guericke,* German scientist; invented the *Magdeburg hemispheres* for demonstration of pressure of the atmosphere; credited with development of first *electrical generating machine.* [d. May 11, 1686]

1725 *Oliver Wolcott,* American Revolutionary leader; Governor of Connecticut, 1796–97; signer of the Declaration of Independence. [d. December 1, 1797]

1752 *Thomas Chatterton,* English poet; creator of *Thomas Rowley,* an imaginary 15th-century monk, whose works were the subject of debate for nearly 100 years; committed suicide in desperation over failure of his own literary works. [d. August 24, 1770]

1761 *Pope Pius VIII,* pope 1829–30. [d. November 30, 1830]

1841 *Sir Wilfrid Laurier,* Canadian statesman; Prime Minister of Canada, 1896–1911. [d. February 17, 1919]

1855 *Josiah Royce,* U.S. idealist philosopher; professor of philosophy, Harvard University, 1882–1916. Noted for his contributions to logic, religion, metaphysics, and the philosophy of mathematics; developed system of philosophy based on concepts of the Absolute. [d. September 14, 1916]

1858 *Selma Lagerlöf,* Swedish novelist, short-story writer; the first woman to win the Nobel Prize in literature, 1909. [d. March 16, 1940]

1866 *Judge Kenesaw Mountain Landis,* U.S. jurist, sports executive; first commissioner of professional baseball. [d. November 25, 1944]

1873 *William Weber Coblentz,* U.S. physicist, pioneer in *infrared spectrophotometry.* [d. September 15, 1962]

1884 *Norman (Mattoon) Thomas,* U.S. socialist leader, reformer, editor, clergyman; a founder of *American Civil Liberties Union,* 1920; leader of *American Socialist Party,* 1926–48; conscience candidate for American liberals in numerous elections. [d. December 19, 1968]

1885 *Albert Kesselring,* German Air Force field marshal; commanded German invasions of Poland, 1939, and France, 1940; condemned as German war criminal; committed to life imprisonment. [d. July 16, 1960]

1886 *Karl von Frisch,* German zoologist; Nobel Prize in physiology or medicine for research in *ethology* (with K. Lorenz and N. Tinbergen), 1973. [d. June 12, 1982]

november

1889 *Edwin Powell Hubble,* U.S. astronomer; developed *Hubble's constant,* a numerical value applied to the speed of recession of distant galaxies; contributed greatly to development of cosmology and concept of *expanding universe.* [d. September 28, 1953]

1908 *(Alfred) Alistair Cooke,* U.S. journalist, broadcaster, born in England; chief correspondent of Manchester *Guardian,* 1948–72; master of ceremonies of *Masterpiece Theatre,* a dramatic series, produced by the BBC, on National Public Television.

1914 *Emilio Pucci,* Italian fashion designer. [d. November 29, 1992]

1917 *Robert Carlyle Byrd,* U.S. politician, lawyer; Senator, 1958–; Senate Majority Leader, 1977–81, 1987–89.

1920 *Gene Tierney,* U.S. actress. [d. November 6, 1991]

1923 *Nadine Gordimer,* South African writer; Nobel Prize for Literature in 1991.

1925 *Maya Michailovna Plisetskaya,* Soviet prima ballerina; Artistic Director, Theatro Lirico National, 1987–90.

Robert Francis Kennedy, U.S. politician, lawyer; Attorney General, 1961–64; brother of U.S. President John F. Kennedy (May 29). Assassinated. [d. June 6, 1968]

1926 *Kaye Ballard (Catherine Gloria Balotta),* U.S. singer, actress, comedienne, writer; starred in the television series, *The Mothers-in-Law,* 1967–69.

1927 *Estelle Parsons,* U.S. actress; Oscar winner for *Bonnie and Clyde,* 1967.

1938 *Dick Smothers,* U.S. folksinger, comedian; with brother Tom (February 2) became center of controversy during 1960s when their program was edited by television censors.

1942 *Joseph Robinette Biden, Jr.,* U.S. politician, lawyer; Senator, 1972–; withdrew from 1988 presidential race after charges of plagiarism appeared in the press.

1945 *Veronica Hamel,* U.S. model, actress; known for her role as Joyce Davenport on the television series, *Hill Street Blues,* 1981–87.

1946 *(Howard) Duane Allman,* U.S. singer, musician; member of the *Allman Brothers Band;* known as one of the great U.S. rock guitarists. [d. October 29, 1971]

Judy Carline Woodruff, U.S. broadcast journalist, author.

1947 *Joseph Fidler (Joe) Walsh,* U.S singer, musician; member of the rock groups, *The James Gang* and *The Eagles;* known for his guitar style.

1948 *Richard Masur,* U.S. actor.

1956 *Marcus D. (Mark) Gastineau,* U.S. football player; defensive end, New York Jets; known for his inflammatory dances after quarter-back sacks.

1959 *Sean Young,* U.S. actress.

HISTORICAL EVENTS

1541 *John Calvin* establishes a theocratic government at Geneva, creating a base for Protestantism in Europe.

1759 Engish defeat French off *Quiberon, France (Seven Years' War).*

1910 *Francisco I. Madero* leads a rebellion that overthrows the government of Mexican dictator of *Porfirio Díaz.*

1917 First demonstration of effectiveness of *tanks* in warfare is made as British attack German lines during *Battle of Cambrai (World War I).*

1921 Madame *Marie Spaak-Janson,* Belgian socialist, becomes first woman elected to Belgian parliament.

1922 *Lausanne Conference,* to conclude peace between Turkey and the Allies of World War I, opens in Switzerland.

1924 The Beatrice Creamery Co. (later *Beatrice Companies Inc.)* is incorporated in Delaware.

1942 U.S., British, and French troops begin the first battle against Nazi forces in *Tunisia (World War II).*

Willi Pep defeats *Chalky Wright* to win the world featherweight boxing title.

1943 U.S. infantry invades *Makin Island,* one of the Gilbert Islands in the Central Pacific *(World War II).*

1945 *Nuremburg Trials* begin in Germany, an international military tribunal, trying Nazi offenders for crimes against peace, humanity, and the laws of war.

1953 French forces capture *Dien Bien Phu,* a Viet Minh fortress in nothern Vietnam.

1962 The U.S.S.R. agrees to withdraw all IL-28 jet bombers from *Cuba,* prompting the U.S. to end its naval blockade.

U.S. President John Kennedy signs executive order prohibiting *racial discrimination* in housing built or purchased with federal funds.

1964 The *Vatican II Ecumenical Council* exonerates Jews of any special guilt in the crucifixion of Christ.

1966 John Kander and Frank Ebb's musical, *Cabaret,* premieres in New York.

1969 U.S. Department of Agriculture orders a halt in the use of the pesticide *DDT* in residential areas.

Native Americans occupy *Alcatraz Island* for nineteen months.

1978 *Ethiopia* signs a 20-year treaty of friendship and cooperation with the U.S.S.R. which insures a foothold for the Soviet Union in the Horn of Africa.

1986 British scientists report the rising of the Earth's temperature by one degree Fahrenheit in the past 123 years. Excessive atmospheric pollutants are thought to be the cause of this warming trend, known as the *greenhouse effect.*

1993 The *North American Free Trade Agreement (NAFTA)* is approved by the Senate. It goes into effect January 1, 1994.

1994 The government of *Angola* and rebel forces sign a peace treaty aimed at ending the nineteen-year-old civil war.

november

NOVEMBER
21

RELIGIOUS CALENDAR

Feasts

The Presentation of the Blessed Virgin Mary. Commemorates Mary's being brought by her parents to the Temple at Jerusalem. Of 6th-century origin; formally recognized in 1585. Obligatory Memorial.

The Saints

St. Gelasius I, pope. Elected 492. [d. 496]

St. Albert of Louvain, Bishop of Liège and martyr. [d. 1192]

BIRTHDATES

1495 *John Bale,* English bishop, reformer, anti-quary, and dramatist; author of several controversial works on Protestantism. [d. November 1563]

1694 *François Marie Arouet de Voltaire,* French philosopher, writer; master of satire; champion of victims of religious intolerance; author of *La Siècle de Louis XIV,* 1751. [d. May 30, 1778]

1729 *Josiah Bartlett,* American physician, Revolutionary War patriot; representative to Continental Congress; signer of Declaration of Independence; Chief Justice of Superior Court of New Hampshire, 1788–90;

President of New Hampshire, 1790–92; first governor of New Hampshire, 1793–94. [d. May 19, 1795]

1785 *William Beaumont,* US. surgeon, known for his study of the stomach and digestion. [d. April 25, 1853]

1787 *Sir Samuel Cunard,* Canadian shipowner; founder of Cunard Shipping Co., 1839; with others, established Royal Mail Steam Packet Co., the first regularly scheduled trans-Atlantic mail service, 1839. [d. April 28, 1865]

1789 *Cesare Balbo,* Italian author, statesman; first premier of Piedmont, 1848. [d. June 3, 1853]

1834 *(Henrietta Howland) Hettie Green,* U.S. financier; reputedly the richest woman of her time in the U.S.; shrewd, eccentric, financial genius; investments in real estate, railroad securities, and government bonds estimated at $100 million at her death. [d. July 3, 1916]

1851 *Désiré Joseph Mercier,* Belgian cardinal; the spokesman for Belgians during German occupation (World War I). [d. January 23, 1926]

1854 *Pope Benedict XV,* pope 1914–22; a strict neutral

during World War I, he refrained from condemning any actions of the belligerents. [d. January 22, 1922]

1867 *Vladimir Nikolaevich Ipatieff,* U.S. chemist, born in Russia; developed numerous high-pressure catalytic reactions; important in synthesis of hydrocarbons; head of Russian chemical works during World War I. [d. November 29, 1952]

1869 *William Henry Murray,* U.S. politician; U.S. Congressman, 1913–17; Governor of Oklahoma, 1931–35. [d. October 15, 1956]

1886 *Sir Harold George Nicolson,* British diplomat, biographer, historian; husband of *Victoria Mary Sackville West.* [d. May 1, 1968]

1893 *(Arthur) Harpo Marx,* U.S. comedian, screen actor; silent member of *Marx Brothers* comedy team. [d. September 28, 1964]

1898 *René François-Ghislain Magritte,* Belgian surrealist painter. [d. August 15, 1967]

1907 *Jim Bishop,* U.S. journalist, author; known for his detailed portrayals of deaths of Jesus, Abraham Lincoln, and John F. Kennedy. [d. July 26, 1987]

1912 *Eleanor Powell,* U.S. dancer. [d. February 11, 1982]

1920 *Stan(ley Frank) "the Man" Musial,* U.S. baseball player; Baseball Hall of Fame, 1960.

1927 *Joseph Mario Campanella,* U.S. actor; starred in the television series, *The Lawyer,* 1969–72.

1929 *Marilyn French,* U.S. author; wrote *The Women's Room,* 1977.

1938 *Margaret (Marlo) Thomas,* U.S. actress; starred in *That Girl,* 1966–71; Emmy Award for *Free to Be...You and Me,* 1977; daughter of Danny Thomas; wife of Phil Donahue.

1940 *Natalia Romanovna Makarova,* U.S. ballerina; defected from Russia, 1970.

1941 *Juliet Mills,* British actress; known for her performance in the television series, *Nanny and the Professor,* 1970–71; daughter of John Mills.

1944 *Harold Ramis,* U.S. actor, writer, director. Starred in *Ghostbusters,* 1984.

1945 *Goldie Hawn,* U.S. actress, comedienne, singer, dancer, producer; 1969 Academy Award for best supporting actress in *Cactus Flower.*

1952 *Lorna Luft,* U.S. singer, daughter of Judy Garland and Sid Luft.

1953 *Tina Brown,* British editor, journalist; editor-in-chief, *Vanity Fair,* 1984–98.

1961 *Mariel Hemingway,* U.S. actress, starred in the films, *Lipstick,* 1976, and *Manhattan,* 1979.

1965 *Bjork (Gundmundsdottir),* Icelandic singer.

1966 *Troy Aikman,* U.S. football player with the Dallas Cowboys.

1969 *Ken Griffey, Jr.,* U.S. baseball player.

HISTORICAL EVENTS

1620 *Mayflower Compact,* a preliminary plan of government for the Pilgrims, is signed in the cabin of *The Mayflower,* near Provincetown, Massachusetts.

1783 Two Frenchmen, *Jean François Pilâtre de Rozier* and the *Marquis d'Arlandes,* make first successful *balloon ascent,* lasting 25 minutes and covering more than five miles.

1789 *North Carolina* becomes the twelfth state to ratify the U.S. Constitution.

1916 *Emperor Franz Josef* of Austria-Hungary dies and is succeeded by his nephew, Karl.

1918 The German High Seas Fleet is surrendered to the British near Rosyth, Scotland, for internment at *Scapa Flow (World War I).*

1920 Fourteen secret British agents in Dublin are slain by the I.R.A. in what is henceforth called *Bloody Sunday.*

1922 *Rebecca Felton* becomes the first female U.S. senator.

1934 Cole Porter's musical comedy, *Anything Goes,* opens in New York, including title song and *I Get a Kick Out of You.*

1938 Gene Kelly's first play *Leave it to Me* premieres in New York.

1945 Sergei Prokofiev's opera ballet, *Cinderella,* opens in Moscow.

1946 *Harry S. Truman* becomes first U.S. president to travel underwater in a submarine.

1953 The *Piltdown skull,* allegedly belonging to an early hominid, is found to be a hoax.

1963 Ecumenical Council of Roman Catholic Church (Vatican II) authorizes use of *vernacular languages* in all churches.

1964 *Verrazano-Narrows Bridge* between Brooklyn and Staten Island, then the world's longest suspension bridge, is formally opened.

1976 *Einstein at the Beach,* an opera by Philip Glass and Robert Wilson, premieres in New York.

1985 *Paias Wingti* is inaugurated as prime minister of Papua New Guinea.

1988 *Brian Mulroney* wins a second term as Prime Minister of Canada.

1990 *Michael Milken,* also known as the "junk bond king," enters a plea of guilty to insider trading and is sentenced to a ten-year prison term.

1993 *District of Columbia* is denied statehood.

1995 Leaders of *Bosnia-Herzegovina, Serbia,* and *Croatia* agree on a peace accord.

november

NOVEMBER
22

HOLIDAYS

Republic of Georgia
St. George's Day

Guinea
National Day or Day of 1970 Invasion

Lebanon
Independence Day
Commemorates Lebanon's achievement of independence from France, 1941.

RELIGIOUS CALENDAR

The Saints
SS. Philemon and Apphia, martyrs. Apphia also called *Apphis*, or *Appia*. [d. 1st cent.]
St. Cecilia, virgin and martyr. Patron of church music, musicians, makers of musical instruments, and of music generally. Also called *Cecily*. [death date unknown] Obligatory Memorial.

The Beatified
Blessed Maria de Jesus Sacramentado Venegas. [beatified 1992]
Blessed Cristobal Magellanes. [beatified 1992]

BIRTHDATES

1643 *René Robert Cavelier, Sieur de La Salle,* French explorer in North America; expeditions of wilderness south of Lakes Ontario and Erie helped him to eventually take possession of the waterway region of the Mississippi River, dubbed Louisiana, and to claim it for France; killed by mutinous companions while exploring for the mouth of the Mississippi River. [d. March 19, 1687]

1767 *Andreas Hofer,* Tirolean patriot; led rebellion against Bavarian army; defeated and killed. [d. February 20, 1810]

1808 *Lionel Nathan Rothschild,* British banker; first Jewish member of Parliament. [d. June 3, 1879]

1819 *George Eliot (Mary Ann Evans),* British novelist; known for her irregular lifestyle and humorous descriptions of rural life in England. [d. December 22, 1880]

1842 *José María de Heredia,* French poet, bibliophile, born in Cuba; leading representative of French Parnassians; author of *Les Trophées,* a collection of 50 sonnets, 1893. [d. October 2, 1905]

1852 *Paul H. B. B. d'Estournells de Constant de Rebecque,* French diplomat, politician; Nobel Peace Prize for his work for international conciliation and disarmament, 1909. [d. May 15, 1924]

1857 *George (Robert) Gissing,* British novelist and man of letters; noted for portrayal of middle-class life in England. [d. December 28, 1903]

1868 *John Nance (Cactus Jack) Garner,* U.S. Congressman, 1903–33; U.S. Vice President, 1933–41; two-time running mate of U.S. President Franklin D. Roosevelt; upon retirement became known as a minor political sage. [d. November 7, 1967]

1869 *André (Paul Guillaume) Gide,* French novelist, esssayist; a founder of *Nouvelle Revue Française.* [d. February 19, 1951]

1890 *Charles (André Joseph Marie) De Gaulle,* French statesman, soldier, writer; head of French government in exile during World War II; President of Fifth Republic, 1958–69. [d. November 9, 1970]

1899 *Wiley Post,* U.S. aviator; first solo pilot to successfully circumnavigate the globe; with Will Rogers (November 4), killed on flight across Alaska. [d. August 15, 1935]

Hoagy Carmichael (Hoagland Howard Carmichael), U.S. composer, singer, pianist; wrote *Stardust, Georgia on My Mind,* and *Nearness of You.* [d. December 27, 1981]

1904 *Louis Eugene Felix Neel,* French physicist; Nobel Prize in physics for discoveries in area of magneto-hydrodynamics (with H. O. G. Alfven), 1970.

1913 *(Edward) Benjamin Britten,* British composer; leading figure in development of 20th-century music. [d. December 4, 1976]

1918 *Claiborne Pell,* U.S. politician; Senator, 1960–95.

1921 *Rodney Dangerfield,* U.S. comedian.

1924 *Geraldine Page,* U.S. actress; Academy Award for *A Trip to Bountiful,* 1986. [d. June 13, 1987]

1925 *Gunther Schuller,* U.S. composer, conductor; founder of the New England Conservatory Ragtime Ensemble; known for his arrangements of Scott Joplin's works which were featured in the movie, *The Sting.*

1932 *Robert Vaughn,* U.S. actor; known for his role as Napoleon Solo in the television series, *The Man from U.N.C.L.E.,* 1964–67.

1940 *Terry Gilliam,* U.S. illustrator, cartoonist; member of *Monty Python's Flying Circus;* directed the award-winning movie, *Brazil,* 1985.

1941 *Thomas Antonio (Tom) Conti,* Scottish actor; Tony Award for *Whose Life is It Anyway?,* 1978–79.

Nicholas Dante, U.S. dramatist; Pulitzer Prize and Tony Award for *A Chorus Line,* 1976.

1943 *Billie Jean King,* U.S. tennis player.

1958 *Jamie Lee Curtis,* U.S. actress; starred in the movies, *Halloween* and *A Fish Called Wanda;* daughter of Tony Curtis and Janet Leigh.

1967 *Boris Becker,* German tennis player; youngest and first unseeded player to win the Wimbledon Singles Championship, 1985.

HISTORICAL EVENTS

1497 *Vasco da Gama* rounds the *Cape of Good Hope* in Africa, discovering for Portugal an ocean passage to India.

1878 *Second Afghan War* begins when Ali Mujid is shelled and occupied by the British.

1914 *Battle of Ypres* ends with the failure of a second massive German offensive (*World War I*).

1917 *National Hockey League* is established at Montreal.

1927 George and Ira Gershwin's musical, *Funny Face,* premieres in New York.

1928 Ravel's *Bolero* opens at Paris Opera with *Ida Rubenstein* dancing.

1931 Ferde Grofé's *Grand Canyon Suite* premieres in Chicago.

1938 *Henry C. Lee,* Chinese-born forensic scientist; testified for the defense during the O. J. Simpson trial, 1995.

1941 *Lebanon* achieves independence from France, which has maintained control under a mandate from the League of Nations.

1942 The U.S. petroleum industry war council announces that *tubeless tires* have successfully passed government testing and been approved for use.

1943 *First Cairo Conference* begins as U.S. President Franklin Roosevelt, British Prime Minister Churchill, and Chinese Premier Chiang Kai-shek confer.

1944 *Metz* in France falls to U.S. Third Army under Patton (*World War II*).

1963 *John F. Kennedy,* 35th President of the U.S., is assassinated in Dallas, Texas. Vice-President *Lyndon Baines Johnson* is sworn in as president.

1965 *Cassius Clay* retains his world heavyweight championship by defeating Floyd Patterson in the 12th round in Las Vegas, Nevada.

Mitch Leigh and Joe Darion's musical, *Man of La Mancha,* premieres in New York.

1975 *Juan Carlos I* takes oath as the king of Spain, two days after the death of Geralissimo *Francisco Franco.*

1989 *René Moawad,* newly-elected president of Lebanon, is assassinated.

1990 *Margaret Thatcher* resigns as Britain's prime minister.

1993 The Mexican senate approves the *North American Free Trade Agreement (NAFTA)* (November 20, 1993).

november

NOVEMBER
23

HOLIDAYS

Japan
Labor Thanksgiving Day or Kinro-Kansha-No-Hi
A day of rest for workers in Japan on which they reflect on the dignity of labor and express gratitude for success and abundance.

RELIGIOUS CALENDAR

The Saints
St. Clement I, pope and martyr. Elected 88. First of the Apostolic Fathers. Patron of the Gild, Fraternity, and Brotherhood House of the Most Glorious and Undivided Trinity of London, or Trinity House; patron of boatmen, hatters, tanners, and stonecutters. Invoked to aid sick children. [d. c. 99]

St. Amphilochius, Bishop of Iconium. [d. c. 400]

St. Gregory, Bishop of Girgenti. [d. c. 603]

St. Columban, Abbot of Luxeuil and Bobbio, and missionary-monk. [d. 615] Optional Memorial.

St. Trudo, missionary. Also called *Tron,* or *Trond.* [d. c. 690]

BIRTHDATES

912 *Otto I, (the Great),* King of Germany and Holy Roman Emperor, 936–973; consolidated the German state and decisively defeated the Magyars in 955. [d. May 7, 973]

1221 *Alfonso X (the Wise),* King of Castile and Leon. [d. April 4, 1284]

1608 *Francisco Manuel de Melo,* Portuguese moralist, historian, playwright, and poet; accused of attempted assassination of *King John IV* of Portugal; exiled to Brazil, 1653–59. [d. August 24, 1666]

1712 *Andrew Foulis,* Scottish publisher, printer; with his brother, Robert, noted for editions of Thomas Gray's poetry and Milton's *Paradise Lost.* [d. September 18, 1775]

1749 *Edward Rutledge,* American patriot, lawyer; member of the Continental Congress, 1774–77; signer of the Declaration of Independence, 1776; Governor of South Carolina, 1798–1800. [d. January 23, 1800]

1803 *Theodore Dwight Weld,* U.S. social reformer; called the *Great Abolitionist.* [d. February 3, 1895]

1804 *Franklin Pierce,* U.S. lawyer; 14th President of the U.S., 1853–57. [d. October 8, 1869]

1837 *Johannes D. van der Waals,* Dutch physicist; discovered *van der Waals forces;* Nobel Prize in physics for research on mathematical equations describing the continuity of gaseous and liquid states of matter, electrolytic dissociation, and the thermodynamic theory of capillarity, 1910. [d. March 9, 1923]

1859 *Billy the Kid (William H. Bonney),* U.S. outlaw; one of most highly publicized outlaws in U.S. history; killed 21 men before being shot to death at age of 21. [d. July 15, 1881]

1860 *Karl Hjalmar Branting,* Swedish statesman, diplomat; awarded Nobel Peace Prize for his conciliatory international diplomacy from 1900–1920, 1921. [d. February 24, 1925]

1869 *Valdemar Poulsen,* Danish scientist; developed methods of recording of sound with magnetization, 1898; invented *arc generator* for high-frequency oscillations used in *wireless telegraphy.* [d. July 1942]

1876 *Manuel de Falla,* Spanish composer; known for his nationalistic and impressionistic themes; wrote *The Three-Cornered Hat.* [d. November 14, 1946]

1878 *Ernest Joseph King,* U.S. admiral; first man to act as commander of the Combined

Fleet (COMINCH), simultaneously acting as chief of naval operations; as such he commanded the largest fleet of ships, planes, and men in the history of the Navy; also acted as adviser to U.S. President Franklin Roosevelt on naval issues. [d. June 25, 1956]

1883 *José Clemente Orozco,* Mexican painter; master of fresco painting. [d. September 7, 1949]

1887 *Henry Gwyn-Jeffreys Moseley,* British physicist; noted for research on x-ray elements; killed during World War I. [d. August 10, 1915]

Boris Karloff (William Henry Pratt), British actor. [d. February 3, 1969]

1892 *Erte (Romain De Tirtoff),* Russian fashion designer; created costumes for theater and film; designs used in the movie, *Ben Hur,* and for the Folies Bergere, 1919–30; noted for his covers for *Harper's Bazaar* in the 1920s and 1930s. [d. April 22, 1990]

1913 *Carlos Bulosan,* U.S. author, labor organizer. [d. 1956]

1926 *Jose Napoleon Duarte,* Salvadoran political leader;

exiled after staging an abortive coup, 1972–79; President, 1981–82, 1984–89. [d. February 23, 1990]

1927 *Otis Chandler,* U.S. newspaper publisher; publisher of *Los Angeles Times,* 1960–80.

1930 *William Emerson (Bill) Brock,* U.S. politician; Congressman, 1962–70; Senator, 1970–77; Chairman, Republican National Committee, 1977–81; U.S. Special Trade Representative.

1939 *Susan Anspach,* U.S. actress; appeared in the films, *Play It Again Sam,* 1972, and *Five Easy Pieces,* 1970.

HISTORICAL EVENTS

1890 *Grand Duchy of Luxembourg* is separated from the Netherlands.

1914 *Turkey* issues a formal declaration of war against the Allies (*World War I*).

1938 *The Boys from Syracuse,* Richard Rodgers' musical comedy based on Shakespeare's *A Comedy of Errors,* premieres in New York.

1943 U.S. captures Makin Island from Japan in the *Battle of the Gilbert Islands (World War II).*

1961 The name of the capital of the Dominican Republic is changed from *Ciudád Trujillo* to *Santo Domingo.*

1970 *Pope Paul VI* issues a decree barring cardinals over age 80 from voting for a new pope.

1979 The assassin of Earl Mountbatten of Burma, *Thomas McMahon,* is convicted by a special criminal court in Dublin and sentenced to life imprisonment.

1980 A violent *earthquake* devastates southern *Italy,* killing 3,000 and leaving 200,000 homeless.

1983 Two Soviet cosmonauts return to earth safely after spending 150 days in the *Salyut* 7 space station.

1986 *Mike Tyson* wins the world heavyweight boxing title by defeating Trevor Berbic.

1997 *Milan Kucanis* is re-elected President of Slovenia.

november

NOVEMBER 24

HOLIDAYS

Democratic Republic of the Congo
Anniversary of the New Regime
Marks the beginning of the new government, 1964.

RELIGIOUS CALENDAR

The Saints
St. Chrysogonus, martyr. [d. c. 304]
St. Colman of Cloyne, bishop. [d. 6th century]
St. Minver, virgin and nun. Also called *Menefreda*. [d. c. 6th century]
St. Enfleda, Abbess of Whitby. Also called *Eanflaed*. [d. c. 704]
SS. Flora and Mary, virgins and martyrs. [d. 851]

The Beatified
Blessed Maria Anna Sala. [beatified 1982]
Blessed Salvator Lilli and his Seven Companions. [beatified 1982]
Blessed Jakob Gapp. [beatified 1996]
Blessed Catherine Jarrige. [beatified 1996]
Blessed Otto Neururer. [beatified 1996]

BIRTHDATES

1394 *Charles, duc de Orléans*, French poet. [d. January 5, 1465]

1632 *Baruch Spinoza*, Dutch philosopher; pre-eminent pantheistic philosopher of 17th century. [d. February 21, 1677]

1655 *Charles XI*, King of Sweden, 1660–97; responsible for establishment of an absolute monarchy. [d. April 5, 1697]

1713 *Laurence Sterne*, English novelist; author of *Tristram Shandy*. [d. March 18, 1768]

Junipero Serra (Miguel José Serra), Spanish Franciscan missionary in Mexico; ascetic, founder of *Mission San Diego*, the first European settlement in Upper California; also responsible for missions at *San Francisco, Santa Barbara, San Luis Obispo, Santa Clara*, and *San Juan Capistrano*. [d. August 28, 1784]

1784 *Zachary Taylor*, U.S. soldier; 12th President of the U.S., 1849–50; hero of the War with Mexico; favored annexation of California. [d. July 9, 1850]

1826 *Carlo Collodi (Carlo Lorenzini)*, Italian author, journalist; creator of *Pinocchio*. [d. October 26, 1890]

1848 *Lilli Lehmann*, German operatic soprano, lieder singer; known for her interpretations of Wagner and Mozart. [d. May 17, 1929]

1849 *Frances Eliza Hodgson Burnett*, U.S. novelist, born in England; author of *Little Lord Fauntleroy* and *The Secret Garden*. [d. October 29, 1924]

1853 *William Barclay (Bat) Masterson*, U.S. lawman; Marshal of Dodge City, Kansas; friend of Wyatt Earp. [d. October 25, 1921]

1859 *Cass Gilbert*, U.S. architect; designed the Woolworth Building, New York, 1913; the Supreme Court Building, Washington, D.C., 1935. [d. May 17, 1934]

1864 *Henri de Toulouse-Lautrec*, French artist; known primarily for his paintings of Parisian life and his poster drawings. [d. September 9, 1901]

1868 *Scott Joplin*, U.S. pianist; gained significant place in history of American music as pioneer of *ragtime;* the *Maple Leaf Rag* is his most famous composition. [d. April 1, 1917]

1877 *Alben William Barkley*, U.S. lawyer; Vice-President of U.S., 1949–53; U.S. Senator, 1927–49, 1954–56. [d. April 30, 1956]

1888 *Dale Carnegie*, U.S. writer, teacher of public speaking, author of *How to Win Friends and Influence*

People. [d. November 1, 1955]

Cathleen (Mary) Nesbitt, British actress; known as a grande dame of the stage, having portrayed numerous characters in more than 300 roles on the London and Broadway stages and in films. [d. August 2, 1982]

1892 *Konstantin Aleksandrovich Fedin,* Soviet novelist. [d. July 15, 1977]

1912 *Garson Kanin,* U.S. playwright, director, author, screenwriter; husband of Ruth Gordon (October 30).

1914 *Geraldine Fitzgerald,* Irish actress.

1921 *John V(liet) Lindsay,* U.S. politician, lawyer, author; U.S. Congressman, 1959–65; Mayor of New York City, 1966–74.

1925 *Simon van der Meere,* Dutch physicist; Nobel Prize in physics for demonstrating the existence of subatomic particles called intermediate vector bosons (with Carlo Rubbia), 1984.

1926 *Tsung-Dao Lee,* U.S. physicist, born in China; Nobel Prize in physics for disproving law of parity conservation in nuclear physics (with C. N. Yang), 1957.

1929 *George Richard Moscone,* U.S. government official; Mayor of San Francisco, 1976–78; murdered by Daniel

White. [d. November 27, 1978]

1935 *Ronald Dellums,* U.S. politician; Congressman, 1970–84.

1940 *Paul Tagliabue,* U.S. lawyer; commissioner of the National Football League, 1989– .

1946 *Theodore Robert (Ted) Bundy,* U.S. murderer; convicted of killing two Florida sorority sisters; managed to postpone his death sentence through complicated legal maneuvers. [d. January 24, 1989]

1948 *Stephen Wayne (Steve) Yeager,* U.S. baseball player.

HISTORICAL EVENTS

1642 *Abel Tasman,* Dutch explorer, discovers *Tasmania,* which he names Van Diemen's Land.

1865 *Mississippi* is first of Southern state legislatures to enact a *Black Code,* a body of apprenticeship laws binding freedmen to the land.

1918 *United Kingdom of the Serbs, Croats, and Slovenes* is proclaimed at Zagreb with *King Peter* of Serbia as king (World War I).

1935 *George II* of Greece returns from exile in England.

1946 *Thomas Berreta* is elected president of Uruguay.

1950 Frank Loesser's musical *Guys and Dolls,* based on

characters from Damon Runyon's stories, premieres in New York.

1963 *Lee Harvey Oswald,* accused by Dallas police of assassinating President John F. Kennedy, is shot and killed by *Jack Ruby* in the basement of the Dallas municipal building while in police custody.

1964 Belgian paratroopers are flown to the *Democratic Republic of the Congo,* to rescue the rebel-controlled city of *Stanleyville.*

1965 *Sheikh Abdullah of Kuwait* dies and is succeeded by his younger brother, *Sabah as-Salim as-Sabah.*

1972 *Finland* becomes the first Western state to formally recognize *East Germany,* and the first to establish ties with both Germanys.

UN grants permanent observer status to *East Germany* based on UNESCO's approval of East German membership in that body on November 21; this effectively gives East Germany the same status as West Germany.

1976 *Earthquake* in eastern *Turkey* takes an estimated 4,000 lives; relief efforts in the mountain villages are hampered by blizzards

1995 Irish voters decide to end the ban on *divorce.*

november

NOVEMBER
25

HOLIDAYS

Madagascar
Thanksgiving Day

Suriname
Independence Day
Celebrates achievement of independence from The Netherlands, 1975.

U.S. (New York)
Evacuation Day
Commemorates the day British troops left the U.S. after the American Revolution.

Yugoslavia
Bosnian State Day

RELIGIOUS CALENDAR

The Saints
St. Moses, priest and martyr. [d. 251]
St. Catherine of Alexandria, virgin and martyr; patron of Christian philosophers and students of philosophy. Also called *Catharine,* or *Katherine.* [death date unknown]
St. Mercurius, martyr. Also called *Abu Saifain, the Father of Swords,* or *Mercury.* [death date unkown]

BIRTHDATES

1562 *Lope (Felix) de Vega El Fenix de España,* Spanish dramatist, poet; developed the comic character *gracioso* or clown; author, reputedly, of more than 1,800 plays and several hundred other works. [d. August 27, 1635]

1778 *Joseph Lancaster,* English educator; founder of a free school based on man's conventional principles that competed with the system supported by the Church of England; emigrated to U.S., 1818. [d. October 24, 1838]

1814 *Julius von Mayer,* German physicist; pioneer in thermodynamic investigations, 1842. [d. March 20, 1878]

1835 *Andrew Carnegie,* U.S. industrialist, philanthropist, born in Scotland; founder of Carnegie Steel Company. [d. August 11, 1919]

1844 *Karl Friedrich Benz,* German engineer; pioneer in design and development of the automobile; founder of automobile manufacturing company that makes *Mercedes Benz,* named for his daughter. [d. April 4, 1929]

1846 *Carrie (Amelia) Nation,* U.S. temperance advocate; famed for her hatchet-wielding rampages through the saloons of Kansas; always appeared dressed in deaconess garb. [d. June 9, 1911]

1869 *Benjamin Barr Lindsey,* U.S. jurist, publicist; pioneer in handling of juvenile delinquents; established a conciliation court to deal with divorce cases; espoused principle of *compassionate marriage,* or trial marriage. [d. March 26, 1943]

1877 *Harley Granville-Barker,* British playwright, actor, director, and critic; a major figure in the London theater of the early 1900s. [d. August 31, 1946]

1878 *Georg Kaiser,* German playwright; leader in Expressionist movement in Germany. [d. June 4, 1945]

1881 *John XXIII,* pope 1958–63; convened the *Second Vatican Council,* 1959–65. [d. June 3, 1963]

1894 *Laurence Stallings,* U.S. playwright. [d. February 28, 1968]

Lawrence Mario Giannini, U.S. banker; President, Transamerica Corporation, 1930–32; President, Bank of America, 1936–52. [d. August 19, 1952]

1895 *Helen Hooven Santmyer,* U.S. author; republication of her novel, *...And Ladies of the Club,* made her a best-selling writer at the age of 88. [d. February 21, 1986]

1896 *Virgil Thomson,* U.S. composer, music critic. [d. September 30, 1989]

1897 *Willie (The Lion) Smith (William Henry Bertholoff),* U.S. musician; a major contributor to development of ragtime music in U.S. [d. April 18, 1973]

1900 *Helen Gahagan Douglas,* U.S. politician, actress; U.S. Congresswoman, 1945–51; candidate for U.S. Senate in opposition to Richard Nixon, 1951 (defeated); wife of Melvyn Douglas (April 5). [d. June 28, 1980]

1914 *Joe DiMaggio,* U.S. baseball player.

1915 *Augusto Pinochet Ugarte,* President, Republic of Chile, 1973–90.

1920 *Ricardo Montalban,* U.S. actor, born in Mexico.

1923 *Mauno Koivisto,* President, Republic of Finland, 1982–94.

1925 *William F(rank) Buckley, Jr.,* U.S. publisher, editor, writer, television interviewer; political conservative; unsuccessful candidate for mayor of New York City, 1965.

1933 *Kathryn Crosby (Kathryn Grandstaff),* U.S. actress; leading lady during the 1950s under the name *Kathryn Grant;* married Bing Crosby, 1957.

1942 *Tracey Walter,* U. S. actress.

1947 *John Larroquette,* U.S. actor; Emmy Awards for *Night Court,* 1985, 1986, 1987.

1960 *John Fitzgerald Kennedy, Jr.,* son of John Fitzgerald Kennedy, 35th U.S. President.

HISTORICAL EVENTS

1034 *Malcolm II,* King of Scots dies and is succeeded by *Duncan,* his grandson.

1542 *Henry VIII* of England is victorious over the forces of *James V* of Scotand at the *Battle of Solvay Moss.*

1758 British forces led by Washington take *Fort Duquesne* (Pittsburgh) from French (*French and Indian War*).

1783 Last British troops leave New York City (*American Revolution*).

1863 Confederates are driven from Tennessee and roads are opened into Georgia by the *Battle of Chattanooga* (*U.S. Civil War*).

1882 Gilbert and Sullivan's comic opera *Iolanthe* opens simultaneously in London and New York.

1885 *King Alfonso XII* of Spain dies and is succeeded by his mother, Maria Christina, who reigns as regent for Alfonso's son, born posthumously, who ascends to the throne in 1902.

1901 *Gustav Mahler* conducts the world premiere, in Munich, of his *Fourth Symphony in G Major.*

1904 Russian sailors of the Black Sea Fleet mutiny at *Sevastopol.*

1918 *Strasbourg, Alsace,* is occupied by the French (*World War I*).

1922 *Benito Mussolini* assumes dictatorial powers in Italy.

1943 Five U.S. destroyers sink three Japanese destroyers and severely damage two others at the *Battle of Cape St. George* (*World War II*).

1950 Hurricane winds cause severe damage on the eastern seaboard, while a record blizzard, killing more than 100 persons, paralyzes western Pennsylvania, Ohio, and West Virginia.

1961 *U.S.S. Enterprise,* nuclear-powered aircraft carrier, the largest, fastest, and most powerful warship built to date, is commissioned at Newport News, Virginia.

1962 Supporters of French President *Charles De Gaulle* win control of national assembly in run-off elections; it is the first time in modern French history that one group has gained a clear majority.

1970 Japanese poet and writer *Yukio Mishima* commits ritual suicide in Tokyo in protest against Japan's westernization and the weakness of the post-World War II Japanese Constitution.

1971 Denmark and Norway become the first NATO members to establish full diplomatic relations with *North Vietnam.*

1973 Lieutenant General *Phaidon Gizikis* assumes power in Greece after a bloodless coup d'etat.

1975 Aluminum-producing South American territory of *Suriname* becomes independent after 308 years of Dutch colonial rule and promulgates a constitution.

1976 *Rene Levesque,* leader of the separatist *Parti Quebecois,* is inaugurated as prime minister of Quebec.

1984 *Julio Maria Sanguinetti* is elected president of Uruguay in the first national election in 13 years.

november

1986 President Ronald Reagan accepts the resignation of Admiral *John Poindexter* and fires Lieutenant Colonel *Oliver North* for their involvement in the *Iran-contra affair*.

1990 The first free elections since World War II are held in *Poland*.

HOLIDAYS

São Tomé and Príncipe
Anniversary of Signing of Argel Agreement

RELIGIOUS CALENDAR

The Saints
St. Peter, Bishop of Alexandria, and martyr. [d. 311]
St. Siricius, pope. Elected 384. [d. 399]
St. Basolus, monk and hermit. Also called *Basle.* [d. c. 620]
St. Conrad, Bishop of Constance. [d. 975]
St. Nikon (Metanoeite) missionary. Also called *Nicon.* [d. 998]
St. Silvester Gozzolini, abbot and founder of the Silvestrine Benedictines. Also called *Sylvester.* [d. 1267]
St. John Berchmans, patron of altar boys. [d. 1621]
St. Leonard of Port Maurice, Franciscan friar and missionary. [d. 1751]

The Beatified
Blessed Pontius of Faucigny, abbot. [d. 1178]
Blessed James, Bishop of Mantua. [d. 1338]

BIRTHDATES

1731 *William Cowper,* English poet; despite periods of great mental instability, produced numerous significant poems, including *Olney Hymns,* with John Newton, 1779; *The Task;* early proponent of break with strict guidelines of classicism; foreshadowed Romantic movement in English poetry. [d. April 25, 1800]

1792 *Sarah Moore Grimké,* U.S. reformer, abolitionist, and women's rights advocate; sister of Angelina Grimké (February 20). [d. December 23, 1873]

1832 *Mary Walker,* U.S. physician, women's rights advocate, assistant surgeon of Union Army (U.S. Civil War), 1864–65; only woman to receive Medal of Honor, 1865. [d. February 21, 1919]

1842 *Prince Peter Alexeyevich Kropotkin,* Russian geographer, social philosopher; after escape from prison, lived in England, 1886–1914, and Russia, 1917–21; author of numerous books on social subjects. [d. February 8, 1921]

1861 *Albert Bacon Fall,* U.S. politician, lawyer, rancher; U.S. Senator, 1912–21; U.S. Secretary of the Interior, 1921–23; convicted in *Teapot Dome* scandal; imprisoned, 1931–32. [d. November 30, 1944]

1894 *Norbert Wiener,* U.S. mathematician; creator of the field of *cybernetics.* [d. March 18, 1964]

1895 *William Griffith Wilson,* U.S. reformer; founder of *Alcoholics Anonymous,* 1935. [d. January 24, 1971]

1898 *Karl Ziegler,* German chemist; Nobel Prize in chemistry for research in plastics (with G. Natta), 1963. [d. August 12, 1973]

1901 *Melville Bell Grosvenor,* U.S. editor; member of the founding family of the *National Geographic Society;* editor in chief, *National Geographic Magazine,* 1967–77; led the society to be the largest private educational and scientific association in the world. [d. April 22, 1982]

1907 *Ruth Patrick,* U.S. botanist; discovered diatoms.

1910 *Cyril Cusack,* Irish actor; member of the Abbey Players, 1932–46; appeared in the movies, *Odd Man Out, Fahrenheit 451,* and *Harold and Maude.* [d. October 7, 1993]

1912 *(Arnold) Eric Sevareid,* U.S. broadcast journalist; correspondent with CBS News, 1939–77. [d. July 9, 1992]

Eugene Ionesco, French playwright, born in Romania; author of absurdist dramas,

november

incuding *Rhinoceros,* 1959, *The Bald Soprano,* 1950, and *Exit the King,* 1963. [d. March 28, 1994]

1922 *Charles M(onroe) Schulz,* U.S. cartoonist; creator of *Peanuts,* a cartoon strip.

1924 *George Segal,* U.S. sculptor; known for his life-size sculpture done in plaster.

1925 *Gregorio Conrodo Alvarez Armelino,* President, Oriental Republic of Uruguay, 1981–85.

1933 *Robert Goulet,* U.S. actor, singer; made his Broadway debut in *Camelot,* 1960; Tony Award for *The Happy Time,* 1968.

1938 *Richard Caruthers (Rich) Little,* Canadian-born entertainer; can do 160 different impressions of famous personalities.

Tina Turner (Anna Mae Bullock), U.S. singer; Grammy Awards for *Proud Mary,* 1972, and *What's Love Got to Do With It?,* 1984.

1942 *Olivia Cole,* U.S. actress; Emmy Award for the mini-series, *Roots,* 1977.

1946 *John McVie,* British musician; member of the rock group, *Fleetwood Mac.*

1948 *Elizabeth H. Blackburn,* Australian biochemist; known for her research on DNA.

1952 *Wendy Turnbull,* Australian tennis player; partner of John Lloyd; French Open Doubles Champion, 1982; Wimbledon Doubles Champion, 1983; called *Rabbit.*

1969 *Shawn Kemp,* U.S. basketball player; member of the Olympic Dream Team II, 1994.

HISTORICAL EVENTS

1917 *Bolshevik* government abolishes all class privileges in the Russian Republic.

1946 Jean-Paul Sartre's play, *No Exit,* premiere in New York.

1950 *Andres Martinez Trueba* is elected president of Uruguay.

1965 France places its first space satellite in orbit from its test center in the Algerian Sahara.

1966 U.S. military authorities in Vietnam announce the end of *Operation Attleboro,* the biggest U.S. offensive of the war (*Vietnam War*).

1969 U.S. President Richard Nixon authorizes legislation establishing a *draft lottery.*

1974 Japan's Prime Minister *Kakuei Tanaka* resigns under pressure.

1979 More than 300,000 Afghan refugees flee into Pakistan as a result of civil war between Muslim rebels and government troops; Soviet military personnel are used against rebel positions.

1982 *Yasuhiro Nakasone* is elected prime minister of Japan.

1990 Singapore Prime Minister *Lee K. Yew* resigns after 31 years in office.

RELIGIOUS CALENDAR

The Saints

St. James Intercisus, martyr. Also called *James Intercisius.* [d. c. 421]

St. Secundinus, bishop. Also called *Seachnal, Sechnall,* or *Secundin.* [d. 447]

St. Maximus, Bishop of Riez; patron of the Diocese of Boulogne in Picardy. Also called *Masse.* [d. c. 460]

St. Cungar, abbot. Also called *Congar,* or *Cyngar.* [d. 6th century]

St. Virgil, Bishop of Salzburg; apostle of the Slovenes. Also called *Feargal, Fergal,* or *Ferghil.* [d. 784]

St. Fergus, bishop and missionary. Also called *the Pict.* [d. c. 8th century]

SS. Barlaam and Josaphat. Josaphat also called *Joasaph.* [death date unknown]

The Beatified

Blessed Bernardino of Fossa, Friar Minor of the Observance. [d. 1503]

Blessed Humilis of Bisignano, lay brother. [d. 1637]

BIRTHDATES

1701 *Anders Celsius,* Swedish astronomer; the originator of the Celsius scale, also called centigrade, in which the freezing point of water is 0 (degrees) and the boiling point is 100 (degrees). [d. April 25, 1744]

1746 *Robert R. Livingston,* U.S. diplomat, lawyer; a drafter of the Declaration of Independence, 1776; administered the oath of office to President George Washington; with Robert Fulton, built first steamboat; U.S. Minister to France, 1801–04. [d. February 26, 1813]

1754 *Johann George Adam Forster,* German traveler, scientist, author, and revolutionary; accompanied Captain James Cook (October 27) on his voyage around the world, 1772. [d. January 10, 1794]

1809 *Fanny Kemble,* British author, actress; her 1829 debut as Juliet in Shakespeare's Romeo and Juliet brought prosperity to the Covent Garden theatre; her *Journals,* 1835 and 1863, contain valuable information of 19th-century stage and social history. [d. January 15, 1893]

1857 *Sir Charles Scott Sherrington,* British neurologist; Nobel Prize in physiology or medicine for studies on physiology of the nervous system (with E. D. Adrian), 1932. [d. March 4, 1952]

1870 *Joseph Sanford Mack,* U.S. silk manufacturer, trucking executive; with his brothers, founded Mack Brothers Wagon Co., 1889, builders of gasoline-powered buses and trucks. [d. July 25, 1953]

1874 *Charles A(ustin) Beard,* U.S. historian; a founder of the *New School for Social Research,* 1919; author of *The Rise of American Civilization,* 1927–39; severe critic of policies of Franklin D. Roosevelt. [d. September 1, 1948]

Chaim Weizmann, Zionist leader, biochemist, born in Russia; first president of Israel, 1949–52. [d. November 9, 1952]

1879 *Vito Genovese,* Italian-born organized crime figure; rose to power in the underworld through narcotics trafficking; ordered the murder of Albert Anastasia. [d. February 14, 1969]

1903 *Lars Onsager,* U.S. chemist; Nobel Prize in chemistry for developing theory of irreversible chemical processes, 1968. [d. October 5, 1976]

1909 *James Agee,* U.S. writer, film critic; Pulitzer Prize, 1958. [d. May 16, 1955]

1912 *David Merrick (David Margulois),* U.S. theatrical producer.

november

1917 *Bob Smith (Buffalo Bob),* U.S. entertainer; best known for his role in the *Howdy Doody Show,* a television program popular in the early 1950s. [d. July 30, 1998]

1932 *Benigno Simeon (Ninoy) Aquino, Jr.,* Philippine politician; bitter rival of Ferdinand Marcos; assassinated upon return to Manila after three years of exile; husband of Corazon Aquino. [d. August 21, 1983]

1937 *Gail (Henion) Sheehy,* U.S. journalist, writer; author of *Passages* and *Predictable Crises of Adult Life.*

1940 *Bruce Lee (Lee Yuen Kam),* U.S. actor; best known for his martial arts films; starred in *Enter the Dragon,* 1973. [d. July 30, 1973]

1941 *Edward Thomas (Eddie) Rabbitt,* U.S. singer, songwriter; wrote over 300 songs; songs include *Kentucky Rain* and *I Love a Rainy Night.* [d. May 7, 1998]

1942 *James Marshall (Jimi) Hendrix,* U.S. musician, singer; considered to be one of the greatest of rock guitarists; songs include *Purple Haze,* 1967, and *Hey Joe,* 1967; died of a drug overdose. [d. September 18, 1970]

1943 *Jil Sanders,* German fashion designer.

1944 *Danny Michael DeVito,* U.S. actor; Emmy Award for *Taxi,* 1981, starred in the movies, *Ruthless People, Throw Momma From the Train,* and *Twins.*

1957 *Caroline Bouvier Kennedy,* daughter of John Fitzgerald Kennedy, 35th U.S. President.

1964 *Robin Givens,* U.S. actress.

1976 *Jaleel White,* U.S. actor.

HISTORICAL EVENTS

1295 *Model Parliament* meets in England, granting money for French and Scottish wars.

1308 *Henry VII,* Count of Luxembourg is elected German king.

1919 *Treaty of Neuilly* is signed by Bulgaria, ending World War I with the Allies and recognizing the independence of *Yugoslavia.*

1942 French fleet is scuttled at *Toulon* to prevent its being taken by the Germans (*World War II*).

1950 *German Suarez Flamerich* is inaugurated as the first civilian president of Venezuela's junta.

1962 California governor, Edmund Brown, announces that *California* has replaced *New York* as the most populous U.S. state.

1963 South Vietnamese president, *Ngo Dinh Diem,* is overthrown in a violent coup d'etat.

1965 Between 15,000 and 35,000 persons take part in a march on Washington for peace in Vietnam, initiated by the Committee for a Sane Nuclear Policy.

1970 *Antonio Ortiz Mena* is elected president of the *Inter-American Development Bank (IDB).*

1977 *Upper Volta (Burkina Faso)* promulgates a new constitution.

1978 San Francisco mayor *George Moscone* and City Supervisor *Harvey Milk* are assassinated in City Hall.

Masayoshi Ohira becomes the President of the ruling Liberal-Democratic Party and Prime Minister of Japan.

1990 *John Major* replaces Margaret Thatcher as prime minister of Britain.

1992 President *Carlos Andres Perez* of Venezuela is able to halt a coup attempt on his government.

HOLIDAYS

Albania

Independence Proclamation Day
Commemorates Albania's declaration of independence from Turkey, 1912.

Chad

Proclamation of the Republic
Commemorates the proclamation which established Chad as a member state in the French community, 1958.

Mauritania

Independence Day
Celebrates achievement of independence from France, 1960.

Panama

Independence from Spain
Celebrates Panama's achievement of independence from Spain, 1821.

RELIGIOUS CALENDAR

The Saints

St. Stephen the Younger, martyr. [d. 764]

St. Simeon Metaphrastes, principal compiler of the legends of the saints found in the menologies of the Byzantine church [d. c. 1000]

St. James of the March, priest. [d. 1476]

St. Joseph Pignatelli, Jesuit. [d. 1811]

St. Catherine Labouré, virgin, nun and visionary. Also called *Katherine.* [d. 1876]

St. Juthwara, virgin and martyr. Also called *Aude.* [death date unknown]

The Beatified

Blessed James Thompson, priest and martyr. [d. 1582]

BIRTHDATES

1632 *Jean-Baptiste Lully,* French composer, born in Italy; primarily known for his operas and ballets; called the *Founder of the French National Opera.* [d. March 22, 1687]

1757 *William Blake,* English poet, artist; noted for mystical nature of his poetry; author of *Songs of Innocence* and *Songs of Experience;* his engravings illustrated a famous edition of Milton's *Paradise Lost.* [d. August 12, 1827]

1792 *Victor Cousin,* French philosopher, educational administrator; leader of Eclectic School. [d. January 13, 1867]

1820 *Friedrich Engels,* German philosopher, businessman; with Karl Marx, regarded as the founder of modern Communism; with Marx, co-authored *The Communist Manifesto.* [d. August 5, 1895]

1829 *Anton Grigorievich Rubinstein,* Russian composer, pianist. [d. November 20, 1894]

1832 *Sir Leslie Stephen,* British author, critic, editor; first editor of *Dictionary of National Biography;* father of Virginia Woolf (January 25). [d. February 22, 1904]

1847 *Prince Taro Katsura,* Japanese military leader and statesman; Premier of Japan, 1901–06; 1908–11; 1912–13. [d. October 10, 1913]

1851 *Albert Henry George Grey, 4th Earl Grey,* British official; Governor-General of Canada, 1904–11. [d. August 29, 1917]

1857 *Alfonso XII,* King of Spain, 1875–85; his short reign led to hopes for a constitutional Spanish monarchy. [d. November 25, 1885]

1858 *Sir Robert Abbott Hadfield,* British metallurgist; developer of *manganese steel.* [d. September 30, 1940]

1866 *Henry Bacon,* U.S. architect; designer of the *Lincoln Memorial.* [d. February 16, 1924]

1873 *Frank Phillips,* U.S. oilman; a founder of Phillips Petroleum Co. [d. August 23, 1950]

1880 *Aleksandr Aleksandrovich Blok,* Russian poet; leader of Symbolist School in Russian poetry. [d. August 9, 1921]

1887 *Ernst Röhm,* German soldier; National Socialist Workers

november

leader; commander of Hitler's *Brown Shirts;* acted as Reich's Secretary of State for Bavaria; executed by Hitler's troops, 1934. [d. June 30, 1934]

1895 *José Iturbi,* U.S. pianist, born in Spain; began his professional career at the age of seven; noted for his flamboyant lifestyle and enormous energy during his long history of concerts. [d. June 28, 1980]

1904 *James O. Eastland,* U.S. politician, lawyer, farmer; Senator, 1941–78; President Protempore of the U.S. Senate, 1972–78. [d. February 19, 1986]

Nancy Mitford, British novelist, biographer, editor; noted for her biographies of Voltaire and Louis XIV of France. [d. June 30, 1973]

1907 *Alberto Moravia (Alberto Pincherle),* Italian author, playwright; known for his recurring theme of life's absurdity and treatment of sex in his work; author of *The Woman of Rome* and *Two Women.* [d. September 26, 1990]

1908 *Claude Levi-Strauss,* French anthropologist, university professor, writer; developed concept of *structural anthropology.*

1928 *Margaret (Midge) Costanza,* U.S. presidential aide; Special Assistant to Jimmy Carter; acted as liaison to special interest groups.

1929 *Berry Gordy, Jr.,* U.S. record executive, film executive; founded Motown Records, 1959; signed the musical groups, *The Temptations* and *The Supremes.*

1933 *Hope Elise Ross Lange,* U.S. actress; Academy Award nominee for *Peyton Place,* 1957; starred in the television series, *The Ghost* and *Mrs. Muir;* appeared in the movie, *Blue Velvet,* 1987.

1936 *Gary Warren Hart (Gary Warren Hartpence),* U.S. politician; Senator, 1975–87; vied for Democratic presidential nomination, 1984; withdrew from the 1988 presidential race amidst allegations of marital infidelity.

1938 *Michael Ritchie,* U.S. director. Directed the *Bad News Bears* movies.

1942 *Paul Warfield,* U.S. football player; receiver, Cleveland Browns and Miami Dolphins.

1943 *Randy Newman,* U.S. singer, songwriter; known for his satirical lyrics and melodic abilities; Gold Record Award for *Short People,* 1978.

1949 *(Boris) Alexander Godunov,* Russian-born ballet dancer, actor; first member of the Bolshoi Ballet to defect to the U.S., 1979. [d. May 18, 1995]

1950 *Ed Harris,* U.S. actor; starred in *Apollo 13,* 1995.

Russell A. Hulse, U.S. physicist; Nobel Prize for Physics with Joseph H. Taylor for the discovery of the binary pulsar, 1993.

1958 *David Allen (Dave) Righetti,* U.S. baseball player; pitched a no-hitter, July 4, 1983.

1959 *Judd Nelson,* U.S. actor.

HISTORICAL EVENTS

1821 *Panama* declares its independence from Spain and joins *Republic of Colombia.*

1855 Russians capture Turkish fortress of *Kars* in the Caucasus (*Crimean War*).

1885 British forces occupy *Mandalay* in the *Third Burmese War.*

1888 *Gambia* becomes a separate British Crown Colony.

1895 First recorded automobile race in America is held, sponsored by *Chicago Times Herald,* over a 54-mile course.

1902 *Lord Horatio Herbert Kitchener,* distinguished British soldier, becomes the new commander in chief of the Indian army.

1912 *Albania* proclaims its independence from Turkey.

1919 *Lady Nancy Witcher Astor* becomes first woman to be elected to the British Parliament.

1922 Polish President *Józef Pilsudski* convokes new national assembly.

1925 *Grand Ole Opry,* a medley of cowboy tunes and ballads, is first broadcast as *Barn Dance.*

1941 *Benjamin Britten's Scottish Ballad* is first performed by the Cincinnati Symphony Orchestra.

1943 *Teheran Conference* begins; Roosevelt, Churchill, and Stalin meet to plan Allied invasion of Europe (*World War II*).

1950 U.S. and Chinese troops clash for the first time in the *Korean War.*

1960 *Mauritania* gains independence from France.

1963 President Lyndon Johnson announces that *Cape Canaveral,* Florida, will be renamed *Cape Kennedy.*

1966 *Dominican Republic* promulgates a new constitution.

1971 Jordanian prime minister, *Wasfi Tal,* is assassinated by three Palestinian guerrillas in Cairo.

1975 *Timor* gains its independence from Portugal.

1989 *Helmut Kohl,* Chancellor of West Germany, announces a plan to unify East and West Germany.

1995 The *U.S. federal speed limit* is repealed; most states raise their speed limits to 65 m.p.h. on highways, while Montana enacts no daytime speed limit.

november

HOLIDAYS

Albania
Liberation Day
Continuation of the celebration of November 28, commemorating the withdrawal of occupation troops, 1944.

Grenada
Thanksgiving Day

Liberia
President Tubman's Birthday
Celebrates the birthday of William Tubman, the nation's president, 1944–71.

U.N. Member Nations
International Day of Solidarity with the Palestinian People
Sponsored by the United Nations.

U.S. (Wyoming)
Nellie Taylor Ross' Birthday

Vanuatu
Unity Day

Yugoslavia
Day of the Republic
Commemorates the proclamation of the Republic, 1945.

RELIGIOUS CALENDAR

St. Saturninus, first bishop of Toulouse, and martyr. Also called *Sernin.* [d. c. 3rd century]
St. Saturninus, priest and martyr. [d. c. 309]
St. Brendan of Birr, abbot and chief of the prophets of Ireland. [d. 573]

St. Ethelwin, monk and hermit. Also called *Ailwin,* or *Egelwin.* [d. 7th century]
St. Radbod, Bishop of Utrecht. [d. 918]

The Beatified
Blessed Frederick of Regensburg, lay brother. [d. 1329]
Blessed Dionysius, Carmelite priest, and *Redemptus,* lay brother; martyrs. [d. 1638]
Blessed Francis Antony of Lucera, priest. Also called *Padre Maestro, Father Master.* [d. 1742]

BIRTHDATES

1607 *John Harvard,* American colonial clergyman, baptized on this date; his library and estate, left to a Massachusetts college, became the foundation of *Harvard University.* [d. September 14, 1638]

1781 *Andrés Bello,* Chilean poet, statesman, scholar; one of Chile's greatest poets; edited the Civil Code of Chile. [d. October 15, 1865]

1797 *Gaetano Donizetti,* Italian opera composer; composer of *Lucrezia Borgia* and *Lucia di Lammermoor.* [d. April 8, 1848]

1799 *Amos Bronson Alcott,* U.S. philosopher, teacher, reformer; a leader of the Transcendentalist movement in New England; father of Louisa May Alcott (November 29). [d. March 4, 1888]

1803 *Christian Johann Doppler,* Austrian physicist, mathematician; first to explain the change in sound frequencies when a source approaches and departs from a listener (later called the *Doppler effect*). [d. March 17, 1853]

1811 *Wendell Phillips,* U.S. orator, reformer; eloquent advocate of abolition of slavery. [d. February 2, 1884]

1816 *Morrison Remick Waite,* U.S. lawyer; Chief Justice of the U.S. Supreme Court, 1874–88. [d. March 23, 1888]

1825 *Jean-Martin Charcot,* French neurologist, known for his research in areas of *hysteria* and *hypnosis.* [d. August 16, 1893]

1832 *Louisa May Alcott,* U.S. novelist; author of *Little Women;* daughter of Amos Bronson Alcott (November 29). [d. March 6, 1888]

1834 *George Holmes Howison,* U.S. mathematician and philosopher; one of chief exponents of *personalism.* [d. December 31, 1916]

1849 *John Ambrose Fleming,* British electrical engineer;

inventor of the *diode thermionic valve (radio tube)*, 1904. [d. April 18, 1945]

1856 *Theobald von Bethmann-Hollweg,* German politician; Chancellor of Germany, 1909–17. [d. January 1, 1921]

1866 *Ernest William Brown,* U.S. astronomer, mathematician; professor of mathematics, Yale University, 1907–32; noted for his investigations of celestial mechanics. [d. July 22, 1938]

1874 *Antonio Caetano de Abreu Freire Egas Moniz,* Portuguese surgeon, statesman; Nobel Prize in physiology or medicine for development of technique of *prefrontal lobotomy* in treatment of psychoses (with W. R. Hess), 1949. [d. December 13, 1955]

1876 *Nellie Taylor Ross,* U.S. government official; first woman governor in the U.S.; Governor of Wyoming, 1925–27; first woman director of the U.S. Mint, 1933–53. [d. December 19, 1977]

1898 *C(live Hamilton) S(taples) Lewis,* British novelist, critic, scholar; known for his science fiction works and allegories. [d. November 22, 1963]

1908 *Adam Clayton Powell, Jr.,* U.S. politician, clergyman; prominent black leader; U.S. Congressman, 1945–67; removed from U.S. Congress for improper activities. [d. April 4, 1972]

1916 Sir *Sydney Douglas Gun-Munro,* Governor-General, Saint Vincent and the Grenadines, 1977–85.

1917 *Merle Travis,* U.S. musician; elected to the Country Music Hall of Fame, 1977; compositions include *16 Tons* and *Old Mountain Dew.* [d. October 20, 1983]

1918 *Madeleine L'Engle,* U.S. writer; author of the *Time Fantasy* series.

1920 *Elmo Russell Zumwalt, Jr.,* U.S. naval officer; Commander of U.S. naval forces in Vietnam Conflict, 1968–70; Chief of Naval Operations, 1970–74.

1923 *Frank Reynolds,* U.S. broadcast journalist; chief anchorman, *ABC World News Tonight,* 1978–83. [d. July 20, 1983]

1927 *Vince(nt Edward) Scully,* U.S. sportscaster.

1928 *Paul Simon,* U.S. politician, author; Senator, 1974–97; presidential candidate, 1987–88.

1932 *Jacques Rene Chirac,* French politician; Mayor of Paris, 1977–83; Prime Minister, 1974–76, 1986–88; President, 1995– .

1933 *John Brumwell Mayall,* British-born jazz musician; considered the originator of the British rock-blues movement in the 1960s; founded the rock group, *The Bluesbreakers,* 1963; fronted other groups which included Eric Clapton, Mick Taylor, and Jack Bruce.

David Robert Reuben, U.S. psychiatrist, author; became known for series of *Everything You Wanted to Know* books.

1934 *Willie Morris,* U.S. editor, novelist, nonfiction writer;

executive editor and editor-in-chief of *Harper's Magazine.* 1965–71.

1935 *Lucio Pozzi,* Italian-born artist, educator.

1936 *Yuan Tseh Lee,* Japanese-born chemist; Nobel Prize in chemistry for his research in reaction dynamics (with Dudley Robert Herschbach and John C. Polanyi), 1986.

1939 *George Gilder,* U.S. economist, author; wrote *Wealth and Poverty,* 1981; known for his controversial views of capitalism and the role of women in society.

Diane Ladd, U.S. actress; Oscar nominee for *Wild At Heart,* 1990.

1940 *Charles Frank (Chuck) Mangione,* U.S. composer, jazz musician; Platinum Album Award for *Feels So Good,* 1978.

1941 *William Ashley (Bill) Freehan,* U.S. baseball player; catcher, Detroit Tigers, 1961–76; American League All- Star Team, 1965–73.

1943 *David (Dave) Bing,* U.S. basketball player; career average of over 20 points per game, 1967–78.

1946 *Suzy Chaffee,* U.S. skier; Captain, U.S. Olympic Ski Team, 1968; World Free-Style Champion, 1971–73.

1947 *Petra Karin Kelly,* German politician; spokesperson and strategist for West Germany's Green Party.

1949 *Garry Shandling,* U.S. comedian, actor; star of *The Larry Sanders Show,* 1992–1998.

1957 *Janet Napolitano,* U.S. lawyer; represented Anita Hill

november

before the Senate Judiciary Committee regarding the Supreme Court nominee Clarence Thomas.

1962 *Andrew McCarthy,* U.S. actor; known for roles in *St. Elmo's Fire* and *Weekend at Bernies'* movies.

HISTORICAL EVENTS

1314 *Philip IV,* King of France, dies and is succeeded by *Louis X.*

1864 Cavalrymen attack Cheyenne and Arapaho Indians gathered near Fort Lyon, Colorado, for a parley with the U.S. government. Three hundred Indians are killed in the *Sand Creek massacre.*

1890 First *Japanese Diet* opens, seating first freely elected public officials in Japan's history.

1900 *Lord Horatio Herbert Kitchener* becomes supreme commander of British forces during the *Boer War.*

1914 The Serbs evacuate their capital of *Belgrade* in the face of the Austrian advance (*World War I*).

1916 *Sir David Beatty* succeeds Admiral Jellicoe as commander-in-chief of the British fleet (*World War I*).

1922 *Tomb of Tutankhamun* is discovered in Egypt by British archaeologists *Howard Carter* and *Lord Carnarvon.*

1929 *Richard E. Byrd* and *Bernt Balchen* pilot *The Floyd Bennett* in the first flight over the *South Pole.*

1932 Cole Porter's musical *Gay Divorce* premieres in New York.

1944 Drs. *Helen Taussig* and *Alfred Blalock* perform the first successful surgery to oxygenate the blood of babies afflicted with *cyanotic heart disease.*

1945 Federal People's Republic of *Yugoslavia* is proclaimed.

1947 UN approves the partition of *Palestine.*

1950 *National Council of the Churches of Christ* [in the U.S.] is formally established by delegates of 25 Protestant denominations and 4 Eastern Orthodox churches.

1951 Generals *Phin Chunhawan* and *Pho Suriyanond* stage a bloodless military coup in Thailand.

1962 The Algerian government bans the Communist Party and declares the *National Liberation Front (FLN)* to be the only legitimate party.

1963 President Lyndon B. Johnson creates a special commission headed by Chief Justice Earl Warren to investigate the assassination of President Kennedy and the murder of his presumed assassin, *Lee Harvey Oswald (Warren Commission).*

1964 Revolutionary changes in the Roman Catholic liturgy, including the use of English in many prayers and responses, become effective in the U.S.

1974 Great Britain outlaws *Irish Republican Army* in the wake of bombings and terrorist attacks.

France's National Assembly votes to legalize *abortion,* overturning a 1920 law.

1975 The *Education for All Handicapped Children Act* passes.

1987 Gangs loyal to former Haitian dictator, *Jean-Claude Duvalier,* reemerge to sabotage the country's first free elections in 30 years.

1989 *Rajiv Gandhi,* Prime Minister of India, resigns.

1990 Bulgarian Prime Minister *Andrei Lukanov* announces his resignation.

The *United Nations Security Council* votes in favor of using force to remove Iraqi forces from Kuwait.

Premier *Andrei Lukanov* of Bulgaria resigns.

HOLIDAYS

Barbados
Independence Day
Commemorates the achievement of independence from Great Britain, 1966.

Benin
National Day
Commemorates the establishment of the country, formerly *Dahomey*, 1975.

Burkina Faso
Youth Day

Philippines
Bonifacio Day
Celebrates the birthday of revolutionary leader *Andres Bonifacio*, 1863.

Republic of Yemen (Southern Yemen)
Independence Day
Commemorates the establishment of the new government and achievement of independence from Great Britain, 1967.

Yugoslavia
Day of the Republic
Continuation of the celebration of November 29.

RELIGIOUS CALENDAR

Feasts
St. Andrew, apostle and first-called of the followers of Christ. Patron of Scotland, Russia, the Order of the Golden Fleece of Burzmund, the Order of the Cross of St. Andrew, fishermen, and fish dealers. Invoked for motherhood. [d. 1st century] [major holy day, Episcopal Church; minor festival, Lutheran Church]

The Saints
SS. Sapor and Isaac, bishops and martyrs. [d. 339]

The Beatified
Blessed Andrew of Antioch, Augustinian canon regular. [d. c. 1348]

BIRTHDATES

1468 *Andrea Doria*, Italian admiral, statesman. [d. November 25, 1560]

1508 *Andrea Palladio (Andrea di Pietro della Gondola)*, Italian architect; his designs exerted great influence on later European domestic architecture. [d. August 19, 1580]

1554 *Sir Philip Sidney*, English poet, courtier, scholar, soldier; author of *Arcadia* and *Astrophel and Stella*, an early sonnet sequence. [d. October 17, 1586]

1667 *Jonathan Swift*, English satirist, clergyman; author of *Gulliver's Travels.* [d. October 19, 1745]

1699 *Christian VI*, King of Denmark and Norway. [d. August 6, 1746]

1756 *Ernst Florens Friedrich Chladni*, German physicist; authority in *acoustics;* did extensive experimentation in measuring *velocity of sound.* [d. April 3, 1827]

1817 *Theodor Mommsen*, German historian, writer; Nobel Prize in literature for his history of Rome, 1902. [d. November 1, 1903]

1819 *Cyrus West Field*, U.S. businessman, science promoter; used his fortune to promote laying of first transatlantic cable. [d. July 12, 1892]

1835 *Samuel Langhorne Clemens (Mark Twain)*, U.S. humorist and novelist; among his books are: *Huckleberry Finn* and *The Adventures of Tom Sawyer.* [d. April 21, 1910]

1858 *Charles Allerton Coolidge*, U.S. architect; designed *Chicago Public Library* and *Rockefeller Institute* in New York. [d. April 1, 1936]

1869 *Nils G. Dalén*, Swedish physicist; Nobel Prize in physics for his invention of the *automatic sun valve* in lighting, 1912. [d. December 9, 1937]

1872 *John McCrae*, Canadian physicist, poet; surgeon to

november

first brigade of Canadian artillery, World War I; author of poem *In Flanders Field*. [d. January 28, 1918]

1874 *Sir Winston Churchill,* British statesman, author; guided British policy during the World War II years; Prime Minister, 1939–45; 1951–55; Nobel Prize in literature, 1953. [d. January 24, 1965]

1889 *Edgar Douglas Adrian, Baron of Cambridge,* British physiologist; Nobel Prize in physiology or medicine for studies in physiology of the nervous system (with C. S. Sherrington), 1932. [d. August 4, 1977]

1894 *Donald Ogden Stewart,* U.S. actor and author; member of the famous *Algonquin Round Table* of the 1920s; one of the most successful scriptwriters in Hollywood during the 1930s and 1940s; blacklisted during the McCarthy anti-Communist era; moved to England where he continued to write movie scripts and books of humor. [d. August 2, 1980]

1904 *Clyfford Still,* U.S. artist; although a recluse, exerted a profound influence on contemporary American artists; the subject of the largest one-man exhibition the Metropolitan Museum of Art ever devoted to a living artist. [d. June 23, 1980]

1907 *Jacques Barzun,* U.S. educator, historian, born in France; author of several books on music, art, and education.

1915 *Henry Taube,* Canadian-born chemist, educator; Nobel Prize in chemistry for his

research of electron transference in inorganic compounds, 1983.

1920 *Virginia Mayo (Virginia Jones),* U.S. actress; glamorous star of the 1940s and 1950s; starred in *The Secret Life of Walter Mitty* and *Best Years of Our Lives.*

1923 *Efrem Zimbalist, Jr.,* U.S. actor.

1924 *Shirley Anita St. Hill Chisholm,* U.S. Congresswoman, author; first black woman elected to Congress, 1968; wrote *Good Fight,* 1973.

1926 *Andrew Schally,* U.S. biochemist, born in Poland; Nobel Prize in physiology or medicine for research in pituitary hormones (with R. C. L. Guillemin and R. S. Yalow), 1977.

1927 *Richard Crenna,* U.S. actor; starred in the television series, *Our Miss Brooks* and *The Real McCoys;* featured in the film, *The Flamingo Kid,* 1985.

1929 *Richard Wagstaff (Dick) Clark,* U.S. entertainer; host of the television series, *American Bandstand,* 1952–89.

1930 *G(eorge) Gordon Liddy,* U.S. lawyer, government official; one of original conspirators in *Watergate Incident.*

1936 *Abbott (Abbie) Hoffman,* U.S political activist, author; defendent in the Chicago Seven trial; wrote *Revolution for the Hell of It,* 1968, and *Woodstock Nation,* 1969. [d. April 12, 1989]

1937 *Robert Guillaume (Robert Peter Williams),* U.S. actor;

two Emmy Awards for his role as Benson on *Soap* and *Benson.*

(Noel) Paul Stookey, U.S. singer, songwriter; member of the folk group, *Peter, Paul, and Mary.*

Richard D. Threlkeld, U.S. broadcast journalist.

1945 *Jay D. Hair,* U.S. environmentalist; president of the National Wildlife Federation, 1981– .

1947 *David Mamet,* U.S. dramatist; Obie Award for Best New Playwright for *Sexual Perversity in Chicago* and *American Buffalo,* 1976; Pulitzer Prize for *Glengarry Glen Ross,* 1984; wrote the screenplay for the film, *The Verdict,* 1982.

1949 *James S. Williamson,* U.S. solar power scientist; developed one of the first solar-powered electricity-generating plants in the U.S.

1952 *Mandel (Mandy) Patinkin,* U.S. actor, singer; Tony Award for his role as Che Guevara in *Evita,* 1980; appeared in the movies, *Ragtime, Yentl,* and *The Princess Bride.*

1955 *Billy Idol (William Board),* British singer; punk rock teen idol; songs include *Eyes Without a Face* and *Catch My Fall.*

1962 *Vincent Edward (Bo) Jackson,* U.S. football player, baseball player; Heisman Trophy, 1985; first modern athlete to play professional baseball and football in the same year, 1987.

HISTORICAL EVENTS

1016 *Edmund Ironside,* King of England, dies; *Cnut of Denmark* is recognized as King of England.

1554 *Roman Catholicism* is restored in England as *Queen Mary I* achieves reconciliation with Rome.

1700 *Peter the Great* of Russia is decisively defeated at *Narva* by *Charles XII* of Sweden (*Great Northern War*).

1718 *Charles XII* of Sweden is killed near *Frederikshall* and is succeeded by his sister, *Ulrika Eleanora.*

1853 Russia destroys Turkish fleet at *Sinope,* precipitating *Crimean War.*

1864 *Battle of Franklin, Tennessee* results in costly Confederate defeat (*U.S. Civil War*).

1914 *Battle of Lowicz* between Russia and Germany begins in Poland (*World War I*).

1918 *Iceland* is granted autonomy by Denmark.

1939 Soviet planes attack *Finland,* beginning the *Winter War.*

1954 *Johannes Strydom* succeeds *Daniel Malan* as prime minister of South Africa.

1956 First videotaped television program is broadcast.

Floyd Patterson knocks out *Archie Moore* for the World Boxing Association heavyweight title.

1962 *U Thant* is elected secretary general of the United Nations.

1965 *Declaration of Rio* is signed at Second Special Inter-American Conference.

1966 *Barbados* achieves complete independence from Great Britain.

1967 *South Yemen People's Republic,* formerly the *South Arabian Federation,* is declared independent of Great Britain.

1970 South Yemen changes its name to the *People's Democratic Republic of Yemen.*

1972 The first commercial atomic *breeder reactor* begins operation at Shevchenko, U.S.S.R.

1974 Anthropologists *Don Johanson* and *Tom Gray* discover the remains of a 3 million-year-old hominid near *Hadar, Ethiopia.* The skeleton is the most complete ever found and revolutionizes ideas about man's ancestors.

Ridder Publications merges with Knight Newspapers to form *Knight-Ridder Newspapers.* The new corporation controls 35 U.S. daily newspapers in 16 states.

1975 *Dahomey* changes its name to the People's Republic of *Benin.*

1988 *Kohlberg Kravis Roberts and Co.* agrees to acquire *RJR Nabisco Inc.* for $25.07 billion.

1992 United Nations secretary *Boutros Boutros-Ghali* endorses military intervention in Somalia to help distribute food and medical aid to the famine-stricken population.

1993 U.S. President *Bill Clinton* signs the *Brady Bill* into law, which requires a waiting period before purchasing a handgun.

november

DECEMBER

December is the twelfth month of the Gregorian calendar and has 31 days. The Latin *decem* 'ten,' in the name of this month, refers to December's original position as the final month in the early Roman 10-month calendar. The name remained as December even after the Roman adoption of a 12-month calendar, with December still the final month. (See also at **September**.)

The Romans celebrated the Saturnalia in late December, a festival of great merriment dedicated to the god Saturn, marked by exchange of gifts, temporary liberty for slaves, and the playful honoring of a mock king, the Lord of Misrule, known by the Romans as *Saturnalicius princeps*. The Anglo-Saxons celebrated the great Yule feast, associated with Christmas but probably originating in an ancient, pre-Christian festival.

The occurrence of the winter solstice—the shortest day of the year—approximately on December 22 in the northern hemisphere is very likely the reason that many ancient religions celebrated important festivals at this time. The lengthening of daylight after the solstice was a reassurance that the solar cycle was continuing and that warmer weather would return.

In the astrological calendar, December spans the zodiac signs of Sagittarius, the Archer (November 22–December 21) and Capricorn, the Goat (December 22–January 19).

The birthstone for December is the turquoise or zircon, and the flower is the holly or narcissus

STATE, NATIONAL, AND INTERNATIONAL HOLIDAYS

Nine Days of Posada
(Mexico)
Third Week

Christmas Day
December 25

Boxing Day
(Great Britain)
December 26

SPECIAL EVENTS AND THEIR SPONSORS

Tinsel Day
December 5

Tandem Day
December 13
Puns Corp. c/o Robert L. Birch

DECEMBER
1

HOLIDAYS

Angola
Pioneers' Day

Central African Republic
Anniversary of the Proclamation of the Republic
Celebrates the achievement of independence from France, 1958.

Portugal
Restoration of Independence

RELIGIOUS CALENDAR

The Saints
St. Ansanus, martyr and first apostle of Siena. Also called the *Baptizer.* [d. 304]

St. Agericus, Bishop of Verdun. Also called *Airy.* [d. 588]

St. Tudwal, bishop. Also called *Pabu, Tugdual,* or *Tutwal.* [d. 6th cent.]

St. Eligius, Bishop of Noyon; patron of all kinds of smiths and metalworkers. Invoked on behalf of horses. Also called *Eloi,* or *Eloy.* [d. 660]

The Beatified
Blessed Bentivoglia, Franciscan friar minor. [d. 1232]

Blessed John of Vercelli, 6th master general of the Dominican Order of Preachers. [d. 1283]

Blessed Gerard Gagnoli, Franciscan lay brother. [d. 1345]

Blessed Antony Bonfadini, Franciscan friar minor. [d. 1482]

Blessed Hugh Faringdon, abbot of Reading, and his Companions, martyrs. [d. 1539]

Blessed John Beche, Abbot of Colchester and martyr. Also called *Thomas Marshall.* [d. 1539]

Blessed Richard Whiting, Abbot of Glastonbury, and his Companions, martyrs. [d. 1539]

BIRTHDATES

1751 *Johan Henrik Kellgren,* Swedish poet, critic; private secretary and literary advisor to *King Gustavus III* of Sweden. [d. April 20, 1795]

1766 *Nikolai Mikhaylovich Karamzin,* Russian writer; author of a 12-volume *History of Russia;* brought about reforms in the literary language of Russia; exerted significant influence on development of the language and literature. [d. May 22, 1826]

1792 *Nikolai Ivanovich Lobachevsky,* Russian mathematician; an early developer of non-Euclidean geometries. [d. February 24, 1856]

1830 *Luigi Cremona,* Italian mathematician; known for his work in geometry and graphical statistics;

reorganized technical schools in major cities in Italy. [d. June 10, 1903]

1846 *William Henry Holmes,* U.S. anthropologist; Chief, Bureau of American Ethnology, 1902–09; Head Curator of Anthropology, U.S. National Museum, 1910–20; Director, National Gallery of Art, 1920–33. [d. April 20, 1933]

1854 *William Temple Hornaday,* U.S. zoologist, wild life conservator; early promoter of game preserves and protection of wild life through conservation laws. [d. March 6, 1937]

1879 *Lane Bryant (Lena Himmelstein),* U.S. merchant, born in Lithuania; founder of Lane Bryant chain of stores that cater to larger-size women's clothes and maternity clothes. [d. September 26, 1951]

1886 *Rex (Todhunter) Stout,* U.S. novelist; known for his creation of *Nero Wolfe* detective stories. [d. October 27, 1975]

1897 *Cyril Ritchard,* Australian actor, director. [d. December 18, 1977]

1906 *Berta Scharrer,* German-born biologist; known for her contributions to the field of neuroendocrinology. [d. 1995]

1910 *Dame Alicia Markova (Lilian Alicia Marks),* British ballerina; first prima ballerina of Vic-Wells Ballet (now Royal Ballet Company), 1933–35; Vice-President, Royal Academy of Dancing, 1958–; Governor, Royal Ballet, 1973–.

1912 *Minoru Yamasaki,* U.S. architect. [d. 1986]

1913 *Mary Martin,* U.S. actress, singer. [d. November 3, 1990]

1925 *Martin Rodbell,* U.S. biochemist, and Alfred G. Gilman; Nobel Prize for Medicine in 1994 for the discovery of G proteins.

1929 *David Fitzgerald Doyle,* U.S. actor; known for his role as Bosley on television series, *Charlie's Angels.* [d. February 26, 1997]

Dick Shawn (Richard Schulefand), U.S. actor. [d. April 17, 1987]

1935 *Lou Rawls,* U.S. rhythm and blues singer.

Woody Allen (Allen Stewart Konigsberg), U.S. comedian, film maker; Academy Award (Best Picture, Director) for *Annie Hall,* 1977.

1939 *Dianne Lennon,* U.S. singer; member of the singing group, *Lennon Sisters.*

Lee Trevino, U.S. golfer.

1940 *Richard Pryor,* U.S. comedian, actor.

1941 *Dennis Wilson,* U.S. musician, singer; member of the rock group, *The Beach Boys.* [d. December 28, 1983]

1945 *Bette Midler,* U.S. singer, actress.

1946 *Gilbert O'Sullivan (Raymond Edward O'Sullivan),* Irish singer; known for his songs, *Alone Again Naturally* and *Claire.*

1951 *Treat Williams,* U.S. actor.

1958 *Charlene Tilton,* U.S. actress; known for her role as Lucy Ewing on television series, *Dallas,* 1978–85.

HISTORICAL EVENTS

1135 *Henry I* of England dies and is succeeded by his nephew, *Stephen of Blois.*

1145 *Pope Eugene III* proclaims the *Second Crusade.*

1640 *Portugal* gains independence from Spain.

1887 The infant *King Alfonso XIII* is crowned king of Spain.

China cedes *Macao* to Portugal.

1918 British and American troops begin the occupation of Germany following *World War I.*

1924 George Gershwin's musical revue, *Lady Be Good,* containing *Fascinating Rhythm,* opens in New York.

1925 *Locarno Treaties* are signed with Germany; Belgium, France, Britain, and Italy mutually guarantee peace in Western Europe, and Germany promises arbitration in any disputes with Poland, France, Belgium, and Czechoslovakia.

1934 *Serge Kirov,* a close collaborator of Stalin, is assassinated in Russia, followed by an outbreak of terror and purges within the Communist Party.

1940 *Manuel Avila Camacho* is inaugurated as president of Mexico.

1942 Nationwide *gasoline rationing* goes into effect in the U. S.

1943 *Declaration of Cairo* by U.S., Great Britain, and China, clarifies goals of war against Japan (*World War II*).

1945 *The Lost Weekend,* a film featuring Ray Milland, premieres in New York.

1946 *Miguel Aleman Valdes* is inaugurated as president of Mexico.

1950 U.S. Marines rescue 1,200 American soldiers at *Chosin, Korea (Korean War.)*

1951 Benjamin Britten's opera *Billy Budd* premieres in London.

1952 *Adolfo Ruiz Cortines* is inaugurated as president of Mexico.

Danish doctors perform a sex-change operation, transforming George Jorgensen, Jr., into *Christine Jorgensen.*

1955 *Rosa Parks,* a black seamstress in Montgomery, Alabama, is arrested for refusing to give up her bus seat to a white passenger.

1956 Leonard Bernstein's musical comedy *Candide* premieres in New York.

1958 Richard Rodgers and Oscar Hammerstein's musical, *The Flower Drum Song,* premieres in New York.

1959 *Antarctic Treaty* is signed in Washington, D.C., guaranteeing international use of continent for peaceful purposes only.

december

1960 Congolese forces arrest Premier *Patrice Lumumba* for instigating rebellion in the *Republic of the Congo.*

1963 *Queen Elizabeth II* officially opens the Commonwealth Pacific submarine telephone cable extending from Vancouver Island to Australia.

1964 *Gustavo Diaz* is inaugurated as president of Mexico.

1966 *Kurt-Georg Kiesinger* is elected chancellor of West Germany.

1970 *Luis Echeverria Alvarez* is inaugurated as president of Mexico.

Divorce is legalized in Italy.

1988 *Carlos Salinas de Gortari* is inaugurated as president of Mexico.

1989 For the first time, a Soviet leader, *President Mikhail Gorbachev,* meets with a pope, *John Paul II.* The Pope praises the ongoing democratic reforms in the Soviet Union.

1990 President *Hissene Habré* of Chad is overthrown by a rebel force led by *Idris Deby.*

1994 The U.S. congress approves the *General Agreement on Tariffs and Trade (GATT).*

1997 The United Nations conference on global warming ends successfully with the passage of the *Kyoto Protocol* that aims at reducing the amount of greenhouse gases.

HOLIDAYS

Kyrgyzstan
National Day

Laos
National Day

United Arab Emirates
National Day
Commemorates the achievement of independence from Great Britain, 1971.

RELIGIOUS CALENDAR

The Saints
St. Chromatius, Bishop of Aquileia. [d. c. 407]
St. Bibiana, virgin and martyr. Also called *Bibiania,* or *Viviana.* [death date unknown]

The Beatified
Blessed John Ruysbroeck, priest and contemplative. Also called *Jan Van Ruysbroeck,* or *Joannes Rusbrochius.* [d. 1381]

BIRTHDATES

1738 *Richard Montgomery,* American Revolutionary general; killed leading assault on Quebec. [d. December 31, 1775]

1813 *Matthias Alexander Castrén,* Finnish linguist and ethnologist; pioneer in *Ural-Altaic philology.* [d. May 7, 1852]

1825 *Pedro II,* second and last Emperor of Brazil; forced to abdicate in 1889 when federal republic was established. [d. December 5, 1891]

1842 *Enos Melancthon Barton,* U.S. manufacturer; founder of Western Electric Co. [d. May 3, 1916]

1859 *Georges Seurat,* French painter; a pioneer of *Neo-impressionism;* creator of *pointillism.* [d. March 29, 1891]

1863 *Charles Ringling,* U.S. circus owner; co-founder, Ringling Brothers. [d. December 3, 1926]

1866 *Harry Thacker Burleigh,* U.S. singer, composer; noted for his exquisite voice, as well as his renditions of the Negro spiritual which he popularized during numerous European concert tours. [d. September 12, 1949]

1883 *Nikos Kazantzakis,* Greek author; wrote *Zorba the Greek,* 1952, and *The Odyssey: A Modern Sequel,* 1958. [d. October 26, 1957]

1885 *George R. Minot,* U.S. physician; Nobel Prize in physiology or medicine for new discoveries in the treatment of *pernicious anemia,* at that time a uniformly fatal disease (with

W. P. Murphy and G. H. Whipple), 1934. [d. February 25, 1950]

1904 *Donald Woods (Ralph L. Zink),* U.S. actor, realtor; known for his role in *True Grit,* 1969. [d. March 5, 1998]

1906 *Peter Carl Goldmark,* U.S. inventor, born in Hungary; credited with invention of *color television.* [d. December 7, 1977]

1914 *Alexander (Meigs) Haig, Jr.,* U.S. Army general; NATO Supreme Allied Commander in Europe, 1974–79; White House chief of staff, 1973–74; U.S. Secretary of State, 1980–82.

1915 *Marais Viljoen,* State President of the Republic of South Africa, 1979–85.

1916 *David W. Hearst,* U.S. publisher; published *Los Angeles Herald-Express,* 1950. [d. May 13, 1986]

1922 *Charles Coles Diggs, Jr.,* U.S. politician; Congressman, 1954–80; convicted of defrauding government in payroll kickback, 1980. [d. August 24, 1998]

1925 *Julie Harris,* U.S. actress.

1931 *Edwin Meese, III,* U.S. government official; Attorney General, 1985–88.

1940 *Dwight Lee Chapin,* U.S. government official; convicted of perjury in Watergate incident, April 5, 1974.

1955 *Dennis Christopher (Dennis Carelli),* U.S. actor; known for his starring roles in *Breaking Away,* 1979, and *Chariots of Fire,* 1981.

1958 *Randy Gardner,* U.S. figure skater; teamed with Tai Babilonia to win five national championships and 1979 world title.

1960 *Rick Savage,* British musician; member of the rock group, *Def Leppard.*

1962 *Tracy Austin,* U.S. tennis player.

1973 *Monica Seles,* Yugoslavian-born tennis player.

HISTORICAL EVENTS

1254 *Manfred,* King of Sicily retains his kingdom against claims of *Charles of Anjou* at the *Battle of Foggia.*

1804 *Napoleon Bonaparte* is crowned French Emperor *Napoleon I* of France.

1805 *Napoleon* scores one of his greatest victories in the *Battle of Austerlitz,* defeating the combined Russian and Austrian armies.

1823 *Monroe Doctrine* is expressed by U.S. President James Monroe in his annual message to Congress.

1848 *Emperor Ferdinand* of Holy Roman Empire abdicates in favor of his nephew, *Franz Joseph.*

1851 *Napoleon III* is proclaimed emperor of France following a coup d'etat.

1859 *John Brown* is hanged at Charlestown for treason against the state of Virginia.

1903 *First Panama Canal Treaty* is ratified.

1911 *King George V* and *Queen Mary* arrive at Bombay, the first British sovereigns to visit India.

1942 Scientists at the University of Chicago achieve the first self-sustaining *nuclear reaction.*

1943 *Carmen Jones,* Oscar Hammerstein II's Americanization of Bizet's *Carmen,* premieres in New York.

1957 A *nuclear power plant* in Shippingport, Pennsylvania, begins producing electricity. This represents the first non-military use of nuclear power in the U.S.

1960 Archbishop of Canterbury, *Geoffrey Fisher,* meets with Pope *John XXIII* in the Vatican. It is the first meeting between leaders of the Anglican and Roman Catholic faiths since the founding of the Church of England in 1534.

1962 Record *thorium* deposits in the White Mountains of New Hampshire are found by geologists; they constitute a reserve for nuclear fuel equal to the nation's uranium deposits.

1966 *U.S. Catholic Bishops Conference* abolishes rule of

abstinence from meat except on Ash Wednesday and Fridays during Lent.

1971 Six Persian Gulf sheikdoms proclaim their independence as the *United Arab Emirates.*

1979 Iranians approve a new constitution that establishes *Shi'ite Islam* as the state religion and makes *Ayatollah Rubollah Khomeini* the political and religious leader for life.

1982 *Dr. William DeVries* and a team of surgeons at Utah Medical Center successfully implant an *artificial heart* in *Barney Clark,* a Washington State dentist (who lives for 112 days after the surgery).

1986 President Ronald Reagan requests an independent counsel to investigate the *Iran-contra affair.*

1988 *Benazir Bhutto* is inaugurated as president of Pakistan. She becomes the first woman in modern history to govern a Moslem nation.

1989 *Vishwanath Pratap Singh* is selected as the new prime minister of India following the resignation of Rajiv Gandhi.

1991 *Joseph Cicippio* and *Alann Steen,* hostages held by the Islamic Jihad, are freed.

1993 Canada approves the *North American Free Trade Agreement (NAFTA).*

1997 *Farooq Leghari* resigns as President of Pakistan.

RELIGIOUS CALENDAR

The Saints

St. Cassian, martyr. Also called *Cassian of Tangier;* patron of stenographers. [d. c. 298]

St. Birinus, first bishop of Dorchester, and Apostle of Wessex. Also called *Berin,* or *Birin.* Feast formerly December 5. [d. c. 650]

St. Sola, priest and solitary. Also called *Sualo.* [d. 794]

St. Francis Xavier, apostle of India and one of the first Jesuits. Patron saint of the East Indies and of Roman Catholic missionaries in foreign parts as well as all works for the spreading of the faith. Invoked against plague. [d. 1552] Obligatory Memorial.

SS. Claudius, Hilaria, and their Companions, martyrs. [death date unknown]

St. Lucius, king. [death date unknown]

BIRTHDATES

1368 *Charles VI* of France, the *Well-Beloved;* also known as *Charles the Mad* because of his periods of insanity beginning in 1392. [d. October 21, 1422]

1684 *Baron Ludvig Holberg,* Danish writer, historian, philosopher; known as the father of Danish literature; claimed also by Norway as the founder of its literature. [d. January 28, 1754]

1753 *Samuel Crompton,* English inventor; in 1779 developed the *mule,* a spinning machine which revolutionized the cotton industry. [d. June 26, 1827]

1755 *Gilbert Charles Stuart,* U.S. painter; created the *Athenaeum Head,* the most popular, romantic portrait ever done of George Washington. [d. July 9, 1828]

1764 *Mary Ann Lamb,* English author; sister of Charles Lamb (February 10); with her brother wrote various poems, especially children's verses. [d. May 20, 1847]

1795 *Sir Rowland Hill,* British postal authority; creator of the first *postage stamp,* the *Penny Black;* responsible for the reform of the British postal system; Secretary to the Post office, 1854–64. [d. August 27, 1879]

1805 *Ernest Adolphe Hyacinthe Constantin Guys,* French artist; noted for his detailed sketches of life during the Second Empire. [d. March 13, 1892]

1812 *Hendrik Conscience,* Flemish novelist; regarded as the *Founder of Modern Flemish Literature.* [d. September 10, 1883]

1826 *George Brinton McClellan,* Union Army general, public official; Commander of the Army of the Potomac during U.S. Civil War, 1861–62. [d. October 29, 1885]

1830 *Frederick Leighton, Baron Leighton,* British artist; noted for his detailed draftsmanship, especially in *Venus Disrobing for the Bath.* [d. January 25, 1896]

1838 *Cleveland Abbe,* U.S. astronomer; the first meteorologist to issue daily *weather forecasts;* advocate of *standard time system.* [d. October 28, 1916]

1842 *Charles Alfred Pillsbury,* U.S. milling executive; founder of Charles A. Pillsbury & Co., 1872. [d. September 17, 1899]

1845 *Henry Bradley,* British philologist, lexicographer; became editor and eventually senior editor of *Oxford English Dictionary,* 1889–1923. [d. May 23, 1923]

1857 *Joseph Conrad (Jozef Teodor Konrad Korzeniowski),* British novelist, short-story writer, born in Poland; one of the master stylists of English literature. [d. August 3, 1924]

1864 *Herman Heijermans (Koos Habbema, Samuel Falkland),*

Dutch dramatist, short-story writer; author of numerous works of fiction, especially of Dutch small-town life. [d. November 22, 1924]

1880 *(Moritz Albert Franz Friedrich) Fedor von Bock,* German field marshal, World War II; chief of northern armies during invasion of Poland; commanded armies on Russian front, 1941. [d. c. May 1, 1945]

1886 *Karl Manne Georg Siegbahn,* Swedish physicist; Nobel Prize in physics for discovery of M series in the x-ray spectrum, 1925. [d. September 30, 1978]

1895 *Anna Freud,* Austro-English psychoanalyst; considered the definitive interpreter of the theories of her father, Sigmund Freud. [d. October 9, 1982]

1896 *Carlo Schmid,* West German statesman; leader of the Social Democrat Party; helped reshape West Germany after World War II. [d. December 11, 1979]

1899 *Hayoto Ikeda,* Japanese statesman; signed the treaty of peace with U.S. ending *World War II.* [d. August 13, 1965]

1900 *Richard Kuhn,* German chemist; Nobel Prize in chemistry for work on *carotenoids* and *vitamins,* 1938. [d. August 1, 1967]

1923 *Maria Callas (Cecilia Sophia Anna Maria Kalogeropoulos),* U.S. prima donna operatic soprano. [d. September 16, 1977]

1930 *Jean-Luc Godard,* French film director; leader of the nouvelle vague cinéma.

Andy Williams, U.S. singer.

1933 *Paul Crutzen,* Dutch chemist; Nobel Prize for Chemistry in 1995. Crutzen shares the award with fellow chemists, Mario Molina and F. Sherwood Rowland. The three chemists researched atmospheric chemistry.

1937 *Robert Arthur (Bobby) Allison,* U.S. auto racer.

1949 *John (Ozzy) Osbourne,* British singer; member of the rock group, *Black Sabbath;* known for killing animals in solo performances before he was reprimanded by the Humane Society.

1951 *Alberto Juantorena,* Cuban middle-distance runner; Olympic gold medalist, 1976.

1956 *Hart Bochner,* Canadian actor; known for his role on the television series, *War and Remembrance;* appeared in *Die Hard,* 1988.

1960 *Julianne Moore,* U.S. actress.

1968 *Brendan Fraser,* U.S. actor.

HISTORICAL EVENTS

1170 *Thomas Becket,* Archbishop of Canterbury, returns to Canterbury after exile in France.

1800 *Battle of Hohenlinden,* in Upper Bavaria, results in great French victory over the Austrians (*War of the Second Coalition*).

1818 *Illinois* is admitted to Union as the 21st state.

1833 *Oberlin College,* the first college to admit women, is founded in Oberlin, Ohio.

1849 *Mt. Kenya* in Africa is discovered by *Dr. Lewis Krapf.*

1909 *Housing and Town Planning Act* goes into effect in Great Britain.

1912 *First Balkan War* ends with armistice between Turkey, Bulgaria, Serbia, and Montenegro.

1914 *Battle of the Kolubara River* opens between the Austrians and the Serbs (*World War I*).

1915 *General Joseph Joffre* is named commander in chief of all French armies (*World War I*).

1917 Negotiations are opened at *Brest-Litovsk* between Russia and Germany in an attempt at peace (*World War I*).

1944 Civil war breaks out in *Greece* between the government in power, backed by British troops, and its Communist-dominated opposition group.

1951 Colonel *Fawzi Silo* is installed as Syrian head of state, premier, and defense minister following a coup led by Army Chief-of-Staff *Adeeb Shishekly.*

1953 Robert Wright's and George Forrest's musical, *Kismet,* opens in New York.

1960 Frederick Loewe's *Camelot* premieres in New York.

1967 *Christiaan Barnard* of South Africa performs first successful human *heart transplant* operation at a Cape Town hospital.

1973 *Pioneer 10,* U.S. unmanned spacecraft, reaches its closest approach to *Jupiter,* 21 months after its launch.

1974 U.S. space vehicle *Pioneer 11* begins a five-year journey to *Saturn.*

1977 *Karen Farmer* becomes the first black member of the

Daughters of the American Revolution.

1979 *Iran* adopts an Islamic constitution.

1984 A gas leak from a Union Carbide plant in *Bhopal, India,* causes the worst industrial accident in history. Twenty-five hundred people are killed by toxic fumes and fifty thousand are injured.

1992 *Famine disaster* accounts for more than 300,000 deaths in *Somalia,* as political unrest plagues the country.

DECEMBER
4

HOLIDAYS

Mexico
Day of the Artisans
Set aside to honor the workers of
the nation.

Tonga
Tupou I Day

RELIGIOUS CALENDAR

The Saints
St. Clement of Alexandria. Feast
    suppressed 1969. [d. c. 215]
St. Maruthas, bishop of Maiferkat.
    Considered one of the chief
    Syrian doctors. [d. c. 415]
St. John Damascene, Doctor of the
    Church. Last of the Greek
    fathers and one of the two
    greatest poets of the Eastern
    church. Also called *Mansur.*
    Feast formerly March 27. [d.
    c. 749] Optional Memorial.
St. Anno, Archbishop of Cologne. [d.
    1075]
St. Osmund, Bishop of Salisbury. [d.
    1099]
St. Bernard, Bishop of Parma, and
    cardinal. [d. 1133]
St. Barbara, virgin and martyr;
    patron of gunners, miners,
    mathematicians, architects,
    smelters, brewers, oilers,
    masons, and captives.
    Invoked against lightning, fire,
    and sudden death. [death
    date unknown]Feast
    suppressed 1969.

BIRTHDATES

34 *Persius,* Roman satirist; wrote
    six satires expaining stoicism.
    [d. November 24, 62]

1585 *John Cotton,* American
    colonial leader; Puritan leader
    of Massachusetts Bay Colony;
    responsible for expulsion of
    Anne Hutchinson (July 20)
    and Roger Williams from the
    colony. [d. December 23,
    1652]

1595 *Jean Chapelain,* French poet,
    critic; one of founders of
    Académie Française. [d.
    February 22, 1674]

1730 *William Moultrie,* American
    Revolutionary general; his
    defense of Charleston, 1776,
    delayed British infiltration of
    the South for years. [d.
    September 27, 1805]

1795 *Thomas Carlyle,* British
    essayist, philosopher,
    historian. [d. February 5,
    1881]

1835 *Samuel Butler,* British
    novelist, satirist; known for
    his novels, *The Way of All
    Flesh* and *Erewhon.* [d. June
    18, 1902]

1860 *George Albert Hormel,* U.S.
    businessman; founder of
    George A. Hormel & Co., first
    company to produced canned
    hams in U.S. [d. June 5, 1946]

1861 *Lillian Russell (Helen Louise
    Leonard),* U.S. entertainer,
    actress. [d. June 6, 1922]

1865 *Luther Halsey Gulick,* U.S.
    educator; co-founder of
    Camp Fire Girls of America.
    [d. August 13, 1918]

    Edith Cavell, British nurse;
    executed by German soldiers
    in Brussels for harboring
    Allied soldiers. [d. October
    12, 1915]

1866 *Wassily Kandinsky,* Russian
    artist; one of the founders of
    abstract art. [d. December 17,
    1944]

1875 *Rainer Maria Rilke,* German
    lyric poet, author; known for
    his somewhat mystical works,
    often dealing with death. [d.
    December 29, 1926]

1892 *Francisco Franco,* Spanish
    government leader; dictator
    of Spain, 1936–75. [d.
    November 20, 1975]

1904 *Harry N(athan) Abrams,* U.S.
    publisher; founder and
    Chairman of the Board, Harry
    N. Abrams Inc., the largest
    American publisher of art
    books. [d. November 25,
    1979]

1908 *Alfred Day Hershey,* U.S.
    biologist; Nobel Prize in
    physiology or medicine for
    research into *genetic
    structure of viruses* (with M.
    Delbruck and S. E. Luria),
    1969. [d. May 22, 1997]

1911 *Robert Payne,* British-American author, linguist; produced over 100 books, including biographies of Karl Marx and Charlie Chaplin; founding director, Columbia University translation center. [d. February 18, 1983]

1912 *Gregory (Pappy) Boyington,* U.S. pilot; leader of a Marine Fighter Squadron called Blacksheep that shot down 98 Japanese planes in 84 days of combat, 1943. [d. January 11, 1988]

1918 *John Bell Williams,* U.S. politician; U.S. Congressman, 1947–67; Governor of Mississippi, 1968–72; staunch segregationist. [d. March 26, 1983]

1922 *Deanna Durbin (Edna Mae Durbin),* U.S. singer, actress.

1931 *Alex Delvecchio,* Canadian hockey player, hockey coach; elected to Hall of Fame, 1977.

1934 *Winston Conrad (Wink) Martindale,* U.S. television host.

1935 *Robert Lee Vesco,* U.S. financier.

1949 *Jeff Bridges,* U.S. actor; known for his starring roles in *The Last Picture Show, Against All Odds,* and *The Jagged Edge.*

1964 *Marisa Tomei,* U.S. actress; Academy Award (Best Supporting Actress) for *My Cousin Vinny,* 1992.

1973 *Tyra Banks,* U.S. model, actress.

HISTORICAL EVENTS

963 Roman synod deposes *Pope John XII.*

1214 *William the Lion,* King of Scotland, dies and is succeeded by *Alexander II.*

1867 *The Grange* (The Order of Patrons of Husbandry), is founded at Washington, D.C.

1920 The French colony of Upper Senegal-Niger is renamed the *French Sudan.*

1942 In its first aerial attack on Italy, the U.S. bombs *Naples. (World War II)*

1961 *Floyd Patterson* knocks out *Tom McNeeley* to retain the world heavyweight boxing title.

1965 U.S. spacecraft *Gemini 7,* with Frank Borman and James A. Lovell, Jr., aboard, is successfully launched into orbit from Cape Kennedy, Florida.

1972 General *Oswaldo Lopez Arellano* assumes power in Honduras after a bloodless coup d'etat.

1974 Church of England *Worship and Doctrine Measure* is passed, giving power to change Anglican liturgy.

1976 *Jean-Bédel Bokassa* declares himself emperor of the Central African Republic in a $20 million extravaganza. Though the country is one of the world's poorest, it is believed to have great undeveloped mineral deposits.

1983 *Jaime Lusinchi* is elected president of Venezuela.

1984 *Herbert Blaize* is inaugurated as prime minister of Grenada.

1985 The first joint U.S.-Vietnamese search for the remains of U.S. servicemen missing in action ends. The search team excavated the site of a U.S. plane crash outside of Hanoi. *(Vietnam War)*

1991 *Charles Keating* is found guilty of fraud resulting from the Lincoln Savings & Loan scandal.

Terry Anderson, the last American held hostage, is released from captivity by the Islamic Jihad in Lebanon after seven years.

DECEMBER
5

HOLIDAYS

Haiti
Discovery Day
Celebrates the discovery of the island by Christopher Columbus, 1492.

Thailand
King's Birthday

U.S.
Tinsel Day

RELIGIOUS CALENDAR

The Saints
St. Crispina, martyr. [d. 304]
St. Sabas, abbot and one of the most renowned patriarchs of the monks of Palestine. Founded the monastery called *Mar Saba* near Jerusalem, one of the oldest occupied monasteries in the world. Also called *Sebas.* [d. 532]
St. Nicetius, Bishop of Trier. [d. c. 566]
St. Justinian, priest, hermit, and martyr. Also called *Jestin.* [d. 6th cent.]
St. Sigiramnus, abbot. Also called *Cyran,* or *Siran.* [d. c. 655]
St. Christina of Markyate, virgin. Also called *Theodora.* [d. c. 1161]

The Beatified
Blessed Nicholas of Sibenik, Franciscan friar minor and martyr. [d. 1391]
Blessed Bartholomew of Mantua, Dominican preacher. [d. 1495]

BIRTHDATES

1443 *Julius II, pope,* 1503–13; greatest art patron of all the popes; commissioned Michelangelo's Sistine chapel frescoes. [d. February 21, 1513]

1753 *Phillis Wheatley,* U.S. poet. [d. 1784]

1782 *Martin Van Buren,* U.S. Senator, 1821–28; U.S. Secretary of State, 1829–31; U.S. Vice-President, 1833–37; 8th President of U.S., 1837–41. [d. July 24, 1862]

1803 *Fyodor Tyutchev,* Russian lyric poet, essayist. [d. August 8, 1873]

1830 *Christina (Georgina) Rossetti,* British poet; noted chiefly for her sacred poetry. [d. December 29, 1894]

1839 *George Armstrong Custer,* U.S. cavalry officer; known primarily for his defeat by Sitting Bull and Crazy Horse at the *Battle of Little Bighorn,* which is often called *Custer's Last Stand.* [d. June 25, 1876]

1841 *Marcus Daly,* U.S. miner, businessman; founder of the Anaconda Mining Co.; exerted great influence on Democratic politics in Montana. [d. November 12, 1900]

1859 *Sir Sidney Lee,* British scholar, editor; editor-in-chief of

Dictionary of National Biography, 1891–1917. [d. March 3, 1926]

John Rushworth Jellicoe, Earl Jellicoe, British naval officer in World War I; commander of the grand fleet in *Battle of Jutland,* 1916. [d. November 20, 1935]

1867 *Joseph Pilsudski,* Polish military officer, statesman; Chief of State, 1920; Dictator of Poland, 1921; 1926–28; 1930; Minister of War and Commander in Chief of Army, 1930–35. [d. May 12, 1935]

1879 *Clyde Vernon Cessna,* U.S. aircraft manufacturer; founder of Cessna Airplane Co., 1927. [d. November 20, 1954]

1890 *Fritz Lang,* Austrian director; known for his direction of *Dr. Mabuse* and *Big Heat.* [d. August 2, 1976]

1894 *P(hilip) K(night) Wrigley,* U.S. manufacturer; President and Chairman of the Board of William Wrigley & Co., the world's largest *chewing gum* manufacturer; son of W. Wrigley, Jr. (September 30). [d. April 12, 1977]

1896 *Carl Ferdinand Cori,* U.S. biochemist, born in Czechoslovakia; Nobel Prize in physiology or medicine for research in *carbohydrate metabolism* (with G. T. Cori), 1947. [d. October 26, 1957]

1901 *Werner Karl Heisenberg,* German physicist; known for the *uncertainty principle,* which maintains that observations are affected by the observer; Nobel Prize in physics for discoveries in study of *hydrogen,* 1932. [d. February 1, 1976]

Walt(er Elias) Disney, U.S. film producer; pioneer in *movie animation;* creator of *Mickey Mouse,* 1928; produced first feature length cartoon, *Snow White,* 1938. [d. December 15, 1966]

1902 *(James) Strom Thurmond,* U.S. politician, farmer, lawyer; Governor of South Carolina, 1947–51; U.S. Senator, 1954–.

1903 *Cecil Frank Powell,* British physicist; Nobel Prize in physics for development of photographic method of tracking nuclear particles, 1950. [d. August 9, 1969]

1905 *Mohammad Abdullah,* Kashmiri statesman; known as the *Lion of Kashmir;* Chief Minister, Kashmir, 1947–53; 1975–82. [d. September 8, 1982]

1906 *Otto Preminger,* Austrian-born film director. [d. April 23, 1986]

1908 *Lin Piao (Lin Biao),* Chinese communist military leader; reported to have died in airplane crash, 1971. [d. September 12, 1971]

1925 *Anastasio Somoza Debayle,* Nicaraguan political leader; President, 1967–72; 1974–79. [d. September 17, 1980]

1927 *Bhumibol Adulyadej,* King of Thailand, 1946–.

1932 *Sheldon L. Glashow,* U.S. physicist; Nobel Prize in physics for formulating theory concerning interaction of elementary particles (with S. Weinberg), 1979.

1934 *Joan Didion,* U.S. novelist, journalist.

1935 *Calvin Marshall Trillin,* U.S. author; wrote *If You Can't Say Something Nice,* 1987.

1946 *Jose Carreras,* Spanish opera singer.

1947 *Jim Messina,* U.S. rock musician.

James William (Jim) Plunkett, Jr., U.S. football player; Heisman Trophy, 1970.

1957 *Art Monk,* U.S. football player.

1968 *Margaret Cho,* U.S. comedienne, actress.

HISTORICAL EVENTS

1189 *King Richard I* of England acknowledges independence of *Scotland* and sells Roxburgh and Berwick to *William the Lion,* of Scotland.

1301 *Pope Boniface VIII* issues papal bull against *Philip IV* of France over issue of king's right to tax the clergy.

1484 *Pope Innocent VIII* issues papal bull against witchcraft and sorcery.

1560 *Francis II* of France dies and is succeeded by *Charles IX,* his brother, under regency of Catherine de' Medici, their mother.

1776 *Phi Beta Kappa* fraternity is founded at William and Mary College as a social fraternity; in 1831, it becomes an honorary fraternity for students achieving academic distinction.

1870 *Rome* is declared the capital of Italy.

1892 Tchaikovsky's ballet *The Nutcracker* premieres at St. Petersburg, Russia.

1897 The authority of the British South Africa Company under *Cecil Rhodes* is extended over Northern Rhodesia.

1919 *Yugoslavia* signs treaties of peace with Austria and Bulgaria ending *World War I.*

1930 *The Swedish National Socialist Party* (Fascist) holds its first meeting.

1933 21st Amendment, revoking the *18th (Prohibition) Amendment,* is ratified in the U.S.

1936 U.S.S.R. adopts a new constitution recasting the Soviet federation.

1947 *Joe Louis* defeats *Jersey Joe Walcott* to retain the world heavyweight boxing title.

1955 Civil rights leader, *Martin Luther King, Jr.,* organizes the *Montgomery bus boycott* to protest racial segregation on municipal buses.

1967 More than 1,000 persons, including numerous nationally known personalities, are arrested during a *Stop the Draft Week* demonstration in New York City.

1972 *Gough Whitlam* is inaugurated as prime minister of Australia.

1977 *Tripoli Declaration* is issued by Arab critics of President *Anwar Sadat* of Egypt; Sadat, in retaliation, breaks off diplomatic relations with Algeria, Iraq, Libya, Yemen, and Syria.

december

1987 *Penaia Ganilau* is appointed the first president of the new republic of Fiji.

HOLIDAYS

Ecuador
Day of Quito
Commemorates the founding of the city, 1534.

Finland
Independence Day
Commemorates Finland's declaration of independence from Russia, 1917.

Ivory Coast Republic
Independence Day
Commemorates Ivory Coast's achievement of independence from France, 1960.

Spain
Constitution Day

RELIGIOUS CALENDAR

The Saints
St. Nicholas, called *St. Nicholas of Bari,* Bishop of Myra; patron of Russia, Greece, Sicily, Lorraine, mariners, children, virgins, merchants, pawnbrokers, coopers, brewers, those who lose in lawsuits unjustly, scholars, dock workers, and the worshipful company of parish clerks of the city of London. Invoked by and on behalf of prisoners. Also called *Santa Claus, Sint Klaes,* or *Sinta Klaas.* [d. 4th century] Optional Memorial.
SS. Dionysia, Majoricus, and other martyrs. [d. 484]

St. Abraham, Bishop of Kratia. [d. c. 558]

The Beatified
Blessed Peter Pascual, Bishop of Jaén, martyr; commonly called *saint.* [d. 1300]

BIRTHDATES

1478 *Count Baldassare Castiglione,* Italian diplomat, soldier, and author; known for his writings on courtly life; author of *The Courtier.* [d. February 7, 1529]

1637 *Sir Edmund Andros,* English governor of New England, 1674–86. [d. February 24, 1714]

1719 *John Phillips,* U.S. merchant, educational benefactor; founded *Phillips Exeter Academy,* New Hampshire, 1781. [d. April 21, 1795]

1732 *Warren Hastings,* English administrator; first governor-general of British India. [d. August 22, 1818]

1778 *Joseph Louis Gay-Lussac,* French chemist; developer of *Gay-Lussac's Law* of volumes of gases, 1808. [d. May 9, 1850]

1792 *William II,* King of the Netherlands, 1840–49; his reign saw the Netherlands transformed into a constitutional monarchy. [d. March 17, 1849]

1810 *Robert Cornelis Napier, 1st Baron Napier of Magdala,* British Army field marshal, administrator; Commander in Chief in India, 1770–76; Governor of Gibraltar, 1876–82. [d. January 14, 1890]

1824 *Emmanuel Frémiet,* French sculptor; a leading sculptor of animals. [d. September 10, 1910]

1863 *Charles Martin Hall,* U.S. chemist; discovered an inexpensive method for the isolation of pure *aluminum* from its compounds. [d. December 27, 1914]

1878 *John Sargent Pillsbury,* U.S. manufacturer; Chairman, Pillsbury Mills, Inc., 1932. [d. January 31, 1968]

1886 *(Alfred) Joyce Kilmer,* U.S. poet; best known for his poem *Trees.* [d. July 30, 1918]

1887 *Lynn Fontanne,* U.S. actress, born in England. [d. July 30, 1983]

1892 *Sir (Francis) Osbert Sacheverell Sitwell, 5th Baronet Sitwell,* British poet, author, critic; brother of Edith Sitwell (September 7). [d. May 4, 1969]

1896 *Ira Gershwin,* U.S. lyricist; frequent collaborator with brother George (September 26) on Broadway musicals; wrote *Porgy and Bess* and *Of*

Thee I Sing, first musical to win Pulitzer Prize, 1932. [d. August 17, 1983]

1897 *Milton R. Young,* U.S. politician, farmer; U.S. Senator, 1945–81; served the longest continuous Senate term of any Republican. [d. May 31, 1983]

1898 *Alfred Eisenstaedt,* U.S. photojournalist; has over ninety *Life* cover photographs to his credit. [d. August 23, 1995]

Gunnar Myrdal, Swedish economist, sociologist, public official; Nobel Prize in economics (with F. von Hajek), 1974. [d. May 17, 1986]

1906 *Agnes Moorehead,* U.S. actress. [d. April 30, 1974]

1908 *George (Baby Face) Nelson,* U.S. bank robber; member of the Dillinger gang. [d. November 28, 1934]

1920 *George Porter,* British chemist; Nobel Prize in chemistry for studies of chemical reactions affected by energy pulsations (with M. Eigen and R. G. W. Norrish), 1967.

Dave (David Warren) Brubeck, U.S. musician; a prime mover in the development of modern jazz.

1924 *Wally Cox,* U.S. comedian. [d. February 15, 1973]

1932 *Donald (Don) King,* U.S. boxing promoter; ex-convict who became a millionaire by arranging fights such as the Ali-Frazier *Thrilla in Manila,* 1975.

1935 *Bobby Van (Robert Van Stein),* U.S. actor. [d. July 31, 1980]

1941 *Bruce Nauman,* U.S. artist.

Richard Franklin Speck, U.S. murderer; killed eight student nurses in Chicago, July 13–14, 1966.

1953 *Thomas Hulce,* U.S. actor; known for his starring role in *Amadeus,* 1984.

Dwight Stones, U.S. track athlete.

1963 *Janine Turner,* U.S. actress; played Maggie O'Donnell on the TV series *Northern Exposure.*

1971 *Ryan White,* U.S. AIDS activist. [d. April 8, 1990]

HISTORICAL EVENTS

1506 *Macchiavelli* creates *Florentine Militia,* first national Italian troops.

1822 *Republic of Mexico* is established following achievement of independence from Spain.

Britain extends suffrage to agricultural workers.

1907 Mononagh, West Virginia, *coal mine disaster,* one of worst in U.S. history, kills 361 men.

1914 *Łódź, Poland* falls to Germans (*World War I*).

Battle of the Kolubara River ends in an Austrian defeat and flight from Serbia (*World War I*).

1916 *David Lloyd George* replaces *Herbert Henry Asquith* as prime minister of Great Britain.

German army enters *Bucharest (World War I).*

1917 *Finland* declares its independence from Russia.

1921 *Irish Peace Treaty* is signed, giving Ireland dominion status and establishing *Irish Free State.*

1948 *Arthur Godfrey's Talent Scouts* makes its television debut.

1953 Italy and Yugoslavia begin withdrawing their troops from *Trieste* after Marshal Tito renounces Yugoslavian claims to the city.

1957 The American Federation of Labor-Congress of Industrial Organizations (AFL-CIO) votes to expel the *Teamsters Union* after it refuses to oust *Jimmy Hoffa* and other leaders accused of corruption.

1971 *India* recognizes the Bangladesh rebel government as the government of *East Pakistan;* Pakistan breaks diplomatic relations with India.

1973 *Gerald Ford* is inaugurated as the 40th U.S. vice president, becoming the first non-elected vice president to take office under the 25th Amendment.

1977 South African government officially grants independence to the black homeland of *Bophuthatswana.*

1978 A new constitution is approved in *Spain,* providing for a constitutional monarchy, a parliamentary system of government, and general individual liberties.

1992 *Milan Kucan* is elected President of Slovenia.

HOLIDAYS

Armenia
Day of Remembrance
Armenians remember those who perished in the earthquake catastrophe of 1988.

Ivory Coast
Independence Day
Commemorates achievement of independence from France, 1960

U.S. (Delaware)
Delaware Day

U.S.
Pearl Harbor Day
Honors the Americans who died in the attack.

RELIGIOUS CALENDAR

The Saints
St. Eutychian, pope. Elected 275. [d. 283]

St. Ambrose, Bishop of Milan and Doctor of the Church; patron of Milan, bees, and domestic animals. Introduced Ambrosian chant. Obligatory Memorial [d. 397]

St. Diuma, Bishop of Middle Angles and Mercians. Also called *Diona.* [d. 658]

St. Josepha Rossello, virgin and founder of the Daughters of Our Lady of Mercy. [d. 1880]

BIRTHDATES

1598 *Giovanni Lorenzo Bernini,* Italian sculptor, architect, painter, designer; the *Father of Italian Baroque Style.* [d. November 28, 1680]

1760 *Madame (Marie Gresholtz) Tussaud,* Swiss wax modeler; famous for her museum of waxwork figures of famous people, in London. [d. April 15, 1850]

1784 *Allan Cunningham,* Scottish poet; close associate of Sir Walter Scott; edited Robert Burns's work, 1834. [d. October 30, 1842]

1801 *Johann Nepomuk Edward Ambrosius Nestroy,* Austrian dramatist, actor; leading actor of his time. [d. May 25, 1862]

1804 *Noah Swayne,* U.S. judge; Supreme Court Justice, 1862–81. [d. June 8, 1884]

1810 *Theodor Schwann,* German physiologist; developed the *cell theory of life.* [d. January 11, 1882]

1823 *Leopold Kronecker,* German mathematician; known for his work in algebra and theory of numbers. [d. December 29, 1891]

1830 *Judah Loeb Gordon,* Hebrew poet; the leading Hebrew poet of the 19th century. [d. September 16, 1892]

1841 *Michael Cudahy,* U.S. meat packer; founder of Cudahy Packing Co., 1890. [d. November 27, 1910]

1876 *Willa Cather,* U.S. novelist, short-story writer; Pulitzer Prize in fiction, 1923. [d. April 24, 1947]

1879 *(Charles) Rudolf Friml,* U.S. composer, born in Czechoslovakia; composer of several popular operettas. [d. November 12, 1972]

1888 *(Arthur) Joyce Lunel Cary,* British novelist; author of *The Horse's Mouth.* [d. March 29, 1957]

Heywood Campbell Broun, U.S. journalist, founder of the Newspaper Guild; the *Heywood Campbell Broun Award* is named for him. [d. December 18, 1939]

1893 *Virginia Kirkus,* U.S. literary critic, author; founder of *Kirkus Service,* which was later sold to the *New York Review of Books.* [d. September 10, 1980]

1894 *Stuart Davis,* U.S. artist; leading exponent of abstract art in the U.S. [d. June 24, 1964]

1910 *Vere Cornwall Bird,* Prime Minister, Antigua and Barbuda, 1981–93.

1915 *Eli Wallach,* U.S. actor.

1923 *Ted Knight (Tadeus Wladyslaw Konopka),* U.S. actor; two Emmy Awards for his role as Ted Baxter on television series, *The Mary Tyler Moore Show.* [d. August 26, 1986]

1924 *Mario Soares,* Portuguese political leader; Prime Minister, 1976–78, 1983–85; President, 1986–96.

1928 *Noam Chomsky,* U.S. linguist, writer, political activist; father of *transformational grammar.*

1932 *Ellen Burstyn,* U.S. actress.

1933 *Rosemary Rogers,* U.S. author; known for romance novels; wrote *Sweet Savage Love, Wicked Loving Lies,* and *The Crowd Pleasers.*

1936 *Martha Layne Hall Collins,* U.S. politician; Governor of Kentucky, 1983–87.

1937 *Thad Cochran,* U.S. politician; Senator, 1978–.

1942 *Harry Foster Chapin,* U.S. singer; known for his song, *Taxi,* 1972. [d. July 16, 1981]

1947 *Gregory Lenoir (Gregg) Allman,* U.S. singer, musician; member of the rock group, *Allman Brothers Band.*

Johnny Lee Bench, U.S. baseball player; Most Valuable Player, 1976 World Series.

1949 *Tom Waits,* U.S. singer.

1956 *Larry Joe Bird,* U.S. basketball player, coach; three-time Most Valuable Player.

1966 *C. Thomas Howell,* U.S. actor.

HISTORICAL EVENTS

1767 *John Street Theatre,* America's leading theater until 1797, opens in New York City.

1787 *Delaware* votes to adopt the newly created federal constitution, thus becoming the first state of the United States.

1829 The custom of *suttee,* or self-immolation of widows on their husbands' funeral pyres, is outlawed in parts of India under the control of the British East India Company.

1835 *Steam locomotive* is first used in Germany when a railroad opens from Nürnberg to Fürth.

1842 *New York Philharmonic Society* is formed in the U.S.

1889 *The Gondoliers,* a comic opera by Sir Arthur Sullivan and W. S. Gilbert, premieres in London.

1906 The National Board of *Young Women's Christian Associations (YWCA)* is founded in New York City.

1916 *Lloyd George* of Great Britain forms a war cabinet after the resignation of the Asquith coalition cabinet (*World War I*).

1917 *Battle of Cambrai* ends with the British losing much of what they had gained in the initial offensive (*World War I*).

U.S. declares war on Austria-Hungary (*World War I*).

1937 *Romansch* is recognized as a fourth national language in Switzerland.

1941 Japanese carrier-based planes make a surprise attack on U.S. fleet at *Pearl Harbor,* Hawaii, destroying 188 U.S. aircraft and many ships and precipitating U.S. declaration of war on Japan. (*World War II*)

1945 American military commission sentences Japanese general *Tomoyuki Yamashita* to be hanged.

1955 *Sultan Sidi Mohammed ben Youssef* becomes French Morocco's first constitutional monarch; *M'barek Bekkai* is named to form a government.

1965 *Pope Paul VI* and the Ecumenical Patriarch, *Athenagoras I* of the Greek Church, issue a joint declaration constituting an act of reconciliation between their two churches.

1971 A capsule launched from the Soviet Union's *Mars 3* space probe on December 2 makes soft landing on Mars.

1972 Reverend *W. Sterling Cary* is elected president of the National Council of Churches. He is the first black to hold the office.

1977 *Gordie Howe* becomes the first hockey player in history to score one thousand goals.

1987 Transport ministers agree to deregulate the *European airline industry.*

1988 More than fifty thousand people are killed when an earthquake strikes the Soviet republic of Armenia.

Miklos Nemeth becomes premier of Hungary.

1989 *Lithuania,* acting on the democratic changes sweeping across Eastern Europe, approves a multiple party political system.

1990 *Dimitar Popov* is elected premier of Bulgaria.

HOLIDAYS

Immaculate Conception Day
Celebrated in many Catholic
countries.

Panama

Mother's Day
Consistent with the celebration of
the Immaculate Conception, the
people of Panama honor mothers
on this day.

Uruguay

Blessing of the Waters

RELIGIOUS CALENDAR

Feasts

*Feast of the Immaculate Conception
of the Blessed Virgin Mary;*
celebrates the conception of
Mary, the Mother of Christ, in
the womb of St. Anne; prior
to 1854, the feast was known
as the *Conception of St.
Anne.* A public holiday in
many Catholic countries.

The Saints

St. Budoc, abbot. Also called *Beuzec,
Budeaux,* or *Buoc.* Feast
formerly December 7 [d. c.
6th century]
St. Romaric, abbot. Also called
Romaricus. [d. 653]

BIRTHDATES

65BC *Horace (Quintus Horatius
Flaccus),* the great lyric poet
of Rome; under the
patronage of Maecenas, wrote
numerous works describing
the Age of Augustus; known
for his *Odes, Satires, Epistles,*
and *Ars Poetica.* [d.
November 27, 8 B.C.]

1542 *Mary, Queen of Scots (Mary
Stuart),* Queen of Scotland;
unpopular with her subjects
owing to her *Roman
Catholicism* and possible
involvement in death of her
husband, Lord Darnley;
forced to abdicate, 1567;
imprisoned in England by
Elizabeth I; executed. [d.
February 8, 1587]

1626 *Christina,* Queen of Sweden,
1632–44; her reign was
disturbed by the *Thirty Years'
War* and great civil unrest;
abdicated in favor of her
cousin, *Charles X Gustavus.*
[d. April 19, 1689]

1708 *Francis I,* Holy Roman
Emperor, 1745–65;
overshadowed by his wife,
Maria Theresa of Austria. [d.
August 18, 1765]

1730 *Jan Ingenhousz,* Dutch
physician, plant physiologist;
early developer of theory of
photosynthesis. [d. September
7, 1799]

1765 *Eli Whitney,* U.S. inventor;
invented the *cotton gin,*
which revolutionized the
cotton growing industry; used
early form of *assembly line*
method of manufacturing in
his musket factory. [d.
January 8, 1925]

1826 *Friedrich Siemens,* German
inventor; industralist; together
with his brother, Sir William
Siemens (April 4) developed
the *regenerative furnace*
used in steel manufacturing.
[d. April 24, 1904]

1856 *Henry Thomas Mayo,* U.S.
naval commander in World
War I; Commander in Chief,
Atlantic Fleet, 1916–18. [d.
February 23, 1937]

1861 *William Crapo Durant,* U.S.
auto manufacturer; founder of
the Buick Motor Co., General
Motors Company, Chevrolet
Motor Co.; President of
General Motors Co., 1916–20;
founder of Durant Motors,
1921. [d. March 17, 1947]

Aristide Maillol, French
sculptor, designer, and
illustrator; best known for
monument to Cézanne. [d
October 5, 1944]

1862 *Georges Leon Jules Marie
Feydeau,* French dramatist;
known for his bedroom
farces; wrote *Le Tailleur pour
Dames,* 1887. [d. June 5,
1921]

1865 *Jean Sibelius,* Finnish
composer; pioneer of Finnish
national music; composed

Finlandia, 1900. [d.
September 20, 1957]

1881 *Padraic Colum,* Irish-
American poet, dramatist, a
founder of the Irish theater.
[d. January 11, 1972]

1885 *Kenneth Lewis Roberts,* U.S.
novelist; Pulitzer Prize
(Special Citation) for
historical novels that
increased interest in early
American history, 1957. [d.
July 21, 1957]

1886 *Diego Rivera,* Mexican
painter, muralist; his work
was controversial because of
his communist sympathies,
resulting in his murals at
Rockefeller Center, New York,
being removed. [d. November
25, 1957]

1894 *James (Grover) Thurber,* U.S.
humorist, cartoonist; known
for his numerous
contributions to *The New
Yorker,* 1927–52. [d.
November 2, 1961]

1898 *Emmett Kelly,* U.S. clown. [d.
March 28, 1979]

1901 *Manuel Urrutia Lleo,* Cuban
statesman; President of Cuba,
1959. Defected to U.S., 1963,
where he headed Anti-Castro
Democratic Revolutionary
Alliance. [d. July 5, 1981]

1906 *Richard Llewellyn (Richard
David Vivian Llewellyn
Lloyd),* Welsh author,
dramatist; wrote *How Green
Was My Valley,* 1940. [d.
November 30, 1983]

1908 *Adele Simpson,* U.S. fashion
designer. [d. August 23, 1995]

1911 *Lee J. Cobb,* U.S. actor. [d.
February 11, 1976]

1925 *Sammy Davis, Jr.,* U.S.
entertainer. [d. May 16, 1990]

1930 *Maximilian Schell,* Austrian
actor.

1932 *Bjørnstjerne Bjørnson,*
Norwegian poet, novelist,
playwright; political and social
leader; the national poet of
Norway; Nobel Prize in
literature, 1903. [d. April 26,
1910]

1933 *Clerow (Flip) Wilson,* U.S.
actor, comedian; known for
his television series, *The Flip
Wilson Show.*

1937 *James MacArthur,* U.S. actor;
known for his role on
television series, *Hawaii
Five-0,* 1968–80; son of Helen
Hayes.

1939 *James Galway,* Irish virtuoso
flautist.

1943 *Jim Morrison,* U.S. musician;
a leading rock vocalist of the
1960s. [d. July 3, 1971]

1946 *John Rubinstein,* U.S. actor;
Tony Award for *Children of a
Lesser God,* 1980.

1947 *Thomas Robert Cech,* U.S.
biochemist; Nobel Prize in
Chemistry along with Sidney
Altman, 1989.

Margaret Joan Geller, U.S.
astrophysicist, educator;
discovered the "Great Wall"
(number of galaxies) with
John Huchra, 1989.

1953 *Kim Basinger,* U.S. actress,
model; known for her starring
roles in *The Natural, 9 1/2
Weeks,* and *Batman*; Academy
Award (Best Supporting
Actress) for *L. A.
Confidential.*

1966 *Sinead O'Connor,* Irish pop
singer.

HISTORICAL EVENTS

1795 *Gagging Act* is passed to
protect king and government
of Great Britain from
seditious meetings.

1854 Dogma of the *Immaculate
Conception* is made an article
of faith in Roman Catholic
Church.

1886 *American Federation of
Labor* is organized at
Columbus, Ohio, with *Samuel
Gompers* as first president.

1907 *King Oscar II* of Sweden dies
and is succeeded by his son,
Gustavus V.

1911 *San Francisco Symphony
Orchestra* is established.

1914 *Battle of the Falkland Islands*
between Great Britain and
Germany results in victory for
the British. German Admiral
Maximilian von Spee dies
when his ship is sunk (*World
War I*).

1940 U.S. professional
championship football game
is first broadcast on radio,
with Chicago defeating
Washington, 73-0.

Japanese troops land on
Bataan, the east coast of
Malaya, and invade *Thailand*
(*World War II*).

1941 *Great Britain* declares war on
Japan. (*World War II*)

President *Franklin Roosevelt*
calls the Japanese bombing of
Pearl Harbor "a date which
will live in infamy" during a
speech to the U.S. Congress.

Russian-born aeronautical
engineer, *Igor Sikorsky,* tests
his VS-300 helicopter. It
becomes the prototype for
others used during World War
II.

U.S. declares war on Japan (*World War II*).

U.S.S. Wake becomes the only American warship to surrender during World War II as it surrenders to the Japanese near Shanghai.

1948 *Anne of the Thousand Days,* a Maxwell Anderson play based on Henry VIII's marriage to Anne Boleyn, premieres on Broadway.

1949 *Chinese Nationalists* flee the Chinese mainland, moving their capital to *Formosa (Taiwan).*

Jule Styne's musical comedy *Gentlemen Prefer Blondes* premieres in New York.

1966 Canada adopts a *medicare* program providing for payment by federal

government of one half of medical costs.

28 world nations, including the U.S. and U.S.S.R., reach agreement on a treaty to prohibit use of *outer space* for placement of weapons of mass destruction.

1967 Major *Robert Lawrence,* the first black astronaut, is killed when his training plane crashes.

1980 Rock star *John Lennon,* originally the leader of the Beatles, is shot and killed in New York City.

1987 President *Ronald Reagan* and General Secretary *Mikhail Gorbachev* sign a historic bilateral agreement to destroy all *intermediate-range nuclear force* weapons. The

INF treaty is considered an important step toward world peace.

A traffic accident involving an Israeli army truck, which kills four Arabs, touches off Palestinian violence in the Israeli-held *Gaza Strip* and *West Bank.* It is the beginning of months of unrest, known as the *Intifada.*

1987 U.S. President *Ronald Reagan* and Soviet President *Mikhail Gorbachev* sign treaty to eliminate medium-range nuclear weapons.

1993 U.S. President Bill Clinton signs the *North American Free Trade Agreement (NAFTA)* into law.

1997 *Jenny Shipley* is elected as the first female Prime Minister of New Zealand.

DECEMBER
9

HOLIDAYS

Lesotho
Mourning Day

Tanzania
Independence/Republic Day
Commemorates the achievement of complete independence from Great Britain, 1961, and the establishment of the Republic, 1962.

RELIGIOUS CALENDAR

The Saints
SS. Hipparchus and his Companions, the *Seven Martyrs of Samosata.* [d. c. 297]

St. Leocadia, virgin and martyr. [d. c. 304]

St. Gorgonia, matron. [d. c. 372]

St. Peter Fourier, co-founder of the Augustinian Canonesses Regular of Our Lady. [d. 1640]

The Beatified
Blessed Francis Antony Fasani, priest. [d. 1742]

BIRTHDATES

1594 *Gustavus II Adolphus,* King of Sweden, 1611–32; called the *Lion of the North;* responsible for making Sweden a major European power. [d. November 6, 1632]

1608 *John Milton,* English poet, essayist; one of the masters of English literature; wrote *Paradise Lost,* 1665–74, considered the greatest epic in English language; blind from 1652. [d. November 8, 1674]

1717 *Johann Joachim Winckelmann,* German archeologist; founder of the history of ancient art and scientific archaeology. [d. June 8, 1768]

1742 *Karl Wilhelm Scheele,* Swedish pharmacist-chemist; among many of his discoveries were: *chlorine, ammonia, prussic acid,* and *oxygen;* his work on oxygen done independently of Joseph Priestley (March 13). [d. May 21, 1786]

1748 *Claude Louis Berthollet,* French chemist; with Lavoisier, established system of *chemical nomenclature* still in use today. [d. November 6, 1822]

1848 *Joel Chandler Harris,* U.S. journalist, short-story writer, novelist; creator of *Uncle Remus,* the cartoon character whose stories became extremely popular in the late 19th and early 20th centuries. [d. July 3, 1908]

1868 *Fritz Haber,* German physical chemist; Nobel Prize in chemistry for development of process for synthesizing *ammonia* from nitrogen and hydrogen. [d. January 29, 1934]

1886 *Clarence Birdseye,* U.S. businessman, inventor; developed the quick freeze process of food preservation; founder of General Foods Corporation. [d. October 7, 1956]

1895 *Dolores Ibarruri,* Spanish politician, journalist; Secretary General of Spanish Communist Party (Partido Communista Español), 1942–60; President in exile 1960–77; returned to Spain, 1977. [d. November 12, 1989]

1905 *Dalton Trumbo,* U.S. screenwriter, author; wrote *Johnny Got His Gun,* 1939. [d. September 10, 1976]

1909 *Douglas Fairbanks, Jr.,* U.S. actor, television producer; son of silent-film star Douglas Fairbanks (May 23).

1911 *Broderick Crawford,* U.S. actor; Oscar Award for *All the King's Men.* [d. April 26, 1986]

1912 *Thomas P. (Tip) O'Neill,* U.S. politician; Congressman, 1952–86; Speaker of the U.S. House of Representatives, 1976–86. [d. January 5, 1994]

1915 *Elisabeth Schwarzkopf,* German operatic soprano.

1917 *L. James Rainwater,* U.S. physicist; Nobel Prize in physics for development of theory of *structure of the atomic nucleus* (with B.R. Mottelson and A.N. Bohr), 1975. [d. May 31, 1986]

1918 *Kirk Douglas,* U.S. actor.

1919 *Roy DeCarava,* U.S. photographer.

William N. Lipscomb, U.S. chemist; Nobel Prize in chemistry for investigation of the *structure of boranes,* 1976.

1922 *Redd Foxx (John Elroy Sanford),* U.S. comedian, actor; known for his role as Fred Sanford on television series, *Sanford and Son,* 1972–77. [d. October 11, 1991]

1925 *Dina Merrill (Nedenia Hutton),* U.S. actress; heiress to the Post cereal fortune.

1926 *Henry Kendall,* U.S. nuclear physicist; Nobel Prize for Physics with Jerome Freidman and Richard E. Taylor, for their study of quarks, 1990.

1928 *Dick Van Patten,* U.S. actor; known for his role as Tom Bradford on television series, *Eight Is Enough.*

1929 *John Cassavetes,* U.S. actor, director, screenwriter. [d. February 3, 1989]

Robert James Lee (Bob) Hawke, Australian politician; Prime Minister, 1983–91.

1930 *Buck Henry,* U.S. actor, author; co-directed *Heaven Can Wait* with Warren Beatty, 1978.

1932 *George Bass,* U.S. archaeologist; founder of the Institute of Nautical Archaeology and known for his contributions to underwater archaeology.

Bill Hartack, U.S. jockey; rode five Kentucky Derby winners, in 1957, 1960, 1962, 1964, 1969.

1935 *Stephen Scott (Steve) Bell,* U.S. broadcast journalist.

1941 *Lloyd Vernet (Beau) Bridges, III,* U.S. actor; known for *The Other Side of the Mountain,* 1975, and *Norma Rae,* 1979.

1942 *Richard J. (Dick) Butkus,* U.S. football player, actor; elected to Hall of Fame, 1979.

Joe McGinniss, U.S. author; wrote *The Selling of the President,* 1968.

1943 *Michael Ondaatje,* Ceylon educator, writer; author of *The English Patient,* 1992.

1949 *Thomas O. Kite, Jr.,* U.S. golfer.

1950 *Joan Armatrading,* British singer, songwriter.

1953 *John Malkovich,* U.S. actor, producer; starred in *Dangerous Liaisons,* 1988; produced *The Accidental Tourist,* 1988.

1958 *Donald Clark (Donny) Osmond,* U.S. actor, singer; known for his co-starring role on television series, *Donny and Marie Show,* 1976–79; comeback hit, *Soldier of Love,* 1989.

HISTORICAL EVENTS

1165 *Malcolm IV,* King of Scotland dies and is succeeded by his brother, *William the Lion.*

1625 *Treaty of the Hague* is signed, in which England and the Netherlands agree to subsidize Denmark against the Holy Roman Emperor, *Ferdinand.*

1865 *Leopold I* of Belgium dies and is succeeded by *Leopold II.*

1905 Richard Strauss's one-act opera, *Salome,* opens at the Dresden Opera.

1913 Richard Strauss's *Der Rosenkavalier* premieres in New York.

1917 *Cossacks* revolt against the Bolshevick government in the Ural and Don regions of Russia.

British troops capture *Jerusalem* from the Turks. Muslims had held the city for almost seven hundred years *(World War I).*

1918 *Romania* signs treaties of peace with Austria and Bulgaria, ending *World War I.*

1953 *Moshe Sharett* is named prime minister of Israel following the resignation of *David Ben-Gurion.*

1958 *John Birch Society* is founded in Boston for the purpose of combatting Communism.

1961 *Tanganyika* gains its independence from Great Britain with *Julius Nyerere* as Prime Minister.

1962 *Tanganyika* changes to a republic, with *Julius Nyerere* as first president.

1966 *Barbados* becomes the 122nd member of the UN.

1974 Greek Parliament is re-established after seven years; *King Constantine* is stripped of his title.

Takeo Miki is elected premier of Japan.

1985 Five former members of the Argentine military junta, including *Jorge Videla* and *Roberto Viola,* receive prison sentences for their participation in the "Dirty War" of the 1970s.

1987 *Palestinians* revolt against the Israeli occupation of West Bank and Gaza Strip.

1990 *Lech Walesa* is elected president of Poland.

1992 British Prime Minister *John Major* announces the separation of *Prince Charles* and *Princess Diana.*

U.S. troops arrive in Somalia to calm the unrest and provide famine relief.

U.S. marines and other *U.N. forces* enter Somalia to deliver relief aid to the starving people.

HOLIDAYS

Angola
M.P.L.A. Foundation Day
Commemorates the founding of the *Popular Movement for the Liberation of Angola.*

Thailand
Constitution Day
Commemorates the promulgation of the first Thai constitution, 1932.

UN Member Nations
Human Rights Day
Commemorates the adoption of the *Universal Declaration of Human Rights* by the UN, 1948.

U.S. (Wyoming)
Wyoming Day
Commemorates Wyoming's admission to the Union, 1890.

RELIGIOUS CALENDAR

The Saints
St. Eulalia of Mérida, virgin and martyr. Most celebrated virgin martyr of Spain. [d. c. 304]
St. Miltiades, pope and martyr. Elected 311. Also called *Melchiades,* [d. 314]
St. Gregory III, pope. Elected 731. [d. 741]
The London Martyrs of 1591 SS. Mennas, Hermogenes, and Eugraphus, martyrs. Mennas also called *Menas.* [death date unknown]

The Beatified
Blessed Thomas Somers, Benedictine priest and martyr. [d. 1610]

BIRTHDATES

1787 *Thomas Hopkins Gallaudet,* U.S. educator; founder of first free school for the deaf, *American Asylum,* 1817; *Gallaudet College* in Washington, D.C., is named in his honor. [d. September 10, 1851]

1804 *Karl Gustav Jacobi,* German mathematician; known for his work in theoretical mathematics, differential equations, and calculus. [d. February 18, 1851]

1805 *William Lloyd Garrison,* U.S. journalist, abolitionist leader; editor of *The Liberator,* the chief abolitionist publication of the pre-Civil War period in America, 1831–65. [d. May 24, 1879]

1813 *Zachariah Chandler,* U.S. government official; U.S. Senator, 1857–63; 1863–69; 1877–79. [d. November 1, 1879]

1822 *César Auguste Franck,* French composer, organist, born in Belgium; regarded as the founder of the modern French instrumental school. [d. November 8, 1890]

1830 *Emily Dickinson,* U.S. poet; known only posthumously for her highly unorthodox, whimsical yet profound poetry; lived a reclusive life. [d. May 15, 1886]

1843 *Queen Elizabeth* of Rumania (Carmen Sylvia), 1881–1914; writer and folk tale collector. [d. March 2, 1916]

1851 *Melvil Dewey,* U.S. librarian; developer of the *Dewey Decimal System,* 1876. [d. December 26, 1931]

1891 *Nelly Leonie Sachs,* German poet, dramatist; Nobel Prize in literature (with S. Y. Agnon), 1966. [d. May 12, 1970]

Harold Rupert Leofric George Alexander, 1st Earl Alexander of Tunis, British Army general; in charge of evacuation of British forces from Dunkirk, 1940; Commander in Chief of Allied Forces, Italy, 1944–45. [d. June 16, 1969]

1905 *Hellmut Wilhelm,* German scholar; known for his books on Chinese history and literature.

1906 *Walter Henry Zinn,* U.S. physicist, born in Canada, developer of the *breeder reactor,* 1951.

1911 *Chester (Chet) Huntley,* U.S. television newscaster, best known for his news program with David Brinkley (July 10), 1956–70. [d. March 20, 1974]

1912 *Philip A. Hart,* U.S. politician, lawyer; U.S. Senator, 1959–76. [d. December 26, 1976]

december

1914 *Dorothy Lamour,* U.S. actress. [d. September 22, 1996]

1923 *Michael Norman Manley,* Jamaican politician; Prime Minister, 1972–80, 1989–92. [d. March 6, 1997]

1934 *Howard Martin Temin,* U.S. molecular biologist; Nobel Prize in physiology or medicine for discoveries in area of tumor viruses (with D. Baltimore and R. Dulbecco), 1975. [d. February 9, 1994]

1946 *Gloria Jean Loring,* U.S. singer, actress; known for her starring role on television soap opera, *Days of Our Lives.*

1952 *Susan Hallock Dey,* U.S. model, actress; known for her starring roles on television series, *The Partridge Family* and *L.A. Law.*

1960 *Kenneth C. Branagh,* Irish actor, director; Academy Award nominee for *Henry V,* 1989.

HISTORICAL EVENTS

1508 *League of Cambrai* is formed between Holy Roman Emperor *Maximilian I, Louis XII* of France, and *Ferdinand of Aragon,* against Venice.

1520 *Martin Luther* burns the papal bull excommunicating him.

1710 French defeat Austrians at *Villa Viciosa,* leaving *Philip V* as master of Spain (*War of the Spanish Succession*).

1817 *Mississippi* is admitted to the Union as the 20th state.

1848 *Louis Napoleon* is elected President of the French Republic.

Second Sikh War between Great Britain and rebel Indian leaders begins.

1869 *Territory of Wyoming* grants *women's suffrage,* becoming first U.S. possession to do so.

1896 First *intercollegiate basketball game* is played, at New Haven, Connecticut, between Wesleyan University and Yale; Yale wins, 39 to 4.

1898 *Treaty of Paris* between U.S. and Spain settles *Spanish-American War,* with U.S. gaining Cuba, Puerto Rico, Guam, and the Philippines.

1904 *Bethlehem Steel Corp.* is founded in Pennsylvania.

1905 O. Henry's short story *Gift of the Magi* is published.

1910 Giacomo Puccini's opera, *The Girl of the Golden West,* premieres at the Metropolitan Opera in New York City.

1916 Sergei Prokofiev's *The Ugly Duckling* premieres.

1936 *Edward VIII* of Great Britain abdicates in order to marry *Wallis Warfield Simpson,* becoming the first monarch to abdicate voluntarily in British history. He becomes known as the *Duke of Windsor,* and is succeeded on the throne by his brother, *George VI.*

1941 Japanese troops capture *Guam (World War II).*

1950 *Ralph Bunche* becomes the first black to win the Nobel Peace Prize.

William Faulkner is awarded the Nobel Prize in literature.

1963 *Zanzibar* becomes an independent member of the Commonwealth of Nations.

1964 *Martin Luther King, Jr.,* accepts the Nobel Peace Prize in Oslo, Norway.

1970 *Lee Iacocca* is named president of Ford Motor Co.

1983 *Raul Ricardo Alfonsin* is inaugurated as president of Argentina.

1997 *Kim Dae Jung* is elected President of South Korea.

Nelson Mandela, president of South Africa, signs the new constitution into law (May 8, 1996).

HOLIDAYS

Burkina Faso
National Holiday
Commemorates the attainment of independent standing within the French community, 1958.

UN Member Nations
UNICEF Anniversary Day

U.S. (Indiana)
Indiana Day
Commemorates the date Indiana was admitted as a state.

RELIGIOUS CALENDAR

The Saints
St. Damasus, pope. Elected 366. Also called *Damascus I.* [d. 384] Optional Memorial.
St. Daniel the Stylite, priest. Best known of the disciples of St. Simeon the Stylite. [d. 493]
St. Barsabas, abbot and martyr. Also called *Barsabias.* [death date unknown]
SS. Fuscian, Victoricus, and Gentian, martyrs. [death date unknown]
Blessed Peter of Siena, Franciscan tertiary. [d. 1289]
Blessed Franco of Grotti, Carmelite lay brother. [d. 1291]
Blessed Hugolino Magalotti, Franciscan tertiary. [d. 1373]
Blessed Jerome Ranuzzi, Servite priest. [d. 1455]

BIRTHDATES

1475 *Pope Leo X,* pope 1513–21. [d. December 1, 1521]

1803 *(Louis) Hector Berlioz,* French composer; leader in the Romantic movement in French music; known as a pioneer in *modern orchestration.* [d. March 8, 1869]

1810 *(Louis Charles) Alfred de Musset,* French dramatist and poet; intimate of George Sand (July 1); some of his best poetry was composed at end of their liaison. [d. May 2, 1857]

1838 *Emil Rathenau,* German industrialist; founder of Deutsche Edison Gesellschaft, which eventually became Telefunken, a leading German electronics firm. [d. June 20, 1915]

1843 *Robert Koch,* German physician, bacteriologist; Nobel Prize in physiology or medicine for developments in *bacteriology* and discoveries related to *tuberculosis,* 1905. [d. May 27, 1910]

1847 *Michel Joseph Maunoury,* French army commander; commanded the French 6th Army that checked the German offensive on Paris during World War I. [d. March 28, 1923]

1849 *Ellen Karoline Sofia Key,* Swedish sociologist, author, feminist. [d. April 24, 1926]

1856 *Georgi Plekhanov,* Russian political philosopher; proponent of Marxism and chief advocate of development of socialist thought. [d. May 30, 1918]

1863 *Annie Jump Cannon,* U.S. astronomer; developed a spectral classification system by which she eventually cataloged hundreds of thousands of stars; her work published as the *Henry Draper Catalogue,* 1918–24, consisted of 9 volumes, and effected a great evolution in the science of *astronomy.* [d. April 13, 1941]

1874 *James Lewis Kraft,* U.S. manufacturer; invented pasteurizing process for cheese. [d. February 16, 1953]

1882 *Max Born,* British physicist; Nobel Prize in physics for his statistical studies of *wave functions,* 1954. [d. January 5, 1970]

Fiorello H(enry) LaGuardia, U.S. politician; Congressman, 1916–17; 1918–20; 1922–32; Mayor of New York City, 1933–45; noted for his honesty; well-loved by his constituents and the people of the city. [d. September 20, 1947]

1889 *Walter Knott,* U.S. businessman; founded Knott's Berry Farm amusement park, 1940; coined the term boysenberrry. [d. December 3, 1981]

1911 *Naguib Mahfouz,* Egyptian author; recognized as the "Father of the Modern Arab Novel"; Nobel Prize in literature, 1988.

1913 *Carlo Ponti,* Italian film producer.

1918 *Alexander Isayevich Solzhenitsyn,* Soviet novelist; Nobel Prize in literature (declined), 1970; deported to the West, 1974; awarded the Nobel Prize when he arrived in Switzerland, 1974.

1931 *Rita Moreno,* U.S. singer, actress; only woman to win the four top entertainment awards: Oscar, Grammy, Tony, and Emmy.

Bhagwan Shree Rajneesh, Indian religious leader; cult leader who was deported from the U.S. after he was charged with immigration fraud for arranging false marriages to bring Indian cult followers to the U.S. [d. January 19, 1990]

1939 *Thomas Emmett (Tom) Hayden,* U.S. political activist; co-founded students for Democratic Society, 1961.

1943 *Donna Mills (Donna Jean Miller),* U.S. actress; known for her role as Abby Ewing on television series, *Knot's Landing.*

1944 *Brenda Lee (Brenda Mae Tarpley),* U.S. singer.

1945 *Teri Garr,* U.S. actress; known for her roles in *Tootsie* and *Mr. Mom.*

1946 *Lynda Day George,* U.S. actress; known for her role on television series, *Mission Impossible,* 1971–73.

1950 *Christina Onassis,* Greek shipping executive; daughter of Aristotle Onassis; chief executive, Olympic Maritime Enterprises. [d. November 19, 1988]

1952 *Susan Seidelman,* U.S. director, producer; known for her direction of *Desperately Seeking Susan,* 1984.

1953 *Elizabeth Key (Bess) Armstrong,* U.S. actress; known for her roles in *Four Seasons,* 1981, and *High Road to China,* 1983.

1954 *Jermaine La Jaune Jackson,* U.S. singer, musician; member of the rock group, *The Jacksons.*

HISTORICAL EVENTS

1205 *John de Grey* is elected Archbishop of Canterbury but is rejected by *Pope Innocent III.*

1776 U.S. General *George Washington* retreats across the Delaware, escaping capture by the British (*American Revolution*).

1816 *Indiana* is admitted to the Union as the 19th state.

1845 *Sonderbund* is formed in Switzerland by the seven Catholic cantons to support education by the Jesuits and to protect their interests against the Liberal cantons.

1901 First *transatlantic radio signal* is transmitted by *Guglielmo Marconi* from Cornwall to St. John's, Newfoundland.

1917 *Lithuania* proclaims its independence from Russia.

1930 *Bank of the United States* in New York, with more than 400,000 depositors, fails, another indication of the *Great Depression* in the U.S.

1941 Germany and Italy declare war on U.S. (*World War II*).

U.S. declares war on *Germany* and *Italy (World War II).*

1946 United Nations International Children's Emergency Fund (*UNICEF*) is established by the United Nations General Assembly.

1951 *Joe Di Maggio* retires from baseball after 13 seasons with the New York Yankees.

1961 Thirty-three U.S. Army helicopters and 400 crewmen arrive in Saigon, marking the first overt U.S. action in the Vietnam conflict.

1965 *Philip Johnson* is chosen by Dallas officials to design the *Kennedy Memorial.*

1973 *Czechoslovakia* and *West Germany* sign a treaty establishing diplomatic relations and voiding the 1938 Munich pact.

1983 Lieutenant General *Hossein Mohammed Ershad* names himself president of Bangladesh and dissolves the cabinet.

1994 Russian troops invade *Chechnya* when the independence movement in the country gains momentum.

HOLIDAYS

Kenya

Independence Day
Commemorates the achievement of independence from Great Britain, 1963.

Mexico

Our Lady of Guadalupe
Commemorates the appearance of the Blessed Virgin to a young Indian, 1531.

RELIGIOUS CALENDAR

The Saints

SS. Epimachus and Alexander and other Martyrs. [d. 250]
St. Finnian of Clonard, bishop. Also called *Finan,* or *Finian.* [d. c. 549]
St. Edburga, Abbess of Minster and virgin. Also called *Eadburge,* or *Eadburh.* [d. 751]
St. Vicelin, Bishop of Staargard, evangelizer of the Wends. [d. 1154]
St. Jane Frances de Chantal, widow and co-founder of the Order of the Visitation. Feast formerly August 21. [d. 1641] Optional Memorial.

The Beatified

Blessed Thomas Holland, Jesuit priest and martyr. [d. 1642]

BIRTHDATES

1520 *Pope Sixtus V,* pope 1585–90. [d. August 27, 1590]

1731 *Erasmus Darwin,* English physician, poet, and speculative thinker; grandfather of Charles Darwin (February 12). [d. April 18, 1802]

1745 *John Jay,* American public official, jurist; President of Continental Congress, 1778; first Chief Justice of the U.S. Supreme Court, 1789–94. [d. May 17, 1829]

1786 *William Learned Marcy,* U.S. politician; first to articulate the concept of the spoils system; Governor of New York, 1833–39; U.S. Secretary of War, 1844–50; U.S. Secretary of State, 1853–57. [d. July 4, 1857]

1803 *James Challis,* British astronomer; one of first to observe the planet *Neptune.* [d. December 3, 1882]

1805 *William Lloyd Garrison,* U.S. abolitionist, author; founded American Anti-Slavery Society. [d. May 24, 1879]

Henry William Dwight Wells, U.S. transportation executive; with his partner, William George Fargo (May 20), formed the Wells, Fargo & Co., 1852, express and commercial transportation company. [d. December 10, 1878]

1821 *Gustave Flaubert,* French novelist; author of *Madame Bovary,* a classic of French literature. [d. May 8, 1880]

1838 *Sherburne Wesley Burnham,* U.S. astronomer; noted for his discovery and cataloging of double stars. [d. March 11, 1921]

1849 *William Kissam Vanderbilt,* U.S. financier; with his brother Cornelius, managed the assets and investments of the Vanderbilt empire, 1878–1903. [d. July 12, 1920]

1863 *Edvard Munch,* Norwegian artist. [d. January 23, 1944]

1864 *Arthur Brisbane,* U.S. journalist; noted for his exploitation of the media and use of *yellow journalism* to build his fortune. [d. December 25, 1936]

Paul Elmer More, U.S. philosopher, editor, critic; founder, with Irving Babbitt (August 2), of the *neo-humanist* movement in the U.S. [d. March 4, 1937]

1866 *George Swinnerton Parker,* U.S. games manufacturer; founder of Parker Brothers, manufacturers of *Monopoly.* [d. September 26, 1952]

Alfred Werner, Swiss chemist; Nobel Prize in chemistry for studies of molecular structure, 1913. [d. November 15, 1919]

december

1872 *Albert Payson Terhune,* U.S. novelist; known for his novels about collies, including *Lad, a Dog.* [d. February 18, 1942]

1875 *Karl Rudolf von Rundstedt,* German Army field marshal; Chief of General Staff, World War I; Commander in Chief on Western Front, 1942–45. [d. February 24, 1953]

1881 *Harry Warner,* U.S. motion picture executive; co-founder of Warner Brothers movie empire with his brothers Jack (August 2) and Albert (July 23). [d. July 25, 1958]

1893 *Edward G. Robinson (Emanuel Goldenburg),* U.S. actor, born in Hungary; noted for gangster roles during 1930s. [d. January 26, 1973]

1915 *Curt Jurgens,* German actor; known for his roles in over 150 films, including *The Enemy Below,* 1957, and *The Spy Who Loved Me,* 1977. [d. June 18, 1982]

Frank (Francis Albert) Sinatra, U.S. singer, actor. [d. May 15, 1998]

1917 *Dan Dailey,* U.S. actor. [d. October 17, 1978]

1918 *Eugene Burdick,* U.S. novelist, political theorist. [d. July 26, 1965]

Joe Williams (Joseph Goreed), U.S. singer; known for hits with Count Basie, including the song, *Everyday I Have the Blues,* 1955; appeared as Grandpa Huxtable on *The Cosby Show.*

1923 *Robert William (Bob) Barker,* U.S. television personality; host of television game show, *Truth or Consequences* and *The Price Is Right.*

1924 *Edward Irving Koch,* U.S. politician, lawyer; U.S. Congressman, 1969–76; Mayor of New York City, 1978–90.

Charles Louis Schultze, U.S. economist; Chairman, Council of Economic Advisers, 1977–81.

1927 *Robert Noyce,* U.S. physicist; invented an improved integrated circuit and founder of the Intel Corporation. [d. June 3, 1990]

1928 *Helen Frankenthaler,* U.S. painter.

1929 *John James Osborne,* British playwright, screenwriter. [d. December 24, 1994]

1934 *Miguel de la Madrid Hurtado,* Mexican politician; President, 1982–88.

1938 *Connie Francis (Concetta Maria Franconero),* U.S. singer and actress; known for her starring role in *Where the Boys Are,* 1963.

1941 *Dionne Warwick,* U.S. singer; three Grammy Awards.

1943 *Grover Washington, Jr.,* U.S. musician.

1946 *Emerson Fittipaldi,* Brazilian-born race car driver; Indianapolis 500 winner, 1992.

1952 *Cathy Rigby,* U.S. gymnast.

1957 *Ana Alicia (Ana Alicia Ortez),* U.S. actress; known for her role as Melissa Cumson Gioberti on television series, *Falcon Crest.*

1959 *Sheila E (Sheila Escovedo),* U.S. singer, musician; known for her song, *The Glamorous Life,* 1984.

1975 *Mayim Bialik,* U.S. actress, best known for title role on TV's *Blossom,* 1991–95

HISTORICAL EVENTS

1417 *Sir John Oldcastle, Lord Cobham,* leader of the Lollards, is burned and hanged. He is later portrayed as *Falstaff* by Shakespeare.

1787 *Pennsylvania* ratifies the Constitution and becomes the second state in the Union.

1901 The first *radio transmission* across the Atlantic Ocean occurs. The message begins in Cornwall, England and is received in Newfoundland, Canada.

1903 *Marie* and *Pierre Curie* and *Henri Becquerel* receive the Nobel Prize for their studies of *radioactivity.*

1906 *Oscar Solomon Straus* becomes the first Jew to receive a U.S. cabinet appointment when he is named Secretary of Commerce.

1911 The capital of British India is changed from Calcutta to *Delhi.*

1914 *Dow Jones average* drops 24.4%, the largest one-day percentage decline in history.

1926 New York defeats Philadelphia in the first professional interleague *football game.*

1936 *Chiang Kai-shek,* Chinese leader, declares war on Japan.

1963 *Kenya* gains independence from Great Britain.

1966 *Francis Chichester,* British yachtsman, completes a solo voyage from England to Sydney, Australia, a distance of more than 14,000 miles, in 107 days.

1972 *Orange soil* is discovered by *Apollo 17* astronauts Eugene

A. Cernan and Harrison H. Schmitt during their second day of exploration on the lunar surface.

1975 *Robert David Muldoon* is inaugurated as prime minister of New Zealand.

1984 Army Chief of Staff *Maaouya Ould Sidi Ahmed Taya* overthrows the government of Lieutenant Colonel *Mohamed Khouna Ould Haidalla* in Mauritania.

1985 President Ronald Reagan signs the *Gramm-Rudman-Hollings budget-balancing bill*. The new law is intended to reduce government spending for the next five years.

december

DECEMBER
13

HOLIDAYS

Japan
Sosubarai or Soot Sweeping Day
A time of traditional year-end house cleaning.

Malta
Repubic Day
Commemorates the establishment of the Republic, 1974.

St. Lucia, Sweden
St. Lucia Day

U.S.
Tandem Day
Sponsored by Puns Corp.

RELIGIOUS CALENDAR

The Saints
St. Lucy, virgin and martyr. Patron of Syracuse, Sicily. Invoked against eye diseases, dysentery, and hemorrhages. Also called *Lucia.* [d. 304] Obligatory Memorial.
St. Judoc, priest and hermit. Also called *Jodoc,* or *Josse.* [d. 668]
St. Aubert, Bishop of Cambrai and Arras. Also called *Autbertus.* [d. c. 669]
St. Odilia, virgin and abbess; patron of Alsace. Invoked for sore eyes and other ophthalmic troubles. Also called *Odile, Othilia, Othilla,* or *Ottilia.* [d. c. 720]
St. Eustratius and his Companions, martyrs. [death date unknown]

The Beatified
Blessed John Marinoni, priest. [d. 1562]
Blessed Antony Grassi, priest. [d. 1671]

BIRTHDATES

1553 *Henry IV,* King of France, 1589–1610; first of the *Bourbon line;* made enemies by giving tolerance to Protestants in the *Edict of Nantes;* assassinated. [d. May 14, 1610]

1720 *Count Carlo Gozzi,* Italian dramatist; author of many fairy plays. [d. April 4, 1806]

1797 *Heinrich Heine (Chaim Harry Heine),* German lyric poet; his lyrics are among the best loved in German music. [d. February 17, 1856]

1804 *Joseph Howe,* Nova Scotian official, editor; Governor of Nova Scotia, 1873. [d. June 1, 1873]

1810 *Clark Mills,* U.S. sculptor; best known for his equestrian statues of George Washington and Andrew Jackson. [d. January 12, 1883]

1816 *(Ernst) Werner von Siemens,* brother of Friedrich Siemens (December 8), German inventor, industrialist; a pioneer in producing telegraphic equipment and the *open-hearth process* used in steel manufacturing. [d. December 6, 1892]

1818 *Mary Todd Lincoln,* U.S. First Lady; wife of Abraham Lincoln, 16th President. [d. July 16, 1882]

1835 *Phillips Brooks,* U.S. Episcopal clergyman, hymn writer; author of *O Little Town of Bethlehem,* 1868. [d. January 23, 1893]

1844 *John Henry Patterson,* U.S. manufacturer; founder of the National Cash Register Co. [d. May 7, 1922]

1856 *Abbott Lawrence Lowell,* U.S. political scientist, educational administrator; President, Harvard University, 1909–33; responsible for establishment of schools of architecture, business administration, education, and public health. [d. January 6, 1943]

1879 *Eleanor Robson Belmont,* U.S. socialite, actress; legendary *grande dame* of New York society; wife of August Belmont (February 18); subject of George Bernard Shaw's play, *Major Barbara.* [d. October 24, 1979]

1887 *Alvin Cullum York,* U.S. soldier; one of most popular and decorated heroes of World War I; the subject of the movie *Sergeant York.* [d. December 2, 1964]

1890 *Marc(us Cook) Connelly,* U.S. dramatist; Pulitzer Prize in drama, 1930. [d. December 21, 1980]

1897 *Drew Pearson,* U.S. columnist; known for his muckraking column, (*Washington Merry-Go-Round*) which exposed and caused the retirement of numerous corrupt public figures. [d. September 1, 1969]

1902 *Talcott Parsons,* U.S. sociologist; Professor of Sociology, Harvard University, 1927–73; first chairman of Department of Social Relations. [d. May 8, 1979]

1903 *Younghill Kang,* U.S. author. [d. 1972]

1905 *Carey McWilliams,* U.S. author, editor; social critic; editor, *The Nation,* 1955–75; author of more than 20 books on U.S. social problems. [d. June 27, 1980]

1910 *Lillian Roth (Lillian Rutstein),* U.S. singer of 1920s and 1930s. [d. May 12, 1980]

Van (Emmett Evan) Heflin, U.S. actor; Oscar Award for *Johnny Eager,* 1942. [d. July 23, 1971]

1911 *Trygve Haavelmo,* Norwegian economist; Nobel Prize for Economics (1989) for his work on econometrics.

1913 *Archie Moore (Archibald Lee Wright),* U.S. boxer; World light-heavyweight champion, 1952–61.

1915 *Ross MacDonald (Kenneth Millar),* U.S. novelist, mystery writer; creator of fictional detective *Lew Archer.* [d. July 11, 1983]

Balthazar Johannes Vorster, South African political leader; noted for his extremist policies; Prime Minister, 1966–78. [d. September 10, 1983]

1920 *George Pratt Shultz,* U.S. government official; Secretary of State, 1982–89.

1923 *Philip Warren Anderson,* U.S. physicist; Nobel Prize in physics for developments in *solid state circuitry* and *theories of magnetism and conduction* (with J. H. Van Vleck and N. F. Mott), 1977.

1925 *Dick Van Dyke,* U.S. actor, comedian; three Emmy Awards for his starring role on television series, *The Dick Van Dyke Show,* 1961–66; also stars in the series *Diagnosis Murder,* 1993– .

1929 *(Arthur) Christopher Plummer,* Canadian actor; known for his role as Baron von Trapp in *The Sound of Music,* 1965; Tony Award, 1974.

1930 *Robert J. Prosky,* U.S. actor; played Sergerant Stan Jablonski on TV drama *Hill Street Blues.*

1936 *Aga Khan IV (Prince Karim Khan),* Arabic religious leader; descendant of Mohammed; spiritual leader of Ismaili Muslims, 1957–.

1941 *John Davidson,* U.S. singer, actor; known as host of television series, *That's Incredible,* 1980–85.

1948 *Ted Nugent,* U.S. rock singer, disk jockey, hunters' rights activist

1959 *Johnny Whitaker,* U.S. actor; known for his role as Jody on television series, *Family Affair,* 1966–71.

1969 *Sergei Federov,* Russian hockey player.

HISTORICAL EVENTS

1250 *Frederick II* of Germany dies and is succeeded by *Conrad IV.*

1545 *Council of Trent* is opened, during which Roman Catholics deal with doctrinal issues raised by Protestants.

1577 *Sir Francis Drake* embarks on voyage to circumnavigate the globe.

1642 *New Zealand* is discovered by the Dutch navigator *Abel Jansen Tasman.*

1664 *New Haven General Court* holds last meeting as the *Colony of New Haven* becomes part of *Connecticut.*

1769 *Dartmouth College,* the first college to admit American Indians, is founded in Hanover, New Hampshire.

1843 *Basutoland,* a native state under British protection, is established.

1862 *Battle of Fredericksburg* ends in defeat of Union troops by Confederate General *Robert E. Lee (U.S. Civil War).*

1928 George Gershwin's *American in Paris* premieres in New York.

1937 Chinese city of *Nanking* falls to Japanese after heavy fighting (*World War II*).

1951 *Bogotá Charter* creating *Organization of American States* goes into effect.

december

1960 Guatemala, Honduras, Nicaragua, and El Salvador sign a treaty creating a trade organization, the *Central American Common Market (CACM)*.

1974 *Malta* becomes a federal republic, and Governor General Sir *Anthony Malmo* is inaugurated as president.

1981 Martial law is declared in *Poland* in response to increasing demands for independence by *Solidarity Union*.

1983 *Turkut Ozal* becomes prime minister of Turkey after President Kenan Evren grants approval to a cabinet.

1988 Angola, Cuba, and South Africa sign an agreement providing for the withdrawal of Cuban troops from *Angola* and the Independence of *Namibia*.

RELIGIOUS CALENDAR

The Saints

St. Spiridion, Bishop of Tremithus. Also called *Spyridon.* [d. 4th century]

St. Nicasius, Bishop of Rheims, and his Companions, martyrs. [d. c. 451]

St. Venantius Fortunatus, Bishop of Poitiers. [d. c. 605]

St. Hybald, abbot. Also called *Hibald,* or *Higbald.* [d. 7th century]

St. John of the Cross, Doctor of the Church, and co-founder of the Barefooted Carmelite Friars. Feast formerly November 24. [d. 1591] Obligatory Memorial.

The Beatified

Blessed Bartholomew of San Gimignano, priest. Also called *Bartolo.* [d. 1300]

Blessed Conrad of Offida, priest. [d. 1306]

Blessed Bonaventure Buonaccorsi, priest. [d. 1315]

Blessed Nicholas Factor, Friar Minor of the Observance. [d. 1583]

BIRTHDATES

1503 *Nostradamus (Michel de Nostradame),* French astrologer, physician; wrote rhymed astrological predictions [d. July 2, 1566]

1546 *Tycho Brahe,* Danish astronomer; with Johannes Kepler (December 27), made numerous significant discoveries which aided in the development of modern scientific *astronomy.* [d. October 24, 1601]

1739 *Pierre Samuel Du Pont de Nemours,* French economist; exponent of Physiocratic school of thought; member of States-General, 1789–92; emigrated to U.S.; developed a national scheme for education, which was never adopted in U.S., but parts of which were incorporated in French national plan. [d. August 6, 1817]

1775 *Thomas Cochrane, 10th Earl of Dundonald,* British admiral noted for his capture of foreign sailing vessels, 1800–06; member of Parliament, 1806–09; expelled from Navy because of political jealousies; led Chilean navy in fight for freedom from Spain; led Brazilian navy in war for independence, 1819–22; one of first to utilize *screw propeller* on warships; pioneered in use of *steamship* in combat; reinstated in English navy, 1832. [d. October 31, 1860]

1829 *John Mercer Langston,* U.S. public official; the first black elected to public office in the U.S., 1855; Minister to Haiti, 1877–85; President, Virginia Normal and Collegiate Institute, 1885–88; U.S. Congressman, 1888–90. [d. November 15, 1897]

1856 *Louis Marshall,* U.S. lawyer, political leader; known for his pioneer work in securing better conditions for blacks and Jews in the U.S.; led fight for international tolerance; founder and president of *American Jewish Committee;* founder and head of *American Jewish Relief Committee.* [d. September 11, 1929]

1870 *Dirk Jan de Geer,* Dutch statesman; Prime Minister, 1926–29, 1939–40. [d. November 28, 1960]

1893 *John Cowles,* U.S. newspaper publisher; founded a newspaper empire based on education of readers, promotion of tolerance, and provision of unbiased information; adviser to U.S. Presidents Eisenhower, Kennedy, and Johnson. [d. February 25, 1983]

1895 *George VI,* King of Great Britain, 1936–52; acceded upon abdication of his brother, Edward VIII, 1936. [d. February 6, 1952]

Paul Eluard, French poet; a pioneer of *surrealism.* [d. November 18, 1952]

1896 *James Harold Doolittle,* U.S. Army aviator; one of most popular U.S. heroes of World War II; led first bombing raid on Japan, 1942. [d. September 27, 1993]

1897 *Margaret Chase Smith,* U.S. politician, columnist; U.S. Congresswoman, 1940–49; U.S. Senator, 1948–72; first woman to be elected to both houses of Congress. [d. May 29, 1995]

1909 *Edward Lawrie Tatum,* U.S. biochemist; Nobel Prize in physiology or medicine for discovery of role of genes in *heredity* (with G. W. Beadle and J. Lederberg), 1958. [d. November 5, 1975]

1911 *Lindsay Armstrong (Spike) Jones,* U.S. bandleader, musician. [d. May 1, 1964]

1914 *Morey Amsterdam,* U.S. actor, comedian; known for his role as Buddy Sorrell on television series, *The Dick Van Dyke Show,* 1961–66. [d. October 18, 1996]

Karl Carstens, West German statesman; President, West Germany (Federal Republic of Germany), 1979–84. [d. May 30, 1992]

Solomon Spiegelman, U.S. microbiologist; recognized for his extensive research on DNA and RNA. [d. January 21, 1983]

1916 *Priscilla of Boston (Priscilla Kidder),* U.S. fashion designer; known for her bridal gown designs.

1919 *Shirley Jackson,* U.S. short-story writer, novelist. [d. August 8, 1965]

1922 *Nikolai Gennadievich Basov,* Russian physicist; Nobel Prize in physics for research in *quantum electronics* and contributions to development of *maser-laser principle* (with A. Prokhorov and C. H. Townes), 1964.

1932 *Charles Allan (Charlie) Rich,* U.S. musician, singer; known for his song, *Behind Closed Doors,* 1973. [d. July 25, 1995]

1935 *Lee Remick,* U.S. actress; known for her roles in *Days of Wine and Roses,* 1963, and *The Omen,* 1976. [d. July 2, 1991]

1946 *Patty Duke (Anna Marie Duke),* U.S. actress.

Sanjay Gandhi, son of Indira Gandhi, Indian prime minister. [d. June 23, 1980]

Stanley Roger (Stan) Smith, U.S. tennis player.

HISTORICAL EVENTS

1542 *James V* of Scotland dies and is succeeded by *Arran* who is appointed Regent for 6-day-old *Mary, Queen of Scots.*

1788 *Charles III* of Spain dies and is succeeded by *Charles IV.*

1819 *Alabama* is admitted to Union as the 22nd state.

1911 *Roald Amundsen,* Norwegian explorer becomes first to reach the *South Pole.*

1914 Allies launch a general attack along the entire *Western Front* from Nieuport to Verdun (*World War I*).

1918 *President Sidonia da Silva Paes of Portugal* is assassinated.

Women vote for the first time in Great Britain.

1927 New Iraqi-British treaty is signed, recognizing independence of *Iraq* and promising British support for Iraq's admission to the League of Nations in 1932.

1944 *National Velvet,* a film featuring Elizabeth Taylor, premieres in New York.

1946 UN General Assembly votes to accept a gift of $8.5 million from *John D. Rockefeller, Jr.,* to acquire a site on the East River in New York for the *UN Headquarters.*

1951 *San Salvador Charter* creating *Organization of Central American States* becomes effective.

1960 Western European nations and the U.S. and Canada sign agreement for the creation of an *Organization for Economic Cooperation and Development.*

The *United Nations General Assembly* unanimously votes to support the independence of all remaining colonies.

1961 *Tanganyika* is admitted to the UN as the 104th member.

1962 U.S. space probe *Mariner II,* on its 109th day of flight, transmits information about *Venus.*

1964 *Forbes Burnham* is inaugurated as president of British Guiana.

1967 *King Constantine II* of Greece flees to Italy after an abortive attempt to overthrow the military junta in power since earlier that year.

Stanford University biochemists report they have produced a synthetic version of *DNA,* the master chemical of all life.

1978 *The Deer Hunter,* a film starring Robert De Niro and Meryl Streep, premieres in New York.

1981 Israel formally annexes the *Golan Heights,* which had been captured from Syria during the 1967 War.

1984 *Manuel Esquivel* is elected prime minister of Belize.

1989 *Patricio Aylwin* is elected president of Chile, ending the violent era of General *Augusto Pinochet.*

1992 *Viktor Chernomyrdin* is selected as the new Deputy Premier for Russia.

1995 The *Bosnian Peace Treaty* is signed.

DECEMBER
15

HOLIDAYS

Aruba, Netherlands Antilles
Statute Day or Kingdom Day
Commemorates the achievement of autonomy, 1954.

U.S.
Bill of Rights Day
Commemorates the passage of the Bill of Rights, 1791.

RELIGIOUS CALENDAR

The Saints
St. Niō, virgin. [d. 4th century]
St. Valerian and other Martyrs in Africa. [d. 457 and 482]
St. Offa of Essex, king. [d. c. 709]
St. Stephen, Bishop of Surosh. [d. c. 760]
St. Paul of Latros, hermit. [d. 956]
St. Mary di Rosa, virgin, and founder of the Handmaids of Charity of Brescia. Also called *Paula,* or *Pauline.* [d. 1855]

The Beatified
Blessed Mary Margaret d'Youville, founder of the Grey Nuns of Canada. [d. 1771]

BIRTHDATES

37 *Nero Claudius Caesar,* Emperor of Rome, 54–68; last Julio-Claudian emperor. [d. June 9, 68]

1787 *Charles Cowden Clarke,* English critic, bookseller, and lecturer; intimate of Keats, Shelley, Leigh Hunt, and Charles and Mary Lamb; lectured on Shakespeare, 1834–56. [d. March 13, 1877]

1793 *Henry Charles Carey,* U.S. economist; renowned for progressive economic theories that won him recognition in the U.S. and Europe. [d. October 13, 1879]

1802 *János Bolyai,* Romanian mathematician; pioneer in development of *non-Euclidean geometries.* [d. January 27, 1860]

1832 *Alexandre Gustave Eiffel,* French engineer; known chiefly for construction of the *Eiffel Tower,* Paris; also constructed framework of Bartholdi's *Statue of Liberty.* [d. December 27, 1923]

1848 *Edwin Howland Blashfield,* U.S. painter; decorated the central dome of the Library of Congress, Washington, D.C. [d. October 12, 1936]

1852 *Antoine Henri Becquerel,* French physicist; Nobel Prize in physics for discovery of *spontaneous radioactivity* (with M. and P. Curie), 1903. [d. August 25, 1908]

1859 *Ludwik Lazanz Zamenhof,* Polish linguist; developer of *Esperanto,* an artificial language, 1887. [d. April 14, 1917]

1860 *Niels R. Finsen,* Danish physician; Nobel Prize in physiology or medicine for his development of *phototherapy,* the treatment of diseases by light, 1903. [d. September 24, 1904]

1863 *Arthur D(ehon) Little,* U.S. industrial chemist; patented *rayon,* the first successful cellulose fiber. [d. August 1, 1935]

1877 *John Timothy McNichols,* U.S. Roman Catholic archbishop; founder of *National Legion of Decency,* a group established to boycott immoral or obscene films; Archbishop of Cincinnati, 1925–50. [d. April 22, 1950]

1883 *William A. Hinton,* U.S. physician; developed the Hinton test which diagnosed syphilis. [d. August 8, 1959]

1888 *Maxwell Anderson,* U.S. dramatist; famous for verse plays and his drama, *What Price Glory?,* Pulitzer Prize in drama, 1933. [d. February 28, 1959]

1892 *J(ean) Paul Getty,* U.S. oilman; one of the richest men in the world; left a fortune estimated at over $1 billion. [d. June 6, 1976]

1899 *Harold Abrahams,* British track athlete; Gold medal, 1920 Olympic Games; subject of the film, *Chariots of Fire.* [d. January 14, 1978]

1906 *Betty Smith,* U.S. novelist, playwright; author of *A Tree Grows in Brooklyn,* 1948. [d. January 17, 1972]

1913 *Muriel Rukeyser,* U.S. poet; known for her poetry protesting social injustice and reflecting on political and economic issues. [d. February 12, 1980]

1916 *Maurice Hugh Frederick Wilkins,* British molecular biologist; Nobel Prize in physiology or medicine for research into the *molecular structure of DNA* (with J.D. Watson and F.H.C. Crick), 1962.

1922 *Alan Freed,* disk jockey; first to introduce the term *rock-'n'-roll* to the American public. [d. January 20, 1965]

1933 *Tim Conway,* U.S. actor; performed on the TV shows *McHale's Navy* and *The Carol Burnett Show.*

1944 *James Richard Leyland,* U.S. baseball coach; National League Manager of the Year, 1988, 1990; manager of the Florida Marlins, 1997– .

1948 *Patricia S. Cowings,* U.S. psychologist; known for her research on zero-gravity sickness syndrome.

1950 *Don Johnson,* U.S. actor; known for his role as Sonny Crockett on television series *Miami Vice* and *Nash Bridges.*

1963 *Helen Slater,* U.S. actress.

HISTORICAL EVENTS

1791 *Bill of Rights,* the first ten amendments to U.S. Constitution, are passed.

1794 *Revolutionary Tribunal* is abolished in France (*French Revolution*).

1821 U.S. government representatives negotiate the purchase of a strip of land on the West African coast for the establishment of a colony of freed slaves, naming it *Monrovia.*

1914 *Battle of Lódź* ends with Russians falling back toward Warsaw (*World War I*).

1917 *Moldavian Republic* declares its independence from Russia.

1941 *U.S.S. Swordfish* becomes first U.S. submarine to sink a Japanese ship in *World War II.*

1944 *Glenn Miller,* orchestra leader and director of the U.S. Air Force Band, is presumed dead when his plane is lost on a flight from England to France. *(World War II).*

1951 *British Foreign Exchange Market* opens for first time since the end of World War II.

1955 Otto Preminger's film, *The Man With the Golden Arm,* premieres in New York.

1961 *Adolf Eichmann* is convicted by an Israeli court in Jerusalem of war crimes committed during World War II.

1964 *Canada* adopts a national flag with a red maple leaf on a white background with vertical red bars at each end.

1965 U.S. spacecraft *Gemini 6* is launched and effects a rendezvous with *Gemini 7.*

1970 *Venera 7,* Soviet unmanned spacecraft, lands on *Venus.*

1973 *J. Paul Getty III,* grandson of U.S. oil magnate J. Paul Getty, is found in southern Italy more than five months after his disappearance, following payment of a reported $2.8 million ransom.

1981 Peruvian diplomat, *Javier Perez de Cuellar,* is elected to succeed *Kurt Waldheim* as United Nations Secretary-General.

1986 *Chemical New York Corp.* agrees to buy *Texas Commerce Bancshares* for $1.1 billion.

Arthur Robinson replaces *George Chambers* as prime minister of Trinidad and Tobago.

1995 Leaders of the *European Union* announce a new common currency called euro, which will be effective in the year 1999.

A nuclear-free zone is created by the *Association of Southeast Asian Nations (ASEAN),* which covers Vietnam to Indonesia.

North Korea signs a *nuclear accord* with South Korea, Japan, and the United States. The accord stipulates that North Korea's nuclear reactors be replaced with reactors that produce less plutonium.

DECEMBER
16

HOLIDAYS

Bahrain
National Day of Bahrain

Bangladesh
Victory Day or National Day
Commemorates the end of conflict with Pakistan, 1971.

Namibia, South Africa
Day of the Vow or Day of the Covenant

Nepal
Constitution Day
Commemorates the adoption of Nepal's Constitution, 1962.

RELIGIOUS CALENDAR

The Saints
St. Adelaide, widow. Also called *Alice.* [d. 999]

The Beatified
Blessed Ado, first archbishop of Vienne. [d. 875]
Blessed Sebastian of Brescia, preacher. [d. 1496]
Blessed Mary of Turin, virgin, prioress, and mystic. [d. 1717]

BIRTHDATES

1485 *Catherine of Aragon,* 1st wife of *King Henry VIII* of England and mother of *Queen Mary* of England. [d. January 7, 1536]

1742 *Gebhard Liberecht Blücher von Wahlstatt,* Prussian field marshal; known for his role in aiding Wellington in defeat of Napoleon at *Waterloo.* [d. September 12, 1819]

1770 *Ludwig van Beethoven,* German composer; known as one of the foremost musical geniuses of all time. [d. March 26, 1827]

1775 *Jane Austen,* English novelist; noted for her novels of the manners of provincial English men and women, such as *Pride and Prejudice.* [d. July 18, 1817]

1776 *Johann Wilhelm Ritter,* German physicist; discoverer of ultraviolet rays; conducted numerous experiments in electricity that led to various discoveries, as electroplating. [d. 1810]

1790 *Leopold I,* first King of the Belgians; elected king by a national congress in 1831. [d. December 10, 1865]

1792 *Abbott Lawrence,* U.S. manufacturer, government official; U.S. Congressman, 1835–40; U.S. Minister to Great Britain, 1849–52; town of Lawrence, Massachusetts is named for him. [d. August 18, 1855]

1857 *Edward Emerson Barnard,* U.S. astronomer; famed for his photographic surveys of the *Milky Way.* [d. February 6, 1923]

1859 *Francis Thompson,* British poet; known for his poetry on religious themes, especially *The Hound of Heaven.* [d. November 13, 1907]

1863 *George Santayana,* U.S. philosopher, poet, novelist, born in Spain; significant contributions to aesthetics, speculative philosophy, and literary criticism. Wrote *The Life of Reason, Scepticism and Animal Faith,* and other philosophical works. [d. September 26, 1952]

Ralph Adams Cram, U.S. architect; noted for his design of Gothic structures, including the *Cathedral of St. John the Divine,* New York City; Professor of Architecture, Massachusetts Institute of Technology, 1914–21; Chairman of Boston City Planning Board, 1915–22. [d. September 22, 1942]

1882 *Zoltán Kodály,* Hungarian composer, teacher; noted for his collections of classic Hungarian folk tales. [d. March 6, 1967]

1888 *Alexander I,* King of the Serbs, Croats, and Slovenes, 1921–29, and of Yugoslavia, 1929–34; struggled to unite his ethnically divided country. [d. October 9, 1934]

1899 *Sir Noel (Pierce) Coward,* British playwright, actor,

composer, and director. [d. March 26, 1963]

1900 *Sir V(ictor) S(awdon) Pritchett,* British author; wrote *The Spanish Temper,* 1954. [d. March 20, 1997]

1901 *Margaret Mead,* U.S. anthropologist; especially well known for studies of cultural, sexual, and adolescent development in primitive areas and in the U.S. [d. November 15, 1978]

1912 *Robert M(artin) Fouss,* U.S. editor, advertising executive; Editor, *Saturday Evening Post,* 1942–62. [d. January 27, 1980]

1913 *Buddy Parker,* U.S. football coach. [d. March 22, 1982]

1917 *Arthur Charles Clarke,* British author; best known for his science fiction works, including *2001: A Space Odyssey.*

1928 *Bruce N. Ames,* U.S. biochemist; developed the Ames test which identifies cancer-causing chemicals.

1939 *Liv Ullmann,* Norwegian actress.

1941 *Lesley Rene Stahl,* U.S. broadcast journalist; correspondent for the TV news show *60 Minutes,* 1991–.

1943 *Steven Bochco,* U.S. writer, producer; known for the creation of television series,

Hill Street Blues, L.A. Law, and *NYPD Blue.*

1947 *Bernard (Ben) Cross,* British actor; known for his role as Olympic runner Harold Abrahams in *Chariots of Fire,* 1981.

1950 *Ieremia Tabai,* President, Republic of Kiribati, 1979–82, 1983–1991.

1962 *William (The Refrigerator) Perry,* U.S. football player.

1966 *Alberto Tomba,* Italian skier; Olympic gold medalist, 1988, 1992, 1994.

HISTORICAL EVENTS

1653 In England, the *Protectorate* is established with *Oliver Cromwell* as Lord Protector.

1773 A group of American patriots dressed as Indians dumps British tea overboard in Boston Harbor, protesting taxes levied by the British government; the event is referred to as the *Boston Tea Party.*

1815 *Brazil* becomes seat of the empire under *John, Prince Regent of Portugal.*

1835 Great fire in *New York City* destroys $20 million worth of property and levels 674 buildings.

1838 Boers under *Andries Pretorius* defeat the Zulus under Dingaan at *Blood River, Natal.*

1856 *South African Republic (Transvaal)* is established with Pretoria as its capital.

1864 *Battle of Nashville* ends as Confederate army commanded by General John B. Hood is almost destroyed by Union troops under General George Thomas (*U.S. Civil War*).

1944 *Battle of the Bulge,* the major German offensive in the Ardennes, begins (*World War II*).

1962 *Nepal* promulgates its constitution.

1963 *Zanzibar* and *Kenya* are admitted as the 112th and 113th members of the UN.

1966 *Dick Tiger* defeats *Jose Torres* to win the world light heavyweight boxing title.

1968 Spanish government declares void a 1492 decree expelling Jews from Spain.

1971 *Bangladesh* comes into existence, being formed from the old state of *Bengal.*

1987 Former U.S. presidential aide, *Michael Deaver,* is found guilty of perjury for giving false testimony concerning his use of political influence for personal gain.

In the largest *Mafia trial* to date, 338 Sicilians are convicted of drug trafficking and other crimes.

DECEMBER
17

HOLIDAYS

Bhutan
National Day

U.S.
Wright Brothers Day
Commemorates the first flight of the Wright Brothers at Kitty Hawk, North Carolina, 1903.

Venezuela
Bolívar Day
Commemorates the death of Simon Bolívar, 1830.

RELIGIOUS CALENDAR

The Saints
St. Lazarus, Bishop at Kition. Raised from the dead by Jesus. [d. 1st century]
St. Olympias, widow. [d. c. 408]
St. Begga, widow and abbess; patroness of the Béguines of Belgium. [d. 693]
St. Sturmi, abbot and apostle of the Saxons. First German known to have become a Benedictine monk. Also called *Sturm.* [d. 779]
St. Wivina, virgin and abbess. [d. c. 1170]

BIRTHDATES

1571 *Johannes Kepler,* German astronomer; developed Kepler's Laws of planetary motion. [d. November 15, 1630]

1758 *Nathaniel Macon,* U.S. legislator; U.S. Congressman, 1791–1815; U.S. Senator, 1815–19. [d. June 29, 1837]

1778 *Sir Humphrey Davy,* English chemist; first to isolate *potassium, sodium, calcium;* discovered that chlorine is an element; discovered that a diamond is carbon; identified role of hydrogen in acids; developed miners' safety lamp known as the *Davy lamp.* [d. May 29, 1829]

1787 *Jan Evangelista Purkinje,* Czech physiologist; renowned for basic discoveries in physiology and microscopic anatomy; named for him are the *Purkinje cells* in the brain and *Purkinje tissue* in the heart. [d. July 18, 1869]

1797 *Joseph Henry,* U.S. physicist; pioneer in development of *electromagnetism;* did extensive research in coil behavior; developed early versions of the telegraph and the electric motor; first secretary and director of the Smithsonian Institution, 1846; developed method of tracking and recording weather which led to establishment of *U.S. Weather Bureau.* [d. May 13, 1878]

1807 *John Greenleaf Whittier,* U.S. poet, social reformer. [d. September 7, 1892]

1853 *Sir Herbert (Draper) Beerbohm Tree,* British actor, producer, playwright; noted for his Shakespearean roles; half-brother of Sir Max Beerbohm (August 24). [d. July 2, 1917]

1860 *James Herbert McGraw,* U.S. publisher; a founder of McGraw-Hill Publishing Co., 1916. [d. February 21, 1948]

1861 *Arthur Edwin Kennelly,* U.S. electrical engineer, born in India; assistant to Thomas A. Edison, 1887–94; discovered, in conjunction with Oliver Heaviside, the *Kennelly-Heaviside Layer* in the upper atmosphere. [d. June 18, 1939]

1873 *Ford Madox Ford (Ford Madox Heuffer,)* British novelist, editor, critic. [d. July 26, 1939]

1874 *William Lyon Mackenzie King,* Canadian statesman; Prime Minister, 1921–26; 1926–30; 1935–48. [d. July 22, 1950]

1894 *Arthur Fiedler,* U.S. conductor; conducted the *Boston Pops Orchestra,* 1930–79. [d. July 10, 1979]

1903 *Erskine (Breston) Caldwell,* U.S. novelist; known especially for his novels of the rural south, including *God's Little Acre,* 1933. [d. April 11, 1987]

1908 *Willard Frank Libby,* U.S. chemist; Nobel Prize in chemistry for development of a technique of radioactive carbon dating that determines geological age by measuring *carbon 14* in organic objects, 1960. [d. September 8, 1980]

1927 *Richard Long,* U.S. actor; known for his starring roles on television series, *Big Valley,* 1965–69, and *Nanny and the Professor,* 1970–71. [d. December 22, 1974]

1929 *William L. Safire,* U.S. author, journalist.

1930 *Bob Guccione (Robert Charles Joseph Edward Sabatini),* U.S. publisher; founder of magazines, *Penthouse,* 1965, *Omni,* 1978, and *Spin,* 1985.

1938 *Peter Snell,* New Zealand distance runner; Olympic gold medalist, 1960, 1964.

HISTORICAL EVENTS

1819 *Republic of Colombia* is established with *Simon Bolívar* as president.

1903 *Wright Brothers* at *Kitty Hawk, North Carolina* make first successful flight of self-powered heavier-than-air craft, lasting 12 seconds.

1917 The confiscation of the property of the Russian church and abolition of religious instruction in schools is announced by the Bolshevik government.

1933 First *National Football League* championship game is played at Wrigley Field, Chicago, between the New York Giants and the Chicago Bears; the Bears win 23–21.

1943 The United States repeals the *Chinese Exclusion Acts.*

1944 German troops execute 71 U.S. prisoners of war near *Malmedy, Belgium (World War II).*

1962 *Monaco* promulgates restoration of the National Council and a new constitution.

1968 Sir *Georg Solh* is named musical director of the Chicago Symphony.

1973 Arab guerrillas kill 31 persons at Rome airport and hijack a West German airliner to Athens where they demand the release of Palestinian terrorists being held there.

1978 *Rwanda* promulgates a new constitution.

1981 U.S. army officer, *James Dozier,* is abducted by *Red Brigade* gunmen in Verona, Italy.

1983 A car bomb explodes outside *Harrods* department store in London, killing 5 and injuring 91. The *Irish Republican Army (IRA)* later acknowledged responsibility.

1985 Doctors at Flinders Medical Centre in Adelaide, Australia announce the first successful use of a frozen egg for *in-vitro fertilization.*

1995 *René Préval* is elected president of Haiti after Jean-Bertrand Aristide announces that he will not seek another term.

HOLIDAYS

Niger

National Day
Celebrates the establishment of the constitutional government and achievement of independence from France, 1960.

RELIGIOUS CALENDAR

The Saints

SS. Rufus and Zosimus, martyrs. Zosimus also called *Zozimus.* [d. c. 107]

St. Gatian, Bishop of Tours. [d. c. 301]

St. Flannan, first bishop of Killaloe. [d. c. 7th century]

St. Samthann, nun. [d. 739]

St. Winebald, abbot. Also called *Wynbald.* [d. 761]

St. Mawnan. Also called *Maunanus.* [death date unknown]

BIRTHDATES

1709 *Elizabeth,* Empress of Russia, 1741–61; daughter of *Peter the Great.* [d. January 5, 1762]

1819 *Isaac Thomas Hecker,* U.S. Roman Catholic priest; founder of Congregation of the Missionary Priests of St. Paul the Apostle (*Paulist Fathers*). [d. December 22, 1888]

1835 *Lyman Abbott,* U.S. clergyman, author; editor of *The Outlook.* [d. October 22, 1922]

1856 *Sir Joseph John Thomson,* British physicist; Nobel Prize in physics for investigations into *conductivity of gases,* 1906. [d. August 30, 1940]

1861 *Edward Alexander MacDowell,* U.S. composer, pianist, teacher; the *Edward MacDowell Medal* is presented annually to recognize individual contributions in the arts. [d. January 3, 1908]

1863 *Francis Ferdinand,* Archduke of Austria; heir to the Austrian throne whose assassination was the immediate cause of *World War I.* [d. July 28, 1914]

1870 *H(ector) H(ugh) Munro (Saki),* British short-story writer, journalist, born in Burma. [d. November 14, 1916]

1879 *Paul Klee,* Swiss painter, etcher; Surrealist artist known for his works showing strong African influence. [d. June 29, 1940]

1886 *Ty(rus Raymond) Cobb,* U.S. baseball player; inducted into Baseball Hall of Fame, 1936. [d. July 17, 1961]

Chu Teh, Chinese military leader; commander in chief of Chinese Communist Army; led his army to victory over Nationalist Chinese forces, 1949. [d. July 6, 1976]

1888 *Robert Moses,* U.S. public official; known as the master builder of New York City. [d. July 29, 1981]

1890 *Edwin Howard Armstrong,* U.S. engineer, inventor; invented the *regenerative circuit,* which revolutionized the field of radio; developed system of frequency modulation (FM) radio transmission; also responsible for development of *multiplexing system* that allowed more than one FM transmission on the same frequency. [d. February 1, 1954]

1904 *George Stevens,* U.S. film director. [d. March 8, 1975]

1907 *Christopher Fry,* British dramatist.

1912 *Benjamin Oliver Davis, Jr.,* U.S. Air Force general; first black graduate of West Point, 1936; first black general in the Air Force.

1913 *Betty Grable,* U.S. actress. [d. July 2, 1973]

Willy Brandt (Karl Herbert Frahn), German politician; Chancellor of Federal Republic of Germany, 1969–74; Nobel Peace Prize, 1971. [d. October 8, 1992]

1916 *Douglas Andrew Fraser,* Scottish-born labor union official; President, United Auto Workers, 1977–83.

1917 *Ossie Davis,* U.S. actor, dramatist; wrote, directed, and starred in *Purlie Victoria,* 1961.

1923 *Arturo Cruz (Arturo Jose Cruz Porras),* Nicaraguan politician; Ambassador to U.S., 1981– .

1927 *(William) Ramsey Clark,* U.S. lawyer, government official; U.S. Attorney General, 1967–69.

Peter W. Stroh, U.S. brewer; Chairman, Stroh Brewery, 1982–.

1929 *Jozef Glemp,* Polish Roman Catholic cardinal; head of Polish Catholic Church, 1981–; Cardinal, 1983–.

1932 *Roger Smith,* U.S. actor; husband and manager of Ann-Margret.

1939 *Harold E. Varmus,* U.S. virologist; Nobel Prize for Medicine in 1989, with J. Michael Bishop for their cancer research.

1943 *Keith Richards,* British musician, singer; member of the rock group, *The Rolling Stones.*

1946 *Steven Biko,* South African political activist. [d. September 12, 1977]

1947 *Steven Spielberg,* U.S. director; known for his direction of *Jaws, ET, The Color Purple, Jurassic Park,* and *Saving Private Ryan*; Academy Award for *Schindler's List,* 1993.

1950 *Janie Frickie,* U.S. singer, musician; known for song,

Down to My Last Broken Heart, 1980.

Leonard Maltin, U.S. movie critic.

1955 *Ray Liotta,* U.S. actor; known for roles in *Something Wild,* 1986 and *GoodFellas,* 1990.

1963 *Brad Pitt,* U.S. actor.

1966 *Kiefer Sutherland,* U.S. actor.

1971 *Arantxa Sanchez-Vicario,* Spanish tennis player.

HISTORICAL EVENTS

1398 *Timur Lenk (Tamerlane),* ruler of Mongols, conquers *Delhi.*

1437 *Albert V* of Austria becomes King of Hungary.

1787 *New Jersey* becomes the third state to ratify the U.S. Constitution.

1865 *13th Amendment* to U.S. Constitution, prohibiting slavery, is ratified.

1914 British declare a protectorate over *Egypt* and begin to provide for its defense (*World War I*).

1916 *Battle of Verdun,* a German offensive and the longest battle of *World War I,* ends with little gain for the Germans and combined casualties of about 750,000.

1933 The government of *Newfoundland* collapses; Great Britain establishes a commission to govern.

1940 *Hitler* orders full military preparations for German invasion of Russia (*World War II*).

1957 *The Bridge on the River Kwai,* a film starring Alec

Guiness, premieres in New York.

1964 Organization of American States Council approves the *Act of Washington,* establishing procedures for admission of new members.

1965 *Japan* and *South Korea* establish formal diplomatic relations.

1968 *Intelsat 3A,* first in a series of communications satellites, is launched from Cape Kennedy, Florida.

1969 *Capital punishment* is abolished in the *United Kingdom.*

Kuwait and *Saudi Arabia* sign an agreement formally establishing new international boundaries.

1971 The United States passes the *Alaska Native Claims Act.*

1971 *Jesse Jackson* announces the formation of *People United to Save Humanity (PUSH),* a Chicago-based black political and economic rights organization.

1986 *Nguyen Van Linh* is named secretary general of the Vietnamese Communist Party.

1987 U.S. securities speculator, *Ivan Boesky,* is sentenced to five years in prison for filing false stock trading records with the Securities and Exchange Commission.

1990 *Jean-Bertrand Aristide* is elected president of Haiti in that country's first free election in 33 years.

1992 *Kim Young Sam* is elected president of South Korea.

1995 U.S. troops land in *Bosnia and Herzegovina* to ensure the peace accord agreed to earlier in the year (November 21, 1995).

HOLIDAYS

Anguilla
Separation Day

RELIGIOUS CALENDAR

The Saints
SS. Nemesius and other Martyrs. [d. 250]
St. Anastasius I, pope. Elected 399. [d. 401]

The Beatified
Blessed William of Fenoli, Carthusian lay brother. [d. 1205]
Blessed Urban V, pope. Elected c. 1361. [d. 1370]

BIRTHDATES

1683 *Philip V,* King of Spain, 1700–1746; first of the *Spanish Bourbon dynasty.* [d. July 9, 1746]

1790 *Sir William Edward Parry,* British naval officer; famous for his discovery of an entrance to the *Northwest Passage* in the Arctic as well as for development of *polar survival techniques.* [d. July 8, 1855]

1814 *Edwin McMasters Stanton,* U.S. statesman; U.S. Secretary of War, 1862–68. [d. December 24, 1869]

1820 *Mary Ashton Livermore,* U.S. social reformer; noted for her ardent advocacy of suffrage for women and temperance; editor of *The Agitator,* a suffragist paper, 1869–72; editor of *Woman's Journal,* 1872–82. [d. May 23, 1905]

1849 *Henry Clay Frick,* U.S. industrialist; Chairman, Carnegie Steel Co., 1889–1900; leader in negotiations that resulted in formation of United States Steel Corporation; his art collection and home donated to New York City as the *Frick Museum.* [d. December 2, 1919]

1852 *Albert Abraham Michelson,* U.S. physicist; received first U.S. Nobel Prize in physics for development of *spectroscopic and meteorological measuring equpment,* 1907. [d. May 9, 1931]

1865 *Minnie Madern Fiske,* U.S. actress; noted for her brilliant performances on the New York stage; managed the Manhattan Theater, 1901–07. [d. February 15, 1932]

1875 *Carter Godwin Woodson,* U.S. educator, historian, publisher; known as the *Father of Negro History in the U.S.* [d. April 3, 1950]

1888 *Fritz Reiner,* U.S. conductor, born in Hungary; conductor of Metropolitan Opera, 1948–53; noted for his interpretations of Wagner and Strauss. [d. November 15, 1963]

1894 *Ford Frick,* U.S. baseball executive; professional baseball commissioner, 1951–65. [d. April 8, 1978]

1899 *Martin Luther (Daddy) King, Sr.,* U.S. clergyman; pastor of Ebenezer Baptist Church, Atlanta, Georgia, who preached nonviolence; father of Martin Luther King, Jr. [d. November 11, 1984]

1901 *Oliver Lafarge,* U.S. novelist, anthropologist; Pulitzer Prize in fiction, 1930. [d. August 2, 1963]

1902 *Sir Ralph David Richardson,* British actor; noted for his Shakespearean roles; his career spanned over 50 years in the theater, as well as in films. [d. October 10, 1983]

1903 *George Snell,* U.S. geneticist; Nobel Prize in physiology or medicine for his work dealing with the relationship between heredity and transplants, 1980. [d. June 6, 1996]

1906 *Leonid I. Brezhnev,* Soviet leader; Chairman of Presidium of Supreme Soviet of U.S.S.R., 1960–64, 1977–82. [d. November 12, 1982]

1910 *Jean Genet,* French dramatist, essayist, existentialist; a founder of the *theater of the absurd.* [d. April 13, 1986]

1915 *Edith Piaf (Edith Giovanna Gassion),* French singer; renowned as a song stylist. [d. October 11, 1963]

1920 *David (Howard) Susskind,* U.S. producer, television host.

1924 *William Chapoton, Jr.,* U.S. financier; partner in William C. Roney and Co., 1949–84. [d. April 26, 1984]

Doug Harvey, Canadian hockey player.

1929 *Howard Sackler,* U.S. playwright; Pulitzer Prize in drama, 1969. [d. October 13, 1982]

1934 *Albert William (Al) Kaline,* U.S. baseball player, sportscaster; elected to Hall of Fame, 1980.

1939 *Cicely Tyson,* U.S. actress; co-founder of the *Dance Theatre of Harlem.*

1940 *Philip David (Phil) Ochs,* U.S. singer, political activist. [d. April 9, 1976]

1943 *William Castle DeVries,* U.S. surgeon; implanted artificial heart in Barney Clark, 1982, and William Schroeder, 1984.

1944 *Richard E(rskine) F. Leakey,* British paleontologist, born in Nairobi, Kenya; with his parents, Louis S. B. Leakey (August 7) and Mary Leakey (February 6), made significant discoveries regarding the origins of man; Director of National Museum of Kenya.

Tim Reid, U.S. actor; known for his roles on the television series, *WKRP in Cincinnati, Simon and Simon,* and *Frank's Place.*

1945 *Elaine Joyce (Elaine Joyce Pinchot),* U.S. actress, dancer.

Robert Urich, U.S. actor; known for his starring roles on television series, *Vega$,* 1978–80, and *Spencer for Hire,* 1985–88.

1960 *Daryl Hannah,* U.S. actress.

1961 *Reggie White,* U.S. football player.

1963 *Jennifer Beals,* U.S. actress; known for her starring roles in *Flashdance* and *The Bride.*

1972 *Alyssa Milano,* U.S. actress; known for her role as Samantha Micelli on television series, *Who's the Boss,* 1984–92.

HISTORICAL EVENTS

1777 American Continental Army establishes camp at *Valley Forge,* Pennsylvania.

1915 *Sir Douglas Haig* replaces *Sir John French* as supreme commander of the British Army in France (*World War I*).

1917 The *National Hockey League* begins its first professional season with four teams.

1946 Vietnamese independence forces in *Hanoi* attack the French garrison, beginning an eight-year war for independence from France which ends with defeat of the French in 1954.

1957 Meredith Willson's musical, *The Music Man,* premieres in New York.

1961 New transatlantic submarine cable between Britain and Canada (first link in a proposed around-the-world Commonwealth system) is inaugurated by a telephone conversation between Queen Elizabeth II and Prime Minister Diefenbaker of Canada.

1962 *Nyasaland* secedes from the *Central African Federation.*

1974 *Catfish Hunter* becomes the first free agent in major league professional baseball history.

1975 *John Paul Stevens* is named to the U.S. Supreme Court, taking the seat of retired justice *William O. Douglas.*

1976 Women are awarded *Rhodes Scholarships* for the first time.

1984 Great Britain signs an accord with the People's Republic of China providing for the return of *Hong Kong* to Chinese control after 1997.

The U.S. announces that it is withdrawing from the *United Nations Educational, Scientific, and Cultural Organization (UNESCO)* due to the group's alleged mishandling of funds and anti-Western bias.

1986 A panel of federal judges select *Lawrence Walsh* as the independent counsel to investigate the *Iran-contra affair.*

Soviet dissident, *Andrei Sakharov,* is released from internal exile in the city of *Gorky.*

1988 Former U.S. representative *Jack Kemp* is named the new Secretary of Housing and Urban Development (HUD) by president-elect George Bush.

U.S. forces invade Panama. *General Manuel Noriega* uses the Vatican's mission to gain asylum. (January 3, 1990)

RELIGIOUS CALENDAR

The Saints

SS. Ammon and his Companions, martyrs. [d. 250]

St. Philogonius, Bishop of Antioch. [d. 324]

St. Ursicinus, abbot. Also called Ursinus. [d. c. 625]

St. Dominic of Silos, abbot. [d. 1073]

BIRTHDATES

1743 *James Rumsey,* U.S. inventor; ran first steamboat on the Potomac. [d. December 20, 1792]

1805 *Thomas Graham,* Scottish chemist; discovered *dialysis process;* known for his research in *colloids.* [d. September 16, 1869]

1813 *Samuel Jordan Kirkwood,* U.S. politician; U.S. Senator, 1866–67; 1877–81; U.S. Secretary of the Interior, 1881–82. [d. September 1, 1894]

1833 *Samuel Alexander Mudd,* U.S. physician; treated broken leg of John Wilkes Booth following the assassination of President Lincoln; convicted as a conspirator in the assassination plot but maintained his innocence. [d. January 10, 1883]

1841 *Ferdinand Edouard Buisson,* French educator; Nobel Peace Prize for his work with the *League of Human Rights* and efforts for Franco-German friendship after World War I (with Ludwig Quidde), 1927. [d. February 16, 1932]

1849 *Harry Pratt Judson,* U.S. educator; President of Chicago University, 1907–23. [d. March 4, 1927]

1851 *Theodore Elijah Burton,* U.S. lawyer, legislator; U.S. Senator, 1909–15. [d. October 28, 1929]

1853 *Husayn Kamil,* Sultan of Egypt, 1914–17. [d. October 9, 1917]

1856 *Baron Shibasaburo Kitazato,* Japanese bacteriologist; responsible for isolation of bacilli for *tetanus, anthrax, dysentery,* and *bubonic plague.* [d. June 13, 1931]

1865 *Maude Gonne,* Irish patriot; impassioned advocate of Irish freedom; subject of various literary works by William Butler Yeats (June 13). [d. April 27, 1953]

1868 *Harvey Samuel Firestone,* U.S. tire manufacturer; founder of Firestone Tire & Rubber Co., 1900. [d. February 7, 1938]

1871 *Henry Kimball Hadley,* U.S. orchestral composer, conductor; Conductor, San Francisco Orchestra, 1911–15; Conductor, Manhattan Symphony, 1929–37. [d. September 6, 1937]

1876 *Walter Sidney Adams,* U.S. astronomer, born in Turkey; ascertained velocities and distances of thousands of stars by spectroscopic analysis; contributed to planning of *Mt. Palomar Observatory* in California. [d. May 11, 1956]

1881 *Branch (Wesley) Rickey,* U.S. baseball executive. [d. December 9, 1965]

1890 *Jaroslav Heyrovsky,* Czech chemist; Nobel Prize in chemistry for discovery and development of *polarography,* 1959. [d. March 27, 1967]

1893 *Richard Paul Carlton,* U.S. manufacturer; President, Minnesota Mining and Manufacturing Co. 1949–53. [d. June 17, 1953]

1894 *Robert Gordon Menzies,* Prime Minister of Australia, 1939–41; responsible for industrial growth of Australia after World War II. [d. May 14, 1978]

1899 *John J. Sparkman,* U.S. politician, lawyer; Congressman, 1937–46; Senator, 1946–79. [d. November 16, 1985]

Finn Ronne, U.S. arctic explorer, engineer; member

of nine expeditions to Antarctica; member of Admiral Richard Byrd's expedition, 1933. Author of several books dealing with his explorations. [d. January 2, 1980]

1902 *Max Lerner,* U.S. journalist. [d. June 5, 1992]

1904 *Irene Dunne,* U.S. actress. [d. September 4, 1990]

1914 *Harry (Flood) Byrd,* U.S. politician; U.S. Senator, 1965–81.

1922 *George Roy Hill,* U.S. director; Academy Award for *The Sting,* 1973.

1935 *William Julius Wilson,* U.S. educator, writer, sociologist; author of *The Declining Significance of Race, The Truly Disadvantaged,* and *When Work Disappears.*

1946 *Andrei Codrescu,* Romanian-born writer.

Uri Geller, Israeli psychic; known for his ability to bend metal and start and stop watches.

1952 *Jenny Agutter,* British actress; known for her starring roles in *Walkabout* and *Logan's Run.*

1956 *Blanche Baker,* U.S. actress; Emmy Award for her role on television movie, *Holocaust,* 1978.

HISTORICAL EVENTS

1046 Holy Roman Emperor *Henry III* deposes both antipope *Silvester II* and *Pope Gregory VI.*

1803 U.S. takes formal possession of the *Louisiana Territory.*

1848 *Prince Louis Napoleon (Napoleon III)* takes oath as President of the French Republic.

1852 *Pegu (Lower Burma)* is annexed to the Indian Empire.

1860 *South Carolina* secedes from the Union (*U.S. Civil War*).

1914 *First Battle of Champagne* opens with a French attack on the Western Front between Verdun and Reims (*World War I*).

1917 *Lenin* creates the *Revolutionary Tribunal (Cheka)* for suppression of counter-revolutionary activity, marking the beginning of the *red terror.*

1928 *Nanking* government of China is recognized by the British.

1946 *(Sugar) Ray Robinson* defeats *Tommy Bell* to win the world welterweight boxing title.

1968 U.S. government lifts its ban on cultural exchanges with the U.S.S.R.

1971 *Zulfikar Ali Bhutto* is inaugurated as president of Pakistan.

1973 *Spanish Premier Carrero* is assassinated in Madrid.

1979 *Kim Jae Kyu,* former head of the Korean Central Intelligence Agency, and five of his aides are sentenced to death for the assassination of President *Park Chung Hee* and five of his bodyguards.

1981 *Romauld Spasowski,* the Polish Ambassador to the U.S., is granted political asylum in the U.S.

1982 The *Boland amendment* is passed by the U.S. Congress. It prohibits defense funds from being used to support forces seeking to overthrow the Sandinista government of *Nicaragua.*

1983 Four thousand *Palestine Liberation Organization* troops are evacuated to Tunis under United Nations protection after a six-week siege of their fortifications in Tripoli by Syrian-supported Palestinian rebels.

1987 A Philippine passenger ferry collides with an oil tanker off the coast of Manila. Over 1,600 people are killed, making this the worst *maritime accident* in the twentieth century.

1989 *U.S. troops* invade Panama after *Manuel Noriega* refuses to give up power.

1992 *Slobodan Milosevic* is reelected president of Serbia.

1997 *Janet Jagan* is elected president of Guyana.

HOLIDAYS

Malawi
National Tree Planting Day

São Tomé and Príncipe
Anniversary of the Coming into Power of the Transition Government

U.S.
Forefathers' Day

RELIGIOUS CALENDAR

The Saints

St. Thomas, apostles of the Indies and martyr patron of architects, builders, and divines. Surnamed *Didymus,* or *the Twin.* [d. 1st century] Celebrated by Episcopal and Lutheran churches on this date. Roman Catholic Church celebrates this Memorial on July 3.

St. Anastasius II, Patriarch of Antioch and martyr. [d. 609]

St. Peter Canisius, Jesuit priest, writer, educator, and Doctor of the Church; second Apostle of Germany. Feast formerly April 27. [d. 1597] Optional Memorial.

BIRTHDATES

1118 *Thomas Becket,* British religious leader; Archbishop of Canterbury, 1162–70; murdered in Canterbury Cathedral by knights of Henry II. [d. December 29, 1170]

1401 *Masaccio (Tommaso Guidi),* Italian painter; his works mark the beginning of Renaissance painting in Italy. [d. 1428]

1795 *Leopold von Ranke,* German historian; founder of the modern school of history, utilizing writings based on fact and source material rather than tradition and legend. [d. May 23, 1886]

1804 *Benjamin Disraeli,* Earl of Beaconsfield, British statesman; Prime Minister of England, 1868; 1874–80; responsible for British involvement in *Suez Canal;* one of founders of modern *conservatism* in Great Britain. [d. April 19, 1881]

1823 *Jean Henri Fabre,* French entomologist; noted for his direct observation and study of insects; author of 10-volume *Souvenirs Entomologiques,* 1879–1907. [d. October 11, 1915]

1860 *Henrietta Szold,* U.S. Zionist leader; founder of *Hadassah,* U.S. Women's Zionist organization. [d. February 13, 1945]

1879 *Joseph Stalin (Josif Vissarionovich Dzhugashvili),* Russian political leader; after death of Lenin, established himself as virtual dictator, 1929–53; responsible for establishment of Russia as a world power. [d. March 5, 1953]

1886 *Maria Cadilla de Martinez,* Puerto Rican author, educator, and feminist. [d. 1951]

1890 *Herman Joseph Muller,* U.S. biologist; Nobel Prize in physiology or medicine for discovering use of *x-rays in genetics,* 1946. [d. April 5, 1967]

1891 *John W. McCormack,* U.S. politician, lawyer; Congressman, 1928–71. [d. November 22, 1980]

1892 *Walter Hagen,* U.S. golfer; P.G.A. champion, 1921; 1924–27; British Open Champion, 1922, 1924, 1928–29. [d. October 5, 1969]

1908 *Luigi Giorgio Barzini, Jr.,* Italian author; wrote *Americans Are Alone in the World* and *The Italians.* [d. March 30, 1984]

1909 *George Ball,* U.S. lawyer, diplomat; UN Ambassador, 1968–69. [d. May 26, 1994]

1917 *Heinrich Boll,* German novelist, short-story writer; Nobel Prize in literature, 1972. [d. July 16, 1985]

1918 *Donald Thomas Regan,* U.S. government official; Secretary of Treasury, 1981–86; White House Chief of Staff, 1986–87.

Kurt Waldheim, Austrian statesman; Secretary-General, United Nations, 1972–81; elected President of Austria in spite of allegations of Nazi involvement, 1986–92.

1921 *Alicia Alonso,* Cuban prima ballerina.

1926 *Joe Paterno,* U.S. football coach; head coach at Pennsylvania State University, 1966– .

1935 *Philip John (Phil) Donahue,* U.S. television personality; host of talk show, *Donahue,* 1967–96; Emmy Awards, 1977, 1979.

Edward Richard Schreyer, Canadian politician; Governor-General of Canada, 1979–84; youngest person to hold that position.

1937 *Jane Fonda,* U.S. actress, social activist; daughter of Henry Fonda (May 16).

1940 *Francis Vincent (Frank) Zappa, Jr.,* U.S. musician, singer; member of the rock group, *The Mothers of Invention.* [d. December 4, 1993]

1944 *Michael Tilson Thomas,* U.S. conductor. [d. December 4, 1993]

1946 *Carl Dean Wilson,* U.S. singer; member of the rock group, *The Beach Boys.* [d. February 6, 1998]

1948 *Samuel L. Jackson,* U.S. actor; known for roles in *Menace II Society* and *Pulp Fiction.*

1954 *Chris Evert,* U.S. tennis player.

1959 *Florence (Flo-Jo) Griffith Joyner,* U.S. track athlete; won three Gold Medals and one Silver Medal in the 1988 Olympics. [d. September 21, 1998]

1960 *Andrew (Andy) Van Slyke,* U.S. baseball player.

1975 *Paloma Herrera,* Argentine ballerina.

HISTORICAL EVENTS

1192 *Richard I* of England, having returned from Palestine on the *Third Crusade,* is captured by *Leopold,* Duke of Austria.

1620 *Mayflower* lands at Plymouth Rock, after completing its 3-month voyage from England to the New World.

1864 *General William Sherman* and his Union Army take Savannah, Georgia, concluding Sherman's famous *March to the Sea (U.S. Civil War).*

1902 First *wireless telegraph* message is exchanged between Canada and England.

1913 The first *crossword puzzle* is printed in a New York newspaper.

1914 First air raid on *England* by German planes occurs near *Dover (World War I).*

1923 *Nepal* gains independence from Great Britain.

Dirigible *Dixmude,* largest airship in the world, disappears over Tunis.

1937 Walt Disney's *Snow White and the Seven Dwarfs* premieres. It is the first animated feature-length film with sound and color.

1943 U.S. General *Joe Stilwell* begins campaign against the Japanese in northern Burma *(World War II).*

1951 119 miners are killed in a *coal mine explosion* near West Frankfort, Illinois.

1956 The *Montgomery bus boycott* ends when officials agree to end racial segregation on municipal buses.

1958 *Charles De Gaulle* is named President of the Fifth French Republic.

1968 *Apollo 8,* first manned flight around the moon, with astronauts Frank Borman, William A. Anders, and James A. Lovell Jr. aboard, is launched from Cape Kennedy.

1973 First peace conference between Israel and Arab countries is opened in Geneva.

1975 *Madagascar* promulgates a constitution.

1976 Liberian-registered tanker *Argo Merchant* spills 7.5 million gallons of crude oil into the North Atlantic.

Patricia Roberts Harris is named Secretary of Housing and Urban Development, becoming the first U.S. black woman to fill a cabinet position.

1978 *Fred De Gazon* is elected the first president of Dominica.

1979 The U.S. Congress approves a $1.5 billion loan to the financially troubled *Chrysler Corp.*

1987 *British Airways* wins a takeover bid for *British Caledonian Airways.* The merger creates one of the largest airlines in the world.

1988 Pan Am Flight 103 explodes over *Lockerbie, Scotland,* killing all 259 people on board. Eleven people on the ground are also killed.

1991 The *Soviet Union* no longer exists when the leaders of the eleven remaining republics create the *Commonwealth of Independent States.*

1997 *Milan Milutinovic* is elected president of Serbia.

DECEMBER
22

HOLIDAYS

Japan
Toji or Winter Solstice
Marks the beginning of the solar new year.

RELIGIOUS CALENDAR

The Saints
SS. Chaeremon, Ischyrion and other Martyrs. [d. 250]

The Beatified
Blessed Jutta of Diessenberg, virgin and recluse. [d. 1136]
Blessed Adam of Loccum, priest. [d. c. 1210]

BIRTHDATES

1400 *Luca della Robbia,* Italian sculptor; creator of *della Robbia* reliefs. [d. September 22, 1482]

1639 *Jean Racine,* French dramatist; known for his classical drama; intimate of La Fontaine (July 8) and Molière (January 15). [d. April 21, 1699]

1696 *James Edward Oglethorpe,* English colonist of America; founder of colony of *Georgia.* [d. July 1, 1785]

1755 *Georges Couthon,* French revolutionist; associate of Robespierre (May 6); guillotined with him. [d. July 28, 1794]

1768 *John Crome (Old Crome),* English landscape painter; founder of *Norwich school of painting.* [d. April 22, 1821]

1807 *Johan Sebastian Welhaven,* Norwegian poet, critic; champion of conservatism in literature. [d. October 21, 1873]

1823 *Thomas Wentworth Storrow Higginson,* U.S. writer; advocate of woman's suffrage; a confidant of Emily Dickinson. [d. May 9, 1911]

1842 *Joseph Bernard Bloomingdale,* U.S. merchant; a founder of Bloomingdale's department store, 1872. [d. November 21, 1904]

1857 *Frank Billings Kellogg,* U.S. politician, diplomat, lawyer; author of the *Kellogg-Briand Pact;* U.S. Senator, 1917–23; U.S. Ambassador to Great Britain; U.S. Secretary of State, 1925–29; Nobel Peace Prize, 1929. [d. December 21, 1937]

1858 *Giacomo Puccini,* Italian opera composer. [d. November 19, 1924]

1862 *Connie Mack (Cornelius Alexander McGillicuddy),* U.S. baseball manager; won nine pennants with the Philadelphia A's, 1901–50; elected to Hall of Fame, 1937. [d. February 8, 1956]

1869 *Edward Arlington Robinson,* U.S. poet; Pulitzer Prize in poetry, 1925, 1928. [d. April 6, 1935]

1883 *Arthur W. Mitchell,* U.S. politician; U.S. Congressman, 1934–42; first black Democrat elected to Congress. [d. May 1968]

1901 *André Kostelanetz,* U.S. conductor, born in Russia. [d. January 14, 1980]

1903 *Haldan Keffer Hartline,* U.S. physiologist; Nobel Prize in physiology or medicine for discoveries in physiology of the eye (with G. Wald and R.A. Granit), 1967. [d. March 15, 1983]

1905 *Kenneth Rexroth,* U.S. poet, historian, critic; elder statesman of the American *beat generation.* [d. June 6, 1982]

1907 *Dame Peggy Ashcroft (Edith Margaret Emily),* British actress; Academy Award for *A Passage to India,* 1984. [d. June 4, 1991]

1912 *Claudia Alta (Ladybird) Johnson,* U.S. First Lady; wife of Lyndon B. Johnson, 36th President of the U.S.

1917 *Gene Rayburn (Eugene Rubessa),* U.S. television personality; host of television game show, *Match Game.*

1921 *Clifton Canter Garvin, Jr.,* U.S. oil executive; Chairman of the Board and Chief Executive Officer, Exxon Corporation, 1975–.

1922 *James Claud (Jim) Wright, Jr.,* U.S. politician; Congressman, 1955–89; Speaker of the U.S. House of Representatives, 1987–89.

1927 *Peggie Castle,* U.S. actress; known for her roles in *I the Jury,* and *Jesse James' Women.* [d. August 11, 1973]

1935 *Tomás Rivera,* U.S. author and educator. [d. 1984]

1936 *Hector Elizondo,* U.S. actor; known for his role in *American Gigolo,* 1980, and the TV drama *Chicago Hope.*

1944 *Steven Norman (Steve) Carlton,* U.S. baseball player; only major league pitcher to win Cy Young Award four times; four thousand career strikeouts.

1945 *Diane K. Sawyer,* U.S. broadcast journalist; special assistant to President Nixon; correspondent on television news show, *60 Minutes,* 1984–89; anchor for the news show *Primetime Live,* 1989– .

1948 *Steve Patrick Garvey,* U.S. baseball player; first baseman, 1969–87; holds many fielding records.

1949 *Maurice Gibb,* British singer, songwriter; member of the rock group, *The Bee Gees.*

Robin Gibb, British musician; member of the rock group, *The Bee Gees.*

1951 *Jan Stephenson,* U.S. golfer; Rookie of the Year, 1974.

1962 *Ralph Fiennes,* British actor; Academy Award nominee for *Schindler's List,* 1994 and Tony Award winner for *Hamlet,* 1995.

HISTORICAL EVENTS

640 *Saracens* conquer *Alexandria, Egypt.*

1807 *Thomas Jefferson,* U.S. President, gets Congress to pass *Embargo Act,* to force France and Britain to withdraw restrictions on American trade.

1894 *U.S. Golf Association* is founded.

1917 Peace negotiations begin at *Brest-Litovsk* between Germany and Russia (*World War I*).

1928 *Mahatma Gandhi* regains leadership at the *All-Parties Conference* in Calcutta and calls for mass *civil disobedience* if dominion status is not given India in one year.

1929 *Russia* and *China* reach agreement, ending prolonged dispute over conflicting claims to the *Chinese Eastern Railway.*

1930 *Oslo Agreement,* concerning tariffs between Scandinavian countries, the Netherlands, Belgium, and Luxembourg is signed.

1941 Japanese capture *Wake Island (World War II).*

1947 *Italy* adopts a new constitution which includes provisions for a seven-year presidential term, equal rights for women, and universal suffrage.

1950 *U.S.S. Meredith Victory* evacuates 14,000 refugees from Hungnam, Korea, establishing world's passenger carrying record.

1968 83-man crew of the *U.S.S. Pueblo,* captured in the Sea of Japan on January 23, are released by North Korea.

1969 *Bernadette Devlin,* Irish activist, is found guilty of inciting to riot and riotous behavior during Catholic-Protestant clashes in Londonderry in August.

1984 Dr. *Carmello Mifsud Bonnici* replaces *Dom Mintoff* as prime minister of Malta.

Ted Hughes is named poet laureate of Great Britain.

1994 *Silvio Berlusconi* announces his resignation as premier of Italy.

DECEMBER
23

HOLIDAYS

Egypt
Victory Day

Japan
Birthday of Emperor Akihito

RELIGIOUS CALENDAR

The Saints

The Ten Martyrs of Crete. [d. 250]

St. Servulus, paralytic beggar. [d. c. 590]

St. Dagobert II of Austrasia, king. [d. 679]

St. Frithebert, Bishop of Hexham. [d. 766]

St. Thorlac, Bishop of Skalholt. [d. 1193]

St. John of Kanti, priest and scholar. Also called *John Cantius.* Feast formerly October 20. [d. 1473] Optional Memorial.

SS. Victoria and Anatolia, virgins and martyrs. [death date unknown]

The Beatified

Blessed Hartman, Bishop of Brixen. [d. 1164]

Blessed Margaret of Savoy, widow. [d. 1464]

BIRTHDATES

1597 *Martin Opitz von Boberfeld,* German poet, literary theorist; founder of the first *Silesian school of poets.* [d. August 20, 1639]

1732 *Sir Richard Arkwright,* English textile manufacturer; inventor of a spinning machine called the *water frame.* [d. August 3, 1792]

1777 *Alexander I,* Emperor of Russia, 1801–25; founded the coalition that defeated Napoleon I. [d. December 1, 1825]

1783 *Giovanni Berchet,* Italian romantic poet; author of *Lettera Semiseria,* the manifesto of the Italian Romantic movement. [d. December 23, 1851]

1790 *Jean François Champollion,* French archaeologist; founded the Egyptian museum at the Louvre; from study of trilingual *Rosetta Stone,* established principles for deciphering Egyptian hieroglyphics. [d. March 4, 1832]

1805 *Joseph Smith,* U.S. religious leader; founder of the *Church of Jesus Christ of Latter-Day Saints* or *Mormon Church.* [d. June 27, 1844]

1815 *Henry Highland Garnet,* U.S. clergyman, orator, and political activist; leader in abolition movement among blacks; called upon slaves to rise up and kill their masters; U.S. Minister to Liberia, 1881–82. [d. 1882]

1854 *Victoriano Huerta,* Mexican revolutionary politician; responsible for the rise to power of *Porfirio Diaz* and for the overthrow of Francisco Madero's government, 1913; provisional president of Mexico, 1913–14. [d. January 13, 1916]

1856 *James Buchanan Duke,* U.S. industrialist, philanthropist; founder of American Tobacco Company; major benefactor of *Duke University.* [d. October 10, 1925]

1867 *Sarah Breedlove Walker (Madame C. J. Walker),* U.S. businesswoman; invents and profits from straighting kinky hair. [d. 1919]

1911 *Niels Kai Jerne,* British-born immunologist; Nobel Prize in physiology or medicine for his theories concerning the immune system, 1984. [d. October 7, 1994]

1918 *Helmut Schmidt,* German political leader; Chancellor of West Germany, 1974–82.

1924 *Dan(iel John) Devine,* U.S. football coach.

1926 *Robert Bly,* U.S. poet; gained political prominence by helping found the *American Writers Against the Vietnam War.*

1935 *Paul Hornung,* U.S. football player, broadcaster.

1947 *Bill Rodgers,* U.S. distance runner; winner of Boston Marathon, 1975; 1978–79.

1972 *Corey Haim,* U.S. actor.

HISTORICAL EVENTS

1861 *Moldavia* and *Wallachia* are united as the principality of *Romania* under *Alexander Cuza.*

1893 *Hansel und Gretel,* by Humperdinck premieres in Weimar, Germany.

1910 *Padlock Bill* is passed in Spain, prohibiting the establishment of any new religious houses without the consent of the government in an attempt to curb the power of the Roman Catholic Church.

1913 *Glass-Owen Act* authorizes the creation of the *Federal Reserve System* as part of a major reform of banking and finance in the U.S.

1914 The Russians are forced to end their siege of *Cracow (World War I).*

1919 *Government of India Act* introduces the *Montagu-Chelmsford reforms* and establishes a system of government called "dyarchy."

1938 Spanish insurgents begin great drive in *Catalonia (Spanish Civil War).*

Boogie-woogie music is first performed in a public demonstration at Carnegie Hall, in a historical review, *From Spiritual to Swing.*

1941 *Wake Island* is captured by the Japanese *(World War II).*

1947 Scientists at the Bell Telephone Laboratories announce the invention of the *transistor,* a device which will revolutionize electronic circuit construction.

1950 *Pope Pius XII* confirms that the *tomb of St. Peter* has been discovered beneath St. Peter's Basilica in Rome.

1961 All foreign-owned land in *Egypt* is nationalized.

1972 Massive *earthquake* devastates the city of *Managua, Nicaragua.*

1975 *Richard S. Welch,* station chief of the U.S. Central Intelligence Agency, is shot and killed outside his suburban Athens residence.

1983 *Jeanne Sauve* is appointed the first woman governor-general of Canada.

1986 U.S. pilots, *Dick Rutan* and *Jeanna Yeager,* land the experimental aircraft *Voyager* in California after a record nine-day trip around the world without refueling.

DECEMBER
24

RELIGIOUS CALENDAR

Feasts

*The Vigil of the Nativity of Jesus
 Christ.*

The Saints

St. Gregory of Spoleto, priest and
 martyr. [d. c. 304]

St. Delphinus, Bishop of Bordeaux.
 [d. 403]

SS. Tharsilla and Emiliana, virgins.
 [d. c. 550]

St. Mochua of Timahoe, monk. [d.
 c. 657]

SS. Irmina, virgin, and *Adela,*
 widow. [d. c. 710 and c. 734]

The Beatified

Blessed Paula Cerioli, widow and
 founder of the Institute of the
 Holy Family of Bergamo. [d.
 1865]

BIRTHDATES

1167 *John (Lackland),* King of
 England, 1199–1216; forced
 by the English barons to sign
 the *Magna Carta;* brother of
 Richard I. [d. October 19,
 1216]

1737 *Silas Deane,* American
 diplomat, lawyer, merchant.
 [d. September 23, 1789]

1745 *Benjamin Rush,* American
 physician, educator; first
 surgeon general of American
 Army, 1777; established first
 free dispensary in America,

1786; Treasurer of the U.S.,
 1797–1813; author of *Medical
 Inquiries and Observations
 upon the Diseases of the
 Mind,* the first systematic
 study of the subject in
 America. [d. April 19, 1813]

1754 *George Crabbe,* English poet.
 [d. February 3, 1832]

1798 *Adam (Bernard) Mickiewicz,*
 Polish poet, playwright, and
 scholar; author of epic *Pan
 Tadeusz;* first professor of
 Slavic literature, Coll ège de
 France, 1840–44. [d.
 November 26, 1855]

1809 *Kit Carson,* U.S. frontiersman,
 soldier, Indian agent; best
 known as Indian scout in
 Mexican War. [d. May 23,
 1868]

1818 *James Prescott Joule,* English
 physicist; discoverer (with
 William Thomson, Baron
 Kelvin) of the *Joule-Thomson
 effect* of expanding gases. [d.
 October 11, 1889]

1822 *Matthew Arnold,* British poet,
 critic. [d. April 15, 1888]

 Charles Hermite, French
 mathematician; first to solve
 equations to fifth degree. [d.
 January 14, 1901]

1845 *George I,* King of Greece. [d.
 March 18, 1913]

1868 *Scott Joplin,* U.S. composer of
 ragtime music. [d. 1917]

1881 *Juan Ramón Jiménez,*
 Spanish lyric poet; Nobel
 Prize in literature, 1956. [d.
 May 29, 1958]

 Charles Wakefield Cadman,
 U.S. composer; best known
 for his studies of *North
 American Indian songs.* [d.
 December 30, 1946]

1893 *Harry Warren,* U.S.
 composer; composed the
 popular songs: *Lullaby of
 Broadway* and *You'll Never
 Know.* [d. September 22,
 1981]

1894 *Georges M. Guynemer,*
 French aviator; the
 outstanding air ace of France
 in World War I. [d. September
 11, 1917]

1895 *Maurice (Richard) Robinson,*
 U.S. publisher, editor;
 founder of Scholastic
 Magazine, Inc. publishers of
 magazines for young people.
 [d. February 7, 1982]

1905 *Howard (Robard) Hughes,
 Jr.,* U.S. industrialist; was one
 of the world's richest men
 and became an eccentric
 recluse. [d. April 5, 1976]

1907 *I(sidor) F(einstein) Stone,*
 U.S. journalist. [d. June 18,
 1989]

 John Patrick, Cardinal Cody,
 U.S. Roman Catholic
 Archbishop of Chicago. [d.
 April 25, 1982]

1922 *Ava Gardner (Lucy Johnson),* U.S. actress. [d. January 25, 1990]

1929 *Mary Higgins Clark,* U.S. author.

1930 *Robert Joffrey,* U.S. dancer, choreographer, ballet director; founder of the *Joffrey Ballet,* 1956. [d. March 25, 1988]

1940 *Anthony S. Fauci,* U.S. physician; known for his contributions to understanding and treating AIDS (acquired immunodeficiency syndrome).

1944 *Michael Charles (Mike) Curb,* U.S. politician; President, MGM Records, 1968–74; Lieutenant Governor of California, 1979–83.

HISTORICAL EVENTS

1046 *Clement II* is elected pope at the *Synod of Rome.*

1800 *Bank of France* is founded by Napoleon, aided by *Count Mollien.*

1814 *Treaty of Ghent* is signed between the U.S. and Great Britain, ending the *War of 1812.*

1851 Two-thirds of the collection of the *Library of Congress* and a portion of the Capitol are destroyed by fire.

1859 First *iron-clad ship* is launched at Toulon, France.

1865 *Ku Klux Klan* is first formed in Pulaski, Tennessee.

1941 British Prime Minister Winston Churchill and U.S. President Franklin Roosevelt meet in Washington to discuss fundamental war strategy (*World War II*).

1942 French West African leader, *Jean Louis Darlan,* is assassinated by a follower of Charles de Gaulle.

1943 U.S. Air Force makes first major raid on German secret weapon targets near the *Pas de Calais (World War II).*

1949 *Adam's Rib,* a film starring Spencer Tracy and Katharine Hepburn, premieres in New York.

1951 Gian Carlo Menotti's opera *Amahl and the Night Visitors* premieres on NBC television; it is the first opera written for television.

Libya declares its independence and proclaims a constitutional and hereditary monarchy under *King Idris I.*

1952 The *McCarran-Walter Immigration and Nationality Act* goes into effect. The law is criticized for discriminating against Asians and blacks from Third World countries.

1953 Soviet officials reveal the execution of *Lavrenti Beriya,* former head of internal security forces.

1974 *Pope Paul VI* inaugurates Holy Year 1975.

1976 *Takeo Fukuda* is elected premier by the Japanese parliament.

1992 U.S. President *George Bush* grants pardons to Caspar Weinberger, Clair George, Duane Clarridge, Alan Fiers, Robert McFarlane, and Elliott Abrams for their part in the Iran-Contra affair.

DECEMBER
25

HOLIDAYS

Christmas Day
Celebrated in all the Christian
countries of the world;
commemorates the birth of Jesus
Christ; the feast was instituted in the
mid 4th century.

Angola, São Tomé and Príncipe
Family Day

Congo
Children's Day

Mozambique
National Family Day

Pakistan
Birthday of Quaid-es-Azam

Taiwan (Republic of China)
Constitution Day
Commemorates the adoption of the
constitution, 1946.

RELIGIOUS CALENDAR

Feasts
*The Birthday of Our Lord Jesus
    Christ,* commonly called
    Christmas Day.

The Saints
Many Martyrs of Nicomedia. [d.
    303]
St. Anastasia, martyr. [d. c. 304]
St. Alburga, founder of Wilton
    nunnery. [d. c. 810]
St. Eugenia, virgin and martyr.
    [death date unknown]

The Beatified
Blessed Jacopone of Todi, Franciscan
    lay brother. [d. 1306]

BIRTHDATES

1564 *Johannes Buxtorf (the Elder),*
German Protestant scholar; an
authority on Hebrew and
rabbinical literature. [d.
September 13, 1629]

1642 *Sir Isaac Newton,* English
scientist, mathematician;
discovered the law of
universal *gravitation;* one of
the fathers of modern
science. [d. March 20, 1727]

1709 *Julien Offroy de La Mettrie,*
French philosopher,
physician; espoused
materialistic philosophy;
believed that the only
pleasures are sensual and that
the soul ceases to exist after
the death of the body. [d.
November 11, 1751]

1717 *Pope Pius VI,* pope 1775–99.
[d. August 29, 1799]

1721 *William Collins,* English poet;
best known for his ode on
the death of his friend, James
Thomson, *Elegy on Thomson,*
1749. [d. June 12, 1759]

1730 *Filippo Mazzei,* Italian author
and supporter of the
American Revolution. [d.
1810]

1763 *Claude Chappe,* French
engineer; developed the first
semaphore, 1793. [d. January
23, 1805]

1821 *(Clarissa Harlowe) Clara
Barton,* U.S. humanitarian;

founder of the *American Red
Cross.* [d. April 12, 1912]

1829 *Patrick Sarsfield Gilmore,*
U.S. bandmaster, born in
Ireland; author, under
pseudonym *Louis Lambert;*
wrote *When Johnny Comes
Marching Home Again.* [d.
September 24, 1892]

1851 *Herman Frasch,* U.S.
chemical engineer, born in
Germany; developed process
for mining deep-lying sulfur
deposits. [d. May 1, 1914]

1865 *Evangeline Cory Booth,*
British social reformer;
seventh child of William
Booth (April 10), founder of
Salvation Army; national
commander of Salvation Army
in U.S., 1904–34; international
leader of Salvation Army,
1934. [d. July 17, 1950]

1870 *Rosa Luxemburg (Red Rosa),*
German socialist
revolutionary; associated with
Karl Liebknecht (August 3); a
founder of the *Spartacus
Union.* [d. 1919]

1876 *Giuseppe de Luca,* Italian
operatic baritone. [d. August
26, 1950]

Mohammed Ali Jinnah,
Muslim leader; first governor-
general of Pakistan, 1947–48.
[d. September 11, 1948]

Adolf Windaus, German
chemist; Nobel Prize in

chemistry for research on *steroids* and *vitamins*, 1928. [d. June 9, 1959]

1883 *Maurice Utrillo,* French artist; known for his paintings of Parisian street scenes. [d. November 5, 1955]

1886 *(Edward) Kid Ory,* U.S. musician; chief exponent of New Orleans jazz. [d. January 23, 1973]

1887 *Conrad (Nicholson) Hilton,* U.S. hotelier; founder of Hilton Hotels Corporation, 1946. [d. January 3, 1979]

1888 *David Lawrence,* U.S. journalist; editor of *U.S. News & World Report,* 1948–73. [d. February 11, 1973]

1889 *Lila Acheson Wallace,* U.S. publisher; with her husband, Dewitt Wallace (November 12), founded *Readers' Digest,* 1921. [d. May 8, 1984]

1892 *Dame Rebecca West (Cicily Isabel Fairfield),* British novelist, critic; noted for her writing on Yugoslavia, as well as her reports on the Nuremberg trials. [d. March 16, 1983]

1893 *Robert Leroy Ripley,* U.S. cartoonist; best known for his syndicated feature *Believe It or Not,* which described curiosities. [d. May 27, 1949]

1899 *Humphrey Bogart,* U.S. actor, known for his romantic tough guy image; won 1951 Academy Award for role in *The African Queen.* [d. January 14, 1957]

1904 *Gladys Swarthout,* U.S. mezzo-soprano; primarily known for her interpretation of *Carmen.* [d. July 7, 1969]

Gerhard Herzberg, Canadian chemist; Nobel Prize in

chemistry for work in determining the electronic structure and geometry of molecules, 1971.

1906 Sir *Lew Grade,* British media executive; Chairman, Embassy Communications International.

Ernst Ruska, German scientist; Nobel Prize in physics for his invention of the electron microscope, 1986. [d. May 27, 1988]

1907 *Cab(ell) Calloway,* U.S. musician. [d. November 18, 1994]

1913 *Tony Martin (Alfred Norris, Jr.),* U.S. singer.

1914 *Oscar Lewis,* U.S. anthropologist; author of *The Children of Sanchez,* 1961. [d. December 16, 1971]

1918 *Anwar Sadat,* Egyptian leader; known for his peace efforts with Israel; assassinated. [d. October 6, 1981]

1924 *Rod Serling,* U.S. author, producer; known for the creation and production of the television series, *Twilight Zone* and *Night Gallery.* [d. June 28, 1975]

Atal Bihari Vajpayee, Indian politician; Prime Minister of India, 1998– .

1931 *Carlos Castaneda,* U.S. anthropologist, born in Brazil; best known for his writings about his apprenticeship to a Yaqui Indian sorcerer. [d. April 27, 1998]

1935 *Little Richard (Richard Penniman),* U.S. singer; known for songs, *Tutti Frutti* and *Good Golly Miss Molly.*

1940 *Philip Harvey (Phil) Spector,* U.S. record producer; known

for his "wall of sound" technique of sound arrangement.

1946 *Jimmy Buffet,* U.S. singer, songwriter; known for his song, *Margaritaville,* 1977.

Larry Richard Csonka, U.S. football player.

Gary Sandy, U.S. actor; known for his role as Andy Travis on the television series, *WKRP in Cincinnati,* 1978–82.

1948 *Barbara Ann Mandrell,* U.S. singer, musician.

1949 *Dan Pastorini,* U.S. football player.

Mary Elizabeth (Sissy) Spacek, U.S. actress; Academy Award for *Coal Miner's Daughter,* 1980.

1954 *Annie Lennox,* British singer; member of the rock group, *Eurythmics;* Grammy Award nominee for *Diva,* 1992.

1958 *Ricky Henley Henderson,* U.S. baseball player.

HISTORICAL EVENTS

503 *Clovis,* King of the Franks, is baptized a Christian.

800 *Charlemagne* is crowned Holy Roman Emperor by *Pope Leo III* at Rome.

1066 *William I (the Conqueror)* is crowned King of England.

1100 *Baldwin I* is crowned King of Jerusalem at Bethlehem.

1130 *Roger II* is crowned King of Sicily.

1194 *Henry VI,* Holy Roman Emperor, is crowned King of Sicily.

1196 *Frederick II* is elected King of Germany.

1492 Columbus's flagship, the *Santa Maria,* is wrecked on northern coast of Hispaniola.

1497 *Vasco da Gama* sights the entrance to Durban harbor in South Africa and names the country *Terra Natalis (Natal).*

1776 *George Washington,* American general, crosses the Delaware River, staging a surprise attack on the British and Hessian troops in Trenton, New Jersey (*American Revolution*).

1926 *Hirohito* becomes emperor of Japan on the death of his father, *Yoshihito.*

1940 Richard Rodgers and Moss Hart's musical, *Pal Joey,* premieres in New York.

1941 *Hong Kong* surrenders to *Japan (World War II).*

1944 U.S. forces capture the last remaining Japanese stronghold on Leyte Island in the Philippines, successfully completing the *Leyte-Samar operation (World War II).*

1950 *Stone of Scone,* symbol of the union of the English and Scottish thrones, is stolen from Westminster Abbey in London.

1957 Walt Disney's film, *Old Yeller,* premieres in New York.

1961 *Pope John XXIII* issues a papal bull convening the Roman Catholic Church's 21st ecumenical council, to be held in 1962.

1973 *The Sting,* a film starring Paul Newman and Robert Redford, premieres in New York.

1974 *Darwin, Australia,* is devastated by a *cyclone.*

1989 *Nicolae Ceausescu,* Romanian leader, and wife Elena are found guilty of genocide against the Romanian people. They are sentenced to death and immediately shot.

1991 *Mikhail Gorbachev* resigns as Soviet president.

HOLIDAYS

Boxing Day
Celebrated in many Christian countries; traditionally the first weekday after Christmas, but generally on this day; a day when gifts (boxes) are given to servants or others who provide services.

Andorra, Austria, Czech Republic, Ireland, Italy, Liechtenstein, San Marino, Switzerland
St. Stephen's Day
Commemorates the feast of St. Stephen, first martyr of the Christian Church.

Luxembourg, Netherlands, Norway
Second Day of Christmas

Namibia
Family Day

South Africa
Day of Good Will

U.S.
Kwanzaa

Vatican City
Christmas Holiday

RELIGIOUS CALENDAR

Feasts

St. Stephen, the first martyr and one of the first seven deacons; patron of smelters and stonecutters. Also called Proto-Martyr of the Church. [d. c. 34]

The Saints

St. Dionysius, pope. Elected 259. [d. 269]

St. Zosimus, pope. Elected 417. [d. 418]

St. Tathai, founder of the Monastery of Llantathan. Also called *Atheus, Tathan,* or *Tathar.* [d. 5th–6th century]

St. Archelaus, Bishop of Kashkar. [death date unknown]

The Beatified

Blessed Vincentia Lopez y Vicuña, virgin and founder of the Daughters of Mary Immaculate. [d. 1890]

BIRTHDATES

1194 *Frederick II,* Holy Roman Emperor, 1220–50; pursued many policies opposing papal authority. [d. December 13, 1250]

1542 *Iyeyasu Tokugawa,* Japanese feudal lord, general; founder of the *Tokugawa* shogunate, which lasted 1603–1867; made numerous attempts to open Japan to commercial trade with the West. [d. 1616]

1716 *Thomas Gray,* English poet; best known for his melancholy lyrics; wrote *Elegy Written in a Country Churchyard,* 1751. [d. July 30, 1771]

1738 *Thomas Nelson,* American merchant; member of Continental Congress, 1775–77; signer of the Declaration of Independence; Governor of Virginia, 1781. [d. January 4, 1789]

1769 *Ernest Moritz Arndt,* German poet, historian; his writings led to abolition of *serfdom* in Sweden; led opposition to Napoleonic movements in Germany. [d. January 29, 1860]

1792 *Charles Babbage,* English mathematician, inventor; a pioneer in development of calculating machines which ultimately resulted in the creation of the computer; also developed the *ophthalmoscope,* the *speedometer,* and the *skeleton key.* [d. October 18, 1871]

1820 *Dion Boucicault (Dionysius Lardner Boursiquot),* U.S. actor, playwright, born in Ireland; a leading figure in New York and London theater, 1853–69. [d. September 18, 1890]

1825 *Ernst Felix Hoppe-Seyler,* German biochemist, physiologist; noted for his articulation of *biochemistry* as a separate science. [d. August 10, 1895]

1837 *George Dewey,* U.S. naval officer; hero of the *Spanish-American War;* responsible for the destruction of the Spanish fleet in *Manila Bay,* Philippines. [d. January 16, 1917]

1859 *Robert Hawley Ingersoll,* U.S. manufacturer; with his brother, C. H. Ingersoll, founded the Ingersoll Watch Co., manufacturers of the *one dollar Ingersoll watch.* [d. September 4, 1928]

1872 *Sir Norman Thomas Angell (Ralph Norman Angell Lane),* British economist, author; Nobel Peace Prize, 1933. [d. October 7, 1967]

1878 *Isaiah Bowman,* U.S. geographer; President, Johns Hopkins University, 1935–49. [d. January 6, 1950]

1891 *Henry (Valentine) Miller,* U.S. author; because of the explicit sexual nature of his novels (*Tropic of Cancer, Tropic of Capricorn,*) his work was banned in the U.S. until the 1960s; a 1964 Supreme Court ruling allowed publication of his novels in the U.S. [d. June 6, 1980]

1893 *Mao Tse-tung,* Chinese communist leader; Chairman of the Chinese Communist Party, 1949–76; Chairman of the People's Republic of China, 1949–59. [d. September 9, 1976]

1901 *Georgy Rimsky-Korsakov,* Russian musician; an exponent of quarter-tone music; grandson of Nikolai Rimsky-Korsakov (March 18).

1905 *William Loeb,* U.S. publisher; known for his conservative position and brutal attacks on liberal Democrats; editor of *The Manchester Union*

Leader. [d. September 13, 1981]

1907 *Albert Arnold Gore,* U.S. coal industry executive, politician; U.S. Congressman, 1939–53; U.S. Senator, 1953–70.

1914 *Richard Widmark,* U.S. actor.

1917 *Rose Mary Woods,* U.S. secretary; executive secretary to Richard Nixon, 1969–75; erased parts of the Watergate tapes.

1920 *Emmet John Hughes,* U.S. journalist, author; chief foreign correspondent, Time-Life Corporation, 1957–60. [d. September 20, 1982]

1921 *Steve Allen,* U.S. humorist, composer; the originator of the *Tonight Show,* 1950.

1927 *Alan King (Irwin Kniberg),* U.S. comedian.

1929 *Regine (Regina Zylberberg),* French businesswoman; owner of nightclubs bearing her name in cities all over the world.

1930 *Donald Moffat,* British actor; known for his roles in *Rachel, Rachel, Eleanor and Franklin,* and *Popeye.*

1935 *Norm(an Victor Alexander) Ullman,* Canadian hockey player; elected to Hall of Fame, 1982.

1937 *Gnassingbe Eyadema,* President, Republic of Togo, 1967–.

1947 *Carlton Ernest Fisk,* U.S. baseball player.

1949 *José Ramos-Horta,* Timor political activist; Nobel Prize for Peace in 1996, Ramos-Horta shares the prize with

Bishop Carlos F. X. Belo for their work toward peace in Timor.

1954 *Osborne Earl (Ozzie) Smith,* U.S. baseball player.

HISTORICAL EVENTS

1776 *Washington* and his Continental troops defeat Hessian mercenaries at the *Battle of Trenton (American Revolution).*

1836 First settlers arrive at British colony of *South Australia.*

1900 *Ollanta,* by José Maria Valle-Riestra, the first truly national Peruvian opera, premieres in Lima.

1908 *Jack Johnson* defeats *Tommy Burns* to win the world heavyweight boxing title.

1917 American pilots of the *Lafayette Escadrille* transfer from the French to the American service (*World War I*).

1928 A.A. Milne's classic *House at Pooh Corner* is published.

1941 *Manila* is declared an open city (*World War II*).

1973 *The Exorcist,* a film starring Linda Blair and Ellen Burstyn, premieres in New York.

Soyuz 13, Soviet-manned spacecraft, ends an eight-day flight orbiting the earth.

1989 *Ion Iliescu* is selected as the interim president of *Romania* after the execution of President Nicolae Ceausescu (December 25, 1989).

1995 *Tansu Ciller,* prime minister of Turkey, announces his resignation.

HOLIDAYS

North Korea
Constitution Day

Vatican City
Christmas Holiday

Zimbabwe
Public Holiday

RELIGIOUS CALENDAR

Feasts
St. John the Evangelist, apostle; patron of Sweden and theologians. Invoked against poisons and burns and for forming friendships. Also called *the Divine, the Theologian.* [d. c. 100] [major holy day, Episcopal Church; minor festival, Lutheran church]

The Saints
St. Fabiola, matron. [d. 399]
St. Nicarete, virgin. [d. c. 410]
SS. Theodore and Theophanes, monks. Surnamed *Graptoi,* that is, *the written-on.* [d. c. 841 and 845]

BIRTHDATES

1571 *Johannes Kepler,* German astronomer; discovered the three laws of planetary action called *Kepler's Laws;* pioneered in research in optics; contributed to the invention of *calculus.* [d. November 15, 1630]

1654 *Jakob Bernoulli,* Swiss mathematician; developed calculus of variations; the *Bernoulli numbers* are named for him. [d. August 16, 1705]

1714 *George Whitefield,* British religious leader; his evangelical tours through America initiated spiritual revival known as the Great Awakening. [d. September 30, 1770]

1741 *Jean Etienne Boré,* U.S. sugar planter; the father of the sugar industry in Louisiana; Mayor of New Orleans, 1803. [d. February 2, 1820]

1769 *Alexander John Forsyth,* Scottish clergyman, inventor; invented the *percussion lock,* an improvement in the explosive mechanism of firearms. [d. June 11, 1843]

1798 *William Wilson Corcoran,* U.S. banker, philanthropist; founded the *Corcoran Art Gallery,* Washington, D.C. [d. February 24, 1888]

1822 *Louis Pasteur,* French chemist; proponent of the *germ theory of disease;* through research discovered the basic principle of *inoculation* as a method of preventing disease. [d. September 28, 1845]

1879 *Sydney Greenstreet,* British actor; known for his performances on stage and in the films; his film career began at age 62. [d. January 18, 1954]

1883 *Cyrus Stephen Eaton,* U.S. industrialist, financier; founder of Republic Steel Corporation, 1930; sponsored the annual *Pugwash Conference* for the international exchange of scholarly, scientific, and business information; supported improved relations with Russia; awarded Lenin Peace Prize, 1960. [d. May 9, 1979]

1896 *Louis Bromfield,* U.S. writer; Pulitzer prize in fiction, 1927. [d. March 18, 1956]

1901 *Marlene Dietrich (Maria Magdalena von Losch),* U.S. actress, born in Germany. [d. may 6, 1992]

1906 *Oscar Levant,* U.S. concert pianist, comedic actor. [d. August 14, 1972]

1910 *Charles Olson,* U.S. poet. [d. 1970]

1915 *William Howell Masters,* U.S. physician, educator; with his wife, Virginia E. Johnson, contributed significant research to the understanding of *human sexual characteristics.*

1926 *Lee Salk,* U.S. psychologist, author. [d. May 2, 1992]

1927 *Anne Legendre Armstrong,* U.S. government official; Ambassador to Great Britain, 1976–77.

1930 *Meg Greenfield,* U.S. journalist, editor; *Newsweek* columnist; Pulitzer Prize for editorial writing.

1942 *John Amos,* U.S. actor; known for his role as James Evans on television series, *Good Times.*

1943 *Cokie Roberts,* U.S. broadcast journalist.

1948 *Gerard Depardieu,* French actor; known for his lead roles in *The Return of Martin Guerre, Danton,* and *Cyrano de Bergerac.*

1951 *Ernesto Zedillo (Ponce de Leon),* Mexican politician; president of Mexico, 1994– .

1952 *Karla Bonoff,* U.S. singer, songwriter.

Tovah Feldshuh, U.S. actress; known for her roles in television movies, *Amazing Howard Hughes* and *Holocaust.*

1953 *Arthur Kent,* U.S. television journalist; best known for his live coverage of the Persian Gulf War, 1991.

HISTORICAL EVENTS

1882 600th anniversary of the establishment of the *House of Hapsburg* is celebrated throughout Austrian Empire.

1917 Independent *Ukrainian Soviet Socialist Republic* is proclaimed.

Bolshevik government of Russia nationalizes all banks and confiscates all private accounts.

1927 *Jerome Kern's* musical comedy, *Show Boat,* with book and lyrics by Oscar Hammerstein II, based on Edna Ferber's novel, opens in New York.

Soviet Communist Congress expels *Leon Trotsky* and his followers from the Communist Party, marking final victory of *Joseph Stalin* in Soviet power struggle.

1932 *Radio City Music Hall* opens in New York City as the world's largest indoor theater with seating for 6,200 people.

1939 Severe *earthquakes* destroy city of *Erzincan, Turkey,* with about 100,000 casualties.

1941 *Rubber rationing* begins in the U.S. with restrictions placed on rubber tires.

1945 *Indonesia* becomes a new and independent state as The Netherlands relinquishes its sovereignty.

1947 First episode of the popular children's television program, *Howdy Doody,* is aired.

1948 *Jozef Cardinal Mindszenty,* Primate of Hungary, is arrested for anti-Communist statements. Later sentenced to death, the sentence is commuted to life imprisonment.

1972 Belgium becomes the first NATO nation to extend full diplomatic recognition to *East Germany.*

1978 *Abdel Fattah Ismail* is elected president of South Yemen.

1979 *Soviet Union* invades *Afghanistan.* President Hafizullah Amin is denounced and executed; *Babrak Karmal* is installed as president.

1992 *U.S. air forces* shoot down an Iraqi fighter plane that encroached upon the established "*no-fly zone*" in southern Iraq.

HOLIDAYS

Costa Rica (San Jose)
Public Holiday

Nepal
National Day

RELIGIOUS CALENDAR

Feasts

The Holy Innocents. Commemorates the suffering of the children of Bethlehem two years old and younger. Also called *Childermas.* [major holy day, Episcopal Church; minor festival, Lutheran Church]

The Saints

St. Theodore the Sanctified, abbot. [d. 368]

St. Antony of Lérins, monk and hermit. [d. c. 520]

BIRTHDATES

1619 *Abbé Antoine Furetière,* French poet, editor; compiled the *Dictionnaire Universel* over a 40-year period; was forbidden permission by the French government to publish it. [d. May 14, 1688]

1798 *Thomas Henderson,* Scottish astronomer; one of first to measure *stellar parallax* [d. November 23, 1844]

1818 *Carl Remigius Fresenius,* German chemist; known for research and writing in field of *analytical chemistry.* [d. June 11, 1897]

1856 *(Thomas) Woodrow Wilson,* U.S. political scientist, educator; 28th President of the U.S.; responsible for the *Fourteen Points* plan for peace after World War I; Nobel Peace Prize, 1919. [d. February 23, 1924]

1862 *Morris Rosenfeld (Moshe Jacob Alter),* foremost early Yiddish poet. [d. June 22, 1923]

1873 *William Draper Harkins,* U.S. chemist, known for his work on *atomic structure* and *isotopes.* [d. March 7, 1951]

1882 *Sir Arthur Stanley Eddington,* British scientist; with others, verified Einstein's prediction concerning bending of light rays, 1919; known for research on motion of stars and their evolution. [d. November 22, 1944]

1896 *Roger (Huntington) Sessions,* U.S. composer, teacher. [d. March 16, 1985]

1903 *John von Neumann,* U.S. mathematician, born in Hungary; invented the *von Neumann algebras;* leader in movement to integrate all mathematics; contributed to the development of *atomic bomb* through his work in computer science; the *Father of Game Theory.* [d. February 8, 1957]

1905 *Cliff Arquette (Charley Weaver),* U.S. actor; known for his appearances on television game show, *Hollywood Squares.* [d. September 23, 1974]

Earl (Fatha) Hines, U.S. jazz musician; a profound influence on American jazz music particularly such jazz stars as Dizzy Gillespie and Sarah Vaughan. [d. April 22, 1983]

1908 *Lew Ayres,* U.S. actor; leading film star of the 1930s. [d. December 30, 1996]

1911 *Sam(uel) Levenson,* U.S. comedian, author. [d. August 27, 1980]

1917 *Ellis E.I. Clarke,* President, Republic of Trinidad and Tobago, 1976–87.

1925 *Hildegarde Neff,* German actress.

Milton Obote, President, Republic of Uganda, 1980–85.

1929 *Owen Frederick Bieber,* U.S labor union official; President, United Auto Workers, 1983–.

Terry Sawchuk, Canadian hockey player; elected to Hall of Fame, 1971.

1931 *Martin Sam Milner,* U.S. actor; known for his role as

Pete Malloy on television series, *Adam-12,* 1968–75.

1934 *Maggie Smith,* British actress.

1944 *Sandra M. Faber,* U.S. astronomer; known for her research on the evolution of galaxies.

Kary B. Mullis, U.S. biochemist; one-half of the Nobel Prize for Chemistry in 1993. Mullis invented the polymerase chain reaction. Michael Smith, British biochemist; other half of the prize for his work on oligonucleotide-based site-directed mutagenesis.

1945 *Birendra Bir Bikram Shah Dev,* King of Nepal, 1972–.

1946 *Edgar Holand Winter,* U.S. singer, musician; member of the rock groups, *White Trash* and *Edgar Winter Group.*

1953 *Richard Clayderman,* French musician; pianist with 177 gold records.

1954 *Denzel Washington,* U.S. actor; Academy Award (Best Supporting Actor) for *Glory,* 1989.

1960 *Ray Bourque,* Canadian hockey player.

HISTORICAL EVENTS

1846 *Iowa* is admitted to the Union as the 29th state.

1885 The first *Indian National Congress* opens at Bombay.

1902 Syracuse defeats Philadelphia at Madison Square Garden in the first indoor professional *football game.*

1908 *Earthquake* in *Calabria* and *Sicily* destroys towns on both sides of Straits of Messina.

1937 First radio transmission of a musical score is made between Leipzig and Boston, transmitting last portions of Jean Sibelius' *Origin of Fire.*

1944 Leonard Bernstein's musical, *On the Town,* premieres in New York.

1949 *Hungary* nationalizes all major industries.

1950 Chinese troops cross over the 38th parallel in Korea, posing the threat of war between China and the U.S. (*Korean War*)

1973 Alexander Solzhenitsyn's account of Soviet repression, *Gulag Archipelago,* is published in Paris.

Comet *Kohoutek* makes its closest approach to the sun.

1974 Severe *earthquake* in northern *Pakistan* kills more than 5,000 persons.

1989 *Vaclav Havel* is elected president of *Czechoslovakia.*

1992 The second *Strategic Arms Reduction Treaty (START II)* is announced in Geneva, Switzerland.

Fernando Collor de Mello, president of Brazil, resigns amidst corruption charges. Itamar Franco, then vice-president, is sworn in as the new leader.

1996 The *Guatemalan government* signs a peace treaty with rebel forces aimed at ending the 36-year-old civil war that had ravaged the country.

1997 *Terry Nichols* is found guilty of conspiracy and manslaughter stemming from the Oklahoma City bombing (April 19, 1995).

HOLIDAYS

Costa Rica (San Jose)
Civic Holiday

RELIGIOUS CALENDAR

The Saints

St. Trophimus, first bishop of Arles. [d. c. 3rd cent.]

St. Marcellus Akimetes, abbot. Also called *Marcellus the Righteous.* [d. c. 485]

St. Ebrulf, abbot. Also called *Evroul,* or *Evroult.* [d. 596]

St. Thomas Becket, archbishop of Canterbury, and martyr. Patron of secular clergy, blind men, eunuchs, and sinners. Also called *Thomas àBecket.* [d. 1170] Optional Memorial.

The Beatified

Blessed Peter the Venerable, abbot. [d. 1156]

BIRTHDATES

1721 *Madame de Pompadour (Jeanne Antoinette Poisson),* mistress of *Louis XV* of France; exerted enormous influence over the king and the political affairs of the country; responsible for France's involvement in the Seven Years' War. [d. April 15, 1764]

1766 *Charles Macintosh,* Scottish chemist; inventor of process of bonding rubber to cloth to produce raincoats (*macintoshes*), 1823. [d. July 25, 1843]

1796 *Ferdinand Petrovich, Baron von Wrangel,* Russian explorer; commander of Russian Polar expedition, 1820–24; Governor-General of Russian America (Alaska), 1829–34. *Wrangel Island* in the East Siberian Sea is named for him although he did not discover it. [d. June 6, 1870]

1800 *Charles Goodyear,* U.S. inventor; developed the *vulcanization process* which revolutionized the rubber industry; in spite of his discovery, he died deeply in debt because of infringement of his patent. [d. July 1, 1860]

1808 *Andrew Johnson,* U.S. tailor, politician; military governor of Tennessee, 1862–64; Vice-President, 1865; 17th President of the U.S., 1865–69, succeeding Abraham Lincoln after his assassination. [d. July 31, 1875]

1809 *William Ewart Gladstone,* British statesman; Prime Minister, 1868–74; 1880–85; 1886; 1892–94; advocate of Irish Home Rule. [d. May 19, 1898]

1816 *Carl Ludwig,* German physiologist; perfected the *kymograph,* an instrument for measuring blood pressure and circulation. [d. April 23, 1895]

1833 *John James Ingalls,* U.S. politician, lawyer, farmer; U.S. Senator, 1873–91. [d. August 16, 1900]

1859 *Venustiano Carranza,* Mexican revolutionist, political leader; opposed Victoriano Huerta (December 23); proclaimed First Chief of Mexico, 1914; President of Mexico, 1917–20; assassinated. [d. May 21, 1920]

1876 *Pablo Casals,* Spanish cellist, conductor; considered the greatest cellist of the 20th century. [d. October 22, 1973]

1879 *William (Billy) Mitchell,* U.S. Army Air Corps general, aviation pioneer; hero of World War I; court-martialed for criticism of U.S. Navy and War Departments regarding their neglect of air power; later vindicated by events during World War II. [d. February 19, 1936]

1891 *Joyce Clyde Hall,* U.S. manufacturer; founder, President and Chairman of the Board, Hallmark Cards, Inc., 1913–66, largest manufacturer of greeting cards in the world. [d. October 29, 1982]

1900 *Thomas Gardiner Corcoran,* U.S. lawyer; assisted in the drafting of the *Securities Act of 1933,* the *Securities Exchange Act of 1934* and other New Deal legislation. [d. December 6, 1981]

1907 *Robert C. Weaver,* U.S. economist, government official; first black cabinet member in U.S. history as Secretary of Housing and Urban Development, 1966–68; Professor of Urban Affairs, Hunter College. [d. July 17, 1997]

1910 *Ronald H. Coase,* U.S. economist; Nobel Prize for Economics, 1991.

1915 *Robert (Chester) Ruark,* U.S. novelist, journalist. [d. June 30, 1965]

1917 *Thomas Bradley,* U.S. politician, lawyer; mayor of Los Angeles, 1973–93.

1925 *Luis Alberto Monge Alvarez,* President, Republic of Costa Rica, 1982–86.

1936 *Mary Tyler Moore,* U.S. actress; known for her starring roles on television series, *The Dick Van Dyke Show* and *The Mary Tyler Moore Show*; Television Hall of Fame inductee, 1985.

1938 *Jon Voight,* U.S. actor.

1939 *Maumoon Abdul Gayoom,* President, Republic of Maldives, 1978–.

1946 *Marianne Faithful,* British singer, actress.

1947 *Edward Bridge (Ted) Danson, III,* U.S. actor; known for his role as Sam Malone on television series, *Cheers,* 1982–1993; starred in the films, *Three Men and a Baby,* 1987, and *Three Men and a Little Lady.*

1952 *Gelsey Kirkland,* U.S. ballerina.

1953 *Yvonne Elliman,* U.S. singer.

HISTORICAL EVENTS

1170 *Thomas Becket,* Archbishop of Canterbury, is murdered by four Norman knights.

1778 General Clinton and British forces crush Americans and take *Savannah, Georgia (American Revolution).*

1845 *Texas* is admitted to the Union as the 28th state.

1874 The Spanish army proclaims *Alfonso,* son of the deposed Queen Isabella, king.

1890 U.S. authorities, seeking to curb religious rites of the Teton Sioux, massacre Indians at the *Battle of Wounded Knee.*

1911 *Sun Yat-sen* is elected President of the *United Provinces of China* by the revolutionary provisional assembly at Nanking.

1914 *Battle of Sarikamish* opens in the Caucasus between Russia and Turkey (*World War I*).

1937 *Irish Free State* is renamed *Eire.*

1941 Japanese bomb *Corregidor* for the first time (*World War II*).

1954 *Paris Pacts* abolish all economic ties between *Laos* and France.

1958 *Project HOPE,* an organization for the promotion of world health, is founded.

1975 Bomb explosion at New York's *La Guardia Airport* kills 11 people and injures 75.

1982 U.S. scientists unearth the oldest human bones yet found in North America at Anzick, Montana. The discovery of the skeleton, that of a woman estimated to be more than 12,000 years old, concludes 80 years of searching for ancient human remains.

1983 U.S. announces that it intends to end its membership in the *United Nations Educational Scientific and Cultural Organization (UNESCO)* by the end of 1984.

HOLIDAYS

Costa Rica (San Jose)
Civic Holiday

Madagascar
*Anniversary of the Democratic
Republic of Madagascar*

Philippines
Rizal Day
Commemorates the death of José
Mercado Rizal, Philippine nationalist,
1896.

Romania
Republic Day

St. Kitts
Carnival

RELIGIOUS CALENDAR

The Saints
SS. Sabinus and his Companions,
martyrs. [d. c. 303]
St. Anysius, Bishop of Thessalonica.
[d. c. 410]
St. Peter of Canterbury, first abbot
of St. Augustine's. [d. 607]
St. Egwin, Bishop of Worcester. [d.
717]

BIRTHDATES

1844 *Charles Albert Coffin,* U.S.
manufacturer; founder of
General Electric Corporation,
1892. [d. July 14, 1926]

1847 *John Peter Altgeld,* U.S.
politician; governor of Illinois,
1892–96; defended industrial
strikers against federal
intervention. [d. March 12,
1902]

1850 *John Milne,* British geologist;
developed the first accurate
seismograph. [d. July 30,
1913]

1851 *Asa Griggs Candler,* U.S.
businessman; founder of
Coca-Cola Corporation, 1873;
mayor of Atlanta, Georgia,
1917–18. [d. March 12, 1929]

1865 *(Joseph) Rudyard Kipling,*
British poet, novelist, born in
India; primarily known for his
writings about India; Nobel
Prize in literature, 1907. [d.
January 18, 1936]

1867 *John Simon Guggenheim,*
U.S. industrialist,
philanthropist; son of Meyer
Guggenheim (February 1);
established the *Guggenheim
Foundation,* 1925. [d.
November 2, 1941]

1869 *Stephen Butler Leacock,*
Canadian humorist,
economist, and political
scientist. [d. March 28, 1944]

1872 *William Augustus Larned,*
U.S. champion lawn-tennis
player; seven-time national
singles champion. [d.
December 16, 1926]

1873 *Alfred E(mmanuel) Smith,*
U.S. politician; governor of
New York, 1918–20; 1922–28;
first man to serve four terms
as governor of New York;
twice a candidate for U.S.
President. [d. October 4,
1944]

1884 *Hideki (Eiki) Tojo,* Japanese
leader, military officer; Prime
Minister of Japan, 1941–44;
responsible for ordering
Japanese attack on *Pearl
Harbor.* [d. December 23,
1948]

1906 *Sir Carol Reed,* British film
director. [d. April 25, 1976]

1914 *Bert Parks,* U.S. actor; known
for hosting the Miss America
Pageant, 1954–79. [d.
February 2, 1992]

1928 *Bo Diddley (Elias McDaniel),*
U.S. musician; one of early
leaders in *rock-'n'-roll* music.

1930 *Jack Lord,* U.S. actor,
producer, artist; known for
his production of and starring
role on television series,
Hawaii Five-O, 1969–80. [d.
January 21, 1998]

1934 *Nicholas Daniloff,* U.S.
journalist; reporter, *U.S.
World and News Report;*
jailed and accused of spying
in the Soviet Union, 1986.

1935 *Albert-Bernard (Omar)
Bongo,* President of Gabon,
1967– .

Sanford (Sandy) Koufax, U.S.
baseball player, sportscaster;

december

youngest player elected to Hall of Fame at age 36, 1971.

1940 *Philippe Cousteau,* French oceanographer, producer; known for his production of television sereies, *Undersea World of Jacques Cousteau,* 1970–75. [d. June 28, 1979]

1942 *Mike Nesmith,* U.S. singer, songwriter; member of the rock group, *The Monkees,* and star of the television series of the same name, 1966–69.

1946 *David (Davy) Jones,* British musician; member of the rock group, *The Monkees,* and star of the television series of the same name, 1966–69.

1959 *Tracey Ullman,* British singer, actress; stars in the television series, *The Tracey Ullman Show,* 1986–90.

1975 *Tiger Woods,* U.S. golfer.

HISTORICAL EVENTS

1460 *Queen Margaret* of England defeats and kills *Richard* of York at Wakefield (*War of the Roses*).

1880 Revolt of the *Transvaal Boers* breaks out against the British with the proclamation of a republic by Boer leaders Kruger, Pretorius, and Joubert.

1895 *Dr. Starr Jameson* of the Cape Colony begins his famous *Jameson Raid,* an effort to bring support to rebellious Uitlanders.

1903 Disastrous *Iroquois Theatre fire* in Chicago kills 588 but leads to new and better fire codes in most cities.

1916 *Rasputin* is assassinated in the house of Prince Felix Yussopov in St. Petersburg, Russia.

1917 Foreign intervention in Russia's *Bolshevik revolution* begins with the arrival of Japanese warships at Vladivostok.

1922 *Union of Soviet Socialist Republics* is established by confederation of Russia, Ukraine, White Russia, and Transcaucasia.

1947 *King Michael* of Romania abdicates under Communist pressure.

1948 Cole Porter's musical, *Kiss Me Kate,* premieres in New York. It is based on Shakespeare's *Taming of the Shrew.*

1953 *The wild One,* a film starring Marlon Brando, premieres in New York.

1954 Runner *Malvin Whitfield* becomes the first black honored as U.S. Amateur Athlete of the Year.

1957 *Carlos Garcia* is inaugurated as president of the Philippines.

1961 *Diosdado Macapagal* is inaugurated as president of the Philippines.

1971 Anglican-Roman Catholic International Commission announces agreement on essential teachings about the Eucharist.

1978 Ohio State University fires football coach *Woody Hayes* after he punches a Clemson player.

1983 Former Argentine president, *Leopoldo Galtieri,* is indicted on torture and murder charges related to the "Dirty War" of the 1970s. A military commission had earlier recommended that he be court-martialed for mismanagement of the Falkland Islands War.

HOLIDAYS

New Year's Eve
Traditionally, the vigil celebration ushering out the old year and in with the new.

Azerbaijan
Universal Azeri Solidarity Day

Benin
Feed Yourself Day or Production Day

Congo
Proclamation of the Republic

Costa Rica (San Jose)
Public Holiday

Ghana
Revolution Day

Japan
Omisoka or Grand Last Day

Lebanon
Foreign Troops Evacuation Day

Scotland
Hogmanay Day
Traditional name given to New Year's Eve, celebrated by children who visit from house to house gathering sweets.

RELIGIOUS CALENDAR

Feasts
New Year's Eve [minor festival, Lutheran Church]

The Saints
St. Silvester I, pope. Elected 314. Also called *Sylvester*. [d. 335]

St. Melania the Younger, widow. [d. 439]
St. Columba of Sens, virgin and martyr. [death date unknown]

The Beatified
Blessed Israel, Augustinian precentor. [d. 1014]

BIRTHDATES

1320 *John Wycliffe*, British theologian; directed the first translation of the Latin Vulgate Bible into English; major force behind the Protestant Reformation. [d. 1384]

1378 *Pope Calixtus III*, pope 1455–58; his heroic crusade to recover Constantinople from the Turks failed. [d. August 6, 1458]

1491 *Jacques Cartier*, French navigator, explorer; discovered the St. Lawrence Seaway. [d. September 1, 1557]

1514 *Andreas Vesalius*, Flemish anatomist. [d. October 15, 1564]

1668 *Hermann Boerhaave*, Dutch physician, philosopher; author of several encyclopedic medical books; responsible for systemizing *physiology*. [d. September 23, 1738]

1712 *Peter Bochler*, U.S. Moravian theologian, born in Prussia;

leader of Moravians of Georgia in migration to *Bethlehem, Pennsylvania*. [d. April 27, 1775]

1738 *Charles, 1st Marquis Cornwallis*, British Army general; a primary force in the British presence in the American Revolution; Governor-General of India, 1786; 1805; Viceroy of Ireland, 1798–1801. [d. October 5, 1805]

1803 *José Maria Heredia*, French poet, born in Cuba; leader in French Parnassian movement. [d. May 2, 1939]

1815 *George Gordon Meade*, U.S. soldier; commander of the *Army of the Potomac*, 1863–65; victorious over Confederate forces at the *Battle of Gettysburg*. [d. November 6, 1872]

1830 *Ismail Pasha*, Viceroy of Egypt, 1866–79; his rule led directly to British occupation of Egypt, 1882. [d. March 2, 1895]

1853 *Tasker Howard Bliss*, U.S. soldier, diplomat; first commandant of U.S. Army War College; U.S. Army Chief of Staff, 1915–20. [d. November 9, 1930]

1869 *Henri-Emile Benoit Matisse*, French painter; leader of the Fauvist school. [d. November 3, 1954]

1880 *George Catlett Marshall,* U.S. Army general, statesman; U.S. Army Chief of Staff, 1939–45; U.S. Envoy to China, 1945–47; U.S. Secretary of State, 1947–49; U.S. Secretary of Defense, 1950–51; formulated plan for economic relief of war-ravaged Europe (*Marshall Plan*); Nobel Peace Prize, 1953. [d. October 16, 1959]

1884 *Elizabeth Arden (Florence Nightingale Graham),* U.S. businesswoman; opened her own luxury salons and developed the line of Elizabeth Arden cosmetics. [d. October 18, 1966]

Stanley F(orman) Reed, U.S. jurist; Associate Justice, U.S. Supreme Court, 1938–57. [d. April 3, 1980]

1892 *Jason Robards,* U.S. actor; leading actor in over one hundred films, 1921–61. [d. April 4, 1963]

1894 *Pola Negri (Barbara Appolonia Chalupiec),* Polish-born actress. [d. August 1, 1987]

1905 *Jule Styne (Julius Kerwin Stein),* U.S. composer, producer. [d. September 20, 1994]

1908 *Simon Wiesenthal,* Austrian author; survivor of Nazi death camps who founded Jewish Documentation Center; wrote *The Murderers Among Us,* 1967.

1930 *Odetta (Felious Gordon),* U.S. folk singer, known for the African motifs in her songs.

1937 *Anthony Hopkins,* Welsh actor; Oscar winner for *Silence of the Lambs,* 1991

1943 *John Denver (Henry John Deutschendorf),* U.S. singer, songwriter, actor; known for his songs, *Take Me Home Country Road,* 1971, and *Rocky Mountain High,* 1972. [d. October 12, 1997]

Ben Kingsley (Krishna Bhanji), British actor; Academy Award for *Ghandhi,* 1983.

Sarah Miles, British actress; known for her role in *Ryan's Daughter,* 1970.

1946 *Diane von Furstenberg,* Belgium-born fashion designer.

Patti Smith, U.S. singer, poet, songwriter.

Diane (Simone Michelle) von Furstenberg, U.S. fashion designer, born in Belgium.

1947 *Burton Cummings,* Canadian singer, musician; member of the rock group, *Guess Who.*

1948 *Tim Matheson,* U.S. actor; known for his role in *Animal House,* 1978.

Donna Summer (LaDonna Andrea Gaines), U.S. singer; known for her disco songs, *Hot Stuff* and *She Works Hard for the Money.*

1959 *Val Kilmer,* U.S. actor; starred in *Batman Forever,* 1995.

HISTORICAL EVENTS

1584 In France the Guises and *Philip II* form *League of Joinville* against the Huguenots.

1600 *East India Company (London Company)* is chartered.

1908 *Sergei Prokofiev* makes first professional appearance at age 17 in St. Petersburg, Russia.

1941 *Chester W. Nimitz* assumes command of U.S. Pacific Fleet (World War II).

1946 French troops evacuate *Lebanon.*

1963 Federation of *Rhodesia* and *Nyasaland* is dissolved; the two territories gain independence from Great Britain as the *Republic of Zambia* and *Malawi.*

1968 U.S.S.R. conducts the world's first test of a commercial supersonic jetliner.

1970 Proceedings are begun in a London court to end *The Beatles'* partnership.

1974 *Gold* sales become legal in the U.S. after 40 years of restriction.

1983 Major General *Mohammed Buhari* is named Nigerian chief of state in a military coup which deposes President *Alhaji Shehu Shagari.*

1997 *Mohammad Rafiq Tara* becomes the new president of Pakistan, replacing Farooq Leghari, who had resigned (December 2, 1997).

Index of Names, Terms, and Events

A

A.R.E. National Day (Libya), Jul. 23.
Aachen (Germany), Oct. 2, 1944; falls to Allies, Oct. 21, 1944.
Aaland Islands, May 25, 1921.
Aalto, Alvar, Feb. 3, 1898.
Aames, Willie, Jul. 15, 1960.
Aaron, Henry Louis (Hank), Feb. 5, 1934; Apr. 8, 1974; May 1, 1975.
Abacha, Sani, dies, Jun. 8, 1998.
Abbe, Cleveland, Dec. 3, 1838.
Abbey, Edwin Austin, Apr. 1, 1852.
Abbey Theater (Dublin), Jul. 18, 1951.
Abbot, George, Jun. 25, 1887.
Abbott, Bud (William A.) Oct. 2, 1900.
Abbott, Grace, Nov. 17, 1878.
Abbott, Jack, Jan. 21, 1944.
Abbott, Lyman, Dec. 18, 1835.
Abbyssinia, Oct. 18, 1896.
Abdoulaya Issa Day (Popular Republic of Benin), Apr. 1.
Abdul, Paula, Jun. 19, 1963.
Abdul-Jabbar, Kareem, Apr. 16, 1947.
Abdullah (Sheikh of Kuwait): dies, Nov. 24, 1965.
Abdullah, Mohammad, Dec. 5, 1905.
Abdullah, Seyyid Iamshid bin, Jul. 2, 1963.
Abel, Niels Henrik, Aug. 5, 1802.
Abel, Rudolf, Feb. 10, 1962.
Abel, Sid, Feb. 22, 1918.
Abel, Sir Frederick, Augustus, Jul. 17, 1827.
Abenaki Indians, Feb. 28, 1704.
Abercromby, Sir Ralph, Oct. 7, 1734.
Aberdeen, patron of, Nov. 13.
Aberdeen University, Feb. 10, 1495.
Aberfan (Wales): colliery slag disaster, Oct. 21, 1966.
Abernathy, Ralph, Mar. 11, 1926.

Abertondo, Antonio, Sep. 22, 1961.
Able, May 28, 1959.
Abolhassan, Bani-Sadr, Mar. 22, 1933.
Abolition Day (Puerto Rico), Mar. 22.
abortion, Jan. 22, 1973; Feb. 13, 1973; legalized in Italy, May 18, 1978; legalized in Canada, Jan. 28, 1988; restrictions on, Jul. 3, 1989; new legislation in Pennsylvania, Nov. 18, 1989.
Aboukir, H.M.S.: sunk, Sep. 22, 1914.
Abourezk, James George, Feb. 24, 1931.
Abraham, F. Murray, Oct. 24, 1940.
Abrahams, Harold, Dec. 15, 1899.
Abram, Morris Berthold, Jun. 19, 1918.
Abrams, Creighton Williams, Sep. 15, 1914.
Abrams, Harry N(athan), Dec. 4, 1904.
Abruzzo, Ben, Aug. 17, 1978.
Abscam investigation, May 1, 1981.
Abu Simbel temples, Jan. 4, 1966.
Abyssinia, Oct. 26, 1896.
Abzug, Bella, Jul. 14, 1920.
Academie Francaise, Jan. 29, 1635.
Academy of Arts and Letters, American, Apr. 17, 1916.
Academy of Arts and Sciences, American, May 4, 1780.
Academy of Motion Picture Arts and Sciences, Nov. 7, 1941.
Academy of Radio and Television Arts and Sciences, Mar. 21, 1950.
Acadia, Mar. 29, 1632.
Acadians: expelled, Oct. 7, 1755.
Accession of H.M. King Hussein (Jordan), Aug. 11.

Accession of Sheik Zaid Bin Sultan Al-Nahayan Anniversary of the (United Arab Emirates), Aug. 6.
Accession of the Sultan (Oman), Jul. 23.
Ace, Goodman, Jan. 15, 1899.
Acheson, Dean G., Apr. 11, 1893. Sep. 8, 1950.
Achille Lauro, Oct. 7, 1985.
Achonry Ireland, patron of, Aug. 11.
acid rain, Aug. 14, 1984.
Acquired Immune Deficiency Syndrome See: AIDS.
Acre: captured, Jul. 12, 1191; May 18, 1291; Mar. 19, 1799.
act of reconciliation: Roman Catholic and Greek Churches, Dec. 71 1965.
Act of Supremacy, May 8, 1559.
Actium, Battle of, Sep. 2, 31 b.c.
actors, patroness of, Jan. 3.
Actors' Equity Union, May 26, 1913.
actresses: first, Jan. 3, 1661.
Acuff, Roy, Sep. 15, 1903.
Adair, Frank, Apr. 9, 1887.
Adalberto Rivera, Julio: inaugurated, Jul. 1, 1962.
Adam, Robert, Jul. 3, 1728.
Adam's Rib: premiere, Dec. 24, 1949.
Adami, Eddie French: inaugurated, May 12, 1907.
Adamic, Louis, Mar. 23, 1899.
Adamkus, Valdas, Jan. 4, 1998.
Adams, Abigail, Nov. 11, 1744.
Adams, Ansel, Feb. 20, 1902.
Adams, Brock(man), Jan. 13, 1927.
Adams, Brooke, Feb. 8, 1949.
Adams, Brooks, Jun. 24, 1848.
Adams, Bryan, Nov. 5, 1959.
Adams, Charles Francis, Aug. 18, 1807; May 27, 1835.
Adams, Don, Apr. 19, 1927.

Adams, Douglas Noel, Mar. 11, 1952.

Adams, Edie, Apr. 16, 1929.

Adams, Henry Brooks, Feb. 16, 1838.

Adams, Herbert Baxter, Apr. 16, 1850.

Adams, James Truslow, Oct. 18, 1878.

Adams, Joey, Jan. 6, 1911.

Adams, John Couch, Jun. 5, 1819.

Adams, John M. G., Sep. 24, 1931.

Adams, John, Oct. 30, 1735; Feb. 24, 1785; Feb. 4, 1789; Mar. 4, 1793; inaugurated, Mar. 4, 1797.

Adams, John Quincy, Jul. 11, 1767; inaugurated, Mar. 4, 1825.

Adams, Lee, Apr. 14, 1960.

Adams, Louisa, Feb. 12, 1775.

Adams, Maud, Feb. 12, 1945.

Adams, Maude, Nov. 11, 1872.

Adams, Samuel, Sep. 27, 1722.

Adams, Sherman Llewellyn, Jan. 8, 1899.

Adams, Walter Sidney, Dec. 20, 1876.

Adamson, Joy, Jan. 20, 1910.

Addams, Charles (Samuel), Jan. 7, 1912.

Addams, Jane, Sep. 6, 1869.

Adderley, Cannonball, Sep. 9, 1928.

Addis Ababa, May 5, 1936; Apr. 6, 1941.

Addis Ababa, Treaty of: signed, Oct. 26, 1896.

Addison, Joseph, May 1, 1672.

Addman, Kenneth Lee, Jun. 9, 1946.

Ade, George, Feb. 9, 1866.

Aden, Jan. 18, 1963.

Adenauer, Konrad, Jan. 5, 1876.

Adjani, Isabelle, Jun. 27, 1955.

Adler, Alfred, Feb. 7, 1870.

Adler, Cyrus, Sep. 13, 1863.

Adler, Kurt, Jul. 10, 1902.

Adler, Richard, May 13, 1954; May 5, 1955.

Admission Day (Alaska), Jan. 3.

Admission Day (Arizona), Feb. 14.

Admission Day (California), Sep. 9.

Admission Day (Hawaii), Aug. intro.

Admission Day (Kansas), Jan. 29.

Admission Day (Maine), Mar. 15.

Admission Day (Michigan), Jan. 26.

Admission Day (New Mexico), Jan. 6.

Admission Day (Oregon), Feb. 14.

Admission Day (Rhode Island), May 29.

Admission Day (Utah), Jan. 4.

Admission Day (Vermont), Mar. 4.

Adolf (Count of Nassau), May 5, 1292.

Adolf Frederick (Sweden), May 14, 1710.

Adolphus, William, Jul. 24, 1817.

Adoption Week, National, Nov. intro.

Adrian, Edgar Douglas, Nov. 30, 1889.

Adrian I (pope), Feb. 1, 772.

Adrian VI (pope), Mar. 2, 1459.

Adrianople, Jul. 22, 1913.

Adrianople, Peace of, Sep. 14, 1829.

Adults' Day (Japan), Jan. 15.

Adundet, Phumiphon, May 5, 1950.

Aduwa, Battle of, Mar. 1, 1896.

The Adventures of Augie March: published, Sep. 18, 1953.

Adzhubei, Aleksei I., Jan. 30, 1962.

aerial bombing of U.S.: only, Sep. 9, 1942.

aerial reconnaissance, Oct. 22, 1911.

Aeronautical Society of Great Britain, Jan. 12, 1866.

affirmative action: women, Mar. 25, 1987; Jan. 23, 1989.

The Affluent Society: published, May 27, 1958.

Afghan New Year (Afghanistan), Mar. intro.

Afghan War, First, Nov. 2, 1841.

Afghan War, Second: begins, Nov. 22, 1878.

Afghanistan, Aug. 8, 1919; Jan. 17, 1929; Sep. 6, 1961; monarchy abolished, Jul. 17, 1973; Apr. 27, 1978; Feb. 14, 1979; invaded by Soviet Union, Dec. 27, 1979; Feb. 22, 1980; Soviet troop withdrawal, May 15, 1988; withdrawal of Soviet forces, Jan. 20, 1989, Feb. 5, 1989, Feb. 15, 1989; earthquake, Feb. 4, 1998.

AFL *See*: American Federation of Labor.

Africa Day (Gabon), May 25.

Africa Day (Zambia), Mar. 24.

Africa Freedom Day (Zambia), May intro.

Africa, German East (Tanganyika), Jan. 10, 1920.

Africa, North: German and Italian surrender, May 12, 1943.

African American Marketing & Media Association, Oct. 26, 1990.

African famine rdief, Mar. 7, 1985; Jul. 13, 1985.

African Kraal: premieres, Jun. 30, 1903.

African National Congress (ANC), Apr. 5, 1960; victorious in free elections, Nov. 1, 1995.

African Nuclear Weapons Free Zone Treaty, Apr. 11, 1996.

The African Queen: premiere, Feb. 20, 1952.

African Unity, Organization of, May 26, 1963; concludes meeting, Jul. 5, 1977.

Afridi uprising, Mar. 11, 1898.

Afro-American (Hlack) History Month, National, Feb. intro.

Afro-American Unity Organization, Feb. 21, 1965.

Afro-Asian People's Solidarity Conference, Third, Feb. 10, 1963.

Agar, Herbert (Sebastian), Sep. 29, 1897.

Agassi, Andre, Apr. 28, 1970.

Agassiz, Jean Louis Rodolphe, May 28, 1807.

Agattu (Aleutian Islands): seized by Japan, Jun. 14, 1942.

Agca, Mehmet Ali, Jul. 22, 1981.

The Age of Innocence, May 29, 1921.

The Age of Reform, May 7, 1956.

Agee, James, Nov. 27, 1909; May 5, 1958.

Agee, William McReynolds, Jan. 5, 1938.

Agency for International Development, Sep. 4, 1961.

Agincourt, Battle of, Oct. 25, 1415.

Agnadello, Battle of, May 14, 1509.

Agnew, Spiro, Nov. 9, 1918; Jan. 20, 1969; resigns, Oct. 10, 1973; May 2, 1974.

Agnon, Shmuel Yosef Halevi, Jul. 17, 1888.

Agreement on Tariffs and Trade (GATT), Jan. 1, 1995.

Agricola, Georgius, Mar. 24, 1494.

agricultural fair: first in U.S., Oct. 1, 1810.

Agricultural Adjustment Act, May 12, 1933.

Agricultural Fair Day (U.S), Oct. 1.

Agriculture Day, Mar. intro.

Agronsky, Martin Zama, Jan. 12, 1915.

Agt, Andreas van, Feb. 2, 1931.

Aguinaldo, Emilio, Mar. 23, 1901.

Agutter, Jenny, Dec. 20, 1952.

Ahern, Bertie, Jun. 26, 1997.

Aherne, Brian, May 2, 1902.

Ahidjo, Ahmadou, Aug. 5, 1924.

AIDS, Jan. 4, 1984; Jan. 11, 1984; Apr. 21, 1984; Apr. 23, 1984; Mar. 2, 1985; Sep. 19, 1986; Jan. 16, 1987; Mar. 4, 1987; Jun. 24, 1987; Nov. 12, 1987.

Aiken, Conrad (Potter), Aug. 5, 1889.

Aiken, Howard Hathaway, Mar. 8, 1900.

Aiken, Joan Delano, Sep. 4, 1924.

Aikin, Howard, Aug. 6, 1944.

Aikman, Troy, Nov. 21, 1966.

Ailey, Alvin, Jan. 5, 1931.

Aimee, Anouk, Apr. 27, 1932.

air attack: first U.S. on Germany, Jan. 27, 1943.

air mail service: first established, Nov. 10, 1919.

Air Force Academy (U.S.): established, Apr. 1, 1954; dedicated, Jul. 11, 1955.

Air Force Day (Nicaragua), Feb. 1.

aircraft crossing of Atlantic: first, Jun. 15, 1919.

airline industry, European, Dec. 7, 1987.

airplane trip around the world: first, Jul. 1, 1931.

airship passenger service: first, Jun. 22, 1910.

Airy, Sir George Biddell, Jul. 27, 1801.

Aisne, First Battle of, Sep. 15, 1914.

Aisne, Second Battle of, Apr. 16, 1917.

Aisne, Third Battle of, May 27, 1918; May 31, 1918; Jun. 1, 1918.

Aix, France, patron of, Jun. 8.

Aix-la-Chapelle, Peace of, Oct. 18, 1748.

Akbar (Emperor of Hindustan), Oct. 15, 1542.

Akbar the Great (Mogul), Nov. 5, 1556.

Akeley, Carl, May 19, 1864.

Akers, Michelle, Feb. 1, 1966.

Aki, Heiiti, Mar. 3, 1930.

Akihito: ascension, Jan. 7, 1989.

Akins, Zoe, Oct. 30, 1886.

Akufo-Addo, Edward: inaugurated, Aug. 31, 1970.

Al-Massira Celebration Day (Morocco), Nov. 6.

Alabama, University of, Feb. 6, 1956.

Alabama: admitted to Union, Dec. 14, 1819; secedes from Union, Jan. 11, 1861; May 20, 1961.

Alain-Fournier, Oct. 3, 1886.

Alais, Peace of, Jun. 28, 1629.

Alam El Halfa, Battle of: begins, Aug. 31, 1942.

Alamo, Mar. 6, 1836.

Alamogordo (New Mexico), Jul. 16, 1945.

Alarcon, Fabian, Feb. 9, 1997.

Alarcon, Pedro Antonio de, Mar. 10, 1833.

Alaska Day (Alaska), Oct. 18.

Alaska Native Claims Act, Dec. 18, 1971.

Alaska: purchased by U.S., Mar. 30, 1867; purchase, May 15, 1867; admitted to Union, Jan. 3, 1959.

Alaskan oil pipeline, Jan. 13, 1971; work begins, Mar. 9, 1975; first oil, Jul. 28, 1977.

Albania, Nov. 28, 1912; Jan. 23, 1916; Jan. 21, 1925; Apr. 7, 1939; Apr. 8, 1939; Jul. 11, 1967; Sep. 13, 1968.

Albany (New York State), Jan. 6, 1797.

Albee, Edward Franklin, Mar. 12, 1928.

Alberghetti, Anna, Maria, May 15, 1936.

Albert (Sweden), Feb. 24, 1389.

Albert, Carl, May 10, 1908.

Albert, Eddie, Feb. 22, 1908.

Albert I (Belgium), Apr. 8, 1875; dies, Feb. 17, 1934.

Albert II (Germany), Aug. 16, 1397.

Albert of Saxe-Coburg-Gotha, Prince, Aug. 26, 1819.

Albert, Prince (England), Feb. 10, 1840.

Albert, Prince (Monaco), Mar. 14, 1958.

Albert V (Austria), Dec. 18, 1437; King of Germany, Mar. 18, 1438.

Albert: named Prince Consort, Jun. 25, 1857.

Alberta (Canada), Sep. 1, 1905.

Alberti, Leon Battista, Feb. 14, 1401.

Albertson, Jack, Jun. 16, 1910.

Albright, Madeleine, May 15, 1937, Jan. 23, 1997.

Albright, William F., May 24, 1891.

Albright, William, Oct. 20, 1944.

Albuquerque, Afonso de, Mar. 4, 1510.

Alcala Zamora y Torres, Niceto, Apr. 7, 1936.

Alcatraz Island, Mar. 21, 1963; occupied by Native Americans, Nov. 20, 1969.

Alcock, John W., Nov. 6, 1892; Jun. 15, 1919.

Alcohol Education Month, Nov. intro.

Alcohol, Tobacco, and Firearms (ATF), Department of, Apr. 19, 1993.

Alcoholics Anonymous: established, Jun. 10, 1935.

Alcott, Amos Bronson, Nov. 29, 1799.

Alcott, Louisa, May, Nov. 29, 1832.

Alda, Alan, Jan. 28, 1936.

Alda, Robert, Feb. 26, 1914.

Aldershot, Feb. 22, 1972.

Aldington, Richard, Jul. 8, 1892.

Aldiss, Prian (Wilson), Aug. 18, 1925.

Aldrich, Thomas Bailey, Nov. 11, 1836.

Aldridge, Ira, Aug. 7, 1805.

Aldrin, Edwin Eugene (Buzz) Jr., Jan. 20, 1930; Nov. 13, 1966; Jul. 20, 1969.

Aleardi, Aleardo, Nov. 4, 1812.

Alegre, S , Apr. 13, 1913.

Aleichem, Sholem, Feb. 18, 1859.

Aleixandre, Vicente, Apr. 26, 1898.

Aleman, Arnoldo, elected, Oct. 20, 1996.

Aleman Valdes, Miguel: inaugurated, Dec. 1, 1946.

Aleppo, Jan. 1, 1925.

Alessandri Rodriguez, Jorge: inaugurated, Nov. 3, 1958.

Aleutians: Japanese carrier attack, Jun. 3, 1942.

Alexander (King of Greece), Jul. 20, 1893; Jun. 11, 1917; Jul. 2, 1917.

Alexander (Lithuania), Jun. 7, 1492.

Alexander (Russia), Apr. 30, 1815.

Alexander (Serbia), Mar. 6, 1889; massacred, Jun. 10, 1903.

Alexander Cuza, King (Rumania), Feb. 23, 1866.

Alexander, Grover Cleveland, Feb. 26, 1887.

Alexander, Harold Rupert Leofric George, Dec. 10, 1891.

Alexander I (Russia), Dec. 23, 1777; Mar. 23, 1801.

Alexander I (Scotland), Jan. 8, 1107; dies, Apr. 22, 1124.

Alexander I (Yugoslavia), Dec. 16, 1888; Aug. 16, 1921; Jan. 5, 1929; Mar. 22, 1929.

Alexander II (Russia), Apr. 29, 1818; Mar. 2, 1855; Sep. 7, 1856; Jan. 15, 1858; Apr. 3, 1861; Apr. 14, 1879; Feb. 17, 1880; assassinated, Mar. 13, 1881.

Alexander II (Scotland), Aug. 24, 1198; Dec. 4, 1214.

Alexander III (Russia), Mar. 10, 1845; May 27, 1883; dies, Nov. 1, 1894.

Alexander III (Scotland), Sep. 4, 1241; dies, Mar. 19, 1286.

Alexander IV (pope), May 4, 1256.

Alexander, Jane, Oct. 28, 1939.

Alexander, Lamar, Jul. 3, 1940.

Alexander, Shana, Oct. 6, 1925.

Alexander, Sir William, Feb. 4, 1629.

Alexander the Great, Sep. 20, 356 b.c.

Alexander V (pope), Jun. 29, 1408.

Alexander VI (pope), May 4, 1493.

Alexander VII (pope), Feb. 13, 1599.

Alexanderson, Ernst Frederick Werner, Jan. 25, 1878.

Alexandr Pushkin: Soviet liner, Apr. 26, 1966.

Alexandra (Denmark), Mar. 10, 1863.

Alexandri, Vasile, Jul. 21, 1821.

Alexandria (Egypt), Dec. 22, 640.

alexandrite, Jun. intro.

Alexian Brothers, patron saint of the, Jul. 17

Alexis, (Czarevitch of Russia), Aug. 12, 1904.

Alexius I Comnenus (Byzantine Emperor), Apr. 29, 1091.

Alfieri, Count Vittorio, Jan. 16, 1749.

Alfonsin, Raul Ricardo: inaugurated, Dec. 10, 1983, Jun. 8, 1987; resigns, Jun. 12, 1989.

Alfonso (Aragon), Feb. 26, 1443.

Alfonso (King of Spain), Dec. 29, 1874.

Alfonso VI (Castile), May 25, 1085.

Alfonso X (Castile), Sep. 14, 1262; Jan. 15, 1950.

Alfonso X (Germany, Holy Roman Emperor), Nov. 23, 1221.

Alfonso XI (Castile), Oct. 30, 1340.

Alfonso XII (Spain), Nov. 28, 1857; Jun. 25, 1870; Jan. 9, 1875; Jan. 14, 1875; dies, Nov. 25, 1885.

Alfonso XIII (Spain), Apr. 17, 1886; May 17, 1886; crowned, Dec. 1, 1887; May 17, 1902; Apr. 13, 1913.

Alfred Hitchcock Presents: television debut, Oct. 2, 1955.

Alfred P. Murrah federal building, bombed, Apr. 19, 1995.

Alfven, Hannes, May 30, 1908.

Alger, Horatio, Jan. 13, 1832.

Algeria, Nov. 1, 1954; Jan. 24, 1960; Jan. 29, 1960; Feb. 19, 1962; independence, Jul. 3, 1962; Jul. 5, 1962; first regular government, Sep. 26, 1962; Oct. 8, 1962; Jun. 15, 1964; Feb. 11, 1965; Feb. 24, 1971; Nov. 19, 1976.

Algeria-Morocco Campaign: begins, Nov. 8, 1942.

Algerian Home Guard, Feb. 10, 1960.

Algiers, Mar. 3, 1815; capture by French, Jul. 5, 1830; Jan. 24, 1960.

Algiers Treaty, Sep. 17, 1980.

Algren, Nelson, Mar. 28, 1909.

Ali Bhutto, Zulfikar: inaugurated, Dec. 20, 1971.

Ali Khan, Liaqual: assassinated, Oct. 16, 1951.

Ali, Muhammad (Cassius Clay), Jan. 18, 1942; Apr. 18, 1953. Feb. 25, 1964. May 25, 1965; May 5, 1967; May 8, 1967; Mar. 8, 1971; Jun. 26, 1971; Oct. 30, 1974; Sep. 15, 1978.

Ali Nasser Muhammad, Jan. 13, 1986.

Ali of Arabia, Caliph: murdered, Jan. 24, 661.

Ali Razmara, Premier (Iran): assassinated, Mar. 7, 1951.

Alia, Ramiz, Apr. 11, 1985; Feb. 22, 1991.

Alice (Mary Victoria Augusta Pauline), Princess, Feb. 25, 1883.

Alicia, Ana, Dec. 12, 1957.

aliens, illegal, May 5, 1987.

Alinsky, Saul David, Jan. 30, 1909.

All Fools' Day, Apr. 1.

All Hallow's Eve, Oct. 31.

All in the Family: television debut, Jan. 12, 1971.

All People's Congress (Sierra Leone), Jun. 14, 1978.

All Prayer's Day (Denmark), Apr. 25.

All Saints of Ireland, Feast of, Nov. 6.

All Saints' Day ,(Sweden), Nov. 5.

All Saints' Day, Nov. 1.

All Souls' Day, Nov. 2.

Allais, Maurice, May 31, 1911.

Allama Iqbal Day (Pakistan), Nov. 9.

Allan, Yigal, Oct. 10, 1918.

Allen, Bryan, Jun. 12, 1979.

Allen, Deborah, Jan. 16, 1950. Sep. 30, 1953.

Allen, Ethan, Jan. 10, 1738; May 10, 1775.

Allen, Florence Ellinwood, Mar. 23, 1884.

Allen, Fred, May 31, 1894.

Allen, Gracie, Jul. 26, 1906.

Allen, Irwin, Jun. 12, 1916.

Allen, Joan, Aug. 20, 1956.

Allen, Karen, Oct. 5, 1951.

Allen, Mel, Feb. 14, 1913.

Allen, Nancy, Jun. 24, 1949.

Allen, Peter Woolnough, Feb. 10, 1944.

Allen, Red, Jan. 1, 1895.

Allen, Richard, Feb. 14, 1760.

Allen, Richard Vincent, Jan. 1, 1936.

Allen, Steve, Dec. 26, 1921.

Allen, Tim, Jun. 13, 1953.

Allen, Woody, Dec. 1, 1935; Apr. 3, 1978; Apr. 24, 1979.

Allenby, Edmund Henry Hynman, Apr. 23, 1861.

Allende, Salvador, Jul. 26, 1908; inaugurated Nov. 4, 1970; Sep. 11, 1973.

Alley, Kirstie, Jan. 12, 1955.
Alliance for Progress, Aug. 17, 1961.
Allies, Supreme Council of, May 7, 1919.
Alliluyeva, Svetlana, Mar. 6, 1967; Nov. 2, 1984.
Allison, Robert Arthur *(Bobby)*, Dec. 3, 1937.
Allman, Duane, Nov. 20, 1946.
Allman, Gregory Lenoir *(Gregg),* Dec. 7, 1947.
Allston, Washington, Nov. 5, 1779.
Allward, Walter Seynnour, Nov. 18, 1875.
Allyson, June, Oct. 7, 1923.
Almeida, Francisco de, Feb. 2, 1509.
Almeida Neves, Tancredo de: elected, Jan. 15, 1985.
Alomar, Roberto, Feb. 5, 1968.
Alonso, Alicia, Dec. 21, 1921.
Alpert, Herb, Mar. 31, 1935.
Alpinists, patron of, May 28.
Alsace, patron of, Dec. 13.
Alsop, Joseph Wright, Oct. 11, 1910.
Alsop, Stewart Johonnot Oliver, May 17, 1914.
Altagracia Day (Dominican Republic), Jan. 21.
Altgeld, John Peter, Dec. 30, 1847.
Alting: world's oldest parliament (Iceland), Jun. 23, 1930.
Altman, Robert, Feb. 20, 1925.
Altman, Sidney, May 7, 1939.
Altmark, Truce of, Sep. 25, 1629.
Alton, Treaty of, Jul. 19, 1101.
Altranstadt, Feb. 13, 1706.
Alvarado, General Juan Velasco (Peru): overthrown, Aug. 29, 1975.
Alvarez Armelino, Gregorio Conrodo, Nov. 26, 1925.
Alvarez de Toledo, Fernando, Oct. 29, 1507.
Alvarez, Luis Walter, Jun. 13, 1911.
Alvarino, Angeles, Oct. 3, 1916.
Alvensleben Convention, Feb. 8, 1863.
Amadeo I (Spain), Nov. 17, 1870; Feb. 11, 1873.
Amadeus, Duke of Aosta, Nov. 17, 1870.
Amadeus I (Spain), May 30, 1845.
Amahl and the Night Visitors: premiere, Dec. 24, 1951.

Amalrik, Andrei Alekseyevich, May 12, 1938.
Amanulla (King of Afganistan): abdicates, Jan. 14, 1929.
Ambers, Lou, Aug. 17, 1938.
Ambler, Eric, Jun. 28, 1909.
Amboise, Edict of, Mar. 19, 1563.
Ameche, Don, May 31, 1908.
Amerasinghe, Hamilton Shirley, Mar. 18, 1915.
America's Cup, Aug. 22, 1851; Sep. 26, 1983; Feb. 4, 1987.
America, Aug. 22, 1851.
American Astronomical Society, Jan. 8, 1998, Jan. 9, 1998.
American Bar Association: created, Aug. 21, 1878.
American Baseball League, Jan. 29, 1900.
American Basketball Association: formed, Feb. 2, 1967; Jun. 17, 1976.
American Bell, Inc., Jan. 6, 1983.
American Broadcasting Companies, Mar. 18, 1985.
American Buffalo: opens, Feb. 16, 1977.
American Cancer Society, May 22, 1913.
American Canoe Association: organized, Aug. 3, 1880.
The American Challenge: published, Jul. 15, 1968.
American Civil Liberties Union, Jan. 20, 1920.
American Council on Education, Mar. 26, 1919.
American Dental Association, Feb. 26, 1950.
American Dictionary of the English Language, Apr. 14, 1828.
American Family Day (Arizona, Minnesota), Aug. intro.
American Federation of Labor, Nov. 9, 1935.
American Federation of Teachers, May 9, 1916.
American Football League, Jun. 8, 1966.
American Free Trade Agreement (NAFTA), approved by U.S. Senate, Nov. 20, 1993; Mexico approves, Nov. 22, 1993;

Canada North Atlantic
Americans with Disabilities Act, Jul. 26, 1990.
American Heart Association, Jun. 8, 1963.
American History Month, Feb. intro.
American hostages: freed, Jan. 20, 1981.
American in Paris: premiere, Dec. 13, 1928; film premiere, Oct. 4, 1951.
American Indian Movement, Feb. 27, 1973; Apr. 5, 1973.
American Legion, Mar. 15, 1919.
American Library Association: founded, Oct. 6, 1876.
American Lung Association, Jun. 6, 1904.
American Motors Corp., Mar. 9, 1987.
American Nazi Party: leader killed, Aug. 25, 1967; Apr. 21, 1983.
American Philatelic Society, Sep. 14, 1886.
American Professional Football Association, Jun. 24, 1922.
American Revolution, Jun. 2, 1774; May 10, 1775; Jul. 3, 1775; Sep. 22, 1776; Dec. 11, 1776; Dec. 25, 1776; Dec. 26, 1776; Jul. 6, 1777; Aug. 16, 1777; Oct. 3, 1777; Oct. 4, 1777; Oct. 17, 1777; Dec. 29, 1778; May 25, 1780; Sep. 23, 1780; Sep. 25, 1780; Oct. 7, 1780; Jan. 17, 1781; Oct. 19, 1781; Nov. 25, 1783.
American Society for the Prevention of Cruelty to Animals: founded, Apr. 10, 1866.
American Society of Composers, Authors, and Publishers, Feb. 13, 1914
American Telephone & Telegraph Co., May 15, 1951; Jan. 1, 1984.
American Tobacco Co., May 1, 1911.
Amerson, Lucius, Jan. 16, 1967.
Ames, Bruce N., Dec. 16, 1928.
Ames, Ed, Jul. 9, 1927.
amethyst, Feb. intro.
Amiens, Peace of, Mar. 27, 1802.
Amin, Hafizullah (Afghanistan): Jan. 17, 1929; inaugurated, Sep. 16, 1979. Dec. 27, 1979.

Amin, Idi (Uganda), Jan. 25, 1971;
Feb. 2, 1971.

Amini, Ali, May 9, 1961.

Amir, Yigal, life imprisonment, Mar.
27, 1996.

Amis, Kingsley, Apr. 16, 1922.

Ammann, Othmar H., Mar. 26, 1879.

Amoco Cadiz, Mar. 17, 1978; Apr.
19, 1984.

Amory, Cleveland, Sep. 2, 1917.

Amos 'n' Andy: television debut,
Jun. 28, 1951.

Amos, John, Dec. 27, 1942.

Amos, Tori, Aug. 22, 1963.

Amos, Wally, Jul. 1, 1936.

Ampere, Andre Marie, Jan. 22, 1775.

Amritsar, Golden Temple of, Jun. 6,
1984.

Amritsar Massacre, Apr. 13, 1919.

Amsterdam, Morey, Dec. 14, 1914.

Amtrak, May 1, 1971; Jan. 4, 1987;
Sep. 22, 1993.

Amundsen, Roald, Jul. 16, 1872; Dec.
14, 1911; May 12, 1926.

amyotrophic lateral sclerosis (Lou
Gehrig's Disease), Mar. 4, 1993.

Anastasia, Albert, Sep. 26, 1902.

Anaya, Rudolfo, Oct. 30, 1937.

Ancestors Day (Haiti), Jan. 1.

Anchorage: earthquake, Mar. 27,
1964.

Ancon, Peace of, Oct. 20, 1883.

Andean Development Corporation,
Feb. 7, 1968.

Anders, William A., Dec. 21, 1968.

Andersen, Hans Christian, Apr. 2,
1805.

Anderson, Bonnie Marie, Oct. 22,
1955.

Anderson, Carl David, Sep. 3, 1905.

Anderson, Dame Judith, Feb. 10,
1898.

Anderson, Eddie *(Rochester),* Sep.
18, 1905.

Anderson, George Lee *(Sparky),*
Feb. 22, 1934.

Anderson, Gilbert *(Bronco Billy),*
Mar. 21, 1882.

Anderson, Gillian, Aug. 9, 1968.

Anderson, Harry, Oct. 14, 1952.

Anderson, Ian, Aug. 10, 1947.

Anderson, Jack, Oct. 19, 1922.

Anderson, Loni, Aug. 5, 1946.

Anderson, Lynn, Sep. 26, 1947

Anderson, Marian, Feb. 17, 1902;
Apr. 9, 1939; Oct. 7, 1954.

Anderson, Max(ie Leroy), Aug. 17,
1978. May 15, 1980. Jun. 27,
1983.

Anderson, Maxwell, Dec. 15, 1888;
Dec. 8, 1948.

Anderson, Melissa Sue, Sep. 26,
1962.

Anderson, Philip Warren, Dec. 13,
1923.

Anderson, Robert Orville, Apr. 13,
1917.

Anderson, Sherwood, Sep. 13, 1876.

Anderson, Terry, released from
captivity, Dec. 4, 1991.

Andersonville, May 7, 1956.

Andersson, Bibi, Nov. 11, 1935.

Andes (Peru): earthquake, May 31,
1970.

Andorra la Vieja, Fiesta de
(Andorra), Aug intro.

Andre, John, May 2, 1750; Sep. 23,
1780.

Andrea Doria: sinks, Jul. 25, 1956.

Andree, (Salomon) August, Oct. 18,
1854; body found, Aug. 6, 1930.

Andreotti, Giulio, Jan. 14, 1919.

Andres Perez, Carlos: inaugurated,
Mar. 12, 1974.

Andress, Ursula, Mar. 19, 1936.

Andrew (Albert Christian Edward),
Prince, Feb. 19, 1960; Mar. 18,
1986; Jul. 23, 1986.

Andrews, (Carver) Dana, Jan. 1,
1909.

Andrews, Julie, Oct. 1, 1935.

Andrews, LaVerne, Jul. 6, 1915.

Andrews, Maxine, Jan. 3, 1918.

Andrews, Patricia *(Patti),* Feb. 16,
1920.

Andric, Ivo, Feb. 10, 1892; Oct. 10,
1892.

Andropov, Yuri Vladimirovich, Jun.
15, 1914. Nov. 12, 1982. dies,
Feb. 9, 1984; Feb. 13, 1984.

Andros, Sir Edmund, Dec. 6, 1637.

Andrus, Cecil D., Aug. 25, 1931.

The Andy Griffith Show: television
debut, Oct. 3, 1960.

Anfinsen, Christian Boehmer, Mar.
26, 1916.

Angam Day (Nauru), Oct. intro.

Angell, Sir Norman Thomas, Dec. 26,
1872.

Angelou, Maya Marguerita, Apr. 4,
1928.

Angle, Edward Hartley, Jun. 1, 1855.

Anglesey, patron of, Feb. 1.

Anglican-Roman Catholic
International Commission, Dec.
30, 1971.

Anglund, Joan Walsh, Jan. 3, 1926.

Angola, Jan. 31, 1975; independence,
Nov. 11, 1975; Apr. 10, 1977;
Jan. 8, 1984; Apr. 17, 1985; Dec.
13, 1988; peace treaty, Nov. 20,
1994.

Angola, National Union for the Total
Independence of, Apr. 4, 1978.

Angola, Popular Movement for
Liberation of, Feb. 11, 1976.

Angora, Battle of (Ankara), Jul. 20,
1402; Jul. 28, 1402.

Angora, Mar. 28, 1930.

Angostura Bridge, Jan. 6, 1967.

Angstrom, Anders Jonas, Aug. 13,
1814.

Anguilla Day (Anguilla), May 30.

Anguilla, Feb. 16, 1967.

Anheuser-Busch Companies:
incorporated, Jul. 7, 1875.

Animal Farm: published, Aug. 26,
1946.

Aniston, Jennifer, Feb. 11, 1969.

Anka, Paul, Jul. 30, 1941.

Ankara, Mar. 28, 1930.

Ankara, Treaty of, Oct. 30, 1930.

Ankerstrom, Count, Mar. 16, 1792.

Ankrah, Joseph, Feb. 24, 1966.

Ann-Margret (Ann Margret Olsson),
Apr. 28, 1941.

Anna (Empress of Russia), Feb. 7,
1693; Feb. 11, 1730.

Annabella, Oct. 31, 1965.

Annam: French control established,
Jun. 6, 1884.

Anne (Queen of England), Feb. 6,
1665; Mar. 8, 1702; dies, Aug. 1,
1714.

*Anne Frank: The Diary of a Young
Girl:* published, Jun. 12, 1952.

Anne of Austria, May 14, 1643.

Anne of Cleves, Jan. 6, 1540; Jul. 6,
1540; Jul. 29, 1540.

Anne of the Thousand Days:
premiere, Dec. 8, 1948.

Anne, Princess (England), Aug. 15, 1950; Nov. 14, 1973.

Annenberg, Walter Hubert, Mar. 13, 1908.

Annie Get Your Gun: premiere, May 16, 1946.

Annie Hall, Apr. 3, 1978.

Annie: premiere, Apr. 21, 1977.

Anniversary Day (Albania), Jan. 1.

Anniversary Day (Auckland, New Zealand), Jan. 29.

Anniversary Day (Wellington, New Zealand), Jan. 22.

Anniversary of Liberation (Czech Republic), May 9.

Anniversary of the 1985 Coup Attempt (Liberia), Nov. 12.

Anniversary of the Battle of Vonnu (1919) (Estonia), Jun. 23.

Anniversary of the Coronation of Grand Duke Mindaugas (Lithuania), Jul. 6.

Anniversary of the Death of Chiang Kai-shek (Taiwan), Apr. 5.

Anniversary of the Enlightenment of Sakyamuni, founder of Buddhism (Tibet), Apr. 15.

Anniversary of the First Postage Stamp (U.S.), May 6.

Anniversary of the Green March (Morocco), Nov. 6.

Anniversary of the Popular Movement of the Revolution (Democratic Republic of the Congo), May 20.

Anniversary of the Royal Brunei Regiment (Brunei), May 31.

Anniversary of the Slovak National Uprising Day (Slovakia), Aug. 29.

Anniversary of Women's Revolt (Guinea), Aug. 27.

Anniversary of Zaire (Democratic Republic of the Congo), Oct. 27.

Annunciation, Mar. intro.

Annunciation of our Lord to the Blessed Virgin, Mary, Mar. 25.

Anouilh, Jean, Jun. 23, 1910.

Ansermet, Ernest Alexandre, Nov. 11, 1883.

Anson, (Adrian) Cap, Apr. 17, 1851.

Anson, George, Apr. 23, 1697.

Anspach, Susan, Nov. 23, 1939.

Ant, Adam, Nov. 3, 1954.

Antarctic Treaty, Dec. 1, 1959.

Antarctica, Mar. 2, 1958; Mar. 4, 1962.

Anthony, Susan Brownell, Feb. 15, 1820; Jun. 18, 1872.

Anti-Defamation League, Oct. 13, 1913.

Anti-Semitic Day (Germany), Apr. 1, 1933.

anti-war demonstration: Wall Street (New York City), May 8, 1970.

antiapartheid groups, protests in South African, Jun. 6, 1988.

Antietam, Battle of, Sep. 17, 1862.

Antigua and Barbuda: become a single independent nation, Oct. 31, 1981.

Antigua, Nov. 1, 1964; Feb. 16, 1967; Feb. 27, 1967; independence, Nov. 1, 1981.

Antin, Mary, Jun. 13, 1881.

Antioch College, May 14, 1852.

Antioch, Jun. 3, 1098; Jun. 28, 1098.

Antipiracy agreement, Jun. 17, 1996.

Anton, Susan, Oct. 12, 1950.

Antonescu, Ion, Jun. 15, 1882; Oct. 6, 1940; overthrown, Aug. 23, 1944; Jun. 1, 1946.

Antonio, Reynaldo Benito, Jan. 21, 1928.

Antonioni, Michelangelo, Sep. 29, 1912.

Antony and Cleopatra: premiere, Sep. 16, 1966.

Antwerp (Belgium): German siege of, Sep. 28, 1914; falls to Germany, Oct. 9, 1914; reoccupied by Belgium, Nov. 19, 1918; Scp. 4, 1944.

Antwerp, Truce of, Apr. 9, 1609.

Anything Goes: premiere, Nov. 21, 1934.

ANZAC Day (Australia, New Zealand, Samoa, Tonga), Apr. 25.

Anzick (Montana): oldest human bones found at, Dec. 29, 1982.

Anzio (Italy), Jan. 22, 1944.

ANZUS Treaty: signed, Sep. 1, 1951.

aortic valve, Sep. 11, 1952.

Apaches, May 17, 1885.

apartheid, Feb. 3, 1960; Apr. 13, 1961; Feb. 10, 1963.

aperire, Apr. intro.

Apess, William, Jan. 31, 1798.

Apollo spacecraft, Jan. 27, 1967.

Apollo 4, Nov. 9, 1967.

Apollo 7, Oct. 22, 1968.

Apollo 8, Dec. 21, 1968.

Apollo 9, Mar. 3, 1969; Mar. 13, 1969.

Apollo 10, Mar. 18, 1969; May 22, 1969.

Apollo 11, Jul. 16, 1969; Jul. 20, 1969.

Apollo 12, Nov. 14, 1969; Nov. 19, 1969.

Apollo 13, launched, Apr. 11, 1970.

Apollo 14, launched, Jan. 31, 1971.

Apollo 15, Jul. 26, 1971; Jul. 31, 1971; Aug. 2, 1971.

Apollo 16, moon walk, Apr. 21, 1972; Apr. 27, 1972.

Apollo 17, Dec. 12, 1972.

Apollo 18, Jul. 17, 1975; Jul. 24, 1975.

Apollo, May intro.

Appearing of Our Lady at Lourdes, Feast of, Feb. 11.

Appearing of St. Michael the Archangel, Feast of the, May 8.

Apple Month, National, Oct. intro.

Appleton, Sir Edward Victor, Sep. 6, 1892.

Appomattox Court House, Apr. 9, 1865.

April Fools' Day, Apr. 1.

Aprilis, Apr. intro.

Aqaba (Jordan): captured by Arabia, Jul. 6, 1917.

aquamarine, Mar. intro.

Aquarius, Jan. intro; Feb. intro.

Aquino, Benigno S., Jr.: Nov. 27, 1932; Aug. 3, 1976; assassinated, Aug. 21, 1983; murder investigation, Oct. 23, 1984; Jan. 23, 1985.

Aquino, Corazon Cojuangco (*Cory*), Jan. 25, 1933 Feb. 7, 1986; inaugurated, Feb. 25, 1986.

Aquitaine, Jan. 11, 1360.

Arab commandos, Sep. 6, 1970.

Arab countries: first peace conference with Israel, Dec. 21, 1973.

Arab Federation of Iraq and Jordan, Feb. 14, 1958.

Arab guerrillas: attack at Rome airport, Dec. 17, 1973.

Arab League Day (Arab League Countries), Mar. 22.

Arab nations: policy regarding Israel, Jan. 12, 1965.

Arab oil embargo: begins, Oct. 17, 1973; Oct. 21, 1973.

Arab-Israeli War of 1947, May 15, 1947.

Arab-Israeli War of 1967, Jun. 5, 1975.

Arabi Pasha, Jan. 10, 1883.

Arafat, Yasir, Aug. 24, 1929; Feb. 3, 1969. May 2, 1989; signs an accord with Rabin, May 5, 1994; elected, Jan. 20, 1996.

Arago, Francois, Feb. 26, 1786.

Aragon, Jan. 19, 1497.

Aragon, Louis, Oct. 3, 1897.

Aragon, patron of, Mar. 26.

Aramburu, Pedro Eugenio, Nov. 13, 1955.

Arana, Diego Barros, Aug. 16, 1830.

Arana Osorio, Carlos: inaugurated, Jul. 1, 1970.

Arango, Andres Pastrana, Aug. 17, 1954; elected, Jun. 21, 1998.

Arany, Janos, Mar. 2, 1817.

Aras, Second Battle of, Sep. 3, 1918.

Arbor Day (Arizona), Feb. 6.

Arbor Day (Delaware, Nebraska, Wyoming, Utah), Apr. intro.

Arbor Day (Delaware, Nebraska), Apr. 22.

Arbor Day (Jordan), Jan. 15.

Arbor Day (Spain), Mar. 26.

Arbor Day (Taiwan), Mar. 12.

Arbor Day, Apr. intro.

Arbuckle, Fatty, Mar. 24, 1887.

Arcaro, Eddie, Feb. 19, 1916.

Archbasilica of the Most Holy Savior Dedication of the, Feast of, Nov. 9.

Archer, Anne, Aug. 25, 1947.

Archer, Jeffrey Howard, Apr. 15, 1940.

archers, patron of, Jan. 20; Jul. 25.

Archipenko, Alexander, May 30, 1887.

architects, patron of, Jul. 2; Dec. 4; Dec. 21.

Arden, Elizabeth, Dec. 31, 1884.

Arden, Eve, Apr. 30, 1912.

Ardennes, Jan. 6, 1945.

Ardizzone, Edward (Jeffrey Irving), Oct. 16, 1906.

Ardrey, Robert, Oct. 16, 1908.

Arendt, Hannah, Oct. 14, 1906.

Aretino, Pietro, Apr. 20, 1492.

Arezzo, patrons of, Jun. 3.

Argentina, May 25, 1810; independence, Jul. 9, 1816; Sep. 4, 1939; Oct. 17, 1945; Sep. 23, 1947; May 20, 1955; Mar. 24, 1976; Jan. 7, 1977; May 4, 1982; new currency, Jan. 6, 1983; divorce legalized, Jun. 8, 1987.

Argo Merchant: oil spill, Dec. 21, 1976.

Argonne, Feb. 20, 1915.

Argonne Forest, Battle of: begins, Sep. 26, 1918; ends, Oct. 10, 1918.

Arguello, Leonardo, May 26, 1947.

Arianism, Feb. 27, 380.

Arias, Arnulfo, May 9, 1951.

Arias Navarro, Carlos, Jan. 3, 1974; Jul. 3, 1976.

Arias, Oscar: inaugurated, May 8, 1986; Aug. 7, 1987.

Aries, Mar. intro; Apr. intro.

Ariosto, Ludovico, Sep. 8, 1474.

Aristide, Jean-Bertrand, Jul. 15, 1953; elected, Dec. 18, 1990; overthrown, Sep. 29, 1991; Oct. 19, 1993; ousted, Sep. 19, 1994.

Aristides: first Kentucky Derby winner, May 17, 1875.

Arizona: purchased from Mexico, Jun. 30, 1854; admitted to Union, Feb. 14, 1912.

Arkansas: admitted to Union, Jun. 15, 1836; secedes, May 6, 1861.

Arkin, Alan Wolf, Mar. 26, 1934.

Arktika, Aug. 16, 1977.

Arkwright, Sir Richard, Dec. 23, 1732.

Arlandes, Marquis d', Nov. 21, 1783.

Arledge, Roone Pinckney, Jul. 8, 1931.

Arliss, George, Apr. 10, 1868.

Armada, Spanish, May 19, 1588; dispersed, Jul. 28, 1588.

Armatrading, Joan, Dec. 9, 1950.

Armed Forces Day (Angola), Aug. 1.

Armed Forces Day (Benin, Rwanda), Oct. 26.

Armed Forces Day (Burma), Mar. 27.

Armed Forces Day (Chile), Sep. 19.

Armed Forces Day (Egypt), Oct. 6.

Armed Forces Day (Equatorial Guinea), Aug. 3.

Armed Forces Day (Honduras), Oct. 21.

Armed Forces Day (Liberia), Feb. 11.

Armed Forces Day (Mauritania), Jul. 10.

Armed Forces Day (United States), May intro.

Armenia, May 28, 1918; Dec. 7, 1988; independence, Aug. 23, 1990.

Armenian Republic, Jan. 26, 1920.

Armenian revolt, Apr. 20, 1915.

Armenian Soviet Socialist Republic, Apr. 2, 1921.

Armenians: Turkish persecution, Apr. 8, 1915; Feb. 11, 1988.

Armida: premiere, Mar. 25, 1904.

The Armies of the Night: published, May 6, 1968.

Armilustrium, Oct. intro.

Arminius, Jacob, Oct. 10, 1560.

Armistice Day, Nov. 11.

armistice: signed, ends World War I, Nov. 3, 1918; goes into effect, Nov. 11, 1918.

Armour, Philip Danforth, May 16, 1832.

Armstrong, (Daniel) Louis (Satchmo), Jul. 4, 1900.

Armstrong, Anne Legendre, Dec. 27, 1927.

Armstrong, Bess, Dec. 11, 1953.

Armstrong, Edwin H., Dec. 18, 1890; Nov. 6, 1935; Jan. 5, 1940.

Armstrong, Henry, Oct. 29, 1937; May 31, 1938; Aug. 17, 1938.

Armstrong, Louis, Aug. 4, 1901.

Armstrong, Neil A.: first man to set foot on the moon, Aug. 5, 1930; Jul. 20, 1969.

Armstrong, Otis, Nov. 11, 1950.

Armstrong-Jones, Antony, Mar. 7, 1930. May 6, 1960.

Army Day (Azerbaijan), Oct. 9.

Army Day (Democratic Republic of the Congo), Nov. 17.

Army Day (Guatemala), Jun. 30.

Army Day (Haiti), Nov. 18.

Army Day (Iraq), Jan. 6.

Army Day (Lesotho), Jan. 21.

Army Day (People's Republic of China), Aug. 1.

Army Day (Republic of Mali), Jan. 20.

Army Day (Tajikistan), Feb. 23.

Army Nurse Corps: organized, Feb. 2, 1901.

Arnason, Jon, Aug. 17, 1819.

Arnaz, Desi, Mar. 2, 1917.

Arnaz, Desi(derio Alberto), Jr., Jan. 19, 1953.

Arnaz, Lucie Desiree, Jul. 17, 1951.

Arndt, Ernest Moritz, Dec. 26, 1769.

Arne, Thomas, Augustine, Mar. 12, 1710.

Arness, James, May 26, 1923.

Arno, Peter, Jan. 8, 1904.

Arnold, Benedict, Jan. 14, 1741; Sep. 25, 1780.

Arnold, Eddy, May 15, 1918.

Arnold, Henry Harley (Hap), Jun. 25, 1886.

Arnold, Matthew, Dec. 24, 1822.

Arnold, Thomas, Jun. 13, 1795.

Arnold, Tom, Mar. 6, 1959.

Arnoldson, Klas P., Oct. 27, 1844.

Arnow, Harriette Louisa Simpson, Jul. 7, 1908.

Arnulf (Holy Roman Emperor), Sep. 1, 891.

Arosemena, Alcibiades, May 9, 1951.

Arosemena Monroy, Carlos: overthrown, Jul. 11, 1963.

Arosemena Monroy, Julio: inaugurated, Nov. 9, 1961.

Arp, Hans (Jean), Sep. 16, 1887.

Arquette, Cliff, Dec. 28, 1905.

Arquette, Rosanna, Aug. 10, 1959.

Arran (Regent of Scotland), Dec. 14, 1542.

Arras, Peace of, Sep. 21, 1435; May 17, 1597.

Arras, Second Battle of the: opens, Aug. 21, 1918.

Arrau, Claudio, Feb. 6, 1903.

Arrhenius, Svante August, Feb. 19, 1859.

Arrow, Kenneth J., Aug. 23, 1921.

Arrow War, Oct. 7, 1856.

Art Week, Mar. intro.

arteriosclerosis, Oct. 9, 1951.

Arthritis Month, May intro.

Arthur, Bea(trice), May 13, 1926.

Arthur, Chester A., Oct. 5, 1829; Mar. 4, 1881; Sep. 19, 1881.

Arthur, Ellen, Aug. 30, 1837.

Arthur Godfrey and His Friends: television debut, Jan. 12, 1949.

Arthur Godfrey Time, Apr. 30, 1945.

Arthur Godfrey's Talent Scouts: television debut, Dec. 6, 1948.

Articles of Confederation: adopted, Nov. 15, 1777.

Articles of Religion: published, Jun. 8, 1536.

artificial heart: implanted in human, Apr. 4, 1969; first successful, Dec. 2, 1982; Mar. 21, 1983.

Artigas Day (Uruguay), Jun. 19.

Artisans, Day of the (Mexico), Dec. 4.

artists, patron of, Oct. 18.

Artois, First Battle of, Sep. 27, 1914.

Artois, Second Battle of, May 9, 1915; ends, Jun. 18, 1915.

Artois, Third Battle of, Sep. 25, 1915; ends, Oct. 15, 1915.

Arts and Letters, American Academy of, Apr. 23, 1904.

Arts and Letters, National Institute of, Apr. 23, 1904.

Aruba, Jan. 1, 1986.

Asbjornsen, Peter Christen, Jan. 15, 1812.

Asbury, Francis, Aug. 20, 1745.

Ascalon: Crusaders defeat Egyptians, Aug. 12, 1099.

ASCAP See: American Society of Composers, Authors, and Publishers.

Asch, Sholem, Nov. 1, 1880.

ASEAN See: Association of Southeast Asian Nations.

Ash, Mary Kay, May 12, c. 1915.

Ashanti War, Apr. 5, 1873; Feb. 4, 1874.

Ashanti: annexed by Great Britain, Sep. 26, 1901.

Ashantis (West Africa), Mar. 25, 1900.

Ashcroft, Dame Peggy, Dec. 22, 1907.

Ashdod, Apr. 30, 1979.

Ashdown, Battle of, Jan. 6, 871.

Ashe, Arthur, Jul. 10, 1943; Sep. 9, 1968; Jan. 28, 1970; Jul. 5, 1975.

Asher, Peter, Jun. 22, 1944.

Ashford, Evelyn, Apr. 15, 1957.

Ashkenazy, Vladimir, Jul. 6, 1937.

Ashley, Elizabeth, Aug. 30, 1939.

Ashley, Laura Mountney, Sep. 7, 1925.

Ashton, Sir Frederick, Sep. 17, 1904.

Asia-Pacific Economic Cooperation (APEC), Nov. 19, 1995.

Asimov, Isaac, Jan. 2, 1920.

Askew, Reubin O'Donovan, Sep. 11, 1928.

Asner, Edward, Nov. 15, 1929.

aspartame, Jul. 15, 1981.

Aspin, Les, women in aerial combat, Apr. 28, 1993.

Aspin, Les(lie), Jr., Jul. 21, 1938.

aspirin, Jan. 26, 1988.

Asquith, Herbert Henry, Sep. 12, 1852; Dec. 6, 1916.

Assad, Hafez al, Oct. 6, 1930. Mar. 12, 1971.

Assam, India: earthquake, Aug. 15, 1950.

Assante, Armand, Oct. 4, 1949.

Asser, Tobias M. C., Apr. 28, 1838.

Associated Press: founded, May 22, 1900.

Association of Caribbean States, Aug. 17, 1995

Association of Southeast Asian Nations (ASEAN), Dec. 15, 1995.

Association of Southeast Asian Nations (ASEAN): formed, Feb. 24, 1967; established, Aug. 8, 1967.

assumption of the Virgin Mary: proclaimed dogma, Nov. 1, 1950.

Assumption Day (Lebanon), Aug. 15.

Assumption Day (Malta), August 15.

Assumption Day (Roman Catholic Communities), Aug. 15.

Assumption Day (Senegal), August 15.

Assumption of Power by the Supreme Military Council (Niger), Apr. 15.

Assumption of the Blessed Virgin Mary, Cathedral of: first U.S. catholic cathedral, May 31, 1821.

Astaire, Adele, Sep. 10, 1898.

Astaire, Fred, May 10, 1899.

aster, Sep. intro.

Astin, John Allen, Mar. 30, 1930.

Astin, Mackenzie Alexander, May 12, 1973.

Aston, Francis William, Sep. 1, 1877.

Astor, John Jacob, Jul. 17, 1763.

Astor, Mary, May 5, 1906.

Astor Place Riot, May 10, 1849.

Astor, Viscountess Nancy Witcher Langhorne, May 19, 1879. Nov. 28, 1919.

Astro-dome (Houston), Apr. 12, 1965.

astronauts (U.S.): three die, Jan. 27, 1967.

Asturias, Miguel Angel, Oct. 19, 1899.

Aswan High Dam, Jan. 9, 1960; Jan. 4, 1966; dedicated, Jan. 15, 1971.

Atassi, Hashem al-, Sep. 5, 1950.

Ataturk, Kemal, Mar. 12, 1880; Jan. 23, 1913; Jan. 20, 1921; Nov. 1, 1922; Oct. 29, 1923; dies, Nov. 10, 1938.

Athenagoras I (Patriarch of Constantinople), Jan. 5, 1964; Dec. 7, 1965.

Athens (Greece): bombarded, Sep. 26, 1687; Apr. 6, 1896; Apr. 27, 1941.

Atherton, Gertrude Franklin, Oct. 30, 1857.

athletes, patron of, Jan. 20.

Atkins, Chet, Jun. 20, 1924.

Atkins, Christopher, Feb. 21, 1961.

Atkinson, (Justin) Brooks, Nov. 18, 1894.

Atlanta (Georgia): occupied, Sep. 2, 1864; Archdiocese of, Jun. 10, 1962.

Atlantic cable: completed, Aug. 5, 1857.

Atlantic Charter: signed, Aug. 14, 1941; Jan. 1, 1942.

Atlantic City (New Jersey), May 26, 1978.

Atlantic Richfield Co.: incorporated, Apr. 29, 1870.

Atlantic telegraph cable: completed, Jul. 27, 1866.

Atlantis: German raider, Apr. 16, 1941.

Atlantis, (space shuttle): launched, May 5, 1989; *Galileo* aboard,

Oct. 18, 1989; docks with *Mir,* Jun. 29, 1995; repairs to *Mir,* Sep. 25, 1997.

Atlas I, Dec. 18, 1958.

atomic bomb: possibilities of developing, Oct. 11, 1939; first test, Jul. 16, 1945; secrets, Apr. 5, 1951.

atomic explosion: first underground, Sep. 19, 1957.

atomic power plant: Antarctica, Mar. 4, 1962.

atomic weapon: Great Britain explodes its first, Oct. 3, 1945; development, Jan. 31, 1950.

Atomic Energy Commission: formed, Aug. 1, 1946; Jan. 31, 1950; Apr. 5, 1963.

Attas, Haydar Abu Bakr al-, Feb. 8, 1986.

Attenborough, David Frederick, May 8, 1926.

Attenborough, Sir Richard (Samuel), Aug. 29, 1923.

Attica (New York): prison riot, Sep. 13, 1971.

Attlee, Clement Richard, Jan. 3, 1883. Jul. 26, 1945.

Attu (Aleutian Islands): seized by Japan, Jun. 14, 1942; Apr. 26, 1943; May 11, 1943.

Atwood, Margaret Eleanor, Nov. 18, 1939.

Auberjonois, Rene Murat, Jun. 1, 1940.

Auberoche, Battle of, Oct. 21, 1345.

Aubrey, John, Mar. 12, 1626.

Auburn Prison, Aug. 6, 1890.

Auchincloss, Louis Stanton, Sep. 27, 1917.

Auchinleck, Sir Claude (John Eyre), Jun. 21, 1884

Audacious H.M.S.: sunk, Oct. 27, 1914.

Auden, W. H., Feb. 21, 1907.

Audubon, John James, Apr. 26, 1785.

Audubon Societies, National Association of, Jan. 5, 1905.

Auel, Jean Marie, Feb. 18, 1936.

Auerbach, Red, Sep. 20, 1917.

Augsburg Confession, presentation of, Jun. 25.

Augsburg, League of: created, Jul. 9, 1686.

Augsburg, Religious Peace of, Sep. 25, 1555.

August Monday (Dominica), Aug. First Monday.

Auguste, Jean Marie Mathias Philippe, Nov. 7, 1838.

Augustine Hermits, Order of, May 4, 1256.

Augustinian nuns, patron of, Aug. 27.

Augustovo Forest, Battle of, Mar. 15, 1915.

Augustus Caesar (Octavius), Sep. 23, 63 b.c.; Sep. 2, 31 b.c.; Aug. intro.

Augustus, Aug. intro.

Aumont, Jean-Pierre, Jan. 5, 1913.

Aung San Suu Kyi, Jun. 19, 1945.

Auntie Mame: opens, Oct. 31, 1956.

Aurangzeb (Emperor of Hindustan), Oct. 24, 1618; May 26, 1659.

Aurelius, Marcus, Apr. 26, 121 a.d..

Auschwitz, Jun. 14, 1940. Jan. 27, 1945.

Austen, Jane, Dec. 16, 1775.

Austerlitz, Battle of, Dec. 2, 1805.

Austin, Alfred: named poet laureate, Oct. 6, 1892.

Austin, Patti, Aug. 10, 1948.

Austin, Stephen Fuller, Nov. 3, 1793.

Austin, Tracy, Dec. 2, 1962.

austral, Jun. 14, 1985.

Australia, Apr. 19, 1770; Apr. 28, 1770; Jan. 1, 1901; first parliament, May 9, 1901; Mar. 2, 1986; bans Japanese fishing boats, Jan. 22, 1998.

Australia Day, Jan. 26.

Australia, patron of, Feb. 1.

Australia, South: first settlers arrive, Dec. 26, 1836.

Australian Air Force, Royal: established, Sep. 1, 1923.

Australian Constitution Act, Aug. 5, 1850.

Australian Gold Rush, Aug. 9, 1851.

Australian-New Zealand troops, Apr. 25, 1915.

Austria, Jan. 26, 1699; serfdom abolished, Sep. 7, 1848; Apr. 14, 1849; May 3, 1859; declares war on Russia, Aug. 6, 1914; proclaimed a republic, Nov. 12, 1918; Apr. 30, 1934; invaded by

Germany, Mar. 12, 1938; Soviet invasion, Mar. 30, 1945; Apr. 13, 1945; Russian occupation ends, May 15, 1955; becomes free and independent, Oct. 25, 1955; Apr. 21, 1970.

Austria, patron of, Nov. 15.

Austria-Hungary: declares war on Serbia, Jul. 28, 1914; general mobilization, Jul. 31, 1914; declares war on Belgium, Aug. 22, 1914; May 23, 1915; Mar. 15, 1916; Apr. 8, 1917; Greece declares war on, Jul. 2, 1917; U.S. declares war on, Dec. 7, 1917; Nov. 12, 1918.

Austrian State Treaty, Oct. 25, 1955

Austrian Succession, War of the, Mar. 15, 1744; ends, Oct. 18, 1748.

Austrians, Jan. 26, 1915.

Austro-Hungarians, May 15, 1916.

autogyro: first, Jan. 10, 1923.

automobile insurance, Aug. 24, 1970.

automobile race: first in U.S., Nov. 28, 1895.

Autry, (Orvon) Gene, Sep. 29, 1907.

autumnal equinox, Sep. intro.

Autumnal Equinox (Japan), Sep. 23.

Avalon, Frankie, Sep. 18, 1940.

Avedon, Richard, May 15, 1923.

Avery, Ostwald T., Oct. 21, 1877.

Avignon, patron of, Apr. 14; Jul. 2.

Avignonese papacy, Jan. 17, 1377.

Avila Camacho, Manuel: inaugurated, Dec. 1, 1940.

Avogadro, Count Amedeo, Jun. 9, 1776.

Avril, Prosper, Sep. 17, 1988.

Awadallah, Abubakr, May 25, 1969.

Awami League, Feb. 24, 1975.

Award Day (Mali), Jan. 20.

Awardene, Junius Richard Jay (Sri Lanka), Feb. 4, 1978.

Awolowo, Obafemi, Mar. 6, 1909.

Axelrod, Julius, May 30, 1912.

Axton, Hoyt Wayne, Mar. 25, 1938.

Ayala, Eligio (Paraguay): overthrown, Feb. 17, 1936.

Ayckbourn, Alan, Apr. 12, 1939.

Ayer, Francis Wayland, Feb. 4, 1848.

Ayer, Harriet Hubbard, Jun. 27, 1849.

Aykroyd, Dan, Jul. 1, 1952.

Aylwin, Patricio, elected, Dec. 14, 1989.

Ayres, Lew, Dec. 28, 1908.

Ayrshire, May 10, 1307.

Ayub Khan, Mohammed, Oct. 27, 1958; inaugurated, Feb. 17, 1960.

Azam, Khaled el, Mar. 27, 1951.

Azcona, Jose: inaugurated, Jan. 27, 1986.

Azerbaijan, May 28, 1918.

Azerbaijan, Soviet troops in, Jan. 20, 1990; independence, Oct. 18, 1991.

azidothymidine (AZT), Sep. 19, 1986. Jan. 16, 1987. Mar. 4, 1987.

Azikiwe, Nnamdi: inaugurated, Oct. 1, 1963.

Azinger, Paul, Jan. 6, 1960.

Aznar, Jose Maria, May 4, 1996.

Azores, Sep. 6, 1951.

B

B'nai B'rith International, Oct. 13, 1843.

B'nai B'rith Month, National, Oct. intro.

B-50, Mar. 2, 1949.

B-52 bombers: crashes, Jan. 22, 1968; first used, Jul. 18, 1968.

B-58: jet bomber, May 26, 1961.

Baath Party (Syria), Feb. 23, 1966.

Babangida, Ibrahim, Aug. 27, 1985.

Babbage, Charles, Dec. 26, 1792.

Babbitt, Bruce Edward, Jun. 27, 1938.

Babbitt, Irving, Aug. 2, 186S

Babbitt, Isaac, Jul. 26, 1799.

Babcock & Wilson Co., Jan. 27, 1983.

Babes in Arms: premiere, Apr. 14, 1937.

Babes in Toyland: premiere, Jun. 17, 1903.

Babilonia, Tai Reina, Sep. 22, 1960.

baboon heart: transplant, Oct. 26, 1984.

Babson, Roger Ward, Jul. 6, 1875.

Baby Fae, Oct. 26, 1984.

Baby M, Mar. 31, 1987.

Bacall, Lauren, Sep. 16, 1924; Jul. 16, 1948.

Baccouche, Salah Eddine, Apr. 15, 1952.

Bach, Barbara, Aug. 27, 1947.

Bach, Catharine, Mar. 1, 1954.

Bach, Johann Christian, Sep. 5, 1735.

Bach, Johann Sebastian, Mar. 21, 1685.

Bach, Karl Philipp Emanuel, Mar. 8, 1714.

Bach, Richard (Davis), Jun. 23, 1936.

Bacha-i-Saquao, Jan. 17, 1929.

Bacharach, Burt, May 12, 1929.

Bachelors' Day, Feb. 29.

Bachman, Randy, Sep. 27, 1943.

Backhaus, Wilhelm, Mar. 26, 1884.

Backus, James Gilmore *(Jim),* Feb. 25, 1913.

Bacon, Henry, Nov. 28, 1866.

Bacon, Kevin, Jul. 8, 1958.

Bacon, Nathaniel, Jan. 2, 1647.

Bacon, Sir Francis, Jan. 22, 1561; Oct. 28, 1909.

bacteria, drug-resistant, Sep. 5, 1984.

Badajoz, Treaty of, Jun. 6, 1801.

Baden, Peace of, Sep. 7, 1714.

Baden-Powell, Robert, Feb. 22, 1857.

Badge of Military Merit, Apr. 7, 1782.

Badr, Saif-al-lslam Mohammed Bin Ahmed al-, Sep. 26, 1962.

Baeck, Leo, May 23, 1873.

Baedeker, Karl, Nov. 3, 1801.

Baekeland, Leo Hendrik, Nov. 14, 1863.

Baer, George Frederick, Sep. 26, 1842.

Baer, Karl Ernst von, Feb. 29, 1792.

Baer, Max, Jun. 14, 1934; Jun. 13, 1935.

Baeyer, Adolph von, Oct. 31, 1835.

Baez, Albert, Nov. 15, 1912.

Baez, Joan, Jan. 9, 1941.

Bagaza, Jean Baptiste, Aug. 29, 1946; Nov. 1, 1976.

Baghdad, Mar. 11, 1917.

Bagnold, Enid, Oct. 27, 1889.

Baha'u'llah, Nov. 12, 1817.

Bahadur Shah II (India), Mar. 9, 1858.

Bahamas: independence, Jan. 7, 1964; Jan. 16, 1967; Jul. 10, 1973; U.N. membership, Sep. 15, 1973.

Bahrain: independence, Aug. 15, 1971.

Bailey, F(rancis) Lee, Jun. 10, 1933.

Bailey, Liberty Hyde, Mar. 15, 1858.

Bailey, Pearl, Mar. 29, 1918.

Bain, Barbara, Sep. 13, 1932.

Bain, Conrad Stafford, Feb. 4, 1923.

Baio, Scott Vincent, Sep. 22, 1961.

Baird, John Logie, Aug. 13, 1888.

Baiul, Oksana, Nov. 16, 1977.

Bajazet I (Ottoman ruler), Jul. 28, 1402.

Bajer, Fredrik, Apr. 21, 1837.

Baker, Blanche, Dec. 20, 1956.

Baker, Carroll, May 28, 1935.

Baker, Diane, Feb. 25, 1938.

Baker, George Pierce, Apr. 4, 1866.

Baker, Ginger, Aug. 19, 1940.

Baker, Howard Henry, Nov. 15, 1925; Feb. 27, 1987.

Baker, James Addison, III, Apr. 28, 1930.

Baker, Joe Don, Feb. 12, 1936.

Baker, Josephine, Jun. 3, 1906.

Baker, May 28, 1959.

Baker, Russell (Wayne), Aug. 14, 1925.

Baker, Sir Samuel White, Mar. 14, 1864.

Bakhtiar, Shahpur: inaugurated, Jan. 6, 1979.

Bakke, Allan Paul, Feb. 4, 1940. Nov. 15, 1976. Jun. 28, 1978.

Bakker, James Orsen (Jim), Jan. 2, 1939. Mar. 19, 1987; Oct. 5, 1989; Oct. 24, 1989.

Bakr, Ahmed Hassan al-, Jul. 16, 1979.

Bakshi, Ralph, Oct. 26, 1938.

Bakunin, Mikhail Aleksandrovitch, May 18, 1814.

Balaclava, Battle of: begins, Oct. 25, 1854.

Balaguer. Joaquin, Sep. 1, 1907, Jan. 18 1962. Jun 1, 1966; May 26, 1978.

Balanchine, George, Jan. 9, 1904.

Balbo, Cesare, Nov. 21, 1789.

Balbo, Italo, Jun. 6, 1896.

Balch, Emily Green, Jan. 8, 1867.

Balchen, Bernt, Oct. 23, 1899; Nov. 29, 1929.

bald eagle, Apr. 8, 1940.

Bald Eagle Days, Aug. intro.

Baldasare, Fred, Jul. 11, 1962.

Baldrige, Malcolm, Jr., Oct. 4, 1922.

Baldwin, Alec, Apr. 3, 1958.

Baldwin, Billy, May 30, 1904.

Baldwin, Faith (Cuthrell), Oct. 1, 1893.

Baldwin I (Jerusalem), Dec. 25, 1100.

Baldwin, James, Aug. 2, 1924; May 18, 1953.

Baldwin, Robert, May 12, 1804.

Baldwin, Roger Nash, Jan. 21, 1884.

Baldwin, Stanley, Aug. 3, 1867.

Bale, John, Nov. 21, 1495.

Balenciaga, Cristobal, Jan. 21, 1895.

Balewa, Abubakar Tafawa, Sep. 2, 1957.

Balfe, Michael William, May 15, 1808.

Balfour, Arthur James, Jul. 25, 1848.

Balfour, Declaration, Nov. 2, 1917.

Balfour, Lord, Apr. 1, 1925.

Balikiapen (Borneo), Apr. 23, 1945.

Balin, Marty, Jan. 30, 1943.

Baliol, John, Nov. 17, 1292.

Balkan Pact, Feb. 9, 1934.

Balkan War, Mar. 6, 1912; begins, Oct. 7, 1912; Oct. 18, 1912; ends, Dec. 3, 1912; Mar. 26, 1913; May 30, 1913; begins, Jun. 30, 1913; Jul. 10, 1913; Jul. 22, 1913.

Ball, Ernest, Jul. 22, 1878.

Ball, George, Dec. 21, 1909.

Ball, Hugo, Feb. 22, 1886.

Ball, Lucille, Aug. 6, 1911.

Ball, Thomas, Jun. 3, 1819.

Ballante, Maurice, Sep. 2, 1930.

Ballantine, Ian Keith, Feb. 15, 1916.

Ballard, Florence, Jun. 30, 1943.

Ballard, Kaye, Nov. 20, 1926.

Ballard, Robert D., Jun. 30, 1942.

Ballesteros, Severiano, Apr. 9, 1957.

Ballet Comique de la Reine: first ballet, Oct. 15, 1581.

Ballinger, Richard Achilles, Jul. 9, 1858.

Balliol, Edward (Scotland): assumes throne, Aug. 11, 1332; Jul. 19, 1333.

balloon ascent: first, Nov. 21, 1783.

balloon flight: first U.S., Jan. 9, 1793.

balloon: first to carry cargo, Sep. 19, 1783.

Ballou, Hosea, Apr. 30, 1771.

Balmaceda, Jose Manuel, Jul. 19, 1840.

Balmain, Pierre Alexandre, May 18, 1914.

Balmat, Jacques, Aug. 8, 1786.

Balsam, Martin Henry, Nov. 4, 1919.

Balthus, Feb. 29, 1908.

Baltic Pact, Sep. 12, 1934.

Baltimore and Ohio Railroad, Mar. 4, 1828; Jul. 4, 1828.

Baltimore, David, Mar. 7, 1938.

Baltimore Orioles (baseball), Sep. 30, 1953.

Baltimore: fire, Feb. 7, 1904.

Balzac, Honore de, May 20, 1799.

Bamberger, Louis, May 15, 1855.

Ban the Bomb rally (London), Apr. 15, 1963.

Banana, Cannan, Mar. 5, 1936.

Bancroft, Ann, Sep. 17, 1931; May 1, 1986.

Bancroft, George, Oct. 3, 1800.

Bancroft, Hubert Howe, May 5, 1832.

Band Aid, Jan. 6, 1985.

Banda, H. Kamazu, Apr. 14, 1906; Feb. 1, 1963; Jul. 6, 1964; inaugurated, Jul. 6, 1966; Aug. 20, 1971.

Bandaranaike, Sirimavo, Apr. 17, 1916; first woman prime minister of Ceylon, Jul. 21, 1960.

Bandaranaike, Solomon: inaugurated, Apr. 12, 1956; assassinated, Sep. 25, 1959.

Banderas, Antonio, Aug. 10, 1960.

Bandinelli, Baccio, Nov. 12, 1493.

Bandung Conference, Apr. 18, 1955.

Bangalore, Mar. 21, 1791.

Bangao Islands, Apr. 2, 1945.

Bangladesh, Mar. 26, 1971; Apr. 12, 1971; Dec. 6, 1971; formed, Dec. 16, 1971; Jan. 24, 1972; Feb. 4, 1972; treaty with India, Mar. 19, 1972; Feb. 24, 1974; Apr. 9, 1974; Jan. 25, 1975; May 30, 1981; Mar. 24, 1982; cyclone hits, Apr. 20, 1991.

Bani-Sadr, Abolhassan, Jan. 25, 1980; dismissed, Jun. 22, 1981.

Bank Employees Day (Guatemala), Jul. 1.

Bank Holiday (Bangladesh), Jul. 1.

Bank Holiday (Botswana, Canada, Fiji, Grenada, Guyana, Hong Kong, Ireland, Malawi), Aug. intro.

Bank Holiday (Iceland), Aug. 1; Aug. 8.

Bank Holiday (Ireland), Jun. intro.; Oct. intro.

Bank Holiday (Japan), Jan. 2.

Bank Holiday (San Marino), Aug. 14; Aug. 15; Aug. 16.

Bank Holiday (Seychelles), Jan. 2.

Bank Holiday (Somalia), Jan. 1.

Bank Holiday (St. Lucia), Aug. First Monday.

Bank Holiday (Taiwan), Jul. 1.

Bank of Canada, Mar. 11, 1935.

Bank of England: incorporated, Jul. 27, 1694; nationalized, Feb. 14, 1946.

Bank of North America: first U.S. commercial bank, Jan. 7, 1782.

Bank of the United States: fails, Dec. 11, 1930.

BankAmerica Corp., Jun. 22, 1983.

bankers, patron of, Sep. 21.

Bankhead, Tallulah, Jan. 31, 1903.

Banks, Ernie, Jan. 31, 1931.

Banks, Jeffrey, Nov. 3, 1953.

Banks, Nathaniel Prentiss, Jan. 30, 1816.

Banks, Tyra, Dec. 4, 1973.

Banneker, Benjamin, Nov. 9, 1731.

Bannister, Roger, Mar. 23, 1929; May 6, 1954.

Bannockburn, Battle of, Jun. 24, 1314; Jun. 11, 1488.

Banque de France: founded, Apr. 14, 1800.

Bante, Teferi (Ethiopia): assassinated, Feb. 3, 1977.

Banting, Sir Frederick Grant, Nov. 14, 1891.

Banzer Suarez, Hugo, Jul. 10, 1926; Aug. 22, 1971; Jul. 21, 1978.

Bao Dai, Feb. 7, 1950; May 21, 1955.

Baptista da Figueiredo, Gen. Joao (Brazil), Oct. 15, 1978; Mar. 15, 1979.

Bara, Theda, Jul. 20, 1890.

Barangay Day (Philippines), Sep. 11.

Barany, Robert, Apr. 22, 1876.

Barbados, Nov. 1, 1964; independence, Nov. 30, 1966; admitted to U.N., Dec. 9, 1966; Mar. 11, 1985.

Barbarossa, Frederick (Germany), May 28, 1167.

Barbeau, Adrienne, Jun. 11, 1945.

Barbecue Month, National, May intro.

barbed wire, Feb. 15, 1876.

Barber, Samuel, Mar. 9, 1910; Sep. 16, 1966.

Barber, Walter Lanier (Red), Feb. 17, 1908.

barbers, patron of, Aug. 25.

Barbie, Klaus, Jan. 25, 1983; Feb. 5, 1983; May 11, 1987; Jul. 4, 1987.

Barbosa, Jose Celso, Jul. 27, 1857.

Barbosa's Birthday (Puerto Rico), Jul. 27.

Barbuda and Antigua: become a single independent nation, Oct. 31, 1981.

Barbuda: independence, Nov. 1, 1981.

Barcelona (Spain): captured, Oct. 14, 1705; Jan. 9, 1875; Jan. 24, 1919; Jan. 26, 1936.

Barcelona, Peace of, Jan. 19, 1493.

Barco Vargas, Virgilio: inaugurated, Aug. 7, 1986.

Bardeen, John, May 23, 1908; Nov. 1, 1956; Oct. 20, 1972.

Bardi, Giovanni de', Feb. 5, 1534.

Bardot, Brigitte, Sep. 28, 1934.

Baretti, Giuseppe, Marc'antonio, Apr. 24, 1719.

Barfield, Jesse Lee, Oct. 29, 1951.

Barghash (Sultan of Zanzibar), Jun. 5, 1873.

Baring, Sir Francis, Apr. 18, 1740.

Barker, Leonard Harold, II (Len), Jul. 7, 1955.

Barker, Robert William (Bob), Dec. 12, 1923.

Barkla, Charles G., Jun. 7, 1877.

Barkley, Alben W., Nov. 24, 1877; Jul. 12, 1948; Jan. 20, 1949.

Barkley, Charles, Feb. 20, 1963.

Barlow, Joel, Mar. 24, 1754.

Barnard, Christiaan (Neethling), Nov. 8, 1922; Dec. 3, 1967.

Barnard, Edward Emerson, Dec. 16, 1857.

Barnard, Frederick Augustus Porter, May 5, 1809.

Barnard, George Grey, May 24, 1863.

Barnes, Clive Alexander, May 13, 1927.

Barnes, Thomas, Sep. 16, 1785.

Barneveldt, Jan van, May 14, 1619.

Barney, Joshua, Jul. 6, 1759.

Barnum and Bailey Circus: debut, Mar. 16, 1881.

Barnum, P(hineas) T(aylor), Jul. 5, 1810.

Barnveldt, Jan van Olden, Sep. 14, 1547.

Baron Bliss Day (Belize), Mar. 9.

Barras, Count Paul Francois Jean Nicolas, Jun. 30, 1755.

Barre, Mohammed Siad, ousted, Jan. 26, 1991.

Barre, Raymond, Apr. 12, 1924; Aug. 25, 1976.

barrelmakers, patron of, Nov. 6.

Barrett, Rona, Oct. 8, 1936.

Barrie, Sir J. M., May 9, 1860; Apr. 24, 1954.

Barrientos, Rene, Nov. 4, 1964; inaugurated, Aug. 6, 1966; Apr. 27, 1969.

Barrier Treaty, Nov. 15, 1715.

Barris, Chuck, Jun. 2, 1929.

Barrow, Clyde, Mar. 24, 1909.

Barrow, Errol: elected, May 29, 1986.

Barrow, Sir John, Jun. 19, 1764.

Barrows, Isabel, Apr. 17, 1845.

Barry, Gene, Jun. 4, 1922.

Barry, Marion, Mar. 6, 1936.

Barry, Sir Charles, May 23, 1795.

Barrymore, Drew, Feb. 22, 1975.

Barrymore, Ethel, Aug. 15, 1879.

Barrymore, John, Feb. 15, 1882.

Barrymore, Lionel, Apr. 28, 1878.

Barth, Heinrich, Feb. 16, 1821.

Barth, John Simmons, May 27, 1930.

Barth, Karl, May 10, 1886.

Barthelme, Donald, Apr. 7, 1931.

Barthes, Roland, Nov. 12, 1915.

Bartholdi, Frederic, Apr. 2, 1834.

Bartholin, Thomas, Oct. 20, 1616.

Bartholomew, Frederick Llewellyn (Freddie), Mar. 28, 1924.

Bartlett, Edward Louis, Apr. 20, 1904.

Bartlett, John, Jun. 14, 1820.

Bartlett, Josiah, Nov. 21, 1729.

Bartlett, Robert Abram, Aug. 15, 1875.

Bartok, Bela, Mar. 25, 1881; Jan. 13, 1904; Feb. 26, 1913; Jul. 1, 1927; First Piano Concerto: premiere, Jul. 1, 1927.

Bartoli, Cecilia, Jun. 4, 1966.

Bartolommeo, Fra, Mar. 28, 1475.

Barton, Clara, Dec. 25, 1821; May 21, 1881.

Barton, Derek Harold Richard, Sep. 18, 1918.

Barton, Enos Melancthon, Dec. 2, 1842.

Bartram, John, Mar. 23, 1699.

Baruch, Bernard M(annes), Aug. 19, 1870.

Baryshnikov, Mikhail, Jan. 28, 1948.

Barzini, Luigi Giorgio, Jr., Dec. 21, 1908.

Barzun, Jacques, Nov. 30, 1907.

Baseball Hall of Fame, Jan. 29, 1936; dedicated, Jun. 12, 1939.

baseball: first game, Jun. 19, 1846; longest major league game, May 1, 1920; first all-star game, Jul. 6, 1933; first night game, May 24, 1935; first indoor game, Apr. 12, 1965; first players' strike, Apr. 13, 1972; first free agent, Dec. 19, 1974.

Basedow, Johann Bernhard, Sep. 11, 1723.

Basehart, Richard, Aug. 31, 1914.

Basel Council, Sep. 4, 1439.

Basel, Peace of, Apr. 12, 1500.

Basel, Treaty of, Sep. 22, 1499.

Basie, Count, Aug. 21, 1904.

Basilica of St., Mary Major Dedication of the, Aug. 5.

Basilicas of St. Peter and of St. Paul Dedication of the, Feast of the, Nov. 18.

Basinger, Kim, Dec. 8, 1953.

basketball: first game, Jan. 20, 1892; first intercollegiate game, Dec. 10, 1896.

Basov, Nikolai Gennadievich, Dec. 14, 1922.

Basra (Iraq), Jan. 9, 1987.

Bass, George, Dec. 9, 1932.

Bass, Sam, Jul. 21, 1851.

Bassey, Shirley, Jan. 8, 1939.

Bastille (Paris): falls to revolutionaries, Jul. 14, 1789.

Bastille Day, Jul. 14.

Basutoland: established, Dec. 13, 1843; Mar. 12, 1868; Feb. 2, 1884; Apr. 30, 1965; Oct. 4,

1966; BAT missles, Apr. 23, 1945.

Bataan (Philippines): Japanese landing, Dec. 8, 1941; falls, Apr. 9, 1942; May 6, 1942; Death March, May 7, 1942.

Bateman, Justine, Feb. 19, 1966.

Bates, Alan Arthur, Feb. 17, 1934.

Bates, Edward, Sep. 4, 1793.

Bates, Henry Walter, Feb. 8, 1825.

Bates, Katherine Lee, Aug. 12, 1859.

Bates, Kathy (Kathleen Doyle Bates), Jun. 28, 1948.

Bateson, Gregory, May 9, 1904.

Batista, Fulgencio (Cuba), Jul. 14, 1940; Mar. 10, 1952; Jan. 2, 1959.

Baton Rouge (Louisiana), Sep. 8, 1935.

Battista, Giovanni: elected pope, Jun. 3, 1963.

Battle, Kathleen, Aug. 13, 1948.

Battle of Boyacá (Colombia), Aug. 7.

Battle of Boyaca (Colombia), Aug. 7.

Battle of the Sexes: tennis match, Sep. 20, 1973.

Batu, Apr. 9, 1241.

Baudelaire, Charles, Apr. 9, 1821.

Baudouin I (Belgium), Sep. 7, 1930; Aug. 11, 1950; Jul. 17, 1951.

Bauer, Eddie, Oct. 19, 1899.

Baum, L. Frank, May 15, 1856.

Baum, Vicki, Jan. 24, 1888.

Baur, Ferdinand Christian, Jun. 21, 1792.

Baxter, Anne, May 7, 1923.

Baxter-Birney, Meredith, Jun. 21, 1947.

Bay Area Rapid Transit (San Francisco): rapid transit system, Sep. 11, 1972.

Bay of Pigs invasion, Apr. 17, 1961; Apr. 20, 1961; Apr. 7, 1962.

Bayar, Celal, May 14, 1950.

Bayh, Birch Evans, Jan. 22, 1928.

Bayle, Pierre, Nov. 18, 1647.

Baylis, Dame Lilian, May 9, 1874.

Bayliss, Sir William Maddock, May 2, 1860.

Bazalgette, Sir Joseph William, Mar. 28, 1819.

Bazazid I (Sultan of Turkey), Jul. 20, 1402.

bazooka, Mar. 27, 1943.

Be Kind to Animals Week, May intro.

Be Late for Something Day (U.S.), Sep. intro; Sep. 5.

Beacham, Stephanie, Feb. 28, 1947.

Beadle, Erastus Flavel, Sep. 11, 1821.

Beadle, George Wells, Oct. 22, 1903.

Beal, John, Aug. 13, 1909.

Beale, Dorothea, Mar. 21, 1831.

Beals, Jennifer, Dec. 19, 1963.

Bean, Alan L., Mar. 15, 1932; Nov. 19, 1969; Jul. 28, 1973.

Bean, Orson, Jul. 22, 1928.

Bean-throwing Festival (Japan), Feb. intro; Feb. 3; Feb. 3.

Beanmont, William, Nov. 21, 1785.

Bear Flag Revolt: begins, Jun. 14, 1846.

Beard, Charles A(ustin), Nov. 27, 1874.

Beard, Daniel Carter, Jun. 21, 1850.

Beard, James, May 5, 1903.

Beardsley, Aubrey (Vincent), Aug. 21, 1872.

Beatles: first recording, Sep. 11, 1962; Oct. 19, 1963; Feb. 7, 1964; Feb. 9, 1964; last concert, Aug. 30, 1966; Jun. 1, 1967; Apr. 10, 1970; May 8, 1970; Dec. 31, 1970.

Beaton, Cecil, Jan. 14, 1904.

Beatrice Companies Inc.: incorporated, Nov. 20, 1924.

Beatrix (Netherlands), Apr. 30, 1980.

Beattie, David Stuart, Feb. 29, 1924.

Beatty, David Earl, Jan. 17, 1871.

Beatty, Ned, Jul. 6, 1937.

Beatty, Sir David, Nov. 29, 1916.

Beatty, Warren, Mar. 30, 1937.

Beaufort, Pierre Roger de, Jan. 5, 1371.

Beauharnais, Josephine de, Mar. 9, 1796.

Beaumarchais, Pierre-Augustin Caron de, Jan. 24, 1732; Apr. 27, 1784.

Beauregard, Pierre Gustave Toutant, May 28, 1818; Apr. 6, 1862.

Beauty Queen Week, Aug. intro.

Beauvoir, Simone de, Jan. 9, 1908.

Beaverbrook, William Maxwell Aitken Lord, May 25, 1879.

Bechuanalnnd (Botswana), Oct. 3, 1895; Mar. 8, 1950; independence, Sep. 30, 1966.

Beck, Dave: indicted, May 2, 1957.

Beck, Jeff, Jun. 24, 1944.

Becker, Boris, Nov. 22, 1967; JuL 7, 1985.

Becket, Thomas, Dec. 21, 1118. Nov. 2, 1164; Dec. 3, 1170; murdered, Dec. 29, 1170; Jul. 12, 1174.

Beckett, Samuel, Apr. 13, 1906; Apr. 19, 1956; Jun. 17, 1970.

Beckett, Sir Edmund, May 12, 1816.

Beckor, Carl Lotus, Sep. 7, 1873.

Becquerel, Antoine Menri, Dec. 15, 1,852; Dec. 12, 1903.

Bedelia, Bonnie, Mar. 25, 1948.

Bedey, Ed, Jr., Sep. 16, 1949.

Beecham, Sir Thomns, Apr. 29, 1879.

Beecher, Catharine Esther, Sep. 6, 1800.

Beecher, Henry Ward, Jun. 24, 1813.

Beecher, Lyman, Oct. 12, 1775.

Beene, Geoffrey, Aug. 30, 1927.

Beeoh, Olive Ann, Sep. 25, 1903.

Beerbohm, Sir Max, Aug. 24, 1872.

Beernaert, Auguste Marie Francois, Jul. 26, 1829.

Beers, Clifford Whittingham, Mar. 30, 1876.

Beersheba (Palestine): captured by British, Nov. 1, 1917.

Beery, Noah, Jan. 17, 1884.

Beery, Noah, Jr. , Aug. 10, 1913.

Beery, Wallace, Apr. 1, 1886.

bees, patron, of, Dec. 7.

Beethoven, Ludwig van, Dec. 16, 1770.

Begay, Fred, Jul. 2, 1932.

Begelman, David, Au. 26, 1921.

Begin, Menachem, Aug. 16, 1913; Jun. 21, 1977; Sep. 17, 1978; Oct. 17, 1978; Mar. 26, 1979; resigns, Sep. 15, 1983.

Begley, Ed(ward James), Mar. 25, 1901.

Beguines of Delgium, patroness of the, Dec. 17.

Behnn, Brendan, Feb. 9, 1923.

Behrens, Peter, Apr. 14, 1868.

Behring, Emil von, Mar. 15, 1854.

Beiderbecke, Leon Bismarck (Bix), Mar. 10, 1903.

Beijing Apr. 5, 1976.

Beirut (Lebanon), Oct. 5, 1918; Oct. 28, 1975; U.S. embassy

destroyed, Apr. 12, 1983; attack on Marine headquarters, Oct. 23, 1983; Feb. 26, 1984.

Bekesy, Georg van, Jun. 3, 1899.

Bekkai, M'barek, Dec. 7, 1955.

Bel Geddes, Barbara, Oct. 31, 1922.

Bel Geddes, Norman, Apr. 27, 1893.

Belafonte, Harry, Mar. 1, 1927.

Belafonte-Haper, Shari, Sep. 22, 1954.

Belasco, David, Jul. 25, 1853.

Belaunde Terry, Fernando, Oct. 7, 1912; inaugurated, Jul. 28, 1963.

Belcher, Jonathan, Jan. 8, 1682.

Belgian Congo. *See*: Congo, Belgian; Congo, Democratic Republic of the; Congo Free State; Zaire, Republic of.

Belgium: independence, Oct. 4, 1830; Apr. 19, 1839; Jan. 1, 1922; May 10, 1940; May 28, 1940; Apr. 3, 1979.

Belgrade, Nov. 29, 1914; falls to Germany and Austria, Oct. 9, 1915; recapture by Serbs, Nov. 1, 1918; Apr. 20, 1941; captured, Oct. 20, 1944.

Belinski, Vissarion Grigorievich, Jul. 12, 1811.

Beliveau, Jean, Aug. 31, 1931.

Belize, Jun. 1, 1973; independcnce, Sep. 21, 1981.

Belknap, Jeremy, Jun. 4, 1744.

Bell, Alexander Graham, Mar. 3, 1847; telephone patent, Mar. 7, 1876; Mar. 10, 1876; Feb. 12, 1877; Jan. 14, 1878; Jan. 25, 1915.

Bell, Andrew, Mar. 27, 1753.

Bell, Clive, Sep. 16, 1881.

Bell, Elliott V(allance), Sep. 25, 1902.

Bell, Gertrude, Jul. 14, 1868.

Bell, Griffin Boyette, Oct. 31, 1918.

Bell, John, Feb. 1, 1797.

Bell, Marilyn, Sep. 9, 1954.

The Bell of Amherst: opens, Apr. 28, 1976.

Bell, Ricky Lynn, Apr. 8, 1955.

Bell, Stephen Scott (*Steve*), Dec. 9, 1935.

Bell, Tommy, Dec. 20, 1946.

Bell, Vanessa, May 30, 1879.

Bell X-1: breaks sound barrier, Oct. 14, 1947.

bell-makers, patron of, Feb. 5.

Bellamy, Edward, Mar. 26, 1850.

Bellamy, Ralph, Jun. 17, 1904.

Bellarmine, Robert (Cardinal), May 19, 1923.

Belle, Albert, Aug. 25, 1966.

Belleau Wood, Hattle of: begins, Jun. 6, 1918; captured, Jun. 25, 1918.

Bellerophon, Jul. 15, 1815.

Belli, Melvin (Mouron), Jul. 29, 1907.

Bellingham, John, May 11, 1812.

Bellingshausen, Fabian Gottlieb von, Sep. 9, 1778.

Bellini, Vincenzo, Nov. 3, 1801.

Bello, Andres, Nov. 29, 1781.

Belloc, (Joseph-Pierre) Hilaire, Jul. 27, 1870.

Bellow, Saul, Jun. 10, 1915; Sep. 18, 1953; Oct. 21, 1976.

Bellows, George Wesley, Aug. 12, 1882.

Bellwood, Pamela, Jun. 26, 1946.

Belmondo, Jean-Paul, Apr. 9, 1933.

Belmont, August, Feb. 18, 1853.

Belmont, Eleanor Robson, Dec. 13, 1879.

Belo, Bishop Carlos F. X., Feb. 3, 1948.

Belsen, Apr. 15, 1945.

Belushi, James, May 15, 1954.

Belushi, John, Jan. 24, 1949.

Bembo, Pietro, May 20, 1470.

Bemelmans, Ludwig, Apr. 27, 1898.

Ben Ali, Zine el- Abidine, Nov. 7, 1987.

Ben Arafa, Moulay Mohammed, Aug. 21, 1953.

Ben Bella, Ahmed, Sep. 26, 1962; Sep. 15, 1963; Jun. 19, 1965; Jul. 4, 1979.

Ben Hur: premiere, Nov. 18, 1959; Apr. 4, 1960.

Ben Youssef, Mohammed, Aug. 15, 1953; Aug. 21, 1953. Dec. 7, 1955.

Ben-Gurion, David, Oct. 16, 1886; Dec. 9, 1953; May 23, 1960; Jun. 19, 1963.

Benacerraf, Baruj, Oct. 29, 1920.

Benatar, Pat, Jan. 10, 1952.

Benavante y Martinez, Jacinto, Aug. 12, 1866.

Bench, Johnny Lee, Dec. 7, 1947.

Benchley, Nathaniel (Goddard), Nov. 13, 1915.

Benchley, Peter, May 8, 1940.

Benchley, Robert Charles, Sep. 15, 1889.

Bendix, Vincent, Aug. 12, 1882.

Bendix, William, Jan. 14, 1906.

Bendjedid, Chadli, Apr. 14, 1929.

Benedict, Dirk, Mar. 1, 1945.

Benedict IX (Boy Pope): resigns, Jul. 16, 1048.

Benedict, Ruth (Fulton), Jun. 5, 1887.

Benedict the Black, Apr. 4.

Benedict XII (pope), Jun. 29, 1408.

Benedict XIII (pope), Feb. 2, 1649.

Benedict XIV (pope), Mar. 31, 1675.

Benedict XV (pope), Nov. 21, 1854; Sep. 3, 1914.

Benedictine nuns and nunneries, patron of, Feb. 10.

Benedictine oblates, patron of, Jul. 13.

Benelux Economic Union: established, Feb. 3, 1958.

Benes, Edvard, May 28, 1884.

Benet, Stephen Vincent, Jul. 22, 1898.

Benet, William Rose, Feb. 2, 1886.

Benevente (Portugal), Apr. 23, 1909.

Bengal, Apr. 23, 1795; becomes Bangladesh, Dec. 16, 1971.

Bengali New Year (Bangladesh), Apr. 15.

Benghazi (Libya), Feb. 7, 1941; Apr. 3, 1941.

Benguela-Katanga railway, Jul. 1, 1931.

Benin: independence, Aug. 1, 1960; Nov. 30, 1975.

Bening, Annette, May 5, 1958.

Benito Juarez Memorial Day (Mexico), Jul. 18.

Benjamin Franklin's Birthday (U.S.), Jan. 17.

Benjamin, Judah Philip, Aug. 6, 1811.

Benjedid, Chadli, Feb. 2, 1979; Jan. 11, 1992.

Benn, Tony, Apr. 3, 1925.

Bennet, Joan, Feb. 27, 1910.

Bennett, Arnold, May 27, 1867.

Bennett, Constance, Oct. 22, 1904.

Bennett, Floyd, Oct. 25, 1890; May 9, 1926.

Bennett, Harry Herbert, Jan. 17, 1892.

Bennett, James Gordon, Sep. 1, 1795; May 10, 1841.

Bennett, Michael, Apr. 8, 1943.

Bennett, Richard Bedford, Jul. 5, 1870.

Bennett, Robert Russell, Jun. 15, 1894.

Bennett, Tony, Aug. 3, 1926.

Bennett, William John, Jul. 31, 1943.

Bennett, William Richards, Apr. 14, 1932.

Bennington Battle Day (Vermont), Aug. 16.

Bennington, Battle of, Aug. 16, 1777.

Benny, Jack, Feb. 14, 1894.

Benoit, Joan, Mar. 16, 1957.

Benso, Camillo, Aug. 10, 1810.

Benson, Edward White, Jul. 14, 1829.

Benson, Ezra Taft, Aug. 4, 1899.

Benson, Frank Weston, Mar. 24, 1862.

Benson, George, Mar. 22, 1943.

Benson, Sally, Sep. 3, 1900.

Bentham, Jeremy, Feb. 15, 1748.

Benton, Thomas Hart, Mar. 1, 1782; Apr. 15, 1889.

Bentsen, Lloyd Millard, Jr., Feb. 11, 1921.

Benumont, Hugh, Feb 16, 1909.

Benvenuti, Nino, Nov. 7, 1970.

Benz, Karl Friedrich, Nov. 25, 1844.

Beobe, (Charles) WIlliam, Jul. 29, 1877.

Berchet, Giovanni, Dec. 23, 1783.

Berchtoldstag (Switzerland), Jan. 2.

Beregovoy, Pierre, Apr. 2, 1992.

Berenger, Thomas (Tom), May 31, 1950.

Berenson, Bernard, Jun. 26, 1865.

Berg, Alan, Apr. 15, 1985.

Berg, Gertrude, Oct. 3, 1889.

Berg, Paul, Jun. 30, 1926.

Bergamo, Apr. 19, 1428.

Bergen, Candice, May 9, 1946.

Bergen, Edgar, Feb. 16, 1903.

Bergen, John J(oseph), Aug. 7, 1896.

Bergen, Polly, Jul. 14, 1930.

Berger, Victor, Nov. 8, 1910.

Bergerac, Cyrano de, Mar. 6, 1619.

Bergius, Friedrich Karl Rudolf, Oct. 11, 1884.

Bergland, Bob Selmer, Jul. 22, 1928.

Bergman, (Ernst) Ingmar, Jul. 14, 1918.

Bergman, Ingrid, Aug. 29, 1915.

Bergson, Henri, Oct. 18, 1859.

Bergstrom, Sune K., Jan. 10, 1916.

Bering Expedition, Feb. 5, 1725.

Beriosova, Svetlana, Sep. 24, 1932.

Berisha, Sali, resigns, Jul. 23, 1997.

Beriya, Lavrenti Pavlovich, Mar. 18, 1899; Jul. 10, 1953; Dec. 24, 1953.

Berkeley, George, Mar. 12, 1685.

Berkeley, University of California at, May 15, 1969.

berkelium, Jan. 17, 1950.

Berkowitz, David, Aug. 10, 1977.

Berle, Adolf Augustus, Jan. 29, 1895.

Berle, Milton, Jul. 12, 1908.

Berlin (Germany), British bombing begins, May 20, 1943; Mar. 6, 1944; Russian troops enter, Apr. 24, 1945; May 2, 1945; Jun. 5, 1945 Soviet blockade, Jun. 24, 1948.

Berlin air lift: ends, Sep. 30, 1949.

Berlin Congress, Jul. 13, 1878.

Berlin, East, Oct. 27, 1961; Jan. 31, 1971.

Berlin, Irving, May 11, 1888; Jun. 16, 1919; May 16, 1946.

Berlin Wall: construction begins, Aug. 13, 1961; taken down, Nov. 9, 1989.

Berlin, West, Jun. 26, 1963; Jan. 31, 1971.

Berliner, Emile, May 20, 1851.

Berliner, Henry, Jun. 16, 1922.

Berlinguer, Enrico, May 25, 1922.

Berlioz, (Louis) Hector, Dec. 11, 1803.

Berlusconi, Silvio, resigns, Dec. 22, 1994.

Berman, Emile Zola, Nov. 2, 1903.

Berman, Sheldon Leonard (Shelley), Feb. 3, 1926.

Bermuda Day (Bermuda), May 25.

Bermuda, May 26, 1968.

Bermudez, Francisco Morales, Oct. 4, 1921.

Bern (Switzerland): Protestant victory, Jul. 25, 1712.

Bernadette, Jan. 7, 1844.

Bernadotte, Folke (Count), Jan. 2, 1895; assassinated, Sep. 17, 1948.

Bernadotte, Marshall, Feb. 5, 1818.

Bernard, Claude, Jul. 12, 1813.

Bernardi, Hershel, Oct. 30, 1923.

Bernhard (Leopold Friedrich Eberhard Julius Kurt Karl Gottfried Peter), Prince, Jun. 29, 1911.

Bernhard, Prince (Netherlands): bribery scandal, Aug. 26, 1976.

Bernhard, Sandra, Jun. 6, 1955.

Bernhardi, Friedrich von, Nov. 2, 1849.

Bernhardt, Sarah, Oct. 22, 1844.

Bernini, Giovanni Lorenzo, Dec. 7, 1598.

Bernoulli, Jakob, Dec. 27, 1654.

Bernsen, Corbin, Sep. 7, 1954.

Bernstein, Carl, Feb. 14, 1944.

Bernstein, Elmer, Apr. 4, 1922.

Bernstein, Leonard, Aug. 25, 1918; Jan. 28, 1944; Dec. 28, 1944; Dec. 1, 1956; Sep. 26, 1957; Nov. 19, 1957.

Bernstorff, Count Andreas Peter von, Aug. 28, 1735.

Bernstorff, Count Johann-Heinrich von, Nov. 14, 1862.

Berra, Yogi, May 12, 1925.

Berreta, Thomas, Nov. 24, 1946.

Berrigan, Daniel J., May 9, 1921.

Berrigan, Philip Francis, Oct. 5, 1923.

Berry, Chuck, Jan. 15, 1926; Oct. 18, 1926.

Berry, Halle, Aug. 14, 1968.

Berry, Ken, Nov. 3, 1933.

Berryman, John, Oct. 25, 1914.

Berthelot, (Pierre Eugene), Marcelin, Mar. 18, 1827; Oct. 27, 1827.

Berthollet, Claude Louis, Dec. 9, 1748.

Berthoud, Ferdinand, Mar. 19, 1727

Berillon, Alphonse, Apr. 23, 1853.

Bertinelli, Valerie, Apr. 23, 1960.

Bertolucci, Bernardo, Mar. 16, 1940.

Bertrand, Louis Jacques Napoleon, Apr. 20, 1807.

Berwanger, Jay, Feb. 8, 1936.

Berzelius, Baron Jons Jakob, Aug. 20, 1779.

Besant, Annie, Oct. 1, 1847.

Besant Pancami (India), Jan. 26.

Besnard, Paul Albert, Jun. 2, 1849.

Besoyan, Rick, Nov. 18, 1959.

Bessarabia, Apr. 9, 1918.

Bessel, Friedrich Wilhelm, Jul. 22, 1784.

Bessell, Ted, May 20, 1935.

Bessemer, Sir Henry, Jan. 19, 1813.

Betances, Ram n, Apr. 8, 1827.

Betancourt, Romulo, Feb. 22, 1908; inaugurated, Feb. 13, 1959; Mar. 11, 1964.

Betancur, Belisario: elected, May 31, 1982.

Bethe, Hans Albrecht, Jul. 2, 1906.

Bethlehem Steel Corp.: founded, Dec. 10, 1904.

Bethmann-Hollweg, Theobald von, Nov. 29, 1856.

Bethune, Mary McLeod, Jul. 10, 1875.

Betjeman, Sir John, Apr. 6, 1906; Oct. 10, 1972.

Bettelheim, Bruno, Aug. 28, 1903.

Better Business Bureaus, Council of, Jul 21, 1970.

Better Hearing and Speech Month, May intro.

Bevan, Aneurin, Nov. 15, 1897.

Beveridge, Albert Jeremiah, Oct. 6, 1862.

Beveridge, William Henry, Mar. 5, 1879.

The Beverly Hillbillies: television debut, Sep. 26, 1962.

Bevin, Ernest, Mar. 9, 1881.

Bewick, Thomas, Aug. 12, 1753.

Bewitched: television debut, Sep. 17, 1964.

Bhave, Vinoba, Sep. 11, 1895.

Bhopal (India), Dec. 3, 1984; Apr. 8, 1985; Feb. 14, 1989.

Bhumibol Adulyadej (King of Thailand), Dec. 5, 1927.

Bhutan, Apr. 5, 1964.

Bhutto, Benazir, Jun. 21, 1953; Jan. 10, 1984; inaugurated, Dec. 2, 1988; removed from office, Aug. 6, 1990; re-elected, Oct. 19, 1993; removed from power, Nov. 5, 1996.

Bhutto, Zulfikar Ali, Jan. 5, 1928; Jul. 5, 1977; sentenced, Mar. 18, 1978; hanged, Apr. 4, 1979; Jan. 10, 1984.

Biafra: Republic of, May 30, 1967; declares independence, Jul. 6, 1967; Apr. 13, 1968; Jan. 11, 1970; Jan. 12, 1970.

Jan. 15, 1970.

Biaggi, Mario, Oct. 26, 1917.

Biak: U.S. troops land on, May 27, 1944.

Bialik, Hayyim Nahman, Jan. 9, 1873.

Bialik, Mayim, Dec. 12, 1975.

Bias, Len, Nov. 18, 1963.

Bible, Revised Version, Feb. 10, 1899.

Bible Week, National, Nov. intro.

Bicentennial, American Revolution, Apr. 18, 1975.

Bicentennial, U.S., Jul. 4, 1976.

Bich, Marcel, Jul. 29, 1914.

Bichat, Marie Francois Xavier, Nov. 11, 1771.

bicycle race: first official, May 31, 1868.

Biddle, Francis Beverly, May 9, 1886.

Biddle, Nicholas, Jan. 8, 1786.

Biden, Joseph Robinette, Jr., Nov. 20, 1942.

Bieber, Owen Frederick, Dec. 28, 1929. May 18, 1983.

Bienville, Jean-Baptiste Le Moyne, sieur de, Feb. 23, 1680.

Bierce, Ambrose (Gwinett), Jul. 24, 1842.

Bierstadt, Albert, Jan. 7, 1830.

Big Bang theory, Smoot, George, Apr. 23, 1992.

The Big Bopper, Oct. 24, 1930.

Bigelow, Erastus Brigham, Apr. 2, 1814.

Biggers, Earl Derr, Aug. 26, 1884.

Biggs, E. Power, Mar. 29, 1906.

Bignone, Reynaldo Benito Antonio, Jan. 21, 1928.

Bike Safety Month, May intro.

Bike Safety Week, National, Apr. intro.

Biko, Steven, Dec. 18, 1946; Sep. 12, 1977; Sep. 15, 1977; funeral, Sep. 25, 1977; Jul. 27, 1979.

Bilbo, Theodore Gilmore, Oct. 13, 1877.

Bill of Rights Day (U.S.), Dec. 15.

Bill of Rights: passed, Dec. 15, 1791.

billiards championship: first U.S., Apr. 12, 1859.

Billings, John Shaw, Apr. 12, 1:838.

Billings, William, Oct. 7, 1746.

Billy Budd: opera premieres, Dec. 1, 1951.

Billy the Kid (ballet): opens, Oct. 16, 1938.

Biloxi (Mississippi): riots, Apr. 24, 1960.

Binaisa, Godfrey, May 30, 1920; Jun. 20, 1979.

Binet, Alfred, Jul. 8, 1857.

Bing, David (Dave), Nov. 29, 1943.

Bing, Sir Rudolph, Jan. 9, 1902.

Bingham, George Caleb, Mar. 20, 1811.

Binnig, Gerd, Jul. 20, 1947.

Binyon, Laurence, Aug. 10, 1869.

biological weapons: treaty, Apr. 10, 1972.

Biosphere 2, Sep. 26, 1991; Sep. 26, 1993.

Birch, Thomas, Jul. 26, 1779.

Bird Day (Oklahoma), May intro.; May 1.

Bird Day (U.S.), Apr. intro.

Bird, Larry Joe, Dec. 7, 1956.

Bird, Vere: first Prime Minister of Antigua and Barbuda, Dec. 7, 1910; Nov. 1, 1981.

Birdseye, Clarence, Dec. 9, 1886.

Birendra Bir Bikram Shah Dev (King of Nepal), Dec. 28, 1945; crowned, Feb. 24, 1975.

Birkenhead (England), Jan. 20, 1885.

Birkoff, George David, Mar. 21, 1884.

Birmingham, Stephen, May 28, 1931.

Birney, David Edwin, Apr. 23, 1940.

Birney, James Gillespie, Feb. 4, 1792.

birth control clinic: first, Oct. 16, 1917.

birth control devices: sale of, Jun. 7, 1965.

birth control pills, May 9, 1960.

Birth of a Nation, Feb. 8, 1915.

Birthday of Atatürk (Turkey), May 19.

Birthday of Emperor Akihito (Japan), Dec. 23.

Birthday of His Majesty the King (Bhutan), Nov. 11.

Birthday of King Sobhuza II (Swaziland), Jul. 22.

Birthday of President Mobutu (Democratic Republic of the Congo), Oct. 14.

Bishop, Hazel (Gladys), Aug. 17, 1906.

Bishop, J. Michael, Feb. 22, 1936.

Bishop, Jim, Nov. 21, 1907.

Bishop, Joey, Feb. 3, 1918.

Bishop, Maurice, May 29, 1944; Mar. 13, 1979; killed, Oct. 19,1983.

Bishop, Sir Henry Rowley, Nov. 18, 1786.

Bismarck, Otto von, Apr. 1, 1815; Sep. 23, 1862; Mar. 18, 1890.

Bismarck Sea, Battle of, Mar. 2, 1943.

Bismarck, Feb. 14, 1939; May 24, 1941.

Bissell, Emily Perkins, May 31, 1861.

Bissell, George Henry, Nov. 8, 1821.

Bisset, Jacqueline Fraser, Sep. 13, 1944.

Bitar, Salah al-, Feb. 23, 1966.

Bitzius, Albrecht (Jeremias Gotthelf), Oct. 4, 1797.

Bixby, Bill, Jan. 22, 1934.

Biya, Paul, re-elected, Oct. 23, 1997.

Biyogo, Masie Nguema: overthrown, Aug. 3, 1979.

Bizet, Georges, Oct. 25, 1838; Mar. 3, 1875; Feb. 26, 1935; First Symphony premiere, Feb. 26, 1935.

Bjerknes, Jacob Aall Bonnevie, Nov. 2, 1879.

Bjork (Gundmundsdottir), Nov. 21, 1965.

Bjorling, Jussi, Feb. 2, 1911.

Bjornson, Bjornsqerne, Dec. 8, 1932.

Bjornsson, Sveinn, Feb. 27, 1881; Jun. 17, 1944.

black majority rule, Mar. 14, 1978.

black rule in Rhodesia, Jul. 5, 1977.

Black Academy of Arts and Letters, Jul. 13, 1970.

Black and Tans, May 15, 1920.

Black Christ Festival (Guatemala), Jan. intro; Jan. 15.

Black, Clint, Feb. 4, 1962.

Black Code: enacted, Nov. 24, 1865.

Black, Davidson, Jul. 25, 1884.

Black Friday: financial panic, Sep. 24, 1869; Germany, May 13, 1927.

Black Hand, The, Jun. 28, 1914.

Black Hole of Calcutta, The, Jun. 20, 1756.

Black, Hugo Lafayette, Feb. 27, 1886.

Black January or Martyr's Day (Azerbaijan), Jan. 20.

Black, Joseph, Apr. 16, 1728.

Black, Karen, Jul. 1, 1942.

Black Monday: stock market decline, Oct. 19, 1987.

Black Prince (England), Sep. 19, 1370.

Black Sea, Jan. 9, 1792.

Black, September: terrorists, Sep. 5, 1972.

Black, Shirley Temple, Apr. 23, 1928.

Black, Sir James W., Jun. 14, 1924.

Black Thursday, Oct. 24, 1929.

Black Tuesday, Oct. 29, 1929.

Blackburn, Elizabeth H., Nov. 26, 1948.

Blackett, Lord Patrick Maynard Stuart, Nov. 18, 1897.

Blackmer, Sidney, Jul. 13, 1898.

Blackmun, Harry Andrew, Nov. 12, 1908; Jun. 9, 1970.

Blackout: New York City, Jul. 13, 1977.

blacks disenfranchised: Louisiana, May 12, 1898.

Blacks, North American: patron of, Apr. 4.

blacksmiths: patron of, Nov. 6.

Blackstone (Virginia): meteor, May 12, 1922.

Blackstone, Sir William, Jul. 10, 1723.

Blackwell, Antoinette Louisa, May 20, 1825.

Blackwell, Earl, Jr., May 3, 1913.

Blackwell, Elizabeth, Feb. 3, 1821.

Blackwell, Henry Browne, May 4, 1825.

Blades, Ruben, Jul. 16, 1948.

Blaiberg, Philip, Jan. 2, 1968.

Blaine, James Gillespie, Jan. 31, 1830.

Blair, Bonnie, Mar. 18, 1964.

Blair, Francis Preston, Apr. 12, 1791.

Blair, Frank, May 30, 1915.

Blair, Linda, Jan. 22, 1959. Dec. 26, 1973.

Blair, Montgomery, May 10, 1813.

Blair, Tony, May 6, 1953; May 1, 1997.

Blaize, Herbert: inaugurated, Dec. 4, 1984.

Blake, Amanda, Feb. 20, 1931.

Blake, Eubie, Feb. 7, 1883; Mar. 2, 1976.

Blake, Robert (Admiral), Apr. 20, 1657.

Blake, Robert, Sep. 18, 1938.

Blake, William, Nov. 28, 1757.

Blakelock, Ralph Albert, Oct. 15, 1847.

Blakely, Susan, Sep. 7, 1948.

Blalock, Alfred, Nov. 29, 1944.

Blalock, Jane, Sep. 19, 1945.

Blanc, (Jean Joseph Charles) Louis, Oct. 29, 1811.

Blanc, Mel(vin Jerome), May 30, 1908.

Blanchard, Francois, Jan. 7, 1785; Jan. 9, 1793.

Blanchard, James J., Aug. 8, 1942.

Blanco, Salvador Jorge, Jul. 5, 1926.

Blanqui, Louis, Auguste, Feb. 1, 1805.

Blasco Ibanez, Vincente, Jan. 29, 1867.

Blashfield, Edwin Howland, Dec. 15, 1848.

Blass, Bill, Jun. 22, 1922.

Blatty, William Peter, Jan. 7, 1928.

Bledsoe, Drew, Feb. 14, 1972.

Bleek, Friedrich, Jul. 4, 1793.

Bleier, Robert Patrick (Rocky), Mar. 5, 1946.

Blenheim, Battle of, Aug. 13, 1704.

Bleriot, Louis, Jul. I, 1872.

Blessed Adam of Loccum, Dec. 22.

Blessed Ado, Dec. 16.

Blessed Adolph Kolping, Oct. 27.

Blessed Adrian Fortescue, Jul. 11.

Blessed Agathangelo, Aug. 7.

Blessed Agnello of Pisa, Mar. 13.

Blessed Agnes de Jesus Galand, Nov. 20.

Blessed Agnes of Bohemia, Mar. 2.

Blessed Alanus de Solminihac, Jan. 3.

Blessed Albert of Bergamo, May 11.

Blessed Alberto Hurtado Cruchaga, Oct. 16.

Blessed Alcuin, May 19.

Blessed Alda, Apr. 26.

Blessed Alexander Rawlins, Apr. 7.

Blessed Alfredo Ildefonso Schuster, May 12.

Blessed Alix le Clercq, Jan. 9.

Blessed Aloisius Scrosoppi, Oct. 5.

Blessed Aloysius Palazzolo, Jun. 15.

Blessed Aloysius Rabata, May 11.

Blessed Alpais, Nov. 3.

Blessed Alphonsus de Orozco, Sep. 19.

Blessed Alvarez of Cordova, Feb. 19.

Blessed Amadeus IX of Savoy, Mar. 30.

Blessed Amata, Jun. 9.

Blessed Ambrose of Camaldoli, Nov. 20.

Blessed Ambrose of Siena, Mar. 20.

Blessed Andrew, May 30.

Blessed Andrew Abellon, May 17.

Blessed Andrew Bessette, Jan. 6.

Blessed Andrew Hilbernon, Apr. 18.

Blessed Andrew of Anagni, Feb. 17.

Blessed Andrew of Antioch, Nov. 30.

Blessed Andrew of Borgo San Sepolcro, Sep. 3.

Blessed Andrew of Montereale, Apr. 12.

Blessed Andrew of Peschiera, Jan. 19.

Blessed Andrew of Rinn, Jul. 12.

Blessed Andrew of Siena, Mar. 19.

Blessed Andrew of Spello, Jun. 3.

Blessed Andrew of Strumi, Mar. 10.

Blessed Angela de la Cruz Guerrero Gonzalez, Mar. 2.

Blessed Angela of Foligno, Feb. 28.

Blessed Angela Salawa, Aug. 13.

Blessed Angelina of Marsciano, Jul. 21.

Blessed Angelo Augustine of Florence, Aug. 18.

Blessed Angelo of Acri, Oct. 30.

Blessed Angelo of Borgo San Sepolcro, Feb. 15.

Blessed Angelo of Chivasso, Apr. 12.

Blessed Angelo of Foligno, Aug. 27.

Blessed Angelo of Furcio, Feb. 6.

Blessed Angostino Roscelli, May 7.

Blessed Anne Mary Javouhey, Jul. 15.

Blessed Anne Mary Taigi, Jun. 9.

Blessed Anne of St. Bartholomew, Jun. 7.

Blessed Annunciata Cocchetti, Apr. 21.

Blessed Anthony Middleton, May 6.

Blessed Anthony Pavoni, Apr. 9.

Blessed Anthony Primaldi, Aug. 14.

Blessed Anthony Pucci, Jan. 12.

Blessed Antonia of Florence, Feb. 28.

Blessed Antonius Gonzdez, Sep. 24.

Blessed Antony Baldinucci, Nov. 7.

Blessed Antony Bonfadini, Dec. 1.

Blessed Antony Della Chiesa, Jul. 28.

Blessed Antony Grassi, Dec. 13.

Blessed Antony Neyrot, Apr. 10.

Blessed Antony of Siena, Apr. 27.

Blessed Antony of Stroncone, Feb. 7.

Blessed Antony the Pilgrim, Feb. 1.

Blessed Apollinaris Franco, Charles Spinola, Sep. 10.

Blessed Archangeklo of Bologna, Apr. 16.

Blessed Archangela Girlani, Feb. 13.

Blessed Archangelo of Calatafimi, Jul. 30.

Blessed Arnold Janssen, Jan. 15.

Blessed Arnulf of Villers, Jun. 30.

Blessed Augustine, Aug. 3.

Blessed Augustine Novello, May 19.

Blessed Augustine of Biella, Jul. 24.

Blessed Avertanus, Feb. 25.

Blessed Ayrald, Jan. 2.

Blessed Balthasar of Chiavari, Oct. 25.

Blessed Baptist of Mantua, Mar. 20.

Blessed Baptista Varani, Jun. 7.

Blessed Bartholomew, Oct. 23.

Blessed Bartholomew of Cervere, Apr. 22.

Blessed Bartholomew of Mantua, Dec. 5.

Blessed Bartholomew of Montepulciano, May 23.

Blessed Bartholomew of San Gimignano, Dec. 14.

Blessed Beatrice D'Este of Ferrara, Jan. 18.

Blessed Beatrice da Silva, Aug. 18.

Blessed Beatrice of Este, May 10.

Blessed Beatrice of Ornacieu, Feb. 13.

Blessed Benedict of Coltiboni, Jan. 20.

Blessed Benedict of Urbino, Apr. 30.

Blessed Benedict XI, Jul. 7.

Blessed Benincasa, May 11.

Blessed Benno, Jul. 22.

Blessed Bentivoglia, Dec. 1.

Blessed Benvenuta of Cividale, Oct. 30.

Blessed Benvenuto of Gubbio, Jun. 27.

Blessed Benvenuto of Recanati, May 21.

Blessed Bernard of Baden, Jul. 15.

Blessed Bernard of Corleone, Jan. 19.

Blessed Bernard of Offida, Aug. 26.

Blessed Bernard Scammacca, Feb. 16.

Blessed Bernard the Penitent, Apr. 19.

Blessed Bernard Tolomei, Aug. 21.

Blessed Bernardina Maria Jablonski, Jun. 6

Blessed Bernardino of Feltre, Sep. 28.

Blessed Bernardino of Fossa, Nov. 27.

Blessed Bernhard Lichtenberg, Jun. 23.

Blessed Berthold of Garsten, Jul. 27.

Blessed Bertrand of Garrigues, Sep. 6.

Blessed Boleslava Lament, Jun. 5

Blessed Bonaventure Buonaccorsi, Dec. 14.

Blessed Bonaventure of Barcelona, Sep. 11.

Blessed Bonaventure of Forli, Mar. 31.

Blessed Bonaventure of Peraga, Jun. 10.

Blessed Bonaventure of Potenza, Oct. 26.

Blessed Bonavita, Mar. 1.

Blessed Boniface of Savoy, Jul. 14.

Blessed Bronislava, Aug. 30.

Blessed Candida Maria de Jesus Cipitria y Barriola, May 12.

Blessed Caspar de Bono, Jul. 14.

Blessed Cassian, Aug. 7.

Blessed Castora Gabrielli, Jun. 14.

Blessed Catherine Jarrige, Nov. 24

Blessed Catherine of Pallanza, Apr. 6.

Blessed Catherine of Parc-aux-Dames, May 4.

Blessed Catherine of Racconigi, Sep. 4.

Blessed Cecilia, Jun. 9.

Blessed Ceferino Gimenez Malla, May 4.

Blessed Ceslaus, Jul. 17.

Blessed Charlemagne, Jan. 28.

Blessed Charles of Blois, Sep. 29.

Blessed Charles the Good, Mar. 2.

Blessed Christian, Mar. 18.

Blessed Christina of Aquila, Jan. 18.

Blessed Christina of Spoleto, Feb. 13.

Blessed Christina of Stommeln, Nov. 6.

Blessed Christopher Bales, Mar. 4.

Blessed Christopher Macassoli, Mar. 11.

Blessed Christopher of Romagnola, Oct. 25.

Blessed Clara Bosatta, Apr. 21.

Blessed Clare of Pisa, Apr. 17.

Blessed Clare of Rimini, Feb. 10.

Blessed Claud la Colombiere, Feb. 15.

Blessed Claudio Granzotto, Nov. 20.

Blessed Clement of Osimo, Apr. 8.

Blessed Columba Gabriel, May 16.

Blessed Columba of Rieta, May 20.

Blessed Conrad of Ascoli, Apr. 19.

Blessed Conrad of Offlda, Dec. 14.

Blessed Conrad of Seldenburen, May 2.

Blessed Constantius of Fabrino, Feb. 25.

Blessed Contardo Ferrini, Oct. 27.

Blessed Crescentia of Kaufbeuren, Apr. 5.

Blessed Cristobal Magellanes, Nov. 22

Blessed Dalmatius Moner, Sep. 26.

Blessed Damian of Finario, Oct. 26.

Blessed Damien de Veuster, Jun. 4.

Blessed Daniel Comboni, Mar. 17.

Blessed Desiderius, Jan. 20.

Blessed Diana, Jun. 9.

Blessed Didacus of Cadiz, Mar. 24.

Blessed Diemoda, Mar. 29.

Blessed Dina Belanger, Mar. 20.

Blessed Dionysius, Nov. 29.

Blessed Dodo, Mar. 30.

Blessed Dominic, Apr. 26.

Blessed Dominic Barberi, Aug. 27.

Blessed Dominic Spadafora, Oct. 3.

Blessed Dorothy of Montau, Oct. 30.

Blessed Eberhard of Marchthal, Apr. 17.

Blessed Edmund Catherick, Apr. 13.

Blessed Edmund Rice, Oct. 6.

Blessed Edoardo Giuseppe Rosaz, Jun. 14.

Blessed Edward Jones, May 6.

Blessed Edward Oldcorne, Apr. 7.

Blessed Edward Powell, Jul. 30.

Blessed Edward Stransham, Jan. 21.

Blessed Edward Waterson, Jan. 7.

Blessed Elisabeth Vendramini, Nov. 4.

Blessed Elizabeth Canori Mora, Apr. 24.

Blessed Elizabeth of Mantua, Feb. 20.

Blessed Elizabeth the Good, Nov. 17.

Blessed Emeric, Nov. 4.

Blessed Emily of Vercelli, Aug. 19.

Blessed Emmanuel Ruiz, Jul. 10.

Blessed Enrico Rebuschini, May 4.

Blessed Ermengard, Jul. 16.

Blessed Eugenia Joubert, Nov. 20.

Blessed Eugenia Smet, Feb. 7.

Blessed Eugenius III, Jul. 8.

Blessed Eustochium of Messina, Feb. 16.

Blessed Eustochium of Padua, Feb. 13.

Blessed Eva of Liege, May 26.

Blessed Evangelist, Mar. 20.

Blessed Everard Hanse, Jul. 30.

Blessed Faustina Kowalska, Apr. 18.

Blessed Felicia of Milan, Jul. 24.

Blessed Felix of Nicosia, Jun. 1.

Blessed Ferdinand of Portugal, Jun. 5.

Blessed Ferreolus, Jan. 16.

Blessed Filippo Smaldone, May 12.

Blessed Florentino Asensio Barroso, May 4.

Blessed Florida Cevoli, May 16.

Blessed Frances D'Ambrose, Nov. 4.

Blessed Francesco Spinelli, Jun. 21.

Blessed Francis Antony Fasani, Dec. 9.

Blessed Francis Antony of Lucera, Nov. 29.

Blessed Francis Coll, Apr. 2.

Blessed Francis de Capillas, Jan. 15.

Blessed Francis de Montmorency-Laval, May 6.

Blessed Francis de Posadas, Sep. 20.

Blessed Francis Dickenson, Apr. 30.

Blessed Francis Masabki, Jul. 10.

Blessed Francis of Calderola, Sep. 28.

Blessed Francis of Fabriano, Apr. 22.

Blessed Francis Page, Apr. 20.

Blessed Francis Patrizzi, May 12.

Blessed Franco of Grotti, Dec. 11.

Blessed Frederic Ozanam, Aug. 22.

Blessed Frederick of Regensburg, Nov. 29.

Blessed Fulco of Neuily, Mar. 2.

Blessed Gabra Michael, Sep. 1.

Blessed Gabriel Mary, Aug. 27.

Blessed Gabriel of Ancona, Nov. 12.

Blessed Gaetano Catanoso, May 4.

Blessed Gandulf of Binasco, Apr. 2.

Blessed Gemma of Solmona, May 12.

Blessed Gennaro Sarnelli, May 12.

Blessed Genoveva Torres Morales, Jan. 29.

Blessed Gentilis, Sep. 5.

Blessed George Gervase, Apr. 11.

Blessed George Napper, Nov. 9.

Blessed George Swallowell, Jul. 24.

Blessed Gerard Gagnoli, Dec. 1.

Blessed Gerard of Clairvaux, Jun. 13.

Blessed Gerard of Monza, Jun. 6.

Blessed Gerard of Villamagna, May 23.

Blessed Gertrude of Altenberg, Aug. 13.

Blessed Gertrude of Delft, Jan. 6.

Blessed Gianna Beretta Molla, Apr. 24.

Blessed Giles Mary, Feb. 7.

Blessed Giles of Assisi, Apr. 23.

Blessed Giles of Lorenzana, Jan. 14.

Blessed Giles of Portugal, May 14.

Blessed Giuseppe Marello, Sep. 26.

Blessed Godfrey of Kappenberg, Jan. 13.

Blessed Gomidas Keumurgian, Nov. 5.

Blessed Gonsalo of Amarante, Jan. 16.

Blessed Gratia of Cattaro, Nov. 16.

Blessed Gregory, Apr. 26.

Blessed Gregory X, Jan. 10.

Blessed Gregory Lopez, Jul. 20.

Blessed Gregory of Verucchio, May 4.

Blessed Grimoaldo of the Purification, Jan. 29.

Blessed Guala, Sep. 3.

Blessed Guido Maria Conforti. Mar. 17.

Blessed Guillelmus Courtet, Sep. 29.

Blessed Guiseppina Bonino, May 7.

Blessed Gunther, Oct. 9.

Blessed Guy Maramaldi, Jun. 25.

Blessed Guy of Cortona, Jun. 16.

Blessed Hanibal Maria De Francia, Oct. 7.

Blessed Hartman, Dec. 23.

Blessed Haymo of Savigliano, Aug. 18.

Blessed Hedwig of Poland, Feb. 28.

Blessed Helen Guerra, Apr. 11.

Blessed Helen of Arcella, Nov. 7.

Blessed Helen of Bologna, Sep. 23.

Blessed Helen of Udine, Apr. 23.

Blessed Henry de Osso y Cervello, Jan. 27.

Blessed Henry of Treviso, Jun. 10.

Blessed Henry Suso, Mar. 2.

Blessed Henry the Shoemaker, Jun. 9.

Blessed Henry Walpole, Apr. 7.

Blessed Henry Zdik, Jun. 25.

Blessed Herculanus of Piegaro, Jun. 1.

Blessed Herluin, Aug. 26.

Blessed Herman Joseph, Apr. 7.

Blessed Herman the Cripple, Sep. 25.

Blessed Hildegard, Apr. 30.

Blessed Hippolytus Galantini, Mar. 20.

Blessed Hroznata, Jul. 14.

Blessed Hugh Faringdon, Dec. 1.

Blessed Hugh More, Sep. 1.

Blessed Hugh of Anzy, Apr. 20.

Blessed Hugh of Fosses, Feb. 10.

Blessed Hugolino Magalotti, Dec. 11.

Blessed Hugolino of Cortona, Mar. 22.

Blessed Hugolino of Gualdo, Jan. 1.

Blessed Humbeline, Aug. 21.

Blessed Humbert III of Savoy, Mar. 4.

Blessed Humbert of Romans, Jul. 14.

Blessed Humilis of Bisignano, Nov. 27.

Blessed Hyacintfius Ansalone, Nov. 17.

Blessed Hyacinthe Marie Cormier, Nov. 20.

Blessed Ida of Boulogne, Apr. 13.

Blessed Ida of Toggenburg, Nov. 3.

Blessed Ignatius Azevedo, Jul. 15.

Blessed Imelda, May 13.

Blessed Innocent of Berzo, Mar. 3.

Blessed Innocent V, Jun. 22.

Blessed Innocent XI, Aug. 11.

Blessed Isabel of France, Feb. 26.

Blessed Isaiah of Cracow, Feb. 8.

Blessed Isidore Bakanja, Apr. 24.

Blessed Isnardo of Chiampo, Mar. 22.

Blessed Jacopino of Canepaci, Mar. 3.

Blessed Jacopone of Todi, Dec. 25.

Blessed Jakob Gapp, Nov. 24.

Blessed James, Jan. 28; Mar. 14; Nov. 26.

Blessed James Bell, Apr 20.

Blessed James Bertoni, May 30.

Blessed James Bird, Mar. 25.

Blessed James D. Laval, Sep. 9.

Blessed James Duckett, Apr. 19.

Blessed James of Bevagna, Aug. 23.

Blessed James of Bitetto, Apr. 27.

Blessed James of Cerqueto, Apr. 17.

Blessed James of Certaldo, Apr. 13.

Blessed James of Lodi, Apr. 18.

Blessed James of Ulm, Oct. 11.

Blessed James of Voragine, Jul. 13.

Blessed James Sales, Feb. 7.

Blessed James Strepar, Oct. 21.

Blessed James the Venetian, May 31.

Blessed James Thompson, Nov. 28.

Blessed Jane of Portugal, May 12.

Blessed Jane of Reggio, Jul. 9.

Blessed Jermyn Gardiner, Mar. 11.

Blessed Jerome Ranuzzi, Dec. 11.

Blessed Joachim of Siena, Apr. 16.

Blessed Joan Mary de Maill'e, Nov. 6.

Blessed Joan of Aza, Aug. 8.

Blessed Joan of Orvieto, Jul. 23.

Blessed Joan of Signa, Nov. 17.

Blessed Joan of Toulouse, Mar. 31.

Blessed Joan Soderini, Sep. 1.

Blessed Joanna Jugan, Aug. 29.

Blessed Johann Nepomuk von Tschiderer, Apr. 30.

Blessed John, Mar. 16; Jun. 3.

Blessed John I, Apr. 26.

Blessed John Amias, Mar. 16.

Blessed John Angelo Porro, Oct. 23.

Blessed John Baptist of Fabriano, Mar. 11.

Blessed John Baptist Turpin du Cormier, Oct. 17.

Blessed John Beche, Dec. 1.

Blessed John Bodey, Nov. 2.

Blessed John Boste, Jul. 24.
Blessed John Buoni, Oct. 23.
Blessed John Colombini, Jul. 31.
Blessed John Cornelius, Jul. 4.
Blessed John Della Pace, Nov. 12.
Blessed John Dominici, Jun. 10.
Blessed John du Lau, Archbishop of Arles, Sep. 2.
Blessed John Duckett, Sep. 7.
Blessed John Duns Scotus, Mar. 20.
Blessed John Felton, Aug. 8.
Blessed John Forest, May 22.
Blessed John Gabriel Perboyre, Sep. 11.
Blessed John Haile, May 11.
Blessed John Ingram, Jul. 24.
Blessed John Ireland, Mar. 11.
Blessed John Larke, Mar. 11.
Blessed John Liccio, Nov. 14.
Blessed John Lockwood, Apr. 13.
Blessed John Marinoni, Dec. 13.
Blessed John Martin Moye, May 4.
Blessed John Massias, Sep. 18.
Blessed John Nelson, Feb. 3.
Blessed John of Alvernia, Aug. 13.
Blessed John of Avila, May 10.
Blessed John of Dukla, Sep. 28.
Blessed John of Parma, Mar. 20.
Blessed John of Penna, Apr. 2.
Blessed John of Perugia, Sep. 1.
Blessed John of Prado, May 24.
Blessed John of Rieti, Aug. 9.
Blessed John of Salerno, Aug. 9.
Blessed John of Tossignano, Jul. 24.
Blessed John of Vallombrosa, Mar. 10.
Blessed John of Vercelli, Dec. 1.
Blessed John of Warneton, Jan. 27.
Blessed John Pelingotto, Jun. 1.
Blessed John Pibush, Feb. 18.
Blessed John Rainuzzi, Jun. 8.
Blessed John Ruysbroeck, Dec. 2.
Blessed John Sarkander, Mar. 17.
Blessed John Slade, Oct. 30.
Blessed John Soreth, Jul. 30.
Blessed John Speed, Jul. 24.
Blessed John Storey, Jun. 1.
Blessed John the Spaniard, Jun. 25.
Blessed Jolenta of Hungary, Jun. 15.
Blessed Jordan of Pisa, Mar. 6.
Blessed Jordan of Saxony, Feb. 15.
Blessed Jose Maria de Yermo y Porres, May 6.

Blessed Josemarie Escriva de Balaguer, May 17.
Blessed Joseph Allamano, Oct. 7.
Blessed Joseph de Anchieta, Oct. 5.
Blessed Joseph Freinademetz, Jan. 22.
Blessed Joseph Tommasi, Jan. 1.
Blessed Joseph Vaz, Jan. 21.
Blessed Josephine Bakhita, May 17.
Blessed Josephine Vannini, Oct. 16.
Blessed Jozef Sebastian Pelczar, Jun. 2.
Blessed Juan Diego, Apr. 9.
Blessed Julia Billart, Apr. 8.
Blessed Julia of Certaldo, Feb. 15.
Blessed Julian Maunoir, Jan. 28.
Blessed Julian of Norwich, May 13.
Blessed Juliana of Mount Cornillon, Apr. 5.
Blessed Justin de Jacobis, Jul. 31.
Blessed Justina of Arezzo, Mar. 12.
Blessed Jutta of Diessenberg, Dec. 22.
Blessed Jutta of Huy, Jan. 13.
Blessed Juvenal Ancina, Aug. 31.
Blessed Karl Leisner, May 23.
Blessed Kateri Tekakwitha, Apr. 17.
Blessed Léonie Françoise de Sales Aviat, Sep. 27.
Blessed Ladislaus of Gielniow, May 11.
Blessed Lanfranc, May 24; Jun. 23.
Blessed Lanvinus, Apr. 14.
Blessed Laurence Imbert, Sep. 21.
Blessed Laurence Loricatus, Aug. 16.
Blessed Laurence Nerucci, Aug. 31.
Blessed Laurence of Ripafratta, Sep. 28.
Blessed Laurence of Villamagna, Jun. 6.
Blessed Laurentius Ruiz, Sep. 29.
Blessed Lazarus de Kyoto, Sep. 29.
Blessed Leo Ignatius Mangin, Ann Wang, and their companions, Jul. 20.
Blessed Leo of Saint-Bertin, Feb. 26.
Blessed Liberatus of Loro, Sep. 6.
Blessed Louis Allemand, Sep. 16.
Blessed Louis Morbioli, Nov. 16.
Blessed Louis of Thuringia, Sep. 11.
Blessed Louisa Albertoni, Feb. 28.
Blessed Louisa of Savoy, Sep. 9.

Blessed Louise Therese de Montaignac de Chauvance, Nov. 4.
Blessed Luchesio, Apr. 28.
Blessed Lucy of Amelia, Jul. 27.
Blessed Lucy of Caltagirone, Sep. 26.
Blessed Lucy of Narni, Nov. 16.
Blessed Ludovic Pavoni, Apr. 1.
Blessed Ludovico of Casoria, Apr. 18.
Blessed Luke Belludi, Feb. 17.
Blessed Maddalena Caterina Morano, Nov. 5.
Blessed Madeleine Fontaine and her companions, Jun. 27.
Blessed Magdalen di Canossa, May 14.
Blessed Magdalen Panattieri, Oct. 13.
Blessed Magdalena de Nagasaki, Oct. 15.
Blessed Mannes, Jul. 30.
Blessed Manuel Barbal Cosan, Apr. 29.
Blessed Marcelina Darowski, Oct. 6.
Blessed Marcellinus Champagnat, Jun. 6.
Blessed Marcolino of Forli, Jan. 24.
Blessed Margaret Bourgeoys, Jan. 12; Jan. 19.
Blessed Margaret Colonna, Nov. 7.
Blessed Margaret of Cittaea-di-Castello, Apr. 13.
Blessed Margaret of Lorraine, Nov. 6.
Blessed Margaret of Louvain, Sep. 2.
Blessed Margaret of Ravenna, Jan. 23.
Blessed Margaret of Savoy, Dec. 23.
Blessed Margaret Pole, May 28.
Blessed Marguerite Bays, Oct. 29.
Blessed Maria Alvarado Cardoza, May 7.
Blessed Maria Ana Mogas Fontcuberta, Oct. 6.
Blessed Maria Anglea Astorch, Jan. 6.
Blessed Maria Anna Sala, Nov. 24.
Blessed Maria Antonia Bandres, May 12.
Blessed Maria Bernarda Butler, Oct. 29.
Blessed Maria Catherine Kasper, Feb 2.
Blessed Maria de Jesus Sacramentado Venegas, Nov. 22
Blessed Maria Domenica Brun Barbantini, May 7.

Blessed Maria Francesca Rubatto, Oct. 10.

Blessed Maria Helena Stollenwerk, May 7.

Blessed Maria Josefa Sancho de Guerra, Sep. 27

Blessed Maria Karlowska, Jun. 6.

Blessed Maria Raffaella Cimatti, May 12.

Blessed Maria Rafols, Oct. 16.

Blessed Maria Rivier, Jan. 14; Feb. 3.

Blessed Maria Rosa Durocher, Oct. 6.

Blessed Maria Satellico, Oct. 10.

Blessed Maria Schinina, Nov. 4.

Blessed Marianus Scotus, Feb. 9.

Blessed Marie Poussepin, Nov. 20.

Blessed Marie Therese Haze, Apr. 21.

Blessed Marie-Louise Trichet, May 16.

Blessed Mark, Sep. 7.

Blessed Mark Barkworth, Feb. 27.

Blessed Mark Fantucci, Apr. 10.

Blessed Mark of Modena, Sep. 23.

Blessed Mark of Montegallo, Mar. 20.

Blessed Marthe Aimee LeBouteiller, Nov. 4.

Blessed Mary Angela Truszkowska, Apr. 18.

Blessed Mary Asunta Pallotta, Apr. 7.

Blessed Mary Bartholomea of Florence, May 28.

Blessed Mary de Mattias, Aug. 20.

Blessed Mary L'Huilier, Oct. 17.

Blessed Mary Magdalen, Martinengo, Jul. 27.

Blessed Mary, Margaret d'Youville, Dec. 15.

Blessed Mary of Oignies, Jun. 23.

Blessed Mary of Pisa, Jan. 28.

Blessed Mary of the Incarnation, Apr. 18.

Blessed Mary of Turin, Dec. 16.

Blessed Mary Soledad, Oct. 11.

Blessed Mary Teresa de Soubiran, Oct. 20.

Blessed Mary Theresa Scherer, Oct. 29.

Blessed Matthew, Oct. 21.

Blessed Matthew of Mantua, Oct. 7.

Blessed Matthia of Matelica, Nov. 7.

Blessed Maurice of Hungary, Mar. 20.

Blessed Maurice Tornay, May 16.

Blessed Meinwerk, Jun. 5.

Blessed Melchior, Sep. 7.

Blessed Mercedes Prat, Apr. 29.

Blessed Michael de Aozaraza, Sep. 29.

Blessed Michael Giedroye, May 4.

Blessed Michelina of Pesaro, Jun. 20.

Blessed Miles Gerard, Apr. 30.

Blessed Milo of Selincourt, Jul. 16.

Blessed Modestino of Jesus and Mary, Jan. 29.

Blessed Mother Mary of the Cross MacKillop, Jan. 19

Blessed Narcisa Martillo Moran, Oct. 25.

Blessed Nazaria Ignacia March Mesa, Sep. 27.

Blessed Neol Pinot, Feb. 21.

Blessed Nicholas, Jul. 24.

Blessed Nicholas Albergati, May 9.

Blessed Nicholas Factor, Dec. 14.

Blessed Nicholas of Forca Palena, Oct. 1.

Blessed Nicholas of Sibenik, Dec. 5.

Blessed Nicolas Roland, Oct. 16.

Blessed Nonius, Nov. 6.

Blessed Notker Balbulus, Apr. 6.

Blessed Novellone, Aug. 13.

Blessed Oddino of Fossano, Jul. 21.

Blessed Odo, Jun. 19.

Blessed Odo of Novara, Jan. 14.

Blessed Odoric of Pordenone, Jan. 14.

Blessed Olive of Palermo, Jun. 10.

Blessed Oliver Plunket, Jul. 1.

Blessed Oringa, Jan. 4.

Blessed Osanna of Cattaro, Apr. 27.

Blessed Otto Neururer, Nov. 24.

Blessed Pacifico of Cerano, Jun. 8.

Blessed Paula Cerioli, Dec. 23.

Blessed Paula Frassinetti, Jun. 11.

Blessed Paula Gambara-Costa, Jan. 31.

Blessed Paula Montal Fornes, Apr. 18.

Blessed Pauline of the Heart of Jesus in Agony Visintainer, Oct. 18.

Blessed Pepin of Landen, Feb. 21.

Blessed Peregrine, Mar. 20.

Blessed Peregrine of Falerone, Sep. 6.

Blessed Peter, Apr. 4.

Blessed Peter Armengol, Apr. 27.

Blessed Peter de Betancur, Apr. 25.

Blessed Peter Donders, Jan. 14.

Blessed Peter Favre, Aug. 11.

Blessed Peter Geremia, Mar 10.

Blessed Peter Gonzalez, Apr. 14.

Blessed Peter Igneus, Feb. 8.

Blessed Peter of Castelnau, Jan. 15.

Blessed Peter of Gubbio, Mar. 23.

Blessed Peter of Jully, Jun. 23.

Blessed Peter of Luxemburg, Jul. 2.

Blessed Peter of Mogliano, Jul. 30.

Blessed Peter of Pisa, Jun. 17.

Blessed Peter of Ruffla, Nov. 7.

Blessed Peter of Sassoferrato, Sep. 1.

Blessed Peter of Siena, Dec. 11.

Blessed Peter of Tiferno, Oct. 21.

Blessed Peter of Treia, Feb. 17.

Blessed Peter Pascual, Dec. 6.

Blessed Peter Petroni of Siena, May 29.

Blessed Peter Rene Roque, Mar. 1.

Blessed Peter Sanz, May 26.

Blessed Peter the Venerable, Dec. 29.

Blessed Peter To Rot, Jan. 17.

Blessed Peter Wright, May 19.

Blessed Petra of St. Joseph Perez Florido, Oct. 16.

Blessed Petronilla of Moncel, May 14.

Blessed Philip Powell, Jun. 30.

Blessed Philip Rinaldi, Apr. 29.

Blessed Philippa Mareri, Feb. 16.

Blessed Philippine Duchesne, Nov. 17.

Blessed Pierre Giorgio Frassati, May 20.

Blessed Pietro Casini, Oct. 1

Blessed Placid Riccardi, Mar. 15.

Blessed Placida Viel, Mar. 4.

Blessed Pontius of Faucigny, Nov. 26.

Blessed Prudence, May 6.

Blessed Rabanus Maurus, Feb. 4.

Blessed Rafael Arnáiz Baron, Sep. 27.

Blessed Rafael Chylinski, Jun. 9.

Blessed Rafael Guizar Valencia, Jan. 29.

Blessed Rainerius Inclusis of Osnabruck, Apr. 11.

Blessed Rainerius of Arezzo, Nov. 12.

Blessed Ralph Ashley, Apr. 7.

Blessed Ralph Corby, Sep. 7.

Blessed Ratho of Andechs, May 17.

Blessed Raymund Lull, Sep. 5.

Blessed Raymund of Capua, Oct. 5.

Blessed Raymund of Fitero, Feb. 6.

Blessed Reginald of Orleans, Feb. 17.

Blessed Richard Fetherston, Jul. 30.

Blessed Richard Herst, Aug. 29.

Blessed Richard Kirkman, Aug. 22.

Blessed Richard Newport, May 30.

Blessed Richard of Hampole, Sep. 29.

Blessed Richard Pampuri, Feb. 3.

Blessed Richard Thirkeld, May 29.

Blessed Richard Whiting, Dec. 1.

Blessed Rizzerio, Feb. 7.

Blessed Robert Anderton, Apr. 25.

Blessed Robert Dalby, Mar. 16.

Blessed Robert of Arbrissel, Feb. 25.

Blessed Robert of Knaresborough, Sep. 24.

Blessed Roger Dickenson, Jul. 7.

Blessed Roger Le Fort, Mar. 1.

Blessed Roger of Ellant, Jan. 4.

Blessed Roger of Todi, Jan. 14.

Blessed Romaeus, Feb. 25.

Blessed Roque Gonzalez, Nov. 17.

Blessed Rose Venerini, May 7.

Blessed Roseline, Jan. 17.

Blessed Rudolf Aquaviva, Jul. 27.

Blessed Sadoc, Jun. 2.

Blessed Salome, Nov. 17

Blessed Salvator Lilli, Nov 24.

Blessed Santuccia, Mar. 21.

Blessed Sebastian Aparicio, Feb. 25.

Blessed Sebastian of Brescia, Dec 16

Blessed Sebastian Valfre, Jan. 30.

Blessed Seraphina Sforza, Sep. 9.

Blessed Serapion, Nov. 14

Blessed Serlo, Mar 3.

Blessed Sibyllina of Pavia, Mar. 23.

Blessed Simon de Rojas, Sep. 28.

Blessed Simon of Cascia, Feb. 3.

Blessed Simon of Lipnicza, Jul. 30.

Blessed Simon of Rimini, Nov. 3.

Blessed Simon of Todi, Apr. 20.

Blessed Sr. Maria Enarnacion Rosal of the Sacred Heart, May 4.

Blessed Stephana Quinzani, Jan. 2.

Blessed Stephen, Sep. 7.

Blessed Stephen Bandelli, Jun. 12.

Blessed Stephen Bellesini, Feb. 3.

Blessed Stilla, Jul. 19.

Blessed Teresa Couderc, Sep. 26.

Blessed Teresa Jornet Ibars, Aug. 20.

Blessed Teresa Verzani, Mar. 3.

Blessed Thaddeus, Oct. 25.

Blessed Thomas Abel, Jul. 30.

Blessed Thomas Alfield, Jul. 6.

Blessed Thomas Corsini, Jun. 23.

Blessed Thomas Hemerford, Feb. 12.

Blessed Thomas Hioji Rokuzayemon Nishi, Nov. 17.

Blessed Thomas Holland, Dec. 12.

Blessed Thomas Maxfield, Jul. 1.

Blessed Thomas of Bioille, Oct. 19.

Blessed Thomas of Cori, Jan. 19.

Blessed Thomas of Florence, Oct. 25.

Blessed Thomas of Walden, Nov. 2.

Blessed Thomas Percy, Aug. 26.

Blessed Thomas Plumtree, Feb. 4.

Blessed Thomas Reynolds, Jan. 21.

Blessed Thomas Sherwood, Feb. 7.

Blessed Thomas Somers, Dec. 10.

Blessed Thomas Tunstal, Jul. 13.

Blessed Thomas Welbourn, Aug. 1.

Blessed Thomas Woodhouse, Jun. 19.

Blessed Thomasius, Mar. 25.

Blessed Timothy of Montecchio, Aug. 26.

Blessed Torello, Mar. 16.

Blessed Ubald of Florence, Apr. 9.

Blessed Urban II, Jul. 29.

Blessed Urban V, Dec. 19.

Blessed Ursalina, Apr. 7.

Blessed Verdiana, Feb. 16.

Blessed Veronica of Binasco, Jan. 13.

Blessed Victor III, Sep. 16.

Blessed Victoria Fornari-Strata, Sep. 12.

Blessed Villana of Florence, Feb. 28.

Blessed Vincent, Mar. 8.

Blessed Vincentia Lopez y Vicuna, Dec. 26.

Blessed Vincentius Schiwozuka, Sep. 29.

Blessed Vitalis of Savigny, Sep. 16.

Blessed Vivaldo, May 11.

Blessed Waltman, Apr. 11.

Blessed William Andleby, Jul. 4.

Blessed William Brown, Aug. 1.

Blessed William Freeman, Aug. 13.

Blessed William Harringron, Feb. 18.

Blessed William Hart, Mar. 15.

Blessed William Lacey, Aug. 22.

Blessed William Marsden, Apr. 25.

Blessed William of Fenoli, Dec. 19.

Blessed William of Hirschau, Jul. 4.

Blessed William of Polizzi, Apr. 16.

Blessed William of Scicli, Apr. 7.

Blessed William of Toulouse, May 18.

Blessed William Patenson, Jan. 22.

Blessed William Richardson, Feb. 17.

Blessed William Scott, May 30.

Blessed William Tempier, Mar. 27.

Blessed William Ward, Jul. 26.

Blessed Wincenty Lewoniuk, Oct. 6

Blessed Wolfhelm, Apr. 22.

Blessing of the Waters (Uruguay), Dec. 8.

Blffsed Magdalen Albrizzi, May 15.

Blffsed Osanna of Mantua, Jun. 20.

Bligh, William (Captain), Sep. 9, 1754; Apr. 28, 1789.

blindmen, patron of, Dec. 29.

Bliss, Tasker Howard, Dec. 31, 1853.

Blizzard of '88, Mar. 12, 1888.

Bloch, Felix, Oct. 23, 1905.

Bloch, Konrad Emil, Jan. 21, 1912.

Bloch, Oscar, May 8, 1877.

Block, Herbert Lawrence, Oct. 13, 1909.

Block Island, U.S.S.: torpedoed, May 29, 1944.

Blodgett, Katharine Burr, Jan. 10, 1898.

Bloembergen, Nicolaas, Mar. 11, 1920.

Bloemfontein, Convention of, Feb. 17, 1854.

Bloemfontein, Mar. 13, 1900.

Blok, Aleksandr Aleksandrovich, Nov. 28, 1880.

Blon, Karl, Aug. 28, 1894.

Blondell, Joan, Aug. 30, 1909.

Blondin, Charles, Feb. 28, 1824.

blood vessels, artificial, Jan. 17, 1986.

Blood River (Natal), Dec. 16, 1838.

bloodstone, Mar. intro.

Bloodworth-Thomason, Linda, Apr. 15, 1947.

Bloody Sunday (Dublin, Ireland), Nov. 21, 1920.

Bloody Sunday (Russia), Jan. 22, 1905.

Bloom, Claire, Feb. 15, 1931.

Bloomer, Amelia, May 27, 1818.

Bloomfield, Leonard, Apr. 1, 1887.

Bloomingdale, Alfred S., Apr. 15, 1916.

Bloomingdale, Joseph Bernard, Dec. 22, 1842.

Blotlingk, Otto von, Jun. 11, 1815.

Blount College, Sep. 10, 1794.

Blount, William, Mar. 26, 1749.

Blucher: sunk, Jan. 24, 1915.

blue laws: upheld, May 29, 1961.

Blue, Ben, Sep. 12, 1901.

Blue, Vida Rochelle, Jul. 28, 1949.

Bluford, Guion, Aug. 30, 1983.

Blum, Leon (France), Apr. 9, 1872; Mar. 13, 1938.

Blumberg, Baruch S., Jul. 28, 1925.

Blume, Judy, Feb. 12, 1938.

Blumenbach, Johann Friedrich, May 11, 1752.

Blunt, Sir Anthony: discovered to be a spy, Nov. 15, 1979.

Blunt, Wilfrid Scawen, Aug. 17, 1840.

Bly, Nellie, May 5, 1867.

Bly, Robert, Dec. 23, 1926.

Blyleven, Bert (Rikalbert), Apr. 6, 1951.

Blyth, Ann, Aug. 16, 1928.

Boas, Franz, Jul. 9, 1858.

boat people: Indochinese people admitted into U.S., Jul. 15, 1977; problem addressed, May 16, 1979.

boatmen, patron of, Feb. 12; Nov. 23.

Bobbies (London Police), Sep. 29, 1829.

Bocage, Manuel Maria Barbosa du, Sep. 15, 1765.

Bocca, Julio, Mar. 7, 1967.

Boccherini, Luigi, Feb. 19, 1743.

Bochler, Peter, Dec. 31, 1712.

Bochner, Hart, Dec. 3, 1956.

Bochco, Steven, Dec. 16, 1943.

Bock, (Moritz Albert Franz Friedrich) Fedor von, Dec. 3, 1880.

Bock, Jerry, Sep. 22, 1964.

Bocuse, Paul, Feb. 11, 1926.

Bode, Johann Elert, Jan. 19, 1747.

Bodmer, Johann Jakob, Jul. 19, 1698.

Bodoni, Giambattista, Feb. 16, 1740.

Boeing 707, South Korean, Apr. 20, 1978.

Boeing 747: first trans-atlantic proving flight, Jan. 12, 1970; first commercial flight, Jan. 22, 1970.

Boeing Co.: incorporated, Jul. 19, 1934.

Boeing, William Edward, Oct. 1, 1881.

Boer War, Apr. 5, 1881; Jan. 2, 1896; Oct. 9, 1899; begins, Oct. 11, 1899; Oct. 20, 1899; Nov. 2, 1899; Jan. 10, 1900; Feb. 27, 1900; Feb. 28, 1900; Mar. 13, 1900; May 21, 1900; May 31, 1900; Jun. 5, 1900; Nov. 29, 1900; May 31, 1902; ends, Feb. 3, 1915.

Boerhaave, Hermann, Dec. 31, 1668.

Boers, Jan. 17, 1837; Dec. 16, 1838.

Boesky, Ivan, Nov. 14, 1986; Dec. 18, 1987.

Boetie, Etienne de La, Nov. 1, 1530.

Boganda, Barthelemy (Central African Republic), Mar. 29, 1959.

Boganda Day (Central African Republic), Mar. 29.

Bogarde, Dirk, Mar. 28, 1921.

Bogart, Humphrey, Dec. 25, 1899; Jul. 16, 1948; Feb. 20 1952.

Bogata, Declaration of: issued, Aug. 16, 1966.

Bogdanovich, Peter, Jul. 30, 1939.

Boggs, (Thomas) Hale, Feb. 15, 1914.

Boggs, Lindy, Mar. 13, 1916.

Boggs, Wade Anthony, Jun. 15, 1958.

Bogor (Indonesia), Jul. 25, 1988.

Bogosian, Eric, Apr. 24, 1953.

Bogota Charter, Dec. 13, 1951.

Bohemia, May 23, 1611; Apr. 5, 1897; Mar. 15, 1939.

Bohemia, patron of, Jun. 15.

Bohlen, Charles E., Aug. 30, 1904.

Bohr, (Aage) Niels, Jun. 19, 1922.

Bohr, Niels Henrik David, Oct. 7, 1885.

Boileau-Despreaux, Nicolas, Nov 1, 1636.

Boitano, Brian, Oct. 22, 1963.

Boito, Arrigo, Feb. 24, 1842.

Bok, Derek Curtis, Mar. 22, 1930.

Bok, Edward William, Oct. 9, 1863.

Bokassa, Jean Bedel (Central African Republic), Feb. 21, 1921, Jan. 1, 1966; Feb. 22, 1972; Jan. 2, 1975; crowns self, Dec. 4, 1976; Sep. 20,1979.

Bol, Ferdinand, Jun. 24, 1616.

Bolan, Marc, May 8, 1948.

Boland amendment, Dec. 20, 1982.

Bolero opens, Nov. 22, 1928.

Boleyn, Anne, Nov. 14, 1532; Jan. 25, 1533; beheaded, May 19, 1536.

Bolger, Ray, Jan. 10, 1904.

Bolingbroke, 1st Viscount (Henry St. John), Sep. 16, 1678.

Bolivar Day (Venezuela), Dec. 17.

Bolivar's Birthday (Ecuador, Venezuela), Jul. 24.

Bolivia: independence, Aug. 6, 1825; Apr. 5, 1879; Apr. 4, 1884; Chaco War ends, Jun. 12, 1935; new constitution, Aug. 5, 1961; Mar. 17, 1978; military coup, Jul. 21, 1978.

Bolivian revolution, Apr. 9, 1952.

boliviano, Jan. 1, 1987.

Boljvar, Simon, Jul. 24, 1783; Dec. 17, 1819; Jul. 5, 1821.

Boll, Heinrich, Dec. 21, 1917.

Bolshevik government: confiscation of Russian Church property, Dec. 17, 1917; nationalizes banks, Dec. 27, 1917.

Bolshevik Revolution, Feb. 18, 1918.

Bolsheviks: defeated, Jul. 16, 1917; Nov. 7, 1917; Nov. 26, 1917; foreign intervention, Dec. 30, 1917; Jul. 16, 1918; Jan. 5, 1919; Apr. 19, 1919; Jan. 30, 1920.

Bolt, Robert (Oxton), Aug. 15, 1924.

Bolton (Bolotin), Michael, Feb. 26, 1953.

Boltzmann, Ludwig, Feb. 20, 1844.

Bolyai, Janos, Dec. 15, 1802.

Bombeck, Erma, Feb. 21, 1927.

Bon or Feast of Fortune (Japan), Jul. 10.

Bon Oum, Jan. 19, 1962.

Bonanza Creek: gold discovered, Aug. 16, 1896.

Bonanza television debut, Sep. 12, 1959.

Bonaparte, Joseph, King of Naples, Jan. 7, 1768; Mar. 30, 1806.

Bonaparte, Louis, Sep. 2, 1778; Jun. 5, 1806; (Holland): abdicates, Jul. 1, 1810; Jul. 9, 1810.

Bonaparte, Napoleon, May 10, 1796; May 18, 1804; Dec. 2, 1804; abdicates, Jun. 22, 1815.

Bonaparte: family excluded from France, Jan. 12, 1816.

Bond, Julian, chairman of the NAACP, Mar. 21, 1998.

Bond, Julian, Jan. 14, 1940; Jan. 10, 1966.

Bond, Ward, Apr. 9, 1903.

Bond, William Cranch, Sep. 9, 1789.

Bondfield, Margaret Grace, Mar. 17, 1873.

Bonds, Barry, Jul. 24, 1964.

Bonds, Gary, Jun. 6, 1939.

Bongo, Albert-Bemard (Omar), Dec. 30, 1935.

Bonham, John Henry, May 31, 1949.

Bonham-Carter, Helena, May 25, 1966.

Bonheur, Rosa, Mar. 16, 1822.

Boniface VIII (pope), Dec. 5, 1301.

Bonifacio Day or National Heroes' Day (Philippines), Nov. 30.

Bonilla, Bobby (Roberto), Feb. 23, 1963.

Bonin Islands, Jun. 26, 1968.

Bonn (Germany), Mar. 7, 1945.

Bonnat, Leon Joseph Florentin, Jun. 20, 1833.

Bonnelly, Rafael, Jan. 18, 1962.

Bonnet, Charles, Mar. 13, 1720.

Bonney, (Billy the Kid) William H., Nov. 23, 1859.

Bonnici, Carmello Mifsud, Dec. 22, 1984.

Bono, Mary, Apr. 7, 1998.

Bono, Salvatore Phillip (Sonny), Feb. 16, 1940.

Bonoff, Karla, Dec. 27, 1952.

Bonstelle, Jessie, Nov. 18, 1871.

Bonus, March, Jul. 28, 1932.

boogie-woogie music: first performed, Dec. 23, 1938.

book and print sellers, patron of, Mar. 8.

Book of Common Prayer, May 8, 1559.

Book of Concord: published, Jun. 25, 1580.

bookbinders, patron of, Aug. 24.

booksellers and publishers, patron of, Apr. 19.

booksellers, patron of, May 6.

Boole, George, Nov. 2, 1815.

Boone, Daniel, Nov. 2, 1734.

Boone, Deborah Ann (Debby), Sep. 22, 1956.

Boone, Pat, Jun. 1, 1934.

Boone, Richard, Jun. 18, 1917.

Boorstin, Daniel J., Oct. 1, 1914.

Boost Your Home Town Month, Apr. intro.

Booth, Ballington, Jul. 28, 1859.

Booth, Charles, Mar. 30, 1840.

Booth, Edwin, Nov. 13, 1833.

Booth, Evangeline Cory, Dec. 25, 1865.

Booth, John Wilkes, May 10, 1838; Apr. 14, 1865; shot, Apr. 26, 1865.

Booth, Shirley, Aug. 30, 1907.

Booth, William, Apr. 10, 1829; Jul. 2, 1865.

Boothe, Powers, Jun. 1, 1949.

Bophuthatswana: independence, Dec. 6, 1977.

Bopp, Franz, Sep. 14, 1791.

Bopp, Thomas, discover Hale-Bopp Comet, Jul. 22, 1995.

Boqueron Day Battle of (Paraguay), Sep. 29.

Bora, Catherine von, Jun. 13, 1515.

Borah, William Edgar, Jun. 29, 1865.

Bordaberry, Juan Maria: inaugurated, Mar. 1, 1972.

Bordeaux (France), Oct. 23, 1452; Sep. 2, 1914.

Borden, Gail, Nov. 9, 1801.

Borden, Lizzie (Andrew), Jul. 19, 1860.

Borden, Robert Laird, Jun. 26, 1854.

Bordet, Jules Jean Baptiste Vincent, Jun. 13, 1870.

Bore, Jean Etienne, Dec. 27, 1741.

Borelli, Giovanni, Jan. 28, 1608.

Boren, David Lyle, Apr. 21, 1941.

Borg, Bjorn, Jun. 6, 1956.

Borge, Victor, Jan. 3, 1909.

Borges, Jorge Luis, Aug. 24, 1899.

Borgia, Lucrezia, Apr. 18, 1480.

Borglum, Gutzon, Mar. 25, 1871.

Borgnine, Ernest, Jan. 24, 1917.

Boris III (Bulgaria), Jan. 30, 1894; Aug. 28, 1943.

Borja Cevallos, Rodrigo: elected, May 8, 1988.

Bork, Robert Heron, Mar. 1, 1927. Oct. 23, 1987.

Borlaug, Norman E., Mar. 25, 1914.

Borman, Frank, Dec. 4, 1965; Dec. 21, 1968.

Born, Max, Dec. 11, 1882; Nov. 3, 1954.

Borneo, North, May 12, 1888.

Borodin, Aleksandr Profiryevich, Nov. 12, 1833.

Borodino, Battle of, Sep. 7, 1812.

Borormke, Brian (King of Ireland): slain, Apr. 23, 1014.

Boroughbridge, Mar. 16, 1322.

Borromeo, Federigo, Aug. 18, 1564.

Borromini, Francesco, Sep. 25, 1599.

Borrow, George Henry, Jul. 5, 1803.

Bosch, Carl, Aug. 27, 1874.

Bosch, Juan, Jun. 30, 1909; Feb. 27, 1963.

Bosley, Tom, Oct. 1, 1927.

Bosnia, independence of, Feb. 29, 1992; UN member, May 22, 1992; U.S. aid for, Feb. 28, 1993; formation of federation, Mar. 1, 1994.

Bosnia-Herzegovina, as independent republic, Apr. 7, 1992; peace accord, Nov. 21, 1995; U.S. troops in, Dec. 18, 1995.

Bosnian Peace Treaty, Dec. 14, 1995.

Bosnian State Day (Yugoslavia), Nov. 25.

Bosporous Bridge, Feb. 20, 1970.

Boss's Day, Oct. intro.

Bossano, Joe, Mar. 24, 1988.

Bossuet, Jacques Benigne, Sep. 27, 1627.

Bossy, Mike, Jan. 22, 1957.

Boston Latin School, Feb. 13, 1635.

Boston, Mar. 17, 1776.

Boston Massacre, Mar. 5, 1770.

Boston News-Letter, Apr. 24, 1704.

Boston Strangler, Jan. 18, 1967.

Boston Symphony Orchestra: founded, Oct. 22, 1881; Oct. 15, 1900.

Boston Tea Party, Apr. 27, 1773; Dec. 16, 1773.

Boston University, Feb. 11, 1875.

Boston Weekly Journal: first use of wood-pulp paper, Jan. 14, 1868.

Bostwick, Barry, Feb. 24, 1945.

Boswell, James, Oct. 29, 1740; May 16, 1763.

Botero, Fernando (Angulo), Apr. 19, 1932.

Botha, General, Mar. 20, 1915.

Botha, Louis, Sep. 27, 1862.

Botha, P(ieter) W(illem), Jan. 12, 1916; Sep. 28, 1978; Jan. 18, 1989; Aug. 14, 1989.

Botha, Roelof Pik, Apr. 27, 1932.

Bothe, Walther Wilhelm Georg Franz, Jan. 8, 1891; Nov. 3, 1954.

Bothwell, Earl of (James Hepburn), May 15, 1567.

Botswana (Bechuanaland): independence, Sep. 30, 1966; admitted to UN, Oct. 17, 1966.

Botswana Day (Botswana), Sep. 30; Oct. 1.

Bottoms, Joseph, Apr. 22, 1954.

Bottoms, Sam, Oct. 17, 1955.

Bottoms, Timothy, Aug. 30, 1951.

Bouabid, Maati, Nov. 11, 1927.

Boucher, Francois, Sep. 29, 1703.

Boucicault, Dion, Dec. 26, 1820.

Boudiaf, Mohammed, Jan. 16, 1992; Jun. 29, 1992; Jul. 2, 1992.

Bougainville, Louis Antoine de, Nov. 11, 1729.

Boulanger, Nadia Juliette, Sep. 16, 1887.

Boulder Dam, Sep. 17, 1930.

Boulding, Renneth Ewart, Jan. 18, 1910.

Boulez, Pierre, Mar. 26, 1925.

Boull, Sir Adrian Cedric, Apr. 8, 1889.

Boulle, Pierre Francois Marie-Louis, Feb. 20, 1912.

Boulogne Diocese of (Picardy) patron of, Nov. 27.

Boumedienne, Houari, Aug. 23, 1932; Jun. 19, 1965.

boundary set: between Canada and U.S., Oct. 20, 1818.

Bounet Island, Jan. 18, 1928.

Bounty, H.M.S., Apr. 28, 1789.

Bourassa, Robert, Jul. 14, 1933.

Bourdaloue, Louis, Aug. 20, 1632.

Bourdelle, Emile Antoine, Oct. 30, 1861.

Bourgeois, Leon V. A., May 21, 1851.

Bourguiba, Habib, Aug. 3, 1903; Apr. 9, 1938; Jul. 25, 1957; Mar. 18, 1975; Jan. 26, 1978; overthrown, Nov. 7, 1987.

Bourke-White, Margaret, Jun. 14, 1906.

Bourque, Ray, Dec. 28, 1960.

Bouton, James Alan *(Jim),* Mar. 8, 1939.

Boutros-Ghali, Boutros, Nov. 14, 1922; Jan. 1, 1992; Nov. 30, 1992.

Bouvines, Battle of: establishes France as European power, Jul. 27, 1214.

Bovet, Daniel, Mar. 23, 1907.

Bow, Clara, Aug. 6, 1905.

Bowditch, Nathaniel, Mar. 26, 1773.

Bowe, Riddick, Nov. 11, 1993.

Bowen, Elizabeth, Jun. 7, 1899.

Bowers, J. O., Apr. 22, 1953.

Bowie, David, Jan. 8, 1947.

Bowie, James, Mar. 6, 1836.

Bowles, Chester, Apr. 5, 1901.

Bowling Congress, American, Sep. 9, 1895.

bowling: first ten-pin match, Jan. 1, 1840.

Bowman, Isaiah, Dec. 26, 1878.

Boxer Protocol, Sep. 7, 1901.

Boxer Rebellion, Jan. 7, 1895; Jun. 20, 1900 war declared, Jun. 26, 1900; Aug. 14, 1900; Aug. 17, 1900; ends, Sep. 7, 1901; Jan. 3, 1903.

boxing match: first modern, Sep. 7, 1892.

Boxing Day, Dec. 26.

boxing: last bare-knuckles championship, Jul. 8, 1889.

Boxleitner, Bruce, May 12, 1951.

Boy George, Jun. 14, 1961.

Boy Scout Day (U.S.), Feb. 8.

Boy Scouts of America: incorporated, Feb. 8, 1910.

Boy Scouts, patron of, Apr. 23.

Boycott, Charles Cunningham, Mar 12, 1832.

Boyd, Julian (Parks), Nov. 3, 1903.

Boyd, William, Jun. 5, 1895.

Boyd-Orr of Brechin Mearns, Lord John, Sep. 23, 1880.

Boyer, Charles, Aug. 28, 1899.

Boyes, Sir Brian Barratt, Jan. 13, 1924.

Boyington, Pappy, Dec. 4, 1912.

Boyle, Lara Flynn, Mar. 24, 1970.

Boyle, Peter, Oct. 18, 1935.

Boyle, Robert, Jan. 25, 1627.

Boyle, Tony, Sep. 11, 1975.

Boyne, Battle of the, Jul. 12, 1690.

The Boys from Syracuse: premiere, Nov. 23, 1938.

Boys' Clubs of America, Federated, May 19, 1906.

Brabham, Sir John Arthur, Apr. 2, 1926.

Brackley, patron of, Nov. 3.

Brackman, Robert, Sep. 25, 1898.

Bracy, Arnold, Mar. 27, 1987.

Bradbury, Ray, Aug. 22, 1920.

Braddock, Edward, Jul. 9, 1755.

Braddock, James J., Jun. 13, 1935. Jun. 22, 1937.

Brademas, John, Mar. 2, 1927.

Bradford, Gamaliel, Oct. 9, 1863.

Bradford, Roark, Aug. 21, 1896.

Bradford, William, Mar. 19, 1589.

Bradlee, Ben(jamin Crouninshield), Aug. 26,1921.

Bradley, Bill, Jul. 28, 1943.

Bradley, Ed, Jan. 22, 1941.

Bradley, Henry, Dec. 3, 1845.

Bradley, Milton, Nov. 8, 1836.

Bradley, Omar N., Feb. 12, 1893; appointed chairman, Joint Chiefs of Staff, Aug. 11, 1949, promoted, Sep. 18, 1950.

Bradley, Thomas, Dec. 29, 1917.

Bradshaw, Terry Paxton, Sep. 2, 1948.

Brady Bill, Nov. 30, 1993.

Brady, James Buchanan *(Diamond Jim),* Aug. 12, 1856.

Brady, James S., Aug. 29, 1940.

Brady, Sarah, Feb. 6, 1942.

Braga (Portugal), patron of, Apr. 26.

Bragg, Braxton, Mar. 22, 1817.

Bragg, Sir William Henry, Jul. 2, 1862.

Bragg, Sir William Lawrence, Mar. 31, 1890.

Brahe, Tycho, Dec. 14, 1546.

Brahms, Johannes, May 7, 1833.

Braille, Louis, Jan. 4, 1809.

Brailer, John: first professional football player, Aug. 31, 1895.

Bramah, Joseph, Apr. 13, 1748.

Branagh, Kenneth C., Dec. 10, 1960.

Branch Davidians, Feb. 28, 1993.

Brancusi, Constantin, Feb. 21, 1876.

Brand, Max, Mar. 20, 1892.

Brandeis, Louis (Dembitz), Nov. 13, 1856.

Brando, Marlon, Apr. 3, 1924; Dec. 30, 1953; Mar. 15, 1972.

Brandt, Willy, Dec. 18, 1913; Oct. 3, 1957; Mar. 19, 1970; resigns, May 6, 1974.

Brandy (Norwood), Feb. 11, 1979.

Braniff International Corp., May 13, 1983.

Branigan, Laura, Jul. 3, 1957.

Branson, Richard, Jul. 3, 1987.

Branting, Karl Hjalmar, Nov. 23, 1860.

Braque, Georges, May 13, 1882.

Brasilia (Brazil), Apr. 21 1960.

Bratianu, Ion, Aug. 20, 1864.

Brattain, Walter Houser, Feb. 10, 1902. Nov. 1, 1956.

Brauchitsch, Heinrich Alfred Walther, Oct. 4, 1881.

Braudel, Fernand Paul, Aug. 24, 1902.

Braun, Carol Moseley, Aug. 16, 1947.

Braun, Eva, Feb. 6, 1912.

Braun, Karl F., Jun. 6, 1850.

Braun, Werner von, Mar. 23, 1912.

Brautigan, Richard, Jan. 30, 1933.

Brazelton, T(homas) Berry, May 10, 1918.

Brazil: discovered, Apr. 22, 1500, claimed for Portugal, Jun. 23, 1501, becomes empire Dec. 16, 1815; independence from Portugal, Sep. 7, 1822; declares independence, Oct. 12, 1822; independence, Aug. 29, 1825; serfdom abolished, May 13, 1888; extradition treaty with U.S., Jan. 13, 1961; Jan. 18, 1963; Jan. 22, 1967; Feb. 24, 1976.

Brazzaville, Mar. 18, 1977.

Breakfast at Tiffany's: published, Oct. 28, 1958.

Bream, Julian, Jul. 15, 1933.

breast cancer: X-ray treatment of, Jan. 29, 1896.

Breasted, James Henry, Aug. 27, 1865.

Brecht, Bertolt, Feb. 10, 1898.

Breck, John Henry, Jun. 5, 1877.

Breckinridge, John Cabell, Jan. 21, 1821; Mar. 4, 1857.

Breckinridge, Sophonisba, Apr. 1, 1866.

Breed's Hill, Jun. 17, 1775.

breeder reactor, Nov. 30, 1972.

Breidfjord, Sigurdur Eirikson, Mar. 4, 1798.

Breitenfeld, Battle of, Sep. 17, 1631; Nov. 2, 1642.

Breitinger, Johann Jakob, Mar. 1, 1701.

Brel, Jacques, Apr. 8, 1929.

Bremer, Arthur Herman, Aug. 21, 1950. found guilty of attempted assassination of George Wallace, Aug. 4, 1972.

Bremer, Fredrika, Aug. 17, 1801.

Brendel, Alfred, Jan. 5, 1931.

Brennan, Eileen Regina, Sep. 3, 1937.

Brennan, Walter, Jul. 25, 1894.

Brennan, William Joseph, Jr., Apr. 25, 1906. Mar. 19, 1957; Jul. 20, 1990.

Brenner, David, Feb. 4, 1945.

Brenner Pass, Jan. 4, 1945.

Brentano, Clemens, Maria, Sep. 8, 1778.

Bresci, Gaetano, Jul. 29, 1900.

Brescia, Apr. 19, 1428.

Brescia, patrons of, Feb. 15.

Breslau, Jan. 20, 1918.

Breslin, Jimmy, Oct. 17, 1930.

Bresse, Jan. 17, 1601.

Brest-Litovsk: negotiations between Russia and Germany, Dec. 3, 1917; peace negotiations begin, Dec. 22, 1917; Treaty of, Mar. 3, 1918; Mar. 16, 1918.

Breton, Andre, Feb. 18, 1896.

Breton, Jules Adolphe, May 1, 1827.

Brett, George Howard, May 15, 1953.

Brett, William Howard, Jul. 1, 1846.

Bretton Woods Conference: begins, Jul. 1, 1944.

Breuer, Josef, Jan. 15, 1842.

Breuer, Marcel Lajos, May 21, 1902.

Breuil, Henri Edouard-Prosper, Feb. 28, 1877.

Brewer, Theresa, May 7, 1931.

brewers, patron of, Dec. 4; Dec. 6.

Brewster, Kingman, Jun. 17, 1919.

Breyer, Stephen G., Aug. 15, 1938.

Brezhnev Doctrine, Feb. 24, 1972.

Brezhnev, Leonid I., Dec. 19, 1906; May 7, 1960; Oct. 15, 1964; Jun. 16, 1977; Jun. 18, 1979. Nov. 12, 1982.

Briand, Aristide, Mar. 28, 1862.

Brice, Fanny, Oct. 29, 1891.

Brickell, Edie, Mar. 10, 1966.

Brico, Antonia, Jun. 26, 1902.

The Bridge on The River Kwai: premiere, Dec. 18, 1957.

Bridge Over Troubled Water, Feb. 14, 1970.

Bridger, James, Mar. 17, 1804.

Bridges, Calvin Blackman, Jan. 11, 1889.

Bridges, Jeff, Dec. 4, 1949.

Bridges, Lloyd, Jan. 15, 1913.

Bridges, Lloyd Vernet, III *(Beau)*, Dec. 9, 1941.

Bridges, Roben Seymour, Oct. 23, 1844.

Bridgman, Percy Williams, Apr. 21, 1882.

Brigadoon: premiere, Mar. 13, 1947.

Briggs, Walter Owen, Jr., Jan. 20, 1912.

Bright, John, Nov. 16, 1811.

Brill, Abraham Arden, Oct. 12, 1874.

Brillat-Savarin, Anthelme, Apr. 1, 1755.

Brimsek, Frankie *(Mr. Zero)*, Sep. 26, 1915.

Brindisi (Italy): destruction of Byzantine fleet, May 28, 1156.

Brinkley, Christie, Feb. 2, 1953.

Brinkley, David (McClure), Jul. 10, 1920.

Brisbane, Arthur, Dec. 12, 1864.

Brisebois, Danielle, Jun. 28, 1969.

Bristol (England), Jan. 9, 1969.

Bristow, Benjamin Helm, Jun. 20, 1832.

Bristow, Lonnie, Apr. 6, 1930.

Britain. *See:* Great Britain.

British air force, Jan. 13, 1993.

British Air Training Corps, Feb. 1, 1941.

British Airways, Dec. 21, 1987.

British Association for the Advancement of Science: formed, Sep. 27, 1831.

British Broadcasting Company: established, Oct. 18, 1922;

begins transmission, Nov. 11, 1922.

British Caledonian Airways, Dec. 21, 1987.

British East India Company, Mar. 9, 1846; Aug. 2, 1858.

British Expeditionary Force: arrives in France, Aug. 7, 1914.

British Gazette and Sunday Monitor, The, Mar. 26, 1780.

British Honduras (Belize), Mar. 3, 1964; Jun. 1, 1973; Sep. 21, 1981.

British Museum: opens, Jan. 15, 1759.

British Nationality Bill, Oct. 30, 1981.

British North America Act, Jul. 1, 1867; Apr. 17, 1982.

British Road Traffic Act, Mar. 26, 1934.

British South Africa Company: granted charter, Oct. 29, 1889; May 3, 1895; Dec. 5, 1897.

Britten, (Edward) Benjamin, Nov. 22, 1913; Aug. 18, 1938; First Piano Concerto: premiere, Aug. 18, 1938; Nov. 28, 1941; Dec. 1, 1951; Jun. 8, 1953.

Britton, Nathaniel Lord, Jan. 15, 1859.

Broca, Philippe Claude Alex de, Mar. 15, 1933.

Broca, Pierre Paul, Jun. 28, 1824.

Brock, Lou, Sep. 23, 1979.

Brock, Sir Isaac, Oct. 6, 1769.

Brock, William Emerson (Bill), Nov. 23, 1930.

Brockhouse, Bertram N., Jul. 15, 1918.

Broda, Walter (Turk), May 15, 1914.

Broderick, Matthew, Aug. 21, 1962.

Brodie, Fawn McKay, Sep. 15, 1915.

Brodsky, Joseph Alexandrovich, May 24, 1940.

Brody, Jane Ellen, May 5, 1941.

Broglie, Prince Louis-Victor de, Aug. 15, 1892.

Brokaw, Thomas John (Tom), Feb. 6, 1940.

Brolin, James, Jul. 18, 1941.

Bromfield, Louis, Dec. 27, 1896.

Bromsebro, Peace of: signed, Aug. 23, 1645.

Bronfman, Edgar Miles, Jun. 20, 1929.

Brongniart, Alexandre, Feb. 5, 1770.

Bronk, Detlev Wulf, Aug. 13, 1897.

Bronson, Charles, Nov. 13, 1922.

Bronte, Anne, Jan. 17, 1820.

Bronte, Charlotte, Apr. 21, 1816.

Bronte, Emily Jane (Ellis Bell), Jul. 30, 1818.

Brook, Alexander, Jul. 14, 1898.

Brook, Peter, Mar. 21, 1925.

Brooke, Edward W., Oct. 26, 1919.

Brooke, Rupert, Aug. 3, 1887.

Brooke, Sir Alan Francis, Jul. 23, 1883.

Brookings, Robert Somers, Jan. 22, 1850.

Brooklyn Bridge: construction begins, Jan. 3, 1870; opens, May 24, 1883.

Brooklyn Dodgers (baseball), Oct. 8, 1957.

Brooklyn-Battery Tunnel: opens, May 25, 1950.

Brooks, Foster Murrell, May 11, 1912.

Brooks, Garth, Feb. 7, 1962.

Brooks, Gwendolyn (Elizabeth), Jun. 7, 1917; May 5, 1950.

Brooks, James L., May 9, 1940.

Brooks, Louise, Nov. 14, 1906.

Brooks, Mel, Jun. 28, 1926.

Brooks, Phillips, Dec. 13, 1835.

Brooks, Richard, May 18, 1912.

Brooks, Van Wyck, Feb. 16, 1886.

broommakers, patron of, Jul. 26.

Brosio, Manlio (Giovanni), Jul. 10, 1897.

Brosnan, Pierce, May 16, 1953.

Brotherhood-Sisterhood Week, Feb. intro.

Brothers, Joyce Diane Bauer, Oct. 20, 1928.

Broun, Heywood, Mar. 10, 1918; Dec. 7, 1888.

Browder, Earl Russell, May 20, 1891.

Brower, David, Jul. 1, 1912.

Brown, Arthur W., Jul. 23, 1886.

Brown, Bryan, Jun. 23, 1947.

Brown, David, Jul. 28, 1916.

Brown, Dee, Feb. 28, 1908.

Brown, Edmund G., Jr., Jul. 7, 1938.

Brown, Ernest William, Nov. 29, 1866.

Brown, Ford Madox, Apr. 16, 1821.

Brown, George Scratchley, Aug. 17, 1918.

Brown, H(ubert) Rap, Oct. 4, 1943. May 12, 1967.

Brown, Harold, Sep. 19, 1927.

Brown, Helen Gurley, Feb. 18, 1922.

Brown, Herben, May 22, 1912.

Brown, Ian, Jan. 1 1998.

Brown, Jacob Jennings, May 9, 1775.

Brown, James, Jun. 17, 1928.

Brown, James, May 3, 1934.

Brown, James Nathaniel (Jim), Feb. 17, 1936.

Brown, Jerry, Jr., Apr. 7, 1938.

Brown, Joe E., Jul. 28, 1892.

Brown, John, May 9, 1800; May 24, 1856; Oct. 16, 1859; hanged, Dec. 2, 1859.

Brown, Joseph, Jan. 26, 1810.

Brown, Les(ter Raymond), Mar. 12, 1912.

Brown, Louise Joy, Jul. 25, 1978.

Brown, Michael Stuart, Apr. 13, 1941.

Brown, Moses, Sep. 23, 1738.

Brown, Pat, Apr. 21, 1905.

Brown, Paul, Jul. 9, 1908.

Brown, Ronald, Aug. 1, 1941; Feb. 10, 1989; Apr. 3, 1996.

Brown, Tina, Nov. 21, 1953.

Brown, William, Jan. 5, 1975.

Brown, Willie, Jr., Mar. 20, 1934.

Brown-Sequard, Charles Edouard, Apr. 8, 1817.

Brown vs. Board of Education, May 17, 1954.

Browne, Charles Farrar, Apr. 26, 1834.

Browne, Jackson, Oct. 9, 1950.

Browne, Leslie, Jun. 29, 1957.

Browne, Sir Thomas, Oct. 19, 1605.

Browning, Elizabeth Barrett, Mar. 6, 1806.

Browning, Roben, May 7, 1812.

Brownmiller, Susan, Feb. 15, 1935.

Brubeck, Dave, Dec. 6, 1920.

Bruce, Blanche Kelso, Mar. 1, 1841.

Bruce, David K. E., Feb. 12, 1898.

Bruce, Edward (King of Ireland), May 2, 1316.

Bruce, Jack, May 15, 1943.

Bruce, Lenny, Oct. 13, 1925.

Bruce, Nigel, Feb. 4, 1895.

Bruce, Robert de (King of Scotland),
Mar. 25, 1306; Jun. 26, 1306;
May 10, 1307; Jun. 24, 1314;
May 4, 1328; dies, Jun. 7, 1329.
Bruce, Virginia, Sep. 29, 1910.
Bruckner, Anton, Sep. 4, 1824.
Bruges, Truce of, Jun. 27, 1375.
Bruhn, Erik, Oct. 3, 1928.
Brum, Baltasar, Jun. 18, 1883.
Brumidi, Constantino, Jul. 26, 1805.
Brummell, George Bryan (Beau),
Jun. 7, 1778.
Brundage, Avery, Sep. 28, 1887.
Brundtland, Gro Harlem (Norway):
first woman premier, Feb. 4,
1981. May 9, 1986.
Brunei, May 12, 1888; Jan. 1, 1984.
Brunel, Isambard Kingdom, Apr. 9,
1806.
Brunel, Sir, Marc Isambard, Apr. 25,
1769.
Bruning, Heinrich, Apr. 13, 1932.
Brunn, Treaty of, Feb. 10, 1364.
Brush, Charles Francis, Mar. 17,
1849.
brushmakers, patron of, Jan. 17.
Brusilov, Aleksei Akekseevich, Aug.
19, 1853.
Brussels (Belgium), Nov. 18, 1918;
Sep. 4, 1944.
Brussels Pact: signed, Mar. 17, 1948.
Brussels, patron of, Jan. 8.
Brutus, Mar. 15, 44.
Bryan, William Jennings, Mar. 19,
1860; Jul. 8, 1896; resigns, Jun.
8, 1915.
Bryant, Anita, Mar. 25, 1940.
Bryant, Lane, Dec. 1, 1879.
Bryant, Paul (Bear), Sep. 11, 1913.
Bryant, William Cullen, Nov. 3, 1794.
Bryce, James Wares, Mar. 27, 1880.
Bryn Mawr College, Oct. 23, 1885.
Brynjulfsson, Gisli, Sep. 3, 1827.
Brynner, Yul, Jul. 11, 1920.
Bryson, Peabo, Apr. 13, 1951.
Brzezinski, Zbigniew, Mar. 28, 1928.
Bubblin' Brown Sugar: opens, Mar.
2, 1976.
Buber, Martin, Feb. 8, 1878.
Bucaram, Abdal , removed from
office, Feb. 9, 1997.
Bucer, Manin, Nov. 11, 1491.
Buch, Leopold von, Apr. 26, 1774.
Buchan, Sir John, Aug. 26, 1875.

Buchanan, Franklin, Sep. 17, 1800.
Buchanan, James, Apr. 23, 1791;
inaugurated, Mar. 4, 1857.
Buchanan, James M., Oct. 2, 1919.
Buchanan, Ken, Jun. 26, 1972.
Buchanan, Patrick Joseph, Nov. 2,
1938.
Bucharest, Treaty of, Mar. 3, 1886;
signed, Aug. 10, 1913; May 7,
1918.
Bucharest: Germans enter, Dec. 6,
1916; earthquake, Mar. 4, 1977.
Buchenwald concentration camp,
Jul. 16, 1937. liberated, Apr. 19,
1945.
Bucher, Giovanni Enrico, Jan. 16,
1969.
Buchner, Eduard, May 20, 1860.
Buchwald, Art, Oct. 20, 1925.
Buck, Frank, Mar. 17, 1884.
Buck, Pearl (Sydenstricker), Jun. 26,
1892.
Buckingham, Lindsey, Oct. 3, 1947.
Buckle, George Earle, Jun. 10, 1854.
Buckley, Betty, Jul. 3, 1947.
Buckley, James Lane, Mar. 9, 1923.
Buckley, Tim, Feb. 17, 1947.
Buckley, William F(rank), Nov. 25,
1925.
Buckley, William, Mar. 16, 1984.
Buckminster, Joseph Stevens, May
26, 1784.
Buckner, Simon Bolivar, Apr. 1,
1823.
Budapest (Hungary), Jan. 13, 1904;
Sep. 5, 1942; Russians enter,
Dec. 29, 1944; Feb. 13, 1945.
Buddha Gautama, Apr. 8, 563 b.c.
Buddha's Birthday (Japan), Apr. 8.
Buddha's Birthday (Korea), May 24.
Buddhism, Aug. 26, 1961.
Bude, Guillaume, Jan. 26, 1468.
Budge, Don, Jun. 13, 1915.
Budge, Sir Ernest Alfred Wallis, Jul.
27, 1857.
Buena Vista, Battle of, Feb. 22, 1847.
Bueno, Maria, Oct. 11, 1939.
Buffet, Jimmy, Dec. 25, 1946.
Buffet, Warren, Aug. 30, 1930.
Buffon, Georges Louis Leclerc du,
Sep. 7, 1707.
Buford, John, Mar. 4, 1826.
Buganda, Kingdom of, Jun. 10, 1966.
Bugenhagen, Johann, Jun. 24, 1485.

Bugey, Jan. 17, 1601.
Bugliosi, Vincent T., Aug. 18, 1934.
Buhan, Mohammed, Dec. 31, 1983;
Jan. 1, 1984.
Buick, David Dunbar, Sep. 17, 1854.
builders, patron of, Jul. 2; Aug. 25;
Dec. 21.
Buisson, Ferdinand Edouard, Dec.
20, 1841.
Bujold, Genevieve, Jul. 1, 1942.
Bukhari, Mohammed ibn Ismail al-,
Jul. 21, 810.
Bukharin, Nikolai Ivanovich, Oct. 9,
1888; Feb. 4, 1988.
Bulatovic, Momir, May 19, 1998.
Bulfinch, Charles, Aug. 8, 1763.
Bulfinch, Thomas, Jul. 15, 1796.
Bulganin, Nikolai Aleksandrovich,
Jun. 11, 1895.
Bulgaria: proclaims independence,
Oct. 5, 1908; war with Romania,
Jul. 10, 1913; declares war on
Romania, Sep. 1, 1916; Greece
declares war on, Jul. 2, 1917;
armistice with Allies, Sep. 30,
1918; May 19, 1934; Mar. 1,
1941; surrenders, Sep. 8, 1944.
Bulge, Battle of the: begins, Dec. 16,
1944; ends, Jan. 16, 1945.
Bull Moose Party, Jun. 22, 1912.
Bull Run, First Battle of, Jul. 21,
1861.
Buller, Redvers, Feb. 28, 1900; Jun.
5, 1900.
Bullinger, Heinrich, Jul. 18, 1504.
Bullitt, William Christian, Jan. 25,
1891.
Bulosan, Carlos, Nov. 23, 1913.
Bulova, Arde, Oct. 24, 1889.
Bulow, Prince Bernhard von, May 3,
1849.
Bulwer-Lytton, Edward George (Earl
Lytton), May 15, 1803.
Bumble Bee Seafoods, Apr. 12, 1990.
Bumbry, Grace Ann Jaeckel, Jan. 4,
1937.
Bumpers, Dale, Aug. 12, 1925.
Bunau-Varilla, Philippe Jean, Jul. 26,
1860.
Bunche, Ralph, Aug. 7, 1904; Dec.
10, 1950; Mar. 21, 1965.
Bundy, McGeorge, Mar. 30, 1919.
Bundy, Theodore Robert (Ted), Nov.
24, 1946; Jan. 24, 1989.

Bunin, Ivan Alekseyevich, Oct. 10, 1870.

Bunker, Ellsworth, May 11, 1894.

Bunker Hill, Battle of, Jun. 17, 1775.

Bunker Hill Day (Massachusetts), Jun. 17.

Bunning, Jim, Jun. 21, 1964.

Bunon Island, U.S.S., Sep. 4, 1954.

Bunsen, Roben Wilhelm, Mar. 31, 1811.

Buntline, Ned, Mar. 20, 1823.

Bunuel, Luis, Feb. 22, 1900.

Bunyan, John, Feb. 18, 1678.

Burbank, Luther, Mar. 7, 1849.

Burbidge, E. Margaret, Aug. 12, 1919.

Burbidge, Geoffrey, Sep. 24, 1925.

Burdick, Eugene, Dec. 12, 1918; Oct. 1, 1958.

Burdon, Eric, Apr. 5, 1941.

Bureau of Indian Affairs: created, Mar. 11, 1824.

Bureau of the Census: created, Mar. 6, 1902.

Burford, Anne McGill Gorsuch, Apr. 21, 1942. Mar. 9, 1983.

Burger, Warren Earl, Sep. 17, 1907; Jun. 23, 1969.

Burgess, Anthony, Feb. 25, 1917.

Burgess, Thornton W., Jan. 4, 1874.

Burgesses, House of: convenes, Jul. 30, 1619.

Burghley, Baron (William Cecil), Sep. 13, 1520.

Burghoff, Gary, May 24, 1943.

Burgoyne, General John, Oct. 17, 1777.

Burgundy, Duke of, May 18, 1412.

Burke, Arleigh, Oct. 19, 1901.

Burke, Billie, Aug. 7, 1886.

Burke, Edmund, Jan. 12, 1729.

Burke, Johnny, Oct. 3, 1908.

Burke, Martha Jane (*Calamity Jane*), May 1, 1852.

Burke, Thomas, May 6, 1882.

Burkina Faso, Aug. 3, 1983.

Burleigh, Harry Thacker, Dec. 2, 1866.

Burlingame, Anson, Nov. 14, 1820.

Burlington Arcade, Mar. 20, 1819.

Burma (Upper): annexed by British, Jan. 1, 1886.

Burma, Lower (Pegu), Dec. 20, 1852.

Burma, Mar. 9, 1942; independence, Jan. 4, 1948; Apr. 5, 1960; Aug. 26, 1961; coup d'etat, Mar. 2, 1962; new constitution, Jan. 4, 1974; military rule ends, Mar. 2, 1974.

Burma Road, Apr. 29, 1942.

Burma, Socialist Republic of the Union of, Jan. 3, 1974.

Burma War, First, May 4, 1824.

Burmese War, Third, Nov. 28, 1885.

Burnc-Jones, Sir Edward Coley, Aug. 28, 1833.

Burnell, Jocelyn Bell, Jul. 15, 1943.

Burnet, Sir Frank Macfarlane, Sep. 3, 1899.

Burnett, Carol, Apr. 26, 1936.

Burnett, Frances Eliza Hodgson, Nov. 24, 1849.

Burney, Frances (Fanny), Jun. 13, 1752.

Burnham, Daniel Hudson, Sep. 4, 1846.

Burnham, Linden Forbes, Feb. 20, 1923; inaugurated, Dec. 14, 1964.

Burnham, Sherburne Wesley, Dec. 12, 1838.

Burns, Arthur, Apr. 27, 1904.

Burns, George, Jan. 20, 1896.

Burns, Kenneth L., Jul. 29, 1953.

Burns Night (Scotland), Jan. 25.

Burns, Robert, Jan. 25, 1759.

Burns, Tommy, Dec. 26, 1908.

Burnside, Ambrose Everett, May 23, 1824.

Burpee, David, Apr. 5, 1893.

Burpee, W. Atlee, Apr. 5, 1858.

Burr, Aaron, Feb. 6, 1756; Mar. 4, 1801; Jul. 11, 1804.

Burr, Raymond, May 21, 1917.

Burroughs, Edgar Rice, Sep. 1, 1875; Oct. 1, 1912.

Burroughs, John, Apr. 3, 1837.

Burroughs, William, Feb. 5, 1914.

Burroughs, William Seward, Jan. 28, 1855.

Burrows, Millar, Oct. 26, 1889.

Burstyn, Ellen, Dec. 7, 1932; Dec. 26, 1973.

Burton, Charles, Apr. 11, 1982.

Burton, Harold Hitz, Jun. 22, 1888.

Burton, LeVar(dis Robert Martyn), Jr., Feb. 16, 1957.

Burton, Michael, Jul. 3, 1947.

Burton, Richard, Nov. 10, 1925; Mar. 15, 1964.

Burton, Robert, Feb. 8, 1577.

Burton, Sir Richard Francis, Mar. 19, 1821; Feb. 13, 1858.

Burton, Theodore Elijah, Dec. 20, 1851.

Burundi: independence, Jul. 1, 1962; Jan. 30, 1965; Nov. 1, 1976.

Bus Stop: premiere; Aug. 21, 1956.

Busby, Richard, Sep. 22, 1606.

Buscaglia, Leo(nardo), Mar. 31, 1925.

Busch, Adolphus, Jul. 10, 1839.

Busch, Wilhelm, Apr. 15, 1832.

Busey, Gary, Jun. 29, 1944.

Bush, Barbara, Jun. 8, 1925.

Bush, George Walker, Jul. 6, 1946; Jan. 20, 1981; Jan. 20, 1985; elected, Nov. 8, 1988; sworn in, Jan. 20, 1989; Americans with Disabilities Act, Jul. 26, 1990; Clean Air Act, Nov. 15, 1990; Martin Luther King, Jr. holiday, Jan. 17, 1992; nuclear arsenals agreement, Jun. 16, 1992; Cuban Democracy Act, Oct. 23, 1992; Iran-Contra affair, Dec. 24, 1992; Strategic Arms Reduction Treaty (START II), Jan. 3, 1993; plot to assassinate, Jun. 26, 1993.

Bush, Kate, Jul. 30, 1958.

Bush, Vannevar, Mar. 11, 1890.

Bushell, John, Mar. 23, 1752.

Bushman, Francis X., Jan. 10, 1883.

business and professional women, patron of, Nov. 17.

Busoni, Ferruccio Benvenuto, Apr. 1, 1866.

Bustamente Rivero, Jose Luis, Jul. 28, 1945.

butchers, patron of, Jan. 17; Aug. 24; Sep. 8.

Butenandt, Adolf Friedrich Johann, Mar. 24, 1903.

Butkus, Richard J. *(Dick)*, Dec. 9, 1942.

Butler, Alban, Oct. 24, 1710.

Butler, Benjamin Franklin, Nov. 5, 1818.

Butler, James (Marquis of Ormonde), Sep. 11, 1649.

Butler, Joseph, May 18, 1692.

Butler, Nicholas Murray, Apr. 2, 1862.

Butler, Pierce, Mar. 17, 1866.

Butler, Samuel, Dec. 4, 1835.

Butler, Smedley Darlington, Jul. 30, 1881.

Butlerov, Aleksandr Mikhailovich, Sep. 6, 1828.

Butterfield, Alexander Porter, Apr. 6, 1926.

Butterick, Ebenezer, May 29, 1826.

Buttigieg, Anton, Feb. 19, 1912.

Button, Dick, Jul. 18, 1929.

Buttons, Red, Feb. 5, 1919.

Butz, Earl: resigns, Oct. 4, 1976.

Buu Loc, Jan. 12, 1954; Jun. 4, 1954.

Buxtorf, Johannes (the Elder), Dec. 25, 1564.

Buynak, Eugene, Jun. 26, 1966.

Buzzi, Ruth Ann, Jul. 24, 1936.

Bye, Bye Birdie: premiere, Apr. 14, 1960.

Byland, Oct. 14, 1322.

Byng, Julian (Sir), May 28, 1916.

Byrd, Harry (Flood), Jr., Jun. 10, 1887; Dec. 20, 1914.

Byrd, Richard E., Oct. 25, 1888; May 9, 1926; Nov. 29, 1929.

Byrd, Robert Carlyle, Nov. 20, 1917; Jan. 15, 1918.

Byrne, David, May 14, 1952.

Byrne, Jane, May 24, 1934.

Byrnes, James Francis, May 2, 1879; Jun. 12, 1941.

Byron, Lord *See*: Gordon, George (Lord Byron).

C

Caan, James, Mar. 26, 1939.

cab drivers in Paris, patron of, Sep. 1.

Caballe, Montserrat, Apr. 12, 1933.

Caballo Island, Mar. 27, 1945.

Cabaret: premiere, Nov. 20, 1966.

Cabell, James Branch, Apr. 14, 1879.

cabinetmakers, patron of, Jul. 21.

cable, transatlantic submarine: inaugurated, Dec. 19, 1961.

Cable, George Washington, Oct. 12, 1844.

Cable TV Month, Sep. intro.

Cabot, John, Jun. 24, 1450; Mar. 5, 1496; Jun. 24, 1497.

Cabot, Sebastian, Jul. 6, 1918.

Cabral, Pedro, Apr. 22, 1500; Jun. 23, 1501.

Cabrini, Frances Xavier: first American canonized, Jul. 7, 1946.

Caddell, Pat(rick Hayward), May 19, 1950.

Cade, Jack, Jun. 27, 1450.

Cade's Insurrection, Jun. 27, 1450.

Cadillac, Antoine de la Mothe, Mar. 5, 1658.

Cadiz (Spain): captured from Moors, Sep. 14, 1262; Apr. 19, 1587.

Cadman, Charles Wakefield, Dec. 24, 1881.

Caen (France), Jul. 9, 1944.

Caernarvon Castle (Wales), Apr. 25, 1284.

Caesar, Julius, Jul. 12, 100 b.c.; Feb. 6, 46 b.c.; Mar. 17, 45 b.v.; assassinated, Mar. 15, 44 b.c.; Feb. 15, 44 b.c.; Jul. intro.; Aug. intro.

Caesar, Nero Claudius, Dec. 15, 37.

Caesar, Sid, Sep. 8, 1922.

Caetano, Marcelo, Jul. 6, 1955; Apr. 25, 1974.

Cafe Filho, Joao, Aug. 24, 1954.

Cagayan and Sibutu Islands (Philippines): ceded to U.S., Nov. 7, 1900.

Cage, John Milton, Jr., Sep. 5, 1912.

Cage Nicolas, Jan. 7, 1964.

Cagliari Harbor, Apr. 1, 1943.

Cagliostro, Count Alessandro, Jun. 2, 1743.

Cagney, James, Jul. 17, 1899.

Cahn, Sammy, Jun. 18, 1913.

Cailletet, Louis Paul, Sep. 21, 1832.

Cain, Richard Harvey, Apr. 12, 1825.

Caine, Michael, Mar. 14, 1933.

Caine, Sir Thomas Henry Hall, May 14, 1853.

Cairo Conference, First: begins, Nov. 22, 1943.

Cairo, Declaration of, Dec. 1, 1943.

Caithness, patron of, Oct. 8.

Cakobau, George, Nov. 6, 1912.

Calabria (Italy): earthquake, Dec. 28, 1908.

Calais, patron of, Jun. 20.

Calais, Peace of, Oct. 24, 1360.

Calais: surrenders to Edward III (England), Aug. 3, 1347; Jan. 7, 1558; Jan. 20, 1558; Jan. 7, 1785.

Calatafimi, Battle of, May 15, 1860.

calculator, Aug. 6, 1944.

Calcutta (India): captured, Jun. 20, 1756; Dec. 12, 1911.

Calcutta, University of (India), Jan. 24, 1857.

Caldecott, Randolph, Mar. 22, 1846.

Calder, Alexander, Jul. 22, 1898.

Caldera Rodriguez: inaugurated, Mar. 11, 1969.

Calderon de la Barca, Pedro, Jan. 17, 1600.

Caldicott, Helen, Aug. 7, 1938.

Caldron Guardia, Rafael Angel: inaugurated, May 8, 1940.

Caldwell, Erskine, Dec. 17, 1903.

Caldwell, Sarah, Mar. 6, 1924; Jan. 13, 1976.

Caldwell, Taylor, Sep. 7, 1900.

calendar, Gregorian, Feb. 24, 1582.

calendar, Julian, Feb. 24, 1582.

calendula, Oct. intro.

Calhoun, John C., Mar. 18, 1782; Mar. 4, 1825; Mar. 4, 1829.

Calhoun, Rory, Aug. 8, 1923.

Calicut (India), May 20, 1498.

Califano, Joseph A., Apr. 28, 1977.

California, May 30, 1848; admitted to Union, Sep. 9, 1850; Nov. 27, 1962; earthquake, Feb. 9, 1971; right to die recognized, Sep. 30, 1976.

California, Republic of: proclaimed, Jun. 14, 1846.

California, University of, Jan. 6, 1971.

californium: identified, Mar. 17, 1950.

Caligula (Roman emperor), Aug. 31, 12.

Calixtus III (pope), Dec. 31, 1378; May 15, 1455.

Callaghan, James (England), Mar. 27, 1912; Apr. 5, 1976; Mar. 1, 1979.

Callas, Maria, Dec. 3, 1923.

Calles, Plutarco Elias, Sep. 25, 1877.

Calley, Lt. William L.: charged, Nov. 12, 1969; found guilty, Mar. 29, 1971; sentenced, Mar. 31, 1971.

Calloway, Cab(ell), Dec. 25, 1907.

Calve, Emma, Aug. 15, 1858.

Calvin, John, Jul. 10, 1509; Apr. 21, 1538; Jun. 13, 1541; Nov. 20, 1541.

Calving, Italo, Oct. 15, 1923.

Cambodia, Jan. 29, 1950; Feb. 7, 1950; Jan. 31, 1964; May 3, 1965; Mar. 1, 1975; Apr. 17, 1975; seizure of the Mayaguez May 12, 1975; Jan. 5, 1976; peace talks begin, Jul. 25, 1988; UN peace proposal, Sep. 10, 1990.

Cambodia, National Union of, Apr. 25, 1975.

Cambrai, Battle of, Nov. 20, 1917; ends, Dec. 7, 1917.

Cambrai, League of: formed, Dec. 10, 1508; May 14, 1509.

Cambrai, Oct. 9, 1918.

Cambrai, Peace of: signed, Aug. 5, 1529.

Cambridge, Godfrey, Feb. 26, 1933.

Camden, William, May 2, 1551.

Camelot: premiere, Dec. 3, 1960.

Cameron, James, Aug. 16, 1954.

Cameron, Kirk, Oct. 12, 1970.

Cameron, Sir David Young, Jun. 28, 1865.

Cameroon, Feb. 18, 1916; independence, Jan. 1, 1960; admitted to the U.N., Jan. 26, 1960; May 20, 1972.

Cameroon, Northern, Jun. 1, 1961.

Cammaerts, Emile, Mar. 16, 1878.

Camoens and Portuguese Communities Day (Macao), Jun. 10.

Camoes, Dia de, Jun. intro.

Camp David Agreement, Apr. 25, 1982.

Camp David, Middle East Summit at, Sep. 17, 1978.

Camp Fire Birthday Week, Mar. intro.

Camp Fire Founders Day (U.S.), Mar. 17.

Camp Fire Girls: established, Mar. 17, 1910.

Camp, Walter Chauncey, Apr. 17, 1859.

Campanella, Joseph Mario, Nov. 21, 1927.

Campanella, Roy, Nov. 19, 1921.

Campanella, Tommaso, Sep. 5, 1568.

Campanile (Venice), Apr. 25, 1903.

Campbell, (Ignatius) Roy (Dunnachie), Oct. 2, 1901.

Campbell, Alexander, Sep. 12, 1788.

Campbell, Ben Nighthorse, Apr. 13, 1933.

Campbell, Douglas, Apr. 14, 1918.

Campbell, Glen, Apr. 22, 1938.

Campbell, James B., Apr. 18, 1963.

Campbell, Kim, Jun. 12, 1993.

Campbell, Sir Malcolm, Mar. 11, 1885.

Campbell, Mrs. Patrick, Feb. 9, 1865.

Campbell, Naomi, May 22, 1970.

Campbell, Neve, Oct. 3, 1973.

Campbell, Thomas, Jul. 27, 1777.

Campbell, William Wallace, Apr. 11, 1862.

Camper, Pieter, May 11, 1722.

Campion, Thomas, Feb. 12, 1567.

Campo Formio, Peace of, Oct. 17, 1797.

Campobello Island, Jan. 22, 1964.

Campora, Hector Jose, Mar. 26, 1909. Mar. 11, 1973.

Camus, Albert, Nov. 7, 1913; Jan. 11, 1954.

Can-Cam: premiere, May 7, 1953.

Canada and U.S.S.R.: first direct air service between, Jul. 11, 1966.

Canada Constitution Act: passed, Jun. 10, 1791.

Canada Day (Canada), Jul. 1.

Canada, Dominion of: created, Jul. 1, 1867.

Canada, Jan. 22, 1964; flag adopted, Dec. 15, 1964; new flag, Feb. 15, 1965; Feb. 7, 1968; official languages, Jul. 7, 1969; Oct. 16, 1970; Progressive Conservatives, May 22, 1979.

Canada, Lower, Jun. 10, 1791; Jul. 23, 1840; Jul. 1, 1867.

Canada, Upper, Jun. 10, 1791; Jul. 23, 1840; Jul. 1, 1867.

Canada-U.S. Goodwill Week, Apr. intro.

Canadian Corps, May 28, 1916.

Canadian government: admission of U.S. deserters, May 22, 1969.

Canalejas, Jose (Spain): assassinated, Nov. 12, 1912.

Canaletto (Giovanni Antonio Canal), Oct. 18, 1697.

Canaris, Wilhelm Franz, Jan. 1, 1887.

Canary Islands, Mar. 6, 1480.

Canby, Henry Seidel, Sep. 6, 1878.

Canby, Vincent, Jul. 27, 1924.

cancer, lung, May 26, 1950.

Cancer, Jun. intro; Jul. intro.

The Cancer Ward: U.S. publication, Oct. 15, 1968.

Candid Camera: television debut, Aug. 10, 1948.

Candide: premiere, Dec. 1, 1956.

Candlemas (Liechtenstein), Feb. 2.

Candler, Asa Griggs, Dec. 30, 1851.

Candolle, Augustine Pyrame, Feb. 4, 1778.

Candy, John, Oct. 31, 1950.

Canetti, Elias, Jul. 25, 1905.

Canfield, Cass, Apr. 26, 1897.

Canicula, Jul. intro.

Canis Major, Jul. intro.

Cannell, Stephen J., Feb. 5, 1943.

Canning, George, Apr. 11, 1770.

Cannizzaro, Stanislao, Jul. 13, 1826.

Cannon, Annie Jump, Dec. 11, 1863.

Cannon, Clarence, Apr. 11, 1879.

Cannon, Dyan, Jan. 4, 1938.

Cannon, Joseph Curney, May 7, 1836.

Cannonball, Apr. 30, 1900.

Cano, Alonso, Mar. 19, 1601.

Canossa, Jan. 28, 1077.

Canova, Antonio, Nov. 1, 1757.

Canova, Diana, Jun. 2, 1953.

Canseco, Jose, Jul. 2, 1964.

Cantemir, Prince Dimitrie, Sep. 21, 1708.

Canterbury (England), May 31, 1942.

Canterbury, 100th Archbishop of (Arthur Michael Ramsey), Jun. 27, 1961.

Canterbury, Archbishop of, Mar. 23, 1966.

Canterbury Cathedral, Jul. 11, 1946.

Canterbury, Martyrs, Oct. 1, 1588.

Cantigny (France), May 28, 1918.

Canton (China): British blockade, Jun. 28, 1840; Jan. 20, 1924; Oct. 21, 1938.

Canton (Ohio), Sep. 17, 1920.

Cantor, Eddy, Jan. 31, 1892.

Cantor, Georg, Mar. 3, 1845.

cantus tradionalis, Jan. 8, 1904.

Canute II (Denmark), Feb. 3, 1014.

Canute II (Norway), Jul. 29, 1030.

Canutes Day (Sweden), Jan. 13.

Cape Canaveral (Florida); Jan. 31, 1961; May 5, 1961; Apr. 26, 1962; Nov. 28, 1963. *See also*: Cape Kennedy (Florida).

Cape Cod Canal: opens, Oct. 7, 1915.

Cape Colony, Apr. 6, 1652; Jan. 17, 1837; Jan. 12, 1879; Jul. 17, 1890; Jan. 6, 1896.

Cape Esperance, Battle of, Oct. 11, 1942.

Cape Kennedy (Florida), Nov. 28, 1963; Jan. 27, 1967. *See also*: Cape Canaveral (Florida).

Cape of Good Hope, Feb. 3, 1488; British occupation of, Jan. 8, 1806; Colony of: ceded to British, Aug. 13, 1814; May 31, 1910.

Cape St. George, Battle of, Nov. 25, 1943.

Cape Town, Jan. 10, 1900.

Cape Verde Islands: independence, Jul. 5, 1975.

Capetown, University of, Apr. 27, 1916.

capital punishment: abolished in United Kingdom, Dec. 18, 1969; reinstated in U.S., Jan. 17, 1977; Jun. 6, 1977.

Capital Cities Communications Inc., Mar. 18, 1985.

Capodistrias, Ioannes (Greece): assassinated, Oct. 9, 1831.

Capone, Al, Jan. 17, 1899.

Caporetto, Battle of: ends, Oct. 24, 1917.

Capote, Truman, Sep. 30, 1924; Oct. 28, 1958; Jan. 17, 1966.

Capp, Al, Sep. 28, 1909.

Capra, Frank, May 18, 1897.

Capriati, Jennifer, Mar. 29, 1976.

Capricorn, Jan. intro; Dec. intro.

Captain Regents Day (San Marino), Apr. 1; Oct. 1.

captives, patron of, Dec. 4.

Caputo, Philip Joseph, Jan. 10, 1941.

Cara, Irene, Mar. 18, 1959.

Carabobo Battle of (Venezuela), Jun. 24.

Caravaggio, Sep. 28, 1573.

Caraway, Hattie Wyatt, Feb. 1, 1878.

Carcaterra, Lorenzo, Oct. 16, 1954.

Cardano, Girolamo, Sep. 24, 1501.

C rdenas, L zaro, May 21, 1895.

cardiac message, Apr. 19, 1950.

cardiac pacemaker, Oct. 23, 1950.

Cardin, Pierre, Jul. 7, 1922.

Cardinale, Claudia, Apr. 15, 1938.

Cardoso, Fernando, Jan. 18, 1931; elected, Oct. 2, 1994.

Cardozo, Benjamin Nathan, May 24, 1870.

Carducci, Giosue, Jul. 27, 1835.

Carew, Rod(ney Cline), Oct. 1, 1945.

Carey, George, Nov. 13, 1935.

Carey, Henry Charles, Dec. 15, 1793.

Carey, Henry Dewitt, II *(Harry)*, Jan. 16, 1878.

Carey, Hugh, Apr. 11, 1919.

Carey, MacDonald, Mar. 15, 1914.

Carey, Mariah, Mar. 27, 1970.

Caribbean Day (Barbados, Guyana), Jul. intro.

Caribbean Day (Guyana), Jun. 26.

Caricom Day (Antigua and Barbuda), Jul. 3.

Caricom Day (Barbados), Aug. 4.

Caricom Day (Dominica), Jul. 2.

Cariou, Leonard *(Len)*, Sep. 30, 1939.

Carl XVI Gustaf (Sweden), Apr. 30, 1946; Sep. 15, 1973.

Carletonville (South Africa): wage riot, Sep. 12, 1973.

Carlin, George, May 12, 1937.

Carlisle, Belinda, Aug. 17, 1958.

Carlisle, Kitty, Sep. 3, 1915.

Carlos, Don, Apr. 22, 1834; Mar. 4, 1876.

Carlos I (Portugal): assassinated, Feb. 1, 1908.

Carlos, John, Oct. 16, 1968.

Carlota (Mexico), Jun. 7, 1840.

Carlsbad Caverns, May 14, 1930.

Carlsbad, Decrees (Germany), Sep. 20, 1819.

Carlson, Chester, Feb. 8, 1906; Oct. 22, 1938.

Carlsson, Ingvar: inaugurated, Mar. 12, 1986.

Carlton, Richard Paul, Dec. 20, 1893.

Carlton, Steve(n Norman), Dec. 22, 1944.

Carlucci, Frank Charles, III, Oct. 18, 1930.

Carlyle, Thomas, Dec. 4, 1795.

Carmelite, Martyrs of Compiegne, Jul. 17.

Carmen Jones: premiere, Dec. 2, 1943.

Carmen: premiere, Mar. 3, 1875.

Carmer, Carl, Oct. 16, 1893.

Carmichael, Hoagy, Nov. 22, 1899.

Carmichael, Stokely, Jun. 29, 1941; May 16, 1966; May 12, 1967; calls for black revolution, Aug. 17, 1967.

Carmina Burana: premiere, Jun. 8, 1937.

Carnarvon, Lord, Nov. 29, 1922.

carnation, Jan. intro.

Carnation Day, Jul. intro; Jul. 4.

Carnaval des Animaux: premiere, Feb. 25, 1922.

Carne, Judy, Apr. 27, 1939.

Carnegie, Andrew, Nov. 25, 1835.

Carnegie, Dale, Nov. 24, 1888.

Carnegie Hall, Jan. 16, 1938.

carnelian, Aug. intro.

Carnera, Primo, Jun. 29, 1933; Jun. 14, 1934.

Carnes, Kim, Jul. 20, 1946.

Carney, Art, Nov. 4, 1918.

Carnival (St. Kitts), Dec. 30.

Carnival Rest Day (Bonaire), Feb. 27.

Carnot, Lazare Nicolas, May 13, 1753.

Carnot, Marie Francois Sadi, Aug. 11, 1837.

Carnot, Nicolas Leonard Sadi, Jun. 1, 1796.

Caro, Miguel Antonio, Nov. 10, 1843.

Carol I (Romania), Apr. 20, 1839.

Carol II (Rumania), Jun. 9, 1930.

Carolina, South: secedes, Dec. 20, 1860.

Caroline (Louise Marguerite), Princess, Jan. 23, 1957.

Caron, Leslie Clare Margaret, Jul. 1, 1931.

Carothers, Wallace Hume, Apr. 27, 1896.

Carousel: premiere, Apr. 19, 1945.

Carpathian Passes, Battles of, Jan. 26, 1915.

Carpatho-Ukraine, Mar. 15, 1939.

Carpeaux, Jean Baptiste, May 14, 1827.

Carpenter, Bobby, Jul. 13, 1963.

Carpenter, Elizabeth Sutherland *(Liz)*, Sep. 1, 1920.

Carpenter, John, Jan. 16, 1948.

Carpenter, Karen Ann, Mar. 2, 1950.

Carpenter, M(alcolm) Scott, May 1, 1925; May 24, 1962.

Carpenter, Richard Lynn, Oct. 15, 1946.

carpenters, patron of, Mar. 11; Mar. 19; Jul. 26.

Carpentier, Georges, Jan. 12, 1894; Sep. 24, 1922.

Carr, Vikki, Jul. 19, 1941.

Carracci, Agostino, Aug. 16, 1557.

Carracci, Annibale, Nov. 3, 1560.

Carracci, Ludovico, Apr. 21, 1555.

Carradine, David, Oct. 8, 1940.

Carradine, John Richmond, Feb. 5, 1906.

Carradine, Keith lan, Aug. 8, 1950.

Carradine, Robert Reed, Mar. 24, 1954.

Carranza, Venustiano, Dec. 29, 1859; Oct. 19, 1915.

Carrel, Alexis, Jun. 28, 1873.

Carreras, Jose, Dec. 5, 1946.

Carrero Blanco, Luis (Spain), Jun. 8, 1973; assassinated, Dec. 20, 1973; Jan. 3, 1974.

Carrey, Jim, Jan. 17, 1962.

Carroll, Charles, Sep. 20, 1737.

Carroll, Diahann, Jul. 17, 1935.

Carroll, James, Jun. 5, 1854.

Carroll, John, Jan. 8, 1735; Nov. 6, 1789.

Carroll, Leo G., Oct. 25, 1892.

Carroll, Lewis, Jan. 27, 1832.

Carroll, Pat, May 5, 1927.

Carson, Benjamin S., Sep. 18, 1951.

Carson, Jack, Oct. 27, 1910.

Carson, Johnny, Oct. 23, 1925; retires, May 22, 1992.

Carson, Kit, Dec. 24, 1809.

Carson, Rachel, May 27, 1907.

Carstens, Karl, Dec. 14, 1914.

Carter, Amy, Oct. 19, 1967.

Carter, Anthony, Sep. 17, 1960.

Carter, Benny, Aug. 8, 1907.

Carter, Billy, Mar. 29, 1937.

Carter, Hodding, III, Apr. 7, 1935.

Carter, Howard, May 9, 1873; Nov. 29, 1922; Feb. 16, 1923.

Carter, Jack, Jun. 24, 1923.

Carter, Jimmy, Oct. 1, 1924; inaugurated, Jan. 20, 1977; Jan.

21, 1977; Mar. 5, 1977; Apr. 6, 1977; Jul. 15, 1977; Apr. 6, 1978; Sep. 17, 1978; Jun. 18, 1979.

Carter, Joe, Mar. 7, 1960.

Carter, Lillian (Miss Lillian), Aug. 15, 1898.

Carter, Lynda, Jul. 24, 1951.

Carter, Maybell (Mother), May 10, 1909.

Carter, Nell, Sep. 13, 1948.

Carter, Rosalynn, Aug. 18, 1927.

Carter, Violet Bonham, Apr. 15, 1887.

Cartier, Jacques, Dec. 31, 1491; Apr. 20, 1534.

Cartier, Sir George Etienne, Sep. 6, 1814.

Cartier-Bresson, Henri, Aug. 22, 1908.

Cartland, Barbara Hamilton, Jul. 9, 1901.

Cartwright, Angela, Sep. 9, 1952.

Cartwright, Edmund, Apr. 24, 1743.

Cartwright, John, Sep. 17, 1740.

Caruso, Enrico, Feb. 25, 1873; Feb. 1, 1904; Apr. 9, 1909.

Carver Day, George Washington (U.S.), Jan. intro; Jan. 5.

Carver, George Washington, Jan. 5, 1864.

Carver, John, Mar. 22, 1621.

Carvey, Dana, Apr. 2, 1955.

Carville, James, Oct. 25, 1944.

Cary, (Arthur) Joyce Lunel, Dec. 7, 1888.

Cary, W. Sterling, Dec. 7, 1972.

Casablanca (Morocco): U.S. attacks French naval forces, Nov. 10, 1942.

Casablanca Conference, Jan. 14, 1943.

Casadesus, Robert, Apr. 7, 1099.

Casals, Pablo, Dec. 29, 1876.

Casanova de Seingalt, Giovanni, Apr. 2, 1725.

Case, Steve, Aug. 21, 1958.

Casement, Sir Roger, Sep. 1, 1864; Apr. 20, 1916; Jun. 29, 1916; hanged for treason, Aug. 3, 1916; Mar. 1, 1965.

Casey, Dan(iel Maurice), Oct. 2, 1865.

Casey, Warren, Feb. 14, 1972.

Casey, William Joseph, Mar. 13, 1913.

Cash, Gerald C., May 28, 1917.

Cash, Johnny, Feb. 26, 1932.

Cash, Norm(an Dalton), Nov. 10, 1934.

Cash, Roseanne, May 24, 1955.

Casimir III (Poland), Apr. 30, 1309.

Casimir IV (Poland), May 27, 1471; Apr. 6, 1490; dies, Jun. 7, 1492.

Cass, Lewis, Oct. 9, 1782.

Cass, Peggy, May 21, 1925.

Cassatt, Mary, May 22, 1844.

Cassavetes, John, Dec. 9, 1929.

Cassel, Battle of, Apr. 11, 1677; Nov. 1, 1762.

Cassidy, Butch, Apr. 6, 1867.

Cassidy, David Bruce, Apr. 12, 1950.

Cassidy, Jack, Mar. 5, 1927.

Cassidy, Shaun Paul, Sep. 27, 1958.

Cassin, Rene, Oct. 5, 1887.

Cassini de Thury, Cesar, Jun. 17, 1714.

Cassini, Oleg Lolewski, Apr. 11, 1913.

Cassini (spacecraft), Oct. 15, 1997.

Cassino (Italy), May 17, 1944.

Cassius, Mar. 15, 44.

Castaneda, Carlos, Dec. 25, 1931.

Castelbuono, patron of, Apr. 16.

Castello Branco, Camillo, Mar. 16, 1825.

Castiglione, Baldassare, Dec. 6, 1478.

Castile, Jan. 19, 1497.

Castilla, Ramon, Aug. 27, 1797.

Castillo Armas, Carlos, Jul. 8, 1954; Jul. 26, 1957.

Castillo, Ramon, Aug. 29, 1940; Jun. 4, 1943.

Castillon, Jul. 17, 1453.

Castle, Irene, Apr. 7, 1893.

Castle, Peggie, Dec. 22, 1927.

Castle, Vernon, May 2, 1887.

Castren, Matthias Alexander, Dec. 2, 1813.

Castro, Fidel, Aug. 13, 1926; Jul. 26, 1953; Jan. 2, 1959; Feb. 16, 1959; Feb. 20, 1960; Apr. 20, 1961; Apr. 30, 1961; May 1, 1961; Jan. 3, 1962.

Castro, Raul, Jun. 3, 1931.

Castro y Bellvis, Guillen de, Nov. 4, 1569.

Cat on a Hot Tin Roof: premiere, Mar. 24, 1955.

Catalonia (Spain): autonomy, Sep. 25, 1932; Dec. 23, 1938.

Catalonian Union, Jan. 24, 1919.

Catania (Sicily), patron of, Feb. 5.

The Catcher in the Rye: published, Jul. 16, 1951.

Cateau-Cambresis, Treaty of, Apr. 3, 1559.

Cather, Willa, Dec. 7, 1876.

Catherine Cornaro (Cyprus), Mar. 14, 1489.

Catherine I (Russia), Apr. 5, 1684; Feb. 8, 1725.

Catherine of Aragon, Dec. 16, 1485; May 23, 1533.

Catherine of France, Jun. 2, 1420.

Catherine the Great (Russia), Apr. 21, 1729; May 2, 1729; dies, Nov. 17, 1796.

Catholic Bishops Conference, U.S.: rule of abstinence from meat abolished, Dec. 2, 1966.

Catholic Church,; Jan. 3, 1521; first meeting of Pope with Orthodox Patriarch, Jan. 5, 1964; revised calendar, May 9, 1969; May 9, 1983. *See also*: Roman Catholic Church.

Catholic college: first in U.S., Mar. 1, 1815.

Catholic youth, patron of, Jun. 21.

Catlin, George, Jul. 26, 1796.

Cato Street Conspiracy, Feb. 23, 1820.

Cats, Jacob, Nov. 10, 1577.

Catt, Carrie Chapman, Jan. 9, 1859.

Catton, Bruce, Oct. 8, 1899; May 3, 1954.

Catulli Carmina: premiere, Nov. 6, 1943.

Caucasus, Jan. 2, 1915; May 7, 1925.

Cauchy, Augustin-Louis, Aug. 21, 1789.

Caulkin, Macaulay, Aug. 26, 1980.

Cauthen, Steve, May 1, 1960.

Cavaco Silva, Anibal: inaugurated, Nov. 6, 1985.

Cavazos, Lauro, Aug. 10, 1988.

Cave, George, Feb. 23, 1856.

Cavell, Edith, Dec. 4, 1865; Oct. 12, 1915.

Cavendish, Henry, Oct. 10, 1731.

Cavendish, Lord Frederick, May 6, 1882.

Cavett, Dick, Nov. 19, 1936.

Caxton, William, Aug. 13, 1422.

Cayce, Edgar, Mar. 18, 1877.

Cayley, Arthur, Aug. 16, 1821.

Ceausescu, Nicolae (Romania), Jan. 26, 1918; Mar. 19, 1965, Mar. 28, 1974; dies, Dec. 25, 1989.

Cech, Thomas Robert, Dec. 8, 1947.

Cecil, Lord Robert (1st Viscount Cecil of Chelwood), Feb. 3, 1830; Sep. 14, 1864.

Cédras, Raoul, Oct. 19, 1993; Sep. 19, 1994.

Cela, Camilo Jose, May 11, 1916.

Celebration of the Second Republic (Guinea), Apr. 3.

Celeste, Richard F., Nov. 11, 1937.

celibacy, Oct. 20, 1928.

celibacy, priestly, Jun. 23, 1967.

Celine, Louis-Ferdinand, May 27, 1894.

Celler, Emmanuel, May 6, 1888.

Cellini, Benvenuto, Nov. 3, 1500.

Celsius, Anders, Nov. 27, 1701.

cemetary workers, patron of, Jan. 17.

Centennial Exposition, U.S., May 10, 1876.

Centennial Olympic park, bombing, Jul. 27, 1996.

Central African Federation, Dec. 19, 1962.

Central African Republic: independence, Aug. 13, 1960; Jan. 2, 1975; Sep. 1, 1981.

Central America, Apr. 27, 1983.

Central American Common Market (CACM), Dec. 13, 1960.

Central American States, Organization of: created, Dec. 14, 1951.

Central Intelligence Agency (CIA), Feb. 13, 1967; experiments revealed, Jul. 20, 1977; Nicholson, Harold, Mar. 3, 1997.

Central Planning Board (Cuba), Feb. 20, 1960.

Central provinces (Poland), Apr. 30, 1815.

Cerdagne, Jan. 19, 1493.

Cerdan, Marcel, Sep. 21, 1948; Jun. 16, 1949.

Cerezo Arevalo, Marco Vinicio: inaugurated, Jan. 14, 1986.

Cerf, Bennett, May 25, 1898.

Cermak, Anton, Feb. 15, 1933.

Cernan, Eugene A., Jun. 6, 1966; Dec. 12, 1972.

Cerro Gordo, Battle of, Apr. 18, 1847.

Cervantes (Saavedra), Miguel, Sep. 29, 1547.

Cessna, Clyde Vernon, Dec. 5, 1879.

Cetera, Peter, Sep. 13, 1944.

Ceylon,; Mar. 27, 1802; Jan. 10, 1883; Apr. 4, 1942; Feb. 4, 1948; Jul. 21, 1960; May 22, 1972; name changed to Sri Lanka, Sep. 7, 1978. *See also*: Sri Lanka.

Cezanne, Paul, Jan. 19, 1839.

Ch'ien Lung, Sep. 25, 1711.

Chávez, Dennis, Apr. 8, 1888.

Chaco War: ends, Jun. 12, 1935.

Chad, Apr. 22, 1900; independence, Aug. 13, 1960; Apr. 14, 1962; Apr. 13, 1975; civil war ends, Mar. 15, 1979.

Chadwick, Florence, Nov. 8, 1918; Oct. 9, 1953

Chadwick, George Whitefield, Nov. 13, 1854.

Chadwick, Henry, Oct. 6, 1824.

Chadwick, Sir Edwin, Jan. 24, 1800.

Chadwick, Sir James, Oct. 20, 1891.

Chaffee, Adna Romanza, Sr., Apr. 14, 1842.

Chaffee, Roger, Feb. 15, 1935.

Chaffee, Suzy, Nov. 29, 1946.

Chaflee, Adna Romanza, Jr., Sep. 23, 1884.

Chagall, Marc, Jul. 7, 1887.

Chain, Ernst Boris, Jun. 19, 1906.

Chaing Kai-shek, Jun. 11, 1926.

Chair of Peter, Feb. 22.

Chakri Memorial Day (Thailand), Apr. 6.

Chaliapin, Fyodor Ivanovich, Feb. 13, 1873.

Challe, Maurice (General), Jan. 24, 1960.

Challenger (U.S. space shuttle): launched, Apr. 4, 1983; Jun. 24, 1983; explosion, Jan. 28, 1986; Mar. 21, 1986; Jun. 9, 1986.

Challis, James, Dec. 12, 1803.

Chalmers, Thomas, Mar. 17, 1780.

Chama Cha Mapenduzi (CCM Day) (Tanzania), Feb. 5.

Chamberlain, Neville, Mar. 18, 1869.

Chamberlain, Owen, Jul. 10, 1920.

Chamberlain, Sir Joseph Austen, Oct. 16, 1863.

Chamberlain, Wilt, Aug. 20, 1936; Feb. 16, 1972.

Chambers, George, Dec. 15, 1986.

Chambers, Whittaker, Apr. 1, 1901; Jan. 21, 1950.

Chambord, Treaty of, Jan. 15, 1552.

Chamorro, Violetta Barrios de, Feb. 25, 1990.

Chamoun, Camille, Sep. 23, 1952.

Champagne, Battle of, Feb. 1, 1915; Feb. 16, 1915; Sep. 25, 1915.

Champagne, First Battle of: opens, Dec. 20, 1914; Mar. 17, 1915.

Champagne, Philippe de, May 26, 1602.

Champagne, Second Battle of, Sep. 22, 1915; ends, Nov. 6, 1915.

Champion, Gower, Jun. 22, 1921.

Champion, Marge, Sep. 2, 1923.

Champlain, Samuel de, Jul. 3, 1608.

Champollion, Jean Francois, Dec. 23, 1790.

Chan, Jackie, Apr. 7, 1954.

Chan, Sir Julius, Aug. 29, 1939.

Chancellor, John (William), Jul. 14, 1927.

Chancellorsville, Battle of, May 4, 1863.

Chandler, Dorothy Buffum, May 19, 1901.

Chandler, Harry, May 17, 1864.

Chandler, Otis, Nov. 23, 1927.

Chandler, Raymond (Thornton), Jul. 23, 1888.

Chandler, Zachariah, Dec. 10, 1813.

Chandrasekhar, Subrahmanyan, Oct. 19, 1910.

Chanel, Coco, Aug. 19, 1882.

Chaney, Lon, Apr. 1, 1883.

Chaney, Lon, Jr., Feb. 10, 1905.

Chang, Michael, Feb. 22, 1972.

Channing, Carol, Jan. 31, 1923.

Channing, Edward, Jun. 15, 1856.

Channing, Stockard, Feb. 13, 1944.

Channing, William Ellery, Apr. 7, 1780.

Chapelain, Jean, Dec. 4, 1595.

Chapin, Dwight Lee, Dec. 2, 1940.

Chapin, Harry Foster, Dec. 7, 1942.

Chaplin, Charlie, Apr. 16, 1889; Feb. 2, 1914; Aug. 16, 1925.

Chaplin, Geraldine, Jul. 31, 1944.

Chapman, Frank Michler, Jun. 12, 1864.

Chapman, Graham, Jan. 8, 1941.

Chapman, John (Johnny Appleseed), Sep. 26, 1774.

Chapman, Mark David, May 10, 1955.

Chapoton, William, Jr., Dec. 19, 1924.

Chappaquiddick Island, Jul. 19, 1969.

Chappe, Claude, Dec. 25, 1763.

Chapultepec, Battle of, Sep. 13, 1846.

charcoal burners, patron of, Aug. 11.

Charcot, Jean-Martin, Nov. 29, 1825.

Chardin, Jean Baptiste Simeon, Nov. 2, 1699.

Chardonnet, Louis Marie, May 1, 1839.

Charge of the Light Brigade, Oct. 25, 1854.

Charing Cross Railway Station, Jan. 11, 1864.

Charisse, Cyd, Mar. 8, 1923.

Charlemagne (Holy Roman Emperor), Apr. 2, 742; Dec. 25, 800.

Charlemagne, Apr. intro.

Charleroi, Hattle of: opens, Aug. 21, 1914.

Charles (Prince of Denmark), Nov. 18, 1905.

Charles Albert (Sardinia), Jul. 25, 1848; Mar. 23, 1849.

Charles, duc d'Orleans, Nov. 24, 1394.

Charles, Duke of Burgundy, Nov. 10, 1433.

Charles, Ezzard, Jun. 22, 1949; Sep. 27, 1950; Jul. 18, 1951.

Charles I (Austria), Aug. 17, 1887; abdicates, Nov. 12, 1918.

Charles I (England), Nov. 19, 1600; Mar. 27, 1625; Apr. 13, 1640; Sep. 2, 1644; Jan. 21, 1645; May 5, 1645; beheaded, Jan. 30, 1649; Sep. 3, 1651.

Charles I (Spain), Jun. 28, 1519.

Charles II (England), May 29, 1630; May 29, 1660; crowned, Apr. 23,

1661; Oct. 27, 1662; Mar. 4, 1681; Feb. 6, 1685.

Charles II (Scotland), Jan. 1, 1651.

Charles II (Spain), Nov. 6, 1661; Sep. 17, 1665; dies, Nov. 1, 1700.

Charles II (the Bald), Jun. 13, 823.

Charles III (France), Sep. 17, 879.

Charles III (Holy Roman Emperor), Feb. 12, 881.

Charles III (Naples), Feb. 27, 1386.

Charles III (Spain), Jan. 20, 1716; Aug. 10, 1759; dies, Dec. 14, 1788; Mar. 1, 1797.

Charles IV (France), Jan. 3, 1322; dies, Feb. 1, 1328.

Charles IV (Holy Roman Emperor), May 14, 1316; Apr. 7, 1348; Apr. 5, 1355; Jan. 10, 1356.

Charles IV (Spain), Nov. 11, 1748; Dec. 14, 1788; Mar. 19, 1808; May 1, 1808.

Charles IX (France), Jun. 27, 1550; Dec. 5, 1560; dies, May 30, 1574.

Charles IX (Sweden), Oct. 4, 1550; Mar. 20, 1604; dies, Oct. 30, 1611.

Charles, Jacques Alexandre Cesar, Nov. 12, 1746.

Charles of Anjou, Dec. 2, 1254.

Charles, Prince of Hohenzollern, Feb. 23, 1866.

Charles, Prince of Wales, Nov. 14, 1948; Jul. 1, 1969; Jun. 23, 1970; Jul. 29, 1981; announcement of separation, Dec. 9, 1992; divorce of, Feb. 28, 1996.

Charles, Ray, Sep. 23, 1930.

Charles the Bold (Burgundy), Mar. 2, 1476.

Charles V (France), Jan. 21, 1337; Apr. 8, 1364; May 21, 1369; dies, Sep. 16, 1380.

Charles V (Holy Roman Emperor), Feb. 24, 1500; Jan. 23, 1516; Jun. 28, 1519; Apr. 28, 1521; May 22, 1526; May 6, 1527; Jan. 21, 1528; Aug. 5, 1529; Feb. 1, 1539; Apr. 19, 1539; Sep. 18, 1544; Mar. 9, 1551; Oct. 25, 1555; Jan. 16, 1556.

Charles VI (France), Dec. 3, 1368; Sep. 16, 1380; dies, Oct. 21, 1422.

Charles VII (France), Feb. 22, 1403;
     Oct. 21, 1422; Sep. 21, 1435;
     Nov. 2, 1439; dies, Jul. 28, 1461.
Charles VII (Holy Roman Emperor),
     Aug. 6, 1697; Jan. 24, 1742.
Charles VIII (France), Jun. 30, 1470;
     Aug. 30, 1483; Sep. 1, 1494;
     Mar. 31, 1495.
Charles VI (Holy Roman Emperor),
     Oct. 1, 1685; Apr. 17, 1711; Apr.
     19, 1713; Mar. 6, 1714; dies,
     Oct. 20, 1740.
Charles X (France), Oct. 9, 1757;
     Sep. 16, 1824; abdicates, Jul. 29,
     1830.
Charles X (Sweden), Nov. 8, 1622;
     Jun. 6, 1654; dies, Feb. 23,
     1660.
Charles XI (Sweden), Nov. 24, 1655;
     Feb. 23, 1660.
Charles XII (Sweden), Jun. 17, 1682;
     Nov. 30, 1700; May 1, 1703;
     Feb. 13, 1706; Jul. 8, 1709;
     killed, Nov. 30, 1718.
Charles XIII (Sweden and Norway),
     Oct. 7, 1748; Mar. 13, 1806;
     Mar. 29, 1809.
Charles XIV John (Sweden and
     Norway), Jan. 26, 1763; Feb. 5,
     1818; dies, Mar. 8, 1844.
Charles XV (Sweden and Norway),
     May 3, 1826; Jul. 8, 1859.
Charleston (South Carolina), Apr. 10,
     1861; Feb. 18, 1865.
Charlestown (South Carolina), Jan.
     12, 1773.
Charlie Brown: command ship, May
     22, 1969.
Charlottetown Conference, Sep. 1,
     1864.
Charnin, Martin, Apr. 21, 1977.
Charo, Jan. 15, 1951.
Charpak, Georges, Aug. 1, 1924.
Charpentier, Gustave, Jun. 25, 1860.
Charter Oath, Apr. 6, 1868.
Chartres Cathedral: consecrated,
     Oct. 24, 1260.
Chase, Chevy, Oct. 8, 1943.
Chase, Lucia, Mar. 27, 1907.
Chase Manhattan Corp., merger,
     Aug. 28, 1995.
Chase, Salmon Portland, Jan. 13,
     1808; Oct. 12, 1864.
Chase, Samuel, Apr. 17, 1741.

Chase, Sylvia, Feb. 23, 1938.
Chateau-Thierry, Jun. 1, 1918.
Chateaubriand, Francois-Rene,
     Vicomte de, Sep. 4, 1768.
Chatham, Russell, Oct. 27, 1939.
Chattanooga, Battle of, Nov. 25,
     1863.
Chatterjee, Bankim Chandra, Jun.
     27, 1838.
Chatterton, Thomas, Nov. 20, 1752.
Chauri Chaura, Feb. 12, 1922.
Chaves, Federico: inaugurated, Aug.
     15, 1950; May 5, 1954.
Chavez, Carlos, Jun. 13, 1899.
Chavez, Cesar, Mar. 31, 1927; Sep. 1,
     1966; Sep. 24, 1973; Aug. 8,
     1994.
Chavis, Benjamin, May 22, 1948.
Chayefsky, Paddy, Jan. 29, 1923.
Chechnya, invaded by Soviet troops,
     Dec. 11, 1994; Russian troops
     in, Jan. 19, 1995; pullout accord
     signed, Jun. 10, 1996.
Checker, Chubby, Oct. 3, 1941.
Cheer Up the Lonely Day, National,
     Jul. intro.
Cheever, John, May 27, 1912.
Cheka (Revolutionary Tribunal):
     established, Dec. 20, 1917.
Cheke, Sir John, Jun. 16, 1514.
Chekhov, Anton Pavlovich, Jan. 17,
     1860; Jan. 31, 1901.
chemical toxins, Feb. 14, 1970.
chemical weapons Jan. 13, 1993.
Chemical Banking Corp., merger,
     Aug. 28, 1995.
Chemical New York Corp., Dec. 15,
     1986.
Chen, Joan, Apr. 26, 1961.
Cheney, Benjamin Pierce, Aug. 12,
     1815.
Chenier, Andre Marie, Oct. 20, 1762.
Chenik, Mohammed, Apr. 15, 1952.
Chennault, Claire Lee, Sep. 6, 1890.
Cher, May 20, 1946.
Cherbourg (France), Jun. 25, 1944.
Cherenkov, Pavel Alekseyevich, Aug.
     10, 1904.
Chernenko, Konstantin, Sep. 24,
     1911; Feb. 13, 1984; Mar. 11,
     1985.
Chernobyl, Apr. 26, 1986; Jul. 29,
     1987.

Chernomyrdin, Viktor, Deputy
     Premier, Dec. 14, 1992; cease-
     fire agreement, May 27, 1996.
Chernyshevsky, Nikolay Gavrilovich,
     Jul. 12, 1828.
Cherokee Phoenix, published, Feb.
     21, 1828.
Cherokee Strip (U.S.): opened for
     settlement, Sep. 16, 1893.
Cherokee Strip Day (Oklahoma),
     Sep. 16.
Cherry Month, National, Feb. intro.
Chesapeake Bay Bridge, Jul. 30,
     1952.
Chesapeake Bay, May 21, 1964.
Cheshire, Maxine, Apr. 5, 1930.
Chessman, Caryl Whittier, May 27,
     1921.
Chester, Earl of, Jul. 1, 1969.
Chester, patron of, Feb. 3.
Chesterfield, 4th Earl of (Philip
     Dormer Stanhope), Sep. 22,
     1694.
Chesterton, G. K., May 29, 1874.
Chestnutt, Charles Waddell, Jun. 20,
     1858.
Chevalier, Maurice, Sep. 12, 1888.
Chevy Chase, Battle of, Aug. 19,
     1388.
chewing tobacco, Jan. 15, 1986.
Chiang Ch'ing: arrested, Oct. 12,
     1976.
Chiang Ching-Kuo, Mar. 18, 1910;
     May 20, 1978; Jul. 14, 1987; Jan.
     13, 1988.
Chiang Kai-shek, Oct. 31, 1887; Mar.
     21, 1927; Apr. 15, 1927; Apr. 18,
     1927; Sep. 20, 1927;
     inaugurated, Oct. 10, 1928;
     declares war on Japan, Dec. 12,
     1936; resigns, May 31, 1945; Jan.
     21, 1949; Mar. 1, 1950; May 20,
     1978.
Chiang Kai-shek, President, Birthday
     of (Taiwan), Oct. 31.
Chiano, Leroy, Aug. 28, 1960.
Chiari, Roberto: inaugurated, Oct. 1,
     1960.
Chicago (Illinois): fire, Oct. 7, 1871;
     May 4, 1886; May 1, 1893; Feb.
     14, 1929; Apr. 12, 1983.
Chicago, Judy, Jul. 20, 1939.

Chicago Seven: trial begins, Sep. 24, 1969; trial begins, Sep. 24, 1969; Feb. 18, 1970.

Chicago Tribune, Nov. 3, 1948.

Chicago, University of, Dec. 2, 1942.

Chichester, Sir Francis Charles, Sep. 17, 1901. Dec. 12, 1966.

Chichoner, El: erupts, Mar. 29, 1982.

Chico and the Man: television debut, Sep. 13, 1974.

Chihuly, Dale P., Sep. 20, 1941.

Child Health Day (United States), Oct. intro.

Child, Julia, Aug. 15, 1912.

Child Labor Act *(Keating-Own Act),* Sep. 1, 1916.

Child, Marriage Act (India), Apr. 1, 1930.

Childe, Vere Gordon, Apr. 14, 1892.

children in convulsions, patron of, Feb. 10.

children, little, patron of, Aug. 31.

children, patron of, Dec. 6.

Children's Book Week, National, Nov. intro.

Children's Day (Congo), Dec. 25.

Children's Day (South Korea), May 5.

Children's Day (Turkey), Apr. 23.

Children's Day (Uruguay), Jan. 6.

Children's Day (Verde Islands), Jun. 1.

Children's Day or Kodomo-No-Hi (Japan), May 5.

Children's Dental Health Month, National, Feb. intro.

Children's Protection Day (Japan), Apr. 17.

Childs, Marquis William, Mar. 17, 1903.

Childs, Samuel Shannon, Apr. 4, 1863.

Chile: patron saint of, Jul. 25; independence, Sep. 18, 1810; Feb. 12, 1818; Apr. 5, 1879; Apr. 4, 1884; Jan. 5, 1971; military coup, Sep. 11, 1973; Sep. 13, 1973; Mar. 17, 1978.

Chiles, Lawton Mainor, Jr., Apr. 3, 1930.

Chiluba, Frederick, Apr. 30, 1943; elected, Oct. 31, 1991.

China, People's Republic of, Dec. 29, 1911; Feb. 12, 1912; Mar. 10, 1912; May 2, 1913; Oct. 6, 1913; civil war, Apr. 21, 1922; Jan. 6, 1946; Oct. 1, 1949; recall of U.S. personnel from, Jan. 14, 1950; May 3, 1950; May 18, 1951; Jan. 10, 1957; May 25, 1960; Jul. 23, 1960; May 17, 1962; Jan. 27, 1964; Jan. 31, 1964; Oct. 16, 1964; Jan. 30, 1965; Jun. 18, 1966; Jun. 17, 1967; Jan. 24, 1969; first satellite, Apr. 24, 1970; Jan. 5, 1971; U.S. travel to, Mar. 15, 1971; U.S. trade embargo removed, Jun. 10, 1971; admitted to U.N., Oct. 25, 1971; assumes seat in U.N., Nov. 15, 1971; Feb. 21, 1972; Feb. 27, 1972; Mar. 13, 1972; Sep. 29, 1972; Feb. 2, 1974; Jan. 19, 1975; earthquakes, Jul. 28, 1976; Feb. 3, 1978; prisoners released, Jun. 5, 1978; Jan. 1, 1979; May 14, 1979; Apr. 19, 1985; May 16, 1989; May 18, 1989.

China, Empire, Jan. 20, 1841; Jan. 7, 1895; Boxer Rebellion, Sep. 7, 1901; Jan. 30, 1902; slavery abolished, Jan. 31, 1910.

China, Nationalist, Feb. 10, 1964.

Chinaglia, Giorgio, Jan. 24, 1947.

Chinese boycott of Japanese goods, Jan. 28, 1932.

Chinese Civil War, Oct. 30, 1948.

Chinese Communists, Jan. 4, 1951.

Chinese Eastern Railway, Dec. 22, 1929.

Chinese Exclusion Acts, Dec. 17, 1943.

Chinese Imperial Court, Jan. 7, 1902.

Chinese Nationalists, Dec. 8, 1949.

Chinese railroads nationalized, May 9, 1911.

Chinese Republic, Jan. 1, 1912; first parliament, Apr. 8, 1913.

Chinese Revolution: begins, Oct. 10, 1911.

Ching Ming (Hong Kong), Apr. 5.

Ching Ming (Taiwan), Apr. 5.

Chinh Truong, Jul. 14, 1986.

Chios, Feb. 17, 1916.

Chippendale, Thomas, Jun. 5, 1718.

Chirac, Jacques Rene, Nov. 29, 1932; Aug. 25, 1976; Mar. 20,1986; May 7, 1995; Jan. 29, 1996.

Chisholm, Shirley Anita St. Hill, Nov. 30, 1924.

Chissano, Joaquim Alberto: elected, Nov. 3, 1986.

Chisum, John Simpson, Aug. 15, 1824.

chivalry, patron of, Oct. 8.

Chladni, Ernst Florens Friedrich, Nov. 30, 1756.

chlorofluorocarbons (CFCs), Sep. 16, 1987; Mar. 14, 1988; Mar. 2, 1989.

chloroform: first used as anesthetic, Nov. 14, 1847.

Cho, Margaret, Dec. 5, 1968.

Choate, Rufus, Oct. 1, 1799.

Cholame Valley (California), Apr. 5, 1985.

cholera, outbreak in Peru, Jan. 23, 1991.

Chomsky, Noam, Dec. 7, 1928.

Choonhaven, Chatichai, Feb. 23, 1991.

Chopin, Frederic, Feb. 22, 1810; Mar. 1, 1810.

Chopin, Kate O'Flaherty, Feb. 8, 1851.

A Chorus Line: premiere, Jul. 25, 1975.

Chosin (Korea), Dec. 1, 1950.

Chou En-lai, Oct. 1, 1949; Jun. 18, 1966.

Chouteau, Auguste, Feb. 15, 1764.

Choxo-no-Sekku or Chrysanthemum Day (Japan), Sep. 9.

Chretien, Jean, Jan. 11, 1934; Nov. 4, 1993.

Christ Birthday of Our Lord Jesus, Dec. 25.

Christ of Esquipulas, Feast of (Guatemala), Jan. intro.

Christ of the Andes: dedicated, Mar. 13, 1904.

Christian Democrats (Italy), May 3, 1979.

Christian I (Denmark), Mar. 5, 1460.

Christian II (Denmark), Jul. 1, 1481; Nov. 4, 1520; Nov. 8, 1520.

Christian III (Denmark and Norway), Aug. 12, 1503.

Christian IV (Denmark and Norway), Apr. 12, 1577; May 22, 1629.

Christian IX (Denmark), Apr. 8, 1818; Nov. 15, 1863.

Christian philosophers, patron of, Nov. 25.

Christian V (Denmark and Norway), Apr. 15, 1646.

Christian VII (Denmark and Norway), Jan. 29, 1749.

Christian VIII (Denmark), Sep. 18, 1786; dies, Jan. 20, 1848.

Christian Vl (Denmark and Norway), Nov. 30, 1699.

Christian X (Denmark), Sep. 26, 1870; dies, Apr. 20, 1947.

Christiana, Jan. 1, 1925.

Christianborg Palace (Denmark): burned, Oct. 3, 1884.

Christiani, Alfredo, Mar. 19, 1989.

Christie, Agatha, Sep. 15, 1890.

Christie, Julie, Apr. 14, 1940.

Christina (Queen of Sweden), Dec. 8, 1626; abdicates, Jun. 6, 1654.

Christmas (Ethiopia), Jan. 6.

Christmas Day (Armenia), Jan. 6.

Christmas Day, Dec. 25.

Christmas Holiday (Vatican City State), Dec. 26; Dec. 27.

Christmas Island, May 6, 1962.

Christmas Seal Campaign, Nov. intro.

Christo, Jun. 13, 1935.

Christofer, Michael, Jan. 22, 1945; Mar. 31, 1977.

Christophe, Henri, Oct. 6, 1767.

Christopher, Dennis, Dec. 2, 1955.

Christopher, Warren, Oct. 27, 1925.

chrysanthemum, Nov. intro.

Chryse, Plain of (Mars), Jul. 20, 1976.

Chrysler Corporation, May 4, 1950; Dec. 21, 1979; Mar. 9, 1987; May 7, 1998.

Chrysler, Walter Percy, Apr. 2, 1875.

Chu Teh, Dec. 18, 1886.

Chulalongkorn Day (Thailand), Oct. 23.

Chun Doo Hwan, Jan. 18, 1931.

Chung, Arthur, Mar. 17, 1970.

Chung, Connie, Aug. 20, 1946.

Chunhawan, Phin, Nov. 29, 1951.

church music, patron of, Nov. 22.

Church, Frank, Jul. 25, 1924.

Church, Frederick Edwin, May 4, 1826.

Church of Christ, Scientist, Jun. 10, 1906.

Church of England, Jan. 14, 1604; Worship and Doctrine Measure passed, Dec. 4, 1974; Jan. 24, 1989; approves women priests, Nov. 11, 1992; first women priests, Mar. 12, 1994.

Church of Ireland: established, Jan. 1, 1871.

Church of Jesus Christ of Latter-Day Saints, Apr. 6, 1830; Jun. 9, 1978.

Church, Sam, Jr., Sep. 20, 1936.

Churchill, John, May 26, 1650.

Churchill, Lord Randolph, Feb. 13, 1849.

Churchill, Sarah, Oct. 17, 1914.

Churchill, Winston, Nov. 30, 1874; appointed First Lord of Admiralty, Oct. 24, 1911; May 10, 1940; Dec. 24, 1941; May 12, 1943; iron curtain speech, Mar. 5, 1946; appointed Prime Minister, Oct. 26, 1951; Oct. 15, 1953; Apr. 9, 1963; dies, Jan. 24, 1965.

Churubusco, Battle of, Aug. 20, 1846.

Ciano, Galeazzo, Jan. 11, 1944.

Ciardi, John Anthony, Jun. 24, 1916.

Cibber, Colley, Nov. 6, 1671.

Cicero, Marcus Tullius, Jan. 3, 106 b.c.

Cicippio, Joseph, Dec. 2, 1991.

Cierva, Juan de la, Sep. 21, 1895; Jan. 10, 1923.

cigarette advertising, Jun. 2, 1967; Apr. 1, 1970.

cigarette smoking: first drive against, Jun. 8, 1963.

Ciller, Tansu, Dec. 26, 1995.

Cincinnati (Ohio), May 24, 1935.

Cincinnati Reds, May 24, 1935; Oct. 21, 1976.

Cincinnati, Society of the, May 13, 1783.

Cinco de Mayo (Mexico), May 5.

Cinderella: premiere, Nov. 21, 1945.

CIO. *See*: Congress of Industrial Organizations.

Ciorbea, Victor, resigns, Mar. 30, 1998.

Cipollone, Rose, Jun. 13, 1988.

Cisneros, Henry G., Jun. 11, 1947.

Citadel, admits women, Jul. 2, 1994.

Citeaux Monastery: founded, Mar. 21, 1098.

Citizenship Day (U.S.), Sep. 17.

Citrine, Walter McLennan, Baron, Aug. 22, 1887.

city commission government: first in U.S., Sep. 8, 1900.

City of Glasgow, Apr. 6, 1929.

Ciudad Trujillo, Nov. 23, 1961.

Civic Holiday (San Jose, Costa Rica), Dec. 29; Dec. 30.

civil disobedience: India, Mar. 30, 1919; Mar. 18, 1922; Dec. 22, 1928; Mar. 12, 1930; May 5, 1930; Mar. 4, 1931; Mar. 5, 1931.

civil rights, Apr. 28, 1941; Apr. 3, 1944; march on White House, Aug. 28, 1963.

civil rights bill: housing, Apr. 11, 1968.

Civil Rights Act, May 6, 1960; signed, Jul. 2, 1964.

Civil Rights Act of 1957, Sep. 9, 1957.

Civil Rights Commission (U.S.), Jan. 3, 1958.

Civil Rights Restoration Act, Mar. 22, 1988.

Civil Servants' Day (Venezuela), Sep. 4.

Civil Service (U.S.), Jan. 6, 1883.

Civil Service Commission (U.S.): established, Mar. 4, 1871.

Civil War (China), Jan. 21, 1949; Jan. 22, 1949.

Civil War, (U.S.): begins, Apr. 12, 1861; Dec. 13, 1862; ends, Apr. 9, 1865; centennial, Jan. 8, 1961.

Civiletti, Benjamin R., Jul. 17, 1935.

Civilian Conservation Corps: established, Mar. 31, 1933.

civilians, patron of, Apr. 24.

Civita Vecchia, Apr. 26, 1849.

Claiborne, Craig, Sep. 4, 1920.

Claiborne, Elisabeth *(Liz),* Mar. 31, 1929.

Clair, Rene, Nov. 11, 1891.

Clairaut, Alexis, May 13, 1713.

Clairvaux, Abbey of: founded, Jun. 25, 1115.

Clancy, Frank (King), Feb. 25, 1903.

Clantarf, Battle of, Apr. 23, 1014.

Clanton Gang, Oct. 26, 1881.

Clapper, Victor (Dit), Feb. 9, 1907.

Clapperton, Hugh, May 18, 1788.

Clapton, Eric, Mar. 30, 1945.

Clare, John, Jul. 13, 1793.

Clark, (William) Ramsey, Dec. 18, 1927.

Clark, Barney, Jan. 21, 1922; artificial heart implanted, Dec. 2, 1982; Mar. 21, 1983.

Clark, Champ (James Beauchamp), Mar. 7, 1850.

Clark, Dick, Nov. 30, 1929.

Clark, George Rogers, Nov. 19, 1752.

Clark, Joe, Jun. 5, 1939; May 22, 1979; Mar. 3, 1980.

Clark, Kenneth Bancroft, Jul. 24, 1914.

Clark, Mark Wayne, May 1, 1896; Sep. 9, 1943. Apr. 28, 1952.

Clark, Mary Higgins, Dec. 24, 1929.

Clark, Petula, Nov. 15, 1932.

Clark, Robert, Jan. 2, 1968.

Clark, Roy Linwood, Apr. 15, 1933.

Clark, Septima, May 3, 1898.

Clark, Thomas Campbell, Sep. 23, 1899; Aug. 24, 1949.

Clark, Walter van Tilburg, Aug. 3, 1909.

Clark, Wendel, Oct. 25, 1966.

Clark, William, Aug. 1, 1770; May 14, 1804; Sep. 23, 1806.

Clarke, Arthur Charles, Dec. 16, 1917.

Clarke, Charles Cowden, Dec. 15, 1787.

Clarke, Ellis E. I., Dec. 28, 1917.

Clarke, John Hessin, Sep. 18, 1857.

Clarke, Samuel, Oct. 11, 1675.

Classified Advertising Week, International, May intro.

Claude, Albert, Aug. 24, 1899.

Claudel, Paul (Louis-Marie), Aug. 6, 1868.

Claudius, Matthias, Aug. 15, 1740.

Clausewitz, Karl Maria von, Jun. 1, 1780.

Clavell, James Dumaresq, Oct. 10, 1924.

Clay, Cassius. See: Ali, Muhammad.

Clay, Henry, Apr. 12, 1777.

Clay, Lucius, Apr. 23, 1897.

Clayburgh, Jill, Apr. 30, 1944.

Clayderman, Richard, Dec. 28, 1953.

Clayton-Bulwer Treaty, Apr. 19, 1850.

Clean Air Act, Nov. 15, 1990.

Cleaner Air Week, National, Oct. intro.

Cleaver, Eldridge, Feb. 12, 1968.

Cleese, John, Oct. 27, 1939.

Clemenceau, Georges, Sep. 28, 1841; Jan 1919.

Clemens, Roger, Aug. 4, 1962.

Clemens, Samuel Langhorne. See: Twain, Mark.

Clement II (pope), Dec. 24, 1046.

Clement III (anti pope), Jun. 25, 1080; Mar. 31, 1084.

Clement III (pope), Apr. 3, 1189.

Clement IV (pope), Feb. 5, 1265.

Clement IX (pope), Jan. 28, 1600.

Clement V (pope), Mar. 22, 1312.

Clement VI (pope), Apr. 13, 1346.

Clement VII (pope), May 26, 1478;

Clement VIII (pope), Feb. 24, 1536.

Clement X (pope), Jul. 12, 1590.

Clement XI (pope), Jul. 23, 1649.

Clement XII (pope), Apr. 7, 1652.

Clement XIII (pope), Mar. 7, 1693.

Clement XIV (pope), Oct. 31, 1705; Jul. 21, 1773; expells Jesuits from Rome, Aug. 16, 1773.

Clemente, Roberto, Aug. 18, 1934.

Clemson College, Jan. 28, 1963.

Clerides, Glafcos, elected, Feb. 15, 1998.

Clermont: begins regular service, Aug. 9, 1807.

Cleveland (Ohio), Jan. 10, 1870; Nov. 7, 1967.

Cleveland, Frances, Jul. 21, 1864.

Cleveland, Grover, Mar. 18, 1837; inaugurated, Mar. 4, 1885; dedicates Statue of Liberty, Oct. 28, 1886; second term, Mar. 4, 1893.

Cliburn, Van, Jul. 12, 1934; Apr. 11, 1958.

Cliff, Jimmy, Apr. 1, 1948.

Clift, Montgomery, Oct. 17, 1920.

Clinch River Breeder Reactor, Oct. 26, 1983.

Cline, Patsy, Sep. 8, 1932.

Clinton, Dewitt, Mar. 2, 1769.

Clinton, George, Jul. 22, 1940.

Clinton, George, Jul. 26, 1739.

Clinton, Hillary Rodham, Oct. 26, 1947; testifies, Jan. 26, 1996; Whitewater, Mar. 11, 1996.

Clinton, William Jefferson (Bill), Aug. 19, 1946; elected, Nov. 3, 1992; sworn in, Jan. 20, 1993; abortion, Jan 21, 1993; signs Revenue Reconciliation Act, Aug. 10, 1993; signs Brady Bill, Nov. 30, 1993; signs NAFTA, Dec. 8, 1993; trade embargo, Feb. 3, 1994; aid to Mexico, Jan. 31, 1995; diplomatic recognition to Vietnam, Jul. 11, 1995; government shutdown, Jan. 6, 1996; Telecommunications Bill, Feb. 8, 1996; embargo against Cuba, Mar. 2, 1996; Whitewater, trial begins, Mar. 11, 1996; signs Line-Item Veto, Apr. 9, 1996; Grand Staircase-Escalante National Monument Act, Sep. 18, 1996; sworn in, Jan. 20, 1997; Lewinsky, Monica, Jan 21, 1998; balanced budget, Feb. 1, 1998; Jones lawsuit dismissed, Apr. 1, 1998; testifies before grand jury, Aug. 17, 1998.

Clive, Robert, Sep. 29, 1725.

cloning, Jan. 20, 1998.

Clooney, George, May 5, 1961.

Clooney, Rosemary, May 23, 1928.

Close, Glenn, May 19, 1947.

clothing industry workers, patron of, Jan. 15.

clothmakers, patron of, Nov. 13.

Clovis (King of the Franks), Dec. 25, 503.

Clown Week, National, Aug. intro.

clowns, patron of, Feb. 12.

Clurman, Harold, Sep. 18, 1901.

Clymer, George, Mar. 16, 1739.

Cnut of Denmark, Nov. 30, 1016.

Coachman, Alice, Aug. 7, 1948.

coal mine disaster: Mononagh (West Virginia), Dec. 6, 1907.

coal mine explosion: West Frankfort (Illinois), Dec. 21, 1951.

coalminers, patron of, Nov. 6.

Coase, Ronald H., Dec. 29, 1910.

Coast Guard, United States, Jan. 28, 1915; Nov. 1, 1941.

coastal fishing zone, U.S.: extended, Oct. 14, 1966.

Cobb, Henry Ives, Aug. 19, 1859.

Cobb, Irvin S(hrewsbury), Jun. 23, 1876.

Cobb, Lee J., Dec. 8, 1911.

Cobb, Ty(rus Raymond), Dec. 18, 1886.

cobblers, patron of, Jun. 29.

Cobden, Richard, Jun. 3, 1804.

Coblentz, William Weber, Nov. 20, 1873.

Coblenz, Alliance of, Sep. 5, 1338.

Coburn, Charles, Jun. 19, 1877.

Coburn, James, Aug. 31, 1928.

cocaine, Sep. 15, 1884.

Cochin-China, Apr. 13, 1862.

Cochran, Eddie, Oct. 3, 1938.

Cochran, Jacqueline, May 18, 1953.

Cochran, Johnnie L., Oct. 2, 1937.

Cochran, Thad, Dec. 7, 1937.

Cochrane, Thomas, Dec. 14, 1775.

Cockburn, Bruce, May 27, 1945.

Cockcroft, Sir John Douglas, May 27, 1897.

Cocker, Joe, May 20, 1944.

Coco, James, Mar. 21, 1929.

Cocos Islands, Apr. 6, 1984.

Cocteau, Jean, Jul. 5, 1889.

code of ethics, Mar. 2, 1977.

Codex Juris Canonici, May 19, 1918.

Codrescu, Andrei, Dec. 20, 1946.

Cody, John Patrick Cardinal, Dec. 24, 1907.

Cody, William Frederick *(Buffalo Bill),* Feb. 26, 1846.

Coe, Sebastian, Sep. 29, 1956.

Coercive Acts, Mar. 28, 1774.

Coffey, Paul, Jun. 1, 1961.

Coffin, Charles Albert, Dec. 30, 1844.

Coffin, Robert Peter Tristram, Mar. 18, 1892.

Coffin, William Sloane, Jun. 1, .1924.

Coggan, Donald (Archbishop of Canterbury), May 14, 1974.

Cognac, League of, May 22, 1526.

Cohan, George M., Jul. 3, 1878; Apr. 6, 1917.

Cohen, Alexander H., Jul. 24, 1920.

Cohen, Leonard, Sep. 21, 1934.

Cohen, Morris Raphael, Jul. 25, 1880.

Cohen, Stanley, Nov. 17, 1922.

Cohen, William, Aug. 28, 1940.

Cohn, Ferdinand Julius, Jan. 24, 1828.

Cohn, Roy Marcus, Feb. 20, 1927.

Coke, Sir Edward, Feb. 1, 1552; Jan. 6, 1622.

Colbert, Claudette, Sep. 18, 1905.

Colbert, Jean Baptiste, Aug. 29, 1619.

Colby, William Egan, Jan. 4, 1920.

Cole, Cozy, Oct. 17, 1909.

Cole, Johnetta B., Oct. 19, 1936.

Cole, Nat *King,* Mar. 17, 1919.

Cole, Natalie Maria, Feb. 6, 1949.

Cole, Olivia, Nov. 26, 1942.

Cole, Thomas, Feb. 1, 1801.

Cole, Timothy, Apr. 6, 1852.

Cole, Tina, Aug. 4, 1943.

Coleman, Cy, Jan. 29, 1966.

Coleman, Dabney, Jan. 3, 1932.

Coleman, Gary, Feb. 8, 1968.

Coleman, Lonnie (William), Aug. 2, 1920.

Coleman, Ornette, Mar. 19, 1930.

Coleridge, Samuel Taylor, Oct. 21, 1772.

Colette (Sidonie Gabrielle Colette), Jan. 28, 1873.

Colfax, Schuyler, Mar. 23, 1823.

Colgate, William, Jan. 25, 1783.

Colijn, Hendrik, Jun. 22, 1869.

Collamer, Jacob, Jan. 8, 1791.

Collazo, Oscar, Apr. 6, 1951.

Collett, Camilla, Jan. 23, 1813.

Collier, Barron Gift, Mar. 23, 1873.

Collier, Peter, Jun. 2, 1939.

Collingwood, Charles Cummings, Jun. 4, 1917.

Collins, Anthony, Jun. 21, 1676.

Collins, Gary, Aug. 30, 1934.

Collins, Joan, May 23, 1933.

Collins, Judith *(Judy),* May 1, 1939.

Collins, Larry, Sep. 14, 1929.

Collins, Martha Layne Hall, Dec. 7, 1936.

Collins, Marva Deloise Nettles, Aug. 31, 1936.

Collins, Michael (Irish Free State), Oct. 16, 1890; killed, Aug. 22, 1922.

Collins, Michael, Oct. 31, 1930; Jul. 21, 1966.

Collins, Phil, Jan. 30, 1951.

Collins, Wilkie, Jan. 8, 1824.

Collins, William, Dec. 25, 1721.

Collodi, Carlo, Nov. 24, 1826.

Colman, Ronald, Feb. 9, 1891.

Cologne, patrons of, Jul. 23.

Cologne: Archbishop of, Jan. 24, 1446; British air raids, May 18, 1918; May 30, 1942; Mar. 6, 1945.

Colombia: patron of, Oct. 9; declares independence, Jul. 20, 1810; established, Dec. 17, 1819; Nov. 28, 1821; Jan. 26, 1827; Sep. 27, 1947.

Colombo, Joseph Anthony, Jun. 16, 1923.

Colonial Dames of America, May 23, 1890.

Colorado Day (Colorado), Aug. intro.

Colorado, May 30, 1848; admitted to Union, Aug. 1, 1876.

Colson, Charles W., Oct. 16, 1931.

Colt, Samuel, Jul. 19, 1814.

Colter, Jessie, May 25, 1947.

Coltrane, Trane, Sep. 26, 1926.

Colum, Padraic, Dec. 8, 1881.

Columbia Broadcasting System (CBS), Sep. 28, 1928; Oct. 11, 1950; Jan. 14, 1987; Nov. 18, 1987.

Columbia, District of, Jan. 29, 1850; residents vote for the first time, Nov. 5, 1974; denied statehood, Nov. 21, 1993.

Columbia Inc., Jan. 10, 1949; space shuttle first launched, Apr. 12, 1981; first lands, Apr. 14, 1981; Nov. 12, 1981; Mar. 22, 1982.

Columbia River, Sep. 1, 1836; Jan. 13, 1964; Jan. 22, 1964.

Columbia, S.C., Feb. 17, 1865.

Columbia University, Oct. 31, 1754; Jan. 5, 1887.

Columbian Exhibition, May 1, 1893.

Columbus, Christopher, Apr. 17, 1492; begins first voyage, Aug. 3, 1492; first landfall in New World, Oct. 12, 1492; discovers Cuba, Oct. 28, 1492; Mar. 4, 1493; second voyage, Sep. 25, 1493; Sep. 18, 1502.

Columbus Day, Oct. intro; Oct. 12.

Colvin, Shawn, Jan. 10, 1958.

Colvin, Sir Sidney, Jun. 18, 1845.

Comaneci, Nadia, Nov. 12, 1961; Jul. 22, 1976.

Combat of Angamos (Peru), Oct. 8.

combatants against Communism, patron of, Mar. 19.

Comet Kohoutek, Dec. 28, 1973.

Cominform (Communist Information Bureau), Jun. 28, 1948.

Coming into Power of the Transition Government Anniversary of the (Sao Tome and Principe), Dec. 21.

Commager, Henry Steele, Oct. 25, 1902.

Commemoration Day (Turkmenistan), Jan. 12.

Commemoration of All the Faithful Departed, Nov. 2.

Commemoration of September 3, 1934 (Tunisia), Sep. 3.

Commencement of the Armed Struggle (Angola), Feb. 4.

commercial flight: first around-the-world, Jan. 6, 1942.

Committee for a Sane Nuclear Policy, Nov. 27, 1965.

Committee of Public Safety (France), Apr. 6, 1793.

Commodity Credit Corporation: established, Oct. 18, 1933.

Common Cause: founded, Aug. 18, 1970.

Common Market: established, Mar. 25, 1957; Jan. 1, 1958; Jan. 4, 1960; Jan. 1, 1973; Jun. 5, 1975; Mar. 13, 1979.

Common Sense, Jan. 10, 1776.

Commonwealth of Independent States, Dec. 21, 1991; Jan. 19, 1995. See also Russia; U.S.S.R.

Commoner, Barry, May 28, 1917.

Commons, John Rogers, Oct. 13, 1862.

Commonwealth Day (Belize), May intro.

Commonwealth Day (British Virgin Islands), Mar. 8.

Commonwealth Day (Emancipation Day), (Belize), May 24.

Commonwealth Day (Gibraltar), Mar. 9.

Commonwealth Day (Swaziland), Mar. intro; Mar. 8.

Commonwealth of Independent States, formed, Sep. 5, 1991.

communication through space: first, Jan. 10, 1946.

Communications Commission, U.S. Federal: created, Jun. 19, 1934.

Communist Labor Party of America: founded, Aug. 31, 1919.

Communist organizations: required registration in U.S., Jun. 5, 1961.

Communist Party, American, Jan. 12, 1962.

Communist Party, Cambodian: 17th anniversary, Sep. 28, 1977.

Communist Party, China, May 4, 1919; Apr. 15, 1927; Jun. 29, 1981; Sep. 6, 1982.

Communist Party, Czechoslovak, Jul. 29, 1968.

Communist Party, East German, May 3, 1971.

Communist Party, Soviet, Jan. 15, 1925; Dec. 1, 1934; Jul. 29, 1968; Jun. 4, 1977.

Communist Party: legalized in Spain, Apr. 9, 1977.

Communists, French, May 27, 1966.

Como, Perry, May 18, 1912.

Comoros Islands: independence, Jul. 6, 1975.

Compiegne, May 23, 1430; armistice between France and Germany, Jun. 22, 1940.

Compiegne, Treaty of: signed, Jun. 20, 1624.

Compromise of 1850, Sep. 20, 1850.

Compton, Ann, Jan. 19, 1947.

Compton, Arthur Holly, Sep. 10, 1892.

Compton, Karl Taylor, Sep. 14, 1887.

Compton-Burnett, Dame Ivy, Jun. 5, 1892.

computer security, Aug. 11, 1983.

Comstock, Anthony, Mar. 7, 1844.

Comstock, Elizabeth L., Oct. 30, 1815.

Comte, Auguste, Jan. 19, 1798.

Conant, James Bryant, Mar. 26, 1893.

Conaway, Jeff, Oct. 5, 1950.

Concord, battle of, Apr. 19, 1775.

Concorde: first test, Jan. 9, 1969; May 24, 1976; Oct. 17, 1977.

Condillac, Etienne Bonnot de, Sep. 30, 1714.

Condon, Richard, Mar. 18, 1915.

condor, Apr. 19, 1987; Apr. 29, 1988.

Condorcet, Marquis de (Marie-Jean-Antoine-Nicolas Caritat), Sep. 17, 1743.

Confederal Agreement Day (Gambia, Senegal), Feb. 1.

Confederate Heroes Day (Texas), Jan. intro; Jan. 19.

Confederate Memorial Day: (Alabama, Florida, Georgia, Mississippi), Apr. intro; (Florida, Georgia), Apr. 26; (North Carolina, South Carolina, Virginia), May intro.; (North Carolina, South Carolina), May 10; (Virginia), May 30; (Kentucky), Jun. 3.

Confederate ports: blockade of, Apr. 19, 1861.

Confederate States of America: organized, Feb. 4, 1861; Feb. 8, 1861; Feb. 9, 1861.

Confederation of Arab Republics: formed, Aug. 20, 1971; Oct. 4, 1971.

Confession of St. Peter the Apostle, Jan. 18.

The Confessions of Nat Turner: published, Sep. 9, 1967.

Confucius, Aug. 27, 551 b.c.

Confucius, Birthday of (Taiwan), Sep. 28.

Congo, Belgian, Feb. 5, 1885; Nov. 15, 1908; civil unrest, Jan. 6, 1959; first government, Jun. 21, 1960; independence, Jun. 30, 1960.

Congo, Democratic Republic of the, Feb. 12, 1961; Jan. 15, 1963; Jun. 30, 1964; Aug. 5, 1964; Nov. 24, 1964; named Republic of Zaire, Oct. 27, 1971.

Congo Free State: name change, Nov. 15, 1908.

Congo, French, Jan. 15, 1910; independence, Aug. 13, 1960.

Congo, International Association of, Apr. 22, 1884.

Congo National Liberation Front, May 11, 1978.

Congo, Nov. 4, 1608; Jul. 1, 1885.

Congo, People's Republic of the, Jan. 3, 1970.

Congo, Republic of the, Jul. 11, 1960; Jul. 14, 1960;

independence, Aug. 15, 1960;
Dec. 1, 1960.

Congress (U.S.): first meeting, Mar.
4, 1789; first Washington
meeting, Nov. 17, 1800; Jan. 28,
1915.

Congress of Industrial Organizations:
created, Nov. 9, 1935. Feb. 15,
1950.

Congress of Racial Equality:
organized, Jun. 6, 1942.

Congress of Vienna, Mar. 20, 1815.

congressional districts, Feb. 17,
1964.

Congressional Medal of Honor:
authorized, Jul. 12, 1862.

Congreve, William, Jan. 24, 1670.

Conigliaro, Anthony Richard *(Tony)*,
Jan. 7, 1945.

Conn, Billy, Oct. 8, 1917; Jun. 18,
1941.

Connally, John Bowden, Feb. 27,
1917.

Connally, Thomas Terry *(Tom)*, Aug.
19, 1877.

Connecticut, Jan. 9, 1788.

Connelly, Marc(us Cook), Dec. 13,
1890.

Conner, Dennis, Feb. 4, 1987.

Connery, Sean, Aug. 24, 1930.

Connery, Sean, Aug. 25, 1930.

Conniff, Ray, Nov. 6, 1916.

Connolly, Harold, Aug. 1, 1931.

Connolly, James, Apr. 6, 1896.

Connolly, Maureen, Sep. 17, 1934.

Connor, Theophilus Eugene *(Bull)*,
Jul. 11, 1897.

Connors, Chuck, Apr. 10, 1921.

Connors, Jimmy, Sep. 2, 1952.

Connors, Mike, Aug. 15, 1925.

Conombo, Joseph, Jul. 7, 1978.

Conrad, Charles (Pete) Jr., Jun. 2,
1930; Nov. 19, 1969; Jun. 22,
1973.

Conrad II (Holy Roman Emperor),
Mar. 26, 1027; May 28, 1037.

Conrad III (Germany), Mar. 7, 1138.

Conrad IV (Holy Roman Emperor),
Apr. 25, 1228; Dec. 13, 1250.

Conrad, Joseph, Dec. 3, 1857.

Conrad, Robert, Mar. 1, 1935.

Conrad, William, Sep. 27, 1920.

Conradin (Holy Roman Emperor),
Mar. 25, 1252; beheaded, Aug.
29, 1268.

Conrail, Mar. 26, 1987.

Conscience, Hendrik, Dec. 3, 1812.

conscription: British, Apr. 27, 1939.

Conservative Party, Great Britain,
May 3, 1979.

Considine, Robert Bernard, Nov. 4,
1906.

Constable, John, Jun. 11, 1776.

Constance (Sicily), Jan. 27, 1186.

Constance, Council of: convenes,
Nov. 5, 1414.

Constant de Rebecque, Henri
Benjamin, Oct. 25, 1767.

Constantine (Byzantine Emperor):
killed, May 29, 1453.

Constantine I (Greece), Aug. 2,
1868; Mar. 18, 1913; abdicates,
Jun. 11, 1917; Mar. 6, 1964.

Constantine II (Greece): flees, Dec.
14, 1967; stripped of title, Dec.
9, 1974.

Constantine, Learie Nicholas, Mar.
26, 1969.

Constantine, Michael, May 22, 1927.

Constantinescu, Emil, elected, Nov.
17, 1996.

Constantinople, May 11, 330; Apr.
12, 1204; May 29, 1453; May 15,
1455; Mar. 28, 1930.

Constantinople, Peace of, Apr. 16,
1712.

Constantinople, Sixth Council of:
convenes, Nov. 7, 680.

Constanza (Romania), Oct. 22, 1916.

Constitution Act (Canada), Apr. 17,
1982.

Constitution Day (Anguilla), Apr. 1.

Constitution Day (Belarus), Mar. 15.

Constitution Day (Brunei), Sep. 29.

Constitution Day (Cayman Islands),
Jul. intro.

Constitution Day (Cook Island), Aug.
4.

Constitution Day (Democratic
Republic of the Congo), Jun. 24.

Constitution Day (Denmark), Jun. 5.

Constitution Day (Dominican
Republic), Nov. 6.

Constitution Day (Fiji), july 24.

Constitution Day (Hungary), Aug.
20.

Constitution Day (Japan), May intro.

Constitution Day (Kosrae,
Micronesia), Jan. 11.

Constitution Day (Kyrgyzstan), May
5.

Constitution Day (Mexico), Feb. 5.

Constitution Day (Nauru), May 17.

Constitution Day (Nepal), Nov. 9.

Constitutis Day (North Korea),
Dec. 27.

Constitution Day (Norway), May 17.

Constitution Day (Paraguay), Aug.
25.

Constitution Day (Philippines)
(1935), Feb. 8.

Constitution Day (Poland), May 3.

Constitution Day (Puerto Rico), Jul.
25.

Constitution Day (South Korea), Jul.
17.

Constitution Day (Spain), Dec. 6.

Constitutis Day (Taiwan), Dec. 25.

Constitution Day (Thailand), Dec.
10.

Constitution Day (Tonga), Nov. 4.

Constitution Day (U.S.), Mar. 4; Sep.
17.

Constitution Day (Uruguay), Jul. 18.

Constitution Day (Vanuatu), Oct. 5.

Constitution Day or Victory Day
(Tunisia)

Constitution Day or Victory Day
(Tunisia), Jun. 1.

Constitution Day, Sep. intro.

Constitution Memorial Day (Japan),
May 3.

Constitution, U.S.: signed, Sep. 17,
1787.

Constitution, U.S.S, Aug. 19, 1812;
Feb. 20, 1815.

Constitution Week, Sep. intro.

Constitutional Convention, May 25,
1787.

Constitutis de Feudis, May 28, 1037.

Contadora Peace Proposal, Jan. 8,
1984.

Conti, Bill, Apr. 13, 1942.

Conti, Thomas Antonio *(Tom)*, Nov.
22, 1941.

Continental Airlines, Sep. 24, 1983.

Continental Army: formed, May 31,
1775; Jun. 15, 1775; Jul. 3, 1775;
Valley Forge camp, Dec. 19,
1777.

Continental Congress: First, Sep. 5, 1774; Second, May 10, 1775; Jul. 4, 1776; Nov. 15, 1777; Jan. 14, 1784.

Continental Illinois Corp., May 17, 1984.

contraception, Jul. 29, 1968.

contraceptive advertising, Jan. 16, 1987.

Conventional Forces in Europe Treaty, Nov. 19, 1990.

Converse, Marquis M., Oct. 23, 1861.

Conversion of St. Paul, Feast of, Jan. 25.

Convy, Bert, Jul. 23, 1934.

Conway, Lynn, Jan. 2, 1938.

Conway, Tim, Dec. 15, 1933.

Cooder, Ry(land Peter), Mar. 15, 1947.

Coogan, Jackie, Oct. 26, 1914.

Cook, Frederick Albert, Apr. 21, 1865.

Cook, James (Captain), Oct. 27, 1728; landfall in New Zealand, Oct. 30, 1769; Apr. 19, 1770; Apr. 28, 1770; murdered, Feb. 13, 1779.

Cook, Robin, May 4, 1940.

Cooke, (Alfred) Alistair, Nov. 20, 1908.

Cooke, Jay, Aug. 10, 1821.

Cooke, Sam, Jan. 22, 1935.

Cooke, Terence James, Mar. 21, 1921.

Cooke, William F., May 4, 1806.

cooks, patron of, Jul. 29; Aug. 10.

Cooley, Denton A., Apr. 4, 1969.

Coolidge, (John) Calvin, Jul. 4, 1872; Mar. 4, 1921; Aug. 3, 1923. May 26, 1924; inaugurated, Mar. 4, 1925.

Coolidge, Charles Allerton, Nov. 30, 1858.

Coolidge, Grace, Jan. 3, 1879.

Coolidge, Rita, May 1, 1945.

Coolidge, William David, Oct. 23, 1873.

Coolio (Artis Ivey, Jr.), Aug. 1, 1963.

Coon, Carleton S(tevens), Jun. 23, 1904.

Cooney, Gerald Arthur (Gerry), Aug. 24, 1956.

Cooper, Alice, Feb. 4, 1948.

Cooper, Gary, May 7, 1901.

Cooper, Gordon, Mar. 6, 1927; May 16, 1963.

Cooper, Jackie, Sep. 15, 1922.

Cooper, James Fenimore, Sep. 15, 1789.

Cooper, John Sherman, Aug. 23, 1901.

Cooper, Leon N., Feb. 28, 1930.

Cooper, Peter, Feb. 12, 1791.

coopers, patron of, Dec. 6.

Cooperstown (New York), Jan. 29, 1936.

Coors, Joseph, Nov. 12, 1917.

Coover, Robert, Feb. 4, 1932.

Copeland, Stewart, Jul. 16, 1952.

Copenhagen, patron of, Mar. 4.

Copenhagen, Treaty of: signed, Jun. 6, 1660.

Copernicus, Nicolas, Feb. 19, 1473.

Copland, Aaron, Nov. 14, 1900; Symphony: premiere, Jan. 11, 1925; Oct. 16, 1938; Jan. 28, 1941.

Copley, John Singleton, Jul. 3, 1738.

coppersmiths, patron of, Nov. 6.

Coppola, Francis Ford, Apr. 7, 1939.

Coptic Orthodox Church, Apr. 12, 1983.

Coral Sea, Battle of, May 4, 1942; May 8, 1942.

Coralli, Jean, Jun. 28, 1841.

Corbeil, Treaty of, May 11, 1258.

Corbett, James J. (Gentleman Jim), Sep. 1, 1866. Sep. 7, 1892.

Corbusier, Le, Oct. 6, 1887.

Corby, Ellen, Jun. 3, 1913.

Corcoran, Thomas Gardiner, Dec. 29, 1900.

Corcoran, William Wilson, Dec. 27, 1798.

Corday, Charlotte, Jul. 27, 1768; Jul. 13, 1793.

Cordero, Angel Thomas, May 8, 1942.

Cordero Rivadeneira, Leon Febres: elected, May 6, 1984.

Cordoba, Jun. 29, 1236.

Corea, Armando (Chick), Jun. 12, 1941.

Corelli, Franco, Apr. 8, 1921.

Corey, Elias James, Jul. 12, 1928.

Corey, William Ellis, May 4, 1866.

Corfu, Jan. 11, 1916; Jan. 13, 1916.

Corfu, Pact of, Jul. 20, 1917.

Cori, Carl Ferdinand, Dec. 5, 1896.

Cori, Gerty Theresa, Aug. 15, 1896.

Corinth (Greece), Jun. 12, 1917.

Cormack, Allan MacLeod, Feb. 23, 1924.

Corneille, Pierre, Jun. 6, 1606.

Cornelius, Peter Joseph von, Sep. 27, 1783.

Cornell, Ezra, Jan. 11, 1807.

Cornell, Katharine, Feb. 16, 1898.

Cornfeld, Bernard, Aug. 17 1927.

Cornforth, John, Sep. 7, 1917.

Cornwallis, Charles 1st Marquis, Dec. 31, 1738; Jan. 3, 1777.

Coronation Day (Thailand), May 5.

Corot, Jean Baptiste Camille, Jul. 16, 1796.

Correct Posture Month, Apr. intro.

Corrective Move Day (People's Democratic Republic of Yemen), Jun. 22.

Correggio, Antonio Allegri da, Aug. 30, 1494.

Corregidor: first Japanese bombing, Dec. 29, 1941; (Philippines), May 6, 1942; Feb. 16, 1945.

Correll, Charles, Feb. 2, 1890.

Corrigan, Mairead, Jan. 27, 1944.

Cortes, Hernando, Nov. 8, 1519.

Cortina, May 30, 1915.

Cortona, Pietro Berretini da, Nov. 1, 1596.

Corvette, Jun. 30, 1953.

Corwin, Thomas, Jul. 29, 1794.

Cosby, Bill, Jul. 12, 1937.

Cosell, Howard, Mar. 25, 1920.

cosmetics manufacturers, Oct. 11, 1973.

cosmos, Oct. intro; Oct. 26, 1967.

Cosmos 954, Jan. 24, 1978.

Cossacks: revolt, Dec. 9, 1917; Jan. 10, 1918; Jan. 7, 1920.

Cossiga, Francesco: elected, Jun. 24, 1985.

Costa e Silva, Artur: inaugurated, Mar. 15, 1967.

Costa Gomes Francisco da, Sep. 30, 1974.

Costa Rica: discovered, Sep. 18, 1502; independence, Sep. 15, 1821; Jan. 19, 1921; Nov. 9, 1949.

Costa-Gavras, Henri, May 23, 1969.

Costain, Thomas B., May 8, 1885.

Costanza, Midge, Nov. 28, 1928.
Costanzi Theater (Rome), Jan. 14, 1900.
Coste, Dieudonne (Captain), Sep. 2, 1930.
Costello, Elvis, Aug. 25, 1955.
Costello, Lou, Mar. 6, 1906.
Costner, Kevin, Jan. 18, 1955.
Cotman, John Sell, May 16, 1782.
Cotten, Joseph, May 15, 1905.
cotton gin: patented, Mar. 14, 1794.
Cotton Bowl, Jan. 1, 1937.
Cotton, Charles, Apr. 28, 1630.
Cotton, John, Dec. 4, 1585.
Coty, Franeois, May 3, 1874.
Coubertin, Pierre, Jan. 1, 1863.
Coughlin, Charles Edward, Oct. 25, 1891.
Coulanges, Numa Denis Fustel de, Mar. 18, 1830.
Coulomb, Charles Augustin de, Jun. 14, 1736.
Council of Europe, May 2, 1951; Apr. 29, 1965.
Council of Four, Mar. 25, 1919.
Country Music Month, Oct. intro.
Countryman's Day (Peru), Jun. 24.
Couperin, Francois, Nov. 10, 1668.
Couples, Fred, Oct. 3, 1959.
Courbet, Gustave, Jun. 10, 1819.
Couric, Katherine (Katie), Jan. 7, 1957.
Courier, Jim, Aug. 17, 1970.
Cournand, Andre F., Sep. 24, 1895.
Court, Margaret, Jul. 16, 1942.
Courtenay, Tom, Feb. 25, 1937.
Cousin, Victor, Nov. 28, 1792.
Cousins, Norman, Jun. 24, 1915.
Cousteau, Jacques Ives, Jun. 11, 1910.
Cousteau, Philippe, Dec. 30, 1940.
Cousy, Bob, Aug. 9, 1928.
Couthon, Georges, Dec. 22, 1755.
Couzens, James Joseph, Jr., Aug. 26, 1876; Jul. 19, 1919.
Covenant, Day of the (Namibia, South Africa), Dec. 16.
Coward, Sir Noel (Pierce), Dec. 16, 1899.
Cowell, Henry Dixon, Mar. 11, 1897.
Cowen, Joshua Lionel, Aug. 25, 1880.
Cowings, Patricia S., Dec. 15, 1948.
Cowles, John, Dec. 14, 1893.
Cowley, Malcolm, Aug. 24, 1898.

Cowpens (South Carolina), Jan. 17, 1781.
Cowper, William, Nov. 26, 1731.
Cox, Allyn, Jun. 5, 1896.
Cox, Archibald, May 17, 1912; May 18, 1973; Oct. 20, 1973.
Cox, Courteney, Jun. 15, 1964.
Cox, Edward Finch, Oct. 2, 1946; Jun. 12, 1971.
Cox, Kenyon, Oct. 27, 1856.
Cox, Wally, Dec. 6, 1924.
Coxey, Jacob Sechler, Apr. 16, 1854.
Coysevox, Antoine, Sep. 29, 1640.
Cozzens, James Gould, Aug. 19, 1903.
Crabbe, Buster, Feb. 7, 1909.
Crabbe, George, Dec. 24, 1754.
Cracow, Battle of: begins, Nov. 15, 1914; siege ends, Dec. 23, 1914.
Cracow, Jan. 9, 1493.
Craddock, Billy (Crash), Jun. 16, 1940.
Craig, Jim, May 31, 1957.
Craig, Roger Timothy, Jul. 10, 1960.
Cram, Donald J., Apr. 22, 1919.
Cram, Ralph Adams, Dec. 16, 1863.
Cranach, Lucas, Oct. 4, 1472.
Crandall, Prudence, Sep. 3, 1803.
Crane, (Harold) Hart, Jul. 21, 1899.
Crane, Bob, Jul. 13, 1928.
Crane, Philip Miller, Nov. 3, 1930.
Crane, Stephen (Townley), Nov. 1, 1871.
Cranmer, Thomas, Jul. 2, 1489; burned at stake, Mar. 21, 1556.
Cranston, Alan MacGregor, Jun. 19, 1914.
Craven, Wes, Aug. 2, 1939.
Crawford, Broderick, Dec. 9, 1911.
Crawford, Francis Marion, Aug. 2, 1854.
Crawford, Joan, Mar. 23, 1908.
Crawford, Michael (Patrick Dumble-Smith), Jan. 19, 1942.
Craxi, Bettino: Feb. 24, 1934; inaugurated, Aug. 4, 1983; Mar. 3, 1987; Jul. 29, 1987.
Cray, Robert, Aug. 1, 1953.
Cray, Seymour, Sep. 28, 1925.
Crazy Blues, Aug. 10, 1920.
Crazy Horse: surrenders, May 6, 1877.
Creach, John (Papa), May 17, 1917.
creationism, Jun. 19, 1987.

Crecy, Battle of, Aug. 26, 1346.
Credit-Anstalt: bank failure, May 11, 1931.
crematorium: first municipal, Jan. 2, 1901.
Cremer, Sir William Randal, Mar. 18, 1838.
Cremona, Italy, patron of, Nov. 13.
Cremona, Luigi, Dec. 1, 1830.
Crenna, Richard, Nov. 30, 1927.
Crenshaw, Ben Daniel, Jan. 11, 1952.
Crenshaw, Marshall, Nov. 11, 1953.
Crespy, Treaty of, Sep. 18, 1544.
Cresson, Edith, Jan. 27, 1934; May 15, 1991; Apr. 2, 1992.
Cressy, H.M.S.: sunk, Sep. 22, 1914.
Crete (Greece), Mar. 18, 1897; May 20, 1941.
Crevecoeur, Michael-Guillaume-Jean de, Jan. 31, 1735.
Crichton, (John) Michael, Oct. 23, 1942.
Crichton, James, Aug. 19, 1560.
Crichton, Michael, Oct. 24, 1942.
Crichton, Robert, Jan. 29, 1925.
Crick, Francis H.C., Apr. 25, 1953.
Crime Prevention Week, National, Feb. intro.
Crimea, Jan. 9, 1792.
Crimean War, Apr. 19, 1853; begins, Jul. 2, 1853; begins, Oct. 5, 1853; Nov. 30, 1853; Mar. 12, 1854; Mar. 27, 1854; Mar. 28, 1854; Sep. 14, 1854; Oct. 17, 1854; Oct. 25, 1854; Nov. 4, 1854; Sep. 11, 1855; Nov. 28, 1855; treaty ending, Mar. 30, 1856.
Crisler, Herbert Orin (Fritz), Jan. 12, 1899.
Crispi, Francesco, Oct. 4, 1819.
Cristal, Linda, Feb. 24, 1936.
Cristofori, Bartolommeo, May 4, 1655.
Crittenden, John Jordan, Sep. 10, 1787.
Croatia, Jan. 26, 1699; Jan. 14, 1972; independence, Jun. 25, 1991; UN member, May 22, 1992; peace accord, Nov. 21, 1995.
Croatian and Bosnian Uprising Day (Yugoslavia), Jul. 27.
Croce, Benedetto, Feb. 25, 1866.
Croce, Jim, Jan. 10, 1943.

Crocker, Charles, Sep. 16, 1822.

Crockett, Davy, Aug. 17, 1786; Mar. 6, 1836.

Crome, John, Dec. 22, 1768.

Crompton, Samuel, Dec. 3, 1753.

Cromwell, Oliver, Apr. 25, 1599; defeats Scots, Aug. 17, 1648; Jan. 30, 1649; Sep. 11, 1649; Sep. 3, 1650; Sep. 3, 1651; Apr. 20, 1653; Dec. 16, 1653; Sep. 3, 1654; Mar. 31, 1657; dies, Sep. 3, 1658; May 25, 1659.

Cromwell, Richard, Oct. 4, 1626; Sep. 3, 1658; May 25, 1659.

Cromwell, Thomas (Earl of Essex), Apr. 12, 1533; beheaded, Jul. 28, 1540.

Cronenberg, David, May 15, 1943.

Cronin, A(rchibald) J(oseph), Jul. 19, 1896.

Cronin, James, Sep. 29, 1931.

Cronkite, Walter (Leland), Jr., Nov. 4, 1916.

Cronyn, Hume, Jul. 18, 1911.

Crook, George, Sep. 23, 1829.

Crookes, Sir William, Jun. 17, 1832.

crops, patron of, Mar. 13.

Crosby, Bing, May 2, 1904.

Crosby, David, Aug. 14, 1941.

Crosby, Kathryn, Nov. 25, 1933.

Crosby, Mary Frances, Sep. 14, 1959.

Crosby, Norm(an Lawrence), Sep. 15, 1927.

Crosley Field (Cincinnati), May 24, 1935.

Crosley, Powel, Jr., Sep. 18, 1886.

Cross, Bernard (Ben), Dec. 16, 1947.

Cross, James R., Oct. 5, 1970.

Cross of Gold: speech, Jul. 8, 1896.

Cross, Wilbur Lucius, Apr. 10, 1862.

cross-country flight: first U.S., Nov. 5, 1912.

crossword puzzle: first printed, Dec. 21, 1913.

Crothers, Benjamin Sherman (Scatman), May 23, 1910.

Crouse, Lindsay Ann, May 12, 1948.

Crow, Sheryl, Feb. 11, 1964.

Crowdy, Oliver, Apr. 6, 1830.

Crowley, Leo T., Aug. 15, 1889.

Crowley, Pat, Sep. 17, 1929.

Crown Imperial: first performed, May 9, 1937.

Crown of St. Stephen, Jan. 6, 1978.

Crown Prince Harald's Birthday (Norway), Feb. 21.

Crowther, F. Bosley, Jul. 13, 1905.

The Crucible: premiere, Jan. 22, 1953.

Cruikshank, George, Sep. 27, 1792.

Cruise, Tom, Jul. 3, 1962.

Crummell, Alexander, Mar. 3, 1819.

Crump, Diana, Feb. 7, 1969.

Crusade, First, Jul. 1, 1097; Jun. 3, 1098; Jun. 28, 1098; Jul. 15, 1099.

Crusade, Fourth, Apr. 12, 1204.

Crusade, Second: proclaimed, Dec. 1, 1145; Mar. 31, 1146; (Louis Vll), Mar. 24, 1267.

Crusade, Sixth, Mar. 18, 1229; Jun. 4, 1249.

Crusade, Third, Jul. 1, 1190; Jul. 12, 1191; Sep. 1, 1192; Dec. 21, 1192.

Crutzen, Paul, Dec. 3, 1933.

Cruz, Arturo, Dec. 18, 1923.

Cruz, Ramon Ernesto: inaugurated, Jun. 6, 1971.

Crystal, Billy, Mar. 14, 1947.

Crystal Night (Kristal-nacht), Nov. 9, 1938.

Csonka, Larry Richard, Dec. 25, 1946.

Cuba, Oct. 18, 1854; U.S. protectorate, Mar. 2, 1901; Jun. 12, 1901; independence, May 20, 1902; May 20, 1902; Jun. 9, 1940; Jun. 30, 1951; Mar. 10, 1952; Feb. 13, 1960; May 27, 1960; Jul. 23, 1960; embargo, Oct. 19, 1960; Jan. 3, 1961; Jan. 16, 1961; expulsion from O.A.S., Jan. 31, 1961; Mar. 15, 1961; Apr. 17, 1961; May 1, 1961; Aug. 29, 1961; Sep. 14, 1961; Feb. 3, 1962; U.S. naval blockade, Oct. 22, 1962; Oct. 28, 1962; Nov. 20, 1962; U.S. bans financial transactions, Jul. 8, 1963; Jul. 26, 1964; Jan. 9, 1970; Jul. 29, 1975; Sep. 1, 1977; shoots down U.S. planes, Feb. 24, 1996.

Cuban Democracy Act, Oct. 23, 1992.

Cudahy, Edward Aloysius, Feb. 1, 1859.

Cudahy, Michael, Dec. 7, 1841.

Cugat, Xavier, Jan. 1, 1900.

Cugnot, Nicholas, Sep. 25, 1725.

Cukor, George, Jul. 7, 1899.

Culbertson, Ely, Jul. 22, 1891.

Culloden, Battle of, Apr. 16, 1746.

Culp, Robert, Aug. 13, 1930.

Cultural Revolution, Chinese, Jun. 18, 1966; Feb. 2, 1974; Jun. 5, 1978; condemned, Sep. 29, 1979; Jan. 25, 1981.

Culture Day (Japan), Nov. 3.

Culture Day (Slovenia), Feb. 8.

Cumana (Venezuela), patron of, Jan. 21.

Cumberland, Mar. 8, 1862.

Cummingham, Ouinn, Aug. 13, 1967.

Cummings, Burton, Dec. 31, 1947.

Cummings, Constance, May 15, 1910.

Cummings, E. E., Oct. 14, 1894.

Cunard, Sir Samuel, Nov. 21, 1787.

Cunningham, Allan, Dec. 7, 1784.

Cunningham, Imogen, Apr. 12, 1883.

Cunningham, Merce, Apr. 16, 1919; Aug 19, 1919.

Cunningham, Randall, Mar. 27, 1963.

Cuomo, Mario Matthew, Jun. 15, 1932; Aug. 14, 1984.

Cuppy, Will(iam Jacob), Aug. 23, 1884.

Curb, Michael Charles (Mike), Dec. 24, 1944.

Curie, Marie, Nov. 7, 1867; Apr. 20, 1902; Dec. 12, 1903.

Curie, Pierre, May 15, 1859; Apr. 20, 1902; Dec. 12, 1903.

Curl, Robert F., Jr., Aug. 23, 1933.

Curran, Joseph Edwin, Mar. 1, 1906.

Currier, Nathaniel, Mar. 27, 1813.

curriers, patron of, Oct. 28.

Curry, Tim, Apr. 19, 1946.

Curtin, Jane Therese, Sep. 6, 1947.

Curtin, John, Jan. 8, 1885.

Curtis, Benjamin Robbins, Nov. 4, 1809.

Curtis, Charles, Jan. 25, 1860; Mar. 4, 1929.

Curtis, Cyrus Hermann Kotzschmar, Jun. 18, 1850.

Curtis, Jamie Lee, Nov. 22, 1958.

Curtis, Tony, Jun. 3, 1925; Mar. 29, 1959.

Curtiss, Glenn, May 21, 1878.

Curzon, Clifford, May 18, 1907.

Curzon, George Nathaniel, Jan. 11, 1859.

Cusack, Cyril, Nov. 26, 1910.

Cusack, Joan, Oct. 11, 1962.

Cusack, John, Jun. 26, 1966.

Cushing, Harvey Williams, Apr. 8, 1869.

Cushing, Peter, May 26, 1913.

Cushing, Richard James, Aug. 24, 1895.

Cushing, U.S.S.: bombed. Apr. 28, 1915.

Cushman, Charlotte Saunders, Jul. 23, 1816.

Custer, George A(rmstrong), Dec. 5, 1839; massacred, Jun. 25, 1876.

customs officers, patron of, Sep. 21.

Custozza, Battle of, Jul. 25, 1848.

Cuvier, Baron Georges (Jean-Leopold-Nicolas Frederic), Aug. 23, 1769.

Cuza, Alexander, Dec. 23, 1861.

Cyane, Feb. 20, 1815.

cyanotic heart disease, Nov. 29, 1944.

cyclamates, Aug. 14, 1970.

cyclone: Darwin (Australia), Dec. 25, 1974.

cyclosporin, Jul. 30, 1981.

Cyprus: independence, Aug. 16, 1960; Mar. 4, 1964; Jul. 15, 1974; Feb. 13, 1975.

Czech language, Apr. 5, 1897.

Czech Republic, formation of, Jan. 1, 1993.

Czechoslovakia: patron of, Sep. 28; proclaimed a republic, Oct. 28, 1891; declares war on Germany, Aug. 13, 1918; Sep. 2, 1918; declares independence, Oct. 21, 1918; Nov. 10, 1918; Nov. 2, 1938; deprives Germans and Hungarians of citizenship, Aug. 3, 1945; Feb. 25, 1948; Mar. 17, 1951; Jun. 2, 1951; communist Party of, Jan. 5, 1968; Apr. 5, 1968; invaded by Warsaw Pact troops, Aug. 20, 1968; federal government, Jan. 1, 1969; Jan. 16, 1969; treaty with West Germany, Dec. 11, 1973; Jan. 6, 1977; Havel, Vaclav, Dec. 29, 1989; free elections in, Jun. 8, 1990.

Czerny, Karl, Feb. 20, 1791.

Czolgosz, Leon, Sep. 6, 1901.

D

d'Albert, Eugen Francis Charles, Apr. 10, 1864.

d'Alembert, Jean Le Rond, Nov. 17, 1717.

D'Amato, Alfonse Marcello, Aug. 1, 1937.

d'Annunzio, Gabriele, Mar. 12, 1863; Sep. 12, 1919.

D'Aquino, Iva Toguri, Jan. 19, 1977.

D'Arvy, Terence Trent, Mar. 15, 1962.

d'Aubigne, Jean Henri Merle, Aug. 16, 1794.

d'Estournells de Constant de Rebecque, Paul H. B. B., Nov. 22, 1852.

d'Indy, Vincent, Mar. 27, 1851.

D'Oyly Carte, Richard, May 3, 1844.

da Costa e Silva, Arthur, Oct. 3, 1902.

da Los Santos, Emilio, Sep. 26, 1963.

da Ponte, Lorenzo, Mar. 10, 1749.

da Silva Quadros, Janio: inaugurated, Jan. 31, 1961; Sep. 7, 1961.

Da Nang, Mar. 30, 1975.

Dachau: liberated, Apr. 24, 1945.

Dacko, David, Sep. 20, 1979; Sep. 1, 1981.

Daedalrls 88, Apr. 23, 1988.

daffodil, Mar. intro.

Dafoe, Willem, Jul. 22, 1955.

Daguerre, Louis Iacques Mande, Nov. 18, 1789.

Dahab, Abdel Rahman Siwar el-, Apr. 6, 1985.

Dahl, Arlene, Aug. 11, 1928.

Dahl, Roald, Sep. 13, 1916.

Dahomey, Jun. 22, 1894; Nov. 30, 1975.

Dailey, Dan, Dec. 12, 1917.

Dailey, Irene, Sep. 12, 1920.

Dailey, Janet, May 21, 1944.

Daimler, Gottlieb Wilhelm, Mar. 17, 1834.

Daimler-Benz, Jun. 11, 1988; May 7, 1998.

Daimler-Chrysler, merger, May 7, 1998.

dairy workers, patron of, Feb. 1.

Dairy Month, National, Jun. intro.

daisy, Apr. intro.

Daladier, Edouard, Jun. 18, 1884.

Dalai Lama, May 27, 1951; Mar. 31, 1959; Oct. 6, 1989.

Dalberg-Acton, John Emerich Edward, 1st Baron Acton, Jan. 10, 1834.

Dale, Sir Henry H., Jun. 9, 1875.

Dalen, Nils G., Nov. 30, 1869.

Daley, Richard J., May 15, 1902; Apr. 5, 1955.

Daley, Richard M., Apr. 24, 1942; inaugurated, Apr. 24, 1989.

Dali, Salvador, May 11, 1904.

Dalkon Shield, Apr. 2, 1985.

Dallas Cowboys, Jan. 31, 1993; Jan. 30, 1994.

Dallas, George M., Jul. 10, 1792; Mar. 4, 1845.

Dallas: television debut, Apr. 2, 1978.

Dallmeier, Francisco, Feb. 15, 1953.

Dalls, Alexander James, Jun. 21, 1757.

Dalton, Abby, Aug. 15, 1935.

Dalton, John, Sep. 6, 1766.

Dalton, Lacy J., Oct. 13, 1946.

Dalton, Timothy, Mar. 21, 1944.

Daltrey, Roger, Mar. 1, 1945.

Daly, Marcus, Dec. 5, 1841.

Daly, Tyne, Feb. 21, 1944.

Dam, Henrik C. P., Feb. 21, 1895.

Damansky (Chanpao) Island, Mar. 2, 1969.

Damao, Mar. 14, 1962.

Damascus, Mar. 24, 1401; seized by British and Arabs, Oct. 1, 1918; Jan. 1, 1925. Jun. 20, 1941.

Damashek, William, Jun. 13, 1959.

Damn Yankees: premiere, May 5, 1955.

Damon, Stuart, Feb. 5, 1937.

Damone, Vic, Jun. 12, 1928.

Damrosch, Walter Johannes, Jan. 30, 1862.

Dana, Richard Henry, Jr., Aug. 1, 1815.

Danatbank: failure, Jul. 13, 1931.

Dandridge, Dorothy, Nov. 9, 1922.

Danes, Jan. 6, 871.

Danforth, John Claggett, Sep. 5, 1936.

Dangerfield, Rodney, Nov. 22, 1921.

Daniel, Clifton, Jr., Sep. 19, 1912.

Daniels, Charlie, Oct. 28, 1936.

Daniels, Jeff, Feb. 19, 1955.

Daniels, Jonathan Worth, Apr. 26, 1902.

Daniels, William, Mar. 31, 1927.

Danielson, Gary, Sep. 10, 1951.

Daniken, Erich von, Apr. 14, 1935.

Daniloff, Nicholas, Dec. 30, 1934; Sep. 29, 1986; Sep. 30, 1986.

Danilova, Alexandra, Jan. 20, 1904.

Danish Constitution: adopted, Jun. 5, 1953.

Danish West Indies, Aug. 4, 1916; Mar. 31, 1917.

Danish West Indies Emancipation Day (Virgin Islands), Jul. 3.

Dankworth, John Philip William, Sep. 20, 1927.

Dannay, Frederic, Oct. 20, 1905.

Dannecker, Johann Heinrich von, Oct. 15, 1758.

Danner, Blythe Katharine, Feb. 3, 1943.

The Danny Thomas Show: television debut, Sep. 29, 1953.

Danson, Ted, III, Dec. 29, 1947.

Dante Alighieri, May 27, 1265.

Dante, Nicholas, Nov. 22, 1941.

Dantley, Adrian Delano, Feb. 26, 1956.

Danton, Georges Jacques, Oct. 26, 1759.

Danza, Tony, Apr. 21, 1951.

Danzig, Jun. 2, 1734. Aug. 29, 1939.

Daphnis et Chloe: premiere, Jun. 8, 1912.

Daradzic, Kadovan, Nov. 16, 1995.

Darby, Kim, Jul. 8, 1948.

Dardanelles, Feb. 23, 1905; Oct. 1, 1914; Feb. 19, 1915.

Dare, Virginia, Aug. 18, 1587.

Darin, Bobby, May 14, 1936.

Dario, Ruben, Jan 18, 1867.

Darion, Joe, Nov. 22, 1965.

Darktown Strutters' Ball, Jan. 30, 1917.

Darlan, Jeon Louis: assassinated, Dec. 24, 1942.

Darling, Ron(ald Maurice), Jr., Aug. 19, 1960.

Darnell, Linda, Oct. 16, 1921.

Darnley, Lord (Henry Stuart), Jul. 29, 1565; Feb. 10, 1567.

Darren, James, Jun. 8, 1936.

Darrow, Clarence, Apr. 18, 1857; Jul. 10, 1925.

Dart, Raymond Arthur, Feb. 4, 1893.

Dartmoor Prison, Mar. 20, 1806.

Dartmouth College, Dec. 13, 1769.

Darwin (Australia), Dec. 25, 1974.

Darwin, Charles Robert, Feb. 12, 1809.

Darwin, Erasmus, Dec. 12, 1731.

Darwin, Sir George Howard, Jul. 9, 1845.

DaSilva, Howard, May 4, 1909.

Dato, Eduardo, Mar. 8, 1921.

Daubigny, Charles Francois, Feb. 15, 1817.

Daud Khan, Sardar Mohammad, Apr. 27, 1978.

Daughters of the American Revolution, Aug. 8, 1890; Apr. 9, 1939; Dec. 3, 1977.

Daumier, Honore, Feb. 26, 1808.

Dauphin, Claude Le Grand Maria Eugene, Aug. 19, 1903.

Dausset, Jean, Oct. 19, 1916.

Davenport, James, Feb. 14, 1764.

David, Hal, May 25, 1921.

David I (Scotland), Apr. 22, 1124; Apr. 27, 1124; Aug. 22, 1138; dies, May 24, 1153.

David II (Scotland), Jun. 7, 1329; deposed, Aug. 11, 1332; Oct. 17, 1346.

David, Jacques-Louis, Aug. 30, 1748.

David, Sep. 21, 1971.

Davidson, Jo, Mar. 30, 1883.

Davidson, John, Dec. 13, 1941.

Davies, Arthur B(owen), Sep. 26, 1862.

Davies, Hunter, Jan. 7, 1936.

Davies, Marion, Jan. 3, 1897.

Davies, Ray(mond Douglas), Jun. 21, 1944.

Davis, Adelle, Feb. 25, 1904.

Davis, Alice Brown, Sep. 10, 1852.

Davis, Benjamin Oliver, Jr., Dec. 18, 1912.

Davis, Benjamin Oliver, Jul. 1, 1877.

Davis, Bette, Apr. 5, 1908; Nov. 7, 1941.

Davis, Billy, Jr., Jun. 26, 1940.

Davis, Clifton, Oct. 4, 1945.

Davis, Dwight Filley, Jul. 5, 1879.

Davis, Geena, Jan. 21, 1957.

Davis, James Robert *(Jim)*, Jul. 28, 1945.

Davis, Jan, Sep. 12, 1992.

Davis, Jefferson, Birthday (U.S. southern states), Jun. intro.

Davis, Jefferson, Jun. 3, 1808; Feb. 8, 1861; Oct. 17, 1978.

Davis, Jim, Aug. 26, 1916.

Davis, Loyal, Jan. 17, 1896.

Davis, Miles, Jr., May 25, 1926.

Davis, Ossie, Dec. 18, 1917.

Davis, Patti, Oct. 21, 1952.

Davis, Richard Harding, Apr. 18, 1864.

Davis, Sammy, Jr., Dec. 8, 1925.

Davis, Stuart, Dec. 7, 1894.

Davis, Terrell, Oct. 28, 1972.

Davis, William Morris, Feb. 12, 1850.

Davisson, Clinton Joseph, Oct. 22, 1881.

Davout, Louis Nicolas, May 10, 1770.

Davy, Sir Humphrey, Dec. 17, 1778.

Dawber, Pam, Oct. 18, 1951.

Dawes, Charles Gates, Aug. 27, 1865; Mar. 4, 1925.

Dawes General Allotment Act, Feb. 8, 1887.

Dawkins, Darryl, Jan. 11, 1957; May 31, 1975.

Dawson, Andre Nolan, Jul. 7, 1954.

Dawson, William L., Apr. 26, 1886.

Day, Clarence (Shepard), Nov. 18, 1874.

Day, Doris, Apr. 3, 1924.

Day, Dorothy, Nov. 8, 1897.

Day of 1970 Invasion (Guinea), Nov. 22.

Day of Andalucia (Spain), Feb. 28.

Day of Association (Senegal), Jul. 14.

Day of Commemoration (Belarus), Nov. 2.

Day of Goodwill (Nambia), Oct. 7.

Day of Independence Restored (Lithuania), Mar. 11.

Day of International Socialism (Chechnia), May 1.

Day of Liberation and Renewal (Suriname), Feb. 25.

Day of National Revival (Azerbaijan), Nov. 17.

Day of Referendum (Macedonia), Sep. 8.

Day of Remembrance (Armenia), Dec. 7.

Day of State Sovereignty
(Azerbaijan), Oct. 18.
Day of Supreme Sacrifice (The
Congo), Mar. 18.
Day of the Americas (Honduras),
Apr. 14.
Day of the Apostles, St. Cyril and St.
Methodius Day (Czech,
Republic), Jul. 6.
Day of the Armeal Forces
(Mozambique), Sep. 25.
Day of the Army (Laos), Jan. 20.
Day of the Covenant (Namibia,
South Africa), Dec. 16.
Day of the Dead (Mexico), Nov. 2.
Day of the Hispanidad, Oct. 12.
Day of the Public Functionary
(Venezuela), Sep. 24.
Day of the Republic (Azerbaijan),
May 28.
Day of the Slav Apostles, St. Cyril
and St. Methodius (Slovakia),
Jul. 5.
Day, Pat, Oct. 13, 1953.
Day, Thomas, Jun. 22, 1748.
Day, William Rufus, Apr. 17, 1849.
Day-Lewis, Daniel, Apr. 28, 1957.
Dayan, Moshe, May 20, 1915; Oct.
21, 1979.
Daylight Saving Time, Mar. 31, 1918;
Sep. 30, 1974.
Dayton, Jonathan, Oct. 16, 1760.
DC-10 jetliner: crashes, May 25,
1979.
DDT: banned in residential areas,
Nov. 20, 1969; Jan. 7, 1971.
De Carlo, Yvonne, Sep. 1, 1924.
de Diego's Birthday (Puerto Rico),
Apr. 16.
de Duve, Christian Rene, Oct. 2,
1917.
De Forest, Lee, Aug. 26, 1873; Mar.
5, 1907; Apr. 9, 1909.
De Gaulle, Charles, Nov. 22, 1890;
Jun. 1, 1958; named president
of Fifth Republic, Dec. 21, 1958;
Jan. 29, 1960; Apr. 14, 1962;
Nov. 25, 1962; Jan. 31, 1964;
Apr. 28, 1969.
de Havilland, Olivia, Jul. 1, 1916.
De Hostos' Birthday (Puerto Rico),
Jan. intro.; Jan. 11.
de Klerk, F. W., elected, Jan. 18,
1989; Mar. 18, 1936.

De La Beckwith, Byron, murder of
Evers, Medgar, Jun. 12, 1963;
convicted, Feb. 5, 1994; life
imprisonment of, Mar. 4, 1994.
De la Guardia, Ernesto, Oct. 1, 1956.
de la Guardia Ricardo Adolfo, Oct. 9,
1941.
De La Hoya, Oscar, Feb. 4, 1973.
de la Madrid, Miguel: elected, Jul. 4,
1982.
de la Renta, Oscar, Jul. 22, 1932.
De Larrocha, Alicia, May 23, 1923.
De Laurentiis, Dino, Aug. 8, 1919.
de Luca, Giuseppe, Dec. 25, 1876.
De Mille, Cecil B(lount), Aug. 12,
1881.
de Neve, Felipe, Feb. 3, 1777.
De Niro, Robert, Aug. 17, 1943.
de Paul, Gene, Nov. 15, 1956.
De Sanctis, Francesco, Mar. 28, 1817.
De Sica, Vittorio, Jul. 7, 1901.
De Valera, Eamon, Oct. 14, 1882;
Apr. 5, 1919; Jun. 13, 1951.
De Voto, Bernard A., Jan. 11, 1897.
De Wet, Christiaan Rudolph, Oct. 7,
1854.
De Witt, Jan, Sep. 24, 1625.
deaconate: married men admitted to
Roman Catholic, Sep. 29, 1964.
Dead or All Saints' Day, Day of the,
Nov. 1.
Deak, Ferencz, Oct. 17, 1803.
dealers in used clothing, patron of,
Jul. 26.
Dean, Dizzy, Jan. 16, 1911.
Dean, James, Feb. 8, 1931; Mar. 9,
1955; dies, Sep. 30, 1955.
Dean, John W., III, Oct. 15, 1938;
Apr. 30, 1973; Aug. 2, 1974.
Dean, William F(riske), Aug. 1, 1899.
Deane, Silas, Dec. 24, 1737.
A Death in the Family, May 5, 1958.
death penalty: restoration in
U.S.S.R., Jan. 12, 1950.
Death Anniversary of Eleanor
Roosevelt (U.S.), Nov. 7.
Death March (Bataan), May 7, 1942.
Death of a Salesman: premiere,
Feb. 10, 1949.
Death of General San Martin
Anniversary of the (Argentina),
Aug. 17.
Death of Quaid-e-Azam Anniversary
of the (Pakistan), Sep. 11.

Death to America Day (Iran), Nov. 4.
Deaver, Michael, Dec. 16, 1987.
Debakey, Michael Ellis, Sep. 7, 1908.
Oct. 27, 1963; May 17,1966.
DeBarge, James, Aug. 22, 1963.
DeBarge, Randy, Aug. 6, 1958.
Debs, Eugene V(ictor), Nov. 5, 1855.
Debussy, Claude, Aug. 22, 1862; Apr.
30, 1902; Mar. I, 1907.
Deby, Idris, Dec. 1, 1990.
Debye, Peter J. W., Mar. 24, 1884.
DeCarava, Roy, Dec. 9, 1919.
Decatur, Stephen, Feb. 16, 1804;
Oct. 25, 1812; Jun. 30, 1815.
decem, Dec. intro.
Decentralization Day (Sudan), Jul. 1.
decimal currency: Britain, Feb. 15,
1971.
Declaration of Independence:
adopted, Jul. 4, 1776.
Declaration of the Rights of Man
(France): adopted, Aug. 4, 1789.
DeConcini, Dennis Webster, May 8,
1937.
Decoration Day (Liberia), Mar. 8.
Decoration Day (Liberia), Mar. intro.
Decoration Day (U.S.), Jul. intro.
Dedekind, Richard, Oct. 6, 1831.
Dee, Kiki, Mar. 6, 1947.
Dee, Ruby, Oct. 27, 1924.
Dee, Sandra, Apr. 23, 1942.
The Deer Hunter: premiere, Dec. 14,
1978.
Deere, John, Feb. 7, 1804.
Deerneld, Massachusetts, Feb. 28,
1704.
Defender of the Faith, Feb. 2, 1522.
Defenders of Freedom Day
(Lithuania), Jan. 13.
Defenders' Day (Missouri), Sep. 12.
Defenders' Day, Sep. intro.
Defense of Pakistan Day (Pakistan),
Sep. 6.
Defense Production Administration,
Jan. 3, 1951.
Defoe, Daniel, Apr. 26, 1661.
DeFreeze, Donald David, Nov. 16,
1943.
Degas, (Hilaire Germaine) Edgar,
Jul. 19, 1834.
DeGazon, Fred, Dec. 21, 1978.
DeHartog, Jan, Apr. 22, 1914.
DeHaven, Gloria, Jul. 23, 1925.
Dehmelt, Hans Georg, Sep. 9, 1922.

Deighton, Leonard Cyril (Len), Feb. 18, 1929.

Deisenhofer, Johann, Sep. 30, 1943.

Dekker, Eduard Douwes (*Multatuli*), Mar. 2, 1820.

DeKooning, Willem, Apr. 24, 1904.

del Sarto, Andrea, Jul. 16, 1486.

Del Monaco, Mario, Jul. 25, 1915.

Del Rey, Lester, Jun. 2, 1915.

Del Rio, Dolores, Aug. 3, 1905.

Delacroix, Eugene, Apr. 26, 1798.

Delagoa Bay Railway, Jul. 8, 1875.

Delaney, Dana, Mar. 13, 1956.

Delano, Jane, Mar. 12, 1862.

Delany, Martin, May 6, 1812.

Delarge, Robert C., Mar. 15, 1842.

Delaroche, Hippolyte Paul, Jul. 17, 1797.

Delaunay, Sonia, Nov. 14, 1885.

Delavigne, Jean Francois Casimir, Apr. 4, 1793.

Delaware (U.S.): first state, Dec. 7, 1787.

Delaware Day (Delaware), Dec. 7.

Delbruck, Max, Sep. 4, 1906.

Delderfield, Ronald Frederick, Feb. 12, 1912.

Deledda, Grazia, Sep. 27, 1875.

Delgado Chalbaud, Carlos: assassinated, Nov. 13, 1950.

Delhi, Dec. 18, 1398; Jan. 3, 1399; Dec 12, 1911.

Delhi Pact, Mar. 5, 1931.

Deliverance: published, Apr. 23, 1970.

Dellums, Ronald, Nov. 24, 1935.

Delmonico, Lorenzo, Mar. 13, 1813.

Delon, Alain, Nov. 8, 1935.

DeLorean, John Zachary, Jan. 6, 1925. Oct. 19, 1982; Aug. 16, 1984.

DeLorean Motor Co., Feb. 19, 1982.

Deloria, Ella Cara, Jan. 31, 1889.

Delors, Jacques, Jul. 20, 1925.

DeLuise, Dom, Aug. 1, 1933.

Delvalle, Eric Arturo, Feb. 26, 1988.

Delvecchio, Alex, Dec. 4, 1931.

Demarest, William, Feb. 27, 1892.

Demaret, James N., May 25, 1910.

Demerol, Apr. 1, 1942.

Demers, Jaques, Aug. 25, 1944.

DeMille, Agnes George, Sep. 18, 1905.

DeMille, Cecil B(lount), Nov. 8, 1956.

DeMita, Ciriaco: inaugurated, Apr. 13, 1988.

Demme, Jonathan, Feb. 22, 1944.

Democracy Day (Nepal), Feb. 18.

Democracy Day (Rwanda), Jan. 28.

Democratic convention: rioting, Aug. 28, 1968.

Democratic Republic of Madagascar Anniversary of the (Madagascar), Dec. 30.

Democratic Republic of the Congo, formation of, May 17, 1997; new political system, May 27, 1998.

Dempsey, Jack, Jun. 24, 1895; Jul. 4, 1919; Sep. 23, 1926; Sep. 22, 1927.

Dempsey, Rick, Sep. 13, 1949.

Deneuve, Catherine, Oct. 22, 1943.

Deng Xiaoping, Apr. 5, 1976; Jul. 22, 1977.

DeNiro, Robert, Dec. 14, 1978.

Denmark, Apr. 4, 1611; Sep. 14, 1770; Jan. 14, 1814; May 8, 1852; Jan. 17, 1917; Apr. 22, 1918; Mar. 8, 1920; Apr. 9, 1940; new constitution, Mar. 30, 1953; Jan. 15, 1969.

Denmark, patron of, Feb. 3.

Denmark, patron saint of, Jan. 19.

Dennehy, Brian, Jul. 9, 1939.

Dennis, Sandy, Apr. 27, 1937.

Dennison, Aaron Lufkin, Mar. 6, 1812.

Dennison, Robert Lee, Apr. 13, 1901.

dentists, patron of, Feb. 9.

Denver, Bob, Jan. 9, 1935.

Denver International Airport, Mar. 1, 1995.

Denver, John, Dec. 31, 1943.

DePalma, Brian Russell, Sep. 11, 1940.

Depardieu, Gerard, Dec. 27, 1948.

Department of Defense (U.S.): created, Aug. 10, 1949.

Department of Energy (U.S.): created, Aug. 4, 1977.

Department of Labor and Commerce (U.S.), Feb. 14, 1903.

Department of State (U.S.), Jul. 27, 1789.

Department of Transportation (U.S.): created, Oct. 15, 1966.

Depp, Johnny, Jun. 9, 1963.

DeQuincy, Thomas, Aug. 15, 1785.

Derby, Earl of, Oct. 21, 1345.

Derek, Bo, Nov. 16, 1956.

Derek, John, Aug. 12, 1926.

Deringer, Henry, Oct. 26, 1786.

Dern, Bruce MacLeish, Jun. 4, 1936.

Dern, Laura, Feb. 10, 1966.

Derne (Tripoli), Apr. 27, 1805.

DeRoburt, Hammer, Sep. 25, 1922.

Derzhavin, Gavrila, Jul. 14, 1743.

Desai, Morarji R. (India), Mar. 24, 1977.

DeSalvo, Albert, Jan. 18, 1967.

Descartes, Rene, Mar. 31, 1596.

desegregation: Nashville (Tennessee), May 10, 1960; Sep. 8, 1964; Sep. 14, 1964.

desert wanderers, patrons of, Oct. 8.

DeShannon, Jackie, Aug. 21, 1944.

DeSoto (automobile), Nov. 18, 1960.

Dessalines, Jean Jacques, Mar. 29, 1804.

Dessalines Memorial Day (Haiti), Oct. 17.

Detroit (Michigan), Jan. 21, 1915; racial violence, Jul. 23, 1967.

Dett, Robert Nathaniel, Oct. 11, 1882.

Dettingen, Jun. 27, 1743.

Deukmejian, George, Jr., Jun. 6, 1928.

Deutch, John, Jul. 27, 1938.

Deutsch, Helen, Oct. 9, 1884; Mar. 21, 1906.

Deutschland, Jun. 22, 1910.

Deux Images: premiere, Feb. 26, 1913.

Devane, William, Sep. 5, 1937.

Devers, (Yoland) Gail, Nov. 19, 1966.

Devesi, Baddeley, Oct. 16, 1941.

Devine, Andy, Oct. 7, 1905.

Devine, Dan(iel John), Dec. 23, 1924.

DeVito, Danny Michael, Nov. 27, 1944.

Devlin, Bernadette, Apr. 23, 1947; Dec. 22, 1969.

DeVries, Peter, Feb. 27, 1910.

DeVries, William Castle, Dec. 19, 1943, Dec. 2, 1982.

Dewar, Sir James, Sep. 20, 1842.

Dewey, George, Dec. 26, 1837; May 1, 1898.

Dewey, John, Oct. 20, 1859.

Dewey, Melvil, Dec. 10, 1851.

Dewey, Thomas E., Mar. 24, 1902. Nov. 3, 1948.

Dewhurst, Colleen, Jun. 6, 1926.

Dey, Susan Hallock, Dec. 10, 1952.

Dhlakama, Afonso, Jan. 1, 1953.

Di Mucci, Dion, Jul. 18, 1939.

Dia de la Candelaria (Mexico), Feb. 2.

Dia de Muertos (Mexico), Nov. 2.

Diaghilev, Sergei Pavlovich, Mar. 19, 1872.

Dial M for Murder: premiere, May 28, 1954.

diamond, Apr. intro.

Diamond, Neil, Jan. 24, 1941.

Diana, Princess of Wales, Jul. 1, 1961; Jul. 29, 1981; announcement of separation, Dec. 9, 1992; divorce of, Feb. 28, 1996; death of, Aug. 31, 1997; funeral of, Sep. 6, 1997; Jan. 5, 1998.

Dias, Bartholomeu, Feb. 3, 1488.

Diaz de la Pena, Narcisse Virgile, Aug. 20, 1808.

Diaz, Gustavo: inaugurated, Dec. 1, 1964.

Diaz, Porfirio, Sep. 15, 1830; Nov. 20, 1910; May 25, 1911.

DiCaprio, Leonardo, Nov. 11, 1974.

Dick, Albert Blake, Apr. 16, 1856.

Dick Tracy: debut, Oct. 4, 1931.

The Dick Van Dyke Show: television debut, Oct. 3, 1961.

Dickens, Charles, Feb. 7, 1812.

Dickerson, Eric Demetric, Sep. 2, 1960.

Dickey, James, Feb. 2, 1923; Apr. 23, 1970.

Dickinson, Angie, Sep. 30, 1931.

Dickinson, Emily, Dec. 10, 1830.

Dickinson, John, Nov. 8, 1732; Nov. 5, 1767.

Diddley, Bo, Dec. 30, 1928.

Diderot, Denis, Oct. 5, 1713.

Didi, Al Amir Mohammed Farid, Mar. 7, 1954.

Didion, Joan, Dec. 5, 1934.

Die Kluge: opens, Feb. 18, 1943.

Die Meistersinger: premiere, Jun. 21, 1868.

Diefenbaker, John George, Sep. 18, 1895; Jun. 17, 1957.

Diego Gestido, Oscar (Uruguay), Mar. 1, 1967.

Diego, José de, Apr. 16, 1866.

Diels, Otto Paul Hermann, Jan. 23, 1876.

Diem, Ngo Dinh, Jan. 3, 1901; overthrown, Nov. 27, 1963.

Dien Bien Phu, Feb. 3, 1954; Mar. 13, 1954; May 7, 1954; May 7, 1975; Jul. 2, 1976.

Dieppe, Aug. 19, 1942.

Dierx, Leon, Mar. 31, 1838.

Dies, Martin, Nov. 5, 1901.

Diesel, Rudolf, Mar. 18, 1858.

Dietrich, Marlene, Dec. 27, 1901.

Diez, Friedrich Christian, Mar. 15, 1794.

Diggs, Charles Coles, Jr., Dec. 2, 1922.

Dillard, Annie Doak, Apr. 30, 1945.

Diller, Phyllis, Jul. 17, 1917.

Dillinger, John, Jun. 22, 1903.

Dillon, John, Sep. 4, 1851.

Dillon, Matt, Feb. 18, 1964.

Dillon, Melinda, Oct. 31, 1939.

DiMaggio, Joe, Nov. 25, 1914; Dec. 11, 1951.

Dinant, Battle of, Aug. 15, 1914.

Dinesen, Isak, Apr. 17, 1885.

Dingell, John David, Jr., Jul. 8, 1926.

Dini, Lamberto, elected, Jan. 18, 1989.

Dinkins, David N., Jul. 10, 1927.

Dinnyes, Lajos, May 31, 1947.

Diomedes, Alexander, Jun. 30, 1949.

Dion, Celine, Mar. 30, 1968.

Dionne Quintuplets, May 28, 1934.

Dior, Christian, Jan. 21, 1905.

Diori, Hamani, Apr. 15, 1974; Apr. 17, 1974.

Diouf, Abdou, Sep. 7, 1935; Jan. 1, 1981.

dioxin, Jan. 3, 1983; Feb. 22, 1983.

Dirac, Paul Adrien Maurice, Aug. 8, 1902.

direct primary system: adoption of, May 23, 1903.

dirigible: first use in warfare, Mar. 6, 1912; first Atlantic crossing, Jul. 6, 1919.

Dirksen, Everett McKinley, Jan. 4, 1896.

Disaster, "The Great Flood of 1993," Jul. 26, 1993.

Discoverers' Day (Hawaii), Oct. intro.

Discovery Day (Bahamas), Oct. 12.

Discovery Day (Cayman Islands), May intro.

Discovery Day (Guam), Mar. 6.

Discovery Day (Haiti), Dec. 5.

Discovery Day (Honduras), Oct. 12.

Discovery Day (St. Vincent), Jan. 22.

Discovery Day (Trinidad and Tobago), Aug. intro.

Discovery, Jan. 24, 1985.

Discovery of Puerto Rico (Puerto Rico), Nov. 19.

Discovery. launched, Mar. 13, 1989; Hubble Space Telescope, Apr. 24, 1990; launched, Feb. 3, 1994; Glenn, John, Jan. 16, 1998.

Disney, Walt, Dec. 5, 1901; Nov. 18, 1928; May 25, 1933; Dec. 21, 1937; Nov. 13, 1940; Jun. 23, 1955; Dec. 25, 1957; Aug. 27, 1964.

Disneyland: television debut, Oct. 27, 1954; Jul. 17, 1955; Mar. 24, 1987.

Disraeli, Benjamin, Dec. 21, 1804; Feb. 29, 1868; Aug. 12, 1876.

distillers, patron of, Aug. 25.

Distinguished Flying Cross, Jun. 11, 1927.

Distinguished Service Medal, Mar. 7, 1918.

Ditka, Mike, Oct. 18, 1939.

Diu, Battle of, Feb. 2, 1509.

Diu, Mar. 14, 1962.

divines, patron of, Jul. 2; Dec. 2.

divorce, ban on, ended in Ireland, Nov. 24, 1995.

Dix, Dorothea, Apr. 4, 1802.

Dix, John Adams, Jul. 24, 1798.

Dixiecrats, Jul. 17, 1948.

Dixmude, Dec. 21, 1923.

Dixon, Dean, Jan. 10, 1915; Aug. 10, 1941.

Dixon, Jeane Pinckert, Jan. 5, 1918.

Djibouti, Jun. 27, 1977; Sep. 20, 1977.

Djukanovic, Milo, Jan. 15, 1998.

Dlamini, Bhekimpi, Mar. 25, 1983.

Dlamini, Mabandla, Mar. 25, 1983.

DNA: structure, Apr. 25, 1953; synthesized, Dec. 14, 1967.

Dobie, James Frank, Sep. 26, 1888.

Dobrolyubov, Nikolai, Jan. 24, 1836.

Dobrovolsky, Georgi T., Jun. 30, 1971.

Dobrynin, Anatoliy F., Nov. 16, 1919.

Dobson, Kevin, Mar. 18, 1944.

dock workers, patron of, Dec. 6.

Doctor's Day (Georgia), Mar. 30.

Doctor's Day, Mar. intro.

Doctorow, E. L., Jan. 6, 1931. Jan. 8, 1976.

doctors, patron of, Jul. 27; Oct. 18.

Dodd, Christopher John, May 27, 1944.

Dodd, William Edward, Oct. 21, 1869.

Dodds, Harold Willis, Jun. 28, 1889.

Dodecanese Islands, Mar. 31, 1947.

Dodge, Cleveland, Feb. 5, 1888.

Dodge, Horace Elgin, May 17, 1868.

Dodge, John Francis, Oct. 25, 1864.

Dodge, Mary Elizabeth, Jan. 26, 1831.

Dodik, Milorad, elected, Jan. 18, 1989.

Doe, Samuel K., May 6, 1952; Apr. 12, 1980; Sep. 9, 1990.

Doenitz, Karl, Sep. 16, 1891; May 23, 1945.

dog days, Jul. intro.

Dogger Bank, Battle of (World War I), Jan. 24, 1915.

Doheny, Edward Lawrence, Aug. 10, 1856.

Doherty, Henry Latham, May 15, 1870.

Doherty, Peter C., Oct. 15, 1940.

Doherty, Shannen, Apr. 12, 1971.

Dohrn, Bernadine Rae, Jan. 12, 1942.

Doisy, Edward A., Nov. 13, 1893.

Dolby, Ray Milton, Jan. 18, 1933.

Dolby, Thomas, Oct. 14, 1958.

Dole, Elizabeth (Liddy) Hanford, Jul. 20, 1936; Oct. 24, 1990.

Dole, Robert J., Jul. 22, 1923.

Dole, Sanford Ballard, Apr. 23, 1844; May 14, 1900.

Dolenz, Mickey, Mar. 8, 1945.

Dollfuss, Engelbert, Oct. 4, 1892; Apr. 30, 1934; Jul. 25, 1934.

Dolls' Day (Japan), Mar. 3.

Dolly Sisters (Rosie and Jenny), Oct. 25, 1892.

"Dolly" (sheep), cloned, Jul. 5, 1996.

Domagk, Gerhard, Oct. 30, 1895.

Domenici, Pete V(ichi), May 7, 1932.

domestic animals, patron saint of, Jan. 17.

domestic workers, patron of, Apr. 27.

Domingo, Placido, Jan. 21, 1941.

Dominica, Nov. 1, 1964; Feb. 16, 1967; Nov. 2, 1978.

Dominican Republic, Feb. 27, 1844; May 30, 1961; Jan. 4, 1962; Feb. 27, 1963; Apr. 25, 1965; May 2, 1965; Jun. 1, 1966; Nov. 28, 1966; May 26, 1978.

Dominion Day (Canada), Jul. 1.

Domino, Antoine (Fats), Feb. 26, 1928.

Domitien, Elizabeth, Jan. 2, 1975.

Don, Republic of, Jan. 10, 1918,

Don River (Russia), Aug. 20, 1942.

Donahue, Elinor, Apr. 19, 1937.

Donahue, Phil(ip John), Dec. 21, 1935.

Donahue, Troy, Jan. 27, 1937.

Donaldson, Mary, Sep. 29, 1983.

Donaldson, Sam(uel Andrew), Mar. 11, 1934.

Donat, Robert, Mar. 18, 1905.

Donati, Giovanni Battista, Oct. 16, 1826.

Donelson, Fort, Feb. 16, 1862.

Donizetti, Gaetano, Nov. 29, 1797.

Donleavy, J. P., Apr. 23, 1926.

Donnall, Thomas E., Mar. 15, 1920.

Donovan, Feb. 10, 1946; May 10, 1946.

Donovan, Raymond James, Aug. 31, 1930.

Donovan, Robert John, Aug. 21, 1912.

Donovan, William Joseph (Wild Bill), Jan. 1, 1883.

Doolittle, Hilda, Sep. 10, 1886.

Doolittle, James (Col.), Dec. 14, 1896; Apr. 18, 1942.

Doornkop (South African Republic), Jan. 2, 1896.

Doppler, Christian Johann, Nov. 29, 1803.

Dorati, Antal, Apr. 9, 1906.

Dorchester Heights, Mar. 17, 1776.

Doria, Andrea, Nov. 30, 1468.

Doriot, Georges Frederic, Sep. 24, 1899.

Dorji, Jigme, Apr. 5, 1964.

Dornberger, Walter R(obert), Sep. 6, 1895.

Dorpat, Treaty of, Feb. 2, 1920; signed, Oct. 14, 1920.

Dorrington, Arthur, Nov. 15, 1950.

Dors, Diana, Oct. 23, 1931.

Dorsett, AntLony Drew (Tony), Apr. 7, 1954.

Dorsey, Jimmy, Feb. 29, 1904.

Dorsey, Thomas A., Jan. 23, 1899.

Dorsey, Tommy, Nov. 19, 1905.

Dorylaeum, Jul. 1, 1097.

Dos Passos, John, Jan. 14, 1896.

Dostoyevsky, Fyodor Mikhailovich, Nov. 11, 1821.

Double Eagle II, Aug. 17, 1978.

Double Tenth Day (Taiwan), Oct. 10.

Doubleday, Abner, Jun. 26, 1819.

Doubleday, Frank Nelson, Jan. 8, 1862.

Doubleday, Nelson, Jun. 16, 1889.

Doughty, Charles Montagu, Aug. 19, 1843.

Douglas, Donald Willis, Apr. 6, 1892.

Douglas, Helen Gahagan, Nov. 25, 1900.

Douglas, James (Buster), Feb. 10, 1990.

Douglas, James, Nov. 4, 1837.

Douglas, Kirk, Dec. 9, 1918.

Douglas, Lloyd (Cassel), Aug. 27, 1877.

Douglas MacArthur Day (Arkansas), Jan. 26.

Douglas, Michael, Sep. 25, 1944.

Douglas, Mike, Aug. 11, 1925.

Douglas, Molvyn, Apr. 5, 1901.

Douglas, Paul, Apr. 11, 1907.

Douglas, Paul Howard, Mar. 26, 1892.

Douglas, Stephen A., Apr. 23, 1813.

Douglas, William O., Oct. 16, 1898; Nov. 12, 1975; Dec. 19, 1975.

Douglas-Home, Alexander Frederick, Jul. 2, 1903.

Douglass, Frederick, Feb. 14, 1817.

Doullens, Conference of, May 8, 1918.

Doumer, Paul, Mar. 22, 1857.

Doumergue, Gaston, Aug. 1, 1863.

Dove, Rita, Aug. 28, 1952.

Dover (England), Jan. 7, 1785; first German air raid, Dec. 21, 1914.

Dow, Charles Henry, Nov. 6, 1851.

Dow, Herbert Henry, Feb. 26, 1866.

Dow Jones average: largest decline, Dec. 12, 1914; passes 1000, Mar. 11, 1976; passes 2,000, Jan. 8, 1987.

Dow, Tony, Apr. 13, 1945.

Dowding, Hugh Caswall Tremenheere, Apr. 24, 1882.

Dowie, John Alexander, May 25, 1847.

Down, Lesley-Anne, Mar. 17, 1954.

Downey, Robert, Jr., Apr. 4, 1965.

Downhearted Blues, Feb. 16, 1923.

Downs, Hugh, Feb. 14, 1921.

Doyle, David Fitzgerald, Dec. 1, 1929.

Doyle, Sir Arthur Conan, May 22, 1859.

Dozier, James Lee, Apr. 10, 1931, Dec. 17, 1981; Jan. 28, 1982.

Dr. Zhivago: published, Sep. 5, 1958.

Drabble, Margaret, Jun. 5, 1939.

Dracula, Nov. 8, 1847.

draft evaders: pardoned, Jan. 21, 1977.

draft lottery (U.S.): established, Nov. 26, 1969.

draft regulations (U.S.), Jan. 19, 1970.

draft: first peacetime in U.S., Oct. 29, 1940.

Drafting Week, National, Apr. intro.

Draga (Serbia): massacred, Jun. 10, 1903.

Dragnet: television debut, Jan. 3, 1952.

Drago, Luis Maria, May 6, 1859.

Drake, Alfred, Oct. 7, 1914.

Drake, Betsy, Sep. 11, 1923.

Drake, Edwin Laurentine, Mar. 29, 1819; Aug. 27, 1859.

Drake, Francis, Feb. 11, 1573; Dec. 13, 1577; Apr. 4, 1581; Apr. 19, 1587.

Draper, Henry, Mar. 7, 1837.

Dravecky, David, Feb. 14, 1956.

Dreadnought: first British nuclear submarine, Oct. 21, 1960.

Dred Scott decision, Mar. 7, 1857.

Dreiser, Theodore, Aug. 27, 1871.

Dresden Opera, Jan. 25, 1909; Jan. 26, 1911.

Dresden: sunk, Mar. 14, 1915.

Dressler, Marie, Nov. 9, 1869.

Drew, Charles, Jun. 3, 1904.

Drexler, Clyde, Jun. 22, 1962.

Dreyfus, Alfred, Oct. 19, 1859; Jul. 12, 1906.

Dreyfus case, Jan. 13, 1898; ends, Jul. 12, 1906.

Dreyfuss, Richard (Stephen), Oct. 29, 1947.

Driegroschenoper, Die (The Three Penny Opera): premiere, Aug. 31, 1928.

Driesch, Hans, Oct. 28, 1891.

Drinkwater, John, Jun. 1, 1882.

driving tests, Mar. 26, 1934.

Drogheda (Ireland): sack of, Sep. 11, 1649.

druggists, patrons of, Sep. 26.

Druids, May intro.

Drury, Allen Stuart, Sep. 2, 1918.

Dryden, John, Aug. 9, 1613.

Dryden, Ken, Aug. 8, 1947.

Drysdale, Don(ald Scott), Jul. 23, 1936.

du Maurier, Sir Gerald, Mar. 26, 1873.

Du Barry, Comtesse (Marie Jeanne Bhecu), Aug. 19, 1743.

Du Maurier, Daphne, May 13, 1907.

Du Pont de Nemours, Eleuthere Irenee, Jun. 24, 1771.

Du Pont de Nemours, Pierre Samuel, Dec. 14, 1739.

Du Pont, Pierre Sunuel, Jan. 15, 1870.

Duarte, Jose Napoleon, Nov. 23, 1926; Mar. 25, 1984. May 6, 1984.

Duarte Nuna, Dom (Portugal), Apr. 17, 1922.

Duarte's Hirthday (Dominican Republic), Jan. 26.

Dubcek, Alexander, Jan. 5, 1968; Apr. 5, 1968; Apr. 17, 1969.

Dubinsky, David, Feb. 22, 1892.

Dublin (Ireland), Jan. 21, 1950.

Dubno, Jun. 2, 1916.

Dubois, W. E. B., Feb. 23, 1868; Jul. 13, 1970.

Dubos, Rene, Feb. 20, 1901.

Dubs, Adolph: assassinated, Feb. 14, 1979.

Duchamp, Marcel, Jul. 28, 1887; Feb. 17, 1913.

Duchin, Eddy, Apr. 1, 1909.

Duchin, Peter (Oelrichs), Jul. 28, 1937.

Duchovny, David, Aug. 7, 1960.

Ducommun, Elie, Feb. 19, 1833.

Duffy, Karen, May 23, 1962.

Duffy, Patrick, Mar. 17, 1949.

Dufy, Rwul, Jun. 3, 1877.

duGran, Claurene, Mar. 21, 1927.

Duguay, Ron(ald), Jul. 6, 1957.

Dukakis, Michael, Nov. 3, 1933; Nov. 8, 1988.

Dukakis, Olympia, Jun. 20, 1931.

Dukas, Paul Abraham, Oct. 1, 1865.

Duke, Benjamin Newton, Apr. 27, 1855.

Duke, Charles, Apr. 21, 1972; Apr. 27, 1972.

Duke, James Buchanan, Dec. 23, 1856.

Duke, Patty, Dec. 14, 1946.

The Dukes of Hazzard: television debut, Jan. 26, 1979.

Dukhouskaya, Battle of, Aug. 24, 1918.

Dulbecco, Renata, Feb. 2, 1914.

Dulles, Allen, Apr. 7, 1893.

Dulles, John Foster, Feb. 25, 1888.

Dulong, Pierre-Louis, Feb. 12, 1785.

Duma, Apr. 1, 1906.

Dumas, Alexandre (fils), Jul. 27, 1824.

Dumas, Alexandre (pere), Jul. 24, 1802.

Dumbarton Oaks Con-erence, Aug. 21, 1944.

Dunant, Jean Henri, Birthday Anniversary of, May intro.; May 8, 1828.

Dunaway, Faye, Jan. 14, 1941.

Dunbar, Battle of, Apr. 27, 1296; Sep. 3, 1650.

Dunbar, Charles Franklin, Jul. 28, 1830.

Dunbar, Paul Lawrence, Jun. 27, 1872.

Dunbar-Nelson, Alice, Jul. 19, 1875.

Dunblane, Scotland, shooting of school children, Mar. 13, 1996.

Duncan (King of Scotland), Nov. 25, 1034.

Duncan, Isadora, May 27, 1878.

Duncan, Sandy, Feb. 20, 1946.

Dunham, Katherine, Jun. 22, 1910.

Dunkirk: sold to France, Oct. 27, 1662; bombed, Jan. 10, 1915.

Dunlop, John Boyd, Feb. 5, 1840.

Dunn, James, Nov. 2, 1905.

Dunne, Dominick, Oct. 29, 1925.

Dunne, Finley Peter, Jul. 10, 1867.

Dunne, Irene, Dec. 20, 1904.

Dunne, John Gregory, May 25, 1932.

Dunning, William Archibald, May 12, 1857.

Dunsinane (Scotland), Jul. 27, 1054.

Dunster, Rev. Henry, Oct. 28, 1636.

Dupes, Day of, Nov. 11, 1630.

Dupleix, Joseph, Jan. 1, 1697.

DuPont, Pierre Samuel, III, Jan. 1, 1911.

DuPont, Pierre Samuel, IV *(Pete),* Jan. 22, 1935.

Dupre, Jules, Apr. 5, 1811.

Duran, Roberto, Jun. 16, 1951; Jun. 26, 1972.

Durand Agreement: signed, Nov. 12, 1893.

Durand, Asher Brown, Aug. 21, 1796.

Durant, Ariel, May 10, 1898.

Durant, Thomas Clark, Feb. 6, 1820.

Durant, Will(iam James), Nov. 5, 1885.

Durant, William Crapo, bec. 8, 1861.

Durante, Jimmy, Feb. 10, 1893.

Duras, Marguerite Donnadieu, Apr. 4, 1914.

Durban (South Africa), Jan. 21, 1898.

Durbin, Deanna, Dec. 4, 1922.

Durenberger, David Ferdinand, Aug. 19, 1934.

Durer, Albrecht, May 21, 1471.

Durham, Martyrs of 1594, Jul. 24.

Durkheim, Emile, Apr. 15, 1858.

Durnan, Bill, Jan. 22, 1916.

Durning, Charles, Feb. 28, 1923.

Durocher, Leo Ernest, Jul. 27, 1906.

Durrell, Gerald, Jan. 7, 1925.

Durrell, Lawrence, Feb. 27, 1912.

Durrenmatt, Friedrich, Jan: 5, 1921.

Duse, Eleanora, Oct. 3, 1859.

Dussault, Nancy, Jun. 30, 1936.

Dutch army, May 15, 1940.

Dutch East India Company: established, Mar. 20, 1602; Apr. 6, 1652.

Dutch War of Liberation, Nov. 8, 1576; Aug. 17, 1585; May 17, 1597.

Dutch West Indies Company: chartered, Jun. 3, 1621.

Dutra, Eurico Gaspar: inaugurated, Jan. 31, 1946.

Dutton, E(dward) P(ayson), Jan. 4, 1831.

Duvalier, Francois, Apr. 14, 1907; inaugurated, Oct. 22, 1957; Jun. 21, 1964; May 21, 1968; dies, Apr. 22, 1971.

Duvalier, Jean-Claude, Jul. 3, 1951; Apr. 22, 1971; Jan. 31, 1986; Feb. 7, 1986; Nov. 29, 1987.

Duvall, Robert Seldon, Jan. 5, 1931.

Duvall, Shelley, Jul. 7, 1949.

Dvinsk, Jan. 4, 1920.

Dvorak, Antonin, Sep. 8, 1841; Sep. 18, 1841; Mar. 25, 1904.

Dwight, Timothy, May 14, 1752.

dyarchy: established in India, Dec. 23, 1919.

Dyer, Wayne, May 10, 1940.

Dykstra, Lenny, Feb. 10, 1963.

Dylan, Bob, May 24, 1941.

Dynasty Day (Belgium), Nov. 15.

Dystel, Oscar, Oct. 31, 1912.

Dzundza, George, Jul. 19, 1945.

E

E., Sheila, Dec. 12, 1959.

Eagle, Jul. 20, 1969.

Eagleton, Thomas Francis, Sep. 5, 1929.

Eakins, Thomas (Cowperthwait), Jul. 25, 1844.

Eames, Charles, Jun. 17, 1907.

Earhart, Amelia, Jul. 24, 1898; May 21, 1932; disappears, Jul. 2, 1937.

Earl, Steve, Jan. 17, 1955.

Earle, Sylvia A., Aug. 30, 1935.

Early Bird: launched, Apr. 6, 1965; begins transmission, May 2, 1965.

Early, Jubal Anderson, Nov. 3, 1816.

Earp, Wyatt, Mar. 19, 1848; Oct. 26, 1881.

Earth Day, Apr. intro.; Apr. 22; Apr. 22, 1970.

Earth Summit, Jun. 3, 1992.

earthquake: Japan, Oct. 28, 1891; northern India, Apr. 4, 1905; Calabria (Italy), Dec. 28, 1908; Sicily (Italy), Dec. 28, 1908; Japan, Sep. 1, 1923; Quetta (India), May 31, 1935; Erzincan (Turkey), Dec. 27, 1939; Alaska, Mar. 27, 1964; Turkey, Mar. 28, 1969; Andes (Peru), May 31, 1970; Managua (Nicaragua), Dec. 23, 1972; Pakistan, Dec. 28, 1974; Turkey, Sep. 6, 1975; Italy, May 6, 1976; China, Jul. 28, 1976; Turkey, Nov. 24, 1976; Italy, Nov. 23, 1980; Francisco, California, Oct. 17, 1989; Iran, Jun. 21, 1990; Kobe, Japan, Jan. 17, 1995; Afghanistan, Feb. 4, 1998.

East Africa, British, Jul. 23, 1920.

East Beirut (Lebanon), Sep. 23, 1988.

East Berlin. *See*: Berlin, East.

East Germany. *See*: Germany, East.

East India Company: chartered, Dec. 31, 1600; Sep. 5, 1698; Sep. 1, 1858.

East India Railway, Apr. 2, 1895; Mar. 5, 1928.

East Indies, patron saint of, Dec. 3.

East of Eden: premiere, Mar. 9, 1955.

Easter Sunday: holiday established, Aug. 25, 325.

Eastern Air Lines: incorporated, Mar. 29, 1938.

Eastern Solomons, Battle of the: begins, Aug. 23, 1942.

Eastland, James O., Nov. 28, 1904.

Eastman, George, Jul. 12, 1854.

Eastman Kodak Co.: incorporated, Oct. 24, 1901.

Easton, Sheena, Apr. 27, 1959.

Eastwood, Clint, May 31, 1930.

Eaton, Cyrus Stephen, Dec. 27, 1883; May 3, 1960.

Eaues, Antonio dos Santos Ramalho, Jan. 25, 1935.

Eban, Abba, Feb. 2, 1915.

Ebb, Frank, Nov. 20, 1966.

Eberhart, Richard Ghormley, Apr. 5, 1904.

Ebers, Georg Moritz, Mar. 1, 1837.

Ebert, Friedrich, Feb. 4, 1871.

Ebsen, Buddy, Apr. 2, 1908.

Eccles, Sir John Carew, Jan. 27, 1903.

Echegaray y Eizaguirre, Jose, Apr. 19, 1832.

Echeverria Alvarez, Luis, Jan. 17, 1922; inaugurated, Dec. 1, 1970; Jul. 28, 1972.

Echo I, Aug. 12, 1960; Apr. 24, 1962.

Echo II, Feb. 21, 1964.

Eckermann, Johann Peter, Sep. 21, 1792.

Economic Cooperation and Development, Organization for: created, Dec. 14, 1960; Apr. 28, 1964.

Economic Liberation Day (Togo), Jan. 24.

Ecuador: independence, May 24, 1822; Sep. 27, 1947; earthquake, Aug. 5, 1949; Apr. 29, 1979.

Ecumenical Council: convenes, Dec. 25, 1961; Sep. 29, 1964; Mar. 7, 1965; Nov. 19, 1965.

Ed Sullivan Show: television show, Jun. 20, 1948.The

Eddington, Sir Arthur Stanley, Dec. 28, 1882.

Eddy, Mary (Morse) Baker, Jul. 16, 1821.

Eddy, Nelson, Jun. 9, 1901.

Edelman, Gerald Maurice, Jul. 1, 1929.

Edelman, Marian Wright, June 6, 1939.

Eden, Anthony, Jun. 12, 1897; Apr. 6, 1955; Jan. 9, 1957; resigns, Jan. 10, 1957.

Eden, Barbara, Aug. 23, 1934.

Ederle, Gertrude, Oct. 23, 1906; swims English Channel, Aug. 6, 1926.

Edgar (King of England), May 11, 973.

Edict of Nantes: revoked, Oct. 18, 1685.

Edinburgh, patron of, Sep. 1.

Edison, Thomas Alva, Feb. 11, 1847; Jul. 31, 1877; Feb. 19, 1878; Oct. 21, 1879; Sep. 4, 1882.

Edmund Fitzgerald, Nov. 10, 1975.

Edmund Ironside (England): dies, Nov. 30, 1016.

Edmunds, Dave, Apr. 15, 1944.

Edo (Tokyo), Apr. 25, 1867.

Edo Bay, Jul. 8, 1853.

Edo, Jul. 17, 1868.

Edo, Treaty of, Aug. 26, 1858.

Edsel (automobile), Sep. 4, 1957; Nov. 19, 1959.

Education for All Handicapped Children Act, Nov. 29, 1975.

educators of young girls, patron of, Oct. 21.

Edward (Prince of Wales), May 4, 1471.

Edward I (England), Jun. 17, 1239; Nov. 16, 1272; Apr. 25, 1284; Oct. 7, 1290; Nov. 17, 1292; Oct. 12, 1297; Jul. 22, 1298; dies, Jul. 7, 1307.

Edward II (England), Apr. 25, 1284; Apr. 27, 1296; Jul. 7, 1307; Feb. 25, 1308; Jun. 24, 1314; Mar. 16, 1322; defeated, Oct. 14, 1322; Sep. 24, 1326; Jan. 20, 1327.

Edward III (England), Nov. 13, 1312; Jan. 20, 1327; Jan. 25, 1327; Jul. 19, 1333; Sep. 5, 1338; Jan. 5, 1340; defeats Calais, Aug. 3, 1347; Apr. 23, 1348; Jan. 11, 1360; Oct. 24, 1360; dies, Jun. 21, 1377; Jun. 22, 1377.

Edward IV (England), Apr. 28, 1442; Mar. 4, 1461; Mar. 29, 1461; Apr. 14, 1471; May 21, 1471; dies, Apr. 9, 1483.

Edward, Prince (England), Aug. 4, 1265; Jul. 1, 1543.

Edward, the Black Prince, Jun. 15, 1330.

Edward the Confessor (England), Jun. 8, 1042.

Edward the Martyr (England): murdered, Mar. 18, 979.

Edward V (England), Apr. 9, 1483; Jun. 26, 1483.

Edward VI (England), Jan. 28, 1547; Feb. 20, 1547; dies, Jul. 6, 1553.

Edward VII (England), Nov. 9, 1841; Mar. 10, 1863; Jan. 22, 1901; Jan. 1, 1902; dies, May 6, 1910.

Edward VIII (England), Jun. 23, 1894; Jan. 20, 1936; May 12, 1936; abdicates, Dec. 10, 1936.

Edwards, Anthony, Jul. 19, 1962.

Edwards, Blake, Jul. 26, 1922.

Edwards, Bob, May 16, 1947.

Edwards, Douglas, Jul. 14, 1917.

Edwards, Edwin Washington, Aug. 7, 1927.

Edwards, Jonathan, Oct. 5, 1703.

Edwards, Vince, Jul. 7, 1928.

Eggar, Samantha, Mar. 5, 1940.

Egypt, Jan. 10, 1883; declares war on Turkey, Nov. 6, 1914; British protectorate declared, Dec. 18, 1914; Feb. 28, 1922; Apr. 26, 1922; first parliament, Mar. 15, 1924; Jul. 30, 1952; declared republic, Jun. 18, 1953; nationalization of land, Dec. 23, 1961; Jan. 4, 1966; May 30, 1967; Apr. 6, 1972; Jan. 18, 1974; peace treaty with Israel, Mar. 26, 1979; Feb. 26, 1980; Apr. 25, 1982.

Egypt, Sultan of, Mar. 15, 1922.

Egyptian Revolution Day (Syria), Jul. 23.

Ehrenberg, Christian, Apr. 19, 1795.

Ehrlich, Paul Ralph, May 29, 1932.

Ehrlichman, John, Mar. 20, 1925; Apr. 30, 1973; Jan. 1, 1975; Feb. 21, 1975.

Eichelberger, Clark M(ell), Jul. 29, 1896.

Eichendorff, Joseph Karl, Mar. 10, 1788.

Eichmann, Adolf, Mar. 19, 1906; May 23, 1960; Apr. 11, 1961; convicted, Dec. 15, 1961.

Eiffel Tower, May 6, 1889.

Eifrel, Alexandre Gustave, Dec. 15, 1832.

Eigen, Manfred, May 9, 1927.

Eighteenth Amendment (U.S. Constitution), Jan. 16, 1920; (Prohibition) revoked, Dec. 5, 1933.

Eighth Air Force, Jan. 27, 1943.

Eighth Army, British, Jan. 24, 1943; Sep. 3, 1943; Jan. 1, 1945.

Eighth of February Revolution (Iraq), Feb. 8.

Eighth Symphony, Nov. 4, 1943.

Eijkman, Christiaan, Aug. 11, 1858.

Eikenberry, Jill, Jan. 21, 1947.

Einstein, Albert, Mar. 14, 1879; Apr. 15, 1912; Oct. 11, 1939.

Einstein at the Beach: premiere, Nov. 21, 1976.

Einthoven, Willem, May 21, 1860.

Eire: named, Dec. 29, 1937.

Eiseley, Loren C(orey), Sep. 3, 1907.

Eisenhower, David, Apr. 1, 1947.

Eisenhower, Dwight D., Oct. 14, 1890; Feb. 6, 1943; Feb. 21, 1943; Jan. 16, 1944; Apr. 28, 1952; inaugurated, Jan. 20 1953; Sep. 24, 1957; May 6, 1960; Jan. 14, 1961; Jan. 17, 1961.

Eisenhower, John Sheldon Doud, Aug. 3, 1922.

Eisenhower, Julie Nixon, Jul. 5, 1948.

Eisenhower, Mamie Doud, Nov. 14, 1896.

Eisenman, Peter, Aug. 11, 1932.

Eisenstaedt, Alfred, Dec. 6, 1898.

Eisenstein, Sergei Mikhailovich, Jan. 23, 1898.

Ekberg, Anita, Sep. 29, 1931.

Ekland, Britt, Oct. 6, 1942.

El Alamein, Battle of, Oct. 23, 1942; Nov. 24, 1942.

El Salvador, Jan. 19, 1921; Jan. 8, 1962; May 24, 1984; Jan. 16, 1992.

El-Majali, Hazza (Jordan): assassinated, Aug. 29, 1960.

Elam, Jack, Nov. 13, 1916.

Elba (Italy), Apr. 11, 1814; French troops land, Jun. 17, 1944.

Elbegdorj, Tsakhiagiin, Apr. 23, 1998.

Elders, Joycelyn, Sep. 7, 1993; Feb. 10, 1998.

Eldfell Volcano, Jan. 23, 1973.

Eldridge, Florence, Sep. 5, 1901.

Eleanor Roosevelt's Birthday (U.S.), Oct. 11; electric chair, Jan. 1, 1889.

electric lighting industry: begins, Sep. 4, 1882.

electric shaver: first patent, Nov. 6, 1923.

Electric Kool-Aid Acid Test: published, Aug. 19, 1968.The electron microscope, Jul. 25, 1941.

Elektra: premiere, Jan. 25, 1909.

Eleventh Amendment: (U.S. Constitution) ratified, Jan. 8, 1798.

Elfheah (Archbishop): murdered, Apr. 19, 1012.

Elgar, Sir Edward William, Jun. 2, 1857.

El as, Jorge Serrano, elected, Jun. 1, 1993.

Elion, Gertrude, Jan. 23, 1918.

Eliot, Charles William, Mar. 20, 1834.

Eliot, Feld, Jul. 5, 1942.

Eliot, George, Nov. 22, 1819.

Eliot, T(homas) S(tearns), Sep. 26, 1888.

Elizabeth (Empress of Russia), Dec. 18, 1709; Jan. 5, 1762.

Elizabeth Cady Stanton Day (U.S.), Nov. 12.

Elizabeth I (England), Sep. 7, 1533; Nov. 17, 1558; crowned, Jan. 15, 1559; May 8, 1559; excommunicated, Feb. 25, 1570; Apr. 4, 1581; dies, Mar. 24, 1603.

Elizabeth II (England), Apr. 21, 1926; Feb. 6, 1952; crowned, Jun. 2, 1953; Jan. 12, 1954; Dec. 1, 1963; May 14, 1965; Jul. 4, 1966; Jul. 1, 1969; Oct. 20, 1973; May 14, 1974; Feb. 6, 1977; Apr. 17, 1982; Mar. 2, 1986.

Elizabeth, Queen of Rumania (Carmen Sylvia), Dec. 10, 1843.

Elizabeth, the Queen Mother, Aug. 4, 1900.

Elizondo, Hector, Dec. 22, 1936.

Elks, Benevolent and Protective Order of: founded, Feb. 16, 1868.

Ellerbee, Linda, Aug. 15, 1944.

Elliman, Yvonne, Dec. 29, 1953.

Ellington, Duke, Apr. 29, 1899.

Ellington, Mercer, Mar. 11, 1919.

Elliot, Bob, Mar. 26, 1923.

Elliott, Cass, Sep. 19, 1941.

Elliott, Sam, Aug. 9, 1944.

Ellis, Havelock, Feb. 2, 1859.

Ellis Island, New York, Jan. 1, 1892; Nov. 12, 1954.

Ellis, Jimmy, Feb. 16, 1970.

Ellis, Perry Edwin, Mar. 3, 1940.

Ellison, Harlan Jay, May 27, 1934.

Ellison, Ralph Waldo, Mar. 1, 1914.

Ellsberg, Daniel, Apr. 7, 1931; Jun. 13, 1971.

Ellsworth, Lincoln, May 12, 1880; May 12, 1926.

Ellsworth, Oliver, Apr. 29, 1745.

Elphin, patron of, Apr. 27.

Elrom, Ephraim, May 23, 1971.

Elsheimer, Adam, Mar. 18, 1578.

Eluard, Paul, Dec. 14, 1895.

Elway, John Albert, Jun. 28, 1960.

Elwes, Cary, Oct. 26, 1962.

Elytis, Odysseus, Nov. 2, 1911.

Emancipation Day (Bahamas), Aug. First Monday.

Emancipation Day (Grenada), Aug. 3.

Emancipation Day (Guyana, St. Lucia, St. Vincent, Turks, Caicos Islands), Aug. 2.

Emancipation Day (Puerto Rico), Mar. 22.

Emancipation Day (Texas), Jun. 19.

Emancipation Day (Tonga), Jun. 4.

Emancipation Edict (Russia), Apr. 3, 1861.

Emancipation Proclamation, Jan. 1, 1863.

Embargo Act (U.S.), Dec. 22, 1807; repealed, Mar. 15, 1808.

embroidery workers, patron of, Aug. 11; Aug. 25.

embryo, donated, Feb. 3, 1984.

embryo transfer, Mar. 10, 1987.

emerald, May intro.

Emergency Banking Relief Act: passed, Mar. 9, 1933.

Emergency Economic Powers Act, Apr. 8, 1988.

Emergency Quota Act, May 15, 1924.

Emergency Relief Appropriation Act, Apr. 8, 1934.

Emergency War Measures Act, Oct. 16, 1970.

Emerson, Faye, Jul. 8, 1917.

Emerson, Keith, Nov. 1, 1944.

Emerson, Ralph Waldo, May 25, 1803.

Emerson, Roy, Nov. 3, 1936.

Emmett, Daniel, Decatur, Oct. 29, 1815.

Emperor's Birthday (Japan), Apr. 29.

Empire Day (Japan), Feb. 11.

Empire State Building, May 1, 1931.

Employee's Day (El Salvador), Aug. 3.

Empress of Britain: sunk, Oct. 2, 1940.

Empress of China, Feb. 22, 1785.

Ems, Punctuation of, Aug. 25, 1786.

endangered wildlife species: treaty, Mar. 2, 1973.

Endangered Species Act, Jun. 15, 1978.

Endara, Guillermo, elected, May 7, 1989.

Endeavor, carries first married couple, Sep. 12, 1992; Jemison, Mae, Sep. 12, 1992.

Enders, John Franklin, Feb. 10, 1897.

engaged couples, patron of, Feb. 14.

Engel, Georgia Bright, Jul. 28, 1948.

Engels, Friedrich, Nov. 28, 1820.

Engineer's Week, Feb. intro.

England, Jan. 20, 1301; Jan. 21, 1528; Jan. 21, 1645; Apr. 12, 1654; Jan. 23, 1668; May 4, 1702; union with Scotland, May 1, 1707; Jan. 4, 1717; Jan. 16, 1756; Jan. 4, 1762; first German air raid, Dec. 21, 1914.

England, Kingdom of, Protector of, Apr. 23.

Engler, John, Oct. 12, 1948.

English Carthusian, Martyrs, May 11.

English Channel: first air crossing, Jan. 7, 1785; first swimmer, Aug. 25, 1875; Apr. 16, 1912; first two-way, non-stop swim, Sep. 22, 1961; first underwater crossing, Jul. 11, 1962.

English Civil War: begins, Aug. 22, 1642; Sep. 2, 1644; Jan. 21, 1645; May 5, 1645.

English language in India, Feb. 17, 1965.

English, Martyrs of the Oates Plot, Jun. 20.

Englund, Robert, Jun. 6, 1949.

Eniwetok Atoll, Nov. 1, 1952.

Eno, Brian, May 15, 1948.

Entebbe Airport (Uganda), Jul. 3, 1976.

Entente Cordiale, Apr. 8, 1904.

Enterprise, U.S.S.: launched, Sep. 24, 1960; Nov. 25, 1961; Jan. 14, 1969.

Entwistle, John, Sep. 10, 1944.

Environmental Protection Agency (EPA), Oct. 2, 1970; Mar. 9, 1983.

Enya (Eithne Ni Bhraonain), May 17, 1961.

Ephron, Nora, May 19, 1941.

Epilepsy Month, National, Nov. intro.

Epiphany, Jan. 6.

Episcopal Chureh: woman priests and bishops, Sep. 16, 1976; first woman priest, Jan. 1, 1977.

Episcopal School Month, Oct. intro.

Epstein, Brian, Sep. 19, 1934.

equal pay for equal work: law signed, Jun. 10, 1963.

Equal Rights Amendment: passed by U.S. Senate, Mar. 22, 1972; ratification vote extended, Oct. 6, 1978.

Equatorial Guinea: independence, Oct. 12, 1968; Nov. 12, 1968; Sep. 29, 1979.

Equus October, Oct. intro.

Erasmus, Desiderius, Oct. 26, 1466.

Erbakan, Necmettin, resigns, Jun. 1, 1997.

Erben, Karel Jaromir, Nov. 7, 1811.

Erdrnan, Paul E., May 19, 1932.

Ereilla y Zuniga, Alonso de, Aug. 7, 1533.

Erhard, Ludwig, Feb. 4, lB97; Oct. 16, 1963.

Erhard, Werner, Sep. 5, 1935.

Erie Canal: construction begins, Jul. 4, 1817; opens, Oct. 26, 1825.

Eriekson, Leif, Oct. 27, 1911.

Eriesson, John, Jul. 31, 1803.

Eriksen, Erik, Oct. 28, 1950.

Eritrea, Jan. 1, 1890; Nov. 14, 1962; Feb. 15, 1975; May 23, 1993.

Eritrean Liberation Front, Feb. 10, 1975.

Erlanger, Joseph, Jan. 5, 1874.

Erne, Frank, May 12, 1902.

Ernst, Max, Apr. 2, 1891.

Ernst, Richard R., Aug. 14, 1933.

Errol Barrow Day (Barbados), Jan. 21.

Ershad, Hossein Mohammed, Dec. 11, 1983.

Ertegilford, Nov. 23, 1892.

Ervin, Sam, Sep. 17, 1896; Feb. 8, 1973.

Erving, Julius Winfield (*Doctor J*), Feb. 22, 1950.

Erzerum, Feb. 16, 1916.

Erzincan (Turkey): earthquake, Dec. 27, 1939.

Esaki, Leo, Mar. 12, 1925.

Escoffier, Georges Auguste, Oct. 28, 1846.

escudo, gold, May 22, 1911.

Esenin, Sergei Aleksandrovich, Oct. 3, 1895.

Eshkol, Levi, Jun. 19, 1963.

Esiason, Norman (*Boomer*), Apr. 17, 1961.

Esposito, Anthony James (*Tony*), Apr. 23, 1944.

Esposito, Phil(ip), Feb. 20, 1942.

Espriella, Ricardo de la, Sep. 5, 1934.

Espy, James Pollard, May 9, 1785.

Esquivel, Juan, Jan. 20, 1918.

Esquivel, Manuel: elected, Dec. 14, 1984.

Essex, David, Jul. 23, 1947.

Establishment of the Republic (Guinea-Bissau), Sep. 24.

Estefan, Gloria, Sep. 1, 1957.

Estevez, Emilio, May 12, 1962.

Estime, Dumarasais, May 10, 1950.

Estonia, Feb. 2, 1920; Mar. 12, 1934; incorporated into U.S.S.R., Aug. 25, 1940; Aug. 20, 1991; Sep. 17, 1991; Jan. 16, 1998.

Estonia Independence Day (Lithuania), Feb. 24.

Estonian ferry, capsizes, Sep. 28, 1994.

Estrada, Erik (Henry Enrique), Mar. 16, 1949.

Estrada, Joseph, elected, May 11, 1998.

Estrada Palma, Tomas, Jul. 9, 1835.

Etaples, Peace of: signed, Nov. 3, 1492.

Ethan Allen: U.S. nuclear submarine, May 6, 1962.

Ethelred II (England), Mar. 18, 979; Apr. 14, 979; Nov. 13, 1002; Apr. 19, 1012.

ether, Oct. 16, 1846.

Etheridge, Melissa, May 29, 1961.

Ethiopia, Apr. 3, 1930; invaded by Italy, Oct. 3, 1935; May 9, 1936; drought, Oct. 28, 1973; Feb. 15,

1975; treaty with U.S.S.R., Nov. 20, 1978; Communist government, Sep. 10, 1984; new constitution, Feb. 1, 1987; treaty with Somalia, Apr. 3, 1988.

Ethiopian New Year and Reunion of Eritrea with Ethiopia, Sep. 11.

Ethiopian resistance: to Italy, May 5, 1936.

Etpison, Ngiratkel, Nov. 2, 1988.

Eucken, Rudolph Christoph, Jan. 5, 1846.

Eugene III (pope), Dec. 1, 1145.

Eugene IV (pope), May 31, 1433; Sep. 4, 1439; Jan. 24, 1446.

Euler, Leonhard, Apr. 15, 1707.

Euler, Ulf Svante von, Feb. 7, 1905.

Euler-Chelpin, Hans Karl August Simon, Feb. 15, 1873.

eunuchs, patron of, Dec. 29.

Euripides, Sep. 23, 480 b.c.

European Coal and Steel Community, Mar. 19, 1951.

European Community, Jan. 1, 1984; Feb. 1, 1985; Jan. 1, 1986; Mar. 2, 1989; Jan. 15, 1992; Jan. 1, 1993.

European economic union, Apr. 18, 1951.

European Economic Community: established, Mar. 25, 1957; Jan. 1, 1958; tariffs abolished, Jun. 28, 1967; Feb. 6, 1970; May 10, 1972; Jan. 1, 1973; Feb. 3, 1978; May 28, 1979; Jan. 1, 1981.

European Free Trade Association, Jan. 4, 1960; Jan. 1, 1984.

European Monetary System, Mar. 13, 1979.

European Parliamentary Assembly, Jun. 7, 1979.

European Research Organization, Jun. 14, 1962.

European Social Charter, Feb. 26, 1965.

European Space Agency, May 30, 1975.

European Union, Dec. 15, 1995.

European War, Jun. 15, 1866.

Eurotunnel, opens, May 6, 1994.

Evacuation Day (British), Apr. 28.

Evacuation Day (Egypt), Jun. 18.

Evacuation Day (Libya), Mar. 28.

Evacuation Day (New York, U.S.), Nov. 25.

Evacuation Day (Syria), Apr. 17.

Evacuation Day (Tunisia), Oct. 15.

Evangelical United Brethren, Nov.

Evans, Alice, Jan. 29, 1881.

Evans, Bergen, Sep. 19, 1904.

Evans, Dale, Oct. 31, 1912.

Evans, Dame Edith, Feb. 8, 1888.

Evans, Linda, Nov. 18, 1942.

Evans, Luther H(arris), Oct. 13, 1902.

Evans, Maurice, Jun. 3, 1901.

Evans, Oliver, Sep. 13, 1755.

Evans, Robert L. *(Bob)*, Mar. 30, 1918 Jun. 29, 1930.

Eve of Epiphany (England). Jan. 5.

Everest, Mt., May 29, 1953; May 25, 1960; May 14, 1978.

Everett, Chad, Jun. 11, 1937.

Everett, Edward, Apr. 11, 1794.

Everly, Don, Feb. 1, 1937.

Everly, Phil, Jan. 19, 1939.

Evers, James Charles, Sep. 11, 1922.

Evers, Medgar, Jul. 2, 1925; murdered, Jun. 12, 1963; De La Beckwith, Byron, Feb. 5, 1994, Mar. 4, 1994.

Evers-Williams, Myrlie, Mar. 17, 1933; Feb. 18, 1995; Mar. 21, 1998.

Evert, Chris, Dec. 21, 1954.

Evita: opens, Jun. 21, 1978.

evolutionism, Jun. 19, 1987.

Evren, Kenan (General), Sep. 10, 1980.

Ewald, Johannes, Nov. 18, 1743.

Ewart-Briggs, Christopher T. E., Jul. 21, 1976.

Ewing, Patrick Aloysius, May 5, 1962.

Ewing, William Maurice, May 12, 1906.

Ewry, Ray, Oct. 14, 1873.

Exaltation of the Holy Cross, Sep. 14.

Exclusion Act, Chinese, May 6, 1882.

exclusionary rule, Jul. 5, 1984.

Exercise Desert Rock, Nov. 1, 1951.

Exorcist: premiere, Dec. 26, 1973.The

Expeditionary Force, American: arrives in France, Jun. 13, 1917.

Expeditionary Force, First U.S. (World War II), Jan. 26, 1942.

Explorer I: launched, Jan. 31, 1958; Mar. 31, 1970.

Expo 70, Mar. 14, 1970.

Extension Homemaker Council Week, National, May intro.

Exxon Corp., Nov. 1, 1972.

Exxon Valdez, Mar. 24, 1989; Mar. 22, 1990.

Eyadema, Etienne, Jan. 13, 1967.

Eyadema, Gnassingbe, Dec. 26, 1937.

Eyck, Jan van, May 6, 1432.

eye transplant, Apr. 22, 1969.

Eye Safety Month, Jul. intro.

Eylan, Battle of, Feb. 7, 1807.

Eyre, Governor Edward John: recalled, Oct. 11, 1865.

Eyskens, Gaston: resigns, Mar. 27, 1961.

F

Fabares, Michelle Marie *(Shelley),* Jan. 19, 1944.

Faber, Sandra M., Dec. 28, 1944.

Faberge, Peter Carl, May 30, 1846.

Fabian, Feb. 6, 1943.

Fabius, Laurent, Jul. 17, 1984; Mar. 20, 1986.

Fabray, Nanette, Oct. 27, 1920.

Fabre, Jean Henri, Dec. 21, 1823.

Fabricius, Hieronymous, May 20, 1537.

Factory Act (Great Britain): passed, Jul. 2, 1819.

Fadiman, Clifton, May 15, 1904.

Faenza, patron of, Feb. 23.

Fahrenheit, Gabriel Daniel, May 14, 1686.

Fair Labor Standards Act, Jun. 25, 1938.

Fairbanks, Charles W., May 11, 1852.

Fairbanks, Charles Warren, Mar. 4, 1905.

Fairbanks, Douglas, Jr., Dec. 9, 1909.

Fairbanks, Douglas, May 23, 1883.

Fairchild, Morgan, Feb. 3, 1950.

Fairclough, Ellen, Jan. 19, 1962.

Fairfax, Thomas, Third Baron Fairfax, Jan. 17, 1612; Jan. 21, 1645.

Fairness Doctrine, Aug. 4, 1987.

Faisal (Saudi Arabia), Nov. 2, 1964; assassinated, Mar. 25, 1975.

Faisal I (Syria), Mar. 11, 1920.

Faisal ibn Musad, Prince, Mar. 25, 1975.

Faisal II (Iraq), Apr. 4, 1939; May 2, 1953.

Faith 7, May 16, 1963; May 16, 1963.

Faithfull, Marianne, Dec. 29, 1946.

Falaise-Argentan Gap, Aug. 20, 1944.

Falana, Lola, Sep. 11, 1943.

Falashas, Jan. 4, 1985.

Faldo, Nick, Jul. 18, 1957.

Falk, Peter, Sep. 16, 1927.

Falkenhayn, General von, Sep. 14, 1914.

Falkirk, Jul. 22, 1298.

Falkland Islands, Jan. 22, 1771; British sovereignty, Jan. 1, 1833; Battle of the, Dec. 8, 1914; seized by Argentina, Apr. 2, 1982; Apr. 25, 1982; May 4, 1982; Argentine troops surrender, Jun. 14, 1982.

Falkopping, Feb. 24, 1389.

Fall, Albert Bacon, Nov. 26, 1861.

Falla, Manuel de, Nov. 23, 1876.

Fallaci, Oriana, Jun. 29, 1930.

Fallersleben, August Heinrich Hoffmann von, Apr. 2, 1798.

Falstaff: portrayal of Sir John Oldcastle, Dec. 12, 1417.

Falwell, Jerry, Aug. 11, 1933.

Family and Medical Leave Act, Feb. 5, 1993.

Family Day (Angola, Sao Tome and Principe), Dec. 25.

Family Day (Canada (Alberta), Feb. 16.

Family Day (Lesotho), Jul. intro.

Family Day (Namibia), Dec. 26.

Family Day (U.S.), Aug. 7.

Family Day, Aug. intro.

Famine disaster, Dec. 3, 1992.

Fan Fair Celebration, Jun. intro.

Faneuil, Peter, Jun. 20, 1700.

Fanfani, Amintore: inaugurated, Apr. 18, 1987.

Fantasia: premiere, Nov. 13, 1940.

The Fantastics: premiere, May 3, 1960.

Faraday, Michael, Sep. 22, 1791.

Faraday, Michael, Sep. 27, 1791.

Farentino, James, Feb. 24, 1938.

Fargo, Donna, Nov. 10, 1949.

Fargo, William George, May 20, 1818.

Farley, Chris, Feb. 15, 1964.

Farley, James A., May 30, 1888.

Farm City Week, National, Nov. intro.

Farm Credit Act, Jun. 16, 1933.

Farm Safety Week, National, Sep. intro.

Farm Workers Union, Sep. 1, 1966.

Farmer, Fannie, Mar. 23, 1857.

Farmer, Frances, Sep. 19, 1914.

Farmer, James Leonard, Jan. 12, 1920.

Farmer, Karen, Dec. 3, 1977.

Farmer, Philip Jose, Jan. 26, 1918.

Farmer's Day (Zambia), Aug. 5.

Farmers' Day (Florida), Oct. intro.

Farnese, Alessandro (Duke of Parma), Aug. 27, 1545.

Farouk I (Egypt), Feb. 11, 1920; Apr. 28, 1936; Jul. 23, 1952.

Farr, Jamie, Jul. 1, 1934.

Farragut, Adm. David, Jul. 5, 1801; May 1, 1862; Aug. 5, 1864.

Farrakhan, Louis, Apr. 8, 1984.

Farrakhan, Louis, May 11, 1933.

Farrell, Edelmiro, Mar. 10, 1944.

Farrell, Eileen, Feb. 13, 1920.

Farrell, James Thomas, Feb. 27, 1904.

Farrell, Mike, Feb. 6, 1939.

Farrell, Suzanne, Aug. 16, 1945.

Farrow, Mia Villiers, Feb. 9, 1945.

Fasci del Combattimento, Mar. 23, 1919.

Fascinating Rhythm, Dec. 1, 1924.

Fascist Charter of Labor, Apr. 21, 1927.

Fascist movement (Italy): founded, Mar. 23, 1919.

Fascist party, Mar. 27, 1927.

Fascists, Apr. 4, 1928.

Fassbinder, Rainer Werner, May 31, 1946.

Fast and Prayer Day (Lesotho, Liberia), Apr. intro.

Fast and Prayer Day (Liberia), Apr. 11.

Fast and Prayer Day (Liberia), Apr. 14.

Fast, Howard, Nov. 11, 1914.

Fatah, al-, Jun. 24, 1983.

Father's Day, Jun. intro; first, Jun. 19, 1910.

Faubus, Orval, Jan. 7, 1910; Sep. 4, 1957; Sep. 30, 1958.

Fauci, Anthony S., Dec. 24, 1940.

Faulkner, Shannon, Aug. 14, 1995.

Faulkner, William (Harrison), Sep. 25, 1897.

Faulkner, William, Dec. 10, 1950.

Fauntroy, Walter E., Feb. 6, 1933.

Faunus, Feb. intro.

Faure, Gabriel Urbain, May 13, 1845.

Faust, Gerald Anthony, Jr. *(Gerry)*, May 21, 1935.

Fawcett, Farrah Leni, Feb. 2, 1947.

Fawkes, Guy, Nov. 5, 1605.

Faye, Alice, May 5, 1915.

Fayette (New York), Apr. 6, 1830.

Fearing, Kenneth Flexner, Jul. 28, 1902.

Feast of Christ of Esquipulas (Guatemala), Jan. 15.

Feast of Fortune (Japan), Jul. 10.

Feast of Our Lady, Mary (Dominican Republic, Peru), Sep. 24.

Feast of SS. Peter and Paul (Chile), Jun. 29.

Feast of SS. Peter and Paul (Italy), Jun. 29.

Feast of SS. Peter and Paul (Malta), Jun. 29.

Feast of SS. Peter and Paul (Spain), Jun. 29.

Feast of St. Charles Borromeo (Andorra), Nov. 4.

Feast of St. George (Spain), Apr. 23.

Feast of St. John (Andorra), Jun. 24.

Feast of St. Maron (Lebanon), Feb. 9.

Feast of St. Matthias, Aug. 9.

Feast of the Annunciation (Liechtenstein), Mar. 25.

Feast of the Assumption into heaven of the Blessed Virgin, Mary, Aug. 15.

Feast of the Finding of the True Cross (Ethiopia), Sep. 27.

Feast of the Redeemer (Venice), Jul. 17.

Feast of the Throne (Morocco), Mar. 3.

Februa, Feb. intro.

Februaritus, Jan. intro.; Feb. intro.

February Revolution: ends, Mar. 1, 1917.

Fechter, Peter: killed at Berlin Wall, Aug. 17, 1962.

federal debt ceiling, U.S., Sep. 29, 1981.

Federal Bureau of Investigation (FBI), May 11, 1972; Apr. 27, 1973; May 8, 1976.

Federal Communications Commission (U.S.), Jun. 14, 1934; Jan. 19, 1961.

Federal Election Campaign Act, May 11, 1976.

Federal Home Loan Bank Act: adopted, Jul. 22, 1932.

Federal Music Project: organized, Aug. 1, 1935.

Federal Radio Commission, Feb. 23, 1927.

Federal Republic of Germany Repetence Day, Nov. 22.

Federal Reserve System, Dec. 23, 1913.

Federal Securities Act, May 27, 1933.

Federal Territory Day (Malaysia), Feb. 1.

Federal Trade Commission: established, Sep. 26, 1914.

Federation of Labor, American, Dec. 8, 1886.

Federation of Rhodesia and Nyasaland, Mar. 29, 1963.

Federov, Sergei, Dec. 13, 1969.

Fedin, Konstantin Aleksandrovich, Nov. 24, 1892.

Fedor I (Russia), May 31, 1557.

Feed Yourself Day (Henin), Dec. 31.

Feiffer, Jules, Jan. 26, 1929; Jun. 17, 1970.

Feinstein, Dianne, Jun. 22, 1933.

Felder, Don(ald William), Sep. 21, 1947.

Feldman, Corey, Jul. 16, 1971.

Feldman, Marty, Jul. 8, 1933.

Feldon, Barbara, Mar. 12, 1941.

Feldshuh, Tovah, Dec. 27, 1952.

Feliciano, Jose, Sep. 10, 1945.

Felipe (Spain), Jan. 30, 1986.

Fell, Norman, Mar. 24, 1925.

Fellini, Federico, Jan. 20, 1920.

Felton, Rebecca, Nov. 21, 1922.

Fenelon, Fania, Sep. 2, 1918.

Fenelon, Francois de Salignac de la Mothe, Aug. 6, 1651.

Fenians, May 6, 1882.

Fenn, Sherilyn, Feb. 1, 1965.

Fenwick, Millicent Hammond, Feb. 25, 1910.

Ferber, Edna, Aug. 15, 1885; Dec. 27, 1927.

Ferdinand (Austria), Apr. 28, 1521.

Ferdinand (Holy Roman Emperor), Dec. 9, 1625; abdicates, Dec. 2, 1848.

Ferdinand I (Austria), Apr. 19, 1793; Mar. 2, 1835.

Ferdinand I (Bohemia), Mar. 10, 1503.

Ferdinand I (Bulgaria), Feb. 26, 1861.

Ferdinand I (Holy Roman Emperor), Mar. 14, 1558; dies, Jul. 25, 1564.

Ferdinand I (Romania), Aug. 24, 1865; dies, Jul. 20, 1927.

Ferdinand II (Holy Roman Emperor), Jul. 9, 1578; May 23, 1618; Aug. 28, 1619; May 22, 1629; dies, Feb. 15, 1637.

Ferdinand II (Naples), Jan. 12, 1810; Nov. 8, 1830.

Ferdinand II (Sicily), Jan. 12, 1848.

Ferdinand III (Castile), Jun. 29, 1236.

Ferdinand III (Holy Roman Emperor), Jul. 13, 1608; Feb. 15, 1637.

Ferdinand of Aragon (Spain), Oct. 18, 1469; Jan. 19, 1497; Dec. 10, 1508; Apr. 5, 1513; dies, Jan. 23, 1516.

Ferdinand of Naples, Jan 2, 1751.

Ferdinand V (Castile), Mar. 10, 1452.

Ferdinand V (Spain): dies, Aug. 10, 1759.

Ferdinand VI (Spain), Sep. 23, 1713.

Ferdinand VII (Spain), Oct. 14, 1784; Mar. 19, 1808; May 1, 1808; Aug. 31, 1823; dies, Sep. 29, 1833.

Ferguson, Maynard, May 4, 1928.

Ferguson, Sarah, Mar. 18, 1986; Jul. 23, 1986.

Ferguson, Sarah, Oct. 15, 1959.

Ferlinghetti, Lawrence, Mar. 24, 1919.

Fermat, Pierre de, Aug. 17, 1601.

Fermi Award, Apr. 5, 1963.

Fermi, Enrico, Sep. 29, 1901.

Ferragamo, Vince, Apr. 24, 1954.

Ferran, Enzo, Feb. 20, 1898.

Ferrante, Arthur, Sep. 7, 1921.

Ferrara, Peace of, Apr. 19, 1428.

Ferraro, Geraldine Anne, Aug. 26, 1935; Jul. 12, 1984.

Ferrer, Jose, Jan. 8, 1912.

Ferrer, MeL, Aug. 25, 1917.

Ferrigno, Lou, Nov. 9, 1952.

Ferry, Bryan, Sep. 26, 1945.

Ferry, Jules Francois Camille, Apr. 5, 1832.

ferrymen, patron of, Feb. 12.

fertilization, in-vitro, Dec. 17, 1985.

Fessenden, William Pitt, Oct. 16, 1806.

Festival of the Tricolor (Italy), May 12.

Fete du Trone (Morocco), Mar. 3.

Fetzer, John Earl, Mar. 25, 1901.

Feuerbach, Ludwig Andreas, Jul. 28, 1804.

Feuillet, Octave, Aug. 11, 1821.

Feydeau, Georges Leon Jules Marie, Dec. 8, 1862.

Feynman, Richard Philips, May 11, 1918.

FFA Week, National, Feb. intro.

FHA/HERO Week, Feb. intro.

fiber-optics system, laser, Feb. 10, 1983.

Fibiger, Johannes A. G., Apr. 23, 1867.

Fichte, Johann, May 19, 1762.

Fiddler on the Roof: premiere, Sep. 22, 1964.

Fidrych, Mark *(The Bird)*, Aug. 14, 1954.

Fiedler, Arthur, Dec. 17, 1894.

Fiedler, Leslie, Mar. 8, 1917.

Field, Cyrus West, Nov. 30, 1819.

Field, Ebbets, Oct. 30, 1956.

Field, Eugene, Sep. 2, 1850.

Field, Marshall, Aug. 18, 1834.

Field, Marshall III, Sep. 28, 1893.

Field, Rachel, Sep. 19, 1894.

Field, Sally Margaret, Nov. 6, 1946.

Field, Winston J., Apr. 13, 1964.

Fielder, Cecil, Sep. 21, 1963.

Fielding, Henry, Apr. 22, 1707.

Fields, Dorothy, Jan. 29, 1966.

Fields, Gracie, Jan. 9, 1898.

Fields, Totie, May 7, 1930.

Fields, W. C., Jan. 29, 1880.

Fiennes, Ralph, Dec. 22, 1962.

Fiennes, Ranulph (Sir), Apr. 11, 1982.

Fierstein, Harvey Forbes, Jun. 6, 1954.

Fiesta de Menendez (Florida), Feb. 13.

Fiesta del Arbol (Spain), Mar. 26.

Fiesta St. Blas (Puerto Rico), Feb. 3.

Fifteenth Amendment (U.S. Constitution): ratified, Mar. 30, 1869.

Fifth Army, U S., Sep. 9, 1943.

Fifth Republic: France, Sep. 28, 1958.

Figueiredo, Joao Baptista de Oliveira, Jan. 15, 1918.

Figueres Ferrer, Jose: inaugurated, Nov. 8, 1953; inaugurated, May 8, 1970.

Fiji Day (Fiji), Oct. intro.

Fiji, Oct. 10, 1874; Oct. 25, 1874; Oct. 10, 1970; Oct. 13, 1970.

Filene, Edward Albert, Sep. 3, 1860.

Fillmore, Abigail, Mar. 13, 1798.

Fillmore, Caroline, Oct. 21, 1813.

Fillmore, Millard, Jan. 7, 1800; Mar. 4, 1849; Jul. 9, 1850.

Finch, Peter, Sep. 28, 1916.

Finding of St. Stephen, Feast of, Aug. 3.

Finian's Rainbow: opens, Jan. 10, 1923.

Finland, patron saint of, Jan. 19.

Finland: ceded to Russia, Sep. 17, 1806; Mar. 21, 1917; independence, Dec. 6, 1917; war with Russia, Jun. 6, 1919; May 25, 1921; Nov. 30, 1939; Apr. 13, 1962; Jan. 15, 1969; Nov. 24, 1972.

Finlandia: premiere, Jul. 2, 1900.

Finlay, Frank, Aug. 6, 1926.

Finley, Martha, Apr. 26, 1828.

Finnbogadottir, Vigdis, Apr. 15, 1930.

Finney, Albert, May 9, 1936.

Finney, John Miller Turpin, Jun. 20, 1863.

Finsen, Niels R., Dec. 15, 1860.

Fire Prevention Week, National, Oct. intro.

The Firebird: premiere, Jun. 25, 1910.

fireside chat: first, Mar. 12, 1933.

Fireside Chat Anniversary Day, Mar. intro.

Fireside Theatre: television debut, Apr. 5, 1949.

Firestone, Harvey Samuel, Dec. 20, 1868.

Firkusny, Rudolf, Feb. 11, 1912.

first female in space: Valentina V. Tereshkova, Jun. 16, 1963.

First Crusade: Ascalon, Aug. 12, 1099.

First Cry of Independence Anniversary of (El Salvador), Nov. 5.

First Navigation Act (England): established, Oct. 9, 1651.

First Opium War, Feb. 23, 1841.

First Postage Stamp, Anniversary of the, May intro.

First Republic Day (Ghana), Jul. 1.

Fischer, Bobby, defeats Spassky, Boris, Nov. 5, 1992.

Fischer, Bobby, Mar. 9, 1943; Sep. 1, 1972.

Fischer, Edmond H., Apr. 6, 1920.

Fischer, Emil Hermann, Oct. 9, 1852.

Fischer, Ernst Otto, Nov. 10, 1918.

Fischer, Hays, Jul. 27, 1881.

Fischer von Erlach, Johann Bernard, Jul. 20, 1656.

Fischer-Dieskau, Dietrich, May 28, 1925.

Fish, Hamilton, Aug. 3, 1808.

Fishburne, Laurence, Jul. 30, 1961.

Fisher, Andrew, Aug. 29, 1862.

Fisher, Carrie Frances, Oct. 21, 1956.

Fisher, Eddie, Aug. 10, 1928.

Fisher, Gail, Aug. 18, 1935.

Fisher, Geoffrey, Dec. 2, 1960.

Fisher, Mary, Apr. 6, 1948.

fishermen and fish dealers, patron of, Nov. 30.

fishermen, patron of, Jun. 29.

fishmongers, patron saint of, Apr. 16.

Fisk, Carlton Ernest, Dec. 26, 1947.

Fisk, James, Apr. 1, 1834. Sep. 24, 1869.

Fisk University, Apr. 4, 1953.

Fiske, Minnie Madern, Dec. 19, 1865.

Fitch, John, Jan. 21, 1743; demonstrates steamboat, Aug. 22, 1787; patents steamboat, Aug. 26, 1791.

Fitch, Val, Mar. 10, 1923.

Fittipaldi, Emerson, Dec. 12, 1946.

Fitzgerald, Barry, Mar. 10, 1888.

Fitzgerald, Edward, Mar. 31, 1809.

Fitzgerald, Ella, Apr. 25, 1918.

Fitzgerald, F(rancis) Scott, Sep. 24, 1896.

Fitzgerald, Geraldine, Nov. 24, 1914.

Fitzgerald, John, Feb. 11, 1863.

Fitzgerald, Zelda, Jul. 24, 1900.

Fitzsimmons, Frank, Apr. 7, 1908; Jul. 8, 1971.

Fiume (Italy), Sep. 12, 1919.

Five Forks, Battle of, Apr. 1, 1865.

Five-Year Plan: inaugurated by U.S.S R., Oct. 1, 1928.

The Fixer, Mar. 8, 1967.

Fixx, James Fuller, Apr. 23, 1932.

Fizeau, Armand, Sep. 23, 1819.

Fjartende, Februar (Denmark), Feb. 14.

Flack, Roberta, Feb. 10, 1940.

flag, U.S. 50-star: flown for first time, Jul. 4, 1960; Jul. 7, 1968.

Flag Day (American Samoa), Apr. 17.

Flag Day (Argentina), Jun. 20.

Flag Day (Finland), Jun. 4.

Flag Day (Haiti), May 18.

Flag Day (Mexico), Feb. 24.

Flag Day (Panama), Nov. 4.

Flag Day (Sweden), Jun. 6.

Flag Day (Turkmenistan), Feb. 19.

Flag Day (U.S.), Jun. intro.; June 14.

Flagg, Fannie, Sep. 21, 1944.

Flagstad, Kirsten, Jul. 12, 1895.

Flamborough Head, Mar. 30, 1406.

flamethrower: first, Feb. 20, 1915.

Flamsteed, John, Aug. 19, 1646.

Flanagan, Edward Joseph, Jul. 13, 1886.

Flanders: British offensive, Jul. 31, 1917; Apr. 9, 1918.

Flanner, Janet, Mar. 13, 1892.

Flannery, Susan, Jul. 31, 1943.

Flatt, Lester Raymond, Jun. 28, 1914.

Flaubert, Gustave, Dec. 12, 1821.

Flaxman, John, Jul. 6, 1755.

Fleck, Sir Alexander, Nov. 11, 1889.

Fleet Financial Corp., Mar. 18, 1987.

Fleetwood, Mick, Jun. 24, 1942.

Fleischmann, Charles Louis, Nov. 3, 1834.

Fleming, Ian, May 28, 1908.

Fleming, John Ambrose, Nov. 29, 1849.

Fleming, Peggy, Jul. 27, 1948.

Fleming, Rhonda, Aug. 10, 1922.

Fleming, Sir Alexander, Aug. 6, 1881; Aug. 27, 1942.

Flemming, Walther, Apr. 21, 1843.

Flensburg (West Germany), May 23, 1945.

Flers-Courcelette, Sep. 15, 1916.

Fletcher, Alice Cunningham, Mar. 15, 1838.

Fletcher, Frank Jack, Apr. 29, 1885.

Fleurus, Jun. 26, 1794.

Flexner, Simon, Mar. 25, 1863.

The Flip Wilson Show: television debut, Sep. 17, 1970.

Flodden Field, Battle of, Sep. 9, 1513.

Flood, Curt(is Charles), Jan. 18, 1938.

Flora, May intro.

Floralia, May intro.

Florence (Italy), Sep. 6, 1512.

Florence, patron of, May 25.

Florentine Militia: created, Dec. 6, 1506.

Flores, Carlos, Facusse sworn in, Jan. 27, 1998.

Flores, Juan Jose, Jul. 19, 1800.

Florey, Howard Walter, Sep. 24, 1898.

Florida (confederate cruiser), Jan. 15, 1863.

Florida Appreciation Month, Aug. intro.

Florida, Apr. 2, 1513; Jun. 3, 1539; Feb. 22, 1819; Mar. 3, 1845; Jan. 10, 1861.

Florio, James J., Aug. 29, 1937.

florists, patron of, Feb. 6.

Flory, Paul J., Jun. 19, 1910.

The Flower Drum Song: premiere, Dec. 1, 1958.

Flower Festival (Japan), Apr. 8.

Flowers, Tiger, Feb. 26, 1926.

fluoridation of drinking water, Jul. 23, 1956.

fluoride, Jun. 16, 1951.

Flutie, Doug(las Richard), Oct. 23, 1962.

Flygare-Carlen, Emilie, Aug. 8, 1807.

Flynn, Elizabeth Gurley, Aug. 7, 1890.

Flynn, Errol, Jun. 20, 1909.

Flynt, Larry Claxton, Nov. 1, 1942; Feb. 8, 1977.

FM radio, Jan. 5, 1940.

FM radio transmission: first demonstration, Nov. 6, 1935.

Fntz, John, Aug. 21, 1823.

Fo, Dario, Mar. 24, 1926.

Foat, Ginny, Jun. 21, 1941.

Foch, Ferdinand, Oct. 2, 1851; May 8, 1918; Aug. 6, 1918.

Foch, Nina, Apr. 20, 1924.

Fodor, Eugene Nicholas, Mar. 5, 1950.

Fodor, Eugene, Oct. 5, 1905.

Fogarty, Anne, Feb. 2, 1919.

Fogel, Robert W., Jul. 1, 1926.

Fogelberg, Dan(iel Grayling), Aug. 13, 1951.

Fogerty, John, May 28, 1945.

Foggia, Battle of, Dec. 2, 1254.

Fokine, Michel, Apr. 26, 1880.

Fokker, Anthony Herman Gerard, Apr. 6, 1890.

Foley, Thomas S., Mar. 6, 1929.

Folger, Henry Clay, Jun. 18, 1857.

Foligno (Italy), patron of, Jan. 24.

Folkestone (England): German raid on, May 25, 1915.

Folklore Day (South, Korea), Feb. 15.

Follett, Ken(neth Martin), Jun. 5, 1949.

Follies of 1907, Jul. 8, 1907.

Folsom, Frank, May 14, 1894.

Folsom, Jim, Jr., Apr. 22, 1993.

Fonda, Bridget, Jan. 27, 1964.

Fonda, Henry, May 16, 1905.

Fonda, Jane, Dec. 21, 1937.

Fonda, Peter, Feb. 23, 1939.

Fonseca, Manuel Deodoro da, Aug. 5, 1829.

Fontaine, Joan, Oct. 22, 1917.

Fontainebleau, Treaty of, Oct. 27, 1807.

Fontanne, Lynn, Dec. 6, 1887.

Fonteyn, Margot, May 18, 1919.

food stamps: first introduced, May 16, 1939.

Food and Drug Administration (FDA), U.S., Sep. 4, 1969; AZT, Mar. 20, 1987; AZT, May 3, 1990; approves DDI, Oct. 10, 1991; cloning, Jan. 19, 1998; approves sucralose, Apr. 1, 1998.

Food for Peace agreement: signed, Aug. 21, 1961.

Food Stamp Act: signed, Aug. 31, 1964.

fools, patron of, Nov. 1.

Foot, Michael, Jul. 23, 1913.

football game: first American, Nov. 6, 1869; first professional game, Aug. 31, 1895; first indoor, Dec. 28, 1902; first interleague, Dec. 12, 1926; first broadcast of pro championship, Dec. 8, 1940; sudden death overtime, Aug. 28, 1955.

Football Association, American Professional: formed, Sep. 17, 1920.

Foote, Andrew Hull, Sep. 12, 1806.

Forbes, (Malcolm) Steve(nson), Jr., Jul. 18, 1947.

Forbes, Kathryn, Mar. 20, 1909.

Forbes, Malcolm Stevenson, Aug. 19, 1919.

forces, Dec. 20, 1989; Jan. 3, 1990; asylum, Dec. 19, 1990; found guilty of drug trafficking, Apr. 9, 1992.

Forcheim, Diet of, Mar. 15, 1077.

Ford, Benson, Jul. 20, 1919.

Ford, Edsel Bryant, Nov. 6, 1893.

Ford, Eileen, Mar. 25, 1922.

Ford, Elizabeth *(Betty)*, Apr. 8, 1918.

Ford, Ford Madox, Dec. 17, 1873.

Ford Foundation, Jan. 15, 1936.

Ford, Gerald, Jul. 14, 1913; Dec. 6, 1973; Aug. 9, 1974; Sep. 8, 1974; Sep. 16, 1974; Mar. 1, 1975; Apr. 18, 1975; Sep. 5, 1975; Sep. 22, 1975; Feb. 17, 1976; Aug. 19, 1976; Jan. 19, 1977.

Ford, Glenn, May 1, 1916.

Ford, Harold, May 20, 1945.

Ford, Harrison, Jul. 13, 1942.

Ford, Henry II, Sep. 4, 1917; Nov. 9, 1960.

Ford, Henry, Jul. 30, 1863; Jul. 19, 1919.

Ford, John, Apr. 17, 1586; Feb. 1, 1895.

Ford Motor Co., Jan. 12, 1914; reincorporated, Jul. 19, 1919; Sep. 13, 1978.

Ford, Ruth Elizabeth, Jul. 7, 1915.

Ford, Susan Elizabeth, Jul. 6, 1957.

Ford, Tennessee Ernie, Feb. 13, 1919.

Ford, Whitey, Oct. 21, 1928.

Ford, William Clay, Mar. 14, 1925.

Ford's Theater, Apr. 14, 1865.

Forefathers' Day (U.S.), Dec. 21.

foreign aid bill: first U.S., Mar. 3, 1812.

Foreign Exchange Market, British: opens, Dec. 15, 1951.

Foreign Language Week, National, Mar. intro.

Foreign Troops Evacuation Day (Lebanon), Dec. 31.

Foreman, George, heavyweight title, Nov. 5, 1994.

Foreman, George, Jan. 10, 1949; Jan. 22, 1973; Oct. 30, 1974.

Forest Hills (New York), Sep. 9, 1968.

Forester, C(ecil) S(cott), Aug. 27, 1899.

foresters, patron of, Jul. 12.

Forman, Milos, Feb. 18, 1932.

Formidable: sunk, Jan. 1, 1915.

Formigny, Battle of, Apr. 15, 1450.

Formosa, Dec. 8, 1949.

Forrest, Edwin, Mar. 9, 1806.

Forrest, George, Dec. 3, 1953.

Forrest, Nathan Bedford, Jul. 13, 1821.

Forrest, Sir John, Aug. 22, 1847.

Forrestal, James V., Feb. 15, 1892; first Secretary of Defense, Sep. 17, 1947.

Forrestal. U.S.S., Jul. 29, 1967.

Forsch, Ken(neth Roth), Sep. 8, 1946.

Forssmann, Werner, Aug. 29, 1904.

Forster, E. M., Jan. 1, 1879.

Forster, Johann George Adam, Nov. 27, 1754.

Forsyth, Alexander John, Dec. 27, 1769.

Forsyth, Frederick, Aug. 25, 1938.

Forsythe, John, Jan. 29, 1918.

Fort Christiana, Delaware, Mar. 29, 1638.

Fort Dearborn: Indian massacre, Aug. 15, 1812.

Fort Duquesne (Pittsburgh), Jul. 9, 1755; Nov. 25, 1758.

Fort Flemalle (Belgium): falls to Germans, Aug. 16, 1914.

Fort Henry, Battle of, Feb. 6, 1862.

Fort Monmouth (New Jersey), Jan. 10, 1946.

Fort Peck Dam, Oct. 24, 1933.

Fortas, Abe, Jun. 19, 1910; Oct. 4, 1965; May 15, 1969.

Fortress of Peter and Paul, Oct. 23, 1917.

Forty, Martyrs of Sebastea, Mar. 10.

41st International Eucharistic Congress, Aug. 1, 1976.

Fosbury, Dick, Mar. 6, 1947.

Fosdick, Harry Emerson, May 24, 1878.

Fosse, Bob, Jun. 23, 1927.

Fossey, Dian, Jan. 16, 1932.

fossils, Feb. 5, 1998.

Foster, Bob, May 24, 1968.

Foster, Jodie, Nov. 19, 1962.

Foster, Preston, Aug. 24, 1901.

Foster, Stephen (Collins), Jul. 4, 1826.

Foucault, Jean Bernard Leon, Sep. 18, 1819.

Fouche, Joseph, May 21, 1759.

Fougeres (France), Mar. 24, 1449.

Foulis, Andrew, Nov. 23, 1712.

Foundation of the German Democratic Republic Day of, Oct. 7.

Foundation of the Republic Day (Somalia), Jul. 1.

Foundation of Workers's Party (North Korea), Oct. intro.

Founders Day (Republic of South Africa), Apr. 6.

Founding Day (Vietnam), Feb. 3.

Founding of Panama City (Panama), Aug. 15.

Founding of Sao Paulo Day (Brazil), Jan. 25.

Founding of the Republic of China (Taiwan), Jan. 1.

Fountain, Peter Dewey (Pete), Jul. 2, 1930.

Four Chaplains Memorial Day (U.S.), Feb. 3.

Four Crowned Ones, Nov. 8.

4-H Week, National, Oct. intro.

Fourier, Francois Marie, Apr. 7, 1772.

Fourier, Joseph Jean Baptiste, Mar. 21, 1768.

Fourneyron, Benoit, Oct. 31, 1802.

Fourteen Holy Helpers, Aug. 8.

Fourteen Points: U.S. peace demands, Nov. 4, 1918.

Fourteenth Amendment (U.S. Constitution): ratified, Jul. 28, 1868.

Fourteenth of July Revolution (Iraq), Jul. 14.

Fourth Republic (France): collapse, Jun. 1, 1958.

Fouss, Robert M(artin), Dec. 16, 1912.

Fowler, Mark Stephen, Oct. 6, 1941.

Fowler, Sir John, Jul . 15, 1817.

Fowler, William A., Aug. 9, 1911.

Fowles, John, Mar. 31, 1926.

Fox, Carol, Jun. 15, 1920.

Fox, Charles James, Jan. 24, 1749.

Fox, Edward, Apr. 13, 1937.

Fox James, May 19, 1939.

Fox, Michael J., Jun. 9, 1961.

Fox, Sir William, Jan. 20, 1812; Jan. 1, 1879.

Fox, Terrance Stanley *(Terry)*, Jul. 28, 1958.

Fox, Virgil, May 3, 1912.

Foxworth, Robert, Nov. 1, 1941.

Foxworthy, Jeff, Sep. 6, 1958.

Foxx, Redd, Dec. 9, 1922.

Foy, Eddie, Mar. 9, 1857.

Foyt, A. J., Jan. 16, 1935.

Fracci, Carla, Aug. 20, 1936.

Fragonard, Jean-Honore, Apr. 5, 1732.

Fragrance Day (U.S.), Mar. 21.

Frampton, Peter, Apr. 22, 1950.

Franca, Celia, Jun. 25, 1921.

France, Jan. 20, 1558; Jan. 17, 1601; allied with Swedes, Jul. 26, 1648; Jan. 23, 1668; May 4, 1702; Jan. 4, 1717; Jan. 22, 1760; annexes Geneva, Apr. 26, 1798; becomes Empire, May 18, 1804; May 5, 1811; war with Spain, Apr. 7, 1823; declares war on Austria, May 3, 1859; Apr. 23, 1860; mobilizes army, Jul. 31, 1914; declares war on

Germany, Aug. 3, 1914; declares war on Austria-Hungary, Aug. 13, 1914; declares war on Turkey, Nov. 5, 1914; Mar. 20, 1915; May 10, 1917; U.S. troops arrive, Jun. 26, 1917; May 6, 1919; Jan. 21, 1930; declares war on Germany, Sep. 3, 1939; Jun. 21, 1940; women vote, Apr. 30, 1945; Fifth Republic, Jan. 8, 1959; first atomic weapon test, Feb. 13, 1960; accord with Mali Federation, Apr. 4, 1960; Jan. 27, 1964; explodes its first hydrogen bomb, Aug. 24, 1968; Jan. 7, 1969; nuclear testing, Sep. 5, 1995, Oct. 2, 1995; 35-hour work week, May 19, 1998.

France, Anatole, Apr. 16, 1844.

France, Bank of: founded, Dec. 24, 1800.

France, patron of, May 30.

France, Republic of, Feb. 24, 1848.

Frances E. Willard Memorial Day (U.S.), Feb. 17.

Frances Willard Day (Minnesota), Sep. 28.

Franche-Conte, Apr. 3, 1559.

Franciosa, Anthony, Oct. 25, 1928.

Francis, Anne, Sep. 16, 1930.

Francis, Arlene, Oct. 20, 1908.

Francis, Connie, Dec. 12, 1938.

Francis Ferdinand (Archduke of Austria), Dec. 18, 1863; Jun. 28, 1914; Jul. 25, 1914.

Francis, Genie, May 26, 1962.

Francis I (Austria): dies, Mar. 2, 1835.

Francis I (France), Sep. 12, 1494; Jan. 1, 1515; Feb. 24, 1525; Aug. 5, 1529; Feb. 1, 1539; Sep. 18, 1544; dies, Mar. 31, 1547.

Francis I (Holy Roman Emperor), Dec. 8, 1708; dies, Aug. 18, 1765.

Francis II (France), Jan. 19, 1544; dies, Dec. 5, 1560.

Francis II (Holy Roman Emperor), Feb. 12, 1768; Mar. 1, 1792.

Francis Joseph I (Austria-Hungary), Aug. 18, 1830.

Francis, Kay, Jan. 13, 1905.

Francis of France (Dauphin), Apr. 24, 1558.

Francis of Padua, May 23, 1474.

Francis, Sir Philip, Oct. 22, 1740.

Francisco Morazan's Birthday (Honduras), Oct. 3.

Franciscus, James, Jan. 31, 1934.

Franck, Cesar Auguste, Dec. 10, 1822.

Franck, James, Aug. 26, 1882.

Franco, Augusto Cautiero, Sep. 29, 1992.

Franco, Francisco, Dec. 4, 1892; Jan. 26, 1936; Jul. 18, 1936; Oct. 1, 1936; Feb. 8, 1937; Feb. 15, 1938; Apr. 15, 1938; Feb. 27, 1939; Mar. 28, 1939; Apr. 1, 1939; Jun. 8, 1973.

Franco, Rafael, Mar. 11, 1936.

Franco-German peace treaty, May 10, 1871.

Franco-German War, May 10, 1871.

Franco-Prussian War, Sep. 2, 1830; Jul. 19, 1870; Jan. 28, 1871.

Frank, Anne, Jun. 12, 1929.

Frank E. Evans: U.S. destroyer, Jun. 3, 1969.

Frank, Ilya Mikhaylovich, Oct. 23, 1908.

Frank, Robert, Nov. 9, 1924.

Frank, Waldo, Aug. 25, 1889.

Frankenheimer, John, Feb. 19, 1930.

Frankenthaler, Helen, Dec. 12, 1928.

Frankfort, Truce of, Apr. 19, 1539.

Frankfurt, Diet at, Sep. 5, 1338.

Frankfurter, Felix, Feb. 15, 1882.

Frankfurter, Felix, Nov. 15, 1882.

Frankland, Edward, Jan. 18, 1825.

Frankland, Percy Faraday, Oct. 3, 1858.

Franklin (Tennessee), Battle of, Nov. 30, 1864.

Franklin, Aretha, Feb. 14, 1967.

Franklin, Benjamin, Birthday, Jan. intro; Jan. 17, 1706; Feb. 3, 1766.

Franklin, Bonnie Gail, Jan. 6, 1944.

Franklin D. Roosevelt Birthday Anniversary (U.S.), Jan. 30.

Franklin, Rosalind, Jul. 25, 1920.

Franklin, Sir John, Apr. 16, 1786.

Franz, Dennis, Oct. 28, 1944.

Franz Josef (Austria-Hungary): Aug. 9, 1830; Dec. 2, 1848. dies, Nov. 21, 1916.

Franz Josef II (Liechtenstein), Aug. 16, 1906; Aug. 26, 1984.

Franz Josef, Pnnce: Birthday of (Liechtenstein), Aug. 16.

Frasch, Herman, Dec. 25, 1851.

Fraser, Brendan, Dec. 3, 1968.

Fraser, Bruce Austin, Feb. 5, 1888.

Fraser, Dawn, Sep. 4, 1937.

Fraser, Donald Mackay, Feb. 20, 1924.

Fraser, Douglas Andrew, Dec. 18, 1916.

Fraser, James (Earle), Nov. 4, 1876.

Fraser, John Malcolm, Mar. 21, 1930; Mar. 21, 1930; inaugurated, Nov. 11, 1975.

Fraser, Lady Antonia, Aug. 27, 1932.

Fraternal Day (Alabama), Oct. intro.

Fratianne, Linda, Aug. 2, 1960.

Fraunhofer, Joseph von, Mar. 6, 1787.

Frazer, Sir James George, Jan. 1, 1854.

Frazetta, Frank, Feb. 9, 1928.

Frazier, Joe *(Smokin' Joe),* Jan. 17, 1944; Feb. 16, 1970, Mar. 8, 1971; Jan. 22, 1973.

Frazier, Walt, Mar. 29, 1945.

Frechette, Louis-Honore, Nov. 16, 1839.

Frederick Charles of Prussia, (Prince), Mar. 20, 1828.

Frederick Henry (Dutch Stadholder), Apr. 23, 1625; Mar. 14, 1647.

Frederick I (Denmark), Oct. 7, 1471.

Frederick I (Prussia), Jul. 11, 1657; Jan. 18, 1701.

Frederick I (Sweden), Apr. 17, 1676; Feb. 29, 1720.

Frederick I Barbarossa (Holy Roman Emperor), Mar. 4, 1152; Jun. 18, 1155; May 28, 1167; Apr. 16, 1175; Jul. 30, 1178; Apr. 3, 1189; drowns, Jun. 10, 1190.

Frederick II (Denmark, Norway), Jul. 1, 1534.

Frederick II (Holy Roman Emperor), Dec. 26, 1194; Dec. 25, 1196; May 17, 1198; Mar. 18, 1229; Mar. 20, 1239; deposed, Jul. 17, 1245; Feb. 18, 1248; dies, Dec. 13, 1250.

Frederick II (Prussia), Jan. 24, 1712; May 31, 1740; Apr. 10, 1741; May 6, 1757.

Frederick III (Denmark and Norway), Mar. 18, 1609.

Frederick III (Germany), Mar. 9, 1888; dies, Jun. 15, 1888.

Frederick III (Holy Roman Emperor), Sep. 21, 1415; Feb. 1, 1440; Jan. 24, 1446; Mar. 19, 1452; dies, Aug. 19, 1493.

Frederick III, Oct. 18, 1831.

Frederick IV (Denmark), Oct. 11, 1671.

Frederick IX (Denmark), Mar. 11, 1899; Apr. 20, 1947; dies, Jan. 15, 1972.

Frederick of Brandenburg, Jan. 18, 1701.

Frederick, Prince of Wales: dies, Mar. 20, 1751.

Frederick the Great (Prussia), Nov. 3, 1760; dies, Aug. 17, 1786.

Frederick V (Denmark and Norway), Mar. 31, 1723.

Frederick VI (Denmark), Jan. 28, 1768.

Frederick VII (Denmark), Oct. 6, 1808; Jan. 20, 1848; dies, Nov. 15, 1863.

Frederick VIII (Denmark), Jun. 3, 1843.

Frederick William I (Prussia): Aug. 15, 1688; dies, May 31, 1740.

Frederick William II (Prussia), Sep. 25, 1744; dies, Nov. 16, 1797.

Frederick William III (Prussia), Aug. 3, 1770; Aug. 17, 1786; Nov. 16, 1797; dies, Jun. 7, 1840.

Frederick William IV (Prussia), Oct. 15, 1795; Jun. 7, 1840; Mar. 28, 1849; dies, Jan. 2, 1861.

Fredericksburg, Battle of: ends, Dec. 13, 1862.

Frederika (Greece), Apr. 18, 1918.

Frederikshamm, Peace of, Sep. 17, 1806.

Fredro, Count Alexander, Jun. 20, 1793.

Free Trade Area of the Americas (FTAA), Apr. 18, 1998.

Freed, Alan, Dec. 15, 1922.

Freedom 7, May 5, 1961.

Freedom Day (Guyana), Aug. 7.

Freedom Day (Guyana), Aug. First Monday.

Freedom Day (Malta), Mar. 31.

Freedom Day (Philippines), Feb. 25.

Freedom Day (St. Lucia, St. Vincent, Turks and Caicos Islands), Aug. 2.

Freedom, Day of (Republic of Surinam), Jul. 1.

Freedom Journal, Mar. 16, 1827.

Freedom Rides, May 4, 1961.

Freedom Shrine Month, Apr. intro.

Freeh, Louis J., Jan. 6, 1950.

Freehan, William Ashley *(Bill)*, Nov. 29, 1941.

Freeman, Edward Augustus, Aug. 2, 1823.

Freeman, Harry Lawrence, Jun. 30, 1903.

Freeman, Mary Eleanor Wilkins, Oct. 31, 1852.

Freeman, Morgan, Jun. 1, 1937.

Freer, Charles Lang, Feb. 25, 1856.

Frege, Gottlob, Nov. 8, 1848.

Frei, Eduard, Jan. 16, 1911; inaugurated, Nov. 3, 1964.

Frei, Eduardo, Mar. 11, 1994.

Fremiet, Emmanuel, Dec. 6, 1824.

Fremont, John Charles, Jan. 21, 1813.

French Academy, Oct. 20, 1928.

French air force, Jan. 13, 1993.

French and Indian War, Sep. 8, 1700; Jul. 9, 1755; Sep. 8, 1755; Jul. 26, 1757; Fort William Henry captured by French, Aug. 9, 1757; Jul. 24, 1758; Nov. 25, 1758; treaty ending, Feb. 10, 1763.

French, Daniel Chester, Apr. 20, 1850.

French Directory: installed, Nov. 2, 1795.

French Equatorial Africa, Jan. 15, 1910.

French Guinea, Mar. 10, 1893.

French Indochina, Feb. 7, 1950.

French, John, Dec. 19, 1915.

French language in Canada, Feb. 7, 1968.

French, Marilyn, Nov. 21, 1929.

French Republic: proclaimed, Sep. 22, 1792.

French Revolution, Jun. 17, 1789; Jul. 14, 1789; Jun. 21, 1791; Mar. 7, 1792; Jun. 20, 1792; Tuilenes stormed, Aug. 10, 1792; Sep. 22, 1792; Jan. 21, 1793; Mar. 7, 1793; Apr. 6, 1793; Jun. 2, 1793; Jul. 28, 1794; Dec. 15, 1794.

French-Indo-Chinese War, Apr. 7, 1951.

Freneau, Philip Morin, Jan. 2, 1752.

Frere, Sir Henry I3artle, Mar. 29, 1815.

Fresenius, Carl Remigius, Dec. 28, 1818.

Fresnel, Augustin, May 10, 1788.

Freteval, Jul. 22, 1194.

Freud, Anna, Dec. 3, 1895.

Freud, Sigmund, May 6, 1856.

Frey, Glenn, Nov. 6, 1948.

Freycinet, Charles Louis de Saulces de, Nov. 14, 1828.

Freytag, Gustav, Jul. 13, 1816.

Frick, Ford, Dec. 19, 1894.

Frick, Henry Clay, Dec. 19, 1849.

Frickie, Janie, Dec. 18, 1950.

Fried, Alfred H., Nov. 11, 1864.

Friedan, Betty, Feb. 4, 1921.

Friedkin, William, Aug. 29, 1939.

Friedman, Eruce, Apr. 26, 1930.

Friedman, Jerome I., Mar. 28, 1930.

Friedman, Milton, Jul. 31, 1912.

Friend, Charlotte, Mar. 11, 1921.

Friend, John (Sir), Apr. 3, 1696.

Friendly, Fred W., Oct. 30, 1915.

Friendship VII, Feb. 20, 1962.

Friml, (Charles) Rudolf, Dec. 7, 1879.

Frisch, Karl von, Nov. 20, 1886.

Frisch, Otto Robert, Oct. 1, 1904.

Frisch, Ragnar, Mar. 3, 1895.

Froebel, Friedrich Wilhelm, Apr. 21, 1872.

Frohman, Charles, Jun. 17, 1860.

From Here to Eternity: premiere, Aug. 5, 1953

From Spiritual to Swing, Dec. 23, 1938.

Fromm, Erich, Mar. 23, 1900.

Fromme, Lynette *(Squeaky)*, Sep. 5, 1975.

Frost, David, Apr. 7, 1939.

Frost, Robert, Mar. 26, 1874.

fruit dealers, patron of, Jul. 25.

Fry, Christopher, Dec. 18, 1907.

Fuad I (Egypt), Feb. 28, 1922; Mar. 15, 1922; Mar. 15, 1924; dies, Apr. 28, 1936.

Fuad Pasha, Ahmed (Egypt), Mar. 26, 1868.

Fuchs, Klaus, Feb. 10, 1950; May 23, 1950.

Fuchs, Leonhard, Jan. 17, 1501.

Fuchs, Sir Vivian, Mar. 2, 1958.

Fuentes, Carlos, Nov. 11, 1928.

Fuentes d'Onoro (Portugal), May 5, 1811.

Fugard, Athol, Jun. 11, 1932.

Fuhr, Grant, Sep. 28, 1962.

Fujimori, Alberto, Apr. 5, 1992.

Fujimori, Alberto, Jul. 28, 1938.

Fujita, Tetsuya Theodore, Oct. 23, 1920.

Fukuda, Takeo, Jan. 14, 1905; elected, Dec. 24, 1976.

Fukui, Kenichi, Oct. 4, 1918.

Fulbright Act, Aug. 1, 1946.

Fulbright, J. William, Apr. 9, 1905.

Fulbright Scholarships: created, Aug. 1, 1946.

Fulford, Battle of, Sep. 20, 1966.

Fulgencio, Batista, Jan. 28, 1955.

Fulghum, Robert, Jun. 4, 1937.

Fuller Brush Co.: incorporated, Sep. 29, 1913.

Fuller, Carl Alfred, Jan. 13, 1885.

Fuller, John Frederick Charles, Sep. 1, 1878.

Fuller, Melville Weston, Feb. 11, 1833.

Fuller, R(ichard) Buckminster, Jul. 12, 1895.

Fuller, Sarah Margaret, May 23, 1810.

Fullmer, Gene, Oct. 23, 1962.

Fulton, Robert, Nov. 14, 1765; Feb. 11, 1809.

Fulton, U.S.S.: first U.S. steam warship, Oct. 29, 1814.

Fundamental Orders of Connecticut: first constitution in America, Jan. 14, 1639.

Funeral Music: first performance, Jan. 22, 1936.

Funicello, Annette, Oct. 22, 1942.

Funk, Casimir, Feb. 23, 1884.

Funk, Isaac, Sep. 10, 1839.

Funny Face: premiere, Nov. 22, 1927.

A Funny Thing Happened: premiere, May 8, 1962.

Funston, Frederick, Nov. 9, 1865.

Funt, Allen, Sep. 16, 1914.

Furetiere, Abbe Antoine, Dec. 28, 1619.

Furness, Elizabeth Mary *(Betty)*, Jan. 3, 1916.

furriers, patron of, Nov. 3.

Furstenberg, Diane (Simone Michelle) von, Dec. 31, 1946.

Future Shock: published, Jul. 29, 1970.

G

Gabelentz, Hans Conon von der, Oct. 13, 1807.

Gabin, Jean, May 17, 1904.

Gable, Clark, Feb. 1, 1901.

Gabon, Feb. 21, 1961.

Gabon Republic: independence, Jul. 15, 1960.

Gabor, Dennis, Jun. 5, 1900.

Gabor, Eva, Feb. 11, 1921.

Gabor, Jolie, Sep. 29, 1896.

Gabor, Magda, Jul. 10, 1917.

Gabor, Zsa Zsa, Feb. 6, 1919.

Gabriel, Peter, May 13, 1950.

Gabrovo's Biannual Comedic Extravaganza (Bulgaria), May intro.

Gadsden, James, May 15, 1788.

Gadsden Purchase, Jun. 30, 1854.

Gaetano, Marcello (Jose), Aug. 17, 1906.

Gagarin, Yuri, Mar. 9, 1934; first man in space, Apr. 12, 1961.

Gagging Act (Great Britain), Dec. 8, 1795.

Gail, Max(well Towbridge), Jr., Apr. 5, 1943.

Gaines, Ernest J., Jan. 15, 1933.

Gainsborough, Thomas, May 14, 1727.

Gairy, Sir Eric (Grenada), Mar. 13, 1979.

Gajdusek, Daniel C., Sep. 9, 1923.

Galanos, James, Sep. 20, 1924.

Galapagos Islands, Feb. 12, 1832.

Galaup, Jean Francois de, Aug. 22, 1741.

Galbraith, John Kenneth, Oct. 15, 1908; May 27, 1958; Jun. 26, 1967.

Galella, Ron, Jan. 10, 1927.

Galicia: Austro-German offensive, May 3, 1915.

Galilee, Sea of, May 5, 1964.

Galileo, Feb. 15, 1564; Jan. 7, 1610; May 9, 1983.

Gallagher, Capt. James, Mar. 2, 1949.

Gallagher, Peter, Aug. 19, 1955.

Gallagher, Rory, Mar. 2, 1949.

Gallatin, Albert, Jan. 29, 1761.

Gallaudet, Thomas Hopkins, Dec. 10, 1787.

Gallaudet University, Mar. 13, 1988.

Galle, Johann, Jun. 9, 1812.

Gallegos, Romulo, Aug. 2, 1884; inaugurated, Feb. 15, 1948.

Gallico, Paul William, Jul. 26, 1897.

Gallipoli Campaign, Apr. 25, 1915; ends, Aug. 21, 1915.

Gallo, Robert, Mar. 23, 1937.

Galloway, Don, Jul. 27, 1937.

Gallup, George Horace, Nov. 18, 1901.

Galois, Evariste, Oct. 25, 1811.

Galsworthy, John, Aug. 14, 1867.

Galt, Alexander Tilloch, Sep. 6, 1817.

Galtieri, Leopoldo, Dec. 30, 1983.

Galton, Sir Francis, Feb. 16, 1822.

Galvani, Luigi, Sep. 9, 1737.

Galveston (Texas): hurricane, Sep. 8, 1900.

Galvin, John R., May 13, 1929.

Galway, James, Dec. 8, 1939.

Gama, Vasco da, Jul. 8, 1497; Nov. 22, 1497; Dec. 25, 1497; Mar. 1, 1498; May 20, 1498.

Gambetta, Leon, Apr. 2, 1838.

Gambia, Nov. 28, 1888; Feb. 18, 1965; admitted to U.N., Sep. 21, 1965; Apr. 23, 1970; Apr. 24, 1970; Feb. 1, 1982.

gambling, casino: legalized in Atlantic City, May 26, 1978.

Gamow, George, Mar. 4, 1904.

Gandamak, Treaty of, May 26, 1879.

Gandhi, Indira, Nov. 19, 1917; Jan. 19, 1966; Jan. 24, 1966; Jan. 19, 1970; Feb. 14, 1970; convicted, Jun. 12, 1975; Jun. 26, 1975; Jan. 18, 1977; Mar. 24, 1977; assassinated, Oct. 31, 1984.

Gandhi, Mahatma, Oct. 2, 1869; Mar. 30, 1919; Feb. 12, 1922; Mar. 10, 1922; Mar. 18, 1922; Feb. 4, 1924; Dec. 22, 1928; Mar. 12, 1930; Jan. 26, 1931; Mar. 4, 1931; Mar. 5, 1931; Jan. 4, 1932; Aug. 9, 1942; assassinated, Jan. 30, 1948.

Gandhi, Rajiv Ratna, Aug. 20, 1944; inaugurated, Oct. 31, 1984; resigns, Nov. 29, 1989; assassinated, May 21, 1991.

Gandhi, Sanjay, Dec. 14, 1946.

Gandhi's Birthday (India), Oct. 2.

Gang of Four: arrested, Oct. 12, 1976.

Ganilau, Penaia, Dec. 5, 1987.

Gann, Ernest K(ellogg), Oct. 13, 1910.

Gannett, Frank Ernest, Sep. 15, 1876.

Gannett, Henry, Augu 24, 1846.

Gans, Joe, May 12, 1902.

Gantt, Harvey, Jan. 28, 1963.

Garagiola, Joseph Henry (Joe), Feb. 12, 1926.

Garand, John Cantius, Jan. 1, 1888.

Garbo, Greta, Sep. 18, 1905.

Garborg, Arne Evenson, Jan. 25, 1851.

Garcia, Andy, Apr. 12, 1956.

Garcia, Carlos: inaugurated, Dec. 30, 1957.

Garcia, Cristina, Jul. 4, 1958.

Garcia Gutierrez, Antonio, Oct. 5, 1813.

Garcia, Jerome John (Jerry), Aug. 1, 1942.

Garcia Lorca, Federico, Jun. 5, 1899.

Garcia Perez, Alain: inaugurated, Jul. 28, 1985.

Garcia-Marquez, Gabriel, Mar. 6, 1928.

Garcilaso de la Vega (El Inca), Apr. 12, 1539.

Gard, Roger Martin du, Mar. 23, 1881.

gardeners, patron of, Feb. 6.

Gardenia, Vincent, Jan. 7, 1922.

Gardner, Ava, Dec. 24, 1922.

Gardner, Erle Stanley, Jul. 17, 1889.

Gardner, John (Champlin), Jul. 20, 1933.

Gardner, John William, Oct. 8, 1912.

Gardner, Randy, Dec. 2, 1958.

Garfield, James, Nov. 19, 1831; inaugurated, Mar. 4, 1881; Jul. 2, 1881; dies, Sep. 19, 1881.

Garfield, John, Mar. 4, 1913.

Garfield, Lucretia, Apr. 19, 1832.

Garfunkel, Art(hur), Oct. 13, 1941; Feb. 14, 1970.

Gargan, William, Jul. 17, 1905.

Garibaldi, Giuseppe, Jul. 4, 1807; May 5, 1860; May 15, 1860; May 27, 1860; Sep. 7, 1860; Jul. 19, 1862.

Garifuna Settlement Day (Belize), Nov. 19.

Garland, Beverly, Oct. 17, 1926.

Garland, Hamlin, Sep. 14, 1860.

Garland, Judy, Jun. 10, 1922.

Garn, Jake, Oct. 12, 1932.

Garner, Erroll, May 15, 1921.

Garner, James, Apr. 7, 1928.

Garner, John Nance (Cactus Jack), Nov. 22, 1868; Mar. 4, 1933.

Garnerin, Andre Jacques: first parachute jump, Oct. 22, 1797.

garnet, Jan. intro.

Garnet, Henry Highland, Dec. 23, 1815.

Garnier, Francis, Jul. 25, 1839.

Garnier, Jean Louis Charles, Nov. 6, 1825.

Garofalo, Janeane, Sep. 28, 1964.

Garr, Teri, Dec. 11, 1945.

Garrett, Leif, Nov. 8, 1961.

Garrick, David, Feb. 19, 1717.

Garriott, Owen K, Jul. 28, 1973.

Garrison, William Lloyd, Dec. 10, 1805; Dec. 12,1805.

Garroway, Dave, Jul. 13, 1913.

Garson, Greer, Sep. 29, 1908.

Garter, Order of the: established, Apr. 23 1348.

Garvey, Marcus (Moziah), Aug. 17, 1887.

Garvey, Steve Patrick, Dec. 22, 1948.

Garvin, Clifton Canter, Jr., Dec. 22, 1921.

Gary, Elbert Henry, Oct. 8, 1846.

gas, chlorine: first use as weapon, Apr. 22, 1915.

gas street-lights: introduced in London, Aug. 16, 1807.

Gashmi, Ahmen Hussein al-: assassinated, Jun. 24, 1978.

Gaskell, Elizabeth Cleghorn, Sep. 29, 1865.

gasoline rationing: begins in U.S., Dec. 1, 1942.

Gasparri, Pietro, May 5, 1852.

Gasperi, Alcide de, Apr. 2, 1881; Jun. 2, 1946; Jan. 28, 1950.

Gassendi, Pierre, Jan. 22, 1592.

Gasser, Herbert Spencer, Jul. 5, 1888.

Gassman, Vittorio, Sep. 1, 1922.

Gastineau, Marcus D. (Mark), Nov. 20, 1956.

Gates III, William (Bill) Henry, Oct. 28, 1955.

Gates, Robert M., Sep. 25, 1943.

Gates, Thomas S., Jr., Apr. 10, 1906.

Gatlin, Larry Wayne, May 2, 1949.

Gatling, Richard Jordan, Sep. 12,1818.

Gatty, Harold, Jul. 1, 1931.

Gaudier-Brzeska, Henri, Oct. 4, 1891.

Gauguin, (Eugene-Henri-) Paul, Jun. 7, 1848.

Gaultier, Jean-Paul, Apr. 24, 1952.

Gauss, Karl Friedrich, Apr. 30, 1777.

Gautier, Dick, Oct. 30, 1937.

Gautier, Theophile, Aug. 30, 1811.

Gavin, James Maurice, Mar. 22, 1907.

Gavin, John, Apr. 8, 1932.

Gavutu, Solomon Islands: captured by U.S., Aug. 8, 1942.

Gay Divorce, Nov. 29, 1932.

Gay, John, Sep. 16, 1685.

Gay-Lussac, Joseph Louis, Dec. 6, 1778.

Gaye, Marvin (Pentz), Apr. 2, 1939.

Gayle, Crystal, Jan. 9, 1951.

Gayle, Helene D., Aug. 16, 1955.

Gaynor, Gloria, Sep. 7, 1949.

Gaynor, Janet, Oct. 6, 1906.

Gaynor, Mitzi, Sep. 4, 1931.

Gayoom, Maumoon Abdul, Dec. 29, 1939.

Gaza, Battle of, Mar. 26, 1917.

Gaza, Second Battle of, Apr. 19, 1917.

Gaza Strip, Dec. 8, 1987.

Gaza, Third Battle of, Nov. 1, 1917; Nov. 7, 1917.

Gazzara, Ben, Aug. 28, 1930.

Geary, Anthony, May 29, 1948.

Gedda, Nikolai, Jul. 11, 1925.

Geddes, Patrick, Oct. 20, 1854.

Geer, Dirk Jan de, Dec. 14, 1870.

Geer, Will, Mar. 9, 1902.

Geffen, David, Feb. 21, 1943.

Gegenbauer, Karl, Aug. 21, 1826.

Gehrig, (Henry) Lou(is), Jun. 19, 1903.

Geiger, (Johannes) Hans Wilhelm, Sep. 30, 1882.

Geiger, Abraham, May 24, 1810.

Geisel, Emesto: inaugurated, Mar. 15, 1974.

Geisel, Theodore Seuss (Dr. Seuss), Mar. 2, 1904.

Geissler, Hanrich, May 26, 1814.

Gelasius II (pope), Apr. 7, 1118.

Gelb, Barbara Stone, Feb. 6, 1926.

Gelbart, Larry, Feb. 25, 1928.

Geldof, Bob, Oct. 5, 1954; Jan. 6, 1985.

Gell-Mann, Murray, Sep. 15, 1929.

Geller, Margaret Joan, Dec. 8, 1947.

Geller, Uri, Dec. 20, 1946.

Gemayel, Amin, Sep. 21, 1982; Sep. 23, 1988.

Gemayel, Bashir, Nov. 10, 1947.

Gemini, May intro; Jun. intro.

Gemini 4, Jun. 3, 1965.

Gemini 5, Aug. 21, 1965.

Gemini 6, Dec. 15, 1965.

Gemini 7, Dec. 4, 1965; Dec. 15, 1965.

Gemini 9, Jun. 6, 1966.

Gemini 10, Jul. 21, 1966.

Gemini 11, Sep. 12, 1966.

Gemini 12, Nov. 11, 1966; Nov. 13, 1966.

gene, Jun. 3, 1970.

gene splicing, Apr. 16, 1987.

gene therapy, May 22, 1989.

General Accounting Office (GAO), Jun. 10, 1921.

General Agreement on Tariffs and Trade (GATT), Dec. 1, 1994.

General Election Day (United States), Nov. intro.

General Electric Co.: incorporated, Apr. 15, 1892; May 21, 1986.

General Electric Theater television debut, Feb. 1, 1953.

General Federation of Women's Clubs Day (U.S.), Apr. 24.

General Motors Corp.: incorporated, Sep. 16, 1908; Apr. 11, 1984.

General Pulaski Memorial Day (Indiana), Oct. 11.

Genet, Jean, Dec. 19, 1910.

genetic engineering, Apr. 16, 1987.

Geneva (Switzerland): theocratic state, Jun. 13, 1541; Apr. 26, 1798; Apr. 11, 1919; Jun. 10, 1969.

Geneva Agreement, Jul. 2, 1976.

Geneva Conventions: updated, Jun. 10, 1977.

Geneva Protocol: signed, Jun. 17, 1925.

Gennes, Pierre-Gilles de, Oct. 24, 1932.

Genoa Conference, Apr. 10, 1922.

Genocide Memorial Day (Armenia), Apr. 24.

Genovese, Vito, Nov. 27, 1879.

Genscher, Hans-Dietrich, Mar. 21, 1927.

Genseric the Vandal, Jul. 15, 455.

Genshi-Sai (Japan), Jan. 3.

Gentlemen Prefer Blondes: premiere, Dec. 8, 1949; premiere, Jul. 15, 1953.

Gentry, Bobbie, Jul. 27, 1942.

Geoffrey, Count of Anjou, Aug. 24, 1113.

Geography Awareness Week (U.S.), Nov. intro.

George I (England), Mar. 28, 1660; May 28, 1660; Aug. 1, 1714; dies, Jun. 12, 1727.

George I (Greece), Dec. 24, 1845; assassinated, Mar. 18, 1913.

George II (England), Nov. 10, 1683; Jun. 12, 1727; Jun. 27, 1743; Oct. 31, 1754; dies, Oct. 25, 1760.

George II (Greece), Jul. 20, 1890; May 1, 1924; Nov. 24, 1935; Apr. 20, 1941; Apr. 1, 1947.

George III (England), Jun. 4, 1738; Mar 20, 1751; Oct. 25, 1760; Oct. 7, 1763; May 4, 1776; Feb. 5, 1811; dies, Jan. 29, 1820.

George IV (England), Aug. 12, 1762; Jan. 29, 1820; Jul. 19, 1821; dies, Jun. 26, 1830.

The George Burns and Gracie Allen Show: television debut, Oct. 12, 1950.

George Cross of Great Britain, Apr. 15, 1942.

George, Henry, Sep. 2, 1839.

George, Lloyd, Dec 7, 1916.

George, Lynda Day, Dec. 11, 1946.

George V (England), Jun. 3, 1865; May 6, 1910; Dec. 2, 1911; Jun. 22, 1921; dies, Jan. 20, 1936; Jan. 22, 1936.

George VI (England), Dec. 14, 1895; May 12, 1936; Dec. 10, 1936; May 9, 1937; Jul. 11, 1946; Oct. 26, 1951; dies, Feb. 6, 1952.

George Washington Carver Day (U.S.), Jan. 5.

George Washington, U.S.S.: first thermonuclear missiles, Nov. 15, 1960.

Georgetown College, Mar. 1, 1815.

Georgia (U.S.): colony formed, Jun. 9, 1732; Jan. 2, 1788; Jan. 27, 1961.

Georgia Day (U.S.), Feb. 12.

Georgia Tech, Oct. 7, 1916.

Georgian Sidres (Uranus), Mar. 13, 1781.

Georgs Phyllis. Jun. 25, 1949.

Gerber, Daniel, May 6, 1898.

Gerber, Frank, Jan. 12, 1873.

Gere, Richard, Aug. 29, 1949.

Gericault, (Jean Louis Andre) Theodore, Sep. 26, 1791.

German air raid: first over England, Jan. 19, 1915; England (World War I), Jan. 31, 1915.

German Democratic Republic. See: Germany, East.

German East Africa (Tanganyika), May 7, 1919.

German High Command: surrenders, May 8, 1945.

German Naval Law, Second, Jun. 12, 1900.

German Unity Day (Germany), Oct. 3.

German Unity, Day of (West Germany), Jun. 17.

German war debt, Apr. 25, 1961.

German-Italian-Japanese pact, Sep. 27, 1940.

Germanic Confederation of 1815: end, Aug. 23, 1866.

Germans, Emperor of, Mar. 28, 1849.

Germantown, Battle of, Oct. 3, 1777; Oct. 4, 1777.

Germany, East, Oct. 7, 1949; Oct. 11, 1949; Jun. 23, 1950; Sep. 20, 1955; Mar. 5, 1950; Nov. 24, 1972; May 11, 1973; U.N. membership, Sep. 15, 1973; Sep. 4, 1974; Nov. 1, 1989; May 18, 1990; Jul. 1, 1990; Oct. 3, 1990.

Germany, Federal Republic of, *See:* Germany, West.

Germany, patron of, Jun. 15.

Germany, Mar. 6, 1629; war with Russia, Jul. 31, 1914; invades France, Aug. 2, 1914; declares war on France, Aug. 3, 1914; declares war on Belgium, Aug. 4, 1914; declares war on Romania, Aug. 28, 1916; unrestricted submarine warfare, Jan. 31, 1917; Greece declares war on, Jul. 2, 1917; occupation, Dec. 1, 1918; Jan. 30, 1933; abrogates Versailles Treaty, Mar. 16, 1935, attacks Poland, Sep. 1, 1939; May 10, 1940; May 15, 1940, prepares to invade Russia, Dec 18, 1940; Apr. 17, 1941; Sep. 6, 1941; declares war on U.S; Dec. 11, 1941; Dec. 11, 1941; Jan. 27, 1943; surrender in Italy, May 2, 1945; divided into occupation zones, Jun. 5, 1945; Mar. 19, 1970; reunited, Oct. 3, 1990.

Germany, West: established, Sep. 20, 1949; May 13, 1965; Jan. 31, 1968;: May 11, 1973; U.N. membership, Sep. 15, 1973; treaty with Czechoslovakia, Dec. 11, 1973; shared monetary economy, May 18, 1990; shared monetary system begins, Jul. 1, 1990; reunited with East Germany, Oct. 3, 1990.

Gernreich, Rudi, Aug 8, 1922.

Geronimo, May 17, 1885.

Gerry, Elbridge, Jul. 17, 1744; Mar. 4, 1809.

Gershwin *Second Rhapsody:* premiere, Jan. 29, 1932.

Gershwin, George, Sep. 26, 1898; Feb. 14, 1918; Feb. 12, 1924;

Dec. 1, 1924; Nov. 22, 1927; Dec. 13, 1928; Oct. 14, 1930; Jan. 29, 1932; Sep. 30, 1935.

Gershwin, Ira, Dec. 6, 1896; Nov. 22, 1927.

Gerstungen, Peace of, Feb. 2, 1074.

Gerulaitis, Vitas, Jul. 26, 1954.

Gesell, Arnold Lucius, Jun. 21, 1880.

Gesner, Konrad von, Mar. 26, 1516.

Gessner, Salomon, Apr. 1, 1730.

Getty, J. Paul, Dec. 15, 1892.

Getty, J. Paul III, Dec. 15, 1973.

Getty Oil Co., Feb. 13, 1984.

Gettysburg Address: delivered, Nov. 19, 1863.

Gettysburg, Battle of: begins, Jul. 1, 1863.

Getz, Stan, Feb. 2, 1927.

Gex, Jan. 17, 1601.

Ghana, Mar. 5, 1952; independence, Jul. 1, 1960; Jun. 16, 1979.

Ghanaian National Liberahon Council, Mar. 1, 1966.

Ghazi I (Iraq): dies, Apr. 4, 1939.

Ghent (Belgium), May 6, 1432.

Ghent and Haarlem, patron of, Oct. 1.

Ghent, Pacification of, Nov. 8, 1576.

Ghent, Treaty of, Dec. 24, 1814.

Gheorghiu-Dej, George, Jun. 2, 1952.

GI Bill of Rights, Jun. 22, 1944.

Giacometti, Alberto, Oct. 10, 1901.

Giaevar, Ivar, Apr. 5, 1929.

Giamatti, A. Bartlett, Apr. 4, 1938.

Giannini, Amadeo Peter, May 6, 1870.

Giannini, Giancarlo, Aug. 1, 1942.

Giannini, Lawrence Mario, Nov. 25, 1894.

Giauque, William Francis, May 12, 1895.

Gibb, Andy, Mar. 5, 1958.

Gibb, Barry, Sep. 1, 1946.

Gibb, Maruice, Dec. 22, 1949.

Gibb, Robin, Dec. 22, 1949.

Gibbon, Edward, Apr. 27, 1737.

Gibbons, Euell, Sep. 8, 1911.

Gibbons, Grnling, Apr. 4, 1648.

Gibbons, James, Jul. 23, 1834.

Gibbs, Josiah Willard, Feb. 11, 1839.

Gibraltar, Aug. 4, 1704; Sep. 10, 1967; Apr. 20, 1982.

Gibran, Khalil, Jan. 6, 1883.

Gibson, Althea, Aug. 25, 1927; Aug. 29, 1950; Jul. 6, 1957.

Gibson, Bob, Jul. 18, 1974.

Gibson, Charles Dana, Sep. 14, 1867.

Gibson, Hoot, Augu. 6, 1892.

Gibson, Kirk, May 28, 1957.

Gibson, Mel, Jan. 3, 1933.

Gibson, Violet, Apr. 7, 1926.

Gibson, William, Mar. 17, 1948.

Giddings, Joshua Reed, Oct. 6, 1795.

Gide, Andre (Paul Guillanume), Nov. 22, 1869.

Gielgud, Sir John, Apr. 14, 1904.

Gierek, Edward, Jan. 6, 1913.

Giffard, Henri, Jan. 8, 1825.

Gifford, Frank, Aug. 16, 1930.

Gifford, Kathie Lee, Aug. 16, 1953.

Gift of the Magi,: Dec. 10, 1905; Apr. 10, 1906.

Gigi: premiere, May 15, 1958.

Gigli, Beniamino Mar. 20, 1890.

Gijon (Spain) captured, Oct. 21, 1937.

Gilbert and Sullivan, Mar. 14, 1885.

Gilbert, Cass, Nov. 24, 1859.

Gilbert, Grove Karl, May 6, 1843.

Gilbert Islands, Battle of the, Nov. 18, 1943; Nov. 23, 1943.

Gilbert, John, Jul. 10, 1897.

Gilbert, Melissa, May 8, 1964.

Gilbert, Sir William Schwenck, Nov. 18, 1836; Nov. 25, 1882; Dec. 7, 1889.

Gilbert, Walter, Mar. 21, 1932.

Gilbert, William, May 24, 1544.

Gild, Fraternity, and Brotherhood House of the Most Glorious and Undivided Trinity of London, patron of, Nov. 23.

Gilder, George, Nov. 29, 1939.

Gildersleeve, Basil Lanneau, Oct. 23, 1831.

Gill, Eric, Feb. 22, 1882.

Gill, Hrendan, Oct. 4, 1914.

Gill, Vince, Apr. 5, 1957.

Gillespie, Dizzy, Oct. 21, 1917.

Gillett, Frederick Huntington, Oct. 16, 1851.

Gillette, King C., Jan. 5, 1855.

Gillette, William (Hooker), Jul. 24, 1855.

Gilley, Mickey Leroy, Mar. 9, 1936.

Gilliam, Terry, Nov. 22, 1940.

Gillooly, Jeff, Jan. 14, 1994.

Gilman, Alfred G., Jul. 1, 1941.

Gilman, Daniel Coit, Jul. 6, 1831.

Gilmer, Elizabeth Meriwhether, Nov. 18, 1870.

Gilmore, Gary, Jan. 17, 1977.

Gilmore, Patrick Sarsfield, Dec. 25, 1829.

Gilmour, David, Mar. 6, 1947.

Gilmour, Doug, Jun. 25, 1963.

Gimbel, Bernard Feustman, Apr. 10, 1885.

The Gin Game: opens, Oct. 6, 1977.

Gingrich, Newt, Jun. 17, 1943; Jan. 7, 1997.

Ginsburg, Allen, Jun. 3, 1926.

Ginsburg, Ruth Bader, Mar. 15, 1933; Aug. 3, 1993.

Ginzberg, Asher, Aug. 5, 1856.

Gioberti, Vincenzo, Apr. 5, 1801.

Giolitti, Giovanni, Oct. 27, 1842.

Giovanni, Nikki, Jun. 7, 1943.

Girardon, Francois, Mar. 17, 1628.

Giraudoux, (Hippolyte) Jean, Oct. 29, 1882.

Giri, V(arahagiri) V(enkata), Aug. 10, 1894.

Girl Crazy: opens, Oct. 14, 1930.

The Girl of the Golden West: premiere, Dec. 10, 1910.

girl scouts, patron of, Jan. 21.

Girl Guides, Mar. 12, 1912.

Girl Scout Birthday, Mar. intro; Mar. 12.

Girl Scout Week, Mar. intro.

Girl Scouts: forerunner, Mar. 12, 1912.

Girls Club Week, National, May intro.

Girls' Fair (Romania), Jul. intro.

Girondist deputies: arrested, Jun. 2, 1793.

Giroux, Robert, Apr. 8, 1914.

Giscard D'Estaing, Valery, Feb. 2, 1926.

Giselle: premiere, Jun. 28, 1841.

Gish, Dorothy, Mar. 11, 1898.

Gish, Lillian, Oct. 14, 1896.

Gissing, George (Robert), Nov. 22, 1857.

Giuliani, Rudolph, May 28, 1944.

Givenchy, Hubert de, Feb. 21, 1927.

Givens, Robin, Nov. 27, 1964.

Gizikis, Phaidon, Nov. 25, 1973.

Gjellerup, Karl Adolf, Jun. 2, 1857.

Glacier National Park: established, May 11, 1910.

gladiolus, Aug. intro.

Gladstone, William Ewart, Dec. 29, 1809.

Glaser, Donald Arthur, Sep. 21, 1926.

Glaser, Paul Michael, Mar. 25, 1942.

Glasgow, Ellen, Apr. 22, 1874.

Glasgow, University of, Jan. 7, 1450.

Glashow, Sheldon L., Dec. 5, 1932.

Glass, Carter, Jan. 4, 1858.

Glass, Charles, Aug. 18, 1987.

The Glass Menagerie: premiere, Mar. 31, 1945.

Glass, Philip, Jan. 31, 1937; Nov. 21, 1976.

Glass, Ron, Jul. 10, 1945.

Glass-Owen Act, Dec. 23, 1913.

glassmakers, patron of, Oct. 18.

Glasspole, Florizel A., Sep. 25, 1909.

Glaucoma Alert Month, Apr. intro.

Glazer, Nathan, Feb. 25, 1923.

glaziers, patron of, Apr. 25.

Glazunov, Aleksandr Konstantinovich, Aug. 10, 1865.

Gleason, Jackie, Feb. 26, 1916.

Gleason, James, May 23, 1886.

Glemp, Jozef, Dec. 18, 1929.

Glencoe Massacre (Scotland), Feb. 13, 1692.

Glenn, John, Jul. 18, 1921; Feb. 20, 1962; Jan. 16, 1998.

Glenn, Scott, Jan. 26, 1942.

Glennon, John Joseph, Jun. 14, 1862.

Gless, Sharon, May 31, 1943.

Glidden, Joseph Farwell, Jan. 18, 1813.

Glinka, Mikhail Ivanovich, Jun. 1, 1804.

Global Forum of Women, Jul. 13, 1992.

Gloriana: premiere, Jun. 8, 1953.

Glorification of the Heroes of Independence, Day of the (Haiti), Jan. 1.

glovemakers, patron of, Jul. 21.

Glover, Danny, Jul. 22, 1947.

Glover, Savion, Nov. 19, 1973.

Gluck, Christoph Willibald (Ritters von), Jul. 2, 1714.

Glueck, (Sol) Sheldon, Aug. 15, 1896.

Gneisenau, Wilhelm August Count Neithardt von, Oct. 27, 1760.

Go Tell It on the Mountain: published, May 18, 1953.

Goa, Mar. 4, 1510; Mar. 14, 1962.

Gobat, Charles A., May 21, 1843.

Gobel, George Leslie, May 20, 1919.

Gobineau, Joseph Arthur, Jul. 14, 1816.

God Bless America, Nov. 11, 1939.

Godard, Jean-Luc, Dec. 3, 1930.

Goddard, John, Jan. 20, 1724.

Goddard, Paulette, Jun. 3, 1911.

Goddard, Robert Hutchings, Oct. 5, 1882; Mar. 16, 1926.

Godey, Louis Antoine, Jun. 6, 1804.

The Godfather premiere, Mar. 15, 1972.

Godfrey, Arthur, Aug. 31, 1903.

Godse, Nathuram, Jan. 30, 1948.

Godunov, Alexander, Nov. 28, 1949; Aug. 23, 1979.

Godwin, Mary Wollstonecraft, Apr. 27, 1759.

Godwin, William, Mar. 3, 1756.

Goebbels, Joseph (Paul), Oct. 29, 1897.

Goeben, Jan. 20, 1918.

Goeppert-Mayer, Marie, Jun. 28, 1906.

Goering, Hermann, Oct. 16, 1946.

Goethals, George Washington, Jun. 29, 1858.

Goethe, Johann Wolfgang von, Aug. 28, 1749.

Goetz, Bernhard, Jun. 16, 1987.

Gogol, Nikolai Vasilyevich, Mar. 31, 1809.

Goheen, Robert Francis, Aug. 15, 1919.

Goiania (Brazil), Sep. 13, 1987.

Golan Heights, Dec. 14, 1981.

Gold, Andrew, Aug. 2, 1951.

Gold Coast (Africa), Feb. 1, 1642; Denmark cedes to Great Britain, Aug. 17, 1850; Feb. 25, 1871; Feb. 2, 1872; Apr. 5, 1873; Jan. 13, 1886.

Gold Coast Colony, Sep. 26, 1901.

Gold Creek (Montana), Sep. 8, 1883.

Gold, Harry, May 23, 1950.

Gold Rush (California), Jan. 24, 1848.

The Gold Rush, Aug. 16, 1925.

gold standard: adopted by U.S., Mar. 14, 1900; Great Britain abandons, Sep. 21, 1930; Apr. 19, 1932.

gold-backed currency, U.S.: eliminated, Mar. 19, 1968.

Goldberg, Arthur Joseph, Aug. 8, 1908. Jul. 20, 1965.

Goldberg, Leonard, Jan. 24, 1934.

Goldberg, Reuben Lucius *(Rube),* Jul. 4, 1883.

Goldberg, Sol Harry, Apr. 20, 1880.

Goldberg, Whoopi, Nov. 13, 1949.

Goldblum, Jeff, Oct. 22, 1952.

Golden Bull, Jan. 10, 1356.

Golden Fleece, Order of, Jan. 10, 1429.

Golden Gate Bridge: opened, May 27, 1937.

Golden, Harry Lewis, May 6, 1902.

Golden Spike: first transcontinental railroad, May 10, 1869.

Goldhaber, Maurice, Apr. 18, 1911.

Goldie, Sir George Dashwood Taubman, May 20, 1846.

Golding, William, Sep. 19, 1911; Oct. 13, 1955.

Goldman, Emma, Jun. 27, 1869.

Goldman, William, Aug. 12, 1931.

Goldmann, Nahum, Jul. 10, 1895.

Goldmark, Karl, May 18, 1830.

Goldmark, Peter Carl, Dec. 2, 1906; Jun. 18, 1948.

Goldoni, Carlo, Feb. 25, 1707.

Goldsboro, Bobby, Jan. 18, 1941.

Goldsmith, Oliver, Nov. 10, 1728.

Goldstein, Joseph L(eonard), Apr. 18, 1940.

Goldwater, Barry (Morris), Jan. 1, 1909.

Goldwyn, Samuel, Aug. 27, 1884.

golf club: first American, Nov. 14, 1888.

Golf Association, U.S.: founded, Dec. 22, 1894.

Golf Hall of Fame, Apr. 9, 1941.

Golgi, Camillo, Jul. 7, 1843.

Golino, Valeria, Oct. 22, 1966.

Gomer Pyle, U.S.M.C: television debut, Sep. 25, 1964.

Gomez Castro, Laureano: inaugurated, Aug. 6, 1950.

Gomez, Jose Miguel, Jul. 6, 1858; inaugurated, Jan. 28, 1909.

Gomez, Juan Vincente, Jul. 24, 1857.

Gomez, Laureano, Jun. 13, 1953.

Gomide, Aloysio Dias (Brazil), Feb. 21, 1971.

Gompers, Samuel, Jan. 27, 1850; Dec. 8, 1886.

Gomulka, Wladyslaw, Feb. 6, 1905.

Goncourt, Edmond Louis Antoine Huot de, May 26, 1822.

Gondoliers: premiere, Dec. 7, 1889.

Gonne, Maude, Dec. 20, 1865.

Gonzalez, Richard Alonzo (Pancho), May 9, 1928.

Good Bears of the World Day, Oct. intro; Oct. 27.

Good Hope, Cape of: discovered, Jul. 8, 1497; Nov. 22, 1497.

Good Neighbor Day, National, Sep. intro.

Good Thief, Mar. 25.

Good Will Day of (South Africa), Dec. 26.

Goodall, Jane (Baroness, Jane Van Lawick-Goodall), Apr. 3, 1934.

Goode, Wilson, Aug. 19, 1938; elected, Nov. 8, 1983.

Gooden, Dwight Eugene, Nov. 16, 1964.

Goodhue, Bertram Grosvenor, Apr. 28, 1869.

Gooding, Cuba, Jr., Jan. 2, 1968.

Goodman, Benny, May 30, 1909; Jan. 16, 1938.

Goodman, Dody, Oct. 28, 1929.

Goodman, Ellen Holtz, Apr. 11, 1941.

Goodman, John, Jun. 20, 1952.

Goodrich, B(enjamin) F(ranklin), Nov. 4, 1841.

Goodrich Co., H. F.: incorporated, May 2, 1912.

Goodrich, Samuel Griswold, Aug. 19, 1793.

Goodson, Mark, Jan. 24, 1915.

Goodyear, Charles, Dec. 29, 1800; Jun. 15, 1844.

Goodyear Tire & Rubber Co.: incorporated, Aug. 29, 1898.

Goolagong, Evonne, Jul. 31, 1951.

Gorbachev, Mikhail S., Mar. 2, 1931; Mar. 11, 1985; Apr. 7, 1985; signs INF treaty, Dec. 8, 1987; Oct. 1, 1988; coup attempt,

Aug. 19, 1991; resigns, Aug. 24, 1991; nuclear weapons treaty, Dec. 8, 1987; meets with John Paul II, Dec. 1, 1989; and Lithuania, Mar. 11, 1990; resigns, Dec. 25, 1991.

Gorbachev, Raisa Maximovna, Jan. 5, 1932.

Gorboduc: first English tragedy, Jan. 18, 1562.

Gordimer, Nadine, Nov. 20, 1923.

Gordon, Charles George, Jan. 28, 1833; Feb. 18, 1884; Jan. 26, 1885.

Gordon, Gale, Feb. 2, 1906.

Gordon, George (Lord Byron), Jan. 22, 1788.

Gordon, Jeff, Aug. 4, 1971.

Gordon, Judah Loeb, Dec. 7, 1830.

Gordon, Richard F., Oct. 5, 1929.

Gordon, Ruth, Oct. 30, 1896.

Gordone, Charles, Oct. 12, 1927.

Gordy, Berry, Jr., Nov. 28, 1929.

Gore, Albert Arnold, Dec. 26, 1907.

Gore, Lesley, May 2, 1946.

Goren, Charles Henry, Mar. 4, 1901.

Gorgas, William Crawford, Oct. 3, 1854.

Goria, Giovanni: inaugurated, Jul. 29, 1987.

Gorin, Igor, Oct. 26, 1909.

Goring, Hermann Wilhelm, Jan. 12, 1893.

Gorki, Maksim, Mar. 16, 1868.

Gorky (U.S.S.R.), Dec. 19, 1986.

Gorlice-Tarnow, Battle of, May 2, 1915.

Gorme, Eydie, Aug. 16, 1932.

Gorran (Cornwall), patron of, Apr. 7.

Gortari, Carlos Salinas de, Apr. 3, 1948.

Gortner, Marjoe, Jan. 14, 1945.

Gosden, Freeman, May 5, 1899.

Goslin, Goose, Oct. 16, 1900.

Gossage, Richard Michael *(Goose),* Jul. 5, 1951.

Gossamer Albatross: first flight across English Channel, Jun. 12, 1979.

Gosse, Sir Edmund William, Sep. 21, 1849.

Gosset, Lou(is), Jr., May 27, 1936.

Gotthard Railway Tunnel, Feb. 29, 1880.

Gotthard Railway: first scheduled trip, Jun. 1, 1882.

Gotti, John, found guilty, Apr. 4, 1992.

Gottschalk, Louis Moreau, May 8, 1829.

Gottwald, Klement, Jul. 3, 1946.

Goudy, Frederic William, Mar. 8, 1865.

Goulart, Joao, Sep. 7, 1961.

Gould, Chester, Oct. 4, 1931.

Gould, Elliott, Aug. 29, 1938.

Gould, Glenn, Sep. 25, 1932.

Gould, Jay, May 27, 1836; Sep. 24, 1869.

Gould, Stephen Jay, Sep. 10, 1941.

Goulding, Ray Walter, Mar. 20, 1922.

Goulet, Robert, Nov. 26, 1933.

Gounod, Charles Francois, Jun. 17, 1818.

Gourand, Henri Joseph Eugene, Nov. 17, 1867.

Gourdine, Meredith, Sep. 26, 1929.

Government of India Act, Dec. 23, 1919; Aug. 2, 1935.

Government Printing Office (U.S.): established, Mar. 4, 1861.

Gowan, Yakubu, Aug. 1, 1966; Jan. 15, 1969; overthrown, Jul. 29, 1975.

Gowdy, Curt, Jul. 31, 1919.

Goya, Mar. 30, 1746.

Gozzi, Count Carlo, Dec. 13, 1720.

Grable, Betty, Dec. 18, 1913.

Grace, Joseph Peter, May 25, 1913.

Grace of Monaco (Grace Keily), Nov. 12, 1929.

Grade, Sir Lew, Dec. 25, 1906.

Graetz, Heinrich, Oct. 31, 1817.

Graf, Steffi, Jun. 14, 1969.

Graf Zeppelin, Oct. 31, 1928; Sep. 1, 1929.

Graham, Bill, Jan. 8, 1931.

Graham, Billy, Nov. 17, 1918.

Graham, Bob, Nov. 9, 1936.

Graham, George, Jul. 7, 1673.

Graham, Katharine (Meyer), Jun. 16, 1917.

Graham, Martha, May 11, 1893.

Graham, Philip Leslie, Jul. 18, 1915.

Graham, Robert, Aug. 19, 1938.

Graham, Sir Robert, Feb. 20, 1437.

Graham, Thomas, Dec. 20, 1805.

Graham, Virginia, Jul. 4, 1912.

Grahame, Kenneth, Mar. 8, 1859.

Gramm, Phil, Jul. 8, 1942.

Gramm-Rudman-Hollings budget-balancing bill, Dec. 12, 1985.

Gramme, Zenobe Theophile, Apr. 4, 1826.

Grammer, Kelsey, Feb. 21, 1945.

gramophone: patent, Feb. 19, 1878.

Granada, Jan. 2, 1492.

Granada, Treaty of: signed, Nov. 11, 1500.

Grand Alliance, Mar. 13, 1813.

Grand Armee, Jun. 22, 1812.

Grand Army (France), Sep. 7, 1812.

Grand Canyon National Park, Feb. 26, 1919.

Grand Canyon Suite: premiere, Nov. 22, 1931.

Grand Central Station, Feb. 2, 1913.

Grand Coulee Dam, May 11, 1950.

Grand Last Day (Japan), Dec. 31.

Grand Ole Opry, Nov. 28, 1925.

Grand Staircase-Escalante National Monument Act, Sep. 18, 1996.

Grand Teton National Park, Feb. 26, 1929.

grandfather clause, May 12, 1898.

Grandmother_s Day (Bulgaria), Jan. 21.

Grandparents' Day, National, Sep. intro.

Grange (Order of Patrons of Husbandry): founded, Dec. 4, 1867.

Grange, Harold Edward (Red), Jun. 13, 1903.

Grange Week, Apr. intro.

Granger, Farley, Jul. 1, 1925.

Granger, Lester B., Sep. 16, 1896.

Granger, Stewart, May 6, 1913.

Granit, Ragnar, Oct. 30, 1900.

Granson, Battle of, Mar. 5, 1476.

Granson, Mar. 3, 1476.

Grant, Cary, Jan. 18, 1904.

Grant, Hugh, Sep. 9, 1960.

Grant, Julia, Jan. 26, 1826.

Grant, Lee, Oct. 31, 1931.

Grant, Ulysses S., Apr. 27, 1822; Feb. 6, 1862, Feb. 16, 1862; Apr. 6, 1862; Apr. 7, 1862; Mar. 9, 1864; Apr. 3, 1865; Apr. 9, 1865; inaugurated, Mar. 4, 1869; Mar. 4, 1871.

Granville-Barker, Harley, Nov. 25, 1877.

Graphics Communication Week, Jan. intro.

Grappelli, Stephane, Jan. 26, 1908.

Grass, Gunter, Oct. 16, 1927.

Grass Month, Apr. intro.

Grasse-Tilly, Marquis de (Francois Joseph), Sep. 13, 1722.

Grassmann, Hermann Gunther, Apr. 15, 1809.

Grasso, Ella Tambussi, May 10, 1919.

Grattan, Henry, Jul. 3, 1746.

Grau San Martin, Ramon: inaugurated, Oct. 10, 1944.

Grau, Shirley Ann, Jul. 8, 1929.

Grav, Raul Cubas, elected, May 10, 1998.

Graves, Peter, Oct. 21, 1911; Mar. 18, 1926.

Graves, Robert Ranke, Jul. 26, 1895.

Gray, Asa, Nov. 18, 1810.

Gray, Elisha, Aug. 2, 1835.

Gray, Hanna Holborn, Oct. 25, 1930.

Gray, Horace, Mar. 24, 1828.

Gray, L. Patrick, May 3, 1972; resigns, Apr. 27, 1973.

Gray, Linda, Sep. 12, 1941.

Gray, Robert, May 10, 1755.

Gray, Thomas, Dec. 26, 1716.

Gray, Tom, Nov. 30, 1974.

Graziano, Rocky, Jun. 7, 1922.

Grease: premiere, Feb. 14, 1972.

Great Blood Purge: Germany, Jun. 30, 1934.

Great Britain, May 1, 1707; Jan. 22, 1760; Jan. 22, 1771; May 5, 1811; suffrage to agricultural workers, Dec. 6, 1822; Jan. 20, 1841; Jan. 20, 1874; Mar. 10, 1900; Jan. 30, 1902; treaty with Masai, Apr. 4, 1911; declares war on Germany, Aug. 4, 1914; declares war on Austria-Hungary, Aug. 12, 1914; declares war on Turkey, Nov. 5, 1914; Mar. 20, 1915; declares war on Bulgaria, Oct. 15, 1915; Jan. 4, 1916; women vote, Dec. 14, 1918; May 6, 1919; first Labour Cabinet, Jan. 22, 1924; Jan. 21, 1930; Jan. 26, 1931; declares war on Germany, Sep.

3, 1939; Dec. 8, 1941; Jan. 1,
1947; Jan. 1, 1948; Jan. 4, 1948;
Jan. 6, 1950; Apr. 5, 1967; Jan.
19, 1968; Jan. 29, 1968; Jan. 1,
1970; Jan. 30, 1972; Mar. 30,
1972; first national referendum,
Jun. 5, 1975; adopts metric
system, Oct. 1, 1995; peace
settlement with Ireland, Apr. 10,
1998.

Great Chicago Fire, Oct. 7, 1871.

Great Depression: begins, Dec. 11,
1930.

Great Easter Rebellion, Apr. 24,
1916.

Great Exhibition, May 1, 1851.

"Great Flood of 1993," Jul. 26, 1993.

Great Northern War, Nov. 30, 1700;
Jul. 8, 1709; ends, Aug. 30,
1721.

Great Seal of the United States:
adopted, Jun. 20, 1782.

Great Society, Jan. 4, 1965.

Great Train Robbery: convictions,
Mar. 26, 1964.

Great Trek, Jan. 17, 1837.

The Great Union: first U.S. flag, Jan.
1, 1776.

Great Western, Apr. 8, 1838.

Great Western Railroad: opened,
Sep. 17, 1838.

Greb, Harry, Feb. 26, 1926.

Greece, patron of, Dec. 6.

Greece: civil war, Mar. 25, 1821;
independence from Turkey, Jan.
27, 1822; Apr. 18, 1897; declares
neutrality, Aug. 31, 1914; Jan.
13, 1916; proclaimed republic,
May 1, 1924; German invasion,
Apr. 6, 1941; Oct. 30, 1944; civil
war, Dec. 3, 1944; coup, Apr.
21, 1967; May 28, 1979; Jan. 1,
1981.

Greek army: surrender, Apr. 23,
1941.

Greek Independence Day (Cyprus),
Mar. 25.

Greek monarchy: abolished, Jun. 1,
1973.

Greek National Day (Greece,
Cyprus), Oct. 28.

Greek Parliament: re-established,
Dec. 9, 1974.

Greeks, May 4, 1041.

Greeley, Horace, Feb. 3, 1811.

Greely, Adolphus Washington, Mar.
27, 1844.

Green, (Henrietta Howland) *Hettie,*
Nov. 21, 1834.

Green, Al, Apr. 13, 1946.

Green, Charles, Jan. 31, 1785.

Green, Julian, Jun. 3, 1971.

Green Monday (Cyprus), Feb. 19.

Green Mountain Boys, May 10, 1775.

Green, William, Mar. 3, 1873.

Greenaway, Kate, Mar. 17, 1846.

Greenberg, Hank, Jan. 1, 1911.

Greene, Graham, Oct. 2, 1904; Mar.
9, 1956.

Greene, Joseph *(Joe),* Sep. 24, 1946

Greene, Lorne, Feb. 12, 1915.

Greene, Nathanael, Aug 7, 1742.

Greene, Robert Bernard, Jr., *(Bob),*
Mar. 10, 1947.

Greenfield, Meg, Dec. 27, 1930.

greengrocers, patron of, Nov. 6.

greenhouse effect, Nov. 21, 1986.

Greenland, May 10, 1921; becomes
part of Denmark, Jun. 5, 1953;
Feb. 1, 1985.

Greenough, Horatio, Sep. 6, 1805.

Greensboro, N.C., Feb. 2, 1960.

Greenspan, Alan, Mar. 6, 1926.

Greenstreet, Sydney, Dec. 27, 1879.

Greenwich, Peace of, Jul. 1, 1543.

Greenwich time: adopted by France,
Mar. 10, 1911.

Greenwood, Lee, Oct. 27, 1942.

Greer, Germaine, Jan. 29, 1939.

Gregorian calendar: introduced, Oct.
4, 1582; Jan. 12, 1701; adopted
by England, Sep. 14, 1752;
adopted by Japan, Jan. 1, 1873;
adopted by Egypt, Jan. 1, 1876;
adopted in Russia, Jan. 31, 1918.

Gregorian chant, Jan. 8, 1904.

Gregorian, Vartan, Apr. 8, 1934.

Gregory, Bettina Louise, Jun. 4,
1946.

Gregory, Cynthia Kathleen, Jul. 8,
1946.

Gregory, Dick, Oct. 12, 1932.

Gregory I (pope), Feb. 3, 590.

Gregory IX (pope), Mar. 20, 1239.

Gregory, Lady Isabella, Mar. 5, 1852.

Gregory VI (pope): deposed, Dec.
20, 1046.

Gregory VII (pope), Jan. 24, 1076;
Jan. 28, 1077; Mar. 7, 1080; Jun.
25, 1080; Jun. 3, 1083.

Gregory XI (pope), Jan. 5, 1371; Jan.
17, 1377.

Gregory XII (pope), Jun. 29, 1408;
Jan. 7, 1502.

Gregory XIII (pope), Jun. 7, 1502;
Feb. 24, 1582.

Gregory XIV (pope), Feb. 11, 1535.

Gregory XV (pope), Jan. 9, 1554.

Gregory XVI (pope), Sep. 18, 1765.

Grenada, Feb. 16, 1967; Mar. 3,
1967; independence, Feb. 7,
1974; invaded by U.S. Marines
and Army Rangers, Oct. 25,
1983.

Grenfell, Sir Wilfred, Feb. 28, 1865

Grenville, George, Oct. 14, 1712;
Apr. 7, 1763

Grenville, William Wyndham, Oct.
25, 1759

Gretzky, Wayne, Jan. 26, 1961.

Greville, Sir Fulke, Oct. 3, 1554.

Grevy, Francois Paul Jules, Aug. 15,
1807.

Grey, Albert Henry George, Nov. 28,
1851.

Grey, Charles, Mar. 13, 1764.

Grey, Jennifer, Mar. 26, 1960.

Grey, Joel, Apr. 11, 1932.

Grey, John de: elected Archbishop
of Canterbury, Dec. 11, 1205.

Grey, Lady Jane: beheaded, Feb. 12,
1554.

Grey, Sir George, Apr. 14, 1812.

Grey, Zane, Jan. 31, 1872.

Griboedov, Aleksandr Sergeievich,
Jan. 15, 1795.

Grieg, Edward (Hagerup), Jun. 15,
1843.

Grier, Pamela Suzette, May 26, 1949.

Grier, Roosevelt *(Rosey),* Jul. 14,
1932.

Griese, Robert Allen *(Bob),* Feb. 3,
1945.

Griffes, Charles Tomlinson, Sep. 7,
1884.

Griffey, Ken, Jr., Nov. 21, 1969.

Griffin, Archie, Aug. 21, 1954.

Griffin, John Howard, Jun. 16, 1920.

Griffin, Merv, Jul. 6, 1925.

Griffin, Robert P., Nov. 6, 1923.

Griffith, Andrew *(Andy)*, Jun. 1, 1926.

Griffith, D. W., Jan. 22, 1875.

Griffith, Emile, Apr. 1, 1961.

Griffith, Melanie, Aug. 9, 1957.

Griffith, Nanci, Jul. 16, 1954.

Griffiths, Martha Wright, Jan. 29, 1912.

Grimké, Charlotte Forten, Aug. 17, 1837.

Grimke, Angelina Emily, Feb. 20, 1805.

Grimke, Sarah Moore, Nov. 26, 1792.

Grimm, Jacob, Jan. 4, 1785.

Grimm, Wilhelm Carl, Feb. 24, 1786.

Grinnel, George Bird, Sep. 20, 1849.

Gris, Carlotta, Jun. 28, 1819.

Gris, Juan, Mar. 23, 1887.

Grissom, Virgil (Gus), Apr. 3, 1926; Mar. 23, 1965.

Grito de Lares, Sep. 23.

Grock (Adrien Wettach), Jan. 10, 1880.

Grodin, Charles, Apr. 21, 1935.

Grofe, Ferde, Mar. 27, 1892; Nov. 22, 1931.

Groh, David Lawrence, May 21, 1939.

Grolier Club: founded, Feb. 5, 1884.

Gromyko, Andrei, Jul. 6, 1909; Apr. 25, 1989.

Gropius, Walter, May 18, 1883.

Grosfontein diamond field, Mar. 4, 1927.

Gross, Michael, Jun. 21, 1947.

Gross, Robert Ellsworth, May 11, 1897.

Grossinger, Jennie, Jun. 16, 1892.

Grosvenor, Melville Bell, Nov. 26, 1901.

Grosz, Karoly, May 22, 1988.

Grote, George, Nov. 17, 1794.

Grotius, Hugo, Apr. 10, 1583.

Groton (Connecticut), Sep. 30, 1954.

Groundhog Day (Canada), Feb. 2.

Groundhog Day (U.S.), Feb. 2.

Grove, Sir George, Aug. 13, 1820.

growth hormone, human: synthesized, Jan. 6, 1967.

Grube, Emil H., Jan. 29, 1896.

Gruber, Franz Xavier, Nov. 5, 1787.

Gruen, Victor (David), Jul. 18, 1903.

Gruenberg, Louis, Jan. 7, 1933.

Gruening, Ernest, Feb. 6, 1887.

Gruenther, Alfred M., Mar. 3, 1899.

Grumman, Leroy Randle, Jan. 4, 1895.

Grunitzky, Nikolas, Jan. 13, 1963.

Guadalcanal, Battle of, Aug. 8, 1942.

Guadalcanal: U.S. land offensive begins, Aug. 7, 1942; naval battle begins, Nov. 12, 1942; battle ends, Nov. 15, 1942; Jan. 15, 1943; Feb. 9, 1943.

Guadalupe Hidalgo, Treaty of, Feb. 2, 1848.

Guadeloupe, May 7, 1902.

Guam: captured by Japanese, Dec. 10, 1941; U.S. naval bombardment begins, Jul 8, 1944; U.S. troops land, Jul. 21, 1944; U.S. regains control, Jul. 27, 1944; recaptured by U.S., Aug. 10, 1944; Aug. 1, 1950, Jan. 23, 1960; Jan. 24, 1972.

Guanacaste Annexation of (Costa Rica), Jul. 25.

Guantanamo, (Cuba): taken by U.S., Jun. 15, 1898

Guantanamo Bay Cuba, Oct. 15, 1943.

Guardian Angels, Feast of the, Oct. 2.

Guardian Angels, Feb. 13, 1979.

Guatemala, Jan. 19, 1921; Apr. 5, 1970; earthquake, Feb. 4, 1976; Dec. 29, 1996.

Guccione, Bob, Dec. 17, 1930.

Guderian, Heinz Wilhelm, Jun. 17, 1888.

Guericke, Otto von, Nov. 20, 1602.

Guernica (Spain), Apr. 26, 1937.

Guerorguiev, Kimon, May 19, 1934.

Guerriere, H.M.S., Aug. 19, 1812.

Guesde, Jules, Nov. 11, 1845.

Guest, Edgar A(lbert), Aug. 20, 1881.

Guest, Judith, Mar. 29, 1936.

Guevara, Che, Jun. 14, 1928; Feb. 24, 1961. dies, Oct. 9, 1967.

Guggenheim, Daniel, Jul. 9, 1856.

Guggenheim, John Simon, Dec. 30, 1867.

Guggenheim, Meyer, Feb. 1, 1828.

Guggenheim Museum of Art: opens, Oct. 21, 1959.

Guggenheim, Peggy, Aug. 26, 1898.

Guiana: part ceded to Spain, Jun. 6, 1801.

Guicciardini, Francesco, Mar. 6, 1483.

guided missile: first submarine launching, Feb. 12, 1947.

Guido, Jose Maria, Mar. 30, 1962.

Guidry, Ron(ald Ames), Aug. 28, 1950.

guilders, patron of, Aug. 11.

Guilford Courthouse, Battle at, Mar. 15, 1781.

Guillén, Nicolás, Jul. 10, 1902.

Guillaume, Charles Edouard, Feb. 15, 1861.

Guillaume, Robert, Nov. 30, 1937.

Guillemin, Roger, Jan. 11, 1924.

Guillon, Treaty of, Jan. 11, 1360.

Guillotin, Joseph Ignace, May 28, 1738.

guillotine, Mar. 7, 1792; first use, Apr. 25, 1792.

Guinea: independence, Oct. 2, 1958; Nov. 12, 1958; Mar. 5, 1960.

Guinean Democratic Party, Anniversary of the (Guinea), May 14.

Guinean Democratic Party, Apr. 3, 1984.

Guinean Independence, Anniversary of (Guinea), Oct. 2.

Guinness, Sir Alec, Apr. 2, 1914; Dec. 18, 1957.

Guise, Duke of (France), Jan. 20, 1558.

Guisewaite, Cathy Lee, Sep. 5, 1950.

Guiteau, Charles J., Jul. 2, 1881.

Guizot, Francois Pierre Guillaume, Oct. 4, 1787.

Gujarat, Battle of, Feb. 21, 1849.

Gulag Archipelago: published, Dec. 28, 1973.

Gulf Corp., Mar. 5, 1984.

Gulflight: sunk, May 1, 1915

Gulick, Luther Halsey, Dec. 4, 1865.

Gullstrand, Allvar, Jun. 5, 1862.

Gumbel, Bryant Charles, Sep. 29, 1948.

Gumbleton, Thomas, Jan. 26, 1930.

Gun-Munro, Sir Sydney Douglas, Nov. 29, 1916.

gunners, patron of, Dec. 4.

Gunpowder Plot, Nov. 5, 1605.

Gunsmoke: television debut, Sep. 10, 1955.

Gunther, John, Aug. 30, 1901.

Gursel, Cemal, May 27, 1960.

Gustav VI Adolf (Sweden), Nov. 11, 1882; Oct. 29, 1950. dies, Sep. 15, 1973.

Gustavus Adolphus Day (Sweden), Nov. 6.

Gustavus I (Sweden), Jun. 7, 1523.

Gustavus II Adolphus (Sweden), Dec. 9, 1594; Oct. 30, 1611; Sep. 17, 1631; Nov. 16, 1632.

Gustavus III (Sweden), Jan. 24, 1746; Aug. 19, 1772; assassinated, Mar. 16, 1792; dies, Mar. 29, 1792.

Gustavus IV Adolphus (Sweden), Nov. 1, 1778; Mar. 29, 1792; Mar. 13, 1806; abdicates, Mar. 29, 1806.

Gustavus V (Sweden), Jun. 16, 1858; Dec. 8, 1907; dies, Oct. 29, 1950.

Guston, Philip, Jun. 27, 1913.

Gutenberg, Johannes, Feb. 23, 1400.

Guthrie, Arlo, Jul. 10, 1947.

Guthrie, Janet, Mar. 7, 1938.

Guthrie, Woody, Jul. 14, 1912.

Guttenberg, Steve, Aug. 24, 1958.

Guttmacher, Alan Frank, May 19, 1898.

Guy Fawkes Day (Great Britain), Nov. 5.

Guyana, May 26, 1966; Sep. 19, 1966; Feb. 23, 1970.

Guynemer, Georges M., Dec. 24, 1894.

Guys and Dolls: premiere, Nov. 24, 1950.

Guys, Ernest Adolphe Hyacinthe Constantin, Dec. 3, 1805.

Guzman Fernandez, Antonio, May 26, 1978.

Gwinear (Cornwall), patron of, Mar. 23.

Gwyn, Nell, Feb. 2, 1650.

Gwynn, Tony, May 9, 1960.

Gwynne, Fred, Jul. 10, 1926.

Gwythian, patron of, Nov. 1.

Gypsy: premiere, May 21, 1959.

H

Haakon VII (Norway), Aug. 3, 1872; Nov. 18, 1905; dies, Sep. 21, 1957.

Haavelmo, Trygve, Dec. 13, 1911.

Habeas Corpus Act (England), May 27, 1679.

Habeas Corpus Constitution (Poland), Jan. 9, 1493.

Haber, Fritz, Dec. 9, 1868.

haberdashers, patron of, Aug. 25.

Habib, Philip Charles, Feb. 25, 1920.

Habibe, Bacharuddin Jusuf, Jun. 25, 1936; May 21, 1998.

Habré, Hissene, overthrown, Dec. 1, 1990.

Habyarimana, Juvenal, Mar. 8, 1937; Apr. 6, 1994.

Hack, Shelley, Jul. 6, 1952.

Hackett, Bobby, Jan. 31, 1915.

Hackett, Buddy, Aug. 31, 1924.

Hackett, Joan, Mar. 1, 1934.

Hackman, Gene, Jan. 30, 1931.

Hadar (Ethinpia), Nov. 30. 1974.

Haddon, Alfred Cort. May 24, 1855.

Hadfield, Sir Rabert Abbott, Nov. 28, 1858.

Hadley, Arthur Twining, Apr. 23, 1856.

Hadley, Henry Kimball, Dec 20, 1871.

Hadrian, Jan. 24, 74.

Haeckel, Emst Hrinrich, Feb. 16, 1834.

Hagar, Sammy, Oct. 13, 1949.

Hagaru (Korea): U.S. occupies, Nov. 15, 1950.

Hagen, Uta, Jun. 12, 1919.

Hagen, Walter, Dec. 21, 1892.

Haggard, Sir Henry Rider, Jun 22, 1856.

Haggard, Merle Ronald, Apr. 6, 1937.

Haggerty, Dan, Nov. 19, 1941.

Hagler, *(Marvelous)* Marvin Nathaniel, May 23, 1952.

Hagman, Larry, Sep. 21, 1931.

Hague, Alliance of the, Jan. 23, 1668.

Hague (Holland), Jan. 29, 1914.

Hague, Treaty of, Dec. 9, 1625.

Hahn, Otto, Mar. 8, 1879.

Hahnemann, Samuel Christian Friedrich, Apr. 10, 1755.

Haidalla, Mohamed Khouna Ould, Dec. 12, 1984.

Haig, Alexander (Meigs), Jr., Dec. 2, 1914.

Haig, Douglas, Jun. 19, 1861; Dec. 19, 1915.

Haile I Selassie (Emperor of Ethiopia), Jul. 23; Apr. 3, 1930; Nov. 2, 1930; exiled, Oct. 3, 1935; address to League of Nations, Jun. 30, 1936; deposed, Sep. 12, 1974.

Hailey, Arthur, Apr. 5, 1920.

Haim, Corey, Dec. 23, 1972.

Hainan Island, Apr. 23, 1950.

Haiphong: bombed, Sep. 22, 1940; Jun. 29, 1966.

Hair: opens, Oct. 29, 1967.

Hair, Jay D., Nov. 30, 1945.

hairdressers, patron of, Aug. 25.

Haise, Fred W. Jr., Apr. 11, 1970.

Haiti: independence, Jan. 1, 1804; Mar. 29, 1804; U.S. occupation, Sep. 16, 1915; May 21, 1968; Haitian refugees, Feb. 3, 1992; refugees returned, May 24, 1992; embargo against, Oct. 19, 1993.

Haka Road, Apr. 20, 1890.

Hakim, Albert, Mar. 16, 1988.

Halas, George, Feb. 2, 1895.

Halberstam, David, Apr. 10, 1934.

Haldane, J(ohn) B(urdon) S(anderson), Nov. 5, 1892.

Haldane, Richard Burdon, Jul. 30, 1856.

Haldeman, H. R., Oct. 27, 1926; Apr. 30, 1973; Jan. 1, 1975; Feb. 21, 1975.

Hale, Alan, Feb. 10, 1892.

Hale, Alan: discovers Hale-Bopp Comet, Jul. 22, 1995.

Hale, Alan, Jr., Mar. 8, 1918.

Hale, Edward Everett, Apr. 3, 1822.

Hale, George Ellery, Jun. 29, 1868.

Hale, Sir Matthew, Nov. 1, 1609.

Hale, Nathan, Jun. 6, 1755; executed, Sep. 22, 1776.

Hale, Sarah Josepha Buell, Oct. 24, 1788.

Halek, Vitezslav, Apr. 5, 1835.

Hales, Stephen, Sep. 7, 1677.

Halevy, Ludovic, Jan. 1, 1834.

Haley, Alex (Palmer), Aug. 11, 1921.

Haley, Bill, Jul. 6, 1925.

Haley, Jack, Aug. 10, 1900.

Half-year Holiday (Hong Kong), Jul. 1.

Halidon Hill, Jul. 19, 1333.

Halifx Gazette, Mar. 23, 1752.

Halifax Resolves, Anniversary of the Signing of (North Carolina), April 12.

Hall, Anthony Michael, Apr. 14, 1968.

Hall, Arsenio, Feb. 12, 1955.

Hall, Asaph, Oct. 15, 1829.

Hall, Charles Martin, Dec. 6, 1863

Hall of Fame for Great Americans, May 30, 1901.

Hall of the Golden Fleece, Oct. 25, 1555.

Hall, Franville Stanley, Feb. 1, 1844.

Hall, Glenn (Mr. Goalie), Oct. 3, 1931.

Hall, Lloyd A., Jun. 20, 1894.

Hall, Sir James, Jan. 17, 1761; Apr. 22, 1887.

Hall, Joyce Clyde, Dec. 29, 1891.

Hall, Marshall, Feb. 18, 1790.

Hall, Monty, Aug. 25, 1924.

Hall, Paul, Aug. 21, 1914.

Hall, Tom T., May 25, 1936.

Hallam, Henry, Jul. 9, 1777.

Halleck, Charles A., Aug. 22, 1900.

Halleck, Henry Wager, Jan. 16, 1815.

Haller, Albrecht von, Oct. 8, 1708; Oct. 16, 1708.

Halley, Edmund, Nov. 8, 1656.

Halley's comet, Mar. 6, 1986.

Hallgrimsson, Jonas, Nov. 16, 1807.

Halliburton, Richard, Jan. 9, 1900.

Halloween, Oct. 31.

Hallstein, Walter, Nov. 17, 1901.

Hallstrom, Ivar Christian, Jun. 5, 1826.

Halsey, William Frederick (Bull), Oct. 30, 1882.

Halsted, William Stewart, Sep. 23, 1852.

Halston, Apr. 23, 1932.

Ham: chimpanzee, Jan. 31, 1961.

Hamadan, Mar. 2, 1917.

Hamadi, Mohammed Shamte (Zanzibar), Jun. 24, 1963.

Hamann, Johann Georg, Aug. 27, 1730.

Hamburg (Germany), May 4, 1942; Jul. 24, 1943.

Hamburger Hill: Vietnam War, May 20, 1969.

Hamdi, Ibrahim al-, Jun. 13, 1974; assassinated, Oct. 11, 1977.

Hamel, Veronica, Nov. 20, 1945.

Hamer, Fannie Lou, Oct. 6, 1917.

Hamill, Mark, Sep. 25, 1952.

Hamill, Pete, Jun. 24, 1935.

Hamilton, Alexander, Jan. 11, 1755; dies, Jul. 11, 1804.

Hamilton, Edith, Aug. 12, 1867.

Hamilton, George, Aug. 12, 1939.

Hamilton, Linda, Sep. 26, 1957.

Hamilton, Margaret, Sep. 12, 1902.

Hamilton, Scott, Aug. 28, 1958.

Hamilton, Thomas, Mar. 13, 1996.

Hamilton, Sir William Rowan, Aug. 4, 1805.

Hamlet: film premiere, Sep. 29, 1948.

Hamlin, Hannibal, Aug. 27, 1809; Mar. 4, 1861.

Hamlin, Harry, Oct. 30, 1951.

Hamlisch, Marvin, Jun. 2, 1944; Jul. 25, 1975.

Hammarskjold, Dag, Jul. 29, 1905; Apr. 7, 1953; killed, Sep. 18, 1961.

Hammer, Armand, May 21, 1898.

Hammerstein, Oscar, May 8, 1847

Hammerstein, Oscar 11, Jul. 12, 1895; Dec. 27, 1927; Dec. 2, 1943; Apr. 19, 1945; Apr. 7, 1949; Dec. 1, 1958.

Hammett, Dashiell, May 27, 1894.

Hammond, James Bartlett, Apr. 23, 1839.

Hamner, Earl Henry, Jr., Jul. 10, 1923.

Hampshire, Susan, May 12, 1942.

Hampton Court Conference, Jan. 14, 1604.

Hampton, Lionel, Apr. 12, 1913.

Hampton Roads, Mar. 8, 1862.

Hampton Roads Conference, Feb. 7, 1865.

Hampton, Wade, Mar. 28, 1818.

Hamstrom (Switzerland), Feb. intro.

Hamsun, Knut, Aug. 4, 1859.

Han, Suyin, Sep. 12, 1917.

Hana, Mar. 13, 1915.

Hana Matsuri (Japan), Apr. 8.

Hanauer, Lee Edward *(Chip)*, Jul. 1, 1954.

Hancock, Herbert Jeffrey *(Herbie)*, Apr. 12, 1940.

Hancock, John, Jan. 12, 1737.

Hancock, Winfield Scott, Feb. 14, 1824.

Handel, George Frederick, Feb. 23, 1685.

Handicapped Awareness Week, National, Oct. intro.

handicapped, discrimination, Apr. 28, 1977.

Handler, Philip, Aug. 13, 1917.

Handlin, Oscar, Sep. 19, 1915.

Hands Across America, May 25, 1986.

Handsel Monday (Scotland), Jan. intro.

Handwriting Day, Jan. intro; Jan. 23.

Handwriting Day (U.S.), Jan. 23.

Handy, Thomas Troy, Mar. 11, 1892.

Handy, W(illiam) C(hristopher), Nov. 16, 1873.

hanging, Jul. 13, 1965.

Hani, Chris, assassinated, Apr. 10, 1993.

Hankow, Mar. 15, 1927.

Hanks, Tom, Jul. 9, 1956.

Hanna, Marcus Alonzo, Sep. 24, 1834.

Hanna, William Denby, Jul. 14, 1910.

Hannah, Daryl, Dec. 19, 1960.

Hanoi: attack on French garrison, Dec. 19, 1946; Jul. 28, 1954; Jun. 29, 1966; Feb. 19, 1972.

Hanotaux, Albert Auguste Gabriel, Nov. 19, 1853.

Hanover: separated from England, Jun. 20, 1837.

Hans Adam (Liechtenstein), Aug. 26, 1984.

Hansberry, Lorraine, May 19, 1930; Mar. 11, 1959.

Hanseatic League, Feb. 24, 1664.

Hansel und Gretel: premiere, Dec. 23, 1893.

Hanson, Howard Harold, Oct. 28, 1896.

Hanson, John, Apr. 3, 1715.

Hansson, Per Albin, Oct. 28, 1885.

Happy Days: television debut, Jan. 15, 1974.

Hapsburg, House of: 600th anniversary celebrated, Dec. 27, 1882.

Hapsburg-Valois Wars, Feb. 24, 1525; Feb. 1, 1539; Feb. 5, 1556; Apr. 3, 1559.

Hapsburgs, Feb. 10, 1364.

Hara, Takashi (Japan): assassinated, Nov. 4, 1921.

Harald Haardraade (King of Norway), Sep. 20, 1066; Sep. 25, 1066.

Haraldson, Olaf, Jul. 29, 1030.

Harburg, E. Y., Apr. 8, 1896.

Hardaway, Anfernee (Penny), Jul. 18, 1971.

Hardecanute (Denmark), Jun. 17, 1040.

Hardecanute (England): dies, Jun. 8, 1042.

Harden, Sir Arthur, Oct. 12, 1865.

Hardenberg, Prince Karl August von, May 31, 1750.

Hardie, Keir, Jan. 13, 1893.

Harding, Chester, Sep. 1, 1792.

Harding, Florence, Aug. 15, 1860.

Harding, Warren G., Nov. 2, 1865; inaugurated, Mar. 4, 1921; dies, Aug. 2, 1923; Aug. 3, 1923.

Hardouin-Mansart, Jules, Apr. 16, 1646.

Hardwick, Elizabeth, Jul. 27, 1916.

Hardwicke, Sir Cedric, Feb. 19, 1893.

Hardy, Oliver, Jan. 18, 1892.

Hardy, Thomas, Jun. 2, 1840.

Hari, Mata, Feb. 9, 1917.

Hari Raya Puasa (Singapore), Jan. 29.

Haring, Bernard, Nov. 10, 1912.

Harkes, John, Mar. 8, 1967.

Harkins, Paul, Apr. 25, 1964.

Harkins, William Draper, Dec. 28, 1873.

Harkness, Rebekah, Apr. 17, 1915.

Harlan, John Marshall, Jun. 1, 1833; May 20, 1899.

Harlem River (New York), Sep. 30, 1877.

Harlow, Jean, Mar. 3, 1911.

Harmel, Pierre, Jul. 27, 1965.

Harmon, Thomas D. (Tom), Sep. 28, 1919.

Harmon, Mark, Sep. 2, 1951.

Harmsworth, Alfred Charles William, Jul. 15, 1865.

Harmsworth, Harold Sidney, Apr. 26, 1868.

Harnack, Adolf von, May 7, 1851.

Harnett, William Michael, Aug. 10, 1848.

Harnick, Sheldon, Sep. 22, 1964.

Harold II (England), Jan. 6, 1066; Sep. 20, 1066; Sep. 25, 1066; killed, Oct. 14, 1066.

Harper, Frances Ellen Watkins, Sep. 24, 1825.

Harper, James, Apr. 13, 1795.

Harper, Valerie, Aug. 22, 1941.

Harper, William Rainey, Jul. 26, 1856.

Harper's Ferry, Oct. 16, 1859.

Harrelson, Woody, Jul. 23, 1961.

Harriman, Edward Henry, Feb. 25, 1848.

Harriman, W(illiam) Averell, Nov. 15, 1891.

Harriman, Pamela, Mar. 20, 1920.

Harrington, Michael, Feb. 24, 1928.

Harrington, Pat, Aug. 13, 1929.

Harris, Barbara, Jan. 24, 1989.

Harris, Chapin Aaron, May 6, 1806.

Harris, Ed, Nov. 28, 1950.

Harris, Elisha, Mar. 5, 1824.

Harris, Emmylou, Apr. 2, 1948.

Harris, Franco, Mar. 7, 1950.

Harris, Frank, Feb. 14, 18,56.

Harris, Fred Roy, Nov. 13, 1930.

Harris, Jean, Feb. 24, 1981.

Harris, Joel Chandler, Dec. 9, 1848.

Harris, Julie, Dec. 2, 1925.

Harris, Louis, Jan. 6, 1921.

Harris, Patricia Roberts, May 31, 1924; Dec. 21, 1976.

Harris, Richard (St. John), Oct. 1, 1930.

Harris, Rosemary, Sep. 19, 1930.

Harris, Sydney Justin, Sep. 14, 1917.

Harris, Townsend, Oct. 3, 1804.

Harris, William Torrey, Sep. 10, 1835.

Harrison, Anna, Jul. 25, 1775.

Harrison, Benjamin, Aug. 20, 1833; inaugurated, Mar. 4, 1889.

Harrison, Caroline, Oct. 1, 1832.

Harrison, Faustino: inaugurated, Mar. 1, 1962.

Harrison, George, Feb. 25, 1943.

Harrison, Gregory, May 31, 1950.

Harrison, Mary (Mamie), Apr. 30, 1858.

Harrison, Rex, May 5, 1908.

Harrison, Ross Granville, Jan. 13, 1870.

Harrison, Wallace Kirkman, Sep. 28, 1895.

Harrison, William Henry, Feb. 9, 1773; Nov. 7, 1811; inaugurated, Mar. 4, 1841; dies, Apr. 4, 1841; Jan. 3, 1951.

Harrods department store: bomb explodes, Dec. 17, 1983.

Harry, Debbie, Jul. 1, 1945.

Harsanyi, John C., May 29, 1920.

Hart, Albert Bushnell, Jul. 1, 1854.

Hart, B(asil) H(enry) Liddell, Oct. 31, 1895.

Hart, Gary Warren, Nov. 28, 1936; May 8, 1987.

Hart, Lorenz, May 2, 1895; Apr. 14, 1937; May 11, 1938.

Hart, Moss, Oct. 24, 1904; Dec. 25, 1940.

Hart, Philip A., Dec. 10, 1912.

Hartack, Bill, Dec. 9, 1932.

Harte, Bret(t), Aug. 25, 1836.

Hartford (Connecticut), May 31, 1639.

Hartke, Vance, May 31, 1919.

Hartley, David, Aug. 30, 1705.

Hartley, Mariette, Jun. 21, 1940.

Hartline, Haldan Keffer, Dec. 22, 1903.

Hartman, David, May 19, 1935.

Hartman, Phil, Sep. 24, 1948.

Hartzenbusch, Juan Eugenio, Sep. 6, 1806.

Harvard College, Oct. 28, 1636.

Harvard, John, Nov. 29, 1607.

Harvard University: medical school, Sep. 25, 1944.

Harvey, Doug, Dec. 19, 1924.

Harvey, Laurence, Oct. 1, 1928.

Harvey, Paul, Sep. 4, 1918.

Harvey, William, Apr. 1, 1578.

Harwell, Ernie, Jan. 25, 1918.

Hasek, Jaroslav, Apr. 30, 1883.

Hashimoto, Ryutaro, Jan. 11, 1995.

Hassam, Childe, Oct. 17, 1859.

Hassan II (Morocco), Jul. 9, 1929; Jan. 2, 1962; Aug. 19, 1972.

Hassan, Mulay (Morocco), Feb. 26, 1961.

Hassel, Odd, May 17, 1897.

Hasselhof, David, Jul. 17, 1952.

Hastenbeck, Jul. 26, 1757.

Hastings: Battle of, Oct. 14, 1066.

Hastings, Warren, Dec. 6, 1732; Feb. 13, 1788; Apr. 23, 1795.

Hatch Act, Mar. 2, 1887; Aug. 2, 1939.

Hatch, Orrin Grant, Mar. 22, 1934.

Hatfield, Mark, Jul. 12, 1922.

hatters, patron of, Nov. 23.

Haughey, Charles, Mar. 10, 1987.

Hauptman, Herbert A(aron), Feb. 14, 1917.

Hauptmann, Gerhart, Nov. 15, 1862.

Haussmann, Georges Eugene, Mar. 27, 1809.

Havana, Feb. 15, 1898.

Have Gun Will Travel: television debut, Sep. 14, 1957.

Havel, Vaclav, Oct. 5, 1936; elected, Dec. 29, 1989; resigns, Jul. 17, 1992; elected, Jan. 26, 1996; re-elected, Jan. 20, 1998.

Havelock, Sir Henry, Apr. 5, 1795.

Havens, Richie, Jan. 21, 1941.

Haverhill Massacre, Aug. 29, 1708.

Havlicek, John, Apr. 8, 1940.

Havlicek, Karl, Oct. 31, 1821.

Havoc, June, Nov. 8, 1916.

Havre (France), Oct. 13, 1914.

Hawaii, Jan. 20, 1887; Feb. 14, 1893; declared U.S. territory, Jul. 6, 1898; first governor, May 14, 1900; admitted to Union, Aug. 21, 1959.

Hawaii Five-O: television debut, Sep. 26, 1968.

Hawaii, Territory of: becomes part of U.S., Jun. 14, 1900.

Hawaiian Islands: annexed by U.S., Aug. 12, 1898; Jun. 14, 1900.

Hawke, Ethan, Nov. 6, 1970.

Hawke, Robert James Lee *(Bob)*, Dec. 9, 1929.

Hawke, Robert, Mar. 5, 1983.

Hawking, Stephen, Jan. 8, 1942.

Hawkins, Paula Fickes, Jan. 24, 1927.

Hawks, Howard, May 30, 1896.

Hawley, Sandy, Sep. 1, 1980.

Hawn, Goldie, Nov. 21, 1945.

Haworth, Sir Walter N., Mar. 19, 1883.

hawthorn, May intro.

Hawthorne, Nathaniel, Jul. 4, 1804.

Hay, John, Oct. 8, 1838.

Hay-Pauncefote Treaty, Nov. 18, 1901.

Hayakawa, Samuel Ichiye, Jul. 18, 1906.

Hayden, Carl Trumbull, Oct. 2, 1877; Feb. 19, 1962.

Hayden, Thomas Emmett *(Tom)*, Dec. 11, 1939.

Hayden, Melissa, Apr. 25, 1923.

Hayden, Sterling, Mar. 26, 1916.

Haydn, Joseph, Mar. 31, 1732; Jun. 9, 1951.

Hayek, Friedrich August von, May 8, 1899.

Hayes, Gabby, May 7, 1885.

Hayes, Helen, Oct. 10, 1900.

Hayes, Isaac, Aug. 20, 1942.

Hayes, Janet Gray, Nov. 6, 1974.

Hayes, Lucy Webb, Aug. 28, 1831.

Hayes, Roland, Jun. 3, 1887.

Hayes, Rutherford B., Oct. 4, 1822; Mar. 2, 1877; inaugurated, Mar. 4, 1877.

Hayes, Wayne Woodrow *(Woody)*, Feb. 14, 1913.

Hayes, Woody, Dec. 30, 1978.

Haymarket Riot, May 4, 1886.

Haymarket Theater, Apr. 9, 1705; Jan. 3, 1895.

Haymes, Richard *(Dick)*, Sep. 13, 1917.

Haynes, Elwood, Oct. 14, 1857.

Haynes, George Edmund, May 11, 1880.

Haynsworth, Clement Furman, Jr., Oct. 30, 1912.

Hays, Anna Mae, Jun. 11, 1970.

Hays, (Lawrence) Brooks, Aug. 9, 1898.

Hayward, Brooke, Jul. 5, 1937.

Hayward, George, Mar. 9, 1791.

Hayward, Leland, Sep. 13, 1902.

Hayward, Susan, Jun . 30, 1919.

Hayworth, Rita, Oct. 17, 1918.

Hazelwood, Joseph, guilty of negligence, Mar. 22, 1990.

Hazen, Aldrich, arrested for spying, Feb. 20, 1994.

Hazen, Maria, arrested for spying, Feb. 20, 1994.

Hazlitt, William, Apr. 10, 1778.

Head, Edith, Oct. 28, 1907.

health insurance (universal), Apr. 12, 1988.

Healy, George Peter Alexander, Jul. 15, 1813.

Healy, Timothy Michael, May 17, 1855.

Heaney, Seamus, Apr. 13, 1939.

Heard, John, Mar. 7, 1946.

Hearn, Lafcadio, Jun. 27, 1850.

Hearns, Thomas *(Tommy)*, Oct. 18, 1958.

Hearst, David W., Dec. 2, 1916.

Hearst, Millicent Wilson, Jul. 16, 1882.

Hearst, Patricia, Feb. 20, 1954. Feb 4, 1974; Sep. 18, 1975; Mar. 20, 1976.

Hearst, William Randolph, Apr. 29, 1863.

Hearst, William Randolph, Jr., Jan. 27, 1908.

heart bypass pump, May 17, 1966.

heart-liver transplant, Feb. 14, 1984.

heart transplant: first successful, Dec. 3, 1967.

Heartbreak Hotel, Jan. 10, 1956.

heartpumping device, Oct. 27, 1963.

Heath, Edward, Jul. 9, 1916; Feb. 10, 1974.

Heatherton, Joey, Sep. 14, 1944.

Heathrow Airport, Jan. 12, 1970.

Heaviside, Oliver, May 13, 1850.

Hebert, F(elix) Edward, Oct. 12, 1901.

Hebrew University (Jerusalem), Jul. 24, 1918; Apr. 1, 1925.

Hecht, Ben, Feb. 28, 1894.

Hecht, George Joseph, Nov. 1, 1895.

Hecker, Isaac Thomas, Dec. 18, 1819.

Heckler, Margaret, Jun. 21, 1931.

Hedaya, Dan, Jul. 24, 1940.

Hedin, Sven Anders, Feb. 19, 1865.

Hedren, Natalie Kay *(Tippi)*, Jan. 19, 1935.

Heflin, Van (Emmett Evan), Dec. 13, 1910.

Hefner, Christine Ann *(Christie)*, Nov. 8, 1952.

Hefner, Hugh, Apr. 9, 1926.

Hegel, Georg Wilhelm Friedrich, Aug. 27, 1770.

Heiberg, Peter Andreas, Nov. 16, 1758.

Heidegger, Martin, Sep. 26, 1889.

Heiden, Eric, Jun. 14, 1958.

Heidenstam, Verner von, Jul. 6, 1859.

Heifetz, Jascha, Feb. 2, 1901.

Heijermans, Herman, Dec. 3, 1864.

Heilbroner, Robert Louis, Mar. 24, 1919; Jul. 29, 1953.

Heilbronn, League of, Apr. 23, 1633.

Heine, Heinrich, Dec. 13, 1797.

Heinemann, Gustav, May 17, 1971.

Heinlein, Robert A(nson), Jul. 7, 1907.

Heinz Co, H. J.: incorporated, Jul. 27, 1900; Apr. 12, 1990.

Heinz, Henry John, Oct. 11, 1844.

Heinz, John, III, Oct. 23, 1938.

Heisenberg, Werner Karl, Dec. 5, 1901.

Heisman, John William, Oct. 23, 1869.

helicopter: first successful, Sep. 14, 1939.

Heligoland: British and German naval forces clash, Aug. 28, 1914.

Heller, Joseph, May 1, 1923.

Heller, Stephen, May 15, 1814.

Heller, Walter Wolfgang, Aug. 27, 1915.

Hellman, Lillian, Jun. 20, 1905.

Hello Dolly: premiere, Jan. 16, 1964.

Helm, Levon, May 26, 1943.

Helmholtz, Hermann Ludwig Ferdinand von, Aug. 31, 1821.

Helmond, Katherine, Jun. 5, 1933.

Helmont, Jan Baptist van, Jan. 12, 1580.

Helms, Jesse A., Oct. 18, 1921.

Helms, Richard McGarrah, Mar. 30, 1913.

Helmsley, Leona, convicted, Aug. 30, 1989.

Heloise, May 4, 1919.

Helou, Charles: inaugurated, Sep. 23, 1964.

Helsinki accords, Jul. 30, 1975.

Helsinki Agreement, Jan. 6, 1977.

Helvetian Confession: first, May 27, 1536.

Helvetic Republic: established, Feb. 9, 1798; Feb. 28, 1803.

Helvetius, Claude Adrien, Jan. 26, 1715.

Hemingway, Ernest, Jul. 21, 1899; Sep. 8, 1952; Oct. 28, 1954.

Hemingway, Mariel, Nov. 21, 1961.

Hemmings, David, Nov. 2, 1941.

Hemsley, Sherman, Feb. 1, 1938.

Hench, Philip Showalter, Feb. 28, 1896.

Henderson, Arthur, Sep. 13, 1863.

Henderson Field, Aug. 8, 1942.

Henderson, Florence, Feb. 14, 1934.

Henderson, Rickey Henley, Dec. 25, 1958.

Henderson, Thomas, Dec. 28, 1798.

Hendricks, Thomas, Sep. 7, 1819.

Hendricks, Thomas A., Mar. 4 1885.

Hendrix, James Marshall (Jimi), Nov. 27, 1942.

Henie, Sonja, Apr. 8, 1912.

Henley, Beth, May 8, 1952.

Henley, Don, Jul. 22, 1947.

Henley, William Ernest, Aug. 23, 1849.

Hennepin, Louis, Apr. 7, 1640.

Henner, Marilu, Apr. 6, 1953.

Henning, Doug, May 3,.1947.

Henreid, Paul, Jan. 10, 1908.

Henri, Robert, Jun. 25, 1865.

Henriques, Alfonso (Portugal), Jul. 25, 1139.

Henry I (England), Aug. 2, 1100; Jul. 19, 1101; dies, Dec. 1, 1135.

Henry I (France): dies, Aug. 4, 1060.

Henry II (England), Mar. 5, 1133; Nov. 7, 1153; Oct. 25, 1154; Jan. 6, 1169; Oct. 16, 1171; Jul. 12, 1174; Sep. 30, 1174; Nov. 18, 1188; dies, Jul. 6, 1189.

Henry II (France), Mar. 19, 1519; Mar. 31, 1547; Jan. 15, 1552; Feb. 5, 1556.

Henry II (Holy Roman Emperor), May 15, 1004; Feb. 14, 1014.

Henry III (England), Oct. 1, 1207; Oct. 19, 1216; Jun. 11, 1258; dies, Nov. 16, 1272.

Henry III (France), Sep. 19, 1551; May 30, 1574; murdered, Aug. 2, 1589; Mar. 14, 1590.

Henry III (Holy Roman Emperor), Oct. 28, 1017; Apr. 14, 1028; Dec. 20, 1046.

Henry IV (England), Apr. 3, 1367; Sep. 30, 1399; Mar. 30, 1406; May 18, 1412; dies, Mar. 21, 1413.

Henry IV (France), Dec. 13, 1553; Apr. 13, 1598.

Henry IV (King of Germany, Holy Roman Emperor), Nov. 11,

1050; Feb. 2, 1074; Jan. 24, 1076; Oct. 16, 1076; Jan. 28, 1077; Mar. 15, 1077; Mar. 7, 1080; Oct. 15, 1080; Jun. 3, 1083; Mar. 31, 1084.

Henry V (England), Sep. 16, 1387; Mar. 21, 1413; May 23, 1414; Oct. 25, 1415; Jan. 19, 1419; Jun. 2, 1420; dies, Aug. 31, 1422.

Henry V (Holy Roman Emperor), Jan. 8, 1081; Nov. 8, 1086; Jan. 6, 1099; Feb. 4, 1111; Feb. 12, 1111; Apr. 13, 1111; Apr. 7, 1118; Sep. 23, 1122.

Henry VI (England), Aug. 31, 1422; Jun. 27, 1450; Jul. 10, 1460; Mar. 4, 1461; Mar. 29, 1461; May 4, 1471; dies, May 21, 1471.

Henry VI (Holy Roman Emperor), Jan. 27, 1186; Apr. 14, 1191; Feb. 3, 1194; Dec. 25, 1194; Mar. 8, 1198.

Henry VI (Rome), Aug. 15, 1169.

Henry VII (England), Jan. 28, 1457; Mar. 5, 1496; Jan. 25, 1502; dies, Apr. 21, 1509; Aug. 16, 1513.

Henry VII (Holy Roman Emperor), Jun. 29, 1312.

Henry VII (Count of Luxembourg), Nov. 27, 1308.

Henry VIII (England), Jun. 28, 1491; Apr. 21, 1509; Apr. 5, 1513; Feb. 2, 1522; Nov. 14, 1532; Jan. 25, 1533; May 23, 1533; Jul. 11, 1533; Jul. 6, 1535; May 19, 1536; May 30, 1536; Jan. 6, 1540; Jul. 6, 1540; Jul. 28, 1540; Jul. 29, 1540; Jul. 12, 1542; Nov. 25, 1542; dies, Jan. 28, 1547.

Henry, Buck, Dec. 9, 1930.

Henry of Carinthia, Aug. 15, 1307.

Henry *(Harry)*, Prince of Wales, Sep. 15, 1984

Henry, Joseph, Dec. 17, 1797.

Henry the Navigator, (Prince), Mar. 4, 1394; Jul. 25, 1415.

Henry, O., Sep. 11, 1862; Dec. 10, 1905; Apr. 10, 1906.

Henry, Patrick, May 29, 1736; May 29, 1765; Mar. 23, 1775.

Henry, Prince de Conde, May 3, 1616.

Henryk II (Duke of Silesia), Apr. 9, 1241.

Henschel, George, Oct. 22, 1881.

Henson, James (Maury), Sep. 24, 1936.

Hepburn, Audrey, May 4, 1929.

Hepburn, James (Earl of Bothwell), May 15, 1567.

Hepburn, Katharine, Nov. 8, 1909; Dec. 24, 1949; Feb. 20, 1952.

Hepworth, Barbara, Jan. 10, 1903.

Herbert, Frank Patrick, Oct. 8, 1920.

Herbert, George, Apr. 3, 1593.

Herbert, Victor, Feb. 1, 1859; Jun. 17, 1903; Oct. 24, 1910.

Herder, Johann Gottfried von, Aug. 25, 1744.

Heredia, Jose Maria de, Dec. 31, 1803; Nov. 22, 1842.

Hereros, Jan. 11, 1904.

Heritage Day (Canada (Yukon)), Feb. 20.

Herman, Jerry, Jan. 16, 1964; May 24, 1966.

Herman, Pee-Wee, Aug. 27, 1952.

Herman, Woody, May 16, 1913.

Hermite, Charles, Dec. 24, 1822.

Hermits of St. Francis of Assisi, Order of, May 23, 1474.

Hernandez Colon, Rafael: inaugurated, Jan. 2, 1973.

Hernandez, Keith, Oct. 20, 1953.

Hernandez, Willie, Nov. 14, 1955.

Heroes Day (Haiti), Jan. 1.

Heroes' Day (Jamaica), Oct. intro.

Heroes' Day (Mozambique), Feb. 3.

Heroes Day (Paraguay), Mar. 1.

Heroes' Day (St. Vincent and the Grenadines), Jan. 22.

Heroes' Day (Tanzania), Sep. 1.

Heroes' Day (Zambia), Jul. intro.; Jul. 5.

Heroes' Day (Zimbabwe), Aug. 11.

Heroes of Independence Day (Haiti), Jan. 2.

Herrera Campins, Luis, May 4, 1925; Mar. 12, 1979.

Herrera, Caroline, Jan. 8, 1939.

Herrera, Felipe, Feb. 5, 1960.

Herrera, Paloma, Dec. 21, 1975.

Herrick, Myron Timothy, Oct. 9, 1854.

Herriot, Edouard, Jul. 5, 1872.

Herriot, James, Oct. 3, 1916.

Herrmann, Edward, Jul. 21, 1943.

Herschbach, Dudley Robert, Jun. 18, 1932.

Herschel, Sir John Frederick, Mar. 7, 1792.

Herschel, Sir William, Nov. 15, 1738; Mar. 13, 1781.

Hersey, John (Richard), Jun. 17, 1914.

Hersh, Seymour, Apr. 8, 1937.

Hershey, Alfred Day, Dec. 4, 1908.

Hershey, Barbara, Feb. 5, 1948.

Hershey, Lewis Blaine, Sep. 12, 1893.

Hershey, Milton Snavely, Sep. 13, 1857.

Herter, Christian Archibald, Mar. 28, 1895.

The Hertz Corp.: incorporated, Apr. 17, 1923.

Hertz, Gustav Ludwig, Jul. 22, 1887.

Hertz, Heinrich Rudolf, Feb. 22, 1857.

Hertzog, James Barry Munnik, Apr. 3, 1866.

Hertzsprung, Ejnar, Oct. 8, 1873.

Herzberg, Gerhard, Dec. 25, 1904.

Herzegovina, independence of, Feb. 29, 1992; formation of federation, Mar. 1, 1994; UN member, May 22, 1992.

Herzl, Theodor, May 2, 1860.

Herzog, Chaim, Sep. 17, 1918.

Hesburgh, Theodore Martin, May 25, 1917.

Hess, Rudolf, Apr. 26, 1894; May 10, 1941.

Hess, Victor F., Jun. 24, 1883.

Hess, Walter, Mar. 17, 1881.

Hesse, Hermann, Jul. 2, 1877.

Hesseman, Howard, Feb. 27, 1940.

Heston, Charlton, Oct. 4, 1924; Nov. 18, 1959.

Hevesy, Georg, Aug. 1, 1885.

Hewes, Joseph, Jan. 23, 1730.

Hewish, Antony, May 11, 1924.

Hewitt, Abram Stevens, Jul. 31, 1822.

Hewlett-Packard Co.: incorporated, Aug. 18, 1947.

Hewlett, William, May 20, 1913.

Hexum, Jon-Erik, Nov. 5, 1958.

Heydrich, Reinhard, Mar. 7, 1904; dies, Jun. 4, 1942; Jun. 10, 1942.

Heyerdahl, Thor, Oct. 6, 1914.

Heymans, Corneille J. F., Mar. 28, 1892.

Heyrovsky, Jaroslav, Dec. 20, 1890.

Heyse, Paul Johann Ludwig von, Mar. 15, 1830.

Heyward, Du Bose, Aug. 31, 1885.

Hickok, James Butler, May 27, 1837.

Hicks, Edward, Apr. 4, 1780.

Hicks, Granville, Sep. 9, 1901.

Hicks, Sir John R., Apr. 8, 1904.

Hidalgo y Costilla, Miguel, May 8, 1753.

Higginbotham, Jay C., May 11, 1906.

Higgins, Marguerite, Sep. 3, 1920.

Higgins, William, death of, Jul. 30, 1989.

Higginson, Thomas Wentworth Storrow, Dec. 22, 1823.

High Council of the Revolution (Portugal), Mar. 15, 1975.

High Court of Parliament, Apr. 23, 1952.

Hijaz and Nejd, Kingdom of (Saudi Arabia), Sep. 23, 1932.

Hijaz (Saudi Arabia), Jan. 8, 1926.

Hilbert, David, Jan. 23, 1862.

Hildebrand, Joel, Nov. 16, 1881.

Hildebrandt, Johann Lucus von, Nov. 14, 1668.

Hildegarde, Feb. 1, 1906.

Hill, Ambrose Powell, Nov. 9, 1825.

Hill, Anita, Jul. 30, 1956.

Hill, Archibald Vivian, Sep. 26, 1886.

Hill, David Jayne, Jun. 10, 1850.

Hill, Benjamin (Benny), Jan. 21, 1925.

Hill, Faith, Sep. 21, 1967.

Hill, George Roy, Dec. 20, 1922.

Hill, Grace Livingstone, Apr. 16, 1865.

Hill, Grant, Oct. 5, 1971.

Hill, James Jerome, Sep. 16, 1838.

Hill, Sir Rowland, Dec. 3, 1795.

Hill Street Blues: television debut, Jan. 15, 1981.

Hillary, Sir Edmund (Percival), Jul. 20, 1919; May 29, 1953.

Hilleman, Maurice, Jun. 26, 1966.

Hillenkoetter, Roscoe H., May 8, 1897.

Hillery, Patrick J., May 2, 1923.

Hillman, Bessie, May 15, 1889.

Hillman, Sidney, Mar. 23, 1887.

Hills, Carla Anderson, Jan. 3, 1934.

Hilo (Hawaii), Jul. 25, 1934.

Hilton, Conrad (Nicholson), Dec. 25, 1887.

Hilton, James, Sep. 9, 1900.

Himmler, Heinrich, Oct. 7, 1900; Jun. 21, 1943.

Hina Matsuri (Japan), Mar. 3.

Hinckley, John W., Jr., May 29, 1955; Mar. 30, 1981; Jun. 21, 1982.

Hindemith, Paul, Nov. 16, 1895; Jan. 22, 1936.

Hindenburg: first air-born piano recital, May 7, 1936; burns, May 6, 1937.

Hindenburg Line, Feb. 24, 1917; Mar. 14, 1917; Apr. 5, 1917; Sep. 3, 1918; Sep. 29, 1918.

Hindenburg, Paul von, Oct. 2, 1847; Sep. 18, 1914; Aug. 29, 1916; Apr. 10, 1932.

Hindi language, Jan. 26, 1965.

Hines, Earl *(Fatha)*, Dec. 28, 1905.

Hines, Duncan, Mar. 26, 1880.

Hines, Gregory Oliver, Feb. 14, 1946.

Hines, Jerome, Nov. 8, 1921.

Hingle, Pat, Jul. 19, 1924.

Hinshelwood, Sir Cyril Norman, Jun. 19, 1897.

Hinton, Sir Christopher, May 12, 1901.

Hinton, William A., Dec. 15, 1883.

Hipper, Baron Franz von, Sep. 13, 1863.

Hipple, Eric Ellsworth, Sep. 16, 1957.

Hirobumi Ito, Prince, Sep. 2, 1841.

Hirohito (Emperor of Japan), Apr. 29, 1901; world tour, Mar. 3, 1921; Dec. 25, 1926; first public appearance, Sep. 27, 1946; Nov. 10, 1976. dies, Jan. 7, 1989.

Hiroshima, Japan, Aug. 6, 1945.

Hiroshima Mon Amour: premiere, May 16, 1960.

Hirsch, Emil Gustav, May 22, 1851.

Hirsch, Judd, Mar. 15, 1935.

Hirschfeld, Albert, Jun. 21, 1903.

Hirshhorn, Joseph (Herman), Aug. 1, 1899.

Hirt, Al, Nov. 7, 1922.

Hiss, Alger, Nov. 11, 1904; Jan. 21, 1950.

Histoires Naturelles: premiere, Jan. 12, 1907.

Historic Preservation Week, National, May intro.

Historical Association, American: founded, Sep. 9, 1884.

Hitch Hiking Month, Jul. intro.

Hitchcock, Alfred (Joseph), Aug. 13, 1899; May 28, 1954; Aug. 4, 1954; Aug. 4, 1955; May 16, 1956; Aug. 6, 1959, Jun. 16, 1960.

Hitchings, George, Apr. 18, 1905.

Hite, Shere D., Nov. 2, 1942.

Hitler, Adolf, Apr. 20, 1889; Apr. 10, 1932; Jan. 30, 1933; Mar. 23, 1933; Jun. 30, 1934; Mar. 16, 1935; Mar. 29, 1936; Oct. 27, 1936; Feb. 4, 1938; Dec. 18, 1940; assassination attempt, Jul. 20, 1944; Oct. 14, 1944; suicide, Apr. 30, 1945.

Hitler-Stalin Pact (1939), anniversary of, Aug. 23, 1989.

H. M. King Hussein's Birthday (Jordan), Nov. 14.

Ho, David, Nov. 3, 1952.

Ho Chi Minh, May 19, 1890; Sep. 2, 1945; Apr. 7, 1951.

Ho Chi Minh City, Apr. 30, 1975.

Ho, Don, Aug. 13, 1930.

Hoar, George Frisbie, Aug. 29, 1826.

Hobart, Garret Augustus, Jun. 3, 1844; Mar. 4, 1897.

Hobbes, Thomas, Apr. 5, 1588.

Hobbit Day, Sep. intro.; Sep. 22.

Hobby Month, National, Feb. intro.

Hobby, Ovetta Culp, Jan. 19, 1905.

Hoboken (New Jersey): first baseball game, Jun. 19, 1846.

Hobson, Laura Z(ametkin), Jun. 19, 1900.

Hoche, Lazare, Jun. 25, 1768.

Hocking, William E., Aug. 10, 1873.

Hockney, David, Jul. 9, 1937.

Hodges, Courtney Hicks, Jan. 5, 1887.

Hodges, Gil, Apr. 4, 1924.

Hodges, Johnny, Jul. 25, 1906.

Hodgkin, Sir Alan Lloyd, Feb. 5, 1914.

Hodgkin, Dorothy C., May 12, 1910.

Hoe, Richard March, Sep. 12, 1812.

Hoess, Rudolf, Apr. 15, 1947.

Hofer, Andreas, Nov. 22, 1767.

Hoffa, James R., Feb. 14, 1913; Dec. 6, 1957; becomes head of Teamsters Union, Jan. 23, 1958; Mar. 4, 1964; Jul. 31, 1975.

Hoffer, Eric, Jul. 25, 1902.

Hoffman, Abbott *(Abbie)*, Nov. 30, 1936.

Hoffman, Dustin, Aug. 8, 1937.

Hoffman, Julius Jennings, Jul. 7, 1895.

Hoffmann, Ernst Theodor, Jan. 24, 1776.

Hoffmann, Roald, Jul. 18, 1937.

Hofmann, August Wilhelm von, Apr. 8, 1818.

Hofmannsthal, Hugo von, Feb. 1, 1874.

Hofmeyr, Jan Hendrik, Jul. 4, 1845.

Hofstadter, Richard, Aug. 6, 1916; May 7, 1956.

Hofstadter, Robert, Feb. 5, 1915.

Hogan, (William) Ben(jamin), Aug. 13, 1912.

Hogan, Paul, Oct. 8, 1939.

Hogarth, William, Nov. 10, 1697.

Hogmanay Day (Scotland), Dec. 31.

Hogue, H.M.S.: sunk, Sep. 22, 1914.

Hogwood, Christopher, Sep. 10, 1941.

Hohenlinden, Battle of, Dec. 3, 1800.

Hoisington, Elizabeth, Jun. 11, 1970.

Hokusai, Katsushika, Oct. 21, 1760.

Holberg, Baron Ludvig, Dec. 3, 1684.

Holbrook, Harold Rowe, Jr. *(Hal)*, Feb. 17, 1925.

Holden, William, Apr. 17, 1918.

Holder, Geoffrey, Sep. 1, 1930.

Holderlin, Johann Friedrich, Mar. 20, 1770.

Holdren, Judd Clifton, Oct. 16, 1915.

Holiday, Billie, Apr. 7, 1915.

Holidays are Pickle Days, Nov. intro.

Holland, Jan. 23, 1668; May 4, 1702; Jan. 4, 1717; Jul. 9, 1810; Jan. 13, 1916; Jan. 23, 1920.

Holland, Clifford Milburn, Mar. 3, 1883.

Holland Festival (Netherlands), Jun. intro.

Holland, John Philip, Feb. 29, 1840; Feb. 24, 1842.

Holland, U.S.S.: first U.S. submarine, Apr. 11, 1900.

Holley, George Malvin, Apr. 14, 1878.

Holley, Robert William, Jan. 28, 1922.

Holliday, Jennifer Yvette, Oct. 19, 1960.

Holliday, Judy, Jun. 21, 1921.

Holliday, Polly Dean, Jul. 2, 1937.

Holliman, Earl, Sep. 11, 1936.

Hollings, Ernest Frederick (Fritz), Jan. 1, 1922.

Holloway, Sterling, Jan. 4, 1905.

holly, Dec. intro.

Holly, Buddy, Sep. 7, 1936.

Holly, Lauren, Oct. 28, 1966.

Holm, Celeste, Apr. 29, 1919.

Holm, Ian, Sep. 12, 1931.

Holman, Nat, Feb. 1, 1896.

Holmes, Larry, Nov. 3, 1949.

Holmes, Oliver Wendell, Aug. 29, 1809.

Holmes, Oliver Wendell, Jr., Mar. 8, 1841.

Holmes, Rupert, Feb. 24, 1947.

Holmes, William Henry, Dec. 1, 1846.

Holocaust, Aug. 19, 1953.

Holocaust (Israeli-Albanian concert), Nov. 4, 1995.

Holocaust Victims Fund, Mar. 5, 1997.

Holst, Gustav Theodore, Sep. 21, 1874.

Holstein, Jan. 24, 1867.

Holt, Harold, Jan. 20, 1966.

Holtzman, Elizabeth, Aug. 11, 1941.

Holy Day of the Three Hierarchs, Jan. 30.

Holy Eucharist, Feb. 23, 1970.

Holy Innocents, Feast of, Dec. 28.

Holy League, Mar. 31, 1495; Oct. 4, 1511; May 20, 1591.

Holy League, War of the, Jun. 6, 1513.

Holy Machabees, Aug. 1.

Holy Name of Mary, Feast of, Sep. 12.

Holy Roman Empire, May 4, 1702; Feb. 9, 1801.

Holyfield, Evander, Oct. 25, 1990; Nov. 11, 1993.

Home Decorating Month, National, May intro.

Home and Family Month, Nov. intro.

Home, John, Sep. 21, 1722.

The Homecoming: opens, Jan. 5, 1967.

Homer, Arthur Bartlett, Apr. 14, 1896.

Homer, Winslow, Feb. 24, 1836.

Homestead Act, May 20, 1862.

Homestead (Steel) Plant: strike ends, Jun. 30, 1892.

Honduras, Jan. 19, 1921; Feb. 11, 1922; 18, 1960; Jan. 5, 1982; Mar. 16, 1988.

Honecker, Erich, Aug. 25, 1912; May 3, 1971; Sep. 7, 1987.

Honegger, Arthur Oscar, Mar. 10, 1892.

The Honeymooners: television debut, Oct. 1955.

honeysuckle, Jun. intro.

Hong Kong, Nov. 3, 1839; Jan. 20, 1841; ceded to Britain, Aug. 29, 1842; Dec. 25, 1941; May 17, 1962; Jan. 9, 1972; British withdrawal announced, Apr. 20, 1984; Dec. 19, 1984; Jul. 1, 1997.

Hong Kong University, Mar. 16, 1910.

Honolulu, Declaration of, Feb. 8, 1966.

Hood: British battle cruiser, May 24, 1941.

Hood, John Bell, Jun. 1, 1831; Dec. 16, 1864.

Hooft, Pieter Corneliszoon, Mar. 16, 1581.

Hooke, Robert, Jul. 18, 1635.

Hooker, John Lee, Aug. 22, 1917.

Hooker, Joseph, Nov. 13, 1814.

Hooker, Thomas, Jul. 7, 1586; May 31, 1639.

Hooks, Robert, Apr. 18, 1937.

Hooper, Bishop John, Feb. 9, 1555.

Hoover Dam, Sep. 17, 1930.

Hoover, Herbert (Clark), Aug. 10, 1874; inaugurated, Mar. 4, 1929.

Hoover, J. Edgar, Jan. 1, 1895; May 3, 1972.

Hoover, Lou, Mar. 29, 1875.

Hope, Bob, May 29, 1903.

Hope Chest Month, National, May intro.

Hope Diamond, Nov. 8, 1958.

Hope (Wales) patron of, Nov. 7.

Hopkins, Anthony, Dec. 31, 1937.

Hopkins, Bo, Feb. 2, 1942.

Hopkins, Esek, Apr. 26, 1718.

Hopkins, Sir Frederick Gowland, Jun. 30, 1861.

Hopkins, Gerard Manley, Jul. 28, 1844.

Hopkins, Harry (Lloyd), Aug. 17, 1890.

Hopkins, Johns, May 19, 1795.

Hopkins, Mark, Feb. 4, 1802; Sep. 1, 1813.

Hopkins, Sam (Lightnin'), Mar. 15, 1912.

Hopkins, Samuel: first patent, Jul. 31, 1790.

Hopkins, Stephen, Mar. 7, 1707.

Hopkins, Telma Louise, Oct. 28, 1948.

Hopkinson, Francis, Sep. 21, 1737.

Hoppe-Seyler, Ernst Felix, Dec. 26, 1825.

Hoppe, Willie, Oct. 11, 1887.

Hopper, Dennis, May 17, 1936.

Hopper, Edward, Jul. 22, 1882.

Hopper, Hedda, Jun. 2, 1890.

Hora de la Prisiop (Romania), Aug. intro.

Horace, Dec. 8, 65 b.c.

Hormel, George Albert, Dec. 4, 1860.

Hormuz, Strait of, Jul. 22, 1987.

Hornaday, William Temple, Dec. 1, 1854.

Horne, Lena, Jun. 30, 1917.

Horne, Marilyn, Jan. 16, 1934.

Horner, Bob, Aug. 6, 1957.

Horney, Karen, Sep. 16, 1885.

Hornsby, Rogers, Apr. 27, 1896.

Hornung, Paul, Dec. 23, 1935.

Horowitz, David Joel, Jan. 10, 1939.

Horowitz, Vladimir, Oct. 1, 1904; Apr. 14, 1986.

horses and their riders, patron of, Aug. 13.

horseshoe pitching: first national championship, Oct. 23, 1915.

Horsley, Lee, May 15, 1955.

Horstmann, Dorothy, Jul. 2, 1911.

Horthy, Miklos von Nagybanya, Jun. 18, 1869.

Horton, Miles Gilbert (Tim), Jan. 12, 1930.

Horton, William Wattison (Willie), Oct. 18, 1942.

Hosenfus, Eugene, Oct. 5, 1986.

Hosiery Week, National, Aug. intro.

Hoskins, Bob, Oct. 26, 1942.

Hosokawa, Morihiro, Jan. 14, 1938; Apr. 8, 1994.

hospitality and hotelkeepers, patron of, Jan. 9.

hospitals, patron of, Mar. 8.

Hostak, Al, Jul. 19, 1940.

Hostos, Eugenio Maria De, Jan. 11, 1839.

hot-air balloon, Aug. 17, 1978; May 1980; Jul. 3, 1987.

Hot Dog Month, National, Jul. intro.

hot line, Aug. 3Q 1963.

hotelkeepers, patron of, Jul. 29.

Hotzendorf, Franz Conrad von, Nov. 11, 1852.

Houdek, Vladimir, May 16, 1950.

Houdini, Harry, Mar. 24, 1874; performs most famous magic act, Aug. 6, 1926.

Houdon, Jean Antoine, Mar. 20, 1741.

Hounsfield, Godfrey Newbold, Aug. 28, 1919.

Houphouet-Boigny, Felix, Oct. 18, 1905.

Housatonic, Feb. 17, 1864.

Housatonic, S.S., Feb. 3, 1917.

House of Assembly, South African, May 3, 1968.

House at Pooh Corner: published, Dec. 26, 1928.

House, Edward Mandell, Jul. 26, 1858.

House of Representatives (U.S.), Mar. 2, 1977.

House Un-American Activities Committee, Mar. 7, 1951.

Houseman, John, Sep. 22, 1902.

Houser, Theodore V., Sep. 8, 1892.

housewives, patron of, Jul. 29.

Housing Act, National *(Wagner-Steagall Act),* Sep. 1, 1937.

Housing Administration, Federal: created, Jun. 28, 1934.

Housing Authority, U.S.: established, Sep. 1, 1937.

Housing and Town Planning Act (Great Britain), Dec. 3, 1909.

Housing and Urban Development, Department of, Jan. 13, 1966.

Housman, A. E., Mar. 26, 1859; May 26, 1859.

Houssay, Bernardo Alberto, Apr. 10, 1887.

Houston, Sam, Mar. 2, 1793; Apr. 21, 1836; Oct. 22, 1836.

Houston, U.S.S., Jul. 25, 1934.

Houston (Texas), May 8, 1967.

Houston, Whitney, Aug. 9, 1963.

How to Marry a Millionaire: premiere, Nov. 10, 1953.

How to Succeed in Business Without Really Trying: premiere, Oct. 14, 1961.

Howard, Catherine, Jul. 28, 1540; beheaded, Feb. 13, 1542.

Howard, Desmond, May 15, 1970.

Howard, Elston, Nov. 7, 1963.

Howard, John Galen, May 8, 1864.

Howard, Ken(neth Joseph), Jr., Mar. 28, 1944.

Howard, Leslie, Apr. 3, 1893.

Howard, Moe, Jun. 19, 1897.

Howard, Oliver Otis, Nov. 8, 1830.

Howard, Ron, Mar. 1, 1954.

Howard, Roy Wilson, Jan. 1, 1883.

Howard, Sidney (Coe), Jun. 26, 1891.

Howard, Susan, Jan. 28, 1943.

Howard, Trevor (Wallace), Sep. 29, 1916.

Howdy Doody: television debut, Dec. 27, 1947.

Howe, Elias, Jul. 9, 1819; Sep. 10, 1846.

Howe, Geoffrey, Apr. 20, 1984.

Howe, Gordie, Mar. 31, 1928; Dec. 7, 1977.

Howe, Irving, Jun. 11, 1920.

Howe, James Wong, Aug. 28, 1898.

Howe, Joseph, Dec. 13, 1804.

Howe, Julia Ward, May 27, 1819; May 10, 1908.

Howe, Richard, Mar. 19, 1725; Mar. 8, 1726.

Howe, Samuel Gridley, Nov. 10, 1801.

Howe, Syd(ney Harris), Sep. 28, 1911.

Howe, William, Aug. 10, 1729. Sep. 15, 1776.

Howell, C. Thomas, Dec. 7, 1966.

Howells, William Dean, Mar. 1, 1837.

Howes, Sally Ann, Jul. 20, 1934.

Howison, George Holmes, Nov. 29, 1834.

Howland, Beth, May 28, 1941.

Howser, Richard Dalton *(Dick),* May 14, 1937.

Hoxha, Enver, Apr. 11, 1985.

Hoyte, Desmond, Aug. 11, 1984; inaugurated, Aug. 6, 1985.

Hrdlihcka, Ales, Mar. 29, 1869.

Hu Yaobang, Jun. 29, 1981; Jan. 16, 1987.

Hua Guofeng, Oct. 12, 1976; Jun. 29, 1981.

Hubbard, L. Ron, Mar. 13, 1911.

Hubbard, Orville Liscum, Apr. 2, 1903.

Hubbell, Carl, Jun. 22, 1903.

Hubble, Edwin Powell, Nov. 20, 1889.

Hubble Space Telescope, launched on *Discovery,* Apr. 24, 1990.

Hubel, David H., Feb. 27, 1926.

Huber, Robert, Feb. 20, 1937.

Hubertusburg, Treaty of, Feb. 15, 1763.

Hubley, Season, May 14, 1951.

Hubmaier (Austrian Anabaptist), Mar. 10, 1528.

Huc, Evariste Regis, Jun. 1, 1813.

Hudson Bay Company, May 2, 1670; Mar. 9, 1869.

Hudson, Brett Stuart Patrick, Jan. 18, 1953.

Hudson, Henry, Sep. 12, 1575; Sep. 13, 1609.

Hudson, William Louis, II *(Bill),* Oct. 17, 1949.

Hudson, Mark Jeffrey Anthony, Aug. 23, 1951.

Hudson River: claimed for Netherlands, Sep. 13, 1609.

Hudson River Revival, Great, Jun. intro.

Hudson, Rock, Nov. 17, 1925.

Hudson, William Henry, Aug. 4, 1841.

Hue, Mar. 26, 1975.

Hue, Treaty of: signed, Aug. 25, 1883; Jun. 6, 1884.

Huerta, Dolores, Apr. 10, 1930.

Huerta, Victoriano, Dec. 23, 1854.

Huey P. Long Day (Louisiana), Jul. 30; Aug. 30.

Hufnagel, Charles, Sep. 11, 1952.

Hufstedler, Shirley, Aug. 24, 1925.

Huggins, Charles Brenton, Sep. 22, 1901.

Huggins, Miller, Mar. 27, 1879.

Huggins, Sir William, Feb. 7, 1824.

Hughes, Charles Evans, Apr. 11, 1862; Apr. 25, 1910; resigns, Jun. 2, 1941.

Hughes, David Edward, May 16, 1831.

Hughes, Emmet John, Dec. 26, 1920.

Hughes, Howard, Dec. 24, 1905; autobiography hoax, Mar. 13, 1972.

Hughes, John, Feb. 18, 1950.

Hughes, Langston, Feb. 1, 1902.

Hughes, Richard, Apr. 19, 1900.

Hughes, Ted, Dec. 22, 1984.

Hughes, Thomas, Oct. 20, 1822.

Hugo, Victor, Feb. 26, 1802.

Huguenot War, First: ends, Mar. 19, 1563.

Huguenot Wars, Mar. 1, 1562; end, Jun. 28, 1629.

Huguenots, Apr. 13, 1598.

Huguenots, Massacre of the: begins, Aug. 24, 1572.

Huidobro, Vicente, Jan. 10, 1893.

Hulce, Thomas, Dec. 6, 1953.

Hull, Brett, Aug. 9, 1964.

Hull, Cordell, Oct. 2, 1871.

Hull (England), Jan. 2, 1901.

Hull, Isaac, Mar. 9, 1773; Aug. 19, 1812.

Hull, Robert Martin (Bobby), Jan. 3, 1939.

Hull, William, Jun. 24, 1753.

Hulme, T(homas) E(rnest), Sep. 16, 1883.

Hulse, Russell A., Nov. 28, 1950.

Hulst, Hendrik van de, Nov. 19, 1918.

human bones, oldest in North America, Dec. 29, 1982.

Human Rights Day, Dec. 10.

Humanae Vitae: encyclical, Jul. 29, 1968.

Humane Society, Sep. 3, 1903.

Humayun (Sultan of Delhi), May 17, 1540.

Humbard, Rex, Aug. 13, 1919.

Humbert I (Italy), Jan. 9, 1878; assassinated, Jul. 29, 1900.

Humberto Romero, Carlos: overthrown, Oct. 15, 1979.

Humble Petition and Advice, Mar. 31, 1657.

Humboldt, Alexander von, Sep. 14, 1769.

Humboldt, Wilhelm von, Jun. 22, 1767.

Hume, David, Apr. 26, 1711.

Humperdinck, Engelbert, Sep. 1, 1854; Dec. 23, 1893.

Humperdinck, Engelbert (singer), May 3, 1936.

Humphrey, Doris, Oct. 17, 1895.

Humphrey, George Magoffin, Mar. 8, 1890.

Humphrey, Hubert H., May 27, 1911; Democratic candidate for Vice-President, Aug. 26, 1964; Jan. 20, 1965; Democratic nomination for President, Aug. 28, 1968.

Humphreys, David, Jul. 10, 1752.

Hun, Koh, Mar. 4, 1997.

Hun Sen, Jan. 14, 1985.

The Hundred Days: begins, Mar. 20, 1815.

The Hundred Days (Roosevelt): begins, Mar. 9, 1933.

Hundred Years War, May 20, 1303; Jan. 5, 1340; Jun. 24, 1340; Mar. 15, 1341; Oct. 21, 1345; Aug. 26, 1346; Aug. 3, 1347; Jan. 11, 1360; Oct. 24, 1360; Mar. 14, 1369; May 21, 1369; Sep. 19, 1370; Jun. 23, 1372; Jun. 27, 1375; May 18, 1412; Oct. 25, 1415; Jan. 19, 1419; Mar. 24, 1449; Apr. 15, 1450; Aug. 12, 1450; Oct. 23, 1452; Jul. 17, 1453; Oct. 19, 1453.

Hung Hsiu Ch'uan, Jan. 11, 1851.

Hungarian Republic: proclaimed, Nov. 16, 1918.

Hungarian Revolution Anniversary (Hungary), Mar. 15.

Hungary, Aug. 26, 1541; Jan. 26, 1699; Apr. 14, 1849; Oct. 17, 1918; Nov. 1, 1918; Nov. 12, 1918; Mar. 22, 1919; Sep. 18, 1922; Apr. 11, 1939; Anti-Jewish laws, May 3, 1939; Jun. 27, 1941; Feb. 1, 1946; Dec. 28,

1949; Nov. 1, 1956; Nov. 3, 1956; Sep. 15, 1964; Feb. 24, 1972; May 2, 1989; Oct. 23, 1989.

Hungnam (Korea): evacuated, Dec. 22, 1950.

Hunley, Feb. 17, 1864.

Hunt, E(verette) Howard, Oct. 9, 1918.

Hunt, Guy, Apr. 22, 1993.

Hunt, H. L., Feb. 7, 1889.

Hunt, Helen, Jun. 15, 1963.

Hunt, (James Henry) Leigh, Oct. 19, 1784.

Hunt, Linda, Apr. 2, 1945.

Hunt, Richard Morris, Oct. 31, 1827.

Hunt, (William) Holman, Apr. 2, 1827.

Hunter, Catfish, Apr. 18, 1946; May 8, 1968; Dec. 19, 1974.

Hunter, Evan, Oct. 15, 1926.

Hunter, Holly, Mar. 20, 1958.

Hunter, John, Feb. 13, 1728.

Hunter, Kim, Nov. 12, 1922.

Hunter, Ross, May 6, 1926.

Hunter, Tab, Jul. 11, 1931.

Hunter, Thomas, Oct. 18, 1831.

hunters, patron of, Sep. 20; Nov. 3.

Hunting and Fishing Day, National, Sep. intro.

Huntington, Henry Edwards, Feb. 27, 1850.

Huntington, Samuel, Jul. 5, 1731.

Huntington's Disease, Mar. 26, 1993.

Huntley, Chester (Chet), Dec. 10, 1911.

Huong, Tran Van, Jan. 26, 1965.

Huppert, Isabelle, Mar. 16, 1955.

Hurok, Sol, Apr. 9, 1888.

Hurrah, David, Aug. 7, 1950.

Hurricane Andrew, Aug. 22, 1992, Aug. 24, 1992.

Hurricane Camille, Aug. 17, 1969.

Hurricane Fifi, Sep. 20, 1974.

Hurricane Hugo, Sep. 21, 1989.

Hurricane Iniki, Sep. 11, 1992.

Hurst, Fannie, Oct. 18, 1889.

Hurston, Zora Neale, Jan. 7, 1903.

Hurt, John, Jan. 22, 1940.

Hurt, William, Mar. 20, 1950.

Hurtado, Miguel de la Madrid, Dec. 12, 1934.

Hus, John, Nov. 5, 1414; Jul. 6, 1415; Feb. 22, 1418.

Husak, Gustav, Jan. 10, 1913.

Husayn Kamil (Egypt), Dec. 20, 1853.

Hussein, Abdullah ibn (Jordan): crowned, May 25, 1946; assassinated, Jul. 20, 1951.

Hussein ibn Talal (King of Jordan), Nov. 14, 1935; May 2, 1953.

Hussein (King of the Hejaz), Jan. 13, 1919.

Hussein, Saddam, Apr. 28, 1937; crowned, May 25, 1946; Jul. 16, 1979.

Husserl, Edmund, Apr. 8, 1859.

Hussey, Olivia, Apr. 17, 1951.

Hussey, Ruth, Oct. 30, 1917.

Hustler, Feb. 8, 1977.

Huston, Angelica, Jul. 9, 1951.

Huston, John, Aug. 5, 1906; Feb. 20, 1952.

Huston, Walter, Apr. 6, 1884.

Hutcheson, Francis, Aug. 8, 1694.

Hutchins, Robert Maynard, Jan. 17, 1899.

Hutchinson, Anne, Jul. 20, 1591; Nov. 17, 1637.

Hutchinson, Thomas, Sep. 9, 1711.

Hutson, Don, Jan. 31, 1913.

Hutten, Ulrich von, Apr. 21, 1488.

Hutton, Barbara, Nov. 14, 1912.

Hutton, Betty, Feb. 26, 1921.

Hutton, E. F., May 2, 1985.

Hutton, James, Jun. 3, 1726.

Hutton, Jim, May 31, 1938.

Hutton, Lauren, Nov. 17, 1943.

Hutton, Timothy James, Aug. 16, 1960.

Huxley, Aldous (Leonard), Jul. 26, 1894.

Huxley, Andrew Fielding, Nov. 2, 1917.

Huxley, Julian, Jun. 22, 1887.

Huxley, Thomas Henry, May 4, 1825.

Huygens, Christian, Apr. 14, 1629.

Huysmans, Joris Karl, Feb. 5, 1848.

Huzak, Gustav, Apr. 17, 1969.

Hyatt, Joel, May 6, 1950.

Hyde, Douglas, Jan. 17, 1860; May 4, 1938.

Hyde, Edward, Feb. 18, 1609.

Hyde Park (London), May 1, 1851.

Hyde-White, Wilfred, May 12, 1903.

hydrogen bomb, Jul. 6, 1962; first for China, Jun. 17, 1967; first for France, Aug. 24, 1968.

Hynde, Christine Elaine *(Chrissie),* Sep. 7, 1951.

Hyslop, James Hervey, Aug. 18, 1854.

I

I Love Lucy: television debut, Oct. 15, 1951.

I Married an Angel: premiere, May 11, 1938.

I Remember Mama: premiere, Oct. 19, 1944.

I Want to Hold Your Hand: recorded, Oct. 19, 1963.

Iacocca, Lee, Oct. 15, 1920; Dec. 10, 1970; Nov. 2, 1978.

Ian, Janis, May 7, 1950.

Ibanez del Campo, Carlos, Nov. 3, 1952.

Ibarruri, Dolores, Dec. 9, 1895.

Ibn Saud (Saudi Arabia), Jan. 8, 1926; May 20, 1927; Nov. 9, 1953.

Ibsen, Henrik, Mar. 20, 1828.

Ice Cream Week, National, Jul. intro.

Ice Cube, Jun. 15, 1969.

Ice Skating Month, National, Nov. intro.

Iceland, May 18, 1920; Jun. 23, 1930; May 9, 1940; independence, Jun. 17, 1944; Jun. 17, 1944; Jan. 23, 1973; Feb. 19, 1976.

Icelandic Supreme Court: established, Oct. 6, 1919.

The Iceman Cometh: premiere, Oct. 9, 1946.

Ickes, Harold LeClair, Mar. 15, 1874.

Ida, Don, Jun. 27, 1983.

Idaho: admitted to the Union, Jul. 3, 1890; Teton Dam collapses, Jun. 5, 1976.

An Ideal Husband: premieres, Jan. 3, 1895.

Ides of March, Mar. 15, 44 b.c.

Idle, Eric, Mar. 29, 1943.

Idol, Billy, Nov. 30, 1955.

Idris I (Libya), Dec. 24, 1951.

Ie Shima, Apr. 16, 1945.

Ifni: returned to Morocco, Jun. 30, 1969.

Iggy Pop (James Osterberg), Apr. 21, 1947.

Iglesias, Julio, Sep. 23, 1943.

Iglesias, Santiago, Feb. 22, 1872.

Ignatius Loyola, Apr. 4, 1541.

Ikeda, Hayoto, Dec. 3, 1899; inaugurated, Jul. 18, 1960.

Il Palio (Italy), Jul. 2.

Iliescu, Ion, Dec. 26, 1989.

Ilitch, Mike, Jul. 20, 1929.

Illia, Arturo (Umberto), Aug. 4, 1900.

Illinois: admitted to Union, Dec. 3, 1818.

illiterate, patron of, Jun. 13.

Ilq, Frances Lillian, Oct. 11, 1902.

Immaculate Conception of the Blessed Virgin Mary, Feast of, Dec. 8.

Immaculate Conception Day, Dec. 8.

Immaculate Conception, Dogma of, Dec. 8, 1854.

Immaculate Heart of Mary, Feast of the, May 27.

immigration quota system: abolished in U.S., Oct. 3, 1965.

immigration regulations (Canadian), Jan. 19, 1962.

impeachment: Richard M. Nixon, May 9, 1974; three articles against, Jul. 30, 1974.

implant, Sep. 11, 1952.

impossible, patron of the, Oct. 28.

Impression of the Stigmata upon St. Francis, Sep. 17.

Imus, Don, Jul. 23, 1940.

In Cold Blood: published, Jan. 17, 1966.

In the Heat of the Night: premiere, Aug. 2 1967.

Inatome, Rick, Jul. 27, 1953.

Inauguration Day (U.S.), Jan. 20.

Inayatullah (King of Afganistan), Jan. 14, 1929.

incandescent lamp, Oct. 21, 1879.

Inchon, Sep. 15, 1950.

Inclusive Language Lectionary, Oct. 14, 1983.

Independence Anniversary (Gabon Republic), Aug. 16; Aug. 17; Aug. 18.

Independence Anniversary (Venezuela), Jul. 5.

Independence of Cartagena (Colombia), Nov. 11.

Independence Celebration Day (Morocco), Nov. 18.

Independence Commemoration Day (Sri Lanka), Feb. 4.

Independence of Cuenca (Ecuador), Nov. 3.

Independence Day (Algeria), Jul. 5.

Independence Day (Angola), Nov. 11.

Independence Day (Antigua), Nov. 1.

Independence Day (Argentina), Jul. 9.

Independence Day (Armenia), May 28.

Independence Day (Bahamas), Jul. 10.

Independence Day (Bangladesh), Mar. 26.

Independence Day (Barbados), Nov. 30.

Independence Day (Barbuda), Nov. 1.

Independence Day (Belarus), Jul. 27.

Independence Day (Belgium), Jul. 21.

Independence Day (Belize), Sep. 21.

Independence Day (Benin), Aug. 1.

Independence Day (Bolivia), Aug. 6.

Independence Day (Brazil), Sep. 7.

Independence Day (Burkina Faso), Aug. 5.

Independence Day (Burma), Jan. 4.

Independence Day (Burundi), Jul. 1.

Independence Day (Cameroon), Jan. 1.

Independence Day (Cape Verde Islands), Jul. 5.

Independence Day (Central America), Sep. 15.

Independence Day (Chad), Aug. 11.

Independence Day (Chile), Sep. 18.

Independence Day (Colombia), Jul. 20.

Independence Day (Colon, Panama), Nov. 5.

Independence Day (Cyprus), Oct. 1.

Independence Day (Democratic Republic of the Congo), June 30.

Independence Day (Dominica), Nov. 2; Nov. 3.

Independence Day (Dominican Republic), Feb. 27.

Independence Day (Ecuador), Aug. 10.

Independence Day (Eritrea), May 25.

Independence Day, (Estonia), Feb. 24.

Independence Day (Fiji), Oct. 10.

Independence Day (Finland), Dec. 6.

Independence Day (Republic of Georgia), May 26.

Independence Day (Ghana), Mar. 6.

Independence Day (Greece), Mar. 25.

Independence Day (Grenada), Feb. 7.

Independence Day (Haiti), Jan. 1.

Independence Day (Iceland), Jun. 17.

Independence Day (India), Jan. 26; Aug. 15.

Independence Day (Indonesia), Aug. 17.

Independence Day (Israel), May 14.

Independence Day (Ivory Coast), Dec. 6; Dec. 7.

Independence Day (Jamaica), Aug. intro.

Independence Day (Jordan), May 25.

Independence Day (Kazakstan), Oct. 25.

Independence Day (Kenya), Dec. 12.

Independence Day (Kinbati), Jul. 12.

Independence Day (Kyrgyzstan), Aug. 31.

Independence Day (Latvian Community, U.S.), Nov. 18.

Independence Day (Lebanon), Nov. 22.

Independence Day (Lesotho), Oct. 1.

Independence Day (Liberia), Jul. 26.

Independence Day (Lithuania), Feb. 16.

Independence Day (Madagascar), Jun. 26.

Independence Day (Maldives), Jul. 26; Jul. 27.

Independence Day (Mauritania), Nov. 28.

Independence Day (Mauritius), Mar. 12.

Independence Day (Mexico), Sep. 16.

Independence Day (Moldova), Aug. 27.

Independence Day (Morocco), Mar. 2.

Independence Day (Mozambique), Jun. 25.

Independence Day (Nauru), Jan. 31.

Independence Day (Nevis), Sep. 19.

Independence Day (Niger), Aug. 3.

Independence Day (Northern Region, Somalia), Jun. 26.

Independence Day (Norway), May 17.

Independence Day (Pakistan), Aug. 14.

Independence Day (Palau), Jan. 1.

Independence Day (Papua New Guinea), Sep. 16.

Independence Day (Paraguay), May 15.

Independence Day (People's Democratic Republic of Yemen), Nov. 30.

Independence Day (Peru), Jul. 28; Jul. 29.

Independence Day (Philippines), Jun. 12.

Independence Day (Qatar), Sep. 3.

Independence Day (Rhode Island), May intro.; May 4.

Independence Day (Romania), May 10.

Independence Day (Rwanda), Jul. 1.

Independence Day (St. Christopher), Sep. 19.

Independence Day (St. Lucia), Feb. 22; Feb. 22.

Independence Day (Seychelles), Jun. 29.

Independence Day (Sierra Leone), Apr. 27.

Independence Day (Solomon Islands), Jul. 7.

Independence Day (Sudan), Jan. 1.

Independence Day (Suriname), Nov. 25.

Independence Day (Swaziland), Sep. 6.

Independence Day (Syria), Apr. 17.

Independence Day (Tajikistan), Sep. 9.

Independence Day (Texas), Mar. 2.

Independence Day (The Comoros), Jul. 6.

Independence Day (Togo), Apr. 27.

Independence Day (Trinidad and Tobago), Aug. 31.

Independence Day (Tunisia), Mar. 20.

Independence Day (Turkmenistan), Oct. 27.

Independence Day (Uganda), Oct. 9.

Independence Day (Ukraine), Aug. 24.

Independence Day (U.S.), Jul. intro.; Jul. 4.

Independence Day (Uruguay), Aug. 25.

Independence Day (Uzbekistan), Sep. 1.

Independence Day (Vanuatu), Jul. 30.

Independence Day (Venezuela), Apr. 19.

Independence Day (Western Samoa), Jan. 1.

Independence Day (Zambia), Oct. intro.; Oct. 23.

Independence Day (Zimbabwe), Apr. 18; Apr. 18.

Independence Feast Day (Djibouti), Jun. 27.

Independence from Colombia (Panama), Nov. 3.

Independence from Spain (Panama), Nov. 28.

Independence of Guayaquil (Ecuador), Oct. 9.

Independence Hall, Jun. 28, 1948.

Independence Hero Tiradentes (Brazil), Apr. 21.

Independence Holiday (Western Samoa), Jun. 1; Jun. 2.

Independence of India League: founded, Aug. 30, 1928.

Independence Movement Day (South Korea), Mar. 1.

Independence National Historical Park, Jun. 28, 1948.

Independence Proclamation Day (Albania), Nov. 28.

Independence/Republic Day (Tanzania), Dec. 9.

Independence Wars Beginning of (Cuba), Oct. 10.

Independent Labour Party (Great Britain), Jan. 13, 1893.

India, Jan. 3, 1399; Jan. 7, 1761; Jun. 3, 1818; suttee outlawed, Dec.

7, 1829; Jan. 24, 1857; first visit by British sovereign, Dec. 2, 1911; first parliament, Jan. 3, 1921; riots against British rule, May 6, 1930; republic status, Aug. 15, 1947; Jan. 30, 1948; independence, Jan. 26, 1950; Jan. 11, 1960; Jan. 19, 1970; Dec. 6, 1971; Sep. 19, 1973; Apr. 9, 1974; first nuclear device, May 18, 1974; Feb. 24, 1975; state of emergency, Jun. 26, 1975; Jan. 18, 1977; earthquake, Sep. 29, 1993; nuclear testing, May 11, 1998.

India Bill: passed, Aug. 2, 1858.

India Councils Act, May 25, 1909.

Indian Appropriations Act, Mar. 3, 1871.

Indian Day (Massachusetts), Aug. 12.

Indian Independence Act: enacted, Aug. 14, 1947.

Indian Mercantile, Marine, Feb. 9, 1926.

Indian National Congress: first opens, Dec. 28, 1885; Jan. 1, 1930.

Indian railway: first, Apr. 16, 1853.

Indian Reorganization Act, Jun. 18, 1934.

Indian Rights Day (Wisconsin), Jul. 4.

Indian Summer, Oct. intro.

Indiana: admitted to Union, Dec. 11, 1816.

Indiana Day (U.S.), Dec. 11.

Indiana, Robert, Sep. 13, 1928.

Indianapolis, Jan. 6, 1821; Jul. 30, 1945.

Indianapolis Speedway: first 500-mile automobile race, May 30, 1911.

Indians, American, Jan. 7, 1865.

Indians, Canadian, Jun. 21, 1984.

Indo-China, Jan. 19, 1951.

Indonesia, Aug. 17, 1945; independence, Dec. 27, 1945; Mar. 19, 1950; admitted to U.N., Sep. 28, 1950; Jan. 21, 1965; withdraws from U.N., Mar. 1, 1965; Apr. 24, 1965; launches satellite, Jul. 8, 1976.

Indurain, Miguel, Jul. 16, 1964.

Industrial Workers of the World, Jun. 27, 1905.

infantrymen, patron of, Sep. 22.

Infrared Astronomical Satellite, Jan. 25, 1983.

Ingalls, John James, Dec. 29, 1833.

Inge, William Motter, May 3, 1913; May 4, 1953.

Inge, William Ralph, Jun. 6, 1860.

Ingemann, Bernhard Severin, May 28, 1789.

Ingenhousz, Jan, Dec. 8, 1730.

Ingersoll, Charles Henry, Oct. 29, 1865.

Ingersoll, Robert Hawley, Dec. 26, 1859.

Ingersoll, Royal Eason, Jun. 20, 1883.

Ingram, James, Feb. 16, 1956.

Ingres, Jean-Auguste-Dominique, Aug. 29, 1780.

initiative and referendum devices: adopted by Oregon, Jun. 2, 1902.

Inman, Bobby Ray, Apr. 4, 1931.

Inness, George, May 1, 1825.

Innis, Roy, Jun. 6, 1934.

innkeepers, patron of, Feb. 12.

Innocent II (pope), Feb. 14, 1130; Jun. 4, 1133.

Innocent III (pope), Dec. 11, 1205; Nov. 18, 1210; May 15, 1213.

Innocent IV (pope), Jul. 17, 1245.

Innocent VIII (pope), Dec. 5, 1484.

Innocent IX (pope), Jul. 20, 1519.

Innocent X (pope), May 7, 1574; May 31, 1653.

Innocent XI (pope), May 19, 1611.

Innocent XII (pope), Mar. 13, 1615.

Innocent XIII (pope), May 13, 1655.

Inonu, Ismet (Turkey), Sep. 24, 1884; Nov. 10, 1938.

Inouye, Daniel Ken, Sep. 7, 1924.

insider trading, Nov. 14, 1986.

insulin gene, May 23, 1977.

insurance, first auto, Feb. 1, 1898.

integration, Jan. 28, 1963.

integration workers, patron of, Nov. 3.

Intelsat 3A, Dec. 18, 1968.

Inter-American Development Bank (IDB), Nov. 27, 1970.

Inter-Governmental, Maritime Commission/(United Nations), Jan. 13, 1959.

intercontinental ballistic missile, Aug. 26, 1957.

interferon alpha two, Jan. 9, 1986.

Interior, Depanment of, Jan. 13, 1971.

Intermall, Jan. 1, 1965.

intermediate-range nuclear force treaty, Dec. 8, 1987.

Internal Revenue Service, May 24, 1983.

Internal Security Act, Jun. 5, 1961.

International Atomic Energy Agency: first meeting, Oct. 1, 1957.

International Campaign to Ban Landmines, Oct. 10, 1997.

International Cometary Explorer, Sep. 11, 1985.

International Committee of the Red Cross: established, Oct. 26, 1863.

International Conference on Acquired Immune Deficiency Syndrome (AIDS), Jun. 4, 1989.

International Court of Justice, Jun. 27, 1986.

International Criminal Tribunal begins, May 7, 1996.

International Day for the Elimination of Racial Discrimination (UN Member Countries), Mar. 21.

International Day of Peace (U.S.), Sep. 20.

International Day of Solidarity with the Palestinian People (U.N. Member Nations), Nov. 29.

International Day of Solidarity with the Struggling People of South Africa, Jun. 16.

International Friendship Month, Feb. intro.

International Gideons, Jul. 1, 1899.

International Labor Organization, May 20, 1970.

International Law, Academy of, Jan. 29, 1914.

International Literacy Day, Sep. 8.

International Monetary Fund, Mar. 1, 1947; Jan. 8, 1976; Jan. 18, 1983.

International Oceanographic Insitute, Jan. 23, 1911.

International Olympic Committee: bars Rhodesia, Aug. 22, 1972.

International Petroleum Co., Feb. 6, 1969.

International Red Cross: founded, Aug. 22, 1864.

International Solidanty Day (People's Republic of Mongolia), May 1.

International Telephone & Telegraph Corp.: incorporated, Jun. 16, 1920. Jan. 18, 1963.

International Women's Day (Adjarians), Mar. 8.

International Women's Day (Belarus), Mar. 8.

International Women's Day (UN Member Countries), Mar. 8.

Internet, Mar. 4, 1998.

interracial marriage, Apr. 15, 1985.

Interstate Commerce Act, Feb. 4, 1887; Feb. 8, 1887; Jun. 5, 1950.

Interstate Commerce Commission, Jun. 18, 1910; Aug. 9, 1935.

intifada, Dec. 8, 1987.

Inuit, Jun. 21, 1984.

Iolanthe: premiere, Nov. 25, 1882.

Ionesco, Eugene, Nov. 26, 1912.

Ionescu, Take, Oct. 26, 1858.

Ionian Islands: ceded to Greece, Nov. 14, 1863; Apr. 28, 1864; Jun. 5, 1864.

Iowa, U.S.S. Apr. 19, 1989.

Iowa: admitted to Union, Dec. 28, 1846.

Iowa Volunteers, Cavalry of, Jan. 7, 1865.

Ipatieff, Vladimir Nikolaevich, Nov. 21, 1867.

Ippolitov-Ivanov, Mihail Mihailovich, Nov. 19, 1859.

Iquique Battle of (Chile), May 21.

IRA. *See*: Irish Republican Army (IRA).

Iran, Jan. 30, 1915; Mar. 21, 1935; Jan. 28, 1951; Mar. 17, 1951; May 2, 1951; U.S. evacuation, Jan. 30, 1979; Islamic government, Feb. 11, 1979, U.S. embassy seized, Nov. 4, 1979; Nov. 14, 1979; Islamic constitution, Dec. 3, 1979; Apr. 24, 1980; war with Iraq, Sep. 22, 1980; Jan. 20, 1981; Jan. 23, 1984.

Iran-contra affair, Feb. 22, 1986; Nov. 3, 1986; Nov. 13, 1986; Nov. 25, 1986; Dec. 2, 1986; Dec. 19, 1986; Feb. 26, 1987; May 5, 1987; Jul. 7, 1987; Jul. 15, 1987;

Nov. 18, 1987; Mar. 11, 1988; Mar. 16, 1988; earthquake, Jun. 21, 1990.

Iran-Contra affair, trial begins, Feb. 21, 1989; Poindexter, John, Apr. 7, 1990.

Iran-Iraq War, Sep. 17, 1980; Mar. 2, 1983; Jan. 9, 1987; Aug. 20, 1988.

Iran, Islamic Republic of, Jan. 25, 1980.

Iranian embassy, London, Apr. 30, 1980.

Iranian oil industry: nationalization, Mar. 15, 1951.

Iraq, Apr. 25, 1920; independence, Dec. 14, 1927; Oct. 3, 1932; overthrows monarchy, Jul. 14, 1958; nationalizes banks, insurance companies, and industrial and commercial concerns, Jul. 14, 1958; Jan. 31, 1965; Mar. 11, 1970; war with Iran, Sep. 22, 1980; bombs Tel Aviv, Jan. 18, 1989; Operation Desert Storm, Jan. 16, 1991; ground invasion of, Feb. 24, 1991; "no-fly zone," Jan. 13, 1993; blocks UN inspectors, Jan. 13, 1993.

Iraqi Army, Apr. 1, 1929.

IRAS-Araki-Aleoek, May 11, 1983.

Ireland, Apr. 12, 1654; Jul. 29, 1848; Apr. 24, 1916; Apr. 5, 1919; May 15, 1920; May 4, 1938; Nov. 24, 1995; May 22, 1998.

Ireland, Bank of: established, Jun. 1, 1783.

Ireland, Jill, Apr. 24, 1936.

Ireland, Northern: first Parliament opens, Jun. 22, 1921; Jan. 26, 1942; Jan. 14, 1965; Apr. 20, 1969; Feb. 7, 1970; Mar. 30, 1972; Mar. 8, 1973; Oct. 26, 1973; Nov. 15, 1985; peace talks, Jun. 10, 1996; peace settlement with Britain, Apr. 10, 1998.

Ireland, patron of, Feb. 1; Mar. 17.

Ireland, Republic of, Apr. 18, 1949; Jan. 21, 1950; Jan. 14, 1965.

Ireton, Henry, Nov. 3, 1611.

Irigoyen, Hipolito, Jul. 12, 1852.

Irish Free State, Dec. 6, 1921; established, Jan. 14, 1922; Oct. 24, 1922; renamed Eire, Dec. 29, 1937.

Irish National Land League: formed, Oct. 31, 1879.

Irish Nationalist League: first meeting, Feb. 7, 1883.

Irish nuns, patron of, Feb. 1.

Irish Peace Treaty, Dec. 6, 1921.

Irish Republic, Jan. 14, 1965.

Irish Republican Army (IRA), Feb. 26, 1962; Feb. 22, 1972; outlawed in Great Britain, Nov. 29, 1974; hunger strike, May 5, 1981; bomb at Harrods, Dec. 17, 1983; peace talks, Aug. 31, 1994.

Irish Sweepstakes, Feb. 27, 1987.

Irish women, patron of, Feb. 1.

iron-clad ship: first launched, Dec. 24, 1859.

iron curtain, Mar. 5, 1946.

Irons, Jeremy, Sep. 19, 1948.

Iroquois Theater fire, Dec. 30, 1903.

Irvin, Michael, Mar. 5, 1966.

Irving, Amy, Sep. 10, 1953.

Irving, Clifford, Mar. 13, 1972.

Irving, Sir Henry, Feb. 6, 1838.

Irving, John, Mar. 2, 1942.

Irving, Washington, Apr. 3, 1783.

Irwin, Hale, Jun. 3, 1945.

Irwin, James B., Jul. 26, 1971.

Isaak, Chris, Jun. 6, 1956.

Isabella I (Castile), Apr. 22, 1451; Oct. 18, 1469; Jan. 19, 1497.

Isabella II (Spain), Oct. 10, 1830; Sep. 27, 1833; Sep. 29, 1833; Apr. 22, 1834; flees to France, Sep. 29, 1868; abdicates, Jun. 25, 1870; Dec. 29, 1874.

Isabella (Queen of England), Sep. 24, 1326.

Isabey, Eugaeene Louis Gabriel, Jul. 22, 1803.

Isherwood, Christopher, Aug. 26, 1904.

Iskander, Mahmood, Feb. 9, 1984.

Isla, Jose Francisco, Apr. 24, 1703.

Islam, Apr. 9, 1928.

Islamic Alliance of Afghan Mujahedeen, May 23, 1983.

Islamic Conference Organization, Jan. 30, 1984.

Islamic Jihad Organization, Apr. 12, 1983; Jan. 8, 1985.

Islamic Republic Day (Iran), Apr. 1.

Islamic Republic (Pakistan), Feb. 29, 1956.

Isle of Wight: rock festival, Sep. 2, 1969.

Ismail, Abdel Fattah, Dec. 27, 1978.

Ismail Pasha, Dec. 31, 1830.

Isonzo, Second Battle of: begins, Jul. 18, 1915.

Isozaki, Arata, Jul. 23, 1931.

Israel: recognition by U.S., May 14, 1948; Feb. 14, 1949; Apr. 3, 1949; admitted to the United Nations, May 11, 1949; Feb. 1, 1950; Apr. 27, 1950; pipeline opens, May 5, 1964; Apr. 15, 1965; May 13, 1965; May 20, 1966; Soviet Union breaks relations, Jun. 10, 1967; Jan. 7, 1969; first peace conference with Arab countries, Dec. 21, 1973; Jan. 18, 1974; peace treaty with Egypt, Mar. 26, 1979; Feb. 26, 1980; Apr. 25, 1982; invades Lebanon, Jun. 6, 1982; troop withdrawal, May 17, 1983; prisoner exchange, May 20, 1985; completes troop withdrawal, Jun. 10, 1985; peace talks, Feb. 25, 1994; peace treaty, Oct. 26, 1994.

Israeli-Albanian concert, Nov. 4, 1995.

Issa, Abdullah, May 19, 1956.

Istanbul (Turkey), Jan. 21, 1929; Mar. 28, 1930; May 23, 1971.

Isthmian Canal, Nov. 18, 1901.

Italia: dirigible, May 24, 1928.

Italian fleet: surrenders, Sep. 11, 1943.

Italian independence: first efforts, Jul. 25, 1848.

Italian League: formed, Feb. 25, 1455.

Italian nurses, patron of, Apr. 29.

Italian Parliament: first, Apr. 2, 1860.

Italian Popular Movement, Apr. 20, 1979.

Italian Revolution, May 5, 1860.

Italian Tirol, patron of, Jun. 26.

Italy, Mar. 31, 1861; unification, Jul. 3, 1866; capital established, Jul.

2, 1871; war with Turkey, Sep. 29, 1911; secret treaty, Apr. 26, 1915; May 23, 1915; declares war on Turkey, Aug. 21, 1915; declares war on Germany, Aug. 27, 1916; first American troops arrive, May 30, 1918; Jan. 21, 1930; May 5, 1936; annexes Ethiopia, May 9, 1936; war with France and Great Britain, Jun. 10, 1940; declares war on U.S., Dec. 11, 1941; Dec. 11, 1941; British invasion of, Sep. 3, 1943; surrenders, Sep. 8, 1943; May 2, 1945; abolishes monarchy, Jun. 2, 1946; new constitution, Dec. 22, 1947; Jan. 24, 1969; divorce legalized, Dec. 1, 1970.

Italy, Kingdom of, Mar. 17, 1861.

Italy, patron saint of, Jan. 17.

Italy, unification of Kingdom of, Sep. 21, 1870.

Itashimoto, Ryutaro, resigns, Jul. 13, 1998.

Iturbi, Jose, Nov. 28, 1895.

Iturbide, Agustin de, Sep. 27, 1783.

Iulius, Jul. intro.

Ivan IV (Russia), Aug. 25, 1530; Jan. 16, 1547. Jan. 9, 1570.

Ivan VI (Russia), Aug. 13, 1740.

Ives, Burl, Jun. 14, 1909.

Ives, Charles Edward, Oct. 20, 1874.

Ives, James Merritt, Mar. 5, 1824.

Ivory Coast, Mar. 10, 1893; independence, Aug. 7, 1960; Nov. 3, 1960.

Iwo Jima: U.S. attack begins, Aug. 31, 1944; Nov. 11, 1944; Feb. 19, 1945; Feb. 23, 1945; battle ends, Mar. 17, 1945; Jun. 26, 1968.

Izetbegovic, Alija, Aug. 8, 1925.

Izvestia, Jan. 30, 1962.

J

J. B., Apr. 12, 1959.

Jablonski, Henryk, Dec. 27, 1909.

J'accuse: appearance in French newspaper, Jan. 13, 1898.

J'accusel, Jul. 12, 1906.

The Jack Benny Show: television debut, Oct. 28, 1950.

Jack Jouett Day (Virginia), Jun. intro.

The Jackie Gleason Show: television debut, Sep. 20, 1952.

Jackson, Alan, Oct. 17, 1958.

Jackson, Andrew, Mar. 15, 1767; Jan. 8, 1815; inaugurated, Mar. 4, 1829.

Jackson, Anne, Sep. 3, 1936.

Jackson, Bo, Nov. 30, 1962.

Jackson, Charles Thomas, Jun. 21, 1805.

Jackson, Glenda, May 9, 1937.

Jackson, Helen Hunt, Oct. 15, 1830.

Jackson, Henry Martin, May 31, 1912.

Jackson, Thomas Jonathan *(Stonewall)*, Jan. 21, 1824.

Jackson, Janet, May 16, 1966.

Jackson, Jermaine La Jaune, Dec. 11, 1954.

Jackson, Jesse, Oct. 8, 1941; Dec. 18, 1971; Apr. 8, 1984.

Jackson, Joe, Aug. 11, 1955.

Jackson, Kate, Oct. 29, 1948.

Jackson, Mahalia, Oct. 29, 1911.

Jackson, Marlon David, Mar. 12, 1957.

Jackson, Maynard, Mar. 23, 1938.

Jackson, Michael, Aug. 29, 1958.

Jackson, Milt(on), Jan. 1, 1923.

Jackson, Phil(ip), Sep. 17, 1945.

Jackson, Toriano Adaryll *(Tito)*, Oct. 15, 1953.

Jackson, Randy, Oct. 29, 1961.

Jackson, Reggie, May 18, 1946.

Jackson, Rachel, Jun. 15, 1767.

Jackson, Robert, Jul. 27, 1941.

Jackson, Robert Houghwout, Feb. 13, 1892.

Jackson, Samuel L., Dec. 21, 1948.

Jackson, Shirley, Dec. 14, 1919.

Jackson, Shirley Ann, Aug. 5, 1946.

Jackson State College (Mississippi), May 15, 1970.

Jacob, Francois, Jun. 17, 1920.

Jacobi, Derek, Oct. 22, 1938.

Jacobi, Karl Gustav, Dec. 10, 1804.

Jacobs, Jim, Feb. 14, 1972.

Jacobs, W(illiam) W(ymark), Sep. 8, 1863.

Jacquard, Joseph Marie, Jul. 7, 1752.

Jaegar, Andrea, Jun. 4, 1965.

Jaffe, Rona, Jun. 12, 1932.

Jagan, Cheddi: inaugurated, Sep. 5, 1961.

Jagan, Janet, elected, Dec. 20, 1997.

Jagellon Dynasty: ends, Jul. 7, 1572.

Jagger, Dean, Nov. 7, 1905.

Jagger, Jade, Oct. 21, 1971.

Jagger, Mick, Jul. 26, 1943.

Jagr, Jaromir, Feb. 15, 1972.

Jahn, Eiriedrich Ludwig, Aug. 11, 1778.

Jaisohn, Philip (So Jae-P_il), Oct. 28, 1866.

Jakes, John, Mar. 31, 1932.

Jalal ad-Din ar-Rumi, Sep. 30, 1207.

Jam-Zapolski, Peace of, Jan. 15, 1582.

Jamaica, Sep. 19, 1961; independence, Aug. 6, 1962; Jan. 10, 1983.

James I (Aragon), Feb. 2, 1208.

James I (England), Jun. 19, 1566; Mar. 24, 1603; Oct. 24, 1604; Apr. 10, 1606; Jan. 6, 1622; dies, Mar. 27, 1625; Feb. 6, 1685.

James I (Scotland), Mar. 30, 1406; Apr. 4, 1406; May 21, 1424; Feb. 20, 1437.

James II (England), Jul. 12, 1690.

James II (Scotland), Oct. 16, 1430; killed, Aug. 3, 1460; Oct. 14, 1633.

James 111 (Scotland), Aug. 3, 1460; Feb. 20, 1471; murdered, Jun. 11, 1488.

James IV (Scotland), Mar. 17, 1473; Jun. 11, 1488; Jan. 25, 1502; marries Margaret Tudor, Aug. 8, 1502; defeated and killed, Sep. 9, 1513.

James V (Scotland), Apr. 10, 1512; Sep. 9, 1513; Nov. 25, 1542; dies, Dec. 14, 1542.

James VI (Scotland), Jun. 15, 1567; Mar. 24, 1603.

James of Aragon, May 11, 1258.

James Craig Craigavon, 1st viscount, Jan. 8, 1871.

James, Etta (Jamesetta Hawkins), Jan. 25, 1938.

James, Harry, Mar. 15, 1916.

James, Henry, Jun. 2, 1811; Apr. 15, 1843.

James, Jesse, Sep. 5, 1847.

James, P(hyllis) D(orothy), Aug. 3, 1920.

James, Rick, Feb. 1, 1952.

James, Sonny, Mar. 1, 1929.

James, William, Jan. 11, 1842.

Jameson, Sir Leander Starr, Feb. 9, 1853; Dec. 30, 1895; Jan. 2, 1896; Jan. 21, 1898.

Jameson Raid: begins, Dec. 30, 1895; Jan. 2, 1896; Jan. 6, 1896.

Jamestown (Guyana), Nov. 18, 1978.

Jamestown (Virginia): founded, May 14, 1607; Jul. 30, 1619.

Jamison, Judith, May 10, 1934.

Jamkodjian, Mardiros, Jun. 9, 1981.

Jan, Mayen Island, May 8, 1929.

Janacek, Leos, Jul. 3, 1854; Oct. 9, 1921.

Janata Party (India), Jul. 28, 1979.

Janet, Pierre Marie Felix, May 30, 1859.

Janeway, Eliot, Jan. 1, 1913.

Jankau, Mar. 7, 1645.

Janksy, Karl Guthe, Oct. 22, 1905.

Jannings, Emil, Jul. 26, 1886.

Jansen, Cornelis, Oct. 28, 1585; May 31, 1653.

Jansen, Dan, Jun. 17, 1965.

Janssen, David, Mar. 27, 1930.

Januarius, Jan. intro.; Sep. intro.

Janus, Jan. intro.

Japan: first U.S. bid for trade and diplomatic relations, Jul. 8, 1853; Jan. 3, 1868; Feb. 7, 1868; Apr. 6, 1868; Aug. 29, 1871; gold standard, Mar. 1, 1897; Jan. 30, 1902; declares war on Germany, Aug. 23, 1914; declares war on Austria-Hungary, Aug. 25, 1914; Apr. 27, 1919; first imperial census, Mar. 1, 1921; male suffrage, Mar. 29, 1925; Jan. 21, 1930; Jan. 26, 1930; Apr. 13, 1941; U.S. declares war on, Dec. 8, 1941, Dec. 8, 1941; Dec. 25, 1941; Aug. 8, 1945; U.S. occupation begins, Aug. 30, 1945; surrenders to U.S., Sep. 2, 1945; May 3, 1947; U.S. occupation ends, Mar. 20, 1952; U.S. economic assistance, Jan. 9, 1962; Apr. 28, 1964; treaty with Korea, Jun. 22, 1965; relations with South Korea, Dec. 18, 1965; first satellite, Feb. 11, 1970; Sep. 29, 1972; automobile exports, May 1, 1981; nuclear power plant accident, Feb. 9, 1991.

Japan Air Lines, Aug. 12, 1985.

Japan, Sea of, Sep. 1, 1983.

Japanese-American citizens, Feb. 19, 1942; Mar. 23, 1942; Jan. 2, 1945; May 20, 1958; Aug. 10, 1988.

Japanese credit: frozen in U.S., Jul. 26, 1941.

Japanese Diet: opens, Nov. 29, 1890.

Japanese troops, Jan. 28, 1932.

Japanese war criminals, Apr. 20, 1951.

Japanese World Exposition: opens, Mar. 14, 1970.

Jarmusch, Jim, Jan. 22, 1954.

Jarre, Maurice, Sep. 13, 1924.

Jarreau, Al, Mar. 12, 1940.

Jarrell, Randall, May 6, 1914.

Jarrett, Keith, May 8, 1945.

Jaruzelski, Wojciech, Jul. 6, 1923, Feb. 9, 1981; Jul. 19, 1989.

Jarvik, Robert Koffler, May 11, 1946.

Jarvis, Anne, May 10, 1908.

Jarvis, Howard Arnold, Sep. 22, 1902.

Jaspers, Karl Theodor, Feb. 23, 1883.

Jassy, Peace of, Jan. 9, 1792.

Jassy (Romania): captured by Soviets, Aug. 24, 1944.

Jastrow, Robert, Sep. 7, 1925.

Jauregg, Julius Wagner von, Mar. 7, 1857.

Jaures, Jean Leon, Sep. 3, 1859.

Java, Mar. 9, 1942.

Java Sea, Battle of the, Feb. 27, 1942.

Javits, Jacob K., May 18, 1904.

Jawara, Dawda Kairaba, May 16, 1924; inaugurated, Jun. 12, 1962; Mar. 28, 1972.

Jaworski, Leon, Sep. 19, 1905

Jaworski, Ron(ald Vincent), Mar. 23, 1951.

Jay, John, Dec. 12, 1745; Feb. 1, 1790.

Jay, Peter, Feb. 7, 1937.

Jaycees Week, National, Jan. intro.

Jayewardene, Junius Richard, Sep. 17, 1906; inaugurated, Jul. 23, 1977.

Jay's Treaty: concluded, Nov. 19, 1794.

jazz bands: earliest printed mention, Oct. 27, 1916.

jazz recording: first, Mar. 7, 1917.

The Jazz Singer: opens, Oct. 6, 1927.

Jean, (Grand Duke), Jan. 5, 1921.

Jean Henri Dunant's Birthday (U.S.), May 8.

Jeans, Sir James Hopwood, Sep. 11, 1877.

Jeffers, Robinson, Jan. 10, 1887.

Jefferson Davis's Birthday (U.S.), Jun. 3.

Jefferson, Martha, Oct. 19, 1748; Sep. 27, 1772.

Jefferson Memorial, Apr. 13, 1943.

Jefferson, Thomas, Apr. 13, 1743; Mar. 4, 1797; inaugurated, Mar. 4, 1801; Dec. 22, 1807.

Jeffrey, Francis, Oct. 23, 1773.

Jeffreys, Anne, Jan. 26, 1923.

Jeffries, Jim, Jul. 4, 1910.

Jeffries, John, Feb. 5, 1744; Jan. 7, 1785.

Jellicoe, John Rushworth, Dec. 5, 1859.

Jemison, Mae C., Sep. 12, 1992; Oct. 17, 1956.

Jenco, Lawrence Martin, Jan. 8, 1985.

Jenkins, Ray H., Mar. 18, 1897.

Jenkins, Wilfred, May 20, 1970.

Jenner, Bruce, Oct. 28, 1949.

Jenner, Edward, May 17, 1749; May 14, 1796.

Jenney, William Le Baron, Sep. 25, 1832.

Jennings, Peter Charles, Jul. 29, 1938.

Jennings, Waylon, Jun. 15, 1937.

Jenrette, John Wilson, Jr., May 19, 1936.

Jensen, J. Hans Daniels, Jun. 25, 1907.

Jensen, Johannes, Jan. 20, 1873.

Jepsen, Marie, Aug. 30, 1992.

Jeremiah: premiere, Jan. 28, 1944.

Jericho, Feb. 21, 1918.

Jerne, Niels Kai, Dec. 23, 1911.

Jerusalem, Jul. 15, 1099; Oct. 2, 1187; captured by Egyptian Khwarazmi, Aug. 22, 1244; Dec. 9, 1917; Feb. 1, 1949; Apr. 3, 1949; Jan. 23, 1950; Jan. 5, 1964; Jun. 28, 1967; Jan. 15, 1970.

Jerusalem Day (Iran), May 5.

Jervis, John, Jan. 9, 1735.

Jespersen, (Jens) Otto (Harry), Jul. 16, 1860.

Jessel, George, Apr. 3, 1898.

Jesuits: founded, Aug. 15, 1534; Apr. 4, 1541; Jul. 21, 1773; expelled from Rome, Aug. 16, 1773; Mar. 1, 1797.

Jesus Christ: birth year, Apr. 6, 6 b.c.

Jesus Christ Superstar: premiere, Oct. 12, 1971.

jet fighter planes, Nov. 9, 1950.

jet propulsion, Jan. 6, 1944.

jetliner accident, Mar. 3, 1953.

Jett, Joan, Sep. 22, 1960.

Jewel (Jewel Kilcher), May 23, 1974.

Jewett, Sarah Orne, Sep. 3, 1849.

Jewish Book Month, National, Nov. intro.

Jewish Heritage Week, Apr. intro.

Jewison, Norman, Jul. 21, 1926; Aug. 2, 1967.

Jews expelled from Spain, Mar. 30, 1492.

Jhabvala, Ruth Prawer, May 7, 1927.

Jiang Qing, Jan. 25, 1981; Jan. 25, 1983.

Jillette, Penn, Mar. 5, 1955.

Jillian, Ann, Jan. 29, 1951.

Jimenez, Juan Ramon, Dec. 24, 1881.

Jiminez, Marcos Perez, Apr. 25, 1914.

Jimmy the Greek, Sep. 9, 1919.

Jingsheng, Wei, May 20, 1950.

Jinnah, Mohammed Ali, Dec. 25, 1876.

Joachim, Joseph, Jun. 28, 1831.

Joachim, King of Naples, Mar. 15, 1815.

Joan of Arc, Jan. 6, 1412; May 1, 1429; captured, May 23, 1430; burned at the stake, May 30, 1431; beatified, Apr. 18, 1909; canonized, May 16, 1920.

Jobs, Steven, Feb. 24, 1955.

Jochumsson, Matthias, Nov. 11, 1835.

Jodl, Alfred, May 10, 1890.

Joel, Billy, May 9, 1949.

Joergensen, Anker, Jul. 13, 1922.

Joffre, Joseph Jaeques, Jan. 12, 1852; Dec. 3, 1915.

Joffrey, Robert, Dec. 24, 1930.

Johannesburg: British seize, May 31, 1900.

Johansen, David, Jan. 9, 1950.

Johanson, Donald, Jun. 23, 1943.

Johanson, Don, Nov. 30, 1974.

Johansson, Ingemar, Jun. 26, 1959; Jun. 20, 1960; Mar. 13, 1961.

John II Casimir (Poland), May 3, 1660.

John II (Denmark), Oct. 28, 1497.

John II (France), Apr. 16, 1319; Aug. 22, 1350; dies, Apr. 8, 1364.

John III *(the Pious)*, King of Portugal, Jun. 6, 1502.

John III Sobieski (Poland), Aug. 17, 1629; Feb. 14, 1674.

John VI (Portugal), May 13, 1767; Aug. 29, 1820.

John XII (pope): deposed, Dec. 4, 963.

John XXII (pope), Mar. 23, 1324; Apr. 18, 1328.

John XXIII (pope), Nov. 25, 1881; Oct. 28, 1958; Mar. 3, 1960; Mar. 28, 1960; Dec. 2, 1960; Jul. 14, 1961; Dec. 25, 1961; Oct. 11, 1962; Apr. 10, 1963; dies, Jun. 3, 1963.

John Albert (Poland), Jun. 7, 1492.

John Birch Society: founded, Dec. 9, 1958.

John Cantius, Dec. 23.

John Casimir (Poland): abdicates, Jun. 19, 1669.

John of the Cross, Saint, Jun. 24, 1542.

John (Don of Austria), Oct. 7, 1571; May 20, 1591.

John, Elton, Mar. 25, 1947.

John of Gaunt, Sep. 30, 1399.

John, Thomas Edward, Jr., *(Tommy)*, May 22, 1943.

John (King of England), Dec. 24, 1167; May 22, 1200; May 15, 1213; Jun. 15, 1215; dies, Oct. 19, 1216.

John of Lancaster, Jun. 20, 1389.

John Paul I (pope), Oct. 17, 1912; elected, Aug. 26, 1978; dies, Sep. 29, 1978.

John Paul II (pope), May 18, 1920; first non-Italian pope in 456 years, Oct. 16, 1978; arrives in

U.S., Oct. 1, 1979; Oct. 6, 1979; shot, May 13, 1981; Jan. 25, 1983; May 9, 1983; meets with Gorbachev, Mikhail, Dec. 1, 1989; visits Cuba, Jan 21, 1998.

John, Prince Regent of Portugal, Dec. 16, 1815.

John Street Theater: opens, Dec. 7, 1767.

Johns, Glynis, Oct. 5, 1923.

Johns, Jasper, May 15, 1930.

Johnson, Amy, May 24, 1930.

Johnson, Andrew, Dec. 29, 1808; Mar. 4, 1865; impeachment trial, May 16, 1868.

Johnson, Betsey, Aug. 10, 1942.

Johnson, Beverly, Oct. 13, 1951.

Johnson, Byron Bancroft, Jan. 5, 1864.

Johnson, Claudia Alta *(Ladybird)*, Dec. 22, 1912.

Johnson, David Allen *(Dave)*, Jan. 30, 1943.

Johnson, Don, Dec. 15, 1950.

Johnson, Earvin *(Magic)*, Aug. 14, 1959; retires, Nov. 7, 1991; retires, Nov. 2, 1992.

Johnson, Eliza, Oct. 4, 1810.

Johnson, Eyvind, Jul. 29, 1900.

Johnson, Hiram Warren, Sep. 2, 1866.

Johnson, Jack, Mar. 31, 1878; Dec. 26, 1908; Jul. 4, 1910; Apr. 5, 1915.

Johnson, James Weldon, Jun. 17, 1871.

Johnson, Jimmy, Jul. 16, 1943.

Johnson, John, Jan. 19, 1918.

Johnson, Larry, Mar. 14, 1969.

Johnson, Lyndon B., Aug. 27, 1908; Jan. 20, 1961; Nov. 22, 1963; Jul. 2, 1964; Democratic candidate for President, Aug. 26, 1964; Jan. 4, 1965; inaugurated, Jan. 20, 1965; Feb. 8, 1966; Jan. 5, 1967; Mar. 31, 1968; Apr. 11, 1968; dies, Jan. 22, 1973.

Johnson, Mordecai, Jan. 12, 1890.

Johnson, Pamela Hansford, May 29, 1912.

Johnson, Philip *(Cortelyou)*, Jul. 8, 1906; Dec. 11, 1965.

Johnson, Rafer, Aug. 18, 1935.

Johnson, Randall (Randy) David, Sep. 10, 1963.

Johnson, Richard Mentor, Oct. 17, 1780.

Johnson-Reed Immigration Bill, May 26, 1924.

Johnson, Reverdy, May 21, 1796.

Johnson, Richard M., Mar. 4, 1837.

Johnson, Samuel, Oct. 14, 1696; Sep. 18, 1709; May 16, 1763.

Johnson, Sonia, Feb. 27, 1936.

Johnson, Van, Aug. 20, 1916.

Johnson, Virginia E., Feb. 11, 1925.

Johnson, William, Sep. 8, 1755.

Johnson, William Eugene, Mar. 25, 1862.

Johnston, Albert (General), Apr. 6, 1862.

Johnston, Clement D(ixon), Nov. 7, 1895.

Joinville, League of, Dec. 31, 1584.

Joliet, Louis, Sep. 21, 1645.

Joliot-Curie, Irene, Sep. 12, 1897.

Joliot-Curie, Jean Frederic, Mar. 19, 1900; Apr. 28, 1950.

Jolson, Al, May 26, 1886.

Jonathan, Leabua (Lesotho), Jan. 30, 1970; Mar. 31, 1970; Jan. 20, 1986.

Jones, Mary *(Mother Jones)*, May 1, 1830.

Jones, David *(Davy)*, Dec. 30, 1946.

Jones, Brian, Feb. 26, 1943.

Jones, Carolyn, Apr. 28, 1933.

Jones, Casey, Apr. 30, 1900.

Jones, Dean, Jan. 25, 1936.

Jones, Edward Lee *(Too Tall)*, Feb. 23, 1951.

Jones, Ernest, Jan. 1, 1879.

Jones, George, Sep. 12, 1931.

Jones, Grace, May 19, 1952.

Jones, Inigo, Jul. 19, 1573.

Jones, Jack, Jan. 14, 1938.

Jones, James, Nov. 6, 1921.

Jones, James Earl, Jan. 17, 1931.

Jones, Jeffrey, Sep. 28, 1947.

Jones, Jennifer, Mar. 2, 1919.

Jones, Jenny (Janina Stronski), Jun. 7, 1946.

Jones, Jerry (Jerral), Oct. 13, 1942.

Jones, Jim, Nov. 18, 1978.

Jones, John P., Jan. 3, 1946.

Jones, John Paul, Jul. 6, 1747.

Jones, Kenny, Sep. 16, 1948.

Jones, Leroi, Oct. 7, 1934.

Jones, Paula, lawsuit dismissed, Apr. 1, 1998.

Jones, Quincy Delight, Mar. 14, 1933.

Jones, Rickie Lee, Nov. 18, 1954.

Jones, Samuel Milton (Golden Rule), Aug. 8, 1846.

Jones, Shirley, Mar. 31, 1934.

Jones, Spike, Dec. 14, 1911.

Jones, Stormie, Feb. 14, 1984.

Jones, Tom (dramatist), May 3, 1960.

Jones, Tom (singer), Jun. 7, 1940.

Jones, Tommy Lee, Sep. 15, 1946.

Jong, Erica, Mar. 26, 1942.

Jongkind, Johan Barthold, Jun. 3, 1819.

jonquil, Mar. intro.

Jonson, Ben(jamin), Jun. 11, 1572.

Joplin, Janis, Jan. 19, 1943.

Joplin, Scott, Nov. 24, 1868.

Jordaens, Jacob, May 19, 1593.

Jordan, Feb. 20, 1928; formed, Apr. 24, 1950; Jan. 8, 1952; May 30, 1967; Apr. 6, 1972; Oct. 26, 1994.

Jordan, Barbara, Feb. 21, 1936.

Jordan, David Starr, Jan. 19, 1851.

Jordan, Irving, Jr., Mar. 13, 1988.

Jordan, Louis, Jul. 8, 1908.

Jordan, Michael, Feb. 17, 1963; retires, Oct. 6, 1993; return to NBA, Mar. 18, 1994.

Jordan, Richard, Jul. 19, 1938.

Jordan, Vernon E., Jr., Aug. 15, 1935.

Jorgensen, Anker: inaugurated, Feb. 13, 1975.

Jorgensen, Christine, Dec. 1, 1952.

Jorgensen, George, Jr. See: Jorgensen, Christine.

Josef I (Holy Roman Emperor), May 5, 1705; dies, Apr. 17, 1711.

Josef II (Holy Roman Emperor), Mar. 13, 1741; Aug. 18, 1765; dies, Feb. 20, 1790.

Josef Ferdinand (Archduke of Austria), May 3, 1915.

Joseph I (Portugal): dies, Feb. 24, 1777.

Joseph, Chief: surrenders, Oct. 4, 1877; Oct. 5, 1877.

Josephine (Beauharnais), Jun. 23, 1766.

Josephson, Brian David, Jan. 4, 1940.

Jouhaux, Leon, Jul. 1, 1879.

Joule, James Prescott, Dec. 24, 1818.

Jourdan, Louis, Jun. 19, 1921.

Jovellanos, Gaspar Melchor de, Jan. 5, 1744.

Jowett, Benjamin, Apr. 15, 1817.

Joyce, Elaine, Dec. 19, 1945.

Joyce, William (Lord Haw-Haw), Jan. 3, 1946.

Joyce, James, Feb. 2, 1882; Feb. 2, 1922.

Joyner, Wallace Keith (Wally), Jun. 16, 1962.

Joyner, Florence (Flo-Jo) Griffith, Dec. 21, 1959.

Joyner-Kersee, Jackie, Mar. 3, 1962.

Jozef Pilsudski, Nov. 28, 1922.

Juan Carlos I (Spain), Jan. 5, 1938; assumes power, Oct. 30, 1975; Nov. 22, 1975.

Juan Carlos (Alfonso Victor Maria de Borboon y Borbon), Jul. 22, 1969.

Juan Manuel (Infante de Castile), May 5, 1282.

Juan Santamaria Day (Costa Rica), Apr. 11.

Juana Ines de la Cruz, Sor, Nov. 12, 1651.

Juantorena, Alberto, Dec. 3, 1951.

Juarez, Benito, Mar. 21, 1806.

Judd, Ashley, Apr. 19, 1968.

Judd, Naomi, Jan. 11, 1946.

Judd, Wynonna, May 30, 1964.

judicial review, Feb. 24, 1803.

Judson, Harry Pratt, Dec. 20, 1849.

jugglers, patron of, Feb. 12.

Juilliard, Augustus D., Apr. 19, 1836.

Julesburg (Colorado), Jan. 7, 1865.

Julia, Raul, Mar. 9, 1940.

Julian, Percy Lavon, Apr. 11, 1899.

Juliana (Queen of the Netherlands), Apr. 30, 1909; Sep. 4, 1948; abdicates, Apr. 30, visits Indonesia, Aug. 26, 1981.

Julius I (pope), Feb. 6, 337.

Julius II (pope), Dec. 5, 1443.

Julius III (pope), Sep. 10, 1487.

July Belongs to Blueberries, Jul. intro.

Jumblatt, Kamal: assassinated, Mar. 16, 1977.

Junejo, Muhammad Khan: inaugurated, Mar. 23, 1985.

Jung, Carl Gustav, Jul. 26, 1875.

Jungmann, Josef Jakub, Jul. 16, 1773.

Junior Achievement Week, Jan. intro.

Junius, Jun. intro.

Juno, Jun. intro.

Jupiter, Jan. 7, 1610; approached by Pioneer 10, Dec. 3, 1973; Mar. 1, 1979; Mar. 5, 1979.

Jurgens, Curt, Dec. 12, 1915.

Jurgenson, Sonny, Aug. 23, 1934.

Just, Ernest Everett, Aug. 14, 1883.

Justice, U.S. Department of: established, Jun. 22, 1870.

Jutland, Battle of, May 31, 1916.

K

K-k-k-Ka-ty, Beautiful Katy: copyrighted, Oct. 10, 1916.

K Mart Corp.: incorporated, Mar. 8, 1916.

Kabbah, Ahmed Tejan: removed from power, May 25, 1997; return to power, Mar. 10, 1998.

Kabila, Laurent, May 16, 1997; May 17, 1997.

Kabul (Afghanistan): massacre of British, Sep. 3, 1879; Jan. 17, 1929.

Kachingwe, Joe, Feb. 5, 1968.

Kaczynski, Theodore, Jan. 22, 1998; four life prison term, May 4, 1998. See also unabomber.

Kadar, Janos, May 22, 1912; Nov. 4, 1956; May 22, 1988.

Kadooment Day (Barbados), Jul. intro.

Kael, Pauline, Jun. 19, 1919.

Kaesong (North Korea), Jul. 14, 1951.

Kafi, Ali, Jul. 2, 1992.

Kafka, Franz, Jul. 3, 1883.

Kaganovich, Jan. 27, 1962.

Kagitingan Day (Phillipines), May 6.

Kahlo, Frida, Jul. 6, 1907.

Kahn, Albert, Mar. 21, 1869.

Kahn, Louis I., Feb. 2, 1901.

Kahn, Madelrne Gail, Sep. 29, 1942.

Kahn, Otto Hermann, Feb. 21, 1867.

Kaiser, Edgar F(osburgh), Jul. 29, 1908.

Kaiser, Georg, Nov. 25, 1878.

Kaiser, Henry John, May 9, 1882.

Kalakaua, David, Nov. 16, 1836.

Kalanianaole Day, Prince Johan Kuhio (Hawaii), Mar. intro.

Kalb, Baron Johann de, Jun. 29, 1721.

Kalb, Marvin Leonard, Jun. 9, 1930.

Kaledin, Aleksei, Jan. 10, 1918; Feb. 13, 1918.

Kalevala Day (Finland), Feb. 28.

Kaline, Al(bert William), Dec. 19, 1934.

Kalinin, Mikhail Ivanovich, Nov. 19, 1875.

Kalish, Isidore, Nov. 15, 1816.

Kalmbach, Herbert Warren, Oct. 19, 1921.

Kaltenborn, H. V. (Hans von), Jul. 9.

Kamahameha III (Hawaii), Mar. 7, 1814.

Kamali, Norma, Jun. 27, 1945.

Kamarampaka Day (Rwanda), Sep. 25.

Kamehameha Day (Hawaii, U.S.), Jun. 11.

Kamen, Martin David, Aug. 27, 1913.

Kamenev, Lev Borisovich, Jul. 18, 1883.

Kamerlingh-Onnes, Heike, Sep. 21, 1853.

kamikaze attack, Apr. 6, 1945.

Kaminska, Ida, Sep. 4, 1899.

Kampala (Uganda), Apr. 11, 1979.

Kampelman, Max M., Nov. 7, 1920.

Kamuzu Day (Malawi), May 14.

Kanagawa, Treaty of, Mar. 31, 1854.

Kanauj (India), May 17, 1540.

Kander, John, Nov. 20, 1966.

Kandinsky, Wassily, Dec. 4, 1866.

Kane, Carol, Jun. 18, 1952.

Kanellopoulos, Kanellos, Apr. 23, 1988.

Kanemaru, Shin, Aug. 28, 1992.

K'ang-hsi (Manchu Dynasty), May 4, 1654.

K'ang Yu-wei, Mar. 19, 1858.

Kang, Younghill, Dec. 13, 1903.

Kania, Stanislaw, Mar. 8, 1927.

Kanin, Garson, Nov. 24, 1912.

Kansas-Nebraska Act, May 30, 1854.

Kansas (U.S.): admitted to Union, Jan. 29, 1861.

Kant, Immanuel, Apr. 22, 1724.

Kantanga, Jan. 15, 1963.

Kantemir (Cantemir), Dimitrie, Oct. 26, 1673.

Kantner, Dee, Oct. 28, 1997.

Kantner, Paul, Mar. 12, 1942.

Kantor, MacKinlay, Feb. 4, 1904, May 7, 1956.

Kantorovich, Leonid, Jan. 15, 1912.

Kapitsa, Pyotr, Jun. 26, 1894.

Kaplan, Gabriel (Gabe), Mar. 31, 1945.

Kaplan, Dora: executed, Sep. 4, 1918.

Kappel, Battle of: ends, Oct. 11, 1531.

Karachi (India), Apr. 6, 1929.

Karadzic, Vuk Stefanovic, Oct. 26, 1787.

Karajan, Herbert von, Apr. 5, 1908; Apr. 5, 1955.

Karakatoa volcano: explodes, Aug. 26, 1883.

Karamanlis, Constantine, Feb. 23, 1907.

Karameh, Mar. 21, 1968.

Karami, Rashid: resigns, May 4, 1987.

Karamzin, Nikolai Mikhaylovich, Dec. 1, 1766.

Karan, Donna Faske, Oct. 2, 1948.

Karjalainen, Ahti, Apr. 13, 1962.

Karle, Jerome, Jun. 18, 1918.

Karlfeldt, Erik Axel, Jul. 20, 1864.

Karloff, Boris, Nov. 23, 1887.

Karlowitz, Treaty of, Jan. 26, 1699.

Karmal, Babrak, Dec. 27, 1979; May 4, 1986.

Karolyi, Count Michael, Nov. 1, 1918.

Karp, Haskell, Apr. 4, 1969.

Karpov, Anatoly Yevgenyevich, May 23, 1951; Nov. 9, 1985.

Karras, Alex(ander G.), Jul. 15, 1935.

Karrer, Paul, Apr. 21, 1889.

Kartini Day (Indonesia), Apr. 21.

Kasala, Mar. 19, 1896

Kasdan, Lawrence Edward, Jan. 14, 1949.

Kashmir, Mar. 9, 1846.

Kasparov, Gary, Apr. 12, 1963; Nov. 9, 1985.

Kassebaum, Nancy Landon, Jul. 29, 1932.

Kassorla, Irene Chamie, Aug. 18, 1931.

Kastler, Alfred, May 3, 1902.

Katanga Company, Apr. 15, 1891.

Katanga province, Jul. 11, 1960; Jul. 14, 1960.

Katsura, Prince Taro, Nov. 28, 1847.

Katt, William, Feb. 16, 1955.

Katz, Alex, Jul. 24, 1927.

Katz, Sir Bernard, Mar. 26, 1911.

Kauffman, Angelica, Oct. 20, 1741.

Kaufman, Andy, Jan. 17, 1949.

Kaufman, George S(imon), Nov. 16, 1889.

Kaulbach, Wilhelm von, Oct. 15, 1805.

Kaunda, Kenneth D., Apr. 28, 1924; Jan. 22, 1964.

Kavner, Julie Deborah, Sep. 7, 1951.

Kawabata Yasunari, Jun. 11, 1899.

Kay, Hershy, Nov. 17, 1919.

Kaye, Danny, Jan. 18, 1913.

Kaye, Sammy, Mar. 13, 1913.

Kazan, Elia, Sep. 7, 1909; Jul. 28, 1954.

Kazan, Lainie, May 16, 1940.

Kazantzakis, Nikos, Dec. 2, 1883; Apr. 15, 1953.

KDKA, Pittsburgh: first commercial news radio broadcast, Nov. 2, 1920.

Keach, Stacy, Jun. 2, 1941.

Kean, Edmund, Mar. 17, 1787.

Kearny, Philip, Jun. 1, 1814.

Kearny, U.S.S.: sunk, Oct. 17, 1941.

Kearny, Stephen Watts, Aug. 30, 1794.

Keating, Charles, Dec. 4, 1991.

Keating-Owen Act (Child Labor Act), Sep. 1, 1916.

Keaton, Buster, Oct. 4, 1895.

Keaton, Diane, Jan. 5, 1946; Apr. 24, 1979.

Keaton, Michael, Sep. 5, 1951.

Keats, John, Oct. 31, 1795.

Keeler, Christine, Jun. 5, 1963

Keeler, Ruby, Aug. 25, 1909.

Keen, William Williams, Jan. 19, 1837.

Keep America Beautiful Week, Apr. intro.

Keeshan, Bob, Jun. 27, 1927.

Kefauver, (Carey) Estes, Jul. 26, 1903.

Keillor, Garrison, Aug. 7, 1942.

Keita, Mobido: overthrown, Nov. 19, 1968.

Keitel, Harvey, May 13, 1939.

Keitel, Wilhelm, Sep. 22, 1882.

Keith, Brian, Nov. 14, 1921.

Keith, Louis, Apr. 24, 1935.

Keith, Vicki, Aug. 30, 1988.

Kekkonen, Urho K., May 26, 1979.

Kell, George Clyde, Aug. 23, 1922.

Kellaway, Cecil, Aug. 22, 1894.

Keller, Gottfried, Jul. 19, 1819.

Keller, Helen Adams, Jun. 27, 1880.

Kellerman, Sally, Jun. 2, 1937.

Kelley, Clarence M., Oct. 24, 1911; Jul. 9, 1973.

Kelley, Frank Joseph, Dec. 31, 1924.

Kelley, Kitty, Apr. 4, 1942.

Kelley, Virginia Clinton, Jan. 6, 1994.

Kellgren, Johan Henrik, Dec. 1, 1751.

Kellogg-Briand Pact: signed, Aug. 27, 1928.

Kellogg, Frank Billings, Dec. 22, 1857.

Kellogg, John Harvey, Feb. 26, 1852.

Kellogg, Will Keith, Apr. 7, 1860.

Kelly, Clarence M., May 8, 1976.

Kelly, Ellsworth, May 31, 1923.

Kelly, Emmett, Dec. 8, 1898.

Kelly, Gene, Aug. 23, 1912; Nov. 21, 1938.

Kelly, Jim, Feb. 14, 1960.

Kelly, Leonard Patrick (Red), Jul. 9, 1927.

Kelly, Petra Karin, Nov. 29, 1947.

Kelly, R(obert), Jan. 8, 1968.

Kelly, William, Aug. 22, 1811.

Kemble, Fanny, Nov. 27, 1809.

Kemble, John Philip, Feb. 1, 1757.

Kemmerer, Edwin Walter, Jun. 29, 1875.

Kemp, Jack French, Jul. 13, 1935; Dec. 19, 1988.

Kemp, Shawn, Nov. 26, 1969.

Kemp, Steve(n F.), Aug. 7, 1954.

Kemper, James S(cott), Nov. 18, 1886.

Kendall, Edward Calvin, Mar. 8, 1886.

Kendall, Henry, Dec. 9, 1926.

Kendrew, John C., Mar. 24, 1917.

Kennan, George Frost, Feb. 16, 1904.

Kennedy, Anthony, Feb. 18, 1988.

Kennedy, Caroline Bouvier, Nov. 27, 1957.

Kennedy Center for the Performing Arts, John F., Sep. 8, 1971.

Kennedy, Edward M., Feb. 22, 1932; Jul. 19, 1969.

Kennedy, George, Feb. 18, 1925.

Kennedy, Joan Bennett, Sep. 5, 1936.

Kennedy, John F., May 29, 1917; Nov. 4, 1946; Jul. 13, 1960; Sep. 26, 1960; inaugurated, Jan. 20, 1961; Jan. 25, 1961; Mar. 1, 1961; Jan. 30, 1962; Feb. 3, 1962; May 12, 1962; Jun. 10, 1963; Jun. 26, 1963; assassinated, Nov. 22, 1963; Sep. 27, 1964; memorial, May 14, 1965; Jan. 3, 1967.

Kennedy, John Fitzgerald, Jr., Nov. 25, 1960.

Kennedy, Joseph Patrick, Sep. 6, 1888.

Kennedy, Joseph Patrick, III, Sep. 24, 1952.

Kennedy Memorial, Dec. 11, 1965.

Kennedy, Moorehead Cowell, Jr., Nov. 5, 1930.

Kennedy, Robert F., Nov. 20, 1925; shot, Jun. 5, 1968; Apr. 17, 1969; Apr. 23, 1969.

Kennedy, Rose, Jul. 22, 1890.

Kennedy Space Center (Florida), Apr. 12, 1981.

Kennedy, William, Jan. 16, 1928.

Kennedy, William Patrick (Bill), Jan. 20, 1955.

Kennelly, Arthur Edwin, Dec. 17, 1861.

Kennerly, David Hume, Mar. 9, 1947.

Kennesaw Mountain, Battle of, Jun. 27, 1864.

Kenney, George Churchill, Aug. 6, 1889.

Kenny, Sister Elizabeth, Sep. 20, 1886.

Kent (England): German raid on, May 25, 1915.

Kent, Arthur, Dec. 27, 1953.

Kent, James, Jul. 31, 1763.

Kent, Rockwell, Jun. 21, 1882.

Kent State shootings: U.S. Commission report, Oct. 4, 1970.

Kent State University, May 4, 1970.

Kenton, Stan, Feb. 19, 1912.

Kentucky: admitted to Union, Jun. 1, 1792.

Kentucky Derby: first, May 17, 1875; May 12, 1917.

Kentucky Fried Chicken Corp.: incorporated, Mar. 4, 1964; Aug. 10, 1970.

Kenya: made British protectorate, Jun. 15, 1895; Oct. 23, 1952; May 28, 1963; independence, Dec. 12, 1963; admitted to U.N., Dec. 16, 1963; Jan. 31, 1968; May 19, 1977; ban on ivory, May 11, 1989.

Kenya (British East Africa): becomes colony, Jul. 23, 1920.

Kenya, Mt.: discovered, Dec. 3, 1849; first climbed, Sep. 13, 1899.

Kenyatta Day (Kenya), Oct. 20.

Kenyatta, Jomo, Oct. 20, 1891; Oct. 23, 1952; released from prison, Aug. 21, 1961; May 28, 1963.

Keokuk Dam: opened, Aug. 26, 1914.

Kepler, Johannes, Dec. 27, 1571.

Kercheval, Ken, Jul. 15, 1935.

Kerekou, Mathieu, Sep. 2, 1933; Oct. 27, 1972.

Kerenski, Aleksandr Feodorovich, Apr. 22, 1881.

Kern, Jerome, Jan. 27, 1885; Dec. 27, 1927.

Kerouac, Jack, Mar. 12, 1922; Sep. 5, 1957.

Kerr, Deborah Jane, Sep. 30, 1921; Aug. 5, 1953.

Kerr, John, Nov. 15, 1931.

Kerr-McGee Corp., Aug. 22, 1986.

Kerr, Robert Samuel, Sep. 11, 1896.

Kerr, Walter Francis, Jul. 8, 1913.

Kerrey, J. Robert, Aug. 27, 1943.

Kerrigan, Nancy, Oct. 13, 1969; Jan. 6, 1994.

Kershaw, Doug(las James), Jan. 24, 1936.

Kerwin, Joseph P., Jun. 22, 1973.

Kerz, Leo, Nov. 1, 1912.

Kesey, Ken, Sep. 17, 1935.

Keshtmand, Soltan Ali, May 27, 1988.

Kesselring, Albert, Nov. 20, 1885.

Kessler, David, May 31, 1951.

Kettering, Charles Franklin, Aug. 29, 1876.

Kevorkian, Dr. Jack, Mar. 8, 1996.

Key, Ellen Karoline Sofia, Dec. 11, 1849.

Key, Francis Scott, Aug. 1, 1779; Apr. 13, 1814; Sep. 14, 1814.

Key Largo: premieres, Jul. 16, 1948.

Keyes, Alan L., Aug. 7, 1950.

Keyes, Frances Parkinson, Jul. 21, 1885.

Keynes, John Maynard, Jun. 5, 1883.

Khaalis, Hamaas Abdul, Jul. 23, 1977.

Khachaturian, Aram Ilich, Jun. 6, 1903.

Khalid (Saudi Arabia), Mar. 25, 1975.

Khama, Sir Seretse M., Jul. 1, 1921; Mar. 8, 1950.

Khambatta, Persis, Oct. 2, 1950.

Khan, Aga, III, Nov. 2, 1877.

Khan, Aga, IV, Dec. 13, 1936.

Khan, Chaka, Mar. 23, 1953.

Khan, Ghulam Ishaq, Aug. 6, 1990.

Khan, Mohammad Daud, Jul. 17, 1973; Jul. 28, 1973.

Khanh, Hguyen (General), Jan. 26, 1965.

Khartoum, Feb. 18, 1884; Jan. 26, 1885.

Khashoggi, Adnan, Jul. 25, 1935.

Khatami, Mohammed, May 23, 1997.

Khim Tit, Apr. 2, 1956.

Khmer Rouge, Apr. 17, 1975; Apr. 25, 1975; Sep. 2, 1985; Apr. 5, 1989; Sep. 26, 1989.

Khomeini, Ayatollah Ruhollah, May 17, 1900; Feb. 1, 1979; Feb. 11, 1979; Mar. 16, 1979; issues bans, Jul. 23, 1979; Dec. 2, 1979; Jun. 22, 1981; Jun. 3, 1989.

Khorana, Har Gobind, Jan. 9, 1922.

Khruschshev, Nikita S., Apr. 17, 1894; Mar. 20, 1953; Sep. 13, 1953; Secret Speech, Feb. 24, 1956; Oct. 28, 1962; Oct. 15, 1964.

Khyber Pass: massacre, Jan. 13, 1842; May 26, 1879; Mar. 11, 1898; first train through, Nov. 1, 1925.

Kiaochow Bay, Mar. 6, 1898.

Kidd, William, May 23, 1701.

Kidder, Margot, Oct. 17, 1948.

Kidman, Nicole, Jun. 20, 1967.

kidney transplant, Jun. 17, 1950.

Kids' Day, Sep. intro; Sep. 24.

Kiefer, Anselm, Mar. 8, 1945.

Kiel: German naval mutiny, Nov. 3, 1918.

Kiel, Treaty of, Jan. 14, 1814.

Kienzle, William Xavier, Sep. 11, 1928.

Kieran, John, Aug. 2, 1892.

Kierkegaard, Soren, May 5, 1813.

Kiesinger, Kurt-Georg, Dec. 1, 1966.

Kiev, Feb. 18, 1918; Sep. 19, 1941; Nov. 6, 1943.

Kiker, Douglas, Jan. 7, 1930.

Kilimanjaro, Mar. 5, 1916.

Killebrew, Harmon (Clayton), Jun. 29, 1936.

Killiecrankie: Scottish Jacobites defeated, Jul. 27, 1689.

Killy, Jean-Claude, Aug. 30, 1943.

Kilmer, (Alfred) Joyce, Dec. 6, 1886.

Kilmer, Val, Dec. 31, 1959.

Kilpatrick, James Jackson, Nov. 1, 1920.

Kilrain, Jake, Jul. 8, 1889.

Kim Dae Jung, Jan. 6, 1924.

Kim Dae Jung, Dec. 10, 1997; Feb. 25, 1998.

Kim Hyun Chul, Jul. 10, 1962.

Kim Il-Sung, Apr. 15, 1912.

Kim Il-Sung's Birthday (North Korea), Apr. 15.

Kim Jae Kyu, Oct. 26, 1979; sentenced, Dec. 20, 1979.

Kim Jong Il, Feb. 15, 1942.

Kim Young Sam, elected, Dec. 18, 1992.

Kimball, Spencer Woolley, Mar. 28, 1895.

Kimberley (South Africa): diamond fields annexed, Oct. 27, 1871.

Kimmel, Husband Edward, Feb. 26, 1882.

King, Alan, Dec. 26, 1927.

King, Albert, Apr. 24, 1923.

King, Martin Luther, Sr (Daddy), Dec. 19, 1899.

King, B. B., Sep. 16, 1925.

King, Billie Jean, Nov. 22, 1943; Sep. 20, 1973.

King, Carole, Feb. 9, 1941.

King, Clarence, Jan. 6, 1842.

King, Coretta Scott, Apr. 27, 1927.

King David Hotel (Jerusalem), Jul. 22, 1946.

King Day, Martin Luther (U.S.), Jan. 20, 1986.

King, Don(ald), Dec. 6, 1932.

King, Ernest Joseph, Nov. 23, 1878.

King, Evelyn (Champagne), Jul. 1, 1960.

King Juan Carlos' Saint's Day (Spain), Jun. 24.

King Kamehameha Day (Hawaii), Jun. 11.

King, Larry, Nov. 19, 1933.

King, Malcolm, Jul. 19, 1885.

King, Martin Luther, Jr.,: Birthday (U.S.), Jan. intro; Jan. 15, 1929; Dec. 5, 1955; Aug. 28, 1963; Dec. 10, 1964; Feb. 4, 1965; Mar. 21, 1965; calls for civil disobedience, Aug. 15, 1967; assassinated, Apr. 4, 1968; Apr. 5, 1968; Jun. 8, 1968; birthday made federal holiday, Oct. 19, 1983.

King, Perry, Apr. 30, 1948.

King, Richard, Jul. 10, 1825.

King, Rodney, beaten, Mar. 3, 1991; officers acquitted in beating of, Apr. 29, 1992; rioting in Los Angeles, CA, May 2, 1992; beating trial of, begins, Feb. 25, 1993.

King, Rufus, Mar. 24, 1755.

King, Stephen, Sep. 21, 1947.

King, William Lyon Mackenzie, Dec. 17, 1874; Nov. 15, 1948.

King, William R., Mar. 4, 1853.

King, William Rufus de Vane, Apr. 7, 1786.

Kingdom Day (Aruba, Netherlands), Dec. 15.

Kingdom of the Serbs, Croats, and Slovenes, Oct. 3, 1929.

King's Birthday (Lesotho), May intro.

King's Birthday (Swaziland), Apr. 19; Apr. 19.

King's Birthday (Thailand), Dec. 5; Dec. 5.

King's College (Columbia University): chartered, Oct. 31, 1754.

Kings Lynn, Jan. 19, 1915.

King's Mountain, Battle of, Oct. 7, 1780.

Kingsley, Ben, Dec. 31, 1943.

Kingsley, Charles, Jun . 12, 1819.

Kingston, Maxine Hong, Oct. 27, 1940.

Kinnock, Neil Gordon, Mar. 28, 1942.

Kinsey, Alfred Charles, Jun. 23, 1894.

Kinski, Nastassja, Jan. 24, 1960.

Kintner, Robert E(dmonds), Sep. 12, 1909.

Kintradwell, patron of, Oct. 8.

Kipling, (Joseph) Rudyard, Dec. 30, 1865.

Kiplinger, William, Jan. 8, 1891.

Kirby-Smith, Edmund, May 16, 1824.

Kirchner, Leon, Jan. 24, 1919.

Kirchschlaeger, Rudolf, Mar. 20, 1915.

Kiriyenko, Sergie, Jul. 16, 1926; Mar. 27, 1998.

Kirkland, Gelsey, Dec. 29, 1952.

Kirkland, Lane, Mar. 12, 1922; Nov. 19, 1979.

Kirkpatrick, Jeane Duane Jordan, Nov. 19, 1926. Jan. 30, 1985; Mar. 25, 1985.

Kirkus, Virginia, Dec. 7, 1893.

Kirkwood, Samuel Jordan, Dec. 20, 1813.

Kirov, Serge: assassinated, Dec. 1, 1934.

Kirshner, Don, Apr. 17, 1934.

Kisfaludy, Sandor, Sep. 27, 1772.

Kishinev (Romania): captured by Soviets, Aug. 24, 1944.

Kiska (Aleutian Islands): seized by Japan, Jun. 14, 1942; reoccupied by U.S. and Canada, Aug. 15, 1943.

Kismet: opens, Dec. 3, 1953.

Kiss Me Kate: premiere, Dec. 30, 1948.

Kissinger, Henry, May 27, 1923; named Secretary of State, Aug. 22, 1973; Sep. 21, 1973; Feb. 24, 1976; Mar. 10, 1976.

Kitazato, Baron Shibasaburo, Dec. 20, 1856.

Kitchener, Lord Horatio Herbert, Jun. 24, 1850; Mar. 19, 1896; Sep. 2, 1898; Jan. 21, 1899; Jan. 10, 1900; Feb. 27, 1900; Nov. 29, 1900; Nov. 28, 1902; drowned, Jun. 5, 1916.

Kite, Thomas O., Jr., Dec. 9, 1949.

Kitt, Eartha, Jan. 26, 1928.

Kitt Peak, Mar. 15, 1960.

Kitty Hawk (North Carolina), Dec. 17, 1903.

Kiukiang, Mar. 15, 1927.

Kiwanis International, Jan. 21, 1915.

Kiwanis Week, World-wide, Jan. intro.

Kiwanuka, Benedicto (Uganda): first prime minister, Mar. 1, 1962.

Klarsfeld, Beate, Feb. 13, 1931.

Kleban, Edward, Jul. 25, 1975.

Kleber, Jean Baptiste, Mar. 9, 1753.

Klee, Paul, Dec. 18, 1879.

Klein, Anne, Aug. 3, 1923.

Klein, Calvin, Nov. 19, 1942.

Klein, Lawrence R., Sep. 14, 1920.

Klein, Robert, Feb. 8, 1942.

Kleindienst, Richard Gordon, Aug. 5, 1923; Apr. 30, 1973.

Klemperer, Otto, May 14, 1885.

Klemperer, Werner, Mar. 22, 1920.

Klimt, Gustav, Jul. 4, 1862.

Kline, Kevin, Oct. 24, 1947.

Klinghoffer, Leon, Oct. 7, 1985.

Klestil, Thomas, reelected, Apr. 19, 1998.

Klitzing, Klaus von, Jun. 28, 1943.

Klondike gold rush, Aug. 16. 1896.

Klopstock, Friedrich Gottlieb, Jul. 2, 1724.

Kluck, Alexander von, May 20, 1846.

Klug, Aaron, Aug. 11, 1926; Aug. 11, 1926.

Klugman, Jack, Apr. 27, 1922.

Knebel, Fletcher, Oct. 1, 1911.

Kneller, Sir Godfrey (Gottfried Kniller), Aug. 8.

Knickerbocker Baseball Club: first baseball game, Jun. 19, 1846.

Knight, Eric Mowbray, Apr. 10, 1897.

Knight, Gladys Maria, May 28, 1944.

Knight, John S(hively), Oct. 26, 1894.

Knight, Robert Montgomery (Bobby), Oct. 25, 1940.

Knight, Phil(ip H.), Feb. 24, 1938.

Knight-Ridder Newspapers, Nov. 30, 1974.

Knight, Shirley, Jul. 5, 1937.

Knight, Ted, Dec. 7, 1923.

Knights of Columbus: organized, Feb. 2, 1882; chartered, Mar. 29, 1882.

Knights of Pythias: founded, Feb. 19, 1864.

Knopf, Alfred A., Sep. 12, 1892.

Knopfler, Mark, Aug. 12, 1949.

Knott, Walter, Dec. 11, 1889.

Knotts, Don, Jul. 21, 1924.

Knowles, John, Sep. 16, 1926.

Knox, Henry, Jul. 25, 1750.

Knox, Philander Chase, May 6, 1853.

Kobe, Japan, earthquake, Jan. 17, 1995.

Koch, Edward Irving, Dec. 12, 1924.

Koch, Robert, Dec. 11, 1843.

Kocharyan, Robert, Mar. 30, 1998.

Kocher, Emil Theodar, Aug. 25, 1841.

Kodaly, Zoltan, Dec. 16, 1882.

Kodsi, Nazem el-, Jun. 4, 1950.

Koerner, Theodor: inaugurated, Jun. 21, 1951.

Koestler, Arthur, Sep. 5, 1905.

Kohl, Helmut, Oct. 4, 1982; unification plan, Nov. 28, 1989; reelected, Nov. 15, 1994.

Kohlberg Kravis Roberts and Co., Nov. 30, 1988.

Kohler, Georges J. F., Apr. 17, 1946.

Kohler, Kaufmann, May 10, 1843.

Kohler, Wolfgang, Jan. 21, 1887.

Koivisto, Mauno, Nov. 25, 1923; May 26, 1979.

Kokoschka, Oskar, Mar. 1, 1886.

Kolbe, Adolph Wilhelm Hermann, Sep. 27, 1818.

Kolbe, Georg, Apr. 4, 1877.

Kolingba, Andre (General), Aug. 12, 1936; Sep. 1, 1981.

Kollr, Jan, Jul. 29, 1793.

Kollwitz, Kathe, Jul. 8, 1867.

Kolreuter, Josef Gottlieb, Apr. 27, 1733.

Koltsov, Alexey Vasilyevich, Oct. 3, 1809.

Kolubara River, Battle of, Dec. 3, 1914; ends, Dec. 6, 1914.

Komandorskie Islands, Battle of, Mar. 26, 1943.

Komensky, Jan Amos, Mar. 28, 1592.

Koniggratz, Battle of: ends, Jul. 3, 1866.

Konstantinov, Vladimir, Mar. 19, 1967.

Koontz, Dean, Jul. 9, 1945.

Koop, Charles Everett, Oct. 14, 1916.

Koopmans, Tjalling, Aug. 28, 1910.

Kopechne, Mary Jo, Jul. 26, 1940; Jul. 19, 1969.

Kopell, Bernard Morton *(Bernie)*, Jul. 21, 1933.

Kopp, Elizabeth, Oct. 2, 1984.

Koraes, Adamantios, Apr. 27, 1748.

Korbut, Olga, May 16, 1955.

Korda, Sir Alexander, Sep. 16, 1893.

Korda, Michael Vincent, Oct. 8, 1933.

Korea, Feb. 26, 1876; independence, Jan. 7, 1895; Jan. 30, 1902; annexed by Japan, Aug. 22, 1910; Mar. 1, 1919; becomes Japanese province, Aug. 19, 1919; Chinese troops enter, Dec. 28, 1950.

Korea, Democratic People's Republic of, *See* Korea, North.

Korea, North: established, Sep. 9, 1948; Jan. 4, 1951; May 18, 1951; Jan. 23, 1968; Mar. 12, 1993; Dec. 15, 1995.

Korea, South: invaded, Jun. 25, 1950; May 21, 1961; treaty with Japan, Jun. 22, 1965; relations with Japan, Dec. 18, 1965; new constitution, Oct. 27, 1987.

Koreagate scandal, Oct. 24, 1976; Apr. 3, 1978.

Korean Air Lines Flight 007, Sep. 1, 1983.

Korean Alphabet Day or Han'gu Day (South Korea), Oct. 9.

Korean nationalists, Apr. 27, 1919.

Korean War, May 3, 1950; Jun. 25, 1950; Jun. 27, 1950; Jun. 28, 1950; U.S. Marines land in Korea, Aug. 2, 1950; Sep. 6, 1950; Sep. 15, 1950; Sep. 26, 1950; Nov. 9, 1950; Nov. 15, 1950; Nov. 28, 1950; Dec. 1, 1950; Dec. 28, 1950; Jan. 4, 1951; Mar. 14, 1951; Mar. 15, 1951; May 9, 1951; May 8, 1952; Aug. 1, 1952; Oct. 25, 1952; Jul. 12, 1953; armistice signed, Jul. 27, 1953.

Korean War veterans, May 10, 1951.

Koresh, David, Feb. 28, 1993; standoff with ATF, Apr. 19, 1993.

Korietz, Feb. 9, 1904.

Korizis, Alexander, Jan. 29, 1941; Apr. 20, 1941.

Kornberg, Arthur, Mar. 3, 1918.

Kornilov, Lavrenti Georgievich, Jul. 30, 1870.

Koseiusko, Thaddeus, Feb. 4, 1746.

Kosciuszko, Army of, Apr. 4, 1917.

Koseiuszko, Thaddeus, Feb. 12, 1746.

Kossel, Albrecht, Sep. 16, 1853.

Kossuth: first performance, Jan. 13, 1904

Kossuth, Lajos, Sep. 19, 1802.

Kostelanetz, Andre, Dec. 22, 1901.

Kosygin, Aleksei N., Feb. 20, 1904; Oct. 15, 1964; resigns, Oct. 23, 1980.

Kotalawala, John, Oct. 13, 1953.

Kotzebue, August von, Sep. 20, 1819.

Koufax, Sanford *(Sandy)*, Dec. 30, 1935.

Kountche, Seyni (Lt. Col.), Apr. 17, 1974; Nov. 10, 1987.

Koussevitzky, Serge Alexandrovitch, Jul. 26, 1874.

Kovac, Michal, elected, Feb. 15, 1993.

Kovaes, Ernie, Jan. 23, 1919.

Kovel, Battle of, Jul. 28, 1916.

Kozol, Jonathan, Sep. 5, 1936.

Krafft-Ebbing, Baron Richard, Aug. 14, 1840.

Kraft, Charles Herbert, Oct. 17, 1880.

Kraft, Christopher Columbus, Feb. 28, 1924.

Kraft, James Lewis, Dec. 11, 1874.

Kraft, Joseph, Sep. 4, 1924.

Krag, Jens Otto, Sep. 3, 1962.

Kramer, Larry, Jun. 25, 1935.

Kramer, Stanley, Sep. 29, 1913.

Krantz, Judith, Jan. 9, 1928.

Krapf, Lewis (Dr.), Dec. 3, 1849.

Krasicki, Count Ignacy, Feb. 3, 1735.

Kraszewski, Jozef Ignacy, Jul. 28, 1812.

Kraut & Frankfurter Week, National, Feb. intro.

Kravitz, Lenny, May 25, 1964.

Krebs, Edwin G., Jun. 6, 1918.

Krebs, Sir Hans Adolf, Aug. 25, 1900.

Kreisky, Bruno, Jan. 22, 1911; Apr. 21, 1970; May 6, 1979.

Kreisler, Fritz, Feb. 2, 1875.

Krementz, Jill, Feb. 19, 1940.

Kreps, Juanita Morris, Jan. 11, 1921.

Kresge, Sebastian Spering, Jul. 31, 1867.

Kreskin, Jan. 12, 1935.

Kress, Samuel Henry, Jul. 23, 1863.

Kreuger, Ivar, Mar. 2, 1880.

Krickstein, Aaron, Aug. 2, 1967.

Krikalev, Sergei, Feb. 3, 1994.

Kristel, Sylvia, Sep. 28, 1952.

Kristofferson, Kris, Jun. 22, 1936.

Kroc, Ray A., Oct. 5, 1902.

Kroger, Bernard Henry, Jan. 24, 1860.

Krogh, Schack August Steenberg, Nov. 15, 1874.

Krone, Julie, Jul. 24, 1963.

Kronecker, Leopold, Dec. 7, 1823.

Kronstadt (Russia): ship canal, May 27, 1885; Feb. 23, 1921.

Kropotkin, Prince Peter Alexeyevich, Nov. 26, 1842.

Kroto, Harold W., Oct. 7, 1939.

Kruger Day (Namibia, South Africa), Oct. 10.

Kruger, Otto, Sep. 6, 1885.

Kruger, Paul, Oct. 10, 1825; Apr. 16, 1883.

Kruger Telegram, Oct. 9, 1899.

Kruk, John, Feb. 9, 1961.

Krupa, Gene, Jan. 15, 1909.

Krupp, Alfred, Apr. 26, 1812; Jan. 31, 1951.

Krupp Works: French air raid on, Sep. 24, 1916.

Krzyzewski, Mike, Feb. 13, 1947.

Ku Klux Klan: formed, Dec. 24, 1865; Apr. 21, 1983.

Kubler-Ross, Elisabeth, Jul. 8, 1926.

Kubrick, Stanley, Jul. 26, 1928; Apr. 3, 1968.

Kucan, Milan, elected, Dec. 6, 1992.

Kucanis, Milan, re-elected, Nov. 23, 1997.

Kuchma, Leonid, elected, Jul. 10, 1994.

Kudrow, Lisa, Jul. 30, 1963.

Kuhn, Bowie, Oct. 28, 1926.

Kukoc, Toni, Sep. 18, 1968.

Kuhn, Franz Felix Adalbert, Nov. 19, 1812.

Kuhn, Richard, Dec. 3, 1900.

Kula Gulf, Battle of, Jul. 6, 1943.

Kulp, Nancy, Aug. 28, 1921.

Kumasi, Battle of, Feb. 4, 1874.

Kumin, Maxine Winokur, Jun. 6, 1925.

Kun, Bela (Hungary), Mar. 22, 1919.

Kundera, Milan, Apr. 1, 1929.

Kung, Hans, Mar. 19, 1928.

Kunstler, William, Jul. 7, 1919.

Kuo Min Tang National Congress, Jan. 20, 1924.

Kuomintang, Apr. 15, 1927.

Kuralt, Charles Bishop, Sep. 10, 1934.

Kurdish people, Mar. 11, 1970.

Kurdish rebels, Mar. 14, 1974.

Kurosawa, Akira, Mar. 23, 1910.

Kurtis, William Horton (Bill), Sep. 21, 1940.

Kurtz, Swoosie, Sep. 6, 1944.

Kusch, Polykarp, Jan. 26, 1911.

Kuscsik, Nina, Apr. 17, 1972.

Kut-el-Amara, Jan. 4, 1916; Apr. 29, 1916; taken by British, Sep. 28, 1916.

Kutuzov, Prince Mikhail Illarionovich Golenishchev, Sep. 16, 1745.

Kuwait: independence, Jun. 19, 1961; May 14, 1963; boundaries established, Dec. 18, 1969; oil tanker escort, Jul. 22, 1987; invaded, Aug. 2, 1990; U.S. forces enter, Feb. 27, 1991.

Kuwaitly, Shukri al-, Aug. 18, 1955.

Kuyper, Abraham, Oct. 29, 1837.

Kuznets, Simon, Apr. 30, 1901.

Kwan, Nancy Kashen, May 19, 1939.

Kwang-su (Emperor of China), Jan. 12, 1875.

Kwanzaa (U.S.), Dec. 26.

Kwasniewski, Aleksandr, elected, Nov. 19, 1995.

Ky, Nguyen Cao, Jun. 18, 1965; Feb. 8, 1966; Sep. 3, 1967.

Kyd, Thomas, Nov. 5, 1558.

Kyoto Protocol, Dec. 1, 1997.

Kyrpianou, Spyros, Oct. 28, 1932.

Kyushu, Japan, Mar. 18, 1945.

L

La Boheme: premiere, Feb. 1, 1896.

La Bruyere, Jean de, Aug. 16, 1645.

La Farge, John, Mar. 31, 1835.

La Follette, Philip F., May 8, 1897.

La Follette, Robert Marion, Jr., Feb. 6, 1895.

La Follette, Robert Marion, Sr., Jun. 14, 1855; Jan. 21, 1911.

La Fontaine, Henri, Apr. 22, 1854.

La Fontaine, Jean de, Jul. 8, 1621.

La Guardia Airport: bomb at, Dec. 29, 1975.

La Mer: premiere, Mar. 1, 1907.

La Mettrie, Julien Offroy de, Dec. 25, 1709.

La Piedras Battle Day (Uruguay), May 18.

La Rochefoucauld, Francois duc de, Sep. 15, 1613.

La Rochelle, Seige of: ends, Oct. 28, 1628.

La Salle, Eriq, Jul. 23, 1962.

La Salle, Jean Baptiste de, Apr. 30, 1651.

Ia Salle, Sieur de, Feb. 6, 1682; Apr. 9, 1682.

La Tour, Maurice Quentin de, Sep. 5, 1704.

LaBelle, Patti, May 24, 1944.

Labor Congress of China, National, May 1, 1922.

Labor Day, May 1.

Labor Day (Bahamas), Jun. intro.

Labor Day (Belize), May 2.

Labor Day (Bosnia and, Herzegovina), Jul. 27 .

Labor Day (Bulgaria), May 1.

Labor Day (Korea), Mar. 10.

Labor Day (New Zealand), Oct. intro.

Labor Day (U.S.), Sep. intro; established, Jun. 28, 1894; Sep. 6, 1982.

Labor Day (Slovenia), May 1.

Labor Thanksgiving Day or Kinro-Kansha-No-Hi (Japan), Nov. 23.

Labour Day (Jamaica), May 23.

Labour Day (Trinidad and Tobago), Jun. 19.

Labour Government, British: fall, Mar. 28, 1979.

Labrador, Apr. 20, 1534.

lacemakers, patron of, Oct. 18.

Lacey, Robert, Jan. 3, 1944.

Lackland, John (King of England), Apr. 6, 1199.

Laclede, Pierre, Feb. 15, 1764.

Lacoste, Rene, Jul. 2, 1905.

Lacretelle, Pierre Louis, Oct. 9, 1751.

Ladd, Alan, Sep. 3, 1913.

Ladd, Cheryl, Jul. 2, 1952.

Ladd, Diane, Nov. 29, 1939.

Ladislas II (King of Bohemia and Hungary), Mar. 1, 1456; May 27, 1471; Apr. 6, 1490.

Ladislas V (Hungary), Feb. 22, 1440; Nov. 10, 1444.

Ladislaus (King of Naples), Feb. 27, 1386; Apr. 21, 1408.

Lady Be Good: opens, Dec. 1, 1924.

Lady Day (Great Britain), Mar. 25.

Lady of Fatima Day (Portugal), May 13.

Lady and the Tramp: premiere, Jun. 23, 1955.

Ladysmith (Natal): attacked, Oct. 20, 1899.

Ladysmith, Seige of, Nov. 2, 1899; Feb. 28, 1900.

Laemmle, Carl, Jan. 17, 1867.

Laennec, Rene, Feb. 17, 1781; Sep. 13, 1816.

Laettner, Christian, Aug. 17, 1969.

Lafarge, Oliver, Dec. 19, 1901.

Lafayette Escadrille, Dec. 26, 1917.

Lafayette, Marquis de (Marie Joseph Paul), Sep. 6, 1757.

Laffer, Arthur Betz, Aug. 14, 1940.

Laffite, Jean, Aug. 29, 1780.

Lafleur, Guy Damien, Sep. 20, 1951.

Lagerfeld, Karl, Sep. 10, 1938.

Lagerkvist, Par Fabian, May 23, 1891.

Lagerlof, Selma, Nov. 20, 1858.

Lagos, Jan. 13, 1886; Jan. 1, 1900.

Lagrange, Joseph Louis, Jan. 25, 1736.

LaGuardia, Fiorello H(enry), Dec. 11, 1882; Jan. 1, 1934.

Lahore, Treaty of, Mar. 9, 1846.

Lahr, Bert, Aug. 13, 1895.

Lahti, Christine, Apr. 4, 1950.

Laika (dog), Nov. 3, 1957.

Laikipia (East Africa), Apr. 4, 1911.

Laine, Cleo, Oct. 28, 1927.

Laine, Frankie, Mar. 30, 1913.

Laing, Alexander Gordon, Aug. 18, 1825.

Laird, Melvin (Robert), Sep. 1, 1922.

Lajoie, Napoleon, Sep. 5, 1875.

Lake Albert Nyanza, Mar. 14, 1864.

Lake Champlain, Battle of, Sep. 11, 1814.

Lake Erie, Jan. 19, 1977.

Lake Erie, Battle of, Sep. 10, 1813.

Lake George, Battle of, Sep. 8, 1755.
Lake Nios (Cameroon), Aug. 21, 1986.
Lake Ontario, Sep. 9, 1954.
Lake, Veronica, Nov. 14, 1919.
Lake Washington: floating bridge, Jul. 2, 1940
Lakehurst (New Jersey), May 6, 1937.
Laker Airways, Sep. 26, 1977.
Laker, Frederick Alfred *(Freddie)*, Aug. 6, 1922.
Lakeview (Oregon), May 5, 1945.
LaLanne, Jack, Sep. 26, 1914.
Lalas, Alexi, Jun. 1, 1970.
Lamar, Mirabeau Buonaparte, Aug. 16, 1798.
Lamarck, Jean-Baptiste de Monet, Chevalier de, Aug. 1.
Lamarr, Hedy, Sep. 11, 1913.
Lamartine, Alphonse Mane Louis Prat de, Oct. 21, 1790.
Lamas, Fernando, Jan. 9, 1925.
Lamb, Lady Caroline Ponsonby, Nov. 13, 1785.
Lamb, Charles, Feb. 10, 1775.
Lamb, Mary Ann, Dec. 3, 1764.
Lamb, William, Mar. 15, 1779.
Lamb, Willis E., Jul. 12, 1913.
Lambeau, Curly, Apr. 9, 1898.
Lambert, Christopher, Mar. 29, 1957.
Lambert, Johann Heinrich, Aug. 26, 1728.
Lambert, John Harold *(Jack)*, Jul. 8, 1952.
Lamizana, Sangoule, Jan. 4, 1966.
Lamm, Richard D., Aug. 3, 1935.
Lamm, Robert, Oct. 13, 1944.
Lammas Day (England), Aug. 1.
LaMotta, Jacob *(Jake)*, Jul. 10, 1921; Jun. 16, 1949; Feb. 14, 1951.
Lamour, Dorothy, Oct. 10, 1914.
Lamy, John Baptist, Oct. 11, 1814.
Lancaster, Burt, Nov. 2, 1913; Aug. 5, 1953.
Lancaster, Joseph, Nov. 25, 1778.
Lanchester, Elsa, Oct. 28, 1902.
Land, Edwin Herbert, May 7, 1909.
Landau, Lev Davidovitch, Jan. 22, 1908.
Landau, Martin, Jun. 20, 1934.
Lander, Richard and John, Mar. 22, 1830.
Landers, Ann, Jul. 4, 1918.

Landing of the 33 Orientales (Uruguay), Apr. 19.
Landis, John David, Aug. 3, 1950.
Landis, Judge Kenesaw Mountain, Nov. 20, 1866.
Landon, Alf(red Mossman), Sep. 9, 1887.
Landon, Michael, Oct. 31, 1937.
Landor, Walter Savage, Jan. 30, 1775.
Landowska, Wanda, Jul. 5, 1877.
Landrieu, Moon, Jul. 23, 1930.
Landry, Tom, Sep. 11, 1924.
Landsbergis, Vytautas, Oct. 18, 1932.
Landsteiner, Karl, Jun. 14, 1868.
Lane, Sir Allen, Sep. 21, 1902.
Lane, Burton, Jan. 10, 1923.
Lane, Diane, Jan. 22, 1965.
Lane, John Richard, Aug. 12, 1932.
Lane, Nathan, Feb. 3, 1956.
Lang, Andrew, Mar. 31, 1844.
Lang, Eugene M., Mar. 16, 1919.
Lang, Fritz, Dec. 5, 1890.
lang, k. d. (Kathryn Dawn Lang), Nov. 2, 1961.
Lange, Christian Louis, Sep. 17, 1869.
Lange, David, Jul. 14, 1984.
Lange, Helene, Apr. 9, 1848.
Lange, Hope Elise Ross, Nov. 28, 1933.
Lange, Jessica, Apr. 20, 1949.
Langley, Samuel Pierpont, Aug. 22, 1834.
Langley, U.S.S.: first U S aircraft carrier, Mar. 20, 1922.
Langella, Frank, Jan. 1, 1940.
Langmuir, Irving, Jan. 31, 1881.
Langsides, Battle of, May 16, 1568.
Langston, John Mercer, Dec. 14, 1829.
Langtry, Lillie, Oct. 13, 1853.
Laniel, Joseph, Jun. 4, 1954.
Lanier, Robert Jerry, Jr. *(Bob)*, Sep. 10, 1948.
Lanier, Sidney, Feb. 3, 1842.
Lansbury, Angela, Oct. 16, 1925.
Lansing-Ishi Agreement, Nov. 2, 1917.
Lansing, Robert, Oct. 17, 1864.
Lansing, Sherry Lee, Jul. 31, 1944.
Lansky, Meyer, Jul. 4, 1902.
Lantern Festival (Tibet), Jan. 15.
Lanza, Mario, Jan. 31, 1921.

Laos: independence, Jul. 19, 1949; Jan. 29, 1950; Feb. 7, 1950; ties with France, Dec. 29, 1954; Jan. 19, 1962; May 12, 1962; Jan. 31, 1964; Apr. 5, 1974.
Laotian army, Apr. 19, 1961.
Laplante, Andre, Nov. 12, 1949.
Laporte, Pierre (Canada): kidnapped, Oct. 10, 1970.
Lardner, Ring, Mar. 6, 1885.
Lardner, Ring Wilmer, Jr., Aug. 19, 1915.
Larissa (Greece), Jun. 12, 1917.
Larkin, Philip (Arthur), Aug. 9, 1922.
larkspur, Jul. intro.
Larned, William Augustus, Dec. 30, 1872.
LaRosa, Julius, Jan. 2, 1930.
LaRouche, Lyndon H., Jr., Sep. 8, 1922.
Larousse, Pierre Athanase, Oct. 23, 1817.
Larra y Sanchez de Castro, Mariano Jose de, Mar. 24, 1809.
Larroquette, John, Nov. 25, 1947.
Larsen, Don, Oct. 8, 1956.
Larson, April, Oct. 11, 1992.
Larson, Nicolette, Jul. 18, 1952.
Larsson, Carl, May 28, 1853.
Lartet, Edouard Armand Isidore Hippolyte, Apr. 15, 1801.
Las Piedras, Battle of (Uruguay), May intro.
Las Vegas Hilton, Feb. 7, 1981.
Las Vegas (Nevada), Sep. 17, 1930.
LASER, Mar. 22, 1960. May 10, 1962.
Lashio, Apr. 29, 1942.
Lasker, Albert Davis, May 1, 1880.
Laski, Harold Joseph, Jun. 30, 1893.
Lasorda, Thomas Charles *(Tom)*, Sep. 22, 1927.
Lassalle, Ferdinand, Apr. 11, 1825.
Lassie: television debut, Sep. 12, 1954.
The Last Hurrah: published, Feb. 6, 1956.
Lateran Council, Fifth, Mar. 16, 1517.
Lateran Council, First: begins, Mar. 18, 1123.
Lateran Treaty, Feb. 11, 1929.
Lateranesi Anniversary of (Vatican City State), Feb. 11.
Lathrop, Julia Clifford, Jun. 29, 1858.
Latimer, Lewis Howard, Sep. 4, 1848.

Latin American Free Trade Association, May 2, 1961.

Latin American Week, Dec. intro.

Latin Empire, Apr. 12, 1204; overthrown, Jul. 25, 1261.

Latrobe, Benjamin Henry, May 1, 1764.

Latvia: independence, Jan. 12, 1918; proclaimed sovereign free state, Nov. 18, 1918; May 15, 1934; incorporated into U.S.S.R., Aug. 25, 1940; independence, Aug. 21, 1991; North Atlantic Treaty Organization (NATO), Jan. 16, 1998.

Laud, William, Oct. 7, 1573.

Lauder, Estee, Jul. 1, 1908.

Lauder, Sir Harry, Aug. 4, 1870.

Laue, Max von, Oct. 9, !879.

Laugerud Garcia, Kjell: inaugurated, Jul. 1, 1974.

Laughton, Charles, Jul. 1, 1899.

laundresses, patron of, Jul. 29.

Lauper, Cynthia (Cyndi), Jun. 20, 1953.

Laurel, Stan, Jun. 16, 1890.

Lauren, Ralph, Oct. 14, 1939.

Laurier, Sir Wilfrid, Nov. 20, 1841.

Lausanne Conference: opens, Nov. 20, 1622; second, Apr. 23, 1923.

Lausanne, Treaty of, Oct. 18, 1912; concludes, Jul. 24, 1923.

Lausche, Frank J., Nov. 14, 1895.

Lautreamont, Comte de, Apr. 4, 1846.

Laval, Gustav de, May 9, 1845.

Laval, Pierre, Jun. 28, 1883; Apr. 18, 1942; executed, Oct. 15, 1945.

Lavater, Johann Kaspar, Nov. 15, 1741.

Lavelle, Rita Marie, Sep. 8, 1947.

Laver, Rod(ney George), Aug. 9, 1938.

Laveran, Charles Louis Alphonse, Jun. 18, 1845.

Lavin, Linda, Oct. 15, 1939.

Lavoisier, Antoine Laurent, Aug. 26, 1743.

Law, Andrew Bonar, Sep. 16, 1858.

Law Day (U.S.), May intro.; May 1.

Law of the Sea, U.N. conference, Mar. 17, 1960.

Lawes, Lewis Edward, Sep. 13, 1883.

Lawford, Peter, Sep. 7, 1923.

Lawler, Richard, Jun. 17, 1950.

Lawless, Lucy, Mar. 28, 1958.

Lawrence, Abbott, Dec. 16, 1792.

Lawrence, Amos Adams, Jul. 31, 1814.

Lawrence, Carol, Sep. 5, 1935.

Lawrence, David, Dec. 25, 1888.

Lawrence, D(avid) H(erbert), Sep. 11, 1883.

Lawrence, Ernest Orlando, Aug. 8, 1901.

Lawrence, Gertrude, Jul. 4, 1898.

Lawrence, James, Oct. 1, 1781.

Lawrence (Kansas), May 21, 1856.

Lawrence, Robert, Dec. 8, 1967.

Lawrence, Steve, Jul. 8, 1935.

Lawrence, T. E. (Lawrence of Arabia), Aug. 15, 1888; Jul. 6, 1917.

Lawrence, Sir Thomas, Apr. 13, 1769.

Lawrence, Vicki, Mar. 26, 1949.

The Lawrence Welk Show: television debut, Jul. 2, 1955.

lawrencium, Apr. 12, 1961.

lawsuits unjustly, those who lose in, patron of, Dec. 6.

lawyers, patron of, Apr. 24; Apr. 25.

lawyers, patroness of, Jan. 3.

Laxalt, Paul, Aug. 2, 1922.

Laxness, Halldor Kiljan, Apr. 24, 1902.

lay investiture, Mar. 7, 1080.

Lazar, Swifty, Mar. 28, 1907.

Lazarus, Emma, Jul. 22, 1849.

Lazear, Jesse William, May 2, 1866.

Lazy Eye Alert Month, Oct. intro.

Le Brun, Charles, Feb. 24, 1619.

Le Carre, John, Oct. 19, 1931.

Le Chatelier, Henri Louis, Oct. 8, 1850.

Le Duc Tho, Oct. 14, 1911; refuses Nobel Peace Prize, Oct. 23, 1973.

Le Fanu, Joseph Sheridan, Aug. 28, 1814.

Le Goulet, Peace of, May 22, 1200.

Le Mariage de Figaro: premiere, Apr. 27, 1784.

Le Moyne, Pierre, Jul. 16, 1661.

Le Redoutable: French nuclear submarine, Mar. 29, 1967.

Le Verrier, Urbain, Mar. 11, 1811.

Leach, Penelope, Nov. 19, 1937.

Leach, Richard Max (Rick), May 4, 1957.

Leachman, Cloris, Apr. 30, 1925.

Leacock, Stephen Butler, Dec. 30, 1869.

League of Cambrai: formed, Mar. 23, 1509.

League of Nations, Jan. 22, 1917; Jan. 8, 1918; Jan. 25, 1919; first meeting, Feb. 5, 1919; Apr. 11, 1919; Covenant of the, Apr. 28, 1919; founded, Jan. 10, 1920; Mar. 5, 1920; Mar. 8, 1920; Mar. 9, 1920; first meeting of assembly, Nov. 15, 1920; May 25, 1921; May 14, 1938; Apr. 11, 1939; dissolved, Apr. 18, 1945; Jan. 10, 1946.

Leahy, Patrick Joseph, Mar. 31, 1940.

Leahy, William Daniel, May 6, 1875.

Leakey, L(ouis) S(eymour) B(azett), Aug. 7, 1903; Mar. 22, 1962.

Leakey, Maeve, Aug. 17, 1995.

Leakey, Mary, Feb. 6, 1913.

Leakey, Richard E(rskine) F., Dec. 19, 1944.

Lean, David, Mar. 25, 1908.

Leap Year Day, Feb. 29.

Lear, Edward, May 12, 1812.

Lear, Norman, Jul. 27, 1922.

Learned, Michael, Apr. 9, 1929.

Leary, Timothy Francis, Oct. 22, 1920.

Leave it to Beaver: television debut, Oct. 4, 1957.

Leave it to Me, Nov. 21, 1938.

Leavey, Edmond H(arrison), Jul. 20, 1894.

Lebanon: independence, Nov. 22, 1941; French evacuate, Dec. 31, 1946; May 14, 1958; Israeli invasion, Jun. 6, 1982; Israeli troop withdrawal, May 17, 1983; Israeli troop withdrawal, Jan. 14, 1985; Israeli troop withdrawal complete, Jun. 10, 1985.

Lebesque, Henri, Jun. 28, 1875.

LeBon, Simon, Oct. 27, 1958.

Lebowitz, Fran(ces Ann), Oct. 27, 1950.

Lebrun, Albert, Aug. 29, 1871.

Lechfeld, Battle of, Aug. 10, 955.

Ledbetter, Huddie (Leadbelly), Jan. 20, 1889.

Lederberg, Joshua, May 23, 1925.

Lederer, William, Mar. 31, 1912; Oct. 1, 1958.

Lederman, Leon, Jul. 15, 1922.

Lee, Ann, Feb. 29, 1736.

Lee, Brenda, Dec. 11, 1944.

Lee, Bruce, Nov. 27, 1940.

Lee, Christopher, May 27, 1922.

Lee, David M., Jan. 20, 1931.

Lee, Dixie, Nov. 4, 1911.

Lee, Henry C., Nov. 22, 1938.

Lee, Henry (Light-Horse Harry), Jan. 29, 1759.

Lee, Francis Lightfoot, Oct. 14, 1734.

Lee, Gypsy Rose, Jan. 9, 1914.

Lee, Harper, May 1, 1961.

Lee Jackson Day (Virginia), Jan. intro.

Lee, John D.: executed, Mar. 23, 1877.

Lee K'uan Yew, Aug. 16, 1923.

Lee, Manfred Bennington, Oct. 20, 1905.

Lee, Mark, Sep. 12, 1992.

Lee, Martin, (Chu-Ming Lee), Jun. 8, 1938.

Lee, Michele, Jun. 24, 1942.

Lee, (Nelle) Harper, Apr. 28, 1926.

Lee, Peggy, May 20, 1920; May 26, 1920.

Lee, Richard Henry, Jan. 20, 1732.

Lee, Robert E., Jan. 19, 1807, appointed commander, Feb. 6, 1862; Dec. 13, 1862, Apr. 1, 1865; surrender, Apr. 9, 1865.

Lee, Robert E., Birthday (U.S. southern states), Jan. intro.

Lee, Rose Hum, Aug. 20, 1904.

Lee, Sir Sidney, Dec. 5, 1859.

Lee, Spike, Mar. 20, 1956.

Lee Teng-hui: inaugurated, Jan. 13, 1988.

Lee, Tsung-Dao, Nov. 24, 1926.

Lee, Yuan Tseh, Nov. 29, 1936.

Leek, Sybil, Feb. 22, 1917.

Leeuwenhoek, Anton van, Oct. 24, 1632.

Lefebvre, Marcel, Jun. 30, 1988.

LeFlore, Ron(ald), Jun. 16, 1948.

legal aid, Mar. 18, 1963.

Leger, Fernand, Feb. 4, 1881.

Leger, Jules, Apr. 4, 1913.

Leghari, Farooq, resigns, Dec. 2, 1997.

Legion of Honor, French, May 19, 1802.

Legionnaire's Disease, Jul. 21, 1976; Jan. 18, 1977.

Legrand, Michel Jean, Feb. 24, 1932.

Leguia y Salcedo, Augusto Bernardino, Feb. 19, 1863.

LeGuin, Ursula Kroeber, Oct. 21, 1921.

Leguizamo, John, Jul. 22, 1965.

Lehar, Franz, Apr. 30, 1870.

Lehder Rivas, Carlos Enrique, Feb. 4, 1987.

Lehigh: sunk, Oct. 19, 1941.

Lehman Brothers, Apr. 10, 1984.

Lehman, John Francis, Jr., Sep. 14, 1942.

Lehmann, Lilli, Nov. 24, 1848.

Lehn, Jean-Marie, Sep. 30, 1939.

Leibman, Ron, Oct. 11, 1938.

Leibniz, Gottfried Wilhelm von, Jul. 1, 1646.

Leibovitz, Annie, Oct. 2, 1949.

Leif Ericsson Day (U.S.), Oct. 9.

Leigh, Douglas, May 24, 1907.

Leigh, Janet, Jul. 6, 1927.

Leigh, Jennifer Jason, Feb. 5, 1962.

Leigh, Mitch, Nov. 22, 1965.

Leigh, Vivien, Nov. 5, 1913.

Leighton, Frederick, Dec. 3, 1830.

Leinsdorf, Erich, Feb. 4, 1912.

Leinster: sunk, Oct. 10, 1918.

Leipzig, Battle of, Oct. 16, 1813.

Leipzig (Germany), Jan. 10, 1921.

Lekhanya, Justin (Lesotho), Jan. 20, 1986.

Leland, Henry Martyn, Feb. 16, 1843.

Leloir, Luis F., Sep. 6, 1906.

Lelouch, Claude, Oct. 30, 1937.

Lelyveld, Joseph S., Apr. 5, 1937.

Lemaitre, Georges, Jul. 17, 1894.

Lemay, Curtis (Emerson), Nov. 15, 1906.

Lemberg, First Battle of: begins, Aug. 26, 1914.

Lemieux, Claude, Jul. 16, 1965.

Lemieux, Mario, Oct. 5, 1965.

Lemmon, Jack, Feb. 8, 1925; Mar. 29, 1959.

Lemnitzer, Lyman L., Aug. 29, 1899; Jan. 2, 1963.

Lemnos, Feb. 23, 1905.

Lemon, Meadow George, III (Meadowlark), Apr. 25, 1932.

Lenard, Philipp E. A. von, Jun. 7, 1862.

Lend-Lease Act, Sep. 6, 1940; passed, Mar. 11, 1941.

Lendl, Ivan, Mar. 7, 1960.

L'Enfant, Pierre Charles, Aug. 2, 1754.

L'Engle, Madeleine, Nov. 29, 1918.

Lenglen, Suzanne, May 24, 1899.

Lenin, Apr. 9, 1870; Jul. 16, 1917; Nov. 7, 1917; Dec. 20, 1917; Mar. 17, 1921.

Lenin Peace Prize, Jun. 23, 1925; May 3, 1960; Apr. 30, 1961.

Leningrad, May 27, 1703; Mar. 9, 1917; Apr. 22, 1920.

Lenngren, Anna Maria, Jun. 18, 1754.

Lennon, Dianne, Dec. 1, 1939.

Lennon, Janet, Nov. 15, 1946.

Lennon, John, Oct. 9, 1940; Jun. 17, 1970; killed, Dec. 8, 1980.

Lennon, Julian, Apr. 8, 1963.

Lennon, Kathy, Aug. 22, 1942.

Lennon, Peggy, Apr. 8, 1940.

Lennox, Annie, Dec. 25, 1954.

Lennox (Scotland), patron of, Mar. 10.

Leno, Jay, Apr. 28, 1950.

LeNotre, Andre, Mar. 12, 1613.

Lens, patron of, Nov. 3.

Lenski, Lois, Oct. 14, 1893.

Lenya, Lotte, Oct. 18, 1900.

Lenz, Jakob Michael Reinhold, Jan. 12, 1751.

Lenz, Kay, Mar. 4, 1953.

Leo, Jul. intro.; Aug. intro.

Leo III (pope), Dec. 25, 800; Oct. 7, 1883.

Leo X (pope), Dec. 11, 1475; Apr. 5, 1513; Feb. 3, 1518; Jun. 15, 1520; Jan. 3, 1521; Feb. 2, 1522.

Leo XI (pope), Jun. 2, 1535.

Leo XII (pope), Aug. 22, 1760.

Leo XIII (pope), Mar. 2, 1810; Mar. 4, 1878.

Leon Carpio, Ramiro de, elected, Jun. 5, 1993.

Leonard, Dutch, Mar. 25, 1909.

Leonard, Dutch, Jr., Oct. 11, 1925.

Leonard, Ray, May 17, 1956.

Leonard, Robert Sean, Feb. 28, 1969.

Leonard, Sheldon, Feb. 22, 1907.

Leonardo da Vinci, Apr. 15, 1452.

Leone, Giovanni, Nov. 3, 1908; resigns, Jul. 8, 1978.

Leoni, Raul: inaugurated, Mar. 11, 1964; Jan. 6, 1967.

Leone, Sergio, Jan. 23, 1921.

Leonov, Aleksei Arkhipovich, May 30, 1934; Mar. 18, 1965.

Leontief, Wassily, Aug. 5, 1906.

Leontovich, Eugenie, Mar. 21, 1900.

Leopardi, Count Giacomo, Jun. 29, 1798.

Leopold (Austria), Nov. 15, 1315.

Leopold I (Belgium), Dec. 16, 1790; dies, Dec. 9, 1865.

Leopold I (Holy Roman Emperor), Aug. 1, 1658; dies, May 5, 1705.

Leopold II (Belgium), Apr. 9, 1835; Dec. 9, 1865; May 2, 1885; Jul. 1, 1885; Oct. 18, 1908.

Leopold II (Holy Roman Emperor), Feb. 20, 1790; dies, Mar. 1, 1792.

Leopold III (Austria), Jul. 9, 1386.

Leopold III (Belgium), Nov. 3, 1901; Feb. 17, 1934; Jul. 23, 1950; abdicates, Jul. 17, 1951.

Leopold, Duke of Austria, Dec. 21, 1192.

Lepanto, Battle of, Oct. 7, 1571.

Lerdo de Tejada, Sebastian, Apr. 25, 1825.

Lermontov, Mikhail Yurievich, Oct. 15, 1814.

Lerner, Alan Jay, Aug. 31, 1918; Nov. 12, 1951.

Lerner and Loewe, Mar. 15, 1955.

Lerner, Max, Dec. 20, 1902.

Lesage, Alain Rene, May 8, 1668.

Lescot, Elie: inaugurated, May 15, 1941.

Leskov, Nikolai Semyanovich, Feb. 16, 1831.

Leslie, Lisa, Jul. 7, 1972.

Lesotho (Basutoland), Feb. 2, 1884; Apr. 30, 1965; becomes independent, Oct. 4, 1966; admitted to U.N., Oct. 17, 1966; Jan. 30, 1970; Mar. 31, 1970.

Lesseps, Ferdinand de, Nov. 19, 1805; Feb. 1, 1864

Lessing, Doris, Oct. 22, 1919.

Lessing, Gotthold Ephraim, Jan. 22, 1729.

Lester, Mark, Jul. 11, 1958.

Lester, Richard, Jan. 19, 1932.

Leszczinski, Stanislas, Jun. 2, 1734.

Let it Be, May 8, 1970.

Letelier, Orlando, Apr. 13, 1932; killed, Sep. 21, 1976.

Letter Writing Week, International, Oct. intro.

Letterman, David, Apr. 12, 1947.

Letters from a Farmer in Pennsylvania, Nov. 5, 1767.

Levant, Feb. 20, 1815.

Levant, Oscar, Dec. 27, 1906.

Levene, Sam, Aug. 28, 1905.

Levenson, Sam(uel), Dec. 28, 1911.

Lever, William Hesketh (1st Viscount Leverhulme), Sep. 19, 1851.

Levertin, Oscar Ivan, Jul. 17, 1862.

Levertov, Denise, Oct. 24, 1923.

Levesque, Rene, Aug. 24, 1922; inaugurated, Nov. 25, 1976.

Levi, Julian (Edwin), Jun. 20, 1900.

Levi-Montalcini, Rita, Apr. 23, 1909.

Levi-Strauss, Claude, Nov. 28, 1908.

Levin, Carl Milton, Jun. 28, 1934.

Levin, Ira, Aug. 27, 1929; Apr. 13, 1967.

Levin, Meyer, Oct. 8, 1905.

Levine, Irving R., Aug. 26, 1922.

Levine, James, Jun. 23, 1943.

Levingston, Roberto Marcelo (Argentina), Mar. 22, 1971.

Levinson, Barry, Jun. 2, 1932.

Levitt, William Jaird, Feb. 11, 1907.

Levy-Bruhl, Lucien, Apr. 10, 1857.

Levy, Jacques Francois Fromental Elie, May 27, 1799.

Levy, U.S.S., Aug. 22, 1945.

Lewes, George Henry, Apr. 18, 1817.

Lewinsky, Monica, Bill, Aug. 17, 1998.

Lewis, Andrew Lindsay, Jr. *(Drew),* Nov. 3, 1931.

Lewis, Anthony, Mar. 27, 1927.

Lewis, Carl, Jul. 1, 1961.

Lewis, C(ecil) Day, Apr. 27, 1904; Jan. 1, 1968.

Lewis and Clark Expedition, May 14, 1804; Sep. 23, 1806.

Lewis, C(live Hamilton) S(taples), Nov. 29, 1898.

Lewis, Edward B., May 20, 1918.

Lewis, Emmanuel, Mar. 9, 1971.

Lewis, Francis, Mar. 21, 1713.

Lewis, Henry, Oct. 16, 1932.

Lewis, Huey, Jul. 5, 1951.

Lewis, Jerry, Mar. 16, 1926.

Lewis, Jerry Lee, Sep. 29, 1935.

Lewis, Joe E., Jan. 12, 1902.

Lewis, John L., Feb. 12, 1880; Nov. 9, 1935; Mar. 6, 1947; Jan. 14, 1960.

Lewis, Matthew Gregory *(Monk),* Jul. 9, 1775.

Lewis, Meriwether, Aug. 18, 1774; May 14, 1804; Sep. 23, 1806.

Lewis, Oscar, Dec. 25, 1914.

Lewis, (Percy) Wyndham, Nov. 18, 1884.

Lewis, Ramsey, May 27, 1935.

Lewis, Shari, Jan. 17, 1934.

Lewis, Sinclair, Feb. 7, 1885.

Lewis, Ted, Jun. 6, 1892.

Lewis, Sir W. Arthur, Jan. 23, 1915.

Lewis, William, Feb. 1, 1960.

Lewis, Wilmarth Sheldon, Nov. 14, 1895.

Lewis, Winford Lee, May 29, 1878.

Lewisohn, Adolph, May 27, 1849.

Lexington, Battle of, Apr. 19, 1775.

Lexington (Virginia), Jan. 8, 1961.

Leyland, James Richard, Dec. 15, 1944.

Ley, Willy, Oct. 2, 1906.

Leyte Gulf, Battle of, Oct. 24, 1944; ends, Oct. 25, 1944.

Leyte-Samar operation, Dec. 25, 1944.

Li Hung-Chang, Feb. 25, 1823.

Li Xiannian, Jun. 18, 1983.

Libby, Willard Frank, Dec. 17, 1908.

Liberace (Wladziu Valentino), May 16, 1919.

Liberal Party (Canada), Apr. 6, 1968.

Liberation of Africa Day (African nations), May 25.

Liberation Anniversary of (Czechoslovakia), May 9.

Liberation Day (Albania), Nov. 29.

Liberation Day (Bulgaria), Mar. 3.

Liberation Day (Channel Islands, United Kingdom), May 9.

Liberation Day (France), May 8.

Liberation Day (French Polynesia), May 8.

Liberation Day (Guam), Jul. 21.

Liberation Day (Hong Kong), Aug. intro.

Liberation Day (Hungary), Apr. 4.

Liberation Day (Italy), Apr. 25.
Liberation Day (Kampuchea), Jan. 7.
Liberation Day (Kuwait), Feb. 26.
Liberation Day (Mali), Nov. 19.
Liberation Day (Netherlands), May 5.
Liberation Day (Nicaragua), Jul. 19.
Liberation Day (Republic of Korea),
  Aug. 15.
Liberation Day (Seychelles), Jun. 5.
Liberation Day (Slovakia), May 8.
Liberation Day (Togo), Jan. 13.
Liberation Day (Uganda), Jan. 26.
Liberation of Monaco (France,
  Monaco), Sep. 3.
Liberation of the Republic
  Anniversary of the (San
  Marino), Feb. 5.
Liberation of Saigon (Vietnam), Apr.
  30.
liberation theology, Sep. 3, 1984.
Liberation of Xanthi (Xanthi,
  Greece), Oct. 4.
Liberation Day (Cuba), Jan. 1.
Liberia: named, Aug. 15, 1824; first
  republic in Africa, Jul. 26, 1847;
  Jan. 3, 1972; Apr. 25, 1980; Doe,
  Samuel, Sep. 9, 1990.
Liberty Bell Pavilion, Jun. 28, 1948.
Liberty Day (Portugal), Apr. 25.
Liberty Day (U.S. Virgin Islands),
  Nov. 1.
Liberty Trec (Boston), Aug. 14, 1765.
Libra, Sep. intro.; Oct. intro.
libraries, patron of, Nov. 4.
Library of Congress (U.S.):
  established, Apr. 24, 1800; fire,
  Dec. 24, 1851.
library school: first U.S., Jan. 5, 1887.
Library Week, National, Apr. intro.
Libya: declared part of Italy, Oct. 25,
  1938; independence, Dec. 24,
  1951; Feb. 23, 1964; Sep. 1,
  1969; U.S. trade ban, Jan. 7,
  1986; assets frozen, Jan. 8, 1986;
  U.S. air strike, Apr. 14, 1986.
Libyan Arab Republic, Sep. 1, 1969.
Lichfield, Patrick, Apr. 25, 1939.
Lichtenstein, Roy, Oct. 27, 1923.
Liddy, G(eorge) Gordon, Nov. 30,
  1930.
Lidice (Czechoslovakia): destroyed,
  Jun. 10, 1942.
Lie, Jonas Lauritz Idemil, Nov. 6,
  1833.

Lie, Trygve, Jul. 16, 1896; Feb. 2,
  1946.
Lieberman, Nancy, Jul. 1, 1958.
Liebermann, Max, Jul. 20, 1847.
Liebig, Baron Justus von, May 12,
  1803.
Liebknecht, Karl, Aug. 13, 1871.
Liechtenstein, Jan. 23, 1719;
  independence, Sep. 23, 1719;
  Mar. 29, 1923; Feb. 28, 1971;
  Apr. 17, 1977.
Liege, Belgium: German invasion,
  Aug. 7, 1914.
Liege, patron of, Nov. 3.
Liegnitz (Silesia), Apr. 9, 1241.
Life Saving Service, Jan. 28, 1915.
Liggett Group Inc., Jun. 13, 1988;
  Mar. 20, 1997.
Light, Judith, Feb. 8, 1948.
Light, Pageant of (Florida), Feb.
  intro.
Lightfoot, Gordon, Nov. 17, 1938.
lighthouse: first nuclear-powered,
  May 21, 1964.
Lightner, Candy, May 30, 1946.
Li'l Abner: premiere, Nov. 15, 1956.
Lilienthal, David E(li), Jul. 8, 1899.
Lilienthal, Otto, May 23, 1848.
Lille (France): German occupation
  begins, Oct. 12, 1914.
Lille, University of (France):
  authorized, Jul. 31, 1559.
Lillehammer, Norway, Winter
  Olympics, Feb. 12, 1994.
Lillie, Beatrice, May 29, 1898.
Lilly, Eli, Apr. 1, 1885.
Liluokalani, Lydia Kamekeha, Sep. 2,
  1838.
lily of the valley, May intro.
Lima, Peru, patron of, Aug. 23.
Limann, Hilla: inaugurated, Sep. 24,
  1979.
Limerick, Treaty of Irish Rebellion:
  ends, Oct. 3, 1691.
limited test ban treaty, Aug. 5, 1963;
  Aug. 25, 1963.
Limoges (France): sack of, Sep. 19,
  1370.
Limon, Jose Arcadio, Jan. 12, 1908.
Lin Piao, Dec. 5, 1908.
Lin Tse-hsu, Mar. 10, 1839.
Lincoln, Abraham, Feb. 12, 1809;
  elected President, Nov. 6, 1860;

  inaugurated, Mar. 4, 1861; Apr.
  15, 1861; May 20, 1862; frees
  slaves, Sep. 22, 1862; Nov. 19,
  1863; second term, Mar. 4,
  1865; assassinated, Apr. 14,
  1865.
Lincoln Center (New York City),
  Sep. 16, 1966.
Lincoln Day (Arizona), Feb. intro.
Lincoln, Mary Todd, Dec. 13, 1818.
Lincoln Memorial, May 30, 1922.
Lincoln penny: first issued, Aug. 2,
  1909.
Lincoln, Robert Todd, Aug. 1, 1843.
Lincoln University, Apr. 29, 1854.
Lincoln, William Wallace: dies, Feb.
  20, 1862.
Lincoln's Birthday (Delaware,
  Oregon), Feb. intro.
Lincoln's Birthday (U.S.), Feb. 12.
Lind, Jenny, Oct. 6, 1820.
Lindbergh, Ann Morrow, Jun. 22,
  1906.
Lindbergh, Charles A., Feb. 4, 1902;
  May 21, 1927; Jun. 11, 1927;
  Feb. 4, 1929; Mar. 1, 1932.
Linde, Carl von, Jun. 11, 1842.
Linden, Hal, Mar. 20, 1931.
Lindgren, Asfrid, Nov. 14, 1907.
Lindley, Audra, Sep. 24, 1918.
Lindley, John, Feb. 5, 1799.
Lindros, Eric, Feb. 28, 1973.
Lindsay, Howard, Mar. 29, 1889.
Lindsay, John V(liet), Nov. 24, 1921;
  Nov. 2, 1965.
Lindsay, Norman, Feb. 23, 1879.
Lindsay, Vachel, Nov. 10, 1879.
Lindscy, Benjamin Barr, Nov. 25,
  1869.
Lindsey, Ted, Jul. 29, 1925.
Lindstrand, Per, Jul. 3, 1987.
Lindstrom, Pia, Sep. 20, 1938.
Line Item Veto Act (1996), Feb. 12,
  1998; Jun. 25, 1998.
Linh, Nguyen Van, Dec. 18, 1986.
Linkletter, Art, Jul. 17, 1912.
Linnaeus, Carolus, May 23, 1707.
Linnas, Karl, Apr. 20, 1987.
Linoviev, Grigory, Oct. 23, 1927.
Linville, Larry Lavon, Sep. 29, 1939.
Lion's Journey for Sight, Apr. intro.
Liotta, Ray, Dec. 18, 1955.
Lipmann, Fritz Albert, Jun. 12, 1899.

Lippincott, Joshua Ballinger, Mar. 18, 1813.

Lippmann, Gabriel, Aug. 16, 1845.

Lippmann, Walter, Sep. 23, 1889.

Lipscomb, Eugene, Nov. 9, 1931.

Lipscomb, William N., Dec. 9, 1919.

Lipton, Peggy, Aug. 30, 1947.

Lipton, Sir Thomas Johnstone, May 10, 1850.

Lisbon (Portugal), May 19, 1588; Sep. 6, 1951.

Lisle, Charles Marie Rene Leconte de, Oct. 22, 1818.

Lissa (Italy): fleet destroyed, Jul. 20, 1866.

Lister, Joseph, Apr. 5, 1827; Jan. 8, 1870.

Liston, Charles (Sonny), May 8, 1932, Sep. 25, 1962; Jul. 22, 1963; Feb. 25, 1964, May 25, 1965.

Liszt, Franz, Oct. 22, 1811.

Literacy Day (Liberia), Feb. 14.

literacy test, Feb. 4, 1965.

Lithgow, John Arthur, Oct. 19, 1945.

Lithuania, Jan. 18, 1401; Jul. 1, 1569; independence, Dec. 11, 1917; incorporated into U.S.S.R., Aug. 25, 1940; multiple party political system, Dec. 7, 1989; votes to secede, Mar. 11, 1990; North Atlantic Treaty Organization (NATO), Jan. 16, 1998.

Lithuanian Independence Day (U.S. Lithuanian Community), Feb. 16.

Little, Arthur D(ehon), Dec. 15, 1863.

Little Big Horn (South Dakota), Jun. 25, 1876.

Little, Cleavon Jake, Jun. 1, 1939.

Little, Joanne, Aug. 15, 1975.

Little League Baseball, Jun. 6, 1939; Jun. 1974.

Little League Week, National, Jun. intro.

Little Mory Sunshine: premiere, Nov. 18, 1959.

A Little Night Music: premiere, Feb. 25, 1973.

Little Richard, Dec. 25, 1935.

Little, Rich(ard Caruthers), Nov. 26 1938; Little Rock (Arkansas),

Sep. 4, 1957, racial integration, Sep. 24, 1957; four schools closed, Sep. 30, 1958.

Little St. Hugh of Lincoln, Aug. 27.

Littre, Emile, Feb. 1, 1801.

Litvinov, Maxim, Jul. 17, 1871.

Litvinov Protocol, Feb. 9, 1929.

Live Aid, Jul. 13, 1985.

Livermore, Mary Ashton, Dec. 19, 1820.

Liverpool (England), Jan. 20, 1885.

Liverpool and Manchester Railway, Sep. 15, 1830.

Livingston, Edward, May 28, 1764.

Livingston, Philip, Jan. 15, 1716.

Livingston, Robert R., Nov. 27, 1746.

Livingstone, Dr. David, Mar. 19, 1813; Aug. 1, 1849; Nov. 17, 1855; Sep. 16, 1859; Jan. 6, 1871; Mar. 21, 1871; meets H.M. Stanley, Oct. 28, 1871; Mar. 14, 1872.

Livonian War, Jan. 15, 1582.

LL Cool J (James Todd Smith), Aug. 16, 1968.

Llandingat, Wales, patron of, Nov. 1.

Lleras Camargo, Alberto, Aug. 7, 1958.

Lleras Restrepo, Carlos: inaugurated, Aug. 7, 1966.

Llewellyn, Richard, Dec. 8, 1906.

Lloyd, Christopher, Oct. 22, 1938.

Lloyd George, David, Jan. 17, 1863; Dec. 6, 1916.

Lloyd, Harold, Apr. 2, 1893; Apr. 20, 1893.

Lloyd, John, Aug. 27, 1954.

Lloyd, Marie, Feb. 12, 1870.

Lobachevsky, Nikolai Ivanovich, Dec. 1, 1792.

Locarno Pacts, Mar. 7, 1936.

Locarno Treaties, Dec. 1, 1925.

Locke, David Ross, Sep. 20, 1833.

Locke, John, Aug. 29, 1632.

Locke, Sondra, May 28, 1947.

Lockerbie, Scotland, Pan Am Flight 103, Dec. 21, 1988.

Lockhart, John Gibson, Jul. 14, 1794.

Lockhart, June, Jun. 25, 1925.

Lockhart Medical College (Peking): opens, Feb. 13, 1906.

Lockheed Aircraft Corp., Feb. 4, 1976.

Locklear, Heather, Sep. 25, 1961.

Lockridge, Richard, Sep. 26, 1898.

locksmiths, patron of, Jun. 29; Nov. 6.

Lockwood, Belva Anna Bennett, Oct. 24, 1830; Mar. 3, 1879.

Lockwood, Gary, Feb. 21, 1937.

Lockwood, Margaret, Sep. 15, 1916.

Lockyer, Sir Joseph Norman, May 17, 1836.

locomotive, steam: first use, Dec. 7, 1835.

Lodge, Henry Cabot, May 12, 1850.

Lodge, Henry Cabot, Jr., Jul. 5, 1902.

Lodge, Sir Oliver Joseph, Jun. 12, 1851.

Lodi (Austria), May 10, 1796.

Lodi, Peace of, Apr. 9, 1454.

Lodovico the Moor, Sep. 1, 1494.

Lodz, Battle of: begins, Nov. 16, 1914; Dec. 6, 1914, ends, Dec. 15, 1914.

Loeb, Jacques, Apr. 7, 1859.

Loeb, William, Dec. 26, 1905.

Loesser, Frank, Jun. 29, 1910; Nov. 24, 1950; Oct. 14, 1961.

Loewe, Frederick, Jun. 10, 1901; Mar. 13, 1947; Nov. 12, 1951; Dec. 3, 1960.

Loewi, Otto, Jun. 3, 1873.

Lofgren, Nils, Jun. 21, 1951.

Lofting, Hugh, Jan. 14, 1886.

Lofton, Kenny, May 31, 1967.

Lofts, Norah Robinson Aug. 27, 1904.

Logan, Josh, Aug. 21, i956.

Logan, Joshua, Oct. 5, 1908.

Loggins, Kenneth Clarke (Kenny), Jan. 7, 1948.

Lohengrin: premieres, Aug. 28, 1850.

Lokoloko, Tore, Sep. 21, 1930.

Lolich, Michael Stephen (Mickey), Sep. 12, 1940.

Lollards, Dec. 12, 1417.

Lollobrigida, Gina, Jul. 4, 1928.

Lolovic, Vladimir: dies, Apr. 15, 1971.

Lomax, John Avery, Sep. 23, 1867.

Lombard, Carole, Oct. 6, 1908.

Lombard League, Apr. 16, 1175.

Lombardi, Vince, Jun. 11, 1913.

Lombardo, Guy, Jun. 19, 1902.

Lombards, May 4, 1041.

Lombardy, May 15, 1004.

Lomonosov, Mikhail Vasilievich, Nov. 8, 1711.

Lon Nol, Mar. 18, 1970.

London, Conference of: Greek independence, Feb. 4, 1830.

London, Declaration of, Feb. 13, 1920.

London Dock Strike: begins trade unionism in Great Britain, Aug. 13, 1889.

London (England), Jan. 8, 1800; Jan. 7, 1927; Jan. 26, 1930; Aug. 23, 1940.

London General Omnibus Company, Jan. 7, 1857.

London, Great Fire of, Sep. 2, 1666.

London, Jack, Jan. 12, 1876.

London martyrs of 1582, May 28.

London Martyrs of 1588, Aug. 28; Oct. 25.

London Naval Conference, Jan. 21, 1930.

London Naval Conference Treaty, Apr. 10, 1930.

London police, Sep. 29, 1829.

London Stock Exchange, Oct. 20, 1987.

London Symphony Orchestra: inaugural concert, Jun. 9, 1904.

London *Times*: first color Sunday supplement, Feb. 4, 1964.

London, Treaty of, Apr. 19, 1839; May 8, 1852; May 11, 1867.

London, Treaty of (First Balkan War), May 30, 1913.

London University: chartered, Feb. 11, 1826.

Lone Ranger: radio debut, Jan. 30, 1933; television debut, Sep. 15, 1949.

Lonetree, Clayton, Mar. 27, 1987; Aug. 21, 1987.

Long Beach, Sep. 9, 1961.

Long, Crawford Williamson, Nov 1, 1815.

Long Day, Huey P. (Louisiana), Jul. 30.

Long Day's Journey into Night: opens, Nov. 7, 1956.

Long, Earl Kemp, Aug. 26, 1895.

Long, Huey P., Aug. 30, 1893; assassinated, Sep. 8, 1935.

Long, John Davis, Oct. 27, 1838.

Long, Richard, Dec. 17, 1927.

Long, Russell (Billiu), Nov. 3, 1918.

Long, Shelley, Aug. 23, 1949.

Longet, Claudine Georgette, Jan. 29, 1942.

Longfellow, Henry Wadsworth, Feb. 27, 1807.

Longo, Luigi, Mar. 15, 1900.

Longstreet, James, Jan. 8, 1821.

Longworth, Alice Lee Roosevelt, Feb. 12, 1884.

Longworth, Nicholas, Nov. 5, 1869.

Lonnrot, Elias, Apr. 9, 1802.

Loos, Anita, Apr. 26, 1893.

Lopez Aldana, Fernando Schwalb: inaugurated, Jan. 3, 1983.

Lopez, Alfonso: inaugurated, Aug. 7, 1942.

Lopez, Al(fonso Ramon), Aug. 20, 1908.

Lopez Arellano, Oswaldo, Oct. 3, 1963, Dec. 4, 1972; Apr. 22, 1975.

Lopez, Carlos Antonio, Nov. 4, 1790.

Lopez de Ayala y Herrera, Adelardo, May 1, 1828.

Lopez de Santa Anna, Antonio, Feb. 21, 1794.

Lopez, Francisco Solano, Jul. 24, 1827.

Lopez Mateos, Adolfo, Jul. 6, 1958.

Lopez Michelsen, Alfonso: inaugurated, Aug. 7, 1974.

Lopez, Nancy, Jan. 1, 1957.

Lopez Portillo, Jose, Jun. 16, 1920; elected, Jul. 4, 1976.

Lopez Rega, Jan. 3, 1975.

Lopez, Trini(dad), III, May 15, 1937.

Lord of the Flies: published, Oct. 13, 1955.

Lord, Bette Bao, Nov. 3, 1938.

Lord, Jack, Dec. 30, 1930.

Lord, Walter, Oct. 8, 1917.

Loren, Sophia, Sep. 20, 1934.

Lorentz, Hendrik A., Jul. 18, 1853.

Lorenz, Konrad Zacharias, Nov. 7, 1903.

Lorimer, George Horace, Oct. 6, 1867.

Loring, Gloria Jean, Dec. 10, 1946.

Lorraine, patron of, Dec. 6.

Lorre, Peter, Jun. 26, 1904.

Los Angeles (California), Jan. 15, 1939; Jan. 30, 1993.

Losonczi, Pal, Sep. 18, 1919.

The Lost Weekend: premiere, Dec. 1, 1945.

Lostwithiel, Sep. 2, 1644.

Lothair of Saxony, Aug. 30, 1125; Jun. 4, 1133.

Lothrop, Harriet Mulford, Jun. 22, 1844.

Lott, Trent, Oct. 9, 1941.

lottery, Apr. 30, 1963.

Lotze, Rudolf Hermann, May 21, 1817.

Loucheur, Louis, Aug. 12, 1872.

Loudon, John Claudius, Apr. 8, 1783.

Loudun, Treaty of, May 3, 1616.

Louganis, Greg, Jan. 29, 1960; Sep. 27, 1988.

Louis I (Hungary), Mar. 5, 1326.

Louis I (Portugal), Nov. 11, 1861.

Louis II (Anjou), Feb. 27, 1386.

Louis II (Hungary), Jul. 1, 1506.

Louis III (Bavaria), Jan. 7, 1845.

Louis IV (Holy Roman Emperor), Mar. 23, 1324; Jan. 17, 1328; Apr. 18, 1328; Sep. 5, 1338; Mar. 15, 1341; Apr. 13, 1346.

Louis VI (France): dies, Aug. 1, 1137.

Louis VII (France), Aug. 1, 1137; Jan. 6, 1169; Sep. 30, 1174; dies, Sep. 18, 1180.

Louis VIII (France), Jul. 14, 1223.

Louis IX (France), Apr. 25, 1214; Jun. 4, 1249; May 11, 1258; dies, Aug. 25, 1270.

Louis X (France), Oct. 4, 1289; Nov. 29, 1314; dies, Jun. 4, 1316.

Louis XI (France), Jul. 28, 1461; Jun. 19, 1464; dies, Aug. 30, 1483.

Louis XII (France), Jun. 27, 1462; Dec. 10, 1508; dies, Jan. 1, 1515.

Louis XIII (France), Sep. 27, 1601.

Louis XIV (France), Sep. 5, 1638; May 14, 1643; Oct. 18, 1685; Jul. 9, 1686; dies, Sep. 1, 1715.

Louis XV (France), Feb. 15, 1710; Sep. 1, 1715; dies, May 10, 1774.

Louis XVI (France), Aug. 23, 1754; May 16, 1770; May 10, 1774; Jul. 14, 1789; arrested, Jun. 21, 1791; beheaded, Jan. 21, 1793.

Louis XVII (France), Mar. 27, 1785.

Louis XVIII (France), Nov. 17, 1755; dies, Sep. 16, 1824.

Louis of Battenberg (Mountbatten), Oct. 29, 1914.

Louis Charles (Belgium), Feb. 3, 1831.

Louis, the Child (Germany), Feb. 4, 900.

Louis, Edward Antony Richard, Mar. 10, 1964.

Louis, Joe, May 13, 1914; Jun. 22, 1937; Jun. 18, 1941; Dec. 5, 1947; Mar. 1, 1949; Sep. 27, 1950.

Louis Napoleon, Dec. 20, 1848.

Louis-Philippe (France), Oct. 6, 1773; Jul. 29, 1830; Aug. 7, 1830; abdication, Feb. 24, 1848.

Louis, Saint (France), Mar. 24, 1267.

Louisburg (Canada), Jul. 24, 1758.

Louise, Tina, Feb. 11, 1937.

Louisiana, Apr. 9, 1682; admitted to Union, Apr. 30, 1812; May 12, 1898.

Louisiana Purchase, Feb. 22, 1819.

Louisiana Territory, Apr. 30, 1803; U.S. takes possession, Dec. 20, 1803.

Lousma, Jack, E;eb. 29, 1936, Jul. 28, 1973.

Louvain, Battle of, Sep. 1, 891.

Louvain, Belgium: occupied by Germans, Aug. 19, 1914.

Lovastatin, Sep. 1, 1987.

Love Canal (New York), Aug. 7, 1978; May 21, 1980.

Love, James Spencer, Jul. 6, 1896.

Love Me, Do: Beatles first recording, Sep. 11, 1962.

Love, Mike, Mar. 15, 1941.

Lovecraft, H(oward) P(hillips), Aug. 20, 1890.

Lovejoy, Elijah Parish, Nov. 9, 1802; killed, Nov. 7, 1837.

Loveless, Patty, Jan. 4, 1957.

Lovell, Sir Alfred Charles Bernard, Aug. 31, 1913.

Lovell, James A., Jr., Mar. 25, 1928; Dec. 4, 1965; Dec. 21, 1968; Apr. 11, 1970.

Lovelock, James E., Jul. 26, 1919.

lovers, Welsh patron of, Jan. 25.

Lovett, Lyle, Nov. 1, 1957.

Lovett, Robert Abercrombie, Sep. 14, 1895.

Lovitz, Jon, Jul. 21, 1957.

Low, Sir David Alexander Cecil, Apr. 7, 1891.

Low, Juliet, Mar. 12, 1912.

Low, Juliette Gordon, Oct. 31, 1860.

Lowe, Nick, Mar. 25, 1949.

Lowe, Rob(ert Hepler), Mar. 17, 1964.

Lowe, Thaddeus S. C., Aug. 20, 1832.

Lowell, Abbott Lawrence, Dec. 13, 1856.

Lowell, Amy, Feb. 9, 1874.

Lowell, James Russell, Feb. 22, 1819.

Lowell, Percival, Mar. 13, 1855.

Lowell, Robert Traill Spence, Mar. 1, 1917.

Lowicz, Battle of: begins, Nov. 30, 1914.

Lowry Air Force Base, Jul. 11, 1955.

Lowry, Malcolm, Jul. 28, 1909.

Loy, Myrna, Aug. 2, 1905.

Loyalty Day (U.S.), May intro; May 1.

Loyola, Ignatius, Aug. 15, 1534.

Lubeck, Peace of, May 22, 1629.

Lublin, Union of, Jul. 1, 1569.

Luboff, Norman, Apr. 14, 1917.

Lucas, George, May 15, 1944.

Lucas, Robert E., Jr., Sep. 15, 1937.

Lucca (Italy), patron of, Mar. 18.

Luce, Claire Boothe, Apr. 10, 1903; Feb. 7, 1953.

Luce, Henry Robinson, Apr. 3, 1898.

Luciano, Charles (Lucky), Nov. 11, 1896.

Luciano, Ron(ald Michael), Jun. 28, 1937.

Lucky Lady II, Mar. 2, 1949.

The Lucy Show: television debut, Oct. 1, 1962.

Ludden, Allen Ellsworth, Oct. 5, 1918.

Ludendorff, Erich Friedrich Wilhelm, Apr. 9, 1865; resigns, Oct. 27, 1916.

Ludlum, Robert, May 25, 1927.

Ludwig I (Bavaria), Mar. 20, 1848.

Ludwig, Carl, Dec. 29, 1816.

Ludwig, Christa, Mar. 16, 1928.

Luedtke, Kurt Mamre, Sep. 28, 1939.

Luft, Lorna, Nov. 21, 1952.

Lugar, Richard Green, Apr. 4, 1932.

Lugosi, Bela, Oct. 29, 1884.

Luis I (Portugal), Oct. 31, 1838.

Lukanov, Andrei, resigns, Nov. 29, 1990.

Lukas, Paul, May 26, 1891.

Lule, Jusufu (Uganda), Jun. 20, 1979.

Lully, Jean-Baptiste, Nov. 28, 1632.

Lulu, Nov. 3, 1948.

Lumet, Sidney, Jun. 25, 1924.

Lumiere, Auguste, Oct. 19, 1862; Feb. 13, 1895.

Lumiere, Louis Jean, Oct. 5, 1864; Feb. 13, 1895.

Lumumba, Patrice, Jul. 2, 1925; Jun. 21, 1960; Dec. 1, 1960; killed, Feb. 12, 1961.

Luna I, Jan. 2, 1959.

Luna 9: moon landing, Feb. 3, 1966.

Luna 10: first lunar orbiter, Apr. 3, 1966.

Luna 15, Jul. 17, 1969.

Luna 17, Nov. 17, 1970.

Luna 20, Feb. 25, 1972.

lunar eclipse: first recorded, Mar. 19, 72.

lunar module, Mar. 13, 1969.

Lunar Orbiter I: transmits photos of moon's surface, Aug. 18, 1966.

Lunar Orbiter 2, Nov. 18, 1966.

Lunar Orbiter III, Feb. 4, 1967.

Lunceford, Jimmie, Jun. 6, 1902.

Lunden, Joan, Sep. 19, 1951.

Lundgren, Dolph, Nov. 3, 1959.

Lundquist, Steve, Feb. 20, 1961.

Luneville, Peace of, Feb. 9, 1801.

Lunik 5, May 9, 1965.

Lunokhod 2, Jan. 16, 1973.

Lunt, Alfred, Aug. 19, 1892.

Lupercalia, Feb. intro.

Lupino, Ida, Feb. 4, 1918.

LuPone, Patti, Apr. 21, 1949.

Lupus Week, National, Oct. intro.

Lurcat, Jean Marie, Jul. 1, 1892.

Luria, Salvador Edward, Aug. 13, 1912.

Lurie, Alison, Sep. 3, 1926.

Lusinchi, Jaime: elected, Dec. 4, 1983; inaugurated, Feb. 2, 1984.

Lusitania: maiden voyage, Sep. 12, 1908; Feb. 6, 1915; sunk, May 7, i915; Jun. 8, 1915.

Luther, Martin, Feb. 18; Nov. 10, 1483; Jun. 13, 1515; Oct. 31, 1517, interrogated, Oct. 12, 1518; teachings condemned by Leo X, Jun. 15, 1520; Dec. 10, 1520; excommunicated by Pope Leo X, Jan. 3, 1521; excommunicated by Diet of

Worms, Apr. 17, 1521; May 26, 1521.

Lutheran Church, American: formed, Apr. 22, 1960.

Lutheran Church, Evangelical, Apr. 22, 1960.

Lutheran Church, United Evangelical, Apr. 22, 1960.

Lutyens, Sir Edwin Landseer, Mar. 29, 1869.

Lutzen, Battle of, Nov. 16, 1632.

Lutzk: captured by Russians, Jun. 2, 1916.

Luxembourg, May 11, 1867; Nov. 23, 1890; May 10, 1940.

Luxemburg, Rosa *(Red Rasa)*, Dec. 25, 1870.

Luxemburgs, Feb. 10, 1364.

Luzan, Ignacio de, Mar. 28, 1702.

Luzon (Philippines): attack by U.S. carriers, Sep. 21, 1944; Jan. 9, 1945.

Lvov, Prince Georgy Yevgenyevich, Oct. 21, 1861.

Lwoff, Andre Michael, May 8, 1902.

Lydekker, Richard, Jul. 25, 1849.

Lydwina of Schiedam, Apr. 14.

Lyell, Sir Charles, Nov. 14, 1797.

Lyme Disease, Jul. 18, 1976.

Lynch, David K., Jan. 20, 1946.

Lynch, John R., Sep. 10, 1847.

Lynch, Kelly, Mar. 4, 1959.

Lynde, Paul (Edward), Jun. 13, 1926.

Lyndon B. Johnson's Birthday (Texas), Aug. 27.

Lyne, Adrian, Mar. 4, 1941.

Lynen, Feodor, Apr. 6, 1911.

Lynn, Loretta, Jan. 14, 1935.

Lyon, Mary, Feb. 28, 1797.

Lyons, Sir Joseph Aloysius, Sep. 15, 1879.

Lyons, Treaty of, Jan. 17, 1601.

M

M*A*S*H: television debut, Sep. 17, 1972.

Ma, Yo-Yo, Oct. 7, 1955.

Maas, Peter, Jun. 27, 1929.

Maazel, Lorin, Mar. 6, 1930.

Mabley, Jackie *(Moms),* Mar. 19, 1894.

Mac-Mahon, Marie-Edme-Patrice-Maurice, Jul. 13, 1808.

Macao, Dec. 1, 1887; Aug. 15, 1984.

Macapagal, Diosdado: inaugurated, Dec. 30, 1961.

MacArthur, Arthur, Jun. 2, 1845.

MacArthur, Charles G(ordon), Nov. 5, 1895.

MacArthur, Douglas, Jan. 26, 1880; Jul. 26, 1941; Mar. 17, 1942; Oct. 20, 1944; Feb. 5, 1945; Feb. 7, 1945; Sep. 7, 1945; Jul. 8, 1950; Sep. 29, 1950; Apr. 11, 1951; Apr. 19, 1951.

MacArthur, James, Dec. 8, 1937.

MacArthur, John Donald, Mar. 6, 1897.

Macaulay, Rose, Aug. 1, 1881.

Macaulay, Thomas Babington, Oct. 25, 1800.

Macbeth, Jul. 27, 1054; killed, Aug. 15, 1057; May 10, 1849.

MacBride, Sean, Jan. 26, 1904.

Macchiavelli, Dec. 6, 1506.

Macchio, Ralph George, Jr., Nov. 4, 1962.

MacCorkindale, Simon, Feb. 12, 1953.

MacDermott, Galt, Oct. 29, 1967.

Macdiarmid, Hugh, Aug. 1, 1892.

MacDonald, Dwight, Mar. 24, 1906.

MacDonald, Hattie, Jun. 10, 1895.

MacDonald, James Ramsay, Oct. 12, 1866; Jan. 22, 1924.

MacDonald, Jeanette, Jun. 18, 1907.

Macdonald, Sir John, Jan. 11, 1815.

MacDonald, John D., Jul. 24, 1916.

MacDonald, Ross, Dec. 13, 1915.

MacDowell, Andie, Apr. 21, 1958.

MacDowell, Edward Alexander, Dec. 18, 1861.

Macedonia, member UN, Apr. 8, 1993.

Macedonian, H.M.S., Oct. 25, 1812.

Macedonian Uprising Day (Yugoslavia), Aug. 2.

MacGraw, Ali, Apr. 1, 1938.

Mach, Ernst, Feb. 18, 1838.

Macha, Karel Hynek, Nov. 16, 1810.

Machado y Morales, Gerardo, Sep. 29, 1871.

Machel, Samora, Sep. 29, 1933.

Machensen, General von, Apr. 28, 1915.

Machiavelli, Niccolo, May 3, 1469; Jun. 15, 1498.

Macias Nquema: executed, Sep. 29, 1979.

MacInnes, Helen Clark, Oct. 7, 1907.

Macintosh, Charles, Dec. 29, 1766.

Macintosh personal computer, Jan. 24, 1984.

Mack, Connie, Dec. 22, 1862; Oct. 18, 1950.

Mack, Joseph Sanford, Nov. Z7, 1870.

Mack, Ted, Feb. 12, 1904.

Mackay, Charles Hungerford, Apr. 17, 1874.

Mackensen, August von (General), Sep. 6, 1914; Oct. 6, 1915.

Mackenzie, Alexander, Jan. 28, 1822.

Mackenzie, Sir Alexander Campbell, Aug. 22, 1847.

MacKenzie, Gisele, Jan. 10, 1927.

Mackenzie, Henry, Aug. 25, 1745.

Mackenzie, William Lyon, Mar. 12, 1795; Mar. 6, 1834.

Mackie, Robert Gordon *(Bob),* Mar. 24, 1940.

Mackin, Catherine Patricia *(Cassie),* Aug. 28, 1939.

Mackinac Bridge, May 7, 1954; Nov. 1, 1957.

Mackinder, H. J., Sep. 13, 1899.

MacLachlan, Kyle, Feb. 22, 1959.

Maclaine, Shirley, Apr. 24, 1934.

MacLeish, Archibald, May 7, 1892; Apr. 12, 1959.

MacLeish, Rod, Jan. 15, 1926.

MacLeod, Gavin, Feb. 28, 1930.

Macleod, John James Rickard, Sep. 6, 1876.

Macmillan Inc.: incorporated, Jun. 1, 1896.

Macmillan, Donald Baxter, Nov. 10, 1874.

Macmillan, Harold, Feb. 10, 1894; Jan. 10, 1957; Winds of Change, Feb. 3, 1960.

Macmurray, Fred(erick Martin), Aug. 30, 1908.

MacNee, Patrick, Feb. 6, 1922.

MacNeil, Robert Breckenridge Ware, Jan. 19, 1931.

Macon, Nathaniel, Dec. 17, 1758.

MacPhail, Leland Stanford, Jr. *(Lee),* Oct. 25, 1917.

Macpherson, Elle, Mar. 29, 1964.

Macpherson, James, Oct. 27, 1736.

MacRae, Gordon, Mar. 12, 1921.

MacRae, Meredith, May 30, 1944.

MacRae, Sheila, Sep. 24, 1923.

Macready, William Charles, Mar. 3, 1793.

MacSweney, Terence: dies, Oct. 25, 1920.

Macy & Co., R. H.: incorporated, May 28, 1919.

Macy, Bill, May 18, 1922.

mad dogs, patron of, Aug. 3.

mad cow disease, Mar. 28, 1996.

Mad Parliament, Jun. 11, 1258.

Madach, Imre, Jan. 21, 1823.

Madagascar: French colony, Aug. 6, 1896; annexed by France, Aug. 18, 1896; Sep. 10, 1942; Mar. 26, 1960.

Madagasgar. *See also*: Malagasy Republic.

Madame Butterfly: premiere, Feb. 17, 1904.

Madaraka Day (Kenya), Jun. 1.

Madden, John, Apr. 10, 1936.

Maddox, Lester, Sep. 30, 1915.

Maddux, Greg, Apr. 14, 1966.

Madero, Francisco Indalecio, Oct. 30, 1873; Nov. 20, 1910; May 25, 1911; Nov. 6, 1911; assassinated, Feb. 22, 1913.

Madfai, Jamil al-, Jan. 29, 1953.

Madigan, Amy, Sep. 11, 1951.

Madison, Dolley, May 20, 1768.

Madison, James, Mar. 16, 1751; inaugurated, Mar. 4, 1809.

Madlock, William, Jr. *(Bill)*, Jan. 12, 1951.

Madonna, Aug. 16, 1959.

Madrid Convention: signed, Jul. 3, 1880.

Madnd, Treaty of, Nov. 5, 1630.

Madrid, University of: closed, Mar. 17, 1929.

Madsen, Virginia, Sep. 11, 1963.

Maeterlinck, Maurice, Aug. 29, 1862.

Mafia trial (Sicily), Dec. 16, 1987.

Magana, Alvaro Alfredo, Oct. 8, 1925.

Magellan, launched aboard *Atlantis,* May 5, 1989.

Magellan Day (Guam), Mar. 6.

Magellan, Ferdinand, Feb. 3, 1521; killed, Apr. 27, 1521.

Magendie, Francois, Oct. 15, 1783.

Maglich, Bogdan C., Aug. 5, 1928.

Magloire, Paul, May 10, 1950.

Magna Carta: signed, Jun. 15, 1215; final form, Feb. 25, 1225; confirmed, Oct. 12, 1297.

Magnani, Anna, Mar. 7, 1908.

magnetic videotape recording, Oct. 3, 1952.

Magnuson, Warren G., Apr. 12, 1905.

Magritte, Rene Francois-Ghislain, Nov. 21, 1898.

Magruder, Jeb Stuart, Nov. 5, 1934.

Magsaysay, Ramon, Aug. 31, 1907.

Mahan, Alfred Thayer, Sep. 27, 1840.

Maharis, George, Sep. 1, 1933.

Mahdi, Jan. 26, 1885.

Mahendra (King of Nepal), Mar. 14, 1955; dies, Jan. 31, 1972.

Maher, Bill, Jan. 20, 1956.

Mahfouz, Naguib, Dec. 11, 1911.

Mahgoub, Muhammad Ahmed, May 25, 1969.

Mahler, Gustav, Jul. 7, 1860; Nov. 25, 1901; Jun. 9, 1902; Oct. 18, 1904; first American appearance, Jan. 1, 1908.

Mahler's *Fourth Symphony in G Major*: premiere, Nov. 25, 1901.

Mahler's *Third Symphony*: first complete performance of, Jun. 9, 1902.

Mahmud II (Turkey), Jul. 20, 1785.

Mahmud (Emperor of India), Jan. 3, 1399.

Mahovlich, Francis William *(Frank),* Jan. 10, 1938.

Maia, May intro.

Maia Majesta, May intro.

Maida, Adam J., Mar. 18, 1930.

Mailer, Norman, Jan. 31, 1923; May 6, 1968.

Maiman, Theodore, Jul. 11, 1927.

Maillol, Aristide, Dec. 8, 1861.

Maimonides, Moses, Mar. 30, 1135.

Maine, Mar. 3, 1820; admitted to Union, Mar. 15, 1820.

Maine, Henry James Sumner, Aug. 15, 1822.

Maine Memorial Day (U.S.), Feb. 15.

Maine, U.S.S., Feb. 15, 1898.

Maistre, (Joseph Marie) de, Apr. 1, 1753.

Maitland, Frederick Lewis, Jul. 15, 1815.

Maitlisunntig (Switzerland), Jan. intro.

Maiziere, Lothar de, Apr. 12, 1990.

Major, John, Mar. 29, 1943; Nov. 27, 1990; separation of Prince and Princess Dec. 9, 1992.

Majors, Lee, Apr. 23, 1940.

Makarios III (Archbishop, Cyprus), Aug. 13, 1913; deported, Mar. 9, 1956; overthrown, Jul. 15, 1974.

Makarios Memorial Day (Cyprus), May 1.

Makarova, Natalia Romanovna, Nov. 21, 1940.

Makeba, Miriam, Mar. 4, 1932.

makers of precision instruments, patron of, Nov. 3.

Makha Bucha Day (Thailand), Feb. 11.

Makin Island, Nov. 20, 1943.

Making a Living, Feb. 2, 1914.

Makino, Count Nobuaki, Apr. 22, 1861.

Malaga, Feb. 8, 1937.

Malagasy Republic (Madagascar), Mar. 26, 1960; independence, Jun. 26, 1960; Sep. 6, 1970; Feb. 11, 1975.

Malamud, Bernard, Apr. 26, 1914; Mar. 8, 1967.

Malan, Daniel, Nov. 30, 1954.

Malawi, Feb. 1, 1963; independence, Jul. 6, 1964.

Malay Peninsula, Jan. 20, 1874.

Malaya: Japanese landing, Dec. 8, 1941; Feb. 1, 1948; independent member of British Commonwealth, Aug. 31, 1957.

Malaysia, Federation of: created, Jul. 9, 1963; Sep. 16, 1963; Sep. 21, 1963; Mar. 7, 1970.

Malcolm, Jul. 27, 1054.

Malcolm II (Scotland): dies, Nov. 25, 1034.

Malcolm III (Scotland): killed, Nov. 13, 1092.

Malcolm IV (Scotland), May 24, 1153; dies, Dec. 9, 1165.

Malcolm X, May 19, 1925; assassinated, Feb. 21, 1965.

Malczewski, Antoni, Jun. 3, 1793.

Malden, Karl, Mar. 22, 1913.

Maldive Islands: independence, Jul. 26, 1965; admitted to U.N., Sep. 21, 1965.

Malebranche, Nicolas de, Aug. 6, 1638.

Malenkov, Georgi Maximilianovich, Jan. 8, 1902; Jan. 27, 1962.

Mali, Federation of, Apr. 4, 1960; independence, Jun. 20, 1960; Aug. 20, 1960.

Mali, Republic of: independence, Sep. 22, 1960; admitted to U.N., Sep. 28, 1960.

Malinowski, Bronislaw Kasper, Apr. 7, 1884.

Malkovich, John, Dec. 9, 1953.

Mallarme, Stephane, Mar. 18, 1842.

Malle, Louis, Oct. 30, 1932.

Malmaison, Battle of, Oct. 23, 1917.

Malmedy (Belgium), Dec. 17, 1944.

Malmo, Sir Anthony: inaugurated, Dec. 13, 1974.

Malone, Dorothy, Jan. 30, 1925; Jun. 30, 1925.

Malone, Dumas, Jan. 10, 1892.

Malone, Karl, Jul. 24, 1963.

Malone, Moses Eugene, Mar. 23, 1955.

Malpighi, Marcello, Mar. 10, 1628.

Malplaquet, Battle of, Sep. 11, 1700.

Malraux, Andre, Nov. 3, 1901.

Malta, May 30, 1814; Apr. 15, 1942; May 9, 1942; Mar. 3, 1962; independence, Sep. 21, 1964; Apr. 29, 1965; Dec. 13, 1974; Apr. 1, 1979.

Malta, Knights of, patron of, Jan. 23.

Malthus, Thomas Robert, Feb. 14, 1766.

Maltin, Leonard, Dec. 18, 1950.

Malus, Etienne Louis, Jun. 23, 1775.

Mame: premiere, May 24, 1966.

Mameluke, May 18, 1291; Mar. 1, 1811.

Mamet, David, Nov. 30, 1947; Feb. 16, 1977.

The Man in the Gray Flannel Suit: published, Jul. 18, 1955.

Man of La Mancha: premiere, Nov. 22, 1965.

Man Watchers' Compliment Week, Jul. intro.

Man Watchers' Week, Jan. intro.

The Man Who Knew Too Much: premiere, May 16, 1956.

The Man with the Golden Arm: premiere, Dec. 15, 1955.

Managua (Nicaragua): earthquake, Dec. 23, 1972.

Manchester, Melissa Toni, Feb. 15, 1951.

Manchester, William, Apr. 1, 1922.

Manchu Dynasty, Jan. 11, 1851; Feb. 12, 1912.

Manchukuo, Feb. 18, 1932.

Manchuria, Apr. 7, 1907; Apr. 14, 1929; Japanese military action in, Sep. 18, 1931; Oct. 30, 1948.

Manchuria, War Lord of, Apr. 21, 1922.

Mancini, Henry, Apr. 16, 1924.

Mancini, Pasquale Stanislao, Mar. 17, 1817.

Mandalay, Nov. 28, 1885; Mar. 20, 1945.

Mandela, Nelson Rolihlahla, Jul. 18, 1918; released from prison, Feb. 11, 1990; visits New York, Jun. 20, 1990; sworn in, May 10, 1994; new constitution, Dec. 10, 1997.

Mandelshtam, Osip Emilyevich, Jan. 15, 1891.

Mandelstam, Nadezhda Yakovlevna, Oct. 31, 1899.

Mandlikova, Hana, Feb. 19, 1963.

Mandrell, Barbara Ann, Dec. 25, 1948.

Manes, Apr. 24, 216.

Manet, Edouard, Jan. 23, 1832.

Manfred (King of Sicily), Dec. 2, 1254.

Mangione, Chuck, Nov. 29, 1940.

Manhattan, U.S.S., Sep. 14, 1969.

Manhatten: premiere, Apr. 24, 1979.

Manigat, Leslie: inaugurated, Feb. 7, 1988; Jun. 20, 1988.

Manila Bay, Battle of, May 1, 1898.

Manila (Philippines): captured by U.S., Aug. 13, 1898; Dec. 26, 1941; Japanese occupation, Jan. 2, 1942; Feb. 5, 1945; Feb. 7, 1945; becomes capital, Jun. 24, 1976.

Manilow, Barry, Jun. 17, 1946.

Mankiewicz, Frank Fabian, May 16, 1924.

Mankiewicz, Joseph Leo, Feb. 11, 1909.

Manlapit, Pablo, Jan. 17, 1891.

Manley, Michael Norman, Dec. 10, 1923; inaugurated, Mar. 2, 1972; Feb. 13, 1989.

Mann Act (White Slave Traffic Act): passed, Jun. 25, 1910.

Mann-Elkins Act: passed, Jun. 18, 1910.

Mann, Herbie, Apr. 16, 1930.

Mann, Horace, May 4, 1796.

Mann, Thomas, Jun. 6, 1875.

Mannerheim, Carl Gustav Emil, Jun. 4, 1867; Jun. 22, 1941.

Manners, John, Jan. 2, 1721.

Manning, Henry Edward, Jul. 15, 1808.

Mansfield, Jayne, Apr. 19, 1932.

Mansfield, Katherine, Oct. 14, 1888.

Mansfield, Michael Joseph, Mar. 16, 1903.

Mansfield, Richard, May 24, 1854.

Manson, Charles (Milles), Nov. 12, 1934; Aug. 8, 1969; Jan 26, 1971.

Manson, Sir Patrick, Oct. 3, 1844.

Mantegna, Joe, Nov. 13, 1947.

Mantle, Mickey, Oct. 20, 1931.

Mantovani, Annunzio, Nov. 5, 1905.

Mantua, patron of, Mar. 18.

Manuel II (Portugal), Oct. 5, 1910.

Many, Martyrs of Nicomedia, Dec. 25.

Manzoni, Alessandro Francesco Tommaso Antonio de, Mar. 7, 1785.

Mao Tse-tung, Dec. 26, 1893; Oct. 1, 1949; Jan. 19, 1975; Oct. 12, 1976.

Maori insurrection: ends, Mar. 19, 1861.

Maori War: begins, Mar. 17, 1860.

Marantha War: last, ends, Jun. 3, 1818.

Marasesti, Battle of, Jul. 22, 1917.

Marat, Jean Paul, May 24, 1743; assassinated, Jul. 13, 1793.

Maravich, Pete, Jun. 22, 1948.

Marble, Alice, Sep. 28, 1913.

Marbury v. *Madison*, Feb. 24, 1803.

Marceau, Marcel, Mar. 22, 1923.

Marcellus II (pope), May 6, 1501.

March of Dimes, Jan. 3, 1938.

March, Fredric, Aug. 31, 1897.

Marchand, Nancy, Jun. 19, 1928.

Marciano, Rocky, Sep. 1, 1923; Sep. 23, 1952.

Marcqni, Guglielmo, Apr. 25, 1874; Jul. 31, 1897; Dec. 11, 1901.

Marcos, Ferdinand, Sep. 11, 1917; Nov. 10, 1965; Sep. 21, 1972; Feb. 2, 1973; Apr. 7, 1978; Feb. 7, 1986; Apr. 16, 1986.

Marcos, Imelda, Jul. 2, 1931; Nov. 4, 1991.

Marcus Aurelius (Roman Emperor), Apr. 20, 121.

Marcus, Harold Stanley, Apr. 20, 1905.

Marcus, Rudolph A., Jul. 21, 1923.

Marcus Island, Mar. 4, 1942.

Marcus Welby, M.D.: television debut, Sep. 23, 1969.

Marcuse, Herbert, Jul. 19, 1898.

Marcy, William Learned, Dec. 12, 1786.

Mare, Walter de la, Apr. 25, 1873.

Marengo, Jun. 14, 1800.

Marette, Jacques, Jul. 13, 1962.

Margaret, Maid of Norway (Queen of Scotland), Mar. 19, 1286; dies, Oct. 7, 1290.

Margaret of Navarre, Apr. 11, 1492.

Margaret (Queen of England), Mar. 23, 1430; Dec. 30, 1460; Feb. 17, 1461.

Margaret Rose, Princess (England), Aug. 21, 1930; May 6, 1960; May 24, 1978.

Margaret Tudor, Jan. 25, 1502; marries James IV (Scotland), Aug. 8, 1502.

Margarethe Il (Denmark), Apr. 16, 1940; Jan. 15, 1972.

Maria I (Portugal), Feb. 24, 1777.

Maria II (Portugal), Apr. 4, 1819; Sep. 24, 1834; dies, Nov. 15, 1853.

Maria-Luisa (Austria), Feb. 11, 1810.

Maria Theresa (Austria), May 13, 1717; Oct. 20, 1740.

Mariam, Mengistu Haile, resigns, May 21, 1991.

Mariana Islands: Oct. 21 1914; bombed, Jun. 12, 1944; May 23, 1973.

Mariategui, Jose Carlos, Jun. 14, 1895.

Marie Antoinette (France), Nov. 2, 1755; May 16, 1770; beheaded, Oct. 16, 1793.

Marie Louise (Austria), Apr. 1, 1810.

Marignano, Battle of, Sep. 13, 1515.

Marijnen, Victor: inaugurated, Jul. 24, 1963.

Marin, Richard *(Cheech)*, Jul. 13, 1946.

Marinaro, Ed, Mar. 3, 1950.

Marine Memorial (U.S.), Nov. 10, 1954.

Mariner II: launched, Aug. 27, 1962; Dec. 14, 1962; Feb. 26, 1963.

Mariner 9, Nov. 13, 1971; mariners, patron of, Apr. 14; Jul. 25; Nov. 13; Dec. 6.

Marines, U.S., Nov. 10, 1775; Apr. 21, 1914.

Marino, Dan(iel Constantine), Jr., Sep. 15, 1961.

Maris, Roger, Sep. 10, 1934; breaks Babe Ruth's record, Oct. 1, 1961.

Maritain, Jacques, Nov. 18, 1882.

maritime accident: Philippines, Dec. 20, 1987.

Maritime Day, National (U.S.), May intro.

Maritime Day, World, Mar. intro.

Mark Antony, Feb. 15, 44 b.c.; Sep. 2, 31 b.c.

Markevitch, Igor, Jul. 27, 1912.

Markham, Beryl, Oct. 26, 1902.

Markham, Sir Clements Robert, Jul. 20, 1830.

Markham, Edwin Charles, Apr. 23, 1852.

Markham, Monte, Jun. 21, 1935.

Markova, Dame Alicia, Dec. 1, 1910.

Markovic, Ante, Jan. 19, 1989.

Markowitz, Harry M., Aug. 24, 1927.

Marlborough (England), May 23, 1706.

Marley, Robert Nesta *(Bob)*, Feb. 6, 1945.

Marlin, John Mahlon, May 6, 1837.

Marlowe, Christopher, Feb. 6, 1564; Feb. 26, 1564.

Marne, First Battle of the, Sep. 6, 1914; ends, Sep. 9, 1914.

Marne River: reached by U.S. Third Arrny, Aug. 28, 1944.

Marne, Second Battle of the: begins, Jul. 15, 1918; Jul. 18, 1918; ends, Aug. 7, 1918.

Marquand, J(ohn) P(hillips), Nov. 10, 1893.

Marquette, Jacques, Jun. 1, 1637.

Marquez, Felipe Gonzalez, Mar. 5, 1942.

Marquis, Don(ald Robert Perry), Jul. 19, 1878.

married priests: excommunicated, Mar. 9, 1074.

Marriner, Neville, Apr. 15, 1924.

Marriott, John Willard, Sep. 17, 1900.

Mars, Mar. intro; Oct. intro; Jul. 20, 1976; Sep. 3, 1976.

Mars 3: space probe, Dec. 7, 1971.

Marsalis, Branford, Aug. 26, 1960.

Marsalis, Wynton, Oct. 18, 1961.

Marsh, Jean Lyndsey Torren, Jul. 1, 1934.

Marsh, Dame Ngaio, Apr. 23, 1899.

Marsh, Othniel Charles, Oct. 29, 1831.

Marshall, E(verett) G., Jun. 18, 1910.

Marshall, F. Ray, Aug. 22, 1928.

Marshall, Garry Kent, Nov. 13, 1934.

Marshall, George C., Dec. 31, 1880; Sep. 1, 1939; Jun. 5, 1945; Oct. 30, 1953.

Marshall Islands, Jun. 25, 1983.

Marshall, James Wilson, Oct. 8, 1810.

Marshall, John, Sep. 24, 1755.

Marshall, Sir John Hubert, Mar. 19, 1876.

Marshall, Louis, Dec. 14, 1856.

Marshall, Penny, Oct. 15, 1945.

Marshall, Peter, May 27, 1902; Mar. 30, 1930.

Marshall Plan: launched, Jun. 5, 1945; U.S.S.R. rejects, Jul. 2, 1947; passed, Apr. 3, 1948.

Marshall, (Sarah) Catherine, Sep. 27, 1914.

Marshall, Thomas R., Mar. 4, 1913; Mar. 4, 1917.

Marshall, Thurgood, Jul. 2, 1908; first black on U.S. Supreme Court, Jun. 13, 1967; retires, Jun. 27, 1991.

Marshall, Tully, Apr. 13, 1869.

Martel, Charles, Oct. 25, 732.

Martello, Pier Iacopo, Apr. 28, 1665.
Martens, Wilfried, Apr. 3, 1979.
Marti, Jose, Jan. 28, 1853.
Martian atmosphere: nitrogen found, Jul. 26, 1976.
Martin V (pope), Feb. 22, 1418.
Martin, Archer John Porter, Mar. 1, 1910.
Martin, Billy, May 16, 1928.
Martin, Dean, Jun. 17, 1917.
Martin, Dick, Jan. 30, 1923.
Martin, Dino, Jr., Nov. 17, 1953.
Martin, Glenn Luther, Jan. 17, 1886.
Martin, Judith, Sep. 13, 1938.
Martin Luther King Day (U.S.), Jan. 20, 1986.
Martin Luther King's Birthday (U.S. and Virgin Islands), Jan. 15.
Martin, Mary, Dec. 1, 1913.
Martin, Pamela Sue, Jan. 5, 1954.
Martin, Quinn, May 22, 1927.
Martin, Steve, Aug. 14, 1945.
Martin, Strother, Mar. 26, 1919.
Martin, Tony, Dec. 25, 1913.
Martindale, Wink, Dec. 4, 1934.
Martineau, Harriet, Jun. 12, 1802.
Martinez de la Rosa, Francisco, Mar. 10, 1787.
Martinez, Maria Cadilla de, Dec. 21, 1886.
Martinez Trueba, Andres, Nov. 26, 1950.
Martino, Al, Nov. 7, 1927.
Martins, Peter, Oct. 11, 1946.
Martinson, Harry Edmund, May 6, 1904.
Martius, Mar. intro.
Martyrdom of Imam Ali (Iran), Jul. 14.
Martyrs of China, Feb. 17; Jul. 9.
Martyrs of Colonialism Day (Guinea-Bissau), Aug. 3.
Martyrs of Damascus, Jul. 10.
Martyrs' Day (Bangladesh), Feb. 20.
Martyrs' Day (Benin), Jan. 16.
Martyrs' Day (Burma), Jul. 19.
Martyrs' Day (Eritrea), Jun. 20.
Martyrs' Day (Lebanon), May 6.
Martyrs' Day (Malawi), Mar. 3.
Martyrs' Day (Nepal), Jan. 29.
Martyrs' Day (Syria), May 6.
Martyrs' Day (Tunisia), Apr. 9.
Martyrs of Douax, Oct. 29.
Martyrs of Ebsdorf, Feb. 2.

Martyrs of England and Wales, Oct. 25.
Martyrs and Heroes Remembrance Day (Israel), May 2.
Martyrs of Indo-China, Jul. 11; Nov. 6.
Martyrs of Japan, Feb. 5; Jun. 1.
Martyrs and Liberation Days of (Sao Tome and Principe), Feb. 3.
Martyrs of Lyons and Vienne, Jun. 2.
Martyrs of Mar Saba, Mar. 20.
Martyrs of Mount Sinai, Jan. 14.
Martyrs of Nagasaki, Sep. 29.
Martyrs of North America, Sep. 26.
Martyrs of Orange, Jul. 9.
Martyrs in the Plague of Alexandria, Feast of, Feb. 28.
Martyrs of Rome, Jun. 30.
Martyrs of the Serapeum, Mar. 17.
Martyrs of Uganda, Jun. 3.
Martyrs under the Danes, Apr. 10.
Martyrs under the Lombards, Mar. 2
Martyrs under Nero, Jun. 24.
Martyrs of Utica, Aug. 24.
Marvin, Lee, Feb. 19, 1924.
Marx, *(Chico),* Mar. 26, 1891.
Marx, *(Groucho)* Julius, Oct. 2, 1895
Marx, Karl, May 5, 1818.
Marx, Arthur Harpo, Nov. 21, 1893.
Marx, *(Zeppo),* Feb. 25, 1901.
Mary I (England), Feb. 18, 1516; Jul. 6, 1553; Feb. 12, 1554; Nov. 30, 1554; dies, Nov. 17, 1558.
Mary Poppins: premiere, Aug. 27, 1964.
Mary (Queen of England), Dec. 2, 1911.
Mary, Queen of Scots, Dec. 8, 1542; Dec. 14, 1542; Jul. 1, 1543; Apr. 24, 1558; Aug. 19, 1561; Jul. 29, 1565; Feb. 10, 1567; May 15, 1567; abdicates, Jun. 15, 1567; May 13, 1568; May 16, 1568; beheaded, Feb. 8, 1587.
The Mary Tyler Moore Show: television debut, Sep. 19, 1970.
Maryland Day (Maryland), Mar. 25.
Maryland State House, Jan. 14, 1784.
Maryland (U.S.), Mar. 25, 1634; Apr. 28, 1788.
Masaccio (Tommaso Guidi), Dec. 21, 1401.
Masai, Apr. 4, 1911.
Masaryk, Jan, Sep. 14, 1886.

Masaryk, Thomas Garrigue, Mar. 7, 1850; elected president, Oct. 28, 1871; Nov. 10, 1918.
Masefield, John, Jun. 1, 1878.
Masire, Dr. Quett Ketumile Joni, Jul. 23, 1925.
Mason, Dave, May 10, 1946.
Mason, James, May 15, 1909.
Mason, John Young, Apr. 18, 1789.
Mason, Lowell, Jan. 8, 1792.
Mason, Marsha, Apr. 3, 1942.
masons, patron of, Dec. 4.
Massachusetts: state of rebellion, Feb. 2, 1775; joins Union, Feb. 6, 1788.
Massachusetts Bay Colony, Sep. 13, 1635; Jun. 21, 1684.
Massachusetts Circular Letter, Feb. 11, 1768.
Massachusetts Institute of Technology: gene synthesis, Aug. 27, 1976.
Massasoit, Chief, Mar. 22, 1621.
Massena, Duc Andre, May 6, 1758.
Massenet, Jules Emile Frederic, May 12, 1842.
Massey, Raymond, Aug. 30, 1896.
Massey, Vincent, Feb. 20, 1887; Feb. 28, 1952.
Masters, Edgar Lee, Aug. 23, 1869.
Masters, William Howell, Dec. 27, 1915.
Masterson, Bat, Nov. 24, 1853.
Masterson, Mary Stuart, Jun. 28, 1966.
Masterton, Bill *(Bat),* Aug. 16, 1938.
Mastroianni, Marcello, Sep. 28, 1924.
Masur, Richard, Nov. 20, 1948.
Masuria, Battle of, Feb. 4, 1915; Feb. 17, 1915.
Mata Hari, Aug. 7, 1876.
Mater et Magistra: papal encyclical, Jul. 14, 1961.
mathematicians, patron of, Dec. 4.
Mather, Cotton, Feb. 12, 1663.
Mather, Increase, Jun. 21, 1639.
Mathers, Jerry, Jun. 2, 1948.
Matheson, Tim, Dec. 31, 1948.
Mathews, Shailer, May 26, 1863.
Mathewson, Christy, Aug. 12, 1880.
Mathias, Bob, Nov. 17, 1930.
Mathias, Charles McCurdy, Jr., Jul. 24, 1922.
Mathis, Johnny, Sep. 30, 1935.

Matisse, Henri-Emile Benoit, Dec. 31, 1869.

Matlin, Marlee, Aug. 24, 1965.

Matta, Juan Ramon, Apr. 5, 1988.

Matteotti, Giacomo: murdered, Jun. 10, 1924.

Matterhorn: first ascent, Jul. 14, 1865.

Matteucci, Pellegrino, Oct. 13, 1850.

Matthau, Walter, Oct. 1, 1920.

Matthias I (Hungary), Feb. 24, 1440.

Matthias Corvinus (King of Hungary), Apr. 6, 1490.

Matthias (Holy Roman Emperor), May 23, 1611; Jan. 20, 1612.

Mattingly, Don(ald Arthur), Apr. 20, 1961.

Mature, Victor, Jan. 29, 1916.

Matuszak, John, Oct. 25, 1950.

Matzeliger, Jan Ernst, Sep. 15, 1852.

Maudslay, Henry, Aug. 22, 1771.

Maugham, W. Somerset, Jan. 25, 1874; Apr. 20, 1944.

Maunoury, Michel Joseph, Dec. 11, 1847.

Maupassant, Guy de, Aug. 5, 1850.

Maupertius, Pierre Louis Moreau, Jul. 17,–1698.

Mauriac, Francois, Oct. 11, 1885.

Maurice, John Frederick Denison, Aug. 29,–1805.

Maurice, Joseph Henri (Rocket Richard), Aug. 4, 1921.

Maurice of Nassau (Dutch Stadholder), Nov. 13, 1567; Jul. 10, 1584; Apr. 23, 1625.

Mauritania: French colony, Jan. 1, 1921; independence, Nov. 28, 1960; admitted to U.N., Oct. 25, 1961.

Mauritius, Mar. 12, 1968; Apr. 24, 1968.

Maurois, Andre, Jul. 26, 1885.

Maurras, Charles, Apr. 20, 1868.

Maury, Matthew Fontaine, Jan. 14, 1806.

Mauser, Peter Paul, Jun. 27, 1838.

Mawson Antarctic Expedition, Jan. 13, 1930.

Mawson, Sir Douglas, May 5, 1882.

Max, Peter, Oct. 19, 1937.

Max Planck Institute (West Germany), Jan. 19, 1977.

Maxim, Sir Hiram Stevens, Feb. 5, 1840.

Maxim, Hudson, Feb. 3, 1853.

Maximilian I (Holy Roman Emperor), Mar. 22, 1459; Feb. 16, 1486; Aug. 19, 1493; Feb. 13, 1498; Sep. 22, 1499; Oct. 13, 1501; Dec. 10, 1508; Apr. 5, 1513; Aug. 16, 1513.

Maximilian II (Holy Roman Emperor), Jul. 25, 1564; dies, Oct. 12, 1576.

Maximilian II (Mexico), Jul. 6, 1832.

Maximilian (Archduke of Austria), Apr. 10, 1864.

Maximilian (Mexico): executed, Jun. 19, 1867.

Maxwell, Elsa, May 24, 1883.

Maxwell, James, Aug. 7, 1950.

Maxwell, James Clerk, Nov. 13, 1831.

May, Brian, Jul. 19, 1947.

May Day, May intro; May 1.

May Day Eve (Finland), Apr. 30.

May, Elaine, Apr. 21, 1932.

May Fourth Movement, May 4, 1919.

May poles, May intro.

May queens, May intro.

Mayaguez, May 12, 1975.

Mayakovsky, Vladimir Vladimirovich, Jul. 19, 1893

Mayall, John Brumwell, Nov. 29, 1933.

Mayer, Julius von, Nov. 25, 1814.

Mayer, Louis B(urt), Jul. 4, 1885.

Mayer, Nathan 1st Baron Rothschild, Sep. 16, 1777.

Mayer, Oscar Ferdinand, Mar. 29, 1859.

Mayer, Oscar Gottfried, Mar. 10, 1888.

Mayerling (Austria), Jan. 30, 1889.

Mayflower, Sep. 16, 1620; Dec. 21, 1620.

Mayflower Compact: signed, Nov. 21, 1620.

Maynor, Dorothy, Feb. 17, 1952.

Mayo, Charles Horace, Jul. 19, 1865.

Mayo, Henry Thomas, Dec. 8, 1856.

Mayo, Virginia, Nov. 30, 1920.

Mayo, William James, Jun. 29, 1861.

Mayo, William Worrall, May 31, 1819.

Mayron, Melanie, Oct. 20, 1952.

Mays, Willie, May 6, 1931; 600 home runs, Sep. 22, 1969.

Maytag, Elmer Henry, Sep. 18, 1883.

Maytag, Frederick Louis, Jul. 14, 1857.

Mazarin, Jules, Jul. 14, 1602.

Maze Prison (Belfast), May 5, 1981.

Mazursky, Paul, Apr. 25, 1930.

Mazzei, Filippo, Dec. 25, 1730.

Mazzini, Giuseppe, Jun. 22, 1805; Feb. 9, 1849.

Mazzola, Francesco, Jan. 11, 1503.

Mbasogo, Teodoro Obiang Nguema, Jun. 5, 1941; Aug. 3, 1979.

Mboya, Tom, Aug. 15, 1930.

McAdam, John Loudon, Sep. 21, 1756.

McAdoo, William Gibbs, Oct. 31, 1863.

McAfee, Mildred: first U.S. woman naval officer commissioned, Aug. 3, 1942.

McAleese, Mary, elected, Oct. 30, 1997.

McArdle, Andrea, Nov. 4, 1963.

McAuliffe, Anthony Clement, Jul. 2, 1898.

McAuliffe, Christa Corrigan, Sep. 2, 1948.

McAuliffe, Sharon Christa, Jul. 19, 1985.

McBride, Mary Margaret, Nov. 16, 1899.

McBurney, Robert Ross, Mar. 31, 1837.

McCabe, Thomas B(ayard), Jul. 11, 1893.

McCallum, David, Sep. 19, 1933.

McCambridge, Mercedes, Mar. 17, 1918.

McCandless, Bruce, II, Jun. 8, 1937; Feb. 7, 1984.

McCarey, Leo, Oct. 3, 1898.

McCarran, Patrick A., Aug. 8, 1876.

McCarran-Walter Immigration and Nationality Act, Dec. 24, 1952.

McCarron, Chris, Mar. 27, 1955.

McCarthy, Andrew, Nov. 29, 1962.

McCarthy, Eugene, Mar. 29, 1916.

McCarthy, Jenny, Nov. 1, 1972.

McCarthy, J(oseph) P(riestly), Mar. 22, 1934.

McCarthy, Joseph (Raymond), Nov. 14, 1908, Feb. 9, 1950; Mar. 9, 1954.

McCartney, Linda, Sep. 24, 1942.

McCarthy, Mary (Therese), Jun. 21, 1912.
McCarthyism, Jul. 1, 1950.
McCartney, Paul, Jun. 18, 1942; Apr. 10, 1970.
McClellan, George Brinton, Dec. 3, 1826.
McClennan, John Little, Feb. 25, 1896.
McClintock, Barbara, Jun. 16, 1902; May 21, 1971.
McCloskey, John, Mar. 10, 1810.
McCloskey, Paul N., Jr., Sep. 29, 1927.
McClure, Doug, May 11, 1938.
McClure, Michael, Oct. 20, 1932.
McClure Strait (Northwest Passage), Sep. 4, 1954.
McCollum v. *Board of Education*: Supreme Court decision, Mar. 8, 1948.
McConaughey, Matthew, Nov. 4, 1969.
McCoo, Marilyn, Sep. 3, 1947.
McCord, Kent, Sep. 26, 1942.
McCormack, John, Jun. 13, 1884.
McCormack, John W., Dec. 21, 1891.
McCormick, Cyrus Hall, Feb. 15, 1809; Jun. 21, 1834.
McCormick, Robert Rutherford (*Colonel*), Jul. 30, 1880.
McCourt, Frank, Aug. 19, 1930.
McCrae, John, Nov. 30, 1872.
McCrea, Joel, Nov. 5, 1905.
McCullers, Carson, Feb. 19, 1917.
McCullough, Colleen, Jun. 1, 1937.
McCutcheon, John, May 6, 1870.
McDermott, Dylan, Oct. 26, 1962.
McDivitt, James Alton, Jun. 10, 1929.
McDormand, Frances, Jun. 23, 1957.
McDougall, William, May 22, 1871.
McDowall, Roderick Andrew (*Roddy*), Sep. 17, 1928.
McDowell, Ephraim, Nov. 11, 1771.
McDowell, Irvin, Jul. 21, 1861.
McDowell, Malcolm, Jun. 15, 1943.
McDuffie, George, Aug. 10, 1790.
McEnroe, John Patrick, Jr., Feb. 16, 1959.
McEntire, Reba, Mar. 28, 1954.
McFadden, Mary Josephine, Oct. 1, 1938.
McFarlane, Robert Carl (*Bud*), Jul. 12, 1937; Mar. 11, 1988.

McFerrin, Bobby, Mar. 11, 1950.
McGavin, Darren, May 7, 1922.
McGee, Willie Dean, Nov. 2, 1958.
McGill, James, Oct. 6, 1744.
McGill, Ralph E., Feb. 5, 1898.
McGinley, Phyllis, Mar. 21, 1905.
McGinniss, Joe, Dec. 9, 1942.
McGiver, John, Nov. 5, 1913.
McGoohan, Patnck, Mar. 19, 1928.
McGovern, Elizabeth, Jul. 18, 1961.
McGovern, George (Stanley), Jul. 19, 1922.
McGovern, Maureen Therese, Jul. 27, 1949.
McGowan, Robert, Oct. 23, 1890.
McGraw-Hill, Mar. 13, 1972.
McGraw, James Herbert, Dec. 17, 1860.
McGraw, John Joseph, Apr. 7, 1873.
McGraw, Tim, May 1, 1967.
McGraw, Tug, Aug. 30, 1944.
McGuffey, William Holmes, Sep. 23, 1800.
McGuinn, Roger, Jul. 13, 1942.
McGuire, Al, Sep. 7, 1928.
McGuire, Dorothy, Jun. 14, 1918.
McGwire, Mark, Sep. 8, 1998.
McHenry, Donald F., Oct. 13, 1936.
McHenry, Fort, Sep. 14, 1814.
McIntire, Samuel, Jan. 16, 1757.
McKay, Jim, Sep. 24, 1921.
McKean, Michael, Oct. 17, 1947.
McKechnie, Donna Ruth, Nov. 16, 1942.
McKellen, Ian Murray, May 25, 1939.
McKenna, Ronald, Jul. 6, 1863.
McKenna, Siobhan, May 24, 1922.
McKeon, Doug, Jun. 10, 1966.
McKeon, Nancy, Apr. 4, 1966.
McKeon, Philip, Nov. 11, 1964.
McKim, Charles Follen, Aug. 24, 1847.
McKinley, Ida, Jun. 8, 1847.
McKinley, Mount: first ascent, Jun. 6, 1913.
McKinley Tariff Act: passed, Oct. 1, 1890.
McKinley, William, Jan. 29, 1843; inaugurated, Mar. 4, 1897; second term, Mar. 4, 1901; shot, Sep. 6, 1901; dies, Sep. 14, 1901.
McKinney, Cynthia A., Mar. 17, 1955.
McKissick, Floyd Bixler, Mar. 9, 1922.

McKuen, Rod, Apr. 29, 1938.
McLachlan, Sarah, Jan. 28, 1968.
McLain, Dennis Dale (*Denny*), Mar. 29, 1944. Feb. 19, 1970.
McLaughlin, James, Oct. 19, 1784.
McLean, Don, Oct. 2, 1945.
McLowery Brothers, Oct. 26, 1881.
McLuhan, (Herbert) Marshall, Jul. 21, 1911 Mar. 1, 1967.
McMahon Act, Aug. 1, 1946.
McMahon, Brien, Oct. 6, 1903.
McMahon, Ed(ward Lee), Mar. 6, 1923.
McMahon, James Robert (*Jim*), Aug. 21, 1959.
McMahon, Thomas, Nov. 23, 1979.
McMahon, William: inaugurated, Mar. 10, 1971.
McManus, Sean, Feb. 16, 1955.
McMaster, John Bach, Jun. 29, 1852.
McMillan, Edwin Mattison, Sep. 18, 1907.
McMurdo Sound, Mar. 4, 1962.
McMurtry, James, Mar. 18, 1962.
McMurtry, Larry Jeff, Jun. 3, 1936.
McNair, Barbara, Mar. 4, 1937.
McNair, Ronald, Oct. 12, 1950.
McNamara, Robert (Strange), Jun. 9, 1916; Nov. 9, 1960.
McNeeley, Tom, Dec. 4, 1961.
McNeely, Eugene, Jul. 13, 1962.
McNeile, Herman Cyril, Sep. 28, 1888.
McNichol, Jimmy, Jul. 2, 1961.
McNichol, Kristy, Sep. 9, 1962.
McNichols, John Timothy, Dec. 15, 1877.
McPartland, Jimmy, Mar. 15, 1907.
McPartland, Marian Margaret, Mar. 20, 1920.
McPherson, Aimee Semple, Oct. 9, 1890.
McQueen, Thelma (*Butterfly*), Jan. 7, 1911.
McQueen, Steve, Mar. 24, 1930.
McRaney, Gerald, Aug. 19, 1948.
M'Culloch v. *Maryland*: Supreme Court decision, Mar. 6, 1819.
McVeigh, Timothy, indicted, Aug. 10, 1995; Jan. 7, 1998.
McVie, Christine Perfect, Jul. 12, 1943.
McVie, John, Nov. 26, 1946.
McWhirter, Alan Ross, Aug. 12, 1925.

McWhirter, Norris Dewar Aug. 12, 1925.

McWilliams, Carey, Dec. i3, 1905.

Mead, George Houk, Nov. 5, 1877.

Mead, Larkin Goldsmith, Jan. 3, 1835.

Mead, Margaret, Dec. 16, 1901.

Meade, George Gordon, Dec. 31, 1815.

Meade, James E., Jun. 23, 1907.

Meadows, Jayne Cotter, Sep. 27, 1926.

Meany, George, Aug. 16, 1894.

Meara, Anne, Sep. 20, 1924.

Meat Loaf, Sep. 27, 1947.

Mecca, Sep. 20, 622.

Mecham, Evan, Apr. 4, 1988.

Mechlin, Treaty of, Apr. 5, 1513.

Mecklenburg, Declaration of Independence Anniversary of (North Carolina), May 20.

Mecklenburg Independence Day (North Carolina), May intro.

Medawar, Peter Brian, Feb. 28, 1915; Oct. 3, 1953.

Mediation, Act of, Feb. 28, 1803.

Medicaid, Jul. 30, 1965.

Medical Association, American, May 7, 1847.

medical school: first in U.S., May 3, 1765.

Medicare, Jul. 30, 1965.

medicare program: Canada, Dec. 8, 1966.

Medici, Alessandro de', Jan. 5, 1537.

Medici, Catherine de, Apr. 13, 1519; Dec. 5, 1560.

Medici, Cosimo de, Sep. 27, 1389; Jun. 12, 1519; Apr. 17, 1555.

Medici family, Sep. 6, 1512.

Medici, Lorenzo de, Jan. 1, 1449.

Medici, Maria de, Nov. 11, 1630.

medicinal springs, patron of, Mar. 2.

Medina, Sep. 20, 622, Jan. 13, 1919.

Medina Angarita, Isaias: inaugurated, May 5, 1941.

Medina, Ernest L., Mar. 8, 1971.

The Medium is the Message: published, Mar. 1, 1967.

Meere, Simon van der, Nov. 24, 1925.

Meese, Edwin, III, Dec. 2, 1931.

Meet the Press: television debut, Nov. 6, 1947.

Mehta, Zubin, Apr. 29, 1936.

Meighen, Arthur, Jun. 16, 1874.

Meiji (Emperor of Japan), Apr. 6, 1868; Aug. 29, 1871.

Mein, John Gordon: assassinated, Aug. 28, 1968

Meir, Golda, May 3, 1898; Mar. 17, 1969; Jan. 15, 1973; Apr. 10, 1974.

Meisner, Randy, Mar. 8, 1946.

Meitner, Lise, Nov. 7, 1878.

Mejdani, Rexhep, elected, Jul. 24, 1997.

Mejia Victores, Oscar Humberto, Aug. 8, 1983.

Mekong River delta, Jan. 6, 1967.

Melanchthon, Philipp, Feb. 15, 1497.

Melba, Nellie, May 19, 1861.

Melbourne: Australian aircraft carrier, Jun. 3, 1969.

Melbourne (Australia), May 9, 1901.

Melcher, Frederick G., Apr. 12, 1879.

Melchior, Lauritz, Mar. 20, 1890.

Melgar Castro, Juan Alberto, Aug. 7, 1978.

Melgarejo, Mariano, Apr. 15, 1820.

Mellencamp, John Cougar, Oct. 7, 1951.

Mello, Fernando Collor de, Aug. 12, 1949; impeached, Sep. 29, 1992; Dec. 29, 1992.

Mellon, Andrew William, Mar. 24, 1855.

Melo, Francisco Manuel de, Nov. 23, 1608.

Melville, George Wallace, Jun. 10, 1841.

Melville, Herman, Aug. I, 1819.

Memorial Day: first celebrated, May 30, 1868.

Memorial Day (Brazil, Ecuador, El Salvador, Luxembourg, Macao, Mexico, San Marino, Uruguay, Vatican City), Nov. 2.

Memorial Day (Madagascar), May 31.

Memorial Day (Malagasy Republic), Mar. 29.

Memorial Day (New Mexico), May 25.

Memorial Day (Puerto Rico), May 28.

Memorial Day (Puerto Rico, U.S.), May intro.

Memorial Day (South Korea), Jun. 6.

Memorial Day (U.S.), May 30.

Memory Day, Mar. intro.

Memory Day (U.S.), Mar. 21.

Memphis (Tennessee), Apr. 4, 1968.

Mencken, H(enry) L(ouis), Sep. 12, 1880.

Mendel, Gregor Johann, Jul . 22, 1822.

Mendeleev, Dmitri Ivanovich, Feb. 7, 1834.

Mendelssohn, Felix, Feb. 3, 1809.

Mendelssohn, Moses, Sep. 6, 1729.

Menderes, Adnan, May 14, 1950

Mendes-France, Pierre, Jan. 11, 1907.

Mendes, Sergio, Feb. 11, 1941.

Mendez, Nicanor Costa, Oct. 30, 1922.

Menem, Carlos, May 14, 1989.

Menendez de Aviles, Pedro, Feb. 15, 1519; Sep. 8, 1565.

Menendez, Erik, Mar. 20, 1996.

Menendez, Lyle, Mar. 20, 1996.

Menendez Pidal, Ramon, Mar. 13, 1869.

Mengelberg, Willem, Mar. 28, 1871.

Mengele, Josef, Mar. 16, 1911; Jun. 21, 1985.

Mengistu Haile-Mariam (Ethiopia), Feb. 3, 1977.

Menjou, Adolphe, Feb. 18, 1890.

Menninger, Karl Augustus, Jul. 22, 1893.

Menotti, Gian Carlo, Jul. 7, 1911; Dec. 24, 1951.

Men's Day (Adjaria, Republic of Georgia), Feb. 23.

Mental Health Month, National, May intro.

Menuhin, Yehudi, Apr. 22, 1916.

Menzies, Robert Gordon, Dec. 20, 1894; resigns, Jan. 20, 1966.

Mercator, Gerardus, Mar. 5, 1512.

Mercer, Johnny, Nov. 18, 1909; Nov. 15, 1956.

Merchant, Natalie, Oct. 26, 1963.

merchants, patron of, Dec. 6.

Mercier, Desire Joseph, Nov. 21, 1851.

Merciless Parliament, Feb. 3, 1388.

Mercouri, Melina, Oct. 18, 1925.

Mercury, Freddie, Sep. 8, 1946.

Meredith, Burgess, Nov. 16, 1909.

Meredith, Don, Apr. 10, 1938.

Meredith, George, Feb. 12, 1828.

Meredith, James Howard, Jun. 25, 1933; Sep. 30, 1962; first black to graduate from University of Mississippi, Aug. 18, 1963.

Meredith Victory, U.S.S., Dec. 22, 1950.

Mergenthaler, Ottmar, May 11, 1854.

Merimee, Prosper, Sep. 28, 1803.

Merit, Legion of: authorized, Jul. 20, 1942.

Meriwether, Lee, May 27, 1935.

Merman, Ethel, Jan. 16, 1909.

Merrick, David, Nov. 27, 1912.

Merrifield, R(obert) Bruce, Jul. 15, 1921.

Merrill, Dina, Dec. 9, 1925.

Merrill, Gary Franklin, Aug. 2, 1915.

Merrill, Robert, Jun. 4, 1919.

Memmac, Mar. 8, 1862.

Mersen, Treaty of, Aug. 9, 870.

Mersey Tunnel, Jan. 20, 1885.

Mesa Verde National Park: established, Jun. 29, 1906.

Mesmer, Franz Anton, May 23, 1734.

Messerschmitt, Willy (Wilhelm), Jun. 26, 1898.

Messiah (Handel): premiere, Apr. 13, 1742.

Messier, Charles, Jun. 26, 1730.

Messier, Mark, Jan. 18, 1961.

Messina, Jim, Dec. 5, 1947.

Messina, Sicily: captured by U.S., Aug. 16, 1943.

Messines, Battle of, Jun. 7, 1917.

Messmer, Otto, Aug. 16, 1892.

Messner, Reinhold: solo ascent of Mt. Everest, Aug. 20, 1980.

Mesta, Pearl, Oct. 12, 1891.

Metalious, Grace, Sep. 8, 1924; Sep. 24, 1956.

metalworkers, patron of, Dec. 1.

Metastasio, Pietro Antonio Domenico Buonaventura, Jan. 3, 1698.

Metaxas, Ioannis (Greece), Aug. 4, 1936; Jan. 29, 1941.

Metaxas, Johannes, Apr. 12, 1871.

Metcalf, Laurie, Jun. 16, 1955.

Metchnikoff, Elie, May 15, 1845.

meteor: Blackstone (Virginia), May 12, 1922.

meteorites: craters found in northern Siberia, Jun. 30, 1908; China, Mar. 8, 1976.

Meteorological Day, World, Mar. intro.

Methodist Church, Nov. 11, 1966.

Methuen: English victory over Scots, Jun. 26, 1306.

metric system, Oct. 1, 1995.

Metropolitan Museum of Art (N.Y.), Apr. 13, 1870.

Metropolitan Opera Co., Oct. 7, 1954.

Metropolitan Opera House (New York City), Oct. 22, 1873; Apr. 9, 1909; Jan. 7, 1933; Sep. 16, 1966.

Metropolitan University (Peking): opens, Aug. 6, 1927.

Metternich, Klemens Wenzel Nepomuk Lothar von, May 15, 1773.

Metternich, Prince Clemens, Mar. 13, 1848.

Metz, Battle of: begins, Jun. 9, 1918; Jun. 12, 1918; ends, Jun. 14, 1918.

Metz (France), Jan. 15, 1552; occupied by French, Nov. 19, 1918; Nov. 9, 1944; Nov. 22, 1944.

Metzenbaum, Howard M(orton), Jun. 4, 1917.

Meunier, Constantin Emile, Apr. 12, 1831.

Meusnier, Jean Baptiste Marie, Jun. 19, 1754.

Mexia, Ines, May 24, 1879.

Mexican army, May 5, 1867.

Mexican Civil War, May 25, 1911.

Mexican Revolution Anniversary (Mexico), Nov. 20.

Mexican War, Jan. 13, 1846; May 8, 1846; May 9, 1846; U.S. declares, May 12, 1846, May 24, 1846; Aug. 4, 1846; U.S. occupies Santa Fe, Aug. 18, 1846; Sep. 13, 1846; Sep. 25, 1846; Feb. 22, 1847; Mar. 29, 1847; Apr. 18, 1847; Sep. 8, 1847; treaty ending, Feb. 2, 1848.

Mexico: claims independence, Sep. 16, 1810; May 30, 1848; constitution, Feb. 5, 1917; expropriates oil companies,

Mar. 18, 1938; aid from U.S., Jan. 31, 1995.

Mexico, Bank of, Sep. 6, 1982.

Mexico City: capture of, Sep. 14, 1846.

Mexico, Republic of: established, Dec. 6, 1822; proclaimed, Mar. 26, 1825.

Meyer, Adolf, Sep. 13, 1866.

Meyer, Debbie, Aug. 14, 1952.

Meyer, Julius Lothar, Aug. 19, 1830.

Meyer, Nathan, Jul. 26, 1858.

Meyer, Viktor, Sep. 8, 1848.

Meyerhof, Otto F., Apr. 12, 1884.

Meynell, Alice, Aug. 17, 1847.

Mfume, Kweisi, Oct. 24, 1948; president of (NAACP), Feb. 20, 1996.

Michael III Obrenovihc (Serbia): assassinated, Jun. 10, 1868.

Michael VIII Palaeologus (Byzantine emperor), Jul. 25, 1261.

Michael, George, Jun. 25, 1963.

Michael, Grand Duke (Russia), Mar. 15, 1917.

Michael Romanov (Russia), Feb. 21, 1613.

Michael (Rumania), Jul. 20, 1927; abdicates, Dec. 30, 1947.

Michel, Clemence Louise, May 29, 1830.

Michel, Hartmut, Jul. 18, 1948.

Michelangelo (Buonarrotti), Mar. 6, 1475; Jan. 1, 1547.

Michelet, Jules, Aug. 21, 1798.

Michelin, Andre, Jan. 16, 1853.

Michelson, Albert Abraham, Dec. 19, 1852.

Michener, James A., Feb. 3, 1907.

Michigan (U.S.): admitted to Union, Jan. 26, 1837.

Mickey Mouse, Nov. 18, 1928.

Mickiewicz, Adam (Bernard), Dec. 24, 1798.

microwave relay system: first call placed, Aug. 18, 1951.

Mid-August Holiday (Vatican City State), Aug. 14; Aug. 15; Aug. 16.

Midas II: satellite, May 24, 1960.

Middlecoff, Cary, Jan. 6, 1921.

Middleton, Arthur, Jun. 26, 1742.

Midgley, Thomas, May 18, 1889.

Midler, Bette, Dec. 1, 1945.

Midnight Cowboy: premiere, May 25, 1969.

Midsummer Celebrations (Finland, Sweden), Jun. intro.

Midsummer's Day (Great Britain), Jun. intro; Jun. 24

Midway, Battle of: begins, Jun. 4, 1942; ends, Jun. 6, 1942.

midwives, patron of, Jan. 28; Jul. 27; Aug. 31; Sep. 26.

Mielziner, Jo, Mar. 19, 1901.

Mifune, Toshiro, Apr. 1, 1920.

MiG-25 jet, Soviet, Sep. 6, 1975.

Mignard, Pierre, Nov. 17, 1612.

Migrants' Rights Pact, May 5, 1996.

Miguel, Dom (Portugal), Oct. 26, 1802; May 26, 1834,

Miguel of Portugal, Dom, Apr. 17, 1922.

Mihajlovic, Draza, Mar. 27, 1893.

The Mikado: premiere, Mar. 14, 1885.

Miki, Takeo, Dec. 9, 1974.

Mikulski, Barbara Ann, Jul. 20, 1938.

Milan, Mar. 18, 1848.

Milan IV (Serbia), Mar. 6, 1882.

Milan, Cathedral of, May 26, 1805.

Milan (Italy), Aug. 13, 1943.

Milan, patron of, Dec. 7.

Milan (Serbia), Mar. 6, 1889.

Milano, Alyssa, Dec. 19, 1972.

Miles, Nelson Appleton, Aug. 8, 1839.

Miles, Sarah, Dec. 31, 1943.

Miles, Sylvia, Sep. 9, 1932.

Miles, Vera, Aug. 23, 1930.

Military Academy, U.S.: opens, Jul. 4, 1804.

military service bill (British), Jan. 6, 1916.

Milius, John, Apr. 11, 1944.

Milk, Harvey, Nov. 27, 1978.

Milken, Michael, Apr. 24, 1990; Nov. 21, 1990.

Mill, James, Apr. 6, 1773.

Mill, John Stuart, May 20, 1806.

Milland, Ray(mond Alton), Jan. 3, 1908; Dec. 1, 1945.

Millay, Edna St. Vincent, Feb. 22, 1892.

Miller, Ann, Apr. 12, 1923.

Miller, Arnold Ray, Apr. 25, 1923.

Miller, Arthur, Oct. 17, 1915; Feb. 10, 1949; Jan. 22, 1953.

Miller, Betty, May 12, 1963.

Miller, Dennis, Nov. 3, 1953.

Miller, Glenn, Mar. 1, 1904; Dec. 15, 1944.

Miller, Henry (Valentine), Dec. 26, 1891.

Miller, Jason, Apr. 22, 1939.

Miller, Joaquin, Sep. 8, 1837.

Miller, Jonathan Wolfe, Jul. 21, 1934.

Miller, Kelly, Jul. 23, 1863.

Miller, Merton H., May 16, 1923.

Miller, Penelope Ann, Jan. 13, 1964.

Miller, Reggie, Aug. 24, 1965.

Miller, Richard, Oct. 2, 1984.

Miller, Roger Dean, Jan. 2, 1936.

Miller, Shannon, Mar. 10, 1977.

Miller, Steve, Oct. 5, 1943.

Miller, William, Feb. 15, 1782.

Millet, Jean-Francois, Jan. 20, 1814; Oct. 4, 1814.

Millett, Katherine Murray *(Kate)*, Sep. 14, 1934.

Milligan, Spike, Apr. 16, 1918.

Millikan, Robert Andrews, Mar. 22, 1868.

Milliken, William G(rawn), Mar. 26, 1922.

Million Man March, Oct. 16, 1995.

Million Woman March, Oct. 25, 1997.

Mills, Clark, Dec. 13, 1810.

Mills, Donna, Dec. 11, 1943.

Mills, Hayley, Apr. 18, 1946.

Mills, Sir John, Feb. 22, 1908.

Mills, Juliet, Nov. 21, 1941.

Mills, Robert, Aug. 12, 1781; Feb. 2

Mills, Stephanie, Mar. 22, 1957.

Mills, Wilbur Daigh, May 24, 1909.

Milne, A. A., Jan. 18, 1882; Oct. 14, 1926; Dec. 26, 1928.

Milne, Christopher Robin, Aug. 21, 1920.

Milne, John, Dec. 30, 1850.

Milner, Martin Sam, Dec. 28, 1931.

Milnes, Sherrill Eustace, Jan. 10, 1935.

Milosevic, Slobodan, Aug. 20, 1941; reelected, Dec. 20, 1992; Jul. 23, 1997.

Milosz, Czeslaw, Jun. 30, 1911.

Milsap, Ronnie, Jan. 16, 1944.

Milstein, Cesar, Oct. 8, 1927.

Milton, John, Dec. 9, 1608.

Milutinovic, Milan, elected, Dec. 21, 1997.

Mimieux, Yvette Carmen M., Jan. 8, 1939.

Mindanao, Philippines: earthquake, Aug. 17, 1976.

Mindszenty, Joseph (Jozsef Pehm) (Cardinal), Mar. 29, 1892; arrested, Dec. 27, 1948; Feb. 8, 1949; arrives at the Vatican, Sep. 28, 1971.

Mineo, Sal, Jan. 10, 1939.

miners, patron of, Jul. 26; Dec. 4.

Minghetti, Marca, Nov. 8, 1818.

Mingus, Charles, Apr. 22, 1922.

minimum wage, increase, Nov. 8, 1988.

Minneapolis: first U.S. direct primary election, Sep. 18, 1900.

Minneapolis Symphony Orchestra, Nov. 5, 1903.

Minnelli, Liza, Mar. 12, 1946.

Minnelli, Vincente, Feb. 28, 1913; Oct. 4, 1951; May 15, 1958.

Minnesota: admitted to Union, May 11, 1858.

Minnesota Day (Minnesota), May intro; May 11.

Minot, George R., Dec. 2, 1885.

Minsky, Marvin, Aug. 9, 1927.

Mint, U.S.: established, Apr. 2, 1792.

Mintoff, Dominic: inaugurated, Jun. 17, 1971; Dec. 22, 1984.

Minuteman (missile), Feb. 1, 1961.

Mir, (space station), accident, Jun. 25, 1997; repaired by *Atlantis* space shuttle, Sep. 25, 1997.

Mirabeau, Gabriel Honore Rigueti, Mar. 9, 1749.

The Miracle Worker: opens, Oct. 19, 1959.

Miranda, Carmen, Feb. 9, 1909.

Miranda, Francisco Antonio Gabriel, Mar. 28, 1750.

Miranda, Francisco de Sa de, Aug. 28, 1481.

Miro, Joan, Apr. 20, 1893.

Mirrlees, James A., Jul. 5, 1936.

Mirza, Iskander, Oct. 7, 1958; Oct. 27, 1958.

Mishima, Yukio, Jan. 14, 1925; ritual suicide, Nov. 25, 1970.

Misrule, Lord of, Dec. intro.

Miss America Pageant, Sep. 10, 1921.

Missionary Day (French Polynesia), Mar. 5.

missionary enterpnses among the Negroes, patron of, Sep. 9.

Mississippi: admitted to Union, Dec. 10, 1817; secedes from Union, Jan. 9, 1861; first southern state to enact a Black Code, Nov. 24, 1865; Jan. 2, 1968.

Mississippi, University of: desegregation, Sep. 30, 1962.

Missouri, Mar. 3, 1820; admitted to Union, Aug. 10, 1821.

Missouri Compromise, Mar. 3, 1820; Mar. 7, 1857.

Missouri, U.S.S., Sep. 2, 1945; Oct. 25, 1952.

Mistral, Frederic, Sep. 8, 1830.

Mistral Gabriela, Apr. 7, 1889.

Mitchell, Arthur W., Dec. 22, 1883.

Mitchell, Arthur, Mar. 27, 1934.

Mitchell, Cameron, Nov. 4, 1918.

Mitchell, Edgar D., Sep. 17, 1930.

Mitchell, George John, Aug. 20, 1933.

Mitchell, John, Jan. 1, 1975; Feb. 21, 1975.

Mitchell, Joni, Nov. 7, 1943.

Mitchell, Margaret, Nov. 8, 1900.

Mitchell, Maria, Aug. 1, 1818.

Mitchell, Martha Elizabeth Beall, Sep. 2, 1918.

Mitchell, Peter, Sep. 29, 1920.

Mitchell, William *(Billy),* Dec. 29, 1879.

Mitchelson, Marvin M(orris), May 7, 1928.

Mitchum, Robert, Aug. 6, 1917.

Mitford, Jessica, Sep. 11, 1917.

Mitford, Nancy, Nov. 28, 1904.

Mitropoulos, Dimitri, Mar. 1, 1896.

Mitscherlich, Eilhardt, Jan. 7, 1794.

Mitterand, Etienne Alexandre, Feb. 10, 1859.

Mitterand, Francois, Oct. 26, 1916; May 10, 1981; reelected, Jul. 8, 1988.

Mix, Tom, Jan. 6, 1880.

Miyazawa, Kiichi, elected, Nov. 5, 1991.

Mladenov, Petar, Jul. 6, 1990; Aug. 1, 1990.

Mladic, Ratko, Nov. 16, 1995.

Moawad, Rene, assassinated, Nov. 22, 1989.

Mobile (Alabama), Jan. 15, 1863.

Mobile Bay, Battle of, Aug. 5, 1864.

Mobius, August Ferdinand, Nov. 17, 1790.

Mobutu, Joseph D. (Congol Leopoldville), Oct. 14, 1930; Mar. 22, 1966.

Mobutu, Seko Sese, Oct. 14, 1920.

Moe, Tommy, Feb. 17, 1970.

Model Parliament, Nov. 27, 1295.

Model T automobile: introduced, Oct. 1, 1908.

Modigliani, Amedeo, Jul. 12, 1884.

Modigliani, Franco, Jun. 18, 1918.

Moffat, Donald, Dec. 26, 1930.

Moffo, Anna, Jun. 27, 1934.

Mogul dynasty, May 26, 1659.

Mogul Empire, Jan. 7, 1761.

Mohajer, Dineh, Sep. 2, 1972.

Mohammed II, May 29, 1453.

Mohammed IV (Turkey): deposed, Nov. 2, 1687.

Mohammed V, Aug. 10, 1910.

Mohammed Ali, Mar. 1, 1811.

Mohammed Ayub Khan (Pakistan), Mar. 1, 1962.

Mohammed, Murtala: assassinated, Feb. 13, 1976.

Mohammed Zahir Shah (Afghanistan), Nov. 8, 1933.

Mohs, Friedrich, Jan. 29, 1773.

Moi, Daniel T. arap, Sep. 2, 1924; Jan. 5, 1998.

Moiseyev, Igor Alexandrovich, Jan. 21, 1906.

Moissan, Henri, Sep. 28, 1852.

Mokhehle, Ntsu, Jan. 30, 1970.

Moldavia, Dec. 23, 1861.

Moldavian Republic: independence, Dec. 15, 1917; Apr. 9, 1918.

Moliere, Jan. 15, 1622.

Molina, Mario, Mar. 19, 1943.

Molinari, Susan, Mar. 27, 1958.

Molino del Rey, Battle of, Sep. 8, 1847.

Mollison, Irvin, Nov. 3, 1948.

Mollwitz, Battle of, Apr. 10, 1741.

Molly Maguire, Mar. 16, 1843.

Molniya 1, Apr. 27, 1965.

Molotov, Vyacheslav Mikhailovich, Mar. 9, 1890; Jan. 27, 1962.

Moltke, General von (the Younger), May 25, 1848; Sep. 14, 1914.

Moltke, Count Helmuth von, Oct. 26, 1800.

Molucca Islands, Apr. 22, 1529.

Mommsen, Theodor, Nov. 30, 1817.

Monaco, Jan. 5, 1911.

Monage Alvarez, Luis Alberto (Costa Rica), Feb. 7, 1982.

Monaghan, Tom, Mar. 25, 1937.

Monastir, Second Battle of, Mar. 10, 1917.

Mondale, Walter, Jan. 5, 1928; Jan. 20, 1977.

Mondrian, Pieter Cornelis, Mar. 7, 1872.

Moneo, Jose Rafael, May 9, 1937.

Monet, Claude, Nov. 14, 1840.

Moneta, Ernesto T., Sep. 20, 1833.

Monge, Luis Alberto, Dec. 29, 1925.

Mongolia: expulsion of Chinese by Russians, Jan. 9, 1912; U.S. steamer, Apr. 19, 1917; independence, Nov. 5, 1921; Jan. 1 1998.

Mongolian Peoples' Republic: established, Jul. 11, 1921; admitted to U.N., Oct. 27, 1961; Jan. 15, 1966.

Moniz, Antonio Caetano de Abreu Freire Egas, Nov. 29, 1874.

Monje Gutierrez, Tomas, Jul. 22, 1946.

Monk, Art, Dec. 5, 1957.

Monnet, Jean Omer Marie Gabriel, Nov. 9, 1888.

Monod, Jacques Lucien, Feb. 9, 1910.

Mononagh (West Virginia): coal mine disaster, Dec. 6, 1907.

Monophysitism, Nov. 7, 680.

Monotheletism, Nov 7, 680.

Monroe Doctrine, Dec. 2, 1823.

Monroe, Elizabeth, Jun. 30, 1768.

Monroe, James, Apr. 28, 1758; inaugurated, Mar. 4, 1817; Dec. 2, 1823.

Monroe, Marilyn, Jun. 1, 1926; Jul. 15, 1953; Nov. 10, 1953; Mar. 29, 1959; dies, Aug. 5, 1962.

Monroe, Vaughn, Oct. 7, 1911.

Monroe, William Blanc, Jr. *(Bill),* Jul. 17, 1920

Monroney, A. S., Mar. 2, 1902.

Monrovia: land purchased, Dec. 15, 1821.

Mons (Belgium), patron of, Apr. 9.

Mont Blanc: first ascent, Aug. 8, 1786.

Mont Blanc Tunnel: opens, Jul. 16, 1965.

Montagu, Ashley, Jun. 28, 1905.

Montagu, Charles, Apr. 16, 1661.

Montagu-Clemsford reforms, Dec. 23, 1919.

Montagu, Lady Mary Wortley, May 26, 1689.

Montaigne, Michel Eyquem de, Feb. 28, 1533.

Montalban, Ricardo, Nov. 25, 1920.

Montale, Eugenio, Oct. 12, 1896.

Montana: admitted to Union, Nov. 8, 1889; first old-age pension, Mar. 5, 1923.

Montana, Joseph C. *(Joe)*, Jun. 11, 1956.

Montand, Yves, Oct. 31, 1921.

Montcalm, Louis Joseph, Feb. 28, 1712.

Monte Cassino, Feb. 15, 1944.

Montebello,Treaty of,Apr. 16, 1175.

Monteil, Mar. 14, 1369.

Montemaggiore, May 4, 1041.

Montenegro: independence, Jul. 13, 1878; declares war on Turkey, Oct. 8, 1912; declares war on Austria-Hungary, Aug. 5, 1914; Jan. 23, 1916; Apr. 20, 1920; formation of new Yugoslavia, Apr. 17, 1992.

Monterey, May 24, 1846; Sep. 25, 1846.

Montessori, Maria, Aug. 31, 1870.

Monteux, Pierre, Apr. 4, 1875.

Monteverdi, Claudio Giovanni Antonio, May 15, 1567.

Montevideo, Treaty of, May 2, 1961.

Montezuma, Nov. 8, 1519.

Montfort, Simon de, Jun. 11, 1258, killed Aug. 4, 1265.

Montgolfier, Jacques Etienne, Jan. 7, 1745.

Montgolfier, Joseph Michel, Aug. 26, 1740.

Montgomery, Bernard Law, Nov. 17, 1887.

Montgomery bus boycott, Dec. 5, 1955, Dec. 21, 1956.

Montgomery, Elizabeth, Apr. 15, 1933.

Montgomery, George, Aug. 29, 1916.

Montgomery, Richard, Dec. 2, 1738.

Montgomery, Robert, May 21, 1904.

months, number of days, Aug. intro.

Montini, Giovanni Battista: elected Pope Paul VI, Jun. 21, 1963.

Montoya, Joseph Manuel, Sep. 24, 1915.

Montreal: captured from French, Sep. 8, 1700.

Montserrat, Nov. 1, 1964.

Monzon, Carlos, Nov. 7, 1970.

Moody, Dwight Lyman, Feb. 5, 1837.

Moog, Robert, May 23, 1934.

Moon, Keith, Aug. 23, 1946.

A Moon for the Misbegotten: opens, May 2, 1957.

Moon, Sung Myung, Jan. 6, 1920; Jul. 16, 1982.

Moon, Warren, Nov. 18, 1956.

Moon, William Least Heat, Aug. 27, 1939.

moonstone, Jun. intro.

Moore, Arch Alfred, Jr., Apr. 16, 1923.

Moore, Archie, Dec. 13, 1913, Nov. 30, 1959.

Moore, Clayton, Sep. 14, 1914.

Moore, Clement (Clarke), Jul. 15, 1779.

Moore, Demi, Nov. 11, 1962.

Moore, Dudley Stuart John, Apr. 19, 1935.

Moore, Garry, Jan. 31, 1915.

Moore, George, Feb. 24, 1852.

Moore, Henry, Jul. 30, 1898.

Moore, James, May 31, 1868.

Moore, James V., Jun. 24, 1987.

Moore, Julianne, Dec. 3, 1960.

Moore, Marianne (Craig), Nov. 15, 1887.

Moore, Mary Tyler, Dec. 29, 1936.

Moore, Melba, Oct. 29, 1945.

Moore, Michael, Nov. 5, 1994.

Moore, Robin, Oct. 31, 1925.

Moore, Roger George, Oct. 14, 1928.

Moore, Sara Jane, Sep. 22, 1975.

Moore, Stanford, Sep. 4, 1913.

Moore, Terry, Jan. 1, 1932.

Moore, Thomas, May 28, 1779.

Moore, William Henry, Oct. 25, 1848.

Moorehead, Agnes, Dec. 6, 1906.

Moran, Erin, Oct. 18, 1961.

Moranis, Rick, Apr. 18, 1954.

Moravia, Mar. 15, 1939.

Moravia, Alberto, Nov. 28, 1907.

More, Paul Elmer, Dec. 12, 1864.

More, Sir Thomas, Feb. 7, 1478; executed, Jul. 6, 1535.

Moreas, Jean, Apr. 15, 1856.

Moreau, Gustave, Apr. 6, 1826.

Moreau, Jean Victor Marie, Feb. 14, 1763.

Moreau, Jeanne, Jan. 23, 1928.

Morelos, Jose, Sep. 30, 1765.

Moreno, Rita, Dec. 11, 1931.

Morenz, Howie, Jun. 21, 1902.

Morgagni, Giovanni Battista, Feb. 25, 1682.

Morgan, Daniel, Jan. 17, 1781.

Morgan, Harry, Apr. 10, 1915.

Morgan, Helen, Aug. 2, 1900.

Morgan, J. P., Jr., Apr. 17, 1837; Sep. 7, 1867.

Morgan, John, Jun. 10, 1735, May 3, 1765.

Morgan, Joseph Leonard *(Joe)*, Sep. 19, 1943.

Morgan, Junius Spencer, Apr. 14, 1813.

Morgan, Marabel, Jun. 25, 1937.

Morgan, Thomas Hunt, Sep. 25, 1866.

Morgarten, Battle of, Nov. 15, 1315.

Morgenthau, Henry, Jr., May 11, 1891.

Morgon, Garrett, Mar. 3, 1877.

Moriarty, Michael, Apr. 5, 1942.

Morison, Samuel Eliot, Jul. 9, 1887.

Morisot, Berthe, Jan. 14, 1841.

Morissette, Alanis, Jun. 1, 1974.

Morita, Pat, Jun. 28, 1936.

Mork and Mindy: television debut, Sep. 14, 1978.

Morley, Edward Williams, Jan. 29, 1838.

Morley, Robert, May 26, 1908.

Mormon Church. *See* Church of Jesus Christ of Latter-Day Saints.

Mormons, Jun. 27, 1844; exodus, Feb. 10, 1846; enter Salt Lake Valley, Jul. 22, 1847.

Mornay, Rebecca de, Aug. 29, 1961.

morning glory, Sep. intro.

Moro, Aldo, Sep. 23, 1916;
kidnapped, Mar. 16, 1978; May
9, 1978.
Morocco, Mar. 6, 1480;
independence, Jul. 3, 1880;
Franco-German agreement, Feb.
9, 1909; Mar. 2, 1956; Apr. 18,
1960.
Morocco National Day (Morocco),
Mar. 3.
Morphy, Paul, Jun. 22, 1837.
Morricone, Ennio, Oct. 11, 1928.
Morrill Act: passed, Jul. 2, 1862.
Morris, Eugene (Mercury), Jan. 5,
1947.
Morris, Gouverneur, Jan. 31, 1752.
Morris, Greg, Sep. 26, 1934.
Morris, John Scott (Jack), May 16,
1956.
Morris, Lewis, Apr. 8, 1726.
Morris, Robert, Jan. 20, 1734; Jan.
31, 1734.
Morris, William, Mar. 24, 1834.
Morris, Willie, Nov. 29, 1934.
Morrison, Jim, Dec. 8, 1943.
Morrison, Norman R., Nov. 2, 1965.
Morrison, Toni, Feb. 18, 1931; Nobel
Prize, Oct. 7, 1993.
Morrison, Van, Aug. 31, 1945.
Morristown (New Jersey), May 25,
1780.
Morrow, Rob, Jul. 21, 1962.
Morrow, Vic, Feb. 14, 1932.
Morse, Jedediah, Aug. 23, 1761.
Morse, Samuel F. B., Apr. 27, 1791,
Jun. 20, 1840; May 24, 1844.
Morse, Wayne, Jan. 6, 1838; Oct. 20,
1900.
Mortimer, Roger, Sep. 24, 1326.
Morton, Joe, Oct. 18, 1948.
Morton, Joy, Sep. 27, 1855.
Morton, Julius Sterling, Apr. 22,
1832.
Morton, Levi P., May 16, 1824; Mar.
4, 1889.
Morton, Rogers C. B., Sep. 19, 1914.
Morton, Thurston Ballard, Aug. 19,
1907.
Morton, William Thomas Green,
Aug. 9, 1819. Oct. 16, 1846.
Moscone, George Richard. Nov. 24,
1929; Nov. 27, 1978.
Moscow: burned, Sep. 15, 1812; Mar.
9, 1917; Jul. 21, 1941; first

official visit of U.S. president,
May 22, 1972.
Moscow Conference of Foreign
Ministers: opens, Oct. 19, 1943.
Moscow State Symphony: first U.S.
performance, Jan. 3, 1960.
Moseley, Henry Gwyn-Jeffreys, Nov.
23, 1887.
Mosely, Mark DeWayne, Mar. 12,
1948.
Mosely, Sir Oswald Ernald, Nov. 16,
1896.
Moses, Anna Mary (Grandma)
Robertson, Sept. 7, 1860.
Moses, Edwin, Aug. 31, 1955.
Moses, Robert, Dec. 18, 1888.
Moshoeshoe II (Lesotho), May 2,
1938; Mar. 31, 1970.
Moshoeshoe's Day (Lesotho), Mar.
12.
Mosilikatze (Chief of Zulus), Jan. 17,
1837.
Moss, Kate, Jan. 16, 1974.
Mossadegh, Mohammed, Apr. 29,
1951; Aug. 22, 1953.
Mossbauer, Rudolf Ludwig, Jan. 31,
1919.
Most, Donny, Aug. 8, 1953.
Mostel, Samuel Joel (Zero), Feb. 28,
1915.
Mother Cabrini, Saint Frances Xavier,
Jul. 15.
Mother-in-Law's Day, Oct. intro.
Motherhood of Our Lady, Feast of
the, Oct. 11.
Mother's Day: first, May 10, 1908.
Mother's Day (Central African
Republic), May intro.
Mother's Day (Guatemala), May 10.
Mother's Day (India), Feb. 22.
Mother's Day (Malawi), Oct. 17.
Mother's Day (Panama), Dec. 8.
Mother's Day (United States), May
intro.
motion picture: first commercial,
Apr. 23, 1896.
motion picture projector, Feb. 13,
1895.
Motley, Constance Baker, Jan. 25,
1966.
Motor Carner Act, U.S.: adopted,
Aug. 9, 1935.
motorists, patron of, Jul. 25.
Mott, Charles Stewart, Jun. 2, 1875.

Mott, John Raleigh, May 25, 1865.
Mott, Lucretia Coffin, Jan. 3, 1793;
Jul. 19, 1848.
Mott, Sir Nevill Francis, Sep. 30,
1905.
Mottelson, Ben Ray, Jul. 9, 1926.
Moultrie, William, Dec. 4, 1730.
Mount Aconcagua, Jan. 14, 1897.
Mount Etna: erupts, Apr. 23, 1910.
Mount Everest: first solo ascent,
Aug. 20, 1980.
Mount Holyoke Seminary, Feb. 11,
1836.
Mount St. Helens: erupts, Mar. 27,
1980.
Mount Soufriere volcano, May 7,
1902.
Mount Suribachi, Feb. 23, 1945.
Mount Vesusius: erupts, Aug. 24, 79.
Mount Whitney, Aug. 18, 1873.
Mount Yerupaja, Aug. 7, 1950.
Mountain Meadow Massacre, Mar.
23, 1877.
mountaineers, patron of, May 28.
Mountbatten, Lord Louis, Jun. 25,
1900; appointed Supreme Allied
Commander, Aug. 25, 1943;
killed, Aug. 27, 1979.
Mountlouis, Treaty of, Sep. 30, 1174.
Mourning, Alonzo, Feb. 8, 1970.
Mourning Day (Lesotho), Dec. 9.
Mourning Day of (Mexico), Feb. 14.
Moussa, Ibrahim, Sep. 30, 1946.
movable holidays, p. xii.
Mowat, Farley McGill, May 12, 1921.
Moyers, Bill, Jun. 5, 1934.
Moynihan, Daniel Patnck, Mar. 16,
1927.
Mozambican Popular Liberation
Forces Day (Mozambique), Sep.
25.
Mozambique, Mar. 1, 1498.
Mozambique, People's Republic of:
independence, Jun. 25, 1975.
Mozart, Wolfgang Amadeus, Jan. 27,
1756.
Mozorewa, Abel, Apr. 14, 1925.
M.P.L.A. Foundation Day (Angola),
Dec. 10.
Mr. T, May 21, 1952.
Mswati III (Swaziland), Apr. 25, 1986.
Mubarak, Hosni, May 4, 1928; Oct.
13, 1981.
Mudd Roger, Feb. 9, 1928.

Mudd Samuel Alexander, Dec. 20, 1833.

Mudros, Armistice of: signed, Oct. 30, 1918.

Mueller, Elizabeth: West German diplomat, Jan. 25, 1970.

Mueller, R(euben) H(erbert), Jun. 2, 1897.

Mugabe, Robert, Feb. 21, 1924; Mar. 4, 1980.

Muhammad: arrives at Yathrib (Medina), Sep. 20, 622; dies, Jun. 8, 632.

Muhammad, Elijah, Oct. 10, 1897.

Muhlenberg, Frederick Augustus Conrad, Jan. 1, 1750.

Muhlenberg, Heinrich Melchior, Sep. 6, 1711.

Muhlenberg, John Peter Gabriel, Oct. 1, 1746.

Muir, John, Apr. 21, 1838.

Mukden, Oct. 30, 1948.

Mukden Incident, Sep. 18, 1931.

Mulai Hafid (Sultan of Morocco), Jan. 4, 1908.

Muldaur, Diana Charlton, Aug. 10, 1938.

Muldaur, Maria, Sep. 12, 1943.

Muldoon, Robert David, Sep. 21, 1921; inaugurated, Dec. 12, 1975; Jul. 14, 1984.

Mull, Martin, Aug. 18, 1943.

Mullavey, Greg, Sep. 10, 1939.

Muller, Friedrich, Jan. 13, 1749.

Muller, Herman Joseph, Dec. 21, 1890.

Muller, Johann (Regiomontanus), Jun. 6, 1436.

Muller, Paul, Jan. 12, 1899.

Mulligan, Gerry, Apr. 6, 1927.

Mulligan, Richard, Nov. 13, 1932.

Mulliken, Robert S., Jun. 7, 1896.

Mullis, Kary B., Dec. 28, 1944.

Mulroney, Brian, Mar. 20, 1939; inaugurated, Sep. 4, 1984; reelected, Nov. 21, 1988; January 2, 1989; resigns, Feb. 24, 1993.

Muluzi, Bakili, elected May 21, 1994.

Mumford, Lewis, Oct. 19, 1895.

mumps vaccine, Jun. 26, 1966.

Munch, Charles, Sep. 26, 1891.

Munch, Edvard, Dec. 12, 1863.

Munchhausen, Baron von, May 11, 1720.

Munda, Mar. 17, 45 b.c.

Muni, Paul, Sep. 22, 1895.

Munich (Germany) Feb. 10. 1970; XX Summer Olympics, Aug. 26, 1972; Sep. 5, 1972.

Munich Pact, Sep. 29, 1938.

Munoz, Marin Luis, Feb. 18, 1898.

Munoz Rivera's Birthday (Puerto Rico), Jul. 17.

Munro, Alice, Jul. 10, 1931.

Munro, H(ector) H(ugh) (Saki), Dec. 18, 1870.

Munsel, Patrice, May 14, 1925.

Munson, Thurman Lee, Jun. 7, 1947.

Murat, Joachim, Mar. 25, 1767.

Murchison, Roderick Impey, Feb. 19, 1792.

Murdoch, (Jean) Iris, Jul. 15, 1919.

Murdoch, Rupert, Mar. 11, 1931.

Murger, Henry, Mar. 24, 1822.

Murillo, Bartolome Esteban, Jan. 1, 1618.

Muroc Dry Lake (California), Oct. 1, 1942.

Muroran (Japan): U.S. warships bombard, Jul. 15, 1945.

Murphy, Audie, Jun. 20, 1924.

Murphy, Ben(jamin Edward), Mar. 6, 1942.

Murphy, Eddie, Apr. 3, 1961.

Murphy, Frank, Jan. 16, 1940.

Murphy, William P., Feb. 6, 1892.

Murray, Anne, Jun. 20, 1945.

Murray, Arthur, Apr. 4, 1895.

Murray, Bill, Sep. 21, 1950.

Murray, Eddie Clarence, Feb. 24, 1956.

Murray, George Gilbert, Jan. 2, 1866.

Murray, James, Jan. 21, 1721.

Murray, Sir James Augustus, Feb. 7, 1837.

Murray, Jan, Oct. 4, 1917.

Murray, John, Mar. 3, 1841.

Murray, Joseph E., Apr. 1, 1919.

Murray, Philip, May 25, 1886.

Murray, William, Mar. 2, 1705.

Murray, William Henry, Nov. 21, 1869.

Murrieta, Luis, Mar. 23, 1994.

Murrow, Edward R(oscoe), Apr. 25, 1908; Mar. 9, 1954.

Musad, Faisal ibn (Prince): beheaded, Jun. 18, 1975.

Musashi: sunk, Oct. 24, 1944.

Musburger, Brent Woody, May 26, 1939.

Muscovy, patrons of, Jul. 24.

museum: first in U.S., Jan. 12, 1773.

Museum of Fine Arts (Boston): incorporated, Feb. 4, 1870.

Museveni, Yoweri: inaugurated, Jan. 29, 1986.

Musial, Stan, Nov. 21, 1920.

The Music Man: premiere, Dec. 19, 1957.

Music in our Schools Week, Mar. intro.

music, patron of, Nov. 22.

musical instruments, makers of, patron of, Nov. 22.

musicians, patron of, Nov. 22.

Muskie, Edmund, Mar. 28, 1914.

Musset, (Louis Charles) Alfred de, Dec. 11, 1810.

Mussolini, Benito, Jul. 29, 1883; Nov. 14, 1914; Mar. 23, 1919; Oct. 28, 1922; Oct. 31, 1922; Nov. 25, 1922; Jan. 3, 1925; Apr. 7, 1926; Apr. 8, 1926; Apr. 21, 1927; ten commandments, Apr. 4, 1928; Oct. 27, 1936; Oct. 25, 1938; resigns, Jul. 25, 1943; killed, Apr. 28, 1945.

Mussorgsky, Modest Petrovitch, Mar. 21, 1839.

Mutsuhito (Emperor of Japan), Nov. 3, 1852; Jan. 9, 1867; Feb. 3, 1867.

Mutter, Anne-Sophie, Jun. 29, 1963.

Mutual Assurance Company: first fire insurance company in U.S., Jun. 15, 1787.

Mutual Defense and Assistance Agreement, Jun. 30, 1971.

Mutual Security and Friendship Pact, Apr. 6, 1948.

Mutual Service Week, World, Nov. intro.

Muybridge, Eadweard (Edward), Apr. 9, 1830.

Muzorewa, Abel (Bishop), Apr. 21, 1979; May 31, 1979.

Mwambutsa, Jul. 8, 1966.

Mwinyi, Ali Hassan: inaugurated, Nov. 5, 985.

My Fair Lady: premiere, Mar. 15, 1955.

My-Khe, Mar. 16, 1968.

My Lai, Mar. 16, 1968; Nov. 12, 1969; Mar. 8, 1971; Mar. 29, 1971; Mar. 31, 1971.

Myers, Mike, May 25, 1963.

Myerson, Bess, Jul. 16, 1924.

Myrdal, Alva Reimer, Jan. 31, 1902.

Myrdal, Gunnar, Dec. 6, 1898.

Mysore War, Third, Mar. 21, 1791.

N

Naber, John, Jan. 20, 1956.

Nabokov, Vladimir, Apr. 22, 1899.

Nabors, Jim, Jun. 12, 1932.

Nabulski, Suleiman, Oct. 27, 1956.

Nader, Michael, Feb. 18, 1945.

Nader, Ralph, Feb. 27, 1934.

Nadir Shah (Afghanistan): assassinated, Nov. 8, 1933.

Nagel, Conrad, Mar. 16, 1897.

Nagoya, Apr. 18, 1942.

Naguib, Mohammed, Jun. 18, 1953; Apr. 18, 1954.

Nagy, Ferenc, Feb. 1, 1946.

Nagy, Imre, Jun. 7, 1896; Jul. 4, 1953; Apr. 14, 1955; Oct. 23, 1956.

nail makers, patron of, Sep. 7.

Naipaul, V(idiadhar) S(urajpresad), Aug. 17, 1932.

Nair, Chengara Veetil Devan, Aug. 5, 1923.

Nairuz (Iraq), Mar. 21.

Naish, J. Carroll, Jan. 21, 1900.

Naismith, James, Nov. 6, 1861.

Najibullah, May 4, 1986.

Nakasone, Yasuhiro, May 27, 1918; elected, Nov. 26, 1982; Nov. 6, 1987.

Namath, Joe, May 31, 1943.

Name Day of Archbishop Makarios (Cyprus), Jan. 19.

Namibia, Jan. 18, 1983; Dec. 13, 1988; independence of, Mar. 21, 1990.

Namibia Day (U.N. Member Nations), Aug. 26.

Namphy, Henri, Jun. 20, 1988; Sep. 17, 1988.

Nanak, Apr. 15, 1469.

Nanking (China), Sep. 20, 1927; government recognized by British, Dec. 20, 1928; falls to Japanese, Dec. 13, 1937; Jan. 21, 1949.

Nanking, Treaty of, Aug. 29, 1842; Mar. 19, 1853; Mar. 24, 1927.

Nano, Fatos, Feb. 22, 1991.

Nansen, Fridtjof, Oct. 10, 1861.

Nantes, Edict of, Apr. 13, 1598.

Napier, Robert Cornelis, Dec. 6, 1810.

Naples (Italy), Jan. 4, 1762; taken by Garibaldi, Sep. 7, 1860; Dec. 4, 1942; U.S. troops enter, Oct. 1, 1943; Aug. 21, 1971.

Naples (Italy), patron of, Jan. 28.

Napoleon, Aug. 15, 1769; Mar. 9, 1796; Jan. 4, 1797; Jan. 14, 1797; Jan. 2, 1799; Mar. 19, 1799; Feb. 19, 1800; defeat of Austrians, Jun. 14, 1800; founds Bank of France, Dec. 24, 1800; crowned, Dec. 2, 1804; Jan. 4, 1805; Apr. 11, 1805; May 26, 1805; Dec. 2, 1805; Feb. 7, 1807; May 1, 1808; May 1, 1809; defeats Austrians, Jul. 5, 1809; Feb. 11, 1810; Apr. 1, 1810; Jun. 22, 1812; Sep. 7, 1812; Sep. 15, 1812; abdicates, Apr. 11, 1814; Mar. 1, 1815; Mar. 20, 1815; defeated, Jun. 18, 1815; surrenders, Jul. 15, 1815; banished to St. Helena, Aug. 8, 1815; Oct. 15, 1815; dies, May 5, 1821.

Napoleon III (France), Apr. 20, 1808; Sep. 2, 1830; Dec. 2, 1851; Nov 2, 1852; Jan. 14, 1858; May 3, 1859; deposed, Mar. 1, 1871.

Napoleon, Louis, Dec. 10, 1848.

Napoleonic Wars, May 10, 1796; Jan. 14, 1797; May 18, 1803; Oct. 21, 1805; Jan. 7, 1807; May 5, 1811; Jun. 21, 1813; Mar. 31, 1814.

Napolitano, Janet, Nov. 29, 1957.

Narasimha, P. V., Rao Jun. 21, 1990.

narcissus, Dec. intro.

narcotic drugs, Mar. 25, 1972.

Narita: Tokyo airport opened, May 21, 1978.

Narock, Battle of, Mar. 18, 1916.

Naruhito, Prince (Japan), marries Masako Owada, Jun. 9, 1993.

Narva, Battle of, Nov. 30, 1700.

Narvaez, Panfilo de, Apr. 14, 1528.

Narvik Sun Pageant (Norway), Feb. 8.

NASA. *See* National Aeronautics and Space Administration.

Nash, Charles William, Jan. 28, 1864.

Nash, Graham, Feb. 2, 1942.

Nash, Johnny, Aug. 19, 1940.

Nash, Ogden, Aug. 19, 1902.

Nashville, Battle of: ends, Dec. 16, 1864.

Nashville (Tennessee): desegregation, May 10, 1960.

Nasmyth, James, Aug. 19, 1808.

Nasrin, Taslima, Aug. 25, 1962.

Nasser, Gamal Abdel, Jan. 15, 1918; Jul. 23, 1952; Apr. 18, 1954; Jun. 19, 1967.

Nast, Conde, Mar. 26, 1874.

Nast, Thomas, Sep. 27, 1840.

Nastase, Ilie, Jul. 19, 1946.

Natal (South Africa), Dec. 25, 1497. May 12, 1843. May 31, 1910; Jun. 12, 1973.

Nathan, George Jean, Feb. 14, 1882.

Nathans, Daniel, Oct. 30, 1928.

Nation, Carrie (Amelia), Nov. 25, 1846.

National Academy of Recording Arts and Sciences: founded, May 28, 1957.

National Academy of Science, Mar. 3, 1863.

National Advisory Commission on Civil Disorders, Jul. 27, 1967.

National Aeronautics and Space Administration (NASA): established, Jul. 29, 1958; Jan. 5, 1972; Jun 9, 1986; Jan. 6, 1998; Jan. 16, 1998.

National Anthem Day (Panama), Nov. 1.

national anthem (U.S.), Mar. 3, 1931.

National Anthem & Flay Day (Aruba), Mar. 18.

National Assembly (China): first meeting, Oct. 3, 1910.

National Association for the Advancement of Colored People: formed, Feb. 12, 1909; Feb. 18, 1995.

National Aviation Day (U.S.), Aug. 19.

National Awami Party, Feb. 10, 1975.

National Banking Act, Feb. 25, 1863.

National Basketball Association, Jun. 17, 1976; Oct. 28, 1997.

National Basketball Players Association, Mar. 31, 1983.

National Broadcasting Co., Sep. 14, 1926.

National Child Labor Committee (NCLC), Apr. 15, 1904.

National Children's Day (Tuvalu), Aug. 4.

National Coming Out March, Oct. 11, 1987.

National Congress of Parents and Teachers: founded, Feb. 17, 1897.

National Contest of Paso Horses (Peru, Lima), Apr. 14.

National Convention of African Americans, Sep. 15, 1830.

National Council of Catholic Bishops, Feb. 13, 1973.

National Council of Churches: family planning, Feb. 23, 1961.

National Council of the Churches of Christ: established, Nov. 29, 1950.

National Day (Antigua), Nov. 1.

National Day (Bahrain), Dec. 16.

National Day (Bangladesh), Dec. 16.

National Day (Barbuda), Nov. 1.

National Day (Belgium), Jul. 21.

National Day (Belize), Sep. 10.

National Day (Benin), Nov. 30.

National Day (Bhutan), Dec. 17.

National Day (Bolivia), Apr. 9.

National Day (Brunei), Feb. 23.

National Day (Burkina Faso), Aug. 4.

National Day (Cameroon), May 20.

National Day (Croatia), Jun. 22.

National Day (Equatorial Guinea), Oct. 12.

National Day (Federal Republic of Germany), Jun. 17.

National Day (Grenada), Mar. 13.

National Day (Guinea), Nov. 22.

National Day (Guinea-Bissau), Sep. 12.

National Day (Iran), Feb. 11.

National Day (Kuwait), Feb. 25.

National Day (Kyrgyzstan), Dec. 2.

National Day (Laos), Mar. 8; Dec. 2.

National Day (Latvia), Nov. 18.

National Day (Latvian Community, U.S.), Nov. 18.

National Day (Libya), Mar. 8; Sep. 1.

National Day (Malaysia), Aug. 31.

National Day (Malta), Mar. 31.

National Day (Mauritius), Mar. 12.

National Day (Mongolia), Jul. 11.

National Day (Nationalist China), Oct. 10.

National Day (Nepal), Dec. 28.

National Day (Niger), Dec. 18.

National Day (Oman), Nov. 18.

National Day (People's Republic of China), Oct. 1, Oct. 2.

National Day (San Marino), Apr. 1.

National Day (Saudi Arabia), Sep. 23; Sep. 23.

National Day (Senegal), Apr. 4.

National Day (Singapore), Aug. 9.

National Day (Spain), Oct. 12.

National Day (Sri Lanka), Feb. 4.

National Day (Switzerland), Aug. 1.

National Day (Syria), Nov. 16.

National Day (United Arab Emirates), Dec. 2.

National Day (Vietnam), Sep. 2; Sep. 3.

National Day (Yemen People's Democratic Republic), Oct. 14.

National Day Eve (Tahiti), Jul. 13.

National Day of Hope and Mourning (Lithuania), Nov. 1.

National Day of Sudan (Libya), May 25.

National Days (Oman), Nov. 19.

National Defense Day (Paraguay), Mar. 1.

National Democracy Day (Nepal), Feb. 19.

National Education Association (NEA), Aug. 26, 1857.

National Family Day (Mozambique), Dec. 25.

National Farm Workers Association founded, Sep. 30, 1962.

National Flag Day (Liberia), Aug. 24.

National Flag Day (Paraguay), May 14.

National Flag Day (Swaziland), Apr. 25.

National Flag of Canada Day (Canada), Feb. 15.

National Football League: Sep. 17, 1920; established, Jun. 24, 1922; first championship, Dec. 17, 1933; Jan. 15, 1939; Jun. 8, 1966; first in-season strike, Sep. 21, 1982.

National Foundation Day (Japan), Feb. 11.

National Foundation Day (Korea), Sep. 9.

National Foundation Day (South Korea), Oct. 3.

National Freedom Day (U.S.), Feb. 1.

National Gallery of Art (Washington): opens, Mar. 17, 1941.

National Guardsmen, May 4, 1970; acquitted, Nov. 8, 1974.

National Hero, Day of the (Angola), Sep. 17.

National Heroes Day (Cape Verde Islands), Jan. 20.

National Heroes Day (Costa Rica), Apr. 11.

National Heroes Day (Guinea-Bissau), Jan. 20.

National Heroes Day (Sao Tome and Principe), Sep. 6.

National Heroes Day (Sri Lanka), May 22.

National Hockey League: established, Nov. 22, 1917; Dec. 19, 1917.

National Holiday (Austria), Oct. 26.

National Holiday (French West Indies, Monaco, Tahiti), Jul. 14.

National Holiday (Liechtenstein), Jan. 23.

National Holiday (Luxembourg), Jun. 23.

National Holiday (Macedonia), Aug. 2.

National Holiday (Nigeria), Oct. 1.

National Holiday (Republic of Mali), Sep. 22.

National Holiday (Revolucion de Mayo) (Argentina), May 25.

National Holiday (Romania), Aug. 24.

National Holiday (Zimbabwe), Aug. 12.

National Independence, Anniversary of (Sao Tome and Principe), Jul. 12.

National Industrial Recovery Act, May 27, 1935.

National Institute of Arts & Letters, Feb. 4, 1913.

National Inventors Day (U.S.), Feb. 11.

National Labor Board: established, Aug. 5, 1933.

National Labor Relations Board, Jul. 5, 1935.

National League of Women Voters, Feb. 14, 1920.

National Liberation Day (Chad), Jun. 7.

National Liberation Day (Chile), Sep. 11.

National Liberation Day (Poland), Jul. 22.

National Liberation Front, Nov. 29, 1962.

National Magic Day (U.S.), Oct. 31.

National, Maritime Day (U.S.), May 22.

National Mourning Day (Bangladesh), Feb. 12.

National Mourning Day of (Mexico), Feb. 14.

National Mourning Day (Panama), Jan. 9.

National Movement (Spain), Jun. 9, 1976; Apr. 1, 1977.

National Notary Public Day (U.S.), Nov. 7.

National Organization of Cypriot Struggle, Feb. 10, 1978.

National Organization of Women (NOW): founded, Oct. 29, 1966.

National Park Service, U.S.: established, Aug. 25, 1916

National Play-Doh Day (U.S.), Sep. 16.

National Portrait Gallery (London), Jan. 15, 1859.

National Progressive Republican League, Jan. 21, 1911.

National Railroad Passenger Corporation, May 1, 1971.

National Rally Day (Liberia), May 13.

National Redemption Day (Liberia), Apr. 12.

National Resistance Day (Slovenia), Apr. 27.

National Revolution Day (Bangladesh), Nov. 7.

National Revolution Day (Tunisia), Jan. 18.

National Revolutionary Festival (Cuba), Jul. 25; Jul. 26; Jul. 27.

National Revolutionary Government (China), Sep. 20, 1927.

National Revolutionary Movement (Bolivia), Apr. 9, 1952.

National Right to Life Committee, May 14, 1973.

National Science Foundation, May 5, 1950.

National Security Act: signed, Aug. 10, 1949.

National Socialist (German Workers) Party (Nazi), Jan. 5, 1919; Sep. 14, 1930; Jul. 14, 1933.

National Sovereignty Day (Turkey), Apr. 23.

National Sovereignty and Thanksgiving Day (Haiti), May 22.

National Sports Day (Lesotho), Oct. 6.

National Statehood Day (Slovenia), Jun. 25.

National Student Association, Feb. 13, 1967.

National Thanksgiving Day (Philippines), Sep. 21.

National Theatre (London), Oct. 25, 1976.

National Traffic Safety Agency (U.S.), Jan. 31, 1967.

National Tree Planting Day (Lesotho), Mar. 21.

National Tree Planting Day (Malawi), Dec. 21.

National UNICEF Day, Oct. 31.

National Unification Day (Liberia), May 14.

National Union Day (Surinam), Jul. 1.

National Unity Day (Italy), Nov. 4.

National Unity Day (Nepal), Jan. 11.

National Unity Day (Rwanda), Jul. 5.

National Unity Day (Yemen), May 22.

National University (Greece), Feb. 11, 1875.

National Velvet: premiere, Dec. 14, 1944.

National Wildlife Federation, Feb. 5, 1936.

National Women in Sports Day (United States), Feb. 4.

National Youth Administration, Jun. 26, 1935.

National Youth Day (Liberia), Oct. 29.

National Zoo (Washington, D.C.), Apr. 16, 1972.

Nationalist China (Taiwan): expelled from U.N., Oct. 25, 1971.

Nationalist Chinese, Mar. 24, 1927; May 20, 1978.

Nationality Day (Cape Verde Islands), Sep. 12.

Nationalization Day (Sao Tome and Principe), Sep. 30.

NATO (North Atlantic Treaty Organization), Sep. 6, 1951; Jan. 2, 1963; Jun. 20, 1963; Mar. 18, 1966; Supreme Military Headquarters opens, Mar. 31, 1967; Aug. 21, 1971.

Natori, Josie, May 9, 1947.

Natta, Giulio, Feb. 26, 1903.

natural gas, Jan. 1, 1984.

Natwick, Mildred, Jun. 19, 1908.

Naughty Marietta: premiere, Oct. 24, 1910.

Nauman, Bruce, Dec. 6, 1941.

Nauru, Nov. 1, 1947; independence, Jan. 29, 1968; independence, Jan. 31, 1968.

Nautilus, U.S.S.: launched, Jan. 21, 1954; commissioned, Sep. 30, 1954; Mar. 4, 1958; Aug. 3, 1958; Aug. 7, 1958; underwater trans-Atlantic crossing, Aug. 24, 1958.

Naval Reserves, U.S.: active duty, Jun. 12, 1941.

Navarino, Battle of, Oct. 20, 1827.

Navarro Madrazo, Ignacio, Sep. 12, 1987.

Navon, Yitzhak, Apr. 19, 1921.

Navratilova, Martina, Oct. 10, 1956.

Navruz (New Day) (Tajikistan), Mar. 21.

Navy, U.S., Apr. 11, 1900; first enlisted women, Jul. 7, 1948.

Navy Day (Chile), May 21.

Nawruz (Iran), Mar. 21.

Nazi leaders: sentenced, Oct. 1, 1946.

Nazi occupation: Denmark, May 5, 1945.

Nazi party: dissolved in Austria, Jun. 18, 1933; wins elections, Mar. 29, 1936.

Nazi war criminals, Jan. 31, 1951; West Germany continues to prosecute, Jul. 3. 1979.

Nazimova, Alla, Jun. 4, 1879.

Nazimuddin, Khwaja: resigns, Apr. 18, 1953.

Ndadaye, Melchior, assassinated, Oct. 21, 1993.

Ndinzeye, Charles (Prince of Burundi), 8, 1966.

Ne Win: inaugurated, Oct. 29, 1958; Apr. 5, 1960. Jul. 23, 1988.

Neal, Patricia, Jan. 20, 1926.

Nebraska: admitted to Union, Mar. 1, 1867.

Nechita, Alexandra, Aug. 27, 1985.

Necker, Jacques, Sep. 30, 1732.

Neel, Louis Eugene Felix, Nov. 22, 1904.

Neeson, Liam, Jun. 7, 1952.

Neff, Hildegarde, Dec. 28, 1925.

Negev Desert, May 5, 1964.

Negri, Pola, Dec. 31, 1894.

Nehemiah, Renaldo, Mar. 24, 1959.

Neher, Erwin, Mar. 20, 1944.

Nehru, Jawaharlal, Nov. 14, 1889; founds Independence of India League, Aug. 30, 1928, Apr. 14, 1930, inaugurated, Jan. 26, 1950, Jun. 2, 1964; Jan. 19, 1966; Jan. 24, 1966.

Neilson, William Allen, Mar. 28, 1869.

Neiman, LeRoy, Jun. 8, 1926.

Nejd-Hejaz (Saudi Arabia), May 20, 1927.

Nejd (Saudi Arabia), Jan. 8, 1926.

Nellie Taylor Ross' Birthday (Wyoming), Nov. 29.

Nelligan, Kate (Patricia Colleen), Mar. 16, 1951.

Nelson, Craig T., Apr. 4, 1946.

Nelson, Harriet, Jul. 18, 1912.

Nelson, Adm. Horatio, Sep. 29, 1758; Aug. 1, 1798; Apr. 2, 1801; Oct. 21, 1805.

Nelson, George (Baby Face), Dec. 6, 1908.

Nelson, Judd, Nov. 28, 1959.

Nelson, Oswald George (Ozzie), Mar. 20, 1906.

Nelson, Rick, May 8, 1940.

Nelson, Thomas, Dec. 26, 1738.

Nelson, Willie, Apr. 30, 1933.

Nemerov, Howard, Mar. 1, 1920.

Nemeth, Miklos, Dec. 7, 1988.

Nenni, Pietro, Feb. 9, 1891.

Nepal: independence, Dec. 21, 1923.

neptunium, Oct. 15, 1946.

Nernst, Walther Hermann, Jun. 24, 1864.

Nero, Apr. intro.

Nero, Peter, May 22, 1934.

Neronius, Apr. intro.

Neruda, Jan, Jul. 10, 1834.

Neruda, Pablo, Jul. 12, 1904.

nerves: first transplants, human, Apr. 18, 1963.

Nervi, Pier (Luigi), Jun. 21, 1891.

Nesbitt, Cathleen (Mary), Nov. 24, 1888.

Nesmith, Mike, Dec. 30, 1942.

Ness, Eliot, Apr. 19, 1903.

Nesselrode, Count Karl Robert, Mar. 23, 1780.

Nessen, Ron(ald Harold), May 25, 1934.

Nestroy, Johann Nepomuk Edward Ambrosius, Dec. 7, 1801.

Netanyahu, Benjamin, Oct. 21, 1949; May 29, 1996.

Netherlands, Jan. 30, 1648; declared kingdom, Jun. 5, 1806; Mar. 9, 1920; Jan. 1, 1921; May 26, 1932; May 10, 1940; May 1, 1943.

Netherlands East Indies, Mar. 19, 1942.

Netherlands, Southern, May 17, 1597.

Netherlands, Spanish, May 23, 1706.

Nettles, Graig, Aug. 20, 1944.

Neturno (Italy), Jan. 22, 1944.

Neuilly, Treaty of: signed, Nov. 27, 1919.

Neumann, Emanuel, Jul. 2, 1893.

Neumann, John von, Dec. 28, 1903.

Neumann, St. John Nepomucene, Mar. 28, 1811; Jun. 19, 1977.

Neutrality Act: amended, Nov. 17, 1941.

Neutrality Act of 1935: signed, Aug. 31, 1935.

Neutrality Act of 1939, U.S., Nov. 4, 1939.

neutrino, Jun. 21, 1956.

neutron weapons: U.S. announces decision to produce, Aug. 10, 1981.

Neuve Chapelle, Battle of, Mar. 10, 1915; ends, Mar. 13, 1915.

Neva River, May 27, 1703.

Nevada, May 30, 1848; admitted to Union, Oct. 31, 1864; first old-age pension, Mar. 5, 1923.

Nevada Day (Nevada), Oct. 31.

Nevado del Ruiz (Colombia), Nov. 13, 1985.

Nevers, Ernie, Jun. 11, 1903.

Neville, Aaron, Jan. 24, 1941.

Neville's Cross, Battle of, Oct. 17, 1346.

Nevins, Allan, May 20, 1890.

New American Bible, Sep. 29, 1970.

New Amsterdam: surrenders to English, Aug. 27, 1664.

New Brunswick, Jul. 1, 1867.

New Connecticut (Vermont), Jan. 15, 1777.

New Deal, Jul. 2, 1932; Mar. 9, 1933.

New England: hurricane, Sep. 21, 1938.

New England Confederation, May 19, 1643.

New Guinea, Mar. 13, 1884; German troops surrender, Sep. 21, 1914.

New Hampshire: separated from Massachusetts, Sep. 18, 1679; Jun. 21, 1788.

New Haven Colony: becomes part of Connecticut, Dec. 13, 1664.

New Haven General Court, Dec. 13, 1664.

New Hebrides, Jul. 30, 1980.

The New Industrial State: published, Jun. 26, 1967.

New Jersey: third state, Dec. 18, 1787.

New Jewel Movement (Grenada), Mar. 13, 1979; Oct. 19, 1983.

New Mexico, May 30, 1848; purchased from Mexico, Jun. 30, 1854; admitted to Union, Jan. 6, 1912.

New Netherlands: annexed by England, Aug. 29, 1664.

New Netherlands Company: chartered, Oct. 11, 1614.

New Orleans, May 1, 1862; segregation, Mar. 27, 1962.

New Orleans, Battle of, Jan. 8, 1815.

New Orleans Day, Battle of, Jan. intro.

New World: divided between Spain and Portugal, Jun. 7, 1494.

new year, beginning of the, Mar. intro.

New Year's Day, Jan. intro.; Jan. 1.

New Year's Day (Burma), Apr. 17.

New Year's Day (Mauritius), Jan. 2.

New Year's Day (New Zealand), Jan. 2.

New Year's Day (Scotland), Jan. 2.

New Year's Day (Slovenia), Jan. 2.

New Year's Day (South Korea), Jan. 2.

New Year's Eve, Dec. 31.

New York: annexed by England, Aug. 29, 1664; seized by British, Sep. 15, 1776; declared federal capital, Sep. 13, 1788; great fire, Dec. 16, 1835; five boroughs joined, Jan. 1, 1898; Jan. 25, 1915; Jan. 17, 1917; Jan. 7, 1927; May 1, 1931; Jan. 8, 1961; Nov. 27, 1962; Sep. 14, 1964; blackout, Jul. 13, 1977.

New York Giants, Jan. 27, 1991.

New York Herald, Jan. 6, 1871.

New York Nine: first baseball game, Jun. 19, 1846.

New York Public Library, May 23, 1895.

New York, state of: becomes 11th American state, Jul. 26, 1788.

New York Stock Exchange, May 17, 1792; panic selling, Oct. 24, 1929.

New York stock market, Mar. 13, 1907.

New York Times, Jun. 5, 1918.

New York University, May 30, 1901.

New York University Medical Center, Apr. 18, 1963.

New York Yacht Club, Jul. 29, 1844.

New York Yankees, Sep. 14, 1953.

New Zealand: discovered, Dec. 13, 1642; Captain Cook arrives, Oct. 30, 1769; first British colonists, Jan. 22, 1840; Feb. 6, 1840; May 3, 1841; first settlers, Mar. 23, 1848; women vote, Sep. 10, 1893; Sep. 26, 1907; parliament opened, Jan. 12, 1954.

New Zealand Day, Feb. 6.

New Zealand, patron of, Feb. 1.

Newcomb, Simon, Mar. 12, 1835.

Newcombe, John, May 23, 1944.

Newfoundland: government collapses, Dec. 18, 1933; Mar. 31, 1949.

Newhart, Bob, Sep. 5, 1929.

Newley, Anthony, Sep. 24, 1931.

Newman, Barnett, Jan. 29, 1905.

Newman, Barry Foster, Nov. 7, 1938.

Newman, Edwin, Jan. 25, 1919.

Newman, Larry, Aug. 17, 1978.

Newman, Paul, Jan. 26, 1925; Dec. 25, 1973.

Newman, Phyllis, Mar. 19, 1935.

Newman, Randy, Nov. 28, 1943.

Newman, St. John Henry, Feb. 21, 1801.

newspaper strike (New York City): ends, Nov. 6, 1978.

Newspaper Week, National, Oct. intro.

Newsweek, Feb. 17, 1933.

Newton, Sir Isaac, Dec. 25, 1642; Jan. 4, 1643.

Newton-John, Olivia, Sep. 26, 1948.

Newton, Juice, Feb. 18, 1952.

Newton, Wayne, Apr. 3, 1942.

Ney, Michel, Jan. 10, 1769.

Nez Perce Indians, Oct. 4, 1877.

NFL Monday Night FootBall, Sep. 21, 1970.

Ngo Dinh Diem, Oct. 23, 1955; Oct. 26, 1955.

Ngouabi, Marien (Congo/Brazzaville): assassinated, Mar. 18, 1977.

Nguyen Van Tam, Jun. 3, 1952.

Niagara Falls, Jul. 22, 1876; Feb. 27, 1950.

Niagara River, Feb. 27, 1950.

Niarchos, Stavros Spyros, Jul. 3, 1909.

Nicaea, Council of: ends, Aug. 25, 325.

Nicaea, Second Council of, Sep. 24, 787.

Nicaragua, Feb. 12, 1978; Feb. 8, 1979; Jul. 17, 1979; Dec. 20, 1982; Apr. 12, 1984; ceasefire agreement, Mar. 25, 1988.

Nicholas I (Russia), Jul. 6, 1796; Sep. 3, 1826; dies, Mar. 2, 1855.

Nicholas II (pope), Apr. 13, 1059.

Nicholas II (Russia), May 6, 1868; Nov. 1, 1894; crowned, May 26, 1896; Oct. 30, 1905; Mar. 14, 1917; Mar. 15, 1917; abdicates, Mar. 17, 1917; Mar. 21, 1917; imprisoned in Siberia, Aug. 15, 1917; executed, Jul. 16, 1918.

Nicholas V (pope), Nov. 15, 1397; Feb. 25, 1455.

Nichols, Mike, Nov. 6, 1931.

Nichols, Red, May 8, 1905.

Nichols, Terry, indicted, Aug. 10, 1995; Dec. 29, 1997; life imprisonment, Jun. 4, 1998.

Nicholson, Ben, Apr. 10, 1894.

Nicholson, Jack, Apr. 28, 1937.

Nicholson, Harold, Mar. 3, 1997.

nickel (coin), May 16, 1866.

Nicklaus, Jaek, Jan. 21, 1940; Apr. 7, 1963.

Nicks, Stephanie (Stevie), May 26, 1948.

Nieolai, Christoph Friedrieh, Mar. 18, 1733.

Nieolle, Charles J. H., Sep. 21, 1866.

Nieolson, Sir Harold George, Nov. 21, 1886.

Niebuhr, Reinhold, Jun. 21, 1892.

Niehaus, Charles Henry, Jan. 24, 1855.

Niekro, Phil(ip Henry), Apr. 1, 1939.

Nielsen, A(rthur) C(harles), Sep. 5, 1897.

Nielsen, Carl August, Jun. 9, 1865.

Nielsen, Leslie, Feb. 11, 1926.

Niemoller, Martin, Jan. 1, 1892.

Niepee, Joseph Nichepore, Mar. 7, 1765.

Nietzsche, Friedrieh, Oct. 15, 1844.

Nieuport (Belgium), Oct. 27, 1914.

Niger, Oct. 13, 1922; independence, Aug. 3, 1960; Apr. 15, 1974; Apr. 17, 1974.

Niger River, Jul. 21, 1796; Mar. 22, 1830.

Nigeria, Mar. 13, 1884; Jan. 1, 1914; Jul. 1, 1951; May 9, 1960; Oct. 1, 1960; admitted to U.N., Oct. 7,

1960; Jun. 1, 1961; civil war begins, Jul. 6, 1967; Jan. 12, 1970; Jan. 15, 1970; Sep. 21, 1978; Jul. 7, 1979; Jan. 17, 1983.

Nigeria (Lower), Jan. 1, 1900.

Nigeria, Southern, Jan. 19, 1904.

Nigeria (Upper), Jan. 1, 1900.

night watchmen, patron of, Oct. 19.

Nightingale, Florence, May 12, 1820; Nov. 4, 1854.

Nijinsky, Vaslav, Mar. 12, 1890.

Nile basin: French right to territory west of, Sep. 8, 1919.

Nile, Battle of the, Aug. 1, 1798.

Nile River, Feb. 23, 1854.

Niles, John Jacob, Apr. 28, 1892.

Nilsson, Birgit, May 17, 1918.

Nilsson, Harry, Jun. 5, 1941.

Nimeiri, Goafar Mohammed, Jan. 1, 1930; inaugurated, Oct. 12, 1971; Apr. 6, 1985.

Nimitz, Chester W., Feb. 24, 1885; Dec. 31, 1941.

Nimoy, Leonard, Mar. 26, 1931.

Nin, Anais, Feb. 21, 1903.

Nineteenth Amendment (U.S. Constitution): ratified, Aug. 26, 1920. Ninety-five Theses, Oct. 31, 1517.

Nirenberg, Marshall Warren, Apr. 10, 1923.

Niven, David, Mar. 1, 1910.

Nix, Robert C., Aug. 9, 1905.

Nixon, Richard M., Jan. 9, 1913; Jan. 20, 1953; Sep. 26, 1960; Sep. 27, 1961; inaugurated, Jan. 20, 1969; Apr. 3, 1970; Jun. 10, 1971; resigns presidency, Jan. 5, 1972; China trip, Feb. 17, 1972; China visit, Feb. 21, 1972; May 22, 1972; address to Russian people, May 28, 1972; Jan. 15, 1973; Jul. 26, 1973; Feb. 6, 1974; May 9, 1974; Jul. 24, 1974; Jul. 30, 1974; Aug. 8, 1974; pardoned, Sep. 8, 1974; second China visit, Feb. 21, 1976; Mar. 10, 1976; disbarred, Jul. 8, 1976.

Nixon, Thelma *(Pat)* Ryan, Mar. 16, 1912.

Nixon, Tricia, Jun. 12, 1971.

Nizer, Louis, Feb. 6, 1902.

Nkrumah, Kwame, Sep. 21, 1909; inauguration, Mar. 5, 1952; inaugurated, Jul. 1, 1960.

No Exit: premiere, Nov. 26, 1946.

"no-fly zone:" enforcement of, Dec. 27, 1992; Iraq, Apr. 9, 1993.

No No Nanette: opens, Mar. 11, 1925.

Noah, Mar. 17.

Noah, Yannick, May 16, 1960.

Nobel, Alfred Bernhard, Oct. 21, 1833.

Nobile, Umberto, Jan. 24, 1885; May 12, 1926; May 24, 1928.

Noble, Edward John, Aug. 8, 1882.

Noble, Richard, Oct. 5, 1983.

Noddack, Ida Tacke, Feb. 25, 1896.

Noel-Baker, Philip J., Nov. 1, 1889.

Nofziger, Lyn, Jun. 8, 1924.

Noguchi, Isamu, Nov. 17, 1904.

Nolte, Nick, Feb. 8, 1942.

Nomo, Hideo, Aug. 31, 1968.

Non-Intercourse Act, Jan. 9, 1809.

Noonan, Peggy, Sep. 7, 1950.

Noone, Peter, Nov. 5, 1947.

Nordenskiold, (Nils) Adolf, Nov. 18, 1832.

Nordhoff, Charles Bernard, Feb. 1, 1887.

Nordic Economic Union, Jan. 15, 1969.

Nordica, Lillian, May 12, 1859.

Norell, Norman, Apr. 20, 1900.

Norfolk County (England), Jan. 19, 1915.

Norgay, Tenzing, May 29, 1953.

Norge: dirigible, May 12, 1926.

Noriega, Manuel, Feb. 5, 1988; Feb. 26, 1988; Apr. 8, 1988; May 5, 1989; May 7, 1989; Oct. 3, 1989.

Norman Conquest of England: begins, Sep. 28, 1066.

Norman, Greg, Feb. 10, 1955.

Normandie, Feb. 9, 1942.

Normandy: invasion, Jun. 6, 1944.

Normans, May 4, 1041.

Norodom Sihanouk, Oct. 31, 1922; Apr. 25, 1975.

Norris, Benjamin Franklin, Mar. 5, 1870.

Norris, George William, Jul. 11, 1861.

Norstad, Lauris, Mar. 24, 1907.

Norstar Bancorp, Mar. 18, 1987.

North, Lord, Mar. 19, 1782.

North America, Mar. 5, 1496.

North American Free Trade Agreement (NAFTA), Dec. 2, 1993; Dec. 8, 1993.

North Atlantic Council, Dec. 19, 1950.

North Atlantic Treaty: signed, Apr. 4, 1949.

North by Northwest: premiere, Aug. 6, 1959.

North Carolina: ratifies Constitution, Nov. 21, 1789.

North Carolina, University of: opens, Feb. 13, 1795.

North Dakota: admitted to Union, Nov. 2, 1889.

North, Douglass C., Nov. 4, 1920.

North, Frederick, Apr. 13, 1732.

North, Jay, Aug. 3, 1952.

North Korea. *See* Korea, North.

North, Oliver, Nov. 25, 1986; Jul. 7, 1987; Mar. 16, 1988; May 4, 1989.

North Pole, Apr. 6, 1909; May 9, 1926; dirigible flight over, May 12, 1926; Aug. 16, 1977.

North Sea, Sep. 21, 1965.

North Sea oil fields: first oil, Jun. 11, 1975.

North, Sheree, Jan. 17, 1933.

North Vietnam. *See*: Vietnam, North.

Northern Ireland. *See*: Ireland, Northern.

Northern Pacific Railroad: completed, Sep. 8, 1883.

Northern Rhodesia. *See*: Rhodesia, Northern.

Northern War, May 3, 1660.

Northhampton, Treaty of, May 4, 1328.

Northrop, John Howard, Jul. 5, 1891.

Northrup, John Knudsen, Nov. 10, 1895.

Northumbria, Earl of (Tostig), Sep. 20, 1966; Sep. 25, 1966.

Northwest Ordinance, Jul. 13, 1787.

Northwest Passage, Sep. 14, 1969.

Northwest Territory (Canada), Jun. 13, 1898; Jan. 24, 1978.

Northwind, U.S.S, Sep. 4, 1954.

Norton, Eleanor Holmes, Jun. 13, 1937.

Norton, Ken, Aug. 9, 1945.

Norton, Thomas, Jan. 18, 1562.

Norvo, Red, Mar. 31, 1908.

Norway: ceded to Sweden, Jan. 14, 1814; independence of, May 17, 1814; independence recognized, Oct. 27, 1905; Mar. 5, 1920; Jan. 18, 1928; May 8, 1929; Apr. 9, 1940; Feb. 1, 1942; Jan. 15, 1969; Oct. 5, 1978.

Norway, patron of, Feb. 3; Jul. 29.

Norway and Sweden, Union of: dissolved, Jun. 7, 1905.

Nostradamus, Dec. 14, 1503.

Notary Public Day, National, Nov. intro.

Notary Public Week, National, Nov. 7.

Notre Dame Cathedral (France): damaged, Oct. 11, 1914.

Notre Dame, University of, Jan. 15, 1844.

Nova Castella, Juan de, May 21, 1502.

Nova Scotia, Oct. 7, 1755; Jul. 1, 1867.

Novak, Kim, Feb. 18, 1933.

Novak, Robert, Feb. 26, 1931.

Novara, Jun. 6, 1513.

Novello, Antonia, Aug. 23, 1944.

Novello, Don, Jan. 1, 1943.

novem, Nov. intro.

Novgorod (Russia), Jan. 9, 1570; Sep. 20, 1862.

novice masters, patron of, Oct. 23.

Novikov, Nikolay Ivanovieh, Apr. 27, 1744.

Novo 'Teherksk, Jan. 7, 1895.

Novotny, Antonin, Jan. 5, 1968.

Novruz Bairam (Turkmenistan), Mar. 21.

Novruz Bayrom (Azerbaijan), Mar. 22.

NOW. *See*: National Organization of Women.

Now Rooz (Afghanistan), Mar. 21.

Noyce, Robert, Dec. 12, 1927.

Noyes, Alfred, Sep. 16, 1880.

Ntaryamira, Cyprien, death of, Apr. 6, 1994.

Nu, Thakin, Jan. 4, 1948.

Nu, U, Apr. 5, 1960.

nuclear accord, signed by North Korea, Dec. 15, 1995.

nuclear engineering, Jun. 12, 1950.

nuclear missiles: intermediate range, Apr. 7, 1985.

nuclear power plant, accident, Feb. 9, 1991.

Nuclear Non-Proliferation Treaty, Jul. 1, 1968; Mar. 12, 1993.

nuclear power plant, Dec. 2, 1957; India's first, Jan. 19, 1970.

nuclear reaction: first self-sustaining, Dec. 2, 1942.

Nuclear Test-Ban Treaty, Sep. 11, 1996.

nuclear tests, May 10, 1984; May 11, 1998.

nuclear warhead: first Soviet detonation, Jul. 10, 1949; first launched from submarine, May 6, 1962; first carried by long-range missile, May 6, 1962.

nuclear weapons, Jul. 15, 1955.

nuclear weapons testing, Feb. 11, 1971.

Nude Descending a Staircase, Feb. 17, 1913.

Nugent, Ted, Dec. 13, 1948.

Nujoma, Samuel D., May 12, 1929; Mar. 21, 1990.

Numa Pompilius, Jan. intro; Feb. intro.

Nunez de Balboa, Vaseo, Sep. 25, 1513.

Nunn, Sam(uel Augustus), Jr., Sep. 8, 1938.

Nuremberg, Jan. 10, 1356; trials begin, Nov. 20, 1945; International Military Tribunal, Oct. 1, 1946; Oct. 16, 1946.

Nuremberg, Bavaria, patron of, Aug. 19.

Nuremberg (Germany), Apr. 21, 1945.

Nureyev, Rudolf, Mar. 17, 1938; Jun. 16, 1961.

Nurmi, Paavo, Jun. 13 1897.

Nurnberg Laws, Sep. 15, 1935.

nurses, patron of, Feb. 5; Mar. 8; Jul. 14.

Nursing Home Week, National, May intro.

Nusslein-Volhard, Christiane, Oct. 20, 1942.

Nutcracker: premiere, Dec. 5, 1892.

Nutrition Time, National, Mar. intro.

Nyad, Diana, Aug. 22, 1949; first swim Bahamas to U.S., Aug. 20, 1979.

Nyasa, Lake (Africa): discovered, Sep. 16, 1859.

Nyasaland, Dec. 19, 1962; Feb. 1, 1963; Dec. 31, 1963, Jul. 6, 1964.

Nyerere, Julius, May 1, 1961; Dec. 9, 1962.

Nyro, Laura, Oct. 18, 1947.

Nystad, Treaty of Nystad, Treaty of, Sep. 10, 1721.

Nystrom, Bob, Oct. 10, 1952.

O

O-Bon (Japan), Jul. 10.

O'Canada: Canada's national anthem, Jul. 1, 1980.

O. K. Corral, Oct. 26, 1881.

Oakley, Annie, Aug. 13, 1860.

Oates, John, Apr. 7, 1949.

Oates, Joyce Carol, Jun. 16, 1938.

Oates, Warren, Jul. 5, 1928.

OAU Day (Equitorial Guinea), May 25.

Obasanjo, Olusegun, Feb. 13, 1976.

Oberhoffer, Emil, Nov. 5, 1903.

Oberlin College, Dec. 3, 1833.

Oberon, Merle, Feb. 19, 1911.

Obote, Milton, Dec. 28, 1925; inaugurated, Apr. 29, 1962; Feb. 22, 1966; Jun. 10, 1966; overthrown, Jul. 27, 1985.

Obregon, Alvaro, Feb. 19, 1880.

O'Brian, Smith, Jul. 29, 1848.

O'Brian's Rebellion, Jul. 29, 1848.

O'Brien, Edmond, Sep. 10, 1915.

O'Brien, Lawrence, Jul. 7, 1917.

O'Brien, Margaret, Jan. 15, 1937.

O'Brien, Pat, Nov. 11, 1899.

O'Casey, Sean, Mar. 30, 1880.

Ocean Pond, Battle of, Feb. 20, 1864.

Ochi Day (Cyprus, Greece), Oct. 28.

Ochoa, Ellen, May 10, 1958.

Ochoa, Severo, Sep. 24, 1905.

Ochs, Adolph Simon, Mar. 12, 1858.

Ochs, Phil(ip David), Dec. 19, 1940.

Ochsner, Alton, May 4, 1896.

O'Connell, Daniel, Aug. 6, 1775.

O'Connell, Helen, May 23, 1920.

O'Connell, Maura, Sep. 16, 1958.

O'Connor, Carroll, Aug. 2, 1924.

O'Connor, Donald, Aug. 28, 1925.

O'Connor, Edwin (Greene), Jul. 29, 1918; Feb. 6, 1956.

O'Connor, Flannery, Mar. 25, 1925.

O'Connor, John Joseph, Jan. 15, 1920.

O'Connor, Sandra Day, Mar. 26, 1930; Jul. 7, 1981.

O'Connor, Sinead, Dec. 8, 1966.

Octave of Christmas, Jan. 1.

Octavian. *See*: Augustus Caesar (Octavius).

octo, Oct. intro.

October Horse, Oct. intro.

October Manifesto, Oct. 30, 1905.

October Revolution Day (Albania, Bulgaria, Hungary, Mongolia), Nov. 7.

October Revolution (Russia), Oct. 23, 1917.

Odd Fellows, Independent Order of, Apr. 26, 1819.

Odessa, Feb. 8, 1920; Oct. 16, 1941.

Odets, Clifford, Jul. 18, 1906.

Odetta, Dec. 31, 1930.

Odoacer, Mar. 5, 493.

O'Donnell, Chris, Jun. 26, 1970.

O'Donnell, Rosie, Mar. 21, 1962.

Oduber Quiros, Daniel: inaugurated, May 8, 1974.

Oe, Kenzaburo, Jan. 31, 1935.

Oehlenschllager, Adam Gottlob, Nov. 14, 1779.

Oerter, Al, Sep. 19, 1936.

O'Faolain, Sean, Feb. 22, 1900.

Offenbach, Jacques, Jun. 20, 1819.

Offcial Language Act (Quebec), Jul. 30, 1974.

Official Languages Act (India), Jan. 26, 1965.

Ogaden, Apr. 3, 1988.

Ogden, Robert Morris, Jul. 6, 1877.

Ogilvy, David MacKenzie, Jun. 23, 1911.

Oglala Sioux reservation, Feb. 27, 1973.

Oglethorpe Day (Georgia), Feb. 12.

Oglethorpe, James, Dec. 22, 1696; Jun. 9, 1732; Feb. 12, 1733.

O'Grady, Scott, Jun. 8, 1995.

Oh, Calcutta: premiere, Jun. 17, 1970.

O'Hair, Madalyn Murray, Apr. 13, 1919; Jan. 26, 1970.

O'Hara, Catherine, Mar. 4, 1954.

O'Hara, Geoffrey, Oct. 10, 1916.

O'Hara, John Henry, Jan. 31, 1905.

O'Hara, Mary, Jul. 10, 1885.

O'Hara, Maureen, Aug. 17, 1921.

O'Hare, Edward Henry, Mar. 13, 1914.

O'Hare International Airport, May 25, 1979.

Ohio: admitted to Union, Mar. 1, 1803.

Ohio, U.S.S., Jun. 17, 1981.

Ohio University, Feb. 18, 1804.

Ohira, Masayoshi, Mar. 12, 1910; Nov. 27, 1978.

Ohm, George Simon, Mar. 16, 1787.

Ohnesorg, Benno, Jun. 2, 1967.

oil embargo against U.S.: ended, Mar. 18, 1974.

Oil Nationalization Day (Iran), Mar. 20.

oil pipeline (U.S.S.R.), Nov. 5, 1974.

oil spill (Brittany Coast), Mar. 17, 1978.

oil spill (Cornwall, England), Mar. 18, 1967.

oilers, patron of, Dec. 4.

O'Keeffe, Georgia, Nov. 15, 1887.

Okello, Basilio Olara, Jul. 27, 1985.

Okello, Tito, Jan. 29, 1986.

Okinawa: bombed, Oct. 10, 1944; U.S. invasion, Apr. 1, 1945; Apr. 6, 1945.

Oklahoma, Apr. 22, 1889; admitted to Union, Nov. 16, 1907.

Oklahoma Day, Apr. intro.; Apr. 22.

Oklahoma Heritage Week, Nov. intro.

Oklahoma Historical Day, Oct. 10.

Oklahoma!: premiere, Mar. 31, 1943.

Okuchi, Nobuo, Mar. 11, 1970.

Olaf V (Norway), Jul. 2, 1903; Sep. 21.

Olah, George A., May 22, 1927.

Olajuwon, Akeem Abdul Ajibola, Jan. 23, 1963.

Old Baldy, Aug. 1, 1952.

The Old Man and the Sea: published, Sep. 8, 1952.

Old Yeller: premiere, Dec. 25, 1957.

Oldcastle, John: burned and hanged, Dec. 12, 1417.

Older Americans Month, May intro.

Oldman, Gary, Mar. 21, 1958.

Olds, Ransom Eli, Jun. 3, 1864.

O'Leary, Hazel, May 17, 1937.

olestra Jan. 24, 1996.

Olin, John Merrill, Nov. 10 1892.

Oliphant, Patrick Bruce, Jui. 24, 1935.

Oliva, Treaty of, May 3, 1660.

Olive Tree coalition, Apr. 21, 1996.

Oliver, James, Aug. 28, 1823.

Olivier, George Borg, Mar. 3, 1962.

Olivier, Laurence, May 22, 1907; Sep. 29, 1948.

Ollanta: premiere, Dec. 26, 1900.

Olmos, Edward James, Feb. 24, 1947.

Olmsted, Frederick Law, Apr. 26, 1822.

Olsen, Merlin, Sep. 15, 1940.

Olson, Charles, Dec. 27, 1910.

Olustee, Battle of, Feb. 20, 1864.

Olympic Games: first modern, Apr. 6, 1896; XVIII Summer, Oct. 10, 1964; black power demonstration, Oct. 16, 1968; Lillehammer, Norway, Feb. 12, 1994; Atlanta, Georgia, Jul. 19, 1996; Feb. 7, 1998.

Olympio, Sylvanus, Jan. 13, 1963.

Oman, Sir Charles, Jan. 12, 1860.

Oman, Sultanate of, Aug. 10, 1970.

Omar Khayyam: horse, May 12, 1917.

Omdurman (Sudan), Battle of, Sep. 2, 1898.

omega-minus sub-atomic particle, Feb. 19, 1964.

Omisoka (Japan), Dec. 31.

Ommegang Pageant (Belgium), Jul. 7.

On the Road: published, Sep. 5, 1957.

On the Town: premiere, Dec. 28, 1944.

On the Waterfront: premiere, Jul. 28, 1954.

On With the Show, May 28, 1929.

Onassis, Aristotle Socrates, Jan. 20, 1906; Oct. 20, 1968.

Onassis, Christina, Dec. 11, 1950.

Onassis, Jacqueline Bouvier Kennedy, Jul. 28, 1929; Oct. 20, 1968; May 19, 1994.

The Once and Future King: published, Aug. 25, 1958.

Ondaatje, Michael, Dec. 9, 1943.

One Flew Over the Cuckoo's Nest, Mar. 29, 1976.

One Nation Under God Month, Nov. intro.

O'Neal, Patrick, Sep. 26, 1927.

O'Neal, Ryan, Apr. 20, 1941.

O'Neal, Tatum, Nov. 5, 1963.

O'Neil, John, May 29, 1962.

O'Neal, Shaquille, Mar. 6, 1972.

O'Neill, Eugene (Gladstone), Oct. 16, 1888 Oct. 9, 1946; Nov. 7, 1956. May 2, 1957.

O'Neill, Thomas P. (Tip), Dec. 9, 1912. Jan. 4, 1977.

O'Neill, James, Nov. 15, 1849.

O'Neill, Jennifer, Feb. 20, 1949.

Ongania, Juan Carlos, Jun. 29, 1966.

Onizuka, Ellison, Jun. 24, 1946.

Ono, Yoko, Feb. 18, 1933.

O'Nolan, Brian, Oct. 5, 1911.

Onsager, Lars, Nov. 27, 1903.

Oort, Jan Hendrik, Apr. 28, 1900.

opal, Oct. intro.

OPEC, Mar. 14, 1983.

Open Door Policy: China, Feb. 4, 1919.

opera written for television, first: Amahl and the Night Visitors Dec. 24, 1951.

Operation Attleboro: ends, Nov. 26, 1966.

Operation Desert Storm, Jan. 16, 1991; ground invasion of Iraq, Feb. 24, 1991.

Operation Junction City, Feb. 22, 1967.

Operation Market-Garden, Sep. 17, 1944.

Operation Shingle, Jan. 22, 1944.

Operation Ten-Go, Apr. 6, 1945.

Ophuls, Marcel, Nov. 1, 1927.

Opitz von Boberfeld, Martin, Dec. 23, 1597.

Opium Conference, Feb. 7, 1925.

Opium Convention, Feb. 12, 1915.

Opium War, First, Mar. 10, 1839; Jul. 7, 1839; Nov. 3, 1839; Jun. 28, 1840; Jan. 7, 1841; Jun. 19, 1842; ends, Aug. 29, 1842.

Oppenheimer, J. Robert, Apr. 22, 1904; Apr. 5, 1963.

Opper, Frederick Burr, Jan. 2, 1857.

Oppurg, Franz, May 14, 1978.

oral contraceptives: approved, Sep. 4, 1969.

Orange Free State (South Africa), Feb. 17, 1854; Feb. 23, 1854; Apr. 10, 1854; May 21, 1900; May 31, 1910.

Orange River Colony, May 21, 1900.

Orangeman's Day (Northern Ireland), Jul. 12.

Orbison, Roy, Apr. 23, 1936.

The Order, Apr. 15, 1985.

Order of the Cross of St. Andrew, patron of, Nov. 30.

Order of the Golden Fleece of Burzmund, patron of, Nov. 30.

Order of Templars: abolished, Mar. 22, 1312.

Ordinance of Union, Apr. 12, 1654.

Ordonez, Jose Batlle, May 21, 1856.

Oregon: admitted to Union, Feb. 14, 1859; first state to adopt initiative and referendum devices, Jun. 2, 1902; only aerial bombing of U.S., Sep. 9, 1942.

Oregon, Territory of Northern, Sep. 1, 1836.

Oregon Treaty: signed, Jun. 15, 1846.

Orfeo et Euridice: premiere, Jun. 9, 1951.

Orff, Carl, Jul. 10, 1895; Jun. 8, 1937; Feb. 18, 1943; Nov. 6, 1943.

organ transplants, Oct. 3, 1953; Jun. 13, 1959.

Organization for African Unity, Feb. 11, 1976.

Organization of American States, Aug. 28, 1950; created, Dec. 13, 1951; Jan. 4, 1962; Jan. 31, 1962; Feb. 14, 1962; Jul. 26, 1964; Feb. 23, 1967; Jul. 29, 1975.

Organization of Arab Petroleum Exporting Countries, Oct. 17, 1973.

Organization of Petroleum Exporting Countries (OPEC), Mar. 14, 1983.

Organization of the Oppressed of the World, Jul. 30, 1989.

Oriani, Alfredo, Aug. 22, 1852.

Orient Express: last regular run, May 22, 1977.

Origin of Fire, Dec. 28, 1937.

Original Dixieland Jazz Band, Jan. 17, 1917; Jan. 30, 1917.

Orinoco River, Jan. 6, 1967.

Orkney Islands: patron of, Jul. I; Feb. 20, 1471.

Orlando, Tony, Apr. 3, 1944.

Orleans: siege of, May 1, 1429.

Orleans, Duke of, May 18, 1412.

Orlich Bolmarcich, Francisco Jose (Costa Rica), Feb. 4, 1962.

Orlov, Yuri, Feb. 10, 1977.

Ormandy, Eugene, Nov. 18, 1899; Jan. 3, 1941.

Ormonde, Marquis of (James Butler), Sep. 11, 1649.

Orozco, Jose Clemente, Nov. 23, 1883.

orphan drug bill, Jan. 4, 1983.

orphans and abandoned children, patron of, Feb. 8.

Orr, Robert Gordon (*Bobby*), Mar. 20, 1948.

Orsini, Jan. 14, 1858.

Ortega, Daniel, Nov. 11, 1945; elected, Nov. 4, 1984; Jan. 10, 1985; reelected, May 1998.

Ortega y Gasset, Jose, May 9, 1883.

Ortelius (Abraham Oertel), Apr. 14, 1527.

Orthodox Church: first meeting of Patriarch with Roman Catholic Pope, Jan. 5, 1964.

Ortiz Mena, Antonio, Nov. 27, 1970.

Ortiz, Roberto: resigns, Aug. 29, 1940

Orwell, George, Jun. 25, 1903; Aug. 26, 1946.

Ory, Kid, Dec. 25, 1886.

Osaka (Japan), Mar. 14, 1945.

Osborn, Frederick Henry, Mar. 21, 1889.

Osborne, John James, Dec. 12, 1929.

Osborne, Joan, Jul. 8, 1962.

Osbourne, Jeffrey, Oct. 9, 1948.

Osbourne, Ozzie, Dec. 3, 1949.

Oscar I (Sweden), Jul. 4, 1799; Mar. 8, 1844; dies, Jul. 8, 1859.

Oscar II (Sweden), Jan. 21, 1829; May 12, 1873; Oct. 27, 1905; dies, Dec. 8, 1907.

Osgood, Charles, Jan. 8, 1933.

Osheroff, Douglass D., Aug. 1, 1945.

Osirak nuclear reactor (Iraq): destroyed, Jun. 7, 1981.

Oslo, Jan. 1, 1925.

Oslo Agreement, Dec. 22, 1930.

Osmena, Sergio, Aug. 1, 1944.

Osmond, Donald Clark *(Donny)*, Dec. 9, 1958.

Osmond, Marie, Oct. 13, 1959.

Osorio, Oscar: inaugurated, Sep. 14, 1950.

Ospina Perez, Mariano: inaugurated, Aug. 7, 1946.

Ossietzky, Carl von, Oct. 3, 1888.

Ostend Manifesto, Oct. 18, 1854.

Ostrogoths, Mar. 5, 493.

Ostrovsky, Alexander Nikolaevich, Apr. 12, 1823.

Ostwald, Friedrich Wilhelm, Sep. 2, 1853.

O'Sullivan, Gilbert, Dec. 1, 1946.

O'Sullivan, Maureen, May 17, 1911.

Oswald, Lee Harvey, Oct. 18, 1939; killed, Nov. 24, 1963.

Othman (Caliph of Arabia): murdered, Jun. 17, 656.

Otira Tunnel: opens, Aug. 6, 1923.

Otis, Elisha Graves, Aug. 3, 1811.

Otis, James, Feb. 5, 1725.

O'Toole, Peter (Seamus), Aug. 2, 193?.

Ott, Mel, Mar. 2, 1909.

Otto I (Holy Roman Emperor), Nov. 23, 912; Aug. 10, 955; Feb. 2, 962.

Otto III (Holy Roman Emperor), May 21, 996.

Otto IV (Holy Roman Emperor), Oct. 4, 1209; excommunicated, Nov. 18, 1210.

Otto, Louise, Mar. 26, 1819.

Otto, Nikolaus August, Jun. 10, 1832.

Ottoman Empire: dissolution, Jul. 13, 1878.

Oued Eddahab Day (Morocco), Aug. 14.

Ouedraogo, Jean-Baptiste, Aug. 5, 1983.

Our Lady of the Angels (Costa Rica), Aug.

Our Lady Aparecida, Patroness of Brazil (Brazil), Oct. 12.

Our Lady of Guadalupe, Dec. 12.

Our Lady of Meritxell (Andorra), Sep. 8.

Our Lady of Mount Carmel, Feast of, Jul. 16.

Our Lady of Ransom, Sep. 24.

Our Lady of the Rosary, Feast of, Oct. 7.

Ourique, Battle of, Jul. 25, 1139.

Outer Mongolia: admitted to U.N., Oct. 25, 1965.

outer space: weapons prohibited, Dec. 8, 1966.

Outer Space Treaty, Jan. 23, 1967.

Ovanda Candia, Alfredo, Apr. 6, 1918.

Over There: composed, Apr. 6, 1917.

Ovett, Steve, Oct. 9, 1955.

Ovid (Publius Ovidius Naso), Mar. 20, 43 b.c.

Owada, Masako, Jun. 9, 1993.

Owen, Robert, May 14, 1771.

Owen, Robert Dale, Nov. 9, 1801.

Owen, Wilfred, Mar. 18, 1893.

Owens, Buek, Aug. 12, 1929.

Owens, Jessie, Sep. 12, 1913; Aug. 9, 1936.

Owens, Michael J., Jan. 1, 1859.

Oxford English Dictionary: first published, Feb. 1, 1884; completed, Apr. 19, 1928.

Oxford, Provisions of: issued, Jun. 11, 1258.

Oxford University, Apr. 13, 1749.

Ozal, Turkut, Dec. 13, 1983.

Ozawa, Seiji, Sep. 1, 1935.

ozone layer, Mar. 14, 1988.

ozone treaty, Sep. 16, 1987.

P

Paar, Jack, May 1, 1918.

Paasikivi, Juho: eleeted, Mar. 9, 1946.

Paccard, Dr. Michel, Aug. 8, 1786.

Pacem in Terris: issued, Apr. 10, 1963.

pacemaker: nuclear powered, Apr. 28, 1970.

pacemaker (heart), Jun. 22, 1962.

Pachelbel, Johann, Sep. 1, 1653.

Pacino, Al, Apr. 25, 1940; Mar. 15, 1972.

Packard (automobile), Aug. 19, 1958.

Packard, David, Sep. 7, 1912.

Packard, James Ward, Nov. 5, 1863.

Packard, Vance, May 22, 1914.

Packwood, Robert William *(Bob)*, Sep. 11, 1932.

Pact of Union, Jan. 19, 1921.

Paderewski Fund, May 15, 1900.

Paderewski, Ignace, Nov. 18, 1860; May 15, 1900; Apr. 3, 1903; Jan. 17, 1919.

padlock bill: passed in Spain, Dec. 23, 1910.

Padua, patron of, Jun. 13.

Paes, Sidonia da Silva (Portugal): assassinated, Dec. 14, 1918.

Paets, Konstantin (Estonia), Mar. 12, 1934.

Paganini, Niceolo, Oct. 27, 1782.

Page, James Patrick *(Jimmy)*, Jan. 9, 1944.

Page, Geraldine, Nov. 22, 1924.

Page, Patti, Nov. 8, 1927.

Pagels, Elaine, Feb. 13, 1943.

Paglia, Camille, Apr. 2, 1947.

Pahlavi dynasty (Iran), Feb. 21, 1921.

Pahlavi, Mohammad Reza (Shah of Iran), Oct. 26, 1919; ADr. 25. 1926, Sep. 16, 1941. Jan. 28, 1951; Aug 22, 1953. May 9, 1961; Oct. 30, 1967; May 11, 1978; Jan. 16, 1979; Jan. 30, 1979; Oct. 22, 1979; dies, Jul. 27, 1980.

Pahlevi, Farah Diba, Oct. 14, 1938.

Paige, Janis, Sep. 16, 1923.

Paige, (Leroy Robert), Jul. 7, 1906.

Paine, John Knowles, Jan. 9, 1839.

Paine, Robert Treat, Mar. 11, 1731.

Paine, Thomas, Jan. 29, 1737; Jan. 10, 1776.

Paint Your Wagon: premiere, Nov. 12, 1951.

painters, patron of, Oct. 18.

Paisley, Ian Richard Kyle, Apr. 6, 1926.

Paixhans, Henri Joseph, Jan. 22, 1783.

The Pajama Game: premiere, May 13, 1954.

Pakistan, Feb. 29, 1956; martial law, Oct. 7, 1958; Jan. 11, 1960; Sep.

6, 1961; Jan. 30, 1972; Sep. 19, 1973; Apr. 9, 1974; earthquake, Dec. 28, 1974; Feb. 24, 1975; Feb. 10, 1979; nuclear testing, May 28, 1998.

Pakistan, East, Apr. 12, 1971; Dec. 6, 1971.

Pakula, Alan Jay, Apr. 7, 1928.

Pal Joey: premiere, Dec. 25, 1940.

Palace of Peace (the Hague): dedicated, Aug. 28, 1913.

Palace of the Senators, Apr. 20, 1979.

Palach, Jan, Jan. 16, 1969.

Palacky, Frantisek, Jun. 14, 1798.

Palade, George Emil, Nov. 19, 1912.

Palance, Jack, Feb. 18, 1920.

Palau Islands, Sep. 16, 1944.

Palembang: sunk, Mar. 18, 1916.

Palermo, patron of, Apr. 4; Sep. 4.

Palermo (Sicily), May 27, 1860; liberated, Jul. 22, 1943.

Palestine, Apr. 25, 1920; May 17, 1930; Peel Report recommendations, Jul. 8, 1937; Nov. 29, 1947; Apr. 24, 1950; Dec. 9, 1987; peace talks, Feb. 25, 1994.

Palestine Liberation Organization (PLO): founded, May 29, 1964; Feb. 3, 1969; recognized by U.N., Oct. 14, 1974; Aug. 21, 1982; Jun. 24, 1983; Dec. 20, 1983; Mar. 11, 1988; Apr. 16, 1988; Jul. 31, 1988; Nov. 15, 1988; May 2, 1989.

Palestine National Council, Apr. 24, 1996.

Palestinian terrorists: Munich, Sep. 5, 1972.

Paley, Barbara Cushing *(Babe)*, Jul. 5, 1915.

Paley, William S., Sep. 28, 1901; Sep. 28, 1928. Jan. 14, 1987.

Palin, Michael, May 5, 1943.

Palinkas, Pat, Aug. 15, 1970.

Palladio, Andrea, Nov. 30, 1508.

Palme, Olof: assassinated, Feb. 28, 1986.

Palmer, Alice Elvira Freeman, Feb. 21, 1855.

Palmer, Arnold, Sep. 10, 1929.

Palmer, Carl, Mar. 20, 1951.

Palmer, James Alvin *(Jim)*, Oct. 15, 1945.

Palmer, Lilli, May 24, 1914.

Palmer, Nathaniel Brown, Aug. 8, 1799.

Palmer, Potter, May 20, 1826.

Palmer, Robert, Jan. 19, 1949.

Palmer, Violet, Oct. 28, 1997.

Palmerston, (Henry John Temple) Viscount, Oct. 20, 1784.

Palminteri, Chazz, May 15, 1951.

Palo Alto, Battle of, May 8, 1846.

Paltrow, Gwyneth, Sep. 28, 1972.

Pan-Africanist Congress (PAC), Apr. 5, 1960.

Pan American Airways, Jan. 6, 1942.

Pan-American Conference: first, Oct. 2, 1889.

Pan American Day, Apr. 14.

Pan American Day (Belize), Oct. 12.

Pan-German League, Apr. 9, 1891.

Panama: independence from Spain, Nov. 28, 1821; independence, Nov. 3, 1903; Feb. 13, 1904; Oct. 5, 1941; Oct. 11, 1972.

Panama Canal, Feb. 1, 1864; opened to international commercial vessels, Aug. 15, 1914; Jul. 28, 1926; Jul. 11, 1934; Oct. 1, 1979.

Panama Canal Treaty: ratified, Dec. 2, 1903; Apr. 18, 1978.

Panama, Isthmus of, Sep. 25, 1513.

Panama-U.S. Treaty: signed, Jul. 28, 1926.

Panchen Lama, May 27, 1951.

pandas, giant, Apr. 16, 1972; Jan. 12, 1985.

Pandit, Vijaya Lakshmi, Aug. 18, 1900.

Panetta, Leon, Jun. 28, 1938.

Pangkor, Treaty of, Jan. 20, 1874.

Panic of 1873, Sep. 18, 1873.

Panic of 1893, May 5, 1893.

Panic of 1907, Mar. 13, 1907.

Panipat (India), Nov. 5, 1556.

Panizzi, Antonio, Sep. 16, 1797.

Pankhurst, Emmeline, Jul. 4, 1858.

Pankow, James, Aug. 20, 1947.

Papadopoulos: Georgios (Greece), Apr. 21, 1967; Jun. 1, 1973; first President, Aug. 19, 1973.

Papagos, Alexander: inaugurated, Nov. 19, 1952.

Papal Chancery: adopts, January 1 as beginning of year, Nov. 16, 1621.

papal infallibility: declared, Jul. 18, 1870.

Papal States, May 1, 1809.

Papandreou, Andreas George, Feb. 5, 1919; Oct. 21, 1981; Jan. 15, 1996.

Papandreou, George, Apr. 23, 1944.

Papanicolaou, George Nicholas, May 13, 1883.

Papas, Irene, Sep. 3, 1926.

Papen, Franz von, Jun. 1, 1932.

Papin, Denis, Aug. 22, 1647.

Papp, Joseph, Jun. 22, 1921.

Pappas, Ike, Apr. 16, 1933.

Papua New Guinea, Jan. 19, 1975; independence, Sep. 16, 1975.

Papua Republic, Jan. 19, 1975.

Paracelsus, Nov. 10, 1493.

parachute, Oct. 22, 1797.

Paraguay: declares independence, Oct. 12, 1811; Chaco War ends, Jun. 12, 1935; Mar. 11, 1936.

Parc de St. Cloud (Paris), May 31, 1868.

Parcel Post (U.S.), Jan. 1, 1913.

Parents' Day (Democratic Republic of the Congo), Aug. 1.

Parents Without Partners Founder's Month, Mar. intro.

Paret, Benny, Apr. 1, 1961.

Pareto, Vilfredo, Jul. 15, 1848.

Parini, Giuseppe, May 23, 1729.

Paris, Mar. 31, 1814; capitulates to Prussia, Jan. 28, 1871; Jan. 23, 1911; German bombardment, Mar. 23, 1918; Jan. 27, 1973.

Paris Commune: uprising, Mar. 18, 1871; established, Mar. 26, 1871.

Paris (France). German troops enter, Jun. 14, 1940; liberated, Aug. 25, 1944; Jul. 8, 1951.

Paris (France), patroness of, Jan. 3.

Paris, Gabriel, May 10, 1957.

Paris, Jerry, Jul. 25, 1925.

Paris Pacts, Dec. 29, 1954.

Paris Peace Conference, Jan. 18, 1919; Apr. 28, 1919; Jul. 29, 1946.

Paris Peace Conference, Supreme Council of, Apr. 25, 1920.

Paris Peace Pact, Mar. 1, 1929.

Paris, Treaty of, May 20, 1303; Feb. 10, 1763; independence of U.S., Sep. 3, 1783; Jan. 14, 1784; Mar. 30, 1856; Spanish-American War, Dec. 10, 1898.

parish clergy throughout the world, principal patron saint of, Aug. 3.

parish clerks, patron of, Nov. 13.

Parizeau, Jacques, Aug. 9, 1930.

Park, Brad, Jul. 6, 1948.

Park Chung Hee, Sep. 30, 1917; Mar. 10, 1976; assassinated, Oct. 26, 1979.

Park, Mungo, Sep. 10, 1771; Jul. 21, 1796.

Park Tong Sun, Jun. 5, 1977; Sep. 6, 1977; Mar. 9, 1978; Apr. 3, 1978.

Parker, Bonnie, Oct. 1, 1910.

Parker, Buddy, Dec. 16, 1913.

Parker, Charlie (Bird), Aug. 29, 1920.

Parker, Dorothy, Aug. 22, 1893.

Parker, Eleanor, Jun. 26, 1922.

Parker, Fess, Aug. 16, 1925.

Parker, George Swinnerton, Dec. 12, 1866.

Parker, Jameson, Nov. 18, 1950.

Parker, Mary-Louise, Aug. 2, 1964.

Parker, Ray, Jr., May 1, 1954.

Parker, Sarah Jessica, Mar. 25, 1965.

Parker, Suzy, Oct. 28, 1933.

Parkhurst, Charles Henry, Apr. 17, 1842.

Parkinson's disease, Sep. 12, 1987.

Parkman, Francis, Sep. 16, 1823.

Parks, Bert, Dec. 30, 1914.

Parks, Rosa Lee, Feb. 4, 1913. Dec. 1, 1955.

Parkyns, William (Sir), Apr. 3, 1696.

Parliament (British), Jan. 6, 1916; Jul. 13, 1965; opening first telecast, Apr. 21, 1966.

Parliament, English, May 20, 1774.

Parliament of Lincoln (England), Jan. 20, 1301.

Parliament, Long, Apr. 20, 1653.

Parliament, Short, Apr. 13, 1640.

Parliamentary army (English Civil War), Jan. 21, 1645.

Parnell, Charles Stewart, Jun. 27, 1846; Oct. 31, 1879.

Parr, Kathrine, Jul. 12, 1542.

Parrish, Lance Michael, Jun. 15, 1956.

Parrish, Maxfield, Jul. 25, 1870.

Parry, Sir William Edward, Dec. 19, 1790.

Parseghian, Ara, May 21, 1923.

Parsons, Sir Charles Algernon, Jun. 13, 1854.

Parsons, David, Oct. 29, 1959.

Parsons, Estelle, Nov. 20, 1927.

Parsons, Gram, Nov. 5, 1946.

Parsons, Louella O., Aug. 6, 1881.

Parsons, Talcott, Dec. 13, 1902.

Parthenon: destroyed, Sep. 26, 1687.

Parti Quebecois, Nov. 25, 1976.

Partition of Poland, Third, Oct. 24, 1795.

Partition Treaty, First, Oct. 11, 1698.

Parton, Dolly, Jan. 19, 1946.

Partridge, Eric Honeywood, Feb. 6, 1894.

Pas de Calais: U.S. raids, Dec. 24, 1943.

Pascal, Blaise, Jun. 19, 1623.

Paschal II (pope), Feb. 4, 1111; Feb. 12, 1111.

Paschal III (antipope), May 28, 1167.

Pascua Florida Day (Florida), Apr. 2.

Pasha, Aly Maher, Jan. 27, 1952.

Pasha, Mustapha el Nahas, Jan. 12, 1950; Jan. 27, 1952.

Pass Law (South Africa), Mar. 21, 1960; Apr. 18, 1986.

Passos, John Dos, Jan. 14, 1898.

Passy, Frederic, May 20, 1822.

Pasta, Giuditta, Apr. 9, 1798.

Pasternak, Boris, Feb. 10, 1890; Sep. 5, 1958; Oct. 29, 1958.

Pasteur, Louis, Dec. 27, 1822.

Pastora Gomez, Eden, Jan. 22, 1937. Apr. 14, 1984.

Pastorini, Dan, Dec. 25, 1949.

Pastrana Borrero, Misael: inaugurated, Aug. 7, 1970.

pastry cooks and confectioners, patron of, Jan. 2.

Pataki, George, Jun. 23, 1945.

Patch, Alexander, Mar. 21, 1944.

Patent Office, U.S.: opens, Jul. 31, 1790.

Pater, Walter Horatio, Aug. 4, 1839.

Paterno, Joe, Dec. 21, 1926.

Pathet Lao Day (Laos), Jan. 6.

Pathfinder (spacecraft), lands on Mars, Jul. 4, 1997.

Patinkin, Mandel (Mandy), Nov. 30, 1952.

Patino, Simon Iturri, Jun. 1, 1862.

Patman, Wright, Aug. 6, 1893.

Patmore, Coventry Kersey Dighton, Jul. 23, 1823.

Paton, Alan Stewart, Jan. 11, 1903.

Patric, Jason, Jun. 27, 1966.

Patrick, John, May 17, 1905.

Patrick, Ruth, Nov. 26, 1907.

Patriot's Day (Maine, Massachusetts), Apr. intro.

Patriots' Victory Day (Ethiopia), Apr. 6.

Patsayev, Vladislav N., Jun. 30, 1971.

Patten, Christopher, May 12, 1944.

Patterson, Floyd, Jan. 4, 1935; Jun. 26, 1959; Nov. 30, 1959; Jun. 20, 1960; Mar. 13, 1961; Dec. 4, 1961; Sep. 25, 1962; Jul. 22, 1963.

Patterson, John Henry, Dec. 13, 1844.

Patton, George S(mith), Nov. 11, 1885; Mar. 21, 1944; Nov. 9, 1944.

Patton, Will, Jun. 14, 1954.

Paul I (Greece), Apr. 1, 1947; Mar. 6, 1964.

Paul I (Russia), Oct. 1, 1754; Nov. 17, 1796; assassinated, Mar. 23, 1801.

Paul II (pope), Feb. 23, 1417.

Paul III (pope), Feb. 29, 1468; Jan. 1, 1547.

Paul IV (pope), Jun. 28, 1476.

Paul V (pope), Sep. 17, 1552.

Paul VI (pope), Sep. 26, 1897; Jun. 3, 1963; Jun. 21, 1963; Jan. 5, 1964; Ecclesiam Suam Aug. 10, 1964; Mar. 7, 1965; addresses U.N., Oct. 5, 1965; Dec. 7, 1965; Feb. 17, 1966; Mar. 23, 1966; Jan. 29, 1967; Mar. 28, 1967; Jun. 23, 1967; Jul. 25, 1967; restructures Curia, Aug. 12, 1967; Jul. 29, 1968; Aug. 22, 1968; priestly celibacy, Feb. 1, 1970; Jul. 3, 1970; Nov. 23, 1970; Jan. 15, 1973; Feb. 2, 1973; Dec. 24, 1974; Sep. 14, 1975; dies, Aug. 6, 1978.

Paul, Alice, Jan. 11, 1885.

Paul (Prince of Yugoslavia), Mar. 28, 1941.

Paul, Wolfgang, Aug. 10, 1913.

Pauley, Jane, Oct. 31, 1950.
Pauli, Wolfgang, Apr. 25, 1900.
Pauling, Linus Carl, Feb. 28, 1901.
Paulsen, Pat, Jul. 6, 1927.
Pavarotti, Luciano, Oct. 12, 1935.
Pavin, Corey, Nov. 16, 1959.
Pavlov, Ivan Petrovich, Sep. 14, 1849.
pawnbrokers, patron of, Dec. 6.
Paxton, Sir Joseph, Aug. 3, 1801.
Paxton, Thomas R. *(Tom)*, Oct. 31, 1937.
Pay Your Bills Week, National, Feb. intro.
Paycheck, Johnny, May 31, 1941.
Payne, Freda, Sep. 19, 1945.
Payne, John Howard, Jun. 9, 1791.
Payne, Robert, Dec. 4, 1911.
Payne system of income tax, Feb. 10, 1944.
Payola Incident, Jan. 2, 1960.
Payson, Joan Whitney, Feb. 5, 1903.
Payton, Walter, Jul. 25, 1954.
Paz Estenssoro, Victor, May 16, 1951; Apr. 9, 1952; Apr. 16, 1952; inaugurated, Aug. 6, 1985.
Paz, Octavio, Mar. 31, 1914.
Peabody, Elizabeth Palmer, May 16, 1804.
Peabody, George, Feb. 18, 1795; Jul. 27, 1852.
Peace of Chaco Day (Paraguay), Jun. 12.
Peace Conference (World War I), Jan. 25, 1919.
Peace Corps: established, Mar. 1, 1961; Sep. 22, 1961.
Peace Day (Armenia), May 9.
Peace Day (Rwanda), Jul. 5.
Peace Officers Memorial Day (U.S.), May 15.
Peace, Palace of, Jul. 30, 1907.
Peace of Trento, Oct. 13, 1501.
Peace with Bolivia Day (Paraguay), Jun. 12.
peace without victory: Wilson's speech, Jan. 22, 1917.
Peach Festival (Japan), Mar. 3.
Peale, Charles Wilson, Apr. 15, 1741.
Peale, Norman Vincent, May 31, 1898.
Peale, Raphael, Feb. 17, 1774.
Peale, Rembrandt, Feb. 22, 1778.
Peale, Titian Ramsay, Nov. 17, 1799.
Peanut Month, National, Mar. intro.

pearl, Jun. intro.
Pearl Harbor, Jan. 20, 1887; Japanese attack on, Dec. 7, 1941.
Pearl Harbor Day (U.S.), Dec. 7.
Pearl, Minnie, Oct. 25, 1912.
Pearson, Ben, Nov. 16, 1898.
Pearson, Drew, Dec. 13, 1897; Jan. 12, 1951.
Pearson, Karl, Mar. 27, 1857.
Pearson, Lester Bowles, Apr. 23, 1897; inaugurated, Apr. 22, 1963.
Peary, Robert (Admiral), May 6, 1856; Apr. 6, 1909.
Peasants Day (Burma), Mar. 2.
peasants, poor, patroness of, Sep. 14.
Peck, Gregory, Apr. 5, 1916.
Peckinpah, Sam, Feb. 21, 1925.
Pedersen, Charles J., Oct. 3, 1904.
Pedro II (Brazil), Dec. 2, 1825; Apr. 7, 1831; abdicates, Nov. 15, 1889.
Pedro IV (Portugal), Oct. 12, 1798.
Pedro V (Portugal), Sep. 16, 1837; Nov. 15, 1853.
Pedro, Dom (Portugal) abdicates, Apr. 7, 1831; Apr. 2, 1832; May 26, 1834; Sep. 24, 1834.
Peel Report, Jul. 8, 1937.
Peel, Sir Robert, Feb. 5, 1788; Sep. 29, 1829.
Peerce, Jan, Jun. 3, 1904.
Pegasus, Feb. 16, 1965.
Pegau, Battle of, Oct. 15, 1080.
Pegu (Lower Burma), Dec. 20, 1852.
Peguy, Charles, Jan. 7, 1873.
Pei, I. M., Apr. 26, 1917.
Peirce, Benjamin, Apr. 4, 1809.
Peirce, Charles Santiago Sanders, Sep. 10, 1839.
Peking (China): occupied, Oct. 12, 1860; Jan. 7, 1895; Apr. 8, 1913; captured, Jun. 8, 1928; Jan. 22, 1949.
Pele (Edson Arantes do Nascimento), Oct. 23, 1940; scores 1000th goal, Nov. 19, 1969, Jul. 18, 1971.
Pell, Claiborne, Nov. 22, 1918.
Pella, Giuseppe, Apr. 18, 1902.
Pelleas et Melisande: premiere, Apr. 30, 1902.
Pelletier, Wilfrid, Jun. 30, 1896.

Pelshe, Arvid Y., Feb. 7, 1899.
Peltier, Leonard, Sep. 12, 1944.
Peltz, Mary Ellis, May 4, 1896.
Penance, Day of (Federal Republic of Germany), Nov. 17.
Pendergrass, Theodore D. *(Teddy)*, Mar. 26, 1950.
Pendleton Act, Jan. 6, 1883.
penicillin, Aug. 27, 1942.
Peninsular War, Feb. 16, 1808; Aug. 21, 1808; Mar. 12, 1814.
penitent women, patron of, Apr. 2.
Penjdeh, Feb. 13, 1886.
Penn, Arthur, Sep. 27, 1922.
Penn, Sean, Aug. 17, 1960.
Penn, William, Oct. 14, 1644; Mar. 4, 1681.
Pennell, Rebecca Mann, Oct. 5, 1853.
Penney, James Cash, Sep. 16, 1875.
Pennsylvania: second state, Dec. 12, 1787.
Penny Blacks: first adhesive postage stamps, May 6, 1840.
Pennzoil, Apr. 12, 1987.
Pentagon Building, Jan. 15, 1943.
Pentagon Papers: published, Jun. 13, 1971.
Penzias, Arno Allan, Apr. 26, 1933.
People United to Save Humanity (PUSH), Dec. 18, 1971.
People's National Congress (Guyana), May 26, 1966.
People's Park: Vietnam War protest, May 15, 1969.
People's Party (Populist Party): formation, Feb. 22, 1892.
People's Redemption Party (Liberia), Apr. 12, 1980.
People's Redemptive Council (Liberia), Apr. 25, 1980.
People's Republic of China. *See*: China, People's Republic of.
People's Temple, Nov. 18, 1978.
Pep, Willie, Nov. 20, 1942.
Peppard, George, Oct. 1, 1928.
Pepper, Claude Denson, Sep. 8, 1900.
Peppercorn Day (Bermuda), Apr. 23.
Pepsi Cola, Nov. 16, 1972.
Pepys, Samuel, Feb. 23, 1633.
Pequot Indians, Jul. 28, 1637.
Pequot War, Jul. 28, 1637.
Perak (Malay Peninsula), Jan. 20, 1874.

Peralta Azurdia, Enrique, Mar. 30, 1963.

Percival, Spencer, May 11, 1812.

Percy, Charles Harting, Sep. 27, 1919.

Percy, Walker, May 28, 1916.

Pereda Asbun, Juan, Jul. 21, 1978.

Pereira, Aristide, Nov. 17, 1923.

Perelman, S. J., Feb. 1, 1904.

Peres, Shimon, Aug. 16, 1923; Apr. 8, 1977; inaugurated, Sep. 14, 1984.

Peretti, Elsa, May 1, 1940.

Peretz, I. L., May 18, 1852.

Perez, Carlos Andres: Oct. 27, 1922; inaugurated, Feb. 2, 1988; coup attempt, Nov. 27, 1992.

Perez de Cuellar, Javier Perez de Cuellar, Javier, Jan. 19, 1920; Dec. 15, 1981.

Perez, Rose, Sep. 6, 1964.

perfumers, patron of, Jul. 21.

Pergaud, Louis, Jan. 22, 1882.

Pergolesi, Giovanni, Jan. 4, 1710.

peridot, Aug. intro.

Perkin, Sir William Henry, Mar. 12, 1838.

Perkins, Anthony, Apr. 4, 1932; Apr. 14, 1932.

Perkins, Carl, Apr. 9, 1932.

Perkins, Elizabeth, Nov. 18, 1960.

Perkins, Frances, Apr. 10, 1882.

Perkins, Marlin, Mar. 28, 1902.

Perkins, Maxwell, Sep. 20, 1884.

Perlman, Itzhak, Aug. 31, 1945.

Perlman, Rhea, Mar. 31, 1946.

Permanent Court of International Justice: opens, Feb. 15, 1922.

Peron, Eva Duarte de, May 7, 1919; dies, Jul. 26, 1952.

Peron, Isabel, Feb. 6, 1931; Sep. 23, 1973; becomes President, Jul. 1, 1974; Jan. 3, 1975; Jul. 8, 1975; returns to office, Oct. 16, 1975; Mar. 24, 1976; Mar. 29, 1976.

Peron, Juan, Oct. 8, 1895; inaugurated, Jun. 4, 1946; May 20, 1955; resigns, Sep. 19, 1955; ends 17-year exile, Nov. 17, 1972; Sep. 23, 1973; Jul. 1, 1974.

Perot, Ross, Jun. 27, 1930.

perpetuation bill, Apr. 20, 1653.

Perrault, Charles, Jan. 12, 1628.

Perrin, Jean Baptiste, Sep. 30, 1870.

Perrine, Valerie, Sep. 3, 1943.

Perry, Antoinette, Jun. 27, 1888.

Perry, Commodore Matthew, Apr. 10, 1794; Jul. 8, 1853; Mar. 31, 1854.

Perry, Gaylord Jackson, Sep. 15, 1938.

Perry, Harold, Oct. 3, 1965.

Perry, Luke, Oct. 11, 1965.

Perry Mason: television debut, Sep. 21, 1957.

Perry, Matthew, Aug. 19, 1969.

Perry, Oliver Hazard, Aug. 23, 1785; Sep. 10, 1813.

Perry, The Refrigerator, Dec. 16, 1962.

Perry, Robert: shot to death, Jun. 10, 1970.

Perry, Steve, Jan. 22, 1949.

Perry, William, Oct. 11, 1927; Feb. 3, 1994.

Perse, Saint-John, Mar. 31, 1887.

Pershing, John J., Sep. 13, 1860; May 10, 1917; Jun. 13, 1917; Sep. 3, 1919.

Persia: declares neutrality, Nov. 1, 1914; Jan. 30, 1915; Mar. 21, 1935.

Persia, Shah of, Apr. 25, 1926.

Persian Empire: 2,500th anniversary begins, Oct. 12, 1971.

Persian Gulf, May 17, 1987; Jul. 22, 1987.

Persian martyrs, Apr. 6.

Persigny, Jean Gilbert Fialin, Jan. 11, 1808.

Persius, Dec. 4, 34.

Persoff, Nehemiah, Aug. 14, 1920.

Perth, Feb. 20, 1437.

Pertini, Alessandro, Sep. 25, 1896; elected, Jul. 8, 1978.

Peru: independence, Jul. 28, 1821; Jan. 26. 1827; declares war on Spain, Jan. 14, 1866; Apr. 5, 1879; cholera, Jan. 23, 1991.

Perutz, Max, May 19, 1914.

Peruvian opera, first: Ollanta. Dec. 26, 1900.

Pesci, Joe, Feb. 9, 1943.

Pescia in Tuscany, patron of, Oct. 23.

Pescow, Donna, Mar. 24, 1954.

Peshtigo (Wisconsin), Oct. 7, 1871.

Pest Control Month, National, Jun. intro.

Pestalozzi, Johann H., Jan. 12, 1746.

Pet Week, National, May intro.

Petain, Henri Philippe Omer, Apr. 24, 1856. Aug. 15, 1945.

Peter II (Russia), Oct. 23, 1715; dies, Feb. 11, 1730.

Peter Il (Yugoslavia), Mar. 28, 1941.

Peter III (Russia), Feb. 21, 1728; Jan. 5, 1762.

Peter V (Portugal): dies, Nov. 11, 1861.

Peter of Castile, Mar. 14, 1369.

Peter the Great (Russia), Jun. 9, 1672; Nov. 30, 1700; May 1, 1703; May 27, 1703; Jul. 8, 1709; Oct. 22, 1721; dies, Feb. 8, 1725.

Peter, Lawrence (Johnston), Sep. 16, 1919.

Peter Pan: premiere, Apr. 24, 1954.

Peter (Serbia), Nov. 24, 1918.

Peter and the Wolf: premiere, May 2, 1936.

Peter (Yugoslavia): dies, Aug. 16, 1921.

Peterloo Massacre, Aug. 16, 1819.

Peters, Bernadette, Feb. 28, 1948.

Peters, Jean, Oct. 15, 1926.

Peters, Roberta, May 4, 1930.

Peters, Thomas J., Nov. 7, 1942.

Peterson, Oscar (Emanuel), Aug. 15, 1925.

Petipa, Marius, Mar. 11, 1822.

Petit, Alexis, Oct. 2, 1791.

Petofi (Petrovics), Sandor, Jan. 1, 1823.

Petrarch, Jul. 20, 1304; Apr. 8, 1341.

Petrograd, Mar. 8, 1917; Apr. 22, 1920.

Petrograd Soviet of Workers and Soldiers Deputies: organized, Mar. 12, 1917.

Petrouchka: premiere, Jun. 13, 1911.

Pettet, Joanna, Nov. 16, 1944.

Petty, Richard, Jul. 2, 1937.

Petty, Tom, Oct. 20, 1952.

Pevensey (England), Sep. 28, 1066.

Peyton Place: published, Sep. 24, 1956.

Pfeiffer, Michelle, Apr. 28, 1959.

Phair, Elizabeth (Liz), Apr. 17, 1967.

Pham van Dong, Mar. 1, 1906.

Phelan, Michael, Apr. 12, 1859.

Phi Beta Kappa: founded, Dec. 5, 1776; Apr. 4, 1953.

Philadelphia, Feb. 16, 1804.

Philadelphia Contributionship, Apr. 13, 1752.

Philadelphia Orchestra: inaugural concert, Nov. 16, 1900; Jan. 3, 1941.

Philadelphia (Pennsylvania), Sep. 5, 1774; May 25, 1787; May 7, 1847.

Philadelphia Phillies, May 24, 1935.

Philarges, Peter: elected Pope Alexander V, Jun. 29, 1408.

Philatelic Exhibitions Month, May intro.

Philatelic Journalists Day (U.S.), Jun. intro; Jun. 6.

Philatelic Literature Month, Mar. intro.

Philatelic Publications Month, Sep. intro.

Philatelic Societies' Month, Apr. intro.

Philatelic Writers' Month, Jun. intro.

Philately Day, Jan. intro; Jan. 20.

Philately Day (U.S.), Jan. 20.

Philby, Harold Kim, Jan. 1, 1912.

Philco TV Playhouse: television debut, Oct. 3, 1948.

Philharmonic Society, New York: formed, Dec. 7, 1842.

Philip I (France), Aug. 4, 1060.

Philip II, Augustus (France), Aug. 21, 1165; Sep. 18, 1180; Nov. 18, 1188; Jul. 1, 1190; Jul. 22, 1194; May 22, 1200; dies, Jul. 14, 1223.

Philip II (Spain), May 21, 1527; Mar. 9, 1551; Oct. 25, 1555; Jan. 16, 1556; Feb. 5, 1556; Dec. 31, 1584; May 17, 1597; dies, Sep. 13, 1598.

Philip III (France), Apr. 3, 1245; Aug. 25, 1270; dies, Oct. 05, 1285.

Philip III (Spain), Apr. 14, 1578; Sep. 13, 1598; dies, Mar. 31, 1621.

Philip IV (France), Oct. 5, 1285; Dec. 5, 1301; Jul. 11, 1302; dies, Nov. 29, 1314.

Philip IV (Spain), Apr. 8, 1605; Mar. 31, 1621; dies, Sep. 17, 1665.

Philip V (France), Jun. 4, 1316; dies, Jan. 3, 1322.

Philip V (Spain), Dec. 19, 1683; Nov. 1, 1700; Dec. 10, 1710.

Philip VI (France), Feb. 1, 1328; Mar. 15, 1341; dies, Aug. 22, 1350.

Philip of Anjou, Nov. 1, 1700.

Philip of Burgundy, Jan. 11, 1360.

Philip, Duke of Swabia (Germany), Mar. 8, 1198.

Philip the Good (Duke of Burgundy), Jan. 10, 1429; Sep. 21, 1435.

Philip, Prince (England), Jun. 10, 1921; Jul. 4, 1966.

Philippa (Queen of England), Oct. 17, 1346.

Philippine-American Friendship Day (Philippines), Jul. 4.

Philippine Sea, Jul. 30, 1945.

Philippine Sea, Battle of: begins, Jun. 18, 1944; ends, Jun. 20, 1944.

Philippines, Apr. 27, 1521; independence, Jun. 12, 1898; Feb. 4, 1899; rebellion ends, Apr. 19, 1901; military rule ends, Jun. 12, 1901; Mar. 24, 1934; first president of, Sep. 17, 1935; Jan. 2, 1942; Apr. 9, 1942; bombed, Oct. 12, 1944; Oct. 20, 1944; martial law, Sep. 21, 1972; Apr. 7, 1978.

Philippines, National Bank of, Feb. 4, 1916.

Philippines, Republic of the: proclaimed, Jul. 4, 1946.

Phillips, Captain Mark, Nov. 14, 1973.

Phillips, Frank, Nov. 28, 1873.

Phillips, John, Dec. 6, 1719.

Phillips, John Sanburn, Jul. 2, 1861.

Phillips, Julia, Apr. 7, 1944.

Phillips, Lou Diamond, Feb. 17, 1962.

Phillips, MacKenzie, Nov. 10, 1959.

Phillips, Mark Anthony Peter, Sep. 22, 1948.

Phillips, Michelle Gillam, Apr. 6, 1944.

Phillips, Sam, Jan. 5, 1923.

Phillips, Wendell, Nov. 29, 1811.

Phipps, Henry, Sep. 27, 1839.

Phnom Penh (Cambodia), Apr. 17, 1975; Jan. 7, 1979.

Phoenix Park (Dublin), May 6, 1882.

Phoenix, River, Aug. 23, 1971.

Pholien, Joseph, Aug. 15, 1950.

phonograph: patented, Jul. 31, 1877.

phonograph record, long-playing: first public demonstration, Jun. 18, 1948.

Phouma, Souvanna. Jan. 19. 1962; Apr. 5, 1974.

Phram Hung, Jun. 18, 1987.

Phram Van Dong, Jun. 18, 1987.

Phu, Dien Bien, Nov. 20, 1953.

Polish Republic Physical Education Day (Japan), Oct. 10.

physicians, patrons of, Sep. 26.

physician-assisted suicide, Mar. 24, 1998.

Piaf, Edith, Dec. 19, 1915.

Piaget, Jean, Aug. 9, 1896.

Piatigorsky, Gregor, Apr. 20, 1903.

Piazzi, Giuseppe, Jul. 16, 1746.

Picado, Teodoro, Feb. 14, 1944.

Picardy, First Battle of, Sep. 22, 1914.

Picasso, Pablo, Oct. 25, 1881.

Picasso, Paloma, Apr. 19, 1949.

Piccard, Auguste, Jan. 28, 1884.

Piccolo, Brian, Oct. 21, 1943; dies, Jun. 16, 1970.

Pichincha Day Battle of (Ecuador), May 24.

Pickens, Slim, Jun. 29, 1919.

Pickens, T(homas) Boone, Jr., May 22, 1928.

Pickett, George Edward, Jan. 25, 1825.

Pickett, Wilson, Mar. 18, 1941.

Pickford, Mary, Apr. 8, 1893.

Pickle Weeks, May intro.

Picnic, May 4, 1953.

Picnic Day, International, Jun. intro.

Picotte, Susan LaFlesche, Jun. 17, 1865.

picture phone, Aug. 22, 1956.

Pidgeon, Walter, Sep. 23, 1898.

Pieck, Wilhelm, Jan. 3, 1876.

Pierce, David Hyde, Apr. 3, 1959.

Pierce, Franklin, Nov. 23, 1804; inaugurated, Mar. 4, 1853.

Pierce, Jane, Mar. 12, 1806.

Pierrot, George Francis, Jan. 11, 1898.

Pike, James Albert, Feb. 14, 1913.

Pike, Zebulon M., Jan. 5, 1779; Nov. 15, 1806.

Pike's Peak, Nov. 15, 1806.

pilgrims, patron of, Feb. 12.

Pilgrim's Progress, Feb. 18, 1678.

Pillsbury, Charles Alfred, Dec. 3, 1842.

Pillsbury, John Sargent, Jul. 29, 1828. Dec. 6, 1878.

pilots: captured U.S. in Vietnam, Jan. 21, 1970.

Pilsudski, Josef (Poland), Dec. 5, 1867; Oct. 15, 1918; Apr. 19, 1919; May 12, 1926.

Piltdown skull, Nov. 21, 1953.

Pinckney, Charles, Oct. 26, 1757.

Pinckney, Charles Cotesworth, Feb. 25, 1746.

Pinckney's Treaty (Treaty of San Lorenzo), Oct. 27, 1795.

Pincus, Gregory, Apr. 9, 1903.

Pindling, Lynden O., Jan. 16, 1967.

Pinel, Philippe, Apr. 20, 1745.

Pinero, Arthur Wing, May 24, 1855.

Piniella, Lou(is Victor), Aug. 28, 1943.

Pinilla, Gustavo Rojas, Apr. 19, 1970.

Pinkerton, Allan, Aug. 25, 1819.

Pinkham, Lydia Estes, Feb. 9, 1819.

Pinkney, William, Mar. 17, 1764.

Pinkowski, Josef (Poland), Feb. 9, 1981.

pinmakers, patron saint of, Jan. 20.

Pinochet Ugarte, Augusto, Nov. 25, 1915; Sep. 13, 1973; Mar. 11, 1981; Oct. 5, 1988; Dec. 14, 1989.

Pintas-Silgo, Maria de Lurdes: inaugurated, Aug. 1, 1979.

Pinter, Harold, Oct. 30, 1930; Jan. 5, 1967.

Pinto: recalled, Mar. 29, 1971; Sep. 13, 1978.

Pinto da Costa, Manuel, Aug. 5, 1937.

Pinyin, Jan. 1, 1979.

Pinza, Ezio, May 18, 1892.

Pioneer V, Mar. 11, 1960.

Pioneer 10, Mar. 2, 1972; Dec. 3, 1973; Apr. 25, 1983; Jun. 13, 1983.

Pioneer 11, Dec. 3, 1974; Sep. 1, 1979.

Pioneer Day (Idaho), Jun. 15.

Pioneer Day (Utah), Jul. 24.

Pioneers' Day (Angola), Dec. 1.

Pioneers' Day (Liberia), Jan. 7.

Pioneers' Day (South Dakota), Oct. intro.

Piper, William Thomas, Jan. 8, 1881.

Pippen, Scottie, Sep. 25, 1965.

Pippin: premiere, Oct. 23, 1972.

Pirandello, Luigi, Jun. 28, 1867.

Pisa, Council of, Jun. 29, 1408.

Pisa, patron saint of, Jun. 17.

Pisces, Feb. intro.; Mar. intro.

Piscopo, Joseph Charles (Joe), Jun. 17, 1951.

Pissarro, Camille, Jul. 10, 1830.

Piston, Walter, Jan. 20, 1894.

Pitcher, Molly (Mary McCauley), Oct. 13, 1754.

Pitkin, Walter Boughton, Feb. 6, 1878.

Pitman, Sir Isaac, Jan. 4, 1813.

Pitt, Brad, Dec. 18, 1963.

Pitt, William, Nov. 15, 1708; May 28, 1759; Feb. 16, 1801.

Pitts, Eliza Susan (Zasu), Jan. 3, 1900.

Pittsburg Landing (Tennessee), Apr. 6, 1862.

Pittsburgh (Pennsylvania), Jan. 28, 1944.

Pittsburgh Steelers football team, Jan. 21, 1979.

Pius II (pope), Oct. 18, 1405.

Pius IV (pope), Mar. 31, 1499.

Pius V (pope), Jan. 17, 1504; Feb. 25, 1570.

Pius VI (pope), Dec. 25, 1717.

Pius VII (pope), Aug. 14, 1742; May 1, 1809.

Pius VIII (pope), Nov. 20, 1761.

Pius IX (pope), May 13, 1792.

Pius X (pope), Jun. 2, 1835; Aug. 9, 1903; Jan. 8, 1904.

Pius XI (pope), May 31, 1857; Jul. 25, 1929.

Pius XII (pope), Mar. 2, 1876; Mar. 2, 1939; Jul. 7, 1946; Nov. 1, 1950; Dec. 23, 1950.

Pizza Festival Time, Oct. intro.

Place, Mary Kay, Sep. 23, 1947.

Planck, Max, Apr. 23, 1858.

Plant, Robert Anthony, Aug. 20, 1948.

Plantagenet, Edward: first Prince of Wales, Apr. 25, 1284.

Plantagenet, House of: established, Oct. 25, 1154.

Plante, Jacques, Jan. 17, 1929.

Plath, Sylvia, Oct. 27, 1932.

Platt Amendment, Mar. 2, 1901.

Plattsburg Bay, Battle of, Sep. 11, 1814.

Play-Doh Day, National, Sep. intro; Sep. 16.

Playa Giron, Apr. 20, 1961.

Player, Gary, Nov. 1, 1935.

The Players (Club), Jan. 7, 1888.

Playfair, John, Mar. 10, 1748.

playing card makers, patron of, Oct. 25.

Pleasence, Donald, Oct. 5, 1919.

Pledge of Allegiance, Sep. 8, 1892; May 28, 1954.

Plehwe, Vyacheslav: assassinated, Jul. 28, 1904.

Plekhanov, Georgi, Dec. 11, 1856.

Pleshette, Suzanne, Jan. 31, 1937.

Plimpton, George, Mar. 18, 1927.

Plimsall, Samuel, Feb. 10, 1824.

Plisetskaya, Maya Michailovna, Nov. 20, 1925.

Ploesti (Romania): bombed, Aug. 1, 1943; Aug. 30, 1944.

Ploughing Ceremony (Thailand), May 9.

Plowright, Joan (Anne), Oct. 28, 1929.

Plumer, Herbert Charles Onslow, Mar. 13, 1857.

Plummer, Amanda, Mar. 23, 1957.

Plummer, Christopher, Dec. 13, 1929.

Plunkett, James William, Jr. *(Jim),* Dec. 5, 1947.

Plunkett, Oliver, Mar. 17, 1918.

Pluto: discovered, Feb. 18, 1930; Apr. 25, 1983.

Plymouth (England), Sep. 16, 1620.

Pocahontas, Apr. 5, 1614.

Podgorica (Montenegro), Jan. 23, 1916.

Podgorny, Nikolai Viktorovich, Feb. 18, 1903; Jan. 29, 1967.

Podhoretz, Norman, Jan. 16, 1930.

Poe, Edgar Allan, Jan. 19, 1809.

Poetry Day, National, Oct. intro.

poets, patron of, Mar. 1.

Poher, Alain, Apr. 28, 1969.

Poincare, Jules Henri, Apr. 29, 1854.

Poincare, Raymond, Aug. 20, 1860.

Poindexter, John, Nov. 25, 1986; Jul. 15, 1987; Mar. 16, 1988; Apr. 7, 1990.

Point Four program, Sep. 8, 1950.

Pointer, Bonnie, Jul. 11, 1951.

poison gas, Feb. 6, 1922.

poison gas prohibited: Geneva Protocol, Jun. 17, 1925.

Poison Prevention Week, National, Mar. intro.

Poisson, Simeon-Denis, Jun. 21, 1781.

Poitier, Sidney, Feb. 20, 1927.

Pol Pot, May 19, 1928; received in Peking (China), Sep. 28, 1977; Sep. 2, 1985; Apr. 5, 1989.

Poland, Jan. 18, 1401, Jul. 1, 1569; Jan. 15, 1582; Jan. 26, 1699, Jun. 2, 1734; Seven Years War, Jan. 10, 1757; Apr. 11, 1764 partition, Jan. 23, 1793; third partition, Oct. 24, 1795; Apr. 30, 1815; Mar. 30, 1917; declares independence, Oct. 15, 1918; independence, Nov. 9, 1918; Jan. 17, 1919; attacked by Germany, Sep. 1, 1939; invaded by U.S.S.R., Sep. 17, 1939; Jan. 6, 1946; thousandth anniversary of Christianity in, Jan. 8, 1966, Mar. 11, 1968; martial law declared, Dec. 13, 1981 martial law lifted, Jul. 22, 1983; May 17, 1989; free elections, Jun. 4, 1989; free-market rules, Jan. 1, 1990; free elections in, Nov. 25, 1990; approves privatization, May 7, 1993. Poland, Bank of: established, Apr. 1, 1924.

Poland, patron of, Mar. 4; Apr. 11; Nov. 13.

Polanski, Roman, Aug. 18, 1933.

Polanyi, John Charles, Jan. 23, 1929.

Polaris missile: launched for first time from submerged submarine, Jul. 20, 1960; May 6, 1962.

Polhill, Robert, Apr. 22, 1990.

polio vaccine, Apr. 12, 1955; Aug. 24, 1960.

Polisario Republic (Saharan Arab Democratic Republic), Feb. 27, 1976.

Polish Falcons Societies, Union Of, Apr. 4, 1917.

Polish Republic, Nov. 3, 1918.

Polish Succession, War of the, Jun. 2, 1734; ends, Oct. 5, 1735.

Polk, James Knox, Nov. 2, 1795; inaugurated, Mar. 4, 1845.

Polk, Ralph Lane, Jul. 21, 1911.

Polk, Sarah Childress, Sep. 4, 1803.

Pollack, Sydney, Jul. 1, 1934.

Pollard, Jonathan, Jun. 4, 1986; Mar. 4, 1987.

Pollock, Jackson, Jan. 28, 1912.

Poltava, Battle of, Jul. 8, 1709.

polygamy, May 3, 1950.

Pompadour, Madame de, Dec. 29, 1721.

Pompidou, Georges, Jul. 5, 1911; Apr. 14, 1962; Jun. 15, 1969.

Ponce de Leon, Juan, Apr. 8, 1460; Apr. 2, 1513.

Pons, Lily, Apr. 16, 1904.

Ponselle, Rosa Melba, Jan. 22, 1897.

Pontano, Giovanni Gioviano, May 7, 1426.

Pontecorvo, Bruno M., Apr. 21, 1963.

Ponti, Carlo, Dec. 11, 1913.

Pontifical College Josephinum, Sep. 1, 1888.

Pontoppidan, Henrik, Jul. 24, 1857.

Pontormo, Jacopo da, May 24, 1494.

Ponty, Jean-Luc, Sep. 29, 1942.

Pony Express: first, Apr. 3, 1860.

Pool, Ernest, Jun. 3, 1918.

poor, patron of, Jun. 13.

Poor People's Campaign, Jun. 19, 1968.

Poor Richard's Universal Life Church, Jan. 26, 1970.

Popcorn Month, National, Oct. intro.

Pope, Alexander, May 21, 1688.

Pope, John, Mar. 16, 1822.

Popolo d'Italia: first issue, Nov. 14, 1914.

Popov, Dimitar, elected, Dec. 7, 1990.

poppy, Aug. intro.

Popular Front (France), Mar. 13, 1938.

Popular Resistance Day, Oct. 24.

Popular Revolution Commemoration Day (Ethiopia), Sep. 12.

Population Registration Act, Jun. 17, 1991.

Porgy and Bess: premiere, Sep. 30, 1935.

Porsche, Ferdinand, Sep. 3, 1875.

Port Arthur, Feb. 4, 1904; Jan. 2, 1905.

Port Nicholson (New Zealand), Jan. 22, 1840.

Porter, Abel Bergaigne, Aug. 31, 1838.

Porter, Cole, Jun. 9, 1892; Nov. 29, 1932; Nov. 21, 1934; Dec. 30, 1948; May 7, 1953.

Porter, Darrell Ray, Jan. 17, 1952.

Porter, Fitz-John, Aug. 31, 1822.

Porter, Gene(ra) Grace Stratton, Aug. 17, 1868.

Porter, George, Dec. 6, 1920.

Porter, Katherine Anne, May 15, 1890.

Porter, Rodney Robert, Oct. 8, 1917.

Porter, Sarah, Aug. 16, 1813.

Porter, Sylvia (Field), Jun. 18, 1913.

porters, patron of, Nov. 6.

Portnoy's Complaint: published, Feb. 21, 1969.

Portsmouth (New Hampshire), Sep. 5, 1905.

Portsmouth Peace Conference, Aug. 9, 1905.

Portugal, Apr. 22, 1500; independence from Spain, Dec. 1, 1640; Feb. 13, 1668; Jan. 20, 1801; May 5, 1811; declared republic, Oct. 5, 1910; separation of church and state, Apr. 20, 1911; official currency, May 22, 1911; declares war on Germany, May 9, 1915; Mar. 15, 1916; Vatican ambassador recalled, Jul. 3, 1970; Apr. 25, 1974; new constitution, Apr. 25, 1976; Jan. 1, 1986; Nov. 14, 1988.

Portugal Day, Apr. 25; Jun. 10.

Portugal, patron of, Jan. 20; Apr. 23.

Portuguese Civil War, May 26, 1834.

Portuguese Day, Jun. intro.

Portuguese East Africa, Jun. 25, 1975.

Posada, Nine Days of (Mexico), Dec. intro.

Post, Charles William, Oct. 26, 1854.

Post, Elizabeth Lindley, May 7, 1920.

Post, Emily, Oct. 27, 1872.

Post, Marjorie Merriweather, Mar. 15, 1887.

Post Office, U.S.: established, May 8, 1794.

Post, Wiley, Nov. 22, 1899; Jul. 1, 1931.

postage stamps: first adhesive, May 6, 1840.

postal reorganization bill, Aug. 12, 1970.

postal service: concept pioneered in France, Jun. 19, 1464.

postal strike: first in United Kingdom, Jan. 20, 1971.

postal workers, patron of, Mar. 24.

postcards: introduced in Austria, Oct. 1, 1869.

Poste Royale (France): established, Jun. 19, 1464.

Potato Lover's Month, Feb. intro.

Potgieter, Everhardus Johannes, Jun. 17, 1808.

Potowski-Rose, Ernestine, Jan. 12, 1910.

Potsdam Conference, Jul. 17, 1945.

Pottawatomie Creek (Kansas), May 24, 1856.

Potter, Beatrix, Jul. 28, 1866.

Potts, Annie, Oct. 28, 1952.

Potvin, Denis, Oct. 29, 1953.

Poulenc, Francis, Jan. 7, 1899.

Poulsen, Valdemar, Nov. 23, 1869.

Pound, Ezra (Loomis), Oct. 30, 1885; May 5, 1945.

Pound, Roscoe, Oct. 27, 1870.

Powell, Adam Clayton, Jr., Nov. 29, 1908; Mar. 1, 1967; Jun. 16, 1969.

Powell, Bud, Sep. 27, 1924.

Powell, Cecil Frank, Dec. 5, 1903.

Powell, Colin, Apr. 5, 1937.

Powell, Dick, Nov. 14, 1904.

Powell, Eleanor, Nov. 21, 1912.

Powell, Jane, Apr. 1, 1929.

Powell, John Wesley, Mar. 24, 1834.

Powell, Lewis F., Jr., Sep. 19, 1907; Jan. 7, 1972.

Powell, William, Jul. 29, 1892.

power failure: largest in history, Nov. 9, 1965.

Power, Tyrone, May 5, 1913.

Powers, Francis Gary, Aug. 17, 1929; May 1, 1960; May 7, 1960; Feb. 10, 1962.

Powers, John Robert, Sep. 14, 1896.

Powers, Stefanie, Nov. 12, 1942.

Powhatan, Apr. 5, 1614.

Pozzi, Lucio, Nov. 29, 1935.

Prado Ugarteche, Manuel, Jul. 28, 1956.

Praetorius, Michael, Feb. 15, 1571.

Pragmatic Sanction, Apr. 19, 1713.

Prague: captured, Jul. 26, 1648.

Prague, Defenestration of, May 23, 1618.

Prague, Treaty of, Aug. 23, 1866.

Prague University, Apr. 7, 1348.

Prandtl, Ludwig, Feb. 4, 1875.

Prasad, Rajendra, Jan. 26, 1950.

Prati, Giovanni, Jan. 27, 1814.

Pratt, Charles, Oct. 2, 1830.

prayer book: first English, Jun. 9, 1549.

Prayer Day (Denmark), May intro.

prayer in public schools, Jun. 25, 1962.

Prayer for Vocations, World Day of, Apr. intro.; May intro.

preachers, patron of, Sep. 13.

Predock, Antoine, Jun. 23, 1936.

Preece, W.H., Jan. 14, 1878.

Pregl, Fritz, Sep. 3, 1869.

Preisand, Sally Jane, Jun. 3, 1972.

Prelog, Vladimir, Jul. 23, 1906.

Premadasa, Ranasinghe: inaugurated, Jan. 2, 1989; assassinated, Apr. 23, 1993.

Preminger, Otto, Dec. 5, 1906; Dec. 15, 1955.

Prentiss, Paula, Mar. 4, 1939.

Presbyterian Church (U.S.A.), Jun. 10, 1983.

Prescott, William, Feb. 20, 1726.

Presentation of the Lord, Feb. 2.

Presentation of the Blessed Virgin, Mary, Nov. 21.

Pre_eren Day (Slovenia), Feb. 8.

President Bourguiba's Birthday (Tunisia), Aug. 3.

President Tubman's Birthday (Liberia), Nov. 29.

Presidential Succession Act: signed, Jul. 18, 1947.

President's Day (Botswana), Jul. intro.; Jul. 15.

Presidents' Day (Congo), Feb. 5.

Presidents' Day (Hawaii, Nebraska, Pennsylvania, South Dakota), Feb. intro.

Presley, Elvis, Jan. 8, 1935; Jul. 5, 1954; Jan. 10, 1956; army induction, Mar. 24, 1958; Aug. 16, 1977.

Presley, Lisa Marie, Feb. 1, 1968.

Presley, Priscilla Ann Beaulieu, May 24, 1946.

Presser, Jackie, Aug. 6, 1926; May 21, 1986.

Pressler, Larry, Mar. 29, 1942.

Preston, Battle of, Aug. 17, 1648.

Preston, Billy, Sep. 9, 1946.

Preston, Kelly, Oct. 13, 1962.

Pretoria Convention, Aug. 8, 1881.

Pretoria (Transvaal): captured by British, Jun. 5, 1900.

Pretoria, Treaty of, Apr. 5, 1881.

Pretorius, Andries, Dec. 16, 1838.

Pretorius, Marthinius, Jan. 6, 1857.

Pretty Girl Is Like a Melody: premiere, Jun. 16, 1919.

Pretzel Month, National, Oct. intro.

Preung, Pho, Apr. 19, 1960.

Preval, Rene, Jan. 17, 1943; elected, Dec. 17, 1995; elected, Feb. 7, 1996.

Previn, Andre, Apr. 6, 1929.

Prevost, Antoine Francois, Apr. 1, 1697.

Price, Byron, Mar. 25, 1891.

Price, George C., Mar. 3, 1964.

Price, H(enry) Ryan, Aug. 16, 1912.

Price, Leontyne, Feb. 10, 1927; Jan. 3, 1985.

Price, Vincent, May 27, 1911.

Pride, Charley, Mar. 18, 1938.

Priest, Oscar de, May 12, 1871.

Priestly, Jason, Aug. 28, 1967.

Priestley, J(ohn) B(oynton), Sep. 13, 1894.

Priestley, Joseph, Mar. 13, 1733.

Prigogine, Ilya, Jan. 25, 1917.

privatization, approved by Poland, May 7, 1993.

Pynchon, Thomas May 8, 1937.

Primary Election Day (Indiana, Pennsylvania), May intro.

Primary Election Day (Wisconsin, Wyoming), Sep. intro.

primary election, direct (Minneapolis): first in U.S., Sep. 18, 1900.

primrose, Feb. intro.

Primrose, William, Aug. 23, 1904.

Prince, Jun. 7, 1958.

Prince Charles' Birthday (Fiji), Nov. intro.

Prince Edward County (Virginia), Sep. 8, 1964.

Prince Edward Island, Jul. 1, 1873.

Prince Eitel Friedrich: German ship, Jan. 28, 1915.

Prince, Harold Smith, Jan. 30, 1928.

Prince Jonah Kuhio Kalanianaole Day (Hawaii), Mar. 26.

Prince of Monaco Holiday (France, Monaco), Nov. 19.

Prince of Wales' Birthday (British Virgin Islands, St. Kitts, Tuvalu), Nov. 14.

Princeton, Battle of, Jan. 3, 1977.

Princip, Gavrilo, Jul. 25, 1895; Jun. 28, 1914.

Principal, Victoria, Jan. 3, 1944.

Principe: independence, Jul. 12, 1975.

Pringle, Thomas, Jan. 5, 1789.

Printing Ink Day, Jan. intro.

Printing Week, International, Jan. intro.

Prinze, Freddie, Jun. 22, 1954.

Prio Socarras, Carlos: inaugurated, Oct. 10, 1948.

Priscilla of Boston, Dec. 14, 1916.

prisoners, patron of, Nov. 6.

prisoners of war, U.S., Feb. 12, 1973.

Pritchett, Sir V(ictor) S(awdon), Dec. 16, 1900.

Pritikin, Nathan, Aug. 29, 1915.

Prix de Rome, Oct. 20, 1928.

Pro Bowl: first game, Jan. 15, 1939.

Proclamation of 1763: issued, Oct. 7, 1763.

Proclamation of Independence (Central African Republic), Aug. 13.

Proclamation Island, Jan. 13, 1930.

Proclamation of the Republic (Brazil), Nov. 15.

Proclamation of the Republic (Chad), Nov. 28.

Proclamation of the Republic (Congo), Dec. 31.

Proclamation of the Republic Day (Hungary), Oct. 23.

Proclamation of the Republic (Italy), Jun. 2.

Proclamation of the Republic (Latvia), Nov. 18.

Proclamation of the Republic Day (Albania), Jan. 11.

Proclamation of the Republic, Anniversary of the (Central African Republic), Dec. 1.

Procrastination Week, National, Mar. intro.

Procter, William Cooper, Aug. 25, 1862.

Prodi, Romano, May 18, 1996.

Production Day (Benin), Dec. 31.

Proell, Annemarie, Mar. 27, 1953.

Professional Golfers Association (PGA), Apr. 10, 1916. Jan. 17, 1916.

Professional Secretaries' Week, Apr. intro.

Profumo, John Dennis: resigns, Jun. 5, 1963.

Progressive Party, Jun. 22, 1912.

Prohibition (18th Amendment), Jan. 16, 1920; revoked, Dec. 5, 1933.

Project HOPE: founded, Dec. 29, 1958.

Prokhorov, Aleksandr, Jul. 11, 1916.

Prokofiev, Sergei, Apr. 23, 1891; first appearance, Dec. 31, 1908; Dec. 10, 1916; May 2, 1936; Jan. 11, 1940; Nov. 21, 1945.

Promontory (Utah): first transcontinental railroad, May 10, 1869.

Proposition 13: endorsed in California, Jun. 6, 1978.

Propylaea: destroyed, Sep. 26, 1687.

Prosky, Robert J., Dec. 13, 1930.

Prost, Alain Marie Pascal, Feb. 24, 1955.

Protectorate: established in England, Dec. 16, 1653; Sep. 3, 1654.

Protestant Church: Germany, Sep. 28, 1935.

Protestant Reformation Day, Oct. 31.

Protestants, Swiss, May 27, 1536.

Proudhoun, Pierre Joseph, Jan. 15, 1809; Jul. 15, 1809.

Proulx, E. Annie, Aug. 22, 1935.

Proust, Marcel, Jul. 10, 1871.

Prout, William, Jan. 15, 1785.

Prowse, Juliet, Sep. 25, 1936.

Proxmire, William, Nov. 11, 1915.

Prudhoe Bay (Alaska), Mar. 13, 1968.

Prudhomme, Sully, Mar. 16, 1839.

Prus, Boleslaw, Aug. 20, 1847.

Prusiner, Stanley B., May 28, 1942.

Prussia: proclaimed kingdom, Jan. 15, 1701; Jan. 16, 1756; Seven Years War, Jan. 10, 1757; Jan. 23, 1793; new constitution, Jan. 31, 1850; Jan. 24, 1867; Jan. 28, 1871.

Prussia, patron of, Nov. 15.

Prussia, patroness of, Oct. 30.

Pryor, Richard, Dec. 1, 1940.

Przasnyz, Battle of, Feb. 27, 1915; Mar. 11, 1915.

Przemysl (Galicia), Mar. 22, 1915.

P.S., I Love You: Beatles first recording, Sep. 11, 1962.

Psycho: premiere, Jun. 16, 1960.

PTL Club, Mar. 19, 1987.

Pu-Yi, Emperor (China), Feb. 12, 1912.

Public Holiday (Armenia), Sep. 21.

Public Holiday (Beni, Bolivia), Nov. 18.

Public Holiday (Botswana), Jan. 2.

Public Holiday (Brunei), May 31.

Public Holiday (Cobija, Bolivia), Sep. 24.

Public Holiday (Cochabamba, Bolivia), Sep. 14.

Public Holiday (Cyprus), Feb. 13.

Public Holiday (Dominican Republic), Jul. 16.

Public Holiday (Guayaquil, Ecuador), Jul. 25.

Public Holiday (La Paz, Bolivia), Jul. 16.

Public Holiday (Macedonia, Yugoslavia), Oct. 11.

Public Holiday (Managua, Nicaragua), Aug. 10.

Public Holiday (Maracaibo, Venezuela), Oct. 24.

Public Holiday (Mexico), Sep. 1.

Public Holiday (Montenegro, Yugoslavia), Jul. 13.

Public Holiday (North Korea), Oct. 10.

Public Holiday (Oruro, Bolivia), Feb. 22.

Public Holiday (Potosi, Bolivia), Nov. 10.

Public Holiday (Qatar), Feb. 22.

Public Holiday (Rwanda), Aug. 1.

Public Holiday (St. Lucia), Jan. 2.

Public Holiday (San Jose, Costa Rica), Dec. 28; Dec. 31.

Public Holiday (San Marino), Jul. 28.

Public Holiday (Santa Cruz, Bolivia), Sep. 24.

Public Holiday (Slovenia, Yugoslavia), Nov. 1.

Public Holiday (Sucre, Bolivia), May 25.

Public Holiday (Syria), Sep. I; Oct. 6.

Public Holiday (Tarija, Bolivia), Apr. 15.

Public Holiday (Uganda), Mar. 25.

Public Holiday (Zimbabwe), Dec. 27.

Public Order Act, Feb. 7, 1970.

Public Relations Week, May intro.

Public Safety Act (India), Apr. 12, 1929.

public school, first in America, Feb. 13, 1635.

public school segregation laws: Georgia, Jan. 27, 1961.

Public Service Co. of New Hampshire, Jan. 28, 1988.

Publicity Stunt Week, Apr. intro.

Pucci, Emilio, Nov. 20, 1914.

Puccini, Giacomo, Dec. 22, 1858; Feb. 1, 1896; Jan. 14, 1900; Feb. 17, 1904; Dec. 10, 1910.

Puck, Wolfgang, Jan. 8, 1949.

Puckett, Kirby, Mar. 14, 1961.

Puebla Battle Day (Mexico), May 5.

Puebla (Mexico), May 5, 1867.

Pueblo U.S.S., Jan. 23, 1968; Dec. 22, 1968.

Puerto Rico: U.S. territory, Mar. 2, 1917; Feb. 14, 1929; Mar. 3, 1952.

Pugin, Augustus Welby, Mar. 1, 1812.

Pulaski, Count Casimir, Mar. 4, 1747.

Pulitzer, Joseph, Apr. 10, 1847.

Pulitzer Prizes, Jun. 6, 1917.

Puller, Lewis Burwell, Jun. 26, 1898.

Pullman, George Mortimer, Mar. 3, 1831.

Pullman strike, May 11, 1894.

pulsar: discovery, Feb. 29, 1968.

Pultusk, May 1, 1703.

Punch: begins publication, Jul. 17, 1841.

Punjab, Feb. 21, 1849; Mar. 29, 1849; Apr. 2, 1849; Mar. 10, 1966.

Punta del Este, Jan. 31, 1962.

Purcell, Edward Mills, Aug. 30, 1912.

Purcell, Sarah, Oct. 8, 1948.

Pure Food and Drug Act, U.S., Jun. 30, 1906.

Purification of the Blessed Virgin, Mary, Feb. 2.

Purim, Flora, Mar. 6, 1942.

Puritans, Jan. 14, 1604.

purity, patron of, Jan. 21.

Purkinje, Jan Evangelista, Dec. 17, 1787.

Purl, Linda, Sep. 2, 1955.

Purple Heart, Apr. 7, 1782.

Push Comes to Shove: premiere, Jan. 9, 1976.

Pushkin, Alexander Sergeyevich, Jun. 6, 1799.

Pushtoonistan Day (Afghanistan), Aug. 31.

Putnam, George Palmer, Feb. 7, 1814.

Putnam, Israel, Jan. 7, 1718.

Puzo, Mario, Oct. 15, 1920.

Pya, Martyrs Day (Togo), Jun. 21.

Pyle, Howard, Mar. 5, 1853.

Pyle, Ernest *(Ernie)*, Aug. 3, 1900.

Pynchon, Thomas, May 8, 1937.

Pyongyang (North Korea): captured, Oct. 20, 1950.

Pyramids, Battle of, Jul. 21, 1798.

Q

Qabus ibn Said (Oman), Nov. 18, 1942; Jul. 23, 1970; Aug. 10, 1970.

Qadhafi, Mu'ammar al-, Sep. 1, 1969; Apr. 15, 1986.

Qatar, Sep. I, 1971.

Quadruple Alliance, Apr. 22, 1834.

quadruplets: first test-tube, Jan. 6, 1984.

Quaid, Dennis, Apr. 9, 1954.

Quaid-es-Azan Birthday of (Pakistan), Dec. 25.

Quaid, Randy, May 11, 1950.

Quaid, Randy, Oct. 1, 1950.

Quakers, Oct. 14, 1656; hanged in Massachusetts, Oct. 27, 1659.

Quang Duc: suicide, Jun. 11, 1963.

Quant, Mary, Feb. 11, 1934.

Quantrill, William Clarke, Jul. 31, 1839.

quantum mechanics, Nov. 3, 1954.

Quarter Day (Great Britain), Mar. 25.

Quartering Act: passed, Jun. 2, 1774.

Quasimodo, Salvatore, Aug. 20, 1901.

Quatro, Suzi, Jun. 3, 1950.

Quayle, Anthony, Sep. 7, 1913.

Quayle, Dan, Feb. 4, 1947; Jan. 20, 1989.

Quebec, Canada, Jul. 3, 1608; Oct. 30, 1995.

Quebec Act, May 20, 1774.

Queen Aishworya's Birthday (Nepal), Nov. 7.

Queen Elizabeth, S.S., Jan. 9, 1972.

Queen Isabella Day (Spain), Apr. 22.

Queen Margrethe's Birthday (Denmark), Apr. 16.

Queen Noor, Aug. 23, 1951.

Queen's Birthday (Fiji), Jun. 15.

Queen's Birthday (Netherlands and Netherlands Antilles), Apr. 30.

Queen's Birthday (Thailand), Aug. 12.

Queen's Official Birthday (U.K.), Jun. intro.

Queen's University (Ireland): founded, Aug. 15, 1850.

Queensboro Bridge, Mar. 30, 1909.

Queensbury, Marquis of: boxing rules, Sep. 7, 1892.

Queenship of Mary, Aug. 22.

Queiroz, Francisco Teixeira de, May 3, 1848.

Quental, Antero de, Apr. 18, 1842.

Quesnay, Francois, Jun. 4, 1694.

Quetelet, Adolphe, Feb. 22, 1796.

Quetta (India): earthquake, May 31, 1935.

Quevedo y Villegas, Francisco Gomez de, Sep. 17, 1580.

Quezon y Molina, Manuel Luis, Aug. 19, 1878; Sep. 17, 1935. Aug. 1, 1944.

Quiberon (France), Nov. 20, 1759.

Quidde, Ludwig, Mar. 23, 1858.

The Quiet American: published, Mar. 9, 1956.

Quiet City: premiere, Jan. 28, 1941.

Quiet Flows the Don: opens, Oct. 22, 1935.

Quill, Timothy E., Apr. 20, 1949.

Quimby, Edith H., Jul. 10, 1891.

Quimby, Harriet, Apr. 16, 1912.

Quindlen, Anna, Jul. 8, 1952.

Quinlan, Karen Ann, Mar. 29, 1954; Mar. 31, 1976.

Quinlan, Kathleen, Nov. 19, 1954.

Quinn, Aidan, Mar. 8, 1959.

Quinn, Anthony, Apr. 21, 1915.

Quinn, Sally, Jul. 1, 1941.

Quintero, Jose, Oct. 15, 1924.

Quintilis, Jul. intro.

Quisling, Vidkun, Jul. 18, 1887; Feb. 1, 1942.

Quito, Day of (Ecuador), Dec. 6.

R

Rabbinical Assembly of Conservative Judaism, Feb. 14, 1985.

Rabbitt, Edward Thomas *(Eddie)*, Nov. 27, 1941.

Rabe, David William, Mar. 10, 1940.

Rabi, I(sidor) I(saac), Jul. 29, 1898.

Rabin, Yitzhak, Mar. 1, 1922. Apr. 8, 1977; Prime Minister, Feb. 16, 1992; signs an accord with Arafat, May 5, 1994; assassinated, Nov. 4, 1995; Amir, Yigal, Mar. 27, 1996.

Rabinowitz, Solomon, Feb. 18, 1854.

Rabuka, Sitiveni, May 14, 1987.

Race, Day of the, Oct. 12.

Race Relations Sunday (U.S.), Feb. intro.

Rachmaninoff, Sergei, Apr. 1, 1873; Feb. 8, 1908; American debut, Nov. 4, 1909; Nov. 7, 1934, Jan. 3, 1941.

Rachmaninoff's *Second Symphony in Minor*: premiere, Feb. 8, 1908.

racial discrimination: prohibited, Jun. 17, 1968.

racial integration: Arkansas, Sep. 24, 1957; begins in U.S. stores, Oct. 17, 1960; National Guard (U.S.), Apr. 3, 1962. racial quotas, Jan. 17, 1984.

racial segregation, Nov. 13, 1956.

racial violence: Detroit (Michigan), Jul. 23, 1967.

Racine, Jean, Dec. 22, 1639.

Rackham, Arthur, Sep. 19, 1867.

Radcliffe, Ann, Jul. 9, 1764.

Radcliffe Library (Oxford University), Apr. 13, 1749.

Radetzky, Joseph Wenzel, Nov. 2, 1766.

Radford, Arthur William, Feb. 27, 1896.

radio: transmission, Dec. 12, 1901; first composition, Mar. 5, 1907; first commercial broadcast, Aug. 20, 1920.

Radio City Music Hall: opens, Dec. 27, 1932.

Radio Corp. of America, Jan. 10, 1949; May 21, 1986.

radio signal: first transatlantic, Dec. 11, 1901.

radio transmission of a musical score, first, Dec. 28, 1937.

radioactivity, Dec. 12, 1903.

radiotelephone: first between plane and ground, Aug. 18, 1917.

Radishchev, Aleksandr Nikolayevich, Aug. 20, 1749.

Radner, Gilda, Jun. 28, 1946.

Rado, James, Oct. 29, 1967.

Rae, Charlotte, Apr. 22, 1926.

Raeder, Erich, Apr. 24, 1876.

Raemaekers, Louis, Apr. 6, 1869.

Raffin, Deborah, Mar. 13, 1953.

Rafsanjani, Ali Akbar, elected, Jul. 28, 1989.

Raft, George, Sep. 26, 1895.

Raglan, Fitzroy James Henry Somerset, Sep. 30, 1788.

Ragni, Gerome, Oct. 29, 1967.

Ragtime, Jan. 8, 1976.

Ragweed Month, National, Jun. intro.

Rahman, Abdul, Aug. 28, 1957; inaugurated, Sep. 16, 1963.

Rahman, Mujibur (Sheikh), Mar. 26, 1971; inaugurated, Jan. 12, 1972; Jan. 25, 1975; Feb. 24, 1975; assassinated, Aug. 15, 1975.

Rahman, Ziaur, Nov. 7, 1975; inaugurated, Apr. 21, 1977; killed, May 30, 1981.

Raikes, Robert, Jul. 4, 1736.

railroad: first locomotive traction, Sep. 27, 1825.

Rainbow Bridge: opens, Nov. 1, 1941.

Raines, Cristina, Feb. 28, 1953.

Raines, Franklin, Jan. 14, 1949.

Raines, Tim(othy), Sep. 16, 1959.

Rainey, Joseph Hayne, Jun. 21, 1832.

Rainey, Ma, Apr. 26, 1886.

Rainier III (Prince of Monaco), May 31, 1923; crowned, Nov. 19, 1949.

Rains, Claude, Nov. 10, 1889.

Rainwater, L. James, Dec. 9, 1917.

A Raisin in the Sun: opens, Mar. 11, 1959.

Raitt, Bonnie, Nov. 8, 1949.

Rajk, Laslo: executed, Oct. 15, 1949.

Rajneesh, Bhagwan Shree, Dec. 11, 1931.

Rakoczi II, Ferenc (Transylvania), Mar. 27, 1676.

Rakowski, Mieczyslaw, Sep. 27, 1988.

Rama IX (Thailand), May 5, 1950.

Ramakrishna, Feb. 18, 1836.

Raman, Sir Chandrasekhara Venkata, Nov. 7, 1888.

Rambo, Dack, Nov. 13, 1941.

Ramillies, Battle of, May 23, 1706.

Ramirez, Pedro, Jun. 4, 1943; Mar. 10, 1944.

Ramis, Harold, Nov. 21, 1944.

Ramo, Roberta Cooper, Aug. 8, 1942.

Ramon y Cajal, Santiago, May 1, 1852.

Ramos, Fidel V., elected, Jun. 30, 1992.

Ramos, Joao de Deus, Mar. 8, 1830.

Ramos-Horta, Jose, Dec. 26, 1949.

Rampal, Jean-Pierre Louis, Jan. 7, 1922.

Ramsay, Sir William, Oct. 2, 1852.

Ramsey, Michael (Archbishop of Canterbury), Jun. 27, 1961; Mar. 23, 1966; May 14, 1974.

Ramsey, Norman F., Aug. 27, 1915.

Rana, Chandra, May 1, 1948.

Rana, Padma, May 1, 1948.

Rand, Ayn, Feb. 2, 1905.

Rand, James Henry, May 29, 1859.

Rand, Sally, Jan. 2, 1904.

Randall, Tony, Feb. 26, 1924.

Randi, James, Aug. 7, 1928.

Randolf, Asa Philip, Apr. 15, 1889.

Randolph, Edmund Jennings, Aug. 10, 1753.

Randolph, Jennings, Mar. 8, 1902.

Randolph, John, Jun. 2, 1773.

Ranger I, Aug. 23, 1961.

Ranger 6, lunar probe, Feb. 2, 1964.

Ranger 7, Jul. 31, 1964.

Ranger 8, Feb. 20, 1965.

Ranger 9, Mar. 24, 1965.

Ranger, U.S.S.: first aircraft carrier, Feb. 25, 1933

Rangoon (Burma), May 4, 1824. May 3, 1945.

Ranier III, (Prince of Monaco), May 31, 1923.

Ranke, Leopold von, Dec. 21, 1795.

Rankin, Jeannette, Jun. 11, 1880; Mar. 4, 1917.

Rankine, William John McQuorn, Jul. 5, 1820.

Ransom, John Crowe, Apr. 30, 1888.

Rao, P. V. Narasimha,

Rapallo, Treaty of, Apr. 16, 1922.

Raphael, Mar. 28, 1483.

Raphael, Sally Jessie, Feb. 25, 1943.

Rapp, George, Nov. 1, 1757.

Rasmussen, Knud Johan Victor, Jun. 7, 1879.

Raspberry, William, Oct. 12, 1935.

Rasputin, Grigori Yefimovich: assassinated, Dec. 30, 1916; Jan. 1, 1917.

Rastatt, Peace of, Mar. 6, 1714.

Rathbone, Basil, Jun. 13, 1892.

Rathenau, Emil, Dec. 11, 1838.

Rather, Dan(iel), Oct. 31, 1931.

Ratification Day (U.S.), Jan. 14.

Ratisbon, Diet of, Feb. 25, 1803.

Ratisbon, Treaty of, Aug. 15, 1684.

Ratsimandrava, Richard: assassinated, Feb. 11, 1975.

Ratsiraka, Didier, Nov. 4, 1936.

Rattigan, Sir Terence (Mervyn), Jun. 10, 1911.

Rau, Sir Bengal Narsing, Feb. 26, 1887.

Rauschenberg, Robert, Oct. 22, 1925.

Rauschning, Hermann, Jul. 8, 1887.

Ravel, Maurice, Mar. 7, 1875; Mar. 5, 1904; May 17, 1904; Jan. 12, 1907; Jun. 8, 1912; Nov. 22, 1928.

Ravel's *String Quartet in F*: premiere, Mar. 5, 1904

Ravenna, Mar. 5, 493.

Ravenna, Battle of, Apr. 11, 1512.

Rawalpindi, Mar. 12, 1849.

Rawalpindi, Treaty of, Aug. 8, 1919.

Rawlings, Jerry, Jun. 22, 1947; Jun. 16, 1979.

Rawlings, Marjorie Kinnan, Aug. 8, 1896.

Rawls, Lou, Dec. 1, 1935.

Rawson, Arturo, Jun. 4, 1943.

Ray, Charlotte, Jan. 12, 1850.

Ray, Dixy Lee, Sep. 3, 1914; Feb. 6, 1973.

Ray, James Earl, Mar. 10, 1928; Jun. 8, 1968; Mar. 10, 1969.

Ray, John Alvin (*Johnnie*), Jan. 10, 1927.

Ray, Man, Aug. 27, 1890.

Ray, Satyajit, May 2, 1921.

Rayburn, Gene, Dec. 22, 1917.

Rayburn, Sam Taliaferro, Jan. 6, 1882.

Raye, Martha, Aug. 27, 1916.

The Razor's Edge: published, Apr. 20, 1944.

Read, A.C., May 27, 1919.

Read, Piers Paul, Mar. 7, 1941.

Reagan, Maureen, Jan. 4, 1941.

Reagan, Nancy Davis, Jul. 6, 1921.

Reagan, Ronald, Feb. 6, 1911; inaugurated, Jan. 20, 1981; shot, Mar. 30, 1981; Jun. 21, 1982; reelected, Nov. 6, 1984; Jan. 20, 1985. Nov. 13, 1986; Jan. 5, 1987; Nov. 18, 1987; signs INF treaty Dec. 8, 1987; nuclear weapons treaty, Dec. 8, 1987; January 2, 1989.

reaper: patented, Jun. 21, 1834.

Rear Window: premiere, Aug. 4, 1954.

Reasoner, Harry, Apr. 17, 1923.

Reaumur, Rene A. F. de, Feb. 28, 1683.

The Rebel: published, Jan. 11, 1954.

Rebel Without a Cause: premiere, Oct. 26, 1955.

Rebildfest (Denmark), Jul. 4.

Rebozo, Bebe, Nov. 17, 1912.

Reconciliation Day (Slovakia), Nov. 1.

Reconstruction Act: passed, Mar. 2, 1867.

Reconstruction Finance Corporation: established, Feb. 2, 1932.

Red Army, Aug. 26, 1924.

Red Baron, Apr. 21, 1918.

Red Brigade, Mar. 16, 1978; May 9, 1978; May 3, 1979; Dec. 17, 1981; Jan. 28, 1982.

Red Cross Day, May 8.

Red Cross Month, Apr. intro.

Red Cross Society, American, May 21, 1881.

Red Dye No. 2, Jan. 19, 1976.

The Red Skeleton Show: television debut, Sep. 30, 1951.

red terror: begins, Dec. 20, 1917.

Redding, Otis, Sep. 9, 1941.

Reddy, Helen, Oct. 25, 1941.

Redemption Day (Ghana), Jan. 13.

Redentore, II (Venice), Jul. intro.

Redford, Robert, Aug. 18, 1937; Dec. 25, 1973.

Redgrave, Lynn, Mar. 8, 1943.

Redgrave, Sir Michael, Mar. 20, 1908.

Redgrave, Vanessa, Jan. 30, 1937.

Redshirts, May 5, 1860.

Redwood National Park, Oct. 2, 1968.

Reed, Sir Carol, Dec. 30, 1906.

Reed Dance Day (Swaziland), Aug. 24.

Reed, Donna, Jan. 27, 1921.

Reed, Frank, Apr. 30, 1990.

Reed, Jerry, Mar. 20, 1937.

Reed, John, Oct. 22, 1887.

Reed, Lou, Mar. 2, 1944.

Reed, Oliver, Feb. 13, 1938.

Reed, Pamela, Apr. 2, 1949.

Reed, Rex, Oct. 2, 1939.

Reed, Robert, Oct. 19, 1932.

Reed, Stanley F(orman), Dec. 31, 1884.

Reed, Walter, Sep. 13, 1851.

Reese, Della, Jul. 6, 1932.

Reese, Pee Wee, Jul. 23, 1919.

Reeve, Christopher, Sep. 25, 1952.

Reeves, Keanu, Sep. 2, 1964.

Reeves, Martha, Jul. 18, 1941.

Referendum Day (Guinea), Sep. 28.

referendum and initiative devices: adopted by Oregon, Jun. 2, 1902.

Reform Act: passed in Great Britain, Jun. 4, 1832.

Reform Movement's Anniversary (Yemen Arab Republic), Jun. 13.

Reformation Day, Oct. 31.

Reformation Day (Slovenia), Oct. 31.

reformed drunkards, patron of, Nov. 11.

refugees: South Vietnam, May 1, 1975.

Regan, Donald Thomas, Dec. 21, 1918; Feb. 27, 1987.

Regatta Day (Hawaii), Mar. 26.

Regency Act, Feb. 5, 1811.

Regine, Dec. 26, 1929.

Rehabilitation Act, Sep. 26, 1973.

Rehabilitation Week, National, Sep. intro.

Rehnquist, William, Oct. 1, 1924; Jan. 7, 1972; Sep. 17, 1986; Sep. 26, 1986.

Reich, Wilhelm, Mar. 24, 1897.

Reich, Robert, Jun. 23, 1946.

Reichelderfer, F(rancis) W(ilton), Aug. 6, 1895.

Reichstag: first opens, Mar. 21, 1871; Feb. 27, 1933.

Reichstein, Tadeusz, Jul. 20, 1897.

Reid, Ptolemy, Aug. 11, 1984.

Reid, Tim, Dec. 19, 1944.

Reid, Wallace, Apr. 15, 1891.

Reign of Terror, May 31, 1793; Jun. 2, 1793; Jun. 4, 1793; Jul. 28, 1794.

Reilly, Charles Nelson, Jan. 13, 1931.

Reims Cathedral: bombardment of, Sep. 19, 1914.

Reiner, Carl, Mar. 20, 1922.

Reiner, Fritz, Dec. 19, 1888.

Reiner, Rob(ert), Mar. 6, 1947.

Reines, Frederick, Mar. 16, 1918.

Reinhold, Judge, May 21, 1956.

Reinking, Ann, Nov. 10, 1949.

Reisenweber's Restaurant, Jan. 17, 1917.

Reiser, Paul, Mar. 30, 1957.

Reitman, Ivan, Oct. 27, 1946.

religious education, patron of, Nov. 4.

Remagen Bridge, Mar. 7, 1945.

Remarque, Erich Maria, Jun. 22, 1898.

Rembrandt, Jul. 15, 1606.

Remembrance Day (Canada, Bermuda), Nov. 11.

Remembrance Day (Cayman Islands), Nov. intro.

Remembrance Day (Papua New Guinea), Jul. 23.

Remembrance Day (Turks and Caicos Islands), Nov. 9.

Remick, Lee, Dec. 14, 1935.

Remington, Frederic, Oct. 4, 1861.

Remon, Jose Antonio: assassinated, Jan. 2, 1955.

Remsen, Ira, Feb. 10, 1846.

Renaissance, Roman, May 6, 1527.

Renan, Ernest, Feb. 28, 1823.

Renault, Mary, Sep. 4, 1905.

Rene, France-Albert, Nov. 16, 1935.

Renewal Anniversary of (Gabon Republic), Mar. 12.

Reni, Guido, Nov. 4, 1575.

Renner, Karl, Apr. 13, 1945.

Rennie, John, Jun. 7, 1761.

Reno, Janet, Jul. 21, 1938; Mar. 12, 1993.

Renoir, Jean, Sep. 15, 1894.

Renoir, Pierre Auguste, Feb. 25, 1841.

Renovation Day (Gabon Republic), Mar. 12.

Renwick, James, Nov. 1, 1818.

repentant women, patron of, Jul. 22.

Representatives, U.S. House of, May 9, 1974.

Republic Anniversary Day (Sierra Leone), Apr. 19.

Republic Day (Croatia), May 30.

Republic Day (Cyprus, Turkey), Oct. 29.

Republic Day (Gambia), Feb. 18.

Republic Day (Guyana), Feb. 23.

Republic Day (Macao), Sep. 5.

Republic Day (Malawi), Jul. 6.

Republic Day (Maldives), Nov. 11; Nov. 12.

Republic Day (Malta), Dec. 13.

Republic Day (Portugal), Oct. 5.

Republic Day (Republic of South Africa, Namibia), May 31.

Republic Day (Romania), Dec. 30.

Republic Day (Trinidad, Tobago), Sep. 24.

Republic Day (Tunisia), Jul. 25.

Republic, Day of the (Yugoslavia), Nov. 29; Nov. 30.

Republic of Togo, Apr. 27, 1960.

Republican National Committee: first woman head of, Sep. 16, 1974.

Republican Party: first state convention, Jul. 6, 1854.

Resaca de la Palma, Battle of, May 9, 1846.

Resistance Day (Burma), Mar. 27.

Resnais, Alain, Jun. 3, 1922; May 16, 1960.

Resnik, Judith (Judy), Apr. 5, 1949.

Respect: recorded, Feb. 14, 1967.

Respect for Ancestors Day (China), Apr. 5.

Respect for the Aged Day (Japan), Sep. 15.

restaurateurs, patron of, Aug. 10.

Restif Nicolas-Edme, Oct. 23, 1734.

Restitution, Edict of, Mar. 6, 1629.

Reston, James Barrett, Nov. 3, 1909.

Restoration of Independence (Portugal), Dec. 1.

Restoration of the Republic (Dominican Republic), Aug. 16.

retirement age, mandatory, Apr. 6, 1978.

retirement plans, Jul. 6, 1983.

retreats, patron of, Jul. 31.

Retton, Mary Lou, Jan. 24, 1968.

Reuben, David Robert, Nov. 29, 1933.

Reuben James, U.S.S.: sunk, Oct. 31, 1941.

Reuss, Henry S., Feb. 22, 1912.

Reuter, Baron Paul Julius von, Jul. 21, 1816.

Reuther, Walter (Philip), Sep. 1, 1907.

Revels, Hiram Rhodes, Sep. 1, 1822.

Revenue Cutter Service, Jan. 28, 1915.

Revenue Reconciliation Act, Aug. 10, 1993.

revenue sharing, Mar. 31, 1983.

Revere, Paul, Jan. 1, 1735; Apr. 18, 1775.

Revolution of 1830 (France), Jul. 29, 1830.

Revolution of 1905 (Russia), Jan. 22, 1905.

Revolution of 1917 (Russia), Nov. 6, 1917.

Revolution, American: begins, Apr. 19, 1775; Sep. 15, 1776.

Revolution, Anniversary of the
(Algeria), Nov. 1.

Revolution Anniversary (Egypt), Jul.
23.

Revolution Anniversary (Panama),
Oct. 11.

Revolution Anniversary (Somali
Democratic Republic), Oct. 21;
Oct. 22.

Revolution Day (Congo), Jul. 31.

Revolution Day (El Salvador), Oct.
15.

Revolution Day (Ghana), Dec. 31.

Revolution Day (Guatemala), Oct.
20.

Revolution Day (Iran), Feb. 15; Apr.
2.

Revolution Day (Libya), Sep. 1.

Revolution Day (Sudan), May 25.

Revolution Day (Syria), Mar. 8.

Revolution Day (Yemen Arab
Republic), Sep. 26.

Revolutionary Council of Iran, Mar.
16, 1979.

Revolutionary Recovery Day
(Algeria), Jun. 19.

Revolutionary Tribunal (Cheka):
established, Dec. 20, 1917.

Revolutionary Tribunal (France):
abolished, Dec. 15, 1794.

Revson, Charles (Haskell), Oct. 11,
1906.

Revson, Peter Jeffrey, Feb. 27, 1939.

Rexroth, Kenneth, Dec. 22, 1905.

Rey, Alejandro, Feb. 8, 1930.

Reymont, Wladislaw Stanislaw, May
6, 1867.

Reynaud, Paul, Oct. 15, 1878.

Reynolds, Burt, Feb. 11, 1936.

Reynolds, Debbie (Marie Frances),
Apr. 1, 1932.

Reynolds, Frank, Nov. 29, 1923.

Reynolds, Sir Joshua, Jul. 16, 1723.

Reza Khan, Feb. 21, 1921.

Rhapsody in Blue: premiere, Feb.
12, 1924.

Rhapsody on a Theme by Paganini:
premiere, Nov. 7, 1934.

Rhee, Syngman (Republic of Korea):
first President, Apr. 26, 1875;
Aug. 15, 1948; Jun. 28, 1950;
Sep. 29, 1950; Mar. 15, 1960.

Rheims (France): bombarded, Sep.
18, 1914.

Rhine, Mar. 7, 1945.

Rhine, J(oseph) B(anks), Sep. 19,
1895.

Rhineland Campaign, Sep. 15, 1944.

Rhode Island, Sep. 13, 1635; Mar.
24, 1644; slavery law, May 18,
1652; May 4, 1776 May 29, 1790.

Rhodes, Cecil, Jul. 5, 1853; Oct. 29,
1889; Jul. 17, 1890; Jan. 6, 1896;
Dec. 5, 1897.

Rhodes, John J., Sep. 18, 1916.

Rhodes Scholarships, Dec. 19, 1976.

Rhodes, Zandra, Sep. 11, 1940.

Rhodesia: name given, May 3, 1895;
Dec. 31, 1963; Nov. 11, 1965;
Jan. 5, 1967; Apr. 10, 1968; Mar.
2, 1970; Apr. 4, 1975; Jul. 5,
1977; Mar. 14, 1978; Apr. 12,
1978; Feb. 28, 1979; Apr. 21,
1979; May 31, 1979; Apr. 17,
1980.

Rhodesia, Northern (Zambia), Mar.
29, 1963; Jan. 22, 1964.

Rhodesia, Southern: becomes self-
governing colony, Oct. 1, 1923;
Apr. 11, 1963; Apr. 13, 1964.

Rhys, Jean, Aug. 24, 1894.

Ribbentrop, Joachim von, Apr. 30,
1893; executed, Oct. 16, 1946.

Ribicoff, Abraham A., Apr. 9, 1910.

Ricardo, David, Apr. 19, 1772.

Ricci, Christina, Feb. 12, 1980.

Rice, Anne, Oct. 4, 1941.

Rice, Elmer (Leopold), Sep. 28,
1892.

Rice, (Henry) Grantland, Nov. 1,
1880.

Rice, Jerry, Oct. 13, 1962.

Rice, Tim, Oct. 12, 1971.

Rice, Tom, Jun. 21, 1978.

Rich, Adam, Oct. 12, 1968.

Rich, Adrienne, May 16, 1929.

Rich, Buddy, Jun. 30, 1917.

Rich, Charles Allan *(Charlie)*, Dec.
14, 1932.

Rich Man, Poor Man: television
debut, Feb. 1, 1976.

Richard I (England), Sep. 8, 1157;
Nov. 18, 1188; Jul. 6, 1189; Dec.
5, 1189 Jul. 1, 1190; Oct.4, 1190;
Jul. 12, 1191; Aug. 1, 1192; Dec.
21, 1192; Feb. 3, 1194; Apr. 17,
1194; Jul. 22, 1194; dies, Apr. 6,
1199.

Richard II (England), Jan. 6, 1367;
Jun. 21, 1377; Jun. 22, 1377;
Feb. 3, 1388; Sep. 30, 1399;
murdered, Feb. 14, 1400.

Richard III (England), Oct. 2, 1452;
Jun. 26, 1483; killed, Aug. 22,
1485.

Richard, Cliff, Oct. 14, 1940.

Richard (Duke of York), May 22,
1455. Jul. 10, 1460; killed, Dec.
30, 1460.

Richard, Gabriel, Oct. 15, 1767.

Richard of Gloucester (England),
Jun. 26, 1483.

Richards, Keith, Nov. 18, 1943.

Richards, Dickinson W., Jr., Oct. 30,
1895.

Richards, Laura Elizabeth, Feb. 27,
1850.

Richards, Renee, Aug. 19, 1934.

Richards, Theodore William, Jan. 31,
1868.

Richardson, Elliott, Jul. 20, 1920;
resigns, Oct. 20, 1973.

Richardson, Henry Hobson, Sep. 29,
1838.

Richardson, Miranda, Mar. 3, 1958.

Richardson, Miranda, Mar. 3, 1958.

Richardson, Sir Owen Willans, Apr.
26, 1879.

Richardson, Sir Ralph David, Dec.
19, 1902.

Richardson, Robert C., Jun. 26, 1937.

Richardson, Samuel, Aug. 19, 1689.

Richardson, Sid, Apr. 25, 1891.

Richardson, Tony, Jun. 5, 1929.

Richelieu, Cardinal de: becomes first
Chief Minister of France, Aug.
13, 1624; Nov. 11, 1630; Jan. 29,
1635.

Richelieu, Duc de (Armand Jean de
Plessis), Sep. 9, 1585.

Richet, Charles R., Aug. 25, 1850.

Richman, Harry, Aug. 10, 1895.

Richmond (Virginia): surrender, Apr.
3, 1865.

Richter, Burton, Mar. 22, 1931.

Richter, Charles Francis, Apr. 26,
1900.

Richter, Gerhard, Feb. 9, 1932.

Richter, Hans, Apr. 4, 1843; Jun. 9,
1902.

Richter, Jean Paul Friedrich, Mar. 21,
1763.

Richthofen, Manfred von, May 2, 1892; dies Apr. 21, 1918.

Rickenbacker, Edward (Vernon), Oct. 8, 1890.

Rickey, Branch (Wesley), Dec. 20, 1881.

Rickles, Don, May 8, 1926.

Rickover, Hyman George, Jan. 27, 1900.

Riddle, Nelson, Jun. 1, 1921.

Ride, Sally, May 26, 1951; Jun. 24, 1983.

Ridgway, Matthew B., Mar. 3, 1895; May 9, 1951. Apr. 28, 1952.

Riebeeck, Jan van, Apr. 21, 1634; Apr. 6, 1652.

Riegart, Peter, Apr. 11, 1947.

Riegle, Donald Wayne, Jr., Feb. 4, 1938.

Riemann, Georg Friedrich Bernhard, Sep. 17, 1826.

Riga (Latvia), Jan. 4, 1919.

Riga, Treaty of, Mar. 18, 1921.

Rigby, Cathy, Dec. 12, 1952.

Rigg, Diana, Jul. 20, 1938.

Riggins, John, Aug. 4, 1949.

Riggs, Robert Larimore (Bobby), Feb. 25, 1918. Sep. 20, 1973.

Righetti, David Allen (Dave), Nov. 28, 1958.

right to privacy, Jun. 7, 1965.

Righting Day (Algeria), Jun. 19.

Riis, Jacob August, May 3, 1849.

Riley, James Whitcomb, Oct. 7, 1849.

Riley, Jeannie C., Oct. 19, 1945.

Riley, Pat(rick) James, Mar. 20, 1945.

Riley, Richard W., Jan. 3, 1933.

Rilke, Rainer Maria, Dec. 4, 1875.

Rimbaud, (Jean Nicolas) Arthur, Oct. 20, 1854.

Rimes, LeAnn, Aug. 28, 1982.

Rimski-Korsakov, Nicolai, Mar. 6, 1844.

Rimsky-Korsakov, Georgy, Dec. 26, 1901.

Rinaldi, Kathy, Mar. 24, 1967.

Rinehart, Mary Roberts, Aug. 12, 1876.

Ringling, Charles, Dec. 2, 1863.

Ringwald, Molly, Feb. 18, 1968.

Rio de Janeiro, Jan. 1, 1531.

Rio de Janeiro, Treaty of, Aug. 27, 1828.

Rio, Declaration of: signed, Nov. 30, 1965.

Rios, Juan Antonio: inaugurated, Apr. 2, 1942.

Romanovs Rios Montt, Efrain, Mar. 23, 1982; Aug. 8, 1983.

Riotous Assemblies Act (South Africa), Sep. 15, 1977.

Riperton, Minnie, Nov. 8, 1948.

Ripkin, Cal(vin Edwin), Jr., Aug. 24, 1960; Sep. 6, 1995.

Ripley, George, Oct. 3, 1802.

Ripley, Robert Leroy, Dec. 25, 1893.

Ritchard, Cyril, Dec. 1, 1897.

Ritchie, Michael, Nov. 28, 1938.

Rite of Spring, May 29, 1913.

Ritter, Johann Wilhelm, Dec. 16, 1776.

Ritter, Jonathan Southworth (John), Sep. 17, 1948.

Ritter, Tex, Jan. 12, 1907.

Ritter, Thelma, Feb. 14, 1905.

Rivadavia, Bernardino, May 20, 1780.

Rivas Day, Battle of (Costa Rica), Apr. 11.

River Salado, Battle of, Oct. 30, 1340.

Rivera, Chita, Jan. 23, 1933.

Rivera, Diego, Dec. 8, 1886.

Rivera, Geraldo, Jul. 4, 1943.

Rivera, Luis Muñoz, Jul. 17, 1859.

Rivera, Tomas, Dec. 22, 1935.

Rivers, Joan, Oct. 12, 1935.

Rivers, Johnny, Nov. 7, 1942.

Rivers, Larry, Aug. 17, 1923.

Rivers, L(ucius) Mendel, Sep. 28, 1905.

Rivers, William Halse, Mar. 12, 1864.

Rivieres du Sud, Mar. 10, 1893.

Rivlin, Alice Mitchell, Mar. 4, 1931.

Rivoli, Battle of, Jan. 14, 1797.

Rizal Day (Philippines), Dec. 30.

Rizal, Jose Mercado, Jun. 19, 1861.

RJR Nabisco Inc., Nov. 30, 1988.

Roa y Garci, Raul, Apr. 18, 1907.

Roach, Hal, Jan. 14, 1892.

Roanoke Island, North Carolina, Feb. 8, 1862.

Robards, Jason, Dec. 31, 1892. Jul. 22, 1922.

Robb, Charles Spittal, Jun. 26, 1939.

Robbe-Grillet, Alain, Aug. 18, 1922.

Robbia, Luca della, Dec. 22, 1400.

Robbins, Frederick Chapman, Aug. 25, 1916.

Robbins, Harold, May 21, 1916.

Robbins, Jerome, Oct. 11, 1918.

Robbins, Marty, Sep. 26, 1925.

Robbins, Tim, Oct. 16, 1958.

Robert II (Scotland), Mar. 2, 1316; Feb. 22, 1370.

Robert III (Scotland): dies, Apr. 1, 1406.

Robert Bruce (Scotland), Oct. 14, 1322.

Robert E. Lee Day (Kentucky), Feb. 19.

Robert Green, Aug. 11, 1833.

Robert, Henry Martyn, May 2, 1837.

Robert of Normandy, Jul. 19, 1101.

Roberts, Cokie, Dec. 27, 1943.

Roberts, Field Marshal Lord, Jan. 10, 1900.

Roberts, Lord Frederick, Mar. 13, 1900.

Robert's, J.J., Birthday (Liberia), Mar. 15.

Roberts, Julia, Oct. 28, 1967.

Roberts, Kenneth Lewis, Dec. 8, 1885.

Roberts, Oral, Jan. 24, 1918.

Roberts, Pernell, May 18, 1930.

Roberts, Richard J., Sep. 6, 1943.

Roberts, Tony, Oct. 22, 1939.

Robertson, Jaime (Robbie), Jul. 5, 1944.

Robertson, Cliff, Sep. 9, 1923.

Robeson, Paul Leroy, Apr. 9, 1898.

Robespierre, Maximilien Francois Marie Isidore de, May 6, 1758; Jun. 4, 1793; guillotined, Jul. 28, 1794.

Robin Moore: U.S. freighter sunk, May 21, 1941.

Robins A. H. Co., Apr. 2, 1985.

Robinson, Arthur, Dec. 15, 1986.

Robinson, Bill (Bojangles), May 25, 1878.

Robinson, Brooks Calbert, Jr., May 18, 1937.

Robinson, David, Aug. 6, 1965.

Robinson, Edward Arlington, Dec. 22, 1869.

Robinson, Edward G., Dec. 12, 1893.

Robinson, Frank, Aug. 31, 1935; Oct. 3, 1974.

Robinson, Jackie Roosevelt, Jan. 31, 1919. Apr. 11, 1947.

Robinson, James Harvey, Jun. 29, 1863.

Robinson, Larry, Jun. 2, 1951.

Robinson, Mary, May 21, 1944; elected, Nov. 7, 1990.

Robinson, Maurice (Richard), Dec. 24, 1895.

Robinson, Sir Robert, Sep. 13, 1886.

Robinson, *(Sugar)* Ray, May 3, 1920. Dec. 20, 1946; Feb. 14, 1951.

Robinson, William, Jr. *(Smokey),* Feb. 19, 1940.

Robl, James, Jan. 20, 1998.

Robles, Alfonso Garcia, Mar. 20, 1911.

Robson, May, Apr. 19, 1865.

Rocard, Michel, May 10, 1988.

Rochambeau, Comte de, Jul. 1, 1725.

Rochas, Alphonse Beau de, Apr. 9, 1815.

Rochefort, Victor-Henri, Jan. 31, 1830.

Rochelle, La (France), Jun. 23, 1372.

Rochester (Eddie Anderson), Sep. 18, 1905.

Rock and Roll Hall of Fame and Museum, Sep. 1, 1995.

Rockefeller, David, Jun. 12, 1915.

Rockefeller Foundation, May 14, 1913.

Rockefeller, John D., Jr., Jan. 29, 1874; Dec. 14, 1946.

Rockefeller, John D(avison), Jul. 9, 1839.

Rockefeller, John D(avison) IV, Jun. 18, 1937.

Rockefeller, Laurance Spelman, May 26, 1910.

Rockefeller, Nelson, Jul. 8, 1908; nominated as Vice-President, Aug. 20, 1974.

Rockefeller, Winthrop, May 1, 1912.

rocket: first liquid-fuel, Mar. 16, 1926; first to leave atmosphere, Mar. 22, 1946.

Rockne, Knute, Mar. 4, 1888.

Rockwell, George Lincoln, Mar. 9, 1918; killed, Aug. 25, 1967.

Rockwell, Norman, Feb. 3, 1894.

Rocky, Mar. 28, 1977.

Rocky Mountain National Park, Jan. 26, 1915.

Rocroi, Battle of, May 19, 1643.

Rod, Edouard, Mar. 31, 1857.

Rodbell, Martin, Dec. 1, 1925.

Roddenberry, (Eu)gene (Wesley), Aug. 19, 1921.

Rodeo (ballet): premiere, Oct. 16, 1942.

Rodgers, Bill, Dec. 23, 1947.

Rodgers and Hammerstein, Mar. 31, 1943; Mar. 30, 1951.

Rodgers, Richard, Jun. 28, 1902; Apr. 14, 1937; May 11, 1938; Nov. 23, 1938; Dec. 25, 1940; Apr. 19, 1945; Apr. 7, 1949; Dec. 1, 1958.

Rodin, Auguste, Nov. 12, 1840.

Rodino, Peter Wallace, Jr., Jun. 7, 1909.

Rodman, Dennis, May 13, 1961.

Rodney, Caesar, Oct. 7, 1728.

Rodriguez, Andres: inaugurated, Feb. 3, 1989.

Rodriguez, Chi-Chi, Oct. 23, 1934.

Rodriguez, Miguel Angel, elected, Feb. 1, 1998.

Rodriguez Lara, Guillermo, Feb. 15, 1972; overthrown, Jan. 11, 1975.

Roebling, John Augustus, Jun. 12, 1806.

Roebling, Washington Augustus, May 26, 1837.

Roer River (Germany), Nov. 16, 1944.

Roethke, Theodore, May 25, 1908.

Roger II (Sicily), Dec. 25, 1130.

Roger Williams Day (U.S.), Feb. 5.

Rogers, Buddy, Aug. 13, 1904.

Rogers, Carl Ransom, Jan. 8, 1902.

Rogers, Darryl D., May 28, 1935.

Rogers, Don(ald Lavert), Sep. 17, 1962.

Rogers, Fred McFeely, Mar. 20, 1928.

Rogers, Ginger, Jul. 16, 1911.

Rogers, Kenny, Aug. 21, 1938.

Rogers, Mimi, Jan. 27, 1956.

Rogers, Rosemary, Dec. 7, 1933.

Rogers, Roy, Nov. 5, 1912.

Rogers, Wayne, Apr. 7, 1933.

Rogers, Will, Nov. 4, 1879.

Rogers, William Charles *(Bill),* Sep. 10, 1951.

Roget, Peter Mark, Jan. 18, 1779.

Roh Tae Woo: inaugurated, Feb. 25, 1988.

Rohde, Ruth Bryan, Oct. 2, 1885.

Rohm, Ernst, Nov. 28, 1887.

Rohmer, Eric, Mar. 21, 1920.

Rohrer, Heinrich, Jun. 6, 1933.

Rojas Pinilla, Gustavo, Jun. 13, 1953. May 10, 1957.

Roker, Roxie, Aug. 28, 1929.

Roldos Aguilera, Jaime, Apr. 29, 1979; inaugurated, Aug. 10, 1979.

Rolfe, John, Apr. 5, 1614.

Rolland, Romain, Jan. 29, 1866.

Rolle, Esther, Nov. 8, 1933.

Rollin, Betty, Jan. 3, 1936.

Rolling Stones, May 13, 1965.

Rollins, Howard Ellsworth, Jr., Oct. 17, 1950.

Rollins, Sonny, Sep. 7, 1930.

Rolls, Charles Stewart, Aug. 27, 1877.

Rolls-Royce, Ltd.: bankruptcy, Feb. 4, 1971; nationalized, Feb. 23, 1971.

Rolvaag, O. E., Apr. 22, 1876.

Roman Catholic Church, Mar. 17, 19SI; May 26, 1967; Jul. 11, 1967; May 17, 1989; Nov. 16, 1992.

Roman Catholic Mass, Nov. 13, 1962; first in English, Aug. 24, 1964; Jul. 6, 1978.

Roman Catholic missionaries in foreign parts, patron of, Dec. 3.

Roman Catholicism: restored in England, Nov. 30, 1554; religion of Spain, Mar. 16, 1851.

Roman Empire, May 11, 330.

Roman National Assembly, Feb. 8, 1849.

Roman, Petre, resigns, Sep. 27, 1991.

Roman y Reyes, Manuel, Aug. 14, 1947.

Romania: formed, Dec. 23, 1861; independence, Jul, 13, 1878; war with Bulgaria, Jul. 10, 1913; declares war on Austria-Hungary, Aug. 27, 1916; Apr. 9, 1918; Apr. 9, 1918; Dec. 9, 1918; Jan. 10, 1919; Aug. 23, 1944; Apr. 25, 1950; Feb. 24, 1972; Dec. 26, 1989.

Romano, Umberto, Feb. 26, 1906.

Romanovs, Feb. 21, 1613.

Romansch: fourth national language in Switzerland, Dec. 7, 1937.

Romberg, Sigmund, Jul. 29, 1887.

Rome airport: Arab guerilla attack, Dec. 17, 1973.

Rome-Berlin Axis, Oct. 27, 1936.

Rome, Bishop of: authority declared void in England, Jul. 18, 1536.

Rome, Harold Jacob, May 27, 1908.

Rome (Italy): sacked by Alaric, Aug. 24, 410; pillaged, Jul. 15, 455; sack of, May 6, 1527; invaded, Sep. 21, 1870; incorporated with Italy, Oct. 9, 1870; declared capital, Dec. 5, 1870; first governor appointed, Oct. 28, 1925; Jul. 19, 1943; liberated, Jun. 4, 1944; seized by Germans, Sep. 10, 1944; XVII Summer Olympics, Aug. 25, 1960. Rome (Italy), patron of, Jan. 30; Jun. 29.

Rome, Synod of, Dec. 24, 1046.

Rome, Treaty of: signed, Mar. 25, 1957.

Romeo and Juliet (ballet): premiere, Jan. 11, 1940.

Romero, Cesar, Feb. 15, 1907.

Romero, George, Feb. 4, 1940.

Romero, Oscar: assassinated, Mar. 24, 1980.

Romero Pereira, Tomas, May 5, 1954.

Romero y Galdamez, Oscar Arnulfo, Aug. 15, 1917.

Romilly, Sir Samuel, Mar. 1, 1747.

Rommel, Erwin (Johannes Eugin), Nov. 15, 1891; Feb. 9, 1941; Mar. 24, 1941; Jun. 21, 1942; dies, Oct. 14, 1944.

Romney, George Wilcken, Jul. 8, 1907.

Rongji, Zhu, Oct. 1, 1928; Mar. 17, 1998.

Ronne, Finn, Dec. 20, 1899.

Ronsard, Pierre de, Sep. 11, 1524.

Ronstadt, Linda, Jul. 15, 1946.

Rontgen, Wilhelm Konrad, Mar. 27, 1845.

Rooney, Andy, Jan. 14, 1919.

Rooney, Mickey, Sep. 23, 1920.

Roosevelt, Alice, Jul. 29, 1861.

Roosevelt, Edith Kermit Carow, Aug. 16, 1861.

Roosevelt, Eleanor, Oct. 11, 1884.

Roosevelt, Eleanor, Birthday Anniversary, Oct. intro; Oct. 11.

Roosevelt, Eleanor, Death Anniversary of, Nov. intro; Nov. 7.

Roosevelt, Elliot, Sep. 23, 1910.

Roosevelt, Franklin D., Jan. 30, 1882; Jul. 2, 1932; Feb. 15, 1933; inaugurated, Mar. 4, 1933; Mar. 6, 1933; Mar. 12, 1933; May 12, 1933; Jul. 10, 1934; Jul. 11, 1934; Jul. 25, 1934; May 11, 1935; Jun. 26, 1935; Four Freedoms speech, Jan. 6, 1941; Jan. 20, 1941; May 27, 1941; Jul. 26, 1941, Sep. 11, 1941; Nov. 1, 1941; Pearl Harbor speech, Dec. 8, 1941; Dec. 24, 1941; May 12, 1943; Mar. 24, 1944; elected for fourth term, Nov. 7, 1944; dies, Apr. 12, 1945.

Roosevelt, Franklin D., Birthday Anniversary, Jan. intro; Jan. 30.

Roosevelt, Franklin D., Death Anniversary of, Apr. intro; Apr. 12.

Roosevelt, Franklin Delano, Jr., Aug. 17, 1914.

Roosevelt, Theodore, Oct. 27, 1858; Jul. 1, 1898; Mar. 4, 1901; Sep. 14, 1901; Apr. 3, 1903; inaugurated, Mar. 4, 1905; Nov. 9, 1906; Apr. 23, 1909.

Root, Elihu, Feb. 15, 1845.

Root, Elisha, May 10, 1808.

Root, John Wellborn, Jan. 10, 1850.

Root, Waverley L., Apr. 15, 1903.

Roots: television debut, Jan. 23, 1977; Feb. 9, 1977.

ropemakers, patron of, Jun. 29.

Rorem, Ned, Oct. 23, 1923.

Rorschach, Hermann, Nov. 8, 1884.

rose, Jun. intro; U.S. emblem, Oct. 7, 1986.

Rose, Billy, Sep. 6, 1899.

Rose Bowl: first game, Jan. 1, 1902.

Rose Harvest Festival (Bulgaria), Jun. intro.

Rose, Pete(r Edward), Apr. 14, 1941; Aug. 24, 1989.

Rose of Tralee Festival (Ireland), Sep. intro.

Roseanne, Nov. 3, 1953.

Rosecrans, William Starke, Sep. 6, 1819.

Rosemary's Baby: published, Apr. 13, 1967.

Rosen, Moishe, Apr. 12, 1932.

Rosenberg, Ethel, Sep. 28, 1915; Apr. 5, 1951.

Rosenberg, Julius, May 12, 1918; Apr. 5, 1951.

Rosencrantz and Guildenstern: opens, Oct. 16, 1967.

Rosencrantz and Guildenstern Are Dead: premiere, Apr. 11, 1967.

Rosenfeld, Morris, Dec. 28, 1862.

Rosenkavalier, Der: premieres at Dresden Opera, Jan. 26, 1911; premieres in New York, Dec. 9, 1913.

Rosewall, Ken, Nov. 2, 1934.

Ross, Barney, May 31, 1938.

Ross, Betsy, Jan. 1, 1752.

Ross, Diana, Mar. 26, 1944; Jan. 15, 1970.

Ross, Diocese of (Ireland) patron of, Aug. 14.

Ross, Herbert David, May 13, 1927.

Ross, Sir James Clark, Apr. 15, 1800.

Ross, Jerry, May 13, 1954; May 5, 1955.

Ross, Katharine, Jan. 29, 1943.

Ross, Lee Bouvier Radziwill, Mar. 3, 1933.

Ross, Nellie Taylor, Nov. 29, 1876; first U.S. woman governor, Jan. 5, 1925.

Ross, Nellie Taylor, Birthday (Illinois, Nebraska, New Hampshire, Wyoming), Nov. intro.

Ross, Sir Ronald, May 13, 1857.

Rossellini, Isabella, Jun. 18, 1952.

Rossellini, Roberto, May 3, 1906.

Rossen, Robert, Mar. 16, 1908.

Rossetti, Christina (Georgina), Dec. 5, 1830.

Rossetti, Dante Gabriel, May 12, 1828.

Rossini, Gioacchino Antonio, Feb. 29, 1792.

Rossner, Judith, Mar. 1, 1935.

Rostand, Edmond, Apr. 1, 1868.

Rostenkowski, Dan(iel David), Jan. 2, 1928.

Rostow, Eugene Victor, Aug. 25, 1913.

Rostow, Walt Whitman, Oct. 7, 1916.

Rostropovich, Mstislav, Mar. 27, 1927.

Rotary Club International: founded, Feb. 23, 1905.

Rotary Foundation Month, Nov. intro.

Roth, David Lee, Oct. 10, 1955.

Roth, Joe, Jun. 13, 1948.

Roth, Lillian, Dec. 13, 1910.

Roth, Philip, Mar. 19, 1933; Feb. 21, 1969.

Roth, Tim, May 14, 1961.

Rothenbaerg, Susan, Jan. 20, 1945.

Rothko, Mark, Sep. 25, 1903.

Rothschild, Baron Alain de, Jan. 7, 1910.

Rothschild, Baron Guy Edouard Alphonse Paul de, May 21, 1909.

Rothschild, Lionel Nathan, Nov. 22, 1808.

Rothschild, Meyer, Feb. 23, 1743.

Rothschild, Walter Nathan, Apr. 28, 1892.

Rotron, Jean de, Aug. 21, 1609.

Rouen, France, May 30, 1431; first U.S. strategic bombing in Europe, Aug. 17, 1942.

Rough Riders, Jul. 1, 1898.

Roundtree, Richard, Sep. 7, 1942.

Rourke, Mickey, Jul. 16, 1953.

Rous, Francis Peyton, Oct. 5, 1879.

Rousseau, Henri, May 21, 1844.

Rousseau, Jean-Baptiste, Apr. 6, 1671.

Rousseau, Jean-Jacques, Jun. 28, 1712.

Roussillon, Jan. 19, 1493.

Roux, Wilhelm, Jun. 9, 1850.

Rovere, Richard H., May 5, 1915.

Rowan, Carl T., Aug. 11, 1925.

Rowan, Dan, Jul. 2, 1922.

Rowan and Martin's Laugh-In: television debut, Jan. 22, 1968.

Rowe, James Henry, Jr., Jun. 1, 1909.

Rowland, F. Sherwood, Jun. 28, 1927.

Rowlands, Gena, Jun. 19, 1936.

Rowlatt Acts, Mar. 18, 1919; passed in India, Mar. 21, 1919; Mar. 30, 1919.

Roxas y Acuna, Manuel, Jan. 1, 1892; Jul. 4, 1946.

Roy, Patrick, Oct. 5, 1965.

Royal Academy of Italy: created, Jan. 2, 1926.

Royal Air Force, Apr. 1, 1912.

Royal Albert Hall, London: opened, Mar. 29, 1871.

Royal Flying Corps, Apr. 1, 1912.

Royal Indian Navy, Feb. 9, 1926.

Royal Society for the Improvement of Science: chartered, Jul. 15, 1662.

Royal Society of London, Jul. 15, 1662.

Royal University (Italy), Feb. 11, 1875.

Royce, Sir Frederick Henry, Mar. 27, 1863.

Royce, Josiah, Nov. 20, 1855.

Royko, Mike, Sep. 19, 1932.

Rozanov, (General), Jan. 30, 1920.

Rozelle, Pete, Mar. 1, 1926.

Rozema, David Scott *(Dave)*, Aug. 5, 1956.

Rozier, Jean Francois Pilatre de, Nov. 21, 1783; first balloon ascent, Oct. 15, 1788.

Ruark, Robert (Chester), Dec. 29, 1915.

Rub a Bald Head Week, National, Sep. intro.

rubber rationing: begins in U.S., Dec. 27, 1941.

rubber vulcanization: patented, Jun. 15, 1844.

Rubbia, Carlo, Mar. 31, 1934.

Rubens, Peter Paul, Jun. 28, 1577.

Rubenstein, Ida, Nov. 22, 1928.

Rubin, Jerry, Jul. 14, 1938.

Rubin, Robert, Jan. 10, 1995.

Rubinstein, Anton Grigorievich, Nov. 28, 1829.

Rubinstein, Arthur, Jan. 28, 1887.

Rubinstein, John, Dec. 8, 1946.

ruby, Jul. intro.

Ruby, Jack, Nov. 24, 1963; Mar. 14, 1964; Jan. 3, 1967.

Ruehl, Mercedes, Feb. 28, 1945.

Ruekleshaus, William Doyle, Jul. 24, 1934.

Rudolf I (Germany), May 1, 1218.

Rudolf II (Holy Roman Emperor), Oct. 12, 1576; May 23, 1611; dies, Jan. 20, 1612.

Rudolf (Duke of Swabia), Mar. 15, 1077; killed, Oct. 15, 1080.

Rudolph (Archduke of Austria), Jan. 30, 1889.

Rudolph, Wilma, Jun. 23, 1940.

Ruggles, Charles, Feb. 8, 1886.

Ruiz Cortines, Adolfo: inaugurated, Dec. 1, 1952.

Rukeyser, Louis Richard, Jan. 30, 1933.

Rukeyser, Muriel, Dec. 15, 1913.

Rukeyser, William Simon, Jun. 8, 1939.

Rumania. *See*: Romania.

Rummel, Archbishop Joseph Francis, Mar. 27, 1962.

Rumsey, James, Dec. 20, 1743.

Rumsfeld, Donald, Jul. 9, 1932.

Runcie, Robert (Archbishop of Canterbury), Oct. 2, 1921; Sep. 7, 1979.

Rundstedt, Karl Rudolf von, Dec. 12, 1875.

Runeberg's Day (Finland), Feb. 5.

Runnymede (England), May 14, 1965.

Runyon, (Alfred) Damon, Oct. 4, 1884.

Ruppee, Loret Miller, Jan. 3, 1936.

Rural Electrifieation Administration, May 11, 1935.

rural free delivery: begins, Oct. 1, 1896.

Rush, Barbara, Jan. 4, 1929.

Rush, 8enjamin, Dec. 24, 1745.

Rushdie, Salman, Feb. 15, 1989.

Rushing, Jimmy, Aug. 26, 1903.

Rusk, Dean, Feb. 9, 1909.

Ruska, Ernst, Dec. 25, 1906.

Ruskin, John, Feb. 8, 1819.

Russell, Bertrand, May 18, 1872.

Russell, George William, Apr. 10, 1867.

Russell, Henry Norris, Oct. 25, 1877.

Russell, Jane, Jun. 21, 1921.

Russell, Ken, Jul. 3, 1927.

Russell, Kurt (Von Vogel), Mar. 17, 1951.

Russell, Leon, Apr. 2, 1941.

Russell, Lillian, Dec. 4, 1861.

Russell, Mark, Aug. 23, 1932.

Russell, Nipsey, Oct. 13, 1924.

Russell, Pee Wee, Mar. 27, 1906.

Russell, Richard B., Nov. 2, 1897.

Russell, Rosalind, Jun. 4, 1911.

Russell, William Felton *(Bill)*, Feb. 12, 1934.

Russell, William Hepburn, Jan. 31, 1812.

Russia, Jan. 15, 1582; Seven Years War, Jan. 10, 1757; Jan. 9, 1792; Jan. 23, 1793; French invasion, Jun. 22, 1812; emancipation of serfs, Mar. 3, 1861; May 15, 1867; first parliamentary elections, Apr. 1, 1906; declares war on Turkey, Nov. 2, 1914; Mar. 20, 1915; provisional government recognized, Mar. 22, 1917; Jan. 12, 1918; Jan. 28, 1918. *See also*: U.S.S.R.

Russia, patron of, Nov. 13; Nov. 30; Dec. 6.

Russian Christmas, Jan. 7.

Russian Church: confiscation by Bolsheviks, Dec. 17, 1917

Russian monarchy: 1,000th anniversary, Sep. 20, 1862.

Russian Orthodox Church, Jun. 12, 1988.

Russian Revolution, Jan. 7, 1895; Mar. 8, 1917; Mar. 10, 1917; Mar. 17, 1917; Mar. 27, 1917; May 24, 1917; Czar imprisoned in Siberia, Aug. 15, 1917; Nov. 7, 1917; Jan. 10, 1918; Jan. 4, 1919; Jan. 5, 1919; Jan. 30, 1920.

Russian serfs: liberation of, Apr. 3, 1861.

Russian State Bank: opens, Nov. 15, 1921.

Russian workers: establish first soviet, Oct. 26, 1905.

Russians, Jan. 26, 1915.

Russo-Finnish War, Nov. 30, 1939; ends, Mar. 12, 1940.

Russo-Japanese War, Feb. 4, 1904; Feb. 9, 1904; Jan. 2, 1905; May 27, 1905; ends, Aug. 9, 1905; ends, Sep. 5, 1905.

Russo-Turkish War, Sep. 14, 1829; treaty ending, Mar. 3, 1878.

Rustin, Bayard, Mar. 17, 1910.

Rutan, Dick, Dec. 23, 1986.

Rutgers, Henry, Oct. 7, 1745.

Ruth, Babe, Feb. 6, 1895; Sep. 22, 1969.

Rutherford, Ann, Nov. 2, 1917.

Rutherford, Dame, Margaret, May 11, 1892.

Rutherford, Ernest (1st Baron Rutherford of Nelson), Aug. 30, 1871.

Rutherford, Joseph Franklin, Nov. 8, 1869.

Rutledge, Edward, Nov. 23, 1749.

Rutledge, Wiley, Feb. 8, 1943.

Ruyter, Michiel Adriaanszoon de, Mar. 24, 1607.

Ruzicka, Leopold, Sep. 13, 1887.

Rwanda, Republic of: independence, Jul. 1, 1962; refugees flee, Mar. 30, 1994; civil war, Jul. 4, 1994; killing of Hutu civilians, Apr. 22, 1995.

Ryan, Cornelius John, Jun. 5, 1920.

Ryan, Irene Noblette, Oct. 17, 1903.

Ryan, Leo Joseph, May 5, 1925.

Ryan, Meg, Nov. 19, 1961.

Ryan, Nolan, Jan. 31, 1947; Jul. 11, 1985.

Ryan, Paddy, Feb. 7, 1883.

Ryan, Thomas Fortune, Oct. 17, 1851.

Ryan, Tubal Claude, Jan. 3, 1898.

Rydell, Bobby, Apr. 26, 1942.

Rydell, Mark, Mar. 23, 1934.

Ryder, Albert Pinkham, Mar. 19, 1847.

Ryder, Mitch, Feb. 26, 1945.

Ryder, Winona, Oct. 29, 1971.

Ryle, Sir Martin, Sep. 27, 1918.

Rypien, Mark, Oct. 2, 1962.

Ryswyck, Treaty of, Sep. 20, 1697.

Ryuku Islands, Apr. 16, 1945.

Rzewuski, Count Henryk, May 3, 1791.

S

Saar, Jan. 1, 1951.

Saarinen, Eero, Aug. 20, 1910.

Saarinen, Eliel, Aug. 20, 1873.

Saarland, Jan. 1, 1957.

Saavedra Lamas, Carlos de, Nov. 1, 1878.

Saavedra (Ramirez de Baquendano) Angel de, Mar. 10, 1791.

Saba Saba Peasants Day, Jul. 7.

Sabah as-Salim as-Sabah (Kuwait), Nov. 24, 1965.

Sabah, Jaber al-Ahmed al-, May 31, 1966.

Sabater, Francisco: killed, Jan. 5, 1960.

Sabatier, Paul, Nov. 5, 1854.

Sabatini, Gabriela, May 16, 1970.

Sabatini, Rafael, Apr. 29, 1875.

Saberhagen, Bret William, Apr. 13, 1964.

Sabin, Albert Bruce, Aug. 26, 1906; Aug. 24, 1960.

Sabin, Florence R., Nov. 9, 1871.

Sabra and Shatila refugee camps, Sep. 16, 1982.

Sacco, Nicola, Apr. 22, 1891; Jul. 14, 1921.

Sacerdotalis Caelibatus: encyclical, Jun. 23, 1967.

Sacher-Masoch, Leopold von, Jan. 27, 1836.

Sachs, Hans, Nov. 5, 1494.

Sachs, Nelly Leonie, Dec. 10, 1891.

Sackler, Howard, Dec. 19, 1929.

Sacks, Oliver Wolf, Jul. 9, 1933.

Sackville, Thomas, Jan. 18, 1562.

Sackville-West, Victoria Mary, Mar. 9, 1892.

Sacramento (California), Sep. 5, 1975.

Sadat, Anwar, Dec. 25, 1918; Oct. 15, 1970; Oct. 4, 1971; Mar. 28, 1973; Nov. 19, 1977; Dec. 5, 1977; Sep. 17, 1978; Oct. 17, 1978; Mar. 26, 1979; assassinated, Oct. 6, 1981.

Sade, Jan. 16, 1960.

Sade, Donatien Alphonse Francois de, Jun. 2, 1740.

Sadie Hawkins Day (United States), Nov. intro.

Sadler's Wells Theater, Jan. 6, 1931.

Sadowa, Battle of: ends, Jul. 3, 1866.

Safe Boating Week, National, Jun. intro.

Safer, Morley, Nov. 8, 1931.

Safety on the Streets Week, National, Oct. intro.

Safety Sabbath, National, Feb. intro.

Safire, William L., Dec. 17, 1929.

Sagan, Carl, Nov. 9, 1934.

Sagan, Francoise, Jun. 21, 1935.

Sage, Margaret Olivia, Sep. 8, 1828.

Sage, Russell, Aug. 4, 1816.

Sager, Carole Bayer, Mar. 8, 1947.

Sagittarius, Nov. intro; Dec. intro.

Sahara: French right to, Sep. 8, 1919.

Sahl, Mort, May 11, 1927.

Sa'id ibn Taimur (Oman), Jul. 23, 1970.

Saigon, Apr. 30, 1975; May 7, 1975.

Saigon, Treaty of, Apr. 13, 1862.

sailors in Ireland, patron of, Mar. 24.

sailors, patron of, Apr. 2; Jun. 2; Sep. 22.

Saint Aubin, Stephanie Felicite du Crest de, Jan. 25, 1746.

Saint-Denis, Charles de Marguetel de, Apr. 1, 1616.

Saint, Eva Marie, Jul. 4, 1924.

Saint-Exupery, Antoine (Marie-Roger) de, Jul. 31, 1900.

Saint-Gaudens, Augustus, Mar. 1, 1848.

Saint-Hilaire, Etienne Geoffroy, Apr. 15, 1672.

Saint James, Susan, Aug. 14, 1946.

Saint John, Jill, Aug. 9, 1940.

Saint-Leger Leger, Alexis, May 31, 1887.

Saint-Pierre, Jacques Henri Bernardin de, Jan. 19, 1737.

Saint-Saens, (Charles) Camille, Oct. 9, 1835; Feb. 25, 1922.

Sainte-Marie, Beverly (Buffy), Feb. 20, 1941.

St. Abachum, Jan. 19.

St. Abbo of Fleury, Nov. 13, 1048.

St. Abdon, Jul. 30.

St. Abercius, Oct. 22.

St. Abibus, Nov. 14.

St. Abraham Kidunaia, Mar. 16.

St. Abraham of Rostov, Oct. 29.

St. Abraham of Smolensk, Aug. 21.

St. Acacius, Mar. 31; May 8; Jun. 22.

St. Acca, Oct. 20.

St. Achilleus, Apr. 23; May 12.

St. Acisclus, Nov. 17.

St. Adalbald of Ostrevant, Feb. 2.

St. Adalbert, Apr. 23; Jun. 20.

St. Adalbert of Egmond, Jun. 25.

St. Adalhard, Jan. 2.

St. Adam, Sep. 15.

St. Adamnan, Sep. 23.

St. Adamnan of Coldingham, Jan. 31.

St. Adauetus, Aug. 30.

St. Adaueus, Feb. 7.

St. Addai, Aug. 5.

St. Adela, Dec. 23.

St. Adelaide, Feb. 5; Dec. 16.

St. Adelemus, Jan. 30.

St. Adolf, Feb. 14.

St. Adrian, Jan. 9; Mar. 4; Mar. 5; Sep. 8.

St. Adrian III, Jul. 8.

St. Aedh Mac Bricc, Nov. 10.

St. Aelred, Mar. 3.

St. Aemilius, May 22.

St. Afan, Nov. 16.

St. Afra, Aug. 5.

St. Agape, Feb. 15; Apr. 2.

St. Agapitus, Aug. 18.

St. Agapitus I, Apr. 22.

St. Agapius, Aug. 19.

St. Agatha, Feb. 5.

St. Agathangelus, Jan. 23.

St. Agatho, Jan. 10.

St. Agathonice, Apr. 13.

St. Agathopus, Apr. 4.

St. Agericus, Dec. 1.

St. Agilbert, Apr. 1; Oct. 11.

St. Agnes, Jan. 21.

St. Agnes of Assisi, Nov. 16.

St. Agnes Eve (Great Britain), Jan. 20.

St. Agnes of Montepulciano, Apr. 20.

St. Agrecius, Jan. 13.

St. Agricola, Mar. 17; Nov. 4.

St. Agricolus, Sep. 2.

St. Agrippina, Jun. 23.

St. Aichardus, Sep. 15.

St. Aidan, Aug. 31.

St. Aidan of Ferns, Jan. 31.

St. Aigulf, May 22; Sep. 3.

St. Ailbhe, Sep. 12.

St. Alban, Jun. 22.

St. Alban of Mainz, Jun. 21.

St. Alban Roe, Jan. 21.

St. Albans, May 22, 1455; Feb. 17, 1461.

St. Albans, Council of, Aug. 4, 1213.

St. Albenc, Jan. 26.

St. Albert, Apr. 5; Sep. 25.

St. Albert of Cashel, Jan. 19.

St. Albert the Great, Nov. 15.

St. Albert of Louvain, Nov. 21.

St. Albert of Trapani, Aug. 7.

St. Albinus, Mar. 1.

St. Alburga, Dec. 25.

St. Alcmund, Mar. 19.

St. Aldate, Feb. 4.

St. Aldegundis, Jan. 30.

St. Aldemar, Mar. 24.

St. Aldhelm, May 25.

St. Aldric, Jan. 7.

St. Aled, Aug. 1.

St. Alexander, Feb. 26; Mar. 18; Apr. 22; May 3; May 29; Aug. 28.

St. Alexander Akimetes, Feb. 23.

St. Alexander the Charcoal-Burner, Aug. 11.

St. Alexander Sauli, Oct. 11.

St. Alexis, Jul. 17.

St. Aleydis, Jun. 15.

St. Alferius, Apr. 12.

St. Alfwold, Mar. 25.

St. Alipius, Aug. 18.

St. Allucio, Oct. 23.

St. Almachius, Jan. 1.

St. Alnoth, Feb. 27.

St. Alodia, Oct. 22.

St. Aloisius Orione, Mar. 12.

St. Aloysius, Jun. 21.

St. Alphaeus, Nov. 17.

St. Alphege, Mar. 12; Apr. 19.

St. Alphonsus de'Liguori, Aug. 1.

St. Alphonsus Rodriguez, Oct. 30.

St. Altman, Aug. 8.

St. Alto, Feb. 9.

St. Amadeus, Jan. 28.

St. Amadour, Aug. 20.

St. Amalburga of Sustern, Jul. 10.

St. Amandus, Jun. 18.

St. Amator, May 1.

St. Amatus, Sep. 13.

St. Ambrose, Dec. 7.

St. Ambrose Autpert, Jul. 19.

St. Amicus, Nov. 3.

St. Ammon, Oct. 4.

St. Amphilochius, Nov. 23.

St. Anastasia, Apr. 15; Oct. 28; Dec. 25.

St. Anastasia Patricia, Mar. 10.

St. Anastasius I, Apr. 21; Dec. 19.

St. Anastasius II, Dec. 21.

St. Anastasius of Cluny, Oct. 16.

St. Anastasius the Persian, Jan. 22.

St. Anatolius, Jul. 3.

St. Andrew Avellino, Nov. 10.

St. Andrew Bobola, May 21.

St. Andrew Corsini, Feb. 4.

St. Andrew of Crete, Jul. 4; Oct. 20.

St. Andrew, Feast of, Nov. 30.

St. Andrew of Fiesole, Aug. 22.

St. Andrew Hubert Fournet, May 13.

St. Andrew the Tribune, Aug. 19.

St. Andrew's Golf Club (Yonkers, New York): first American golf club, Nov. 14, 1888.

St. Andronicus, Oct. 9; Oct. 11.

St. Angadrisma, Oct. 14.

St. Angela Merici, Jan. 27; Jun. 1.

St. Angelo, May 5.

St. Angilbert, Feb. 18.

St. Anianus, Apr. 25; Nov. 17.

St. Anicetus, Apr. 17.

St. Anne, Jul. 23; Jul. 26.

St. Annemund, Sep. 28.

St. Anno, Dec. 4.

St. Ansanus, Dec. 1.

St. Ansbert, Feb. 9.

St. Ansegisus, Jul. 20.

St. Anselm, Mar. 18; Apr. 21.

St. Anselm of Nonantola, Mar. 3.

St. Ansfrid, May 11.

St. Anskar, Feb. 3.

St. Ansovinus, Mar. 13.

St. Anstrudis, Oct. 17.

St. Anthelm, Jun. 26.

St. Antherus, Jan. 3.

St. Anthimus, Apr. 27.

St. Anthony, Jul. 10.

St. Anthony the Abbot, Jan. 17.

St. Anthony Kausleas, Feb. 12.

St. Anthony, Mary Claret, Oct. 23.

St. Anthony of Padua, Jun. 13.

St. Anthony Pucci, Jan. 14.

St. Anthony's Day (Portugal), Jun. 13.

St. Antonina, Jun. 12.

St. Antoninus, May 10; Sep. 2.

St. Antoninus of Sorrento, Feb. 14.

St. Antony Claret, Oct. 23.

St. Antony Gianelli, Jun. 7

St. Antony of Lerins, Dec. 28.

St. Antony Zaccaria, Jul. 5.

St. Anysius, Dec. 30.

St. Aphraates, Apr. 7.

St. Apollinaris, Jan. 5, Jan. 8; Jul. 23; Oct. 5.

St. Apollo, Jan. 25.

St. Apollonia, Feb. 9.

St. Apollonius, Mar. 8.

St. Apollonius the Apologist, Apr. 18.

St. Apphian of Palestine, Apr. 2.

St. Aquila, Jul. 8.

St. Aquilina, Jun. 13.

St. Aquilinus, Oct. 19.

St. Arbogast, Jul. 21.

St. Arcadius, Jan. 12; Nov. 13.

St. Archelaus, Dec. 26.

St. Archinimus, Mar. 29.

St. Ardalion, Apr. 14.

St. Ardo, Mar. 7.

St. Aretas, Oct. 23.

St. Arild, Jul. 20.

St. Armel, Aug. 16.

St. Armogastes, Mar. 29.

St. Arnulf, Jul. 18; Aug. 15; Aug. 22.

St. Arsacius, Aug. 16.

St. Arsenius the Great, Jul. 19.

St. Artaldus, Oct. 7.

St. Artemas, Jan. 25.

St. Artemius, Oct. 20.

St. Arthelais, Mar. 3.

St. Asaph, May 11.

St. Asclas, Jan. 23.

St. Asicus, Apr. 27.

St. Asterius, Aug. 23; Oct. 30.

St. Astrik, Nov. 12.

St. Astyrius, Mar. 3.

St. Athanasia, Aug. 14; Oct. 9.

St. Athanasius, Jul. 15.

St. Athanasius, Archbishop of Alexandria, May 2.

St. Athanasius the Athonite, Jul. 5.

St. Athenogenes, Jul. 16.

St. Attalas, Mar. 10.

St. Chainoaldus, Sep. 6.

St. Attracta, Aug. 11.

St. Aubert, Sep. 10; Dec. 13.

St. Audifax, Jan. 19.

St. Audoenus, Aug. 24.

St. Audomarus, Sep. 9.

St. Augustine, May 26; Aug. 28; Nov. 13, 354.

St. Augustine (Florida): first colony, Sep. 8, 1565; founded, Feb. 13, 1566.

St. Aumand, Feb. 6.

St. Aunacharius, Sep. 25.

St. Aurea, Mar. 11.

St. Aurelian, Jun. 16.

St. Aurelius, Jul. 20.

St. Aurelius and St. Natalia, Jul. 27.

St. Austel, Jun. 28.

St. Austreberta, Feb. 10.

St. Austregisilus, May 20.

St. Austremonius, Nov. 1.

St. Auxentius, Feb. 14.

St. Avertinus, May 5.

St. Avitus, Feb. 5; Jun. 17.

St. Aybert, Apr. 7.

St. Babylas, Jan. 24.

St. Bagnus, Jun. 20.

St. Balbina, Mar. 31.

St. Baldemus, Apr. 10.

St. Baldomerus, Feb. 27.

St. Balred, Mar. 6.

St. Barachisius, Mar. 29.

St. Baradates, Feb. 22.

St. Barbara, Dec. 4.

St. Barbasymas, Jan. 14.

St. Barbatus, Feb. 19.

St. Barhadbesaba, Jul. 15.

St. Barlaam, Nov. 19; Nov. 27.

St. Barlaam of Khutyn, Nov. 6.

St. Barloc, Sep. 10.

St. Barnabas, Jun. 11.

St. Barontius, Mar. 25.

St. Barry, Sep. 27.

St. Barsabas, Dec. 11.

St. Barsanuphius, Apr. 11.

St. Bartholomea Capitanio, Jul. 26.

St. Bartholomew, Aug. 24.

St. Bartholomew of Farne, Jun. 24.

St. Bartholomew of Grottaferrata, Nov. 11.

St. Bartholomew's Day Massacre, Aug. 24, 1572.

St. Basil of Ancyra, Mar. 22.

St. Basil the Great, Jan. 2.

St. Basil the Younger, Mar. 26.

St. Basilides, Jun. 12.

St. Basilissa, Jan. 9; Apr. 15.

St. Basilla, May 20.

St. Basolus, Nov. 26.

St. Bathan, Jan. 18.

St. Bathildis, Jan. 30.

St. Baudelius, May 20.

St. Bavo, Oct. 1.

St. Bean, Oct. 26.

St. Beatrice, Jul. 29.

St. Beatus, May 9.

St. Bede the Venerable, May 25.

St. Bega, Sep. 6; Oct. 31.

St. Begga, Dec. 17.

St. Benedict, Jan. 12; Mar. 11; Jul. 11; Nov. 12.

St. Benedict II, May 8.

St. Benedict of Aniane, Feb. 11.

St. Benedict the Hermit, Mar. 23.

St. Benedict Joseph Labre, Apr. 16.

St. Benezet, Apr. 14.

St. Benignus, Nov. 9.

St. Benignus of Dijon, Nov. 1.

St. Benildus, Aug. 13.

St. Benjamin, Mar. 31.

St. Benno, Jun. 16.
St. Benvenuto, Mar. 22.
St. Berard, Jan. 16.
St. Bercharius, Oct. 16.
St. Berhtwald, Jan. 9; Jan. 22.
St. Bernadette, Apr. 16.
St. Bernard, Jan. 23; Aug. 20; Dec. 4.
St. Bernard of Capua, Mar. 12.
St. Bernard of Clairvaux, Mar. 31,
    1146.
St. Bernard of Montjoux, May 28.
St. Bernard of Tiron, Apr. 14.
St. Bernard Tunnel, Great: opens,
    Mar. 19, 1964.
St. Bernardino Realino, Jul. 3.
St. Bernardino of Siena, May 20.
St. Berno, Jan. 13.
St. Bernward, Nov. 20.
St. Bersimaeus, Jan. 30.
St. Bertha, May 15; Jul. 4.
St. Berthold, Mar. 28.
St. Bertilia of, Mareuil, Jan. 3.
St. Bertilla, Nov. 5.
St. Bertilla Boscardin, Oct. 20.
St. Bertinus, May 15.
St. Bertrand, Jun. 30; Oct. 16.
St. Bertulf, Feb. 5; Aug. 19.
St. Besas, Feb. 27.
St. Bessarion, Jun. 17.
St. Bettelin, Aug. 10; Sep. 9.
St. Beuno, Apr. 21.
St. Bibiana, Dec. 2.
St. Bilfrid, Mar. 6.
St. Birinus, Dec. 3.
St. Blaan, Aug. 11.
St. Blaise, Feb. 3.
St. Blas (Paraguay), Feb. 3.
St. Blesilla, Jan. 22.
St. Bodo, Sep. 22.
St. Bogumilus, Jun. 10.
St. Boisil, Jul. 7.
St. Bonaventure, Jul. 15.
St. Boniface, Feb. 19; Jun. 5.
St. Boniface I, Sep. 4.
St. Boniface IV, May 8.
St. Boniface of Tarsus, May 14.
St. Bonitus, Jan. 15.
St. Bonosus, Aug. 21.
St. Bordo, Jun. 15.
St. Boris, Jul. 24.
St. Bosa, Mar. 9.
St. Botulf, Jun. 17.
St. Botvid, Jul. 28.
St. Braulio, Mar. 26.

St. Bregwine, Aug. 24.
St. Brendan, May 16.
St. Brendan of Birr, Nov. 29.
St. Briavel, Jun. 17.
St. Brice, Nov. 13.
St. Brice (England), Nov. 13, 1002.
St. Bridget of Sweden, Jul. 23.
St. Brieue, May 1.
St. Brigid, Feb. 1; Jul. 13.
St. Brocard, Sep. 2.
St. Bruno, May 17; Jul. 18; Oct. 6.
St. Bruno the Great, Oct. 11.
St. Bruno of Querfurt, Jun. 19.
St. Brychan, Apr. 6.
St. Budoc, Dec. 8.
St. Burehard, Oct. 14.
St. Burgondofara, Apr. 2.
St. Cadfan, Nov. 1.
St. Cadoc, Sep. 25.
St. Cadroe, Mar. 6.
St. Cadwaladr, Nov. 12.
St. Caedmon, Feb. 11.
St. Caedwalla, Apr. 20.
St. Caesarius, Aug. 27; Nov. 1.
St. Caesarius of Nazianzus, Feb. 25.
St. Cajetan, Aug. 7.
St. Calepodius, May 10.
St. Callistus I, Oct. 14.
St. Caloeerus, May 19.
St. Camerinus, Aug. 21.
St. Camillus de Lellis, Jul. 14.
St. Canice, Oct. 11.
St. Cantianella, May 31.
St. Cantianus, May 31.
St. Cantius, May 31.
St. Canute of Denmark, Jan. 19.
St. Canute Lavard, Jan. 7.
St. Caprasius, Jun. 1; Oct. 20.
St. Caradoc, Apr. 14.
St. Carantoc, May 16.
St. Carilefus, Jul. 1.
St. Carol Melchiori, Jan. 6.
St. Carpus, Apr. 13.
St. Carthage, May 14.
St. Casimir of Poland, Mar. 4.
St. Caspar del Bufalo, Jan. 2.
St. Cassian, Dec. 3.
St. Cassian of Imola, Aug. 13.
St. Cassius, Jun. 29.
St. Cassyon, Aug. 5.
St. Castor, Sep. 2.
St. Castulus, Mar. 26.
St. Castus, May 22.
St. Catald, May 10.

St. Catherine of Alexandria, Nov. 25.
St. Catherine of Bologna, Mar. 9.
St. Catherine dei Ricci, Feb. 13.
St. Catherine of Genoa, Sep. 15.
St. Catherine Laboure, Nov. 28.
St. Catherine of Palma, Apr. 1.
St. Catherine of Siena, Apr. 29.
St. Catherine of Vadstena, Mar. 24.
St. Cecilia, Nov. 22.
St. Cecilius, Jun. 3.
St. Cedd, Oct. 26.
St. Celestine I, Apr. 6.
St. Celestine V, May 19.
St. Celsus, Apr. 7; Jul. 28.
St. Ceolfrid, Sep. 25.
St. Ceolwolf, Jan. 15.
St. Ceratius, Jun. 6.
St. Cerbonius, Oct. 10.
St. Chad, Mar. 2.
St. Chainoaldus, Sep. 6.
St. Charles Borromeo, Nov. 4.
St. Charles of Sezze, Jan. 19.
St. Chelidonius, Mar. 3.
St. Chiona, Apr. 2.
St. Christina, Jul. 24.
St. Christina the Astonishing, Jul. 24.
St. Christina of, Markyate, Dec. 5.
St. Christopher, Jul. 25.
St. Chrodegang, Mar. 6.
St. Chromatius, Dec. 2.
St. Chrysanthus, Oct. 25.
St. Chrysogonus, Nov. 24.
St. Cisellus, Aug. 21.
St. Clair, Arthur, Apr. 3, 1737.
St. Clare, Aug. 11.
St. Clare of Montefalco, Aug. 17.
St. Clarus, Nov. 4.
St. Claud, Jun. 6.
St. Claudia, Aug. 7.
St. Claudius, Aug. 23.
St. Clement, Jan. 23.
St. Clement I, Nov. 23.
St. Clement of Alexandria, Dec. 4
St. Clement of Hofbauer, Mar. 15.
St. Clement of Okhrida and his
    companions, Jul. 17.
St. Clether, Nov. 4.
St. Cletus, Apr. 26.
St. Clodoald, Sep. 7.
St. Clodulf, Jun. 8.
St. Clotilda, Jun. 3.
St. Clydog, Nov. 3.
St. Codratus, Mar. 10.
St. Colette, Mar. 6.

St. Collen, May 21.
St. Colman, Feb. 18; Jun. 7.
St. Colman of Cloyne, Nov. 24.
St. Colman of Kilmacduagh, Oct. 29.
St. Colman of Lann Elo, Sep. 26.
St. Coloman, Oct. 13.
St. Columba, Jun. 9; Sep. 17.
St. Columba of Sens, Dec. 31.
St. Columban, Nov. 23.
St. Comgall, May 11.
St. Comgan, Oct. 13.
St. Conan, Jan. 26.
St. Concordius, Jan. 1.
St. Condedus, Oct. 21.
St. Congar, Nov. 7.
St. Conleth, May 10.
St. Conrad, Nov. 26.
St. Conrad of Parzham, Apr. 21.
St. Conrad of Piacenza, Feb. 19.
St. Conran, Feb. 14.
St. Constantine, Mar. 11.
St. Contardo, Apr. 16.
St. Convoyon, Jan. 5.
St. Corbinian, Sep. 8.
St. Corde Jesu, Jan. 6.
St. Corentin, May 1.
St. Cornelius, Sep. 16.
St. Credan, Aug. 19.
St. Crescentia, Jun. 15.
St. Crispin, Oct. 25.
St. Crispin of Viterbo, May 21.
St. Crispina, Dec. 5.
St. Crispinian, Oct. 25.
St. Cronan of Roscrea, Apr. 28.
St. Cronion, Feb. 27.
St. Cumian, Nov. 12.
St. Cunegund, Mar. 3; Jul. 24.
St. Cungar, Nov. 27.
St. Cunibert, Nov. 12.
St. Cuthbert, Mar. 20.
St. Cuthburga, Aug. 31.
St. Cuthman, Feb. 8.
St. Cybi, Nov. 8.
St. Cyneburga, Mar. 6.
St. Cyneburga of Gloucesterz, Jun. 25.
St. Cyneswide, Mar. 6.
St. Cyprian, Sep. 16.
St. Cyriacus, May 4.
St. Cyricus, Jun. 16.
St. Cyril, Feb. 14; Mar. 6; Mar. 18; Mar. 29; Apr. 28; Jun. 27; Oct. 28.
St. Cyril of Caesarea, May 29.

St. Cyrus, Jan. 31.
St. Dagobert II of Austrasia, Dec. 23.
St. Damasus, Dec. 11.
St. Daniel, Feb. 16; Oct. 10.
St. Daniel the Stylite, Dec. 11.
St. Daria, Oct. 25.
St. Dasius, Nov. 20.
St. Datius, Jan. 14.
St. Dativus, Feb. 11.
St. David, Mar. 1.
St. David I of Scotland, May 24.
St. David of Munktorp, Jul. 15.
St. David's Day (Wales, United Kingdom), Mar. 1.
St. Declan, Jul. 24.
St. Decuman, Aug. 27.
St. Deicola, Apr. 18.
St. Deicolus, Jan. 18.
St. Deiniol, Sep. 11.
St. Delphinus, Dec. 23.
St. Demetrian, Nov. 6.
St. Demetrius, Oct. 8; Oct. 9.
St. Denis, Ruth, Jan. 20, 1879.
St. Denys, Oct. 9.
St. Deodatus, Jun. 19.
St. Deogratias, Mar. 22.
St. Derfel Gadarn, Apr. 5.
St. Dermot Dairmaid, Jan. 10.
St. Desideratus, May 8.
St. Desiderius, May 23.
St. Deusdedit, Jul. 14; Nov. 8.
St. Devote (Monaco), Jan. 26.
St. Didacus, Nov. 13.
St. Didymus, Apr. 28.
St. Dimitrios Day (Thessaloniki, Greece), Oct. 26.
St. Dingad, Nov. 1.
St. Dionysius, Apr. 8; May 25; Nov. 17; Dec. 26.
St. Dionysius the Areopagite, Oct. 9.
St. Disibod, Sep. 8.
St. Disiderius, Nov. 15.
St. Diuma, Dec. 7.
St. Dogmael, Jun. 14.
St. Dometius the Persian, Aug. 7.
St. Dominic, Aug. 8.
St. Dominic of the Causeway, May 12.
St. Dominic Loricatus, Oct. 14.
St. Dominic Savio, Mar. 9.
St. Dominic of Silos, Dec. 20.
St. Dominic of Sora, Jan. 22.
St. Dominica, Feb. 5; Jul. 6.
St. Domitian, May 7.

St. Domitilla, May 12.
St. Domnina, Aug. 23.
St. Domnolus, May 16.
St. Donald, Jul. 15.
St. Donatian, May 24.
St. Donatus, Oct. 22.
St. Donnan, Apr. 17.
St. Dontius, Mar. 8.
St. Dorotheus, Mar. 12.
St. Dorotheus of Tyre, Jun. 5.
St. Dorotheus the Younger, Jan. 5.
St. Dorothy, Feb. 6.
St. Dositheus, Feb. 23.
St. Drausius, Mar. 7.
St. Drithelm, Sep. 1.
St. Droctoveus, Mar. 10.
St. Drogo, Apr. 16.
St. Drostan, Jul. 11.
St. Dubricius, Nov. 14.
St. Dunchad, Mar. 24.
St. Dunstan, May 19.
St. Duthac, Mar. 8.
St. Dwyn, Jan. 25.
St. Dympna, May 15.
St. Eanswida, Sep. 12.
St. Eata, Oct. 26.
St. Ebba, Aug. 25.
St. Ebbe the Younger, Jun. 22.
St. Eberhard, Jun. 22.
St. Ebrulf, Dec. 29.
St. Edbert, May 6.
St. Edburga, Dec. 12.
St. Edburga of Bicester, Jul. 18.
St. Edburga of Winchester, Jun. 15.
St. Edfrith, Jun. 4.
St. Edith of Polesworth, Jul. 15.
St. Edith of Wilton, Sep. 16.
St. Edmund of Abingdon, Nov. 16.
St. Edmund the Martyr, Nov. 20.
St. Edward the Confessor, Oct. 13.
St. Edward the Martyr, Mar. 18; Jun. 20.
St. Edwin, Oct. 12.
St. Edwold of Cerne, Aug. 29.
St. Egbert, Apr. 24.
St. Egwin, Dec. 30.
St. Elesbaan, Oct. 23.
St. Eleusippus, Jan. 17.
St. Eleutherius, Feb. 20; Apr. 18; May 30; Sep. 6; Oct. 2; Oct. 9.
St. Elfleda, Feb. 8.
St. Elgiva, May 18.
St. Elias, Feb. 16.
St. Eligius, Dec. 1.

St. Elizabeth, Jul. 4; Nov. 5.

St. Elizabeth Ann Seton, Jan. 4.

St. Elizabeth Biehier des Ages, Aug. 26.

St. Elizabeth of Hungary, Nov. 17.

St. Elizabeth of Schonau, Jun. 18.

St. Elstan, Apr. 6.

St. Elwin, Jun. 29.

St. Elzear, Sep. 27.

St. Emerentiana, Jan. 23.

St. Emeterius, Mar. 3.

St. Emilian Cucullatus, Nov. 12.

St. Emily de Rodat, Sep. 19.

St. Emily de Vialar, Jun. 17.

St. Emma, Jun. 29.

St. Emmeramus, Sep. 22.

St. Encratis, Apr. 16.

St. Enda, Mar. 21.

St. Endellion, Apr. 29.

St. Eneco, Jun. 1.

St. Enfleda, Nov. 24.

St. Engelbert, Nov. 7.

St. Engelmund, Jun. 21.

St. Ennodius, Jul. 17.

St. Eoban, Jun. 5.

St. Eparchius, Jul. 1.

St. Ephraem, Jun. 9.

St. Epimachus, May 10.

St. Epiphanius, Jan. 21; May 12.

St. Epipodius, Apr. 22.

St. Episteme, Nov. 5.

St. Equitius, Aug. 11.

St. Erasmus, Jun. 2.

St. Erc, Nov. 2.

St. Ercongota, Jul. 7.

St. Erconwald, May 13.

St. Erembert, May 14.

St. Erentrude, Jun. 30.

St. Erhard, Jan. 8.

St. Eric of Sweeden, May 18.

St. Ermelandus, Mar. 25.

St. Ermenburga, Nov. 19.

St. Ermengild, Feb. 13.

St. Errninold, Jan. 6.

St. Ernin, Nov. 2.

St. Eskil, Jun. 12.

St. Esterwine, Mar. 7.

St. Ethbin, Oct. 19.

St. Ethelbert, Feb. 25; May 20.

St. Ethelburga, Apr. 5; Jul. 7; Sep. 8; Oct. 12.

St. Etheldreda, Jun. 23.

St. Etheldritha, Aug. 2.

St. Ethelfleda, Oct. 23.

St. Ethelnoth, Oct. 30.

St. Ethelwald, Feb. 12.

St. Ethelwald the Hermit, Mar. 23.

St. Ethelwin, Nov. 29.

St. Ethelwold, Aug. 1.

St. Eubulus, Mar. 5.

St. Eucherius, Feb. 20; Nov. 16.

St. Eugendus, Jan. 1.

St. Eugene, Aug. 23.

St. Eugenia, Dec. 25.

St. Eugenius, Jul. 13; Nov. 13.

St. Eugenius I, Jun. 2.

St. Eulalia of Merida, Dec. 10.

St. Eulampia, Oct. 10.

St. Eulampius, Oct. 10.

St. Eulogius, Sep. 13.

St. Eulogius of Cordova, Mar. 11.

St. Euphemia, Sep. 16.

St. Euphrasia, Mar. 13.

St. Euphrosyne, Jan. 1.

St. Euphrosyne of Polotsk, May 23.

St. Euplus, Aug. 12.

St. Eurosia, Jun. 25.

St. Eusebia, Mar. 16.

St. Eusebius, Jan. 31; Jun. 21; Aug. 17; Sep.

St. Eusebius of Cremona, Mar. 5.

St. Eusebius (Vercelli) of Rome, Aug. 14.

St. Eustace, Apr. 14; Sep. 20.

St. Eustathius, Jul. 16.

St. Eustochium, Sep. 28.

St. Eustorgius II, Jun. 6.

St. Eustratius and his Companions, Dec. 13.

St. Euthymius the Enlightener, May 13.

St. Euthymius the Great, Jan. 20.

St. Euthymius the Younger, Oct. 15.

St. Eutropius, Jan. 12; Apr. 30; May 27.

St. Eutychian, Dec. 7.

St. Eutychius, Mar. 14; Apr. 6.

St. Evaristus, Oct. 26.

St. Eventius, May 3.

St. Evergislus, Oct. 23.

St. Everild, Jul. 9.

St. Evermod, Feb. 17.

St. Evodius, May 6.

St. Evurtius, Sep. 7.

St. Exsuperius, May 2, Sep. 28.

St. Exuperantius, May 30.

St. Eystein, Jan. 26.

St. Fabian, Jan. 20.

St. Fabiola, Dec. 27.

St. Fachanan, Aug. 14.

St. Faith, Oct. 6.

St. Fantinus, Aug. 30.

St. Faro, Oct. 28.

St. Faustinus, Feb. 15; Jul. 29.

St. Faustus, Sep. 28; Oct. 13.

St. Febronia, Jun. 25.

St. Fechin, Jan. 20.

St. Felician, Jan. 24; Jun. 9.

St. Felicity, Mar. 7; Jul. 10.

St. Felicula, Jun. 13.

St. Felim, Aug. 9.

St. Felix, Mar. 26; Apr. 23; Jun. 11; Jul. 7; Jul. 12; Aug. 30; Oct. 23.

St. Felix I, May 30.

St. Felix II, Jul. 29.

St. Felix II (III), Mar. 1.

St. Felix III (IV), Sep. 22.

St. Felix of Bourges, Jan. 1.

St. Felix of Cantalice, May 18.

St. Felix of Dunwich, Mar. 8.

St. Felix of Nola, Jan. 14.

St. Felix of Valois, Nov. 20.

St. Ferdinand III of Castile, May 30.

St. Fergus, Nov. 27.

St. Ferminus, Sep. 25.

St. Ferreolus, Jun. 16, Sep. 18.

St. Ferrutio, Jun. 16.

St. Fiacre, Sep. 1.

St. Fidelis of Como, Oct. 28.

St. Fidelis of Signaringen, Apr. 24.

St. Fillan, Jan. 19.

St. Fina, Mar. 12.

St. Finan, Feb. 17.

St. Finan of Aberdeen, Mar. 18.

St. Finbar, Sep. 25.

St. Finnian of Clonard, Dec. 12.

St. Finnian Lobhar Mar. 16.

St. Finnian of Moville, Sep. 10.

St. Fintan, Feb. 17.

St. Fintan of Rheinau, Nov. 15.

St. Fintan of Taghmon, Oct. 21.

St. Flannan, Dec. 18.

St. Flavian, Feb. 18; Jul. 20.

St. Flora, Nov. 24.

St. Flora of Beaulieu, Oct. 5.

St. Florentius, Nov. 7.

St. Florian, May 4.

St. Floribert, Apr. 27.

St. Foillan, Oct. 31.

St. Forannan, Apr. 30.

St. Fortunatus, Apr. 23; Jun. 11.

St. Franca of Piacenza, Apr. 26.

St. Frances of Rome, Mar. 9.
St. Frances Xavier Cabrini, Nov. 13.
St. Franchea, Mar. 21.
St. Francis of Assisi, Oct. 4.
St. Francis Borgia, Oct. 10.
St. Francis of Camporosso, Sep. 26.
St. Francis Caraeeiolo, Jun. 4.
St. Francis de Sales, Jan. 24.
St. Francis di Girolamo, May 11.
St. Francis of Paola, Apr. 2.
St. Francis of Pesaro, Oct. 1.
St. Francis Solano, Jul. 13.
St. Francis Xavier, Dec. 3; Apr. 7,
    1506.
St. Francis Xavier Bianchi, Jan. 31.
St. Frederick, Jul. 18.
St. Fremund, May 11.
St. Frideswide, Oct. 19.
St. Fridolin, Mar. 6.
St. Frigidian, Mar. 18.
St. Frithebert, Dec. 23.
St. Frithestan, Sep. 10.
St. Froilan, Oct. 3.
St. Fronto, Oct. 25.
St. Fructuosus, Jan. 21; Apr. 16.
St. Frumentius, Oct. 27.
St. Fulbert, Apr. 10.
St. Fulgentius, Jan. 1.
St. Fulrad, Jul. 16.
St. Fursey, Jan. 16.
St. Gabriel the Archangel, Mar. 24.
St. Gabriel Possenti, Feb. 27.
St. Gaius, Apr. 22.
St. Galation, Nov. 5.
St. Galdinus, Apr. 18.
St. Gall, Jul. 1; Oct. 16.
St. Gallicanus, Jun. 25.
St. Gatian, Dec. 18.
St. Gaucherius, Apr. 9.
St. Gaudentius, Oct. 25.
St. Gaurinus, Feb. 6.
St. Gelasius I, Nov. 21.
St. Gemma Galgani, Apr. 11.
St. Genesius, Jun. 3.
St. Genesius of Arles, Aug. 25.
St. Genesius the Comedian, Aug. 25.
St. Genevieve, Jan. 3.
St. Gengulf, May 11.
St. Genulf, Jan. 17.
St. George, Feb. 21; Apr. 23; Oct. 25.
St. George Mtsmindeli, Jun. 27.
St. George the Younger, Apr. 7.
St. Georges Cay Day (Belize), Sep.
    10.

St. George's Day (England), Apr. 23.
St. Gerald of Aurillac, Oct. 13.
St. Gerald of, Mayo, Mar. 13.
St. Gerard, Apr. 23; Sep. 24.
St. Gerard of Brogne, Oct. 3.
St. Gerard Majella, Oct. 16.
St. Gerardin, Nov. 8.
St. Gerasimus, Mar. 5.
St. Gerebernus, May 15. 1052
St. Geremarus, Sep. 24.
St. Gereon and his Companions,
    Oct. 10.
St. Gerlac, Jan. 5.
St. Gerland, Feb. 25.
St. Germain, Edict of, Jan. 17, 1562.
St. Germain-en-Laye, Treaty of, Mar.
    29, 1632.
St. Germain, Peace of, Aug. 8, 1570.
St. Germain, Treaty of, Sep. 10,
    1919.
St. Germaine of Pibrac, Jun. 15.
St. Germanicus, Jan. 19.
St. Germanus, May 12; May 28; Jun.
    28; Jul. 31; Oct. 30.
St. Germanus of Granfel, Feb. 21.
St. Germanus of Man, Jul. 3.
St. Germerius, May 16.
St. Geroldus, Apr. 19.
St. Gerontius, May 9.
St. Gertrude the Great, Nov. 16.
St. Gertrude of Nivelles, Mar. 17.
St. Gervase, Jun. 19.
St. Gervinus, Mar. 3.
St. Getulius, Jun. 10.
St. Gibrian, May 8.
St. Gilbert of Caithness, Apr. 1.
St. Gilbert of Sempringham, Feb. 4.
St. Gildas the Wise, Jan. 29.
St. Giles, Sep. 1.
St. Gislenus, Oct. 9.
St. Gleb, Jul. 24.
St. Glyceria, May 13.
St. Glywys, May 3.
St. Goar, Jul. 6.
St. Goban, Jun. 20.
St. Gobnet, Feb. 11.
St. Godeberta, Apr. 11.
St. Godehard, May 4.
St. Godeleva, Jul. 6.
St. Godfrey, Nov. 8.
St. Godric, May 21.
St. Goericus, Sep. 19.
St. Gohard, Jun. 25.
St. Goran, Apr. 7.

St. Gordian, May 10.
St. Gorgonia, Dec. 9.
St. Gorgonius, Mar. 12; Sep. 9.
St. Gotthard Tunnel, May 20, 1882.
St. Gottschalk, Jun. 7.
St. Govan, Mar. 26.
St. Gregory, Jan. 4; Mar. 9; Nov. 17;
    Nov. 23.
St. Gregory III, Dec. 10.
St. Gregory VII, May 25.
St. Gregory Barbarigo, Jun. 17.
St. Gregory the Enlightener, Sep. 30.
St. Gregory Makar, Mar. 16.
St. Gregory Nazianzen, Jan. 2.
St. Gregory of Spoleto, Dec. 23.
St. Gregory of Utrecht, Aug. 25.
St. Gregory the Wonderworker, Nov.
    17.
St. Grimbald, Jul. 8.
St. Grimonia, Sep. 7.
St. Gualfardus, Apr. 30.
St. Guarinus, Bishop of Sion, Jan. 6.
St. Gudula, Jan. 8.
St. Gudwal, Jun. 6.
St. Guibert, May 23.
St. Guinoch, Apr. 13.
St. Gummarus, Oct. 11.
St. Gundleus, Mar. 29.
St. Guntramnus, Mar. 28.
St. Gurius, Nov. 15.
St. Guthlac, Apr. 11.
St. Guy of Anderlecht, Sep. 12.
St. Guy of Pomposa, Mar. 31.
St. Gwen of Cornwall, Oct. 18.
St. Gwen Teirbron of Brittany, Jun.
    1.
St. Gwinear, Mar. 23.
St. Gwladys, Mar. 29.
St. Gwythian, Nov. 1.
St. Hallvard, May 15.
St. Hedda, Jul. 7.
St. Hedwig, Oct. 16.
St. Hegesippus, Apr. 7.
St. Heimrad, Jun. 28.
St. Heldrad, Mar. 13.
St. Helen, Aug. 18.
St. Helen of Skovde, Jul. 31.
St. Helena, May 21, 1502; Jan. 1,
    1673; Napoleon arrives, Oct. 15,
    1815; May 5, 1821; Apr. 22,
    1834.
St. Helens, Mount: erupts, May 18,
    1980.
St. Helier, Jul. 16.

St. Heliodorus, Jul. 3.

St. Helladius, Feb. 18.

St. Henry, Jan. 19.

St. Henry of Cocket, Jan. 16.

St. Henry the Emperor, Jul. 13.

St. Herbert, Mar. 20.

St. Herculanus, Nov. 7.

St. Heribald, Apr. 25.

St. Heribert, Mar. 16.

St. Hermagoras, Jul. 12.

St. Hermenegild, Apr. 13.

St. Hermenland, Mar. 25.

St. Hermes, Aug. 28.

St. Herve, Jun. 17.

St. Hesychius, Jun. 15; Oct. 3.

St. Hilarion, Oct. 21.

St. Hilarius, Feb. 28.

St. Hilary, Jan. 13; May 5.

St. Hilary of Galeata, May 15.

St. Hilda, Nov. 17.

St. Hildegard, Sep. 17.

St. Hildegund, Feb. 6; Apr. 20.

St. Hildelitha, Sep. 3.

St. Hildulf, Jul. 11.

St. Himelin, Mar. 10.

St. Hipparchus, Dec. 9.

St. Hippolytus, Aug. 13; Aug. 22.

St. Holy Simeon, Oct. 8.

St. Homobonus, Nov. 13.

St. Honoratus, Jan. 16; May 16.

St. Honorius, Sep. 30.

St. Hormisdas, Aug. 6; Aug. 8.

St. Hubert, Nov. 3.

St. Hugh, Apr. 1; Apr. 9; Nov. 17.

St. Hugh the Great, Apr. 29.

St. Humility, May 22.

St. Humphrey, Mar. 8.

St. Huna, Feb. 13.

St. Hunna, Apr. 15.

St. Hyacinth, Aug. 17.

St. Hyacintha, Mariscotti, Jan. 30.

St. Hybald, Dec. 14.

St. Hydroc, May 5.

St. Hyginus, Jan. 11.

St. Hypathius, Jun. 17.

St. Ia, Feb. 3.

St. Ia and her companions, Aug. 4.

St. Ibar, Apr. 23.

St. Ida of Herzfeld, Sep. 4.

St. Idesbald, Apr. 18.

St. Ignatius, May 28; Oct. 17; Oct. 23.

St. Ignatius of Laconi, May 11.

St. Ignatius of Loyola, Jul. 31.

St. Ildefonsus, Jan. 23.

St. Illtud, Nov. 6.

St. Indractus, Feb. 5.

St. Innocent, Apr. 17.

St. Innocent I, Jul. 28.

St. Irenaeus, Mar. 24; Jun. 28.

St. Irene, Apr. 2.

St. Irmina, Dec. 23.

St. Isaac, Sep. 9; Nov. 30.

St. Isaac of Constantinople, May 30.

St. Isaac of Cordova, Jun. 3.

St. Isaac of Spoleto, Apr. 11.

St. Isaias, Feb. 16.

St. Isias, May 15.

St. Isidore, Apr. 4.

St. Isidore of Alexandria, Jan. 15.

St. Isidore of Chios, May 15.

St. Isidore the Husbandman, May 15.

St. Isidore of Pelusium, Feb. 4.

St. Ismael, Jun. 16.

St. Issac Jogues and his Companions, Oct. 19.

St. Ita, Jan. 15.

St. Ithamar, Jun. 10.

St. Ive (England), patron of, Apr. 24.

St. Ivo, Apr. 24; May 23.

St. Ivo of Kermartin, May 19.

St. Iwi, Oct. 8.

St. Jambert, Aug. 12.

St. James, Apr. 30; Jul. 15.

St. James Day (Spain), Jul. 25.

St. James the Greater, Feast of, Jul. 25.

St. James Intercisus, Nov. 27.

St. James of Jerusalem, Feast of, Oct. 23.

St. James of the, March, Nov. 28.

St. James, Lyn, Mar. 13, 1947.

St. Jane Frances de Chantal, Dec. 12.

St. Januarius, Oct. 13.

St. Januarius, Bishop of Benevento, and his Companions, Sep. 19.

St. Jarlath, Jun. 6.

St. Jason, Jul. 12.

St. Jean Day (Quebec), Jun. 24.

St. Jean de Brebeuf, Oct. 19.

St. Jeremy, Feb. 16.

St. Jerome, Sep. 30.

St. Jerome Emiliani, Feb. 8.

St. Joachim, Jul. 26.

St. Joachima des Mas y de Vedruna, May 22.

St. Joan Antide-Thouret, Aug. 25.

St. Joan of Arc, May 30.

St. Joan de Lestonnac, Feb. 2.

St. Joan Delanoue, Aug. 17.

St. Joan of France, Feb. 4.

St. Joannicius, Nov. 4.

St. Joans, Mar. 29.

St. Joavan, Mar. 2.

St. John, Jan. 31; Jun. 26; Jun. 26; Jul. 11.

St. John I, May 18; May 27.

St. John III, Aug. 28.

St. John the Almsgiver, Jan. 23.

St. John Antony, Apr. 14.

St. John the Baptist; the nativity of, Jun. 24; beheading of, Aug. 29.

St. John Baptist de la Salle, Apr. 7.

St. John Baptist Rossi, May 23.

St. John before the Latin Gate, May 6.

St. John Berchmans, Nov. 26.

St. John, Bemard, Mar. 11, 1985.

St. John of Beverly, May 7.

St. John of Bridlington, Oct. 21.

St. John Calybites, Jan. 15.

St. John of Capistrano, Oct. 23.

St. John Cassian, Jul. 23.

St. John of Chinon, Jun. 27.

St. John Chrysostom, Sep. 13.

St. John Climacus, Mar. 30.

St. John of the Cross, Dec. 14.

St. John Damascene, Dec. 4.

St. John de Britto, Feb. 4.

St. John de Ribera, Jan. 6.

St. John the Dwarf, Oct. 17.

St. John of Egypt, Mar. 27.

St. John Eudes, Aug. 19.

St. John the Evangelist, Feast of, Dec. 27.

St. John Fisher, Jun. 22.

St. John Francis Regis, Jun. 16.

St. John of God, Mar. 8.

St. John the Good, Jan. 10.

St. John of Gorze, Feb. 27.

St. John of the Grating, Feb. 1.

St. John Gualbert, Jul. 12.

St. John the Iberian, Jul. 12.

St. John of Jerusalem, Order of, patron of, Jan. 23.

St. John, Jill, Aug. 19, 1940.

St. John Joseph of the Cross, Mar. 5.

St. John of Kanti, Dec. 23.

St. John Leonardi, Oct. 9.

St. John of Maltha, Feb. 8.

St. John of Matera, Jun. 20.

St. John of Meda, Sep. 26.

St. John Nepomucen, May 16.
St. John Nepomucen Neumann, Jan. 5.
St. John of Nicomedia, Sep. 7.
St. John Ogilvie, Mar. 10.
St. John of Panaca, Mar. 19.
St. John Reomay, Jan. 28.
St. John the Sage, Jan. 28.
St. John of Sahagun, Jun. 12.
St. John the Silent, May 13.
St. John Vianney, Aug. 4.
St. John Zedazneli and his Companions, Nov. 4.
St. John's Day (Ireland), Jun. 24.
St. John's Day (Latvia), Jun. 24.
St. John's (Ghent), May 6, 1432.
St. Johns, Adela Rogers, May 20, 1894.
St. Josaphat, Nov. 12; Nov. 27.
St. Joseph, Mar. 19; Nov. 13, 1962.
St. Joseph of Arimathea, Mar. 17.
St. Joseph Barsabas, Jul. 20.
St. Joseph Cafasso, Jun. 23.
St. Joseph Calasanctius, Aug. 25.
St. Joseph Cottolengo, Apr. 29.
St. Joseph of Cupertino, Sep. 18.
St. Joseph, Feast of (Spain), Mar. intro.
St. Joseph of Leonessa, Feb. 4.
St. Joseph Oriol, Mar. 23.
St. Joseph of Palestine, Jul. 22.
St. Joseph Pignatelli, Nov. 28.
St. Joseph the Worker Day (Spain, Vatican City), May 1.
St. Josepha Rossello, Dec. 7.
St. Joseph's Day, Mar. 19.
St. Jovita, Feb. 15.
St. Juan Bosco, Jan. 31.
St. Jude, Oct. 28.
St. Judith, Jun. 29.
St. Judoc, Dec. 13.
St. Julia, May 22.
St. Julian, Jan. 9; Jan. 27; Feb. 17; Feb. 27; Mar. 8; Nov. 1.
St. Julian of Antioch, Mar. 16.
St. Julian of Brioude, Aug. 28.
St. Julian the Hospitaller, Feb. 12.
St. Julian Sabas, Jan. 17.
St. Juliana, Feb. 16.
St. Juliana Falconieri, Jun. 19.
St. Julitta, Jun. 16; Jul. 30.
St. Julius, May 27; Jul. 3.
St. Julius I, Apr. 12.
St. Justa, Jul. 19.

St. Justice, Nov. 10.
St. Justin, Jun. 1.
St. Justina, Oct. 7.
St. Justinian, Dec. 5.
St. Justus, May 28; Aug. 6; Oct. 14.
St. Justus of Beauvais, Oct. 18.
St. Juthwara, Nov. 28.
St. Jutta, May 5.
St. Juvenal, May 3.
St. Juventinus, Jan. 25.
St. Kea, Nov. 5.
St. Kenelm, Jul. 17.
St. Kentigern, Jan. 14.
St. Kentigerna, Jan. 7.
St. Kessog, Mar. 10.
St. Kevin, Jun. 3.
St. Kew (Cornwall), patron of, Feb. 8.
St. Keyne, Oct. 8.
St. Kieran, Sep. 9.
St. Kieran of Saighir, Mar. 5.
St. Kilian, Jul. 8, Nov. 13.
St. Kinemark, Sep. 8.
St. Kitts, Nov. 1, 1964.
St. Kitts-Nevis, Feb. 16, 1967; Sep. 19, 1983.
St. Kyned, Aug. 1.
St. Ladislaus of Hungary, Jun. 27.
St. Lambert, Apr. 14; May 26; Sep. 17.
St. Landelinus, Jun. 15.
St. Landericus, Jun. 10.
St. Landoald, Mar. 19.
St. Laserian, Apr. 18.
St. Laudus, Sep. 22.
St. Laurence, Aug. 10.
St. Laurence, Archbishop of Canterbury, Feb. 3.
St. Laurence, Bishop of Spoleto, Feb. 3.
St. Laurence Giustiniani, Sep. 5.
St. Laurence O'Toole, Nov. 14.
St. Laurent, Louis, Nov. 15, 1948.
St. Laurent, Louis Stephen, Feb. 1, 1882; Jun. 17, 1957.
St. Laurent, Yves (Mathieu), Aug. 1, 1936.
St. Laurentius, Jun. 3.
St. Lawrence of Brindisi, Jul. 21.
St. Lawrence River, Feb. 4, 1629; Mar. 29, 1632.
St. Lawrence Seaway: opens, Jun. 26, 1959.
St. Lazarus, Feb. 11; Dec. 17.

St. Leander, Feb. 27.
St. Lebuin, Nov. 12.
St. Lelia, Aug. 11.
St. Leo, Feb. 18; May 25.
St. Leo II, Jul. 3.
St. Leo III, Jun. 12.
St. Leo IV, Jul. 17.
St. Leo IX, Apr. 19.
St. Leo the Great, Nov. 10.
St. Leobinus, Mar. 14.
St. Leocadia, Dec. 9.
St. Leocritia, Mar. 15.
St. Leodegarius, Oct. 2.
St. Leonard of Noblac, Nov. 6.
St. Leonard of Port Maurice, Nov. 26.
St. Leonard of Vandoeuvre, Oct. 15.
St. Leonides, Apr. 22.
St. Leontius, May 23.
St. Leopold of Austria, Nov. 15.
St. Leopold of Gaiche, Apr. 2.
St. Leutfridus, Jun. 21.
St. Lewina, Jul. 24.
St. Liberatus, Aug. 17.
St. Liborius, Jul. 23.
St. Licinius, Feb. 13.
St. Lide, Aug. 8.
St. Lietbertus, Jun. 23.
St. Limnaeus, Feb. 22.
St. Linus, Sep. 23.
St. Lioba, Sep. 28.
St. Liphardus, Jun. 3.
St. Liudhard, May 7.
St. Livinus, Nov. 12.
St. Loman, Feb. 17.
St. Longinus, Mar. 15.
St. Louis of Anjou, Aug. 19.
St. Louis Bertrand, Oct. 9.
St. Louis Browns (baseball), Sep. 30, 1953.
St. Louis of France, Aug. 25.
St. Louis, Mary of Montfort, Apr. 28.
St. Louis, Missouri, Feb. 15, 1764.
St. Louis, Sons of, Apr. 7, 1823.
St. Louisa de, Marillac, Mar. 15.
St. Lucia, Nov. 1, 1964; Feb. 16, 1967; Feb. 21, 1979.
St. Lucia Day (St. Lucia, Sweden), Dec. 13.
St. Lucian, Oct. 26.
St. Lucian of Antioch, Jan. 7.
St. Lucian of Beauvais, Jan. 8.
St. Lucillian, Jun. 3.
St. Lucius, Feb. 11; Feb. 24; Mar. 4; Oct. 19; Dec. 3.

St. Lucy, Dec. 13.
St. Lucy Filippini, Mar. 25.
St. Ludan, Feb. 12.
St. Ludger, Mar. 26.
St. Ludmila, Sep. 16.
St. Ludolf, Mar. 29.
St. Lufthildis, Jan. 23.
St. Luke, Feast of, Oct. 18.
St. Luke the Younger, Feb. 7.
St. Lull, Oct. 16.
St. Lupicinus, Feb. 28.
St. Lupus, Jul. 29; Sep. 1.
St. Lutgardis, Jun. 16.
St. Luxorius, Aug. 21.
St. Mabyn, Nov. 18.
St. Maeanisius, Sep. 3.
St. Maearius, Mar. 10.
St. Maearius of Alexandria, Jan. 2.
St. Maearius the Elder, Jan. 15.
St. Maearius of Ghent, Apr. 10.
St. Macarius the Wonder-worker,
    Apr. 1.
St. Macartan, Mar. 26.
St. Macedonius, Jan. 24.
St. Maehan, Sep. 28.
St. Maehar, Nov. 12.
St. Maerina the Elder, Jan. 14.
St. Maerina the Younger, Jul. 19.
St. Madelgisilus, May 30.
St. Madron, May 17.
St. Maelruain, Jul. 7.
St. Mafalda, May 2.
St. Magenulf, Oct. 5.
St. Maglorius, Oct. 23.
St. Magnencus, Jul. 25.
St. Magnus of Orkney, Apr. 16.
St. Maharsapor, Oct. 10.
St. Maimbod, Jan. 23.
St. Majolus, May 11.
St. Malaehy, Nov. 3.
St. Malehus, Oct. 21.
St. Mallonus, Oct. 22.
St. Malo, Nov. 15.
St. Mamas, Aug. 17.
St. Mamertus, May 11.
St. Manaeea, Oct. 14.
St. Manaeeus, Aug. 3.
St. Maneehildis, Oct. 14.
St. Mappalicus, Apr. 17.
St. Marcella, Jan. 31.
St. Marcellian, Jun. 18.
St. Marcellina, Jul. 17.
St. Mareellinus, Apr. 6; Apr. 20; Jun.
    2.

St. Mareellus, Aug. 14; Aug. 27; Sep.
    4; Nov. 1.
St. Mareellus I, Jan. 16.
St. Mareellus Akimetes, Dec. 29.
St. Marcellus the Centunon, Oct. 30.
St. Marchelm, Jul. 14.
St. Marcian, Jan. 10; Apr. 20; Jun. 17;
    Oct. 26; Nov. 2.
St. Mareiana, Jan. 9.
St. Mareulf, May 1.
St. Mardellinus, Apr. 26.
St. Margaret, Jul. 20.
St. Margaret of Cortona, Feb. 22.
St. Margaret of England, Feb. 3.
St. Margaret of Hulme, May 22.
St. Margaret of Hungary, Jan. 26.
St. Margaret Mary, Oct. 17.
St. Margaret Mary Alacoque, Oct. 16.
St. Margaret of Seotland, Nov. 16.
St. Mari, Aug. 5.
St. Marian, Apr. 30.
St. Mariana of Quito, May 26.
St. Marina, Feb. 12.
St. Marinus, Mar. 3; Sep. 4.
St. Marinus Day (San Manno), Sep.
    3.
St. Marius, Jan. 19; Jan. 27.
St. Mark, Mar. 29; Apr. 25; Jun. 18;
    Oct. 7.
St. Maro, Feb. 14.
St. Maron's Day (Lebanon), Feb. 9.
St. Martha, Jan. 19; Jul. 29.
St. Martial, Jun. 30; Oct. 13.
St. Martin, Mar. 20; Oct. 23; Nov. 11
St. Martin I, Apr. 13.
St. Martin de Porres, Nov. 3.
St. Martin of Vertou, Oct. 23.
St. Martina, Jan. 30.
St. Martinian, Oct. 16.
St. Martinian the Hermit, Feb. 13.
St. Martius, Apr. 13.
St. Martyrius, May 29.
St. Maruthas, Dec. 4.
St. Mary, Nov. 1; Nov. 24.
St. Mary of Cerevellon, Sep. 19.
St. Mary of Cleophas, Apr. 9.
St. Mary di Rosa, Dec. 15.
St. Mary of Egypt, Apr. 2.
St. Mary Euphrasia Pelletier, Apr. 2
St. Mary Frances of Naples, Oct. 6.
St. Mary Goretti, Jul. 6.
St. Mary Magdalen, Jul. 22.
St. Mary Magdalen Postel, Jul. 16.
St. Mary Mazzarello, May 14.

St. Mary Michaela Desmaisieres, Aug.
    25.
St. Maternus, Sep. 14.
St. Matilda, Mar. 14.
St. Matrona, Mar. 15.
St. Matthew, Feast of, Sep. 21.
St. Matthias the Apostle, Feb. 24.
St. Matthias, Feast of, May 14.
St. Maturinus, Nov. 1.
St. Maughold, Apr. 27.
St. Maura, May 3; Jul. 13.
St. Maura of Troyes, Sep. 21.
St. Maurice, Sep. 22.
St. Maurice of Carnoet, Oct. 13.
St. Maurilius, Sep. 13.
St. Mauruntius, May 5.
St. Maurus, Oct. 5.
St. Mawes, Nov. 18.
St. Mawnan, Dec. 18.
St. Maxellendis, Nov. 13.
St. Maxentia, Nov. 20.
St. Maxentius, Jun. 26.
St. Maximian, Aug. 21.
St. Maximilian, Mar. 12; Oct. 12.
St. Maximilian Kolbe, Aug. 14.
St. Maximinus, Jan. 25; May 29.
St. Maximinus of Aix, Jun. 8.
St. Maximus, Apr. 14; Apr. 30; Jun.
    25; Nov. 27.
St. Maximus the Confessor, Aug. 13.
St. Mechtildis, Nov. 16.
St. Mechtildis of Edelstetten, May 31.
St. Medard, Jun. 8.
St. Medericus, Aug. 29.
St. Meen, Jun. 21.
St. Meingold, Feb. 8.
St. Meinrad, Jan. 21.
St. Mel, Feb. 6.
St. Melaine, Nov. 6.
St. Melangell, May 27.
St. Melania the Younger, Dec. 31.
St. Melchu, Feb. 6.
St. Meletius, Feb. 12.
St. Meleusippus, Jan. 17.
St. Melito, Apr. 1.
St. Mellitus, Apr. 24.
St. Melorus, Oct. 1.
St. Mennas, Aug. 25; Nov. 11.
St. Mercurius, Nov. 25.
St. Merewenna, Feb. 10.
St. Meriadoc, Jun. 7.
St. Mesrop, Feb. 19.
St. Methodius, Feb. 14.
St. Methodius I, Jun. 14.

St. Methodius of Olympus, Sep. 18.
St. Metrophanes, Jun. 4.
St. Michael and All the Angels, Feast of, Sep. 29.
St. Michael of Chernigov, Sep. 21.
St. Michael de Sanctis, Apr. 10.
St. Michael Garicoits, May 14.
St. Milburga, Feb. 23.
St. Mildgyth, Jan. 17.
St. Mildred, Jul. 13.
St. Miltiades, Dec. 10.
St. Minver, Nov. 24.
St. Mirin, Sep. 15.
St. Mochoemoc, Mar. 13.
St. Mochta, Aug. 19.
St. Mochua of Timahoe, Dec. 23.
St. Modan, Feb. 4.
St. Modestus, Jun. 15.
St. Modoaldus, May 12.
St. Modomnoc, Feb. 13.
St. Modwenna, Jul. 6.
St. Molaug, Jun. 25.
St. Moling, Jun. 17.
St. Mommolinus, Oct. 16.
St. Monegundis, Jul. 2.
St. Monenna, Jul. 6.
St. Monica, Aug. 27.
St. Montanus, Feb. 24.
St. Morand, Jun. 3.
St. Moses, Feb. 7; Nov. 25.
St. Moses the Black, Aug. 28.
St. Mucius, May 13.
St. Mura, Mar. 12.
St. Murtagh, Aug. 12.
St. Nabor, Jul. 12.
St. Narcissus, Oct. 29.
St. Natalia, Sep. 8.
St. Nathalan, Jan. 19.
St. Nathy, Aug. 9.
St. Nazaire, Mar. 28, 1942.
St. Nazarius, Jul. 28.
St. Nectan, Jun. 17.
St. Nectarius, Oct. 11.
St. Nemesius, Dec. 19.
St. Nemesius and many Companions, Sep. 10.
St. Neon, Aug. 23.
St. Neot, Jul. 31.
St. Nereus, May 12.
St. Nerses, Nov. 20.
St. Nerses I, Nov. 19.
St. Nerses Klaietsi, Aug. 13.
St. Nerses Lampronatsi, Jul. 17.
St. Nestabus, Sep. 8.

St. Nestor, Feb. 26; Sep. 8.
St. Nicander, Jun. 17.
St. Nicarete, Dec. 27.
St. Nicasius, Dec. 14.
St. Nicephorus, Feb. 9; Mar. 13.
St. Nicetas, Jan. 31; Apr. 2; Jun. 22.
St. Nicetas of Constantinople, Oct. 6.
St. Nicetas the Goth, Sep. 15.
St. Nicetas of Pereaslau, May 24.
St. Nicetius, Feb. 8; Apr. 2; Dec. 5.
St. Nicholas, Dec. 6.
St. Nicholas I, Nov. 13.
St. Nicholas Pieck and his companions, Jul. 9.
St. Nicholas the Pilgrim, Jun. 2.
St. Nicholas Studites, Feb. 4.
St. Nicholas of Tolentino, Sep. 10.
St. Nicholas von Flue, Mar. 22.
St. Nicomedes, Sep. 15.
St. Nikon (Metanoeite), Nov. 26.
St. Nilus the Elder, Nov. 12.
St. Nilus of Rossano, Sep. 26.
St. Ninian, Sep. 16.
St. Ninnoc, Jun. 4.
St. Nio, Dec. 15.
St. Non, Mar. 3.
St. Nonna, Aug. 5.
St. Norbert, Jun. 6.
St. Notburga, Sep. 14.
St. Nothelm, Oct. 17.
St. Nunilo, Oct. 22.
St. Nympha, Nov. 10.
St. Oda, Jul. 4.
St. Odilia, Dec. 13.
St. Odilio, Jan. 1.
St. Odo of Cluny, Nov. 18.
St. Odulf, Jun. 12.
St. Oengus, Mar. 11.
St. Offa of Essex, Dec. 15.
St. Olaf, Jul. 29.
St. Olga, Jul. 11.
St. Ollegarius, Mar. 6.
St. Olympias, Dec. 17.
St. Onesimus, Feb. 16.
St. Onuphnus, Jun. 12.
St. Opatatus, Apr. 16.
St. Opportuna, Apr. 22.
St. Optatus, Jun. 4.
St. Orsiesius, Jun. 15.
St. Osburga, Mar. 30.
St. Osmund, Dec. 4.
St. Oswald, Aug. 9.
St. Oswald of Worcester, Feb. 28.
St. Oswin, Aug. 20.

St. Osyth, Oct. 7.
St. Otger, May 8.
St. Otteran, Oct. 27.
St. Otto, Jul. 2.
St. Pachomius, May 9.
St. Pacian, Mar. 9.
St. Pacifico of San Severino, Sep. 24.
St. Palladius, Jul. 7.
St. Pambo, Jul. 18.
St. Pammachius, Aug. 30.
St. Pamphilus, Apr. 28; Jun. 1.
St. Pancras, Apr. 2; May 12.
St. Pandonia, Aug. 26.
St. Pantaenus, Jul. 7.
St. Pantaleon, Jul. 27.
St. Paphnutius, Sep. 11.
St. Papylus, Apr. 13.
St. Paregorius, Feb. 18.
St. Parisio, Jun. 11.
St. Parthenius, May 19.
St. Paschal I, Feb. 11.
St. Paschal Baylon, May 17.
St. Paschasius Radbertus, Apr. 26.
St. Pastor, Aug. 6.
St. Paternus, Apr. 16.
St. Paternus of Abdinghof, Apr. 10.
St. Patiens, Sep. 11.
St. Patricia, Aug. 25.
St. Patrick, Mar. 17.
St. Patrick's Day, Mar. intro; Irish bank holiday, Mar. 23, 1903.
St. Patrick's Day (Ireland), Mar. 17.
St. Patroclus, Jan. 21.
St. Paul, Jan. 15; Jun. 26; Jun. 29; Jul. 25.
St. Paul I, Jun. 7; Jun. 28.
St. Paul IV, Aug. 28.
St. Paul Aurelian, Mar. 12.
St. Paul of the Cross, Oct. 19.
St. Paul of Cyprus, Mar. 17.
St. Paul of Latros, Dec. 15.
St. Paul Miki, Feb. 6.
St. Paul of Narbonne, Mar. 22.
St. Paul the Simple, Mar. 7.
St. Paula, Jan. 26.
St. Paulinus, Jan. 28; Aug. 31; Oct. 10.
St. Paulinus of Nola, Jun. 22.
St. Paul's Shipwreck (Malta), Feb. 10.
St. Pega, Jan. 8.
St. Pelagia of Antioch, Jun. 9.
St. Pelagia the Penitent, Oct. 8.
St. Pelagia of Tarsus, May 4.
St. Pelagius, Jun. 26.

St. Peleus, Sep. 19.

St. Peregrine, May 16.

St. Peregrine Laziosi, May 1.

St. Pergentinus, Jun. 3.

St. Perpetua, Mar. 7.

St. Perpetuus, Apr. 8.

St. Peter, Jan. 9; Mar. 12; Apr. 26; May 8; Jun. 2; Jun. 29; Nov. 26.

St. Peter ad Vincula, Aug. 1.

St. Peter of Alcantara, Oct. 19.

St. Peter Arbues, Sep. 17.

St. Peter of Atroa, Jan. 1.

St. Peter Balsam, Jan. 3.

St. Peter Canisius, Dec. 21.

St. Peter of Canterbury, Dec. 30.

St. Peter of Cava, Mar. 4.

St. Peter of Chavanon, Sep. 11.

St. Peter Chrysologus, Jul. 30.

St. Peter Claver, Sep. 9.

St. Peter Damian, Feb. 21; Feb. 23.

St. Peter Fourier, Dec. 9.

St. Peter Julian Eymard, Aug. 3.

St. Peter of Lampsacus, May 15.

St. Peter Mary Chanel, Apr. 28.

St. Peter of Mount Athos, Jun. 12.

St. Peter Nolasco, Jan. 28.

St. Peter Orseolo, Jan. 10.

St. Peter Regalatus, May 13.

St. Peter Thomas, Jan. 28.

St. Peter of Verona, Apr. 29.

St. Peter's Kaiserwerth, patron of, Mar. 1.

St. Petersburg (Russia), May 27, 1703; ship canal, May 27, 1885; Jan. 22, 1905; Apr. 22, 1920.

St. Petroc, Jun. 4.

St. Petronax, May 6.

St. Petronilla, May 31.

St. Petronius, Oct. 4.

St. Pharaidis, Jan. 4.

St. Philastrius, Jul. 18.

St. Phileas, Feb. 4.

St. Philemon, Mar. 8.

St. Philibert, Aug. 20.

St. Philip Benizi, Aug. 23.

St. Philip, Bishop of Heraclea, Oct. 22.

St. Philip the Deacon, Jun. 6.

St. Philip Neri, May 26.

St. Philip of Zell, May 3.

St. Philogonius, Dec. 20.

St. Philomena, Aug. 10.

St. Phocas, Sep. 22.

St. Phocas of Antioch, Mar. 5.

St. Phoebe, Sep. 3.

St. Photina, Mar. 20.

St. Pierius, Nov. 4.

St. Pionius, Feb. 1.

St. Piran, Mar. 5.

St. Pirrninus, Nov. 3.

St. Pius I, Jul. 11.

St. Pius V, Apr. 30.

St. Pius X, Aug. 21.

St. Placid, Oct. 5.

St. Plato, Apr. 4.

St. Plechelm, May 8.

St. Plegmund, Aug. 2.

St. Poemen, Aug. 27.

St. Pollio, Apr. 28.

St. Polycarp, Feb. 23.

St. Polyeuctus, Feb. 13.

St. Pompilio Pirrotti, Jul. 15.

St. Pontian, Aug. 13.

St. Pontius, May 14.

St. Poppo, Jan. 25.

St. Porcarius, Aug. 12.

St. Porphyry, Feb. 26.

St. Possidius, May 16.

St. Potamon, May 18.

St. Pothinus, Jun. 2.

St. Praejectus, Jan. 25.

St. Praetextatus, Feb. 24.

St. Praxedes, Jul. 21.

St. Primus, Jun. 9.

St. Prisca, Jan. 18; Jul. 8.

St. Priscilla, Jan. 16.

St. Priscus, May 26.

St. Priscus of Capua, Sep. 1.

St. Probus, Oct. 11.

St. Processus and Martinian, Jul. 2.

St. Proclus, Oct. 23.

St. Procopius, Jul. 8.

St. Proculus, Jun. 1.

St. Prosper, Jun. 25.

St. Prosper of Aquitaine, Jun. 25.

St. Proterius, Feb. 28.

St. Prudentius, Apr. 6.

St. Ptolemaeus, Oct. 19.

St. Publia, Oct. 9.

St. Publius, Jan. 25.

St. Pudens, May 19.

St. Pudentiana, May 19.

St. Pulcheria, Sep. 10.

St. Quadratus, May 26.

St. Quenburga, Aug. 31.

St. Quentin, Battle of, Aug. 10, 1557.

St. Quintinus, Oct. 31.

St. Quirinus, Jun. 4.

St. Quiteria, May 22.

St. Radbod, Nov. 29.

St. Radegund, Aug. 13.

St. Rainerius, Jun. 17.

St. Ralph, Jun. 21.

St. Raphaela Mary, Jan. 6.

St. Raymond of Penafort, Jan. 7.

St. Raymund Nonnatus, Aug. 31.

St. Raymund of Toulouse, Jul. 8.

St. Regina, Sep. 7.

St. Regulus, Mar. 30.

St. Reineldis, Jul. 16.

St. Reinold, Jan. 7.

St. Rembert, Feb. 4.

St. Remigius, Oct. 1.

St. Reparata, Oct. 8.

St. Respicius, Nov. 10.

St. Restituta of Sora, May 27.

St. Revocatus, Mar. 7.

St. Richard, Feb. 7; Jun. 9.

St. Richard of Wyche, Apr. 2.

St. Richardis, Sep. 18.

St. Richarius, Apr. 26.

St. Richimir, Jan. 17.

St. Rictrudis, May 12.

St. Rigobert, Jan. 4.

St. Rita of Cascia, May 22.

St. Robert, Jun. 7.

St. Robert Ballarrnine, Sep. 17.

St. Robert of Chaise-Dieu, Apr. 17.

St. Robert of Molesmes, Apr. 29.

St. Rock, Aug. 16.

St. Roderic, Mar. 13.

St. Rogatian, May 24.

St. Romanus, Feb. 28; May 22; Aug. 9; Oct. 23.

St. Romanus of Antioch, Nov. 18.

St. Romanus the Melodist, Oct. 1.

St. Romaric, Dec. 8.

St. Romualdo, Jun. 19.

St. Romula and her companions, Jul. 23.

St. Romulus, Jul. 6.

St. Ronan, Feb. 7; Jun. 1.

St. Rosalia, Sep. 4.

St. Rose of Lima (Peru), Aug. 23; Aug. 30.

St. Rose of Viterbo, Sep. 4.

St. Ruadan of Lothra, Apr. 15.

St. Rudesind, Mar. 1.

St. Ruffin, Jul. 24.

St. Rufina, Jul. 10; Jul. 19.

St. Rufinus, Jun. 14.

St. Rufus of Capua, Aug. 27.

St. Rumold, Jul. 3.
St. Rumon, Aug. 30.
St. Rumwald, Nov. 3.
St. Rupert, Mar. 29; May 15.
St. Rusticus, Oct. 9; Oct. 26.
St. Sabas, Dec. 5.
St. Sabas the Goth, Apr. 12.
St. Sabian, Jan. 29.
St. Sabina, Aug. 29.
St. Sabinus, Jan. 17; Feb. 9; Dec. 30.
St. Sadoth, Feb. 20.
St. Saethrith, Jan. 10.
St. Salaberga, Sep. 22.
St. Salome, Jun. 29.
St. Salvator of Horta, Mar. 18.
St. Salvius, Jan. 11; Jun. 26; Oct. 28.
St. Samonas, Nov. 14.
St. Samson, Jul. 28.
St. Samson of Constantinople, Jun. 27.
St. Samthann, Dec. 18.
St. Samuel, Feb. 16.
St. Sanchia, Jun. 17.
St. Sanctius, Jun. 5.
St. Sapor, Nov. 30.
St. Saturninus, Feb. 11; Mar. 7; Nov. 29.
St. Saturus, Mar. 7; Mar. 29.
St. Satyrus, Sep. 17.
St. Sava, Jan. 14.
St. Savin, Oct. 9.
St. Scholastica, Feb. 10.
St. Sebald, Aug. 19.
St. Sebastian, Jan. 20.
St. Sebastian Day (Rio de Janeiro, Brazil), Jan. 20.
St. Sebbe, Sep. 1.
St. Secunda, Jul. 10.
St. Secundinus, Nov. 27.
St. Secundulus, Mar. 7.
St. Seirol, Feb. 1.
St. Senan of Scattery Island, Mar. 8.
St. Senator, May 28.
St. Sennen, Jul. 30.
St. Senoch, Oct. 23.
St. Sequanus, Sep. 19.
St. Seraphino, Oct. 17.
St. Serapion, Mar. 21; Oct. 30.
St. Serenicus, May 7.
St. Serenus, May 7.
St. Serenus the Gardener, Feb. 23.
St. Serf, Jul. 1.
St. Sergius, Jun. 28.
St. Sergius I, Sep. 8.

St. Sergius of Radonezh, Sep. 25.
St. Servatius, May 13.
St. Servulus, Dec. 23.
St. Sethrida, Jul. 7.
St. Severian, Feb. 21.
St. Severinus, Jan. 8; Feb. 11; Oct. 23.
St. Severinus Boethius, Oct. 23.
St. Severinus of Noricum, Jan. 8.
St. Sexburga, Jul. 6.
St. Shenute, Jul. 1.
St. Sidonius Apollinaris, Aug. 21.
St. Sidwell, Jul. 31.
St. Sigebert, Feb. 1.
St. Sigfrid, Feb. 15; Aug. 22.
St. Sigiramnus, Dec. 5.
St. Sigismund of Burgundy, May 1.
St. Silas, Jul. 13.
St. Silverius, Jun. 20.
St. Silvester I, Dec. 31.
St. Silvester Gozzolini, Nov. 26.
St. Silvin, Feb. 17.
St. Simeon, Feb. 18.
St. Simeon the Armenian, Jul. 26.
St. Simeon Barsabae, Apr. 21.
St. Simeon, Holiday of, Feb. 2.
St. Simeon Metaphrastff, Nov. 28.
St. Simeon Salus, Jul. 1.
St. Simeon Stylites the Younger, Sep. 3.
St. Simeon of Syracuse, Jun. 1.
St. Simon, Oct. 28.
St. Simon of Crepy, Sep. 30.
St. Simon Stock, May 16.
St. Simon the Stylite, Jan. 5.
St. Simon of Trent, Mar. 24.
St. Simplicius, Mar. 10; Jun. 24; Jul. 29.
St. Siricius, Nov. 26.
St. Sisinnius, May 29.
St. Sisoes, Jul. 6.
St. Sithney, Aug. 4.
St. Sixtus, Apr. 2.
St. Sixtus II, Aug. 7.
St. Sixtus III, Aug. 19.
St. Socrates, Sep. 17.
St. Sola, Dec. 3.
St. Solangia, May 10.
St. Solomon, Mar. 13.
St. Sophronius, Mar. 11.
St. Soter, Apr. 22.
St. Soteris, Feb. 10.
St. Sozon, Sep. 7.
St. Speratus, Jul. 17.

St. Speusippus, Jan. 17.
St. Spiridion, Dec. 14.
St. Stanislaus, Apr. 11.
St. Stanislaus Kostka, Nov. 13.
St. Stephen, Apr. 26; Jun. 2; Sep. 17; Dec. 15.
St. Stephen I, Aug. 2.
St. Stephen, Feast of, Dec. 26.
St. Stephen Harding, Apr. 17.
St. Stephen of Hungary, Aug. 16.
St. Stephen of Muret, Feb. 8.
St. Stephen of Obazine, Mar. 8.
St. Stephen Pechersky, Apr. 27.
St. Stephen of Rieti, Feb. 13.
St. Stephen the Younger, Nov. 28.
St. Stephen's Day, Dec. 26.
St. Sturmi, Dec. 17.
St. Sulian, Jul. 29.
St. Sulpicius, Jan. 29.
St. Sulpicius II, Jan. 17.
St. Sunniva, Jul. 8.
St. Superius, Jun. 26.
St. Swithbert, Mar. 1.
St. Swithin, Jul. 15.
St. Syagrius, Aug. 27.
St. Symmachus, Jul. 19.
St. Symphorian, Aug. 22.
St. Symphorosa and her seven sons, Jul. 18.
St. Syncletica, Jan. 5.
St. Tanco, Feb. 15.
St. Tancred, Sep. 30.
St. Tarachus, Oct. 11.
St. Tarasius, Feb. 25.
St. Tarsicius, Aug. 15.
St. Tathai, Dec. 26.
St. Tatian Dulas, Jun. 15.
St. Teilo, Feb. 9.
St. Telesphorus, Jan. 5.
St. Tenenan, Jul. 16.
St. Teresa, Jun. 17.
St. Teresa of Avila, Oct. 15.
St. Teresa Margaret Redi, Mar. 11.
St. Ternan, Jun. 12.
St. Tewdric, Apr. 1.
St. Thais, Oct. 8.
St. Thalassius, Feb. 22.
St. Thalelaceus, May 20.
St. Thalelaeus the Hermit, Feb. 27.
St. Thea, Jul. 25.
St. Thecla, Aug. 19; Oct. 15.
St. Thecla of Iconium, Sep. 23.
St. Theobald of Alba, Jun. 1.
St. Theobald of Marly, Jul. 27.

St. Theobald of Provins, Jun. 30.

St. Theoctista, Nov. 10.

St. Theodard, May l; Sep. 10.

St. Theodata, Aug. 2.

St. Theodolus, May 3.

St. Theodora of Alexandria, Sep. 11.

St. Theodore, Sep. 19; Sep. 21; Dec. 27.

St. Theodore of Heraclea, Feb. 7.

St. Theodore the Sanctified, Dec. 28.

St. Theodore the Studite, Nov. 11.

St. Theodore of Sykeon, Apr. 22.

St. Theodore Tiro, Nov. 9.

St. Theodoret, Oct. 23.

St. Theodoric, Jul. 1.

St. Theodosia, Apr. 2; May 29.

St. Theodosius the Cenobiarch, Jan. 11.

St. Theodosius Perchersky, Jul. 10.

St. Theodulus, Feb. 17.

St. Theonilla, Aug. 23.

St. Theophanes, Dec. 27.

St. Theophanes the Chronicler, Mar. 12.

St. Theophilus of Corte, May 21.

St. Theophilus the Penitent, Feb. 4.

St. Theophylact, Mar. 7.

St. Theotonius, Feb. 18.

St. Therese of Lisieux, Oct. 1; May 17, 1925.

St. Theuderius, Oct. 29.

St. Thodora, Apr. 28.

St. Thomas, Dec. 21.

St. Thomas Acquinas, Jan. 28.

St. Thomas Becket, Dec. 29.

St. Thomas Cantelupe, Oct. 3.

St. Thomas of Dover, Aug. 2.

St. Thomas, Feast of, Jul. 3.

St. Thomas More, Jun. 22.

St. Thomas of Villanova, Sep. 22.

St. Thorfinn, Jan. 8.

St. Thorlac, Dec. 23.

St. Tibba, Mar. 6.

St. Tiburtius, Apr. 14.

St. Tigernach, Apr. 4.

St. Tigrius, Jan. 12.

St. Tillo, Jan. 7.

St. Timothy, Jan. 24; Jan. 26; May 3; Aug. 19; Aug. 22.

St. Titus, Jan. 26.

St. Torquatus, May 15.

St. Torthred, Sep. 30.

St. Tova, Sep. 30.

St. Triduana, Oct. 8.

St. Triphyllius, Jun. 13.

St. Trophimus, Dec. 29.

St. Trudo, Nov. 23.

St. Trumwin, Feb. 10.

St. Trypho, Nov. 10.

St. Tuda, Oct. 21.

St. Tudwal, Dec. 1.

St. Tudy, May 11.

St. Turbibius, Apr. 16.

St. Turibius, Apr. 27.

St. Turibius of Mongrovejo, Mar. 23.

St. Tutlio, Mar. 28.

St. Tychon, Jun. 16.

St. Tyrannio, Feb. 20.

St. Tysilio, Nov. 8.

St. Ubald, May 16.

St. Ulphia, Jan. 31.

St. Ulric, Jul. 4.

St. Ulric of Zell, Jul. 14.

St. Ultan, May 2; Sep. 4.

St. Urban I, May 25.

St. Urbicius, Jun. 3.

St. Urho's Day, Mar. intro.; Mar. 16.

St. Urith of Chittlehampton, Jul. 8.

St. Ursicinus, Dec. 20.

St. Ursmar, Apr. 19.

St. Ursula and her Maidens, Oct. 21.

St. Ursula's Day (British Virgin Islands), Oct. 21.

St. Valentina, Jul. 25.

St. Valentine, Jan. 7; Feb. 14.

St. Valentine's Day, Feb. 14.

St. Valentine's Day Massacre, Feb. 14, 1929.

St. Valeria, Apr. 28.

St. Valerian, Sep. 4.

St. Valerian and other Martyrs in Africa, Dec. 15.

St. Valerius, Apr. 14; Jun. 14.

St. Varus, Oct. 19.

St. Vedast, Feb. 6.

St. Venantius, May 18.

St. Venantius Fortunatus, Dec. 14.

St. Venerius, May 4.

St. Veremund, Mar. 8.

St. Verena, Sep. 1.

St. Veronica, Jul. 12.

St. Veronica Giuliani, Jul. 9.

St. Vicelin, Dec. 12.

St. Victor I, Jul. 28.

St. Victor the Hermit, Feb. 26.

St. Victor of Marseilles, Jul. 21.

St. Victor Maurus, May 8.

St. Victoria, Nov. 17.

St. Victorian, Mar. 23.

St. Victorinus, Feb. 25; Nov. 2.

St. Victricius, Aug. 7.

St. Vigilius, Jun. 26.

St. Vigor, Nov. 1.

St. Vincent, Nov. 1, 1964.

St. Vincent of Agen, Jun. 9.

St. Vincent de Paul, Sep. 27.

St. Vincent Ferrer, Apr. 5.

St. Vincent and the Grenadines, Oct. 27, 1979.

St. Vincent of Lerins, May 24.

St. Vincent Madelgarius, Sep. 20.

St. Vincent Pallotti, Jan. 22.

St. Vincent of Saragossa, Jan 22.

St. Vincent Strambi, Sep. 25.

St. Vincentia Gerosa, Jun. 4.

St. Vincentian, Jan. 2.

St. Vindician, Mar. 11.

St. Virgil, Mar. 5; Nov. 27.

St. Vitalian, Jan. 27.

St. Vitalis, Apr. 28; Nov. 4.

St. Vitonus, Nov. 9.

St. Vitus, Jun. 15.

St. Vladimir of Kiev, Jul. 15.

St. Vodalus, Feb. 5.

St. Volusian, Jan. 18.

St. Vulflagius, Jun. 7.

St. Vulmar, Jul. 20.

St. Walaricus, Apr. 1.

St. Walburga, Feb. 25.

St. Waldebert, May 2.

St. Waldetrudis, Apr. 9.

St. Walfrid, Feb. 15.

St. Walstan, May 30.

St. Walter of L'Esterp, May 11.

St. Walter of Pontoise, Apr. 8.

St. Waltheof, Aug. 3.

St. Wandregisilus, Jul. 22.

St. Waningus, Jan. 9.

St. Wenceslaus of Bohemia, Sep. 28.

St. Werburga, Feb. 3.

St. Wiborada, May 2.

St. Wigbert, Aug. 13.

St. Wilfrid the Younger, Apr. 29.

St. Wilgefortis, Jul. 20.

St. Willehad, Nov. 8.

St. William, Jan. 10; Jun. 8; Sep. 2.

St. William of Eskill, Apr. 6.

St. William Firmatus of Tours, Apr. 24.

St. William of Gellone, May 28.

St. William of Maleval, Feb. 10.

St. William of Norwich, Mar. 24.

St. William Pinchon, Jul. 29.

St. William of Rochester, May 23.

St. William of Saint Benignus, Jan. 1.

St. William of Vercelli, Jun. 25.

St. Willibald, Jun. 7.

St. Willibrord, Nov. 7.

St. Willigis, Feb. 23.

St. Wiltrudis, Jan. 6.

St. Winebald, Dec. 18.

St. Winifred, Nov. 3.

St. Winnoc, Nov. 6.

St. Winwaloe, Mar. 3.

St. Wiro, May 8.

St. Wistan, Jun. 1.

St. Wite, Jun. 1.

St. Withburga, Jul. 8.

St. Wivina, Dec. 17.

St. Wolfgang, Oct. 31.

St. Wulfhad, Jul. 24.

St. Wulfhilda, Sep. 9.

St. Wulfram, Mar. 20.

St. Wulfric, Feb. 20.

St. Wulfstan, Jan. 19.

St. Wulganus, Nov. 3.

St. Wulsin, Jan. 8.

St. Zachaeus, Nov. 17.

St. Zachary, Mar. 15; Nov. 5.

St. Zeno, Apr. 12; Sep. 8.

St. Zenobius, Feb. 20; May 25.

St. Zephyrinus, Aug. 26.

St. Zita, Apr. 27.

St. Zoe, May 2.

St. Zoilus and his companions, Jun. 27.

St. Zosimus, Mar. 30; Dec. 26.

SS. Abundius, Abundantius, Sep. 16.

SS. Alcmund and Tilbert, Sep. 7.

SS. Alphius, May 10.

SS. Ammon, Dec. 20.

SS. Apphia and Philemon, Nov. 22.

SS. Chaeremon and Ischyrion, Dec. 22.

SS. Charles Lwanga and Joseph Mkasa, Jun. 3.

SS. Claudius and Hilaria, Dec. 3.

SS. Cosmas and Damian, Sep. 26.

SS. Cyprian and Justina, Sep. 26.

SS. Cyril & Methodius Day (Bulgaria), May 24.

SS. Dionysia and Majorieus, Dec. 6.

SS. Donatian and Laetus, Sep. 6.

SS. Epimachus and Alexander, Dec. 12.

SS. Faith, Hope, Charity, and Wisdom, Aug. 1.

SS. Felix and Cyprian, Oct. 12.

SS. Florus and Laurus, Aug. 18.

SS. Fuscian and Victoricus, and Gentian, Dec. 11

SS. James and Philip, Feast of, May 1.

SS. Marcellus and Apuleius, Oct. 8.

SS. Mennas, Hermogenes, and Eugraphus, Dec. 10.

SS. Peter and Paul, Feast of, Jun. 29.

SS. Philemon and Apphia, Nov. 22.

SS. Philip and James, Feast of, May 1.

SS. Plutarch and Potamiaena, Jun. 28.

SS. Protus and Hyacinth, Sep. 11.

SS. Rhipsime and Gaiana, Sep. 29.

SS. Rugus and Zosimus, Dec. 18.

SS. Sergius and Bacchus, Oct. 8.

SS. Tharsilla and Emiliana, Dec. 23.

SS. Thecusa and Theodotus, May 18.

SS. Theodore, David, and Constantine, Sep. 19.

SS. Theodotus and Theeusa, May 18.

SS. Tiburtius and Susanna, Aug. 11.

SS. Victoria and Anatolia, Dec. 23.

SS. William, Stephen and Raymund, May 29.

Saipan (Mariana Islands): U.S. Marines land, Jun. 15, 1944; Jul. 8, 1944.

Sakharov, Andrei, May 21, 1921; Oct. 9, 1975; Jan. 22, 1980; Dec. 19, 1986; Apr. 20, 1989.

Sakmann, Bert, Jun. 12, 1942.

Saks, Gene Michael, Nov. 8, 1921.

Saladin (Damascus): takes Jerusalem, Oct. 2, 1187; Sep. 1, 1192; dies, Mar. 4, 1193.

Salal, Abdullah al-, Nov. 5, 1967.

Salam, Abdus, Jan. 29, 1926.

Salamanca, Battle of: ends, Jul. 22, 1812.

Salant, Richard, Apr. 14, 1914.

Salazar, Antonio de Oliveira, Apr. 28, 1889; Jul. 5, 1932.

Saldanha, Joao Carlos, Nov. 17, 1790.

Salem Witch Trials: begin, Mar. 1, 1692.

Salerno (Italy): U.S. landing, Sep. 9, 1943.

Sales, Soupy, Jan. 8, 1930.

Salic Law, Jun. 20, 1837.

Salidivar, Yolanda, Oct. 23, 1995.

Salinas de Gortari, Carlos: inaugurated, Dec. 1, 1988.

Salinger, J. D., Jan. 1, 1919; Jul. 16, 1951.

Salinger, Pierre, Jun. 14, 1925.

Salisbury, Harrison (Evans), Nov. 14, 1908.

Salk, Jonas Edward, Oct. 28, 1914. Apr. 12, 1955.

Salk, Lee, Dec. 27, 1926.

Salli, Lazarus: inaugurated, Oct. 25, 1985.

Salome (opera): premiere, Dec. 9, 1905. Jan. 22, 1907.

Salonika (Greece), Jun. 3, 1916.

Salonika, patron of, Oct. 8.

SALT II: agreements, May 9, 1979; Jun. 18, 1979.

Salt, Barbara, Nov. 3, 1962.

Salt Lake Valley, Jul. 22, 1847.

Saltonstall, Leverett, Sep. 1, 1892.

Saltpetre War, Apr. 5, 1879; ends, Oct. 20, 1883.

Saluzzo, Apr. 3, 1559.

Salvation Army, Jul. 2, 1865; Mar. 10, 1880.

Salvation Army Week, National, May intro.

Salyut, Apr. 24, 1971; Jun. 7, 1971.

Salyut 6, Nov. 2, 1978.

Salyut 7, Nov. 23, 1983.

Salzburg: union with Germany, May 29, 1921.

Samaranch, Juan Antonio, Jul. 20, 1920.

Samoa (Western): independence, Jan. 1, 1962.

Samora (Portugal), Apr. 23, 1909.

Sampras, Pete, Aug. 12, 1971; Jul. 5, 1998.

Sampson, Edith, Aug. 24, 1950.

Sampson, Ralph, Jul. 7, 1960.

Samuelson, Paul Anthony, May 15, 1915.

Samuelsson, Bengt I., May 21, 1934.

San, Battle of the, May 16, 1915.

San Domingo: blacks revolt, Aug. 22, 1791.

San Fermin, Feria de (Spain), Jul. intro.

San Francisco, Jan. 3, 1847; earthquake, Apr. 18, 1906; Oct. 11, 1906; Jan. 25, 1915.

San Francisco 49ers, Jan. 29, 1995.

San Francisco Symphony Orchestra: established, Dec. 8, 1911.

San Francisco Treaty of Peace, Sep. 8, 1951.

San Jacinto, Apr. 21, 1836.

San Jacinto, Battle of (Nicaragua), Sep. 14.

San Jacinto Day (Texas), Apr. 21.

San Joaquin Valley, Jan. 24, 1848.

San Jose (Costa Rica), Sep. 24, 1950.

San Juan Day (Puerto Rico), Jun. 24.

San Juan del Norte (Nicaragua), Apr. 14, 1984.

San Juan Hill, Battle of, Jul. 1, 1898.

San Lorenzo, Treaty of (Pinckney's Treaty), Oct. 27, 1795.

San Martin, Jose de, Feb. 25, 1778; Jul. 28, 1821.

San Miguel Triangle, Sep. 27, 1947.

San Salvador Charter, Dec. 14, 1951.

San Salvador's Feast (El Salvador), Aug. 4; Aug. 5; Aug. 6.

San Stefano, Mar. 3, 1878.

Sanchez, George I., Oct. 4, 1906.

Sanchez Hernandez, Fidel, Mar. 5, 1967.

Sanchez, Oscar Arias, Sep. 13, 1941.

Sand Creek massacre, Nov. 29, 1864.

Sand, George, Jul. 1, 1804.

Sand, Karl Ludwig, Sep. 20, 1819.

Sand, Paul, Mar. 5, 1941.

Sand River Convention, Jan. 17, 1852.

Sandburg, Carl, Jan. 6, 1878.

Sanders, Barry, Jul. 16, 1968.

Sanders, Deion, Aug. 9, 1967.

Sanders, George, Aug. 3, 1906.

Sanders, Harland, Sep. 9, 1890; Aug. 10, 1970.

Sanders, Jil, Nov. 27, 1943.

Sanders, Marlene, Jan. 10, 1931.

Sanderson, Derek Michael, Jun. 16, 1946.

Sandinista National Liberation Front, Feb. 12, 1978; seizes national palace in Managua, Nicaragua, Aug. 22, 1978; Jul. 17, 1979.

Sandinista Revolution, Anniversary of the (Nicaragua), Jul. 19.

Sandler, Adam, Sep. 9, 1966.

Sands, Bobby, May 5, 1981.

Sandy, Gary, Dec. 25, 1946.

Sanford, Isabel Gwendolyn, Aug. 29, 1933.

Sanford, Terry, Aug. 20, 1917.

Sang, Samantha, Aug. 5, 1953.

Sanga Sanga, Apr. 2, 1945.

Sanger, Frederick, Aug. 13, 1918.

Sanger, Margaret, Sep. 14, 1883; Oct. 16, 1917.

Sangster, Donald B. (Jamaica), Feb. 22, 1967.

Sanguinetti, Julio Maria: elected, Nov. 25, 1984; inaugurated, Mar. 1, 1985.

Sankara, Thomas, Aug. 5, 1983.

Santa Anna, Mar. 6, 1836; Apr. 21, 1836; Feb. 22, 1847.

Santa Barbara (California): captured by U.S., Aug. 4, 1846.

Santa Clara de Asis, Mission: established, Jan. 12, 1777.

Santa Cruz de Tenerife, Apr. 20, 1657.

Santa Cruz (Philippines), May 3, 1945.

Santa Fe: occupied by U.S., Aug. 18, 1846.

Santa Maria: wrecked, Dec. 25, 1492.

Santana, Carlos, Jul. 20, 1947.

Santana, Pedro (Santo Dominto), Mar. 18, 1861.

Santander (Spain), patrons of, Mar. 3.

Santayana, George, Dec. 16, 1863.

Santiago (Cuba): Jul. 10, 1898, surrenders, Jul. 17, 1898; Jan. 2, 1959.

Santillana, Marquis of (Inigo Lopez de Mendoza), Aug. 19, 1398.

Santmyer, Helen Hooven, Nov. 25, 1895.

Santo Domingo, Mar. 18, 1861; Nov. 23, 1961.

Santos, Jose Eduardo dos, Jun. 22, 1989.

Santos-Dumont, Alberto, Jun. 20, 1873.

Sao Tome: independence, Jul. 12, 1975.

Sao Tome and Principe, Nov. 5, 1975.

Sapoa (Nicaragua), Mar. 25, 1988.

sapphire, Sep. intro.

Saracens, Dec. 22, 640.

Saragossa, Treaty of, Apr. 22, 1529.

Sarajevo (Bosnia), Jun. 28, 1914; Mar. 19, 1996.

Saralegui, Cristina, Jan. 29, 1948.

Sarandon, Chris, Jul. 24, 1942.

Sarandon, Susan Abigail, Oct. 4, 1946.

Saratoga, Oct. 17, 1777.

Sarawak, May 12, 1888.

Sardi, Vincent, Sr., Jul. 23, 1885.

sardonyx, Aug. intro.

Sargent, Dick, Apr. 19, 1933.

Sargent, Francis W., Apr. 2, 1970.

Sargent, John Singer, Jan. 12, 1856.

Sarikamish, Battle of, Dec. 29, 1914; Jan. 2, 1915.

Sarkis, Elias, Jul. 20, 1924; inaugurated, Sep. 23, 1976.

Sarney, Jose: inaugurated, Mar. 15, 1985.

Sarnoff, David, Feb. 27, 1891.

Sarnoff, Robert William, Jul. 2, 1918.

Saroyan, William, Aug. 31, 1903.

Sarrazin, Michael, May 22, 1940.

Sarron, Petey, Oct. 29, 1937.

Sarton, May, May 3, 1912.

Sartre, Jean-Paul, Jun. 21, 1905; Nov. 26, 1946; rejects Nobel Prize for literature, Oct. 22, 1964.

Sartzetakis, Christos: inaugurated, Mar. 30, 1985.

Saskatchewan (Canada), Sep. 1, 1905.

Sasser, James Ralph *(Jim)*, Sep. 30, 1936.

Sassoon, Siegfried (Lorraine), Sep. 8, 1886.

Sassoon, Vidal, Jan. 17, 1928.

Sassou-Nguesso,, Denis, Oct. 25, 1997.

Satanic Verses, Feb. 15, 1989.

Satcher, David, Feb. 10, 1998.

satellite broadcast: first, Aug. 14, 1960.

satellite communications, Jan. 19, 1961.

satellite, international: first, Apr. 26, 1962.

satellite systems: Indonesian domestic, Jul. 8, 1976.

Satie, Erik Alfred-Leslie, May 17, 1866.

Satisfaction (I Can't Get No): recorded, May 13, 1965.

Sato, Eisako, Mar. 27, 1901; Nov. 9, 1964.

Satsuma Rebellion, Oct. 13, 1877.

Sattahid, Thailand: U.S. air base dedicated, Aug. 10, 1966.

Saturday Evening Post: published, Aug. 18, 1821; suspends publication, Jan. 10, 1969; Feb. 8, 1969.

Saturn, Feb. 2, 1982.

Saturn V, Nov. 9, 1967.

Saturn Corp., Jan. 8, 1985.

Saturnalia, Dec. intro.

Saturnalicius princeps, Dec. intro.

Saud (Saudi Arabia), Jan. 15, 1902; Nov. 9, 1953; deposed, Nov. 2, 1964.

Saudi Arabia: named, Sep. 23, 1932; Jan. 18, 1963; boundaries established, Dec. 18, 1969.

Saund, Dilip Sindh, Sep. 20, 1899.

Saur Revolution Day (Afghanistan), Apr. 27.

Sauve, Jeanne, Dec. 23, 1983.

Savage, Michael Joseph, Mar. 23, 1872.

Savage, Richard, Jan. 16, 1697.

Savage, Riek, Dec. 2, 1960.

Savalas, Telly, Jan. 21, 1927.

Savannah: first steamship to cross Atlantic, Aug. 22, 1818; Mar. 23, 1962; completes maiden voyage, Aug. 22, 1962.

Savannah (Georgia): taken by British, Dec. 29, 1778; captured by General Sherman, Dec. 21, 1864.

Save Your Vision Week, National, Mar. intro.

Savimbi, Jonas Malheiro, Aug. 3, 1934; Jun. 22, 1989.

Savitch, Jessica Beth, Feb. 2, 1948.

Savitskaya, Svetlana, Jul. 25, 1984.

Savonarola, Girolamo, Sep. 21, 1452; executed, May 23, 1498.

Savoy, Jan. 17, 1601; Apr. 23, 1860.

Saw Maung, Sep. 18, 1988.

Sawchuk, Terry, Dec. 28, 1929.

Sawyer, Diane K. Dec. 22, 1945.

Saxbe, William Bart, Jun. 25, 1916.

Saxon, John, Aug. 5, 1935.

Saxons, Jan. 6, 871.

Saxony, patron of, Jun. 15.

Sayer, Leo (Gerald), May 21, 1948.

Sayers, Dorothy L(eigh), Jun. 13, 1893.

Scaggs, William Royee *(Boz),* Jun. 8, 1944.

Scalia, Antonin, Mar. 11, 1936; Sep. 26, 1986.

Scaliger, Joseph Justus, Aug. 5, 1540.

Scaliger, Julius Caesar, Apr. 23, 1484.

Scandinavian Star, Apr. 7, 1990.

Scandinavian Union, Oct. 28, 1497.

Scapa Flow, Nov. 21, 1918; German fleet scuttled, Jun. 21, 1919.

Scarlatti, Alessandro, May 2, 1660.

Scarlatti, (Giuseppe) Domenico, Oct. 26, 1685.

Scarron, Paul, Jul. 4, 1610.

Scavullo, Francesco, Jan. 16, 1929.

Schacht, Hjalmar, Jan. 22, 1877.

Schaefer, Rudolph Jay, Feb. 21, 1863.

Schaerf, Adolf, May 5, 1957.

Schally, Andrew, Nov. 30, 1926.

Scharrer, Berta, Dec. 1, 1906.

Schawlow, Arthur L., May 5, 1921; Mar. 22, 1960.

Schechter Poultry Corp. vs. *United States,* May 27, 1935.

Scheele, Karl Wilhelm, Dec. 9, 1742.

Scheider, Roy (Richard), Nov. 10, 1935.

Schell, Maximilian, Dec. 8, 1930.

Schelling, Friedrich Wilhelm Joseph von, Jan. 27, 1775.

Schembechler, Bo, Apr. 1, 1929.

Schenectady, Feb. 8, 1690.

Schenkel, Chris(topher Eugene), Aug. 21, 1924.

Scherman, Harry, Feb. 1, 1887.

Schiaparelli, Elsa, Sep. 10, 1890.

Schick, Col. Jacob, Sep. 16, 1877; Nov. 6, 1923.

Schiller, Johann Christoph Friedrich, Nov. 10, 1759.

Schippers, Thomas, Mar. 9, 1930.

Schirach, Baldur von: released from prison, Oct. 1, 1966.

Schirra, Walter M., Jr., Mar. 12, 1923; Oct. 3, 1962.

Schlafly, Phyllis, Aug. 15, 1924.

Schlegel, August Wilhelm, Sep. 8, 1767.

Schlegel, Friedrich von, Mar. 10, 1772.

Schleiden, Matthias, Apr. 5, 1804.

Schlesinger, Arthur M(eier), Jr., Oct. 15, 1917; May 2, 1966.

Schlesinger, James Rodney, Feb. 15, 1929.

Schlesinger, John, May 25, 1969.

Schlesinger, John, Feb. 16, 1926.

Schleswig and Holstein, Mar. 5, 1460; Jan. 24, 1867.

Schlieffen, Alfred Graf von, Feb. 28, 1833.

Schliemann, Heinrich, Jan. 6, 1822.

Schmeling, Max, Sep. 28, 1905; Jun. 12, 1930; Jun. 21, 1932.

Schmid, Carlo, Dec. 3, 1896.

Schmidt, Harvey, May 3, 1960.

Schmidt, Helmut, Dec. 23, 1918; May 16, 1974.

Schmidt, Mit, Mar. 5, 1918.

Schmitt, Harrison H. *(Jack),* Jul. 3, 1935; Dec. 12, 1972.

Schnabel, Julian, Oct. 26, 1951.

Schnabel, Karl Ulrich, Aug. 6, 1909.

Schneider, John, Apr. 8, 1954.

Schneider, Rob, Oct. 31, 1965.

Schneider, Romy, Sep. 23, 1938.

Schnitzler, Arthur, May 15, 1862.

Schoelcher Day (French West Indies), Jul. 21.

Schoenbrun, David Franz, Mar. 15, 1915.

scholars, patron of, Aug. 28; Dec. 6.

Schomburg, Arthur Alfonso, Jan. 24, 1874.

Schonberg, Arnold, Sep. 13, 1874.

Schoolcraft, Henry Rowe, Mar. 28, 1793.

schools, private, May 24, 1983.

Schoonover, Lawrence Lovell, Mar. 6, 1906.

Schopenhauer, Arthur, Feb. 22, 1788.

Schorr, Daniel, Aug. 13, 1916; Feb. 23, 1976.

Schreiber, Avery, Apr. 9, 1935.

Schreyer, Edward Richard, Dec. 21, 1935.

Schrieffer, John Robert, May 31, 1931.

Schroder, Ricky, Apr. 13, 1970.

Schrodinger, Erwin, Aug. 12, 1887.

Schroeder, Pat(ricia Scott), Jul. 30, 1940.

Schroeder, William, Feb. 14, 1932.

Schubart, Christian Friedrich Daniel, Apr. 13, 1739.

Schubert, Franz Peter, Jan. 31, 1797.

Schulberg, Budd, Mar. 27, 1914.

Schuller, Gunther, Nov. 22, 1925; Aug. 15, 1966.

Schuller, Robert Harold, Sep. 16, 1926.

Schultz, Dutch, Aug. 6, 1902.

Schultz, George, Jul. 16, 1982.

Schultz, Theodore W., Apr. 30, 1902.

Schultze, Charles Louis, Dec. 12, 1924.

Schulz, Charles M., Nov. 26, 1922.

Schurz, Carl, Mar. 2, 1829.

Schwab, Charles Michael, Feb. 18, 1862.

Schwabe, Heinrich Samuel, Oct. 25, 1789.

Schwann, Theodor, Dec. 7, 1810.

Schwartz, Melvin, Nov. 2, 1932.

Schwartz, Robert, Jun. 13, 1959.

Schwartz, Stephen, Oct. 23, 1972.

Schwarzenegger, Arnold, Jul. 30, 1947.

Schwarzkopf, Elisabeth, Dec. 9, 1915.

Schwarzkopf, H. Norman, Aug. 22, 1934.

Schweitzer, Albert, Jan. 14, 1875; Oct. 30, 1953.

Schwinger, Julian Seymour, Feb. 12, 1918.

Scobee, Francis Richard (Dick), May 19, 1939.

Scofield, Paul, Jan. 21, 1922.

Scone, May 21, 1424.

Scoon, Paul, Jul. 4, 1935.

Scopes, John, Jul. 10, 1925.

Scopes, John Thomas, Aug. 3, 1900.

Scorpio, Oct. intro; Nov. intro.

Scorsese, Martin, Nov. 17, 1942; May 28, 1976.

Scotland: independence acknowledged, Dec. 5, 1189; Jan. 20, 1301; Jul. 19, 1333; Apr. 12, 1654; Union with England, May 1, 1707; Mar. I, 1979.

Scotland, patron of, Nov. 16; Nov. 30.

Scott, David R., Jul. 26, 1971.

Scott, George C., Oct. 18, 1927.

Scott, G.H., Jul. 6, 1919.

Scott, Hazel (Dorothy), Jun. 11, 1920.

Scott, Hugh Doggett, Jr., Nov. 11, 1900.

Scott, Michael Warren (Mike), Apr. 26, 1955.

Scott, Lizbeth, Sep. 29, 1922.

Scott, Paul Mark, Mar. 25, 1920.

Scott, Randolph, Jan. 23, 1903.

Scott, Robert, Jan. 17, 1912.

Scott, Robert Falcon, Jun. 6, 1868.

Scott, Sir Walter, Aug. 15, 1771.

Scott, Willard Herman, Jr., May 7, 1934.

Scott, Winfield, Jun. 13, 1786; Sep. 13, 1846; Sep. 14, 1846; Apr. 18, 1847.

Scott, Zachary, Feb. 21, 1914.

Scottish Ballad: first performance, Nov. 28, 1941.

Scottish College of Justice: established, May 13, 1532.

Scottish Jacobites, Jul. 27, 1689.

Scottish National Gallery: opens, Mar. 21, 1859.

Scottish Quarter Day (Scotland), Feb. 2.

Scotto, Renata, Feb. 24, 1934.

Scourby, Alexander, Nov. 13, 1913.

Scouting Anniversary, Feb. intro.

Scranton, George Whitfield, May 11, 1811.

Scranton, William Warren, Jul. 19, 1917.

Scribner, Charles, Feb. 21, 1821.

Scripps, E(dward) W(yllis), Jun. 18, 1854.

Scripps, Ellen Browning, Oct. 18, 1836.

Scruggs, Earl, Jan. 6, 1924.

Scully, Vince(nt Edward), Nov. 29, 1927.

Scutaria (Albania), Jan. 23, 1916.

Seaborg, Glenn T., Apr. 19, 1912, Oct. 15, 1946.

Seabrook Nuclear Power Plant, Jan. 28, 1988.

Seabury, Samuel, Nov. 14, 1784.

Seafirst Corp., Jun. 22, 1983.

Seaga, Edward Phillip George, May 28, 1930.

Seagal, Steven, Apr. 10, 1951.

Seagram, Joseph Edward Frowde, Aug. 11, 1903.

Sealab II, Oct. 12, 1965.

Sealsfield, Charles, Mar. 3, 1793.

seamstresses, patron of, Jul. 26.

Searles, Joseph L., III, Feb. 13, 1970.

Sears, John Patrick, Jul. 3, 1940.

seatbelts, Jun. 27, 1955, Feb. 24, 1961.

Seaver, Tom, Nov. 17, 1944.

Sebastian, John, Mar. 17, 1944.

Sebastopol: capitulates to Allies, Sep. 11, 1855.

Sebastopol, Siege of: begins, Oct. 17, 1854.

Seberg, Jean, Nov. 13, 1938.

Sebour (Archbishop of Paris), Jan. 3, 1857.

Second Balkan War: ends, Aug. 10, 1913.

Second Coalition, War of, Mar. 12, 1799; Mar. 25, 1799; Dec. 3, 1800.

Second Day of Christmas (Luxembourg), Dec. 26.

Second Day of Christmas (Netherlands), Dec. 26.

Second Day of Christmas (Norway), Dec. 26.

Second Empire (France), Nov. 2, 1852.

Second, Maratha War, Aug. 7, 1803.

Second Reform Act (Great Britain), Aug. 15, 1867.

Second World War, The, Oct. 15, 1953.

Secondat, Charles-Louis de, Jan. 18, 1689.

Secord, Richard, Mar. 16, 1988.

Secretariat: Triple Crown winner, Jun. 9, 1973.

secretaries, patron of, Jan. 3.

Secular Affairs Institute: seized, Jun. 23, 1966.

secular clergy, patron of, Dec. 29.

Securities & Exchange Commission: created, Jun. 6, 1934.

Sedaka, Neil, Mar. 13, 1939.

Sedan (France), Nov. 6, 1918.

Sedgwick, Adam, Mar. 22, 1785.

Sedition Act, May 16, 1918.

Seeger, Alan, Jun. 22, 1888.

Seeger, Pete, May 3, 1919.

Seereiter, John, Apr. 12, 1859.

Seferis, Giorgos, Mar. 13, 1900.

Segal, Erich, Jun. 16, 1937.

Segal, George, Nov. 26, 1924; Feb. 13, 1934.

Seger, Bob, May 6, 1945.

Segovia, Andres, Feb. 18, 1894.

Segre, Emilio, Feb. 1, 1905.

segregation, Oct. 11, 1906; ruled illegal in railroad cars, Jun. 5, 1950.

Seguin, Marc, Apr. 20, 1786.

Seibert, Florence, Oct. 6, 1897.

Seidelman, Susan, Dec. 11, 1952.

Seifert, Jaroslav, Sep. 23, 1901.

Seko, Mobutu Sese, dies, Sep. 7, 1997.

Seldes, George, Nov. 16, 1890.

Selective Service Act, May 18, 1917; signed Jun. 24, 1948.

Selective Service System, Jan. 19, 1970.

Selena (Quintanliaa Perez) killed, Mar. 31, 1995.

Seles, Monica, Dec. 2, 1973.

Selfridge, Harry Gordon, Jan. 11, 1864.

Selfridge, Thomas, Sep. 17, 1908.

Selig, Bud (Allan H.), Jul. 30, 1934; Sep. 14, 1994.

Sellecca, Connie, May 25, 1955.

Selleck, Tom, Jan. 29, 1945.

Sellers, Peter, Sep. 8, 1925.

Selma (Alabama), Mar. 21, 1965; Mar. 21, 1965.

Selten, Reinhard, Oct. 5, 1930.

Selznick, David O., May 10, 1902.

Semenov, Nikolay Nikolaevich, Apr. 15, 1896.

Semmes, Raphael, Sep. 27, 1809.

Sempach, Jul. 9, 1386.

Senate, U.S., Apr. 18, 1978.

Sendak, Maurice, Jun. 10, 1928.

Sending Off the Kitchen God Day (China), Jan. 22.

Senefelder, Aloys, Nov. 6, 1771.

Senegal: French government established, Oct. 16, 1904; Apr. 4, 1960; admitted to U.N., Sep. 28, 1960; Mar. 3, 1963; Feb. 1, 1982.

Senegal-Niger, Upper (French Sudan), Dec. 4, 1920.

Senegal and Sudanese Republic: independence, Jun. 20, 1960.

Senegambia: confederation, Feb. 1, 1982.

Senegambia Confederation Day (The Gambia, Senegal), Feb. 1.

Senghor, Leopold Sedar, Oct. 9, 1906.

Senior Citizens Day (Oklahoma), Jun. 9.

Senlis, City and Diocese of, patron of, Mar. 30.

Senlis, Treaty of, May 23, 1493.

Sennett, Mack, Jan. 17, 1880.

Seoul (Korea): captured, Jun. 28, 1950; falls to U.S., Sep. 26, 1950; handed over to Republic of Korea, Sep. 29, 1950; Jan. 4, 1951; Mar. 14, 1951; Jun. 29, 1996.

Separation Day (Anguilla), Dec. 19.

Separation Day (Delaware), Jun. 15.

Sepoy Mutiny, Mar. 9, 1858.

septem, Sep. intro.

septuplets, May 21, 1985.

Serbia, Mar. 3, 1878; independence, Jul. 13, 1878; Jul. 28, 1914; declares war on Germany, Aug. 6, 1914; invaded by Austria-Hungary, Aug. 11, 1914; invasion begins, Oct. 6, 1915; occupies Vukovar, Croatia, Nov. 19, 1991; formation of new Yugoslavia, Apr. 17, 1992; peace accord, Nov. 21, 1995.

Serbia, patron, Jan. 14.

Serbian Uprising Day (Yugoslavia), Jul. 7.

serfdom (Austnar): abolished, Sep. 7, 1848.

Sgt. Pepper's Lonely Hearts Club Band, Jun. 1, 1967.

Serge, Grand Duke (Russia): killed, Feb. 17, 1905.

Serkin, Rudolf, Mar. 28, 1903.

Serling, Rod, Dec. 25, 1924.

Serpico, Francisco Vincent *(Frank),* Apr. 14, 1936.

Serra, Junipero, Nov. 24, 1713.

Serra, Richard Anthony, Nov. 2, 1939.

Sert, Jose Luis, Jul. 1, 1902.

Servan Schreiber, Jean-Jacques, Jul. 15, 1968.

servants, hired, partron of, Sep. 14.

Servetus, Michael: convicted and executed, Oct. 27, 1553.

service to the needy, patron of those of, Jul. 29.

Service, Robert W., Jan. 16, 1874.

Sesame Street: television debut, Nov. 10, 1969.

Sessions, Roger (Huntington), Dec. 28, 1896.

Seton, Elizabeth Ann, Aug. 28, 1774; beatified, Mar. 17, 1963; Sep. 14, 1975.

Seton, Ernest Thompson, Aug. 14, 1860.

Setsubun (Japan), Feb. intro., Feb. 3.

Settlers' Day (Namibia, South Africa), Sep. 5.

Seurat, Georges, Dec. 2, 1859.

Sevareid, Eric, Nov. 26, 1912.

Sevastopol: Russian sailors mutiny, Nov. 25, 1904; falls to Germany, Jul. 1, 1942, Soviets regain, May 9, 1944.

Seven Apostles of Bulgaria, Jul. 17.

Seven Brothers, Jul. 10.

Seven Founders of the Servite Order, Feb. 12; Feb. 17.

Seven oaks, Jun. 27, 1450.

Seven Sisters of Ephesus, Jul. 27.

Seven Sorrows of the Blessed Virgin, Mary, Sep. 15.

Seven Weeks War, Jul. 3, 1866; Jul. 30, 1866; ends, Oct. 3, 1866.

Seven Years War, Jan. 16, 1756; begins, Aug. 29, 1756; Jan. 10, 1757; May 6, 1757; Jul. 26, 1757; Aug. 30, 1757; Nov. 20, 1759; Nov. 3, 1760; Jan. 4, 1762; Nov. 1, 1762; ends, Feb. 10, 1763.

Seventeenth Amendment: U.S. Constitution, May 31, 1913.

Seventeenth of July Revolution or Baath Revolution Day (Iraq), Jul. 17.

Seventeenth Summer Olympics: open in Rome, Aug. 25, 1960.

Severinsen, Carl H. (Doc), Jul. 7, 1927.

Severndroog, Feb. 11, 1755.

Sevier, John, Sep. 23, 1745.

Sevres, Treaty of, Aug. 10, 1920.

Sewall, Samuel, Mar. 28, 1652.

Seward, William Henry, May 16, 1801.

Seward's Day (Alaska), Mar. intro.

Seward's Folly, Mar. 30, 1867.

Sewell, Anna, Mar. 30, 1820.

sewing machine: first patented, Sep. 10, 1846.

Sextilis, Aug. intro.

Sexton, Anne, Nov. 9, 1928.

Seybou, Ali, Nov. 10, 1987.

Seychelles: independence, Jun. 29, 1976.

Seymour, Anne Eckert, Sep. 11, 1909.

Seymour, Jane, May 30, 1536.

Seyss-lnquart, Arthur, Jul. 22, 1892.

Sforim, Mendele Mokher,

Shaba (Zaire), May 11, 1978.

Shabazz, Attalah, Nov. 16, 1958.

Shackelford, Ted, Jun. 23, 1946.

The Shadow Box: opens, Mar. 31, 1977.

Shaffer, Peter, May 15, 1926.

Shaftesbury, Anthony Ashley Cooper, Jul. 22, 1621.

Shaftesbury Factory Act: passed, Aug. 29, 1833.

Shagari, Alhaji Shehu, Apr. 25, 1925; Oct. 1, 1979; Dec. 31, 1983.

Shah Jahan, Jan. 5, 1592; May 26, 1659.

Shah, Mohammad Zahir, Jul. 17, 1973.

Shah Rokh, Feb. 18, 1405.

Shaheed Day (Bangladesh), Feb. 20.

Shahn, Ben(jamin), Sep. 12, 1898.

Shaiba, Battle of, Apr. 12, 1915; ends, Apr. 14, 1915.

Shakespeare, Frank Joseph, Jr., Apr. 9, 1925.

Shakespeare, William, Apr. 23, 1564; Apr. 26, 1564; dies, Apr. 23, 1616; anniversary, Apr. 23, 1964.

Shalala, Donna, Feb. 14, 1941.

Shales, Thomas William *(Tom),* Nov. 3, 1948.

Shalikashvili, John, Jun. 27, 1936.

Sham el Nassim (Sudan), Apr. 27.

Shamir, Yitzhak, Nov. 3, 1914; inaugurated, Oct. 20, 1986.

Shandling, Garry, Nov. 29, 1949.

Shange, Ntozake, Oct. 18, 1948.

Shanghai: seized by British, Jun. 19, 1842; Jan. 3, 1903; Mar. 21, 1927; Jan. 28, 1932.

Shanghai Communique, Feb. 27, 1972.

Shankar, Ramsewak: inaugurated, Jan. 25, 1988.

Shankar, Ravi, Apr. 7, 1920.

Shanker, Albert, Sep. 14, 1928.

Shannon, Claude Elwood, Apr. 30, 1916.

Shantung, Mar. 6, 1898.

Shantung Concessions, Jun. 28, 1919.

Shantung Province (China), May 20, 1929.

Shapiro, Jacob, May 5, 1897.

Shapiro, Karl Jay, Nov. 10, 1913.

Shapiro, Stanley, Jul. 16, 1959.

Shapley, Harlow, Nov. 2, 1885.

Sharett, Moshe, Dec. 9, 1953.

Sharg, Mohammed Hassan, May 27, 1988.

Sharif, Nawaz, elected, Feb. 3, 1997.

Sharif, Omar, Apr. 10, 1932.

Shark Island, Feb. 3, 1521.

Sharkey, Jack, Jun. 12, 1930; Jun. 21, 1932; Jun. 29, 1933.

Sharon, Ariel, Jun. 22, 1983.

Sharp, William, Sep. 12, 1855.

Sharpe, Sterling, Apr. 6, 1965.

Sharpe, William F., Jun. 16, 1934.

Sharpeville Massacre, Mar. 21, 1960.

Shastri, Lal Bahadun, Jun. 2, 1964; Jan. 24, 1966.

Shatner, William, Mar. 22, 1931.

Shaver, Helen, Feb. 24, 1951.

Shaw, Anna Howard, Feb. 14, 1847.

Shaw, Artie, May 23, 1910.

Shaw, George Bernard, Jul. 26, 1856.

Shaw, Irwin, Feb. 27, 1913.

Shaw, Robert, Aug. 9, 1927.

Shawn, Dick, Dec. 1, 1929.

Shays, Daniel, Feb. 4, 1787.

Shay's Rebellion, Feb. 4, 1787.

Shcharansky, Anatoly Borisovich, Jan. 20, 1948, sentenced, Jul. 14, 1978; Jan. 7, 1986, Feb. 11, 1986.

Shearer, Moira, Jan. 17, 1926.

Shearer, Norma, Aug. 10, 1904.

Shearing, George, Aug. 13, 1919.

Shearson/American Express Inc., Apr. 10, 1984.

Shedd, John Graves, Jul. 20, 1850.

Sheed, Frank, Mar. 20, 1897.

Sheehy, Gail (Henion), Nov. 27, 1937.

Sheen, Charlie, Sep. 3, 1965.

Sheen, Fulton J., May 8, 1895.

Sheen, Martin, Aug. 3, 1940.

Sheffield: British destroyer, May 4, 1982.

Sheffield, England, Apr. 15, 1989.

Sheffield, Gary, Nov. 18, 1968.

Sheherazade: premiere, May 17, 1904.

Shehu, Mehmet, Jan. 10, 1913.

Sheldon, Sidney, Feb. 11, 1917.

Shelley, Mary Wollstonecraft, Aug. 30, 1797.

Shelley, Percy Bysshe, Aug. 4, 1792.

Shenouda III, Apr. 12, 1983, Jan. 4, 1985.

Shepard, Alan B., Nov. 18, 1923; first American in space, May 5, 1961.

Shepard, Sam, Nov. 5, 1943.

Shepherd, Cybill, Feb. 18, 1950.

shepherds, patron of, Feb. 12; Apr. 16.

Sher Shah, May 17, 1540.

Sheridan, Ann, Feb. 21, 1915.

Sheridan, Philip Henry, Mar. 6, 1831.

Sheridan, Richard Brinsley (Butler), Nov. 4, 1751.

Sherman Anti-Trust Act, Jul. 2, 1890; passed, Jul. 14, 1890, May 1, 1911.

Sherman Anti-Trust Law, Apr. 6, 1964.

Sherman, Bobby, Jul. 22, 1945.

Sherman, Cynthia, Jan. 19, 1954.

Sherman, James S., Oct. 24, 1855; Mar. 4, 1909.

Sherman, John, May 10, 1823.

Sherman, Roger, Apr. 19, 1721.

Sherman, William Tecumseh (General), Feb. 8, 1820; Sep. 2, 1864; Nov. 15, 1864; Dec. 21, 1864.

Sherrill, Henry Knox, Nov. 6, 1890.

Sherrington, Sir Charles Scott, Nov. 27, 1857.

Sherry Wine Harvest (Jerez de la Frontera, Spain), Sep. intro.

Sherwood, Robert, Apr. 4, 1896.

Shetland Islands, Feb. 20, 1471.

Shevardnadze, Eduard Amvrosiyevich, Jan. 25, 1928; Nov. 5, 1995; Feb. 9, 1998.

Shevchenko, Arkady Nikolayevich, Oct. 11, 1930, Apr. 10, 1978.

Shevchenko, Taras Grigorievich, Mar. 9, 1814.

Shield, Lansing Peter, Apr. 8, 1896.

Shields, Brooke, May 31, 1965.

Shih-Chieh Wang, Mar. 10, 1891.

Shi'ite Islam, Dec. 2, 1979.

Shiloh, Battle of, Apr. 6, 1862; Apr. 7, 1862.

Shimonoseki, Treaty of, Apr. 17, 1895.

Shinto, Feb. 7, 1868.

Shipley, Jenny, elected, Dec. 8, 1997.

Shire, Talia, Apr. 25, 1946.

Shirer, William, Feb. 23, 1904.

Shirley, George, Apr. 18, 1934.

Shishekly, Adeeb, Dec. 3, 1951.

Shockley, William Bradford, Feb. 13, 1910, Nov. 1, 1956.

Shoemaker, Willie, Aug. 19, 1931.

Sholes, Christopher Latham, Feb. 14, 1819.

Sholokhov, Mikhail Aleksandrovich, May 24, 1905; Oct. 22, 1935; Oct. 15, 1965.

Shore, Dinah, Mar. 1, 1921.

Shore, Eddie, Nov. 25, 1902.

Short, Martin, Mar. 26, 1950.

Short, Robert Waltrip (Bobby), Sep. 15, 1926.

Shorter, Frank, Oct. 31, 1947.

Shostakovich, Dimitri, Sep. 25, 1906; Nov. 4, 1943.

Show Boat: opens, Dec. 27, 1927.

Shreve, Henry Miller, Oct. 21, 1785.

Shrimpton, Jean Rosemary, Nov. 6, 1942.

Shriner, Herb, May 29, 1918.

Shriners, Sep. 26, 1872.

Shriver, Maria Owings, Nov. 6, 1955.

Shriver, Pam(ela), Jul. 4, 1962.

Shriver, R. Sargent, Nov. 9, 1915.

Shubert, Lee, Mar. 18, 1875.

Shubert, Jacob, Feb. 21, 1950.

Shue, Elisabeth, Oct. 6, 1963.

Shula, Don Francis, Jan. 4, 1930.

Shull, Clifford G., Sep. 23, 1915.

Shultz, George Pratt, Dec. 13, 1920.

Shunki-Koreisan (Japan), Mar. 23.

Shut-in Day, National, Oct. intro.

Shute, Nevil, Jan. 17, 1899.

Siam: declares war, Jul. 22, 1917; May 11, 1949.

Sibelius, Jean, Dec. 8, 1865; Jul. 2, 1900; Apr. 25, 1905; Feb. 19, 1923; Dec. 28, 1937.

Siberia: meteorite craters found, Jun. 30, 1908; oil pipeline opens, Jun. 27, 1971.

Sicilian Vespers, Mar. 31, 1282.

Sicily, Apr. 13, 1848; earthquake, Dec. 28, 1908.

Sicily, patron of, Jun. 15; Dec. 6.

sick, patron of the, Jul. 14.

sick people, patron of, Mar. 8.

Siddons, Sarah (Kemble), Jul. 5, 1755.

Sidey, Hugh Swanson, Sep. 3, 1927.

Sidney, Sir Philip, Nov. 30, 1554; Sep. 22, 1586.

Sidney, Sylvia, Aug. 8, 1910.

Sidon (Lebanon), Feb. 16, 1985.

Sidra, Gulf of, Mar. 24, 1986.

Siegbahn, Kai M., Apr. 20, 1918.

Siegbahn, Karl Manne Georg, Dec. 3, 1886.

Siegel, Benjamin (Bugsy), Feb. 28, 1906.

Siegel, Don, Oct. 26, 1912.

Siemens, Friedrich, Dec. 8, 1826.

Siemens, Werner von, Dec. 13, 1816.

Siemens, Sir William, Apr. 4, 1823.

Siena, Apr. 17, 1555.

Sienkiewicz, Henryk, May 5, 1846.

Sierra Club, May 28, 1892; Jun. 4, 1892.

Sierra Leone, Feb. 22, 1787; becomes British colony, Jan. 1, 1808; independence, Apr. 27, 1961; admitted to U.N., Sep. 27, 1961; Apr. 19, 1971.

Sieyes, Emmanuel Joseph, May 3, 1748.

Sight Saving Month, Sep. intro.

Sigismund II (Poland): dies, Jul. 7, 1572.

Sigismund III (Poland), Aug. 19, 1587.

Sigismund of Germany (Holy Roman Emperor), Feb. 15, 1368; May 31, 1433.

Signing of Argel Agreement, Anniversary of (Sao Tome and Principe), Nov. 26.

Signoret, Simone, Mar. 25, 1921.

Sigsbee, Charles Dwight, Jan. 16, 1845.

Sigurjonsson, Johann, Jun. 19, 1880.

Sihanouk, Norodom, Apr. 19, 1960; Sep. 24, 1993.

Sikh War, First: treaty ending, Mar. 9, 1846.

Sikh War, Second: begins, Dec. 10, 1848; Feb. 21, 1849; Mar. 14, 1849.

Sikhs, Mar. 12, 1849.

Siki, Battling, Sep. 24, 1922.

Sikorsky, Igor, May 25, 1889; Sep. 14, 1939; Dec. 8, 1941.

Silent Ones, the (Nigeria), Mar. 14, 1904.

Siles Salinas, Luis Adolfo, Apr. 27, 1969.

Siles Zuazo, Hernan, Aug. 6, 1956.

Silesia, Apr. 10, 1741; Feb. 15, 1763.

Silesian War, First, Jun. 27, 1743.

Silk, Karen, Nov. 13, 1974; Aug. 22, 1986.

Sillanpaa, Frans Eemil, Sep. 16, 1888.

Sillitoe, Alan, Mar. 4, 1928.

Sills, Beverly, May 25, 1929.

Silo, Fawzi, Dec. 3, 1951.

silver: eliminated from U.S. coins, Jun. 3, 1965.

Silver, Horace Ward Martin Tavares, Sep. 2, 1928.

Silverman, Fred, Sep. 13, 1937.

Silverman, Jonathan, Aug. 5, 1966.

Silvers, Phil, May 11, 1911.

Silverstone, Alicia, Oct. 4, 1976.

Silvester II (antipope): deposed, Dec. 20, 1046.

Simbra Oiler at Oas (Romania), May intro.

Simcon II, Aug. 28, 1943.

Simitis, Costas, Jan. 15, 1996.

Simmons, Al, May 22, 1902.

Simmons, Gene, Aug. 25, 1949.

Simmons, Jean, Jan. 31, 1929.

Simmons, Richard, Jul. 12, 1948.

Simms, William Gilmore, Apr. 17, 1806.

Simon, Carly, Jun. 25, 1945.

Simon, Claude, Oct. 10, 1913.

Simon, Herbert A., Jun. 15, 1916.

Simon, Neil, Jul. 4, 1927.

Simon, Paul, Nov. 29, 1928; Feb. 14, 1970.

Simon, Paul, (singer) Nov. 5, 1942.

Simon, Pierre, Mar. 23, 1749.

Simplesse, Feb. 22, 1990.

Simplon Tunnel, May 19, 1906.

Simpson, Adele, Dec. 8, 1908.

Simpson, Sir James Young, Jun. 7, 1811, Nov. 14, 1847.

Simpson, Louis, Mar. 27, 1923.

Simpson, O(renthal) J(ames): Jul. 9, 1947; car chase, Jun. 17, 1994; trial begins, Jan. 24, 1995; acquitted of murder, Oct. 3, 1995.

Simpson, Wallis Warfield, May 12, 1936; Dec. 10, 1936.

Sims, Billy Ray, Sep. 18, 1955.

Sims, James Marion, Jan. 25, 1813.

Sinai, Jan. 26, 1915; Apr. 25, 1982.

Sinai Liberation Day (Egypt), Apr. 26.

Sinatra, Frank, Dec. 12, 1915.

Sinbad, Nov. 10, 1957.

Sinclair, Upton, Sep. 20, 1878.

Singapore, Feb. 15, 1942; secedes from Malaysia, Aug. 9, 1965; admitted to U.N., Sep. 21, 1965; Oct. 16, 1965.

Singer, Isaac Bashevis, Jul. 14, 1904, Oct. 5, 1978.

Singer, Isaac M., Oct. 27, 1811.

Singer, Lori, Nov. 6, 1962.

Singer, Maxine, Feb. 15, 1931.

Singh, Giani Zail, May 5, 1916.

Singh, Guru Gobind, Jan. 15, 1666.

Singh, Jarnail, Jun. 6, 1984.

Singh, Vishwanath Pratap: Dec. 2, 1989; resigns, Nov. 7, 1990.

Singleton, John, Jan. 6, 1968.

Sinhalese, Jan. 10, 1961.

Sinn Fein, Apr. 24, 1916; Apr. 5, 1919; Jun. 22, 1922.

sinners, patron of, Dec. 29.

Sino-American treaty: immigration, Mar. 14, 1888.

Sino-German Convention, Mar. 6, 1898.

Sino-Japanese War, Aug. 1, 1894; ends, Feb. 12, 1895.

Sino-Tebetan convention, Apr. 27, 1914.

Sinowatz, Fred: inaugurated, May 24, 1983.

Sinph, Charan, Jul. 28, 1979.

Sioux Nation, Jun. 13, 1979.

Siphandon, Khamtai, Feb. 8, 1924; Feb. 24, 1998.

Sirhan, Sirhan Beshara, Mar. 19, 1944, Jun. 5, 1968; convicted, Apr. 17, 1969; sentenced, Apr. 23, 1969.

Sirica, John Joseph, Mar. 19, 1904.

Sirius, Jul. intro.

Siskel, Eugene Karl *(Gene)*, Jan. 26, 1946.

Sisler, George, Mar. 24, 1893.

Sisley, Alfred, Oct. 30, 1839.

Sisters of Charity of St. Joseph, Mar. 17, 1963.

Sithney, patron of, Aug. 3.

Sithole, Ndabaningi, Mar. 4, 1975; Apr. 4, 1975.

"Sit-Ins," Feb. 1, 1960.

Sitting Bull, Jun. 25, 1876.

Sittler, Darryl Glen, Sep. 18, 1950.

Sitwell, Dame Edith, Sep. 7, 1887.

Sitwell, Sir (Francis) Osbert Sacheverell, Dec. 6, 1892.

Siward of Northumbria, Jul. 27, 1054.

Six-Day War, May 30, 1967; Jun. 5, 1967; Jun. 6, 1967; Jun. 11, 1967; Jan. 23, 1968.

Sixteenth Amendment (U.S. constitution): adopted, Feb. 25, 1913.

Sixth Symphony: premiere, Feb. 19, 1923.

Sixtus IV (pope), Jul. 21, 1414; May 23, 1474.

Sixtus V (pope), Dec. 12, 1520.

The $64,000 Question: television debut, Jun. 7, 1955.

60 Minutes: television debut, Sep. 24, 1968.

Skaggs, Ricky, Jul. 18, 1954.

Skelton, Red, Jul. 18, 1913.

Skerritt, Thomas Roy (Tom), Aug. 25, 1933.

Skidmore, Louis, Apr. 8, 1897.

Skinner, B. F., Mar. 20, 1904.

Skinner, Cornelia, May 30, 1901.

Skinner, Otis, Jun. 28, 1858.

Skinner, Samuel K., June 10, 1938.

Skoblikova, Lidiya, Feb. 2, 1964.

Skoda, Emil von, Nov. 19, 1839.

Skylab: launched, May 14, 1973; Jul. 28, 1973; Jul. 11, 1979.

Skylab 2, Jun. 22, 1973; Sep. 25, 1973.

Skylab 3, Nov. 16, 1973.

Skylab 4, Feb. 8, 1974.

Skytrain: Laker Airways, Sep. 26, 1977.

Slaney, Mary Decker, Aug. 4, 1958.

Slater, Christian, Aug. 18, 1969.

Slater, Helen, Dec. 15, 1963.

Slater, Rodney E., Feb. 23, 1955.

Slater, Samuel, Jun. 9, 1768.

Slatkin, Leonard, Sep. 1, 1944.

Slaughter, Frank G., Feb. 25, 1908.

Slaughterhouse Five: published, Mar. 31, 1969.

Slav Letters or Education Day, Day of (Bulgaria), May 24.

slave trade: banned in U.S., Jan. 1, 1808; Jan. 29, 1850; abolished in Washington, D.C., Sep. 20, 1850; abolished in Zanzibar, Jun. 5, 1873; outlawed, Mar. 31, 1901.

Slavery: abolition in British Empire, Aug. 1, 1834.

slavery prohibited: 13th Amendment, Dec. 18, 1865.

Slavonia, Jan. 26, 1699.

Sledge, Debbie, Jul. 9, 1954.

Sledge, Joni, Sep. 13, 1956.

Sledge, Kim, Aug. 21, 1957.

Slezak, Erika, Aug. 5, 1946.

Slezak, Walter, May 3, 1902.

Slick, Grace Wing, Oct. 30, 1943.

Sliwa, Curtis, Mar. 26, 1954; Feb. 13, 1979.

Sloan, John French, Aug. 2, 1871.

Sloan Kettering Cancer Center, Aug. 11, 1983.

Sloane, Eric, Feb. 27, 1910.

Sloane, Sir Hans, Apr. 16, 1660.

Slocum, Joshua, Feb. 20, 1844.

Slovakia, independence, Jun. 25, 1991; member of UN, Apr. 23, 1992; UN member, May 22, 1992; formation of, Jan. 1, 1993.

Slovenian Liberation Front Day (Yugoslavia), Apr. 27.

Sluys: English defeat French, Jun. 24, 1340.

Small Fry Club, Apr. 14, 1947.

Smalls, Charlie, Jan. 5, 1975.

Smalls, Robert, Apr. 5, 1839.

Smathers, George Armistead, Nov. 14, 1913.

Smeal, Eleanor Cutri, Jan. 30, 1939.

smelters, patron of, Nov. 3; Dec. 4; Dec. 26.

Smetana, Bedrich, Mar. 2, 1824.

Smiley, Jane, Sep. 26, 1949.

Smith, Adam, Jun. 5, 1723.

Smith, Adam (economist), Jul. 4, 1921.

Smith, Albert Merriman, Feb. 10, 1913.

Smith, Alfred E(mmanuel), Dec. 30, 1873.

Smith, Bessie, Apr. 15, 1894; Sep. 26, 1894; Feb. 16, 1923.

Smith, Betty, Dec. 15, 1906.

Smith, Bob (Buffalo Bob), Nov. 27, 1917.

Smith, Sir C(harles) Aubrey, Jul. 21, 1863.

Smith, Clarence (Pinetop), Jun. 11, 1904.

Smith, Dean, retires, Oct. 9, 1997.

Smith, Emmitt, May 15, 1969.

Smith, Francis Hopkinson, Oct. 23, 1838.

Smith, George, Mar. 26, 1840.

Smith, Hamilton O., Aug. 23, 1931.

Smith, Charles Aaron (Bubba), Feb. 28, 1945.

Smith, Holland McTyeire, Apr. 20, 1882.

Smith, Howard K., May 12, 1914.

Smith, Ian, Apr. 8, 1919; Apr. 13, 1964; Apr. 4, 1975; Apr. 12, 1978.

Smith, Willie (The Lion), Nov. 25, 1897.

Smith, Jaclyn, Oct. 26, 1948.

Smith, Jedediah Strong, Jan. 6, 1799.

Smith, Joseph, Dec. 23, 1805; Apr. 6, 1830; murdered, Jun. 27, 1844.

Smith, Kate, May 1, 1909; Nov. 11, 1939.

Smith, Maggie, Dec. 28, 1934.

Smith, Margaret Chase, Dec. 14, 1897; Jan. 20, 1949; Jul. 1, 1950.

Smith, Martin Cruz, Nov. 3, 1942.

Smith, Mary Elizabeth (Liz), Feb. 2, 1923.

Smith, Mary Louise: first woman head of Republican National Committee, Sep. 16, 1974.

Smith, Michael, Apr. 26, 1932.

Smith, Osborne Earl (Ozzie), Dec. 26, 1954.

Smith, Patti, Dec. 31, 1946.

Smith, Robert H., Aug. 8, 1879; Jun. 10, 1935.

Smith, Robyn Caroline, Aug. 14, 1944.

Smith, Roger, Dec. 18, 1932.

Smith, Samantha, Jun. 29, 1972.

Smith, Stan(ley Roger), Dec. 14, 1946.

Smith, Theobald, Jul. 31, 1859.

Smith, Tommie, Oct. 16, 1968.

Smith, Walter Wellesley (Red), Sep. 25, 1905.

Smith, Will(ard), Jr., Sep. 25, 1968.

Smith, Willi Donnell, Feb. 29, 1948.

Smith, William, Mar. 23, 1760.

Smithers, Jan, Jul. 3, 1949.

smiths, patron of, Dec. 1.

Smits, Jimmy, Jul. 9, 1955.

Smithsonian Institution, May 1, 1847; Apr. 23, 1909; May 1, 1947; Apr. 7, 1983.

smoking, passive, May 23, 1984.

Smolensk: liberated, Sep. 25, 1943.

Smollett, Tobias George, Mar. 19, 1721.

Smoot, George F., Feb. 20, 1945; Apr. 23, 1992.

Smothers, Dick, Nov. 20, 1938.

Smothers, Thomas Bolyn, III (Tommy), Feb. 2, 1937.

Smuts, Jan Christiaan, May 24, 1870; Mar. 5, 1916.

Snack a Pickle Time, Sep. intro.

snail darter, Jun. 15, 1978.

Snead, Sam, May 27, 1912.

Snell, George, Dec. 19, 1903.

Snell, Peter, Dec. 17, 1938.

Sneva, Thomas Edsol (Tom), Jun. 1, 1948.

Snider, Dee, Mar. 15, 1955.

Snipes, Wesley, Jul. 31, 1962.

Snodgrass, William Dewitt, Jan. 5, 1926.

Snodgress, Carrie, Oct. 27, 1946.

Snoopy: lunar module, May 22, 1969.

Snow, C(harles) P(ercy), Oct. 15, 1905.

Snow, Hank, May 9, 1914.

Snow, Phoebe Lamb, Jul. 17, 1952.

Snow White and the Seven Dwarfs: premiere, Dec. 21, 1937.

Snowden, Earl of, May 24, 1978.

Snowden, Philip, Jul. 18, 1864.

snowdrop, Jan. intro.

snuff, Jan. 15, 1986.

Snyder, Tom, May 12, 1936.

Soane, Sir John, Sep. 10, 1753.

Soap Box Derby, All American, Aug. intro.

Soares, Mario, Dec. 7, 1924; inaugurated, Jul. 23, 1976; Apr. 25, 1983; inaugurated, Jun. 9, 1983; inaugurated, Mar. 9, 1986.

Sobell, Morton, Apr. 11, 1917.

Sobhuz II (Swaziland), Jul. 22.

Sobieski, John III (Poland), Jun. 2, 1624; Sep. 12, 1683.

Social Christian Party (Belgium), Jul. 27, 1965; Apr. 3, 1979.

Social Democratic Party (Britain), Mar. 26, 1981.

Social Democratic Party (Portugal), Apr. 25, 1983.

Social Democratic Party (Sweden), Sep. 20, 1976.

social justice, patron of, Nov. 3.

Social Security Act: signed, Aug. 14, 1935.

Socialist Party, U.S., May 21, 1932.

Societe Nationale de Musique, Jan. 12, 1907.

Soddy, Frederick, Sep. 2, 1877.

Soderbert, Carl Richard, Feb. 3, 1895.

Soderblom, Nathan, Jan. 15, 1866.

Soil Conservation Service, U.S., Apr. 27, 1935.

Soissons, Battle of, Jan. 8, 1915; Jan. 14, 1915.

Solar Challenger, Jul. 7, 1981.

solar telescope: largest, Mar. 15, 1960.

Soldau (East Prussia), Nov. 18, 1914.

soldier vote bill, Mar. 31, 1944.

soldiers, patron of, Jan. 20; Sep. 8; Oct. 8.

Solemnity of, Mary, Jan. 1.

Solidarity Day: march, Jun. 19, 1968.

Solidarity (Poland): ruled legal, Nov. 10, 1980; Dec. 13, 1981; banned, Oct. 8, 1982; Apr. 5, 1989.

Solidarity with South African Political Prisoners, Oct. 11.

Solis Parma, Manuel: inaugurated, Feb. 26, 1988.

Solomon, Elijah Ben, Apr. 23, 1720.

Solomon Islands: U.S. troops land, Jun. 30, 1934; U.S. offensive begins, Aug. 7, 1942; Mar. 6, 1943; independence, Jul. 7, 1978.

Solomos, Dionysius, Apr. 8, 1798.

Solovieff, Alexander, Apr. 14, 1879.

Solow, Robert M., Aug. 23, 1924.

Solti, Sir Georg, Oct. 21, 1912; Dec. 17, 1968.

Solvay, Ernest, Apr. 16, 1838.

Solvay Mass, Battle of, Nov. 25, 1542.

Solzhenitsyn, Alexander, Dec. 11, 1918; Oct. 15, 1968; Dec. 28, 1973; Feb. 13, 1974.

Somali Coast, Mar. 13, 1884.

Somali Democratic Republic: formed, Jul. 1, 1960.

Somalia, Jan. 31, 1968; treaty with Ethiopia, Apr. 3, 1988; famine, Dec. 3, 1992; UN forces removed, Mar. 3, 1995.

Somaliland, Jan. 27, 1950; independence, Jun. 26, 1960.

Somaliland, British, Jul. 1, 1960.

Somaliland, Italian, Jul. 1, 1960.

Some Like It Hot: premiere, Mar. 29, 1959.

Somers, Suzanne, Oct. 16, 1946.

Somes, Michael, Sep. 28, 1917.

Somhlolo Day (Swaziland), Sep. 6.

Somme, Battle of the, Jun. 24, 1916; Jul. 1, 1916; Sep. 15, 1916; ends, Apr. 6, 1918.

Somme offensive: begins, Mar. 21, 1918.

Somme, Second Battle of the: opens, Aug. 21, 1918; Sep. 3, 1918.

Sommer, Elke, Nov. 5, 1941.

Somoza Debayle, Anastasio, Dec. 5, 1925; elected, Feb. 2, 1967; Jul. 17, 1979; assassinated, Sep. 17, 1980.

Somoza Debayle, Luis Anastasio, May 1, 1957.

Somoza Garcia, Anastasio, Feb. 1, 1896; May 26, 1947; May 21, 1950; May 21, 1950; Sep. 21, 1956.

Somport Tunnel: opens, Jul. 18, 1928.

Son of Sam, Aug. 10, 1977.

Son Sen, Sep. 2, 1985.

Sonderbund: formed in Switzerland, Dec. 11, 1845.

Sondheim, Stephen, Mar. 22, 1930; May 21, 1959; May 8, 1962; Feb. 25, 1973.

Sontag, Susan, Jan. 28, 1933.

Sony Corp., Jun. 6, 1961; Nov. 18, 1987.

Soo, Jack, Oct. 28, 1915.

Soong, T. V., May 31, 1945.

Sophia (Sweden), May 12, 1873.

Sophoulis, Themisto Cles, Jun. 30, 1949.

Sopwith, Sir Thomas, Jan. 18, 1888.

Sora, Italy, patron of, May 27.

Sorby, Henry Clifton, May 10, 1826.

Sorensen, Theodore Chaikin (Ted), May 8, 1928.

Sorge, Reinhard Johannes, Jan. 29, 1892.

Sorolla y Bastida, Joaquin, Feb. 27, 1863.

Sosuharai or Soot Sweeping Day (Japan), Dec. 13.

Sothern, Ann, Jan. 22, 1912.

Soto, Fernando de, Jun. 3, 1539.

Soul, David, Aug. 28, 1946.

Soul on Ice: published, Feb. 12, 1968.

souls on journey from this world to the next, patron of, Mar. 17.

souls in purgatory, patron of, Sep. 10.

Soult, Nicolas Jean de Dieu, Mar. 29, 1769.

sound barrier, Jun. 10, 1948; broken by land vechicle, Oct. 13, 1997.

The Sound of Music: premiere, Nov. 16, 1959.

sound, speed of, May 27, 1986.

soup kitchen: first, Jan. 8, 1800.

Souphanouvrong, Jan. 19, 1962.

Sousa, John Philip, Nov. 6, 1854.

Souter, David, Oct. 7, 1990.

South Africa: first European settlement, Apr. 6, 1652; Jan. 21, 1898; Aug. 27, 1952; Mar. 11, 1964; sports ban, Jul. 22, 1976; Catholic Schools in, Jan. 17, 1977; Sep. 15, 1977; Nov. 4, 1977; tricameral parliament, Nov. 2, 1983; interracial marriage legalized, Apr. 15,

1985; U.S. trade sanctions, Sep. 9, 1985; new constitution, Nov. 18, 1993; blacks votes for first time, Apr. 26, 1994; new constitution, May 8, 1996; U.S. ends weapons moratorium, Feb. 27, 1998.

South Africa, Union of, May 31, 1910; Mar. 5, 1916; Apr. 27, 1916; May 31, 1961.

South Africa, University of, Apr. 27, 1916.

South African Nationalist Party, Jun. 29, 1949.

South African Republic (Transvaal): established, Dec. 16, 1856; Jan. 6, 1857; Apr. 16, 1883; Jan. 2, 1896; Sep. 1, 1900; Oct. 25, 1900.

South African Students' Organization, Jul. 16, 1969.

South African Union, Convention of the: opens, Oct. 12, 1908.

South America, Jul. 10, 1934.

South Arabian Federation, Nov. 30, 1967.

South Bend (Indiana), Jan. 15, 1844.

South Carolina: admitted to Union, May 23, 1788; Apr. 12, 1861; Jan. 28, 1963.

South Dakota: admitted to Union, Nov. 2, 1889.

South Georgia Island (Falkland Islands), Apr. 25, 1982.

South Pacific: premiere, Apr. 7, 1949.

South Pole, Dec. 14, 1911; Jan. 17, 1912; first flight over, Nov. 29, 1929.

South Vietnam. *See*: Vietnam, South.

South Yemen People's Republic. *See*: Yemen People's Republic, South.

Southeast Asia Treaty Organization: founded, Sep. 8, 1954; dissolved, Jun. 30, 1977.

Southeast Asian Nations, Association of, May 16, 1979.

Southern Rhodesia. *See*: Rhodesia, Southern.

Sovereignty Day (Argentina), Jun. 10.

Soviet Socialist Republics, Union of *See*: U.S.S.R.

Soviet Union *See*: U.S.S.R.

Soviets, Second Congress of: convenes, Nov. 8, 1917.

Soweto Day, Jun. 16.

Soyinka, Wole, Jul. 13, 1934.

Soyuz 9, Jun. 19, 1970.

Soyuz 10, Apr. 24, 1971.

Soyuz 11, Jun. 7, 1971; Jun. 30, 1971.

Soyuz 11, Dec. 26, 1973.

Soyuz 19, Jul. 17, 1975.

Soyuz 25, Oct. 10, 1977.

Soyuz 27, Mar. 16, 1978.

Soyuz 31, Nov. 2, 1978.

Soyuz spacecraft, Jan. 16, 1969.

Spaak-Janson, Marie: first woman elected to Belgian parliament, Nov. 20, 1921.

Spaak, Paul Henri, Jan. 25, 1899.

Spaatz, Carl, Jun. 28, 1891.

space: peaceful use of, Jan. 27, 1967.

space endurance record, Jun. 30, 1971.

space shuttle, manned, Jan. 5, 1972.

space walk: *Gemini 4,* Jun. 3, 1965.

space walk, first, Mar. 18, 1965.

Spacek, Sissy, Dec. 25, 1949.

Spacey, Kevin, Jul. 26, 1959.

Spader, James, Feb. 7, 1960.

Spahn, Warren, Apr. 23, 1921.

Spain, Jan. 2, 1492; Jan. 30, 1648; Jan. 4, 1762; Jan. 22, 1771; Jan. 20, 1801; Jan. 4, 1805; war with France, Apr. 7, 1823; concordat with papacy, Mar. 16, 1851; jury trial introduced, May 29, 1889; universal suffrage, Mar. 27, 1890; Apr. 4, 1892; declares war on U.S., Apr. 24, 1898; Cuban independence from, May 20, 1902; Republic of, Apr. 14, 1931, expulsion of Jews voided, Dec. 16, 1968; trade with U.S.S.R., Sep. 15, 1972; Mar. 5, 1976; free elections, Jun. 15, 1977; first free elections in 41 years, Jun. 15, 1977; new constitution, Dec. 6, 1978; joins NATO, May 30, 1982; Jan. 1, 1986; Nov. 14, 1988.

Spain, patron of, Jul. 25; Nov. 12.

Spalding, Albert Goodwill, Sep. 2, 1850.

Spallanzani, Lazzaro, Jan. 12, 1729.

Spanish-American War, Apr. 24, 1898, May 1, 1898; Jun. 15, 1898; Jul. 1, 1898; Jul. 10, 1898; Jul. 17, 1898; ends, Aug. 12, 1898; Aug. 13, 1898; Treaty of Paris, Dec. 10, 1898; Feb. 6, 1899.

Spanish Armada: defeated, Aug. 8, 1588.

Spanish Civil War, Jan. 26, 1936; Apr. 7, 1936; begins, Jul. 18, 1936; Oct. 1, 1936; Nov. 18, 1936; Apr. 26, 1937; Oct. 21, 1937; Apr. 15, 1938; Dec. 23, 1938; ends, Mar. 28, 1939; Apr. 1, 1939; May 20, 1939.

Spanish government, Jan. 26, 1977.

Spanish Inquisition, Oct. 17, 1483; Jews expelled, Mar. 30, 1492.

Spanish Netherlands, Nov. 15, 1715.

Spanish Sahara, Feb. 27, 1976; Apr. 14, 1976.

Spanish Succession, War of the: begins, Nov. 1, 1700; Aug. 13, 1704; Oct. 14, 1705; Dec. 10, 1710; Apr. 11, 1713.

Spano, Joe, Jul. 7, 1946.

Spark, Muriel, Feb. 1, 1918.

Sparkman, John J., Dec. 20, 1899.

Spasowski, Romauld, Dec. 20, 1981.

Spassky, Boris, Jan. 30, 1937; Sep. 1, 1972.

Speaker, Tristram, Apr. 4, 1888.

Speakes, Larry Melvin, Sep. 13, 1939.

Special Olympics, Jul. 19, 1968.

Speck, Richard Franklin, Dec. 6, 1941.

Spector, Phil(ip Harvey), Dec. 25, 1940.

Spee, Count Maximilian von, Jun. 22, 1861; dies, Dec. 8, 1914.

speed limit (federal), repealed, Nov. 28, 1995.

Speedwell Iron Works, Jan. 6, 1838.

Speer, Albert, Mar. 19, 1905; released from prison, Oct. 1, 1966.

Speke, John Hanning, May 3, 1827; Feb. 23, 1854; Feb. 13, 1858; discovers Lake Victoria, Aug. 3, 1858.

Spelling, Aaron, Apr. 22, 1925.

Spellman, Francis Joseph, May 4, 1889.

Spelterina, Maria, Jul. 22, 1876.

Spemann, Hans, Jun. 27, 1869.

Spencer-Churchill, Lady, Feb. 19, 1977.

Spencer, Herbert, Apr. 27, 1820.

Spender, Stephen, Feb. 28, 1909.

Spengler, Oswald, May 29, 1880.

Sperry, Elmer A(mbrose), Oct. 12, 1860.

Sperry, Roger W., Aug. 20, 1913.

Spiegelman, Solomon, Dec. 14, 1914.

Spielberg, Steven, Dec. 18, 1947.

Spillane, Mickey, Mar. 9, 1918.

Spinal Health Month, National, Oct. intro.

Spindletop: first Texas oil strike, Jan. 10, 1901.

Spingarn, Joel Elias, May 17, 1875.

Spinks, Leon, Jul. 11, 1953; Sep. 15, 1978.

Spinks, Michael, Jul. 29, 1956.

spinning and carding machine, Feb. 14, 1764.

Spinning and Weaving Week, National, Oct. intro.

Spinola, Antonio de (Portugal), Apr. 11, 1910; Apr. 25, 1974; Sep. 30, 1974, Mar. 15, 1975.

Spinoza, Baruch, Nov. 24, 1632.

spiritual exercises, patron of, Jul. 31.

Spitz, Mark, Feb. 10, 1950; Sep. 4, 1972.

Spock, Benjamin, May 2, 1903.

Spohr, Louis, Apr. 5, 1784.

Sports Day (Japan), Oct. 10.

Sports' Day, National (Lesotho), Oct. intro; Oct. 7.

Sports Illustrated, Aug. 12, 1954.

Spreti, Karl von (Count): slain, Apr. 5, 1970.

Spring Day (Iraq), Mar. 21.

Spring Day (Turkey), May 1.

Spring Festival (China), Feb. 15.

Spring Festival (Mauritius), Feb. 5.

Spring Imperial Festival (Japan), Mar. 23.

Springfield, Dusty, Apr. 16, 1939.

Springfield (Massachusetts), Jan. 20, 1892.

Springfield, Rick, Aug. 23, 1949.

Springsteen, Bruce, Sep. 23, 1949.

Sproul, Mary, Jan. 1, 1950.

Spruance, Raymond Ames, Jan. 3, 1886.

Spruce Goose, The, Nov. 2, 1947.

Spurs, Battle of, Aug. 16, 1513.

Sputnik I, Oct. 4, 1957; Jan. 4, 1958.

Sputnik II, Nov. 3, 1957.

Spyri, Johanna Heuser, Jun. 12, 1827.

Squaw Winter, Oct. intro.

Squibb, Edward Robinson, Jul. 4, 1819.

Squier, Billy, May 12, 1950.

Sri Lanka,; Feb. 4, 1948; May 22, 1972; Feb. 4, 1978; adopts constitution, Sep. 7, 1978. *See also*: Ceylon.

S.S. France, May 11, 1960.

stablemen, patron of, Jul. 26.

Stack, Robert, Jan. 13, 1919.

Stade, Frederica von, Jun. 1, 1945.

Stael, Madame de (Anne Louise Germaine), Apr. 22, 1766.

Stafford, Humphry: slain, Jun. 27, 1450.

Stafford, Jo, Nov. 12, 1918.

Stafford, patron of, Aug. 10; Sep. 9.

Stafford, Thomas Patten, Sep. 17, 1930.

Stagg, (Amos) Alonzo, Aug. 16, 1862.

Stahl, Georg Ernst, Oct. 21, 1660.

Stahl, Lesley Rene, Dec. 16, 1941.

Stalin, Joseph, Dec. 21, 1879; Dec. 27, 1927; Jan. 21, 1929; Aug. 19, 1936; Aug. 21, 1940; May 6, 1941; Mar. 6, 1967.

Stalingrad: German army enters, Sep. 13, 1942; front, Nov. 19, 1942; Feb. 2, 1943; renamed Volgograd, Nov. 11, 1961.

Stallings, Laurence, Nov. 25, 1894.

Stallone, Sylvester, Jul. 6, 1946; Mar. 28, 1977.

Stamford, Battle of, Mar. 13, 1470.

Stamford Bridge, Battle of, Sep. 25, 1066.

Stamp Act: passed, Mar. 2, 1765; passed, Mar. 23, 1765; Feb. 3, 1766; repealed, Mar. 18, 1766.

Stamp Act Congress, Oct. 7, 1765.

Stamp Collecting Month, National, Nov. intro.

Stamp Collector's Month, Jan. intro.

Stamp, Terence, Jul. 22, 1940.

Standard, Battle of the, Aug. 22, 1138.

Standard Oil Company: incorporated, Jan. 10, 1870; May 1, 1911; Mar. 5, 1984; Apr. 19, 1984.

Stanford, A. Leland, Mar. 9, 1824.

Stanford Linear Collider, Apr. 15, 1987.

Stanford, Sally, May 5, 1903.

Stanford University, Nov. 11, 1885; DNA synthesized, Dec. 14, 1967.

Stanislas II (Poland), Jan. 17, 1732.

Stanislavsky, Konstantin, Jan. 7, 1863.

Stankiewicz, Richard (Peter), Oct. 18, 1922.

Stanley, Francis Edgar, Jun. 1, 1849.

Stanley, Sir Henry Morton, Jan. 28, 1841; Jan. 6, 1871; Mar. 21, 1871; meets David Livingstone, Oct. 28, 1871; Mar. 14, 1872; reaches Congo River, Aug. 12, 1877.

Stanley, Paul, Jan. 20, 1949.

Stanley, Wendell Meredith, Aug. 16, 1904.

Stanleyville (Congo), Aug. 5, 1964, Nov. 24, 1964.

Stans, Maurice Hubert, Mar. 22, 1908.

Stanton, Edwin McMasters, Dec. 19, 1814.

Stanton, Elizabeth Cady, Nov. 12, 1815; Jul. 19, 1848.

Stanton, Frank Lebby, Feb. 22, 1857.

Stanton, Frank Nicholas, Mar. 20, 1908.

Stanwyck, Barbara, Jul. 16, 1907.

Stapleton, Jean, Jan. 19, 1923.

Stapleton, Maureen, Jun. 21, 1925.

Star of India, Order of: instituted, Jun. 25, 1861.

Star Spangled Banner, Sep. 14, 1814; Mar. 3, 1931.

Star Trek: television debut, Sep. 8, 1966.

Stargell, Willie, Mar. 6, 1941.

Stark, Johannes, Apr. 15, 1874.

Stark, John, Aug. 28, 1728.

Stark, U.S.S., May 17, 1987.

Starling, Ernest Henry, Apr. 17, 1866.

Starr, Belle, Feb. 5, 1848.

Starr, Kay, Jul. 21, 1924.

Starr, Ringo, Jul. 7, 1940.

Starr, Bryan B. (Bart), Jan. 9, 1934.

Stars and Stripes, Mar. 3, 1988.

Stars and Stripes: first published, Apr. 17, 1942; Feb. 4, 1987.

Stassen, Harold Edward, Apr. 13, 1907.

State Security Ministry, Feb. 8, 1950.

State Sovereignty Day (Russia), June 12.

State of the Union Message: first, Jan. 8, 1790.

Statehood Day (St. Kitts-Nevis), Feb. 27.

States-General: first meeting, Apr. 10, 1302.

States Rights Party: formed, Jul. 17, 1948.

Statue of Liberty: formally presented, Jul. 4, 1884; cornerstone laid, Aug. 5, 1884; dedicated, Oct. 28, 1886; 100th anniversary, Jul. 3, 1986.

Statute Day (Aruba, Netherlands Antilles), Dec. 15.

Staubach, Roger Thomas, Feb. 5, 1942.

Staudinger, Hermann, Mar. 23, 1881.

Stauffenberg, Klaus Von, Jul. 20, 1944.

Stead, Christina Ellen, Jul. 17, 1902.

steam ferry, free: London, Mar. 23, 1889.

steamboat: demonstrated, Aug. 22, 1787; patented, Aug. 26, 1791; Feb. 11, 1809.

Steamboat Willie: premiere, Nov. 18, 1928.

Steel Seafarer: first U.S. merchant ship lost to enemy air attack, Sep. 7, 1941.

Steen, Alann, Dec. 2, 1991.

Steenburgen, Mary, Feb. 8, 1953.

Stefani, Gwen, Oct. 3, 1969.

Stefansson, Vilhjalmur, Nov. 3, 1879.

Steffens, Lincoln, Apr. 6, 1866.

Stegner, Wallace Earle, Feb. 18, 1909.

Steichen, Edward, Mar. 27, 1879.

Steiger, Rod, Apr. 14, 1925.

Stein, Gertrude, Feb. 3, 1874.

Stein, Joseph, Sep. 22, 1964.

Stein, Jules, Apr. 26, 1896.

Stein, William Howard, Jun. 25, 1911.

Steinbeck, John, Feb. 27, 1902.

Steinberg, David, Aug. 9, 1942.

Steinberg, Saul, Jun. 15, 1914.

Steinberger, Jack, May 25, 1921.

Steinbrenner, George Michael, III, Jul. 4, 1930.

Steinem, Gloria, Mar. 25, 1934.

Steiner, Max, May 10, 1888.

Steiner, Rudolph, Feb. 27, 1861.

Steinmetz, Charles Proteus, Apr. 9, 1865.

Steinway, Henry Engelhard, Feb. 15, 1797.

Steinway, William, Mar. 5, 1836.

Stella, Frank, May 12, 1936.

Stellenbosch University, Apr. 27, 1916.

Stendahl (Marie Henri Beyle), Jan. 23, 1783.

Stengel, Casey (Charles Dillon), Jul. 30, 1891.

Stenmark, Ingemar, Mar. 18, 1956.

Stennis, John Cornelius, Aug. 3, 1901.

stenographers, patron of, Dec. 3.

Stepanakert (U.S.S.R.), Feb. 11, 1988.

Stephanie (Marie Elisabeth), Princess, Feb. 1, 1965.

Stephen of Blois, Dec. 1, 1135.

Stephen (England), Aug. 22, 1138; Nov. 7, 1153; dies, Oct. 25, 1154.

Stephen Foster Memorial Day (U.S.), Jan. 13.

Stephen, Sir Leslie, Nov. 28, 1832.

Stephens, Alexander H., Feb. 11, 8, 1861.

Stephenson, George, Jun. 9, 1781.

Stephenson, Jan, Dec. 22, 1951.

Steptoe, Patrick Christopher, Jun. 9, 1913.

stereophonic sound, Apr. 9, 1940.

Sterling Bridge, Battle of, Sep. 11, 1297.

Sterling, Bruce, Apr. 14, 1954.

Sterling, Jan, Apr. 3, 1923.

Sterling, Robert, Nov. 13, 1917.

Stern, Isaac, Jul. 21, 1920.

Stern, Howard, Jan. 12, 1954.

Sterne, Laurence, Nov. 24, 1713.

stethoscope, Sep. 13, 1816.

Stettinius, Edward Reilly, Jr., Oct. 22, 1900.

Steuben, Baron Friedrich Wilhelm, Augustus von, Sep. 17, 1730.

Stevens, Andrew, Jun. 10, 1955.

Stevens, Cat, Jul. 21, 1947.

Stevens, Connie, Aug. 8, 1938.

Stevens, George, Dec. 18, 1904.

Stevens, John Paul, Apr. 20, 1920; Dec. 19, 1975.

Stevens, Ray, Jan. 24, 1939.

Stevens, Rise, Jun. 11, 1913.

Stevens, Robert T(en Broeck), Jul. 31, 1899

Stevens, Siaka P., Aug. 24, 1905.

Stevens, Stella, Oct. 1, 1938.

Stevens, Thaddeus, Apr. 4, 1792.

Stevens, Theodore Fulton, Nov. 18, 1923.

Stevens, Wallace, Oct. 2, 1879.

Stevenson, Adlai E., Oct. 23, 1835; Mar. 4, 1893.

Stevenson, Adlai E(wing), II, Feb. 5, 1900; Jul. 20, 1965.

Stevenson, Adlai E(wing), III, Oct. 10, 1930.

Stevenson, Karen, Sep. 9, 1979.

Stevenson, McLean, Nov. 14, 1929.

Stevenson, Parker, Jun. 4, 1951.

Stevenson, Robert Louis (Balfour), Nov. 13, 1859.

Stevenson, Teofilo, Mar. 23, 1952.

Stewart, David, Sep. 19, 1952.

Stewart, Donald Ogden, Nov. 30, 1894.

Stewart, Jackie, Jun. 11, 1939.

Stewart, James, May 20, 1908.

Stewart, John (Black Jack), May 6, 1917.

Stewart, Mary, Sep. 17, 1916.

Stewart, Patrick, Jul. 13, 1940.

Stewart, Potter, Jan. 23, 1915; May 5, 1959.

Stewart, Robert, Jun. 18, 1769.

Stewart, Robert (King of Scotland), Apr. 1, 1406.

Stewart, Rod(erick David), Jan. 10, 1945.

Stice, Steven, Jan. 20, 1998.

Stieglitz, Alfred, Jan. 1, 1864.

Stiernhielm, Georg, Aug. 7.

Stiers, David Ogden, Oct. 31, 1942.

Stigler, George J., Jan. 17, 1911.

Stigwood, Robert C., Apr. 16, 1934.

Stiklestad, Battle of, Jul. 29, 1030.

Still, Clyfford, Nov. 30, 1904.

Still, William Grant, May 11, 1895.

Stiller, Jerry, Jun. 8, 1926.

Stillness at Appomattox, May 3, 1954.

Stills, Stephen, Jan. 3, 1945.

Stilwell, Joseph Warren, Mar. 19, 1883; Dec. 21, 1943.

Stimson, Henry Lewis, Sep. 21, 1867.

Sting, Oct. 2, 1951; premiere, Dec. 25, 1973.

Stock Exchange, New York, May 5, 1893; May 25, 1970.

Stockholm, Jul. 25, 1956.

Stockholm, Blood Bath of, Nov. 8, 1520.

Stockman, David Allen, Nov. 10, 1946.

Stockton, David (Dave), Nov. 2, 1941.

Stockton, Dick, Feb. 18, 1951.

Stockton, John, Mar. 26, 1962.

Stokach, Mar. 25, 1799.

Stoker, Bram, Nov. 8, 1847.

Stokes, Carl, Nov. 7, 1967.

Stokes, Carl Burton, Jun. 21, 1927.

Stokowski, Leopold, Apr. 18, 1882; Oct. 11, 1912.

Stolypin, Peter, Sep. 14, 1911.

stomach patients, patron of, Jan. 26.

Stone, Amasa, Apr. 27, 1818.

Stone, Edward Durell, Mar. 9, 1902.

Stone, Harlan Fiske, Oct. 11, 1872; Jun. 27, 1941.

Stone, Irving, Jul. 14, 1903.

Stone, I(sidor F(einstein), Dec. 24, 1907.

Stone, Lucy, Aug. 13, 1818.

stone masons, patron of, Jan. 7.

Stone, Oliver, Sep. 15, 1946.

Stone, Richard, Aug. 13, 1913.

Stone of Scone: stolen, Dec. 25, 1950.

Stone, Sharon, Mar. 10, 1958.

Stone, Sly, Mar. 15, 1944.

stonecutters, patron of, Nov. 23; Dec. 26.

Stonehenge: sold, Sep. 21, 1915.

Stones, Dwight, Dec. 6, 1953.

Stony Tunguska River (Siberia): meteorite craters found, Jun. 30, 1908.

Stookey, Paul, Nov. 30, 1937.

Stop the Draft Week, Dec. 5, 1967.

Stoph, Willi, Mar. 19, 1970.

Stoppard, Tom, Jul. 3, 1937; Apr. 11, 1967; Oct. 16, 1967.

Storch, Larry, Jan. 8, 1923.

Story, Joseph, Sep. 18, 1779.

Storytelling Festival, National, Oct. intro.

Stout, Rex (Todhunter), Dec. 1, 1886.

Stowe, Harriet (Elizabeth) Beecher, Jun. 14, 1811.

Stowe, Madeleine, Aug. 18, 1958.

Stoyanov, Petar, elected, Nov. 3, 1996.

Strachey, Lytton, Mar. 1, 1880.

Stradonitz, Friedrich, August Kekule von, Sep. 7, 1829.

Strait, George, May 18, 1952.

Straits Convention: signed, Jul. 13, 1841.

Stralsund, Peace of, May 24, 1370.

Strangest Love Story of All: premiere, Feb. 14, 1927.

Strasberg, Lee, Nov. 17, 1901.

Strasberg, Susan, May 22, 1938.

Strasbourg (Alsace): occupied by France, Nov. 25, 1918.

Strasbourg, Peace of, Apr. 3, 1189.

Strategic Air Command: established, Mar. 21, 1946.

Strategic Arms Reduction Treaty (START II), Dec. 29, 1992.

Stratemeyer, Edward L., Oct. 4, 1862.

Stratford-on-Avon, Apr. 23, 1964.

Stratigic Arms Limitation Treaty (SALT) II, Jun. 18, 1979.

Stratten, Dorothy, Feb. 28, 1960.

Straus, Isidor, Feb. 6, 1845.

Straus, Nathan, Jan. 31, 1848.

Straus, Oscar, Apr. 6, 1870.

Straus, Oscar Solomon, Dec. 12, 1906.

Straus, Percy Selden, Jun. 27, 1876.

Strauss, Franz Josef, Sep. 6, 1915.

Strauss, Johann, Oct. 25, 1825.

Strauss, Levi, Feb. 26, c. 1829.

Strauss, Richard, Jun. 11, 1864; Dec. 9, 1905; Jan. 22, 1907; Jan. 25, 1909; Jan. 26, 1911.

Strauss, Robert Schwarz, Oct. 9, 1918.

Stravinsky, Igor, Jun. 17, 1882; Jun. 25, 1910; Jun. 13, 1911; May 29, 1913.

Strawberry, Darryl Eugene, Mar. 12, 1962.

Streep, Meryl, Jun. 22, 1949; Dec. 14, 1978.

Streisand, Barbara, Apr. 24, 1942.

Stresemann, Gustav, May 10, 1878.

Strindberg, August, Jan. 22, 1849.

Stroessner, Alfredo, Nov. 3, 1912; May 5, 1954; Apr. 8, 1987; Feb. 3, 1989; Feb. 2, 1989.

Stroh, Peter W., Dec. 18, 1927.

Stroheim, Erich von, Sep. 22, 1885.

Strouse, Charles, Jun. 7, 1928; Apr. 14, 1960; Apr. 21, 1977.

Strug, Kerri, Nov. 19, 1977.

Struthers, Sally Anne, Jul. 28, 1948.

Strutt, John William, Nov. 12, 1842.

Struve, Friedrich Georg Wilson von, Apr. 15, 1793.

Strydom, Johannes, Nov. 30, 1954.

Stuart, Charles, Apr. 28, 1795.

Stuart, Elbridge Amos, Sep. 10, 1856.

Stuart, Gilbert Charles, Dec. 3, 1755.

Stuart, Henry (Lord Darnley), Jul. 29, 1565.

Stuart, Jeb, Feb. 6, 1833.

Stuart, Jesse, Aug. 8, 1907.

Stuart, John (Earl of Bute), Apr. 7, 1763.

Stubbs, George, Aug. 24, 1724.

Stuber, William George, Apr. 9, 1864.

Stuck, Hudson: first ascent of Mount McKinley, Jun. 6, 1913.

Studebaker, Clement, Mar. 12, 1831.

Studebaker, John Mohler, Oct. 10, 1833.

student newspapers, Jan. 13, 1988.

Student Nonviolent Coordinating Committee, May 16, 1966, May 12, 1967.

Students for a Democratic Society, Jun. 11, 1962; Apr. 2, 1970.

students of the natural sciences, patron of, Nov. 15.

students, patron of, Sep. 30.

students of philosophy, patron of, Nov. 25.

Sturgeon, William, May 22, 1783.

Styne, Jule, Dec. 31, 1905; Dec. 8, 1949; May 21, 1959.

Styron, William Clark, Jr., Jun. 11, 1925, Sep. 9, 1967.

Suan (Korea), May 8, 1952.

Suarez Flamerich, German: inaugurated, Nov. 27, 1950.

Suarez Gonzales, Adolfo (Spain), Sep. 25, 1932; Jul. 3, 1976, Mar. 1, 1979.

Suazo Cordova, Roberto, Jan. 5, 1982.

submarine attack, first, Feb. 17, 1864.

submarine blockade, German, Feb. 18, 1915.

submarine telephone cable, Trans-Tasman: opens, Jul. 9, 1962.

submarine warfare, Jan. 16, 1915; Feb. 1, 1917; Feb. 6, 1922; regulation of, Apr. 10, 1930.

subway: first section opens in New York, Oct. 27, 1904; Chicago's first, Oct. 17, 1944; Los Angeles, Cal., Jan. 30, 1993; opens in Shanghai, Apr. 10, 1995.

sucralose, approved by FDA, Apr. 1, 1998.

Sucre, Jose Antonio de, Feb. 3, 1793.

Sudan, Jan. 26, 1885; Sep. 2, 1898; Oct. 22, 1952; independence, Jan. 1, 1956; civilian government overthrown, Nov. 17, 1958; Apr. 4, 1960; Feb. 26, 1972.

Sudan, French (Upper Senegal-Niger), Dec. 4, 1920.

Sudanese Republic, Sep. 22, 1960.

Sudanese Republic and Senegal: independence as Federation of Mali, Jun. 20, 1960.

sudden death overtime, Aug. 28, 1955.

Sudetenland, Jun. 23, 1950.

Suez Canal, Apr. 25, 1859; opens, Nov. 17, 1869; Oct. 29, 1888; Oct. 30, 1951; Jun. 14, 1956; nationalized, Jul. 26, 1956; Oct. 31, 1956; Jun. 6, 1967; Jan. 18, 1974; reopens, Jun. 5, 1975; Apr. 30, 1979.

Suez National Day (Egypt), Oct. 23.

Suggs, Louise, Sep. 7, 1923.

Suharto, Mar. 12, 1966; re-elected, Mar. 11, 1998; resigns, May 21, 1998.

Sukarno, Ahmed, Jun. 6, 1901; Jan. 13, 1959; Mar. 5, 1960; Sep. 21, 1963; Mar. 12, 1966.

Sukarno government, Apr. 24, 1965.

Suleiman I (Turkey): conquers Belgrade, Aug. 29, 1521.

Suleiman III (Turkey), Nov. 2, 1687.

Sullavan, Margaret, May 16, 1911.

Sullivan, A(loysius) M(ichael), Aug. 9, 1896.

Sullivan, Anne, Apr. 14, 1866.

Sullivan, Sir Arthur S., May 13, 1842; Nov. 25, 1882, Dec. 7, 1889.

Sullivan, Barry, Aug. 29, 1912.

Sullivan, Ed(ward Vincent), Sep. 28, 1902.

Sullivan, John L., Oct. 15, 1858; Feb. 7, 1883; Jul. 8, 1889; Sep. 7, 1892, Jun. 16, 1899.

Sullivan, Louis, Nov. 3, 1933.

Sullivan, Louis H., Sep. 3, 1856.

Sullivan Ordinance, Jan. 21, 1908.

Sullivan, Susan, Nov. 18, 1944.

Sully, Thomas, Jun. 19, 1783.

Sultan's Birthday (Brunei), Jul. 15.

Sulzberger, Arthur Hays, Sep. 12, 1891.

Sumarokov, Aleksandr Petrovic, Jun. 4, 1718.

Sumatra, Jan. 1, 1596.

Summer, Donna, Dec. 31, 1948.

Summer Holiday (San Marino), Aug. 14; Aug. 15; Aug. 16.

summer solstice, Jun. intro.

Summerskill, Edith Clara, Apr. 19, 1901.

Summit of the Americas, Apr. 18, 1998.

Sumner, Charles, Jan. 6, 1811.

Sumner, James Batcheller, Nov. 19, 1887.

Sumner, William Graham, Oct. 30, 1840.

Sumter, Fort, Apr. 10, 1861; Apr. 12, 1861.

Sun Yat-sen, Nov. 12, 1866; Dec. 29, 1911; Jan. 1, 1912; Feb. 15, 1912; Apr. 7, 1921; Jan. 20, 1924.

Sun Yat-sen, Dr., Birthday of (Taiwan), Nov. 12.

Sun Yun-suan, Nov. 11, 1913.

Sunay, Cevdet, Feb. 10, 1900.

Sunday, Billy, Nov. 18, 1862.

Sundberg, James Howard (Jim), May 18, 1951.

Sunshine Week, National, Oct. intro.

Super Bowl, Jan. 15, 1967; Jan. 21, 1979; Jan. 27, 1991; Jan. 26, 1992; Jan. 31, 1993; Jan. 30, 1994; Jan. 29, 1995.

superconductivity, Oct. 20, 1972.

superfund: law, Jan. 4, 1983.

supersonic jetliner: first test, Dec. 31, 1968.

Supremacy, Act of, Jan. 15, 1535.

Supreme Council of National Economy (U.S.S.R.), Mar. 13, 1963.

Supreme Court, Canada: rules on abortion, Jan. 28, 1988.

Supreme Court, U.S.: first meeting, Feb. 1, 1790; Jan. 8, 1798; Mar. 3, 1879; May 1, 1911; May 27, 1935; civil rights, Apr. 3, 1944; rules on segregation, Jun. 5, 1950; Jan. 15, 1951; May 17, 1954; ruling against segregation, Sep. 30, 1958; May 29, 1961; search or seizure, Jun. 19, 1961; Feb. 18, 1963; Feb. 17, 1964; Apr. 6, 1964; Mar. 29, 1965; rules on sale of birth control devices, Jun. 7, 1965; rules on poll tax, Mar. 25, 1966; rules on children's rights, May 15, 1967; first black seated, Jun. 13, 1967; rules on racial discrimination, Jun. 17, 1968; Apr. 21, 1969; Jun. 16, 1969; Jan. 19, 1970; Jan. 22, 1973; death penalty, Jul. 2, 1976; rules on capital punishment, Jun. 6, 1977; Jun. 15, 1978; reverse discrimination, Jun. 28, 1978; first woman member, Jul. 7, 1981, May 24, 1983; rules on legislative veto, Jun. 23, 1983; rules on retirement plans, Jul. 6, 1983; rules on aliens, Jun. 5, 1984; affirmative action, Mar. 25, 1987; Jun. 19, 1987; student newspaper censorship, Jan. 13, 1988; sex discrimination, Jun. 20, 1988; special prosecutor law upheld, Jun. 29, 1988; restrictions on abortion, Jul. 3, 1989.

Supreme Soviet, ends religious repression, Sep. 26, 1990.

surgeons, patron of, Aug. 16.

Suriname, Jan. 20, 1950; independent, Nov. 25, 1975.

Suriyanond, Pho, Nov. 29. 1951.

Surrey Iron Railway: first public freight- carrying railway, Jul. 26, 1803.

surrogate parenting, Jun. 27, 1988.

surrogate parenting contracts, Mar. 31, 1987.

Surveyor, Jun. 2, 1966.

Surveyor VII, Jan. 7, 1968; Jan. 9, 1968.

Susan B. Anthony Day (U.S.), Feb. 15.

Susann, Jacqueline, Aug. 20, 1921.

Susskind, David (Howard), Dec. 19, 1920.

Sutcliffe, Richard Lee (Rick), Jun. 21, 1956.

Sutherland, Donald, Jul . 17, 1934.

Sutherland, Earl Wilbur, Nov. 19, 1915.

Sutherland, Graham Vivian, Aug. 24, 1903.

Sutherland, Dame Joan, Nov. 7, 1926.

Sutherland, Kiefer, Dec. 18, 1966.

Sutri, Treaty of, Feb. 4, 1111.

suttee: outlawed, Dec. 7, 1829.

Sutter, John Augustus, Feb. 15, 1803.

Sutter's Mill, Jan. 24, 1848.

Suttner, Baroness Bertha von, Jun. 9, 1843.

Sutton, Don(ald Howard), Apr. 2, 1945.

Suvorov, Aleksandr Vasilievich, Nov. 13, 1729.

Suzman, Janet, Feb. 9, 1939.

Suzuki, Zenko, Jan. 11, 1911

Svedberg, Theodor H. E., Aug. 30, 1884.

Swaggert, Jimmy, Feb. 21, 1988.

Swahili language, Jan. 4, 1967.

Swallow Day (California), Mar. 19.

Swan, Sir Joseph Wilson, Oct. 31, 1828.

Sweeney, John J., elected, Oct. 25, 1995.

Swan Lake: opens, Jan. 15, 1895.

Swanee: premiere, Feb. 14, 1918.

Swanson, Gloria, Mar. 27, 1899.

Swap Ideas Day, Sep. intro, Sep. 10.

Swarthout, Gladys, Dec. 25, 1904.

Swayne, Noah, Dec. 7, 1804.

Swayze, John Cameron, Apr. 4, 1906.

Swayze, Patrick, Aug. 18, 1955.

Swaziland: independence, Sep. 6, 1968; admitted to U.N., Sep. 24, 1968.

sweatshops, Mar. 25, 1911.

Sweden, Apr. 4, 1611; May 3, 1660; Jan. 23, 1668; Seven Years War, Jan. 10, 1757; Jan. 14, 1814; May 17, 1814; universal suffrage, May 13, 1907; women's suffrage, May 26, 1919; Mar. 9, 1920; Jan. 10, 1969; Jan. 15, 1969; Feb. 27, 1974.

Sweden, patron of, Feb. 3; Jul. 23; Dec. 27.

Swedenborg, Emanuel, Jan. 29, 1688.

Swedes: allied with French, Jul. 26, 1648.

Swedish Colonial Day (Delaware), Mar. 29.

Swedish National Socialist Party (Fascist), Dec. 5, 1930.

Sweet Bird of Youth: opens, Mar. 10, 1959.

Sweet Charity: premiere, Jan. 29, 1966.

sweet pea, Apr. intro.

Sweetest Day, Oct. intro.

Swenson, May, May 28, 1919.

Sweyn Forkbeard (Denmark): dies, Feb. 3, 1014.

Swicky, Fritz, Feb. 14, 1898.

Swift, Gustavus Franklin, Jun. 24, 1839.

Swift, Jonathan, Nov. 30, 1667.

swimming championship: first U.S., Sep. 30, 1877.

Swinburne, Algernon Charles, Apr. 5, 1837.

Swinburne, Laurence, Jul. 2, 1924.

Swing, Raymond Gram, Mar. 25, 1887.

Swipert, John L., Apr. 11, 1970.

Swiss Army, Apr. 12, 1907.

Swiss Confederation: formed, Aug. 1, 1291; independence, Nov. 4, 1307; dissolved, Feb. 9, 1798.

Swiss infantry, Nov. 15, 1315.

Swiss women: right to vote, Feb. 7, 1971; elected to parliament, Oct. 31, 1971.

Swit, Loretta, Nov. 4, 1937.

Switzerland: independence, Jul. 9, 1386; Jul. 25, 1712; Feb. 28, 1803; Mar. 20, 1815; civil war begins, Nov. 14, 1847; constitution, Sep. 12, 1848; Feb. 13, 1920; Mar. 8, 1920; Mar. 29, 1923; neutrality, May 14, 1938.

Switzerland, patron of, Oct. 16.

Swoopes, Sheryl, Mar. 25, 1971.

Swope, Herbert Bayard, Jan. 5, 1882.

sword-makers, patron of, Sep. 22.

Swordfish, U.S.S., Dec. 15, 1941.

Sydney (Australia): first settlers, Jan. 26, 1788.

Sydney (Australia) Opera House: opens, Oct. 20, 1973.

Sydow, Max von, Apr. 10, 1929.

Sykes, Richard: assassinated, Mar. 22, 1979.

Symbionese Liberation Army, Feb. 4, 1974; Sep. 18, 1975.

Symington, Stuart, Jun. 26, 1901.

Symms, Steven Douglas, Apr. 23, 1938.

Symons, Julian Gustave, May 30, 1912.

Symphonic Dances, Jan. 3, 1941.

Synge, John Millington, Apr. 16, 1871.

Synge, Richard Laurence Millington, Oct. 28, 1914.

Synod of Brixen, Jun. 25, 1080.

Syracuse, (Sicily), patron of, Dec. 13.

Syria, Jan. 2, 1799; Apr. 25, 1920; Jan. 1, 1925; British forces occupy, Jul. 12, 1941; independence, Apr. 17, 1946; Mar. 8, 1963.

Szent-Gyorgyi, Albert, Sep. 16, 1893.

Szilard, Leo, Feb. 11, 1898.

Szoka, Edmund Casimir Sep. 14, 1927.

Szold, Henrietta, Dec. 21, 1860.

Szuros, Matyas, Oct. 23, 1989.

Szymborsha, Wislawa, Jul. 2, 1923.

T

Tabai, Ieremia, Dec. 16, 1950.

Tabriz (Persia), Jan. 8, 1915, Jan. 30, 1915.

Tactical Air Command: established, Mar. 21 1946.

Tafari, Ras (Haile Selassie I), Apr. 3, 1930.

Taft-Hartley Act: adopted, Jun. 23, 1947 Feb. 6, 1950.

Taft, Helen, Jun. 2, 1861.

Taft, Lorado, Apr. 29, 1860.

Taft Memorial Bell Tower, Apr. 14, 1959.

Taft, Robert A(lphonso), Sep. 8, 1889; Apr. 14, 1959.

Taft, Robert Alphonso, Jr., Feb. 26, 1917.

Taft, William Howard, Sep. 15, 1857; inaugurated, Mar. 4, 1909; Jun. 30, 1921; Apr. 14, 1959.

Tagliabue, Paul, Nov. 24, 1940.

Taglioni, Maria, Apr. 23, 1804.

Tagore, Rabindranath, May 7, 1861.

Tahiti: annexed by France, Jun. 29, 1880.

TailHook Association convention, Apr. 23, 1993.

tailors, patron of, Nov. 13.

Taine, Hippolyte Adolphe, Apr. 21, 1828.

Taiping Rebellion, Jan. 11, 1851; Mar. 19, 1853.

Taiwan, May 19, 1949, May 20, 1978.

Taiwan Restoration Day, Oct. 25.

Takada, Kenzo, Feb. 28, 1940.

Takeover Day (Nauru), Jul. 1.

Takeshita, Noboru: elected, Nov. 6, 1987 Apr. 25, 1989.

Taklamakan Desert, Oct. 16, 1964.

Tal, Wasfi: assassinated, Nov. 28, 1971.

Talal (King of Jordan), Jul. 20, 1951; Sep. 6, 1951, Jun. 6, 1952.

Talbot, John (Earl of Shrewsbury), Jul. 17, 1453.

Talbot, William, Feb. 11, 1800.

Tales of Wells Fargo: television debut, Mar. 18, 1957.

Talese, Gay, Feb. 7, 1932.

Tallchief, Maria, Jan. 24, 1925.

Talleyrand-Perigord, Charles Maurice de, Feb. 2, 1754.

Talmadge, Eugene, Sep. 23, 1884.

Talmadge, Herman Eugene, Aug. 9, 1913.

Talmadge, Norma, May 26, 1897.

Tamil Thai Pongal Day (Sri Lanka), Jan. 15.

Tamm, Igor Yevgenyevich, Jul. 8, 1895.

Tampa (Florida), Apr. 14, 1528.

Tanaka, Kakuei, May 4, 1918; elected, Jul. 5, 1972; resigns, Nov. 26, 1974; bribery conviction, Oct. 12, 1983.

Tanambogo, Solomon Islands: captured by U.S., Aug. 8, 1942.

Tanana, Frank Daryl, Jul. 3, 1953.

Tancred the Bastard (Sicily), Nov. 18, 1189.

Tandem Day, Dec. intro, Dec. 13.

Tandy, Jessica, Jun. 7, 1909.

Taney, Roger Brooke, Mar. 17, 1777.

Tanganyika, Feb. 25, 1885; Jan. 10, 1920; Feb. 1, 1950; May 1, 1961; Dec. 09, 1961; admitted to UN, Dec. 14, 1961; Dec. 9, 1962; Apr. 26, 1964.

Tanganyika, Lake, Feb. 13, 1858.

Tangier, Apr. 18, 1960; Jan. 2, 1962.

Tangier Zone, Feb. 7, 1924.

Tangiers Convention, Feb. 7, 1924.

Tanguy, Yves, Jan. 5, 1900.

tanks: first, Feb. 2, 1916; first use of, Sep. 15, 1916; first demonstration of effectiveness, Nov. 20, 1917.

Tannenberg, Battle of, Aug. 26, 1914; Aug. 30, 1914.

Tanner, Henry, Jul. 13, 1970.

Tanner, Roscoe, III, Oct. 15, 1951.

tanners, patron of, Jul. 21; Aug. 24; Nov. 23.

Tannhauser: premiere, Mar. 13, 1861.

Tanzania, Apr. 26, 1964, Jan. 4, 1967; Apr. 13, 1968.

Tanzanian constitution, Apr. 26, 1977.

Tara, Mohammad Rafiq, Dec. 31, 1997.

Tarantino, Quentin, Mar. 27, 1963.

Taranto, Malta: British attack, Nov. 11, 1941.

Taras Bulba: premiere, Oct. 9, 1921.

Tarbell, Ida Minerva, Nov. 5, 1857.

tariff of abominations, May 19, 1828.

Tarkanian, Jerry, Aug. 8, 1930.

Tarkenton, Fran(cis Asbury), Feb. 3, 1940.

Tarkington, (Newton) Booth, Jul. 29, 1869.

Tarnow, May 3, 1915.

Tarnower, Herman, Mar. 18, 1910; Feb. 24, 1981.

Tarrytown (New York), Sep. 23, 1780.

Tartikoff, Brandon, Jan. 13, 1949.

Tarzan: published, Oct. 1, 1912.

Tasman, Abel, Nov. 24, 1642; discovers New Zealand, Dec. 13, 1642.

Tasmania: discovered, Nov. 24, 1642.

Tasso, Torquato, Mar. 11, 1544.

Tate, (John Orley) Allen, Nov. 19, 1899.

Tate, Sharon, Aug. 8, 1969; Jan. 26, 1971.

Tati, Jacques, Oct. 9, 1908.

Tatum, Edward Lawrie, Dec. 14, 1909.

Taube, Henry, Nov. 30, 1915.

Tauber, Richard, May 16, 1892.

Taufa'ahau Tupou IV His Majesty, King Birthday of (Tonga), Jul. 4.

Taufa'ahau Tupou IV, (Tonga), Jul. 4, 1918.

Taupin, Bernie Taupin, Bernie, May 22, 1950.

Taurus, Apr. intro; May intro.

Taussig, Helen Brooke, May 24, 1898, Nov. 29, 1944.

tax collectors, patron of, Sep. 21.

taxi cabs, metered, May 1, 1907.

Taxi Driver, May 28, 1976.

Taya, Maaouya Ould Sidi Ahmed, Dec. 12, 1984.

Taylor, Billy, Jul. 24, 1921.

Taylor, Brook, Aug. 18, 1685.

Taylor, Charles, elected, Jul. 19, 1997.

Taylor, Elizabeth, Feb. 27, 1932; Dec. 14, 1944; Mar. 15, 1964.

Taylor, Frederick Winslow, Mar. 20, 1856.

Taylor, Graham, May 2, 1851.

Taylor, James, Mar. 12, 1948.

Taylor, Joseph H., Mar. 24, 1941.

Taylor, Margaret, Sep. 21, 1788.

Taylor, Maxwell, Aug. 26, 1901.

Taylor, Mick, Jan. 17, 1948.

Taylor, Paul (Belville), Jul. 29, 1930.

Taylor, Richard E., Nov. 2, 1929.

Taylor, Robert, Aug. 5, 1911.

Taylor, Zachary, Nov. 24, 1784; May 8, 1846; May 9, 1846; May 24, 1846; Sep. 25, 1846; Feb. 22, 1847; inaugurated, Mar. 4, 1849; dies, Jul. 9, 1850.

Tchaikovsky International Piano and Violin Competition, Apr. 11, 1958.

Tchaikovsky, Peter Ilyich, May 7, 1840; Dec. 5, 1892; Jan. 15, 1895.

Tcherkassky, Marianna Alexsavena, Oct. 28, 1952.

Te Kanawa, Dame Kiri, Mar. 6, 1947.

Tea Act, Apr. 27, 1773.

Teachers' Day (China), Sep. 9.

Teachers' Day (Taiwan), Sep. 28.

Teachers' Day (Venezuela), Jan. intro; Jan. 15.

Teagarden, Jack Weldon Lee, Aug. 20, 1905.

Teague, Olin E., Apr. 6, 1910.

Teale, Edwin Way, Jun. 2, 1899.

Teamsters, International Brotherhood of, Dec. 6, 1957; Jan. 23, 1958. Jul. 8, 1971.

Tearle, Sir Godrey, Oct. 12, 1884.

Teasdale, Sara, Aug. 8, 1884.

Tebaldi, Renata, Jan. 2, 1922.

Tecumseh, Oct. 5, 1813.

Tedder, Arthur William, Jul. 11, 1890.

Tegner, Esaias, Nov. 13, 1782.

Teheran Conference: begins, Nov. 28, 1943.

Tcicher, Louis, Aug. 24, 1924.

Teilhard de Chardin, Pierre, May 1, 1881.

Tel-el Aqqaqir, Nov. 2, 1942.

telecast address: first from White House, Oct. 5, 1947.

Telecommunications bill, Feb. 8, 1996.

telegraph, Jan. 6, 1838; patented, Jun. 20, 1840; first message, May 24, 1844.

telegraph cable: first submarine, Nov. 13, 1851; first Pacific, Jul. 4, 1903.

telegraph communications: established between U.S. and England, Jul. 27, 1866.

telegraph service, wireless: opened, Jan. 26, 1930.

telegraph workers, patron of, Mar. 24.

telegraphic line: London to New Zealand, Feb. 18, 1876.

telephone: patented, Mar. 7, 1876; first demonstration, Feb. 12, 1877; first demonstration to Queen Victoria, Jan. 14, 1878; inter-city link, Mar. 27, 1884; communication between London and Paris, Mar. 18, 1891; first transcontinental call, Jan. 25, 1915; first mechanical switchboard, Oct. 14, 1923; transatlantic service, Jan. 7, 1927.

telephone cable: first trans-Atlantic, Sep. 25, 1956; Commonwealth Pacific submarine opened, Dec. 1, 1963.

telephone line: first submarine, Mar. 14, 1891.

telephone workers, patron of, Mar. 24.

television, Apr. 20, 1939; first network, Feb. 1, 1940, Nov. 30, 1956, Apr. 24, 1962.

television broadcasts, color, Oct. 11, 1950; first broadcast, Jun. 28, 1951.

Telford, Thomas, Aug. 9, 1757.

Teller, Feb. 13, 1948.

Teller, Edward, Jan. 15, 1908.

Tellico Dam, Jun. 15, 1978.

Telstar I, Jul. 10, 1962; Jul. 13, 1962.

Temin, Howard Martin, Dec. 10, 1934.

Temple Beth Israel, Jan. 26, 1951.

Templer, Sir Gerald Walter Robert, Sep. 11, 1898.

Ten Boom, Corrie, Apr. 15, 1892.

The Ten Commandments: premiere, Nov. 8, 1956.

Ten, Martyrs of Crete, Dec. 23.

Tenerife: air disaster, Mar. 27, 1977.

Tennant, Veronica, Jan. 15, 1946.

Tennessee: admitted to Union, Jun. 1, 1796.

Tennessee Valley Authority, May 18, 1933.

Tenniel, Sir John, Feb. 28, 1820.

Tennille, Toni, May 8, 1943.

Tennis Court Oath, Jun. 17, 1789.

Tennyson, Alfred Lord, Aug. 6, 1809; Apr. 23, 1850; Oct. 6, 1892.

Teo, Penitala Fiatau, Jul. 23, 1911.

Ter-Petrossian, Levon, resigns, Feb. 3, 1998.

Teresa of Avila, Mar. 28, 1515.

Teresa of Calcutta, Mother, Aug. 27, 1910.

Tereshkova, Valentina Vladimirovna, Mar. 6, 1937; first female in space, Jun. 16, 1963.

Terhune, Albert Payson, Dec. 12, 1872.

Terkel, Studs, May 16, 1912.

Terman, Lewis Madison, Jan. 15, 1877.

Terni (Umbria), patron of, Feb. 15.

Terra Natalis (Natal), Dec. 25, 1497.

Terrell, Mary Church, Sep. 23, 1863.

Territorial Day (New Caledonia), Sep. 24.

Territory Day (British Virgin Islands), Jul. 1.

Terry, Dame Ellen Alice, Feb. 27, 1847.

Terry, Fernando Belaunde, Feb. 1, 1969.

Teruel (Spanish Civil War), Feb. 15, 1938.

Tesh, John, Jul. 9, 1952.

Tesla, Nikola, Jul. 9, 1856.

Test Act (England), Mar. 22, 1673.

test-tube baby: first is born, Jul. 25, 1978.

test-tube fertilization, Mar. 10, 1987.

Tet Offensive, Jan. 31, 1968.

Teton Dam: collapses, Jun. 5, 1976.

tetracycline, Sep. 24, 1953.

Tetrazzini, Luisa, Jun. 29, 1871.

Tewksbury, Battle of, May 4, 1471.

Texaco Inc., Apr. 12, 1987.

Texaco Star Theater: television debut, Jun. 8, 1948.

Texas: independence, Mar. 1, 1836; annexed to U.S., Mar. 1, 1845; admitted to Union, Dec. 29, 1845; May 30, 1848; Koresh, David, Apr. 19, 1993.

Texas Commerce Bancshares, Dec. 15, 1986.

Texas Republic, Oct. 22, 1836.

Thackeray, William Makepeace, Jul. 18, 1811.

Thailand: Japanese invasion of, Dec. 8, 1941; May 11, 1949; Mar. 6, 1962; May 12, 1962; Feb. 5, 1965; Mar. 7, 1970; Jan. 26, 1975; government falls, Oct. 6, 1976; new constitution, Sep. 27, 1997.

Thalberg, Irving Grant, May 30, 1899.

thalidomide, Feb. 23, 1962.

Thames, Battle of, Oct. 5, 1813.

Thanarat, Sarit, Oct. 20, 1958.

Thani, Khalifa Bin Hamad Al-, Feb. 22, 1972.

Thanksgiving Day (Canada), Oct. intro.

Thanksgiving Day (Grenada), Nov. 29.

Thanksgiving Day (Liberia), Nov. intro.

Thanksgiving Day (Madagascar), Nov. 25.

Thanksgiving Day (St. Lucia), Oct. intro.

Thanksgiving Day (United States), Nov. intro.

Thanksgiving and Independence Day (St. Vincent), Oct. 27.

Thanksgiving Salute to Older Americans, National, Nov. intro.

Thant, U, Jan. 22, 1909.

Thapsus, Feb. 6, 46.

Tharp, Twyla, Jul. 1, 1941, Jan. 9, 1976.

Thatcher, Margaret, Oct. 13, 1925; Feb. 11, 1975; May 3, 1979; Nov. 22, 1990.

That's Incredible!: television debut, Mar. 3, 1980.

Thayer, Sylvanus, Jun. 9, 1785.

Theiler, Max, Jan. 30, 1899.

Theismann, Joseph Robert *(Joe)*, Sep. 9, 1949.

Theodoric, Mar. 5, 493.

Theodosius, Emperor, Feb. 27, 380.

theologians, patron of, Aug. 28; Dec. 27.

Theorell, (Alex) Hugo (Teodor), Jul. 6, 1903.

thermonuclear missiles: first on U.S. submarine, Nov. 15, 1960.

Theroux, Paul, Apr. 10, 1941.

Thiers, Louis Adolphe, Apr. 15, 1797.

Thiessen, Tiffani-Amber, Jan. 23, 1974.

Thieu, Nguyen Van, Apr. 5, 1923; Jun. 13, 1965; Jun. 18, 1965; Sep. 3, 1967; Sep. 27, 1969; Apr. 21, 1975.

thieves, patron of, Nov. 13.

Third Coalition, Apr. 11, 1805.

Third Coalition, War of, Feb. 7, 1807.

Third Crusade, Oct. 4, 1190.

Third Republic Day (Ghana), Sep. 24.

Third Togolese Republic, Jan. 13, 1967.

Thirteenth Amendment (U.S. Constitution): slavery prohibited, Dec. 18, 1865; Mississippi adopts, Mar. 16, 1995.

Thirty-three Immortals (Uruguay), Apr. 19.

Thirty Years War, May 23, 1618; Mar. 10, 1624; Jun. 20, 1624; Nov. 5, 1630; Sep. 17, 1631; Mar. 29, 1632; Nov. 16, 1632; May 19, 1635; Nov. 2, 1642; May 19, 1643; Mar. 7, 1645; Mar. 14, 1647; Jan. 30, 1648; Jul. 26, 1648; ends, Oct. 24, 1648.

Torres, Jose Thomas, Betty, Jul. 27, 1948.

Thomas, B(illy) J(oe), Aug. 7, 1942.

Thomas, Clarence, Jun. 23, 1948; Nov. 1, 1991.

Thomas, Danny, Jan. 6, 1914.

Thomas, Dave, Jul. 2, 1932.

Thomas, Debi, Feb. 8, 1986; Mar. 21, 1986.

Thomas, Dylan (Marlais), Oct. 27, 1914.

Thomas, Frank, May 27, 1968.

Thomas, George, Jul. 31, 1816; Dec. 16, 1864.

Thomas, Helen A., Aug. 4, 1920.

Thomas, Henry, Sep. 9, 1971.

Thomas, Isiah, Apr. 30, 1961.

Thomas, Thurman, May 16, 1966.

Thomas Jefferson's Birthday (Alabama, Oklahoma, Virginia), Apr. 13.

Thomas, Kurt, Mar. 29, 1956.

Thomas of Lancaster, Mar. 16, 1322.

Thomas, Lowell, Apr. 6, 1892.

Thomas, Marlo, Nov. 21, 1938.

Thomas, Martha Carey, Jan. 2, 1857.

Thomas, Michael Tilson, Dec. 21, 1944.

Thomas, Norman, Nov. 20, 1884; May 21, 1932.

Thomas, Philip Michael, May 26, 1949.

Thomas, Richard Earl, Jun. 13, 1951.

Thomas, Terry, Jul. 14, 1911.

Thomas, William Miles Webster, Mar. 2, 1897.

Thompkins, Daniel, Jun. 21, 1774.

Thompson, Sir Benjamin, Mar. 26, 1753.

Thompson, Daley, Jul. 30, 1958.

Thompson, David, Apr. 30, 1770.

Thompson, Dorothy, Jul. 9, 1894.

Thompson, Emma, Apr. 15, 1959.

Thompson, Francis, Dec. 16, 1859.

Thompson, Fred, Aug. 19, 1942.

Thompson, Hunter S(tockton), Jul. 18, 1939.

Thompson, James Robert, May 8, 1936.

Thompson, J(ames) Walter, Oct. 28, 1847.

Thompson, Lea, May 31, 1961.

Thompson, Sada Carolyn, Sep. 27, 1929.

Thomson, Charles Wyville, Mar. 5, 1830.

Thomson, Elihu, Mar. 29, 1853.

Thomson, Sir George Paget, May 3, 1892.

Thomson, Joseph, Feb. 14, 1858.

Thomson, Sir Joseph John, Dec. 18, 1856.

Thomson, Virgil, Nov. 25, 1896.

Thomson, William, Jun. 26, 1824.

Thorbecke, Jan Rudolf de, Jan. 14, 1798.

Thoreau, Henry David, Jul. 12, 1817.

Thorild, Thomas, Apr. 18, 1759.

thorium: deposits found, Dec. 2, 1962.

Thorndike, Dame Sybil, Oct. 24, 1882.

Thornton, Charles B(ates), Jul. 22, 1913.

Thornton, William, May 20, 1759.

Thoroddsen, Jon, Oct. 5, 1819.

Thorpe, Jeremy, Apr. 29, 1929.

Thorpe, Jim, May 28, 1888; Jul. 7, 1912.

A Thousand Days, May 2, 1966.

Three Glorious Days (Congo), Aug. 13; Aug. 14; Aug. 15.

Three Kings Day (D a de los Tr¤s Magos) (Puerto Rico), Jan. 6.

Three Little Pigs: premiere, May 25, 1933.

Three Mile Island, Mar. 28, 1979; Jan. 27, 1983.

Three Sisters: premiere, Jan. 31, 1901.

Three Wise Men, Jul. 23.

Three's Company: television debut, Mar. 15, 1977.

Threlkeld, Richard D., Nov. 30, 1937.

Thresher, U.S.S.: lost, Apr. 10, 1963.

Thrust Oct. 13, 1997.

Thule (Greenland), Jan. 22, 1968.

Thulin, Ingrid, Jan. 27, 1929.

Thumb, General Tom, Jan. 4, 1838.

Thunderbirds (U.S. Air Force flying team), Jan. 18, 1982.

Thurber, James (Grover), Dec. 8, 1894.

Thurman, Uma, Apr. 28, 1970.

Thurmond, (James) Strom, Dec. 5, 1902; Jul. 17, 1948; sets filibuster record, Aug. 30, 1957.

Thurow, Lester Carl, May 7, 1938.

Thyssen, Fritz, Nov. 9, 1873.

Tiananmen Square, Hu Yaobang, Apr. 15, 1989; massacre at, Jun. 4, 1989.

Tiberius (Roman emperor), Nov. 16, 42 b.c.

Tibet, Apr. 21, 1912; Oct. 25, 1950; incorporated into China, May 27, 1951; independence demonstration, Mar. 5, 1989.

Ticonderoga, Fort, May 10, 1775; captured by British, Jul. 6, 1777.

Tiegs, Cheryl, Sep. 25, 1947.

Tientsin, Treaty of: signed, Jun. 26, 1858.

Tiepolo, Giambattista, Mar. 5, 1696.

Tierney, Gene, Nov. 20, 1920.

Tiffany, Charles Lewis, Feb. 15, 1812.

Tiffany, Louis Comfort, Feb. 18, 1848.

Tiger, Dick, Oct. 23, 1962; Dec. 16, 1966; May 24, 1968.

Tilden, William Tatem, Jr. *(Bill),* Feb. 10, 1893.

Tilden, Samuel Jones, Feb. 9, 1814.

Tildy, Zoltan, Feb. 1, 1946.

tile makers, patron of, Aug. 16.

Tillich, Paul, Aug. 20, 1886.

Tillis, Mel(vin), Aug. 8, 1932.

Tilly, Count of, Sep. 17, 1631.

Tilly, Jennifer, Sep. 16, 1962.

Tilly, Meg, Feb. 14, 1960.

Tilsit, Treaty of: signed, Jul. 7, 1807.

Tilton, Charlene, Dec. 1, 1958.

Time Inc., Mar. 4, 1989.

Times Beach, Missouri, Jan. 3, 1983, Feb. 22, 1983.

Timket (Ethiopia), Jan. 19.

Timmerman, Jacobo, Jan. 6, 1923.

Timor, Nov. 28, 1975.

Timur (Tamerlane): conquers Delhi, Dec. 18, 1398; Jan. 3, 1399; Mar. 24, 1401; Jul. 20, 1402; Jul. 28, 1402; Feb. 18, 1405; Jun. 20, 1941.

Tio, Lola Rodr guez de, Sep. 14, 1843.

Tinbergen, Jan, Apr. 12, 1903.

Tinbergen, Nikolaas, Apr. 15, 1907.

Tindemans, Leo: inaugurated, Oct. 20, 1978.

Ting, Samuel Chao Chung, Jan. 26, 1936.

Tinker, Grant A., Jan. 11, 1926.

Tinsel Day, Dec. intro., Dec. 5.

Tiny Tim, Apr. 12, 1922.

Tippecanoe, Battle of, Nov. 7, 1811.

Tippin, Aaron, Jul. 3, 1958.

tipsy people, patron of, May 25.

tires, tubeless, Nov. 22, 1942.

Tiris el-Gharbia: annexed by Morocco, Aug. 11, 1979.

Tiros I: launched, Apr. 1, 1960.

Tirpitz, Admiral Alfred von, Mar. 19, 1849; Mar. 16, 1916.

Tisch, Laurence, Jan. 14, 1987.

Tiselius, Arne W. K., Aug. 10, 1902.

tissue plasminogen activator, Nov. 13, 1987.

Titan, Feb. 24, 1960.

Titanic: sinks, Apr. 15, 1912; Sep. 1, 1985; remains of found, Sep. 1, 1985.

Tito, Marshal, May 7, 1892; May 25, 1944; Nov. 11, 1945; Apr. 7, 1963.

Tituba, Mar. 1, 1692.

To Catch a Thief: premiere, Aug. 4, 1955.

To Kill a Mockingbird, May 1, 1961.

Tobacco industry, settlement, Oct. 10, 1997.

Tobias, Andrew, Apr. 20, 1947.

Tobin, James, Mar. 5, 1918.

Tobruk (Libya), Jun. 21, 1942.

Tocqueville, Alexis de, Jul. 29, 1805.

Todd, Alexander Robertus, Oct. 2, 1907.

Todd, Michael, Jun. 2, 1909.

Todd, Richard, Jun. 11, 1919.

Toffler, Alvin, Oct. 4, 1928; Jul. 29, 1970.

Togliatti, Palmiro, Mar. 26, 1893.

Togo, Jan. 13, 1963; Jan. 13, 1967.

Togoland, May 6, 1919; Apr. 27, 1960.

Toji or Winter Solstice (Japan), Dec. 22.

Tojo, Hideki *(Eiki)*, Dec. 30, 1884.

Toklas, Alice B(abette), Apr. 30, 1877.

Tokugawa, Iyeyasu, Dec. 26, 1542.

Tokyo (Japan), Apr. 25, 1867; becomes capital of Japan, Jul. 17, 1868; Sep. 1, 1923; Apr. 18, 1942; allied bombing, Apr. 13, 1945; Sep. 7, 1945; XVIII Summer Olympics, Oct. 10, 1964; May 21, 1978; subway gas attack, Mar. 20, 1995.

Tokyo Rose, Jul. 4, 1916; Jan. 19, 1977.

Tokyo Stock Exchange, Oct. 20, 1987.

Toland, John Willard, Jun. 29, 1912.

Tolbert, William R., Jr., May 13, 1913; Jul. 23, 1971; Jan. 3, 1972; Apr. 14, 1979; Apr. 12, 1980.

Toledo (Spain), May 25, 1085.

Toledo, Treaty of, Mar. 6, 1480; Feb. 1, 1539.

Toler, Sidney, Apr. 28, 1874.

Tolkien, J. R. R., Jan. 3, 1892.

Tolkien Week, Sep. intro.

Tolman, Edward Chace, Apr. 14, 1886.

Tolstoi, Aleksei Nikolaevich, Jan. 10, 1882.

Tolstoi, Leo Nikolayevich, Count, Sep. 9, 1828.

tomb of St. Peter: discovered, Dec. 23, 1950.

Tomb of the Unknown Soldier: dedicated, Nov. 11, 1921; May 28, 1984.

Tomb Sweeping Day (Taiwan), Apr. 5.

Tomba, Alberto, Dec. 16, 1966.

Tombalbaye, Francois (Chad): assassinated, Apr. 13, 1975.

Tombaugh, Clyde, Feb. 18, 1930.

Tomei, Marisa, Dec. 4, 1964.

Tomlin, Lily, Sep. 1, 1936.

Tomonaga, Sin-ltiro, Mar. 31, 1906.

Tompkins, Daniel D., Mar. 4, 1817.

Tone, Wolfe, Jan. 20, 1763.

Tonegawa, Susumu, Sep. 5, 1939.

Tonga: independence, Jun. 4, 1970.

Tonga Islands, May 18, 1900.

Tongoland, Apr. 23, 1895.

The Tonight Show: television debut, Sep. 27, 1954.

Tonkin: made French protectorate, Jun. 6, 1884.

Tonkin, Gulf of, Aug. 5, 1964.

Tonkin Gulf Resolution, Aug. 7, 1964.

top quark, Jul. 3, 1984.

topaz, Nov. intro.

Topper, Sir Charles, Jul. 2, 1821.

Torah, Oct. 22, 1952.

Tordesillas, Treaty of: divides New World, Jun. 7, 1494.

Torgau, Battle of, Nov. 3, 1760.

Torgau (Germany), Apr. 25, 1945.

Tork, Peter, Feb. 13, 1944.

Torme, Mel, Sep. 13, 1925.

Torn, Elmore, Jr. *(Rip)*, Feb. 6, 1931.

Toronto: incorporated, Mar. 6, 1834.

Torp, Oscar: inaugurated, Nov. 19, 1951.

Torre, Joe, Jul. 18, 1940.

Torres, Jose, Dec. 16, 1966.

Torrey Canyon, Mar. 18, 1967.

Torrieelli, Evangelista, Oct. 15, 1608.

Torrijos-Herrera, Omar, Feb. 13, 1929.

Torstenson, Lennart, Count of Ortala, Aug. 17, 1603.

Tosca: premiere, Jan. 14, 1900.

Toseanini, Arturo, Mar. 25, 1867; Nov. 16, 1908.

Tosh, Peter, Oct. 9, 1944.

Tosovsky, Josef, January 2, 1998.

Tostig (Earl of Northumbria), Sep. 20, 1066; Sep. 25, 1066.

Totenberg, Nina, Jan. 14, 1944.

Toul, Jan. 15, 1552.

Toulet, Paul Jean, Jun. 5, 1867.

Toulon (Franee), Nov. 27, 1942.

Toulouse-Lautrec, Henri de, Nov. 24, 1864.

Toure, Sekou, Oct. 2, 1958.

Touring Theater Month, May intro.

tourmaline, Oct. intro.

Towens, Charles Hard, Mar. 22, 1960.

Tower Commission, Feb. 26, 1987.

Tower, John Goodwin, Sep. 29, 1925.

Tower of London, May 21, 1471.

Town, Ithiel, Oct. 3, 1784.

Town Meeting Day (Vermont), Mar. intro.

Townes, Charles Hard, Jul. 28, 1915.

Townsend, Francis Everett, Jan. 13, 1867.

Townshend Acts passed, Jun. 29, 1767; Feb. 11, 1768.

Townshend, Pete(r Dennis Blanford), May 19, 1945.

Toxic Substances Control Act, Sep. 28, 1976.

Toynbee, Arnold, Apr. 14, 1889.

Toyota Motors Corp., Apr. 11, 1984.

Tracy, Spencer, Apr. 5, 1900; Dec. 24, 1949.

Trades Disputes Act (India), Apr. 12, 1929.

Trafalgar, Battle of, Oct. 21, 1805.

tram cars: first in London, Mar. 23, 1861.

Trammel, Alan Stuart, Feb. 21, 1958.

Tran Van Huu, Mar. 3, 1951; Jun. 3, 1952.

Tranquillity, Sea of, Feb. 20, 1965.

trans-Alaska oil pipeline: construction authorized, Nov. 16, 1973; first oil, Jun. 20, 1977.

Trans-Caucasian Soviet Socialist Republic: organized, Mar. 12, 1922.

Trans-Siberian Railway, May 31, 1891.

Trans-Tasman submarine telephone cable: opens, Jul. 9, 1962.

transatlantic passenger service: first commercial, Jun. 28, 1939.

transatlantic radio broadeast: first, Mar. 12, 1922.

transatlantie radio-telephone transmission: first, Oct. 21, 1915.

transcontinental automobile trip: first U.S., Aug. 18, 1903.

Transfer Day (Virgin Islands), Mar. intro.

Transfiguration of Our Lord Jesus Christ, Feast of, Aug. 6.

transistor, Dec. 23, 1947; Nov. 1, 1956; Oct. 20, 1972.

Transit I-B: space lighthouse, Apr. 13, 1960.

Transjordan, Feb. 20, 1928; Mar. 22, 1946; Apr. 3, 1949, Apr. 24, 1950.

Transkei, Republic of: given independenee, Oct. 26, 1976.

Transportation Corps, U.S.: created, Jul. 31, 1942.

Transvaal Boers: revolt breaks out, Dec. 30, 1880.

Transvaal Colony, Oct. 25, 1900.

Transvaal (South African Republic), Jan. 17, 1852; established, Dec. 16, 1856; Jan. 6, 1857; Apr. 12, 1877; declared British territory, Sep. 29, 1879; Jan. 6, 1896; Jan. 21, 1898.

Transylvania, Jan. 26, 1699; Romanian invasion begins, Aug. 28, 1916; Jan. 10, 1919.

Traore, Moussa, Sep. 25, 1936.

Trapp, Maria Augusta von, Jan. 26, 1905.

Traubel, Helen, Jun. 20, 1899.

Travanti, Daniel J(ohn), Mar. 7, 1940.

travelers, patron of, Feb. 12; Mar. 17; Jul. 25.

Travers, Mary, Nov. 7, 1937.

Travis, Merle, Nov. 29, 1917.

Travis, Randy, May 4, 1959.

Travis, William Barret, Aug. 9, 1809.

Travolta, John, Feb. 18, 1954.

Treacher, Arthur, Jul. 23, 1894.

Treasury, U.S. Department of, Sep. 2, 1789.

Treaty on the Final Settlement with Respect to Germany, Sep. 12, 1990

Treaty Organization (NATO), Jan. 16, 1998.

Trebek, Alex, Jul. 22, 1940.

Trebizond, Apr. 18, 1916.

Trebur (Germany), Oct. 16, 1076.

Tree, Sir Herbert (Draper) Beerbohm, Dec. 17, 1853.

Tree Planting Day (Lesotho), Mar. intro.

Treitschke, Heinrich Gotthard von, Sep. 15, 1834.

Trenchard, Hugh Montague, Feb. 3, 1873.

Trent, Nov. 3, 1918.

Trent, Council of: opens, Dec. 13, 1545.

Trentino (Italy), May 15, 1916.

Trentino, patron of, Jun. 26.

Trenton, Battle of, Dec. 26, 1776.

Treseder, Peter, Jan. 1 1998.

Trevino, Lee, Dec. 1, 1939.

Trevithick, Richard, Apr. 13, 1771.

Trevor, Claire, Mar. 8, 1909.

Triangle Shirtwaist Co.: fire, Mar. 25, 1911.

Tribhubana (King of Nepal), Mar. 14, 1955.

tricameral parliament (South Africa), Nov. 2, 1983.

Trident II, Jan. 15, 1987.

Trident Conference, May 12, 1943.

Trier: Archbishop of, Jan. 24, 1446.

Trieste, Nov. 3, 1918; Dec. 6, 1953, Oct. 26, 1954; U.S. bathyscaphe, Sep. 19, 1957; Jan. 23, 1960.

Trifon Zarenzan (Bulgaria), Feb. 14.

Trillin, Calvin Marshall, Dec. 5, 1935.

Trilling, Diana Rubin, Jul. 21, 1905.

Trilling, Lionel, Jul. 4, 1905.

Trinidad, Mar. 27, 1802.

Trinidad and Tobago: independent member of Commonwealth of Nations, Aug. 31, 1962; Feb. 23, 1967; becomes republic, Aug. 31, 1976.

Trinity House, patron of, Nov. 23.

Triple Alliance, Jan. 4, 1717.

Triple Crown: Secretariat wins, Jun. 9, 1973.

Tripoli: annexed by Italy, Nov. 5, 1911; Mar. 6, 1912; Apr. 8, 1926; Jan. 24, 1943.

Tripoli, Declaration, Dec. 5, 1977.

Tripolitan War, May 14, 1801.

Trippe, Juan (Terry), Jun. 27, 1899.

Tripucka, Kelly, Feb. 16, 1959.

Trissino, Giangiorgio, Jul. 8, 1478.

Triton: U.S. atomic submarine, May 10, 1960.

Tritt, Travis, Feb. 9, 1963.

Triumph of the Revolution Anniversary of the (Cuba), Jan. 1.

Trivia Day, Jan. intro; Jan. 4.

TRNC Day (Cyprus), Nov. 15.

Trocadero, Battle of, Aug. 31, 1823.

Trollope, Anthony, Apr. 24, 1815.

Trotsky, Leon, Oct. 26, 1879; Jul. 16, 1917; Jan. 15, 1925; May 7, 1925; Sep. 30, 1927; Oct. 23, 1927; expelled from Communist Party, Dec. 27, 1927; Jan. 3, 1928; Jan. 19, 1929; Jan. 21, 1929; assassinated, Aug. 21, 1940.

Trottier, Bryan, Jul. 17, 1956.

Troup, Robert William *(Bobby)*, Oct. 18, 1918.

Troutt, Kenneth A., Jan. 8, 1948.

Trower, Robin, Mar. 9, 1945.

Trudeau, Margaret Joan Sinclair, Sep. 10, 1948.

Trudeau, Pierre Elliott, Oct. 18, 1919; Apr. 6, 1968; May 22, 1979; Mar. 3, 1980; resigns, Feb. 29, 1984.

Truffaut, Francois, Feb. 6, 1932.

Truitt, Anne, Mar. 16, 1921.

Trujillo, Cesar Gaviria, elected, May 27, 1990.

Trujillo Molina, Rafael Leonidas, Oct. 24, 1891; May 16, 1942; assassinated, May 30, 1961.

Truk, Feb. 16, 1944, Apr. 29, 1944.

Truman, Bess, Feb. 13, 1885.

Truman Day (Missouri), May intro.

Truman, Harry S, Birthday (Missouri), May 8.

Truman, Harry S, May 8, 1884; Apr. 12, 1945; Nov. 21, 1946; Jul. 12, 1948; Jul. 17, 1948; Nov. 3, 1948; inaugurated, Jan. 20, 1949; Jan. 31, 1950; Feb. 6, 1950; May 11, 1950; Jun. 27, 1950; Nov. 1, 1950; Jan. 3, 1951; Apr. 6, 1951; Apr. 11, 1951; Apr. 29, 1952, May 8, 1964.

Truman, Margaret, Feb. 17, 1924.

Trumbo, Dalton, Dec. 9, 1905.

Trumbull, John, Jun. 6, 1756.

Trumbull, Jonathan, Oct. 12, 1710.

Trump, Ivana, Feb. 20, 1949.

Truong Chinh, Jun. 18, 1987.

Truth-in-Lending Law, U.S., Jul. 1, 1969.

Tryon, Thomas, Jan. 14, 1926.

Tsedenbal, Yumzhagiyen, Sep. 17, 1916, Aug. 23, 1984.

Tshombe, Moise (Kapenda), Nov. 10, 1919; Jul. 11, 1960.

Tsingtao (China), Nov. 7, 1914.

Tsiolkovsky, Konstantin Eduardovich, Sep. 17, 1857.

Tsiranana, Philibert, Sep. 6, 1970.

Tsongas, Paul Efthemios, Feb. 14, 1941.

Tsushima Strait, Battle of, May 27, 1905.

Tsvett, Mikhail Semenovich, May 14, 1872.

TU-144: Soviet supersonic jetliner, May 25, 1971.

Tubb, Ernest *(Ernie)*, Feb. 9, 1914.

Tubman, William V.S., May 4, 1943; Jan 1960; Jul. 23, 1971.

Tuchman, Barbara, Jan. 30, 1912.

Tucker, Forrest Meredith, Feb. 2, 1919.

Tucker, Henry (Sir), May 26, 1968.

Tucker, Karla Faye, Feb. 3, 1998.

Tucker, Richard, Aug. 28, 1914.

Tucker, Sophie, Jan. 13, 1884.

Tucker, Tanya, Oct. 10, 1958.

Tudjman, Franjo, May 14, 1922; Jun. 15, 1997.

Tudor, Antony, Apr. 4, 1908.

Tuileries: mob marches, Jun. 20, 1792; stormed by Parisian mob, Aug. 10, 1792.

Tukhachevski, Michael: executed, Jun. 12, 1937.

Tulagi, Solomon Islands: captured by U.S., Aug. 8, 1942.

Tune, Thomas James *(Tommy)*, Feb. 28, 1939.

Tunisia, Apr. 9, 1938; Nov. 20, 1942; May 10, 1943; Mar. 20, 1956; Jan. 10, 1957; monarchy abolished, Jul. 25, 1957; independence, Jun. 1, 1959.

Tunisian workers rising, Jan. 26, 1978.

Tunney, Gene, May 25, 1898; May 25, 1898; Sep. 23, 1926; Sep. 22, 1927.

Tunney, John Varick, Jun. 26, 1934.

Tupou I Day (Tonga), Dec. 4.

Tupouto'a Crown Prince Birthday of (Tonga), May 4.

Turajlic, Hakija, Jan. 8, 1993.

Turbay Ayala, Julio Cesar: inaugurated, Aug. 7, 1978.

turbo-prop: first airliner, Feb. 1, 1957.

Turenne, Vicomte de (Henri de La Tour d'Auvergne), Sep. 11, 1611.

Turgenev, Ivan Sergeyevich, Nov. 9, 1818.

Turin (Italy), Aug. 13, 1943.

Turing, Alan, Jun. 23, 1912.

Turkey, Jan. 9, 1792; Jan. 27, 1822; independence, Jul. 13, 1841; invaded by Russia, Jul. 2, 1853; Apr. 18, 1897; Oct. 7, 1912; coup d'etat, Jan. 23, 1913; recaptures Adrianople, Jul. 22, 1913; declares war against Allies, Nov. 23, 1914; invasion of, Apr. 25, 1915; declares war on Romania, Aug. 30, 1916; Greece declares war on, Jul. 2, 1917; Jan. 20, 1921; Jan. 2, 1922; Jul. 24, 1923; Apr. 9, 1928; U.S. aid cut, Feb. 5, 1975; coup d'etat, Sep. 10, 1980.

Turkish Caliphate: abolished, Mar. 3, 1924.

Turkish Cypriots, Feb. 13, 1975.

Turkish forces (World War I), Jan. 26, 1915.

Turkish National Day (Turkey, Cyprus), Oct. 29.

Turkish Republic: proclaimed, Oct. 29, 1923.

Turkish troops (World War I), Jan. 9, 1917.

Turks, Jan. 26, 1699; Jan. 30, 1915; Jan. 4, 1916.

Turnbull, Wendy, Nov. 26, 1952.

Turner, Frederick Jackson, Nov. 14, 1861.

Turner, Henry McNear, Feb. 1, 1831.

Turner, Ike, Nov. 5, 1931.

Turner, J. M. W., Apr. 23, 1775.

Turner, Janine, Dec. 6, 1963.

Turner, John: inaugurated, Jun. 30, 1984.

Turner, Kathleen, Jun. 19, 1954.

Turner, Lana, Feb. 8, 1920.

Turner, Nat, Oct. 2, 1800; slave insurrection begins, Aug. 13, 1831.

Turner, Stansfield, Feb. 1, 1923.

Turner, Ted, III, Nov. 19, 1938.

Turner, Tina, Nov. 26, 1938.

turquoise, Dec. intro.

Turturro, John, Feb. 28, 1957.

Tushingham, Rita, Mar. 14, 1942.

Tuskeegee Institute, Jul. 4, 1881.

Tussaud, Madame, Dec. 7, 1760.

Tutankhamen's sarcophagus, Nov. 29, 1922; Feb. 16,1923, Feb. 12, 1924.

Tutsi rebel forces, declare victory in Rwanda, Jul. 4, 1994.

Tutu, Desmond Mpilo, Oct. 7, 1931, Feb 3, 1985.

Tuvalu Day (Tuvalu), Oct. 1; Oct. 2.

TWA Flight 800, Jul. 17, 1996.

Twain, Mark, Nov. 30, 1835.

Twain, Shania, Aug. 28, 1965.

Tweed, William Marcy, Apr. 3, 1823; Nov. 19, 1873.

Twelfth Amendment (U.S. Constitution), Sep. 25, 1804.

Twelfth Imam's Birthday (Iran), Jun. 9.

Twelfth Night (England), Jan. 5.

Twelve Brothers, Sep. 1.

Twentieth Amendment (U.S. Constitution), Feb. 6, 1933.

Twentieth Summer Olympics: open in Munich, Aug. 26, 1972.

Twenty-fifth Amendment (U.S. Constitution): ratified, Feb. 10, 1967.

Twenty-first Amendment (U.S. Constitution): revokes Prohibition (18th Amendment), Dec. 5, 1933.

Twenty-fourth Amendment (U.S. Constitution), Feb. 4, 1964.

Twenty-fourth Infantry Regiment: disbanded, Jul. 26, 1951.

Twenty-second Amendment (U.S. Constitution): ratified, Feb. 25, 1951.

Twenty-sixth Amendment (U.S. Constitution): ratified, Jun. 30, 1971.

Twenty-third Amendment (U.S. Constitution): ratified, Mar. 29, 1961.

The Twilight Zone: television debut, Oct. 2, 1959.

Twining, Nathan Farragut, Oct. 11, 1897.

Twitty, Conway, Sep. 1, 1933.

Two Ewalds, Oct. 3.

Twombly, Cy (Edward Parker), Apr. 25, 1928.

2001: A Space Odyssey: premiere, Apr. 3, 1968.

Tydings-McDuffie Act, Mar. 24, 1934.

Tylenol capsule, Feb. 8, 1986.

Tyler, Anne, Oct. 25, 1941.

Tyler, Bonnie, Jun. 8, 1953.

Tyler, John, Mar. 29, 1790; Mar. 4, 1841; Apr. 4, 1841.

Tyler, Julia, May 4, 1820.

Tyler, Letitia, Nov. 12, 1790.

Tyler, Liv (Rundgren), Jul. 1, 1978.

Tyler, Royall, Jul. 18, 1757.

Tynan, Kenneth, Apr. 2, 1927; Jun. 17, 1970.

Tyndall, John, Aug. 2, 1820.

Tynwald Day (United Kingdom), Jul. 5.

typewriter: first patent, Jan. 7, 1714.

Tyrol, Apr. 24, 1921.

Tyson, Cicely, Dec. 19, 1939.

Tyson, Laura D'Andrea, June 28, 1947.

Tyson, Mike, Nov. 23, 1986.

Tyus, Wyomia, Aug. 29, 1945.

Tyutchev, Fyodor, Dec. 5, 1803.

Tyvendedagen (Norway), Jan. 13.

U

U-2 reconnaissance plane: shot down, May 1, 1960.

U Ne Win, Mar. 2, 1974.

U Nu, Mar. 2, 1962.

U Thant, Nov. 30, 1962; Mar. 5, 1967.

Udall, Morris (King), Jun. 15, 1922.

Ueberroth, Peter Victor, Sep. 2, 1937.

Uecker, Robert George *(Bob),* Jan. 26, 1935.

Uganda, Apr. 11, 1894; Mar. 10, 1900; independence, Oct. 9, 1962; admitted to UN, Oct. 25, 1962; businesses nationalized, May 1, 1970.

Uganda, Second Republic of, Jan. 25, 1971.

Uggams, Leslie, May 25, 1943.

The Ugly American: published, Oct. 1, 1958.

The Ugly Duckling: premiere, Dec. 10, 1916.

Ukraine, Jan. 28, 1918; Feb. 18, 1918; Jan. 2, 1922; Jun. 1, 1996.

Ukranian Soviet Socialist Republic: independence, Dec. 27, 1917.

ukulele: patented, Sep. 18, 1917.

Ulanova, Galina Sergeyevna, Jan. 8, 1910.

Ullman, Norm(an Victor Alexander), Dec. 26, 1935.

Ullman, Tracey, Dec. 30, 1959.

Ullmann, Liv, Dec. 16, 1939.

Ullsten, Ola, Oct. 13, 1978.

Ulm, Mar. 14, 1647.

Ulmanis, Karlis, May 15, 1934.

Ulrika Eleanora (Sweden), Jan. 23, 1688, Nov. 30, 1718; Feb. 29, 1720.

Ulysses: published, Feb. 2, 1922.

Umberto II (Italy), Sep. 15, 1904; Jun. 5, 1944.

Umhlanga (Swaziland), Aug. 24.

U.N. *See*: United Nations.

unabomber bombings, Kaczynski, Theodore, sentenced, May 4, 1998.

Unamuno y Jugo, Miguel de, Sep. 2, 1864.

Understanding and Peace Day, World, Feb. intro.

Underwood, John Thomas, Apr. 12, 1857.

Undset, Sigrid, May 20, 1882.

Unemployment Relief Act, Mar. 31, 1933.

UNESCO. *See* United Nations Educational, Scientific, and Cultural Organization.

UNICEF. *See* United Nations International Children's Emergency Fund.

unidentified flying objects, Jun. 24, 1947.

Unification Church, Jul. 16, 1982.

Unification of Italy, May 27, 1860.

unified field theory, Jul. 3, 1984.

Uniformity Act, Jan. 15, 1549.

U9: German submarine, Sep. 22, 1914.

Union Act: passed, Jul. 23, 1840.

Union Carbide Corp., Apr. 8, 1985; Feb. 14, 1989.

Union of Central American Republics: formed, Mar. 21, 1847.

Union Day (Burma), Feb. 12.

Union Day (Romania), Jan. 24.

Union Day (Tanzania), Apr. 26.

Union of the Democratic Center (Spain), Jun. 15, 1977.

Union Nationale Camerounaise Day (Cameroon), Sep. 1.

Union of Soviet Socialist Republics. See U.S.S.R.

Union of Sweden and Norway: ended, Oct. 26, 1905.

Unitas, Johnny, May 7, 1933.

United African National Couneil (Rhodesia), Apr. 21, 1979.

United Arab Emirates United Arab Emirates: formation, Dec. 2, 1971.

United Arab Republic: formation, Feb. 1, 1958; Jun. 19, 1967.

United Automobile Workers (UAW), Aug. 26, 1935, May 4, 1950; May 22, 1970; May 18, 1983.

United Church of Christ, Jun. 25, 1957.

United Farm Workers, Sep. 24, 1973.

United Front (Cambodia), Jan. 7, 1979.

United Independent Broadcasters, Sep. 18, 1927.

United Kingdom, Jan. 1, 1801; capital punishment abolished, Dec. 18, 1969; Jan. 20, 1971; Mar. 13, 1972; Mar. 8, 1973.

United Kingdom of England and Ireland: first parliament, Feb. 2, 1801.

United Kingdom of the Serbs, Croats, and Slovenes: proclaimed, Nov. 24, 1918.

United Methodist Church, Nov. 11, 1966.

United Mine Workers, Mar. 6, 1947; Jan. 14, 1960; Jan. 5, 1970; strike ends, Jun. 8, 1981.

United Nations, Jan. 1, 1942; Apr. 18, 1945; charter signed, Jun. 26, 1945; Rockefeller gift accepted, Dec. 14, 1946; May 11, 1949; Apr. 27, 1960; Jan. 27, 1967; use of force in Kuwait, Nov. 29, 1990; Yugoslavia voted out, Sep. 22, 1992; naval blockade, Nov. 16, 1992; in Somalia, Dec. 9, 1992; creation of international court, Feb. 22, 1993; embargo against Haiti, Oct. 19, 1993; sends troops to Haiti, Jan. 29, 1995; forces removed from Somalia, Mar. 3, 1995; attacks Bosnian Serb targets, Aug. 30, 1995; fiftieth anniversary, Oct. 22, 1995; ban on weapons to Yugoslavia, Mar. 31, 1998.

United Nations Charter Day, Jun. 26.

United Nations Day, Oct. 23.

United Nations' Day (Barbados), Oct. intro.

United Nations Disarmament Commission, Feb. 4, 1952.

United Nations Educational, Scientific, and Cultural Organization (UNESCO): formed, Nov. 4, 1946; U.S. ends membership, Dec. 29, 1983; U.S. withdrawal, Dec. 19, 1984.

United Nations Food and Agriculture Organization, Apr. 2, 1951.

United Nations General Assembly: first, Jan. 10, 1946; Dec. 14, 1960.

United Nations International Children's Emergency Fund, Anniversary Day, Dec. 11.

United Nations International Children's Emergency Fund (UNICEF): established, Dec. 11, 1946, Jul. 20, 1953.

United Nations Relief and Rehabilitation Administration: formed, Nov. 9, 1943.

United Nations Security Council, Mar. 26, 1946.

United Negro College Fund: founded, Apr. 25, 1944.

United Presbyterian Church in the U.S.A., May 28, 1958.

United Provinces (Netherlands), Apr. 9, 1609.

United Service Organization: founded, Feb. 4, 1941.

United Somali Congress, revolt, Jan. 26, 1991.

United States, U.S.S. Oct. 25, 1812.

U.S. census: first, Mar. 1, 1790.

U.S. Civil War, Dec. 20, 1860; Jul. 1, 1863; Jul. 4, 1863; Nov. 25, 1863; Jun. 27, 1864; Aug. 5, 1864; Nov. 15, 1864; Nov. 30, 1864; Dec. 16, 1864.

U.S. Congress, Jun. 26, 1986.

U.S. copyright law: amended, Feb. 3, 1831.

U.S. declares neutrality, Nov. 6, 1914.

U.S. Defense Department, TailHook report released, Apr. 23, 1993.

U.S. embassies, Aug. 7, 1998.

U.S. First Army: begin operations in Germany, Oct. 2, 1944.

United States Football League, Mar. 5, 1983.

U.S. Golfers Association Open: first, Oct. 4, 1895.

U.S. Marine Corps headquarters: suicide attack in Beirut (Lebanon), Oct. 23, 1983.

U.S.-Mexico Binational Commission, May 5, 1996.

U.S. military, invades Panama, Dec. 20, 1989; invasion of Iraq, Feb. 24, 1991; Somalia, Dec. 9, 1992; "no-fly zone," Dec. 27, 1992; Jan. 13, 1993; occupy Haiti, Sep. 19, 1994; bomb Sudan and Afghanistan, Aug. 20, 1998.

U.S. Naval Academy. *See* U.S. Naval School.

U.S. Naval School: opens, Oct. 10, 1845.

U.S. Naval War College: established, Oct. 6, 1884.

U.S. Navy: established, Mar. 27, 1794; Jun. 26, 1993.

U.S. Open tennis tournament, Sep. 9, 1968.

U.S. Senate, approves women pilots, Jul. 31, 1991.

U.S. Steel Corp., Mar. 3, 1901.

U.S. Supreme Court. *See* Supreme Court, U.S.

U.S. and Canadian trade accord, Jan. 2, 1988.

U.S. and South Africa, Feb. 27, 1998.

U.S. and U.S.S.R.: first direct air service between, Jul. 15, 1968.

U.S. women's hockey, Feb. 17, 1998.

United Steelworkers of America, Jul. 6, 1936.

Unity Day (Egypt), Feb. 22.

Unity Day (Syria), Feb. 22.

Unity Day (Vanuatu), Nov. 29.

Unity Day (Zambia), Jul. intro.

Universal Azeri Solidarity Day (Azerbaijan), Dec. 31.

Universal Children's Day, Oct. 6.

Universal Church, patron of, Mar. 19.

Universal Exhibition (Paris), May 6, 1889.

Universal Postal Union Day, Oct. 9.

universal suffrage: Portugal, Mar. 11, 1918.

Universal Vote Day (San Marino), Mar. 25.

universities, colleges and schools, patron of, Jan. 28.

University of Budapest: opens, Nov. 15, 1635.

University of Georgia, Jan. 10, 1961.

University of Heidelberg: founded, Oct. 23, 1385.

Unlearned Parliment (England), Oct. 6, 1404.

unmanned rocket, Jun. 4, 1989.

unnilpentium, Apr. 27, 1970.

Uno, Sousuke, elected, Jun. 2, 1989; resigns, Jul. 24, 1989.

Unser, Al, May 29, 1939.

Unser, Al, Jr., Apr. 19, 1962.

Unser, Bobby, Feb. 20, 1924; Feb. 20, 1934.

Untermeyer, Louis, Oct. 1, 1885.

Unyamwize, Mar. 14, 1872.

Updike, John, Mar. 18, 1932.

Upjohn, Richard, Jan. 22, 1802.

Upper Volta, Mar. 1, 1919; independence, Aug. 5, 1960; Nov. 27, 1977; renamed, Aug. 3, 1983.

Uprising of Los Santos (Panama), Nov. 10.

Upshaw, (Eu)gene, Aug. 15, 1945.

Uranus, Mar. 13, 1781; Jan. 24, 1986; Sep. 6, 1997.

Urban VI (pope), Oct. 23, 1385.

Urban VII (pope), Aug. 4, 1521.

Urey, Harold Clayton, Apr. 29, 1893.

Urich, Robert, Dec. 19, 1945.

Uris, Leon (Marcus), Aug. 13, 1924.

Urquhart, Sir Brian, Feb. 28, 1919.

Urriolagoiti, Mamerto, May 16, 1951.

Urrutia Lleo, Manuel, Dec. 8, 1901.

Ursuline, Martyrs of Valenciennff, Oct. 17.

Uruguay: independence, Aug. 25, 1825.

USAir jet, crashes, Sep. 8, 1994.

USO Anniversary (U.S.), Feb. intro.; Feb. 4.

Ussher, Jamff, Jan. 4, 1581.

U.S.S.R,; established, Dec. 30, 1922; name adopted, Jan. 1, 1923; Nov. 2, 1923; Jan. 3, 1928; Jan. 21, 1929; joins League of Nations, Sep. 18, 1934; new constitution, Dec. 5, 1936; invades Poland, Sep. 17, 1939; Apr. 13, 1941; German invasion, Jun. 22, 1941; May 15, 1955; Feb. 13, 1960; Jan. 27, 1962; Jan. 27, 1967; Jan. 19, 1968; cultural exchange ban lifted by U.S., Dec. 20, 1968; satellite station agreement with Cuba, Jan. 9, 1970; Jan. 24, 1972; trade with Spain, Sep. 15, 1972; constitution, Jun. 4, 1977; adopts new constitution, Oct. 7, 1977; Feb. 15, 1989; Mar. 26, 1989; Apr. 25, 1989; May 16, 1989; withdrawal of forces, Jan. 20, 1989; Afghanistan, Feb. 5, 1989; troops in Azerbaigan, Jan. 20, 1990; property law, Mar. 6, 1990; union intact, Mar. 1, 1991; Commonwealth of Independent States, Dec. 21, 1991. *See also* Russia.

U.S.S.R. and Canada: first direct air service between, Jul. 11, 1966.

U.S.S.R. and U.S.: first direct air service between, Jul. 15, 1968.

Ustinov, Peter, Apr. 16, 1921.

Utah, May 30, 1848; admitted to Union, Jan. 4, 1896.

Utah Medical Center, Dec. 2, 1982.

Utah State Prison, Jan. 17, 1977.

Utrecht, Peace of, Feb. 28, 1474; Apr. 11, 1713.

Utrillo, Maurice, Dec. 25, 1883.

V

V-1 rocket: first used, Jun. 12, 1944.

V-2 rocket: first fired on London, Sep. 7, 1944; first launch from ship, Sep. 6, 1947.

V-E Day, May 8.

V-J Day, Aug. 14, 1945.

Vaccaro, Brenda, Nov. 18, 1939.

vaccination: development of, May 14, 1796.

Vadim, Roger, Jan. 26, 1928.

Vail, Theodore Newton, Jul. 16, 1845.

Vajpayee, Atal Bihari, Dec. 25, 1924; Mar. 19, 1998.

Val d'Isere: avalanche, Feb. 9, 1970.

Valachi, Joseph M. *(Joe)*, Sep. 22, 1904.

Valdez (Alaska), Jul. 28, 1977.

Vale, Jerry, Jul. 8, 1932.

Valence, patron of, Oct. 5.

Valens, Richie, May 13, 1941.

Valens (Roman Emperor): killed, Aug. 9, 378.

Valenti, Jack Joseph, Sep. 5, 1921.

Valentine, Karen, May 25, 1947.

Valentino, May 11, 1932.

Valentino, Rudolph, May 6, 1895.

Valenzuela, Fernando, Nov. 1, 1960.

Valera y Alcala Galiano, Juan, Oct. 18, 1824.

Valery, Paul Ambroise Toussainl Jules, Oct. 30, 1871.

Vallandigham, Clement Laird, Jul. 29, 1820.

Valle-Riestra, Jose Maria, Dec. 26, 1900.

Vallee, Rudy, Jul. 28, 1901.

Valletta, Carnival in (Malta), May intro.

Valley Forge, Dec. 19, 1777.

Valli, Frankie, May 3, 1937.

Valois (Edris Stannus), Ninette de, Jun. 6, 1898.

Valromey, Jan. 17, 1601.

Valse Triste: premiere, Apr. 25, 1905.

Van Allen, James Alfred, Sep. 7, 1914.

Van Ark, Joan, Jun. 16, 1946.

Van, Bobby, Dec. 6, 1935.

Van Brocklin, Norm, Mar. 15, 1926.

Van Buren, Abigail, Jul. 4, 1918.

Van Buren, Hannah, Mar. 8, 1783.

Van Buren, Martin, Dec. 5, 1782; inaugurated, Mar. 4, 1837.
Van Camp Seafood, ban on tuna netting, Apr. 12, 1990.
Van (Caucasus), Apr. 20, 1915.
Van Damme, Jean-Claude, Oct. 18, 1961.
van der Rohe, Miff, Mar. 27, 1886.
Van Devere, Trish, Mar. 9, 1945.
Van Doren, Carl, Sep. 10, 1885.
Van Doren, Charles, Jan. 19, 1962.
Van Doren, Mamie, Feb. 6, 1933.
Van Doren, Mark, Jun. 13, 1894.
Van Druten, John, Oct. 19, 1944.
Van Duyn, Mona, May 9, 1921.
Van Dyke, Sir Anthony, Mar. 22, 1599.
Van Dyke, Dick, Dec. 13, 1925.
Van Dyken, Amy, Feb. 1, 1973.
van Gogh, Vincent, Mar. 30, 1853.
Van Halen, Alex, May 8, 1955.
Van Halen, Edward (Eddie), Jan. 26, 1957.
Van Heusen, Jimmy, Jan. 26, 1913.
Van Houtte, Jean, Jan. 15, 1952.
Van Loon, Hendrik, Jan. 14, 1882.
Van Patten, Dick, Dec. 9, 1928.
Van Patten, Vince(nt), Oct. 17, 1957.
Van Peebles, Mario, Jan. 15, 1957.
Van Rensselaer, Stephen, Nov. 1, 1764.
Van Riebeeck Day (Republic of South Africa), Apr. 6.
Van Slyke, Andrew (Andy), Dec. 21, 1960.
Van Slyke, Helen Lenore Vogt, Jul. 9, 1919.
Van Vleck, John Hasbrouck, Mar. 13, 1899.
Van Zeeland, Paul (Belgium), Mar. 25, 1935.
Vance, Cyrus, Mar. 27, 1917; Jan. 6, 1978.
Vance, Vivian, Jul. 26, 1912.
Vancouver, George, Jun. 22, 1757.
Vandegrift, Alexander Archer, Mar. 13, 1887.
Vandenberg, Arthur Hendrick, Mar. 22, 1884.
Vanderbilt, Amy, Jul. 22, 1908.
Vanderbilt, Cornelius, May 27, 1794.
Vanderbilt, Gloria Morgan, Feb. 20, 1924.

Vanderbilt, William Henry, May 8, 1821.
Vanderbilt, William Kissam, Dec. 12, 1849.
Vandeweghe, Kiki, Aug. 1, 1958.
Vandross, Luther, Apr. 20, 1951.
VanDyke, Jerry, Jul. 27, 1931.
Vane, John R(obert), Mar. 29, 1927.
Vangelis, Mar. 29, 1943.
Vanguard I, Mar. 17, 1958.
Vannelli, Gino, Jun. 16, 1952.
Vanocur, Sander, Jan. 8, 1928.
Van't Hoff, Jacobus H., Aug. 30, 1852.
Vanuatu, Republic of: independence, Jul. 30, 1980.
Vanunu, Mordechai, Mar. 24, 1988.
Vanzetti, Bartolomeo, Jul. 11, 1888; Jul. 14, 1921.
Vardon, Harry, May 7, 1870.
Varennes: French royal family arrested, Jun. 21, 1791.
Varennes, Pierre Gaultier de, Nov. 17, 1685.
Vargas, Getulio Dorneles, Apr. 19, 1883; inaugurated, Jan. 31, 1951; Aug. 24, 1954.
Vargas Llosa, Mario, Mar. 28, 1936.
Variag, Feb. 9, 1904.
Varmus, Harold E., Dec. 18, 1939.
Varna, Battle of, Nov. 10, 1444.
Vasa, Gustavus, Jun. 7, 1523.
Vasari, Giorgio, Jul. 30, 1511.
Vasile, Radu, Apr. 1, 1998.
Vassiliou, George: elected, Feb. 21, 1988.
Vassy, Mar. 1, 1562.
Vatican, Oct. 22; Sep. 15, 1964; exonerates Jews, Nov. 20, 1964; Jan. 8, 1966; abolition of book censure, Feb. 8, 1966; Jan. 29, 1967; Jan. 25, 1970; May 18, 1978; Jan. 16, 1982; Jan. 10, 1984; report on liberation theology, Sep. 3, 1984.
Vatican City, Feb. 11, 1929.
Vatican Council, Second: opens, Oct. 11, 1962.
Vauban, Sebastien le Prestre de, May 15, 1633.
Vaucanson, Jacques de, Feb. 24, 1709.
Vaucelles, Truce of, Feb. 5, 1556.
Vaughan, Henry, Apr. 17, 1622.

Vaughan, Sarah, Mar. 27, 1924.
Vaughan, Stevie Ray, Oct. 3, 1954.
Vaughn, Robert, Nov. 22, 1932.
Veblen, Thorstein (Bunde), Jul. 30, 1857.
Vedrines, J., Feb. 22, 1912.
Vega I, Mar. 6, 1986.
Vega Day (Sweden), Apr. 24.
Vega, Lope (Felix) de, Nov. 25, 1562.
Veil, Simone, Jul. 13, 1927.
Veit, Philipp, Feb. 13, 1793.
Velasco Alvarado, Juan, Oct. 3, 1968; Feb. 6, 1969.
Velasco Ibarra, Jose Maria: inaugurated, Aug. 31, 1952.
Velazquez, Diego Rodriguez de Silva y, Jun. 6, 1599.
Velikovsky, Immanuel, Jun. 10, 1895.
Venda, Sep. 13, 1979.
Venera 7, Dec. 15, 1970.
Venetia, Jul. 3, 1866.
Venetian Republic, Mar. 22, 1848.
Veneto, Vittorio, Nov. 3, 1918.
Venezuela: independence, Jul. 5, 1821; Jan. 23, 1961; Jan. 23, 1961; Jan. 6, 1967.
Venice (Italy), Jan. 26, 1699; Apr. 25, 1903.
Venice, patron of, Apr. 25.
Venizelos, Eleutherios, Aug. 23, 1864.
Venizelos, Sophocles, Apr. 23, 1944; inaugurated, Mar. 23, 1950.
Venus, Feb. 12, 1961; information from Mariner II, Dec. 14, 1962; temperature, Feb. 26, 1963 Soviet spacecraft lands, Dec. 15, 1970.
Venus 3, Mar. 1, 1966.
Venus with the Mirror, Mar. 10, 1914.
Ver, Fabian, Jan. 23, 1985.
Vera-Ellen, Feb. 16, 1926.
Veracruz (Mexico), Mar. 29, 1847, Apr. 21, 1914.
Verdaguer, Jacinto, May 17, 1845.
Verdi, Giuseppe, Oct. 10, 1813.
Verdon, Gwen, Jan. 13, 1925.
Verdun, Jan. 15, 1552.
Verdun, Battle of, Feb. 20, 1916; Mar. 6, 1916; Apr. 20, 1916; ends, Dec. 18, 1916.
Vereen, Bob, Oct. 10, 1946.
Vereeniging, Treaty of, May 31, 1902.

Verga, Giovanni, Sep. 2, 1840.

Verger, Jan. 3, 1857.

Vergil, Oct. 15, 70 b.c.

Verhoeven, Paul, Jul. 18, 1938.

Verlaine, Paul, Mar. 30, 1844.

Vermeer, Jan, Oct. 30, 1632.

Vermeil, Richard Albert (Dick), Oct. 30, 1936.

Vermont, Jan. 15, 1777; admitted to Union, Mar. 4, 1791.

vernacular languages: authorized use in all Roman Catholic churches, Nov. 21, 1963.

Vernal Equinox Day (Japan), Mar. intro.

Vernal Equinox (Japan), Mar. 20.

Verne, Julff, Feb. 8, 1828.

Verrazano Day (New York), Apr. 7.

Verrazano-Narrows Bridge: opens, Nov. 21, 1964.

Versaillff, May 16, 1770.

Versaillff, Treaty of: signed, Jun. 28, 1919; ratified by Germany, Jul. 7, 1919; ratified by France, Oct. 13, 1919; ratified by Britain and Italy, Oct. 15, 1919; Japan ratifies, Oct. 30, 1919; U.S. rejects, Mar. 19, 1920; abrogated by Germany, Mar. 1935.

Vertierff Day (Haiti), Nov. 18.

Verwoerd, Hendrik: assassinated, Sep. 6, 1966.

Vesak Day (Singapore), May 1.

Vesalius, Andreas, Dec. 31, 1514.

Vesco, Robert Lee, Dec. 4, 1935.

Vespucci, Amerigo, Mar. 9, 1451.

Vestmannaeyjax (Iceland), Jan. 23, 1973.

Veterans Administration Act, Jul. 3, 1930.

Veterans Administration, U.S.: created, Jul. 3, 1930.

Veterans Day (France), Nov. 11.

Veterans Day (U.S., Guam, Puerto Rico, Virgin Islands), Nov. 11.

veto, legislative, Jun. 23, 1983.

Vetsera, Marie, Jan. 30, 1889.

Veuster Joseph Damie de (Father Damien), Jan. 3, 1840.

Vicario, Arantxa, Dec. 18, 1971.

Vickers, Jon, Oct. 29, 1926.

Vickrey, William, Jun. 21, 1914.

Vicksburg: surrenders, Jul. 4, 1863.

Vico, Giovanni Battista, Jun. 23, 1668.

Victims' Rights Week, National, Apr. intro.

Victor, Alfred, Mar. 27, 1797.

Victor Emmanuel II, Mar. 31, 1861; Sep. 21, 1870.

Victor Emmanuel III (Italy), Nov. 11, 1869; Jun. 1, 1936; Jun. 5, 1944.

Victor Emmanuel (Italy), Mar. 23, 1849; Nov. 7, 1860; Mar. 17, 1861; dies, Jan. 9, 1878.

Victoria (Australia), Jul. 1, 1851.

Victoria Cross, Order of, Jan. 29, 1857.

Victoria Day (Canada, Scotland), May intro.

Victoria Day (Poland), May 9.

Victoria (England), May 24, 1819; Jun. 20, 1837; Feb. 10, 1840; May 1, 1876; Jan. 1, 1877; Jan. 14, 1878; golden jubilee, Jun. 21, 1887; dies, Jan. 22, 1901.

Victoria Falls: discovered, Nov. 17, 1855.

Victoria Falls Bridge, Apr. 11, 1905.

Victory of Aduwa Day (Ethiopia), Mar. 2.

Victory Day, Nov. 11.

Victory Day (Angola), Mar. 27.

Victory Day (Bangladesh), Dec. 16.

Victory Day (Belarus), May 9.

Victory Day (Bashkir, Russia), May 9.

Victory Day (Egypt), Dec. 23.

Victory Day (Ethiopia), Mar. 6.

Victory Day (Mozambique), Sep. 7.

Victory Day (Rhode Island), Aug. intro.

Victory Day (Togo), Apr. 24.

Victory Day (Tunisia), Jun. 2.

Victory of Uprona (Burundi), Sep. 18.

Victory over American Imperialism Day (Cambodia), Apr. 17.

Vidal, Gore, Oct. 3, 1925.

Videla, Jorge Rafael, Aug. 2, 1925; Mar. 24, 1976; Mar. 29, 1976; Jul. 31, 1978; Dec. 9, 1985.

videotape recording machine, Apr. 14, 1956.

Vidor, King Wallis, Feb. 8, 1894.

Vienna: Turkish siege of, Sep. 12, 1683; Mar. 13, 1938, Apr. 13, 1945.

Vienna, Peace of: signed, Oct. 14, 1809; Oct. 30, 1864.

Vienna, Treaty of, Oct. 5, 1735.

Viet Cong, Jan. 6, 1967.

Viet-Minh, Jan. 19, 1951; Mar. 13, 1954.

Vietnam Day (Vietnam), Jan. 27.

Vietnam: Japanese attack French, Sep. 22, 1940; Sep. 2, 1945; Jan. 29, 1950; Jun. 4, 1954; Jul. 21, 1954; Jan. 31, 1964; U.S. P.O.W.'s released, Mar. 29, 1973; end of U.S. presence, Apr. 29, 1975; unification, Apr. 25, 1976; last U.S. personnel are withdrawn, Jun. 5, 1976; admitted to U.N., Sep. 20, 1977; Chinese invasion, Feb. 17, 1979; Chinese troop withdrawal, Mar. 5, 1979; troops removed from Cambodia, Apr. 5, 1989; army exits Cambodia, Sep. 26, 1989; trade embargo, Feb. 3, 1994.

Vietnam, North, Aug. 5, 1964; Feb. 8, 1965; Mar. 5, 1967; Jan. 10, 1969; Jan. 21, 1970; Jul. 2, 1976.

Vietnam, South, Aug. 10, 1950; Oct. 23, 1955; Republic of, established, Oct. 26, 1955; Mar. 9, 1962; Jan. 26, 1965; Feb. 24, 1965; U.S. combat activity first acknowledged, Jun. 5, 1965; Feb. 8, 1966; Jan. 6, 1967; Sep. 3, 1967; U.S. troops withdrawn, Mar. 29, 1973; Mar. 1, 1975; Communist victory, May 1, 1975; Jul. 2, 1976.

Vietnam Veterans' Day (U.S.), Mar. 29.

Vietnam War, Dec. 11, 1961; Apr. 25, 1964; Aug. 5, 1964; Feb. 24, 1965; first U.S.-Viet Cong skirmish, Mar. 12, 1965; Jul. 28, 1965; Jun. 23, 1966; Jun. 29, 1966, Nov. 26, 1966; Jan. 6, 1967; Feb. 22–May 13, 1967; Jul. 29, 1967; Jan. 31, 1968; U.S. casualties exceed those of Korean War, Mar. 14, 1968; Mar. 16, 1968; peace negotiations begin, May 13, 1968; Jul. 18, 1968; May 20, 1969; Jun. 8, 1969, Sep. 27, 1969; May 8,

1972; Aug. 12, 1972; Jan. 15, 1973; cease fire, Jan. 27, 1973; deserters clemency, Sep. 16, 1974; Mar. 26, 1975; May 28, 1984; MIA search, Dec. 4, 1985.

Vietnam War Memorial: groundbreaking, Mar. 26, 1982, Nov. 9, 1984.

Vietnam War protest: (Washington), Apr. 17, 1965.

Vietnam War protest (N.Y), Apr. 15, 1967; Berkeley (California), May 15, 1969.

Vigil of the Nativity of Jesus Christ, Dec. 23.

Vigneaud, Vincent Du, May 18, 1901.

Vigoda, Abe, Feb. 24, 1921.

Viking 1, Jul. 20, 1976; Jul. 26, 1976.

Viking 2, Sep. 3, 1976.

Vilas, Guillermo, Aug. 17, 1952.

Vilijoen, Marais, Dec. 2, 1915.

Villa, Celso Torrelio, Jun. 3, 1931.

Villa-Lobos, Hector, Mar. 5, 1887.

Villa, Francisco *(Pancho),* Jun. 5, 1878; Mar. 15, 1916.

Villa Viciosa, Dec. 10, 1710.

Villard, Henry, Apr. 10, 1835.

Villard, Oswald Garrison, Mar. 13, 1872.

Villarroel, Gualberto: assassinated, Jul. 22, 1946.

Villechaize, Herve Jean Pierre, Apr. 23, 1943.

Villella, Edward, Oct. 1, 1936.

Villeneuve, Jacques, Apr. 9, 1971.

Villiers, George (1st Duke of Buckingham), Aug. 28, 1592; assassinated, Aug. 23, 1628.

Villmergen, Battle of, Jul. 25, 1712.

Vilna (Poland), Jan. 5, 1919; Apr. 19, 1919; Apr. 18, 1922.

Vimiera, Battle of, Aug. 21, 1808.

Vimy Ridge, Apr. 9, 1917.

Vinaroz, Apr. 15, 1938.

Vincennes, U.S.S., Jul. 3, 1988.

Vincent, Francis (Fran) T., Jr., May 29, 1938.

Vincent, Jan-Michael, Jul. 15, 1944.

Vincent, John Heyl, Feb. 23, 1832.

vine growers, patron of, Jun. 16.

Vinje, Aasmund Olavssen, Apr. 6, 1818.

Vinland Map: existence disclosed, Oct. 10, 1965.

Vinson, Carl, Nov. 18, 1883.

Vinson, Frederick, Jun. 20, 1946.

Vinson, Frederick Moore, Jan. 22, 1890.

vintners, patron of, Aug. 10.

Vinton, Bobby, Apr. 16, 1935.

Viola, Roberto, Jul. 31, 1978; Jun. 22, 1984; Dec. 9, 1985.

violet, Feb. intro.

violinists, patron of, Feb. 12.

Viorst, Judith (Stahl), Feb. 2, 1931.

Virchow, Rudolph, Oct. 13, 1821.

Virgen de la Candelaria - Puno (Peru), Feb. 8.

Virgin Islands: ceded to U.S., Aug. 4, 1916 Jan. 17, 1917.

Virgin Islands Transfer Day (U.S.), Mar. 31.

Virgin Mary, Birthday of the Blessed Feast of, Sep. 8.

Virgina, Jun. 25, 1788.

Virginia, Charter of, Apr. 10, 1606.

Virginia schools: desegregation, Feb. 2, 1959.

Virginia, West: admitted to the Union, Jun. 20, 1863.

virginity, patron of, Jan. 21.

virgins, patron of, Nov. 3; Dec. 6.

Virgo, Aug. intro.; Sep. intro.

Virtanen, Artturi I., Jan. 15, 1895.

Visconti, Luchino, Nov. 2, 1906.

Vishnevskaya, Galina (Pavlovna), Oct. 25, 1926.

Visitation of the Virgin Mary, Feast of the, May 31.

Vitale, Dick, Jun. 9, 1939.

Viticulturists Day (Bulgaria), Feb. 14.

Vitoria: French defeated by British, Jun. 21, 1813.

Vittorio Veneto, Oct. 28, 1871.

Vittono Veneto, Hattle of: begins, Oct. 25, 1918.

Vivaldi, Antonio, Mar. 4, 1678.

Vivff, Juan Luis, Mar. 6, 1492.

Vladislav II (Poland), Jan. 9, 1493.

Vlajkovic, Radovan: inaugurated, May 15, 1985.

Vo Chi Cong, Jun. 18, 1987.

Vocation Awareness Week, National, Oct. intro.

Vocational Service Month, Oct. intro.

Voight, Jon, Dec. 29, 1938.

volcano: Colombia, Nov. 13, 1985.

Volcker, Paul A., Sep. 5, 1927.

Volgograd (U.S.S.R), Nov. 11, 1961.

Volkov, Victor I., Jun. 30, 1971.

Volstead, Andrew Jpseph, Oct. 31, 1860.

Volta, Conte Alessandro Giuseppe, Feb. 18, 1745.

Voltaire, Francois Marie Arouet de, Nov. 21, 1694.

Volunteers of America Week, Mar. intro.

Von Bulow, Claus, Aug. 11, 1926.

von Furstenberg, Diane, Dec. 31, 1946.

Von Zell, Harry, Jul. 11, 1906.

VonHoffman, Nicholas, Oct. 16, 1929.

Vonnegut, Kurt, Jr., Nov. 11, 1922, Mar. 31, 1969.

Voroshilov, Kliment Efremovich, Feb. 4, 1881; Jan. 27, 1962.

Vorster, Balthazar Johannes, Dec. 13, 1915; Sep. 13, 1966.

Voskhod: first multi-seat spacecraft, Oct. 13, 1964.

Voskhod 2, Mar. 18, 1965.

Vostok I, Apr. 12, 1961.

Vostok VI, Jun. 16, 1963.

voting age: lowered to 18 in U.S., Mar. 12, 1970.

Voting Rights Act, Aug. 6, 1965.

Vow, Day of the (Namibia, South Africa), Dec. 16.

Voyager, Dec. 23, 1986.

Voyager I, Mar. I, 1979; Mar. 5, 1979.

Voyager 2: passes Saturn, Aug. 25, 1981; Feb. 2, 1982; passes Uranus, Jan. 24, 1986.

Vries, Hugo Marie De, Feb. 16, 1848.

Vuillard, (Jean) Edouard, Nov. 11, 1868.

W

W particles, Jan. 26, 1983; Jun. 1, 1983.

Waals, Johannes D. van der, Nov. 23, 1837.

Wade, Virginia, Jul. 10, 1945.

wage freeze, Apr. 8, 1943.

Waggoner, Lyle, Apr. 13, 1935.

Wagner-Connery Act, Jul. 5, 1935.

Wagner, Franz: first air-born piano recital, May 7, 1936.

Wagner, Jack Peter, Oct. 3, 1959.

Wagner, Lindsay, Jun. 22, 1949.

Wagner, Richard, May 22, 1813; Aug. 28, 1850; Mar. 13, 1861; Jun. 21, 1868.

Wagner, Robert F., Jr., Apr. 20, 1910.

Wagner, Robert John, Jr., Feb. 10, 1930.

Wagon Train: television debut, Sep. 18, 1957.

Wagoner, Porter, Aug. 12, 1927.

Wahlberg, Mark, Jun. 5, 1971.

Wahlstatt, Gebhard Liberecht Blucher von, Dec. 16, 1742.

Washington, Dinah Wainwright, Jonathan (Mayhew), Aug. 23, 1883, May 6, 1942.

Wait, William Bell, Mar. 25, 1839.

Waitangi Day (New Zealand), Feb. 6.

Waitangi, Treaty of, Feb. 6, 1840.

Waite, John, Jul. 4, 1955.

Waite, Morrison Remick, Nov. 29, 1816; Jan. 19, 1874.

Waite, Ralph, Jun. 22, 1928.

Waite, Terence Hardy *(Terry)*, May 31, 1939, Jan. 20, 1987; Nov. 18, 1991.

Waiting for Godot: opens, Apr. 19, 1956.

Waits, Tom, Dec. 7, 1949.

Waitz, Grete, Oct. 1, 1953.

Wake Island, Dec. 22, 1941; captured by Japanese, Dec. 23, 1941; Sep. 3, 1944.

Wake, U.S.S.: surrender of, Dec. 8, 1941.

Wakefield, Battle of, Dec. 30, 1460.

Wakefield, Edward Gibbon, Mar. 20, 1796.

Wakeman, Rick, May 18, 1949.

Waksman, Selman Abraham, Jul. 22, 1888.

Walcott, Derek, Jan. 23, 1930.

Walcott, Jersey Joe, Jan. 31, 1914; Dec. 5, 1947; Jun. 22, 1949; Jul. 18, 1951; Sep. 23, 1952.

Wald, George, Nov. 18, 1906.

Wald, Lillian D., Mar. 10, 1867.

Waldemar I, King of Denmark, Jan. 14, 1131.

Walden, Robert, Sep. 25, 1943.

Waldeyer, Heinrich Wilhelm Gottfried von, Oct. 6, 1836.

Waldheim, Kurt, Dec. 21, 1918; inaugurated, Jan. 1, 1972; Dec.

15, 1981; Mar. 4, 1986; inaugurated, Jul. 8, 1986; Apr. 27, 1987; Feb. 9, 1988.

Wales, Mar. 1, 1979.

Wales, patron of, Feb. 1; Mar. 1.

Wales, Prince of, Jul. 1, 1969.

Wales, Statute of: enacted, Mar. 19, 1284.

Walesa, Lech: awarded Nobel Peace Prize, Oct. 5, 1983; elected, Dec. 9, 1990; defeated, Nov. 19, 1995.

Walgreen, Charles Rudolph, Oct. 9, 1873.

Walid, Khalil, Apr. 16, 1988.

Walken, Christopher, Mar. 31, 1943.

Walker, Alice, Feb. 9, 1944.

Walker, Herschel, Mar. 3, 1962.

Walker, Hiram, Jul. 4, 1816.

Walker, James Carter *(Jimmie)*, Jun. 25, 1948.

Walker, James (John), Jun. 19, 1881.

Walker, John, Jan. 12, 1952; May 20, 1985.

Walker, Mary, Nov. 26, 1832.

Walker, Nancy, May 10, 1921.

Walker, Sarah Breedlove (Madame C. J. Walker), Dec. 23, 1867.

Walla Walla, Fort, Sep. 1, 1836.

Wallace, Alfred Russel, Jan. 8, 1823.

Wallace, Chris, Oct. 12, 1947.

Wallace, Dewitt, Nov. 12, 1889.

Wallace, George Corley, Aug. 25, 1919; inaugurated, Jan. 14, 1963; Jun. 11, 1963; assassination attempt, May 15, 1972.

Wallace, Henry Agard, Oct. 7, 1888.

Wallace, Irving, Mar. 19, 1916.

Wallace, Lew(is), Apr. 10, 1827.

Wallace, Lila Acheson, Dec. 25, 1889.

Wallace, Lurleen Burns, Sep. 19, 1926.

Wallace, Mike, May 9, 1918.

Wallace, William, Sep. 11, 1297; Jul. 22, 1298; executed, Aug. 23, 1305.

Wallach, Eli, Dec. 7, 1915.

Wallach, Otto, Mar. 27, 1847.

Wallachia, Dec. 23, 1861.

Wallechinsky, David, Feb. 5, 1948.

Wallenberg, Rauol Gustav, Aug. 4, 1912.

Wallenda, Karl, Mar. 22, 1978.

Wallenstein, Alfred, Oct. 7, 1898.

Waller, Edmund, Mar. 3, 1606.

Waller, Fats, May 21, 1904.

Waller, Frederic, Mar. 10, 1886.

Wallingford, Treaty of: signed, Nov. 7, 1153.

Wallis, Hal, Sep. 14, 1898.

Walpole, Horace, Sep. 24, 1717.

Walpole, Hugh, Mar. 13, 1884.

Walpole, Robert, Aug. 26, 1676.

Walpurgis Night (Germany and Scandinavia), Apr. 30.

Walsh, Joseph Fidler *(Joe)*, Nov. 20, 1947.

Walsh, Lawrence, Dec. 19, 1986.

Walsh, M. Emmet, Mar. 21, 1935.

Walsh, Raoul, Mar. 11, 1892.

Walsh, Stella, Apr. 11, 1911.

Walter, Bruno, Sep. 15, 1876.

Walter, C. F. W., Feast of, May 7.

Walter, Jessica, Jan. 31, 1944.

Walter, Tracey, Nov. 25, 1942.

Walters, Barbara, Sep. 25, 1931.

Walters, Vernon Anthony, Jan. Mar. 25, 1985.

Walton, Bill, Nov. 5, 1952.

Walton, Ernest Thomas Sinton, Oct. 6, 1903.

Walton, Izaak, Aug. 9, 1593.

Walton, Sam Moore, Mar. 29, 1918.

Walton, Sir William, Mar. 29, 1902; May 9, 1937.

The Waltons: television debut, Sep. 14, 1972.

Wambaugh, Joseph, Jan. 22, 1937.

Wanamaker, John, Jul. 11, 1838.

Wandiwash, Battle of, Jan. 22, 1760.

Wang, An, Feb. 7, 1920.

Wang, Wayne, Jan. 12, 1949.

Wangchuk, Jigme Dorji, Oct. 27, 1952.

Wangchuk, Jigme Singye: crowned, Jul. 24, 1972.

Wannsee Conference, Jan. 20, 1942.

War of 1812: declared, Jun. 18, 1812; British capture Detroit, Aug. 16, 1812; Aug. 19, 1812; Oct. 25, 1812; Sep. 10, 1813; Oct. 5, 1813; Washington burned, Aug. 24, 1814; Sep. 11, 1814; Sep. 14, 1814; Jan. 8, 1815; Feb. 20, 1815.

War Claims Commission (U.S.), Feb. 8, 1950.

War Conference Rules of, Jun. 10, 1977.

War of the Holy League, Sep. 13, 1515.

War of Independence (Estonia), Jun. 23, 1919.

War of Italian Unification, May 15, 1860.

War of the League of, Augsburg, Sep. 20, 1697.

War of the Oranges, Jan. 20, 1801; Mar. 2, 1801.

War of the Roses: begins, May 22, 1455; Jul. 10, 1460; Dec. 30, 1460; Feb. 17, 1461; Mar. 29, 1461; Apr. 14, 1471; May 4, 1471.

War of the Spanish Succession, Sep. 11, 1700; Aug. 4, 1704; May 23, 1706.

War of the Third Coalition, Jan. 4, 1805.

War Trials (German Supreme Court), Jan. 10, 1921.

War of the Worlds: broadcast, Oct. 30, 1939.

Warburg, Otto Heinrich, Oct. 8, 1883.

Ward, Barbara Mary, May 23, 1914.

Ward, Deighton, May 16, 1909.

Ward, Montgomery, Feb. 17, 1843.

Ward, Simon, Oct. 19, 1941.

Warden, Jack, Sep. 18, 1920.

Warfield, (Bessie) Wallis, Jun. 19, 1896.

Warfield, Paul, Nov. 28, 1942.

Warhol, Andy, Aug. 6, 1927.

Waring, Fred M., Jun. 9, 1900.

Warner, Albert, Jul. 23, 1884.

Warner Communications Inc., Mar. 4, 1989.

Warner, Harry, Dec. 12, 1881.

Warner, H(erbert) B(ryan), Oct. 26, 1876.

Warner, Jack, Aug. 2, 1892.

Warner, John William, Feb. 18, 1927.

Warner, Malcolm-Jamal, Aug. 18, 1970.

Warner, Sam(uel Louis), Aug. 10, 1887.

Warner-Steagall Act (National Housing Act), Sep. 1, 1937.

Warren Commission, Nov. 29, 1963.

Warren, Earl, Mar. 19, 1891; Oct. 5, 1953.

Warren, Harry, Dec. 24, 1893.

Warren, Joseph, Jun. 10, 1741.

Warren, Leonard, Apr. 21, 1911.

Warren, Lesley Ann, Aug. 16, 1946.

Warren, Mercy Otis, Sep. 23, 1728.

Warren Report: issued, Sep. 27, 1964.

Warren, Robert Penn, Apr. 24, 1905; Feb. 26, 1986.

Warren, Shields, Feb. 26, 1898.

Warren, Whitney, Jan. 29, 1864.

warriors, patron of, Nov. 1.

Warsaw, Battle of: opens, Oct. 9, 1914.

Warsaw ghetto, Apr. 20, 1943.

Warsaw Pact, May 14, 1955; Sep. 13, 1968.

Warsaw (Poland), Oct. 4, 1914; German occupation, Aug. 5, 1915; falls to Germans, Sep. 27, 1939; Jan. 17, 1945.

Warsaw Treaty Organization. *See*: Warsaw Pact.

Warwick, Dionne, Dec. 12, 1941.

Warwick (Duke of), Apr. 14, 1471.

Washburn, William Drew, Jan. 14, 1831.

washerwomen, patron of, Aug. 1|.

Washington: admitted to Union, Nov. 11, 1889.

Washington, Act of, Dec. 18, 1964.

Washington Admission Day (U.S.), Nov. 11.

Washington Armament Conference: begins, Nov. 12, 1921.

Washington, Booker T., Apr. 5, 1856; Jul. 4, 1881.

Washington Conference, Feb. 4, 1919; Feb. 6, 1922.

Washington Day (Arizona), Feb. intro.

Washington, Denzel, Dec. 28, 1954.

Washington, D.C., Mar. 4, 1801; burned by British, Aug. 24, 1814.

Washington, Dinah, Aug. 29, 1924.

Washington, George, Feb. 22, 1732; Jun. 15, 1775; Jul. 3, 1775; Jan. 1, 1776; Dec. 11, 1776; Dec. 25, 1776; Dec. 26, 1776; Jan. 3, 1777; Oct. 3, 1777; Jan. 7, 1789;

elected president, Feb. 4, 1789; inaugurated, Apr. 30, 1789; Jan. 8, 1790; second term, Mar. 4, 1793; Apr. 22, 1793; farewell address, Sep. 17, 1796.

Washington, Grover, Jr., Dec. 12, 1943.

Washington, Harold, Apr. 15, 1922; Apr. 12, 1983.

Washington-Lincoln Day (Ohio, Wisconsin, Wyoming), Feb. intro.

Washington, Martha, Jun. 21, 1731.

Washington Monument, Feb. 21, 1885.

Washington, Walter, Apr. 16, 1915.

Washington Redskins, Jan. 26, 1992.

Washington's Birthday (U.S.), Feb. intro. Feb. 22.

Wasp: U.S. carrier, May 9, 1942.

Wassail Eve (England), Jan. 5.

Wasserman, August von, Feb. 21, 1866.

Watchet, patron of, Aug. 27.

water molecules: discovery outside earth's galaxy, Jan. 19, 1977.

Water Quality Improvement Act, Apr. 3, 1970.

Watergate Incident, Jun. 17, 1972; Feb. 8, 1973; Apr. 30, 1973; May 17, 1973; May 18, 1973; Jul. 26, 1973; Oct. 12, 1973; Oct. 20, 1973; indictments, Mar. 1, 1974; Jul. 24, 1974; Jul. 30, 1974; John Dean sentenced to prison, Aug. 2, 1974; Nixon resignation, Aug. 8, 1974; trial begins, Oct. 1, 1974; Jan. 1, 1975; Feb. 21, 1975.

Waterhouse, Benjamin, Mar. 4, 1754.

Waterloo, Battle of, Jun. 18, 1815.

Waters, Ethel, Oct. 31, 1900.

Waters, John, Apr. 22, 1946.

Waters, Muddy, Apr. 4, 1915.

Waterston, Sam(uel Atkinson), Nov. 15, 1940.

Watkins, Levi, Jr., Jun. 13, 1945.

Watson, James Dewey, Apr. 6, 1928; Apr. 25, 1953.

Watson, John Broadus, Jan. 9, 1878.

Watson, John Thomas, Jr., Jan. 8, 1914.

Watson, Lucile, May 27, 1879.

Watson, Thomas A., Jan. 25, 1915.

Watson, Tom, Sep. 4, 1949.

Watson-Watt, Sir Robert Alexander, Apr. 13, 1892.

Watson-Wentworth, Charlff (Marquis of Rockingham), Mar. 19, 1782.

Watt, Jamff, Jan. 19, 1736.

Watteau, (Jean) Antoine, Oct. 10, 1684.

Wattenberg, Ben J., Aug. 26, 1933.

Watts, Alan Wilson, Jan. 6, 1915.

Watts, Andre, Jun. 20, 1946.

Watts, George Frederic, Feb. 23, 1817.

Watts, Charles Robert (Charlie), Jun. 2, 1941.

Watts (Los Angeles, Calfornia): race riots begin, Aug. 11, 1965.

Waugh, Alec (Alexander Raban), Jul. 8, 1898.

Waugh, Evelyn (Arthur St. John), Oct. 18, 1903.

WAVE (Women Appointed for Voluntary Emergency): sworn into U.S. Navy, Jul. 7, 1948.

Wavell, Archibald Percival, May 5, 1883.

Wayans, Keenen Ivory, Jun. 8, 1958.

Wayne, Anthony (Mad Anthony), Jan. 1, 1745.

Wayne, David, Jan. 30, 1914.

Wayne, John, May 26, 1907.

Wayne, Patrick, Jul. 15, 1939.

We Are the World, Mar. 7, 1985.

Weather Bureau (U.S.): established, Feb. 9, 1870.

Weatherman faction, Apr. 2, 1970.

Weaver, Dennis, Jun. 4, 1925.

Weaver, Earl, Aug. 14, 1930.

Weaver, Fritz William, Jan. 19, 1926.

Weaver, Robert C., Dec. 29, 1907; Jan. 13, 1966.

Weaver, Sigourney, Oct. 8, 1949.

weavers, patron of, Jan. 15; Sep. 22.

Webb, Captain Matthew: first swimmer of English Channel, Aug. 25, 1875.

Webb, Clifton, Nov. 19, 1896.

Webb, Jack, Apr. 2, 1920.

Webb, Jamff H(enry), Feb. 9, 1946.

Webb (Potter) Beatrice, Jan. 22, 1858.

Webb, Sidney Jamff, Jul. 13, 1859.

Webber, Andrew Lloyd, Mar. 22, 1948; Oct. 12, 1971; Jun. 21, 1978.

Weber, Carl Maria von, Nov. 18, 1768.

Webber III, Mayce Edward Christopher (Chris), Mar. 1, 1973.

Weber, Ernst Heinrich, Jun. 24, 1795.

Weber, Max, Apr. 21, 1864.

Webster-Ashburton Treaty, Aug. 9, 1842.

Webster, Daniel, Jan. 18, 1782.

Webster, Noah, Oct. 16, 1758; Apr. 14, 1828.

Webster, William Hedgcock, Mar. 6, 1924.

Weckherin, Georg Rodolf, Sep. 15, 1584.

Weddell, James, Aug. 24, 1787.

Wedgwood, Josiah, Jul. 12, 1730.

Weeks' Week, Jan. intro.

Wegener, Alfred, Nov. 1, 1880.

Weicker, Lowell Palmer, Jr., May 16, 1931.

Weidman, Jerome, Aug. 4, 1913.

Weierstrass, Karl, Oct. 31, 1815.

weight-lifting: first world championship, Mar. 28, 1891.

Weihaiwei, Battle of, Feb. 12, 1895.

Weil, Andrew, Jun. 8, 1942.

Weil, Simone, Feb. 3, 1909.

Weill, Kurt, Mar. 2, 1900.

Weimar Constitution: adopted, Jul. 31, 1919.

Weinberg, Steven, May 3, 1933.

Weinberger, Casper Willard (Cap), Aug. 18, 1917.

Weingarten, Violet, Feb. 23, 1915.

Weir, Peter, Aug. 8, 1944.

Weismann, August, Jan. 17, 1834.

Weiss, Peter, Nov. 8, 1916.

Weiss, Ted, Sep. 17, 1927.

Weissmuller, Johnny, Jun. 2, 1904.

Weitz, Bruce Peter, May 27, 1943.

Weitz, Paul J., Jun. 22, 1973.

Weizmann, Chaim (Israel), Nov. 27, 1874; Jul. 24, 1918; Feb. 14, 1949.

Welch, Bob, Jul. 31, 1946.

Welch, Raquel, Sep. 5, 1940.

Welch, Richard S., Dec. 23, 1975.

Welch, Robert Lynn (Bob), Nov. 3, 1956.

Welch, William Henry, Apr. 8, 1850.

Weld, Theodore Dwight, Nov. 23, 1803.

Weld, Tuffday, Aug. 27, 1943.

Welhaven, Johan Sebastian, Dec. 22, 1807.

Welk, Lawrence, Mar. 11, 1903.

Weller, Peter, Jun. 23, 1947.

Weller, Thomas Huckle, Jun. 15, 1915.

Welles, (Benjamin) Sumner, Oct. 14, 1892.

Wellff, Orson, May 6, 1915; Oct. 30, 1939.

Wellington, Arthur Wellesley (Duke), May 1, 1769; Mar. 12, 1814.

Wells, Henry William Dwight, Dec. 12, 1805.

Wells, H(erbert) G(eorge), Sep. 21, 1866.

Wells, Horace, Jan. 21, 1815.

Wells, Mary, May 13, 1943.

Wells-Barnet, Ida B., Jul. 16, 1862.

Welty, Eudora, Apr. 13, 1909.

Wenceslas: elected King of the Romans, Jun. 10, 1376.

Wendorf, Fred, Apr. 7, 1983.

Wendt, George, Oct. 17, 1948.

Wenner, Jann, Jan. 7, 1947.

Wentworth, Sir Thomas, Apr. 13, 1593.

Werfel, Franz, Sep. 10, 1890.

Wergeland, Henrik Arnold, Jun. 17, 1808.

Werner, Alfred, Dec. 12, 1866.

Werner, Oskar, Nov. 13, 1922.

Werner, Zacharias, Nov. 18, 1768.

Wertheimer, Max, Apr. 15, 1880.

Wertmuller, Lina von Eigg, Aug. 14, 1928.

Wesley, John, Jun. 17, 1703.

Wesleyan University, Dec. 10, 1896.

West Bank, Apr. 3, 1949; Dec. 8, 1987; Jul. 31, 1988.

West Beirut (Lebanon), Sep. 23, 1988.

West, Benjamin, Oct. 10, 1738.

West, Cornel, Jun. 2, 1953.

West, Dottie, Oct. 11, 1932.

West Germany, Apr. 15, 1965.

West Indies Federation: formed Nov. 1, 1964.

West, Jessamyn, Jul. 18, 1902.

West, Mae, Aug. 17, 1892.

West, Morris L., Apr. 26, 1916.

West, Nathanael, Oct. 17, 1903.

West Point (U.S. Military Academy): founded, Mar. 16, 1802; Jul. 4, 1804.

West, Dame Rebecca, Dec. 25, 1892.

West Side Story: premiere, Sep. 26, 1957.

West Virginia Day (West Virginia), Jun. 20.

Western Deep Levels gold mine (South Africa), Sep. 12, 1973.

Western Front (World War I): allied attack, Dec. 14, 1914; Jan. 8, 1915.

Westheimer, Irvin Ferdinand, Sep. 19, 1879.

Westinghouse Electric Corp., Jan. 4, 1983.

Westinghouse, George, Oct. 6, 1846.

Westminster Palace, Jul. 6, 1978.

Westminster, Treaty of, Feb. 9, 1674; Jan. 16, 1756.

Westmoreland, William Childs, Mar. 26, 1914. Apr. 25, 1964.

Weston, Edward, Mar. 24, 1886.

Westphalia, patrons of, Oct. 3.

Westphalia, Peace of, Oct. 24, 1648.

Westwood, Jean, Jul. 14, 1972.

Wexler, Nancy S., Jul. 19, 1945.

Whalley-Kilmer, Joanne, Aug. 25, 1964.

Wharton, Edith, Jan. 24, 1862; May 29, 1921.

Wharton, Joseph, Mar. 3, 1826.

What's My Line?: television debut, Feb. 16, 1950.

Wheatley, Phillis, Dec. 5, 1753.

Wheatstone, Sir Charlff, Feb. 6, 1802.

Wheeler, Burton K., Feb. 27, 1882.

Wheeler-Howard Act, Jun. 18, 1934.

Wheeler, Joseph, Sep. 10, 1836.

Wheeler, William A., Mar. 4, 1877.

Wheelock, Eleazar, Apr. 22, 1711.

Wheelwrights, patron of, Mar. 19.

Whelchel, Lisa, May 29, 1963.

Whipple, George H., Aug. 28, 1878.

Whipple, William, Jan. 14, 1730.

Whistler, James (Abott) McNeill, Jul. 10, 1834.

Whitaker, Forest, Jul. 15, 1961.

Whitaker, Johnny, Dec. 13, 1959.

Whitaker, Lou(is Rodman), May 12, 1957.

White, Andrew Dickson, Nov. 7, 1832.

White, Byron, Mar. 19, 1993.

White, Hetty, Jan. 17, 1917.

White Cane Safety Day (U.S.), Oct. 15.

White Cane Week, National, May intro.

White, Edward Douglass, Nov. 3, 1845.

White, Edward H. II, Nov. 14, 1930, Jun. 3, 1965.

White, E(lwyn) B(rooks), Jul. 11, 1899.

White House: cornerstone laid, Oct. 13, 1792; musicales, Apr. 3, 1903.

White, Jaleel, Nov. 27, 1976.

White, Kevin Hagan, Sep. 25, 1929.

White, Mark Wells, Jr., Mar. 17, 1940.

White Mountains (New Hampshire): thorium found, Dec. 2, 1962.

White, Patrick, May 28, 1912.

White, Paul Dudley, Jun. 6, 1886.

White, Randy Lee, Jan. 15, 1953.

White, Reggie, Dec. 19, 1961.

White, Robert M., Oct. 11, 1961.

White, Ryan, Dec. 6, 1971.

White Russian government, Jan. 30, 1920.

White Shirt Day (Michigan), Feb. 11.

White Slave Traffic Act, Jun. 25, 1910.

White, Stanford, Nov. 9, 1853.

White, T(erence) H(anbury), May 29, 1906; Aug. 25, 1958.

White, Theodore H., May 6, 1915.

White, Walter Francis, Jul. 1, 1893.

White, William, Feb. 3, 1897.

White, William Allen, Feb. 10, 1868.

Whitefield, George, Dec. 27, 1714.

Whitehead, Alfred North, Feb. 15, 1861.

Whitehead, Donald Ford, Apr. 8, 1908.

Whitehead, Robert, Jan. 3, 1823.

Whiteman, Paul, Mar. 28, 1891.

Whitewater, Mar. 11, 1996.

Whitfield, Malvin, Dec. 30, 1954.

Whiting, Margaret, Jul. 22, 1924.

Whitlam, Gough: inaugurated, Dec. 5, 1972.

Whitman, Marcus, Sep. 4, 1802; Sep. 1, 1836.

Whitman, Stuart, Feb. 1, 1926.

Whitman, Walt, May 31, 1819.

Whitmore, Jamff (Allcn), Oct. 1, 1921.

Whitney, Dwight Morrow, Jan. 11, 1873.

Whitney, Eli, Dec. 8, 1765; Mar. 4, 1794; patents cotton gin, Mar. 14, 1794.

Whitney, Gertrude Vanderbilt, Apr. 19, 1877.

Whitney, John Hay, Aug. 17, 1904.

Whitney, William Collins, Jul. 5, 1841.

Whittaker, Charles, Mar. 19, 1957.

Whitten-Brown, A., Jun. 15, 1919.

Whittier, John Greenleaf, Dec. 17, 1807.

Whittle, Frank, Jun. 1, 1930.

Who's Afraid of the Big Bad Wolf, May 25, 1933.

Why Marry?, Nov. 1, 1917.

Whymper, Edward, Jul. 14, 1865.

Wicker, Thomas Grey *(Tom),* Jun. 18, 1926.

Wickman, Carl Eric, Aug. 7, 1887.

Widener, Paul Arrell Brown, Nov. 3, 1834.

Widmark, Richard, Dec. 26, 1914.

Wido of Spoleto (Holy Roman Emperor), Feb. 21, 891.

Wieland, Christoph Martin, Sep. 5, 1733.

Wieland, Heinrich Otto, Jun. 4, 1877.

Wiener, Norbert, Nov. 26, 1894.

Wiesbaden (Germany), Jan. 20, 1981.

Wieschaus, Eric F., Jun. 8, 1947.

Wiest, Dianne, Mar. 28, 1948.

Wiffel, Elie(zer), Sep. 30, 1928.

Wiffel, Torsten N., Jun. 3, 1924.

Wiesenthal, Simon, Dec. 31, 1908.

Wiggin, Kate (Douglas), Sep. 28, 1856.

Wigglesworth, Michael, Oct. 18, 1631.

Wigner, Eugene Paul, Nov. 17, 1902.

Wijetunge, Dingiri Banda, Apr. 23, 1993.

Wilberforce, William, Aug. 24, 1759.

Wilbur, Richard Purdy, Mar. 1, 1921.

Wilcox, Larry Dec., Aug. 8, 1947.

wild animals, patron of, Feb. 3.

The Wild One: premiere, Dec. 30, 1953.

Wilde, Cornel(ius Louis), Oct. 13, 1918.

Wilde, Oscar, Oct. 16, 1854; Jan. 3, 1895.

Wilder, Alec, Feb. 16, 1907.

Wilder, Billy, Jun. 22, 1906.

Wilder, Gene, Jun. 11, 1935.

Wilder, Laura Ingalls, Feb. 7, 1867.

Wilder, L. Douglas, Jan. 17, 1931.

Wilder, Robert Ingersoll, Jan. 25, 1901.

Wilder, Thornton, Apr. 17, 1897.

Wilderness, Battle of the: ends, Jul. 9, 1755.

Wilderness Society, Apr. 30, 1937.

Wilding, Michael, Jul. 23, 1912.

Wildlife Week, National, Mar. intro.

Wiley, Harvey W., Oct. 18, 1844.

Wilhelm, Hellmut, Dec. 10, 1905.

Wilhelmina (Queen of the Netherlands), Aug. 31, 1880; Sep. 6, 1898; abdicates, Sep. 4, 1948.

Wilhemshaven (Germany), Jan. 27, 1943.

Wilkes, Charles, Apr. 3, 1798.

Wilkins, Dominique, Jan. 12, 1960.

Wilkins, Sir George Hubert, Oct. 31, 1888.

Wilkins, Maurice Hugh Frederick, Dec. 15, 1916.

Wilkins, Roy, Aug. 30, 1901.

Wilkinson, Sir Geoffrey, Jul. 14, 1921.

Wilkens, Lenny (Leonard Randolph), Oct. 28, 1937.

Will, George F., May 4, 1941.

Willander, Mats, Aug. 22, 1964.

Willard, Daniel, Jan. 28, 1861.

Willard, Emma, Feb. 23, 1787.

Willard, Frances, Sep. 28, 1839.

Willard, Jffs, Apr. 5, 1915; Jul. 4, 1919.

Willard Memorial Day, Frances E. (U.S.), Feb. 17.

Willebrands, Johannes, Sep. 4, 1909.

Willem-Alexander Claus, Prince (Netherlands), Apr. 27, 1967.

William I (England), Dec. 25, 1066.

William I (Germany), Mar. 9, 1888.

William I (Prince of Orange), Apr. 24, 1533; assassinated, Jul. 10, 1584.

William I (Prussia), Mar. 22, 1797; Jan. 2, 1861; Jan. 18, 1871.

William I (Scotland), Aug. 24, 1772.

William I (Sicily), May 28, 1156.

William II (England): killed, Aug. 2, 1100.

William II (Germany), Jan. 27, 1859; Jun. 15, 1888; Mar. 18, 1890; forced to aWicate, Nov. 9, 1918; Jan. 23, 1920.

William II (Netherlands), Dec. 6, 1792.

William II (Prince of Orange), Mar. 14, 1647.

William II (Sicily): dies, Nov. 18, 1189.

William III (England), Nov. 14, 1650; Apr. 11, 1677; Jul. 12, 1690; Apr. 3, 1696; diff, Mar. 8, 1702.

William III (Netherlands), Feb. 19, 1817.

William III (Prince of Orange), Jul. 12, 1690.

William IV (England), Jun. 26, 1830; dies, Jun. 20, 1837.

William the Lion (King of Scotland), Dec. 9, 1165; Dec. 5, 1189; dies, Dec. 4, 1214.

William and Mary, College of: chartered, Feb. 8, 1693.

William and Mary (England), Feb. 13, 1689.

William of Normandy, Sep. 28, 1066.

William P. Frye: sunk, Jan. 28, 1915.

William, Prince (Britain), Jun. 21, 1982.

William (Prince of Denmark): King of Greece, Mar. 30, 1863.

Williams, Andy, Dec. 3, 1930.

Williams, Betty, May 22, 1943.

Williams, Billy Dee, Apr. 6, 1937.

Williams, Cindy, Aug. 22, 1948.

Williams, Daniel Hale, Jan. 18, 1858.

Williams, Dar, Apr. 19, 1967.

Williams, Deniece, Jun. 3, 1951.

Williams, Edward Bennett, May 31, 1920.

Williams, Eric (Eustace), Sep. 25, 1911.

Williams, Esther, Aug. 8, 1923.

Williams, Sir George, Oct. 11, 1821; Jun. 6, 1844.

Williams, G(erhard) Mennen, Feb. 23, 1911.

Williams, Hank, Sep. 15, 1923.

Williams, Hank, Jr., May 26, 1949.

Williams, Harrison, May 1, 1981; Mar. 11, 1982.

Williams, Jesse Lynch, Nov. 1, 1917.

Williams, Joe, Dec. 12, 1918.

Williams, John, Feb. 8, 1932.

Williams, John Bell, Dec. 4, 1918.

Williams, Keith, Jan. 1 1998.

Williams, Mary Lou, May 8, 1910.

Williams, Paul, Sep. 19, 1940.

Williams, Ralph Vaughan, Oct. 12, 1872; Oct. 13, 1872.

Williams, Robin, Jul. 21, 1952.

Williams, Roger: banished from Massachusetts, Sep. 13, 1635; Mar. 24, 1644.

Williams, Ted, Aug. 31, 1918; .406 batting average, Sep. 28, 1941.

Williams, Tennessee, Mar. 26, 1911; Mar. 31, 1945; Mar. 24, 1955; Mar. 10, 1959.

Williams, Terry, May 5, 1973.

Williams, Tex, Aug. 23, 1917.

Williams, Treat, Dec. 1, 1951.

Williams, Vanessa, Mar. 18, 1963.

Williams, Venus, Jun. 17, 1980.

Williams, Wayne B., Jul. 17, 1981; Feb. 27, 1982.

Williams, William Carlos, Sep. 17, 1883.

Williamson, Alexander William, May 1, 1824.

Williamson, James S., Nov. 30, 1949.

Williamson, Nicol, Sep. 14, 1938.

Willis, Bruce, Mar. 19, 1955.

Willkie, Wendell Lewis, Feb. 18, 1892.

Willoch, Kaare Isaachson, Oct. 3, 1928.

Wills, Chill, Jul. 18, 1902.

Wills, Garry, May 22, 1934.

Wills, Helen, Oct. 6, 1905.

Willson, Meredith, May 18, 1902; Dec. 19, 1957.

Willstatter, Richard M., Aug. 13, 1872.

Willys, John North, Aug. 25, 1873.

Wilmut, Ian, Jul. 5, 1996.

Wilson, Alexander, Jul. 6, 1766.

Wilson, Bill, Jun. 10, 1935.
Wilson, Brian Douglas, Jun. 20, 1942.
Wilson, Carl Dean, Dec. 21, 1946.
Wilson, Charles Erwin, Jul. 18, 1890.
Wilson, Charles T. R., Feb. 14, 1869.
Wilson, David, Jan. 16, 1987.
Wilson, Dennis, Dec. 1, 1941.
Wilson, Don, Sep. 1, 1900.
Wilson, Earl, May 3, 1907.
Wilson, Edith, Oct. 15, 1872.
Wilson, Edmund, May 8, 1895.
Wilson, Edward O., Jun. 10, 1929.
Wilson, Ellen Louise, May 15, 1860.
Wilson, Flip, Dec. 8, 1933.
Wilson, Harold, Mar. 11, 1916;
     inaugurated, Oct. 16, 1964; Apr.
     5, 1976.
Wilson, Henry, Feb. 16, 1812; Mar. 4,
     1869; murdered, Jun. 22, 1922.
Wilson, Jackie, Jun. 9, 1932.
Wilson, James, Sep. 14, 1742.
Wilson, James Harrison, Sep. 2,
     1837.
Wilson, Kemmons, Jan. 5, 1913.
Wilson, Nancy, Feb. 20, 1937.
Wilson, Peter B., Aug. 23, 1933.
Wilson, Robert, Jan. 10, 1936; Nov.
     21, 1976.
Wilson, Sloan, May 8, 1920; Jul. 18,
     1955.
Wilson, William Griffith, Nov. 26,
     1895.
Wilson, William Julius, Dec. 20, 1935.
Wilson, Woodrow, Dec. 28, 1856;
     inaugurated, Mar. 4, 1913; Jan.
     22, 1917; second term, Mar. 4,
     1917; Apr. 2, 1917; Jan. 8, 1918;
     Jan. 25, 1919; Feb. 5, 1919;
     paralyzed, Sep. 26, 1919.
Winchell, Walter, Apr. 7, 1897.
Winchester, Jesse, May 17, 1944.
Winchester, patron of, Jul. 15.
Winckelmann, Johann Joachim, Dec.
     9, 1717.
Windaus, Adolf, Dec. 25, 1876.
Winfrey, Oprah, Jan. 29, 1954.
Windmill Day (Netherlands), May
     intro.
wine growers, patron of, Jun. 3.
wine industry, patron of, Jan. 22.
Winebrenner, John, Mar. 25, 1797.
Winfield, David Mark *(Dave)*, Oct. 3,
     1951.
Winfield, Paul Edward, May 22, 1941.

Wingate, Orde Charles, Feb. 26,
     1903.
Winger, Debra, May 17, 1955.
Wingti, Paias: inaugurated, Nov. 21,
     1985.
Winkler, Henry (Franklin), Oct. 30,
     1945.
Winnie-the-Pooh: published, Oct. 14,
     1926.
Winninger, Charles, May 26, 1884.
Winningham, Mare, May 6, 1959.
Winslow, Edward, Oct. 18, 1595.
Winsor, Justin, Jan. 2, 1831.
Winter, Alex, Jul. 17, 1965.
Winter, Edgar Holand, Dec. 28,
     1946.
Winter, Ella, Mar. 17, 1898.
Winter, John Dawson, III *(Johnny)*,
     Feb. 23, 1944.
Winter Olympics, VIII, Feb. 18, 1960.
Winter Olympics, XI, Feb. 3, 1972.
Winter Olympics, XII, Feb. 4, 1976.
Winter Palace (St. Petersburg), Mar.
     13, 1917.
Winter, Paul, Aug. 31, 1939.
winter solstice, Dec. intro.
Winter War, Nov. 30, 1939.
Winter, William Forrest, Feb. 21,
     1923.
Winters, Jonathan, Nov. 11, 1925.
Winters, Shelley, Aug. 18, 1922.
Winther, Christian, Jul. 29, 1796.
Winthrop, John, Jan. 12, 1588.
Winwood, Steve *(Stevie)*, May 12,
     1948.
wireless telegraph: patented, Jul. 31,
     1897; Mar. 27, 1899; first
     message, Dec. 21, 1902;
     newspaper service begins
     between England and U.S., Oct.
     17, 1907.
wireless telephone service: between
     Ireland and Canada, Mar. 20,
     1919.
Wisconsin (U.S.): admitted to Union,
     May 29, 1848; adoption of
     direct primary, May 23, 1903.
Wise, Isaac Mayer, Mar. 29, 1819.
Wise, Robert (Earl), Sep. 10, 1914.
Wise, Stephen Samuel, Mar. 17,
     1874.
Wiseman, Frederick, Jan. 1, 1930.
Wisniowiecki, Michael (Poland), Jun.
     19, 1669.

Wister, Owen, Jul. 14, 1869.
witchcraft and sorcery: papal bull
     against, Dec. 5, 1484.
Withers, Bill, Jul. 4, 1938.
Witherspoon, John, Feb. 5, 1723.
Witkin, Joel-Peter, Sep. 13, 1939.
Witt, Jamal Mahuad, elected, Jul. 12,
     1998.
Witte, Edwin Emil, Jan. 4, 1887.
Witte, Count Sergei Yulievich, Jun.
     29, 1849.
Wittenmyer, Annie Turner, Aug. 26,
     1827.
Wittgenstein, Ludwig Josef Johann,
     Apr. 26, 1889.
Wittig, Georg, Jun. 16, 1897.
Witwatersrand, University of:
     established, Oct. 4, 1922.
Wives Feast, Feb. 2.
The Wiz: premiere, Jan. 5, 1975.
Wladyslaw I, *The Short* (Poland), Jan.
     20, 1320.
Wodehouse, Sir P(elham)
     G(renville), Oct. 15, 1881.
Wojtyla, Karol (Cardinal). *See*: John
     Paul 11 (pope).
Wolcott, Oliver, Nov. 20, 1725.
Wold, Emma, Sep. 29, 1871.
Wolf, Howlin', Jun. 10, 1910.
Wolf, Hugo, Mar. 13, 1860.
Wolf, Peter, Mar. 7, 1946.
Wolfe, James, Jan. 2, 1727.
Wolfe, Thomas (Clayton), Oct. 3,
     1900.
Wolfe, Tom, Mar. 2, 1931; Aug. 19,
     1968.
Wolff-Bekker, Elisabeth, Jul. 24,
     1738.
Wolfman Jack, Jan. 21, 1938.
Wollaston, William Hyde, Aug. 6,
     1766.
Wollenstein, Albrecht Eusebius
     Wenzel von, Sep. 24, 1583.
women in labor, patron of, Jul. 26;
     Aug. 31; Nov. 6.
women, patron of, Jul. 20.
women pilots, Jul. 31, 1991.
Women's Air Force, Jun. 12, 1948.
Women's Army Corps, Jun. 12, 1948,
     Oct. 20, 1978.
Women's Army Corps, patroness of,
     Jan. 3.
Womens' Clubs Day, General
     Federation of, Apr. intro.

Women's Clubs, General Federation of: founded, Mar. 20, 1890.

Womens' Clubs Week, General Federation of, Apr. intro.

Women's Day (Afghanistan), Mar. 8.

Women's Day (Azerbaijan), Mar. 8.

Women's Day (Cape Verde Islands), Mar. 8.

Women's Day (China), Mar. 8.

Women's Day (Ginea-Bissau), Mar. 8.

Women's Day, International, Mar. intro.

Women's Holiday (Kyrgyzstan), Mar. 8.

Women's Day (Mauretania), Mar. 8.

Women's Day (Nepal), Mar. 8.

Women's Day (People's Republic of Mozambique), Apr. 7.

Women's Day (Tunisia), Aug. 13.

Women's Equality Day (U.S.), Aug. 26.

Women's National Basketball Association (WNBA) Jun. 21, 1997.

women's rights convention: first, Jul. 19, 1848.

women's suffrage: Territory of Wyoming, Dec. 10, 1869.

Wonder, Stevie, May 13, 1950.

Wong, Bradley D., Oct. 4, 1962.

Wong, George S. K., May 27, 1986.

Wonsan, Mar. 15, 1951; air and sea attack, Jul. 12, 1953.

Woo, Roh Tae, Nov. 16, 1995.

Wood, Edward, Apr. 16, 1881; Mar. 5, 1931.

Wood, Elijah, Jan. 28, 1981.

Wood, Grant, Feb. 13, 1892.

Wood, Sir Henry Joseph, Mar. 3, 1869.

Wood, Jethrow, Mar. 16, 1774.

Wood, Leonard, Oct. 9, 1860.

Wood, Natalie, Jul. 20, 1938.

Wood, Robert Elkington, Jun. 13, 1879.

Wood, Ron(ald), Jun. 1, 1947.

Woodcock, George, Oct. 20, 1904.

Woodcock, Leonard, Feb. 15, 1911; May 22, 1970.

Woodhouse, Barbara Blackburn, May 9, 1910.

Woodhull, Victoria, Sep. 23, 1838.

Woodiwiss, Kathleen E., Jun. 3, 1939.

Woodruff, Judy Carline, Nov. 20, 1946.

Woods, Donald, Dec. 2, 1904.

Woods, George D(avid), Jul. 27, 1901.

Woods, Granville T., Jan. 30, 1856.

Woods, James, Apr. 18, 1947.

Woods, Rose Mary, Dec. 26, 1917.

Woods, Tiger, Dec. 30, 1975; U.S. Amateur Golf Tournament, Aug. 25, 1996; Aug. 28, 1994; Masters Tournament, Apr. 13, 1997.

Woodson, Carter Godwin, Dec. 19, 1875; Jul. 13, 1970.

Woodson, Rod, Mar. 10, 1965.

Woodstock Music and Art Fair: begins, Aug. 15, 1969.

Woodard, Alfre, Nov. 8, 1953.

Woodward, Joanne, Feb. 27, 1930.

Woodward, Robert Burns, Apr. 10, 1917.

Woodward, Robert Upshur, Mar. 26, 1943.

wool combers, patron of, Feb. 3.

Woolf, Virginia, Jan. 25, 1882.

Woollcott, Alexander, Jan. 19, 1887.

Woolley, Sir Charles Leonard, Apr. 17, 1880.

Woolley, Monty, Aug. 17, 1888.

Woolworth, Frank Winfield, Apr. 13, 1852.

Wopat, Tom, Sep. 9, 1951.

Worcester, Battle of, Sep. 3, 1651.

Worden, Alfred M., Jul. 26, 1971.

Wordsworth, William, Apr. 7, 1770.

work for interracial justice and harmony, patron of, Nov. 3.

Workers' Day, May 1.

Workers' Party of Ethiopia, Sep. 10, 1984.

Workmen's Compensation Act: India, Mar. 5, 1923.

Works Progress Administration, Apr. 8, 1934.

works for the spreading of the faith, patron of, Dec. 3.

World Conference on Women, Sep. 4, 1995.

World Council of Churches, Aug. 22, 1948; Feb. 13, 1970.

World Development Information Day, Oct. 23. 1079

World Environment Day, Jun. 5.

World Food Day, Oct. 16.

World Food Program, Jan. 6, 1998

World Health Day, Apr. 7.

World Health Organization, Apr. 7, 1948; Nov. 15, 1993.

World, Maritime Day (UN Member Countries), Mar. 17.

World Meteorological Day (UN Member Countries), Mar. 23.

World Meteorological Organization: established, Mar. 23, 1950.

World Poetry Day, Oct. 15.

World Series, Sep. 14, 1994.

World Summit for Children, Sep. 30, 1990.

World Telecommunications Day, May 17.

World Trade Center Building, bombed, Feb. 26, 1993.

World Trade Organization, Jan. 1, 1995.

World Understanding Month, Feb. intro.

The Worldly Philosophers: published, Jul. 29, 1953.

Worley, Jo Anne, Sep. 6, 1937.

Worms, City of, Jan. 18, 1074.

Worms, Concordat of, Sep. 23, 1122.

Worms, Diet of, Apr. 17, 1541.

Worms, Edict of, May 26, 1521.

Worms, Synod of, Jan. 24, 1076.

Worship and Doctrine Measure (Church of England), Dec. 4, 1974.

Worshipful Company of Parish Clerks of the City of London, patron of, Dec. 6.

Worsley, Lorne (Gump), May 14, 1929.

Wouk, Herman, May 27, 1915.

Wounded Knee, Battle of, Dec. 29, 1890.

Wounded Knee (South Dakota), Feb. 27, 1973; Apr. 5, 1973; siege of, May 8, 1973.

Wrangel, Baron Petr Nikolayevich, Aug. 27, 1878.

Wrangel, Baron von, Dec. 29, 1796.

Wray, Fay, Sep. 10, 1907.

Wren, Sir Christopher, Oct. 20, 1632.

Wreyford, Ronald George, Nov. 9, 1897.

Wright, Sir Almroth E., Aug. 10, 1861.

Wright, James Claud *(Jim),* Dec. 22, 1922.

Wright Brothers, Dec. 17, 1903.

Wright Brothers Day (U.S.), Dec. 17.

Wright, Chalky, Nov. 20, 1942.

Wright, Frances (Fanny), Sep. 6, 1795.

Wright, Frank Lloyd, Jun. 8, 1867; Oct. 21, 1959.

Wright, Gary, Apr. 26, 1943.

Wright, Jim, resigns, May 31, 1989.

Wright, Orville, Aug. 19, 1871.

Wright, Richard, Sep. 4, 1908.

Wright, Robert, Dec. 3, 1953.

Wright, Robin, Apr. 8, 1966.

Wright, Teresa, Oct. 27, 1918.

Wright, Wilbur, Apr. 16, 1867.

Wrigley Field, Aug. 8, 1988.

Wrigley, P(hilip) K(night), Dec. 5, 1894.

Wrigley, William, Jr., Sep. 30, 1861.

Wu, Chien-Shiung, May 31, c.1912.

Wu, Harry (Hongda), Feb. 8, 1937.

Wundt, Wilhelm, Aug. 16, 1832.

Wurlitzer, Rudolph, Jan. 31, 1831.

Wyatt, James, Aug. 3, 1746.

Wyatt, Jane, Aug. 13, 1912.

Wycliffe, John, Dec. 31, 1320; Nov. 5, 1414; Feb. 22, 1418.

Wyeth, Andrew, Jul. 12, 1917.

Wyeth, N(ewell) C(onvers), Oct. 22, 1882.

Wyle, Noah, Jun. 4, 1971.

Wyler, William, Jul. 1, 1902.

Wylie, Philip, May 12, 1902.

Wyman, William George *(Bill),* Oct. 24, 1941.

Wyman, Jane, Jan. 4, 1914.

Wynette, Tammy, May 4, 1942.

Wynn, Ed, Nov. 9, 1886.

Wynn, Keenan, Jul. 27, 1916.

Wyoming, May 30, 1848; admitted to Union, Jul. 11, 1890; raises drinking age, Jul. 1, 1988.

Wyoming Day (Wyoming), Dec. 10.

Wyoming, Territory of: women's suffrage, Dec. 10, 1869.

Wyss, Johann Rudolf, Mar. 4, 1782.

Wyszynski, Stephen (Cardinal), Aug. 3, 1901; Sep. 28, 1953, Jan. 8, 1966.

X

X-15 rocket plane, Oct. 11, 1961.

X-ray treatment: breast cancer, Jan. 29, 1896.

xerographic image: first, Oct. 22, 1938.

Xiaoping, Deng, dies, Feb. 19, 1997.

Y

Yablans, Frank, Aug. 27, 1935.

Yablonski, Joseph A., Jan. 5, 1970; Sep. 11, 1975.

Yahya Khan, Agha Muhammad, Feb. 4, 1917.

Yale, Elihu, Apr. 5, 1649.

Yale, Linus, Apr. 5, 1821.

Yale University, Oct. 9, 1701; Dec. 10, 1896; Nov. 14, 1968.

Yalow, Rosalyn, Jul. 19, 1921.

Yalta Conference: begins, Feb. 4, 1945; ends, Feb. 11, 1945.

Yamagata Aritomo, Jun. 14, 1838.

Yamaguchi, Kristi, Jul. 12, 1971.

Yamamoto, Isoroku, Apr. 4, 1884.

Yamasaki, Minoru, Dec. 1, 1912.

Yamashita, Tomoyuki, Nov. 8, 1885; Dec. 7, 1945.

Yamato: sunk, Apr. 7, 1945.

Yandarbiyev, Zelimkhan, May 27, 1996.

Yang, Chen Ning, Sep. 22, 1922.

Yangtze, War Lord of, Apr. 21, 1922.

Yankee Clipper, Jun. 28, 1939.

Yankee Stadium: opens, Apr. 18, 1923.

Yankovic, Weird Al, Oct. 23, 1959.

Yaobang, Hu, Apr. 15, 1989.

Yarborough, Glenn, Jan. 12, 1930.

Yarmouth, Jan. 19, 1915.

Yarmuk, Battle of, Aug. 20, 636.

Yarrow, Peter, May 31, 1938.

Yastrzemski, Carl, Aug. 22, 1939.

Yates, Peter, Jul. 24, 1929.

Yat-sen, Sun, Mar. 12, 1866.

Yazykov, Nikolay, Mar. 16, 1803.

Yeager, Charles Elwood *(Chuck),* Feb. 13, 1923, Jun. 10, 1948.

Yeager, Jeanna, Dec. 23, 1986.

Yeager, Stephen Wayne *(Steve),* Nov. 24, 1948.

year, beginning of the, Jan. intro.; Mar. intro.

Yearwood, Trisha, Sep. 19, 1964.

Yeats, William Butler, Jun. 13, 1865.

Yeh, George K(ung) C(hao), Sep. 12, 1904.

Yellowstone National Park: established, Mar. 1, 1872.

Yeltsin, Boris: Feb. 1, 1931; Nov. 11, 1987; elected, May 29, 1990; elected, Jun. 12, 1991; resistance against coup, Aug. 19, 1991; nuclear arsenals agreement, Jun. 16, 1992; Strategic Arms Reduction Treaty (START II), Jan. 3, 1993; peace plan for Chechnya, Mar. 31, 1996; reelected, Jul. 3, 1996.

Yemen, Apr. 28, 1964.

Yemen, People's Democratic Republic of, Nov. 30, 1970; Jan. 13, 1986.

Yemen People's Republic, South, Nov. 30, 1967.

Yemn, Republic of: formation of, May 23, 1990.

Yen Chia-kan: inaugurated, Apr. 6, 1975.

Yerba Buena, Jan. 3, 1847.

Yerby, Frank (Garvin), Sep. 5, 1916.

Yerkes, Robert Merans, May 26, 1876.

Yevtushenko, Yevgeny Aleksandrovich, Jul. 18, 1933.

Yew, Lee Kuan, Sep. 16, 1923; Nov. 26, 1990.

Yip, Yip, Yaphank: premiere, Aug. 19, 1918.

YMCA: organized, Jun. 6, 1844.

Yoakam, Dwight, Oct. 23, 1956.

Yokohama (Japan), Sep. 1, 1923; Apr. 18, 1942.

Yokoi, Shoichi, Jan. 24, 1972.

Yombi-Opango, Joachim, Apr. 3, 1977.

Yongchong (Korea), Sep. 6, 1950.

York, Alvin Cullum, Dec. 13, 1887.

York, Richard Allen *(Dick),* Sep. 4, 1928.

York, Michael, Mar. 27, 1942.

York, Parliament of, May 2, 1322.

York, Susannah, Jan. 9, 1941.

Yorktown, Oct. 19, 1781.

Yoshihito (Emperor of Japan): Aug. 30, 1879; dies, Dec. 25, 1926.

Yost, Charles W(oodruff), Nov. 6, 1907.

Yothers, Tina, May 5, 1973.

You Bet Your Life: television debut, Oct. 5, 1950.

Youman Nabi (Guyana), Jan. 19.

Youmans, Vincent (Millie), Sep. 27, 1898; Mar. 11, 1925.

Young, Andrew, Mar. 12, 1932; resigns, Aug. 15, 1979.

Young, Brigham, Jun. 1, 1801; Apr. 6, 1868.

Young Child, Week of the, Apr. intro.

young children, patron of, Mar. 7.

Young, Coleman A(lexander), May 24, 1918.

Young, Cy, Mar. 29, 1867; May 5, 1904.

Young, Ella Flagg, Jan. 15, 1845.

Young, Gig, Nov. 4, 1917.

young girls, patron of, Jan. 21.

Young, John (Watts), Sep. 24, 1930; Mar. 23, 1965; Jul. 21, 1966; Apr. 21, 1972, Apr. 27, 1972.

Young, Lester, Aug. 27, 1909.

Young, Loretta Gretchen, Jan. 6, 1913.

Young Men's Hebrew Association: first meeting, Mar. 22, 1847.

Young, Milton R., Dec. 6, 1897.

Young, Neil, Nov. 12, 1945.

Young, Robert, Feb. 22, 1907.

Young, Sean, Nov. 20, 1959.

Young, Sheila, Oct. 14, 1950.

Young, Steve, Oct. 11, 1961.

Young, Thomas, Jun. 13, 1773.

Young Turks, Jan. 23, 1913.

Young, Whitney Moore, Jr., Jul. 31, 1921.

Younger, Thomas Coleman *(Cole)*, Jan. 15, 1844.

Your Hit Parade, Apr. 20, 1935.

Yousef, Mohammed: inaugurated, Mar. 19, 1963.

Yousef, Ramzi Ahmed, Nov. 12, 1997; Jan. 8, 1998.

Youth Activities Month, Sep. intro.

Youth Art Month, National, Mar. intro.

Youth Day (Angola), Apr. 14.

Youth Day (Cameroon), Feb. 11.

Youth Day (Congo), Feb. 8.

Youth Day (Democratic Republic of the Congo), Oct. 14.

Youth Day (Kiribati), Aug. 4.

Youth Day (Oklahoma), Mar. intro.

Youth Day (Popular Republic of Benin), Apr. 1.

Youth Day (Taiwan), Mar. intro.

Youth Day (Tunisia), Jun. 2.

Youth Day (Zambia), Mar. intro.

Youth Day (Zambia), Mar. 8.

Youth and Martyrs' Day (Taiwan), Mar. 29.

Youth and Sports Day (Cyprus, Turkey), May 19.

Youth's Companion, Sep. 8, 1892.

Ypres, First Battle of: opens, Oct. 19, 1914.

Ypres, Second Battle of, Apr. 22, 1915; May 25, 1915.

Yuan Shih-K'ai, Feb. 15, 1912; Mar. 10, 1912.

Yugoslav Republic Day (Yugoslavia), Apr. 7.

Yugoslav War Crimes Tribunal, Nov. 16, 1995.

Yugoslavia: formation, Jul. 20, 1917; Apr. 20, 1920; Oct. 3, 1929; Mar. 24, 1941; German invasion, Apr. 6, 1941; Apr. 17, 1941; National Front wins elections, Nov. 11, 1945; Federal People's Republic of, Nov. 29, 1945, constitution, Jan. 31 1946 expelled from Cominform, Jun. 28, 1948; Socialist Federal Republic of, Apr. 7, 1963, Jan. 31, 1968; Feb. 6, 1970; independence of, Feb. 29, 1992; Serbia and Montenegro, Apr. 17, 1992; voted out of United Nations, Sep. 22, 1992; UN ban on weapons to, Mar. 31, 1998.

Yugov, Anton, Nov. 19, 1962.

Yukawa, Hideki, Jan. 23, 1907.

Yukon Territory: formed, Jun. 13, 1898.

Yule, Dec. intro.

Yusef, Pasha of Tripoli, May 14, 1801.

Yutang, Lin, Oct. 10, 1895.

YWCA: founded, Dec. 7, 1906.

YWCA Day, World, Apr. intro.

YWCA Teen Week, National, Oct. intro.

YWCA Week, National, Apr. intro.

Yzerman, Stevie, May 9, 1965.

Z

Z, May 23, 1969.

Z-zero sub-nuclear particle, Jun. 1, 1983.

Zablocki, Clement John, Nov. 18, 1912.

Zaharias, Babe Didrickson, Jun. 26, 1914.

Zahn, Paula, Feb. 24, 1956.

Zaire, Republic of (Congo), Oct. 27, 1971; Apr. 10, 1977; May 11, 1978. *See also*: Congo, Belgian; Congo, Democratic Republic of; Congo Free State.

Zakharov, Gennadi, Sep. 30, 1986.

Zakrzewska, Marie E., Sep. 6, 1820.

Zaldivar, Fulgencio Batista y, Jan. 16, 1901.

Zale, Tony, Jul. 19, 1940; Sep. 21, 1948.

Zambia, Republic of: independence, Dec. 31, 1963; independence, Oct. 24, 1964; Feb. 25, 1972.

Zamenhof, Ludwik Lazanz, Dec. 15, 1859.

Zanaibar, Feb. 25, 1885.

Zanardi, Alex, Oct. 23, 1966.

Zane, Billy, Feb. 24, 1966.

Zangara, Giuseppe, Feb. 15, 1933.

Zanuck, Darryl F(rancis), Sep. 5, 1902.

Zanzibar, Mar. 10, 1862; British protectorate, Nov. 4, 1890; self-government, Jun. 24, 1963; independence, Dec. 10, 1963; admitted to UN, Dec. 16, 1963; Jan. 12, 1964; Feb. 23, 1964; Apr. 26, 1964.

Zanzibar Revolution Day (Tanzania), Jan. 12.

Zapata, Emiliano, Aug. 8, 1883.

Zapatista National Liberation Army, Jan. 1, 1994; Mar. 2, 1994.

Zappa, Francis Vincent, Jr. *(Frank),* Dec. 21, 1940.

Zaragoza, Ignacio (General), May 5, 1867.

Zatopek, Emil, Nov. 19, 1922.

Zebon, Warren, Jan. 24, 1947.

Zedillo, Ernesto, (Ponce de Le n), Dec. 27, 1951; Aug. 21, 1994.

Zeeman, Pieter, May 25, 1865.

Zefflrelli, Franco, Feb. 12, 1923.

Zemeckis, Robert, May 14, 1951.

Zemin, Jiang, Aug. 17, 1926; elected, Mar. 27, 1993.

Zemstous (Russian provincial assemblies), Jan. 13, 1864.

Zeppelin, Count Ferdinand von, Jul. 8, 1838; Jun. 22, 1910.

Zeppelins (German), May 31, 1915.

Zernike, Frits, Jul. 16, 1888.

Zeroul, Liamine, reelected, Nov. 16, 1995.

Zesen, Philipp von, Oct. 8, 1619.

Zhao Ziyang, Jan. 16, 1987.

Zhdanov, Andrei Alexandrovich, Feb. 14, 1896.

Zhelov, Zhelyu, Aug. 1, 1990.

Zhirinovsky, Vladimir, Apr. 26, 1946.

Zhivkov, Todor, Sep. 7, 1911; Nov. 19, 1962; Nov. 10, 1989.

Zia ul-Haq, Mohammad, Aug. 12, 1924; Jul. 5, 1977.

Ziegfeld, Florenz, Mar. 21, 1869.

Ziegfeld Follies, Jul. 8, 1907; Jul. 22, 1944.

Ziegler, Karl, Nov. 26, 1898.

Zigler, Edward, Mar. 1, 1930.

Zimbabwe, May 31, 1979; independence, Apr. 17, 1980.

Zimbabwe African National Union, Mar. 4, 1975; Apr. 4, 1975.

Zimbalist, Efrem, Apr. 9, 1889.

Zimbalist, Efrem, Jr., Nov. 30, 1923.

Zimbalist, Stephanie, Oct. 8, 1956.

Zimmerman, Paul Lionel, Oct. 23, 1932.

Zindel, Paul, May 15, 1936.

Zingarelli, Nicola Antonio, Apr. 4, 1752.

Zinkernagel, Rolf M., Jan. 6, 1944.

Zinn, Walter Henry, Dec. 10, 1906.

Zinnemann, Fred, Apr. 29, 1907.

Zinoviev, Grigori Evsevich, Sep. 11, 1883.

Zinser, Elizabeth, Mar. 13, 1988.

Zionism, Nov. 10, 1975.

zircon, Dec. intro.

Zitkala-Sa (Gertrude Bonnin), Feb. 22, 1876.

zloty: polish currency, Jan. 23, 1924.

Zmed, Adrian, Mar. 14, 1954.

Zoeller, Fuzzy, Nov. 11, 1951.

Zog (King of Albania): abdicates, Apr. 8, 1939; Jan. 2, 1946.

Zola, Emile, Apr. 2, 1840; Jan. 13, 1898; Jul. 12, 1906.

Zond 6, Nov. 17, 1968.

Zorba the Greek: published, Apr. 15, 1953.

Zorinsky, Edward, Nov. 11, 1928.

Zsigmondy, Richard Adolf, Apr. 1, 1865.

Zucker, Jerry, Mar. 11, 1950.

Zug, Switzerland, patron of, Aug. 9.

Zuider Zee, Jan. 13, 1916; May 26, 1932.

Zukor, Adolph, Jan. 7, 1873.

Zuloaga y Zabaleta, Ignacio, Jul. 26, 1870.

Zulu War, Jan. 12, 1879.

Zululand: annexed to British Empire, Jun. 21, 1887.

Zulus: defeated by Boers, Dec. 16, 1838.

Zumwalt, Elmo Russell, Jr., Nov. 29, 1920.

Zuniga, Daphne, Oct. 28, 1963.

Zurbaran, Francisco de, Nov. 7, 1598.

Zurbriggen, Mattias, Jan. 14, 1897.

Zutphen, Battle of, Sep. 22, 1586.

Zweig, Arnold, Nov. 10, 1887.

Zwilich, Ellen, Apr. 30, 1939.

Zwingli, Huldrych (Ulrich), Jan. 1, 1484; Jan. 1, 1519; dies, Oct. 11, 1531.

Zworykin, Vladimir Kosma, Jul. 30, 1889.